Dodd-Frank Wall Street Reform and Consumer Protection Act

Law, Explanation and Analysis

CCH Attorney-Editor Publication

This publication is designed to provide accurate and authoritative information in regard to the subject matter covered. It is sold with the understanding that the publisher is not engaged in rendering legal, accounting, or other professional service. If legal advice or other expert assistance is required, the services of a competent professional person should be sought.

ISBN 978-0-8080-2164-3

©2010 CCH. All Rights Reserved.

4025 W. Peterson Ave.
Chicago, IL 60646-6085
1 800 248 3248
business.cch.com

No claim is made to original government works; however, within this Product or Publication, the following are subject to CCH's copyright: (1) the gathering, compilation, and arrangement of such government materials; (2) the magnetic translation and digital conversion of data, if applicable; (3) the historical, statutory and other notes and references; and (4) the commentary and other materials.

Printed in the United States of America

Foreword

Dodd-Frank Wall Street Reform and Consumer Protection Act: Law, Explanation and Analysis provides comprehensive analysis of this sweeping new banking and securities legislation. Passed by the House of Representatives on June 30 and by the Senate on July 15, the Dodd-Frank Wall Street Reform and Consumer Protection Act was signed into law by the President on July 21, 2010.

These historic reforms will transform the way banks, broker-dealers, hedge funds, investment advisers, credit rating agencies, accountants, public companies and other financial institutions—and the attorneys who advise these entities—operate. Thus, a comprehensive understanding of these changes will be vital to all participants in the U.S. financial system. This definitive publication provides immediate insight into the impact of the new law.

Written by the CCH editorial staff of banking and securities attorneys, the 1,600-plus page book explains every provision of this complex legislation, providing the analysis you need to understand the impact of this historic legislation. Commentary includes discussion of the relevant legislative history, including committee reports, colloquies and floor remarks, detailed citations to new and amended law sections, and editorial comments and caution notes. This publication also features the full text of the legislation and committee reports, tables of effective dates and statutes amended, and a topical index.

The legislation's far-reaching reforms include the creation of an independent Bureau of Consumer Financial Protection housed within the Federal Reserve Board and new federal government power to wind down large, failing financial institutions. The Act establishes a 10-member Financial Stability Oversight Council to oversee systemic risk, strengthen regulation of financial holding companies and abolish the Office of Thrift Supervision, transferring its functions to the Fed, Office of the Comptroller of the Currency and Federal Deposit Insurance Corporation.

The Act introduces a new Volcker Rule that will limit the amount of money a bank can invest in hedge funds. The legislation also discourages financial institutions from excessive risk-taking by imposing tough new capital and leverage requirements. The Act effectively ends new lending under the Troubled Asset Relief Program. Further, it allows the Government Accountability Office to conduct a one-time audit of the Fed's emergency lending activities during the financial crisis and would establish the Federal Insurance Office to supervise insurance products, other than health insurance, at the federal level.

In addition, the legislation imposes stricter oversight of the over-the-counter derivatives market, including mandatory clearing and trading and real-time reporting of derivatives trades. Among other measures, the Act institutes numerous investor protections, including greater oversight of credit rating agencies, important securitization reforms and expanded SEC enforcement powers. It also mandates strong mortgage protections requiring lenders to ensure that their borrowers can repay their loans by establishing a simple federal standard for all home loans.

These and all other measures contained in the Dodd-Frank Act are explained in full detail.

July 2010

Wolters Kluwer Law & Business Publishing
EDITORIAL STAFF

Mark Dorman, *Vice President, Legal Markets Group*
Malcolm D. Conner, *General Manager, Securities and Banking Practice Area*
Susan Chazin, *Associate Publisher, Securities and Banking Practice Area*, J.D.
Peggy L. Hayner, *Product Manager, Securities and Banking Practice Area*

EXPLANATION and ANALYSIS

James Hamilton, *Principal Analyst, Securities Law*, J.D., LL.M.
Andrew A. Turner, *Managing Editor, Banking Law*, J.D.
Ted Trautmann, *Portfolio Managing Editor, Securities Law*, J.D.

Katalina M. Bianco, J.D.	Amy L. Leisinger, J.D.	N. Peter Rasmussen, J.D.
J. Preston Carter, J.D., LL.M.	Mark S. Nelson, J.D.	Richard A. Roth, J.D.
John M. Jascob, J.D.	John M. Pachkowski, J.D.	Anne M. Sherry, J.D.
Gregg D. Killoren, J.D.	Lene Powell, J.D.	

OTHER EDITORIAL CONTRIBUTORS

John Filar Atwood
Associate Managing Editor

Laurel Binder-Arain, J.D.

Kristine Chung, J.D.

Peter Feltman

Jay Fishman, J.D.
Associate Managing Editor

Matthew Garza, J.D.
Associate Managing Editor

Lisa M. Goolik, J.D.

Rachel Jennens, J.D.
Associate Managing Editor

Nicholas Kaster, J.D.

Melanie King, J.D.

Jacquelyn Leatherman

Serena Lynn

Amanda Maine, J.D.

Doreen Meinck, J.D.
Associate Managing Editor

Svetlana Meltser, J.D.

Charles A. Menke, J.D.

Linda Panszczyk, J.D.

Elizabeth Pope, J.D.

Avram L. Sacks, J.D.

Stephen R. Streich, J.D.

Rodney Tonkovic, J.D.

Thomas G. Wolfe, J.D.

ELECTRONIC and PRINT PRODUCTION

Matthew Court
Production Coordinator

Daniel J. Dalaly
Production Coordinator

Matthew E. DuVall
Senior Manager, Product Services

Doris M. Heaney
Senior Workflow Analyst

Shannon D. Jaronik
Manager, Technology Liaison Group

Carmen Kane
Senior Production Specialist

Frank R. Kellner
Production Supervisor

Ellen Kuksuk
Conversion Services Leader

Amy Mathews
Production Coordinator

Kathleen M. McEnroe
Production Manager

Danford A. Miller
Production Supervisor

Justin Miller
Production Specialist

Leslie Stoken
Senior Production Specialist

Brandy Vavrock
Content Associate

Nicholas Waleszonia
Technology Liaison

Kathleen E. Watts
Production Coordinator

¶1 Features of This Publication

This publication is your complete guide to the Dodd-Frank Wall Street Reform and Consumer Protection Act, signed into law by President Barack Obama on July 21, 2010. The core feature of this work is the Explanation portion. Written by the CCH staff of attoney-editors, the explanations discuss and analyze all sections of the Dodd-Frank Act, explaining the changes, the historical context, the congressional intent and the practical impact. To clarify the law's purpose and effect, the explanations integrate relevant pieces of the legislative history—committee reports, statements, floor remarks, colloquies and congressional testimony—that bring meaning to the statutory text. CCH editorial comments and caution notes throughout the explanations alert readers to statutory inconsistencies, uncertainties, related provisions and other concerns.

The publication reproduces the full text of the Dodd-Frank Act. It also reproduces the relevant committee reports: the Conference Committee's joint explanatory statement, the Senate Banking Committee report, the House Financial Services Committee report on the mortgage reform provisions (Title XIV), as well as a letter from Senators Christopher Dodd and Blanche Lincoln explaining the derivatives provisions in Title VII.

The book also contains numerous other features designed to help you locate and understand the changes made by this legislation. These features include cross references to related materials, detailed effective dates, and numerous tables and indexes. A more detailed description of these features appears below.

EXPLANATIONS

Explanations are designed to give you a complete and accessible understanding of the new laws. Explanations are arranged by subject and follow the organizational structure of the law for ease of use. There are several options for locating explanations on a given topic. These are:

- A detailed table of contents at the beginning of the publication listing all of the explanations of the new laws;
- A table of contents preceding each chapter; and
- An extensive topical index covering the subject matter of the legislation.

The explanations contain special features to aid in your complete understanding of the new laws. These include:

- A brief overview of the new laws;
- Discussion of background or prior law, as applicable, that puts the law changes into perspective;
- Analysis of legislative history (committee reports, statements, floor remarks, colloquies and congressional testimony) where available and appropriate;
- Editorial aids, including cautions and comments, that highlight the law's impact, related provisions, inconsistencies in the statutory text, and other concerns;

¶1

- Captions at the end of each explanation identifying the law sections added, amended or repealed, as well as the Act sections containing the changes;
- Cross references to the law and committee report paragraphs related to the explanation; and
- A caption highlighting the effective date of each law change, marked by an arrow symbol.

The Explanations begin at ¶ 55.

LAW TEXT

The full text of the Dodd-Frank Wall Street Reform and Consumer Protection Act appears at ¶ 10,001 *et seq.* Cross references to explanation paragraphs related to each provision are also provided.

The online version of this book will, shortly after publication, include the existing laws as amended or repealed. This presentation will display the amendments to existing laws in context, giving a fuller sense of how existing laws will appear after the changes are integrated. These will include the added, amended and repealed provisions of the major banking and securities laws, *e.g.*, the Bank Holding Company Act, the Commodity Exchange Act, the Federal Deposit Insurance Act, the Federal Reserve Act, the Investment Advisers Act, the Investment Company Act, the National Bank Act, the Securities Act, the Securities Exchange Act, and the Securities Investor Protection Act.

COMMITTEE REPORTS

The publication reproduces the relevant committee reports and related materials. These include: the Conference Committee's joint explanatory statement discussing the final bill (see ¶ 50,001 *et seq*); the Senate committee report (S. Rep. No. 111-176) explaining the Senate bill (see ¶ 54,000 *et seq*); the House committee report (H. Rep. No. 111-94) on the separate legislation from which the Title XIV mortgage reform provisions originated (see ¶ 55,000 *et seq*); and a joint letter from Senators Christopher Dodd and Blanche Lincoln explaining the derivatives provisions in Title VII (see ¶ 56,001).

The Conference Committee Report for the Dodd-Frank Act consists only of the Act itself. The Act text is reproduced in the "Law Text" portion of this publication. There is no narrative conference report explaining the Act's purpose and its individual provisions apart from the Conference Committee's joint explanatory statement noted above.

TABLES and INDEX

The publication also contains tables and other finding devices. A Table of Effective Dates listing provisions containing major effective dates offers a reference bridge between existing or new law sections and Act sections. The table also indicates the retroactive or prospective nature of the laws. Compliance dates for prescribed rules and regulations, as well as mandated studies and reports, also are included. The effective dates table begins at ¶ 60,001.

A Table of Statutes Added, Amended or Repealed lists the existing law provisions changed by the Dodd-Frank Act. It contains an alphabetically organized list of existing laws (*e.g.*, Bank Holding Company Act, Commodity Exchange Act, etc.) and the new, amended or repealed provisions. This table is located at ¶61,001.

A Table of Act Sections Not Amending Existing Laws lists all the Dodd-Frank Act provisions that do not change existing laws but are new, stand-alone sections that, as of enactment, have not been codified. This table is located at ¶62,001.

Finally, a Topical Index provides an alternate means of finding information in the explanations. It lists major topics and subtopics, with references to the paragraph number of explanations on point. The index appears at the end.

¶2 Table of Contents

¶1 Features of This Publication

EXPLANATION

¶55	Introduction	
¶105	Chapter 1	Financial Stability Oversight
¶505	Chapter 2	Orderly Liquidation Authority
¶1005	Chapter 3	Supervision of Depository Institutions
¶1505	Chapter 4	Private Fund Advisers
¶2005	Chapter 5	Insurance
¶2505	Chapter 6	Bank and Thrift Regulatory Improvements
¶3005	Chapter 7	OTC Derivatives
¶3505	Chapter 8	Clearing and Settlement
¶4005	Chapter 9	Investor Protection and Securities Regulation
¶4505	Chapter 10	Consumer Financial Protection
¶5005	Chapter 11	Strengthening the Federal Reserve
¶5505	Chapter 12	Access to Mainstream Finance
¶6005	Chapter 13	Pay It Back Act
¶6505	Chapter 14	Mortgage Reform and Anti-Predatory Lending
¶7005	Chapter 15	Miscellaneous Provisions

LAW TEXT

¶10,001 Dodd-Frank Wall Street Reform and Consumer Protection Act

COMMITTEE REPORTS

¶50,001 Conference Committee Explanatory Statement
¶54,000 Senate Report 111-176
¶55,000 House Report 111-94
¶56,001 Dodd-Lincoln Letter on Title VII (June 30, 2010)

TABLES

¶60,001 Table of Effective Dates
¶61,001 Table of Statutes Added, Amended or Repealed
¶62,001 Table of Act Sections Not Amending Existing Laws

Page 1607 Topical Index

¶3 Detailed Table of Contents

INTRODUCTION

- ¶55   Background
- ¶60   Overview
- ¶65   General Provisions

CHAPTER 1. FINANCIAL STABILITY OVERSIGHT

FINANCIAL STABILITY OVERSIGHT COUNCIL

- ¶105   Introduction
- ¶110   Creation of Council
- ¶115   Council Authority
- ¶120   Regulation of Nonbank Financial Companies
- ¶125   Enhanced Prudential Standards
- ¶130   Reports
- ¶135   Companies Ceasing to Be Bank Holding Companies
- ¶140   Dispute Resolution
- ¶145   Recommendations to Primary Regulators
- ¶150   Mitigation of Risks to Financial Stability

OFFICE OF FINANCIAL RESEARCH

- ¶160   Introduction
- ¶165   Creation of Office
- ¶170   Purpose, Powers and Duties
- ¶175   Data Collection and Research Centers
- ¶180   Funding

ADDITIONAL FED AUTHORITY

- ¶190   Introduction
- ¶195   Reports and Examination of Nonbank Financial Companies
- ¶200   Examination and Enforcement
- ¶205   Acquisitions
- ¶210   Management Interlock Prohibition
- ¶215   Enhanced Supervision and Prudential Standards
- ¶220   Early Remediation of Financial Distress

¶225 Affiliations
¶230 Safe Harbor
¶235 Leverage and Risk-Based Capital Requirements
¶240 Foreign Firm Access to U.S. Market
¶245 Holding Company Capital Requirement Studies
¶250 International Policy Coordination

CHAPTER 2. ORDERLY LIQUIDATION AUTHORITY

¶505 Introduction
¶510 FDIC Appointment as Receiver
¶515 Systemic Risk Determination
¶520 Orderly Liquidation Authority
¶525 Receiver's Powers and Duties
¶530 Claims and Contracts
¶535 Officers, Directors, Employees and Agents
¶540 Bridge Financial Companies
¶545 Orderly Liquidation Fund
¶550 Inspector General Review and Reports

CHAPTER 3. SUPERVISION OF DEPOSITORY INSTITUTIONS

TRANSFER OF OTS FUNCTIONS AND POWERS

¶1005 Introduction
¶1010 OTS Abolished
¶1015 OTS Functions Transferred
¶1020 OCC Reestablished
¶1025 Federal Information Policy Amended
¶1030 Continuation of OTS Regulations
¶1035 References in Federal Law to Federal Banking Agencies
¶1040 Agency Funding
¶1045 Contracting and Leasing Authority

TRANSITIONAL PROVISIONS

¶1050 Introduction
¶1055 Interim Use of Funds, Personnel and Property
¶1060 Transfer of Employees
¶1065 Property Transferred

¶1070	Funds Transferred
¶1075	Disposition of Affairs
¶1080	Continuation of Services
¶1085	Implementation Plan and Reports

DEPOSIT INSURANCE REFORM

¶1090	Introduction
¶1095	Deposit Insurance Assessments
¶1100	Permanent Increase in Deposit Insurance Limits
¶1105	FDIC Board of Directors

OTHER MATTERS

¶1110	Branching
¶1115	Office of Minority and Women Inclusion
¶1120	Insurance of Transaction Accounts

TECHNICAL AND CONFORMING AMENDMENTS

¶1125	Amendments to the Balanced Budget and Emergency Deficit Control Act of 1985
¶1130	Amendments to the Bank Enterprise Act
¶1135	Amendments to the Bank Holding Company Act
¶1140	Amendments to the Bank Holding Company Act Amendments of 1970
¶1145	Amendments to the Bank Protection Act
¶1150	Amendments to the Bank Service Company Act
¶1155	Amendments to the Community Reinvestment Act
¶1160	Amendments to the Crime Control Act of 1990
¶1165	Amendments to the Depository Institution Management Interlocks Act
¶1170	Amendments to the Emergency Homeowners' Relief Act
¶1175	Amendments to the Federal Credit Union Act
¶1180	Amendments to the Federal Deposit Insurance Act
¶1185	Amendments to the Federal Home Loan Bank Act
¶1190	Amendments to the Federal Housing Enterprises Financial Safety and Soundness Act
¶1195	Amendments to the Federal Reserve Act
¶1200	Amendments to the Financial Institutions Reform, Recovery, and Enforcement Act
¶1205	Amendments to the Flood Disaster Protection Act
¶1210	Amendments to the Home Owners' Loan Act
¶1215	Amendments to the Housing Act of 1948
¶1220	Amendments to the Housing and Community Development Act of 1992
¶1225	Amendments to the Housing and Urban-Rural Recovery Act of 1983

¶1230	Amendments to the National Housing Act
¶1235	Amendments to the Neighborhood Reinvestment Corporation Act
¶1240	Amendments Pertaining to Investment in State Housing Corporations
¶1245	Amendments to the Securities and Exchange Act
¶1250	Amendments to Criminal Laws
¶1255	Amendments to Title 31, United States Code

CHAPTER 4. PRIVATE FUND ADVISERS

¶1505	Introduction
¶1510	Definitions
¶1515	Adviser Registration
¶1520	Reports and Records
¶1525	SEC Rulemaking
¶1530	Family Offices
¶1535	State Oversight of Mid-Sized Advisers
¶1540	Custody of Client Assets
¶1545	Accredited Investors
¶1550	Commodity Pool Operators, Trading Advisors
¶1555	Qualified Client Standard
¶1560	Studies and Reports

CHAPTER 5. INSURANCE

FEDERAL INSURANCE OFFICE

¶2005	Introduction
¶2010	Establishment of the Federal Insurance Office

STATE-BASED INSURANCE REFORM

¶2015	Introduction
¶2020	Surplus Lines Insurance
¶2025	Regulation by Insured's Home State
¶2030	Participation in National Producer Database
¶2035	Surplus Lines Eligibility
¶2040	Application for Commercial Purchasers
¶2045	GAO Study Required
¶2050	Nonadmitted Insurance Definitions
¶2055	Reinsurance
¶2060	Regulation of Solvency

¶2065	Reinsurance Definitions
¶2070	Rule of Construction
¶2075	Severability

CHAPTER 6. BANK AND THRIFT REGULATORY IMPROVEMENTS

¶2505	Introduction
¶2510	Deposit Insurance and Change in Bank Control Moratorium
¶2515	GAO Study of Bank Holding Company Act Exceptions
¶2520	Holding Company Examination Improvements
¶2525	Functionally Regulated Subsidiaries
¶2530	Acquisitions
¶2535	Oversight of Depository Institution Subsidiary Activities
¶2540	Enhanced Capitalization and Management
¶2545	Transactions with Affiliates and Insiders
¶2550	Lending Limits
¶2555	Charter Conversions
¶2560	De Novo Branching
¶2565	Source of Strength
¶2570	Investment and Securities Holding Companies
¶2575	Proprietary Trading, Hedge Funds and Private Equity Funds—Volcker Rule
¶2580	Study of Bank Investment Activities
¶2585	Conflicts of Interest Relating to Securitizations
¶2590	Concentration Limits
¶2595	Interstate Bank Mergers and Acquisitions
¶2600	Thrift Dividends
¶2605	Mutual Holding Company Dividends
¶2610	Intermediate Holding Companies
¶2615	Payment of Interest on Demand Deposits
¶2620	Credit Card Bank Small Business Lending

CHAPTER 7. OTC DERIVATIVES

GENERAL PROVISIONS

¶3005	Introduction
¶3010	Definitions
¶3015	Jurisdiction

¶3020	CFTC-SEC Coordination
¶3025	Portfolio Margining
¶3030	Prohibition Against Bailout of Swaps Entities
¶3035	CFTC-SEC Jurisdiction; New Product Approval
¶3040	Novel Derivative Products
¶3045	Conflicts of Interest
¶3050	Studies and Reports

SWAPS MARKETS

¶3060	Clearing
¶3065	Swaps, Segregation and Bankruptcy Treatment
¶3070	Derivatives Clearing Organizations
¶3075	Public Reporting of Swap Transaction Data
¶3080	Swap Data Repositories
¶3085	Reporting and Recordkeeping (CFTC)
¶3090	Large Swap Trader Reporting
¶3095	Swap Dealers and Major Swap Participants
¶3100	Swap Execution Facilities
¶3105	Derivatives Transaction Execution Facilities and EBOTs
¶3110	Designated Contract Markets
¶3115	Position Limits
¶3120	Foreign Boards of Trade
¶3125	Legal Certainty for Swaps
¶3130	Enforcement
¶3135	Retail Commodity Transactions
¶3140	Enhanced Compliance for Registered Entities
¶3145	Whistleblowers
¶3150	International Harmonization
¶3155	Anti-Manipulation Authority

SECURITY-BASED SWAP MARKETS

¶3160	Securities Law Amendments
¶3165	Regulation of Dealers and Major Participants
¶3170	Reporting and Recordkeeping (SEC)
¶3175	State Gaming and Bucket Shop Laws

CHAPTER 8. CLEARING AND SETTLEMENT

¶3505	Introduction
¶3510	Systemic Importance

¶3515 Risk Management Standards
¶3520 Operations of Financial Market Utilities
¶3525 Examination and Enforcement—Financial Market Utilities
¶3530 Examination and Enforcement—Financial Institutions
¶3535 Requests for Information, Reports and Records

CHAPTER 9. INVESTOR PROTECTION AND SECURITIES REGULATION

INVESTOR PROTECTION

¶4005 Introduction
¶4010 Investor Advisory Committee
¶4015 Consumer Testing
¶4020 Fiduciary Standard for Broker-Dealers and Advisers
¶4025 Office of the Investor Advocate
¶4030 SRO Rule Changes
¶4035 Pre-Purchase Disclosures
¶4040 Studies and Reports

ENFORCEMENT AND REMEDIES

¶4050 Introduction
¶4055 Mandatory Arbitration Clauses
¶4060 Whistleblowers
¶4065 Collateral Bars
¶4070 Regulation D Offerings
¶4075 Self-Regulatory Organization Rules
¶4080 State-Registered Investment Advisers
¶4085 Margin Lending
¶4090 Fair Fund Provision
¶4095 SIPA Amendments
¶4100 Lost, Stolen, Counterfeit and Cancelled Securities
¶4105 Nationwide Service of Process
¶4110 Formerly Associated Persons
¶4115 Hiring Authority for Market Specialists
¶4120 Confidential and Privileged Information
¶4125 Transactions Not Conducted on Exchanges
¶4130 Aiding-and-Abetting Violations
¶4135 SEC Enforcement Authority
¶4140 Custody and Recordkeeping

¶4145	Reporting Obligations
¶4150	Fingerprinting
¶4155	Enforcement Deadlines
¶4160	Notice to Missing Shareholders
¶4165	Short-Sale Disclosures
¶4170	Aiding-and-Abetting Study

CREDIT RATING AGENCIES

¶4180	Introduction
¶4185	Enhanced Regulation and Transparency
¶4190	Assigned Credit Ratings
¶4195	State of Mind in Private Actions
¶4200	Information from Third-Party Sources
¶4205	Professional Standards for Rating Analysts
¶4210	Universal Rating Symbols
¶4215	Whistleblowers
¶4220	Removal of Statutory References to Ratings
¶4225	Regulation FD Exemption
¶4230	Section 11 Liability
¶4235	Studies and Reports

SECURITIZATION

¶4250	Introduction
¶4255	Credit Risk Retention
¶4260	Issuer Disclosure and Reporting
¶4265	Real Estate Mortgage Notes Exemption
¶4270	Due Diligence Analysis
¶4275	Macroeconomic Effects of Risk Retention

EXECUTIVE COMPENSATION and GOVERNANCE

¶4290	Introduction
¶4295	Shareholder Advisory Vote
¶4300	Independent Compensation Committees
¶4305	"Pay vs. Performance" Disclosure
¶4310	Recovery of Erroneously-Awarded Compensation
¶4315	Hedging by Directors and Employees
¶4320	Incentive-Based Compensation Arrangements
¶4325	Proxy Voting by Brokers
¶4330	Shareholder Proxy Access
¶4335	Bifurcation of Chair and CEO Role

SEC ORGANIZATION AND FUNDING

¶4350	Introduction
¶4355	Studies and Reports
¶4360	Examination Staff
¶4365	SEC Employee Hotline
¶4370	SEC Funding

MUNICIPAL SECURITIES

¶4380	Introduction
¶4385	Municipal Advisor Registration
¶4390	Broker-Dealer Regulation
¶4395	Municipal Securities Rulemaking Board
¶4400	Office of Municipal Securities
¶4405	Governmental Accounting Standards Board Funding
¶4410	Studies and Reports

PUBLIC COMPANY ACCOUNTING OVERSIGHT BOARD

¶4420	Introduction
¶4425	Audit Information to be Produced and Exchanged
¶4430	Information Sharing with Foreign Regulators
¶4435	Auditors of Broker-Dealers

ADDITIONAL SECURITIES REFORMS

¶4450	Introduction
¶4455	Portfolio Margining
¶4460	Securities Lending and Borrowing
¶4465	Deposit Insurance Fund Loss Reviews
¶4470	Study of Proprietary Trading
¶4475	Senior Investor Protection
¶4480	SEC and CFTC Inspectors General
¶4485	Person-to-Person Lending
¶4490	Internal Controls Auditor Attestation
¶4495	NAIC Model Regulations

CHAPTER 10. CONSUMER FINANCIAL PROTECTION

INTRODUCTION AND DEFINITIONS

¶4505	Introduction and Short Title
¶4510	Definitions

BUREAU OF CONSUMER FINANCIAL PROTECTION

¶4515	Creation of the Bureau

¶4520 Executive and Administrative Powers
¶4525 Bureau Personnel and Internal Organization
¶4530 Consumer Advisory Board
¶4535 Coordination with Other Agencies
¶4540 Reports to Congress
¶4545 Funding the Bureau; Fines and Penalties
GENERAL BUREAU POWERS
¶4550 Goals and Functions of the Bureau
¶4555 Rulemaking Authority
¶4560 Financial Stability Oversight Council Review of Regulations
¶4565 Bureau Supervision of Nondepository Institutions
¶4570 Supervision of Large Institutions
¶4575 Supervision of Smaller Institutions
¶4580 Limits on the Bureau's Authority
¶4585 Arbitration Agreements
¶4590 Exclusion for Motor Vehicle Dealers
SPECIFIC BUREAU AUTHORITIES
¶4595 Unfair, Deceptive or Abusive Acts or Practices
¶4600 Disclosures
¶4605 Consumers' Right to Information
¶4610 Response to Consumers
¶4615 Private Education Loan Ombudsman
¶4620 Prohibited Acts and Assisting Prohibited Acts
PREEMPTION OF STATE LAW AND STATE ENFORCEMENT
¶4625 Effect on State Law
¶4630 State Enforcement Authority
¶4635 Preservation of Existing Contracts
¶4640 Preemption Standards for National Banks and Subsidiaries
¶4645 Preemption for Nondepositary National Bank Subsidiaries and Affiliates
¶4650 Preemption for Federal Thrifts and Subsidiaries
¶4655 State Visitorial Authority over Federal Institutions
BUREAU ENFORCEMENT POWERS
¶4660 Definitions
¶4665 Investigations and Administrative Discovery
¶4670 Hearings and Adjudications
¶4675 Litigation
¶4680 Relief Available for Violations

| ¶4685 | Criminal Prosecution Referrals |
| ¶4690 | Whistleblower Protections |

TRANSFER OF FUNCTIONS AND PERSONNEL

¶4695	Transfer of Bureau Functions
¶4700	Designated Transfer Date
¶4705	Savings Provisions
¶4710	Personnel Transfers
¶4715	Incidental Transfers of Assets and Liabilities
¶4720	Interim Operations
¶4725	Oversight of the Transition

REGULATORY IMPROVEMENTS—AMENDMENTS TO OTHER LAWS

¶4730	Lending to Women- or Minority-Owned Small Businesses
¶4735	Assistance for Economically Vulnerable Persons
¶4740	Remittance Transfers
¶4745	Government Sponsored Enterprise Study
¶4750	Payment Card Transaction Fees and Rules
¶4755	Reverse Mortgage Rules
¶4760	Private Education Loans and Lenders
¶4765	Credit Scores Study and Report
¶4770	Exchange Facilitators
¶4775	Financial Fraud

CONFORMING AMENDMENTS

¶4780	Amendments to the Inspector General Act
¶4785	Amendments to the Privacy Act
¶4790	Amendments to the Alternative Mortgage Transaction Parity Act
¶4795	Amendments to the Electronic Fund Transfer Act
¶4800	Amendments to the Equal Credit Opportunity Act
¶4805	Amendments to the Expedited Funds Availability Act
¶4810	Amendments to the Fair Credit Billing Act
¶4815	Amendments to the Fair Credit Reporting Act and the Fair and Accurate Credit Transactions Act of 2003
¶4820	Amendments to the Fair Debt Collection Practices Act
¶4825	Amendments to Federal Deposit Insurance Act
¶4830	Amendments to the Federal Financial Institutions Examination Council Act
¶4835	Amendments to the Federal Trade Commission Act
¶4840	Amendments to the Gramm-Leach-Bliley Act

¶4845	Amendments to the Home Mortgage Disclosure Act
¶4850	Amendments to the Homeowners Protection Act
¶4855	Amendments to the Home Ownership and Equity Protection Act
¶4860	Amendments to the Omnibus Appropriations Act, 2009
¶4865	Amendments to the Real Estate Settlement Procedures Act
¶4870	Amendments to Interstate Land Sales Full Disclosure Act
¶4875	Amendments to the Right to Financial Privacy Act
¶4880	Amendments to the Secure and Fair Enforcement for Mortgage Licensing Act of 2008
¶4885	Amendments to the Truth in Lending Act
¶4890	Amendments to the Truth in Savings Act
¶4895	Amendments to the Telemarketing and Consumer Fraud and Abuse Prevention Act
¶4900	Amendments to the Paperwork Reduction Act
¶4905	Adjustments for Inflation in the Truth in Lending Act
¶4910	Adverse Action Notices and Credit Reports
¶4915	Small Business Fairness and Regulatory Transparency

CHAPTER 11. STRENGTHENING THE FEDERAL RESERVE

¶5005	Overview
¶5010	Emergency Lending Authority
¶5015	GAO Review of Credit Facilities
¶5020	One-Time GAO Audit
¶5025	Public Access to Fed Information
¶5030	Fed Transparency and Release of Information
¶5035	Liquidity Event Guarantees
¶5040	Federal Reserve Governance

CHAPTER 12. ACCESS TO MAINSTREAM FINANCE

¶5505	Introduction
¶5510	Program Eligibility and Account Activities
¶5515	Low-Cost Alternatives to Small Dollar Loans
¶5520	Grants to Establish Loan-Loss Reserves
¶5525	Program Funding and Oversight

CHAPTER 13. PAY IT BACK ACT

¶6005 Overview
¶6010 TARP Wind Down
¶6015 Public Debt Reduction
¶6020 FHFA Reporting
¶6025 Recovery Act Funds

CHAPTER 14. MORTGAGE REFORM AND ANTI-PREDATORY LENDING

INTRODUCTION
¶6505 Introduction
¶6510 Consumer Law

RESIDENTIAL MORTGAGE LOAN ORIGINATION STANDARDS
¶6515 Definitions
¶6520 Residential Mortgage Loan Origination
¶6525 Prohibition of Steering Incentives
¶6530 Mortgage Originator Liability
¶6535 Discretionary Regulatory Authority
¶6540 Study of Shared Appreciation Mortgages

MINIMUM STANDARDS FOR MORTGAGES
¶6545 Ability to Repay
¶6550 Safe Harbor and Rebuttable Presumptions
¶6555 Defense to Foreclosure
¶6560 Additional Standards and Requirements
¶6565 Rule of Construction
¶6570 Amendments to Civil Liability Provisions
¶6575 Lender Rights as to Borrower Deception
¶6580 Notice Prior to Reset of Hybrid Adjustable Rate Mortgages
¶6585 Required Disclosures
¶6590 Monthly Statement Disclosures
¶6595 Government Accountability Office Report
¶6600 State Attorney General Enforcement Authority

HIGH-COST MORTGAGES
¶6605 Definitions Relating to High-Cost Mortgages
¶6610 Amendments to Existing Requirements
¶6615 Additional Requirements for Certain Mortgages

¶3

OFFICE OF HOUSING COUNSELING

¶6620 Establishment of Housing Counseling Office
¶6625 Counseling Procedures
¶6630 Grants for Housing Counseling
¶6635 Requirements to Use HUD-Certified Counselors
¶6640 Study of Defaults and Foreclosures
¶6645 Default and Disclosure Database
¶6650 Definitions for Counseling-Related Programs
¶6655 Accountability and Transparency for Grant Recipients
¶6660 Mortgage Information Booklet
¶6665 Home Inspection Counseling
¶6670 Warnings to Homeowners of Foreclosure Rescue Scams

MORTGAGE SERVICING

¶6675 Escrow and Impound Accounts
¶6680 Disclosure Notice for Consumers Who Waive Escrow Services
¶6685 Real Estate Settlement Procedures Act Amendments
¶6690 Truth in Lending Act Amendments
¶6695 Escrows Included in Repayment Analysis

APPRAISAL ACTIVITIES

¶6700 Property Appraisal Requirements
¶6705 Appraisal Independence Requirements
¶6710 FIRREA Amendments
¶6715 Equal Credit Opportunity Act Amendment
¶6720 Real Estate Settlement Procedures Act Amendment
¶6725 GAO Study

MORTGAGE RESOLUTION and MODIFICATION

¶6730 Mulitfamily Mortgage Resolution Program
¶6735 Home Affordable Modification Program Guidelines
¶6740 Public Availability of Information of Making Home Affordable Program
¶6745 Extension and Clarification of Protecting Tenants at Foreclosure Act

MISCELLANEOUS PROVISIONS

¶6750 Sense of Congress on Government Sponsored Enterprises Reform
¶6755 GAO Study Report on Mortgage Foreclosure Scams and Loan Modification Fraud
¶6760 Study of Effect of Drywall Presence on Foreclosures
¶6765 Emergency Mortgage Relief
¶6770 Additional Assistance for Neighborhood Stabilization Program

¶3

¶6775   Legal Assistance for Foreclosure-Related Issues

CHAPTER 15. MISCELLANEOUS PROVISIONS

¶7005   Introduction
¶7010   Section 1256 Contracts
¶7015   U.S. Funds for Foreign Governments
¶7020   Conflict Minerals
¶7025   Mine Safety Violations
¶7030   Payments by Resource Extraction Issuers
¶7035   Report on Inspectors General
¶7040   Study of Core and Brokered Deposits

Introduction

¶55 Background
¶60 Overview
¶65 General Provisions

¶55 Background

The events leading up to the passage of this historic financial reform legislation were unique and unprecedented. The financial crisis that gripped the United States and led to this massive overhaul of federal financial regulation was unprecedented in type and magnitude. It began with an asset bubble in housing, expanded into the subprime mortgage crisis and the attendant securitization of subprime mortgages and other assets, and escalated into a severe freeze-up of the interbank lending market, culminating in intervention by the United States and other countries to rescue their financial systems from systemic collapse (Congressional Oversight Panel Report, December 9, 2009).

In the years leading up to these market events, a dramatic shift in the financial regulatory system was occurring. Vigorous governmental oversight was abandoned as regulators and policy makers placed their faith in the ability of markets to self-police and self-correct. The prevailing view was that too much regulation, rather than too little, was eroding the competitiveness of U.S. markets.

The roots of the crisis go back decades. Years without a serious economic recession bred complacency among financial intermediaries and investors. At some of the most sophisticated financial firms, risk management systems did not keep pace with the complexity of new financial products. The lack of transparency and standards in markets for securitized loans helped to weaken underwriting standards. Market discipline broke down as investors relied excessively on credit rating agencies. Compensation practices throughout the financial services industry rewarded short-term profits at the expense of long-term value (*Financial Regulatory Reform, A New Foundation: Rebuilding Financial Supervision and Regulation*, Treasury Department (June 17, 2009), FED. BANK. L. REP. ¶ 75-201).

Securitization.—In many ways the financial crisis was a crisis of securitization. Rapid financial innovation led to securitization techniques with unknown complexities and uncontrollable chains of intermediaries between originators and final investors.

Securitization, by breaking down the traditional relationship between borrowers and lenders, created conflicts of interest that market discipline failed to correct. Loan originators failed to require sufficient documentation of income and ability to pay. Securitizers failed to set high standards for the loans they were willing to buy, encouraging underwriting standards to decline. Investors placed undue reliance on credit ratings, which often failed to describe the true risk of rated products. In each case, lack of transparency prevented market participants from understanding the full nature of the risks they were taking.

OTC Derivatives.—Although many factors led to the financial sector's unraveling and the subsequent government intervention, a major contributor to the financial crisis was the unregulated over-the-counter (OTC) derivatives market. Derivatives can trade either over-the-counter where contracts are often customized and privately negotiated between counterparties, or through regulated central clearinghouses and exchanges that establish rules for trading contracts among many different counterparties (S. Rep. No. 111-176, p. 29).

The dangers posed by the OTC derivatives market have been known for many years. In 1994, the GAO produced a report titled, Financial Derivatives: Actions Needed to Protect the Financial System. At the time of the report, the GAO determined the size of the derivatives market to be $12.1 trillion. Included in GAO's findings in 1994 were concerns about risks to taxpayers arising from the interconnectedness between dealers and end users and the rapid growth and increasing complexity of derivatives activities, as well as increasing risks to the financial system, participants, and U.S. taxpayers. A broader concern is that the relationships between the major U.S. dealers that handle most derivatives activities, the end users, and the exchange-traded markets makes the failure of any one of them potentially damaging to the entire financial market.

By the time of the 2008 crisis, the derivatives market had grown to almost 50 times larger than when the GAO raised a red flag. Much of this growth can be attributed to the Commodity Futures Modernization Act of 2000, which explicitly exempted OTC derivatives, to a large extent, from regulation by the Commodity Futures Trading Commission and limited the Securities and Exchange Commission's authority to regulate certain types of OTC derivatives (S. Rep. No. 111-176, p. 29).

Credit default swaps, a type of derivative, were essentially insurance policies written against a default in the financial markets. While originally used as counterparty insurance, they became a highly efficient way to short an institution by entering into a swap where one party paid a relatively small premium but would receive a large payout on failure. The markets for credit default swaps quickly became illiquid.

According to the Obama administration, the downside of this lax regulatory regime became disastrously clear during the financial crisis when many institutions and investors had substantial positions in credit default swaps, particularly tied to asset-backed securities. The sheer volume of these contracts overwhelmed some firms that had promised to provide payment on the credit default swaps and left institutions with losses that they believed they had been protected against. Lacking authority to regulate the OTC derivatives market, regulators were unable to identify or mitigate the enormous systemic threat that had developed (*Financial Regulatory Reform, A New Foundation: Rebuilding Financial Supervision and Regulation, supra*).

Credit Rating Agencies.—Ratings agencies gained global power as the pricing of securitization tranches was largely based on their assessments. Credit rating agencies were issuing more and more downgrades of securitized instruments composed of souring subprime mortgages. Rating agencies downgraded a large number of asset-backed securities and collateralized debt obligations. Even AAA-rated tranches declined below par value.

As the financial crisis unfolded, credit rating agencies were seen to have failed to reflect early enough in their ratings the worsening market conditions and to adjust their credit ratings in time. There were issues involving conflicts of interest, lack of transparency and the internal governance of the credit rating agencies. In essence, credit rating agencies had become a de facto oligopoly that underestimated the credit risk inherent in structured and securitized products and did not adapt their ratings when the markets fell.

Hedge Funds.—At the same time, leverage mounted ever higher and a shadow banking system composed of hedge funds and other private funds developed largely unregulated. The crisis demonstrated that a significant part of credit intermediation was channeled outside the regulated financial sector and off the radar screen into hedge funds and other entities comprising the non-regulated shadow banking system. Moreover, little was known about the exposures between this shadow system and the regulated one, which turned out to be substantial. Information on non-banking institutions, potentially of systemic importance, such as hedge funds, was scattered, not quality-checked and provided on a voluntary basis (*Financial Regulatory Reform, A New Foundation: Rebuilding Financial Supervision and Regulation, supra; G-30 Report on Financial Reform: A Framework for Financial Stability*, Jan 15, 2009).

Corporate Governance.—The financial crisis also revealed a failure of corporate governance and massive gaps in risk management. Executive compensation that rewarded short-term success with annual bonuses without penalizing the long-term consequences of decisions that were taken enhanced procyclicality. Executive compensation also often led to excessive risk taking.

Subprime Lending Crisis.—The subprime mortgage crisis came to the public's attention when a steep rise in home foreclosures in 2006 spiraled seemingly out of control in 2007, triggering a national financial crisis that went global within the year. With consumer spending down, the housing market plummeted, foreclosure numbers continued to rise and the stock market was shaken. Initially, many experts believed that the crisis would be contained within the arena of mortgage issuers who had overloaded on subprime loans, but ultimately the subprime fallout would be so severe as to pose a significant threat to the economy

Financial Meltdown.—By the end of June 2007, the three biggest rating agencies had downgraded their ratings on 2,012 tranches, or slices, of mortgage-backed securities. Just 16 days later, that number had climbed to 3,079. Initially the downgrades were largely confined to the securities' lower-rated tranches. But soon even the safest pieces of these mortgage-backed bonds, those rated AAA, were being downgraded (Congressional Oversight Panel Report, December 9, 2009).

The first major casualty was Bear Stearns. In addition to its exposure to risky mortgages, the investment bank had come to rely heavily on short-term loans. These factors made Bear Stearns especially vulnerable to a run, which came in March 2008. As the firm lost assets, its ability to borrow deteriorated. On March 14, the Federal Reserve agreed to lend $29 billion as part of a deal that allowed JPMorgan Chase to buy Bear Stearns. The government's rescue of Bear Stearns established a new precedent. Previously, the government had allowed faltering investment banks, which are not insured by the federal government or regulated like commercial banks, to go bankrupt, as

¶55

Drexel Burnham Lambert did in 1990 (Congressional Oversight Panel Report, December 9, 2009).

At the same time, securitization markets, which had provided the funding that fueled the housing boom, were severely contracting. Fear in the financial markets, which had been building, evolved into a full-blown panic in September 2008. During a 19-day stretch, the federal government took over the two largest players in the mortgage market, allowed a large investment bank to go bankrupt, bailed out one of the world's largest insurance companies, and steered a major financial institution through the largest bank failure in U.S. history (Congressional Oversight Panel Report, December 9, 2009).

Fair Value Accounting.—The application of fair value accounting contributed to procyclicality in the financial markets. Compared with the historical cost approach, fair value accounting intensifies market fluctuations. While the fair value approach can better reflect the real time value of assets and liabilities, it also magnifies the changes in their values and increases the volatility of returns through the profit and loss account as a consequence. As a result of the massive collateralized securities they held, financial institutions registered mounting unrealized losses that actually involved no cash flow under the fair value rule. Although these losses were only meaningful in accounting, such astronomical book losses distorted investors' expectations and formed a vicious cycle of tumbling prices and asset write-downs.

Both generally accepted accounting principles (GAAP) and International Financial Reporting Standards (IFRS) defined fair value in a similar way, which is a price at which an asset and liability can be traded with a willing counterparty in an orderly manner. Both accounting frameworks also provided measurement approaches at differentiated levels:

- Level 1—Prices can be observed on active market, which are used to measure the value of assets and liabilities—a practice called mark-to-market.
- Level 2—When assets could no longer be marked-to-market because there was no active market for them, firms had no choice but to use internal modeling processes, whose quality and adequacy was sometimes flawed. This is mark-to-model.
- Level 3—The measurement approach used on Level 3 is similar to the mark-to-model approach, but it involves unobservable parameters and model assumptions as inputs.

The poorly guided adoption of fair value in non-active markets exacerbated market volatility. As defined, the use of fair value approaches must be based on the prerequisite of orderly trading. At times of crisis, as a large number of institutions were forced to liquidate their assets, prices developed under this situation did not meet the prerequisite for fair value measurement. However, due to the lack of specific guidelines on dealing with such circumstances, reporting entities had to conduct fair value measurement on the basis of unreasonable market prices, which magnified book losses and exacerbated the vicious cycle—the phenomenon of procyclicality.

At the same time that mark-to-market accounting rules became increasingly widespread, unsustainable external deficits and surpluses in some major economies paved the way for macro-economic imbalances at the global level. Information began to flow instantaneously around the globe and raised competitive pressure on all financial market participants. In this environment, banks and other investors engaged in a search for yield with the help of the new credit products and investment vehicles, circum-

¶55

venting existing regulations. The pace of this herd behavior into ever more complicated forms of securitization far exceeded the market's capacity to solve the issues of valuation, risk management and incentives (Remarks of Zhou Xiaochuan, Governor of the Central Bank of China, before G-20 central bankers, Nov. 15, 2008).

This resulted in widespread financial instabilities in the form of a highly complex, opaque and illiquid system of credit risk distribution. Many investors were either ignorant or imprudent with regard to the risks that they had acquired. Contrary to conventional wisdom, this distribution led to much less diversification than thought and to some surprising concentrations of risks in a number of large and complex financial institutions. Although mortgage market exposures, including those in U.S. sub-prime mortgages, were part of the problem, it later became clear that the problem of bad assets was more widespread.

Administration's Principles for Reform.—On February 25, 2009, President Obama outlined seven broad principles involving transparency, systemic risk management, and investor protection to guide Congress in passing this historic legislation to reform the nation's outdated financial regulatory regime (Remarks by the President After Regulatory Reform Meeting, February 25, 2009).

The first and second principles center on systemic risk. The first is to enforce the strict oversight of financial institutions that pose systemic risks to the markets. The second and related principle is to strengthen markets so they can withstand both system-wide stress and the failure of one or more large institutions. These principles dovetailed with recommendations of the G-30 report for a systemic risk regulator, a concept endorsed by the legislation.

It is crucial that a systemic risk regulator be created so that there is in place an effective early warning mechanism to detect signs of weaknesses in the financial system as soon as they emerge. Also essential is a graduated risk warning framework for ensuring that, in the future, the identification of risks translates into appropriate action (*Financial Regulatory Reform, A New Foundation: Rebuilding Financial Supervision and Regulation, supra*).

A third principle is to encourage transparency in the financial system. This is a goal of several past blueprints for reform. In conjunction with systemic reform, a fourth principle seeks to regulate financial products based on actual data on how actual people make financial decisions.

A fifth principle that must guide financial regulation reform is accountability, starting at the top. This principle incorporates "tone at the top" and the need to create a culture of compliance, effective risk management and sound corporate governance.

A sixth broad principle is to overhaul regulations so they are comprehensive and free of gaps. This principle appears to portend the regulation of hedge funds and other entities that have historically evaded regulation. There is also a growing consensus to regulate large financial firms that may affect systemic market risk.

Finally, the regulatory overhaul must be informed by the recognition that the financial markets are global. This will mean cooperating and coordinating with financial regulators in the European Union and elsewhere (Remarks by the President After Regulatory Reform Meeting, *supra*).

White House Proposal.—In June 2009, the Obama Administration integrated these principles into a comprehensive proposal to Congress calling for sweeping reform of the

¶55

U.S. financial and securities markets (*Financial Regulatory Reform, A New Foundation: Rebuilding Financial Supervision and Regulation, supra*). The proposal identified as key objectives the goals of regulating systemic risk, enhancing transparency and disclosure, delinking executive compensation from excessive risk, improving investor protection and preventing regulatory arbitrage.

Detailed recommendations in the proposal included a measure to establish a Financial Services Oversight Council that would facilitate information sharing and coordination, identify emerging risks, advise the Federal Reserve on the identification of firms whose failure could pose a threat to financial stability due to their combination of size, leverage and interconnectedness, and provide a forum for resolving jurisdictional disputes between regulators.

The plan also recommended expanded regulation of hedge funds and over-the-counter derivatives, including credit default swaps, as well as a new resolution authority to unwind failing financial firms. In addition, the Administration recommended major corporate governance reforms, such as shareholder advisory votes on compensation and enhanced compensation committees.

The proposal envisioned a completely reformed securitization process playing an important role in the financial markets. Further, the plan proposed new authority for the SEC to protect investors, improve disclosure, raise standards and increase enforcement. The SEC would be directed to establish a fiduciary duty for broker-dealers offering investment advice and also to harmonize the regulation of investment advisers and broker-dealers. A new independent regulator, the Consumer Financial Protection Agency, would have authority to ensure that consumer protection regulations are written and enforced.

These and other key elements of the White House proposal informed and shaped the legislation that ultimately emerged more than one year later, the Dodd-Frank Wall Street Reform and Consumer Protection Act.

¶60 Overview

Passage of the Dodd-Frank Wall Street Reform and Consumer Protection Act culminated an 18-month struggle to enact reforms in the wake of the greatest financial crisis since the Great Depression with an historic overhaul of U.S. financial regulation. The landmark legislation touches many aspects of banking and securities regulation.

The Dodd-Frank Act institutes far-reaching reforms, including the creation of an independent Bureau of Consumer Financial Protection housed within the Federal Reserve Board and new federal government power to wind down large, failing financial institutions. The Act establishes a 10-member Financial Stability Oversight Council to oversee systemic risk, strengthens regulation of financial holding companies and abolishes the Office of Thrift Supervision (OTS), transferring its functions to the Federal Reserve Board (Fed), Office of the Comptroller of the Currency (OCC) and Federal Deposit Insurance Corporation (FDIC).

The Act includes significant limitations on proprietary trading and sponsoring or investing in hedge funds or private equity funds by banking entities through the Volcker Rule. The legislation also discourages financial institutions from excessive risk-taking by imposing tough new capital and leverage requirements. The Act effectively ends new lending under the Troubled Asset Relief Program. Further, it allows the Government Accountability Office to conduct a one-time audit of the Fed's emergency lending activities during the financial crisis and establishes the Federal Insurance Office to supervise insurance products, other than health insurance, at the federal level.

Other provisions establish strict oversight of the over-the-counter derivatives market, including mandatory clearing and trading and real-time reporting of derivatives trades. The Act also institutes numerous investor protections, including stricter oversight of credit rating agencies, securitization reforms and expanded SEC enforcement powers. Further, the legislation prescribes strong mortgage protections requiring lenders to ensure that their borrowers can repay their loans by establishing a simple federal standard for all home loans.

FINANCIAL STABILITY: Oversight Council.—Title I, Subtitle A (discussed at ¶ 105 et seq.), creates an independent agency charged with monitoring and responding to systemic risks posed by large, complex companies, products and activities. The new Financial Stability Oversight Council, chaired by the Treasury Secretary and composed of key regulators such as the Fed, OCC, FDIC, SEC and CFTC, has the following enumerated purposes: (1) identifying risks to U.S. financial stability that could arise from the financial distress or failure of large, interconnected bank holding companies or nonbank financial companies; (2) promoting market discipline by eliminating expectations on the part of shareholders, creditors and counterparties of those companies that the government will shield them from losses in the event of failure; and (3) responding to emerging threats to the stability of U.S. financial markets.

Office of Financial Research.—Title I, Subtitle B (discussed at ¶ 160 et seq.), establishes an executive agency to collect and standardize data on financial firms and their activities to aid and support the work of the federal financial regulators. The Office of Financial Research, headed by a director appointed by the President for a six-year term, is intended to provide the Council and financial regulators with the data and analytic tools needed to prevent and contain future financial crises by measuring and monitoring systemic risk. The logic behind the Office is that it makes no sense to create a systemic risk regulator when there are no standardized tools for measuring systemic risk.

Additional Fed Authority.—Title I, Subtitle C (discussed at ¶ 190 et seq.), gives additional authority to the Fed to help it carry out its obligation to supervise nonbank financial companies. These additional powers include authority to require reporting by, and examination of, nonbank financial companies and to bring enforcement proceedings against companies for violation of Fed rules. In addition, the Fed must establish heightened prudential standards—including risk-based capital requirements, leverage limits, liquidity requirements, resolution plan and credit exposure report requirements, and concentration limits—for nonbank financial companies and large, interconnected bank holding companies.

ORDERLY LIQUIDATION AUTHORITY.— Title II (discussed at ¶ 505 et seq.) establishes an orderly liquidation authority for large, failing financial institutions. This authority gives the U.S. government a viable alternative to the undesirable choice it faced during the financial crisis: (1) allow a large, complex financial company to file for bankruptcy protection, disrupting markets and damaging the economy; or (2) bail out the company, exposing taxpayers to losses and undermining market discipline. The new orderly liquidation authority allows the FDIC to safely unwind failing nonbank financial

¶60

firms or bank holding companies, an option that was not available during the financial crisis. The process includes several steps intended to discourage the use of this authority. There is a strong presumption that the Bankruptcy Code will continue to apply to most failing financial companies.

SUPERVISION of DEPOSITORY INSTITUTIONS: Transfer of OTS Functions.— Title III (discussed at ¶ 1005 *et seq.*) transfers the functions of the Office of Thrift Supervision to the Office of the Comptroller of the Currency, which will now supervise federal thrifts, to the Federal Deposit Insurance Corporation, which will supervise state-chartered thrifts, and to the Federal Reserve Board, which will supervise thrift holding companies.

Deposit Insurance Reform.—Title III, Subtitle C (discussed at ¶ 1090 *et seq.*), revises the FDIC's assessment base for deposit insurance, maintaining the risk-based nature of the assessment structure but transitioning to a broader assessment base for bank premiums based on total assets (minus tangible equity). The title makes permanent the increase in deposit insurance to $250,000, and makes the increase retroactive to January 1, 2008.

Office of Minority and Women Inclusion.—Title III, Subtitle D (discussed at ¶ 1115), requires each federal agency to establish an Office of Minority and Women Inclusion not later than six months after the date of enactment that will be responsible for all matters of the agency relating to diversity in management, employment and business activities.

PRIVATE FUND ADVISERS.—Title IV (discussed at ¶ 1505 *et seq.*) subjects advisers to hedge funds and other private funds to SEC registration and disclosure requirements. Private fund advisers come under SEC oversight by eliminating the exemption in Advisers Act Section 203(b)(3) for advisers with fewer than 15 clients. Under former law, a hedge fund was counted as a single client, allowing private fund advisers to avoid SEC registration. Among other reforms, the title includes measures that: subject private fund advisers to SEC registration requirements; impose recordkeeping and disclosure duties; clarify the SEC's rulemaking powers; codify the Commission's long-standing position that family offices are not "investment advisers"; raise the asset-under-management threshold for federal regulation of advisers from $25 million to $100 million; and raise the net worth threshold for accredited investor status.

INSURANCE: Federal Insurance Office.—Title V, Subtitle A (discussed at ¶ 2005 *et seq.*), creates a Federal Insurance Office (FIO) within the Treasury Department with authority over all types of insurance, other than health, long-term care and crop insurance. The Office would not be accompanied by the establishment of a national insurance charter. Its functions include collecting information about the insurance industry; monitoring for systemic risk in the insurance industry, including serving in an advisory capacity to the Financial Stability Oversight Council; and administering the Terrorism Risk Insurance Program.

State-Based Insurance Reform.—Title V, Subtitle B (discussed at ¶ 2015 *et seq.*), is intended to reform and modernize two sectors of the commercial insurance marketplace—nonadmitted (surplus lines) insurance and reinsurance—through state-based reforms.

BANK and THRIFT REGULATORY IMPROVEMENTS.— Title VI (discussed at ¶ 2505 *et seq.*) seeks to improve prudential regulation of banks, saving associations and their holding companies. New limits, known as the Volcker Rule, are placed on the amount of money a bank can invest in hedge funds and private equity funds. A new supervisory regime for "securities holding companies" restricts the capital market activities of banks and bank holding companies and imposes concentration limits on large financial firms.

OTC DERIVATIVES.—Title VII (discussed at ¶ 3005 *et seq.*) subjects over-the-counter derivatives to greater oversight. Designed to address the systemic risk to financial markets posed by OTC derivatives, the legislation mandates their regulation under a dual SEC-CFTC regime that emphasizes transparency. Specifically, the legislation gives the CFTC jurisdiction over swaps and gives the SEC oversight over security-based swaps. Oversight of certain prudential issues goes to the prudential regulators.

CLEARING and SETTLEMENT.—Title VIII (discussed at ¶ 3505 *et seq.*) reforms the clearing and settlement activities of financial institutions. The SEC or other supervisory agency with primary jurisdiction over a designated financial market utility must conduct safety and soundness examinations of the utility at least annually and may take enforcement action against it. The Fed can participate in the examinations and may recommend enforcement action against a designated financial market utility. The appropriate financial regulator may examine a financial institution engaged in designated payment, clearing or settlement activities and may enforce the legislation's provisions or its underlying rules and orders against such an institution.

INVESTOR PROTECTION and SECURITIES REGULATION: Investor Protection.—Title IX, Subtitle A (discussed at ¶ 4005 *et seq.*), establishes mechanisms to assist investors in their dealings with the SEC by creating an Office of Investor Advocate and an Ombudsman. It directs the SEC to study the standards of care applicable to broker-dealers and investment advisers giving investment advice to retail customers, and it authorizes the SEC to promulgate rules imposing a fiduciary duty on broker-dealers and investment advisers to protect retail customers. In addition, the subtitle streamlines filing procedures for self-regulatory organizations. Subtitle A also clarifies the authority of the SEC to require investor disclosures before purchase of investment products and services.

Enforcement and Remedies.—Title IX, Subtitle B (discussed at ¶ 4050 *et seq.*), strengthens the SEC's authority to conduct investigations, impose liability on control persons, and assess penalties for violations of the securities laws. It also makes clear that the intent standard in SEC enforcement actions for aiding and abetting is recklessness, and it requires a study regarding the issue of aiding and abetting liability in private actions. Under Subtitle B, the SEC has the authority to restrict pre-dispute mandatory arbitration. The subtitle further enhances incentives and protections for whistleblowers providing information leading to successful SEC enforcement actions. Awards to whistleblowers will range from 10 percent to 30 percent of the amounts collected by the SEC in actions where the SEC obtained monetary sanctions exceeding $1 million. The subtitle also works to protect the confidentiality of whistleblowers.

Credit Rating Agencies.—Title IX, Subtitle C (discussed at ¶ 4180 *et seq.*), institutes reforms to the governance and operations of the credit rating industry. An independent office is established within the SEC dedicated to improving the quality of regulation of credit rating agencies. The Office of Credit Ratings, headed by a person reporting directly to the SEC Chair, is intended to promote accuracy in credit ratings and keep conflicts of interest from unduly influencing ratings.

¶60

Securitization.—Title IX, Subtitle D (discussed at ¶ 4250 *et seq.*), reforms the process of securitization by requiring companies that sell asset-backed securities to retain a portion of the risk. Companies that sell products like mortgage-backed securities are required to keep some "skin in the game" by retaining at least 5 percent of the credit risk. Thus, if the investment collapses, the company that made, packaged and sold the product would lose out right along with the buyers. Subtitle D also requires enhanced disclosure by issuers of asset-backed securities, including data related to the underlying loans or assets.

Executive Compensation and Governance.—Title IX, Subtitles E and G (discussed at ¶ 4290 *et seq.*), institute an array of corporate governance reforms. The provisions are designed to help rein in excessive compensation and shift management's focus from short-term profits to long-term growth and stability by, among other measures, giving shareholders a "say on pay" and proxy access to nominate directors and requiring companies to set "clawback" policies to recover compensation payouts based on inaccurate financial statements. Other reforms include a shareholder advisory vote on executive compensation, greater independence of compensation committees, and disclosure of hedging by directors and employees. In addition, the legislation authorizes SEC rulemaking on shareholder access to proxy materials.

SEC Organization and Funding.—Title IX, Subtitles F and J (discussed at ¶ 4350 *et seq.*), include several provisions designed to improve the SEC's organization, management, funding and overall effectiveness. Subtitle F requires several reports designed to assess SEC performance and provide recommendations for improvements. Subtitle J maintains the role of the Appropriations Committees in setting the SEC's annual budgets on and after fiscal year 2012.

Municipal Securities.—Title IX, Subtitle H (discussed at ¶ 4380 *et seq.*), includes measures to reform the regulation and stability of the municipal securities industry. It requires the registration of municipal financial advisors and subjects them to rules to be promulgated by the Municipal Securities Rulemaking Board, which will be enforced by the SEC.

Public Company Accounting Oversight Board.—Certain provisions in Title IX (discussed at ¶ 4420 *et seq.*) affect the Public Company Accounting Oversight Board (PCAOB). One such provision enhances the PCAOB's ability to access the audit work papers and documentation of foreign public accounting firms when they perform material services on which a registered public accounting firm relies in conducting an audit. Another allows the PCAOB to examine the auditors of broker-dealers. A third provision authorizes the PCAOB to share information with foreign authorities.

Additional Securities Reforms.—Title IX, Subtitle I (discussed at ¶ 4450 *et seq.*), provides additional reforms of the securities regulatory structure and other investor protection measures. It authorizes portfolio margining for accounts that hold both securities and futures. In response to problems related to securities borrowing and lending, the Dodd-Frank Act requires more transparency. It also raises the dollar threshold that triggers a full "material loss review" by federal banking regulators' inspectors general. Subtitle I improves the coordination, activities, flexibility, and accountability of inspectors general at Federal financial agencies. Subtitle I also exempts small issuers (those with less than $75 million in market capitalization) from the external audit of internal controls requirements of Sarbanes-Oxley Section 404(b), and requires studies on the impact of such an exemption and the exemption for mid-sized companies.

BUREAU of CONSUMER FINANCIAL PROTECTION.—Title X (discussed at ¶ 4505 *et seq.*) establishes the Bureau of Consumer Financial Protection (BFCP or Bureau), which will be an independent bureau within the Federal Reserve System. The task of the Bureau is to "regulate the offering and provision of consumer financial products or services under the Federal consumer financial laws." The Bureau has nearly exclusive authority to adopt rules implementing the federal consumer financial protection laws (nearly exclusive because the Federal Trade Commission retains some authority to adopt rules under the Federal Trade Commission Act). The Bureau also has authority to supervise many nonbank companies that provide financial products or services. Its authority extends to all nonbank consumer mortgage loan originators, brokers and servicers, and to mortgage loan modification and foreclosure relief service providers. Also, the BCFP has supervisory authority over any company that is "a larger participant of a market for other consumer financial products or services."

The Bureau has primary supervisory and enforcement authority over larger institutions—those with total assets of more than $10 billion. However, supervisory and enforcement authority over institutions that do not reach that threshold remains with those institutions' prudential regulators. Exclusions from supervision and enforcement are provided for nonfinancial companies, including attorneys, accountants, and real estate brokers, and merchants and retailers that finance the purchase of their nonfinancial consumer products and services under certain conditions and where the nonfinancial company is not significantly engaged in such financing. There is also an exclusion from the authority of the Bureau for automobile dealers.

The Bureau will share with the FTC the ability to adopt and enforce regulations against unfair or deceptive acts or practices. It also will be able to act against abusive acts or practices—those that interfere with a consumer's ability to understand a financial transaction or that take "unreasonable advantage" of a consumer's lack of understanding or belief that the financial company will act in the consumer's best interest. The Bureau is specifically empowered to require specified disclosures and to draft model disclosure forms.

Title X, Subtitle D (discussed at ¶ 4625 *et seq.*), declares that state laws are preempted only to the extent that they are inconsistent with federal law and that state laws offering higher degrees of protection to consumers are not considered to be inconsistent. However, it also establishes that different preemption standards will apply for national banks and federal savings associations. State attorneys general are given the power to enforce the Dodd-Frank Act and the Bureau's regulations in either federal or state court.

STRENGTHENING the FEDERAL RESERVE.—Title XI (discussed at ¶ 5005 *et seq.*) is intended to strengthen the Federal Reserve System, increase transparency and eliminate conflicts of interest. The Federal Reserve will be able to make emergency loans only through widely available programs approved by the Secretary of the Treasury, and not to individual firms. FDIC programs to guarantee short-term debt during financial crises will be limited to solvent depository institutions and their holding companies, and can be created only after meeting several conditions including Congressional approval. The GAO is also to conduct a one-time audit of all loans and other

¶60

financial assistance provided by the Federal Reserve Board between Dec. 1, 2007, and the date of enactment of the Dodd-Frank Act.

ACCESS to MAINSTREAM FINANCE.—Title XII (discussed at ¶ 5505 *et seq.*) encourages initiatives that help Americans who are currently unable to participate fully in mainstream finance to gain access to appropriate financial services and products. This title seeks to expand access to safe and affordable bank accounts, credit and financial information for low-income, minority and other underserved families.

PAY IT BACK ACT.—Title XIII (discussed at ¶ 6005 *et seq.*), the TARP Pay it Back Act, reduces the amount authorized under the Troubled Asset Repurchase Program to $475 billion, from the original $700 billion; prohibits Treasury from using repaid TARP funds; and prohibits Treasury from initiating new programs under TARP.

MORTGAGE REFORM and ANTI-PREDATORY LENDING: Loan Origination Standards.—Title XIV, Subtitle A (discussed at ¶ 6515 *et seq.*), prohibits steering incentives for creditors. For any mortgage loan, the mortgage originator may not receive compensation that varies based on the terms of the loan, other than the amount of the principal. In general, a mortgage originator may not receive an origination fee or charge from any person other than the consumer except bona fide third-party charges. No person other than the consumer who knows, or has reason to know, that the consumer has directly compensated the originator may pay any origination fee or charge except bona fide third-party charges.

Mortgage Standards.—Title XIV, Subtitle B (discussed at ¶ 6545 *et seq.*), sets minimum standards for mortgages by requiring lenders to establish that consumers have a reasonable ability to repay at the time the mortgage is consummated. It provides that certain high-quality, low-cost loans (defined as "qualified mortgages") are presumed to meet this standard.

High-Cost Mortgages.—The Act prescribes standards for points and fees related to high-cost mortgages, open-end consumer credit plans and bona fide discount points and prepayment penalties (discussed at ¶ 6605 *et seq.*).

Office of Housing Counseling.—Title XIV, Subtitle D (discussed at ¶ 6620 *et seq.*), establishes, within the Department of Housing and Urban Development (HUD), the Office of Housing Counseling (OFC). Under Title XIV, a Director of Housing Counseling is appointed by and reports to the HUD Secretary. The director has primary responsibility for all activities and matters relating to homeownership and rental housing counseling.

Mortgage Servicing.—Title XIV, Subtitle E (discussed at ¶ 6675 *et seq.*), provides that a creditor in a consumer credit transaction secured by a first lien on the principal dwelling of the consumer must establish an escrow or impound account for the payment of taxes and hazard insurance and any other applicable required periodic payments or premiums. This provision would not apply to a consumer credit transaction under an open-end credit plan or a reverse mortgage.

Appraisal Activities.—Title XIV, Subtitle F (discussed at ¶ 6700 *et seq.*), includes provisions on appraisal activities. A creditor is prohibited from making a higher-risk mortgage loan without first obtaining a written appraisal of the property to be mortgaged. The appraiser must be certified and licensed, and must conduct a physical property visit of the interior of the mortgaged property. The Act also creates appraisal independence standards.

Mortgage Resolution and Modification.—Title XIV, Subtitles G and H (discussed at ¶ 6730 *et seq.*), include "Emergency Mortgage Relief," in the form of loans to homeowners who lose their jobs, to help make mortgage payments while the homeowner is out of work. The Act also provides $1 billion for a third round of funding for the Neighborhood Stabilization Program to enable state and local governments to finance the purchase and redevelopment of foreclosed homes and residential properties. In addition, the Act authorizes a HUD-administered grant-making program to help entities that provide legal assistance to low- and moderate income recipients on home ownership preservation, foreclosure prevention, and the rights of tenants associated with home foreclosure.

MISCELLANEOUS PROVISIONS.—Titles XV and XVI (discussed at ¶ 7005 *et seq.*) contain several miscellaneous provisions. Most significant among them is the lone provision in Title XVI to address the recharacterization of income as a result of increased exchange-trading of derivatives contracts by clarifying that section 1256 of the Internal Revenue Code does not apply to certain derivatives contracts transacted on exchanges (see ¶ 7010).

Title XV (discussed at ¶ 7015 *et seq.*) requires public disclosure to the SEC of any payment relating to the commercial development of oil, natural gas, and minerals made by any person to the U.S. or a foreign government, and includes as a "payment" taxes, royalties, fees, licenses, production entitlements, bonuses, and other material benefits, as determined by the SEC. The Act also requires disclosure to the SEC by all persons otherwise required to file with the SEC for whom minerals originating in the Democratic Republic of Congo and adjoining countries are necessary to the functionality or production of a product manufactured by such person.

¶65 General Provisions

The Dodd-Frank Wall Street Reform and Consumer Protection Act is divided into sixteen separate titles, each addressing a discrete area of financial reform. Sections 1–6 of the Dodd-Frank Act contain provisions of general applicability.

The Act name and table of contents are provided (Sec. 1 of the Dodd-Frank Wall Street Reform and Consumer Protection Act). Definitions are provided in Act Section 2, which generally incorporates meanings and references in existing law, clarifies ambiguities and accommodates new terminology (Sec. 2 of the Dodd-Frank Act). It defines the following terms:

- affiliate
- appropriate Federal banking agency
- Board of Governors
- Bureau
- Commission
- commodity futures terms
- Corporation
- Council
- credit union

- Federal banking agency
- functionally regulated subsidiary
- primary financial regulatory agency
- prudential standards
- Secretary
- securities terms
- State
- transfer date
- other incorporated definitions

Severability.—A severability provision makes clear that, if any provision in the Dodd-Frank Act is held to be unconstitutional, the remainder of the Act is unaffected (Sec. 3 of the Dodd-Frank Act).

General Effective Date.—Most provisions in the Dodd-Frank Act are subject to the general effective date provision, which states that, unless otherwise specifically provided, the Act and the amendments made by it take effect one day after the date of enactment (Sec. 4 of the Dodd-Frank Act). The President signed the Dodd-Frank Act into law on July 21, 2010. Provisions subject to the general effective date of Section 4 therefore take effect July 22, 2010.

Budgetary Effects.—The budgetary effects of the Dodd-Frank Act, for the purpose of complying with the Statutory Pay-As-You-Go-Act of 2010, are to be determined by reference to the latest statement titled "Budgetary Effects of PAYGO Legislation" for the Act, jointly submitted for printing in the Congressional Record by the Chairmen of the House and Senate Budget Committees (Sec. 5 of the Dodd-Frank Act).

Antitrust Savings Clause.—The Act does not modify, impair or supersede the operation of any of the antitrust laws, unless otherwise specified (Sec. 6 of the Dodd-Frank Act).

▶ **Effective date.** Except as otherwise specifically provided, Act sections and amendments take effect one day after the date of enactment (Sec. 4 of the Dodd-Frank Wall Street Reform and Consumer Protection Act). The President signed the Dodd-Frank Act into law on July 21, 2010. Provisions subject to the general effective date of Section 4 therefore take effect July 22, 2010.

Law source: Law at ¶10,001, ¶10,002, ¶10,003, ¶10,004, ¶10,005 and ¶10,006.

— Sec. 1(a) of the Dodd-Frank Wall Street Reform and Consumer Protection Act, providing the short title of the Act;

— Sec. 1(b), providing the table of contents;

— Sec. 2, defining terms;

— Sec. 3, addressing severability;

— Sec. 5, referencing budgetary effects determination;

— Sec. 6, providing the antitrust savings clause;

— Sec. 4, providing the effective date.

Financial Stability Oversight

FINANCIAL STABILITY OVERSIGHT COUNCIL

¶105 Introduction
¶110 Creation of Council
¶115 Council Authority
¶120 Regulation of Nonbank Financial Companies
¶125 Enhanced Prudential Standards
¶130 Reports
¶135 Companies Ceasing to Be Bank Holding Companies
¶140 Dispute Resolution
¶145 Recommendations to Primary Regulators
¶150 Mitigation of Risks to Financial Stability

OFFICE of FINANCIAL RESEARCH

¶160 Introduction
¶165 Creation of Office
¶170 Purpose, Powers and Duties
¶175 Data Collection and Research Centers
¶180 Funding

ADDITIONAL FED AUTHORITY

¶190 Introduction
¶195 Reports and Examination of Nonbank Financial Companies
¶200 Examination and Enforcement
¶205 Acquisitions
¶210 Management Interlock Prohibition
¶215 Enhanced Supervision and Prudential Standards
¶220 Early Remediation of Financial Distress
¶225 Affiliations
¶230 Safe Harbor
¶235 Leverage and Risk-Based Capital Requirements
¶240 Foreign Firm Access to U.S. Market

¶245 Holding Company Capital Requirement Studies
¶250 International Policy Coordination

FINANCIAL STABILITY OVERSIGHT COUNCIL

¶105 Introduction

Title I of the Dodd-Frank Wall Street Reform and Consumer Protection Act is called the "Financial Stability Act of 2010" (Sec. 101 of the Dodd-Frank Act). The title is designed to monitor and prevent systemic risk to the entire financial system through a combination of holistic oversight, transparency and macro-prudential regulation in coordination with the primary federal financial regulators. Subtitle A, the focus of this subchapter, creates the Financial Stability Oversight Council (Council). Chaired by the Treasury Secretary and consisting of the key financial regulators, the Council will monitor emerging risks to U.S. financial stability, recommend heightened prudential standards for large, interconnected financial companies, and require nonbank financial companies to be supervised by the Board of Governors of the Federal Reserve System (the Fed) if their failure poses a risk to financial stability (S. Rep. No. 111-176, p. 2).

Background.—The regulatory framework was not equipped to handle a financial crisis of the magnitude that occurred. While most interconnected and highly leveraged financial firms were subject to some form of federal regulation, the forms of regulation proved inadequate and inconsistent. On a systemic basis, regulators did not take into account the harm that large, interconnected, and highly leveraged institutions could inflict on the financial system and on the economy if they failed (*Financial Regulatory Reform, A New Foundation: Rebuilding Financial Supervision and Regulation*, Treasury Department (June 17, 2009), at FED. BANK. L. REP. ¶ 75-201).

The significant size and growth of unsupervised financial activities outside the traditional banking system, in what is termed the "shadow" financial system, made it difficult for regulators or market participants to understand the real dynamics of either bank credit markets or public capital markets. The macro-prudential oversight of system-wide risks requires the integration of insights from different regulatory perspectives, including banks, securities firms and holding companies. It is only through these differing perspectives that there can be a holistic view of developing risks to the financial system (Testimony of FDIC Chair Sheila Bair before the Senate Banking Committee, July 23, 2009).

According to Sen. Susan Collins (R-ME), the legislation implements a strategy that regulates the financial system as a whole, in a holistic way, not just its individual components. To ensure this holistic approach to federal financial regulation, the legislation creates the Council to serve as a systemic-risk regulator. The Council will fill regulatory gaps, facilitate coordination of policy, and identify emerging risks in firms and market activities. Accordingly, the Council will maintain comprehensive oversight of all potential risks to the financial system and has the power to act to prevent or mitigate those risks (Cong. Rec., March 23, 2009, p. S3612, upon the introduction of S. 664, the Financial System Stabilization and Reform Act of 2009, creating a financial stability oversight council on which the current council is modeled).

Although some commenters had suggested that the Fed should play the role of systemic-risk regulator, that is not what the legislation contemplates. In the view of Sen. Collins, the Fed already had enough on its plate and did not need additional, heavy responsibilities. Rather, the creation of an independent council with regulatory agency participation provides an appropriate system of checks and balances to ensure that decisions reflect the various interests of public and private stakeholders (Testimony of FDIC Chair Sheila Bair before the Senate Banking Committee, July 23, 2009). The Fed Chair is a member of the Council, however, and plays a critical role in how the Council discharges its responsibilities. Moreover, nothing in the legislation alters the Fed's role with respect to monetary policy (Cong. Rec., March 23, 2009, p. S3612).

Systemic Risk.—"Systemic risk" means the risk of a significant reduction in the effectiveness of the financial system caused by a chain reaction of failures of major financial institutions. There are two different kinds of systemic risk: (1) the risk of sudden, near-term systemic seizures or cascading failures; and (2) the longer-term risk that the financial system will unintentionally favor large systemically important institutions over smaller, more nimble competitors, reducing the system's ability to innovate and adapt to change (Testimony of SEC Chair Mary Schapiro before the Senate Banking Committee, July 23, 2009).

There are two different kinds of systemic risk regulation: (1) the traditional oversight, regulation, market transparency and enforcement provided by primary regulators that helps keep systemic risk from developing in the first place; and (2) the new macro-prudential regulation designed to identify and minimize systemic risk. The legislation embodies an amalgam of the two types of systemic risk regulation, with new strict prudential standards working in tandem with traditional "block and tackle" oversight and regulation performed by the SEC and other primary federal financial regulators (Testimony of SEC Chair Mary Schapiro, above).

The financial crisis developed as a systemic breakdown of the financial system that triggered massive damages to the real economy. One major cause of this development was the failure of large and interconnected institutions. The financial system is composed of intermediaries, markets and the infrastructure of payment, settlement and trading mechanisms that support them. Intermediaries are connected with each other through direct transactions, as in interbank markets, and through similar investment and financing decisions with third parties such as other intermediaries or end investors. Financial markets, in turn, are connected with each other through the trading activities of financial intermediaries and through end investors active in more than one market.

Systemic risk within the financial system relates to the risk that these interconnections and similarities render emerging financial instability widespread in the system. Even if the original problem seems more contained, important amplification mechanisms can be at work. Systemic risk spreads throughout the financial system through contagion, which is when the failure of one financial intermediary can lead to failures of other financial intermediaries, even when the latter have not invested in the same risks and are not subject to the same original shock as the former. For example, intermediaries' losses can trigger fire sales of already largely illiquid assets, which reduce their values and cause losses to other intermediaries.

Detecting systemic risks early is the task of macro-prudential regulation, which is embodied in the legislation. The old approach focused too much on individual risks and too little on interconnections across intermediaries and markets. In addition, the traditional approach generated a great deal of information about some types of in-

¶105

termediaries but much less on others, including the shadow banking system of hedge funds and other private equity funds. This made it difficult to understand fully the procyclical behavior of the financial system in the aggregate.

Procyclicality refers to the tendency of financial variables to fluctuate around a trend during the economic cycle. Procyclicality of capital occurs when financial institutions are profitable and their strong capital base allows them to take larger positions in the markets. This mechanism has been amplified by mark-to-market accounting. In a mark-to-market environment, an increase in asset prices quickly translates into stronger capital for financial institutions. In turn, this triggers additional demand for assets and a further increase in their prices. Procyclicality in leverage is more subtle. It has been shown that financial institutions' balance sheets expand and contract with the economic cycle (Remarks by Jean-Pierre Landau, Deputy Governor of the Bank of France, at the Bank of Spain's conference on Procyclicality and the Role of Financial Regulation, Madrid, May 4, 2009).

The pervasive problem of procyclicality in the financial system requires efforts across financial sectors. The Council will address these issues and conduct macro-prudential analysis and coordinate oversight of the financial system as a whole (Testimony of Federal Reserve Board Governor Daniel Tarullo before the Senate Banking Committee, July 23, 2009).

More specifically, the legislation answers the challenge of collecting the information that is necessary to identify systemic risks early and break the vicious procyclical cycle of tumbling prices and asset write-downs. It requires combining some micro-level data with aggregate data from components of the financial system. This means covering major types of intermediaries, in particular large and complex ones. To contain systemic risk, macro-prudential regulators need to have a good understanding of all parts of the financial system that are relevant for the risks of contagion, the build-up and unraveling of widespread imbalances, and macro shocks. There must also be a measuring of the interconnectedness among the systemically most important intermediaries.

In addition, the legislation fosters an effective exchange of information between macro-prudential regulators and micro-prudential regulators since this cooperation is an essential element of identifying and containing systemic risk. There will be strong demands on both micro- and macro-prudential regulators to ensure a smooth exchange of information under the post-crisis regulatory regime that the Dodd-Frank Act establishes.

Macro-prudential regulation designed to detect systemic risk and propose remedial action has been devised because, in a highly integrated and complex financial system, micro-prudential regulation alone can no longer guarantee financial stability. The main challenge in systemic risk analysis is therefore to integrate all relevant perspectives, including those of regulators, accountants, securitization experts, rating experts, risk managers and others, to take a holistic view on the system, its dynamics and its interlinkages.

Congressional Intent.—Legislative history appears to indicate that this new regulatory structure is not intended to replace or duplicate the regulation of securities or derivative exchanges that are already subject to regulation by the SEC or the Commodity Futures Trading Commission (CFTC). The Senate Banking Committee Report states that it is not intended that a securities or futures exchange regulated by the SEC and the CFTC that acts as an administrator of a marketplace be considered a significant nonbank financial company, a term used in Title I with respect to counterparty exposure, to the extent the exchange does not act as a counterparty and thus does not create credit exposure.

In addition, a colloquy in the House indicates that, in looking at the statutory criteria for determining whether a financial company should face stricter prudential standards, it is hard to visualize the application of these criteria to derivatives and securities exchanges. Exchanges do not trade, but administer the marketplace where trading occurs. Thus, while derivatives and securities exchanges would technically meet the definition of a financial company under Title I, the House intended the legislation to address the players in the marketplace rather than the administration of the marketplace (Peterson-Frank colloquy, Cong. Rec., Dec. 9, 2009, p. H14425).

Also, in a colloquy with House Financial Services Committee Chair Barney Frank (D-MA), Rep. Mary Jo Kilroy (D-OH) clarified that it is the not the legislation's intent to subject nondepository captive finance companies to strict prudential standards because they do not pose the types of risks that warrant heightened treatment. Nondepository captive finance companies typically provide financing on a nonrevolving basis only to customers and to dealers who sell and lease the products of their parent or affiliate. As such, they are involved in only a narrow scope of financial activity. Equally important, their loans are made on a depreciating asset, a fact taken into account when the loans are entered into. If they are not depository institutions, they have no access to the federal deposit insurance safety net (Kilroy-Frank colloquy, Cong. Rec., Dec. 9, 2009, p. H14431).

Definitions.—Section 102 of the Dodd-Frank Act defines terms used in Title I. The term "bank holding company" has the same meaning as in Bank Holding Company Act (BHCA) Section 2 (12 U.S.C. § 1841). A foreign bank or company treated as a bank holding company under the BHCA, pursuant to Section 8(a) of the International Banking Act of 1978, will be treated as a bank holding company for Title I purposes (Sec. 102(a)(1) of the Dodd-Frank Act).

"Foreign nonbank financial company" means a company (other than a bank holding company) that is: (1) incorporated or organized in a country other than the United States; and (2) predominantly engaged in financial activities (Sec. 102(a)(4)(A) of the Dodd-Frank Act).

"U.S. nonbank financial company" means, with certain exceptions, a company (other than a bank holding company), or a national securities exchange, clearing agency, security-based swap data repository registered with the SEC, or a board of trade designated as a contract market, or a derivatives clearing organization, swap execution facility or a swap data repository registered with the CFTC, that is: (1) incorporated or organized under laws of the United States; and (2) predominantly engaged in financial activities (Sec. 102(a)(4)(B) of the Dodd-Frank Act).

A company is "predominantly engaged in financial activities" if: (1) the annual gross revenues derived by the company and its subsidiaries from activities that are financial in nature (as defined in Bank Holding Company Act Section 4(k)) and, if applicable, from the ownership or control of one or more insured depository institutions, represents 85 percent or more of the company's consolidated annual gross revenues; or (2) the consolidated assets of the company and its subsidiaries related to activities that are financial in nature and, if applicable, related to the ownership or control of one or more

¶105

insured depository institutions, represents 85 percent or more of the company's consolidated assets (Sec. 102(a)(6) of the Dodd-Frank Act).

Economic Impact Study.—The Council Chair must conduct a study of the economic impact of possible financial services regulatory limitations intended to reduce systemic risk. The study must estimate the benefits and costs on capital market efficiency, on the financial sector and on national economic growth of several enumerated limits. Among others, these include: limits on the maximum size of banks, bank holding companies and other large financial institutions; limits on the organizational complexity and diversification of large financial institutions; limits on risk transfer between business units; limits on commingling commercial and financial activities; and segregation requirements between traditional financial activities and trading or other high-risk operations (Sec. 123(a)(1) of the Dodd-Frank Act).

The Council's report must include recommendations for the optimal structure of these limits in order to maximize their effectiveness and minimize their economic impact (Sec. 123(a)(2) of the Dodd-Frank Act). The Council must issue a report to Congress on the results of this study within 180 days of enactment, and not later than every five years thereafter (Sec. 123(b) of the Dodd-Frank Act).

▶ **Effective date.** The provision takes effect one day after the date of enactment (Sec. 4 of the Dodd-Frank Wall Street Reform and Consumer Protection Act).

Law source: Law at ¶10,101, ¶10,102, ¶10,123 and ¶10,004. Committee Report at ¶50,011, ¶54,005 and ¶54,022.

— Sec. 101 of the Dodd-Frank Wall Street Reform and Consumer Protection Act, providing the short title of Title I;
— Sec. 102, defining terms used in Title I;
— Sec. 123, requiring an economic impact study and report;
— Sec. 4, providing the effective date.

¶110 Creation of Council

Section 111 of the Dodd-Frank Wall Street Reform and Consumer Protection Act establishes the Financial Stability Oversight Council, consisting of ten voting members and five advisory members. The Council must meet at least quarterly and must make all decisions by majority vote, unless otherwise specified. The Council may appoint advisory, technical or professional committees to carry out its functions, and any federal department or agency may provide the Council with support services the Council deems advisable.

Membership.—The Council will consist of the following voting members:

- the Treasury Secretary, who will serve as Council Chair;
- the Fed Chair;
- the Comptroller of the Currency;
- the Director of the new Bureau of Consumer Financial Protection;
- the SEC Chair;
- the FDIC Chair;
- the CFTC Chair;
- the Director of the Federal Housing Finance Agency;
- the Chair of the National Credit Union Administration Board; and
- an independent insurance expert appointed by the President, with the Senate's advice and consent (Sec. 111(b)(1) of the Dodd-Frank Wall Street Reform and Consumer Protection Act).

Unless otherwise specified, the Council must make all its decisions by a majority vote of the members then serving (Sec. 111(f) of the Dodd-Frank Act). Nonvoting members, who serve in an advisory capacity, include: the Director of the Office of Financial Research (discussed at ¶ 160); the Director of the Federal Insurance Office (discussed at ¶ 2010); a designated state insurance commissioner; a designated state banking supervisor; and a designated state securities commissioner (Sec. 111(b)(2) of the Dodd-Frank Act).

The independent member having insurance expertise must serve for a term of six years. The nonvoting members who are designated state regulators must serve for a term of two years. Any vacancy on the Council must be filled in the same manner that the original appointment was made. In the event of a vacancy in the office of the head of a member agency or department, and pending the appointment of a successor, the acting head of the member agency or department must serve as a Council member in the place of that agency or department head (Sec. 111(c) of the Dodd-Frank Act).

Meetings, Committees and Support Services.—The Council must meet at the call of the Chair or a majority of the members then serving, but not less frequently than quarterly (Sec. 111(e)(1) of the Dodd-Frank Act). Any federal government employee may be detailed to the Council, and any federal department or agency may provide the Council support services the Council deems advisable (Sec. 111(h) of the Dodd-Frank Act).

The Council may appoint any special advisory, technical or professional committees that may be useful in carrying out its functions, including an advisory committee consisting of state regulators, and the members of those committees may be Council members or other persons, or both (Sec. 111(d) of the Dodd-Frank Act). The Federal Advisory Committee Act (5 U.S.C. App.) does not apply to the Council or to any special advisory, technical or professional committee appointed by the Council, except that, if an advisory, technical or professional committee has one or more members who are not employees of or affiliated with the federal government, the Council must publish a list of the names of the committee members (Sec. 111(g) of the Dodd-Frank Act).

Council members who are also federal officers or employees must serve without compensation in addition to that received for their services as federal officers or employees. Federal employees may be detailed to the Council without reimbursement, and this detail must be without interruption or loss of the employee's civil service status or privilege. Federal employees detailed to the Council are subject to Council oversight during the assignment, but must be compensated by the department or agency from which they were detailed (Sec. 111(i)(1) and (j) of the Dodd-Frank Act). The independent Council member must be compensated according to the executive schedule pay rates for federal employees (5 U.S.C. § 5314, as amended by the Dodd-Frank Act).

Council Funding.—Any expenses of the Council must be treated as expenses of, and paid by, the Office of Financial Research (Sec. 118 of the Dodd-Frank Act). For discussion of the Office of Financial Research, see ¶ 160 *et seq.*

GAO Audit.—The Government Accountability Office (GAO) may audit the Council and any person or entity acting under its authority (Sec. 122(a) of the Dodd-Frank Act). In aid of its audit, the GAO must have access to Council records and other information under the Council's control or under the control of a person acting under the Council's authority. The GAO must also have access to the officers, directors, employees, financial advisors, staff, working groups and agents and representatives of the Council (Sec. 122(b)(1) of the Dodd-Frank Act). The GAO may make and retain copies of any books, accounts and other records to which it has been granted access (Sec. 122(b)(2) of the Dodd-Frank Act).

▶ **Effective date.** The provision takes effect one day after the date of enactment (Sec. 4 of the Dodd-Frank Wall Street Reform and Consumer Protection Act).

Law source: Law at ¶10,111, ¶10,118 and ¶10,122 and ¶10,004. Committee Report at ¶54,040 and ¶54,047.

— Sec. 111(a), of the Dodd-Frank Wall Street Reform and Consumer Protection Act, establishing the Financial Stability Oversight Council;
— Secs. 111(b) and (c), establishing the Council's membership, terms of service and means for filling vacancies;
— Sec. 111(d), providing for appointment of technical and professional advisory committees;
— Sec. 111(e), requiring meetings and providing for rules for conducting business;
— Sec. 111(f), requiring decisions by majority vote, unless otherwise specified;
— Sec. 111(g), excepting Council committees from the Federal Advisory Committee Act;
— Secs. 111(h)–(j), providing for support services, compensation and employees;
— Sec. 118, treating expenses of the Council as expenses of the Office of Financial Research;
— Sec. 122, providing for GAO audits of the Council;
— Sec. 4, providing the effective date.

¶115 Council Authority

The Dodd-Frank Wall Street Reform and Consumer Protection Act enumerates the purposes of the Financial Stability Oversight Council, which include identifying risks to U.S. financial stability that could arise: (1) from the material financial distress or failure, or ongoing activities, of large, interconnected bank holding companies or private funds and other nonbank financial companies; or (2) from outside the financial services marketplace. The Council must also promote market discipline by eliminating expectations on the part of shareholders, creditors and counterparties of those companies that the government will shield them from losses in the event of failure. Finally, the Council must respond to emerging threats to U.S. financial system stability (Sec. 112(a)(1) of the Dodd-Frank Wall Street Reform and Consumer Protection Act).

Duties.—The Dodd-Frank Act enumerates several duties of the Council, including collecting information from member agencies, other financial regulatory agencies, the Federal Insurance Office (see ¶ 2005) and, if necessary to assess risks to the U.S. financial system, directing the Office of Financial Research (see ¶ 160) to collect information from bank holding companies and nonbank financial companies. The Council must provide direction to, and request data and analyses from, the Office to support its work. The Council must also monitor the financial services marketplace to identify threats to financial stability, monitor domestic and international regulatory proposals, facilitate information sharing among the member agencies, and recommend to member agencies general supervisory priorities and principles reflecting the outcome of discussions among the member agencies (Sec. 112(a)(2)(A)–(F) of the Dodd-Frank Act).

In addition, the Council must identify gaps in regulation that could pose risks to U.S. financial stability and require supervision by the Fed for nonbank financial companies that may pose risks to financial stability in the event of their material financial distress or failure. The Council must make recommendations to the Fed concerning the establishment of heightened prudential standards for risk-based capital, leverage, liquidity, contingent capital, resolution plans and credit exposure reports, concentration limits, enhanced public disclosures and overall risk management for nonbank financial companies and large, interconnected bank holding companies (Sec. 112(a)(2)(G)–(I) of the Dodd-Frank Act).

Further, the Council must identify systemically important financial market utilities and payment, clearing and settlement system activities (as defined in Title VIII, discussed at ¶ 3510). The Council must make recommendations to the SEC, CFTC and other primary financial regulatory agencies to apply new or heightened standards and safeguards for financial activities or practices that could create or increase risks of significant liquidity, credit or other problems spreading among bank holding companies, nonbank financial companies and U.S. financial markets. The SEC is the primary financial regulator for registered brokers, dealers, investment companies, investment advisers and clearing agencies (Sec. 112(a)(2)(J) and (K) of the Dodd-Frank Act).

The Council must review and, as appropriate, may submit comments to the SEC and any standard-setting body regarding accounting principles, standards or procedures. The Council must also provide a forum for discussion and analysis of emerging market developments and financial regulatory issues, and for resolution of jurisdictional disputes among member agencies. Finally, the Council must annually report to and testify before Congress (Sec. 112(a)(2)(L)–(N) of the Dodd-Frank Act).

Voting Member Statements; Testimony.—When the Council submits a report required above, each voting member must submit a signed statement to Congress. If the member believes the Council, the government and the private sector are taking all reasonable steps to ensure financial stability and to mitigate systemic risk, the mem-

¶115

ber's statement must declare that belief. If the member does not believe all reasonable steps are being taken, the statement must describe what actions he or she believes should be taken (Sec. 112(b) of the Dodd-Frank Act).

After the Council submits a report required above, the Council Chair must appear before the House Financial Services Committee and the Senate Banking Committee at an annual hearing. The hearing's purpose is to discuss the Council's activities, objectives and plans, and to discuss and answer questions concerning the report (Sec. 112(c) of the Dodd-Frank Act).

Data and Information Gathering.—The Council may request and receive data from the Office of Financial Research, member agencies, and the Federal Insurance Office to carry out its duties (Sec. 112(d)(1) of the Dodd-Frank Act). The Council, acting through that Office, may also require the submission of reports from financial companies to help assess whether a financial company, activity or market poses a threat to U.S. financial stability. Before requiring those reports, the Council must coordinate with the SEC and the CFTC and other appropriate primary financial regulators. Whenever possible, the Council must rely on information already available from these primary regulators. In the case of a foreign nonbank financial company or a foreign-based bank holding company, Congress intends for the Council, acting through the Office of Financial Research, to consult with the applicable foreign regulator for the company and rely on information already being collected, with English translations (Sec. 112(d)(3) of the Dodd-Frank Act).

If the Council cannot determine whether the financial activities of a U.S. nonbank financial company pose a threat to financial stability based on information or reports and discussions with management, the Council may request the Fed to conduct an examination of the company for the sole purpose of determining whether it should be supervised by the Fed. The Fed has specific authority to conduct such an examination (Sec. 112(d)(4) of the Dodd-Frank Act).

The Council, the Office and the other member agencies of the Council must maintain the confidentiality of any data, information and reports submitted by these firms. The submission of any nonpublicly available data or information will not constitute a waiver of, or otherwise affect, any privilege arising under federal or state law, including the rules of any federal or state court to which the data is otherwise subject (Sec. 112(d)(5) of the Dodd-Frank Act).

▶ **Effective date.** The provision takes effect one day after the date of enactment (Sec. 4 of the Dodd-Frank Wall Street Reform and Consumer Protection Act).

Law source: Law at ¶10,112 and ¶10,004. Committee Report at ¶54,041.

— Sec. 112(a) of the Dodd-Frank Wall Street Reform and Consumer Protection Act, stating the Council's purpose and duties;

— Sec. 112(b), authorizing the Council to obtain information;

— Sec. 4, providing the effective date.

¶120 Regulation of Nonbank Financial Companies

The Dodd-Frank Wall Street Reform and Consumer Protection Act authorizes the Financial Stability Oversight Council to determine that a nonbank financial company will be supervised by the Fed and subjected to heightened prudential standards if the Council determines that material financial distress at the company would pose a threat to U.S. financial stability (Secs. 113(a)(1) and (b)(1) of the Dodd-Frank Wall Street Reform and Consumer Protection Act). The Council may also subject a company's financial activities to supervision under the prudential standards if it determines that the activities pose a threat to financial stability and that the company is organized or operated in a way designed to evade the application of the systemic risk provisions (Sec. 113(c) of the Dodd-Frank Act).

Definitions.—"Nonbank financial company" means a U.S. nonbank financial company or a foreign nonbank financial company, as defined below (Sec. 102(a)(4)(C) of the Dodd-Frank Act). "U.S. nonbank financial company" means, with certain exceptions, a company (other than a bank holding company), or a national securities exchange, clearing agency, security-based swap data repository registered with the SEC, or a board of trade designated as a contract market, or a derivatives clearing organization, swap execution facility or a swap data repository registered with the CFTC, that is: (1) incorporated or organized under laws of the United States; and (2) predominantly engaged in financial activities, as defined below (Sec. 102(a)(4)(B) of the Dodd-Frank Act).

"Foreign nonbank financial company" means a company (other than a bank holding company) that is: (1) incorporated or organized in a country other than the United States; and (2) predominantly engaged in financial activities, as defined below (Sec. 102(a)(4)(A) of the Dodd-Frank Act).

A company is "predominantly engaged in financial activities" if (1) the annual gross revenues derived by the company and its subsidiaries from activities that are financial in nature (as defined in Bank Holding Company Act Section 4(k)) and, if applicable, from the ownership or control of one or more insured depository institutions, represents 85 percent or more of the company's consolidated annual gross revenues; or (2) the consolidated assets of the company and its subsidiaries related to activities that are financial in nature and, if applicable, related to the ownership or control of one or more insured depository institutions, represents 85 percent or more of the company's consolidated assets (Sec. 102(a)(6) of the Dodd-Frank Act).

Considerations.—The Council may, by a two-thirds vote, including an affirmative vote by the Chair, determine that a U.S. nonbank financial company will be supervised by the Fed and subjected to heightened prudential standards if the Council determines that material financial distress at the company—or the company's nature, scope, size, scale, concentration, interconnectedness or mix of activities—could pose a threat to U.S. financial stability (Sec. 113(a)(1) of the Dodd-Frank Act).

In making such a determination, the Council must consider:

- the extent of the company's leverage (a typical mutual fund could be an example of a nonbank financial company with a low degree of leverage);
- the extent and nature of its off-balance-sheet exposures;

- the extent and nature of the company's transactions and relationships with other significant nonbank financial companies and bank holding companies;
- the company's importance as a source of credit for households, businesses and state and local governments and as a source of liquidity for the financial system;
- the company's importance as a source of credit for low income, minority or underserved communities, and the impact that its failure would have on the availability of credit in those communities;
- the extent to which assets are managed rather than owned and the extent to which ownership of assets under management is diffuse;
- the company's nature, scope, size, scale, concentration, interconnectedness and mix of activities;
- the degree to which the company is already regulated by one or more primary financial regulator;
- the amount and nature of its financial assets;
- the amount and types of liabilities, including the degree of reliance on short-term funding; and
- any other risk-related factors the Council deems appropriate (Sec. 113(a)(2) of the Dodd-Frank Act).

Size alone should not be dispositive in the Council's determination. In considering the listed factors, the Council should also take into account other indicia of the overall risk posed to U.S. financial stability, including the extent of the nonbank financial company's interconnections with other significant financial companies and the complexity of the nonbank financial company (S. Rep. No. 111-176, pp. 48–49).

Congress does not intend for a Council determination to be based on the exchange functions of securities or futures exchanges regulated by the SEC and the CFTC, to the extent that as part of these functions the exchanges act as administrators of marketplaces and not as counterparties. Further, Congress does not intend the activities of securities and futures exchanges overseen by the SEC and the CFTC that consist of, or occur prior to, trade execution to be considered a clearing, settlement or payment business, provided that these activities do not include functioning as a counterparty (S. Rep. No. 111-176, p. 49).

The Council should consult with the SEC or other primary financial regulator for each nonbank financial company or subsidiary of a nonbank financial company that is being considered for supervision by the Fed before the Council makes any final determination regarding that firm (Sec. 113(g) of the Dodd-Frank Act). In the case of a foreign nonbank financial company, Congress intends for the Council to consult to the extent appropriate with the applicable foreign regulator for the company (S. Rep. No. 111-176, p. 49).

The Council must consider a similar set of factors in the case of a foreign nonbank financial company (Sec. 113(b)(2) of the Dodd-Frank Act).

Notice, Hearing and Judicial Review.—The Council must provide to a nonbank financial company written notice of a proposed determination of the Council, including an explanation of the basis of the proposed determination that the company must be supervised by the Fed and be subject to prudential standards (Sec. 113(e)(1) of the Dodd-Frank Act).

Within 30 days of receipt of any notice of a proposed determination, the nonbank financial company may request, in writing, an opportunity for a written or oral hearing before the Council to contest the proposed determination. Upon receipt of a timely request, the Council must fix a time, not later than 30 days after receipt of the request, and place at which the company may appear, personally or through counsel, to submit written materials or, at the Council's discretion, oral testimony and oral argument (Sec. 113(e)(2) of the Dodd-Frank Act).

Within 60 days of the hearing, the Council must notify the nonbank financial company of its final determination and include a statement of the basis for the decision (Sec. 113(e)(3) of the Dodd-Frank Act). The final determination can be appealed to the federal court for the judicial district in which the home office of the nonbank financial company is located, or in the U.S. District Court for the District of Columbia. The court must, upon review, dismiss the action or direct the final determination to be rescinded. The review of such an action is limited to whether the final determination was arbitrary and capricious (Sec. 113(h) of the Dodd-Frank Act).

If a nonbank financial company does not make a timely request for a hearing, the Council must give the company written notice of its final determination within ten days of the date by which the company may have requested a hearing (Sec. 113(e)(4) of the Dodd-Frank Act).

A nonbank financial company must register with the Fed within 180 days of the Council's final determination that the company poses a systemic risk and must be supervised by the Fed (Sec. 114 of the Dodd-Frank Act).

Anti-Evasion Provisions.—To prevent the evasion of systemic risk supervision, the Council may determine, on a two-thirds vote with the Chair in affirmance, that: (1) material financial distress related to—or the nature, scope, size, scale, concentration, interconnectedness or mix of—a company's financial activities would pose a threat to financial stability; (2) the company is organized or operated in a way designed to evade the application of systemic risk provisions; and (3) the company must be supervised by the Fed and subject to prudential standards (Sec. 113(c)(1) of the Dodd-Frank Act). Upon making such a determination, the Council must submit a report to the appropriate congressional committees detailing its reasons (Sec. 113(c)(2) of the Dodd-Frank Act).

The term "financial activities" for purposes of the anti-evasion provisions: (1) means activities that are financial in nature, as defined by Bank Holding Company Act Section 4(k); (2) includes the ownership or control of one or more insured depository institutions; and (3) does not include internal financial activities conducted by the company or an affiliate, including internal treasury, investment and employee benefit operations (Sec. 113(c)(5) of the Dodd-Frank Act).

The company that is the subject of the anti-evasion determination may establish an intermediate holding company in which its financial activities must be conducted in compliance with any Fed regulations or guidance. The intermediate holding company must be subject to Fed supervision and prudential standards as if the intermediate holding company were a nonbank financial company supervised by the Fed (Sec. 113(c)(3)(A) of the Dodd-Frank Act). Also, the Fed can require a company to establish

¶120

an intermediate holding company subject to its supervision and to prudential standards as if the intermediate holding company were a nonbank financial company supervised by the Fed (Sec. 113(c)(3)(B) of the Dodd-Frank Act).

Reevaluation and Rescission.—The Council must annually reevaluate systemic risk supervision determinations and, for a nonbank financial company supervised by the Fed, rescind any such determination if the Council finds by a two-thirds vote, including an affirmative vote by the Chair, that the company no longer meets the standards for supervision (Sec. 113(d) of the Dodd-Frank Act).

Under an emergency exception, the Council may waive or modify this requirement for a nonbank financial company, if the Council determines, by a two-thirds vote with the Chair affirming, that waiver or modification is necessary or appropriate to prevent or mitigate threats posed by the company to U.S. financial stability. The affected company must be notified as soon as practicable, but not later than 24 hours after granting a waiver or modification. In making a determination, the Council must consult with the appropriate home country supervisor, if any, of a foreign nonbank financial company under consideration for such a determination. Also, the affected company must, on request, be afforded a hearing to contest the waiver or modification. The Council must notify the company of its final determination within 30 days after any hearing and must provide the basis for its decision (Sec. 113(f) of the Dodd-Frank Act).

International Coordination.—In exercising its duties under the systemic risk provisions with respect to foreign nonbank financial companies, foreign-based bank holding companies and cross-border activities and markets, the Council must consult with appropriate foreign regulatory authorities to the extent appropriate (Sec. 113(i) of the Dodd-Frank Act).

▶ **Effective date.** The provisions take effect one day after the date of enactment (Sec. 4 of the Dodd-Frank Wall Street Reform and Consumer Protection Act).

Law source: Law at ¶10,113, ¶10,114 and ¶10,004. Committee Report at ¶54,042 and ¶54,043.

— Sec. 113(a) of the Dodd-Frank Wall Street Reform and Consumer Protection Act, authorizing the Financial Stability Oversight Council to require Fed supervision of U.S. nonbank financial companies;

— Sec. 113(b), granting authority to require Fed supervision of foreign nonbank financial companies;

— Sec. 113(c), prescribing anti-evasion provisions;

— Sec. 113(d), providing for reevaluation and rescission of determinations;

— Sec. 113(e), requiring notice and an opportunity for hearing;

— Sec. 113(f), providing for emergency waivers and modifications;

— Sec. 113(g), requiring consultation with primary financial regulators;

— Sec. 113(h), providing for judicial review;

— Sec. 113(i), requiring coordination with foreign regulatory authorities;

— Sec. 114, requiring nonbank financial companies posing a systemic risk to register with the Fed;

— Sec. 4, providing the effective date.

¶125 Enhanced Prudential Standards

The Financial Stability Oversight Council may make recommendations to the Fed concerning the establishment and refinement of prudential standards and reporting and disclosure requirements applicable to nonbank financial companies supervised by the Fed and large, interconnected bank holding companies (Sec. 115(a)(1) of the Dodd-Frank Wall Street Reform and Consumer Protection Act). These standards and requirements must be more stringent than those applicable to other nonbank financial companies and certain bank holding companies that do not present similar risks to financial stability and they must increase in stringency as appropriate in relation to certain characteristics of the company, including its size and complexity (Sec. 115(a)(1)(A) and (B) of the Dodd-Frank Act).

In making its recommendations, the Council may differentiate among companies that are subject to heightened standards on an individual basis or by category. It may also recommend an asset threshold higher than $50 billion for the application of any particular standard (Sec. 115(a)(2) of the Dodd-Frank Act).

Development of Standards.—The prudential standards recommended by the Council may include:

- risk-based capital requirements;
- leverage limits;
- liquidity requirements;
- resolution plan and credit exposure report requirements;
- concentration limits;
- a contingent capital requirement;
- enhanced public disclosures;
- short-term debt limits; and
- overall risk management requirements (Sec. 115(b)(1) of the Dodd-Frank Act).

The Council must consider several factors in making its recommendations, including those factors considered in determining whether a nonbank financial company should be subject to Fed supervision and prudential standards. These factors include the amounts and types of assets and liabilities, the degree of leverage and the extent of off-balance-sheet exposures, and whether the company owns an insured depository institution (Sec. 115(b)(3) of the Dodd-Frank Act).

The Council must give due regard to the principle of national treatment and competitive equity when recommending prudential standards for foreign nonbank financial companies and foreign-based bank holding companies. The Council must also consider the extent to which these foreign companies are subject on a consolidated basis to home country standards comparable to those applied to financial companies in the United States (Sec. 115(b)(2) of the Dodd-Frank Act).

Contingent Capital.—Contingent capital is a hybrid of debt and equity that is institutionalized by the legislation. There has been concern that contingent capital can reduce core capital. But contingent capital, which automatically converts to equity when a financial institution begins to run out of money, can be an important part of capital structure because it provides a way to decrease dependency on a regulator working out precisely the correct Basel ratio for capital adequacy. Contingent capital creates a cushion of capital that can be converted to equity when necessary. Moreover, creditors will know that there are circumstances when they would bear the burden and would not just be bailed out by government.

Broadly, contingent capital places more risk back on to the financial market rather than on government. In addition, contingent capital gives its holders an incentive to monitor the firm in which they are invested, with the result that movements in the price of the debt on the market would be a source of information for both the firm and its regulators.

With respect to the contingent capital requirement, the Council must conduct a study of the feasibility, benefits, costs and structure of such a requirement and report to Congress within two years after the date of enactment. The study must include an evaluation of the degree to which the requirement would enhance the safety and soundness of companies subject to the requirement, promote financial stability and reduce risks to taxpayers, as well as an evaluation of the characteristics and amounts of contingent capital that should be required. The study must also analyze potential prudential standards that should be used to determine whether a company's contingent capital would be converted to equity in times of financial stress (Sec. 115(c)(1) and (2) of the Dodd-Frank Act).

The study must also evaluate the costs to companies, the effects on the structure and operation of credit and other financial markets, and other economic effects of requiring contingent capital. There must be an additional evaluation of the effects of the requirement on the international competitiveness of companies subject to the requirement and the prospects for international coordination in establishing the requirement. Finally, the study must make recommendations for implementing regulations (Sec. 115(c)(1) of the Dodd-Frank Act).

After submitting the study to Congress, the Council may recommend that the Fed require supervised nonbank financial companies and certain bank holding companies to maintain a minimum amount of contingent capital that is convertible to equity in times of financial stress. In making its recommendations, the Council must consider: (1) an appropriate transition period for implementation of a conversion; (2) the factors used by the Council in making recommendations concerning prudential standards; (3) capital requirements; (4) the study results; and (5) any other factors the Council deems appropriate (Sec. 115(c)(3) of the Dodd-Frank Act).

Resolution Plans and Credit Exposure Reports.—The Council may make recommendations to the Fed concerning the requirement that each nonbank financial company supervised by the Fed and certain bank holding companies report periodically to the Council, the Fed and the FDIC the company's plan for rapid and orderly resolution in the event of material financial distress or failure (Sec. 115(d)(1) of the Dodd-Frank Act).

The Council may also make recommendations to the Fed for requiring reports on: (1) the nature and extent to which the company has credit exposure to other significant nonbank financial companies and significant bank holding companies; and (2) the nature and extent to which other significant nonbank financial companies and signifi-

¶125

cant bank holding companies have credit exposure to that company (Sec. 115(d)(2) of the Dodd-Frank Act).

Concentration Limits and Public Disclosure.—To limit the risks that the failure of any individual company could pose to nonbank financial companies supervised by the Fed or certain bank holding companies, the Council may make recommendations to the Fed to adopt standards to limit those risks, as set forth in Section 165 (discussed at ¶ 215) (Sec. 115(e) of the Dodd-Frank Act).

The concentration standards the Fed must prescribe are designed to limit the risks that the failure of any company could pose to a nonbank financial company or certain bank holding companies. The regulations must prohibit the nonbank financial companies and bank holding companies from having credit exposure to any unaffiliated company that exceeds 25 percent of the company's capital stock and surplus, or any lower amount the Fed may determine to be necessary to mitigate risks to financial stability.

The legislation defines "credit exposure" to mean:

- all extensions of credit to the company, including loans, deposits and lines of credit;
- all repurchase agreements and reverse repurchase agreements, and all securities borrowing and lending transactions with the company to the extent that the transactions create credit exposure for the nonbank financial company or certain bank holding companies;
- all guarantees, acceptances or letters of credit;
- all purchases of or investments in securities issued by the company;
- counterparty credit exposure to the company in connection with a derivative transaction between the nonbank financial company or certain bank holding companies and the company; and
- any other similar transactions that the Fed determines to be a credit exposure (Sec. 165(e)(3) of the Dodd-Frank Act).

The Council may also make recommendations to the Fed to require periodic public disclosures by certain bank holding companies and by nonbank financial companies supervised by the Fed in order to support market evaluation of the risk profile, capital adequacy and risk management capabilities of those firms (Sec. 115(f) of the Dodd-Frank Act).

Finally, the Council may recommend that the Fed require short-term debt limits to mitigate the risks that an over-accumulation of short-term debt could pose to covered bank holding companies, nonbank financial companies supervised by the Fed, or the financial system (Sec. 115(g) of the Dodd-Frank Act).

▶ **Effective date.** The provision takes effect one day after the date of enactment (Sec. 4 of the Dodd-Frank Wall Street Reform and Consumer Protection Act).

Law source: Law at ¶10,115 and ¶10,004. Committee Report at ¶54,044.

— Sec. 115(a) of the Dodd-Frank Wall Street Reform and Consumer Protection Act, stating the purpose of prudential standards;

— Sec. 115(b), providing for the development of prudential standards and listing considerations;

— Sec. 115(c), requiring a study of contingent capital requirement;

¶125

- Sec. 115(d), providing for recommendations concerning resolution plans and credit exposure reports;
- Sec. 115(e)–(g), providing for recommendations concerning concentration limits, enhanced public disclosures and short-term debt limits;
- Sec. 4, providing the effective date.

¶130 Reports

The Financial Stability Oversight Council, acting through the Office of Financial Research (see ¶160), may require certified reports from: (1) bank holding companies with total consolidated assets of $50 billion or more; and (2) nonbank financial companies supervised by the Fed pursuant to a systemic risk determination. The Council may also require these reports from any subsidiary of such a company (Sec. 116(a) of the Dodd-Frank Wall Street Reform and Consumer Protection Act).

The reports are designed to keep the Council informed of: (1) the company's financial condition; (2) its risk management systems; (3) transactions with any subsidiary that is a depository institution; and (4) the extent to which the company's activities could, under adverse circumstances, disrupt the financial markets and affect overall financial stability (Sec. 116(a) of the Dodd-Frank Act).

To mitigate the reporting burden on financial companies, the Council must use existing reports provided to primary domestic and foreign financial regulators to the fullest extent possible, as well as externally audited financial statements. The Council must maintain the reports' confidentiality (Sec. 116(b) of the Dodd-Frank Act).

▶ **Effective date.** The provision takes effect one day after the date of enactment (Sec. 4 of the Dodd-Frank Wall Street Reform and Consumer Protection Act).

Law source: Law at ¶10,116 and ¶10,004. Committee Report at ¶54,045.

- Sec. 116(a) of the Dodd-Frank Wall Street Reform and Consumer Protection Act, requiring certified reports to the Financial Stability Oversight Council;
- Sec. 116(b), requiring the Council to use existing reports to the extent possible and maintain confidentiality;
- Sec. 4, providing the effective date.

¶135 Companies Ceasing to Be Bank Holding Companies

The Dodd-Frank Wall Street Reform and Consumer Protection Act ensures that a bank holding company that could pose a risk to financial stability if it experiences material financial distress will remain supervised by the Fed and subject to prudential standards even if it sells or closes its bank. The Financial Stability Oversight Council must consider if the company meets the standards for determining that a company poses a systemic risk to financial stability by examining such factors as the degree of leverage, the amount and nature of the company's financial assets, and the amount and types of liabilities. The company may request a hearing and appeal to the Council its treatment as a nonbank financial company supervised by the Fed.

Applicability and Treatment.—A bank holding company that could pose a risk to financial stability if it experienced material financial distress will remain supervised by the Fed and subject to the prudential standards authorized by the legislation even if it sells or closes its bank (Sec. 117(b) of the Dodd-Frank Wall Street Reform and Consumer Protection Act). This assurance of continuity would apply to any entity or a successor entity that: (1) was a bank holding company having total consolidated assets equal to or greater than $50 billion as of January 1, 2010; and (2) received financial assistance under or participated in the Capital Purchase Program established by the Troubled Asset Relief Program (TARP) (Sec. 117(a) of the Dodd-Frank Act).

If the entity ceases to be a bank holding company at any time after January 1, 2010, the entity will be treated as a nonbank financial company supervised by the Fed as if the Council had made a determination that the firm posed a systemic risk to financial stability. The firm may request a hearing and appeal to the Council its treatment as a nonbank financial company supervised by the Fed (Sec. 117(b) of the Dodd-Frank Act).

Appeals.—If the firm requests a hearing, the Council must fix a hearing time and place within 30 days of the request (Sec. 117(c)(1) of the Dodd-Frank Act). A Council decision to grant an appeal requires a two-thirds vote, including an affirmative vote by the Chair. Within 60 days after the hearing, the Council must submit a report of its proposed decision and the reasons for its decision to the Senate Banking Committee and the House Financial Services Committee, and may testify before those committees (Sec. 117(c)(2)(A) of the Dodd-Frank Act). Within 60 days of filing a report to its oversight committees, or within 60 days of a hearing by the oversight committee on the report, whichever is later, the Council must notify the firm of its final decision and provide the basis for that decision (Sec. 117(c)(2)(B) of the Dodd-Frank Act).

Each determination must be based on a consideration by the Council of factors listed in Sections 113(a) or (b) (discussed at ¶ 120), as applicable, including:

- the extent of the company's leverage (a typical mutual fund could be an example of a nonbank financial company with a low degree of leverage);
- the extent and nature of its off-balance-sheet exposures;
- the extent and nature of the company's transactions and relationships with other significant nonbank financial companies and bank holding companies;
- the company's importance as a source of credit for households, businesses and state and local governments and as a source of liquidity for the financial system;
- the company's importance as a source of credit for low income, minority or under-served communities, and the impact that its failure would have on the availability of credit in those communities;
- the extent to which assets are managed rather than owned and the extent to which ownership of assets under management is diffuse;
- the company's nature, scope, size, scale, concentration, interconnectedness and mix of activities;
- the degree to which the company is already regulated by one or more primary financial regulator;

¶135

- the amount and nature of its financial assets;
- the amount and types of liabilities, including the degree of reliance on short-term funding; and
- any other risk-related factors the Council deems appropriate (Sec. 117(c)(2)(C) of the Dodd-Frank Act).

If the Council denies an appeal, it must review and reevaluate its decision annually (Sec. 117(c)(3) of the Dodd-Frank Act).

▶ **Effective date.** The provision takes effect one day after the date of enactment (Sec. 4 of the Dodd-Frank Wall Street Reform and Consumer Protection Act).

Law source: Law at ¶10,117 and ¶10,004. Committee Report at ¶54,046.

— Sec. 117(a) of the Dodd-Frank Wall Street Reform and Consumer Protection Act, governing applicability;

— Sec. 117(b), providing for treatment as nonbank financial companies;

— Sec. 117(c), providing for appeals;

— Sec. 4, providing the effective date.

¶140 Dispute Resolution

The Dodd-Frank Wall Street Reform and Consumer Protection Act authorizes a nonbinding dispute resolution function for the Financial Stability Oversight Council. Under the resolution mechanism, the Council must seek to resolve disputes among member agencies about the respective jurisdiction over a particular financial company, activity or product if the agencies, after a good faith effort, cannot resolve the dispute without the Council's intervention (Sec. 119(a) of the Dodd-Frank Wall Street Reform and Consumer Protection Act).

The legislation prescribes the procedures for dispute resolution and makes the Council's recommendation nonbinding on the member agencies that are parties to the dispute (Sec. 119(d) of the Dodd-Frank Act). The Council's recommendation must be by two-thirds vote, be in writing and include an explanation of its underlying reasons (Sec. 119(c) of the Dodd-Frank Act). The Council must attempt to resolve the dispute within a reasonable time after receipt of a dispute resolution request, after considering relevant information provided by the disputants, and by agreeing entirely with one disputant or reaching a compromise position (Sec. 119(b) of the Dodd-Frank Act).

▶ **Effective date.** The provision takes effect one day after the date of enactment (Sec. 4 of the Dodd-Frank Wall Street Reform and Consumer Protection Act).

Law source: Law at ¶10,119 and ¶10,004. Committee Report at ¶54,048.

— Sec. 119 of the Dodd-Frank Wall Street Reform and Consumer Protection Act, authorizing the Council to seek resolution of supervisory jurisdictional disputes among member agencies;

— Sec. 4, providing the effective date.

¶145 Recommendations to Primary Regulators

The Dodd-Frank Wall Street Reform and Consumer Protection Act authorizes the Financial Stability Oversight Council to issue recommendations to the SEC, CFTC and other primary financial regulators to apply new or heightened prudential standards and safeguards for a financial activity or practice conducted by bank holding companies or nonbank financial companies under their jurisdiction. The Council may make such a recommendation if it determines the conduct, scope, nature, size, scale, concentration or interconnectedness of that activity or practice could create or increase the risk of significant liquidity, credit or other problems spreading among bank holding companies and nonbank financial companies, U.S. financial markets, or low income, minority or underserved communities (Sec. 120(a) of the Dodd-Frank Wall Street Reform and Consumer Protection Act).

Procedure and Implementation.—The Council must consult with the relevant primary financial regulators and provide notice to the public and opportunity for comment on any proposed recommendations that the regulators apply new or heightened standards or safeguards for a financial activity or practice (Sec. 120(b)(1) of the Dodd-Frank Act). The new or heightened standards or safeguards must take into account the costs to long-term economic growth and may include prescribing the conduct of the activity or practice in specific ways, such as limiting its scope or applying particular capital or risk management requirements, or prohibiting the activity (Sec. 120(b)(2) of the Dodd-Frank Act).

The primary financial regulator must impose the standards recommended by the Council, or similar standards acceptable to the Council, or explain in writing within 90 days why it chose not to follow the recommendations (Sec. 120(c)(2) of the Dodd-Frank Act).

Reports to Congress.—The Council must report to Congress on any recommendations it issues and the primary regulator's implementation of the recommendations or failure to implement them. If there is no primary regulator for the firm, the report must make legislative recommendations (Sec. 120(d) of the Dodd-Frank Act).

Effect of Rescission.—The Council may recommend to a primary financial regulator that a bank holding company or nonbank financial company, activity or practice no longer requires any heightened standards (Sec. 120(e)(1) of the Dodd-Frank Act). The primary financial regulator may determine whether to keep those standards in effect, and must promulgate regulations to establish a procedure by which entities under its jurisdiction may appeal the determination of the primary financial regulator (Sec. 120(e)(2) of the Dodd-Frank Act).

▶ **Effective date.** The provision takes effect one day after the date of enactment (Sec. 4 of the Dodd-Frank Wall Street Reform and Consumer Protection Act).

Law source: Law at ¶10,120 and ¶10,004. Committee Report at ¶54,049.

— Sec. 120(a) of the Dodd-Frank Wall Street Reform and Consumer Protection Act, authorizing the Financial Stability Oversight Council to issue recommendations to primary financial regulators;

— Sec. 120(b), setting forth the procedure for recommendations;

— Sec. 120(c), governing implementation;

— Sec. 120(d), requiring reports to Congress;

— Sec. 120(e), concerning the effect of rescission of identification;

— Sec. 4, providing the effective date.

¶150 Mitigation of Risks to Financial Stability

Upon determining that a nonbank financial company it supervises or a bank holding company with total consolidated assets of $50 billion or more poses a grave threat to financial stability, the Fed must order the company to: (1) limit its ability to merge with, acquire, consolidate with or otherwise become affiliated with another company; (2) restrict its ability to offer a financial product; (3) terminate certain activities; (4) comply with conditions on the conduct of certain activities; or (5) sell or transfer assets or off-balance-sheet items to unaffiliated entities, if the Fed determines that the other actions are inadequate to mitigate a threat to financial stability (Sec. 121(a) of the Dodd-Frank Wall Street Reform and Consumer Protection Act). To give such orders, the Fed must have an affirmative vote of two-thirds of the voting members of the Financial Stability Oversight Council then serving. This provision is intended to provide additional authority for regulators to address grave threats to financial stability if the prudential standards established by the Dodd-Frank Act would not otherwise do so (S. Rep. No. 111-176, p. 51).

Notice and Hearing.—The Fed, in consultation with the Council, must provide notice and an opportunity for hearing to a company that it is being considered for risk mitigation treatment. The notice must be in writing and must include an explanation of the basis for, and a description of, the proposed mitigatory action (Sec. 121(b)(1) of the Dodd-Frank Act). Within 30 days of receipt of the notice, the company may request, in writing, an opportunity for a written or oral hearing before the Fed to contest the proposed mitigatory action. Upon receipt of a timely request, the Fed must fix, within 30 days, a time and place at which the company may appear, personally or through counsel, to submit written materials. The Fed, at its discretion and in consultation with the Council, may hear oral testimony and oral argument (Sec. 121(b)(2) of the Dodd-Frank Act). Within 60 days of the hearing, the Fed must issue a final decision (Sec. 121(b)(3) of the Dodd-Frank Act).

Considerations.—The Fed and the Council must consider several factors in any decision under Section 121. These factors essentially parallel the factors needed to take a firm into systemic risk supervision, including the degree of leverage, the amount and nature of the company's financial assets, the amount and types of the liabilities, the extent and types of the off-balance sheet exposures, and the extent and types of the company's transactions and relationships with other significant nonbank financial companies and significant bank holding companies. Additionally, the Fed and the Council must consider the company's importance as a source of credit for households, businesses and state and local governments and as a source of liquidity for the financial system. Finally, the company's importance as a source of credit for low-income, minority or underserved communities must be taken into consideration, as well as the impact that the company's failure would have on the availability of credit in those communities (Sec. 121(c) of the Dodd-Frank Act).

Foreign Financial Companies.—The Fed may adopt regulations on the application of these risk mitigatory provisions to supervised foreign nonbank financial companies and foreign-based bank holding companies. In adopting the regulations, the Fed must give due regard to the principles of national treatment and equality of competitive opportunity. The Fed must also take into account the extent to which the foreign nonbank financial company or foreign-based bank holding company is subject on a consolidated basis to home country standards that are comparable to those applied to U.S. financial companies (Sec. 121(d) of the Dodd-Frank Act).

▶ **Effective date.** The provision takes effect one day after the date of enactment (Sec. 4 of the Dodd-Frank Wall Street Reform and Consumer Protection Act).

Law source: Law at ¶10,121 and ¶10,004. Committee Report at ¶54,050.

— Sec. 121(a) of the Dodd-Frank Wall Street Reform and Consumer Protection Act, authorizing the Fed to require subject companies to mitigate risks to financial stability;

— Sec. 121(b), requiring notice and an opportunity for hearing;

— Sec. 121(c), listing considerations in subjecting a company to risk mitigation treatment;

— Sec. 121(d), governing the application of regulations to foreign financial companies;

— Sec. 4, providing the effective date.

OFFICE of FINANCIAL RESEARCH

¶160 Introduction

Title I, Subtitle B, of the Dodd-Frank Wall Street Reform and Consumer Protection Act establishes an executive agency to collect and standardize data on financial firms and their activities to aid and support the work of the federal financial regulators. The Office of Financial Research (Office), headed by a director appointed by the President for a six-year term, will provide the Financial Stability Oversight Council (Council) and financial regulators with the intelligence needed to prevent and contain future financial crises by developing tools for measuring and monitoring systemic risk (Sec. 152 of the Dodd-Frank Wall Street Reform and Consumer Protection Act).

The Office must help the Council fulfill its duties by collecting data on the Council's behalf and providing that data to the Council and member agencies, standardizing the types and formats of data reported and collected, and performing applied research and essential long-term research (Sec. 153(a) of the Dodd-Frank Act). Before requesting a report from any financial company regulated by a member agency, any primary financial regulator or a foreign supervisory authority, the Office must coordinate with that regulator and, whenever possible, rely on information available from the primary regulator. This will mitigate the reporting burden on financial firms (Sec. 154(b)(1)(B) of the Dodd-Frank Act).

Congressional Intent.—The rationale behind the Office is that it makes no sense to pass legislation creating a systemic risk regulator if there are no standardized tools for measuring systemic risk. The Office would not only develop the metrics and tools financial regulators need to monitor systemic risk, it would also help policymakers by conducting studies and providing advice on the impact of government policies on systemic risk. The Office is patterned on an executive agency envisioned by the National Institute of Finance Act of 2010, S. 3005, sponsored by Sen. Jack Reed (D-RI), Chair of the Securities Subcommittee.

At the behest of Sen. Reed, the National Academy of Sciences conducted a study and found that the U.S. currently lacks the technical tools to monitor and manage systemic financial risk with sufficient comprehensiveness and precision. The Academy also found that market efficiency, in addition to regulatory capacity, would be enhanced by improved intelligence about what is going on in the system as a whole. Existing capabilities are not a sufficient foundation for systemic risk management (Cong. Rec., Feb. 4, 2010, p. S496).

According to Sen. Reed, the financial crisis revealed that federal financial regulators do not have the appropriate tools or knowledge to address risks that cut across different markets and sectors of the financial system. Although the bill then under consideration was an important step in filling this huge regulatory gap by establishing centralized systemic risk oversight, he reasoned, any new regulatory structure will be ineffective unless it has a strong, independent and well-funded data, research and analytic capacity to fulfill its mission (Cong. Rec., Feb. 4, 2010, p. S496).

▶ **Effective date.** The provisions take effect one day after the date of enactment (Sec. 4 of the Dodd-Frank Wall Street Reform and Consumer Protection Act).

Law source: Law at ¶10,152, ¶10,153, ¶10,154 and ¶10,004. Committee Report at ¶54,061, ¶54,062 and ¶54,063.

— Sec. 152 of the Dodd-Frank Wall Street Reform and Consumer Protection Act, establishing the Office of Financial Research;

— Sec. 153(a), stating the Office's purpose and duties;

— Sec. 154(b)(1)(B), requiring coordination with primary regulators;

— Sec. 4, providing the effective date.

¶165 Creation of Office

The legislation establishes the Office of Financial Research within the Treasury Department (Sec. 152(a) of the Dodd-Frank Wall Street Reform and Consumer Protection Act). The Office will be headed by a director appointed for a six-year term by the President, with the Senate's advice and consent (Sec. 152(b)(1) and (2) of the Dodd-Frank Act). The director cannot, during his or her term, also serve as the head of any financial regulatory agency (Sec. 152(b)(4) of the Dodd-Frank Act). The director will have sole discretion in how he or she fulfills the responsibilities and duties of the position and exercises the authorities granted by the statute (Sec. 152(b)(5) of the Dodd-Frank Act).

The director, in consultation with the Council Chair, may fix the number of, and appoint and direct, all Office employees (Sec. 152(d)(1) of the Dodd-Frank Act).

Agency Assistance.—Any federal department or agency may provide to the Office, and to any special advisory, technical or professional committees appointed by the Office, any services, funds, facilities, staff and other support services that the Office deems advisable. Any federal government employee may be detailed to the Office without reimbursement, and that detail will be without interruption or loss of civil service status or privilege (Sec. 152(e) of the Dodd-Frank Act).

Temporary and Intermittent Services.—The director may procure temporary and intermittent services under 5 U.S.C. § 3109(b), at rates for individuals that do not exceed the daily equivalent of the annual rate of basic pay prescribed for level V of the Executive Schedule under 5 U.S.C. § 5316 (Sec. 152(f) of the Dodd-Frank Act).

Post-Employment Restriction.—The director and any Office employee with access to the transaction or position data maintained by the Data Center or other business confidential information about financial entities that report to the Office are subject to a non-compete restriction. The Treasury Secretary, with the concurrence of the Director of the Office of Government Ethics, must issue regulations prohibiting the director or staff member from being employed by or providing advice or consulting services to a financial company for a one-year period after last having access to that transaction or position data or business confidential information in the course of official duties, regardless of whether that entity must report to the Office. For staff whose access to business confidential information was limited, the regulations may provide, on a case-by-case basis, for a shorter period of post-employment prohibition, as long as the shorter period does not compromise business confidential information (Sec. 152(g) of the Dodd-Frank Act).

Advisory Committees.—The Office, in consultation with the Council Chair, may appoint any special advisory, technical or professional committees that may be useful in carrying out its functions. The committee members may consist of Office staff, other persons, or both (Sec. 152(h) of the Dodd-Frank Act).

Transitional Period.—The legislation provides for an orderly transitional period as the Office of Financial Research gets underway. The provision attempts to ensure that the Office: (1) has an orderly and organized startup; (2) attracts and retains a qualified workforce; and (3) establishes a comprehensive employee training and benefits programs (Sec. 156(a) of the Dodd-Frank Act).

The Office must submit an annual report to the Senate Banking Committee and the House Financial Services Committee that includes a training and workforce development plan, a workplace flexibilities plan and a recruitment and retention plan (Sec. 156(b) of the Dodd-Frank Act). The reporting requirement will terminate five years after the date of enactment (Sec. 156(c) of the Dodd-Frank Act).

Nothing in the transition provision should be construed to affect a collective bargaining agreement or the rights of employees under 5 U.S.C. Chapter 71 (Sec. 156(d) of the Dodd-Frank Act).

▶ **Effective date.** The provisions take effect one day after the date of enactment (Sec. 4 of the Dodd-Frank Wall Street Reform and Consumer Protection Act).

Law source: Law at ¶10,152, ¶10,156 and ¶10,004. Committee Report at ¶54,061 and ¶54,065.

— Sec 152 of the Dodd-Frank Wall Street Reform and Consumer Protection Act, establishing the Office of Financial Research;

— Sec. 156, providing for an orderly transitional period;

— Sec. 4, providing the effective date.

¶165

¶170 Purpose, Powers and Duties

The purpose of the Office of Financial Research is to support the Financial Stability Oversight Council in fulfilling its duties and to support the Council's member agencies (Sec. 153(a) of the Dodd-Frank Wall Street Reform and Consumer Protection Act). The Office will accomplish this purpose by:

(1) collecting data on the Council's behalf and providing that data to the Council and member agencies;

(2) standardizing the types and formats of data reported and collected;

(3) performing applied research and essential long-term research;

(4) developing tools for risk measurement and monitoring;

(5) performing other related services;

(6) making the results of Office activities available to financial regulatory agencies; and

(7) assisting member agencies in determining the types and formats of data that they may collect (Sec. 153(a) of the Dodd-Frank Act).

The Office would not only develop the metrics and tools financial regulators need to monitor systemic risk, it would also help policymakers by conducting studies and providing advice on the impact of government policies on systemic risk. The Office is patterned on an executive agency envisioned by the National Institute of Finance Act of 2010, S. 3005, sponsored by Sen. Jack Reed (D-RI), Chair of the Securities Subcommittee.

Administrative Powers.—The Office may share data and information, including software that it develops, with the Council, member agencies and the Bureau of Economic Analysis. The shared data, information and software must be maintained with at least the same level of security as is used by the Office and cannot be shared with any individual or entity without the Council's permission (Sec. 153(b)(1) of the Dodd-Frank Act). The Office may also sponsor and conduct research projects (Sec. 153(b)(2) of the Dodd-Frank Act). In addition, the Office may assist, on a reimbursable basis, with financial analyses undertaken at the request of other federal agencies that are not member agencies (Sec. 153(b)(3) of the Dodd-Frank Act).

Rulemaking Powers.—The Office, in consultation with the Council Chair, must issue rules, regulations and orders only to the extent necessary to carry out the purposes and duties described in paragraphs (1), (2) and (7) of subsection (a), listed above (Sec. 153(c)(1) of the Dodd-Frank Act).

Member agencies, in consultation with the Office, must implement these Office regulations to standardize the types and formats of data reported and collected on the Council's behalf. If a member agency fails to implement these regulations within three years after their publication, the Office, in consultation with the Council Chair, may implement the regulations with respect to the financial entities under the member agency's jurisdiction (Sec. 153(c)(2) of the Dodd-Frank Act).

Testimony.—The director must report to and testify before the Senate Committee on Banking, Housing, and Urban Affairs and the House Committee on Financial Services annually on Office activities, including the work of the Data Center and the Research and Analysis Center, and the Office's assessment of significant financial market developments and potential emerging threats to U.S. financial stability (Sec. 153(d)(1) of the Dodd-Frank Act).

No federal officer or agency can require the director to submit this or other congressional testimony for approval, comment or review prior to its submission. Any such testimony must include a statement that the views expressed are those of the director and do not necessarily represent the President's views (Sec. 153(d)(2) of the Dodd-Frank Act).

Additional Reports.—The director may provide additional reports to Congress concerning U.S. financial stability. The director must notify the Council of any such additional reports (Sec. 153(e) of the Dodd-Frank Act).

Subpoena Powers.—The director may require a financial company, by subpoena, to produce data, but only upon a written finding by the director that: (1) the data is necessary to carry out the Office functions; and (2) the Office has coordinated with the agency as required under Section 154(b)(1)(B)(ii) (discussed at ¶175) (Sec. 153(f)(1) of the Dodd-Frank Act).

Subpoenas must bear the director's signature and will be served by any person or class of persons designated by the director for that purpose (Sec. 153(f)(2) of the Dodd-Frank Act).

In the case of contumacy or failure to obey a subpoena, the subpoena will be enforceable by order of the appropriate federal district court. Any failure to obey the court's order may be punished as a contempt of court (Sec. 153(f)(3) of the Dodd-Frank Act).

▶ **Effective date.** The provision takes effect one day after the date of enactment (Sec. 4 of the Dodd-Frank Wall Street Reform and Consumer Protection Act).

Law source: Law at ¶10,153 and ¶10,004. Committee Report at ¶54,062.

— Sec 153(a) of the Dodd-Frank Wall Street Reform and Consumer Protection Act, stating the purpose of the Office of Financial Research;

— Sec. 153(b), listing the Office's administrative powers;

— Sec. 153(c), describing the Office's rulemaking authority;

— Sec. 153(d), providing for congressional testimony;

— Sec. 153(e), allowing additional reports to Congress;

— Sec. 153(f), describing subpoena powers;

— Sec. 4, providing the effective date.

¶175 Data Collection and Research Centers

The Dodd-Frank Wall Street Reform and Consumer Protection Act establishes two programmatic units within the Office of Financial Research to carry out the Office's programmatic responsibilities. As discussed below, they are the Data Center and the Research and Analysis Center (Sec. 154(a) of the Dodd-Frank Wall Street Reform and Consumer Protection Act).

Data Center.—The Data Center must collect, validate and maintain all data necessary to carry out its duties, as described below. The data assembled must be obtained from member agencies, commercial data providers, publicly available data sources and financial entities (Sec. 154(b)(1)(A) of the Dodd-Frank Act).

Periodic and Other Reports. The Office may, as determined by the Council or by the director in consultation with the Council, require periodic and other reports from any financial company to assess the extent to which a financial activity or financial market in which the company participates, or the financial company itself, poses a threat to U.S. financial stability (Sec. 154(b)(1)(B)(i) of the Dodd-Frank Act).

The legislation includes a provision to mitigate the report burden. Before requiring the submission of a report from any financial company that is regulated by a member agency, any primary financial regulatory agency or a foreign supervisory authority, the Office must coordinate with the agencies and must, whenever possible, rely on information available from those agencies (Sec. 154(b)(1)(B)(ii) of the Dodd-Frank Act).

The Office must promulgate regulations under Section 153(a)(1), (a)(2), (a)(7) and (c)(1) (discussed at ¶170) regarding the type and scope of the data to be collected by the Data Center under this paragraph (Sec. 154(b)(1)(C) of the Dodd-Frank Act).

Publication of Data. The Data Center must prepare and publish, in a manner that is easily accessible to the public, and without disclosing confidential data:

- a financial company reference database;
- a financial instrument reference database; and
- formats and standards for Office data, including standards for reporting financial transaction and position data to the Office (Sec. 154(b)(2)(A) of the Dodd-Frank Act).

Catalog of Entities and Instruments. The Data Center must maintain a catalog of the financial entities and instruments reported to the Office (Sec. 154(b)(4) of the Dodd-Frank Act).

Information Availability, Security. The Data Center must make data collected and maintained by the Data Center available to the Council and member agencies, as necessary to support their regulatory responsibilities (Sec. 154(b)(5) of the Dodd-Frank Act). The director must ensure that data collected and maintained by the Data Center are kept secure and protected against unauthorized disclosure (Sec. 154(b)(3) of the Dodd-Frank Act).

Other Authority. The Office must, after consultation with the member agencies, provide certain data to financial industry participants and to the general public to increase market transparency and facilitate research on the financial system, to the extent that intellectual property rights are not violated, business confidential information is properly protected, and sharing this information poses no significant threat to the U.S. financial system (Sec. 154(b)(6) of the Dodd-Frank Act).

Research and Analysis Center.—The Research and Analysis Center, on the Council's behalf, must develop and maintain independent analytical capabilities and computing resources. These include capabilities and resources:

- to develop and maintain metrics and reporting systems for risks to U.S. financial stability;

- to monitor, investigate and report on changes in system-wide risk levels and patterns to the Council and Congress;
- to conduct, coordinate and sponsor research to support and improve regulation of financial entities and markets;
- to evaluate and report on stress tests or other stability-related evaluations of financial entities overseen by the member agencies;
- to maintain expertise in any areas that may be necessary to support specific requests for advice and assistance from financial regulators;
- to investigate disruptions and failures in the financial markets, report findings and make recommendations to the Council based on those findings;
- to conduct studies and provide advice on the impact of policies related to systemic risk; and
- to promote best practices for financial risk management (Sec. 154(c) of the Dodd-Frank Act).

Report to Congress.—Within two years after the date of enactment, and within 120 days after the end of each subsequent fiscal year, the Office must prepare and submit a report to Congress (Sec. 154(d)(1) of the Dodd-Frank Act). Each report must assess the state of the U.S. financial system, including: (1) an analysis of any threats to U.S. financial stability; (2) the status of the Office's efforts in meeting its mission; and (3) key findings from the research and analysis of the financial system by the Office (Sec. 154(d)(2) of the Dodd-Frank Act).

▶ **Effective date.** The provision takes effect one day after the date of enactment (Sec. 4 of the Dodd-Frank Wall Street Reform and Consumer Protection Act).

Law source: Law at ¶10,154 and ¶10,004. Committee Report at ¶54,063.

— Sec 154(a) of the Dodd-Frank Wall Street Reform and Consumer Protection Act, establishing programmatic units of the Office;
— Sec. 154(b), listing duties of the **Data Center**;
— Sec. 154(c), listing duties of the **Research and Analysis Center**;
— Sec. 154(d), providing for a report to Congress;
— Sec. 4, providing the effective date.

¶180 Funding

The legislation creates a Financial Research Fund within the Treasury to support the operations of the Office of Financial Research (Sec. 155(a)(1) of the Dodd-Frank Wall Street Reform and Consumer Protection Act). Funding provided to the Office, and assessments received by the Office, must be deposited into the new fund (Sec. 155(a)(2) of the Dodd-Frank Act).

Amounts obtained by, transferred to, or credited to the fund must be immediately available to the Office, and must remain available until expended, to pay the Office's expenses in carrying out its duties (Sec. 155(b)(1) of the Dodd-Frank Act). Amounts obtained by, transferred to, or credited to the fund cannot be construed to be government funds or appropriated money (Sec. 155(b)(2) of the Dodd-Frank Act). Similarly, the amounts in the fund are not subject to apportionment for purposes of 31 U.S.C. Chapter 15 or under any other authority (Sec. 155(b)(3) of the Dodd-Frank Act).

The funding for the Office will be in two steps: interim and permanent. The Fed must provide interim funding during the two-year period following the date of enactment (Sec. 155(c) of the Dodd-Frank Act). After this initial two-year period, the Treasury Secretary must establish by regulation, with the Council's approval, an assessment schedule applicable to bank holding companies with total consolidated assets of $50 billion or more and nonbank financial companies supervised by the Fed that takes into account differences among those companies based on considerations for establishing the prudential standards for the companies under Section 115 (discussed at ¶ 125) The assessments must be sufficient to cover the Office's expenses (Sec. 155(d) of the Dodd-Frank Act).

▶ **Effective date.** The provision takes effect one day after the date of enactment (Sec. 4 of the Dodd-Frank Wall Street Reform and Consumer Protection Act).

Law source: Law at ¶10,155 and ¶10,004. Committee Report at ¶54,064.

— Sec. 155(a) of the Dodd-Frank Wall Street Reform and Consumer Protection Act, establishing the Financial Research Fund;

— Sec. 155(b), stating the allowable use of funds;

— Sec. 155(c), providing for interim funding;

— Sec. 155(d), providing for permanent self-funding;

— Sec. 4, providing the effective date.

ADDITIONAL FED AUTHORITY

¶190 Introduction

Title I, Subtitle C, of the Dodd-Frank Wall Street Reform and Consumer Protection Act gives additional authority to the Board of Governors of the Federal Reserve System (the Fed) to help it carry out its obligation under Subtitle A to supervise nonbank financial companies. These additional powers include authority to require reporting by, and examination of, nonbank financial companies (discussed at ¶ 195) and to bring enforcement proceedings against companies for violation of Fed rules (discussed at ¶ 200).

In addition, the Fed must issue heightened prudential standards—including risk-based capital requirements, leverage limits, liquidity requirements, resolution plan and credit exposure report requirements and concentration limits—for nonbank financial companies and large, interconnected bank holding companies (discussed at ¶ 215). The Fed, in consultation with the Financial Stability Oversight Council (Council) and the Federal Deposit Insurance Corporation (FDIC), must prescribe regulations establishing requirements to provide for the early remediation of financial distress of a nonbank financial company supervised by the Fed or a large, interconnected bank holding company (discussed at ¶ 220).

The Fed also must promulgate regulations on behalf of, and in consultation with, the Council specifying the criteria for exempting certain types or classes of U.S. nonbank financial companies or foreign nonbank financial companies from Fed supervision (discussed at ¶ 230).

Further, the federal banking agencies must impose minimum leverage and risk-based capital requirements on a consolidated basis for banks, bank holding companies and nonbank financial firms such as investment banks and private funds that are identified by the Council for enhanced Fed supervision (discussed at ¶ 235).

Rulemaking.—Except as otherwise specified in Subtitles A or C, the Fed must issue final regulations to implement Subtitles A and C, and the amendments made by them, within 18 months after the Dodd-Frank Act's effective date (Sec. 168 of the Dodd-Frank Act).

Regulations and standards imposed under Title I cannot be construed in a manner that would weaken the requirements of any applicable primary financial regulator or any other federal or state agency that otherwise apply. This title, and the regulations or orders prescribed under it, do not divest any such agency of its authority under other applicable law (Sec. 176 of the Dodd-Frank Act).

Avoidance of Duplication.—The Fed must take any action it deems appropriate to avoid imposing requirements under Subtitle C that duplicate requirements for bank holding companies and nonbank financial companies under other provisions of law (Sec. 169 of the Dodd-Frank Act).

▶ **Effective date.** Section 165(e) takes effect three years after the date of enactment (Sec. 165(e)(7) of the Dodd-Frank Wall Street Reform and Consumer Protection Act). Section 171 provides special effective dates and phase-in periods for certain entities and instruments, discussed at ¶235 (Sec. 171(b)(4) of the Dodd-Frank Act). The remaining provisions in Subtitle C take effect one day after the date of enactment (Sec. 4 of the Dodd-Frank Act).

Law source: Law at ¶10,161, ¶10,165, ¶10,168, ¶10,169, ¶10,176 and ¶10,004. Committee Report at ¶54,080, ¶54,087 and ¶54,088.

— Sec. 161 *et seq.* of the Dodd-Frank Wall Street Reform and Consumer Protection Act, giving the Fed additional authority to carry out its supervision duties under Subtitle A;

— Sec. 165(e)(7), providing the effective date for Sec 165(e);

— Sec. 168, imposing a deadline for Fed rulemaking;

— Sec. 169, requiring the Fed to avoid issuing duplicative requirements;

— Sec. 176, stating the rule of construction as to regulations, standards and orders issued under Title I;

— Sec. 4, providing the effective date.

¶195 Reports and Examination of Nonbank Financial Companies

The Dodd-Frank Wall Street Reform and Consumer Protection Act gives the Board of Governors of the Federal Reserve System (the Fed) authority to require reports from, and to examine, nonbank financial companies supervised by the Fed under a Section 113 determination (discussed at ¶ 120) (Secs. 161(a) and (b) of the Dodd-Frank Act). It also provides for coordination with the company's primary financial regulator (Sec. 161(c) of the Dodd-Frank Act).

To the fullest extent possible, the Fed must rely on reports and information that these companies and their subsidiaries have provided to other federal and state regulatory agencies, and on reports of examination of functionally-regulated subsidiaries made by their primary regulators (or in the case of foreign nonbank financial companies, reports provided to the home country supervisor to the extent appropriate) (S. Rep. No. 111-176, p. 53-54).

Reports.—The Fed may require each nonbank financial company that it supervises, and any subsidiary, to submit reports under oath, to keep the Fed informed as to: (1) the financial condition of the company or subsidiary; (2) systems of the company or subsidiary for monitoring and controlling financial, operating and other risks; and (3) the extent to which the company's activities and operations pose a threat to U.S. financial stability (Sec. 161(a)(1)(A) of the Dodd-Frank Act). The report may also address the company's or subsidiary's compliance with the requirements of Dodd-Frank Act Title I (Sec. 161(a)(1)(B) of the Dodd-Frank Act).

The legislation requires the Fed to rely on existing information to ease the reporting burden. The Fed must, to the fullest extent possible, use:

- reports and supervisory information that a nonbank financial company or subsidiary must provide to other federal or state regulatory agencies;
- information otherwise obtainable from federal or state agencies;
- information that must otherwise be reported publicly; and
- externally audited financial statements of the company or subsidiary (Sec. 161(a)(2) of the Dodd-Frank Act).

A Fed-supervised nonbank financial company or subsidiary must, upon request, promptly provide to the Fed any information listed above (Sec. 161(a)(3) of the Dodd-Frank Act).

Examinations.—The Fed may examine any nonbank financial company it supervises, and any subsidiary of that company, to inform the Fed of: (1) the nature of its operations and financial condition; (2) the financial, operational and other risks of the company or subsidiary that may pose a threat to its safety and soundness or to U.S. financial stability; (3) the systems for monitoring and controlling those risks; and (4) the company's or subsidiary's compliance with the requirements of Title I (Sec. 161(b)(1) of the Dodd-Frank Act).

The legislation requires the Fed to rely on existing information to ease the examination burden. To the fullest extent possible, the Fed must rely on reports of examination of any subsidiary depository institution or functionally-regulated subsidiary made by the primary financial regulatory agency for that subsidiary, and on other existing information sources (Sec. 161(b)(2) of the Dodd-Frank Act).

Coordination with Primary Regulator.—The Fed must: (1) provide reasonable notice to, and consult with, the primary financial regulatory agency for any subsidiary before requiring a report or commencing an examination of the subsidiary; and (2) avoid duplication of examination activities, reporting requirements and information requests, to the fullest extent possible (Sec. 161(c) of the Dodd-Frank Act).

▶ **Effective date.** The provision takes effect one day after the date of enactment (Sec. 4 of the Dodd-Frank Wall Street Reform and Consumer Protection Act).

Law source: Law at ¶10,161 and ¶10,004. Committee Report at ¶54,080.

— Sec. 161(a) of the Dodd-Frank Wall Street Reform and Consumer Protection Act, providing for reports by Fed-supervised nonbank financial companies and their subsidiaries;
— Sec. 161(b), providing for examination of Fed-supervised nonbank financial companies and their subsidiaries;
— Sec. 161(c), requiring coordination with the primary financial regulator;
— Sec. 4, providing the effective date.

¶200 Examination and Enforcement

The Dodd-Frank Wall Street Reform and Consumer Protection Act prescribes the Fed's enforcement authority over nonbank financial companies that it supervises. These companies will be subject to the enforcement provisions under Federal Deposit Insurance Act (FDIA) Section 8. If the Fed determines that a depository institution or functionally regulated subsidiary does not comply with the Fed's regulations or otherwise poses a threat to U.S. financial stability, the Fed may recommend to the primary financial regulator that it initiate enforcement proceedings. If the agency does not initiate proceedings within 60 days, the Fed may take the recommended action.

General Authority.—In general, a nonbank financial company supervised by the Fed and any subsidiaries of the company (other than any depository institution subsidiary) is subject to FDIA Section 8(b)–(n) (12 U.S.C. § 1818(b)–(n)), in the same manner and to the same extent as if the company were a bank holding company (Sec. 162(a) of the Dodd-Frank Wall Street Reform and Consumer Protection Act).

Functionally Regulated Subsidiaries.—If the Fed determines that a condition, practice or activity of a depository institution subsidiary or functionally regulated subsidiary of a nonbank financial company supervised by the Fed does not comply with the Fed's regulations or orders, or otherwise poses a threat to U.S. financial stability, the Fed may recommend, in writing, to the primary regulator that the regulator initiate a supervisory action or enforcement proceeding. The recommendation must be accompanied by a written explanation of the Fed's concerns (Sec. 162(b)(1) of the Dodd-Frank Act).

If, within 60 days after the primary financial regulatory agency receives such a recommendation, the primary regulator does not take appropriate action against a subsidiary, the Fed (upon a vote of its members) may take the recommended supervisory or enforcement action as if the subsidiary were a bank holding company subject to Fed supervision (Sec. 162(b)(2) of the Dodd-Frank Act).

Insurance and Resolution Purposes.—Special requirements apply to examinations for insurance and resolution purposes (see Sec. 172 of the Dodd-Frank Act). The FDIC may conduct a special examination of any nonbank financial company supervised by the Fed or bank holding company described in Section 165(a) (discussed at ¶ 215) for the purpose of implementing its authority to provide for orderly liquidation of any such company under Title II (discussed in Chapter 2, at ¶ 520 and ¶ 525) (12 U.S.C. § 1820(b)(3)(A), as amended by the Dodd-Frank Act).

Special examinations are subject to limitations. For example, the FDIC cannot use this power to examine a company that is in a generally sound condition (12 U.S.C.

§ 1820(b)(3)(A), as amended by the Dodd-Frank Act). In addition, before conducting the special examination, the FDIC must review any available and acceptable resolution plan that the company has submitted in accordance with Section 165(d) (discussed at ¶ 215), consistent with the plan's nonbinding effect, and available reports of examination, and must coordinate as much as practicable with the Fed to minimize duplicative or conflicting examinations (12 U.S.C. § 1820(b)(3)(B), as amended by the Dodd-Frank Act).

▶ **Effective date.** The provision takes effect one day after the date of enactment (Sec. 4 of the Dodd-Frank Wall Street Reform and Consumer Protection Act).

Law source: Law at ¶ 10,162, ¶ 10,172 and ¶ 10,004. Committee Report at ¶ 54,081.

— Sec. 162(a) of the Dodd-Frank Wall Street Reform and Consumer Protection Act, subjecting Fed-supervised nonbank financial companies and their subsidiaries to enforcement under 12 U.S.C. § 1818;

— Sec. 162(b)(1), providing for Fed referral of enforcement action against a functionally-regulated subsidiary to the primary financial regulator;

— Sec. 162(b)(2), prescribing Fed back-up authority;

— Sec. 172, authorizing special examinations for insurance and resolution purposes;

— Sec. 4, providing the effective date.

¶205 Acquisitions

The Dodd-Frank Wall Street Reform and Consumer Protection Act imposes restrictions on acquisitions by supervised nonbank financial holding companies. A nonbank financial company supervised by the Fed under Section 113 (discussed at ¶ 120) must be treated as a bank holding company for purposes of Bank Holding Company Act (BHCA) Section 3 (12 U.S.C. § 1842), which governs bank acquisitions (Sec. 163(a) of the Dodd-Frank Wall Street Reform and Consumer Protection Act). A nonbank financial company supervised by the Fed or a bank holding company with total consolidated assets of $50 billion or more cannot acquire direct or indirect ownership or control of any voting shares of a company engaged in nonbanking activities described in BHCA Section 4(k) having total consolidated assets of $10 billion or more without providing advanced written notice to the Fed (Sec. 163(b)(1) of the Dodd-Frank Act). BHCA Section 4(k) lists financial holding company activities that are financial in nature and do not pose a substantial risk to safety or soundness of depository institutions or the financial system generally.

Exemptions.—The prior notice requirement does not apply to the acquisition of shares that would qualify for the exemptions in BHCA Sections 4(c) or 4(k)(4)(E) (12 U.S.C. § 1843(c) and (k)(4)(E)) (Sec. 163(b)(2) of the Dodd-Frank Act).

Notice Procedure.—The notice procedures in BHCA Section 4(j)(1) (12 U.S.C. § 1843(j)(1)) apply to an acquisition of any company (other than an insured depository institution) by a bank holding company with total consolidated assets equal to or greater than $50 billion or a nonbank financial company supervised by the Fed, including any such company engaged in activities described in BHCA Section 4(k) (Sec. 163(b)(3) of the Dodd-Frank Act).

Standards for Review.—In addition to the standards for reviewing acquisitions in BHCA Section 4(j)(2) (12 U.S.C.§ 1843(j)(2)), the Fed must consider the extent to which the proposed acquisition would result in greater or more concentrated risks to global or U.S. financial stability or to the U.S. economy (Sec. 163(b)(4) of the Dodd-Frank Act).

Hart-Scott-Rodino Filings.—Transactions under this provision must, solely for purposes of Clayton Act Section 7A(c)(8) (15 U.S.C. § 18a(c)(8)), be treated as if Fed approval is not required (Sec. 163(b)(5) of the Dodd-Frank Act).

▶ **Effective date.** The provision takes effect one day after the date of enactment (Sec. 4 of the Dodd-Frank Wall Street Reform and Consumer Protection Act).

Law source: Law at ¶10,163 and ¶10,004. Committee Report at ¶54,082.

— Sec. 163(a) of the Dodd-Frank Wall Street Reform and Consumer Protection Act, subjecting Fed-supervised nonbank financial companies to BHCA Sec. 3 governing bank acquisitions;

— Sec. 163(b)(1), imposing a notice requirement for certain acquisitions;

— Sec. 163(b)(2), creating an exemption for certain acquisitions;

— Sec. 163(b)(3), prescribing the notice procedure;

— Sec. 163(b)(4), providing standards for reviewing acquisitions;

— Sec. 163(b)(5), describing treatment of Hart-Scott-Rodino filings;

— Sec. 4, providing the effective date.

¶210 Management Interlock Prohibition

A nonbank financial company supervised by the Fed must be treated as a bank holding company for purposes of the Depository Institutions Management Interlocks Act (12 U.S.C. § 3201 *et seq.*). The Fed cannot, however, exercise the authority provided in Section 7 of that Act (12 U.S.C. § 3207) to permit service by a management official of a Fed-supervised nonbank financial company as a management official of any bank holding company with total consolidated assets equal to or greater than $50 billion, or of any other Fed-supervised, nonaffiliated nonbank financial company (other than to provide a temporary exemption for interlocks resulting from a merger, acquisition or consolidation) (Sec. 164 of the Dodd-Frank Wall Street Reform and Consumer Protection Act).

> **CCH Comment:** Congress did not intend that a registered investment company sponsored by a nonbank financial company be deemed unaffiliated with its sponsor for the purpose of this section (S. Rep. No. 111-176, p. 54).

▶ **Effective date.** The provision takes effect one day after the date of enactment (Sec. 4 of the Dodd-Frank Wall Street Reform and Consumer Protection Act).

Law source: Law at ¶10,164 and ¶10,004. Committee Report at ¶54,083.

— Sec. 164 of the Dodd-Frank Wall Street Reform and Consumer Protection Act, prohibiting management interlocks between certain nonbank financial companies;

— Sec. 4, providing the effective date.

¶215 Enhanced Supervision and Prudential Standards

The Dodd-Frank Wall Street Reform and Consumer Protection Act requires the Fed to issue heightened prudential standards for nonbank financial companies and large, interconnected bank holding companies. To prevent or mitigate risks to U.S. financial stability that could arise from the material financial distress or failure, or ongoing activities, of large, interconnected financial institutions, the Fed must, on its own or pursuant to Council recommendations under Section 115 (discussed at ¶125), establish prudential standards for nonbank financial companies under its supervision and bank holding companies with total consolidated assets of at least $50 billion. These standards and requirements must:

- be more stringent than the standards and requirements applicable to nonbank financial companies and bank holding companies that do not present similar risks to U.S. financial stability; and

- increase in stringency, based on the considerations discussed below in subsection (b)(3) (Sec. 165(a)(1) of the Dodd-Frank Wall Street Reform and Consumer Protection Act).

Tailored Application.—In prescribing more stringent prudential standards under this section, the Fed may, on its own or pursuant to a recommendation by the Council in accordance with Section 115, differentiate among companies on an individual basis or by category, taking into consideration their capital structure, riskiness, complexity, financial activities (including the financial activities of their subsidiaries), size, and any other risk-related factors that the Fed deems appropriate (Sec. 165(a)(2)(A) of the Dodd-Frank Act). The Fed may establish an asset threshold greater than $50 billion for application of any particular standard under subsections (c) through (g) (Sec. 165(a)(2)(B) of the Dodd-Frank Act).

Prudential Standards.—The Fed must establish prudential standards as described above that include:

- risk-based capital requirements and leverage limits (unless the Fed deems these requirements not appropriate);
- liquidity requirements;
- overall risk management requirements;
- resolution plan and credit exposure report requirements; and
- concentration limits (Sec. 165(b)(1)(A) of the Dodd-Frank Act).

The Fed may establish additional prudential standards that include: (1) a contingent capital requirement; (2) enhanced public disclosures; (3) short-term debt limits; and (4) any other requirements the Fed deems appropriate (Sec. 165(b)(1)(B) of the Dodd-Frank Act).

Foreign Financial Companies. In applying the above standards to any foreign nonbank financial company supervised by the Fed or foreign-based bank holding company, the Fed must: (1) give due regard to the principles of national treatment and equality of competitive opportunity; and (2) consider the extent to which the foreign financial company is subject on a consolidated basis to home country standards comparable to those applied to U.S. financial companies (Sec. 165(b)(2) of the Dodd-Frank Act).

Considerations. In prescribing prudential standards, the Fed must consider differences among nonbank financial companies supervised by the Fed and bank holding companies, based on:

- the factors described in Dodd-Frank Act Section 113(a) and (b) (discussed at ¶ 120);
- whether the company owns an insured depository institution;
- the company's nonfinancial activities and affiliations; and
- any other risk-related factors the Fed deems appropriate (Sec. 165(b)(3)(A) of the Dodd-Frank Act).

The Fed must also, to the extent possible, ensure that small changes in the factors listed in Section 113(a) and (b) would not result in sharp, discontinuous changes in the prudential standards established under this provision. In addition, the Fed must consider any recommendations of the Council under Section 115 (discussed at ¶ 125). Finally, the Fed must adapt the required standards as appropriate in light of any predominant line of business of the company for which particular standards may not be appropriate (Sec. 165(b)(3)(B)–(D) of the Dodd-Frank Act).

Consultation. Before imposing prudential standards or other requirements (including notices of deficiencies in resolution plans and more stringent requirements or divestiture orders resulting from those notices) likely to have a significant impact on a functionally regulated subsidiary or depository institution subsidiary of a nonbank financial company supervised by the Fed or a covered bank holding company, the Fed must consult with each Council member that primarily supervises any such subsidiary regarding the standard or requirement in question (Sec. 165(b)(4) of the Dodd-Frank Act).

Report. The Fed must submit an annual report to Congress regarding the implementation of the prudential standards, including their use to mitigate risks to U.S. financial stability (Sec. 165(b)(5) of the Dodd-Frank Act).

Contingent Capital.—The legislation allows the Fed to impose contingent capital requirements. After the Council submits its report to Congress under Section 115(c) (discussed at ¶ 125), the Fed may issue regulations that require each nonbank financial company under its supervision and covered bank holding companies to maintain a minimum amount of contingent capital that is convertible to equity in times of financial stress (Sec. 165(c)(1) of the Dodd-Frank Act). In developing these regulations, the Fed must consider:

- the results of the Council study, and any Council recommendations, under Section 115(c);
- an appropriate transition period for contingent capital implementation;
- the factors described above in subsection (b)(3)(A);
- capital requirements applicable to the affected companies and their subsidiaries; and
- any other factor the Fed deems appropriate (Sec. 165(c)(2) of the Dodd-Frank Act).

Resolution Plan and Credit Exposure Reports.—The legislation mandates periodic reporting on the company's resolution plan and credit exposure. The Fed must require each nonbank financial company under its supervision and covered bank holding company to report periodically to the Fed, the Council and the FDIC the company's plan for rapid and orderly resolution in the event of material financial distress or failure. The plan must include:

- information on how any insured depository institution affiliated with the company is protected from risks arising from any nonbank subsidiary's activities;
- a full description of the company's ownership structure, assets, liabilities and contractual obligations;
- identification of cross-guarantees tied to different securities, major counterparties, and a process for determining to whom the company's collateral is pledged; and
- any other information the Fed and FDIC jointly require (Sec. 165(d)(1) of the Dodd-Frank Act).

The Fed must also require these companies to report periodically to the Fed, the Council and the FDIC on the nature and extent to which: (1) the company has credit exposure to other significant nonbank financial companies and significant bank holding companies; and (2) other significant nonbank financial companies and significant bank holding companies have credit exposure to that company (Sec. 165(d)(2) of the Dodd-Frank Act).

Review and Notice. The Fed and FDIC must review the information provided in these periodic reports (Sec. 165(d)(3) of the Dodd-Frank Act). If they jointly determine, based on this review, that the resolution plan is not credible or would not facilitate the company's orderly resolution under the bankruptcy code (11 U.S.C.), the Fed and FDIC must notify the company, as applicable, of the plan's deficiencies. The company must resubmit the resolution plan within a timeframe determined by the Fed and FDIC, with revisions demonstrating that the plan is credible and would result in an orderly resolution under the bankruptcy code, including any proposed changes in business operations and corporate structure to facilitate the plan's implementation (Sec. 165(d)(4) of the Dodd-Frank Act).

Failure to Resubmit Credible Plan. If a nonbank financial company supervised by the Fed or a covered bank holding company fails to timely resubmit the resolution plan as required under paragraph (4), with such revisions as are required under subparagraph (B), the Fed and the FDIC may jointly impose more stringent capital, leverage, or liquidity requirements, or restrictions on the growth, activities or operations of the company, or any subsidiary, until the company resubmits a plan that remedies the deficiencies (Sec. 165(d)(5)(A) of the Dodd-Frank Act).

Divestiture. The Fed and the FDIC, in consultation with the Council, may order a nonbank financial company supervised by the Fed and a covered bank holding company to divest certain assets or operations identified by the Fed and the FDIC to facilitate the company's orderly resolution under the bankruptcy code in the event of its failure. Divestiture is appropriate if:

- the Fed and the FDIC have jointly imposed more stringent requirements on the company under Section 165(d)(5)(A); and

- the company has failed, within two years after imposition of those requirements, to resubmit the resolution plan with any required revisions (Sec. 165(d)(5)(B) of the Dodd-Frank Act).

Effect on Other Authorities. A resolution plan submitted in accordance with this subsection is not binding on a bankruptcy court, a receiver appointed under Title II, or any other authority authorized or required to resolve the nonbank financial company supervised by the Board, any bank holding company, or a subsidiary or affiliate (Sec. 165(d)(6) of the Dodd-Frank Act).

Private Action. There is no private right of action based on any resolution plan submitted under this provision (Sec. 165(d)(7) of the Dodd-Frank Act).

Rulemaking. Within 18 months after the date of enactment, the Fed and the FDIC must jointly issue final rules implementing this subsection (Sec. 165(d)(8) of the Dodd-Frank Act).

Concentration Limits.—To limit the risks that the failure of any individual company could pose to a nonbank financial company supervised by the Fed or a covered bank holding company, the Fed must prescribe regulations that limit these risks (Sec. 165(e)(1) of the Dodd-Frank Act). The regulations must: (1) prohibit each nonbank financial company supervised by the Fed and covered bank holding company from having credit exposure to any unaffiliated company that exceeds 25 percent of its capital stock and surplus (or any lower amount the Fed deems necessary to mitigate risks to U.S. financial stability) (Sec. 165(e)(2) of the Dodd-Frank Act).

Credit Exposure. "Credit exposure" to a company means:

- all extensions of credit to the company, including loans, deposits, and lines of credit;
- all repurchase agreements and reverse repurchase agreements with the company, and all securities borrowing and lending transactions with the company, to the extent that these transactions create credit exposure for the nonbank financial company supervised by the Fed or covered bank holding company;
- all guarantees, acceptances, or letters of credit (including endorsement or standby letters of credit) issued on the company's behalf;
- all purchases of or investment in securities issued by the company;
- counterparty credit exposure to the company in connection with a derivative transaction between the nonbank financial company supervised by the Fed or covered bank holding company and the company; and
- any other similar transactions that the Fed, by regulation, determines to be a credit exposure (Sec. 165(e)(3) of the Dodd-Frank Act).

Attribution Rule. Any transaction by a Fed-supervised nonbank financial company or a covered bank holding company with any person is a transaction with a company, to the extent that the transaction proceeds are used for the benefit of, or transferred to, that company (Sec. 165(e)(4) of the Dodd-Frank Act).

Rulemaking. The Fed may issue any regulations and orders, including definitions consistent with this section, necessary to administer and carry out this subsection (Sec. 165(e)(5) of the Dodd-Frank Act).

Exemptions. This provision does not apply to any federal home loan bank. The Fed may, by regulation or order, exempt transactions, in whole or in part, from the definition of

¶215

"credit exposure" if the Fed finds that the exemption is in the public interest and is consistent with the purpose of this provision (Sec. 165(e)(6) of the Dodd-Frank Act).

Transition Period. This provision and any related Fed regulations and orders will not take effect until three years after the date of enactment. The Fed may extend the transition period for up to two additional years (Sec. 165(e)(7) of the Dodd-Frank Act).

Enhanced Public Disclosure.—The Fed may issue regulations requiring periodic public disclosures by nonbank financial companies under its supervision and covered bank holding companies to improve market evaluation of the company's risk profile, capital adequacy and risk management capabilities (Sec. 165(f) of the Dodd-Frank Act).

Short-Term Debt Limits.—To mitigate the risks that an over-accumulation of short-term debt could pose to financial companies and to U.S. financial stability, the Fed may issue regulations limiting the amount of short-term debt, including off-balance sheet exposures, that may be accumulated by any covered bank holding company and any nonbank financial company supervised by the Fed (Sec. 165(g)(1) of the Dodd-Frank Act).

Any such limit must be based on the company's short term debt as a percentage of its capital stock and surplus or on any other measure the Fed deems appropriate (Sec. 165(g)(2) of the Dodd-Frank Act). "Short-term debt" means any liabilities with short-dated maturity that the Fed identifies, by regulation, except that the term does not include insured deposits (Sec. 165(g)(3) of the Dodd-Frank Act).

Risk Committee.—The Fed must require each nonbank financial company under its supervision that is a publicly traded company to establish a risk committee within one year after the company receives a notice of final determination under Section 113(d)(3) (discussed at ¶ 120) (Sec. 165(h)(1) of the Dodd-Frank Act).

As for bank holding companies, the Fed must issue regulations requiring each bank holding company that is a publicly traded company and that has total consolidated assets of at least $10 billion to establish a risk committee. The Fed may require each bank holding company that is a publicly traded company and that has total consolidated assets of less than $10 billion to establish a risk committee, as the Fed deems necessary or appropriate to promote sound risk management practices (Sec. 165(h)(2) of the Dodd-Frank Act).

A risk committee required by this subsection must:

- be responsible for overseeing the company's enterprise-wide risk management practices;
- include the number of independent directors that the Fed deems appropriate, based on the nature of operations, size of assets and other appropriate criteria related to the company; and
- include at least one risk management expert having experience in identifying, assessing and managing risk exposures of large, complex firms (Sec. 165(h)(3) of the Dodd-Frank Act).

The Fed must issue final rules to carry out this subsection within one year after the transfer date, to take effect not later than 15 months after the transfer date (Sec. 165(h)(4) of the Dodd-Frank Act).

¶215

Stress Tests.—The Fed must conduct annual analyses in which nonbank financial companies under its supervision and covered bank holding companies are subject to evaluation of whether the companies have the capital, on a total consolidated basis, necessary to absorb losses as a result of adverse economic conditions (Sec. 165(i)(1)(A) of the Dodd-Frank Act). The tests are subject to several enumerated parameters. For example, the Fed must provide for at least three different sets of conditions under which the test will be conducted, including baseline, adverse and severely adverse. In addition, the Fed must require the companies to update their resolution plans, as the Fed deems appropriate, based on the results of the analyses. The Fed may develop and apply any other analytic techniques necessary to identify, measure and monitor risks to U.S. financial stability (Sec. 165(i)(1)(B) of the Dodd-Frank Act).

A nonbank financial company supervised by the Fed and a covered bank holding company must conduct semiannual stress tests. All other financial companies that have total consolidated assets of more than $10 billion and are regulated by a primary federal financial regulatory agency must conduct annual stress tests (Sec. 165(i)(2)(A) of the Dodd-Frank Act). A company required to conduct a stress test must submit a report to the Fed and to its primary regulator at the times and in the format required by the regulator (Sec. 165(i)(2)(B) of the Dodd-Frank Act).

Each federal primary financial regulator, in coordination with the Fed and the Federal Insurance Office, must issue consistent and comparable regulations that: (1) define the term "stress test"; (2) establish methodologies for the conduct of required stress tests that provide for at least three different sets of conditions, including baseline, adverse and severely adverse; (3) establish the form and content of the company's stress test report; and (4) require companies to publish a summary of the results of the required quarterly stress tests (Sec. 165(i)(2)(C) of the Dodd-Frank Act).

Leverage Limit.—The Fed must require a bank holding company with total consolidated assets of at least $50 billion or a nonbank financial company supervised by the Fed to maintain a debt-to-equity ratio of no more than 15 to 1, upon the Council's determination that the company poses a grave threat to U.S. financial stability and that imposing the limit is necessary to mitigate that risk. Nothing in this paragraph applies to a federal home loan bank (Sec. 165(j)(1) of the Dodd-Frank Act).

In making its determination, the Council must consider the factors described in Section 113(a) and (b) (discussed at ¶ 120) and any other risk-related factors it deems appropriate (Sec. 165(j)(2) of the Dodd-Frank Act). The Fed must prescribe regulations to establish procedures and timelines for compliance (Sec. 165(j)(3) of the Dodd-Frank Act). A separate provision requiring federal banking regulators to impose additional leverage limitations is discussed at ¶ 235.

Off-Balance-Sheet Activities.—In the case of any covered bank holding company or nonbank financial company supervised by the Fed, the computation of capital for purposes of meeting capital requirements must consider the company's off-balance-sheet activities (Sec. 165(k)(1) of the Dodd-Frank Act). If the Fed determines that an exemption from this requirement is appropriate, it may exempt a company, or any transaction or transactions engaged in by the company (Sec. 165(k)(2) of the Dodd-Frank Act).

The term "off-balance-sheet activities" means an existing liability of a company that is not currently a balance sheet liability, but may become one upon the happening of some future event, including the following transactions, to the extent that they may create a liability:

- direct credit substitutes in which a bank substitutes its own credit for a third party, including standby letters of credit;
- irrevocable letters of credit that guarantee repayment of commercial paper or tax-exempt securities;
- risk participations in bankers' acceptances;
- sale and repurchase agreements;
- asset sales with recourse against the seller;
- interest rate swaps;
- credit swaps;
- commodities contracts;
- forward contracts;
- securities contracts; and
- any other activities or transactions that the Fed defines by rule (Sec. 165(k)(3) of the Dodd-Frank Act).

▶ **Effective date.** Subsection (e) takes effect three years after the date of enactment (Sec. 165(e)(7) of the Dodd-Frank Wall Street Reform and Consumer Protection Act). The remainder of this provision takes effect one day after the date of enactment (Sec. 4 of the Dodd-Frank Act).

Law source: Law at ¶10,165 and ¶10,004. Committee Report at ¶54,084.

— Sec. 165(a) of the Dodd-Frank Wall Street Reform and Consumer Protection Act, requiring heightened prudential standards for Fed-supervised nonbank financial companies and certain large, interconnected bank holding companies;
— Sec. 165(b), prescribing requirements for heightened prudential standards;
— Sec. 165(c), allowing the Fed to impose contingent capital requirements;
— Sec. 165(d), mandating periodic reporting on a company's resolution plan and credit exposure;
— Sec. 165(e), requiring Fed regulations imposing concentration limits;
— Sec. 165(f), allowing Fed regulations requiring periodic public disclosures;
— Sec. 165(g), authorizing the Fed to impose short-term debt limits;
— Secs. 165(h)–(k), providing for risk committees, stress testing, leverage limit and off-balance-sheet activities;
— Sec. 4, providing the effective date.

¶220 Early Remediation of Financial Distress

The Fed, in consultation with the Council and the FDIC, must prescribe regulations establishing requirements to provide for the early remediation of financial distress of a nonbank financial company supervised by the Fed or a bank holding company described in Section 165(a) (*i.e.*, a "covered bank holding company," as discussed in ¶215). Nothing in this subsection, however, authorizes the provision of financial assistance from the federal government (Sec. 166(a) of the Dodd-Frank Wall Street Reform and Consumer Protection Act).

Purpose.—The purpose of the early remediation requirements is to establish a series of specific remedial actions to be taken by a nonbank financial company supervised by the Fed or a covered bank holding company that is experiencing increasing financial distress, in order to minimize the risk of insolvency and the resulting harm to U.S. financial stability (Sec. 166(b) of the Dodd-Frank Act).

Contents.—The Fed's remediation regulations must define measures of the company's financial condition, including regulatory capital, liquidity measures and other forward-looking indicators (Sec. 166(c)(1) of the Dodd-Frank Act). The regulations must also establish requirements that increase in stringency as the company's financial condition declines, including:

- requirements in the initial stages of financial decline, *e.g.*, limits on capital distributions, acquisitions and asset growth; and
- requirements at later stages of financial decline, *e.g.*, a capital restoration plan and capital-raising requirements, limits on transactions with affiliates, management changes and asset sales (Sec. 166(c)(2) of the Dodd-Frank Act).

  CCH Comment: Congress intended that the requirements take into account the structure and operations of, and any existing regulatory regime applicable to, different types of nonbank financial companies, including whether certain structures impose legal or structural limits on the ability of the nonbank financial company to hold capital (S. Rep. No. 111-176, p. 56).

▶ **Effective date.** The provision takes effect one day after the date of enactment (Sec. 4 of the Dodd-Frank Wall Street Reform and Consumer Protection Act).

Law source: Law at ¶10,166 and ¶10,004. Committee Report at ¶54,085.

— Sec. 166(a) of the Dodd-Frank Wall Street Reform and Consumer Protection Act, requiring Fed regulations imposing early remediation requirements;

— Sec. 166(b), stating the purpose of early remediation requirements;

— Sec. 166(c), prescribing contents of regulations;

— Sec. 4, providing the effective date.

¶225 Affiliations

Nothing in Subtitle C requires a nonbank financial company supervised by the Fed, or a company that controls such a company, to conform its activities to the requirements of Bank Holding Company Act (BHCA) Section 4 (12 U.S.C. § 1843), relating to ownership or control of nonbank companies and engagement in nonbanking activities (Sec. 167(a) of the Dodd-Frank Wall Street Reform and Consumer Protection Act).

Creation of Intermediate Holding Company.—If a nonbank financial company supervised by the Fed conducts activities other than those determined to be financial in nature or incidental thereto under BHCA Section 4(k), the Fed may require the company to establish and conduct all or a portion of those activities determined to be financial in nature or incidental thereto in or through an intermediate holding company established under Fed regulation. The Fed may impose this requirement within 90 days (or any longer period that the Fed deems appropriate) after the nonbank financial company receives notice of the Fed's determination under this provision (Sec. 167(b)(1)(A) of the Dodd-Frank Act).

The Fed must, however, require a nonbank financial company under its supervision to establish an intermediate holding company if the Fed determines that doing so is necessary: (1) to appropriately supervise activities determined to be financial in nature or incidental thereto; or (2) to ensure that Fed supervision does not extend to the company's commercial activities (Sec. 167(b)(1)(B) of the Dodd-Frank Act).

Internal Financial Activities.—Activities determined to be financial in nature or incidental thereto under BHCA Section 4(k) do not include internal financial activities, including internal treasury, investment and employee benefit functions. With respect to any internal financial activity engaged in for the company or an affiliate and a non-affiliate during the year prior to the date of enactment, the company may continue to engage in that activity as long as at least two-thirds of the assets or two-thirds of the revenues generated from the activity are from or attributable to the company or an affiliate, subject to Fed review, to determine whether engaging in the activity presents undue risk to the company or to U.S. financial stability (Sec. 167(b)(2) of the Dodd-Frank Act).

Source of Strength.—A company that directly or indirectly controls an intermediate holding company established under this section must serve as a "source of strength" to its subsidiary intermediate holding company (Sec. 167(b)(3) of the Dodd-Frank Act). The Fed may require such a company, and its officers or directors, to provide reports under oath for purposes of ensuring compliance with this section, including assessing the company's ability to serve as a source of strength to its subsidiary intermediate holding company and enforcing compliance (Sec. 167(b)(4) of the Dodd-Frank Act).

Fed Regulations.—The Fed must issue regulations prescribing the criteria for determining whether to require a nonbank financial company under its supervision to establish an intermediate holding company as described above (Sec. 167(c)(1) of the Dodd-Frank Act).

The Fed may issue regulations to establish restrictions on transactions between an intermediate holding company or a nonbank financial company supervised by the Fed and its affiliates, as necessary to prevent unsafe and unsound practices in connection with transactions between the company, or any subsidiary, and its parent company or affiliates that are not subsidiaries of the company. These regulations cannot, however, restrict or limit any transaction in connection with the bona fide acquisition or lease by an unaffiliated person of assets, goods or services (Sec. 167(c)(2) of the Dodd-Frank Act).

▶ **Effective date.** The provision takes effect one day after the date of enactment (Sec. 4 of the Dodd-Frank Wall Street Reform and Consumer Protection Act).

Law source: Law at ¶10,167 and ¶10,004. Committee Report at ¶54,086.

— Sec. 167(a) of the Dodd-Frank Wall Street Reform and Consumer Protection Act, stating the rule of construction concerning Subtitle C and the impact of BHCA Sec. 4;

— Sec. 167(b), requiring creation of an intermediate holding company for the conduct of financial activities;

— Sec. 167(c)(1), requiring regulations for determining the need for an intermediate holding company;
— Sec. 167(c)(2), allowing regulations restricting certain transactions with affiliates;
— Sec. 4, providing the effective date.

¶230 Safe Harbor

The Dodd-Frank Wall Street Reform and Consumer Protection Act requires the development of criteria for exempting certain types or classes of nonbank financial companies from Fed supervision. Specifically, the Fed must promulgate regulations on behalf of, and in consultation with, the Council specifying the criteria for exempting certain types or classes of U.S. nonbank financial companies or foreign nonbank financial companies from Fed supervision (Sec. 170(a) of the Dodd-Frank Wall Street Reform and Consumer Protection Act).

In developing these criteria, the Fed must consider the factors described in Dodd-Frank Act Section 113(a) and (b) (discussed at ¶ 120) in determining whether a U.S. or foreign nonbank financial company must be supervised by the Fed (Sec. 170(b) of the Dodd-Frank Act).

> **CCH Comment:** Congress intended that these regulations take into account potential duplication between the requirements under this title and Title VIII of the Dodd-Frank Act for financial market utilities (S. Rep. No. 111-176, p. 56). For discussion of Title VIII, see ¶ 3505 *et seq.*

Rule of Construction.—This section cannot be construed to require Fed supervision of a U.S. or foreign nonbank financial company if that company does not meet the Fed's criteria for exemption described above (Sec. 170(c) of the Dodd-Frank Act).

Revisions.—The Fed must, in consultation with the Council, review its exemption criteria regulations at least every five years. Based on the review, the Fed may revise the regulations on behalf of, and in consultation with, the Council to update as necessary the exemption criteria (Sec. 170(d)(1) of the Dodd-Frank Act). Any revisions cannot take effect until two years after the date of their publication in final form (Sec. 170(d)(2) of the Dodd-Frank Act; S. Rep. No. 111-176, p. 56).

Report to Congress.—The Fed Chair and the Treasury Secretary must submit a joint report to the Senate Committee on Banking, Housing, and Urban Affairs and the House Committee on Financial Services within 30 days after issuing final exemption criteria regulations, or any subsequent revision to those regulations. The report must include, at a minimum, the rationale for exemption and empirical evidence to support the exemption criteria (Sec. 170(e) of the Dodd-Frank Act).

▶ **Effective date.** The provision takes effect one day after the date of enactment (Sec. 4 of the Dodd-Frank Wall Street Reform and Consumer Protection Act).

Law source: Law at ¶ 10,170 and ¶ 10,004. Committee Report at ¶ 54,089.

— Sec. 170(a) of the Dodd-Frank Wall Street Reform and Consumer Protection Act, requiring the Fed to establish criteria for exempting certain nonbank financial companies from supervision;
— Sec. 170(b), listing factors to consider in determining whether Fed supervision is necessary;

— Sec. 170(c), stating the rule of construction;

— Sec. 170(d), providing for revision of the exemption criteria;

— Sec. 170(e), requiring a report to Congress after issuing exemption criteria;

— Sec. 4, providing the effective date.

¶235 Leverage and Risk-Based Capital Requirements

The Dodd-Frank Wall Street Reform and Consumer Protection Act includes minimum leverage and risk-based capital requirements for banks, bank holding companies and nonbank financial companies. Section 171, authored by Sen. Susan Collins (R-ME), and inserted by way of amendment on the Senate floor, requires financial firms to have adequate amounts of cash and other liquid assets to survive financial crisis. Federal regulators must impose minimum leverage and risk-based capital requirements on banks, bank holding companies and nonbank financial firms such as investment banks and private funds that are identified by the Financial Stability Oversight Council for enhanced Fed supervision (Cong. Rec., May 10, 2010, p. S3460).

Background and Congressional Intent.—According to Sen. Collins, before this provision, no federal law required regulators to adjust capital standards for risk factors as financial institutions grew in size and engaged in risky practices. The provision ensures that bank holding companies and large nonbanks are held to the same capital and risk standards applied to insured banks in order to protect against excessive leverage that could destabilize the financial system (Cong. Rec., May 10, 2010, p. S3460).

The provision tightens the standards for larger financial institutions by requiring them to meet, at a minimum, the standards that already apply to small banks. According to Sen. Collins, this makes sense because, if a small bank fails, the FDIC can close down that bank over a weekend, allow it to operate, avoid a run on the bank, and deal with it in an orderly way. But if a large bank holding company or nonbank financial firm fails, it is so interconnected with the economy that its failure sets off a cascade of dire economic consequences (Cong. Rec., May 10, 2010, p. S3460).

Senator Dodd's Remarks. According to Sen. Christopher Dodd (D-CT), the heightened standards for leverage and risk-based capital will serve as speed bumps to keep financial companies from growing too large and risky and threatening financial stability. The Collins provision would prevent regulators from weakening risk-based capital and leverage standards. It effectively sets a floor for those standards going forward that would apply to all banks, bank holding companies, and nonbank financial companies supervised by the Fed. The Collins provision also reinforces the legislation's requirement that capital for large, interconnected financial companies should reflect the risks that their failure may pose to financial stability. The financial crisis revealed how dangerously overleveraged many large investment banks and other nonbank financial companies were. The provision will ensure that the largest, most interconnected financial companies maintain a robust level of capital and eliminate gaps in capital standards between banks and other financial companies that could undermine financial stability (Cong. Rec., May 14, 2010, p. S3774).

FDIC Chair Statement. In a May 7, 2010 letter to Sen. Collins, FDIC Chair Shelia Bair described the provision as a critical element in ensuring that U.S. financial institutions hold sufficient capital to absorb losses during future periods of financial stress. With the new resolution authority in the legislation, taxpayers will no longer bail out large financial institutions. This makes it imperative that firms have sufficient capital to stand on their own in times of adversity (Cong. Rec., May 10, 2010, p. S3460, Exhibit 1 (letter to Sen. Collins dated May 7, 2010)).

In the FDIC Chair's view, the crisis also demonstrated the dangers of excessive leverage undertaken by large nonbanks outside of the scope of federal bank regulation. Notable examples included the excessive leverage of the largest investment banks during the run-up to the crisis. To remedy this and prevent regulatory gaps and arbitrage, large nonbank financial institutions deemed to be systemic must be held to the same, or higher, capital standards as those applicable to banks and bank holding companies. The Collins provision accomplishes this goal simply and directly (Cong. Rec., May 10, 2010, p. S3460, Exhibit 1 (letter to Sen. Collins dated May 7, 2010)).

Finally, and more broadly, the crisis identified the dangers of a regulatory mindset focused exclusively on the soundness of individual banks without reference to the big picture. For example, an individual overnight "repo" may be safe, but widespread financing of illiquid securities with overnight repos left the system vulnerable to a liquidity crisis. A financial system-wide view requires regulators, working in conjunction with the Council, to develop capital regulations to address the risks of activities that affect the broader financial system, beyond the bank that is engaging in the activity (Cong. Rec., May 10, 2010, p. S3460, Exhibit 1 (letter to Sen. Collins dated May 7, 2010)). Repos are repurchase agreements with the legal characteristics of both a sale and a secured transaction that economically function as a loan to the counterparty in which the securities purchased serve as collateral for the loan (see SEC Release No. IC-25058 (July 17, 2001).

Leverage Capital Requirements.—The appropriate federal banking agencies must establish minimum leverage capital requirements on a consolidated basis for insured depository institutions, depository institution holding companies and nonbank financial companies supervised by the Fed. The minimum leverage capital requirements established under this paragraph cannot be: (1) less than the "generally applicable leverage capital requirements" (as defined below), which must serve as a floor for any capital requirements the agency may require; or (2) quantitatively lower than the generally applicable leverage capital requirements in effect for insured depository institutions as of the date of enactment (Sec. 171(b)(1) of the Dodd-Frank Wall Street Reform and Consumer Protection Act).

Risk-Based Capital Requirements.—The appropriate federal banking agencies must establish minimum risk-based capital requirements on a consolidated basis for insured depository institutions, depository institution holding companies and nonbank financial companies supervised by the Fed. The minimum risk-based capital requirements established under this paragraph cannot be: (1) less than the "generally applicable risk-based capital requirements" (as defined below), which must serve as a floor for any capital requirements that the agency may require; or (2) quantitatively lower than the generally applicable risk-based capital requirements in effect for insured depository institutions as of the date of enactment (Sec. 171(b)(2) of the Dodd-Frank Act).

¶235

Definitions.—The term "generally applicable leverage capital requirements" means the minimum ratios of tier 1 capital to average total assets, as established by the appropriate federal banking agencies to apply to insured depository institutions under the prompt corrective action regulations implementing Federal Deposit Insurance Act Section 38, regardless of total consolidated asset size or foreign financial exposure (Sec. 171(a)(1)(A) of the Dodd-Frank Act). The term includes the regulatory capital components in the numerator of that capital requirement, average total assets in the denominator of that capital requirement, and the required ratio of the numerator to the denominator (Sec. 171(a)(1)(B) of the Dodd-Frank Act).

The term "generally applicable risk-based capital requirements" means the risk-based capital requirements, as established by the appropriate federal banking agencies to apply to insured depository institutions under the prompt corrective action regulations implementing Federal Deposit Insurance Act Section 38, regardless of total consolidated asset size or foreign financial exposure (Sec. 171(a)(2)(A) of the Dodd-Frank Act). The term includes the regulatory capital components in the numerator of those capital requirements, the risk-weighted assets in the denominator of those capital requirements, and the required ratio of the numerator to the denominator (Sec. 171(a)(2)(B) of the Dodd-Frank Act).

Investments in Subsidiaries.—For purposes of this section, investments in financial subsidiaries that insured depository institutions have to deduct from regulatory capital under federal law need not be deducted from regulatory capital by depository institution holding companies or nonbank financial companies supervised by the Fed unless that capital deduction is required by the Fed or the primary financial regulator in the case of nonbank financial companies (Sec. 171(b)(3) of the Dodd-Frank Act).

Effective Dates and Phase-In.—For debt or equity instruments issued on or after May 19, 2010, this provision is deemed effective as of May 19, 2010 (Sec. 171(b)(4)(A) of the Dodd-Frank Act). For debt or equity instruments issued before May 19, 2010, any regulatory capital deductions required under this section must be phased in incrementally over a three-year period, with the phase-in period to begin on January 1, 2013 (Sec. 171(b)(4)(B) of the Dodd-Frank Act). The capital deductions are not required for debt or equity instruments issued before May 19, 2010 by bank holding companies with total consolidated assets of less than $15 billion and by organizations that were mutual holding companies on May 19, 2010 (Sec. 171(b)(4)(C) of the Dodd-Frank Act).

For bank holding companies that were not supervised by the Fed as of May 19, 2010, the Section 171 requirements will be effective five years after the date of enactment (Sec. 171(b)(4)(D) of the Dodd-Frank Act). Similarly, for bank holding company subsidiaries of foreign banking organizations that have relied on the Fed's Supervision and Regulation Letter SR-01-1 (as in effect on May 19, 2010), the requirements of this section will be effective five years after the date of enactment (Sec. 171(b)(4)(E) of the Dodd-Frank Act).

Exceptions.—This provision does not apply to debt or equity instruments issued to the United States or any U.S. agency or instrumentality under the Emergency Economic Stabilization Act of 2008, and prior to October 4, 2010. Nor does it apply to any federal home loan bank or any small bank holding company subject to the Fed's Small Bank Holding Company Policy Statement, as in effect on May 19, 2010 (Sec, 171(b)(5) of the Dodd-Frank Act).

¶235

Study of Smaller Bank Access to Capital.—The Comptroller General of the United States must conduct a study of access to capital by smaller banks with consolidated assets of $5 billion or less and report to Congress 18 months after enactment summarizing the results of the study, together with recommendations for legislative or regulatory action that would enhance small banks' access to capital in a manner consistent with safety and soundness (Sec. 171(b)(6) of the Dodd-Frank Act).

Activities Posing Financial System Risks.—Subject to the Council's recommendations, in accordance with Dodd-Frank Act Section 120 (discussed at ¶ 145), the federal banking agencies must develop capital requirements applicable to insured depository institutions, depository institution holding companies and nonbank financial companies supervised by the Fed that address the risks posed by the institution's activities, not only to the institution itself, but to other public and private stakeholders in the event of adverse performance, disruption or failure of the institution or the activity (Sec. 171(b)(7)(A) of the Dodd-Frank Act). These rules must address, at a minimum, the risks arising from:

- significant volumes of activity in derivatives, securitized products purchased and sold, financial guarantees purchased and sold, securities borrowing and lending, and repurchase agreements and reverse repurchase agreements;
- concentrations in assets for which the values presented in financial reports are based on models rather than historical cost or prices deriving from deep and liquid two-way markets; and
- concentrations in market share for any activity that would substantially disrupt financial markets if the institution is forced unexpectedly to cease the activity (Sec. 171(b)(7)(B) of the Dodd-Frank Act).

▶ **Effective date.** The provision takes effect one day after the date of enactment (Sec. 4 of the Dodd-Frank Wall Street Reform and Consumer Protection Act). However, for bank holding companies that were not supervised by the Fed as of May 19, 2010, the requirements of this provision will be effective five years after the date of enactment (Sec. 171(b)(4)(D) of the Dodd-Frank Act). Similarly, for bank holding company subsidiaries of foreign banking organizations that have relied on the Fed's Supervision and Regulation Letter SR-01-1 (as in effect on May 19, 2010), the requirements of this provision will be effective five years after the date of enactment (Sec. 171(b)(4)(E) of the Dodd-Frank Act). In the case of certain debt and equity instruments, special phase-in dates apply, as discussed above (see Sec. 171(b)(4)(A)–(C) of the Dodd-Frank Act).

Law source: Law at ¶ 10,171 and ¶ 10,004.

— Sec. 171(a) of the Dodd-Frank Wall Street Reform and Consumer Protection Act, defining terms;

— Sec. 171(b), requiring federal banking agencies to establish minimum capital requirements;

— Sec. 4, providing the effective date.

¶240 Foreign Firm Access to U.S. Market

The Dodd-Frank Wall Street Reform and Consumer Protection Act restricts the access of foreign institutions to the U.S. market. The legislation includes amendments to the International Banking Act of 1978 (12 U.S.C. §3105) concerning the establishment and termination of foreign bank branch offices in the United States. The Dodd-Frank Act also amends the Securities Exchange Act of 1934 (15 U.S.C. § 78o) concerning foreign person registration as a broker or dealer in the United States.

Bank Branch, Acquisition or Subsidiary.—The Fed may consider risk to U.S. financial stability in deciding whether to approve a foreign bank's application to establish a branch or to acquire a commercial lending company. Specifically, the Fed may take into account, for a foreign bank that presents a risk to U.S. financial system stability, whether the bank's home country has adopted, or is making demonstrable progress toward adopting, an appropriate system of financial regulation to mitigate that risk (12 U.S.C. § 3105(d)(3)(E), as added by the Dodd-Frank Wall Street Reform and Consumer Protection Act).

The legislation also amends the standards for terminating a branch or subsidiary in the United States. The Fed, after notice and opportunity for hearing and notice to any appropriate state bank supervisor, may order a foreign bank that operates a state branch or agency or commercial lending company subsidiary in the United States to terminate the activities of the branch, agency or subsidiary if the Fed finds, in the case of a foreign bank that presents a risk to U.S. financial system stability, that the bank's home country has not adopted, or made demonstrable progress toward adopting, an appropriate system of financial regulation to mitigate that risk (12 U.S.C. § 3105(e)(1)(C), as added by the Dodd-Frank Act).

Broker-Dealer Registration.—The SEC may consider the same factor in deciding whether to permit or terminate a foreign person's broker-dealer registration. In determining whether to permit a foreign person or affiliate to register as a U.S. broker or dealer, or succeed to the registration of a U.S. broker or dealer, the Commission may consider whether, for a foreign person or an affiliate that presents a risk to U.S. financial system stability, the person's home country has adopted, or made demonstrable progress toward adopting, an appropriate system of financial regulation to mitigate that risk (Exchange Act Sec. 15(k), as added by the Dodd-Frank Act).

For a foreign person or an affiliate that presents a risk to U.S. financial system stability, the SEC may terminate the person's registration as a broker or dealer in the United States if the Commission determines that the person's home country has not adopted, or made demonstrable progress toward adopting, an appropriate system of financial regulation to mitigate that risk (Exchange Act Sec. 15(l), as added by the Dodd-Frank Act).

▶ **Effective date.** The provision takes effect one day after the date of enactment (Sec. 4 of the Dodd-Frank Wall Street Reform and Consumer Protection Act).

Law source: Law at ¶ 10,173 and ¶ 10,004.

— Sec. 173(a) of the Dodd-Frank Wall Street Reform and Consumer Protection Act, adding 12 U.S.C. § 3105(d)(3)(E);

— Sec. 173(b), adding 12 U.S.C. § 3105(e)(1)(C);

— Sec. 173(c), adding Exchange Act Secs. 15(k) and (l);

— Sec. 4, providing the effective date.

¶245 Holding Company Capital Requirement Studies

The Dodd-Frank Wall Street Reform and Consumer Protection Act calls for two studies by the Comptroller General of the United States relating to holding company capital requirements. The first study must examine the use of hybrid capital instruments to comply with Tier 1 capital requirements. The second study must examine capital requirements for U.S. intermediate holding companies of foreign banks (Sec. 174 of the Dodd-Frank Wall Street Reform and Consumer Protection Act).

Hybrid Capital Instruments.—The Comptroller General, in consultation with the Fed, the Comptroller of the Currency, and the FDIC, must conduct a study of the use of hybrid capital instruments as a component of Tier 1 capital for banking institutions and bank holding companies. The study must consider:

- the current use of hybrid capital instruments, such as trust preferred shares, as a component of Tier 1 capital;
- the differences between the components of capital permitted for insured depository institutions and those permitted for firms that control insured depository institutions;
- the benefits and risks of allowing the use of hybrid capital instruments to comply with Tier 1 capital requirements;
- the economic impact of prohibiting the use of these instruments for Tier 1;
- the consequences of disqualifying trust preferred instruments, and whether doing so could lead to the failure or undercapitalization of existing banking organizations;
- the international competitive implications of prohibiting hybrid capital instruments for Tier 1;
- the impact of such a prohibition on the cost and availability of credit;
- the availability of capital for financial institutions with less than $10 billion in total assets; and
- any other relevant factors relating to the safety and soundness of the U.S. financial system and the potential economic impact of such a prohibition (Sec. 174(a) of the Dodd-Frank Act).

Foreign Bank Intermediate Holding Companies.—The Comptroller General, in consultation with the Treasury Secretary, the Fed, the Comptroller of the Currency, and the FDIC, must conduct a study of capital requirements applicable to U.S. intermediate holding companies of foreign banks that are bank holding companies or savings and loan holding companies. The study must consider:

- current Fed policy regarding the treatment of intermediate holding companies;
- the principle of national treatment and equality of competitive opportunity for foreign banks operating in the United States;
- the extent to which foreign banks are subject on a consolidated basis to home country capital standards comparable to U.S. capital standards;
- potential effects on U.S. banking organizations operating abroad caused by changes to U.S. policy regarding intermediate holding companies;

- the impact on the cost and availability of credit in the United States from a change in U.S. policy regarding intermediate holding companies; and
- any other relevant factors relating to the safety and soundness of the U.S. financial system and the potential economic impact of such a prohibition (Sec. 174(b) of the Dodd-Frank Act).

Report.—Within 18 months of the date of enactment, the Comptroller General must submit reports to the Senate Banking Committee and the House Financial Services Committee summarizing the results of the studies. The reports must include specific recommendations for legislative or regulatory action regarding the treatment of hybrid capital instruments, including trust preferred shares, and must explain the basis for those recommendations (Sec. 174(c) of the Dodd-Frank Act).

▶ **Effective date.** The provision takes effect one day after the date of enactment (Sec. 4 of the Dodd-Frank Wall Street Reform and Consumer Protection Act).

Law source: Law at ¶10,174 and ¶10,004.

— Sec. 174(a) of the Dodd-Frank Wall Street Reform and Consumer Protection Act, requiring a study of the use of hybrid capital instruments to comply with Tier 1 requirements;

— Sec. 174(b), requiring a study of capital requirements for U.S. intermediate holding companies of foreign banks;

— Sec. 174(c), requiring a report to Congress;

— Sec. 4, providing the effective date.

¶250 International Policy Coordination

The Dodd-Frank Wall Street Reform and Consumer Protection Act calls for improved coordination with foreign states, foreign regulators and international organizations to protect global financial stability and reduce systemic risk to the international financial system.

President.—The President, or a designee of the President, may coordinate through all available international policy channels, similar policies as those found in U.S. laws limiting the scope, nature, size, scale, concentration and interconnectedness of financial companies, in order to protect financial stability and the global economy (Sec. 175(a) of the Dodd-Frank Wall Street Reform and Consumer Protection Act).

Council.—The Chair of the Financial Stability Oversight Council, in consultation with the other Council members, must regularly consult with foreign financial regulatory entities and other appropriate foreign or international organizations on matters relating to systemic risk to the international financial system (Sec. 175(b) of the Dodd-Frank Act).

Fed and Treasury Secretary.—The Fed and the Treasury Secretary must consult with their foreign counterparts and through appropriate multilateral organizations to encourage comprehensive and robust prudential supervision and regulation for all highly leveraged and interconnected financial companies (Sec. 175(c) of the Dodd-Frank Act).

▶ **Effective date.** The provision takes effect one day after the date of enactment (Sec. 4 of the Dodd-Frank Wall Street Reform and Consumer Protection Act).

Law source: Law at ¶10,175 and ¶10,004.

— Sec. 175(a) of the Dodd-Frank Wall Street Reform and Consumer Protection Act, providing for presidential coordination of financial stability policies as applied to the global economy;
— Sec. 175(b), requiring Council coordination with foreign regulators and organizations;
— Sec. 175(c), requiring Fed and Treasury consultation with foreign counterparts;
— Sec. 4, providing the effective date.

Orderly Liquidation Authority

¶505	Introduction
¶510	FDIC Appointment as Receiver
¶515	Systemic Risk Determination
¶520	Orderly Liquidation Authority
¶525	Receiver's Powers and Duties
¶530	Claims and Contracts
¶535	Officers, Directors, Employees and Agents
¶540	Bridge Financial Companies
¶545	Orderly Liquidation Fund
¶550	Inspector General Review and Reports

¶505 Introduction

Title II of the Dodd-Frank Wall Street Reform and Consumer Protection Act (Sections 201 *et seq.*) establishes a mechanism for the orderly liquidation of large, failing financial institutions that threaten U.S. financial stability. In response to recent market events and the deficiencies that they revealed, Title II creates a resolution authority to wind down large, interconnected financial companies in an orderly manner. Under this legislation, firms that are supposedly "too big to fail" can be shut down and liquidated before their systemic failure endangers the financial markets (Remarks of Sen. John Kerry (D-MA), Cong. Rec., May 20, 2010, p. S4067). The new orderly liquidation authority gives federal authorities a viable alternative to the undesirable choice between bankruptcy and bailout (S. Rep. No. 111-176, p. 4). The FDIC will be able to unwind a failing firm so that existing contracts can be dealt with and creditors' claims can be addressed. Unlike traditional bankruptcy, which does not account for complex interrelationships of such large firms and may endanger financial stability, this more flexible process will help prevent disruption to the entire system and the overall economy.

Background.—The lack of a federal regulatory regime and resolution authority for large systemic financial institutions contributed to the financial crisis and, unless addressed with legislation, will constrain the federal response to future crises. As demonstrated by the failure of AIG, severe distress at any large global financial institution—not just banks—can pose systemic risks to the financial markets. The current bankruptcy framework available to resolve large, complex non-bank financial entities and financial holding companies was not designed to protect the stability of the financial system (Testimony of FDIC Chair Sheila Bair, Senate Banking Committee, May 6, 2009).

The financial crisis demonstrated the need for a resolution mechanism for financial firms to preserve stability and encourage market discipline. Such a mechanism would enable the financial markets to continue to function smoothly, while providing for an orderly transfer or unwinding of the firm's operations. It would also ensure that shareholders and creditors of the failed firm, not taxpayers, would bear any losses and that senior management and directors would be replaced. The resolution process would ensure that there would be the necessary liquidity to complete transactions in process at the time of failure, addressing the potential for systemic risk without creating the expectation of a bailout (Testimony of FDIC Chair Shelia Bair, Senate Banking Committee, July 23, 2009).

The federal government's responses to the then-impending bankruptcies of Bear Stearns, Lehman Brothers and AIG were complicated by the lack of a statutory framework for winding down failing securities firms and other non-bank financial firms, including affiliates of banks or other insured depository institutions. In the absence of such a framework, the government's only option to avoid the disorderly failures of Bear Stearns and AIG was to use the lending authority of the Federal Reserve. This authority could not prevent the bankruptcy of Lehman Brothers, however, which demonstrated how disruptive the disorderly failure of a non-bank financial firm could be to the financial system and the larger economy (*Financial Regulatory Reform, A New Foundation: Rebuilding Financial Supervision and Regulation*, Treasury Department (June 17, 2009), FED. BANK. L. REP. ¶ 75-201).

It can now be seen that the perception of some firms as being "too big to fail" leads to reckless behavior that endangers the economy. Large firms able to raise large amounts of debt and equity are given access to the credit markets at favorable terms without consideration of the firms' risk profile. Investors invest more and creditors lend more, both groups believing their exposure to be minimal since they also believe the government will not allow these firms to fail. The large firms leverage these funds and become even larger, which makes investors and creditors more complacent and more likely to extend credit and funds without fear of losses. In some respects, investors, creditors and the firms themselves are making a bet that they are immune from the risks of failure and loss because they have become too big, believing that regulators will avoid taking action for fear of repercussions to the broader market and economy (Testimony of FDIC Chair Shelia Bair, Senate Banking Committee, July 23, 2009).

Overview.—Title II of the Dodd-Frank Act establishes an orderly liquidation authority to unwind complex, systemically important financial firms whose failure could put the entire financial system in jeopardy. The provision was intended to give the government a viable alternative to the undesirable choice it faced during the financial crisis: (1) allow a large, complex financial company to file for bankruptcy protection, disrupting markets and damaging the economy; or (2) bail out the company, exposing taxpayers to losses and undermining market discipline (S. Rep. No. 111-176, p. 4). According to Sen. Mark Warner (D-VA), a co-author of Title II, the orderly liquidation authority title embodies three key principles: (1) firms will not be rescued because they are thought to be too big to fail; (2) the regime will be used rarely, with bankruptcy remaining the preferred method for resolving financial-institution failures; and (3) taxpayers will not be burdened. Senator Christopher Dodd (D-CT) said that the liquidation authority will wind down failing financial firms, eliminate shareholder interests, cause culpable management to be fired, impose losses on creditors and require clawback of any payment to creditors above liquidation value. In limiting the definition of "financial company" to companies with 85 percent of revenues coming from financial activities, Congress intended to exclude nonfinancial commercial firms (House-Senate Conference Committee Meeting, June 17, 2010).

The new legislation includes several hurdles intended to limit the use of the orderly liquidation authority to only those financial companies whose failure would threaten U.S. financial stability (S. Rep. No. 111-176, p. 4). Triggering the orderly liquidation authority requires: (1) a recommendation by a two-thirds vote of the Board of Governors of the Federal Reserve System; (2) a recommendation by a two-thirds vote of the FDIC; (3) a determination and approval by the Treasury Secretary after consultation with the President; and (4) a review and determination by a judicial panel (S. Rep. No. 111-176, p. 4; Sec. 203 of the Dodd-Frank Wall Street Reform and Consumer Protection Act). Once a failing financial company is placed under this authority, liquidation is the only option; the company cannot be kept open or rehabilitated. The firm's business operations must be wound down and its assets must be liquidated and the proceeds distributed pursuant to the priority scheme of Section 210 of the Dodd-Frank Act. The culpable management must be discharged, equity must be eliminated, and unsecured creditors and counterparties must bear losses (S. Rep. No. 111-176, p. 4).

The legislation allows regulators to bar culpable management and directors of failed firms from working in the financial sector (Sec. 213 of the Dodd-Frank Act). It also requires post-resolution reviews to determine if regulators did all they were supposed to do to prevent the failure of a systemically significant institution. According to Sen. Richard Shelby (R-AL), these reviews are essential to hold regulators accountable for their actions or inactions, as the case may be (Cong. Rec., May 5, 2010, p. S3140).

The Boxer Amendment, Section 214 (discussed at ¶ 545), clarifies that no financial company will be kept alive with taxpayer money. If a financial company needs to be liquidated, the costs of liquidation will be recovered from the disposition of the company's assets or will be the responsibility of the financial sector, through assessments (Remarks of Sen. Barbara Boxer (D-CA), Cong. Record, May 4, 2010, p. S3063).

Definitions.—In addition to the definitions discussed where relevant throughout this chapter, Section 201 of the Dodd-Frank Act defines various other terms used in Title II:

"Administrative expenses of the receiver" includes the actual, necessary costs and expenses incurred by the FDIC as receiver in liquidating a covered financial company and any obligations that the FDIC determines are necessary and appropriate to facilitate a smooth and orderly liquidation (Sec. 201(a)(1) of the Dodd-Frank Act).

"Bankruptcy Code" means Title 11 of the U.S. Code (Sec. 201(a)(2) of the Dodd-Frank Act).

"Bridge financial company" means a new financial company organized by the FDIC in accordance with Section 210(h) for the purpose of resolving a covered financial company (Sec. 201(a)(3) of the Dodd-Frank Act).

"Claim" means any right of payment, whether or not reduced to judgment, liquidated, unliquidated, fixed, contingent, matured, unmatured, disputed, undisputed, legal, equitable, secured or unsecured (Sec. 201(a)(4) of the Dodd-Frank Act).

"Company" has the same meaning as in Bank Holding Company Act Section 2(b), except that it includes any company defined by Title II as a "financial company," the majority of the securities of which are owned by the United States or any state (Sec. 201(a)(5) of the Dodd-Frank Act).

"Court" means the U.S. District Court for the District of Columbia (except where context requires otherwise) (Sec. 201(a)(6) of the Dodd-Frank Act).

"Covered broker or dealer" means a covered financial company that is a broker or dealer that is registered with the SEC under Exchange Act Section 15(b) and is a member of the SIPC (Sec. 201(a)(7) of the Dodd-Frank Act).

"Covered subsidiary" means a subsidiary of a covered financial company, other than an insured depository institution, an insurance company or a covered broker or dealer (Sec. 201(a)(9) of the Dodd-Frank Act).

"Customer," "customer name securities," "customer property" and "net equity" in the context of a covered broker or dealer have the same meanings as in SIPA Section 16 (Sec. 201(a)(10) of the Dodd-Frank Act).

"Fund" means the Orderly Liquidation Fund established under Dodd-Frank Act Section 210(n) (Sec. 201(a)(12) of the Dodd-Frank Act).

"Insurance company" means any entity that is engaged in the business of insurance, subject to regulation by a state insurance regulator and covered by a state law designed to specifically deal with the rehabilitation, liquidation or insolvency of an insurance company (Sec. 201(a)(13) of the Dodd-Frank Act). A colloquy between House Financial Services Committee Chairman Barney Frank (D-MA) and Rep. Andre Carson (D-IN) confirmed that mutual insurance holding companies are included in the definition of "insurance company." Thus, under Title II of the Dodd-Frank Act, all insurance companies, specifically including mutual insurance holding companies, remain subject to resolution under their existing state insurance insolvency and liquidation regimes. Chairman Frank noted that Congress has no intention of disturbing the well-run state insurance regime in this area (Cong. Rec., June 30, 2010, p. H5216).

"Nonbank financial company" has the same meaning as in Section 102(a)(4)(C) of the Dodd-Frank Act (Sec. 201(a)(14) of the Dodd-Frank Act), and "nonbank financial company supervised by the Board of Governors" has the same meaning as in Section 102(a)(3)(D) of the Dodd-Frank Act (Sec. 201(a)(15) of the Dodd-Frank Act).

"SIPC" means the Securities Investor Protection Corporation (Sec. 201(a)(16) of the Dodd-Frank Act).

Effect on Bankruptcy Proceedings.—Section 208 of the Dodd-Frank Act provides for dismissal of any case or proceeding with respect to the covered financial company under the Bankruptcy Code or the SIPA, effective as of the date of the FDIC's appointment as receiver (or the SIPC's appointment as trustee, in the case of a covered broker or dealer), upon notice to the bankruptcy court or the SIPC, as applicable. No such case or proceeding can be commenced at any time while the orderly liquidation is pending (Sec. 208(a) of the Dodd-Frank Act). Effective as of the date of the receivership, the assets of a covered financial company that have vested in any other entity as a result of a case under the Bankruptcy Code, SIPA or other similar liquidation or insolvency provisions will revest in the covered financial company (Sec. 208(b) of the Dodd-Frank Act). However, notwithstanding the above, any order entered or other relief granted by a bankruptcy court prior to the date of the receivership will continue with the same validity as if an orderly liquidation had not begun (Sec. 208(c) of the Dodd-Frank Act).

Regulations.—Section 209 of the legislation requires the FDIC to make rules and regulations, in consultation with the Financial Stability Oversight Council, as it considers necessary or appropriate to implement Title II. These may include rules and regulations with respect to the rights of creditors, counterparties, security entitlement holders or other persons with respect to any covered financial company or assets held by a covered financial company, and may address the potential for conflicts of interest between or among individual receiverships established under Title II or under the Federal Deposit Insurance Act. Where possible, the FDIC must seek to harmonize these rules and regulations with the insolvency laws that would otherwise apply to a covered financial company (Sec. 209 of the Dodd-Frank Act).

Circumvention and Conflicts of Interest.—The legislation prohibits governmental entities from taking any action to circumvent the purposes of Title II (Sec. 212(b) of the Dodd-Frank Act). The FDIC may take appropriate action to avoid any conflicts of interest that arise in the event that it is appointed receiver for more than one covered financial company or for a covered financial company and its insured depository institution affiliate (Sec. 212(c) of the Dodd-Frank Act).

Conforming Change.—The legislation makes a conforming change to 18 U.S.C. § 1032 relating to the concealment of assets from the FDIC as receiver (Secs. 211(a)–(b) of the Dodd-Frank Act). It also makes a conforming change to the netting provisions contained in the Federal Deposit Insurance Corporation Improvement Act of 1991 by expanding the exceptions to include Section 210(c) of the Dodd-Frank Act and Section 1367 of the Federal Housing Enterprises Financial Safety and Soundness Act of 1992 (Sec. 211(c) of the Dodd-Frank Act; S. Rep. No. 111-176, p. 65).

▶ **Effective date.** The provisions take effect one day after the date of enactment (Sec. 4 of the Dodd-Frank Wall Street Reform and Consumer Protection Act).

Law source: Law at ¶10,201, ¶10,203, ¶10,208, ¶10,209, ¶10,210, ¶10,211, ¶10,212, ¶10,213 and ¶10,004. Committee Report at ¶54,100.

— Sec. 201 of the Dodd-Frank Wall Street Reform and Consumer Protection Act, defining terms;

— Sec. 203, establishing the process for triggering the orderly liquidation authority;

— Sec. 208, providing for dismissal of bankruptcy proceedings;

— Sec. 209, requiring the FDIC to make rules and regulations;

— Sec. 210, establishing the priority of claims;

— Sec. 211, making conforming changes to 18 U.S.C. § 1032 and to the Federal Deposit Insurance Corporation Improvement Act of 1991;

— Sec. 212, prohibiting governmental entities from circumventing the purposes of Title II and authorizing the FDIC to avoid conflicts of interest;

— Sec. 213, authorizing an officer/director bar;

— Sec. 4, providing the effective date.

¶510 FDIC Appointment as Receiver

Section 202 of the Dodd-Frank Wall Street Reform and Consumer Protection Act prescribes the procedural and judicial review requirements for FDIC receivership. This provision establishes the mechanism for appointing the FDIC as receiver of a covered financial company, as well as the appeals process, rules and procedures to be established, the respective roles of the receivership process and the Bankruptcy Code as they relate to financial companies, the time limit for the receivership, and studies and reports to be conducted.

Procedure.—If the Treasury Secretary determines that a financial company satisfies the criteria for FDIC receivership in Section 203(b) of the Dodd-Frank Act, the Secretary must so notify the FDIC and the covered financial company. If the board of directors (or similar body) of the covered financial company acquiesces, the Secretary must appoint the FDIC as receiver. However, if the board of directors or other body does not consent to the receivership, the Secretary must petition the district court for the District of Columbia for an order authorizing the Secretary to appoint the FDIC as receiver (Sec. 202(a)(1)(A)(i) of the Dodd-Frank Wall Street Reform and Consumer Protection Act). The petition must be filed under seal and must present all relevant findings and the recommendation made pursuant to Section 203(a) (Sec. 202(a)(1)(A)(ii) of the Dodd-Frank Act).

Under strict confidentiality and without any prior public disclosure, the court, after notice to the covered financial company and a hearing, must determine whether the Secretary's determination that the covered financial company is in default or in danger of default and satisfies the definition of a financial company under Section 201(a)(11) is arbitrary and capricious (Sec. 202(a)(1)(A)(iii) of the Dodd-Frank Act). If the court finds that the determination is not arbitrary and capricious, it must issue an order immediately authorizing the Secretary to appoint the FDIC as receiver (Sec. 202(a)(1)(A)(iv)(I) of the Dodd-Frank Act). If the court finds the determination arbitrary and capricious, it must immediately provide to the Secretary a written statement of each reason supporting its determination and afford the Secretary an immediate opportunity to amend and refile the petition (Sec. 202(a)(1)(A)(iv)(II) of the Dodd-Frank Act). If the court does not make any determination within 24 hours of receipt of the petition, the petition will be granted by operation of law, the Secretary must appoint the FDIC as receiver, liquidation must begin automatically and without further notice, and the FDIC may immediately take all actions authorized under Title II of the Dodd-Frank Act (Sec. 202(a)(1)(A)(v) of the Dodd-Frank Act).

Immediately upon the conclusion of the proceedings, the court must provide for the record a written statement of each reason supporting its decision, and must provide copies thereof to the Secretary and to the covered financial company. The court's determination is final and appealable only as set forth in Section 202(a)(2). The decision is not subject to any stay or injunction pending appeal (Sec. 202(a)(1)(B) of the Dodd-Frank Act).

The legislation provides for criminal penalties for violating confidentiality. A person who recklessly discloses a determination of the Secretary under Section 203(b), a petition of the Secretary under Section 202(a)(1)(A), or the pendency of court proceedings under

Section 202(a)(1)(A) will be fined not more than $250,000, imprisoned for not more than five years, or both (Sec. 202(a)(1)(C) of the Dodd-Frank Act).

Directors Not Liable.—Section 207 of the Dodd-Frank Act expressly provides that the members of the board of directors (or similar body) of a covered financial company are not liable to the company's shareholders or creditors for acquiescing in good faith to the FDIC's appointment as receiver (Sec. 207 of the Dodd-Frank Act).

Definitions.—The term "financial company" means:

(1) a bank holding company;

(2) a nonbank financial company supervised by the Board of Governors of the Federal Reserve System (the Fed);

(3) any company predominantly engaged in activities that the Fed has determined are financial in nature, or incidental to activities that are financial in nature, for purposes of Bank Holding Company Act Section 4(k); or

(4) a subsidiary of any company described in (1)–(3) above, other than an insured depository institution or insurance company (Sec. 201(a)(11) of the Dodd-Frank Act).

Congress did not intend that an investment company registered under the Investment Company Act of 1940 would be deemed a subsidiary of a company described in (1)–(3) above because of the company's provision of services to the investment company, unless the company (including through all of its affiliates) owned 25 percent or more of the investment company's shares (S. Rep. No. 111-176, p. 57). The definition of "financial company" also excludes Farm Credit System institutions charted under and subject to the provisions of the Farm Credit Act of 1971, government entities, and regulated entities as defined under Section 1303 of the Federal Housing Enterprises Financial Safety and Soundness Act of 1992 (Sec. 201(a)(11)(C) of the Dodd-Frank Act).

A company cannot be deemed predominantly engaged in activities that the Fed has determined are financial in nature if its consolidated revenues from these activities constitute less than 85 percent of its total consolidated revenues, as the FDIC, in consultation with the Treasury Secretary, establishes by regulation (Sec. 201(b) of the Dodd-Frank Act). This 85-percent requirement was designed to exclude commercial firms from the definition of "financial company". (House-Senate Conference Committee Meeting, June 17, 2010). In determining whether a company is a financial company, the consolidated revenues derived from the ownership or control of a depository institution must be included (Sec. 201(b) of the Dodd-Frank Act).

The legislation defines a "covered financial company" as a financial company, other than an insured depository institution, for which a determination has been made under Section 203(b) (Sec. 201(a)(8) of the Dodd-Frank Act).

Appeals.—The Treasury Secretary or the covered financial company, through its board of directors, may appeal a final decision of the district court to the U.S. Court of Appeals for the District of Columbia Circuit within 30 days after the date on which the district court's decision is rendered or deemed to be rendered (Sec. 202(a)(2)(A)(i) of the Dodd-Frank Act). The Court of Appeals has jurisdiction only if the covered financial company did not acquiesce or consent to the appointment of a receiver by the Secretary under Section 202(a)(1)(A). The Court of Appeals must consider any appeal on an

¶510

expedited basis, and review is limited to whether the Secretary's determination that a company is in default or danger of default and meets the definition of "financial company" is arbitrary and capricious (Secs. 202(a)(2)(A)(iii)–(iv) of the Dodd-Frank Act).

The Treasury Secretary or the covered financial company, through its board of directors, may petition the U.S. Supreme Court for a writ of certiorari within 30 days from the final decision of the Court of Appeals (Sec. 202(a)(2)(B)(i) of the Dodd-Frank Act). If a petition is filed, the Court of Appeals must immediately provide for the record a written statement of each reason for its decision (Sec. 202(a)(2)(B)(ii) of the Dodd-Frank Act). The Supreme Court must consider any petition on an expedited basis, and its review is limited to whether the Secretary's determination that a company is in default or danger of default and satisfies the definition of "financial company" is arbitrary and capricious (Secs. 202(a)(2)(B)(iii)–(iv) of the Dodd-Frank Act).

Court Rules and Procedures.—Within six months after the date of enactment, the district court must establish such rules and procedures as may be necessary to ensure the orderly conduct of proceedings, including rules and procedures to ensure that the 24-hour deadline is met and that the Secretary has an ongoing opportunity to amend and refile petitions (Sec. 202(b)(1) of the Dodd-Frank Act). The rules and procedures must be recorded and must be transmitted to the Senate Judiciary Committee, the Senate Banking Committee, the House Judiciary Committee and the House Financial Services Committee (Sec. 202(b)(2) of the Dodd-Frank Act).

Bankruptcy Code.—Except as expressly provided in Title II, the Bankruptcy Code and the underlying rules, and not Title II, apply to financial companies that are not covered financial companies for which the FDIC has been appointed as receiver. Conversely, Title II, not the Bankruptcy Code and rules, exclusively applies to and governs all matters relating to covered financial companies for which the FDIC is appointed as receiver (Sec. 202(c) of the Dodd-Frank Act).

Time Limit.—An FDIC receivership must terminate after three years (Sec. 202(d)(1) of the Dodd-Frank Act). The FDIC may extend its appointment by up to two additional periods of up to one year each, and there may be an additional extension to conclude ongoing litigation. To extend the time limit, the FDIC Chairperson must determine and certify in writing to the Senate Banking Committee and the House Financial Services Committee that continuation of the receivership is necessary: (1) to maximize the net present value return from, or to minimize the amount of loss realized upon, the disposition of the assets of the covered financial company; and (2) to protect the stability of the U.S. financial system (Sec. 202(d)(2) of the Dodd-Frank Act). In the case of a second extension, in addition to this certification, the FDIC must submit a report to the Senate Banking Committee and the House Financial Services Committee describing the need for the extension and the FDIC's specific plan to conclude the receivership before the end of the second extension (Sec. 202(d)(3) of the Dodd-Frank Act).

Finally, the time limit may be extended for the purpose of completing ongoing litigation to which the FDIC as receiver is a party if: (1) the Financial Stability Oversight Council (Council) determines that the FDIC used its best efforts to conclude the receivership within the extended time limit; (2) the Council determines that the completion of ongoing litigation justifies the need for an extension; and (3) the FDIC submits a report approved by the Council within 30 days after the Council's determinations to the Senate Banking Committee and the House Financial Services Committee describing the ongoing litigation and the FDIC's specific plan to complete the litigation and conclude the receivership. The receivership must terminate within 90 days after the date of completion of litigation (Sec. 202(d)(4) of the Dodd-Frank Act).

The FDIC may issue regulations governing the termination of receiverships under Title II. The FDIC and the Deposit Insurance Fund are not liable for unresolved claims arising from the receivership after its termination (Secs. 202(d)(5)–(6) of the Dodd-Frank Act).

Studies and Reports.—The Administrative Office of the U.S. Courts and the Comptroller General of the United States must each monitor the activities of the district court and must conduct separate studies regarding the bankruptcy and orderly liquidation process for financial companies under the Bankruptcy Code. The studies must evaluate the effectiveness of Bankruptcy Code Chapter 7 or 11 in facilitating the orderly liquidation or reorganization of financial companies, ways to maximize the efficiency and effectiveness of the district court, and ways to make the orderly liquidation process for financial companies under the Bankruptcy Code more effective. Within the first year after enactment of the Dodd-Frank Act, in each successive year until the third year, and every fifth year after the date of enactment, the Administrative Office and the Comptroller General must submit to the Senate Banking Committee, the Senate Judiciary Committee, the House Financial Services Committee, and the House Judiciary Committee separate reports summarizing the results of their studies (Sec. 202(e) of the Dodd-Frank Act).

Upon enactment of the Dodd-Frank Act, the Fed, in consultation with the Administrative Office of the U.S. Courts, must conduct a study regarding the resolution of financial companies under Bankruptcy Code Chapters 7 and 11. The study must evaluate (1) the effectiveness of Chapters 7 and 11 in facilitating the orderly resolution or reorganization of systemic financial companies; (2) whether a special financial resolution court or panel should be established to oversee cases involving financial companies, to provide for their resolution with minimal adverse impacts on financial markets and without creating "moral hazard"; (3) whether the Bankruptcy Code should be amended to enhance the resolution of financial companies with minimal adverse impacts on financial markets and without creating "moral hazard"; (4) whether the Bankruptcy Code, the Federal Deposit Insurance Act and other insolvency laws should be amended to address the treatment of qualified financial contracts; and (5) the implications, challenges and benefits of creating a new Bankruptcy Code chapter or subchapter to deal with financial companies (Sec. 216(a) of the Dodd-Frank Act). The Administrative Office must report the study results to the Senate Banking Committee, the Senate Judiciary Committee, the House Financial Services Committee and the House Judiciary Committee within one year of enactment and every year thereafter until the fifth year after enactment (Sec. 216(b) of the Dodd-Frank Act).

The Comptroller General must also conduct a study regarding international coordination relating to the orderly liquidation of financial companies under the Bankruptcy Code. The study must evaluate the extent to which international coordination of the bankruptcy process currently exists, current mechanisms and structures for facilitating international cooperation, barriers to effective international coordination, and ways to increase and improve international coordination. Within one year from the enactment of the Dodd-Frank Act, the Comptroller General must submit to the Senate Banking Committee, Senate Judiciary Committee, the House Financial Services Committee, the House Judiciary Committee and the Treasury Secretary a report summarizing the study's results (Sec. 202(f) of the Dodd-Frank Act).

The Fed, in consultation with the Administrative Office of the U.S. Courts, must conduct a study regarding international coordination relating to the resolution of systemic financial companies under the Bankruptcy Code and applicable foreign law. The study must consider the extent to which international coordination currently exists, current mechanisms and structures for facilitating coordination, barriers to effective coordination and ways to increase and improve coordination of the resolution of financial companies so as to minimize the impact on the financial system without creating "moral hazard" (Sec. 217(a) of the Dodd-Frank Act). The Administrative Office must report the findings of the study to the Senate Banking and Judiciary Committees and the House Financial Services and Judiciary Committees within one year of enactment (Sec. 217(b) of the Dodd-Frank Act).

Finally, the Comptroller General must conduct a study regarding the implementation of prompt corrective action by the appropriate federal banking agencies. The study must evaluate: (1) the effectiveness of implementation of prompt corrective action by the appropriate federal banking agencies and the resolution of insured depository institutions by the FDIC; and (2) ways to improve prompt corrective action as a tool to resolve the insured depository institutions at the least possible long-term cost to the Deposit Insurance Fund. Within one year of enactment of the Dodd-Frank Act, the Comptroller General must submit to the Council a report on the results of the study. Within six months of receipt of the report, the Council must submit a report to the Senate Banking Committee and the House Financial Services Committee on actions taken in response to the report, including any recommendations made to the primary financial regulators under Section 120 of the Dodd-Frank Act (Sec. 202(g) of the Dodd-Frank Act).

▶ **Effective date.** The provisions take effect one day after the date of enactment (Sec. 4 of the Dodd-Frank Wall Street Reform and Consumer Protection Act).

Law source: Law at ¶10,201, ¶10,202, ¶10,207, ¶10,216, ¶10,217 and ¶10,004. Committee Report at ¶54,100, ¶54,101 and ¶54,106.

— Sec. 201(a) of the Dodd-Frank Wall Street Reform and Consumer Protection Act, defining key terms;
— Sec. 202(a), establishing receivership procedure and appeal process;
— Sec. 202(b), requiring court rules and procedures for receivership proceedings;
— Sec. 202(c), describing the bankruptcy code's scope in relation to Title II;
— Sec. 202(d), prescribing the receivership time limit;
— Secs. 202(e)–(f), requiring studies and reports;
— Sec. 207, shielding directors from liability for acquiescing in receivership;
— Sec. 216, requiring studies and reports on the resolution of financial companies under the Bankruptcy Code;
— Sec. 217, requiring a study and report on international coordination relating to bankruptcies;

— Sec. 4, providing the effective date.

¶515 Systemic Risk Determination

Section 203 of the Dodd-Frank Wall Street Reform and Consumer Protection Act establishes the process for triggering the orderly liquidation authority. There is a strong presumption that the Bankruptcy Code will continue to apply to most failing financial companies, and the legislation includes several steps intended to make the use of the orderly liquidation authority rare (S. Rep. No. 111-176, p. 58).

Overview.—First, the Board of Governors of the Federal Reserve System (the Fed) and the FDIC Board of Directors (or, in a case involving a broker or dealer, the Fed and the SEC, and in the case of an insurance company, the Fed in consultation with the FDIC and with the approval of the Federal Insurance Office) must each, by a two-thirds vote, provide to the Treasury Secretary a written recommendation of actions to be taken. Then, upon receiving the recommendation, the Treasury Secretary (in consultation with the President) may make a written determination of systemic risk. After making this determination, the Secretary may appoint the FDIC receiver or petition the court for authorization to do so if the financial company does not consent to the receivership. The Secretary must take into consideration the effectiveness of the action in mitigating adverse effects on the financial system, any cost to the Treasury, and the potential to encourage creditors, counterparties and shareholders in the covered financial company to take excessive risk (S. Rep. No. 111-176, pp. 58–59).

The Secretary must provide written notice of the determination to Congress within 24 hours. The FDIC must submit a report to Congress within 60 days of its appointment as receiver of the covered financial company and must update the information contained in the report at least quarterly. The Government Accountability Office must review and report on the Secretary's determination (S. Rep. No. 111-176, p. 59).

The FDIC must establish policies and procedures acceptable to the Treasury Secretary governing the use of funds available to the FDIC to carry out Title II of the Dodd-Frank Act. If an insurance company is a covered financial company or subsidiary or affiliate of a covered financial company, its liquidation or rehabilitation must be conducted as provided under state law. The FDIC must have backup authority to file appropriate judicial action in state court to place the company into liquidation under state law if the state regulator fails to act within 60 days (S. Rep. No. 111-176, p. 59).

Written Recommendation.—To trigger the orderly liquidation authority, the FDIC Board of Directors and the Fed, on their own initiative or at the Treasury Secretary's request, must each, by a two-thirds vote, provide a written recommendation to the Secretary (Sec. 203(a)(1)(A) of the Dodd-Frank Wall Street Reform and Consumer Protection Act). The recommendation must include:

- an evaluation of whether the financial company is in default or in danger of default;
- a description of the effect that default would have on U.S. financial stability;
- a description of the effect that default would have on economic conditions or financial stability for low-income, minority or underserved communities;

- a recommendation regarding the nature and extent of actions to be taken regarding the financial company;
- an evaluation of the likelihood of a private-sector alternative to default;
- an evaluation of why a bankruptcy case is not appropriate;
- an evaluation of the effects on creditors, counterparties and shareholders of the financial company and other market participants; and
- an evaluation of whether the company satisfies the definition of a financial company under Section 201 of the legislation (Sec. 203(a)(2) of the Dodd-Frank Act).

With respect to a broker or dealer, or a financial company whose largest U.S. subsidiary is a broker or dealer, the recommendation must be made by the SEC and the Fed by a two-thirds vote, in consultation with the FDIC (Sec. 203(a)(1)(B) of the Dodd-Frank Act). With respect to an insurance company, or a financial company whose largest U.S. subsidiary is an insurance company, the recommendation must be made by the Fed by a two-thirds vote, with the approval of the Director of the Federal Insurance Office and in consultation with the FDIC (Sec. 203(a)(1)(C) of the Dodd-Frank Act).

Secretary's Determination.—Upon receiving the recommendation, the Treasury Secretary must: (1) notify the FDIC and the covered financial company that it recommends receivership and appoint the FDIC receiver (if the board of directors of the covered financial company acquiesces); or (2) petition the district court for the District of Columbia for an order authorizing the Secretary to appoint the FDIC as receiver (if the board does not acquiesce), as set forth in Section 202(a)(1)(A)(i) (Sec. 203(b) of the Dodd-Frank Act). The Secretary must do so if it determines, in consultation with the President, that:

- the financial company is in default or in danger of default;
- the company's failure and its resolution under otherwise applicable federal or state law would have serious adverse effects on U.S. financial stability;
- no viable private-sector alternative is available to prevent default;
- any effect on the claims or interests of the company's creditors, counterparties and shareholders and other market participants as a result of actions to be taken under Title II is appropriate, given the impact that any action taken under Title II would have on U.S. financial stability;
- any action under Section 204 of the Dodd-Frank Act would avoid or mitigate those adverse effects, taking into consideration the effectiveness of the action in mitigating potential adverse effects on the financial system, the cost to the general fund of the Treasury, and the potential to increase excessive risk taking on the part of creditors, counterparties, and shareholders in the financial company;
- a federal regulatory agency has ordered the financial company to convert all of its convertible debt instruments that are subject to the regulatory order; and
- the company satisfies the definition of a financial company under Section 201 of the legislation (Sec. 203(b) of the Dodd-Frank Act).

The Secretary must document any determination, retain the documentation for review and notify the covered financial company and the FDIC of the determination (Sec.

203(c)(1) of the Dodd-Frank Act). Within 24 hours after the FDIC's appointment as receiver, the Treasury Secretary must provide written notice of the recommendations and determinations to the Senate Majority and Minority Leaders, the House Speaker and Minority Leader, the Senate Banking Committee and the House Financial Services Committee. The Secretary's report must consist of a summary of the basis for the determination, including, to the extent available at the time of the determination:

- the size and financial condition of the covered financial company;
- the sources of capital and credit support that were available to the covered financial company;
- the operations of the covered financial company that could have had a significant impact on financial stability, markets, or both;
- identification of the banks and financial companies that may be able to provide the services offered by the covered financial company;
- any potential international ramifications of resolution of the covered financial company under other applicable insolvency law;
- an estimate of the potential effect on U.S. financial stability of the resolution of the covered financial company under other applicable insolvency law;
- the potential effect of the appointment of a receiver on consumers and on the financial system, financial markets, and banks and other financial companies; and
- whether resolution of the covered financial company under other applicable insolvency law would cause banks or other financial companies to experience severe liquidity distress (Sec. 203(c)(2) of the Dodd-Frank Act).

Default or Danger of Default.—A financial company is "in default or in danger of default" if one of the following has occurred or is likely to occur: (1) a case has been commenced with respect to the financial company under the Bankruptcy Code; (2) the financial company has incurred losses that will deplete all or substantially all of its capital, and there is no reasonable prospect for the company to avoid this depletion; (3) the assets of the financial company are less than its obligations to creditors and others; or (4) the financial company is unable to pay its obligations (other than those subject to a bona fide dispute) in the normal course of business (Sec. 203(c)(4) of the Dodd-Frank Act).

FDIC Reports and Testimony.—Within 60 days after its appointment as receiver, the FDIC must file a report with the Senate Banking Committee and the House Financial Services Committee (Sec. 203(c)(3)(A) of the Dodd-Frank Act). The report must:

- provide information on the financial condition of the covered financial company as of the date of the appointment, including a description of its assets and liabilities;
- describe the FDIC's plan and actions taken to wind down the covered financial company;
- explain each instance in which the FDIC waived applicable requirements of Part 366 of 12 CFR, with respect to conflicts of interest by any person in the private sector who was retained to provide services to the FDIC in connection with the receivership;

¶515

- describe the reasons for the provision of any funding to the receivership out of the Orderly Liquidation Fund established under Section 210(n);
- state the expected costs of the liquidation; and
- include the identity of any claimant that is treated differently from similarly situated claimants under Section 210(b)(4), (d)(4) or (h)(5)(E), the amount of any additional payment to the claimant under subsection (d)(4), and the reason for the action.

The FDIC must publish the report on a website maintained by the FDIC, subject to appropriate confidentiality (Sec. 203(c)(3)(A) of the Dodd-Frank Act). The FDIC must, timely and at least quarterly, amend or revise and resubmit the reports as necessary (Sec. 203(c)(3)(B) of the Dodd-Frank Act). The FDIC and the primary financial regulatory agency, if any, of the financial company under receivership must appear before Congress, if requested, within 30 days after the FDIC first files its required reports (Sec. 203(c)(3)(C) of the Dodd-Frank Act).

GAO Reports.—The Comptroller General of the United States must review and report to Congress on any determination of the Treasury Secretary that results in the FDIC's appointment as receiver. The report must include: the basis for the determination; the purpose for which the action was taken; the likely effect of the determination and action on the incentives and conduct of financial companies and their creditors, counterparties and shareholders; and the likely disruptive effect of the determination and action on the reasonable expectations of creditors, counterparties and shareholders, taking into account the impact on U.S. financial stability and the rights of these parties (Sec. 203(c)(5) of the Dodd-Frank Act).

FDIC Policies and Procedures.—As soon as practicable after enactment of the Dodd-Frank Act, the FDIC must establish policies and procedures acceptable to the Treasury Secretary governing the use of funds available to the FDIC to carry out Title II. The policies and procedures must include the terms and conditions for the provision and use of funds under Sections 204(d) (funding for orderly liquidation), 210(h)(2)(G)(iv) (operating funds for a bridge financial company) and 210(h)(9) (funding of certain transactions with respect to bridge financial companies) (Sec. 203(d) of the Dodd-Frank Act).

Insurance Companies.—If an insurance company is a covered financial company or a subsidiary or affiliate of a covered financial company, its liquidation or rehabilitation and that of any subsidiary or affiliate that is itself an insurance company must be conducted under state law (Secs. 203(e)(1)–(2) of the Dodd-Frank Act). If the applicable regulatory agency has not filed the appropriate state judicial action to place the insurance company into orderly liquidation within 60 days after a Section 202(a) determination is made, the FDIC may file the state action in the place of the regulatory agency (Sec. 203(e)(3) of the Dodd-Frank Act).

▶ **Effective date.** The provision takes effect one day after the date of enactment (Sec. 4 of the Dodd-Frank Wall Street Reform and Consumer Protection Act).

Law source: Law at ¶10,203 and ¶10,004. Committee Report at ¶54,102.

— Sec. 203 of the Dodd-Frank Wall Street Reform and Consumer Protection Act, establishing procedures for triggering the use of the orderly liquidation authority;
— Sec. 4, providing the effective date.

¶515

¶520 Orderly Liquidation Authority

Section 204 of the Dodd-Frank Wall Street Reform and Consumer Protection Act describes the purpose of the orderly liquidation authority, authorizes the FDIC to act as receiver and to consult with federal agencies and third parties, and allows the FDIC to make funding available to the receivership.

Purpose.—The orderly liquidation authority's purpose is to provide the necessary authority to liquidate failing financial companies that pose a significant risk to U.S. financial stability in a manner that mitigates that risk and minimizes "moral hazard" (Sec. 204(a) of the Dodd-Frank Wall Street Reform and Consumer Protection Act). The section provides that, in the exercise of orderly liquidation authority, creditors and shareholders will bear losses; management responsible for the company's financial condition will not be retained; and the FDIC and other agencies must take steps to ensure that all parties responsible for the company's financial condition bear losses consistent with their responsibility through actions for damage, restitution and clawbacks (Sec. 204(a) of the Dodd-Frank Act; S. Rep. No. 111-176, p. 59).

FDIC Receivership and Consultations.—The FDIC must act as receiver upon its appointment under Section 202 of the Dodd-Frank Act, with all of the rights and obligations set forth in Title II (Sec. 204(b) of the Dodd-Frank Act). As receiver, the FDIC must consult with the primary financial regulatory agencies of: (1) the covered financial company and its covered subsidiaries to ensure an orderly liquidation; and (2) any subsidiaries other than covered subsidiaries to coordinate the treatment of solvent subsidiaries and the separate resolution of insolvent subsidiaries under other governmental authority (Secs. 204(c)(1) and (3) of the Dodd-Frank Act). The FDIC must also consult with the SEC and the SIPC if the company is a broker or dealer registered with the SEC and a member of the SIPC, for the purpose of determining whether to transfer customer accounts to a bridge financial company without the consent of any customer (Sec. 204(c)(4) of the Dodd-Frank Act). The FDIC may also consult with or acquire the services of any outside experts, as appropriate, to assist the FDIC in the orderly liquidation process (Sec. 204(c)(2) of the Dodd-Frank Act).

Funding.—The FDIC may make funds available to the receivership for the orderly liquidation of the covered financial company. Its authority to make funds available is subject to the conditions listed in Section 206 applicable to all orderly liquidation actions, and to the orderly liquidation plan (Sec. 204(d) of the Dodd-Frank Act).

All funds provided have claims priority and may include funds used for:

- making loans to, or purchasing the debt of, the covered financial company or covered subsidiary;
- purchasing, or guaranteeing against loss, the assets of the financial company or subsidiary;
- assuming or guaranteeing the company's or subsidiary's third-party obligations;
- taking a lien on assets of the company or subsidiary, including a first-priority lien on unencumbered assets to secure repayment of any transactions conducted under this subsection;

- selling or transferring all or any part of the acquired assets, liabilities or obligations of the company or subsidiary; and
- making payments to similarly-situated creditors pursuant to Sections 210(b)(4), (d)(4) and (h)(5)(E) (Sec. 204(d) of the Dodd-Frank Act).

Brokers and Dealers.—Section 205 of the Dodd-Frank Act authorizes the application of orderly liquidation authority, if necessary, to a covered broker or dealer while preserving the powers and duties of the Securities Investor Protection Corporation (SIPC) with respect to a liquidation under the Securities Investor Protection Act of 1970 (SIPA) (S. Rep. No. 111-176, p. 59). Upon the FDIC's appointment as receiver for a covered broker or dealer, the FDIC must appoint, without the need for court approval, the SIPC to act as liquidation trustee under the SIPA (Sec. 205(a)(1) of the Dodd-Frank Act). Upon its appointment as trustee, the SIPC must promptly file an application for a protective decree under the SIPA as to the covered broker or dealer with any federal district court specified in Exchange Act Section 21 or 27. The SIPC and FDIC, in consultation with the SEC, must jointly determine the protective decree's terms (Sec. 205(b)(3) of the Dodd-Frank Act). The court must accept and approve the filing and immediately issue the protective decree (Sec. 205(a)(2)(A) of the Dodd-Frank Act).

Following entry of the protective decree, the determination of claims and liquidation of assets of the covered broker or dealer retained in the receivership must be administered under the SIPA by SIPC as trustee (Sec. 205(a)(2)(B) of the Dodd-Frank Act). As trustee, the SIPC must determine and satisfy claims arising on or before the filing date, consistent with Title II of the Dodd-Frank Act and with the SIPA (Sec. 205(a)(2)(D) of the Dodd-Frank Act). "Filing date" means the date on which the FDIC is appointed receiver (Sec. 205(a)(2)(C) of the Dodd-Frank Act).

The SEC and the FDIC, after consulting with SIPC, must jointly issue rules to implement Section 205 (Sec. 205(h) of the Dodd-Frank Act).

Powers and Duties of SIPC and FDIC. As trustee for the liquidation of a covered broker or dealer, the SIPC must conduct the liquidation in accordance with the SIPA and has all of the powers and duties provided by the SIPA, including rights of action against third parties, but does not have any powers or duties with respect to assets and liabilities transferred by the FDIC to a bridge financial company (Sec. 205(b)(1) of the Dodd-Frank Act). Furthermore, the SIPC, in exercising its powers and functions as trustee, cannot impair or impede the FDIC's exercise of its powers and duties with regard to determining claims under Section 205(e) or any action: to make funds available under Section 204(d); to organize, establish, operate or terminate a bridge financial company; to transfer assets and liabilities; to enforce or repudiate contracts; or to take any other action relating to a bridge financial company under Section 210 (Sec. 205(b)(2) of the Dodd-Frank Act). The rights and obligations of any counterparty to a qualified financial contract to which a covered broker or dealer is a party are governed exclusively by Section 210 of the Dodd-Frank Act, notwithstanding any contrary SIPA provision (Sec. 205(b)(4) of the Dodd-Frank Act).

Except as otherwise provide in Title II, no court may take any action, including an action pursuant to the SIPA or the Bankruptcy Code, to restrain or affect the FDIC's powers or functions as receiver of the covered broker or dealer (Sec. 205(c) of the Dodd-Frank Act; S. Rep. No. 111-176, p. 60).

¶520

Rights of Customers. The FDIC cannot take any action as receiver with respect to a covered broker or dealer that would adversely affect the rights of a customer to customer property or customer-name securities, diminish the amount or timely payment of net equity claims of customers, or otherwise impair the recovery provided to a customer under the SIPA (Sec. 205(d)(1) of the Dodd-Frank Act). The net proceeds from any transfer, sale or disposition of assets by the FDIC as receiver are for the benefit of the estate of the covered broker or dealer (Sec. 205(d)(2) of the Dodd-Frank Act).

Claims against the FDIC as receiver arising from broker-dealer assets transferred to a bridge financial company must be determined in accordance with Section 210(a)(2) and may be reviewed by the appropriate U.S. district or territorial court as provided in Section 210(a)(5) (Sec. 205(e) of the Dodd-Frank Act).

Customers of a covered broker or dealer that is placed into receivership, or with respect to which a bridge financial company is established, are to receive securities or payment that result in treatment at least as beneficial as if the covered broker or dealer had been subject to a proceeding under the SIPA (Sec. 205(f)(1) of the Dodd-Frank Act). The SIPC, as trustee, must satisfy customer claims as if the SIPA applied and the FDIC receivership had not occurred, and the FDIC must satisfy customer claims to the extent the customer would have received more securities or cash with respect to the allocation of customer property in a SIPA proceeding (Sec. 205(f)(2) of the Dodd-Frank Act). The SIPC must allocate customer property and deliver customer name securities in accordance with SIPA Section 8(c), and all other claims (including any unpaid claim for the allowed net equity claim from customer property) must be paid in accordance with the priorities in Section 210(b) of the Dodd-Frank Act (Sec. 205(g) of the Dodd-Frank Act).

Nonmember Brokers. In liquidating any covered financial company or bridge financial company that either is a stockbroker that is not a member of SIPC or is a commodity broker, the FDIC must apply the applicable liquidation provisions of the Bankruptcy Code pertaining to stockbrokers and commodity brokers (as those terms are defined in Bankruptcy Code Section 101) (Sec. 210(m) of the Dodd-Frank Act; S. Rep. No. 111-176, pp. 62–63).

Terms and Conditions for All Liquidations.—The FDIC may take action under Title II only as it determines necessary for U.S. financial stability and not for the purpose of preserving the covered financial company. The FDIC must also ensure that shareholders do not receive any payment until after all other claims are fully paid, that unsecured creditors bear losses in accordance with the claims priority provisions in Section 210, and that management and directors responsible for the company's failure are removed (if they have not already been removed at the time of the FDIC's appointment as receiver). The FDIC cannot take an equity interest in or become a shareholder of any covered financial company or covered subsidiary (Sec. 206 of the Dodd-Frank Act; S. Rep. No. 111-176, p. 60).

▶ **Effective date.** The provisions take effect one day after the date of enactment (Sec. 4 of the Dodd-Frank Wall Street Reform and Consumer Protection Act).

Law source: Law at ¶10,204, ¶10,205, ¶10,206, ¶10,210 and ¶10,004. Committee Report at ¶54,103, ¶54,104, ¶54,105 and ¶54,109.

- Sec. 204(a) of the Dodd-Frank Wall Street Reform and Consumer Protection Act, setting forth the purpose of the orderly liquidation authority;
- Secs. 204(b)–(d), authorizing the FDIC to act as receiver and fund the receivership;
- Sec. 205, providing for the orderly liquidation of covered brokers and dealers;
- Sec. 206, prescribing terms and conditions applicable to all orderly liquidations;
- Sec. 210(m), providing for the liquidation of nonmember brokers;
- Sec. 4, providing the effective date.

¶525 Receiver's Powers and Duties

Section 210(a) of the Dodd-Frank Wall Street Reform and Consumer Protection Act defines the FDIC's powers and duties as receiver of a covered financial company, including its powers and duties: (1) to succeed to the rights, title, powers and privileges of the covered financial company and its stockholders, members, officers and directors; (2) to operate the company with all the powers of shareholders, members, directors and officers; (3) to liquidate the company through the sale of assets or transfer of assets to a bridge financial company established under Section 210(h); (4) to merge the company with another company or transfer assets or liabilities; (5) to pay valid obligations that come due, to the extent that funds are available; (6) to exercise subpoena powers; (7) to use private-sector services to manage and dispose of assets; (8) to terminate rights and claims of stockholders and creditors (except for the right to payment of claims consistent with the priority of claims provision under this section); and (9) to determine and pay claims. The subsection also prescribes the FDIC's authorities to avoid fraudulent or preferential transfers of interests of the covered financial company (Sec. 210(a) of the Dodd-Frank Wall Street Reform and Consumer Protection Act; S. Rep. No. 111-176, pp. 60–61).

Provisions of Section 210 regarding the claims process and priority of claims and provisions relating to contracts (including qualified financial contracts) are discussed at ¶ 530.

General Powers.—Upon its appointment as receiver for a covered financial company, the FDIC will succeed to all rights, titles, powers and privileges of the covered financial company and its assets and of any shareholder, member, office or director of the company; and to title to the books, records and assets of any previous receiver or other legal custodian of the company (Sec. 210(a)(1)(A) of the Dodd-Frank Act). In operating the covered financial company, the receiver may:

- take over the assets of and operate the company with all of the powers of the company's members or shareholders, directors and officers, and conduct all the company's business;
- collect all obligations and money owed to the company;
- perform all company functions in the name of the company;
- manage the company's assets and property consistent with maximizing the value of its assets in the context of the orderly liquidation; and

- provide by contract for assistance in fulfilling any function, activity, action or duty of the FDIC as receiver (Sec. 210(a)(1)(B) of the Dodd-Frank Act).

The FDIC may provide for the exercise of any function by any member or stockholder, director or officer of the covered financial company (Sec. 210(a)(1)(C) of the Dodd-Frank Act).

Notwithstanding any other provision of law, the FDIC as receiver will succeed by operation of law to the rights, titles, powers and privileges described above and must terminate all rights and claims that the covered financial company's shareholders and creditors may have against the company's assets or the FDIC arising out of their status as stockholders or creditors, except to their right to payment, resolution or other satisfaction of their claims. The FDIC must ensure that shareholders and unsecured creditors bear losses consistent with the priority-of-claims provisions under Section 210 (Sec. 210(a)(1)(M) of the Dodd-Frank Act).

Subject to valid perfected security interests and enforceable security entitlements, the FDIC may liquidate and wind up the affairs of the covered financial company, including realizing upon the company's assets, as it deems appropriate, including through the sale of assets or transfer of assets to a bridge financial company, or exercising any other rights or privileges granted to the receiver under Section 210 (Sec. 210(a)(1)(D) of the Dodd-Frank Act).

The FDIC may appoint itself receiver of a domestic covered subsidiary of the covered financial company in receivership if the FDIC and the Treasury Secretary jointly determine that the subsidiary is in default or in danger of default and that receivership would avoid or mitigate serious adverse effects on U.S. financial stability or economic conditions and would facilitate the orderly liquidation of the covered financial company (Sec. 210(a)(1)(E)(i) of the Dodd-Frank Act). The covered subsidiary must thereafter be considered a covered financial company under Title II, and the FDIC will have all powers and rights with respect to the subsidiary as it has with respect to any other covered financial company under Title II (Sec. 210(a)(1)(E)(ii) of the Dodd-Frank Act).

The FDIC as receiver may organize a bridge financial company under Section 210(h) (Sec. 210(a)(1)(F) of the Dodd-Frank Act).

Merger and Transfer. Subject to antitrust review and any rights of setoff, the FDIC may merge the covered financial company with another company or transfer any asset or liability of the covered financial company (including those held for security entitlement holders or associated with any trust or custody business and including customer property) without obtaining any approval, assignment or consent to transfer (Sec. 210(a)(1)(G)(i) of the Dodd-Frank Act). With respect to transfers, any transferee, including a bridge financial company, must be subject to the same claims or rights as would prevail under applicable noninsolvency law (Sec. 210(a)(1)(G)(iii) of the Dodd-Frank Act).

With respect to mergers, if a proposed merger requires approval by a federal agency, the merger cannot be consummated before the fifth calendar day after the agency approves the merger (Sec. 210(a)(1)(G)(ii)(I) of the Dodd-Frank Act). If a report on competitive factors is required, the agency must promptly notify the U.S. Attorney General of the proposed merger, and the Attorney General must provide the required

¶525

report within 10 days of the request (Sec. 210(a)(1)(G)(ii)(II) of the Dodd-Frank Act). Finally, if notification is required under Clayton Act Section 7A with respect to the proposed merger, the required waiting period will end on the 15th day after the Attorney General and the FTC receive that notification, unless terminated earlier under Section 7A(b)(2) or extended under Section 7A(e)(2) (Sec. 210(a)(1)(G)(ii)(III) of the Dodd-Frank Act).

Payment of Claims. The FDIC as receiver must, to the extent funds are available, pay all valid obligations of the covered financial company that are due and payable at the time of the FDIC's appointment as receiver, in accordance with the prescriptions and limitations of Title II (Sec. 210(a)(1)(H) of the Dodd-Frank Act).

Applicable Noninsolvency Law. Except as otherwise provided in Title II, the applicable noninsolvency law must be determined by the noninsolvency choice of law rules otherwise applicable to the claims, rights, titles, persons or entities at issue (Sec. 210(a)(1)(I) of the Dodd-Frank Act).

Subpoena Authority. The FDIC as receiver may, for purposes of carrying out any power, authority or duty (including determining claims against, and collecting money due to, the covered financial company), exercise any power established under Federal Deposit Insurance Act (FDIA) Section 8(n) as if the FDIC were the appropriate federal banking agency for the covered financial company and the covered financial company were an insured depository institution (Sec. 210(a)(1)(J)(i) of the Dodd-Frank Act). This requirement cannot be construed as limiting any rights that the FDIC (in any capacity) otherwise has to exercise these powers or under any other provision of law (Sec. 210(a)(1)(J)(ii) of the Dodd-Frank Act).

Incidental Powers. The FDIC as receiver may exercise all powers and authorities specifically granted to receivers under Title II and any incidental powers necessary to carry out the powers under Title II (Sec. 210(a)(1)(K) of the Dodd-Frank Act).

Private-sector Services. In carrying out its responsibilities, the FDIC may use the services of private persons, including real-estate and loan portfolio management, property management, auction marketing, legal and brokerage services, if these services are available in the private sector and the FDIC determines that using those services is practicable, efficient and cost-effective (Sec. 210(a)(1)(L) of the Dodd-Frank Act).

Coordination with Foreign Authorities. The FDIC must coordinate as much as possible with the appropriate foreign financial authorities regarding the orderly liquidation of any covered financial company that has assets or operations outside of the United States (Sec. 210(a)(1)(N) of the Dodd-Frank Act). Section 210(k) authorizes the receiver to request the assistance of, and provide assistance to, any foreign financial authority in accordance with FDIA Section 8(v) as if the covered financial company were an insured depository institution, the FDIC were the appropriate federal banking agency and the foreign financial authority were the foreign banking authority (Sec. 210(k)(1) of the Dodd-Frank Act). The receiver may maintain an office to coordinate foreign investigations or investigations on behalf of foreign financial authorities (Sec. 210(k)(2) of the Dodd-Frank Act).

Restriction on Transfers. If the FDIC establishes one or more bridge financial companies with respect to a covered broker or dealer, the FDIC must transfer to one of those bridge financial companies all customer accounts of the covered broker or dealer and all associated customer name securities and customer property, unless the FDIC, after consulting with the SEC and SIPC, determines that the customer accounts and associated property are likely to be promptly transferred to another broker or dealer registered with the SEC and a member of SIPC, or the transfer of the accounts to the bridge financial company would materially interfere with the FDIC's ability to avoid or mitigate serious adverse effects on U.S. financial stability or economic conditions (Sec. 210(a)(1)(O)(i) of the Dodd-Frank Act). SIPC, as trustee in the liquidation of the covered broker or dealer, and the SEC must provide reasonable assistance necessary to complete the transfers (Sec. 210(a)(1)(O)(ii) of the Dodd-Frank Act). Customer consent to and court approval of the transfers are not required (Sec. 210(a)(1)(O)(iii) of the Dodd-Frank Act). The FDIC must identify to SIPC the customer accounts and associated property transferred, and the FDIC and SIPC must share information necessary for each entity to fulfill its obligations under Title II of the Dodd-Frank Act and under the SIPA, including by providing access to the books and records of the covered financial company and any bridge financial company (Sec. 210(a)(1)(O)(iv) of the Dodd-Frank Act).

Suspension of Actions.—After the FDIC is appointed receiver, it may request, and the court must grant, a stay of up to 90 days in any judicial action or proceeding in which the covered financial institution is or becomes a party (Sec. 210(a)(8) of the Dodd-Frank Act).

Additional Rights and Duties.—The FDIC must abide by any final, nonappealable judgment of a court of competent jurisdiction rendered before the FDIC's appointment as receiver (Sec. 210(a)(9)(A) of the Dodd-Frank Act). In the event of an appealable judgment, the FDIC as receiver has all the rights and remedies available to the covered financial company and the FDIC, including removal to a federal court and all appellate rights, and need not post a bond (Sec. 210(a)(9)(B) of the Dodd-Frank Act). Courts cannot issue any attachment or execution on assets in the FDIC's possession as receiver (Sec. 210(a)(9)(C) of the Dodd-Frank Act). Except as otherwise provided in Title II, no court has jurisdiction over any claim or action with respect to the assets of the covered financial company, including any assets that the FDIC may acquire from itself, or any claim relating to any act or omission of the company or the receiver (Sec. 210(a)(9)(D) of the Dodd-Frank Act).

Finally, the FDIC as receiver must exercise its rights and conduct its operations to, as much as possible, maximize the net present value return from the sale or disposition of assets, minimize the amount of loss realized in resolving cases, mitigate the potential for serious adverse effects to the financial system, ensure timely and adequate competition and fair and consistent treatment of offerors and prohibit discrimination on the basis of race, sex or ethnic group in the solicitation and consideration of offers (Sec. 210(a)(9)(E) of the Dodd-Frank Act).

Statute of Limitations.—Notwithstanding any contractual provision, the statute of limitations applicable to any action brought by the receiver is the longer of six years or the applicable state law limitations period, for contract claims, and the longer of three years or the applicable state law limitations period, for tort claims (Sec. 210(a)(10)(A) of the Dodd-Frank Act). The statute of limitations begins to run on the later of the date of the FDIC's appointment as receiver or the date on which the cause of action accrues (Sec. 210(a)(10)(B) of the Dodd-Frank Act). The receiver may bring an action without regard to the expiration of the statute of limitations with respect to a tort claim arising from fraud, intentional misconduct resulting in unjust enrichment or intentional misconduct resulting in substantial loss to the covered financial company, provided the state statute of limitations has expired not more than five years before the receivership (Sec. 210(a)(10)(C) of the Dodd-Frank Act).

Avoidable Transfers.—The legislation allows the receiver to recover certain preferential and fraudulent transfers made prior to the receivership and unauthorized transfers made during the receivership (Sec. 210(a)(11) of the Dodd-Frank Act).

Fraudulent Transfers. The FDIC as receiver may avoid a transfer of an interest of the covered financial company in property, or an obligation incurred by the company, made within two years before the receivership if:

- the company, voluntarily or involuntarily: (1) made the transfer with actual intent to hinder, delay or defraud any entity to which the company was or became indebted; or (2) received less than a reasonably equivalent value in exchange for the obligation; and
- the company, voluntarily or involuntarily: (1) was insolvent on the date of the transfer or obligation or became insolvent as a result of it; (2) was engaged in or about to engage in business or a transaction for which any property remaining with the company was an unreasonably small capital; (3) intended to incur or believed that it would incur debts that it would be unable to pay as they matured; or (4) made the transfer or incurred the obligation to or for the benefit of an insider under an employment contract and not in the ordinary course of business (Sec. 210(a)(11)(A) of the Dodd-Frank Act).

Preferential Transfers. The FDIC as receiver may avoid certain transfers made to or for the benefit of a creditor, for or on account of an antecedent debt, made while the covered financial company was insolvent. Such a transfer may be avoided if it was made in the 90 days before the receivership began (or within one year prior to the receivership, if the transfer recipient was an insider) and it enabled the creditor to receive more than it would have if the company had been liquidated under Bankruptcy Code Chapter 7, the transfer had not been made and the creditor received payment under Chapter 7 (Sec. 210(a)(11)(B) of the Dodd-Frank Act).

With respect to fraudulent and preferential transfers:

- the term "insider" has the same meaning as in Bankruptcy Code Section 101(31);
- a transfer is made when it is so perfected that a bona fide purchaser from the covered financial company against whom applicable law permits the transfer to be perfected cannot acquire an interest in the property superior to the transferee's interest, but if the transfer is not so perfected before the receivership, the transfer is made immediately before the date of the receivership; and
- the term "value" means property, or satisfaction or securing of a present or antecedent debt of the covered financial company, but does not include an unperformed promise to furnish support to the company (Sec. 210(a)(11)(H)(i) of the Dodd-Frank Act).

With respect to preferential transfers, the term "insolvent" has the same meaning as in Bankruptcy Code Section 101(32), and the covered financial company is presumed to have been insolvent on and during the 90-day period immediately preceding the receivership (Sec. 210(a)(11)(H)(ii) of the Dodd-Frank Act).

Post-receivership Transfers. The FDIC as receiver may avoid an unauthorized transfer that occurred after it was appointed receiver (Sec. 210(a)(11)(C) of the Dodd-Frank Act).

If a transfer described above is avoided, the FDIC may recover, for the benefit of the covered financial company, the property avoided or the value of the property (if so ordered by a court) from the initial transferee or any immediate or mediate transferee of the initial transferee (Sec. 210(a)(11)(D) of the Dodd-Frank Act). The FDIC cannot recover from any transferee that takes for value (including in satisfaction of or to secure a debt), in good faith, and without knowledge of the transfer's avoidability, or from any immediate or mediate good-faith transferee of such a transferee (Sec. 210(a)(11)(E) of the Dodd-Frank Act).

A transferee or obligee from which the FDIC seeks to recover a transfer or avoid an obligation has the same defenses available to a transferee or obligee from which a bankruptcy trustee seeks to recover or avoid an obligation under the Bankruptcy Code, and the FDIC's authority to recover a transfer or avoid an obligation is subject to Bankruptcy Code Sections 546(b) and (c), 547(c) and 548(c) (Sec. 210(a)(11)(F) of the Dodd-Frank Act).

The FDIC's rights as receiver under Section 210 are superior to any rights of a trustee or any other party (other than a federal agency) under the Bankruptcy Code (Sec. 210(a)(11)(G) of the Dodd-Frank Act).

Setoff.—Except as otherwise provided in Title II, a creditor may assert any right to offset a mutual debt owed by the creditor that arose before the receivership against its claim against the covered financial company, provided that this setoff right is enforceable under applicable noninsolvency law. The creditor cannot exercise this right of setoff, however, to the extent that:

- the claim of the creditor against the financial company is disallowed;
- the claim was transferred to the creditor by an entity other than the covered financial company either: (1) after the receivership began; or (2) within 90 days before the receivership began and while the covered financial company was insolvent (except for a setoff in connection with a qualified financial contract); or
- the debt owed to the covered financial company was incurred within the 90-day period preceding the receivership, while the financial company was insolvent and for the purpose of obtaining a right of setoff (except for a setoff in connection with a qualified financial contract) (Sec. 210(a)(12)(A) of the Dodd-Frank Act).

Insufficiency. Except for a setoff in connection with a qualified financial contract, if a creditor offsets a mutual debt within the 90-day period preceding the receivership, the FDIC may recover the amount offset, to the extent that any insufficiency on the date of the setoff is less than the insufficiency on the later of:

- the date that is 90 days before the FDIC's appointment as receiver; or

- the first day on which there is an insufficiency during the 90-day period preceding the receivership (Sec. 210(a)(12)(B)(i) of the Dodd-Frank Act).

"Insufficiency" means the amount by which a claim against the covered financial company exceeds a mutual debt owed by the holder of the claim (Sec. 210(a)(12)(B)(ii) of the Dodd-Frank Act).

Insolvency. The term "insolvent" has the same meaning as in Bankruptcy Code Section 101(32) (Sec. 210(a)(12)(C) of the Dodd-Frank Act). For purposes of Section 210(a)(12), the covered financial company is presumed to have been insolvent during the 90-day period preceding the receivership (Sec. 210(a)(12)(D) of the Dodd-Frank Act).

Nothing in Section 210(a)(12) provides a basis for any right of setoff where no such right exists under applicable noninsolvency law (Sec. 210(a)(12)(E) of the Dodd-Frank Act).

Except as otherwise provided in Title II, the receiver may sell or transfer any assets free and clear of the setoff rights of any party, except that the party is entitled to a claim, subordinate to the claims payable under Sections 210(b)(1)(A)–(D), but senior to all other unsecured liabilities defined in Section 210(b)(1)(E), in an amount equal to the value of the setoff rights (Sec. 210(a)(12)(F) of the Dodd-Frank Act).

Attachment of Assets.—A court of competent jurisdiction may, at the request of the receiver, issue an order in accordance with Rule 65 of the Federal Rules of Civil Procedure, including an order placing the assets of any person designated by the FDIC under the control of the court and appointing a trustee to hold those assets (Sec. 210(a)(13) of the Dodd-Frank Act). Rule 65 applies without regard to the requirement that the FDIC show that injury, loss or damage is irreparable and immediate (Sec. 210(a)(14)(A) of the Dodd-Frank Act). If the proceeding is in state court and the court determines that the state rules offer protections substantially similar to those under Rule 65, the receiver may request relief under the state rules (Sec. 210(a)(14)(B) of the Dodd-Frank Act).

Contract Claims Against Receiver.—Any final, nonappealable judgment for monetary damages against the receiver for the breach of an agreement executed or approved by the receiver must be paid as an administrative expense. This requirement cannot be construed to limit the power of a receiver to exercise any rights under contract or law, including to terminate, breach, cancel or otherwise discontinue its agreements (Sec. 210(a)(15) of the Dodd-Frank Act).

Accounting and Recordkeeping.—The FDIC must maintain a full accounting of each receivership or other disposition of a covered financial company and must make an annual accounting or report available to the Treasury Secretary and the Comptroller General of the United States (Secs. 210(a)(16)(A)–(B) of the Dodd-Frank Act). Any such report, and any report prepared pursuant to Section 203(c)(3), must be made available to the public (Sec. 210(a)(16)(C) of the Dodd-Frank Act).

The FDIC must prescribe regulations and establish retention schedules necessary to maintain the documents and records generated in exercising the authorities of Title II and the records of the covered financial company, with due regard for the avoidance of duplicative retention and the expected evidentiary needs of the receiver and the public regarding the records of covered financial companies (Sec. 210(a)(16)(D)(i) of the Dodd-Frank Act). Unless otherwise required by federal law or court order, the FDIC cannot destroy these records (Sec. 210(a)(16)(D)(ii) of the Dodd-Frank Act). "Records" and "records of a covered financial company" include any document, book, paper, map, photograph, microfiche, microfilm, computer or electronically-created record generated or maintained by the covered financial company in the course of and necessary to its transaction of business (Sec. 210(a)(16)(D)(iii) of the Dodd-Frank Act).

Subsection 210(e) of the Dodd-Frank Act precludes a court from taking action to restrain or affect the exercise of powers or functions of the receiver. Any remedy against the FDIC or receiver is limited to money damages determined in accordance with Title II (Sec. 210(e) of the Dodd-Frank Act).

Section 210(l) prohibits the FDIC from entering into any agreement, or approving any protective order, that would prohibit it from disclosing the terms of a settlement of an administrative or other action for damages or restitution brought by the FDIC as receiver (Sec. 210(l) of the Dodd-Frank Act).

Standstill Prohibition.—Section 210(p) prohibits any term in a standstill, confidentiality, or other agreement that affects or restricts the ability of a person to acquire, prohibits a person from offering to acquire, or prohibits a person from using any previously disclosed information in connection with an offer to acquire, all or part of any covered financial company, including any liabilities, assets or interest therein, in connection with any transaction in which the FDIC exercises its authority under Title II (Sec. 210(p)(2) of the Dodd-Frank Act). Such a provision is unenforceable as against public policy (Sec. 210(p)(1) of the Dodd-Frank Act).

Tax Exemptions.—Section 210(q) provides certain exemptions to the FDIC from taxes and levies. The FDIC, when acting as receiver, is exempt from all state and local taxation, except for real property taxes (Sec. 210(q)(1)(A) of the Dodd-Frank Act). None of the FDIC's property is subject to levy, attachment, garnishment, foreclosure or sale without its consent and no involuntary lien may attach to the FDIC's property (Sec. 210(q)(1)(B) of the Dodd-Frank Act). The FDIC is not liable for penalties or fines, including those arising from failure to pay taxes or recording or filing fees (Sec. 210(q)(1)(C) of the Dodd-Frank Act). Finally, the FDIC is exempt from prosecution by the United States or any state or local authority for any criminal offense arising under federal, state or local law that was allegedly committed by the covered financial company or persons acting on its behalf prior to the FDIC's appointment as receiver (Sec. 210(q)(1)(D) of the Dodd-Frank Act). The FDIC is not exempt from any tax imposed under, or other amount arising under, the Internal Revenue Code (Sec. 210(q)(2) of the Dodd-Frank Act).

▶ **Effective date.** The provision takes effect one day after the date of enactment (Sec. 4 of the Dodd-Frank Wall Street Reform and Consumer Protection Act).

Law source: Law at ¶10,210 and ¶10,004. Committee Report at ¶54,109.

— Sec. 210(a) of the Dodd-Frank Wall Street Reform and Consumer Protection Act, establishing the powers and duties of the receiver;

— Sec. 210(e), precluding courts from restraining the receiver and limiting damages;

— Sec. 210(h), authorizing the receiver to establish bridge financial companies;

¶525

— Sec. 210(k), authorizing coordination with foreign authorities;
— Sec. 210(l), prohibiting the FDIC from agreeing not to disclose settlement terms;
— Sec. 210(p), prohibiting standstill agreements;
— Sec. 210(q), providing tax exemptions;
— Sec. 4, providing the effective date.

¶530 Claims and Contracts

The Dodd-Frank Wall Street Reform and Consumer Protection Act, in enumerating the receiver's rights and duties, establishes procedures for claims resolution and priority. It also prescribes the rights of counterparties to certain contracts with the covered financial company, which the receiver may elect to continue or to repudiate.

Section 210(b) of the Dodd-Frank Act defines the priority of expenses and unsecured claims against the covered financial company. All claimants that are similarly situated must be treated in a similar manner, except where the FDIC determines that doing otherwise would maximize the value of the company's assets or maximize the present value of the proceeds (or minimize any loss) from disposing of the assets. Claimants that are similarly situated in the expenses and claims priority cannot receive less than the maximum liability amount defined in Section 210(d). The section also defines the priority of expenses and unsecured claims in those cases where the FDIC is appointed receiver for a covered broker or dealer (S. Rep. No. 111-176, p. 61).

Section 210(c) authorizes the FDIC to repudiate and enforce contracts and handle the financial company's qualified financial contracts (including derivatives) (S. Rep. No. 111-176, p. 61).

Determination of Claims.—The FDIC must report on claims as set forth in Section 203(c)(3) of the Dodd-Frank Act. Subject to Section 210(a)(4), the receiver must determine claims in accordance with the requirements of Section 210(a) and the regulations prescribed under Section 209 (Sec. 210(a)(2)(A) of the Dodd-Frank Wall Street Reform and Consumer Protection Act). In any case involving the liquidation or winding up of the affairs of a covered financial company, the FDIC must issue a notice to the company's creditors to present their claims and proofs of claims by a date specified in the notice, which cannot be earlier than 90 days after the publication of the notice. The FDIC must publish this notice promptly and must republish it one and two months after the initial publication (Sec. 210(a)(2)(B) of the Dodd-Frank Act). The FDIC must also mail a similar notice at the time of publication to any creditor on the books and records of the covered financial company. It must do so at the last address of the creditor appearing in the books or in any claim filed by the claimant, or within 30 days after the discovery of the name and address of a claimant not appearing in the books and records (Sec. 210(a)(2)(C) of the Dodd-Frank Act).

Claim Resolution Procedures.—The FDIC must notify a claimant whether it accepts or objects to the claim within 180 days after the claim is filed, unless the claimant and the FDIC agree in writing within the 180 days to extend this period. Failure to notify the claimant of a disallowance within the original or extended time period is deemed a disallowance, entitling the claimant to file or continue an action in court (Secs. 210(a)(3)(A)(i)–(ii) of the Dodd-Frank Act). Notification is sufficient if mailed to the last address appearing on the books and records of the covered financial company, in the claim filed or in documents submitted in proof of the claim (Sec. 210(a)(3)(A)(iii) of the Dodd-Frank Act).

A notice of disallowance must include a statement of each reason for the disallowance and the procedures required to file or continue an action in court (Sec. 210(a)(3)(A)(iv) of the Dodd-Frank Act). The receiver must allow any claim received by the bar date set forth in the notice that is proved to the satisfaction of the receiver (Sec. 210(a)(3)(B) of the Dodd-Frank Act). Claims filed after the bar date will be disallowed, and that disallowance will be final, unless the claimant did not receive notice of the receivership in time to file a timely claim and the late-filed claim is filed in time to permit payment of the claim (Sec. 210(a)(3)(C) of the Dodd-Frank Act).

The FDIC may object to any portion of a claim that is not proved to its satisfaction (Sec. 210(a)(3)(D)(i) of the Dodd-Frank Act). If a claim is undersecured, the FDIC may treat the portion of the claim that exceeds the fair market value of the collateral as an unsecured claim and cannot make any payment with respect to that unsecured claim other than in connection with the disposition of all claims of unsecured creditors (Sec. 210(a)(3)(D)(ii) of the Dodd-Frank Act). The above provisions do not apply with respect to any extension of credit from any federal reserve bank or from the FDIC to any covered financial company, or any legally enforceable and perfected security interest in the company's assets securing the extension of credit (subject to Section 210(a)(3)(D)(ii) with respect to an undersecured claim) (Sec. 210(a)(3)(D)(iii) of the Dodd-Frank Act).

The filing of a claim is considered commencement of an action for purposes of any applicable statute of limitations (Sec. 210(a)(3)(E)(i) of the Dodd-Frank Act). The filing of a claim will not, however, prejudice any right of the claimant to continue an action filed before the receivership (Sec. 210(a)(3)(E)(ii) of the Dodd-Frank Act).

Judicial Determination of Claims.—A claimant may file suit on a claim or continue a suit brought before the receivership in the district or territorial court for the district in which the covered financial company has its principal place of business (Sec. 210(a)(4)(A) of the Dodd-Frank Act). If a claimant fails to file suit or continue an action within 60 days of the bar date set forth in the FDIC's notice to claimants (or the later bar date established by agreement) or within 60 days of the date of any notice of disallowance of the claim, whichever comes first, the claim will be deemed disallowed on a final basis as of the end of that period (Secs. 210(a)(4)(B)–(C) of the Dodd-Frank Act).

Expedited Determination.—The FDIC must establish an expedited claims procedure for any claimant that alleges that it has (or is an entitlement holder that has control of) a legally valid and enforceable or perfected security interest in property of a covered financial company and that irreparable injury will occur if the regular claims procedure is followed (Sec. 210(a)(5)(A) of the Dodd-Frank Act). Within 90 days after a claim is filed in accordance with the expedited claims procedures, the FDIC must determine whether to allow or disallow the claim or portions thereof or whether the claim should be determined pursuant to the nonexpedited claims procedures, notify the claimant of the determination and, if the claim is disallowed, provide each reason for the disallow-

¶530

ance and the procedure for obtaining a judicial determination (Sec. 210(a)(5)(B) of the Dodd-Frank Act).

If a claimant requesting expedited relief fails to file suit, or to continue a suit filed before the receivership, within 30 days after the end of the 90-day period after the filing of the expedited claim or after the date on which the FDIC denies the claim or portions thereof, whichever comes first, the claim will be deemed disallowed on a final basis as of the end of that period (Secs. 210(a)(5)(C)–(D) of the Dodd-Frank Act). The filing of a claim is considered commencement of an action for purposes of any applicable statute of limitations (Sec. 210(a)(5)(E)(i) of the Dodd-Frank Act). But, subject to Section 210(a)(8) (discussed below), filing of a claim will not prejudice any right of the claimant to continue an action filed before the receivership (Sec. 210(a)(5)(E)(ii) of the Dodd-Frank Act).

Agreements Against Receiver's Interest.—An agreement that tends to diminish or defeat the receiver's interest in any asset acquired by it under Section 210 is not valid unless it is in writing, was executed by an authorized officer or representative of the covered financial company or was confirmed by the company in the ordinary course of business, and has been an official record of the company since its execution or the party claiming under the agreement provides acceptable documentation of the agreement and its authorized execution or confirmation by the company (Sec. 210(a)(6) of the Dodd-Frank Act).

Payment of Claims.—The FDIC may, in its discretion, to the extent funds are available, pay creditor claims that are allowed by the receiver, approved by the receiver pursuant to a final determination, or determined by the final judgment of a court (Sec. 210(a)(7)(A) of the Dodd-Frank Act). In no event will a creditor receive less than the amount it is entitled to receive under Section 210(d)(2) or (3) (Sec. 210(a)(7)(B) of the Dodd-Frank Act). The FDIC may, in its discretion, pay dividends on proven claims at any time, and it will have no liability for paying dividends on proven claims or for failing to pay dividends on unproven claims (Sec. 210(a)(7)(C) of the Dodd-Frank Act). Finally, the FDIC may prescribe rules and define terms to establish an interest rate for or to make payments of post-insolvency interest to creditors holding proven claims, but no interest may be paid until the FDIC has satisfied the principal amount of all creditor claims (Sec. 210(a)(7)(D) of the Dodd-Frank Act).

Priority of Claims.—Unsecured claims have priority in the following order:

1. Administrative expenses of the receiver.
2. Any amounts owed to the United States (unless the United States agrees otherwise).
3. Wages, salaries or commissions, including vacation, severance and sick leave pay earned by an individual (other than a senior executive or director of the covered financial company) of up to $11,725 per individual (and indexed for inflation by FDIC regulation) earned within 180 days before the receivership.
4. Contributions owed to employee benefit plans arising from services rendered within 180 days before the receivership, to the extent of the number of employees covered by each plan multiplied by $11,725 (and indexed for inflation by FDIC regulation), less the aggregate amount paid to the employees as wages, salaries or commis-

sions, plus the aggregate amount paid by the receivership on behalf of the employees to any other employee benefit plan.

5. Any other general or senior liability of the covered financial company.
6. Any obligation subordinated to general creditors.
7. Any wages, salaries or commissions, including vacation, severance and sick leave pay, owed to a senior executive or director of the covered financial company.
8. Any obligation to shareholders, members, general partners, limited partners or other persons with interests in the equity of the covered financial company arising as a result of their status as shareholders, members, general partners, limited partners or other persons with interests in the equity of the covered financial company (Sec. 210(b)(1) of the Dodd-Frank Act).

If the receiver cannot obtain unsecured credit for the covered financial company from commercial sources, it may obtain credit or incur debt on the part of the covered financial company, which must have priority over administrative expenses (Sec. 210(b)(2) of the Dodd-Frank Act). Unsecured claims of the United States must at a minimum have a higher priority than liabilities of the covered financial company that count as regulatory capital (Sec. 210(b)(3) of the Dodd-Frank Act).

Similarly-Situated Creditors. All claimants that are similarly situated under Section 210(b)(1)'s priority structure must be treated in a similar manner. However, the FDIC may take any action (including making payments) that does not treat similarly-situated creditors similarly if it determines that this action is necessary to maximize the value of the assets of the covered financial company, to initiate and continue operations essential to implementing the receivership or any bridge financial company, to maximize the present value return from, or minimize the loss realized upon, the sale or other disposition of assets of the covered financial company (Sec. 210(b)(4)(A) of the Dodd-Frank Act). Even so, all claimants that are similarly situated must receive at least the maximum liability amount provided in Sections 210(d)(2) and (3) (Sec. 210(b)(4)(B) of the Dodd-Frank Act).

Secured Claims. The priority structure for administrative expenses and unsecured claims will not affect secured claims or security entitlements respecting assets or property held by the covered financial company except to the extent that the security is insufficient to satisfy the claim (Sec. 210(b)(5) of the Dodd-Frank Act).

Priority in Broker-Dealer Liquidations. In a broker-dealer receivership, claims that are proven to the FDIC's satisfaction as receiver under Section 205(e) must have the same priority as in a non-broker-dealer receivership, except that:

- the SIPC may recover administrative expenses incurred under Section 205 on an equal basis with the FDIC;
- the FDIC may recover any amounts paid to customers or to the SIPC under Section 205(f) as claims owed to the United States;
- the SIPC may recover any amounts paid out of the SIPC Fund to meet its obligations under Section 205 and under the SIPA, which claim will be subordinate to administrative expenses (Sec. 210(b)(1)(A) of the Dodd-Frank Act) and claims owed to the

¶530

United States (Sec. 210(b)(1)(B) of the Dodd-Frank Act) but senior to all other claims; and

- the FDIC may, after paying any proven claims to customers under SIPA Section 205, pay dividends on other proven claims in accordance with the priorities set forth in Section 210(b)(1) (Sec. 210(b)(6) of the Dodd-Frank Act).

Repudiation of Contracts.—The FDIC may repudiate contracts entered into by the covered financial company before the receivership if the FDIC determines: (1) the contract's performance would be burdensome; and (2) disaffirmance or repudiation would promote the orderly administration of the company's affairs (Sec. 210(c)(1) of the Dodd-Frank Act). The FDIC must determine whether or not to repudiate contracts within a reasonable time (Sec. 210(c)(2) of the Dodd-Frank Act).

The FDIC's liability as receiver for a covered financial company is limited to actual direct compensatory damages determined as of the date of the FDIC's appointment as receiver or, in the case of a qualified financial contract, the date of the contract's disaffirmance or repudiation (Sec. 210(c)(3)(A) of the Dodd-Frank Act). "Actual direct compensatory damages" does not include punitive or exemplary damages, damages for lost profits or opportunity, or damages for pain and suffering (Sec. 210(c)(3)(B) of the Dodd-Frank Act).

Debt Obligations. Actual direct compensatory damages for repudiation or disaffirmance of debt obligations must be no less than the amount loaned plus accrued interest and any credited original issue discount as of the date the FDIC was appointed receiver. The damages must also include accrued interest through the date of repudiation or disaffirmance, in the case of an allowed secured claim that is secured by property worth more than the amount of the claim and accrued interest (Sec. 210(c)(3)(D) of the Dodd-Frank Act).

Contingent Obligations. The FDIC may issue a rule or regulation prescribing that damages for repudiation of a contingent obligation of a covered financial company under a guarantee, letter of credit or loan commitment, or any similar obligation, be no less than the estimated value of the claim as of the date the FDIC was appointed receiver. This value must be measured based on the likelihood that the contingent claim would become fixed and on the probable magnitude of the claim (Sec. 210(c)(3)(E) of the Dodd-Frank Act).

Leases under which Company is Lessee. If the FDIC repudiates a lease under which the financial company is the lessee, damages must be limited to the contractual rent accruing before the date on which the notice of repudiation is mailed or the date on which the repudiation becomes effective (unless the lessor is in default or breach of the lease), whichever is later (Sec. 210(c)(4)(B)(i) of the Dodd-Frank Act). The lessor will not have a claim for damages under any acceleration clause or other penalty provision in the lease, but will have a claim for unpaid rent, subject to all appropriate offsets and defenses, due as of the date of the FDIC's appointment as receiver (Secs. 210(c)(4)(B)(ii)–(iii) of the Dodd-Frank Act).

Real-Estate Leases under which Company is Landlord. If the FDIC repudiates an unexpired, written real-estate lease under which the financial company is the landlord, and the tenant is not in default as of the date of repudiation, the tenant may choose to treat the lease as terminated by the repudiation or remain in possession for the balance of the lease term, unless the tenant defaults after the date of repudiation (Sec. 210(c)(5)(A) of the Dodd-Frank Act). If the tenant chooses to remain in possession, the tenant must continue to pay the contractual rent and may offset against any rent payment accruing after repudiation any damages accruing after repudiation as a result of the nonperformance of the financial company's obligations under the lease (Sec. 210(c)(5)(B)(i) of the Dodd-Frank Act). The FDIC is not liable for damages arising after repudiation as a result of repudiation, other than the offset (Sec. 210(c)(5)(B)(ii) of the Dodd-Frank Act).

Real-Estate Sales Contracts. If the FDIC repudiates a written real-estate sale contract, and the purchaser under the contract is in possession and is not in default as of the date of repudiation, the purchaser may choose to treat the contract as terminated or remain in possession (Sec. 210(c)(6)(A) of the Dodd-Frank Act). If the purchaser remains in possession, the purchaser must continue to make all payments due under the contract after repudiation, and may offset against those payments any damages accruing after repudiation due to the post-repudiation nonperformance of the financial company's obligations (Sec. 210(c)(6)(B)(i) of the Dodd-Frank Act). The FDIC is not liable for damages arising after repudiation as a result of repudiation, other than the offset, and will have no obligation under the contract other than to deliver title to the purchaser in accordance with the contract's provisions (Sec. 210(c)(6)(B)(ii) of the Dodd-Frank Act). The above provisions do not limit any right of the FDIC to assign the contract and sell the property, and the FDIC has no further liability under the contract after the assignment and sale is consummated (Sec. 210(c)(6)(C) of the Dodd-Frank Act).

Contracts for Services. In the case of any contract for services under which the financial company is a party, any claim of the counterparty for services performed before the date the FDIC was appointed receiver will be a claim to be paid in accordance with Sections 210(a), (b) and (d), and will be deemed to have arisen as of the date of the receiver's appointment (Sec. 210(c)(7)(A) of the Dodd-Frank Act). The FDIC may repudiate a contract for services even after it has accepted performance of some services under the contract (Sec. 210(c)(7)(C) of the Dodd-Frank Act). Services provided after the FDIC's appointment as receiver, but before repudiation, will be paid for under the contract terms as an administrative expense of the receivership (Sec. 210(c)(7)(B) of the Dodd-Frank Act).

Qualified Financial Contracts.—Section 210(c)(8) describes the rights of parties to qualified financial contracts with a covered financial company. Compensatory damages for repudiation of qualified financial contracts include normal and reasonable costs of cover or other reasonable measures of damages typical in the relevant industry (Sec. 210(c)(3)(C) of the Dodd-Frank Act). Damages must be paid in accordance with Sections 210(c)(3) and 210(d).

Definitions. The definitions of terms in Section 210(c) apply to that subsection only and do not affect the terms under any other statute, regulation or rule (Sec. 210(c)(15) of the Dodd-Frank Act). "Qualified financial contract" is defined to mean any securities contract, commodity contract, forward contract, repurchase agreement, swap agreement and any similar agreement that the FDIC determines by regulation, resolution or order to be a qualified financial contract for Section 210(c)(8) purposes (Sec.

¶530

210(c)(8)(D)(i) of the Dodd-Frank Act). Those terms are defined at Sections 210(c)(8)(D)(ii)–(vi), respectively:

"Securities contract" means:

(1) a contract for the purchase, sale or loan of a security, a certificate of deposit, a mortgage loan, any interest in a mortgage loan, a group or index of securities, certificates of deposit, or mortgage loans or interests therein (including any interest therein or based on the value thereof), or any option on any of the foregoing, including any option to purchase or sell any security, certificate of deposit, mortgage loan, interest, group or index, or option, and including any repurchase or reverse repurchase transaction on any security, certificate of deposit, mortgage loan, interest, group or index, or option (whether or not the repurchase or reverse repurchase transaction is a "repurchase agreement" as defined in Section 210(c)(8)(D)(v));

(2) any option entered into on a national securities exchange relating to foreign currencies;

(3) the guarantee (including by novation) by or to any securities clearing agency of any settlement of cash, securities, certificates of deposit, mortgage loans or interests therein, group or index of securities, certificates of deposit or mortgage loans or interests therein (including any interest therein or based on the value thereof) or an option on any of the foregoing, including any option to purchase or sell any such security, certificate of deposit, mortgage loan, interest, group or index, or option (whether or not the settlement is in connection with any agreement or transaction referred to in this list);

(4) any margin loan;

(5) any extension of credit for the clearance or settlement of securities transactions;

(6) any loan transaction coupled with a securities collar transaction, any prepaid securities forward transaction, or any total return swap transaction coupled with a securities sale transaction;

(7) any other agreement or transaction that is similar to any agreement or transaction referred to in this list;

(8) any combination of the agreements or transactions referred to in this list;

(9) any option to enter into any agreement or transaction referred to in this list;

(10) a master agreement, together with all supplements, that provides for an agreement or transaction referred to above, without regard to whether the master agreement provides for an agreement or transaction that is not a securities contract under this definition, except that the master agreement will be considered to be a securities contract only with respect to each agreement or transaction under the master agreement that is referred to in any of the above list items; or

(11) any security agreement or arrangement or other credit enhancement related to any agreement or transaction referred to above, including any guarantee or reimbursement obligation in connection with any such agreement or transaction (Sec. 210(c)(8)(D)(ii) of the Dodd-Frank Act).

The term "securities contract" does not include any purchase, sale or repurchase obligation under a participation in a commercial mortgage loan unless the FDIC determines by regulation, resolution, or order to include the agreement within the meaning of the term (Sec. 210(c)(8)(D)(ii)(II) of the Dodd-Frank Act).

"Commodity contract" means:

(1) with respect to a futures commission merchant, a contract for the purchase or sale of a commodity for future delivery on, or subject to the rules of, a contract market or board of trade;

(2) with respect to a foreign futures commission exchange, a foreign future;

(3) with respect to a leverage transaction merchant, a leverage transaction;

(4) with respect to a clearing organization, a contract for the purchase or sale of a commodity for future delivery on, or subject to the rules of, a contract market or board of trade that is cleared by the clearing organization, or commodity option traded on, or subject to the rules of, a contract market or board of trade that is cleared by the clearing organization;

(5) with respect to a commodity options dealer, a commodity option;

(6) any other agreement or transaction that is similar to any agreement or transaction referred to in this list;

(7) any combination of the agreements or transactions referred to in this list;

(8) any option to enter into any agreement or transaction referred to in this list;

(9) a master agreement, together with all supplements, that provides for an agreement or transaction referred to in any of the list items above, without regard to whether the master agreement provides for an agreement or transaction that is not a commodity contract under this definition, except that the master agreement will be considered to be a commodity contract only with respect to each agreement or transaction under the master agreement that is referred to in any of the list items above; or

(10) any security agreement or arrangement or other credit enhancement related to any agreement or transaction referred to above, including any guarantee or reimbursement obligation in connection with any such agreement or transaction (Sec. 210(c)(8)(D)(iii) of the Dodd-Frank Act).

"Forward contract" means:

(1) a contract (other than a commodity contract) for the purchase, sale or transfer of a commodity or any similar good, article, service, right or interest that is presently or in the future becomes the subject of dealing in the forward contract trade, or product or byproduct thereof, with a maturity date that is more than two days after the date on which the contract is entered into, including a repurchase or reverse repurchase transaction (whether or not it is a "repurchase agreement" as defined in Section 210(c)(8)(D)(v) of the Dodd-Frank Act), consignment, lease, swap, hedge transaction, deposit, loan, option, allocated transaction, unallocated transaction or any other similar agreement;

¶530

(2) any combination of agreements or transactions referred to in items 1 and 3 of this list;

(3) any option to enter into any agreement or transaction referred to in items 1 or 2 of this list;

(4) a master agreement that provides for an agreement or transaction referred to in the above list items, together with all supplements, without regard to whether the master agreement provides for an agreement or transaction that is not a forward contract under this definition, except that the master agreement will be considered to be a forward contract only with respect to each agreement or transaction under the master agreement that is referred to in the list items above; or

(5) any security agreement or arrangement or other credit enhancement related to any agreement or transaction referred to in Section the list items above, including any guarantee or reimbursement obligation in connection with any agreement or transaction referred to in any of those list items (Sec. 210(c)(8)(D)(iv) of the Dodd-Frank Act).

"Repurchase agreement" (or "reverse repurchase agreement") means:

(1) an agreement, including related terms, which provides for the transfer of one or more certificates of deposit, mortgage related securities (as defined in Exchange Act Section 3), mortgage loans, interests in mortgage-related securities or mortgage loans, eligible bankers' acceptances, qualified foreign government securities (meaning a security that is a direct obligation of, or that is fully guaranteed by, the central government of a member of the Organization for Economic Cooperation and Development, as determined by regulation or order adopted by the Board of Governors), or securities that are direct obligations of, or that are fully guaranteed by, the United States or any U.S. agency against the transfer of funds by the transferee of such certificates of deposit, eligible bankers' acceptances, securities, mortgage loans, or interests with a simultaneous agreement by the transferee to transfer to the transferor certificates of deposit, eligible bankers' acceptances, securities, mortgage loans, or interests as described above, at a date certain not later than one year after such transfers or on demand, against the transfer of funds, or any other similar agreement;

(2) any combination of agreements or transactions referred to in items 1 and 3 of this list;

(3) any option to enter into any agreement or transaction referred to in items 1 or 2 of this list;

(4) a master agreement that provides for an agreement or transaction referred to in any of the above list items, together with all supplements, without regard to whether the master agreement provides for an agreement or transaction that is not a repurchase agreement under this definition, except that the master agreement will be considered to be a repurchase agreement only with respect to each agreement or transaction under the master agreement that is referred to in any of the above list items; and

(5) any security agreement or arrangement or other credit enhancement related to any agreement or transaction referred to above, including any guarantee or

reimbursement obligation in connection with any agreement or transaction referred to above (Sec. 210(c)(8)(D)(v) of the Dodd-Frank Act).

The term "repurchase agreement" does not include any repurchase obligation under a participation in a commercial mortgage loan, unless the FDIC determines, by regulation, resolution or order, to include such a participation within the meaning of the term (Sec. 210(c)(8)(D)(v)(II) of the Dodd-Frank Act).

"Swap agreement" means:

(1) any agreement, including the terms and conditions incorporated by reference, that is an interest rate swap, option, future or forward agreement, including:

— a rate floor, rate cap, rate collar, cross-currency rate swap and basis swap;

— a spot, same day-tomorrow, tomorrow-next, forward or other foreign exchange, precious metals or other commodity agreement;

— a currency swap, option, future or forward agreement;

— an equity index or equity swap, option, future or forward agreement;

— a debt index or debt swap, option future or forward agreement;

— a total return, credit spread or credit swap, option, future or forward agreement;

— a commodity index or commodity swap, option, future or forward agreement;

— a weather swap, option, future or forward agreement;

— an emissions swap, option, future or forward agreement; or

— an inflation swap, option, future or forward agreement;

(2) any agreement or transaction that is similar to any other agreement or transaction referred to in this list and that is of a type that has been, is, or becomes the subject of recurrent dealings in the swap or other derivatives markets (including terms and conditions incorporated by reference) and that is a forward, swap, future, option or spot transaction on one or more rates, currencies, commodities, equity securities or other equity instruments, debt securities or other debt instruments, quantitative measures associated with an occurrence, extent of an occurrence, or contingency associated with a financial, commercial, or economic consequence, or economic or financial indices or measures of economic or financial risk or value;

(3) any combination of agreements or transactions referred to in this list;

(4) any option to enter into any agreement or transaction referred to in this list;

(5) a master agreement that provides for an agreement or transaction referred to in the above list items, together with all supplements, without regard to whether the master agreement contains an agreement or transaction that is not a swap agreement under this definition, except that the master agreement will be considered to be a swap agreement only with respect to each agreement or transaction under the master agreement that is referred to in the list items above; and

(6) any security agreement or arrangement or other credit enhancement related to any agreement or transaction referred to in Sections the above list items, including any guarantee or reimbursement obligation in connection with any agreement or

¶530

transaction referred to in any of the above items (Sec. 210(c)(8)(D)(vi) of the Dodd-Frank Act).

The section also defines "default" and "in danger of default" when those terms are used in Sections 210(c)(8) and 210(c)(10). "Default" means, with respect to a covered financial company, any adjudication or other official decision by any court of competent jurisdiction, or other public authority under which the FDIC was appointed receiver. "In danger of default" means that the FDIC or appropriate state authority has, in its opinion, determined that a covered financial company:

- is not likely to be able to pay its obligations in the normal course of business and there is no reasonable prospect that it will be able to pay those obligations without federal assistance, or
- has incurred or is likely to incur losses that will deplete all or substantially all of its capital, and there is no reasonable prospect that the capital will be replenished without federal assistance (Sec. 210(c)(8)(D)(vii) of the Dodd-Frank Act).

The term "transfer" means every mode of disposing of or parting with property or with an interest in property, whether direct or indirect, absolute or conditional, voluntary or involuntary. It includes retention of title as a security interest and foreclosure of the equity of redemption of the covered financial company (Sec. 210(c)(8)(D)(ix) of the Dodd-Frank Act). "Person" includes any governmental entity in addition to any entity included in the definition of "person" in 1 U.S.C. § 1 (Sec. 210(c)(8)(D)(x) of the Dodd-Frank Act).

Master Agreements. Any master agreement, together with supplements, will be treated as a single agreement and a single qualified financial contract. If a master agreement contains provisions relating to agreements or transactions that are not qualified financial contracts, it will be deemed to be a qualified financial contract only with respect to the transactions that are themselves qualified financial contracts (Sec. 210(c)(8)(D)(viii) of the Dodd-Frank Act).

Stay of Exercise of Rights. Section 210(c)(8)(A) provides that, subject to Sections 210(a)(8) and 210(c)(9) and (10), no person will be stayed or prohibited from exercising any right to terminate, liquidate or accelerate a qualified financial contract with a covered financial company arising upon the date of the FDIC's appointment as receiver; any right under any security agreement or arrangement or other credit enhancement related to one or more such qualified financial contracts; or any right to offset or net out any termination value, payment amount, or other transfer obligation arising under or in connection with one or more such qualified financial contracts (including any master agreement) (Sec. 210(c)(8)(A) of the Dodd-Frank Act). Section 210(a)(8) applies to any judicial action or proceeding brought against the FDIC as receiver referred to above, or against the financial company, by any counterparty to a qualified financial contract described in Section 210(c)(8)(A)(i) (Sec. 210(c)(8)(B) of the Dodd-Frank Act).

Certain Transfers and Interests Not Avoidable. The FDIC, whether acting as the FDIC or as receiver, cannot avoid any transfer of money or other property in connection with any qualified financial contract with a covered financial company, unless the transferee had actual intent to hinder, delay or defraud the company, its creditors or the FDIC as receiver (Sec. 210(c)(8)(C) of the Dodd-Frank Act). No provision of Section 210(c) can be construed as permitting the avoidance of any legally enforceable or perfected security interest in any of the assets of any covered financial company, except in accordance with Section 210(c)(11), or any legally enforceable interest in customer property, security entitlements respecting assets or property held by the covered financial company for any security entitlement holder (Sec. 210(c)(12) of the Dodd-Frank Act).

Walkaway Clauses. Notwithstanding Section 210(c)(8)(A) of the Dodd-Frank Act and Sections 403 and 404 of the Federal Deposit Insurance Corporation Improvement Act of 1991, no walkaway clause is enforceable in a qualified financial contract of a covered financial company in default (Sec. 210(c)(8)(F)(i) of the Dodd-Frank Act). But any payment or delivery obligations otherwise due from a party under the contract must be suspended from the time at which the FDIC is appointed as receiver until the time at which the party receives notice that the contract has been transferred pursuant to Section 210(c)(10)(A) or 5:00 p.m. (eastern time) on the business day following the FDIC's appointment as receiver, whichever comes first (Sec. 210(c)(8)(F)(ii) of the Dodd-Frank Act). "Walkaway clause" means any provision in a qualified financial contract that suspends, conditions or extinguishes a payment obligation of a party (or does not create an obligation that would otherwise exist) solely because of the status of that party as a nondefaulting party in connection with the insolvency of a covered financial company or the exercise of rights or powers by the FDIC as receiver, and not as a result of the exercise by a party of a right to offset, setoff, or net obligations that exist under the contract, any other contract between those parties, or applicable law (Sec. 210(c)(8)(F)(iii) of the Dodd-Frank Act).

Obligations to Clearing Organizations. If the covered financial company is a party to any qualified financial contract cleared by or subject to the rules of a clearing organization (as defined in Section 210(c)(9)(D) of the Dodd-Frank Act), the FDIC must use its best efforts to meet all margin, collateral and settlement obligations of the covered financial company that arise under qualified financial contracts (unless those obligations are not enforceable against the receiver under Section 210(c)(8)(F)(i) or Section 210(c)(10)(B) of the Dodd-Frank Act), as required by the rules of the clearing organization when due. If the receiver fails to satisfy any such obligation, the clearing organization is not stayed from exercising its rights and remedies under its rules and applicable law, including the right to liquidate all positions and collateral of the covered financial company and suspend or cease to act for the financial company (Sec. 210(c)(8)(G) of the Dodd-Frank Act).

Recordkeeping. The primary federal financial regulatory agencies must, within 24 months of enactment, jointly prescribe regulations requiring that financial companies maintain records with respect to qualified financial contracts, including market valuations, as the agencies determine to be necessary or appropriate to assist the FDIC as receiver in exercising its rights and fulfilling its obligations under Sections 210(c)(8), (9) or (10) (Secs. 210(c)(8)(H)(i)–(ii) of the Dodd-Frank Act). The regulations must, as appropriate, differentiate among financial companies by their size, risk, complexity, leverage, frequency and dollar amount of qualified financial contracts, interconnectedness to the financial system and any other appropriate factors (Sec. 210(c)(8)(H)(iv) of the Dodd-Frank Act). If the agencies do not prescribe joint final or interim final regulations within the 24-month period, the Chairperson of the Financial Stability

¶530

Oversight Council must do so in consultation with the FDIC (Sec. 210(c)(8)(H)(iii) of the Dodd-Frank Act).

Transfer of Qualified Financial Contracts. No law can be construed as limiting, or authorizing a court or agency to limit or delay, the FDIC's power to transfer a qualified financial contract in accordance with Section 210(c)(9) or (10) or to disaffirm or repudiate the contract in accordance with Section 210(c) (Sec. 210(c)(8)(E) of the Dodd-Frank Act).

Section 210(c)(9) provides that, in transferring any assets or liabilities of a covered financial company in default (including any qualified financial contract), the FDIC must transfer to one financial institution that is not itself under a conservator, receiver, trustee in bankruptcy or other legal custodian or otherwise the subject of a bankruptcy or insolvency proceeding either all of the following, or none of the following:

- the qualified financial contracts between any person or any affiliate of that person and the covered financial company in default;
- the claims of the person or affiliate against the covered financial company under any such contract (other than any claim that is subordinated to the claims of general unsecured creditors under the contract terms);
- the claims of the covered financial company against the person or affiliate under the contract; and
- the property securing or any other credit enhancement for any contract described above or under any such contract (Sec. 210(c)(9)(A) of the Dodd-Frank Act).

For purposes of this paragraph, a bridge financial company cannot be considered a covered financial company for which a conservator, receiver, trustee in bankruptcy or other legal custodian has been appointed or which is otherwise the subject of a bankruptcy or insolvency proceeding (Sec. 210(c)(10)(C) of the Dodd-Frank Act). The FDIC as receiver cannot make a transfer to a foreign bank, financial institution organized under the laws of a foreign country, or branch or agency of a foreign bank or financial institution unless, under the law applicable to such institution, to the financial contracts, and to any netting contract, any security agreement or arrangement or other credit enhancement related to one or more qualified financial contracts, the parties' contractual rights are enforceable substantially to the same extent as permitted under Section 210 of the Dodd-Frank Act (Sec. 210(c)(9)(B) of the Dodd-Frank Act).

If the qualified financial contract and related claims, property or credit enhancement transferred are cleared by or subject to the rules of a clearing organization, the clearing organization cannot be required to accept the transferee as a member by virtue of the transfer (Sec. 210(c)(9)(C) of the Dodd-Frank Act).

"Financial institution" means a broker or dealer, depository institution, futures commission merchant, bridge financial company or any other institution determined by the FDIC, by regulation, to be a financial institution (Sec. 210(c)(9)(D)(i) of the Dodd-Frank Act). "Clearing organization" has the same meaning as in Section 402 of the Federal Deposit Insurance Corporation Improvement Act of 1991 (Sec. 210(c)(9)(D)(ii) of the Dodd-Frank Act).

Notification of Transfer. If the FDIC as receiver for a covered financial company in default or in danger of default transfers any assets or liabilities of the covered financial company that include any qualified financial contract, the FDIC must notify any party to the contract of the transfer before 5:00 p.m. (eastern time) on the business day following the FDIC's appointment as receiver (Sec. 210(c)(10)(A) of the Dodd-Frank Act). A party to a qualified financial contract with a covered financial company is stayed from exercising any right to terminate, liquidate or net such contract under Section 210(c)(8)(A) solely by reason of or incidental to the FDIC's appointment as receiver or the company's insolvency or financial condition until 5:00 p.m. (eastern time) on the business day following the appointment, or until after the person has received notice of the contract's transfer under Section 210(c)(9)(A) (Sec. 210(c)(10)(B)(i) of the Dodd-Frank Act).

The FDIC will be deemed to have notified a party to a qualified financial contract if the FDIC has taken steps reasonably calculated to provide such notice in time (Sec. 210(c)(10)(B)(ii) of the Dodd-Frank Act). "Business day" means any day other than any Saturday, Sunday or any day on which either the New York Stock Exchange or the Federal Reserve Bank of New York is closed (Sec. 210(c)(10)(D) of the Dodd-Frank Act).

Disaffirmance or Repudiation. In exercising its rights of disaffirmance or repudiation, the FDIC must disaffirm or repudiate either all or none of the qualified financial contracts between the covered financial company in default and any person or affiliate of such person (Sec. 210(c)(11) of the Dodd-Frank Act).

Authority to Enforce Contracts.—The FDIC as receiver may enforce any contract, other than a liability insurance contract of a director or officer, a financial institution bond entered into by the covered financial company, notwithstanding any contract provision for termination, default, acceleration or exercise of rights upon, or solely because of, insolvency, the appointment of or exercise of rights or powers by the FDIC as receiver, the filing of the petition pursuant to Section 202(a)(1), or the issuance of the recommendations or determination, or any related actions or events, under Section 203 (Sec. 210(c)(13)(A) of the Dodd-Frank Act). The FDIC as receiver retains any right to enforce or recover under a liability insurance contract of a director or officer or financial institution bond under other applicable law (Sec. 210(c)(13)(B) of the Dodd-Frank Act).

Ipso Facto Clauses. Except as otherwise provided, no person may exercise any right or power to terminate, accelerate, or declare a default under any contract to which the covered financial company is a party (and no provision in any such contract providing for such default, termination or acceleration is enforceable), or to obtain possession of or exercise control over any property of the covered financial company or affect any contractual rights of the covered financial company, without the consent of the FDIC as receiver during the first 90 days of the receivership (Sec. 210(c)(13)(C)(i) of the Dodd-Frank Act). No provision of Section 210(c)(13)(C), however, applies to a director or officer liability insurance contract or a financial institution bond, to the rights of parties to certain qualified financial contracts pursuant to Section 210(c)(8), or to the rights of parties to netting contracts pursuant to Subtitle A of Title IV of the Federal Deposit Insurance Corporation Improvement Act of 1991, nor will any provision be construed as permitting the FDIC as receiver to fail to comply with otherwise enforceable provisions of the contract (Sec. 210(c)(13)(C)(ii) of the Dodd-Frank Act).

Contracts to Extend Credit. Notwithstanding any other provision in Title II of the Dodd-Frank Act, if the FDIC as receiver enforces any contract to extend credit to the covered financial company or bridge financial company, any valid and enforceable obligation to repay the debt will be paid by the FDIC as an administrative expense of the receivership (Sec. 210(c)(13)(D) of the Dodd-Frank Act).

Contracts Subject to Guarantee. The FDIC may enforce contracts of subsidiaries or affiliates of the covered financial company, the obligations under which are guaranteed or otherwise supported by or linked to the covered financial company, notwithstanding any contractual right to cause the termination, liquidation or acceleration of those contracts based only on the insolvency, financial condition or receivership of the covered financial company, if the guarantee or other support and all related assets and liabilities are transferred to and assumed by a bridge financial company or a third party that is not itself under a conservator, receiver, trustee in bankruptcy or other legal custodian or otherwise the subject of a bankruptcy or insolvency proceeding within the same time period as the FDIC is entitled to transfer the qualified financial contracts of the financial company and the FDIC otherwise provides adequate protection (Sec. 210(c)(16)(A) of the Dodd-Frank Act). For purposes of this paragraph, a bridge financial company will not be considered a third party for which a conservator, receiver, trustee in bankruptcy or other legal custodian has been appointed or that is otherwise the subject of a bankruptcy or insolvency proceeding (Sec. 210(c)(16)(B) of the Dodd-Frank Act).

Exception.—No provision of Section 210(c) will apply with respect to an extension of credit from any federal reserve bank or the FDIC to any covered financial company or any security interest in the company's assets securing any such extension of credit (Sec. 210(c)(14) of the Dodd-Frank Act).

Maximum Liability.—Section 210(d) of the Dodd-Frank Act establishes the FDIC's maximum liability for claims against the covered financial company or against the FDIC as receiver. The maximum liability is the amount that the claimant would have received if the FDIC had not been appointed receiver and instead the company were liquidated under Chapter 7 of the Bankruptcy Code or any state insolvency law (S. Rep. No. 111-176, p. 61). The FDIC, with the Treasury Secretary's approval, may make additional payments to claimants if the FDIC determines this to be necessary to minimize losses from the orderly liquidation of the covered financial company (S. Rep. No. 111-176, pp. 61–62).

The FDIC's maximum liability, whether acting as receiver or in any other capacity, to a person having a claim against the receiver or the covered financial company will equal the amount that the claimant would have received if the FDIC had not been appointed receiver and the covered financial company had been liquidated under chapter 7 of the Bankruptcy Code or any similar provision of state insolvency law (Sec. 210(d)(2) of the Dodd-Frank Act). In broker-dealer receiverships, the FDIC's maximum liability will be determined as of the close of business on the day the FDIC is appointed receiver and will equal the amount that the customer would have received in a case initiated by the SIPC under the SIPA (Sec. 210(d)(3) of the Dodd-Frank Act).

The FDIC may, with the Treasury Secretary's approval, make additional payments or credit additional amounts to any claimant or category of claimants if the FDIC determines that these payments or credits will minimize losses from the orderly liquidation (Sec. 210(d)(4)(A) of the Dodd-Frank Act). The FDIC cannot, however, make any payments that would result in any claimant receiving more than the face value of its proven claim (Sec. 210(d)(4)(B)(i) of the Dodd-Frank Act). Additional payments may be made directly to the claimants or to a company (other than a covered financial company or its associated bridge financial company) to induce this company to accept liability for the claims (Sec. 210(d)(4)(C) of the Dodd-Frank Act). Making an additional payment or credit will not obligate the FDIC to make payments to any other claimant or category of claimants (Sec. 210(d)(4)(B)(ii) of the Dodd-Frank Act).

The maximum liability requirements govern the rights of creditors notwithstanding any other provision of federal or state law and regardless of the method used by the FDIC for a covered financial company, including transactions authorized under Section 210(h) (Sec. 210(d)(1) of the Dodd-Frank Act).

▶ **Effective date.** The provision takes effect one day after the date of enactment (Sec. 4 of the Dodd-Frank Wall Street Reform and Consumer Protection Act).

Law source: Law at ¶10,210 and ¶10,004. Committee Report at ¶54,109.

— Sec. 210(a) of the Dodd-Frank Wall Street Reform and Consumer Protection Act, establishing procedures for determining and resolving claims against the receivership estate;

— Sec. 210(b), establishing the priority of expenses and claims;

— Sec. 210(c), authorizing the receiver to repudiate contracts and establishing damages for repudiation;

— Sec. 210(d), establishing the maximum liability of the FDIC;

— Sec. 4, providing the effective date.

¶535 Officers, Directors, Employees and Agents

Title II of the Dodd-Frank Wall Street Reform and Consumer Protection Act contains several provisions that hold culpable officers and directors responsible or otherwise affect parties that contributed to the failure of the covered financial company. The receiver may remove culpable management and directors, bar officers and directors from serving in the financial industry, recoup compensation paid to officers and directors, recover damages and enjoy expedited consideration of cases against officers, directors, employees or agents of the covered financial company. Also, officers and directors may be subject to personal liability for their actions, and certain parties are prohibited from purchasing the company's assets due to their role in its failure.

Removal of Management and Directors.—The legislation provides that the FDIC as receiver will remove management and directors responsible for the company's failure, if they are still serving at the beginning of the receivership (Sec. 206 of the Dodd-Frank Wall Street Reform and Consumer Protection Act).

Personal Liability.—Section 210(f) of the Dodd-Frank Act permits the FDIC to take actions holding directors and officers personally liable (S. Rep. No. 111-176, p. 62). A director or officer may be held personally liable for monetary damages in a civil action for gross negligence brought by, on behalf of, or at the request of, the FDIC for its benefit acting as receiver, acting based on a cause of action conveyed by the FDIC as receiver, or acting based on a cause of action conveyed by the covered financial company or its affiliate. In addition, the FDIC retains any other rights under other applicable law (Sec. 210(f) of the Dodd-Frank Act).

Damages.—In any proceeding against a party employed by or providing services to a covered financial company, recoverable damages determined to result from the improvident or otherwise improper use or investment of any assets of the covered financial company must include principal losses and appropriate interest (Sec. 210(g) of the Dodd-Frank Act).

Expedited Litigation.—Section 210(j) of the Dodd-Frank Act expedites federal courts' consideration of cases brought by the FDIC against the officers, directors, employees or agents of a covered financial company. The notice of appeal of a case brought by the FDIC against any person employed by or providing services to a covered financial company must be filed within 30 days after the entry of the order. The appeal must be heard within 120 days, and decided within 180 days, after the notice of appeal (Sec. 210(j)(1) of the Dodd-Frank Act). The court must expedite the consideration of any case brought by the FDIC against a person employed by or providing services to a covered financial company and must give the case priority on its docket as far as practicable (Sec. 210(j)(2) of the Dodd-Frank Act). The court may modify these schedules and limitations based on a specific finding that the ends of justice served by making a modification would outweigh the public interest in having the case resolved expeditiously (Sec. 210(j)(3) of the Dodd-Frank Act).

Ban on Purchasing Assets.—Section 210(r) of the Dodd-Frank Act prohibits certain parties that defaulted on obligations to the covered financial company or otherwise caused a loss from purchasing assets of the company. The FDIC must prescribe regulations that prohibit the sale of a covered financial company's assets to:

- any person who defaulted, or was a member of a partnership or an officer or director of a corporation that defaulted, on one or more obligations to the covered financial company in the aggregate amount of over $1 million; engaged in fraudulent activity in doing so; and proposes to purchase any company asset through the use of the proceeds of a loan or credit advance from the FDIC or any covered financial company;

- any person who participated, as an officer or director of the covered financial company or its affiliate, in a material way in any transaction that resulted in a substantial loss to the covered financial company; or

- any person who has demonstrated a pattern or practice of defalcation regarding obligations to the covered financial company (Sec. 210(r)(1) of the Dodd-Frank Act).

Additionally, a person cannot purchase any asset of a covered financial company from the receiver if the person: (1) has been convicted of an offense under 18 U.S.C. §§ 215, 656, 657, 1005, 1006, 1007, 1008, 1014, 1032, 1341, 1343 or 1344, or of conspiring to commit such an offense, affecting any covered financial company; and (2) is in default on any loan or other extension of credit from the covered financial company which, if unpaid, will cause substantial loss to the Orderly Liquidation Fund or the FDIC (Sec. 210(r)(2) of the Dodd-Frank Act).

¶535

"Default" for purposes of this provision means a failure to comply with the terms of a loan or other obligation to such an extent that the property securing the obligation is foreclosed on (Sec. 210(r)(4) of the Dodd-Frank Act). These prohibitions will not apply if the sale or transfer of the asset resolves or settles, or is part of the resolution or settlement of, one or more claims that have been or could have been asserted by the FDIC against the person (Sec. 210(r)(3) of the Dodd-Frank Act).

"Clawback."— Section 210(s) of the Dodd-Frank Act authorizes the receiver to recoup compensation from senior executives and directors who were responsible for the failure of the covered financial company. The FDIC as receiver may recover from any current or former senior executive or director substantially responsible for the failed condition of the covered financial company any compensation received during the two years preceding the receivership. In the case of fraud, no time limit will apply (Sec. 210(s)(1) of the Dodd-Frank Act). The FDIC must weigh the financial and deterrent benefits of recoupment against the cost of executing the recovery (Sec. 210(s)(2) of the Dodd-Frank Act). The FDIC must prescribe regulations to implement the recoupment, including defining "compensation" to mean any financial remuneration, including salary, bonuses, incentives, benefits, severance, deferred compensation or golden parachute benefits and any profits realized from the sale of the securities of the covered financial company (Sec. 210(s)(3) of the Dodd-Frank Act).

Industry Ban.—Section 213 of the Dodd-Frank Act authorizes a ban on a senior executive or director of the covered financial company from further participation in the financial industry for two years or longer. The Board of Governors of the Federal Reserve System (the Fed) or, if the covered financial company was not supervised by the Fed, the FDIC may provide written notice to a senior executive or director of the agency's intent to ban that person from any further participation in the conduct of the affairs of any financial company for a time period determined by the agency commensurate with the executive's or director's violation, practice or breach, but for at least two years (Secs. 213(a) and (c)(1) of the Dodd-Frank Act). The agency may send this notice if it determines that the executive or director, prior to the receivership:

- violated any law or regulation, any final cease-and-desist order, any condition imposed in writing by a federal agency in connection with any action on any application, notice, or request by such company or senior executive, or any written agreement between such company and such agency;
- engaged or participated in any unsafe or unsound practice in connection with any financial company; or
- committed or engaged in any act, omission or practice which constitutes a breach of the fiduciary duty of such senior executive or director (Sec. 213(b) of the Dodd-Frank Act).

To subject the executive or director to the ban, the conduct must have involved personal dishonesty or demonstrated willful or continuing disregard for the company's safety or soundness; the violation, practice or breach must have contributed to the failure of the company; and the executive or director must have received financial gain or other benefit because of the violation, practice or breach (Sec. 213(b) of the Dodd-Frank Act).

¶535

The due process requirements under the Federal Deposit Insurance Act apply as if the covered financial company were an insured depository institution and the senior executive or director were an institution-affiliated party, as those terms are defined in that statute (Sec. 213(c)(2) of the Dodd-Frank Act). The FDIC and the Fed, in consultation with the Financial Stability Oversight Council, must jointly prescribe rules or regulations to administer and carry out these provisions, including defining the term "senior executive" (Sec. 213(d) of the Dodd-Frank Act).

Other Incidental Provisions.—Officers and directors are treated less favorably than other parties in some other provisions of Title II. For example, as insiders of the corporation they are subject to a longer look-back period with respect to recovery of preferential transfers (see discussion at ¶ 525), and their compensation claims against the receivership estate have lower priority than those of other employees (see ¶ 530).

▶ **Effective date.** The provisions take effect one day after the date of enactment (Sec. 4 of the Dodd-Frank Wall Street Reform and Consumer Protection Act).

Law source: Law at ¶ 10,210, ¶ 10,213 and ¶ 10,004. Committee Report at ¶ 54,109.

— Sec. 206 of the Dodd-Frank Wall Street Reform and Consumer Protection Act, requiring that the FDIC remove culpable management and directors;

— Sec. 210(f), authorizing the FDIC to hold officers and directors personally liable for gross negligence;

— Sec. 210(g), establishing damages for improper investments;

— Sec. 210(j), providing for expedited litigation of cases against employees or agents of the covered financial company;

— Sec. 210(r), prohibiting certain parties from purchasing assets;

— Sec. 210(s), authorizing the receiver to recoup compensation paid to senior executives and directors;

— Sec. 213, authorizing an industry ban;

— Sec. 4, providing the effective date.

¶540 Bridge Financial Companies

Section 210(h) of the Dodd-Frank Wall Street Reform and Consumer Protection Act authorizes the FDIC, as receiver, to establish one or more bridge financial companies to assume liabilities and purchase assets of the covered financial company and perform other temporary functions that the FDIC may prescribe (S. Rep. No. 111-176, p. 62).

Formation.—The FDIC as receiver, or in anticipation of becoming receiver, for one or more covered financial companies may organize one or more bridge financial companies (Sec. 210(h)(1)(A) of the Dodd-Frank Wall Street Reform and Consumer Protection Act). Upon its creation, a bridge financial company may assume liabilities (excluding regulatory capital) and purchase assets of the covered financial company as the FDIC determines in its discretion to be appropriate and may perform any other temporary function that the FDIC prescribes in its discretion and in accordance with Section 210 (Sec. 210(h)(1)(B) of the Dodd-Frank Act).

Except as provided in Section 210(h)(2)(H) for covered brokers or dealers, the FDIC as receiver may grant a federal charter to and approve articles of association for one or more bridge financial companies. The bridge financial company will, by operation of law and immediately upon issuance of its charter and approval of its articles of association, be established and operate in accordance with and subject to the charter and articles and Section 210 (Sec. 210(h)(2)(A) of the Dodd-Frank Act). Upon its establishment, the bridge financial company will be under the management of a board of directors appointed by the FDIC (Sec. 210(h)(2)(B) of the Dodd-Frank Act). The FDIC must provide the terms of, and designate representatives to execute, the articles of association and organization certificate (Sec. 210(h)(2)(C) of the Dodd-Frank Act). The FDIC also must establish the charter's terms and the rights, powers, authorities and privileges of a bridge financial company granted by the charter and provide for, and establish, the terms and conditions governing the management (including bylaws and number of directors) and operations of the bridge financial company (Sec. 210(h)(2)(D) of the Dodd-Frank Act).

The FDIC may provide for a bridge financial company to succeed to and assume any rights, powers, authorities or privileges of the covered financial company (Sec. 210(h)(2)(E)(i) of the Dodd-Frank Act). The succession and assumption will then by operation of law take effect without any further approval under federal or state law, assignment or consent required (Sec. 210(h)(2)(E)(ii) of the Dodd-Frank Act).

To the extent permitted by the FDIC and consistent with Section 210 and its associated rules and regulations, a bridge financial company may elect to follow the corporate governance practices and procedures applicable to Delaware corporations or to corporations in the state of incorporation or organization of the covered financial company (Sec. 210(h)(2)(F) of the Dodd-Frank Act).

To fund the bridge financial company's operation, the FDIC may in its discretion cause capital stock or other securities to be issued and offered for sale (Sec. 210(h)(2)(G)(iii) of the Dodd-Frank Act) or may make funds available in lieu of capital, subject to the orderly liquidation plan (Sec. 210(h)(2)(G)(iv) of the Dodd-Frank Act). The FDIC need not, however, pay capital into the bridge financial company or issue any capital stock on the bridge company's behalf (Sec. 210(h)(2)(G)(ii) of the Dodd-Frank Act), and a bridge company may operate without any capital or surplus if permitted in the FDIC's discretion (Sec. 210(h)(2)(G)(i) of the Dodd-Frank Act).

Covered Brokers and Dealers.—Section 210(h)(2)(H) addresses bridge financial companies established with respect to a covered broker or dealer. The FDIC as receiver for the broker or dealer may approve articles of association for a bridge financial company that will by operation of law, immediately upon approval of its articles of association, be established and deemed registered with the SEC and a member of the SIPC, operate in accordance with its articles and Section 210, and succeed to any and all registrations and memberships of the covered financial company with any self-regulatory organizations (Sec. 210(h)(2)(H)(i) of the Dodd-Frank Act). The bridge financial company is otherwise subject to the federal securities laws and all requirements with respect to membership in a self-regulatory organization, unless exempted by the SEC in the public interest or for the protection of investors (Sec. 210(h)(2)(H)(ii) of the Dodd-Frank Act).

Unless otherwise provided in Title II, any customer of the covered broker or dealer whose account is transferred to a bridge financial company has all the rights, privileges and protections under Section 205(f) of the Dodd-Frank Act and under the SIPA as if the account had not been transferred (Sec. 210(h)(2)(H)(iii) of the Dodd-Frank Act). The FDIC cannot operate any bridge financial company created with respect to a covered broker or dealer in a way that interferes in customers' ability to promptly access their customer property according to applicable law (Sec. 210(h)(2)(H)(iv) of the Dodd-Frank Act).

Assets and Obligations of Financial Companies.—A bridge financial company must assume, acquire or succeed to the assets or liabilities of a covered financial company only to the extent that the assets and liabilities are transferred to the bridge financial company in accordance with, and subject to the restrictions of, Section 210(h)(1)(B) (Sec. 210(h)(3)(A) of the Dodd-Frank Act). The bridge financial company cannot assume, acquire or succeed to any obligation to an equity holder that arises as a result of the person having an equity interest in the covered financial company (Sec. 210(h)(3)(B) of the Dodd-Frank Act).

Default.—A bridge financial company must be treated as a covered financial company in default as the FDIC determines in its discretion (Sec. 210(h)(4) of the Dodd-Frank Act).

Transfer of Assets and Liabilities.—The receiver may make initial and subsequent transfers of any assets and liabilities of a covered financial company to one or more bridge financial companies in accordance with and subject to the restrictions of Section 210(h)(1) (Secs. 210(h)(5)(A)–(B) of the Dodd-Frank Act). Transfers may include assets or liabilities associated with a trust or custody business, including fiduciary appointments, held by the covered financial company (Sec. 210(h)(5)(C) of the Dodd-Frank Act). Transfers are effective without any further federal or state law approval, assignment or consent (Sec. 210(h)(5)(D) of the Dodd-Frank Act).

In exercising its authority to transfer assets or liabilities, the FDIC must treat creditors that are situated similarly under the priority structure of Section 210(b)(1) similarly. However, the FDIC may do otherwise if it determines necessary to maximize the value of the assets of the covered financial company or to maximize the present value return from, or minimize the loss realized upon, the sale or other disposition of assets, and as long as all similarly-situated creditors receive at least the maximum liability amount set forth in Sections 210(d)(2) and (3) (Sec. 210(h)(5)(E) of the Dodd-Frank Act). The aggregate amount of liabilities transferred to the bridge financial company cannot exceed the aggregate amount of assets transferred (Sec. 210(h)(5)(F) of the Dodd-Frank Act).

Stay of Judicial Action.—Any judicial action to which a bridge financial company becomes a party by virtue of its acquisition of assets or assumption of liabilities of the covered financial company will be stayed for up to 45 days (or a longer period if agreed to by all parties) at the request of the bridge financial company (Sec. 210(h)(6) of the Dodd-Frank Act).

Agreements Against Interest.—No agreement that tends to diminish or defeat the bridge financial company's interest in any asset it acquires will be valid unless the agreement is in writing, was executed by an authorized officer or representative of the covered financial company or was confirmed by the company in the ordinary course of business, and has been an official record of the company since its execution or the party claiming under the agreement provides acceptable documentation of the agreement and its authorized execution or confirmation by the company (Sec. 210(h)(7) of the Dodd-Frank Act).

No Federal Status.—A bridge financial company is not a U.S. agency, establishment or instrumentality and its representatives, directors, officers, employees and agents are not, solely by virtue of their capacity as such, U.S. officers or employees (Secs. 210(h)(8)(A)–(B) of the Dodd-Frank Act). Any employee of the FDIC or other federal instrumentality who serves at the request of the FDIC with respect to a bridge financial company will not lose any existing status as an officer or employee of the United States solely by virtue of that service and will not receive any salary or benefits for service with respect to a bridge financial company in addition to the salary or benefits obtained through employment with the FDIC or other federal instrumentality (Sec. 210(h)(8)(B) of the Dodd-Frank Act).

Funding.—The FDIC may, subject to the orderly liquidation plan, provide funding to facilitate any transaction described in Sections 210(h)(13)(A)–(D) with respect to a bridge financial company and may facilitate the acquisition by a bridge financial company of any assets, or the assumption of any liabilities, of a covered financial company (Sec. 210(h)(9) of the Dodd-Frank Act).

Obtaining Credit.—A bridge financial company may obtain unsecured credit and issue unsecured debt (Sec. 210(h)(16)(A) of the Dodd-Frank Act). If it is unable to do so, the FDIC may authorize the bridge financial company to obtain credit or issue debt with priority over any or all of the obligations of the bridge financial company, secured by a lien on property that is not otherwise subject to a lien, or secured by a junior lien on property that is otherwise subject to a lien (Sec. 210(h)(16)(B) of the Dodd-Frank Act).

After notice and a hearing before a U.S. court with jurisdiction to conduct the hearing and to authorize the bridge financial company to obtain secured credit, the FDIC may also authorize credit or debt secured by a senior or equal lien on property that is already subject to a lien if the bridge financial company otherwise cannot obtain credit or issue debt and there is adequate protection of the existing lienholder's interest (Sec. 210(h)(16)(C) of the Dodd-Frank Act). The FDIC has the burden of proof on the issue of adequate protection (Sec. 210(h)(16)(D) of the Dodd-Frank Act). No credit or debt obtained or issued by a bridge financial company may contain terms that impair a counterparty's rights to a qualified financial contract upon a default by the bridge company, other than the priority of the counterparty's resulting unsecured claim relative to the priority of the bridge company's obligations respecting the credit or debt, unless the counterparty consents in writing to the impairment (Sec. 210(h)(16)(E) of the Dodd-Frank Act).

The reversal or modification on appeal of an authorization to obtain credit or issue debt, or of a grant of a priority or a lien, does not affect the validity of the debt or priority of the lien to an entity that extended the credit in good faith, whether or not the entity knew of the pendency of the appeal, unless the authorization and issuance of the debt or the granting of the priority or lien were stayed pending appeal (Sec. 210(h)(17) of the Dodd-Frank Act).

¶540

Tax-Exempt Status.—A bridge financial company and its franchise, property and income are exempt from all present and future federal, state and local taxes (Sec. 210(h)(10) of the Dodd-Frank Act).

Agency Approval and Antitrust Review.—If a transaction involving the merger or sale of a bridge financial company requires approval by a federal agency, the merger cannot be consummated before the fifth calendar day after the agency approves the merger. If a report on competitive factors is required, the agency must promptly notify the U.S. Attorney General of the proposed merger, and the Attorney General must provide the required report within 10 days of the request. Finally, if notification is required under Clayton Act Section 7A, the required waiting period will end on the 15th day after the Attorney General and the FTC receive that notification, unless terminated earlier under Section 7A(b)(2) or extended under Section 7A(e)(2) (Sec. 210(h)(11) of the Dodd-Frank Act).

Duration.—The status of a bridge financial company as such will end two years after the date on which it was granted a charter. The FDIC may extend the status in its discretion for no more than three additional one-year periods (Sec. 210(h)(12) of the Dodd-Frank Act). In any event, the status of the bridge financial company as such will end upon the earliest of:

- the date of the merger or consolidation of the bridge financial company with a company that is not a bridge financial company;
- at the election of the FDIC, the sale of a majority of the capital stock of the bridge financial company to a person other than the FDIC or another bridge financial company;
- the sale of 80 percent or more of the capital stock of the bridge financial company to a person other than the FDIC or another bridge financial company;
- at the election of the FDIC, either the assumption of all or substantially all of the liabilities of, or the acquisition of all or substantially all of the assets of, the bridge financial company by a company that is not a bridge financial company, or other entity as permitted under applicable law; and
- the end of the two-year period after the date the bridge financial company was granted a charter, as extended if applicable, pursuant to Section 210(h)(12) (Sec. 210(h)(13) of the Dodd-Frank Act).

A merger or consolidation must be conducted in accordance with applicable law, and the bridge financial company must be treated as a Delaware corporation (unless the bridge financial company has selected the law of another state in accordance with Section 210(h)(2)(F)) with the FDIC as its sole shareholder (Sec. 210(h)(14)(A) of the Dodd-Frank Act).

After the sale of a majority of the capital stock as provided in Section 210(h)(13)(B), the FDIC may amend the charter of the bridge financial company to reflect the termination of its status as a bridge financial company. After such an amendment, or following the sale of 80 percent or more of the capital stock as provided in Section 210(h)(13)(C), the company will then have all of the rights, powers and privileges under its constituent documents and applicable federal or state law. The FDIC may take steps to reincorporate the bridge financial company under state law and the state-chartered

¶540

corporation will be deemed to succeed by operation of law to the rights, titles, powers and interests of the bridge financial company as the FDIC provides, with the same effect as if the bridge financial company had merged with the state-chartered corporation under state corporate law (Secs. 210(h)(14)(B)–(C) of the Dodd-Frank Act).

After the assumption of all or substantially all of the liabilities or the sale of all or substantially all of the assets of the bridge financial company, at the election of the FDIC, the company may retain its status as a bridge financial company for the time period provided in Section 210(h)(12) or may be dissolved (Sec. 210(h)(14)(D) of the Dodd-Frank Act).

After consummation of a transaction that results in the termination of the status of a bridge financial company as such, the charter of the resulting company must be amended to reflect this change in status (Sec. 210(h)(14)(E) of the Dodd-Frank Act).

Dissolution of Bridge Financial Companies. If the status of a bridge financial company as such has not been previously terminated by an event specified in Sections 210(h)(13)(A)–(D), the corporation may in its discretion dissolve the bridge financial company, and must do so upon the expiration of the two-year period following the date on which the bridge financial company was chartered, or any extension of that period, as provided in Section 210(h)(12) (Sec. 210(h)(15)(A) of the Dodd-Frank Act). The FDIC will remain receiver for the purpose of dissolving the bridge financial company, and in that capacity will wind up the company's affairs in accordance with the provisions regarding the liquidation of covered financial companies under Title II. The FDIC as receiver will have all the rights, powers and privileges and will perform the duties related to the exercise of the rights, powers or privileges granted by law to the FDIC as receiver, and in its exercise of those rights, powers and privileges the FDIC will not be subject to the direction or supervision of any state agency or other federal agency (Sec. 210(h)(15)(B) of the Dodd-Frank Act).

Information Sharing.—Section 210(i) requires other federal regulators to make their records relating to the covered financial company available to the FDIC. The FDIC may use shared records in any manner that it determines to be appropriate (Sec. 210(i) of the Dodd-Frank Act).

▶ **Effective date.** The provision takes effect one day after the date of enactment (Sec. 4 of the Dodd-Frank Wall Street Reform and Consumer Protection Act).

Law source: Law at ¶10,210 and ¶10,004. Committee Report at ¶54,109.

— Sec. 210(h) of the Dodd-Frank Wall Street Reform and Consumer Protection Act, authorizing the FDIC to establish bridge financial companies;

— Sec. 210(i), requiring other federal regulators to share their information relating to the covered financial company;

— Sec. 4, providing the effective date.

¶545 Orderly Liquidation Fund

Section 210(n) establishes an Orderly Liquidation Fund in the Treasury Department to be made available to the FDIC to carry out the authorities in Title II and to pay the costs of actions authorized by Title II (Sec. 210(n)(1) of the Dodd-Frank Wall Street Reform and Consumer Protection Act). Amounts received by the FDIC, including assessments received under Section 210(o), proceeds of obligations issued under Section 210(n)(5), interest and other earnings from investments and repayments to the FDIC by covered financial companies will be deposited into the Fund (Sec. 210(n)(2) of the Dodd-Frank Act). The FDIC must manage the Fund in accordance with Sections 210(n) and 203(d) (Sec. 210(n)(3) of the Dodd-Frank Act). At the request of the FDIC, the Treasury Secretary may invest amounts held in the fund that are not, in the FDIC's judgment, required to meet the FDIC's current needs in government bonds with suitable maturities, the proceeds of which must be credited to the Fund (Sec. 210(n)(4) of the Dodd-Frank Act).

Authority to Issue Obligations.—The FDIC may issue obligations to the Treasury Secretary upon its appointment as receiver (Sec. 210(n)(5)(A) of the Dodd-Frank Act), and the Secretary may purchase or agree to purchase these obligations under such terms and conditions as the Secretary may require (Sec. 210(n)(5)(B) of the Dodd-Frank Act). The Secretary cannot provide funding to the FDIC except under an agreement providing a specific plan and schedule for repayment and demonstrating that income to the FDIC from the liquidated assets of the covered financial company and assessments under Section 210(o) will be sufficient to amortize the outstanding balance within the repayment period and pay the interest within the time provided in Section 210(o)(1)(B) (Sec. 210(n)(9)(B)(i) of the Dodd-Frank Act). The Secretary and the FDIC must consult with the Senate Banking Committee and the House Financial Services Committee on the terms of the repayment agreement and must submit a copy of the agreement to the committees within 30 days of funding by the Secretary (Sec. 210(n)(9)(B)(ii) of the Dodd-Frank Act). The Secretary may use the proceeds of the sale of any securities issued under 31 U.S.C. Chapter 31 as a public debt transaction to purchase obligations from the FDIC (Sec. 210(n)(5)(B) of the Dodd-Frank Act).

The purchase of obligations must be on terms and conditions that will yield a return at a rate determined by the Secretary taking into consideration the current average yield on outstanding U.S. government bonds of comparable maturity, plus an interest surcharge to be determined by the Secretary that must be greater than the difference between the current average rates of an index of corporate bonds and on government bonds of comparable maturity (Sec. 210(n)(5)(C) of the Dodd-Frank Act). The Secretary may sell the obligations it acquires (Sec. 210(n)(5)(D) of the Dodd-Frank Act). All of the Secretary's purchases and sales of obligations will be treated as public debt transactions of the United States, and the proceeds from any sales must be deposited into the Treasury as miscellaneous receipts (Sec. 210(n)(5)(E) of the Dodd-Frank Act).

Maximum Obligation Limitation.—The FDIC cannot issue or incur any obligation if it would mean the aggregate amount of obligations outstanding for each covered financial company would exceed:

- an amount equal to 10 percent of the total consolidated assets of the covered financial company during the 30-day period following the FDIC's appointment as receiver, or a shorter time period if the FDIC has calculated the 90-percent figure described immediately below, and

- the amount equal to 90 percent of the fair value of the total consolidated assets of the covered financial company that are available for repayment, after the time period described immediately above (Sec. 210(n)(6)(A) and (B) of the Dodd-Frank Act). The FDIC and Treasury Secretary, in consultation with the Financial Stability Oversight Council (Council), must jointly prescribe regulations governing the calculation of the maximum obligation limitation (Sec. 210(n)(7) of the Dodd-Frank Act). For purposes of determining the amount of obligations under Section 210(n), the FDIC must include contingent liabilities of the FDIC pursuant to Title II and must value any contingent liability at its expected cost to the FDIC (Sec. 210(n)(8)(B) of the Dodd-Frank Act).

Rule of Construction.—Nothing in Section 210 may be construed to affect the FDIC's authority under Federal Deposit Insurance Act Section 14(a) or (b) or 15(c)(5), the management of the Deposit Insurance Fund by the FDIC, or the resolution of insured depository institutions, provided that the FDIC's authorities under Title II will not be used to assist the Deposit Insurance Fund or any financial company under applicable law other than the Dodd-Frank Act. Conversely, the FDIC's authorities relating to the Deposit Insurance Fund or any other responsibilities under applicable law other than in Title II cannot be used to assist a covered financial company under Title II. The Deposit Insurance Fund cannot be used to circumvent the purposes of Title II (Sec. 210(n)(8)(A) of the Dodd-Frank Act).

Orderly Liquidation and Repayment Plans.—The FDIC may use amounts in the Fund after it has developed an orderly liquidation plan acceptable to the Treasury Secretary, including the provision and use of funds, including taking any actions specified under Sections 204(d) and 210(h)(2)(G)(iv) and (h)(9), and including payments to third parties. The plan must take into account actions to avoid or mitigate potential adverse effects on low-income, minority or underserved communities affected by the failure of the covered financial company and must provide for coordination with the appropriate primary financial regulatory agencies to ensure that these actions are taken. The FDIC may amend an orderly liquidation plan approved by the Secretary at any time with the agreement of the Secretary (Sec. 210(n)(9)(A) of the Dodd-Frank Act).

The Secretary cannot provide to the FDIC, pursuant to Section 210(n)(5) (authority to issue obligations, discussed above), any amount authorized under Section 210(n)(6)(B) (the maximum obligation limitation, discussed above), unless the two have an agreement that:

- provides a specific plan and schedule to achieve the repayment of the outstanding amount of any borrowing under Section 210(n)(5); and
- demonstrates that income to the FDIC from the company's liquidated assets and assessments under Section 210(o) will be sufficient to amortize the outstanding balance within the period established in the repayment schedule and pay the interest accruing on that balance within the time provided in Section 210(o)(l)(B) (Sec. 210(n)(9)(B)(i) of the Dodd-Frank Act).

The Secretary and the FDIC must: (1) consult with the Senate Banking Committee and the House Financial Services Committee on the terms of any repayment schedule agreement; and (2) submit a copy of the repayment schedule agreement to the

Committees before the end of the three-day period beginning on the date on which any amount is provided by the Secretary to the FDIC under Section 210(n)(5) (Sec. 210(n)(9)(B)(ii) of the Dodd-Frank Act).

Implementation Expenses.—The FDIC's reasonable implementation expenses incurred after enactment of the Dodd-Frank Act must be treated as expenses of the Council (Sec. 210(n)(10)(A) of the Dodd-Frank Act). "Implementation expenses" means costs incurred by the FDIC beginning on the date of enactment to implement Title II that do not relate to a particular covered financial company, and includes the costs incurred in developing policies, procedures, rules and regulations and other planning activities (Sec. 210(n)(10)(C) of the Dodd-Frank Act). The FDIC must periodically submit a request for reimbursement for these expenses to the Chairperson of the Council, who must arrange for prompt reimbursement to the FDIC of reasonable expenses (Sec. 210(n)(10)(B) of the Dodd-Frank Act).

Assessments.—Section 210(o) requires the FDIC to charge risk-based assessments to eligible financial companies. Eligible financial companies are bank holding companies with total consolidated assets equal to or greater than $50 billion and nonbank financial companies supervised by the Board of Governors (Sec. 210(o)(1)(A) of the Dodd-Frank Act).

The FDIC must charge assessments if necessary to pay in full the obligations issued by the FDIC to the Treasury Secretary within 60 months of the date of issuance (Sec. 210(o)(1)(B) of the Dodd-Frank Act). The FDIC may extend this time period as it determines is necessary to avoid a serious adverse effect on the U.S. financial system (Sec. 210(o)(1)(C) of the Dodd-Frank Act).

The FDIC must impose assessments, as soon as practicable, on any claimant that received additional payments or amounts from the FDIC under Sections 210(b)(4), (d)(4) or (h)(5)(E), except for payments or amounts necessary to initiate and continue operations essential to implementing the receivership or any bridge financial company. The assessments must be imposed to recover, on a cumulative basis, the entire difference between the aggregate value the claimant received on a claim under Title II as of the date on which value was received and the value the claimant was entitled to receive solely from the proceeds of the liquidation of the covered financial company. If the amounts to be recovered on a cumulative basis are insufficient to repay the FDIC's obligations to the Treasury, the FDIC must impose assessments on eligible financial companies and financial companies with total consolidated assets equal to or greater than $50 billion that are not eligible financial companies (Sec. 210(o)(1)(D) of the Dodd-Frank Act).

The FDIC must notify each financial company of its assessment. The financial company must pay the assessment in accordance with Section 210(o)(6) (Sec. 210(o)(3) of the Dodd-Frank Act). The FDIC must impose assessments on a graduated basis, with financial companies having greater assets and risk being assessed at a higher rate (Sec. 210(o)(2) of the Dodd-Frank Act). In imposing assessments, the FDIC must use a risk matrix. The Council must recommend a risk matrix to the FDIC, and the FDIC must take into account this recommendation in establishing the risk matrix (Sec. 210(o)(4) of the Dodd-Frank Act). In recommending and establishing the risk matrix, the Council and the FDIC, respectively, must take into account:

- economic conditions generally affecting financial companies, so as to allow for higher assessments during more favorable economic conditions and lower assessments during less favorable economic conditions;
- any assessments imposed on a financial company or affiliate that is an insured depository institution pursuant to the Federal Deposit Insurance Act, a member of the SIPC pursuant to the SIPA, an insured credit union assessed pursuant to the Federal Credit Union Act or an insurance company assessed pursuant to state law to cover the costs of state insolvency proceedings;
- the risks presented by the financial company to the financial system and the extent to which the company has benefitted (or likely would benefit) from the orderly liquidation, including
  — the amount, categories, and concentrations of assets of the financial company and its affiliates, including on- and off-balance-sheet assets;
  — the activities of the company and its affiliates;
  — the relevant market share of the company and its affiliates;
  — the extent to which the company is leveraged;
  — the potential of sudden calls on liquidity precipitated by economic distress;
  — the amount, maturity, volatility and stability of the company's financial obligations to and relationship with other financial companies;
  — the amount, maturity, volatility and stability of the company's liabilities, including its reliance on short-term funding, taking into consideration existing systems for measuring a company's risk-based capital;
  — the stability and variety of the company's sources of funding;
  — the company's importance as a source of credit for households, businesses and state and local governments and as a source of liquidity to the financial system;
  — the extent to which assets are simply managed and not owned by the company and the extent to which ownership of assets under management is diffuse; and
  — the amount, categories and concentrations of liabilities, both insured and uninsured, contingent and non-contingent, including on- and off-balance-sheet liabilities, of the company and its affiliates;
- any risks presented by the company in the 10 years prior to the receivership that contributed to the company's failure; and
- any other risk-related factors that the FDIC or the Council, as applicable, deems appropriate (Sec. 210(o)(4) of the Dodd-Frank Act).

A colloquy between House Financial Services Chairman Barney Frank (D-MA) and Rep. Luis Gutierrez (D-IL) clarified that the risk matrix considerations regarding the scope and nature of an institution's activity mean that these assessments should be made in light of their impact on the ability of a tax-exempt, not-for-profit organization to carry out its legally required charitable and educational activities. Chairman Frank said that a firm should not be assessed on the basis of a tax exemption it received for charitable activity. An underlying principle of the Dodd-Frank Act is to discourage excessive risk (Cong. Rec., June 30, 2010, p. H5218).

Prohibition of Outside Funding or Bailouts.—Section 212 of the Dodd-Frank Act prohibits any funding for the orderly liquidation of a covered financial company other than as specified in Title II (Sec. 212(a) of the Dodd-Frank Act). Furthermore, Section 214 prohibits financial company bailouts. This section clarifies that all financial companies put into receivership under Title II will be liquidated and that no taxpayer funds will be used to prevent liquidation (Sec. 214(a) of the Dodd-Frank Act). All funds expended in liquidating a financial company under Title II must be recovered from the company's assets or will be the responsibility of the financial sector, through assessments (Sec. 214(b) of the Dodd-Frank Act). Taxpayers cannot bear any losses from the exercise of Title II authority (Sec. 214(c) of the Dodd-Frank Act).

Study on Secured Creditor Haircuts.—The Council must conduct a study evaluating the importance of maximizing taxpayer protections and promoting market discipline with respect to the effect of the orderly liquidation authority on fully secured creditors (Sec. 215(a) of the Dodd-Frank Act). The Council must:

- not be prejudicial to current or past laws or regulations with respect to secured creditor treatment in a resolution process;
- study the similarities and differences between the resolution mechanisms authorized by the Bankruptcy Code, the FDIC Improvement Act of 1991 and the orderly liquidation authority of Title II;
- determine how secured creditors are treated in the resolution mechanisms and how a haircut could improve market discipline and protect taxpayers;
- compare the benefits and dynamics of prudent secured lending practices by depository institutions for consumers and small businesses to the lending practices for secured creditors of large, interconnected financial firms;
- consider whether credit differs according to different types of collateral and different terms and timing of the extension of credit; and
- examine stakeholders who were unsecured or undersecured and seek collateral when a firm is failing and the impact this behavior has on financial stability and an orderly resolution that protects taxpayers if the firm fails.

Within one year of enactment, the Council must issue a report to Congress containing its findings and conclusions (Sec. 215(a) of the Dodd-Frank Act).

Collection of Information.—The FDIC may impose on covered financial companies any collection-of-information requirements that it deems necessary after its appointment as receiver (Sec. 210(o)(5) of the Dodd-Frank Act).

Rulemaking.—The FDIC, in consultation with the Treasury Secretary, must prescribe regulations to carry out Section 210(o) (Sec. 210(o)(6)(A) of the Dodd-Frank Act). These regulations must take into account the differences in risks posed by different financial companies, the differences in liability structures of financial companies and the different bases for other assessments that financial companies may be required to pay, to ensure that assessed financial companies are treated equitably and that assessments reflect these differences (Sec. 210(o)(6)(B) of the Dodd-Frank Act).

▶ **Effective date.** The provisions take effect one day after the date of enactment (Sec. 4 of the Dodd-Frank Wall Street Reform and Consumer Protection Act).

¶545

Law source: Law at ¶10,210, ¶10,212, ¶10,214, ¶10,215 and ¶10,004. Committee Report at ¶54,109.

— Sec. 210(n) of the Dodd-Frank Wall Street Reform and Consumer Protection Act, establishing the Orderly Liquidation Fund;

— Sec. 210(o), requiring the FDIC to charge assessments;

— Sec. 212(a), prohibiting outside funding;

— Sec. 214, providing that no taxpayer funds may be used in liquidating a financial company or to prevent liquidation;

— Sec. 215, requiring the Council to conduct a study on secured creditor haircuts;

— Sec. 4, providing the effective date.

¶550 Inspector General Review and Reports

The Dodd-Frank Wall Street Reform and Consumer Protection Act requires periodic review and reporting on the supervision and liquidation of financial companies under Title II. This responsibility falls to the inspectors general of the FDIC, the Treasury and the primary financial regulatory agencies, as well as the Fed (Secs. 211(d)–(f) of the Dodd-Frank Wall Street Reform and Consumer Protection Act).

FDIC.—Within the first six months of the receivership and every six months thereafter until one year after the date of termination of the receivership, the FDIC Inspector General must conduct, supervise and coordinate audits and investigations of the liquidation of any covered financial company by the FDIC as receiver. The review must include:

- a description of actions taken by the FDIC as receiver;

- a description of any material sales, transfers, mergers, obligations, purchases and other material transactions entered into by the FDIC;

- an evaluation of the adequacy of the FDIC's policies and procedures under Section 203(d) and orderly liquidation plan;

- an evaluation of the use by the FDIC of the private sector in carrying out its functions, including the adequacy of any conflict-of-interest reviews; and

- an evaluation of the FDIC's overall performance in liquidating the covered financial company, including administrative costs, timeliness of the liquidation process and impact on the financial system (Secs. 211(d)(1)–(2) and (5) of the Dodd-Frank Act).

The FDIC Inspector General must include a summary of its findings and evaluations in the semiannual reports required of it by the Inspector General Act of 1978 and must appear before the appropriate committees of Congress, if requested, to present those reports (Sec. 211(d)(3) of the Dodd-Frank Act). The expenses incurred in conducting the reviews and issuing the reports must be administrative expenses of the receivership, and if the FDIC's funding under Title II is insufficient, the FDIC must pay additional amounts needed from assessments imposed under Section 210 (Sec. 211(d)(4) of the Dodd-Frank Act).

Treasury.—Within the first six months of the receivership and every six months thereafter until one year after the date on which the obligations purchased by the Treasury Secretary from the FDIC under Section 210 are fully redeemed, the Treasury Inspector General must conduct, supervise and coordinate audits of its actions related to the liquidation of any covered financial company. The review must include:

- a description of actions taken by the Secretary under Title II;
- an analysis of the approval by the Secretary of the FDIC's policies and procedures under Section 203 and acceptance of the FDIC's orderly liquidation plan under Section 210; and
- an assessment of the terms and conditions underlying the purchase by the Secretary of the FDIC's obligations under Section 210 (Secs. 211(e)(1)–(2) and (4) of the Dodd-Frank Act).

The Treasury Inspector General must include a summary of its findings and evaluations in the semiannual reports required of it by the Inspector General Act of 1978 and must appear before the appropriate congressional committees, if requested, to present those reports (Sec. 211(e)(3) of the Dodd-Frank Act).

Primary Financial Regulator and Fed.—Within the first year of the receivership, the inspector general of the primary financial regulator supervising the covered financial company, or the Board of Governors of the Federal Reserve System (the Fed) under Section 165, must make a written report reviewing the supervision by the agency or the Fed of the covered financial company. The report must: (1) evaluate the effectiveness of the agency or the Fed in carrying out its supervisory responsibilities; (2) identify any acts or omissions by agency or Fed officials that contributed to the covered financial company being in default or in danger of default; (3) identify any actions that they could have taken to prevent the company from being in default or in danger of default; and (4) recommend appropriate administrative or legislative action (Sec. 211(f)(1) of the Dodd-Frank Act). The inspector general or Fed must appear before the appropriate committees of Congress, if requested, to present the report (Sec. 211(f)(2) of the Dodd-Frank Act). Within 90 days of receipt of the report, the primary federal regulatory agency or the Fed, as applicable, must provide a written report to Congress describing any actions taken in response to the report's recommendations or explaining why no such actions were taken (Sec. 211(f)(2) of the Dodd-Frank Act).

▶ **Effective date.** The provision takes effect one day after the date of enactment (Sec. 4 of the Dodd-Frank Wall Street Reform and Consumer Protection Act).

Law source: Law at ¶10,211 and ¶10,004.

— Sec. 211(d) of the Dodd-Frank Wall Street Reform and Consumer Protection Act, requiring the FDIC Inspector General to review and report on FDIC actions related to the liquidation of financial companies;

— Sec. 211(e), requiring the Treasury Inspector General to review and report on Treasury actions related to liquidation of financial companies;

— Sec. 211(f), requiring the inspector general of the primary financial regulator or the Fed to review and report on the supervision of financial companies;

— Sec. 4, providing the effective date.

Supervision of Depository Institutions

TRANSFER of OTS FUNCTIONS AND POWERS
- ¶1005 Introduction
- ¶1010 OTS Abolished
- ¶1015 OTS Functions Transferred
- ¶1020 OCC Reestablished
- ¶1025 Federal Information Policy Amended
- ¶1030 Continuation of OTS Regulations
- ¶1035 References in Federal Law to Federal Banking Agencies
- ¶1040 Agency Funding
- ¶1045 Contracting and Leasing Authority

TRANSITIONAL PROVISIONS
- ¶1050 Introduction
- ¶1055 Interim Use of Funds, Personnel and Property
- ¶1060 Transfer of Employees
- ¶1065 Property Transferred
- ¶1070 Funds Transferred
- ¶1075 Disposition of Affairs
- ¶1080 Continuation of Services
- ¶1085 Implementation Plan and Reports

DEPOSIT INSURANCE REFORM
- ¶1090 Introduction
- ¶1095 Deposit Insurance Assessments
- ¶1100 Permanent Increase in Deposit Insurance Limits
- ¶1105 FDIC Board of Directors

OTHER MATTERS
- ¶1110 Branching
- ¶1115 Office of Minority and Women Inclusion
- ¶1120 Insurance of Transaction Accounts

TECHNICAL and CONFORMING AMENDMENTS
- ¶1125 Amendments to the Balanced Budget and Emergency Deficit Control Act of 1985
- ¶1130 Amendments to the Bank Enterprise Act

¶1135 Amendments to the Bank Holding Company Act
¶1140 Amendments to the Bank Holding Company Act Amendments of 1970
¶1145 Amendments to the Bank Protection Act
¶1150 Amendments to the Bank Service Company Act
¶1155 Amendments to the Community Reinvestment Act
¶1160 Amendments to the Crime Control Act of 1990
¶1165 Amendments to the Depository Institution Management Interlocks Act
¶1170 Amendments to the Emergency Homeowners' Relief Act
¶1175 Amendments to the Federal Credit Union Act
¶1180 Amendments to the Federal Deposit Insurance Act
¶1185 Amendments to the Federal Home Loan Bank Act
¶1190 Amendments to the Federal Housing Enterprises Financial Safety and Soundness Act
¶1195 Amendments to the Federal Reserve Act
¶1200 Amendments to the Financial Institutions Reform, Recovery, and Enforcement Act
¶1205 Amendments to the Flood Disaster Protection Act
¶1210 Amendments to the Home Owners' Loan Act
¶1215 Amendments to the Housing Act of 1948
¶1220 Amendments to the Housing and Community Development Act of 1992
¶1225 Amendments to the Housing and Urban-Rural Recovery Act of 1983
¶1230 Amendments to the National Housing Act
¶1235 Amendments to the Neighborhood Reinvestment Corporation Act
¶1240 Amendments Pertaining to Investment in State Housing Corporations
¶1245 Amendments to the Securities and Exchange Act
¶1250 Amendments to Criminal Laws
¶1255 Amendments to Title 31, United States Code

TRANSFER of OTS FUNCTIONS AND POWERS

¶1005 Introduction

"The Enhancing Financial Institution Safety and Soundness Act of 2010," Title III of the Dodd-Frank Wall Street Reform and Consumer Protection Act, seeks to:

(1) provide for the safe and sound operation of the U.S. banking system;

(2) preserve the dual banking system of federal and state charters for depository institutions;

(3) ensure fair supervision of depository institutions, regardless of their size or type of charter; and

(4) streamline and rationalize the supervision of depository institutions and financial holding companies (Sec. 301 of the Dodd-Frank Act).

To accomplish these goals the Dodd-Frank Act:

- abolishes one of the many banking regulators;
- consolidates supervision of state banks into a single federal regulator; and
- consolidates supervision of bank holding companies with less than $50 billion in total consolidated assets so that the regulator for the bank and thrift will also be the regulator for the holding company.

Specifically, the Dodd-Frank Act eliminates the Office of Thrift Supervision (OTS), transferring its regulatory and rulemaking authority to the Office of the Comptroller of the Currency (OCC) and the Federal Reserve Board (Fed), primarily, with some functions being absorbed by the Federal Deposit Insurance Corporation (FDIC) and the newly created Consumer Financial Protection Bureau. However, federal savings association charters are allowed to continue.

Background.—The OTS is responsible for regulating state and federal thrifts and their holding companies. The Senate Banking Committee found that savings and loan associations suffered disproportionate losses during the financial crisis, due in part to lax supervision by the OTS. The most serious of these losses were the failures of mortgage giants Washington Mutual and Indy Mac Bank and the near-failure, but for federal assistance, of American International Group. Moreover, from the start of 2008 through the date the legislation was introduced, 73 percent of failed institution assets were attributable to thrifts regulated by the OTS, even though the agency only supervised 12 percent of all financial institution assets at the beginning of the period (S. Rep. No. 111-76, p. 25).

The Committee also cited the White Paper on reforming the financial regulatory system issued by the Obama administration in which the administration asserted that advances in the financial industry had diminished the need to reserve the federal thrift charter as a special class of depository institutions focused on residential mortgage lending. That focus, the administration argued, made federal thrifts particularly susceptible to the housing downturn. The Committee noted that total assets of OTS-supervised institutions declined 36 percent between 2006 and 2009, compared to an increase of 11 percent of all FDIC-insured banks and thrifts over the same period (S. Rep. No. 111-76, p. 26).

Transfer Date.—The transfer of powers and duties provisions generally take effect one year after the date of enactment. This effective date is defined as the "transfer date." The legislation allows for the transfer date to be extended up to 18 months past the date of enactment by the Treasury Secretary, in consultation with the heads of the OCC, OTS, Fed and FDIC (Sec. 311 of the Dodd-Frank Act). Other than the repeal of the administrative expenses provision in Sec. 18(c) of the Federal Home Loan Bank Act that is effective 90 days after the transfer date, technical and conforming amendments take effect on the transfer date (Sec. 351 of the Dodd-Frank Act).

▶ **Effective date.** The provisions take effect one day after the date of enactment (Sec. 4 of the Dodd-Frank Wall Street Reform and Consumer Protection Act).

Law source: Law at ¶10,300, ¶10,301, ¶10,311, ¶10,351 and ¶10,004. Committee Report at ¶54,005, ¶54,120 and ¶54,140.

— Sec. 300 of the Dodd-Frank Wall Street Reform and Consumer Protection Act, providing the short title of Title III;

— Sec. 301, providing the purposes;

— Sec. 311, providing the transfer date;

— Secs. 4 and 351, providing the effective date.

¶1010 OTS Abolished

The Dodd-Frank Act abolishes the OTS and the position of Director of the OTS. There is no impact on the federal thrift charter, however.

> **CCH Comment:** The Senate version of financial reform would also have abolished all new federal thrift charters without placing limits on existing federal savings associations.

▶ **Effective date.** The abolishment of the OTS takes effect 90 days after the transfer date (one year after the date of enactment) (Sec. 311 and Sec. 313 of the Dodd-Frank Wall Street Reform and Consumer Protection Act).

Law source: Law at ¶10,313 and ¶10,311. Committee Report at ¶54,142 and ¶54,140.

— Sec. 313 of the Dodd-Frank Wall Street Reform and Consumer Protection Act;

— Sec. 311, providing the transfer date;

— Sec. 313, providing the effective date.

¶1015 OTS Functions Transferred

All functions of the OTS are transferred to the OCC, Fed and FDIC.

Supervision of Thrift Holding Companies.—Under the Dodd-Frank Act, the Fed acquires regulatory and rulemaking authority over savings and loan holding companies, in addition to its present oversight of national and state bank holding companies, state member banks and certain other entities (Sec. 312(b) of the Dodd-Frank Act).

Supervision of Thrifts.—The OCC will supervise federal savings associations, adding to its present oversight of national banks and federal branches and agencies of foreign banks. The FDIC will supervise federally insured state nonmember banks, insured branches of foreign banks and state-chartered savings associations (Federal Deposit Insurance Act Sec. 3(q), as amended by Sec. 312(c) of the Dodd-Frank Act).

Federal Deposit Insurance Act Amended.—Definitional provisions in the Federal Deposit Insurance Act (FDIA) are amended to reflect the OTS powers transferred to the OCC, Fed and FDIC (FDIA Sec. 3, as amended by Sec. 312(c) of the Dodd-Frank Act).

Fed Holding Company Regulatory Authority.—The Senate legislation, as originally drafted by Senate Banking Committee Chairman Chris Dodd, D-Conn., called for a shift in the regulation of financial holding companies. The Dodd version called for all national bank and federal savings and loan holding companies with total consolidated assets of less than $50 billion (the threshold for being designated a "systemically significant firm") to be supervised by the OCC, rather than the Fed or OTS, respectively, and for state member banks and thrifts to be supervised by the FDIC, rather than the Fed. Thus, all bank and thrift holding companies with less than $50 billion in total consolidated assets would have experienced a change in their primary federal regulator at the holding company level. However, an amendment introduced by Sen. Kay Bailey Hutchison, R-Texas, restored the Fed's regulatory dominion over financial holding companies. The Hutchison amendment was incorporated into the Dodd-Frank Act. Thus, the major changes with respect to bank supervision in the Dodd-Frank Act, in addition to provisions for "systemically significant firms," deal with the abolition of the OTS and the transfer of its regulatory and rulemaking authority.

Transfer of OTS Rulemaking Authority.—In addition, all rulemaking authority of the OTS and the Director of the OTS under Sec. 11 of the Home Owners' Loan Act (HOLA), relating to transactions with affiliates and extensions of credit to executive officers, directors and principal shareholders, and under Sec. 5(q) of HOLA, relating to tying arrangements is transferred to the Fed. The OCC receives all rulemaking authority of the OTS and the Director of the OTS relating to savings associations. The FDIC picks up OTS rulemaking authority over state savings associations (Sec. 312(b)(2) of the Dodd-Frank Act). None of these provisions limits or otherwise affects the transfer of powers to the new Consumer Financial Protection Bureau under Title X (Sec. 312(d) of the Dodd-Frank Act).

> **CCH Comment:** The House version of financial reform differed significantly in its restructuring of depository institution supervision. All powers, authorities, rights and duties that were invested in the Director of the OTS would transfer to the OCC under the House version, with three exceptions:
>
> 1. powers, rights, authorities and duties pertaining to savings and loan holding companies and their affiliates would transfer to the FDIC;
>
> 2. powers, rights, authorities and duties pertaining to savings and loan holding companies that are, on a consolidated basis, predominantly engaged in the business of insurance would transfer to the Federal Reserve Board; and
>
> 3. consumer financial protection functions of both the OTS and OCC would shift to the new Consumer Financial Protection Bureau.

▶ **Effective date.** The provision takes effect on the transfer date, which is one year after the date of enactment (Sec. 311 and Sec. 312(a) of the Dodd-Frank Wall Street Reform and Consumer Protection Act).

Law source: Law at ¶10,312 and ¶10,311. Committee Report at ¶54,141 and ¶54,140.

— Secs. 312(b) and (d) of the Dodd-Frank Wall Street Reform and Consumer Protection Act;

— Sec. 312(c), amending Federal Deposit Insurance Act Sec. 3(q);

— Sec. 311, providing the transfer date;

— Sec. 312(a), providing the effective date.

¶1015

¶1020 OCC Reestablished

The Dodd-Frank Act reestablishes the OCC as an independent agency housed within the Treasury Department. The OCC's directives are modified to include assuring the safety and soundness of financial institutions under its supervision as well as those institutions' compliance with laws and regulations. In addition, the OCC is to assure its supervised institutions provide fair access to financial institutions and fair treatment of customers (12 USC 1, as amended by Sec. 314(a) of the Dodd-Frank Act). Previously, the OCC's primary responsibilities were to execute all federal laws relating to the issue and regulation of national currency secured by U.S. bonds and, under the general supervision of the Fed, of all Federal Reserve notes, except for the cancellation and destruction, and accounting with respect to such cancellation and destruction, of Federal Reserve notes unfit for circulation. The OCC's financial institution supervisory responsibilities were governed by HOLA Sec. 3(b)(3).

The Dodd-Frank Act requires the Comptroller of the Currency to designate a Deputy Comptroller responsible for the supervision and examination of federal savings associations (Revised Statutes 327B, as added by Sec. 314(b) of the Dodd-Frank Act). The Comptroller or Deputy Comptroller is barred from holding an interest in a federal savings association (12 USC 11, as amended by Sec. 314(c) of the Dodd-Frank Act).

▶ **Effective date.** The provision takes effect on the transfer date, which is one year after the date of enactment (Sec. 311 and Sec. 314(d) of the Dodd-Frank Wall Street Reform and Consumer Protection Act).

Law source: Law at ¶10,314 and ¶10,311. Committee Report at ¶54,143 and ¶54,140.

— Sec. 314(a) of the Dodd-Frank Wall Street Reform and Consumer Protection Act, amending 12 USC 1;

— Sec. 314(b), adding Revised Statutes Sec. 327B;

— Sec. 314(c), amending 12 USC 11;

— Sec. 311, providing the transfer date;

— Sec. 314(d), providing the effective date.

¶1025 Federal Information Policy Amended

The Federal Information Policy is amended to include the OCC in the definition of "independent regulatory agency."

▶ **Effective date.** The provision takes effect one day after the date of enactment (Sec. 4 of the Dodd-Frank Wall Street Reform and Consumer Protection Act).

Law source: Law at ¶10,315 and ¶10,004. Committee Report at ¶54,144.

— Sec. 315 of the Dodd-Frank Wall Street Reform and Consumer Protection Act, amending 44 USC 3502(5);

— Sec. 4, providing the effective date.

¶1030 Continuation of OTS Regulations

All regulations promulgated by the OTS will remain in effect and be transferred to the Fed, OCC and FDIC, as appropriate (Sec. 316(b) of the Dodd-Frank Act). By the transfer date, the Fed, OCC and FDIC, in consultation with one another, are required to determine the existing OTS regulations that will be enforced by each agency and publish those regulations in the *Federal Register* (Sec. 316(c) of the Dodd-Frank Act).

Further, any legal action or proceeding commenced by or against the OTS before the transfer date will continue with the appropriate agency substituted for the OTS. In addition, all orders, resolutions, determinations, agreements, interpretative rules, other interpretations, guidelines, procedures and other advisory materials that have been issued, made, prescribed or allowed to become effective by the OTS that will be transferred by the legislation, and that are in effect on the day before the transfer date, will continue in effect according to the terms of those materials and are enforceable by or against the Fed, OCC or FDIC, as appropriate, until modified, terminated, set aside or superseded in accordance with applicable law by the appropriate agency, by any court of competent jurisdiction or by operation of law (Sec. 316(a) of the Dodd-Frank Act).

Any regulation proposed but not yet published by the OTS before the transfer date will be deemed to be a proposed regulation of the OCC or Fed, as appropriate. Any interim or final OTS regulation published before the transfer date but not yet effective will become effective as a regulation of the OCC or Fed, as appropriate (Sec. 316(d) of the Dodd-Frank Act).

▶ **Effective date.** The provision takes effect one day after the date of enactment (Sec. 4 of the Dodd-Frank Wall Street Reform and Consumer Protection Act).

Law source: Law at ¶10,316, ¶10,311 and ¶10,004. Committee Report at ¶54,145 and ¶54,140.

— Sec. 316 of the Dodd-Frank Wall Street Reform and Consumer Protection Act;
— Sec. 311, providing the transfer date.
— Sec. 4, providing the effective date.

¶1035 References in Federal Law to Federal Banking Agencies

On and after the transfer date, references to the OTS or the Director of the OTS will be deemed to be references to the Comptroller of the Currency, the OCC, the FDIC Chair, the FDIC, the Fed Chairman or the Fed, as appropriate and consistent with conforming amendments made in Subtitle E.

▶ **Effective date.** The provision takes effect one day after the date of enactment (Sec. 4 of the Dodd-Frank Wall Street Reform and Consumer Protection Act).

Law source: Law at ¶10,317 and ¶10,004. Committee Report at ¶54,140.

— Sec. 317 of the Dodd-Frank Wall Street Reform and Consumer Protection Act;
— Sec. 4, providing the effective date.

¶1040 Agency Funding

The Hutchison amendment altered language in the original Senate bill with regard to how each agency is funded. Those changes were incorporated into the final legislation as follows:

OCC.—The Comptroller of the Currency is authorized to collect an assessment, fee or other charge from any entity the OCC supervises as necessary to carry out its responsibilities, including with respect to holding companies, federal thrifts and non-bank affiliates (that are not functionally regulated) that engage in bank permissible activities. In establishing the amount of the assessment, fee or other charge collected from an entity, the OCC may take into account the funds transferred to the OCC, the nature and scope of the activities of the entity, the amount and types of assets held by the entity, the financial and managerial condition of the entity and any other factor that the OCC deems appropriate (Revised Statutes Sec. 5240A, as added by Sec. 318(b) of the Dodd-Frank Act).

Fed.—The Fed is directed to collect assessments, fees and other charges that are equal to the expenses incurred by the Fed to carry out its responsibilities with respect to such companies from:

(1) bank holding companies and savings and loan holding companies with assets equal to or greater than $50 billion; and

(2) all non-bank financial companies supervised by the Fed (Federal Reserve Act Sec. 11(s), as added by Sec. 318(c) of the Dodd-Frank Act).

FDIC.—The FDIC also is authorized to charge for its supervision of non-bank affiliates (FDIA Sec. 10(e), as amended by Sec. 318(d) of the Dodd-Frank Act).

▶ **Effective date.** The provision takes effect on the transfer date, which is one year after the date of enactment (Sec. 311 and Sec. 318(e) of the Dodd-Frank Wall Street Reform and Consumer Protection Act).

Law source: Law at ¶10,318 and ¶10,004. Committee Report at ¶54,147 and ¶54,140.

— Sec. 318(a) of the Dodd-Frank Wall Street Reform and Consumer Protection Act, amending 12 USC 481;

— Sec. 318(b), adding Revised Statutes Sec. 5240A;

— Sec. 318(c), adding 12 USC 248(s);

— Sec. 318(d), amending Federal Deposit Insurance Act Sec. 10(e)(1);

— Sec. 311, providing the transfer date;

— Sec. 318(e), providing the effective date.

¶1045 Contracting and Leasing Authority

The Dodd-Frank Act provides the OCC with the power to acquire, hold, maintain, sell, lease or otherwise dispose of real property as necessary to carry out its duties and responsibilities.

▶ **Effective date.** The provision takes effect one day after the date of enactment (Sec. 4 of the Dodd-Frank Wall Street Reform and Consumer Protection Act).

Law source: Law at ¶10,319 and ¶10,004. Committee Report at ¶54,148.

— Sec. 319 of the Dodd-Frank Wall Street Reform and Consumer Protection Act;
— Sec. 4, providing the effective date.

TRANSITIONAL PROVISIONS

¶1050 Introduction

Subtitle B to Title III of the Dodd-Frank Wall Street Reform and Consumer Protection Act generally provides for the orderly transfer of functions from the OTS to the OCC, Fed and FDIC by guiding on how funds, personnel and property of the OTS should be transferred.

▶ **Effective date.** The provisions generally take effect one day after the date of enactment (Sec. 4 of the Dodd-Frank Wall Street Reform and Consumer Protection Act).

Law source: Law at ¶10,321, ¶10,322, ¶10,323, ¶10,324, ¶10,325 and ¶10,004. Committee Report at ¶54,160, ¶54,161, ¶54,162, ¶54,163, ¶54,164 and ¶54,165.

— Secs. 321—326 of the Dodd-Frank Wall Street Reform and Consumer Protection Act, providing transitional provisions;
— Sec. 4, providing the effective date.

¶1055 Interim Use of Funds, Personnel and Property

The Dodd-Frank Act provides procedures for the use of OTS funds, personnel and property during the period between the date of enactment and the transfer date.

Funds.—Before the transfer date, the OCC, Fed and FDIC may jointly require the OTS to pay funds to the agencies for expenses associated with the transfer of functions during the period beginning on the date of enactment and ending on the transfer date (Sec. 321(b)(1) of the Dodd-Frank Act).

Personnel.—The OCC, Fed and FDIC may jointly require the OTS to provide a detailed list of personnel appropriate to facilitate the orderly transfer of functions to the agencies (Sec. 321(b)(2) of the Dodd-Frank Act).

Property.—The OTS must also provide property and administrative services to the OCC, Fed and FDIC that the agencies jointly determine to be necessary to implement an orderly transfer of OTS functions (Sec. 321(b)(3) of the Dodd-Frank Act).

Notice.—Reasonable notice must be provided to the OTS of any request for funds, personnel or property (Sec. 321(c) of the Dodd-Frank Act).

▶ **Effective date.** The provision takes effect one day after the date of enactment (Sec. 4 of the Dodd-Frank Wall Street Reform and Consumer Protection Act).

Law source: Law at ¶10,321 and ¶10,004. Committee Report at ¶54,160.

— Sec. 321 of the Dodd-Frank Wall Street Reform and Consumer Protection Act;
— Sec. 4, providing the effective date.

¶1060 Transfer of Employees

The Dodd-Frank Act requires that all OTS employees be transferred to the OCC or the FDIC, with exceptions for provisions in Title X relating to staffing for the Consumer Financial Protection Bureau (Secs. 302 and 322(a) of the Dodd-Frank Act).

Allocation of Employees.—The Director of the OTS, the Comptroller of the Currency and the FDIC Chairman must jointly determine and identify the OTS employees to be transferred to the OCC and FDIC (Sec. 322(a) of the Dodd-Frank Act).

Service Periods Credit and Appointment Authority for Excepted Service.—Periods of service with a Federal Home Loan Bank, a joint office of Federal Home Loan Banks or a Federal Reserve Bank will be credited as periods of service with a federal agency. The Dodd-Frank Act also includes provisions for transferring the appointment authority of the OTS under federal law for filling the positions of employees in the excepted service to the Comptroller of the Currency or the FDIC Chairman, as appropriate (Sec. 322(a) of the Dodd-Frank Act).

Timing.—Each employee is to be transferred not later than 90 days after the transfer date and must receive notice of the position assignment no later than 120 days after the effective date of the transfer (Sec. 322(b) of the Dodd-Frank Act).

Deemed Transfer of Functions.—The transfer of employees is deemed a transfer of functions (Sec. 322(c) of the Dodd-Frank Act).

Equal Status and Tenure Positions.—Each transferred employee is to be placed in a position at the OCC or FDIC with the same status and tenure as the position the employee held at the OTS (Sec. 322(d) of the Dodd-Frank Act).

No Additional Certification Requirements.—A transferred examiner will not be subject to additional certification requirements before being placed in a comparable position at the OCC or FDIC (Sec. 322(e) of the Dodd-Frank Act).

Personnel Protection.—The Dodd-Frank Act bars any action, with some exceptions, to involuntarily separate or reassign an employee outside his or her locality pay area during the 30-month period beginning on the transfer date. This provision covers both transferred OTS employees and OCC and FDIC employees holding a permanent position the day before the transfer date (Sec. 322(g) of the Dodd-Frank Act).

Pay.—In addition to the position protection, a transferred employee, during the 30-month period beginning on the date the employee is transferred, must be paid at a rate that is not less than the basic rate of pay that the transferred employee received during the pay period immediately preceding the date on which the employee was transferred, with certain exceptions. The pay protection only applies so long as the transferred employee remains employed by the OCC or FDIC. Also, pay increases are permitted (Sec. 322(h) of the Dodd-Frank Act).

Benefits.—Each transferred employee's existing retirement plan must continue so long as the transferred employee is employed by the OCC or FDIC. Other benefits may be retained by the transferred employee during the one-year period following the transfer date. Special provisions are included in the Dodd-Frank Act with regard to dental, vision, long-term care and life insurance benefit programs (Sec. 322(i) of the Dodd-Frank Act).

Incorporation Into Agency Pay System.—Not later than two years following the transfer date, the Comptroller of the Currency and the FDIC Chairman must place each transferred employee into the established pay system and structure of the agency (Sec. 322(j) of the Dodd-Frank Act).

Equitable Treatment.—The Dodd-Frank Act provides for the equitable treatment of transferred employees by barring the Comptroller of the Currency and the FDIC Chairman from taking certain actions, and requires the two agency heads to conduct a study detailing the position assignments of all transferred employees, describing the procedures and safeguards adopted to ensure equitable treatment and demonstrating that the Act's requirements on equitable treatment have been met. The study must be completed and submitted to Congress not later than 365 days after the transfer date (Sec. 322(k) of the Dodd-Frank Act).

Reorganization.—Any reorganization required by the Comptroller of the Currency or the FDIC Chairman during the two-year period beginning one year after the transfer date will be deemed a "major reorganization" for purposes of affording affected employees retirement (Sec. 322(l) of the Dodd-Frank Act).

▶ **Effective date.** The provision takes effect one day after the date of enactment (Sec. 4 of the Dodd-Frank Wall Street Reform and Consumer Protection Act).

Law source: Law at ¶10,302, ¶10,322, ¶10,311 and ¶10,004. Committee Report at ¶54,161 and ¶54,140.

— Sec. 302 of the Dodd-Frank Wall Street Reform and Consumer Protection Act;
— Sec. 322, providing for transfer of employees;
— Sec. 311, providing the transfer date;
— Sec. 4, providing the effective date.

¶1065 Property Transferred

The Dodd-Frank Act defines the term "property" and prescribes deadlines for transferring OTS property, among other requirements.

"Property" Defined.—Under the Dodd-Frank Act, the term "property" includes all real property and all personal property, including computers, furniture, fixtures, equipment, books, accounts, records, reports, files, memoranda, paper, reports of examination and correspondence related to such reports, work papers and any other information or materials (Sec. 323(a) of the Dodd-Frank Act).

Property of the OTS.—No later than 90 days after the transfer date, all property of the OTS determined jointly by the Comptroller of the Currency and the FDIC Chairman to be property used to perform or support the function of the OTS must be transferred to the OCC or FDIC. In addition, certain personal property jointly determined by the Comptroller of the Currency, the FDIC Chair and the Fed Chairman to be property used to perform or support OTS functions transferred to the Fed must be transferred to the Fed (Sec. 323(b) of the Dodd-Frank Act).

Contracts Related to Property Transferred.—Contracts, agreements, leases, licenses, permits and similar arrangements transfer with property transferred to the OCC or FDIC (Sec. 323(c) of the Dodd-Frank Act).

Preservation of Property.—Property to be transferred must not be altered, destroyed or deleted prior to transfer (Sec. 323(d) of the Dodd-Frank Act).

▶ **Effective date.** The provision takes effect one day after the date of enactment (Sec. 4 of the Dodd-Frank Wall Street Reform and Consumer Protection Act).

Law source: Law at ¶10,323, ¶10,311 and ¶10,004. Committee Report at ¶54,162 and ¶54,140.

— Sec. 323(a) of the Dodd-Frank Wall Street Reform and Consumer Protection Act;

— Sec. 311, providing the transfer date;

— Sec. 4, providing the effective date.

¶1070 Funds Transferred

OTS funds available on the day before the transfer date must be transferred to the OCC, FDIC and Fed on the transfer date, as appropriate to the functions transferred to the respective agencies.

▶ **Effective date.** The provision takes effect one day after the date of enactment (Sec. 4 of the Dodd-Frank Wall Street Reform and Consumer Protection Act).

Law source: Law at ¶10,324, ¶10,311 and ¶10,004. Committee Report at ¶54,163 and ¶54,140.

— Sec. 324 of the Dodd-Frank Wall Street Reform and Consumer Protection Act;

— Sec. 311, providing the transfer date;

— Sec. 4, providing the effective date.

¶1075 Disposition of Affairs

During the 90-day period beginning on the transfer date, the Director of the OTS may manage employees and property not yet transferred and take other action only for the purpose of winding up the affairs of the OTS. The OTS Director may exercise any authority vested in the position on the day before the transfer date, but only to the extent necessary to wind up the OTS and carry out the transfer. In addition, during the 90-day period, the OTS Director will continue to be treated as an officer of the United States and is entitled to receive compensation as the Director received the day before the transfer date.

▶ **Effective date.** The provision takes effect one day after the date of enactment (Sec. 4 of the Dodd-Frank Wall Street Reform and Consumer Protection Act).

Law source: Law at ¶10,325, ¶10,311 and ¶10,004. Committee Report at ¶54,164 and ¶54,140.

— Sec. 325 of the Dodd-Frank Wall Street Reform and Consumer Protection Act;

— Sec. 311, providing the transfer date;

— Sec. 4, providing the effective date.

¶1080 Continuation of Services

Any federal agency, department or other instrumentality that, prior to the transfer date, was providing services to the OTS related to functions transferred must continue to provide such services to the OCC, FDIC or Fed until the transfer of functions is complete.

▶ **Effective date.** The provision takes effect one day after the date of enactment (Sec. 4 of the Dodd-Frank Wall Street Reform and Consumer Protection Act).

Law source: Law at ¶10,326, ¶10,311 and ¶10,004. Committee Report at ¶54,165 and ¶54,140.

— Sec. 326 of the Dodd-Frank Wall Street Reform and Consumer Protection Act;
— Sec. 311, providing the transfer date;
— Sec. 4, providing the effective date.

¶1085 Implementation Plan and Reports

The Fed, FDIC, OCC and OTS are required to jointly submit a plan, within 180 days of the date of enactment, to the Senate Banking Committee and the House Financial Services Committee and certain inspectors general detailing the steps the agencies will take to implement the transfer of functions from the OTS (Sec. 327(a) of Dodd-Frank Act). The inspectors general must, within 60 days of receiving the plan, provide a written report to the agencies and the Senate and House Committees detailing whether the plan conforms with the Dodd-Frank Act (Sec. 327(b) of Dodd-Frank Act).

Not later than six months after the inspectors general report is delivered to Congress, and every six months thereafter until all aspects of the plan have been implemented, the inspectors general must provide a written report on the status of the implementation of the plan to the agencies, with a copy to the Senate and House Committees (Sec. 327(c) of Dodd-Frank Act).

▶ **Effective date.** The provision takes effect one day after the date of enactment (Sec. 4 of the Dodd-Frank Wall Street Reform and Consumer Protection Act).

Law source: Law at ¶10,327, ¶10,311 and ¶10,004.

— Sec. 327 of the Dodd-Frank Wall Street Reform and Consumer Protection Act;
— Sec. 311, providing the transfer date;
— Sec. 4, providing the effective date.

DEPOSIT INSURANCE REFORM

¶1090 Introduction

Subtitle C to Title III of the Dodd-Frank Wall Street Reform and Consumer Protection Act addresses deposit insurance reform and makes technical amendments to the provisions of the Federal Deposit Insurance Act (FDIA) relating to the composition of the FDIC's Board of Directors.

¶1095 Deposit Insurance Assessments

The Dodd-Frank Act removes a provision in the Federal Deposit Insurance Act, dealing with deposit insurance assessments, that states no institution may be denied the lowest-risk category solely because of its size (FDIA Sec. 7(b)(2), as amended by Sec. 331(a) of the Dodd-Frank Act).

Assessment Base.—Section 331(b) of the Dodd-Frank Act also directs the FDIC to amend its regulations to define the term "assessment base" of an insured depository institution for purposes of deposit insurance assessments.

The assessment base is to be an amount equal to the average consolidated total assets of the insured depository institution during the assessment period, minus the sum of the average tangible equity of the insured depository institution during the assessment period and an amount that the FDIC determines is necessary to establish assessments consistent with the risk-based assessment system found in FDIA 7(b)(1) for a "custodial bank" or a "banker's bank" (Sec. 331(b) of the Dodd-Frank Act).

The FDIC is to define the term "custodial bank" based on factors including the percentage of total revenues generated by custodial businesses and the level of assets under custody. A "banker's bank" is defined in 12 USC 24 as a bank or company that is engaged exclusively in providing services to or for other depository institutions (Sec. 331(b)(2) of the Dodd-Frank Act).

Procyclical Assessments.—The Dodd-Frank Act also eliminates procyclical assessments. This is accomplished by allowing the FDIC, in its sole discretion, to suspend or limit a payment of dividends if the Deposit Insurance Fund (DIF) reserve ratio is in excess of 1.5 percent of estimated insured deposits. The payment of a prorated dividend if the reserve ratio is between 1.35 percent and 1.5 percent is also eliminated to address procyclical assessments (FDIA Sec. 7(e)(2)(B) as amended by Sec. 332(1)(A) of the Dodd-Frank Act).

As part of the elimination of procyclical assessments, the FDIC is also required to issue regulations addressing the method for the declaration, calculation, distribution and payment of dividends (FDIA Sec. 7(e)(2)(C) as amended by Sec. 332(1)(B) of the Dodd-Frank Act). This regulatory requirement replaces a more elaborate statutory scheme that was codified at FDIA Section 7(e)(2)(D)–(G) (Sec. 332(1)(C) of the Dodd-Frank Act).

Enhanced Access to Information.—The Dodd-Frank Act also amends the assessment provisions of the FDIA to enhance the access to information for deposit insurance purposes. This is accomplished by allowing the FDIC's Board of Directors to require any insured depository institution to periodically file additional reports that are deemed "advisable for insurance purposes." The FDIC's Board of Directors is to consult with the other banking agencies before requiring these additional reports (FDIA Sec. 7(a)(2)(B), as amended by Sec. 333(a) of the Dodd-Frank Act).

Reserve Ratio.—A transition reserve ratio requirement is also established to reflect the new risk-focused assessment base. This new minimum reserve ratio for any year may not be less than 1.35 percent of estimated insured deposits, or the comparable percentage of the assessment base (FDIA Sec. 7(b)(3)(B), as amended by Sec. 334(a) of the Dodd-Frank Act). An amendment to the definition of "Deposit Insurance Fund" also reflects the establishment of the reserve ratio (FDIA Sec. 3(y)(3), as amended by Sec. 334(b) of the Dodd-Frank Act).

Target Date. The Dodd-Frank Act also requires that the FDIC must take "such steps as may be necessary" to increase the level of the DIF to 1.35 percent of estimated insured deposits. The FDIC is given until Sept. 30, 2020, to meet the 1.35 reserve ratio target (Sec. 334(d) of the Dodd-Frank Act).

Small Banks. Banks with assets under $10 billion would be exempt from the increase in the reserve ratio to 1.35 percent (Sec. 334(e) of the Dodd-Frank Act).

> **CCH Comment:** The Conference Committee had originally agreed to set the reserve ratio a 1.15 percent, however, the ratio was increased to 1.35 percent following a reopening of the Conference Committee, on June 29, 2010, to address opposition to a $19 billion tax on large financial institutions to pay for the costs of the Dodd-Frank Act. Commenting on the increased reserve ratio, the American Bankers Association said it had "deep concerns" about the approach taken by the conferees. The ABA added that "manipulating FDIC premiums as a budget 'pay for,' and doing so without any hearing or chance for debate, risks undermining the integrity of the basis for insurance premiums." It added that consumer confidence in the FDIC would be undermined if it is seen as a "political pot to be used for other purposes."

Finally, the FDIC is required to make available to the public the reserve ratio and the designated reserve ratio using both estimated insured deposits and the assessment base under FDIA section 7(b)(2)(C) for a period of at least five years after the date of enactment of the Dodd-Frank Act (Sec. 334(c) of the Dodd-Frank Act).

▶ **Effective date.** The provision takes effect one day after the date of enactment (Sec. 4 of the Dodd-Frank Wall Street Reform and Consumer Protection Act).

Law source: Law at ¶10,331, ¶10,332, ¶10,333, ¶10,334 and ¶10,004. Committee Report at ¶54,180.

— Sec. 331(a) of the Dodd-Frank Wall Street Reform and Consumer Protection Act, amending Federal Deposit Insurance Act Sec. 7(b)(2);

— Sec. 331(b), requiring the term "assessment base" to be defined;

— Sec. 332(1), amending Federal Deposit Insurance Act Sec. 7(e)(2);

— Sec. 332(2), amending Federal Deposit Insurance Act Sec. 7(e)(4)(A);

— Sec. 333(a), amending Federal Deposit Insurance Act Sec. 7(a)(2)(B);

— Sec. 333(b), amending Federal Deposit Insurance Act Sec. 7(b)(1)(E);

— Sec. 334(a), amending Federal Deposit Insurance Act Sec. 7(b)(3)(B);

— Sec. 334(b), amending Federal Deposit Insurance Act Sec. 3(y)(3);

— Sec. 334(c)–(e), setting transition reserve ratio requirements;

— Sec. 4, providing the effective date.

¶1100 Permanent Increase in Deposit Insurance Limits

The standard maximum deposit insurance amount of $100,000, found in FDIA Section 11, is increased to $250,000. During the height of the financial crisis, the standard maximum deposit insurance amount was temporarily increased to $250,000 by Section 136(a) of the Emergency Economic Stabilization Act of 2008. This temporary increase originally was to last until Dec. 31, 2009, but was extended until Dec. 31, 2013, by the Helping Families Save Their Homes Act of 2009 (FDIA Sec. 11(a)(1)(E), as amended by Sec. 335(a) of the Dodd-Frank Act).

The increase in the standard maximum deposit insurance amount to $250,000 is to apply to depositors in any institution for which the FDIC was appointed as receiver or conservator on or after Jan. 1, 2008, and before Oct. 3, 2008. Any payment on a deposit claim made by the FDIC to a depositor above the standard maximum deposit insurance amount in effect at the time of the FDIC's appointment as receiver or conservator is deemed to be part of the net amount due to the depositor under FDIA Section 11(a)(1)(B).

The Dodd-Frank Act also increases the standard maximum share insurance amount to $250,000 for credit union share accounts (Federal Credit Union Act Sec. 207(k)(5), as amended by Sec. 335(b) of the Dodd-Frank Act).

▶ **Effective date.** The provision takes effect one day after the date of enactment (Sec. 4 of the Dodd-Frank Wall Street Reform and Consumer Protection Act).

Law source: Law at ¶10,335 and ¶10,004.

— Sec. 335(a) of the Dodd-Frank Wall Street Reform and Consumer Protection Act, amending Federal Deposit Insurance Act Sec. 11(a)(1)(E);

— Sec. 335(b), amending Federal Credit Union Act Sec. 207(k)(5);

— Sec. 4, providing the effective date.

¶1105 FDIC Board of Directors

The Dodd-Frank Wall Street Reform and Consumer Protection Act replaces the position of the Director of the Office of Thrift Supervision on the FDIC Board of Directors with the Director of the Consumer Financial Protection Bureau (FDIA Sec. 2(a)(1)(B), as amended by Sec. 336(a)(1) of the Dodd-Frank Act).

Vacancies.—If there is a vacancy on the FDIC's Board, the Dodd-Frank Act provides that the acting Comptroller of the Currency or the acting Director of the Consumer Financial Protection Bureau is to be a member of the FDIC's Board in the place of the Comptroller or Director. This is to address the situation in which there is vacancy in the Comptroller of the Currency or the office of Director of the Consumer Financial Protection Bureau and the appointment of a successor is pending, as well as the absence or disability of the Comptroller of the Currency or the Director of the Consumer Financial Protection Bureau (FDIA Sec. 2(d)(2), as amended by Sec. 336(a)(2) of the Dodd-Frank Act).

Corporation Employees.—Finally, the Dodd-Frank Act provides that the term "employee of the Corporation" includes any employee of the Consumer Financial Protection Bureau. The phrase "Office of Thrift Supervision" is removed due to that agency's abolishment (FDIA Sec. 2(f)(2), as amended by Sec. 336a)(3) of the Dodd-Frank Act).

▶ **Effective date.** The provision becomes effective on the "transfer date" provided in Section 311 of the Dodd-Frank Act. The "transfer date," which occurs one year after the date of the enactment of the Dodd-Frank Act, is the time frame in which the supervisory functions of the OTS are transferred to the OCC, Fed and FDIC (Sec. 336(b) of the Dodd-Frank Wall Street Reform and Consumer Protection Act).

Law source: Law at ¶10,336. Committee Report at ¶54,181.

— Sec. 336(a)(1) of the Restoring American Financial Stability Act of 2010, amending Federal Deposit Insurance Act Sec. 2(a)(1)(B);

— Sec. 336(a)(2), amending Federal Deposit Insurance Act Sec. 2(d)(2);

— Sec. 336(a)(3), amending Federal Deposit Insurance Act Sec. 2(f)(2);

— Sec. 336(b), providing the effective date.

OTHER MATTERS

¶1110 Branching

Under the Dodd-Frank Wall Street Reform and Consumer Protection Act, a savings association that becomes a bank may:

- continue to operate any branch or agency the savings association operated immediately before becoming a bank; and
- establish, acquire and operate additional branches and agencies at any location in any state in which the savings association operated a branch immediately before becoming a bank as long as the law of the branch's state would permit the branch to be opened if the bank were state-chartered.

▶ **Effective date.** The provision takes effect one day after the date of enactment (Sec. 4 of the Dodd-Frank Wall Street Reform and Consumer Protection Act).

Law source: Law at ¶10,341 and ¶10,004. Committee Report at ¶54,201.

— Sec. 341 of the Dodd-Frank Wall Street Reform and Consumer Protection Act;

— Sec. 4, providing the effective date.

¶1115 Office of Minority and Women Inclusion

The Dodd-Frank Act requires each federal agency to establish an Office of Minority and Women Inclusion not later than six months after the date of enactment that will be responsible for all matters of the agency relating to diversity in management, employment and business activities. The new Consumer Financial Protection Bureau is also required to establish an Office of Minority and Women Inclusion, but not later than six months after the designated transfer date (Sec. 342(a) of the Dodd-Frank Act).

Director.—A Director of each Office of Minority and Women Inclusion must be appointed by, and will report to, the agency administrator. Each Director is to establish standards for equal employment opportunity, increased participation of minority-and women-owned businesses in the programs and contracts of the agency and assessing the diversity policies and practices of entities supervised by the agency (Sec. 342(b) of the Dodd-Frank Act).

Inclusion in All Levels of Business Activities.—Each Director must develop and implement standards and procedures to ensure the fair inclusion of minorities, women and minority- and women-owned businesses in all activities of the agency at all levels (Sec. 342(c) of the Dodd-Frank Act).

Applicability.—The provision applies to all contracts of an agency for services of any kind, including the services of financial institutions, investment banking firms, mortgage banking firms, asset management firms, brokers, dealers, financial services entities, underwriters, accountants, investment consultants and providers of legal services (Sec. 342(d) of the Dodd-Frank Act).

Reports.—Each Office of Minority and Women Inclusion must submit an annual report to Congress regarding the action taken by the agency and the Office (Sec. 342(e) of the Dodd-Frank Act).

Diversity in Agency Workforce.—Each agency is required to take affirmative steps to seek diversity at all levels in the agency's workforce (Sec. 342(f) of the Dodd-Frank Act).

▶ **Effective date.** The provision takes effect one day after the date of enactment (Sec. 4 of the Dodd-Frank Wall Street Reform and Consumer Protection Act).

Law source: Law at ¶10,342 and ¶10,004.

— Sec. 342 of the Dodd-Frank Wall Street Reform and Consumer Protection Act;
— Sec. 4, providing the effective date.

¶1120 Insurance of Transaction Accounts

The FDIA and Federal Credit Union Act (FCUA) are amended to require that the FDIC and National Credit Union Administration, respectively, fully insure the net amount that any depositor at an insured depository institution maintains in a noninterest-bearing transaction account (FDIA Sec. 11(a)(1) and FCUA Sec. 207(k)(1), as amended by Sec. 343(a)(1) and Sec. 343(b) of the Dodd-Frank Act).

Noninterest-bearing Transaction Account Defined.—The Dodd-Frank Act provides that, for purposes of the amendments, a noninterest-bearing transaction account is a deposit or account maintained at an insured depository institution that does not accrue or pay interest, allows the depositor to make withdrawals by negotiable or transferable instrument, payment orders of withdrawal, telephone or electronic media transfers or other similar items and on which the depository institution or credit union does not reserve the right to require advance notice of an intended withdrawal (FDIA Sec. 11(a)(1)(B)(iii) and FCUA Sec. 207(k)(1)(A)(iii), as added by Sec. 343(a)(1)(A)(ii) and Sec. 343(b)(1)(A)(ii) of the Dodd-Frank Act).

Prospective Repeal.—Both amendments are repealed effective Jan. 1, 2013 (FDIA Sec. 11(a)(1) and FCUA Sec. 207(k)(1), as amended by Sec. 343(a)(3) and Sec. 343(b)(3) of the Dodd-Frank Act).

> **CCH Comment:** With the enactment of Section 343(a)(1) of the Dodd-Frank Act, it appears that Congress is statutorily extending deposit insurance coverage to noninterest-bearing transaction accounts covered by the FDIC's Transaction Account Guarantee (TAG) Program until Dec. 31, 2012. The TAG Program was established by the FDIC in the fall 2008, during the financial crisis, to offset the migration of traditional transaction account relationships, such as municipal and small business payroll accounts, from smaller banks to larger competitors due to uncertainties in the financial system at that time. Once the December 2012 deadline passes, it could be posited that the TAG Program would end. It should also be noted that Section 1106 of the Dodd-Frank Act prohibits the FDIC from "establish[ing] any widely available debt guarantee program" pursuant to the systemic risk provision of FDIA Section 13(c)(4)(G).

▶ **Effective date.** The effective date of the amendment to the Federal Deposit Insurance Act is Dec. 31, 2010. The effective date of the amendment to the Federal Credit Union Act is the date of enactment. (Secs. 343(a)(2) and (b)(2) of the Dodd-Frank Wall Street Reform and Consumer Protection Act). The prospective repeal of the amendments is effective Jan. 1, 2013 (Secs. 343(a)(3) and (b)(3) of the Dodd-Frank Wall Street Reform and Consumer Protection Act).

Law source: Law at ¶10,343.

— Sec. 343(a)(1) of the Dodd-Frank Wall Street Reform and Consumer Protection Act, amending Federal Deposit Insurance Act Sec. 11(a)(1);

— Sec. 343(a)(3), prospectively repealing the amendment in Sec. 343(a)(1);

— Sec. 343(b), amending Federal Credit Union Act Sec. 207(k)(1);

— Sec. 343(b)(3), prospectively repealing the amendment in Sec. 343(b)(1);

— Secs. 343(a)(2) and 343(b)(2), providing the effective dates.

TECHNICAL and CONFORMING AMENDMENTS

¶1125 Amendments to the Balanced Budget and Emergency Deficit Control Act of 1985

The Dodd-Frank Act removes references to the OTS and the Resolution Trust Corporation in the Balanced Budget and Emergency Deficit Control Act of 1985.

▶ **Effective date.** The provision takes effect on the transfer date, which is one year after the date of enactment (Sec. 311 and Sec. 351 of the Dodd-Frank Wall Street Reform and Consumer Protection Act).

Law source: Law at ¶10,352, ¶10,351 and ¶10,311.

— Sec. 352 of the Dodd-Frank Wall Street Reform and Consumer Protection Act, amending Balanced Budget and Emergency Deficit Control Act of 1985 Sec. 256(h);

— Sec. 311, providing the transfer date;

— Sec. 351, providing the effective date.

¶1130 Amendments to the Bank Enterprise Act

References to the Fed are removed and replaced by references to the Comptroller of the Currency for purposes of qualifying lifeline accounts for reduced assessment rates in the Bank Enterprise Act.

▶ **Effective date.** The provision takes effect on the transfer date, which is one year after the date of enactment (Sec. 311 and Sec. 351 of the Dodd-Frank Wall Street Reform and Consumer Protection Act).

Law source: Law at ¶10,353, ¶10,351 and ¶10,311.

— Sec. 353 of the Dodd-Frank Wall Street Reform and Consumer Protection Act, amending Bank Enterprise Act Sec. 232(a);

— Sec. 311, providing the transfer date;

— Sec. 351, providing the effective date.

¶1135 Amendments to the Bank Holding Company Act

The Dodd-Frank Act removes a reference to the Director of the Office of Thrift Supervision in the Bank Holding Company Act. In addition, with regard to the acquisition of a savings association, the amendment requires the Fed to solicit comments and recommendations from the OCC for an acquisition of a federal savings association and the FDIC for an acquisition of a state savings association.

▶ **Effective date.** The provision takes effect on the transfer date, which is one year after the date of enactment (Sec. 311 and Sec. 351 of the Dodd-Frank Wall Street Reform and Consumer Protection Act).

Law source: Law at ¶10,354, ¶10,351 and ¶10,311.

— Sec. 354 of the Dodd-Frank Wall Street Reform and Consumer Protection Act, amending Bank Holding Company Act Secs. 2(j)(3), 4 and 5(f);

— Sec. 311, providing the transfer date;

— Sec. 351, providing the effective date.

¶1140 Amendments to the Bank Holding Company Act Amendments of 1970

The prohibition on certain tying arrangements in the Bank Holding Company Act Amendments of 1970 is amended to require the Fed to consult with the OCC and FDIC in issuing regulations.

▶ **Effective date.** The provision takes effect on the transfer date, which is one year after the date of enactment (Sec. 311 and Sec. 351 of the Dodd-Frank Wall Street Reform and Consumer Protection Act).

Law source: Law at ¶10,355, ¶10,351 and ¶10,311.

— Sec. 355 of the Dodd-Frank Wall Street Reform and Consumer Protection Act, amending Bank Holding Company Act Amendments of 1970 Sec. 106(b)(1);

— Sec. 311, providing the transfer date;
— Sec. 351, providing the effective date.

¶1145 Amendments to the Bank Protection Act

The Dodd-Frank Act removes a reference to the OTS and makes technical amendments to the Bank Protection Act.

▶ **Effective date.** The provision takes effect on the transfer date, which is one year after the date of enactment (Sec. 311 and Sec. 351 of the Dodd-Frank Wall Street Reform and Consumer Protection Act).

Law source: Law at ¶10,356, ¶10,351 and ¶10,311.

— Sec. 356 of the Dodd-Frank Wall Street Reform and Consumer Protection Act, amending Bank Protection Act Secs. 2, 3 and 5;
— Sec. 311, providing the transfer date;
— Sec. 351, providing the effective date.

¶1150 Amendments to the Bank Service Company Act

Amendments to the Bank Service Company Act remove references to the Director of the OTS and the Federal Savings and Loan Insurance Corporation and add "savings association" to the definition of "depository institution."

▶ **Effective date.** The provision takes effect on the transfer date, which is one year after the date of enactment (Sec. 311 and Sec. 351 of the Dodd-Frank Wall Street Reform and Consumer Protection Act).

Law source: Law at ¶10,357, ¶10,351 and ¶10,311.

— Sec. 357 of the Dodd-Frank Wall Street Reform and Consumer Protection Act, amending Bank Service Company Act Secs. 1(b)(4), 1(b)(5) and 7(c)(2);
— Sec. 311, providing the transfer date;
— Sec. 351, providing the effective date.

¶1155 Amendments to the Community Reinvestment Act

The Dodd-Frank Act makes technical amendments to the Community Reinvestment Act to reflect the new supervisory responsibilities of the Fed with respect to savings and loan holding companies, OCC with respect to federal savings associations, and FDIC with respect to state savings associations. The amendment also removes references to the OTS.

▶ **Effective date.** The provision takes effect on the transfer date, which is one year after the date of enactment (Sec. 311 and Sec. 351 of the Dodd-Frank Wall Street Reform and Consumer Protection Act).

Law source: Law at ¶10,358, ¶10,351 and ¶10,311.

— Sec. 358 of the Dodd-Frank Wall Street Reform and Consumer Protection Act, amending Community Reinvestment Act of 1977 Secs. 803 and 806;

— Sec. 311, providing the transfer date;

— Sec. 351, providing the effective date.

¶1160 Amendments to the Crime Control Act of 1990

The Dodd-Frank Act removes references to the OTS and the Resolution Trust Corporation from the list of institutions that are members of the U.S. Attorney General's financial institutions fraud task force in the Crime Control Act.

▶ **Effective date.** The provision takes effect on the transfer date, which is one year after the date of enactment (Sec. 311 and Sec. 351 of the Dodd-Frank Wall Street Reform and Consumer Protection Act).

Law source: Law at ¶10,359, ¶10,351 and ¶10,311.

— Sec. 359 of the Dodd-Frank Wall Street Reform and Consumer Protection Act, amending Crime Control Act of 1990 Sec. 2539(c)(2) and 2554(b)(2);

— Sec. 311, providing the transfer date;

— Sec. 351, providing the effective date.

¶1165 Amendments to the Depository Institution Management Interlocks Act

An amendment to the administration, enforcement and rules and regulations provisions of the Depository Institution Management Interlocks Act removes references to the OTS and adds references to the OCC, Fed and FDIC, as appropriate, to reflect provisions of the Dodd-Frank Act abolishing the OTS and transferring its functions to the other agencies.

▶ **Effective date.** The provision takes effect on the transfer date, which is one year after the date of enactment (Sec. 311 and Sec. 351 of the Dodd-Frank Wall Street Reform and Consumer Protection Act).

Law source: Law at ¶10,360, ¶10,351 and ¶10,311.

— Sec. 360 of the Dodd-Frank Wall Street Reform and Consumer Protection Act, amending Depository Institution Management Interlocks Act Secs. 207, 209 and 210(a);

— Sec. 311, providing the transfer date;

— Sec. 351, providing the effective date.

¶1170 Amendments to the Emergency Homeowners' Relief Act

The Dodd-Frank Act makes a technical amendment to the Emergency Homeowners' Relief Act to remove references to the Home Loan Board and Federal Savings and Loan Insurance Corporation and replace those with the Federal Housing Finance Agency.

▶ **Effective date.** The provision takes effect on the transfer date, which is one year after the date of enactment (Sec. 311 and Sec. 351 of the Dodd-Frank Wall Street Reform and Consumer Protection Act).

Law source: Law at ¶10,361, ¶10,351 and ¶10,311.

— Sec. 361 of the Dodd-Frank Wall Street Reform and Consumer Protection Act, amending Emergency Homeowners' Relief Act Sec. 110;
— Sec. 311, providing the transfer date;
— Sec. 351, providing the effective date.

¶1175 Amendments to the Federal Credit Union Act

An amendment to the Federal Credit Union Act removes references to the OTS and FSLIC, among other technical modifications.

▶ **Effective date.** The provision takes effect on the transfer date, which is one year after the date of enactment (Sec. 311 and Sec. 351 of the Dodd-Frank Wall Street Reform and Consumer Protection Act).

Law source: Law at ¶10,362, ¶10,351 and ¶10,311.

— Sec. 362 of the Dodd-Frank Wall Street Reform and Consumer Protection Act, amending the Federal Credit Union Act Secs. 107(8), 205 and 206(g)(7);
— Sec. 311, providing the transfer date;
— Sec. 351, providing the effective date.

¶1180 Amendments to the Federal Deposit Insurance Act

The Dodd-Frank Act amends the Federal Deposit Insurance Act most notably by replacing references to the Director of the OTS with the OCC, Fed or FDIC to reflect provisions of the Dodd-Frank Act abolishing the OTS and transferring its functions to the other agencies. The amendment also makes numerous technical changes, mostly removing outdated references.

▶ **Effective date.** The provision takes effect on the transfer date, which is one year after the date of enactment (Sec. 311 and Sec. 351 of the Dodd-Frank Wall Street Reform and Consumer Protection Act).

Law source: Law at ¶10,363, ¶10,351 and ¶10,311.

— Sec. 363 of the Dodd-Frank Wall Street Reform and Consumer Protection Act, amending Federal Deposit Insurance Act Secs. 3, 7, 8, 10, 11, 13, 18, 19, 28 and 33;

- Sec. 311, providing the transfer date;
- Sec. 351, providing the effective date.

¶1185 Amendments to the Federal Home Loan Bank Act

Provisions of the Federal Home Loan Bank Act involving OTS administrative expenses and the Thrift Depositor Protection Oversight Board are repealed.

▶ **Effective date.** The repeal of the administrative expenses provision in Federal Home Loan Bank Act Sec. 18(c) takes effect 90 days after the transfer date (Sec. 364(a) of the Dodd-Frank Wall Street Reform and Consumer Protection Act). The repeal of the Thrift Depositor Protection Oversight Board provision in Federal Home Loan Bank Act Sec. takes effect on the transfer date, which is one year after the date of enactment (Sec. 311 and Sec. 351 of the Dodd-Frank Wall Street Reform and Consumer Protection Act).

Law source: Law at ¶10,364, ¶10,351 and ¶10,311.

- Sec. 364(a) of the Dodd-Frank Wall Street Reform and Consumer Protection Act repealing Federal Home Loan Bank Act Sec. 18(c);
- Sec. 364(b), repealing Federal Home Loan Bank Act Sec. 21A;
- Sec. 311, providing the transfer date;
- Secs. 351 and 364(a), providing the effective date.

¶1190 Amendments to the Federal Housing Enterprises Financial Safety and Soundness Act

Amendments to the Federal Housing Enterprises Financial Safety and Soundness Act remove references to the OTS and the Director of the OTS.

▶ **Effective date.** The provision takes effect on the transfer date, which is one year after the date of enactment (Sec. 311 and Sec. 351 of the Dodd-Frank Wall Street Reform and Consumer Protection Act).

Law source: Law at ¶10,365, ¶10,351 and ¶10,311.

- Sec. 365 of the Dodd-Frank Wall Street Reform and Consumer Protection Act, amending Federal Housing Enterprises Financial Safety and Soundness Act of 1992 Secs. 1315(b) and 1317(c);
- Sec. 311, providing the transfer date;
- Sec. 351, providing the effective date.

¶1195 Amendments to the Federal Reserve Act

The Dodd-Frank Act amends the Federal Reserve Act to replace references to the Director of the OTS with the Comptroller of the Currency and to reflect the division of supervision of savings associations, with the Fed overseeing federal savings associations and the FDIC responsible for oversight of state savings associations.

▶ **Effective date.** The provision takes effect on the transfer date, which is one year after the date of enactment (Sec. 311 and Sec. 351 of the Dodd-Frank Wall Street Reform and Consumer Protection Act).

Law source: Law at ¶10,366, ¶10,351 and ¶10,311.

— Sec. 366 of the Dodd-Frank Wall Street Reform and Consumer Protection Act, amending Federal Reserve Act Secs. 11(a)(2) and 19(b);

— Sec. 311, providing the transfer date;

— Sec. 351, providing the effective date.

¶1200 Amendments to the Financial Institutions Reform, Recovery, and Enforcement Act

The Dodd-Frank Act amends the Financial Institutions Reform, Recovery, and Enforcement Act generally to reflect provisions of the Dodd-Frank Act abolishing the OTS and transferring its functions to the other agencies and makes other technical changes.

▶ **Effective date.** The provision takes effect on the transfer date, which is one year after the date of enactment (Sec. 311 and Sec. 351 of the Dodd-Frank Wall Street Reform and Consumer Protection Act).

Law source: Law at ¶10,367, ¶10,351 and ¶10,311.

— Sec. 367 of the Dodd-Frank Wall Street Reform and Consumer Protection Act, amending Financial Reform, Recovery, and Enforcement Act Secs. 203, 302(1), 305, 308, 402, 1103(a), 1205(b), 1206 and 1216;

— Sec. 311, providing the transfer date;

— Sec. 351, providing the effective date.

¶1205 Amendments to the Flood Disaster Protection Act

The Dodd-Frank Act amends the Flood Disaster Protection Act to remove a reference to the OTS.

▶ **Effective date.** The provision takes effect on the transfer date, which is one year after the date of enactment (Sec. 311 and Sec. 351 of the Dodd-Frank Wall Street Reform and Consumer Protection Act).

Law source: Law at ¶10,368, ¶10,351 and ¶10,311.

— Sec. 368 of the Dodd-Frank Wall Street Reform and Consumer Protection Act, amending Flood Disaster Protection Act of 1973, Sec. 3(a)(5);

— Sec. 311, providing the transfer date;

— Sec. 351, providing the effective date.

¶1210 Amendments to the Home Owners' Loan Act

The Dodd-Frank Act amends the Home Owners' Loan Act generally to reflect provisions of the Dodd-Frank Act abolishing the OTS and transferring its functions to the other agencies and makes other technical changes.

▶ **Effective date.** The provision takes effect on the transfer date, which is one year after the date of enactment (Sec. 311 and Sec. 351 of the Dodd-Frank Wall Street Reform and Consumer Protection Act).

Law source: Law at ¶10,369, ¶10,351 and ¶10,311.

— Sec. 369 of the Dodd-Frank Wall Street Reform and Consumer Protection Act, amending Home Owners' Loan Act Secs. 1—5 and 8—13;

— Sec. 311, providing the transfer date;

— Sec. 351, providing the effective date.

¶1215 Amendments to the Housing Act of 1948

The Dodd-Frank Act amends the Housing Act of 1948 to transfer the additional powers and duties vested in the OTS to the OCC and FDIC.

▶ **Effective date.** The provision takes effect on the transfer date, which is one year after the date of enactment (Sec. 311 and Sec. 351 of the Dodd-Frank Wall Street Reform and Consumer Protection Act).

Law source: Law at ¶10,370, ¶10,351 and ¶10,311.

— Sec. 370 of the Dodd-Frank Wall Street Reform and Consumer Protection Act, amending Housing Act of 1948 Sec. 502(c);

— Sec. 311, providing the transfer date;

— Sec. 351, providing the effective date.

¶1220 Amendments to the Housing and Community Development Act of 1992

The Dodd-Frank Act amends the Housing and Community Development Act of 1992 to remove references to the OTS.

▶ **Effective date.** The provision takes effect on the transfer date, which is one year after the date of enactment (Sec. 311 and Sec. 351 of the Dodd-Frank Wall Street Reform and Consumer Protection Act).

Law source: Law at ¶10,371, ¶10,351 and ¶10,311.

— Sec. 371 of the Dodd-Frank Wall Street Reform and Consumer Protection Act, amending Housing and Community Development Act of 1992 Sec. 543;

— Sec. 311, providing the transfer date;

— Sec. 351, providing the effective date.

¶1225 Amendments to the Housing and Urban-Rural Recovery Act of 1983

A technical amendment to the Housing and Urban-Rural Recovery Act of 1983 replaces a reference to the Federal Home Loan Bank Board with the Federal Housing Finance Agency.

▶ **Effective date.** The provision takes effect on the transfer date, which is one year after the date of enactment (Sec. 311 and Sec. 351 of the Dodd-Frank Wall Street Reform and Consumer Protection Act).

Law source: Law at ¶10,372, ¶10,351 and ¶10,311.

— Sec. 372 of the Dodd-Frank Wall Street Reform and Consumer Protection Act, amending Housing and Urban-Rural Recovery Act of 1983 Sec. 469;

— Sec. 311, providing the transfer date;

— Sec. 351, providing the effective date.

¶1230 Amendments to the National Housing Act

The Dodd-Frank Act amends the National Housing Act to modify the notice requirements when a mortgagee is suspended or revoked from participating in certain federal mortgage insurance programs. With regard to federal savings associations and subsidiaries or affiliates of savings associations, the Secretary of Housing and Urban Development is to notify the OCC. With regard to state savings associations, the notice is to be sent to the FDIC. In addition, a reference to the Director of the OTS is removed.

▶ **Effective date.** The provision takes effect on the transfer date, which is one year after the date of enactment (Sec. 311 and Sec. 351 of the Dodd-Frank Wall Street Reform and Consumer Protection Act).

Law source: Law at ¶10,373, ¶10,351 and ¶10,311.

— Sec. 373 of the Dodd-Frank Wall Street Reform and Consumer Protection Act, amending National Housing Act Sec. 202(f);

— Sec. 311, providing the transfer date;

— Sec. 351, providing the effective date.

¶1235 Amendments to the Neighborhood Reinvestment Corporation Act

The Dodd-Frank Act amends the Neighborhood Reinvestment Corporation Act to remove a reference to the FHLBB and replace it with a reference to the FHFA.

▶ **Effective date.** The provision takes effect on the transfer date, which is one year after the date of enactment (Sec. 311 and Sec. 351 of the Dodd-Frank Wall Street Reform and Consumer Protection Act).

Law source: Law at ¶10,374, ¶10,351 and ¶10,311.

— Sec. 374 of the Dodd-Frank Wall Street Reform and Consumer Protection Act, amending Neighborhood Reinvestment Corporation Act Sec. 606(c)(3);

— Sec. 311, providing the transfer date;

— Sec. 351, providing the effective date.

¶1240 Amendments Pertaining to Investment in State Housing Corporations

The Dodd-Frank Act amends Public Law 93-100 (12 USC 1470), relating to investments in state housing corporations, to reflect provisions of the Dodd-Frank Act abolishing the OTS and transferring its functions to the other agencies and makes other technical changes.

▶ **Effective date.** The provision takes effect on the transfer date, which is one year after the date of enactment (Sec. 311 and Sec. 351 of the Dodd-Frank Wall Street Reform and Consumer Protection Act).

Law source: Law at ¶10,375, ¶10,351 and ¶10,311.

— Sec. 375 of the Dodd-Frank Wall Street Reform and Consumer Protection Act, amending 12 USC 1470(a);

— Sec. 311, providing the transfer date;

— Sec. 351, providing the effective date.

¶1245 Amendments to the Securities and Exchange Act

The Dodd-Frank Act amends the Securities and Exchange Act to update definitions to reflect provisions of the Dodd-Frank Act abolishing the OTS and transferring its functions to the other agencies.

▶ **Effective date.** The provision takes effect on the transfer date, which is one year after the date of enactment (Sec. 311 and Sec. 351 of the Dodd-Frank Wall Street Reform and Consumer Protection Act).

Law source: Law at ¶10,376, ¶10,351 and ¶10,311.

— Sec. 376 of the Dodd-Frank Wall Street Reform and Consumer Protection Act, amending Securities and Exchange Act Secs. 3(a)(34), 12(i), 15C(g)(1) and 23(b)(1);

— Sec. 311, providing the transfer date;

— Sec. 351, providing the effective date.

¶1250 Amendments to Criminal Laws

The Dodd-Frank Act amends Title 18, United States Code (Crimes and Criminal Procedure), to remove references to the OTS, the Director of the OTS and the Resolution Trust Corporation.

▶ **Effective date.** The provision takes effect on the transfer date, which is one year after the date of enactment (Sec. 311 and Sec. 351 of the Dodd-Frank Wall Street Reform and Consumer Protection Act)t.

Law source: Law at ¶10,377, ¶10,351 and ¶10,311.

— Sec. 377 of the Dodd-Frank Wall Street Reform and Consumer Protection Act, amending 18 USC Secs. 212(c)(2), 657, 981(a)(1)(D), 982(a)(3), 1006, 1014 and 1032(1);

— Sec. 311, providing the transfer date;

— Sec. 351, providing the effective date.

¶1255 Amendments to Title 31, United States Code

The Dodd-Frank Act amends Title 31, United States Code (Money and Finance), to remove a reference to the OTS and make other technical modifications.

▶ **Effective date.** The provision takes effect on the transfer date, which is one year after the date of enactment (Sec. 311 and Sec. 351 of the Dodd-Frank Wall Street Reform and Consumer Protection Act).

Law source: Law at ¶10,378, ¶10,351 and ¶10,311.

— Sec. 378 of the Dodd-Frank Wall Street Reform and Consumer Protection Act, amending 31 USC Secs. 321 and 714(a);

— Sec. 311, providing the transfer date;

— Sec. 351, providing the effective date.

Private Fund Advisers

¶1505	Introduction
¶1510	Definitions
¶1515	Adviser Registration
¶1520	Reports and Records
¶1525	SEC Rulemaking
¶1530	Family Offices
¶1535	State Oversight of Mid-Sized Advisers
¶1540	Custody of Client Assets
¶1545	Accredited Investors
¶1550	Commodity Pool Operators, Trading Advisors
¶1555	Qualified Client Standard
¶1560	Studies and Reports

¶1505 Introduction

Title IV of the Dodd-Frank Wall Street Reform and Consumer Protection Act, the "Private Fund Investment Advisers Registration Act of 2010," brings advisers of hedge funds and other private funds under SEC regulation (see Sec. 401 *et seq.* of the Dodd-Frank Wall Street Reform and Consumer Protection Act). Among other reforms, the title includes measures that: subject private fund advisers to SEC registration requirements (see ¶ 1515); impose recordkeeping and disclosure duties (see ¶ 1520); clarify the SEC's rulemaking powers (see ¶ 1525); codify the Commission's long-standing position that family offices are not "investment advisers" (see ¶ 1530); raise the asset-under-management threshold for federal regulation of advisers from $25 million to $100 million (see ¶ 1535); and raise the net worth threshold for accredited investor status (see ¶ 1545).

Congressional Purpose.—Private funds are not currently subject to the same set of standards and regulations as banks and mutual funds, reflecting the traditional view that private-fund investors are more sophisticated than retail investors and therefore require less protection. This regulatory exemption has enabled private funds to operate largely outside the framework of the financial regulatory system, even as they have become increasingly interwoven into the financial markets. As a result of the regulatory void, there are no data on the number or nature of these funds and on the risks they pose to the broader markets and the economy.

Congress chose to regulate hedge fund advisers based on systemic risk and retailization. In recent years, hedge funds have indelibly altered the risk and reward landscape of financial investments. These funds are unregulated, opaque investment partnerships that engage in a variety of active investment strategies involving significant leverage. Further, it has become clear that hedge fund liquidations can be a significant source of systemic risk. In addition, pension funds are increasing their allocations to hedge funds, and as the retailization of hedge funds continues, losses in the industry may have more significant implications for individual investors, in some cases threatening retirement wealth and basic living standards.

As the Senate Banking Committee noted:

> [T]he unregulated status of large hedge funds constitutes a serious regulatory gap. No precise data regarding the size and scope of hedge fund activities are available, but the common estimate is that the funds had about $2 trillion under management before the crisis, and that amount may be magnified by leverage. They are significant participants in many financial markets; their trades and strategies can affect prices. While hedge funds are generally not thought to have caused the current financial crisis, information regarding their size, strategies, and positions could be crucial to regulatory attempts to deal with a future crisis. The case of Long-Term Capital Management, a hedge fund that was rescued through Federal Reserve intervention in 1998 because of concerns that it was "too-interconnected-to-fail," indicates that the activities of even a single hedge fund may have systemic consequences (S. Rep. No. 111-176, pp. 71–72).

In response to these trends, the legislation mandates SEC registration for advisers to private funds and subjects them to recordkeeping and disclosure requirements primarily because they can pose a systemic risk to the larger financial system. The legislation gives the Commission the information it needs to understand how these funds operate and whether their actions pose a threat to the financial system as a whole.

Background.—Hedge funds and private equity funds have historically operated within the shadow financial system of unregulated non-bank financial entities. These funds and their managers have been exempt from regulation because of a combination of factors related to the number and relative sophistication of investors they serve and the size of assets under management. Unencumbered by leverage limits, compliance examinations or full disclosure requirements, many private funds operate under the radar. Their ability to take on enormous leverage, in particular, enables them to hold huge positions that can pose a systemic risk to the broader market.

If market trends move against a hedge fund or a private equity fund and it is forced to liquidate at fire-sale prices, prime brokers, banks and other counterparties could face significant losses. Even market participants who have no direct dealings with the fund could be battered by the resulting plunge in asset prices and liquidity squeeze.

The legislation is an acknowledgment that registration would afford a degree of transparency and oversight for these systemically important market players. It would at least ensure disclosure of basic information about the managers and funds and subject them to possible SEC examination.

Over the past two decades, private funds, including hedge, private equity and venture capital funds, have grown to play a significant role in the capital markets, both as a source of capital and as the investment vehicle of choice for many institutional investors. It is estimated that advisers to hedge funds have almost $1.4 trillion under management. Since many hedge funds are active and leveraged traders, this amount understates their impact on the trading markets. Hedge funds reportedly account for 18–22 percent of all trading on the New York Stock Exchange.

The federal securities laws have not kept pace with the growth and market significance of private funds and, as a result, the SEC has limited oversight authority over these vehicles. Sponsors of private funds, typically investment advisers, were able to organize their affairs to avoid registration under federal securities laws. Before this legislation, the Commission only had authority to conduct compliance examinations of those funds and advisers that were registered under one of the statutes the SEC administers. Consequently, advisers to private funds could essentially opt out of SEC oversight.

Moreover, the Commission traditionally has had incomplete information about the advisers and private funds that participate in financial markets. It was therefore not uncommon that the SEC's first contact with a manager of a significant amount of assets was during an investigation by the Enforcement Division. The information gathered by the SEC in this area has usually been based on industry sources, which have proven to be unreliable and inconsistent over the years because neither the private funds nor their advisers had to report even basic census-type information.

The situation presented a significant regulatory gap that Congress has now closed. The Commission tried to close the gap in 2004, at least partially, by adopting a rule requiring all hedge fund advisers to register under the Investment Advisers Act of 1940. That rulemaking was overturned by a federal appeals court in *Goldstein v. SEC* (CA-DofC 2006) FED. SEC. L. REP. ¶ 93,890. Since then, the SEC has continued to bring enforcement actions vigorously against private funds that violate federal securities laws and has continued to conduct compliance examinations of the hedge fund advisers that remain registered under the Advisers Act. But those efforts revealed only a slice of the private fund industry, and the Commission has endorsed legislative action to enhance regulation in this area.

In general, private funds are considered to be professionally managed pools of assets that are not subject to regulation under the Investment Company Act of 1940. Private funds include, but are not limited to, hedge funds, private equity funds and venture capital funds. Hedge funds pursue a wide variety of strategies that typically involve the active management of a liquid portfolio, and often include short selling and leverage.

Private equity funds generally invest in companies to which their advisers provide management or restructuring assistance and use strategies that include leveraged buyouts, mezzanine finance and distressed debt. Venture capital funds typically invest in earlier stage and start-up companies with the goal of either taking the company public or privately selling the company.

Each type of private fund plays an important role in the capital markets. Hedge funds tend to be active traders that contribute to market efficiency and enhance liquidity, while private equity and venture capital funds often help create new businesses, foster innovation and assist businesses in need of restructuring. Moreover, investing in these funds can serve to provide investors with portfolio diversification and returns that may be uncorrelated or minimally correlated to traditional securities indices.

Private funds seek to qualify for one of two exceptions from regulation under the Investment Company Act. They either limit themselves to 100 total investors (as provided in Section 3(c)(1)) or permit only "qualified purchasers" to invest (as provided in Section 3(c)(7)). As a result, the types of safeguards that protect retail investors under the Investment Company Act are the subject of private contracts for investors in private funds. These safeguards include investor redemption rights, application of auditing standards, asset valuation, portfolio transparency and fund governance. The safeguards are typically included in private fund partnership documents, but are not required and vary significantly among funds.

Transition Period.—Except as otherwise provided, this title takes effect one year after the date of enactment. However, any investment adviser may, at its discretion, register with the Commission under the Advisers Act during that one-year period, subject to SEC rules (Sec. 419 of the Dodd-Frank Act).

▶ **Effective date.** The provision takes effect one year after the date of enactment (Sec. 419 of the Dodd-Frank Wall Street Reform and Consumer Protection Act).

Law source: Law at ¶10,401 and ¶10,419. Committee Report at ¶54,220 and ¶54,235.

— Sec. 401 of the Dodd-Frank Wall Street Reform and Consumer Protection Act, providing the short title of Title IV;

— Sec. 419, providing for the effective date and transition period.

¶1510 Definitions

The Dodd-Frank Wall Street Reform and Consumer Protection Act defines key terms used in Title IV: "private fund," "foreign private adviser" and "investment adviser."

Private Fund.—Although the SEC has never explicitly defined "hedge fund," the Dodd-Frank Act defines the term "private fund." A private fund is an issuer that would be an investment company under Section 3 of the Investment Company Act of 1940 but for an exception provided from that definition by either Section 3(c)(1) or Section 3(c)(7) of the 1940 Act (Advisers Act Sec. 202(a)(29), as added by the Dodd-Frank Wall Street Reform and Consumer Protection Act).

Foreign Private Adviser.—The legislation also defines "foreign private adviser." Exempted from the new registration requirements (see ¶1515), a foreign private adviser is an investment adviser who meets four conditions. First, the adviser must have no place of business in the United States (Advisers Act Sec. 202(a)(30)(A), as added by the Dodd-Frank Act). Second, the adviser must have in total fewer than 15 clients and/or investors in the United States in private funds advised by the investment adviser (Advisers Act Sec. 202(a)(30)(B), as added by the Dodd-Frank Act). Third, the adviser must have aggregate assets under management attributable to clients and investors in the United States in private funds advised by the investment adviser of less than $25 million, or any higher amount that the SEC may by rule deem appropriate (Advisers Act Sec. 202(a)(30)(C), as added by the Dodd-Frank Act).

Finally, a foreign private adviser must neither hold itself out generally to the public in the United States as an investment adviser nor act as an investment adviser to any investment company registered under the Investment Company Act or a company that has elected to be a business development company under Investment Company Act Section 54 and has not withdrawn that election (Advisers Act Sec. 202(a)(30)(D), as added by the Dodd-Frank Act).

Investment Adviser.—The term "investment adviser" has the same meaning as in Advisers Act Section 202, as amended by the Dodd-Frank Act.

▶ **Effective date.** The provision takes effect one year after the date of enactment (Sec. 419 of the Dodd-Frank Wall Street Reform and Consumer Protection Act).

Law source: Law at ¶10,402 and ¶10,419. Committee Report at ¶54,221.

— Sec. 402(a) of the Dodd-Frank Wall Street Reform and Consumer Protection Act, adding Advisers Act Secs. 202(a)(29) and (30);

— Sec. 402(b), defining "investment adviser";

— Sec. 419, providing the effective date.

¶1515 Adviser Registration

The Dodd-Frank Wall Street Reform and Consumer Protection Act mandates the registration of advisers to private pools of capital so that regulators can better understand exactly how those entities operate and whether their actions pose a threat to the financial system as a whole. The Act requires investment advisers to hedge funds and other private investment funds to register with the SEC if they have assets under management of at least $150 million and subjects them to significant recordkeeping and disclosure requirements (Advisers Act Sec. 203(b), as amended by the Dodd-Frank Wall Street Reform and Consumer Protection Act). Prior law generally did not require hedge fund and other private fund advisers to register with any federal financial regulator.

The legislation accomplishes the registration of hedge fund advisers by eliminating the Investment Adviser Act's private adviser exemption, which exempts from registration investment advisers that have fewer than 15 clients, do not hold themselves out to the public as investment advisers, and do not act as investment advisers to registered investment companies or business development companies. This was the legislative fix heralded by the D.C. Circuit opinion in *Goldstein v. SEC* (CA-DofC 2006) FED. SEC. L. REP. ¶93,890.

Intrastate Clients.—The legislation excludes investment advisers of private funds from the intrastate exemption from registration (Advisers Act Sec. 203(b)(1), as amended by the Dodd-Frank Act). This exemption is otherwise available to advisers whose clients all reside in the state where the adviser maintains its principal office and place of business.

Foreign Private Funds.—The legislation creates a registration exemption for foreign private advisers (Advisers Act Sec. 203(b)(3), as amended by the Dodd-Frank Act). As discussed elsewhere (see ¶1510), the term "foreign private adviser" is an adviser that meets a three-pronged definition in Advisers Act Sec. 202(a)(30).

Commodity Trading Advisors.—Another exemption is available for any investment adviser registered with the Commodity Futures Trading Commission as a commodity trading advisor that advises a private fund. If the commodity trading advisor's business becomes predominately the provision of securities-related advice, however, it must register with the SEC (Advisers Act Sec. 203(b)(6)(B), as added by the Dodd-Frank Act).

Small Business Investment Companies.—Also exempt from registration are advisers who confine their advice to small business investment companies. Specifically, the legislation exempts an investment adviser, other than any entity that has elected to be regulated or is regulated as a business development company under Investment Company Act Section 54 (15 U.S.C. § 80a-54), who solely advises:

(A) small business investment companies licensed under the Small Business Investment Act of 1958;

(B) entities that have received from the Small Business Administration notice to proceed to qualify for a license, which notice or license has not been revoked; or

(C) applicants that are affiliated with one or more licensed small business investment companies covered in subparagraph (A) that have applied for another license, which application remains pending (Advisers Act Sec. 203(b)(7), as added by the Dodd-Frank Act).

Venture Capital Funds.—The legislation contains a registration exemption for advisers to venture capital funds. Within one year of enactment, the SEC must define the term "venture capital fund." In addition, the Commission must require advisers to venture capital funds to maintain records and provide annual or other reports as the Commission determines necessary or appropriate in the public interest or for the protection of investors (Advisers Act Sec. 203(l), as added by the Dodd-Frank Act).

Congress believes that venture capital funds, a subset of private investment funds specializing in long-term equity investment in small or start-up businesses, do not present the same risks as the large private funds whose advisers are required to register with the SEC under the Act. Their activities are not interconnected with the global financial system, and they generally rely on equity funding, so that losses that may occur do not ripple throughout world markets but are borne by fund investors alone (S. Rep. No. 111-176, pp. 74–75).

Funds Below $150 Million Threshold.—The Commission must provide an exemption from the registration requirements under Advisers Act Section 203 for any investment adviser that acts solely as an adviser to private funds and has assets under management in the United States of less than $150 million (Advisers Act Sec. 203(m)(1), as added by the Dodd-Frank Act). Although exempt from registration, these advisers must maintain any records and provide to the SEC any annual or other reports that the Commission deems necessary or appropriate in the public interest or for investor protection. When adopting regulations to implement these requirements with respect to investment advisers to mid-sized private funds, the SEC must consider the size, governance, and investment strategy of those funds to determine whether they pose systemic risk. The Commission also must provide for registration and examination procedures with respect to the advisers of those funds that reflect the level of systemic risk posed by the funds (Advisers Act Sec. 203(m), as added by the Dodd-Frank Act).

Transition Period.—The registration provisions take effect one year after the date of enactment. However, any investment adviser may, at its discretion, register with the Commission under the Advisers Act during that one-year period, subject to SEC rules (Sec. 419 of the Dodd-Frank Act).

▶ **Effective date.** The provisions take effect one year after the date of enactment (Sec. 419 of the Dodd-Frank Wall Street Reform and Consumer Protection Act).

Law source: Law at ¶10,403, ¶10,407, ¶10,408 and ¶10,419. Committee Report at ¶54,222 and ¶54,226.

— Sec. 403 of the Dodd-Frank Wall Street Reform and Consumer Protection Act, amending Advisers Act Sec. 203(b);
— Sec. 407, adding Advisers Act Sec. 203(l);
— Sec. 408, adding Advisers Act Sec. 203(m);
— Sec. 419, providing for the effective date and transition period.

¶1520 Reports and Records

New recordkeeping and disclosure requirements for private fund advisers will give regulators the information needed to evaluate both individual firms and entire market segments that, until now, have largely escaped any meaningful regulation, without posing undue burdens on those industries. Under the legislation, advisers to hedge funds, private equity firms and other private pools of capital will have to follow some basic ground rules in order to continue to operate in the capital markets. Regulators will have authority to examine the records of these investment advisers.

The legislation authorizes the SEC to require registered investment advisers to: (1) maintain records of, and submit reports regarding, the private funds they advise as the SEC determines is necessary or appropriate in the public interest and for investor protection, or for the assessment of systemic risk by the Financial Stability Oversight Council (Council); and (2) provide or make available to the Council those reports or the information in them (Advisers Act Sec. 204(b)(1), as amended by the Dodd-Frank Wall Street Reform and Consumer Protection Act). The records and reports of any private fund are further deemed to be the records and reports of the registered investment adviser (Advisers Act Sec. 204(b)(2), as amended by the Dodd-Frank Act).

Required Information.—The reports and records required to be maintained by a private fund and subject to SEC inspection must include, for each private fund advised by the investment adviser, a description of:

- the amount of assets under management and use of leverage;
- counterparty credit risk exposure;
- trading and investment positions;
- valuation policies and practices;
- types of assets held;
- side arrangements or side letters in which certain investors in the fund obtain more favorable rights or entitlements than other investors; and
- trading practices (Advisers Act Sec. 204(b)(3)(A)–(G), as amended by the Dodd-Frank Act).

As a catchall, the report also must contain any other information that the SEC, in consultation with the Council, determines is necessary and appropriate in the public interest and for the protection of investors or for the assessment of systemic risk. This may include the establishment of different reporting requirements for different classes of fund advisers, based on the type or size of private fund being advised (Advisers Act Sec. 204(b)(3)(H), as amended by the Dodd-Frank Act).

Recordkeeping and Reports.—The records must be maintained for a period of time set by SEC regulation (Advisers Act Sec. 204(b)(4), as amended by the Dodd-Frank Act). Further, the Commission must issue rules requiring each investment adviser to a private fund to file reports containing information the SEC deems necessary and appropriate in the public interest and for investor protection or for the assessment of systemic risk (Advisers Act Sec. 204(b)(5), as amended by the Dodd-Frank Act).

Examination.—All records of a private fund maintained by a registered investment adviser are subject at any time to periodic, special and other examinations by the SEC or any of its representatives. The investment adviser must make available to the Commission or its representatives any copies or extracts from any records that may be prepared without undue effort, expense or delay as the Commission or its representatives may reasonably request (Advisers Act Sec. 204(b)(6), as amended by the Dodd-Frank Act).

Information Sharing.—The SEC must make available to the Council copies of all reports, documents, records and information filed with or provided to the Commission by an investment adviser that the Council deems necessary for the purpose of assessing the systemic risk of a private fund (Advisers Act Sec. 204(b)(7)(A), as amended by the Dodd-Frank Act). The Council must maintain the confidentiality of all such reports, documents, records and information obtained from the SEC in a manner consistent with the confidentiality established by the SEC. Private fund records, including those containing proprietary information, are not subject to disclosure pursuant to the Freedom of Information Act (Advisers Act Sec. 204(b)(7)(B), as amended by the Dodd-Frank Act).

Proprietary Information.—The legislation erects a confidentiality regime by providing that any proprietary information of an investment adviser ascertained as proprietary by the SEC from any report filed with it under the new disclosure rubric is subject to public disclosure limitations (Advisers Act Sec. 204(b)(10)(A), as amended by the Dodd-Frank Act). As noted above, private fund records, including those containing proprietary information, are not subject to disclosure pursuant to the Freedom of Information Act (Advisers Act Sec. 204(b)(7)(B), as amended by the Dodd-Frank Act). The term "proprietary information" includes sensitive, non-public information regarding the investment adviser's investment or trading strategies, analytical or research methodologies, trading data, computer hardware or software containing intellectual property, and any additional information that the Commission determines to be proprietary (Advisers Act Sec. 204(b)(10)(B), as amended by the Dodd-Frank Act).

The confidentiality provisions do not, however, authorize the SEC to withhold information from Congress. Nor do they prevent the Commission from complying with a request for information from any other federal regulator or any self-regulatory organization requesting the information for purposes within the scope of its jurisdiction, or from complying with a federal court order in an action brought by the United States or the SEC (Advisers Act Sec. 204(b)(8), as amended by the Dodd-Frank Act).

Client Confidentiality Exception.—The legislation authorizes the SEC to require investment advisers to disclose the identity, investments or affairs of any client, if necessary to assess potential systemic risk (Advisers Act Sec. 210(c), as amended by the Dodd-Frank Act; S. Rep. No. 111-176, p. 74). Advisers Act Section 210(c) provides that the Act cannot be construed to require, or authorize the SEC to require, advisers engaged in rendering advisory services to disclose the identity, investments or affairs of any of its clients unless that disclosure is necessary in an enforcement proceeding or investigation. The legislation adds "or for purposes of assessment of potential systemic risk" to the enforcement or investigation exceptions (Advisers Act Sec. 210(c), as amended by the Dodd-Frank Act).

Report to Congress.—The Commission must report annually to Congress on how it has used the data collected from private fund advisers to monitor the markets for the protection of investors and the integrity of the markets (Advisers Act Sec. 204(b)(11), as amended by the Dodd-Frank Act).

▶ **Effective date.** The provisions take effect one year after the date of enactment (Sec. 419 of the Dodd-Frank Wall Street Reform and Consumer Protection Act).

Law source: Law at ¶10,404, ¶10,405 and ¶10,419. Committee Report at ¶54,223 and ¶54,224.

— Sec. 404 of the Dodd-Frank Wall Street Reform and Consumer Protection Act, redesignating Advisers Act Sec. 204(b) and (c) as (c) and (d), respectively, and adding new subsection (b);

— Sec. 405, amending Advisers Act Sec. 210(c);

— Sec. 419, providing the effective date.

¶1525 SEC Rulemaking

The Dodd-Frank Wall Street Reform and Consumer Protection Act clarifies the SEC's authority to define technical, trade and other terms. However, the SEC cannot define "client," for purposes of Advisers Act Sections 206(1) and (2), to include investors in a private fund managed by an investment adviser if the fund has entered into an advisory contract with the adviser (Advisers Act Sec. 211(a), as amended by the Dodd-Frank Wall Street Reform and Consumer Protection Act). The clarification avoids potential conflicts between the fiduciary duty an adviser owes to a private fund and to the individual investors in the fund if those investors are defined as clients of the adviser. Actions in the best interest of the fund may not always be in the best interests of each individual investor (S. Rep. No. 111-176, p. 74).

> **CCH Comment:** This provision was added by Rep. Spencer Bachus (R-AL) so that the SEC would not define the term "client" to include investors in a private fund managed by an investment adviser when that private fund has also entered into an advisory contract with the same adviser. According to Rep. Bachus, the provision will prevent advisers from being subjected to an irresolvable conflict of interest when they manage a pooled investment with the interest of each individual investor in mind.

The measure also directs the SEC and Commodity Futures Trading Commission (CFTC) to issue joint rules governing reports by firms registered with both agencies. Specifically, the two regulators must, after consulting with the Council but not later than 12 months after the date of enactment, jointly promulgate rules to establish the form and content of the reports required to be filed with the SEC under Advisers Act Section 204(b) and with the CFTC by investment advisers that are registered both under the

Advisers Act and the Commodity Exchange Act (Advisers Act Sec. 211(e), as added by the Dodd-Frank Act).

▶ **Effective date.** The provision takes effect one year after the date of enactment (Sec. 419 of the Dodd-Frank Wall Street Reform and Consumer Protection Act).

Law source: Law at ¶10,406 and ¶10,419. Committee Report at ¶54,225.

— Sec. 406 of the Dodd-Frank Wall Street Reform and Consumer Protection Act, amending Advisers Act Sec. 211(a) and adding Sec. 211(e);

— Sec. 419, providing the effective date.

¶1530 Family Offices

Family offices provide investment advice in the course of managing the investments and financial affairs of one or more generations of a single family. Since the enactment of the Investment Advisers Act, the SEC has issued orders to family offices declaring that those family offices are not investment advisers within the intent of the Act and thus not subject to registration.

The legislation essentially codifies the SEC position by excluding family offices from the Advisers Act definition of "investment adviser" (Advisers Act Sec. 202(a)(11), as amended by the Dodd-Frank Wall Street Reform and Consumer Protection Act). The SEC must adopt rules of general applicability defining "family offices" for purposes of the exemption. The rules must provide for an exemption that is consistent with the SEC's previous exemptive policy and that takes into account the range of organizational and employment structures employed by family offices (Sec. 409(b)(1) and (2) of the Dodd-Frank Act).

Congressional Intent.—This provision reflects a congressional belief that family offices are not investment advisers intended to be subject to registration under the Advisers Act. That Act was not designed to regulate the interactions of family members. Registration would unnecessarily intrude on the privacy of the family involved (S. Rep. No. 111-176, pp. 75–76).

Congress recognizes that many family offices have become professional in nature and may have officers, directors and employees who are not family members, and who may be employed by the family office itself or by an affiliated entity. These persons may co-invest with family members, enabling them to share in the profits of investments they oversee, and better aligning their interests with those of the family members served by the family office. Congress expects that these arrangements would not automatically exclude a family office from the definition (S. Rep. No. 111-176, pp. 75–76).

Restriction on Exclusions.—The SEC rules exempting family offices cannot exclude persons not registered under the Advisers Act on January 1, 2010 solely because those persons provided investment advice to officers, directors or employees of the family office who invested with the family office before January 1, 2010 and are accredited investors under Regulation D. Also, the exemptive rules cannot exclude any company controlled by members of the family of the family office. Finally, the rules cannot exclude any registered investment adviser that provides investment advice to the family office and who identifies investment opportunities to the family office, and invests in transactions on substantially the same terms as the family office invests, but does not invest in other funds advised by the family office, and whose assets as to which the family office provides investment advice represent, in the aggregate, not more than five percent of the value of the total assets as to which the family office provides investment advice (Sec. 409(b)(3) of the Dodd-Frank Act).

▶ **Effective date.** The provision takes effect one year after the date of enactment (Sec. 419 of the Dodd-Frank Wall Street Reform and Consumer Protection Act).

Law source: Law at ¶10,409 and ¶10,419. Committee Report at ¶54,228.

— Sec. 409(a) of the Dodd-Frank Wall Street Reform and Consumer Protection Act, amending Advisers Act Sec. 202(a)(11);

— Sec. 409(b), providing for SEC rules and orders regarding the definition of "family office";

— Sec. 419, providing the effective date.

¶1535 State Oversight of Mid-Sized Advisers

The Dodd-Frank Wall Street Reform and Consumer Protection Act could move the regulation of thousands of investment advisers from the SEC to the states by raising the assets-under-management trigger for federal regulation from $25 million to $100 million and authorizing the SEC to move the threshold even higher. The Act mandates state oversight of investment advisers with up to $100 million in assets under management. If application of the $100 million asset threshold would result in an adviser having to register with 15 or more states, the adviser may maintain its registration with the SEC (Advisers Act Sec. 203A(a)(2), as amended by the Dodd-Frank Wall Street Reform and Consumer Protection Act).

> **CCH Comment:** The $25 million trigger for state regulation was set in the National Securities Markets Improvement Act of 1996. As part of the 1996 Act, Congress determined that the SEC should regulate larger investment advisers while states should oversee smaller advisers.

▶ **Effective date.** The provision takes effect one year after the date of enactment (Sec. 419 of the Dodd-Frank Wall Street Reform and Consumer Protection Act).

Law source: Law at ¶10,410 and ¶10,419. Committee Report at ¶54,229.

— Sec. 410 of the Dodd-Frank Wall Street Reform and Consumer Protection Act, amending Advisers Act Sec. 203A(a);

— Sec. 419, providing the effective date.

¶1540 Custody of Client Assets

The Dodd-Frank Wall Street Reform and Consumer Protection Act requires registered investment advisers to comply with SEC rules for safeguarding client assets and to use independent public accountants to verify assets. Specifically, the law requires a registered investment adviser to take any steps to safeguard client assets in the adviser's custody, including verification of those assets by an independent public accountant, that the Commission may prescribe by rule (Advisers Act Sec. 223, as added by the Dodd-Frank Wall Street Reform and Consumer Protection Act).

CCH Comment: The SEC recently adopted rules imposing heightened standards for custody of client assets (see Release No. IA-2968 (Dec. 30, 2009), amending Rule 206(4)-2).

This provision attempts to reduce the risks of Ponzi schemes and theft by requiring money managers to keep client assets at a qualified custodian (S. Rep. No. 111-176, pp. 76–77, citing testimony before the Senate Subcommittee on Securities, Insurance, and Investment, 111th Congress, 1st sess., p. 18 (2009) (testimony of Mr. James Chanos)). Professor John Coffee of Columbia Law School wrote in testimony for the Senate Banking Committee that the custodian requirement largely removes an adviser's ability to pay the proceeds invested by new investors to old investors. The custodian will take the instructions to buy or sell securities but not to remit the sales proceeds of sales to the adviser or to others (except in return for share redemptions by investors). This requirement eliminates the manager's ability to "recycle" funds from new to old investors (S. Rep. No. 111-176, p. 77).

The GAO must conduct a study and submit a report to Congress, within three years of enactment, on the compliance costs associated with current SEC rules under the Investment Advisers Act regarding the custody of funds or securities of clients by investment advisers (Sec. 412 of the Dodd-Frank Act). For additional details, see ¶ 1560.

▶ **Effective date.** The provisions take effect one year after the date of enactment (Sec. 419 of the Dodd-Frank Wall Street Reform and Consumer Protection Act).

Law source: Law at ¶ 10,411, ¶ 10,412 and ¶ 10,419. Committee Report at ¶ 54,230.

— Sec. 411 of the Dodd-Frank Wall Street Reform and Consumer Protection Act, adding Advisers Act Sec. 223;

— Sec. 412, requiring a GAO study and report on the cost of complying with rules for custody of client assets;

— Sec. 419, providing the effective date.

¶1545 Accredited Investors

A person must have accredited investor status, defined in SEC regulations, to invest in hedge funds and other private securities offerings. Accredited investors are presumed to be sophisticated and therefore not in need of the investor protections afforded by SEC registration and disclosure requirements (S. Rep. No. 111-176, p. 77).

The legislation raises the net worth needed to attain accredited investor status by making the test $1 million of net worth, excluding the person's primary residence (Sec. 413(a) of the Dodd-Frank Wall Street Reform and Consumer Protection Act). Specifically, it requires the SEC to adjust the net-worth standard for an accredited investor, as set forth in rules under the Securities Act of 1933, so that the individual net worth of any natural person, or joint net worth with the spouse of that person, at the time of purchase, is more than $1 million (as adjusted periodically by SEC rule), excluding the value of the person's primary residence. However, during the first four years after the date of enactment, the net-worth standard must be $1 million, excluding the primary residence (Sec. 413(a) of the Dodd-Frank Act).

Background and Purpose.—The current test includes the primary residence in the net-worth threshold. Congress noted that the net-worth test has not been adjusted since 1982. Some observers believe that because of inflation and real estate price appreciation many individuals who now meet the accredited investor standard may lack the degree of financial expertise that was implied by the thresholds when they were established nearly three decades ago (S. Rep. No. 111-176, p. 77). For example, the North American Securities Administrators Association wrote in a 2007 comment letter to the SEC:

> NASAA has long advocated for adjusting the definition of "accredited investor" in light of inflation and has expressed concern at the length of time the thresholds contained in the definition have not been adjusted ... [I]nflation has seriously eroded the efficacy of the existing thresholds in the definition of "accredited investor" since their adoption in 1982. NASAA further supports an inflation adjustment every five years [S. Rep. No. 111-176, p. 77, quoting NASAA comment letter in response to SEC proposed rule *Revisions of Limited Offering Exemptions in Regulation D*, Release No. 33-8828; IC-27922 (October 26, 2007)].

Review and Adjustment.—The legislation calls for periodic review and adjustment of the "accredited investor" definition, apart from the net-worth test, with separate requirements for the initial review and for subsequent reviews.

Initial Review. The Commission may review the definition of "accredited investor" as applied to natural persons to determine whether adjustment of the requirements, excluding the net-worth standard, is appropriate for investor protection, in the public interest, and in light of the economy (Sec. 413(b)(1)(A) of the Dodd-Frank Act).

After completing the initial review, the Commission may, by notice and comment rulemaking, adjust the definition of "accredited investor" (excluding the net-worth standard), as applied to natural persons, if it deems the adjustment appropriate for investor protection, in the public interest, and in light of the economy (Sec. 413(b)(1)(B) of the Dodd-Frank Act).

Subsequent Reviews. Not earlier than four years after the date of enactment, and not less frequently than once every four years thereafter, the SEC must review the definition, in its entirety, of the term "accredited investor" in Securities Act Rule 215 (17 CFR § 230.215), as applied to natural persons, to determine whether adjustments are appropriate for investor protection, in the public interest, and in light of the economy (Sec. 413(b)(2)(A) of the Dodd-Frank Act).

After completing the review, the Commission may, by notice and comment rulemaking, adjust the Rule 215 definition of "accredited investor," as applied to natural persons, if it deems the adjustment appropriate for investor protection, in the public interest, and in light of the economy (Sec. 413(b)(2)(B) of the Dodd-Frank Act).

State and Local Governments.—Senators Mark Begich (D-AK) and Lisa Murkowski (R-AK) engaged in a colloquy with Senator Christopher Dodd (D-CT) over whether the SEC has authority under existing law to amend the definitions of "accredited investor" in Regulation D and related SEC rules and "qualified institutional buyer" in Rule 144A (17 CFR § 230.144A) to expressly include state and local government bodies within those definitions, and whether the SEC should take the opportunity presented by

¶1545

Section 413 to include governmental entities within those definitions (Cong. Rec., May 20, 2010, pp. S4063-4064).

Senator Murkowski said that it is in the interests of state and local governments for the SEC to add governmental entities to the definitions of "accredited investor" and "qualified institutional buyer" when it promulgates rules under the legislation. Governments are large, sophisticated investors with professional treasury management staffs that manage large amounts of the government's own money and seek to invest in securities to diversify their portfolios and obtain a favorable return. Many of the most attractive investments are offered only in private placements to institutional investors conducted under Regulation D or Rule 144A. Without access to these investments, the government earns a lower return and has less diversification in its investments than would be optimal. The senators asked Chairman Dodd if he agreed that when the SEC promulgates its rules under the legislation, it should address, while taking care to ensure appropriate minimum asset protections are in place, the inclusion of state and local governments in the definitions of "accredited investor" and "qualified institutional buyer" (Cong. Rec., May 20, 2010, pp. S4063-4064).

In response, Senator Dodd agreed that it would be appropriate for the SEC to take the opportunity presented by the rulemakings under Section 413 to consider whether to include state and local government bodies within those definitions (Cong. Rec., May 20, 2010, p. S4064).

GAO Study.—A separate provision calls for a Government Accountability Office study on the appropriate financial thresholds or other criteria for "accredited investor" status (Sec. 415 of the Dodd-Frank Act). For additional details, see ¶ 1560.

▶ **Effective date.** The provision takes effect one year after the date of enactment (Sec. 419 of the Dodd-Frank Wall Street Reform and Consumer Protection Act).

Law source: Law at ¶10,413 and ¶10,419. Committee Report at ¶54,231.

— Sec. 413(a) of the Dodd-Frank Wall Street Reform and Consumer Protection Act, requiring adjustment of the net-worth test for accredited investors;

— Sec. 413(b)(1), providing for initial SEC review and adjustment of the "accredited investor" definition;

— Sec. 413(b)(2), providing for subsequent reviews and adjustment of the definition;

— Sec. 419, providing the effective date.

¶1550 Commodity Pool Operators, Trading Advisors

The Dodd-Frank Wall Street Reform and Consumer Protection Act clarifies that its provisions do not affect any duties, rights or remedies under the Commodity Exchange Act governing commodity pools, commodity pool operators or commodity trading advisors. Specifically, nothing in Title IV of the Dodd-Frank Act will act to relieve any person of any obligation or duty, or affect the availability of any right or remedy available to the Commodity Futures Trading Commission or any private party, arising under the Commodity Exchange Act governing commodity pools, commodity pool operators, or commodity trading advisors (Advisers Act Sec. 224, added by the Dodd-Frank Wall Street Reform and Consumer Protection Act).

▶ **Effective date.** The provision takes effect one year after the date of enactment (Sec. 419 of the Dodd-Frank Wall Street Reform and Consumer Protection Act).

Law source: Law at ¶10,414 and ¶10,419.

— Sec. 414 of the Dodd-Frank Wall Street Reform and Consumer Protection Act, adding Advisers Act Sec. 224;

— Sec. 419, providing the effective date.

¶1555 Qualified Client Standard

The Dodd-Frank Wall Street Reform and Consumer Protection Act mandates inflation-based adjustments to the "qualified client" standard for exemption under Advisers Act Section 205(e). With respect to any factor used in any SEC rule in making a determination under Advisers Act Section 205(e), if the Commission uses a dollar amount test in connection with that factor, such as a net asset threshold, the SEC must, by order, within one year of enactment, and every five years thereafter, adjust for the effects of inflation on that test. Any adjustment that is not a multiple of $100,000 must be rounded to the nearest multiple of $100,000 (Advisers Act Sec. 205(e), as amended by the Dodd-Frank Wall Street Reform and Consumer Protection Act).

Advisers Act Section 205(e) permits the SEC to exempt any person or transaction from the investment advisory contract requirements of Section 205(a)(1) if the Commission finds that the person does not need the statute's protections. As amended, the law provides:

> The Commission, by rule or regulation, upon its own motion, or by order upon application, may conditionally or unconditionally exempt any person or transaction, or any class or classes of persons or transactions, from subsection (a)(1), if and to the extent that the exemption relates to an investment advisory contract with any person that the Commission determines does not need the protections of subsection (a)(1), on the basis of such factors as financial sophistication, net worth, knowledge of and experience in financial matters, amount of assets under management, relationship with a registered investment adviser, and such other factors as the Commission determines are consistent with this section. With respect to any factor used in any rule or regulation by the Commission in making a determination under this subsection, if the Commission uses a dollar amount test in connection with such factor, such as a net asset threshold, the Commission shall, by order, not later than 1 year after the date of enactment of the Private Fund Investment Advisers Registration Act of 2010, and every 5 years thereafter, adjust for the effects of inflation on such test. Any such adjustment that is not a multiple of $100,000 shall be rounded to the nearest multiple of $100,000 [Advisers Act Sec. 205(e), as amended by the Dodd-Frank Act].

▶ **Effective date.** The provision takes effect one year after the date of enactment (Sec. 419 of the Dodd-Frank Wall Street Reform and Consumer Protection Act).

Law source: Law at ¶ 10,418 and ¶ 10,419.

— Sec. 418 of the Dodd-Frank Wall Street Reform and Consumer Protection Act, amending Advisers Act Sec. 205(e);

— Sec. 419, providing the effective date.

¶ 1560 Studies and Reports

The Dodd-Frank Wall Street Reform and Consumer Protection Act calls for several studies to gather further information on private funds. The studies will focus on: (1) the costs of complying with SEC rules on custody of client assets; (2) the appropriate criteria for accredited investor status; (3) the feasibility of creating a self-regulatory organization for private funds; and (4) short selling practices.

Custody of Client Assets.—The Government Accountability Office (GAO) Comptroller General of the United States must conduct a study of the compliance costs associated with current SEC Rules 204-2 and 206(4)-2 under the Investment Advisers Act regarding the custody of funds or securities of clients by investment advisers. The study must also examine the additional costs if Advisers Act Rule 206(4)-2(b)(6), relating to operational independence, was eliminated. Within three years of enactment, the Comptroller General must submit a report to the Senate Committee on Banking, Housing, and Urban Affairs and the House Committee on Financial Services on the results of the study (Sec. 412 of the Dodd-Frank Wall Street Reform and Consumer Protection Act). For discussion of new client asset custody requirements imposed by the legislation, see ¶ 1540.

Accredited Investors.—The Comptroller General must also conduct a study on the appropriate criteria for determining the financial thresholds or other criteria for accredited investor status and eligibility to invest in private funds. Within three years of enactment, the Comptroller General must submit a report to the Senate Committee on Banking, Housing, and Urban Affairs and the House Committee on Financial Services on the results of the study (Sec. 415 of the Dodd-Frank Act).

The goal of the exemptions for accredited investors is to identify a category of investors who have sufficient knowledge and expertise to fend for themselves in making investment decisions. Currently, this category is identified by salary or wealth. However, Congress recognizes that these are imperfect standards. For example, a wealthy person may be a widow or widower with a large inheritance but have little investment expertise. Accordingly, Congress asks the GAO to determine whether other measures would be more appropriate (S. Rep. No. 111-176, p. 78). For discussion of accredited investor threshold changes imposed by the legislation, see ¶ 1545.

SRO for Private Funds.—The Comptroller General must also conduct a study on the feasibility of creating a self-regulatory organization to oversee private funds, including hedge funds, private equity funds and venture capital funds. Within one year of enactment, the Comptroller General must submit a report to the Senate Committee on Banking, Housing, and Urban Affairs and the House Committee on Financial Services on the results of the study (Sec. 416 of the Dodd-Frank Act).

Short Selling.—The SEC Division of Risk, Strategy, and Financial Innovation must conduct two studies. The first study will, taking into account current scholarship, examine the state of short selling on national securities exchanges and in the over-the-counter markets, with particular attention to the impact of recent rule changes and the incidence of: (1) failure to deliver shares sold short; or (2) delivery of shares on the fourth day following the short sale transaction (Sec. 417(a)(1) of the Dodd-Frank Act).

The second study will examine the feasibility, benefits and costs of:

- requiring public reporting, in real time, of short-sale positions of publicly-listed securities, or, in the alternative, reporting of those short positions in real time only to the Commission and the Financial Industry Regulatory Authority; and
- conducting a voluntary pilot program in which public companies will agree to have all trades of their shares marked "short," "market maker short," "buy," "buy-to-cover" or "long" and reported in real time through the Consolidated Tape (Sec. 417(a)(2) of the Dodd-Frank Act).

The SEC must submit a report to the Senate Banking Committee and the House Financial Services Committee on the results of the first study, including recommendations for market improvements, within two years after the date of enactment (Sec. 417(b)(1) of the Dodd-Frank Act). The Commission must submit a report to the same committees on the results of the second study within one year after the date of enactment (Sec. 417(b)(2) of the Dodd-Frank Act).

▶ **Effective date.** The provisions take effect one year after the date of enactment (Sec. 419 of the Dodd-Frank Wall Street Reform and Consumer Protection Act).

Law source: Law at ¶10,412, ¶10,415, ¶10,416, ¶10,417 and ¶10,419. Committee Report at ¶54,232, ¶54,233 and ¶54,234.

— Sec. 412 of the Dodd-Frank Wall Street Reform and Consumer Protection Act, requiring a GAO study and report on the cost of complying with rules for custody of client assets;
— Sec. 415, requiring a GAO study and report on accredited-investor requirements;
— Sec. 416, requiring a GAO study and report on the feasibility of an SRO for private funds;
— Sec. 417, requiring two SEC studies and reports on short selling;
— Sec. 419, providing the effective date.

Insurance

FEDERAL INSURANCE OFFICE

¶2005 Introduction
¶2010 Establishment of the Federal Insurance Office

STATE-BASED INSURANCE REFORM

¶2015 Introduction
¶2020 Surplus Lines Insurance
¶2025 Regulation by Insured's Home State
¶2030 Participation in National Producer Database
¶2035 Surplus Lines Eligibility
¶2040 Application for Commercial Purchasers
¶2045 GAO Study Required
¶2050 Nonadmitted Insurance Definitions
¶2055 Reinsurance
¶2060 Regulation of Solvency
¶2065 Reinsurance Definitions
¶2070 Rule of Construction
¶2075 Severability

FEDERAL INSURANCE OFFICE

¶2005 Introduction

To promote national coordination in the insurance sector, Title V of the Dodd-Frank Wall Street Reform and Consumer Protection Act creates a Federal Insurance Office (FIO) within the Treasury Department with authority over all types of insurance, other than health, long-term care and crop insurance (31 USC 313(a) and (d), as added by Sec. 502 of the Dodd-Frank Act). Subtitle A may be cited as the "Federal Insurance Office Act of 2010" (Sec. 501 of the Dodd-Frank Act).

CCH Comment: The Federal Insurance Office is the first office ever created in the federal government focused on insurance (other than deposit insurance).

▶ **Effective date.** The provision takes effect one day after the date of enactment (Sec. 4 of the Dodd-Frank Wall Street Reform and Consumer Protection Act).

Law source: Law at ¶10,501, ¶10,502 and ¶10,004. Committee Report at ¶54,241.

— Sec. 501 of the Dodd-Frank Wall Street Reform and Consumer Protection Act, providing the short title of Subtitle V-A;

— Sec. 502(a)(3), adding 31 USC 313 and 31 USC 314;

— Sec. 4, providing the effective date.

¶2010 Establishment of the Federal Insurance Office

The Federal Insurance Office is not accompanied by the establishment of a national insurance charter. It is headed by a Director, appointed by the Treasury Secretary (31 USC 313(b), as added by Sec. 502(a) of the Dodd-Frank Wall Street Reform and Consumer Protection Act).

Its principal functions are to:

- monitor the insurance industry, with the authority to gather information and issue reports;
- identify issues or gaps in the regulation of insurers that could contribute to a systemic crisis;
- monitor the extent to which minorities, low- and moderate-income persons and underserved communities have access to affordable insurance products, except health insurance;
- recommend which insurance companies should be designated as entities subject to regulation as nonbank financial companies supervised by the Federal Reserve Board;
- recommend which insurance companies should be subject to stricter standards;
- assist in the administration of the Terrorism Insurance Program;
- coordinate international insurance issues and assist in negotiating covered agreements;
- determine whether state insurance measures are preempted by covered agreements;
- consult with states regarding insurance matters of national and international importance; and
- conduct a study on ways to modernize insurance regulation and provide Congress with recommendations (31 USC 313(c), as added by Sec. 502(a) of the Dodd-Frank Act).

Collection of Information.—The FIO may require an insurer or affiliate to submit data or information it reasonably requires in carrying out its functions. This does not apply to small insurers—those that meet a minimum size threshold that the FIO may establish. Before collecting the data or information, the FIO must coordinate with each relevant federal agency and state insurance regulator and any publicly available sources to determine if the information is available from those sources. If it is not available, the

FIO must comply with requirements of the Paperwork Reduction Act to collect it (31 USC 313(e), as added by Sec. 502(a) of the Dodd-Frank Act).

> **CCH Comment:** The final measure adds the House provision requiring the FIO to make a Paperwork Reduction Act showing before requiring insurers to produce information. The Senate measure required the FIO to "coordinate" with state and federal agencies/regulators to determine if desired information is available through sources other than directly from insurers, but the Senate version did not require the FIO to get information from an alternate source if available.

Confidentiality.—The submission of any nonpublicly available data and information to the FIO does not affect any privilege arising under federal or state law to which the material is otherwise subject (31 USC 313(e), as added by Sec. 502(a) of the Dodd-Frank Act).

Information-Sharing Agreement.—Any data or information obtained may be made available to state insurance regulators through an information-sharing agreement that complies with applicable federal law and does not affect any privilege under federal or state law to which the material is otherwise subject (31 USC 313(e), as added by Sec. 502(a) of the Dodd-Frank Act).

Subpoena Power.—The FIO has the power to subpoena information from insurers that it needs to carry out its functions. Prior to issuing a subpoena, the FIO must coordinate with the relevant state insurance regulator to determine if the information is available from the regulator or publicly available sources (31 USC 313(e), as added by Sec. 502(a) of the Dodd-Frank Act).

> **CCH Comment:** The Senate Committee Report stated that the subpoena authority is intended to be an option of last resort that would very rarely be used, since it is expected that the relevant regulator or agency and the insurers would cooperate with reasonable requests for data or information by the FIO.

Preemption.—In carrying out its duties that relate to international insurance, the FIO has limited authority to declare that inconsistent state laws or regulations are pre-empted. A state insurance measure would be preempted if it results in less favorable treatment of a non-U.S. insurer domiciled in a foreign jurisdiction that is subject to a covered agreement than a U.S. insurer admitted in that state, and it is inconsistent with a covered agreement (31 USC 313(f)(1) as added by Sec. 502 of the Dodd-Frank Act). Before making any determination of inconsistency, the FIO must:

- notify the state;
- notify the United States Trade Representative;
- publish a notice of the issue in the *Federal Register*; and
- provide interested parties an opportunity for comment and consider the effect of preemption.

There is a minimum 30-day period before a notice of determination of inconsistency becomes effective. Any preemption determination is limited to the subject matter contained in the covered agreement and receives a level of protection for insurance or reinsurance consumers that is substantially equivalent to the level of protection achieved under state insurance or reinsurance regulation (31 USC 313(f)(2) as added by Sec. 502 of the Dodd-Frank Act). Determinations of inconsistency are subject to the Administrative Procedures Act, except that in any action for judicial review of a determination, the court will determine the matter de novo. (31 USC 313(g), as added by Sec. 502(a) of the Dodd-Frank Act).

Regulations and Consultation.—The Treasury Secretary may issue orders, regulations, policies and procedures to implement these provisions (31 USC 313(h), as added by Sec. 502(a) of the Dodd-Frank Act). Also, the Director will consult with state insurance regulators in carrying out the functions of the office (31 USC 313(i), as added by Sec. 502(a) of the Dodd-Frank Act).

Retention of Authority of Federal Financial Regulatory Agencies and Unites States Trade Representative.—These provisions do not limit the authority of any federal financial regulatory agency to develop and coordinate policy, negotiate and enter into agreements with foreign governments, authorities, regulators and multinational regulatory committees, or preempt state measures to affect uniformity with international regulatory agreements (31 USC 313(l), as added by Sec. 502(a) of the Dodd-Frank Act). Also, these provisions do not affect the authority of the United States Trade Representative over the development and coordination of U.S. international trade policy and the administration of the U. S. trade agreements program (31 USC 313(m), as added by Sec. 502(a) of the Dodd-Frank Act).

Reports.—Beginning Sept. 30, 2011, an annual report must be submitted to Congress on the insurance industry, any actions taken by the office regarding preemption determinations, and any other relevant or requested information (31 USC 313(n), as added by Sec. 502(a) of the Dodd-Frank Act). Beginning in 2012, reports must be submitted to Congress on the U.S. and global reinsurance market (31 USC 313(o), as added by Sec. 502(a) of the Dodd-Frank Act).

Within 18 months of enactment, a report must be submitted to Congress containing any legislative, administrative or regulatory recommendations to modernize and improve the system of insurance regulation. Issues to be considered as part of the required study include:

- systemic risk regulation for insurance;
- capital standards and an appropriate match between capital allocation and liabilities for risk;
- consumer protection for insurance products and practices, including gaps in state regulation;
- the degree of national uniformity of state insurance regulation;
- regulation of insurance companies and affiliates on a consolidated basis;
- international coordination of insurance regulation;
- costs and benefits of potential federal regulation across various lines of insurance; and
- consequences of subjecting insurance companies to a federal resolution authority (31 USC 313(p), as added by Sec. 502(a) of the Dodd-Frank Act).

International Agreements.—The Dodd-Frank Act authorizes the Treasury Secretary and the United States Trade Representative to negotiate and enter into covered agreements on behalf of the United States (31 USC 314(a), as added by Sec. 502(a) of the Dodd-Frank Act). A "covered agreement" is a written bilateral or multilateral agreement entered into between the United States and a foreign government, authority or regulatory entity regarding prudential measures applicable to the business of insurance or reinsurance that achieves a level of protection for consumers that is substantially equivalent to the level of protection achieved under state insurance or reinsurance regulation (31 USC 313(r), as added by Sec. 502(a) of the Dodd-Frank Act). Covered agreement negotiations may be entered into only after consultation with Congress and after submitting to Congress the final legal text of the agreement (31 USC 314(b) and (c), as added by Sec. 502(a) of the Dodd-Frank Act).

> **CCH Comment:** The final measure replaces the Senate definition of "International Insurance Agreement on Prudential Measures" with the House "covered agreement" definition that requires international agreements to provide for regulatory protection "substantially equivalent" to regulatory protection as currently provided by state insurance measures.

Duties of Treasury Secretary.—The Dodd-Frank Act amends 31 USC 321(a) to add that the Treasury Secretary will advise the President on major domestic and international prudential policy issues in connection with all lines of insurance except health insurance (Sec. 502(b) of the Dodd-Frank Act).

▶ **Effective date.** The provision takes effect one day after the date of enactment (Sec. 4 of the Dodd-Frank Wall Street Reform and Consumer Protection Act).

Law source: Law at ¶10,502 and ¶10,004. Committee Report at ¶54,241.

— Sec. 502(a) of the Dodd-Frank Wall Street Reform and Consumer Protection Act, adding 31 USC 313 and 31 USC 314;

— Sec. 502(b), prescribing duties of the Treasury Secretary;

— Sec. 502(b), adding 31 USC 321(a)(9);

— Sec. 4, providing the effective date.

STATE-BASED INSURANCE REFORM

¶2015 Introduction

Title V of the Dodd-Frank Wall Street Reform and Consumer Protection Act contains provisions that are intended to streamline the regulation of surplus lines insurance and reinsurance through state-based reforms. Subtitle B may be cited as the "Nonadmitted and Reinsurance Reform Act of 2010."

▶ **Effective date.** The provision is effective one year after the date of enactment, which is the effective date for Subtitle B—State-Based Insurance Reform, except as otherwise specifically provided (Sec. 512 of the Dodd-Frank Wall Street Reform and Consumer Protection Act).

Law source: Law at ¶10,511 and ¶10,512. Committee Report at ¶54,260.

— Sec. 511 of the Dodd-Frank Wall Street Reform and Consumer Protection Act, providing the short title of Title V-B;

— Sec. 512, providing the effective date.

¶2020 Surplus Lines Insurance

The Dodd-Frank Act gives the home state of the insured (policyholder) sole regulatory authority over the collection and allocation of premium tax obligations related to nonadmitted (surplus lines) insurance (Sec. 521(a) of the Dodd-Frank Act). States are authorized to enter into a compact or other agreement to establish uniform allocation and remittance procedures (Sec. 521(b) of the Dodd-Frank Act).

The insured's home state can require surplus lines brokers and insureds to file tax allocation reports detailing the portion of premiums attributable to properties, risks or exposures located in each state (Sec. 521(c) of the Dodd-Frank Act).

▶ **Effective date.** The provision is effective one year after the date of enactment (Sec. 512 of the Dodd-Frank Wall Street Reform and Consumer Protection Act).

Law source: Law at ¶10,521 and ¶10,512. Committee Report at ¶54,265.

— Sec. 521 of the Dodd-Frank Wall Street Reform and Consumer Protection Act;

— Sec. 512, providing the effective date.

¶2025 Regulation by Insured's Home State

The placement of nonadmitted insurance is subject to the law and regulations of the insured's home state (Sec. 522(a) of the Dodd-Frank Act). Only the insured's home state can require a surplus lines broker to be licensed in order to sell, solicit or negotiate nonadmitted insurance with respect to the insured (Sec. 522(b) of the Dodd-Frank Act). The home state's laws and rules preempt those of other states (Sec. 522(c) of the Dodd-Frank Act). However, workers' compensation laws and rules are not preempted (Sec. 522(d) of the Dodd-Frank Act).

▶ **Effective date.** The provisions are effective one year after the date of enactment (Sec. 512 of the Dodd-Frank Wall Street Reform and Consumer Protection Act).

Law source: Law at ¶10,522 and ¶10,512. Committee Report at ¶54,266.

— Sec. 522 of the Dodd-Frank Wall Street Reform and Consumer Protection Act;

— Sec. 512, providing the effective date.

¶2030 Participation in National Producer Database

Two years after enactment, states will not be allowed to collect fees relating to licensing of nonadmitted brokers unless the states participate in the national insurance producer database of the National Association of Insurance Commissioners (NAIC).

▶ **Effective date.** The provision is effective one year after the date of enactment (Sec. 512 of the Dodd-Frank Wall Street Reform and Consumer Protection Act).

Law source: Law at ¶10,523 and ¶10,512. Committee Report at ¶54,267.

— Sec. 523 of the Dodd-Frank Wall Street Reform and Consumer Protection Act;

— Sec. 512, providing the effective date.

¶2035 Surplus Lines Eligibility

The Dodd-Frank Act streamlines eligibility requirements for nonadmitted insurance providers with the eligibility requirements set forth in the NAIC's Nonadmitted Insurance Model Act. Also, a state may not prohibit a surplus lines broker from placing nonadmitted insurance with, or procuring nonadmitted insurance from, a nonadmitted insurer domiciled outside the United States that is listed on the Quarterly Listing of Alien Insurers maintained by the NAIC.

▶ **Effective date.** The provision is effective one year after the date of enactment (Sec. 512 of the Dodd-Frank Wall Street Reform and Consumer Protection Act).

Law source: Law at ¶10,524 and ¶10,512. Committee Report at ¶54,268.

— Sec. 524 of the Dodd-Frank Wall Street Reform and Consumer Protection Act;

— Sec. 512, providing the effective date.

¶2040 Application for Commercial Purchasers

The Dodd-Frank Act allows exempt commercial purchasers easier access to the nonadmitted marketplace by waiving certain requirements. A surplus lines broker seeking to procure or place nonadmitted insurance in a state for an exempt commercial purchaser need not satisfy any state requirement to make a due diligence search to determine whether the full amount or type of insurance can be obtained from admitted insurers if:

(1) the broker has disclosed that the insurance may or may not be available from the admitted market that may provide greater protection with more regulatory oversight; and

(2) the exempt commercial purchaser has subsequently requested in writing that the broker procure or place the insurance from a nonadmitted insurer.

▶ **Effective date.** The provision is effective one year after the date of enactment (Sec. 512 of the Dodd-Frank Wall Street Reform and Consumer Protection Act).

Law source: Law at ¶10,525 and ¶10,512. Committee Report at ¶54,269.

— Sec. 525 of the Dodd-Frank Wall Street Reform and Consumer Protection Act;

— Sec. 512, providing the effective date.

¶2045 GAO Study Required

The Government Accountability Office, in consultation with the NAIC, must conduct a study, within 30 months of enactment, of the nonadmitted insurance market to determine the effect of the new law on the size and market share of the nonadmitted market.

▶ **Effective date.** The provision is effective one year after the date of enactment (Sec. 512 of the Dodd-Frank Wall Street Reform and Consumer Protection Act).

Law source: Law at ¶10,526 and ¶10,512. Committee Report at ¶54,270.

— Sec. 526 of the Dodd-Frank Wall Street Reform and Consumer Protection Act;
— Sec. 512, providing the effective date.

¶2050 Nonadmitted Insurance Definitions

The term "admitted insurer" means, with respect to a state, an insurer licensed to engage in the business of insurance in the state.

The term "exempt commercial purchaser" means any person purchasing commercial insurance that, at the time of placement:

(1) employs or retains a qualified risk manager to negotiate insurance coverage;

(2) has paid aggregate nationwide commercial property and casualty insurance premiums in excess of $100,000 in the immediately preceding 12 months; and

(3) meets at least one of the five criteria set out in the Dodd-Frank Act regarding net worth, annual revenues, number of employees, being a nonprofit or public entity exceeding a certain size, or being a municipality of a certain size.

The term "nonadmitted insurance" means any property and casualty insurance permitted to be placed directly or through a surplus lines broker with a nonadmitted insurer eligible to accept such insurance.

The term "nonadmitted insurer" means an insurer not licensed to engage in the insurance business in the state but does not include a risk retention group.

The term "premium tax" means any tax, fee, assessment or other charge imposed by a government directly or indirectly based on any payment made as consideration for an insurance contract, including premium deposits, assessments and registration fees.

The term "surplus lines broker" means an individual, form or corporation licensed in a state to sell, solicit or negotiate insurance on properties, risks or exposures located or to be performed in a state with nonadmitted insurers.

▶ **Effective date.** The provision is effective one year after the date of enactment (Sec. 512 of the Dodd-Frank Wall Street Reform and Consumer Protection Act).

Law source: Law at ¶10,527 and ¶10,512. Committee Report at ¶54,271.

— Sec. 527 of the Dodd-Frank Wall Street Reform and Consumer Protection Act;
— Sec. 512, providing the effective date.

¶2055 Reinsurance

The Dodd-Frank Act prohibits non-domiciliary states from denying credit for reinsurance if the state of domicile of a ceding insurer is an NAIC-accredited state or has solvency requirements substantially similar to those required for NAIC accreditation (Sec. 531(a) of the Dodd-Frank Act). It also prohibits non-domiciliary states from:

- restricting or eliminating the rights of reinsurers to resolve disputes pursuant to contractual arbitration clauses;
- ignoring or eliminating contractual agreements on choice of law determinations; and
- enforcing reinsurance contracts on terms different from those set forth in the reinsurance contract (Sec. 531(b) of the Dodd-Frank Act).

▶ **Effective date.** The provisions are effective one year after the date of enactment (Sec. 512 of the Dodd-Frank Wall Street Reform and Consumer Protection Act).

Law source: Law at ¶10,531 and ¶10,512. Committee Report at ¶54,275.

— Sec. 531 of the Dodd-Frank Wall Street Reform and Consumer Protection Act;

— Sec. 512, providing the effective date.

¶2060 Regulation of Solvency

The state of domicile of the reinsurer is solely responsible for regulating the financial solvency of the reinsurer (Sec. 532(a) of the Dodd-Frank Act). Non-domiciliary states cannot require a reinsurer to provide any financial information other than the information required by the state of domicile. Non-domiciliary states also get copies of the financial information that is required to be filed with the state of domicile (Sec. 532(b) of the Dodd-Frank Act).

▶ **Effective date.** The provisions are effective one year after the date of enactment (Sec. 512 of the Dodd-Frank Wall Street Reform and Consumer Protection Act).

Law source: Law at ¶10,532 and ¶10,512. Committee Report at ¶54,276.

— Sec. 532 of the Dodd-Frank Wall Street Reform and Consumer Protection Act;

— Sec. 512, providing the effective date.

¶2065 Reinsurance Definitions

The term "ceding insurer" means an insurer that purchases reinsurance.

The term "reinsurance" means the assumption by an insurer of all or part of a risk undertaken originally by another insurer.

The term "reinsurer" means an insurer to the extent that the insurer is principally engaged in the business of reinsurance, does not conduct significant amounts of direct insurance as a percentage of its net premiums and is not routinely engaged in the business of soliciting direct insurance (Sec. 533 of the Dodd-Frank Act).

▶ **Effective date.** The provision is effective one year after the date of enactment (Sec. 512 of the Dodd-Frank Wall Street Reform and Consumer Protection Act).

Law source: Law at ¶10,533 and ¶10,512. Committee Report at ¶54,277.

— Sec. 533 of the Dodd-Frank Wall Street Reform and Consumer Protection Act;

— Sec. 512, providing the effective date.

¶2070 Rule of Construction

The Dodd-Frank Act clarifies that this subtitle will not modify, impair or supersede the application of antitrust laws and confirms that any potential conflict between this subtitle and the antitrust laws will be resolved in favor of the operation of the antitrust laws.

▶ **Effective date.** The provision is effective one year after the date of enactment (Sec. 512 of the Dodd-Frank Wall Street Reform and Consumer Protection Act).

Law source: Law at ¶10,541 and ¶10,512. Committee Report at ¶54,280.

— Sec. 541 of the Dodd-Frank Wall Street Reform and Consumer Protection Act;
— Sec. 512, providing the effective date.

¶2075 Severability

The Dodd-Frank Act provides that, if any of these provisions are held to be unconstitutional, the remainder of them, and their application to any other person or circumstance, is not to be affected.

▶ **Effective date.** The provision is effective one year after the date of enactment (Sec. 512 of the Dodd-Frank Wall Street Reform and Consumer Protection Act).

Law source: Law at ¶10,542 and ¶10,512. Committee Report at ¶54,281.

— Sec. 542 of the Dodd-Frank Wall Street Reform and Consumer Protection Act;
— Sec. 512, providing the effective date.

Bank and Thrift Regulatory Improvements

¶2505	Introduction
¶2510	Deposit Insurance and Change in Bank Control Moratorium
¶2515	GAO Study of Bank Holding Company Act Exceptions
¶2520	Holding Company Examination Improvements
¶2525	Functionally Regulated Subsidiaries
¶2530	Acquisitions
¶2535	Oversight of Depository Institution Subsidiary Activities
¶2540	Enhanced Capitalization and Management
¶2545	Transactions with Affiliates and Insiders
¶2550	Lending Limits
¶2555	Charter Conversions
¶2560	De Novo Branching
¶2565	Source of Strength
¶2570	Investment and Securities Holding Companies
¶2575	Proprietary Trading, Hedge Funds and Private Equity Funds—Volcker Rule
¶2580	Study of Bank Investment Activities
¶2585	Conflicts of Interest Relating to Securitizations
¶2590	Concentration Limits
¶2595	Interstate Bank Mergers and Acquisitions
¶2600	Thrift Dividends
¶2605	Mutual Holding Company Dividends
¶2610	Intermediate Holding Companies
¶2615	Payment of Interest on Demand Deposits
¶2620	Credit Card Bank Small Business Lending

¶2505 Introduction

Title VI of the Dodd-Frank Wall Street Reform and Consumer Protection Act—The Bank and Savings Association Holding Company and Depository Institution Regulatory

Improvements Act of 2010—seeks to improve the regulation and supervision of bank and savings association holding companies and depository institutions to assure these financial institutions do not pose a threat to the country's financial stability.

Title VI also makes a number of amendments to various statutes to reflect the abolishment of the Office of Thrift Supervision (OTS) and transfer of that agency's supervisory powers to the Office of the Comptroller of the Currency (OCC) and Federal Deposit Insurance Corporation (FDIC).

Finally, Title VI creates a supervisory regime for "securities holding companies," restricts the capital market activities of banks and bank holding companies and imposes concentration limits on large financial firms.

▶ **Effective date.** The provision takes effect one day after the date of enactment (Sec. 4 of the Dodd-Frank Wall Street Reform and Consumer Protection Act).

Law source: Law at ¶10,601 and ¶10,004. Committee Report at ¶54,290.

— Sec. 601 of the Dodd-Frank Wall Street Reform and Consumer Protection Act, providing the short title of Title VI;

— Sec. 4, providing the effective date.

¶2510 Deposit Insurance and Change in Bank Control Moratorium

The Dodd-Frank Act imposes a three-year moratorium on the approval of a deposit insurance application by the FDIC. This moratorium applies to deposit insurance applications received after Nov. 23, 2009, for an industrial bank, credit card bank or trust bank that is controlled by a "commercial firm" (Sec. 603(a)(2) of the Dodd-Frank Act).

A "commercial firm" is defined as any entity that derives not less than 15 percent of its consolidated annual gross revenues, including all affiliates, from engaging in activities that are not financial in nature or incidental to activities that are financial in nature, as provided in Section 4(k) of the Bank Holding Company Act of 1956 (BHCA) (Sec. 602 of the Dodd-Frank Act).

The moratorium also provides that the OCC, Federal Reserve Board (Fed) and FDIC cannot approve a change in control of an industrial bank, credit card bank or trust bank that is controlled by a commercial firm (Sec. 603(a)(2) of the Dodd-Frank Act). The moratorium on a change of bank control does not apply if the bank is in danger of default or if the change of control:

- is the result of the merger or whole acquisition of a commercial firm that directly or indirectly controls the bank in a bona fide merger with or acquisition by another commercial firm; or

- results from an acquisition of voting shares of a publicly traded company that controls the bank, if, after the acquisition, the acquiring shareholder (or group of shareholders acting in concert) holds less than 25 percent of any class of the voting shares of the company.

In each of these cases in which a change in control is permitted, the applicant must have obtained all regulatory approvals (Sec. 603(a)(3) of the Dodd-Frank Act).

CCH Comment: The moratorium is similar to a 2006 moratorium that the FDIC imposed on deposit insurance applications and change in bank control notices filed by industrial loan companies.

▶ **Effective date.** The provision takes effect one day after the date of enactment (Sec. 4 of the Dodd-Frank Wall Street Reform and Consumer Protection Act).

Law source: Law at ¶10,602, ¶10,603 and ¶10,004. Committee Report at ¶54,291 and ¶54,292

— Secs. 602 and 603(a) of the Dodd-Frank Wall Street Reform and Consumer Protection Act;

— Sec. 4, providing the effective date.

¶2515 GAO Study of Bank Holding Company Act Exceptions

The Government Accountability Office (GAO) is required to conduct a study to determine whether to eliminate the BHCA exceptions for six specific institutions that are not currently considered to be bank holding companies or banks. This study is to be submitted to the House Financial Services Committee and the Senate Banking Committee within 18 months after the enactment of the Dodd-Frank Act (Sec. 603(b)(1) of the Dodd-Frank Act).

These six institutions are:

1. companies that own any state-chartered bank or trust company that is wholly owned by one or more thrift institutions or savings banks and has restricted deposit-taking abilities;
2. FDIC-insured trust companies or mutual savings banks that are permitted by state law to have limited control of one bank in the same state;
3. trust banks;
4. credit card banks;
5. industrial banks; and
6. thrift institutions.

The GAO's study is to:

- identify which institutions held by holding companies are commercial firms;
- ascertain whether the institutions have any affiliates that are commercial firms;
- identify the federal banking agency responsible for supervision;
- determine whether the regulatory framework, especially regarding affiliate transactions, is adequate; and
- evaluate the potential consequences of subjecting these institutions to the BHCA, with particular attention to credit availability, financial stability and safety and soundness (Sec. 603(b)(2)(A) of the Dodd-Frank Act).

For thrift institutions currently excepted from BHCA coverage, the GAO would determine the adequacy of the federal bank regulatory framework and evaluate the potential consequences of subjecting thrift institutions to the BHCA (Sec. 603(b)(2)(B) of the Dodd-Frank Act).

▶ **Effective date.** The provision takes effect one day after the date of enactment (Sec. 4 of the Dodd-Frank Wall Street Reform and Consumer Protection Act).

Law source: Law at ¶10,603 and ¶10,004. Committee Report at ¶54,292.

— Sec. 603(b) of the Dodd-Frank Wall Street Reform and Consumer Protection Act;

— Sec. 4, providing the effective date.

¶2520 Holding Company Examination Improvements

Section 604 of the Dodd-Frank Act makes a number of changes to the examination provisions of the BHCA and the holding company provisions of the Home Owners' Loan Act (HOLA).

With the abolishment of the OTS, the Fed gains sole responsibility for the supervision of bank holding companies (BHCs) and savings and loan holding companies (SLHCs), as well as any non-depository institution subsidiaries.

> **CCH Comment:** An earlier version of the Dodd-Frank Act would have made the OCC responsible for BHCs and SLHCs with consolidated assets of less than $50 billion and a federally chartered depository institution subsidiary. BHCs and SLHCs with consolidated assets of less than $50 billion and a state-chartered depository institution subsidiary were to be supervised by the FDIC. Finally, the Fed was to have the supervisory authority for BHCs with consolidated assets of more than $50 billion and any non-depository institution subsidiaries.

Use of Existing Reports.—The Fed, as the "appropriate Federal banking agency" for BHCs, is required to use the reports and other supervisory information that the BHC or any subsidiary has been required to provide to other federal or state regulatory agencies. The agencies are also to use, to the fullest extent possible, externally audited financial statements and any other information available from other federal or state regulatory agencies (BHCA Sec. 5(c)(1), as amended by Sec. 604(a) of the Dodd-Frank Act).

Examinations.—The examination provisions of the BHCA are amended to provide that one of the goals of an examination is to inform the Fed of the financial, operational and other risks the BHCs and any subsidiaries may pose to the financial stability of the United States (BHCA Sec. 5(c)(2), as amended by Sec. 604(b) of the Dodd-Frank Act).

The other purposes of the examination authority, such as: informing the Fed of the operations and financial condition of the holding company and the subsidiary; any risks within the holding company's organization; and systems to monitor and control the risk, are unaffected by Section 604(b) amendments.

The Fed is also required to use examination reports made by other federal and state regulators relating to the holding company and subsidiary. In addition, the Fed is to notify and consult with other regulators before requesting a report or conducting an examination of a depository institution subsidiary or a functionally regulated subsidiary to avoid duplication of reporting requirements and requests for information (BHCA Sec. 5(c)(5)(B) as amended by the Dodd-Frank Act).

Savings and Loan Holding Companies.—Finally, the Dodd-Frank Act addresses the examination of SLHCs by amending provisions of HOLA. One of the amendments to HOLA addresses the supervisory role that the Fed plays once the OTS is abolished. The other provision amends the SLHC examination provisions found in HOLA Section 10(b). This amendment mirrors the examination provisions found in BHCA Section 5(c)(2), which deal with using existing reports and ensuring that the activities of the SLHC and its subsidiaries do not pose a risk to the financial stability of the United States (HOLA Sec. 10(b), as amended by Sec. 604(g) of the Dodd-Frank Act).

The Dodd-Frank Act also amends the definition of savings and loan holding company. Specifically, the Dodd-Frank Act amends the portion of the definition that excludes certain entities as savings and loan holding companies (HOLA Sec. 10(a)(1)(D)(ii), as amended by Sec. 604(h)(2) of the Dodd-Frank Act).

▶ **Effective date.** The provision is effective on the "transfer date" provided in Section 311 of the Dodd-Frank Act. The "transfer date," which occurs one year after the date of the enactment of the Dodd-Frank Act, is the time frame in which the supervisory functions of the OTS are transferred to the OCC, Fed and FDIC (Sec. 604(i) of the Dodd-Frank Wall Street Reform and Consumer Protection Act).

Law source: Law at ¶10,604. Committee Report at ¶54,293.

— Sec. 604(a) of the Dodd-Frank Wall Street Reform and Consumer Protection Act, amending Bank Holding Company Act Sec. 5(c)(1);

— Sec. 604(b), amending Bank Holding Company Act Sec. 5(c)(2);

— Sec. 604(g), amending Home Owners' Loan Act Secs. 10(b)(2);

— Sec. 604(h)(1), adding Home Owners' Loan Act Sec. 2(10) and (11);

— Sec. 604(h)(2), amending Home Owners' Loan Act Sec. 10(a)(1)(D)(ii);

— Sec. 604(h)(i), amending Home Owners' Loan Act Sec. 10(b)(4);

— Sec. 604(j), providing the effective date.

¶2525 Functionally Regulated Subsidiaries

The Dodd-Frank Act removes the "back-door" enforcement provision found in BHCA Section 10A, which limited the Fed's rulemaking and enforcement authority with respect to functionally regulated subsidiaries. The Fed was only able to take action against a functionally regulated subsidiary if its actions posed a threat to the safety and soundness of a depository institution affiliate or the domestic or international payment system (BHCA, Sec. 10A, as removed by Sec. 604(c)(2) of the Dodd-Frank Act).

▶ **Effective date.** The provision becomes effective on the "transfer date" provided in Section 311 of the Dodd-Frank Act. The "transfer date," which occurs one year after the date of the enactment of the Dodd-Frank Act, is the time frame in which the supervisory functions of the OTS are transferred to the OCC, Fed and FDIC (Sec. 604(j) of the Dodd-Frank Wall Street Reform and Consumer Protection Act).

Law source: Law at ¶10,604. Committee Report at ¶54,293.

— Sec. 604(c)(2) of the Dodd-Frank Wall Street Reform and Consumer Protection Act, striking Bank Holding Company Act Sec. 10A;

— Sec. 604(j), providing the effective date.

¶2530 Acquisitions

The factors to be considered for bank acquisitions under BHCA Section 3 and the nonbank acquisitions under BHCA Section 4 are amended by the Dodd-Frank Act.

In the case of a Section 3 acquisition, the Fed is to consider whether the acquisition would result in greater or more concentrated risks to the stability of the U.S. banking or financial system (BHCA Sec. 3(c)(7), as added by Sec. 604(d) of the Dodd-Frank Act).

For Section 4 acquisitions, the general standards for reviewing the acquisition require the Fed to determine whether the acquisition poses any risk to the stability of the U.S. banking or financial system (BHCA Sec. 4(j)(2)(A), as added by Sec. 604(e)(1) of the Dodd-Frank Act).

Financial Holding Company Acquisitions.—The Dodd-Frank Act retains the "no prior approval" provisions of BHCA Section 4(k)(6) whenever a financial holding company (FHC) acquires a company that engages in an activity that is financial in nature. The FHC will now need prior approval from the Fed if the acquisition exceeds $10 billion in total consolidated assets. The Dodd-Frank Act also addresses the application of the Hart-Scott-Rodino filing requirements of the Clayton Act (BHCA Sec. 4(k)(6)(B), as added by Sec. 604(e)(2) of the Dodd-Frank Act).

> **CCH Comment:** In an earlier version of the Dodd-Frank Act, the threshold for the Fed's prior approval was $25 billion.

Bank Merger Act.—Finally, the Bank Merger Act (BMA) provisions, found in Section 18 of the Federal Deposit Insurance Act (FDIA), are also amended to require that the reviewing banking agency consider whether the transactions conducted under the BMA pose any risk to the stability of the U.S. banking or financial system.

▶ **Effective date.** The provision becomes effective on the "transfer date" provided in Section 311 of the Dodd-Frank Act. The "transfer date," which occurs one year after the date of the enactment of the Dodd-Frank Act, is the time frame in which the supervisory functions of the OTS are transferred to the OCC, Fed and FDIC (FDIA Sec. 18(c)(5), as amended by Sec. 604(f) of the Dodd-Frank Act) (Sec. 604(j) of the Dodd-Frank Wall Street Reform and Consumer Protection Act).

Law source: Law at ¶10,604. Committee Report at ¶54,293.

— Sec. 604(d) of the Dodd-Frank Wall Street Reform and Consumer Protection Act, adding Bank Holding Company Act of 1956 Sec. 3(c)(7);

— Sec. 604(e)(1), amending Bank Holding Company Act of 1956 Sec. 4(j)(2)(A);

— Sec. 604(e)(2), amending Bank Holding Company Act of 1956 Sec.4(k)(6)(B);

— Sec. 604(f), amending Federal Deposit Insurance Act Sec. 18(c)(5);

— Sec. 604(j), providing the effective date.

¶2535 Oversight of Depository Institution Subsidiary Activities

The Dodd-Frank Act adds a new Section 26 to the FDIA to assure consistent oversight of permissible activities of depository institution holding company subsidiaries.

CCH Comment: An earlier version of the Dodd-Frank Act had a similar examination provision to be codified at Section 6 of the BHCA.

The Fed is required to examine the activities of a nondepository institution subsidiary of a depository institution holding company. These activities are the same type of activities that are permissible for the holding company's depository institution subsidiaries. The examination is to be done in the same manner, subject to the same standards and with the same frequency as would be required if a nondepository institution subsidiary's activities were conducted in the "lead insured depository institution," which is the largest insured depository institution controlled by the holding company at any time, based on a comparison of the average total risk-weighted assets controlled by each insured depository institution during the previous 12-month period. It should be noted that the FDIA Section 26 examination authority does not apply to the holding company's functionally regulated subsidiaries. (FDIA Sec. 26(b), as added by Sec. 605(a) of the Dodd-Frank Act).

CCH Comment: An earlier version of the Dodd-Frank Act provided that this type of examination was to determine whether the nondepository institution subsidiaries' activities: presented safety and soundness risks to any of the holding company's depository institution subsidiaries; were conducted in accordance with applicable law; and were subject to appropriate internal control systems for monitoring risks, such as financial or operational risk and protecting the depository institution subsidiaries.

Coordinated Examinations.—The Dodd-Frank Act requires the Fed to consult and coordinate with a state regulator if a nondepository institution subsidiary is subject to some sort of state supervision (Federal Deposit Insurance Act Sec. 26(c)(1), as added by Sec. 605(a) of the Dodd-Frank Act).

Alternating Examinations. The Fed is also permitted to conduct a joint or alternating examination with a state regulator if it determines that the examination of the nondepository institution subsidiary conducted by the state regulator carries out the purposes of FDIA Section 26 (Federal Deposit Insurance Act Sec. 26(c)(2), as added by Sec. 605(a) of the Dodd-Frank Act).

Backup Examination Authority.—If the Fed fails to meet its obligation under FDIA Section 26(b) to conduct an examination that meets certain standards, the "appropriate Federal banking agency" for the lead insured depository institution may provide a written explanation of the appropriate federal banking agency's concerns giving rise to the recommendation that the Fed perform the examination as required under FDIA Section 26(b) (FDIA Sec. 26(d)(1), as added by Sec. 605(a) of the Dodd-Frank Act).

Appropriate Federal Banking Agency Examination. The Fed has 60 days following receipt of the appropriate federal banking agency's recommendation to begin the FDIA Section 26(b) examination or provide a written response to the appropriate federal banking agency's concerns. If the Fed fails to fulfill either of these two requirements, the appropriate federal banking agency may examine the nondepository institution subsidiary's permissible activities (FDIA Sec. 26(d)(2), as added by Sec. 605(a) of the Dodd-Frank Act).

The appropriate federal banking agency's examination of the nondepository institution subsidiary's permissible activities are to determine whether the activities: present safety and soundness risks to any of the holding company's depository institution subsidiaries; are conducted in accordance with applicable federal law; and are subject to appropriate internal control systems for monitoring risks, such as financial or operational risk and protecting the depository institution subsidiaries (FDIA Sec. 26(d)(2)(A)–(C), as added by Sec. 605(a) of the Dodd-Frank Act).

Coordination. The appropriate federal banking agency that conducts a backup examination must coordinate the examination with the Fed so as to:

- avoid duplication;
- allow sharing of relevant information;
- achieve the examination objectives of Section 6; and
- ensure that a holding company and its subsidiaries are not subject to conflicting supervisory demands by the lead federal banking agency and the Fed (FDIA Sec. 26(d)(3), as added by Sec. 605(a) of the Dodd-Frank Act).

Fees. Finally, the appropriate federal banking agency may collect an assessment, fee or other charge from the subsidiary as the appropriate federal banking agency determines necessary or appropriate to carry out its backup examination authority (FDIA Sec. 26(d)(4), as added by Sec. 605(a) of the Dodd-Frank Act).

Enforcement Action Referrals.—Once the appropriate federal banking agency examines a nondepository institution subsidiary, under its backup examination authority, and finds that subsidiary's activities pose a material threat to the safety and soundness of any insured depository institution subsidiary of the depository institution holding company, the appropriate federal banking agency may submit a written recommendation that the Fed take enforcement action against the nondepository institution subsidiary. As part of the written recommendation, the appropriate federal banking agency must explain its concerns giving rise to the recommendation (FDIA Sec. 26(e)(1), as added by Sec. 605(a) of the Dodd-Frank Act).

The Fed has 60 days to act on the enforcement action recommendation. If the Fed fails to act or does not provide an acceptable plan for an enforcement action, the lead federal banking agency may take the recommended enforcement action (FDIA Sec. 26(e)(2), as added by Sec. 605(a) of the Dodd-Frank Act).

▶ **Effective date.** The provision becomes effective on the "transfer date" provided in Section 311 of the Dodd-Frank Act. The "transfer date," which occurs one year after the date of the enactment of the Dodd-Frank Act, is the time frame in which the supervisory functions of the OTS are transferred to the OCC, Fed and FDIC (Sec. 605(b) of the Dodd-Frank Wall Street Reform and Consumer Protection Act).

Law source: Law at ¶10,605. Committee Report at ¶54,294.

— Sec. 605(a) of the Dodd-Frank Wall Street Reform and Consumer Protection Act, adding Federal Deposit Insurance Act Sec. 26;

— Sec. 605(b), providing the effective date.

¶2540 Enhanced Capitalization and Management

Several provisions of the Dodd-Frank Act strengthen the operations of holding companies and the standards for interstate acquisitions under the BHCA.

Expanded Financial Activities.—A bank holding company must be "well capitalized and well managed" before undertaking certain activities permissible for financial holding companies, limited non-financial activities and affiliations or grandfathered commodities activities (BHCA, Sec. 4(l)(1), as amended by Sec. 606(a) of the Dodd-Frank Act).

Interstate Acquisitions and Mergers.—The Dodd-Frank Act also requires a bank holding company to be "well capitalized and well managed" before seeking control of a bank located in another state (BHCA Sec. 3(d)(1)(A), as amended by Sec. 607(a) of the Dodd-Frank Act).

There is a similar requirement that applicants seeking approval of an interstate merger under the FDIA be "well capitalized and well managed" (FDIA Sec. 44(b)(4)(B), as amended by Sec. 607(b) of the Dodd-Frank Act).

Regulatory Capital Requirements.—In addition, the Dodd-Frank Act amends the BHCA and the savings and loan holding company provisions of HOLA. In each instance, the supervision and administration of bank holding companies and savings and loan holding companies must take into consideration regulations relating to capital requirements.

Countercyclical Capital Requirements. In establishing capital regulations, the Dodd-Frank Act requires that the Fed make these requirements countercyclical, so that the amount of capital required to be maintained by a company increases in times of economic expansion and decreases in times of economic contraction, consistent with the safety and soundness of the bank holding company (BHCA Sec. 5(b), as amended by Sec. 616(a) of the Dodd-Frank Act).

Exempt SLHC Activities.—Finally, the Dodd-Frank Act amends the list of exempt activities for savings and loan holding companies. The latest exempt activity relates to activity that is permissible for a financial holding company (HOLA Sec. 10(c)(2)(H), as added by Sec. 606(b) of the Dodd-Frank Act).

▶ **Effective date.** The provisions become effective on the "transfer date" provided in Section 311 of the Dodd-Frank Act. The "transfer date," which occurs one year after the date of the enactment of the Dodd-Frank Act, is the time frame in which the supervisory functions of the OTS are transferred to the OCC, Fed and FDIC (Secs. 606(c), 607(c) and 616(d) of the Dodd-Frank Wall Street Reform and Consumer Protection Act).

Law source: Law at ¶10,606, ¶10,607, and ¶10,616. Committee Report at ¶54,295, ¶54,296 and ¶54,305.

— Sec. 606(a) of the Dodd-Frank Wall Street Reform and Consumer Protection Act, amending Bank Holding Company Act Sec. 4(l)(1);

— Sec. 606(b), adding Home Owners' Loan Act Sec. 10(c)(2)(I I);

— Sec. 607(a), amending Bank Holding Company Act Sec. 3(d)(1)(A);

— Sec. 607(b), amending Federal Deposit Insurance Act Sec. 44(b)(4)(B);

— Sec. 616(a), amending Bank Holding Company Act Sec. 5(b);

— Sec. 616(b), amending Home Owners' Loan Act Sec. 10(g)(1);
— Secs. 606(c), 607(c) and 616(d), providing the effective date.

¶2545 Transactions with Affiliates and Insiders

The Dodd-Frank Act makes several important changes to the transactions with affiliate requirements found in Sections 23A and 23B of the Federal Reserve Act (FRA) and the insider lending restriction found in FRA Section 22(h). Each of the amendments made by the Dodd-Frank Act recognize the role derivatives and other credit exposures played in the financial crisis.

Affiliates.—The definition of "affiliate" is amended to include any investment fund in which a member bank or one of its affiliates is an investment adviser (FRA Sec. 23A(b)(1), as amended by Sec. 608(a)(1)(A) of the Dodd-Frank Act).

Covered Transactions.—The definition of "covered transactions" is amended in a number of ways. First, the Dodd-Frank Act provides that a "covered transaction" occurs when a member bank enters into a securities borrowing or lending transaction with an affiliate and that transaction causes the member bank, or one of its subsidiaries, to have credit exposure to that affiliate. The Dodd-Frank Act also provides that a covered transaction arises whenever a member bank enters into a derivatives transaction with an affiliate and that derivatives transaction causes the member bank, or one of its subsidiaries, to have credit exposure to that affiliate (FRA Sec. 23A(b)(7), as amended by Sec. 608(a)(1)(B) of the Dodd-Frank Act).

The Dodd-Frank Act also gives the Fed the authority to issue regulations or interpretations with respect to the manner in which a netting agreement may be taken into account in determining the amount of a covered transaction between a member bank or a subsidiary and an affiliate. This authority can also be used to determine whether a netting agreement is fully secured for purposes of FRA Section 23A(d)(4) (FRA Sec. 23A(f)(4), as amended by Sec. 608(a)(4)(B) of the Dodd-Frank Act).

Interpretive Authority.—If the Fed chooses to exercise its interpretive authority with respect to a specific member bank, subsidiary or affiliate, the agency's interpretation must be issued jointly with the "appropriate Federal banking agency" for the member bank, subsidiary or affiliate (FRA Sec. 23A(f)(2), as amended by Sec. 608(a)(4)(A) of the Dodd-Frank Act).

Exempted Affiliate Transactions.—The Fed's exemptive authority under FRA Section 23A is also affected. Specifically, before the Fed grants an exemption under FRA Section 23A, it must obtain the concurrence of the FDIC chairman. When granting an exemption, the Fed must find that the exemption is in the public interest and consistent with the purposes of FRA Section 23A. In addition, the FDIC chairman's concurrence must be based on a finding that exemption does not present an unacceptable risk to the Deposit Insurance Fund (DIF) (FRA Sec. 23A(f)(2), as amended by Sec. 608(a)(4)(A) of the Dodd-Frank Act).

If the exemption involves a national bank, the Fed must obtain the concurrence of the OCC, as well as the FDIC chairman.

The Dodd-Frank Act also establishes a new mechanism for exempting affiliate transactions involving state-chartered banks with the FDIC having exemptive authority over state nonmember banks and the Fed having authority over state member banks.

The Fed also has to obtain the FDIC chairman's concurrence for any exemption under FRA Section 23B that imposes market terms and conditions on covered transactions. As with FRA Section 23A exemptions, when granting an exemption under FRA Section 23B, the Fed must find that the exemption is in the public interest and consistent with the purposes of FRA Section 23B, and the FDIC chairman must concur with the Fed's findings. This concurrence is based on the FDIC's finding that exemption does not present an unacceptable risk to the DIF.

The OCC is also given new exemptive authority for a federal savings association's transactions with an affiliate. This authority is found in HOLA Section 11(d)(1) and is similar to the limits placed on the Fed in that the OCC must find that the exemption is in the public interest and consistent with purposes of HOLA Section 11(d) and that the FDIC concurs that the exemption does not present an unacceptable risk to the DIF (HOLA Sec. 11(d)(1), as amended by Sec. 608(c) of the Dodd-Frank Act).

Finally, the FDIC has exemptive authority under HOLA Section 11(d)(2). The FDIC can exempt a state-chartered savings association's transaction with affiliates if it and the Fed find that the exemption is in the public interest and consistent with the purposes of HOLA Section 11, and the exemption does not present an unacceptable risk to the DIF (HOLA Sec. 11(d)(2), as amended by Sec. 608(c) of the Dodd-Frank Act).

Financial Subsidiaries.—The Dodd-Frank Act removes the FRA Section 23A(e)(3) exceptions for transactions with financial subsidiaries. Under FRA Section 23A(e)(3), the limitation on covered transactions between the bank and its affiliates to 10 percent of the bank's capital and surplus did not apply to transactions between the bank and any single financial subsidiary. In addition, the retained earnings of a financial subsidiary were not to be considered part of the bank's investment, although they were part of the bank's investment for regulatory capital purposes (FRA Sec. 23A(e), as amended by Sec. 609(a) of the Dodd-Frank Act).

The removal of FRA Section 23A(e)(3) applies with respect to any covered transaction that is entered into on or after the enactment of the Dodd-Frank Act.

Insider Lending.—An amendment to the FRA provisions dealing with loans to insiders explicitly provides that an "extension of credit" would have occurred between a member bank and a person if the member bank has credit exposure to the person arising from a derivatives transaction, repurchase agreement, reverse repurchase agreement, securities lending transaction or securities borrowing transaction between the member bank and the person (FRA Sec. 22(h)(9)(D)(i), as amended by Sec. 614(a) of the Dodd-Frank Act).

Finally, the Dodd-Frank Act amends the Federal Deposit Insurance Act by imposing a general prohibition on asset sales to an executive officer, director or principal shareholder of an insured depository institution. Under this new prohibition, an insured depository institution cannot be involved in the purchase or sale of an asset with these persons and their related interests unless the transaction is on market terms and is approved by a majority of the institution's board of directors who do not have an interest

¶2545

in the transaction. Board approval is only necessary if the transaction represents more than 10 percent of the institution's capital stock and surplus (FDIA Sec. 18(z); as added by Sec. 615(a) of the Dodd-Frank Act).

The Dodd-Frank Act also removes a similar asset purchases prohibition from FRA Section 22(d).

▶ **Effective date.** The provisions become effective on the "transfer date" provided in Section 311 of the Dodd-Frank Act. The "transfer date," which occurs one year after the date of the enactment of the Dodd-Frank Act, is the time frame in which the supervisory functions of the OTS are transferred to the OCC, Fed and FDIC (Sec. 604(i) of the Dodd-Frank Wall Street Reform and Consumer Protection Act) (Secs. 608(d), 609(c), 614(b) and 615(c) of the Dodd-Frank Wall Street Reform and Consumer Protection Act).

Law source: Law at ¶10,608, ¶10,609, ¶10,614 and ¶10,615. Committee Report at ¶54,297, ¶54,298, ¶54,303 and ¶54,304.

— Secs. 608(a) of the Dodd-Frank Wall Street Reform and Consumer Protection Act, amending Federal Reserve Act Secs. 23A(b), (c) (d) and (f);

— Sec. 608(b), amending Federal Reserve Act Sec. 23B(e),

— Sec. 608(c), adding Home Owners' Loan Act Sec. 11(d);

— Sec. 609(a), amending Federal Reserve Act Sec. 23A(e);

— Sec. 614(a), amending Federal Reserve Act Sec. 22(h)(9)(D)(i);

— Sec. 615(a), amending Federal Deposit Insurance Act Sec. 18;

— Sec. 615(b), reserving Federal Reserve Act, Sec. 22(d);

— Secs. 608(d), 609(c), 614(b) and 615(c) providing the effective date.

¶2550 Lending Limits

Section 610 of the Dodd-Frank Act amends the National Bank Act (NBA) lending limits by revising the definition of "loans and extensions of credit" to include credit exposure to a person arising from a derivative transaction, repurchase agreement, reverse repurchase agreement, securities lending transaction or securities borrowing transaction between a national bank and the person (12 USC 84(b), as amended by Sec. 610(a) of the Dodd-Frank Act).

The Dodd-Frank Act also makes a minor revision to the HOLA loan to one borrower provisions. This change reflects the fact that the OCC assumes the responsibility of regulating federal savings associations following the abolishment of the OTS (HOLA, Sec. 5(u)(3), as amended by Sec. 610(b) of the Dodd-Frank Act).

Finally, Section 611 of the Dodd-Frank Act amends the FDIA by requiring consistent treatment of derivative transactions in lending limits. The new provisions allows an insured state bank to engage in a derivative transaction, only if the lending limits law of the bank's chartering state take into consideration credit exposure to derivative transactions (FDIA Sec. 18(y), as added by Sec. 611(a) of the Dodd-Frank Act).

▶ **Effective date.** The amendments made by Sec. 610 to 12 USC 84(b) and HOLA, Sec. 5(u)(3) become effective on the "transfer date" provided in Section 311 of the Dodd-Frank Act. The amendment made by Sec. 611 adding FDIA Sec. 18(y) becomes effective 18 months after the "transfer date" provided in Section 311 of the Dodd-Frank Act. The "transfer date," which occurs one year after the date of the enactment of the Dodd-Frank Act, is the time frame in which the supervisory functions of the OTS are transferred to the OCC, Fed and FDIC (Secs. 610(c) and, 611(b) of the Dodd-Frank Wall Street Reform and Consumer Protection Act).

Law source: Law at ¶10,610 and ¶10,611. Committee Report at ¶54,299 and ¶54,300.

— Sec. 610(a) of the Dodd-Frank Wall Street Reform and Consumer Protection Act, amending 12 USC 84(b);

— Sec. 610(b), amending Home Owners' Loan Act Sec. 5(u)(3);

— Sec. 611(a), amending Federal Deposit Insurance Act Sec. 18;

— Secs. 610(c) and 611(b) providing the effective date.

¶2555 Charter Conversions

Charter conversions by national banks, state banks and federal savings associations would be impacted by amendments made by the Dodd-Frank Act. In each instance, if the converting institution is subject to an enforcement action initiated by its primary state or federal regulator, the conversion transaction would be prohibited (Sec. 10 of Act of Aug. 17, 1950, 12 USC 35 and HOLA, Sec. 5(i), as amended by Sec. 612 of the Dodd-Frank Act).

> **CCH Comment:** This prohibition on charter conversions would end the use of regulatory arbitrage and allow the institution "no place to hide" by switching charters.

Permissible Conversions.—A bank or savings association that is subject to an enforcement action can convert its charter despite the prohibition on conversion. This is possible if:

- the federal banking agency that would be the appropriate federal banking agency after the proposed conversion gives the appropriate federal banking agency or state bank supervisor that issued the enforcement action written notice of the proposed conversion including a plan to address the significant supervisory matter in a manner that is consistent with the safe and sound operation of the converting bank or savings association;

- the banking agency that issued the enforcement action does not object to the conversion plan or the plan to address the significant supervisory matter; and

- after the conversion is completed, the plan to address the significant supervisory matter is implemented.

In the case of a final enforcement action by a state attorney general, approval of the conversion is conditioned on compliance by the bank or savings association with the terms of that final enforcement action.

Access to Information.—When a bank or savings association that is subject to an enforcement action seeks to convert its charter, the institution must transmit a copy of its conversion application to its appropriate federal banking agency and the federal banking agency that would become the appropriate federal banking agency upon completion of the charter conversion. Once the appropriate federal banking agency for the bank or savings association receives the conversion application, it must notify the federal banking agency that would become the appropriate federal banking agency upon completion of the charter conversion in writing of any ongoing supervisory or investigative proceedings that are likely to result in enforcement action with respect to a significant supervisory matter. The federal banking agency that would be the appropriate federal banking agency for the institution after the proposed conversion must also be provided access to all investigative and supervisory information relating to the enforcement action.

▶ **Effective date.** The provision takes effect one day after the date of enactment (Sec. 4 of the Dodd-Frank Wall Street Reform and Consumer Protection Act).

Law source: Law at ¶10,612 and ¶10,004. Committee Report at ¶54,301.

— Sec. 612(a) of the Dodd-Frank Wall Street Reform and Consumer Protection Act, adding Sec. 10 to Act of Aug. 17, 1950;

— Sec. 612(b), amending 12 USC 35;

— Sec. 612(c), amending Home Owners' Loan Act Sec. 5(i);

— Sec. 612(d) and (e) of the Dodd-Frank Wall Street Reform and Consumer Protection Act;

— Sec. 4, providing the effective date.

¶2560 De Novo Branching

The Dodd-Frank Act makes minor changes to the de novo branching requirements of the NBA and FDIA. In each instance, the concept of "host State" is removed (12 USC 36(g)(1)(A) and FDIA Sec. 18(d)(4)(A)(i), as amended by Sec. 613 of the Dodd-Frank Act).

▶ **Effective date.** The provision takes effect one day after the date of enactment (Sec. 4 of the Dodd-Frank Wall Street Reform and Consumer Protection Act).

Law source: Law at ¶10,613 and ¶10,004. Committee Report at ¶54,302.

— Sec. 613(a) of the Dodd-Frank Wall Street Reform and Consumer Protection Act, amending 12 USC 36(g)(1)(A);

— Sec. 613(b), amending Federal Deposit Insurance Act Sec. 18(d)(4)(A)(i);

— Sec. 4, providing the effective date.

¶2565 Source of Strength

The Dodd-Frank Act amends the FDIA by statutorily requiring a BHC or SLHC to serve as a source of financial strength for any depository institution subsidiary (FDIA Sec. 38A(a), as added by Sec. 616(d) of the Dodd-Frank Act).

> **CCH Comment:** Currently, the Fed, in its corporate practices regulation codified at 12 CFR 225.4(a), requires a BHC to "serve as a source of financial and managerial strength to its subsidiary banks and shall not conduct its operations in an unsafe or unsound manner."

CCH Comment: Section 626(b)(3) of the Dodd-Frank Act requires a grandfathered unitary savings and loan holding company that controls an intermediate holding company to serve as a source of strength to its subsidiary intermediate holding company.

Source of Strength Defined.—For purposes of the Dodd-Frank Act, the term "source of strength" means "the ability of a company that directly or indirectly owns or controls an insured depository institution to provide financial assistance to such insured depository institution in the event of the financial distress of the insured depository institution" (FDIA Sec. 38A(e), as added by Sec. 616(d) of the Dodd-Frank Act).

Rulemaking.—To give effect to the new FDIA source-of-strength provision, the federal banking agencies that regulate holding companies must issue final rules within one year after the "transfer date" provided in the Dodd-Frank Act (FDIA Sec. 38A(d), as added by Sec. 616(d) of the Dodd-Frank Act).

Controlling Companies.—If an insured depository institution is not the subsidiary of a BHC or SLHC, the appropriate federal banking agency for the insured depository institution will require any company that directly or indirectly controls the insured depository institution to serve as a source of financial strength for the insured depository institution (FDIA Sec. 38A(b), as added by Sec. 616(d) of the Dodd-Frank Act).

Reports.—The controlling company will also be required to submit a report to the depository institution subsidiary's appropriate federal banking agency. The report is to determine whether the controlling company is acting as a source of strength (FDIA Sec. 38A(c), as added by Sec. 616(d) of the Dodd-Frank Act).

▶ **Effective date.** The provision becomes effective on the "transfer date" provided in Section 311 of the Dodd-Frank Act. The "transfer date," which occurs one year after the date of the enactment of the Dodd-Frank Act, is the time frame in which the supervisory functions of the OTS are transferred to the OCC, Fed and FDIC (Secs. 616(e) of the Dodd-Frank Wall Street Reform and Consumer Protection Act).

Law source: Law at ¶10,616. Committee Report at ¶54,305.

— Sec. 616(d) of the Dodd-Frank Wall Street Reform and Consumer Protection Act, adding Federal Deposit Insurance Act Sec. 38A;

— Sec. 616(e), providing the effective date.

¶2570 Investment and Securities Holding Companies

The Dodd-Frank Act eliminates the investment bank holding company supervisory framework found in Section 17 of the Securities Exchange Act of 1934 (Exchange Act Sec. 17(i), as stricken by Sec. 617(a) of the Dodd-Frank Act). The creation of the investment bank holding company supervisory scheme was one of the many hallmark elements of the Gramm-Leach Bliley Act (GLB Act). Under the GLB Act, securities firms were given the opportunity to be voluntarily supervised by the Securities and Exchange Commission (SEC) as holding companies. It was envisioned that this supervisory regime would have been useful for firms seeking to engage in global financial activities.

In place of the investment bank holding company supervisory framework, the Dodd-Frank Act creates a securities holding company supervisory framework (Sec. 618 of the Dodd-Frank Act).

The Dodd-Frank Act generally defines a "securities holding company" as a person, other than a natural person, that owns or controls one or more brokers or dealers registered with the SEC or a person associated with the securities holding company. There are a number of entities that are excluded under the definition, such as nonbank financial companies and certain foreign banks (Sec. 618(a)(4) of the Dodd-Frank Act).

Under the new supervisory framework, a "securities holding company" can register with the Fed if it is required by a foreign regulator or provision of foreign law to be subject to comprehensive consolidated supervision (Sec. 618(b)(1) of the Dodd-Frank Act).

Registration.—A securities holding company's registration with the Fed becomes effective 45 days after it is received by the agency. The Fed will issue regulations specifying the registration process requirements (Sec. 618(b)(2) of the Dodd-Frank Act).

Recordkeeping and Reporting.—In order to adequately supervise each securities holding company, the Dodd-Frank Act imposes recordkeeping and reporting requirements on each securities holding company and each of its affiliates. These requirements are intended to provide the Fed with information as to the securities holding company's compliance with the Dodd-Frank Act and any other applicable provisions of law (Sec. 618(c)(1) of the Dodd-Frank Act).

Any records submitted to the Fed must be certified by a registered public accounting firm. The types of forms that must be provided to the Fed include:

- balance sheets or income statements;
- assessments of the consolidated capital and liquidity;
- reports by independent auditors attesting to the holding company's risk management and internal control objectives; and
- compliance reports.

The Fed is also required, under the Dodd-Frank Act, to accept reports that the securities holding company or an affiliate is required to provide to another regulatory agency or a self regulatory organization.

Examinations.—When examining a securities holding company, the Fed is to focus on whether there are any evasions of the Section 618 supervisory framework and to monitor the securities holding company's compliance with the framework. The Dodd-Frank Act also requires the Fed to use examination reports made by any other federal or state regulatory authorities with respect to any functionally regulated subsidiary, trust bank, credit card bank or industrial loan company (Sec. 618(c)(3) of the Dodd-Frank Act).

Capital and Risk Management Standards.—The Fed must prescribe capital adequacy and risk management standards to protect the safety and soundness of securities holding companies and address any risks they pose to financial stability (Sec. 618(d) of the Dodd-Frank Act).

In developing the capital and risk management standards, the Fed must take into account:

- the different types of business activities carried out by securities holding companies;
- the nature and amount of the holding companies' financial assets and liabilities, including reliance on short-term funding;
- off-balance sheet exposures;
- the companies' interconnectedness with other financial companies;
- the importance of the companies as a source of credit and liquidity; and
- the companies' mix of activities.

Enforcement Authority.—Finally, the Fed is given the authority to undertake enforcement measures provided in Section 8 of the FDIA. These measures include cease and desist proceedings and Bank Secrecy Act compliance (Sec. 618(e) of the Dodd-Frank Act).

▶ **Effective date.** The amendments made by Section 617 become effective on the "transfer date" provided in Section 311 of the Dodd-Frank Act. The "transfer date," which occurs one year after the date of the enactment of the Dodd-Frank Act, is the time frame in which the supervisory functions of the OTS are transferred to the OCC, Fed and FDIC. Sec. 618 takes effect one day after the date of enactment (Secs. 4 and 618 of the Dodd-Frank Wall Street Reform and Consumer Protection Act).

Law source: Law at ¶10,617, ¶10,618 and ¶10,004. Committee Report at ¶54,306 and ¶54,307.

— Sec. 617(a)(i) of the Dodd-Frank Wall Street Reform and Consumer Protection Act, striking Securities Exchange Act Sec. 17(i);
— Sec. 617(a)(2), redesignating Securities Exchange Act Sec. 17(j) and (k);
— Sec. 618 of the Dodd-Frank Wall Street Reform and Consumer Protection Act;
— Secs. 4 and 618, providing the effective date.

¶2575 Proprietary Trading, Hedge Funds and Private Equity Funds—Volcker Rule

Section 619 of the Dodd-Frank Act prohibits or places restrictions on certain types of financial activity conducted by "banking entities" and nonbank financial companies supervised by the Fed, which are "high-risk or which create significant conflicts of interest between these institutions and their customers" (S. Rep. No. 111-176, p. 8).

These prohibitions and restrictions seek to "reduce potential taxpayer losses at institutions protected by the federal safety net, and reduce threats to financial stability, by lowering their exposure to risk" (S. Rep. No. 111-176, p. 8). In addition, prohibitions and restrictions are intended to "reduce the scale, complexity, and interconnectedness of those banking entities and nonbank financial companies that are now actively engaged in proprietary trading, or have hedge fund or private equity exposure" (S. Rep. No. 111-176, p. 9). Finally, they "reduce the possibility that banking entities and nonbank financial companies will be too big or too complex to resolve in an orderly manner should they fail" (S. Rep. No. 111-176, p. 9).

The prohibitions and restrictions are commonly referred to as the "Volcker Rule" after former Federal Reserve Board Chairman Paul Volcker, who has strongly advocated that beneficiaries of the federal financial safety net—deposit insurance guarantees and discount window borrowing—should be prohibited from engaging in high-risk activities (S. Rep. No. 111-176, p. 91).

Definitions.—Section 619 of the Dodd-Frank Act provides a number of definitions.

Banking Entity. For purposes of the Volcker Rule, a "banking entity" is defined as: any insured depository institution; any company that controls an insured depository institution or that is treated as a bank holding company for purposes of the International Banking Act of 1978; and any affiliate or subsidiary (BHCA Sec. 13(h)(1), as added by Sec. 619 of the Dodd-Frank Act).

Certain institutions that function solely in a trust or fiduciary capacity are not considered to be insured depository institution. These institutions are excluded from the definition of insured depository institution if:

- their deposits are in trust funds and are received in a bona fide fiduciary capacity;
- any FDIC-insured deposits are not offered or marketed by or through an affiliate;
- they do not accept demand deposits; and
- they do not avail themselves of certain services offered by the Federal Reserve Banks.

Hedge Fund/Private Equity Fund. The terms "hedge fund" and "private equity fund" are generally defined to mean an issuer that would be an investment company, as defined in the Investment Company Act of 1940. The appropriate federal banking agencies, SEC and Commodity Futures Trading Commission (CFTC) can also issue a regulation determining that other types of funds also fall within the definition of hedge fund or private equity fund (BHCA Sec. 13(h)(2), as added by Sec. 619 of the Dodd-Frank Act).

During debate on the Conference Report on the Dodd-Frank Act, in the House of Representatives, Rep. Jim Himes, D-Conn., entered into a colloquy with Financial Services Committee Chairman Barney Frank, D-Mass., regarding the application of the Volcker Rule to the terms hedge fund and private equity fund. In particular, Himes was concerned that the definition of those two terms, based on the very broad Investment Company Act definition, "could technically apply to lots of corporate structures, and not just the hedge funds and private equity funds." Himes asked Chairman Frank "to confirm that when firms own or control subsidiaries or joint ventures that are used to hold other investments, that the Volcker Rule won't deem those things to be private equity or hedge funds and disrupt the way the firms structure their normal investment holdings." Frank answered, "The point the gentleman [Himes] makes is absolutely correct." Frank added, "We don't want there to be excessive regulation . . . [and] we are confident that the regulators will appreciate that distinction, maintain it, and we will be there to make sure that they do" (Cong. Record (June 30), H5226).

Nonbank Financial Company Supervised by the Board. The term "nonbank financial company supervised by the Board" means a nonbank financial company supervised by the Fed, as defined in Section 102 of the Dodd-Frank Act (BHCA Sec. 13(h)(3), as added by Sec. 619 of the Dodd-Frank Act).

Proprietary Trading. The term "proprietary trading" generally means engaging as a principal for the trading account of the banking entity or nonbank financial company in any transaction to purchase, sell or otherwise acquire or dispose of any security, derivative, contract of sale of a commodity for future delivery, or option on any security, derivative or contract. The appropriate federal banking agencies, SEC and CFTC can also issue a regulation determining that other types of securities and instruments fall within this definition (BHCA Sec. 13(h)(4), as added by Sec. 619 of the Dodd-Frank Act).

Sponsoring. The term "sponsoring" is used in conjunction with hedge fund and private equity fund. Under the Dodd-Frank Act, "sponsoring" means: serving as a general partner, managing member or trustee of the fund; selecting or controlling a majority of the directors, trustees or management of the fund; or sharing with the fund the same name or a variation of the same name for corporate, marketing, promotional or other purposes (BHCA Sec. 13(h)(5), as added by Sec. 619 of the Dodd-Frank Act).

Trading Account. The term "trading account" means any account used for acquiring or taking positions in the securities and instruments within the proprietary trading definition principally for the purpose of selling in the near term (or otherwise with the intent to resell in order to profit from short-term price movements), and any such other accounts as the appropriate federal banking agencies, the SEC and the CFTC may, by rule, determine (BHCA Sec. 13(h)(6), as added by Sec. 619 of the Dodd-Frank Act).

Prohibited Activities.—Section 619(a)(1) of the Dodd-Frank Act specifically prohibits a banking entity from engaging in proprietary trading and sponsoring and investing in hedge funds and private equity funds (BHCA Sec. 13(a)(1), as added by Sec. 619 of the Dodd-Frank Act).

Capital and Quantitative Limits.—Also, Section 619(a)(2) of the Dodd-Frank Act places new capital requirements and quantitative limits on the proprietary trading and hedge fund and private equity fund activities of certain Fed-supervised nonbank financial companies (BHCA Sec. 13(a)(2), as added by Sec. 619 of the Dodd-Frank Act).

The prohibitions and restrictions placed on banking entities and nonbank financial companies for their proprietary trading and investments in hedge fund and private equity funds "supersede" any other laws permitting the activities (BHCA Sec. 13(g)(1), as added by Sec. 619 of the Dodd-Frank Act).

However, loan securitization activities by banking entities and nonbank financial companies are unaffected by the Volcker Rule. Also, any inherent authority of any federal agency or state regulatory authority is unaffected by the Volcker Rule (BHCA Sec. 13(g)(2) and (3), as added by Sec. 619 of the Dodd-Frank Act).

Regulations.—For the prohibition and restrictions on proprietary trading and sponsoring and investing in hedge funds and private equity funds to take effect, the appropriate federal banking agencies, along with the SEC and CFTC, are required to issue regulations to implement the general prohibition placed on propriety trading and activities relating to hedge funds and private equity funds (BHCA Sec. 13(b)(2)(A), as added by Sec. 619 of the Dodd-Frank Act).

Council Study. However, before the agencies can issue their regulations, the Financial Stability Oversight Council (Council) is required to complete a study within six months after the Dodd-Frank Act's enactment. The study is to determine whether the general prohibition placed on propriety trading and activities relating to hedge funds and private equity funds would:

- promote safety and soundness of banking entities;
- protect taxpayers;
- limit the inappropriate transfer of federal subsidies, such as deposit insurance and liquidity facilities;
- reduce conflicts of interest between banking entities and nonbank financial companies and their customers;
- limit activities that have caused undue risk or loss in banking entities and nonbank financial companies;
- appropriately accommodate the business of insurance within an insurance company while protecting the safety and soundness of a banking entity which is affiliated with that insurance company;
- raise the cost of credit or other financial services; and
- appropriately time the divestiture of illiquid assets (BHCA Sec. 13(b)(1)(A)–(G), as added by Sec. 619 of the Dodd-Frank Act).

Once the study is complete, the Council is to make recommendations to aid the agencies in the development of their regulations.

Consistent and Comparable Rules. In developing and issuing their regulations, the appropriate federal banking agencies, the SEC and CFTC are to consult and coordinate with each other. This is to assure that the regulations are comparable and provide for consistent application to avoid providing advantages to or imposing disadvantages on the companies affected by the prohibition and restrictions on proprietary trading and sponsoring and investing in hedge funds and private equity funds, as well as to protect the safety and soundness of banking entities and nonbank financial companies. (BHCA Sec. 13(b)(2)(B)(ii), as added by Sec. 619 of the Dodd-Frank Act).

Rulemaking Deadline. Following completion of the Council's study, the banking agencies must, within nine months, issue their joint regulations implementing the prohibition and restrictions on proprietary trading and sponsoring and investing in hedge funds and private equity funds (BHCA Sec. 13(b)(2)(A), as added by Sec. 619 of the Dodd-Frank Act).

Permitted Activities.—The Dodd-Frank Act provides a number of exceptions to the general prohibition placed on propriety trading and activities relating to hedge funds and private equity funds. These exceptions are known as "permitted activities." Although the Dodd-Frank Act allows banking entities and nonbank financial companies to conduct these activities, the activities are also subject to other provisions of federal and state law as well as limitations provided in Section 619(d)(2) of the Dodd-Frank Act and any restrictions and limitations imposed by the appropriate federal banking agencies, the SEC and CFTC (BHCA Sec. 13(d)(1), as added by Sec. 619 of the Dodd-Frank Act).

¶2575

CCH Comment: The version of the Volcker Rule originally approved by the Senate in S. 3217, the "Dodd-Frank Wall Street Reform and Consumer Protection Act," provided only four exceptions. The current version of the Volcker Rule expands the number of exceptions to a total of 10.

Governmental Obligations. Banking entities and nonbank financial companies can purchase, sell, acquire or dispose of:

- obligations of the United States and its agencies;
- obligations, participations or other instruments of or issued by the government-sponsored enterprises—Fannie Mae and Freddie Mac, as well the mortgage guarantor Ginnie Mae, the Federal Home Loan Banks, the federal Agricultural Mortgage Corporation (Farmer Mac) or institutions chartered under the Farm Credit Act of 1971; and
- obligations of any state government or one of its political subdivisions (BHCA Sec. 13(d)(1)(A), as added by Sec. 619 of the Dodd-Frank Act).

Securities and Instruments. Another permitted activity is the purchase, sale, acquisition or disposition of any security, derivative, contract of sale of a commodity for future delivery or option on any security, derivative or contract (securities and instruments). This activity must be conducted in connection with underwriting or market making-related activities and must be designed not to exceed the reasonably expected near term demands of clients, customers or counterparties (Bank Holding Company Act Sec. 13(d)(1)(B), as added by Sec. 619 of the Dodd-Frank Act).

The purchase, sale, acquisition or disposition of any security or instrument also is a permitted activity for banking entities and nonbank financial companies if the activity is on behalf of its customers (BHCA Act Sec. 13(d)(1)(D), as added by Sec. 619 of the Dodd-Frank Act).

A banking entity also can participate in the sale or purchase of securities and instruments by insurance companies and their affiliates if the securities and instruments are used for the insurance company's general account.

CCH Comment: A general account is an insurance company's investments and other assets that are available to pay claims and benefits to its policyholders.

This is a permitted activity as long as:

- the transaction complies with the laws, regulations and written guidance of the jurisdiction in which the insurance company is domiciled; and
- the appropriate Federal banking agencies, after consultation with the Financial Stability Oversight Council and the relevant insurance commissioners, have not jointly determined, after notice and comment, that a particular law, regulation or written guidance is insufficient to protect the safety and soundness of the banking entity or the financial stability of the United States (BHCA Sec. 13(d)(1)(F), as added by Sec. 619 of the Dodd-Frank Act).

Hedging Activities. Certain risk-mitigating hedging activities are another permitted activity for banking entities. These risk-mitigating hedging activities must be done in connection with and related to a banking entity's individual or aggregated positions, contracts or other holdings and designed to reduce the specific risks to the banking entity in connection with and related to those positions, contracts or other holdings (BHCA Sec. 13(d)(1)(C), as added by Sec. 619 of the Dodd-Frank Act).

SBIC and Public Welfare Investments. Any investments in small business investment companies and investments designed to promote the public welfare are also considered to be permitted activities (BHCA Act Sec. 13(d)(1)(E), as added by the Dodd-Frank Act).

Private Equity and Hedge Funds. Organizing and offering a private equity or hedge fund is also a permitted activity. This activity includes serving as a general partner, managing member or trustee of the fund and selecting or controlling a majority of the directors, trustees or management of the fund (BHCA Sec. 13(d)(1)(G), as added by Sec. 619 of the Dodd-Frank Act).

To be a permitted activity, the organizing and offering activity must meet eight separate conditions:

1. the banking entity provides bona fide trust, fiduciary or investment advisory services;
2. the fund is organized and offered only in connection with bona fide trust, fiduciary or investment advisory services and only to persons that are customers of those services;
3. the banking entity does not acquire or retain an equity interest, partnership interest or other ownership interest in the funds except for a de minimis investment;
4. the banking entity complies with the limitations on relationships with hedge funds and private equity funds;
5. the banking entity does not guarantee, assume or insure the obligations or performance of the hedge fund or private equity fund;
6. the banking entity does not share with the hedge fund or private equity fund, for corporate, marketing, promotional or other purposes, the same name or a variation of the same name;
7. no director or employee of the banking entity takes or retains an equity interest, partnership interest or other ownership interest in the hedge fund or private equity fund; and
8. the banking entity provides a written disclosure to prospective and actual investors in the fund that any losses in the hedge fund or private equity fund are borne solely by investors (BHCA Sec. 13(d)(1)(G)(i)–(viii), as added by Sec. 619 of the Dodd-Frank Act).

Foreign Bank Proprietary Trading. Proprietary trading conducted by certain foreign-based banking entities is also a permitted activity as long as the trading occurs solely outside of the United States and the foreign-based banking entity is not controlled by a banking entity that is organized in the United States (BHCA Sec. 13(d)(1)(H), as added by Sec. 619 of the Dodd-Frank Act).

Foreign Bank Fund Investments. The acquisition or retention of any equity, partnership, or other ownership interest in, or the sponsorship of, a hedge fund or a private equity fund by a foreign-based banking entity is another permitted activity. This activity is conditioned on the requirement that no ownership interest in the hedge fund or private equity fund is offered for sale or sold to a U.S. resident and the foreign-based banking entity is not controlled by a banking entity that is organized in the United States (BHCA Sec. 13(d)(1)(I), as added by Sec. 619 of the Dodd-Frank Act).

Promotion of Safety and Soundness and Financial Stability. The final permitted activity is a "catch all" in which the appropriate federal banking agencies, the SEC and CFTC permit, by rule, any activity that would promote and protect the safety and soundness of a banking entity and the financial stability of the United States (BHCA Sec. 13(d)(1)(J), as added by Sec. 619 of the Dodd-Frank Act).

Limitations on Permitted Activities.—The Dodd-Frank Act also places a number of other limitations and requirements on the permitted activities allowed under Section 619(d)(1).

A permitted activity cannot:

- involve or result in a "material conflict of interest" between a banking entity and its clients, customers or counterparties (the phrase "material conflict of interest" is to be defined by regulation) (BHCA Sec. 13(d)(2)(A)(i), as added by Sec. 619 of the Dodd-Frank Act);
- result in a "material exposure" by a banking entity to "high-risk assets or high-risk trading strategies" (the phrases "material exposure" and "high-risk assets or high-risk trading strategies" are to be defined by regulation) (BHCA Sec. 13(d)(2)(A)(ii), as added by Sec. 619 of the Dodd-Frank Act); or
- pose a threat to the safety and soundness of a banking entity (BHCA Sec. 13(d)(2)(A)(iii), as added by Sec. 619 of the Dodd-Frank Act).

Capital and Quantitative Limitations.—The appropriate federal banking agencies, the SEC and CFTC are required to adopt rules imposing additional capital requirements and quantitative limitations, including diversification requirements, regarding the permitted activities if the agencies determine that additional capital and quantitative limitations are appropriate to protect the safety and soundness of banking entities engaged in any permitted activity (BHCA Sec. 13(d)(3), as added by Sec. 619 of the Dodd-Frank Act).

For purposes of any additional capital requirements, the aggregate amount of the outstanding investments by a banking entity, including retained earnings, are to be deducted from the assets and tangible equity of the banking entity, and the amount of the deduction is to increase commensurate with the leverage of the hedge fund or private equity fund (BHCA Sec. 13(d)(4)(B)(iii), as added by Sec. 619 of the Dodd-Frank Act).

Fund Investments.—A banking entity is permitted under the Dodd-Frank Act to make and retain an investment in a hedge fund or private equity fund that the banking entity organizes and offers. This investment authority is subject to certain limitations and restrictions.

The banking entity's investment is to be used to establish the fund and provide the fund with sufficient initial equity for investment so as to attract unaffiliated investors. Other than that, the entity can only make a de minimis investment (BHCA Sec. 13(d)(4)(A), as added by Sec. 619 of the Dodd-Frank Act).

Investment Limitations and Restrictions. A banking entity making an investment in a hedge fund or private equity fund is required to actively seek unaffiliated investors to reduce or dilute its investment (BHCA Sec. 13(d)(4)(B)(i), as added by Sec. 619 of the Dodd-Frank Act).

A banking entity has one year from the date the hedge fund or private equity fund was established to reduce its investment to no more than 3 percent of the ownership interests of the fund. The one-year time period to reduce an investment can be extended by the Fed for an additional two years provided the Fed finds that the extension would be consistent with safety and soundness and in the public interest (BHCA Sec. 13(d)(4)(B)(ii)(I) and (d)(4)(C), as added by Sec. 619 of the Dodd-Frank Act).

Also, the banking entity's investment must be "immaterial" and the total of all the banking entity's investments in all hedge funds and private equity funds cannot exceed 3 percent of the banking entity's Tier 1 capital. The term "immaterial" is to be defined by regulation (BHCA Sec. 13(d)(4)(B)(ii)(II), as added by Sec. 619 of the Dodd-Frank Act).

Compliance with Volcker Rule.—A number of provisions of Section 619 of the Dodd-Frank Act ensure compliance with the Volcker Rule.

Internal Controls and Recordkeeping. The federal banking agencies, the SEC and CFTC are required to issue regulations regarding internal controls and recordkeeping in order to insure compliance by banking entities and nonbank financial companies supervised by the Fed (BHCA Sec. 13(e)(1), as added by Sec. 619 of the Dodd-Frank Act).

Termination of Activities or Investments. Whenever an appropriate federal banking agency, the SEC or CFTC has reasonable cause to believe that a banking entity or nonbank financial company supervised by the Fed has made an investment or engaged in an activity in a manner that functions as an evasion of the Volcker Rule or otherwise violates the restrictions under Section 619 of the Dodd-Frank Act, the agency is to order the banking entity or nonbank financial company to terminate the activity and dispose of the investment. Prior to issuing its order, the agency must provide the banking entity or nonbank financial company with due notice and an opportunity for a hearing. This termination authority does not limit the inherent authority of any federal agency or state regulatory authority to further restrict any investments or activities under otherwise applicable provisions of law (BHCA Sec. 13(e)(2), as added by Sec. 619 of the Dodd-Frank Act).

Limitations on Business Relationships.—The Dodd-Frank Act also imposes a number of limitations on banking entities and nonbank financial companies supervised by the Fed regarding their business relationships with hedge funds and private equity funds that they advise, organize or sponsor.

Transactions with Affiliates. The transactions with affiliates restrictions found in Sections 23A and 23B of the FRA are made applicable to transactions between a banking entity and any hedge fund or private equity fund for which the banking entity serves as investment manager or investment adviser. The FRA Section 23A and 23B restrictions also apply to transactions between a banking entity and any hedge fund or private equity fund that the banking entity sponsored or organized. In each instance, any transaction is a covered transaction as defined in FRA Section 23A. The transactions with affiliate restrictions also apply to any of the banking entity's other affiliates. (BHCA Sec. 13(f)(1) and (2), as added by Sec. 619 of the Dodd-Frank Act).

Prime Brokerage Transactions. If a hedge fund or private equity fund that is managed, sponsored or advised by a banking entity or nonbank financial company supervised by the Fed has taken some type of ownership interest in another hedge fund or private equity fund, the first banking entity or nonbank financial company can, with the Fed's permission, enter into a prime brokerage transaction with that other hedge fund or private equity fund (BHCA Sec. 13(f)(3)(A), as added by Sec. 619 of the Dodd-Frank Act).

> **CCH Comment:** Generally, prime brokerage transactions are services offered to hedge funds and other professional investors allowing them to borrow securities and cash.

The prime brokerage transaction is permissible, as long as:

- the banking entity or nonbank financial company is in compliance with the hedge fund and private equity permitted activities requirements (BHCA Sec. 13(f)(3)(A)(i), as added by Sec. 619 of the Dodd-Frank Act Sec. 619(d));
- the banking entity's chief executive officer provides an annual written certification that the banking entity does not provide any type of guarantee regarding the obligations or performance of the hedge fund or private equity fund (BHCA Sec. 13(f)(3)(A)(ii), as added by Sec. 619 of the Dodd-Frank Act); and
- the Fed has determined that a prime brokerage transaction is consistent with the safe and sound operation and condition of the banking entity or nonbank financial company (BHCA Sec. 13(f)(3)(A)(iii), as added by Sec. 619 of the Dodd-Frank Act).

Any prime brokerage transaction entered into by a banking entity is subject to the FRA Section 23B qualitative requirements for affiliate transactions. These qualitative requirements impose market terms and conditions on affiliate transactions (BHCA Sec. 13(f)(3)(A)(iii), as added by Sec. 619 of the Dodd-Frank Act).

Finally, the Dodd-Frank Act requires that the appropriate federal banking agencies and the SEC and CFTC adopt rules imposing additional capital charges or other restrictions for nonbank financial companies to address the risks to and conflicts of interest of banking entities (BHCA Sec. 13(f)(4), as added by Sec. 619 of the Dodd-Frank Act).

Compliance Period.—The Dodd-Frank Act provides a number of provisions setting forth timeframes in which banking entities and nonbank financial companies must bring their activities and investments into compliance with the requirements of the Volcker Rule.

Two-Year Compliance Period. Generally, a banking entity or nonbank financial company is to bring its activities and investments into compliance with the requirements of the Volcker Rule not later than two years after the date on which the requirements become effective or two years after the date on which the entity or company becomes a nonbank financial company supervised by the Fed (BHCA Sec. 13(c)(2), as added by Sec. 619 of the Dodd-Frank Act).

The two-year time period can be extended by the Fed for not more than one year at a time. This extension is based on the Fed's judgment that the extension is consistent with the purposes of Volcker Rule and would not be detrimental to the public interest. The Fed's extensions may not exceed an aggregate of three years (BHCA Sec. 13(c)(2), as added by Sec. 619 of the Dodd-Frank Act).

Not later than six months after the date of enactment of the Volcker Rule the Fed is required to issue rules to implement the compliance provisions (BHCA Sec. 13(c)(6), as added by Sec. 619 of the Dodd-Frank Act).

Illiquid Funds. A banking entity may apply to the Fed seeking an extension of the two-year time frame to conform its investments and activities with the Volcker Rule regarding "illiquid funds." The extension of time would permit the banking entity, to the extent necessary to fulfill a contractual obligation that was in effect on May 1, 2010, to take or retain its equity, partnership or other ownership interest in, or otherwise provide additional capital to, an illiquid fund. The Fed has the discretion to grant an extension that cannot exceed five years. (BHCA Sec. 13(c)(3), as added by the Dodd-Frank Act).

An "illiquid fund" is defined as a hedge fund or private equity fund that:

- as of May 1, 2010, was principally invested in, or contractually committed to principally invest in, illiquid assets, such as portfolio companies, real estate investments and venture capital investments; and
- has an investment strategy to principally invest in illiquid assets (BHCA Sec. 13(h)(7), as added by Sec. 619 of the Dodd-Frank Act).

Not later than six months after the date of enactment of the Volcker Rule the Fed is required to issue rules to implement the illiquid fund provisions (BHCA Sec. 13(c)(6), as added by Sec. 619 of the Dodd-Frank Act).

A banking entity will be required to divest its interests in any illiquid fund either on the date on which the contractual obligation to invest in the illiquid fund terminates or the date on which any extensions granted by the Fed expire, depending upon which occurs first (BHCA Sec. 13(c)(4), as added by Sec. 619 of the Dodd-Frank Act).

▶ **Effective date.** The provision becomes effective on the earlier of 12 months after the date of the issuance of final rules under Section 619(b), or two years after the date of enactment of Bank Holding Company Act Section 13 (Bank Holding Company Act Sec. 13(c)(1), as added by Sec. 619 of the Dodd-Frank Act).

Law source: Law at ¶10,619. Committee Report at ¶54,005 and ¶54,308.

— Sec. 619 of the Dodd-Frank Wall Street Reform and Consumer Protection Act, adding Bank Holding Company Act Sec. 13;
— Sec. 619, providing the effective date.

¶2580 Study of Bank Investment Activities

The appropriate federal banking agencies are required by the Dodd-Frank Act to jointly review and prepare a report on the activities that a banking entity may engage in under federal and state law, including activities authorized by statute and by order, interpretation and guidance. The agencies must complete the report within 18 months of the enactment of the Dodd-Frank Act (Sec 620(a)(1) of the Dodd-Frank Act).

The report is to focus on:

- the type of activities or investments;
- any types of risks, such as financial, operational, managerial or reputation associated with the activity or making the investment; and
- mitigation activities undertaken by the banking entity with regard to the risks (Sec. 620(a)(2) of the Dodd- Frank Act).

One the report is complete, the agencies must submit the report within two months to the House Financial Services Committee and the Senate Banking Committee with recommendations regarding:

- whether each activity or investment has or could have a negative effect on the safety and soundness of the banking entity or the U.S. financial system;
- the appropriateness of the conduct of each activity or type of investment by banking entities; and
- additional restrictions as may be necessary to address risks to safety and soundness arising from the activities or types of investments (Sec 620(b) of the Dodd-Frank Act).

▶ **Effective date.** The provision takes effect one day after the date of enactment (Sec. 4 of the Dodd-Frank Wall Street Reform and Consumer Protection Act).

Law source: Law at ¶10,620 and ¶10,004.

— Sec. 620 of the Dodd-Frank Wall Street Reform and Consumer Protection Act;
— Sec. 4, providing the effective date.

¶2585 Conflicts of Interest Relating to Securitizations

The Dodd-Frank Act imposes a one-year prohibition on any underwriter, placement agent, initial purchaser or sponsor involved in an asset securitization from engaging in any transaction that would involve or result in any material conflict of interest with respect to any investor in a transaction arising out of the securitization. The prohibition also applies to affiliates and subsidiaries (Securities Act Sec. 27B(a), as added by Sec. 621(a) of the Dodd-Frank Act).

The conflicts of interest prohibition does not limit the application of credit risk retention requirements of newly-added Section 15G of the Exchange Act (Securities Act Sec. 27B(d), as added by Sec. 621(a) of the Dodd-Frank Act).

> **CCH Comment:** Section 15G of the Exchange Act was added by Sec. 941(b) of the Dodd-Frank Act.

Excepted Activities.—The prohibition does not apply to:
- certain risk-mitigating hedging activities in connection with the initial asset-backed security transaction;
- purchases or sales of asset-backed securities to provide liquidity for the asset-backed security, or
- bona fide market-making in the asset backed security (Securities Act Sec. 27B(c), as added by Dodd-Frank Act Sec. 621(a)).

Rulemaking.—The SEC is required to issue regulations implementing the conflicts of interest prohibition within 270 days after the enactment of the Dodd-Frank Act (Securities Act Sec. 27B(b), as added by Dodd-Frank Act Sec. 621(a)).

▶ **Effective date.** The provision generally takes effect on the effective date of final rules issued by the SEC. The exceptions to the conflicts of interest prohibition and the application of the credit risk retention requirements of newly-added Section 15G of the Exchange Act take effect on the date of enactment of the Dodd-Frank Act (Sec. 621(b) of the Dodd-Frank Wall Street Reform and Consumer Protection Act).

Law source: Law at ¶10,621.

— Sec. 621(a) of the Dodd-Frank Wall Street Reform and Consumer Protection Act, adding Securities Act Sec. 27B;

— Sec. 621(b), providing the effective date.

¶2590 Concentration Limits

The Dodd-Frank Act provides that a "financial company" cannot merge or consolidate with, acquire the assets of, or otherwise acquire control of, another company if the total consolidated "liabilities" of the acquiring financial company upon consummation of the transaction would exceed 10 percent of the aggregate consolidated liabilities of all financial companies at the end of the calendar year preceding the transaction (BHCA Sec. 14(b), as added by Sec. 622 of the Dodd-Frank Act).

Exceptions.—The concentration limits do not apply to acquisitions of a bank in danger of default, assisted transactions under the FDIA and if the acquisition only results in a de minimis increase in the financial company's liabilities (BHCA Sec. 14(c), as added by Sec. 622 of the Dodd-Frank Act).

In order to avail itself of any of these exceptions, the financial company must obtain the Fed's written approval prior to undertaking the acquisition.

Rulemaking.—The Fed is to issue regulations implementing the concentration limits. These regulations are to take into account any recommendations issued in a study conducted by the Financial Stability Council. This study is to be completed within six months of the enactment of the Dodd-Frank Act and is to ascertain the effects the concentration limits would have on:

- financial stability;
- moral hazard;
- the efficiency and competitiveness of U.S. financial firms and financial markets; and
- the cost and availability of credit and other financial services (BHCA Sec. 14(d), as added by Sec. 622 of the Dodd-Frank Act).

Definitions.—For purposes of the Dodd-Frank Act, a "financial company" is defined as:

- an insured depository institution;
- a bank holding company;
- a savings and loan holding company;
- a company that controls an insured depository institution;
- a nonbank financial company supervised by the Fed; and
- a foreign bank or company that is treated as a bank holding company (BHCA Sec. 14(a)(2), as added by Sec. 622 of the Dodd-Frank Act).

The definition of "liabilities" under the Dodd-Frank Act depends on the location or type of financial company (BHCA Sec. 14(a)(3), as added by Sec. 622 of the Dodd-Frank Act).

For a financial company located in the United States, "liabilities" means the financial company's total risk-weighted assets, as adjusted to reflect exposures that are deducted from regulatory capital, less the total regulatory capital of the financial company under the risk-based capital rules applicable to bank holding companies.

The liabilities of a foreign-based financial company is the total risk-weighted assets of the U.S. operations of the financial company, as adjusted to reflect exposures that are deducted from regulatory capital, less the total regulatory capital of the U.S. operations of the financial company.

Finally, with respect to an insurance company or other nonbank financial company supervised by the Fed, its liabilities are those assets as specified by any regulation issued by the Fed. This treatment is to provide for consistent and equitable treatment of these companies.

▶ **Effective date.** The provision takes effect one day after the date of enactment (Sec. 4 of the Dodd-Frank Wall Street Reform and Consumer Protection Act).

Law source: Law at ¶10,622 and ¶10,004. Committee Report at ¶54,309.

— Sec. 622 of the Dodd-Frank Wall Street Reform and Consumer Protection Act, adding Bank Holding Company Act Sec. 14;

— Sec. 4, providing the effective date.

¶2595 Interstate Bank Mergers and Acquisitions

The interstate merger and acquisitions provisions of the FDIA, HOLA and BHCA are amended to reflect the concentration limits found in Section 622 of the Dodd-Frank Act.

FDIA Bank Mergers.—An application for an "interstate merger transaction" cannot be approved if the resulting insured depository institution, including all insured depository institutions that are affiliates of the resulting insured depository institution, would control more than 10 percent of the total amount of deposits of the insured depository institutions in the United States (FDIA Sec. 18(c)(13)(A), as added by Sec. 623(a) of the Dodd-Frank Act).

An "interstate merger transaction" is a merger transaction involving one or more insured depository institutions that have different home states and that are not affiliates (FDIA Sec. 18(c)(13)(C)(i), as added by Sec. 623(a) of the Dodd-Frank Act).

An interstate merger transaction can occur, even if the 10-percent concentration limit is met, if the transaction involves one or more insured depository institutions in default, or in danger of default, or the transaction is part of assisted acquisition under FDIA Section 13 (FDIA Sec. 18(c)(13)(B), as added by Sec. 623(a) of the Dodd-Frank Act).

The Fed cannot approve a BHC's application to acquire an insured depository institution under the BHCA if the home state of the insured depository institution is a state other than the BHC's home state and the BHC, including all of its insured depository institution affiliates, controls or, upon consummation of the transaction, would control more than 10 percent of the total amount of deposits of insured depository institutions in the United States (BHCA Sec. 4(i)(8)(A), as added by Sec. 623(b)(1)(A) of the Dodd-Frank Act).

The interstate acquisition is permitted, despite the acquisition meeting the 10-percent concentration limit, if the acquisition involves an insured depository institution in default or in danger of default, or the transaction is part of assisted acquisition under FDIA Section 13 (BHCA Sec. 4(i)(8)(B), as added by Sec. 623(b)(1)(A) of the Dodd-Frank Act).

There is a similar restriction on an interstate acquisition of an insured depository institution by a SLHC (HOLA Sec. 10(e)(2)(E), as added by Sec. 623(c)(1) of the Dodd-Frank Act).

▶ **Effective date.** The provision takes effect one day after the date of enactment (Sec. 4 of the Dodd-Frank Wall Street Reform and Consumer Protection Act).

Law source: Law at ¶10,623 and ¶10,004.

— Sec. 623(a) of the Dodd-Frank Wall Street Reform and Consumer Protection Act, amending Federal Deposit Insurance Act Sec. 18(c);

— Sec. 623(b)(1)(A), amending Bank Holding Company Act Sec. 4(i)(8);

— Sec. 623(c)(1)(E), amending Home Owners' Loan Act Sec. 10(e)(2);

— Sec. 4, providing the effective date.

¶2600 Thrift Dividends

If a savings association fails to become or remain a qualified thrift lender (QTL), it becomes subject to new dividends restrictions under the Dodd-Frank Act.

> **CCH Comment:** Congress first established the QTL test as part of the Competitive Equality Banking Act of 1987 (CEBA) which required all savings associations to invest at least 60 percent of their tangible assets in certain housing and related investments—actual thrift investment percentage (ATIP)—to maintain QTL status. Currently, a savings association's ATIP is 65 percent.

Dividend Restrictions.—Specifically, the Dodd-Frank Act will restrict the savings association from paying dividends, except for dividends that:

- would be permissible for a national bank;
- are necessary to meet obligations of a company that controls the savings association; and
- are specifically approved by the OCC and the Fed (HOLA Sec. 10(m)(3)(B)(i)(III), as added by Sec. 624 of the Dodd-Frank Act).

Besides the dividends restrictions, a savings association that fails to become or remain a QTL is deemed to have violated HOLA Section 5 and is subject to enforcement actions authorized by HOLA Section 5(d) (HOLA Sec. 10(m)(3)(B)(i)(IV), as added by Sec. 624 of the Dodd-Frank Act).

▶ **Effective date.** The provision takes effect one day after the date of enactment (Sec. 4 of the Dodd-Frank Wall Street Reform and Consumer Protection Act).

Law source: Law at ¶10,624 and ¶10,004.

— Sec. 624 of the Dodd-Frank Wall Street Reform and Consumer Protection Act, amending Home Owners' Loan Act Sec. 10(m)(3);

— Sec. 4, providing the effective date.

¶2605 Mutual Holding Company Dividends

Section 625 of the Dodd-Frank Act addresses dividends offered by mutual holding companies and their savings association subsidiaries.

Notice of Dividend.—In order for a mutual holding company's savings association subsidiary to pay a dividend, the savings association is required by the Dodd-Frank Act to give the appropriate federal banking agency and the Federal Reserve Board 30 days notice before the savings association's board of directors declares the dividend on the guaranty, permanent or other nonwithdrawable stock of the savings association (HOLA Sec. 10(o)(11)(A)(i), as added by Sec. 625(a) of the Dodd-Frank Act).

Invalid Dividends. Any dividend that is declared without giving the required 30-day notice, or that is declared during the 30-day period preceding the date of a proposed declaration for which notice is given to the appropriate federal banking agency and the Fed, is invalid and confers no rights or benefits on the holder of that stock (HOLA Sec. 10(o)(11)(A)(ii), as added by Sec. 625(a) of the Dodd-Frank Act).

Waiver of Dividends.— A mutual holding company is permitted to waive the right to receive any dividend declared by one of its subsidiaries provided that:

- no mutual holding company insider, associate of an insider, or tax-qualified or non-tax-qualified employee stock benefit plan of the mutual holding company holds any share of the stock in the class of stock to which the waiver would apply; or
- the mutual holding company gives written notice to the Fed of its intent to waive the right to receive dividends (HOLA Sec. 10(o)(11)(B), as added by Sec. 625(a) of the Dodd-Frank Act).

The notice must be given no later than 30 days before the proposed date of the dividend payment and the Fed must not object to the waiver.

Board Resolution. When filing its waiver notice with the Fed, the mutual holding must also include a copy of its board of directors resolution stating that the proposed dividend waiver is consistent with the board's fiduciary duties to the mutual holding company's members' dividends (HOLA Sec. 10(o)(11)(C), as added by Sec. 625(a) of the Dodd-Frank Act).

Fed Objection to Waiver. The Fed may not object to a waiver of dividends if:

- the waiver is not detrimental to the safe and sound operation of the savings association;
- the mutual holding company's board of directors expressly determines that a waiver is consistent with its fiduciary duties to the holding company's mutual members; and
- the mutual holding company had, prior to Dec. 1, 2009: reorganized into a mutual holding company; issued minority stock; and waived dividends it had a right to receive from the subsidiary stock savings association (HOLA Sec. 10(o)(11)(D), as added by Sec. 625(a) of the Dodd-Frank Act).

Exchange Ratio.—Finally, Section 625 of the Dodd-Frank Act requires that the appropriate federal banking agency consider waived dividends in determining an appropriate exchange ratio in the event of a full conversion to stock form (HOLA Sec. 10(o)(11)(E), as added by Sec. 625(a) of the Dodd-Frank Act).

The waiver of dividends is not to be considered in determining an appropriate exchange ratio if a savings association has reorganized into a mutual holding company, issued minority stock from a mid-tier stock holding company or a subsidiary stock savings association of the mutual holding company and waived dividends it had a right to receive from a subsidiary savings association before Dec. 1, 2009.

▶ **Effective date.** The provision becomes effective on the "transfer date" provided in Section 311 of the Dodd-Frank Act. The "transfer date," which occurs one year after the date of the enactment of the Dodd-Frank Act, is the time frame in which the supervisory functions of the OTS are transferred to the OCC, Fed and FDIC (Sec. 625(b) of the Dodd-Frank Wall Street Reform and Consumer Protection Act).

Law source: Law at ¶10,625.

— Sec. 625(a) of the Dodd-Frank Wall Street Reform and Consumer Protection Act, adding Home Owners' Loan Act Sec. 10(o)(11);

— Sec. 625(b), providing the effective date.

¶2610 Intermediate Holding Companies

To better regulate the "financial activities" of a commercial company that controls a "grandfathered unitary savings and loan holding company," the Dodd-Frank Act establishes an intermediate holding company supervisory structure.

During debate of the Conference Report on the Dodd-Frank Act in the House of Representatives, Rep. Jim Himes, D-Conn., entered into a colloquy with Financial Services Committee Chairman Barney Frank, D-Mass., regarding the interaction of the Section 626 intermediate holding company provisions with the provisions of Section 167 of the Dodd-Frank Act regarding the creation of intermediate holding company by a nonbank financial company supervised by the Fed for that company's determined to be financial in nature or incidental thereto. Specifically Himes asked whether the intent of the Dodd-Frank Act is for these sections to be applied in harmony, so that an organization will have a single intermediate holding company. Frank replied Himes was "exactly right." Frank continued, "And just to sum it up, we want regulated some activities and not regulated other activities when you have a hybrid kind of situation, and what the gentleman has described is how you accomplish that" (Cong. Record (June 30), H5226).

For purposes of the new supervisory structure, a "grandfathered unitary savings and loan holding company" is a holding company that was in existence or had filed an application with the OTS on or before May 4, 1999, to acquire a savings association (HOLA Sec. 10A(a)(2), as added by Sec. 626 of the Dodd-Frank Act).

> **CCH Comment:** The definition of "grandfathered unitary savings and loan holding company" makes reference to HOLA Section 10(c)(9)(C).

"Financial activities" are defined by Section 626 of the Dodd-Frank Act with a reference to HOLA Section 10(c)(9)(A)(i) and (ii), which in turn refers to a list of business activities found in HOLA Section 10(c)(1)(C) and (2) (HOLA Sec. 10A(a)(1), as added by Sec. 626 of the Dodd-Frank Act).

These activities include, among other things:

- furnishing or performing management services for a savings association subsidiary;
- conducting an insurance agency or escrow business;
- holding, managing or liquidating assets owned or acquired from a savings association subsidiary;
- acting as trustee under deed of trust; and
- permissible activities for bank holding companies or financial holding companies.

Formation of Intermediate Holding Companies.—If a grandfathered unitary savings and loan holding company conducts activities other than financial activities, the Fed **may** require the grandfathered unitary savings and loan holding company to establish and conduct all or a portion of its financial activities in or through an intermediate holding company, which is to be a savings and loan holding company (HOLA Sec. 10A(b)(1)(A), as added by Sec. 626 of the Dodd-Frank Act).

The grandfathered unitary savings and loan holding company has 90 days after the transfer date to establish the intermediate holding company. The 90-day period can be extended by the Fed.

> **CCH Comment:** The transfer date, which occurs one year after the date of the enactment of the Dodd-Frank Act, is the time frame in which the supervisory functions of the OTS are transferred to the OCC, Fed and FDIC.

On the other hand, a grandfathered unitary savings and loan holding company **is required** to establish an intermediate holding company if the Fed determines that the establishment of intermediate holding company is necessary to:

- appropriately supervise activities that are determined to be financial activities; or
- ensure that supervision by the Fed does not extend to the grandfathered unitary savings and loan holding company's activities that are not financial activities (HOLA Sec. 10A(b)(1)(B), as added Sec. 626 of by the Dodd-Frank Act).

Regulations. The Fed is to promulgate regulations establishing the criteria for determining whether to require a grandfathered unitary savings and loan holding company to establish an intermediate holding company (HOLA Sec. 10A(c)(1), as added by Sec. 626 of the Dodd-Frank Act).

Internal Financial Activities. The "internal financial activities" of a grandfathered unitary savings and loan holding company do not have to be placed in an intermediate holding company (HOLA Sec. 10A(b)(2)(A), as added by Sec. 626 of the Dodd-Frank Act).

The term "Internal financial activities" includes:

- internal financial activities conducted by a grandfathered savings and loan holding company or any affiliate; and
- internal treasury, investment and employee benefit functions (HOLA Sec. 10A(a)(3), as added by Sec. 626 of the Dodd-Frank Act).

A grandfathered unitary savings and loan holding company is not required to conform its activities to permissible activities (Home Owners' Loan Act Sec. 10A(d)(1), as added by Sec. 626 of the Dodd-Frank Act). Moreover, the formation of an intermediate holding

¶2610

company is to be presumed to be a permissible corporate reorganization as described in HOLA Section 10(c)(9)(D) (HOLA Sec. 10A(d)(2), as added by Sec. 626 of the Dodd-Frank Act).

Grandfathered Activities.—A grandfathered unitary savings and loan holding company may continue to engage in an internal financial activity if:

- it engaged in the activity during the year before the date of enactment of Section 626 of the Dodd-Frank Act; and
- it generated at least two-thirds of its assets or two-thirds of its revenues from the activity (HOLA Sec. 10A(b)(2)(B), as added by Sec. 626 of the Dodd-Frank Act).

The Fed is to review the grandfathered activity to determine that the activity presents no undue risk to the grandfathered unitary savings and loan holding company or to the financial stability of the United States.

> **CCH Comment:** Currently, the Fed, in its corporate practices regulation codified at 12 CFR 225.4(a), requires a BHC to "serve as a source of financial and managerial strength to its subsidiary banks and shall not conduct its operations in an unsafe or unsound manner."

> **CCH Comment:** Section 616(d) of the Dodd-Frank Act added a new source of strength requirement for BHCs and SLHCs to be codified as Section 38A of the FDIA.

Reporting Requirements.—The Fed may periodically examine and require reports under oath from a grandfathered unitary savings and loan holding company that controls an intermediate holding company. These reports are to be used to ensure compliance with the intermediate holding company provisions and assess the grandfathered unitary savings and loan holding company's ability to serve as a source of strength to its subsidiary intermediate holding company (HOLA Sec. 10A(b)(4), as added by Sec. 626 of the Dodd-Frank Act).

Enforcement Actions.—For purposes of the enforcement authority provisions found in FDIA Section 8, a grandfathered unitary savings and loan holding company is to be treated as if it were a savings and loan holding company (HOLA Sec. 10A(b)(5)(A), as added by Sec. 626 of the Dodd-Frank Act).

Affiliate Transactions.—The Fed may promulgate regulations to establish any restrictions or limitations on transactions between an intermediate holding company or its parent and its affiliates. The restrictions and limitations are to prevent unsafe and unsound practices in connection with affiliate transactions.

Any regulations promulgated by the Fed cannot restrict or limit any transaction in connection with the bona fide acquisition or lease by an unaffiliated person of assets, goods or services (HOLA Sec. 10A(b)(c), as added by Sec. 626 of the Dodd-Frank Act).

▶ **Effective date.** The provision takes effect one day after the date of enactment (Sec. 4 of the Dodd-Frank Wall Street Reform and Consumer Protection Act).

Law source: Law at ¶10,626 and ¶10,004.

— Sec. 626 of the Dodd-Frank Wall Street Reform and Consumer Protection Act, adding Home Owners' Loan Act Sec. 10A;

— Sec. 4, providing the effective date.

¶2615 Payment of Interest on Demand Deposits

The prohibition of banks paying interest on demand deposits that applies to state member banks has been repealed by the Dodd-Frank Act (FRA Sec. 19(i), as repealed by Sec. 627(a)(1) of the Dodd-Frank Act). Similar prohibitions applying to federal savings associations and insured state nonmember banks were also removed or repealed (HOLA Sec. 5(b)(1)(B), as amended, and FDIA Sec. 18(g), as repealed by Sec. 627(a)(2) and (a)(3) of the Dodd-Frank Act).

▶ **Effective date.** The amendments made by Section 627(a) take effect one year after the date of the enactment of the Dodd-Frank Act (Sec. 627(b) of the Dodd-Frank Wall Street Reform and Consumer Protection Act).

Law source: Law at ¶10,627.

— Sec. 627(a)(1) of the Dodd-Frank Wall Street Reform and Consumer Protection Act, repealing Federal Reserve Act Sec. 19(i);

— Sec. 627(a)(2), amending Home Owners' Loan Act Sec. 5(b)(1)(B);

— Sec. 627(a)(3), repealing Federal Deposit Insurance Act Sec. 18(g);

— Sec. 627(b), providing the effective date.

¶2620 Credit Card Bank Small Business Lending

A portion of the definition of "credit card bank" found in the BHCA is amended by the Dodd-Frank Act allowing certain credit card loans to businesses that meet the criteria to be eligible for business loans under regulations established by the Small Business Administration. The BHCA definition still prohibits a credit card bank from engaging in the business of making commercial loans (BHCA Sec. 2(c)(2)(F)(v), amended by Sec. 628 of the Dodd-Frank Act).

▶ **Effective date.** The provision takes effect one day after the date of enactment (Sec. 4 of the Dodd-Frank Wall Street Reform and Consumer Protection Act).

Law source: Law at ¶10,628 and ¶10,004.

— Sec. 628 of the Dodd-Frank Wall Street Reform and Consumer Protection Act, amending Sec. 2(c)(2)(F)(v);

— Sec. 4, providing the effective date.

OTC Derivatives

GENERAL PROVISIONS

¶3005 Introduction
¶3010 Definitions
¶3015 Jurisdiction
¶3020 CFTC-SEC Coordination
¶3025 Portfolio Margining
¶3030 Prohibition Against Bailout of Swaps Entities
¶3035 CFTC-SEC Jurisdiction; New Product Approval
¶3040 Novel Derivative Products
¶3045 Conflicts of Interest
¶3050 Studies and Reports

SWAP MARKETS

¶3060 Clearing
¶3065 Swaps, Segregation and Bankruptcy Treatment
¶3070 Derivatives Clearing Organizations
¶3075 Public Reporting of Swap Transaction Data
¶3080 Swap Data Repositories
¶3085 Reporting and Recordkeeping (CFTC)
¶3090 Large Swap Trader Reporting
¶3095 Swap Dealers and Major Swap Participants
¶3100 Swap Execution Facilities
¶3105 Derivatives Transaction Execution Facilities and EBOTs
¶3110 Designated Contract Markets
¶3115 Position Limits
¶3120 Foreign Boards of Trade
¶3125 Legal Certainty for Swaps
¶3130 Enforcement
¶3135 Retail Commodity Transactions

¶3140 Enhanced Compliance for Registered Entities
¶3145 Whistleblowers
¶3150 International Harmonization
¶3155 Anti-Manipulation Authority

SECURITY-BASED SWAP MARKETS

¶3160 Securities Law Amendments
¶3165 Regulation of Dealers and Major Participants
¶3170 Reporting and Recordkeeping (SEC)
¶3175 State Gaming and Bucket Shop Laws

GENERAL PROVISIONS

¶3005 Introduction

The Dodd-Frank Wall Street Reform and Consumer Protection Act establishes a comprehensive framework for the regulation of over-the-counter (OTC) derivatives. The provisions are contained in Title VII, the "Wall Street Transparency and Accountability Act of 2010" (Section 701 *et seq.*). The title broadly splits authority between the Commodity Futures Trading Commission (CFTC) and the Securities and Exchange Commission (SEC). Specifically, the legislation gives the CFTC jurisdiction over swaps and gives the SEC oversight over security-based swaps. Oversight of certain prudential issues goes to the prudential regulators.

Title VII provides for regulation of both dealers (swap and security-based swap dealers and major swap and security-based swap participants) and trading and clearing facilities (designated contract markets, swap execution facilities and derivatives clearing organizations, among other entities). It imposes significant governance, margin and reporting and recordkeeping requirements.

Significantly, the legislation requires banks to "spin off" certain types of derivatives trading to affiliates. If they do not, they lose federal assistance, including implicit government guarantees and access to the Federal Reserve discount window.

The legislation also exempts certain end users from major oversight provisions, imposes certain position limits, and creates a heightened duty to special entities.

Background.—One of the most significant developments in the financial system during recent decades has been the substantial growth and innovation in the markets for derivatives, especially OTC derivatives. Because of their enormous volume and the critical role they play in the financial markets, establishing a comprehensive framework of oversight for the OTC derivative markets was seen by the Obama Administration as crucial to laying the foundation for a safer, more stable financial system (*Financial Regulatory Reform, A New Foundation: Rebuilding Financial Supervision and Regulation*, Treasury Department (June 17, 2009), at FED. BANK. L. REP. ¶ 75-201).

It is widely asserted that OTC derivatives played a major part in the financial crisis of 2008. Products currently traded on the OTC swaps market have a net notional value of approximately $300 trillion in the United States—roughly 20 times the size of the U.S. economy (Testimony of CFTC Chair Gary Gensler before Financial Crisis Inquiry Commission, July 1, 2010).

Despite the enormous size of the OTC markets, these markets largely operated without regulatory oversight. The OTC markets began to develop in the early 1980s, away from the regulated exchanges, transacted bilaterally and not subject to regulation. As volume grew, the question of whether to regulate swaps as futures began to surface. In 1989, the CFTC issued a policy statement stating that swap transactions were not appropriately regulated as futures contracts. In 1992, Congress gave the CFTC broad authority to exempt swap agreements and some hybrid products, which the CFTC then did. Subsequently, the CFTC also exempted various energy swaps from regulation, subject to certain conditions (Testimony of CFTC Chair Gary Gensler before Financial Crisis Inquiry Commission, July 1, 2010).

In the 1990s, swaps began to become more standardized. In 1998, the Bank for International Settlements estimated the total notional value of outstanding swaps at approximately $80 trillion—while the notional value of outstanding exchange-traded futures and options was only $13.5 trillion. The CFTC issued a concept release stating its intention to reexamine its approach to the OTC market. A significant policy debate ensued (Testimony of CFTC Chair Gary Gensler before Financial Crisis Inquiry Commission, July 1, 2010).

Various industry groups and other stakeholders argued that swaps should be exempt from regulation. They argued that the derivatives market was an institutional marketplace, not retail, composed of sophisticated traders who did not need the same protections as the wider public. The large financial institutions dealing derivatives were sufficiently expert and self-interested that the markets would discipline themselves. Industry groups further asserted that the institutions that dealt derivatives were already sufficiently regulated and did not need additional regulation. Additionally, they argued that OTC derivatives were so customized and specialized that they were not susceptible to centralized trading and clearing. Finally, the industry asserted, if the United States regulated its OTC markets, capital would just migrate to Europe and Asia to avoid regulation.

The end result of the debate was the Commodity Futures Modification Act of 2000 (CFMA), which continued the broad exemption of swaps from regulation.

According to the Obama Administration, the downside of this lax regulatory regime became disastrously clear during the recent financial crisis, when many institutions and investors had substantial positions in credit default swaps tied to asset-backed securities. Excessive risk taking by AIG and other insurance companies that provided protection against declines in the value of such asset-backed securities, as well as poor counterparty credit risk management by many banks, saddled the financial system with an enormous unrecognized level of risk (*Financial Regulatory Reform, A New Foundation, supra*).

When the value of the asset-backed securities fell, the danger became clear. Individual institutions believed that these derivatives would protect their investments and provide return, even if the market went down. During the crisis, however, the sheer volume of these contracts overwhelmed some firms that had promised to provide payment on the credit default swaps, and left institutions with losses that they believed they had been protected against. Lacking authority to regulate the OTC derivatives market, regulators

¶3005

were unable to identify or mitigate the enormous systemic threat that had developed (*Financial Regulatory Reform, A New Foundation, supra*).

In addition, the SEC and CFTC had different product introduction and approval processes.

OTC derivatives markets directly affect the regulated securities and futures markets by serving as a less regulated alternative for engaging in economically equivalent activity. The regulatory arbitrage possibilities can facilitate a flow of funds out of the regulated markets and into the unregulated shadow markets. The lack of transparency and oversight also enables bad actors to hide trading activities that would be more easily detected if done in the regulated markets (Testimony of SEC Chair Mary Schapiro before Senate Agriculture Committee, Sept. 22, 2009).

The reform legislation is designed to restore stability and confidence in the financial system by providing for the federal regulation of OTC derivatives under a bifurcated SEC-CFTC regime.

Derivatives Markets.—A derivative is a financial instrument whose value is based on the value of an underlying asset, which could be a Treasury bond or a stock, a foreign currency or a commodity, or a corporate loan or a mortgage-backed security. Derivatives can trade either over-the-counter where contracts are often customized and privately negotiated between counterparties, or through regulated central clearinghouses and exchanges that establish rules for trading contracts among many different counterparties (New York Federal Reserve Bank Report: Policy Perspectives on OTC Derivatives Market Infrastructure, January 2010, Revised March 2010).

OTC derivatives generally are bilateral contracts between sophisticated parties. They include interest rate swaps, foreign exchange contracts, equity swaps, commodity swaps, security-based swaps and credit default swaps, along with other types of swaps, contracts and options. It is widely acknowledged that OTC derivatives contracts, particularly credit default swaps, played a significant role in the recent financial crisis.

OTC contracts can be more flexible than standardized contracts, but they suffer from greater counterparty and operational risks and less transparency. Information on prices and quantities is opaque. This can lead to inefficient pricing and risk assessment for derivatives users and leave regulators ill-informed about risks building up throughout the financial system. Lack of transparency in the massive OTC market intensified systemic fears during the crisis about interrelated derivatives exposures from counterparty risk. These counterparty risk concerns played an important role in freezing up credit markets around the failures of Bear Stearns, AIG and Lehman Brothers.

Counterparty Credit Risk.—Even when it performs as intended, an OTC derivatives contract exposes its holders to the risk of loss in two ways: first, through the performance of the underlying asset and second, through the potential default of the counterparty. For example, a forward contract for oil causes a loss to the buyer and a gain to the seller when the price of oil declines, and vice versa when oil prices rise. Any loss to one counterparty is the gain of the other. In addition, each counterparty is exposed to the default of the other. For example, suppose the buyer of the oil forward contract has a position worth $100 million, assuming performance by the seller. If the seller declares bankruptcy, the buyer may lose some of this potential $100 million value, and indeed could lose more than $100 million by the time the contract is terminated and settled. The buyer's position is thus, in some respects, like that of a lender to the seller.

Counterparty credit risk, that is, the risk of holding a contract with a firm that could potentially fail to fulfill its obligations, is a major consideration of participants in the OTC derivatives market (*New York Federal Reserve Bank Report: Policy Perspectives on OTC Derivatives Market Infrastructure,* January 2010, Revised March 2010).

Counterparty credit risk rises to the level of systemic risk when the failure of a market participant with an extremely large derivatives portfolio could trigger large unexpected losses on its derivatives trades, which could seriously impair the financial condition of one or more of its counterparties. Systemic risk also arises when the fear of such a failure could lead counterparties to attempt to avoid potential losses by reducing their exposures to a large weak market participant, possibly contributing to a run that indeed accelerates the failure of that market participant.

An additional form of systemic risk that can arise from the actual or anticipated failure of a large OTC derivatives market participant is the potential for an accompanying fire sale, which can lead to significant price volatility or price distortions (in both derivative markets and underlying asset markets) when counterparties suddenly attempt to replace their positions with the distressed firm, and otherwise attempt to sell risky assets in favor of safer assets, a flight to quality. Through price impacts, such a fire sale or flight to quality could cause failure threatening losses to some market participants, even those with no direct counterparty credit risk to the firm in question.

Counterparty credit risk can often be reduced by clearing, which means obtaining the effect of a guarantee by a central counterparty (CCP), sometimes called a clearing house. The CCP stands between the two original counterparties, acting as the seller to the original buyer, and as the buyer to the original seller. Because its long and short positions are automatically offsetting, a CCP has no losses or gains on a derivatives contract so long as the original counterparties to the trade continue to perform. The CCP is, however, exposed to counterparty credit risk from each of its participants.

Although OTC derivatives can be used to manage risk and increase liquidity, they also increase leverage in the financial system. Traders can take large speculative positions on a relatively small capital base because there are no regulatory requirements for margin or capital. When users negotiate margin bilaterally, they will act in their own interest to manage their risk. These actions may not take into account the spillover risk throughout the system.

Counterparty credit exposure in the derivatives market was largely seen as a source of systemic risk during the failures of both Bear Stearns and Lehman Brothers, and would have brought down AIG but for a massive collateral payment made with taxpayer money. It created the dangerous interconnections that spread and amplified risk across the entire financial system. More collateral in the system, through margin requirements, will help protect taxpayers and the economy from bailing out companies' risky derivatives positions in the future (Testimony of Federal Reserve Board Chair Ben Bernanke before the Senate Banking Committee, December 3, 2009). Mr. Bernanke described margin requirements for derivatives users as an appropriate cost of protecting against counterparty risk.

With certain exceptions, derivatives on securities may be listed on securities exchanges without filing a proposed rule change with the SEC. Instead, these products are listed under previously approved exchange listing rules. The exception is "new derivative products," which consists of any type of option, warrant, hybrid securities product or any other security, other than a single equity option or a security futures product,

¶3005

whose value is based, in whole or in part, on the performance of, or interest in, an underlying instrument (see Exchange Act Rule 19b-4(e)).

Most new derivative products listed on a securities exchange have tended to fall within previously approved generic listing standards and, accordingly, no prior approval has been required before commencement of trading. In these circumstances, the exchange must file a notice with the SEC within five days after trading begins. New derivative products that are novel and therefore do not fit within existing listing standards, however, must be approved by the Commission.

The Commodity Exchange Act, by contrast, generally allows for the introduction of all products to the market upon certification by a designated contract market that the product does not violate the CEA or CFTC regulations. The CFTC conducts due diligence reviews of all self-certified products to ensure compliance with statutory and regulatory requirements. Generally, the level of scrutiny for these reviews is commensurate with the complexity of the product, with innovative or novel products receiving more detailed review. Ultimately, however, the CFTC cannot move to de-list the product unless it determines that the listing violates the CEA (Joint SEC-CFTC Report on Harmonization of Regulation, Oct. 16, 2009).

Credit Default Swaps.—Credit default swaps provide a simple device for banks and other lenders to hedge the risks associated with lending to a particular company, industry or other counterparty, including government entities. A credit default swap is a derivative contract based on one or more assets (*e.g.*, a corporate loan or bond), in which the protection buyer pays a fee, typically on a quarterly basis, through the life of the contract in return for a payment by the protection seller upon the occurrence of a pre-specified credit event relating to a company (*e.g.*, bankruptcy). If no pre-specified event occurs during the life of the transaction, the seller must retain the quarterly payments as compensation for assuming the risk (Testimony of ISDA Vice Chair Robert Pickel, before House Financial Services Committee, April 29, 2010).

Credit default swaps can reduce certain types of risk while causing others. For example, they permit individual firms to obtain or reduce credit risk exposure to a single company or a sector, thereby reducing or increasing that risk. In addition to obtaining or reducing exposure to credit risk, a credit default swap contract participant must take on counterparty and liquidity risk from the other side of the swap. Through a credit default swap, financial institutions and other market participants can shift credit risk from one party to another, and thus the market may be relevant to a particular firm's willingness to participate in an issuer's securities offering or to lend to a firm. However, they can also lead to greater systemic risk by, among other things, concentrating risk in a small number of large institutions and facilitating lax lending standards more generally. These risks are heightened by the lack of regulatory oversight of dealers and other participants in this market. This combination can lead to inadequate capital and risk management standards. Associated failures can cascade through the global financial system.

During the financial crisis, trading practices in the credit default swap market had a direct effect on the underlying securities markets. Both narrow and broad-based index credit default swaps can be used as synthetic alternatives to debt, and even equity, securities of one or more companies. In addition, market participants may use them to establish a short position with respect to the fortunes of a specific company. In particular, a market participant may be able even to use a broad-based index CDS that includes the company as a way to short that company's debt or equity. In brief, debt and equity securities and single-name and narrow- and broad-based index credit default swaps are all economic substitutes, and therefore ripe for regulatory arbitrage (Testimony of ISDA Vice Chair Robert Pickel, before House Financial Services Committee, April 29, 2010).

Sovereign Credit Default Swaps. Although not nearly as widespread as credit default swaps related to corporate exposures, many institutions also use CDS to hedge the risks associated with lending to a sovereign nation or other governmental entity. Sovereign CDS are similar to corporate CDS, but they are based on government-issued debt and subject to a different set of credit event triggers, such as the government's moratorium on payment of its debt. A significant portion of corporate CDS trading is based on indices, while sovereign indices have only recently been developed.

Generally speaking, CDS, whether related to corporate or sovereign debt, help to mitigate credit risk for investors and lenders. Unlike corporate CDS, however, sovereign CDS can also provide effective hedges against the broader economic risk related to a particular country. Investors may use sovereign CDS for a variety of risk management purposes. For example, international banks that extend credit to corporations and banks located in a particular country may use sovereign CDS to hedge credit or counterparty exposures or to provide country-level risk diversification.

Investors in the debt or equity of companies in a specific country may use sovereign CDS as a proxy hedge against potential systemic shocks that would reduce the value of their positions. Investors with large real estate or other corporate holdings in a country may similarly use sovereign CDS. Portfolio managers may use credit default swaps to hedge against country, liquidity and market risk related to a portfolio comprising debt or equity positions and to better diversify their portfolios. Large banks, which typically do not require highly-rated sovereign entities to post collateral for swap arrangements may use sovereign CDS to hedge against the risk posed by these uncollateralized exposures.

Naked Credit Default Swaps. With these hedging and risk mitigation factors in mind, the Senate rejected a proposed amendment to ban the use of synthetic asset-backed securities and naked credit default swaps in which no one had an insurable interest. In vetting a motion to table the amendment, which essentially killed it, Sen. Christopher Dodd (D-CT) expressed concern about unintended consequences of shutting down a $25 trillion credit default swap market without necessary protections for commercial end users and governments and corporations that depend on credit in which to operate.

Overview.—The derivatives title is divided into three parts: (1) regulatory authority; (2) regulation of swap markets; and (3) regulation of security-based swap markets. The legislation brings currently unregulated swaps, swaps dealers and swaps markets under a comprehensive SEC-CFTC regulatory regime, thereby increasing transparency and regulatory oversight. It also facilitates the standardization and central clearing of swaps, thereby fostering a better market and reducing counterparty risk.

The legislation imposes requirements on (1) the *instruments* that are traded (swaps, security-based swaps); (2) the *dealers* who perform the trades (swap and security-based swap dealers); and (3) the *facilities* where the trades are executed, cleared and reported (designated contract markets, swap execution facilities and security-based swap execution facilities, derivatives clearing organizations, swap and security-based swap data

¶3005

repositories). Thus, all the components that make up swap and security-based swap markets are subject to a comprehensive regulatory regime.

Authority over swap markets falls largely to the CFTC, and authority over security-based swap markets to the SEC. Authority over certain prudential issues, including the setting of capital and margin requirements in some instances, falls to the prudential regulators.

The legislation requires clearing and exchange trading of derivatives that can be cleared. It requires margin for uncleared trades, in order to offset the greater risk they pose to the financial system and encourage more trading to take place in transparent, regulated markets. It imposes new reporting and record-keeping requirements, to increase data collection and publication through clearing houses or swap repositories, to improve market transparency and provide regulators important tools for monitoring and responding to risks. The measure also sets out core derivatives clearing organizations, swap execution facilities and swap data repositories. The legislation also creates a heightened code of conduct when dealing with "special entities", including government entities, pension plans, endowments and others. Finally, the legislation increases the CFTC's enforcement authority in market manipulation.

According to the Senate Banking Committee Report, the main tool for regulating contagion and systemic risk is liquidity reserves or margin. In the OTC market, margin requirements are set bilaterally and do not take account of the counterparty risk that each trade imposes on the rest of the system, thereby allowing systemically important exposures to build up without sufficient capital to mitigate associated risks. The problem of under-collateralization is especially apparent in bank transactions with non-financial firms, and regulators should address this problem through the new margin requirements for uncleared derivatives established in the legislation (S. Rep. No. 111-176, p. 33).

With appropriate collateral and margin requirements, a central clearing organization can substantially reduce counterparty risk and provide an organized mechanism for clearing transactions. For uncleared swaps, regulators should establish margin requirements. In addition, regulators should also impose capital requirements on swap dealers and major swap participants. While large losses are to be expected in derivatives trading, if those positions are fully margined there will be no loss to counterparties and the overall financial system and none of the uncertainty about potential exposures that contributed to the panic in 2008 (S. Rep. No. 111-176, p. 33).

Although central clearing helps mitigate counterparty risk, central clearing alone is not enough. Exchange trading is also essential in order to provide price discovery, transparency and meaningful regulatory oversight of trading and intermediaries. Exchange trading can provide pre- and post- trade transparency for end users, market participants and regulators. When swaps are executed on the basis of robust price information, rather than privately quoted, the cost of those transactions can be reduced over time (Testimony of former CFTC Chair Brooksley Born, before Senate Joint Economic Committee, Dec. 1, 2009).

With certain exceptions, the Dodd-Frank Act requires swaps to be cleared with a derivatives clearing organization (DCO) and security-based swaps to be cleared with a clearing agency. DCOs are subject to registration, reporting, and recordkeeping requirements, and must comply with certain core principles. The clearing requirement does not apply if one of the counterparties to the swap is not a financial entity, is using swaps to hedge or mitigate commercial risk, and notifies the CFTC how it generally meets its financial obligations associated with entering into non-cleared swaps.

For swaps subject to the clearing requirement, the counterparties must execute the transaction on a designated contract market or swap execution facility. However, this requirement does not apply if no designated contract market or swap execution facility makes the swap available to trade, or if the swap is subject to a clearing exception. Designated contract markets and swap execution facilities are subject to registration, reporting, and recordkeeping requirements, and must comply with certain core principles.

Derivatives Spin-Off. The legislation prohibits federal assistance (including federal deposit insurance, and access to the Federal Reserve discount window) to swaps entities in connection with their trading in swaps or securities-based swaps. This section would effectively require some derivatives activities to be conducted outside of banks and bank holding companies, with the exception of bona fide hedging activities and some traditional bank activities. The legislation allows banks to set up a swaps entity affiliate under certain conditions. This provision has a two-year effective date.

End-User Exemption. Commercial end users are exempted from mandatory swap clearing. Financial entities cannot claim this exemption. These firms, such as manufacturers, often use the derivatives markets to hedge risks, such as price risks.

Swap Execution Facilities. Swap execution facilities must be registered with the SEC for security-based swaps and the CFTC for swaps under an oversight regime of governance and core principles. Under both SEC and CFTC oversight, the swap execution facility must establish self-regulatory core operational principles. The legislation also requires the swap execution facility to appoint a chief compliance officer and imposes duties to be carried out by such officer, including annual reporting.

Position Limits. The legislation requires the setting of position limits in order to provide an important restriction on market manipulation and the amount of risk that can build up in any one market participant.

▶ **Effective date.** Unless otherwise provided, the provisions of both subtitles take effect on the later of 360 days after the date of enactment (Secs. 754 and 774 of the Dodd-Frank Wall Street Reform and Consumer Protection Act). To the extent a provision requires rulemaking, the provision takes effect not less than 60 days after publication of the final rule or regulation implementing the provision.

Law source: Law at ¶10,701, ¶10,754 and ¶10,774. Committee Report at ¶50,071 and ¶54,321.

— Sec. 701 of the Dodd-Frank Wall Street Reform and Consumer Protection Act, providing the short title of Title VII;

— Secs. 754 and 774, providing the general effective date for Subtitles A and B, respectively.

¶3010 Definitions

The Dodd-Frank Wall Street Reform and Consumer Protection Act amends the Commodity Exchange Act (CEA), Securities Exchange Act of 1934 (Exchange Act), and Securities Act of 1933 (Securities Act) to provide definitions for new terms and amends existing definitions to incorporate new provisions relating to swaps and security-based swaps.

Regulatory Authority.—The following terms have meanings as given in CEA Section 1a: "prudential regulator," "swap," "swap dealer," "major swap participant," "swap data repository," "associated person of a swap dealer or major swap participant," "eligible contract participant," "swap execution facility," "security-based swap," "security-based swap dealer," "major security-based swap participant," "swap data repository" and "associated person of a security-based swap dealer or major security-based swap participant" (Sec. 711 of the Dodd-Frank Wall Street Reform and Consumer Protection Act).

The term "appropriate federal banking agency" has the meaning given in Federal Deposit Insurance Act Section 3. In the case of a noninsured state bank, the term means the Board. For farm credit system institutions, the term refers to the Farm Credit Administration (Sec. 721(a) of the Dodd-Frank Act).

The term "associated person of a security-based swap dealer or major security-based swap participant" has the meaning given in Exchange Act Section 3(a) (Sec. 721(a) of the Dodd-Frank Act).

"Associated person of a swap dealer or major swap participant" means a person who is associated with a swap dealer or major swap participant who is a partner, officer, employee or agent (or occupies similar status), in any capacity that involves the solicitation or acceptance of swaps, or the supervision of persons involved in the solicitation or acceptance of swaps. The term does include persons performing a merely clerical or ministerial function (Sec. 721(a) of the Dodd-Frank Act).

"Board" means the Board of Governors of the Federal Reserve System (Sec. 721(a) of the Dodd-Frank Act).

Swaps.—Meanings are given for the following terms: "cleared swap," "commodity pool," "commodity pool operator," "floor broker," "floor trader," "foreign exchange forward," "forward exchange swap," "futures commission merchant," "introducing broker," "major security-based swap participant," "major swap participant," "prudential regulator," "security-based swap," "security-based swap dealer," "swap," "swap data repository," "swap dealer," and "swap execution facility" (Sec. 721(a) of the Dodd-Frank Act).

The CFTC may define the term "commercial risk" and any other term included in an amendment made by the derivatives title to the CEA (Sec. 721(b) of the Dodd-Frank Act).

The CFTC must adopt rules to further define the terms "swap," "swap dealer," "major swap participant" and "eligible contract participant" (Sec. 721(c) of the Dodd-Frank Act).

Contracts for future delivery dealing in motion picture box office receipts (or any index, measure, value or data related to such receipts), and all services, rights and interests (except motion picture box office receipts or any index, measure, value or data related to such receipts) are specifically excluded from the definition of "commodity". This measure has an effective date of June 1, 2010 (Secs. 721(a)(4) and (f) of the Dodd-Frank Act).

¶3010

A colloquy between House Agriculture Committee Chair Collin Peterson (D-MN) and Rep. Leonard Boswell (D-IA) clarified an important point regarding the intention of one of the exclusions from the definition of "swap" for any sale of a nonfinancial commodity or security for deferred shipment or delivery, so long as the transaction is intended to be physically settled and is intended to be consistent with the forward contract exclusion that is currently in the Commodity Exchange Act and the CFTC's established policy on this subject (Cong. Rec., June 30, 2010, p. 5246).

Chairman Peterson remarked that physical commodity transactions should not be regulated as swaps, as that term is defined in the legislation. This is true even if commercial parties agree to "book-out" their delivery obligations under a forward contract. A book-out is a second agreement between two commercial parties to a forward contract who find themselves in a delivery chain or circle at the same delivery point. The parties can agree to settle their delivery obligations by exchanging a net payment if there has been some change arising since the initial forward contract was entered into. Book-outs can reduce transaction costs (Cong. Rec., June 30, 2010, pp. 5246–5247).

According to Chairman Peterson, the correct interpretation of the exclusionary provision from the definition of "swap" is that the exclusion would apply to transactions in which the parties' delivery obligations are booked-out. The fact that the parties may subsequently agree to settle their obligations with a payment based on a price difference through a book-out does not turn a forward contract into a swap. Excluding physical forward contracts, including book-outs, is consistent with the CFTC's long-standing view that physical forward contracts in which the parties later agree to bookout their delivery obligations for commercial convenience are excluded from its jurisdiction. Nothing in the Dodd-Frank Act changes that result with respect to commercial forward contracts (Cong. Rec., June 30, 2010, pp. 5246–5247).

Security-Based Swaps.—The following definitions are added to the Exchange Act: "eligible contract participant," "major swap participant," "major security-based swap participant," "security-based swap," "swap," "person associated with a security-based swap dealer or major security-based swap participant," "security-based swap dealer," "appropriate federal banking agency," "board," "prudential regulator," "security-based swap data repository," "swap dealer," "security-based swap execution facility," "security-based swap agreement," and other incorporated definitions (Sec. 761(a) of the Dodd-Frank Act).

The SEC may by rule further define the following:

- "Commercial risk";
- "Security-based swap participant" and "eligible contract participant," with regard to security-based swaps;
- Any other term included in an amendment to the Exchange Act made by the derivatives title (Sec. 761(b) of the Dodd-Frank Act).

The Investment Company Act of 1940 and Investment Advisers Act of 1940 are amended to provide that the terms "commodity pool," "commodity pool operator," "commodity trading advisor," "major swap participant," "swap dealer," and "swap execution facility" have the same meanings as in CEA Section 1a (Investment Company Act

¶3010

Sec. 2(a)(54), as added by Sec. 769 of the Dodd-Frank Act; Advisers Act Sec. 202(a)(29), as added by Sec. 770 of the Dodd-Frank Act).

▶ **Effective date.** The provision takes effect 360 days after enactment, except subsection 721(a)(4), which becomes effective June 1, 2010 (Secs. 721(f), 754 and 774 of the Dodd-Frank Wall Street Reform and Consumer Protection Act).

Law source: Law at ¶10,711, ¶10,721, ¶10,761, ¶10,769, ¶10,770, ¶10,754 and ¶10,774. Committee Report at ¶50,071.

— Sec. 711 of the Dodd-Frank Wall Street Reform and Consumer Protection Act, giving certain terms the same meanings given by the CEA;

— Sec. 721, giving definitions;

— Sec. 761, defining terms;

— Sec. 769, adding Investment Company Act Sec. 2(a)(54);

— Sec. 770, adding Advisers Act Sec. 202(a)(29);

— Secs. 754 and 774, providing the general effective date.

¶3015 Jurisdiction

The Dodd-Frank Wall Street Reform and Consumer Protection Act amends the Commodity Exchange Act (CEA) to reaffirm the CFTC's exclusive jurisdiction, excepting any restrictions in the Act, and incorporates swaps into that jurisdiction under the CEA. The legislation also amends the Securities Exchange Act of 1934 (Exchange Act) to clarify the jurisdiction of the CFTC and SEC over swaps and securities-based swaps.

In the view of House Agriculture Committee Chair Collin Peterson (D-MN), the Dodd-Frank Act allocates authority over swaps and security-based swaps as follows. First, the CFTC has exclusive jurisdiction over swaps, including swaps on broad-based security indexes. Within the swap definition is a category of swaps called security-based swap agreements. For this specific category of swaps, the CFTC will continue to exercise its full jurisdictional authority, while the SEC may exercise certain specific authorities over these products. Title VII also clarifies that the SEC has jurisdiction over security-based swaps, which are swaps on narrow-based security indexes and single securities, and that the two agencies share authority over mixed swaps (Cong. Rec., June 30, 2010, p. H5256).

Chairman Peterson emphasized that nothing in the SEC savings clauses, or any other provision of Title VII, alters the existing jurisdictional divide between the CFTC and SEC established by the Johnson-Shad Accord which, among other things, provides the CFTC exclusive jurisdiction over futures (and options on futures) on broad-based security indexes. Nor do these savings clauses, or any other provision of Title VII, divest or limit the authority that the CFTC shares with the SEC over security futures products as authorized by the Commodity Futures Modernization Act of 2000 (Cong. Rec., June 30, 2010, p. H5256).

In the 1980s, disputes arose over whether certain derivatives transactions based on stock prices were best regulated as futures or securities. In 1982, the SEC and CFTC agreed on a regulatory scheme that came to be known as the Shad-Johnson Jurisdictional Accord. The accord reinforced the SEC's jurisdiction over options on securities and recognized the CFTC's jurisdiction over options on certain futures. The accord also delineated jurisdiction between the SEC and CFTC on stock index futures.

Swaps.—The CEA is amended to incorporate the CFTC's exclusive jurisdiction over non-securities based swaps. This does not limit the SEC's jurisdiction over security-based swaps and does not give the CFTC jurisdiction over any security (CEA Sec. 2(a)(1), as amended by Sec. 722(a) of the Dodd-Frank Wall Street Reform and Consumer Protection Act).

Swaps cannot be regulated as insurance under state law. With regard to swaps, the Act does not apply to activities outside the United States, unless they either have a direct and significant connection with the commercial activities of the United States or violate rules promulgated by the Commission to prevent evasion of the requirements of the Act (CEA Secs. 12(h) and (i), as added by Secs. 722(b) and (d) of the Dodd-Frank Act).

The CFTC and SEC have authority to investigate and report on any swap or security-based swap that is found to be detrimental to the stability of financial markets or their participants. The CFTC and SEC may by rule or order collect any information they find necessary to conduct these investigations (Sec. 714 of the Dodd-Frank Act).

Except as provided in CEA Section 4, the CFTC and SEC, in consultation with the Treasury Secretary, can generally bar entities domiciled in a foreign country from participating in U.S. swaps or security-based swaps markets, if it is determined that regulation in the foreign entity's country undermines the U.S. financial system (Sec. 715 of the Dodd-Frank Act).

Security-Based Swaps.—The Act repeals provisions of the Gramm-Leach-Bliley (GLB) Act and the Commodity Futures Modernization Act (CFMA) that prohibited the SEC from regulating security-based swaps. Most notably, GLB Section 206B is repealed. Conforming amendments are made to the GLB Act, Securities Act and Exchange Act (Sec. 762 of the Dodd-Frank Act).

The SEC does not have authority to grant exemptions from specified security-based swaps provisions of the derivatives title, except as expressly authorized by the Dodd-Frank Act. The derivatives title, or regulation under it, does not apply to any person transacting security-based swaps outside U.S. jurisdiction, unless the person is doing so against SEC rules adopted to prevent the evasion of the derivatives provisions of the legislation (Exchange Act Sec. 30(c), as added by Sec. 772(a),(b) of the Dodd-Frank Act).

Unless otherwise provided, the derivatives provisions of the legislation do not divest any appropriate federal banking agency, the SEC or CFTC, or other federal or state agency, of any authority derived from any other applicable law (Secs. 743 and 771 of the Dodd-Frank Act).

Foreign Exchange Swaps (FOREX).—The Treasury Secretary has authority whether to exempt foreign exchange swaps and forwards from the definition of the term "swap." The Secretary must consider certain factors in making a determination. A determination that a contract is not a swap does not exempt foreign exchange swaps and forwards from applicable antifraud and anti-manipulaton provisions (CEA Sec. 1b, as added by Sec. 722(h) of the Dodd-Frank Act).

Energy and Environmental Markets Advisory Committee.—The Act amends the CEA to establish the Energy and Environmental Markets Advisory Committee. A Committee of the same name was formed in 2008 by the CFTC.

The Committee must consist of nine members, who are appointed to three-year terms, and may be removed for cause by the CFTC. The Committee must meet at least twice a year. The Committee's objective is to conduct public meetings, submit reports and recommendations to the Commission, and otherwise serve as a vehicle for discussion on matters of concern to exchanges, firms, end users and regulators regarding energy and environmental markets and their regulation by the Commission. The Committee is not subject to the Federal Advisory Committee Act (CEA Sec. 2(a)(15)(A),(B),(E), as added by Sec. 751 of the Dodd-Frank Act).

FERC Authority.—Since 1935, the Federal Power Act and the Natural Gas Act have required the Federal Energy Regulatory Commission (FERC) to ensure that utility customers are charged just and reasonable rates for electricity and natural gas. State laws require state commissions to do the same for retail customers. FERC also has authority, granted in the Energy Policy Act of 2005, to police market manipulation in electricity and gas markets that would affect the prices customers pay.

The Dodd-Frank Act clarifies the authorities of the CFTC and FERC over financial instruments, both swaps and futures, traded pursuant to FERC- or state-approved tariffs or rate schedules. Section 722 preserves FERC's existing authorities over financial instruments traded pursuant to a FERC or state approved tariff or rate schedule, which under current law does not extend to CFTC-regulated exchanges and clearinghouses, because these are within the CFTC's exclusive jurisdiction. The CFTC's authorities over futures and swaps traded pursuant to FERC or state approved tariffs or rate schedules are also fully preserved (Cong. Rec., June 30, 2010, p. H5256).

The Act further specifies that, outside of regional transmission organizations/independent system operators (RTOs/ISOs) markets, the CFTC must continue to have exclusive jurisdiction over financial instruments traded on CFTC-regulated exchanges, such as NYMEX or ICE, traded through swap execution facilities, or cleared on CFTC-regulated clearinghouses. To avoid the potential for overlapping or duplicative FERC and CFTC authority, the Act provides the CFTC with the authority to exempt financial instruments traded within an RTO/ISO from CFTC regulation if the CFTC determines the exemption would be consistent with the public interest and the purposes of the Commodity Exchange Act. Section 722 also preserves FERC's anti-manipulation authority as it currently exists under the Federal Power Act and the Natural Gas Act prior to enactment of Dodd-Frank (Cong. Rec., June 30, 2010, p. H5256).

Nothing in the Dodd-Frank Act limits or affects any statutory authority of FERC or a state regulatory authority (as defined in section 3(21) of the Federal Power Act with respect to an agreement, contract or transaction entered into pursuant to a tariff or rate schedule approved by FERC or a state regulatory authority, if the transaction is not executed, traded or cleared on a registered entity or trading facility, or executed, traded or cleared on a registered entity or trading facility owned or operated by a regional transmission organization or independent system operator (CEA Sec. 2(a)(1)(I), as added by Sec. 722(e) of the Dodd-Frank Act).

If the CFTC finds that an exemption would be in the public interest, the CFTC must exempt an agreement, contract or transaction entered into under a tariff or rate schedule approved by FERC or a state (CEA Sec. 4(c)(6), as added by Sec. 722(f) of the Dodd-Frank Act).

Nothing in the derivatives title limits or affects any statutory enforcement authority of FERC under Federal Power Act Section 222 and Natural Gas Act Section 4A that existed prior to enactment (Sec. 722(g) of the Dodd-Frank Act).

The CFTC and FERC must negotiate a Memorandum of Understanding to establish procedures for (a) applying the agencies' respective authorities so as to ensure effective and efficient regulation in the public interest; (b) resolving conflicts concerning overlapping jurisdiction between the two agencies; and (c) avoiding conflicting or duplicative regulation. This memorandum and any subsequent amendments must be promptly submitted to the appropriate committees of Congress. The two agencies must also negotiate an additional Memorandum of Understanding to share information requested by either commission conducting an investigation into potential manipulation, fraud or market power abuse in markets subject to the Commission's regulation or oversight. Shared information remains subject to restrictions on disclosure applicable to the Commission initially holding the information. The Memoranda of Understanding must be completed within 180 days after enactment (Sec. 720(a) of the Dodd-Frank Act).

▶ **Effective date.** The provisions take effect 360 days after enactment, except as specified by subsection (Secs. 754 and 774 of the Dodd-Frank Wall Street Reform and Consumer Protection Act).

Law source: Law at ¶10,714, ¶10,715, ¶10,720, ¶10,722, ¶10,743, ¶10,751, ¶10,762, ¶10,772, ¶10,771, ¶10,754 and ¶10,774. Committee Report at ¶50,071.

— Sec. 714 of the Dodd-Frank Wall Street Reform and Consumer Protection Act, giving CFTC and SEC authority to investigate abusive swaps;

— Sec. 715, permitting ban of specific foreign entities from U.S. swaps or security-based swaps markets;

— Sec. 720, requiring CFTC and FERC to enter into Memorandum of Understanding;

— Secs. 722(a)–(f) and (h), amending CEA 2(a)(1)(A); adding CEA Secs. 12(h), 2(i), 2(a)(1)(I) and 5(c)(6), adding CEA Sec. 1b;

— Sec. 722(g), clarifying that nothing in the derivatives title affects any statutory enforcement authority of FERC that existed prior to enactment;

— Secs. 743 and 771, clarifying that the Act's derivatives provisions do not divest authority from federal or state agencies, unless specified;

— Sec. 751, adding CEA Sec. 2(a)(15).

— Sec. 762(a), repealing Secs. 206B and 206C of the Gramm-Leach-Bliley Act;

— Secs. 762(b)–(d), making conforming amendments to Gramm-Leach-Bliley Act Sec. 206A(a), Securities Act Sec. 17, Exchange Act Secs. 3A, 9, 10, 15, 20, 21A;

— Secs. 772(a) and (b), adding Exchange Act Secs. 36(c) and 30(c);

— Secs. 754 and 774, providing the effective date.

¶3015

¶3020 CFTC-SEC Coordination

The Dodd-Frank Wall Street Reform and Consumer Protection Act requires coordination by the CFTC and SEC before issuing rules or orders in connection with swaps or security-based swaps. The legislation also calls for joint rulemaking (Sec. 712 of the Dodd-Frank Wall Street Reform and Consumer Protection Act).

Consultation Between Agencies.—The CFTC must consult and coordinate with the SEC and the prudential regulators before commencing rulemaking or issuing an order regarding the following: swaps; swap dealers or associated persons; major swap participants or associated persons; swap data repositories; derivative clearing organizations with regard to swaps; eligible contract participants; or swap execution facilities pursuant to the derivatives title (Sec. 712(a)(1) of the Dodd-Frank Act).

Similarly, the SEC must consult and coordinate with the CFTC and the prudential regulators before commencing rulemaking or issuing an order regarding the following: security-based swaps; security-based swap dealers or associated persons; major security-based swap participants or associated persons; security-based swap data repositories; clearing agencies with regard to security-based swaps; eligible contract participants with regard to security-based swaps; or security-based swap execution facilities (Sec. 712(a)(2) of the Dodd-Frank Act).

These regulations must be prescribed in accordance with requirements of U.S.C. Title 5, and must be issued in final form within 360 days after the date of enactment (Sec. 712(a)(3) of the Dodd-Frank Act).

However, the consultation provisions do not apply to orders issued (a) in connection with violations of the Commodity Exchange Act (CEA); (b) in connection with violations of the securities laws; or (c) in any proceeding conducted on the record in accordance with 5 U.S.C. §556 and §557. Consultation between the two commissions must be consistent with 5 U.S.C. Ch. 7 and Ch. 5, Subchapter 5 (the Administrative Procedures Act). In promulgating rules and orders under the Act, the commissions must consider the views of the prudential regulators. In adopting rules, the commissions must treat similar products similarly, but not necessarily identically (Secs. 712(a)(4)–(7) of the Dodd-Frank Act).

If necessary to carry out the provisions of the derivatives, title, the commissions must jointly promulgate regulations regarding "mixed swaps", as described in CEA Section 1a(47)(D) and Exchange Act Section 3(a)(68)(D) (Sec. 712(a)(8) of the Dodd-Frank Act).

Limitation.—Unless specifically mentioned elsewhere in the Act, the CFTC does not have jurisdiction over security-based swaps or associated entities, and the SEC does not have jurisdiction over other swaps or associated entities (Secs. 712(b)(1) and (2) of the Dodd-Frank Act).

Similarly, no futures association registered under the CFTC has authority over any security-based swap, and no national securities association registered under the Exchange Act has jurisdiction over any swap (Sec. 712(b)(3) of the Dodd-Frank Act).

Objection to Commission Regulation.—Within 60 days of publication of the final rule, regulation or order, the SEC and the CFTC may appeal to the Court of Appeals for the District of Columbia, if either determines that the other has issued a rule or order that conflicts with their authority. These proceedings must be expedited. Procedures, timelines and standard of review are established (Sec. 712(c) of the Dodd-Frank Act).

Joint Rulemaking.—In consultation with the Board of Governors of the Federal Reserve System (the Fed), the CFTC and SEC must adopt rules to further define the following terms: "swap," "security-based swap," "swap dealer," "security-based swap dealer," "major swap participant," "major security-based swap participant," "eligible contract participant," and "security-based swap agreement" in CEA Section 1a(47)(A)(v) and Exchange Act Section 3(a)(78) (Sec. 712(d)(1) of the Dodd-Frank Act).

The CFTC and SEC, in consultation with the Fed, must jointly adopt other rules regarding definitions as the commissions determine necessary and appropriate, in the public interest and for the protection of investors. The commissions must jointly adopt rules governing books and records required to be kept regarding security-based swap agreements by swap data repositories, including uniform rules that specify the data elements that must be collected and maintained. The commissions must jointly adopt rules governing books and records regarding security-based swap agreements, including daily trading records, for swap dealers, major swap participants, security-based swap dealers and security-based swap participants (Sec. 712(d)(2)(A)–(C) of the Dodd-Frank Act).

Rules prescribed jointly under the derivatives title must be comparable to the maximum extent possible, taking into consideration differences in instruments and applicable statutory requirements. The CFTC must make available to the SEC information relating to uncleared security-based swap agreement transactions. Rules regarding definitions must require the maintenance of records of all activities related to uncleared security-based swap agreement transactions (Sec. 712(d)(2)(D)–(F) of the Dodd-Frank Act).

If the CFTC and SEC fail to jointly prescribe necessary rules in a timely manner, then at the request of either commission, the Financial Stability Oversight Council must resolve the dispute in a prescribed manner. Any interpretation or guidance concerning the derivatives title by either commission is effective only if issued jointly by the CFTC and SEC, in consultation with the Fed, if the title requires the commissions to issue joint regulations to implement the provision (Sec. 712(d)(3)–(4) of the Dodd-Frank Act).

The CFTC or the SEC must individually, not jointly, promulgate rules and regulations required due to enactment of the Act within 360 days after enactment (Sec. 712(e) of the Dodd-Frank Act).

Beginning upon enactment and without regard to the effective date of any provision, the CFTC and SEC may (1) promulgate rules, regulations or orders permitted or required by the Act; (2) conduct studies and prepare reports and recommendations as required by the Act; (3) register persons under the provisions of the Act; and (4) exempt persons, agreements, contracts or transactions from the Act, according to the terms of the Act. However, none of these actions will become effective prior to the effective date applicable to the action under the provisions of the Act (Sec. 712(f)) of the Dodd-Frank Act).

▶ **Effective date.** Subsections (a)–(c) and (f) take effect 360 days after enactment. Subsections (d) and (e) take effect on the later of: (1) 360 days after enactment; or (2) 60 days after publication of the final implementing rules (Sec. 754 of the Dodd-Frank Wall Street Reform and Consumer Protection Act).

Law source: Law at ¶10,712 and ¶10,754. Committee Report at ¶50,071.

— Sec. 712(a) of the Dodd-Frank Wall Street Reform and Consumer Protection Act, requiring regulatory coordination of the CFTC and SEC;

— Sec. 712(b), providing for exclusive jurisdiction of the CFTC over swaps and the SEC over security-based swaps;

— Sec. 712(c), providing for judicial resolution of disputes over SEC and CFTC jurisdiction;

— Sec. 712(d), providing for joint rulemaking;

— Sec. 712(e), requiring for a global rulemaking timeframe;

— Sec. 712(f), providing for actions by the CFTC and SEC;

— Sec. 754, providing the effective date.

¶3025 Portfolio Margining

The Dodd-Frank Wall Street Reform and Consumer Protection Act amends the Securities Exchange Act of 1934 (Exchange Act) and the Commodity Exchange Act (CEA) to provide for portfolio margining of customer accounts.

"Portfolio margining" refers to the ability to reduce the amount of margin required by the holding of one position if another position simultaneously held by the customer would offset the risk posed by the first position. Portfolio margining would release firm and customer capital to be used for other purposes. Portfolio margining may be attained in one of two general ways: by placing the relevant instruments in either a single securities or futures account, or in two separate accounts.

The SEC has approved portfolio margining for positions held in a securities account for equities, securities options, equity-based OTC derivatives, single stock futures and broad-based index futures (Joint SEC-CFTC Report on Harmonization of Regulation, Oct. 16, 2009).

Exchange Act Amendments.—The legislation amends the Exchange Act to permit a broker or dealer who is also registered with the CFTC as a futures commission merchant to hold cash and securities in a portfolio margining account carried as a futures account. The portfolio margining account must be under a portfolio margining program approved by the CFTC and is subject to 11 U.S.C. Ch. 7, subchapter 4. The SEC must consult with the CFTC to adopt rules to ensure that transactions and accounts are subject to comparable requirements to the extent practicable for similar products (Exchange Act Sec. 15(c)(3)(C), as added by Sec. 713(a) of the Dodd-Frank Wall Street Reform and Consumer Protection Act).

CEA Amendments.—The legislation amends the CEA to permit a futures commission merchant who is also registered with the SEC as a broker or dealer to hold, in a portfolio margining account, a commodity futures contract or an option on such a contract, and any money, securities or other property received from a customer to margin the contract, or accruing to a customer as the result of such a contract. The CFTC must consult with the SEC to adopt rules to ensure that transactions and accounts are subject to comparable requirements to the extent practicable for similar products (CEA 4d(h), as added by Sec. 713(b) of the Dodd-Frank Act).

The CFTC must exercise its authority to ensure that securities held in a portfolio margining account carried as a futures account are customer property (CEA Sec. 20(c), as added by Sec. 713(c) of the Dodd-Frank Act).

▶ **Effective date.** The provision takes effect 360 days after enactment (Sec. 754 of the Dodd-Frank Wall Street Reform and Consumer Protection Act).

Law source: Law at ¶10,713 and ¶10,754. Committee Report at ¶50,071.

— Sec. 713(a) of the Dodd-Frank Wall Street Reform and Consumer Protection Act, adding Exchange Act Sec. 15(c)(3)(C);

— Sec. 713(b), adding CEA Sec. 4d(h);

— Sec. 713(c), adding CEA Sec. 20(c);

— Sec. 754, providing the effective date.

¶3030 Prohibition Against Bailout of Swaps Entities

The Dodd-Frank Wall Street Reform and Consumer Protection Act prohibits certain federal assistance to swap entities in connection with trading in swaps or securities-based swaps, including federal deposit insurance and access to the Fed discount window. Moreover, banks are prohibited from acting as a swaps entity for uncleared credit default swaps. Additionally, insured depository institutions must comply with the prohibition on proprietary trading in derivatives as required by Section 619 of the Dodd-Frank Act.

Importantly, however, the term "swap entity" does not include an insured depository institution that is also a major swap participant or security-based swap participant. Further, banks are allowed to engage in bona fide hedging and traditional bank activities. Finally, banks are permitted to have or establish affiliates, to which they may transfer disallowed swaps activities.

Effectively, the provision requires banks to divest the types of derivatives activities considered to carry the greatest risk, while allowing banks to retain the majority of their routine low-risk derivatives activities on behalf of customers.

Congressional Purpose.—According to Sen. Blanche Lincoln (D-AR), the author of the provision, Section 716 has two goals. The first goal is getting banks back to performing the duties they were meant to perform, such as taking deposits and making loans for mortgages, small businesses and commercial enterprise. The second goal is separating out the activities that put these financial institutions in peril. Section 716 makes clear that engaging in risky derivatives dealing is not central to the business of banking (Cong. Rec., May 5, 2010, p. S3140).

Senator Lincoln refuted suggestions that this provision will push derivatives trading off into the dark without oversight. The derivatives title of the Dodd-Frank Act makes it abundantly clear that all swaps activity will be vigorously regulated by the SEC and CFTC (Cong. Rec., May 5, 2010, p. S3140).

Similarly, Sen. Lincoln rejected the argument that Section 716 will prevent banks from using swaps to hedge their risks. Banks that have been acting as banks will be able to continue doing business as they always have under the reform legislation, she assured, with banks using swaps still being allowed to hedge their interest rate risk on their loan portfolio. Most importantly, Congress wants them to do so. Banks offering a swap in connection with a loan to a commercial customer are still in the business of banking and will not be affected (Cong. Rec., May 5, 2010, p. S3140).

According to Sen. Lincoln, using derivatives to manage risk and using them to create exotic swaps that contributed to the financial crisis of 2008 are two very different things. Regulated, transparent swap activity is a necessary part of managing risk, she noted, but it has no place inside a bank, where too many innocent bystanders are put at risk. By quarantining highly risky swaps trading from banking altogether, federally insured deposits will not be put at risk by toxic swaps transactions. Moreover, banks will be forced to behave like banks, focusing on extending credit in a manner that builds economic strength as opposed to fostering worldwide economic instability (Cong. Rec., May 5, 2010, p. S3140).

Federal Assistance Prohibited.—No federal assistance may be provided to any swaps entity with respect to any swap-security-based swap or other activity of the swaps entity (Sec. 716(a) of the Dodd-Frank Act). "Federal assistance" means the use of advances from a Federal Reserve credit facility or discount window that is not part of a program or facility with broad-based eligibility under Section 13(3)(A) of the Federal Reserve Act, Federal Deposit Insurance Corporation insurance or guarantees for the purpose of:

- making a loan to, or purchasing any stock, equity interest or debt obligation of any swaps entity;
- purchasing the assets of any swap entity;
- guaranteeing any loan or debt issuance of any swaps entity;
- entering into any assistance arrangement (including tax breaks), loss sharing or profit sharing with any swaps entity (Sec. 716(b)(1) of the Dodd-Frank Act).

"Swaps entity" means any swap dealer, security-based swap dealer, major swap participant or major security-based swap participant that is registered under the CEA or Exchange Act. The term does not include any major swap participant or security-based swap participant that is an insured depository institution (Sec. 716(b)(2) of the Dodd-Frank Act).

Affiliates of Insured Depository Institutions.—The prohibition on federal assistance does not prevent an insured depository institution from having or establishing an affiliate that is a swaps entity, as long as: (1) the insured depository institution is part of a bank holding company, or savings and loan holding company, that is supervised by the Federal Reserve; and (2) the swaps entity affiliate complies with Federal Reserve Act Sections 23A and 23B and any other requirements the CFTC, SEC and the Board of Governors of the Federal Reserve System (the Fed) deem necessary and appropriate (Sec. 716(c) of the Dodd-Frank Act).

Bona Fide Hedging and Traditional Bank Activities.—The prohibition on federal assistance applies to an insured depository institution unless the institution limits its activities to (1) hedging and other similar risk mitigating activities directly related to the insured depository institution's activities; and (2) acting as a swaps entity for swaps or security-based swaps involving rates or reference assets that are permissible for investment by a national bank, under the paragraph designated as "Seventh." of Section 5136 of the Revised Statutes of the United States (12 U.S.C. §24) (Sec. 716(d) of the Dodd-Frank Act).

Acting as a swaps entity for credit default swaps, including swaps or security-based swaps referencing the credit risk of asset-backed securities as defined in Exchange Act Section 3(a)(77) is not considered a bank permissible activity, unless the swaps or security-based swaps are cleared by a derivatives clearing organization or clearing agency that is registered or exempt from registration (Sec. 716(d) of the Dodd-Frank Act).

Existing Swaps and Security-Based Swaps.—The prohibition on federal assistance applies only to swaps or security-based swaps entered into by an insured depository institution after the end of the transition period (Sec. 716(e) of the Dodd-Frank Act).

Transition Period.—During the two-year transition, banks will be permitted to divest the swaps entity or cease the activities that required registration as a swaps entity. In establishing the appropriate transition period to effect such divestiture or cessation of activities, which may include making the swaps entity an affiliate of the bank, federal banking regulators must take into account and make written findings regarding the potential impact of divestiture or cessation of swap activities on the bank's mortgage lending, small business lending, job creation and capital formation, versus the potential negative impact on banks and the FDIC's deposit insurance fund (Sec. 716(f) of the Dodd-Frank Act).

Banking regulators can impose necessary and appropriate conditions on the divestiture or cessation of activities of the swaps entity. The regulators can extend the transition period for up to one year, after consulting with the SEC and CFTC (Sec. 716(f) of the Dodd-Frank Act).

Excluded Entities.—For purposes of the section, the term "swaps entity" does not include any insured depository institution under the Federal Deposit Insurance Act or covered financial company under Title II that is in conservatorship, receivership or a bridge bank operated by the FDIC (Sec. 716(g) of the Dodd-Frank Act).

Liquidation.—Swaps entities that are FDIC insured institutions put into receivership or declared insolvent as a result of swap or security-based swap activity are subject to the termination or transfer of that swap or security-based swap activity, in accordance with applicable law prescribing the treatment of those contracts. No taxpayer funds may be used to prevent the receivership of any swap entity resulting from swap or security-based swap activity of the swaps entity (Sec. 716(i)(1)(A) of the Dodd-Frank Act).

Swaps entities that are institutions that pose a systemic risk and are subject to heightened prudential supervision as regulated under Section 113 of the Dodd-Frank Act, that are put into receivership or declared insolvent as a result of swap or security-based swap activity are subject to the termination or transfer of that swap or security-based swap activity, in accordance with applicable law prescribing the treatment of those contracts. No taxpayer funds may be used to prevent the receivership of any swap

¶3030

entity resulting from swap or security-based swap activity of the swaps entity (Sec. 716(i)(1)(B) of the Dodd-Frank Act).

No taxpayer resources may be used for the orderly liquidation of any swaps entities that are non-FDIC insured, non-systemically significant institutions not subject to heightened prudential supervision as regulated under Section 113 of the Dodd-Frank Act (Sec. 716(i)(1)(C) of the Dodd-Frank Act).

All funds expended on the termination or transfer of the swap or security-based swap activity of the swaps entity must be recovered in accordance with applicable law from the disposition of assets of that swap entity or through assessments, including on the financial sector as provided under applicable law (Sec. 716(i)(2) of the Dodd-Frank Act).

Taxpayers cannot bear any losses from the exercise of any authority under the derivatives title (Sec. 716(i)(3) of the Dodd-Frank Act).

Unregulated Combination of Swaps Entities and Banking.—After the adoption of rules by the prudential regulator, a bank or bank holding company cannot be or become a swap entity unless it conducts its swap or security-based swap activities in compliance with minimum standards set by its prudential regulator to permit the entity to conduct its activities in a safe and sound manner and mitigate systemic risk (Sec. 716(j) of the Dodd-Frank Act).

Rulemaking Considerations.—In prescribing rules, the prudential regulator for a swaps entity must consider the following factors: (1) the expertise and managerial strength of the swaps entity, including systems for effective oversight; (2) the financial strength of the swaps entity; (3) systems for identifying, measuring and controlling risks arising from the swaps entity's operations; (4) systems for identifying, measuring and controlling the swaps entity's participation in existing markets; and (5) systems for controlling the swaps entity's participation or entry into in new markets and products (Sec. 716(k) of the Dodd-Frank Act).

Financial Stability Oversight Council.—The Financial Stability Oversight Council (Council) may determine that, when other provisions established by the Dodd-Frank Act are insufficient to effectively mitigate systemic risk and protect taxpayers, that swaps entities may no longer access federal assistance with respect to any swap, security-based swap or other activity of the swaps entity. Any such determination by the Financial Stability Oversight Council of a prohibition of federal assistance must be made on an institution-by-institution basis, and requires the vote of not fewer than two-thirds of the members of the Financial Stability Oversight Council. The majority vote must include the vote by the chairs of the Council, the Fed and the Federal Deposit Insurance Corporation. Notice and hearing requirements for such determinations must be consistent with the standards provided in Title I of the Dodd-Frank Act (Sec. 716(l) of the Dodd-Frank Act).

Ban on Proprietary Trading in Derivatives.—An insured depository institution must comply with the prohibition on proprietary trading in derivatives as required by Section 619 of the Dodd-Frank Act (Sec. 716(m) of the Dodd-Frank Act).

▶ **Effective date.** The provision becomes effective two years after enactment (Sec. 716(h) of the Dodd-Frank Wall Street Reform and Consumer Protection Act).

Law source: Law at ¶10,716. Committee Report at ¶50,071.

— Secs. 716(a) and (b) of the Dodd-Frank Wall Street Reform and Consumer Protection Act, prohibiting federal assistance to swap entities;

— Sec. 716(c), allowing insured depository institutions to have or establish affiliates;

— Sec. 716(d), providing that banks must limit their activities to bona fide hedging and traditional bank activities;

— Sec. 716(e), providing that the prohibition on federal assistance applies only to instruments entered into after the transition period;

— Sec. 716(f), providing for a transition period;

— Sec. 716(g), providing that "swaps entity" does not include a bank or covered financial company in conservatorship, receivership or bridge bank operated by the FDIC;

— Sec. 716(h), providing the effective date;

— Sec. 716(i), providing for termination of swaps activity for banks that are in receivership or declared insolvent;

— Sec. 716(j), requiring banks to comply with rules and standards set by the prudential regulator;

— Sec. 716(k), enumerating factors the prudential regulator for a swaps entity must consider when prescribing rules;

— Sec. 716(l), providing for denial of federal assistance upon Council's determination;

— Sec. 716(m), requiring insured depository institutions to comply with Sec. 619.

¶3035 CFTC-SEC Jurisdiction; New Product Approval

The Dodd-Frank Wall Street Reform and Consumer Protection Act amends the Commodity Exchange Act (CEA) and Securities Exchange Act of 1934 (Exchange Act) to clarify overlapping jurisdiction between the Commodities Futures Trading Commission and the Securities and Exchange Commission over securities futures. It also establishes a joint regulatory process to approve new securities futures products.

Jurisdiction.—The CFTC has jurisdiction over accounts, agreements and transactions involving a put, call or other option on securities, as defined in Securities Act Section 2(a)(1) or Exchange Act Section 3(a)(10) on the date of enactment of the Futures Trading Act of 1982. The CFTC may permit the listing for trading of those securities under CEA Section 5c(c). CFTC jurisdiction includes any group or index of those securities exempted by the SEC under Exchange Act Section 36(a)(1), with the condition that the CFTC and SEC exercise concurrent jurisdiction over puts, calls or other options. The Dodd-Frank Act cannot be construed to affect the SEC's jurisdiction and authority over these puts, calls or other options (CEA Sec. 2(a)(1)(C)(i)(II), as added by Sec. 717(a) of the Dodd-Frank Wall Street Reform and Consumer Protection Act).

An agreement, contract or transaction, or class thereof, that is exempted by the CFTC under CEA Section 4(c)(1), but that remains subject to concurrent jurisdiction, is deemed a "security" for purposes of the securities laws (Exchange Act Sec. 3B(a), as added by Sec. 717(b) the Dodd-Frank Act).

New Product Approval Process.—Upon the CFTC's request, the time period within which the SEC must approve a proposed SRO rule change (or initiate proceedings to disapprove the rule change) is stayed, pending the SEC's determination whether the product that is the subject of the proposed rule change is a "security" under Section 718 of the Dodd-Frank Act (Exchange Act Sec. 19(b)(10), as added by Sec. 717(c) of the Dodd-Frank Act).

Similarly, upon the SEC's request, a certification by a self-regulatory organization that a new contract or rule complies with the CEA is stayed, pending the CFTC's determination that the product is a contract of sale of a commodity for future delivery, an option on such a contract or an option on a commodity under Section 718 of the Dodd-Frank Act (CEA Sec. 5c(c)(1), as added by Sec. 717(d) of the Dodd-Frank Act).

▶ **Effective date.** The provision takes effect 360 days after enactment (Sec. 754 of the Dodd-Frank Wall Street Reform and Consumer Protection Act).

Law source: Law at ¶10,717 and ¶10,754.

— Sec. 717(a) of the Dodd-Frank Wall Street Reform and Consumer Protection Act, amending CEA Sec. 2(a)(1)(C);

— Sec. 717(b), adding Exchange Act Sec. 3B;

— Sec. 717(c), adding Exchange Act Sec. 19(b)(10);

— Sec. 717(d), amending CEA Sec. 5c(c)(1);

— Sec. 754, providing the effective date.

¶3040 Novel Derivative Products

The Dodd-Frank Wall Street Reform and Consumer Protection Act establishes a process by which new derivatives instruments may be introduced, evaluated and approved by regulators. The process is in three parts: (1) Notice; (2) Request for Determination; and (3) Determination. The section makes reference to the Commodity Exchange Act (CEA) and Securities Exchange Act of 1934 (Exchange Act).

Notice.—A person filing a proposal to list or trade a novel derivative product that may have elements of both securities and commodity futures contracts (or options on such contracts or commodities) may notify the SEC and the CFTC and furnish a copy of the filing with both commissions. If notice is given, it must state that notice has been made to both commissions (Sec. 718(a)(1)(A) of the Dodd-Frank Wall Street Reform and Consumer Protection Act).

If no notice is given, the SEC or CFTC must notify the other commission within five business days after determining that a proposal that seeks to list or trade a novel derivative product may have elements of both securities and commodity futures contracts (or options on such contracts or commodities). The notifying commission must provide a copy of the filing (Sec. 718(a)(1)(B) of the Dodd-Frank Act).

Request for Determination.—Within 21 days of receipt of notice of a proposal to list or trade a novel derivative product, or on its own initiative if no notice is received, the CFTC may request that the SEC issue a determination as to whether the product is a security under Exchange Act Section 3(a)(10) (Sec. 718(a)(2)(A) of the Dodd-Frank

Act). Similarly, within 21 days of receipt of notice of a proposal to list or trade a novel derivative product, or on its own initiative if no notice is received, the SEC may request that the CFTC issue a determination as to whether the product is a contract of sale of a commodity for future delivery, an option on such a contract, or an on option on a commodity subject to the CFTC's exclusive jurisdiction under CEA Section 2(a)(1)(A) (Sec. 718(a)(2)(B) of the Dodd-Frank Act). Requests for determination must be in writing (Sec. 718(a)(2)(C) of the Dodd-Frank Act).

The Act does not prevent exemptions by the SEC under Exchange Act Section 36(a)(1) or by the CFTC under CEA Section 4(c)(1). Further, exemptions under these statutes are not subject to the judicial review resolution procedure to which novel derivative product determinations are subject. The Act does not require the SEC or CFTC to issue exemptions (Sec. 718(a)(2)(D) of the Dodd-Frank Act).

The SEC or CFTC may withdraw a request for determination at any time before the determination is made by providing written notice to the head of the other commission (Sec. 718(a)(2)(E) of the Dodd-Frank Act).

Determination.—Within 120 days of receiving a request for determination, the SEC or CFTC must make a determination or grant an exemption. If an exemption is not granted, the commission must explain why, except that a decision by the SEC is not reviewable under Exchange Act Section 25 (Sec. 718(a)(3) of the Dodd-Frank Act).

Judicial Review.—The CFTC or SEC may petition the United States Court of Appeals for the District of Columbia Circuit for review of a final order of the other commission regarding a novel derivative product with securities and commodities futures elements, if the commission believes the order may affect its statutory jurisdiction. The petition must be filed within 60 days after the date of entry of the order. The proceeding must be expedited by the Court of Appeals (Sec. 718(b)(1) of the Dodd-Frank Act).

A copy of the petition must be transmitted to the responding commission within one business day. On receipt of the petition, the responding commission must file a copy of the order and any associated documents with the court (Sec. 718(b)(2) of the Dodd-Frank Act).

The court will not give deference to the views of either agency (Sec. 718(b)(3) of the Dodd-Frank Act). The filing of a petition with the court operates as a stay of the order, until the dispute is resolved by the court (Sec. 718(b)(4) of the Dodd-Frank Act).

▶ **Effective date.** The provision takes effect 360 days after enactment (Sec. 754 of the Dodd-Frank Wall Street Reform and Consumer Protection Act).

Law source: Law at ¶10,718 and ¶10,754.

— Sec. 718(a)(1) of the Dodd-Frank Wall Street Reform and Consumer Protection Act, providing for notice to CFTC and SEC;

— Sec. 718(a)(2) providing for requests for determination;

— Sec. 718(a)(3), providing for determination by CFTC and SEC;

— Sec. 718(b), providing for judicial review of commission orders;

— Sec. 754, providing the effective date.

¶3045 Conflicts of Interest

The Dodd-Frank Wall Street Reform and Consumer Protection Act requires the CFTC and SEC to adopt rules on conflicts of interest. The legislation also requires futures commission merchants (FCMs) and introducing brokers (IBs) to reduce conflicts of interest.

> **CCH Comment:** There was concern that, with derivatives trading required to be conducted through clearinghouses, large financial institutions would own and control the clearinghouses and effectively set rules for their own derivatives deals. In a colloquy with Rep. Stephen Lynch (D-MA), House Financial Services Committee Chair Barney Frank (D-MA) agreed that Sections 726 and 765 of the Dodd-Frank Act require the CFTC and SEC to adopt rules eliminating the conflicts of interest arising from the control of clearing and trading facilities by entities such as swap dealers, security-based swap dealers and major swap participants and major security-based swap participants. SEC and CFTC adoption of strong conflict of interest rules on control and governance of clearing and trading facilities is mandatory. According to Rep. Lynch, the rulemaking is necessary because 95 percent of the clearinghouses are owned by just five banks and Congress is relying on the clearinghouses to reduce systemic risk (Cong. Rec., June 30, 2010, p. H5217).

CFTC Rulemaking.—Within 180 days of enactment, the CFTC must adopt rules to mitigate conflicts of interest in specified entities. The rules may include numerical limits on the control of the entities, or voting rights with respect to the entities. Specified entities include any derivatives clearing organization that clears swaps, or swap execution facility or board of trade designated as a contract market that posts swaps or makes swaps available for trading. Restrictions may be imposed on the control of these entities by (1) a bank holding company with assets of $50 billion or more; (2) a nonbank financial company supervised by the Board of Governors of the Federal Reserve System (the Fed); (3) an affiliate of such a bank holding company or nonbank financial company; or (4) a swap dealer, major swap participant or associated person of a swap dealer or major swap participant (Sec. 726(a) of the Dodd-Frank Wall Street Reform and Consumer Protection Act).

The CFTC must adopt rules if it deems it necessary to improve governance, mitigate systemic risk, promote competition or mitigate conflicts of interest in connection with a swap dealer or major swap participant's interaction with a (1) derivatives clearing organization; (2) contract market; or (3) swap execution facility that clears or posts swaps or makes swaps available for trading and in which such swap dealer or major swap participant has a material debt or equity investment (Sec. 726(b) of the Dodd-Frank Act).

In adopting rules, the CFTC must consider conflicts of interest arising from: (1) the amount of equity owned by a single investor; (2) the ability to vote, cause the vote of, or withhold votes entitled to be cast by the holders of the ownership interest; and (3) the governance arrangements of the specified entities (Sec. 726(c) of the Dodd-Frank Act).

SEC Rulemaking.—Within 180 days after enactment, the SEC must adopt rules to mitigate conflicts of interest in specified entities. The rules may include numerical limits on the control of the entities, or voting rights with respect to the entities. Specified entities include any clearing agency that clears security-based swaps, security-based swap execution facility and national securities exchange that posts or makes available for trading security-based swaps. Restrictions may be imposed on the control of these entities by: (1) a bank holding company with total assets of $50 billion or more; (2) a nonbank financial company supervised by the Fed; (3) an affiliate of the bank holding company or nonbank financial company; (4) a security-based swap dealer, major security-based swap participant; or (5) person associated with a security-based swap dealer or major security-based swap participant (Sec. 765(a) of the Dodd-Frank Act).

The SEC must adopt rules if it determines that rules are necessary to improve governance, mitigate systemic risk, promote competition or mitigate conflicts of interest in connection with a security-based swap dealer or major security-based swap participant's dealings with a: (1) clearing agency; (2) national security exchange; or (3) security-based swap execution facility that clears, posts or trades security-based swaps, in which the security-based swap dealer or major security-based swap participant has a material debt or equity investment (Sec. 765(b) of the Dodd-Frank Act).

In adopting rules, the SEC must consider conflicts of interest arising from: (1) the amount of equity owned by a single investor; (2) the ability to vote, cause the vote of, or withhold votes entitled to be cast by the holders of the ownership interest; and (3) the governance arrangements of the specified entities (Sec. 726(c) of the Dodd-Frank Act).

FCMs and IBs.—Futures commission merchants (FCMs) and introducing brokers (IBs) must implement systems and procedures to separate research and analysis functions from review, pressure or oversight by individuals whose involvement in trading or clearing activities might bias their judgment or supervision (CEA Sec. 4d(c), as amended by Sec. 732 of the Dodd-Frank Act).

FCMs must designate a chief compliance officer. The officer must perform duties as set forth in rules to be adopted by the CFTC or a futures association registered under CEA Section 17 (CEA Sect. 4d(d), as amended by Sec. 732 of the Dodd-Frank Act).

▶ **Effective date.** Provisions requiring CFTC and SEC rulemaking take effect on the later of: (1) 360 days after enactment; or (2) 60 days after publication of the final implementing rules. Provisions regarding futures commission merchants and introducing brokers take effect 360 days after enactment (Sec. 754 of the Dodd-Frank Wall Street Reform and Consumer Protection Act).

Law source: Law at ¶10,726, ¶10,732, ¶10,765, ¶10,754 and ¶10,774.

— Sec. 726(a) of the Dodd-Frank Wall Street Reform and Consumer Protection Act, requiring CFTC rules on control of certain swaps entities by certain financial entities;

— Sec. 726(b), requiring CFTC rules as necessary to improve governance, mitigate risk, promote competition or mitigate conflicts of interest;

— Sec. 726(c), listing conflicts of interest the CFTC must consider;

— Sec. 732, redesignating existing CEA Sec. 4d(c) as 4(d)(e) and adding new Secs. 4d(c) and 4(d)(d).

— Sec. 765(a), requiring the SEC to adopt rules on control of certain securities-based swaps entities by certain financial entities;

— Sec. 765(b), requiring the SEC to adopt rules if it finds it necessary to improve governance, mitigate risk, promote competition or mitigate conflicts of interest;

— Sec. 765(c), listing conflicts of interest the SEC must consider;

— Secs. 754 and 774, providing the effective date.

¶3050 Studies and Reports

The Dodd-Frank Wall Street Reform and Consumer Protection Act requires the CFTC and SEC to conduct certain studies.

Position Limits.—The CFTC must consult with designated contract markets to study the effects of position limits on excessive speculation and migration of capital to trading venues abroad (Sec. 719(a) of the Dodd-Frank Wall Street Reform and Consumer Protection Act).

The CFTC must submit a report to Congress within twelve months of the imposition of position limits pursuant to the Dodd-Frank Act. Subsequently, the House of Representatives Committee on Agriculture must hold a hearing examining the report findings, within 30 days of receiving the report (Sec. 719(a) of the Dodd-Frank Act).

In addition, the CFTC Chair must submit to Congress biennial reports on the growth or decline of the derivatives markets in the United States and abroad, including assessments of various factors. In preparing the report, the Chair must consult with market participants, regulators, legislators and other interested parties (Sec. 719(a) of the Dodd-Frank Act).

Standardizing Algorithmic Descriptions.—The CFTC and SEC must conduct a joint study on the feasibility of requiring the derivatives industry to adopt standardized computer-readable algorithmic descriptions that may be used to describe complex and standardized financial derivatives. The agencies must submit a report on the study's findings to certain House and Senate committees within 8 months after enactment (Sec. 719(b) of the Dodd-Frank Act).

International Swap Regulation.—The CFTC and SEC must conduct a joint study on swap, clearing house and clearing agency regulation in the United States, Asia and Europe. The report must identify similar areas of regulation in the three regions that can be harmonized. The study must include examination of certain topics. The agencies must submit a report on the study's findings to certain House and Senate committees within 18 months of enactment (Sec. 719(c) of the Dodd-Frank Act).

Stable Value Contracts.—Within 15 months of enactment, the CFTC and SEC must conduct a joint study to determine whether stable value contracts fall within the definition of a swap. The commissions must consult with certain other agencies. If the commissions determine that stable value contracts fall within the definition of a swap, the commissions must jointly determine if an exemption for stable value contracts is appropriate and in the public interest. The commissions must issue regulations implementing the determinations. Until the effective date of the regulations, the requirements of the derivatives title will not apply to stable value contracts. Stable value contracts in effect prior to the effective date of the new regulations will not be considered swaps. For purposes of the subsection, a definition is provided for the term "stable value contract" (Sec. 719(d) of the Dodd-Frank Act).

Carbon Markets.—The Dodd-Frank Act establishes an interagency working group consisting of the following members: (1) CFTC Chair, who will serve as Chair of the interagency group; (2) Secretary of Agriculture; (3) Treasury Secretary; (4) SEC Chair; (4) Administrator of the Environmental Protection Agency; (5) Chair of the Federal Energy Regulatory Commission; (6) Commissioner of the Federal Trade Commission; and (7) Administrator of the Energy Information Administration (Sec. 750(a) of the Dodd-Frank Act).

The group must conduct a study on the oversight of existing and prospective carbon markets, including spot markets and derivative markets (Sec. 750(d) of the Dodd-Frank Act).

The interagency group must consult with representatives of exchanges, clearinghouses, self-regulatory bodies, major carbon market participants, consumers and the general public, as the group deems appropriate (Sec. 750(c) of the Dodd-Frank Act).

Within 180 days after enactment, the group must submit a report to Congress detailing its findings, including recommendations for the oversight of existing and prospective carbon markets to ensure an efficient, secure and transparent carbon market, including oversight of spot markets and derivative markets (Sec. 750(e) of the Dodd-Frank Act).

▶ **Effective date.** The agencies must complete studies within timeframes as specified by subsection.

Law source: Law at ¶10,719 and ¶10,750. Committee Report at ¶50,071.

— Sec. 719(a) of the Dodd-Frank Wall Street Reform and Consumer Protection Act, requiring the CFTC to study the effect of position limits;

— Sec. 719(b), requiring the CFTC and SEC to study the feasibility of requiring standardized algorithmic descriptions of derivatives products;

— Sec. 719(c), requiring the CFTC and SEC to study certain areas of international regulation relating to swaps and clearing;

— Sec. 719(d), requiring the CFTC and SEC to study whether stable value contracts fall within the definition of a swap;

— Secs. 750(a)–(e), providing for study of the carbon markets by a newly-established interagency working group;

SWAP MARKETS

¶3060 Clearing

The Dodd-Frank Wall Street Reform and Consumer Protection Act amends the Commodity Exchange Act (CEA) to provide for clearing of swaps.

Repeal of Existing Provisions.—Existing provisions regarding the following are repealed: excluded derivatives transactions, excluded electronic trading facilities, swap transactions and transactions in exempt commodities (CEA Secs. 2(d), (e), (g) and (h), as struck by Sec. 723(a) of the Dodd-Frank Wall Street Reform and Consumer Protection Act).

Except for an extensive list of exceptions, the CEA does not govern or apply to swaps (CEA Sec. 2(d), as added by the Sec. 723(a)(2) of the Dodd-Frank Act).

Mandatory Clearing of Swaps.—The legislation makes it unlawful for any person other than an eligible contract participant to enter into a swap unless the swap is entered into, or subject to the rules of, a board of trade designated as a contract market under CEA Section 5 (CEA Sec. 2(e), as added by Sec. 723(a)(2) of the Dodd-Frank Act).

If a swap must be cleared, it is unlawful to engage in a swap without submitting the swap for clearing to a derivatives clearing organization (DCO) registered under the CEA, or to a DCO exempt from registration under CEA Section 5b(h). The rules of a DCO must provide that all swaps with the same terms and conditions are economically equivalent within the DCO and may be offset with each other within the DCO. The rules must also provide for nondiscriminatory clearing of a swap executed bilaterally or on or through the rules of an unaffiliated designated contract market or swap execution facility. These rules do not apply to commodity futures contracts or options (CEA Secs. 2(h)(1)(A) and (B), as added by the Sec. 723(a)(3) of the Dodd-Frank Act).

The CFTC must review on an ongoing basis each swap or group of swaps to determine whether the swap should be required to cleared. The CFTC must provide at least a 30-day public comment period regarding any determination. A DCO must submit to the CFTC any swap or category of swaps the DCO plans to accept for clearing, and provide notice to its members of the submission. Any swap listed as of enactment is deemed submitted. The CFTC must: (1) make submissions available to the public; (2) review each submission and determine whether the swap must be cleared; and (3) provide at least a 30-day public comment period regarding its determination. The CFTC must make its determination within 90 days of receiving a submission, unless the DCO agrees to an extension (CEA Sec. 2(h)(2)(A)–(C), as added by the Sec. 723(a)(3) of the Dodd-Frank Act).

CFTC Determination.—In reviewing a submission, the CFTC must review whether the submission is consistent with CEA Section 5b(c)(2). The CFTC must consider specified factors and may impose conditions on approval. The CFTC must approve, unconditionally or subject to terms and conditions, any request for clearing approval if the CFTC finds it consistent with Section 5(b)(c)(2). The CFTC cannot approve a request without this finding. Within one year of enactment, the CFTC must adopt rules for a DCO's submission of swaps it seeks to accept for clearing (CEA Sec. 2(h)(2)(D)–(E), as added by the Sec. 723(a)(3) of the Dodd-Frank Act).

After making a determination that a swap must be cleared, the CFTC may stay its determination pending review. The CFTC must complete review within 90 days, unless the DCO agrees to an extension. Upon completion of review, the CFTC may determine that the swap or class of swaps must be cleared, if it finds that clearing is consistent with a positive determination. Alternatively, the CFTC may determine that clearing is not required (CEA Sec. 2(h)(3)(A)–(C), as added by Sec. 723(a)(3) of the Dodd-Frank Act).

Within one year of enactment, the CFTC must adopt rules governing review. The CFTC must prescribe rules to prevent evasion of the mandatory clearing requirements. If the CFTC finds that a class of swaps is subject to the clearing requirement but has not been submitted for approval, the CFTC must investigate, issue a public report within 30 days, and take any necessary actions. The Act does not require the CFTC to adopt rules requiring a DCO to list a swap or class of swaps for clearing, if doing so would threaten the financial integrity of the DCO (CEA Sec. 2(h)(3)(D), as added by Sec. 723(a)(3) of the Dodd-Frank Act).

Swaps entered into before enactment must be reported to a swap data repository within 180 days of the effective date of the Act. Swaps entered into on after enactment must be reported to a swap data repository within 90 days of the effective date, or within a time prescribed by the CFTC. Swaps entered into before enactment, and swaps entered into before application of the clearing requirement, are exempt from clearing requirements if reported according to reporting requirements (CEA Sec. 2(h)(5)–(6), as added by Sec. 723(a)(3) of the Dodd-Frank Act).

Exception from Clearing Requirement.—The clearing requirement does not apply to a swap if one of the counterparties to the swap is not a *financial entity*, is using swaps to hedge or mitigate commercial risk, and notifies the CFTC how it generally meets its financial obligations associated with entering into non-cleared swaps. The application of the clearing exception is solely at the discretion of the counterparty that meets these conditions (CEA Sec. 2(h)(7), as added by Sec. 723(a)(3) of the Dodd-Frank Act).

"Financial entity" defined. The term "financial entity" means:

- a swap dealer;
- a security-based swap dealer;
- a major swap participant;
- a major security-based swap participant;
- a commodity pool
- a private fund as defined in Advisers Act Section 202(a);
- an employee benefit plan as defined in Employment Retirement Income Security Act Sections 3(3) and 3(32);
- a person predominantly engaged in the business of banking, or in activities that are financial in nature, as defined in Bank Holding Company Act Section 4(k) (CEA Sec. 2(h)(7), as added by Sec. 723(a)(3) of the Dodd-Frank Act).

The definition of "financial entity" does not include an entity whose primary business is providing financing, and uses derivatives for the purpose of hedging underlying commercial risks related to interest rate and foreign currency exposures, 90 percent or more of which are manufactured by the parent company or another subsidiary (CEA Sec. 2(h)(7), as added by Sec. 723(a)(3) of the Dodd-Frank Act).

Consideration for Exemption. The CFTC must consider whether to exempt small banks, savings associations, farm credit system institutions and credit unions, including:

- depository institutions with total assets of $10 billion or less;
- farm credit system institutions with total assets of $10 billion or less; or
- credit unions with total assets of $10 billion or less (CEA Sec. 2(h)(7), as added by Sec. 723(a)(3) of the Dodd-Frank Act).

In a colloquy with Rep. Tim Holden (D-PA), House Agriculture Chair Collin Peterson (D-MN) agreed that, with regard to language requiring the CFTC to consider exempt-

¶3060

ing small banks, Farm Credit System institutions, and credit unions from provisions requiring that all swaps be cleared, the Act's special emphasis on institutions with less than $10 billion in assets should not in any way be viewed by the CFTC as a limit on the size of the institution that should be considered for an exemption. The language says that institutions to be considered for the exemption must include those with $10 billion or less in assets. According to Chairman Peterson, it is not a firm standard. Some firms with larger assets could qualify, while some with smaller assets may not. The regulators will have maximum flexibility when looking at the risk portfolio of these institutions for consideration of an exemption (Cong. Rec., June 30, 2010, p. H5246).

Affiliates. An affiliate of a person that qualifies for a clearing exception may qualify for the exception only if the affiliate, acting on behalf of the person and as an agent, uses the swap to hedge or mitigate the commercial risk of the person or other affiliate of the person that is not a financial entity (CEA Sec. 2(h)(7), as added by Sec. 723(a)(3) of the Dodd-Frank Act). The affiliate exception does not apply if the affiliate is:

- a swap dealer;
- a security-based swap dealer;
- a major swap participant;
- a major security-based swap participant;
- an issuer that would be an investment company, as defined in Investment Company Act Section 3, but for paragraph (c)(1) or (c)(7);
- a commodity pool; or
- a bank holding company with over $50 billion in consolidated assets (CEA Sec. 2(h)(7), as added by Sec. 723(a)(3) of the Dodd-Frank Act).

An affiliate, subsidiary or a wholly owned entity of a person that qualifies for an exception and is predominantly engaged in providing financing for the purchase or lease of merchandise or manufactured goods of the person is exempt from the margin requirement described in section 4s(e) and the clearing requirement described in paragraph (1) with regard to swaps entered into to mitigate the risk of the financing activities for not less than a 2-year period beginning on the date of enactment (CEA Sec. 2(h)(7), as added by Sec. 723(a)(3) of the Dodd-Frank Act).

For swaps required to be cleared and that are entered into by a swap dealer or major swap dealer with a counterparty that is not a swap dealer, major swap participant, security-based swap dealer, or major security-based swap participant, the counterparty has the sole right to select the DCO at which the swap will be cleared. For swaps that are not required to be cleared, and are entered into by a swap dealer or major swap participant with a counterparty that is not a swap dealer, major swap participant, security-based swap dealer, or major security-based swap participant, the counterparty may elect to require clearing of the swap. If a counterparty chooses to require clearing, it has sole discretion to select the DCO at which the swap will be cleared (CEA Sec. 2(h)(7), as added by Sec. 723(a)(3) of the Dodd-Frank Act).

The CFTC may prescribe such rules or issue interpretations of the rules it deems necessary to prevent abuse of exceptions. The Commission may also request information from persons claiming the clearing exception as necessary to prevent abuse of exceptions (CEA Sec. 2(h)(7), as added by Sec. 723(a)(3) of the Dodd-Frank Act).

For a counterparty that is an issuer of securities registered under Exchange Act Section 12, or must file reports under Exchange Act Section 15(d), executing and clearing exemptions are available only if an appropriate committee of the issuer's board or governing body has reviewed and approved its decision to enter into swaps subject to these exemptions (CEA Sec. 2(j), as added by Sec. 723(b) of the Dodd-Frank Act).

Trade Execution.—For swaps subject to the clearing requirement, the counterparties must execute the transaction on a board of trade designated as a contract market under CEA Section 5, or execute the transaction on a swap execution facility registered or exempt under CEA Section 5h. However, this requirement does not apply if no board of trade or swap execution facility makes the swap available to trade, or if the swap is subject to a clearing exception (CEA Sec. 2(h)(8), as added by Sec. 723(a)(3) of the Dodd-Frank Act).

Grandfather Provisions.—Within 60 days of enactment, a person may petition the CFTC to remain subject to CEA Section 2(h) as in effect on the day before the date of enactment of the Dodd-Frank Act. The CFTC must consider the petition promptly and may allow the person to continue operating subject to the old provisions for up to one year after the effective date of the subtitle (Secs. 723(c)(1) and (2) of the Dodd-Frank Act).

Agricultural Swaps. No person may enter into or confirm execution of an agricultural swap, except under CEA Section 4(c) or CFTC rule permitting these swaps (Sec. 723(c)(3) of the Dodd-Frank Act).

Required Reporting. If no facility makes a swap available to trade, the counterparties must comply with any recordkeeping and transaction reporting requirements prescribed by the CFTC with respect to swaps subject to CEA Section 2(h)(8)(B) (Sec. 723(c)(4) of the Dodd-Frank Act).

▶ **Effective date.** The provision takes effect 360 days after enactment, except for Section 723(a)(3), which takes effect on the later of: (1) 360 days after enactment; or (2) 60 days after publication of the final implementing rules (Sec. 754 of the Dodd-Frank Wall Street Reform and Consumer Protection Act).

Law source: Law at ¶10,723 and ¶10,754. Committee Report at ¶50,071.

— Sec. 723(a)(1) of the Dodd-Frank Wall Street Reform and Consumer Protection Act, striking CEA Secs. 2(d), (e), (g) and (h);

— Sec. 723(a)(2), adding CEA Secs. 2(d), (e) and (h);

— Sec. 723(b), adding CEA Sec. 2(j);

— Sec. 723(c), listing grandfather provisions;

— Sec. 754, providing the effective date.

¶3065 Swaps, Segregation and Bankruptcy Treatment

The Dodd-Frank Wall Street Reform and Consumer Protection Act amends the Commodity Exchange Act (CEA) to provide for treatment of swap customer funds held by futures commission merchants (FCMs). The legislation also provides for bankruptcy treatment of cleared swaps.

Treatment of Swap Customer Funds.—A person that holds assets from or for customers to margin or guarantee swaps cleared by a derivatives clearing organization (DCO) must register as an FCM (CEA Sec. 4d(f)(1), as added by Sec. 724(a) of the Dodd-Frank Wall Street Reform and Consumer Protection Act).

FCMs must segregate funds belonging to the swaps customer. FCMs must separately account for property of a swap customer. Swap funds cannot be commingled with the FCM's funds or used to margin or guarantee trades of any other customer (CEA Sec. 4d(f)(2), as added by Sec. 724(a) of the Dodd-Frank Act).

Property of a swaps customer may, for convenience, be commingled or deposited in the same account or accounts with any bank, trust company or DCO. This property may be withdrawn in the normal course of business and applied to purposes lawfully accruing in connection with the cleared swap, or as permitted by CFTC rule. Property of a swaps customer may be invested in certain government debt instruments or other investments in accordance with CFTC rules (CEA Secs. 4d(f)(3) and (4), as added by Sec. 724(a) of the Dodd-Frank Act).

A swap cleared by or through a DCO is considered a commodity contract as defined under 11 U.S.C. §761, with regard to all property of a swaps customer received by an FCM to margin or guarantee the swap. It is unlawful for any person, including a DCO or depository institution, that has received property for deposit in a separate account or accounts, to hold or use this money as belonging to the FCM or any person other than the swaps customer of the FCM (CEA Secs. 4d(f)(5) and (6), as added by 724(a) of the Dodd-Frank Act).

The legislation amends the U.S. Bankruptcy Code to include contracts cleared by clearing organizations, and with respect to FCMs, expands the term "commodity futures account" to "commodity contract account" (11 U.S.C. §761, as amended by Sec. 724(b) of the Dodd-Frank Act).

Segregation Requirements for Uncleared Swaps.—A swap dealer or major swap participant must notify the counterparty at the beginning of a swap transaction that the counterparty has the right to require segregation of the funds provided to margin or guarantee the swap. If the counterparty requests it, the swap dealer or major swap participant must segregate the funds. Segregated accounts must be carried by an independent third-party custodian and designated as a segregated account for the behalf of the counterparty (CEA Sec. 4s(l)(1),(3) as added by Sec. 724(c) of the Dodd-Frank Act).

These requirements apply only to a swap between a swap dealer or major swap participant that is not submitted for clearing to a DCO. Segregation requirements also do not apply to variation margin payments, and do not preclude a commercial arrangement regarding investment of segregated funds, or the allocation of gains and losses resulting from investment of the funds. If the counterparty chooses not to require segregation of the funds, the swap dealer or major swap participant must quarterly report to the counterparty that its back office procedures relating to margin and collateral requirements are in compliance with the agreement of the counterparties (CEA Secs. 4s(l)(2) and (4), as added by Sec. 724(c) of the Dodd-Frank Act).

▶ **Effective date.** The provision takes effect 360 days after enactment (Sec. 754 of the Dodd-Frank Wall Street Reform and Consumer Protection Act).

Law source: Law at ¶10,724 and ¶10,754. Committee Report at ¶50,071.

— Sec. 724(a) of the Dodd-Frank Wall Street Reform and Consumer Protection Act, adding CEA Sec. 4d(f);

— Sec. 724(b), amending 11 U.S.C. §761;

— Sec. 724(c), adding CEA Sec. 4s(l);

— Sec. 754, providing the effective date.

¶3070 Derivatives Clearing Organizations

The Dodd-Frank Wall Street Reform and Consumer Protection Act amends the Commodity Exchange Act (CEA) to provide for registration and governance of derivatives clearing organizations (DCOs).

Registration.—A clearinghouse that clears non-exempt non-security-based swaps must register with the CFTC as a DCO. A clearinghouse that clears swaps not required to be cleared may voluntarily register as a DCO (CEA Secs. 5b(a) and (b) as amended by Sec. 725(a) of the Dodd-Frank Wall Street Reform and Consumer Protection Act).

An existing depository institution or clearing agency is deemed registered to the extent that, before enactment, a depository institution cleared swaps as a multilateral clearing organization or the clearing agency cleared swaps. A depository institution meeting this requirement may, by vote of shareholders owning at least 51 percent of the voting interests, be converted into a state corporation, partnership, limited liability company or similar legal form, if the conversion does not contravene applicable state law (CEA Sec. 5b(g), as added by Sec. 725(b) of the Dodd-Frank Act).

The SEC must make available to the CFTC all information it determines relevant regarding a clearing agency deemed registered under this section (CEA Sec. 5b(g), as added by Sec. 725(b) of the Dodd-Frank Act).

The CFTC may exempt a DCO from registration requirements if it finds the DCO is subject to comparable supervision and regulation by the SEC or appropriate government authorities in the organization's home country (CEA Sec. 5b(h), as added by Sec. 725(b) of the Dodd-Frank Act).

Core Principles.—DCOs must comply with a series of core principles in the following areas: (1) compliance; (2) financial resources; (3) participant and product eligibility; (4) risk management; (5) settlement procedures; (6) treatment of funds and assets; (7) default rules and procedures; (8) rule enforcement; (9) system safeguards; (10) reporting; (11) recordkeeping; (12) public disclosure of information; (13) information-sharing; (14) antitrust considerations; (15) governance fitness standards; (16) conflicts of interest; (17) composition of governing boards; and (18) legal risk (CEA Sec. 5b(c)(2), as amended by Sec. 725(c) of the Dodd-Frank Act).

DCOs must designate a chief compliance officer, who, among other duties, must prepare and sign an annual compliance report in accordance with CFTC rules (CEA Sec. 5b(j), as added by Sec. 725(b) of the Dodd-Frank Act).

The CFTC must adopt rules mitigating conflicts of interest involving the interaction of a swap dealer or major swap participant with a DCO, board of trade or swap execution facility that clears or trades swaps in which the swap dealer or major swap participant has a material debt or equity investment (Sec. 725(d) of the Dodd-Frank Act).

Reporting Requirements.—DCOs that clear swaps must provide all information to the CFTC deemed necessary by the CFTC. The CFTC must adopt data collection and maintenance requirements for swaps cleared by DCOs comparable to the corresponding requirements for swaps data reported to swap data repositories and swaps traded on swap execution facilities (CEA Secs. 5b(k)(1) and (2), as added by Sec. 725(e) of the Dodd-Frank Act).

A DCO that clears security-based swaps as defined in Exchange Act Section 1a(47)(A)(v) must, upon request, open its books and records to the SEC, consistent with confidential and disclosure requirements of Section 8. This does not affect the exclusive jurisdiction of the CFTC to prescribe recordkeeping and reporting requirements for a DCO registered with the CFTC (CEA Sec. 5b(k)(3), as added by Sec. 725(e) of the Dodd-Frank Act).

Subject to confidentiality and disclosure provisions and upon request, the CFTC must share information collected above with the following: the Fed; the SEC; each prudential regulator; the Financial Stability Oversight Council; the Department of Justice; and any other person the CFTC deems appropriate, including foreign regulators, foreign central banks and foreign ministries (CEA Sec. 5b(k)(4), as added by Sec. 725(e) of the Dodd-Frank Act).

Before the CFTC may share this information, it must receive a written agreement from each entity stating that it will abide by the confidentiality requirements of CEA Section 8, and that it will indemnify the CFTC for any expenses arising from litigation relating to the information provided (CEA Sec. 5b(k)(5), as added by Sec. 725(e) of the Dodd-Frank Act).

DCOs that clear swaps must provide to the CFTC information in form and frequency as necessary to comply with public reporting requirements specified in CEA Section 2(a)(13) (CEA Sec. 5b(k)(6), as added by Sec. 725(e) of the Dodd-Frank Act).

Legal Certainty for Identified Banking Products.—There was legislative and regulatory concern that if only federal banking agencies could except identified banking products from exclusion, then foreign banks not subject to oversight by any federal banking regulator could offer OTC derivatives to U.S. persons in the guise of "bank products." Therefore, the SEC Chair urged that the legislation clarify that the same exceptions from exclusion are not available to foreign banks or their subsidiaries not subject to federal banking oversight (Testimony of SEC Chair Mary Schapiro before the Senate Agriculture Committee, Sept. 22, 2009).

The legislation amends the Legal Certainty for Bank Products Act of 2000 (7 U.S.C. § 27 *et seq.*) to provide that the CEA does not apply to identified banking products, and the CFTC will not exercise regulatory authority over these products (Sec. 403(a)(1) of the

Legal Certainty for Bank Products Act of 2000, as amended by Sec. 725(g) of the Dodd-Frank Act).

The definitions of "security-based swap" in Exchange Act Section 3(a)(68) and "security-based swap agreement" in CEA Section 1a(47)(A)(v) and Exchange Act. Section 3(a)(78) do not include any identified banking product (Sec. 403(a)(2) of the Legal Certainty for Bank Products Act of 2000, 7 U.S.C. §27a, as amended by the Sec. 725(g) of the Dodd-Frank Act).

An appropriate federal banking agency may except an identified banking product from the above exclusion if the agency determines, in consultation with the CFTC and SEC, that: (1) the product meets the definition of a "swap" under CEA Section 1a(47) or "security-based swap" under Exchange Act Section 3(a)(68); or (2) has become known to the trade as a swap or security-based swap, or has been structured as an identified banking product for the purposes of evading the CEA, Exchange Act or Securities Act (Sec. 403(b) of the Legal Certainty for Bank Products Act of 2000, 7 U.S.C. §27a, as amended by the Sec. 725(g) of the Dodd-Frank Act).

The above exclusions do not apply to an identified banking product that: (1) is a product of a bank not under the regulatory jurisdiction of an appropriate federal banking agency; (2) meets the definition of "swap" under CEA Section 1a(47) or "security-based swap" under Exchange Act Section 3(a)(68); and (3) has become known to the trade as a swap or security-based swap, or has been structured as an identified banking product for the purposes of evading the CEA, Exchange Act or Securities Act of 1933 (Sec. 403(c) of the Legal Certainty for Bank Products Act of 2000, 7 U.S.C. §27a, as amended by the Sec. 725(g) of the Dodd-Frank Act).

Under no circumstances may a DCO be forced to accept the counterparty credit risk of another clearing organization (CEA Sec. 5b(f)(1), as added by Sec. 725(g) of the Dodd-Frank Act).

The legislation repeals certain provisions of the Federal Deposit Insurance Corporation Improvement Act of 1991 governing multilateral clearing organizations (Sec. 740 of the Dodd-Frank Act).

▶ **Effective date.** The provision takes effect 360 days after enactment, except for Section 725(d), which takes effect on the later of: (1) 360 days after enactment; or (2) 60 days after publication of the final implementing rules (Sec. 754 of the Dodd-Frank Wall Street Reform and Consumer Protection Act).

Law source: Law at ¶10,725, ¶10,740 and ¶10,754. Committee Report at ¶50,071.

— Sec. 725(a) of the Dodd-Frank Wall Street Reform and Consumer Protection Act, amending CEA Sec. 5b(a), 5b(b);

— Sec. 725(b), adding CEA Secs. 5b(g)–(j);

— Sec. 725(c), amending CEA Sec. 5b(c)(2);

— Sec. 725(d), requiring the CFTC to adopt rules mitigating conflict of interest involving certain entities;

— Sec. 725(e), adding CEA Secs. 5b(k)(1)–(6);

— Sec. 725(g), amending Legal Certainty for Bank Products Act Sec. 403 and making conforming amendments;

— Sec. 725(h), amending CEA Sec. 5b(f)(1).

— Sec. 740, repealing provisions of the Federal Deposit Insurance Corporation Improvement Act of 1991;

— Sec. 754, providing the effective date.

¶3075 Public Reporting of Swap Transaction Data

The Dodd-Frank Wall Street Reform and Consumer Protection Act amends the Commodity Exchange Act (CEA) to provide for public reporting of swap transaction data. The purpose of the provision is to authorize the CFTC to make swap transaction and pricing data available to the public, in a form and timeframe the CFTC determines appropriate to enhance price discovery (CEA Sec. 2(a)(13)(B), as added by Sec. 727 of the Dodd-Frank Wall Street Reform and Consumer Protection Act).

The CFTC must provide by rule for the public availability of swap transaction and pricing. The CFTC must require real-time reporting for the following transactions: (1) swaps subject to mandatory clearing requirements; (2) swaps not subject to mandatory clearing that are cleared at a registered DCO; and (3) swaps exempt from the requirements of subsection of (h)(1). For swaps not subject to the mandatory clearing requirement that are reported to a swap repository or the CFTC, the CFTC must make aggregate data publicly available in a manner that does not disclose any participant's business transactions or market positions (CEA Sec. 2(a)(13)(C), as added by Sec. 727 of the Dodd-Frank Act).

"Real time reporting" means the reporting of data on the swap transaction as soon as technologically practicable after its execution (CEA Sec. 2(a)(13)(A), as added by Sec. 727 of the Dodd-Frank Act).

The CFTC may require registered entities to publicly disseminate swap transaction and pricing data. The CFTC must include rule provisions to ensure that participants are not identified. The CFTC must also specify criteria for determining what constitutes a large notional swap transaction for particular markets, with appropriate time delays of the reporting of such large notional swap transactions. Additionally, the CFTC must take into account when promulgating the rule whether the public disclosure would materially reduce market liquidity (CEA Secs. 2(a)(13)(D) and (E), as added by Sec. 727 of the Dodd-Frank Act).

Parties to a swap transaction and their agents are responsible for the timely reporting of swap transaction information to the proper registered entity under CFTC rules (CEA Sec. 2(a)(13)(F), as added by Sec. 727 of the Dodd-Frank Act).

The CFTC must issue semiannual and annual reports on the trading and clearing of major swap categories, market participants and development of new products. In preparing these reports, the Commission must use information from swap data repositories and derivatives clearing organizations and consult with the Office of the Comptroller of the Currency and the Bank for International Settlements, and such other regulators as necessary. The CFTC may delegate its public reporting responsibilities as deems appropriate and in the public interest (CEA Sec. 2(a)(14), as added by Sec. 727 of the Dodd-Frank Act).

▶ **Effective date.** The provision takes effect on the later of: (1) 360 days after enactment; or (2) 60 days after publication of the final implementing rules (Sec. 754 of the Dodd-Frank Wall Street Reform and Consumer Protection Act).

Law source: Law at ¶10,727 and ¶10,754. Committee Report at ¶50,071.

— Sec. 727 of the Dodd-Frank Wall Street Reform and Consumer Protection Act, adding CEA Sec. 2(a)(13);

— Sec. 727, adding CEA Sec. 2(a)(14);

— Sec. 754, providing the effective date.

¶3080 Swap Data Repositories

The Dodd-Frank Wall Street Reform and Consumer Protection Act amends the Commodity Exchange Act (CEA) to set forth requirements for swap data repositories.

Swap data repositories must register with the CFTC and are subject to inspection and examination. Swap data repositories must comply with core principles. A derivatives clearing organization may register as a swap data repository. A person required to register as a swap data repository must register with the CFTC whether or not it is also licensed as a bank or registered as a swap data repository with the SEC (CEA Secs. 21(a) and (g), as added by Sec. 728 of the Dodd-Frank Wall Street Reform and Consumer Protection Act).

The CFTC must adopt rules governing registered swap data repositories The CFTC must set standards for data identification, collection and maintenance. The data standards for swap data repositories must be comparable standards for derivatives clearing organizations that clear swaps (CEA Secs. 21(b) and (h), as added by Sec. 728 of the Dodd-Frank Act).

A swap data repository must accept data; confirm data to both counterparties; maintain data according to standards set by the CFTC; provide direct electronic access to the CFTC and provide information as required by the CFTC; establish automated systems for monitoring and analyzing data, including use of end user clearing exemptions; maintain user privacy; make data available to specified regulators; and establish emergency procedures. The CFTC may develop additional duties, taking into consideration evolving standards of the United States and international community, and must establish additional duties for registrants described in CEA Section 1a(48) in order to minimize conflicts of interest, protect data, ensure compliance and guarantee the safety and security of the swap data repository (CEA Sec. 21(c), as added by Sec. 728 of the Dodd-Frank Act).

Before a swap data repository may share information with specified regulators, it must receive a written agreement from each regulator stating that it will abide by confidentiality requirements and indemnify the swap data repository and the CFTC for any litigation expenses relating to the information (CEA Sec. 21(d), as added by Sec. 728 of the Dodd-Frank Act).

Each data repository must have a chief compliance officer who must report directly to the board or a senior officer of the repository. The chief compliance officer must review compliance with the core principles, resolve conflicts of interest in consultation with the board, administer policies and procedures, establish procedures for the handling, remediation and closing of non-compliance issues identified through office review, internal or external audit, look-back self-reported error or validated complaint. The chief compliance officer must also annually prepare, sign and certify as accurate a report describing the swap data repository's compliance and the policies and procedures of the repository, including its code of ethics and conflict of interest policies. The report must accompany the financial statements that the swap data repository must file with the CFTC (CEA Sec. 21(e), as added by Sec. 728 of the Dodd-Frank Act).

A swap data repository must abide by core principles including antitrust considerations, governance arrangements and conflicts of interest (CEA Sec. 21(f), as added by Sec. 728 of the Dodd-Frank Act).

▶ **Effective date.** The provision takes effect on the later of: (1) 360 days after enactment; or (2) 60 days after publication of the final implementing rules (Sec. 754 of the Dodd-Frank Wall Street Reform and Consumer Protection Act).

Law source: Law at ¶10,728 and ¶10,754.

— Sec. 728 of the Dodd-Frank Wall Street Reform and Consumer Protection Act, adding CEA Secs. 21(a)–(g);

— Sec. 754, providing the effective date.

¶3085 Reporting and Recordkeeping (CFTC)

The Dodd-Frank Wall Street Reform and Consumer Protection Act amends the Commodity Exchange Act (CEA) to prescribe reporting and recordkeeping requirements for uncleared swaps.

Swaps not accepted for clearing by a derivatives clearing organization must be reported to a swap data repository, or if no swap data repository accepts the swap, to the CFTC, within a time period prescribed by CFTC rule (CEA Sec. 4r(a)(1), as added by Sec. 729 of the Dodd-Frank Wall Street Reform and Consumer Protection Act).

Reporting provisions are effective upon enactment. Unexpired swaps entered into before enactment must be reported to a registered swap data repository or the CFTC within 30 days after issuance of the interim final rule or other deadline set by the CFTC. The CFTC must promulgate an interim final rule within 90 days of enactment providing for the reporting of swaps entered into before enactment (CEA Sec. 4r(a)(2), as added by Sec. 729 of the Dodd-Frank Act).

For swaps in which only one counterparty is a swap dealer or major swap participant, that counterparty must report the swap. Where one counterparty is a swap dealer and the other is a major swap participant, the swap dealer must report the swap. For swaps not meeting either of these criteria, the counterparties must select a counterparty to report the swap (CEA Sec. 4r(a)(3), as added by Sec. 729 of the Dodd-Frank Act).

An individual or entity entering into a swap must meet certain reporting and recordkeeping requirements if it did not clear the swap under Section 2(h)(1) or did not have the data regarding the swap accepted by a swap repository. These requirements include: (1) providing reports upon written request by the CFTC; and (2) maintaining books and records as required by the CFTC and making these available for inspection by the CFTC, appropriate prudential regulator, SEC, Financial Stability Oversight Council and the Department of Justice (CEA Sec. 4r(b), 4r(c), as added by Sec. 729 of the Dodd-Frank Act).

CFTC rules must require reports under this section to be at least as comprehensive as data required to be collected by swap data repositories (CEA Sec. 4r(d), as added by Sec. 729 of the Dodd-Frank Act).

▶ **Effective date.** Reporting provisions become effective upon enactment (CEA Sec. 4r(a)(2)(C), as added by Sec. 729 of the Dodd-Frank Wall Street Reform and Consumer Protection Act).

Law source: Law at ¶10,729.

— Sec. 729 of the Dodd-Frank Wall Street Reform and Consumer Protection Act, adding CEA Sec. 4r.

¶3090 Large Swap Trader Reporting

The Dodd-Frank Wall Street Reform and Consumer Protection Act amends the Commodity Exchange Act (CEA) to prescribe large swap trader reporting requirements, to be implemented by regulation by the CFTC.

Position Limits.—For swaps that the CFTC determines to perform a significant price discovery function with respect to registered entities, it is unlawful for a person to enter into the swap during any one day in an amount equal or greater to an amount established by the CFTC. It is also unlawful for a person to directly or indirectly obtain a position in the swap equal to or greater than the permitted amount (CEA Sec. 4t(a)(1), as added by Sec. 730 of the Dodd-Frank Wall Street Reform and Consumer Protection Act).

However, this restriction is waived if: (1) the person files reports regarding the transactions or positions as required by CFTC rules; and (2) the person keeps books and records of the swaps transactions and positions in related commodities, and of cash or spot transactions, inventories of, and purchase and sale commitments of the commodity (CEA Sec. 4t(a)(2), as added by Sec. 730 of the Dodd-Frank Act).

Books and Records.—Books and records must show complete details of transactions and positions as the CFTC prescribes by rule, and must be open to inspection and examination by the CFTC (CEA Sec. 4t(b), as added by Sec. 730 of the Dodd-Frank Act).

Books and records must also be open to inspection and examination by the SEC to the extent they relate to security-based swap agreements, as defined in Exchange Act Section 3(a)(79), and consistent with confidentiality and disclosure requirements. This does not affect the exclusive jurisdiction of the CFTC to prescribe recordkeeping and reporting requirements for large swap traders (CEA Sec. 4t(b), as added by Sec. 730 of the Dodd-Frank Act).

For purposes of the provision, swaps, futures and cash or spot transactions and positions include transactions and positions of any persons directly or indirectly controlled by the person (CEA Sec. 4t(c), as added by Sec. 730 of the Dodd-Frank Act).

Significant Price Discovery Function.—In determining whether a swap performs or affects a significant price discovery function with respect to registered entities, the CFTC must consider the factors described in CEA Section 4a(a)(3) (CEA Sec. 4t(d), as added by Sec. 730 of the Dodd-Frank Act).

▶ **Effective date.** The provision takes effect 360 days after enactment (Sec. 754 of the Dodd-Frank Wall Street Reform and Consumer Protection Act).

Law source: Law at ¶10,730 and ¶10,754.

— Sec. 730 of the Dodd-Frank Wall Street Reform and Consumer Protection Act, adding CEA Sec. 4t;

— Sec. 754, providing the effective date.

¶3095 Swap Dealers and Major Swap Participants

The Dodd-Frank Wall Street Reform and Consumer Protection Act amends the Commodity Exchange Act (CEA) to provide for registration requirements and other regulation of swap dealers and major swap participants.

End-User Exemption.—The Act does not specifically define "commercial end user" or provide for a specific exemption of those entities from the registration, capital and margin requirements applicable to swap dealers and major swap participants. However, the Dodd-Frank Act does not authorize regulators to impose margin on end users that use derivatives to hedge or mitigate commercial risk.

Senators Christopher Dodd (D-CT) and Blanche Lincoln (D-AR), respective chairs of the Senate Banking and Agriculture committees, sent a letter to the Chairs of the House Financial Services and Agriculture Committees that clarified exemptions for end users. The senators emphasized that Congress does not intend to regulate end users as major swap participants or swap dealers just because they use swaps to hedge or manage the commercial risks associated with their business. Just as Congress has heard the end user community, said the senators, regulators must carefully consider the impact of regulation and capital and margin on end users (Letter of Sen. Christopher Dodd and Sen. Blanche Lincoln to the Chairs of the House Financial Services and Agricultural Committees, June 30, 2010, reproduced at ¶56,001).

Echoing these comments, House Agriculture Committee Chair Colin Peterson (D-MN) said that Congress focused on creating a regulatory approach that permits end users to continue using derivatives to hedge risks associated with their underlying businesses, whether it is energy exploration, manufacturing or commercial activities. He stated that it is "patently false" to imply that capital and margin requirements apply to end users of derivatives. The section in question governs the regulation of major swap participants and swap dealers, and its provisions apply only to major swap participants and swap dealers. Regulators cannot impose capital and margin requirements on end users (Cong. Rec., June 30, 2010, p. H5425).

The Dodd-Lincoln letter emphasized that Congress clearly stated in the Dodd-Frank Act that margin and capital requirements are not to be imposed on end users, nor can the regulators require clearing for end user trades. If regulators raise the costs of end user transactions, they may create more risk. It is imperative that the regulators do not unnecessarily divert working capital from the economy into margin accounts in a way that would discourage hedging by end users or impair economic growth. Whether swaps are used by an airline hedging its fuel costs or a global manufacturing company hedging its interest rates, derivatives are an important toll that companies use to manage costs and market volatility (Dodd-Lincoln Letter, *supra*, at ¶ 56,001).

SEC and CFTC Rulemaking. The SEC and CFTC are charged with setting rules for capital and margin requirements for uncleared trades. But the senators cautioned that the rules cannot be set in a way that requires the imposition of margin requirements on the end user side of a lawful transaction. In cases where a swap dealer enters into an uncleared swap with an end user, margin on the dealer side on the transaction should reflect the counterparty risk of the transaction (Dodd-Lincoln Letter, *supra*, at ¶ 56,001).

Congress strongly encourages regulators to set margin rules for such swaps or security-based swaps in a manner that is consistent with the congressional intent to protect end users from burdensome costs. A consistent congressional directive throughout all the drafts of the Dodd-Frank Act, and in congressional debate, has been to protect end users from burdensome costs associated with margin requirements and mandatory clearing. Thus, changes made by the conference committee to the section of the bill regulating capital and margin requirements for swap dealers and major swap participants should not be construed as changing this important congressional intent to protect end users. Capital and margin standard should be set to mitigate risks in the financial system, not punish those who are trying to hedge their own commercial risk (Dodd-Lincoln Letter, *supra*, at ¶ 56,001).

Non-Cash Collateral. Congress recognized that the individualized credit arrangements worked out between counterparties in a bilateral transaction can be important components of business risk management. That is why Congress specifically mandates that regulators permit the use of non-cash collateral for counterparty arrangements with swap dealers and major swap participants to allow flexibility. Mitigating risk is one of the most important reasons for passing the Dodd-Frank Act (Dodd-Lincoln Letter, *supra*, at ¶ 56,001).

Clearing. Clearing is at the heart of the reform as it brings transactions and counterparties into a robust, conservative and transparent risk management framework. Congress also said that clearing may not be suitable for every transaction or every counterparty. End users who hedge their risks may find it challenging to use a standard derivative contract to exactly match their risks with counterparties willing to purchase their specific exposures. Standardized derivative contracts may not be suitable for every transaction. Congress recognized that imposing the clearing and exchange trading requirements on commercial end users could raise transaction costs where there is a public interest in keeping such costs low in order to provide consumers with stable process and promote investment (Dodd-Lincoln Letter, *supra*, at ¶ 56,001).

Congress met these concerns by creating a robust end user exemption for those entities using swaps to hedge commercial risk. These entities range from car companies to airlines to energy companies to makers of farm machinery. The end user exemption may also apply to smaller financial entities, credit unions, community banks and farm credit institutions, who did not get the United States into the crisis and should not be punished for Wall Street excesses. That is why Congress provided regulators the authority to exempt these institutions (Dodd-Lincoln Letter, *supra*, at ¶ 56,001).

Narrow Definitions. That is also why the Dodd-Frank Act narrows the scope of the swap dealer and major swap participant definitions. Firms that are properly managing their risks should not be inadvertently pulled in. When implementing these definitions, Congress expects the regulators to adopt rules maintaining that the definition of major swap participant does not capture companies simply because they use swaps to hedge risk in their ordinary course of business. For example, the definitions are not intended to include an electric utility that purchases commodities used either as a source of fuel to produce electricity and that uses swaps to hedge the commercial risks associated with its business. Congress incorporated a de minimis exception to the swap dealer definition to ensure that smaller institutions that are responsibly managing their commercial risk are not inadvertently pulled into more regulation (Dodd-Lincoln Letter, *supra*, at ¶ 56,001).

Differing Risk Profiles. It is also imperative that the SEC and CFTC not assume that all OTC transactions share the same risk profile. Although uncleared swaps should be looked at closely, regulators must carefully analyze the risk associated with cleared and uncleared swaps and apply that analysis when setting capital standards for swap dealers and major swap participants, noted the senators, adding that capital and margin standards must be set relative to the risks associated with trading (Dodd-Lincoln Letter, *supra*, at ¶ 56,001).

Regulators must also consider the potential burdens that swap dealers and major swap participants may impose on end user counterparties, especially if those requirements will discourage the use of swaps by end users. Regulators should impose margins to the extent they are necessary to ensure the safety and soundness of the swap dealers and major swap participants (Dodd-Lincoln Letter, *supra*, at ¶ 56,001).

Congress determined that end users must be empowered in their counterparty relationships, especially relationships with swap dealers. This is why Congress expressly gave end users the option to clear swaps contracts, the option to choose their clearinghouse or clearing agency and the option to segregate margin with an independent third-party custodian (Dodd-Lincoln Letter, *supra*, at ¶ 56,001).

In implementing Title VII, Congress encourages the CFTC to clarify through rulemaking that the exclusion from the definition of swap for any sale of a non-financial commodity or security for deferred shipment or delivery, so long as the transaction is intended to be physically settled, is intended to be consistent with the existing forward contract exclusion in the CEA and the CFTC's established policy and orders on this subject, including situations where commercial parties agree to book-out their physical delivery obligations under a forward contract (Dodd-Lincoln Letter, *supra*, at ¶ 56,001).

Registration.—Swap dealers and major swap participants must register with the CFTC (CEA Sec. 4s(a), as added by Sec. 731 of the Dodd-Frank Act). With certain exceptions, the CFTC may prescribe rules applicable to non-bank major swap dealers and non-bank major swap participants, including rules that limit the activities of swap dealers and major swap participant (CEA Sec. 4s(b), as added by Sec. 731 of the Dodd-Frank Act).

Rules must be adopted for the registration of swap dealers and major swap participant within one year after enactment (CEA Sec. 4s(b), as added by Sec. 731 of the Dodd-Frank Act).

It is unlawful for a swap dealer or major swap participant to permit any associated person subject to statutory disqualification to effect swaps on behalf of the swap dealer or major swap participant (CEA Sec. 4s(b), as added by Sec. 731 of the Dodd-Frank Act).

Swap dealers and major swap participants must register with the CFTC whether or not they are a depository institution and whether or not they also register with the SEC as a security-based swap dealer or major security-based swap participant (CEA Sec. 4s(c), as added by Sec. 731 of the Dodd-Frank Act).

Capital and Margin Requirements.—For banks for which there is a prudential regulator, capital and margin requirements must be set by the prudential regulator. Swap dealers and major swap participants that are not banks and do not have a prudential regulator must have capital and margin requirements set by the CFTC. The prudential regulators, CFTC and SEC must adopt rules providing for certain capital and margin requirements are prescribed (CEA Sec. 4s(e), as added by Sec. 731 of the Dodd-Frank Act).

Business Conduct Standards.—Registered swap dealers and major swap participants must conform with business conduct standards prescribed by CFTC rule, relating to fraud, manipulation and other abusive practices; diligent supervision; adherence to position limits; and other matters the CFTC deems appropriate (CEA Sec. 4s(h)(1), as added by Sec. 731 of the Dodd-Frank Act).

Business conduct requirements adopted by the CFTC must: (1) establish a duty for a swap dealer or major swap participant to verify that a counterparty meets the standards for an eligible contract participant; (2) require swap dealers and major swap participants to disclose certain information to counterparties; (3) establish a duty for swap dealers and major swap participants to communicate in a manner based on principles of fair dealing and good faith; (4) establish certain suitability requirements; and (5) establish other standards as the CFTC determines appropriate. The CFTC must prescribe rules governing business conduct standards (CEA Sec. 4s(h)(3), as added by Sec. 731 of the Dodd-Frank Act).

Certain heightened standards of conduct are established for a swap dealer advising or acting as a counterparty to a special entity. Those providing advice or sale of swaps to any governmental entity (state, state agency, city, county, municipality or other political subdivision or a federal agency), or to pension plans, endowments and retirement plans, have a fiduciary duty to those entities (CEA Sec. 4s(h)(2), as added by Sec. 731 of the Dodd-Frank Act).

Other Requirements.—Registered swap dealers and major swap participants must conform with standards set by CFTC rule regarding timely and accurate confirmation, processing, netting, documentation and valuation of all swaps. The CFTC must adopt rules governing documentation standards. Registered swap dealers and major swap participants must comply with certain additional requirements, including (1) monitoring of trading, (2) risk management procedures, (3) disclosure of general information, (4) ability to obtain information, (5) management of conflicts of interest, and (6) antitrust considerations. The CFTC must adopt rules governing the duties of swap dealers and major swap participants. Swap dealers and major swap participants must designate a chief compliance officer. The duties of the chief compliance officer are enumerated (CEA Secs. 4s(i)–(k), as added by Sec. 731 of the Dodd-Frank Act).

Registered swap dealers and major swap participants must make reports and maintain records as required by the CFTC. Entities without a prudential regulator must also make books and records available for inspection by the CFTC. The CFTC must adopt rules governing reporting and recordkeeping. Certain reporting and recordkeeping requirements are prescribed (CEA Secs. 4s(f) and (g), as added by Sec. 731 of the Dodd-Frank Act).

The CFTC must adopt rules for swap dealers and major swap participants, except that the CFTC cannot prescribe rules imposing prudential requirements on swap dealers or major swap participants for which there is a prudential regulator. This does not limit the CFTC's authority to prescribe rules as directed (CEA Sec. 4s(d), as added by Sec. 731 of the Dodd-Frank Act).

▶ **Effective date.** The provision takes effect on the later of: (1) 360 days after enactment; or (2) 60 days after publication of the final implementing rules (Sec. 754 of the Dodd-Frank Wall Street Reform and Consumer Protection Act).

Law source: Law at ¶10,731 and ¶10,754. Committee Report at ¶56,001.

— Sec. 731 of the Dodd-Frank Wall Street Reform and Consumer Protection Act, adding CEA Sec. 4s(a)–(k);

— Sec. 754, providing the effective date.

¶3100 Swap Execution Facilities

The Dodd-Frank Wall Street Reform and Consumer Protection Act amends the Commodity Exchange Act (CEA) to provide for the registration and regulation of swap execution facilities by the CFTC.

Registration.—An entity that operates a facility for the processing or trading of swaps must register with the CFTC as a swap execution facility or designated contract market. The swap execution facility must register with the CFTC regardless of whether it is also registered with the SEC (CEA Sec. 5h(a), as added by Sec. 733 of the Dodd-Frank Wall Street Reform and Consumer Protection Act).

A swap execution facility may make available or facilitate trade processing of any swap, but cannot list for trading or confirm execution of a swap in an agricultural commodity except as allowed by CFTC rule. A board of trade that operates as a contract market and uses the same electronic trade and execution for listing and executing swaps must identify whether the electronic trade of swaps is taking place on the facility (CEA Secs. 5h(b) and (c), as added by Sec. 733 of the Dodd-Frank Act).

The SEC and CFTC may promulgate rules to define the universe of swaps that can be traded on a swap execution facility. Rules must take into account price and nonprice consideration of counterparties to a swap and the goal of the section, which is to promote the trading of swaps on swap execution facilities and to promote pre-trade price transparency in the swaps market. Swaps not required to be executed through a swap execution facility, may be executed through any other available means of interstate commerce (CEA Sec. 5h(d), 5h(e), as added by Sec. 733 of the Dodd-Frank Act).

Core Principles.—A swap execution facility must comply with certain core principles. The facility has reasonable discretion in how it complies (CEA Sec. 5h(d)(1), as added by Sec. 733 of the Dodd-Frank Act).

A swap execution facility must establish, monitor and enforce compliance with trading, trade processing and participation rules that deter and detect abuses. The rules must provide that a swap dealer or major swap participant subject to a mandatory clearing requirement is responsible for compliance with the mandatory trading requirement of the Dodd-Frank Act (CEA Sec. 5h(f)(2), as added by Sec. 733 of the Dodd-Frank Act).

The swap execution facility may only permit trading in swaps that are not readily susceptible to manipulation. The swap execution facility must establish and enforce rules detailing procedures for entering and processing of swap trades. The facility must also monitor trades to prevent manipulation, price distortion and disruptions of the delivery or cash settlement process, through surveillance, compliance and disciplinary practices and procedures. Methods must include real-time trade monitoring and comprehensive trade reconstruction (CEA Secs. 5h(f)(3) and (4) as added by Sec. 733 of the Dodd-Frank Act).

The swap execution facility must establish and enforce rules to obtain information necessary to carry out core responsibilities, including carrying out international information-sharing as the CFTC may require (CEA Sec. 5h(f)(5), as added by Sec. 733 of the Dodd-Frank Act).

The swap execution facility must establish position limits or accountability levels for speculators. For any contract subject to a position limitation by the CFTC, the facility cannot set its own position limit higher than the CFTC's limit. The facility must monitor trades for compliance with its own accountability levels and CFTC position limits (CEA Sec. 5h(f)(6), as added by Sec. 733 of the Dodd-Frank Act).

The swap execution facility must establish and enforce rules and procedures for ensuring the financial integrity of swaps entered on its facility, including the clearance and settlement of the swaps pursuant to Section 2(h)(1). The swap execution facility must adopt rules for the exercise of emergency authority, in consultation with the CFTC, including the authority to liquidate or transfer open positions or to suspend or curtail trading in a swap (CEA Secs. 5h(f)(7) and (8) as added by Sec. 733 of the Dodd-Frank Act).

The swap execution facility must make public timely information on price, trading volume and other trading data as prescribed by the CFTC. The facility must have the capacity to electronically capture and transmit trade information. The swap execution facility must maintain records of activities, including a complete audit trail, in a form acceptable to the CFTC for a period of five years, and report information the CFTC

¶3100

deems necessary. The facility must also keep its records open to inspection by the SEC. The CFTC must adopt data collection and reporting requirements for swap execution facilities comparable to corresponding requirements for derivatives clearing organizations and swap data repositories (CEA Secs. 5h(f)(9) and (10), as added by Sec. 733 of the Dodd-Frank Act).

Unless necessary to achieve the purposes of the Dodd-Frank Act, the swap facility cannot adopt any rules or take any actions resulting in unreasonable restraint of trade, nor impose any material anti-competitive burden on trading or clearing. The swap execution facility must establish and enforce rules to minimize conflicts in its decision-making processes, and establish a process for resolving conflicts of interest (CEA Sec. 5h(f)(11), 12), as added by Sec. 733 of the Dodd-Frank Act).

The swap execution facility must have adequate financial, operational and managerial resources to discharge its responsibilities. Financial resources sufficient to cover one year's operating costs are considered adequate (CEA Sec. 5h(f)(13), as added by Sec. 733 of the Dodd-Frank Act).

The swap execution facility also must:

- establish and maintain a program of risk oversight and analysis to minimize sources of operational risk, through the development of appropriate controls and automated systems that are reliable, secure and have adequate scalable capacity;
- establish and maintain emergency procedures, backup facilities and disaster recovery plans that allow for timely recovery of operations and fulfillment of obligations; and
- periodically conduct tests of backup resources to ensure continued order processing and trade matching, price reporting, market surveillance and maintenance of a comprehensive audit trail (CEA Sec. 5h(f)(14), as added by Sec. 733 of the Dodd-Frank Act).

The swap execution facility must designate a chief compliance officer, who must fulfill duties as prescribed (CEA Sec. 5h(f)(15), as added by Sec. 733 of the Dodd-Frank Act).

Rulemaking; Exemptions.—The CFTC must prescribe rules governing the regulation of swap execution facilities. The CFTC may exempt a swap execution facility from registration if the CFTC finds that the facility is subject to comparable supervision and regulation by the SEC, a prudential regulator or the appropriate regulators in the facility's home country (CEA Secs. 5h(g) and (h), as added by Sec. 733 of the Dodd-Frank Act).

▶ **Effective date.** The provision takes effect on the later of: (1) 360 days after enactment; or (2) 60 days after publication of the final implementing rules (Sec. 754 of the Dodd-Frank Wall Street Reform and Consumer Protection Act).

Law source: Law at ¶10,733 and ¶10,754.

— Sec. 733 of the Dodd-Frank Wall Street Reform and Consumer Protection Act, adding CEA Sec. 5h;
— Sec. 754, providing the effective date.

¶3105 Derivatives Transaction Execution Facilities and EBOTs

The Dodd-Frank Wall Street Reform and Consumer Protection Act repeals and amends sections of the Commodity Exchange Act (CEA) relating to derivatives transaction execution facilities and exempt boards of trade (EBOTs) and sets forth transitional provisions pertaining to these entities (CEA Secs. 5a, 5d, as repealed by Sec. 734(a) of the Dodd-Frank Wall Street Reform and Consumer Protection Act).

The legislation also makes conforming amendments to reflect the repeal (CEA Sec. 2, Exchange Act Sec. 6(g)(1)(A), as amended by Sec. 734(b) of the Dodd-Frank Act).

Transition Period.—Prior to final effective dates in Dodd-Frank Act Title VII, a person may petition the CFTC to remain subject to CEA Section 5d, as it existed prior to the effective date. The CFTC must consider any such petition in a prompt manner and may allow a person to continue operating subject to CEA Section 5d for up to one year after the Title VII effective date (Sec. 734(c) of the Dodd-Frank Act).

▶ **Effective date.** The provision takes effect on the later of: (1) 360 days after enactment; or (2) 60 days after publication of the final implementing rules (Sec. 754 of the Dodd-Frank Wall Street Reform and Consumer Protection Act).

Law source: Law at ¶10,734 and ¶10,754.

— Sec. 734(a) of the Dodd-Frank Wall Street Reform and Consumer Protection Act, repealing CEA Secs. 5a and 5d;

— Sec. 734(b), making conforming amendments;

— Sec. 734(c), providing for transition;

— Sec. 754, providing the effective date.

¶3110 Designated Contract Markets

The Dodd-Frank Wall Street Reform and Consumer Protection Act amends the Commodity Exchange Act (CEA) to revise core principles governing operations of designated contract markets (DCMs). To be designated as a contract market, a board of trade must comply with core principles prescribed by the CEA and rules promulgated by the CFTC under CEA Section 8a(5).

Core Principles.—A board of trade has reasonable discretion in how it complies. The board of trade must establish, monitor and enforce compliance with the rules of the contract market, including access requirements, terms and conditions of contracts, and rules prohibiting abusive trade practices. The board of trade may investigate and sanction violations of the contract market rules and obtain information necessary to carry out these functions, as well as comply with information-sharing agreements required by the CFTC (CEA Secs. 5(d)(1) and (2), as amended by Sec. 735(b) of the Dodd-Frank Wall Street Reform and Consumer Protection Act).

The board of trade may list only contracts that are not readily susceptible to manipulation. The board of trade has authority and responsibility to prevent manipulation, price distortion and disruptions of the delivery or cash-settlement process through market surveillance, compliance and enforcement procedures, including real-time monitoring of trading and comprehensive trade reconstructions (CEA Secs. 5(d)(3) and (4), as amended by Sec. 735(b) of the Dodd-Frank Act).

As appropriate for each contract, the board of trade must adopt position limits or position accountability for speculators. For any contract subject to a position limit established by the CFTC under CEA Section 4a(a), the board of trade cannot set its position limit higher than the limit established by the CFTC. The board of trade must adopt rules to provide for the exercise of emergency authority, including the authority to liquidate or transfer open positions, suspend or curtail trading, and require market participants to meet special margin requirements (CEA Secs. 5(d)(5) and (6) as amended by Sec. 735(b) of the Dodd-Frank Act).

The board of trade must make available to market authorities, market participants and the public: (1) information concerning contract terms and conditions; (2) rules, regulations and mechanisms for executing transactions; and (3) rules and specifications describing the contract market's electronic matching platform or trade execution facility. The board of trade must make public daily information on settlement prices, volume, open interest and opening and closing ranges for actively traded contracts. The board of trade must provide a competitive, open and efficient market for executing transactions that protects the price discovery process. The rules of the board of trade may authorize certain types of trades, exchanges and agency (CEA Secs. 5(d)(7)–(9), as amended by Sec. 735(b) of the Dodd-Frank Act).

In addition, the board of trade must maintain rules and procedures for the recording and safe storage of identifying trade information, in a manner that enables the contract market to assist in the prevention of customer and market abuses and provide evidence of violations of the rules of the contract market (CEA Sec. 5(d)(10), as amended by Sec. 735(b) of the Dodd-Frank Act).

The board of trade must establish and enforce rules and procedures to ensure the financial integrity of transactions, including the clearance and settlement of the transactions with a derivatives clearing organization. The rules must also ensure the financial integrity of futures commission merchants and introducing brokers and the protection of customer funds. The board of trade must establish and enforce rules to protect markets and market participants from abusive practices and to promote fair and equitable trading. The board of trade must have adequate financial, operational and managerial resources to discharge its responsibilities. Financial resources sufficient to cover operating costs for one year are adequate (CEA Secs. 5(d)(11), (12) and (21), as amended by Sec. 735(b) of the Dodd-Frank Act).

Further, the board of trade must establish and enforce disciplinary procedures authorizing the board of trade to discipline, suspend or expel members or market participants that violate its rules. The board of trade may use alternate methods for the same functions, including delegating the functions to third parties. The board of trade must establish rules and facilities for alternative dispute resolution as appropriate for market participants and intermediaries (CEA Secs. 5(d)(13) and (14) as amended by Sec. 735(b) of the Dodd-Frank Act).

The board of trade must establish and enforce appropriate fitness standards for directors, members of disciplinary committees, contract market members and any other person with direct access to the facility, including affiliates of any of the above. The board of trade must establish and enforce rules to minimize conflicts of interest in decision-making processes and must establish a process for resolving conflicts of interest. The board of trade must design governance arrangements to promote the objectives of market participants (CEA Secs. 5(d)(15)–(17), as amended by Sec. 735(b) of the Dodd-Frank Act).

The board of trade must maintain records for at least five years, in a form acceptable to the CFTC. The board of trade must keep any such records relating to swaps defined in CEA Sec. 1a(47)(A)(v) open to inspection (CEA Secs. 5(d)(18) and (23) as amended by Sec. 735(b) of the Dodd-Frank Act).

Unless necessary to achieve the purposes of the Dodd-Frank Act, the board of trade cannot adopt a rule or take an action resulting in unreasonable restraint of trade, nor impose any material anti-competitive burden on trading (CEA Sec. 5(d)(19), as added by Sec. 735(b) of the Dodd-Frank Act).

The board of trade must: (1) maintain a program of risk oversight and analysis to minimize sources of operational risk, through the development of appropriate controls and automated systems that are reliable, secure and have adequate scalable capacity; (2) maintain emergency procedures, backup facilities and disaster recovery plans that allow for timely recovery of operations and fulfillment of obligations; and (3) periodically conduct tests of backup resources to ensure continued order processing and trade matching, price reporting, market surveillance and maintenance of a comprehensive audit trail (CEA Sec. 5(d)(20), as added by Sec. 735(b) of the Dodd-Frank Act).

If the board of trade is a publicly traded company, it must endeavor to recruit individuals for the board of directors and other decision-making bodies from, and have the board reflect, a broad and culturally diverse pool of qualified candidates (CEA Sec. 5(d)(22), as added by Sec. 735(b) of the Dodd-Frank Act).

Margin.—The CFTC may alter rules of contract markets pertaining to margin requirements. The rules must be limited to protecting the financial integrity of the derivatives clearing organization; must be designed for risk management purposes to protect the financial integrity of transactions; and cannot set specific margin amounts (CEA Sec. 8a(7), as amended by Sec. 736 of the Dodd-Frank Act).

▶ **Effective date.** The provision takes effect 360 days after enactment (Sec. 754 of the Dodd-Frank Wall Street Reform and Consumer Protection Act).

Law source: Law at ¶10,735, ¶10,736 and ¶10,754.

— Sec. 735(a), repealing CEA Sec. 5(b);

— Sec. 735(b), amending CEA Sec. 5(d);

— Sec. 736, amending CEA Sec. 8a(7);

— Sec. 754, providing the effective date.

¶3115 Position Limits

The Dodd-Frank Wall Street Reform and Consumer Protection Act amends the Commodity Exchange Act (CEA) to authorize the CFTC to establish position limits for swaps and commodity futures.

Rulemaking.—The CFTC must establish position limits for futures contracts on physical commodities or options on those contracts, except for excluded commodities and positions meeting bona fide hedging requirements. The CFTC must strive to ensure that trading on foreign boards of trade (FBOTs) are subject to comparable limits and that any limits imposed by the CFTC do not cause price discovery in the commodity to shift to trading on FBOTs (CEA Sec. 4a(a), as amended by Sec. 737(a) of the Dodd-Frank Wall Street Reform and Consumer Protection Act).

The CFTC must establish position limits for exempt commodities within 180 days after enactment and within 270 days after enactment for agricultural commodities (CEA Sec. 4a(a), as amended by Sec. 737(a) of the Dodd-Frank Act).

As appropriate, the CFTC must set limits on the number of positions that may be held by any person by the spot month, each other month, and the aggregate number of positions that may be held by any person for all months. The position limits should be designed to diminish or prevent excessive speculation and market manipulation, squeezes and corners; to ensure sufficient market liquidity for bona fide hedgers; and to ensure that the price discovery function of the underlying market is not disrupted (CEA Sec. 4a(a), as amended by Sec. 737(a) of the Dodd-Frank Act).

Notwithstanding any other provision, the CFTC must establish limits on the amount of positions that may be held by any person with respect to swaps that are economically equivalent to contracts of sale for future delivery, or options on the contracts, or commodities traded on or subject to the rules of a designated contract market. The CFTC must develop these limits concurrently with limits established for futures contracts, and the limits must have similar requirements (CEA Sec. 4a(a), as amended by Sec. 737(a) of the Dodd-Frank Act).

In determining if swaps perform a significant price discovery function, the CFTC must consider a swap's price linkage to traded contracts, potential for price arbitrage between the swap and a contract on a traded platform, whether the price is frequently referenced, whether the contracts are significantly liquid, and any other factor the Commission determines is relevant (CEA Sec. 4a(a), as amended by Sec. 737 of the Dodd-Frank Act).

Aggregate Limits.—The CFTC must establish limits, including related hedge exemption positions, on the aggregate number or amount of positions in contracts based on the same underlying commodity held by a person or group of traders, for each month, across (a) contracts listed by designated contract markets; (b) contracts traded on an FBOT that provides direct U.S. access, for contracts that settle against the price of a contract listed by a U.S. registered entity; and (c) swap contracts that perform or affect a significant price discovery function (CEA Sec. 4a(a), as amended by Sec. 737(a) of the Dodd-Frank Act).

The CFTC has broad authority to exempt persons or swaps from position limits (CEA Sec. 4a(a), as amended by Sec. 737(a) of the Dodd-Frank Act).

Bona Fide Hedging Transaction.—The CFTC must define a bona fide hedging transaction as a transaction or position that: (1) is a substitute for transactions made at a later time in a physical marketing channel; (2) is economically appropriate to risk reduction in the management of a commercial enterprise; and (3) arises from the potential change in the value of certain assets, liabilities or services. Alternatively, a bona fide hedging transaction may be defined as a position that reduces risks attendant to a position resulting from a swap that was executed opposite a counterparty and for which the transaction would qualify as a bona fide hedging transaction under the first definition (CEA Sec. 4a(c), as amended by Sec. 737(c) of the Dodd-Frank Act).

▶ **Effective date.** The provision takes effect upon enactment (Sec. 737(d) of the Dodd-Frank Wall Street Reform and Consumer Protection Act).

Law source: Law at ¶10,737. Committee Report at ¶50,071.

— Sec. 737(a) of the Dodd-Frank Wall Street Reform and Consumer Protection Act, amending CEA Sec. 4a(a);

— Sec. 737(c), amending CEA Sec. 737(c);

— Sec. 737(d), providing the effective date.

¶3120 Foreign Boards of Trade

The Dodd-Frank Wall Street Reform and Consumer Protection Act amends the Commodity Exchange Act (CEA) to establish oversight of foreign boards of trade (FBOTs).

Registration.—The Commission may adopt rules and regulations requiring an FBOT to register with the CFTC if it gives its members or other participants located in the United States direct access to its electronic trading and order matching system, including rules prescribing requirements applicable to the registration of FBOTs. "Direct access" refers to an explicit grant of authority by a FBOT to an identified member or other participant located in the United States to enter trades directly into its trade matching system (CEA Sec. 4b(1)(A), as amended by Sec. 738(a) of the Dodd-Frank Wall Street Reform and Consumer Protection Act).

In adopting these rules, the CFTC must consider whether an FBOT is subject to comparable supervision and regulation by the appropriate governmental authorities in the FBOT's home country, and any previous CFTC findings on that issue (CEA Sec. 4b(1)(A), as amended by Sec. 738(a) of the Dodd-Frank Act).

The CFTC cannot permit an FBOT to give its members or other participants located in the United States direct access to its trade systems for contracts that settle against prices for contracts traded on CFTC-registered entities, unless the FBOT adheres to regulatory standards addressing daily publication of pricing information, position limits and authority over market participants comparable to U.S. standards. The FBOT also must promptly notify the CFTC of changes to these standards (CEA Sec. 4(b)(1)(B), as amended by Sec. 738(a) of the Dodd-Frank Act).

The FBOT must provide large trader information comparable to that provided by registered entities and must provide the CFTC with aggregate trader data comparable to the data provided by registered entities (CEA Sec. 4(b)(1)(B)(ii)(IV), as amended by Sec. 738(a) of the Dodd-Frank Act).

Existing FBOTs may continue to provide direct access under existing standards until 180 days after the date of enactment (CEA Sec. 4(b)(1)(C), as amended by Sec. 738(a) of the Dodd-Frank Act).

Registered entities trading on a FBOT are not liable for an FBOT's violations if the person has reason to believe the transaction is made on an FBOT that meets certain conditions. This does not imply that a board of trade, exchange or market is located outside the United States (CEA Sec. 4(e), as added by Sec. 738(b) of the Dodd-Frank Act).

Contract Enforcement.—A contract of sale of a commodity for future delivery traded or executed on or through the facilities of a board of trade, exchange or market located outside the United States is not void, voidable or unenforceable, and a party to such a contract cannot rescind or recover any payment made with respect to the contract, based on the FBOT's failure to comply with the Act (CEA Sec. 22(a)(6), as added by Sec. 738(c) of the Dodd-Frank Act).

▶ **Effective date.** The provision takes effect 360 days after enactment (Sec. 754 of the Dodd-Frank Wall Street Reform and Consumer Protection Act).

Law source: Law at ¶10,738 and ¶10,754.

— Sec. 738(a) of the Dodd-Frank Wall Street Reform and Consumer Protection Act, amending CEA Sec. 4(b);

— Sec. 738(b), adding CEA Sec. 4(e);

— Sec. 738(c), adding CEA Sec. 22(a)(6);

— Sec. 754, providing the effective date.

¶3125 Legal Certainty for Swaps

The Dodd-Frank Wall Street Reform and Consumer Protection Act amends the Commodity Exchange Act (CEA) to clarify the status of instruments entered into before enactment.

A hybrid instrument sold to an investor is not void or rescindable solely because it does not comply with CEA Section 2(f) or CFTC rules (CEA Sec. 22(a)(4)(A), as amended by Sec. 739 of the Dodd-Frank Wall Street Reform and Consumer Protection Act).

A swap agreement between eligible contract participants, or persons reasonably believed to be eligible contract participants, is not void or rescindable solely because the agreement does not meet the definition of a swap under CEA Section 1a, or because it is not cleared in compliance with CEA Section 2(h)(1) (CEA Sec. 22(a)(4)(B), as amended by Sec. 739 of the Dodd-Frank Act).

Unless specifically reserved in a swap, neither the enactment of Dodd-Frank Act Title VII, nor any requirement under or amendment made by the Act, constitutes a termination event, or similar event under a swap that would permit a party to terminate, renegotiate, modify, amend or supplement transactions under the swap (CEA Sec. 22(a)(5)(A), as added by Sec. 739 of the Dodd-Frank Act).

A position limit newly established by the derivatives title does not apply to a position acquired in good faith prior to the effective date of any rule or order that establishes the position limit. However, these positions will be attributed to the trader if the trader increases the position after the effective date of the rule or order (CEA Sec. 22(a)(5)(B), as added by Sec. 739 of the Dodd-Frank Act).

▶ **Effective date.** The provision takes effect 360 days after enactment (Sec. 754 of the Dodd-Frank Wall Street Reform and Consumer Protection Act).

Law source: Law at ¶10,739 and ¶10,754.

— Sec. 739 of the Dodd-Frank Wall Street Reform and Consumer Protection Act, amending CEA Sec. 22(a)(4);

— Sec. 739, adding CEA Sec. 22(a)(5);

— Sec. 754, providing the effective date.

¶3130 Enforcement

The Dodd-Frank Wall Street Reform and Consumer Protection Act amends the Commodity Exchange Act (CEA) to give the CFTC exclusive enforcement authority over swaps, except as provided below (CEA Sec. 4b-1(a), as added by Sec. 741(a) of the Dodd-Frank Wall Street Reform and Consumer Protection Act). The prudential regulators have exclusive authority to enforce the provisions of CEA Section 4s(e) with respect to swap dealers or major swap participants for which they are the prudential regulators (CEA Sec. 4b-1(b), as added by Sec. 741(a) of the Dodd-Frank Act).

The CFTC and the prudential regulators have referral authority to each other for violations within the other regulator's jurisdiction (CEA Sec. 4b-1(c), as added by Sec. 741(a) of the Dodd-Frank Act). If either regulator does not begin an enforcement proceeding relating to a referred matter within 90 days, the referring regulator may begin an enforcement proceeding (CEA Sec. 4b-1(d), as added by Sec. 741(a) of the Dodd-Frank Act).

Federal courts may award restitution and disgorgement in actions for Act violations brought by the CFTC. The legislation defines standards for restitution of losses proximately caused and for disgorgement of gains received (CEA Sec. 6c(d)(3), as added by Sec. 744 of the Dodd-Frank Act).

A clearing agency that knowingly or recklessly evades or participates in or facilitates an evasion of the clearing requirements is liable for a civil money penalty in twice the amount otherwise available for a violation of Section 3C. Similarly, any security-based swap dealer or major security-based swap participant that knowingly or recklessly evades, or participates in or facilitates an evasion of, the requirements of section 3C is liable for a civil money penalty in twice the amount otherwise available for a violation of Section 3C (Exchange Act Sec. 21B(f), as added by Sec. 773 of the Dodd-Frank Act).

▶ **Effective date.** The provision takes effect 360 days after enactment (Sec. 754 of the Dodd-Frank Wall Street Reform and Consumer Protection Act).

Law source: Law at ¶10,741, ¶10,744, ¶10,754, ¶10,773 and ¶10,774. Committee Report at ¶50,071.

— Sec. 741(a) of the Dodd-Frank Wall Street Reform and Consumer Protection Act, adding CEA Sec. 4b-1;

— Sec. 744, adding CEA Sec. 6c(d)(3);

— Sec. 773, adding Exchange Act Sec. 21B(f).

— Secs. 754 and 774, providing the effective date.

¶3135 Retail Commodity Transactions

The Dodd-Frank Wall Street Reform and Consumer Protection Act amends the Commodity Exchange Act (CEA) to clarify the CFTC's jurisdiction over certain retail commodity transactions.

This section grants CFTC antifraud authority over contracts offered to or entered into with persons who are not eligible contract participants or eligible commercial entities, and over retail contracts that are leveraged, margined or financed by the offeror or counterparty or a person acting in concert with the offeror or counterparty on a similar basis (CEA Sec. 2(c)(2)(D)(i), as amended by Sec 742 of the Dodd-Frank Wall Street Reform and Consumer Protection Act).

CFTC jurisdiction over retail commodity transactions does not extend to (1) securities; (2) futures contracts; (3) any sales contract that results in actual delivery within 28 days (or other time as determined by the CFTC); (4) any sales contract that creates an enforceable obligation to deliver between a seller and buyer that have the ability to accept delivery in connection with the line of business of the seller and buyer; (5) contracts listed on a national securities exchange; or (6) an identified banking product, as defined in Section 402(b) of the Legal Certainty for Bank Products Act of 2000 (CEA Sec. 2(c)(2)(D)(ii), as amended by Sec. 742 of the Dodd-Frank Act).

▶ **Effective date.** The provision takes effect 360 days after enactment (Sec. 754 of the Dodd-Frank Wall Street Reform and Consumer Protection Act).

Law source: Law at ¶10,742 and ¶10,754.

— Sec. 742 of the Dodd-Frank Wall Street Reform and Consumer Protection Act, amending CEA Sec. 2(a)(1)(C);

— Sec. 742, adding Exchange Act Sec. 3B;

— Sec. 742, adding Exchange Act Sec. 19(b)(10);

— Sec. 742, amending CEA Sec. 5c(c)(1);

— Sec. 754, providing the effective date.

¶3140 Enhanced Compliance for Registered Entities

The Dodd-Frank Wall Street Reform and Consumer Protection Act amends the Commodity Exchange Act (CEA) to give the CFTC enhanced rulemaking and interpretive authority over compliance with core principles and rule amendments by derivatives clearing organizations (DCOs) and designated contract markets (DCMs).

A CFTC interpretation regarding acceptable business practices under core principles may provide the exclusive means for complying with certain sections (CEA Sec. 5c(a)(2), as amended by Sec. 745(a) of the Dodd-Frank Wall Street Reform and Consumer Protection Act).

A registered entity may provide a written certification to the CFTC that the new contract or rule complies with the CEA. The entity must give notice of the certification to its members. The new rule becomes effective 10 business days after the CFTC receives the certification, unless the CFTC notifies the entity that it is staying the certification (CEA Secs. 5c(c)(1) and (2), as amended by Sec. 745(b) of the Dodd-Frank Act).

A stay by the CFTC delays effectiveness of the rule for up to 90 days after the date of notification. The new rule becomes effective after a stay expires, unless the CFTC withdraws the stay before expiration, or notifies the registered entity that it objects to the rule on the basis that the rule is inconsistent with the Dodd-Frank Act. If the CFTC reviews a rule or amendment in this manner, the CFTC must provide a public comment period of at least 30 days, within the 90-day period in which the stay is in effect (CEA Sec. 5c(c)(3), as amended by Sec. 745(b) of the Dodd-Frank Act).

Prior Approval.—A registered entity may ask the CFTC to grant prior approval to a new contract or other instrument, rule or rule amendment (CEA Sec. 5c(c)(4)(A), as amended by Sec. 745(b) of the Dodd-Frank Act).

A designated contract market must request prior approval for a rule that materially changes the terms and conditions in a contract of sale for future delivery of a commodity under CEA Section 1a(10), or option on such a commodity, if the rule amendment applies to contracts and delivery months that have already been listed for trading and have open interest. If prior approval is required, the CFTC must take final action on the request within 90 days of submission of the request, unless the requestor agrees to an extension (CEA Secs. 5c(c)(4)(B) and (C), as amended by Sec. 745(b) of the Dodd-Frank Act).

Mandatory Approval.—The CFTC must approve a new rule or rule amendment unless it finds the rule or amendment is inconsistent with the derivatives title of the Dodd-Frank Act, including regulations. The CFTC must approve a new contract or other instrument unless the CFTC finds that it would violate the Dodd-Frank Act (CEA Sec. 5c(c)(5), as amended by Sec. 745(b) of the Dodd-Frank Act).

The CFTC may determine that certain agreements, contracts or transactions are contrary to the public interest. Conditions or subjects contrary to the public interest include (1) activity that is unlawful under any federal or state law; (2) terrorism; (3) assassination; (4) war; (5) gaming; or (6) other similar activity the CFTC determines, by rule or regulation, to be contrary to the public interest. No agreement, contract or transaction determined by the CFTC to be contrary to the public interest may be listed or made available for clearing or trading on or through a registered entity (CEA Sec. 5c(c)(5)(C), as amended by Sec. 745(b) of the Dodd-Frank Act).

The CFTC must determine the initial eligibility or continuing qualification of a derivatives clearing organization to list a swap for clearing, under criteria that the CFTC

¶3140

determines. Any such criteria, conditions or rules must consider the financial integrity of the derivatives clearing organization; and any other factors the CFTC determines appropriate. The CFTC must take final action with regard to event contracts within 90 days after the start of its review, unless the party seeking to offer the contract or swap agrees to an extension (CEA Sec. 5c(c)(5)(C), as amended by Sec. 745(b) of the Dodd-Frank Act).

Violation of Core Principles.—The legislation repeals a section specifying procedures the CFTC must take before it can take enforcement action against a registered entity for violation of a core principle (CEA Sec. 5(c)(d), as repealed by Sec. 745(d) of the Dodd-Frank Act).

▶ **Effective date.** The provision takes effect 360 days after enactment (Sec. 754 of the Dodd-Frank Wall Street Reform and Consumer Protection Act).

Law source: Law at ¶10,745 and ¶10,754.

— Sec. 745(a) of the Dodd-Frank Wall Street Reform and Consumer Protection Act, amending CEA Sec. 5c(a)(2);

— Sec. 745(b), amending CEA Sec. 5c(c);

— Sec. 745(c), repealing CEA Sec. 5c(d);

— Sec. 754, providing the effective date.

¶3145 Whistleblowers

The Dodd-Frank Wall Street Reform and Consumer Protection Act amends the Commodity Exchange Act (CEA) to provide for awards and protection for whistleblowers in the commodities industry.

Amount of Award.—Under certain circumstances, the CFTC will pay whistleblowers not less than 10 percent and not more than 30 percent of the monetary sanctions imposed in a successful enforcement action (CEA Sec. 23(b), as added by Sec. 748 of the Dodd-Frank Act).

Within those guidelines, the amount of the award is at the CFTC's discretion, taking into account certain criteria. Certain types of whistleblowers are excluded from eligibility for award (CEA Sec. 23(c), as added by Sec. 748 of the Dodd-Frank Act).

Award Process.—Whistleblowers making a claim for an award may be represented by counsel. Prior to payment of the award, the whistleblower must disclose his or her identity to the CFTC and other information the CFTC requires (CEA Sec. 23(d), as added by Sec. 748 of the Dodd-Frank Act). The whistleblower does not need to enter into a contract to collect an award, unless otherwise provided by law or regulation (CEA Sec. 23(e), as added by Sec. 748 of the Dodd-Frank Act).

The legislation establishes an appeal process for review of decisions regarding whistleblower awards (CEA Sec. 23(f), as added by the Dodd-Frank Act).

In addition, the Dodd-Frank Act creates a fund with which to pay whistleblower awards (CEA Sec. 23(g), as added by Sec. 748 of the Dodd-Frank Act).

Whistleblower Protections.—Retaliation against whistleblowers is prohibited. Employers cannot discriminate in any way against an individual for providing information or assisting with investigations. Individuals may bring an action for unlawful discharge or other discrimination in district court, except for federal government employees, who may only bring an action under 5 U.S.C.§ 1221. Methods of relief are provided (CEA Sec. 23(h)(1), as added by the Dodd-Frank Act).

Information given to the CFTC by a whistleblower is confidential and privileged and is not subject to discovery in federal or state court or administrative proceeding, or Freedom of Information Act (FOIA) requests, until disclosed to a defendant or respondent in a public proceeding by the CFTC. Notwithstanding these confidentiality protections, at the CFTC's discretion, the information may be disclosed to various federal and state government entities, as well as registered entities, registered futures associations, self-regulatory organizations and foreign futures authorities (CEA Sec. 23(h)(2), as added by the Dodd-Frank Act).

The CFTC Inspector General must conduct a study on whether the FOIA exemption aids whistleblowers in disclosing information to the CFTC, and on the impact the exemption has had on the public's ability to access information about the CFTC's regulation of commodity futures and option markets. The Inspector General must determine whether to make any recommendations on whether the CFTC should continue to use the exemption. Within 30 months of enactment, the Inspector General must report on its findings to the Senate Banking Committee and the House Financial Services Committee and must publish the report on the CFTC's website (CEA Sec. 23(h)(2), as added by the Dodd-Frank Act).

The CFTC may issue rules necessary to implement the whistleblower provisions. The CFTC must issue rules implementing the whistleblower provisions within 270 days of enactment (CEA Sec. 23(i), as added by the Dodd-Frank Act).

Information does not lose its status as "original information" solely because it was submitted before the effective date of the section, as long as it was submitted after enactment of the Act. Awards may be given for information provided about violations of laws or regulations that occurred before enactment (CEA Secs. 23(k) and (l), as added by Sec. 748 of the Dodd-Frank Act).

A whistleblower who knowingly gives false information is not entitled to an award and is subject to prosecution under 18 U.S.C.§ 1001 (CEA Sec. 23(m), as added by Sec. 748 of the Dodd-Frank Act).

Definitions.—The legislation defines the terms "covered judicial or administrative action", "fund", "monetary sanctions", "original information", "related action", "successful resolution" and "whistleblower" (CEA Sec. 23(a), as added by Sec. 748 of the Dodd-Frank Act).

Unwaivability.—The rights and remedies provided cannot be waived by any agreement, policy form or condition of employment, including by a predispute arbitration agreement. Additionally, a predispute arbitration agreement is not valid or enforceable if it requires arbitration of a dispute under the section (CEA Sec. 23(n), as added by Sec. 748 of the Dodd-Frank Act).

¶3145

▶ **Effective date.** The provision takes effect on the later of: (1) 360 days after enactment; or (2) 60 days after publication of the final implementing rules (Sec. 754 of the Dodd-Frank Wall Street Reform and Consumer Protection Act).

Law source: Law at ¶10,748 and ¶10,754.

— Sec. 748 of the Dodd-Frank Wall Street Reform and Consumer Protection Act, adding CEA Sec. 23;

— Sec. 754, providing the effective date.

¶3150 International Harmonization

The Dodd-Frank Wall Street Reform and Consumer Protection Act directs the CFTC, SEC and the prudential regulators, as defined in CEA Section 1a(39), to consult and coordinate with foreign regulators on the establishment of consistent international standards with respect to the regulation of swaps and security-based swaps (Sec. 752(a) of the Dodd-Frank Wall Street Reform and Consumer Protection Act).

The SEC and CFTC may enter into information-sharing arrangements with foreign regulators that the commissions deem appropriate in the public interest or for the protection of investors, swap counterparties and security-based swap counterparties (Sec. 752(a) of the Dodd-Frank Act).

The CFTC must consult and coordinate with foreign regulators to establish consistent international standards and regulation of contracts of sale of a commodity for future delivery (commodity futures). The CFTC may enter into information-sharing arrangements with foreign regulators as deemed appropriate in the public interest for the protection of users of commodity futures (Sec. 752(b) of the Dodd-Frank Act).

▶ **Effective date.** The provision takes effect 360 days after enactment (Sec. 754 of the Dodd-Frank Wall Street Reform and Consumer Protection Act).

Law source: Law at ¶10,752 and ¶10,754.

— Sec. 752(a) of the Dodd-Frank Wall Street Reform and Consumer Protection Act, providing for international regulatory coordination and information-sharing regarding swaps and security-based swaps;

— Sec. 752(b), requiring the CFTC to coordinate with foreign regulators regarding regulation of commodity futures contracts;

— Sec. 754, providing the effective date.

¶3155 Anti-Manipulation Authority

The Dodd-Frank Wall Street Reform and Consumer Protection Act amends the Commodity Exchange Act (CEA) to add new prohibitions against market manipulation and other fraud involving swaps and commodity futures, and prescribes procedural requirements for CFTC enforcement proceedings in those cases.

Background and Purpose.—The anti-manipulation provisions were authored by Sen. Maria Cantwell (D-WA) to strengthen enforcement powers over commodity and derivatives trading. According to Sen. Cantwell, current law makes it difficult for the CFTC to prove that someone had specific intent to manipulate, and that is a difficult standard to prove. Most individuals do not write an e-mail, for example, saying they intend to manipulated prices, but that is currently what the law requires the CFTC to prove, specific intent to manipulate. As a result of this, the federal courts have recognized that with the CFTC's weaker anti-manipulation standard, market manipulation cases generally have not fared so well. In fact, the law is so weak that in the CFTC's 35-year history, it has only had one successfully prosecuted case of market manipulation (Cong, Rec., May 6, 2010, p. S3348).

The language is patterned after the law that the SEC uses to prosecute fraud and manipulation, *i.e.*, that there can be no manipulative devices or contrivances. It is a strong and clear legal standard that allows regulators to pursue reckless and manipulative behavior successfully. The provision tracks the Securities Act in part because federal case law is clear that when the Congress uses language identical to that used in another statute, Congress intended for the courts and the Commission to interpret the new authority in a similar manner, and Congress has made sure that its intention is clear. In the 75 years since enactment of the Securities and Exchange Act, a substantial body of case law has developed around the words "manipulative or deceptive devices or contrivances" (Cong, Rec., May 6, 2010, p. S3348).

Speaking in support of the Cantwell provision, Sen. Blanche Lincoln (D-AR), Chair of the Senate Agriculture Committee, noted that market manipulation is an ever present danger in derivatives trading. Derivatives are leveraged transactions, she noted, and there are numerous opportunities for traders to abuse their positions in order to game the market to their advantage. Section 747 strengthens existing law to target specific market abuses that have arisen in recent years. It takes the significant step of adding a new and versatile standard for deceptive and manipulative practices under the Commodity Exchange Act. It also addresses false reporting and authorizes private rights of action that will aid the CFTC in its enforcement effort (Cong, Rec., May 6, 2010, p. S3349).

Insider Trading.—Federal government employees cannot trade in futures, options or swaps based on insider information not yet available to the trading public (CEA Sec. 4c(a)(3), as added by Sec. 746(a) of the Dodd-Frank Wall Street Reform and Consumer Protection Act).

The legislation also prohibits federal government employees from imparting such information to others, in their personal capacity or for personal gain. It is unlawful for any person from knowingly using such information acquired from federal government employees for trading purposes. Finally, it is unlawful to steal information held by a federal agency that may affect the price of a commodity futures contract or swap, when the information has not been publicly disseminated, and to use this information for trading purposes (CEA Sec. 4c(a)(4), as added by Sec. 746(b) the Dodd-Frank Act).

Antidisruptive Practices Authority.—It is unlawful for any person to engage in certain trading practices on a registered entity, including (1) violating bids or offers; (2) demonstrating intentional or reckless disregard of the orderly execution of transactions during the closing period; or (3) "spoofing". "Spoofing" is defined as bidding or offering

¶3155

with the intent to cancel the bid or offer before execution (CEA Sec. 4c(a)(5), as added by Sec. 747 of the Dodd-Frank Act).

The CFTC may issue rules prohibiting these and any other trading practices disruptive of fair and equitable trading (CEA Sec. 4c(a)(6), as added by Sec. 747 of the Dodd-Frank Act).

It is unlawful to enter into a swap knowing that a counterparty will use the swap as a device to defraud either third parties or the public or to violate any provision of law (CEA Sec. 4c(a)(7), as added by Sec. 747 of the Dodd-Frank Act).

Unlawful Manipulation.—It is unlawful to use a swap or commodity futures contract in violation of rules promulgated by the CFTC. The CFTC must adopt rules within one year of enactment. It cannot, however, issue rules that require any person to disclose to another person nonpublic information that may be material to the market price, rate or level of the commodity transaction, except as necessary to make any statement made to the other person in connection with the transaction not misleading in any material respect (CEA Sec. 6(c)(1), as amended by Sec. 753(a) of the Dodd-Frank Act).

For the purposes of the section, unlawful manipulation includes disseminating a false, misleading or inaccurate report concerning crop or market information or conditions that affect the price of any commodity in interstate commerce, while knowing or acting in reckless disregard of the fact that the report is false, misleading or inaccurate. This does not affect the applicability of CEA Section 9(a)(2). Mistakenly transmitting false information to a price reporting service in good faith does not constitute unlawful manipulation (CEA Sec. 6(c)(1), as amended by Sec. 753(a) of the Dodd-Frank Act).

It is unlawful to make a false or misleading statement of material fact to the CFTC or to omit any fact if the omission would be misleading. In addition, it is unlawful to manipulate or attempt to manipulate the price of any swap, commodity in interstate commerce or contract for future delivery (CEA Secs. 6(c)(2) and (3), as amended by Sec. 753(a) of the Dodd-Frank Act).

Certain procedures are established for enforcement proceedings in cases involving market manipulation, including provisions regarding complaint, hearing, subpoena, service, witnesses, refusal to obey a subpoena or order of court, sanctions and court orders (CEA Secs. 6(c)(4)–(11), as amended by Sec. 753(a) of the Dodd-Frank Act).

The CFTC may issue cease and desist orders in anti-manipulation cases and impose fines for failing to obey these orders (CEA Sec. 6(d), as amended by Sec. 753(b) of the Dodd-Frank Act).

Private Right of Action.—Swaps are added to the type of instruments for which a private right of action arising out of market manipulation is available (CEA Sec. 22(a)(1)(c), as amended by Sec. 753(b) of the Dodd-Frank Act).

▶ **Effective date.** Provisions concerning insider trading and antidisruptive practices authority take effect 360 days after enactment. Provisions concerning unlawful manipulation and private right of action take effect on the date on which the final rule promulgated pursuant to the Dodd-Frank Act takes effect. This does not preclude the CFTC from undertaking rulemaking prior to the effective date as necessary to implement amendments (Secs. 753(d) and 754 of the Dodd-Frank Wall Street Reform and Consumer Protection Act).

Law source: Law at ¶ 10,746, ¶ 10,747, ¶ 10,753 and ¶ 10,754.

— Sec. 746(a) of the Dodd-Frank Wall Street Reform and Consumer Protection Act, adding CEA Sec. 4c(a)(3);
— Sec. 746(b), adding CEA Sec. 4c(a)(4).
— Sec. 747, adding CEA Secs. 4c(a)(5), 4c(a)(6) and 4c(a)(7).
— Sec. 753, amending CEA Secs. 6(c), 6(d) and 22(a)(1)(D);
— Secs. 753(d) and 754, providing for the effective date.

SECURITY-BASED SWAP MARKETS

¶3160 Securities Law Amendments

The Dodd-Frank Wall Street Reform and Consumer Protection Act amends the Securities Exchange Act of 1934 (Exchange Act) to accommodate regulation of security-based swaps.

The legislation adds a new section providing for clearing of security-based swaps. The section provides for (a) standard for clearing; (b) SEC review; (c) stay of clearing requirement; (d) prevention of evasion; (e) reporting; (f) clearing transition rules; (g) exceptions, (h) trade execution; (i) board approval; and (j) designation of chief compliance officer (Exchange Act Sec. 3C, as added by Sec. 763(a) of the Dodd-Frank Wall Street Reform and Consumer Protection Act).

Clearing agency requirements are amended to provide for clearing securities-based swaps. New provisions include requirements relating to registration, voluntary registration, standards for clearing, rules, exemptions, existing depository institutions and derivatives clearing organizations, and modification of core principles (Exchange Act Secs. 17A(g)–(m), as added by Sec. 763(b) of the Dodd-Frank Act).

A new section is added providing for security-based swap execution facilities. The section provides for (a) registration; (b) trading and trade processing; (c) identification of security-based execution; (d) core principles; (e) exemptions; and (f) rules (Exchange Act Sec. 3D, as added by Sec. 763(c) of the Dodd-Frank Act).

Segregation of collateral held in security-based swap transactions is required. The section provides for collateral segregation requirements relating to (a) registration; (b) cleared security-based swaps; (c) exceptions; (d) permitted investments; (e) prohibition; (f) uncleared security-based swaps; and (g) bankruptcy (Exchange Act Sec. 3E, as added by Sec. 763(d) of the Dodd-Frank Act).

Conforming amendments are made to accommodate trading of security-based swaps (Exchange Act Sec. 6(l), as added by Sec. 763(e) of the Dodd-Frank Act).

Certain enforcement provisions are amended to incorporate provisions relating to securities-based swaps (Exchange Act Secs. 9(b)(1)–(3), as amended by Sec. 763(f) of the Dodd-Frank Act).

The SEC may issue rules to prevent fraud, manipulation and deceptive conduct in relation to security-based swaps (Exchange Act Sec. 9(j), as added by Sec. 763(g) of the

Dodd-Frank Act). The SEC must adopt position limits in security-based swaps, as appropriate. Provisions include (a) instruments eligible for position limits; (b) exemptions; (c) SRO rules; and (d) large trader reporting (Exchange Act Sec. 10B, as added by Sec. 763(h) of the Dodd-Frank Act).

Provisions are made for the public availability of security-based swap transaction data. Provisions include definition of real-time reporting; purpose; general rule; dissemination of public information by registered entities; required rulemaking; timeliness of reporting; reporting to security-based swap data repository; registration of clearing agencies; and public reporting of aggregate data (Exchange Act Sec. 13(m), as added by Sec. 763(i) of the Dodd-Frank Act).

The legislation adds provisions governing security-based swap repositories. Provisions include (1) registration; (2) inspection and examination; (3) compliance with core principles; (4) standard setting; (5) duties; (6) designation of chief compliance officer; (7) core principles; (8) dual registration; and (9) rules (Exchange Act Sec. 13(n), as added by Sec. 763(i) of the Dodd-Frank Act).

The Securities Act of 1933 is amended to include security-based swaps within a definition of "security" (Securities Act Sec. 2(a), as amended by Sec. 768(a) of the Dodd-Frank Act).

The legislation also amends Securities Act registration provisions to prohibit offers to sell or purchase a security-based swap without an effective registration statement by any person other than an eligible contract participant, as defined in the CEA (Securities Act Sec. 5(d), as added by Sec. 768(b) of the Dodd-Frank Act).

▶ **Effective date.** The provisions take effect 360 days after enactment, except for subsection (h), which takes effect on the later of: (1) 360 days after enactment; or (2) 60 days after publication of the final implementing rules (Sec. 774 of the Dodd-Frank Wall Street Reform and Consumer Protection Act).

Law source: Law at ¶10,763, ¶10,768 and ¶10,774.

— Secs. 763(a)–(e) of the Dodd-Frank Wall Street Reform and Consumer Protection Act, adding Exchange Act Secs. 3C, 17A(g)–(m), 3D, 3E and 6(l);

— Sec. 763(f), amending Exchange Act Secs. 9(b)(1)–(3);

— Secs. 763(g)–(i), adding Exchange Act Secs. 9(j), 10B, 13(m) and (n);

— Sec. 768(a), amending Securities Act Sec. 2(a);

— Sec. 768(b), adding Securities Act Sec. 5(d);

— Sec. 774, providing the effective date.

¶3165 Regulation of Dealers and Major Participants

The Dodd-Frank Wall Street Reform and Consumer Protection Act amends the Securities Exchange Act of 1934 (Exchange Act) to provide for registration requirements and other regulation of security-based swap dealers and major security-based swap participants.

Registration.—Security-based swap dealers and major security-based swap participants must register with the SEC within one year of the date of enactment. Registration is required whether or not they also register with the CFTC as a swap dealer or major swap participant (Exchange Act Sec. 15F(a)–(c), as added by Sec. 764(a) of the Dodd-Frank Wall Street Reform and Consumer Protection Act).

Within one year of the date of enactment, the SEC must adopt rules to provide for the registration of security-based swap dealers and major security-based swap participants (Exchange Act Sec. 15F(b), as added by Sec. 764(a) of the Dodd-Frank Act).

Except as permitted by the SEC, it is unlawful for a security-based swap dealer or major security-based swap participant to permit an associated person subject to a statutory disqualification to effect security-based swaps on its behalf, if it knew or should have known of the statutory disqualification (Exchange Act Sec. 15F(b), as added by Sec. 764(a) of the Dodd-Frank Act).

The SEC cannot prescribe rules imposing prudential requirements on security-based swap dealers or major security-based swap participants for which there is a prudential regulator. However, the SEC may prescribe rules as directed (Exchange Act Sec. 15F(d), as added by Sec. 764(a) of the Dodd-Frank Act).

Capital and Margin Requirements.—For security-based swap dealers and major security-based swap participants that are banks and do not have a prudential regulator, capital and margin requirements must be set by the prudential regulator. Security-based swap dealers and major security-based swap participants that are not banks and do not have a prudential regulator must have capital and margin requirements set by the SEC. Certain guidelines for capital and margin requirements are prescribed (Exchange Act Sec. 15F(e), as added by Sec. 764(a) of the Dodd-Frank Act).

Reporting and Recordkeeping.—Registered security-based swap dealers and major security-based swap participants must make reports and maintain records as required by the SEC. Entities without a prudential regulator must also make books and records available for inspection by the SEC. The SEC must adopt rules governing reporting and recordkeeping (Exchange Act Sec. 15F(f), as added by Sec. 764(a) of the Dodd-Frank Act).

Certain requirements are imposed for daily trading records. The SEC must adopt rules governing daily trading records (Exchange Act Sec. 15F(g), as added by Sec. 764(a) of the Dodd-Frank Act).

Business Conduct Standards.—Registered security-based swap dealers and major security-based swap participants must conform with business conduct standards prescribed by SEC rule, relating to fraud, manipulation and other abusive practices; diligent supervision; adherence to position limits; and other matters the SEC deems appropriate. Certain guidelines for business conduct standards are given (Exchange Act Sec. 15F(h), as added by Sec. 764(a) of the Dodd-Frank Act).

A security-based swap dealer providing advice or sale of security-based swaps to "special entities" must adhere to certain business conduct standards. The term "special entity" includes governmental entities (federal agency, state, state agency, city, county, municipality or other political subdivision of a state), employee benefit plans, government retirement plans and endowments. Business conduct standards applicable to persons advising or acting as counterparties to these entities are heightened and

¶3165

include specified extra responsibilities (Exchange Act Sec. 15F(h), as added by Sec. 764(a) of the Dodd-Frank Act).

Other Requirements.—Registered security-based swap dealers and major security-based swap participants must conform with standards set by SEC rule regarding timely and accurate confirmation, processing, netting, documentation and valuation of all security-based swaps. The SEC must adopt rules governing documentation standards. Registered security-based swap dealers and major security-based swap participants must comply with certain requirements, including monitoring of trading, risk management procedures, disclosure of general information, ability to obtain information, management of conflicts of interest and antitrust consideration. The SEC must prescribe rules governing duties of security-based swap dealers and major security-based swap participants (Exchange Act Sec. 15F(i), as added by Sec. 764(a) of the Dodd-Frank Act).

Security-based swap dealers and major security-based swap participants must designate a chief compliance officer. The duties of the chief compliance officer are enumerated (Exchange Act Sec. 15F(k), as added by Sec. 764(a) of the Dodd-Frank Act).

The SEC has primary authority to enforce Subtitle B of the derivatives title. The prudential regulators have exclusive authority to enforce capital and margin and other prudential requirements, including risk-management standards, for security-based swap dealers and major security-based swap participants for which there is no prudential regulator. Provisions are made for referral authority, censure, denial, suspension, notice and hearing, associated persons and unlawful conduct (Exchange Act Sec. 15F(l), as added by Sec. 764(a) of the Dodd-Frank Act).

Savings Clause.—Notwithstanding any other provision of the derivatives title, nothing in Subtitle B of the derivatives subtitle will be construed as divesting any appropriate federal banking agency of any authority it may have to establish or enforce, with respect to a person for which that agency is the appropriate federal banking agency, prudential or other standards under federal law other than this title (Sec. 764(b) of the Dodd-Frank Act).

▶ **Effective date.** The provision takes effect on the later of: (1) 360 days after enactment; or (2) 60 days after publication of the final implementing rules (Sec. 774 of the Dodd-Frank Wall Street Reform and Consumer Protection Act).

Law source: Law at ¶10,764, ¶10,774. Committee Report at ¶50,071.

— Sec. 764(a) of the Dodd-Frank Wall Street Reform and Consumer Protection Act, adding Securities Exchange Act Sec. 15F;

— Sec. 764(b), clarifying that the derivatives title does divests any appropriate federal banking agency of any authority to establish prudential or other standards under other law, for persons for which it is the appropriate federal banking agency;

— Sec. 774, providing the effective date.

¶3170 Reporting and Recordkeeping (SEC)

The Dodd-Frank Wall Street Reform and Consumer Protection Act amends the Securities Exchange Act of 1934 (Exchange Act) to prescribe reporting and recordkeeping requirements for uncleared security-based swaps.

Uncleared Security-Based Swaps.—Security-based swaps not accepted for clearing by a derivatives clearing organization must be reported to a security-based swap data repository (Sec. 10B(n)), or if no repository accepts the swap, then to the SEC, within a time period prescribed by SEC rule (Exchange Act Sec. 13A(a), as added by Sec. 766(a) of the Dodd-Frank Wall Street Reform and Consumer Protection Act).

Transition Rule.—Unexpired swaps entered into before enactment must be reported to a registered security-based swap data repository or the SEC within 30 days after issuance of the interim final rule or other deadline set by the SEC (Exchange Act 13A(a), as added by Sec. 766(a) of the Dodd-Frank Act).

The SEC must promulgate an interim final rule within 90 days of enactment providing for the reporting of swaps entered into before enactment (Exchange Act Sec. 13A(a), as added by Sec. 766(a) of the Dodd-Frank Act).

Choice of Reporting Entity.—For swaps in which only one counterparty is a security-based swap dealer or major security-based swap participant, the dealer or participant must report the security-based swap. Where one counterparty is a security-based swap dealer and the other is a major security-based swap participant, the security-based swap dealer must report the swap. For security-based swaps not meeting either of these criteria, the counterparties must select a counterparty to report the security-based swap (Exchange Act Sec. 13A(a), as added by Sec. 766(a) of the Dodd-Frank Act).

Requirements.—An individual or entity entering into a security-based swap must meet certain reporting and recordkeeping requirements if it did not clear the security-based swap under Section 3C(a)(1) or possess the data regarding the security-based swap accepted by a security-based swap repository (Exchange Act Sec. 13A(b), as added by Sec. 766(a) of the Dodd-Frank Act).

These requirements include: (1) providing reports as the SEC prescribes; and (2) maintaining books and records as required by the SEC, and making these available for inspection by the SEC, appropriate prudential regulator, Financial Stability Oversight Council and the Department of Justice (Exchange Act Sec. 13A(c), as added by Sec. 766(a) of the Dodd-Frank Act).

SEC rules must require reports under this section to be at least as comprehensive as data required to be collected by security-based swap data repositories (Exchange Act Sec. 13A(d), as added by Sec. 766(a) of the Dodd-Frank Act).

Beneficial Ownership Reporting.—The legislation includes conforming amendments to expand beneficial ownership reporting requirements to incorporate security-based swaps (Exchange Act Sec. 13(d)(1), 13(g)(1), as amended by Sec. 766(b) of the Dodd-Frank Act).

The legislation expands reporting requirements by institutional investment managers to include beneficial ownership of a security upon the purchase or sale of a security-based swap (Exchange Act 13(f)(1), as amended by Sec. 766(c) of the Dodd-Frank Act).

The legislation defines "beneficial ownership" with regard to security-based swaps (Exchange Act 13(o), as added by Sec. 766(e) of the Dodd-Frank Act).

Administrative Proceeding Authority.—The legislation expands the SEC's administrative proceeding authority to cover security-based swaps (Exchange Act 15(b)(4), as amended by Sec. 766(d) of the Dodd-Frank Act).

¶3170

▶ **Effective date.** Reporting provisions are effective upon enactment (Exchange Act Sec. 13A(a)(1)(C), as added by Sec. 766(a) of the Dodd-Frank Act).

Law source: Law at ¶10,766.

— Sec. 766(a) of the Dodd-Frank Wall Street Reform and Consumer Protection Act, adding Exchange Act Secs. 13A(a)–(d);

— Sec. 766(b), amending Exchange Act Secs. 13(d)(1) and 13(g)(1);

— Sec. 766(c), amending Exchange Act Sec. 13(f)(1);

— Sec. 766(d), amending Exchange Act Sec. 15(b)(4);

— Sec. 766(e), adding Exchange Act Sec. 13(o).

¶3175 State Gaming and Bucket Shop Laws

The Dodd-Frank Wall Street Reform and Consumer Protection Act amends the Securities Exchange Act of 1934 (Exchange Act) to clarify the applicability of state laws to security-based swaps.

Jurisdiction.—The derivatives provisions of the legislation do not affect the jurisdiction of state securities commissions over any security or any person, insofar as state jurisdiction does not conflict with the provisions of the Act or regulations adopted under it. A person pursuing a suit for damages under the derivatives title cannot recover a total amount in excess of actual damages (Exchange Act Sec. 28(a), as amended by Sec. 767 of the Dodd-Frank Wall Street Reform and Consumer Protection Act).

Rights and remedies provided by the Dodd-Frank Act are in addition to any existing rights and remedies (Exchange Act Sec. 28(a)(2), as amended by Sec. 767 of the Dodd-Frank Act).

Applicability.—State laws prohibiting or regulating the making or promoting of wagering or gaming contracts, or the operation of bucket shops or other similar or related activities do not invalidate:

- a put, call, straddle, option, privilege or other security subject to the derivatives title, and do not apply to any activity related to the offer, purchase, sale, exercise, settlement or closeout of any such security, any security-based swap between eligible contract participants, or any security-based swap effected on a national securities exchange (however, an exception is made for any security that has a pari-mutuel payout, or is otherwise determined by the SEC to be appropriately subject to those state laws);

- a security-based swap between eligible contract participants; or

- any security-based swap effected on a national securities exchange registered under Section 6(b) (Exchange Act Sec. 28(a)(3), as amended by Sec. 767 of the Dodd-Frank Act).

No provision of state law regarding the offer, sale or distribution of securities will apply to any transaction in a security-based swap or security futures product. This does not limit any state antifraud law. A security-based swap cannot be regulated as an insurance contract under state law (Exchange Act Sec. 28(a)(4), as amended by Sec. 767 of the Dodd-Frank Act).

▶ **Effective date.** The provision takes effect 360 days after enactment (Sec. 774 of the Dodd-Frank Wall Street Reform and Consumer Protection Act).

Law source: Law at ¶10,767 and ¶10,774.

— Sec. 767 of the Dodd-Frank Wall Street Reform and Consumer Protection Act, amending Security Exchange Act Sec. 28(a);

— Sec. 774, providing the effective date.

Clearing and Settlement

¶3505 Introduction
¶3510 Systemic Importance
¶3515 Risk Management Standards
¶3520 Operations of Financial Market Utilities
¶3525 Examination and Enforcement—Financial Market Utilities
¶3530 Examination and Enforcement—Financial Institutions
¶3535 Requests for Information, Reports and Records

¶3505 Introduction

The Payment, Clearing and Settlement Supervision Act, contained in Title VIII of the Dodd-Frank Wall Street Reform and Consumer Protection Act, reforms the clearing and settlement activities of financial institutions (Secs. 801 *et seq.* of the Dodd-Frank Wall Street Reform and Consumer Protection Act). In its legislative proposal to strengthen the oversight of payment, clearing and settlement systems, the Obama Administration had observed that arrangements for settling payment obligations and financial transactions were a key determinant of the risk posed by the interconnectedness of financial institutions. "The safety and efficiency of financial institutions and markets depend critically on the strength of the infrastructure of the financial system, specifically the payment, clearing and settlement systems that are used to clear and settle financial transactions. In particular, confidence in financial markets and financial market participants rests on the ability of the payment, clearing and settlement systems used by the markets to meet their financial obligations to participants without delay" (*Financial Regulatory Reform, A New Foundation: Rebuilding Financial Supervision and Regulation*, Treasury Department (June 17, 2009), FED. BANK. L. REP. ¶ 75-201; see also Sec. 802(a)(1) of the Dodd-Frank Act).

Senator Christopher Dodd (D-CT) said that Title VIII preserves the role of the front line regulators like the SEC and Commodity Futures Trading Commission (CFTC), while also providing for robust prudential standards for entities designated as systemically important by the Financial Stability Oversight Council (Council). The legislation requires tough and heightened regulation of systemically important financial market utilities because no safety valve otherwise exists if they cannot perform their functions. As financial market utilities provide critical services to the financial system, such as the clearing and settlement of government and municipal securities and derivatives, they could not be carved out of systemic risk oversight. In Sen. Dodd's view, the legislation reduces systemic risk by complementing existing regulations of the SEC and the CFTC. The statute also provides a safeguard for financial market utilities that run into extraordinary liquidity problems by authorizing the Board of Governors of the Federal Reserve System (the Fed) to provide account and settlement services to utilities that are not depository institutions. Finally, Title VIII harmonizes federal legislation with the international consensus that gives central banks a role in payment, clearing and settlement oversight (Comments by Sen. Christopher Dodd, House-Senate Conference Committee meeting, June 17, 2010).

According to Sen. Richard Shelby (R-AL), the Dodd-Frank Act provides for enormous new duties for central clearinghouses. For example, the provisions in Title VII concerning derivatives mandate the clearing of many over-the-counter derivatives for the first time. In this regard, Sen. Shelby said that it was not possible to have an effective derivatives title without an effective payment, clearance and settlement title. Accordingly, it was important for Congress to provide a risk oversight role for the Fed and discount window access for clearinghouses in a liquidity crunch in order to ensure the stability of the financial system (Comments by Sen. Richard Shelby, House-Senate Conference Committee meeting, June 17, 2010).

Congressional Purpose.—Congress found that financial market utilities that conduct or support multilateral payment, clearing or settlement activities may reduce risks to their participants and the broader financial system, but may also concentrate and create new risks (Sec. 802(a)(2) of the Dodd-Frank Act). In addition, the payment, clearing and settlement activities conducted by financial institutions also present important risks both to the institutions themselves and to the financial system (Sec. 802(a)(3) of the Dodd-Frank Act). Accordingly, Congress determined that enhancements to the regulation of systemically important financial market utilities and payment, clearing and settlement activities were necessary to: (1) provide consistency; (2) promote strong risk management and safety and soundness; (3) reduce systemic risks; and (4) support the stability of the financial system (Sec. 802(a)(4) of the Dodd-Frank Act).

To mitigate systemic risk in the financial system and promote financial stability, the legislation gives the Council a role in identifying systemically important financial market utilities or payment, clearing or settlement activities (Sec. 804(a)(1) of the Dodd-Frank Act). It also gives the Fed authority to promote uniform risk management standards while providing the Fed an enhanced role in supervising risk management standards for systemically important financial market utilities and for systemically important payment, clearing and settlement activities conducted by financial institutions. Finally, the legislation seeks to strengthen the liquidity of systemically important financial market utilities (Sec. 802(b) of the Dodd-Frank Act).

> **CCH Comment:** The language of Title VIII draws from proposed legislation drafted by the Obama Administration and includes regulatory features for derivatives market reform endorsed by the G-20.

Rulemaking and Other Authority.—The legislation authorizes the Fed, the supervisory agencies and the Council to prescribe rules and issue orders as may be necessary to administer and carry out the purposes of Title VIII and prevent evasion of its provisions (Sec. 810 of the Dodd-Frank Act).

Unless otherwise provided by its terms, Title VIII does not divest any appropriate financial regulator, supervisory agency or other federal or state agency of any authority derived from any other applicable law. The risk management standards prescribed by the Fed under Section 805, however, will supersede any less stringent requirements established under any other authority to the extent that any conflict exists (Sec. 811 of the Dodd-Frank Act).

▶ **Effective date.** The provision is effective as of the date of enactment (Sec. 814 of the Dodd-Frank Wall Street Reform and Consumer Protection Act).

Law source: Law at ¶10,801, ¶10,802, ¶10,804, ¶10,810, ¶10,811 and ¶10,814. Committee Report at ¶54,421, ¶54,423, ¶54,429 and ¶54,430.

— Sec. 801 of the Dodd-Frank Wall Street Reform and Consumer Protection Act, providing the short title of Title VIII;

— Sec. 802, describing congressional findings and purpose;

— Sec. 804(a)(1), requiring the Council to identify systemically important clearing and settlement activities;

— Sec. 810, providing the Fed and Council with rulemaking authority;

— Sec. 811, preserving the authority of federal and state agencies unless otherwise provided;

— Sec. 814, providing the effective date.

¶3510 Systemic Importance

The Dodd-Frank Wall Street Reform and Consumer Protection Act requires the Financial Stability Oversight Council (Council) to designate those financial market utilities or payment, clearing or settlement activities by financial institutions that the Council determines are, or are likely to become, systemically important. The Council must make any designations on a nondelegable basis and by a vote of two-thirds of its members, including an affirmative vote by the Chairperson of the Council (Sec. 804(a)(1) of the Dodd-Frank Wall Street Reform and Consumer Protection Act).

Definitions.—The term "systemic importance" means a situation where the failure of, or disruption to, either a financial market utility or the conduct of a payment, clearing or settlement activity creates or increases the risk of significant liquidity or credit problems spreading across financial institutions or markets and threatening the stability of the U.S. financial system (Sec. 803(9) of the Dodd-Frank Act).

The term "financial market utility" means any person that manages or operates a multilateral system for the purpose of transferring, clearing or settling payments, securities or other financial transactions either: (1) among financial institutions; or (2) between financial institutions and the person (Sec. 803(6)(A) of the Dodd-Frank Act).

The term "financial market utility" does not, however, include: (1) designated contract markets, regulated futures associations, swap data repositories, and swap execution facilities registered under the Commodity Exchange Act; or (2) national securities exchanges, national securities associations, alternative trading systems, security-based swap data repositories and swap execution facilities registered under the Exchange Act, solely by reason of these entities providing facilities for comparison of data respecting the terms of settlement of securities or futures transactions effected either on an exchange or on electronic systems that they operate and control. These exclusions apply only with respect to activities that require the entity to be registered (Sec. 803(6)(B)(i) of the Dodd-Frank Act).

The term also does not include any broker, dealer, transfer agent, investment company, futures commission merchant, introducing broker, commodity trading advisor or commodity pool operator, solely by reason of functions performed by these institutions as part of brokerage, dealing, transfer agency or investment company activities, or solely by reason of acting on behalf of a financial market utility or participant in connection with the utility's services to its participants, provided that the services performed by the institution do not constitute critical risk management or processing functions of the utility (Sec. 803(6)(B)(ii) of the Dodd-Frank Act).

The term "financial institution" means:

- a depository institution, as defined in Federal Deposit Insurance Act Section 3;
- a branch or agency of a foreign bank, as defined in International Banking Act Section 1(b);
- an organization operating under Federal Reserve Act Section 25 or 25A;
- a credit union, as defined in Federal Credit Union Act Section 101;
- a broker or dealer, as defined in Exchange Act Section 3;
- an investment company, as defined in Investment Company Act Section 3;
- an insurance company, as defined in Investment Company Act Section 2;
- an investment adviser, as defined in Advisers Act Section 202;
- a futures commission merchant, commodity trading advisor or commodity pool operator, as defined in Commodity Exchange Act Section 1a; and
- any company engaged in financial activities, as described in Bank Holding Company Act Section 4 (Sec. 803(5)(A) of the Dodd-Frank Act).

The term "financial institution" does not, however, include: (1) designated contract markets, regulated futures associations, swap data repositories, and swap execution facilities registered under the Commodity Exchange Act; (2) national securities exchanges, national securities associations, alternative trading systems, securities information processors, security-based swap data repositories and swap execution facilities registered under the Exchange Act; or (3) designated clearing entities. These exclusions apply only with respect to activities that require these entities to be registered (Sec. 803(5)(B) of the Dodd-Frank Act).

The term "designated clearing entity" means: (1) a designated financial market utility that is a derivatives clearing organization registered under Commodity Exchange Act Section 5b; or (2) a clearing agency registered with the SEC under Exchange Act Section 17A (Sec. 803(3) of the Dodd-Frank Act).

The phrase "payment, clearing, or settlement activity" means, in general, an activity carried out by one or more financial institutions to facilitate the completion of financial transactions (Sec. 803(7)(A) of the Dodd-Frank Act). When conducted with respect to financial transactions, payment, clearing or settlement activities may include:

- the calculation and communication of unsettled financial transactions between counterparties;

¶3510

- the netting of transactions;
- provision and maintenance of trade, contract or instrument information;
- the management of risks and activities associated with continuing financial transactions;
- transmittal and storage of payment instructions;
- the movement of funds;
- the final settlement of financial transactions; and
- other similar functions that the Council may determine (Sec. 803(7)(C) of the Dodd-Frank Act).

The term "payment, clearing, or settlement activity" excludes, however, any offer or sale of a security under the Securities Act, or any quotation, order, entry, negotiation, or other pre-trade activity (Sec. 803(7)(A) of the Dodd-Frank Act). The term also excludes the public reporting of swap transaction data under new Commodity Exchange Act Section 2(a)(13) or Exchange Act Section 3C(i), as added by the Dodd-Frank Act (Sec. 803(7)(D) of the Dodd-Frank Act).

The term "financial transaction" includes:

- funds transfers;
- securities contracts;
- contracts of sale of a commodity for future delivery;
- forward contracts;
- repurchase agreements;
- swaps, security-based swaps, swap agreements and security-based swap agreements;
- foreign exchange contracts;
- financial derivatives contracts; and
- any similar transaction that the Council determines to be a financial transaction (Sec. 803(7)(B) of the Dodd-Frank Act).

Considerations.—The Council must take the following considerations into account when determining whether a financial market utility or payment, clearing or settlement activity is, or is likely to become, systemically important:

- the aggregate monetary value of transactions processed by the financial market utility or carried out through the payment, clearing or settlement activity;
- the aggregate exposure of the financial market utility or financial institution engaged in the activities to its counterparties;
- the relationship, interdependencies or other interactions of the financial market utility or activity with other financial market utilities and activities;
- the effect that a failure or disruption would have on critical markets, financial institutions or the broader financial system; and
- any other factors that the Council deems appropriate (Sec. 804(a)(2) of the Dodd-Frank Act).

¶3510

Rescission of Designations.—The Council must rescind a designation of systemic importance if the Council determines, by a two-thirds vote of its members, including an affirmative vote by the Chairperson of the Council, that the utility or activity no longer meets the standards for systemic importance. After the rescission of a designation, the financial market utility or financial institution conducting the activity will no longer be subject to Title VIII of the Dodd-Frank Act or any underlying regulations prescribed by the Council (Sec. 804(b) of the Dodd-Frank Act).

Consultation.—The Council must consult with the relevant supervisory agency and Board of Governors of the Federal Reserve System (the Fed) before making or rescinding a designation of systemic importance (Sec. 804(c)(1) of the Dodd-Frank Act). A "supervisory agency" for purposes of Title VIII means the federal agency that has primary jurisdiction over a designated financial market utility under federal banking, securities or commodity futures laws, as follows:

- The SEC has primary jurisdiction over a utility registered with the SEC as a clearing agency.
- The Commodity Futures Trading Commission has primary jurisdiction with respect to registered derivatives clearing organizations.
- Institutions described in Federal Deposit Insurance Act Section 3(q) fall under the primary jurisdiction of the appropriate federal banking agency.

The Fed has primary jurisdiction over any designated financial market utility not otherwise subject to the jurisdiction of the above agencies. Agencies that share jurisdictional supervision of a designated financial market utility should agree on one agency to act as the supervisory agency. If the agencies cannot agree, the Council will determine the supervisory agency for purposes of Title VIII (Sec. 803(8) of the Dodd-Frank Act).

Notice and Hearing.—The Council must provide advance notice to a financial market utility or the financial institutions conducting a payment, clearing or settlement activity before making or rescinding a designation of systemic importance. The Council must publish advance notice to financial institutions in the *Federal Register* (Secs. 804(c)(2)(A) and (B) of the Dodd-Frank Act).

A financial market utility or financial institution may request, in writing and within 30 days, an opportunity for a written or oral hearing before the Council to demonstrate that substantial evidence does not support a proposed designation or a rescission of a designation (Sec. 804(c)(2)(C) of the Dodd-Frank Act). The Council must then fix a time, not more than 30 days after receipt of a timely request, and a place at which the financial market utility or financial institution may appear to submit written materials. The financial market utility or financial institution may appear personally or through counsel. Oral testimony or oral argument may be heard at the sole discretion of the Council (Sec. 804(c)(2)(D) of the Dodd-Frank Act).

The Council may waive or modify the notice and hearing requirements if the Council determines, by a two-thirds vote of its members, including an affirmative vote by the Chairperson, that the waiver or modification is necessary to prevent or mitigate an immediate threat to the financial system. The Council must provide notice of the waiver or modification as soon as practicable. In the case of financial market utilities, the Council must provide notice of the emergency exception no later than 24 hours after the waiver or modification. The Council must notify financial institutions no later that three business days after the waiver or modification by posting a notice on the Council's website and by publishing a notice in the *Federal Register* (Sec. 804(c)(3) of the Dodd-Frank Act).

The Council must notify the financial market utility or financial institution of its final determination within 60 days of any hearing. The notification must be in writing and must include findings of fact on which the Council based its determination. If the Council does not receive a timely request for a hearing, it must notify the financial market utility or financial institution of its determination no later than 30 days after the final date on which a hearing could have been requested. The Council must publish all such notices to financial institutions in the *Federal Register* (Sec. 804(d) of the Dodd-Frank Act).

The Council may extend the time periods established for the notice and hearing requirements as the Council deems necessary (Sec. 804(e) of the Dodd-Frank Act).

▶ **Effective date.** The provision is effective as of the date of enactment (Sec. 814 of the Dodd-Frank Wall Street Reform and Consumer Protection Act).

Law source: Law at ¶10,803, ¶10,804 and ¶10,814. Committee Report at ¶54,423.

— Sec. 803 of the Dodd-Frank Wall Street Reform and Consumer Protection Act, providing definitions;
— Sec. 804(a)(1), requiring designations of systemically important financial market utilities and activities;
— Sec. 804(a)(2), listing considerations in determining systemic importance;
— Sec. 804(b), providing for rescission of designations;
— Sec. 804(c)(1), requiring the Council to consult with the Fed and supervisory agencies;
— Sec. 804(c)(2), requiring advance notice and an opportunity for a hearing;
— Sec. 804(c)(3), providing an exception for emergency waivers and modifications;
— Sec. 804(d), requiring notification of final determinations;
— Sec. 804(e), providing for an extension of notice and hearing periods;
— Sec. 814, providing the effective date.

¶3515 Risk Management Standards

The Board of Governors of the Federal Reserve System (the Fed), in consultation with the Financial Stability Oversight Council (Council) and the supervisory agencies, generally has the authority to prescribe the risk management standards governing the operations of designated financial market utilities and the conduct of designated payment, clearing and settlement activities by financial institutions. The statute sets out the objectives, principles and scope of those standards. The Commodity Futures Trading Commission (CFTC) and the SEC, however, may prescribe risk management standards for designated clearing entities and designated activities of certain financial institutions which fall under their supervisory or regulatory authority.

Authority.—Except for the special procedures for certain entities falling under the supervision of the CFTC or the SEC, the legislation requires the Fed to prescribe risk management standards by rule or order. The Fed's risk management standards must govern: (1) the operations related to the payment, clearing and settlement activities of designated financial market utilities; and (2) the conduct of designated activities by financial institutions. The Fed must consult with the Council and the supervisory agencies and must take into consideration relevant international standards and existing prudential requirements (Sec. 805(a)(1) of the Dodd-Frank Wall Street Reform and Consumer Protection Act).

Objectives and Principles.—The risk management standards should: (1) promote robust risk management; (2) promote safety and soundness; (3) reduce systemic risks; and (4) support the stability of the broader financial system (Sec. 805(b) of the Dodd-Frank Act).

Scope.—The risk management standards may address such areas as:

- risk management policies and procedures;
- margin and collateral requirements;
- participant or counterparty default policies and procedures;
- the ability to complete timely clearing and settlement of financial transactions;
- capital and financial reserve requirements of financial market utilities; and
- other areas that are necessary to achieve the objectives and principles (Sec. 805(c) of the Dodd-Frank Act).

The risk management standards must, where appropriate, establish a threshold as to the level or significance of a financial institution's engagement in a payment, clearing or settlement activity that will subject the financial institution to the standards with respect to that activity (Sec. 805(e) of the Dodd-Frank Act).

Except as provided in Sections 807(e) and (f), nothing in Title VIII permits the Council or the Fed to take any action or exercise any authority granted to the CFTC under Commodity Exchange Act Section 2(h) or to the SEC under Exchange Act Section 3C(a). These prohibited actions include:

- the approval, disapproval, or stay of the clearing requirement for any group, category, type or class of swaps that a designated clearing entity may accept for clearing;
- the determination that any group, category, type or class of swaps will be subject to the mandatory clearing requirement of Commodity Exchange Act Section 2(h)(1) or Exchange Act 3C(a)(1);
- the determination that any person is exempt from the mandatory clearing requirement of Commodity Exchange Act Section 2(h)(1) or Exchange Act 3C(a)(1); or
- any authority granted to the CFTC or the SEC with respect to transaction reporting or trade execution (Sec. 805(d) of the Dodd-Frank Act).

Compliance.—Designated financial market utilities and financial institutions subject to the risk management standards must conduct their operations in compliance with those standards (Sec. 805(f) of the Dodd-Frank Act). To the extent any conflict exists, any standards prescribed by the Fed under Section 805 will supersede any less stringent requirements established under any other authority (Sec. 811 of the Dodd-Frank Act).

Special Procedures.—Section 805(a)(2) permits the CFTC and the SEC, in consultation with the Council and the Fed, to prescribe regulations containing risk management standards for those designated clearing entities and financial institutions engaged in designated activities for which they are the supervisory agency or the appropriate financial regulator. The regulations, which must take into consideration relevant international standards and existing prudential requirements, are permitted for the purpose of governing: (1) the operations related to the payment, clearing and settlement activities of designated clearing entities; and (2) the conduct of designated activities by those financial institutions (Sec. 805(a)(2)(A) of the Dodd-Frank Act).

The Fed may determine that the existing prudential requirements of the CFTC or the SEC with respect to these designated clearing agencies and financial institutions, including the requirements prescribed under Section 805(a)(2)(A), are insufficient to prevent or mitigate significant liquidity, credit, operational or other risks to the financial markets or to financial stability (Sec. 805(a)(2)(B) of the Dodd-Frank Act). The Fed must provide any such determination in writing to the CFTC or the SEC, as applicable, and the Council. The determination must contain a detailed analysis supporting the Fed's findings and must identify the specific prudential requirements that are insufficient (Sec. 805(a)(2)(C) of the Dodd-Frank Act).

Within 60 days, the CFTC or the SEC must either: (1) object to the Fed's determination with a detailed analysis as to why the existing prudential requirements are sufficient; or (2) submit an explanation to the Council and the Fed describing the actions to be taken in response to the Fed's determination (Sec. 805(a)(2)(D) of the Dodd-Frank Act). Upon an affirmative vote of vote of at least two-thirds of its members, the Council must either find: (1) that the response is sufficient; or (2) require the CFTC or the SEC, as applicable, to prescribe the risk management standards deemed necessary by the Council to address the specific prudential requirements that are determined to be insufficient (Sec. 805(a)(2)(E) of the Dodd-Frank Act).

Consultation.—The CFTC must consult with the Fed:

- prior to exercising its authorities under Commodity Exchange Act Sections 2(h)(2)(C), 2(h)(3)(A), 2(h)(3)(C), 2(h)(4)(A), and 2(h)(4)(B), as amended by Title VII of the Dodd-Frank Act;
- with respect to any rule or rule amendment of a derivatives clearing organization for which a stay of certification has been issued under Section 745(b)(3); and
- prior to exercising its rulemaking authority under Section 728 (Sec. 812(a) of the Dodd-Frank Act).

The SEC must consult with the Fed:

- prior to exercising its authorities under Exchange Act Sections 3C(a)(2)(C), 3C(3)(A), 3C(a)(3)(C), 3C(a)(4)(A), and 3C(a)(4)(B), as amended by Title VII of the Dodd-Frank Act;
- with respect to any proposed rule change of a clearing agency for which an extension of the time for review has been designated under Exchange Act Section 19(b)(2); and
- prior to exercising its rulemaking authority under Exchange Act Section 13(n), as added by Section 763(i) (Sec. 812(b) of the Dodd-Frank Act).

¶3515

Designated Clearing Agency Risk Management.—The CFTC and the SEC must coordinate with the Fed to develop jointly risk management programs for designated clearing entities. Not later than one year after the date of enactment, the agencies must submit a joint report to the Senate Banking Committee, the Senate Agriculture Committee, the House Financial Services Committee and the House Agriculture Committee. The report must contain recommendations for:

- improving consistency in the designated clearing entity oversight programs of the SEC and the CFTC;
- promoting robust risk management oversight by regulators of designated clearing entities; and
- improving regulators' ability to monitor the potential effects of designated clearing entity risk management on the stability of U.S. financial system (Sec. 813 of the Dodd-Frank Act).

▶ **Effective date.** The provisions are effective as of the date of enactment (Sec. 814 of the Dodd-Frank Wall Street Reform and Consumer Protection Act).

Law source: Law at ¶10,805, ¶10,811, ¶10,812, ¶10,813 and ¶10,814. Committee Report at ¶54,424 and ¶54,430.

— Sec. 805(a) of the Dodd-Frank Wall Street Reform and Consumer Protection Act, providing authority for establishing risk management standards;
— Sec. 805(b), stating objectives and principles;
— Sec. 805(c), providing the scope;
— Sec. 805(d), setting a limitation on the scope;
— Sec. 805(e), requiring establishment of a threshold level for payment, clearing and settlement activities;
— Sec. 805(f), requiring compliance;
— Sec. 811, concerning other authority;
— Sec. 812, requiring consultation with the Fed;
— Sec. 813, requiring development of a common framework for designated clearing entity risk management;
— Sec. 814, providing the effective date.

¶3520 Operations of Financial Market Utilities

The Board of Governors of the Federal Reserve System (the Fed) may authorize a Federal Reserve Bank to maintain an account for a designated financial market utility (defined at ¶3510) and modify or provide an exemption from reserve requirements that would otherwise apply to the utility. A designated financial market utility must provide advance notice of and obtain approval of material changes to its rules, procedures or operations.

Federal Reserve Account and Services.—The Fed may authorize a Federal Reserve Bank to establish and maintain an account for a designated financial market utility. Subject to any applicable Fed rules, orders or standards, the Federal Reserve Bank may provide to the utility: (1) the services that it provides to depository institutions under Federal Reserve Act Section 11A(b); and (2) deposit accounts authorized under the first undesignated paragraph of Federal Reserve Act Section 13 (Sec. 806(a) of the Dodd-Frank Wall Street Reform and Consumer Protection Act).

In unusual or exigent circumstances, the Fed may also authorize a Federal Reserve Bank to provide discount and borrowing privileges to the financial market utility under Federal Reserve Act Section 10B. The Fed may grant authorization for advances only following: (1) an affirmative vote of either a majority of the Fed or other such number as required by Federal Reserve Act Section 11r(2); (2) consultation with the Treasury Secretary; and (3) a showing by the utility that it cannot secure adequate credit accommodations from other banking institutions. All discounts and borrowing privileges are subject to any limitations, restrictions and regulations that the Fed may prescribe. Access to discount and borrowing privileges under Federal Reserve Act Section 10B does not require a designated financial market utility to be or become a bank or bank holding company (Sec. 806(b) of the Dodd-Frank Act).

The Federal Reserve Bank may pay earnings on account balances in the same manner as it pays earnings to depository institutions, subject to the Fed's requirements (Sec. 806(c) of the Dodd-Frank Act). The Fed may exempt a designated financial market utility from, or modify, any reserve requirements applicable to the utility under Federal Reserve Act Section 19 (Sec. 806(d) of the Dodd-Frank Act).

Changes to Rules, Procedures or Operations.—*Advance Notice.* The legislation requires a designated financial market utility to provide advance notice of any proposed change to its rules, procedures or operations that could materially affect, as defined in the rules of its supervisory agency, the nature or level of the risks presented by the utility. The financial market utility must provide the notice to its supervisory agency 60 days in advance of the proposed change. The statute requires each supervisory agency to prescribe regulations defining and establishing standards for determining when the financial market utility must provide notice (Secs. 806(e)(1)(A) and (B) of the Dodd-Frank Act).

The notice of a proposed change must describe the nature of the change and the expected risks to either the financial market utility, its participants or the market. The notice must also address how the financial market utility plans to manage any identified risks (Sec. 806(e)(1)(C) of the Dodd-Frank Act). If requested by the supervisory agency, the financial market utility must provide any additional information necessary to assess the effect that the proposed change would have on the risks associated with the utility's payment, clearing or settlement activities (Sec. 806(e)(1)(D) of the Dodd-Frank Act).

Notice of Objection. The supervisory agency must notify the financial market utility of any objection regarding the proposed change within 60 days of either: (1) the date the notice is received; or (2) the date the supervisory agency receives any further information requested for consideration (Sec. 806(e)(1)(E) of the Dodd-Frank Act). The utility may implement the proposed change if it has not received an objection within the applicable 60 day period (Sec. 806(e)(1)(G) of the Dodd-Frank Act). A financial market utility may not implement a change, however, to which the supervisory agency has an objection (Sec. 806(e)(1)(F) of the Dodd-Frank Act).

¶3520

Extension for Novel or Complex Issues. The supervisory agency may extend the 60-day review period for an additional 60 days if the proposed change raises novel or complex issues, provided that the supervisory agency or the Fed provides prompt written notice to the utility. Any extension of the review period must also extend the time periods for the supervisory agency to provide notice of objection and for the utility to implement the proposed change (Sec. 806(e)(1)(H) of the Dodd-Frank Act). A designated financial market utility may implement a proposed change in less than 60 days if the supervisory agency notifies the utility that it does not object and authorizes implementation, subject to any conditions imposed by the supervisory agency (Sec. 806(e)(1)(I) of the Dodd-Frank Act).

Emergency Changes. The statute permits a designated financial market utility to implement a change that would otherwise require advance notice if the utility determines: (1) an emergency exists; and (2) the change requires immediate implementation in order for the utility to provide its services in a safe and sound manner. The financial market utility must provide notice to its supervisory agency as soon as practicable, but not later than 24 hours after implementation of the change (Secs. 806(e)(2)(A) and (B) of the Dodd-Frank Act).

The notice of the emergency change must include all of the information otherwise prescribed for changes requiring advance notice, as well as a description of both the nature of the emergency and the reason for the emergency change. The supervisory agency may require modification or rescission of the change if it finds that the change is not consistent with the purposes of the Dodd-Frank Act or any rules, orders or standards prescribed under Section 805(a) (Secs. 806(e)(2)(C) and (D) of the Dodd-Frank Act).

Consultation with Fed. A supervisory agency must provide the Fed with a complete copy of any notice, request or other information it issues or receives concerning proposed changes to a financial market utility's rules, operations or procedures. The supervisory agency must also consult with the Fed before taking any action on, or completing its review of, a proposed change (Secs. 806(e)(3) and (4) of the Dodd-Frank Act).

▶ **Effective date.** The provision is effective as of the date of enactment (Sec. 814 of the Dodd-Frank Wall Street Reform and Consumer Protection Act).

Law source: Law at ¶10,806 and ¶10,814. Committee Report at ¶54,425.

— Sec. 806(a) of the Dodd-Frank Wall Street Reform and Consumer Protection Act, providing for the establishment of Federal Reserve accounts by financial market utilities;

— Sec. 806(b), permitting discount and borrowing privileges under unusual or exigent circumstances;

— Sec. 806(c), permitting the payment of earnings on balances;

— Sec. 806(d), providing exemptions from, or modifications to, reserve requirements;

— Sec. 806(e), requiring advance notice of changes to a financial market utility's rules, procedures or operations;

— Sec. 814, providing the effective date.

¶3525 Examination and Enforcement—Financial Market Utilities

The SEC or other supervisory agency with primary jurisdiction over a designated financial market utility (defined at ¶ 3510) must conduct safety and soundness examinations of the utility at least annually and may take enforcement action against it. The Board of Governors of the Federal Reserve System (the Fed) can participate in the examinations and may recommend enforcement action against a designated financial market utility. The Fed itself may also take emergency enforcement actions directly if there is an imminent risk of substantial harm to financial institutions or the broader financial system.

Examinations.—The supervisory agency with primary jurisdiction over a designated financial market utility must conduct an examination of the utility at least annually. The examination must enable the supervisory agency to determine:

- the nature of the financial utility's operations and the risks the utility bears;
- the financial and operational risks presented by the financial market utility to financial institutions, critical markets or the broader financial system;
- the resources and capabilities of the financial market utility to monitor and control these risks;
- the financial market utility's safety and soundness; and
- the financial market utility's compliance with Title VIII of the Dodd-Frank Wall Street Reform and Consumer Protection Act and its underlying rules and orders (Sec. 807(a) of the Dodd-Frank Act).

The supervisory agency may also examine service providers integral to a financial market utility's operations to determine whether the provision of that service complies with applicable laws, rules and standards. The supervisory agency may examine service providers, even off site providers not affiliated with the financial market utility, to the same extent as if the utility were performing the service on its own premises (Sec. 807(b) of the Dodd-Frank Act).

Enforcement.—The supervisory agency has authority under Federal Deposit Insurance Act Sections 8(b) through 8(n) to enforce the examination provisions against the financial market utility in the same manner and to the same extent as if the financial market utility was an insured depository institution and the supervisory agency was the depository institution's appropriate federal banking agency (Sec. 807(c) of the Dodd-Frank Act).

Fed Involvement.—The supervisory agency must consult annually with the Fed regarding the scope and methodology of any examination of a designated financial market utility that it conducts. The supervisory agency must lead all such examinations, although the Fed may participate in any examination at its discretion (Sec. 807(d) of the Dodd-Frank Act).

The Fed may, after consulting with the Financial Stability Oversight Council (Council) and the supervisory agency, recommend at any time that a supervisory agency take enforcement action against a financial market utility in order to prevent or mitigate significant liquidity, credit, operational or other risks to the financial markets or to financial stability. The recommendation must include a detailed analysis supporting the Fed's recommendation. The supervisory agency must consider the recommendation and submit a response to the Fed within 60 days (Secs. 807(e)(1) and (2) of the Dodd-Frank Act).

If the supervisory agency rejects the recommendation, in whole or in part, the Fed may refer the recommendation to the Council for a binding decision on whether an enforcement action is warranted. If the Council approves the Fed's recommendation by a majority vote, the Council may require the supervisory agency to: (1) exercise the enforcement authority under Federal Deposit Insurance Act Sections 8(b) through 8(n); and (2) take enforcement action against the utility (Secs. 807(e)(3) and (4) of the Dodd-Frank Act).

The Fed may, after consulting with the supervisory agency and upon a majority vote by the Council, take direct enforcement action against a designated financial market utility if the imminent risk of substantial harm precludes the Fed from using the procedures for recommending an enforcement action to the supervisory agency. To take such action, the Fed must have reasonable cause to believe that either an action or contemplated action by the financial market utility or the utility's condition poses an imminent risk of substantial harm to financial institutions, critical markets or the broader financial system (Sec. 807(f)(1) of the Dodd-Frank Act).

If the Fed takes emergency enforcement action against a designated financial market utility, the legislation provides the Fed with authority under Federal Deposit Insurance Act Sections 8(b) through 8(n) in the same manner and to the same extent as if the utility was an insured depository institution and the Fed was the depository institution's appropriate federal banking agency (Sec. 807(f)(2) of the Dodd-Frank Act).

▶ **Effective date.** The provision is effective as of the date of enactment (Sec. 814 of the Dodd-Frank Wall Street Reform and Consumer Protection Act).

Law source: Law at ¶10,807 and ¶10,814. Committee Report at ¶54,426.

— Sec. 807(a) of the Dodd-Frank Wall Street Reform and Consumer Protection Act, requiring examinations of financial market utilities by supervisory agencies;

— Sec. 807(b), permitting examinations of service providers;

— Sec. 807(c), granting enforcement authority to supervisory agencies;

— Sec. 807(d), requiring consultation on examination planning and permitting participation by the Fed;

— Sec. 807(e), permitting enforcement recommendations by the Fed;

— Sec. 807(f), providing for emergency enforcement actions by the Fed;

— Sec. 814, providing the effective date.

¶3530 Examination and Enforcement—Financial Institutions

Under the Dodd-Frank Wall Street Reform and Consumer Protection Act, the appropriate financial regulator may examine a financial institution engaged in designated payment, clearing or settlement activities and may enforce the legislation's provisions or its underlying rules and orders rules against such an institution. The Board of Governors of the Federal Reserve System (the Fed) must collaborate with the appropriate financial regulator to ensure consistent application of the rules. The Fed has back-up authority to conduct examinations and take enforcement action if it has reasonable cause to believe a violation of Title VIII of the Dodd-Frank Act has occurred.

Definitions.—The term "appropriate financial regulator" means:

- the primary financial regulator, as defined in Section 2 of the Dodd-Frank Act;
- the National Credit Union Administration, with respect to any insured credit union under the Federal Credit Union Act; and
- the Fed, with respect to organizations operating under Federal Reserve Act Section 25A (Sec. 803(1) of the Dodd-Frank Wall Street Reform and Consumer Protection Act).

Examinations.—The appropriate financial regulator may examine a financial institution engaged in a designated payment, clearing or settlement activity in order to determine the following:

- the nature and scope of the designated activities engaged in by the financial institution;
- the financial and operational risks the designated activities may pose to the financial institution's safety and soundness;
- the financial and operational risks the designated activities may pose to other financial institutions, critical markets or the broader financial system;
- the financial institution's available resources and capabilities to monitor and control the risks;
- the financial institution's compliance with Title VIII of the Dodd-Frank Act and its underlying rules and orders (Sec. 808(a) of the Dodd-Frank Act).

Enforcement.—The appropriate financial regulator has authority under Federal Deposit Insurance Act Sections 8(b) through 8(n) to enforce the examination provisions against the financial institution in the same manner and to the same extent as if the financial institution was an insured depository institution and the financial regulator was the depository institution's appropriate federal banking agency (Sec. 808(b) of the Dodd-Frank Act).

Technical Assistance.—The Fed must consult with the appropriate financial regulator and provide any technical assistance necessary to ensure that the Fed's rules and orders are interpreted and applied in a consistent manner (Sec. 808(c) of the Dodd-Frank Act).

Delegation to Fed.—The appropriate financial regulator may request that the Fed conduct or participate in an examination of a financial institution in order to assess the financial institution's compliance with either the provisions of Title VIII of the Dodd-Frank Act or its underlying rules or orders. After receiving an appropriate written request, the Fed must conduct an examination under the terms and conditions mutually agreed on by the Fed and the appropriate financial regulator (Sec. 808(d)(1) of the Dodd-Frank Act).

The appropriate financial regulator may also ask the Fed to enforce either the provisions of Title VIII or the statute's underlying rules and orders. After receiving such a request in writing, the Fed must determine whether an enforcement action is warranted. If so, the Fed will have authority under Federal Deposit Insurance Act Sections 8(b) through 8(n) to enforce compliance against the financial institution in the same manner and to the same extent as if the financial institution was an insured depository institution and the Fed was the depository institution's appropriate federal banking agency (Sec. 808(d)(2) of the Dodd-Frank Act).

Fed Back-up Authority.—Notwithstanding any other law provision, the Fed may: (1) conduct an examination of the type described in Section 808(a) of a financial institution that is subject to the standards for designated activities; and (2) enforce the provisions of Title VIII or any of the statute's underlying rules and orders against that institution (Sec. 808(e)(1) of the Dodd-Frank Act).

The Fed may exercise its back-up examination authority, however, only if: (1) the Fed has reasonable cause to believe that the financial institution is not in compliance with the provisions of Title VIII and the Fed's rules; (2) the Fed has provided notice of its belief to both the appropriate financial regulator and the Financial Stability Oversight Council (Council), along with supporting documentation; (3) the Fed has requested that the appropriate financial regulator conduct a prompt examination; (4) either the Fed has not been afforded a reasonable opportunity to participate in an examination within 30 days of providing notice, or the Fed has reasonable cause to believe that the financial institution's non-compliance poses a substantial risk to other financial institutions, critical markets or the broader financial system; and (5) obtained the Council's approval by a majority vote (Sec. 808(e)(2)(A) of the Dodd-Frank Act).

The Fed may exercise its back-up enforcement authority only if the Fed: (1) has reasonable cause to believe that a financial institution is not in compliance with Title VIII or its underlying rules and orders; (2) has notified the appropriate financial regulator of its belief in writing, along with supporting documentation and a recommendation that the financial regulator take one or more specific enforcement actions against the financial institution; and (3) either has not been notified by the appropriate financial regulator of the enforcement action within 60 days of the Fed's notice, or has reasonable cause to believe that the financial institution's non-compliance poses significant liquidity, credit, operational or other risks to the financial markets or to financial stability, subject to the Fed's notifying the financial regulator of the enforcement action; and (4) obtained the Council's approval by a majority vote (Sec. 808(e)(2)(B) of the Dodd-Frank Act).

For purposes of taking action under its back-up enforcement authority, the Fed will have authority under Federal Deposit Insurance Act Sections 8(b) through 8(n) to enforce compliance against the financial institution in the same manner and to the same extent as if the financial institution was an insured depository institution and the Fed was the depository institution's appropriate federal banking agency (Sec. 808(e)(3) of the Dodd-Frank Act).

▶ **Effective date.** The provision is effective as of the date of enactment (Sec. 814 of the Dodd-Frank Wall Street Reform and Consumer Protection Act).

Law source: Law at ¶ 10,808, ¶ 10,803 and ¶ 10,814. Committee Report at ¶ 54,427.

— Sec. 803 of the Dodd-Frank Wall Street Reform and Consumer Protection Act, providing definitions;

— Sec. 808(a), providing for examinations of financial institutions;

— Sec. 808(b), granting enforcement authority to supervisory agencies;

— Sec. 808(c), providing for technical assistance by the Fed;

— Sec. 808(d), permitting delegation of examination and enforcement authority to the Fed;

— Sec. 808(e), providing back-up enforcement authority to the Fed;

— Sec. 814, providing the effective date.

¶ 3535 Requests for Information, Reports and Records

The Financial Stability Oversight Council (Council) may require any financial market utility or financial institution to submit information needed by the Council to assess systemic importance. Once a financial market utility or a payment, clearing or settlement activity has been designated as systemically important, the Board of Governors of the Federal Reserve System (the Fed) or the Council may require the utility and the financial institutions engaging in the activity to submit reports or data for the purposes of assessing safety and soundness, risks to the financial system, and compliance. The Fed or the Council must coordinate any requests for information and the establishment of any reporting requirements with other federal agencies.

Information to Assess Systemic Importance.—The Council may require any financial market utility or financial institution to submit information needed by the Council to assess the systemic importance of either the financial market utility or a payment, clearing or settlement activity engaged in, or supported by, the financial institution. The Council may request this information only for the purpose of assessing systemic importance and only if the Council has a reasonable belief that the financial utility or activity meets the standards for systemic importance set forth under Section 804 (Sec. 809(a) of the Dodd-Frank Wall Street Reform and Consumer Protection Act).

Reporting After Designations of Systemic Importance.—The Fed or the Council may require a designated financial market utility to submit reports or data in the frequency and form the Fed or the Council deem necessary in order to assess the utility's safety and soundness and the systemic risks that the utility's operations pose to the financial system (Sec. 809(b)(1) of the Dodd-Frank Act).

The Fed and the Council may require one or more financial institutions that are subject to the standards prescribed for a designated payment, clearing or settlement activity to submit reports or data with respect to the conduct of that activity. The Fed and Council may request reports and data only to assess whether: (1) the rules, orders and standards prescribed under Title VIII of the Dodd-Frank Act appropriately address the risks that the activity presents to the financial system; and (2) the financial institutions are in compliance with Title VIII and its underlying rules and orders (Sec. 809(b)(2) of the Dodd-Frank Act).

Upon an affirmative vote by a majority of the Council, the Fed may prescribe regulations imposing a recordkeeping or reporting requirement on designated clearing agencies or financial institutions engaged in designated activities that are subject to the risk management standards (Sec. 809(b)(3) of the Dodd-Frank Act).

Coordination with Agencies.—The Fed or the Council must coordinate in advance with the supervisory agency or the appropriate financial regulator before making any requests for material information or imposing any reporting requirements on a financial market utility or financial institution. Advance coordination is required in order to determine if the information is available from, or may be obtained by, the agency in the form, format or detail required by the Fed or the Council. The legislation authorizes the supervisory agency, the appropriate financial regulator and the Fed to provide each other and the Council with copies of examination reports or other similar reports regarding any financial market utility or any financial institution engaged in payment, clearing or settlement activities (Sec. 809(c) of the Dodd-Frank Act).

If the information, reports or data requested by the Fed or the Council under Section 809(c)(1) are not provided in full by the supervisory agency or the appropriate financial regulator in less than 15 days after the request, the Fed or the Council may request the information or impose the recordkeeping or reporting requirements directly, with notice to the agency (Sec. 809(d) of the Dodd-Frank Act).

Information Sharing.—The legislation authorizes the Fed, the Council, the appropriate financial regulator and any supervisory agency to promptly notify each other of material concerns about a designated financial market utility or any financial institution engaged in a designated activity. The agencies may share appropriate reports, information or data relating to such concerns (Sec. 809(e)(1) of the Dodd-Frank Act).

The agencies may also provide confidential supervisory information and other information obtained under the provisions of Title VIII to each other and to the Treasury Secretary, Federal Reserve Banks, state financial institution supervisory agencies, foreign financial supervisors, foreign central banks and foreign finance ministries, subject to reasonable assurances of confidentiality. No person or entity receiving this information, however, may disseminate it to anyone other than these specified persons without complying with applicable law, including Commodity Exchange Act Section 8 (Sec. 809(e)(2) of the Dodd-Frank Act).

Privilege.—Neither the Fed, the Council, the appropriate financial regulator, nor any supervisory agency will be deemed to have waived any privilege with respect to those reports or data that the agencies provide to another person under Section 809 or permit another person to use under that section (Sec. 809(f) of the Dodd-Frank Act).

Disclosure Exemption.—The information obtained by the Fed, the supervisory agencies or the Council under Section 809 in connection with their supervision of designated financial market utilities and designated activities, as well as any materials they have prepared regarding the assessment of systemic importance in connection with that supervision, will be confidential supervisory information exempt from disclosure under 5 U.S.C. § 552. This disclosure exemption will be considered a statute described in 5 U.S.C. § 552(b)(3) (Sec. 809(g) of the Dodd-Frank Act).

▶ **Effective date.** The provision is effective as of the date of enactment (Sec. 814 of the Dodd-Frank Wall Street Reform and Consumer Protection Act).

Law source: Law at ¶10,809 and ¶10,814. Committee Report at ¶54,428.

— Sec. 809(a) of the Dodd-Frank Wall Street Reform and Consumer Protection Act, requiring the submission of information to assess systemic importance;
— Sec. 809(b), providing for reporting after designations of systemic importance;
— Sec. 809(c), requiring coordination with federal agencies;
— Sec. 809(d), permitting direct requests for information and reports by the Fed;
— Sec. 809(e), authorizing the sharing of information;
— Sec. 809(f), maintaining privileged status for reports and data;
— Sec. 809(g), providing an exemption from disclosure;
— Sec. 814, providing the effective date.

Investor Protection and Securities Regulation

INVESTOR PROTECTION

¶4005	Introduction
¶4010	Investor Advisory Committee
¶4015	Consumer Testing
¶4020	Fiduciary Standard for Broker-Dealers and Advisers
¶4025	Office of the Investor Advocate
¶4030	SRO Rule Changes
¶4035	Pre-Purchase Disclosures
¶4040	Studies and Reports

ENFORCEMENT and REMEDIES

¶4050	Introduction
¶4055	Mandatory Arbitration Clauses
¶4060	Whistleblowers
¶4065	Collateral Bars
¶4070	Regulation D Offerings
¶4075	Self-Regulatory Organization Rules
¶4080	State-Registered Investment Advisers
¶4085	Margin Lending
¶4090	Fair Fund Provision
¶4095	SIPA Amendments
¶4100	Lost, Stolen, Counterfeit and Cancelled Securities
¶4105	Nationwide Service of Process
¶4110	Formerly Associated Persons
¶4115	Hiring Authority for Market Specialists
¶4120	Confidential and Privileged Information
¶4125	Transactions Not Conducted on Exchanges
¶4130	Aiding-and-Abetting Violations
¶4135	SEC Enforcement Authority

¶4140 Custody and Recordkeeping
¶4145 Reporting Obligations
¶4150 Fingerprinting
¶4155 Enforcement Deadlines
¶4160 Notice to Missing Shareholders
¶4165 Short-Sale Disclosures
¶4170 Aiding-and-Abetting Study

CREDIT RATING AGENCIES

¶4180 Introduction
¶4185 Enhanced Regulation and Transparency
¶4190 Assigned Credit Ratings
¶4195 State of Mind in Private Actions
¶4200 Information from Third-Party Sources
¶4205 Professional Standards for Rating Analysts
¶4210 Universal Rating Symbols
¶4215 Whistleblowers
¶4220 Removal of Statutory References to Ratings
¶4225 Regulation FD Exemption
¶4230 Section 11 Liability
¶4235 Studies and Reports

SECURITIZATION

¶4250 Introduction
¶4255 Credit Risk Retention
¶4260 Issuer Disclosure and Reporting
¶4265 Real Estate Mortgage Notes Exemption
¶4270 Due Diligence Analysis
¶4275 Macroeconomic Effects of Risk Retention

EXECUTIVE COMPENSATION and GOVERNANCE

¶4290 Introduction
¶4295 Shareholder Advisory Vote
¶4300 Independent Compensation Committees
¶4305 "Pay vs. Performance" Disclosure
¶4310 Recovery of Erroneously-Awarded Compensation
¶4315 Hedging by Directors and Employees

¶4320	Incentive-Based Compensation Arrangements
¶4325	Proxy Voting by Brokers
¶4330	Shareholder Proxy Access
¶4335	Bifurcation of Chair and CEO Role

SEC ORGANIZATION and FUNDING

¶4350	Introduction
¶4355	Studies and Reports
¶4360	Examination Staff
¶4365	SEC Employee Hotline
¶4370	SEC Funding

MUNICIPAL SECURITIES

¶4380	Introduction
¶4385	Municipal Advisor Registration
¶4390	Broker-Dealer Regulation
¶4395	Municipal Securities Rulemaking Board
¶4400	Office of Municipal Securities
¶4405	Governmental Accounting Standards Board Funding
¶4410	Studies and Reports

PUBLIC COMPANY ACCOUNTING OVERSIGHT BOARD

¶4420	Introduction
¶4425	Audit Information to be Produced and Exchanged
¶4430	Information Sharing with Foreign Regulators
¶4435	Auditors of Broker-Dealers

ADDITIONAL SECURITIES REFORMS

¶4450	Introduction
¶4455	Portfolio Margining
¶4460	Securities Lending and Borrowing
¶4465	Deposit Insurance Fund Loss Reviews
¶4470	Study of Proprietary Trading
¶4475	Senior Investor Protection
¶4480	SEC and CFTC Inspectors General
¶4485	Person-to-Person Lending
¶4490	Internal Controls Auditor Attestation

¶ 4495   NAIC Model Regulations

INVESTOR PROTECTION

¶ 4005 Introduction

Title IX, Subtitle A, of the Dodd-Frank Wall Street Reform and Consumer Protection Act (Sections 911 *et seq.*) addresses a number of investor-protection issues and specifically responds to events of the financial crisis caused by a lack of transparency and inadequate disclosure regimes (S. Rep. No. 111-176, pp. 35–36). In the changing marketplace, investors require greater protections from the firms with which they engage in securities transactions, and the provisions made by Subtitle A are designed to give investors the protections and resources they need to make informed investment decisions and to maintain their confidence in the integrity of the marketplace.

As recommended by the Treasury Department in its proposal for financial regulatory reform, the legislation requires the establishment of an investor advisory committee within the SEC to advise and consult with the Commission on issues regarding securities products, financial firm operations, disclosures and investor protection (see ¶ 4010). The legislation also authorizes the SEC to engage in consumer testing in order to gather information about investors and their habits and how they make decisions regarding investments (see ¶ 4015). These provisions offer a means by which to evaluate the effectiveness of disclosures and other investment information provided to consumers and an opportunity for the Commission to make policy and rule changes to foster an environment of better-educated investors (S. Rep. No. 111-176, pp. 104–105).

In addition, the Commission must consider the effectiveness and efficacy of the standards of care applicable to brokers and investment advisers. The SEC must conduct a study to evaluate whether there are regulatory gaps in the protection of retail customers with regard to these standards. The legislation also authorizes the Commission to impose a uniform federal fiduciary standard of care on brokers and investment advisers as necessary or appropriate for the protection of investors (see ¶ 4020).

The legislation also establishes the Office of the Investor Advocate within the SEC. The Senate determined the creation of this office was necessary to strengthen the Commission's authority to take action to protect investors and to ensure that the interests of retail customers are adequately represented. In general, the Office is tasked with making policy recommendations aimed at increasing SEC transparency and accountability (S. Rep. No. 111-176, p. 105). The Investor Advocate must also assist retail investors in resolving conflicts with financial firms and issues with their products and identify areas in which investors would benefit from regulatory changes. The Investor Advocate must report annually to the Senate Banking Committee and the House Financial Services Committee (see ¶ 4025).

In response to industry concerns, the Dodd-Frank Act amended Exchange Act Section 19(b)(2) to update the procedures applicable to rule changes proposed by self-regulatory organizations (SROs). The changes alter the timeframe within which the Commission must approve or disapprove a rule change. According to Congress, a more expedient turnaround is necessary in light of the rapid changes occurring daily in the marketplace (see ¶ 4030).

To provide additional protection for retail investors, Exchange Act Section 15 was amended to clarify that the Commission may issue rules designating specific documents or information that brokers or dealers must provide to retail investors prior to purchases of investment products or services (see ¶ 4035). At present, most prospectuses are delivered after a sale has taken place, and Congress determined that more advance disclosures are necessary to enable investors to make informed investment decisions (S. Rep. No. 111-176, pp. 107–108).

The Dodd-Frank Act also mandates several studies on investment issues and investor protections to be performed by the SEC and the Comptroller General. According to Congress, collection of more information is necessary before it can make certain legislative decisions. To this end, the legislation requires studies concerning: the effectiveness of the existing standards of care imposed on financial intermediaries; the financial literacy of the investing public; mutual fund advertising practices and existing marketing regulations; internal conflicts of interest at financial firms and the impact they have on investors; investor access to information about financial intermediaries and whether additional information should be provided; and the role of financial planners in providing investment advice and whether existing professional designations mislead consumers (see ¶ 4040).

▶ **Effective date.** The provisions take effect one day after the date of enactment (Sec. 4 of the Dodd-Frank Wall Street Reform and Consumer Protection Act).

Law source: Law at ¶ 10,911 and ¶ 10,004. Committee Report at ¶¶ 50,091 and ¶ 54,440.

— Sec. 911 *et seq.* of the Dodd-Frank Wall Street Reform and Consumer Protection Act, containing investor protection provisions of Title IX, Subtitle A;
— Sec. 4, providing the effective date.

¶4010 Investor Advisory Committee

As recommended in the Treasury Department's legislative proposal concerning financial regulatory reform, new Exchange Act Section 39 requires the establishment of an investor advisory committee within the SEC and authorizes appropriations as necessary for its implementation and operation. The committee must advise and consult with the SEC on regulatory priorities and issues regarding securities products, trading strategies, fee structures and the effectiveness of disclosures, as well as initiatives to protect investors' interests and to promote investor confidence. The committee must submit its findings and make recommendations, including proposed legislative changes, to the Commission as it deems appropriate (Exchange Act Sec. 39(a), as added by the Dodd-Frank Wall Street Reform and Consumer Protection Act).

> **CCH Comment:** In June 2009, the SEC formed an Investor Advisory Committee to perform functions similar to those described in the legislation. However, the legislation gives the committee a statutory basis and specifically provides guidance concerning the committee's composition and activities (S. Rep. No. 111 176, pp. 103–104).

Members, Officers and Terms.—The Investor Advocate (see ¶ 4025), a representative of the states' securities commissions and a representative of senior citizens' interests must serve on the committee. The SEC must also appoint 10-20 other individuals who can adequately represent the interests of individual equity and debt investors (including mutual fund investors) and institutional investors (including pension funds and registered investment companies) and who have reputations of integrity and individualized expertise concerning investment issues and decisions. Committee members must serve for four-year terms and will not be considered employees or agents of the SEC solely by reason of committee membership (Exchange Act Sec. 39(b), as added by the Dodd-Frank Act). However, any committee member who is not a full-time federal employee is entitled to compensation for service and travel expenses as described in Section 39(e).

Once selected or appointed, the investor advisory committee must elect officers for three-year terms. The officers elected must include a chairman and a vice chairman (who may not be employed by an issuer), as well as a secretary and an assistant secretary (Exchange Act Sec. 39(c), as added by the Dodd-Frank Act). The committee must meet at least semiannually. The chairman must provide all committee members with two-weeks' written notice of an upcoming meeting (Exchange Act Sec. 39(d), as added by the Dodd-Frank Act).

The SEC must provide staff for the committee as the chairman finds necessary to carry out the committee's duties (Exchange Act Sec. 39(f), as added by the Dodd-Frank Act).

SEC Oversight.—The Commission must review the committee's findings and recommendations. Each time the committee submits a finding or recommendation, the SEC must promptly issue a public statement assessing the committee's determinations and disclosing what action, if any, the Commission intends to take in response (Exchange Act Sec. 39(g), as added by the Dodd-Frank Act). However, the SEC does not have to agree with or take action on any committee finding or recommendation (Exchange Act Sec. 39(h), as added by the Dodd-Frank Act).

> **CCH Comment:** The Federal Advisory Committee Act (5 U.S.C. App.) will not apply to the committee or with respect to any of its activities (Exchange Act Sec. 39(i), as added by the Dodd-Frank Act).

▶ **Effective date.** The provision takes effect one day after the date of enactment (Sec. 4 of the Dodd-Frank Wall Street Reform and Consumer Protection Act).

Law source: Law at ¶10,911 and ¶10,004. Committee Report at ¶54,440.

— Sec. 911 of the Dodd-Frank Wall Street Reform and Consumer Protection Act, adding Exchange Act Sec. 39;

— Sec. 4, providing the effective date.

¶4015 Consumer Testing

For the purposes of evaluating its existing rules and programs and considering, proposing or adopting new rules or programs, the SEC may engage in investor testing. As amended, Securities Act Section 19 now authorizes the Commission to gather information, to communicate with investors and the public, and to engage in temporary or experimental programs that it determines to be in the public interest or necessary for investor protection. The SEC may also confer with academics and other consultants when making its considerations (Securities Act Sec. 19(e), as added by the Dodd-Frank Wall Street Reform and Consumer Protection Act).

In the past, the Commission has conducted programs designed to gather information regarding the knowledge and views of the public concerning the financial industry. However, some have questioned whether this practice is legally sound. The legislation now gives the SEC clear authority to engage in consumer testing, presenting it with a means by which to evaluate the effectiveness of disclosures and other investment information provided to consumers (S. Rep. No. 111-176, p. 104).

Elaborating on the purpose and scope of this authority, the Senate Banking Committee added:

> Mr. James Hamilton, Principal Analyst, CCH Federal Securities Law Reporter has said "The SEC can better evaluate the effectiveness of investor disclosures if it can meaningfully engage in consumer testing of those disclosures. The SEC should be better enabled to engage in field testing, consumer outreach and testing of disclosures to individual investors, including by providing budgetary support for those activities" (S. Rep. No. 111-176, pp. 104–105) (quoting *Obama Reform Proposal Would Enhance SEC Investor Protection Role*, Jim Hamilton's World of Securities Regulation, jimhamiltonblog.blogspot.com, June 17, 2009).

Any action taken in the process of investor testing will not be construed as a collection of information for the purposes of the Paperwork Reduction Act (44 U.S.C. § 3501 *et seq.*) (Securities Act Sec. 19(f), as added by the Dodd-Frank Act).

▶ **Effective date.** The provision takes effect one day after the date of enactment (Sec. 4 of the Dodd-Frank Wall Street Reform and Consumer Protection Act).

Law source: Law at ¶ 10,912 and ¶ 10,004. Committee Report at ¶ 54,441.

— Sec. 912 of the Dodd-Frank Wall Street Reform and Consumer Protection Act, adding Securities Act Secs. 19(e) and (f);

— Sec. 4, providing the effective date.

¶ 4020 Fiduciary Standard for Broker-Dealers and Advisers

The Dodd-Frank Wall Street Reform and Consumer Protection Act includes measures designed to harmonize the fiduciary standard for broker-dealers and investment advisers. These include a mandated SEC study on the effectiveness of, and regulatory shortcomings relating to, existing legal standards of care for brokers, dealers and investment advisers for providing personalized investment advice to retail customers. The Commission must also submit a report to Congress on its findings. Further, it may impose a uniform federal fiduciary standard of care on brokers and investment advisers. Finally, it must harmonize enforcement of fiduciary standard violations under the Exchange Act and Investment Advisers Act (Sec. 913 of the Dodd-Frank Wall Street Reform and Consumer Protection Act).

Congressional Intent.—The existing regulatory regime treats brokers and advisers differently and subjects them to different standards of care, even though the services they provide investors are similar and investors view their roles as essentially the same.

This regime was established during the New Deal and, although amended many times since, remains rooted in the last century. The primary goal of financial regulatory reform has been to allow the SEC to align duties for financial intermediaries across financial products. Thus, Congress determined that the standard of care applicable to brokers when providing investment advice about securities to retail investors should be raised to the fiduciary standard of investment advisers.

The House bill would have imposed a uniform federal fiduciary duty on brokers and advisers, while the Senate bill directed the SEC to conduct a study on the matter. The House-Senate conference committee struck a compromise, vetted by Sen. Tim Johnson (D-SD), a senior member of the Banking Committee, under which the SEC will conduct a study within what Sen. Johnson called "strict parameters" and may impose a uniform federal fiduciary standard on brokers and investment advisers (Sec. 913 of the Dodd-Frank Act).

According to Rep. Spencer Bachus (R-AL), Ranking Member on the House Financial Services Committee, the provision directs the SEC to conduct a study to evaluate the effectiveness of current standards, both at the state and federal levels, with respect to investment advisers and broker-dealers when providing personalized investment advice and recommendations about securities to retail customers. Before the SEC proceeds with any new regulations in this area, said Rep. Bachus, it is critically important that the unique roles of different financial professionals, their distinct relationships with their customers, and the nature of the services and disclosures they provide be fully examined and well understood. These definitive factors should provide information to guide the SEC in determining if any new regulations are needed and defining the details of any such measures that might be proposed. The House-Senate conferees included the requirement for a comprehensive study for these purposes, said Rep. Bachus, and it is the intent of Congress that the SEC follow with a thorough and objective analysis in this regard (Cong. Rec., June 30, 2010, p. H5255).

Rep. Paul Kanjorski (D-PA), Chair of the Capital Markets Subcommittee, emphasized that a chief reform in the area of investor protection is that the Dodd-Frank Act provides that the SEC, after it conducts a study, may issue new rules establishing that every financial intermediary who provides personalized investment advice to retail customers will have a fiduciary duty to the investor. According to Rep. Kanjorski, a traditional fiduciary duty includes an affirmative duty of care, loyalty and honesty; an affirmative duty to act in good faith; and a duty to act in the client's best interests. Through this harmonized standard of care, both broker and investment advisers will place customers' interests first. Rep. Kanjorski noted that regulators, practitioners and investor advocates have become increasingly concerned that investors are confused by the legal distinction between broker-dealers and investment advisers. The two professions currently owe investors different standards of care, even though their services and marketing techniques have become increasingly indistinguishable to retail investors. The issuance of new rules will fix this longstanding problem, in his view (Cong. Rec., June 30, 2010, p. H5237).

Background.— Currently, the fiduciary duty imposed by the Advisers Act requires advisers to act solely with the client's investment goals and interests in mind, free from any conflicts of interest that would tempt them to make recommendations that would also benefit them. Unlike investment advisers, brokers are not categorically bound by statute, regulation or precedent to a *per se* rule imposing fiduciary obligations toward clients. Instead, the existence of fiduciary duties within a broker-client relationship has historically been significantly more contingent, turning ultimately on the factual nature of the relationship as interpreted by courts.

The practices of brokers and advisers have increasingly converged, and the SEC has attempted to calibrate the regulation of these securities professionals in a flexible and innovative manner consistent with investor protection. More practically, the SEC and Congress are trying to accommodate a regulatory regime created in the 1930s with the realities of 2010. Because of the distinct regulatory structures placed on investment advisers and broker-dealers, the dividing line between them has always been elusive. However, Congress excluded brokers from the Advisers Act so long as the advice they give clients is solely incidental to their business as a broker and they do not receive any special compensation for rendering such advice.

As investor confusion over the roles of brokers and advisers deepened, the SEC commissioned the Rand Center for Corporate Ethics, Law and Governance to prepare a report on investor and industry perspectives on investment advisers and broker-dealers. The report, entitled *Investor and Industry Perspectives on Investment Advisers and Broker-Dealers* (Rand Report), was released in January 2008.

The Rand Report's essential conclusion is that the regulatory environment for brokers and investment advisers is eroding along with the distinctions between the two types of financial professionals on which it is based. More broadly, the Report found that the current regulatory regime treats brokers and advisers differently when, in practice, their role is essentially the same, especially from the investor's viewpoint.

The Report found that the bright line between brokers and investment advisers that may have existed in the 1930s has become increasingly blurred. Indeed, whether a financial services professional is a broker or an investment adviser is indistinguishable to most investors. One reason cited in the Report for the blurring of the line between brokers and investment advisers is that much of the marketing by brokers focuses on the ongoing relationship between the broker and the investor as brokers have adopted such titles as financial advisor and financial manager. Many investors believe that brokers and advisers offer the same products and services and do not recognize the operational differences between these intermediaries and are not generally aware that regulatory standards may be different.

Study.—The Dodd-Frank Act requires the SEC to conduct a study to evaluate the effectiveness and efficacy of the existing standards of care for brokers and investment advisers and whether there are regulatory gaps in the protection of retail customers with regard to the standards (Sec. 913(b) of the Dodd-Frank Act). "Retail customer" means a natural person who receives personalized investment advice about securities from a broker or investment adviser and uses the advice primarily for personal, family or household purposes (Sec. 913(a) of the Dodd-Frank Act).

During the study, the SEC must consider whether retail customers understand that there are different standards of care applied to brokers and advisers in the provision of personalized investment advice and whether retail customers are confused about the quality of the personalized investment advice they receive. The SEC study must also

¶4020

examine the regulatory and enforcement resources available to enforce the standards of care for brokers and advisers when providing personalized investment advice about securities to retail customers, including the frequency and effectiveness of examinations. The substantive differences in the regulation of brokers and investment advisers when advising and recommending securities to retail customers must also be examined, and any specific instances when the oversight of brokers provided greater protection to retail investors than the oversight of advisers, and the converse. The existing state regulatory standards for protecting retail securities customers must also be considered (Sec. 913(c) of the Dodd-Frank Act).

The study must also examine the potential impact on retail customers and their access to a range of services and products of imposing the investment adviser standard of care on brokers, as well as the impact of eliminating the broker and dealer exclusion from the Advisers Act definition of "investment adviser," including on retail customers and state and federal resources. The varying level of services provided by brokers and investment advisers must be reviewed, as well as the varying scope and terms of retail customer relationships of brokers, dealers, investment advisers, persons associated with brokers or dealers, and persons associated with investment advisers (Sec. 913(c) of the Dodd-Frank Act).

Finally, the SEC must consider the impact that could result from potential changes in the regulatory requirements or legal standards of care affecting brokers and investment advisers relating to their obligations to retail customers regarding the provision of investment advice, including any potential impact on protection from fraud, access to personalized investment advice and recommendations about securities to retail customers or the availability of such advice and recommendations (Sec. 913(c) of the Dodd-Frank Act).

Report to Congress.—Within six months of enactment, the SEC must submit a report on the study to Congress describing its findings and conclusions and recommendations. The report must set forth the considerations, analysis and public and industry input that the Commission considered, as required by the statute, and include an analysis of regulatory gaps in the protection of retail investors relating to the standard of care of brokers and advisers (Sec. 913(d) of the Dodd-Frank Act).

Rulemaking and Authority.—The Commission may also commence a rulemaking concerning the standards of care applicable to brokers and investment adviser as necessary or appropriate in the public interest and for the protection of consumers (Sec. 913(f) of the Dodd-Frank Act).

The legislation gives the SEC the necessary authority to impose a uniform federal fiduciary standard of care on brokers and investment advisers. The receipt of compensation based on commission or other standard compensation for the sale of securities will not, in and of itself, be considered a violation of such standard applied to a broker or dealer. Moreover, there will be no continuing duty of care or loyalty owed by the broker to the retail customer after the providing of personalized investment advice about securities (Exchange Act Sec. 15(k) and Advisers Act Sec. 211(g), as added by the Dodd-Frank Act).

The Commission may require a broker selling only proprietary or a limited range of products to provide notice to each retail customer and obtain the consent or acknowledgment of the customer. However, the sale of only proprietary or other limited range of products will not, in and of itself, be considered a violation of the standard of care (Exchange Act Sec. 15(k)(2), as added by the Dodd-Frank Act).

The SEC must facilitate the provision of simple and clear disclosures to investors regarding the terms of their relationships with brokers and investment advisers, including any material conflicts of interest and, where appropriate, promulgate rules prohibiting or restricting sales practices, conflicts of interest and compensation schemes for brokers and investment advisers that are contrary to the public interest and the protection of investors (Exchange Act Sec. 15(l) and Advisers Act Sec. 211(h), as added by the Dodd-Frank Act).

Harmonization of Enforcement.—The Commission's enforcement authority with respect to violations of the standard of conduct applicable to a broker or dealer providing personalized investment advice about securities to a retail customer must include:

- the SEC's enforcement authority regarding those violations provided under the Exchange Act; and
- the SEC's enforcement authority regarding violations of the standard of conduct for an investment adviser under the Advisers Act, including the authority to impose sanctions.

The Commission must seek to prosecute and sanction violators of the standard of conduct applicable to a broker or dealer providing personalized investment advice about securities to a retail customer under the Exchange Act to same extent as it prosecutes and sanctions violators of the standard applicable to an investment adviser under the Advisers Act (Exchange Act Sec. 15(m) and Advisers Act Sec. 211(i), as added by the Dodd-Frank Act).

▶ **Effective date.** The provision takes effect one day after the date of enactment (Sec. 4 of the Dodd-Frank Wall Street Reform and Consumer Protection Act).

Law source: Law at ¶10,913 and ¶10,004. Committee Report at ¶54,442.

— Sec. 913(a) of the Dodd-Frank Wall Street Reform and Consumer Protection Act, defining "retail customer";

— Sec. 913(b), requiring an SEC study on the standards of care applicable to brokers, dealers and investment advisers;

— Sec. 913(c), outlining the considerations for the study;

— Sec. 913(d), requiring the SEC to submit a report on its findings;

— Sec. 913(e), requiring the SEC to seek public comment in conducting the study;

— Sec. 913(f), authorizing an SEC rulemaking concerning standards of care;

— Secs. 913(g) and (h), adding Exchange Act Secs. 15(k)–(m) and Adviser Act Secs. 211(g)–(i);

— Sec. 4, providing the effective date.

¶4025 Office of the Investor Advocate

The Dodd-Frank Wall Street Reform and Consumer Protection Act establishes the Office of the Investor Advocate within the SEC (Exchange Act Sec. 4(g)(1), as added by the Dodd-Frank Act). The Senate determined that creation of this office was necessary to strengthen the SEC's authority to take action to protect investors and to ensure that the interests of retail customers are adequately represented. In general, the Office is tasked with making policy recommendations designed to increase transparency within and the accountability of the Commission (S. Rep. No. 111-176, p. 105). According to Sen. Daniel Akaka (D-HI), the Office's mission also includes identifying areas where investors would benefit from changes in the policies of the SEC and self-regulatory organizations (Cong. Rec., May 20, 2010, p. S4068). This mission differs from that of the existing Office of Investor Education and Advocacy, the senator explained, because the new Office will be better equipped to respond to investor feedback and to more effectively evaluate information that could potentially expose inappropriate practices by firms in a timelier manner (Cong. Rec., May 20, 2010, p. S4069).

The head of the Office, the Investor Advocate, must be appointed by the SEC Chair, in consultation with the rest of the Commission, and must be an individual with specific experience in advocating for the interests of securities investors and general investor protection from the perspective of investors. The individual serving as the Investor Advocate may not have been employed by the SEC during the two-year period ending on the date of appointment or be employed by the agency during the five-year period following completion of the term. The Investor Advocate must report directly to the Chair and must be compensated at a rate equal to the highest rate of annual pay for other senior executives who report to the Chair of the Commission (Exchange Act Sec. 4(g)(2), as added by the Dodd-Frank Act).

Duties and Obligations.—The Investor Advocate has responsibility for:

- assisting retail investors in resolving significant problems they may have with the SEC or other self-regulatory organizations;
- identifying areas in which investors would benefit from regulatory changes;
- recognizing problems that investors have with financial service providers and investment products;
- analyzing the potential impact regulations proposed by the SEC and rules proposed by self-regulatory organizations have on investors; and
- to the extent practicable, proposing regulatory changes to the SEC and legislative changes to Congress that may help to mitigate problems discovered by the Office and to promote the interests of investors (Exchange Act Sec. 4(g)(4), as added by the Dodd-Frank Act).

The Investor Advocate may retain or employ staff to act as independent counsel, researchers and service providers as needed to carry out the functions and duties of the Office, and the Commission must ensure that the Investor Advocate has full access to all of the documentation necessary for the Office to effectively operate (Exchange Act Secs. 4(g)(3) and (5), as added by the Dodd-Frank Act).

Ombudsman.—Within 180 days of appointment, the first Investor Advocate must appoint an Ombudsman to act as a liaison between the Commission and retail investors to resolve problems those investors may have with the SEC or with self-regulatory organizations (Exchange Act Sec. 4(g)(8)(A), as added by the Dodd-Frank Act). The Ombudsman must review and make recommendations regarding policies and procedures designed to encourage industry professionals and members of the public to present compliance questions to the Investor Advocate while safeguarding the confidentiality of communications between those individuals and the Ombudsman (Exchange Act Sec. 4(g)(8)(B), as added by the Dodd-Frank Act). The Ombudsman must report directly to the Investor Advocate and use Commission personnel to the extent practicable (Exchange Act Sec. 4(g)(8)(C), as added by the Dodd-Frank Act).

The Ombudsman must submit a semiannual report to the Investor Advocate describing its activities and evaluating its effectiveness during the preceding year, and the Investor Advocate must include these reports in its reports to Congress (Exchange Act Sec. 4(g)(8)(D), as added by the Dodd-Frank Act).

Reporting.—Before June 30 of each year after 2010, the Investor Advocate must complete and submit a report on its objectives for the following fiscal year to the Senate Banking Committee and the House Financial Services Committee (Exchange Act Sec. 4(g)(6)(A)(i), as added by the Dodd-Frank Act). In addition, not later than December 31 of each year after 2010, the Investor Advocate must submit a report on its activities during the immediately preceding fiscal year to the committees (Exchange Act Sec. 4(g)(6)(B)(i), as added by the Dodd-Frank Act). Each of these reports must include:

- appropriate statistical information and substantive analysis;
- information on the measures the Investor Advocate has taken to improve investor services and responsiveness of regulators to investor concerns;
- a summary of the most serious problems encountered by investors during the reporting period;
- an inventory of these problems that specifically states the length of time for which the problem has been ongoing and identifies any action or lack of action by the SEC or a self-regulatory organization and the result of those decisions; and
- recommendations for administrative and legislative actions that may be effective in resolving difficulties encountered by investors (Exchange Act Sec. 4(g)(6)(B)(ii), as added by the Dodd-Frank Act).

The report must be provided to the committees directly by the Office without prior review by the Commission and cannot contain confidential information (Exchange Act Secs. 4(g)(6)(B)(iii) and (iv), as added by the Dodd-Frank Act).

The SEC must establish procedures requiring a formal response to all recommendations by the Investor Advocate to the Commission within three months of a submission (Exchange Act Sec. 4(g)(7), as added by the Dodd-Frank Act).

▶ **Effective date.** The provision takes effect one day after the date of enactment (Sec. 4 of the Dodd-Frank Wall Street Reform and Consumer Protection Act).

¶4025

Law source: Law at ¶10,915, ¶10,919D and ¶10,004. Committee Report at ¶54,443.

— Sec. 915 of the Dodd-Frank Wall Street Reform and Consumer Protection Act, adding Exchange Act Secs. 4(g)(1)–(7);
— Sec. 919D, adding Exchange Act Sec. 4(g)(8)
— Sec. 4, providing the effective date.

¶4030 SRO Rule Changes

Many self-regulatory organizations (SROs) have expressed concern that the SEC's responses to their proposed rule changes have been slow, and given the rapid nature of changes in the securities markets, the Commission's consideration and approval process must become more efficient (S. Rep. No. 111-176, p. 106). The Dodd-Frank Wall Street Reform and Consumer Protection Act amends Exchange Act Section 19(b)(2) to update the filing and approval procedures applicable to rule changes proposed by SROs. Under the amended section, the Commission must approve a proposed rule change or institute proceedings to determine whether it should be disapproved within 45 days after publication of the filing of the proposed rule change. This time period may be extended for up to an additional 45 days if the SEC determines that a longer period is appropriate and publishes the reasons for its decision or if the SRO consents to the longer period (Exchange Act Sec. 19(b)(2)(A), as amended by the Dodd-Frank Wall Street Reform and Consumer Protection Act).

Approval and Disapproval.—The SEC must approve a rule change proposed by an SRO if it finds that the change is consistent with laws and regulations applicable to the SRO. If it does not make this finding, the Commission must disapprove the proposed change. The SEC cannot approve a proposed rule change earlier than 30 days after the date of publication of the filing of the proposed change unless it publishes its reasons for finding good cause to do so (Exchange Act Sec. 19(b)(2)(C), as amended by the Dodd-Frank Act).

If the Commission does not approve the proposed change, it must provide the SRO with notice of the grounds for disapproval under consideration and an opportunity for hearing. Within 180 days after the date of publication of the rule-change notice, the SEC must have completed any required hearing and issued an order approving or disapproving the proposed rule change. This time period can be extended for up to 60 days if the Commission determines that a longer period is appropriate and publishes the reasons for its decision or if the SRO consents to the longer period (Exchange Act Sec. 19(b)(2)(B), as amended by the Dodd-Frank Act).

A proposed rule change will be deemed approved if the SEC fails to approve it or begin proceedings, or if it fails to issue an order approving or disapproving the change, within the prescribed time periods (Exchange Act Sec. 19(b)(2)(D), as amended by the Dodd-Frank Act).

Filing and Effective Dates.—The Act also added a provision to Section 19(b) to clarify that the date of filing of a proposed rule change is the date on which the Commission receives it. However, a proposed rule change will not be deemed to have been "received" if the SEC notifies the SRO within seven days that its proposal does not comply with the Commission's rules concerning the required form. In addition, if the SEC finds that a particular proposed change is unusually lengthy or complex or raises novel regulatory issues, it must inform the SRO of this within seven business days after original receipt of the proposal, and the proposal will not be deemed "received" if the Commission notifies the SRO that its proposal does not comply with SEC rules within 21 days (Exchange Act Sec. 19(b)(10), as added by the Dodd-Frank Act).

A proposed rule change takes effect immediately upon filing with the SEC if the change involves establishing or altering a due, fee or charge imposed by the SRO, regardless of whether the person responsible for payment is a member of the SRO (Exchange Act Sec. 19(b)(3)(A), as amended by the Dodd-Frank Act).

If an SRO, after filing a proposed rule change with the SEC, publishes a notice of the filing along with the terms of the change on a publicly accessible website, the SEC must send the notice to the *Federal Register* for publication within 15 days of the online publication. If the Commission fails to properly complete this process, the official publication date for the proposed rule change will be the date of the original online publication (Exchange Act Sec. 19(b)(2)(E), as amended by the Dodd-Frank Act).

Temporary Suspension of Rule Change.—The Commission may no longer summarily abrogate and require refiling of a proposed rule change if it finds that action necessary or appropriate. Under an amendment to Section 19(b)(3)(C), the SEC may only temporarily suspend the change in order to conduct proceedings to further consider the matter (Exchange Act Sec. 19(b)(3)(C), as amended by the Dodd-Frank Act). A similar change applies to the rules governing rejection of a proposed rule change filed by a clearing agency (Exchange Act Sec. 19(b)(4)(D), as amended by the Dodd-Frank Act).

Procedural Rules.—Within 180 days of enactment, after consultation with other regulatory agencies, the Commission must promulgate rules stating the procedural requirements for proposed SRO rule change proceedings. Any rules adopted by the SEC under this requirement need not include republication of proposed changes or solicitation of public comment (Exchange Act Sec. 19(b)(2)(F), as amended by the Dodd-Frank Act).

▶ **Effective date.** The provision takes effect one day after the date of enactment (Sec. 4 of the Dodd-Frank Wall Street Reform and Consumer Protection Act).

Law source: Law at ¶10,916 and ¶10,004. Committee Report at ¶54,444.

— Sec. 916(a) of the Dodd-Frank Wall Street Reform and Consumer Protection Act, amending Exchange Act Sec. 19(b)(2);

— Sec. 916(b), adding Exchange Act Sec. 19(b)(10);

— Sec. 916(c), amending Exchange Act Sec. 19(b)(3);

— Sec. 916(d), amending Exchange Act Sec. 19(b)(4)(D);

— Sec. 4, providing the effective date.

¶4035 Pre-Purchase Disclosures

The Dodd-Frank Wall Street Reform and Consumer Protection Act amends Exchange Act Section 15 to clarify that the SEC may issue rules designating specific documents or information that brokers or dealers must provide to retail investors prior to purchases of investment products or services. Currently, most prospectuses are not delivered until after a sale has been completed. Congress, however, determined that investors need to be provided with relevant and timely disclosures about financial products and services in advance of purchase so that they can make better, more informed investment decisions (S. Rep. No. 111-176, pp. 107–108).

In adopting rules relating to pre-purchase disclosures, the SEC must consider whether the rules will promote efficiency, competition and capital formation and will improve investor protection. However, any documents or information the SEC requires to be disclosed must be in a summary format and contain clear and concise information about the objectives, strategies, costs and risks involved with the individual investment. The documents and information must also describe any financial incentive that the financial intermediary will receive in connection with the purchase (Exchange Act Sec. 15(n), as added by the Dodd-Frank Wall Street Reform and Consumer Protection Act).

▶ **Effective date.** The provision takes effect one day after the date of enactment (Sec. 4 of the Dodd-Frank Wall Street Reform and Consumer Protection Act).

Law source: Law at ¶10,919 and ¶10,004. Committee Report at ¶54,447.

— Sec. 919 of the Dodd-Frank Wall Street Reform and Consumer Protection Act, adding Exchange Act Sec. 15(n);
— Sec. 4, providing the effective date.

¶4040 Studies and Reports

The Dodd-Frank Wall Street Reform and Consumer Protection Act requires the SEC and the Comptroller General to perform several studies on investor-protection issues. By requiring these studies, Congress acknowledged that further research is necessary to help inform a proper legislative response. As discussed in more detail below, the Dodd-Frank Act requires studies and reports to Congress on:

- the need for enhanced examination of, and enforcement resources for, investment advisers;
- the financial literacy of retail investors, including their understanding of the investment process and their ability to make informed investment decisions;
- advertising practices engaged in by mutual funds, including whether existing and proposed regulatory requirements for open-end investment company advertisements and current marketing practices effectively protect investors;
- conflicts of interest that exist among the various staffs in an individual firm and the impact that these conflicts have on investors;

- investor access to information about the registration of and proceedings against investment advisers, brokers, dealers and their associated persons and whether additional information outside of these systems should be publicly available; and
- the role of financial planners in providing advice to investors regarding financial-resource management and whether certain professional designations mislead consumers.

In addition, the Dodd-Frank Act calls for a study of the effectiveness of the legal and regulatory standards of care imposed on brokers, dealers, investment advisers and persons associated with these entities when providing personalized investment advice to retail customers, and whether new standards are necessary. This provision is discussed elsewhere, at ¶ 4020.

Adviser Examinations.—The SEC must conduct a study to assess the need for enhanced examination of and enforcement resources for investment advisers (Sec. 914(a)(1) of the Dodd-Frank Act). During the study, the Commission and its staff must review the number and frequency of examinations over the five years preceding the Act and analyze current and potential approaches to examining the advisory activities of dually registered broker-dealers and investment advisers and affiliated broker-dealers and investment advisers. The Commission must also consider the extent to which congressional authorization to designate self-regulatory organizations to augment SEC efforts in overseeing investment advisers would improve the frequency of adviser examinations (Sec. 914(a)(2) of the Dodd-Frank Act).

The SEC must report its findings to the House Financial Services Committee and the Senate Banking Committee within 180 days after the date of enactment. The report must discuss the SEC's findings and recommend regulatory and legislative steps to address concerns identified in the study. The Commission must use the findings to revise existing rules and regulations as necessary (Sec. 914(b) of the Dodd-Frank Act).

Financial Literacy of Investors.—The Commission must conduct a study reviewing retail customers' understanding of the investment process and their ability to make informed investment decisions. During the study, the SEC must consider:

- the level of financial literacy among retail investors and individualized subgroups of investors;
- methods that would improve the timing, content and format of disclosures made available to investors relating to financial intermediaries, investment products and investment services;
- the information that would be most useful and relevant to retail investors to assist them in making informed decisions concerning engagement of financial intermediaries or purchases of investment products or services, including shares of open-end investment companies;
- means by which to increase the transparency of expenses and potential conflicts of interest that may result from completing transactions involving investment services and products;
- public and private efforts that would be effective in providing investor education; and

¶4040

- in consultation with the Financial Literacy and Education Commission, strategies that would increase financial literacy of investors to a point that would bring about positive changes in investor behavior (Sec. 917(a) of the Dodd-Frank Act).

Within two years after the date of enactment, the Commission must complete and submit a report on its findings to the Senate Banking Committee and the House Financial Services Committee (Sec. 917(b) of the Dodd-Frank Act).

Mutual Fund Advertising.—The Comptroller General must conduct a study on the advertising practices engaged in by mutual funds. During the study, the Comptroller General must analyze existing and proposed regulatory requirements for open-end investment company advertisements and current marketing practices used in the sale of mutual fund shares and must consider the impact of fund advertising on consumers. At the study's conclusion, the Comptroller General must make recommendations as necessary to improve investor protections in relation to fund advertising and must detail what additional information investors should receive to make informed investment decisions (Sec. 918(a) of the Dodd-Frank Act).

Within 18 months after the date of enactment, the Comptroller General must complete and submit a report on its findings to the Senate Banking Committee and the House Financial Services Committee (Sec. 918(b) of the Dodd-Frank Act).

Internal Conflicts of Interest.—The Comptroller General must conduct a study to identify and examine any conflicts of interest that may exist among various staffs within the same firm (*i.e.*, between investment banking staff and fixed-income securities staff) and make recommendations designed to protect investors from these conflicts (Sec. 919A(a) of the Dodd-Frank Act). During the study, the Comptroller General must consider:

- the potential for investor harm resulting from internal conflicts, including an analysis of the misconduct engaged in by the firms and individuals involved in the Global Analyst Research Settlements of 2003;
- the nature and benefits of the undertakings the firms and individuals involved in the settlements agreed to in enforcement proceedings, which included firewalls between research and investment banking and dedicated legal and compliance staffs, as well as separation of reporting obligations, budget allocation, compensation, performance evaluations and other business decisions;
- whether any of these undertakings should be applied permanently to securities firms by legislation or by Commission rule; and
- additional regulatory or legislative measures that may serve to mitigate any adverse impact that conflicts of interest may have on investors or to enhance investor protection and confidence in the integrity of the securities markets.

In making these determinations, the Comptroller General must consult with the states' attorneys general and other state securities officials, as well as the SEC, FINRA, NYSE Regulation, financial intermediaries, investor advocate groups, investors and academics (Sec. 919A(b) of the Dodd-Frank Act).

The Comptroller General must submit a report on the study's results to the Senate Banking Committee and the House Financial Services Committee within 18 months after the date of enactment (Sec. 919A(c) of the Dodd-Frank Act).

¶4040

Access to Adviser and Broker-Dealer Information.—Within six months after the date of enactment, the Commission must complete a study and issue recommendations on improving investor access to information about the registration of and proceedings against investment advisers, brokers, dealers and their associated persons located on the Central Registration Depository and Investment Adviser Registration Depository systems. The study must analyze the advantages and disadvantages of enabling investor access to the information contained in these systems, must determine what data is most relevant to investors and must determine the most effective and efficient format in which to present the data. The SEC must also consider whether additional information outside of these systems should be made publicly available (Sec. 919B(a) of the Dodd-Frank Act).

The Commission must implement any recommendations made as a result of the study within 18 months after the date of enactment (Sec. 919B(b) of the Dodd-Frank Act).

Financial Planners.—The Comptroller General must also conduct a study evaluating the effectiveness of existing laws and regulations designed to protect investors and other consumers from individuals holding themselves out as financial planners through misleading titles, designations or marketing materials. The study must consider current state and federal oversight of financial planners and must identify any legal or regulatory gaps in the structures governing financial planners and others providing consumers with financial planning services (Sec. 919C(a) of the Dodd-Frank Act).

In conducting the study, the Comptroller General must consider:

- financial planners' role in providing advice regarding personalized management of financial resources (*e.g.*, investment planning, income tax planning, education planning, retirement planning, estate planning and risk management planning);
- adequacy of ethical and professional standards for financial planners found in current state and federal regulations;
- potential risks posed to investors and other consumers by individuals holding themselves out as financial planners or as otherwise providing financial planning services in connection with the sale of financial products, including insurance and securities;
- potential risks posed to investors and other consumers by individuals who use titles, designations or marketing materials in a misleading way in connection with the delivery of financial advice;
- investors' understanding of the licensing requirements and standards of care applicable to those holding themselves out as financial planners or as otherwise providing financial planning services;
- possible benefits of enhanced regulation and professional oversight of financial planners; and
- any other factor the Comptroller General deems appropriate in conducting the study (Sec. 919C(b) of the Dodd-Frank Act).

Following the study, the Comptroller General must make recommendations concerning the appropriate manner in which to regulate financial planners and others providing financial planning services. These recommendations must consider the appropriate

¶4040

regulatory structure as well as the appropriate scope of regulation, including the need to establish competency and practice standards, ethical guidelines, disciplinary authority or transparency to consumers. The recommendations, along with the general findings of and determinations made during the study, must be organized into a report for submission to the Senate Banking Committee, the Senate Special Committee on Aging, and the House Financial Services Committee. The report must describe the considerations made and analysis used during the study and the public, industry and consumer input considered by the Comptroller General in making its findings and recommendations. The report is due within 180 days after the date of enactment (Sec. 919C(c) of the Dodd-Frank Act).

▶ **Effective date.** The provisions take effect one day after the date of enactment (Sec. 4 of the Dodd-Frank Wall Street Reform and Consumer Protection Act).

Law source: Law at ¶10,914, ¶10,917, ¶10,918, ¶10,919A, ¶10,919B, ¶10,919C and ¶10,004. Committee Report at ¶54,445, ¶54,446, ¶54,448, ¶54,449 and ¶54,450.

— Sec. 914 of the Dodd-Frank Wall Street Reform and Consumer Protection Act, requiring an SEC study of investment adviser examinations;

— Sec. 917, requiring an SEC study of financial literacy;

— Sec. 918, requiring a Comptroller General study of mutual fund advertising;

— Sec. 919A, requiring a Comptroller General study of conflicts of interest within financial firms;

— Sec. 919B, requiring an SEC study of investor access to information regarding advisers and broker-dealers;

— Sec. 919C, requiring a Comptroller General study of financial planners and the use of financial designations;

— Sec. 4, providing the effective date.

ENFORCEMENT and REMEDIES

¶4050 Introduction

The Dodd-Frank Wall Street Reform and Consumer Protection Act expands the scope of enforcement tools that the SEC may use to respond to securities law violations. Several enforcement provisions and remedies are located in Title IX, Subtitle B, the focus of this subchapter. These include, for example, a measure authorizing the SEC to restrict or prohibit the use of mandatory arbitration clauses in contracts with broker-dealers and investment advisers (see ¶ 4055). Brokers are also now subject to more restrictive margin lending requirements (see ¶ 4085).

The Commission may compensate whistleblowers for useful tips. The statute provides for bounty payments paid from penalties and disgorgement amounts collected, and authorizes a direct cause of action against employers for retaliation (see ¶ 4060). The SEC may also issue "collateral bars," under which a violator active in one area of the securities industry will be barred from all other securities industry conduct (see ¶ 4065).

As amended, the Sarbanes-Oxley Act "Fair Fund" provisions are available to compensate injured investors even when the defendant did not personally benefit from the conduct (see ¶ 4090). In addition, felons and other "bad actors" will be prohibited from taking advantage of the Regulation D registration exemption (see ¶ 4070).

The legislation also brings more categories of persons and offenses within the SEC's enforcement jurisdiction. The statute affirmatively defines the extraterritorial reach of the securities laws with regard to actions brought by the SEC and the U.S. government. The original statutes were silent on the question, and the courts over the years developed several (and somewhat inconsistent) tests for determining the reach of the securities laws (see ¶ 4135).

The U.S. Supreme Court held in June 2010 that Exchange Act Section 10(b) did not apply to a "foreign-cubed" private action involving foreign conduct, exchanges and purchasers (*Morrison v. National Australia Bank, Ltd.* (U.S. Sup. Ct. 2010), FED. SEC. L. REP. ¶ 95,776). As Justice Scalia wrote for the Court, "there is no affirmative indication in the Exchange Act that § 10(b) applies extraterritorially, and we therefore conclude that it does not." The Dodd-Frank Act fills that statutory void in enforcement actions and affirmatively expresses Congress' intent for the federal courts to have jurisdiction over claims brought by the SEC or the United States if there is conduct within the United States that constitutes significant steps in furtherance of a violation, even if the securities transaction occurs outside the United States and involves only foreign investors. The statute does not apply to private actions, such as *Morrison*, but does require an SEC study of the issue of extraterritoriality in private actions (see ¶ 4135).

The Dodd-Frank Act also clarifies that the SEC may file cases against persons formerly associated with regulated entities and expands the Commission's authority to sue and recover penalties from persons who aid and abet violations (see ¶ 4110). In addition, the Act expands the scope of several antifraud provisions by eliminating the exchange-traded requirement (see ¶ 4125).

Finally, the subtitle amends the Securities Investor Protection Act (SIPA), the law that returns money to the customers of insolvent fraudulent broker-dealers. The Act increases the Securities Investor Protection Corporation's borrowing limit. Although SIPC has not needed to borrow funds to meet its commitments to date, the collapse of Lehman Brothers and the Madoff funds indicated that a higher lending limit may be necessary to deal with future large-scale failures. SIPC members must also pay an annual assessment based on a percentage of their revenues. The bill also increases the maximum cash advance amount to harmed customers as well as various penalty amounts for misconduct (see ¶ 4095).

Treated Elsewhere.—One remaining provision in Subtitle B, Section 929J, is discussed elsewhere (see ¶ 4425). That measure gives the Public Company Accounting Oversight Board (PCAOB) greater ability to access the audit work papers and audit documentation of foreign public accounting firms when they perform material services on which a registered public accounting firm relies in conducting an audit.

▶ **Effective date.** The provisions take effect one day after the date of enactment (Sec. 4 of the Dodd-Frank Wall Street Reform and Consumer Protection Act).

Law source: Law at ¶10,921 and ¶10,004. Committee Report at ¶50,091 and ¶54,460.
— Sec. 921 *et seq.* of the Dodd-Frank Wall Street Reform and Consumer Protection Act, instituting broader enforcement powers and remedies;
— Sec. 4, providing the effective date.

¶4055 Mandatory Arbitration Clauses

Broker-dealers generally require their customers to agree contractually to arbitrate all disputes. Although arbitration may be a reasonable option for many consumers, mandating a particular venue and method of adjudicating disputes while eliminating access to the courts may undermine investor interests.

The Obama administration recommended legislation that would give the SEC clear authority to prohibit mandatory arbitration clauses in broker-dealer and investment advisory contracts with retail customers (*Financial Regulatory Reform, A New Foundation: Rebuilding Financial Supervision and Regulation*, Treasury Department (June 17, 2009), FED. BANK. L. REP. ¶ 75-201). The Dodd-Frank Wall Street Reform and Consumer Protection Act incorporates many of the administration's recommendations. The SEC may restrict or prohibit the use of mandatory arbitration clauses in contracts with broker-dealers and investment advisers. To act on mandatory arbitration provisions, the Commission must determine that any prohibition, condition or limitation is in the public interest and serves to protect investors (Exchange Act Sec. 15(o) and Advisers Act Sec. 205(f), as added by the Dodd-Frank Wall Street Reform and Consumer Protection Act).

Historically, claims for violations of the federal securities laws were considered non-arbitrable based on the doctrine enunciated by the U.S. Supreme Court in *Wilko v. Swan* (U.S. Sup. Ct. 1953), FED. SEC. L. REP. [1952–1956 Transfer Binder] ¶ 90,640. In *Wilko*, the Court held that an agreement to arbitrate claims under Securities Act Section 12(a)(2) was not enforceable. However, as arbitration gained increasing judicial favor, the Court began to chip away at the *Wilko* doctrine and in 1989 expressly overruled it. The Court ruled that a pre-dispute agreement to arbitrate an investor's securities claims against a brokerage firm was enforceable in view of the strong federal policy favoring arbitration (*Rodriguez de Quijas v. Shearson/American Express, Inc.* (U.S. Sup. Ct. 1989), FED. SEC. L. REP. [1989 Transfer Binder] ¶ 94,407).

The securities industry has previously opposed the mandatory arbitration restrictions. As the Securities Industry and Financial Markets Association (SIFMA) stated in a 2007 white paper, "securities arbitration affords investors the opportunity to have their claims heard close to home, before highly trained and experienced arbitrators, in a forum that has proven to resolve disputes at least as fairly as the judicial system, and much faster and less expensively." The group believes "that enforceable contracts between the parties on issues governing their relationship are not only standard, but are essential, and that in particular, contract provisions that provide certainty of process in advance of a dispute that may arise are in the best interests of both parties." However, FINRA Chairman and CEO Richard G. Ketchum testified in October 2009 that the regulatory authority believes that the use of mandatory arbitration agreements "is a decision best made by Congress and the SEC." He stated that "our view is that Congressional or SEC action is necessary in light of Supreme Court precedent that upholds the ability of firms to contract in this way with customers. As such, we do not object to the Administration's proposal" (http://www.house.gov/apps/list/hearing/financialsvcs_dem/ketchum_testimony.pdf).

▶ **Effective date.** The provision takes effect one day after the date of enactment (Sec. 4 of the Dodd-Frank Wall Street Reform and Consumer Protection Act).

Law source: Law at ¶10,921 and ¶10,004. Committee Report at ¶54,460.

— Sec. 921(a) of the Dodd-Frank Wall Street Reform and Consumer Protection Act, adding Exchange Act Sec. 15(o);

— Sec. 921(b), adding Advisers Act Sec. 205(f);

— Sec. 4, providing the effective date.

¶4060 Whistleblowers

The Dodd-Frank Wall Street Reform and Consumer Protection Act allows the SEC to reward whistleblowers who provide the Commission with information on a wide range of securities law violations. Under new Exchange Act Section 21F, the Commission may use funds collected as sanctions in judicial or administrative proceedings to pay rewards for information that leads to successful enforcement actions. This Investor Protection Fund will also pay for an employee "hotline" to allow SEC staff to pass on confidential tips and suggestions to the agency's inspector general. Whistleblowers also receive greater protections from retaliation (Exchange Act Sec. 21F, as added by the Dodd-Frank Wall Street Reform and Consumer Protection Act).

Under prior law, the SEC had limited authority to pay bounties to individuals who reported violations. Exchange Act Section 21A(e) authorized the agency to reward individuals for providing information leading to the recovery of civil penalties for insider trading. That section was limited to insider trading violations, however, and the Commission has rarely used this authority. Since 1989, the SEC has made only seven payouts to five whistleblowers, for a total of $159,537.

In contrast, the SEC may now pay rewards for information that leads to the successful enforcement of any judicial or administrative action brought by the SEC under any provisions of the securities laws. For example, whistleblowers in financial fraud and Foreign Corrupt Practices Act cases, which often generate substantial civil penalties, would be eligible for awards (Exchange Act Sec. 21F(b)(1), as added by the Dodd-Frank Act).

The SEC may reward one or more whistleblowers who voluntarily provided original information to the Commission that leads to the successful prosecution of specified enforcement actions. This authority applies to any judicial or administrative action brought by the SEC under the securities laws that results in monetary sanctions exceeding $1 million (Exchange Act Secs. 21F(a)(1) and (b)(1), as added by the Dodd-Frank Act).

Under new Section 21F, the minimum award is 10 percent of the monetary sanctions collected in the action or in related actions, and any amount paid cannot exceed 30 percent of the collected monetary sanctions (Exchange Act Sec. 21F(b)(1), as added by the Dodd-Frank Act). The statute does not require a whistleblower to enter into a contract with the SEC to receive an award. The Commission may, however, by rule or regulation require claimants to enter into contractual agreements with the agency to receive awards (Exchange Act Sec. 21F(e), as added by the Dodd-Frank Act).

The SEC may, in its discretion, determine the amount of all awards, subject to the 10- and 30-percent limits. The SEC may take into account the significance of the whistleblower's information to the success of the action, the degree of assistance provided by the whistleblower and the Commission's programmatic interest in deterring violations of the securities laws. The Commission may not, however, take the balance available in the Investor Protection Fund into consideration when determining whether to grant an award or the amount of any payout (Exchange Act Sec. 21F(c)(1), as added by the Dodd-Frank Act).

To receive an award, the whistleblower must provide "original information" to the SEC. Qualifying information must be based on the direct and independent knowledge or analysis of the whistleblower. If the SEC became aware of the information from other sources, whistleblowers cannot recover unless they were the initial source of the information. Similarly, the SEC will not pay awards based on allegations in specified government proceedings unless the whistleblower was the initial source of the information that resulted in the governmental action (Exchange Act Sec. 21F(a)(3), as added by the Dodd-Frank Act). As described in the Senate Banking Committee report, in circumstances where "bits and pieces" of the whistleblower's information were known to the media prior to the emergence of the whistleblower, but the critical components of the information were supplied by the whistleblower, the SEC should be able to reward all informants in accordance with the degree of assistance provided (S. Rep. No. 111-176, p. 111).

Information provided to the SEC in writing by a whistleblower will not lose the status of "original information" solely because the whistleblower provided the information prior to the effective date of the regulations, if the whistleblower provides the information after the date of enactment (Sec. 924(b) of the Dodd-Frank Act).

A whistleblower who submits a claim for award under Section 21F(a) may be represented by counsel. Whistleblowers must be represented by counsel if they submit the information anonymously to the SEC. Prior to the payment of any awards, whistleblowers must disclose their identity and provide any other information required by the Commission (Exchange Act Sec. Sec. 21F(d), as added by the Dodd-Frank Act).

Exclusions.—The legislation specifically prohibits award payments to certain whistleblowers. Claimants cannot receive an award under Section 21F(b) if they:

- obtained the information while they were a member, officer, or employee of a regulatory agency, the Department of Justice, the Public Company Accounting Oversight Board, a law enforcement agency or a self-regulatory organization;
- were convicted of a crime related to the judicial or administrative action in question;
- obtained the information through the performance of an audit of financial statements required under the securities laws; or

- otherwise failed to submit information under SEC rules (Exchange Act Sec. 21F(c)(2), as added by the Dodd-Frank Act).

Whistleblowers are also ineligible for compensation if they made any false or fraudulent statements or representations, or knowingly used any false documents in seeking an award (Exchange Act Sec. 21F(i), as added by the Dodd-Frank Act).

Appeals Process.—Claimants may appeal SEC decisions on whether to grant awards to the appropriate federal circuit court of appeals. The standard of review is found in 5 U.S.C. § 706, which allows the court to set aside agency actions that are "arbitrary, capricious, an abuse of discretion, or otherwise not in accordance with law" (Exchange Act Sec. 21F(f), as added by the Dodd-Frank Act).

> **CCH Comment:** The conference committee made a significant change to the appeals process language. The base text of the legislation debated by the conference committee provided that claimants could appeal all aspects of a Commission decision. However, the conference committee added restrictive language providing that "the determination of the amount of an award" was not subject to appeal.

This provision resembles other federal whistleblower statutes. For example, the Internal Revenue Code establishes a minimum award of 15 percent of the collected proceeds. Tax claimants may also appeal the IRS award determination to the Tax Court (I.R.C. § 7623(b)).

> **CCH Comment:** The version of the bill passed by the House established no minimum award, and did not allow claimants to appeal the SEC's initial determination. The Senate Banking Committee report stated, however, that the minimum payout was a "critical component" of the program. The committee noted that whistleblowers often face the difficult choice between telling the truth and the risk of committing "career suicide." The committee determined that the enforceability and relatively predictable level of payout resulting from a minimum award and a review process would significantly encourage potential whistleblowers to come forward (S. Rep. No. 111-176, pp. 111–112).

Confidentiality.—The SEC may generally not disclose information provided by whistleblowers that could reasonably be expected to reveal that person's identity. The Act does provide for a limited exception for disclosures in accordance with the Privacy Act, 5 U.S.C. § 552a. The information is also generally not subject to Freedom of Information Act disclosure. These restrictions apply until the SEC is required by law to disclose the information to a defendant or respondent in connection with a proceeding instituted by the Commission or other entity (Exchange Act Sec. 21F(h)(2)(A), as added by the Dodd-Frank Act).

There are several exceptions, however. For example, Section 21F(h)(2)(C) provides that the section does not limit the Attorney General's ability to present the evidence to a grand jury or to share the evidence with potential witnesses or defendants in the course of an ongoing criminal investigation (Exchange Act Sec. 21F(h)(2)(C), as added by the Dodd-Frank Act).

The Commission may disclose the information in its discretion, and if necessary to protect investors, to other government entities, including the U.S. Attorney General, other regulators, self-regulatory organizations, state attorneys general in connection with criminal investigations and other appropriate state authorities, the Public Company Accounting Oversight Board and foreign securities regulators and law enforcement

¶4060

authorities. Any information provided under this subsection retains its status as confidential in the hands of the Commission (Exchange Act Sec. 21F(h)(2)(D), as added by the Dodd-Frank Act).

The domestic entities that receive information from the SEC under Exchange Act Section 21F(h)(2)(D) must refrain from further disclosure in accordance with Section 21F(h)(2)(A), and the foreign entities must maintain the information in accordance with the assurances of confidentiality as the Commission deems appropriate (Exchange Act Sec. 21F(h)(2)(D), as added by the Dodd-Frank Act).

Investor Protection Fund.—The legislation establishes a special fund to be held by the U.S. Treasury (Exchange Act Section 21F(g), as added by the Dodd-Frank Act). The SEC may use this Investor Protection Fund, without further appropriation or fiscal year limitations, to pay whistleblower awards and to fund the employee hotline program for SEC employees to submit confidential suggestions and information to the Commission's Inspector General as established in Section 966 of the Dodd-Frank Act (Exchange Act Secs. 21F(g)(1) and (2), as added by the Dodd-Frank Act).

> **CCH Comment:** Under the House version of the bill, the fund could be used for investor education programs rather than for an Inspector General tip hotline. It is likely that Exchange Act Section 21F(g)(2)(B) contains a typographical error, as it refers to the activities of the Inspector General under Exchange Act Section 4(i). These provisions are contained in the new Exchange Act Section 4D added in Section 966 of the Dodd-Frank Act. This follows the addition of Exchange Act Section 4(h) in Section 965 of the Dodd-Frank Act, and Section 4(i) as amended does not deal with whistleblower issues.

The SEC will, with specified exceptions, deposit all amounts collected as sanctions in judicial or administrative actions into the Investor Protection Fund. The SEC also cannot make deposits into the fund when the account's balance at the time of collection exceeds $300 million. The monies actually distributed to harmed investors, such as under the Sarbanes-Oxley Act "Fair Fund" provision, cannot become part of the Investor Protection Fund. The SEC will deposit undistributed "Fair Fund" amounts into the Investor Protection Fund, unless the fund's balance exceeds $200 million. If the fund is not sufficient to pay an award, the SEC must deposit an amount equal to the unpaid portion of the award from any monetary sanction collected by the Commission in the action on which the award is based (Exchange Act Secs. 21F(g)(3)(A) and (B), as added by the Dodd-Frank Act).

The fund may also realize income from specified investments. If the fund's balance exceeds current needs, the SEC may request the Treasury Secretary to invest the surplus in obligations issued or guaranteed by the United States (Exchange Act Sec. 21F(g)(4), as added by the Dodd-Frank Act).

Whistleblower Protection.—The Dodd-Frank Act expands the whistleblower protections in the Sarbanes-Oxley Act. Although the two statutes prohibit similar conduct, there are significant differences in both the scope of the measures and in the available relief.

Initially, the Dodd-Frank Act amends Sarbanes-Oxley Section 806(a) to clarify that the whistleblower protections apply to both parent companies and their subsidiaries and affiliates if their financial information is included in the consolidated financial statements of the parent company (Sarbanes-Oxley Act Sec. 806(a), as amended by the Dodd-Frank

Act). The Act also includes employees of nationally recognized statistical rating organizations within the Sarbanes-Oxley Act whistleblower provisions (Sarbanes-Oxley Act Sec. 806(a), as amended by the Dodd-Frank Act).

The victims of retaliatory discrimination also have significantly different relief available under the Dodd-Frank Act. Individuals may immediately and directly file suit against their employer in federal district court, bypassing the Sarbanes-Oxley Act administrative proceeding (Exchange Act Sec. 21F(h)(1)(B), as added by the Dodd-Frank Act). Under Sarbanes-Oxley Section 806, claimants must file a complaint with the Department of Labor, and may only seek district court review if the Secretary of Labor fails to reach a determination within 180 days.

> **CCH Comment:** The Dodd-Frank Act appears to provide an alternative route to the process prescribed by Sarbanes-Oxley Section 806. Aggrieved whistleblowers who would otherwise have to use the Section 806 mechanism—which relies initially on the Department of Labor—now appear to have an attractive federal court option.

Both statutes provide for the reinstatement of claimants with no loss of seniority, and for the recovery of lost wages with interest, litigation costs, expert witness fees and reasonable attorney fees. Under the Dodd-Frank Act, however, injured persons may recover twice their lost wages (Exchange Act Sec. 21F(h)(1)(C), as added by the Dodd-Frank Act), while the Sarbanes-Oxley Act allows only the recovery of actual wages lost.

The statute provides for nationwide service of subpoenas on witnesses. Plaintiffs have six years from the date of the violation to bring suit, or three years from the date when the injured party knew or should reasonably have known of facts material to the right of action. A statute of repose forecloses all actions, regardless of when the individual became aware of the potential claim, that are filed 10 years after the date of the violation (Exchange Act Sec. 21F(h)(1)(B), as added by the Dodd-Frank Act).

> **CCH Comment:** The six-year limitations period is a significant change from Sarbanes-Oxley Act practice. Section 806 initially provided whistleblowers with 90 days from the date of the retaliatory event to initiate an action. The Dodd-Frank bill does extend the Sarbanes-Oxley Act limitation to 180 days from the date of discovery. Even with this extension, however, the new Exchange Act cause of action limitations period is more than 12 times as long as that of the Sarbanes-Oxley Act administrative procedure.

The SEC must also establish a new office to administer and enforce the provisions of Section 21F. The whistleblower office must report annually to Congress on its activities, whistleblower complaints, and the Commission's response to those complaints (Sec. 924(d) of the Dodd-Frank Act). Rep. Ed Royce (R-CA) and Rep. Spencer Bachus (R-AL) introduced the whistleblower office amendment to improve the stature of whistleblower complaints within the SEC and ensure their concerns are being acted upon by the agency. According to Rep. Bachus, this amendment will ensure that the SEC will have a high-ranking official and office to coordinate and pursue the huge volume of whistleblower tips that very well could prevent future frauds like Bernard Madoff and Allen Stanford. Complaints within the industry or by investors are the cheapest, most effective way to identify fraudsters, Rep. Bachus said.

Waiver Provisions.—The statute amends Section 806 of the Sarbanes-Oxley Act to provide that the rights and remedies available to whistleblowers cannot be waived by any agreement, policy form, or condition of employment, including a predispute arbitration agreement. In addition, predispute arbitration agreements cannot compel the arbitration of disputes under the Sarbanes-Oxley Act whistleblower provisions (Sarbanes-Oxley Act Sec. 806(e), as added by the Dodd-Frank Act).

Reports to Congress.—By October 30 of each year, the SEC must submit a report on its whistleblower program to the Senate Banking Committee and the House Financial Services Committee. The report must describe the whistleblower awards granted during the preceding fiscal year. In addition, the report must include financial information concerning the Investor Protection Fund and its transactions. The report must be accompanied by a complete set of audited financial statements, including a balance sheet, income statement and cash flow analysis (Exchange Act Sec. 21F(g)(5), as added by the Dodd-Frank Act).

The SEC Inspector General must conduct a comprehensive one-time study and report on the whistleblower program. The study must assess whether the program is clearly defined and user-friendly, and whether the SEC has adequately promoted and publicized the program. The Inspector General must also examine whether the Commission responds in a timely manner to information it receives, and administers the program efficiently (Sec. 922(d) of the Dodd-Frank Act).

The Inspector General must also examine the effectiveness of several structural aspects of the program, including

- the minimum and maximum award levels;
- the appeals process;
- the funding mechanism; and
- the Freedom of Information Act exemption.

Finally, the Inspector General must review whether individuals who have already attempted to pursue a case through the Commission should have a right of action to sue violators on behalf of the government and themselves. The report is due to the congressional oversight committees and must be published on the SEC website within 30 months from the statute's enactment (Sec. 922(d) of the Dodd-Frank Act).

Rulemaking.—The SEC may issue rules and regulations as necessary or appropriate to implement the statute (Exchange Act Sec. 21F(j), as added by the Dodd-Frank Act). The SEC must adopt final rules to implement the whistleblower provisions within 270 days after enactment (Sec. 924(a) of the Dodd-Frank Act).

Conforming Amendments.—The Dodd-Frank Act makes minor conforming changes to Securities Act Section 20(d), Investment Company Act Section 42(e), Advisers Act Section 209(e) and Exchange Act Section 21(d) to reflect the payment of sanctions funds into the Investor Protection Fund (Sec. 923(a) of the Dodd-Frank Act). The statute also removes the insider-trading bounty language in Exchange Act Section 21A (Sec. 923(b) of the Dodd-Frank Act). That provision is no longer necessary after the establishment of the inclusive bounty provisions in Exchange Act Section 21F.

▶ **Effective date.** The provisions take effect one day after the date of enactment (Sec. 4 of the Dodd-Frank Wall Street Reform and Consumer Protection Act).

Law source: Law at ¶10,922, ¶10,923, ¶10,924, ¶10,929A and ¶10,004. Committee Report at ¶54,461, ¶54,464 and ¶54,470.

— Sec. 922(a) of the Dodd-Frank Wall Street Reform and Consumer Protection Act, adding Exchange Act Sec. 21F;

- Secs. 922(b) and (c), amending Sarbanes-Oxley Act Secs. 806(a) and (b) and adding Sec. 806(e);
- Sec. 922(d), requiring the Inspector General to study and report on the whistleblower program;
- Sec. 923, making conforming amendments to Securities Act Sec. 20(d), Exchange Act Secs. 21(d) and 21A, Investment Company Act Sec. 42(e) and Advisers Act Sec. 209(e);
- Sec. 924, requiring the SEC to adopt implementing regulations;
- Sec. 929A, amending Sarbanes-Oxley Act Sec. 806(a);
- Sec. 4, providing the effective date.

¶4065 Collateral Bars

Under prior law, a securities professional barred from being an investment adviser for serious misconduct could still participate in the industry as a broker-dealer. Noting that expanded sanctions would better enable the SEC to enforce the federal securities laws, the Obama administration sought authority for the SEC to impose collateral bars against regulated persons across all aspects of the industry, rather than in a specific segment of the industry. The interrelationship among the securities activities under the Commission's jurisdiction, the similar grounds for exclusion from each, and the SEC's overarching responsibility to regulate these activities support the imposition of collateral bars.

The Dodd-Frank Wall Street Reform and Consumer Protection Act overturns a 1999 decision by the D.C. Circuit Court of Appeals. In *Teicher v. SEC*, the court held that Exchange Act Section 15(b)(6) did not authorize the Commission to bar an individual from associating with an investment adviser. The court stated that "the SEC believes that once the threshold requirement of any of the particular provisions has been satisfied, it should be able to use the 'place limitations' language to move seamlessly from one licensing regime to another, imposing unlimited sanctions throughout all the branches of the industry within its bailiwick." Such an interpretation would conflict with a "congressional determination to create separate sets of sanctions, each triggered by an individual's satisfying the industry-specific nexus," concluded the court (*Teicher v. SEC* (CA-DofC 1999), FED. SEC. L. REP. [1999 Transfer Binder] ¶ 90,486).

The legislation authorizes the SEC to impose collateral bars against regulated persons. The Commission may bar a regulated person who violates the securities laws in one part of the industry, such as a broker-dealer who misappropriates customer funds, from access to customer funds in another part of the securities industry, for example, by acting as an investment adviser. As stated by SEC Chair Mary Schapiro in July 2009 congressional testimony, the authority to impose broad prophylactic relief in one action in the first instance will enable the Commission to protect investors and the markets more effectively while using SEC resources more efficiently (Exchange Act Secs. 15(b), 15B(c) and 17A(c) and Advisers Act Sec. 203(f), as amended by Sec. 925 of the Dodd-Frank Wall Street Reform and Consumer Protection Act).

▶ **Effective date.** The provision takes effect one day after the date of enactment (Sec. 4 of the Dodd-Frank Wall Street Reform and Consumer Protection Act).

Law source: Law at ¶10,925 and ¶10,004. Committee Report at ¶54,465.

— Sec. 925(a)(1) of the Dodd-Frank Wall Street Reform and Consumer Protection Act, amending Exchange Act Sec. 15(b)(6)(A);

— Sec. 925(a)(2), amending Exchange Act Sec. 15B(c)(4);

— Sec. 925(a)(3), amending Exchange Act Sec. 17A(c)(4);

— Sec. 925(b), amending Advisers Act Sec. 203(f);

— Sec. 4, providing the effective date.

¶4070 Regulation D Offerings

The Dodd-Frank Wall Street Reform and Consumer Protection Act incorporates "bad actor" provisions into the private placement arena. The SEC must, within one year of enactment, adopt rules disqualifying any securities offerings under Rule 506 of Regulation D by a person convicted of any felony or misdemeanor in connection with the purchase or sale of any security or involving the making of any false filing with the SEC or subject to a final order of a state securities commission, or state or federal banking authority barring the person from the financial industry (Sec. 926 of the Dodd-Frank Wall Street Reform and Consumer Protection Act).

As originally drafted, this section would have restored certain authority to the states over Regulation D offerings. In addition, it provided a 120-day period for the SEC to determine whether to review a filing before it would then go to the state regulator. Critics of the measure asserted that the waiting period and state law compliance requirements would unduly hinder the ability of start-up companies to raise capital, particularly from so-called "angel investors." A bipartisan amendment eliminated the 120-day period and stripped out the state authority provisions. As Sen. Mark Warner (D-VA) stated, "[L]imiting access to start-up capital does nothing to encourage innovation or boost our nation's competitiveness . . . [O]ur bipartisan amendment ensures that angel investors will be able to continue to provide critical financing for new entrepreneurs and promising young companies."

▶ **Effective date.** The provision takes effect one day after the date of enactment (Sec. 4 of the Dodd-Frank Wall Street Reform and Consumer Protection Act).

Law source: Law at ¶10,926 and ¶10,004. Committee Report at ¶54,466.

— Sec. 926 of the Dodd-Frank Wall Street Reform and Consumer Protection Act, requiring SEC rulemaking on Regulation D offerings;

— Sec. 4, providing the effective date.

¶4075 Self-Regulatory Organization Rules

The Dodd-Frank Wall Street Reform and Consumer Protection Act makes a technical amendment to Exchange Act Section 29(a) to provide equal treatment for the rules of all self-regulatory organizations. Section 29(a) voids contractual provisions that waive compliance with the statute or rules. Previously, the statute applied to rules issued by the SEC and the exchanges. As amended, Section 29(a) applies to Commission rules as well as to rules issued by all SROs, rather than just the exchanges (Exchange Act Sec. 29(a), as amended by the Dodd-Frank Wall Street Reform and Consumer Protection Act).

> **Caution Note:** The legislation contains duplicate provisions. The amendment to Exchange Act Section 29(a) appears both in Section 927 and Section 929T of the Dodd-Frank Act.

▶ **Effective date.** The provision takes effect one day after the date of enactment (Sec. 4 of the Dodd-Frank Wall Street Reform and Consumer Protection Act).

Law source: Law at ¶10,927, ¶10,929T and ¶10,004. Committee Report at ¶54,467.

— Sec. 927 of the Dodd-Frank Wall Street Reform and Consumer Protection Act, amending Exchange Act Sec. 29(a);

— Sec. 929T, amending Exchange Act Sec. 29(a);

— Sec. 4, providing the effective date.

¶4080 State-Registered Investment Advisers

An amendment to Investment Advisers Act Section 205 clarifies that this provision, which restricts the terms of investment adviser contracts, does not apply to state-registered investment advisers. This is a clarification of changes to the Advisers Act made in the 1996 National Securities Markets Improvement Act (NSMIA).

Previously, the Section 205 contractual term restrictions did not apply to advisers exempted under Advisers Act Section 203(b). The NSMIA amended the Advisers Act to authorize state regulation and preclude SEC registration of advisers managing less than $25 million in client assets. However, NSMIA did not add state registration to the list of Section 203(b) exemptions. The Advisers Act Section 205 contract restrictions apply only to advisers registered with or required to register with the SEC (Advisers Act Sec. 205(a), as amended by the Dodd-Frank Wall Street Reform and Consumer Protection Act).

▶ **Effective date.** The provision takes effect one day after the date of enactment (Sec. 4 of the Dodd-Frank Wall Street Reform and Consumer Protection Act).

Law source: Law at ¶10,928 and ¶10,004. Committee Report at ¶54,468.

— Sec. 928 of the Dodd-Frank Wall Street Reform and Consumer Protection Act, amending Advisers Act Sec. 205(a);

— Sec. 4, providing the effective date.

¶4085 Margin Lending

The Dodd-Frank Wall Street Reform and Consumer Protection Act imposes greater restrictions on margin lending. Under previous law, it was unlawful for any member of a national securities exchange or any broker or dealer to provide margin lending to or for any customer on any non-exempt security unless the loan: (1) complied with the

Federal Reserve's margin regulations; and (2) was properly collateralized. Now, either of these two infractions is unlawful by itself (Exchange Act Sec. 7(c)(1)(A), as amended by Sec. 929 of the Dodd-Frank Wall Street Reform and Consumer Protection Act).

▶ **Effective date.** The provision takes effect one day after the date of enactment (Sec. 4 of the Dodd-Frank Wall Street Reform and Consumer Protection Act).

Law source: Law at ¶10,929 and ¶10,004. Committee Report at ¶54,469.

— Sec. 929 of the Dodd-Frank Wall Street Reform and Consumer Protection Act, amending Exchange Act Sec. 7(c)(1)(A);

— Sec. 4, providing the effective date.

¶4090 Fair Fund Provision

The Fair Fund provisions of the Sarbanes-Oxley Act take the civil penalties levied by the SEC as a result of an enforcement action and direct them to a disgorgement fund for harmed investors. More money will be available to compensate defrauded investors by revising the Fair Fund provisions, as the SEC may use penalties to compensate victims of the fraud even if the Commission does not obtain an order requiring the defendant to disgorge ill-gotten gains. Under previous law, a defendant could engage in a securities law violation that harmed investors, but the SEC could not obtain disgorgement from the defendant if the defendant did not personally benefit from the violation (Sarbanes-Oxley Act Sec. 308, as amended by the Dodd-Frank Wall Street Reform and Consumer Protection Act).

▶ **Effective date.** The provision takes effect one day after the date of enactment (Sec. 4 of the Dodd-Frank Wall Street Reform and Consumer Protection Act).

Law source: Law at ¶10,929B and ¶10,004. Committee Report at ¶54,471.

— Sec. 929B of the Dodd-Frank Wall Street Reform and Consumer Protection Act, amending Sarbanes-Oxley Act Sec. 308;

— Sec. 4, providing the effective date.

¶4095 SIPA Amendments

The Dodd-Frank Wall Street Reform and Consumer Protection Act makes several significant changes to the Securities Investor Protection Act (SIPA). The Securities Investor Protection Corporation (SIPC) fund is revised to permit assessments based on a percentage of a member's gross revenues from the securities business. The maximum cash advance payable from the SIPC fund has been increased from $100,000 to $250,000 and may be adjusted for inflation every five years. The penalties for prohibited acts have been increased and a new penalty has been created to address misrepresentation of SIPC membership or protection. The measure also increases the SIPC's borrowing limit from $1 billion to $2.5 billion.

Minimum Assessments.—The amended SIPA eliminates the annual minimum assessment of $150 and instead requires that members be assessed based on a percentage of revenues. In particular, SIPA Section 4(d) now requires a SIPC member to pay a minimum assessment equal to 0.02 percent of the gross revenues from the member's securities business. As a result, a SIPC member must pay an assessment of 2 basis points of its gross revenues from the securities business (SIPA Sec. 4(d), as amended by the Dodd-Frank Act). The legislative history states that the increased minimum assessment is necessary to update SIPA to reflect the dual impacts of inflation and securities industry growth since the law's enactment in 1970 (Rep. Kanjorski (D-PA), *Discussion Draft of the Investor Protection Act of 2009 Section-by-Section Analysis* (October 1, 2009)).

SIPA Section 16(9) currently defines "gross revenues from the securities business" as the sum (without duplication) of the following:

- commissions earned in connection with securities transactions effected as agent for customers (subject to certain additions and subtractions);
- charges for executing or clearing securities transactions for other brokers or dealers;
- net realized gain (if any) from principal securities transactions in trading accounts;
- net profit from the management of or participation in underwriting or distributing securities;
- interest earned on customers' securities accounts;
- fees for investment advisory services or account supervision of securities (other than certain activities regarding investment companies and separate accounts of insurance companies);
- fees for the solicitation of proxies in tenders or exchanges of securities;
- income from service charges regarding securities;
- dividends and interest received on securities in investment accounts of the broker or dealer;
- fees in connection with puts, calls and other options transactions in securities;
- commissions earned from transactions in certificates of deposit, Treasury bills and other specified instruments with maturities of nine months (subject to SIPC bylaws regarding loss experience); and
- fees and other income from other categories established by the SIPC.

The term "gross revenues from the securities business" also captures fees and other income from other categories of the securities business set forth in the SIPC's bylaws. This catch-all provision now includes revenues earned by a broker or dealer from transactions in customers' portfolio margining accounts carried as securities accounts under a portfolio margining program approved by the SEC (SIPA Sec. 16(9), as amended by the Dodd-Frank Act). For discussion of "gross revenues from the securities business" regarding portfolio margining, see ¶ 4455.

Penalty for Prohibited Acts.—Penalties may be imposed under SIPA Section 14(c)(1) against any person who, in connection with, or in contemplation of, a liquidation proceeding or direct payment procedure:

- employs any device, scheme or artifice to defraud;
- engages in any act, practice or course of business which operates or would operate as a fraud or deceit on any person; or

- fraudulently or with intent to defeat the SIPA engages in specific prohibited acts.

The penalty for these prohibited acts has been increased from $50,000 to $250,000. A violator also may be imprisoned for up to five years or fined and imprisoned (SIPA Sec. 14(c)(1), as amended by the Dodd-Frank Act).

In addition, the penalty for fraudulent conversion has been increased from $50,000 to $250,000. A person who commits fraudulent conversion may be fined or imprisoned for a maximum of five years, or both (SIPA Sec. 14(c)(2), as amended by the Dodd-Frank Act). The legislative history states that the increased fines for various prohibited acts and fraudulent conversion are necessary because these penalties have not been updated since they were enacted more than 30 years ago (Rep. Kanjorski (D-PA), *Discussion Draft of the Investor Protection Act of 2009 Section-by-Section Analysis* (October 1, 2009)).

The Dodd-Frank Act created a new penalty for misrepresentation of SIPC membership or protection. This provision bars misrepresentation by a person that the person or another person is a member of the SIPC or that the person or an account is protected or is eligible for protection under the SIPA. To be penalized, a person must falsely represent SIPC membership or protection by any means (including, without limitation, through the Internet or any other medium of mass communication), with actual knowledge of the falsity of the representation and with intent to deceive or cause injury to another. Violators are liable for any damages caused by the misrepresentation and may be fined up to $250,000 or imprisoned for up to five years (SIPA Sec. 14(d)(1), as added by the Dodd-Frank Act). The legislative history states that the provision is intended to bring false advertising and misrepresentation of SIPC membership or protection within the range of prohibited acts under the SIPA (Rep. Kanjorski (D-PA), *Discussion Draft, supra*).

In addition, injunctive relief may be obtained in misrepresentation cases. Any court that has jurisdiction of a civil action under the SIPA may issue temporary and final injunctions on any terms the court deems reasonable to prevent the misrepresentation of SIPC membership or protection. An injunction may be served anywhere in the United States, is operative throughout the United States, and may be enforced in any U.S. court that has jurisdiction over the person who is subject to the injunction. The clerk of the court that issues an injunction must promptly transmit certified copies of all papers on file in the case to any requesting court in which the injunction is to be enforced (SIPA Sec. 14(d)(2), as added by the Dodd-Frank Act).

Standard Maximum Cash Advance.—SIPA Section 9(a)(1) now provides that if any part of a customer's net equity claim is for cash, as distinct from securities or options on futures contracts, the amount of the advance cannot exceed the standard maximum cash advance. Section 9(d) now fixes the maximum cash advance at $250,000, subject to periodic adjustment for inflation after December 31, 2010 (SIPA Sec. 9(a)(1), as amended, and Sec. 9(d), as added by the Dodd-Frank Act). Previously, cash advances were limited to $100,000 per customer and there was no inflation adjustment. The legislative history states that the increased cash advance amount and the ability to make adjustments for inflation will ensure SIPA coverage for customers of securities brokerage firms that is consistent with the coverage extended to customers of federally-insured banks (Rep. Kanjorski (D-PA), *Discussion Draft, supra*).

The standard maximum cash advance amount fixed by Section 9(a)(1) must now be adjusted for inflation. Beginning no later than January 1, 2011, and every five years going forward, the SIPC board of directors must determine if an inflation adjustment is required. The SIPC board's determination is subject to Commission approval (SIPA Sec. 9(e)(1), as added by the Dodd-Frank Act). The SIPC must consider the following items in making an inflation adjustment determination to increase the standard maximum cash advance:

- the overall state of the SIPC fund and the economic conditions affecting SIPC members;
- the potential problems affecting SIPC members; and
- any other factors the SIPC board deems appropriate (SIPA Sec. 9(e)(5), as added by the Dodd-Frank Act).

An inflation adjustment becomes effective on January 1 of the year following the calendar year in which the SIPC makes its determination (SIPA Sec. 9(e)(4), as added by the Dodd-Frank Act). In addition, no later than April 5 of any calendar year in which an inflation-adjustment determination must be made, the SEC must publish the amount of the standard maximum cash advance in the *Federal Register*. The SIPC board also must submit a report to Congress stating the amount of the standard maximum cash advance (SIPA Sec. 9(e)(3), as added by the Dodd-Frank Act).

SIPC Borrowing Limits.—Under the Securities Investor Protection Act, the SEC may make loans to the SIPC funded by notes issued to the Treasury by the Commission. To make such a loan, the SEC must determine that the transaction is necessary to protect customers of brokers or dealers and to maintain confidence in the U.S. securities markets. The line of credit had not been increased since the enactment of SIPA in 1970 (SIPA Sec. 4(h), as amended by the Dodd-Frank Act). The amendment increases the Securities Investor Protection Corporation's borrowing limit from $1 billion to $2.5 billion.

In testimony before the Senate Banking Committee in January 2009, SIPC CEO Stephen P. Harbeck stated that SIPC has never used any of the available public funds or borrowed under its commercial line of credit. However, Mr. Harbeck said that the recent failures of such large entities as Lehman Brothers and the Madoff funds could "call into question the sufficiency of SIPC's statutory line of credit" (http://banking.senate.gov/public/_files/HarbeckStatementSenateBanking12709.pdf).

Conforming Amendments.—The Act makes conforming changes to SIPA Section 5 to reflect the Title II orderly liquidation provisions. Title II authorizes the application of orderly liquidation authority, if necessary, to a SIPC-member broker or dealer while generally preserving SIPC's powers and duties under SIPA. The Federal Deposit Insurance Corporation must appoint SIPC, without any need for court approval, to act as trustee for the liquidation proceeding. The statute provides that no SIPC member may enter into a federal or state insolvency, receivership or bankruptcy proceeding without SIPA's consent, except as provided in Title II (SIPA Sec. 5, as amended by the Dodd-Frank Act).

▶ **Effective date.** The provisions take effect one day after the date of enactment (Sec. 4 of the Dodd-Frank Wall Street Reform and Consumer Protection Act).

¶4095

Law source: Law at ¶10,929C, ¶10,929H, ¶10,929V, ¶10,983 and ¶10,004. Committee Report at ¶54,472.

— Sec. 929C of the Dodd-Frank Wall Street Reform and Consumer Protection Act, amending SIPA Sec. 4(h);

— Sec. 929H(a), amending SIPA Sec. 9;

— Sec. 929H(b), amending SIPA Sec. 5(a)(3);

— Sec. 929V, amending SIPA Sec. 14;

— Sec. 983, amending SIPA Sec. 16(9);

— Sec. 4, providing the effective date.

¶4100 Lost, Stolen, Counterfeit and Cancelled Securities

The Dodd-Frank Wall Street Reform and Consumer Protection Act updates provisions governing lost and stolen securities. Exchange Act Section 17(f)(1) now requires reports of "cancelled" securities. As a result, every national securities exchange (and its members), registered securities association, broker, dealer, municipal securities dealer, government securities broker, government securities dealer, registered transfer agent, registered clearing agency (and participants), member of the Federal Reserve System and bank whose deposits are insured by the Federal Deposit Insurance Corporation must report missing, lost, counterfeit, stolen, cancelled or any other category of securities identified in Commission rules. Reports generally must be made to the SEC, but reports about government securities are made to the U.S. Treasury (Exchange Act Sec. 17(f)(1)(A), as amended by the Dodd-Frank Wall Street Reform and Consumer Protection Act). The legislative purpose of these amendments is to expand the scope of securities that must be reported to the Commission (Rep. Kanjorski (D-PA), *Discussion Draft of the Investor Protection Act of 2009 Section-by-Section Analysis* (October 1, 2009)).

The Act similarly adds "cancelled" securities to the list of items that these organizations must inquire about to determine whether securities in their custody or control, for which they are responsible, or in which they are effecting, clearing or settling a transaction, have been reported as missing, lost, counterfeit, stolen, cancelled or reported in any other manner stated in SEC rules (Exchange Act Sec. 17(f)(1)(B), as amended by the Dodd-Frank Act).

▶ **Effective date.** The provision takes effect one day after the date of enactment (Sec. 4 of the Dodd-Frank Wall Street Reform and Consumer Protection Act).

Law source: Law at ¶10,929D and ¶10,004.

— Sec. 929D of the Dodd-Frank Wall Street Reform and Consumer Protection Act, amending Exchange Act Sec. 17(f)(1);

— Sec. 4, providing the effective date.

¶4105 Nationwide Service of Process

Subpoenas may be served nationwide in SEC enforcement actions in federal court. Previously, the SEC could use nationwide service of process only in administrative proceedings. In civil enforcement actions in federal court, the SEC could issue a subpoena only within the federal district where the trial took place or within 100 miles of the courthouse. Witnesses in civil cases brought by the Commission are, however, often located outside of a trial court's subpoena range.

The SEC has sought this authority for several years. For example, former Enforcement Director Stephen M. Cutler testified in 2003 that when witnesses are found in distant locations and do not voluntarily appear, the staff must travel to take their depositions and use those depositions at trial. According to Cutler, depositions are more expensive and less effective than live testimony. Director Cutler stated that nationwide service would provide several advantages, including cost savings, staff time savings and more frequent live-witness testimony before trial courts in Commission cases. Nationwide service of process would be available in enforcement actions under the Securities Act, Exchange Act, Investment Company Act and Advisers Act (Securities Act Sec. 22(a), Exchange Act Sec. 27, Investment Company Act Sec. 44 and Advisers Act Sec. 214, as amended by the Dodd-Frank Wall Street Reform and Consumer Protection Act).

▶ **Effective date.** The provision takes effect one day after the date of enactment (Sec. 4 of the Dodd-Frank Wall Street Reform and Consumer Protection Act).

Law source: Law at ¶10,929E and ¶10,004.

— Sec. 929E(a) of the Dodd-Frank Wall Street Reform and Consumer Protection Act, amending Securities Act Sec. 22(a);

— Sec. 929E(b), amending Exchange Act Sec. 27;

— Sec. 929E(c), amending Investment Company Act Sec. 44;

— Sec. 929E(d), amending Advisers Act Sec. 214;

— Sec. 4, providing the effective date.

¶4110 Formerly Associated Persons

The SEC may bring actions against persons formerly associated with a regulated or supervised entity, such as an investment company or an SRO, for misconduct that occurred during that association. This provision closes a loophole in the securities laws that had allowed those who engaged in misconduct while working for a regulated entity to resign and avoid being held accountable for their wrongdoing (Exchange Act Secs. 15B(c), 15C(c), 19(h) and 21(a), Investment Company Act Sec. 36(a) and Sarbanes-Oxley Act Secs. 2(a)(9), 105(c) and 107(d), as amended by the Dodd-Frank Wall Street Reform and Consumer Protection Act).

Many provisions of the federal securities laws that authorize sanctions against persons who engage in misconduct while associated with a regulated or supervised firm explicitly provide that such authority exists even if these persons are no longer associated with that firm or organization. Several provisions, however, do not explicitly address this issue.

As Rep. Kevin McCarthy (R-CA) noted in a written floor statement in July 2009, "Congress must ensure that the SEC has unambiguous statutory authority to investigate individuals suspected of violating the securities laws, to bring enforcement cases, and have those cases considered on the merits and not be dismissed on an ambiguity because a statute is confusing. No one should be able to violate the securities laws and resign their position knowing that the SEC cannot proceed against them." Rep. McCarthy cited the case of Salvatore F. Sodano, the former CEO of the American Stock Exchange LLC. An administrative law judge dismissed charges against Sodano under Exchange Act Section 19(h)(4) because he was not an officer or director at the time of the action. The administrative law judge concluded that "Section 19(h)(4) of the Exchange Act is unambiguous on its face, referring to the officers and directors of an SRO only in the present" (SEC Initial Decision Release No. 333).

Although the SEC subsequently reversed the dismissal and found that it could censure both current and former SRO officers and directors (see Release No. 34-59141), doubt remained concerning the Commission's authority to act against former officers, directors and associated persons in the absence of specific legislative authority. The Act amends those provisions that do not explicitly address this issue to make it clear that the SEC, or in applicable cases the Public Company Accounting Oversight Board, may sanction or discipline persons who engage in misconduct while associated with a regulated or supervised entity even if they are no longer associated with that firm or organization.

▶ **Effective date.** The provisions take effect one day after the date of enactment (Sec. 4 of the Dodd-Frank Wall Street Reform and Consumer Protection Act).

Law source: Law at ¶10,929F and ¶10,004.

— Secs. 929F(a)–(e) of the Dodd-Frank Wall Street Reform and Consumer Protection Act, amending Exchange Act Secs. 15B(a), 15C(c), 19(h) and 21(a);

— Sec. 929F(f), amending Investment Company Act Sec. 36(a);

— Secs. 929F(g)-(i), amending Sarbanes-Oxley Act Secs. 2(a)(9), 105(c) and 107(d) and Exchange Act Sec. 21(a)(1);

— Sec. 4, providing the effective date.

¶4115 Hiring Authority for Market Specialists

The Dodd-Frank Wall Street Reform and Consumer Protection Act authorizes the SEC to set the rate of pay for experts and consultants it uses in the same manner in which it sets the rate of pay for Commission employees. This provision applies with respect to any position of accountant, economist and securities compliance examiner at the SEC, and any position at the Commission requiring specialized knowledge of financial and capital market formation or regulation, financial market structures or surveillance, or information technology (5 U.S.C. §3114, as amended by the Dodd-Frank Wall Street Reform and Consumer Protection Act).

The provision was authored by Sen. Jack Reed (D-RI). It was partially inspired by recommendations of the Investors Working Group to the effect that the SEC and other financial regulators should acquire deeper knowledge and expertise needed to police the complex and rapidly changing financial markets. The Investors Working Group said that the speed with which financial products and services have proliferated and grown more complex has outpaced the ability of regulators to monitor the financial waterfront. Staffing levels have failed to keep pace with the growing work load, and many agencies lack staff with the necessary expertise to grapple with emerging issues. Staff at the SEC should have a wide range of financial backgrounds. Compensation should be sufficient to attract top-notch talent. In particular, agencies should explore ways of recruiting individuals from the private sector to improve the regulators' ability to understand and keep up with complex financial innovations (*Report on U.S. Financial Regulatory Reform: The Investors' Perspective*, July 2009).

▶ **Effective date.** The provision takes effect one day after the date of enactment (Sec. 4 of the Dodd-Frank Wall Street Reform and Consumer Protection Act).

Law source: Law at ¶10,929G and ¶10,004.

— Sec. 929G of the Dodd-Frank Wall Street Reform and Consumer Protection Act, amending 5 U.S.C. §3114;

— Sec. 4, providing the effective date.

¶4120 Confidential and Privileged Information

The Dodd-Frank Wall Street Reform and Consumer Protection Act amends the Exchange Act, the Investment Company Act and the Advisers Act to protect the confidentiality of information or records obtained by the SEC from persons registered under those statutes. The Commission cannot be compelled to disclose this material (or related records or information) if the SEC obtained the material for use in its surveillance, risk assessments or other regulatory and oversight activities.

The revised provisions permit the SEC to disclose some confidential information, however. With regard to information obtained from persons registered under the Exchange Act, the SEC cannot withhold information from Congress and must comply with federal court orders in cases brought by the United States or by the Commission. The SEC must observe the same exceptions with regard to information obtained from persons registered under the Investment Company or the Advisers Act. In addition, the SEC must comply with requests from other federal departments or agencies for this information. In addition, the amended laws are deemed to be statutes that establish particular criteria for withholding or refer to particular types of matters to be withheld under the Freedom of Information Act, 5 U.S.C. §552 (Exchange Act Sec. 24(g), Investment Company Act Sec. 31(c) and Advisers Act Sec. 210(d), as amended by the Dodd-Frank Wall Street Reform and Consumer Protection Act).

The SEC may share privileged information with domestic and foreign regulators and law enforcement agencies engaged in the investigation and prosecution of violations of applicable securities laws without waiving any privileges the SEC may have with respect to this information. This provision is modeled on language in the Federal Deposit

Insurance Act that enables the federal bank regulatory agencies to share information with other regulators without waiving their privileges with respect to this information (Exchange Act Sec. 24(f), as added by the Dodd-Frank Act).

The SEC cannot be compelled to disclose privileged information obtained from any foreign securities regulator or law enforcement authority if that authority has in good faith determined and represented to the Commission that the information is privileged. In addition, federal agencies, state securities or law enforcement authorities, SROs and the Public Company Accounting Oversight Board (PCAOB) cannot be deemed to have waived any applicable privilege by sharing information with the SEC, with the exception of information provided by the PCAOB or an SRO that the SEC uses in an action against these organizations (Exchange Act Sec. 24(f), as added by the Dodd-Frank Act).

▶ **Effective date.** The provision takes effect one day after the date of enactment (Sec. 4 of the Dodd-Frank Wall Street Reform and Consumer Protection Act).

Law source: Law at ¶10,929I, ¶10,929K and ¶10,004.

— Sec. 929I(a) and Sec. 929K of the Dodd-Frank Wall Street Reform and Consumer Protection Act, amending Exchange Act Sec. 24;

— Sec. 929I(b), amending Investment Company Act Sec. 31;

— Sec. 929I(c), amending Advisers Act Sec. 210;

— Sec. 4, providing the effective date.

¶4125 Transactions Not Conducted on Exchanges

Several of the Exchange Act's antifraud provisions, including the manipulation prohibition in Section 9, the short-sale restrictions in Sections 10(a)(1) and the broker-dealer antifraud restrictions in Section 15(c)(1)(A), previously applied only to transactions in exchange-traded securities. The Dodd-Frank Wall Street Reform and Consumer Protection Act amends those sections to broaden the SEC's authority to apply the antifraud provisions to securities transactions not conducted on exchanges. As stated by the House Financial Services Committee, "in today's trading environment, the same standards should apply to transactions whether they involve securities registered on an exchange or not registered on an exchange" (Exchange Act Secs. 9, 10(a)(1) and 15(c)(1)(A), as amended by the Dodd-Frank Wall Street Reform and Consumer Protection Act).

The amendments exclude government securities in order to avoid any possible impact of SEC rules on that market. The general antifraud provisions for these transactions would continue to apply.

▶ **Effective date.** The provision takes effect one day after the date of enactment (Sec. 4 of the Dodd-Frank Wall Street Reform and Consumer Protection Act).

Law source: Law at ¶10,929L and ¶10,004.

— Sec. 929L of the Dodd-Frank Wall Street Reform and Consumer Protection Act, amending Exchange Act Secs. 9, 10(a)(1) and 15(c)(1)(A);

— Sec. 4, providing the effective date.

¶4130 Aiding-and-Abetting Violations

The Dodd-Frank Wall Street Reform and Consumer Protection Act authorizes the SEC to pursue aiding-and-abetting violations in more cases, and makes penalties available in more cases. It also clarifies that recklessness satisfies the mental state element of aiding-and-abetting liability.

Enforcement Authority.—The Exchange Act allows the SEC to bring claims and seek monetary penalties against persons who knowingly or recklessly aid and abet violations of the statute, and Advisers Act Section 209(d) authorizes the Commission to seek injunctive relief against aiders and abettors. Under prior law, however, the Commission could not bring aiding-and-abetting claims under either the Securities Act or the Investment Company Act, and the Advisers Act limited the available relief to injunctions. As amended, the Securities Act and the Investment Company Act now permit the SEC to bring actions for aiding-and-abetting violations, and the Advisers Act expressly permits the imposition of penalties on aiders and abettors (Securities Act Sec. 15(b), Investment Company Act Sec. 48(b) and Advisers Act Sec. 209(f), as added by the Dodd-Frank Wall Street Reform and Consumer Protection Act).

Mental State.—The Act clarifies that the mental state requirement for aiding-and-abetting liability may be satisfied by recklessness as well as by knowing misconduct. Several courts have held that the "knowingly" aspect of aiding-and-abetting liability meant actual knowledge, rather than recklessness. This interpretation resulted in a standard that is higher for aiding-and-abetting violations than for the primary fraud violation, which would include recklessness (Securities Act Sec. 15(b), Investment Company Act Sec. 48(b) and Advisers Act Sec. 209(f), as added by the Dodd-Frank Act; Exchange Act Sec. 20(e), as amended by the Dodd-Frank Act).

> **CCH Comment:** It should be noted that the expansion of aiding-and-abetting liability applies only to SEC actions. The legislation did not disturb the Supreme Court's 1994 holding in *Central Bank of Denver, N.A. v. First Interstate Bank of Denver, N.A.* (FED. SEC. L. REP. [1993-1994 Transfer Binder] ¶ 98,178) that private plaintiffs cannot recover on aiding-and-abetting claims.

SEC Study.—A separate provision requires an SEC study and report on aiding-and-abetting liability in private actions. For further discussion, see ¶ 4170.

▶ **Effective date.** The provisions take effect one day after the date of enactment (Sec. 4 of the Dodd-Frank Wall Street Reform and Consumer Protection Act).

Law source: Law at ¶ 10,929M, ¶ 10,929N, ¶ 10,929O and ¶ 10,004.

— Sec. 929M(a) of the Dodd-Frank Wall Street Reform and Consumer Protection Act, adding Securities Act Sec. 15(b);

— Sec. 929M(b), adding Investment Company Act Sec. 48(b);

— Sec. 929N, adding Advisers Act Sec. 209(f);

— Sec. 929O, amending Exchange Act Sec. 20(e);

— Sec. 4, providing the effective date.

¶4135 SEC Enforcement Authority

The Dodd-Frank Wall Street Reform and Consumer Protection Act enhances the Commission's enforcement authority in several key areas. The SEC may now impose civil money penalties in cease-and-desist proceedings and bring enforcement actions against controlling persons. The statute also defines the extraterritorial reach of the securities laws in enforcement actions and prosecutions.

Cease-and-Desist Penalties.—The Act allows the SEC to impose civil money penalties in cease-and-desist proceedings. This provision eliminates the need for the Commission to seek a court order imposing civil penalties following the entry of a cease-and-desist order against several categories of market participants. As Enforcement Director Robert Khuzami stated in congressional testimony, this authority will enhance the effectiveness and efficiency of the division's enforcement programs.

This provision amends Securities Act Section 8A, Exchange Act Section 21B(a), Investment Company Act Section 9(d)(1) and Advisers Act Section 203(i)(1). Under prior law, the SEC only had authority under Exchange Act Sec. 21B(a)(1) to impose civil money penalties against securities firms and professionals for various Exchange Act violations, including Sections 15(b), 15B-15E and 17A. This amendment allows the SEC to request a penalty award from an administrative law judge (rather than a federal district court) against virtually all market participants (Securities Act Sec. 8A, Exchange Act Sec. 21B(a), Investment Company Act Sec. 9(d)(1) and Advisers Act Sec. 203(i)(1), as amended by the Dodd-Frank Wall Street Reform and Consumer Protection Act).

Extraterritorial Reach.—The rapid globalization of financial markets in recent years has cast into stark relief issues surrounding the international reach of U.S. securities laws. Since the federal securities laws are silent on their international reach, federal courts have developed tests, including the conduct test, which focuses on the nature of the conduct within the United States as it relates to carrying out the alleged fraudulent scheme.

The SEC and the United States may bring civil and criminal law enforcement proceedings involving transnational securities frauds, which are securities frauds in which not all of the fraudulent conduct occurs within the United States and not all of the wrongdoers are located domestically (Securities Act Sec. 22(c), Exchange Act Sec. 27(b) and Advisers Act Sec. 214(b), as added by the Dodd-Frank Act). Specifically, the legislation would amend the Securities Act and the Exchange Act to provide that U.S. district courts have jurisdiction over violations of the antifraud provisions that involve a transnational fraud if there is conduct within the United States that constitutes significant steps in furtherance of the violation, even if the securities transaction occurs outside the United States and involves only foreign investors.

> **CCH Comment:** The statute provides for the extraterritorial application of the securities laws solely to claims brought by the SEC or the U.S. government. Therefore, the U.S. Supreme Court holding in June 2010 that Exchange Act Section 10(b) did not apply to a "foreign-cubed" action involving foreign conduct, exchanges and purchasers (see *Morrison v. National Australia Bank. Ltd.* (U.S. Sup. Ct. 2010), FED. SEC. L. REP. ¶ 95,776) is now confined to claims by private litigants. However, the Dodd-Frank Act does require the SEC to study the extrater-

ritorial application of the securities laws in private actions. The Commission must consider the scope of such a private right of action, including whether it should extend to all private plaintiffs or be limited to a sub-group, such as to institutional investors. The SEC must also examine the costs and impacts of such a change, and report its findings to the congressional oversight committees within 18 months from enactment (Sec. 929Y of the Dodd-Frank Act).

According to Rep. Paul Kanjorski (D-PA), Dodd-Frank Act Section 929P is intended to rebut the recently announced Supreme Court presumption against extraterritorial application of the federal securities laws (Cong Record, June 30, 2010, p. H5237). In *Morrison v. National Australia Bank* (*supra*), a private securities fraud action, the Court ruled that Exchange Act Section 10(b) applies only to transactions in securities listed on U.S. exchanges and transactions in other securities that occur in the United States. As Justice Scalia wrote for the Court, "there is no affirmative indication in the Exchange Act that § 10(b) applies extraterritorially, and we therefore conclude that it does not."

In floor comments on the day the House passed the Dodd-Frank Act, Rep. Kanjorski, said that the Act's provisions concerning extraterritoriality of the federal securities laws are intended to rebut that presumption by clearly indicating that Congress intends extraterritorial application in cases brought by the SEC or the Justice Department. More specifically, the purpose of the Section 929P, which he authored, is to clarify that in actions and proceedings brought by the SEC or the Justice Department, the specified provisions of the Securities Act, the Exchange Act and the Investment Advisers Act may have extraterritorial application, and that extraterritorial application is appropriate irrespective of whether the securities are traded on a domestic exchange or whether the transactions occurred domestically, when the conduct within the United States is significant or when conduct outside the United States has a foreseeable substantial effect domestically (Cong Rec., June 30, 2010, p. H5237).

Rep. Kanjorski explained that transnational securities frauds are those in which not all of the fraudulent conduct occurs within the United States or not all of the wrongdoers are located domestically. The Dodd-Frank Act creates a single national standard for protecting investors affected by transnational frauds by codifying the authority to bring proceedings under both the "conduct" and the "effects" tests developed by the federal courts regardless of the jurisdiction of the proceedings. Under the effects test, courts inquire whether the wrongful conduct had a substantial effect in the United States or upon U.S. citizens, while the conduct test asks whether the wrongful conduct occurred in the United States (Cong Rec., June 30, 2010, p. H5237).

Control Person Liability.—The statute amends Exchange Act Section 20(a) to clarify that the SEC has standing to sue under this provision, which imposes joint and several liability on control persons in the absence of an affirmative defense (Exchange Act Sec. 20(a), as amended by the Dodd-Frank Act). While private litigants file most control person claims, the Commission has recently increased its use of the control person provision. For example, in August 2009, the SEC filed control person charges against Maurice Greenberg, the former AIG CEO, without charging him with any direct securities law violations. Without admitting or denying liability, Greenberg settled the charges and agreed to pay disgorgement and penalties totaling $15 million.

Few reported cases deal directly with the issue of SEC standing under Section 20(a). Some courts have allowed agency claims for control person liability to proceed, but standing questions remained in this rarely-litigated area. The Dodd-Frank Act removes

¶4135

any doubt concerning the SEC's ability to sue under Section 20(a), and may enhance the Commission's ability to hold senior management responsible for corporate wrongdoing. Under Section 20(a), the SEC need not prove that senior management participated in the fraud and acted with fraudulent intent to prevail.

▶ **Effective date.** The provisions take effect one day after the date of enactment (Sec. 4 of the Dodd-Frank Wall Street Reform and Consumer Protection Act).

Law source: Law at ¶10,929P, ¶10,929Y and ¶10,004.

— Sec. 929P(a) of the Dodd-Frank Wall Street Reform and Consumer Protection Act, adding Securities Act Sec. 8A(g), amending Exchange Act Sec. 21B(a), Investment Company Act Sec. 9(d)(1) and Advisers Act Sec. 203(i)(1);

— Sec. 929P(b), adding Securities Act Sec. 22(c), Exchange Act Sec. 27(b) and Advisers Act Sec. 214(b)

— Sec. 929P(c), amending Exchange Act Sec. 20(a);

— Sec. 929Y, requiring the SEC to study the extraterritorial application of the securities laws in private actions.

— Sec. 4, providing the effective date.

¶4140 Custody and Recordkeeping

Persons with custody or use of a registered investment company's securities, deposits or credits must maintain and preserve all records relating to custody or use for any period prescribed by the Commission (Investment Company Act Sec. 31(a)(1), as amended by the Dodd-Frank Wall Street Reform and Consumer Protection Act). Persons with custody or use of a registered investment company's securities, deposits or credits will also be subject to reasonable examinations and requests for information and documents by the SEC as the Commission deems necessary or appropriate in the public interest or for the protection of investors (Investment Company Act Sec. 31(b)(4)(A) and Advisers Act Sec. 204(d)(1), as added by the Dodd-Frank Act).

In addition, persons subject to regulation and examination by another federal financial institution regulatory agency may satisfy any examination request, information request or document request by providing the Commission with a detailed listing of the registered investment company's securities, deposits or credits within the person's custody or use (Investment Company Act Sec. 31(b)(4)(B) and Advisers Act Sec. 204(d)(2), as added by the Dodd-Frank Act).

▶ **Effective date.** The provision takes effect one day after the date of enactment (Sec. 4 of the Dodd-Frank Wall Street Reform and Consumer Protection Act).

Law source: Law at ¶10,929Q and ¶10,004.

— Sec. 929Q(a) of the Dodd-Frank Wall Street Reform and Consumer Protection Act, amending Investment Company Act Sec. 31(b);

— Sec. 929Q(b), adding Advisers Act Sec. 204(d);

— Sec. 4, providing the effective date.

¶4145 Reporting Obligations

The Dodd-Frank Wall Street Reform and Consumer Protection Act makes changes to stock ownership reporting. It amends Exchange Act Sections 13(d) and 13(g), concerning beneficial ownership reporting by substantial shareholders, and Section 16(a), concerning reporting of short-swing profits by insiders (Exchange Act Secs. 13(d), 13(g) and 16(a), as amended by the Dodd-Frank Wall Street Reform and Consumer Protection Act).

Beneficial Ownership.—Persons who have acquired beneficial ownership of more than a five-percent interest in a class of equity securities registered pursuant to Exchange Act Section 12, exempt from registration under Section 12(g)(2)(G), issued by a closed-end investment company registered under the Investment Company Act or any equity security by a Native Corporation pursuant to Section 37(d)(6) of the Alaska Native Claims Settlement Act, no longer have to send statements concerning the change to the security's issuer or any exchange on which the security is traded. Beneficial owners of more than five percent of such a class must still file a statement with the Commission within 10 days or any shorter period that the SEC may require (Exchange Act Sec. 13(d)(1), as amended by the Dodd-Frank Act).

Short-Swing Profits.—In addition, corporate officers, directors and principal shareholders holding more than 10 percent of any class of equity securities registered under Exchange Act Section 12, and all directors and officers of the issuer of that class of equity securities, no longer have to file statements concerning holdings and ownership changes with national securities exchanges on which the security is registered (Exchange Act Sec. 16(a)(1), as amended by the Dodd-Frank Act). However, these parties must report their holdings and non-exempt transactions to the SEC within 10 days of acquiring a 10-percent interest or becoming a director or officer. The Commission may establish a shorter filing time by regulation (Exchange Act Sec. 16(a)(2)(B), as amended by the Dodd-Frank Act).

▶ **Effective date.** The provision takes effect one day after the date of enactment (Sec. 4 of the Dodd-Frank Wall Street Reform and Consumer Protection Act).

Law source: Law at ¶10,929R and ¶10,004.

— Sec. 929R(a) of the Dodd-Frank Wall Street Reform and Consumer Protection Act, amending Exchange Act Secs. 13(d) and 13(g);

— Sec. 929R(b), amending Exchange Act Sec. 16(a);

— Sec. 4, providing the effective date.

¶4150 Fingerprinting

The Dodd-Frank Wall Street Reform and Consumer Protection Act updates the fingerprinting requirement for market participants. Exchange Act Section 17(f)(2) requires every member of a national securities exchange, broker, dealer, registered transfer agent and registered clearing agency to be fingerprinted. Exchange Act Section 17(f)(2) now applies the fingerprinting requirement to members of registered securities information processors and national securities associations. As a result, the amended law mandates that every member of a national securities exchange, broker, dealer, registered transfer agent, registered clearing agency, registered securities information processor, national securities exchange and national securities association must fingerprint each of its partners, directors, officers and employees (Exchange Act Sec. 17(f)(2), as amended by the Dodd-Frank Wall Street Reform and Consumer Protection Act). The legislative history states that the amendment treats registered securities information processors and national securities associations the same as other entities already subject to the fingerprint requirement. The amendment also will help to ensure that these entities are more aware of employees who may have criminal backgrounds (Rep. Kanjorski (D-PA), *Discussion Draft of the Investor Protection Act of 2009 Section-by-Section Analysis* (October 1, 2009)).

▶ **Effective date.** The provision takes effect one day after the date of enactment (Sec. 4 of the Dodd-Frank Wall Street Reform and Consumer Protection Act).

Law source: Law at ¶10,929S and ¶10,004.

— Sec. 929S, amending Exchange Act Sec. 17(f)(2);

— Sec. 4, providing the effective date.

¶4155 Enforcement Deadlines

The Dodd-Frank Wall Street Reform and Consumer Protection Act creates two different 180-day standards for the SEC. The first standard applies to enforcement investigations and requires the Commission, with limited exceptions for complex cases, to either file an action or to inform the Enforcement Director of its intent not to file a case within 180 days of providing a "Wells Notice" (a notification that the SEC staff intends to recommend enforcement action) to a potential defendant. The second standard covers compliance examinations and inspections. Under this provision, the 180-day period begins upon completion of the on-site visit or the receipt of all requested records, whichever is later. By the end of the 180-day period, the SEC staff must issue a written notification that the examination or inspection has concluded without findings or that the entity must undertake corrective action. To address complex cases, the second provision allows for one additional 180-day extension (Exchange Act Sec. 4E, as added by the Dodd-Frank Wall Street Reform and Consumer Protection Act).

CCH Comment: This section differs significantly from the measure originally introduced by Rep. Paul Kanjorski (D-PA). His Investor Protection Act (H.R. 3817) would have required the completion of enforcement actions, as well as investigations and examinations, within a 180-day period.

▶ **Effective date.** The provision takes effect one day after the date of enactment (Sec. 4 of the Dodd-Frank Wall Street Reform and Consumer Protection Act).

Law source: Law at ¶10,929U and ¶10,004.

— Sec. 929U of the Dodd-Frank Wall Street Reform and Consumer Protection Act, adding Exchange Act Sec. 4E;

— Sec. 4, providing the effective date.

¶4160 Notice to Missing Shareholders

Exchange Act Section 17A established a national system for the clearance and settlement of securities transactions. The Dodd-Frank Wall Street Reform and Consumer Protection Act amends these provisions to direct the SEC to revise Rule 240.17Ad-17 regarding notice to missing security holders. In particular, the new rule must require a paying agent to provide a single written notice to each missing security holder stating that the missing security holder has been sent a check that has not yet been negotiated. Notice may be sent with a check or other mailing that is subsequently sent to the missing security holder, but not later than seven months after sending the not-yet-negotiated check. A paying agent is not subject to the new rule if the value of the not-yet-negotiated check is under $25. The rules must provide that the notice requirement has no effect on state escheatment laws (Exchange Act Sec. 17A(g)(1)(A)–(C), as added by the Dodd-Frank Wall Street Reform and Consumer Protection Act).

New Exchange Act Section 17A(g)(1)(D) also defines key terms. "Missing security holder" means a security holder to whom a check is sent that is not negotiated before the earlier of: (1) the paying agent sending the next regularly scheduled check, or (2) six months after sending the not-yet-negotiated check. "Paying agent" includes any issuer, transfer agent, broker, dealer, investment adviser, indenture trustee, custodian or any other person that accepts payments from the issuer of a security and distributes the payments to holders (Exchange Act Secs. 17A(g)(1)(D)(i) and (ii), as added by the Dodd-Frank Act).

The Commission must adopt the rules, regulations and orders necessary to implement Exchange Act Section 17A(g) within one year of enactment. The SEC must propose these rules in a manner that minimizes disruptions to paying agents' current systems for processing payments to account holders. The Commission's proposed rules also must seek to avoid a situation where multiple paying agents send written notice to a missing security holder for the same not-yet-negotiated check (Exchange Act Sec. 17A(g)(2), as added by the Dodd-Frank Act).

▶ **Effective date.** The provision takes effect one day after the date of enactment (Sec. 4 of the Dodd-Frank Wall Street Reform and Consumer Protection Act).

Law source: Law at ¶10,929W and ¶10,004.

— Sec. 929W of the Dodd-Frank Wall Street Reform and Consumer Protection Act, adding Exchange Act 17A(g);
— Sec. 4, providing the effective date.

¶4165 Short-Sale Disclosures

The practice of selling short is controversial because of the potential for abuse. In 1938, the SEC adopted Rule 10a-1 and instituted a sale price test or "tick" test to curb short sales. The Commission removed Rule 10a-1 in July 2007. As the financial crisis unfolded, there were reports of significant short sales of securities issued by financial services companies. The SEC has now reinstituted limited short-sale curbs (see Release

No. 34-61595 (reciting history of Rule 10a-1)). In response to these events, the Dodd-Frank Wall Street Reform and Consumer Protection Act requires short-sellers of equity securities to file periodic reports, bans manipulative short sales and requires brokers and dealers to notify investors of their short-sale practices regarding loaned securities.

Short-Sale Reports.—Exchange Act Section 13(f)(2) now requires public disclosure, at least monthly, of information regarding the short sales of institutional investment managers. The Commission must adopt rules to provide for public disclosure of the name of the issuer and the title, class, CUSIP number, aggregate amount of the number of short sales of each security and any additional information the SEC requires, following the end of the reporting period. The final bill did not include a House provision requiring institutional investment managers to file daily reports with the SEC of all short sales effected (Exchange Act Sec. 13(f)(2), as added by the Dodd-Frank Wall Street Reform and Consumer Protection Act).

Enforcement.—The Dodd-Frank Act updates Exchange Act Section 9 to ban manipulative short sales. Exchange Act Section 9(d) now makes it unlawful for any person to use the mails, any means or instrumentality of interstate commerce or any facility of any national securities exchange, or for any member of a national securities exchange, to effect, alone or with others, a manipulative short sale of any security. The SEC must adopt rules to ensure that appropriate enforcement options and remedies exist to deal with violations (Exchange Act Sec. 9(d), as added by the Dodd-Frank Act).

Investor Notice.—Exchange Act Section 15 governs the registration of brokers and dealers. Exchange Act Section 15(e) now requires that every registered broker or dealer notify its customers that they may elect not to allow their fully paid securities to be used in connection with short sales. If a broker or dealer does use a customer's securities in connection with short sales, the broker or dealer must notify the customer that the broker or dealer may be compensated for lending the customer's securities. The Commission may adopt rules for the form, content, time and delivery of notice (Exchange Act Sec. 15(e), as added by the Dodd-Frank Act).

▶ **Effective date.** The provision takes effect one day after the date of enactment (Sec. 4 of the Dodd-Frank Wall Street Reform and Consumer Protection Act).

Law source: Law at ¶10,929X and ¶10,004.

— Sec. 929X(a) of the Dodd-Frank Wall Street Reform and Consumer Protection Act, amending Exchange Act Sec. 13(f);

— Sec. 929X(b), amending Exchange Act Sec. 9(d);

— Sec. 929X(c), amending Exchange Act Sec. 15(e);

— Sec. 4, providing the effective date.

¶4170 Aiding-and-Abetting Study

The Dodd-Frank Wall Street Reform and Consumer Protection Act mandates a study and report on aiding-and-abetting liability in private actions. The Comptroller General of the United States must conduct a study on the impact of authorizing a private right of action against any person who aids or abets another person in violation of the securities laws (Sec. 929Z(a) of the Dodd-Frank Wall Street Reform and Consumer Protection Act).

> **CCH Comment:** As noted elsewhere (see ¶ 4130), the expansion of aiding-and-abetting liability contained in the Act applies only to SEC actions and does not disturb the Supreme Court's 1994 holding in *Central Bank of Denver, N.A. v. First Interstate Bank of Denver, N.A.* (FED. SEC. L. REP. [1993-1994 Transfer Binder] ¶ 98,178) that private plaintiffs cannot recover on aiding-and-abetting claims.

The study must examine (1) the role of secondary actors in the process of issuing securities, (2) the interpretation by the courts of the scope of liability for secondary actors after the Supreme Court's 2008 decision in *Stoneridge Investment Partners, LLC v. Scientific-Atlanta, Inc.*, FED. SEC. L. REP. [2007-2008 Transfer Binder] ¶ 94,556; and (3) the types of lawsuits decided under the Private Securities Litigation Act of 1995 (Sec. 929Z(a) of the Dodd-Frank Act). Within a year from the date of enactment, the Comptroller General must report to Congress on the findings of the study (Sec. 929Z(b) of the Dodd-Frank Act).

▶ **Effective date.** The provision takes effect one day after the date of enactment (Sec. 4 of the Dodd-Frank Wall Street Reform and Consumer Protection Act).

Law source: Law at ¶ 10,929Z and ¶ 10,004.

— Sec. 929Z(a) of the Dodd-Frank Wall Street Reform and Consumer Protection Act, requiring a Comptroller General study of aiding-and-abetting liability in private actions;

— Sec. 929Z(b), requiring a report to Congress;

— Sec. 4, providing the effective date.

CREDIT RATING AGENCIES

¶4180 Introduction

Credit rating agencies, *i.e.*, nationally recognized statistical ratings organizations (NRSROs), have assumed a central role in the global capital markets. They have faced growing criticism over the past years that reached a crescendo in the recent financial crisis. In response, Congress added Title IX, Subtitle C, to the Dodd-Frank Wall Street Reform and Consumer Protection Act. This subtitle, consisting of Sections 931 through 939H, greatly strengthens the SEC's oversight of credit rating agencies and provides for heightened transparency of rating methodologies in structured and non-structured financial products.

Particular reforms include conflict-of-interest requirements designed to strengthen the independence of rating organization boards, improve disclosure of potential conflicts, and impose duties on compliance officers to help avoid, report and resolve any conflicts (see ¶ 4185). The legislation also requires the SEC to study the feasibility of assigning a rating agency to issue ratings on structured products and, if no better method is found, to implement a mechanism contained in the Senate bill for assigning rating agencies (see ¶ 4190).

Background.—A credit rating is a rating agency's assessment of an issuer's ability and willingness to make timely payments on a financial instrument over the life of that instrument. Investors use ratings to help price the credit risk of securities. To determine an appropriate rating, credit analysts use publicly available information and market and economic data, and often engage in discussions with the issuer's senior management. Rating agencies earn their revenues pursuant to one of two business models: (1) by receiving a fee from an issuer to give a rating to that issuer, which is the predominant model; or (2) by charging investors to subscribe for access to the ratings of issuers who do not pay the rating agency.

Credit rating agencies played a large role in the financial crisis by giving high ratings to subprime asset-backed securities and not downgrading those ratings fast enough when it became apparent that the securities were toxic. The rating agencies failed to sufficiently consider the risks inherent in these complex financial instruments. As a consequence, they underestimated the risk posed by the instruments. Once the rating agencies gave the highest possible ratings to many of those innovative instruments, investors felt confident in purchasing them without properly assessing the risks involved. As market conditions worsened, the rating agencies failed to reflect those conditions promptly in their ratings. Their failure to produce accurate ratings exacerbated the imprudent approach taken by investors, who relied blindly on credit ratings, which in turn failed to accurately describe the risks of rated products. In each case, lack of transparency prevented market participants from understanding the full nature of the risks they were taking (*Financial Regulatory Reform, A New Foundation: Rebuilding Financial Supervision and Regulation,* Treasury Department (June 17, 2009), at FED. BANK. L. REP. ¶ 75-201).

It seems unlikely that a liquid mortgage-backed securities market would have existed without market-accepted credit agency ratings. In many cases, investors had limited information about the actual loans included in mortgage-backed securities pools, and even if they had received detailed information, analyzing the underlying pool risk characteristics would have been costly for individual investors.

Once a rating was accepted, and as long as the securities performed well, few investors found cause to question the rating's accuracy or the rating agencies' opaque, proprietary risk-assessment methodologies. With high ratings, mortgage-backed securities and collateralized debt obligations were readily purchased by institutional investors because they paid higher yields compared to similarly-rated securities. Only when housing prices stopped appreciating did important flaws in ratings methodologies become apparent.

After nearly a century of self-regulation, the rating agencies came under SEC oversight with enactment of the Credit Rating Agency Reform Act of 2006. The 2006 Act authorized the SEC to oversee credit rating agencies registered with the Commission as NRSROs. Previously, credit rating agencies operated under a voluntary system of registration with the SEC. The legislation changed that by mandating registration with the SEC.

However, long before the 2006 Act, in the mid-1970s, the SEC began to make explicit reference to credit ratings in its rules and regulations, using credit ratings by market-recognized rating agencies to delineate grades of creditworthiness for various purposes under the federal securities laws. The Commission originally adopted the term NRSRO in 1975 solely for determining capital charges on different grades of debt securities under the net capital rule for broker-dealers.

Over time, however, the NRSRO concept was incorporated into a number of additional SEC rules and regulations, including rules issued under the Securities Act, the Exchange Act and the Investment Company Act. Congress also began to use the NRSRO concept in legislation, as have other regulatory bodies, including banking regulators both at home and abroad.

Thus, the Commission has referred to credit ratings for over three decades. Although it is quite understandable why they were first incorporated into the net capital rule and in subsequent rules, it has become evident over time that there are considerable unintended consequences to the regulatory use of credit ratings. For example, it was never intended to establish and preserve a valuable franchise for the large rating agencies, while simultaneously inoculating them from market competition. Nor was it intended to serve as a substitute for adequate due diligence by investors, managers, directors and others. Unfortunately, as recent events have demonstrated, regulatory reliance on credit ratings has led to these results (see *Summary Report of Issues Identified in the Commission Staff's Examinations of Select Credit Rating Agencies* (July 8, 2008), FED. SEC. L. REP. ¶ 88,244).

In its 2008 study, the SEC found that credit rating agencies did not properly manage conflicts of interest in rating asset-backed securities during the subprime era. The Commission also found that the rating agencies neither fully disclosed nor properly documented their procedures for rating mortgage-backed securities and collateralized debt obligations. The SEC uncovered serious shortcomings at the firms, including a lack of public disclosure and of policies to manage the rating process, as well as insufficient attention to conflicts of interest (see *Summary Report of Issues Identified in the Commission Staff's Examinations of Select Credit Rating Agencies, supra*).

The SEC study evolved from an extensive 10-month examination of three major credit rating agencies. Broadly, the study found that as the securitization process exploded with a substantial increase in the number and complexity of mortgage-backed securities and collateralized debt obligations, the rating agencies could not keep pace with the growth.

Congressional Findings.—Congress made several findings in support of the new legislation. First, because credit ratings are systemically important and are relied on by investors, financial institutions and regulators, the activities and performances of credit rating agencies, including NRSROs, are matters of national public interest, as credit rating agencies are central to capital formation, investor confidence and the efficient performance of the U.S. economy (Sec. 931(1) of the Dodd-Frank Wall Street Reform and Consumer Protection Act).

Second, credit rating agencies play a critical "gatekeeper" role in the debt market that is functionally similar to that of securities analysts, who evaluate the quality of securities in the equity market, and auditors, who review the financial statements of companies. This role justifies a similar level of public oversight and accountability (Sec. 931(2) of the Dodd-Frank Act).

Third, because credit rating agencies perform evaluative and analytical services on behalf of clients, much as other financial "gatekeepers" do, the activities of credit rating agencies are fundamentally commercial in character and should be subject to the same standards of liability and oversight as apply to auditors, securities analysts and investment bankers (Sec. 931(3) of the Dodd-Frank Act).

Fourth, in certain activities, particularly in advising arrangers of structured financial products on potential ratings of those products, credit rating agencies face conflicts of interest that require careful monitoring. Legislation should explicitly address these conflicts to give the SEC clearer authority (Sec. 931(4) of the Dodd-Frank Act).

Finally, in the recent financial crisis, the ratings on structured financial products have proven to be inaccurate. This inaccuracy contributed significantly to the mismanagement of risks by financial institutions and investors, which in turn harmed the national and global economy. Improved accountability on the part of credit rating agencies is, therefore, necessary (Sec. 931(5) of the Dodd-Frank Act).

SEC Rulemaking.—Unless otherwise specifically provided, the SEC must issue final regulations, as required by Subtitle C and the resulting amendments, not later than one year after the date of enactment (Sec. 937 of the Dodd-Frank Act).

Congress expressed the view that the SEC should exercise its rulemaking authority under Exchange Act Section 15E(h)(2)(B) to prevent improper conflicts of interest arising from employees of NRSROs providing services to issuers of securities that are unrelated to the issuance of credit ratings, including consulting, advisory and other services (Sec. 939H of the Dodd-Frank Act).

▶ **Effective date.** The provision takes effect one day after the date of enactment (Sec. 4 of the Dodd-Frank Wall Street Reform and Consumer Protection Act).

Law source: Law at ¶10,931, ¶10,937, ¶10,939H and ¶10,004. Committee Report at ¶50,091, ¶54,480 and ¶54,486.

— Sec. 931 of the Dodd-Frank Wall Street Reform and Consumer Protection Act, listing congressional findings;

— Sec. 937, providing the general rulemaking deadline;

— Sec. 939H, stating the sense of Congress regarding SEC rulemaking authority to prevent conflicts of interest;

— Sec. 4, providing the effective date.

¶4185 Enhanced Regulation and Transparency

The Dodd-Frank Wall Street Reform and Consumer Protection Act provides for heightened SEC regulation of nationally recognized statistical ratings organizations, greater accountability on the part of rating agencies that fail to produce accurate ratings, and more disclosure to help investors better understand credit ratings and their limitations. The measure also enhances the corporate governance at rating agencies (Exchange Act Sec. 15E, as amended by the Dodd-Frank Wall Street Reform and Consumer Protection Act).

Internal Controls.—Rating agencies must establish, enforce and document an effective internal control structure governing the implementation of and adherence to policies, procedures and methodologies for determining credit ratings, taking into consideration any factors the SEC may prescribe by rule (Exchange Act Sec. 15E(c)(3)(A), as added by the Dodd-Frank Act). The rating agency must submit an annual internal controls report to the SEC containing: (1) a description of management's role in establishing an effective internal control structure; (2) an assessment of the effectiveness of its internal controls; and (3) the CEO's attestation (Exchange Act Sec. 15E(c)(3)(B), as added by the Dodd-Frank Act).

Associated Persons.—The SEC now has greater authority with regard to any person who is associated with, or is seeking to become associated with—or, at the time of an alleged misconduct, was associated with—a credit rating agency. The Commission, by order, must censure, place limitations on the activities or functions of that person, suspend for a period of up to one year, or bar the person from being associated with an NRSRO (Exchange Act Sec. 15E(d), as amended by the Dodd-Frank Act).

Registration Suspension or Revocation.—The legislation authorizes the SEC to temporarily suspend or permanently revoke the registration of an NRSRO with respect to a particular class or subclass of securities, if the SEC finds, on the record after notice and opportunity for hearing, that the rating agency does not have adequate financial and managerial resources to consistently produce credit ratings with integrity (Exchange Act Sec. 15E(d)(2)(A), as added by the Dodd-Frank Act). In determining whether an NRSRO lacks resources, the SEC must consider an agency's failure to consistently produce accurate ratings over a sustained period of time (Exchange Act Sec. 15E(d)(2)(B), as added by the Dodd-Frank Act).

Sales and Marketing.—The legislation includes a measure designed to separate the ratings process from sales and marketing considerations. Congress intended the provision to counter the inherent conflict of interest in the "issuer pays" model of the credit rating industry, under which issuers have an incentive to use the rating agency that provides the highest rating and the rater wants to provide the highest rating to keep the issuer's business (S. Rep. No. 111-176, p. 116). Under the provision, the SEC must adopt rules preventing sales and marketing considerations from influencing the production of ratings (Exchange Act Sec. 15E(h)(3)(A), as added by the Dodd-Frank Act). Violation of these rules will lead to suspension or revocation of NRSRO status if the violation affects a rating. The rules must contain an exception for small rating agencies upon an SEC determination that the separation of ratings and sales and marketing is not appropriate (Exchange Act Sec. 15E(h)(3)(B), as added by the Dodd-Frank Act).

Look-Back Requirement.—Each NRSRO must establish, maintain and enforce policies and procedures reasonably designed to ensure that, if an employee of a person subject to a credit rating of the NRSRO or the issuer, underwriter or sponsor of a security or money market instrument subject to a credit rating of the NRSRO was employed by the NRSRO and participated in determining credit ratings for the person or the securities or money market instruments during the one-year period preceding the date an action was taken with respect to the credit rating, the NRSRO must:

- conduct a review to determine whether any conflicts of interest of the employee influenced the rating; and

¶4185

- take action to revise the rating if appropriate, in accordance with any rules that the SEC may prescribe (Exchange Act Sec. 15E(h)(4)(A), as added by the Dodd-Frank Act).

The SEC must conduct periodic reviews of the policies described above and their implementation at each NRSRO to ensure they are reasonably designed and implemented to eliminate conflicts of interest (Exchange Act Sec. 15E(h)(4)(B), as added by the Dodd-Frank Act) The Commission must review each NRSRO's code of ethics and conflict-of-interest policy: (1) at least annually; and (2) whenever those policies are materially modified (Exchange Act Sec. 15E(h)(4)(B), as added by the Dodd-Frank Act).

Employment Transitions Report.—Each NRSRO must, under certain conditions, report to the SEC any case of which the organization knows or can reasonably be expected to know where a person associated with the organization within the previous five years becomes employed by any obligor, issuer, underwriter or sponsor of a security or money market instrument for which the NRSRO issued a credit rating during the 12-month period prior to that employment. The reporting duty applies if the employee in question:

(1) was a senior officer of the organization;

(2) participated in any capacity in determining credit ratings for the obligor, issuer, underwriter or sponsor; or

(3) supervised an employee described in (2) above (Exchange Act Sec. 15E(h)(5), as added by the Dodd-Frank Act)

Compliance Officers.—The position of "NRSRO compliance officer" was created by the Credit Rating Agency Reform Act of 2006. The legislation enhances this role by prohibiting compliance officers from: (1) performing credit ratings; (2) participating in the development of ratings methodologies; (3) performing marketing or sales functions; or (4) setting compensation for NRSRO employees, other than those working for the compliance officer (Exchange Act Sec. 15E(j)(2)(A), as added by the Dodd-Frank Act). The SEC may exempt small NRSROs on a finding that compliance would impose an unreasonable burden (Exchange Act Sec. 15E(j)(2)(B), as added by the Dodd-Frank Act).

NRSRO compliance officers must establish procedures for the receipt, retention and treatment of complaints about the rating agency or its ratings, including confidential, anonymous complaints by employees and end users (Exchange Act Sec. 15E(j)(3), as added by the Dodd-Frank Act). They must also submit to their rating agencies an annual report on the agency's compliance with the securities laws and the agency's related policies and procedures. The report must also describe any material changes to the agency's code of ethics and conflicts of interest policies, and include a certification that the report is accurate and complete. The NRSRO must submit this report to the SEC along with its required financial report (Exchange Act Sec. 15E(j)(5), as added by the Dodd-Frank Act).

The compensation of each compliance officer cannot be linked to the NRSRO's financial performance and must be arranged so as to ensure the independence of the officer's judgment (Exchange Act Sec. 15E(j)(4), as added by the Dodd-Frank Act).

Office of Credit Ratings.—In recognition of the unique nature of rating agency oversight, the legislation creates the independent Office of Credit Ratings within the SEC to protect investors, to promote accuracy in credit ratings, and to prevent conflicts of interest from unduly influencing credit ratings (Exchange Act Sec. 15E(p)(1)(A), as added by the Dodd-Frank Act). The Office will be adequately staffed to fulfill its statutory role and will include persons with knowledge of and expertise in corporate, municipal and structured debt (Exchange Act Sec. 15E(p)(2), as added by the Dodd-Frank Act).

The Office of Credit Ratings must conduct annual examinations of each NRSRO (Exchange Act Sec. 15E(p)(3)(A), as added by the Dodd-Frank Act). Each examination must include a review of the NRSRO's: (1) adherence to its own policies, procedures and rating methodologies; (2) management of conflicts of interest; (3) implementation of ethics policies; (4) internal supervisory controls; (5) governance; (6) compliance officer activities; (7) processing of complaints; and (8) policies governing the post-employment activities of former staff (Exchange Act Sec. 15E(p)(3)(B), as added by the Dodd-Frank Act).

The SEC will make public, in an easily understandable format, an annual report summarizing the essential findings of all NRSRO examinations conducted that year. The report must include the responses of NRSROs to material regulatory deficiencies identified by the SEC and to recommendations made by the SEC (Exchange Act Sec. 15E(p)(3)(C), as added by the Dodd-Frank Act).

Transparency of Rating Performance.—The legislation mandates substantial disclosures designed to give investors and other market participants more information about the credit risk of a debt issue and the reliability of a rating. Thus, the SEC must require rating agencies to publicly disclose information on their initial credit ratings for each type of obligor, security and money market instrument and any subsequent changes to those credit ratings. The purpose of this disclosure is to allow users of credit ratings to compare the performance and accuracy of ratings issued by different rating agencies (Exchange Act Sec. 15E(q)(1), as added by the Dodd-Frank Act). The disclosures must:

- be comparable among NRSROs so that end users can compare rating performance across NRSROs;
- be clear and informative for investors who use or might use credit ratings;
- include performance information over a range of years and for a variety of types of credit ratings, including for credit ratings withdrawn by the rating agency;
- be published and made freely available by the rating organization on an easily accessible portion of its website, and in writing, when requested;
- be appropriate to the business model of an NRSRO; and
- include an attestation with any credit rating issued by the NRSRO affirming that: (1) no part of the rating was influenced by any other business activities; (2) the rating was based solely on the merits of the instruments being rated; and (3) the rating was an independent evaluation of the instrument's risks and merits (Exchange Act Sec. 15E(q)(2), as added by the Dodd-Frank Act).

This provision seeks to address the lack of market competition in the credit rating industry by allowing investors to compare NRSRO performance. Industry analysts often identify the lack of competition as one reason why the industry performed poorly in rating securities, such as mortgage-backed securities, and thus contributed to the recent economic crisis (S. Rep. No. 111-176, p. 118).

The legislation accommodates subscriber-pay NRSROs by mandating that the disclosure be appropriate to the business model of an NRSRO. For these NRSROs, the publication of rating performance would likely be unsustainable because they rely on credit rating users to pay them for ratings (S. Rep. No. 111-176, p. 119).

Rating Methodologies.—The SEC must adopt rules requiring rating agencies to ensure that credit ratings are determined using procedures and methodologies approved by the board of directors (Exchange Act Sec. 15E(r)(1)(A), as added by the Dodd-Frank Act). The SEC rules must also require that material changes to ratings procedures and methodologies be applied consistently and disclosed publicly. The changes must be applied to all credit ratings to which they apply within a reasonable time period, to be determined by the SEC (Exchange Act Sec. 15E(r)(2), as added by the Dodd-Frank Act). Each NRSRO must notify users of credit ratings when a material change is made to a procedure or methodology, and when a significant error is identified in a procedure or methodology that may result in credit rating actions (Exchange Act Sec. 15E(r)(3), as added by the Dodd-Frank Act).

Qualitative and Quantitative Information.—NRSROs must publish a form with each rating that discloses qualitative and quantitative information that is intended to enable investors and users of credit ratings to better understand the main principles and assumptions that underlie the rating (Exchange Act Sec. 15E(s)(1), as added by the Dodd-Frank Act). The form must be easy to use, directly comparable across different classes of securities, and readily available in either paper or electronic form, as the SEC determines (Exchange Act Sec. 15E(s)(2), as added by the Dodd-Frank Act).

Qualitative Content. The qualitative content of the form must include:

- the credit ratings produced;
- the main assumptions and principles used in constructing procedures and methodologies, including qualitative methodologies and quantitative inputs and assumptions about the correlation of defaults across obligors used in rating structured products;
- the potential limitations of the credit ratings and the types of risks excluded from them that the NRSRO does not comment on;
- information on the uncertainty of the credit rating, including: (1) information on the reliability, accuracy and quality of the data relied on in determining the credit rating; and (2) a statement on the reliability and limitations of the data relied on and any other data accessibility limitations;
- whether and to what extent third-party due diligence services have been used by the NRSRO, including a description of the information that the third party reviewed in conducting due diligence services and a description of the findings or conclusions of that third party;
- a description of the data about any obligor, issuer, security or money market instrument that were relied on for purposes of determining the credit rating;

¶4185

- an overall assessment of the quality of information available and considered in producing a rating in relation to the quality of information available to the NRSRO in rating similar issuances;
- information on conflicts of interest of the rating agency; and
- any additional information the SEC may require (Exchange Act Sec. 15E(s)(3)(A), as added by the Dodd-Frank Act).

Quantitative Content. The quantitative content of the form must include an explanation or measure of the credit rating's potential volatility, including any factors that might lead to a change in the ratings and the magnitude of the change that a user can expect under different market conditions. There must also be disclosure of information on the content of the rating, including historical performance and the probability of default and the expected loss in the event of default. Also required is information on the rating's sensitivity to assumptions made by the rating agency, including five assumptions made in the ratings process that, without accounting for any other factor, would have the greatest impact on a rating if the assumptions were proven false or inaccurate, and an analysis, using specific examples, of how each of the five assumptions affects a rating (Exchange Act Sec. 15E(s)(3)(B), as added by the Dodd-Frank Act).

Third-Party Due Diligence.—Another disclosure that the NRSROs will have to make regards third-party due diligence services. The findings and conclusions of any third-party due diligence report obtained by the issuer or underwriter of an asset-backed security must be made public, in a format to be determined by the SEC (Exchange Act Sec. 15E(s)(4)(A), as added by the Dodd-Frank Act). The person providing the due diligence services must give a written certification to the rating agency and the agency must disclose the certification at the time it produces a rating in a manner that allows the public to determine the adequacy and level of due diligence services provided by the third party (Exchange Act Sec. 15E(s)(4)(B), as added by the Dodd-Frank Act). The SEC must establish the format and content for the certification to ensure that the due diligence providers have conducted a thorough review of data and documentation necessary for the agency to produce an accurate rating (Exchange Act Sec. 15E(s)(4)(C), as added by the Dodd-Frank Act).

Corporate Governance.—At least one-half of an NRSRO's board—but no fewer that two members—must be independent directors (Exchange Act Sec. 15E(t)(2)(A), as added by the Dodd-Frank Act). Directors are deemed independent if they: do not accept consulting, advisory or other fees from the rating agency; are not associated with the agency; and do not participate in any deliberation involving a rating in which the independent director has a financial interest (Exchange Act Sec. 15E(t)(2)(B), as added by the Dodd-Frank Act).

The compensation of independent board members cannot be linked to the business performance of the rating agency and must be arranged to ensure the independence of their judgment. The term of office of the independent directors must be for a pre-agreed fixed period, not to exceed five years, and cannot be renewable (Exchange Act Sec. 15E(t)(2)(C), as added by the Dodd-Frank Act).

An NRSRO board has several enumerated duties. These include: responsibility for establishing, maintaining and enforcing policies and procedures for determining credit ratings; managing conflicts of interests; ensuring the effectiveness of internal control systems; and overseeing compensation practices (Exchange Act Sec. 15E(t)(3), as added by the Dodd-Frank Act).

The SEC may grant an exemption from the independence rules for small NRSROs where compliance would present an unreasonable burden, provided that the board delegates its responsibilities to a committee including at least one user of NRSRO ratings (Exchange Act Sec. 15E(t)(5), as added by the Dodd-Frank Act).

▶ **Effective date.** The provision takes effect one day after the date of enactment (Sec. 4 of the Dodd-Frank Wall Street Reform and Consumer Protection Act).

Law source: Law at ¶10,932 and ¶10,004. Committee Report at ¶54,481.

— Sec. 932 of the Dodd-Frank Wall Street Reform and Consumer Protection Act, amending Exchange Act Secs. 15E(c)(2) and (d), repealing Sec. 15E(p) and adding Secs. 15E(c)(3), (d)(2), (h)(3), (j)(1)–(j)(4) and (p)–(t);

— Sec. 4, providing the effective date.

¶4190 Assigned Credit Ratings

The legislation that passed the Senate on May 20, 2010 contained a provision, Section 939D, authored by Sen. Al Franken (D-MN) that would have created a self-regulatory organization charged with assigning credit rating agencies, on a rotating basis, to provide initial ratings for asset-backed securities and structured financial products. There was no comparable provision in the legislation the House passed on December 11, 2009. The House-Senate conference committee that produced the Dodd-Frank Wall Street Reform and Consumer Protection Act reached a compromise that directs the SEC to conduct a study on the feasibility of assigning a rating agency to issue ratings on structured products and, if no better method is found, to implement Exchange Act Section 15E(w) as authored by Sen. Franken (Sec. 939F of the Dodd-Frank Wall Street Reform and Consumer Protection Act).

Study.—The SEC must conduct a study examining:

- the credit rating process for "structured finance products" (as defined) and the conflicts of interest associated with the issuer-pay and the subscriber-pay models;
- the feasibility of establishing a system in which a public or private utility or a self-regulatory organization assigns nationally recognized statistical rating organizations (NRSROs) to determine the credit ratings of structured finance products, including—
    - an assessment of potential mechanisms for determining fees for the NRSROs;
    - appropriate methods for paying fees to the NRSROs;
    - the extent to which the creation of such a system would be viewed as the creation of "moral hazard" by the federal government; and
    - any constitutional or other issues concerning the establishment of such a system;
- the range of metrics that could be used to determine the accuracy of credit ratings; and

- alternative means for compensating NRSROs that would create incentives for accurate credit ratings (Sec. 939F(b) of the Dodd-Frank Act).

The term "structured finance product" means an asset-backed security, as defined in Exchange Act Section 3(a)(77), as added by Dodd-Frank Act Section 941 (see ¶ 4255), and any structured product based on an asset-backed security, as determined by SEC rule (Sec. 939F(a) of the Dodd-Frank Act).

Report and Recommendation.—Within two years of enactment, the SEC must report to the Senate Banking Committee and the House Financial Services Committee on the study's findings. The report must include any recommendations for regulatory or statutory changes that the SEC deems appropriate to implement those findings (Sec. 939F(c) of the Dodd-Frank Act).

Rulemaking.—After submitting the report, the SEC must establish a system for assigning NRSROs to determine the initial credit ratings of structured finance products in a manner that prevents the product's issuer, sponsor or underwriter from selecting the rating agency that will determine the initial credit ratings and monitor those ratings. In issuing rules, the Commission must give "thorough consideration" to the Franken-authored Exchange Act Section 15E(w) and must implement the system described in that provision unless the SEC decides that an alternative system would better serve the public interest and protect investors (Sec. 939F(d) of the Dodd-Frank Act).

> **CCH Comment:** As noted above, the SEC must give thorough consideration to implementing the Senate bill provision authored by Sen. Al Franken. Under that provision, a oversight body would assign credit rating agencies to provide initial ratings for asset-backed securities and structured financial products on a rotating basis. The SEC would create the Credit Rating Agency Board, a self-regulatory organization tasked with developing a system under which the Board randomly assigns a credit rating agency to provide a product's initial rating (Exchange Act Sec. 15E(w)(2)(A), as proposed by HR 4173 and passed on May 20, 2010).
>
> **Background and Purpose.**—Requiring an initial credit rating by an agency not of the issuer's choosing, but randomly selected by the Board, will put a check on the accuracy of ratings and end forum shopping, in the senator's view. The provision does not prohibit an issuer from then seeking a second or third or fourth rating from an agency of its choosing. The provision leaves flexibility to the Board to determine the assignment process. Thus, the new Board may design the assignment process as it sees fit, which can be at random or based on a formula, as long as the issuer cannot choose its initial rating agency. This should eliminate the current incentive for a rating agency to give an inflated rating in the hope of getting repeat business (Cong. Rec., May 10, 2010, S3465).
>
> Senator Franken has emphasized that the Credit Rating Agency Board will be a self-regulatory organization (SRO) that will eliminate the current rating shopping process and the conflict of interest inherent in that process. Since the Board can take past performance into account in handing out rating assignments to agencies, the new process will incentivize accuracy in the market (Cong. Rec., May 19, 2010, p. S3955).
>
> Another key element of the new SRO regime is that the Board will regularly evaluate the performance of credit rating agencies must take that performance into account in developing an assignment mechanism. In Sen. Franken's view, there is

¶4190

no better way to obtain accurate ratings than giving more initial rating jobs to the most accurate raters and fewer jobs to those that repeatedly do shoddy work. The Board will also be able to prevent raters from charging unreasonable fees, which discourages deals in which a rater asks for more money for a better rating (Cong Record, May 5, 2010, p. S3155).

Senator Franken noted that the provision establishing the Board does not conflict with the section of the Dodd-Frank Act eliminating provisions in federal laws requiring reliance on ratings from NRSROs. The latter section does not eliminate the NRSRO designation or abolish credit rating agencies. Ending federally mandated reliance on NRSRO credit ratings does not change the fact that state laws, pension fund policies and other private market actors will continue to rely on NRSRO ratings. Many states incorporate NRSRO ratings into their laws. Thus, NRSRO ratings will not disappear. The provision ending reliance on ratings has no effect on those requirements, the senator concluded. The simple fact is that credit rating agencies have a place in the market and they perform a needed function, he added (Cong. Rec., May 19, 2010, p. S3956).

Further, most institutional investors lack the capacity to perform the analysis that credit rating agencies perform. For many small institutional investors, such as a school district's pension fund, researching their own investments would be cost prohibitive. These investors must rely at least in part on credit ratings issued by a rating agency. It is also likely that federal regulators will continue to use credit ratings as part of their new creditworthiness standards. Thus, the credit rating agencies will remain very much a part of the market (Cong. Rec., May 19, 2010, p. S3956).

Creating the Board will end the rating-shopping process and implement a system that rewards accuracy instead of grade inflation. The provision ending federal endorsement of ratings and the one creating the Board each tackle a different part of the problem, and there is nothing about them that would prevent them from both being implemented. Working in tandem, these two provisions will both reduce excessive reliance on credit ratings and ensure that the ratings demanded by the marketplace will be accurate (Cong. Rec., May 19, 2010, p. S3956).

Board Members, Funding.—Under the Franken amendment, the SEC must select the initial members of the Board for a four-year term and the SEC has discretion to decide how many members will serve on the Board so long as it is an odd number. A majority of the Board must be investor industry representatives who do not represent issuers. One member must be from the issuer community and one must be from the credit rating agency industry. Finally, one member must be independent. The SEC must adopt rules for the nomination and election of future Board members (Exchange Act Sec. 15E(w)(2)(C), as proposed by HR 4173 and passed on May 20, 2010).

The Board would be composed of industry experts: investors, issuers, raters and independents. A majority of its members would be investors, including institutional investors who have experience managing pension funds and university endowments. According to Sen. Franken, they would have a vested interest in accurate credit ratings because they depend on them when making investments (Cong Record, May 5, 2010, p. S3155).

The Board may levy fees on qualified NRSROs to fund its expenses (Exchange Act Sec. 15E(w)(2)(D), as proposed by HR 4173 and passed on May 20, 2010).

Definitions.—The term "qualified nationally recognized statistical rating organization" (qualified NRSRO) with respect to a category of structured finance products means an NRSRO that the Board determines, using statutory criteria, to be qualified to issue initial credit ratings with respect to that category (Exchange Act Sec. 15E(w)(1)(B), as proposed by HR 4173 and passed on May 20, 2010).

The term "category of structured finance products" includes any asset-backed security and any structured product based on an asset-backed security. The SEC may expand on the definition as necessary, but in issuing regulations the Commission must consider the types of issuers that issue structured finance products and the types of investors who purchase them, as well as the different categories of structured finance products according to capital flow and legal structure, underlying products, terms used in debt securities, the different values of debt securities, and the different numbers of units of debt securities issued together (Exchange Act Sec. 15E(w)(1)(C)(i), as proposed by HR 4173 and passed on May 20, 2010).

Schedule.—The SEC must adopt a schedule ensuring that the Board begins assigning rating agencies to provide initial ratings within one year of selection of the members. The schedule must set forth when the Board will conduct a study of the securitization and rating process and provide recommendations to the SEC and when the Board will begin accepting applications to select qualified NRSROs and begin assigning initial ratings (Exchange Act Sec. 15E(w)(2), as proposed by HR 4173 and passed on May 20, 2010).

Qualification of Rating Agencies.—The Franken amendment provides the Board process for qualifying a rating agency. The rating agency must submit an application to the Board on a form prescribed by the Board to become a qualified NRSRO with respect to a category of structured finance products. The application must contain: (1) information regarding the institutional and technical capacity of the NRSRO to issue credit ratings; (2) information on whether the NRSRO has been exempted by the SEC from any requirements under any other provisions; and (3) any additional information the Board may require. The Board may reject an application if the NRSRO has been exempted by the Commission from any requirements under any other provision of this section (Exchange Act Sec. 15E(w)(3)(A), as proposed by HR 4173 and passed on May 20, 2010).

The Board must select qualified rating agencies with respect to each category of structured finance products from among NRSROs that submit applications. An entity selected as a qualified NRSRO must retain its status and obligations under the law as an NRSRO and neither the SEC nor the Board may exempt qualified NRSROs from obligations or requirements otherwise imposed by federal law on NRSROs (Exchange Act Secs. 15E(w)(3)(B) and (C), as proposed by HR 4173 and passed on May 20, 2010).

Request for Initial Rating.—An issuer seeking an initial credit rating for a structured finance product cannot request an initial credit rating from an NRSRO. Rather, the issuer must submit a request for an initial credit rating to the Board in a form and manner prescribed by the Board (Exchange Act Sec. 15E(w)(4), as proposed by HR 4173 and passed on May 20, 2010).

¶4190

Selection Methods.—Issuer requests for ratings will be given to a rating agency selected by the Board under a system determined by the Board based on statutory selection guidelines (Exchange Act Sec. 15E(w)(5)(A), as proposed by HR 4173 and passed on May 20, 2010). The Board must evaluate a number of selection methods, including a lottery or rotating assignment system, incorporating factors to reduce the conflicts of interest that exist under the issuer-pays model and prescribe and publish a selection method (Exchange Act Sec. 15E(w)(5)(B)(i), as proposed by HR 4173 and passed on May 20, 2010).

In evaluating a selection method, the Board must consider: (1) the information submitted by the qualified NRSRO regarding its institutional and technical capacity to issue credit ratings; (2) performance evaluations conducted by the Board; (3) formal feedback from institutional investors; and (4) information to implement a mechanism that increases or decreases assignments based on past performance. In choosing a selection method, the Board cannot use a method that would allow for the solicitation or consideration of the issuer's preferred NRSRO (Exchange Act Secs. 15E(w)(5)(B)(ii) and (iii), as proposed by HR 4173 and passed on May 20, 2010).

The Board must also issue rules describing the process by which it can modify the assignment of ratings process (Exchange Act Sec. 15E(w)(5)(B)(iv), as proposed by HR 4173 and passed on May 20, 2010).

A rating agency selected by the Board to give an initial rating on a structured product can refuse to accept selection for a particular request by notifying the Board of its refusal and submitting a written explanation for that refusal. Upon receipt of the refusal notification, the Board must select another rating agency. The Board must also annually submit any explanations of refusals it receives to the SEC and these explanatory submissions must be published in the required annual inspection reports (Exchange Act Sec. 15E(w)(5)(C), as proposed by HR 4173 and passed on May 20, 2010).

Fees Charged to Issuer.—A rating organization must charge an issuer a reasonable fee, as determined by the Commission, for an initial credit rating on a structured financial product. Fees may be determined by the qualified NRSRO unless the Board determines it is necessary to issue rules on fees (Exchange Act Sec. 15E(w)(8), as proposed by HR 4173 and passed on May 20, 2010). The Board must issue regulations to define the term "reasonable fee" (Exchange Act Sec. 15E(w)(1)(C)(ii), as proposed by HR 4173 and passed on May 20, 2010).

Disclaimer.—Each initial credit rating issued for a structured financial product must include, in writing, the following disclaimer: "This initial rating has not been evaluated, approved, or certified by the Government of the United States or by a Federal agency" (Exchange Act Sec. 15E(w)(6), as proposed by HR 4173 and passed on May 20, 2010).

Performance Evaluation.—The Board must adopt rules by which it will evaluate the performance of each qualified NRSRO, including rules that require, at a minimum, an annual evaluation of each NRSRO. The Board, in conducting an evaluation, must consider the results of the annual examination, surveillance of credit ratings conducted by the rating agency after the credit ratings are issued, including how the rated instruments perform, the accuracy of the ratings provided compared to the other rating agencies, and the effectiveness of the methodologies used to arrive at the rating. The Board must make any evaluations it conducts available to Congress. A rating agency may request a reevaluation at least once per year (Exchange Act Sec. 15E(w)(7), as proposed by HR 4173 and passed on May 20, 2010).

Conflicts of Interest.—A Board member or employee cannot accept any loan of money or securities, or anything above nominal value, from any NRSRO, issuer or investor. An exception exists for: (1) loans made in the context of disclosed, routine banking and brokerage agreements, and (2) loans that are clearly motivated by a personal or family relationship. Board members or employees cannot engage in employment negotiations with any rating agency, issuer or investor unless they disclose the negotiations immediately upon initiation and recuse themselves from all proceedings concerning the entity involved until termination of negotiations or until termination of their employment by the Board, if an offer of employment is accepted (Exchange Act Sec. 15E(w)(14)(A), as proposed by HR 4173 and passed on May 20, 2010).

A credit analyst of a qualified NRSRO cannot accept any loan of money or securities, or anything above nominal value, from any issuer or investor. An exception exists for: (1) loans made in the context of disclosed, routine banking and brokerage agreements; or (2) loans that are clearly motivated by a personal or family relationship (Exchange Act Sec. 15E(w)(14)(B), as proposed by HR 4173 and passed on May 20, 2010).

▶ **Effective date.** The provision takes effect one day after the date of enactment (Sec. 4 of the Dodd-Frank Wall Street Reform and Consumer Protection Act).

Law source: Law at ¶10,939F and ¶10,004.

— Sec. 939F(a) of the Dodd-Frank Wall Street Reform and Consumer Protection Act, defining "structured finance product";

— Sec. 939F(b), requiring an SEC study of conflicts of interest in the credit rating process;

— Sec. 939F(c), requiring the SEC to report on its findings and make recommendations;

— Sec. 939F(d), requiring the SEC to implement a system for assigning initial credit ratings;

— Sec. 4, providing the effective date.

¶4195 State of Mind in Private Actions

The legislation provides that the enforcement and penalty provisions applicable to statements made by a credit rating agency must apply in the same manner and to the same extent as to statements made by a registered public accounting firm or a securities analyst, and that those statements will not be deemed forward-looking statements (Exchange Act Sec. 15E(m), as amended by the Dodd-Frank Wall Street Reform and Consumer Protection Act).

Further, in actions for money damages brought against a credit rating agency, it is sufficient for pleading any required state of mind in relation to that action to state facts giving rise to a strong inference that the credit rating agency knowingly or recklessly failed: (1) to conduct a reasonable investigation of the factual elements of the rated security; or (2) to obtain reasonable verification of the factual elements from independent sources that it considered to be competent (Exchange Act Sec. 21D(b)(2), as amended by the Dodd-Frank Act).

Essentially, the provision specifies that, for purposes of passing the pleading test of the Private Securities Litigation Reform Act, plaintiffs need not plead that the rating agency knowingly or recklessly engaged in a deceptive misrepresentation or omission in communicating with investors, but instead must only plead that the agency knowingly or recklessly failed to conduct a reasonable investigation with respect to factual elements or to obtain reasonable verification of those elements. The provision thus enables plaintiffs to survive the motion to dismiss stage of litigation more easily. It does not change the ultimate standard used by a fact-finder in determining whether the claim meets the basic elements of Exchange Act Rule 10b-5 (S. Rep. No. 111-176, p. 122).

▶ **Effective date.** The provision takes effect one day after the date of enactment (Sec. 4 of the Dodd-Frank Wall Street Reform and Consumer Protection Act).

Law source: Law at ¶10,933 and ¶10,004. Committee Report at ¶54,482.

— Sec. 933(a) of the Dodd-Frank Wall Street Reform and Consumer Protection Act, amending Exchange Act Sec. 15E(m);

— Sec. 933(b), amending Exchange Act Sec. 21D(b)(2);

— Sec. 4, providing the effective date.

¶4200 Information from Third-Party Sources

The Dodd-Frank Wall Street Reform and Consumer Protection Act requires consideration of credible, relevant information from third parties. It provides that rating agencies must consider information about an issuer that the agency has or receives from a source other than the issuer that is credible and potentially significant to a rating decision (Exchange Act Sec. 15E(v), as added by the Dodd-Frank Wall Street Reform and Consumer Protection Act).

Rating agencies need not, however, initiate a search for this kind of information. Rating agencies should evaluate third-party information on its own merits as to whether it indeed should affect the rating. Congress believes that if the rating agency possesses credible information that is significant to a rating decision about an issuer, it should consider it even if it has not undertaken to independently verify information received from an issuer (S. Rep. No. 111-176, p. 123). Elaborating, the Senate Banking Committee noted:

> Mr. James Gellert, Chairman of Rapid Ratings International, Inc., wrote in congressional testimony that "we believe that, if a rating agency's business model is to provide qualitative assessments of an entity or pool of assets collateralizing a structured product, it should take into account all data it can reasonably attain and qualify as being reliable" (S. Rep. No. 111-176, p. 123 (quoting *Examining Proposals to Enhance the Regulation of Credit Rating Agencies: Testimony before the U.S. Senate Committee on Banking, Housing, and Urban Affairs*, 111th Congress, 1st sess., p. 18 (2009) (Testimony of Mr. James Gellert)).

▶ **Effective date.** The provision takes effect one day after the date of enactment (Sec. 4 of the Dodd-Frank Wall Street Reform and Consumer Protection Act).

Law source: Law at ¶10,935 and ¶10,004. Committee Report at ¶54,484.

— Sec. 935 of the Dodd-Frank Wall Street Reform and Consumer Protection Act, adding Exchange Act Sec. 15E(v);

— Sec. 4, providing the effective date.

¶4205 Professional Standards for Rating Analysts

The legislation calls for professional standards for credit rating analysts. The SEC must, within one year of enactment, issue rules reasonably designed to ensure that any person employed by an NRSRO to perform credit ratings: (1) meets standards of training, experience and competence necessary to produce accurate ratings; and (2) is tested for knowledge of the credit rating process (Sec. 936 of the Dodd-Frank Wall Street Reform and Consumer Protection Act).

According to Congress, the devastating impact of faulty ratings on investors, the economy and families during the recent credit crisis has demonstrated the need to improve the analysis underlying those ratings. This requirement is intended to improve the quality of ratings by increasing the skills of those who formulate them. Under this provision, credit rating analysts would have to meet high professional standards for their industry, just as investment advisers, registered representatives and auditors do for theirs (S. Rep. No. 111-176, p. 123).

▶ **Effective date.** The provision takes effect one day after the date of enactment (Sec. 4 of the Dodd-Frank Wall Street Reform and Consumer Protection Act).

Law source: Law at ¶10,936 and ¶10,004. Committee Report at ¶54,485.

— Sec. 936 of the Dodd-Frank Wall Street Reform and Consumer Protection Act, requiring SEC rules establishing professional standards for rating analysts;

— Sec. 4, providing the effective date.

¶4210 Universal Rating Symbols

The legislation requires credit rating agencies to clearly define any symbols used to denote a credit rating and to apply any such symbols in a consistent manner to all types of securities and money market instruments to which they are applied. Specifically, the SEC must adopt rules requiring credit rating agencies to establish and enforce written policies and procedures that: (1) assess the probability that an issuer of a security or money market instrument will default or fail to make timely payments to investors; (2) clearly define and disclose the meaning of any symbol used to denote a credit rating; and (3) apply any such symbol in a consistent manner (Sec. 938(a) of the Dodd-Frank Wall Street Reform and Consumer Protection Act). However, distinct sets of symbols can be used to denote credit ratings for different types of securities or money market instruments (Sec. 938(b) of the Dodd-Frank Act).

Congress believes that a credit rating symbol should have the same meaning about creditworthiness when it is applied to any issuer, that is, the same symbol should not have a different meaning depending on the issuer. This provision does not dictate the meaning of any credit rating, whether it refers to an issuer's likelihood of default, ability to pay on time or other factors (S. Rep. No. 111-176, p. 124).

▶ **Effective date.** The provision takes effect one day after the date of enactment (Sec. 4 of the Dodd-Frank Wall Street Reform and Consumer Protection Act).

Law source: Law at ¶10,938 and ¶10,004. Committee Report at ¶54,487.

— Sec. 938(a) of the Dodd-Frank Wall Street Reform and Consumer Protection Act, requiring SEC rulemaking on universal rating symbols;

— Sec. 938(b), allowing distinct sets of symbols for different securities;

— Sec. 4, providing the effective date.

¶4215 Whistleblowers

The legislation provides that each credit rating agency must refer to the appropriate law enforcement or regulatory authorities any information that the agency receives and finds credible that alleges that an issuer of securities rated by the agency has committed or is committing a violation of law that has not been adjudicated by a federal or state court (Exchange Act Sec. 15E(u)(1), as added by the Dodd-Frank Wall Street Reform and Consumer Protection Act). This requirement does not impose a duty to verify the accuracy of this information (Exchange Act Sec. 15E(u)(2), as added by the Dodd-Frank Act).

The rating agency must determine whether it believes the information is credible, but need not undertake extensive fact finding or analysis or determine whether a violation of law has occurred. This is in effect a mandatory whistleblower provision, and exceptions could be created to cover circumstances when a compliance officer concludes that the information was false or unreliable (S. Rep. No. 111-176, p. 122).

A separate provision in Title IX, Subtitle B, extends the whistleblower protections of Sarbanes-Oxley Act Section 806 to the employees of credit rating agencies (18 U.S.C. §1514A(a), as amended by the Dodd-Frank Act). For more detailed discussion, see ¶4060.

▶ **Effective date.** The provision takes effect one day after the date of enactment (Sec. 4 of the Dodd-Frank Wall Street Reform and Consumer Protection Act).

Law source: Law at ¶10,922, ¶10,934 and ¶10,004. Committee Report at ¶54,461.

— Sec. 922(b) of the Dodd-Frank Wall Street Reform and Consumer Protection Act, amending 18 U.S.C. §1514A(a);

— Sec. 934, adding Exchange Act Sec. 15E(u);

— Sec. 4, providing the effective date.

¶4220 Removal of Statutory References to Ratings

The Dodd-Frank Wall Street Reform and Consumer Protection Act removes numerous statutory references to credit ratings. Authored by Sen. George LeMieux (R-FL) and Sen. Maria Cantwell (D-WA), the provision eliminates statutory protections for national credit ratings agencies and applies new standards of creditworthiness. It essentially removes the federal government's seal of approval from investment rating agencies. The effect will be to force federal regulators to develop more diverse and accurate measures of creditworthiness.

According to Sen. LeMieux, the provision eliminates the sanctioned monopoly that holds out the rating agencies as the entities that determine creditworthiness. The provision does not take effect until two years after enactment (Sec. 939(g) of the Dodd-Frank Act). There is a two-year waiting period so the market can have time to adjust. The waiting period will give the market time to divest itself from relying on a handful of rating agencies and allow banks time to augment their staffs for the due diligence necessary to prove creditworthiness (Cong Record, May 13, 2010, pp. 3675-3676).

Specifically, the provision eliminates statutory references to credit rating agencies in the Federal Deposit Insurance Act Sections 7(b)(1)(E)(i), 28(d) and 28(e), Federal Housing Enterprises Safety and Soundness Act Section 1319 (12 U.S.C. §4519), Investment Company Act Section 6(a)(5)(A), Section 5136A of Revised Statutes of the United States Title LXII (12 U.S.C. §24a) and Exchange Act Sections 3(a)(41) and (53)(A) (Secs. 939(a)–(e) of the Dodd-Frank Act).

Study and Report.—The legislation also directs the SEC to study the feasibility of standardizing credit ratings terminology so that all rating agencies issue credit ratings using identical terms and across asset classes so that named ratings correspond to a standard range of default probabilities and expected losses independent of asset class and issuing entity, as well as standardizing the market stress conditions under which ratings are evaluated. The study must also examine the feasibility of requiring a quantitative correspondence between credit ratings and a range of default probabilities and loss expectations under standardized conditions of economic stress (Sec. 939(h)(1) of the Dodd-Frank Act).

Within one year after enactment, the Commission must submit a report to Congress on the study's findings and any recommendations (Sec. 939(h)(2) of the Dodd-Frank Act).

Agency Review.—A separate provision requires each federal agency to review any of its regulations that require the use of an assessment of the creditworthiness of a security or money market instrument and any reference in the regulations to credit ratings. The agency must then remove any reference to or requirement of reliance on credit ratings and must substitute a standard of creditworthiness that it deems appropriate (Sec. 939A of the Dodd-Frank Act). For further discussion, see ¶ 4235.

▶ **Effective date.** The amendments made by the provision take effect two years after the date of enactment (Sec. 939(g) of the Dodd-Frank Wall Street Reform and Consumer Protection Act). Subsection (h), relating to the SEC study, takes effect one day after the date of enactment (Sec. 4 of the Dodd-Frank Act).

Law source: Law at ¶10,939 and ¶10,004. Committee Report at ¶54,488.

— Sec. 939(a) of the Dodd-Frank Wall Street Reform and Consumer Protection Act, amending FDIA Secs. 7(b)(1)(E)(i), 28(d) and 28(e);
— Sec. 939(b), amending 12 U.S.C. §4519;
— Sec. 939(c), amending Investment Company Act Sec. 6(a)(5)(A);
— Sec. 939(d), amending 12 U.S.C. §24a;
— Sec. 939(e), amending Exchange Act Secs. 3(a)(41) and (53)(A);
— Sec. 939(g), providing the effective date of the statutory amendments;
— Sec. 939(h), requiring an SEC study and report on the feasibility of standardized credit ratings terminology;
— Sec. 4, providing the effective date for Sec. 939(h).

¶4225 Regulation FD Exemption

The Dodd-Frank Wall Street Reform and Consumer Protection Act requires rulemaking to eliminate the fair disclosure rule exemption for credit rating agencies. Specifically, the SEC must revise Regulation FD to remove the exemption at 17 CFR §243.100(b)(2)(iii) for entities whose primary business is the issuance of credit ratings. The Commission must adopt this change not later than 90 days after the date of enactment (Sec. 939B of the Dodd-Frank Wall Street Reform and Consumer Protection Act).

Background.—Regulation FD is an issuer disclosure rule that addresses the practice of "selective disclosure." It provides that when a company, or person acting on its behalf, discloses material, nonpublic information to securities market professionals, or to company shareholders who may well trade on the basis of the information, the company must make public disclosure of that information (17 CFR §243.100(a)).

The timing of the required public disclosure depends on whether the selective disclosure was intentional. If the selective disclosure was intentional, the company must make public disclosure simultaneously, while for a non-intentional disclosure the public disclosure must be made promptly (17 CFR 243.100(a)). The regulation defines "promptly" to mean as soon as reasonably practicable after a senior company official learns that there has been a non-intentional disclosure of information that the official knows or is reckless in not knowing is both material and nonpublic. The regulation further states that "promptly" can in no event be the later of 24 hours or the commencement of the next day's trading on the New York Stock Exchange (17 CFR 243.101(d)). The company may make the required public disclosure by filing or furnishing a Form 8-K, or by another method or combination of methods reasonably designed to effect broad, non-exclusionary distribution of the information to the public (17 CFR §243.101(e)).

When it adopted Regulation FD, the SEC exempted credit rating agencies and the news media from the regulation's coverage based on the belief that there is a significant difference between analysts, on the one hand, and news reporters and rating agencies, on the other. Reporters gather information for the purpose of reporting the news and informing the public; generally, their reports are widely disseminated. Similarly, credit rating agencies make their ratings reports public when completed. Analysts, by contrast, gather and report information to be used for securities trading; their reports are typically available to a limited, usually paying, audience (see SEC Release No. 33-7881, Part II.B.1.a (Aug. 15, 2000), FED. SEC. L. REP. ¶ 86,319).

▶ **Effective date.** The provision takes effect one day after the date of enactment (Sec. 4 of the Dodd-Frank Wall Street Reform and Consumer Protection Act).

Law source: Law at ¶ 10,939B and ¶ 10,004.

— Sec. 939B of the Dodd-Frank Wall Street Reform and Consumer Protection Act, requiring the SEC to remove the exemption in 17 CFR § 243.100(b)(2)(iii);

— Sec. 4, providing the effective date.

¶4230 Section 11 Liability

The Dodd-Frank Wall Street Reform and Consumer Protection Act nullifies Securities Act Rule 436(g) (17 CFR § 230.436(g)), a special provision that exempts credit rating agencies from liability under Securities Act Section 11 (Sec. 939G of the Dodd-Frank Act).

At the core of the Securities Act is the idea that a company should provide investors with basic information about the securities it is issuing. It requires issuers to publicly disclose significant information about themselves and the terms of the securities. Those who make material misstatements or omissions of fact in a registration statement can be held accountable under Securities Act Section 11. This provision applies to many experts in the financial world, such as accountants, lawyers, investment bankers, directors, officers and executives of the issuers. Credit rating agencies, however, are exempt from Section 11 liability by virtue of Rule 436(g).

The legislation levels the playing field by stating that Rule 436(g) will have no force, effectively removing the "expert" exemption for credit ratings included in a registration statement. Thus, rating agencies will now face greater liability under the securities laws if a rating is included in a registration statement. Rating agencies will be liable for omitting information from a registration statement, giving them the same accountability as other experts like accountants, auditors and lawyers.

▶ **Effective date.** The provision takes effect one day after the date of enactment (Sec. 4 of the Dodd-Frank Wall Street Reform and Consumer Protection Act).

Law source: Law at ¶ 10,939G and ¶ 10,004.

— Sec. 939G of the Dodd-Frank Wall Street Reform and Consumer Protection Act, nullifying Securities Act Rule 436(g);

— Sec. 4, providing the effective date.

¶4235 Studies and Reports

The Dodd-Frank Wall Street Reform and Consumer Protection Act calls for further study of particular aspects of the credit rating industry. As discussed below, the Act mandates a study and report on: (1) regulations that rely on credit ratings; (2) credit rating agency independence; (3) alternative means of compensation; and (4) the feasibility of creating an independent professional organization for rating analysts. A separate study and report on the feasibility of standardized credit ratings terminology is discussed elsewhere, at ¶ 4220.

Reliance on Ratings.—Within one year after enactment, each federal agency must, to the extent applicable, review: (1) any of its regulations that require the use of an assessment of the credit-worthiness of a security or money market instrument; and (2) any references to or requirements in those regulations regarding credit ratings (Sec. 939A(a) of the Dodd-Frank Wall Street Reform and Consumer Protection Act).

Each such agency must modify any such regulations identified by the review to remove any reference to or requirement of reliance on credit ratings and to substitute a standard of credit-worthiness that the agency determines is appropriate for those regulations. In making this determination, the agencies must seek to establish, to the extent feasible, uniform standards of credit-worthiness for use by each agency, taking into account the entities regulated by the agency and the purposes for which those entities would rely on standards of credit-worthiness (Sec. 939A(b) of the Dodd-Frank Act).

Upon conclusion of the review required above, each federal agency must transmit a report to Congress containing a description of any regulation changes the agency made (Sec. 939A(c) of the Dodd-Frank Act).

Rating Agency Independence.—The SEC must conduct a study on the independence of NRSROs and how that independence affects the ratings they issue (Sec. 939C(a) of the Dodd-Frank Act). In conducting the study, the Commission must evaluate:

- the management of conflicts of interest raised by an NRSRO providing other services, including risk management advisory services, ancillary assistance or consulting services;
- the potential impact of rules prohibiting an NRSRO that provides a rating to an issuer from providing other services to the issuer; and
- any other issue relating to NRSROs that the SEC Chair determines is appropriate (Sec. 939C(b) of the Dodd-Frank Act).

Congress intends that this study should include an identification of the types and scope of services provided by NRSROs and which of these services raises a potential for raising a conflict that could change a rating (S. Rep. No. 111-176, p. 126).

Within three years after the date of enactment, the SEC must submit a report on the study's results to the Senate Banking Committee and the House Financial Services Committee. The report must include recommendations, if any, for improving the integrity of ratings issued by NRSROs (Sec. 939C(c) of the Dodd-Frank Act).

Alternative Compensation Means.—The Government Accountability Office (GAO) Comptroller General must conduct a study on alternative means of compensating credit rating agencies in order to create incentives for them to provide more accurate ratings, including any statutory changes needed to facilitate these changes (Sec. 939D(a) of the Dodd-Frank Act).

The predominant NRSRO business model involves the issuer paying for the rating, while a small number of NRSROs rely on subscription fees from users. Congress asks the GAO to analyze which model is likely to produce the most accurate ratings. Recognizing that conflicts of interest exist for rating agencies, Congress seeks an analysis of how and whether these organizations are effectively managed so that conflicts do not unfairly influence ratings decisions (S. Rep. No. 111-176, p. 126).

Within one year after the date of enactment, the GAO must submit a report on the study's results to the Senate Banking Committee and the House Financial Services Committee. The report must include recommendations, if any, for providing incentives for credit rating agencies to improve the credit rating process (Sec. 939D(b) of the Dodd-Frank Act).

Professional Organization for Rating Analysts.—The GAO must also conduct a study on the feasibility and merits of creating an independent professional organization for NRSRO rating analysts that would:

- establish independent standards for governing the rating analyst profession;
- establish a code of ethical conduct; and
- oversee the rating analyst profession (Sec. 939E(a) of the Dodd-Frank Act).

In the aftermath of the recent financial crisis caused in part by poor credit ratings, Congress seeks to explore means of improving the skills of the professionals who produce credit ratings (S. Rep. No. 111-176, p. 127).

Within one year after the date of enactment, the GAO must submit a report on the study's results to the Senate Banking Committee and the House Financial Services Committee (Sec. 939E(b) of the Dodd-Frank Act).

▶ **Effective date.** The provisions take effect one day after the date of enactment (Sec. 4 of the Dodd-Frank Wall Street Reform and Consumer Protection Act).

Law source: Law at ¶10,939A, ¶10,939C, ¶10,939D, ¶10,939E and ¶10,004. Committee Report at ¶54,488, ¶54,489, ¶54,490 and ¶54,491.

— Sec. 939A of the Dodd-Frank Wall Street Reform and Consumer Protection Act, requiring federal agencies to review and modify regulations that rely on credit ratings;

— Sec. 939C, requiring an SEC study and report on rating agency independence;

— Sec. 939D, requiring a GAO study and report on alternative means of compensation;

— Sec. 939E, requiring a GAO study and report on creating an independent professional organization for rating analysts;

— Sec. 4, providing the effective date.

SECURITIZATION

¶4250 Introduction

Title IX, Subtitle D, of the Dodd-Frank Wall Street Reform and Consumer Protection Act (Section 941 *et seq.*) reforms the process of securitization. Despite the role of securitization in the subprime crisis, there is a general consensus that securitization remains essential to the global financial markets. In other words, there will be no return to the originate-and-hold model. The Act therefore imposes various oversight, risk-retention, disclosure and due diligence reforms on the securitization process and industry.

Background.—Securitization is a financing technique in which financial assets, in many cases themselves relatively illiquid, are pooled and converted into instruments that may be offered and sold in the capital markets. In a typical securitization, a sponsor initiates a securitization transaction by selling or pledging to a specially created issuing entity, such as a trust, a group of financial assets that the sponsor either has originated itself or has purchased. The trust or other issuing entity sells securities. The money from the sale of the securities is used to purchase the financial assets from the sponsor. The financial assets are pooled and the pool typically is designed to cover a wide range of obligors on the underlying assets. The securities pay a return based on the assets in the trust (Testimony of Paula Dubberly, Associate Director, SEC Division of Corporation Finance, before House Financial Services Committee, Sept. 24, 2009).

Examples. A typical structured securitized product would be a mortgage-backed securities package with three to six tranches of securities to fund the mortgage pool of assets it purchased. Each tranche had an associated par value and yield and all but perhaps the most junior tranches were rated by a credit rating agency. The most senior mortgage investments (typically AAA-rated) would be paid in full before the next priority tranche would be paid, and so on through the priority structure. As mortgages defaulted, the lowest priority tranche suffered losses first. If the mortgage pool losses were large enough, the claims of the lowest tranche would be wiped out completely and the second-lowest priority tranche would begin to bear losses. As losses grew, they spread to sequentially higher-priority tranches.

When the lack of demand for the high-risk tranches limited the growth of mortgage-backed securities, the financial industry developed two other investment structures: collateralized debt obligations (CDOs) and structured investment vehicles. These structures were critical in creating investor demand for the high-risk tranches of mortgage-backed securities and for creating the credit-market excesses that fueled the housing boom.

CDOs are complex debt securities similar in many ways to mortgage-backed securities but with different collateral. While mortgage-backed securities are based on the cash flows from a pool of individual mortgage loans, CDOs are collateralized by pools of other debt securities, which could be (and in many cases were) mortgage-backed securities. Like mortgage-backed securities, CDOs might have numerous tiers and issue corresponding tranches of securities with different claims priorities and credit ratings.

Financial Crisis. In many ways, the financial meltdown was at root a crisis of securitization. Although traditionally securitization was a successful tool for bundling loans into asset-backed securities, in the last decade, it has become a method of short-term financing of complex, illiquid securities whose value had to be determined by theoretical models. The inherent fragility of this new securitization model was masked by the actions of market intermediaries, particularly credit rating agencies. The collapse of structured securitization revealed that, far from managing and dispersing risk, structured securitization had increased leverage and concentrated risk in a small group of financial institutions.

One of the most significant problems in the securitization markets was the lack of sufficient incentives for lenders and securitizers to consider the performance of the underlying loans after asset-backed securities were issued. Lenders and securitizers had weak incentives to conduct due diligence regarding the quality of the underlying assets being securitized. This problem was exacerbated as the structure of asset-backed securities became more complex and opaque. Inadequate disclosure regimes exacerbated the gap in incentives between lenders, securitizers and investors (*Financial Regulatory Reform, A New Foundation: Rebuilding Financial Supervision and Regulation*, Treasury Department (June 17, 2009) at FED. BANK. L. REP. ¶ 75-201).

The congressional investigation into the causes of the financial crisis identified abuses of the securitization process as a major contributing factor. Two problems emerged in the crisis. First, under the originate to distribute model, loans were made expressly to be sold into securitization pools, which meant that the lenders did not expect to bear the credit risk of borrower default. This led to significant deterioration in credit and loan underwriting standards, particularly in residential mortgages. Second, it proved impossible for investors in asset-backed securities to assess the risks of the underlying assets, particularly when those assets were resecuritized into complex instruments like collateralized debt obligations. With the onset of the crisis, there was widespread uncertainty regarding the true financial condition of holders of asset-backed securities, freezing interbank lending and constricting the general flow of credit. Complexity and opacity in securitization markets created the conditions that allowed the financial shock from the subprime mortgage sector to spread into a global financial crisis (S. Rep. No. 111-176, p. 128).

Overview.—Title IX, Subtitle D, of the legislation reforms the process of securitization. It requires companies that sell products like mortgage-backed securities to retain five percent of the credit risk, discouraging them from selling junk assets because they would have an economic interest in the product (see ¶ 4255). In addition, the SEC must adopt regulations requiring issuers of asset-backed securities to disclose for each tranche or class of security information regarding the assets backing that security. In adopting these regulations, the Commission must set standards for the format of the data provided by issuers to facilitate comparison across securities in similar types of asset classes (see ¶ 4260). The legislation also repeals an exemption from Securities Act registration for mortgage-related securities notes (see ¶ 4265). Issuers must also perform and disclose a due diligence analysis (see ¶ 4270). Finally, the Financial Stability Oversight Council must conduct a study of the macroeconomic effects of the legislation's risk-retention requirements (see ¶ 4275).

¶4250

▶ **Effective date.** The provisions take effect one day after the date of enactment (Sec. 4 of the Dodd-Frank Wall Street Reform and Consumer Protection Act).

Law source: Law at ¶10,941. Committee Report at ¶50,091 and ¶54,500.

— Sec. 941 *et seq.* of the Dodd-Frank Wall Street Reform and Consumer Protection Act, reforming the asset-backed securitization process;

— Sec. 4, providing the effective date.

¶4255 Credit Risk Retention

The legislation requires securitizers, defined as those who issue or organize and initiate asset-backed securities, to retain part of the credit risk for any asset that they transfer, sell or convey to a third party (Exchange Act Sec. 15G(b), as added by the Dodd-Frank Wall Street Reform and Consumer Protection Act). Specifically, within 270 days of enactment, the federal banking agencies and the SEC must jointly prescribe regulations to require any securitizer to retain a material portion of the credit risk of any asset that the securitizer, through the issuance of an asset-backed security, transfers, sells or conveys to a third party (Exchange Act Sec. 15G(b)(1), as added by the Dodd-Frank Act).

A similar provision applies to residential mortgages. Within 270 days after the date of the enactment, the federal banking agencies, the SEC, the Secretary of Housing and Urban Development, and the Federal Housing Finance Agency, must jointly prescribe regulations to require any securitizer to retain an economic interest in a portion of the credit risk for any residential mortgage asset that the securitizer, through the issuance of an asset-backed security, transfers, sells or conveys to a third party (Exchange Act Sec. 15G(b)(2), as added by the Dodd-Frank Act).

The Council Chair must coordinate all joint rulemaking required under this provision (Exchange Act Sec. 15G(h), as added by the Dodd-Frank Act).

Congressional Purpose.—The retention requirement is designed to create incentives that will prevent a recurrence of the excesses and abuses that preceded the crisis, restore investor confidence in asset-backed finance, and permit securitization markets to resume their important role as sources of credit for households and businesses. When securitizers retain a material amount of risk, they have "skin in the game," aligning their economic interests with those of investors in asset-backed securities. Securitizers who retain risk have a strong incentive to monitor the quality of the assets they purchase from originators, package into securities and sell (S. Rep. No. 111-176, pp. 128–129).

Definitions.—"Federal banking agencies" means the Office of the Comptroller of the Currency, the Board of Governors of the Federal Reserve System (the Fed), and the Federal Deposit Insurance Corporation (Exchange Act Sec. 15G(a)(1), as added by the Dodd-Frank Act).

"Securitizer" means (1) an issuer of an asset-backed security; or (2) a person who organizes and initiates an asset-backed securities transaction by selling or transferring assets, either directly or indirectly, including through an affiliate, to the issuer (Exchange Act Sec. 15G(a)(3), as added by the Dodd-Frank Act).

"Asset-backed security" means a fixed-income or other security collateralized by any type of self-liquidating financial asset, including a loan, a lease, a mortgage or a secured or unsecured receivable, that allows the holder of the security to receive payments depending primarily on cash flow from the asset, including collateralized mortgage or debt obligations (Exchange Act Sec. 3(a)(77)(A), as added by the Dodd-Frank Act). The term "asset-backed security" does not include a security issued by a finance subsidiary held by the parent company or a company controlled by the parent company, if none of the securities issued by the finance subsidiary are held by an entity that is not controlled by the parent company (Exchange Act Sec. 3(a)(77)(B), as added by the Dodd-Frank Act).

"Originator" means a person who: (1) through the extension of credit or otherwise, creates a financial asset that collateralizes an asset-backed security; and (2) sells an asset directly or indirectly to a securitizer (Exchange Act Sec. 15G(a)(4), as added by the Dodd-Frank Act).

Hedging Prohibition.—Securitizers cannot hedge or otherwise transfer the credit risk they have to retain. Specifically, regulations must prohibit a securitizer from directly or indirectly hedging or otherwise transferring the credit risk that the securitizer is required to retain with respect to an asset (Exchange Act Sec. 15G(c)(1)(A), as added by the Dodd-Frank Act). This prohibition does not extend to hedging risks other than credit risk (such as interest rate risk) associated with the retained assets or position (S. Rep. No. 111-176, p. 129).

In determining how to allocate risk-retention obligations between a securitizer and an originator, the SEC and the banking agencies must reduce the percentage of risk retention required of the securitizer by the percentage of risk-retention obligations required of the originator and must consider whether: (1) assets being securitized do not have characteristics of low credit risk; (2) conditions in securitization markets are creating incentives for imprudent origination; and (3) allocating part of the risk-retention obligation to originators would prevent consumers and businesses from obtaining credit on reasonable terms (Exchange Act Sec. 15G(d), as added by the Dodd-Frank Act).

Percentage Retained.—The law provides a baseline risk-retention amount of five percent of the credit risk in any securitized asset. Congress believes that regulators should have flexibility in setting risk-retention levels, to encourage recovery of securitization markets and to accommodate future market developments and innovations, but that, in all cases, the amount of risk retained should be material in order to create meaningful incentives for sound and sustainable securitization practices (S. Rep. No. 111-176, pp. 130–131).

Specifically, the mandated regulations must require a securitizer to retain the following risk percentages:

- not less than five percent of the credit risk for any asset:
    - that is not a qualified residential mortgage that is transferred, sold or conveyed through the issuance of an asset-backed security by the securitizer; or

¶4255

— that is a qualified residential mortgage that is transferred, sold or conveyed through the issuance of an asset-backed security by the securitizer, if one or more of the assets that collateralize the asset-backed security are not qualified residential mortgages; or
- less than five percent of the credit risk for an asset that is not a qualified residential mortgage that is transferred, sold or conveyed through the issuance of an asset-backed security by the securitizer, if the originator of the asset meets certain underwriting standards (Exchange Act Sec. 15G(c)(1)(B), as added by the Dodd-Frank Act).

The definition of, and exemption for, qualified residential mortgages is discussed further below.

Form and Duration.—The risk-retention regulations must specify the permissible forms of risk retention (Exchange Act Sec. 15G(c)(1)(C)(i), as added by the Dodd-Frank Act). They must also specify the minimum duration of the risk retention (Exchange Act Sec. 15G(c)(1)(C)(ii), as added by the Dodd-Frank Act).

Commercial Mortgages.—The regulations must, with respect to a commercial mortgage, specify the permissible types, forms and amounts of risk retention that would meet the above risk-retention percentage requirement, such as:

- retention of a specified amount or percentage of the asset's total credit risk;
- retention of the first-loss position by a third-party purchaser that specifically negotiates for the purchase of the first-loss position, holds adequate financial resources to back losses, provides due diligence on all individual assets in the pool before the issuance of the asset-backed securities, and meets the same risk retention standards as those governing the securitizer;
- a determination by the federal banking agency and the SEC that the underwriting standards and controls for the asset are adequate; and
- provision of adequate representations and warranties and related enforcement mechanisms (Exchange Act Sec. 15G(c)(1)(E), as added by the Dodd-Frank Act).

Collateralized Debt Obligations.—The regulations must also establish appropriate standards for retention of an economic interest in collateralized debt obligations, securities collateralized by collateralized debt obligations, and similar instruments collateralized by other asset-backed securities (Exchange Act Sec. 15G(c)(1)(F), as added by the Dodd-Frank Act).

Asset Classes.—Congress believes that implementation of risk-retention obligations should recognize the differences in securitization practices for various asset classes. Accordingly, the legislation requires that the initial joint rulemaking establish asset classes with separate rules for securitizers of different classes of assets, including residential mortgages, commercial mortgages, commercial loans, auto loans, and any other class of assets that the federal banking agencies and the Commission deem appropriate (Exchange Act Sec. 15G(c)(2)(A), as added by the Dodd-Frank Act). Congress expects that these regulations will recognize differences in the assets securitized, in existing risk management practices and in the structure of asset-backed securities, and that regulators will make appropriate adjustments to the amount of risk retention required (S. Rep. No. 111-176, pp. 129–130).

¶4255

For each asset class so established, the regulations must include underwriting standards established by the federal banking agencies that specify the terms, conditions and characteristics of a loan within the asset class that indicate a low credit risk with respect to the loan (Exchange Act Sec. 15G(c)(2)(B), as added by the Dodd-Frank Act).

Exemptions, Exceptions and Adjustments.—The federal banking agencies and the Commission may jointly adopt or issue exemptions, exceptions or adjustments to the risk-retention regulations (Exchange Act Sec. 15G(e)(1), as added by the Dodd-Frank Act). Any such exemption, exception or adjustment must: (1) help ensure high-quality underwriting standards for the securitizers and originators of assets that are securitized or available for securitization; and (2) encourage appropriate risk management practices by the securitizers and originators of assets, improve the access of consumers and businesses to credit on reasonable terms, or otherwise be in the public interest and for investor protection (Exchange Act Sec. 15G(e)(2), as added by the Dodd-Frank Act).

Farm Credit System Institutions. The requirements of this provision do not apply to any loan or other financial asset made, insured, guaranteed or purchased by any institution supervised by the Farm Credit Administration, including the Federal Agricultural Mortgage Corporation (Exchange Act Sec. 15G(e)(3)(A), as added by the Dodd-Frank Act).

U.S. Government Loans. The requirements also do not apply to any residential, multi-family or health care facility mortgage loan asset, or securitization based directly or indirectly on such an asset, that is insured or guaranteed by the United States or a U.S. agency. For this purpose, the Federal National Mortgage Association (Fannie Mae), the Federal Home Loan Mortgage Corporation (Freddie Mac) and the federal home loan banks are not deemed U.S. agencies (Exchange Act Sec. 15G(e)(3)(B), as added by the Dodd-Frank Act).

Government-Issued or Backed Securities. The regulations must provide a total or partial exemption for the securitization of an asset issued or guaranteed by the United States or a U.S. agency, as the federal banking agencies and the Commission jointly determine appropriate in the public interest and for investor protection. For this purpose, Fannie Mae and Freddie Mac are not deemed U.S. agencies (Exchange Act Sec. 15G(c)(1)(G)(ii), as added by the Dodd-Frank Act).

> **CCH Comment:** The legislative history shows that Congress expects asset-backed securities backed by the full faith and credit of the United States, or those that have underlying assets guaranteed by a U.S. agency, to qualify for an exemption (S. Rep. No. 111-176, p. 130).

The regulations must also provide a total or partial exemption for any asset-backed security that is a security issued or guaranteed by any U.S. state, or by any political subdivision of a state or territory, or by any public instrumentality of a state or territory that is exempt from registration under Securities Act Section 3(a)(2), or a security defined as a "qualified scholarship funding bond" in I.R.C. Section 150(d)(2), as may be appropriate in the public interest and for investor protection (Exchange Act Sec. 15G(c)(1)(G)(iii), as added by the Dodd-Frank Act).

Qualified Residential Mortgages. The federal banking agencies, the Commission, the Secretary of Housing and Urban Development, and the Director of the Federal Housing Finance Agency must jointly issue regulations to exempt qualified residential mortgages

¶4255

from the risk-retention requirements (Exchange Act Sec. 15G(e)(4)(A), as added by the Dodd-Frank Act). These agencies must jointly define the term "qualified residential mortgage" for purposes of this exemption, taking into consideration underwriting and product features that historical loan performance data indicate result in a lower risk of default, such as:

- documentation and verification of the financial resources relied on to qualify the mortgagor;
- standards with respect to:
  — the mortgagor's residual income after all monthly obligations;
  — the ratio of the mortgagor's housing payments to his or her monthly income;
  — the ratio of mortgagor's total monthly installment payments to his or her income;
- mitigation of the potential for payment shock on adjustable rate mortgages through product features and underwriting standards;
- mortgage guarantee insurance or other insurance or credit enhancement obtained at the time of origination, to the extent that the insurance or credit enhancement reduces the default risk; and
- prohibition or restriction of the use of balloon payments, negative amortization, prepayment penalties, interest-only payments and other features shown to exhibit a higher risk of borrower default (Exchange Act Sec. 15G(e)(4)(B), as added by the Dodd-Frank Act).

The definition of "qualified residential mortgage" is subject to a limitation. The federal banking agencies, the SEC, the Secretary of Housing and Urban Development, and the Director of the Federal Housing Finance Agency cannot define the term to be any broader than the definition of "qualified mortgage" under Truth in Lending Act Section 129C(b)(2), as amended by Dodd-Frank Act Section 1412 (discussed at ¶ 6550), and the underlying regulations (Exchange Act Sec. 15G(e)(4)(C), as added by the Dodd-Frank Act).

The qualified residential mortgage exemption must provide that an asset-backed security that is collateralized by tranches of other asset-backed securities is not exempt from the risk-retention requirements (Exchange Act Sec. 15G(e)(5), as added by the Dodd-Frank Act).

The Commission must require an issuer to certify, for each issuance of an asset-backed security collateralized exclusively by qualified residential mortgages, that the issuer has evaluated the effectiveness of the internal supervisory controls of the issuer with respect to the process for ensuring that all assets that collateralize the asset-backed security are qualified residential mortgages (Exchange Act Sec. 15G(e)(6), as added by the Dodd-Frank Act).

> **CCH Comment:** Sponsored by Senators Mary Landrieu (D-LA) and Johnny Isakson (R-GA), the carve-out for qualified residential mortgages ensures that originators of mortgages with a high FICO rating will not have to retain the five-percent amount required of other securitized assets. According to Sen. Isakson, the only risk retention that will be required is when someone is making a bad loan. The amendment embodies the principle that underwriting, not risk retention, is the cure-all to good lending (Cong. Rec., May 12, 2010, p. S3576). Although "skin in the game" is important, acknowledged Sen. Mark Warner (D-VA), more important

is the underlying quality of the mortgage. Senator Warner added that the amendment remains true to the legislation's intent to ensure that the mortgage securitization process requires mortgages originators to have a financial stake (Cong. Rec., May 12, 2010, p. S3576).

Enforcement.—The risk-retention regulations must be enforced by: (1) the appropriate federal banking agency, with respect to any securitizer that is an insured depository institution; and (2) the Commission, with respect to any securitizer that is not an insured depository institution (Exchange Act Sec. 15G(f), as added by the Dodd-Frank Act). The SEC's authority under this provision is in addition to its existing authority to enforce the securities laws (Exchange Act Sec. 15G(g), as added by the Dodd-Frank Act).

Regulation Deadline.—The regulations issued under this section must become effective: (1) with respect to securitizers and originators of asset-backed securities backed by residential mortgages, within one year after the date on which final rules under this section are published in the *Federal Register*; and (2) with respect to securitizers and originators of all other classes of asset-backed securities, within two years after the date on which final rules under this section are published in the *Federal Register* (Exchange Act Sec. 15G(i), as added by the Dodd-Frank Act).

Study and Report.—Within 90 days of enactment, the Fed must conduct a study and report to Congress on the combined impact on each individual class of asset-backed security of the new credit-risk-retention requirements and FASB Standards 166 and 167. In doing the study, the Fed must consult and coordinate with the SEC and FDIC, among others. The report to Congress must include statutory and regulatory recommendations for eliminating any negative impacts on the continued viability of the asset-backed securitization markets and on the availability of credit for new lending (Sec. 941(c) of the Dodd-Frank Act).

FAS 166 and 167, which took effect on January 1, 2010, eliminated the use of qualifying special purpose entities to achieve true sales of assets to move them off a securitizer's balance sheet. As a result, many previously securitized assets moved from off-balance sheet to on-balance sheet as of the beginning of this year.

According to Comptroller of the Currency John Dugan, FAS 166 and 167 make it considerably more difficult to structure securitization transactions to qualify as true sales to move assets off the balance sheet. Although the control test used in the new standards is not exactly the same as a risk transfer test, noted Mr. Dugan, the results are conceptually similar. The assumption is that the more control the securitizer retains over assets after securitization the greater the likelihood of ongoing exposure to risk of loss in the securitized assets, and the less likely it is that the risk of loss has adequately shifted to purchasers. As a result, the new accounting standards effectively require the books of securitizers to capture more ongoing risk from securitizations than the old standards (Remarks before American Securitization Forum, Feb. 2, 2010).

▶ **Effective date.** The provision takes effect one day after the date of enactment (Sec. 4 of the Dodd-Frank Wall Street Reform and Consumer Protection Act).

Law source: Law at ¶10,941. Committee Report at ¶54,500.

— Sec. 941(a) of the Dodd-Frank Wall Street Reform and Consumer Protection Act, adding Exchange Act Sec. 3(a)(77);

— Sec. 941(b), adding Exchange Act Sec. 15G;

— Sec. 941(c), requiring a study and report on the impact of the credit-risk-retention requirements and FASB Standards 166 and 167;

— Sec. 4, providing the effective date.

¶4260 Issuer Disclosure and Reporting

To improve transparency in asset-backed securities, the legislation requires expanded issuer disclosure of information regarding the underlying assets. Specifically, the Commission must adopt regulations requiring each issuer of an asset-backed security to disclose, for each tranche or class of security, information regarding the assets backing that security (Securities Act Sec. 7(c)(1), as added by the Dodd-Frank Wall Street Reform and Consumer Protection Act).

In adopting these regulations, the Commission must set standards for the format of the data provided by asset-backed security issuers. The standards must, to the extent feasible, facilitate comparison of the data across securities in similar types of asset classes (Securities Act Sec. 7(c)(2)(A), as added by the Dodd-Frank Act). The standards must also require issuers of asset-backed securities, at a minimum, to disclose asset-level or loan-level data, if such data are necessary for investors to independently perform due diligence, including:

- data having unique identifiers relating to loan brokers or originators;
- the nature and extent of the compensation of the broker or originator of the assets backing the security; and
- the amount of risk retention by the originator and the securitizer of such assets (Securities Act Sec. 7(c)(2)(B), as added by the Dodd-Frank Act).

Congress does not expect that disclosure of data about individual borrowers would be required in cases such as securitizations of credit card or automobile loans or leases, where asset pools typically include many thousands of credit agreements, where individual loan data would not be useful to investors and where disclosure might raise privacy concerns (S. Rep. No. 111-176, p. 131).

> **CCH Comment:** The Investors' Working Group reported that the SEC should develop a regulatory regime for asset-backed securities that would require issuers to make prospectuses available for potential investors in advance of their purchasing decisions. These prospectuses should disclose important information about the securities, including the terms of the offering, information about the sponsor, the issuer and the trust, and details about the collateral supporting the securities. These rules would give investors critical information they need to perform due diligence on offerings prior to investing. They would also create better opportunities for due diligence by the underwriters, thus increasing oversight of the quality and appropriateness of structured offerings (*U.S. Financial Regulatory Reform: An Investor's Perspective*, Investors' Working Group (July 2009), p. 14).

Representations and Warranties.—The legislation mandates SEC regulations on the use of representations and warranties in offerings of asset-backed securities. Within 180 days after the date of enactment, the Commission must prescribe regulations on the use of representations and warranties in the market for asset-backed securities that require each nationally recognized statistical rating organization to include in any report accompanying a credit rating a description of: (1) the representations, warranties and enforcement mechanisms available to investors; and (2) how they differ from the representations, warranties and enforcement mechanisms in issuances of similar securities (Sec. 943 of the Dodd-Frank Act).

The regulations must also require any securitizer to disclose fulfilled and unfulfilled repurchase requests across all trusts aggregated by the securitizer so that investors may identify asset originators with clear underwriting deficiencies (Sec. 943 of the Dodd-Frank Act).

> **CCH Comment:** Congress believes that enhanced disclosure will allow investors to better evaluate representations and warranties and create incentives for issuers to insist that originators back up their representations and warranties with real financial resources (S. Rep. No. 111-176, p. 133).

Suspension of Duty to File.—The Commission may, by rule or regulation, provide for the suspension or termination of the duty to file under this subsection for any class of asset-backed security, on such terms and conditions and for such period or periods as the Commission deems necessary or appropriate in the public interest or for the protection of investors (Exchange Act Sec. 15(d)(2)(A), as added by the Dodd-Frank Act). The Commission may, for purposes of this subsection, classify issuers and prescribe requirements appropriate for each class of issuers of asset-backed securities (Exchange Act Sec. 15(d)(2)(B), as added by the Dodd-Frank Act).

▶ **Effective date.** The provisions take effect one day after the date of enactment (Sec. 4 of the Dodd-Frank Wall Street Reform and Consumer Protection Act).

Law source: Law at ¶10,942. Committee Report at ¶54,501 and ¶54,502.

— Sec. 942(a) of the Dodd-Frank Wall Street Reform and Consumer Protection Act, amending Exchange Act Sec. 15(d);

— Sec. 942(b), adding Securities Act Sec. 7(c);

— Sec. 943, requiring disclosure of representations and warranties;

— Sec. 4, providing the effective date.

¶4265 Real Estate Mortgage Notes Exemption

The Dodd-Frank Wall Street Reform and Consumer Protection Act repeals an exemption from Securities Act registration for transactions involving mortgage-related securities (Securities Act Sec. 4(5), as repealed by the Dodd-Frank Wall Street Reform and Consumer Protection Act). Added by the Securities Reform Act of 1975, Securities Act Section 4(5) exempted transactions involving offers or sales of one or more promissory notes directly secured by a first lien on a single parcel of real estate that has a dwelling or other residential or commercial structure. Specifically, the former provision stated that Section 5 does not apply to the following transactions:

> (A) Transactions involving offers or sales of one or more promissory notes directly secured by a first lien on a single parcel of real estate upon which is located a dwelling or other residential or commercial structure, and participation interests in such notes—

(i) where such securities are originated by a savings and loan association, savings bank, commercial bank, or similar banking institution which is supervised and examined by a Federal or State authority, and are offered and sold subject to the following conditions:

    (a) the minimum aggregate sales price per purchaser shall not be less than $250,000;

    (b) the purchaser shall pay cash either at the time of the sale or within sixty days thereof; and

    (c) each purchaser shall buy for his own account only; or

(ii) where such securities are originated by a mortgagee approved by the Secretary of Housing and Urban Development pursuant to sections 203 and 211 of the National Housing Act and are offered or sold subject to the three conditions specified in subparagraph (A)(i) to any institution described in such subparagraph or to any insurance company subject to the supervision of the insurance commissioner, or any agency or officer performing like function, of any State or territory of the United States or the District of Columbia, or the Federal Home Loan Mortgage Corporation, the Federal National Mortgage Association, or the Government National Mortgage Association.

(B) Transactions between any of the entities described in subparagraph (A)(i) or (A)(ii) hereof involving non-assignable contracts to buy or sell the foregoing securities which are to be completed within two years, where the seller of the foregoing securities pursuant to any such contract is one of the parties described in subparagraph (A)(i) or (A)(ii) who may originate such securities and the purchaser of such securities pursuant to any such contract in any institution described in subparagraph (A)(i) or any insurance company described in subparagraph (A)(ii), the Federal Home Loan Mortgage Corporation, Federal National Mortgage Association, or the Government National Mortgage Association and where the foregoing securities are subject to the three conditions for sale set forth in subparagraphs (A)(i)(a) through (c).

(C) The exemption provided by subparagraphs (A) and (B) hereof shall not apply to resales of the securities acquired pursuant thereto, unless each of the conditions for sale contained in subparagraphs (A)(i)(a) through (c) are satisfied.

As a conforming amendment, the legislation renumbers the following exemption at subsection (6) of Section 4 as new subsection (5) (Securities Act Sec. 4(5), as amended by the Dodd-Frank Act). That provision exempts transactions involving offers or sales by an issuer solely to one or more accredited investors, subject to certain conditions.

¶4265

▶ **Effective date.** The provision takes effect one day after the date of enactment (Sec. 4 of the Dodd-Frank Wall Street Reform and Consumer Protection Act).

Law source: Law at ¶10,944. Committee Report at ¶54,503.

— Sec. 944 of the Dodd-Frank Wall Street Reform and Consumer Protection Act, striking Securities Act Sec. 4(5);

— Sec. 4, providing the effective date.

¶4270 Due Diligence Analysis

The legislation requires asset-backed security issuers to perform and disclose a due diligence analysis. Within 180 days after the date of enactment, the Commission must issue rules relating to the registration statement required to be filed by any issuer of an asset-backed security that require the issuer: (1) to perform a review of the assets underlying the asset-backed security; and (2) to disclose the nature of the review (Securities Act Sec. 7(d), as added by the Dodd-Frank Wall Street Reform and Consumer Protection Act).

In the legislative history, Congress cited testimony by Professor John Coffee of Columbia Law School calling for action to "re-introduce due diligence into the securities offering process" (S. Rep. No. 111-176, p. 133, citing testimony before the U.S. Senate Committee on Banking, Housing, and Urban Affairs, 111th Congress, 1st sess. (2009), p. 53 (testimony of Professor John Coffee)).

▶ **Effective date.** The provision takes effect one day after the date of enactment (Sec. 4 of the Dodd-Frank Wall Street Reform and Consumer Protection Act).

Law source: Law at ¶10,945. Committee Report at ¶54,504.

— Sec. 945 of the Dodd-Frank Wall Street Reform and Consumer Protection Act, adding Securities Act Sec. 7(d);

— Sec. 4, providing the effective date.

¶4275 Macroeconomic Effects of Risk Retention

The Dodd-Frank Wall Street Reform and Consumer Protection Act directs the Financial Stability Oversight Council to conduct a study of the macroeconomic effects of the risk-retention requirements of the Dodd-Frank Act, with emphasis on the potential beneficial effects with respect to stabilizing the real estate market. The study must include an analysis of the effects of risk retention on real estate asset bubble prices, including a retrospective estimate of what fraction of real estate losses may have been averted had such requirements been in force in recent years (Sec. 946(a) of the Dodd-Frank Wall Street Reform and Consumer Protection Act).

The study must also include an analysis of the feasibility of minimizing real estate price bubbles by proactively adjusting the percentage of risk retention that must be borne by creditors and securitizers of real estate debt, as a function of regional or national market conditions, as well as a comparable analysis for proactively adjusting mortgage origination requirements. The study must assess whether such proactive adjustments should be made by an independent regulator, or in a formulaic and transparent manner, and whether those adjustments should take place independently or in concert with monetary policy (Sec. 946(a) of the Dodd-Frank Act).

Within 180 days after enactment, the Council Chair must submit a report to Congress on the study's findings (Sec. 946(b) of the Dodd-Frank Act).

▶ **Effective date.** The provision takes effect one day after the date of enactment (Sec. 4 of the Dodd-Frank Wall Street Reform and Consumer Protection Act).

Law source: Law at ¶10,946 and ¶10,004.

— Sec. 946(a) of the Dodd-Frank Wall Street Reform and Consumer Protection Act, requiring a Council study on the macroeconomic effects of risk retention;

— Sec. 946(b), requiring a report to Congress;

— Sec. 4, providing the effective date.

EXECUTIVE COMPENSATION and GOVERNANCE

¶4290 Introduction

The Dodd-Frank Wall Street Reform and Consumer Protection Act institutes an array of measures reforming the compensation and governance practices of public companies and financial institutions. The provisions fall under Title IX, Subtitles E (Sections 951–956) and G (Sections 971–973). Among other measures, the legislation requires a shareholder advisory vote on executive compensation, greater independence of compensation committees, and disclosure of hedging by directors and employees. In addition, the legislation authorizes SEC rulemaking on shareholder access to proxy materials.

Background.—The financial crisis was, in part, a failure of corporate governance to orient executive compensation methods away from short-term risk taking and toward long-term value creation. The legislative reforms are designed to end the short-term focus of executive compensation and place compensation on a sound footing that fosters long-term value creation. Governance is the key to ensuring that business decisions are aligned with the company's long-term interest. This, in turn, requires giving shareholders an active role in holding executives accountable.

As part of enhancing corporate governance, the Obama administration called for executive compensation reforms, such as "say on pay" rules that require shareholder votes on executive compensation packages. Although nonbinding, these votes send a strong message to management and boards and help to reinforce a culture of performance, transparency and accountability in executive compensation (*Financial Regulatory Reform, A New Foundation: Rebuilding Financial Supervision and Regulation*, Treasury Department (June 17, 2009), FED. BANK. L. REP. ¶ 75-201).

Shareholders have raised concerns about large corporate bonus plans in situations in which they, as the company's owners, have experienced losses. Currently, these decisions are often not directly reviewed by shareholders, leaving them with limited

¶4290

rights to voice their concerns about compensation through an advisory vote (*Financial Regulatory Reform, A New Foundation, supra*).

Overview.—To facilitate greater communication between shareholders and management regarding executive compensation, public companies must now include on their proxies a nonbinding shareholder vote on executive compensation. Thus, the legislation authorizes SEC "say on pay" rules for public companies that promote greater shareholder participation and increased accountability of board members and management. This measure is explained at ¶ 4295.

A separate measure, discussed at ¶ 4300, ensures greater independence of board compensation committees. Public companies must have a compensation committee composed of independent directors. Similarly, compensation committees must consider independence factors when employing compensation consultants, attorneys and other advisors.

The SEC must adopt rules requiring a company to disclose whether it allows any employee or director to purchase financial instruments, including derivatives such as equity swaps, designed to hedge or offset any decrease in the market value of equity securities granted to the director or employee. This requirement is discussed at ¶ 4315.

In addition, the legislation authorizes the SEC to issue "proxy access" regulations regarding the nomination of directors by shareholders to serve on a company's board of directors, thereby further democratizing corporate governance. For a detailed discussion, see ¶ 4330.

▶ **Effective date.** The provisions take effect one day after the date of enactment (Sec. 4 of the Dodd-Frank Wall Street Reform and Consumer Protection Act).

Law source: Law at ¶ 10,951 and ¶ 10,971. Committee Report at ¶ 50,091, ¶ 54,520 and ¶ 54,560.

— Secs. 951 *et seq.* of the Dodd-Frank Wall Street Reform and Consumer Protection Act, providing executive compensation reforms;

— Secs. 971 *et seq.*, providing corporate governance reforms;

— Sec. 4, providing the effective date.

¶4295 Shareholder Advisory Vote

The Dodd-Frank Wall Street Reform and Consumer Protection Act gives shareholders an advisory vote on executive compensation and "golden parachutes." The "say on pay" measure does not set any limits on pay but ensures that shareholders have an advisory vote on their company's executive pay practices without micromanaging the company. Congress believes that shareholders, as the owners of the corporation, have a right to express their opinion collectively on the appropriateness of executive pay. The vote must be tabulated and reported, but the result is not binding on the board or management (S. Rep. No. 111-176, p. 133).

Purpose.—Explaining the purpose of this provision, the Senate Banking Report quoted the testimony of Ann Yerger, representing the Council of Institutional Investors:

[A]n annual, advisory shareowner vote on executive compensation would efficiently and effectively provide boards with useful information about whether investors view the company's compensation practices to be in shareowners' best interests. Nonbinding shareowner votes on pay would serve as a direct referendum on the decisions of the compensation committee and would offer a more targeted way to signal shareowner discontent than withholding votes from committee members. They might also induce compensation committees to be more careful about doling out rich rewards, to avoid the embarrassment of shareowner rejection at the ballot box. In addition, compensation committees looking to actively rein in executive compensation could use the results of advisory shareowner votes to stand up to excessively demanding officers or compensation consultants (S. Rep. No. 111-176, p. 134).

Executive Compensation.—The Dodd-Frank Act requires any proxy, consent or authorization for a shareholder meeting to elect directors must provide for a separate advisory vote to approve the compensation of executives as disclosed under the SEC compensation disclosure rules for named executive officers (Exchange Act Sec. 14A(a)(1), as added by the Dodd-Frank Wall Street Reform and Consumer Protection Act). The shareholder vote is not binding on either the company or its board and cannot be construed as overruling a decision of the company or board, nor as creating or implying any additional fiduciary duty of the company or board. Similarly, the vote cannot be construed to restrict the shareholders' ability to make proposals for inclusion in the proxy materials related to executive compensation (Exchange Act Sec. 14A(c), as added by the Dodd-Frank Act). This provision applies to shareholder meetings occurring at least six months after the date of enactment (Exchange Act Sec. 14A(a)(3), as added by the Dodd-Frank Act).

Golden Parachutes.—In addition to this non-binding annual shareholder advisory vote on executive compensation, there must also be a shareholder advisory vote on golden parachutes. The proxy on golden parachutes must disclose in clear and simple form as determined by SEC rules any agreements or understandings with named executive officers concerning any type of compensation, whether present, contingent or deferred, that relates to a merger, consolidation or sale of all or almost all of the company's assets. The proxy must also disclose the aggregate total of all such compensation that may be paid and the conditions on which it may be paid. The golden parachute vote must be a separate vote unless the agreements or understandings have been subject to a shareholder vote on executive compensation (Exchange Act Sec. 14A(b), as added by the Dodd-Frank Act).

Frequency of Vote.—The frequency of the shareholder advisory vote on executive compensation must be not less frequently than once every three years (Exchange Act Sec. 14A(a)(1), as added by the Dodd-Frank Act). Moreover, not less frequently than once every six years, a proxy solicitation on compensation disclosure must include a separate shareholder resolution allowing the shareholders to vote on whether there should be an advisory vote on executive compensation every one, two or three years (Exchange Act Sec. 14A(a)(2), as added by the Dodd-Frank Act). In addition, the proxy for the first annual or other shareholder meeting occurring after the end of the six-month period from the date of enactment must include a shareholder advisory vote on executive compensation and a shareholder vote to determine whether shareholder advisory votes will occur every one, two or three years (Exchange Act Sec. 14A(a)(3), as added by the Dodd-Frank Act).

Institutional Investment Managers.—Institutional investment managers must report at least annually how they voted on any shareholder advisory vote on executive compensation or on golden parachutes unless such vote is otherwise required to be reported publicly by SEC rule (Exchange Act Sec. 14A(d), as added by the Dodd-Frank Act).

Exemption.—The SEC may by rule or order exempt an issuer or class of issuers from the required shareholder advisory votes on executive compensation or golden parachutes, taking into account whether the shareholder advisory vote requirements burden small issuers (Exchange Act Sec. 14A(e), as added by the Dodd-Frank Act).

▶ **Effective date.** The provision takes effect one day after the date of enactment (Sec. 4 of the Dodd-Frank Wall Street Reform and Consumer Protection Act).

Law source: Law at ¶10,951 and ¶10,004. Committee Report at ¶54,520.

— Sec. 951 of the Dodd-Frank Wall Street Reform and Consumer Protection Act, adding Exchange Act Sec. 14A;

— Sec. 4, providing the effective date.

¶4300 Independent Compensation Committees

The Dodd-Frank Wall Street Reform and Consumer Protection Act mandates that the members of board compensation committees be independent. The SEC must adopt rules requiring the national securities exchanges and associations to prohibit the listing of any equity security of an issuer that does not comply with the Act's compensation committee independence requirements (Exchange Act Secs. 10C(a)(1) and (2), as added by the Dodd-Frank Wall Street Reform and Consumer Protection Act).

The legislation does not define "independence" and leaves that determination to the exchanges and associations. In defining independence, the exchanges and associations must consider "relevant factors," including: (1) the sources of the director's compensation, including any consulting, advisory or other compensatory fees paid by the issuer; and (2) whether the director is affiliated with the issuer, a subsidiary of the issuer, or an affiliate of a subsidiary of the issuer (Exchange Act Sec. 10C(a)(3), as added by the Dodd-Frank Act).

Exclusions and Exemptions.—The Dodd-Frank Act excludes several categories of issuers from the independence requirement. The excluded issuers are:

- controlled companies (companies in which more than 50 percent of the voting power is held by one individual, group or other issuer);
- limited partnerships;
- companies in bankruptcy;
- Investment Company Act-registered open-ended management investment companies; and

- foreign private issuers that annually disclose to shareholders why they do not have an independent compensation committee (Exchange Act Sec. 10C(a)(1), as added by the Dodd-Frank Act).

The exchanges or associations may exempt a particular relationship from the independence requirements. When granting exemptions, the exchanges and associations must consider the size of an issuer and any other relevant factors (Exchange Act Sec. 10C(a)(4), as added by the Dodd-Frank Act).

Compensation Consultants.—The compensation committee may, in its sole discretion, retain and obtain the advice of a compensation consultant meeting certain independence standards. The SEC must identify factors that affect the independence of a compensation consultant. Issuers must consider these factors before employing any consultants or similar advisors (Exchange Act Sec. 10C(b)(1), as added by the Dodd-Frank Act). The factors must be competitively neutral among the categories of consultants, legal counsel or other advisers and preserve the ability of compensation committees to retain the services of members of any of these categories (Exchange Act Sec. 10C(b)(2), as added by the Dodd-Frank Act). The independence factors must include:

- the provision of other services to the issuer by the person that employs the compensation consultant;
- the amount of fees received from the issuer by the person that employs the compensation consultant, legal counsel or other adviser, as a percentage of the total revenue of the person that employs the compensation consultant;
- the policies and procedures of the person that employs the compensation consultant;
- any business or personal relationship of the compensation consultant with a member of the compensation committee; and
- any stock of the issuer owned by the compensation consultant (Exchange Act Sec. 10C(b)(2), as added by the Dodd-Frank Act).

The compensation committee is directly responsible for the consultant's appointment, compensation and oversight. This oversight cannot be construed to require the compensation committee to implement or follow the consultant's advice, and cannot otherwise affect the committee's ability or obligation to exercise its own judgment (Exchange Act Sec. 10C(c)(1), as added by the Dodd-Frank Act).

Starting one year after enactment, proxies sent in connection with the annual shareholders meeting must disclose whether the compensation committee retained or obtained the advice of a compensation consultant. The proxy must also disclose whether the work of the compensation consultant raised any conflicts of interest and, if so, the nature of the conflict and how the conflict is being addressed (Exchange Act Sec. 10C(c)(2), as added by the Dodd-Frank Act).

Legal Counsel and Other Advisers.—The compensation committee may also, in its sole discretion, retain and obtain the advice of independent counsel and other advisers upon consideration of the same independence factors mentioned above for compensation consultants. The compensation committee must be directly responsible for the appointment, compensation and oversight of the independent counsel and other advisers. This oversight cannot, however, be construed to require the compensation committee to implement or act consistently with the advice or recommendations of the independent counsel and other advisers, and cannot otherwise affect the compensation committee's ability or obligation to exercise its own judgment (Exchange Act Sec. 10C(d), as added by the Dodd-Frank Act).

Funding.—Companies must provide for appropriate funding, as determined by the compensation committee, to pay for compensation consultants and any independent legal counsel or other adviser hired by the committee (Exchange Act Sec. 10C(e), as added by the Dodd-Frank Act).

Rulemaking.—The SEC has 360 days from the date of enactment to adopt the required rules. The final rules must direct the exchanges and securities associations to prohibit the listing of any non-compliant issuer's securities, and must allow an issuer a reasonable opportunity to cure any defects resulting in the prohibition (Exchange Act Secs. 10C(f)(1) and (2), as added by the Dodd-Frank Act).

The rules also must grant the exchanges and associations authority to exempt categories of issuers from the independence requirements. The SROs must evaluate the potential impact of the requirements on smaller reporting issuers when considering any exemptions (Exchange Act Sec. 10C(f)(3), as added by the Dodd-Frank Act).

SEC Study.—The conference committee added an amendment requiring the SEC to study the use and impact of compensation consultants and report to Congress within two years from the statute's enactment (Sec. 952(b) of the Dodd-Frank Act).

▶ **Effective date.** The provision takes effect one day after the date of enactment (Sec. 4 of the Dodd-Frank Wall Street Reform and Consumer Protection Act).

Law source: Law at ¶10,952 and ¶10,004. Committee Report at ¶54,521.

— Sec. 952(a) of the Dodd-Frank Wall Street Reform and Consumer Protection Act, adding Exchange Act Sec. 10C;

— Sec. 952(b), requiring a Commission study of compensation consultants;

— Sec. 4, providing the effective date.

¶4305 "Pay vs. Performance" Disclosure

The Dodd-Frank Wall Street Reform and Consumer Protection Act includes a "pay vs. performance" disclosure requirement for proxy statements. Specifically, the SEC must require companies to disclose in their annual proxy statement a clear description of any compensation required to be disclosed under Regulation S-K Item 402, including information that shows the relationship between executive compensation actually paid and the company's financial performance, taking into account the change in the value of the shares, dividends and distributions (Exchange Act Sec. 14(i), as added by the Dodd-Frank Wall Street Reform and Consumer Protection Act).

Congress believes that a significant concern of shareholders is the relationship between executive pay and the company's financial performance for the benefit of shareholders. Shareholders are keenly interested when executive compensation is increasing sharply at the same time as financial performance is falling. It is expected that these disclosures will add to corporate responsibility as firms will have to more clearly disclose and explain executive pay (S. Rep. No. 111-176, p. 135).

This disclosure about the relationship between executive compensation and the financial performance of the company may include a clear graphic comparison of the amount of executive compensation and the financial performance of the issuer or return to investors and may take many forms. For example, a graph could have a horizontal axis of a number of years and a vertical axis with two scales, one for executive compensation and a second for financial performance of the issuer for each year (S. Rep. No. 111-176, p. 135).

In addition, the SEC must amend Regulation S-K Item 402 to mandate new disclosures in annual reports and proxy statements, among other filings. Under the rule as amended, issuers must disclose:

- the median of the annual total compensation of all employees, except the CEO;
- the annual total compensation of the CEO; and
- the ratio of the two (Sec. 953(b)(1) of the Dodd-Frank Act).

The annual total compensation of an employee must be determined by reference to Regulation S-K Item 402(c)(2)(x) in effect on the date of enactment (Sec. 953(b)(2) of the Dodd-Frank Act).

▶ **Effective date.** The provision takes effect one day after the date of enactment (Sec. 4 of the Dodd-Frank Wall Street Reform and Consumer Protection Act).

Law source: Law at ¶10,953 and ¶10,004. Committee Report at ¶54,522.

— Sec. 953(a) of the Dodd-Frank Wall Street Reform and Consumer Protection Act, adding Exchange Act Sec. 14(i);

— Sec. 953(b), requiring the SEC to amend Regulation S-K Item 402;

— Sec. 4, providing the effective date.

¶4310 Recovery of Erroneously-Awarded Compensation

The Dodd-Frank Wall Street Reform and Consumer Protection Act imposes an executive compensation "clawback" requirement on public companies. Under listing standards mandated by SEC rule, public companies must set policies to recover incentive-based compensation that was paid out based on inaccurate financial statements that do not comply with accounting standards (Exchange Act Sec. 10D, as added by the Dodd-Frank Wall Street Reform and Consumer Protection Act). The clawback is not conditioned on an adjudication of misconduct in connection with the problematic accounting that required restatement. Compensation, including stock options, can be recovered from a current or former executive officer under a three-year look-back period from the date the company has to prepare an accounting restatement based on the erroneous data. The company must recover compensation in excess of what would have been paid to the executive officer if correct accounting procedures had been followed (Exchange Act Sec. 10D(b)(2), as added by the Dodd-Frank Act).

Congress believes that it is unfair to shareholders for companies to allow executives to retain compensation that they were awarded erroneously. The legislation requires companies to establish and implement a policy to recover compensation based on inaccurate accounting so that shareholders do not have to embark on costly litigation to recoup their losses (S. Rep. No. 111-176, p. 136).

▶ **Effective date.** The provision takes effect one day after the date of enactment (Sec. 4 of the Dodd-Frank Wall Street Reform and Consumer Protection Act).

Law source: Law at ¶10,954 and ¶10,004. Committee Report at ¶54,523.

— Sec. 954 of the Dodd-Frank Wall Street Reform and Consumer Protection Act, adding Exchange Act Sec.10D;

— Sec. 4, providing the effective date.

¶4315 Hedging by Directors and Employees

The Dodd-Frank Wall Street Reform and Consumer Protection Act requires disclosure of hedging by directors and employees. The SEC must adopt rules requiring a company to disclose whether it allows any employee or director to purchase financial instruments, including derivatives such as equity swaps, designed to hedge or offset any decrease in the market value of equity securities:

- granted to the employee or director by the company as compensation; or
- held directly or indirectly by the employee or director (Exchange Act Sec. 14(j), as added by the Dodd-Frank Wall Street Reform and Consumer Protection Act).

This provision is designed to allow shareholders to know if executives are allowed to purchase financial instruments to effectively avoid compensation restrictions that they hold stock long-term, so that they will receive their compensation even in the case that their firm does not perform (S. Rep. No. 111-176, p. 136).

▶ **Effective date.** The provision takes effect one day after the date of enactment (Sec. 4 of the Dodd-Frank Wall Street Reform and Consumer Protection Act).

Law source: Law at ¶10,955 and ¶10,004. Committee Report at ¶54,524.

— Sec. 955 of the Dodd-Frank Wall Street Reform and Consumer Protection Act, adding Exchange Act Sec. 14(j);

— Sec. 4, providing the effective date.

¶4320 Incentive-Based Compensation Arrangements

The Dodd-Frank Wall Street Reform and Consumer Protection Act requires enhanced disclosure of incentive-based compensation arrangements offered by banks, credit unions, brokerage firms, investment advisers and other financial institutions. It also mandates regulations prohibiting certain incentive-based compensation arrangements that pose excessive risks.

Enhanced Disclosure.—Within nine months of enactment, the "appropriate federal regulators" must jointly adopt regulations or guidelines to require each "covered financial institution" to disclose the structures of all incentive-based compensation arrangements offered by the firm sufficient to determine whether the compensation structure: (1) provides an executive officer, employee, director or principal shareholder with excessive compensation, fees or benefits; or (2) could lead to material financial loss to the financial institution (Sec. 956(a)(1) of the Dodd-Frank Wall Street Reform and Consumer Protection Act).

A financial institution that does not have an incentive-based payment arrangement need not make these disclosures. Further, disclosure of the actual compensation of particular individuals cannot be required (Sec. 956(a)(2) of the Dodd-Frank Act).

Prohibited Compensation.—Within nine months of enactment, the appropriate federal regulators must jointly adopt regulations or guidelines that prohibit any types of incentive-based payment arrangement, or any feature of any such arrangement, that they determine encourages inappropriate risks by covered financial institutions: (1) by providing an executive officer, employee, director or principal shareholder with excessive compensation, fees or benefits; or (2) that could lead to material financial loss to the firm (Sec. 956(b) of the Dodd-Frank Act).

Standards.—The appropriate federal regulators embraced by these mandates must ensure that any compensation standards they establish by regulation or guideline are comparable to the standards established under the section of the Federal Deposit Insurance Act (12 U.S.C. § 1831p-1) for insured banks and in establishing the compensation standards take into consideration the compensation standards described in FDIA Section 39(c) (12 U.S.C. § 1831p-91(c)) (Sec. 956(c) of the Dodd-Frank Act).

Enforcement.—Regulations issued under this section must be enforced under Gramm-Leach-Bliley Act (GLB) Section 505. A violation of this provision or any regulations adopted under it is treated as a violation of GLB Title V, Subtitle A (Sec. 956(d) of the Dodd-Frank Act).

Definitions.—The term "appropriate federal regulator" means the Board of Governors of the Federal Reserve System, the Office of the Comptroller of the Currency, the Board of Directors of the Federal Deposit Insurance Corporation, the Director of the Office of Thrift Supervision, the National Credit Union Administration Board, the Securities and Exchange Commission, and the Federal Housing Finance Agency (Sec. 956(e)(1) of the Dodd-Frank Act).

The term "covered financial institution" means:

- a depository institution or depository institution holding company, as those terms are defined in Federal Deposit Insurance Act Section 3 (12 U.S.C. § 1813);
- a broker-dealer registered under Exchange Act Section 15;
- a credit union, as described in Federal Reserve Act Section 19(b)(I)(A)(iv);
- an investment adviser, as defined in Advisers Act Section 202(a)(11);
- the Federal National Mortgage Association;
- the Federal Home Loan Mortgage Corporation; and
- any other financial institution that the appropriate federal regulators jointly determine, by rule, should be covered (Sec. 956(e)(2) of the Dodd-Frank Act).

Exempt Firms.—Financial institutions with assets of less than $1 billion are exempt from the mandated regulations and guidelines on incentive-based compensation (Sec. 956(f) of the Dodd-Frank Act).

▶ **Effective date.** The provision takes effect one day after the date of enactment (Sec. 4 of the Dodd-Frank Wall Street Reform and Consumer Protection Act).

Law source: Law at ¶10,956 and ¶10,004. Committee Report at ¶54,525.

— Sec. 956(a) of the Dodd-Frank Wall Street Reform and Consumer Protection Act, requiring regulations mandating incentive-based compensation disclosures;

— Sec. 956(b), requiring regulations prohibiting certain incentive-based compensation arrangements;

— Sec. 956(c), prescribing standards for compensation;

— Sec. 956(d), providing for enforcement;

— Sec. 956(e), defining terms;

— Sec. 956(f), exempting smaller financial institutions;

— Sec. 4, providing the effective date.

¶4325 Proxy Voting by Brokers

The legislation mandates that exchange rules prohibit members that are not beneficial owners of a security from granting a proxy to vote the security in connection with a shareholder vote for the election of directors, executive compensation, or any other significant matter as the SEC may determine by rule, unless the beneficial owner of the security has instructed the member to vote the proxy in accordance with the beneficial owner's voting instructions (Exchange Act Sec. 6(b)(10)(A), as added by the Dodd-Frank Wall Street Reform and Consumer Protection Act).

This provision is designed to ensure that brokers who are not beneficial owners of a security cannot vote through company proxies unless the beneficial owner has instructed the broker to do so. The final vote tallies should reflect the wishes of the beneficial owners of the stock and not be affected by the wishes of the broker that holds the shares (S. Rep. No. 111-176, p. 136).

Nothing in this provision prevents an exchange from prohibiting a member that is not the beneficial owner of a security from granting a proxy to vote the security in connection with a shareholder vote not described in subparagraph (A) (Exchange Act Sec. 6(b)(10)(C), as added by the Dodd-Frank Act).

▶ **Effective date.** The provision takes effect one day after the date of enactment (Sec. 4 of the Dodd-Frank Wall Street Reform and Consumer Protection Act).

Law source: Law at ¶10,957 and ¶10,004. Committee Report at ¶54,526.

— Sec. 957 of the Dodd-Frank Wall Street Reform and Consumer Protection Act, amending Exchange Act Sec. 6(b);

— Sec. 4, providing the effective date.

¶4330 Shareholder Proxy Access

The legislation authorizes the SEC to issue "proxy access" regulations giving shareholders greater influence over the director-nomination process (Exchange Act Sec. 14(a)(2), as added by the Dodd-Frank Wall Street Reform and Consumer Protection Act). The term "proxy access" is shorthand for a framework of rules under which a shareholder may require the corporation to include in its proxy statement and proxy card a person nominated by the shareholder—but not by the board of directors—for election to the board. With this explicit statutory authority, the SEC can more successfully avoid or defend potential litigation by companies and industry groups challenging its power to grant this right.

Past efforts to implement proxy access rules faced strong opposition questioning the Commission's authority. For example, the Business Roundtable stated in a comment letter dated January 19, 2010, "mandatory federal proxy access disregards the 200 years of state corporate law that, through its enabling nature, has permitted the growth and prosperity of corporations of all sizes." In remarks at a May 20, 2009 SEC open meeting, Commissioner Troy Paredes stated that the shareholder access proposal under consideration:

> ... especially proposed Rule 14a-11 dictating a direct right of access to the company's proxy materials, encroaches far too much on internal corporate affairs, the traditional domain of state corporate law. The whole of the proposal is about far more than the driving goal of the '34 Act to empower investors by putting information in their hands. The proposal reaches too far past the point of being about disclosure or even about the voting process. Rather, the fundamental essence of the proposal is to realign corporate control at the federal level.

The provision is a general grant of rulemaking authority to the SEC, and does not include any substantive requirements for shareholder proxy access. Rather, the provision authorizes the SEC to adopt access rules "under such terms and conditions as the Commission determines are in the interests of shareholders and for the protection of investors" (Sec. 971(b) of the Dodd-Frank Act). If the SEC exempts issuers, which it may, the SEC must consider the burden on small issuers (Sec. 971(c) of the Dodd-Frank Act). The powers granted by this provision reduce the possibility of legal challenges to future proxy access rules on the grounds that the SEC exceeded its statutory authority in adopting the measures.

The House Financial Services Committee explained in its summary of the provision that "the SEC will have the clear authority to issue proxy access regulations regarding the nomination of directors by shareholders to serve on a company's board of directors, thereby further democratizing corporate governance." As described by Rep. Maxine Waters (D-CA), Congress believes that proxy access is necessary for shareholders to have a meaningful choice in exercising their right to vote for board members and to hold boards accountable. She noted that the regulation of proxy access and disclosure is a core function of the SEC and is one of the original responsibilities that Congress assigned to the Commission in 1934 (Statement by Rep. Maxine Waters, Nov. 4, 2009).

▶ **Effective date.** The provision takes effect one day after the date of enactment (Sec. 4 of the Dodd-Frank Wall Street Reform and Consumer Protection Act).

Law source: Law at ¶10,971 and ¶10,004. Committee Report at ¶54,561.

— Sec. 971(a) of the Dodd-Frank Wall Street Reform and Consumer Protection Act, amending Exchange Act Sec. 14(a);

— Sec. 971(b), authorizing SEC rulemaking on proxy access;

— Sec. 971(c), providing for exemptions;

— Sec. 4, providing the effective date.

¶4335 Bifurcation of Chair and CEO Role

Bifurcation of the roles of board chairman and CEO is widely acknowledged as a sound governance practice to ensure independence. The legislation calls for rulemaking that requires companies to disclose why they have chosen, or not chosen, to bifurcate the two roles. Specifically, the SEC must adopt rules requiring a company to disclose in the annual proxy sent to investors the reasons why it has chosen:

- the same person to serve as chairman of the board of directors and chief executive officer; or

- different individuals to serve as board chair and chief executive officer (Exchange Act Sec. 14B, as added by the Dodd-Frank Wall Street Reform and Consumer Protection Act).

Congress recognizes that different companies may have good reasons for having the same person as CEO and Chairman or different persons in those positions. Thus, the legislation does not endorse or prohibit either method (S. Rep. No. 111-176, p. 147).

The deadline for rulemaking is 180 days after the date of enactment (Exchange Act Sec. 14B, as added by the Dodd-Frank Act).

▶ **Effective date.** The provision takes effect one day after the date of enactment (Sec. 4 of the Dodd-Frank Wall Street Reform and Consumer Protection Act).

Law source: Law at ¶10,972 and ¶10,004. Committee Report at ¶54,562.

— Sec. 972 of the Dodd-Frank Wall Street Reform and Consumer Protection Act, adding Exchange Act Sec. 14B;

— Sec. 4, providing the effective date.

SEC ORGANIZATION and FUNDING

¶4350 Introduction

The Dodd-Frank Wall Street Reform and Consumer Protection Act includes several provisions designed to improve the Securities and Exchange Commission's organization, management, funding and overall effectiveness. These changes are found in Title IX, Subtitles F (Sections 961 *et seq.*) and J (Section 991).

¶4350

Subtitle F.—This subtitle contains provisions designed to improve SEC management and operations, including several mandated studies of various aspects of the Commission's regulatory regime. For example, the SEC must submit a report on its examinations of registered entities, enforcement investigations and corporate filing reviews to the House and Senate oversight committees (see ¶ 4355). According to the Senate Banking Committee, the purpose of this requirement is to promote complete and consistent performance of SEC staff oversight and to foster appropriate supervision of oversight activities through internal supervisory controls. The committee, citing the Bernard Madoff fraud, stated that "there have been numerous examples where securities misconduct has flourished and investors have been harmed due to failure to follow reasonable procedures" (S. Rep. No. 111-176, p. 137).

In addition, the Comptroller General must submit a report every three years to the congressional oversight committees on personnel management by the SEC (see ¶ 4355). The Commission must report annually to Congress on the agency's internal control structure and procedures for financial reporting, and every three years, the Comptroller General must report to Congress on the SEC's oversight of national securities associations (see ¶ 4355).

The Trading and Markets and Investment Management Division must each establish a staff of examiners to perform compliance inspections and examinations of entities under their jurisdictions and report to the division directors (see ¶ 4360). The Inspector General must establish a hotline for SEC employees to submit confidential suggestions for improving the efficiency and effectiveness of the agency, as well as information concerning waste, abuse, misconduct or mismanagement within the SEC (see ¶ 4365).

The Dodd-Frank Act requires an extensive review of the current securities regulatory regime. The Commission must retain an independent organizational consultant to examine its regulatory practices and to identify necessary reform measures (see ¶ 4355).

Finally, the Comptroller General must study and report to the relevant congressional committees on the so-called "revolving door" at the SEC. The revolving door describes the situation where Commission staff leave the SEC for positions in industries regulated by the Commission (see ¶ 4355).

Subtitle J.—This subtitle deals with changes to the SEC funding mechanism (see ¶ 4370). With regard to its regular appropriation, the SEC's funding level will increase from $1.3 billion in fiscal year 2011 to $2.25 billion in fiscal year 2015. The conference committee decided against granting the SEC's request for self-funding, but did provide for regular authorized appropriations increases and a $100 million reserve fund that the SEC may use in any one fiscal year to pay for items such as technology initiatives and capital improvements.

The Act also made changes to the Exchange Act transaction and Securities Act registration fees. These provisions change the due date for certain fee payments and modify the calculation of mid-year fee adjustments for covered transactions.

▶ **Effective date.** The provisions of Subtitle F take effect one day after the date of enactment (Sec. 4 of the Dodd-Frank Wall Street Reform and Consumer Protection Act). In Subtitle J, Section 991(a) takes effect on the *later* of either October 1, 2011 or the date the SEC's regular appropriation for fiscal year 2012 is enacted. Sections 991(b) and (e) take effect on

October 1, 2011. Sections 991(c) and (d) take effect one day after the date of enactment (Sec. 4 of the Dodd-Frank Act).

Law source: Law at ¶10,961, ¶10,991 and ¶10,004. Committee Report at ¶50,091 and ¶54,540.

— Sec. 961 *et seq.* of the Dodd-Frank Wall Street Reform and Consumer Protection Act, requiring studies and reports on SEC organization and management;

— Sec. 991(a)(1), amending Exchange Act Sec. 31;

— Sec. 991(b), amending Securities Act Sec. 6(b) and Exchange Act Secs. 13(e) and 14(g);

— Sec. 991(c), amending Exchange Act Sec. 35;

— Sec. 991(d), amending Exchange Act Sec. 31;

— Sec. 991(e), adding Exchange Act Sec. 4(i);

— Sec. 4, providing the effective date for Subtitle F and Secs. 991(c) and (d).

¶4355 Studies and Reports

The Dodd-Frank Wall Street Reform and Consumer Protection Act requires the SEC and other entities to review several aspects of the Commission's oversight regime and report their findings to Congress. As discussed below, the required studies and reports relate to SEC supervisory controls, personnel management practices, internal controls, oversight of national securities associations and the so-called SEC "revolving door." Also, an independent consultant must review the overall regulatory structure.

Both the House and Senate were critical of the SEC's performance during the Madoff scandal and the financial crisis. According to the discussion draft released by Rep. Paul Kanjorski, "the failures to detect the Madoff and Stanford Financial frauds demonstrated deep deficiencies and flaws in our existing securities regulatory structure" (Rep. Kanjorski (D-PA), *Discussion Draft of the Investor Protection Act of 2009 Section-by-Section Analysis*, October 1, 2009). The Senate Banking Committee similarly noted that the SEC's failure to detect the Madoff fraud "seriously damaged investor confidence in the effectiveness and competence of regulators" (S. Rep. No. 111-176, p. 137).

Supervisory Controls.—The SEC must report on its examinations of registered entities, enforcement investigations and corporate filings review and assess the effectiveness of the agency's internal supervisory controls and examination procedures. The Commission must report their findings to the House Financial Services Committee and the Senate Banking Committee within 90 days after the end of each fiscal year. The directors of the Divisions of Enforcement and Corporation Finance and the Office of Compliance Inspections and Examinations must certify that the agency has adequate supervisory controls or that they have disclosed any significant deficiencies in the controls to the Commission. If any of these directors have been in their positions for less than 90 days on the reporting date, the Commission may wait and submit the report on the date that the director has served for 90 days. Any acting directors may make the required certification in the case of vacancies in the directorships (Secs. 961(a)–(d) of the Dodd-Frank Act).

The Senate Banking Committee stated that the provision's purpose is to promote the complete and consistent performance of SEC staff examinations, investigations and reviews, and to ensure the appropriate supervision of these activities through internal supervisory controls. The committee also suggested that there may be problems with the agency's rulemaking program and its litigation management practices. According to the committee report, the incidents of courts overturning SEC rulemakings in recent years calls into question whether the process by which the SEC is promulgating final rules should be reexamined and refined (S. Rep. No. 111-176, p. 139).

In addition, the committee noted that the SEC's process for reaching settlement recommendations may need to be re-examined in light of the Bank of America case involving the Merrill Lynch acquisition (S. Rep. No. 111-176, p. 139). In that case, a federal district court rejected an SEC-negotiated settlement and criticized the staff's preparation of the case. Judge Jed Rakoff of the Southern District of New York found that the settlement was neither fair, nor reasonable, nor adequate. It was not fair because it did not comport "with the most elemental notions of justice and morality" because the shareholders who were the victims of the bank's alleged misconduct would pay the penalty for that conduct (*SEC v. Bank of America Corp.* (SD NY 2009), FED. SEC. L. REP. ¶ 95,366).

At least every three years, the Comptroller General must report to the congressional oversight committees on the SEC's control structure and attest to the adequacy and effectiveness of the agency's internal supervisory control structure and procedures. The Comptroller General may hire independent consultants with specialized expertise in any area relevant to assist in these studies and reports (Sec. 961(e) of the Dodd-Frank Act).

Personnel Management Practices.—The Comptroller General must review and report on SEC personnel management practices to the congressional oversight committees every three years. The Comptroller General must evaluate such factors as: supervisory effectiveness, promotion practices, staff competency, communication channels, turnover rates and management structure, including whether the agency employs an excessive number of managerial personnel (Secs. 962(a) and (b) of the Dodd-Frank Act).

The Senate Banking Committee expressed concerns about the Commission's promotion practices and the competence of its investigative personnel. The report noted that the SEC Inspector General's report on the Madoff investigation questioned whether some employees who had been promoted to serve as mid-level supervisors had the "necessary judgment, commitment or temperament to be effective supervisors." According to the committee, this raised questions about the appropriateness of the promotion of these employees to supervisory positions (S. Rep. No. 111-176, p. 140).

Regulated entities also informed the Banking Committee that SEC inspectors have conducted inquiries with a limited knowledge of the business they are reviewing (S. Rep. No. 111-176, p. 141). Because the SEC has been aware of these issues for several years, the committee urged an independent review of the personnel questions by the Comptroller General.

The Act directs the Comptroller General to consult with current and former SEC employees, employee unions, the SEC inspector general, persons that have business before the Commission, private management consultants, academics and any other source that the Comptroller General deems appropriate (Sec. 962(c) of the Dodd-Frank Act).

Within 90 days after the Comptroller General submits its findings, the SEC must report to the oversight committees on its actions taken in response to the report's findings. The Commission must also reimburse the GAO for the costs billed by the Comptroller General in connection with the studies and reports (Secs. 962(d) and (e) of the Dodd-Frank Act).

Internal Controls.—The SEC must submit an annual report to Congress on its internal control structure and procedures for financial reporting. These reports are due within six months from the end of each fiscal year. The Comptroller General must also review the financial reporting controls and the report submitted by the Commission, with the SEC to bear the costs of the Comptroller General's study (Sec. 963 of the Dodd-Frank Act).

The Senate Banking Committee noted that the GAO had found material weaknesses in the SEC's internal control structure. The significant deficiencies involved: (1) information security; (2) financial reporting processes; (3) fund balances with the Treasury; (4) registrant deposits; (5) budgetary resources; and (6) risk assessment and monitoring processes. According to the Banking Committee, the internal control weaknesses raised questions about the security and reliability of the data processed by SEC's information systems. In light of these weaknesses, the committee concluded that an annual review would be appropriate and beneficial (S. Rep. No. 111-176, pp. 141-142).

Oversight of National Securities Associations.—Within two years from the date of enactment, and after that every three years, the Comptroller General must study and report to Congress on the SEC's oversight of national securities associations. The report is intended to promote regular and effective oversight by the SEC of the national securities associations and to inform the Congress in its oversight role of the securities markets (Sec. 964 of the Dodd-Frank Act).

The Senate Banking Committee stated that the SEC should oversee specifically several important functions, including governance and conflicts of interest, examinations, executive compensation practices, cooperation with state securities administrators, funding, arbitration services and association review of member advertising (S. Rep. No. 111-176, p. 142).

One key area of potential conflict highlighted by the Banking Committee involved national securities associations with boards including officers of broker-dealers. Former SEC Chief Accountant Lynn Turner testified that this structure poses an inherent conflict, and he urged Congress to consider creating an independent board comparable to the Public Company Accounting Oversight Board.

Independent Consultant Review.—The SEC must hire an independent consultant to conduct a comprehensive study of the present structure of securities regulation. The study must identify structural and operational reforms and offer administrative and regulatory recommendations designed to identify further modifications aimed at enhancing investor protection at the SEC, FINRA and other self-regulatory organizations. The consultant must examine:

- the possible elimination of unnecessary or redundant agency units;

- the communications systems between offices and divisions;
- the chain-of-command structure, particularly for examinations and inspections;
- the impact of high-frequency trading and other technology-driven issues;
- SEC hiring practices, including appropriate skill sets, diversity and pay issues; and
- the proper relationship between the SEC and SROs and the role of SROs in the regulatory scheme (Sec. 967(a) of the Dodd-Frank Act).

Within 150 days after being retained, the independent consultant must issue a report to the SEC and the Congress containing: (1) a detailed description of any findings and conclusions made while carrying out the study; and (2) recommendations for legislative, regulatory or administrative action that the consultant determines appropriate to enable the SEC and other entities on which it reports to perform their missions (Sec. 967(b) of the Dodd-Frank Act).

The SEC must, within six months from the study's release, report to the House Financial Services Committee and the Senate Banking Committee on its progress in implementing the report's recommendations. For the next two years, the SEC must report on its progress to the two committees (Sec. 967(c) of the Dodd-Frank Act).

Revolving Door Study.—The Comptroller General must study and report to the relevant congressional committees on the so-called "revolving door" at the SEC. The revolving door describes the situation where Commission staff leave the SEC for positions in industries regulated by the Commission. The study must examine:

- the number of employees who leave the Commission to work for financial institutions regulated by the SEC;
- how many departing employees worked on cases that involved financial institutions regulated by the SEC;
- the length of time employees work for the Commission before leaving for jobs with financial institutions regulated by the SEC;
- the SEC's existing internal controls and recommend stricter controls to ensure that employees who later take jobs with financial institutions regulated by the Commission did not help those institutions to violate the SEC's rules while employed at the SEC;
- whether greater post-employment restrictions are necessary to prevent former Commission employees from working for firms regulated by the SEC;
- whether the volume of departing Commission employees taking jobs with SEC-regulated firms has led to inefficiencies in enforcement;
- whether SEC employees who later work for firms regulated by the SEC assisted those firms in circumventing federal rules and regulations while employed by the SEC;
- any information that may address the volume of Commission employees who leave for jobs at SEC-regulated firms and to make recommendations to Congress; and
- additional issues raised during the course of the study (Sec. 968(a) of the Dodd-Frank Act).

¶4355

The comptroller's report must be submitted to the congressional oversight committees within a year following the statute's enactment Reform Act (Sec. 968(b) of the Dodd-Frank Act).

▶ **Effective date.** The provision takes effect one day after the date of enactment (Sec. 4 of the Dodd-Frank Wall Street Reform and Consumer Protection Act).

Law source: Law at ¶10,961, ¶10,962, ¶10,963, ¶10,964, ¶10,967, ¶10,968 and ¶10,004. Committee Report at ¶54,540, ¶54,541, ¶54,542 and ¶54,543.

— Sec. 961 of the Dodd-Frank Wall Street Reform and Consumer Protection Act, requiring the SEC to review and report on its regulatory regime;

— Sec. 962, requiring the GAO to review and report on SEC personnel practices;

— Sec. 963, requiring an annual financial controls audit;

— Sec. 964, requiring the Comptroller General to review and report on SEC oversight of national securities associations;

— Sec. 967, requiring an independent consultant review of the overall securities regulatory structure;

— Sec. 968, requiring the Comptroller General to review and report on the SEC "revolving door";

— Sec. 4, providing the effective date.

¶4360 Examination Staff

The Dodd-Frank Wall Street Reform and Consumer Protection Act includes a measure to strengthen the SEC's examination resources. The Trading and Markets and Investment Management Divisions, and any successors, must employ a staff of examiners to perform compliance inspections and examinations, and to report directly to the division directors (Exchange Act 4(h), as added by the Dodd-Frank Act). According to the Banking Committee, this measure will provide each division internally with experts in inspections and in the regulations of that division. These examiners will be closely acquainted with and have access to the staff who write and interpret those regulations, according to the committee report (S. Rep. No. 111-176, p. 143).

▶ **Effective date.** The provision takes effect one day after the date of enactment (Sec. 4 of the Dodd-Frank Wall Street Reform and Consumer Protection Act).

Law source: Law at ¶10,965 and ¶10,004. Committee Report at ¶54,544.

— Sec. 965 of the Dodd-Frank Wall Street Reform and Consumer Protection Act, adding Exchange Act Sec. 4(h);

— Sec. 4, providing the effective date.

¶4365 SEC Employee Hotline

The Dodd-Frank Wall Street Reform and Consumer Protection Act directs the SEC Inspector General to establish a hotline for SEC employees to submit confidential suggestions for improving agency effectiveness and allegations of waste, misconduct or mismanagement within the Commission (Exchange Act Sec. 4D(a), as added by the Dodd-Frank Act). The Inspector General must report to Congress annually on the suggestions and misconduct allegations received. This report should include the Inspector General's recommendations and actions taken in response to the allegations, and any actions taken in response by the SEC (Exchange Act Sec. 4D(d), as added by the Dodd-Frank Act).

The Senate Banking Committee noted that the Office of the Inspector General has a tradition of analyzing agency activity to prevent abuse and promote effective operations. In addition, the committee report stated that Inspector General is sufficiently independent from the SEC and would have few potential conflicts of interest in reviewing suggestions (S. Rep. No. 111-176, p. 144). The costs of the program will be funded by the SEC Investor Protection Fund established in the whistleblower provisions of the Act.

> **CCH Comment:** Under the House version of the bill, the fund could be used for investor education programs rather than for an Inspector General tip hotline.

▶ **Effective date.** The provision takes effect one day after the date of enactment (Sec. 4 of the Dodd-Frank Wall Street Reform and Consumer Protection Act).

Law source: Law at ¶10,966 and ¶10,004. Committee Report at ¶54,545.

— Sec. 966 of the Dodd-Frank Wall Street Reform and Consumer Protection Act, adding Exchange Act Sec. 4D.

— Sec. 4, providing the effective date.

¶4370 SEC Funding

Title IX, Subtitle J, of Dodd-Frank Wall Street Reform and Consumer Protection Act contains a measure to strengthen SEC funding (Sec. 991 of the Dodd-Frank Act). The Commission's regular appropriation level will increase. In addition, the legislation establishes an SEC Reserve Fund. It also makes changes to the Exchange Act transaction and Securities Act registration fees.

Background.—Late in the resolution process, the House and Senate conferees rejected a provision calling for SEC self-funding. This measure would have allowed the SEC to fund its own operations by using the transaction and registration fees it collects in place of a congressionally-mandated budget and appropriation.

Sen. Richard Shelby (R-AL) proposed an amendment that would leave the SEC subject to the appropriations process. The Act as adopted will, however, provide the SEC with some new budgetary resources. With regard to its regular appropriation, the SEC's funding level will increase from $1.3 billion in fiscal year 2011 to $2.25 billion in fiscal year 2015. The enhanced funding authorization would allow the SEC to expand its enforcement programs and to hire additional staff with industry expertise. Congress will also establish a $100 million reserve fund that the SEC may use in any one fiscal year to pay for items such as technology initiatives and capital improvements. In addition, the Commission will be able to submit its budget directly to Congress, and need not seek prior White House approval.

The SEC has long sought self-funding, which would give the SEC more control over its own budget and funding level. In a June 2010 letter to the conference committee members, the executive council of the Federal Bar Association's securities law committee stated that self-funding was "critical" to reversing the "chronic underfunding" of the SEC. According to the council, the previous appropriations-based funding system severely impeded the SEC's ability to keep pace with market and technology changes.

Sen. Shelby, in questioning self-funding, called the inclusion of the measure "surprising" because it would give the SEC virtual budget autonomy from congressional oversight after the SEC dropped the ball in the Madoff and Stanford frauds. Commenting on his appropriations amendment, Sen. Shelby noted that the revised provision allows the SEC the funding it needs while requiring the agency to be accountable to Congress.

Effective Dates.—Unlike most provisions of Title IX, the SEC funding amendments contains specified effective dates. The changes to Exchange Act Section 31 concerning fees payable by national securities exchanges and associations are effective on the *later* of either October 1, 2011, or the date the SEC's regular appropriation for fiscal year 2012 is enacted (Sec. 991(a) of the Dodd-Frank Act). The Securities Act Section 6(b) registration fee and the Exchange Act Section 13(e) and 14(g) amendments take effect October 11, 2011. For fiscal year 2012, the SEC must publish the Section 6(b) rate on August 31, 2011 (Sec. 991(b) of the Dodd-Frank Act).

The amendments concerning SEC appropriations authorizations and the Commission's budget request do not specify an effective date, and are presumed to take effect one day after the date of enactment (Secs. 4 and 991(c) and (d) of the Dodd-Frank Act). The provisions creating the SEC Reserve Fund are effective October 11, 2011 (Sec. 991(e) of the Dodd-Frank Act).

Appropriations and Budgeting.—Congress may appropriate an increasing amount of money to the SEC for each year for the next five years. The authorized amounts are:

- $1.3 billion for fiscal year 2011;
- $1.5 billion for fiscal year 2012;
- $1.75 billion for fiscal year 2013;
- $2 billion for fiscal year 2014; and
- $2.25 billion for fiscal year 2015 (Exchange Act Sec. 35, as amended by the Dodd-Frank Act).

Beginning in fiscal year 2012, the SEC must simultaneously submit a budget estimate or request to the president and to the congressional oversight and appropriations committees. The budget request must include: (1) an itemization of the amount of the funds necessary to carry out agency function; (2) an amount designated as contingency funding to address unanticipated needs; and (3) a designation of any activities for which multi-year budget authority would be suitable.

The President will submit the SEC budget annually to Congress without changes, along with the administration's annual budget proposal. This change allows the SEC to provide Congress with its budget request without obtaining prior White House approval (Exchange Act Sec. 31(m), as added by the Dodd-Frank Act).

SEC Reserve Fund.—The Act establishes a separate fund in the Treasury for use by the Commission. The SEC will deposit any registration fees it collects under Securities Act Section 6(b) and Investment Company Act Section 24(f) into this account, known as the Securities and Exchange Commission Reserve Fund. The maximum amount to be deposited into the reserve fund in any one fiscal year is $50 million, and the overall balance of the reserve fund cannot exceed $100 million. If the SEC collects fees subject to deposit in excess of these limitations, the fees will be transferred to the Treasury's general fund.

The SEC may use available amounts in the reserve fund, up to a total of $100 million in any one fiscal year, as it deems necessary to carry out its functions. Unused amounts in the reserve fund remain available to the SEC until expended. Within 10 days from the date the SEC draws upon the reserve fund, the agency must notify Congress of the date, amount and purpose of the withdrawal. The amounts deposited in the reserve fund cannot be construed to be government funds or appropriated monies and are not subject to apportionment (Exchange Act Sec. 4(i), as added by the Dodd-Frank Act).

Fee Provisions.—The Act makes changes to the transaction fee provisions in Exchange Act Sections 13(e), 14(g) and 31, and the registration fee language in Securities Act Section 6(b). Under Exchange Act Section 31, each exchange and association must pay the Commission twice annually a fee based on the aggregate dollar amount of certain sales of securities. The Act states that the SEC must collect transaction fees and assessments that are designed to recover the costs to the government of the SEC's annual appropriation. The SEC must publish notice of the fee and assessment rates for each fiscal year. As amended, the SEC must publish its fee notice within 30 days from the enactment of its regular appropriation, as compared to the previous deadline of April 30 of the preceding fiscal year. This change will allow the SEC to more accurately set its fees and assessments to recover the amount of its appropriation. Finally, the Act modifies the formula for computing mid-year adjustments to the Section 31 fee rates (Exchange Act Sec. 31, as amended by the Dodd-Frank Act).

The annual publication deadline for the notice of Securities Act Section 6(b) registration fee rates is now August 31 of the preceding year, rather than the previous April 30 deadline. The later deadline is intended to give the Commission a better picture of the level of market activity and the projected amount of securities that will be registered during the period. Transaction fees for issuer purchases and tender offers Exchange Act Sections 13(e) and 14(g) are pegged to the Section 6(b) rate, and must be published and will take effect in accordance with the Section 6(b) provisions (Exchange Act Secs. 13(e) and 14(g), and Securities Act Sec. 6(b), as amended by the Dodd-Frank Act).

▶ **Effective date.** Section 991(a) takes effect on the *later* of either October 1, 2011 or the date the SEC's regular appropriation for fiscal year 2012 is enacted (Sec. 991(a)(2) of the Dodd-Frank Wall Street Reform and Consumer Protection Act). Subsections (b) and (e) take effect October 1, 2011 (Secs. 991(b)(4) and (e)(2) of the Dodd-Frank Act). Subsections (c) and (d) take effect one day after the date of enactment (Sec. 4 of the Dodd-Frank Act).

Law source: Law at ¶10,991. Committee Report at ¶50,091.

— Sec. 991(a) of the Dodd-Frank Wall Street Reform and Consumer Protection Act, amending Exchange Act Sec. 31;

— Sec. 991(b), amending Exchange Act Secs. 13(e) and 14(g), and Securities Act Sec. 6(b), making conforming amendments to Exchange Act Sec. 31;
— Sec. 991(c), amending Exchange Act Sec. 35;
— Sec. 991(d), adding Exchange Act Sec. 31(m);
— Sec. 991(e), establishing the SEC Reserve Fund.

MUNICIPAL SECURITIES

¶4380 Introduction

The Dodd-Frank Wall Street Reform and Consumer Protection Act includes measures to reform the regulation and stability of the municipal securities industry. These provisions fall under Title IX, Subtitle H (Sec. 975 *et seq.* of the Dodd-Frank Wall Street Reform and Consumer Protection Act). The $3 trillion municipal securities market has historically been subject to substantially less supervision than the corporate securities markets, and given the less stringent regulation of the municipal securities industry generally, market participants have less information on which to base investment decisions (S. Rep. No. 111-176, p. 38).

Many municipalities suffered significant losses during the financial crisis as a result of investment in complex derivatives products marketed by unregulated financial intermediaries. Thus, Subtitle H is designed to strengthen oversight of the municipal securities industry and broaden municipal securities market protections to cover those unregulated market participants and their financial transactions with municipal entities (S. Rep. No. 111-176, p. 147).

To increase federal oversight, the Dodd-Frank Act requires municipal advisors to register with the SEC. The term "municipal advisors" refers to those entities that provide advice to municipal entities regarding the issuance of municipal securities and the use of municipal derivatives, as well as advice concerning the investment of proceeds. The SEC must adopt the rules and forms necessary for municipal advisor registration and any additional rules necessary to implement the antifraud prohibitions imposed on these advisors. Registered municipal advisors are also subject to sanctions and recordkeeping procedures as determined by the Commission. These provisions are intended to provide more equivalent regulatory structures for municipal advisors and other financial intermediaries (discussed at ¶ 4385).

The Dodd-Frank Act also requires changes to the rules governing the composition and operation of the Municipal Securities Rulemaking Board (MSRB). The amendments bring certain additional activities under MSRB oversight and provide the MSRB with additional rulemaking authority. The activities of previously unregulated municipal advisors are now subject to MSRB regulation to the same extent as brokers, dealers and municipal securities dealers engaging in municipal securities transactions, and the MSRB may adopt rules concerning the operations of these entities and their professional standards. According to the legislative history, the MSRB is better suited to provide the necessary level of oversight, given its municipal securities expertise.

¶4380

However, the SEC must continue to oversee MSRB operations and has responsibility for disciplinary actions involving violations of MSRB rules (discussed at ¶ 4395).

In addition, the legislation creates a new Office of Municipal Securities within the SEC to administer the Commission's rules regarding municipal securities transactions and market participants. The Office must coordinate with the MSRB, and legislators intend for this new office to help the SEC monitor the municipal securities industry more effectively (discussed at ¶ 4400).

Subject to the limitations of Exchange Act Section 15B, the SEC now may also require registered national securities associations to establish reasonable annual accounting support fees designed to provide adequate funding for the Governmental Accounting Standards Board. The Commission may also require these associations to consult with state and local representatives when adopting procedures providing for assessment, collection and remittance of these fees from association members (discussed at ¶ 4405).

The Dodd-Frank Act also mandates studies by the SEC and the Comptroller General to obtain further information regarding certain aspects of municipal securities market participants and their transactions with each other. The studies include consideration of the sufficiency of disclosures by municipal securities issuers, investor protection in the municipal securities markets and the adequacy of the funding available to the Government Accounting Standards Board to oversee the municipal securities industry (discussed at ¶ 4410).

▶ **Effective date.** Section 975 and the amendments made by that section take effect on October 1, 2010 (Sec. 975(i) of the Dodd-Frank Wall Street Reform and Consumer Protection Act). The remaining provisions in Subtitle H take effect one day after the date of enactment (Sec. 4 of the Dodd-Frank Act).

Law source: Law at ¶¶10,975 and ¶10,004. Committee Report at ¶¶50,091 and ¶54,580.

— Sec. 975 *et seq.* of the Dodd-Frank Wall Street Reform and Consumer Protection Act, implementing registration, disclosure and other requirements for the municipal securities industry;

— Sec. 975(i), providing the effective date of Sec. 975;

— Sec. 4, providing the general effective date.

¶4385 Municipal Advisor Registration

The Dodd-Frank Wall Street Reform and Consumer Protection Act establishes municipal advisors as a new category of SEC registrant. In general, municipal advisors are those individuals and firms that provide advice to municipal entities regarding the issuance of municipal securities and the use of municipal derivatives. Previously, municipal advisors did not have to register with the Commission, but Congress found that registration is, in fact, necessary to level the regulatory playing field and provide additional investor protection (S. Rep. No. 111-176, p. 147–148).

Under the amended provisions, no municipal advisor may provide advice to, or on behalf of, a municipal entity or obligated person regarding municipal financial products or the issuance of municipal securities, or undertake a solicitation of a municipal entity or obligated person, without properly registering (Exchange Act Sec. 15B(a)(1)(B), as added by the Dodd-Frank Wall Street Reform and Consumer Protection Act).

Municipal advisors must register with the SEC by filing an application for registration in the form prescribed by the Commission. The SEC must decide whether to grant registration or institute proceedings to determine whether registration should be denied (Exchange Act Sec. 15B(a)(2), as amended by the Dodd-Frank Act). The Commission may also exempt any municipal advisor or class of advisors from the registration requirements if it determines that exemption is consistent with the public interest and investor protection (Exchange Act Sec. 15B(a)(4), as amended by the Dodd-Frank Act).

Antifraud Provision.—The amendments also contain an antifraud provision prohibiting municipal advisors from making use of the mails or other means of interstate commerce to provide advice to or on behalf of a municipal entity regarding municipal financial products or participation in the issuance of municipal securities, or to undertake a solicitation of a municipal entity, if the advisor uses any fraudulent, deceptive, or manipulative act or practice to do so (Exchange Act Sec. 15B(a)(5), as added by the Dodd-Frank Act).

"Municipal Advisor."— The term "municipal advisor" means a person who is not a municipal entity or an employee of a municipal entity that:

- provides advice to or on behalf of a municipal entity or obligated person with respect to municipal financial products or the issuance of municipal securities, including advice with respect to the structure, timing, terms and other similar matters concerning such financial products or issues; or
- undertakes a solicitation of a municipal entity (Exchange Act Sec. 15B(e)(4)(A), as added by the Dodd-Frank Act).

The term also includes any financial advisors, guaranteed investment contract brokers, third-party marketers, placement agents, solicitors, finders and swap advisors that fall within the categories described above (Exchange Act Sec. 15B(e)(4)(B), as added by the Dodd-Frank Act). However, the following do not qualify as municipal advisors:

- brokers, dealers or municipal securities dealers serving as underwriters;
- investment advisers registered under the Advisers Act;
- any commodity trading advisor registered under the Commodity Exchange Act or persons associated with a commodity trading advisor who are providing advice related to swaps; and
- persons associated with investment advisers, including attorneys providing services of a traditional legal nature and engineers providing engineering advice (Exchange Act Sec. 15B(e)(4)(C), as added by the Dodd-Frank Act).

The terms "person associated with a municipal advisor" and "associated person of an advisor" refer to:

- any partner, officer, director or branch manager of a municipal advisor, as well as any person occupying a similar status or performing similar functions;

¶4385

- any other employee of a municipal advisor who is engaged in the management or performance of activities relating to the provision of investment advice to or on behalf of a municipal entity or obligated person with respect to municipal financial products and the issuance of municipal securities; and
- any person directly or indirectly controlling, controlled by or under common control with a municipal advisor (Exchange Act Sec. 15B(e)(7), as added by the Dodd-Frank Act).

"Municipal Entity."— The following qualify as "municipal entities":

- states, political subdivisions of states, or municipal corporate instrumentalities of states;
- agencies, authorities or instrumentalities of states, political subdivisions or municipal corporate instrumentalities;
- plans, programs or pools of assets sponsored or established by any of the foregoing entities; and
- any other issuers of municipal securities (Exchange Act Sec. 15B(e)(8), as added by the Dodd-Frank Act).

Other Definitions.—A "solicitation of a municipal entity or obligated person" is a direct or indirect communication made by a person who, for compensation, contacts a municipal entity or obligated person on behalf of a broker, dealer, municipal securities dealer, municipal advisor or investment adviser not associated with the solicitor for the purpose of obtaining an engagement by the municipal entity or obligated person in connection with municipal financial products or the issuance of municipal securities or, in the case of an investment adviser, investment advisory services for the municipal entity (Exchange Act Sec. 15B(e)(9), as added by the Dodd-Frank Act).

An "obligated person" is any person (including an issuer of municipal securities) who is either generally, or through an enterprise, fund, or account, committed by contract to support the payment of obligations on municipal securities sold in an offering (Exchange Act Sec. 15B(e)(10), as added by the Dodd-Frank Act).

A "guaranteed investment contract" is any investment that has specified withdrawal or reinvestment provisions and a specifically negotiated or bid interest rate and any agreement to supply investments on two or more future dates, such as a forward supply contract (Exchange Act Sec. 15B(e)(2), as added by the Dodd-Frank Act).

The term "investment strategies" includes plans or programs for the investment of the proceeds of municipal securities that are not municipal derivatives, guaranteed investment contracts and the recommendation of and brokerage of municipal escrow investments (Exchange Act Sec. 15B(e)(3), as added by the Dodd-Frank Act).

The more general "municipal financial product" refers to municipal derivatives, guaranteed investment contracts and investment strategies (Exchange Act Sec. 15B(e)(5), as added by the Dodd-Frank Act).

▶ **Effective date.** The provision and the amendments made by it take effect on October 1, 2010 (Sec. 975(i) of the Dodd-Frank Wall Street Reform and Consumer Protection Act).

Law source: Law at ¶10,975. Committee Report at ¶54,580.

— Sec. 975(a) of the Dodd-Frank Wall Street Reform and Consumer Protection Act, amending Exchange Act Sec. 15B(a);

— Sec. 975(e), adding Exchange Act Sec. 15B(e);

— Sec. 975(i), providing the effective date.

¶4390 Broker-Dealer Regulation

The Dodd-Frank Wall Street Reform and Consumer Protection Act extends the requirements of Exchange Act Section 15(b) to municipal advisors. Section 15(b) provides for censure, bar, suspension or revocation of the registration of broker-dealers for enumerated activities and violations by the broker-dealer or an associated person. As amended, the law permits the SEC to impose sanctions if it finds that the broker-dealer or an associated person has been convicted within 10 years preceding registration or at any time thereafter of any felony or misdemeanor, within or without the United States, that arose out of the conduct of a municipal advisor (Exchange Act Sec. 15(b)(4)(B)(ii), as amended by the Dodd-Frank Act). The Commission may also impose sanctions if a broker or dealer has been permanently or temporarily enjoined by a court from acting as a municipal advisor (Exchange Act Sec. 15(b)(4)(C), as amended by the Dodd-Frank Act).

The legislation amends Exchange Act Section 15(c), an antifraud provision governing the activities of broker-dealers and associated persons. The amendments clarify that all brokers and dealers are prohibited from engaging in manipulative, deceptive and other fraudulent behavior to the same extent as municipal securities dealers (Exchange Act Sec. 15(c), as amended by the Dodd-Frank Act).

The legislation amends Exchange Act Section 17(a)(1) to require that any national securities exchange or exchange member, broker or dealer who transacts business in securities through a registered municipal advisor must make and keep records for any period as prescribed by the SEC and furnish copies as requested. Those transacting business in securities through a municipal advisor must also complete and disseminate reports as the Commission may deem necessary or appropriate in the public interest (Exchange Act Sec. 17(a)(1), as amended by the Dodd-Frank Act).

▶ **Effective date.** The provision and the amendments made by it take effect on October 1, 2010 (Sec. 975(i) of the Dodd-Frank Wall Street Reform and Consumer Protection Act).

Law source: Law at ¶10,975. Committee Report at ¶54,580.

— Sec. 975(g) of the Dodd-Frank Wall Street Reform and Consumer Protection Act, amending Exchange Act Secs. 15(b) and (c);

— Sec. 975(h), amending Exchange Act Sec. 17(a)(1);

— Sec. 975(i), providing the effective date.

¶4395 Municipal Securities Rulemaking Board

The Dodd-Frank Wall Street Reform and Consumer Protection Act imposes requirements on the composition and operations of the Municipal Securities Rulemaking Board (MSRB). It also brings certain activities under MSRB oversight and provides the MSRB with additional authority. According to Ronald A. Stack, the current MSRB Chair, investors in the municipal securities market will benefit from more stringent standards to govern market professionals and to limit fraudulent activities by requiring fair treatment of investors and issuers and increasing transparency and applicable professional standards (S. Rep. No. 111-176, p. 148). The legislators determined that this responsibility for new regulations should be assigned directly to the MSRB because the SEC has very few staff members with expertise in municipal securities and because the MSRB has more resources at its disposal (S. Rep. No. 111-176, p. 149).

The amendments also change the requirements pertaining to MSRB membership and provide the MSRB with additional rulemaking authority to effectively govern the municipal securities activities of brokers, dealers, municipal securities dealers and municipal advisors; the activities of previously unregulated municipal advisors are now subject to MSRB regulation to the same extent as brokers, dealers and municipal securities dealers engaging in municipal securities transactions. The MSRB may adopt rules concerning the operations of these entities and may also set professional standards for their employees. In connection with these rules, the MSRB must collect data regarding the business operations of entities engaging in municipal securities transactions and must also conduct compliance examinations. The SEC must continue to maintain oversight of the MSRB and is responsible for disciplinary actions involving violations of MSRB rules.

Composition.—The MSRB must be composed of 15 members or another number of members if specified by the Board's rules (Exchange Act Sec. 15B(b)(1), as amended by the Dodd-Frank Act). Of these 15 members, eight individuals must be independent of any municipal securities broker, municipal securities dealer or municipal advisor. Of those eight individuals, at least one member must represent the interests of institutional or retail municipal securities investors, and one member must represent the interests of municipal entities. These eight members must also include at least one member of the public that has specialized knowledge of or experience involving the municipal securities industry (Exchange Act Sec. 15B(b)(1), as amended by the Dodd-Frank Act).

The other seven members must be individuals who are associated with brokers, dealers, municipal securities dealers or municipal advisors, including at least one individual associated with and a representative of brokers, dealers or municipal securities dealers that are not banks or divisions of banks, at least one individual associated with and a representative of municipal securities dealers that are banks or divisions of banks, and at least one individual associated with a municipal advisor. Each member of the MSRB must be knowledgeable of matters related to the municipal securities markets (Exchange Act Sec. 15B(b)(1), as amended by the Dodd-Frank Act).

The MSRB must adopt rules governing the nomination and election of the above-discussed public representatives, broker and dealer representatives, bank representatives and advisor representatives and must ensure fair representation during all nominations and elections. These rules must distinctly provide that the MSRB's membership be as evenly divided as possible between those subject to its oversight and those that are not. However, a majority of the members must always qualify as public representatives. The MSRB must adopt rules specifying the length of terms to be served by members and establishing specific requirements regrading the independence of public representatives. The MSRB has discretion concerning increasing the number of its members provided that it is always an odd number (Exchange Act Sec. 15B(b)(2)(B), as amended by the Dodd-Frank Act).

MSRB members must serve for three-year terms or for any other terms specified by the MSRB rules (Exchange Act Sec. 15B(b)(1)(B), as amended by the Dodd-Frank Act).

Rulemaking Authority.—In addition to distinctly retaining the MSRB's authority to adopt rules governing municipal securities transactions, the amendments also permit it to adopt rules pertaining to the advice provided to or on behalf of municipal entities or obligated persons by brokers, dealers, municipal securities dealers and municipal advisors with respect to municipal financial products, the issuance of municipal securities or participation in the issuance of municipal securities, as well as solicitations of municipal entities or obligated persons undertaken by brokers, dealers, municipal securities dealers and municipal advisors (Exchange Act Sec. 15B(b)(2), as amended by the Dodd-Frank Act).

At a minimum, new rules adopted pursuant to these amendments must state that no broker, dealer, municipal securities dealer or municipal advisor may provide advice on these issues without meeting preset standards of operational capability and training, experience and competence. In creating these standards, the MSRB may classify municipal securities brokers, municipal securities dealers and municipal advisors by type and apply specific rules on the basis of these classifications (Exchange Act Sec. 15B(b)(2)(A), as amended by the Dodd-Frank Act).

All MSRB rules must be designed to prevent fraud and promote cooperation and coordination among regulators, transaction facilitators and information gatherers dealing with municipal securities and municipal financial products in order to protect investors and municipal entities and to discourage unfair discrimination among customers, municipal entities, obligated persons, municipal securities brokers, municipal securities dealers and municipal advisors (Exchange Act Sec. 15B(b)(2)(C), as amended by the Dodd-Frank Act).

The MSRB may also establish the terms and conditions under which a broker, dealer or municipal securities dealer may sell or be prohibited from selling any part of a new issue of municipal securities to a related account of a broker, dealer or municipal securities dealer (Exchange Act Sec. 15B(b)(2)(K), as amended by the Dodd-Frank Act).

The amendments also authorize the adoption of rules designed to prevent acts, practices and courses of business inconsistent with a municipal advisor's fiduciary duty to its clients and the adoption of professional standards and continuing education requirements for municipal advisors. However, in adopting rules, the MSRB cannot impose any regulatory burden on small municipal advisors that is not necessary or appropriate in the public interest or for investor protection (Exchange Act Sec. 15B(b)(2)(L), as added by the Dodd-Frank Act).

Other Authority.—The amendments also provide for MSRB determination as to whether arbitration of issues involving the provision of advice regarding municipal financial products is appropriate. However, no person other than a municipal securities broker, municipal securities dealer or municipal advisor may be compelled to submit to arbitration (Exchange Act Sec. 15B(b)(2)(D), as amended by the Dodd-Frank Act).

The MSRB must also issue rules that provide for periodic examination of municipal securities brokers, municipal securities dealers and municipal advisors (Exchange Act Sec. 15B(b)(2)(E), as amended by the Dodd-Frank Act). In addition, the MSRB must determine what records should be made and kept by municipal securities brokers, municipal securities dealers and municipal advisors and for how long those records should be preserved (Exchange Act Sec. 15B(b)(2)(G), as amended by the Dodd-Frank Act). In general, the MSRB cannot require an issuer of municipal securities to furnish the MSRB or prospective purchasers with any application, report or document through a municipal securities broker, municipal securities dealer or municipal advisor. However, it may require disclosure of applications, reports or documents that are generally available from a source other than the issuer (Exchange Act Sec. 15B(d)(2), as amended by the Dodd-Frank Act).

Municipal securities brokers, municipal securities dealers and municipal advisors may also be required to pay fees as necessary to defray the MSRB's operational costs. The MSRB must specify the amount of any fees and charges imposed, which may include charges for failure to submit any items of information or documents required under MSRB rules in a timely manner (Exchange Act Sec. 15B(b)(2)(J), as amended by the Dodd-Frank Act).

The MSRB may provide guidance and assistance to the Commission or other appropriate regulatory agency or association concerning the enforcement of, and examination for, compliance with the Board's rules (Exchange Act Sec. 15B(b)(4), as added by the Dodd-Frank Act).

Information Systems and Fees.—The MSRB, in conjunction with other financial regulators or self-regulatory organizations, may establish information systems to manage the data received from municipal market participants and assess reasonable fees and charges for the submission of information to, or the receipt of information from, these systems for the purposes of continuing to serve as an information repository for market participants or otherwise operate in furtherance of regulatory purposes (Exchange Act Sec. 15B(b)(3), as amended by the Dodd-Frank Act).

No fees may be charged to municipal entities or obligated persons to submit documents or information to the MSRB or to any person seeking to obtain documents or information submitted by municipal entities, obligated persons, brokers, dealers, municipal securities dealers or municipal advisors directly from the MSRB's website. However, the MSRB is not prohibited from charging commercially reasonable fees for any automated subscription-based feeds or similar services or from charging for other data or document-based services containing this information that are customized on the request of any person or made available to commercial enterprises, municipal securities market professionals or the general public, regardless of whether the information is delivered online or through other means. These fees are subject to Commission approval (Exchange Act Sec. 15B(b)(3)(B), as amended by the Dodd-Frank Act).

¶4395

CCH Comment: According to Section 975(b)(3) of the Dodd-Frank Act, the existing text of Exchange Act Section 15B(b)(3) is to be redesignated as Section 15B(b)(7). However, the Dodd-Frank Act does not note any amendments for subparagraph (6). It is likely that this is a technical error and that Section 15B(b)(3) should be redesignated as Section 15B(b)(6).

Meetings.—The MSRB, the Commission, and a registered securities association, or their designees, must meet at least twice a year to describe their work concerning regulation of municipal securities and to share information regarding interpretation of their rules. The group must also discuss examinations concerning, and enforcement of, compliance with MSRB rules (Exchange Act Sec. 15B(b)(5), as added by the Dodd-Frank Act).

Discipline by SEC.—Exchange Act Section 15B(c) establishes the supremacy of the MSRB and prohibits transactions made in contravention of its rules. The section also describes the SEC's authority to sanction municipal securities dealers by censure and placing limitations on activities. The Commission may also suspend or revoke a dealer's registration. To impose sanctions, the SEC must find that the dealer has:

- made willful misstatements in applications for registration or in other required SEC filings, or during SEC registration proceedings, or omitted a required material fact from an application or report;
- been convicted within the preceding 10 years of certain felonies and misdemeanors;
- been permanently or temporarily enjoined from acting in certain financial capacities, including as an investment adviser, an underwriter, a broker, or a dealer;
- willfully violated the federal securities laws and regulations or the MSRB rules;
- willfully aided, abetted, counseled, commanded, induced or procured a violation of any of the federal securities laws by another person or failed to reasonably supervise a subordinate; or
- violated foreign securities laws (Exchange Act Sec. 15B(c)(2), as amended by the Dodd-Frank Act).

Registration may also be voluntarily withdrawn by the entity or cancelled by the Commission due to inactivity (Exchange Act Sec. 15B(c)(3), as amended by the Dodd-Frank Act).

The Commission may censure or place limitations on the activities or functions of any person who is, or at the time of the alleged misconduct was, associated with or seeking to become associated with a municipal securities dealer (Exchange Act Sec. 15B(c)(4), as amended by the Dodd-Frank Act).

The Dodd-Frank Act makes municipal advisors subject to these same obligations and disciplinary procedures and provides municipal entities and obligated persons with the same protections afforded to investors generally. In addition, the amendments to Section 15B(c) prohibit brokers, dealers, municipal securities dealers and municipal advisors from using the mails or any means or instrumentality of interstate commerce to provide advice to or on behalf of a municipal entity or obligated person regarding municipal financial products or the issuance of municipal securities or to undertake a solicitation of a municipal entity or obligated person in contravention of MSRB rules (Exchange Act Sec. 15B(c)(1), as amended by the Dodd-Frank Act).

Any fines collected by the Commission for violations of MSRB rules must be equally divided between the Commission and the MSRB. Fines collected by a registered securities association under Exchange Act Section 15A(7) with respect to MSRB rule violations must be accounted for separately by the association and allocated between the association and the MSRB. This allocation must involve the registered securities association paying to the Board one-third of all fines reasonably allocable to violations of MSRB rules or any other portion as directed by the Commission upon agreement between the association and the MSRB (Exchange Act Sec. 15B(c)(9), as added by the Dodd-Frank Act).

The Commission may administer any competency and skill tests required by the Board for municipal advisors (Exchange Act Sec. 15B(c)(7), as amended by the Dodd-Frank Act).

Fiduciary Duty.—A municipal advisor and its associated persons is deemed to owe a fiduciary duty to any municipal entity for whom the advisor acts as a municipal advisor and cannot engage in any act, practice or course of business inconsistent with this duty or in contravention of MSRB rules (Exchange Act Sec. 15B(c)(1), as amended by the Dodd-Frank Act).

Registered Securities Associations.—An association of brokers and dealers cannot register as a national securities association unless the Commission determines that the association's rules require it to request guidance from the MSRB when interpreting MSRB rules and to provide information directly to the MSRB about enforcement actions and examinations executed by the association under Exchange Act Section 15B(b)(2)(E). This change was made to enable the MSRB to more readily assist in enforcement actions and examinations undertaken by associations and to properly evaluate the ongoing effectiveness of its rules (Exchange Act Sec. 15A(b)(15), as added by the Dodd-Frank Act).

▶ **Effective date.** The provision and the amendments made by it take effect on October 1, 2010 (Sec. 975(i) of the Dodd-Frank Wall Street Reform and Consumer Protection Act).

Law source: Law at ¶10,975. Committee Report at ¶54,580.

— Sec. 975(b) of the Dodd-Frank Wall Street Reform and Consumer Protection Act, amending Exchange Act Sec. 15B(b);

— Sec. 975(c), amending Exchange Act Sec. 15B(c);

— Sec. 975(d), amending Exchange Act Sec. 15B(d)(2);

— Sec. 975(f), adding Exchange Act Sec. 15A(b)(15);

— Sec. 975(i), providing the effective date.

¶4400 Office of Municipal Securities

The Dodd-Frank Wall Street Reform and Consumer Protection Act establishes a new Office of Municipal Securities within the SEC (Sec. 979 of the Dodd-Frank Act). Over the last few years, the Commission has reduced the staff devoted to the existing municipal securities office within the SEC. Congress expects that the creation of the new office will enable the SEC to monitor the municipal markets more effectively (S. Rep. No. 111-176, p. 152).

The Office has responsibility for administering SEC rules concerning the practices of municipal securities brokers and dealers, municipal securities advisors, municipal securities investors and municipal securities issuers. For the purposes of engaging in rulemakings and enforcement actions related to these rules, the Office must coordinate with the Municipal Securities Rulemaking Board as required by law (Sec. 979(a) of the Dodd-Frank Act).

The director of the Office must report to the SEC Chair and is responsible for the staff necessary to sufficiently to carry out the Office's responsibilities. The Office staff must include individuals with specific knowledge of, and expertise in, municipal finance (Secs. 979(b) and (c) of the Dodd-Frank Act).

▶ **Effective date.** The provision takes effect one day after the date of enactment (Sec. 4 of the Dodd-Frank Wall Street Reform and Consumer Protection Act).

Law source: Law at ¶10,979 and ¶10,004. Committee Report at ¶54,584.

— Sec. 979 of the Dodd-Frank Wall Street Reform and Consumer Protection Act, establishing the Office of Municipal Securities within the SEC;

— Sec. 4, providing the effective date.

¶4405 Governmental Accounting Standards Board Funding

The Dodd-Frank Wall Street Reform and Consumer Protection Act provides for funding of the Governmental Accounting Standards Board (GASB). Subject to the limitations of Exchange Act Section 15B, the SEC may require registered national securities associations to establish reasonable annual accounting support fees designed to provide adequate funding for the GASB. The Commission may also require these associations to consult with representatives of state and local officials and financial officers in order to adopt rules and procedures providing for equitable allocation, assessment, collection and remittance of these fees from association members (Securities Act Sec. 19(g)(1), as added by the Dodd-Frank Act).

Any fees or funds collected in this manner must be used to support the GASB's efforts in establishing financial accounting and reporting standards to be recognized as generally accepted accounting principles applicable to state and local governments. However, the amount of fees collected in a fiscal year cannot exceed the recoverable annual budgeted GASB expenses, including operating expenses, capital and accrued items (Securities Act Secs. 19(g)(3) and (4), as added by the Dodd-Frank Act).

Rules of Construction.—Collection of accounting support fees cannot be construed as placing the SEC or the national securities associations in a position of oversight concerning the GASB's agenda or its budget or as affecting the setting of generally accepted accounting principles by the GASB. These fees cannot be considered public monies of the United States. State and local governments will continue to have the authority to establish accounting and financial reporting standards (Securities Act Sec. 19(g)(5), as added by the Dodd-Frank Act).

Study and Report.—The legislation also calls for a study and report on the role and importance of GASB in the municipal securities markets (see discussion at ¶ 4410).

▶ **Effective date.** The provision takes effect one day after the date of enactment (Sec. 4 of the Dodd-Frank Wall Street Reform and Consumer Protection Act).

Law source: Law at ¶ 10,978 and ¶ 10,004. Committee Report at ¶ 54,583.

— Sec. 978 of the Dodd-Frank Wall Street Reform and Consumer Protection Act, adding Securities Act Sec. 19(g);

— Sec. 4, providing the effective date.

¶4410 Studies and Reports

The Dodd-Frank Wall Street Reform and Consumer Protection Act requires a number of studies concerning municipal securities professionals and the municipal securities industry generally. The studies include consideration of:

- the sufficiency of disclosures by municipal securities issuers to regulators and investors and whether recent innovations in the municipal securities industry require more stringent disclosure obligations (Sec. 976 of the Dodd-Frank Act);
- the municipal securities markets and their operations generally and whether additional regulations are necessary to protect investors in the industry (Sec. 977 of the Dodd-Frank Act); and
- funding of the Government Accounting Standards Board and whether that funding is sufficient for the role it plays in governing the municipal securities markets (Sec. 978 of the Dodd-Frank Act).

Issuer Disclosures.—The Comptroller General of the United States must conduct a study and review of the disclosures that must be made by issuers of municipal securities. In executing the study, the Comptroller General must consider and describe the size and scope of the municipal securities markets, as well as the issuers and investors that participate in them, and provide details concerning the disclosures that municipal securities issuers make to investors (Secs. 976(a) and (b) of the Dodd-Frank Act).

During the study, the Comptroller General must also:

- compare the amount, frequency and quality of disclosures municipal securities issuers must provide to shareholders, including the amount and frequency of disclosures actually provided, with the amount and frequency of disclosures that issuers of corporate securities provide for the benefit of their shareholders, taking into account the differences between the two types of issuers;
- evaluate the costs and benefits that could accrue to the different types of municipal securities issuers if issuers of municipal bonds had to provide additional financial disclosures;
- consider the potential benefit to investors if they were presented with additional financial disclosures made by issuers of municipal bonds; and

- make recommendations relating to disclosure requirements for municipal issuers, including the advisability of repealing or retaining Exchange Act Section 15B(d) (the Tower Amendment), which states that the SEC and the MSRB cannot require a municipal issuer to furnish any application, report or document through a municipal securities broker or dealer except to the extent the information is generally available from another source (Sec. 976(b) of the Dodd-Frank Act).

Within 24 months following enactment of the Dodd-Frank Act, the Comptroller General must submit a report to Congress that describes and explains the results of the study and makes recommendations concerning improvement of the disclosures made available by municipal securities issuers (Sec. 976(c) of the Dodd-Frank Act).

Municipal Securities Markets.—The Comptroller General must also conduct a general study of the municipal securities markets (Sec. 977(a) of the Dodd-Frank Act). Within 18 months of enactment, the Comptroller General must submit a report on the study's results to the Senate Banking Committee and the House Financial Services Committee, with copies to the Senate Special Committee on Aging and the Commission. The report must include:

- an analysis of the existing mechanisms providing for and governing trading, quality of trade executions, market transparency, trade reporting, price discovery, settlement clearing and credit enhancements;

- a discussion of market and investor needs and the impact of recent innovations in the industry;

- potential uses of derivatives in the municipal securities markets; and

- recommendations concerning improvement of the transparency, efficiency, fairness and liquidity of trading in the municipal securities markets (Sec. 977(b) of the Dodd-Frank Act).

Within 180 days after receiving its copy of the report, the Commission must submit a response explaining the actions it has taken in response to the report. A copy of the response must also be sent to the Senate Special Committee on Aging (Sec. 977(c) of the Dodd-Frank Act).

GASB Funding.—The Comptroller General must also conduct a study to evaluate the role of the Government Accounting Standards Board (GASB) and its importance in the municipal securities markets and whether the procedures for its funding are adequate (Sec. 978(b)(1) of the Dodd-Frank Act). According to the legislative history, the GASB establishes accounting principles that are used by many state and local governments and thereby plays an important role in the municipal securities markets. The GASB is currently funded by voluntary contributions, resulting in a minimal budget and general uncertainty that compromises its standard-setting process (S. Rep. No. 111-176, p. 151).

During the study, the Comptroller General must review the manner in which the GASB is funded and must also consider the advisability of making changes to the process of funding the GASB. In making these determinations, the Comptroller General must consult with state and local governments and officials, as well as their financial officers (Secs. 978(b)(1) and (2) of the Dodd-Frank Act).

¶4410

Within 180 days after enactment, the Comptroller General must submit a report on its findings to the Senate Banking Committee and the House Financial Services Committee (Sec. 978(b)(3) of the Dodd-Frank Act).

▶ **Effective date.** The provisions take effect one day after the date of enactment (Sec. 4 of the Dodd-Frank Wall Street Reform and Consumer Protection Act).

Law source: Law at ¶10,976, ¶10,977, ¶10,978 and ¶10,004. Committee Report at ¶54,581, ¶54,582 and ¶54,583.

— Sec. 976 of the Dodd-Frank Wall Street Reform and Consumer Protection Act, requiring a Comptroller General study of the disclosures made by municipal securities issuers to regulators and investors;

— Sec. 977, requiring a Comptroller General study of the municipal securities markets and their operations;

— Sec. 978(b), requiring a Comptroller General study of GASB funding in relation to the municipal securities markets;

— Sec. 4, providing the effective date.

PUBLIC COMPANY ACCOUNTING OVERSIGHT BOARD

¶4420 Introduction

The Dodd-Frank Wall Street Reform and Consumer Protection Act includes provisions that expand the powers and jurisdiction of the Public Company Accounting Oversight Board (PCAOB). One such measure enhances the PCAOB's ability to access the audit work papers and documentation of foreign public accounting firms when they perform material services on which a registered public accounting firm relies in conducting an audit (discussed at ¶ 4425). Another provision allows the PCAOB to share information with its foreign counterparts (discussed at ¶ 4430). A third measure broadens the PCAOB regulatory reach to include registered public accounting firms' audit reports of brokers and dealers (discussed at ¶ 4435).

▶ **Effective date.** The provisions take effect one day after the date of enactment (Sec. 4 of the Dodd-Frank Wall Street Reform and Consumer Protection Act).

Law source: Law at ¶10,929J, ¶10,981, ¶10,982 and ¶10,004. Committee Report at ¶54,600 and ¶54,601.

— Sec. 929J of the Dodd-Frank Wall Street Reform and Consumer Protection Act, adding Sarbanes-Oxley Act Sec. 106(e);

— Sec. 981, adding Sarbanes-Oxley Act Secs. 2(a)(17) and 105(b)(5)(C);

— Sec. 982, amending Sarbanes-Oxley Act Secs. 101–106 and 109 and adding Sec. 110;

— Sec. 4, providing the general effective date.

¶4425 Audit Information to be Produced and Exchanged

The Dodd-Frank Wall Street Reform and Consumer Protection Act gives the Public Company Accounting Oversight Board (PCAOB) greater ability to access the audit work papers and audit documentation of foreign public accounting firms when they perform material services on which a registered public accounting firm relies in conducting an audit (Sarbanes-Oxley Act Sec. 106(b)(1), as amended by the Dodd-Frank Wall Street Reform and Consumer Protection Act). This statutory change will resolve international conflicts that have impaired the Board's ability to fulfill its statutory obligation to inspect non-U.S. registered public accounting firms.

Any registered accounting firm that relies on the work of a foreign accounting firm in issuing an audit report or performing audit work must produce the foreign firm's audit work papers and all other audit documents related to any such work in response to a request for production by the Board (Sarbanes-Oxley Act Sec. 106(b)(2)(A), as amended by the Dodd-Frank Act). The accounting firm must also obtain the foreign firm's agreement to produce the documentation as a condition of its reliance on the foreign firm's work (Sarbanes-Oxley Act Sec. 106(b)(2)(B), as amended by the Dodd-Frank Act).

The Act provides that the foreign public accounting firm must be subject to the jurisdiction of the U.S. federal courts for purposes of enforcing a Board request for audit documentation. Any foreign accounting firm that issues an audit report, or performs audit work or other material services on which a registered accounting firm relies in conducting an audit, must designate to the SEC or the Board a U.S. agent on whom may be served any papers in any action to enforce this statute or any request by the SEC or Board under the statute (Sarbanes-Oxley Act Sec. 106(d), as added by the Dodd-Frank Act). A willful refusal to comply, in whole or in part, with any request by the Commission or the Board under this section constitutes a violation of the Act (Sarbanes-Oxley Act Sec. 106(e), as added by the Dodd-Frank Act).

The staff of the SEC or PCAOB may allow foreign public accounting firms subject to this statute to meet their document production obligations through alternate means, for example, through foreign counterparts of the Commission or PCAOB (Sarbanes-Oxley Act Sec. 106(f), as added by the Dodd-Frank Act).

▶ **Effective date.** The provision takes effect one day after the date of enactment (Sec. 4 of the Dodd-Frank Wall Street Reform and Consumer Protection Act).

Law source: Law at ¶10,929J and ¶10,004.

— Sec. 929J of the Dodd-Frank Wall Street Reform and Consumer Protection Act, amending Sarbanes-Oxley Act Sec. 106(b) and adding Secs. 106(d)–(f);

— Sec. 4, providing the effective date.

¶4430 Information Sharing with Foreign Regulators

The Dodd-Frank Wall Street Reform and Consumer Protection Act updates the Sarbanes-Oxley Act to allow the Public Company Accounting Oversight Board (PCAOB) to share information with its foreign counterparts. Sarbanes-Oxley Act Section 105(b) authorizes the PCAOB to conduct investigations of registered public accounting firms and associated persons. The PCAOB's authority includes the power to compel testimony and document production, to assess penalties for non-cooperation with investigations, and to coordinate investigations (including the appropriate referrals). Information collected during an investigation is treated as confidential and privileged in the hands of the PCAOB and cannot be disclosed except for specified purposes.

The PCAOB may now share all information listed in Sarbanes-Oxley Act Section 105(b)(5)(A) related to a public accounting firm that is subject to the inspection of a foreign auditor oversight authority. The PCAOB may provide this information to the foreign regulator, without the information losing its status as confidential and privileged, if:

- the PCAOB finds it necessary to accomplish the purpose of the Sarbanes-Oxley Act or to protect investors;
- the foreign auditor oversight authority provides to the PCAOB: (1) any requested assurance of confidentiality; (2) a description of the foreign authority's information systems and controls; and (3) a description of the relevant laws and regulations of the foreign government that apply to information access; and
- the PCAOB finds that it is appropriate to share the information (Sarbanes-Oxley Act Sec. 105(b)(5)(C), as added by the Dodd-Frank Act).

Definition.—"Foreign auditor oversight authority" means any governmental body or other entity empowered by a foreign government to conduct inspections of public accounting firms or otherwise to administer or enforce laws related to the regulation of public accounting firms (Sarbanes-Oxley Act Secs. 2(a)(17) and 105(b)(5)(C), as added by the Dodd-Frank Act).

Purpose.—The legislative history explains that the PCAOB was previously limited in its ability to share information with foreign regulators. As a result, many non-U.S. audit regulators either refused to cooperate with the PCAOB or discouraged or prohibited PCAOB-registered firms within their jurisdictions from cooperating with the PCAOB. The amended Sarbanes-Oxley Act provision allows the PCAOB to share information if, among other things, a foreign regulator provides assurances of confidentiality. The Senate committee report observed:

> The Committee believes that the Board could accept an assurance of confidentiality as adequate even in circumstances where the foreign auditor oversight authority could disclose the information to relevant law enforcement or regulatory authorities in its jurisdiction, so long as any such authorities are also committed and able to comply with confidentiality limitations comparable to those that apply to the U.S. and state entities with which the Board shares information under Section 105(b)(5)(B) of the Act (S. Rep. No. 111-176, p. 152–153).

▶ **Effective date.** The provision takes effect one day after the date of enactment (Sec. 4 of the Dodd-Frank Wall Street Reform and Consumer Protection Act).

Law source: Law at ¶10,981, ¶10,004. Committee Report at ¶54,600.

— Sec. 981 of the Dodd-Frank Wall Street Reform and Consumer Protection Act, adding Sarbanes-Oxley Act Secs. 2(a)(17) and 105(b)(5)(C);

— Sec. 4, providing the effective date.

¶4435 Auditors of Broker-Dealers

The Dodd-Frank Wall Street Reform and Consumer Protection Act amends the Sarbanes-Oxley Act of 2002 to subject auditors of brokers and dealers to supervision by the Public Company Accounting Oversight Board (PCAOB). The PCAOB also may refer disciplinary matters to self-regulatory organizations (SROs) and impose assessments on brokers and dealers to help fund the PCAOB.

Background.—The Madoff fraud case exposed gaps in the regulation of audit reports of brokers and dealers. Although every broker or dealer was then required under Exchange Act Section 17(e)(1)(A) to file a balance sheet and income statement certified by a public accounting firm registered with the PCAOB, the PCAOB did not have authority to issue standards or to inspect auditors of brokers and dealers. A limited exception applied to a broker or dealer that was also an issuer or whose financial statements were part of an issuer's consolidated financial statements. The Madoff fraud involved investor reliance on the fraudulent audit report of Bernard L. Madoff Securities LLC, and is an example of the harm that can be prevented by closing the regulatory gaps related to audits of brokers and dealers (S. Rep. No. 111-176, p. 155).

Oversight.—The PCAOB now may require registered public accounting firms to provide the names of brokers and dealers they audit in registration applications (Sarbanes-Oxley Act Sec. 102, as amended by the Dodd-Frank Act). The PCAOB's authority to issue ethics and independence standards extends to audits of brokers and dealers (Sarbanes-Oxley Act Sec. 103, as amended by the Dodd-Frank Act).

The PCAOB also has authority to inspect broker-dealer auditors. Specifically, the PCAOB may, by rule, conduct and require a program of inspection of registered public accounting firms that provide one or more audit reports for a broker or dealer. The PCAOB, however, may differentiate among classes of brokers and dealers. If the PCAOB establishes an inspection program, the board must consider whether different inspection schedules are appropriate for registered public accounting firms that issue audit reports only for one or more brokers or dealers that do not receive, handle or hold customer securities or cash, or that are not members of the Securities Investor Protection Corporation. PCAOB rules concerning inspections of broker-dealer auditors are not effective unless the SEC gives its prior approval under Sarbanes-Oxley Act Section 107(b), including an opportunity for public notice and comment. A public accounting firm, Sarbanes-Oxley Act Section 102 notwithstanding, is not required to register with the PCAOB if the firm is exempt from the inspection program for auditors of brokers and dealers (Sarbanes-Oxley Act Sec. 104, as amended by the Dodd-Frank Act).

CCH Comment: The Senate Committee Report notes that the Chairman of the PCAOB addressed a letter to Chairman Christopher Dodd (D-CT) and Ranking Member Richard Shelby (R-AL) recommending that the PCAOB be granted authority to inspect audits of brokers and dealers, and to take disciplinary action to address deficiencies in these audits. The Senate report also notes that the Securities Investor Protection Corporation supported granting the PCAOB oversight of all brokers and dealers, not only those that perform a clearing function or carry customer accounts (S. Rep. No. 111-176, p. 154). The minority view expressed in the Senate report observed that the PCAOB's burden of overseeing brokers and dealers could be minimized if the PCAOB's new authority did not apply to auditors of introducing brokers, who do not handle customer funds (S. Rep. No. 111-176, p. 246).

Definitions.—The Dodd-Frank Act adds Sarbanes-Oxley Act Section 110 specifically to define "broker," "dealer," "audit," "audit report" and "professional standards" in the context of brokers and dealers. The term "self-regulatory organization" has the meaning stated in Exchange Act Section 3(a). A conforming amendment provides that the definitions contained in Sarbanes-Oxley Act Section 2(a) apply generally, unless another definition is specifically provided (Sarbanes-Oxley Act Sec. 2(a), as amended by, and Sec. 110, as added by, the Dodd-Frank Act).

"Broker" or "Dealer." The terms "broker" and "dealer" are now defined in Sarbanes-Oxley Act Sections 110(3) and (4) to mean a broker or dealer as defined in Exchange Act Sections 3(a)(4) and (5) that must file a balance sheet, income statement or financial statement under Exchange Act Section 17(e)(1)(A), which must be certified by a registered public accounting firm (Sarbanes-Oxley Act Secs. 110(3) and (4), as added by, the Dodd-Frank Act).

"Audit." Sarbanes-Oxley Act Section 110(1) defines "audit" to mean an examination of any issuer's, broker's or dealer's financial statements, reports, documents, procedures, controls or notices, by an independent public accounting firm, under PCAOB rules, for the purpose of expressing an opinion on the financial statements or providing an audit report (Sarbanes-Oxley Act Sec. 110(1), as added by, the Dodd-Frank Act).

"Audit Report." The term "audit report" means a document, report, notice or other record that was prepared following a securities law compliance audit of an issuer, broker or dealer, and in which a public accounting firm either: (1) stated the firm's opinion regarding the issuer's, broker's or dealer's financial reports; or (2) asserted that no opinion could be expressed (Sarbanes-Oxley Act Sec. 110(2), as added by, the Dodd-Frank Act).

"Professional Standards." Sarbanes-Oxley Act Section 110(5) defines "professional standards" to mean accounting principles that are: (1) established by the standards-setting body described in Securities Act Section 19(b), by the SEC under Securities Act Section 19(a) or under Exchange Act Section 13(b); and (2) are relevant to audit reports for particular issuers, brokers or dealers, or are dealt with in a particular registered public accounting firm's quality control system. The definition also includes auditing standards, attestation engagement standards, quality control policies and procedures, ethical and competency standards, and independence standards (including Sarbanes-Oxley Act Title II) that the PCAOB has determined: (1) relate to the preparation or issuance of audit reports for issuers, brokers or dealers; and (2) are adopted by the PCAOB under

¶4435

Sarbanes-Oxley Act Section 103(a), or are promulgated as SEC rules (Sarbanes-Oxley Act Sec. 110(5), as added by, the Dodd-Frank Act).

Referrals to SROs.—Sarbanes-Oxley Act Section 105 authorizes the PCAOB to conduct investigations and disciplinary proceedings. The PCAOB generally must coordinate its activities with the Commission. However, in certain matters, the PCAOB may make referrals to the SEC or other federal regulators. As amended, the law permits the PCAOB to refer an investigation regarding the audit report of a broker-dealer to an SRO with jurisdiction (Sarbanes-Oxley Act Sec. 105(b)(4)(B)(ii), as amended by the Dodd-Frank Act).

Assessments on Broker-Dealers.—The PCAOB must be financed through an annual accounting support fee imposed on entities subject to the board's authority (Sarbanes-Oxley Act Section 109(c), as amended by the Dodd-Frank Act). The PCAOB must adopt rules to allocate, assess and collect the fee. Brokers and dealers are subject to the fee as of the first full fiscal year beginning after enactment (Sarbanes-Oxley Act Secs. 109(d)(2) and (3), as amended by the Dodd-Frank Act). Each broker or dealer must pay the fee allocated, and any amount due must be allocated among brokers and dealers, or among classes of brokers and dealers. The fee imposed on a broker or dealer must be in proportion to its net capital (before or after any adjustments) compared to the total net capital of all brokers and dealers (before or after any adjustments). The PCAOB must issue rules to implement the proportionality requirement (Sarbanes-Oxley Act Sec. 109(h), as added by the Dodd-Frank Act).

Effective date. The provision takes effect one day after the date of enactment (Sec. 4 of the Dodd-Frank Wall Street Reform and Consumer Protection Act).

Law source: Law at ¶ 10,982 and ¶ 10,004. Committee Report at ¶ 54,601.

— Sec. 982(a) of the Dodd-Frank Wall Street Reform and Consumer Protection Act, amending Sarbanes-Oxley Act Sec. 2(a) and adding Sec. 110;

— Sec. 982(b), amending Sarbanes-Oxley Act Sec. 101;

— Sec. 982(c), amending Sarbanes-Oxley Act Secs. 102(a) and (b)(2)(A);

— Sec. 982(d), amending Sarbanes-Oxley Act Secs. 103(a)(1), (2)(A)(iii) and (B)(i);

— Sec. 982(e), amending Sarbanes-Oxley Act Sec. 104(a) and providing a conforming amendment to Securities Exchange Act Sec. 17(e)(1)(A);

— Secs. 982(f), (i) and (j), amending Sarbanes-Oxley Act Secs. 105(b)(4)(B), (b)(5)(B)(ii) and (c)(7)(B);

— Sec. 982(g), amending Sarbanes-Oxley Act Sec. 106(a);

— Sec. 982(h), amending Sarbanes-Oxley Act Secs. 109(c)(2) and (d)(2) and adding Sec. 109(h);

— Sec. 4, providing the effective date.

¶4435

ADDITIONAL SECURITIES REFORMS

¶4450 Introduction

Title IX, Subtitle I, of the Dodd-Frank Wall Street Reform and Consumer Protection Act provides additional reforms of the securities regulatory structure and other investor protection measures. The legislation extends the Securities Investor Protection Act to futures contracts and options on futures contracts held in portfolio margining accounts and carried as securities accounts under a portfolio margining program approved by the SEC (see ¶ 4455). The anti-manipulation provisions in Section 10 of the Securities Exchange Act of 1934 now apply to transactions that involve securities lending or borrowing in violation of SEC rules (see ¶ 4460). The Government Accountability Office must study the risks and conflicts associated with proprietary trading at federally insured banks and at bank or financial holding companies (see ¶ 4470). The Office of Financial Literacy within the Bureau of Consumer Financial Protection at the Federal Reserve must establish a grant program to fund state efforts to protect senior citizen investors (see ¶ 4475). The law promotes state adoption of additional model regulations on senior and consumer protection (see ¶ 4495).

The Dodd-Frank Act also updates the Inspector General Act of 1978 to provide that an inspector general may be removed only by a two-thirds vote of their respective full commissions, instead of only by the commission chair. Financial regulatory agencies must take corrective action regarding deficiencies found by inspectors general (see ¶ 4480). The Government Accountability Office must study the person-to-person lending industry (see ¶ 4485). The legislation also exempts non-accelerated filers from Sarbanes-Oxley Act Section 404(b) and mandates a study of Sarbanes-Oxley Act exemptions for smaller issuers (see ¶ 4490).

In addition, the Dodd-Frank Act updates the prompt corrective action laws for national banks and federally chartered credit unions. Specifically, the definition of "material loss" contained in the Federal Deposit Insurance Act and the Federal Credit Union Act has been revised to raise the threshold amount for material loss reports. The inspectors general for each federal banking agency and for the National Credit Union Administration Board must submit semiannual reports on nonmaterial losses (see ¶ 4465).

Treated Elsewhere.—Provisions in Subtitle I involving the Public Company Accounting Oversight Board (PCAOB) are discussed elsewhere. These include Section 981, which allows the PCAOB to share information with its foreign counterparts (see ¶ 4430). Another provision, Section 982, authorizes the PCAOB to inspect registered public accounting firms' audit reports of brokers and dealers (see ¶ 4435).

Conforming and Technical Amendments.—The legislation amends many sections of the securities laws to remove references to the Public Utility Holding Company Act of 1935, which Congress repealed in 2005. These conforming amendments affect the Exchange Act, the Trust Indenture Act, the Investment Company Act and the Advisers Act (Sec. 986 of the Dodd-Frank Act). The legislation also makes numerous technical corrections to the Securities Act, the Exchange Act, the Trust Indenture Act, the Investment Company Act and the Advisers Act (Sec. 985 of the Dodd-Frank Act).

▶ **Effective date.** The provisions take effect one day after the date of enactment (Sec. 4 of the Dodd-Frank Wall Street Reform and Consumer Protection Act).

Law source: Law at ¶10,985, ¶10,986 and ¶10,004. Committee Report at ¶50,091.

— Sec. 985 of the Dodd-Frank Wall Street Reform and Consumer Protection Act, making technical corrections;
— Sec. 986, making conforming amendments;
— Sec. 4, providing the effective date.

¶4455 Portfolio Margining

The Dodd-Frank Wall Street Reform and Consumer Protection Act updates several key definitions in the Securities Investor Protection Act of 1970 (SIPA) to grant protection to futures positions held in portfolio margining accounts. The affected terms include "customer," "customer property," "gross revenues from the securities business" and "net equity." The legislative history states that the revision to these terms is necessary to ensure that, in the event of a broker-dealer's insolvency, a portfolio margining customer will not be treated as a general unsecured creditor regarding futures positions and will have priority regarding securities held in these types of accounts. The changes are also required to allow customers to achieve the economic efficiencies possible by hedging related positions in a single account. These amendments are consistent with recommendations made in the Joint Report on Harmonization of Regulation (October 16, 2009) issued by the SEC and the Commodity Futures Trading Commission (S. Rep. No. 111-176, p. 155).

In addition, Section 9(a)(1) of the SIPA distinguishes between claims for cash and claims for securities. Under this provision, if any or all of a customer's net equity claim is for cash, the customer may receive a cash advance. However, a claim for securities is not eligible for cash advances. The amended SIPA provision clarifies that a claim regarding options on commodities futures contracts is treated like a claim for securities and is, therefore, ineligible for cash advances (SIPA Sec. 9(a)(1), as amended by the Dodd-Frank Act).

Customer.—The revised definition of "customer" of a debtor includes, among other things, any person who has a claim against the debtor for cash, securities, futures contracts or options on futures contracts received, acquired or held in a portfolio margining account carried as a securities account under a portfolio margining program approved by the SEC (SIPA Sec. 16(2), as amended by the Dodd-Frank Act). Existing SIPA Section 16(5) states that a "debtor" is a Securities Investor Protection Corporation (SIPC) member for whom an application for a protective decree has been filed or for whom a direct payment procedure has been instituted. The legislative history states that the revised definition of "customer" ensures that the owner of a portfolio margining account will have the priority of a "customer" regarding futures contracts or options on futures contracts permitted under rules adopted by the SEC for portfolio margining accounts (S. Rep. No. 111-176, p. 156).

Customer Property.—"Customer property" means cash and securities at any time received, acquired or held by or for the account of a debtor from or for the securities accounts of a customer, and the proceeds of any property transferred by the debtor, including property unlawfully converted. The term also includes numerous items sepa-

¶4455

rately identified in SIPA Section 16(4). "Customer property" now includes futures contracts and options on futures contracts received, acquired or held by or for the account of a debtor, from or for these accounts, and the proceeds of these accounts. Futures positions must be held in a customer's portfolio margining account and carried as securities accounts under a portfolio margining program approved by the SEC (SIPA Sec. 16(4), as amended by the Dodd-Frank Act). The legislative history states that the revised definition of "customer property" ensures that the owner of a portfolio margining account will have the priority of a "customer" regarding futures contracts or options on futures contracts permitted under rules adopted by the SEC for portfolio margining accounts (S. Rep. No. 111-176, p. 156).

Gross Revenues from the Securities Business.—Under SIPA Section 16(9), "gross revenues from the securities business" generally includes, among other things, fees and other income from other categories of the securities business as set forth in the SIPC's bylaws. The term now includes revenues earned by a broker or dealer in connection with transactions in customers' portfolio margining accounts carried as securities accounts under a Commission-approved portfolio margining program (SIPA Sec. 16(9), as amended by the Dodd-Frank Act) The legislative history states that the definition of "gross revenues from the securities business" has been revised to specifically include broker or dealer revenues from transactions in portfolio margining accounts that are carried as securities accounts (S. Rep. No. 111-176, p. 156).

Net Equity.—SIPA Section 16(11) now defines "net equity" to include futures portfolio margining accounts. As a result, "net equity" is the dollar amount of a customer's account obtained by calculating the amount owed by a debtor to a customer, if the debtor had liquidated all of the customer's securities positions (other than customer name securities reclaimed by the customer), and all positions in futures contracts and options on futures contracts held in a portfolio margining account carried as securities under a Commission-approved portfolio margining program, including all property collateralizing these positions (to the extent not otherwise included), minus any debts owed by the customer to the debtor on the filing date, plus any payments by a customer on debts owed to the debtor made with the trustee's approval within 60 days of published notice under Section 8(a). The revised provision clarifies that a claim for a commodity futures contract held in a portfolio margining account under an SEC-approved portfolio margining program, or a claim for a security futures contract, is a claim as of the filing date and must be treated as a claim for cash (SIPA Sec. 16(11), as amended by the Dodd-Frank Act).

The legislative history states that the revised definition of "net equity" ensures that the owner of a portfolio margining account will have the priority of a "customer" regarding futures contracts or options on futures contracts permitted under rules adopted by the SEC for portfolio margining accounts. The inclusion of futures and options on futures in "net equity" means that these items will be treated along with cash and securities in the account as securities customer property. The amended definition also provides that a customer's claim for either a commodity futures contract or a security futures contract will be treated as a claim for cash and not as a claim for a security (S. Rep. No. 111-176, p. 156).

¶4455

▶ **Effective date.** The provision takes effect one day after the date of enactment (Sec. 4 of the Dodd-Frank Wall Street Reform and Consumer Protection Act).

Law source: Law at ¶10,983 and ¶10,004. Committee Report at ¶54,602.

— Sec. 983(a) of the Dodd-Frank Wall Street Reform and Consumer Protection Act, amending SIPA Sec. 9(a)(1);

— Sec. 983(b), amending SIPA Secs. 16(2), (4), (9) and (11);

— Sec. 4, providing the effective date.

¶4460 Securities Lending and Borrowing

Section 984 of the Dodd-Frank Wall Street Reform and Consumer Protection Act addresses securities lending. Exchange Act Section 10 provides that it is unlawful for any person to use any means or instrumentality of interstate commerce or of the mails, or of any facility of any national securities exchange, to commit specified manipulative acts. Exchange Act Section 10(c) now extends this prohibition to effecting, accepting, or facilitating a transaction that involves securities lending or borrowing in violation of any applicable SEC rules (Exchange Act Sec. 10(c)(1), as added by the Dodd-Frank Act). The SEC must, within two years following enactment, adopt rules to increase the transparency of information available to brokers, dealers and investors regarding securities lending and borrowing (Sec. 984(b) of the Dodd-Frank Act).

The legislative history states that additional restrictions on securities lending are necessary to curb financial institutions' use of securities lending programs to engage in leveraged and risky trading. The revised law will provide more transparency to brokers, dealers and investors regarding loaned or borrowed securities. The SEC also is encouraged to take action earlier than required if regulatory action is necessary in the public interest (S. Rep. No. 111-176, p. 156).

The amended provision notwithstanding, an appropriate federal banking agency, the National Credit Union Administration, or any other federal department or agency identified by federal law as having a responsibility to issue rules or regulations restricting securities lending or borrowing, may adopt rules to protect the safety and soundness of a financial institution, or to protect the financial system from systemic risk (Exchange Act Sec. 10(c)(2), as added by the Dodd-Frank Act).

▶ **Effective date.** The provision takes effect one day after the date of enactment (Sec. 4 of the Dodd-Frank Wall Street Reform and Consumer Protection Act).

Law source: Law at ¶10,984 and ¶10,004. Committee Report at ¶54,603.

— Sec. 984(a) of the Dodd-Frank Wall Street Reform and Consumer Protection Act, adding Exchange Act Sec. 10(c);

— Sec. 984(b), requiring SEC rulemaking;

— Sec. 4, providing the effective date.

¶4465 Deposit Insurance Fund Loss Reviews

The Dodd-Frank Wall Street Reform and Consumer Protection Act updates the Federal Deposit Insurance Act and the Federal Credit Union Act regarding inspector general reviews of bank and credit union deposit insurance fund losses. Specifically, the amended provisions revise the definition of "material loss" to increase the threshold amount for material loss reports. The provisions also require the inspectors general of each federal banking agency and of the National Credit Union Administration Board to submit semiannual reports on nonmaterial losses.

Federal Deposit Insurance Act.—Section 987 of the Dodd-Frank Act amends the prompt corrective action section of the Federal Deposit Insurance Act (FDIA). "Material loss" now means any estimated loss in excess of:

- $200 million, for losses during the period beginning January 1, 2010 and ending December 31, 2011;
- $150 million, for losses during the period beginning January 1, 2012 and ending December 31, 2013; and
- $50 million, for losses on or after January 1, 2014 (however, the amount is $75 million for a period of one year from the date that the inspector general of a federal banking agency certifies to the Senate Banking Committee and the House Financial Services Committee that the number of projected depository institution failures requiring material loss reviews during the following 12 months will exceed 30 and would hinder oversight function effectiveness) (FDIA Sec. 38(k)(2)(B), as amended by the Dodd-Frank Wall Street Reform and Consumer Protection Act).

Previously, the FDIA defined "material loss" as a loss exceeding the greater of $25 million or two percent of an institution's total assets as of when the Federal Deposit Insurance Corporation (FDIC) initiated assistance or was appointed receiver.

> **CCH Comment:** The legislative history notes that the prior definition, coupled with the rise in bank failures, strained the ability of federal banking regulators to keep pace with the number of required material loss reports. The Senate committee report observed that legislative relief is justified since many banks have failed due to the same exposure to failing mortgages. As a result, the amended prompt corrective action law requires material loss reports based initially on a much higher loss threshold and gradually reduces the threshold amount over time, as the economy recovers and the volume of material loss reports declines. The inspectors general also may conduct a material loss review for a bank failure that does not meet the materiality threshold, if a preliminary assessment shows that the report would be helpful (S. Rep. No. 111-176, p. 156–157).

Nonmaterial Loss Report. The Federal Deposit Insurance Act now requires the inspector general for each federal banking agency to submit semiannual reports on nonmaterial losses. For the six-month period ending on March 31, 2010, and each six-month period thereafter, an inspector general must:

- identify losses to the FDIC fund estimated to have been incurred during the six-month reporting period;

- for nonmaterial losses, determine: (1) the grounds identified by the federal banking agency or state bank supervisor for appointing the FDIC as receiver; and (2) whether any unusual circumstances exist that might warrant in-depth review of the loss;
- prepare and submit a written report to the appropriate federal banking agency and to Congress on the inspector general's determinations regarding: (1) any loss that warrants in-depth review and the reasons for this review or, for any loss that does not warrant review, the reasons for not making a review; and (2) for any loss that warrants in-depth review, the date on which the review, and a report on the review, will be completed and submitted to the federal banking agency and to Congress (FDIA Sec. 38(k)(5)(A), as amended by the Dodd-Frank Act).

The inspector general for each federal banking agency must expeditiously submit semiannual reports, but not later than 90 days following the end of a six-month reporting period. The inspectors general must, upon request, provide a copy of the report to any member of Congress (FDIA Sec. 38(k)(5)(B), as amended by the Dodd-Frank Act).

Federal Credit Union Act.—Section 988 of the Dodd-Frank Act updates the prompt corrective action requirement for federally insured credit unions. "Material loss" to the National Credit Union Share Insurance Fund (fund) is now defined as a loss that exceeds the sum of $25 million and 10 percent of the credit union's total assets on the date the National Credit Union Administration Board (NCUA board) either initiates assistance to the credit union or is appointed liquidating agent (Federal Credit Union Act Sec. 216(j)(2), as amended by the Dodd-Frank Act). Previously, the inspector general of the NCUA board was required to submit a review of the NCUA's supervision of a failed credit union if the loss to the fund exceeded $10 million and equaled 10 percent of the credit union's total assets at the time the NCUA board initiated assistance. The threshold for conducting a material loss review has been raised to ease the inspector general's workload due to the high volume of reviews required by the prior law (S. Rep. No. 111-176, p. 157).

> **Caution Note:** Revised Federal Credit Union Act Section 216(j)(2) defines "material loss" as a loss to the fund that exceeds the sum of $25 million and 10 percent of the failed, insured credit union's total assets. In contrast, the Senate committee report describes the definition of "material loss" using the disjunctive "or" instead of the "and" contained in the amended law (S. Rep. No. 111-176, p. 157).

If the fund has a material loss regarding an insured credit union, the NCUA board's inspector general must submit a written report to the NCUA board. The report must contain a review of the NCUA's supervision of the credit union involved (including the NCUA's implementation of the relevant law), as well as a description of why the credit union's problems resulted in a material loss to the fund, and recommendations to avoid future losses. Copies of the report must be submitted to the U.S. Comptroller General (comptroller), the FDIC, the state supervisor of a state credit union (if applicable), and to any member of Congress, upon request (Federal Credit Union Act Sec. 216(j)(1), as amended by the Dodd-Frank Act).

A material loss report made under the amended law must be publicly disclosed, upon request, under 5 U.S.C. §552, but the law does not require disclosure of customer names (other than an institution-affiliated party), or information from which a customer's identity could reasonably be ascertained (Federal Credit Union Act Sec. 216(j)(3), as amended by the Dodd-Frank Act). The comptroller also may review each

¶4465

report, including the inspector general's compliance with Inspector General Act Section 8L, and recommend improvements to the supervision of insured credit unions. The comptroller's recommendations must include any improvements to the amended law (Federal Credit Union Act Sec. 216(j)(5), as amended by the Dodd-Frank Act). The legislative history states that the comptroller has discretion to review each material loss report and recommend improvements to the supervision of insured credit unions (S. Rep. No. 111-176, p. 157).

Nonmaterial Loss Report. The inspector general of the NCUA board must submit a semiannual report for nonmaterial losses. The first report must cover the six-month period ending March 31, 2010; subsequent reports must be submitted every six months after this date. The inspector general's report must:

- identify any losses estimated to be incurred by the fund regarding insured credit unions during the six-month reporting period;
- determine for each nonmaterial loss: (1) the grounds identified by the NCUA board (or state official, for state credit unions) for appointing the NCUA board liquidating agent; and (2) whether any unusual circumstances exist that might warrant in-depth review of the loss; and
- prepare and submit a written report to the NCUA board and to Congress on the inspector general's determinations, including: (1) the identification of any loss that warrants in-depth review and the reasons for this review or, for any loss that does not warrant review, the reasons for not making a review; and (2) for any loss that warrants in-depth review, the date on which the review, and a report on the review, will be completed (Federal Credit Union Act Sec. 216(j)(4)(A), as amended by the Dodd-Frank Act).

The inspector general must submit semiannual reports expeditiously, but not later than 90 days after the end of a six-month reporting period. Copies of reports on nonmaterial losses must be provided to any member of Congress, upon request (Federal Credit Union Act Sec. 216(j)(4)(B), as amended by the Dodd-Frank Act).

▶ **Effective date.** The provisions take effect one day after the date of enactment (Sec. 4 of the Dodd-Frank Wall Street Reform and Consumer Protection Act).

Law source: Law at ¶10,987, ¶10,988 and ¶10,004. Committee Report at ¶54,606.

— Sec. 987 of the Dodd-Frank Wall Street Reform and Consumer Protection Act, amending Federal Deposit Insurance Act Sec. 38(k);

— Sec. 988, amending Federal Credit Union Act Sec. 216(j);

— Sec. 4, providing the effective date.

¶4470 Study of Proprietary Trading

The Dodd-Frank Wall Street Reform and Consumer Protection Act requires the Comptroller General of the United States to study the risks and conflicts of proprietary trading by covered entities (Sec. 989(b)(1) of the Dodd-Frank Act). "Proprietary trading" is the act of a covered entity to invest as a principal in securities, commodities, derivatives, hedge funds, private equity firms or other financial products or entities as defined by the comptroller (Sec. 989(a)(2) of the Dodd-Frank Act). A "covered entity" is an insured depository institution or an affiliate, a bank or financial holding company or a subsidiary of a bank or financial holding company. The comptroller may deem other entities to be covered entities (Sec. 989(a)(1) of the Dodd-Frank Act).

CCH Comment: For discussion of Dodd-Frank Act Section 619, which contains the "Volcker Rule" and regulates some aspects of proprietary trading by certain financial institutions, see ¶ 2575

Scope of Study.—The comptroller's study must focus on numerous issues associated with proprietary trading, including whether:

- proprietary trading presents material systemic risks to the stability of the U.S. financial system;
- proprietary trading presents material risks to the safety and soundness of covered entities that engage in proprietary trading, and the costs and benefits of mitigating these risks;
- proprietary trading presents material conflicts of interest between covered entities that engage in proprietary trading and clients of institutions that use these firms to execute trades or manage assets, and the costs and benefits of mitigating these risks;
- adequate disclosure of risks and conflicts is made to depositors, trading and management clients, and investors of covered entities, and the costs and benefits of mitigating these risks; and
- banking, securities and commodities regulators have in place adequate systems and controls to monitor and contain any risks and conflicts of interest, and the costs and benefits of mitigating these risks (Sec. 989(b)(1) of the Dodd-Frank Act).

The comptroller's study must consider several factors. It must review current proprietary trading practices and consider the advisability of a complete ban. It must also consider whether covered entities should be subjected to activity limitations, additional capital requirements, restrictions on affiliate transactions, enhanced accounting disclosures, enhanced public disclosures and any other options the comptroller deems appropriate (Sec. 989(b)(2) of the Dodd-Frank Act).

Sources and Confidentiality.—For purposes of conducting the study, the comptroller may interview officers, directors, employees and accountants or other financial advisers of these firms. The comptroller also may request any records that belong to, or are used by, a covered entity that engages in proprietary trading (Sec. 989(d) of the Dodd-Frank Act).

To protect confidentiality, the comptroller cannot disclose any proprietary trading activities of a covered entity unless the information is disclosed at a high enough level of generality to avoid disclosure of specific trading data. Similarly, interviews of individuals cannot be disclosed, except at a level of generality that protects an individual's name or identifying details. The comptroller also cannot reveal the name of an individual third-party provider of professional services to a covered entity believed to be engaged in proprietary trading. An exception to the confidentiality requirement, however, allows the comptroller to reply to an official request from a federal regulatory body, to respond to congressional committees, and to comply with court orders (Sec. 989(e) of the Dodd-Frank Act).

Report to Congress.—The comptroller must submit a report to Congress on the study's results within 15 months after enactment (Sec. 989(c) of the Dodd-Frank Act).

¶4470

▶ **Effective date.** The provision takes effect one day after the date of enactment (Sec. 4 of the Dodd-Frank Wall Street Reform and Consumer Protection Act).

Law source: Law at ¶10,989 and ¶10,004. Committee Report at ¶54,608.

— Sec. 989 of the Dodd-Frank Wall Street Reform and Consumer Protection Act, requiring study of proprietary trading;

— Sec. 4, providing the effective date.

¶4475 Senior Investor Protection

Protection of senior citizen investors falls primarily to state securities authorities under state laws that mandate or permit the adoption of model rules and regulations created by state regulatory associations. The financial reform legislation explicitly references the standards established by the North American Securities Administrators Association (NASAA) and the National Association of Insurance Commissioners (NAIC). Although senior investor protection is not specifically addressed under the federal securities laws, the use of unscrupulous investment practices against seniors often falls within the general anti-fraud authority of the Securities and Exchange Commission.

Section 989A of the Dodd-Frank Wall Street Reform and Consumer Protection Act provides additional resources for states to protect elderly investors. The legislative history indicates that the law seeks to encourage states to adopt standards issued by NASAA and the NAIC to protect seniors from financial advisors who use misleading or fraudulent "senior designations." Financial advisers may obtain these designations online and without significant training (S. Rep. No. 111-176, p. 158).

Against this backdrop, the Dodd-Frank Act requires the Office of Financial Literacy (Office) within the Bureau of Consumer Financial Protection at the Federal Reserve to create a grant program to provide states with additional funds for protecting senior investors.

Definitions.—The Dodd-Frank Act contains definitions of key terms applicable to senior investors. These definitions reflect the purpose of the senior investor provisions, which is to enhance state regulation of the use of misleading certifications and professional designations by salespersons and advisers who market financial products to seniors. "Senior" means an individual who is at least 62 years of age (Sec. 989A(a)(7) of the Dodd-Frank Act). The term "misleading or fraudulent marketing" means the use of a misleading designation by a person who sells to or advises a senior in connection with the sale of a financial product (Sec. 989A(a)(4) of the Dodd-Frank Act). "Financial product" includes securities, insurance products (paying a fixed or variable return), and bank and loan products (Sec. 989A(a)(2) of the Dodd-Frank Act).

"Misleading designation" means a certification, professional designation or other purported credential that indicates or implies special certification or training in advising or servicing seniors. The term "misleading designation," however, excludes certifications and professional designations, licenses and other credentials that:

• are issued or obtained from a regionally accredited academic institution;

- meet the applicable standards created by the NASAA Model Rule on the Use of Senior-Specific Certifications and Professional Designations, or the NAIC Model Regulations on the Use of Senior-Specific Certifications and Professional Designations in the Sale of Life Insurance and Annuities (or successor standards); or
- were issued or obtained from a state (Sec. 989A(a)(3) of the Dodd-Frank Act).

The Office can make grants to states or eligible entities (Sec. 989A(b) of the Dodd-Frank Act). The term "state" means any State of the United States, the District of Columbia, Puerto Rico, the Virgin Islands or any other possession of the United States, as defined in Section 3 of the Exchange Act. "Eligible entity" means: (1) a state securities commission (or equivalent agency) that has adopted rules that meet or exceed the NASAA Model Rule on the Use of Senior-Specific Certifications and Professional Designations; (2) a state insurance commission (or equivalent agency) that has adopted rules that conform, to the extent practicable, to the NAIC Model Regulation on the Use of Senior-Specific Certifications and Professional Designations in the Sale of Life Insurance and Annuities, and has adopted fiduciary or suitability rules for the sale of annuities that meet or exceed the NAIC Suitability in Annuity Transactions Model Regulation; or (3) a state consumer protection agency whose state's securities commission or insurance commission is an eligible entity (Sec. 989A(a)(1) of the Dodd-Frank Act).

Grants to States.—Section 989A(b) of the Dodd-Frank Act directs the Office to establish a grant program to help protect seniors from fraudulent investment schemes. Grants may be used to fund additional investigative and prosecutorial staff; to fund technology, equipment and training for regulators, prosecutors and law enforcement to identify violators and to increase the number of successful prosecutions of violators; to provide educational materials and training to regulators and seniors; to develop comprehensive plans that combat misleading or fraudulent marketing of financial products to seniors; and to enhance state laws that protect seniors against misleading or fraudulent marketing (Sec. 989A(b) of the Dodd-Frank Act).

In addition, the Office may impose performance objectives and reporting requirements for states and eligible entities participating in the grant program (Sec. 989A(d) of the Dodd-Frank Act). Congress has authorized appropriations to provide grants to states for senior investor protection activities in the amount of $8 million for each of the fiscal years 2011 to 2015 (Sec. 989A(h) of the Dodd-Frank Act).

Maximum Grant. A state or eligible entity may be awarded a maximum grant amount of $500,000 for each of three consecutive fiscal years. To receive the maximum amount, the state or eligible entity must adopt rules that:

- meet or exceed the NASAA Model Rule on the Use of Senior-Specific Certifications and Professional Designations;
- to the extent practicable, conform to the minimum requirements of the NAIC Model Regulation on the Use of Senior-Specific Certifications and Professional Designations in the Sale of Life Insurance and Annuities; and
- meet or exceed the fiduciary or suitability requirements of the NAIC Suitability in Annuity Transactions Model Regulation (Sec. 989A(e)(1) of the Dodd-Frank Act).

Reduced Grant. A state or eligible entity may receive a reduced grant of $100,000 for each of three consecutive fiscal years if it has adopted rules that: (1) meet or exceed the NASAA Model Rule on the Use of Senior-Specific Certifications and Professional Designations; or (2) to the extent practicable, conform to the minimum requirements of the NAIC Model Regulation on the Use of Senior-Specific Certifications and Professional Designations in the Sale of Life Insurance and Annuities, and has adopted rules that meet or exceed the fiduciary or suitability requirements in the NAIC's Suitability in Annuity Transactions Model Regulation (Sec. 989A(e)(2) of the Dodd-Frank Act).

Application for Grant.—A state or eligible entity that wishes to obtain a grant must submit an application to the Office and provide details about the proposed use of the grant money. The application must contain a proposal that identifies the scope of the problem, describes how the proposed activities will protect senior investors, and describes how the proposed program will be coordinated with other state efforts. The description of how the state's program will help seniors must explain how the program:

- will proactively identify seniors who are fraud victims;
- can assist in the investigation and prosecution of violators; and
- can help to discourage and reduce cases of misleading or fraudulent marketing (Sec. 989A(c) of the Dodd-Frank Act).

A state or eligible entity may receive federal grants for senior investor protection activities for a three-year period (Sec. 989A(e) of the Dodd-Frank Act). Following the expiration of the original grant, a state may apply for additional funds, regardless of the limits on grant amounts in Section 989A(e) (Sec. 989A(g) of the Dodd-Frank Act). States and other eligible entities may make any subgrants that are necessary to carry out senior investor protection activities (Sec. 989A(f) of the Dodd-Frank Act).

▶ **Effective date.** The provision takes effect one day after the date of enactment (Sec. 4 of the Dodd-Frank Wall Street Reform and Consumer Protection Act).

Law source: Law at ¶10,989A and ¶10,004. Committee Report at ¶54,609.

— Sec. 989A(a) of the Dodd-Frank Wall Street Reform and Consumer Protection Act, defining terms;

— Sec. 989A(b), providing for grants to states and eligible entities;

— Sec. 989A(c), listing application requirements;

— Sec. 989A(d), describing performance objectives and reporting requirements;

— Sec. 989A(e), stating funding amount and duration;

— Sec. 989A(f), allowing subgrants;

— Sec. 989A(g), permitting reapplication;

— Sec. 989A(h), authorizing appropriations;

— Sec. 4, providing the effective date.

¶4480 SEC and CFTC Inspectors General

The Dodd-Frank Wall Street Reform and Consumer Protection Act updates the Inspector General Act of 1978. Specifically, the Dodd-Frank Act enhances the accountability of inspectors general at the Securities Exchange Commission (SEC) and the Commodity Futures Trading Commission (CFTC). The law also makes it more difficult to remove an inspector general. The centerpiece of the amended law creates a Council of Inspectors General of Financial Oversight, which provides the inspectors general at federal financial regulators a forum to discuss topical issues and each others' work. The Dodd-Frank Act requires the heads of establishments to take corrective action in response to deficiencies found by inspectors general. In addition, Section 989B of the Dodd-Frank Act revises the term "head of the designated Federal entity" to include, among other federal regulators, the National Credit Union Administration Board (Inspector General Act Sec. 8G(a)(4)(E), as added by the Dodd-Frank Act).

Accountability.—Section 989C of the Dodd-Frank Act seeks to hold inspectors general accountable. Inspector General Act Section 5(a) requires each federal inspector general to submit semiannual reports to the head of the establishment involved and provide copies to the relevant congressional committees. These reports now must include an appendix stating the results of any peer review conducted by another inspector general during the reporting period. If no peer review was conducted, the report must identify the date of the last peer review. The report also must include a list of any outstanding recommendations from any peer reviews that have not been fully implemented. The list must describe the status of the implementation and why it has not been completed. In addition, the report must list any peer reviews, and any outstanding recommendations from any prior peer review, that remain outstanding or have not been fully implemented (Inspector General Act Secs. 5(a)(14), (15) and (16), as added by the Dodd-Frank Act).

Removal.—Section 989D of the Dodd-Frank Act makes it more difficult for a federal agency to remove an inspector general. A board or commission that is the head of a designated federal entity must now obtain the written concurrence of two-thirds of its members to remove an inspector general (Inspector General Act Sec. 8G(e)(1), as amended by the Dodd-Frank Act).

> **CCH Comment:** According to Sen. Chuck Grassley (R-IA), requiring a two-thirds vote increases the likelihood that some members of a board or commission will dissent from an attempt to remove an inspector general for political reasons (Cong Record, May 18, 2010, p. S3877).

Council of Inspectors General.—Section 989E of the Dodd-Frank Act establishes the Council of Inspectors General on Financial Oversight. The Council is chaired by the U.S. Treasury Inspector General. Its other members are the inspectors general of the:

- Board of Governors of the Federal Reserve System (the Fed);
- CFTC;
- Department of Housing and Urban Development;
- Federal Deposit Insurance Corporation;
- Federal Housing Finance Agency;
- National Credit Union Administration (NCUA);
- SEC; and
- Troubled Asset Relief Program (until the inspector general's powers expire).

¶4480

The Council must hold quarterly meetings, although the chair may schedule more frequent meetings. The Council's purpose is to allow the inspectors general to share information and to discuss each others' ongoing work. Meetings should be focused on concerns for the broader financial sector and ways to improve financial oversight (Secs. 989E(a)(1) and (2)(A) of the Dodd-Frank Act).

Annual Report. The Council must submit an annual report to Congress. The report must include a section edited by each member of the Council discussing the individual inspector general's concerns and recommendations regarding ongoing and completed work, with emphasis on issues that apply to the broader financial sector. The report also must include a summary of the Council's general observations based on the views of the individual members and that focuses on improvements to financial oversight. The council must respond to any concerns raised in the Council's report (Secs. 989E(a)(2)(B) and (b) of the Dodd-Frank Act).

Working Group Evaluation. The Council may convene a Council of Inspectors General Working Group to evaluate the Council's effectiveness and internal operations. The Council must establish such a working group by majority vote. Council members may provide staff and resources to the working group. If established, the working group must submit regular reports of its evaluations to the Council and to Congress (Sec. 989E(a)(3) of the Dodd-Frank Act).

Corrective Action for Deficiencies.—The Dodd-Frank Act requires the heads of the identified establishments to make corrective responses to deficiencies identified by the inspectors general. Specifically, the Fed chair, the CFTC chair, the NCUA chair, the director of the Pension Benefit Guarantee Corporation and the SEC chair must either take action to address identified deficiencies or certify to both houses of Congress that no action is necessary or appropriate regarding an identified deficiency (Sec. 989H of the Dodd-Frank Act).

▶ **Effective date.** The provision takes effect one day after the date of enactment (Sec. 4 of the Dodd-Frank Wall Street Reform and Consumer Protection Act).

Law source: Law at ¶10,989B, ¶10,989C, ¶10,989D, ¶10,989E, ¶10,989H and ¶10,004. Committee Report at ¶54,610.

— Sec. 989B of the Dodd-Frank Wall Street Reform and Consumer Protection Act, amending Inspector General Act Sec. 8G(a)(4);

— Sec. 989C, adding Inspector General Act Secs. 5(a)(14), (15) and (16);

— Sec. 989D, amending Inspector General Act Sec. 8G(e)(1);

— Sec. 989E, creating the Council of Inspectors General for Financial Oversight;

— Sec. 989H, mandating agency response to inspectors general;

— Sec. 4, providing the effective date.

¶4485 Person-to-Person Lending

The Dodd-Frank Wall Street Reform and Consumer Protection Act requires the U.S. Comptroller General to study and report on the person-to-person lending industry. The study's purpose is to determine the optimal federal regulatory regime for these financial services (Sec. 989F(a)(1) of the Dodd-Frank Wall Street Reform and Consumer Protection Act). The comptroller must consult with federal banking agencies, the Commission, consumer groups, outside experts and the person-to-person lending industry (Sec. 989F(a)(2) of the Dodd-Frank Act). Specifically, the study must examine:

- the regulatory structure in existence on the date of enactment, as determined by the SEC, with emphasis on application of the Securities Act, posting of consumer loan information on EDGAR and treatment of privately held person-to-person lending platforms as public companies;
- state and other federal regulators responsible for oversight and regulation of person-to-person lending markets;
- any relevant federal, state or local government or private studies completed or in progress on the date of enactment;
- consumer privacy and data protection, minimum credit standards, anti-money laundering and risk management in the regulatory structure in existence on the date of enactment, and whether new or alternative safeguards are required; and
- the uses of person-to-person lending (Sec. 989F(a)(3) of the Dodd-Frank Act).

In addition, the comptroller must submit a report on the study within one year after enactment to the Senate Banking Committee and the House Financial Services Committee (Sec. 989F(b)(1) of the Dodd-Frank Act). The report must include alternative regulatory options, including the involvement of other federal agencies, and approaches by the SEC with recommendations on the effectiveness of these alternative approaches (Sec. 989F(b)(2) of the Dodd-Frank Act).

> **CCH Comment:** The SEC, in an administrative proceeding, treated notes issued by a person-to-person lending firm as securities under Securities Act Section 2(a)(1). The SEC reasoned that the notes constituted an investment contract under the *Howey* test. The notes also were presumed to be securities as they did not fall within the category of non-security notes, and the notes did not otherwise satisfy the family resemblance test for treatment as non-security notes (*In Re. Prosper Marketplace, Inc.*, Release No. 33-8984 (citing *SEC. v. W.J. Howey Co.*, 328 U.S. 293 (1946) and *Reves v. Ernst & Young, Inc.*, 494 U.S. 56 (1990)). Section 4315 of the House bill would have given the director of the Consumer Financial Protection Agency (CFPA) primary jurisdiction to regulate person-to-person lending and person-to-person lending platforms. An interim provision would have required person-to-person lending platforms that register notes with the SEC to provide any required securities disclosures pending the issuance of regulations by the CFPA (HR 4173 EH, Sec. 4315).

▶ **Effective date.** The provision takes effect one day after the date of enactment (Sec. 4 of the Dodd-Frank Wall Street Reform and Consumer Protection Act).

Law source: Law at ¶10,989F and ¶10,004.

— Sec. 989F(a) of the Dodd-Frank Wall Street Reform and Consumer Protection Act, requiring a study of person-to-person lending;

— Sec. 989F(b), requiring a report to Congress;

— Sec. 4, providing the effective date.

¶4485

¶4490 Internal Controls Auditor Attestation

The Dodd-Frank Wall Street Reform and Consumer Protection Act exempts audit reports of smaller issuers from the internal controls attestation requirement of Sarbanes-Oxley Act Section 404(b). In addition, the legislation requires two related studies: one examining ways to reduce compliance burdens for larger companies; the other examining the impact of the smaller issuer exemption.

Exemption.—Sarbanes-Oxley Act Section 404(b) requires each registered public accounting firm that prepares or issues the audit report for an issuer to attest to, and report on, the assessment made by the issuer's management of the company's internal controls. The Dodd-Frank Act creates an exemption from this requirement for smaller issuers. Specifically, Sarbanes-Oxley Act Section 404(b) does not apply to any audit report prepared for an issuer that is neither a "large accelerated filer" nor an "accelerated filer" under Exchange Act Rule 12b-2 (Sarbanes-Oxley Act Sec. 404(c), as added by the Dodd-Frank Wall Street Reform and Consumer Protection Act).

Studies and Reports.—The SEC must study how to reduce the compliance burdens under Sarbanes-Oxley Act Section 404(b) for companies whose market capitalization is between $75 million and $250 million, while maintaining investor protections for these companies. The study also must consider whether reduced compliance burdens or a complete exemption would encourage companies to list initial public offerings on U.S. exchanges. The Commission must transmit a report of the study to Congress within nine months following enactment of Title IX, Subtitle I (Sec. 989G(b) of the Dodd-Frank Act).

Separately, the Comptroller General of the United States must study the impact of the legislation's amendments to Sarbanes-Oxley Act Section 404. Specifically, the study must examine:

- whether exempt issuers have fewer or more restatements of published accounting statements than nonexempt issuers;
- the cost of capital for exempt issuers versus the capital costs for nonexempt issuers;
- whether there is any difference in investor confidence in the integrity of financial statements of exempt issuers as compared to nonexempt issuers;
- whether issuers that do not receive the attestation for internal controls should have to disclose this fact to investors; and
- the costs and benefits to exempt issuers that voluntarily obtain the attestation of an independent auditor (Sec. 989I(a) of the Dodd-Frank Act).

The Comptroller General must submit a report on its study to the Senate Banking Committee and the House Financial Services Committee within three years after enactment (Sec. 989I(b) of the Dodd-Frank Act).

▶ **Effective date.** The provisions take effect one day after the date of enactment (Sec. 4 of the Dodd-Frank Wall Street Reform and Consumer Protection Act).

Law source: Law at ¶10,989G, ¶10,989I and ¶10,004.

— Sec. 989G(a) of the Dodd-Frank Wall Street Reform and Consumer Protection Act, adding Sarbanes-Oxley Act Sec. 404(c);

- Sec. 989G(b), requiring an SEC study and report on reducing compliance costs;
- Sec. 989I(a), requiring a Comptroller General study of the smaller issuer exemption;
- Sec. 989I(b), requiring a report to Congress;
- Sec. 4, providing the effective date.

¶4495 NAIC Model Regulations

The Dodd-Frank Wall Street Reform and Consumer Protection Act seeks to promote state adoption of model regulations issued by the National Association of Insurance Commissioners (NAIC) for the protection of seniors and other consumers. Specifically, the Dodd-Frank Act promotes adoption of model regulations regarding exempt insurance and annuity products. Securities Act Section 3(a)(8) provides that exempt securities include "any insurance or endowment policy or annuity contract or optional annuity contract, issued by a corporation subject to the supervision of the insurance commissioner, bank commissioner, or any agency or officer performing like functions, of any State or Territory of the United States or the District of Columbia." Section 989J of the Dodd-Frank Act directs the commission to also treat as exempt any insurance or endowment policy or annuity contract or optional annuity contract:

- whose value does not vary according to the performance of a separate account;
- that satisfies either: (1) the nonforfeiture laws or similar requirements of the applicable state law at the time issued; or (2) absent relevant state law, the Model Standard Nonforfeiture Law for Life Insurance or Model Standard Nonforfeiture Law for Individual Deferred Annuities, published by the NAIC; and
- that is issued on or after June 16, 2013, in a state, or by an insurance company domiciled in a state, that either: (1) adopts suitability rules that substantially meet or exceed the minimum requirements of the NAIC Suitability in Annuity Transactions Model Regulation adopted in March 2010, and adopts rules that substantially meet or exceed the minimum requirements of any successor modifications to the model regulations within five years of NAIC's adoption of any successor model regulations; or (2) adopts and implements nationwide practices that meet or exceed the minimum requirements of the NAIC Suitability in Annuity Transactions Model Regulation (Model 275) (or successor) and is thus subject to examination by the insurance company's state of domicile or by any other state where the insurance company conducts sales of subject products, for the purpose of monitoring compliance (Sec. 989J(a) of the Dodd-Frank Act).

In addition, the Dodd-Frank Act states a rule of construction for implementing the provision. Specifically, the provision cannot be construed to affect whether any insurance or endowment policy, annuity contract or optional annuity contract not addressed in the provision is or is not an exempt security under Securities Act Section 3(a)(8) (Sec. 989J(b) of the Dodd-Frank Act).

▶ **Effective date.** The provision takes effect one day after the date of enactment (Sec. 4 of the Dodd-Frank Wall Street Reform and Consumer Protection Act).

Law source: Law at ¶10,989J and ¶10,004.

— Sec. 989J(a) of the Dodd-Frank Wall Street Reform and Consumer Protection Act, directing the SEC to treat certain securities as exempt;
— Sec. 989J(b), stating a rule of construction;
— Sec. 4, providing the effective date.

Consumer Financial Protection

INTRODUCTION and DEFINITIONS

¶4505 Introduction and Short Title
¶4510 Definitions

BUREAU of CONSUMER FINANCIAL PROTECTION

¶4515 Creation of the Bureau
¶4520 Executive and Administrative Powers
¶4525 Bureau Personnel and Internal Organization
¶4530 Consumer Advisory Board
¶4535 Coordination with Other Agencies
¶4540 Reports to Congress
¶4545 Funding the Bureau; Fines and Penalties

GENERAL BUREAU POWERS

¶4550 Goals and Functions of the Bureau
¶4555 Rulemaking Authority
¶4560 Financial Stability Oversight Council Review of Regulations
¶4565 Bureau Supervision of Nondepository Institutions
¶4570 Supervision of Large Institutions
¶4575 Supervision of Smaller Institutions
¶4580 Limits on the Bureau's Authority
¶4585 Arbitration Agreements
¶4590 Exclusion for Motor Vehicle Dealers

SPECIFIC BUREAU AUTHORITIES

¶4595 Unfair, Deceptive or Abusive Acts or Practices
¶4600 Disclosures
¶4605 Consumers' Right to Information
¶4610 Response to Consumers

¶4615 Private Education Loan Ombudsman
¶4620 Prohibited Acts and Assisting Prohibited Acts

PREEMPTION of STATE LAW and STATE ENFORCEMENT

¶4625 Effect on State Law
¶4630 State Enforcement Authority
¶4635 Preservation of Existing Contracts
¶4640 Preemption Standards for National Banks and Subsidiaries
¶4645 Preemption for Nondepositary National Bank Subsidiaries and Affiliates
¶4650 Preemption for Federal Thrifts and Subsidiaries
¶4655 State Visitorial Authority over Federal Institutions

BUREAU ENFORCEMENT POWERS

¶4660 Definitions
¶4665 Investigations and Administrative Discovery
¶4670 Hearings and Adjudications
¶4675 Litigation
¶4680 Relief Available for Violations
¶4685 Criminal Prosecution Referrals
¶4690 Whistleblower Protections

TRANSFER of FUNCTIONS and PERSONNEL

¶4695 Transfer of Bureau Functions
¶4700 Designated Transfer Date
¶4705 Savings Provisions
¶4710 Personnel Transfers
¶4715 Incidental Transfers of Assets and Liabilities
¶4720 Interim Operations
¶4725 Oversight of the Transition

REGULATORY IMPROVEMENTS—AMENDMENTS to OTHER LAWS

¶4730 Lending to Women- or Minority-Owned Small Businesses
¶4735 Assistance for Economically Vulnerable Persons
¶4740 Remittance Transfers
¶4745 Government Sponsored Enterprise Study
¶4750 Payment Card Transaction Fees and Rules

¶4755	Reverse Mortgage Rules
¶4760	Private Education Loans and Lenders
¶4765	Credit Scores Study and Report
¶4770	Exchange Facilitators
¶4775	Financial Fraud

CONFORMING AMENDMENTS

¶4780	Amendments to the Inspector General Act
¶4785	Amendments to the Privacy Act
¶4790	Amendments to the Alternative Mortgage Transaction Parity Act
¶4795	Amendments to the Electronic Fund Transfer Act
¶4800	Amendments to the Equal Credit Opportunity Act
¶4805	Amendments to the Expedited Funds Availability Act
¶4810	Amendments to the Fair Credit Billing Act
¶4815	Amendments to the Fair Credit Reporting Act and the Fair and Accurate Credit Transactions Act of 2003
¶4820	Amendments to the Fair Debt Collection Practices Act
¶4825	Amendments to Federal Deposit Insurance Act
¶4830	Amendments to the Federal Financial Institutions Examination Council Act
¶4835	Amendments to the Federal Trade Commission Act
¶4840	Amendments to the Gramm-Leach-Bliley Act
¶4845	Amendments to the Home Mortgage Disclosure Act
¶4850	Amendments to the Homeowners Protection Act
¶4855	Amendments to the Home Ownership and Equity Protection Act
¶4860	Amendments to the Omnibus Appropriations Act, 2009
¶4865	Amendments to the Real Estate Settlement Procedures Act
¶4870	Amendments to Interstate Land Sales Full Disclosure Act
¶4875	Amendments to the Right to Financial Privacy Act
¶4880	Amendments to the Secure and Fair Enforcement for Mortgage Licensing Act of 2008
¶4885	Amendments to the Truth in Lending Act
¶4890	Amendments to the Truth in Savings Act
¶4895	Amendments to the Telemarketing and Consumer Fraud and Abuse Prevention Act
¶4900	Amendments to the Paperwork Reduction Act
¶4905	Adjustments for Inflation in the Truth in Lending Act
¶4910	Adverse Action Notices and Credit Reports
¶4915	Small Business Fairness and Regulatory Transparency

INTRODUCTION and DEFINITIONS

¶4505 Introduction and Short Title

Title X of the Dodd-Frank Wall Street Reform and Consumer Protection Act is the "Consumer Financial Protection Act of 2010" (Sec. 1001 of the Dodd-Frank Act).

During consideration of financial regulatory reform legislation, perhaps no single topic caused more dispute than the creation of a consumer financial protection regulator. The bill offered by the Obama administration in the summer of 2009 called for the creation of an independent agency, and the House of Representatives adopted this position in its version of the bill. On the other hand, some in Congress wanted no dedicated agency at all. Proposals from this quarter included making no significant change or shifting the responsibility for consumer protection to the Federal Deposit Insurance Corporation. The bill passed by the Senate attempted to reach a compromise among these ideas by creating an independent bureau within the Federal Reserve Board, and this is the choice made by the Dodd-Frank Act.

The major justification offered for the creation of a consumer financial protection agency of some type was that the existing federal regulators had not done an adequate job of regulating irresponsible mortgage lending practices that contributed substantially to the financial system meltdown. To over-simplify the assertion, mortgage brokers and lenders made loans with high loan-to-value ratios (in extreme cases lending as much as 120 percent of a home's appraised value), loans based on the value of the property rather than the borrower's ability to make payments, loans with little or no documentation of the borrower's income and assets (including the infamously named "liar loans"), loans that permitted negative amortization and other loans that, for one reason or another, were far too likely to default when economic conditions deteriorated and that also, often, were abusive to consumers. The securitization of these loans resulted in worldwide economic pain when they began to go into default.

Of course, the establishment of the Bureau of Consumer Financial Protection provided an opportunity to address a number of other practices seen as abusive. It also allowed a chance to strengthen the hand of the state regulators and attorneys general, who often were seen as having tried harder than the federal regulators to protect consumers. Indeed, some state legislatures and regulators had tried to address some of the problematic mortgage lending practices, only to see their efforts blocked by federal regulatory agencies who asserted that the state laws were preempted by federal law.

Structure of the Consumer Protection Act.—In addition to two introductory sections, the Consumer Financial Protection Act comprises eight subtitles:

A. *Bureau of Consumer Financial Protection*—establishes the Bureau of Consumer Financial Protection within the Federal Reserve System and outlines the Bureau's organization and funding.

B. *General Powers of the Bureau*—grants the Bureau the authority to supervise and regulate providers of consumer financial products and services.

C. *Specific Bureau Authorities*—establishes the Bureau's power to act against unfair, deceptive or abusive acts and practices.

D. *Preservation of State Law*—describes the effect of federal law on state law and preserves some regulatory and enforcement powers of state authorities.

E. *Enforcement Powers*—authorizes the Bureau to enforce the Act in court or administratively and to seek remedies for violations of the Act.

F. *Transfer of Functions and Personnel; Transitional Provisions*—provides for the transfer of necessary personnel from the other federal regulatory agencies to the Bureau and establishes protections for the transferred employees.

G. *Regulatory Improvements*—amends a number of the existing federal consumer financial protection laws.

H. *Conforming Amendments*—provides amendments to a number of other federal laws to maintain consistency with the Act.

▶ **Effective date.** The provision takes effect one day after the date of enactment (Sec. 4 of the Dodd-Frank Wall Street Reform and Consumer Protection Act).

Law source: Law at ¶11,001 and ¶10,004. Committee Report at ¶54,640.

— Sec. 1001 of the Dodd-Frank Wall Street Reform and Consumer Protection Act, providing the short title of Title X;

— Sec. 4 providing the effective date;

¶4510 Definitions

No significant legislation is likely to be effective unless it first defines a number of terms. Sec. 1002 of the Dodd-Frank Act provides definitions for more than 25 terms, and many of those definitions have multiple parts and exceptions. The most significant definitions are the following:

Consumer.—A consumer is not just an individual consumer. The definition also includes the individual's agent, trustee or representative (Sec. 1002(4) of the Dodd-Frank Act).

Consumer Financial Product or Service.—This is a financial product or service offered or provided for use by consumers primarily for personal, family or household purposes. It also includes lending activities, real estate settlement services, real or personal property appraisals, consumer reporting activities and debt collection activities if they are delivered, offered or provided in connection with a financial product or service for use by consumers primarily for personal, family or household purposes (Sec. 1002(5) of the Dodd-Frank Act).

Covered Person.—A person that offers or provides financial products or services, or an affiliate that provides services to such a person (Sec. 1002(6) of the Dodd-Frank Act). Generally speaking, these are the entities that are under the supervision of the Bureau and that must comply with its regulations.

Credit.—The right to defer payment of a debt or to incur debt or buy property or services and defer payment (Sec. 1002(7) of the Dodd-Frank Act).

Deposit-Taking Activity.—In addition to the expected meaning of taking or holding deposits by a depository institution, this includes any covered person's receipt of funds to facilitate a payment or transfer value between a consumer and a third party (Sec. 1002(8) of the Dodd-Frank Act).

Designated Transfer Date.—This is the date on which the consumer financial protection functions and authority will be transferred from the other federal regulatory agencies to the Bureau. It is not fixed in the Dodd-Frank Act. Instead, no later than 60 days after Title X is enacted, the Secretary of the Treasury is to consult with the other regulators and select a date no earlier than 180 days and no later than 12 months after enactment. The date can be extended to 18 months after enactment if the Treasury Secretary certifies to Congress that the Title cannot be implemented more quickly (Sec. 1002(9) and Sec. 1062 of the Dodd-Frank Act).

Enumerated Consumer Laws.—These are the federal laws over which the Bureau has regulatory authority (Sec. 1002(12) of the Dodd-Frank Act). There are 18 of them:

(1) Alternative Mortgage Transaction Parity Act;

(2) Consumer Leasing Act;

(3) Electronic Funds Transfer Act;

(4) Equal Credit Opportunity Act;

(5) Fair Credit Billing Act;

(6) Fair Credit Reporting Act (in part);

(7) Fair Debt Collection Practices Act;

(8) Federal Deposit Insurance Act provisions on private deposit insurance;

(9) Gramm-Leach-Bliley Act provisions on consumer financial information privacy and information sharing;

(10) Homeowners Protection Act of 1998;

(11) Home Ownership and Equity Protection Act of 1994;

(12) Home Mortgage Disclosure Act;

(13) Real Estate Settlement Procedures Act;

(14) Secure and Fair Enforcement for Mortgage Licensing Act;

(15) Truth in Lending Act;

(16) Truth in Savings Act;

(17) a portion of the Omnibus Appropriations Act of 2009 (Public Law 111-8) requiring the Federal Trade Commission to adopt a rule addressing unfair or deceptive acts or practices in mortgage lending; and

(18) Interstate Land Sales Full Disclosure Act.

Federal Consumer Financial Law.—This is a more extensive group of laws than the enumerated laws. It includes the enumerated laws and also Title X of the Dodd-Frank Act, the federal laws for which the Bureau has regulatory authority under Subtitles F and H and any rule or order issued by the Bureau. The Federal Trade Commission Act, however, is excluded (Sec. 1002(14) of the Dodd-Frank Act).

Financial Product or Service.—The Dodd-Frank Act lists nearly 30 activities that are considered to be financial products or services and then gives the Bureau the authority to add to the list any activities that are financial in nature or permissible for a bank or a holding company and likely to materially affect consumers, or that are used as a subterfuge to avoid regulation under Title X or any of the enumerated laws (Sec. 1002(15) of the Dodd-Frank Act). The term includes obvious activities such as accepting deposits and extending credit, but also activities such as:

- longer-term leases of property that are functionally equivalent to financing a purchase;
- providing payment or financial data processing services to consumers;
- making consumer reports;
- collecting debts;
- providing credit counseling, debt management or other financial advisory services; and
- providing, issuing or, in some cases, selling stored value cards.

There are specified exceptions as well. These include the business of insurance and electronic conduit services.

Prudential Regulator.—The Federal Reserve Board, Office of the Comptroller of the Currency or National Credit Union Administration, as appropriate for the covered person under consideration (Sec. 1002(24) of the Dodd-Frank Act).

Related Person.—A director, officer, controlling shareholder or managerial employee of a covered person that is not supervised by one of the prudential regulators; a person who materially participates in conducting the affairs of such a covered person; or an independent contractor—including an attorney or accountant—who knowingly or recklessly participates in the violation of any law or regulation or the breach of any fiduciary duty (Sec. 1002(25) of the Dodd-Frank Act).

State.—All of the 50 states plus the District of Columbia, Puerto Rico, Guam, Samoa, the Northern Mariana Islands, the U.S. Virgin Islands and any federally-recognized Indian tribe (Sec. 1002(27) of the Dodd-Frank Act).

Stored Value.—Funds represented in an electronic format in a way that allows them to be retrieved and transferred electronically, other than prepaid, fixed-amount, non-reloadable gift cards issued by and redeemable only with a merchant that sells nonfinancial products or services (Sec. 1002(28) of the Dodd-Frank Act).

▶ **Effective date.** The provision takes effect one day after the date of enactment (Sec. 4 of the Dodd-Frank Wall Street Reform and Consumer Protection Act).

Law source: Law at ¶11,002 and ¶10,004. Committee Report at ¶54,641.

— Sec. 1002 of the Dodd-Frank Wall Street Reform and Consumer Protection Act;

— Sec. 4, providing the effective date.

BUREAU of CONSUMER FINANCIAL PROTECTION

¶4515 Creation of the Bureau

The centerpiece of Title X of the Dodd-Frank Wall Street Reform and Consumer Protection Act, called the Consumer Financial Protection Act of 2010, is the creation of the Bureau of Consumer Financial Protection (the BCFP or the Bureau). The Bureau is an executive agency charged with regulating the offering and providing of consumer financial products and services under the federal consumer financial protection laws. It is an independent bureau within the Federal Reserve System (Sec. 1011(a) of the Dodd-Frank Act).

The structure of, and indeed the need for, the BCFP was one of the most controversial subjects in the financial services regulatory reform debate. On one hand, the version of H.R. 4173 passed by the House of Representatives called for the creation of a completely new agency, to be called (appropriately enough) the Consumer Financial Protection Agency. This was in accord with the proposal put forward by the Obama administration during the summer of 2009. On the other hand, many legislators took the position that consumer financial protection should remain the province of the Federal Reserve Board or that, if a change was necessary, responsibility for consumer protection should be moved to another of the existing regulatory agencies.

Opposition to the creation of a new federal agency was led in the Senate by Banking Committee Ranking Member Richard Shelby, R-Ala. Needing to defeat a Republican filibuster, Banking Committee Chairman Christopher Dodd, D-Conn., crafted a compromise in the Senate—a bureau within the Fed, rather than an independent agency. However, the Senate bill also took considerable steps to attempt to insulate the proposed bureau from interference by the Fed. It was this compromise that was the foundation of the BCFP.

Structure of the Bureau.—The BCFP is to be led by a Director nominated by the President and confirmed by the Senate. The only statutory criterion for eligibility is that the individual must be a U.S. citizen (Sec. 1011(b) of the Dodd-Frank Act). The Director will serve for a term of five years and until a successor is nominated and confirmed Sec. 1011(c) of the Dodd-Frank Act).

The Director has the power to appoint his own Deputy Director. The law specifies no eligibility criteria or term of office for the deputy (Sec. 1011(b) of the Dodd-Frank Act).

Neither the Director nor the Deputy Director may hold any office or job in any Federal Reserve Bank, Federal Home Loan Bank or regulated entity (Sec. 1011(d) of the Dodd-Frank Act).

The main office of the BCFP is to be in Washington, D.C. The Bureau also may establish branch offices as necessary to perform its tasks (Sec. 10011(e) of the Dodd-Frank Act).

▶ **Effective date.** Subtitle A—Bureau of Consumer Financial Protection, is effective on the date of enactment (Sec. 1018 of the Dodd-Frank Wall Street Reform and Consumer Protection Act).

Law source: Law at ¶11,011 and ¶11,018. Committee Report at ¶54,660.

— Sec. 1011 of the Dodd-Frank Wall Street Reform and Consumer Protection Act;
— Sec. 1018, providing the effective date.

¶4520 Executive and Administrative Powers

The Bureau of Consumer Financial Protection is authorized to adopt policies to manage its own executive and administrative functions. These include: policies on adopting rules and issuing orders and guidance; entering into contracts; establishing an internal organization; hiring and supervising personnel; and authorizing expenditures (Sec. 1012(a) of the Dodd-Frank Act). The Bureau Director may delegate any of the Bureau's authority to any of its employees or representatives (Sec. 1012(b) of the Dodd-Frank Act).

Independence of the Bureau.—The Act goes to considerable lengths to insulate the BCFP from interference by the Federal Reserve Board. The Fed can delegate to the BCFP the power to examine institutions under the Fed's authority, but the Fed cannot intervene in any matter before the Bureau, including enforcement proceedings and examinations, unless there is a specific basis under law for doing so. The Fed cannot appoint, give directions to or remove any officer or employee of the Bureau, and cannot take over any part of the Bureau or usurp any of its powers.

Moreover, the Dodd-Frank Act specifies that the Fed has no power to review and no right to approve any rule or order of the Bureau, and that it cannot delay or block the Bureau's issuance of any regulation. (However, the Fed does have a seat on the Financial Stability Oversight Council, which does have such powers.)

The BCFP Director and officers also are shielded from any efforts to control their contacts with Congress, as long as it is made clear that any statements are the views of the Director or the officer, rather than of the Fed or the President.

The Dodd-Frank Act also makes clear that neither the Fed nor the Bureau have any legal liability for the other's action or inaction (Sec. 1012(c) of the Dodd-Frank Act).

▶ **Effective date.** The provision is effective on the date of enactment (Sec. 1018 of the Dodd-Frank Wall Street Reform and Consumer Protection Act).

Law source: Law at ¶11,012 and ¶11,018. Committee Report at ¶54,661.

— Sec. 1012 of the Dodd-Frank Wall Street Reform and Consumer Protection Act;
— Sec. 1018, providing the effective date.

¶4525 Bureau Personnel and Internal Organization

The Director of the Bureau has complete authority over the Bureau's employees, subject to other relevant federal law. He also has considerable power to organize the Bureau as he sees fit, although the Act requires the creation of certain offices and the performance of certain functions.

The BCFP Director can employ whatever attorneys, examiners, other professionals and other employees he determines are needed for the Bureau to be able to perform its assigned tasks. Although these employees are independent of any direction from the Federal Reserve Board, they are to receive the same compensation as other comparable Fed employees. They also have the same rights and protections as other federal employees (Sec. 1013(a) of the Dodd-Frank Act).

The Dodd-Frank Act requires the Bureau to appoint an ombudsman to serve as a liaison between it and any person who has a problem dealing with the Bureau that arises from the Bureau's regulatory activities. The ombudsman also is to create a system that allows individuals to bring confidential complaints against the Bureau. The ombudsman is to be appointed within 180 days after the designated transfer date (Sec. 1013(a) of the Dodd-Frank Act). [The designated transfer date is a date to be fixed by the Treasury Secretary on which the consumer protection functions of the other federal agencies will be transferred to the Bureau. It will be at least 180 days, but no longer than 18 months, after enactment (Sec. 1062(c) of the Dodd-Frank Act)].

Required Functional Units.—Although the BCFP Director can organize the Bureau as he chooses, he is required to establish three specific functional units. These generally are to address research, community affairs and collecting and tracking complaints.

Research—The research unit is responsible for research, analysis and reporting on: market developments; access to fair and affordable credit; effective disclosures; consumer understanding of costs, risks and benefits; consumer behavior and performance; and the experiences of underserved consumers.

Community affairs—The community affairs unit is to provide assistance and information on offering products and services to traditionally underserved consumers.

Complaints—The complaint unit is to establish a toll-free telephone number and a website for collecting and responding to consumer complaints about financial products and services. It also is to maintain a database containing information on these complaints. This unit is to work with the Federal Trade Commission, the federal banking regulators and, when possible, state regulators to ensure that consumer complaints are directed to the proper agency.

The Dodd-Frank Act calls for the BCFP to report to Congress annually on complaints it has received and, when possible, on how those complaints were resolved. All of the federal regulatory agencies, as well as appropriate state agencies, are to share information to be used in this report and to supervise the market for consumer financial products and services generally (Sec. 1013(b) of the Dodd-Frank Act).

Required Offices.—The Bureau Director also is required to establish four specific offices—the Office of Fair Lending and Equal Opportunity, the Office of Financial Education, the Office of Service Member Affairs and the Office of Financial Protection for Older Americans. The first three of these are to be established no later than one year after the designated transfer date (Sec. 1013(f) of the Dodd-Frank Act).

Office of Fair Lending and Equal Opportunity—The Office of Fair Lending and Equal Opportunity is one of the two offices that must be headed by an Assistant Director of the Bureau. It is charged with oversight and enforcement of the Equal Credit Opportunity Act, the Home Mortgage Disclosure Act and any other laws under the BCFP's purview that address fair, equitable and nondiscriminatory access to credit. To do this, it is directed to coordinate with the other federal and state regulators and to work with industry and community groups. The Office also is to make annual reports to Congress on its fair lending enforcement efforts (Sec. 1013(c) of the Dodd-Frank Act).

Office of Financial Education—The main job of the Office of Financial Education is to develop educational programs that will help consumers make better financial decisions. It also is to work to improve consumers' financial literacy through enhancing access to traditional financial products and services and financial counseling. The Act calls for the Office to set "measurable goals and objectives" for this effort. The Bureau Director also is now the Vice Chairman of the Financial Literacy and Education Commission.

Within two years of the designated transfer date, and annually after that, the Office is to report to the House Financial Services Committee and the Senate Banking Committee on its strategy and activities.

The Dodd-Frank Act also requires the Comptroller General to conduct a study on the feasibility of a certification program for the persons who conduct the education programs. The study, which also is to look at tools that can be used to evaluate the programs and make the programs more effective, is to be completed and the results reported to Congress within one year of the enactment of Title X (Sec. 1013(d) of the Dodd-Frank Act)

Office of Service Member Affairs—During the debate over financial services regulatory reform, considerable attention was given to what were seen as undesirable practices that targeted members of the military services and their families. One response to these concerns was the requirement that the Bureau include an Office of Service Member Affairs. This Office is to develop education initiatives targeted specifically to servicemembers and their families, and it is to coordinate with the Bureau's complaint tracking unit to monitor complaints from these individuals and the resolution of those complaints.

The BCFP Director is specifically authorized to establish regional offices near military bases and facilities and to enter into formal agreements with the Defense Department (Sec. 1013(e) of the Dodd-Frank Act).

Office of Financial Protection for Older Americans—The deadline for the creation of the Office of Financial Protection for Older Americans is earlier than for the other agencies—180 days after the designated transfer date, rather than one year. This office, which also is to be headed by an Assistant Director of the Bureau, is to focus on the financial literacy of senior citizens, on protecting them from unfair, deceptive or abusive acts and practices and on their financial choices. It is to develop goals for education and counseling programs and oversee the certification of those who run those programs. Within 18 months of its creation, the Office is to make legislative and regulatory recommendations on how seniors can best select counselors and verify their credentials (Sec. 1013(g) of the Dodd-Frank Act).

▶ **Effective date.** The provision is effective on the date of enactment (Sec. 1018 of the Dodd-Frank Wall Street Reform and Consumer Protection Act).

¶4525

Law source: Law at ¶11,013 and ¶11,018. Committee Report at ¶54,662.

— Sec. 1013 of the Dodd-Frank Wall Street Reform and Consumer Protection Act;

— Sec. 1013(d), amending Financial Literacy and Education Improvement Act Sec. 513;

— Sec. 1018, providing the effective date.

¶4530 Consumer Advisory Board

The Bureau is to be advised by the Consumer Advisory Board, which also is to keep the Bureau informed on emerging national and regional trends in the consumer financial services industry (Sec. 1014(a) of the Dodd-Frank Act). Board members are to be experts in consumer financial protection issues or consumer financial products and services. The Board is to include representatives of financial institutions that primarily serve underserved communities or communities that were significantly affected by higher-priced mortgage loans, but also should include representatives from financial institutions generally. The Act does not specify how many members the Board should have, but does say that at least six members are to be appointed based on the recommendation of the Federal Reserve Bank presidents (Sec. 1014(b) of the Dodd-Frank Act).

The Board is to meet at least twice a year, and more often if the BCFP Director wishes (Dodd-Frank Act Sec. 1014(c)). Members who are not full-time federal employees are to be compensated for their service, and their expenses are to be reimbursed (Sec. 1014(d) of the Dodd-Frank Act).

▶ **Effective date.** The provision is effective on the date of enactment (Sec. 1018 of the Dodd-Frank Wall Street Reform and Consumer Protection Act).

Law source: Law at ¶11,014 and ¶11,018. Committee Report at ¶54,663.

— Sec. 1014 of the Dodd-Frank Wall Street Reform and Consumer Protection Act;

— Sec. 1018, providing the effective date.

¶4535 Coordination with Other Agencies

The BCFP is directed here, as in other places, to coordinate with other federal agencies and also with state regulators. The goal of this cooperation is consistent regulatory treatment of consumer financial and investment products and services (Sec. 1015 of the Dodd-Frank Act).

▶ **Effective date.** The provision is effective on the date of enactment (Sec. 1018 of the Dodd-Frank Wall Street Reform and Consumer Protection Act).

Law source: Law at ¶11,015 and ¶11,018. Committee Report at ¶54,664.

— Sec. 1015 of the Dodd-Frank Wall Street Reform and Consumer Protection Act;

— Sec. 1018, providing the effective date.

¶4540 Reports to Congress

The BCFP is required to submit semi-annual reports to the Senate Banking Committee and the House Financial Services Committee, and the Bureau Director is required to appear before those Committees in connection with the reports (Sec. 1016(a) of the Dodd-Frank Act). This is to begin with the first session of Congress after the designated transfer date—a date to be established by the Treasury Secretary that is between 180 days and 12 months after the enactment of the Act, with a possible extension of an additional six months (Sec. 1062(c) of the Dodd-Frank Act).

These reports must include the following:

- a discussion of the significant problems faced by consumers;
- a justification of the Bureau's budget request;
- a list of the Bureau's significant rules and other actions during the prior year and the Bureau's plans for the following year;
- an analysis of consumer complaints collected by the Bureau during the year;
- a description of the supervisory and enforcement actions in which the BCFP participated during the year;
- a description of actions taken with respect to regulated persons other than banks, thrifts and credit unions;
- an assessment of the significant actions of state regulators;
- an analysis of the Bureau's efforts to promote fair lending; and
- an analysis of the Bureau's efforts to promote diversity among its employees and contractors (Sec. 1016(c) of the Dodd-Frank Act).

▶ **Effective date.** The provision is effective on the date of enactment (Sec. 1018 of the Dodd-Frank Wall Street Reform and Consumer Protection Act).

Law source: Law at ¶11,016 and ¶11,018. Committee Report at ¶54,665.

— Sec. 1016 of the Dodd-Frank Wall Street Reform and Consumer Protection Act;

— Sec. 1018, providing the effective date.

¶4545 Funding the Bureau; Fines and Penalties

The Bureau has the authority to determine its own budget and to claim that amount from the Federal Reserve System, up to a specified percentage of the Fed's 2009 total operating expenses. This is a significant step in maintaining the Bureau's autonomy.

Beginning on the designated transfer date, the Director is to inform the Fed of the funds he has determined the BCFP will need to carry out its duties, on either an annual or quarterly basis. The Fed is required to transfer that amount to the Bureau; however, the amount cannot exceed 10 percent of the Fed's 2009 total operating expenses in 2011, 11 percent in 2012 or 12 percent in or after 2013. The maximum amount is to be adjusted for inflation. Before the designated transfer date, the Treasury Secretary will determine how much the Fed will transfer to the BCFP (Sec. 1017(a) of the Dodd-Frank Act).

The Bureau is subject to standard fiscal controls. Financial operating plans and forecasts and quarterly reports are to be furnished to the Office of Management and Budget. The BCFP is to have the same type of financial management systems as are required of other federal agencies and is to prepare annual financial statements. The financial statement are not to be consolidated with those of the Fed. The Director is to attest to the effectiveness of the Bureau's internal controls, and the Bureau's financial transactions are to be audited annually (Sec. 1017(a) of the Dodd-Frank Act).

Consumer Financial Protection Fund.—The funds transferred to the Bureau are to be deposited in a separate fund at one of the Federal Reserve Banks designated the Consumer Financial Protection Fund. At the Bureau's request, the Fed can invest this money in obligations of or guaranteed by the United States, and any resulting revenue will be credited to the Fund (Sec. 1017(b) of the Dodd-Frank Act).

The Consumer Financial Protection Fund is the source of funds for the BCFP's operations, including compensation. It is not considered to be government funds or appropriated money and is not subject to apportionment (that is, the amount available to the Bureau is not required to be divided on a periodic basis) (Sec. 1017(c) of the Dodd-Frank Act).

Victims Relief Fund.—Civil penalties collected by the BCFP are to be deposited into the Consumer Financial Protection Civil Penalty Fund at one of the Federal Reserve Banks. This fund is not available for the Bureau's operations; instead, it is to be used for payments to victims of activities for which civil penalties have been imposed. The Act does not require explicitly that the proceeds of a civil penalty must be paid to the victims of the specific wrongful activity for which the penalty was imposed, only that the person receiving a payment be a victim of some activity from which a penalty resulted.

If victims cannot be located or payments are impractical, the BCFP may use the fund to pay for consumer education and financial literacy programs. The Act does not specify the mechanics of the payment process, leaving it to be established by regulations adopted by the Board (Sec. 1017(d) of the Dodd-Frank Act).

Additional Appropriations.—In case the funds transferred from the Fed are insufficient for the Bureau's operations, the Act includes an appropriation of $200 million for each of the years 2010 through 2014 (Sec. 1017(e) of the Dodd-Frank Act).

▶ **Effective date.** The provision is effective on the date of enactment (Sec. 1018 of the Dodd-Frank Wall Street Reform and Consumer Protection Act).

Law source: Law at ¶11,017 and ¶11,018. Committee Report at ¶54,666.

— Sec. 1017 of the Dodd-Frank Wall Street Reform and Consumer Protection Act;

— Sec. 1018, providing the effective date.

GENERAL BUREAU POWERS

¶4550 Goals and Functions of the Bureau

The general goal of the Bureau of Consumer Financial Protection is to implement and enforce the federal consumer financial protection laws consistently in order to ensure that consumers have access to the markets and that the markets are "fair, transparent, and competitive" (Sec. 1021(a) of the Dodd-Frank Act).

The Act establishes five objectives for how the BCFP is to use its powers. The Bureau is to ensure that:

- consumers have the information they need to make responsible decisions about financial products and services;
- consumers are protected from discrimination and from unfair, deceptive or abusive acts and practices;
- outdated, unneeded or unnecessarily burdensome regulations are addressed;
- the federal consumer financial protection laws are consistently enforced regardless of whether or not the product or service provider is a depository institution; and
- the consumer financial products and services markets function transparently and efficiently in order to encourage both access and innovation (Sec. 1021(b) of the Dodd-Frank Act).

Primary Functions.—The Act also enumerates six specific functions for the Bureau:

- conducting financial education programs;
- collecting, investigating and addressing consumer complaints;
- collecting, researching and publishing information on the functioning of the markets;
- supervising consumer financial product and service providers that are not supervised by the prudential regulators;
- adopting regulations and issuing orders and guidance to implement the federal consumer financial protection laws; and
- performing activities ancillary to the described activities (Sec. 1021(c) of the Dodd-Frank Act).

▶ **Effective date.** The provision is effective on the designated transfer date, which is a date to be selected by the Treasury Secretary that is at least 180 days, but no longer than 12 months, after enactment, subject to a possible extension of up to an additional six months. Subtitle B—General Powers of the Bureau is effective on the transfer date, except that Secs. 1022 (Rulemaking Authority), 1024 (Supervision of Nondepository Covered Persons) and 1025(e) (Supervision of Very Large Banks, Savings Associations, and Credit Unions—Simultaneous and Coordinated Supervisory Action) are effective on the date of enactment (Secs. 1029A and Sec. 1062(c) of the Dodd-Frank Wall Street Reform and Consumer Protection Act).

Law source: Law at ¶11,021, ¶11,062 and ¶11,029A. Committee Report at ¶54,680.

— Sec. 1021 of the Dodd-Frank Wall Street Reform and Consumer Protection Act;

— Sec. 1062(c), providing the designated transfer date;
— Sec. 1029A, providing the effective date.

¶4555 Rulemaking Authority

The Bureau generally is authorized to use all of its powers to implement the federal consumer financial laws (Sec. 1022(a) of the Dodd-Frank Act). This includes adopting regulations and issuing orders and guidance (Sec. 1022(b) of the Dodd-Frank Act).

The Bureau has nearly exclusive authority to adopt rules implementing federal consumer financial laws (the exception being that the Federal Trade Commission retains the authority to adopt rules that implement the Federal Trade Commission Act (Sec. 1061(b) of the Dodd-Frank Act). Moreover, if adopting a regulation requires interpreting an ambiguous section of a consumer financial law, the BCFP's interpretation is to be accepted by the courts as long as it is reasonable.

Some special considerations apply to rulemaking by the BCFP. It is not only to engage in a traditional cost-benefit analysis but also to consider:

- whether a proposed rule will reduce consumers' access to financial products and services;
- the effect the rule would have on regulated persons; and
- the effect the rule would have on consumers in rural locations.

More significantly, the Bureau also must engage in a meaningful process of consultation with the Federal Reserve Board, Office of the Comptroller of the Currency and other federal regulators on whether a proposed rule is consistent with their prudential, market and systemic regulatory objectives. Should any of these regulators object to a proposed rule in writing, the Bureau must respond to that objection in any release that adopts the proposal.

Exemptions from regulations can be granted on a class-wide basis. The Bureau must consider three factors in deciding to grant an exemption:

- the total assets of the class of covered persons to be exempted;
- the volume of consumer financial product and services transactions in which the covered persons engage; and
- whether other laws or rules exist that provide adequate protection to consumers (Sec. 1022(b) of the Dodd-Frank Act).

Monitoring the Markets.—The Bureau is instructed to monitor the consumer financial products and services markets, and developments in the markets, in search of developing consumer risks. It is to report at least annually on the results of this monitoring process beginning in the calendar year that starts one year after the designated transfer date (a date to be selected by the Treasury Secretary that is at least 180 days, but no longer than 12 months, after enactment, subject to a possible extension of up to an additional six months (Sec. 1062(c) of the Dodd-Frank Act)). The Bureau can require regulated entities to file reports so that it can gain the information it needs, and information obtained in the course of monitoring can be made public as long as steps are taken to protect confidentiality. Regulations on protecting confidentiality must be adopted; however, those regulations must allow the Bureau and the other federal regulators to have access to each other's data as long as appropriate protections are maintained. Proprietary, personal or confidential consumer information must be protected (Sec. 1022(c) of the Dodd-Frank Act).

Registration Requirements.—Registration requirements can be imposed on the persons the Bureau regulates as long as they are not also regulated by one of the prudential regulators. The Bureau has the authority to require businesses to make limited reports and answer specific questions in order to determine whether the businesses are subject to its supervision (Sec. 1022(c) of the Dodd-Frank Act).

Review of Rules.—Within five years of adopting any significant rule or order that implements the consumer financial laws, the BCFP must undertake a review to determine how effective the rule has been in meeting the Act's goals. The rule must consider available evidence and must be open for public comment (Sec. 1022(c) of the Dodd-Frank Act).

▶ **Effective date.** The provision is effective on the date of enactment (Sec. 1029A of the Dodd-Frank Wall Street Reform and Consumer Protection Act).

Law source: Law at ¶11,022 and ¶11,029A. Committee Report at ¶54,681.

— Sec. 1022 of the Dodd-Frank Wall Street Reform and Consumer Protection Act;

— Sec. 1029A, providing the effective date.

¶4560 Financial Stability Oversight Council Review of Regulations

An important constraint on the Bureau's rulemaking power is the ability of the Financial Stability Oversight Council (the Council) to review, stay and even block regulations that impinge on the safety and soundness of the banking system or the stability of the financial system (Sec. 1023(a) of the Dodd-Frank Act).

If a regulatory agency with a seat on the Council believes that a regulation adopted by the Bureau would put the safety and soundness of the banking system or the stability of the financial system at risk, it can file a petition asking the Council to conduct a review. The agency must have attempted to work out its concerns with the Bureau (including, presumably, filing a written objection during the public comment period) and must file its petition within 10 days of when the notice adopting the rule was published in the *Federal Register*. The review petition must be published and also sent to the Senate Banking Committee and House Financial Services Committee (Sec. 1023(b) of the Dodd-Frank Act).

Review Process and Results.— The Council chairperson can stay the effectiveness of a regulation at the request of a single Council member in order to allow an appropriate review. The stay can last until the result of the review is announced or 90 days have passed, whichever is earlier.

A Bureau rule can be blocked only if at least two-thirds of the current Council members vote to do so. If the Council chair has not stayed the rule, the Council must vote within

45 days of the filing of the petition for review; if the rule was stayed, the vote must be taken before the stay elapses. If a vote is not taken within these time limits, the petition is deemed to have been dismissed. A rule or part of a rule that has been set aside is rendered unenforceable.

The review petition must be published in the *Federal Register* when it is filed. However, the review proceedings are not open for public comment. Any person who has suffered a "legal wrong" from the decision can seek legal review, but neither the Bureau nor any of the agencies on the Council may do so (Sec. 1023(c) of the Dodd-Frank Act).

Effect on Other Laws.—Sec. 1023 makes clear that the filing of a petition for review does not affect how any law applies to the regulation in question. It also does not restrict the Bureau's authority to adopt rules; it simply allows the other regulatory agencies to block the enforcement of a rule that has been adopted (Sec. 1023(d) and (e) of the Dodd-Frank Act).

▶ **Effective date.** The provision is effective on the designated transfer date, which is a date to be selected by the Treasury Secretary that is at least 180 days, but no longer than 12 months, after enactment, subject to a possible extension of up to an additional six months (Sec. 1029A and Sec. 1062(c) of the Dodd-Frank Wall Street Reform and Consumer Protection Act).

Law source: Law at ¶11,023, ¶11,062 and ¶11,029A. Committee Report at ¶54,682.

— Sec. 1023 of the Dodd-Frank Wall Street Reform and Consumer Protection Act;
— Sec. 1062(c), providing the designated transfer date;
— Sec. 1029A, providing the effective date.

¶4565 Bureau Supervision of Nondepository Institutions

The BCFP has the authority to require many covered persons who are not depository institutions to file periodic reports and undergo periodic examinations. This authority applies to covered persons who:

- originate, broker or service residential mortgages or who provide mortgage loan modification or foreclosure relief services;
- are "larger participants" (to be defined by regulation) in a market for any other consumer financial product or service;
- have been found by the Bureau to be involved in conduct that poses risks to consumers;
- make private education loans; or
- make payday loans.

The Bureau has one year from the designated transfer date to adopt a rule describing these persons. Insured depository institutions and credit unions cannot be included (Sec. 1024(a) of the Dodd-Frank Act). However, service providers are included to the same extent as the covered person (Sec. 1024(e) of the Dodd-Frank Act).

The Bureau's regulatory and supervisory authority over these persons is exclusive, other than what is shared with the Federal Trade Commission (Sec. 1024(d) of the Dodd-Frank Act). Also, the section has no effect on the authority of the Farm Credit Administration (Sec. 1024(f) of the Dodd-Frank Act).

Supervision.—If a person is covered by the definition and regulation, the Bureau must require periodic reports and make periodic examinations. These are not just to ensure the person's compliance with the consumer financial laws and rules, but also to provide the Bureau with information on risks to consumers and the markets.

The Bureau's supervision regime is to be risk-based, taking into consideration the size of the person being supervised, the risks posed to consumers, the extent to which state authorities also provide supervision and any other relevant factors. Supervision is to be coordinated with the supervisory activities of the other federal agencies and of the state authorities as well. This includes scheduling joint examinations and sharing information when possible.

The regulations the Bureau adopts can include record-keeping and registration obligations. Registration can include background checks for important key individuals, and also bonding or other financial requirements.

The BCFP is directed to inform the Internal Revenue of any information about possible tax law violations that it finds (Sec. 1024(b) of the Dodd-Frank Act).

Enforcement.—The Bureau has the exclusive authority to enforce the federal consumer laws against the persons included in the regulation, except that it shares the authority to enforce the Federal Trade Commission Act with the FTC. The Bureau and the FTC have six months after the designated transfer date to negotiate an agreement to account for this shared authority. These two agencies are forbidden to institute competing enforcement proceedings, but each has the right to participate in a proceeding brought by the other, subject to the agreement they are to negotiate. The other federal regulators can recommend enforcement proceedings to the Bureau (Sec. 1024(c) of the Dodd-Frank Act).

▶ **Effective date.** The provision is effective on the date of enactment (Sec. 1029A of the Dodd-Frank Wall Street Reform and Consumer Protection Act).

Law source: Law at ¶11,024 and ¶11,029A. Committee Report at ¶54,683.

— Sec. 1024 of the Dodd-Frank Wall Street Reform and Consumer Protection Act;

— Sec. 1029A, providing the effective date.

¶4570 Supervision of Large Institutions

The Bureau has exclusive federal consumer law supervisory authority over the largest banks, thrifts and credit unions—those with total assets of more than $10 billion (Sec. 1025(a) of the Dodd-Frank Act). It also has primary, but not exclusive, enforcement authority over these institutions. An institution's service provider is treated the same as the institution itself (Sec. 1025(d) of the Dodd-Frank Act).

Exclusive Supervisory Authority.—Only the BCFP can require reports and conduct examinations of large institutions to determine compliance with the federal consumer financial laws. However, the Bureau is to coordinate its supervisory activities with those of each institution's prudential regulator in an effort to reduce regulatory burden. It also is to rely to the extent possible on reports generated by the other regulators and on publicly available information. Should information about possible tax law violations be learned during the course of the Bureau's supervisory activities, that information is to be given to the Internal Revenue Service (Sec. 1025(b) of the Dodd-Frank Act).

Primary Enforcement Authority.—The Bureau has the primary authority to enforce the consumer financial laws against the largest institutions. However, the prudential regulators have the right to recommend enforcement actions to the Bureau and to act themselves if the Bureau does not take action within 120 days. This includes the right to take related supervisory and support actions (Sec. 1025(c) of the Dodd-Frank Act).

Coordinated Supervisory Activity.—The Dodd-Frank Act has a strong preference for the Bureau and the prudential regulators to coordinate their supervisory activities and even creates a mechanism for institutions to, in some cases, force coordination. The agencies are instructed to schedule simultaneous examinations (unless the institution requests separate examinations) and to share drafts of examination reports and consider each other's comments. The Bureau also is to reach similar arrangement with state enforcement authorities when possible.

If the Bureau and a prudential regulator reach conflicting supervisory determinations, the institution can request that they confer and produce a joint statement. The agencies have 30 days to do so.

If the agencies cannot negotiate a joint statement, or if either agency attempts supervisory action without the agreement of the other, the institution can appeal to a three-member panel comprising one individual from each of the agencies concerned and a third individual from one of the other prudential regulators. Once the panel has received all of the information the institution wishes to provide and all of the information the panel wants, it has 30 days to issue a ruling, to be decided by a majority vote. The rulings are to be publicly available but redacted to protect confidential information.

The regulators all are required to adopt rules prohibiting retaliation against anyone who takes advantage of this appeal process.

The process cannot be used to appeal a prudential regulator's decision to take over or close a financial institution (Sec. 1025(e) of the Dodd-Frank Act).

▶ **Effective date.** The provision is effective on the designated transfer date, which is a date to be selected by the Treasury Secretary that is at least 180 days, but no longer than 12 months, after enactment, subject to a possible extension of up to an additional six months; however, Sec. 1025(e) is effective on the date of enactment (Sec. 1029A and Sec. 1062(c) of the Dodd-Frank Wall Street Reform and Consumer Protection Act).

Law source: Law at ¶11,025, ¶11,062 and ¶11,029A. Committee Report at ¶54,684 and ¶54,761.

— Sec. 1025 of the Dodd-Frank Wall Street Reform and Consumer Protection Act;

— Sec. 1062(c), providing the designated transfer date;

— Sec. 1029A, providing the effective date.

¶4570

¶4575 Supervision of Smaller Institutions

The Bureau has strictly limited authority to supervise banks, thrifts and credit unions with assets of $10 billion or less (Sec. 1026(a) of the Dodd-Frank Act). This essentially is limited to the ability to require reports and to participate in the examinations by an institution's prudential regulator. An institution's service provider is to be treated the same as the institution (Sec. 1026(e) of the Dodd-Frank Act).

Reporting Requirements.—In order to help it perform its regulatory activities and its limited examination activities, the BCFP can require that smaller institutions file periodic reports. However, it must rely on reports submitted to the prudential regulators and on publicly available information to the extent possible. Any information on possible tax law violations must be given to the Internal Revenue Service (Sec. 1026(b) of the Dodd-Frank Act).

Examinations.—The Bureau can choose to include its own examiners in the examinations by the prudential regulators, but may do so only on a "sampling basis." In this case, the Bureau's examiner is to have full access to the entire examination and is to be consulted on the scope and organization of the examination (Sec. 1026(c) of the Dodd-Frank Act).

Enforcement.—The Dodd-Frank Act leaves the Bureau with almost no power to enforce the consumer financial laws and regulations against these smaller institution. The Bureau can enforce its reporting requirements, but the prudential regulators have the exclusive authority to enforce any other laws or rules.

The Bureau can recommend that a prudential regulatory initiate an enforcement action, but the prudential regulator has no obligation to do so. Its only duty is to provide a written response to the recommendation within 60 days (Sec. 1026(d) of the Dodd-Frank Act).

▶ **Effective date.** The provision is effective on the designated transfer date, which is a date to be selected by the Treasury Secretary that is at least 180 days, but no longer than 12 months, after enactment, subject to a possible extension of up to an additional six months (Sec. 1029A and Sec. 1062(c) of the Dodd-Frank Wall Street Reform and Consumer Protection Act).

Law source: Law at ¶11,026, ¶11,062 and ¶11,029A. Committee Report at ¶54,685 and ¶54,761

— Sec. 1026 of the Dodd-Frank Wall Street Reform and Consumer Protection Act;
— Sec. 1062(c), providing the designated transfer date;
— Sec. 1029A, providing the effective date.

¶4580 Limits on the Bureau's Authority

By far the longest section of Subtitle B is the section that excludes various industries and activities from the Bureau's power or places other limits on the Bureau's authority.

Merchants' Exclusion.—Considerable care was taken to prevent retailers and service providers from coming under the Bureau's power if their consumer financial product or service activities are insignificant or if the businesses themselves are too small to require regulation. One often cited example was the need to exempt dentists who permit installment payments from the Bureau's regulation and supervision. The Dodd-Frank Act shields such businesses from both federal and state powers.

To begin with, the BCFP has no authority over a merchant who sells nonfinancial goods or services except to the extent that the merchant also sells financial products or services or is otherwise subject to the consumer financial laws. Moreover, the Bureau has no authority over a merchant who extends credit to a consumer to finance the sale of a nonfinancial product or service to the consumer, collects the debt that results from such a transaction or sells such a debt that is in default. However, if the merchant is significantly engaged in offering consumer financial products or services, the latter exemption does not apply if the merchant sells debts that are not in default, extends credit that significantly exceeds the value of the product or service that was purchased, engages in credit sales to circumvent the Dodd-Frank Act or regularly extends credit that is subject to a finance charge.

Even if the merchant is significantly engaged in offering financial products and services and regularly extends credit that is subject to a finance charge, the Bureau has no authority if standards intended to protect small business are met. Such a business must extend credit only for the sale of nonfinancial products or services, keep the credit on its own books (unless there is a default) and meet relevant industry size thresholds (Sec. 1027(a) of the Dodd-Frank Act).

Other Exempted Activities.—The Act also grants specific exemptions to:

- real estate brokerages (Sec. 1027(b) of the Dodd-Frank Act);
- manufactured or modular home retailers (Sec. 1027(c) of the Dodd-Frank Act);
- accountants and tax return preparers (Sec. 1027(d) of the Dodd-Frank Act);
- attorneys (Sec. 1027(e) of the Dodd-Frank Act);
- persons regulated by a state insurance regulator (Sec. 1027(f) of the Dodd-Frank Act);
- employee benefit and compensation plans (Sec. 1027(g) of the Dodd-Frank Act);
- persons regulated by a state securities regulator (Sec. 1027(h) of the Dodd-Frank Act);
- persons regulated by the Securities and Exchange Commission (Sec. 1027(i) of the Dodd-Frank Act);
- persons regulated by the Commodities Futures Trading Commission (Sec. 1027(j) of the Dodd-Frank Act);
- persons regulated by the Farm Credit Administration (Sec. 1027(k) of the Dodd-Frank Act);
- activities related to charitable contributions (Sec. 1027(l) of the Dodd-Frank Act); or
- the business of insurance (Sec. 1027(m) of the Dodd-Frank Act).

Of course, any of these businesses could fall under the Bureau's authority if it strays from the described activities. The exemption generally is based on the activity, not the nature of the business. Also, many of these businesses remain subject to the Bureau's power to request information (Sec. 1027(n) of the Dodd-Frank Act).

In addition to these activities, a separate section of the Act provides an exclusion for motor vehicle dealers (Sec. 1029 of the Dodd-Frank Act).

Usury.—The Act also explicitly denies the Bureau the ability to establish a national usury limit (Sec. 1027(o) of the Dodd-Frank Act).

▶ **Effective date.** The provision is effective on the designated transfer date, which is a date to be selected by the Treasury Secretary that is at least 180 days, but no longer than 12 months, after enactment, subject to a possible extension of up to an additional six months (Sec. 1029A and Sec. 1062(c) of the Dodd-Frank Wall Street Reform and Consumer Protection Act).

Law source: Law at ¶11,027, ¶11,062 and ¶11,029A. Committee Report at ¶54,686 and ¶54,761.

— Sec. 1027 of the Dodd-Frank Wall Street Reform and Consumer Protection Act;
— Sec. 1062(c), providing the designated transfer date;
— Sec. 1029A, providing the effective date.

¶4585 Arbitration Agreements

The Bureau has the power to limit or ban the use of mandatory arbitration agreements that were entered into between a covered person and a consumer before a dispute arose (Sec. 1028(b) of the Dodd-Frank Act). However, it must first complete a study on the subject and report to Congress on the study findings (Sec. 1028(a) of the Dodd-Frank Act). The ban cannot restrict the use of arbitration agreements voluntarily entered into after a dispute has arisen (Sec. 1028(c) of the Dodd-Frank Act).

Any restriction or ban that is imposed will apply to agreements formed more than 180 days after the regulation's effective date (Sec. 1028(d) of the Dodd-Frank Act).

▶ **Effective date.** The provision is effective on the designated transfer date, which is a date to be selected by the Treasury Secretary that is at least 180 days, but no longer than 12 months, after enactment, subject to a possible extension of up to an additional six months (Sec. 1029A and Sec. 1062(c) of the Dodd-Frank Wall Street Reform and Consumer Protection Act).

Law source: Law at ¶11,028, ¶11,062 and ¶11,029A. Committee Report at ¶54,687 and ¶54,761.

— Sec. 1028 of the Dodd-Frank Wall Street Reform and Consumer Protection Act;
— Sec. 1062(c), providing the designated transfer date;
— Sec. 1029A, providing the effective date.

¶4590 Exclusion for Motor Vehicle Dealers

Motor vehicle dealers are broadly exempted from the Bureau's authority as long as they do not stray into offering other financial products or services. The exemption applies to businesses that are "predominantly engaged in the sale or servicing of motor vehicles, the leasing and servicing of motor vehicles, or both" (Sec. 1029(a) of the Dodd-Frank Act). The definition of "motor vehicle" is very broad, including automobiles, motorcycles, boats, motor homes and "other vehicles that are titled and sold through dealers" (Sec. 1029(f) of the Dodd-Frank Act).

The exclusion does not apply to the extent that a dealer:

- also provides real estate financing services;
- extends credit or leases directly to consumers and does not resell the loans or leases; or
- offers consumer financial products or services that are not related to motor vehicles (Sec. 1029(b) of the Dodd-Frank Act).

Powers of Other Agencies.—Although the Bureau is denied the ability to regulate or supervise motor vehicle dealers, they are not free of federal regulation. Instead, the Federal Reserve Board and Federal Trade Commission retain their existing regulatory powers (Sec. 1029(c) and (d) of the Dodd-Frank Act). Also, these agencies are directed to work with the Bureau's Office of Service Member Affairs to provide education and resolve complaints (Sec. 1029(e) of the Dodd-Frank Act).

▶ **Effective date.** The provision is effective on the designated transfer date, which is a date to be selected by the Treasury Secretary that is at least 180 days, but no longer than 12 months, after enactment, subject to a possible extension of up to an additional six months (Sec. 1029A and Sec. 1062(c) of the Dodd-Frank Wall Street Reform and Consumer Protection Act).

Law source: Law at ¶11,029, ¶11,029A and ¶11,062.

— Sec. 1029 of the Dodd-Frank Wall Street Reform and Consumer Protection Act;

— Sec. 1062(c), providing the designated transfer date;

— Sec. 1029A, providing the effective date.

SPECIFIC BUREAU AUTHORITIES

¶4595 Unfair, Deceptive or Abusive Acts or Practices

The Bureau has the power to take any authorized enforcement action to prevent any person under its authority from engaging in an unfair, deceptive or abusive act or practice in connection with offering a consumer financial product or service or a transaction with a consumer for such a product or service (Sec. 1031(a) of the Dodd-Frank Act). It also has the power to adopt rules that identify acts or practices that are unfair, deceptive or abusive and to prevent those practices (Sec. 1031(b) of the Dodd-Frank Act). However, in adopting rules the Bureau is to consult with the other federal regulators about whether the rules are consistent with prudential, market or systemic objectives (Sec. 1031(e) of the Dodd-Frank Act).

Definitions.—The Dodd-Frank Act defines unfair and abusive acts or practices.

An act or practice cannot be declared to be unfair unless the BCFP has reason to conclude that it causes or is likely to cause substantial injury to consumers that they cannot reasonably avoid, if the injury is not outweighed by benefits to consumers or to competition. The Bureau can consider established public policies, but those cannot be a primary basis for the Bureau's decision (Sec. 1031(c) of the Dodd-Frank Act).

An act or practice cannot be declared to be abusive unless the BCFP has reason to conclude that it materially interferes with a consumer's ability to understand a term or takes unreasonable advantage of:

- the consumer's lack of understanding of the risks, costs or conditions of the product or service;
- the consumer's inability to protect his own interests; or
- the consumer's reasonable reliance on the regulated person to act in the consumer's interests.

The Act does not make benefits to consumers or competition a consideration in whether an act or practice is abusive (Sec. 1031(d) of the Dodd-Frank Act).

The Act does not provide a definition of what constitutes a deceptive act or practice.

Seasonal Income.—When adopting rules on unfair, deceptive or abusive acts and practices, the BCFP is to address the issue of seasonal income and mortgage loan underwriting. In the case of a loan secured by a residence, the regulations must permit the lender to consider whether the consumer's documented income that is to be relied on for repayment is seasonal or irregular. Seasonality and irregularity can be considered both in underwriting the loan and scheduling the loan payments (Sec. 1031(f) of the Dodd-Frank Act).

▶ **Effective date.** Subtitle C—Specific Bureau Authorities is effective on the designated transfer date, which is a date to be selected by the Treasury Secretary that is at least 180 days, but no longer than 12 months, after enactment, subject to a possible extension of up to an additional six months (Sec. 1037 and Sec. 1062(c) of the Dodd-Frank Wall Street Reform and Consumer Protection Act).

Law source: Law at ¶11,031, ¶11,062 and ¶11,037. Committee Report at ¶54,700 and ¶54,761.

— Sec. 1031 of the Dodd-Frank Wall Street Reform and Consumer Protection Act;

— Sec. 1062(c), providing the designated transfer date;

— Sec. 1037, providing the effective date.

¶4600 Disclosures

The Dodd-Frank Act gives the Bureau broad power to require disclosures to consumers. The standards set for the disclosures are high, in that they are to inform consumers of the costs, risks and benefits of the product or service, both at the time of the sale and over the life of the product, "in light of the facts and circumstances" (Sec. 1031(a) of the Dodd-Frank Act).

The Bureau can adopt model disclosure forms, as the Federal Reserve Board has done in the past. Model forms are to be validated through consumer testing (Sec. 1032(b) of the Dodd-Frank Act). Just as with the current model forms, a covered person who uses the proper from will be deemed to have made the required disclosures (Sec. 1032(c) of the Dodd-Frank Act).

Disclosure Trials—In addition to prescribing model consumer disclosures, the Bureau can approve trial disclosure programs by covered persons. These trial programs are to be limited and aimed at gathering information on the effectiveness of consumer disclosures. The Act intends to encourage trial programs by permitting the Bureau to provide a safe harbor for trial disclosure forms or even to temporarily exempt the person conducting the trial from disclosure requirements.

The use of a trial program must be publicly disclosed; however, the Bureau can limit this disclosure if doing so is necessary to encourage consumer financial product and service providers to participate in the program (Sec. 1032(e) of the Dodd-Frank Act).

Mortgage Loan Disclosures.—The Dodd-Frank Act also calls for the eventual adoption of regulations and model disclosures that will combine the requirements of the Truth in Lending Act and the Real Estate Settlement Procedures Act to create a single, integrated disclosure form. The appropriate regulation and forms are to be proposed no later than one year after the designated transfer date. However, the Agency will be relieved of this obligation if the Fed and the Department of Housing and Urban Development have previously issued a proposal for unified disclosures (Sec. 1032(f) of the Dodd-Frank Act).

▶ **Effective date.** The provision is effective on the designated transfer date, which is a date to be selected by the Treasury Secretary that is at least 180 days, but no longer than 12 months, after enactment, subject to a possible extension of up to an additional six months (Sec. 1037 and Sec. 1062(c) of the Dodd-Frank Wall Street Reform and Consumer Protection Act).

Law source: Law at ¶11,032, ¶11,062 and ¶11,037. Committee Report at ¶54,701 and ¶54,761.

— Sec. 1032 of the Dodd-Frank Wall Street Reform and Consumer Protection Act;

— Sec. 1062(c), providing the designated transfer date;

— Sec. 1037, providing the effective date.

¶4605 Consumers' Right to Information

The Dodd-Frank Act gives consumers the right to access to information about the consumer financial products and services they have purchased, and it requires the Bureau to adopt regulations to implement that right. A person who has sold a consumer a financial product or service is to make available to the consumer information that:

- is in the company's control or possession;
- relates to a product or service the consumer bought from the person; and
- relates to a transaction, a series of transactions, or the account costs, charges and usage.

The information is to be furnished electronically, meaning that there is no requirement that printed documents be used (Sec. 1033(a) of the Dodd-Frank Act).

The company cannot be required to:

- provide any confidential commercial information;
- provide any information on programs designed to prevent or detect fraud, money laundering or other illegal activity;
- provide any information it is required by any other law to keep confidential;
- provide any information it cannot retrieve in the ordinary course of business; or
- maintain any specific information about a consumer (Sec. 1033(b) and (c) of the Dodd-Frank Act).

The Agency's regulations should encourage the use of standardized information formats; however, they cannot require or promote the use of any specific technology (Sec. 1033(d) and (e) of the Dodd-Frank Act).

▶ **Effective date.** The provision is effective on the designated transfer date, which is a date to be selected by the Treasury Secretary that is at least 180 days, but no longer than 12 months, after enactment, subject to a possible extension of up to an additional six months (Sec. 1037 and Sec. 1062(c) of the Dodd-Frank Wall Street Reform and Consumer Protection Act).

Law source: Law at ¶11,033, ¶11,062 and ¶11,037. Committee Report at ¶54,702 and ¶54,761.

— Sec. 1033 of the Dodd-Frank Wall Street Reform and Consumer Protection Act;
— Sec. 1062(c), providing the designated transfer date;
— Sec. 1037, providing the effective date.

¶4610 Response to Consumers

The Dodd-Frank Act includes provisions that are intended to keep the consumer complaint resolution process moving. It requires the establishment of standards for timely responses by both regulators and regulated entities.

First, the Bureau is to set procedures for timely responses by regulators to consumers who have filed complaints or made inquiries. The consumer is to be told what the regulator has done, what response the regulator has received from the company and what steps the regulator intends to take next. These procedures are to be followed by all of the federal regulatory agencies (Dodd-Frank Sec. 1034(a)).

Next, the companies that are subject to the Bureau's primary supervision (as opposed to the smaller institutions that continue to be supervised by the federal banking regulatory agencies) are to provide comparable updates to the BCFP. These companies are to tell the Bureau what they have done to respond to the complaint or inquiry, what responses have been received from the consumer and what next steps are planned (Sec. 1034(b) of the Dodd-Frank Act).

Providing Information to Consumers.—The right of the consumer to have access to information first established in Sec. 1033 essentially is repeated here as well. An entity subject to the Bureau's primary supervision and enforcement authority must furnish to a consumer information in the entity's control about products or services the consumer has purchased from the entity, and must do so in a timely manner. The information covered is not spelled out in as much detail as in the earlier section. Also, the exceptions are somewhat different. The company need not furnish:

- confidential commercial information, including algorithms used to derive credit scores or other risk predictors;
- information collected for anti-fraud or anti-money laundering purposes;
- information the company is required by law to keep confidential; or
- other nonpublic or confidential information such as supervisory information (Sec. 1034(c) of the Dodd-Frank Act).

▶ **Effective date.** The provision is effective on the designated transfer date, which is a date to be selected by the Treasury Secretary that is at least 180 days, but no longer than 12 months, after enactment, subject to a possible extension of up to an additional six months (Sec. 1037 and Sec. 1062(c) of the Dodd-Frank Wall Street Reform and Consumer Protection Act).

Law source: Law at ¶11,034, ¶11,062 and ¶11,037. Committee Report at ¶54,703 and ¶54,761.

— Sec. 1034 of the Dodd-Frank Wall Street Reform and Consumer Protection Act;
— Sec. 1062(c), providing the designated transfer date;
— Sec. 1037, providing the effective date.

¶4615 Private Education Loan Ombudsman

A private education loan ombudsman is to be designated within the Bureau. Unusually, the Act says that this person is to be designated by the Treasury Secretary, albeit after consultation with the BCFP Director (Sec. 1035(a) of the Dodd-Frank Act). The Treasury Secretary and the Director are to provide information about the ombudsman's existence and the help he can offer to consumers, schools, lenders, guarantors, loan servicers and others involved in making education loans (Sec. 1035(b) of the Dodd-Frank Act).

The ombudsman is directed to:

- handle and attempt to resolve informally complaints from consumers;
- enter into an agreement with the student loan ombudsman established by The Higher Education Act of 1965 to coordinate their efforts (to be done within 90 days of he designated transfer date);
- collect and analyze data on consumer complaints; and
- make appropriate regulatory and legislative recommendations (Sec. 1035(c) of the Dodd-Frank Act).

The ombudsman also is required to file an annual report on his activities and the effectiveness of his efforts (Sec. 1035(d) of the Dodd-Frank Act).

▶ **Effective date.** The provision is effective on the designated transfer date, which is a date to be selected by the Treasury Secretary that is at least 180 days, but no longer than 12 months, after enactment, subject to a possible extension of up to an additional six months (Sec. 1037 and Sec. 1062(c) of the Dodd-Frank Wall Street Reform and Consumer Protection Act).

Law source: Law at ¶11,035, ¶11,062 and ¶11,037. Committee Report at ¶54,704 and ¶54,761.

— Sec. 1035 of the Dodd-Frank Wall Street Reform and Consumer Protection Act;

— Sec. 1035(c) requiring coordination with the ombudsman under Section 141(f) of The Higher Education Act of 1965;

— Sec. 1062(c), providing the designated transfer date;

— Sec. 1037, providing the effective date.

¶4620 Prohibited Acts and Assisting Prohibited Acts

Section 1036 of the Dodd-Frank Act makes clear that taking any prohibited action is, in fact, a violation of the law. Specifically, it is illegal for any regulated company to:

- offer or provide any consumer financial product or service that is not in compliance with the federal consumer financial protection laws law or to otherwise violate those laws;
- engage in any unfair, deceptive or abusive act or practice;
- refuse to give the BCFP access to its records;
- fail to keep required records; or
- fail to make required reports.

Knowingly or recklessly providing substantial assistance to a regulated person in an unfair, deceptive or abusive act or practice also is a violation, to the same extent as would be committing the act or practice (Sec. 1036(a) of the Dodd-Frank Act).

Selling advertising time or space is not, by itself, a violation (Sec. 1036(b) of the Dodd-Frank Act).

▶ **Effective date.** The provision is effective on the designated transfer date, which is a date to be selected by the Treasury Secretary that is at least 180 days, but no longer than 12 months, after enactment, subject to a possible extension of up to an additional six months (Sec. 1037 and Sec. 1062(c) of the Dodd-Frank Wall Street Reform and Consumer Protection Act).

Law source: Law at ¶11,036, ¶11,062 and ¶11,037. Committee Report at ¶54,705 and ¶54,761.

— Sec. 1036 of the Dodd-Frank Wall Street Reform and Consumer Protection Act;

— Sec. 1062(c), providing the designated transfer date;

— Sec. 1037, providing the effective date.

PREEMPTION of STATE LAW AND STATE ENFORCEMENT

¶4625 Effect on State Law

The basic premise of the Dodd-Frank Wall Street Reform and Consumer Protection Act's provisions on the relationship between federal and state law is that state consumer financial protection laws should not be preempted as long as they do not conflict with federal laws and regulations. The Act also provides that a state law will not be deemed to conflict with federal laws or regulations simply because it offers consumers greater protection (Sec. 1041(a) of the Dodd-Frank Act).

The Bureau of Consumer Financial Protection has the authority to rule on whether a state law is inconsistent. It may make such a ruling on its own or in response to a "nonfrivolous" petition by any other person (Sec. 1041(a) of the Dodd-Frank Act).

The Dodd-Frank Act disclaims any intent to affect how the federal consumer financial protection laws relate to state laws. If a federal consumer financial protection law includes a provision that addresses preemption of state law, the effect of that provision remains unchanged. An example of such a provision would be Fair Credit Reporting Act Sec. 625 (15 USC 1681t) which preserves the effect of a number of specified state statutes. There is one exception to that disclaimer that was needed to address the conforming amendments to the Alternative Mortgage Transaction Parity Act of 1982 made in Title X, Subtitle H, Sec. 1083 (Sec. 1041(b) of the Dodd-Frank Act).

State-Initiated Rulemakings.—The Dodd-Frank Act also gives state governments an unusual ability to initiate regulation amendments and new regulations. If a majority of the states enact resolutions supporting the adoption of a regulation or the amendment of an existing regulation, the Bureau *shall* issue a notice of proposed rulemaking. However, before any final rule is adopted, the Bureau is to consider whether the proposal would enhance consumer protection, whether the costs to consumers would outweigh the benefits to consumers, whether the rule or amendment would discriminate unfairly against any category or class of consumer and whether any of the federal banking regulators has raised safety and soundness concerns (Sec. 1041(c) of the Dodd-Frank Act).

▶ **Effective date.** Subtitle D—Preservation of State Law is effective on the designated transfer date, which is a date to be selected by the Treasury Secretary that is at least 180 days, but no longer than 12 months, after enactment, subject to a possible extension of up to an additional six months (Sec. 1048 and Sec. 1062(c) of the Dodd-Frank Wall Street Reform and Consumer Protection Act).

Law source: Law at ¶11,041, ¶11,062 and ¶11,048. Committee Report at ¶54,720 and ¶54,761.

— Sec. 1041 of the Dodd-Frank Wall Street Reform and Consumer Protection Act;

— Sec. 1062(c), providing the designated transfer date;

— Sec. 1048, providing the effective date.

¶4630 State Enforcement Authority

State attorneys general and state regulatory agencies have some enforcement powers under the Dodd-Frank Act. However, their ability to act against federally chartered institutions is constrained.

The general statement of authority provides that state attorneys general can sue in either federal or state court to enforce the provisions of Title X or any regulations adopted under Title X. It also authorizes state regulators to enforce the title and its implementing regulations against state-chartered companies.

However, the ability of state attorneys general to sue national banks or federal thrifts is restricted. A civil suit can be brought in the name of the state, in federal or state court, to enforce a Bureau of Consumer Financial Protection Agency regulation, but there is no authority granted to enforce the consumer financial protection laws. Instead, Sec. 1042 has no effect on the provisions of any such laws that address state enforcement powers.

The section also does not permit state attorneys general to file *parens patriae* suits, in which the state seeks remedies not for itself but on behalf of its citizens (Sec. 1042(a) of the Dodd-Frank Act).

Consultation Requirement.—A state attorney general who wishes to file an enforcement suit is required first to consult with the Bureau. The Act provides generally that the Bureau is to be given a copy of the proposed complaint and also a notice that sets out the identity of the parties, the factual allegations and whether there is a need for coordinated legal action to avoid conflicts with any other legal actions. In an emergency, the attorney general can file the suit and then notify the Bureau immediately afterwards.

The Bureau can decide whether to intervene in the suit. If it chooses to do so, it can remove a suit that was filed in a state court to the appropriate federal district court and is to be treated as a party for all purposes. The Bureau is not required to take any action in response to a notice (Sec. 1042(b) of the Dodd-Frank Act).

The requirement for consultation is described only in general terms. The Dodd-Frank Act directs the Bureau to adopt regulations that will implement the requirement, which presumably will specify details such as how the notice is to be given and how much notice is required before a suit can be filed (Sec. 1042(c) of the Dodd-Frank Act).

Preservation of Existing Authority.—Section 1042 makes clear that it is not to be interpreted as infringing on the ability of state attorneys general to enforce state laws. It also states that Title X has no effect on the power of state securities or insurance regulators to adopt or enforce rules or take any other regulatory actions authorized by state law (Sec. 1042(d) of the Dodd-Frank Act).

▶ **Effective date.** The provision is effective on the designated transfer date, which is a date to be selected by the Treasury Secretary that is at least 180 days, but no longer than 12 months, after enactment, subject to a possible extension of up to an additional six months (Sec. 1048 and Sec. 1062(c) of the Dodd-Frank Wall Street Reform and Consumer Protection Act).

Law source: Law at ¶11,042, ¶11,062 and ¶11,048. Committee Report at ¶54,721 and ¶54,761.

— Sec. 1042 of the Dodd-Frank Wall Street Reform and Consumer Protection Act;

— Sec. 1062(c), providing the designated transfer date;

— Sec. 1048, providing the effective date.

¶4635 Preservation of Existing Contracts

The Dodd-Frank Act preserves the effectiveness of existing contracts. It provides that neither Title X nor its implementing regulations, nor any subsequent guidance or interpretation, will have any effect on the applicability of prior laws, regulations or legal interpretations of the Office of the Comptroller of the Currency (OCC) or Office of Thrift Supervision (OTS) that address whether state laws apply to contracts entered into before Title X was enacted. National banks, federal thrifts and their subsidiaries that are regulated by the OCC or previously were regulated by the OTS can claim this protection (Sec. 1043 of the Dodd-Frank Act).

▶ **Effective date.** The provision is effective on the designated transfer date, which is a date to be selected by the Treasury Secretary that is at least 180 days, but no longer than 12 months, after enactment, subject to a possible extension of up to an additional six months (Sec. 1048 and Sec. 1062(c) of the Dodd-Frank Wall Street Reform and Consumer Protection Act).

Law source: Law at ¶11,043, ¶11,062 and ¶11,048. Committee Report at ¶54,722 and ¶54,761.

— Sec. 1043 of the Dodd-Frank Wall Street Reform and Consumer Protection Act;

— Sec. 1062(c), providing the designated transfer date;

— Sec. 1048, providing the effective date.

¶4640 Preemption Standards for National Banks and Subsidiaries

The Dodd-Frank Act specifies standards for deciding which state laws are preempted that are somewhat tighter than past standards. It also makes clear that the Act does not alter the determination of whether the application of state laws to national bank subsidiaries or affiliates that are not depositary institutions is preempted. State consumer financial laws apply to nondepositary subsidiaries and affiliates to the same extent that they apply to other persons (Sec. 1044(a) of the Dodd-Frank Act).

The section first defines "state consumer financial laws" as laws that directly and specifically regulate consumer financial transactions or accounts and that do not directly or indirectly discriminate against national banks. Such laws are preempted in only three circumstances:

1. Application of the law would have a discriminatory effect on national banks when compared to its effect on state banks.

2. The law meaningfully interferes with the ability of a national bank to engage in the business of banking as set out in the Supreme Court's opinion in *Barnett Bank v. Nelson*; 517 U.S. 23 (1996).

3. The state law is preempted by a federal law other than the Dodd-Frank Act (Sec. 1044(a) of the Dodd-Frank Act).

Preemption under the second circumstance can result either from a court judgment or from a regulation or order by the Comptroller of the Currency made on a case-by-case basis. Case-by-case basis preemption requires making a determination of the effect that a particular state law, or a particular law of a different state that has substantially the same terms, has on a national bank. There must be substantial evidence supporting the finding that there would be an effect on or interference with the bank's ability to carry out its business, and the Comptroller must make a written finding that a federal law establishes a substantive standard governing the conduct in question. The section provides that a preemption determination is to be made by the Comptroller personally, not delegated to any other individual in the OCC (Sec. 1044(a) of the Dodd-Frank Act).

A regulation or order that arises from a case-by-case determination must be reviewed at least every five years. The result of the review is to be published in the *Federal Register*, and a report is to be made to Congress. A list of determinations that are in effect must be published quarterly (Sec. 1044(a) of the Dodd-Frank Act).

The Dodd-Frank Act disclaims any intent to occupy the field in any area of state law. A determination that a federal law occupies the field in an area of law is usually a basis to determine that any state law in that field is preempted (Sec. 1044(a) of the Dodd-Frank Act).

Review of Preemption Determination.—A court that is called upon to review an OCC determination that a state law is preempted by the Dodd-Frank Act or the Federal Reserve Act is to consider how well supported the agency's ruling was and whether the ruling is consistent with other preemption determinations. The rule that courts should defer to the judgment of the OCC as long as its determinations are reasonable is continued (Sec. 1044(a) of the Dodd-Frank Act).

▶ **Effective date.** The provision is effective on the designated transfer date, which is a date to be selected by the Treasury Secretary that is at least 180 days, but no longer than 12 months, after enactment, subject to a possible extension of up to an additional six months (Sec. 1048 and Sec. 1062(c) of the Dodd-Frank Wall Street Reform and Consumer Protection Act).

Law source: Law at ¶11,044, ¶11,062 and ¶11,048. Committee Report at ¶54,723 and ¶54,761.

— Sec. 1044(a) of the Dodd-Frank Wall Street Reform and Consumer Protection Act, amending Chapter One, Title LXII by adding a new Section 5136C;

— Sec. 1044(b), amending the Table of Contents for Chapter One of Title LXII by adding a new Section 5136C;

— Sec. 1062(c), providing the designated transfer date;

— Sec. 1048, providing the effective date.

¶4640

¶4645 Preemption for Nondepositary National Bank Subsidiaries and Affiliates

Subsidiaries and affiliates of national banks do not receive any beneficial treatment as far as whether state consumer financial protection laws are preempted. As noted in Sec. 1041, nothing in Title X affects the applicability of state laws to these affiliates and subsidiaries (Sec. 1045 of the Dodd-Frank Act).

▶ **Effective date.** The provision is effective on the designated transfer date, which is a date to be selected by the Treasury Secretary that is at least 180 days, but no longer than 12 months, after enactment, subject to a possible extension of up to an additional six months (Sec. 1048 and Sec. 1062(c) of the Dodd-Frank Wall Street Reform and Consumer Protection Act).

Law source: Law at ¶11,045, ¶11,062 and ¶11,048. Committee Report at ¶54,724 and ¶54,761.

— Sec. 1045 of the Dodd-Frank Wall Street Reform and Consumer Protection Act, amending Chapter One, Title LXII, Sec. 5136C;

— Sec. 1062(c), providing the designated transfer date;

— Sec. 1048, providing the effective date.

¶4650 Preemption for Federal Thrifts and Subsidiaries

The Dodd-Frank Act specifies standards for deciding which state laws are preempted that are somewhat tighter than past standards. It also makes clear that the Act does not alter the determination of whether the application of state laws to federal savings association subsidiaries or affiliates that are not depositary institutions is preempted. State consumer financial laws apply to nondepositary subsidiaries and affiliates to the same extent that they apply to other persons.

Rather than creating a section on preemption standards for federal thrifts, the Act simply calls for the use of the same standards that were specified for national banks (Home Owners' Loan Act Sec. 6, as added by Sec. 1046(a) of the Dodd-Frank Act).

The section for national banks, and thus for federal thrifts, first defines "state consumer financial laws" as laws that directly and specifically regulate consumer financial transactions or accounts and that do not directly or indirectly discriminate against the federal institution. These laws are preempted in only three circumstances:

1. Application of the law would have a discriminatory effect on federal thrifts when compared to its effect on state banks.

2. The law meaningfully interferes with the ability of a federal savings association to engage in the business of banking as set out in the Supreme Court's opinion in *Barnett Bank v. Nelson*; 517 U.S. 23 (1996).

3. The state law is preempted by a federal law other than the Dodd-Frank Act (Home Owners' Loan Act Sec. 6, as added by Sec. 1046(a) of the Dodd-Frank Act).

Preemption under the second circumstance can result either from a court judgment or from a regulation or order by the Comptroller of the Currency made on a case-by-case basis. Case-by-case basis preemption requires making a determination of the effect that a particular state law, or a particular law of a different state that has substantially the same terms, has on a federal institution. There must be substantial evidence supporting the finding that there would be an effect on or interference with the federal thrift's ability to carry out its business, and the Comptroller must make a written finding that a federal law establishes a substantive standard governing the conduct in question. The section provides that a preemption determination is to be made by the Comptroller personally, not delegated to any other individual in the OCC (Home Owners' Loan Act Sec. 6, as added by Sec. 1046(a) of the Dodd-Frank Act).

A regulation or order that arises from a case-by-case determination must be reviewed at least every five years. The result of the review is to be published in the *Federal Register*, and a report is to be made to Congress. A list of determinations that are in effect must be published quarterly (Home Owners' Loan Act Sec. 6, as added by Sec. 1046(a) of the Dodd-Frank Act).

The Dodd-Frank Act disclaims any intent to occupy the field in any area of state law. A determination that federal law occupies the field in an area of law is usually a basis to determine that any state law in that field is preempted (Sec. 1046(a) of the Dodd-Frank Act).

Review of Preemption Determination.—A court that is called upon to review an OCC determination that a state law is preempted by the Dodd-Frank Act or the Federal Reserve Act is to consider how well supported the agency's ruling was and whether the ruling is consistent with other preemption determinations. The rule that courts should defer to the judgment of the OCC as long as its determinations are reasonable is continued (Home Owners' Loan Act Sec. 6, as added by Sec. 1046(a) of the Dodd-Frank Act).

▶ **Effective date.** The provision is effective on the designated transfer date, which is a date to be selected by the Treasury Secretary that is at least 180 days, but no longer than 12 months, after enactment, subject to a possible extension of up to an additional six months (Sec. 1048 and Sec. 1062(c) of the Dodd-Frank Wall Street Reform and Consumer Protection Act).

Law source: Law at ¶11,046, ¶11,062 and ¶11,048. Committee Report at ¶54,725 and ¶54,761.

— Sec. 1046 of the Dodd-Frank Wall Street Reform and Consumer Protection Act;

— Sec. 1046(a), amending the Home Owners' Loan Act by adding a new Section 6;

— Sec. 1046(b), amending the Table of Contents for the Home Owners' Loan Act by adding a new Section 6;

— Sec. 1062(c), providing the designated transfer date;

— Sec. 1048, providing the effective date.

¶4655 State Visitorial Authority over Federal Institutions

The otherwise exclusive visitorial authority that federal regulatory agencies have does not prevent state attorneys general from bringing enforcement actions against either national banks or federal savings associations. The Act specifically refers to the U.S. Supreme Court decision in *Cuomo v. Clearing House Assn.*, 129 S.Ct. 2710 (2009), in setting that rule (Chapter One, Title LXII, and Home Owners' Loan Act Sec. 6, as added by Sec. 1047(a) and (b) of the Dodd-Frank Act).

The ability of the OCC to sue to enforce Title X or the Federal Trade Commission Act ban on unfair or deceptive acts and practices does not preclude private enforcement suits, the section adds (Chapter One, Title LXII, and Home Owners' Loan Act Sec. 6, as added by Sec. 1047(a) and (b) of the Dodd-Frank Act).

▶ **Effective date.** The provision is effective on the designated transfer date, which is a date to be selected by the Treasury Secretary that is at least 180 days, but no longer than 12 months, after enactment, subject to a possible extension of up to an additional six months (Sec. 1048 and Sec. 1062(c) of the Dodd-Frank Wall Street Reform and Consumer Protection Act).

Law source: Law at ¶11,047, ¶11,062 and ¶11,048. Committee Report at ¶54,726 and ¶54,761.

— Sec. 1047 of the Dodd-Frank Wall Street Reform and Consumer Protection Act;

— Sec. 1047(a), amending Section 5136C, Chapter One, Title LXII as added by Dodd-Frank Act Sec. Sec. 1044;

— Sec. 1047(b), amending Home Owners' Loan Act Sec. 6 as added by Dodd-Frank Act Sec. Sec. 1046;

— Sec. 1062(c), providing the designated transfer date;

— Sec. 1048, providing the effective date.

BUREAU ENFORCEMENT POWERS

¶4660 Definitions

Subtitle E of Title X sets out the powers that the Bureau of Consumer Financial Protection can use to enforce the federal consumer financial laws and their implementing regulations. The subtitle begins by defining a few terms that are relevant to understanding those powers.

Bureau Investigation.—A Bureau investigation is an inquiry by a Bureau investigator to determine whether anyone has violated or is violating any federal consumer law or regulation (Sec. 1051(1) of the Dodd-Frank Act).

Bureau Investigator.—A Bureau investigator is an attorney or investigator employed by the Bureau who has been charged with the duty of enforcing the federal consumer financial laws (Sec. 1051(2) of the Dodd-Frank Act).

Custodian.—The custodian is the Bureau's custodian or deputy (Sec. 1051(3) of the Dodd-Frank Act).

Documentary Material.—Documentary material is any data or compilation of data. The definition covers both originals and copies, regardless of the storage medium (Sec. 1051(4) of the Dodd-Frank Act).

Violation.—A violation is any act or omission that would constitute a violation of any federal consumer law or implementing regulation (Sec. 1051(5) of the Dodd-Frank Act).

▶ **Effective date.** Subtitle E—Enforcement Powers is effective on the designated transfer date, which is a date to be selected by the Treasury Secretary that is at least 180 days, but no longer than 12 months, after enactment, subject to a possible extension of up to an additional six months (Sec. 1058 and Sec. 1062(c) of the Dodd-Frank Wall Street Reform and Consumer Protection Act).

Law source: Law at ¶11,051, ¶11,062 and ¶11,058. Committee Report at ¶54,740 and ¶54,761.

— Sec. 1051 of the Dodd-Frank Wall Street Reform and Consumer Protection Act;

— Sec. 1062(c), providing the designated transfer date;

— Sec. 1058 providing the effective date.

¶4665 Investigations and Administrative Discovery

The Bureau's investigators have the authority to require that documentary material and tangible objects be produced and to require testimony from witnesses in the course of an investigation. There is no restriction on who can be the subject of such a discovery demand, so a demand can made on not only the financial company under investigation but also its employees, agents, independent contractors and third-party service providers, as well as on independent witnesses (Sec. 1051(b) and (c) of the Dodd-Frank Act).

The Bureau's investigators can act alone or in cooperation with representatives of other agencies. The section mentions explicitly that fair lending investigations can be carried out jointly with the Department of Housing and Urban Development and the Justice Department, but does not impose any restrictions. Thus, the Bureau's investigators can cooperate with other federal agencies and with state agencies to investigate possible violations of any federal consumer law or regulation (Sec. 1052(a) of the Dodd-Frank Act).

The BCFP can act either by issuing subpoenas or by issuing civil investigative demands. Either can be enforced by an order of the appropriate federal district court (Sec. 1052(e) of the Dodd-Frank Act).

Civil Investigative Demands.—A civil investigative demand (CID) can be served on anyone the Bureau reasonably believes has any type of evidence that is relevant to an investigation. It must specify the conduct that is being investigated and the statutory or regulatory provision the Bureau believes is being violated. The class of item to be produced is to be described, a return date must be set and the custodian at the Bureau to whom the items are to be delivered must be identified. A CID can be served personally or by registered mail (Sec. 1052(c) of the Dodd-Frank Act).

If the Bureau wishes oral testimony from an individual, a procedure similar to that of a deposition is to be followed. The testimony is to be under oath and transcribed. Only investigators, the court reporter, the witness and the witness's attorney can be present. Thus, under the statute, a company under investigation has no right to be present for the testimony of a third-party witness (Sec. 1052(c) of the Dodd-Frank Act).

The Bureau is required to establish rules to maintain the confidentiality of any material produced under a CID (Sec. 1052(d) of the Dodd-Frank Act).

Contesting a CID.—A person served with a CID has an opportunity to contest the demand by filing a petition with the BCFP. The deadline for the petition is the earlier of 20 days after the CID was served or the return date.

▶ **Effective date.** The provision is effective on the designated transfer date, which is a date to be selected by the Treasury Secretary that is at least 180 days, but no longer than 12 months, after enactment, subject to a possible extension of up to an additional six months (Sec. 1058 and Sec. 1062(c) of the Dodd-Frank Wall Street Reform and Consumer Protection Act).

Law source: Law at ¶11,052, ¶11,062 and ¶11,058. Committee Report at ¶54,741 and ¶54,761.

— Sec. 1052 of the Dodd-Frank Wall Street Reform and Consumer Protection Act;

— Sec. 1062(c), providing the designated transfer date;

— Sec. 1058 providing the effective date.

¶4670 Hearings and Adjudications

The Bureau has the power to conduct administrative hearings under the same rules of administrative procedure that apply to other agencies (Sec. 1053(a) of the Dodd-Frank Act). The Act requires the BCFP to adopt necessary regulations for these proceedings (Sec. 1053(e) of the Dodd-Frank Act). This authority extends to hearings on temporary and permanent cease-and-desist orders and to adjudications of charged violations. The Act prescribes specific rules for cease-and-desist proceedings.

Cease-and-Desist Proceedings.—A cease-and-desist proceeding begins with the service of a notice of charges on the person who is believed to be in violation. The notice is to contain a statement of facts outlining the violation and is to set a hearing date, which is to be between 30 and 60 days later.

If the respondent does not appear at the hearing, the Bureau is to presume that the person has consented to the entry of a cease-and-desist order. A consent order takes effect at the time the order specifies.

If the respondent appears and contests the charges, a hearing will be conducted according to the standard administrative hearing procedures. The Bureau has 90 days to reach a decision after the hearing is concluded. If a cease-and-desist order results from the hearing, it will take effect 30 days after the order is served and will remain in effect until some further bureau or judicial action is taken.

The U.S. Courts of Appeals have jurisdiction over appeals from cease-and-desist orders or other adjudicatory orders. Appeals must be filed within 30 days of the date the order was served. Unless the appellate court orders a stay of the Bureau's order, the appeal does not operate as a stay (Sec. 1053(b) of the Dodd-Frank Act).

Temporary Cease-and-Desist Proceedings.—The Bureau also has the authority to issue a temporary cease-and-desist order if it believes that the respondent is likely to become insolvent or the interest of consumers are likely to be prejudiced by the continuation of the violation. In addition to requiring that the person halt the challenged conduct, a temporary order also can specify steps the person must take to prevent or remedy the insolvency or consumer harm. Temporary orders are effective as soon as they are served and remain in effect until there is a final ruling in the matter.

A temporary order also can be issued as part of a cease-and-desist proceeding if the Bureau believes that the respondent's books and records are so incomplete or inaccurate that the respondent's financial condition, or the purpose of a transaction relevant to the person's financial condition, cannot be determined. In this case, the order can require the person to halt the conduct that is causing the books and records to be inadequate or inaccurate and to take specified steps to remedy the problems.

To contest a temporary cease-and-desist order, the person must sue the Bureau for an injunction in the appropriate federal district court (Sec. 1053(c) of the Dodd-Frank Act).

Enforcing Orders.—The federal court for the district in which the respondent is located has the jurisdiction to enforce the Bureau's orders. However, the statute denies any court the jurisdiction to interfere with the issuance or enforcement of an order other than a challenge to a temporary cease-and-desist order or an appeal of a permanent order (Sec. 1053(d) of the Dodd-Frank Act).

▶ **Effective date.** The provision is effective on the designated transfer date, which is a date to be selected by the Treasury Secretary that is at least 180 days, but no longer than 12 months, after enactment, subject to a possible extension of up to an additional six months (Sec. 1058 and Sec. 1062(c) of the Dodd-Frank Wall Street Reform and Consumer Protection Act).

Law source: Law at ¶11,053, ¶11,062 and ¶11,058. Committee Report at ¶54,742 and ¶54,761.

— Sec. 1053 of the Dodd-Frank Wall Street Reform and Consumer Protection Act;

— Sec. 1062(c), providing the designated transfer date;

— Sec. 1058 providing the effective date.

¶4675 Litigation

The Consumer Financial Protection Bureau has the authority to sue in its own name, using its own attorneys, anyone who is violating a federal consumer financial law or regulation. It can seek civil penalties, injunctions and any other available relief in such suits, and compromise suits with court approval (Sec. 1054(a), (b) and (c) of the Dodd-Frank Act). With the consent of the Attorney General, the Bureau can even represent itself before the U.S. Supreme Court (Sec. 1054(e) of the Dodd-Frank Act).

The Bureau is required to notify the Attorney General of any suits it files, and also of any suit to which it is a party that does not involve the sale of consumer financial products and services. The Bureau and the Attorney General also are to work out an arrangement to coordinate their litigation activities. In addition to notifying the Attorney General, the Bureau is to notify the appropriate prudential regulator if it sues a depository institution or insured credit union (Sec. 1054(d) of the Dodd-Frank Act).

Venue.—A suit by the Bureau must be brought in the federal district court or state court where the person lives, is located or is doing business (Sec. 1054(f) of the Dodd-Frank Act).

Statute of Limitations.—The Bureau generally must file suit within three years of the date when it discovers the violation. However, any statute of limitations prescribed by the federal consumer financial law under which the Bureau is acting will supersede the three-year limit (Sec. 1054(g) of the Dodd-Frank Act).

▶ **Effective date.** The provision is effective on the designated transfer date, which is a date to be selected by the Treasury Secretary that is at least 180 days, but no longer than 12 months, after enactment, subject to a possible extension of up to an additional six months (Sec. 1058 and Sec. 1062(c) of the Dodd-Frank Wall Street Reform and Consumer Protection Act).

Law source: Law at ¶11,054, ¶11,062 and ¶11,058. Committee Report at ¶54,743 and ¶54,761.

— Sec. 1054 of the Dodd-Frank Wall Street Reform and Consumer Protection Act;

— Sec. 1062(c), providing the designated transfer date;

— Sec. 1058 providing the effective date.

¶4680 Relief Available for Violations

If a violation of any federal consumer law is found, the Bureau or a court hearing an enforcement proceeding has broad power to provide relief. The statute says generally that "any appropriate legal or equitable relief" can be ordered. The Act then lists eight specific remedies:

1. rescission or modification of contracts;
2. refunds of money or returns of real estate;
3. restitution;
4. disgorgement of, or compensation for, unjust enrichment;
5. payment of compensatory damages (punitive damages are prohibited);
6. public notification about the violation;
7. restrictions on the violator's future activities; and
8. civil money penalties (Sec. 1055(a) of the Dodd-Frank Act).

The Dodd-Frank Act also notes that the bureau or any state authority that is successful in an enforcement action can recover the costs it incurred (Sec. 1055(b) of the Dodd-Frank Act).

Civil Money Penalties.—Substantial money penalties are possible in serious cases. The basic penalty for a violation of a federal consumer law or regulation, or of an Bureau order, is up to $5,000 per day. The same penalty is available for the failure to pay an Bureau-imposed fee or assessment. A reckless violation can result in a penalty of up to $25,000 per day, while a knowing violation can carry a penalty of up to $1 million per day.

In setting a civil money penalty, the Bureau or the court is to consider the financial resources and good faith of the violator, the gravity of the violation, the level of the risk of loss to consumers, any prior history of violations by the person and any other factors "as justice may require" (Sec. 1055(c) of the Dodd-Frank Act).

▶ **Effective date.** The provision is effective on the designated transfer date, which is a date to be selected by the Treasury Secretary that is at least 180 days, but no longer than 12 months, after enactment, subject to a possible extension of up to an additional six months (Sec. 1058 and Sec. 1062(c) of the Dodd-Frank Wall Street Reform and Consumer Protection Act).

Law source: Law at ¶11,055, ¶11,062 and ¶11,058. Committee Report at ¶54,744 and ¶54,761.

— Sec. 1055 of the Dodd-Frank Wall Street Reform and Consumer Protection Act;
— Sec. 1062(c), providing the designated transfer date;
— Sec. 1058 providing the effective date.

¶4685 Criminal Prosecution Referrals

If the Bureau finds evidence that anyone has violated a federal criminal law, it is obligated to forward that evidence to the Attorney General for appropriate action. This duty does not affect any other Bureau authority to disclose information (Sec. 1056 of the Dodd-Frank Act).

▶ **Effective date.** The provision is effective on the designated transfer date, which is a date to be selected by the Treasury Secretary that is at least 180 days, but no longer than 12 months, after enactment, subject to a possible extension of up to an additional six months (Sec. 1058 and Sec. 1062(c) of the Dodd-Frank Wall Street Reform and Consumer Protection Act).

Law source: Law at ¶11,056, ¶11,062 and ¶11,058. Committee Report at ¶54,745 and ¶54,761.

— Sec. 1056 of the Dodd-Frank Wall Street Reform and Consumer Protection Act;
— Sec. 1062(c), providing the designated transfer date;
— Sec. 1058 providing the effective date.

¶4690 Whistleblower Protections

The Dodd-Frank Act restricts the ability of persons subject to the Bureau's authority to terminate or otherwise punish employees who have furnished information to the BCFP. The employee protections apply to those who acted as part of their job duties or on their own initiative (Sec. 1057(a) of the Dodd-Frank Act). However, the protection is limited to "covered employees"—those who perform tasks related to offering or providing a consumer financial product or service. This could deny protection to employees whose job functions are ancillary to their employer's lines of business (Sec. 1057(b) of the Dodd-Frank Act).

The protected activities are defined broadly, but covered employees are completely protected from the consequences of revealing an employer's secrets. An employee cannot be punished for:

- providing information to any governmental bureau about violations of the consumer financial protection laws or any rule or other pronouncement of the Bureau;
- testifying in any proceeding resulting from the administration or enforcement of the Act;
- filing personally any proceeding; or
- objecting to or refusing to participate in a violation or in an activity that is unfair, deceptive or abusive, and that is likely to cause specific and substantial injury to at least one consumer.

It should be noted that the Act apparently does not protect employees who provide information to the news media or to private persons who are attempting to sue the employer, or to employees who testify in private civil suits against the employer (Sec. 1057(a) of the Dodd-Frank Act).

Complaint Procedures.—Employees who believe they have been terminated or punished in violation of the Act have 180 days to file a complaint with the Secretary of Labor. The Secretary of Labor is then to notify the employer or other person whose conduct gave rise to the complaint that a complaint has been filed and to describe the allegations and supporting evidence. The notice also should include a description of the rights to contest the complaint.

The employer is to be given the opportunity to respond to the complaint, and both the employee and employer are to have the opportunity to meet with someone from the Labor Department to turn over witness's statements. The Labor Department also is to begin its own investigation within 60 days after it receives a complaint.

If the Department finds reasonable cause to believe the complaint is correct, the employer and employee are to be given a preliminary order setting out the relief deemed to be appropriate. Either then has 30 days to object to the Labor Department's finding and demand a hearing. If no objection to the preliminary order is filed, it becomes a final order that is not subject to judicial review.

If an objection is filed, the Department is to hold a hearing. A final order is to be issued within 120 days of the close of that hearing.

Relief can only be ordered if the protected conduct was a contributing factor in the termination or punishment; moreover, relief cannot be ordered if the employer can show, by clear and convincing evidence, that it would have taken the unfavorable action in the absence of the employee's otherwise protected conduct.

An employee's quest for a remedy will not be excessively delayed if the Labor Department fails to act in a timely manner. If the Department does not issue a final order within 210 days after it received the employee's complaint, or within 90 days after it received a written determination that there is reasonable cause to believe there was a violation, the employee can file suit in the appropriate federal district court. The court's ability to order relief is substantially the same as that of the Bureau (Sec. 1057(c) of the Dodd-Frank Act).

Available Relief.—The Labor Department can order three categories of relief for a successful employee:

1. affirmative action to abate the violation;
2. complete reinstatement, including back pay; and
3. compensatory damages.

The employee also can recover reasonable attorneys' fees and costs of bringing the action.

An employer that successfully defends against a complaint has some small available relief as well. If it is decided that the complaint was brought in bad faith or was frivolous, the employee can be ordered to pay the employer's attorneys' fees. However, the maximum possible award is $1,000 (Sec. 1057(c) of the Dodd-Frank Act).

Appealing and Enforcing Orders.—If either the employee or employer decides to appeal a final order of the Labor Department after a hearing, a petition must be filed in the appropriate U.S. Court of Appeals within 60 days.

Both the Bureau and the prevailing party have the power to enforce a final order by filing suit in the appropriate federal district court (Sec. 1057(c) of the Dodd-Frank Act).

Protecting Employees' Rights.—The Act also attempts to shield employees from actions that employers might consider to avoid these protections. First, it provides that waivers of the right to complain about a discharge or other punishment are unenforceable. Second, it states that arbitration agreements entered into before a dispute arose are unenforceable unless they are part of a collective bargaining agreement. (Sec. 1057(d) of the Dodd-Frank Act).

▶ **Effective date.** The provision is effective on the designated transfer date, which is a date to be selected by the Treasury Secretary that is at least 180 days, but no longer than 12 months, after enactment, subject to a possible extension of up to an additional six months (Sec. 1058 and Sec. 1062(c) of the Dodd-Frank Wall Street Reform and Consumer Protection Act).

Law source: Law at ¶11,057, ¶11,062 and ¶11,058. Committee Report at ¶54,746 and ¶54,761.

— Sec. 1057 of the Dodd-Frank Wall Street Reform and Consumer Protection Act;
— Sec. 1062(c), providing the designated transfer date;
— Sec. 1058 providing the effective date.

TRANSFER of FUNCTIONS and PERSONNEL

¶4695 Transfer of Bureau Functions

The central purpose of the creation of the Bureau of Consumer Financial Protection is, within certain limits, to establish a single entity to regulate the federal consumer protection aspects of financial products and services. To accomplish this, it is necessary to transfer the power and authority of the other regulators to the Bureau.

In most cases, the relevant transfers are accomplished with a simple and straightforward statement. The consumer financial protection functions of the Federal Reserve Board, Office of the Comptroller of the Currency, Office of Thrift Supervision, Federal Deposit Insurance Corporation and National Credit Union Administration all are transferred to the Bureau, along with all of the relevant powers and duties of each regulator. The consumer financial protection functions, powers and duties of the Department of Housing and Urban Development that arise under the Real Estate Settlement Procedures Act and the Secure and Fair Enforcement for Mortgage Licensing Act similarly are transferred (Sec. 1061(b) of the Dodd-Frank Act). The Federal Trade Commission (FTC), however, is treated differently, as described below.

"Consumer financial protection functions" includes: adopting rules, issuing guidance or orders and examining banks, thrifts and credit unions that are large enough to be under the Bureau's examination authority (Sec. 1061(a) of the Dodd-Frank Act).

The transfer does not affect the authority of any of the banking regulatory agencies to examine or enforce the consumer financial protection laws and regulations against the smaller institutions over which they maintain authority. Also, functions related to the Community Reinvestment Act are not transferred.

Federal Trade Commission.—Because the FTC has maintained some of its consumer financial protection authority, the transfer provisions that relate to it are somewhat different. Much of the FTC's power and authority is transferred, but it retains its jurisdiction to implement and enforce the Federal Trade Commission Act (FTC Act), which is a consumer financial law but not one of the enumerated consumer laws. The FTC and the Bureau share these rulemaking and enforcement powers, and they are instructed to negotiate an agreement to avoid duplication of effort and regulation (Sec. 1061(b) of the Dodd-Frank Act).

The Dodd-Frank Act provides that there is to be no mandatory transfer of FTC personnel to the Bureau.

Retained Authority of Prudential Regulators.—The prudential regulators retain some of their authority due to the separation of jurisdiction over smaller and larger institutions. They have the exclusive authority to examine smaller institutions for compliance with the consumer financial laws and, because of their back-up enforcement authority over large institutions, they also have the incidental ability to require reports from and examine them. The same division exists with respect to enforcement authority (Sec. 1061(c) of the Dodd-Frank Act).

▶ **Effective date.** Sec. 1061(b) and Sec. 1061(c) of the provision are effective on the designated transfer date, which is a date to be selected by the Treasury Secretary that is at least 180 days, but no longer than 12 months, after enactment, subject to a possible extension of up to an additional six months (Sec. 1062(c) of the Dodd-Frank Wall Street Reform and Consumer Protection Act). Sec. 1061(a) takes effect one day after the date of enactment (Sec. 4 of the Dodd-Frank Wall Street Reform and Consumer Protection Act).

Law source: Law at ¶11,061 and ¶11,062. Committee Report at ¶54,760 and ¶54,761.

— Sec. 1061 of the Dodd-Frank Wall Street Reform and Consumer Protection Act;

¶4695

— Sec. 1062(c), providing the designated transfer date;
— Sec. 1061(d) providing the effective dates.

¶4700 Designated Transfer Date

The designated transfer date is the date on which the various consumer financial protection regulatory functions and authorities pass from the banking safety and soundness regulators and other agencies to the Bureau of Consumer Financial Protection. Within 60 days of the date that Title X is enacted, the designated transfer date is to be set by the Secretary of the Treasury, after consultation with the heads of a number of other agencies. The parameters are that the date must be at least 180 days, but no longer than 12 months, after the Title is enacted (Sec. 1062(b) of the Dodd-Frank Act). The date can be 18 months after enactment if the Secretary determines that orderly implementation of the implementation of Title X is not feasible within the first 12 months (Sec. 1062(c) of the Dodd-Frank Act).

▶ **Effective date.** The provision takes effect one day after the date of enactment (Sec. 4 of the Dodd-Frank Wall Street Reform and Consumer Protection Act).

Law source: Law at ¶11,062 and ¶10,004. Committee Report at ¶54,761.

— Sec. 1062 of the Dodd-Frank Wall Street Reform and Consumer Protection Act;
— Sec. 4, providing the effective date.

¶4705 Savings Provisions

The effect of contracts, orders, civil suits and other legal activities is preserved by the Dodd-Frank Act. It is, of course, unreasonable to expect that the Bureau will have a "clean plate" on the designated transfer date, so it is necessary to ensure that an agency's loss of authority over consumer financial protection functions does not end the legal effect of any ongoing activity.

To continue the effect of ongoing activities, the Dodd-Frank Act provides, on an agency-by-agency basis, that the transfer of powers and functions does not affect any right duty or obligation of the government or any person that arises from any consumer financial protection law that existed on the day before the designated transfer date. It also provides that the Bureau will take over prosecuting or defending any consumer financial protection-related litigation that was pending on the day before the designated transfer date. Separate subsections preserve ongoing activities of the Federal Reserve Bureau, Office of the Comptroller of the Currency, Office of Thrift Supervision, Federal Deposit Insurance Corporation, National Credit Union Administration, Department of Housing and Urban Development and Federal Trade Commission. However, the FTC provisions do not address pending litigation as it has retained the authority to enforce some consumer financial protection laws and rules (Sec. 1063(a) through (g) of the Dodd-Frank Act).

Effect on Orders and Agreements.—The Dodd-Frank Act provides that orders and agreements made before the designated transfer date will remain in full force and effect.

However, those that relate to banks, thrifts and credit unions will not be enforceable by or against the Bureau (Sec. 1063(h) of the Dodd-Frank Act).

Effect on Regulations.—No later than the designated transfer date, the Bureau is to designate which existing regulations it will enforce and publish a list of those regulations in the *Federal Register*. It is possible, although unlikely, that some of the existing consumer financial protection regulations will essentially be abandoned due to that process (Sec. 1063(i) of the Dodd-Frank Act).

It also is likely that there will be regulations "in the pipeline"—regulations that have been adopted but are not yet effective or that have been proposed and remain under consideration. The Act addresses these as well. A regulation proposed by another regulator before the designated transfer date will be deemed to have been proposed by the Bureau. A regulation that has been published in the *Federal Register* but has not yet taken effect will take effect as if it had been adopted by the Bureau (and presumably would be subject to the requirement that the Bureau include it in the list of regulations to be enforced) (Sec. 1063(j) of the Dodd-Frank Act).

▶ **Effective date.** The provision takes effect one day after the date of enactment (Sec. 4 of the Dodd-Frank Wall Street Reform and Consumer Protection Act).

Law source: Law at ¶11,063 and ¶10,004. Committee Report at ¶54,762.

— Sec. 1063 of the Dodd-Frank Wall Street Reform and Consumer Protection Act;

— Sec. 4, providing the effective date.

¶4710 Personnel Transfers

Personnel will be transferred from the existing regulatory agencies to enable the Bureau of Consumer Financial Protection to get up and running more quickly and to provide it with the institutional knowledge that it needs to do its job properly. Employees will be transferred from the Federal Reserve Board, Office of the Comptroller of the Currency, Office of Thrift Supervision, Federal Deposit Insurance Corporation, National Credit Union Administration and Department of Housing and Urban Development. There is no provision for a mandatory transfer of employees to the Bureau from the FTC.

The Bureau and each of the other affected regulators are directed to confer and determine how many employees need to be transferred in order for the Bureau to do its job. They then are to designate jointly which specific employees will be transferred. If the agencies are unable to reach agreement, the President (or someone to whom he delegates the task) will make the decision.

The other regulatory agencies have the ability to shield some senior employees. If an employee's position is in the excepted service or the "Senior Executive Service," the appointment authority must be transferred with the individual. However, the regulatory agency can block that transfer if that appointment authority relates to a position that is excepted from the competitive service due to its confidential or policy nature. The transfer of appointment authority over non-career positions in the Senior Executive Service also can be blocked (Sec. 1064(a) of the Dodd-Frank Act).

Transfer Procedures.—An employee who is to be transferred must be transferred no later than 90 days after the designated transfer date. Employees must be told of position assignments no later than 120 days after the transfer (Sec. 1064(b) of the Dodd-Frank Act). Any transferred employee must be placed in a position with the same status and tenure as before the transfer. An employee transferred from the Fed or from any Federal Reserve Bank is to be put in a position with the same status and tenure as an employee transferred from the OCC who performed similar functions and had a similar term of service (Sec. 1064(d) of the Dodd-Frank Act).

Many of the transferred employees will be examiners who have been subject to certification regimes at their previous agencies. They are to be placed in a comparable examiner's position at the Bureau, where they will examine the same types of institutions without the need to satisfy any additional certification requirements (Sec. 1064(e) of the Dodd-Frank Act).

Effect of Transfers.—Transferred employees who held permanent positions on the day before the designated transfer date are protected from some job actions for the following two years. They cannot be laid off or be transferred to another locality pay area against their will. However, they can be terminated for cause or for poor performance. An appointment to a position excepted from the competitive service due to its confidential policy nature can be terminated, and a supervisory employee can be relocated if necessary (Sec. 1064(f) of the Dodd-Frank Act).

For two years after the designated transfer date, a transferred employee must have a basic rate of pay, including any geographic adjustment, that is at least equal to the basic pay rate in the year before the transfer. The basic pay rate can be reduced for cause, for unacceptable performance or with the employee's consent. There is no restriction on pay increases (Sec. 1064(g) of the Dodd-Frank Act).

The BCFP also is required to establish a uniform pay and classification system for all transferred employees within the first two years after the designated transfer date. The plan cannot discriminate among employees based on their prior employer (Sec. 1064(j) of the Dodd-Frank Act).

If the Bureau decides during the second or third years after the designated transfer date that a staff reorganization is needed, it is to be considered to be a "major reorganization" for purposes of determining whether affected staff members are to be offered retirement incentives under federal law. All employees in a locality pay area are to be moved into a uniform position classification system and any layoffs are to be governed by federal law. As part of the layoff process, the Bureau will be required to establish competitive areas that include at least all of the employees in the locality pay area and competitive levels that do not consider whether the employees were appointed to their positions in the competitive service or the excepted service. Those appointed to positions in the excepted service must be given the same assignment rights as those appointed to positions in the competitive service, with the exception of employees whose positions were excepted due to a confidential policy nature.

A reorganization that includes layoffs more than three years after the designated transfer date will be handled under the standard terms (Sec. 1064(h) of the Dodd-Frank Act).

¶4710

An employee who has been transferred will remain enrolled in the retirement plan of the prior federal agency. Employees who were transferred from the Fed or from a federal reserve bank will be given the option of changing to the Federal Employee Retirement Program.

Transferred employees can maintain their dental, vision, life or long-term care insurance for the first year after the designated transfer date, with the Bureau reimbursing the prior federal employer for any cost. If the Bureau decides after that not to participate in such insurance plans, the employee is to be given the chance to enroll in existing federal insurance programs.

Time spent as an employee of the prior agency is to be credited as time employed by the Bureau for purposes of insurance plans (Sec. 1064(i) of the Dodd-Frank Act).

▶   **Effective date.** The provision takes effect one day after the date of enactment (Sec. 4 of the Dodd-Frank Wall Street Reform and Consumer Protection Act).

Law source: Law at ¶11,064 and ¶10,004. Committee Report at ¶54,763.

— Sec. 1064 of the Dodd-Frank Wall Street Reform and Consumer Protection Act;
— Sec. 4 providing the effective date.

¶4715 Incidental Transfers of Assets and Liabilities

The Bureau of Consumer Financial Protection will receive other assets and liabilities from other agencies in order to establish itself. For the first five years after the enactment of the Act, the Office of Management and Budget has the authority to transfer assets and liabilities that are related to the transferred consumer financial protection functions (Sec. 1065 of the Dodd-Frank Act).

▶   **Effective date.** The provision takes effect one day after the date of enactment (Sec. 4 of the Dodd-Frank Wall Street Reform and Consumer Protection Act).

Law source: Law at ¶11,065 and ¶10,004. Committee Report at ¶54,764.

— Sec. 1065 of the Dodd-Frank Wall Street Reform and Consumer Protection Act;
— Sec. 4 providing the effective date.

¶4720 Interim Operations

The Secretary of the Treasury will function as the Director of the Bureau until a Director has been nominated by the President and confirmed by the Senate (Sec. 1066(a) of the Dodd-Frank Act).

The Treasury Department can provide any administrative services the Bureau may need until the designated transfer date, which is a date to be selected by the Treasury Secretary that is at least 180 days, but no longer than 12 months, after enactment, subject to a possible extension of up to an additional six months (Sec. 1062(b) and 1066(c) of the Dodd-Frank Act).

▶   **Effective date.** The provision takes effect one day after the date of enactment (Sec. 4 of the Dodd-Frank Wall Street Reform and Consumer Protection Act).

Law source: Law at ¶11,066 and ¶10,004. Committee Report at ¶54,765.

— Sec. 1066 of the Dodd-Frank Wall Street Reform and Consumer Protection Act;
— Sec. 4 providing the effective date.

¶4725 Oversight of the Transition

The Dodd-Frank Act intends to place Congress in a position to oversee the transition of employees and function to the Bureau by requiring a set of annual reports. The goal is to ensure that the BCFP has an orderly and organized start, has a qualified workforce and establishes comprehensive employee training and benefits programs (Sec. 1067(a) of the Dodd-Frank Act).

For the first five years of the Bureau's existence, it is to report annually to the House Financial Service Committee and the Senate Banking Committee on three plans it must establish:

- A training and workforce development plan that addresses identifying and acquiring needed skills, fostering innovation, developing leadership and using technology.
- A workforce flexibility plan that addresses telecommuting, flexible schedules, job sharing and similar initiatives.
- A recruitment and retention plan that addresses workforce diversity, streamlined employment processes and collecting information on the effectiveness of hiring decisions (Sec. 1067(a) and (c) of the Dodd-Frank Act).

The Dodd-Frank Act also allows the Bureau and the prudential regulators to include Bureau examiners in examinations of large banks, thrifts and credit unions before the Bureau assumes responsibility for those examinations. This is to assist the Bureau in readying itself for the task (Sec. 1067(e) of the Dodd-Frank Act).

▶ **Effective date.** The provision takes effect one day after the date of enactment (Sec. 4 of the Dodd-Frank Wall Street Reform and Consumer Protection Act).

Law source: Law at ¶11,067 and ¶10,004. Committee Report at ¶54,766.

— Sec. 1067 of the Dodd-Frank Wall Street Reform and Consumer Protection Act;
— Sec. 4, providing the effective date.

REGULATORY IMPROVEMENTS—AMENDMENTS to OTHER LAWS

¶4730 Lending to Women- or Minority-Owned Small Businesses

A new Sec. 704B is added to the Equal Credit Opportunity Act to focus attention on lending to women-owned, minority-owned and small businesses (Sec. 1071(a) of the Dodd-Frank Act). The new section adds to lenders' existing data collection duties.

If a financial institution receives a small business credit application, it is required to ask whether the business is a women-or minority-owned small business and to keep a record of the responses. These requirements apply to all applications regardless of how they are submitted and regardless of whether the application was solicited by the institution. However, applicants are not required to answer the inquiry.

The response records are to be separated from the application and supporting information and, to the extent possible, no underwriter or other person involved in making a decision about the application is to have access to the responses. If there is a need for such a person to have access, the loan applicant is to be told and also to be told that the institution cannot discriminate on the basis of the information.

A women- or minority-owned business is one in which more than 50 percent of the ownership or control is held by one or more women or members of a minority, or in which more than 50 percent of the net profit or loss accrues to one or more women or members of a minority.

Information to Be Collected.—The Bureau of Consumer Financial Protection is to set standards for the information financial institutions are to collect and how the information should be maintained. The following data is to be collected:

- the identifying number and date of the loan application;
- the type and purpose of the loan;
- the amount of credit or credit limit requested and the amount of credit or limit that was approved;
- the action taken on the application and the date of that action;
- the census tract in which the applicant has its principal place of business;
- the small business's gross annual revenue in the fiscal year before the applications; and
- the race and ethnicity of the business's principal owners.

The Bureau may also require any other information that would be relevant to small business fair lending. All of the data is to be submitted to the Bureau annually and maintained for at least three years. It is to be available to the public in ways specified by the Bureau.

Financial institutions are prohibited from collecting or including in the response records any information that would identify the applicant. This specifically includes the applicant's:

- name;
- address (other than the census tract);
- telephone number; and
- e-mail address.

Public Access to Data.—The Bureau is required to make the data generally available each year. It also may publish data compilations that it has created for its own use.

Regulations and Guidance.—The Bureau is directed to adopt regulations to implement the data collection obligations and to issue any needed guidance. It also has the authority to grant exceptions from the requirements to any financial institution or class of institutions.

The guidance is to assist financial institutions' compliance efforts, and the Act notes specifically that it should cover how institutions can assist applicants in determining whether they are women- or minority-owned businesses.

▶ **Effective date.** The provision is effective on the designated transfer date, which is a date to be selected by the Treasury Secretary that is at least 180 days, but no longer than 12 months, after enactment, subject to a possible extension of up to an additional six months (Secs. 1062(c) and 1071(d) of the Dodd-Frank Wall Street Reform and Consumer Protection Act).

Law source: Law at ¶11,071 and ¶11,062. Committee Report at ¶54,781.

— Sec. 1071 of the Dodd-Frank Wall Street Reform and Consumer Protection Act;
— Sec. 1071(a), amending the Equal Credit Opportunity Act by adding a new Sec .704B;
— Sec. 1071(b), amending the Equal Credit Opportunity Act Sec. 701(b);
— Sec. 1071(c), amending the table of sections for Title VII of the Consumer Credit Protection Act;
— Sec. 1062(c), providing the designated transfer date;
— Sec. 1071(d), providing the effective date.

¶4735 Assistance for Economically Vulnerable Persons

The goal of Sec. 1072 of the Dodd-Frank Wall Street Reform and Consumer Protection Act is to provide financial education and counseling to persons who are identified as economically vulnerable. It does so by amending the Housing and Economic Recovery Act provisions on counseling to include "economically vulnerable individuals and families" after each mention of homebuyers. It also makes tax-exempt organizations with experience in working with such persons eligible for funding as long as the organization is not primarily a credit counseling organization.

The changes are effective only for programs funded with appropriations in 2011 or after.

▶ **Effective date.** The provision takes effect one day after the date of enactment (Sec. 4 of the Dodd-Frank Wall Street Reform and Consumer Protection Act).

Law source: Law at ¶11,072 and ¶10,004. Committee Report at ¶54,784.

— Sec. 1072 of the Dodd-Frank Wall Street Reform and Consumer Protection Act;
— Sec. 1072(a), amending the Housing and Economic Recovery Act Sec 1132;
— Sec. 4, providing the effective date.

¶4740 Remittance Transfers

Lengthy and detailed disclosure requirements for remittance transfer service providers are added by amendments to the Electronic Fund Transfer Act (EFTA) (Sec. 1072(a) of the Dodd-Frank Act). The EFTA amendments speak in terms of actions by the Federal Reserve Board; however, the Fed's authority will be transferred to the Bureau of Consumer Financial Protection as of the designated transfer date (a date to be selected by the Treasury Secretary that is at least 180 days, but no longer than 12 months, after enactment, subject to a possible extension of up to an additional six months (Sec. 1062(c) of the Dodd-Frank Act). For simplicity, this explanation refers only to the Bureau.

A "remittance transfer" is:

- an electronic transfer of funds (which is any transfer using electronic or similar technology, regardless of whether it would be an electronic fund transfer under the EFTA);
- from a person in the United States;
- to a person in a foreign country;
- using a person or financial institution that provides such transfers in the normal course of its business.

The Bureau can, by regulation, set a minimum amount for what will be considered to be a remittance transfer.

A person who provides this service must make described disclosures to consumers at two points in the process: when the consumer requests that a transfer be made and when the consumer makes a payment in connection with the transfer. Of course, these two times could both be part of a continuous transaction and, as noted below, the disclosures may be made in a single written document. All of the disclosures are to be made clearly and conspicuously. If the consumer conducts the transaction electronically, the disclosures are to comply with the Electronic Signatures in Global and National Commerce Act (the E-Sign Act).

Disclosures When Transfer Is Requested.—When a consumer requests a remittance transfer, and before the consumer makes any payment, the service provider must disclose:

- the amount the recipient will receive, using the currency to which the funds will be exchanged;
- the amount the consumer must pay, including any fees; and
- the exchange rate the service provider will use, to the nearest 1/100th of a point.

The Bureau has the ability to make special rules to cover a situation when a foreign nation's laws or local conditions do not permit the service provider to know the precise amount that will be delivered when the disclosures are made.

Disclosures on Payment.—When the consumer makes the required payment, the service provider must give the consumer:

- a receipt that includes the earlier disclosures, the promised delivery date for the funds, the recipient's name and, if provided by the consumer, the recipient's address or telephone number;
- a written statement describing the consumer's error resolution rights and giving contact information for the service provider, any state regulator and the Bureau of

Consumer Financial Protection (including the Bureau's toll-free consumer complaint telephone number).

Possible Exemptions.—The Bureau can adopt rules that change the specified disclosures to account for different circumstances. If a transaction is carried out over the telephone, the first disclosures can be made orally and the latter disclosures by mail. Mailed disclosures must be sent within one business day but, if the transfer is carried out using a deposit account at the service provider, they only need to be included with the next periodic statement. A service provider can include all of the required disclosures in a single document if the information required in the first disclosure is accurate when the payment is made. Also, if the consumer initiates the transaction electronically, the initial disclosures can be made electronically in a form the consumer can retain.

Financial Institution Protections.—Banks, thrifts and credit unions are held to a lower standard when disclosing the amount of currency that will be delivered to a recipient. If the remittance transfer is made through an account the consumer holds with the financial institution and the institution cannot know the precise amount that will be delivered, only a "reasonably accurate estimate" needs to be disclosed. This is not a permanent standard. It is to end in five years, although the Bureau can extend it for an additional five years.

Additional Notices.—The Bureau has the authority, after a study, to require remittance service providers to post "store-front" notices, and is required to establish notices for use on service providers' Internet sites.

If a store-front notice is required, it is to describe a model transfer for at least one amount, showing the amount that will be delivered in the currency to which it will be exchanged. The model will need to be updated in a timely manner. It will be required in every physical location used by the service provider.

The required Internet notices must include the same information as the store-front notices. They must be clear and conspicuous and comply with the E-Sign Act.

Foreign Language Disclosures.—Consumers who use remittance transfers services may not be fluent in English. Thus, the required disclosures are to be made in English and in all other languages principally used by the service provider or its agents to advertise or solicit business at the office where the transaction is carried out.

Error Resolution Procedures.—If a remittance transfer service provider receives notice (written or oral) of an error within 180 days of the promised delivery date, it must comply with the prescribed error resolution procedures. This means that the service provider has 90 days to:

- refund the full amount of the transaction;
- complete the delivery at no additional charge;
- provide any other remedy established by the Bureau's rules; or
- provide an explanation showing that there was no error.

Rules to implement these procedures must be adopted within 18 months of the enactment of the Dodd-Frank Act. The rules must require the service provider to keep a record of the consumer's complaint, the information the consumer furnished and the results of the service provider's investigation.

¶4740

Cancelation and Refunds.—The Dodd-Frank Act does not establish specific cancellation and refund standards. It merely requires the Bureau to adopt rules to create these policies within 18 months of enactment.

Agents' Actions.—A remittance transfer service provider is completely liable for any violations of its agents when they are acting for the service provider. The Bureau is to adopt rules to enforce this liability; however, the rules may include consideration of the service provider's own compliance oversight measures.

Applicability of Standards.—The EFTA amendments distinguish between remittance transfers that are electronic fund transfers under the EFTA and those that are not. If the remittance transfer is not an EFTA-electronic fund transfer, many of the EFTA's consumer protection requirements will not apply and only the requirements of the new EFTA Sec. 919 will apply. If the remittance transfer is also an electronic fund transfer, all of the EFTA standards except the error resolution obligations will apply.

Alternatives to Remittance Transfers.—The Dodd-Frank Act includes several provisions that are intended to encourage the creation of alternatives to the use of traditional remittance service providers. The Fed, federal reserve banks and Treasury Department are instructed to investigate ways to use systems such as the automated clearinghouse system for remittance transfers (Sec. 1073(b) of the Dodd-Frank Act). Also, the prudential regulators are to assist banks, thrifts and credit unions in expanding their ability to provide remittance transfer services (Sec. 1073(c) of the Dodd-Frank Act). The Act includes an amendment to the Federal Credit Union Act to allow these institutions to participate more fully (Sec. 1073(d) of the Dodd-Frank Act).

Credit Scores.—The Act also requires the Bureau to report to Congress within one year of enactment on how a consumer's remittance transfer history could be used to improve that consumer's credit score. The report also is to make recommendations on improvements in how exchange rates are disclosed (Sec. 1073(e) of the Dodd-Frank Act).

▶ **Effective date.** The provision takes effect one day after the date of enactment (Sec. 4 of the Dodd-Frank Wall Street Reform and Consumer Protection Act).

Law source: Law at ¶11,073 and ¶10,004. Committee Report at ¶54,785.

— Sec. 1073 of the Dodd-Frank Wall Street Reform and Consumer Protection Act;
— Sec. 1073(a), amending Electronic Fund Transfer Act Sec. 902;
— Sec. 1073(a), amending Electronic Fund Transfer Act Sec. 904;
— Sec. 1073(a), amending Electronic Fund Transfer Act by renumbering Sec. 919 through Sec. 922;
— Sec. 1073(a), amending Electronic Fund Transfer Act by adding a new Sec. 919;
— Sec. 1073(d), amending Federal Credit Union Act Sec. 107;
— Sec. 4, providing the effective date.

¶4745 Government Sponsored Enterprise Study

The Treasury Department is instructed to conduct a study on how to end the conservatorship of the Federal National Mortgage Association (Fannie Mae) and the Federal

Home Loan Mortgage Corporation (Freddie Mac). This is to be a wide-ranging study to be completed and reported to Congress no later than Jan. 31, 2011 (Sec. 1074(b) of the Dodd-Frank Act).

In addition to options the Treasury may develop on its own, the study is to consider:
- winding-down and liquidating the companies;
- privatizing the companies;
- shifting the functions of the companies to one or more other federal agencies; or
- breaking the companies apart into smaller entities.

Study Topics.—The study is to go beyond ending the conservatorship to consider the full scope of federal government involvement in the housing market. It is to address:
- the appropriate role of the government in supporting the housing finance system and what risks the government should accept;
- how the current housing finance system can be improved;
- how the system should support continued housing credit availability;
- how the system should be structured to ensure continued consumer access to traditional, easy-to-understand mortgage loans;
- the roles of the Federal Housing Administration and the Department of Veterans Affairs;
- the effect of finance system reforms on rental housing;
- the effect of finance system reforms on secondary market liquidity;
- standardization;
- experiences in other countries; and
- how to make the transition to a better system (Sec. 1074(a) of the Dodd-Frank Act).

▶ **Effective date.** The provision takes effect one day after the date of enactment (Sec. 4 of the Dodd-Frank Wall Street Reform and Consumer Protection Act).

Law source: Law at ¶11,074 and ¶10,004.

— Sec. 1074 of the Dodd-Frank Wall Street Reform and Consumer Protection Act;
— Sec. 4, providing the effective date.

¶4750 Payment Card Transaction Fees and Rules

The Dodd-Frank Act attempts to restrict interchange fees that debit card issuers can charge merchants. It also prohibits some practices of debit and credit card networks that are seen as anti-competitive. It does this by adding a new section to the Electronic Fund Transfer Act (EFTA) that requires the Federal Reserve Board to adopt appropriate regulations. Since the EFTA is one of the enumerated consumer laws (Sec. 1002(12) of the Dodd-Frank Act), the Fed's authority will be transferred to the Bureau on the designated transfer date (a date to be selected by the Treasury Secretary that is at least 180 days, but no longer than 12 months, after enactment, subject to a possible extension of up to an additional six months (Sec. 1062(c) of the Dodd-Frank Act).

Within nine months of the enactment of the Dodd-Frank Act, the Fed is to adopt final rules that establish the standards to be used in determining whether a debit card issuer's interchange fees are "reasonable and proportional to the cost incurred by the issuer with respect to the transaction"—the standard for allowable charges. In formulating the rule, the Fed is to consider the similarity between debit card transactions and checks that the Federal Reserve system clears at par. It is to distinguish between the costs incurred by the issuer in handling a specific transaction, which may be recovered, and costs that are not specific to a particular transaction, which may not be recovered. Thus, the charges allowable under the Act would seem to exclude both the recovery of any overhead and any profit for providing debit card services.

The allowable fee may be increased for costs appropriately incurred in preventing fraud. Rules governing these fraud-prevention costs also are to be adopted within nine months of enactment.

The section of the EFTA amendment imposing the interchange fee limits is effective one year after enactment.

Exemptions from the Regulation.—In an effort to shield smaller institutions from the changes, the Act says that debit card issuers with less than $10 billion in total assets, including the assets of all affiliates, will be exempt from the regulation on fee limits. However, these institutions have raised the concern that competition will force them to reduce their interchange fees.

Special provisions are made for debit and prepaid cards that are issued in connection with government benefits programs in order to avoid increasing the costs of those programs. These same provisions apply to general use, reloadable stored value cards that are not marketed as gift cards. In general, the fee-limit regulation will not apply to these cards.

However, two years after the enactment of the Dodd-Frank Act, the fee-limit regulation will apply to these cards if the consumer can be charged a fee for:

- overdrawing the account; or
- the first monthly withdrawal using an automated teller machine that is part of the issuer's ATM network.

Beginning one year after enactment, the Bureau is to make annual reports to Congress on the use of prepaid cards for government programs and the interchange fees charged for the use of the cards.

Network Fees.—Although the Dodd-Frank Act does not seek to limit network fees, it does seek to prevent issuers from imposing network fees to replace the revenue lost due to the limits on interchange fees. Thus, the Fed is to adopt rules to prevent the use of network fees to compensate issuers for transactions or to evade the regulation. These rules are to be adopted within nine months of enactment. "Network fee" is defined broadly to include any fee charged or received by a network for a transaction other than an interchange fee.

Anticompetitive Contract Provisions.—The Act also prohibits several types of anticompetitive provisions in the contacts between merchants and payment card networks. These apply not only to debit cards but to credit cards as well. The prohibited activities include:

¶4750

- exclusivity arrangements;
- banning incentives to use a different payment method; and
- restricting merchants from establishing some maximum or minimum transaction limits.

The Act does provide generally that discriminating between credit and debit card issuers in the same payment network is prohibited.

Exclusivity Arrangements.—Card issuers and payment networks are to be prohibited from, directly or indirectly, restricting the number of networks on which a transaction can be processed. They cannot restrict the transaction to being processed on any one network, or on multiple networks that are operated by affiliated companies. They also cannot restrict the ability of a merchant to choose to which network a transaction will be routed for processing. A regulation to implement this ban is to be adopted within one year of enactment.

Discounts and Incentives.—Payment card networks cannot interfere with a merchant's ability to use discounts or other incentives to induce consumers to use a different payment method. For example, a service station cannot be prevented from offering consumers a discount if they pay with cash instead of using a credit card. However, the merchant cannot discriminate on the basis of the payment network or issuer, or on the basis of credit card network or issuer. Also, the incentive must be clearly and conspicuously disclosed and available to all consumers.

Maximums and Minimums.—Payment card networks cannot interfere with a merchant's decision to impose a minimum transaction amount, as long as the minimum does not exceed $10 and the same minimum applies to all networks and issuers. Also, they cannot interfere with the ability of any federal agency of any institution of higher education to set a maximum limit, if the limit is nondiscriminatory.

Conforming Amendments.—Congress chose to exempt several federal programs from the effect of the changes. Electronic benefit transfer payment programs under these three Acts are exempted:

- the Food and Nutrition Act;
- the Farm Security and Rural Investment;
- the Child Nutrition Act.

▶ **Effective date.** The provision takes effect one day after the date of enactment (Sec. 4 of the Dodd-Frank Wall Street Reform and Consumer Protection Act).

Law source: Law at ¶11,075 and ¶10,004.

— Sec. 1075 of the Dodd-Frank Wall Street Reform and Consumer Protection Act;
— Sec. 1075(a), amending the Electronic Fund Transfer Act by renumbering Sec. 920 and Sec. 921;
— Sec. 1075(a), amending the Electronic Fund Transfer Act by adding a new Sec. 920;
— Sec. 1075(b), amending Food and Nutrition Act Sec. 7;
— Sec. 1075(c), amending Farm Security and Rural Investment Act Sec. 4402;
— Sec. 1075(d), amending Child Nutrition Act Sec. 11;
— Sec. 4, providing the effective date.

¶4750

¶4755 Reverse Mortgage Rules

The Bureau is directed to carry out a study of reverse mortgage transactions within one year of the designated transfer date (Sec. 1076(a) of the Dodd-Frank Act). It can then use the results of the study to adopt regulations governing reverse mortgage transactions. The Dodd-Frank Act expresses special concern over the practice of using reverse mortgage proceeds to fund investments or annuities (Sec. 1076(b) of the Dodd-Frank Act).

The Act suggests that if the Bureau adopts a regulation, it could identify certain acts or practices as unfair, deceptive or abusive and could provide for unified disclosures and model forms to satisfy the Truth in Lending Act, Real Estate Settlement Procedures Act and disclosures required for Home Equity Conversion Mortgages under the National Housing Act.

The study requirement does not, however, interfere with the Bureau's ability to adopt regulations or take any other earlier action (Sec. 1076(c) of the Dodd-Frank Act).

▶ **Effective date.** The provision takes effect one day after the date of enactment (Sec. 4 of the Dodd-Frank Wall Street Reform and Consumer Protection Act).

Law source: Law at ¶11,076 and ¶10,004.

— Sec. 1076 of the Dodd-Frank Wall Street Reform and Consumer Protection Act;

— Sec. 4, providing the effective date.

¶4760 Private Education Loans and Lenders

The Bureau and Department of Education, in consultation with the Attorney General and the Federal Trade Commission, are to carry out an extensive study of private education loans and lenders within two years of the enactment of the Dodd-Frank Act (Sec. 1077(a) of the Dodd-Frank Act). When completed, the study is to be submitted to two committee each in the House and the Senate.

The Act calls for the study to address 10 separate issues:

- growth and changes in the private education loan market;
- factors behind the growth and changes;
- the extent to which students and their parents rely on private education loans;
- characteristics of borrowers;
- characteristics of lenders;
- lenders' underwriting criteria;
- loan terms, conditions and prices;
- disclosures and other consumer protections;
- whether adequate information is available to ensure that fair lending laws are being followed; and
- recommendations for legislative action (Sec. 1077(b) of the Dodd-Frank Act).

▶ **Effective date.** The provision takes effect one day after the date of enactment (Sec. 4 of the Dodd-Frank Wall Street Reform and Consumer Protection Act).

Law source: Law at ¶11,077 and ¶10,004.

— Sec. 1077 of the Dodd-Frank Wall Street Reform and Consumer Protection Act;

— Sec. 4, providing the effective date.

¶4765 Credit Scores Study and Report

The Dodd-Frank Act requires the Bureau to conduct a study to look for credit score discrepancies. The study is to investigate the nature, range and size of variations between credit scores sold to consumers and those sold to creditors, and whether any such differences harm consumers (Sec. 1078(a) of the Dodd-Frank Act). A report to Congress is due within one year of the enactment of the Act (Sec. 1078(b) of the Dodd-Frank Act).

▶ **Effective date.** The provision takes effect one day after the date of enactment (Sec. 4 of the Dodd-Frank Wall Street Reform and Consumer Protection Act).

Law source: Law at ¶11,078 and ¶10,004.

— Sec. 1078 of the Dodd-Frank Wall Street Reform and Consumer Protection Act;

— Sec. 4, providing the effective date.

¶4770 Exchange Facilitators

Exchange facilitators are persons who, for a fee, facilitate like-kind exchanges of property for consumers in a way that allows a consumer to dispose of property and obtain a replacement without immediately paying federal income tax on the capital gains that would result from an outright sale (Sec. 1079(d) of the Dodd-Frank Act). The Act requires the Bureau to undertake a review of the existing federal laws and regulations on these persons and report to Congress within one year of the designated transfer date. The report is to include both legislative and regulatory recommendations (Sec. 1079(a) and (b) of the Dodd-Frank Act).

Within two years after the report is submitted to Congress, the Bureau is to establish a consumer protection program (Sec. 1079(c) of the Dodd-Frank Act).

▶ **Effective date.** The provision takes effect one day after the date of enactment (Sec. 4 of the Dodd-Frank Wall Street Reform and Consumer Protection Act).

Law source: Law at ¶11,079 and ¶10,004.

— Sec. 1079 of the Dodd-Frank Wall Street Reform and Consumer Protection Act;

— Sec. 4, providing the effective date.

¶4775 Financial Fraud

Provisions intended to stiffen penalties for both securities and financial institution financial fraud are included in the Dodd-Frank Act.

First, the United States Sentencing Commission is instructed to review the sentencing guidelines for persons convicted of securities fraud, financial institutions fraud and federally-related mortgage fraud. The Commission is to ensure that the sentencing guidelines give adequate consideration to the seriousness of the offenses and to the harm they can do (Sec. 1079A(a) of the Dodd-Frank Act).

Second, the Act adds a new Sec. 3301 to 18 USC 213 to create a category of "securities fraud offenses" with a six-year statute of limitations (Sec. 1079A(b) of the Dodd-Frank Act).

Finally, the False Claims Act Sec. 3730(h) is amended to enhance the protection for whistleblowing employees (Sec. 1079A(c) of the Dodd-Frank Act).

▶ **Effective date.** The provision takes effect one day after the date of enactment (Sec. 4 of the Dodd-Frank Wall Street Reform and Consumer Protection Act).

Law source: Law at ¶11,079A and ¶10,004.

— Sec. 1079A of the Dodd-Frank Wall Street Reform and Consumer Protection Act;
— Sec. 1079A(b), adding a new 18 USC 3301;
— Sec. 1079A(c), amending 31 USC 3730 of the False Claims Act;
— Sec. 4, providing the effective date.

CONFORMING AMENDMENTS

¶4780 Amendments to the Inspector General Act

An amendment to the Inspector General Act brings the Bureau of Consumer Financial Protection under the oversight of the Federal Reserve Board's Inspector General, which is renamed the Inspector General of the Board of Governors of the Federal Reserve System and the Bureau of Consumer Financial Protection.

> **CCH Comment:** The House version of financial reform (H.R. 4173) would have required the Bureau to establish its own Office of Inspector General by treating the Bureau as a designated federal agency.

▶ **Effective date.** The provision takes effect on the date of enactment (Sec. 1081 of the Dodd-Frank Wall Street Reform and Consumer Protection Act). Except as otherwise provided, Subtitle H—Conforming Amendments is effective on the transfer date, other than Secs. 1081 (Amendments to the Inspector General Act) and 1082 (Amendments to the Privacy Act of 1974), which take effect on the date of enactment (Sec. 1100H of the Dodd-Frank Act).

Law source: Law at ¶11,081 and ¶11,100H. Committee Report at ¶54,800.

— Sec. 1081 of the Dodd-Frank Wall Street Reform and Consumer Protection Act, amending Inspector General Act, Sec. 8G(a)(2), (c) and (g)(3);

— Sec. 1081, providing the effective date.

¶4785 Amendments to the Privacy Act

Conforming amendments make the Privacy Act applicable to the Bureau.

▶ **Effective date.** The provision takes effect on the date of enactment (Sec. 1082 of the Dodd-Frank Wall Street Reform and Consumer Protection Act).

Law source: Law at ¶11,082. Committee Report at ¶54,801.

— Sec. 1082 of the Dodd-Frank Wall Street Reform and Consumer Protection Act, adding 5 USC 552a(w);

— Sec. 1082, providing the effective date.

¶4790 Amendments to the Alternative Mortgage Transaction Parity Act

The Alternative Mortgage Transaction Parity Act was passed in 1982 to preempt state laws and constitutions that prohibited adjustable rate mortgage (ARM) loans for federal- and state-chartered entities. It also preempted state laws with respect to all "alternative" mortgages, including negative amortization loans and interest-only loans. States were unable to regulate terms for mortgages that have proved to have had significant difficulty. The conforming amendment continues to preempt state laws that would prohibit adjustable rate mortgages, but removes this preemption of other types of "alternative" mortgages or features, permitting states to legislate in this area (Alternative Mortgage Transaction Parity Act Sec. 804(c), as amended by Sec. 1083(2)(B) of the Dodd-Frank Act).

> **CCH Comment:** The House version of financial reform would have preempted state laws that would prohibit an alternative mortgage transaction, but removed this preemption where state law regulates mortgage transactions generally, including any restriction on prepayment penalties or late charges.

▶ **Effective date.** The provision is effective on the designated transfer date, which is a date to be selected by the Treasury Secretary that is at least 180 days, but no longer than 12 months, after enactment, subject to a possible extension of up to an additional six months (Secs. 1083(b) and (c) and Sec. 1062(c) of the Dodd-Frank Wall Street Reform and Consumer Protection Act).

Law source: Law at ¶11,083 and ¶11,062. Committee Report at ¶54,802.

— Sec. 1083(a) of the Dodd-Frank Wall Street Reform and Consumer Protection Act, amending Alternative Mortgage Transaction Parity Act Secs. 803 and 804;

— Sec. 1062(c), providing the designated transfer date;

— Secs. 1083(b) and (c), providing the effective date.

¶4795 Amendments to the Electronic Fund Transfer Act

An amendment to the Electronic Fund Transfer Act (EFTA) replaces references to the Federal Reserve System with the Bureau of Consumer Financial Protection. Generally, the Bureau is responsible for prescribing rules to carry out the purposes of the Electronic Fund Transfer Act. However, the Fed retains rulemaking authority to:

- carry out the purposes of the EFTA over a motor vehicle dealer that is predominantly engaged in the sale and servicing of motor vehicles or the leasing and servicing of motor vehicles; and
- with regard to whether a state law relating to electronic fund transfers is inconsistent with federal law (EFTA Sec. 904(a)(2), as amended by Sec. 1084(3)(A) of the Dodd-Frank Act).

▶ **Effective date.** The provision is effective on the designated transfer date, which is a date to be selected by the Treasury Secretary that is at least 180 days, but no longer than 12 months, after enactment, subject to a possible extension of up to an additional six months (Secs. 1062(c) and 1100H and of the Dodd-Frank Wall Street Reform and Consumer Protection Act).

Law source: Law at ¶11,084, ¶11,062 and ¶11,100H. Committee Report at ¶54,803.

— Sec. 1084 of the Dodd-Frank Wall Street Reform and Consumer Protection Act, amending Electronic Fund Transfer Act Secs. 903, 904, 916(d) and 918;

— Sec. 1062(c), providing the designated transfer date;

— Sec. 1100H, providing the effective date.

¶4800 Amendments to the Equal Credit Opportunity Act

The Dodd-Frank Act amends the Equal Credit Opportunity Act (ECOA) by replacing references to the Federal Reserve System with the Bureau of Consumer Financial Protection (Bureau). The ECOA, as amended, clarifies the Federal Trade Commission's enforcement authority by granting the FTC power to enforce rules promulgated by the Bureau (ECOA Sec. 704(c), as amended by Sec. 1085(4)(B) of the Dodd-Frank Act).

▶ **Effective date.** The provision is effective on the designated transfer date, which is a date to be selected by the Treasury Secretary that is at least 180 days, but no longer than 12 months, after enactment, subject to a possible extension of up to an additional six months (Secs. 1062(c) and 1100H and of the Dodd-Frank Wall Street Reform and Consumer Protection Act).

Law source: Law at ¶11,085, ¶11,062 and ¶11,100H. Committee Report at ¶54,804.

— Sec. 1085 of the Dodd-Frank Wall Street Reform and Consumer Protection Act, amending Equal Credit Opportunity Act Secs. 702, 703, 704 and 706;

— Sec. 1062(c), providing the designated transfer date;

— Sec. 1100H, providing the effective date.

¶4805 Amendments to the Expedited Funds Availability Act

The Dodd-Frank Act makes conforming amendments to the Expedited Funds Availability Act and also increases the next-day funds availability amount from $100 to $200 (Expedited Funds Availability Act Sec. 603, as amended by the Dodd-Frank Act). In addition, the Dodd-Frank Act allows for future adjustments to the next-day funds availability amount for inflation (Expedited Funds Availability Act Sec. 607(f), as added by Sec. 1086(f) of the Dodd-Frank Act).

▶ **Effective date.** The provision is effective on the designated transfer date, which is a date to be selected by the Treasury Secretary that is at least 180 days, but no longer than 12 months, after enactment, subject to a possible extension of up to an additional six months (Secs. 1062(c) and 1100H and of the Dodd-Frank Wall Street Reform and Consumer Protection Act).

Law source: Law at ¶11,086, ¶11,062 and ¶11,100H. Committee Report at ¶54,805.

— Sec. 1086 of the Dodd-Frank Wall Street Reform and Consumer Protection Act, amending Expedited Funds Availability Act Secs. 603, 604, 605, 607 and 609;

— Sec. 1062(c), providing the designated transfer date;

— Sec. 1100H, providing the effective date.

¶4810 Amendments to the Fair Credit Billing Act

The Dodd-Frank Act replaces the term "Board" with the term "Bureau" in the Fair Credit Billing Act.

▶ **Effective date.** The provision is effective on the designated transfer date, which is a date to be selected by the Treasury Secretary that is at least 180 days, but no longer than 12 months, after enactment, subject to a possible extension of up to an additional six months (Secs. 1062(c) and 1100H and of the Dodd-Frank Wall Street Reform and Consumer Protection Act).

Law source: Law at ¶11,087, ¶11,062 and ¶11,100H. Committee Report at ¶54,806.

— Sec. 1087 of the Dodd-Frank Wall Street Reform and Consumer Protection Act, amending the Fair Credit Billing Act;

— Sec. 1062(c), providing the designated transfer date;

— Sec. 1100H, providing the effective date.

¶4815 Amendments to the Fair Credit Reporting Act and the Fair and Accurate Credit Transactions Act of 2003

The Dodd-Frank Act makes conforming amendments to the Fair Credit Reporting Act (FCRA) and the Fair and Accurate Credit Transactions Act (FACT Act) granting rulemaking and regulatory authority to the Bureau, but also retaining certain powers in the Federal Trade Commission.

FCRA—Regulations promulgated by the Bureau apply to any person subject to the FCRA regardless of the enforcement authority assigned to other agencies. Among other changes to the FCRA, the Act allows the FTC to retain procedural, investigative and enforcement powers with regard to consumer reporting agencies, including the power to issue procedural rules in enforcing compliance with the FCRA and to require filing of reports, production of documents and appearance of witnesses. The FTC also has authority to bring a civil action to recover a civil penalty in federal court. Such civil penalties are capped at $2,500 per violation (FCRA Sec. 621(a), as amended by Sec. 1088(10)(A) of the Dodd-Frank Act).

FACT Act.—The Act divides regulatory authority under the FACT Act among the Commodity Futures Trading Commission, Securities Exchange Commission and the Bureau (FACT Act Sec. 214(b)(1), as amended by Sec. 1088(b)(3) of the Dodd-Frank Act).

▶ **Effective date.** The provision is effective on the designated transfer date, which is a date to be selected by the Treasury Secretary that is at least 180 days, but no longer than 12 months, after enactment, subject to a possible extension of up to an additional six months (Secs. 1062(c) and 1100H and of the Dodd-Frank Wall Street Reform and Consumer Protection Act).

Law source: Law at ¶11,088, ¶11,062 and ¶11,100H. Committee Report at ¶54,807.

— Sec. 1088(a) of the Dodd-Frank Wall Street Reform and Consumer Protection Act, amending Fair Credit Reporting Act Secs. 603, 604, 605, 611, 615, 621, 623 and 628;

— Sec. 1088(b), amending Fair and Accurate Credit Transactions Act Sec. 214(b)(1);

— Sec. 1062(c), providing the designated transfer date;

— Sec. 1100H, providing the effective date.

¶4820 Amendments to the Fair Debt Collection Practices Act

A conforming amendment to the Fair Debt Collection Practices Act (FDCPA) replaces the FTC with the Bureau as the primary regulator. However, the FTC retains general compliance enforcement responsibility (FDCPA Sec. 814(a), as amended by Sec. 1089(3)(A) of the Dodd-Frank Act).

▶ **Effective date.** The provision is effective on the designated transfer date, which is a date to be selected by the Treasury Secretary that is at least 180 days, but no longer than 12 months, after enactment, subject to a possible extension of up to an additional six months (Secs. 1062(c) and 1100H and of the Dodd-Frank Wall Street Reform and Consumer Protection Act).

Law source: Law at ¶¶11,089, ¶11,062 and ¶11,100H. Committee Report at ¶54,808.

— Sec. 1089 of the Dodd-Frank Wall Street Reform and Consumer Protection Act, amending Fair Debt Collection Practices Act Secs. 803 and 814;

— Sec. 1062(c), providing the designated transfer date;

— Sec. 1100H, providing the effective date.

¶4825 Amendments to Federal Deposit Insurance Act

The Federal Deposit Insurance Act (FDIA) is amended to require each of the prudential federal banking regulators to report to the Bureau when a regulator has a reasonable belief that a violation of a consumer law has been committed by a financial institution under the regulator's supervision (FDIA Sec. 8(t)(6), as added by Sec. 1090(1) of the Dodd-Frank Act).

▶ **Effective date.** The provision is effective on the designated transfer date, which is a date to be selected by the Treasury Secretary that is at least 180 days, but no longer than 12 months, after enactment, subject to a possible extension of up to an additional six months (Secs. 1062(c) and 1100H and of the Dodd-Frank Wall Street Reform and Consumer Protection Act).

Law source: Law at ¶11,090, ¶11,062 and ¶11,100H. Committee Reports at ¶54,809.

— Sec. 1090 of the Dodd-Frank Wall Street Reform and Consumer Protection Act, adding Federal Deposit Insurance Act Sec. 8(t)(6) and amending Sec. 43;

— Sec. 1062(c), providing the designated transfer date;

— Sec. 1100H, providing the effective date.

¶4830 Amendments to the Federal Financial Institutions Examination Council Act

The Dodd-Frank Act amends the Federal Financial Institutions Examination Council Act by replacing a reference to the Director of the Office of Thrift Supervision with a reference to the Director of the Bureau.

▶ **Effective date.** The provision is effective on the designated transfer date, which is a date to be selected by the Treasury Secretary that is at least 180 days, but no longer than 12 months, after enactment, subject to a possible extension of up to an additional six months (Secs. 1062(c) and 1100H and of the Dodd-Frank Wall Street Reform and Consumer Protection Act).

Law source: Law at ¶11,091, ¶11,062 and ¶11,100H.

— Sec. 1091 of the Dodd-Frank Wall Street Reform and Consumer Protection Act, amending Federal Financial Institutions Examination Council Act Sec. 1004(a)(4);

— Sec. 1062(c), providing the designated transfer date;

— Sec. 1100H, providing the effective date.

¶4835 Amendments to the Federal Trade Commission Act

Conforming amendments to the Federal Trade Commission Act to adjust the definitions of banks, savings and loan institutions and federal credit unions and remove rulemaking authority with regard to unfair or deceptive acts or practices from the Fed, the Federal Home Loan Bank Board and National Credit Union Administration Board, respectively, among other technical modifications.

▶ **Effective date.** The provision is effective on the designated transfer date, which is a date to be selected by the Treasury Secretary that is at least 180 days, but no longer than 12 months, after enactment, subject to a possible extension of up to an additional six months (Secs. 1062(c) and 1100H and of the Dodd-Frank Wall Street Reform and Consumer Protection Act).

Law source: Law at ¶11,092, ¶11,062 and ¶11,100H.

— Sec. 1092 of the Dodd-Frank Wall Street Reform and Consumer Protection Act, amending Federal Trade Commission Act Sec. 18(f);

— Sec. 1062(c), providing the designated transfer date;

— Sec. 1100H, providing the effective date.

¶4840 Amendments to the Gramm-Leach-Bliley Act

The Bureau is added to the list of agencies responsible for enforcing the Gramm-Leach-Bliley Act and relevant regulations.

▶ **Effective date.** The provision is effective on the designated transfer date, which is a date to be selected by the Treasury Secretary that is at least 180 days, but no longer than 12 months, after enactment, subject to a possible extension of up to an additional six months (Secs. 1062(c) and 1100H and of the Dodd-Frank Wall Street Reform and Consumer Protection Act).

Law source: Law at ¶11,093, ¶11,062 and ¶11,100H. Committee Report at ¶54,810.

— Sec. 1093 of the Dodd-Frank Wall Street Reform and Consumer Protection Act, amending Gramm-Leach-Bliley Act Secs. 501, 502, 504, 505 and 507;

— Sec. 1062(c), providing the designated transfer date;

— Sec. 1100H, providing the effective date.

¶4845 Amendments to the Home Mortgage Disclosure Act

The Dodd-Frank Act makes conforming and other amendments to the Home Mortgage Disclosure Act (HMDA). Among the modifications are new data fields to be reported to the Bureau, including—

- value of the real property pledged or proposed to be pledged as collateral;

- period of introductory interest rate;
- interest-only or negative amortization information;
- term in months of the loan;
- channel of origination;
- unique originator identification from the Secure and Fair Mortgage Licensing Act of 2008;
- universal loan identifier;
- parcel number to permit geocoding; and
- credit score (HMDA Sec. 304(b)(6), as added by Sec. 1094(3)(A)(iv) of the Dodd-Frank Act).

    CCH Comment: The House version of financial reform also required new data fields to be reported, but did so by requiring two new groupings of disclosures, including mortgage loans grouped by total points and fees, the difference between the annual percentage rate on the mortgage loan and a benchmark rate, and the term in months of any prepayment penalty. In the second additional disclosure group, financial institutions were to report mortgage loans and completed applications grouped by the value of the real property, the actual or proposed introductory interest rate period for adjustable rate loans, actual or proposed contractual terms that would allow for payments other than fully-amortizing payments, the actual or proposed term in months of the mortgage loan, the channel through which the application was made, the unique identifier of the loan originator under the Safe and Fair Enforcement for Mortgage Licensing Act of 2008, a universal loan identifier, the parcel number of the real property and the credit score of the mortgage applicants and mortgagors.

▶ **Effective date.** The provision is effective on the designated transfer date, which is a date to be selected by the Treasury Secretary that is at least 180 days, but no longer than 12 months, after enactment, subject to a possible extension of up to an additional six months (Secs. 1062(c) and 1100H and of the Dodd-Frank Wall Street Reform and Consumer Protection Act).

Law source: Law at ¶11,094, ¶11,062 and ¶11,100H. Committee Report at ¶54,811.

— Sec. 1094 of the Dodd-Frank Wall Street Reform and Consumer Protection Act, amending Home Mortgage Disclosure Act Secs. 303–307;

— Sec. 1062(c), providing the designated transfer date;

— Sec. 1100H, providing the effective date.

¶4850 Amendments to the Homeowners Protection Act

The Dodd-Frank Act makes conforming amendments installing the Bureau as the agency responsible for overseeing compliance with certain provisions of the Homeowners Protection Act.

▶ **Effective date.** The provision is effective on the designated transfer date, which is a date to be selected by the Treasury Secretary that is at least 180 days, but no longer than 12 months, after enactment, subject to a possible extension of up to an additional six months

(Secs. 1062(c) and 1100H and of the Dodd-Frank Wall Street Reform and Consumer Protection Act).

Law source: Law at ¶11,095, ¶11,062 and ¶11,100H. Committee Report at ¶54,812.

— Sec. 1095 of the Dodd-Frank Wall Street Reform and Consumer Protection Act, amending Homeowners Protection Act Sec. 10;

— Sec. 1062(c), providing the designated transfer date;

— Sec. 1100H, providing the effective date.

¶4855 Amendments to the Home Ownership and Equity Protection Act

Conforming amendments are made to the Home Ownership and Equity Protection Act, replacing "Consumer Advisory Council of the Board" with "Advisory Board to the Bureau" and inserting the Bureau in place of the Federal Reserve Board.

▶ **Effective date.** The provision is effective on the designated transfer date, which is a date to be selected by the Treasury Secretary that is at least 180 days, but no longer than 12 months, after enactment, subject to a possible extension of up to an additional six months (Secs. 1062(c) and 1100H and of the Dodd-Frank Wall Street Reform and Consumer Protection Act).

Law source: Law at ¶11,096, ¶11,062 and ¶11,100H. Committee Report at ¶54,813.

— Sec. 1096 of the Dodd-Frank Wall Street Reform and Consumer Protection Act, amending Home Ownership and Equity Protection Act of 1994 Sec. 158;

— Sec. 1062(c), providing the designated transfer date;

— Sec. 1100H, providing the effective date.

¶4860 Amendments to the Omnibus Appropriations Act, 2009

A conforming amendment to the Omnibus Appropriations Act, 2009 provides that the Bureau has rulemaking authority with regard to unfair or deceptive acts or practices relating to mortgage loans, which include unfair or deceptive acts or practices involving loan modification and foreclosure rescue services.

▶ **Effective date.** The provision is effective on the designated transfer date, which is a date to be selected by the Treasury Secretary that is at least 180 days, but no longer than 12 months, after enactment, subject to a possible extension of up to an additional six months (Secs. 1062(c) and 1100H and of the Dodd-Frank Wall Street Reform and Consumer Protection Act).

Law source: Law at ¶11,097, ¶11,062 and ¶11,100H. Committee Report at ¶54,814.

— Sec. 1097 of the Dodd-Frank Wall Street Reform and Consumer Protection Act, amending Omnibus Appropriations Act, 2009 Sec. 626;

— Sec. 1062(c), providing the designated transfer date;

— Sec. 1100H, providing the effective date.

¶4865 Amendments to the Real Estate Settlement Procedures Act

Among conforming amendments to the Real Estate Settlement Procedures Act (RESPA) is a provision requiring the Bureau to publish an integrated model disclosure form for mortgage loan transactions that includes both RESPA and Truth in Lending Act disclosure requirements (RESPA Sec. 4(a), as amended by Sec. 1098(2)(A) of the Dodd-Frank Act).

▶ **Effective date.** The provision takes effect on the designated transfer date. No later than 60 days after Title X is enacted, the Secretary of the Treasury is to consult with the other regulators and select a date no earlier than 180 days after Title X is enacted and no later than 18 months after enactment. The designated transfer date can be extended to 24 months after enactment if the Treasury Secretary certifies to Congress that the Title cannot be implemented more quickly (Sec. 1100H of the Dodd-Frank Wall Street Reform and Consumer Protection Act).

Law source: Law at ¶11,098, ¶11,062 and ¶11,100H. Committee Report at ¶54,815.

— Sec. 1098 of the Dodd-Frank Wall Street Reform and Consumer Protection Act, amending Real Estate Settlement Procedures Act Secs. 3, 4, 5, 7, 8, 10, 16, 18 and 19;

— Sec. 1062(c), providing the designated transfer date;

— Sec. 1100H, providing the effective date.

¶4870 Amendments to Interstate Land Sales Full Disclosure Act

The Dodd-Frank Act amends the Interstate Land Sales Full Disclosure Act to replace the Department of Housing and Urban Development with the Bureau.

▶ **Effective date.** The provision is effective on the designated transfer date, which is a date to be selected by the Treasury Secretary that is at least 180 days, but no longer than 12 months, after enactment, subject to a possible extension of up to an additional six months (Secs. 1062(c) and 1100H and of the Dodd-Frank Wall Street Reform and Consumer Protection Act).

Law source: Law at ¶11,098A, ¶11,062 and ¶11,100H.

— Sec. 1098A of the Dodd-Frank Wall Street Reform and Consumer Protection Act, amending Interstate Land Sales Full Disclosure Act Secs. 1402 and 1416(a);

— Sec. 1062(c), providing the designated transfer date;

— Sec. 1100H, providing the effective date.

¶4875 Amendments to the Right to Financial Privacy Act

Conforming amendments to the Right to Financial Privacy Act exempt from coverage examinations by and disclosures to the Bureau of financial records or information in the exercise of its authority with respect to a financial institution (Right to Financial Privacy Act Sec. 1113(r), as added by Sec. 1099(3) of the Dodd-Frank Act).

▶ **Effective date.** The provision is effective on the designated transfer date, which is a date to be selected by the Treasury Secretary that is at least 180 days, but no longer than 12 months, after enactment, subject to a possible extension of up to an additional six months (Secs. 1062(c) and 1100H and of the Dodd-Frank Wall Street Reform and Consumer Protection Act).

Law source: Law at ¶11,099, ¶11,062 and ¶11,100H. Committee Report at ¶54,816.

— Sec. 1099 of the Dodd-Frank Wall Street Reform and Consumer Protection Act, amending Right to Financial Privacy Act Secs. 1101 and 1112(e) and adding Sec. 1113(r);

— Sec. 1062(c), providing the designated transfer date;

— Sec. 1100H, providing the effective date.

¶4880 Amendments to the Secure and Fair Enforcement for Mortgage Licensing Act of 2008

Conforming amendments to the Secure and Fair Mortgage Licensing Act (SAFE Act), among other provisions, require the Bureau to develop and maintain a system for registering employees of a depository institution, employees of a subsidiary that is owned and controlled by a depository institution and regulated by a federal banking agency or employees of an institution regulated by the Farm Credit Administration as loan originators with the Nationwide Mortgage Licensing System and Registry. The system must be implemented by the end of the one-year period following the date of enactment of the Act (SAFE Act Sec. 1507(a)(1), as amended by Sec. 1100(5)(A)(i) of the Dodd-Frank Act).

▶ **Effective date.** The provision is effective on the designated transfer date, which is a date to be selected by the Treasury Secretary that is at least 180 days, but no longer than 12 months, after enactment, subject to a possible extension of up to an additional six months (Secs. 1062(c) and 1100H and of the Dodd-Frank Wall Street Reform and Consumer Protection Act).

Law source: Law at ¶11,100, ¶11,062 and ¶11,100H. Committee Report at ¶54,817.

— Sec. 1100 of the Dodd-Frank Wall Street Reform and Consumer Protection Act, amending S.A.F.E. Mortgage Licensing Act Secs. 1503, 1507, 1508, 1510 and 1513;

— Sec. 1062(c), providing the designated transfer date;

— Sec. 1100H, providing the effective date.

¶4885 Amendments to the Truth in Lending Act

Conforming amendments to the Truth in Lending Act (TILA) mirror those made to the Real Estate Settlement Procedures Act in that the Bureau is required to publish an integrated model disclosure form for mortgage loan transactions that includes both RESPA and TILA disclosure requirements (TILA Sec. 105(b), as amended by Sec. 1100A(5) of the Dodd-Frank Act).

▶ **Effective date.** The provision is effective on the designated transfer date, which is a date to be selected by the Treasury Secretary that is at least 180 days, but no longer than 12 months, after enactment, subject to a possible extension of up to an additional six months (Secs. 1062(c) and 1100H and of the Dodd-Frank Wall Street Reform and Consumer Protection Act).

Law source: Law at ¶¶11,100A, ¶¶11,062 and ¶11,100H. Committee Report at ¶54,818.

— Sec. 1100A of the Dodd-Frank Wall Street Reform and Consumer Protection Act, amending Truth in Lending Act Secs.103, 105, 108 and, 129;

— Sec. 1062(c), providing the designated transfer date;

— Sec. 1100H, providing the effective date.

¶4890 Amendments to the Truth in Savings Act

Conforming amendments to the Truth in Savings Act transfer regulatory and enforcement powers from the Fed to the Bureau.

▶ **Effective date.** The provision is effective on the designated transfer date, which is a date to be selected by the Treasury Secretary that is at least 180 days, but no longer than 12 months, after enactment, subject to a possible extension of up to an additional six months (Secs. 1062(c) and 1100H and of the Dodd-Frank Wall Street Reform and Consumer Protection Act).

Law source: Law at ¶¶11,100B, ¶¶11,062 and ¶11,100H. Committee Report at ¶54,819.

— Sec. 1100B of the Dodd-Frank Wall Street Reform and Consumer Protection Act, amending Truth in Savings Act Secs. 270, 272 and 274;

— Sec. 1062(c), providing the designated transfer date;

— Sec. 1100H, providing the effective date.

¶4895 Amendments to the Telemarketing and Consumer Fraud and Abuse Prevention Act

Among conforming amendments to the Telemarketing and Consumer Fraud and Abuse Prevention Act (TCFAPA) is a provision requiring the Federal Trade Commission to consult with the Bureau regarding the consistency of a proposed rule with standards, purposes or objectives administered by the Bureau (TCFAPA Sec. 3(b), as amended by Sec. 1100C(a) of the Dodd-Frank Act).

▶ **Effective date.** The provision is effective on the designated transfer date, which is a date to be selected by the Treasury Secretary that is at least 180 days, but no longer than 12 months, after enactment, subject to a possible extension of up to an additional six months (Secs. 1062(c) and 1100H and of the Dodd-Frank Wall Street Reform and Consumer Protection Act).

Law source: Law at ¶11,100C, ¶11,062 and ¶11,100H. Committee Report at ¶54,820.

— Sec. 1100C of the Dodd-Frank Wall Street Reform and Consumer Protection Act, amending Telemarketing and Consumer Fraud Abuse and Prevention Act Secs.3—6;

— Sec. 1062(c), providing the designated transfer date;

— Sec. 1100H, providing the effective date.

¶4900 Amendments to the Paperwork Reduction Act

The Paperwork Reduction Act is amended to reflect the Bureau as an independent agency.

▶ **Effective date.** The provision is effective on the designated transfer date, which is a date to be selected by the Treasury Secretary that is at least 180 days, but no longer than 12 months, after enactment, subject to a possible extension of up to an additional six months (Secs. 1062(c) and 1100H and of the Dodd-Frank Wall Street Reform and Consumer Protection Act).

Law source: Law at ¶11,100D, ¶11,062 and ¶11,100H. Committee Report at ¶54,821.

— Sec. 1100D(a) of the Dodd-Frank Wall Street Reform and Consumer Protection Act, amending Paperwork Reduction Act Sec.2(5);

— Sec. 1100D(b), adding 44 USC 3513(c);

— Sec. 1062(c), providing the designated transfer date;

— Sec. 1100H, providing the effective date.

¶4905 Adjustments for Inflation in the Truth in Lending Act

An amendment to the Truth in Lending Act raises the limit on coverage of credit transactions and consumer leases from $25,000 to $50,000 and allows the Bureau to annually adjust the dollar amounts to account for inflation on and after Dec. 31, 2011.

▶ **Effective date.** The provision is effective on the designated transfer date, which is a date to be selected by the Treasury Secretary that is at least 180 days, but no longer than 12 months, after enactment, subject to a possible extension of up to an additional six months (Secs. 1062(c) and 1100H and of the Dodd-Frank Wall Street Reform and Consumer Protection Act).

Law source: Law at ¶11,100E, ¶11,062 and ¶11,100H. Committee Report at ¶54,822.

— Sec. 1100E(a)(1) of the Dodd-Frank Wall Street Reform and Consumer Protection Act, amending Truth in Lending Act Sec. 104(3);

— Sec. 1100E(a)(2), amending Truth in Lending Act Sec. 181(1);

— Sec. 1100E(b), providing for inflation adjusted amounts;
— Sec. 1062(c), providing the designated transfer date;
— Sec. 1100H, providing the effective date.

¶4910 Adverse Action Notices and Credit Reports

The Dodd-Frank Act amends Sec. 615 of the Fair Credit Reporting Act to expand the range of information that is to be given to a consumer when a consumer report is used as a basis for an adverse action. An adverse action can be a denial of credit, insurance or employment, or an offer of credit on terms that are not as advantageous as the terms available to a substantial portion of consumers.

In such a case, the consumer now is to be told:

- any credit score that was a factor in the adverse action;
- the range of possible credit scores under the system that was used;
- all key factors that adversely affected the credit score (but no more than four factors are to be listed);
- the date on which the credit score was determined; and
- who provided the score or the file on which the score was based.

▶ **Effective date.** The provision is effective on the designated transfer date, which is a date to be selected by the Treasury Secretary that is at least 180 days, but no longer than 12 months, after enactment, subject to a possible extension of up to an additional six months (Secs. 1062(c) and 1100H and of the Dodd-Frank Wall Street Reform and Consumer Protection Act).

Law source: Law at ¶11,100F, ¶11,062 and ¶11,100H.

— Sec. 1100F of the Dodd-Frank Wall Street Reform and Consumer Protection Act, amending Fair Credit Reporting Act, Sec. 615(a) and (h)(5);
— Sec. 1062(c), providing the designated transfer date;
— Sec. 1100H, providing the effective date.

¶4915 Small Business Fairness and Regulatory Transparency

Conforming amendments to federal laws with regard to regulatory functions add the Bureau as a covered agency with respect to procedures for gathering comments on a rule that will have a significant economic impact on a substantial number of small entities. Among other requirements, a covered agency must conduct an initial regulatory flexibility analysis that must include a description of—

- any projected increase in the costs of credit for small entities;
- any significant alternatives to the proposed rule that minimize any increase in the costs of credit for small entities; and

- advice and recommendations of representatives of small entities (5 USC 603(d), as added by Sec. 1100G(b) of the Dodd-Frank Act).

▶ **Effective date.** The provision is effective on the designated transfer date, which is a date to be selected by the Treasury Secretary that is at least 180 days, but no longer than 12 months, after enactment, subject to a possible extension of up to an additional six months (Secs. 1062(c) and 1100H and of the Dodd-Frank Wall Street Reform and Consumer Protection Act).

Law source: Law at ¶11,100G, ¶11,062 and ¶11,100H.

— Sec. 1100G(a) of the Dodd-Frank Wall Street Reform and Consumer Protection Act, amending 5 USC 609(d);
— Sec. 1100G(b), adding 5 USC 603(d);
— Sec. 1100G(c), adding 5 USC 604(a)(6);
— Sec. 1062(c), providing the designated transfer date;
— Sec. 1100H, providing the effective date.

Strengthening the Federal Reserve

¶5005	Overview
¶5010	Emergency Lending Authority
¶5015	GAO Review of Credit Facilities
¶5020	One-Time GAO Audit
¶5025	Public Access to Fed Information
¶5030	Fed Transparency and Release of Information
¶5035	Liquidity Event Guarantees
¶5040	Federal Reserve Governance

¶5005 Overview

By enhancing the supervision of larger, more complex holding companies with assets over $50 billion and other systemically significant financial firms, Title XI of the Dodd-Frank Wall Street Reform and Consumer Protection Act—Sections 1101–1109—is intended to strengthen the Federal Reserve System, increase transparency and eliminate conflicts of interest.

¶5010 Emergency Lending Authority

Given the nearly $2 trillion that the Federal Reserve Board lent under Federal Reserve Act (FRA) Section 13 to address the credit and financial crisis that occurred in late 2008 and early 2009, Section 1101 of the Dodd-Frank Act places a number of new requirements on the Fed's emergency lending programs or facilities.

Broad-Based Eligibility.—The Dodd-Frank Act requires that all of the Fed's emergency lending programs or facilities have a broad-based eligibility requirement so as to prohibit bailing out an individual company (FRA Sec. 13(3)(A), as amended by Sec. 1101(a) of the Dodd-Frank Act).

Policies and Procedures.—As soon as is practicable after the date of enactment of the Dodd-Frank Act, the Fed is to establish policies and procedures to ensure that any emergency lending program or facility:

- provides liquidity to the financial system;
- does not aid a failing financial company;

- requires collateral that is of sufficient quality to protect taxpayers from losses; and
- ends in a timely and orderly fashion.

The Fed is to adopt these policies and procedures in the form of a regulation and act in consultation with the Treasury Department (FRA Sec. 13(3)(B)(i), as added by Sec. 1101(a)(6) of the Dodd-Frank Act).

Insolvent Borrowers.—The Fed is also required to establish procedures to prohibit borrowing from programs and facilities by borrowers that are insolvent. These procedures may include a certification from the borrower's chief executive officer, at the time the borrower initially borrows under the program or facility, that the borrower is not insolvent. The borrower also has a duty to update the certification if the information in the certification materially changes. A borrower is considered insolvent if the borrower is in bankruptcy, resolution under Title II of the Dodd-Frank Act or any other federal or state insolvency proceeding (FRA Sec. 13(3)(B)(ii), as added by Sec. 1101(a)(6) of the Dodd-Frank Act).

> **CCH Comment:** This provision was added during the Conference Committee deliberation on the Dodd-Frank Act and appears to be an effort to avoid a replay of events that occurred with the CIT Group. During the height of the financial crisis in December 2008, the Fed approved CIT Group's application to become a bank holding company, which would allow CIT to avail itself of any of the FRA Section 13(3) emergency lending programs or facilities, as well as programs offered under the Treasury Department's Troubled Asset Relief Program (TARP). Subsequently, CIT filed for bankruptcy in the fall of 2009, creating a $2.3 billion loss for the TARP's Capital Purchase Program.

Targeted Programs.—A program or facility that is structured to remove assets from the balance sheet of a single and specific company, or that is established for the purpose of assisting a single and specific company avoid bankruptcy, resolution under Title II of the Dodd-Frank Act or any other federal or state insolvency proceeding is not considered to be a program or facility with broad-based eligibility (FRA Sec. 13(3)(B)(iii), as added by Sec. 1101(a)(6) of the Dodd-Frank Act).

> **CCH Comment:** This provision was added during the Conference Committee deliberation on the Dodd-Frank Act and appears to be an effort to avoid a replay of the Maiden Lane transactions structured by the Fed and Federal Reserve Bank of New York (FRBank-NY) to facilitate the merger of the Bear Stearns Companies, Inc., and JPMorgan Chase & Co. and the restructuring of the FRBank-NY's financial support to American International Group.

Treasury Approval.—If the Fed were to establish any new lending program or facility it must obtain the Treasury Department's approval (FRA Sec. 13(3)(B)(iv), as added by Sec. 1101(a)(6) of the Dodd-Frank Act).

Reports.—Following the establishment of any new lending program or facility, the Fed also must submit a report to the Senate Banking Committee and the House Financial Services Committee within seven days after providing any loan or financial assistance. This report must include the identity of the recipient and the date, amount and material terms of the assistance. For any outstanding loan or other financial assistance, the Fed is to provide both congressional committees written updates, including: the value of the collateral put up; the amount of interest or items of value received in exchange; and the expected or final costs to taxpayers. This status report must be provided every 30 days (FRA Sec. 13(3)(C), as added by Sec. 1101(a)(6) of the Dodd-Frank Act).

Confidentiality. Although the Fed is submit a report to the Senate Banking Committee and House Financial Services Committee regarding any new lending program or facility, the identity of the participants, the amounts borrowed by each participant, and details concerning the assets or collateral held in connection with a lending program or facility are to remain confidential and can only be disclosed to the Committees' Chairpersons and Ranking Members (FRA Sec. 13(3)(D), as added by Sec. 1101(a)(6) of the Dodd-Frank Act).

GLB Act Privacy Implications. The disclosure of information concerning any individual who is referenced in collateral pledged or assets transferred in connection with a credit facility or covered transaction does not constitute a disclosure of nonpublic personal information as defined under Section 502 of the Gramm-Leach-Bliley Act, unless the person is a borrower, participant or counterparty under the credit facility or covered transaction (FRA Sec. 11(s)(7), as added by Sec. 1103(b) of the Dodd-Frank Act).

CCH Comment: An earlier version of the Dodd-Frank Act provided that the confidential information was to be disclosed one year after the Fed provided assistance under a lending program or facility. The Fed also was given the discretion not to disclose the information if disclosure would have reduced the effectiveness of the lending program or facility in addressing or mitigating financial market disruptions, or have a significant effect on economic or financial market conditions. The Fed was also to provide a report to the Senate Banking Committee and House Financial Services Committee, and the Government Accountability Office was to submit a report to the two congressional committees evaluating whether the Fed's nondisclosure was reasonable.

Priority of Claims.—If an entity that received a loan under FRA Section 13(3) from a Federal Reserve Bank (FRBank) becomes a covered financial company, as defined in Section 203 of the Dodd-Frank Act, while the loan is outstanding, and the FRBank incurs a realized net loss on the loan, then the FRBank has a claim equal to the amount of the net realized loss against the covered entity, with the same priority as an obligation to the Treasury Secretary under orderly liquidity provisions of the Dodd-Frank Act (FRA Sec. 13(3)(E), as added by Sec. 1101(a)(6) of the Dodd-Frank Act).

Bankruptcy Claims. The Dodd-Frank Act also amends the priority of claims under the Bankruptcy Code by giving claims of any Federal Reserve Bank related to loans made through programs or facilities authorized under FRA Section 13(3) second priority in payment. Other second priority claims are administrative expenses allowed under Section 503(b) of the Bankruptcy Code and fees and charges assessed against the estate (Bankruptcy Code Sec. 507(a)(2), as amended by Sec. 1101(b) of the Dodd-Frank Act).

▶ **Effective date.** The provision takes effect one day after the date of enactment (Sec. 4 of the Dodd-Frank Wall Street Reform and Consumer Protection Act).

Law source: Law at ¶10,004, ¶11,101 and ¶11,103. Committee Report at ¶54,840.

— Sec. 1101(a) of the Dodd-Frank Wall Street Reform and Consumer Protection Act, amending Federal Reserve Act Sec. 13(3);

— Sec. 1101(b), amending Bankruptcy Code Sec. 507(a)(2);

— Sec. 1103(b), adding Federal Reserve Act Sec. 11(s)(7);

— Sec. 1103(b), adding Federal Reserve Act Sec. 11(s);
— Sec. 4, providing the effective date.

¶5015 GAO Review of Credit Facilities

Section 1102 of the Dodd-Frank Act expands the Government Accountability Office's (GAO) ability to review credit facilities established by the Fed or a Federal Reserve Bank (FRBank). Currently, 31 USC 714(e) allows the Comptroller General to conduct an on-site examination of "any action taken by the Board under the third undesignated paragraph of Section 13 of the Federal Reserve Act (12 USC 343); with respect to a single and specific partnership or corporation." During the Conference Committee deliberations over the Dodd-Frank Act, the scope of the GAO was expanded to also review "covered transactions."

Definitions.—The Dodd-Frank Act defines "credit facility" and "covered transaction" for purposes of the GAO review.

Credit Facility. A "credit facility" is a program or facility, including any special purpose vehicle or other entity established by the Fed or a FRBank under FRA Section 13(3) emergency lending provisions, that is not subject to a GAO review under 31 USC 714(e) (31 USC 714(f)(1)(A), as added by Sec. 1102(a) of the Dodd-Frank Act).

> **CCH Comment:** In a previous version of the Dodd-Frank Act, the legislation provided an explicit list of the credit facilities that were to be reviewed by the GAO. They were: the Asset-Backed Commercial Paper Money Market Mutual Fund Liquidity Facility (AMLF); the Term Asset-Backed Securities Loan Facility; the Primary Dealer Credit Facility (PDCF); the Commercial Paper Funding Facility (CPFF); and the Term Securities Lending Facility (TSLF).

Covered Transactions. A "covered transaction" is any open market transaction or discount window advance that meets the definition of "covered transaction" in FRA Section 11(s) (31 USC 714(f)(1)(A), as added by Sec. 1102(a) of the Dodd-Frank Act).

The new FRA Section 11(s) definition of "covered transaction" is:

- any open market transaction with a nongovernmental third party conducted under various provisions of FRA Section 14 which authorizes the FRBanks to purchase and sell a variety of assets, such as government obligations and member bank commercial paper; and
- any advance made under FRA Section 10B, which deals with advances to any member bank on its short-term time or demand notes (FRA Sec. 11(s)(4)(B), as added by Sec. 1103(b) of the Dodd-Frank Act).

> **CCH Comment:** The FRA Section 11(s) definition of "covered transactions" is unrelated to the "covered transactions" found in the FRA Section 23A affiliate transaction restrictions. The Section 23A "covered transactions" deal with extensions of credit between a member bank and its affiliates.

Scope of Review.—The review of a credit facility is to assess:

- the facility's operational integrity, accounting, financial reporting and internal controls;

- the effectiveness of the facility's collateral policies that mitigate risk to the relevant FRBank and taxpayers;
- whether the credit facility inappropriately favors one or more specific participants over other institutions; and
- the policies governing the use, selection or payment of third-party contractors by or for any credit facility (31 USC 714(f)(2), as added by Sec. 1102(a) of the Dodd-Frank Act).

Reports.—Once the Comptroller General completes a review of any credit facility, a report must be submitted to Congress within 90 days. The report is to include a detailed description of the findings and conclusions with respect to the scope of review issues—operational integrity, collateral policies, favoritism and use of third-party contractors. The report is also to provide recommendations to Congress and the Fed relating to the findings and conclusions (31 USC 714(f)(3)(A) and (B), as added by Sec. 1102(a) of the Dodd-Frank Act).

Nondisclosure. In conducting its report, the Comptroller General is also subject to a nondisclosure obligation. Information relating to a credit facility's participants, the amounts borrowed and collateral are to be redacted. This nondisclosure obligation expires with respect to any participant on the date the Fed or a FRBank publicly discloses the identity of the participant or the identifying details of the assets or collateral. The nondisclosure obligation specifically does not apply to the three Maiden Lane credit facilities (31 USC 714(f)(3)(C), as added by Sec. 1102(a) of the Dodd-Frank Act).

> **CCH Comment:** Maiden Lane was formed to facilitate the merger of the Bear Stearns Companies, Inc., and JPMorgan Chase & Co. Maiden Lane II and Maiden Lane III were formed to facilitate the restructuring of the New York Federal Reserve Bank's financial support to American International Group.

GLB Act Privacy Implications. The disclosure of information concerning any individual who is referenced in collateral pledged or assets transferred in connection with a credit facility or covered transaction does not constitute a disclosure of nonpublic personal information as defined under Section 502 of the Gramm-Leach-Bliley Act, unless the person is a borrower, participant or counterparty under the credit facility or covered transaction (Federal Reserve Act Sec. 11(s)(7); as added by Sec. 1103(b) of the Dodd-Frank Act).

Non-Redacted Reports. A non-redacted report is to be released one year after a credit facility is terminated by the Fed. A credit facility is considered to be "terminated" 24 months after the date on which the facility ceases to make extensions of credit and loans (31 USC 714(f)(3)(C), as added by the Dodd-Frank Act).

▶ **Effective date.** The provision takes effect one day after the date of enactment (Sec. 4 of the Dodd-Frank Wall Street Reform and Consumer Protection Act).

Law source: Law at ¶10,004, ¶11,102 and ¶11,103. Committee Report at ¶54,841.

— Sec. 1102(a) of the Dodd-Frank Wall Street Reform and Consumer Protection Act, adding 31 USC 714(f);

— Sec. 1102(b), amending 31 USC 714(d);

— Sec. 1103(b), adding Federal Reserve Act Sec. 11(s)(7);

— Sec. 4, providing the effective date.

¶5015

¶ 5020 One-Time GAO Audit

Section 1109 of the Dodd-Frank Act, which was added as an amendment offered by Sen. Bernard Sanders, I-Vt., during Senate deliberation on the Dodd-Frank Act, requires the GAO to conduct a one-time audit of all loans and other financial assistance provided by the Federal Reserve Board between Dec. 1, 2007, and the date of enactment of the Dodd-Frank Act. The audit is to be started within 30 days after the enactment of the Dodd-Frank Act and completed within 12 months of the Dodd-Frank Act's enactment (Sec. 1109(a)(1) and (3) of the Dodd-Frank Act).

The one-time audit is to examine the following credit facilities: the Asset-Backed Commercial Paper Money Market Mutual Fund Liquidity Facility (AMLF); the Term Asset-Backed Securities Loan Facility (TALF); the Primary Dealer Credit Facility (PDCF); the Commercial Paper Funding Facility (CPFF); and the Term Securities Lending Facility (TSLF). The audit will also examine the Maiden Lane transactions undertaken by the Federal Reserve Bank of New York to provide assistance to specific institutions, as well as foreign currency liquidity swap lines and any other program created under Federal Reserve Act Section 13(3).

Scope of GAO Audit.—The review of the Fed programs is to assess: the programs' operational integrity, accounting, financial reporting and internal controls; the effectiveness of the programs' collateral policies that mitigate risk to the relevant FRBank and taxpayers; whether the programs inappropriately favor one or more specific participants over other institutions; the policies governing the use, selection or payment of third-party contractors by or for any of the programs; and whether any conflicts of interest existed (Sec. 1109(a)(2) of the Dodd-Frank Act).

Report. The GAO must submit a report on its audit to Congress within 12 months of the enactment of the Dodd-Frank Act (Sec. 1109(a)(4) of the Dodd-Frank Act).

FRBank Governance.—Section 1109 also calls on the GAO to audit the governance of the FRBanks.

Among other things, this audit is to examine whether the current system of appointing FRBank directors carries out the requirements found in FRA Section 4, which mandate that the FRBank directors represent "the public, without discrimination on the basis of race, creed, color, sex or national origin, and with due but not exclusive consideration to the interests of agriculture, commerce, industry, services, labor, and consumers." The governance audit is also to identify changes to selection procedures for FRBank bank directors to improve how the public is represented and eliminate actual or potential conflicts of interest in bank supervision (Sec. 1109(b)(1) of the Dodd-Frank Act).

Report. The GAO must submit a report on its governance audit to Congress within 90 days after the audit is completed (Sec. 1109(b)(2) of the Dodd-Frank Act).

Publication of Fed Actions.—Finally, the audit provisions require the Fed to publish on its website, not later than Dec. 1, 2010, various items of information relating to its credit facilities, the Maiden Lane Transactions, foreign currency liquidity swap lines and any other program created under FRA Section 13(3).

The required information includes: the identity of each business, individual, entity or foreign central bank to which the Fed has provided assistance; the type of financial assistance provided; the value or amount of that financial assistance; the date on which the financial assistance was provided; the specific terms of any repayment expected including the repayment time period, interest charges, collateral, limitations on executive compensation or dividends and other material terms; and the specific rationale for each facility or program (Sec. 1109(c) of the Dodd-Frank Act).

GLB Act Privacy Implications.—The disclosure of information concerning any individual who is referenced in collateral pledged or assets transferred in connection with a credit facility does not constitute a disclosure of nonpublic personal information as defined under Section 502 of the Gramm-Leach-Bliley Act, unless the person is a borrower, participant or counterparty under the credit facility (FRA Sec. 11(s)(7); as added by Sec. 1103(b) of the Dodd-Frank Act).

▶ **Effective date.** The provision takes effect one day after the date of enactment (Sec. 4 of the Dodd-Frank Wall Street Reform and Consumer Protection Act).

Law source: Law at ¶10,004, ¶11,103 and ¶11,109.

— Sec. 1103(b), adding Federal Reserve Act Sec. 11(s);

— Sec. 1109 of the Dodd-Frank Wall Street Reform and Consumer Protection Act;

— Sec. 4, providing the effective date.

¶5025 Public Access to Fed Information

Section 1103(a) of the Dodd-Frank Wall Street Reform and Consumer Protection Act requires the Federal Reserve Board to place on the homepage of its website a link entitled "Audit" to link to a page serving as a repository of information made available to the public. The information to be posted includes reports prepared by the Comptroller General, annual financial statements and reports submitted to the Senate Banking Committee relating to the Fed's emergency lending authority (FRA Sec. 2B(c), as added by Sec. 1103(a) of the Dodd-Frank Act).

▶ **Effective date.** The provision takes effect one day after the date of enactment (Sec. 4 of the Dodd-Frank Wall Street Reform and Consumer Protection Act).

Law source: Law at ¶10,004 and ¶11,103. Committee Report at ¶54,842.

— Sec. 1103(a) of the Dodd-Frank Wall Street Reform and Consumer Protection Act, adding Federal Reserve Act Sec. 2B(c);

— Sec. 4, providing the effective date.

¶5030 Fed Transparency and Release of Information

The Fed's enumerated powers found in FRA Section 11 are expanded by the Dodd-Frank Wall Street Reform and Consumer Protection Act to ensure transparency concerning the emergency credit facilities, discount window lending programs and open market operations authorized or conducted by the Fed or a FRBank (FRA Sec. 11(s)(1), as added by Sec. 1103(b) of the Dodd-Frank Act).

¶5030

Disclosures.—To accomplish this transparency mandate, the Fed is to timely disclose the following information regarding any "credit facility" or "covered transaction":

- the names and identifying details of each borrower, participant or counterparty;
- the amount borrowed by or transferred by or to a specific borrower, participant or counterparty;
- the interest rate or discount paid by each borrower, participant or counterparty; and
- information identifying the types and amounts of collateral.

Credit Facility. A "credit facility" is a program or facility, including any special purpose vehicle or other entity established by the Fed or a FRBank under FRA Section 13(3) emergency lending provisions, that is not subject to a GAO review under 31 USC 714(e) (FRA Sec. 11(s)(4)(A), as added by Sec. 1103(b) of the Dodd-Frank Act).

Covered Transactions. A "covered transaction" is any:

- open market transaction with a nongovernmental third party conducted under various provisions of FRA Section 14, which authorizes the Federal Reserve Banks to purchase and sell a variety of assets, such as government obligations and member bank commercial paper; and
- advance made under FRA Section 10B, which deals with advances to any member bank on its short-term time or demand notes (FRA Sec. 11(s)(4)(B), as added by Sec. 1103(b) of the Dodd-Frank Act).

> **CCH Comment:** The FRA Section 11(s) definition of "covered transactions" is unrelated to the "covered transactions" found in the FRA Section 23A affiliate transaction restrictions. The Section 23A "covered transactions" deal with extensions of credit between a member bank and its affiliates.

Timing of Disclosures.—The timing of the Fed's disclosures required by Section 1103(b) is dependent upon the type of transaction. In either instance, the disclosure is known as the "mandatory release date."

In addition, the Dodd-Frank Act requires that the information remain confidential until the mandatory release date, unless the Fed Chairman decides that earlier disclosure of the information would be in the public interest and would not harm the effectiveness of the relevant credit facility or covered transaction (FRA Sec. 11(s)(6), as added by Sec. 1103(b) of the Dodd-Frank Act). The Fed's Inspector General is required to conduct a study on the impact that the confidentiality requirement has on the ability of the public to access information about the Fed's administration of emergency credit facilities, discount window lending programs and open market operations and make any recommendations on whether the confidentiality requirement should remain in effect. A report on findings of the Inspector General's study is to be submitted to the Senate Banking Committee and House Financial Services Committee no later than 30 months after the enactment of FRA Section 10(s). The report is also to be posted on the Fed's website (FRA Sec. 10(s)(8), as added by Sec. 1103(b) of the Dodd-Frank Act).

Credit Facilities. For a credit facility, the mandatory release date is the date that is one year after the effective date of the Fed's termination of its authorization of the credit facility (FRA Sec. 11(s)(2)(A), as added by Sec. 1103(b) of the Dodd-Frank Act).

Generally, a credit facility is to be deemed to have terminated as of the end of the 24-month period beginning on the date on which the credit facility ceases to make extensions of credit and loans (FRA Sec. 11(s)(5), as added by Sec. 1103(b) of the Dodd-Frank Act).

Covered Transactions. For covered transactions, the mandatory release date is the last day of the eighth calendar quarter following the calendar quarter in which the covered transaction was conducted (FRA Sec. 11(s)(2)(B), as added by Sec. 1103(b) of the Dodd-Frank Act).

Early Disclosures. The Fed Chairman may publicly release the required information regarding its credit facilities and covered transactions if the Chairman determines that the disclosure would be in the public interest and would not harm the effectiveness of the relevant credit facility or the purpose or conduct of covered transactions (FRA Sec. 11(s)(3), as added by Sec. 1103(b) of the Dodd-Frank Act).

GLB Act Privacy Implications.—The disclosure of information concerning any individual who is referenced in collateral pledged or assets transferred in connection with a credit facility or covered transaction does not constitute a disclosure of nonpublic personal information as defined under Section 502 of the Gramm-Leach-Bliley Act, unless the person is a borrower, participant or counterparty under the credit facility or covered transaction (FRA Sec. 11(s)(7),; as added by Sec. 1103(b) of the Dodd-Frank Act).

FOIA Litigation.—Any pending litigation or lawsuit filed under the Freedom of Information Act on or before the date of enactment of the Dodd-Frank Act is not affected by the FRA Section 11(s) disclosure (FRA Sec. 11(s)(9), as added by Sec. 1103(b) of the Dodd-Frank Act).

▶ **Effective date.** The provision takes effect one day after the date of enactment (Sec. 4 of the Dodd-Frank Wall Street Reform and Consumer Protection Act).

Law source: Law at ¶10,004 and ¶11,103.

— Sec. 1103(b) of the Dodd-Frank Wall Street Reform and Consumer Protection Act, adding Federal Reserve Act Sec. 11(s);

— Sec. 4, providing the effective date.

¶5035 Liquidity Event Guarantees

Sections 1104, 1105 and 1106 of the Dodd-Frank Wall Street Reform and Consumer Protection Act establish a mechanism for the FDIC to create a program to guarantee obligations of solvent insured depository institutions or solvent depository institution holding companies during times of severe economic distress.

Liquidity Event Determination.—The guarantee program is triggered by a request from the Treasury Department that the Federal Deposit Insurance Corporation and Federal Reserve Board determine whether a "liquidity event" exists that warrants use of the program.

A "liquidity event" is defined as a reduction in the usual ability of a financial market participant to either sell a type of financial asset without a significant reduction in price or to borrow using that type of asset as collateral without a significant increase in margin. A significant reduction in the usual ability of financial and nonfinancial market participants to obtain unsecured credit is also considered to be a "liquidity event" (Sec. 1105(g)(3) of the Dodd-Frank Act).

Section 1104 of the Dodd-Frank Act requires that a liquidity event determination be in writing and contain an evaluation that: a liquidity event exists and failure to take actions would have serious adverse effects on financial stability or economic conditions in the United States; and the guarantee program is needed to avoid or mitigate potential adverse effects on the U.S. financial system or economic conditions (Sec. 1104(a)(2) of the Dodd-Frank Act).

The liquidity event determination is also subject to review by the Government Accountability Office (Sec. 1104(c)(2) of the Dodd-Frank Act).

Parallel FDIA Authority.—If the FDIC establishes a guarantee program under Section 1105 of the Dodd-Frank Act, it is prohibited by Section 1106 of the Dodd-Frank Act from exercising its authority under FDIA Section 13(c)(4)(G)(i) to establish any widely available debt guarantee program (Sec. 1106(a) of the Dodd-Frank Act).

> **CCH Comment:** A determination of systemic risk under FDIA Section 13(c)(4)(G) allows the FDIC to take certain actions to avoid or mitigate serious adverse effects on economic conditions and financial stability. The FDIC used this authority during the financial crisis to create the Temporary Liquidity Guarantee Program (TLGP). The TLGP provided two limited guarantee programs: one that guaranteed newly-issued senior unsecured debt of insured depository institutions and most U.S. holding companies (the Debt Guarantee Program), and another that guaranteed certain noninterest-bearing transaction accounts at insured depository institutions (the Transaction Account Guarantee Program).

Determination of Guaranteed Amount.—The Treasury Secretary, in consultation with the President, is required to determine the maximum amount of debt outstanding that the FDIC may guarantee. The President has the discretion to send a written report to Congress stating the FDIC's plan to issue the guarantee up to the maximum amount (Sec. 1105(c)(1) of the Dodd-Frank Act).

Once Congress receives the report, both houses of Congress must pass a joint resolution before the FDIC can issue the guarantee up to the maximum amount of debt outstanding that the FDIC may guarantee. The Dodd-Frank Act provides detailed legislative procedures for enacting this joint resolution (Sec. 1105(d) of the Dodd-Frank Act). These procedures cover fast-track consideration in both houses of Congress and the treatment of companion measures and presidential vetoes. There are similar legislative procedures if it is determined that the maximum guarantee amount should be raised.

Policies and Procedures.—The FDIC is to issue regulations establishing policies and procedures governing the issuance of guarantees under Section 1105 of the Dodd-Frank Act, including the issuance of collateral as a condition for any guarantee. These regulations are to be issued "as soon as practicable" after the date of enactment of the Dodd-Frank Act (Sec. 1105(b)(1) of the Dodd-Frank Act).

The terms and conditions of any guarantee are to be established by the FDIC with concurrence of the Treasury Department (Sec. 1105(b)(2) of the Dodd-Frank Act).

Fees and Charges.—To offset projected losses and administrative expenses, the FDIC is required to charge fees and assessments to all program participants. Once the guarantee program has ended, any excess funds collected from program fees are to be deposited in the General Fund of the Treasury (Sec. 1105(e)(1) and (2) of the Dodd-Frank Act).

FDIC Borrowing. The FDIC is given the ability to borrow funds from the Treasury Department to carry out the program. These borrowed funds can be used to pay reasonable administrative costs of the program. These funds must be repaid to the Treasury in full, with interest. Finally, the Dodd-Frank Act specifically prohibits the FDIC from borrowing funds from the Deposit Insurance Fund (Sec. 1105(e)(3) of the Dodd-Frank Act).

Backup Assessments. If the fees, assessments and FDIC borrowed funds do not meet the program's losses and expenses, the FDIC is required to impose a special assessment on the program's participants (Sec. 1105(e)(4) of the Dodd-Frank Act).

Defaults.—Finally, if a participant in either the Section 1105 guarantee program or a guarantee program established under FDIA Section 13(c)(4)(G) defaults on any obligation, Section 1106(c) of the Dodd-Frank Act provides the FDIC with a course of action.

For any insured depository institution, the FDIC is to appoint itself receiver for the institution. For a depository institution holding company, the FDIC is to consider whether the holding company should be subject to the Orderly Liquidation Authority Panel and resolution provision of Dodd-Frank Act or file for protection under the Bankruptcy Code (Sec. 1106(c) of the Dodd-Frank Act).

▶ **Effective date.** The provision takes effect one day after the date of enactment (Sec. 4 of the Dodd-Frank Wall Street Reform and Consumer Protection Act).

Law source: Law at ¶10,004, ¶11,104, ¶11,105 and ¶11,106. Committee Report at ¶54,843.

— Secs. 1104, 1105 and 1106 of the Dodd-Frank Wall Street Reform and Consumer Protection Act;

— Sec. 4, providing the effective date.

¶5040 Federal Reserve Governance

Sections 1107 and 1108 of the Dodd-Frank Wall Street Reform and Consumer Protection Act make a number of amendments to the Federal Reserve Act (FRA) relating to governance of the Federal Reserve Banks and the supervisory and regulatory policies of the Fed.

FRBank Officers and Directors.—The FRA provisions governing the general powers for the Federal Reserve Bank (FRBanks) in regards to the FRBank presidents are amended. Under the amendment, the FRBank president is the chief executive officer of the bank and is to be appointed by the Class B and Class C directors of the bank, with the approval of the Board of Governors of the Federal Reserve System. The amendment also sets the FRBank president's term of office at five years and provides that the FRBank's executive officers and the employees of the bank are directly responsible to the FRBank president (FRA Sec. 4(4), as amended by Sec. 1107 of the Dodd-Frank Act).

> **CCH Comment:** An earlier version of the Dodd-Frank Act provided that the Federal Reserve Bank of New York President, who is currently appointed by the district board of directors, would be appointed by the President with the advice and

consent of the Senate. The earlier version of the Dodd-Frank Act also provided that no company, subsidiary or affiliate of a company that is supervised by the Fed could vote for FRBank directors. Moreover, all officers, directors and employees of these Fed-supervised companies and their affiliates would have been prohibited from serving as FRBank directors. The intent of these provisions was to eliminate potential conflicts of interest at FRBanks.

Supervisory and Regulatory Policies.—Section 1108 of the Dodd-Frank Act provides that a member of the Board of Governors of the Federal Reserve System is required to serve as Vice Chairman for Supervision. This Vice Chairman will be designated by the President with the advice and consent of the Senate, and will be responsible for developing policy recommendations regarding supervision and regulation for the Fed (FRA Sec. 10(2), as amended by Sec. 1108(a) of the Dodd-Frank Act). The Vice Chairman for Supervision is also required to appear before Congress semi-annually to report on the efforts, objectives and plans of the Fed with respect to the conduct of supervision and regulation (FRA Sec. 10(12), as added by Sec. 1108(b) of the Dodd-Frank Act).

Delegation of Authority.—Finally, Section 1108 of the Dodd-Frank Act provides that the Fed may not delegate to a FRBank its functions for the establishment of policies for the supervision and regulation of depository institution holding companies and other financial firms supervised by the Fed (FRA Sec. 11(k), as amended by Sec. 1108(c) of the Dodd-Frank Act). Section 1108 also provides that no provision of Title I of the Dodd-Frank Act relating to the Fed's authority is to be construed as conferring any decision-making authority on FRBank presidents, and that the Fed cannot delegate its authority to make any voting decision it is authorized or required to make under Title I of the Dodd-Frank Act (Sec. 1108(d) of the Dodd-Frank Act).

> **CCH Comment:** Title I of the Dodd-Frank Act is designed to monitor and prevent systemic risk to the entire financial system through a combination of holistic oversight, transparency and macro-prudential regulation in coordination with the primary federal financial regulators.

▶ **Effective date.** The provision for the establishment of the position of Vice Chairman for Supervision takes effect on the date of enactment of the Dodd-Frank Act and applies to individuals who are designated by the President on or after that date to serve as Vice Chairman of Supervision (Sec. 1108(a)(2) of the Dodd-Frank Wall Street Reform and Consumer Protection Act). No specific effective date is provided by Dodd-Frank Act for the other provisions. The provisions are therefore considered effective one day after the date of enactment. The other provisions take effect one day after the date of enactment (Sec. 4 of the Dodd-Frank Wall Street Reform and Consumer Protection Act).

Law source: Law at ¶10,004, ¶11,107 and ¶11,108. Committee Report at ¶54,845.

— Sec. 1107 of the Dodd-Frank Wall Street Reform and Consumer Protection Act, amending Federal Reserve Act Sec. 4(4);

— Secs. 1108(a)(1), amending Federal Reserve Act Sec. 10(2);

— Secs. 1108(b), adding Federal Reserve Act Sec. 10(12);

— Secs. 1108(c), amending Federal Reserve Act Sec. 11(k);

— Sec. 1108(d) of the Dodd-Frank Act;

— Secs. 4 and 1108(a)(2), providing the effective date.

Access to Mainstream Finance

¶5505 Introduction
¶5510 Program Eligibility and Account Activities
¶5515 Low-Cost Alternatives to Small Dollar Loans
¶5520 Grants to Establish Loan-Loss Reserves
¶5525 Program Funding and Oversight

¶5505 Introduction

Title XII of the Dodd-Frank Wall Street Reform and Consumer Protection Act contains the "Improving Access to Mainstream Financial Institutions Act of 2010" (Sec. 1201 et seq. of the Dodd-Frank Act). The law encourages initiatives that help Americans who are currently unable to participate fully in mainstream finance to gain access to appropriate financial services and products (Sec. 1202 of the Dodd-Frank Act). The legislative history notes that one in four families may be "unbanked" or "underbanked" and, therefore, must rely on non-traditional financing. Reliance on this financing can subject borrowers to predatory financial products and services, which in turn can hinder their ability to save for educational expenses, a down payment on a first home, or other future needs (S. Rep. No. 111-176, p. 184).

The legislation authorizes the Treasury Secretary to create a multi-year grant program designed to: (1) enable low- and moderate-income individuals to establish one or more appropriate accounts in a federally-insured depository institution; and (2) improve access to these accounts on reasonable terms (discussed at ¶ 5510). The legislation also creates low-cost alternatives to high cost small dollar loans and establishes loan-loss reserve funds to enable community development financial institutions to offer small dollar loan programs (discussed at ¶ 5515 and ¶ 5520). In addition, the Act includes requirements for appropriations, rulemaking and reports to Congress (discussed at ¶ 5525).

▶ **Effective date.** The provisions take effect one day after the date of enactment (Sec. 4 of the Dodd-Frank Wall Street Reform and Consumer Protection Act).

Law source: Law at ¶11,201, ¶11,202 and ¶10,004. Committee Report at ¶54,860 and ¶54,861.

— Sec. 1201 of the Dodd-Frank Wall Street Reform and Consumer Protection Act, providing the short title of Title XII;

— Sec. 1202, stating the legislative purpose;

— Sec. 4, providing the effective date.

¶ 5510 Program Eligibility and Account Activities

The Dodd-Frank Wall Street Reform and Consumer Protection Act authorizes the Treasury Secretary to create a multi-year program that consists of grants, cooperative agreements, financial agency agreements and other similar contracts or undertakings. The program's goal is to enable low- and moderate-income individuals to establish one or more appropriate accounts in a federally-insured depository institution and to improve their access to these accounts on reasonable terms (Sec. 1204(a) of the Dodd-Frank Wall Street Reform and Consumer Protection Act). The Secretary must limit participation in these programs to eligible entities. An eligible entity may, subject to regulations issued by the Secretary, participate in one or more programs created by the Secretary (Sec. 1204(b) of the Dodd-Frank Act).

Definitions.—"Eligible entity" means: (1) an organization described in Internal Revenue Code Section 501(c)(3) and exempt from tax under I.R.C. Section 501(a); (2) a federally insured depository institution; (3) a community development financial institution; (4) a state, local or tribal governmental entity; or (5) a partnership or other joint venture comprised of one or more of the designated types of eligible entities (Sec. 1203(3) of the Dodd-Frank Act).

"Federally insured depository institution" means any insured depository institution under Federal Deposit Insurance Act Section 3 and any insured credit union under Federal Credit Union Act Section 101 (Sec. 1203(4) of the Dodd-Frank Act). A "community development financial institution" is an organization that meets the definition in Section 103(5) of the Community Development Banking and Financial Institutions Act of 1994 (Sec. 1203(2) of the Dodd-Frank Act).

Account Activities.—The legislation permits eligible entities to engage in specified account activities. An eligible entity may, subject to regulations adopted by the Secretary, offer small dollar value loans and financial education and counseling regarding conducting transactions in and managing accounts (Sec. 1204(b)(2) of the Dodd-Frank Act). "Account" means an agreement between an individual and an eligible entity under which the individual obtains one or more banking products and services from or through the eligible entity. The term "account" includes deposit accounts, savings accounts (including money market savings accounts), accounts for closed-end loans and any other products or services the Secretary deems appropriate (Sec. 1203(1) of the Dodd-Frank Act). Senator Daniel Akaka (D-HI) clarified that, in the provision, "small dollar-value loans and financial education and counseling relating to conducting transactions and managing accounts are only examples of, and not limitations on, eligible activities" (Cong. Record, May 20, 2010, p. S4069).

Application.—An eligible entity must submit an application to the Secretary to participate in a program or to obtain a grant. The application must be in the form and contain the information required by the Secretary (Sec. 1207 of the Dodd-Frank Act).

▶ **Effective date.** The provisions take effect one day after the date of enactment (Sec. 4 of the Dodd-Frank Wall Street Reform and Consumer Protection Act).

Law source: Law at ¶11,203, ¶11,204, ¶11,207 and ¶10,004. Committee Report at ¶54,863 and ¶54,866.

— Sec. 1203 of the Dodd-Frank Wall Street Reform and Consumer Protection Act, defining terms;

— Sec. 1204, describing program, eligibility and activities;

— Sec. 1207, stating application requirements;

— Sec. 4, providing the effective date.

¶5515 Low-Cost Alternatives to Small Dollar Loans

The Dodd-Frank Wall Street Reform and Consumer Protection Act provides for affordable alternatives to the costly, small-figure loans currently available. It authorizes the Treasury Secretary to create multi-year demonstration programs through grants and other agreements with eligible entities to provide low-cost, small loans to consumers as an alternative to more costly small dollar loans (Sec. 1205(a) of the Dodd-Frank Wall Street Reform and Consumer Protection Act).

Loans subject to the Dodd-Frank Act must be made on terms and conditions, and in accordance with lending practices, that are reasonable for consumers (Sec. 1205(b)(1) of the Dodd-Frank Act). In addition, each eligible entity awarded a grant must promote financial literacy, taking appropriate steps to ensure that each consumer provided with a loan under the law receives educational opportunities such as counseling services, educational courses or wealth-building programs (Sec. 1205(b)(2)(A) of the Dodd-Frank Act). The Secretary may implement reasonable measures or programs to expand access to financial literacy and educational opportunities (Sec. 1205(b)(2)(B) of the Dodd-Frank Act).

> **CCH Comment:** Section 1205 of the Dodd-Frank Act removed references to "payday loans," and instead refers to "small dollar loans" (Sec. 1205 of the Dodd-Frank Act). The Dodd-Frank Act also removed the definition of payday loan contained in the Conference Base Text (Sec. 1203 of the Dodd-Frank Act). "Payday loan" was previously defined to mean any transaction in which a small cash advance is made to a consumer in exchange for the consumer's personal check or share draft under one of two scenarios. Under scenario one, a lender and a consumer agree that presentment or negotiation of the consumer's personal check or share draft, in the amount of the advance plus a fee, will be deferred until a designated future date. In the second scenario, the lender and the consumer agree that the consumer's transaction account or share draft account will be debited, in the amount of the advance plus a fee, at a designated future date (Sec. 1203(5) of the Conference Base Text (HR 4173)).

▶ **Effective date.** The provision takes effect one day after the date of enactment (Sec. 4 of the Dodd-Frank Wall Street Reform and Consumer Protection Act).

Law source: Law at ¶11,205 and ¶10,004. Committee Report at ¶54,864.

— Sec. 1205 of the Dodd-Frank Wall Street Reform and Consumer Protection Act, providing for alternatives to high cost small dollar loans;

— Sec. 4, providing the effective date.

¶5520 Grants to Establish Loan-Loss Reserves

Section 1206 of the Dodd-Frank Wall Street Reform and Consumer Protection Act adds Section 122 to the Community Development Banking and Financial Institutions Act of 1994 (CDBFIA). The law contains provisions to assist institutions that operate small dollar loan programs. One purpose of this provision is to make financial assistance available from the Community Development Banking and Financial Institutions Fund (CDFI fund) to help community development financial institutions create their own loan-loss reserve funds to help defray the costs of operating small dollar loan programs, and to mitigate some losses from these programs. The provision also encourages community development financial institutions to establish small dollar loan programs that help consumers gain access to mainstream financial institutions and to combat high cost small dollar lending (CDBFIA Sec. 122(a), as added by the Dodd-Frank Wall Street Reform and Consumer Protection Act).

> **CCH Comment:** Section 1206 of the Dodd-Frank Act removed references to "payday lending," and instead substituted the term "high cost small dollar lending" (CDBFIA Sec. 122(a)(2), as added by the Dodd-Frank Act). Section 1206 of the Conference Base Text had referred expressly to payday loans.

Definitions.—"Community development financial institution" means an organization that meets the definition set forth in the CDBFIA (Sec. 1203(2) of the Dodd-Frank Act). CDBFIA Section 103(5) states that a person (other than an individual) is a "community development financial institution" if: (1) its primary mission is to promote community development; (2) it serves an investment area or targeted population; (3) it provides development services along with equity investments or loans directly or through a subsidiary or affiliate; (4) it is accountable to the residents of its investment area or targeted population (e.g. through board representation); and (5) it is not a U.S. agency or instrumentality, or a state or local government.

Section 103(5) of the CDBFIA also provides that a depository institution holding company may satisfy the definition if the holding company and its subsidiaries and affiliates collectively meet the above requirements. However, no subsidiary or affiliate of a depository institution holding company will qualify if the consolidated treatment rule has not been satisfied. Similarly, a subsidiary of an insured depository institution will not satisfy the definition unless the insured depository institution and its subsidiaries collectively meet the specific requirements.

"Small dollar loan program" means a loan program through which a community development financial institution (or a partnership of institutions) offers loans to consumers. The loans made to consumers by the institution must: (1) be made in amounts no greater than $2,500; (2) be repaid in installments; (3) have no prepayment penalty; (4) require the institution to report payments to at least one consumer reporting agency that compiles and maintains nationwide consumer data; and (5) meet any other affordability requirements established by the Administrator (CDBFIA Sec. 122(c)(2), as added by the Dodd-Frank Act). "Consumer reporting agency" has the meaning set forth in the Fair Credit Reporting Act Section 603(p) (CDBFIA Sec. 122(c)(1), as added by the Dodd-Frank Act). The Administrator under CDBFIA Section 103(1) is the administrator of the CDFI fund.

Loan-Loss Reserve Fund Grants.—The CDFI fund must make grants to community development financial institutions or to any partnership between these institutions and any federally insured depository institution with a primary mission to serve targeted investment areas. The purpose of the grants is to help community development financial institutions and their partner institutions establish loan-loss reserve funds to defray the costs of operating small dollar loan programs (CDBFIA Sec. 122(b)(1), as added by the Dodd-Frank Act).

Grant recipients must satisfy the matching requirement and comply with the restrictions on the use of grants received. A community development financial institution and its partners must provide non-federal matching funds equal to 50 percent of the grant amount received (CDBFIA Sec. 122(b)(2), as added by the Dodd-Frank Act). Institutions that receive grants are subject to the following rules governing use of funds: (1) grants cannot be used to provide direct loans to consumers; (2) grants may be used to recapture some or all of a defaulted loan made under a small dollar loan program; and (3) grants may be used to designate and use a fiscal agent (CDBFIA Sec. 122(b)(3), as added by the Dodd-Frank Act).

Technical Assistance Grants.—The CDFI fund must make technical-assistance grants to community development financial institutions and their partners. Technical-assistance grants are intended to help support and maintain small dollar loan programs and may be used for technology, staff support and other costs associated with a small dollar loan program (CDBFIA Sec. 122(b)(4), as amended by the Dodd-Frank Act).

▶ **Effective date.** The provisions take effect one day after the date of enactment (Sec. 4 of the Dodd-Frank Wall Street Reform and Consumer Protection Act).

Law source: Law at ¶11,203, ¶11,206 and ¶10,004. Committee Report at ¶54,865.

— Sec. 1203(2) of the Dodd-Frank Wall Street Reform and Consumer Protection Act, defining terms;

— Sec. 1206, adding Community Development Banking and Financial Institutions Act Sec. 122;

— Sec. 4, providing the effective date.

¶5525 Program Funding and Oversight

The Dodd-Frank Wall Street Reform and Consumer Protection Act seeks to achieve program oversight through appropriations of funds, rulemaking and reports to Congress. It authorizes the appropriation of funds to the Treasury Secretary that are necessary to administer and fund the programs and projects authorized under the law (Sec. 1208(a) of the Dodd-Frank Wall Street Reform and Consumer Protection Act). The legislation also authorizes appropriations to the Community Development Banking and Financial Institutions Fund (CDFI fund). The amount of the appropriation must equal the amount of administrative costs of the CDFI fund to operate the grant programs. The appropriation to the CDFI fund is for each fiscal year, beginning in 2010 (Sec. 1208(b) of the Dodd-Frank Act).

The Secretary may issue regulations to implement and administer the grant programs (Sec. 1209(a) of the Dodd-Frank Act). The regulations may contain classifications, differentiations or other provisions, including adjustments and exceptions for any class of grant programs, undertakings or eligible entities. The Secretary may adopt regulations that are necessary and proper to achieve the law's purposes, including the goals of preventing evasion and facilitating compliance (Sec. 1209(b) of the Dodd-Frank Act).

The Secretary must submit a report, for each fiscal year in which a program or project was carried out under the Dodd-Frank Act, to the Senate Committee on Banking, Housing, and Urban Affairs and to the House Committee on Financial Services. The report must describe the activities funded, amounts distributed and measurable results, as appropriate and available (Sec. 1210 of the Dodd-Frank Act).

▶ **Effective date.** The provisions take effect one day after the date of enactment (Sec. 4 of the Dodd-Frank Wall Street Reform and Consumer Protection Act).

Law source: Law at ¶11,208, ¶11,209, ¶11,210 and ¶10,004. Committee Report at ¶54,867, ¶54,868 and ¶54,869.

— Sec. 1208 of the Dodd-Frank Wall Street Reform and Consumer Protection Act, authorizing program funding;

— Sec. 1209, stating Secretary's regulatory authority;

— Sec. 1210, mandating reports to Congress;

— Sec. 4, providing the effective date.

Pay It Back Act

¶6005	Overview
¶6010	TARP Wind Down
¶6015	Public Debt Reduction
¶6020	FHFA Reporting
¶6025	Recovery Act Funds

¶6005 Overview

An amendment offered by Sen. Michael Bennet, D-Colo., during debate on the Restoring American Financial Stability Act of 2010 became Title XIII of the Dodd-Frank Act with the short title the "Pay It Back Act." This amendment had a number of cosposonors from both political parties and is based on legislation introduced by Bennet in September 2009.

The main purpose of the Pay It Back Act, according to a floor statement by Bennet, was to "rebuild the credibility of our financial system, save taxpayers billions of dollars, and finally move to end the [Troubled Asset Relief Program (TARP)]" (Cong. Rec. (May 11), S3511). Bennet added that the Pay It Back Act "prevents further government spending, recaptures taxpayers' investments in financial institutions, and ensures that repaid funds are used for deficit reduction" (Cong. Rec. (May 11), S3512).

In another floor statement, Sen. John Tester, D-Mont., noted that the amendment "will not solve our debt problems, but it is a step in the right direction" (Cong. Rec. (May 11), S3512). Finally, Senate Banking Committee Chairman Chris Dodd, D-Conn., added "the substance of the amendment is critically important" and "dedicates [TARP] resources to deficit reduction" (Cong. Rec. (May 11), S3513).

▶ **Effective date.** The provision takes effect one day after the date of enactment (Sec. 4 of the Dodd-Frank Wall Street Reform and Consumer Protection Act).

Law source: Law at ¶11,301 and ¶10,004.

— Sec. 1301 of the Dodd-Frank Wall Street Reform and Consumer Protection Act, providing short title of Title XIII;

— Sec. 4, providing the effective date.

¶6010 TARP Wind Down

To accomplish winding down TARP, Section 1302(1) of the Pay It Back Act reduces TARP's authority to $475 billion. Under the Emergency Economic Stabilization Act of 2008 (EESA), $700 billion was originally authorized to fund TARP to purchase "toxic assets" from financial institutions (Emergency Economic Stabilization Act of 2008 Sec. 115(a)(3), as amended by Sec. 1302(1) of the Dodd-Frank Act).

As originally agreed to by the Conference Committee on June 25, 2010, Section 1302(1) reduced the TARP funding to $550 billion. The funding figure was changed when the Conference Committee reconvened on June 29, 2010, to address concerns raised by Sen. Scott Brown, R-Mass., over a $19 billion tax on large financial institutions that would have covered the costs of the Dodd-Frank Act.

During the June 29 meeting, Sen. Chris Dodd, D-Conn., noted that the $475 billion figure "effectively ends TARP" since that figure represents the funds already authorized under TARP.

Another change made by the Conference Committee was to prohibit TARP repayments to be used to fund new programs after June 25, 2010 (Emergency Economic Stabilization Act of 2008 Sec. 115(a)(5), as added by Sec. 1302(2) of the Dodd-Frank Act).

During debate of the Dodd-Frank Act in the House of Representatives, Rep. Maxine Waters, D-Calif., entered into colloquy with Financial Services Committee Chairman Barney Frank, D-Mass., regarding the meaning of the word "initiate" in Section 1302(2) of the Act. Specifically, Waters asked,

> "Would 'initiated' include any program or initiative that has been announced by Treasury prior to June 25, 2010? And if so, I assume that that means that programs such as the FHA refinance program, which would address the problem of negative equity and which I understand Treasury and the FHA are working on but is not yet publicly available, would be included as would the Hardest Hit Fund program, which is not fully implemented yet. And this would not prevent, for example, within the $50 billion already allocated for HAMP, perhaps adjusting resources between already-initiated programs based on their effectiveness."

Frank's response was "The answer is a resounding yes." He added, "Nothing new can be started after June 25, but it does not reach back and strangle in the cradle those programs that were under way. I confirm that the conference report would not prevent adjusting resources between already initiated programs based on their effectiveness" (Cong. Record (June 30), H5233).

Finally, the Conference Committee also provided that the amount of authority considered to be exercised by the Treasury Department under EESA is not to be reduced by—

- any amounts received from the repayment of the principal of financial assistance that an entity has received under TARP or any other program enacted by the Treasury Department under the EESA;

- any amounts committed for any guarantees pursuant to TARP that became or become uncommitted; or
- any losses realized by the Treasury Department (Emergency Economic Stabilization Act of 2008 Sec. 115(a)(4), as added by Sec. 1302(2) of the Dodd-Frank Act).

    CCH Comment: The Conference Committee removed a provision permitting the Treasury Department, with concurrence from the Fed Chairman, to purchase troubled assets in an amount equal to amounts received by the Treasury before, on, or after the date of enactment of the Pay It Back Act in the event that there is an immediate and substantial threat to the economy arising from financial instability.

▶ **Effective date.** The provision takes effect one day after the date of enactment (Sec. 4 of the Dodd-Frank Wall Street Reform and Consumer Protection Act).

Law source: Law at ¶11,302 and ¶10,004.

— Sec. 1302(1) of the Dodd-Frank Wall Street Reform and Consumer Protection Act, amending Emergency Economic Stabilization Act of 2008 Sec. 115(a)(3);

— Sec. 1302(2), adding Emergency Economic Stabilization Act of 2008 Sec. 115(a)(4) and (5);

— Sec. 4, providing the effective date.

¶6015 Public Debt Reduction

The Pay It Back Act amends the statutes governing the government-sponsored enterprises (GSEs)—the Federal National Mortgage Association (Fannie Mae) and Federal Home Loan Mortgage Corporation (Freddie Mac)—and the Federal Home Loan Banks (FHLBanks) to address reduction of the public debt.

GSE/FHLBank Obligations.—Under the amended Federal National Mortgage Association Charter Act, Federal Home Loan Mortgage Corporation Act and Federal Home Loan Bank Act, the Treasury Secretary is required to deposit in the Treasury solely for debt reduction any amounts received for the sale of any obligation or security acquired from the GSEs or any FHLBank. The Pay It Back Act also prohibits the use of these amounts as an offset for other spending increases or revenue reductions (Federal National Mortgage Association Charter Act Sec. 304(g)(2); Federal Home Loan Mortgage Corporation Act Sec. 306(l)(2); and Federal Home Loan Bank Act Sec. 11(l)(2), as amended by Sec. 1304 of the Dodd-Frank Act).

Fees and Assessments.—The Pay It Back Act also accomplishes debt reduction by requiring the deposit in the Treasury of any periodic commitment fee or any other fee or assessment paid to the Treasury by the GSEs as a result of any preferred stock purchase agreement, mortgage-backed security purchase program or any other program or activity under the Housing and Economic Recovery Act of 2008 (Sec. 1304(d) of the Dodd-Frank Act).

Report on TARP Proceeds.—Under Section 1303 of the Pay It Back Act, the Treasury is also required to submit a report to Congress every six months on amounts received and transferred to the Treasury's general fund for reduction of the public debt. The report is to be based on the proceeds from the sale of troubled assets purchased under

TARP, or from the sale, exercise or surrender of warrants or senior debt instruments acquired under TARP (Emergency Economic Stabilization Act of 2008 Sec. 106(f), as added by Sec. 1303 of the Dodd-Frank Act).

▶ **Effective date.** The provision takes effect one day after the date of enactment (Sec. 4 of the Dodd-Frank Wall Street Reform and Consumer Protection Act).

Law source: Law at ¶11,303, ¶11,304 and ¶10,004.

— Sec. 1303 of the Dodd-Frank Wall Street Reform and Consumer Protection Act, adding Emergency Economic Stabilization Act of 2008 Sec. 106(f);
— Sec. 1304(a) amending Federal National Mortgage Association Charter Act Sec. 304(g)(2);
— Sec. 1304(b) amending Federal Home Loan Mortgage Corporation Act Sec. 306(l)(2);
— Sec. 1304(c) amending Federal Home Loan Bank Act Sec. 11(l)(2);
— Sec. 1304(d), providing for repayment of fees;
— Sec. 4, providing the effective date.

¶6020 FHFA Reporting

The Director of the Federal Housing Finance Agency (FHFA) is required to report to Congress on the FHFA's plans to continue to support and maintain the nation's vital housing industry, while at the same time guaranteeing that the American taxpayer will not suffer unnecessary losses.

▶ **Effective date.** The provision takes effect one day after the date of enactment (Sec. 4 of the Dodd-Frank Wall Street Reform and Consumer Protection Act).

Law source: Law at ¶11,305 and ¶10,004.

— Sec. 1305 of the Dodd-Frank Wall Street Reform and Consumer Protection Act;
— Sec. 4, providing the effective date.

¶6025 Recovery Act Funds

Finally, the Pay It Back Act makes a number of changes to the American Recovery and Reinvestment Act of 2009 (ARRA).

Funds Sunset.—One change to the ARRA is the sunset of unused funds. Any funds not obligated as of Dec. 31, 2012, are to be returned to the Treasury to pay down the public debt (American Recovery and Reinvestment Act of 2009 Sec. 1603(b), as added by Sec. 1306(c) the Dodd-Frank Act).

As noted by Sen. Bennet, "Congress passed the Recovery Act to jolt our struggling economy back to life and help create and save jobs now. Yet, if funds have not been used by the end of 2012, can we say they have been used to ease our current recession? The taxpayers deserve to see stimulus funds used for real stimulus. If not, they should be used to pay down our debt."

Repayment and Recapture of Funds.—The Pay It Back Act also requires rescission of any ARRA funds offered to but not accepted by the governor or legislature of a state.

These funds are to be deposited in the Treasury solely for public debt reduction (American Recovery and Reinvestment Act of 2009 Sec. 1607(d)(2), as added by Sec. 1306(a) of the Dodd-Frank Act).

There is similar treatment for any funds withdrawn or recaptured by an executive agency head that have not been obligated by a state to a local government or for a specific project (American Recovery and Reinvestment Act of 2009 Sec. 1613, as added by Sec. 1306(b) of the Dodd-Frank Act).

▶ **Effective date.** The provision takes effect one day after the date of enactment (Sec. 4 of the Dodd-Frank Wall Street Reform and Consumer Protection Act).

Law source: Law at ¶11,306 and ¶10,004.

— Sec. 1306(a) of the Dodd-Frank Wall Street Reform and Consumer Protection Act, adding American Recovery and Reinvestment Act of 2009 Sec. 1607(d);

— Sec. 1306(b), adding American Recovery and Reinvestment Act of 2009 Sec. 1613;

— Sec. 1306(c), amending American Recovery and Reinvestment Act of 2009 Sec. 1603;

— Sec. 4, providing the effective date.

Mortgage Reform and Anti-Predatory Lending   14

INTRODUCTION
¶6505 Introduction
¶6510 Consumer Law

RESIDENTIAL MORTGAGE LOAN ORIGINATION STANDARDS
¶6515 Definitions
¶6520 Residential Mortgage Loan Origination
¶6525 Prohibition of Steering Incentives
¶6530 Mortgage Originator Liability
¶6535 Discretionary Regulatory Authority
¶6540 Study of Shared Appreciation Mortgages

MINIMUM STANDARDS for MORTGAGES
¶6545 Ability to Repay
¶6550 Safe Harbor and Rebuttable Presumptions
¶6555 Defense to Foreclosure
¶6560 Additional Standards and Requirements
¶6565 Rule of Construction
¶6570 Amendments to Civil Liability Provisions
¶6575 Lender Rights as to Borrower Deception
¶6580 Notice Prior to Reset of Hybrid Adjustable Rate Mortgages
¶6585 Required Disclosures
¶6590 Monthly Statement Disclosures
¶6595 Government Accountability Office Report
¶6600 State Attorney General Enforcement Authority

HIGH-COST MORTGAGES
¶6605 Definitions Relating to High-Cost Mortgages
¶6610 Amendments to Existing Requirements

¶6615 Additional Requirements for Certain Mortgages

OFFICE of HOUSING COUNSELING

¶6620 Establishment of Housing Counseling Office
¶6625 Counseling Procedures
¶6630 Grants for Housing Counseling
¶6635 Requirements to Use HUD-Certified Counselors
¶6640 Study of Defaults and Foreclosures
¶6645 Default and Disclosure Database
¶6650 Definitions for Counseling-Related Programs
¶6655 Accountability and Transparency for Grant Recipients
¶6660 Mortgage Information Booklet
¶6665 Home Inspection Counseling
¶6670 Warnings to Homeowners of Foreclosure Rescue Scams

MORTGAGE SERVICING

¶6675 Escrow and Impound Accounts
¶6680 Disclosure Notice for Consumers Who Waive Escrow Services
¶6685 Real Estate Settlement Procedures Act Amendments
¶6690 Truth in Lending Act Amendments
¶6695 Escrows Included in Repayment Analysis

APPRAISAL ACTIVITIES

¶6700 Property Appraisal Requirements
¶6705 Appraisal Independence Requirements
¶6710 FIRREA Amendments
¶6715 Equal Credit Opportunity Act Amendment
¶6720 Real Estate Settlement Procedures Act Amendment
¶6725 GAO Study

MORTGAGE RESOLUTION and MODIFICATION

¶6730 Mulitfamily Mortgage Resolution Program
¶6735 Home Affordable Modification Program Guidelines
¶6740 Public Availability of Information of Making Home Affordable Program
¶6745 Extension and Clarification of Protecting Tenants at Foreclosure Act

MISCELLANEOUS PROVISIONS

¶6750 Sense of Congress on Government Sponsored Enterprises Reform
¶6755 GAO Study Report on Mortgage Foreclosure Scams and Loan Modification Fraud
¶6760 Study of Effect of Drywall Presence on Foreclosures
¶6765 Emergency Mortgage Relief
¶6770 Additional Assistance for Neighborhood Stabilization Program
¶6775 Legal Assistance for Foreclosure-Related Issues

INTRODUCTION

¶6505 Introduction

The Dodd-Frank Wall Street Reform and Consumer Protection Act (Dodd-Frank Act) contains a myriad of provisions intended to reform consumer mortgage practices and provide accountability for those practices. Many of these provisions are contained within Title XIV of the Dodd-Frank Act, the "Mortgage Reform and Anti-Predatory Lending Act."

Background.—In part, the financial crisis stemmed from the subprime mortgage crisis, popularly known as the "mortgage mess" or "mortgage meltdown." The subprime crisis came to the public's attention when a steep rise in home foreclosures in 2006 spiraled seemingly out of control in 2007, triggering a national financial crisis that went global within the year.

Commentators have traced the crisis in part to the movement of lenders and mortgage originators away from traditional underwriting practices during the real estate boom, giving rise to risky mortgages and practices, such as "no doc" lending and allowing loans with "negative amortization" features, and to the proliferation of subprime mortgages, especially in refinancing. (H. Rep. No. 111-94, p. 50).

In an effort to prevent reoccurrences of the types of practices that led first to the subprime mortgage crisis and then to the widespread financial crisis, the House of Representatives passed comprehensive mortgage reform legislation on Nov. 15, 2007. The Mortgage Reform and Anti-Predatory Lending Act of 2007, H.R. 3915, passed the House by a vote of 291-127. The Senate did not take action on the bill. However, Title I of the legislation was the S.A.F.E. Mortgage Licensing Act of 2008 (SAFE Act), which provided for national licensing and registration for all mortgage loan originators. The SAFE Act became law as part of the Housing and Economic Recovery Act of 2008 (Public Law 110-289).

On March 26, 2009, Rep. Brad Miller, D-N.C., introduced a second comprehensive mortgage reform bill. The House passed H.R. 1728, the Mortgage Reform and Anti-Predatory Lending Act, on May 7, 2009, by a vote of 300–114 and referred the measure to the Senate on May 12, 2009. The Senate did not take action on the legislation.

The Dodd-Frank Act incorporated H.R. 1728 as Title XIV by amendment. A second amendment revised H.R. 1728 to include reverse mortgages in the Truth in Lending Act (TILA) definition of a "qualified mortgage."

Overview.—Title XIV of the Dodd-Frank Act amends TILA to reform consumer mortgage practices and provide accountability for such practices, to set minimum standards for consumer mortgage loans and for other purposes.

Loan originators are required to offer consumers residential mortgage loans on terms that "reasonably reflect" their ability to repay the loans.

The legislation expands the protections available under federal rules on high-cost loans by lowering the interest rate and the points and fee triggers that define high-cost loans.

The Dodd-Frank Act establishes an Office of Housing Counseling within the U.S. Department of Housing and Urban Development for the purpose of boosting homeownership and rental housing counseling.

Under the Dodd-Frank Act, a creditor in a consumer credit transaction secured by a first lien on the principal dwelling of the consumer must establish an escrow or impound account for the payment of taxes and hazard insurance and any other applicable required periodic payments or premiums.

The legislation also includes provisions on appraisal activities. A creditor is prohibited from extending credit in the form of a subprime mortgage to a consumer without first obtaining a written property appraisal. In addition, the Dodd-Frank Act amends TILA to provide that unfair or deceptive practices in extending credit or providing services for a consumer credit transaction secured by the consumer's principal dwelling are unlawful.

Regulations.—Regulations required by Title XIV must be in final form within 18 months of the designated transfer date and take effect not later than 12 months after issuance of the regulations in final form (Sec. 1400(c)(1) of the Dodd-Frank Wall Street Reform and Consumer Protection Act). The designated transfer date is a date to be selected by the Treasury Secretary that is at least 180 days, but no longer than 12 months, after enactment, subject to a possible extension of up to an additional six months (Secs. 1062(c) and 1495 of the Dodd-Frank Act).

▶ **Effective date.** A section, or provision, of Title XIV takes effect on the date on which the final regulations implementing such section, or provision, take effect. A section for which regulations have not been issued on or before the date that is 18 months after the transfer date will take effect on the date that is 18 months after the transfer date (Sec. 1400(c) of the Dodd-Frank Wall Street Reform and Consumer Protection Act). Title XIV provisions for which regulations are not required to be prescribed take effect one day after the date of enactment except as otherwise specifically provided (Sec. 4 of the Dodd-Frank Act).

Law source: Law at ¶11,400 ¶11,062, ¶11,495 and ¶10,004. Committee Report at ¶55,000A and ¶55,001.

— Sec. 1400(a) of the Dodd-Frank Wall Street Reform and Consumer Protection Act, providing the short title of Title XIV.

— Secs. 1400(c)(1), providing deadlines for regulations;

— Secs. 1062(c) and 1495, providing the transfer date;

— Secs. 4 and 1400(c)(2)-(3), providing the effective date.

¶6510 Consumer Law

The following provisions in the Mortgage Reform and Anti-Predatory Lending Act are enumerated consumer laws that come under the purview of the Bureau of Consumer Financial Protection:

- Subtitle A—Residential Mortgage Loan Origination Standards;
- Subtitle B—Minimum Standards For Mortgages;
- Subtitle C—High-Cost Mortgages;
- Subtitle E—Mortgage Servicing;
- Sec. 1471—Property appraisal requirements;
- Sec. 1472—Unfair and deceptive practices and acts relating to certain consumer credit transactions;
- Sec. 1475—Equal Credit Opportunity Act amendment; and
- Sec. 1476—Real Estate Settlement Procedures Act of 1974 amendment relating to appraisal fees (Sec. 1400(b) of the Dodd-Frank Act).

▶ **Effective date.** The provision takes effect one day after the date of enactment (Sec. 4 of the Dodd-Frank Wall Street Reform and Consumer Protection Act).

Law source: Law at ¶¶ 11,400 and ¶ 10,004.

— Sec. 1400(b) of the Dodd-Frank Wall Street Reform and Consumer Protection Act.
— Sec. 4, providing the effective date.

RESIDENTIAL MORTGAGE LOAN ORIGINATION STANDARDS

¶6515 Definitions

Title XIV, Subtitle A, of the Dodd-Frank Act sets out definitions that relate to mortgage origination and residential mortgage loans (TILA Sec. 103(cc), as added by Sec. 1401 of the Dodd-Frank Act).

The term "Commission" means the Federal Trade Commission, unless otherwise specified (TILA Sec. 103(cc)(1), as added by Sec. 1401 of the Dodd-Frank Act).

The Dodd-Frank Act defines "mortgage originator" as a person who, for compensation:

- takes a residential mortgage application;
- assists a consumer in obtaining or applying to obtain a residential mortgage loan; or
- offers or negotiates terms of a residential mortgage loan (TILA Sec. 103(cc)(2)(A), as added by Sec. 1401 of the Dodd-Frank Act).

A person "assists" a consumer in obtaining or applying to obtain a residential mortgage loan by, among other things, advising on residential mortgage loan terms (including rates, fees and other costs), preparing residential mortgage loan packages, or collecting information on behalf of the consumer with regard to a residential mortgage loan (TILA Sec. 103(cc)(4), as added by Sec. 1401 of the Dodd-Frank Act).

The mortgage originator definition includes persons who represent to the public that they will provide such services through advertising or other means of communication, but eliminates persons who perform administrative or clerical tasks. The Dodd-Frank Act also excludes employees of a retailer of manufactured homes who do not take residential mortgage loan applications or offer or negotiate terms of a residential mortgage loan. This description includes employees who do not advise consumers on loan terms, such as rates and fees (TILA Sec. 103(cc)(2)(B) and (C) as added by Sec. 1401 of the Dodd-Frank Act).

Also excluded from the definition of mortgage originator are those who only perform real estate brokerage activities. An exception to this provision exists for persons who are compensated for brokerage activities by a lender, mortgage broker or other mortgage originator (TILA Sec. 103(cc)(2)(D) as added by Sec. 1401 of the Dodd-Frank Act).

In addition, the definition of mortgage originator does not include a servicer or employees, agents and contractors, including those who offer or negotiate terms of a residential mortgage loan for the purposes of renegotiating, modifying, replacing and subordinating principal of existing mortgages where the borrowers are behind in their payments, in default or have a reasonable likelihood of defaulting (TILA Sec. 103(cc)(2)(G) as added by Sec. 1401 of the Dodd-Frank Act).

Finally, the term does not include a person (or estate or trust) that provides mortgage financing for the sale of three properties in any 12-month period to purchasers who own the properties and are securing the loan with the properties, provided the loan:

- is not made by anyone that has constructed or acted as a contractor for the construction of a residence on the property;
- is fully amortizing;
- is with respect to a sale for which the seller determines in good faith and documents that the buyer has a reasonable ability to repay the loan;
- has a fixed rate or an adjustable rate that is adjustable after five or more years, subject to reasonable annual and lifetime limitations on interest rate increases; and
- meets any other criteria the Federal Reserve Board may require (TILA Sec. 103(cc)(2)(E) as added by Sec. 1401 of the Dodd-Frank Act).

The term "Nationwide Mortgage Licensing System and Registry" has the same meaning as in the Secure and Fair Enforcement for Mortgage Licensing Act (TILA Sec. 103(cc)(3), as added by Sec. 1401 of the Dodd-Frank Act).

In general, "residential mortgage loan" means a consumer credit transaction secured by a mortgage, deed of trust or other equivalent consensual security interest on a dwelling, or residential real property that includes a dwelling, other than a consumer credit transaction under an open-end credit plan (TILA Sec. 103(cc)(5), as added by Sec. 1401 of the Dodd-Frank Act).

The term "Secretary," when used in connection with any transaction or person involved with a residential mortgage loan, means the Secretary of the U.S. Department of

¶6515

Housing and Urban Development (TILA Sec. 103(cc)(6), as added by Sec. 1401 of the Dodd-Frank Act).

▶ **Effective date.** The provisions take effect one day after the date of enactment (Sec. 4 of the Dodd-Frank Wall Street Reform and Consumer Protection Act).

Law source: Law at ¶11,401 and ¶10,004. Committee Report at ¶55,016.

— Sec. 1401 of the Dodd-Frank Wall Street Reform and Consumer Protection Act, adding Truth in Lending Act Sec 103(cc);

— Sec. 4, providing the effective date.

¶6520 Residential Mortgage Loan Origination

The Dodd-Frank Act amends Chapter 2 of TILA by redesignating the second section of Sec. 129 as 129A and adding a new Section 129B that prescribes fiduciary standards for originators of residential mortgages. The amendments are intended to ensure that consumers are offered and receive residential mortgage loans on terms that "reasonably reflect their ability to repay" (TILA Sec. 129B(a)(2), as added by Sec. 1402(a)(2) of the Dodd-Frank Act).

Duty of Care.—Mortgage originators must be qualified and, when required, registered and licensed as a mortgage originator under state and federal law, including the Secure and Fair Enforcement for Mortgage Licensing Act of 2008 (SAFE Act).

Mortgage originators also are required to include on all loan documents any unique identifier of the mortgage originator provided by the Nationwide Mortgage Licensing System and Registry (TILA Sec. 129B(b)(1), as added by Sec. 1402(a)(2) of the Dodd-Frank Act).

Regulations.—The Federal Reserve Board must prescribe rules that require depository institutions to establish and maintain procedures reasonably designed to assure and monitor compliance by the institutions, their subsidiaries, and employees of the institutions and their subsidiaries with the requirements of the section as well as the registration procedures under Sec. 1507 of the SAFE Act (TILA Sec. 129(b)(2), as added by Sec. 1402(a)(2) of the Dodd-Frank Act).

▶ **Effective date.** Based on TILA Sec. 129B(b) as added by Sec. 1402 of the Dodd-Frank Act, and TILA Sec. 129B(e) as added by Sec. 1405 of the Dodd-Frank Act, which both require implementing regulations, TILA Sec. 129B(b) would be effective on the date on which final regulations implementing the section take effect. Regulations must be in final form within 18 months of the designated transfer date and take effect not later than 12 months after issuance of the regulations in final form. If regulations have not been issued on or before the date that is 18 months after the transfer date, the provision will take effect on the date that is 18 months after the transfer date (Sec. 1400(c) of the Dodd-Frank Wall Street Reform and Consumer Protection Act). Amendment provisions that do not require regulations to be prescribed take effect one day after the date of enactment (Sec. 4 of the Dodd-Frank Act).

Law source: Law at ¶11,402, ¶11,400 and ¶10,004. Committee Report at ¶55,017.

— Sec. 1402(a)(2) of the Dodd-Frank Wall Street Reform and Consumer Protection Act, adding Truth in Lending Act Sec. 129B(a) and (b).

— Secs. 4 and 1400(c), providing the effective date.

¶6525 Prohibition of Steering Incentives

The Dodd-Frank Act prohibits steering incentives for creditors. For any mortgage loan, the mortgage originator may not receive compensation that varies based on the terms of the loan, other than the amount of the principal (TILA Sec. 129B(c)(1), as added by Sec. 1403 of the Dodd-Frank Act).

In general, a mortgage originator may not receive an origination fee or charge from any person other than the consumer except bona fide third-party charges. No person other than the consumer who knows, or has reason to know, that the consumer has directly compensated the originator may pay any origination fee or charge except bona fide third-party charges (TILA Sec. 129B(c)(2)(A), as added by Sec. 1403 of the Dodd-Frank Act).

However, a mortgage originator may receive from a person other than the consumer an origination fee or charge if:

- the mortgage originator does not receive any compensation directly from the consumer; and
- the consumer does not make an upfront payment of discount points, origination points or fees other than bona fide third-party charges not retained by the originator, creditor or an affiliate.

The Federal Reserve Board (Fed) may, by rule, waive or provide exemptions to this exemption (TILA Sec. 129B(c)(2)(B), as added by Sec. 1403 of the Dodd-Frank Act).

Regulations.—The Fed must promulgate regulations that prohibit mortgage originators from steering any consumer to a residential mortgage loan that the consumer does not have a "reasonable ability" to repay (TILA Sec. 129B(c)(3)(A)(i), as added by Sec. 1403 of the Dodd-Frank Act).

In addition, the loan must not contain predatory characteristics or effects such as excessive fees or abusive terms (TILA Sec. 129B(c)(3)(A)(ii), as added by Sec. 1403 of the Dodd-Frank Act).

The regulations must prohibit mortgage originators from steering a consumer away from a residential mortgage loan for which the consumer is qualified to a residential mortgage loan that is not a "qualified" mortgage loan (TILA Sec. 129B(c)(3)(B), as added by Sec. 1403 of the Dodd-Frank Act).

The Fed's regulations must ban abusive or unfair lending practices that treat consumers of equal creditworthiness differently based on race, ethnicity, gender or age (TILA Sec. 129B(c)(3)(C), as added by Sec. 1403 of the Dodd-Frank Act).

The regulations must prohibit originators from mischaracterizing the credit history of a consumer, the residential mortgage loans available to the consumer or the appraised value of the property securing the loan (TILA Sec. 129B(c)(3)(D)(i)-(ii), as added by Sec. 1403 of the Dodd-Frank Act).

Finally, the rules must disallow originators from discouraging a consumer from seeking a mortgage loan secured by the consumer's principal dwelling from other mortgage originators if the originator does not have an appropriate loan to offer the consumer (TILA Sec. 129B(c)(3)(D)(iii), as added by Sec. 1403 of the Dodd-Frank Act).

▶ **Effective date.** Based on TILA Sec. 129B(c)(3) as added by Sec. 1403 of the Dodd-Frank Act, and TILA Sec. 129B(e) as added by Sec. 1405 of the Dodd-Frank Act, which both require implementing regulations, TILA Sec. 129B(c)(3) would be effective on the date on which final regulations implementing the section take effect. Regulations must be in final form within 18 months of the designated transfer date and take effect not later than 12 months after issuance of the regulations in final form. If regulations have not been issued on or before the date that is 18 months after the transfer date, the provision will take effect on the date that is 18 months after the transfer date (Sec. 1400(c) of the Dodd-Frank Wall Street Reform and Consumer Protection Act). Amendment provisions that do not require regulations to be prescribed take effect one day after the date of enactment (Sec. 4 of the Dodd-Frank Act).

Law source: Law at ¶11,403, ¶11,400 and ¶10,004. Committee Report at ¶55,018.

— Sec. 1403 of the Dodd-Frank Wall Street Reform and Consumer Protection Act, adding Truth in Lending Act Sec. 129B(c).

— Secs 4 and. 1400(c), providing the effective date.

¶6530 Mortgage Originator Liability

The maximum liability of a mortgage originator to a consumer for violation of the residential mortgage loan origination requirements, in addition to court costs and attorney fees, is the greater of actual damages or three times the total amount of direct and indirect compensation or gain accruing to the originator in connection with the loan (TILA Sec. 129B(d) as added by Sec. 1404 of the Dodd-Frank Act).

▶ **Effective date.** Based on TILA Sec. 129B(d)(1) as added by Sec. 1403 of the Dodd-Frank Act, and TILA Sec. 129B(e) as added by Sec. 1405 of the Dodd-Frank Act, which both require implementing regulations, TILA Sec. 129B(d) would be effective on the date on which final regulations implementing the section take effect. Regulations must be in final form within 18 months of the designated transfer date and take effect not later than 12 months after issuance of the regulations in final form. If regulations have not been issued on or before the date that is 18 months after the transfer date, the provision will take effect on the date that is 18 months after the transfer date (Sec. 1400(c) of the Dodd-Frank Wall Street Reform and Consumer Protection Act). Amendment provisions that do not require regulations to be prescribed take effect one day after the date of enactment (Sec. 4 of the Dodd-Frank Act).

Law source: Law at ¶11,404, ¶11,400 and ¶10,004 Committee Report at ¶55,019.

— Sec. 1404 of the Dodd-Frank Wall Street Reform and Consumer Protection Act, adding Truth in Lending Act Sec.129B(d).

— Secs. 4 and 1400(c), providing the effective date.

¶6535 Discretionary Regulatory Authority

The Federal Reserve Board is required to prohibit or condition terms, acts or practices relating to residential mortgage loans that are abusive, unfair, deceptive or predatory, or as necessary to ensure that responsible, affordable mortgage credit is available to consumers (TILA Sec. 129B(e) as added by Sec. 1405 of the Dodd-Frank Act).

To improve consumer awareness and understanding of transactions involving residential mortgage loans through the use of disclosures, the Fed may, by rule, exempt from or modify disclosure requirements for any class of residential mortgage loans if in the public interest (Sec. 1405(b) of the Dodd-Frank Act).

▶ **Effective date.** Based on TILA Sec. 129B(e) as added by Sec. 1403 of the Dodd-Frank Act, which requires implementing regulations, TILA Sec. 129B(e) would be effective on the date on which final regulations implementing the section take effect. Regulations must be in final form within 18 months of the designated transfer date and take effect not later than 12 months after issuance of the regulations in final form. If regulations have not been issued on or before the date that is 18 months after the transfer date, the provision will take effect on the date that is 18 months after the transfer date (Sec. 1400(c) of the Dodd-Frank Wall Street Reform and Consumer Protection Act). Amendment provisions that do not require regulations to be prescribed take effect one day after the date of enactment (Sec. 4 of the Dodd-Frank Act).

Law source: Law at ¶11,405, ¶11,400 and ¶10,004. Committee Report at ¶55,020.

— Sec. 1405(a) of the Dodd-Frank Wall Street Reform and Consumer Protection Act, adding Truth in Lending Act Sec. 129B(e).

— Secs. 4 and 1400(c), providing the effective date.

¶6540 Study of Shared Appreciation Mortgages

The Secretary of the U.S. Department of Housing and Urban Development (HUD) is required to conduct a comprehensive study and report to Congress on regulatory requirements that would promote widespread use of shared appreciation mortgages intended to strengthen local housing markets, provide new opportunities for affordable homeownership and give homeowners at risk of foreclosure the ability to refinance or modify their mortgages (Sec. 1406(a) of the Dodd-Frank Act).

▶ **Effective date.** The Secretary of HUD must submit a report of the study to Congress within six months of the date of enactment of the Dodd-Frank Wall Street Reform and Consumer Protection Act (Sec. 1406(b) of the Dodd-Frank Act).

Law source: Law at ¶11,406.

— Sec. 1406 of the Dodd-Frank Wall Street Reform and Consumer Protection Act.

MINIMUM STANDARDS for MORTGAGES

¶6545 Ability to Repay

Before making a residential mortgage loan, a creditor is required to make a reasonable and good faith determination, based on verified and documented information, that at the time the loan is consummated the consumer has a reasonable ability to repay the loan, in accordance with regulations prescribed by the Fed. (TILA Sec. 129C(a)(1), as added by Sec. 1411(a)(2) of the Dodd-Frank Act).

If the creditor knows that one or more residential mortgage loans secured by the same dwelling will be made to the same consumer, the creditor must determine that the consumer has a reasonable ability to repay both loans using verified and documented information (TILA Sec. 129C(a)(2), as added by Sec. 1411(a)(2) of the Dodd-Frank Act).

Documented information must include verification of the consumer's credit history, current income, expected income the consumer is reasonably assured of receiving, current obligations, debt-to-income ratio, employment status and other financial resources other than the consumer's equity in the dwelling. A creditor must determine the ability of the consumer to repay using a payment schedule that fully amortizes the loan over the term of the loan. (TILA Sec. 129C(a)(3), as added by Sec. 1411(a)(2) of the Dodd-Frank Act).

If the documented income, including income from a small business, is a repayment source for the loan, a creditor may consider the seasonality and irregularity of the income in the underwriting and scheduling of payments for the loan (TILA Sec. 129C(a)(9), as added by Sec. 1411(a)(2) of the Dodd-Frank Act).

Verification of the consumer's income must be made by Internal Revenue Service transcripts of tax returns or a method that quickly and effectively verifies income documentation by a third party subject to rules prescribed by the Federal Reserve Board (TILA Sec. 129C(a)(4), as added by Sec. 1411(a)(2) of the Dodd-Frank Act).

An exemption exists for loans made, guaranteed or insured by federal departments or agencies. These departments or agencies may exempt refinancings under a streamlined refinancing from the income verification requirement if:

- the consumer is not 30 days or more past due on the prior existing mortgage loan;
- the refinancing does not increase the principal balance outstanding on the prior existing mortgage loan, except to the extent of allowable fees and charges;
- total points and fees, other than bona fide third-party charges not retained by the mortgage originator or creditor, payable in connection with the refinancing do not exceed 3 percent of the new loan amount;
- the interest rate on the refinanced loan is lower than the interest rate of the original loan, unless the borrower is refinancing from an adjustable to a fixed rate loan;
- the refinancing is subject to a payment schedule that will fully amortize the refinancing;
- the terms of the refinancing do not result in a balloon payment; and

- both the mortgage loan being refinanced and the refinancing satisfy the requirements of the department or agency making, guaranteeing or insuring the refinancing (TILA Sec. 129C(a)(5), as added by Sec. 1411(a)(2) of the Dodd-Frank Act).

Nonstandard Loans.—Nonstandard loans require different methods of determining a consumer's ability to repay the loan. For variable rate loans that defer repayment of principal or interest, a creditor must use a fully amortizing repayment schedule (TILA Sec. 129C(a)(6)(A), as added by Sec. 1411(a)(2) of the Dodd-Frank Act). To determine whether a consumer is able to repay an interest-only loan, a creditor must use the payment amount required to amortize the loan by its final maturity (TILA Sec. 129C(a)(6)(B), as added by Sec. 1411(a)(2) of the Dodd-Frank Act).

When making a determination as to a consumer's ability to repay a nonstandard residential mortgage loan, a creditor also must take into consideration any balance increase that may accrue from any negative amortization provision (TILA Sec. 129C(a)(6)(C), as added by Sec. 1411(a)(2) of the Dodd-Frank Act).

To make the determination, a creditor must calculate the monthly payment amount for principal and interest by assuming:

- the loan proceeds are fully disbursed on the date the loan is consummated;
- the loan is to be repaid in substantially equal monthly amortizing payments with no balloon payments; and
- the interest rate over the entire term of the loan is a fixed rate equal to the fully indexed rate—defined as the index rate prevailing on a loan at the time it is made plus the margin that will apply after the expiration of any introductory interest rates—at the time of the loan closing, without considering the introductory fee (TILA Secs. 129C(a)(6)(D) and 129C(a)(7), as added by Sec. 1411(a)(2) of the Dodd-Frank Act).

If the terms of the loan require more rapid repayment, including a balloon payment, the calculation must be made in accordance with federal banking agency regulations or using the contract's repayment schedule. The loan must have an annual percentage rate that does not exceed the prime offer rate for a comparable transaction on the date the interest rate is set by 1.5 or more percentage points for a first-lien residential mortgage loan and by 3.5 or more percentage points for a subordinate-lien residential mortgage loan (TILA Sec. 129C(a)(6)(D), as added by Sec. 1411(a)(2) of the Dodd-Frank Act).

A creditor may consider refinancing an existing hybrid loan into a standard loan when there would be a reduction in monthly payments and the consumer has not been delinquent in any payments. In doing so, the creditor may consider the consumer's good standing on the existing mortgage. The creditor also may consider whether the extension of new credit would prevent a likely default should the original mortgage reset and give this concern a higher priority as an acceptable underwriting practice (TILA Sec. 129C(a)(6)(E), as added by Sec. 1411(a)(2) of the Dodd-Frank Act).

The creditor also may offer the mortgagor rate discounts and other favorable terms that would be available to new customers with high credit ratings based on the underwriting practice (TILA Sec. 129C(a)(6)(E)(iii), as added by Sec. 1411(a)(2) of the Dodd-Frank Act).

¶6545

Reverse Mortgages.—The minimum standards outlined in the subsection do not apply to reverse mortgages, or to a temporary or bridge loan with a term of 12 months or less, including any loan to purchase a new dwelling when the consumer plans to sell a different dwelling within 12 months (TILA Sec. 129C(a)(8), as added by Sec. 1411(a)(2) of the Dodd-Frank Act).

▶ **Effective date.** Based on TILA Sec. 129C(a)(1) as added by Sec. 1411(a)(2) of the Dodd-Frank Act, which requires implementing regulations, TILA Sec. 129C(a)(1) would be effective on the date on which final regulations implementing the section take effect. Regulations must be in final form within 18 months of the designated transfer date and take effect not later than 12 months after issuance of the regulations in final form. If regulations have not been issued on or before the date that is 18 months after the transfer date, the provision will take effect on the date that is 18 months after the transfer date (Sec. 1400(c) of the Dodd-Frank Wall Street Reform and Consumer Protection Act). Amendment provisions that do not require regulations to be prescribed take effect one day after the date of enactment (Sec. 4 of the Dodd-Frank Act).

Law source: Law at ¶11,411, ¶11,400 and ¶10,004. Committee Report at ¶55,025.

— Sec. 1411(a)(2) of the Dodd-Frank Wall Street Reform and Consumer Protection Act, adding Truth in Lending Act Sec.129C;

— Secs. 4 and 1400(c), providing the effective date.

¶6550 Safe Harbor and Rebuttable Presumptions

A creditor may presume that a residential mortgage loan has met the requirements of "ability to repay" if the loan is a "qualified mortgage" (TILA Sec. 129C(b)(1), as added by Sec. 1412 of the Dodd-Frank Act).

"Qualified mortgage" means a residential mortgage loan:

(1) for which the regular periodic payments for the loan may not result in an increase of the principal balance or, except as provided in subparagraph E, allow the consumer to defer repayment of principal;

(2) that does not include a repayment schedule resulting in a balloon payment that is more than twice as large as the average of earlier scheduled payments;

(3) for which the income and financial resources relied on to qualify the consumer for the loan are verified and documented;

(4) that, for a fixed-rate loan, has an underwriting process based on a payment schedule that fully amortizes the loan over the loan term, taking into account taxes, insurance and assessments;

(5) that, in the case of an adjustable rate loan, has underwriting based on the maximum rate permitted under the terms of the loan during the first five years and a payment schedule that fully amortizes the loan over the loan term, taking into account taxes, insurance and assessments;

(6) that complies with Federal Reserve Board guidelines or regulations relating to ratios of total monthly debt to monthly income or alternative measures of ability to

pay expenses after payment of debt each month, taking into account income levels of the borrower and other relevant factors;

(7) for which the total points and fees on the loan do not exceed 3 percent of the total loan amount;

(8) for which the term of the loan does not exceed 30 years, unless extended by regulation; and

(9) that is a reverse mortgage which meets the standards for a qualified mortgage as defined by the Fed in rules implementing the subsection (TILA Sec. 129C(b)(2)(A), as added by Sec. 1412 of the Dodd-Frank Act).

Average Prime Offer Rate.—The term "average prime offer rate" means the average prime offer rate for a comparable transaction as of the date on which the interest rate for the transaction is set, as published by the Fed (TILA Sec. 129C(b)(2)(B), as added by Sec. 1412 of the Dodd-Frank Act).

Points and Fees.—The term "points and fees" means points and fees as defined by TILA Sec. 103(aa)(4), other than bona fide third-party charges not retained by the mortgage originator or creditor (TILA Sec. 129C(b)(2)(C)(i), as added by Sec. 1412 of the Dodd-Frank Act).

For purposes of computing the total points and fees, the total points and fees exclude either of the amounts below but not both:

(1) up to and including two bona fide discount points payable by the consumer, but only if the interest rate from which the mortgage's interest rate will be discounted does not exceed by more than one percentage point the average prime rate offer;

(2) unless two bona fide discounts have been excluded under (1), up to and including one bona fide discount point payable by the consumer, but only if the interest rate from which the mortgage's interest rate will be discounted does not exceed by more than two percentage points the average prime offer rate (TILA Sec. 129C(b)(2)(C)(ii), as added by Sec. 1412 of the Dodd-Frank Act).

These clauses do not apply to discount points used to purchase an interest rate reduction unless the amount of the interest rate reduction purchased is reasonably consistent with industry norms and practices for secondary mortgage market transactions (TILA Sec. 129C(b)(2)(C)(iv), as added by Sec. 1412 of the Dodd-Frank Act).

Bona Fide Discount Points.—The term "bona fide discount points" means loan discount points that are knowingly paid by the consumer for the purpose of reducing, and which in fact do reduce, the interest rate or time-priced differential applicable to the mortgage (TILA Sec. 129C(b)(2)(C)(iii), as added by Sec. 1412 of the Dodd-Frank Act).

Smaller Loans.—The Fed must prescribe rules that adjust the criteria on qualified mortgages as defined in this section in order to permit lenders that extend smaller loans to meet the requirements of the presumption of compliance. The Fed must consider the potential impact of its rules on rural areas and other areas with lower home values (TILA Sec. 129C(b)(2)(D) as added by Sec. 1412 of the Dodd-Frank Act).

Balloon Loans.—The Fed may by regulation provide that the term "qualified mortgage" includes a balloon loan:

¶6550

- that meets all of the criteria for a qualified mortgage with the exceptions as enumerated in the section;

- for which the creditor makes a determination that the consumer is able to make all scheduled payments, except the balloon payment, out of income or assets other than the collateral;

- for which the underwriting is based on a payment schedule that fully amortizes the loan over a period of not more than 30 years and takes into account all applicable taxes, insurance and assessments; and

- that is extended by a creditor who: operates predominantly in rural or underserved areas; together with all affiliates has total annual mortgage loan originations that do not exceed a limit set by the Fed; retains the balloon loans in portfolio; and meets any asset size threshold and other criteria established by the Fed (TILA Sec. 129C(b)(2)(E), as added by Sec. 1412 of the Dodd-Frank Act).

Regulations. The Fed must adopt regulations to carry out the provisions of this subsection. The Fed may prescribe regulations that revise, add to or subtract from the criteria that define a qualified mortgage if it finds that the regulations are necessary to ensure that responsible, affordable mortgage credit is available to consumers.

The following agencies must prescribe regulations under the same standard set for the Fed:

- the Department of Housing and Urban Development, for mortgages insured under the National Housing Act;

- the Department of Veterans Affairs, for loans made or guaranteed by the Secretary of Veterans Affairs;

- the Department of Agriculture, for loans guaranteed by the Secretary of Agriculture;

- the Rural Housing Service, with regard to loans insured by that department (TILA Sec. 129C(b)(3), as added by Sec. 1412 of the Dodd-Frank Act).

▶ **Effective date.** Based on TILA Sec. 129C(b)(3)(A) as added by Sec. 1411(a)(2) of the Dodd-Frank Act, which requires implementing regulations, TILA Sec. 129C(b) would be effective on the date on which final regulations implementing the section take effect. Regulations must be in final form within 18 months of the designated transfer date and take effect not later than 12 months after issuance of the regulations in final form. If regulations have not been issued on or before the date that is 18 months after the transfer date, the provision will take effect on the date that is 18 months after the transfer date (Sec. 1400(c) of the Dodd-Frank Wall Street Reform and Consumer Protection Act). Amendment provisions that do not require regulations to be prescribed take effect one day after the date of enactment (Sec. 4 of the Dodd-Frank Act).

Law source: Law at ¶11,412, ¶11,400 and ¶10,004. Committee Report at ¶55,027.

— Sec. 1412 of the Dodd-Frank Wall Street Reform and Consumer Protection Act, adding Truth in Lending Act Sec.129C(b);

— Secs. 4 and 1400(c), providing the effective date.

¶6550

¶6555 Defense to Foreclosure

When a creditor, assignee or other holder of a residential mortgage loan initiates a judicial or nonjudicial foreclosure, or any other action to collect the debt in connection with the loan, a consumer with the right to rescind is permitted to assert a violation as a defense by recoupment or set-off (TILA Sec. 130(k)(1), as added by Sec. 1413 of the Dodd-Frank Act).

The amount of recoupment or set-off must equal the amount to which the consumer would be entitled under TILA for damages for a valid claim brought in an original action against the creditor, plus costs to the consumer and reasonable attorney's fees (TILA Sec. 130(k)(2)(A), as added by Sec. 1413 of the Dodd-Frank Act).

If the judgment is rendered after the expiration of the time limit on a private action for damages under TILA (15 USC 1640(e)), one year from the date of violation, the amount of recoupment or set-off may not exceed the amount to which the consumer would have been entitled for damages computed up to the day preceding the expiration of the time limit (TILA Sec. 130(k)(2)(B), as added by Sec. 1413 of the Dodd-Frank Act).

▶ **Effective date.** The provisions take effect one day after the date of enactment (Sec. 4 of the Dodd-Frank Wall Street Reform and Consumer Protection Act).

Law source: Law at ¶11,413 and ¶10,004. Committee Report at ¶55,029.

— Sec. 1413 of the Dodd-Frank Wall Street Reform and Consumer Protection Act, adding Truth in Lending Act Sec.130(k);

— Sec. 4, providing the effective date.

¶6560 Additional Standards and Requirements

A residential mortgage loan that is not a "qualified" mortgage may not include terms requiring a consumer to pay a prepayment penalty for paying all or part of the principal after the loan is consummated (TILA Sec. 129C(c)(1)(A), as added by Sec. 1414(a) of the Dodd-Frank Act).

A "qualified" mortgage may not include a residential mortgage loan that has an adjustable rate or has an annual percentage rate that exceeds the average prime offer rate for a comparable transaction as of the date the interest rate is set by:

- 1.5 or more percentage points in the case of a first lien residential mortgage loan having an original principal obligation amount that is equal to or less than the amount of the maximum limitation on the original principal obligation of mortgage in effect for a residence of the applicable size as of the date of the interest rate set;
- 2.5 or more percentage points in the case of a first lien residential mortgage loan having an original principal obligation amount that is more than the amount of the maximum limitation on the original principal obligation of mortgage for a residence of the applicable size as of the date of the interest rate set; and
- 3.5 or more percentage points in the case of a subordinate lien residential mortgage loan (TILA Sec. 129C(c)(1)(B), as added by Sec. 1414(a) of the Dodd-Frank Act).

The Federal Reserve Board must publish and update average prime offer rates at least weekly and adjust the above thresholds as necessary to reflect changes in market conditions (TILA Sec. 129C(c)(2), as added by Sec. 1414(a) of the Dodd-Frank Act).

For one year from the date of loan consummation, the prepayment penalty must not exceed 3 percent of the outstanding balance on the loan. During the second-year period from the date of consummation, the prepayment penalty must not exceed 2 percent of the outstanding balance. The following year (three years from consummation), the prepayment penalty must not exceed 1 percent of the outstanding balance. Finally, no prepayment penalty is allowed after the three-year period beginning on the date of consummation of the loan (TILA Sec. 129C(c)(3), as added by the Dodd-Frank Act).

A creditor may not offer a consumer a residential mortgage loan that has a prepayment penalty without offering the consumer a residential mortgage loan that does not include a prepayment penalty in its terms (TILA Sec. 129C(c)(4), as added by Sec.1414(a) of the Dodd-Frank Act).

Credit Insurance.—A creditor is barred from financing credit life, credit disability, credit unemployment or credit property insurance. This prohibition includes accident, loss-of-income, life or health insurance, as well as any payments for debt cancellation or suspension agreement.

However, there are some exceptions. The Dodd-Frank Act permits insurance premiums or debt cancellation or suspension fees calculated and paid in full on a monthly basis. Also, the prohibition does not apply to credit unemployment insurance if the premiums are reasonable, the creditor does not receive compensation and the premiums are paid pursuant to another insurance contract and not to an affiliate of the creditor (TILA Sec. 129C(d), as added by Sec.1414(a) of the Dodd-Frank Act).

Arbitration.—Residential mortgage loans or extensions of credit under an open-end consumer credit plan secured by the principal dwelling of the consumer may not include terms requiring arbitration.

This provision does not limit the right of the consumer and the creditor to agree to arbitration or any other nonjudicial procedure as the method for resolving any controversy after a dispute or claim under the transaction occurs. In addition, this provision does not bar a consumer from bringing an action for damages or other relief in connection with a violation. (TILA Sec. 129C(e), as added by Sec. 1414(a) of the Dodd-Frank Act).

Negative Amortization.—A creditor is not permitted to extend credit that allows a payment plan that may result in negative amortization.

There are some exceptions. This provision does not apply to reverse mortgages.

In addition, the creditor may extend credit that may result in negative amortization if, before the transaction is consummated, the creditor provides the consumer with a statement that:

- the pending transaction will, or may, result in negative amortization;

- describes negative amortization as prescribed by the Fed; and

¶6560

- negative amortization increases the outstanding principal balance of the account and reduces the consumer's equity in the dwelling or real property secured under the credit.

In addition, a creditor may extend credit that could result in negative amortization if a first-time borrower of a residential mortgage loan that is not qualified provides the creditor with sufficient documentation to demonstrate that the consumer received homeownership counseling from organizations certified by the U.S. Department of Housing and Development (TILA Sec. 129C(f), as added by Sec.1414(a) of the Dodd-Frank Act).

Protection Against Loss of Anti-Deficiency Protection.—If a creditor or mortgage originator provides an application to a consumer, or receives an application from a consumer, for the refinancing of a residential mortgage loan subject to protection under an anti-deficiency law, and the application would cause the loan to lose that protection, the creditor or mortgage originator is required to provide written notice to the consumer describing the protection and its loss before consummation.

The term "anti-deficiency law" means the law of any state that provides that, should there be a foreclosure on residential property secured by a mortgage, the consumer is not liable for any deficiency between the sale price obtained on the property through foreclosure and the outstanding balance of the mortgage.

In addition to a refinancing, a creditor or mortgage loan originator must provide written notice to a consumer in the case of any residential mortgage loan that is, or will be at consummation, subject to protection under an anti-deficiency law. The notice must contain a description of the protection and the significance to the consumer of the loss of the protection. The notice must be provided prior to consummation of the loan (TILA Sec. 129C(g), as added by Sec. 1414(c) of the Dodd-Frank Act).

Partial Payments.—A creditor must disclose prior to settlement of a residential mortgage loan or, in the case of a person becoming a creditor with respect to an existing residential mortgage loan, at the time the person becomes a creditor, the creditor's policy on the acceptance of partial payments. The creditor also must disclose the way in which partial payments will be applied to the mortgage and if the payments will be placed in escrow (TILA Sec. 129C(h), as added by Sec. 1414(d) of the Dodd-Frank Act).

▶ **Effective date.** The provisions take effect one day after the date of enactment (Sec. 4 of the Dodd-Frank Wall Street Reform and Consumer Protection Act).

Law source: Law at ¶11,414 and ¶10,004. Committee Report at ¶55,030.

— Sec. 1414(a) of the Dodd-Frank Wall Street Reform and Consumer Protection Act, adding Truth in Lending Act Sec.129C(c)—(f);

— Sec. 1414(b), adding Truth in Lending Act Sec. 108(a)(7);

— Sec. 1414(c), adding Truth in Lending Act Sec.129C(g);

— Sec. 1414(d), adding Truth in Lending Act Sec.129C(h);

— Sec. 4, providing the effective date.

¶6565 Rule of Construction

Unless provided in Sec. 129B or 129C of the Truth in Lending Act (TILA), as added by the Dodd-Frank Act, no provision supersedes, repeals or affects any duties, rights or remedies under any other provision of TILA, federal or state law (Sec. 1415 of the Dodd-Frank Act).

▶ **Effective date.** The provision takes effect one day after the date of enactment (Sec. 4 of the Dodd-Frank Wall Street Reform and Consumer Protection Act).

Law source: Law at ¶11,415 and ¶10,004. Committee Report at ¶55,031.

— Sec. 1415 of the Dodd-Frank Wall Street Reform and Consumer Protection Act;

— Sec. 4, providing the effective date.

¶6570 Amendments to Civil Liability Provisions

The Dodd-Frank Act doubles Truth in Lending Act (TILA) civil money penalties for certain violations.

Prior to the Dodd-Frank Act, a creditor who failed to comply with any requirement of TILA Chapter 2 was liable in an amount not less than $100 nor greater than $1,000. Under the Dodd-Frank Act, a creditor who fails to comply with the requirements is liable in an amount not less than $200 nor greater than $2,000 (Truth in Lending Act Sec. 130(a)(2), as amended by Sec. 1416(a)(1) of the Dodd-Frank Act).

In a class action, recovery was limited to no more than the lesser of $500,000 or 1 percent of the net worth of the creditor. The Dodd-Frank Act amends TILA to provide that recovery is limited to no more than the lesser of $1,000,000 or 1 percent of the net worth of the creditor (Truth in Lending Act Sec. 130(a)(2), as amended by Sec. 1416(a)(2) of the Dodd-Frank Act).

The Dodd-Frank Act also extends the statute of limitations for Sec. 129 violations from one year from the date of the violation to three years from the occurrence of the violation (Truth in Lending Act Sec. 130(e), as amended by Sec. 1416(b) of the Dodd-Frank Act).

▶ **Effective date.** The provision takes effect one day after the date of enactment (Sec. 4 of the Dodd-Frank Wall Street Reform and Consumer Protection Act).

Law source: Law at ¶11,416 and ¶10,004. Committee Report at ¶55,034.

— Sec. 1416(a) of the Dodd-Frank Wall Street Reform and Consumer Protection Act, amending Truth in Lending Act Sec. 130(a)(2);

— Sec. 1416(b), amending Truth in Lending Act Sec. 130(e);

— Sec. 4, providing the effective date.

¶6575 Lender Rights as to Borrower Deception

A creditor or assignee is not liable to an obligor if the obligor or a co-obligor has been convicted of obtaining the residential mortgage loan by actual fraud.

This provision is in addition to any remedies available by law or contract.

▶ **Effective date.** The provision takes effect one day after the date of enactment (Sec. 4 of the Dodd-Frank Wall Street Reform and Consumer Protection Act).

Law source: Law at ¶11,417 and ¶10,004. Committee Report at ¶55,035.

— Sec. 1417 of the Dodd-Frank Wall Street Reform and Consumer Protection Act, adding Truth in Lending Act Sec. 130(l);

— Sec. 4 providing the effective date.

¶6580 Notice Prior to Reset of Hybrid Adjustable Rate Mortgages

The creditor or servicer of a hybrid adjustable rate mortgage must provide six months notice before the interest rate in effect during the introductory period of the loan resets (TILA Sec. 128A(b), as added by Sec. 1418 of the Dodd-Frank Act). The term "hybrid adjustable rate mortgage" means a consumer credit transaction secured by the consumer's principal residence with a fixed interest rate for an introductory period that adjusts or resets to a variable interest rate after the introductory period (TILA Sec. 128A(a), as added by Sec. 1418 of the Dodd-Frank Act).

The written notice must be separate and distinct from other correspondence to the consumer and include:

- The index or formula used in the adjustment or resetting of the rate, with a source of information about the index or formula;
- An explanation of how the new interest rate and payment would be determined;
- The creditor's or servicer's good faith estimate, using industry standards, of the monthly payment after adjustment or resetting of the rate;
- A list of alternatives consumers can pursue before the date of adjustment or resetting, plus descriptions of the actions consumers must take to pursue the alternatives, including refinancing, renegotiation of loan terms, payment forbearances and pre-foreclosure sales; and
- Information such as addresses and phone numbers of counseling agencies or programs approved by the Housing and Urban Development Secretary or state housing finance authority, along with the contact information for the state housing finance authority for the state in which the consumer resides (TILA Sec. 128A(b), as added by Sec. 1418 of the Dodd-Frank Act).

The Federal Reserve Board may require the notice for adjustable rate mortgage loans that are not hybrid adjustable rate mortgage loans (TILA Sec. 128A(c), as added by Sec. 1418 of the Dodd-Frank Act).

▶ **Effective date.** The provision take effect one day after the date of enactment (Sec. 4 of the Dodd-Frank Wall Street Reform and Consumer Protection Act).

Law source: Law at ¶11,418 and ¶10,004. Committee Report at ¶55,036.

— Sec. 1418 of the Dodd-Frank Wall Street Reform and Consumer Protection Act, adding Truth in Lending Act Sec. 128A;

— Sec. 4, providing the effective date.

¶6585 Required Disclosures

If an escrow or impound account will be created for tax, insurance and assessment payments on a variable rate residential mortgage loan, a creditor must make disclosures to the consumer about the amount of the initial monthly payment due under the loan for the principal and interest and the amount of the payment that will be deposited in the account for payment of taxes, insurance and assessments.

The disclosure must include the amount of the fully indexed monthly payment of principal and interest and the amount of this payment that will be deposited into the escrow or impound account for taxes, insurance and assessments (TILA Sec. 128(a)(16), as added by Sec. 1419 of the Dodd-Frank Act).

For residential mortgage loans not included in the above category, the creditor or servicer must disclose the aggregate amount of settlement charges in connection with the loan, the amount of charges included in the loan and the amount the consumer must pay at closing. The approximate amount of the wholesale rate of funds and the aggregate amount of other fees or required payments in connection with the loan must be included (TILA Sec. 128(a)(17), as added by Sec. 1419 of the Dodd-Frank Act).

In addition, the disclosure must include the aggregate amount of fees paid to the mortgage originator of the loan, the amount of fees paid directly by the consumer and any additional fees the creditor paid to the originator (TILA Sec. 128(a)(18), as added by Sec. 1419 of the Dodd-Frank Act).

Finally, the creditor must disclose the total amount of interest that the consumer will pay over the life of the loan as a percentage of the principal of the loan (TILA Sec. 128(a)(19), as added by Sec. 1419 of the Dodd-Frank Act).

▶ **Effective date.** The provision take effect one day after the date of enactment (Sec. 4 of the Dodd-Frank Wall Street Reform and Consumer Protection Act).

Law source: Law at ¶11,419 and ¶10,004. Committee Report at ¶55,038.

— Sec. 1419 of the Dodd-Frank Wall Street Reform and Consumer Protection Act, adding Truth in Lending Act Secs. 128(a)(16), (17), (18) and (19);

— Sec. 4, providing the effective date.

¶6590 Monthly Statement Disclosures

The creditor, assignee or servicer of a residential mortgage loan must provide to the consumer, for each billing cycle, a statement setting forth certain items, if applicable, in a conspicuous and prominent manner (TILA Sec. 128(f)(1), as added by Sec. 1420 of the Dodd-Frank Act).

These items must include:

- the amount of the principal;
- the current interest rate on the loan;
- the date on which the interest rate may next reset or adjust;
- the amount of the prepayment fee, if any;
- a description of late payment fees;
- contact information the consumer may use to obtain information about the loan;
- contact information for counseling agencies or programs approved by the Department of Housing and Urban Development or state housing finance authority; and
- any information the Federal Reserve Board may require.

These requirements do not apply to any fixed rate residential mortgage loan where the creditor, assignee or servicer provides the obligor with a coupon book containing substantially the same information (TILA Sec. 128(f)(2), as added by Sec. 1420 of the Dodd-Frank Act).

The Fed must adopt a standard form for the required disclosures (TILA Sec. 128(f)(3), as added by Sec. 1420 of the Dodd-Frank Act).

▶ **Effective date.** The provision takes effect one day after the date of enactment (Sec. 4 of the Dodd-Frank Wall Street Reform and Consumer Protection Act).

Law source: Law at ¶11,420 and ¶10,004. Committee Report at ¶55,039.

— Sec. 1420 of the Dodd-Frank Wall Street Reform and Consumer Protection Act, adding Truth in Lending Act Sec. 128(f);

— Sec. 4, providing the effective date.

¶6595 Government Accountability Office Report

The Comptroller General of the Government Accountability Office is required to conduct a study to determine the effects the Dodd-Frank Act will have on the availability and affordability of credit for consumers, small businesses, homebuyers and mortgage lending (Sec. 1421(a) of the Dodd-Frank Act).

The report must also include an analysis of the effect of the Dodd-Frank Act on the capital reserves and funding of lenders of credit risk retention provisions for non-qualified mortgages (Sec. 1421(c) and (d) of the Dodd-Frank Act).

The Comptroller General must submit the report, with recommendations to Congress, within one year of the date of enactment of the Dodd-Frank Act (Sec. 1421(b) of the Dodd-Frank Act).

▶ **Effective date.** The provision takes effect one day after the date of enactment (Sec. 4 of the Dodd-Frank Wall Street Reform and Consumer Protection Act).

Law source: Law at ¶11,421 and ¶10,004. Committee Report at ¶55,042.
— Sec. 1421 of the Dodd-Frank Wall Street Reform and Consumer Protection Act;
— Sec. 4, providing the effective date.

¶6600 State Attorney General Enforcement Authority

The Dodd-Frank Act authorizes state attorneys general to bring an action to enforce the requirements of Title XIV, Subtitle A (residential mortgage loan origination) and Subtitle B (minimum standards for residential mortgage loans) (TILA Sec. 130(e), as amended by Sec. 1422 of the Dodd-Frank Act).

▶ **Effective date.** The provision takes effect one day after the date of enactment (Sec. 4 of the Dodd-Frank Wall Street Reform and Consumer Protection Act).

Law source: Law at ¶11,422 and ¶10,004. Committee Report at ¶55,043.
— Sec. 1422 of the Dodd-Frank Wall Street Reform and Consumer Protection Act, amending Truth in Lending Act Sec. 130(e);
— Sec. 4, providing the effective date.

HIGH-COST MORTGAGES

¶6605 Definitions Relating to High-Cost Mortgages

Title XIV, Subtitle C, of the Dodd-Frank Wall Street Reform and Consumer Protection Act prescribes standards for points and fees related to high-cost mortgages, open-end consumer credit plans and bona fide discount points and prepayment penalties by amending the Truth in Lending Act (TILA).

The term "high-cost mortgage" refers to certain consumer credit transactions, other than reverse mortgages, that are secured by the consumer's principal dwelling (TILA Sec. 103(aa)(1)(A), as amended by Sec. 1431(a) of the Dodd-Frank Act).

If the credit transaction is secured by a first mortgage on the consumer's principal dwelling, the mortgage is high-cost if the annual percentage rate (APR) at consummation of the transaction will exceed by more than 6.5 percentage points (8.5 percent if the dwelling is personal property and the transaction is for less than $50,000) the average prime offer rate for a comparable transaction (TILA Sec. 103(aa)(1)(A)(i)(I), as amended by Sec. 1431(a) of the Dodd-Frank Act).

If the credit transaction is secured by a subordinate or junior lien on the consumer's principal dwelling, the mortgage is high-cost if the APR at the time of consummation of the transaction will exceed by more than 8.5 percentage points the average prime offer rate for a comparable transaction (TILA Sec. 103(aa)(1)(A)(i)(II), as amended by Sec. 1431(a) of the Dodd-Frank Act).

The residential mortgage is high-cost if the total points and fees due in connection with the transaction, other than bona fide third-party charges not retained by the mortgage originator, creditor or an affiliate, exceed 5 percent of the total for transactions of

$20,000 or more, or the lesser of 8 percent of the total or $1,000 for transactions less than $20,000. The Federal Reserve Board may prescribe by regulation a different dollar amount (TILA Sec. 103(aa)(1)(A)(ii), as amended by Sec. 1431(a) of the Dodd-Frank Act).

A mortgage also is considered high-cost if the credit transaction documents allow the creditor to charge or collect prepayment fees or penalties more than 36 months after the closing of the transaction or if the penalties exceed more than 2 percent of the amount prepaid (TILA Sec. 103(aa)(1)(A)(iii), as amended by Sec. 1431(a) of the Dodd-Frank Act).

Introductory Rates.—The APR for purposes of the definition of high-cost mortgage is determined based on the following interest rates:

- for a fixed-rate transaction in which the APR will not vary during the term of the loan, the interest rate is the rate in effect on the date the transaction is consummated.

- in the case of a transaction in which the rate of interest varies solely in accordance with an index, the interest rate is the rate determined by adding the index rate in effect on the date of consummation to the maximum margin permitted at any time during the transaction.

- for any other transactions in which the rate may vary during the life of the loan for any reason, the interest rate is the interest charged on the transaction at the maximum rate that may be charged during the term of the transaction (TILA Sec. 103(aa)(1)(B), as amended by Sec. 1431(a) of the Dodd-Frank Act).

Mortgage Insurance.—For the purpose of calculating total points and fees, the definition of points and fees excludes:

- any premium provided by a federal or state agency;

- any amount not in excess of the amount payable under policies in effect at the time of origination under the National Housing Act, provided that the premium, charge or fee is required to be refundable on a pro-rated basis and the refund is automatically issued on notification of the satisfaction of the mortgage loan; and

- any premium paid by the consumer after closing (TILA Sec. 103(aa)(1)(C), as amended by Sec. 1431(a) of the Dodd-Frank Act).

Adjustment of Percentage Points.—An increase or decrease may not result in the number of percentage points for a first mortgage on the consumer's principal dwelling being less than 6 percentage points or greater than 10 percentage points. In addition, for a subordinate lien on the consumer's principal dwelling, an increase or decrease may not result in the number of percentage points being less than 8 or greater than 12 (TILA Sec. 103(aa)(2)(B), as amended by Sec. 1431(b) of the Dodd-Frank Act).

Points and Fees.—Points and fees include compensation paid directly or indirectly by a consumer to a creditor or mortgage originator from any source, including a mortgage originator that also is the creditor in a table-funded transaction (TILA Sec. 103(aa)(4), as amended by Sec. 1431(c)(1) of the Dodd-Frank Act).

The definition of points and fees also includes:

- premiums or other charges payable at or before closing for credit life, credit disability, credit unemployment, credit property insurance or other insurance, as well as payments for debt cancellation or suspension agreement. Insurance premiums or debt cancellation or suspension fees calculated and paid in full on a monthly basis are not considered financed by the creditor;
- the maximum prepayment fees and penalties that may be charged or collected under the terms of the credit transaction; and
- all prepayment fees or penalties incurred by the consumer if the loan refinances a previous loan made or held by the same creditor or an affiliate of the creditor.

Points and fees for open-end consumer credit plans are calculated by adding the total points and fees known at or before the closing of the transaction, including the maximum prepayment penalties that may be charged under the terms of the credit transaction plus the minimum additional fees the consumer would be required to pay to draw down an amount equal to the credit line (TILA Sec. 103(aa)(5), as added by Sec. 1431(c)(2) of the Dodd-Frank Act).

Bona Fide Discount Points and Prepayment Penalties.—For the purposes of determining the amounts of points and fees, one of the two following amounts are excluded:

(1) An amount up to and including 2 bona fide discount points payable by the consumer, but only if the interest rate from which the mortgage's interest rate will be discounted does not exceed by more than 1 percentage point:

- the average prime offer rate; or
- if secured by a personal property loan, the average rate on a loan in connection with which insurance is provided under Title I of the National Housing Act (TILA Sec. 103(dd)(1), as added by Sec. 1431(d) of the Dodd-Frank Act).

(2) Unless 2 bona fide discount points have been excluded by the previous paragraph, an amount up to and including 1 bona fide discount point payable by the consumer, but only if the interest rate from which the mortgage's interest rate will be discounted does not exceed by more than 2 percentage points:

- the average prime offer rate; or
- if secured by a personal property loan, the average rate on a loan in connection with which insurance is provided under Title I of the National Housing Act (TILA Sec. 103(dd)(2), as added by Sec. 1431(d) of the Dodd-Frank Act).

Neither of these descriptions applies to discount points used to purchase an interest rate reduction unless the amount of the interest rate reduction purchased is reasonably consistent with industry norms and practices for secondary mortgage market transactions (TILA Sec. 103(dd)(4), as added by Sec. 1431(d) of the Dodd-Frank Act).

▶ **Effective date.** The provision takes effect one day after the date of enactment (Sec. 4 of the Dodd-Frank Wall Street Reform and Consumer Protection Act).

Law source: Law at ¶11,431 and ¶10,004. Committee Report at ¶55,045.

— Sec. 1431(a) of the Dodd-Frank Wall Street Reform and Consumer Protection Act, amending Truth in Lending Act Sec.103(aa)(1);

— Sec. 1431(b), amending Truth in Lending Act Sec.103(aa)(2)(B);
— Sec. 1431(c)(1), amending Truth in Lending Act Sec.103(aa)(4);
— Sec. 1431(c)(2), adding Truth in Lending Act Sec.103(aa)(5);
— Sec. 1431(d), adding Truth in Lending Act Sec.103(dd);
— Sec. 4, providing the effective date.

¶6610 Amendments to Existing Requirements

The Dodd-Frank Act repeals an exception to the general rule that a high rate, high fee mortgage may not contain any terms under which a consumer must pay a penalty for prepaying all or part of the principal on the loan before the date on which the principal is due (TILA Sec. 129(c)(2), as repealed by Sec. 1432(a) of the Dodd-Frank Act). Under the prior exception, the mortgage could contain a prepayment penalty if at the time the mortgage was consummated:

- the consumer was not liable for an amount of monthly indebtedness payments that was greater than 50 percent of the monthly gross income of the consumer; and
- the income and expenses of the consumer were verified by a financial statement signed by the consumer, by a credit report, and in the case of employment income, by payment records or by verification from the employer of the consumer.

The Dodd-Frank Act also provides that a high-cost mortgage may not contain a balloon payment—a scheduled payment that is more than twice as large as the average of earlier scheduled payments. This provision does not apply when the payment schedule is adjusted to the seasonal or irregular income of the consumer or in the case of a balance due under the terms of a reverse mortgage (TILA Sec. 129(e), as amended by Sec. 1432(b) of the Dodd-Frank Act).

▶ **Effective date.** The provision takes effect one day after the date of enactment (Sec. 4 of the Dodd-Frank Wall Street Reform and Consumer Protection Act).

Law source: Law at ¶11,432 and ¶10,004. Committee Report at ¶55,046.

— Sec. 1432(a) of the Dodd-Frank Wall Street Reform and Consumer Protection Act, repealing Truth in Lending Act Sec. 129(c)(2);
— Sec. 1432(a), amending Truth in Lending Act Sec. 129(e);
— Sec. 4, providing the effective date.

¶6615 Additional Requirements for Certain Mortgages

A creditor may not recommend or encourage default on a loan or other debt in connection with the closing of a high-cost mortgage that refinances all or part of an existing loan or debt (TILA Sec. 129(j), as added by Sec. 1433(a) of the Dodd-Frank Act).

A creditor may not impose a late payment charge or fee in connection with a high-cost mortgage in an amount in excess of 4 percent of the amount of the payment that is past due unless the loan documents specifically authorize the charge or fee. The creditor is not permitted to impose a charge or fee before the 15-day period following the date the payment is due or, if the interest on each installment is paid in advance, before the 30-day period following the date the payment is due (TILA Sec. 129(k)(1), as added by Sec. 1433(a) of the Dodd-Frank Act).

In addition, a creditor is prohibited from imposing a late payment fee or charge more than once for a single late payment (TILA Sec. 129(k)(1)(D), as added by Sec. 1433(a) of the Dodd-Frank Act).

If a payment is a full payment for the period, paid on its due date or within a stated grace period, and the only delinquency stems from a late fee or delinquency charge assessed on an earlier payment, a creditor cannot impose a late fee or delinquency charge on the payment (TILA Sec. 129(k)(2), as added by Sec. 1433(a) of the Dodd-Frank Act).

If the terms of a loan provide that a payment first be applied to a past-due principal balance, and the consumer fails to make an installment payment but subsequently resumes making installment payments without paying past due installments, the creditor is permitted to impose a separate late payment charge for any principal due—without deduction due to late fees or related fees—until the default is cured (TILA Sec. 129(k)(3), as added by Sec. 1433(a) of the Dodd-Frank Act).

Debt Acceleration.—The provisions of a high-cost mortgage may not permit a creditor to accelerate the debt, except when repayment has been accelerated by default in payment, pursuant to a due-on-sale provision or pursuant to a material violation of the loan unrelated to payment schedule (TILA Sec. 129(l), as added by Sec. 1433(a) of the Dodd-Frank Act).

Financing.—A creditor is barred from directly or indirectly financing any prepayment fee or penalty payable by the consumer in a refinancing transaction if the creditor or an affiliate holds the note being refinanced. A creditor also is prohibited from financing points or fees (TILA Sec. 129(m), as added by Sec. 1433(a) of the Dodd-Frank Act).

Evasions and Structuring.—A creditor may not take any action in connection with a high-cost mortgage to structure a loan transaction as an open-end credit plan or another form of loan or divide a loan transaction into separate parts for the purpose of evading the provisions of Title XIV of the Dodd-Frank Act (TILA Sec. 129(r), as added by Sec. 1433(b) of the Dodd-Frank Act).

Modification or Deferral Fees.—A creditor is prohibited from charging a consumer a fee to modify, renew, extend or amend a high-cost mortgage, or to defer payment on the mortgage (TILA Sec. 129(s), as added by Sec. 1433(c) of the Dodd-Frank Act).

Payoff Statement.—In general, a creditor or servicer cannot charge a fee for providing information on the balance due to pay off an outstanding balance on a high-cost mortgage. However, if the payoff statement is delivered by courier or facsimile, the creditor or servicer is permitted to charge a processing fee to cover the cost in an amount not exceeding an amount comparable to fees for similar services in connection with mortgages that are not high-cost mortgages. Prior to charging a transaction fee, the creditor or servicer must disclose the fee to the consumer.

If a creditor or servicer has provided payoff information without charge, except for a processing fee, on four occasions within a year, the creditor or servicer may charge a reasonable fee for providing the information during the remainder of the year.

A creditor or servicer must provide the payoff statement to the consumer within five business days after receiving a request for the information from the consumer (TILA Sec. 129(t), as added by Sec. 1433(d) of the Dodd-Frank Act).

Pre-Loan Counseling.—A creditor is barred from extending credit to a consumer under a high-cost mortgage without first receiving certification from a counselor approved by the Department of Housing and Urban Development (HUD) or, at the discretion of the HUD Secretary, a state housing finance authority stating that the consumer has received counseling as to the mortgage. The counselor cannot be employed by the creditor or any affiliates.

A counselor may not certify that a consumer has received counseling on the advisability of a high-cost mortgage unless the counselor can verify that the consumer has received the statements required by this section or the Real Estate Settlement Procedures Act (TILA Sec. 129(u), as added by Sec. 1433(e) of the Dodd-Frank Act).

Unintentional Violations.—A creditor in a high-cost loan who, acting in good faith, fails to comply with the TILA Sec. 129 mortgage requirements, will not have committed a violation if the consumer is notified—or discovers—the violation within 30 days of the loan closing and restitution is made along with any necessary adjustments to the loan to, at the consumer's choice, either make the loan satisfy requirements or change the terms in the loan so that it will no longer be a high-cost mortgage (TILA Sec. 129(v)(1), as added by Sec. 1433(f) the Dodd-Frank Act).

In addition, a creditor will not be in violation if within 60 days of the creditor's discovery or receipt of notification of an unintentional or bona fide error, the consumer is notified and offered the choice to make the loan satisfy the requirements of this section or change the terms, so that the loan is no longer a high-cost loan (TILA Sec. 129(v)(2), as added by Sec. 1433(f) the Dodd-Frank Act).

▶ **Effective date.** The provision takes effect one day after the date of enactment (Sec. 4 of the Dodd-Frank Wall Street Reform and Consumer Protection Act).

Law source: Law at ¶11,433 and ¶10,004. Committee Report at ¶55,047.

— Sec. 1433(a) of the Dodd-Frank Wall Street Reform and Consumer Protection Act, adding Truth in Lending Act Secs. 129(j), (k), (l) and (m);

— Sec. 1433(b), adding Truth in Lending Act Sec. 129(r);

— Sec. 1433(c), adding Truth in Lending Act Sec. 129(s);

— Sec. 1433(d), adding Truth in Lending Act Sec. 129(t);

— Sec. 1433(e), adding Truth in Lending Act Sec. 129(u);

— Sec. 1433(f), adding Truth in Lending Act Sec. 129(v);

— Sec. 4, providing the effective date.

OFFICE of HOUSING COUNSELING

¶6620 Establishment of Housing Counseling Office

Title XIV, Subtitle D, of the Dodd-Frank Wall Street Reform and Consumer Protection Act may be cited as the Expand and Preserve Home Ownership Through Counseling Act (Sec. 1441 of the Dodd-Frank Act).

The legislation establishes within the Department of Housing and Urban Development (HUD) the Office of Housing Counseling (OHC). Under Title XIV, a Director of Housing Counseling is appointed by and reports to the HUD Secretary. The Director has primary responsibility for all activities and matters relating to homeownership and rental housing counseling.

The Director will establish rules necessary for, among other things:

- implementing the counseling procedures under Sec. 106(g)(1) of the Housing and Urban Development Act of 1968 (HUD Act);
- executing all other functions of the HUD Secretary under Sec. 106(g) of the HUD Act;
- contributing to the preparation and distribution of home buying information booklets under the Real Estate Settlement Procedures Act;
- implementing the assistance program under Sec. 106(a)(4) of the HUD Act; and
- executing functions concerning abusive, deceptive or unscrupulous lending practices relating to residential mortgage loans. (HUD Act Sec. 4(g), as added by Sec. 1442 of the Dodd-Frank Act).

Advisory Committee.—An advisory committee, appointed by the HUD Secretary, will provide advice on the execution of functions by the Director, but will have no role in reviewing or awarding housing counseling grants.

The advisory committee will consist of a maximum of 12 members, with the membership equally representing the mortgage and real estate industries, including consumers and housing counseling agencies certified by the Secretary. In general, the Secretary will appoint the members for a three-year term (HUD Act Sec. 4(g)(4), as added by Sec. 1442 of the Dodd-Frank Act).

▶ **Effective date.** The provisions take effect one day after the date of enactment (Sec. 4 of the Dodd-Frank Wall Street Reform and Consumer Protection Act).

Law source: Law at ¶11,441, ¶11,442 and ¶10,004. Committee Report at ¶55,055 and ¶55,056.

— Sec. 1441 of the Dodd-Frank Wall Street Reform and Consumer Protection Act, providing the short title of Title VII, Subtitle D;

— Sec. 1442, adding Department of Housing and Urban Development Act Sec. 4(g);

— Sec. 4, providing the effective date.

¶6625 Counseling Procedures

The HUD Secretary is required to establish, coordinate and monitor HUD's counseling procedures for homeownership and rental housing, including all requirements, standards and performance measures relating to homeownership and rental housing counseling.

The term "homeownership counseling" means counseling related to homeownership and residential mortgage loans.

The term "rental housing counseling" means counseling related to rental of residential property, which can include counseling on future homeownership opportunities and referrals for renters and prospective renters to counseling organizations (HUD Act Sec. 106(g)(1), as added by Sec. 1443 of the Dodd-Frank Act).

The HUD Secretary is required to develop standards for materials and forms to be used by homeownership counseling organizations (HUD Act Sec. 106(g)(2), as added by Sec. 1443 of the Dodd-Frank Act).

Mortgage Software.—The HUD Secretary must provide for the certification of computer software programs for consumers to use in evaluating residential mortgage loan proposals. To be certified, mortgage software systems must take into account:

- the consumer's financial situation and the cost of maintaining a home;
- the amount of time the consumer expects to remain in the home or expected time to maturity of the loan; and
- other appropriate factors intended to assist the consumer.

If the HUD Secretary determines that existing software is inadequate to assist consumers during the residential mortgage loan application process, the Secretary is required to arrange for the development of new software mortgage systems by the private sector.

Certified software programs must be used to supplement rather than replace housing counseling. Programs must be initially used only in connection with the assistance of certified housing counselors.

After the period of initial availability, the Secretary is directed to take reasonable steps to make certified mortgage software systems widely available through the Internet and at public locations.

The provisions on mortgage software systems will be effective only to the extent that funds to implement the requirements are available in advance (HUD Act Sec. 106(g)(3), as added by Sec. 1443 of the Dodd-Frank Act).

National Public Service Campaigns.—The Director of Housing Counseling is required to develop, implement and conduct national public service multimedia campaigns intended to make potentially vulnerable consumers—those facing mortgage foreclosure or considering a subprime mortgage loan to purchase a home, elderly persons, those with language barriers, low-income persons and minorities, among others—aware of the need for counseling before seeking or maintaining a residential mortgage loan.

The legislation authorizes appropriations to the Secretary up to $3,000,000 for fiscal years 2009 through 2011 for the development, implementation and maintenance of the national public service media campaigns (HUD Act Sec. 106(g)(4), as added by Sec. 1443 of the Dodd-Frank Act).

Foreclosure Rescue Education.—Ten percent of the appropriations allocated to the HUD Secretary for national public service media campaigns must be used by the Director of Housing Counseling to conduct education programs in areas that have a high density of foreclosure. The programs must include direct mailings to persons in these areas that describe foreclosure rescue scams, predatory lending mortgage agreements, for-profit foreclosure counseling services and local counseling resources approved by HUD.

The program must emphasize service to communities having a high percentage of retirement communities or low-income minorities (HUD Act Sec. 106(g)(4)(D), as added by Sec. 1443 of the Dodd-Frank Act).

The Secretary must provide advice and technical assistance to states, local governments and non-profit organizations on the establishment and operation of educational programs designed to inform consumers about home mortgages, refinancing, home equity loans, home repair loans and flood or other disaster insurance coverage, where appropriate (HUD Act Sec. 106(g)(5), as added by Sec. 1443 of the Dodd-Frank Act).

▶ **Effective date.** The provision take effect one day after the date of enactment.

Law source: Law at ¶11,443 and ¶10,004. Committee Report at ¶55,056.

— Sec. 1443(a) of the Dodd-Frank Wall Street Reform and Consumer Protection Act, adding Department of Housing and Urban Development Act of 1968 Sec. 106(g);

— Sec. 1443(b), adding Department of Housing and Urban Development Act of 1968 Sec. 106(c)(5)(A)(ii)(V);

— Sec. 4, providing the effective date.

¶6630 Grants for Housing Counseling

The HUD Secretary must make financial assistance available to HUD-approved and state housing counseling agencies. The Secretary also must establish standards and guidelines for the eligibility of organizations to receive assistance (HUD Act Sec. 106(a)(4)(A) and (B), as added by Sec. 1444 of the Dodd-Frank Act).

Available assistance must be distributed in a way that encourages successful counseling programs. Methods must ensure adequate distribution in rural areas that have traditionally low levels of access to counseling services. The Secretary must give priority to entities in areas with the highest home foreclosure levels (HUD Act Sec. 106(a)(4)(C), as added by Sec. 1444 of the Dodd-Frank Act).

Funds may not be distributed to organizations that have been convicted of violations relating to an election for federal office or that employ "applicable individuals."

"Applicable individuals" means employees who are employed, contracted or retained by the organization or are acting on behalf of the organization with the authority of the organization and who have been convicted of violating federal law as to an election for federal office (HUD Act Sec. 106(a)(4)(D), as added by Sec. 1444 of the Dodd-Frank Act).

The legislation authorizes appropriations of $45,000,000 for fiscal years 2009 through 2011 for housing counseling assistance (HUD Act Sec. 106(a)(4)(F), as added by the Dodd-Frank Act).

▶ **Effective date.** The provision takes effect one day after the date of enactment.

Law source: Law at ¶11,444 and ¶10,004. Committee Report at ¶55,057.

— Sec. 1444 of the Dodd-Frank Wall Street Reform and Consumer Protection Act, adding Department of Housing and Urban Development Act of 1968 Sec. 106(a)(4);

— Sec. 4, providing the effective date.

¶6635 Requirements to Use HUD-Certified Counselors

An organization that receives assistance for homeownership or rental housing counseling must be certified by the HUD Secretary as competent to provide counseling (HUD Act Sec. 106(e)(1), as amended by Sec. 1445(1) of the Dodd-Frank Wall Street Reform and Consumer Protection Act).

The HUD Secretary is required to take any actions necessary to ensure that individuals and organizations that provide homeownership or rental housing counseling are made aware of certification requirements and standards (HUD Act Sec. 106(e)(4), as added by Sec. 1445(5) of the Dodd-Frank Act).

▶ **Effective date.** The provision takes effect one day after the date of enactment.

Law source: Law at ¶11,445 and ¶10,004. Committee Report at ¶55,058.

— Sec. 1445 of the Dodd-Frank Wall Street Reform and Consumer Protection Act, amending Department of Housing and Urban Development Act of 1968 Sec. 106(e);

— Sec. 4, providing the effective date.

¶6640 Study of Defaults and Foreclosures

The Dodd-Frank Act requires the HUD Secretary to conduct a study examining the causes of home loan defaults and foreclosures using all empirical data available.

The HUD study also must include the role of escrow accounts in aiding prime and nonprime borrowers to avoid defaults and foreclosures, as well as the part played by computer registries of mortgages, including those used for trading mortgage loans (Sec. 1446 of the Dodd-Frank Act).

▶ **Effective date.** The HUD Secretary must submit to Congress a preliminary report on the study no later than 12 months from the date of enactment of the Dodd-Frank Wall Street Reform and Consumer Protection Act. The Secretary must submit to Congress a final report detailing the findings of the study, including the Secretary's recommendations, no later than 24 months from the date of enactment of the Dodd-Frank Act.

Law source: Law at ¶11,446. Committee Report at ¶55,059.

— Sec. 1446 of the Dodd-Frank Wall Street Reform and Consumer Protection Act;

— Sec. 1446, providing the effective date.

¶6645 Default and Disclosure Database

The legislation requires the HUD Secretary to establish and maintain a database of information on foreclosures and defaults on mortgage loans for one- to four-unit residential properties and to make the information available to the public.

In establishing the database, the Secretary is directed to consult with federal banking agencies involved with residential mortgage lending and servicing (Sec. 1447(a) of the Dodd-Frank Act).

The information must include the number and percentage of:

- mortgage loans delinquent by more than 30 days;
- mortgage loans delinquent by more than 90 days;
- properties that are real-estate owned;
- mortgage loans that are within the foreclosure process; and
- mortgage loans that have an outstanding principal amount greater than the value of the property for which the loan was made.

The information also should include any items the Secretary considers appropriate (Sec. 1447(c) of the Dodd-Frank Act).

In establishing and maintaining the database, the Secretary is subject to the standards applicable to federal agencies for the protection and confidentiality of personally identifiable information and for data security and integrity. The Secretary must collect and make this information available, in accordance with monitoring provisions in Sec. 1022(c) of the Dodd-Frank Act for Bureau of Consumer Financial Protection rulemaking, to protect privacy and confidentiality (Sec. 1447(e) of the Dodd-Frank Act).

▶ **Effective date.** The provision takes effect one day after the date of enactment.

Law source: Law at ¶11,447 and ¶10,004. Committee Report at ¶55,059.

— Sec. 1447 of the Dodd-Frank Wall Street Reform and Consumer Protection Act;
— Sec. 4, providing the effective date.

¶6650 Definitions for Counseling-Related Programs

The Dodd-Frank Act sets out various definitions related to counseling programs. The term "nonprofit organization" has the same meaning of the term in the Cranston-Gonzalez National Affordable Housing Act, with the exception of subparagraph D (HUD Act Sec. 106(h)(1), as added by Sec. 1448 of the Dodd-Frank Act).

The Cranston-Gonzalez Act defines, minus subparagraph D, a nonprofit organization as a private nonprofit organization, including a state or locally chartered organization, that is organized under state or local laws, has no part of its net earnings inuring to the benefit of any member, founder, contributor or individual, and complies with standards of financial accountability acceptable to the HUD Secretary.

The legislation defines the term "HUD-approved counseling agency" as a private or public nonprofit organization that is exempt from taxation under Sec. 501(c) of the Internal Revenue Code and certified by the Secretary of HUD.

"State housing finance agency" means a public body, agency or instrumentality created specifically under state law that is authorized to finance activities designed to provide housing and related facilities in the state through land acquisition, construction or rehabilitation (HUD Act Sec. 106(h)(4), as added by Sec. 1448 of the Dodd-Frank Act).

▶ **Effective date.** The provision takes effect one day after the date of enactment.

Law source: Law at ¶11,448 and ¶10,004. Committee Report at ¶55,060.

— Sec. 1448 of the Dodd-Frank Wall Street Reform and Consumer Protection Act, adding Department of Housing and Urban Development Act of 1968 Sec. 106(h);

— Sec. 4, providing the effective date.

¶6655 Accountability and Transparency for Grant Recipients

The HUD Secretary must develop and maintain a system to ensure that an organization that receives "covered assistance" uses all funds in accordance with foreclosure legal assistance and grant recipient provisions (HUD Act Sec. 106(i)(1)(A), as added by Sec. 1449 of the Dodd-Frank Act).

"Covered assistance" means a grant or other financial aid provided under Sec. 1449 of the Dodd-Frank Act (HUD Act Sec. 106(i)(3), as added by Sec. 1449 of the Dodd-Frank Act).

The legislation requires the Secretary to mandate that an organization comply with all requirements that the Secretary establishes as a condition to receiving covered assistance. These requirements include appropriate periodic financial and grant activity reporting, record retention and audits for the period in which the organization receives assistance to ensure compliance (HUD Act Sec. 106(i)(1)(B), as added by Sec. 1449 of the Dodd-Frank Act).

If the Secretary finds that an organization receiving covered assistance has used any of the assistance in a way that is materially in violation of the Dodd-Frank Act or regulations adopted in response to the Act, the Secretary will require that the organization reimburse the Secretary for the amount of the misused amounts and return any unused amounts within 12 months of the finding of misuse. The organization will be ineligible to receive any further covered assistance (HUD Act Sec. 106(i)(2), as added by Sec. 1449 of the Dodd-Frank Act).

▶ **Effective date.** The provision takes effect one day after the date of enactment.

Law source: Law at ¶11,449 and ¶10,004. Committee Report at ¶55,057.

— Sec. 1449 of the Dodd-Frank Wall Street Reform and Consumer Protection Act, adding Department of Housing and Urban Development Act of 1968 Sec. 106(i);

— Sec. 4, providing the effective date.

¶6660 Mortgage Information Booklet

The Director of the Bureau of Consumer Financial Protection must prepare a new mortgage information booklet to assist consumers applying for federally-related mortgages to understand the process and costs of real estate settlement services. The Director must issue the booklet at least once every five years, in various languages and cultural styles.

The Director must distribute the booklet to all lenders that make federally-related mortgage loans. Along with the booklets, the Director must provide lenders with lists organized by location of certified homeownership counselors (RESPA Sec. 5(a) as amended by Sec. 1450(2) of the Dodd-Frank Act).

Contents.—The booklets must be written in plain, understandable language (RESPA Sec. 5(b) as amended by the Dodd-Frank Act).

The booklets must contain:

- a description and explanation of the nature and purpose of the costs related to a real estate settlement or a federally related mortgage loan, including specific information on: balloon payments, prepayment penalties, the advantages of prepayment, and the trade-off between closing costs and the interest rate over the life of the loan;
- an explanation and sample of the uniform settlement statement required by RESPA;
- a list and explanation of lending practices, including those prohibited under the Truth in Lending Act (TILA) and other federal law, as well as other unfair practices and unreasonable or unnecessary charges that a borrower should avoid;
- an explanation of the right of rescission for transactions under TILA Secs. 125 and 129;
- a brief explanation of a variable rate mortgage and a reference to the booklet "Consumer Handbook on Adjustable Rate Mortgages" or to any suitable substitute;
- a brief explanation of a home equity line of credit and a reference to the pamphlet required to be provided under TILA Sec. 127A;
- information about homeownership counseling services, a recommendation that the consumer use the services and a notice that a list of certified providers of homeownership counseling in the area, and their contact information, is available;
- an explanation of escrow accounts as used in residential real estate transactions and the requirements under Subtitle E of Title XIV of the Dodd-Frank Act;
- information on the choices available to buyers of residential real estate when selecting persons to provide necessary services relating to a real estate settlement;
- an explanation of a consumer's responsibilities, liabilities and obligations in a mortgage transaction;
- information on real estate appraisals and the difference between appraisals and home inspections; and
- a notice that HUD's Office of Housing has made available to the public a brochure on loan fraud and contact information to obtain the brochure (RESPA Sec. 5(c) as amended by Sec. 1450(2) of the Dodd-Frank Act).

In preparing the booklet, the Bureau Director must consider differences in real estate procedures among states and U.S. territories, as well as among political subdivisions within states and territories (RESPA Sec. 5(c) as amended by Sec. 1450(2) of the Dodd-Frank Act).

Lenders must include with the booklet a reasonably complete or updated list of certified homeownership counselors located in the lender's area (RESPA Sec. 5(c) as amended by Sec. 1450(3) of the Dodd-Frank Act).

Finally, a lender must provide the HUD-issued booklet in the version most appropriate to the person receiving it (RESPA Sec. 5(d) as amended by Sec. 1450(4) of the Dodd-Frank Act).

▶ **Effective date.** The provision take effect one day after the date of enactment.

Law source: Law at ¶11,450 and ¶10,004. Committee Report at ¶55,061.

— Sec. 1450(1) of the Dodd-Frank Wall Street Reform and Consumer Protection Act, amending Real Estate Settlement Procedures Act Sec. 5 heading;

— Sec. 1450(2), amending Real Estate Settlement Procedures Act Sec. 5(a) and (b);

— Sec. 1450(3), amending Real Estate Settlement Procedures Act Sec. 5(c);

— Sec. 1450(4), amending Real Estate Settlement Procedures Act Sec. 5(d);

— Sec. 4, providing the effective date.

¶6665 Home Inspection Counseling

The HUD Secretary must take whatever steps are necessary to inform potential homebuyers of the availability and importance of obtaining an independent home inspection (Sec. 1451(a)(1) of the Dodd-Frank Act).

These steps must include the following, in both English and Spanish:

- publication of the HUD/Federal Housing Administration (FHA) form HUD 92564-CN and HUD/FHA booklet entitled "For Your Protection: Get a Home Inspection";
- development and publication of a HUD booklet entitled "For Your Protection: Get a Home Inspection" that does not reference FHA-insured homes; and
- publication of the HUD document entitled "Ten Important Questions To Ask Your Home Inspector."

The HUD Secretary must make these materials available for electronic access and, where appropriate, inform potential homebuyers of the availability through home purchase counseling public service announcements and toll-free HUD hotlines. The Secretary must give emphasis to reaching first-time and low-income homebuyers (Sec. 1451(a)(2) of the Dodd-Frank Act).

The HUD Secretary may periodically update the materials as appropriate (Sec. 1451(a)(3) of the Dodd-Frank Act).

A mortgagee approved for participation in the mortgage insurance programs under Title II of the National Housing Act must provide potential homebuyers with the required materials. The materials must be provided at the lender's first contact—pre-qualification, pre-approval or initial application–with the homebuyer (Sec. 1451(b) of the Dodd-Frank Act).

A counseling agency certified by HUD to provide housing counseling services must provide each of its clients with the required materials (Sec. 1451(c) of the Dodd-Frank Act).

Training.—Training provided by HUD for counseling agencies, whether the training is supplied directly by HUD or by an outside source, must include how to provide information about:

- counseling potential homebuyers on the availability and importance of getting an independent home inspection;
- the home inspection process, including the reasons for specific inspections such as radon and lead-based paint testing; and
- advising potential homebuyers on how to locate and select a qualified home inspector.

The training also must include a review of HUD's home inspection public outreach materials (Sec. 1451(d) of the Dodd-Frank Act).

▶ **Effective date.** The provision takes effect one day after the date of enactment.

Law source: Law at ¶11,451 and ¶10,004. Committee Report at ¶55,062.

— Sec. 1451 of the Dodd-Frank Wall Street Reform and Consumer Protection Act;
— Sec. 4, providing the effective date.

¶6670 Warnings to Homeowners of Foreclosure Rescue Scams

Of any amounts made available for a fiscal year under the HUD Act, 10 percent must be used only for assistance to the Neighborhood Reinvestment Corporation (NRC). Funds must be used for activities that inform borrowers who are delinquent on payments on a residential mortgage loan of fraudulent activities associated with foreclosure (Sec. 1452(a) of the Dodd-Frank Act).

The NRC must use the funds to carry out activities that inform borrowers that:

- the foreclosure process is complex and can be confusing;
- borrowers may be approached during the foreclosure process by persons about saving their homes, and borrowers should use caution in dealings with these persons;
- there are federal government and nonprofit agencies that may provide information about the foreclosure process, including HUD;
- borrowers should contact their lender immediately; and
- borrowers should contact HUD to find a counseling agency certified by HUD to assist in avoiding foreclosure or visit HUD's website for tips on avoiding foreclosure.

The information also must include contact information for the loan servicer or successor, HUD's housing counseling line and links to HUD's websites for housing counseling (Sec. 1452(b) of the Dodd-Frank Act).

▶ **Effective date.** The provision takes effect one day after the date of enactment.

Law source: Law at ¶11,452 and ¶10,004.

— Sec. 1452 of the Dodd-Frank Wall Street Reform and Consumer Protection Act;

— Sec. 4, providing the effective date.

MORTGAGE SERVICING

¶6675 Escrow and Impound Accounts

A creditor in connection with a consumer credit transaction secured by a first lien on the principal dwelling of the consumer must establish before consummation of the transaction an escrow or impound account for mandatory periodic payments or premiums including taxes, insurance and ground rents. This Truth in Lending Act (TILA) provision, added by the Dodd-Frank Wall Street Reform and Consumer Protection Act, exempts creditors connected with a consumer credit transaction under an open-end credit plan or a reverse mortgage (TILA Act Sec. 129D(a), as added by Sec. 1461(a) of the Dodd-Frank Act).

The Federal Reserve Board (Fed) may, by regulation, exempt from the requirements of Sec. 129D(a) a creditor that:

- operates predominantly in rural or underserved areas;
- together with all affiliates, has total annual mortgage loan originations that do not exceed a limit set by the Fed;
- retains its mortgage loan originations in portfolio; and
- meets any asset size threshold and any other criteria set by the Fed (TILA Act Sec. 129D(c), as added by Sec. 1461(a) of the Dodd-Frank Act)

Creditors cannot make an escrow or impound account a condition of a real property sale contract or a loan secured by a first deed of trust or mortgage on the consumer's principal dwelling, except when the:

- account is required by federal or state law or by regulation;
- loan is made, guaranteed or insured by a state or federal government lending or insuring agency;
- original principal obligation amount of the loan does not exceed the maximum limitation on the original principal obligation for a residence of the applicable size under the Federal Home Loan Mortgage Corporation Act (Home Loan Act), and the annual percentage rate (APR) will exceed the average prime offer for a comparable transaction by 1.5 or more percentage points; or
- original principal obligation amount of the loan exceeds the maximum limitation on the original principal obligation for a residence of the applicable size under the Home

Loan Act and the APR will exceed the average prime offer for a comparable transaction by 2.5 or more percentage points (TILA Act Sec. 129D(b), as added by Sec. 1461(a) of the Dodd-Frank Act).

An escrow or impound account must remain in existence for at least five years from consummation of the loan until sufficient equity exists so that private mortgage insurance is no longer required, or for a period of time required by regulation, unless the underlying mortgage is terminated (TILA Act Sec. 129D(d), as added by Sec. 1461(a) of the Dodd-Frank Act).

Creditors are not required to establish escrow or impound accounts for loans secured by shares in a cooperative. In addition, insurance premiums need not be included in escrow accounts for loans secured by dwellings or units where the borrower must join an association and that association must maintain a master insurance policy. (TILA Act Sec. 129D(e), as added by Sec. 1461(a) of the Dodd-Frank Act).

Administration of Escrow or Impound Accounts.—Creditors generally must establish escrow or impound accounts in a federally insured depository institution unless directed otherwise by law or regulation.

Except as otherwise provided, an escrow or impound account must be made in accordance with the:

- Real Estate Settlement Procedures Act of 1974 (RESPA) and its regulations;
- Flood Disaster Protection Act of 1973 and its regulations; and
- state law, if applicable, where the property securing the loan is located.

Creditors must pay interest to the consumer on the amount held in an impound, trust or escrow account as required by applicable state or federal law.

If a person has paid a fine, civil money penalty or other damages for an act or omission in violation of RESPA, this section does not apply to additional fines, penalties or other damages unless the act or omission violation also constitutes a direct violation of the section (TILA Act Sec. 129D(g), as added by Sec. 1461(a) of the Dodd-Frank Act).

Disclosures.—A creditor must make certain disclosures to a consumer when an escrow or impound account will be established at consummation of the consumer credit transaction. Disclosure must be by written notice, and the creditor must provide the notice within three business days before consummation.

The notice must include the:

- fact that an escrow or impound account will be established;
- amount required at closing to initially fund the account;
- estimated amount of mandatory periodic payments and premiums, including taxes and insurance, plus the value of improvements on the property, for the first year following consummation;
- estimated monthly amount to be escrowed for required periodic payments or premiums; and
- fact that if the consumer chooses to terminate the account in the future, after the required minimum of five years, the consumer will become responsible for required

¶6675

periodic payments or premiums unless a new account is established (TILA Act Sec. 129D(h), as added by Sec. 1461(a) of the Dodd Frank Act).

▶ **Effective date.** The provision takes effect one day after the date of enactment (Sec. 4 of the Dodd-Frank Wall Street Reform and Consumer Protection Act).

Law source: Law at ¶11,461 and ¶10,004. Committee Report at ¶55,065.

— Sec. 1461(a) of the Dodd-Frank Wall Street Reform and Consumer Protection Act, adding Truth in Lending Act Sec. 129D;

— Sec. 4, providing the effective date.

¶6680 Disclosure Notice for Consumers Who Waive Escrow Services

Creditors are required to provide a disclosure notice to consumers who waive escrow services if an impound, trust or escrow account for required periodic payments and premiums relating to a consumer credit transaction secured by real property is not established. Creditors also must provide a disclosure notice if a consumer chooses, by written notice to the creditor or servicer, to close the account (TILA Act Sec. 129D(j)(1), as added by Sec. 1462 of the Dodd-Frank Act).

The creditor or servicer must provide a timely and clearly written disclosure to the consumer that advises the consumer of the consumer's responsibilities and implications in choosing to waive services or close the account.

The disclosure must include:

- information about fees or costs associated with the waiver of escrow services or closing of the account;

- a clear and prominent notice that the consumer is responsible for directly paying non-escrowed items, in addition to paying the mortgage loan payment, and that the cost of these items can be substantial;

- a clear explanation of the consequences if the consumer fails to pay non-escrowed items, including the possible forced placement of insurance by the creditor or servicer and potentially higher cost or reduced coverage of creditor-placed insurance (TILA Act Sec. 129D(j)(2), as added by Sec. 1462 of the Dodd-Frank Act).

▶ **Effective date.** The provision takes effect one day after the date of enactment (Sec. 4 of the Dodd-Frank Wall Street Reform and Consumer Protection Act).

Law source: Law at ¶11,462 and ¶10,004. Committee Report at ¶55,066.

— Sec. 1462 of the Dodd-Frank Wall Street Reform and Consumer Protection Act, adding Truth in Lending Act Sec. 129D(j);

— Sec. 4, providing the effective date.

¶6685 Real Estate Settlement Procedures Act Amendments

RESPA is amended to prohibit the servicer of a federally-related mortgage loan from engaging in certain practices, including obtaining force-placed hazard insurance, unless there is reason to believe the borrower has failed to comply with the terms of the loan contract.

"Force-placed insurance" means hazard insurance coverage obtained by a servicer of a federally-related mortgage when the borrower has failed to maintain or renew hazard insurance on the property as required under the terms of the mortgage (RESPA Sec. 6(k)(2), as added by Sec. 1463(a) of the Dodd-Frank Act).

A servicer of a federally-related mortgage cannot obtain force-placed hazard insurance unless there is a reasonable basis to believe the borrower has failed to comply with the mortgage's requirement to maintain property insurance (RESPA Sec. 6(k)(1)(A), as added by Sec. 1463(a) of the Dodd-Frank Act).

In addition, the servicer cannot charge fees for responding to valid qualified written requests (to be defined in implementing regulations) (RESPA Sec. 6(k)(1)(B), as added by Sec. 1463(a) of the Dodd-Frank Act).

Servicers must make a timely response to a borrower's requests to correct errors relating to allocation of payments, final balances for paying off the loan or avoiding foreclosure, or other standard servicer's duties (RESPA Sec. 6(k)(1)(C), as added by Sec. 1463(a) of the Dodd-Frank Act).

If a borrower requests the identity and contact information for the owner assignee of the loan, a servicer must respond within 10 business days (RESPA Sec. 6(k)(1)(D), as added by Sec. 1463(a) of the Dodd-Frank Act).

Requirements for Force-Placed Insurance.—A servicer may not impose a charge for force-placed insurance unless the servicer: sends by first-class mail a written notice to the borrower; sends by first-class mail a second written notice at least 30 days after mailing the first notice; and has not received from the borrower proof of hazard insurance for the property by the end of the 15-day period after mailing the second notice (RESPA Sec. 6(l)(1), as added by Sec. 1463(a) of the Dodd-Frank Act).

The first and second notices to the borrower must contain a:

- reminder of the borrower's obligation to maintain hazard insurance on the property securing the federally related mortgage;
- statement that the servicer does not have evidence of insurance coverage of the property;
- clear and conspicuous statement of the procedures by which the borrower can provide evidence of insurance coverage; and
- statement that the servicer may obtain coverage at the borrower's expense if the borrower does not provide proof of insurance in a timely manner.

The servicer must accept as proof of coverage any reasonable form of written confirmation from a borrower of existing insurance coverage if the confirmation includes the insurance policy number and the identity of, and contact information for, the insurance company or agent (RESPA Sec. 6(l)(2), as added by Sec. 1463(a) of the Dodd-Frank Act).

Within 15 days of receiving confirmation of existing insurance coverage, the servicer must terminate the force-placed insurance and refund to the borrower all force-placed insurance premiums paid by the borrower during the period in which both the forced-placed coverage and the borrower's coverage were in effect, as well as any related fees charged to the borrower (RESPA Sec. 6(l)(3), as added by Sec. 1463(a) of the Dodd-Frank Act).

Limitations on Force-Placed Insurance Charges.—All charges, except for those subject to state regulation as the business of insurance, related to force-placed insurance must be bona fide and reasonable (RESPA Sec. 6(m), as added by Sec. 1463(a) of the Dodd-Frank Act).

Penalties.—Penalty amounts are increased for violations. The amendment doubles the maximum statutory RESPA penalties in individual cases from $1,000 to $2,000, and in class action cases from $500,000 to $1,000,000. The changes apply to all RESPA violations (RESPA Sec. 6(f), as amended by Sec. 1463(b) of the Dodd-Frank Act).

Response Times.—The amount of time that a loan servicer has to respond to borrower inquiries is decreased. Specifically, these changes require a servicer to acknowledge receipt of a qualified written request within five days (down from 20 days) and complete action on the inquiry within 30 days (down from 60 days), except that this 30-day period may be extended for not more than 15 days if the servicer notifies the borrower of the extension within the initial 30-day period and details the reasons for the delay in responding (RESPA Sec. 6(e), as amended by Sec. 1463(c) of the Dodd-Frank Act).

Prompt Escrow Refund.—A servicer must return any balance in an escrow account at the time the loan is paid off to the borrower within 20 business days or credit the balance to a similar account for a new mortgage loan with the same lender (RESPA Sec. 6(g), as amended by Sec. 1463(d) of the Dodd-Frank Act).

▶ **Effective date.** The provision takes effect one day after the date of enactment (Sec. 4 of the Dodd-Frank Wall Street Reform and Consumer Protection Act).

Law source: Law at ¶11,463 and ¶10,004. Committee Report at ¶55,067.

— Sec. 1463(a) of the Dodd-Frank Wall Street Reform and Consumer Protection Act, adding Real Estate Settlement Procedures Act of 1974 Secs. 6(k), (l) and (m);

— Sec. 1463(b), amending Real Estate Settlement Procedures Act of 1974 Sec. 6(f);

— Sec. 1463(c) amending Real Estate Settlement Procedures Act of 1974 Sec. 6(e);

— Sec. 1463(d) amending Real Estate Settlement Procedures Act of 1974 Sec. 6(g).

— Sec. 4, providing the effective date.

¶6690 Truth in Lending Act Amendments

TILA is amended to require prompt crediting of home loan payments and payoff statements.

The servicer of a consumer credit transaction secured by the consumer's principal dwelling must credit a payment to the consumer's loan account as of the date of receipt except when a delay in crediting does not result in a charge to the consumer or a report of negative information to a consumer reporting agency (TILA Sec. 129F(a), as added by Sec. 1464(a) of the Dodd-Frank Act).

If a servicer specifies in writing requirements for the consumer to follow when making payments but accepts a payment that does not conform to those requirements, the servicer must credit the payment as of five days after receiving it (TILA Sec. 129F(b), as added by Sec. 1464(a) of the Dodd-Frank Act).

Payoff Balance.—A creditor or servicer of a home loan must send an accurate payoff balance no later than seven business days after receiving a written request for the balance from the borrower (TILA Sec. 129G, as added by Sec. 1464(b) of the Dodd-Frank Act).

▶ **Effective date.** The provision takes effect one day after the date of enactment (Sec. 4 of the Dodd-Frank Wall Street Reform and Consumer Protection Act).

Law source: Law at ¶11,464 and ¶10,004. Committee Report at ¶55,068.

— Sec. 1464(a) of the Dodd-Frank Wall Street Reform and Consumer Protection Act, adding Truth in Lending Act Sec. 129F;

— Sec. 1464(b), adding Truth in Lending Act Sec. 129G.

— Sec. 4, providing the effective date.

¶6695 Escrows Included in Repayment Analysis

Amendments to TILA require that repayment disclosures in connection with a consumer credit transaction secured by a first mortgage or lien on the consumer's principal dwelling take into account the amount of periodic payments or premiums to an escrow account. The requirement does not apply to consumer credit transactions under an open-end credit plan or a reverse mortgage (TILA Sec. 128(b)(4)(A), as added by Sec. 1465 of the Dodd-Frank Act).

The amount taken into account must include the taxable assessed value of the real property securing the transaction after consummation of the transaction, the value of any improvements on the property and the replacement costs of the property for hazard insurance in the initial year after the transaction (TILA Sec. 128(b)(4)(B), as added by Sec. 1465 of the Dodd-Frank Act).

▶ **Effective date.** The provision takes effect one day after the date of enactment (Sec. 4 of the Dodd-Frank Wall Street Reform and Consumer Protection Act).

Law source: Law at ¶11,465 and ¶10,004. Committee Report at ¶55,069.

— Sec. 1465 of the Dodd-Frank Wall Street Reform and Consumer Protection Act, adding Truth Lending Act Sec. 128(b)(4);
— Sec. 4, providing the effective date.

APPRAISAL ACTIVITIES

¶6700 Property Appraisal Requirements

The Dodd-Frank Wall Street Reform and Consumer Protection Act adds new Truth in Lending Act (TILA) provisions that prohibit a creditor from making a higher-risk mortgage loan without first obtaining a written appraisal of the property to be mortgaged. The appraisal must be performed by a certified and licensed appraiser who conducts a physical property visit of the interior of the mortgaged property (TILA Sec. 129H, as added by Sec. 1471 of the Dodd-Frank Act).

The term "certified or licensed appraiser" means a person who, at a minimum, is certified or licensed by the state in which the property to be appraised is located and who performs each appraisal in compliance with the Uniform Standards of Professional Appraisal and Practice and Title XI of the Financial Institutions Reform, Recovery, and Enforcement Act of 1989 and its implementing regulations (TILA Sec. 129H(b)(3), as added by Sec. 1471 of the Dodd-Frank Act).

"Higher-risk mortgage" means a residential mortgage loan (other than a reverse mortgage that is a qualified mortgage) secured by a principal dwelling:

- that is not a qualified mortgage; and
- has an annual percentage rate (APR) that exceeds the average prime offer rate for a comparable transaction as of the date the interest rate is set.

For a first lien residential mortgage loan that has an original principal obligation amount that does not exceed the amount of the maximum limitation on the original principal obligation in effect for a residence of the applicable size as of the date the rate is set, the loan is higher-risk if the APR exceeds the prime offer rate by 1.5 or more percentage points.

If the original principal obligation exceeds the amount of the maximum limitation on the original principal obligation in effect for a comparable residence, the loan is higher-risk if the APR exceeds the average prime offer rate as of the date the interest rate is set by 2.5 percentage points. For a subordinate lien residential mortgage loan, the APR must exceed the annual prime offer rate by 3.5 points to be higher-risk (TILA Sec. 129H(f), as added by Sec. 1471 of the Dodd-Frank Act).

Second Appraisals.—A creditor must obtain a second appraisal if the purpose of the higher-risk mortgage is to finance the purchase or acquisition of the mortgaged property from a person within 180 days of the purchase or acquisition of the property by that person at a price lower than the current sale price of the property.

The second appraisal must be done by a different certified and licensed appraiser and include an analysis of the difference in sale prices, changes in market conditions and any improvements made to the property between the previous sale and the current sale.

The creditor may not charge the cost of the second appraisal to the applicant (TILA Sec. 129H(b)(2), as added by Sec. 1471 of the Dodd-Frank Act).

Regulations.—The Dodd-Frank Act directs the following agencies to jointly prescribe regulations implementing this section: Bureau of Consumer Financial Protection, Federal Reserve Board, Comptroller of the Currency, Federal Deposit Insurance Corporation, National Credit Union Administration and Federal Housing Finance Agency. The agencies may jointly exempt a class of loans from the requirements of this subsection if the agencies determine the exemption is in the public interest and promotes safety and soundness of creditors (TILA Sec. 129H(b)(4), as added by Sec. 1471 of the Dodd-Frank Act).

Additional Provisions.—A creditor must provide one copy of each appraisal of property with a higher-risk mortgage to the applicant without charge at least three days before the closing date (TILA Sec. 129H(c), as added by Sec. 1471 of the Dodd-Frank Act).

A creditor must provide an applicant with a statement at the time of the initial mortgage application that any appraisal prepared for the mortgage is for the sole use of the creditor, and the applicant may have an independent appraisal conducted at the applicant's expense (TILA Sec. 129H(d), as added by Sec. 1471 of the Dodd-Frank Act).

If a creditor willfully fails to obtain an appraisal, the creditor will be liable to the applicant or borrower for the sum of $2,000 (TILA Sec. 129H(e), as added by Sec. 1471 of the Dodd-Frank Act).

▶ **Effective date.** Based on TILA Sec. 129H(b)(4) as added by Sec. 1471 of the Dodd-Frank Act, which requires implementing regulations, TILA Sec. 129H would be effective on the date on which final regulations implementing the section take effect. Regulations must be in final form within 18 months of the designated transfer date and take effect not later than 12 months after issuance of the regulations in final form. If regulations have not been issued on or before the date that is 18 months after the transfer date, the provision will take effect on the date that is 18 months after the transfer date (Sec. 1400(c) of the Dodd-Frank Wall Street Reform and Consumer Protection Act). Amendment provisions that do not require regulations to be prescribed take effect one day after the date of enactment (Sec. 4 of the Dodd-Frank Act).

Law source: Law at ¶11,471 and ¶11,400. Committee Report at ¶55,075.

— Sec. 1471 of the Dodd-Frank Wall Street Reform and Consumer Protection Act, adding Truth in Lending Act Sec.129H;

— Sec. 1400(c), providing the effective date.

¶6705 Appraisal Independence Requirements

When extending credit or providing services for a consumer credit transaction secured by the principal dwelling of a consumer, it is unlawful to engage in acts or practices that violate appraisal independence (TILA Sec. 129E(a), as added by Sec. 1472(a) of the Dodd-Frank Act).

Acts or practices that violate appraisal independence include:

- an appraisal in which a person with an interest in the underlying transaction compensates, coerces, extorts, colludes, instructs, induces, bribes or intimidates a person or firm conducting or involved in the appraisal;
- mischaracterizing, or suborning mischaracterization of, the appraised value of the property;
- attempting to influence an appraiser or encouraging a targeted value to facilitate the transaction; and
- withholding, or threatening to withhold, timely payment for an appraisal report or appraisal services rendered (TILA Sec. 129E(b), as added by Sec. 1472(a) of the Dodd-Frank Act).

A person with an interest in a real estate transaction may ask an appraiser to:

- consider additional, appropriate property information, including the consideration of additional comparable properties in making an appraisal;
- provide further detail, substantiation or explanation for the appraiser's conclusion; or
- correct errors in the appraisal report (TILA Sec. 129E(c), as added by Sec. 1472(a) of the Dodd-Frank Act).

A certified or licensed appraiser conducting an appraisal may not have a direct or indirect interest, financial or otherwise, in the property or transaction involving the appraisal (TILA Sec. 129E(d), as added by Sec. 1472(a) of the Dodd-Frank Act).

Any person involved with an appraisal in connection with a consumer credit transaction secured by the principal dwelling of a consumer who has a reasonable basis to believe the appraiser is not complying with the Uniform Standards of Appraisal Practice, is in violation of applicable laws or is engaging in unethical or unprofessional conduct, must report the appraiser to the state appraiser certifying and licensing agency. "Person" includes mortgage lenders, mortgage brokers, real estate brokers, appraisal management companies and their employees (TILA Sec. 129E(e), as added by Sec. 1472(a) of the Dodd-Frank Act).

If a creditor knows at or before loan consummation of a violation of the appraisal standards established in this section, the creditor is prohibited from extending credit based on the appraisal. An exception exists if the creditor documents that the creditor has acted with reasonable diligence to determine that the appraisal does not materially misstate or misrepresent the value of the dwelling securing the transaction (TILA Sec. 129E(f), as added by Sec. 1472(a) of the Dodd-Frank Act).

Rules and Guidelines.—The federal banking agencies—Federal Reserve Board, Office of the Comptroller of the Currency and Federal Deposit Insurance Corporation—in conjunction with the National Credit Union Administration, Federal Housing Finance Agency and Bureau of Consumer Financial Protection (the agencies), may jointly issue rules, interpretive guidelines and statements of policy with respect to any acts or practices that violate appraisal independence as it relates to mortgage lending or brokerage services for a consumer credit transaction secured by the principal dwelling (TILA Sec. 129E(g)(1), as added by Sec. 1472(a) of the Dodd-Frank Act).

The Fed is required to prescribe interim final regulations within 90 days after the date of enactment. The interim final rules must specifically define acts or practices that violate appraisal independence (TILA Sec. 129E(g)(2), as added by Sec. 1472(a) of the Dodd-Frank Act).

The agencies may also jointly issue regulations that address the issue of appraisal report portability, including regulations that ensure the portability of the appraisal report between lenders for a consumer credit transaction secured by a one- to four-unit single family residence that is the principal dwelling of the consumer, or mortgage brokerage services for such a transaction (TILA Sec. 129E(h), as added by Sec. 1472(a) of the Dodd-Frank Act).

Customary and Reasonable Fee.—Lenders must compensate fee appraisers at a rate that is "customary and reasonable" for appraisal services in the market area of the property being appraised. Lenders may use objective third-party information to establish evidence of the fees. Objective third-party information may include government agency fee schedules, academic studies and independent private sector surveys. However, fee studies must exclude assignments ordered by known appraisal management teams.

The term "fee appraiser" means a person who is not an employee of the mortgage loan originator or the appraisal management company engaging the appraiser. The fee appraiser is:

- a state licensed or certified appraiser who receives a fee for doing an appraisal in accordance with the Uniform Standards of Professional Appraisal Practice; or

- a company not subject to Sec. 1124 of the Financial Institutions Reform, Recovery, and Enforcement Act of 1989 that uses the services of state licensed or certified appraisers and receives a fee for appraisals done in accordance with the Uniform Standards of Professional Appraisal Practice.

An exception to the customary and reasonable standard exists. If the appraisal involves a complex assignment, the customary and reasonable fee may reflect the increased time, difficulty and scope of the work required for the appraisal (TILA Sec. 129E(i) as added by Sec. 1472(a) of the Dodd-Frank Act).

Sunset.—On the date the interim final regulations are adopted, the Home Valuation Code of Conduct announced by the Federal Housing Finance Agency on Dec. 23, 2008, will no longer be in force (TILA Sec. 129E(j) as added by Sec. 1472(a) of the Dodd-Frank Act).

Penalties.—In addition to the enforcement provisions of TILA Sec. 130, a person who violates the provisions of this section must pay a civil penalty of no more than $10,000 for each day the violation continues. For subsequent violations, the civil penalty is a maximum of $20,000 for each day the violation continues (TILA Sec. 129E(k), as added by Sec. 1472(a) of the Dodd-Frank Act).

Deference.—The deference a court awards the Bureau of Consumer Financial Protection as to a determination made by the Bureau on any provision of Title XIV must be applied as if the Bureau were the only agency authorized to apply, enforce, interpret or

¶6705

administer the provisions. This provision does not apply to Sec. 129E or 129H (TILA Sec. 105(h) as added by Sec. 1472(c) of the Dodd-Frank Act).

▶ **Effective date.** Based on TILA Sec. 129E(a) as added by Sec. 1472(a) of the Dodd-Frank Act, which requires implementing regulations, TILA Sec. 129E would be effective on the date on which final regulations implementing the section take effect. Regulations must be in final form within 18 months of the designated transfer date and take effect not later than 12 months after issuance of the regulations in final form. If regulations have not been issued on or before the date that is 18 months after the transfer date, the provision will take effect on the date that is 18 months after the transfer date (Sec. 1400(c) of the Dodd-Frank Wall Street Reform and Consumer Protection Act). The Fed must prescribe interim final regulations defining acts or practices that violate appraiser independence no later than 90 days after the date of enactment. (TILA Sec. 129E(g)(2), as added by Sec. 1472(a) of the Dodd-Frank Act). Amendment provisions that do not require regulations to be prescribed take effect one day after the date of enactment (Sec. 4 of the Dodd-Frank Act).

Law source: Law at ¶11,472 and ¶10,004. Committee Report at ¶55,076.

— Sec. 1472(a) of the Dodd-Frank Wall Street Reform and Consumer Protection Act, adding Truth in Lending Act Sec.129E;

— Sec. 1472(c), adding Truth in Lending Act Sec.105(h);

— Secs. 4 and 1472(a), providing the effective date.

¶6710 FIRREA Amendments

The Financial Institutions Reform, Recovery and Enforcement Act of 1989 (FIRREA) permits federal financial regulatory agencies and the Resolution Trust Corporation (RTC) to establish thresholds at or below which a licensed or certified appraiser is not required to perform appraisals in connection with federally related transactions if the agency determines in writing that the threshold level does not represent a threat to the safety and soundness of financial institutions. The Dodd-Frank Wall Street Reform and Consumer Protection Act amends this provision to add that the Bureau of Consumer Financial Protection must concur that the threshold level provides reasonable protection for consumers who purchase one- to four-unit single-family residences (Sec. 1112(b) as amended by Sec. 1473(a) of the Dodd-Frank Act).

Annual Report.—The Appraisal Subcommittee must provide an annual report to Congress by June 15 of each year. The annual report must describe the manner in which functions assigned to the subcommittee have been carried out during the year. The report also must contain the results of all audits of state appraiser regulatory agencies and an accounting of disapproved actions and warnings taken during the year (FIRREA Sec. 1103(a)(5), as added by Sec. 1473(b) of the Dodd-Frank Act).

Open Meetings.—The Appraisal Subcommittee must meet in public session after notice in the *Federal Register* but may close portions of the meetings related to personnel and review of preliminary state audit reports (FIRREA Sec. 1104(b), as amended by Sec. 1473(c) of the Dodd-Frank Act).

Regulations.—Under the amendments made by these provisions, the Appraisal Subcommittee may prescribe regulations in accordance with Chapter 5, Title 5, of the United States Code (Administrative Procedures Act) after notice and opportunity for comment. Any regulations prescribed by the subcommittee generally must be limited to temporary practice, national registry, information sharing and enforcement.

The Appraisal Subcommittee is required to establish an advisory committee of industry participants—such as appraisers, lenders, consumer advocates, real estate agents and government agencies—for the purpose of prescribing regulations (FIRREA Sec. 1106, as amended by Sec. 1473(d) of the Dodd-Frank Act).

Appraisal Reviews and Complex Appraisals.—Appraisals are subject to review for compliance with the Uniform Standards of Professional Appraisal Practice (FIRREA Sec. 1110, as amended by Sec. 1473(e)(1) of the Dodd-Frank Act).

Appraisal Management Services.—The Appraisal Subcommittee must monitor state requirements for the certification and licensing of individuals who are qualified to perform appraisals in connection with federally related transactions, which includes a code of responsibility. The subcommittee also must monitor state requirements for the registration and supervision of the operations and activities of an appraisal management company.

In addition, the Appraisal Subcommittee is required to maintain a national registry of appraisal management companies that either are:

- registered with, and subject to, supervision of a state appraiser certifying and licensing agency; or
- operating subsidiaries of a federally regulated financial institution (FIRREA Sec. 1103(a), as amended by Sec. 1473(f)(1) of the Dodd-Frank Act).

Appraisal Management Company Minimum Requirements.—The federal banking agencies—Federal Reserve Board, Office of the Comptroller of the Currency and Federal Deposit Insurance Corporation—in conjunction with the National Credit Union Administration, Federal Housing Finance Agency and Bureau of Consumer Financial Protection (the agencies) are required to establish minimum requirements to be applied by a state in the registration of appraisal management companies.

The minimum requirements must state that appraisal management companies must:

- register with a state appraiser certifying and licensing agency in each state in which the company operates;
- verify that only licensed or certified appraisers are used for federally related transactions;
- require that appraisals coordinated by an appraisal management company comply with the Uniform Standards of Professional Appraisals Practice; and
- require that appraisals are conducted independently as set forth in the appraisals independence standards under Sec. 129E of the Truth in Lending Act, as added by the Dodd-Frank Act (FIRREA Sec. 1124(a), as added by Sec. 1473(f)(2) of the Dodd-Frank Act).

These requirements also apply to an appraisal management company that is a subsidiary owned and controlled by a financial institution and regulated by a federal financial institution regulatory agency. However, these appraisal management companies are not required to register with a state (FIRREA Sec. 1124(c), as added by Sec. 1473(f)(2) of the Dodd-Frank Act).

¶6710

States are not prevented from establishing requirements in addition to the rules in this subsection (FIRREA Sec. 1124(b), as added by Sec. 1473(f)(2) of the Dodd-Frank Act).

Registration Limitations.—An appraisal management company cannot be registered by a state or included on the national registry if the company is owned in whole or in part by a person who has had an appraiser license or certificate refused, denied, cancelled, surrendered in lieu of revocation or revoked in any state. Persons that own more than 10 percent of the company must be of good moral character as determined by the state certifying and licensing agency and must submit to a background investigation by the licensing or certifying agency (FIRREA Sec. 1124(d), as added by Sec. 1473(f)(2) of the Dodd-Frank Act).

Reporting.—The agencies must jointly adopt regulations for the reporting of activities of appraisal management companies to the Appraisal Subcommittee in determining the payment of the annual registry fee (FIRREA Sec. 1124(e), as added by Sec. 1473(f)(2) of the Dodd-Frank Act).

Effective Date.—An appraisal management company generally cannot perform services connected to a federally related transaction in a state 36 months after the date on which the agencies' required regulations become final unless the company is registered with the state or subject to oversight by a federal financial institutions regulatory agency (FIRREA Sec. 1124(f)(1), as added by Sec. 1473(f)(2) of the Dodd-Frank Act).

The Appraisal Subcommittee may extend the requirements for the registration and supervision of appraisal management companies by 12 months if the Subcommittee makes a written finding that a state has made substantial progress in establishing a registration and supervision system that appears to conform to the provisions (FIRREA Sec. 1124(f)(2), as added by Sec. 1473(f)(2) of the Dodd-Frank Act).

Certifying and Licensing Authority.—The duties of a state appraiser certifying and licensing agency may include the registration and supervision of appraisal management companies and the addition of information about the company to the national registry (FIRREA Sec. 1117, as amended by Sec. 1473(f)(3) of the Dodd-Frank Act).

"Appraisal management company" means an external third party authorized by a creditor, underwriter or other principal in the secondary mortgage markets that oversees a group of more than 15 certified or licensed appraisers in a state or 25 or more appraisers nationally within a given year to:

- recruit and retain appraisers;
- contract with licensed and certified appraisers to perform appraisal assignments;
- manage the process of having an appraisal performed; or
- review and verify the work of appraisers (FIRREA Sec. 1121(11), as added by Sec. 1473(f)(4) of the Dodd-Frank Act).

State Agency Reporting Requirement.—Reporting requirements are added for state appraiser certifying and licensing agencies. State agencies must provide timely reports on the issuance and renewal of licenses and certifications, sanctions, disciplinary actions, license and certification revocations and suspensions to the national registry of the Appraisal Subcommittee.

In addition, the agencies must submit timely reports on supervisory activities involving appraisal management companies or other third-party providers of appraisals and management services. The report must include any investigations initiated and disciplinary actions taken by the agency (FIRREA Sec. 1109(a), as amended by Sec. 1473(g) of the Dodd-Frank Act).

Registry Fees.—A state appraiser certifying and licensing agency must collect from appraisers involved in federally-related transactions an annual registry fee of not more than $40 (FIRREA Sec. 1109(a)(4)(A), as amended by Sec. 1473(h)(1)(A) of the Dodd-Frank Act).

The state agency also must collect an annual registry fee from appraisal management companies registered with the state certifying and licensing agency or operating as a subsidiary of a federally regulated financial institution (FIRREA Sec. 1109(a)(4)(B), as amended by Sec. 1473(h)(1)(A) of the Dodd-Frank Act).

For a company that has been in existence for more than a year, the fee is $25 multiplied by the number of appraisers working for or contracting with the company in the state during the previous year. Where the $25 amount may be adjusted, the maximum is $50 for each appraiser or contractor.

If the company has not been in existence for over a year, the fee is $25 multiplied by an appropriate number determined by the Appraisal Subcommittee, up to a maximum of $50 (FIRREA Sec. 1109(a)(4)(A), as amended by Sec. 1473(h)(1)(A) of the Dodd-Frank Act).

With the approval of the FFIEC, the Appraisal Subcommittee may adjust the dollar amount of registry fees up to a maximum of $80 per year. The subcommittee must consider whether to adjust the dollar amount at least once every five years to account for inflation. When making a change to the fee, the subcommittee must provide flexibility to the states for multi-year certifications and licenses already in place and a transition period to implement the change (FIRREA Sec. 1109(a)(4), as amended by Sec. 1473(h)(1)(B) of the Dodd-Frank Act).

Incremental revenues collected pursuant to the increases must be placed in a separate account at the Treasury Department entitled "Appraisal Subcommittee Account" (Sec. 1473(h)(2) of the Dodd-Frank Act).

Grants and Reports.—This section authorizes the Appraisal Subcommittee to award grants to state appraiser certifying and licensing agencies in order to support the agencies' compliance with the provisions of the section (FIRREA Sec. 1109(b)(5), as added by Sec. 1473(i)(3) of the Dodd-Frank Act).

The subcommittee is required to report to all state appraiser certifying and licensing agencies when a license or certification is surrendered, revoked or suspended (FIRREA Sec. 1109(b)(6), as added by Sec. 1473(i)(3) of the Dodd-Frank Act).

The authorized obligations may not exceed 75 percent of the fiscal year total of incremental increase in fees collected and deposited in the Appraisal Subcommittee Account (Sec. 1473(i) of Sec. 1473(f) of the Dodd-Frank Act).

Criteria.—The term "state licensed appraiser" means an individual who has satisfied the requirements for state licensing in a state or territory whose criteria for the licensing of a real estate appraiser currently meet or exceed the minimum criteria issued by the Appraisal Qualifications Board of The Appraisal Foundation for the licensing of real estate appraisers (FIRREA Sec. 1116(c), as amended by Sec. 1473(j)(1) of the Dodd-Frank Act).

The Dodd-Frank Act also provides minimum qualifications for state licensed appraisers. Requirements for the positions of "Trainee Appraiser" and "Supervisory Appraiser" must meet or exceed the minimum qualification requirements of the Appraisal Qualifications Board of The Appraisal Foundation. The Appraisal Subcommittee has the authority to enforce the requirements (FIRREA Sec. 1116(e), as amended by Sec. 1473(j)(2) of the Dodd-Frank Act).

Monitoring of Agencies.—The Appraisal Subcommittee is required to monitor each state appraiser certifying and licensing agency to determine whether the agency:

- has policies, practices, funding, staffing and procedures that are consistent with Title XIV of the Dodd-Frank Act;
- processes complaints and completes investigations in a reasonable time period;
- appropriately disciplines sanctioned appraisers and appraisal management companies;
- maintains an effective regulatory program; and
- reports complaints and disciplinary actions on a timely basis to the national registries on appraisers and appraisal management companies maintained by the Appraisal Subcommittee.

The subcommittee has the authority to remove a state licensed or certified appraiser or a registered appraisal management company from a national registry on an interim basis not to exceed 90 days, pending state agency action on licensing, certification, registration and disciplinary proceedings.

The Appraisal Subcommittee may not recognize appraiser certifications and licenses from states with appraisal policies, practices, funding, staffing or procedures that are determined to be inconsistent with Title XIV of the Dodd-Frank Act.

The subcommittee has the authority to impose sanctions against a state agency that fails to have an effective appraiser regulatory program. In determining if the agency's program is effective, the Appraisal Subcommittee must include an analysis of the:

- licensing and certification of appraisers;
- registration of appraisal management companies;
- issuance of temporary appraiser licenses and certifications;
- receiving and tracking of complaints against appraisers and appraisal management companies;
- investigation of complaints; and
- enforcement actions against appraisers and appraisal management companies.

The Appraisal Subcommittee has the authority to impose interim actions and suspensions against a state agency as an alternative to, or in advance of the derecognizing of a state agency (FIRREA Sec. 1118(a), as amended by Sec. 1473(k)(1) of the Dodd-Frank Act).

Additional Provisions.—A federally related transaction may not be appraised by a certified or licensed appraiser unless the state appraiser certifying or licensing agency has a policy of issuing a reciprocal certification or license for an individual from another state when:

- the appraiser licensing and certification program of the other state is in compliance with the provisions of Title XIV; and
- the appraiser holds a valid certification from a state with requirements that meet or exceed the licensure standards of the state where an individual is seeking an appraisal license (FIRREA Sec. 1122(b), as amended by Sec. 1473(k)(2) of the Dodd-Frank Act).

Criteria established by the federal financial institutions regulatory agencies, Federal National Mortgage Association, Federal Home Loan Mortgage Corporation and Resolution Trust Corporation for appraiser qualifications, in addition to state certification or licensing, may include education, experience, sample appraisals and references from prior clients. Membership in a nationally recognized professional organization may be considered, but lack of membership cannot be the sole reason for barring consideration for an assignment (FIRREA Sec. 1122(d), as amended by Sec. 1473(m) of the Dodd-Frank Act).

The Appraisal Subcommittee must monitor state appraiser agencies to determine whether the agency's policies, practices and procedures are consistent with the purpose of maintaining appraiser independence and whether the state has adopted effective laws, regulations and policies intended to maintain appraiser independence (FIRREA Sec. 1122(g), as added by Sec. 1473(n) of the Dodd-Frank Act).

The subcommittee must encourage states to accept appraiser education courses approved by the Appraiser Qualification Board's Course Approval Program (FIRREA Sec. 1122(h), as added by Sec. 1473(o) of the Dodd-Frank Act).

The Appraisal Subcommittee is required to establish and operate a national hotline to receive complaints of non-compliance with appraisal independence standards and Uniform Standards of Professional Appraisal Practice if the subcommittee determines six months after enactment of the section that a national hotline does not exist. The hotline must have a toll-free number and an e-mail address.

The Appraisal Subcommittee must refer complaints from appraisers, individuals and other entities to appropriate government agencies such as state appraiser certifying and licensing agencies and financial institution regulators. The subcommittee has the authority to follow up on complaints forwarded to state certifying and licensing agencies and federal regulators (FIRREA Sec. 1122(i), as added by Sec. 1473(p) of the Dodd-Frank Act).

Automation Valuation Models.—Title XIV of the Dodd-Frank Act amends FIRREA to add a section governing automated valuation models. The term "automated valuation model" means a computerized model used by mortgage originators and secondary market issuers to determine the collateral worth of a mortgage secured by a consumer's principal dwelling (FIRREA Sec. 1125(d), as added by Sec. 1473(q) of the Dodd-Frank Act).

Automated valuation models must comply with quality control standards intended to:

¶6710

- ensure a high level of confidence in the estimates produced by automated valuation models;
- protect against the manipulation of data;
- avoid conflicts of interest;
- require random sample testing and reviews; and
- account for any other factor that the agencies consider appropriate (FIRREA Sec. 1125(a), as added by Sec. 1473(q) of the Dodd-Frank Act).

The agencies must adopt regulations implementing the quality control standards. In proscribing the regulations, the agencies must consult with the staff of the Appraisal Subcommittee and the Appraisal Standards Board of the Appraisal Foundation (FIRREA Sec. 1125(b), as added by Sec. 1473(q) of the Dodd-Frank Act).

Compliance with the regulations will be enforced by the applicable federal regulator with respect to financial institutions and by the Federal Trade Commission, the Bureau and the appropriate state attorney general as to other persons in the market for appraisals of one- to four-unit single family residential real estate (FIRREA Sec. 1125(c), as added by Sec. 1473(q) of the Dodd-Frank Act).

Broker Price Opinions.—Broker price opinions may not be used as the primary basis to evaluate property for a loan origination in connection with a residential mortgage loan secured by the property (FIRREA Sec. 1126(a), as added by Sec. 1473(r) of the Dodd-Frank Act).

"Broker price opinion" is defined as an estimate prepared by a real estate broker, agent or sales person that details the probable selling price of a piece of property. A broker price opinion provides details about the property's condition, market and neighborhood, as well as comparable sales, but does not include an automated valuation model (FIRREA Sec. 1126(b), as added by Sec. 1473(r) of the Dodd-Frank Act).

Appraisal Subcommittee.—Amendments to FIRREA provide that Appraisal Subcommittee members include the Bureau and the Federal Housing Finance Agency.

In addition, at least one member of the Appraisal Subcommittee must have demonstrated knowledge and competence through licensure, certification or professional designation in the appraisal profession (FIRREA Sec. 1011, as amended by Sec. 1473(s) of the Dodd-Frank Act).

▶ **Effective date.** Based on FIRREA Sec. 1124(a) as added by Sec. 1473(f)(2) of the Dodd-Frank Act and FIRREA Sec. 1125(b) as added by Sec. 1473(q) of the Dodd-Frank Act, which requires implementing regulations, FIRREA Sec. 1124(a), which requires federal agencies to establish minimum requirements to be applied by a state in the registration of appraisal management companies, would be effective on the date on which final regulations implementing the section take effect. Regulations must be in final form within 18 months of the designated transfer date and take effect not later than 12 months after issuance of the regulations in final form. If regulations have not been issued on or before the date that is 18 months after the transfer date, the provision will take effect on the date that is 18 months after the transfer date (Sec. 1400(c) of the Dodd-Frank Wall Street Reform and Consumer Protection Act). The amendment provisions that do not require regulations to be prescribed take effect one day after the date of enactment (Sec. 4 of the Dodd-Frank Act).

Law source: Law at ¶11,473, ¶11,400 and ¶10,004. Committee Report at ¶55,077.

— Sec. 1473(a) of the Dodd-Frank Wall Street Reform and Consumer Protection Act, amending Financial Institutions Reform, Recovery, and Enforcement Act of 1989 Sec. 1112(b);

— Sec. 1473(b), adding Financial Institutions Reform, Recovery, and Enforcement Act of 1989 Sec. 1103(a)(5);

— Sec. 1473(c), amending Financial Institutions Reform, Recovery, and Enforcement Act of 1989 Sec. 1104(b);

— Sec. 1473(d), amending Financial Institutions Reform, Recovery, and Enforcement Act of 1989 Sec. 1106;

— Sec. 1473(e), amending Financial Institutions Reform, Recovery, and Enforcement Act of 1989 Sec. 1113;

— Sec. 1473(f)(1)(A), amending Financial Institutions Reform, Recovery, and Enforcement Act of 1989 Sec. 1103(a);

— Sec. 1473(f)(1)(B), adding Financial Institutions Reform, Recovery, and Enforcement Act of 1989 Sec. 1103(a)(6);

— Sec. 1473(f)(2), adding Financial Institutions Reform, Recovery, and Enforcement Act of 1989 Sec. 1124;

— Sec. 1473(f)(3), amending Financial Institutions Reform, Recovery, and Enforcement Act of 1989 Sec. 1117;

— Sec. 1473(f)(4), adding Financial Institutions Reform, Recovery, and Enforcement Act of 1989 Sec. 1121(11);

— Sec. 1473(g), amending Financial Institutions Reform, Recovery, and Enforcement Act of 1989 Sec. 1109(a);

— Sec. 1473(h)(1), amending Financial Institutions Reform, Recovery, and Enforcement Act of 1989 Sec. 1109(a);

— Sec. 1473(h)(2), regarding incremental revenues;

— Sec. 1473(i), adding Financial Institutions Reform, Recovery, and Enforcement Act of 1989 Sec. 1109(b)(5) and (6);

— Sec. 1473(j)(1), amending Financial Institutions Reform, Recovery, and Enforcement Act of 1989 Sec. 1116(c);

— Sec. 1473(j)(2), amending Financial Institutions Reform, Recovery, and Enforcement Act of 1989 Sec. 1116(e);

— Sec. 1473(k)(1), amending Financial Institutions Reform, Recovery, and Enforcement Act of 1989 Sec. 1118(a);

— Sec. 1473(k)(2), amending Financial Institutions Reform, Recovery, and Enforcement Act of 1989 Sec. 1118(b)(2);

— Sec. 1473(l), amending Financial Institutions Reform, Recovery, and Enforcement Act of 1989 Sec. 1122(b);

— Sec. 1473(m), amending Financial Institutions Reform, Recovery, and Enforcement Act of 1989 Sec. 1122(d);

— Sec. 1473(n), adding Financial Institutions Reform, Recovery, and Enforcement Act of 1989 Sec. 1122(g);

— Sec. 1473(o), adding Financial Institutions Reform, Recovery, and Enforcement Act of 1989 Sec. 1122(h);

— Sec. 1473(p), adding Financial Institutions Reform, Recovery, and Enforcement Act of 1989 Sec. 1122(i);

— Sec. 1473(q), adding Financial Institutions Reform, Recovery, and Enforcement Act of 1989 Sec. 1125;

— Sec. 1473(r), adding Financial Institutions Reform, Recovery, and Enforcement Act of 1989 Sec. 1126;

— Sec. 1473(s), amending Federal Financial Institutions Examination Council Act of 1978 Sec. 1011;

— Sec. 1473(t)(1), amending Financial Institutions Reform, Recovery, and Enforcement Act of 1989 Sec. 1119(a)(2);

— Sec. 1473(t)(2), amending Financial Institutions Reform, Recovery, and Enforcement Act of 1989 Sec. 1121(6);

— Sec. 1473(t)(3), amending Financial Institutions Reform, Recovery, and Enforcement Act of 1989 Sec. 1121(8);

— Sec. 1473(t)(4), amending Financial Institutions Reform, Recovery, and Enforcement Act of 1989 Sec. 1122;

— Sec. 4 and 1400(c), providing the effective date.

¶6715 Equal Credit Opportunity Act Amendment

Under an amendment to the Equal Credit Opportunity Act (ECOA), creditors must provide applicants a copy of all written appraisals and valuations developed in connection with a loan secured by a first lien on a dwelling. The creditor must provide the copy on completion of the appraisal, but in no case later than three days before the closing of the loan. The copy of the appraisal and valuation must be given to the applicant whether the creditor grants or denies the credit request or the application is incomplete or withdrawn (ECOA Sec. 701(e)(1), as amended by Sec. 1474 of the Dodd-Frank Act).

The applicant may waive the three-day requirement except where otherwise required by law (ECOA Sec. 701(e)(2), as amended by Sec. 1474 of the Dodd-Frank Act).

At the time of application, the creditor must notify an applicant in writing of the right to receive a copy of each written appraisal and valuation (ECOA Sec. 701(e)(5), as amended by Sec. 1474 of the Dodd-Frank Act).

"Valuation" includes any estimate of the dwelling developed in connection with a creditor's decision to provide credit, including values developed:

- pursuant to a policy of a government-sponsored enterprise;
- by an automated valuation model;
- by a broker price opinion; or
- by any other methodology or mechanism (ECOA Sec. 701(e)(6), as amended by Sec. 1474 of the Dodd-Frank Act).

▶ **Effective date.** The provision takes effect one day after the date of enactment (Sec. 4 of the Dodd-Frank Wall Street Reform and Consumer Protection Act).

Law source: Law at ¶11,474 and ¶10,004. Committee Report at ¶55,079.

— Sec. 1474 of the Dodd-Frank Wall Street Reform and Consumer Protection Act, amending Equal Credit Opportunity Act Sec. 701(e);

— Sec. 4, providing the effective date.

¶6720 Real Estate Settlement Procedures Act Amendment

For an appraisal coordinated by an appraisal management company, the standard real estate settlement form used in transactions that involve federally related mortgage loans may include a clear disclosure of the fee paid directly to the appraiser by the company and the administration fee charged by the company.

▶ **Effective date.** The provision takes effect one day after the date of enactment (Sec. 4 of the Dodd-Frank Wall Street Reform and Consumer Protection Act).

Law source: Law at ¶11,475 and ¶10,004. Committee Report at ¶55,080.

— Sec. 1475 of the Dodd-Frank Wall Street Reform and Consumer Protection Act, adding Real Estate Settlement Procedures Act Sec. 4(c);

— Sec. 4, providing the effective date.

¶6725 GAO Study

The Government Accountability Office (GAO) must conduct a study on the effectiveness and impact of:

- appraisal methods, including the cost approach, comparative sales approach, income approach and other available methods;
- appraisal valuation models, including licensed and certified appraisals, broker-priced opinions and automated valuation models; and
- appraisal distribution channels, including appraisal management companies, independent appraisal operations within mortgage originators and fee-for-service appraisers (Sec. 1476(a)(1) of the Dodd-Frank Act).

The GAO is required to include in the study an examination of appraisal approaches, valuation models and distribution channels. Specifically, the examination must address:

- the prevalence, alone or in combination, of the approaches, models and channels in purchase-money and refinance mortgage transactions;
- the accuracy of the approaches, models and channels in assessing the property as collateral;
- whether and how the approaches, models and channels contributed to price speculation during the previous cycle;
- costs to consumers;
- disclosure of fees to consumers in the appraisal process;

- to what extent the use of the approaches, models and channels may be influenced by a conflict of interest between the mortgage lender and the appraiser, and the mechanism by which the lender chooses and compensates the appraiser; and
- the suitability of the approaches, models and channels in rural versus urban areas (Sec. 1476(c)(1) of the Dodd-Frank Act).

The GAO study also must target the Home Valuation Code of Conduct (HVCC), to determine how the HVCC affects:

- mortgage lenders' selection of appraisers;
- state regulation of appraisers and appraisal distribution channels;
- the quality and cost of appraisals and the length of time to obtain an appraisal; and
- mortgage brokers, small businesses and consumers (Sec. 1476(c)(2) of the Dodd-Frank Act).

The study must be completed within 12 months of enactment and submitted to the Senate Committee on Banking, Housing, and Urban Affairs and House Committee on Financial Services.

Within 90 days of enactment, the GAO must provide a report on the status of the study and any preliminary findings to the House and Senate committees (Sec. 1476(b) of the Dodd-Frank Act).

Additional Study.—Within 18 months of enactment, the GAO must submit a study to the Senate and House committees. The study must include an examination of:

- the Appraisal Subcommittee's ability to monitor and enforce state and federal certification requirements and standards and a summary of enforcement actions taken during the last 10 years;
- whether federal financial institutions regulatory agency exemptions on appraisals for federally related transactions should be revised; and
- whether new means of data collection would benefit the Appraisal Subcommittee's ability to perform its functions.

The report must include recommendations for administrative and legislative action at both the federal and state levels (Sec. 1476(d) of the Dodd-Frank Act).

▶ **Effective date.** The provision takes effect one day after the date of enactment (Sec. 4 of the Dodd-Frank Wall Street Reform and Consumer Protection Act).

Law source: Law at ¶11,476 and ¶10,004.

— Sec. 1476 of the Dodd-Frank Wall Street Reform and Consumer Protection Act, providing for a GAO study;

— Sec. 4, providing the effective date.

MORTGAGE RESOLUTION and MODIFICATION

¶6730 Mulitfamily Mortgage Resolution Program

The Secretary of Housing and Urban Development is required by the Dodd-Frank Wall Street Reform and Consumer ProtectionAct to develop a program intended to ensure the protection of current and future tenants as well as at-risk multifamily properties.

"Multifamily properties" as used in this section means a residential structure consisting of five or more dwelling units (Sec. 1481(c) of the Dodd-Frank Act).

The criteria for the program may include:

- creating sustainable financing of at-risk properties, considering factors such as the rental income generated by the properties and the preservation of adequate operating reserves;
- maintaining the level of federal and state subsidies in effect as of the date of enactment of the Dodd-Frank Act;
- providing funds for rehabilitation; and
- facilitating the transfer of at-risk properties, with the agreement of the owners, to responsible new owners (Sec. 1481(a) of the Dodd-Frank Act).

Criminal Applicants.—No person may receive assistance from any mortgage assistance program under the Emergency Economic Stabilization Act of 2008 on or after 60 days after enactment of the Dodd-Frank Act if the person, in connection with a mortgage or real estate transaction, has been convicted, within the last 10 years, of: felony larceny, theft, fraud or forgery, money laundering, or tax evasion. The Secretary must report to Congress regarding implementation of this provision (Sec. 1481(d) of the Dodd-Frank Act).

▶ **Effective date.** The provision takes effect one day after the date of enactment (Sec. 4 of the Dodd-Frank Wall Street Reform and Consumer Protection Act).

Law source: Law at ¶11,481 and ¶10,004.

— Sec. 1481 of the Dodd-Frank Wall Street Reform and Consumer Protection Act;

— Sec. 4, providing the effective date.

¶6735 Home Affordable Modification Program Guidelines

The Secretary of the Treasury must revise the supplemental directives and other guidelines for the Home Affordable Modification Program (HAMP) to require mortgage servicers participating in the program to provide each borrower whose request for a mortgage modification is denied with all input data related to the borrower and mortgage used in any net present value (NPV) analysis performed in connection with the mortgage (Sec. 1482(a) of the Dodd-Frank Act).

HAMP is a program within the Treasury's Making Home Affordable initiative, authorized under the Emergency Economic Stabilization Act.

The Treasury must establish and maintain a website that provides a calculator for the NPV analyses of a mortgage, based on the Treasury's method of calculation, that mortgagors can use to enter information on their mortgages to get a determination as to whether the mortgage would be accepted for modification under HAMP (Sec. 1482(b)(1) of the Dodd-Frank Act).

The website must prominently disclose that each mortgage servicer participating in HAMP may use a different method of calculation than the one used on the website (Sec. 1482(b)(2) of the Dodd-Frank Act).

Subtitle K requires the Treasury to make a reasonable effort to include on the website a method for homeowners to apply for a mortgage modification under HAMP (Sec. 1482(b)(3) of the Dodd-Frank Act).

Finally, the Treasury must make publicly available its methodology and computer model used for calculating the NPV of a mortgage that is used by the website's calculator as well as all variables used in the NPV analysis (Sec. 1482(c) of the Dodd-Frank Act).

▶ **Effective date.** The provision takes effect one day after the date of enactment (Sec. 4 of the Dodd-Frank Wall Street Reform and Consumer Protection Act).

Law source: Law at ¶11,482 and ¶10,004.

— Sec. 1482 of the Dodd-Frank Wall Street Reform and Consumer Protection Act;

— Sec. 4, providing the effective date.

¶6740 Public Availability of Information of Making Home Affordable Program

The Treasury Department is directed to revise the guidelines for the HAMP to provide that the data being collected by the Secretary from each participating lender and servicer is made publicly available (Sec. 1483(a) of the Dodd-Frank Act).

The Treasury must make the data available according to the following guidelines.

- Within 14 days after each monthly deadline for submission of data by participating servicers and lenders, reports must be made publicly available by posting on the Treasury's website and by submitting a report to Congress that includes the number of requests for mortgage modifications under HAMP that the servicer or lender has received, processed, approved or denied (Sec. 1483(b)(1) of the Dodd-Frank Act).

- Within 60 days after each monthly deadline for data submission, servicers and lenders must make the data available to the public at the individual record level. The Treasury must issue regulations prescribing the procedures for disclosing the data to the public and any deletions it determines are needed to protect the privacy of mortgage modification applicants (Sec. 1483(b)(2) of the Dodd-Frank Act).

▶ **Effective date.** The provision takes effect one day after the date of enactment (Sec. 4 of the Dodd-Frank Wall Street Reform and Consumer Protection Act).

Law source: Law at ¶11,483 and ¶10,004.

— Sec. 1483 of the Dodd-Frank Wall Street Reform and Consumer Protection Act;
— Sec. 4, providing the effective date.

¶6745 Extension and Clarification of Protecting Tenants at Foreclosure Act

The legislation amends Sec. 702(c) of The Protecting Tenants at Foreclosure Act to provide that the date of a notice of foreclosure is the date on which complete title to a property is transferred as a result of a court order or pursuant to a mortgage, deed or trust or security deed. Also, the date of termination in Sec. 704 of that law has been extended from Dec. 31, 2012, to Dec. 31, 2014 (Sec. 1484 of the Dodd-Frank Act).

▶ **Effective date.** The provision takes effect one day after the date of enactment (Sec. 4 of the Dodd-Frank Wall Street Reform and Consumer Protection Act).

Law source: Law at ¶11,484 and ¶10,004.

— Sec. 1484 of the Dodd-Frank Wall Street Reform and Consumer Protection Act;
— Sec. 4, providing the effective date.

MISCELLANEOUS PROVISIONS

¶6750 Sense of Congress on Government Sponsored Enterprises Reform

Title XIV, Subtitle H of the Dodd-Frank Wall Street Reform and Consumer Protection Act expresses the sense of Congress that efforts to enhance the protection, limitation and regulation of residential mortgage credit terms and practices would be incomplete without meaningful structural reforms of the government sponsored enterprises (GSEs) Federal National Mortgage Association (Fannie Mae) and Federal Home Loan Mortgage Corporation (Freddie Mac) (Sec. 1491(b) of the Dodd-Frank Act).

The Dodd-Frank Act outlines the findings by Congress that led to its sense of the importance of GSE reform (Sec. 1491(a) of the Dodd-Frank Act). These findings include the following:

- Congress chartered the GSEs to "ensure a reliable and affordable supply of mortgage funding." Fannie Mae and Freddie Mac have a dual legal status as privately owned corporations with government-mandated affordable housing goals.

- To help reach affordable housing goals, the Department of Housing and Urban Development in 1995 authorized the GSEs to purchase subprime securities, including loans made to low-income borrowers.

- From 2005 through 2007, Fannie Mae and Freddie Mac purchased approximately $1 trillion in subprime and Alt-A loans. Fannie Mae's acquisitions of mortgages with less than 10-percent down payments almost tripled.

- Federal Housing Finance Agency (FHFA) data for the fourth quarter of 2008 revealed that the GSEs own or guarantee 75 percent of newly originated mortgages, and Fannie Mae and Freddie Mac own 13.3 percent of outstanding mortgage debt in the United States. The data also showed that the GSEs have issued mortgage-backed securities for 31 percent of the residential debt market, for a combined total of 44.3 percent of outstanding mortgage debt in the United States.
- The FHFA placed Fannie Mae and Freddie Mac into conservatorship on Sept. 7, 2008. Congress finds that the conservatorship "has potentially exposed taxpayers to upwards of $5,300,000,000,000 worth of risk."
- Congress finds that the dual status of the GSEs "is untenable and must be resolved."

▶ **Effective date.** The provision takes effect one day after the date of enactment (Sec. 4 of the Dodd-Frank Wall Street Reform and Consumer Protection Act).

Law source: Law at ¶11,491 and ¶10,004. Committee Report at ¶55,085.

— Sec. 1491 of the Dodd-Frank Wall Street Reform and Consumer Protection Act;
— Sec. 4, providing the effective date.

¶6755 GAO Study Report on Mortgage Foreclosure Scams and Loan Modification Fraud

The Comptroller General of the United States, as director of the Government Accountability Office (GAO), must conduct a study on inter-agency government efforts—in the form of a task force comprised of the Secretary of the Treasury Department, Secretary of the Department of Housing and Urban Development, Attorney General and Federal Trade Commission—to crack down on mortgage foreclosure rescue scams and loan modification fraud and advise Congress based on the results of the study (Sec. 1492(a) of the Dodd-Frank Act).

The report to Congress must contain recommendations for legislative and administrative actions the Comptroller General determines appropriate. In addition, the report must include an evaluation of the task force's efforts, specific recommendations on agency or legislative actions the Comptroller General believes necessary to protect homeowners from foreclosure rescue and loan modification scams, and whether the financial resources the government is allocating to crack down on the scams and educate homeowners are adequate (Sec. 1492(b) of the Dodd-Frank Act).

The Helping Families Save Their Homes Act is amended to require that certain loan mortgage modification data be reported by state. The Comptroller of the Currency and Director of Office Thrift Supervision must update requirements to reflect the amendments within 60 days after the date of enactment (Sec. 1493 of the Dodd-Frank Act).

▶ **Effective date.** The GAO study provision and the general amendment for reporting of mortgage data by state take effect one day after the date of enactment (Sec. 4 of the Dodd-Frank Wall Street Reform and Consumer Protection Act). The OCC and OTS must update requirements within 60 days of enactment (Sec. 1493(b) of the Dodd-Frank Act).

Law source: Law at ¶11,492, ¶11,493 and ¶10,004.

— Sec. 1492 of the Dodd-Frank Wall Street Reform and Consumer Protection Act;

- Sec. 1493(a) of the Dodd-Frank Wall Street Reform and Consumer Protection Act, amending Helping Families Save Their Homes Act of 2009 Sec. 104(a);
- Sec. 1493(b), amending Helping Families Save Their Homes Act of 2009 Sec. 104(b)(1)(A);
- Sec. 4, providing the effective date.

¶6760 Study of Effect of Drywall Presence on Foreclosures

The Secretary of the Department of Housing and Urban Development (HUD) must conduct a study and report to Congress on the effect on residential mortgage loan foreclosures of the presence of drywall imported from China between 2004 and the end of 2007. The study also must address the availability of property insurance for residential structures in which the drywall is present.

The Secretary must include in the report to Congress its findings, conclusions and recommendations.

▶ **Effective date.** The HUD Secretary must submit to Congress a report on the study no later than the expiration of the 120-day period beginning on the date of enactment of the Dodd-Frank Act.

Law source: Law at ¶11,494.

- Sec. 1494 of the Dodd-Frank Wall Street Reform and Consumer Protection Act;
- Sec. 1494(b), providing the effective date.

¶6765 Emergency Mortgage Relief

Funds are to be made available to the Department of Housing and Urban Development (HUD) as necessary to provide $1,000,000 for emergency mortgage assistance through the Emergency Homeowners' Relief Fund (Relief Fund). The relief fund is to be established by HUD under the Emergency Housing Act of 1975 (Housing Act) (Dodd-Frank Act Sec. 1496(a).

The Housing Act is amended to:

- prohibit assistance with respect to a mortgage unless the mortgagor and the creditor have certified that circumstances make it probable that there will be a foreclosure and that the mortgagor is in need of emergency mortgage relief (Housing Act Sec. 103(2), as amended by Sec. 1496(b)(1)(A) of the Dodd-Frank Act);
- permit emergency mortgage assistance if the mortgagor has incurred a substantial reduction in income as a result of involuntary unemployment or underemployment stemming from medical conditions (Housing Act Sec. 103(4), as amended by Sec. 1496(b)(1)(B) of the Dodd-Frank Act); and
- revise the requirements for emergency mortgage assistance to replace the maximum amount of $250 per month with an amount "reasonably necessary" to supplement what the homeowner is capable of contributing toward the mortgage payment each

month, capping the aggregate amount of assistance to a single homeowner at $50,000 (Housing Act Sec. 104(b), as amended by Sec. 1496(b)(2)(A) of the Dodd-Frank Act).

The rate of interest on a loan or advance of credit is fixed for the life of the loan or advance. The rate may not exceed the rate of interest generally charged for mortgages on single-family housing insured by HUD at the time the loan or advance of credit is made. No interest may be charged on interest deferred on a loan or advance of credit.

In establishing rates, terms and conditions for loans or advances of credit, the Secretary of HUD must take into account a homeowner's ability to repay the loan or advance (Housing Act Sec. 104(d), as amended by Sec. 1496(b)(2)(B) of the Dodd-Frank Act).

A homeowner who receives a grant or advance of credit may repay the loan in full, without penalty, by lump sum or by installment payments at any time before the loan becomes due (Housing Act Sec. 104(e), as amended by Sec. 1496(b)(2)(C) of the Dodd-Frank Act).

The amendments increase from $1.5 billion to $3 billion the cap on the aggregate amount of insured loans and credit advances but include emergency mortgage relief payments in the $3 billion (Housing Act Sec. 104(e), as amended by Sec. 1496(b)(2)(C) of the Dodd-Frank Act).

HUD must establish underwriting guidelines or procedures to allocate amounts available for insured loans and advances and emergency relief payments based on the likelihood that a mortgagor will be able to resume mortgage payments (Housing Act Sec. 105(e), as added by Sec. 1496(b)(3)(D) of the Dodd-Frank Act).

Funds may be administered by a state if the state has an existing program that provides substantially similar assistance to homeowners, as determined by HUD. After HUD makes the determination, the state is not required to modify the program to comply with the provisions of Title XIV (Housing Act Sec. 108(d), as added by Sec. 1496(b)(5) of the Dodd-Frank Act).

The Dodd-Frank Act repeals the authorizations of appropriations for the emergency mortgage relief program, but extends the authority to insure loans and credit advances under the program and to make emergency mortgage relief payments through Fiscal Year 2011 (Housing Act Sec. 109, as amended by Sec. 1496(b)(6) of the Dodd-Frank Act).

▶ **Effective date.** The provision takes effect one day after the date of enactment (Sec. 4 of the Dodd-Frank Wall Street Reform and Consumer Protection Act).

Law source: Law at ¶11,496 and ¶10,004.

— Sec. 1496(a) of the Dodd-Frank Wall Street Reform and Consumer Protection Act;
— Sec. 1496(b)(1), amending Emergency Housing Act of 1975 Sec. 103;
— Sec. 1496(b)(2), amending Emergency Housing Act of 1975 Sec. 104;
— Sec. 1496(b)(3), amending Emergency Housing Act of 1975 Sec. 105;
— Sec. 1496(b)(4), amending Emergency Housing Act of 1975 Sec. 107;
— Sec. 1496(b)(5), adding Emergency Housing Act of 1975 Sec. 108(d);
— Sec. 1496(b)(6), amending Emergency Housing Act of 1975 Sec. 109;
— Sec. 1496(b)(7), striking Emergency Housing Act of 1975 Secs. 110, 111 and 113;

— Sec. 1496(b)(8), redesignating Emergency Housing Act of 1975 Secs. 112 as 110;
— Sec. 4, providing the effective date.

¶6770 Additional Assistance for Neighborhood Stabilization Program

The Treasury Department must transfer to HUD $1 billion to assist states and local government units in the redevelopment of abandoned and foreclosed homes (Sec. 1497(a) of the Dodd-Frank Act). The Treasury Department is authorized to transfer the funds out of funds in the Treasury that are not otherwise appropriated.

The transferred funds will be allocated based on a funding formula established by the Treasury Department under the Housing and Economic Recovery Act of 2008, except that:

- the formula must be established within 30 days after the date of enactment of the Dodd-Frank Act;
- HUD may not establish a minimum grant amount or size for grants to the states. However, HUD may establish a minimum grant amount for allocations to local governments in the amount of $1 million or less; and
- a state or local government that receives a grant must establish procedures to create preferences for the development of affordable rental housing for properties assisted under this section (Sec. 1497(a)(3) of the Dodd-Frank Act).

HUD may not distribute any amounts to an organization that has been convicted of a violation under federal law relating to an election for federal office or employs, or that contracts with or retains any individuals convicted of such violation (Sec. 1497(a)(7) of the Dodd-Frank Act).

Provisions governing emergency assistance for the redevelopment of abandoned and foreclosed homes in the Housing and Economic Recovery Act of 2008 (Housing Act) have been amended. The amendment removes, from the requirement that not less than 25 percent of the available funds be used to house individuals or families whose incomes do not exceed 50 percent of area median income, the additional requirement that those funds also be used for the purchase and redevelopment of abandoned and foreclosed upon homes or residential properties.

That provision of the Housing Act will apply with respect to any unexpended or unobligated balances, including recaptured and reallocated funds made available under this legislation, Sec. 2301 of the Housing Act and a specified portion of the American Recovery and Reinvestment Act of 2009. Moreover, for any funds made available, the date of a notice of foreclosure will be the date on which complete title to a property is transferred to a successor entity or person as a result of a court order or pursuant to a mortgage, deed of trust or security deed (Housing Act Sec. 2301(f)(3)(A)(ii), as amended by Sec. 1497(b)(1) of the Dodd-Frank Act).

▶ **Effective date.** The provision takes effect one day after the date of enactment (Sec. 4 of the Dodd-Frank Wall Street Reform and Consumer Protection Act).

Law source: Law at ¶11,497 and ¶10,004.

— Sec. 1497(a) of the Dodd-Frank Wall Street Reform and Consumer Protection Act;

— Sec. 1497(b), amending Housing and Economic Recovery Act of 2008 Sec. 2301;

— Sec. 4, providing the effective date.

¶6775 Legal Assistance for Foreclosure-Related Issues

The HUD Secretary must establish a grant program providing foreclosure legal assistance to low- and moderate-income homeowners and tenants related to home ownership preservation, home foreclosure prevention and tenancy associated with home foreclosure (Sec. 1498(a) of the Dodd-Frank Act). The Secretary must allocate available amounts to state and local legal organizations on the basis of a competitive process (Sec. 1498(b) of the Dodd-Frank Act). Priority will be given to organizations operating in the 125 metropolitan statistical areas with the highest home foreclosure rates (Sec. 1498(c) of the Dodd-Frank Act). $35,000,000 is authorized to be appropriated for grants for each of the fiscal years 2011 through 2012 (Sec. 1498(f) of the Dodd-Frank Act).

Legal Assistance.—Grant dollars may be used to assist only homeowners of owner-occupied homes with mortgages in default, in danger of default or at risk of foreclosure, or tenants at risk of eviction as a result of foreclosure. Use of grant money must commence within 90 days of receipt. No funds may be used to support class action litigation. Funded legal assistance is limited to mortgage-related default, eviction or foreclosure proceedings, without regard to whether the foreclosure is judicial or nonjudicial. The legal assistance provisions take effect on the date of enactment of the Dodd-Frank Act (Sec. 1498(d) of the Dodd-Frank Act).

Limitation on Funds Distribution.—Grant dollars may not be distributed to any organization that has been convicted of a violation under federal law relating to an election for federal office or any organization that employs an "applicable individual"— one who is employed by, contracted by or acting on behalf of, the organization, or one who has been convicted of a violation under federal law relating to an election for federal office (Sec. 1498(d) of the Dodd-Frank Act).

▶ **Effective date.** The provision takes effect one day after the date of enactment (Sec. 4 of the Dodd-Frank Wall Street Reform and Consumer Protection Act).

Law source: Law at ¶11,498 and ¶10,004.

— Sec. 1498 of the Dodd-Frank Wall Street Reform and Consumer Protection Act;

— Sec. 4, providing the effective date.

Miscellaneous Provisions

¶7005	Introduction
¶7010	Section 1256 Contracts
¶7015	U.S. Funds for Foreign Governments
¶7020	Conflict Minerals
¶7025	Mine Safety Violations
¶7030	Payments by Resource Extraction Issuers
¶7035	Report on Inspectors General
¶7040	Study of Core and Brokered Deposits

¶7005 Introduction

Titles XV and XVI of the Dodd-Frank Wall Street Reform and Consumer Protection Act contain several miscellaneous provisions. Most significant among them is the lone provision in Title XVI, Section 1601, a revenue-raising measure that changes the tax treatment of certain derivatives contracts (discussed at ¶ 7010).

Title XV of the Dodd-Frank Act (Sections 1501 *et seq.*) contains various other measures, including one that requires the Administration to evaluate any proposed loan by the International Monetary Fund if the borrower country's public debt exceeds its annual gross domestic product, and to oppose the loan if it cannot certify to Congress that the loan is likely to be repaid (see ¶ 7015).

Another provision requires disclosure to the SEC by all persons otherwise required to file with the Commission for whom minerals originating in the Democratic Republic of Congo and adjoining countries are necessary to the functionality or production of a product manufactured by that person. The report must describe steps taken to exercise due diligence on the source and chain of custody of the materials, the products manufactured, and other matters (see ¶ 7020).

The Dodd-Frank Act requires certain Exchange Act reporting issuers that operate coal or other mines to include information on mine safety in their periodic reports. Issuers must also disclose on Form 8-K certain information regarding mine shutdowns and patterns of health and safety violations (see ¶ 7025).

The legislation calls for SEC rules requiring resource extraction issuers to include in their annual reports information relating to any payments made to foreign governments or the federal government for the purpose of the commercial development of oil, natural gas or minerals. The term "payment" includes taxes, royalties, fees, licenses, production entitlements, bonuses and other material benefits, as determined by the Commission (see ¶ 7030).

Finally, Title XV mandates two reports: one assessing the relative independence, effectiveness and expertise of presidentially appointed inspectors general and inspectors general of designated federal agencies (see ¶ 7035); the other examining differences between the definitions of core deposits and brokered deposits (see ¶ 7040).

▶ **Effective date.** The provisions in Title XV take effect one day after the date of enactment (Sec. 4 of the Dodd-Frank Wall Street Reform and Consumer Protection Act). The amendments made by Section 1601 apply to taxable years after enactment of the Dodd-Frank Act (Sec. 1601(b) of the Dodd-Frank Act).

Law source: Law at ¶11,501, ¶11,601 and ¶10,004. Committee Report at ¶50,151 and ¶50,161.

— Sec. 1501 *et seq.* of the Dodd-Frank Wall Street Reform and Consumer Protection Act, providing the requirements of Title XV;

— Sec. 1601, amending I.R.C. Sec. 2506(b);

— Sec. 4, providing the general effective date.

¶7010 Section 1256 Contracts

Title XVI (Section 1601) of Dodd-Frank Wall Street Reform and Consumer Protection Act contains a revenue raising amendment to the Internal Revenue Code (I.R.C.). The amendment excludes certain derivatives contracts from I.R.C. Section 1256, which effectively raises the tax on those contracts (I.R.C. Sec. 1256(b)(2), added by the Dodd-Frank Wall Street Reform and Consumer Protection Act).

The Joint Committee on Taxation estimates that exempting swaps and other derivative contracts from the tax consequences of I.R.C. Section 1256 will increase revenues by $120 million over the 2010-2020 period (see *Cost Estimate of the Dodd-Frank Wall Street Reform and Consumer Protection Act*, Congressional Budget Office, June 28, 2010, p. 10).

Background.—Commodities dealers (within the meaning of I.R.C. Section 1402(i)(2)(B)), commodities derivatives dealers (within the meaning of I.R.C. Section 1221(b)(1)(A)), dealers in securities (within the meaning of I.R.C. Section 475(c)(1)) and options dealers (within the meaning of I.R.C. Section 1256(g)(8)), treat the income from certain of their day-to-day dealer activities as giving rise to capital gain. Under I.R.C. Section 1256, these dealers treat 60 percent of their income (or loss) from their dealer activities as long-term capital gain (or loss) and 40 percent of their income (or loss) from their dealer activities as short-term capital gain (or loss). Dealers in other types of property generally treat the income from their day-to-day dealer activities as giving rise to ordinary income.

Section 1256 of requires taxpayers to treat each Section 1256 contract as if it were sold and repurchased for its fair market value on the last day of the year, marked to market. Any gain or loss with respect to a Section 1256 contract that is subject to the mark-to-market rule is treated as short-term capital gain or loss, to the extent of 40 percent of the gain or loss, and long-term capital gain or loss, to the extent of the remaining 60 percent of the gain or loss. Gains and losses upon the termination or transfer of a Section 1256 contract, by offsetting, taking or making delivery, by exercise or by being exercised, by assignment or being assigned, by lapse, or otherwise, also generally are treated as 40 percent short-term and 60 percent long-term capital gains or losses (Report of the Joint Committee on Taxation, June 12, 2009).

The special rule in Section 1256(a) treating gains and losses as 60 percent long-term capital gains and losses and 40 percent short-term capital gains and losses (the "60/40 rule") does not apply to: (1) hedging transactions (as defined in I.R.C. Section 1221(b)(2)(a); (2) a Section 1256 contract that is part of a mixed straddle if the taxpayer elects to have Section 1256 not apply to the Section 1256 contract; or (3) any Section 1256 contract held by a dealer in commodities or by a trader in commodities that makes the mark-to-market election in I.R.C. Section 475 (Report of Joint Committee on Taxation, June 12, 2009).

In general, the 60/40 rule provides a significant tax benefit to certain commodities traders and dealers, allowing them to convert 60 percent of gains from frequent trading that otherwise would be short-term capital gains or ordinary income into long-term capital gains that are taxed at a lower rate (Report of Joint Committee on Taxation, June 12, 2009).

Derivatives Contract Exclusion.—As amended, I.R.C. Section 1256 now excludes certain derivatives transactions from the 60/40 rule. It states that the term "Section 1256 contract" does not include: (1) any securities futures contract or option on such a contract unless the contract or option is a dealer securities futures contract; or (2) any interest rate swap, currency swap, basis swap, interest rate cap, interest rate floor, commodity swap, equity swap, equity index swap, credit default swap or similar agreement (I.R.C. Sec. 1256(b)(2), as added by the Dodd-Frank Act).

▶ **Effective date.** The amendments made by this provision apply to taxable years after enactment of the Dodd-Frank Act (Sec. 1601(b) of the Dodd-Frank Wall Street Reform and Consumer Protection Act).

Law source: Law at ¶11,601. Committee Report at ¶50,161.

— Sec. 1601(a) of the Dodd-Frank Wall Street Reform and Consumer Protection Act, amending I.R.C. Sec. 1256(b);

— Sec. 1601(b), providing the effective date.

¶7015 U.S. Funds for Foreign Governments

Section 1501 of Title XV of the Dodd-Frank Wall Street Reform and Consumer Protection Act requires the Treasury Secretary to instruct the U.S. Executive Director at the International Monetary Fund (IMF) to evaluate any loan proposal to the IMF if the borrowing country's public debt exceeds its gross domestic product. If the evaluation indicates that the proposed loan is not likely to be repaid in full, the Treasury Secretary must instruct the Executive Director to vote against the proposal.

The provision, authored by Sen. John Cornyn (R-TX), is designed to bring needed transparency and accountability to what the IMF is doing with American taxpayer dollars. In discussing the reasoning behind the provision, Sen. Cornyn said that any country that owes more money than its entire economy produces is, by definition, a bad credit risk. Accordingly, the United States should not loan money to such a nation unless absolute confidence exists that the money will be repaid (Cong. Rec., May 17, 2010, p. S3803).

Restrictions on Use.—The legislation amends the Bretton Woods Agreements Act by adding a provision that restricts the use of U.S. funds for foreign governments. The provision has the stated purpose of protecting American taxpayers. The provision requires the Treasury Secretary to instruct the U.S. Executive Director of the IMF to evaluate any proposal submitted to the IMF Board of Executive Directors to make a loan to a country if: (1) the amount of the country's public debt exceeds its gross domestic product as of the most recent year for which the information is available; and (2) the country is not eligible for assistance from the International Development Association. If the evaluation indicates that the proposed loan is not likely to be repaid in full, the Secretary must instruct the Executive Director to vote against the proposal (Bretton Woods Agreements Act Sec. 68(a), as added by the Dodd-Frank Act).

Reports to Congress.—The Treasury Secretary must make a written report to the House Financial Services Committee, the Senate Committee on Foreign Relations, and the Senate Banking Committee within 30 days after the IMF Board of Executive Directors approves a loan proposal evaluated under Bretton Woods Agreements Act Section 68(a). Additionally, the Secretary must make annual reports to these committees by June 30 for the duration of any program approved under the proposal. The reports must assess the likelihood that the loans will be repaid in full, and must include: (1) the borrowing country's current debt status, including the debt's maturity structure, whether it has fixed or floating rates, whether it is indexed, and by whom it is held; (2) the borrowing country's external and internal vulnerabilities that could potentially affect its ability to repay; and (3) the borrowing country's debt management strategy (Bretton Woods Agreements Act Sec. 68(b), as added by the Dodd-Frank Act).

▶ **Effective date.** The provision takes effect one day after the date of enactment (Sec. 4 of the Dodd-Frank Wall Street Reform and Consumer Protection Act).

Law source: Law at ¶11,501 and ¶10,004. Committee Report at ¶50,151.

— Sec. 1501 of the Dodd-Frank Wall Street Reform and Consumer Protection Act, adding Bretton Woods Agreements Act Sec. 68;

— Sec. 4, providing the effective date.

¶7020 Conflict Minerals

Section 1502 of the Dodd-Frank Wall Street Reform and Consumer Protection Act reflects the sense of Congress that the exploitation and trade of conflict minerals originating in the Democratic Republic of the Congo is helping to finance conflict in the eastern part of the country characterized by extreme levels of violence, particularly sexual and gender-based violence (Sec. 1502(a) of the Dodd-Frank Act). The legislation amends the Exchange Act to require persons that manufacture a product containing these minerals as a necessary part of either the product's functionality or its manufacturing process to disclose annually whether the minerals originated in the Democratic

Republic of the Congo or a neighboring country. If the conflict minerals originated in any of these countries, the person must submit to the SEC a report that includes a description of the products manufactured and the measures taken to exercise due diligence on the source and chain of custody of the minerals. These measures must include an independent private sector audit of the report.

The legislation also requires the Secretary of State, in consultation with the Administrator of the United States Agency for International Development, to submit to Congress a strategy to address the illicit minerals trade in the region. The Secretary of State must produce a map showing mineral-rich zones, trade routes and areas under the control of armed groups that addresses linkages between conflict minerals and the armed groups.

> **CCH Comment:** The United Nations Group of Experts has issued reports for several years concerning how parties to the conflict in the eastern Democratic Republic of the Congo continue to benefit and finance themselves by controlling mines or taxing trading routes for these minerals. Despite efforts to curb the violence, mass atrocities and widespread sexual violence have continued at an alarming rate. In response to these reports, the United Nations Security Council adopted Resolution 1857 (2008) encouraging member states to ensure that companies handling minerals from Congo exercise due diligence on their suppliers (Cong. Rec., May 19, 2010, p. S3976).
>
> Authored by Sen. Sam Brownback (R-KS), Section 1502 specifically responds to the continued crisis in eastern Congo. The provision was narrowly crafted in consideration of local economies, however, and thus includes waivers and a sunset clause after five years (Cong. Rec., May 19, 2010, p. S3976).

Definitions.—The term "conflict mineral" means: (1) columbite-tantalite (coltan), cassiterite, gold, wolframite or their derivatives; or (2) any other mineral or its derivatives determined by the Secretary of State to be financing conflict in the Democratic Republic of the Congo or an adjoining country (Sec. 1502(e)(4) of the Dodd-Frank Act).

The term "adjoining country" means a country that shares an internationally recognized border with the Democratic Republic of the Congo (Sec. 1502(e)(1) of the Dodd-Frank Act).

The term "armed group" means an armed group that is identified as being perpetrators of serious human rights abuses in the annual Country Reports on Human Rights Practices issued under Foreign Assistance Act of 1961 Sections 116(d) and 502B(b) relating to the Democratic Republic of the Congo or an adjoining country (Sec. 1502(e)(3) of the Dodd-Frank Act).

The phrase "under the control of armed groups" means areas within the Democratic Republic of the Congo or adjoining countries in which armed groups:

- physically control mines or force labor of civilians to mine, transport or sell conflict minerals;
- tax, extort or control any part of the trade routes for conflict minerals, including the entire trade route from a conflict zone mine to the point of export from the Democratic Republic of the Congo or an adjoining country; or
- tax, extort or control trading facilities, in whole or in part, including the point of export from the Democratic Republic of the Congo or an adjoining country (Sec. 1502(e)(5) of the Dodd-Frank Act).

¶7020

The term "appropriate congressional committees" means:

- the House Committee on Appropriations;
- the House Committee on Foreign Affairs;
- the House Committee on Ways and Means;
- the House Committee on Financial Services;
- the Senate Committee on Appropriations;
- the Senate Committee on Foreign Relations;
- the Senate Committee on Finance; and
- the Senate Committee on Banking, Housing, and Urban Affairs (Sec. 1502(e)(2) of the Dodd-Frank Act).

Disclosures.—Within 270 days after the date of enactment, the SEC must promulgate regulations requiring certain persons who manufacture a product containing conflict minerals to disclose annually whether the conflict minerals originated in the Democratic Republic of the Congo or an adjoining country. The annual disclosures must begin with the person's first full fiscal year that begins after the date of promulgation of the regulations. If the conflict minerals originated in any of these countries, the person must submit to the SEC a report that includes a description of the measures taken to exercise due diligence on the source and chain of custody of the minerals. These measures must include an independent private sector audit of the report that is conducted in accordance with standards established by the Comptroller General, in accordance with rules promulgated by the SEC, in consultation with the Secretary of State (Exchange Act Sec. 13(p)(1)(A)(i), as added by the Dodd-Frank Act).

The report must also include:

- a description of the products either manufactured or contracted be manufactured that are not DRC conflict free, as defined in the statute;
- the entity that conducted the independent private sector audit;
- the facilities used to process the conflict minerals;
- the country of origin of the conflict minerals; and
- the efforts to determine the mine or location of origin with the greatest possible specificity (Exchange Act Sec. 13(p)(1)(A)(ii), as added by the Dodd-Frank Act).

The statute defines "DRC conflict free" to mean products that do not contain minerals that directly or indirectly finance or benefit armed groups in the Democratic Republic of the Congo or an adjoining country (Exchange Act Sec. 13(p)(1)(D), as added by the Dodd-Frank Act).

Covered Persons. A person becomes subject to the disclosure requirements relating to conflict minerals if: (1) the person must file reports with the SEC concerning conflict minerals under Exchange Act Section 13(p)(1)(A); and (2) conflict minerals are necessary to the functionality or production of a product manufactured by that person (Exchange Act Sec. 13(p)(2), as added by the Dodd-Frank Act).

Certification and Unreliable Determination. The person submitting a report concerning conflict minerals must certify the audit that is included in the report. The certified audit will constitute a critical component of due diligence in establishing the source and chain of custody of the minerals (Exchange Act Sec. 13(p)(1)(B), as added by the Dodd-Frank

Act). If a required report relies on a determination of an independent private sector audit or other due diligence processes that have been previously determined by the SEC to be unreliable, the report will not satisfy the reporting requirements of the regulations (Exchange Act Sec. 13(p)(1)(C), as added by the Dodd-Frank Act).

Information Available to the Public. Each person subject to the disclosure requirements for conflict minerals must make the information they have disclosed to the SEC available to the public on their website (Exchange Act Sec. 13(p)(1)(E), as added by the Dodd-Frank Act).

Revisions and Waivers. The SEC must revise or temporarily waive the disclosure requirements for conflict minerals if the President transmits to the SEC a determination that: (1) the revision or waiver is in the U.S. national security interest and the President includes the reasons for the determination; and (2) establishes a date, not later than two years after the initial publication of the exemption, on which the exemption will expire (Exchange Act Sec. 13(p)(3), as added by the Dodd-Frank Act).

Termination of Disclosure Requirements. The disclosure requirements will terminate on the date on which the President determines and certifies to the appropriate congressional committees that no armed groups continue to be directly involved and benefitting from commercial activity involving conflict minerals. The termination date will not be earlier, however, than the date that is one day after the end of the five-year period beginning on the date of enactment (Exchange Act Sec. 13(p)(4), as added by the Dodd-Frank Act).

Strategy and Map to Address Linkages.—*Strategy.* Within 180 days after the date of enactment, the Secretary of State, in consultation with the Administrator of the United States Agency for International Development, must submit to the appropriate congressional committees a strategy to address the linkages between human rights abuses, armed groups, the mining of conflict minerals, and commercial products (Sec. 1502(c)(1)(A) of the Dodd-Frank Act).

The strategy must include a plan to promote peace and security in the Democratic Republic of the Congo by supporting the efforts of that country's government, adjoining countries and the international community to: (1) monitor and stop commercial activities that contribute to the activities of armed groups and human rights violations in the country; and (2) develop stronger governance and economic institutions that can facilitate and improve transparency in the cross-border trade involving the country's natural resources in order to reduce exploitation by armed groups and promote local and regional development (Sec. 1502(c)(1)(B)(i) of the Dodd-Frank Act).

In addition, the strategy must include a plan to provide guidance to commercial entities seeking to exercise due diligence on, and formalize the origin and chain of custody of, the conflict minerals used in their products and the products of their suppliers to ensure that conflict minerals do not directly or indirectly finance armed conflict or result in labor or human rights violations (Sec. 1502(c)(1)(B)(ii) of the Dodd-Frank Act).

Finally, the strategy must include a description of punitive measures that could be taken against individuals or entities whose commercial activities are supporting armed groups and human rights violations in the Democratic Republic of the Congo (Sec. 1502(c)(1)(B)(iii) of the Dodd-Frank Act).

Map. Within 180 days after the date of enactment, the Secretary of State must, in accordance with the recommendation of the United Nations Group of Experts on the

¶7020

Democratic Republic of the Congo in their December 2008 report, produce a map of mineral-rich zones, trade routes and areas under the control of armed groups in the Democratic Republic of the Congo and adjoining countries (Sec. 1502(c)(2)(A)(i) of the Dodd-Frank Act). The map will be known as the "Conflict Minerals Map." The mines depicted on the map that are located in areas under the control of armed groups in the Democratic Republic of the Congo and adjoining countries will be known as "Conflict Zone Mines" (Sec. 1502(c)(2)(B) of the Dodd-Frank Act).

The map must be based on data from multiple sources, including: (1) the United Nations Group of Experts on the Democratic Republic of the Congo; (2) the government of the Democratic Republic of the Congo, the governments of adjoining countries and the governments of other member states of the United Nations; and (3) local and international non-governmental organizations. The Secretary of State must make the map available to the public. The Secretary of State must also provide to the appropriate congressional committees an explanatory note describing the sources of information on which the map is based and identifying, where possible, the armed groups or other forces in control of the mines that are depicted (Sec. 1502(c)(2)(A) of the Dodd-Frank Act).

The Secretary of State must update the map at least once every 180 days until the date on which the disclosure requirements for conflict minerals terminate. The Secretary of State must also add minerals to the list of minerals defined as conflict minerals, as appropriate. In order to declare a mineral as a conflict mineral, the Secretary of State must publish a notice of intent in the *Federal Register* no later than one year before the declaration (Secs. 1502(c)(2)(C) and (D) of the Dodd-Frank Act).

Reports to Congress.—*Baseline Report.* Within one year after the date of enactment, the Comptroller General must submit to appropriate congressional committees a report that includes an assessment of the rate of sexual and gender-based violence in war-torn areas of the Democratic Republic of the Congo and adjoining countries. The Comptroller General must continue to submit the reports annually until the disclosure requirements for conflict minerals terminate (Sec. 1502(d)(1) of the Dodd-Frank Act).

Regular Report on Effectiveness. Within two years after the date of enactment, and annually thereafter, the Comptroller General must submit a report to the appropriate congressional committees that includes the following: (1) an assessment of the effectiveness of Exchange Act Sec. 13(p) in promoting peace and security in the Democratic Republic of the Congo and adjoining countries; (2) a description of the issues encountered by the SEC in carrying out the statute's provisions; (3) a general review of persons who manufacture products for which conflict minerals are necessary, but who do not file reports with the SEC. This general review must state whether information is publicly available about: (1) the use of conflict minerals by these persons; and (2) whether the conflict minerals originate from the Democratic Republic of the Congo or an adjoining country (Sec. 1502(d)(2) of the Dodd-Frank Act).

Report on Private Sector Auditing. Within 30 months after the date of enactment, and annually thereafter, the Secretary of Commerce must submit a report to the appropriate congressional committees that includes the following: (1) an assessment of the accuracy of the independent private sector audits and other due diligence processes described under Exchange Act Section 13(p) to exercise due diligence on conflict minerals; and (2) recommendations for the processes used to carry out audits, including ways to improve accuracy and establish standards of best practices; and (3) a listing of all known conflict mineral processing facilities worldwide (Sec. 1502(d)(3) of the Dodd-Frank Act).

▶ **Effective date.** The provision takes effect one day after the date of enactment (Sec. 4 of the Dodd-Frank Wall Street Reform and Consumer Protection Act).

Law source: Law at ¶11,502 and ¶10,004. Committee Report at ¶50,151.

— Sec. 1502(a), of the Dodd-Frank Wall Street Reform and Consumer Protection Act, expressing the sense of Congress;

— Sec. 1502(b), adding Exchange Act Sec. 13(p);

— Sec. 1502(c), requiring a strategy and map to address linkages;

— Sec. 1502(d), requiring reports to Congress;

— Sec. 1502(e), providing definitions;

— Sec. 4, providing the effective date.

¶7025 Mine Safety Violations

Section 1503 of the Dodd-Frank Wall Street Reform and Consumer Protection Act requires certain Exchange Act reporting issuers that operate coal or other mines, either directly or through subsidiaries, to include information on mine safety in the periodic reports they file with the SEC. Issuers must also disclose on Form 8-K certain information regarding mine shutdowns and patterns of health and safety violations.

Definitions.—The terms "issuer" and "securities laws" have the meanings given to them in Exchange Act Section 3 (Sec. 1503(e)(1) of the Dodd-Frank Act).

The term "coal or other mine" means a coal or other mine as defined in, and subject to, the provisions of Federal Mine Safety and Health Act Section 3 (Sec. 1503(e)(2) of the Dodd-Frank Act).

The term "operator" has the meaning given in Federal Mine Safety and Health Act Section 3 (Sec. 1503(e)(3) of the Dodd-Frank Act).

Periodic Reports.—The legislation requires each issuer reporting under Exchange Act Sections 13(a) or 15(d) that is an operator of a coal or other mine, or that has a subsidiary that is an operator, to include information on mine safety in periodic reports filed with the SEC under the securities laws. The information must be included in each periodic report filed on or after the date of enactment and must be based on the time period covered by the report (Sec. 1503(a) of the Dodd-Frank Act). The reporting requirements do not affect any obligation of a person to make a disclosure under any other applicable law in effect before, on or after the date of enactment (Sec. 1503(c) of the Dodd-Frank Act).

For each coal or other mine of which the issuer or a subsidiary is an operator, each report must include:

- the total number of violations of mandatory health or safety standards that could significantly and substantially contribute to the cause and effect of a coal or other mine safety or health hazard under Federal Mine Safety and Health Act Section 104 for which the operator received a citation from the Mine Safety and Health Administration;

- the total number of orders issued under Federal Mine Safety and Health Act Section 104(b);
- the total number of citations and orders for unwarrantable failure of the mine operator to comply with mandatory health or safety standards under Federal Mine Safety and Health Act Section 104(d);
- the total number of flagrant violations under Federal Mine Safety and Health Act Section 110(b)(2);
- the total number of imminent danger orders issued under Federal Mine Safety and Health Act Section 107(a);
- the total dollar value of proposed assessments from the Mine Safety and Health Administration under the Federal Mine Safety and Health Act; and
- the total number of mining-related fatalities (Sec. 1503(a)(1) of the Dodd-Frank Act).

In addition, each periodic report must also include a list of the mines which the issuer or a subsidiary operate that receive written notice from the Mine Safety and Health Administration of:

- a pattern of violations of mandatory health or safety standards that could have significantly and substantially contributed to the cause and effect of mine health or safety standards under Federal Mine Safety and Health Act Section 104(e); or
- the potential to have such a pattern (Sec. 1503(a)(2) of the Dodd-Frank Act).

Finally, each report must disclose any pending legal action before the Federal Mine Safety and Health Review Commission involving the mines (Sec. 1503(a)(3) of the Dodd-Frank Act).

Shutdowns and Violation Patterns.—Beginning on and after the date of enactment, each issuer that is an operator of a coal or other mine, or that has a subsidiary that is an operator, must file with the SEC a current report on Form 8-K disclosing the following information regarding each mine operated by the issuer or the subsidiary:

- the receipt of an imminent danger order issued under Federal Mine Safety and Health Act Section 107(a);
- the receipt of written notice from the Mine Safety and Health Administration that the coal or other mine has: (1) a pattern of violations of mandatory health and safety standards that could have significantly and substantially contributed to coal or other mine health or safety hazards under Federal Mine Safety and Health Act Section 104(e); or (2) the potential to have such a pattern (Sec. 1503(b) of the Dodd-Frank Act).

SEC Authority.—Violations of Section 1503, or any SEC rule issued under that section, will be treated in the same manner as a violation of the Exchange Act or its underlying rules and regulations. Accordingly, any person violating Section 1503 will be subject to the same penalties, and to the same extent, as for violations of the Exchange Act and its underlying rules and regulations (Sec. 1503(d)(1) of the Dodd-Frank Act).

The SEC may issue regulations that are necessary or appropriate for the protection of investors and to carry out the statute's purposes (Sec. 1503(d)(2) of the Dodd-Frank Act).

▶ **Effective date.** The provision takes effect on the day that is 30 days after the date of enactment (Sec. 1503(f) of the Dodd-Frank Wall Street Reform and Consumer Protection Act).

Law source: Law at ¶11,503. Committee Report at ¶50,151.

— Sec. 1503(a) of the Dodd-Frank Wall Street Reform and Consumer Protection Act, requiring the reporting of mine safety information;

— Sec. 1503(b), requiring reporting of shutdowns and patterns of violations;

— Sec. 1503(c), setting forth the rule of construction;

— Sec. 1503(d), providing for enforcement and rulemaking authority;

— Sec. 1503(e), providing definitions;

— Sec. 1503(f), providing the effective date.

¶7030 Payments by Resource Extraction Issuers

Section 1504 amends the Exchange Act to require the SEC to issue final rules requiring resource extraction issuers to include in their annual reports information relating to any payments made to foreign governments or the federal government for the purpose of the commercial development of oil, natural gas or minerals. The legislation includes as a "payment" taxes, royalties, fees, licenses, production entitlements, bonuses and other material benefits, as determined by the SEC. The rules must require that the information included in the resource extraction issuer's annual report be submitted in an interactive data format, using an interactive data standard that includes electronic tagging of the types and total amount of payments made for each project of the issuer.

According to Sen. Richard Lugar (R-IN), the legislation builds on the findings of a Senate Committee on Foreign Relations staff report, "Petroleum and Poverty Paradox: Assessing U.S. and International Community Efforts to Fight the Resource Curse," which noted that many resource-rich countries that should be well off are, in fact, terribly poor. Senator Lugar observed that transparency is a vital tool in countries abundant in natural resources, corruption and authoritarianism. Accordingly, the increased transparency provided by the legislation will help reverse the "resource curse" by empowering citizens to hold their governments accountable for decisions made in managing valuable oil, gas and mineral resources and revenues. Transparency will also benefit Americans at home, as improved governance of extractive industries will improve investment climates for domestic companies abroad, increase the reliability of commodity supplies and promote greater energy security. Finally, the legislation complements multilateral transparency efforts such as the Extractive Industries Transparency Initiative, under which some countries are beginning to require all extractive companies operating in their territories to publicly report their payments (Cong. Rec., May 17, 2010, pp. S3815–S3816).

Definitions.—The term "resource extraction issuer" means an issuer that: (1) must file an annual report with the SEC; and (2) engages in the commercial development of oil, natural gas or minerals (Exchange Act Sec. 13(q)(1)(D), as added by the Dodd-Frank Wall Street Reform and Consumer Protection Act).

The term "commercial development of oil, natural gas, or minerals" includes exploration, extraction, processing, export and other significant actions relating to oil, natural gas or minerals, or the acquisition of a license for any such activity, as determined by the SEC (Exchange Act Sec. 13(q)(1)(A), as added by the Dodd-Frank Act).

The term "payment" means a payment that: (1) is made to further the commercial development of oil, natural gas or minerals; and (2) is not *de minimis*. The term includes:

- taxes;
- royalties;
- fees, including license fees;
- production entitlements; and
- bonuses.

The term "payment" also includes other material benefits that the SEC, consistent to the extent possible with the guidelines of the Extractive Industries Transparency Initiative, determines to be part of the commonly recognized revenue stream for the commercial development of oil, natural gas or minerals (Exchange Act Sec. 13(q)(1)(C), as added by the Dodd-Frank Act).

The term "foreign government" means: (1) a foreign government; (2) a department, agency or instrumentality of a foreign government; or (3) a company owned by a foreign government, as determined by the SEC (Exchange Act Sec. 13(q)(1)(B), as added by the Dodd-Frank Act).

Rulemaking and Disclosure.—Within 270 days after the date of enactment, the SEC must issue final rules requiring each resource extraction issuer to include in its annual report information relating to any payment made by either the issuer, its subsidiaries or entities under its control to a foreign government or the federal government for the purpose of the commercial development of oil, natural gas or minerals. This information must include: (1) the type and total amount of the payments made for each related project of the issuer; and (2) the type and total amount of payments made to each government (Exchange Act Sec. 13(q)(2)(A), as added by the Dodd-Frank Act).

With respect to each resource extraction issuer, the rules will take effect on the date the issuer must submit an annual report relating to its fiscal year that ends not earlier than one year after the date the SEC issues its final rules (Exchange Act Sec. 13(q)(2)(F), as added by the Dodd-Frank Act).

In issuing the rules governing payments by resource extraction issuers, the SEC may consult with any agency or entity it determines to be relevant (Exchange Act Sec. 13(q)(2)(B), as added by the Dodd-Frank Act). To the extent possible, the rules must also support the commitment of the federal government to international transparency promotion efforts relating to the commercial development of oil, natural gas or minerals (Exchange Act Sec. 13(q)(2)(E), as added by the Dodd-Frank Act).

¶7030

The legislation authorizes appropriations to the SEC as are necessary to carry out the provisions of the statute (Exchange Act Sec. 13(q)(4), as added by the Dodd-Frank Act).

Interactive Data and Public Availability.—The rules issued by the SEC must require that the information included in the resource extraction issuer's annual report be submitted in an interactive data format (Exchange Act Sec. 13(q)(2)(C), as added by the Dodd-Frank Act). For purposes of the statute, the term "interactive data" means an electronic data format in which pieces of information are identified using an interactive data standard. The statute defines "interactive data standard" to mean a standardized list of electronic tags that mark information included in the issuer's annual report (Exchange Act Secs. 13(q)(1)(E) and (F), as added by the Dodd-Frank Act).

The rules must establish an interactive data standard for the information in the resource extraction issuer's annual report. This standard must include electronic tags that identify the following information with respect to any payments made by the resource extraction issuer to a foreign government or the federal government:

- the total amount of the payments, by category;
- the currency used to make the payments;
- the financial period in which the payments were made;
- the business segment of the issuer that made the payments;
- the government that received the payments and the country in which the government is located;
- the project of the issuer to which the payments relate; and
- any other information deemed by the SEC to be necessary or appropriate in the public interest and for investor protection (Exchange Act Sec. 13(q)(2)(D), as added by the Dodd-Frank Act).

To the extent possible, the SEC must make available to the public an online compilation of the information disclosed under the rules. The statute does not require the SEC, however, to make available online any information other than that required to be submitted under the rules (Exchange Act Sec. 13(q)(3), as added by the Dodd-Frank Act).

▶ **Effective date.** The provision takes effect one day after the date of enactment (Sec. 4 of the Dodd-Frank Wall Street Reform and Consumer Protection Act).

Law source: Law at ¶11,504 and ¶10,004. Committee Report at ¶50,151.

— Sec. 1504 of the Dodd-Frank Wall Street Reform and Consumer Protection Act, adding Exchange Act Sec. 13(q);
— Sec. 4, providing the effective date.

¶7035 Report on Inspectors General

The Comptroller General must issue a report under Section 1505 of the Dodd-Frank Wall Street Reform and Consumer Protection Act that assesses the relative independence, effectiveness and expertise of presidentially appointed inspectors general and inspectors general of designated federal entities, as defined under Inspector General

Act Section 8G. The report must also assess the effects on independence of the amendments made to the Inspector General Act by the Dodd-Frank Act (Sec. 1505(a) of the Dodd-Frank Act). The report must be issued no later than one year after the date of enactment to: (1) the House Financial Services Committee; (2) the House Oversight and Government Reform Committee; (3) the Senate Banking, Housing, and Urban Affairs Committee; and (4) the Senate Homeland Security and Governmental Affairs Committee (Sec. 1505(b) of the Dodd-Frank Act).

▶ **Effective date.** The provision takes effect one day after the date of enactment (Sec. 4 of the Dodd-Frank Wall Street Reform and Consumer Protection Act).

Law source: Law at ¶11,505 and ¶10,004. Committee Report at ¶50,151.

— Sec. 1505 of the Dodd-Frank Wall Street Reform and Consumer Protection Act, requiring a report on inspectors general;

— Sec. 4, providing the effective date.

¶7040 Study of Core and Brokered Deposits

Section 1506 requires the Federal Deposit Insurance Corporation (FDIC) to conduct a study on core deposits and brokered deposits. The study must evaluate:

- the definition of core deposits for the purpose of calculating the insurance premiums of banks;
- the potential impact on the Deposit Insurance Fund of revising the definitions of brokered deposits and core deposits to better distinguish between them;
- an assessment of the differences between core deposits and brokered deposits and their role in the economy and banking sector of the United States;
- the potential effect that redefining core deposits might have on stimulating local economies; and
- the competitive parity between large institutions and community banks that could result from redefining core deposits (Sec. 1506(a) of the Dodd-Frank Wall Street Reform and Consumer Protection Act).

Within one year after the date of enactment, the FDIC must submit a report on the results of the study that includes legislative recommendations, if any, to address concerns arising in connection with the definitions of core deposits and brokered deposits. The FDIC must submit the report to the Senate Committee on Banking, Housing, and Urban Affairs and the House Committee on Financial Services (Sec. 1506(b) of the Dodd-Frank Act).

▶ **Effective date.** The provision takes effect one day after the date of enactment (Sec. 4 of the Dodd-Frank Wall Street Reform and Consumer Protection Act).

Law source: Law at ¶11,506 and ¶10,004. Committee Report at ¶50,151.

— Sec. 1506(a) of the Dodd-Frank Wall Street Reform and Consumer Protection Act, requiring a study of core deposits and brokered deposits;

— Sec. 1506(b), requiring a report to Congress;

— Sec. 4, providing the effective date.

Dodd-Frank Wall Street Reform and Consumer Protection Act

H. R. 4173
One Hundred Eleventh Congress of the United States of America
AT THE SECOND SESSION
Begun and held at the City of Washington on Tuesday, the fifth day of January, two thousand and ten

An Act

To promote the financial stability of the United States by improving accountability and transparency in the financial system, to end "too big to fail", to protect the American taxpayer by ending bailouts, to protect consumers from abusive financial services practices, and for other purposes.

Be it enacted by the Senate and House of Representatives of the United States of America in Congress assembled,

[¶ 10,001] ACT SECTION 1. SHORT TITLE; TABLE OF CONTENTS.

(a) SHORT TITLE.—This Act may be cited as the "Dodd-Frank Wall Street Reform and Consumer Protection Act".

(b) TABLE OF CONTENTS.—The table of contents for this Act is as follows:

Sec. 1. Short title; table of contents.
Sec. 2. Definitions.
Sec. 3. Severability.
Sec. 4. Effective date.
Sec. 5. Budgetary effects.
Sec. 6. Antitrust savings clause.
TITLE I—FINANCIAL STABILITY
Sec. 101. Short title.
Sec. 102. Definitions.
Subtitle A—Financial Stability Oversight Council
Sec. 111. Financial Stability Oversight Council established.
Sec. 112. Council authority.
Sec. 113. Authority to require supervision and regulation of certain nonbank financial companies.
Sec. 114. Registration of nonbank financial companies supervised by the Board of Governors.
Sec. 115. Enhanced supervision and prudential standards for nonbank financial companies supervised by the Board of Governors and certain bank holding companies.
Sec. 116. Reports.
Sec. 117. Treatment of certain companies that cease to be bank holding companies.
Sec. 118. Council funding.
Sec. 119. Resolution of supervisory jurisdictional disputes among member agencies.
Sec. 120. Additional standards applicable to activities or practices for financial stability purposes.
Sec. 121. Mitigation of risks to financial stability.
Sec. 122. GAO Audit of Council.
Sec. 123. Study of the effects of size and complexity of financial institutions on capital market efficiency and economic growth.

Subtitle B—Office of Financial Research

Sec. 151. Definitions.
Sec. 152. Office of Financial Research established.
Sec. 153. Purpose and duties of the Office.
Sec. 154. Organizational structure; responsibilities of primary programmatic units.
Sec. 155. Funding.
Sec. 156. Transition oversight.

Subtitle C—Additional Board of Governors Authority for Certain Nonbank Financial Companies and Bank Holding Companies

Sec. 161. Reports by and examinations of nonbank financial companies by the Board of Governors.
Sec. 162. Enforcement.
Sec. 163. Acquisitions.
Sec. 164. Prohibition against management interlocks between certain financial companies.
Sec. 165. Enhanced supervision and prudential standards for nonbank financial companies supervised by the Board of Governors and certain bank holding companies.
Sec. 166. Early remediation requirements.
Sec. 167. Affiliations.
Sec. 168. Regulations.
Sec. 169. Avoiding duplication.
Sec. 170. Safe harbor.
Sec. 171. Leverage and risk-based capital requirements.
Sec. 172. Examination and enforcement actions for insurance and orderly liquidation purposes.
Sec. 173. Access to United States financial market by foreign institutions.
Sec. 174. Studies and reports on holding company capital requirements.
Sec. 175. International policy coordination.
Sec. 176. Rule of construction.

TITLE II—ORDERLY LIQUIDATION AUTHORITY

Sec. 201. Definitions.
Sec. 202. Judicial review.
Sec. 203. Systemic risk determination.
Sec. 204. Orderly liquidation of covered financial companies.
Sec. 205. Orderly liquidation of covered brokers and dealers.
Sec. 206. Mandatory terms and conditions for all orderly liquidation actions.
Sec. 207. Directors not liable for acquiescing in appointment of receiver.
Sec. 208. Dismissal and exclusion of other actions.
Sec. 209. Rulemaking; non-conflicting law.
Sec. 210. Powers and duties of the Corporation.
Sec. 211. Miscellaneous provisions.
Sec. 212. Prohibition of circumvention and prevention of conflicts of interest.
Sec. 213. Ban on certain activities by senior executives and directors.
Sec. 214. Prohibition on taxpayer funding.
Sec. 215. Study on secured creditor haircuts.
Sec. 216. Study on bankruptcy process for financial and nonbank financial institutions.
Sec. 217. Study on international coordination relating to bankruptcy process for nonbank financial institutions.

TITLE III—TRANSFER OF POWERS TO THE COMPTROLLER OF THE CURRENCY, THE CORPORATION, AND THE BOARD OF GOVERNORS

Sec. 300. Short title.
Sec. 301. Purposes.
Sec. 302. Definition.

Subtitle A—Transfer of Powers and Duties

Sec. 311. Transfer date.
Sec. 312. Powers and duties transferred.
Sec. 313. Abolishment.
Sec. 314. Amendments to the Revised Statutes.
Sec. 315. Federal information policy.
Sec. 316. Savings provisions.
Sec. 317. References in Federal law to Federal banking agencies.
Sec. 318. Funding.
Sec. 319. Contracting and leasing authority.

Subtitle B—Transitional Provisions

Sec. 321. Interim use of funds, personnel, and property of the Office of Thrift Supervision.
Sec. 322. Transfer of employees.
Sec. 323. Property transferred.
Sec. 324. Funds transferred.
Sec. 325. Disposition of affairs.
Sec. 326. Continuation of services.
Sec. 327. Implementation plan and reports.

Subtitle C—Federal Deposit Insurance Corporation

Sec. 331. Deposit insurance reforms.
Sec. 332. Elimination of procyclical assessments.
Sec. 333. Enhanced access to information for deposit insurance purposes.
Sec. 334. Transition reserve ratio requirements to reflect new assessment base.
Sec. 335. Permanent increase in deposit and share insurance.
Sec. 336. Management of the Federal Deposit Insurance Corporation.

Subtitle D—Other Matters

Sec. 341. Branching.
Sec. 342. Office of Minority and Women Inclusion.
Sec. 343. Insurance of transaction accounts.

Subtitle E—Technical and Conforming Amendments

Sec. 351. Effective date.
Sec. 352. Balanced Budget and Emergency Deficit Control Act of 1985.
Sec. 353. Bank Enterprise Act of 1991.
Sec. 354. Bank Holding Company Act of 1956.
Sec. 355. Bank Holding Company Act Amendments of 1970.
Sec. 356. Bank Protection Act of 1968.
Sec. 357. Bank Service Company Act.
Sec. 358. Community Reinvestment Act of 1977.
Sec. 359. Crime Control Act of 1990.
Sec. 360. Depository Institution Management Interlocks Act.
Sec. 361. Emergency Homeowners' Relief Act.

Sec. 362. Federal Credit Union Act.
Sec. 363. Federal Deposit Insurance Act.
Sec. 364. Federal Home Loan Bank Act.
Sec. 365. Federal Housing Enterprises Financial Safety and Soundness Act of 1992.
Sec. 366. Federal Reserve Act.
Sec. 367. Financial Institutions Reform, Recovery, and Enforcement Act of 1989.
Sec. 368. Flood Disaster Protection Act of 1973.
Sec. 369. Home Owners' Loan Act.
Sec. 370. Housing Act of 1948.
Sec. 371. Housing and Community Development Act of 1992.
Sec. 372. Housing and Urban-Rural Recovery Act of 1983.
Sec. 373. National Housing Act.
Sec. 374. Neighborhood Reinvestment Corporation Act.
Sec. 375. Public Law 93-100.
Sec. 376. Securities Exchange Act of 1934.
Sec. 377. Title 18, United States Code.
Sec. 378. Title 31, United States Code.

TITLE IV—REGULATION OF ADVISERS TO HEDGE FUNDS AND OTHERS
Sec. 401. Short title.
Sec. 402. Definitions.
Sec. 403. Elimination of private adviser exemption; limited exemption for foreign private advisers; limited intrastate exemption.
Sec. 404. Collection of systemic risk data; reports; examinations; disclosures.
Sec. 405. Disclosure provision amendment.
Sec. 406. Clarification of rulemaking authority.
Sec. 407. Exemption of and reporting by venture capital fund advisers.
Sec. 408. Exemption of and reporting by certain private fund advisers.
Sec. 409. Family offices.
Sec. 410. State and Federal responsibilities; asset threshold for Federal registration of investment advisers.
Sec. 411. Custody of client assets.
Sec. 412. Comptroller general study on custody rule costs.
Sec. 413. Adjusting the accredited investor standard.
Sec. 414. Rule of construction relating to the Commodities Exchange Act.
Sec. 415. GAO study and report on accredited investors.
Sec. 416. GAO study on self-regulatory organization for private funds.
Sec. 417. Commission study and report on short selling.
Sec. 418. Qualified client standard.
Sec. 419. Transition period.

TITLE V—INSURANCE
Subtitle A—Federal Insurance Office
Sec. 501. Short title.
Sec. 502. Federal Insurance Office.
Subtitle B—State-Based Insurance Reform
Sec. 511. Short title.
Sec. 512. Effective date.

¶ 10,001 Act Sec. 1(b)

PART I—NONADMITTED INSURANCE

Sec. 521. Reporting, payment, and allocation of premium taxes.
Sec. 522. Regulation of nonadmitted insurance by insured's home State.
Sec. 523. Participation in national producer database.
Sec. 524. Uniform standards for surplus lines eligibility.
Sec. 525. Streamlined application for commercial purchasers.
Sec. 526. GAO study of nonadmitted insurance market.
Sec. 527. Definitions.

PART II—REINSURANCE

Sec. 531. Regulation of credit for reinsurance and reinsurance agreements.
Sec. 532. Regulation of reinsurer solvency.
Sec. 533. Definitions.

PART III—RULE OF CONSTRUCTION

Sec. 541. Rule of construction.
Sec. 542. Severability.

TITLE VI—IMPROVEMENTS TO REGULATION OF BANK AND SAVINGS ASSOCIATION HOLDING COMPANIES AND DEPOSITORY INSTITUTIONS

Sec. 601. Short title.
Sec. 602. Definition.
Sec. 603. Moratorium and study on treatment of credit card banks, industrial loan companies, and certain other companies under the Bank Holding Company Act of 1956.
Sec. 604. Reports and examinations of holding companies; regulation of functionally regulated subsidiaries.
Sec. 605. Assuring consistent oversight of permissible activities of depository institution subsidiaries of holding companies.
Sec. 606. Requirements for financial holding companies to remain well capitalized and well managed.
Sec. 607. Standards for interstate acquisitions.
Sec. 608. Enhancing existing restrictions on bank transactions with affiliates.
Sec. 609. Eliminating exceptions for transactions with financial subsidiaries.
Sec. 610. Lending limits applicable to credit exposure on derivative transactions, repurchase agreements, reverse repurchase agreements, and securities lending and borrowing transactions.
Sec. 611. Consistent treatment of derivative transactions in lending limits.
Sec. 612. Restriction on conversions of troubled banks.
Sec. 613. De novo branching into States.
Sec. 614. Lending limits to insiders.
Sec. 615. Limitations on purchases of assets from insiders.
Sec. 616. Regulations regarding capital levels.
Sec. 617. Elimination of elective investment bank holding company framework.
Sec. 618. Securities holding companies.
Sec. 619. Prohibitions on proprietary trading and certain relationships with hedge funds and private equity funds.
Sec. 620. Study of bank investment activities.
Sec. 621. Conflicts of interest.
Sec. 622. Concentration limits on large financial firms.
Sec. 623. Interstate merger transactions.
Sec. 624. Qualified thrift lenders.
Sec. 625. Treatment of dividends by certain mutual holding companies.

Sec. 626. Intermediate holding companies.
Sec. 627. Interest-bearing transaction accounts authorized.
Sec. 628. Credit card bank small business lending.

TITLE VII—WALL STREET TRANSPARENCY AND ACCOUNTABILITY

Sec. 701. Short title.

Subtitle A—Regulation of Over-the-Counter Swaps Markets

PART I—REGULATORY AUTHORITY

Sec. 711. Definitions.
Sec. 712. Review of regulatory authority.
Sec. 713. Portfolio margining conforming changes.
Sec. 714. Abusive swaps.
Sec. 715. Authority to prohibit participation in swap activities.
Sec. 716. Prohibition against Federal Government bailouts of swaps entities.
Sec. 717. New product approval CFTC—SEC process.
Sec. 718. Determining status of novel derivative products.
Sec. 719. Studies.
Sec. 720. Memorandum.

PART II—REGULATION OF SWAP MARKETS

Sec. 721. Definitions.
Sec. 722. Jurisdiction.
Sec. 723. Clearing.
Sec. 724. Swaps; segregation and bankruptcy treatment.
Sec. 725. Derivatives clearing organizations.
Sec. 726. Rulemaking on conflict of interest.
Sec. 727. Public reporting of swap transaction data.
Sec. 728. Swap data repositories.
Sec. 729. Reporting and recordkeeping.
Sec. 730. Large swap trader reporting.
Sec. 731. Registration and regulation of swap dealers and major swap participants.
Sec. 732. Conflicts of interest.
Sec. 733. Swap execution facilities.
Sec. 734. Derivatives transaction execution facilities and exempt boards of trade.
Sec. 735. Designated contract markets.
Sec. 736. Margin.
Sec. 737. Position limits.
Sec. 738. Foreign boards of trade.
Sec. 739. Legal certainty for swaps.
Sec. 740. Multilateral clearing organizations.
Sec. 741. Enforcement.
Sec. 742. Retail commodity transactions.
Sec. 743. Other authority.
Sec. 744. Restitution remedies.
Sec. 745. Enhanced compliance by registered entities.
Sec. 746. Insider trading.
Sec. 747. Antidisruptive practices authority.
Sec. 748. Commodity whistleblower incentives and protection.

Sec. 749. Conforming amendments.
Sec. 750. Study on oversight of carbon markets.
Sec. 751. Energy and environmental markets advisory committee.
Sec. 752. International harmonization.
Sec. 753. Anti-manipulation authority.
Sec. 754. Effective date.
Subtitle B—Regulation of Security-Based Swap Markets
Sec. 761. Definitions under the Securities Exchange Act of 1934.
Sec. 762. Repeal of prohibition on regulation of security-based swap agreements.
Sec. 763. Amendments to the Securities Exchange Act of 1934.
Sec. 764. Registration and regulation of security-based swap dealers and major security-based swap participants.
Sec. 765. Rulemaking on conflict of interest.
Sec. 766. Reporting and recordkeeping.
Sec. 767. State gaming and bucket shop laws.
Sec. 768. Amendments to the Securities Act of 1933; treatment of security-based swaps.
Sec. 769. Definitions under the Investment Company Act of 1940.
Sec. 770. Definitions under the Investment Advisers Act of 1940.
Sec. 771. Other authority.
Sec. 772. Jurisdiction.
Sec. 773. Civil penalties.
Sec. 774. Effective date.
TITLE VIII—PAYMENT, CLEARING, AND SETTLEMENT SUPERVISION
Sec. 801. Short title.
Sec. 802. Findings and purposes.
Sec. 803. Definitions.
Sec. 804. Designation of systemic importance.
Sec. 805. Standards for systemically important financial market utilities and payment, clearing, or settlement activities.
Sec. 806. Operations of designated financial market utilities.
Sec. 807. Examination of and enforcement actions against designated financial market utilities.
Sec. 808. Examination of and enforcement actions against financial institutions subject to standards for designated activities.
Sec. 809. Requests for information, reports, or records.
Sec. 810. Rulemaking.
Sec. 811. Other authority.
Sec. 812. Consultation.
Sec. 813. Common framework for designated clearing entity risk management.
Sec. 814. Effective date.
TITLE IX—INVESTOR PROTECTIONS AND IMPROVEMENTS TO THE REGULATION OF SECURITIES
Sec. 901. Short title.
Subtitle A—Increasing Investor Protection
Sec. 911. Investor Advisory Committee established.
Sec. 912. Clarification of authority of the Commission to engage in investor testing.
Sec. 913. Study and rulemaking regarding obligations of brokers, dealers, and investment advisers.

Sec. 914. Study on enhancing investment adviser examinations.

Sec. 915. Office of the Investor Advocate.

Sec. 916. Streamlining of filing procedures for self-regulatory organizations.

Sec. 917. Study regarding financial literacy among investors.

Sec. 918. Study regarding mutual fund advertising.

Sec. 919. Clarification of Commission authority to require investor disclosures before purchase of investment products and services.

Sec. 919A. Study on conflicts of interest.

Sec. 919B. Study on improved investor access to information on investment advisers and broker-dealers.

Sec. 919C. Study on financial planners and the use of financial designations.

Sec. 919D. Ombudsman.

Subtitle B—Increasing Regulatory Enforcement and Remedies

Sec. 921. Authority to restrict mandatory pre-dispute arbitration.

Sec. 922. Whistleblower protection.

Sec. 923. Conforming amendments for whistleblower protection.

Sec. 924. Implementation and transition provisions for whistleblower protection.

Sec. 925. Collateral bars.

Sec. 926. Disqualifying felons and other "bad actors" from Regulation D offerings.

Sec. 927. Equal treatment of self-regulatory organization rules.

Sec. 928. Clarification that section 205 of the Investment Advisers Act of 1940 does not apply to State-registered advisers.

Sec. 929. Unlawful margin lending.

Sec. 929A. Protection for employees of subsidiaries and affiliates of publicly traded companies.

Sec. 929B. Fair Fund amendments.

Sec. 929C. Increasing the borrowing limit on Treasury loans.

Sec. 929D. Lost and stolen securities.

Sec. 929E. Nationwide service of subpoenas.

Sec. 929F. Formerly associated persons.

Sec. 929G. Streamlined hiring authority for market specialists.

Sec. 929H. SIPC Reforms.

Sec. 929I. Protecting confidentiality of materials submitted to the Commission.

Sec. 929J. Expansion of audit information to be produced and exchanged.

Sec. 929K. Sharing privileged information with other authorities.

Sec. 929L. Enhanced application of antifraud provisions.

Sec. 929M. Aiding and abetting authority under the Securities Act and the Investment Company Act.

Sec. 929N. Authority to impose penalties for aiding and abetting violations of the Investment Advisers Act.

Sec. 929O. Aiding and abetting standard of knowledge satisfied by recklessness.

Sec. 929P. Strengthening enforcement by the Commission.

Sec. 929Q. Revision to recordkeeping rule.

Sec. 929R. Beneficial ownership and short-swing profit reporting.

Sec. 929S. Fingerprinting.

Sec. 929T. Equal treatment of self-regulatory organization rules.

Sec. 929U. Deadline for completing examinations, inspections and enforcement actions.

Sec. 929V. Security Investor Protection Act amendments.

Sec. 929W. Notice to missing security holders.
Sec. 929X. Short sale reforms.
Sec. 929Y. Study on extraterritorial private rights of action.
Sec. 929Z. GAO study on securities litigation.
Subtitle C—Improvements to the Regulation of Credit Rating Agencies
Sec. 931. Findings.
Sec. 932. Enhanced regulation, accountability, and transparency of nationally recognized statistical rating organizations.
Sec. 933. State of mind in private actions.
Sec. 934. Referring tips to law enforcement or regulatory authorities.
Sec. 935. Consideration of information from sources other than the issuer in rating decisions.
Sec. 936. Qualification standards for credit rating analysts.
Sec. 937. Timing of regulations.
Sec. 938. Universal ratings symbols.
Sec. 939. Removal of statutory references to credit ratings.
Sec. 939A. Review of reliance on ratings.
Sec. 939B. Elimination of exemption from fair disclosure rule.
Sec. 939C. Securities and Exchange Commission study on strengthening credit rating agency independence.
Sec. 939D. Government Accountability Office study on alternative business models.
Sec. 939E. Government Accountability Office study on the creation of an independent professional analyst organization.
Sec. 939F. Study and rulemaking on assigned credit ratings.
Sec. 939G. Effect of Rule 436(g).
Sec. 939H. Sense of Congress.
Subtitle D—Improvements to the Asset-Backed Securitization Process
Sec. 941. Regulation of credit risk retention.
Sec. 942. Disclosures and reporting for asset-backed securities.
Sec. 943. Representations and warranties in asset-backed offerings.
Sec. 944. Exempted transactions under the Securities Act of 1933.
Sec. 945. Due diligence analysis and disclosure in asset-backed securities issues.
Sec. 946. Study on the macroeconomic effects of risk retention requirements.
Subtitle E—Accountability and Executive Compensation
Sec. 951. Shareholder vote on executive compensation disclosures.
Sec. 952. Compensation committee independence.
Sec. 953. Executive compensation disclosures.
Sec. 954. Recovery of erroneously awarded compensation.
Sec. 955. Disclosure regarding employee and director hedging.
Sec. 956. Enhanced compensation structure reporting.
Sec. 957. Voting by brokers.
Subtitle F—Improvements to the Management of the Securities and Exchange Commission
Sec. 961. Report and certification of internal supervisory controls.
Sec. 962. Triennial report on personnel management.
Sec. 963. Annual financial controls audit.
Sec. 964. Report on oversight of national securities associations.
Sec. 965. Compliance examiners.
Sec. 966. Suggestion program for employees of the Commission.

Sec. 967. Commission organizational study and reform.
Sec. 968. Study on SEC revolving door.
Subtitle G—Strengthening Corporate Governance
Sec. 971. Proxy access.
Sec. 972. Disclosures regarding chairman and CEO structures.
Subtitle H—Municipal Securities
Sec. 975. Regulation of municipal securities and changes to the board of the MSRB.
Sec. 976. Government Accountability Office study of increased disclosure to investors.
Sec. 977. Government Accountability Office study on the municipal securities markets.
Sec. 978. Funding for Governmental Accounting Standards Board.
Sec. 979. Commission Office of Municipal Securities.
Subtitle I—Public Company Accounting Oversight Board, Portfolio Margining, and Other Matters
Sec. 981. Authority to share certain information with foreign authorities.
Sec. 982. Oversight of brokers and dealers.
Sec. 983. Portfolio margining.
Sec. 984. Loan or borrowing of securities.
Sec. 985. Technical corrections to Federal securities laws.
Sec. 986. Conforming amendments relating to repeal of the Public Utility Holding Company Act of 1935.
Sec. 987. Amendment to definition of material loss and nonmaterial losses to the Deposit Insurance Fund for purposes of Inspector General reviews.
Sec. 988. Amendment to definition of material loss and nonmaterial losses to the National Credit Union Share Insurance Fund for purposes of Inspector General reviews.
Sec. 989. Government Accountability Office study on proprietary trading.
Sec. 989A. Senior investor protections.
Sec. 989B. Designated Federal entity inspectors general independence.
Sec. 989C. Strengthening Inspector General accountability.
Sec. 989D. Removal of Inspectors General of designated Federal entities.
Sec. 989E. Additional oversight of financial regulatory system.
Sec. 989F. GAO study of person to person lending.
Sec. 989G. Exemption for nonaccelerated filers.
Sec. 989H. Corrective responses by heads of certain establishments to deficiencies identified by Inspectors General.
Sec. 989I. GAO study regarding exemption for smaller issuers.
Sec. 989J. Further promoting the adoption of the NAIC Model Regulations that enhance protection of seniors and other consumers.
Subtitle J—Securities and Exchange Commission Match Funding
Sec. 991. Securities and Exchange Commission match funding.
TITLE X—BUREAU OF CONSUMER FINANCIAL PROTECTION
Sec. 1001. Short title.
Sec. 1002. Definitions.
Subtitle A—Bureau of Consumer Financial Protection
Sec. 1011. Establishment of the Bureau of Consumer Financial Protection.
Sec. 1012. Executive and administrative powers.
Sec. 1013. Administration.
Sec. 1014. Consumer Advisory Board.

Sec. 1015. Coordination.
Sec. 1016. Appearances before and reports to Congress.
Sec. 1017. Funding; penalties and fines.
Sec. 1018. Effective date.
Subtitle B—General Powers of the Bureau
Sec. 1021. Purpose, objectives, and functions.
Sec. 1022. Rulemaking authority.
Sec. 1023. Review of Bureau regulations.
Sec. 1024. Supervision of nondepository covered persons.
Sec. 1025. Supervision of very large banks, savings associations, and credit unions.
Sec. 1026. Other banks, savings associations, and credit unions.
Sec. 1027. Limitations on authorities of the Bureau; preservation of authorities.
Sec. 1028. Authority to restrict mandatory pre-dispute arbitration.
Sec. 1029. Exclusion for auto dealers.
Sec. 1029A. Effective date.
Subtitle C—Specific Bureau Authorities
Sec. 1031. Prohibiting unfair, deceptive, or abusive acts or practices.
Sec. 1032. Disclosures.
Sec. 1033. Consumer rights to access information.
Sec. 1034. Response to consumer complaints and inquiries.
Sec. 1035. Private education loan ombudsman.
Sec. 1036. Prohibited acts.
Sec. 1037. Effective date.
Subtitle D—Preservation of State Law
Sec. 1041. Relation to State law.
Sec. 1042. Preservation of enforcement powers of States.
Sec. 1043. Preservation of existing contracts.
Sec. 1044. State law preemption standards for national banks and subsidiaries clarified.
Sec. 1045. Clarification of law applicable to nondepository institution subsidiaries.
Sec. 1046. State law preemption standards for Federal savings associations and subsidiaries clarified.
Sec. 1047. Visitorial standards for national banks and savings associations.
Sec. 1048. Effective date.
Subtitle E—Enforcement Powers
Sec. 1051. Definitions.
Sec. 1052. Investigations and administrative discovery.
Sec. 1053. Hearings and adjudication proceedings.
Sec. 1054. Litigation authority.
Sec. 1055. Relief available.
Sec. 1056. Referrals for criminal proceedings.
Sec. 1057. Employee protection.
Sec. 1058. Effective date.
Subtitle F—Transfer of Functions and Personnel; Transitional Provisions
Sec. 1061. Transfer of consumer financial protection functions.
Sec. 1062. Designated transfer date.
Sec. 1063. Savings provisions.

Sec. 1064. Transfer of certain personnel.

Sec. 1065. Incidental transfers.

Sec. 1066. Interim authority of the Secretary.

Sec. 1067. Transition oversight.

Subtitle G—Regulatory Improvements

Sec. 1071. Small business data collection.

Sec. 1072. Assistance for economically vulnerable individuals and families.

Sec. 1073. Remittance transfers.

Sec. 1074. Department of the Treasury study on ending the conservatorship of Fannie Mae, Freddie Mac, and reforming the housing finance system.

Sec. 1075. Reasonable fees and rules for payment card transactions.

Sec. 1076. Reverse mortgage study and regulations.

Sec. 1077. Report on private education loans and private educational lenders.

Sec. 1078. Study and report on credit scores.

Sec. 1079. Review, report, and program with respect to exchange facilitators.

Sec. 1079A. Financial fraud provisions.

Subtitle H—Conforming Amendments

Sec. 1081. Amendments to the Inspector General Act.

Sec. 1082. Amendments to the Privacy Act of 1974.

Sec. 1083. Amendments to the Alternative Mortgage Transaction Parity Act of 1982.

Sec. 1084. Amendments to the Electronic Fund Transfer Act.

Sec. 1085. Amendments to the Equal Credit Opportunity Act.

Sec. 1086. Amendments to the Expedited Funds Availability Act.

Sec. 1087. Amendments to the Fair Credit Billing Act.

Sec. 1088. Amendments to the Fair Credit Reporting Act and the Fair and Accurate Credit Transactions Act of 2003.

Sec. 1089. Amendments to the Fair Debt Collection Practices Act.

Sec. 1090. Amendments to the Federal Deposit Insurance Act.

Sec. 1091. Amendment to Federal Financial Institutions Examination Council Act of 1978.

Sec. 1092. Amendments to the Federal Trade Commission Act.

Sec. 1093. Amendments to the Gramm-Leach-Bliley Act.

Sec. 1094. Amendments to the Home Mortgage Disclosure Act of 1975.

Sec. 1095. Amendments to the Homeowners Protection Act of 1998.

Sec. 1096. Amendments to the Home Ownership and Equity Protection Act of 1994.

Sec. 1097. Amendments to the Omnibus Appropriations Act, 2009.

Sec. 1098. Amendments to the Real Estate Settlement Procedures Act of 1974.

Sec. 1098A. Amendments to the Interstate Land Sales Full Disclosure Act.

Sec. 1099. Amendments to the Right to Financial Privacy Act of 1978.

Sec. 1100. Amendments to the Secure and Fair Enforcement for Mortgage Licensing Act of 2008.

Sec. 1100A. Amendments to the Truth in Lending Act.

Sec. 1100B. Amendments to the Truth in Savings Act.

Sec. 1100C. Amendments to the Telemarketing and Consumer Fraud and Abuse Prevention Act.

Sec. 1100D. Amendments to the Paperwork Reduction Act.

Sec. 1100E. Adjustments for inflation in the Truth in Lending Act.

Sec. 1100F. Use of consumer reports.

Sec. 1100G. Small business fairness and regulatory transparency.

Sec. 1100H. Effective date.
TITLE XI—FEDERAL RESERVE SYSTEM PROVISIONS
Sec. 1101. Federal Reserve Act amendments on emergency lending authority.
Sec. 1102. Reviews of special Federal reserve credit facilities.
Sec. 1103. Public access to information.
Sec. 1104. Liquidity event determination.
Sec. 1105. Emergency financial stabilization.
Sec. 1106. Additional related amendments.
Sec. 1107. Federal Reserve Act amendments on Federal reserve bank governance.
Sec. 1108. Federal Reserve Act amendments on supervision and regulation policy.
Sec. 1109. GAO audit of the Federal Reserve facilities; publication of Board actions.
TITLE XII—IMPROVING ACCESS TO MAINSTREAM FINANCIAL INSTITUTIONS
Sec. 1201. Short title.
Sec. 1202. Purpose.
Sec. 1203. Definitions.
Sec. 1204. Expanded access to mainstream financial institutions.
Sec. 1205. Low-cost alternatives to small dollar loans.
Sec. 1206. Grants to establish loan-loss reserve funds.
Sec. 1207. Procedural provisions.
Sec. 1208. Authorization of appropriations.
Sec. 1209. Regulations.
Sec. 1210. Evaluation and reports to Congress.
TITLE XIII—PAY IT BACK ACT
Sec. 1301. Short title.
Sec. 1302. Amendment to reduce TARP authorization.
Sec. 1303. Report.
Sec. 1304. Amendments to Housing and Economic Recovery Act of 2008.
Sec. 1305. Federal Housing Finance Agency report.
Sec. 1306. Repayment of unobligated ARRA funds.
TITLE XIV—MORTGAGE REFORM AND ANTI-PREDATORY LENDING ACT
Sec. 1400. Short title; designation as enumerated consumer law.
Subtitle A—Residential Mortgage Loan Origination Standards
Sec. 1401. Definitions.
Sec. 1402. Residential mortgage loan origination.
Sec. 1403. Prohibition on steering incentives.
Sec. 1404. Liability.
Sec. 1405. Regulations.
Sec. 1406. Study of shared appreciation mortgages.
Subtitle B—Minimum Standards For Mortgages
Sec. 1411. Ability to repay.
Sec. 1412. Safe harbor and rebuttable presumption.
Sec. 1413. Defense to foreclosure.
Sec. 1414. Additional standards and requirements.
Sec. 1415. Rule of construction.
Sec. 1416. Amendments to civil liability provisions.
Sec. 1417. Lender rights in the context of borrower deception.

Sec. 1418. Six-month notice required before reset of hybrid adjustable rate mortgages.

Sec. 1419. Required disclosures.

Sec. 1420. Disclosures required in monthly statements for residential mortgage loans.

Sec. 1421. Report by the GAO.

Sec. 1422. State attorney general enforcement authority.

Subtitle C—High-Cost Mortgages

Sec. 1431. Definitions relating to high-cost mortgages.

Sec. 1432. Amendments to existing requirements for certain mortgages.

Sec. 1433. Additional requirements for certain mortgages.

Subtitle D—Office of Housing Counseling

Sec. 1441. Short title.

Sec. 1442. Establishment of Office of Housing Counseling.

Sec. 1443. Counseling procedures.

Sec. 1444. Grants for housing counseling assistance.

Sec. 1445. Requirements to use HUD-certified counselors under HUD programs.

Sec. 1446. Study of defaults and foreclosures.

Sec. 1447. Default and foreclosure database.

Sec. 1448. Definitions for counseling-related programs.

Sec. 1449. Accountability and transparency for grant recipients.

Sec. 1450. Updating and simplification of mortgage information booklet.

Sec. 1451. Home inspection counseling.

Sec. 1452. Warnings to homeowners of foreclosure rescue scams.

Subtitle E—Mortgage Servicing

Sec. 1461. Escrow and impound accounts relating to certain consumer credit transactions.

Sec. 1462. Disclosure notice required for consumers who waive escrow services.

Sec. 1463. Real Estate Settlement Procedures Act of 1974 amendments.

Sec. 1464. Truth in Lending Act amendments.

Sec. 1465. Escrows included in repayment analysis.

Subtitle F—Appraisal Activities

Sec. 1471. Property appraisal requirements.

Sec. 1472. Appraisal independence requirements.

Sec. 1473. Amendments relating to Appraisal Subcommittee of FFIEC, Appraiser Independence Monitoring, Approved Appraiser Education, Appraisal Management Companies, Appraiser Complaint Hotline, Automated Valuation Models, and Broker Price Opinions.

Sec. 1474. Equal Credit Opportunity Act amendment.

Sec. 1475. Real Estate Settlement Procedures Act of 1974 amendment relating to certain appraisal fees.

Sec. 1476. GAO study on the effectiveness and impact of various appraisal methods, valuation models and distributions channels, and on the Home Valuation Code of conduct and the Appraisal Subcommittee.

Subtitle G—Mortgage Resolution and Modification

Sec. 1481. Multifamily mortgage resolution program.

Sec. 1482. Home Affordable Modification Program guidelines.

Sec. 1483. Public availability of information of Making Home Affordable Program.

Sec. 1484. Protecting tenants at foreclosure extension and clarification.

Subtitle H—Miscellaneous Provisions

Sec. 1491. Sense of Congress regarding the importance of government-sponsored enterprises reform to enhance the protection, limitation, and regulation of the terms of residential mortgage credit.

Sec. 1492. GAO study report on government efforts to combat mortgage foreclosure rescue scams and loan modification fraud.

Sec. 1493. Reporting of mortgage data by State.

Sec. 1494. Study of effect of drywall presence on foreclosures.

Sec. 1495. Definition.

Sec. 1496. Emergency mortgage relief.

Sec. 1497. Additional assistance for Neighborhood Stabilization Program.

Sec. 1498. Legal assistance for foreclosure-related issues.

TITLE XV—MISCELLANEOUS PROVISIONS

Sec. 1501. Restrictions on use of United States funds for foreign governments; protection of American taxpayers.

Sec. 1502. Conflict minerals.

Sec. 1503. Reporting requirements regarding coal or other mine safety.

Sec. 1504. Disclosure of payments by resource extraction issuers.

Sec. 1505. Study by the Comptroller General.

Sec. 1506. Study on core deposits and brokered deposits.

TITLE XVI—SECTION 1256 CONTRACTS

Sec. 1601. Certain swaps, etc., not treated as section 1256 contracts.

[Explanation at ¶ 65.]

[¶ 10,002] ACT SEC. 2. DEFINITIONS.

As used in this Act, the following definitions shall apply, except as the context otherwise requires or as otherwise specifically provided in this Act:

(1) AFFILIATE.—The term "affiliate" has the same meaning as in section 3 of the Federal Deposit Insurance Act (12 U.S.C. 1813).

(2) APPROPRIATE FEDERAL BANKING AGENCY.—On and after the transfer date, the term "appropriate Federal banking agency" has the same meaning as in section 3(q) of the Federal Deposit Insurance Act (12 U.S.C. 1813(q)), as amended by title III.

(3) BOARD OF GOVERNORS.—The term "Board of Governors" means the Board of Governors of the Federal Reserve System.

(4) BUREAU.—The term "Bureau" means the Bureau of Consumer Financial Protection established under title X.

(5) COMMISSION.—The term "Commission" means the Securities and Exchange Commission, except in the context of the Commodity Futures Trading Commission.

(6) COMMODITY FUTURES TERMS.—The terms "futures commission merchant", "swap", "swap dealer", "swap execution facility", "derivatives clearing organization", "board of trade", "commodity trading advisor", "commodity pool", and "commodity pool operator" have the same meanings as given the terms in section 1a of the Commodity Exchange Act (7 U.S.C. 1 et seq.).

(7) CORPORATION.—The term "Corporation" means the Federal Deposit Insurance Corporation.

(8) COUNCIL.—The term "Council" means the Financial Stability Oversight Council established under title I.

(9) CREDIT UNION.—The term "credit union" means a Federal credit union, State credit union, or State-chartered credit union, as those terms are defined in section 101 of the Federal Credit Union Act (12 U.S.C. 1752).

(10) FEDERAL BANKING AGENCY.—The term—

(A) "Federal banking agency" means, individually, the Board of Governors, the Office of the Comptroller of the Currency, and the Corporation; and

(B) "Federal banking agencies" means all of the agencies referred to in subparagraph (A), collectively.

(11) FUNCTIONALLY REGULATED SUBSIDIARY.—The term "functionally regulated subsidiary" has the same meaning as in section 5(c)(5) of the Bank Holding Company Act of 1956 (12 U.S.C. 1844(c)(5)).

(12) PRIMARY FINANCIAL REGULATORY AGENCY.—The term "primary financial regulatory agency" means—

(A) the appropriate Federal banking agency, with respect to institutions described in section 3(q) of the Federal Deposit Insurance Act, except to the extent that an institution is or the activities of an institution are otherwise described in subparagraph (B), (C), (D), or (E);

(B) the Securities and Exchange Commission, with respect to—

(i) any broker or dealer that is registered with the Commission under the Securities Exchange Act of 1934, with respect to the activities of the broker or dealer that require the broker or dealer to be registered under that Act;

(ii) any investment company that is registered with the Commission under the Investment Company Act of 1940, with respect to the activities of the investment company that require the investment company to be registered under that Act;

(iii) any investment adviser that is registered with the Commission under the Investment Advisers Act of 1940, with respect to the investment advisory activities of such company and activities that are incidental to such advisory activities;

(iv) any clearing agency registered with the Commission under the Securities Exchange Act of 1934, with respect to the activities of the clearing agency that require the agency to be registered under such Act;

(v) any nationally recognized statistical rating organization registered with the Commission under the Securities Exchange Act of 1934;

(vi) any transfer agent registered with the Commission under the Securities Exchange Act of 1934;

(vii) any exchange registered as a national securities exchange with the Commission under the Securities Exchange Act of 1934;

(viii) any national securities association registered with the Commission under the Securities Exchange Act of 1934;

(ix) any securities information processor registered with the Commission under the Securities Exchange Act of 1934;

(x) the Municipal Securities Rulemaking Board established under the Securities Exchange Act of 1934;

(xi) the Public Company Accounting Oversight Board established under the Sarbanes-Oxley Act of 2002 (15 U.S.C. 7211 et seq.);

(xii) the Securities Investor Protection Corporation established under the Securities Investor Protection Act of 1970 (15 U.S.C. 78aaa et seq.); and

(xiii) any security-based swap execution facility, security-based swap data repository, security-based swap dealer or major security-based swap participant registered with the Commission under the Securities Exchange Act of 1934, with respect to the security-based swap activities of the person that require such person to be registered under such Act;

(C) the Commodity Futures Trading Commission, with respect to—

(i) any futures commission merchant registered with the Commodity Futures Trading Commission under the Commodity Exchange Act (7 U.S.C. 1 et seq.), with respect to the activities of the futures commission merchant that require the futures commission merchant to be registered under that Act;

(ii) any commodity pool operator registered with the Commodity Futures Trading Commission under the Commodity Exchange Act (7 U.S.C. 1 et seq.), with respect to the activities of the commodity pool operator that require the commodity pool operator to be registered under that Act, or a commodity pool, as defined in that Act;

(iii) any commodity trading advisor or introducing broker registered with the Commodity Futures Trading Commission under the Commodity Exchange Act (7 U.S.C. 1 et seq.), with respect to the activities of the commodity trading advisor or introducing broker that require the commodity trading adviser or introducing broker to be registered under that Act;

(iv) any derivatives clearing organization registered with the Commodity Futures Trading Commission under the Commodity Exchange Act (7 U.S.C. 1 et seq.), with respect to the activities of the derivatives clearing organization that require the derivatives clearing organization to be registered under that Act;

(v) any board of trade designated as a contract market by the Commodity Futures Trading Commission under the Commodity Exchange Act (7 U.S.C. 1 et seq.);

(vi) any futures association registered with the Commodity Futures Trading Commission under the Commodity Exchange Act (7 U.S.C. 1 et seq.);

(vii) any retail foreign exchange dealer registered with the Commodity Futures Trading Commission under the Commodity Exchange Act (7 U.S.C. 1 et seq.), with respect to the activities of the retail foreign exchange dealer that require the retail foreign exchange dealer to be registered under that Act;

(viii) any swap execution facility, swap data repository, swap dealer, or major swap participant registered with the Commodity Futures Trading Commission under the Commodity Exchange Act (7 U.S.C. 1 et seq.) with respect to the swap activities of the person that require such person to be registered under that Act; and

(ix) any registered entity under the Commodity Exchange Act (7 U.S.C. 1 et seq.), with respect to the activities of the registered entity that require the registered entity to be registered under that Act;

(D) the State insurance authority of the State in which an insurance company is domiciled, with respect to the insurance activities and activities that are incidental to such insurance activities of an insurance company that is subject to supervision by the State insurance authority under State insurance law; and

(E) the Federal Housing Finance Agency, with respect to Federal Home Loan Banks or the Federal Home Loan Bank System, and with respect to the Federal National Mortgage Association or the Federal Home Loan Mortgage Corporation.

(13) PRUDENTIAL STANDARDS.—The term "prudential standards" means enhanced supervision and regulatory standards developed by the Board of Governors under section 165.

(14) SECRETARY.—The term "Secretary" means the Secretary of the Treasury.

(15) SECURITIES TERMS.—The—

(A) terms "broker", "dealer", "issuer", "nationally recognized statistical rating organization", "security", and "securities laws" have the same meanings as in section 3 of the Securities Exchange Act of 1934 (15 U.S.C. 78c);

(B) term "investment adviser" has the same meaning as in section 202 of the Investment Advisers Act of 1940 (15 U.S.C. 80b-2); and

(C) term "investment company" has the same meaning as in section 3 of the Investment Company Act of 1940 (15 U.S.C. 80a-3).

(16) STATE.—The term "State" means any State, commonwealth, territory, or possession of the United States, the District of Columbia, the Commonwealth of Puerto Rico, the Commonwealth of the Northern Mariana Islands, American Samoa, Guam, or the United States Virgin Islands.

(17) TRANSFER DATE.—The term "transfer date" means the date established under section 311.

(18) OTHER INCORPORATED DEFINITIONS.—

(A) FEDERAL DEPOSIT INSURANCE ACT.—The terms "bank", "bank holding company", "control", "deposit", "depository institution", "Federal depository institution", "Federal savings association", "foreign bank", "including", "insured branch", "insured depository institution", "national member bank", "national nonmember bank", "savings association", "State bank", "State depository institution", "State member bank", "State nonmember bank", "State savings association", and "subsidiary" have the same meanings as in section 3 of the Federal Deposit Insurance Act (12 U.S.C. 1813).

(B) HOLDING COMPANIES.—The term—

(i) "bank holding company" has the same meaning as in section 2 of the Bank Holding Company Act of 1956 (12 U.S.C. 1841);

(ii) "financial holding company" has the same meaning as in section 2(p) of the Bank Holding Company Act of 1956 (12 U.S.C. 1841(p)); and

(iii) "savings and loan holding company" has the same meaning as in section 10 of the Home Owners' Loan Act (12 U.S.C. 1467a(a)).

[Explanation at ¶ 65.]

[¶ 10,003] ACT SEC. 3. SEVERABILITY.

If any provision of this Act, an amendment made by this Act, or the application of such provision or amendment to any person or circumstance is held to be unconstitutional, the remainder of this Act, the amendments made by this Act, and the application of the provisions of such to any person or circumstance shall not be affected thereby.

[Explanation at ¶ 65.]

[¶ 10,004] ACT SEC. 4. EFFECTIVE DATE.

Except as otherwise specifically provided in this Act or the amendments made by this Act, this Act and such amendments shall take effect 1 day after the date of enactment of this Act.

[Explanation at ¶ 65.]

[¶ 10,005] ACT SEC. 5. BUDGETARY EFFECTS.

The budgetary effects of this Act, for the purpose of complying with the Statutory Pay-As-You-Go-Act of 2010, shall be determined by reference to the latest statement titled "Budgetary Effects of PAYGO Legislation" for this Act, jointly submitted for printing in the Congressional Record by the Chairmen of the House and Senate Budget Committees, provided that such statement has been submitted prior to the vote on passage in the House acting first on this conference report or amendment between the Houses.

[Explanation at ¶ 65.]

[¶ 10,006] ACT SEC. 6. ANTITRUST SAVINGS CLAUSE.

Nothing in this Act, or any amendment made by this Act, shall be construed to modify, impair, or supersede the operation of any of the antitrust laws, unless otherwise specified. For purposes of this section, the term "antitrust laws" has the same meaning as in subsection (a) of the first section of the Clayton Act, except that such term includes section 5 of the Federal Trade Commission Act, to the extent that such section 5 applies to unfair methods of competition.

[Explanation at ¶ 65.]

TITLE I—FINANCIAL STABILITY

[¶ 10,101] ACT SEC. 101. SHORT TITLE.

This title may be cited as the "Financial Stability Act of 2010".

[Explanation at ¶ 105.]

[¶ 10,102] ACT SEC. 102. DEFINITIONS.

(a) IN GENERAL.—For purposes of this title, unless the context otherwise requires, the following definitions shall apply:

(1) BANK HOLDING COMPANY.—The term "bank holding company" has the same meaning as in section 2 of the Bank Holding Company Act of 1956 (12 U.S.C. 1841). A foreign bank or

company that is treated as a bank holding company for purposes of the Bank Holding Company Act of 1956, pursuant to section 8(a) of the International Banking Act of 1978 (12 U.S.C. 3106(a)), shall be treated as a bank holding company for purposes of this title.

(2) CHAIRPERSON.—The term "Chairperson" means the Chairperson of the Council.

(3) MEMBER AGENCY.—The term "member agency" means an agency represented by a voting member of the Council.

(4) NONBANK FINANCIAL COMPANY DEFINITIONS.—

(A) FOREIGN NONBANK FINANCIAL COMPANY.—The term "foreign nonbank financial company" means a company (other than a company that is, or is treated in the United States as, a bank holding company) that is—

(i) incorporated or organized in a country other than the United States; and

(ii) predominantly engaged in, including through a branch in the United States, financial activities, as defined in paragraph (6).

(B) U.S. NONBANK FINANCIAL COMPANY.—The term "U.S. nonbank financial company" means a company (other than a bank holding company, a Farm Credit System institution chartered and subject to the provisions of the Farm Credit Act of 1971 (12 U.S.C. 2001 et seq.), or a national securities exchange (or parent thereof), clearing agency (or parent thereof, unless the parent is a bank holding company), security-based swap execution facility, or security-based swap data repository registered with the Commission, or a board of trade designated as a contract market (or parent thereof), or a derivatives clearing organization (or parent thereof, unless the parent is a bank holding company), swap execution facility or a swap data repository registered with the Commodity Futures Trading Commission), that is—

(i) incorporated or organized under the laws of the United States or any State; and

(ii) predominantly engaged in financial activities, as defined in paragraph (6).

(C) NONBANK FINANCIAL COMPANY.—The term "nonbank financial company" means a U.S. nonbank financial company and a foreign nonbank financial company.

(D) NONBANK FINANCIAL COMPANY SUPERVISED BY THE BOARD OF GOVERNORS.—The term "nonbank financial company supervised by the Board of Governors" means a nonbank financial company that the Council has determined under section 113 shall be supervised by the Board of Governors.

(5) OFFICE OF FINANCIAL RESEARCH.—The term "Office of Financial Research" means the office established under section 152.

(6) PREDOMINANTLY ENGAGED.—A company is "predominantly engaged in financial activities" if—

(A) the annual gross revenues derived by the company and all of its subsidiaries from activities that are financial in nature (as defined in section 4(k) of the Bank Holding Company Act of 1956) and, if applicable, from the ownership or control of one or more insured depository institutions, represents 85 percent or more of the consolidated annual gross revenues of the company; or

(B) the consolidated assets of the company and all of its subsidiaries related to activities that are financial in nature (as defined in section 4(k) of the Bank Holding Company Act of 1956) and, if applicable, related to the ownership or control of one or more insured depository institutions, represents 85 percent or more of the consolidated assets of the company.

(7) SIGNIFICANT INSTITUTIONS.—The terms "significant nonbank financial company" and "significant bank holding company" have the meanings given those terms by rule of the Board of Governors, but in no instance shall the term "significant nonbank financial company" include those entities that are excluded under paragraph (4)(B).

(b) DEFINITIONAL CRITERIA.—The Board of Governors shall establish, by regulation, the requirements for determining if a company is predominantly engaged in financial activities, as defined in subsection (a)(6).

(c) FOREIGN NONBANK FINANCIAL COMPANIES.—For purposes of the application of subtitles A and C (other than section 113(b)) with respect to a foreign nonbank financial company, references in this title to "company" or "subsidiary" include only the United States activities and subsidiaries of such foreign company, except as otherwise provided.

[Explanation at ¶ 105.]

Subtitle A—Financial Stability Oversight Council

[¶ 10,111] ACT SEC. 111. FINANCIAL STABILITY OVERSIGHT COUNCIL ESTABLISHED.

(a) ESTABLISHMENT.—Effective on the date of enactment of this Act, there is established the Financial Stability Oversight Council.

(b) MEMBERSHIP.—The Council shall consist of the following members:

(1) VOTING MEMBERS.—The voting members, who shall each have 1 vote on the Council shall be—

(A) the Secretary of the Treasury, who shall serve as Chairperson of the Council;

(B) the Chairman of the Board of Governors;

(C) the Comptroller of the Currency;

(D) the Director of the Bureau;

(E) the Chairman of the Commission;

(F) the Chairperson of the Corporation;

(G) the Chairperson of the Commodity Futures Trading Commission;

(H) the Director of the Federal Housing Finance Agency;

(I) the Chairman of the National Credit Union Administration Board; and

(J) an independent member appointed by the President, by and with the advice and consent of the Senate, having insurance expertise.

(2) NONVOTING MEMBERS.—The nonvoting members, who shall serve in an advisory capacity as a nonvoting member of the Council, shall be—

(A) the Director of the Office of Financial Research;

(B) the Director of the Federal Insurance Office;

(C) a State insurance commissioner, to be designated by a selection process determined by the State insurance commissioners;

(D) a State banking supervisor, to be designated by a selection process determined by the State banking supervisors; and

(E) a State securities commissioner (or an officer performing like functions), to be designated by a selection process determined by such State securities commissioners.

(3) NONVOTING MEMBER PARTICIPATION.—The nonvoting members of the Council shall not be excluded from any of the proceedings, meetings, discussions, or deliberations of the Council, except that the Chairperson may, upon an affirmative vote of the member agencies, exclude the nonvoting members from any of the proceedings, meetings, discussions, or deliberations of the Council when necessary to safeguard and promote the free exchange of confidential supervisory information.

(c) TERMS; VACANCY.—

(1) TERMS.—The independent member of the Council shall serve for a term of 6 years, and each nonvoting member described in subparagraphs (C), (D), and (E) of subsection (b)(2) shall serve for a term of 2 years.

(2) VACANCY.—Any vacancy on the Council shall be filled in the manner in which the original appointment was made.

(3) ACTING OFFICIALS MAY SERVE.—In the event of a vacancy in the office of the head of a member agency or department, and pending the appointment of a successor, or during the absence or disability of the head of a member agency or department, the acting head of the member agency or department shall serve as a member of the Council in the place of that agency or department head.

(d) TECHNICAL AND PROFESSIONAL ADVISORY COMMITTEES.—The Council may appoint such special advisory, technical, or professional committees as may be useful in carrying out the functions of the Council, including an advisory committee consisting of State regulators, and the members of such committees may be members of the Council, or other persons, or both.

(e) MEETINGS.—

(1) TIMING.—The Council shall meet at the call of the Chairperson or a majority of the members then serving, but not less frequently than quarterly.

(2) RULES FOR CONDUCTING BUSINESS.—The Council shall adopt such rules as may be necessary for the conduct of the business of the Council. Such rules shall be rules of agency organization, procedure, or practice for purposes of section 553 of title 5, United States Code.

(f) VOTING.—Unless otherwise specified, the Council shall make all decisions that it is authorized or required to make by a majority vote of the voting members then serving.

(g) NONAPPLICABILITY OF FACA.—The Federal Advisory Committee Act (5 U.S.C. App.) shall not apply to the Council, or to any special advisory, technical, or professional committee appointed by the Council, except that, if an advisory, technical, or professional committee has one or more members who are not employees of or affiliated with the United States Government, the Council shall publish a list of the names of the members of such committee.

(h) ASSISTANCE FROM FEDERAL AGENCIES.—Any department or agency of the United States may provide to the Council and any special advisory, technical, or professional committee appointed by the Council, such services, funds, facilities, staff, and other support services as the Council may determine advisable.

(i) COMPENSATION OF MEMBERS.—

(1) FEDERAL EMPLOYEE MEMBERS.—All members of the Council who are officers or employees of the United States shall serve without compensation in addition to that received for their services as officers or employees of the United States.

(2) COMPENSATION FOR NON-FEDERAL MEMBER.—Section 5314 of title 5, United States Code, is amended by adding at the end the following:

"Independent Member of the Financial Stability Oversight Council (1).".

(j) DETAIL OF GOVERNMENT EMPLOYEES.—Any employee of the Federal Government may be detailed to the Council without reimbursement, and such detail shall be without interruption or loss of civil service status or privilege. An employee of the Federal Government detailed to the Council shall report to and be subject to oversight by the Council during the assignment to the Council, and shall be compensated by the department or agency from which the employee was detailed.

[Explanation at ¶110.]

[¶10,112] ACT SEC. 112. COUNCIL AUTHORITY.

(a) PURPOSES AND DUTIES OF THE COUNCIL.—

(1) IN GENERAL.—The purposes of the Council are—

(A) to identify risks to the financial stability of the United States that could arise from the material financial distress or failure, or ongoing activities, of large, interconnected bank holding companies or nonbank financial companies, or that could arise outside the financial services marketplace;

(B) to promote market discipline, by eliminating expectations on the part of shareholders, creditors, and counterparties of such companies that the Government will shield them from losses in the event of failure; and

(C) to respond to emerging threats to the stability of the United States financial system.

(2) DUTIES.—The Council shall, in accordance with this title—

(A) collect information from member agencies, other Federal and State financial regulatory agencies, the Federal Insurance Office and, if necessary to assess risks to the United States financial system, direct the Office of Financial Research to collect information from bank holding companies and nonbank financial companies;

(B) provide direction to, and request data and analyses from, the Office of Financial Research to support the work of the Council;

(C) monitor the financial services marketplace in order to identify potential threats to the financial stability of the United States;

(D) to monitor domestic and international financial regulatory proposals and developments, including insurance and accounting issues, and to advise Congress and make recommendations in such areas that will enhance the integrity, efficiency, competitiveness, and stability of the U.S. financial markets;

(E) facilitate information sharing and coordination among the member agencies and other Federal and State agencies regarding domestic financial services policy development, rulemaking, examinations, reporting requirements, and enforcement actions;

(F) recommend to the member agencies general supervisory priorities and principles reflecting the outcome of discussions among the member agencies;

(G) identify gaps in regulation that could pose risks to the financial stability of the United States;

(H) require supervision by the Board of Governors for nonbank financial companies that may pose risks to the financial stability of the United States in the event of their material financial distress or failure, or because of their activities pursuant to section 113;

(I) make recommendations to the Board of Governors concerning the establishment of heightened prudential standards for risk-based capital, leverage, liquidity, contingent capital, resolution plans and credit exposure reports, concentration limits, enhanced public disclosures, and overall risk management for nonbank financial companies and large, interconnected bank holding companies supervised by the Board of Governors;

(J) identify systemically important financial market utilities and payment, clearing, and settlement activities (as that term is defined in title VIII);

(K) make recommendations to primary financial regulatory agencies to apply new or heightened standards and safeguards for financial activities or practices that could create or increase risks of significant liquidity, credit, or other problems spreading among bank holding companies, nonbank financial companies, and United States financial markets;

(L) review and, as appropriate, may submit comments to the Commission and any standard-setting body with respect to an existing or proposed accounting principle, standard, or procedure;

(M) provide a forum for—

(i) discussion and analysis of emerging market developments and financial regulatory issues; and

(ii) resolution of jurisdictional disputes among the members of the Council; and

(N) annually report to and testify before Congress on—

(i) the activities of the Council;

(ii) significant financial market and regulatory developments, including insurance and accounting regulations and standards, along with an assessment of those developments on the stability of the financial system;

(iii) potential emerging threats to the financial stability of the United States;

(iv) all determinations made under section 113 or title VIII, and the basis for such determinations;

(v) all recommendations made under section 119 and the result of such recommendations; and

(vi) recommendations—

(I) to enhance the integrity, efficiency, competitiveness, and stability of United States financial markets;

(II) to promote market discipline; and

(III) to maintain investor confidence.

(b) STATEMENTS BY VOTING MEMBERS OF THE COUNCIL.—At the time at which each report is submitted under subsection (a), each voting member of the Council shall—

(1) if such member believes that the Council, the Government, and the private sector are taking all reasonable steps to ensure financial stability and to mitigate systemic risk that would negatively affect the economy, submit a signed statement to Congress stating such belief; or

(2) if such member does not believe that all reasonable steps described under paragraph (1) are being taken, submit a signed statement to Congress stating what actions such member believes need to be taken in order to ensure that all reasonable steps described under paragraph (1) are taken.

(c) TESTIMONY BY THE CHAIRPERSON.—The Chairperson shall appear before the Committee on Financial Services of the House of Representatives and the Committee on Banking, Housing, and Urban Affairs of the Senate at an annual hearing, after the report is submitted under subsection (a)—

(1) to discuss the efforts, activities, objectives, and plans of the Council; and

(2) to discuss and answer questions concerning such report.

(d) AUTHORITY TO OBTAIN INFORMATION.—

(1) IN GENERAL.—The Council may receive, and may request the submission of, any data or information from the Office of Financial Research, member agencies, and the Federal Insurance Office, as necessary—

(A) to monitor the financial services marketplace to identify potential risks to the financial stability of the United States; or

(B) to otherwise carry out any of the provisions of this title.

(2) SUBMISSIONS BY THE OFFICE AND MEMBER AGENCIES.—Notwithstanding any other provision of law, the Office of Financial Research, any member agency, and the Federal Insurance Office, are authorized to submit information to the Council.

(3) FINANCIAL DATA COLLECTION.—

(A) IN GENERAL.—The Council, acting through the Office of Financial Research, may require the submission of periodic and other reports from any nonbank financial company or bank holding company for the purpose of assessing the extent to which a financial activity or financial market in which the nonbank financial company or bank holding company participates, or the nonbank financial company or bank holding company itself, poses a threat to the financial stability of the United States.

(B) MITIGATION OF REPORT BURDEN.—Before requiring the submission of reports from any nonbank financial company or bank holding company that is regulated by a member agency or any primary financial regulatory agency, the Council, acting through the Office of Financial Research, shall coordinate with such agencies and shall, whenever possible, rely on information available from the Office of Financial Research or such agencies.

(C) MITIGATION IN CASE OF FOREIGN FINANCIAL COMPANIES.—Before requiring the submission of reports from a company that is a foreign nonbank financial company or foreign-based bank holding company, the Council shall, acting through the Office of Financial Research, to the extent appropriate, consult with the appropriate foreign regulator of such company and, whenever possible, rely on information already being collected by such foreign regulator, with English translation.

(4) BACK-UP EXAMINATION BY THE BOARD OF GOVERNORS.—If the Council is unable to determine whether the financial activities of a U.S. nonbank financial company pose a threat to the financial

stability of the United States, based on information or reports obtained under paragraphs (1) and (3), discussions with management, and publicly available information, the Council may request the Board of Governors, and the Board of Governors is authorized, to conduct an examination of the U.S. nonbank financial company for the sole purpose of determining whether the nonbank financial company should be supervised by the Board of Governors for purposes of this title.

(5) CONFIDENTIALITY.—

(A) IN GENERAL.—The Council, the Office of Financial Research, and the other member agencies shall maintain the confidentiality of any data, information, and reports submitted under this title.

(B) RETENTION OF PRIVILEGE.—The submission of any nonpublicly available data or information under this subsection and subtitle B shall not constitute a waiver of, or otherwise affect, any privilege arising under Federal or State law (including the rules of any Federal or State court) to which the data or information is otherwise subject.

(C) FREEDOM OF INFORMATION ACT.—Section 552 of title 5, United States Code, including the exceptions thereunder, shall apply to any data or information submitted under this subsection and subtitle B.

[Explanation at ¶ 115.]

[¶ 10,113] ACT SEC. 113. AUTHORITY TO REQUIRE SUPERVISION AND REGULATION OF CERTAIN NONBANK FINANCIAL COMPANIES.

(a) U.S. NONBANK FINANCIAL COMPANIES SUPERVISED BY THE BOARD OF GOVERNORS.—

(1) DETERMINATION.—The Council, on a nondelegable basis and by a vote of not fewer than $2/3$ of the voting members then serving, including an affirmative vote by the Chairperson, may determine that a U.S. nonbank financial company shall be supervised by the Board of Governors and shall be subject to prudential standards, in accordance with this title, if the Council determines that material financial distress at the U.S. nonbank financial company, or the nature, scope, size, scale, concentration, interconnectedness, or mix of the activities of the U.S. nonbank financial company, could pose a threat to the financial stability of the United States.

(2) CONSIDERATIONS.—In making a determination under paragraph (1), the Council shall consider—

(A) the extent of the leverage of the company;

(B) the extent and nature of the off-balance-sheet exposures of the company;

(C) the extent and nature of the transactions and relationships of the company with other significant nonbank financial companies and significant bank holding companies;

(D) the importance of the company as a source of credit for households, businesses, and State and local governments and as a source of liquidity for the United States financial system;

(E) the importance of the company as a source of credit for low-income, minority, or underserved communities, and the impact that the failure of such company would have on the availability of credit in such communities;

(F) the extent to which assets are managed rather than owned by the company, and the extent to which ownership of assets under management is diffuse;

(G) the nature, scope, size, scale, concentration, interconnectedness, and mix of the activities of the company;

(H) the degree to which the company is already regulated by 1 or more primary financial regulatory agencies;

(I) the amount and nature of the financial assets of the company;

(J) the amount and types of the liabilities of the company, including the degree of reliance on short-term funding; and

(K) any other risk-related factors that the Council deems appropriate.

(b) FOREIGN NONBANK FINANCIAL COMPANIES SUPERVISED BY THE BOARD OF GOVERNORS.—

(1) DETERMINATION.—The Council, on a nondelegable basis and by a vote of not fewer than ⅔ of the voting members then serving, including an affirmative vote by the Chairperson, may determine that a foreign nonbank financial company shall be supervised by the Board of Governors and shall be subject to prudential standards, in accordance with this title, if the Council determines that material financial distress at the foreign nonbank financial company, or the nature, scope, size, scale, concentration, interconnectedness, or mix of the activities of the foreign nonbank financial company, could pose a threat to the financial stability of the United States.

(2) CONSIDERATIONS.—In making a determination under paragraph (1), the Council shall consider—

(A) the extent of the leverage of the company;

(B) the extent and nature of the United States related off-balance-sheet exposures of the company;

(C) the extent and nature of the transactions and relationships of the company with other significant nonbank financial companies and significant bank holding companies;

(D) the importance of the company as a source of credit for United States households, businesses, and State and local governments and as a source of liquidity for the United States financial system;

(E) the importance of the company as a source of credit for low-income, minority, or underserved communities in the United States, and the impact that the failure of such company would have on the availability of credit in such communities;

(F) the extent to which assets are managed rather than owned by the company and the extent to which ownership of assets under management is diffuse;

(G) the nature, scope, size, scale, concentration, interconnectedness, and mix of the activities of the company;

(H) the extent to which the company is subject to prudential standards on a consolidated basis in its home country that are administered and enforced by a comparable foreign supervisory authority;

(I) the amount and nature of the United States financial assets of the company;

(J) the amount and nature of the liabilities of the company used to fund activities and operations in the United States, including the degree of reliance on short-term funding; and

(K) any other risk-related factors that the Council deems appropriate.

(c) ANTIEVASION.—

(1) DETERMINATIONS.—In order to avoid evasion of this title, the Council, on its own initiative or at the request of the Board of Governors, may determine, on a nondelegable basis and by a vote of not fewer than ⅔ of the voting members then serving, including an affirmative vote by the Chairperson, that—

(A) material financial distress related to, or the nature, scope, size, scale, concentration, interconnectedness, or mix of, the financial activities conducted directly or indirectly by a company incorporated or organized under the laws of the United States or any State or the financial activities in the United States of a company incorporated or organized in a country other than the United States would pose a threat to the financial stability of the United States, based on consideration of the factors in subsection (a)(2) or (b)(2), as applicable;

(B) the company is organized or operates in such a manner as to evade the application of this title; and

(C) such financial activities of the company shall be supervised by the Board of Governors and subject to prudential standards in accordance with this title, consistent with paragraph (3).

(2) REPORT.—Upon making a determination under paragraph (1), the Council shall submit a report to the appropriate committees of Congress detailing the reasons for making such determination.

(3) CONSOLIDATED SUPERVISION OF ONLY FINANCIAL ACTIVITIES; ESTABLISHMENT OF AN INTERMEDIATE HOLDING COMPANY.—

(A) ESTABLISHMENT OF AN INTERMEDIATE HOLDING COMPANY.—Upon a determination under paragraph (1), the company that is the subject of the determination may establish an intermediate holding company in which the financial activities of such company and its subsidiaries shall be conducted (other than the activities described in section 167(b)(2)) in compliance with any regulations or guidance provided by the Board of Governors. Such intermediate holding company shall be subject to the supervision of the Board of Governors and to prudential standards under this title as if the intermediate holding company were a nonbank financial company supervised by the Board of Governors.

(B) ACTION OF THE BOARD OF GOVERNORS.—To facilitate the supervision of the financial activities subject to the determination in paragraph (1), the Board of Governors may require a company to establish an intermediate holding company, as provided for in section 167, which would be subject to the supervision of the Board of Governors and to prudential standards under this title, as if the intermediate holding company were a nonbank financial company supervised by the Board of Governors.

(4) NOTICE AND OPPORTUNITY FOR HEARING AND FINAL DETERMINATION; JUDICIAL REVIEW.—Subsections (d) through (h) shall apply to determinations made by the Council pursuant to paragraph (1) in the same manner as such subsections apply to nonbank financial companies.

(5) COVERED FINANCIAL ACTIVITIES.—For purposes of this subsection, the term "financial activities"—

(A) means activities that are financial in nature (as defined in section 4(k) of the Bank Holding Company Act of 1956);

(B) includes the ownership or control of one or more insured depository institutions; and

(C) does not include internal financial activities conducted for the company or any affiliate thereof, including internal treasury, investment, and employee benefit functions.

(6) ONLY FINANCIAL ACTIVITIES SUBJECT TO PRUDENTIAL SUPERVISION.—Nonfinancial activities of the company shall not be subject to supervision by the Board of Governors and prudential standards of the Board. For purposes of this Act, the financial activities that are the subject of the determination in paragraph (1) shall be subject to the same requirements as a nonbank financial company supervised by the Board of Governors. Nothing in this paragraph shall prohibit or limit the authority of the Board of Governors to apply prudential standards under this title to the financial activities that are subject to the determination in paragraph (1).

(d) REEVALUATION AND RESCISSION.—The Council shall—

(1) not less frequently than annually, reevaluate each determination made under subsections (a) and (b) with respect to such nonbank financial company supervised by the Board of Governors; and

(2) rescind any such determination, if the Council, by a vote of not fewer than $2/3$ of the voting members then serving, including an affirmative vote by the Chairperson, determines that the nonbank financial company no longer meets the standards under subsection (a) or (b), as applicable.

(e) NOTICE AND OPPORTUNITY FOR HEARING AND FINAL DETERMINATION.—

(1) IN GENERAL.—The Council shall provide to a nonbank financial company written notice of a proposed determination of the Council, including an explanation of the basis of the proposed determination of the Council, that a nonbank financial company shall be supervised by the Board of Governors and shall be subject to prudential standards in accordance with this title.

(2) HEARING.—Not later than 30 days after the date of receipt of any notice of a proposed determination under paragraph (1), the nonbank financial company may request, in writing, an opportunity for a written or oral hearing before the Council to contest the proposed determination. Upon receipt of a timely request, the Council shall fix a time (not later than 30 days after the date of receipt of the request) and place at which such company may appear, personally or

through counsel, to submit written materials (or, at the sole discretion of the Council, oral testimony and oral argument).

(3) FINAL DETERMINATION.—Not later than 60 days after the date of a hearing under paragraph (2), the Council shall notify the nonbank financial company of the final determination of the Council, which shall contain a statement of the basis for the decision of the Council.

(4) NO HEARING REQUESTED.—If a nonbank financial company does not make a timely request for a hearing, the Council shall notify the nonbank financial company, in writing, of the final determination of the Council under subsection (a) or (b), as applicable, not later than 10 days after the date by which the company may request a hearing under paragraph (2).

(f) EMERGENCY EXCEPTION.—

(1) IN GENERAL.—The Council may waive or modify the requirements of subsection (e) with respect to a nonbank financial company, if the Council determines, by a vote of not fewer than $2/3$ of the voting members then serving, including an affirmative vote by the Chairperson, that such waiver or modification is necessary or appropriate to prevent or mitigate threats posed by the nonbank financial company to the financial stability of the United States.

(2) NOTICE.—The Council shall provide notice of a waiver or modification under this subsection to the nonbank financial company concerned as soon as practicable, but not later than 24 hours after the waiver or modification is granted.

(3) INTERNATIONAL COORDINATION.—In making a determination under paragraph (1), the Council shall consult with the appropriate home country supervisor, if any, of the foreign nonbank financial company that is being considered for such a determination.

(4) OPPORTUNITY FOR HEARING.—The Council shall allow a nonbank financial company to request, in writing, an opportunity for a written or oral hearing before the Council to contest a waiver or modification under this subsection, not later than 10 days after the date of receipt of notice of the waiver or modification by the company. Upon receipt of a timely request, the Council shall fix a time (not later than 15 days after the date of receipt of the request) and place at which the nonbank financial company may appear, personally or through counsel, to submit written materials (or, at the sole discretion of the Council, oral testimony and oral argument).

(5) NOTICE OF FINAL DETERMINATION.—Not later than 30 days after the date of any hearing under paragraph (4), the Council shall notify the subject nonbank financial company of the final determination of the Council under this subsection, which shall contain a statement of the basis for the decision of the Council.

(g) CONSULTATION.—The Council shall consult with the primary financial regulatory agency, if any, for each nonbank financial company or subsidiary of a nonbank financial company that is being considered for supervision by the Board of Governors under this section before the Council makes any final determination with respect to such nonbank financial company under subsection (a), (b), or (c).

(h) JUDICIAL REVIEW.—If the Council makes a final determination under this section with respect to a nonbank financial company, such nonbank financial company may, not later than 30 days after the date of receipt of the notice of final determination under subsection (d)(2), (e)(3), or (f)(5), bring an action in the United States district court for the judicial district in which the home office of such nonbank financial company is located, or in the United States District Court for the District of Columbia, for an order requiring that the final determination be rescinded, and the court shall, upon review, dismiss such action or direct the final determination to be rescinded. Review of such an action shall be limited to whether the final determination made under this section was arbitrary and capricious.

(i) INTERNATIONAL COORDINATION.—In exercising its duties under this title with respect to foreign nonbank financial companies, foreign-based bank holding companies, and cross-border activities and markets, the Council shall consult with appropriate foreign regulatory authorities, to the extent appropriate.

[Explanation at ¶ 120.]

[¶ 10,114] ACT SEC. 114. REGISTRATION OF NONBANK FINANCIAL COMPANIES SUPERVISED BY THE BOARD OF GOVERNORS.

Not later than 180 days after the date of a final Council determination under section 113 that a nonbank financial company is to be supervised by the Board of Governors, such company shall register with the Board of Governors, on forms prescribed by the Board of Governors, which shall include such information as the Board of Governors, in consultation with the Council, may deem necessary or appropriate to carry out this title.

[Explanation at ¶ 120.]

[¶ 10,115] ACT SEC. 115. ENHANCED SUPERVISION AND PRUDENTIAL STANDARDS FOR NONBANK FINANCIAL COMPANIES SUPERVISED BY THE BOARD OF GOVERNORS AND CERTAIN BANK HOLDING COMPANIES.

(a) IN GENERAL.—

(1) PURPOSE.—In order to prevent or mitigate risks to the financial stability of the United States that could arise from the material financial distress, failure, or ongoing activities of large, interconnected financial institutions, the Council may make recommendations to the Board of Governors concerning the establishment and refinement of prudential standards and reporting and disclosure requirements applicable to nonbank financial companies supervised by the Board of Governors and large, interconnected bank holding companies, that—

(A) are more stringent than those applicable to other nonbank financial companies and bank holding companies that do not present similar risks to the financial stability of the United States; and

(B) increase in stringency, based on the considerations identified in subsection (b)(3).

(2) RECOMMENDED APPLICATION OF REQUIRED STANDARDS.—In making recommendations under this section, the Council may—

(A) differentiate among companies that are subject to heightened standards on an individual basis or by category, taking into consideration their capital structure, riskiness, complexity, financial activities (including the financial activities of their subsidiaries), size, and any other risk-related factors that the Council deems appropriate; or

(B) recommend an asset threshold that is higher than $50,000,000,000 for the application of any standard described in subsections (c) through (g).

(b) DEVELOPMENT OF PRUDENTIAL STANDARDS.—

(1) IN GENERAL.—The recommendations of the Council under subsection (a) may include—

(A) risk-based capital requirements;

(B) leverage limits;

(C) liquidity requirements;

(D) resolution plan and credit exposure report requirements;

(E) concentration limits;

(F) a contingent capital requirement;

(G) enhanced public disclosures;

(H) short-term debt limits; and

(I) overall risk management requirements.

(2) PRUDENTIAL STANDARDS FOR FOREIGN FINANCIAL COMPANIES.—In making recommendations concerning the standards set forth in paragraph (1) that would apply to foreign nonbank financial companies supervised by the Board of Governors or foreign-based bank holding companies, the Council shall—

(A) give due regard to the principle of national treatment and equality of competitive opportunity; and

(B) take into account the extent to which the foreign nonbank financial company or foreign-based bank holding company is subject on a consolidated basis to home country standards that are comparable to those applied to financial companies in the United States.

(3) CONSIDERATIONS.—In making recommendations concerning prudential standards under paragraph (1), the Council shall—

(A) take into account differences among nonbank financial companies supervised by the Board of Governors and bank holding companies described in subsection (a), based on—

(i) the factors described in subsections (a) and (b) of section 113;

(ii) whether the company owns an insured depository institution;

(iii) nonfinancial activities and affiliations of the company; and

(iv) any other factors that the Council determines appropriate;

(B) to the extent possible, ensure that small changes in the factors listed in subsections (a) and (b) of section 113 would not result in sharp, discontinuous changes in the prudential standards established under section 165; and

(C) adapt its recommendations as appropriate in light of any predominant line of business of such company, including assets under management or other activities for which particular standards may not be appropriate.

(c) CONTINGENT CAPITAL.—

(1) STUDY REQUIRED.—The Council shall conduct a study of the feasibility, benefits, costs, and structure of a contingent capital requirement for nonbank financial companies supervised by the Board of Governors and bank holding companies described in subsection (a), which study shall include—

(A) an evaluation of the degree to which such requirement would enhance the safety and soundness of companies subject to the requirement, promote the financial stability of the United States, and reduce risks to United States taxpayers;

(B) an evaluation of the characteristics and amounts of contingent capital that should be required;

(C) an analysis of potential prudential standards that should be used to determine whether the contingent capital of a company would be converted to equity in times of financial stress;

(D) an evaluation of the costs to companies, the effects on the structure and operation of credit and other financial markets, and other economic effects of requiring contingent capital;

(E) an evaluation of the effects of such requirement on the international competitiveness of companies subject to the requirement and the prospects for international coordination in establishing such requirement; and

(F) recommendations for implementing regulations.

(2) REPORT.—The Council shall submit a report to Congress regarding the study required by paragraph (1) not later than 2 years after the date of enactment of this Act.

(3) RECOMMENDATIONS.—

(A) IN GENERAL.—Subsequent to submitting a report to Congress under paragraph (2), the Council may make recommendations to the Board of Governors to require any nonbank financial company supervised by the Board of Governors and any bank holding company described in subsection (a) to maintain a minimum amount of contingent capital that is convertible to equity in times of financial stress.

(B) FACTORS TO CONSIDER.—In making recommendations under this subsection, the Council shall consider—

(i) an appropriate transition period for implementation of a conversion under this subsection;

(ii) the factors described in subsection (b)(3);

(iii) capital requirements applicable to a nonbank financial company supervised by the Board of Governors or a bank holding company described in subsection (a), and subsidiaries thereof;

(iv) results of the study required by paragraph (1); and

(v) any other factor that the Council deems appropriate.

(d) RESOLUTION PLAN AND CREDIT EXPOSURE REPORTS.—

(1) RESOLUTION PLAN.—The Council may make recommendations to the Board of Governors concerning the requirement that each nonbank financial company supervised by the Board of Governors and each bank holding company described in subsection (a) report periodically to the Council, the Board of Governors, and the Corporation, the plan of such company for rapid and orderly resolution in the event of material financial distress or failure.

(2) CREDIT EXPOSURE REPORT.—The Council may make recommendations to the Board of Governors concerning the advisability of requiring each nonbank financial company supervised by the Board of Governors and bank holding company described in subsection (a) to report periodically to the Council, the Board of Governors, and the Corporation on—

(A) the nature and extent to which the company has credit exposure to other significant nonbank financial companies and significant bank holding companies; and

(B) the nature and extent to which other such significant nonbank financial companies and significant bank holding companies have credit exposure to that company.

(e) CONCENTRATION LIMITS.—In order to limit the risks that the failure of any individual company could pose to nonbank financial companies supervised by the Board of Governors or bank holding companies described in subsection (a), the Council may make recommendations to the Board of Governors to prescribe standards to limit such risks, as set forth in section 165.

(f) ENHANCED PUBLIC DISCLOSURES.—The Council may make recommendations to the Board of Governors to require periodic public disclosures by bank holding companies described in subsection (a) and by nonbank financial companies supervised by the Board of Governors, in order to support market evaluation of the risk profile, capital adequacy, and risk management capabilities thereof.

(g) SHORT-TERM DEBT LIMITS.—The Council may make recommendations to the Board of Governors to require short-term debt limits to mitigate the risks that an over-accumulation of such debt could pose to bank holding companies described in subsection (a), nonbank financial companies supervised by the Board of Governors, or the financial system.

[Explanation at ¶125.]

[¶10,116] ACT SEC. 116. REPORTS.

(a) IN GENERAL.—Subject to subsection (b), the Council, acting through the Office of Financial Research, may require a bank holding company with total consolidated assets of $50,000,000,000 or greater or a nonbank financial company supervised by the Board of Governors, and any subsidiary thereof, to submit certified reports to keep the Council informed as to—

(1) the financial condition of the company;

(2) systems for monitoring and controlling financial, operating, and other risks;

(3) transactions with any subsidiary that is a depository institution; and

(4) the extent to which the activities and operations of the company and any subsidiary thereof, could, under adverse circumstances, have the potential to disrupt financial markets or affect the overall financial stability of the United States.

(b) USE OF EXISTING REPORTS.—

(1) IN GENERAL.—For purposes of compliance with subsection (a), the Council, acting through the Office of Financial Research, shall, to the fullest extent possible, use—

(A) reports that a bank holding company, nonbank financial company supervised by the Board of Governors, or any functionally regulated subsidiary of such company has been required to provide to other Federal or State regulatory agencies or to a relevant foreign supervisory authority;

(B) information that is otherwise required to be reported publicly; and

(C) externally audited financial statements.

(2) AVAILABILITY.—Each bank holding company described in subsection (a) and nonbank financial company supervised by the Board of Governors, and any subsidiary thereof, shall provide to the Council, at the request of the Council, copies of all reports referred to in paragraph (1).

(3) CONFIDENTIALITY.—The Council shall maintain the confidentiality of the reports obtained under subsection (a) and paragraph (1)(A) of this subsection.

[Explanation at ¶ 130.]

[¶ 10,117] ACT SEC. 117. TREATMENT OF CERTAIN COMPANIES THAT CEASE TO BE BANK HOLDING COMPANIES.

(a) APPLICABILITY.—This section shall apply to—

(1) any entity that—

(A) was a bank holding company having total consolidated assets equal to or greater than $50,000,000,000 as of January 1, 2010; and

(B) received financial assistance under or participated in the Capital Purchase Program established under the Troubled Asset Relief Program authorized by the Emergency Economic Stabilization Act of 2008; and

(2) any successor entity (as defined by the Board of Governors, in consultation with the Council) to an entity described in paragraph (1).

(b) TREATMENT.—If an entity described in subsection (a) ceases to be a bank holding company at any time after January 1, 2010, then such entity shall be treated as a nonbank financial company supervised by the Board of Governors, as if the Council had made a determination under section 113 with respect to that entity.

(c) APPEAL.—

(1) REQUEST FOR HEARING.—An entity may request, in writing, an opportunity for a written or oral hearing before the Council to appeal its treatment as a nonbank financial company supervised by the Board of Governors in accordance with this section. Upon receipt of the request, the Council shall fix a time (not later than 30 days after the date of receipt of the request) and place at which such entity may appear, personally or through counsel, to submit written materials (or, at the sole discretion of the Council, oral testimony and oral argument).

(2) DECISION.—

(A) PROPOSED DECISION.—A Council decision to grant an appeal under this subsection shall be made by a vote of not fewer than ⅔ of the voting members then serving, including an affirmative vote by the Chairperson. Not later than 60 days after the date of a hearing under paragraph (1), the Council shall submit a report to, and may testify before, the Committee on Banking, Housing, and Urban Affairs of the Senate and the Committee on Financial Services of the House of Representatives on the proposed decision of the Council regarding an appeal under paragraph (1), which report shall include a statement of the basis for the proposed decision of the Council.

(B) NOTICE OF FINAL DECISION.—The Council shall notify the subject entity of the final decision of the Council regarding an appeal under paragraph (1), which notice shall contain a statement of the basis for the final decision of the Council, not later than 60 days after the later of—

(i) the date of the submission of the report under subparagraph (A); or

(ii) if, not later than 1 year after the date of submission of the report under subparagraph (A), the Committee on Banking, Housing, and Urban Affairs of the Senate or the Committee on Financial Services of the House of Representatives holds one or more hearings regarding such report, the date of the last such hearing.

(C) CONSIDERATIONS.—In making a decision regarding an appeal under paragraph (1), the Council shall consider whether the company meets the standards under section 113(a) or 113(b), as applicable, and the definition of the term "nonbank financial company" under section 102. The decision of the Council shall be final, subject to the review under paragraph (3).

(3) REVIEW.—If the Council denies an appeal under this subsection, the Council shall, not less frequently than annually, review and reevaluate the decision.

[Explanation at ¶ 135.]

[¶ 10,118] ACT SEC. 118. COUNCIL FUNDING.

Any expenses of the Council shall be treated as expenses of, and paid by, the Office of Financial Research.

[Explanation at ¶ 110.]

[¶ 10,119] ACT SEC. 119. RESOLUTION OF SUPERVISORY JURISDICTIONAL DISPUTES AMONG MEMBER AGENCIES.

(a) REQUEST FOR COUNCIL RECOMMENDATION.—The Council shall seek to resolve a dispute among 2 or more member agencies, if—

(1) a member agency has a dispute with another member agency about the respective jurisdiction over a particular bank holding company, nonbank financial company, or financial activity or product (excluding matters for which another dispute mechanism specifically has been provided under title X);

(2) the Council determines that the disputing agencies cannot, after a demonstrated good faith effort, resolve the dispute without the intervention of the Council; and

(3) any of the member agencies involved in the dispute—

(A) provides all other disputants prior notice of the intent to request dispute resolution by the Council; and

(B) requests in writing, not earlier than 14 days after providing the notice described in subparagraph (A), that the Council seek to resolve the dispute.

(b) COUNCIL RECOMMENDATION.—The Council shall seek to resolve each dispute described in subsection (a)—

(1) within a reasonable time after receiving the dispute resolution request;

(2) after consideration of relevant information provided by each agency party to the dispute; and

(3) by agreeing with 1 of the disputants regarding the entirety of the matter, or by determining a compromise position.

(c) FORM OF RECOMMENDATION.—Any Council recommendation under this section shall—

(1) be in writing;

(2) include an explanation of the reasons therefor; and

(3) be approved by the affirmative vote of $2/3$ of the voting members of the Council then serving.

(d) NONBINDING EFFECT.—Any recommendation made by the Council under subsection (c) shall not be binding on the Federal agencies that are parties to the dispute.

[Explanation at ¶ 140.]

[¶ 10,120] ACT SEC. 120. ADDITIONAL STANDARDS APPLICABLE TO ACTIVITIES OR PRACTICES FOR FINANCIAL STABILITY PURPOSES.

(a) IN GENERAL.—The Council may provide for more stringent regulation of a financial activity by issuing recommendations to the primary financial regulatory agencies to apply new or heightened standards and safeguards, including standards enumerated in section 115, for a financial activity or practice conducted by bank holding companies or nonbank financial companies under their respective jurisdictions, if the Council determines that the conduct, scope, nature, size, scale, concentration, or interconnectedness of such activity or practice could create or increase the risk of significant liquidity, credit, or other problems spreading among bank holding companies and nonbank financial companies, financial markets of the United States, or low-income, minority, or underserved communities.

(b) PROCEDURE FOR RECOMMENDATIONS TO REGULATORS.—

(1) NOTICE AND OPPORTUNITY FOR COMMENT.—The Council shall consult with the primary financial regulatory agencies and provide notice to the public and opportunity for comment for any proposed recommendation that the primary financial regulatory agencies apply new or heightened standards and safeguards for a financial activity or practice.

(2) CRITERIA.—The new or heightened standards and safeguards for a financial activity or practice recommended under paragraph (1)—

(A) shall take costs to long-term economic growth into account; and

(B) may include prescribing the conduct of the activity or practice in specific ways (such as by limiting its scope, or applying particular capital or risk management requirements to the conduct of the activity) or prohibiting the activity or practice.

(c) IMPLEMENTATION OF RECOMMENDED STANDARDS.—

(1) ROLE OF PRIMARY FINANCIAL REGULATORY AGENCY.—

(A) IN GENERAL.—Each primary financial regulatory agency may impose, require reports regarding, examine for compliance with, and enforce standards in accordance with this section with respect to those entities for which it is the primary financial regulatory agency.

(B) RULE OF CONSTRUCTION.—The authority under this paragraph is in addition to, and does not limit, any other authority of a primary financial regulatory agency. Compliance by an entity with actions taken by a primary financial regulatory agency under this section shall be enforceable in accordance with the statutes governing the respective jurisdiction of the primary financial regulatory agency over the entity, as if the agency action were taken under those statutes.

(2) IMPOSITION OF STANDARDS.—The primary financial regulatory agency shall impose the standards recommended by the Council in accordance with subsection (a), or similar standards that the Council deems acceptable, or shall explain in writing to the Council, not later than 90 days after the date on which the Council issues the recommendation, why the agency has determined not to follow the recommendation of the Council.

(d) REPORT TO CONGRESS.—The Council shall report to Congress on—

(1) any recommendations issued by the Council under this section;

(2) the implementation of, or failure to implement, such recommendation on the part of a primary financial regulatory agency; and

(3) in any case in which no primary financial regulatory agency exists for the nonbank financial company conducting financial activities or practices referred to in subsection (a), recommendations for legislation that would prevent such activities or practices from threatening the stability of the financial system of the United States.

(e) EFFECT OF RESCISSION OF IDENTIFICATION.—

(1) NOTICE.—The Council may recommend to the relevant primary financial regulatory agency that a financial activity or practice no longer requires any standards or safeguards implemented under this section.

(2) DETERMINATION OF PRIMARY FINANCIAL REGULATORY AGENCY TO CONTINUE.—

(A) IN GENERAL.—Upon receipt of a recommendation under paragraph (1), a primary financial regulatory agency that has imposed standards under this section shall determine whether such standards should remain in effect.

(B) APPEAL PROCESS.—Each primary financial regulatory agency that has imposed standards under this section shall promulgate regulations to establish a procedure under which entities under its jurisdiction may appeal a determination by such agency under this paragraph that standards imposed under this section should remain in effect.

[Explanation at ¶145.]

[¶10,121] ACT SEC. 121. MITIGATION OF RISKS TO FINANCIAL STABILITY.

(a) MITIGATORY ACTIONS.—If the Board of Governors determines that a bank holding company with total consolidated assets of $50,000,000,000 or more, or a nonbank financial company supervised by the Board of Governors, poses a grave threat to the financial stability of the United States, the Board of Governors, upon an affirmative vote of not fewer than ⅔ of the voting members of the Council then serving, shall—

(1) limit the ability of the company to merge with, acquire, consolidate with, or otherwise become affiliated with another company;

(2) restrict the ability of the company to offer a financial product or products;

(3) require the company to terminate one or more activities;

(4) impose conditions on the manner in which the company conducts 1 or more activities; or

(5) if the Board of Governors determines that the actions described in paragraphs (1) through (4) are inadequate to mitigate a threat to the financial stability of the United States in its recommendation, require the company to sell or otherwise transfer assets or off-balance-sheet items to unaffiliated entities.

(b) NOTICE AND HEARING.—

(1) IN GENERAL.—The Board of Governors, in consultation with the Council, shall provide to a company described in subsection (a) written notice that such company is being considered for mitigatory action pursuant to this section, including an explanation of the basis for, and description of, the proposed mitigatory action.

(2) HEARING.—Not later than 30 days after the date of receipt of notice under paragraph (1), the company may request, in writing, an opportunity for a written or oral hearing before the Board of Governors to contest the proposed mitigatory action. Upon receipt of a timely request, the Board of Governors shall fix a time (not later than 30 days after the date of receipt of the request) and place at which such company may appear, personally or through counsel, to submit written materials (or, at the discretion of the Board of Governors, in consultation with the Council, oral testimony and oral argument).

(3) DECISION.—Not later than 60 days after the date of a hearing under paragraph (2), or not later than 60 days after the provision of a notice under paragraph (1) if no hearing was held, the Board of Governors shall notify the company of the final decision of the Board of Governors, including the results of the vote of the Council, as described in subsection (a).

(c) FACTORS FOR CONSIDERATION.—The Board of Governors and the Council shall take into consideration the factors set forth in subsection (a) or (b) of section 113, as applicable, in making any determination under subsection (a).

(d) APPLICATION TO FOREIGN FINANCIAL COMPANIES.—The Board of Governors may prescribe regulations regarding the application of this section to foreign nonbank financial companies supervised by the Board of Governors and foreign-based bank holding companies—

(1) giving due regard to the principle of national treatment and equality of competitive opportunity; and

(2) taking into account the extent to which the foreign nonbank financial company or foreign-based bank holding company is subject on a consolidated basis to home country standards that are comparable to those applied to financial companies in the United States.

[Explanation at ¶ 150.]

[¶ 10,122] ACT SEC. 122. GAO AUDIT OF COUNCIL.

(a) AUTHORITY TO AUDIT.—The Comptroller General of the United States may audit the activities of—

(1) the Council; and

(2) any person or entity acting on behalf of or under the authority of the Council, to the extent that such activities relate to work for the Council by such person or entity.

(b) ACCESS TO INFORMATION.—

(1) IN GENERAL.—Notwithstanding any other provision of law, the Comptroller General shall, upon request and at such reasonable time and in such reasonable form as the Comptroller General may request, have access to—

(A) any records or other information under the control of or used by the Council;

(B) any records or other information under the control of a person or entity acting on behalf of or under the authority of the Council, to the extent that such records or other information is relevant to an audit under subsection (a); and

(C) the officers, directors, employees, financial advisors, staff, working groups, and agents and representatives of the Council (as related to the activities on behalf of the Council of such agent or representative), at such reasonable times as the Comptroller General may request.

(2) COPIES.—The Comptroller General may make and retain copies of such books, accounts, and other records, access to which is granted under this section, as the Comptroller General considers appropriate.

[Explanation at ¶ 110.]

[¶ 10,123] ACT SEC. 123. STUDY OF THE EFFECTS OF SIZE AND COMPLEXITY OF FINANCIAL INSTITUTIONS ON CAPITAL MARKET EFFICIENCY AND ECONOMIC GROWTH.

(a) STUDY REQUIRED.—

(1) IN GENERAL.—The Chairperson of the Council shall carry out a study of the economic impact of possible financial services regulatory limitations intended to reduce systemic risk. Such study shall estimate the benefits and costs on the efficiency of capital markets, on the financial sector, and on national economic growth, of—

(A) explicit or implicit limits on the maximum size of banks, bank holding companies, and other large financial institutions;

(B) limits on the organizational complexity and diversification of large financial institutions;

(C) requirements for operational separation between business units of large financial institutions in order to expedite resolution in case of failure;

(D) limits on risk transfer between business units of large financial institutions;

(E) requirements to carry contingent capital or similar mechanisms;

(F) limits on commingling of commercial and financial activities by large financial institutions;

(G) segregation requirements between traditional financial activities and trading or other high-risk operations in large financial institutions; and

(H) other limitations on the activities or structure of large financial institutions that may be useful to limit systemic risk.

(2) RECOMMENDATIONS.—The study required by this section shall include recommendations for the optimal structure of any limits considered in subparagraphs (A) through (E), in order to maximize their effectiveness and minimize their economic impact.

(b) REPORT.—Not later than the end of the 180-day period beginning on the date of enactment of this title, and not later than every 5 years thereafter, the Chairperson shall issue a report to the Congress containing any findings and determinations made in carrying out the study required under subsection (a).

[Explanation at ¶ 105.]

Subtitle B—Office of Financial Research

[¶ 10,151] ACT SEC. 151. DEFINITIONS.

For purposes of this subtitle—

(1) the terms "Office" and "Director" mean the Office of Financial Research established under this subtitle and the Director thereof, respectively;

(2) the term "financial company" has the same meaning as in title II, and includes an insured depository institution and an insurance company;

(3) the term "Data Center" means the data center established under section 154;

(4) the term "Research and Analysis Center" means the research and analysis center established under section 154;

(5) the term "financial transaction data" means the structure and legal description of a financial contract, with sufficient detail to describe the rights and obligations between counterparties and make possible an independent valuation;

(6) the term "position data"—

(A) means data on financial assets or liabilities held on the balance sheet of a financial company, where positions are created or changed by the execution of a financial transaction; and

(B) includes information that identifies counterparties, the valuation by the financial company of the position, and information that makes possible an independent valuation of the position;

(7) the term "financial contract" means a legally binding agreement between 2 or more counterparties, describing rights and obligations relating to the future delivery of items of intrinsic or extrinsic value among the counterparties; and

(8) the term "financial instrument" means a financial contract in which the terms and conditions are publicly available, and the roles of one or more of the counterparties are assignable without the consent of any of the other counterparties (including common stock of a publicly traded company, government bonds, or exchange traded futures and options contracts).

[¶ 10,152] ACT SEC. 152. OFFICE OF FINANCIAL RESEARCH ESTABLISHED.

(a) ESTABLISHMENT.—There is established within the Department of the Treasury the Office of Financial Research.

(b) DIRECTOR.—

(1) IN GENERAL.—The Office shall be headed by a Director, who shall be appointed by the President, by and with the advice and consent of the Senate.

(2) TERM OF SERVICE.—The Director shall serve for a term of 6 years, except that, in the event that a successor is not nominated and confirmed by the end of the term of service of a Director, the Director may continue to serve until such time as the next Director is appointed and confirmed.

(3) EXECUTIVE LEVEL.—The Director shall be compensated at Level III of the Executive Schedule.

(4) PROHIBITION ON DUAL SERVICE.—The individual serving in the position of Director may not, during such service, also serve as the head of any financial regulatory agency.

(5) RESPONSIBILITIES, DUTIES, AND AUTHORITY.—The Director shall have sole discretion in the manner in which the Director fulfills the responsibilities and duties and exercises the authorities described in this subtitle.

(c) BUDGET.—The Director, in consultation with the Chairperson, shall establish the annual budget of the Office.

(d) OFFICE PERSONNEL.—

(1) IN GENERAL.—The Director, in consultation with the Chairperson, may fix the number of, and appoint and direct, all employees of the Office.

(2) COMPENSATION.—The Director, in consultation with the Chairperson, shall fix, adjust, and administer the pay for all employees of the Office, without regard to chapter 51 or subchapter III of chapter 53 of title 5, United States Code, relating to classification of positions and General Schedule pay rates.

(3) COMPARABILITY.—Section 1206(a) of the Financial Institutions Reform, Recovery, and Enforcement Act of 1989 (12 U.S.C. 1833b(a)) is amended—

(A) by striking "Finance Board," and inserting "Finance Board, the Office of Financial Research, and the Bureau of Consumer Financial Protection"; and

(B) by striking "and the Office of Thrift Supervision,".

(4) SENIOR EXECUTIVES.—Section 3132(a)(1)(D) of title 5, United States Code, is amended by striking "and the National Credit Union Administration;" and inserting "the National Credit Union Administration, the Bureau of Consumer Financial Protection, and the Office of Financial Research;".

(e) ASSISTANCE FROM FEDERAL AGENCIES.—Any department or agency of the United States may provide to the Office and any special advisory, technical, or professional committees appointed by the Office, such services, funds, facilities, staff, and other support services as the Office may determine advisable. Any Federal Government employee may be detailed to the Office without reimbursement, and such detail shall be without interruption or loss of civil service status or privilege.

(f) PROCUREMENT OF TEMPORARY AND INTERMITTENT SERVICES.—The Director may procure temporary and intermittent services under section 3109(b) of title 5, United States Code, at rates for individuals which do not exceed the daily equivalent of the annual rate of basic pay prescribed for Level V of the Executive Schedule under section 5316 of such title.

(g) POST-EMPLOYMENT PROHIBITIONS.—The Secretary, with the concurrence of the Director of the Office of Government Ethics, shall issue regulations prohibiting the Director and any employee of the Office who has had access to the transaction or position data maintained by the Data Center or other business confidential information about financial entities required to report to the Office from being employed by or providing advice or consulting services to a financial company, for a period of 1 year after last having had access in the course of official duties to such transaction or position data or business confidential information, regardless of whether that entity is required to report to the Office. For employees whose access to business confidential information was limited, the regulations may provide, on a case-by-case basis, for a shorter period of post-employment prohibition, provided that the shorter period does not compromise business confidential information.

(h) TECHNICAL AND PROFESSIONAL ADVISORY COMMITTEES.—The Office, in consultation with the Chairperson, may appoint such special advisory, technical, or professional committees as may be useful in carrying out the functions of the Office, and the members of such committees may be staff of the Office, or other persons, or both.

(i) FELLOWSHIP PROGRAM.—The Office, in consultation with the Chairperson, may establish and maintain an academic and professional fellowship program, under which qualified academics and professionals shall be invited to spend not longer than 2 years at the Office, to perform research and to provide advanced training for Office personnel.

(j) EXECUTIVE SCHEDULE COMPENSATION.—Section 5314 of title 5, United States Code, is amended by adding at the end the following new item:

"Director of the Office of Financial Research.".

[Explanation at ¶ 160 and ¶ 165.]

[¶ 10,153] ACT SEC. 153. PURPOSE AND DUTIES OF THE OFFICE.

(a) PURPOSE AND DUTIES.—The purpose of the Office is to support the Council in fulfilling the purposes and duties of the Council, as set forth in subtitle A, and to support member agencies, by—

(1) collecting data on behalf of the Council, and providing such data to the Council and member agencies;

(2) standardizing the types and formats of data reported and collected;

(3) performing applied research and essential long-term research;

(4) developing tools for risk measurement and monitoring;

(5) performing other related services;

(6) making the results of the activities of the Office available to financial regulatory agencies; and

(7) assisting such member agencies in determining the types and formats of data authorized by this Act to be collected by such member agencies.

(b) ADMINISTRATIVE AUTHORITY.—The Office may—

(1) share data and information, including software developed by the Office, with the Council, member agencies, and the Bureau of Economic Analysis, which shared data, information, and software—

(A) shall be maintained with at least the same level of security as is used by the Office; and

(B) may not be shared with any individual or entity without the permission of the Council;

(2) sponsor and conduct research projects; and

(3) assist, on a reimbursable basis, with financial analyses undertaken at the request of other Federal agencies that are not member agencies.

(c) RULEMAKING AUTHORITY.—

(1) SCOPE.—The Office, in consultation with the Chairperson, shall issue rules, regulations, and orders only to the extent necessary to carry out the purposes and duties described in paragraphs (1), (2), and (7) of subsection (a).

(2) STANDARDIZATION.—Member agencies, in consultation with the Office, shall implement regulations promulgated by the Office under paragraph (1) to standardize the types and formats of data reported and collected on behalf of the Council, as described in subsection (a)(2). If a member agency fails to implement such regulations prior to the expiration of the 3-year period following the date of publication of final regulations, the Office, in consultation with the Chairperson, may implement such regulations with respect to the financial entities under the jurisdiction of the member agency. This paragraph shall not supersede or interfere with the independent authority of a member agency under other law to collect data, in such format and manner as the member agency requires.

(d) TESTIMONY.—

(1) IN GENERAL.—The Director of the Office shall report to and testify before the Committee on Banking, Housing, and Urban Affairs of the Senate and the Committee on Financial Services of the House of Representatives annually on the activities of the Office, including the work of the Data Center and the Research and Analysis Center, and the assessment of the Office of significant financial market developments and potential emerging threats to the financial stability of the United States.

(2) NO PRIOR REVIEW.—No officer or agency of the United States shall have any authority to require the Director to submit the testimony required under paragraph (1) or other congressional testimony to any officer or agency of the United States for approval, comment, or review prior to the submission of such testimony. Any such testimony to Congress shall include a statement that the views expressed therein are those of the Director and do not necessarily represent the views of the President.

(e) ADDITIONAL REPORTS.—The Director may provide additional reports to Congress concerning the financial stability of the United States. The Director shall notify the Council of any such additional reports provided to Congress.

(f) SUBPOENA.—

(1) IN GENERAL.—The Director may require from a financial company, by subpoena, the production of the data requested under subsection (a)(1) and section 154(b)(1), but only upon a written finding by the Director that—

(A) such data is required to carry out the functions described under this subtitle; and

(B) the Office has coordinated with the relevant primary financial regulatory agency, as required under section 154(b)(1)(B)(ii).

(2) FORMAT.—Subpoenas under paragraph (1) shall bear the signature of the Director, and shall be served by any person or class of persons designated by the Director for that purpose.

(3) ENFORCEMENT.—In the case of contumacy or failure to obey a subpoena, the subpoena shall be enforceable by order of any appropriate district court of the United States. Any failure to obey the order of the court may be punished by the court as a contempt of court.

[Explanation at ¶ 170.]

[¶ 10,154] ACT SEC. 154. ORGANIZATIONAL STRUCTURE; RESPONSIBILITIES OF PRIMARY PROGRAMMATIC UNITS.

(a) IN GENERAL.—There are established within the Office, to carry out the programmatic responsibilities of the Office—

(1) the Data Center; and

(2) the Research and Analysis Center.

(b) DATA CENTER.—

(1) GENERAL DUTIES.—

(A) DATA COLLECTION.—The Data Center, on behalf of the Council, shall collect, validate, and maintain all data necessary to carry out the duties of the Data Center, as described in this subtitle. The data assembled shall be obtained from member agencies, commercial data providers, publicly available data sources, and financial entities under subparagraph (B).

(B) AUTHORITY.—

(i) IN GENERAL.—The Office may, as determined by the Council or by the Director in consultation with the Council, require the submission of periodic and other reports from any financial company for the purpose of assessing the extent to which a financial activity or financial market in which the financial company participates, or the financial company itself, poses a threat to the financial stability of the United States.

(ii) MITIGATION OF REPORT BURDEN.—Before requiring the submission of a report from any financial company that is regulated by a member agency, any primary financial regulatory agency, a foreign supervisory authority, or the Office shall coordinate with such agencies or authority, and shall, whenever possible, rely on information available from such agencies or authority.

(iii) COLLECTION OF FINANCIAL TRANSACTION AND POSITION DATA.—The Office shall collect, on a schedule determined by the Director, in consultation with the Council, financial transaction data and position data from financial companies.

(C) RULEMAKING.—The Office shall promulgate regulations pursuant to subsections (a)(1), (a)(2), (a)(7), and (c)(1) of section 153 regarding the type and scope of the data to be collected by the Data Center under this paragraph.

(2) RESPONSIBILITIES.—

(A) PUBLICATION.—The Data Center shall prepare and publish, in a manner that is easily accessible to the public—

(i) a financial company reference database;

(ii) a financial instrument reference database; and

(iii) formats and standards for Office data, including standards for reporting financial transaction and position data to the Office.

(B) CONFIDENTIALITY.—The Data Center shall not publish any confidential data under subparagraph (A).

(3) INFORMATION SECURITY.—The Director shall ensure that data collected and maintained by the Data Center are kept secure and protected against unauthorized disclosure.

(4) CATALOG OF FINANCIAL ENTITIES AND INSTRUMENTS.—The Data Center shall maintain a catalog of the financial entities and instruments reported to the Office.

(5) AVAILABILITY TO THE COUNCIL AND MEMBER AGENCIES.—The Data Center shall make data collected and maintained by the Data Center available to the Council and member agencies, as necessary to support their regulatory responsibilities.

(6) OTHER AUTHORITY.—The Office shall, after consultation with the member agencies, provide certain data to financial industry participants and to the general public to increase market transparency and facilitate research on the financial system, to the extent that intellectual property rights are not violated, business confidential information is properly protected, and the sharing of such information poses no significant threats to the financial system of the United States.

(c) RESEARCH AND ANALYSIS CENTER.—

(1) GENERAL DUTIES.—The Research and Analysis Center, on behalf of the Council, shall develop and maintain independent analytical capabilities and computing resources—

(A) to develop and maintain metrics and reporting systems for risks to the financial stability of the United States;

(B) to monitor, investigate, and report on changes in systemwide risk levels and patterns to the Council and Congress;

(C) to conduct, coordinate, and sponsor research to support and improve regulation of financial entities and markets;

(D) to evaluate and report on stress tests or other stability-related evaluations of financial entities overseen by the member agencies;

(E) to maintain expertise in such areas as may be necessary to support specific requests for advice and assistance from financial regulators;

(F) to investigate disruptions and failures in the financial markets, report findings, and make recommendations to the Council based on those findings;

(G) to conduct studies and provide advice on the impact of policies related to systemic risk; and

(H) to promote best practices for financial risk management.

(d) REPORTING RESPONSIBILITIES.—

(1) REQUIRED REPORTS.—Not later than 2 years after the date of enactment of this Act, and not later than 120 days after the end of each fiscal year thereafter, the Office shall prepare and submit a report to Congress.

(2) CONTENT.—Each report required by this subsection shall assess the state of the United States financial system, including—

(A) an analysis of any threats to the financial stability of the United States;

(B) the status of the efforts of the Office in meeting the mission of the Office; and

(C) key findings from the research and analysis of the financial system by the Office.

[Explanation at ¶ 175.]

[¶ 10,155] ACT SEC. 155. FUNDING.

(a) FINANCIAL RESEARCH FUND.—

(1) FUND ESTABLISHED.—There is established in the Treasury of the United States a separate fund to be known as the "Financial Research Fund".

(2) FUND RECEIPTS.—All amounts provided to the Office under subsection (c), and all assessments that the Office receives under subsection (d) shall be deposited into the Financial Research Fund.

(3) INVESTMENTS AUTHORIZED.—

(A) AMOUNTS IN FUND MAY BE INVESTED.—The Director may request the Secretary to invest the portion of the Financial Research Fund that is not, in the judgment of the Director, required to meet the needs of the Office.

(B) ELIGIBLE INVESTMENTS.—Investments shall be made by the Secretary in obligations of the United States or obligations that are guaranteed as to principal and interest by the United States, with maturities suitable to the needs of the Financial Research Fund, as determined by the Director.

(4) INTEREST AND PROCEEDS CREDITED.—The interest on, and the proceeds from the sale or redemption of, any obligations held in the Financial Research Fund shall be credited to and form a part of the Financial Research Fund.

(b) USE OF FUNDS.—

(1) IN GENERAL.—Funds obtained by, transferred to, or credited to the Financial Research Fund shall be immediately available to the Office, and shall remain available until expended, to pay the expenses of the Office in carrying out the duties and responsibilities of the Office.

(2) FEES, ASSESSMENTS, AND OTHER FUNDS NOT GOVERNMENT FUNDS.—Funds obtained by, transferred to, or credited to the Financial Research Fund shall not be construed to be Government funds or appropriated moneys.

(3) AMOUNTS NOT SUBJECT TO APPORTIONMENT.—Notwithstanding any other provision of law, amounts in the Financial Research Fund shall not be subject to apportionment for purposes of chapter 15 of title 31, United States Code, or under any other authority, or for any other purpose.

(c) INTERIM FUNDING.—During the 2-year period following the date of enactment of this Act, the Board of Governors shall provide to the Office an amount sufficient to cover the expenses of the Office.

(d) PERMANENT SELF-FUNDING.—Beginning 2 years after the date of enactment of this Act, the Secretary shall establish, by regulation, and with the approval of the Council, an assessment schedule, including the assessment base and rates, applicable to bank holding companies with total consolidated assets of $50,000,000,000 or greater and nonbank financial companies supervised by the Board of Governors, that takes into account differences among such companies, based on the considerations for establishing the prudential standards under section 115, to collect assessments equal to the total expenses of the Office.

[Explanation at ¶ 180.]

[¶ 10,156] ACT SEC. 156. TRANSITION OVERSIGHT.

(a) PURPOSE.—The purpose of this section is to ensure that the Office—

(1) has an orderly and organized startup;

(2) attracts and retains a qualified workforce; and

(3) establishes comprehensive employee training and benefits programs.

(b) REPORTING REQUIREMENT.—

(1) IN GENERAL.—The Office shall submit an annual report to the Committee on Banking, Housing, and Urban Affairs of the Senate and the Committee on Financial Services of the House of Representatives that includes the plans described in paragraph (2).

(2) PLANS.—The plans described in this paragraph are as follows:

(A) TRAINING AND WORKFORCE DEVELOPMENT PLAN.—The Office shall submit a training and workforce development plan that includes, to the extent practicable—

(i) identification of skill and technical expertise needs and actions taken to meet those requirements;

(ii) steps taken to foster innovation and creativity;

(iii) leadership development and succession planning; and

(iv) effective use of technology by employees.

(B) WORKPLACE FLEXIBILITY PLAN.—The Office shall submit a workforce flexibility plan that includes, to the extent practicable

(i) telework;

(ii) flexible work schedules;

(iii) phased retirement;

(iv) reemployed annuitants;

(v) part-time work;

(vi) job sharing;

(vii) parental leave benefits and childcare assistance;

(viii) domestic partner benefits;

(ix) other workplace flexibilities; or

(x) any combination of the items described in clauses (i) through (ix).

(C) RECRUITMENT AND RETENTION PLAN.—The Office shall submit a recruitment and retention plan that includes, to the extent practicable, provisions relating to

(i) the steps necessary to target highly qualified applicant pools with diverse backgrounds;

(ii) streamlined employment application processes;

(iii) the provision of timely notification of the status of employment applications to applicants; and

(iv) the collection of information to measure indicators of hiring effectiveness.

(c) EXPIRATION.—The reporting requirement under subsection (b) shall terminate 5 years after the date of enactment of this Act.

(d) RULE OF CONSTRUCTION.—Nothing in this section may be construed to affect—

(1) a collective bargaining agreement, as that term is defined in section 7103(a)(8) of title 5, United States Code, that is in effect on the date of enactment of this Act; or

(2) the rights of employees under chapter 71 of title 5, United States Code.

[Explanation at ¶ 165.]

Subtitle C—Additional Board of Governors Authority for Certain Nonbank Financial Companies and Bank Holding Companies

[¶ 10,161] ACT SEC. 161. REPORTS BY AND EXAMINATIONS OF NONBANK FINANCIAL COMPANIES BY THE BOARD OF GOVERNORS.

(a) REPORTS.—

(1) IN GENERAL.—The Board of Governors may require each nonbank financial company supervised by the Board of Governors, and any subsidiary thereof, to submit reports under oath, to keep the Board of Governors informed as to—

(A) the financial condition of the company or subsidiary, systems of the company or subsidiary for monitoring and controlling financial, operating, and other risks, and the extent to which the activities and operations of the company or subsidiary pose a threat to the financial stability of the United States; and

(B) compliance by the company or subsidiary with the requirements of this title.

(2) USE OF EXISTING REPORTS AND INFORMATION.—In carrying out subsection (a), the Board of Governors shall, to the fullest extent possible, use

(A) reports and supervisory information that a nonbank financial company or subsidiary thereof has been required to provide to other Federal or State regulatory agencies;

(B) information otherwise obtainable from Federal or State regulatory agencies;

(C) information that is otherwise required to be reported publicly; and

(D) externally audited financial statements of such company or subsidiary.

(3) AVAILABILITY.—Upon the request of the Board of Governors, a nonbank financial company supervised by the Board of Governors, or a subsidiary thereof, shall promptly provide to the Board of Governors any information described in paragraph (2).

(b) EXAMINATIONS.—

(1) IN GENERAL.—Subject to paragraph (2), the Board of Governors may examine any nonbank financial company supervised by the Board of Governors and any subsidiary of such company, to inform the Board of Governors of—

(A) the nature of the operations and financial condition of the company and such subsidiary;

(B) the financial, operational, and other risks of the company or such subsidiary that may pose a threat to the safety and soundness of such company or subsidiary or to the financial stability of the United States;

(C) the systems for monitoring and controlling such risks; and

(D) compliance by the company or such subsidiary with the requirements of this title.

(2) USE OF EXAMINATION REPORTS AND INFORMATION.—For purposes of this subsection, the Board of Governors shall, to the fullest extent possible, rely on reports of examination of any subsidiary depository institution or functionally regulated subsidiary made by the primary financial regulatory agency for that subsidiary, and on information described in subsection (a)(2).

(c) COORDINATION WITH PRIMARY FINANCIAL REGULATORY AGENCY.—The Board of Governors shall—

(1) provide reasonable notice to, and consult with, the primary financial regulatory agency for any subsidiary before requiring a report or commencing an examination of such subsidiary under this section; and

(2) avoid duplication of examination activities, reporting requirements, and requests for information, to the fullest extent possible,

[Explanation at ¶ 190 and ¶ 195.]

[¶ 10,162] ACT SEC. 162. ENFORCEMENT.

(a) IN GENERAL.—Except as provided in subsection (b), a nonbank financial company supervised by the Board of Governors and any subsidiaries of such company (other than any depository institution subsidiary) shall be subject to the provisions of subsections (b) through (n) of section 8 of the Federal Deposit Insurance Act (12 U.S.C. 1818), in the same manner and to the same extent as if the company were a bank holding company, as provided in section 8(b)(3) of the Federal Deposit Insurance Act (12 U.S.C. 1818(b)(3)).

(b) ENFORCEMENT AUTHORITY FOR FUNCTIONALLY REGULATED SUBSIDIARIES.—

(1) REFERRAL.—If the Board of Governors determines that a condition, practice, or activity of a depository institution subsidiary or functionally regulated subsidiary of a nonbank financial company supervised by the Board of Governors does not comply with the regulations or orders prescribed by the Board of Governors under this Act, or otherwise poses a threat to the financial stability of the United States, the Board of Governors may recommend, in writing, to the primary financial regulatory agency for the subsidiary that such agency initiate a supervisory action or enforcement proceeding. The recommendation shall be accompanied by a written explanation of the concerns giving rise to the recommendation.

(2) BACK-UP AUTHORITY OF THE BOARD OF GOVERNORS.—If, during the 60-day period beginning on the date on which the primary financial regulatory agency receives a recommendation under paragraph (1), the primary financial regulatory agency does not take supervisory or enforcement action against a subsidiary that is acceptable to the Board of Governors, the Board of Governors (upon a vote of its members) may take the recommended supervisory or enforcement action, as if the subsidiary were a bank holding company subject to supervision by the Board of Governors.

[Explanation at ¶ 200.]

[¶ 10,163] ACT SEC. 163. ACQUISITIONS.

(a) ACQUISITIONS OF BANKS; TREATMENT AS A BANK HOLDING COMPANY.—For purposes of section 3 of the Bank Holding Company Act of 1956 (12 U.S.C. 1842), a nonbank financial company supervised by the Board of Governors shall be deemed to be, and shall be treated as, a bank holding company.

(b) ACQUISITION OF NONBANK COMPANIES.—

(1) PRIOR NOTICE FOR LARGE ACQUISITIONS.—Notwithstanding section 4(k)(6)(B) of the Bank Holding Company Act of 1956 (12 U.S.C. 1843(k)(6)(B)), a bank holding company with total consolidated assets equal to or greater than $50,000,000,000 or a nonbank financial company supervised by the Board of Governors shall not acquire direct or indirect ownership or control of any voting-shares of any company (other than an insured depository institution) that is engaged in activities described in section 4(k) of the Bank Holding Company Act of 1956 having total consolidated assets of $10,000,000,000 or more, without providing written notice to the Board of Governors in advance of the transaction.

(2) EXEMPTIONS.—The prior notice requirement in paragraph (1) shall not apply with regard to the acquisition of shares that would qualify for the exemptions in section 4(c) or section 4(k)(4)(E) of the Bank Holding Company Act of 1956 (12 U.S.C. 1843(c) and (k)(4)(E)).

(3) NOTICE PROCEDURES.—The notice procedures set forth in section 4(j)(1) of the Bank Holding Company Act of 1956 (12 U.S.C. 1843(j)(1)), without regard to section 4(j)(3) of that Act, shall apply to an acquisition of any company (other than an insured depository institution) by a bank holding company with total consolidated assets equal to or greater than $50,000,000,000 or a nonbank financial company supervised by the Board of Governors, as described in paragraph (1), including any such company engaged in activities described in section 4(k) of that Act.

(4) STANDARDS FOR REVIEW.—In addition to the standards provided in section 4(j)(2) of the Bank Holding Company Act of 1956 (12 U.S.C. 1843(j)(2)), the Board of Governors shall consider the extent to which the proposed acquisition would result in greater or more concentrated risks to global or United States financial stability or the United States economy.

(5) HART-SCOTT-RODINO FILING REQUIREMENT.—Solely for purposes of section 7A(c)(8) of the Clayton Act (15 U.S.C. 18a(c)(8)), the transactions subject to the requirements of paragraph (1) shall be treated as if Board of Governors approval is not required.

[Explanation at ¶ 205.]

[¶ 10,164] ACT SEC. 164. PROHIBITION AGAINST MANAGEMENT INTERLOCKS BETWEEN CERTAIN FINANCIAL COMPANIES.

A nonbank financial company supervised by the Board of Governors shall be treated as a bank holding company for purposes of the Depository Institutions Management Interlocks Act (12 U.S.C. 3201 et seq.), except that the Board of Governors shall not exercise the authority provided in section 7 of that Act (12 U.S.C. 3207) to permit service by a management official of a nonbank financial company supervised by the Board of Governors as a management official of any bank holding company with total consolidated assets equal to or greater than $50,000,000,000, or other nonaffiliated nonbank financial company supervised by the Board of Governors (other than to provide a temporary exemption for interlocks resulting from a merger, acquisition, or consolidation).

[Explanation at ¶ 210.]

[¶ 10,165] ACT SEC. 165. ENHANCED SUPERVISION AND PRUDENTIAL STANDARDS FOR NONBANK FINANCIAL COMPANIES SUPERVISED BY THE BOARD OF GOVERNORS AND CERTAIN BANK HOLDING COMPANIES.

(a) IN GENERAL.—

(1) PURPOSE.—In order to prevent or mitigate risks to the financial stability of the United States that could arise from the material financial distress or failure, or ongoing activities, of large, interconnected financial institutions, the Board of Governors shall, on its own or pursuant to recommendations by the Council under section 115, establish prudential standards for nonbank financial companies supervised by the Board of Governors and bank holding companies with total consolidated assets equal to or greater than $50,000,000,000 that—

(A) are more stringent than the standards and requirements applicable to nonbank financial companies and bank holding companies that do not present similar risks to the financial stability of the United States; and

(B) increase in stringency, based on the considerations identified in subsection (b)(3).

(2) TAILORED APPLICATION.—

(A) IN GENERAL.—In prescribing more stringent prudential standards under this section, the Board of Governors may, on its own or pursuant to a recommendation by the Council in accordance with section 115, differentiate among companies on an individual basis or by category, taking into consideration their capital structure, riskiness, complexity, financial activities (including the financial activities of their subsidiaries), size, and any other risk-related factors that the Board of Governors deems appropriate.

(B) ADJUSTMENT OF THRESHOLD FOR APPLICATION OF CERTAIN STANDARDS.—The Board of Governors may, pursuant to a recommendation by the Council in accordance with section 115, establish an asset threshold above $50,000,000,000 for the application of any standard established under subsections (c) through (g).

(b) DEVELOPMENT OF PRUDENTIAL STANDARDS.—

(1) IN GENERAL.—

(A) REQUIRED STANDARDS.—The Board of Governors shall establish prudential standards for nonbank financial companies supervised by the Board of Governors and bank holding companies described in subsection (a), that shall include—

(i) risk-based capital requirements and leverage limits, unless the Board of Governors, in consultation with the Council, determines that such requirements are not appropriate for a company subject to more stringent prudential standards because of the activities of such company (such as investment company activities or assets under management) or structure, in which case, the Board of Governors shall apply other standards that result in similarly stringent risk controls;

(ii) liquidity requirements;

(iii) overall risk management requirements;

(iv) resolution plan and credit exposure report requirements; and

(v) concentration limits.

(B) ADDITIONAL STANDARDS AUTHORIZED.—The Board of Governors may establish additional prudential standards for nonbank financial companies supervised by the Board of Governors and bank holding companies described in subsection (a), that include

(i) a contingent capital requirement;

(ii) enhanced public disclosures;

(iii) short-term debt limits; and

(iv) such other prudential standards as the Board or Governors, on its own or pursuant to a recommendation made by the Council in accordance with section 115, determines are appropriate.

(2) STANDARDS FOR FOREIGN FINANCIAL COMPANIES.—In applying the standards set forth in paragraph (1) to any foreign nonbank financial company supervised by the Board of Governors or foreign-based bank holding company, the Board of Governors shall—

(A) give due regard to the principle of national treatment and equality of competitive opportunity; and

(B) take into account the extent to which the foreign financial company is subject on a consolidated basis to home country standards that are comparable to those applied to financial companies in the United States.

(3) CONSIDERATIONS.—In prescribing prudential standards under paragraph (1), the Board of Governors shall—

(A) take into account differences among nonbank financial companies supervised by the Board of Governors and bank holding companies described in subsection (a), based on—

(i) the factors described in subsections (a) and (b) of section 113;

(ii) whether the company owns an insured depository institution;

(iii) nonfinancial activities and affiliations of the company; and

(iv) any other risk-related factors that the Board of Governors determines appropriate;

(B) to the extent possible, ensure that small changes in the factors listed in subsections (a) and (b) of section 113 would not result in sharp, discontinuous changes in the prudential standards established under paragraph (1) of this subsection;

(C) take into account any recommendations of the Council under section 115; and

(D) adapt the required standards as appropriate in light of any predominant line of business of such company, including assets under management or other activities for which particular standards may not be appropriate.

(4) CONSULTATION.—Before imposing prudential standards or any other requirements pursuant to this section, including notices of deficiencies in resolution plans and more stringent requirements or divestiture orders resulting from such notices, that are likely to have a significant impact on a functionally regulated subsidiary or depository institution subsidiary of a nonbank financial company supervised by the Board of Governors or a bank holding company described in subsection (a), the Board of Governors shall consult with each Council member that primarily supervises any such subsidiary with respect to any such standard or requirement.

(5) REPORT.—The Board of Governors shall submit an annual report to Congress regarding the implementation of the prudential standards required pursuant to paragraph (1), including the use of such standards to mitigate risks to the financial stability of the United States.

(c) CONTINGENT CAPITAL.—

(1) IN GENERAL.—Subsequent to submission by the Council of a report to Congress under section 115(c), the Board of Governors may issue regulations that require each nonbank financial company supervised by the Board of Governors and bank holding companies described in subsection (a) to maintain a minimum amount of contingent capital that is convertible to equity in times of financial stress.

(2) FACTORS TO CONSIDER.—In issuing regulations under this subsection, the Board of Governors shall consider—

   (A) the results of the study undertaken by the Council, and any recommendations of the Council, under section 115(c);

   (B) an appropriate transition period for implementation of contingent capital under this subsection;

   (C) the factors described in subsection (b)(3)(A);

   (D) capital requirements applicable to the nonbank financial company supervised by the Board of Governors or a bank holding company described in subsection (a), and subsidiaries thereof; and

   (E) any other factor that the Board of Governors deems appropriate.

(d) RESOLUTION PLAN AND CREDIT EXPOSURE REPORTS.—

(1) RESOLUTION PLAN.—The Board of Governors shall require each nonbank financial company supervised by the Board of Governors and bank holding companies described in subsection (a) to report periodically to the Board of Governors, the Council, and the Corporation the plan of such company for rapid and orderly resolution in the event of material financial distress or failure, which shall include—

   (A) information regarding the manner and extent to which any insured depository institution affiliated with the company is adequately protected from risks arising from the activities of any nonbank subsidiaries of the company;

   (B) full descriptions of the ownership structure, assets, liabilities, and contractual obligations of the company;

   (C) identification of the cross-guarantees tied to different securities, identification of major counterparties, and a process for determining to whom the collateral of the company is pledged; and

   (D) any other information that the Board of Governors and the Corporation jointly require by rule or order.

(2) CREDIT EXPOSURE REPORT.—The Board of Governors shall require each nonbank financial company supervised by the Board of Governors and bank holding companies described in subsection (a) to report periodically to the Board of Governors, the Council, and the Corporation on—

   (A) the nature and extent to which the company has credit exposure to other significant nonbank financial companies and significant bank holding companies; and

   (B) the nature and extent to which other significant nonbank financial companies and significant bank holding companies have credit exposure to that company.

(3) REVIEW.—The Board of Governors and the Corporation shall review the information provided in accordance with this subsection by each nonbank financial company supervised by the Board of Governors and bank holding company described in subsection (a).

(4) NOTICE OF DEFICIENCIES.—If the Board of Governors and the Corporation jointly determine, based on their review under paragraph (3), that the resolution plan of a nonbank financial company supervised by the Board of Governors or a bank holding company described in subsection (a) is not credible or would not facilitate an orderly resolution of the company under title 11, United States Code—

   (A) the Board of Governors and the Corporation shall notify the company of the deficiencies in the resolution plan; and

(B) the company shall resubmit the resolution plan within a timeframe determined by the Board of Governors and the Corporation, with revisions demonstrating that the plan is credible and would result in an orderly resolution under title 11, United States Code, including any proposed changes in business operations and corporate structure to facilitate implementation of the plan.

(5) FAILURE TO RESUBMIT CREDIBLE PLAN.—

(A) IN GENERAL.—If a nonbank financial company supervised by the Board of Governors or a bank holding company described in subsection (a) fails to timely resubmit the resolution plan as required under paragraph (4), with such revisions as are required under subparagraph (B), the Board of Governors and the Corporation may jointly impose more stringent capital, leverage, or liquidity requirements, or restrictions on the growth, activities, or operations of the company, or any subsidiary thereof, until such time as the company resubmits a plan that remedies the deficiencies.

(B) DIVESTITURE.—The Board of Governors and the Corporation, in consultation with the Council, may jointly direct a nonbank financial company supervised by the Board of Governors or a bank holding company described in subsection (a), by order, to divest certain assets or operations identified by the Board of Governors and the Corporation, to facilitate an orderly resolution of such company under title 11, United States Code, in the event of the failure of such company, in any case in which—

(i) the Board of Governors and the Corporation have jointly imposed more stringent requirements on the company pursuant to subparagraph (A); and

(ii) the company has failed, within the 2-year period beginning on the date of the imposition of such requirements under subparagraph (A), to resubmit the resolution plan with such revisions as were required under paragraph (4)(B).

(6) NO LIMITING EFFECT.—A resolution plan submitted in accordance with this subsection shall not be binding on a bankruptcy court, a receiver appointed under title II, or any other authority that is authorized or required to resolve the nonbank financial company supervised by the Board, any bank holding company, or any subsidiary or affiliate of the foregoing.

(7) NO PRIVATE RIGHT OF ACTION.—No private right of action may be based on any resolution plan submitted in accordance with this subsection.

(8) RULES.—Not later than 18 months after the date of enactment of this Act, the Board of Governors and the Corporation shall jointly issue final rules implementing this subsection.

(e) CONCENTRATION LIMITS.—

(1) STANDARDS.—In order to limit the risks that the failure of any individual company could pose to a nonbank financial company supervised by the Board of Governors or a bank holding company described in subsection (a), the Board of Governors, by regulation, shall prescribe standards that limit such risks.

(2) LIMITATION ON CREDIT EXPOSURE.—The regulations prescribed by the Board of Governors under paragraph (1) shall prohibit each nonbank financial company supervised by the Board of Governors and bank holding company described in subsection (a) from having credit exposure to any unaffiliated company that exceeds 25 percent of the capital stock and surplus (or such lower amount as the Board of Governors may determine by regulation to be necessary to mitigate risks to the financial stability of the United States) of the company.

(3) CREDIT EXPOSURE.—For purposes of paragraph (2), "credit exposure" to a company means—

(A) all extensions of credit to the company, including loans, deposits, and lines of credit;

(B) all repurchase agreements and reverse repurchase agreements with the company, and all securities borrowing and lending transactions with the company, to the extent that such transactions create credit exposure for the nonbank financial company supervised by the Board of Governors or a bank holding company described in subsection (a);

(C) all guarantees, acceptances, or letters of credit (including endorsement or standby letters of credit) issued on behalf of the company;

(D) all purchases of or investment in securities issued by the company;

(E) counterparty credit exposure to the company in connection with a derivative transaction between the nonbank financial company supervised by the Board of Governors or a bank holding company described in subsection (a) and the company; and

(F) any other similar transactions that the Board of Governors, by regulation, determines to be a credit exposure for purposes of this section.

(4) ATTRIBUTION RULE.—For purposes of this subsection, any transaction by a nonbank financial company supervised by the Board of Governors or a bank holding company described in subsection (a) with any person is a transaction with a company, to the extent that the proceeds of the transaction are used for the benefit of, or transferred to, that company.

(5) RULEMAKING.—The Board of Governors may issue such regulations and orders, including definitions consistent with this section, as may be necessary to administer and carry out this subsection.

(6) EXEMPTIONS.—This subsection shall not apply to any Federal home loan bank. The Board of Governors may, by regulation or order, exempt transactions, in whole or in part, from the definition of the term "credit exposure" for purposes of this subsection, if the Board of Governors finds that the exemption is in the public interest and is consistent with the purpose of this subsection.

(7) TRANSITION PERIOD.—

(A) IN GENERAL.—This subsection and any regulations and orders of the Board of Governors under this subsection shall not be effective until 3 years after the date of enactment of this Act.

(B) EXTENSION AUTHORIZED.—The Board of Governors may extend the period specified in subparagraph (A) for not longer than an additional 2 years.

(f) ENHANCED PUBLIC DISCLOSURES.—The Board of Governors may prescribe, by regulation, periodic public disclosures by nonbank financial companies supervised by the Board of Governors and bank holding companies described in subsection (a) in order to support market evaluation of the risk profile, capital adequacy, and risk management capabilities thereof.

(g) SHORT-TERM DEBT LIMITS.—

(1) IN GENERAL.—In order to mitigate the risks that an over-accumulation of short-term debt could pose to financial companies and to the stability of the United States financial system, the Board of Governors may, by regulation, prescribe a limit on the amount of short-term debt, including off-balance sheet exposures, that may be accumulated by any bank holding company described in subsection (a) and any nonbank financial company supervised by the Board of Governors.

(2) BASIS OF LIMIT.—Any limit prescribed under paragraph (1) shall be based on the short-term debt of the company described in paragraph (1) as a percentage of capital stock and surplus of the company or on such other measure as the Board of Governors considers appropriate.

(3) SHORT-TERM DEBT DEFINED.—For purposes of this subsection, the term "short-term debt" means such liabilities with short-dated maturity that the Board of Governors identifies, by regulation, except that such term does not include insured deposits.

(4) RULEMAKING AUTHORITY.—In addition to prescribing regulations under paragraphs (1) and (3), the Board of Governors may prescribe such regulations, including definitions consistent with this subsection, and issue such orders, as may be necessary to carry out this subsection.

(5) AUTHORITY TO ISSUE EXEMPTIONS AND ADJUSTMENTS.—Notwithstanding the Bank Holding Company Act of 1956 (12 U.S.C. 1841 et seq.), the Board of Governors may, if it determines such action is necessary to ensure appropriate heightened prudential supervision, with respect to a company described in paragraph (1) that does not control an insured depository institution, issue to such company an exemption from or adjustment to the limit prescribed under paragraph (1).

Act Sec. 165(g)(5) ¶10,165

(h) RISK COMMITTEE.—

(1) NONBANK FINANCIAL COMPANIES SUPERVISED BY THE BOARD OF GOVERNORS.—The Board of Governors shall require each nonbank financial company supervised by the Board of Governors that is a publicly traded company to establish a risk committee, as set forth in paragraph (3), not later than 1 year after the date of receipt of a notice of final determination under section 113(e)(3) with respect to such nonbank financial company supervised by the Board of Governors.

(2) CERTAIN BANK HOLDING COMPANIES.—

(A) MANDATORY REGULATIONS.—The Board of Governors shall issue regulations requiring each bank holding company that is a publicly traded company and that has total consolidated assets of not less than $10,000,000,000 to establish a risk committee, as set forth in paragraph (3).

(B) PERMISSIVE REGULATIONS.—The Board of Governors may require each bank holding company that is a publicly traded company and that has total consolidated assets of less than $10,000,000,000 to establish a risk committee, as set forth in paragraph (3), as determined necessary or appropriate by the Board of Governors to promote sound risk management practices.

(3) RISK COMMITTEE.—A risk committee required by this subsection shall—

(A) be responsible for the oversight of the enterprise-wide risk management practices of the nonbank financial company supervised by the Board of Governors or bank holding company described in subsection (a), as applicable;

(B) include such number of independent directors as the Board of Governors may determine appropriate, based on the nature of operations, size of assets, and other appropriate criteria related to the nonbank financial company supervised by the Board of Governors or a bank holding company described in subsection (a), as applicable; and

(C) include at least 1 risk management expert having experience in identifying, assessing, and managing risk exposures of large, complex firms.

(4) RULEMAKING.—The Board of Governors shall issue final rules to carry out this subsection, not later than 1 year after the transfer date, to take effect not later than 15 months after the transfer date.

(i) STRESS TESTS.—

(1) BY THE BOARD OF GOVERNORS.—

(A) ANNUAL TESTS REQUIRED.—The Board of Governors, in coordination with the appropriate primary financial regulatory agencies and the Federal Insurance Office, shall conduct annual analyses in which nonbank financial companies supervised by the Board of Governors and bank holding companies described in subsection (a) are subject to evaluation of whether such companies have the capital, on a total consolidated basis, necessary to absorb losses as a result of adverse economic conditions.

(B) TEST PARAMETERS AND CONSEQUENCES.—The Board of Governors—

(i) shall provide for at least 3 different sets of conditions under which the evaluation required by this subsection shall be conducted, including baseline, adverse, and severely adverse;

(ii) may require the tests described in subparagraph (A) at bank holding companies and nonbank financial companies, in addition to those for which annual tests are required under subparagraph (A);

(iii) may develop and apply such other analytic techniques as are necessary to identify, measure, and monitor risks to the financial stability of the United States;

(iv) shall require the companies described in subparagraph (A) to update their resolution plans required under subsection (d)(1), as the Board of Governors determines appropriate, based on the results of the analyses; and

(v) shall publish a summary of the results of the tests required under subparagraph (A) or clause (ii) of this subparagraph.

(2) BY THE COMPANY.—

(A) REQUIREMENT.—A nonbank financial company supervised by the Board of Governors and a bank holding company described in subsection (a) shall conduct semiannual stress tests. All other financial companies that have total consolidated assets of more than $10,000,000,000 and are regulated by a primary Federal financial regulatory agency shall conduct annual stress tests. The tests required under this subparagraph shall be conducted in accordance with the regulations prescribed under subparagraph (C).

(B) REPORT.—A company required to conduct stress tests under subparagraph (A) shall submit a report to the Board of Governors and to its primary financial regulatory agency at such time, in such form, and containing such information as the primary financial regulatory agency shall require.

(C) REGULATIONS.—Each Federal primary financial regulatory agency, in coordination with the Board of Governors and the Federal Insurance Office, shall issue consistent and comparable regulations to implement this paragraph that shall—

(i) define the term "stress test" for purposes of this paragraph;

(ii) establish methodologies for the conduct of stress tests required by this paragraph that shall provide for at least 3 different sets of conditions, including baseline, adverse, and severely adverse;

(iii) establish the form and content of the report required by subparagraph (B); and

(iv) require companies subject to this paragraph to publish a summary of the results of the required stress tests.

(j) LEVERAGE LIMITATION.—

(1) REQUIREMENT.—The Board of Governors shall require a bank holding company with total consolidated assets equal to or greater than $50,000,000,000 or a nonbank financial company supervised by the Board of Governors to maintain a debt to equity ratio of no more than 15 to 1, upon a determination by the Council that such company poses a grave threat to the financial stability of the United States and that the imposition of such requirement is necessary to mitigate the risk that such company poses to the financial stability of the United States. Nothing in this paragraph shall apply to a Federal home loan bank.

(2) CONSIDERATIONS.—In making a determination under this subsection, the Council shall consider the factors described in subsections (a) and (b) of section 113 and any other risk-related factors that the Council deems appropriate.

(3) REGULATIONS.—The Board of Governors shall promulgate regulations to establish procedures and timelines for complying with the requirements of this subsection.

(k) INCLUSION OF OFF-BALANCE-SHEET ACTIVITIES IN COMPUTING CAPITAL REQUIREMENTS.—

(1) IN GENERAL.—In the case of any bank holding company described in subsection (a) or nonbank financial company supervised by the Board of Governors, the computation of capital for purposes of meeting capital requirements shall take into account any off-balance-sheet activities of the company.

(2) EXEMPTIONS.—If the Board of Governors determines that an exemption from the requirement under paragraph (1) is appropriate, the Board of Governors may exempt a company, or any transaction or transactions engaged in by such company, from the requirements of paragraph (1).

(3) OFF-BALANCE-SHEET ACTIVITIES DEFINED.—For purposes of this subsection, the term "off-balance-sheet activities" means an existing liability of a company that is not currently a balance sheet liability, but may become one upon the happening of some future event, including the following transactions, to the extent that they may create a liability:

(A) Direct credit substitutes in which a bank substitutes its own credit for a third party, including standby letters of credit.

(B) Irrevocable letters of credit that guarantee repayment of commercial paper or tax-exempt securities.

(C) Risk participations in bankers' acceptances.

(D) Sale and repurchase agreements.

(E) Asset sales with recourse against the seller.

(F) Interest rate swaps.

(G) Credit swaps.

(H) Commodities contracts.

(I) Forward contracts.

(J) Securities contracts.

(K) Such other activities or transactions as the Board of Governors may, by rule, define.

[Explanation at ¶190 and ¶215.]

[¶10,166] ACT SEC. 166. EARLY REMEDIATION REQUIREMENTS.

(a) IN GENERAL.—The Board of Governors, in consultation with the Council and the Corporation, shall prescribe regulations establishing requirements to provide for the early remediation of financial distress of a nonbank financial company supervised by the Board of Governors or a bank holding company described in section 165(a), except that nothing in this subsection authorizes the provision of financial assistance from the Federal Government.

(b) PURPOSE OF THE EARLY REMEDIATION REQUIREMENTS.—The purpose of the early remediation requirements under subsection (a) shall be to establish a series of specific remedial actions to be taken by a nonbank financial company supervised by the Board of Governors or a bank holding company described in section 165(a) that is experiencing increasing financial distress, in order to minimize the probability that the company will become insolvent and the potential harm of such insolvency to the financial stability of the United States.

(c) REMEDIATION REQUIREMENTS.—The regulations prescribed by the Board of Governors under subsection (a) shall—

(1) define measures of the financial condition of the company, including regulatory capital, liquidity measures, and other forward-looking indicators; and

(2) establish requirements that increase in stringency as the financial condition of the company declines, including—

(A) requirements in the initial stages of financial decline, including limits on capital distributions, acquisitions, and asset growth; and

(B) requirements at later stages of financial decline, including a capital restoration plan and capital-raising requirements, limits on transactions with affiliates, management changes, and asset sales.

[Explanation at ¶220.]

[¶10,167] ACT SEC. 167. AFFILIATIONS.

(a) AFFILIATIONS.—Nothing in this subtitle shall be construed to require a nonbank financial company supervised by the Board of Governors, or a company that controls a nonbank financial company supervised by the Board of Governors, to conform the activities thereof to the requirements of section 4 of the Bank Holding Company Act of 1956 (12 U.S.C. 1843).

(b) REQUIREMENT.—

(1) IN GENERAL.—

(A) BOARD AUTHORITY.—If a nonbank financial company supervised by the Board of Governors conducts activities other than those that are determined to be financial in nature or incidental thereto under section 4(k) of the Bank Holding Company Act of 1956, the Board of Governors may require such company to establish and conduct all or a portion of such activities that are determined to be financial in nature or incidental thereto in or through an intermediate holding company established pursuant to regulation of the Board of Governors, not later than 90 days (or such longer period as the Board of Governors may deem appropriate) after the date on which the nonbank financial company supervised by the

Board of Governors is notified of the determination of the Board of Governors under this section.

(B) NECESSARY ACTIONS.—Notwithstanding subparagraph (A), the Board of Governors shall require a nonbank financial company supervised by the Board of Governors to establish an intermediate holding company if the Board of Governors makes a determination that the establishment of such intermediate holding company is necessary to—

(i) appropriately supervise activities that are determined to be financial in nature or incidental thereto; or

(ii) to ensure that supervision by the Board of Governors does not extend to the commercial activities of such nonbank financial company.

(2) INTERNAL FINANCIAL ACTIVITIES.—For purposes of this subsection, activities that are determined to be financial in nature or incidental thereto under section 4(k) of the Bank Holding Company Act of 1956, as described in paragraph (1), shall not include internal financial activities, including internal treasury, investment, and employee benefit functions. With respect to any internal financial activity engaged in for the company or an affiliate and a non-affiliate of such company during the year prior to the date of enactment of this Act, such company (or an affiliate that is not an intermediate holding company or subsidiary of an intermediate holding company) may continue to engage in such activity, as long as not less than 2/3 of the assets or 2/3 of the revenues generated from the activity are from or attributable to such company or an affiliate, subject to review by the Board of Governors, to determine whether engaging in such activity presents undue risk to such company or to the financial stability of the United States.

(3) SOURCE OF STRENGTH.—A company that directly or indirectly controls an intermediate holding company established under this section shall serve as a source of strength to its subsidiary intermediate holding company.

(4) PARENT COMPANY REPORTS.—The Board of Governors may, from time to time, require reports under oath from a company that controls an intermediate holding company, and from the appropriate officers or directors of such company, solely for purposes of ensuring compliance with the provisions of this section, including assessing the ability of the company to serve as a source of strength to its subsidiary intermediate holding company pursuant to paragraph (3) and enforcing such compliance.

(5) LIMITED PARENT COMPANY ENFORCEMENT.—

(A) IN GENERAL.—In addition to any other authority of the Board of Governors, the Board of Governors may enforce compliance with the provisions of this subsection that are applicable to any company described in paragraph (1) that controls an intermediate holding company under section 8 of the Federal Deposit Insurance Act, and such company shall be subject to such section (solely for such purposes) in the same manner and to the same extent as if such company were a bank holding company.

(B) APPLICATION OF OTHER ACT.—Any violation of this subsection by any company that controls an intermediate holding company may also be treated as a violation of the Federal Deposit Insurance Act for purposes of subparagraph (A).

(C) NO EFFECT ON OTHER AUTHORITY.—No provision of this paragraph shall be construed as limiting any authority of the Board of Governors or any other Federal agency under any other provision of law.

(c) REGULATIONS.—The Board of Governors—

(1) shall promulgate regulations to establish the criteria for determining whether to require a nonbank financial company supervised by the Board of Governors to establish an intermediate holding company under subsection (b); and

(2) may promulgate regulations to establish any restrictions or limitations on transactions between an intermediate holding company or a nonbank financial company supervised by the Board of Governors and its affiliates, as necessary to prevent unsafe and unsound practices in connection with transactions between such company, or any subsidiary thereof, and its parent company or affiliates that are not subsidiaries of such company, except that such regulations

shall not restrict or limit any transaction in connection with the bona fide acquisition or lease by an unaffiliated person of assets, goods, or services.

[Explanation at ¶ 225.]

[¶ 10,168] ACT SEC. 168. REGULATIONS.

The Board of Governors shall have authority to issue regulations to implement subtitles A and C and the amendments made thereunder. Except as otherwise specified in subtitle A or C, not later than 18 months after the effective date of this Act, the Board of Governors shall issue final regulations to implement subtitles A and C, and the amendments made thereunder.

[Explanation at ¶ 190.]

[¶ 10,169] ACT SEC. 169. AVOIDING DUPLICATION.

The Board of Governors shall take any action that the Board of Governors deems appropriate to avoid imposing requirements under this subtitle that are duplicative of requirements applicable to bank holding companies and nonbank financial companies under other provisions of law.

[Explanation at ¶ 190.]

[¶ 10,170] ACT SEC. 170. SAFE HARBOR.

(a) REGULATIONS.—The Board of Governors shall promulgate regulations on behalf of, and in consultation with, the Council setting forth the criteria for exempting certain types or classes of U.S. nonbank financial companies or foreign nonbank financial companies from supervision by the Board of Governors.

(b) CONSIDERATIONS.—In developing the criteria under subsection (a), the Board of Governors shall take into account the factors for consideration described in subsections (a) and (b) of section 113 in determining whether a U.S. nonbank financial company or foreign nonbank financial company shall be supervised by the Board of Governors.

(c) RULE OF CONSTRUCTION.—Nothing in this section shall be construed to require supervision by the Board of Governors of a U.S. nonbank financial company or foreign nonbank financial company, if such company does not meet the criteria for exemption established under subsection (a).

(d) REVISIONS.—

(1) IN GENERAL.—The Board of Governors shall, in consultation with the Council, review the regulations promulgated under subsection (a), not less frequently than every 5 years, and based upon the review, the Board of Governors may revise such regulations on behalf of, and in consultation with, the Council to update as necessary the criteria set forth in such regulations.

(2) TRANSITION PERIOD.—No revisions under paragraph (1) shall take effect before the end of the 2-year period after the date of publication of such revisions in final form.

(e) REPORT.—The Chairman of the Board of Governors and the Chairperson of the Council shall submit a joint report to the Committee on Banking, Housing, and Urban Affairs of the Senate and the Committee on Financial Services of the House of Representatives not later than 30 days after the date of the issuance in final form of regulations under subsection (a), or any subsequent revision to such regulations under subsection (d), as applicable. Such report shall include, at a minimum, the rationale for exemption and empirical evidence to support the criteria for exemption.

[Explanation at ¶ 230.]

[¶ 10,171] ACT SEC. 171. LEVERAGE AND RISK-BASED CAPITAL REQUIREMENTS.

(a) DEFINITIONS.—For purposes of this section, the following definitions shall apply:

(1) GENERALLY APPLICABLE LEVERAGE CAPITAL REQUIREMENTS.—The term "generally applicable leverage capital requirements" means—

(A) the minimum ratios of tier 1 capital to average total assets, as established by the appropriate Federal banking agencies to apply to insured depository institutions under the prompt corrective action regulations implementing section 38 of the Federal Deposit Insurance Act, regardless of total consolidated asset size or foreign financial exposure; and

(B) includes the regulatory capital components in the numerator of that capital requirement, average total assets in the denominator of that capital requirement, and the required ratio of the numerator to the denominator.

(2) GENERALLY APPLICABLE RISK-BASED CAPITAL REQUIREMENTS.—The term "generally applicable risk-based capital requirements" means—

(A) the risk-based capital requirements, as established by the appropriate Federal banking agencies to apply to insured depository institutions under the prompt corrective action regulations implementing section 38 of the Federal Deposit Insurance Act, regardless of total consolidated asset size or foreign financial exposure; and

(B) includes the regulatory capital components in the numerator of those capital requirements, the risk-weighted assets in the denominator of those capital requirements, and the required ratio of the numerator to the denominator.

(3) DEFINITION OF DEPOSITORY INSTITUTION HOLDING COMPANY.—The term "depository institution holding company" means a bank holding company or a savings and loan holding company (as those terms are defined in section 3 of the Federal Deposit Insurance Act) that is organized in the United States, including any bank or savings and loan holding company that is owned or controlled by a foreign organization, but does not include the foreign organization.

(b) MINIMUM CAPITAL REQUIREMENTS.—

(1) MINIMUM LEVERAGE CAPITAL REQUIREMENTS.—The appropriate Federal banking agencies shall establish minimum leverage capital requirements on a consolidated basis for insured depository institutions, depository institution holding companies, and nonbank financial companies supervised by the Board of Governors. The minimum leverage capital requirements established under this paragraph shall not be less than the generally applicable leverage capital requirements, which shall serve as a floor for any capital requirements that the agency may require, nor quantitatively lower than the generally applicable leverage capital requirements that were in effect for insured depository institutions as of the date of enactment of this Act.

(2) MINIMUM RISK-BASED CAPITAL REQUIREMENTS.—The appropriate Federal banking agencies shall establish minimum risk-based capital requirements on a consolidated basis for insured depository institutions, depository institution holding companies, and nonbank financial companies supervised by the Board of Governors. The minimum risk-based capital requirements established under this paragraph shall not be less than the generally applicable risk-based capital requirements, which shall serve as a floor for any capital requirements that the agency may require, nor quantitatively lower than the generally applicable risk-based capital requirements that were in effect for insured depository institutions as of the date of enactment of this Act.

(3) INVESTMENTS IN FINANCIAL SUBSIDIARIES.—For purposes of this section, investments in financial subsidiaries that insured depository institutions are required to deduct from regulatory capital under section 5136A of the Revised Statutes of the United States or section 46(a)(2) of the Federal Deposit Insurance Act need not be deducted from regulatory capital by depository institution holding companies or nonbank financial companies supervised by the Board of Governors, unless such capital deduction is required by the Board of Governors or the primary financial regulatory agency in the case of nonbank financial companies supervised by the Board of Governors.

(4) EFFECTIVE DATES AND PHASE-IN PERIODS.—

(A) DEBT OR EQUITY INSTRUMENTS ON OR AFTER MAY 19, 2010.—For debt or equity instruments issued on or after May 19, 2010, by depository institution holding companies or by nonbank financial companies supervised by the Board of Governors, this section shall be deemed to have become effective as of May 19, 2010.

(B) DEBT OR EQUITY INSTRUMENTS ISSUED BEFORE MAY 19, 2010.—For debt or equity instruments issued before May 19, 2010, by depository institution holding companies or by nonbank financial companies supervised by the Board of Governors, any regulatory capital deductions required under this section shall be phased in incrementally over a period of 3 years, with the phase-in period to begin on January 1, 2013, except as set forth in subparagraph (C).

(C) DEBT OR EQUITY INSTRUMENTS OF SMALLER INSTITUTIONS.—For debt or equity instruments issued before May 19, 2010, by depository institution holding companies with total consolidated assets of less than $15,000,000,000 as of December 31, 2009, and by organizations that were mutual holding companies on May 19, 2010, the capital deductions that would be required for other institutions under this section are not required as a result of this section.

(D) DEPOSITORY INSTITUTION HOLDING COMPANIES NOT PREVIOUSLY SUPERVISED BY THE BOARD OF GOVERNORS.—For any depository institution holding company that was not supervised by the Board of Governors as of May 19, 2010, the requirements of this section, except as set forth in subparagraphs (A) and (B), shall be effective 5 years after the date of enactment of this Act

(E) CERTAIN BANK HOLDING COMPANY SUBSIDIARIES OF FOREIGN BANKING ORGANIZATIONS.—For bank holding company subsidiaries of foreign banking organizations that have relied on Supervision and Regulation Letter SR-01-1 issued by the Board of Governors (as in effect on May 19, 2010), the requirements of this section, except as set forth in subparagraph (A), shall be effective 5 years after the date of enactment of this Act.

(5) EXCEPTIONS.—This section shall not apply to—

(A) debt or equity instruments issued to the United States or any agency or instrumentality thereof pursuant to the Emergency Economic Stabilization Act of 2008, and prior to October 4, 2010;

(B) any Federal home loan bank; or

(C) any small bank holding company that is subject to the Small Bank Holding Company Policy Statement of the Board of Governors, as in effect on May 19, 2010.

(6) STUDY AND REPORT ON SMALL INSTITUTION ACCESS TO CAPITAL.—

(A) STUDY REQUIRED.—The Comptroller General of the United States, after consultation with the Federal banking agencies, shall conduct a study of access to capital by smaller insured depository institutions.

(B) SCOPE.—For purposes of this study required by subparagraph (A), the term "smaller insured depository institution" means an insured depository institution with total consolidated assets of $5,000,000,000 or less.

(C) REPORT TO CONGRESS.—Not later than 18 months after the date of enactment of this Act, the Comptroller General of the United States shall submit to the Committee on Banking, Housing, and Urban Affairs of the Senate and the Committee on Financial Services of the House of Representatives a report summarizing the results of the study conducted under subparagraph (A), together with any recommendations for legislative or regulatory action that would enhance the access to capital of smaller insured depository institutions, in a manner that is consistent with safe and sound banking operations.

(7) CAPITAL REQUIREMENTS TO ADDRESS ACTIVITIES THAT POSE RISKS TO THE FINANCIAL SYSTEM.—

(A) IN GENERAL.—Subject to the recommendations of the Council, in accordance with section 120, the Federal banking agencies shall develop capital requirements applicable to insured depository institutions, depository institution holding companies, and nonbank financial companies supervised by the Board of Governors that address the risks that the activities of such institutions pose, not only to the institution engaging in the activity, but to other public and private stakeholders in the event of adverse performance, disruption, or failure of the institution or the activity.

(B) CONTENT.—Such rules shall address, at a minimum, the risks arising from—

(i) significant volumes of activity in derivatives, securitized products purchased and sold, financial guarantees purchased and sold, securities borrowing and lending, and repurchase agreements and reverse repurchase agreements;

(ii) concentrations in assets for which the values presented in financial reports are based on models rather than historical cost or prices deriving from deep and liquid 2-way markets; and

(iii) concentrations in market share for any activity that would substantially disrupt financial markets if the institution is forced to unexpectedly cease the activity.

[Explanation at ¶235.]

[¶10,172] ACT SEC. 172. EXAMINATION AND ENFORCEMENT ACTIONS FOR INSURANCE AND ORDERLY LIQUIDATION PURPOSES.

(a) EXAMINATIONS FOR INSURANCE AND RESOLUTION PURPOSES.—Section 10(b)(3) of the Federal Deposit Insurance Act (12 U.S.C. 1820(b)(3)) is amended—

(1) by striking "In addition" and inserting the following:

"(A) IN GENERAL.—In addition"; and

(2) by striking "whenever the board of directors determines" and all that follows through the period and inserting the following: "or nonbank financial company supervised by the Board of Governors or a bank holding company described in section 165(a) of the Financial Stability Act of 2010, whenever the Board of Directors determines that a special examination of any such depository institution is necessary to determine the condition of such depository institution for insurance purposes, or of such nonbank financial company supervised by the Board of Governors or bank holding company described in section 165(a) of the Financial Stability Act of 2010, for the purpose of implementing its authority to provide for orderly liquidation of any such company under title II of that Act, provided that such authority may not be used with respect to any such company that is in a generally sound condition.

"(B) LIMITATION.—Before conducting a special examination of a nonbank financial company supervised by the Board of Governors or a bank holding company described in section 165(a) of the Financial Stability Act of 2010, the Corporation shall review any available and acceptable resolution plan that the company has submitted in accordance with section 165(d) of that Act, consistent with the nonbinding effect of such plan, and available reports of examination, and shall coordinate to the maximum extent practicable with the Board of Governors, in order to minimize duplicative or conflicting examinations.".

(b) ENFORCEMENT AUTHORITY.—Section 8(t) of the Federal Deposit Insurance Act (12 U.S.C. 1818(t)) is amended—

(1) in paragraph (1), by inserting ", any depository institution holding company," before "or any institution-affiliated party";

(2) in paragraph (2)—

(A) by striking "or" at the end of subparagraph (B);

(B) at the end of subparagraph (C), by striking the period and inserting "or"; and

(C) by inserting at the end the following new subparagraph:

"(D) the conduct or threatened conduct (including any acts or omissions) of the depository institution holding company poses a risk to the Deposit Insurance Fund, provided that such authority may not be used with respect to a depository institution holding company that is in generally sound condition and whose conduct does not pose a foreseeable and material risk of loss to the Deposit Insurance Fund;"; and (3) by adding at the end the following:

"(6) POWERS AND DUTIES WITH RESPECT TO DEPOSITORY INSTITUTION HOLDING COMPANIES.—For purposes of exercising the backup authority provided in this subsection—

"(A) the Corporation shall have the same powers with respect to a depository institution holding company and its affiliates as the appropriate Federal banking agency has with respect to the holding company and its affiliates; and

"(B) the holding company and its affiliates shall have the same duties and obligations with respect to the Corporation as the holding company and its affiliates have with respect to the appropriate Federal banking agency.".

(c) RULE OF CONSTRUCTION.—Nothing in this Act shall be construed to limit or curtail the Corporation's current authority to examine or bring enforcement actions with respect to any insured depository institution or institution-affiliated party.

[Explanation at ¶ 200.]

[¶ 10,173] ACT SEC. 173. ACCESS TO UNITED STATES FINANCIAL MARKET BY FOREIGN INSTITUTIONS.

(a) ESTABLISHMENT OF FOREIGN BANK OFFICES IN THE UNITED STATES.—Section 7(d)(3) of the International Banking Act of 1978 (12 U.S.C. 3105(d)(3)) is amended—

(1) in subparagraph (C), by striking "and" at the end;

(2) in subparagraph (D), by striking the period at the end of and inserting "; and"; and

(3) by adding at the end the following new subparagraph:

"(E) for a foreign bank that presents a risk to the stability of United States financial system, whether the home country of the foreign bank has adopted, or is making demonstrable progress toward adopting, an appropriate system of financial regulation for the financial system of such home country to mitigate such risk.".

(b) TERMINATION OF FOREIGN BANK OFFICES IN THE UNITED STATES.—Section 7(e)(1) of the International Banking Act of 1978 (12 U.S.C. 3105(e)(1)) is amended—

(1) in subparagraph (A), by striking "or" at the end;

(2) in subparagraph (B), by striking the period at the end of and inserting "; or"; and

(3) by inserting after subparagraph (B), the following new subparagraph:

"(C) for a foreign bank that presents a risk to the stability of the United States financial system, the home country of the foreign bank has not adopted, or made demonstrable progress toward adopting, an appropriate system of financial regulation to mitigate such risk.".

(c) REGISTRATION OR SUCCESSION TO A UNITED STATES BROKER OR DEALER AND TERMINATION OF SUCH REGISTRATION.—Section 15 of the Securities Exchange Act of 1934 (15 U.S.C. 78o) is amended by adding at the end the following new subsections:

"(k) REGISTRATION OR SUCCESSION TO A UNITED STATES BROKER OR DEALER.—In determining whether to permit a foreign person or an affiliate of a foreign person to register as a United States broker or dealer, or succeed to the registration of a United States broker or dealer, the Commission may consider whether, for a foreign person, or an affiliate of a foreign person that presents a risk to the stability of the United States financial system, the home country of the foreign person has adopted, or made demonstrable progress toward adopting, an appropriate system of financial regulation to mitigate such risk.

"(l) TERMINATION OF A UNITED STATES BROKER OR DEALER.—For a foreign person or an affiliate of a foreign person that presents such a risk to the stability of the United States financial system, the Commission may determine to terminate the registration of such foreign person or an affiliate of such foreign person as a broker or dealer in the United States, if the Commission determines that the home country of the foreign person has not adopted, or made demonstrable progress toward adopting, an appropriate system of financial regulation to mitigate such risk.".

[Explanation at ¶ 240.]

[¶ 10,174] ACT SEC. 174. STUDIES AND REPORTS ON HOLDING COMPANY CAPITAL REQUIREMENTS.

(a) STUDY OF HYBRID CAPITAL INSTRUMENTS.—The Comptroller General of the United States, in consultation with the Board of Governors, the Comptroller of the Currency, and the Corporation, shall conduct a study of the use of hybrid capital instruments as a component of Tier 1 capital for banking institutions and bank holding companies. The study shall consider—

(1) the current use of hybrid capital instruments, such as trust preferred shares, as a component of Tier 1 capital;

(2) the differences between the components of capital permitted for insured depository institutions and those permitted for companies that control insured depository institutions;

(3) the benefits and risks of allowing such instruments to be used to comply with Tier 1 capital requirements;

(4) the economic impact of prohibiting the use of such capital instruments for Tier 1;

(5) a review of the consequences of disqualifying trust preferred instruments, and whether it could lead to the failure or undercapitalization of existing banking organizations;

(6) the international competitive implications prohibiting hybrid capital instruments for Tier 1;

(7) the impact on the cost and availability of credit in the United States from such a prohibition;

(8) the availability of capital for financial institutions with less than $10,000,000,000 in total assets; and

(9) any other relevant factors relating to the safety and soundness of our financial system and potential economic impact of such a prohibition.

(b) STUDY OF FOREIGN BANK INTERMEDIATE HOLDING COMPANY CAPITAL REQUIREMENTS.—The Comptroller General of the United States, in consultation with the Secretary, the Board of Governors, the Comptroller of the Currency, and the Corporation, shall conduct a study of capital requirements applicable to United States intermediate holding companies of foreign banks that are bank holding companies or savings and loan holding companies. The study shall consider—

(1) current Board of Governors policy regarding the treatment of intermediate holding companies;

(2) the principle of national treatment and equality of competitive opportunity for foreign banks operating in the United States;

(3) the extent to which foreign banks are subject on a consolidated basis to home country capital standards comparable to United States capital standards;

(4) potential effects on United States banking organizations operating abroad of changes to United States policy regarding intermediate holding companies;

(5) the impact on the cost and availability of credit in the United States from a change in United States policy regarding intermediate holding companies; and

(6) any other relevant factors relating to the safety and soundness of our financial system and potential economic impact of such a prohibition.

(c) REPORT.—Not later than 18 months after the date of enactment of this Act, the Comptroller General of the United States shall submit reports to the Committee on Banking, Housing, and Urban Affairs of the Senate and the Committee on Financial Services of the House of Representatives summarizing the results of the studies required under subsection (a). The reports shall include specific recommendations for legislative or regulatory action regarding the treatment of hybrid capital instruments, including trust preferred shares, and shall explain the basis for such recommendations.

[Explanation at ¶ 245.]

[¶ 10,175] ACT SEC. 175. INTERNATIONAL POLICY COORDINATION.

(a) BY THE PRESIDENT.— The President, or a designee of the President, may coordinate through all available international policy channels, similar policies as those found in United States law relating to limiting the scope, nature, size, scale, concentration, and interconnectedness of financial companies, in order to protect financial stability and the global economy.

(b) BY THE COUNCIL.—The Chairperson of the Council, in consultation with the other members of the Council, shall regularly consult with the financial regulatory entities and other appropriate organizations of foreign governments or international organizations on matters relating to systemic risk to the international financial system.

(c) BY THE BOARD OF GOVERNORS AND THE SECRETARY.—The Board of Governors and the Secretary shall consult with their foreign counterparts and through appropriate multilateral organizations to encourage comprehensive and robust prudential supervision and regulation for all highly leveraged and interconnected financial companies.

[Explanation at ¶250.]

[¶10,176] ACT SEC. 176. RULE OF CONSTRUCTION.

No regulation or standard imposed under this title may be construed in a manner that would lessen the stringency of the requirements of any applicable primary financial regulatory agency or any other Federal or State agency that are otherwise applicable. This title, and the rules and regulations or orders prescribed pursuant to this title, do not divest any such agency of any authority derived from any other applicable law.

[Explanation at ¶190.]

TITLE II—ORDERLY LIQUIDATION AUTHORITY

[¶10,201] ACT SEC. 201. DEFINITIONS.

(a) IN GENERAL.—In this title, the following definitions shall apply:

(1) ADMINISTRATIVE EXPENSES OF THE RECEIVER.—The term "administrative expenses of the receiver" includes—

(A) the actual, necessary costs and expenses incurred by the Corporation as receiver for a covered financial company in liquidating a covered financial company; and

(B) any obligations that the Corporation as receiver for a covered financial company determines are necessary and appropriate to facilitate the smooth and orderly liquidation of the covered financial company.

(2) BANKRUPTCY CODE.—The term "Bankruptcy Code" means title 11, United States Code.

(3) BRIDGE FINANCIAL COMPANY.—The term "bridge financial company" means a new financial company organized by the Corporation in accordance with section 210(h) for the purpose of resolving a covered financial company.

(4) CLAIM.—The term "claim" means any right to payment, whether or not such right is reduced to judgment, liquidated, unliquidated, fixed, contingent, matured, unmatured, disputed, undisputed, legal, equitable, secured, or unsecured.

(5) COMPANY.—The term "company" has the same meaning as in section 2(b) of the Bank Holding Company Act of 1956 (12 U.S.C. 1841(b)), except that such term includes any company described in paragraph (11), the majority of the securities of which are owned by the United States or any State.

(6) COURT.—The term "Court" means the United States District Court for the District of Columbia, unless the context otherwise requires.

(7) COVERED BROKER OR DEALER.—The term "covered broker or dealer" means a covered financial company that is a broker or dealer that—

(A) is registered with the Commission under section 15(b) of the Securities Exchange Act of 1934 (15 U.S.C. 78o(b)); and

(B) is a member of SIPC.

(8) COVERED FINANCIAL COMPANY.—The term "covered financial company"—

(A) means a financial company for which a determination has been made under section 203(b); and

(B) does not include an insured depository institution.

(9) COVERED SUBSIDIARY.—The term "covered subsidiary" means a subsidiary of a covered financial company, other than—

(A) an insured depository institution;

(B) an insurance company; or

(C) a covered broker or dealer.

(10) DEFINITIONS RELATING TO COVERED BROKERS AND DEALERS.—The terms "customer", "customer name securities", "customer property", and "net equity" in the context of a covered broker or dealer, have the same meanings as in section 16 of the Securities Investor Protection Act of 1970 (15 U.S.C. 78lll).

(11) FINANCIAL COMPANY.—The term "financial company" means any company that—

(A) is incorporated or organized under any provision of Federal law or the laws of any State;

(B) is—

(i) a bank holding company, as defined in section 2(a) of the Bank Holding Company Act of 1956 (12 U.S.C. 1841(a));

(ii) a nonbank financial company supervised by the Board of Governors;

(iii) any company that is predominantly engaged in activities that the Board of Governors has determined are financial in nature or incidental thereto for purposes of section 4(k) of the Bank Holding Company Act of 1956 (12 U.S.C. 1843(k)) other than a company described in clause (i) or (ii); or

(iv) any subsidiary of any company described in any of clauses (i) through (iii) that is predominantly engaged in activities that the Board of Governors has determined are financial in nature or incidental thereto for purposes of section 4(k) of the Bank Holding Company Act of 1956 (12 U.S.C. 1843(k)) (other than a subsidiary that is an insured depository institution or an insurance company); and

(C) is not a Farm Credit System institution chartered under and subject to the provisions of the Farm Credit Act of 1971, as amended (12 U.S.C. 2001 et seq.), a governmental entity, or a regulated entity, as defined under section 1303(20) of the Federal Housing Enterprises Financial Safety and Soundness Act of 1992 (12 U.S.C. 4502(20)).

(12) FUND.—The term "Fund" means the Orderly Liquidation Fund established under section 210(n).

(13) INSURANCE COMPANY.—The term "insurance company" means any entity that is—

(A) engaged in the business of insurance;

(B) subject to regulation by a State insurance regulator; and

(C) covered by a State law that is designed to specifically deal with the rehabilitation, liquidation, or insolvency of an insurance company.

(14) NONBANK FINANCIAL COMPANY.—The term "nonbank financial company" has the same meaning as in section 102(a)(4)(C).

(15) NONBANK FINANCIAL COMPANY SUPERVISED BY THE BOARD OF GOVERNORS.—The term "nonbank financial company supervised by the Board of Governors" has the same meaning as in section 102(a)(4)(D).

(16) SIPC.—The term "SIPC" means the Securities Investor Protection Corporation.

(b) DEFINITIONAL CRITERIA.—For purpose of the definition of the term "financial company" under subsection (a)(11), no company shall be deemed to be predominantly engaged in activities that the Board of Governors has determined are financial in nature or incidental thereto for purposes of section 4(k) of the Bank Holding Company Act of 1956 (12 U.S.C. 1843(k)), if the consolidated revenues of such company from such activities constitute less than 85 percent of the total consolidated revenues of such company, as the Corporation, in consultation with the Secretary, shall establish by regulation. In determining whether a company is a financial company under this title, the consolidated revenues derived from the ownership or control of a depository institution shall be included.

[Explanation at ¶ 505 and ¶ 510.]

[¶ 10,202] ACT SEC. 202. JUDICIAL REVIEW.

(a) COMMENCEMENT OF ORDERLY LIQUIDATION.—

(1) PETITION TO DISTRICT COURT.—

(A) DISTRICT COURT REVIEW.—

(i) PETITION TO DISTRICT COURT.—Subsequent to a determination by the Secretary under section 203 that a financial company satisfies the criteria in section 203(b), the Secretary shall notify the Corporation and the covered financial company. If the board of directors (or body performing similar functions) of the covered financial company acquiesces or consents to the appointment of the Corporation as receiver, the Secretary shall appoint the Corporation as receiver. If the board of directors (or body performing similar functions) of the covered financial company does not acquiesce or consent to the appointment of the Corporation as receiver, the Secretary shall petition the United States District Court for the District of Columbia for an order authorizing the Secretary to appoint the Corporation as receiver.

(ii) FORM AND CONTENT OF ORDER.—The Secretary shall present all relevant findings and the recommendation made pursuant to section 203(a) to the Court. The petition shall be filed under seal.

(iii) DETERMINATION.—On a strictly confidential basis, and without any prior public disclosure, the Court, after notice to the covered financial company and a hearing in which the covered financial company may oppose the petition, shall determine whether the determination of the Secretary that the covered financial company is in default or in danger of default and satisfies the definition of a financial company under section 201(a)(11) is arbitrary and capricious.

(iv) ISSUANCE OF ORDER.—If the Court determines that the determination of the Secretary that the covered financial company is in default or in danger of default and satisfies the definition of a financial company under section 201(a)(11)—

(I) is not arbitrary and capricious, the Court shall issue an order immediately authorizing the Secretary to appoint the Corporation as receiver of the covered financial company; or

(II) is arbitrary and capricious, the Court shall immediately provide to the Secretary a written statement of each reason supporting its determination, and afford the Secretary an immediate opportunity to amend and refile the petition under clause (i).

(v) PETITION GRANTED BY OPERATION OF LAW.—If the Court does not make a determination within 24 hours of receipt of the petition—

(I) the petition shall be granted by operation of law;

(II) the Secretary shall appoint the Corporation as receiver; and

(III) liquidation under this title shall automatically and without further notice or action be commenced and the Corporation may immediately take all actions authorized under this title.

(B) EFFECT OF DETERMINATION.—The determination of the Court under subparagraph (A) shall be final, and shall be subject to appeal only in accordance with paragraph (2). The decision shall not be subject to any stay or injunction pending appeal. Upon conclusion of its proceedings under subparagraph (A), the Court shall provide immediately for the record a written statement of each reason supporting the decision of the Court, and shall provide copies thereof to the Secretary and the covered financial company.

(C) CRIMINAL PENALTIES.—A person who recklessly discloses a determination of the Secretary under section 203(b) or a petition of the Secretary under subparagraph (A), or the pendency of court proceedings as provided for under subparagraph (A), shall be fined not more than $250,000, or imprisoned for not more than 5 years, or both.

(2) APPEAL OF DECISIONS OF THE DISTRICT COURT.—

(A) APPEAL TO COURT OF APPEALS.—

(i) IN GENERAL.—Subject to clause (ii), the United States Court of Appeals for the District of Columbia Circuit shall have jurisdiction of an appeal of a final decision of the Court filed by the Secretary or a covered financial company, through its board of directors, notwithstanding section 210(a)(1)(A)(i), not later than 30 days after the date on which the decision of the Court is rendered or deemed rendered under this subsection.

(ii) CONDITION OF JURISDICTION.—The Court of Appeals shall have jurisdiction of an appeal by a covered financial company only if the covered financial company did not acquiesce or consent to the appointment of a receiver by the Secretary under paragraph (1)(A).

(iii) EXPEDITION.—The Court of Appeals shall consider any appeal under this subparagraph on an expedited basis.

(iv) SCOPE OF REVIEW.—For an appeal taken under this subparagraph, review shall be limited to whether the determination of the Secretary that a covered financial company is in default or in danger of default and satisfies the definition of a financial company under section 201(a)(11) is arbitrary and capricious.

(B) APPEAL TO THE SUPREME COURT.—

(i) IN GENERAL.—A petition for a writ of certiorari to review a decision of the Court of Appeals under subparagraph (A) may be filed by the Secretary or the covered financial company, through its board of directors, notwithstanding section 210(a)(1)(A)(i), with the Supreme Court of the United States, not later than 30 days after the date of the final decision of the Court of Appeals, and the Supreme Court shall have discretionary jurisdiction to review such decision.

(ii) WRITTEN STATEMENT.—In the event of a petition under clause (i), the Court of Appeals shall immediately provide for the record a written statement of each reason for its decision.

(iii) EXPEDITION.—The Supreme Court shall consider any petition under this subparagraph on an expedited basis.

(iv) SCOPE OF REVIEW.—Review by the Supreme Court under this subparagraph shall be limited to whether the determination of the Secretary that the covered financial company is in default or in danger of default and satisfies the definition of a financial company under section 201(a)(11) is arbitrary and capricious.

(b) ESTABLISHMENT AND TRANSMITTAL OF RULES AND PROCEDURES.—

(1) IN GENERAL.—Not later than 6 months after the date of enactment of this Act, the Court shall establish such rules and procedures as may be necessary to ensure the orderly conduct of proceedings, including rules and procedures to ensure that the 24-hour deadline is met and that the Secretary shall have an ongoing opportunity to amend and refile petitions under subsection (a)(1).

(2) PUBLICATION OF RULES.—The rules and procedures established under paragraph (1), and any modifications of such rules and procedures, shall be recorded and shall be transmitted to—

(A) the Committee on the Judiciary of the Senate;

(B) the Committee on Banking, Housing, and Urban Affairs of the Senate;

(C) the Committee on the Judiciary of the House of Representatives; and

(D) the Committee on Financial Services of the House of Representatives.

(c) PROVISIONS APPLICABLE TO FINANCIAL COMPANIES.—

(1) BANKRUPTCY CODE.—Except as provided in this subsection, the provisions of the Bankruptcy Code and rules issued thereunder or otherwise applicable insolvency law, and not the

provisions of this title, shall apply to financial companies that are not covered financial companies for which the Corporation has been appointed as receiver.

(2) THIS TITLE.—The provisions of this title shall exclusively apply to and govern all matters relating to covered financial companies for which the Corporation is appointed as receiver, and no provisions of the Bankruptcy Code or the rules issued thereunder shall apply in such cases, except as expressly provided in this title.

(d) TIME LIMIT ON RECEIVERSHIP AUTHORITY.—

(1) BASELINE PERIOD.—Any appointment of the Corporation as receiver under this section shall terminate at the end of the 3-year period beginning on the date on which such appointment is made.

(2) EXTENSION OF TIME LIMIT.—The time limit established in paragraph (1) may be extended by the Corporation for up to 1 additional year, if the Chairperson of the Corporation determines and certifies in writing to the Committee on Banking, Housing, and Urban Affairs of the Senate and the Committee on Financial Services of the House of Representatives that continuation of the receivership is necessary—

(A) to—

(i) maximize the net present value return from the sale or other disposition of the assets of the covered financial company; or

(ii) minimize the amount of loss realized upon the sale or other disposition of the assets of the covered financial company; and

(B) to protect the stability of the financial system of the United States.

(3) SECOND EXTENSION OF TIME LIMIT.—

(A) IN GENERAL.—The time limit under this subsection, as extended under paragraph (2), may be extended for up to 1 additional year, if the Chairperson of the Corporation, with the concurrence of the Secretary, submits the certifications described in paragraph (2).

(B) ADDITIONAL REPORT REQUIRED.—Not later than 30 days after the date of commencement of the extension under subparagraph (A), the Corporation shall submit a report to the Committee on Banking, Housing, and Urban Affairs of the Senate and the Committee on Financial Services of the House of Representatives describing the need for the extension and the specific plan of the Corporation to conclude the receivership before the end of the second extension.

(4) ONGOING LITIGATION.—The time limit under this subsection, as extended under paragraph (3), may be further extended solely for the purpose of completing ongoing litigation in which the Corporation as receiver is a party, provided that the appointment of the Corporation as receiver shall terminate not later than 90 days after the date of completion of such litigation, if—

(A) the Council determines that the Corporation used its best efforts to conclude the receivership in accordance with its plan before the end of the time limit described in paragraph (3);

(B) the Council determines that the completion of longer-term responsibilities in the form of ongoing litigation justifies the need for an extension; and

(C) the Corporation submits a report approved by the Council not later than 30 days after the date of the determinations by the Council under subparagraphs (A) and (B) to the Committee on Banking, Housing, and Urban Affairs of the Senate and the Committee on Financial Services of the House of Representatives, describing—

(i) the ongoing litigation justifying the need for an extension; and

(ii) the specific plan of the Corporation to complete the litigation and conclude the receivership.

(5) REGULATIONS.—The Corporation may issue regulations governing the termination of receiverships under this title.

(6) NO LIABILITY.—The Corporation and the Deposit Insurance Fund shall not be liable for unresolved claims arising from the receivership after the termination of the receivership.

(e) STUDY OF BANKRUPTCY AND ORDERLY LIQUIDATION PROCESS FOR FINANCIAL COMPANIES.—

(1) STUDY.—

(A) IN GENERAL.—The Administrative Office of the United States Courts and the Comptroller General of the United States shall each monitor the activities of the Court, and each such Office shall conduct separate studies regarding the bankruptcy and orderly liquidation process for financial companies under the Bankruptcy Code.

(B) ISSUES TO BE STUDIED.—In conducting the study under subparagraph (A), the Administrative Office of the United States Courts and the Comptroller General of the United States each shall evaluate—

(i) the effectiveness of chapter 7 or chapter 11 of the Bankruptcy Code in facilitating the orderly liquidation or reorganization of financial companies;

(ii) ways to maximize the efficiency and effectiveness of the Court; and

(iii) ways to make the orderly liquidation process under the Bankruptcy Code for financial companies more effective.

(2) REPORTS.—Not later than 1 year after the date of enactment of this Act, in each successive year until the third year, and every fifth year after that date of enactment, the Administrative Office of the United States Courts and the Comptroller General of the United States shall submit to the Committee on Banking, Housing, and Urban Affairs and the Committee on the Judiciary of the Senate and the Committee on Financial Services and the Committee on the Judiciary of the House of Representatives separate reports summarizing the results of the studies conducted under paragraph (1).

(f) STUDY OF INTERNATIONAL COORDINATION RELATING TO BANKRUPTCY PROCESS FOR FINANCIAL COMPANIES.—

(1) STUDY.—

(A) IN GENERAL.—The Comptroller General of the United States shall conduct a study regarding international coordination relating to the orderly liquidation of financial companies under the Bankruptcy Code.

(B) ISSUES TO BE STUDIED.—In conducting the study under subparagraph (A), the Comptroller General of the United States shall evaluate, with respect to the bankruptcy process for financial companies—

(i) the extent to which international coordination currently exists;

(ii) current mechanisms and structures for facilitating international cooperation;

(iii) barriers to effective international coordination; and

(iv) ways to increase and make more effective international coordination.

(2) REPORT.—Not later than 1 year after the date of enactment of this Act, the Comptroller General of the United States shall submit to the Committee on Banking, Housing, and Urban Affairs and the Committee on the Judiciary of the Senate and the Committee on Financial Services and the Committee on the Judiciary of the House of Representatives and the Secretary a report summarizing the results of the study conducted under paragraph (1).

(g) STUDY OF PROMPT CORRECTIVE ACTION IMPLEMENTATION BY THE APPROPRIATE FEDERAL AGENCIES.—

(1) STUDY.—The Comptroller General of the United States shall conduct a study regarding the implementation of prompt corrective action by the appropriate Federal banking agencies.

(2) ISSUES TO BE STUDIED.—In conducting the study under paragraph (1), the Comptroller General shall evaluate—

(A) the effectiveness of implementation of prompt corrective action by the appropriate Federal banking agencies and the resolution of insured depository institutions by the Corporation; and

(B) ways to make prompt corrective action a more effective tool to resolve the insured depository institutions at the least possible long-term cost to the Deposit Insurance Fund.

(3) REPORT TO COUNCIL.—Not later than 1 year after the date of enactment of this Act, the Comptroller General shall submit a report to the Council on the results of the study conducted under this subsection.

(4) COUNCIL REPORT OF ACTION.—Not later than 6 months after the date of receipt of the report from the Comptroller General under paragraph (3), the Council shall submit a report to the Committee on Banking, Housing, and Urban Affairs of the Senate and the Committee on Financial Services of the House of Representatives on actions taken in response to the report, including any recommendations made to the Federal primary financial regulatory agencies under section 120.

[Explanation at ¶ 510.]

[¶ 10,203] ACT SEC. 203. SYSTEMIC RISK DETERMINATION.

(a) WRITTEN RECOMMENDATION AND DETERMINATION.—

(1) VOTE REQUIRED.—

(A) IN GENERAL.—On their own initiative, or at the request of the Secretary, the Corporation and the Board of Governors shall consider whether to make a written recommendation described in paragraph (2) with respect to whether the Secretary should appoint the Corporation as receiver for a financial company. Such recommendation shall be made upon a vote of not fewer than $2/3$ of the members of the Board of Governors then serving and $2/3$ of the members of the board of directors of the Corporation then serving.

(B) CASES INVOLVING BROKERS OR DEALERS.—In the case of a broker or dealer, or in which the largest United States subsidiary (as measured by total assets as of the end of the previous calendar quarter) of a financial company is a broker or dealer, the Commission and the Board of Governors, at the request of the Secretary, or on their own initiative, shall consider whether to make the written recommendation described in paragraph (2) with respect to the financial company. Subject to the requirements in paragraph (2), such recommendation shall be made upon a vote of not fewer than $2/3$ of the members of the Board of Governors then serving and $2/3$ of the members of the Commission then serving, and in consultation with the Corporation.

(C) CASES INVOLVING INSURANCE COMPANIES.—In the case of an insurance company, or in which the largest United States subsidiary (as measured by total assets as of the end of the previous calendar quarter) of a financial company is an insurance company, the Director of the Federal Insurance Office and the Board of Governors, at the request of the Secretary or on their own initiative, shall consider whether to make the written recommendation described in paragraph (2) with respect to the financial company. Subject to the requirements in paragraph (2), such recommendation shall be made upon a vote of not fewer than $2/3$ of the Board of Governors then serving and the affirmative approval of the Director of the Federal Insurance Office, and in consultation with the Corporation.

(2) RECOMMENDATION REQUIRED.—Any written recommendation pursuant to paragraph (1) shall contain—

(A) an evaluation of whether the financial company is in default or in danger of default;

(B) a description of the effect that the default of the financial company would have on financial stability in the United States;

(C) a description of the effect that the default of the financial company would have on economic conditions or financial stability for low income, minority, or underserved communities;

(D) a recommendation regarding the nature and the extent of actions to be taken under this title regarding the financial company;

(E) an evaluation of the likelihood of a private sector alternative to prevent the default of the financial company;

(F) an evaluation of why a case under the Bankruptcy Code is not appropriate for the financial company;

(G) an evaluation of the effects on creditors, counterparties, and shareholders of the financial company and other market participants; and

(H) an evaluation of whether the company satisfies the definition of a financial company under section 201.

(b) DETERMINATION BY THE SECRETARY.—Notwithstanding any other provision of Federal or State law, the Secretary shall take action in accordance with section 202(a)(1)(A), if, upon the written recommendation under subsection (a), the Secretary (in consultation with the President) determines that—

(1) the financial company is in default or in danger of default;

(2) the failure of the financial company and its resolution under otherwise applicable Federal or State law would have serious adverse effects on financial stability in the United States;

(3) no viable private sector alternative is available to prevent the default of the financial company;

(4) any effect on the claims or interests of creditors, counterparties, and shareholders of the financial company and other market participants as a result of actions to be taken under this title is appropriate, given the impact that any action taken under this title would have on financial stability in the United States;

(5) any action under section 204 would avoid or mitigate such adverse effects, taking into consideration the effectiveness of the action in mitigating potential adverse effects on the financial system, the cost to the general fund of the Treasury, and the potential to increase excessive risk taking on the part of creditors, counterparties, and shareholders in the financial company;

(6) a Federal regulatory agency has ordered the financial company to convert all of its convertible debt instruments that are subject to the regulatory order; and

(7) the company satisfies the definition of a financial company under section 201.

(c) DOCUMENTATION AND REVIEW.—

(1) IN GENERAL.—The Secretary shall—

(A) document any determination under subsection (b);

(B) retain the documentation for review under paragraph (2); and

(C) notify the covered financial company and the Corporation of such determination.

(2) REPORT TO CONGRESS.—Not later than 24 hours after the date of appointment of the Corporation as receiver for a covered financial company, the Secretary shall provide written notice of the recommendations and determinations reached in accordance with subsections (a) and (b) to the Majority Leader and the Minority Leader of the Senate and the Speaker and the Minority Leader of the House of Representatives, the Committee on Banking, Housing, and Urban Affairs of the Senate, and the Committee on Financial Services of the House of Representatives, which shall consist of a summary of the basis for the determination, including, to the extent available at the time of the determination—

(A) the size and financial condition of the covered financial company;

(B) the sources of capital and credit support that were available to the covered financial company;

(C) the operations of the covered financial company that could have had a significant impact on financial stability, markets, or both;

(D) identification of the banks and financial companies which may be able to provide the services offered by the covered financial company;

(E) any potential international ramifications of resolution of the covered financial company under other applicable insolvency law;

(F) an estimate of the potential effect of the resolution of the covered financial company under other applicable insolvency law on the financial stability of the United States;

(G) the potential effect of the appointment of a receiver by the Secretary on consumers;

(H) the potential effect of the appointment of a receiver by the Secretary on the financial system, financial markets, and banks and other financial companies; and

(I) whether resolution of the covered financial company under other applicable insolvency law would cause banks or other financial companies to experience severe liquidity distress.

(3) REPORTS TO CONGRESS AND THE PUBLIC.—

(A) IN GENERAL.—Not later than 60 days after the date of appointment of the Corporation as receiver for a covered financial company, the Corporation shall file a report with the Committee on Banking, Housing, and Urban Affairs of the Senate and the Committee on Financial Services of the House of Representatives—

(i) setting forth information on the financial condition of the covered financial company as of the date of the appointment, including a description of its assets and liabilities;

(ii) describing the plan of, and actions taken by, the Corporation to wind down the covered financial company;

(iii) explaining each instance in which the Corporation waived any applicable requirements of part 366 of title 12, Code of Federal Regulations (or any successor thereto) with respect to conflicts of interest by any person in the private sector who was retained to provide services to the Corporation in connection with such receivership;

(iv) describing the reasons for the provision of any funding to the receivership out of the Fund;

(v) setting forth the expected costs of the orderly liquidation of the covered financial company;

(vi) setting forth the identity of any claimant that is treated in a manner different from other similarly situated claimants under subsection (b)(4), (d)(4), or (h)(5)(E), the amount of any additional payment to such claimant under subsection (d)(4), and the reason for any such action; and

(vii) which report the Corporation shall publish on an online website maintained by the Corporation, subject to maintaining appropriate confidentiality.

(B) AMENDMENTS.—The Corporation shall, on a timely basis, not less frequently than quarterly, amend or revise and resubmit the reports prepared under this paragraph, as necessary.

(C) CONGRESSIONAL TESTIMONY.—The Corporation and the primary financial regulatory agency, if any, of the financial company for which the Corporation was appointed receiver under this title shall appear before Congress, if requested, not later than 30 days after the date on which the Corporation first files the reports required under subparagraph (A).

(4) DEFAULT OR IN DANGER OF DEFAULT.—For purposes of this title, a financial company shall be considered to be in default or in danger of default if, as determined in accordance with subsection (b)—

(A) a case has been, or likely will promptly be, commenced with respect to the financial company under the Bankruptcy Code;

(B) the financial company has incurred, or is likely to incur, losses that will deplete all or substantially all of its capital, and there is no reasonable prospect for the company to avoid such depletion;

(C) the assets of the financial company are, or are likely to be, less than its obligations to creditors and others; or

(D) the financial company is, or is likely to be, unable to pay its obligations (other than those subject to a bona fide dispute) in the normal course of business.

(5) GAO REVIEW.—The Comptroller General of the United States shall review and report to Congress on any determination under subsection (b), that results in the appointment of the Corporation as receiver, including—

(A) the basis for the determination;

(B) the purpose for which any action was taken pursuant thereto;

(C) the likely effect of the determination and such action on the incentives and conduct of financial companies and their creditors, counterparties, and shareholders; and

(D) the likely disruptive effect of the determination and such action on the reasonable expectations of creditors, counterparties, and shareholders, taking into account the impact any action under this title would have on financial stability in the United States, including whether the rights of such parties will be disrupted.

(d) CORPORATION POLICIES AND PROCEDURES.—As soon as is practicable after the date of enactment of this Act, the Corporation shall establish policies and procedures that are acceptable to the Secretary governing the use of funds available to the Corporation to carry out this title, including the terms and conditions for the provision and use of funds under sections 204(d), 210(h)(2)(G)(iv), and 210(h)(9).

(e) TREATMENT OF INSURANCE COMPANIES AND INSURANCE COMPANY SUBSIDIARIES.—

(1) IN GENERAL.—Notwithstanding subsection (b), if an insurance company is a covered financial company or a subsidiary or affiliate of a covered financial company, the liquidation or rehabilitation of such insurance company, and any subsidiary or affiliate of such company that is not excepted under paragraph (2), shall be conducted as provided under applicable State law.

(2) EXCEPTION FOR SUBSIDIARIES AND AFFILIATES.—The requirement of paragraph (1) shall not apply with respect to any subsidiary or affiliate of an insurance company that is not itself an insurance company.

(3) BACKUP AUTHORITY.—Notwithstanding paragraph (1), with respect to a covered financial company described in paragraph (1), if, after the end of the 60-day period beginning on the date on which a determination is made under section 202(a) with respect to such company, the appropriate regulatory agency has not filed the appropriate judicial action in the appropriate State court to place such company into orderly liquidation under the laws and requirements of the State, the Corporation shall have the authority to stand in the place of the appropriate regulatory agency and file the appropriate judicial action in the appropriate State court to place such company into orderly liquidation under the laws and requirements of the State.

[Explanation at ¶ 505 and ¶ 515.]

[¶ 10,204] ACT SEC. 204. ORDERLY LIQUIDATION OF COVERED FINANCIAL COMPANIES.

(a) PURPOSE OF ORDERLY LIQUIDATION AUTHORITY.—It is the purpose of this title to provide the necessary authority to liquidate failing financial companies that pose a significant risk to the financial stability of the United States in a manner that mitigates such risk and minimizes moral hazard. The authority provided in this title shall be exercised in the manner that best fulfills such purpose, so that—

(1) creditors and shareholders will bear the losses of the financial company;

(2) management responsible for the condition of the financial company will not be retained; and

(3) the Corporation and other appropriate agencies will take all steps necessary and appropriate to assure that all parties, including management, directors, and third parties, having responsibility for the condition of the financial company bear losses consistent with their responsibility, including actions for damages, restitution, and recoupment of compensation and other gains not compatible with such responsibility.

(b) CORPORATION AS RECEIVER.—Upon the appointment of the Corporation under section 202, the Corporation shall act as the receiver for the covered financial company, with all of the rights and obligations set forth in this title.

(c) CONSULTATION.—The Corporation, as receiver—

(1) shall consult with the primary financial regulatory agency or agencies of the covered financial company and its covered subsidiaries for purposes of ensuring an orderly liquidation of the covered financial company;

(2) may consult with, or under subsection (a)(1)(B)(v) or (a)(1)(L) of section 210, acquire the services of, any outside experts, as appropriate to inform and aid the Corporation in the orderly liquidation process;

(3) shall consult with the primary financial regulatory agency or agencies of any subsidiaries of the covered financial company that are not covered subsidiaries, and coordinate with such regulators regarding the treatment of such solvent subsidiaries and the separate resolution of any such insolvent subsidiaries under other governmental authority, as appropriate; and

(4) shall consult with the Commission and the Securities Investor Protection Corporation in the case of any covered financial company for which the Corporation has been appointed as receiver that is a broker or dealer registered with the Commission under section 15(b) of the Securities Exchange Act of 1934 (15 U.S.C. 78o(b)) and is a member of the Securities Investor Protection Corporation, for the purpose of determining whether to transfer to a bridge financial company organized by the Corporation as receiver, without consent of any customer, customer accounts of the covered financial company.

(d) FUNDING FOR ORDERLY LIQUIDATION.—Upon its appointment as receiver for a covered financial company, and thereafter as the Corporation may, in its discretion, determine to be necessary or appropriate, the Corporation may make available to the receivership, subject to the conditions set forth in section 206 and subject to the plan described in section 210(n)(9), funds for the orderly liquidation of the covered financial company. All funds provided by the Corporation under this subsection shall have a priority of claims under subparagraph (A) or (B) of section 210(b)(1), as applicable, including funds used for—

(1) making loans to, or purchasing any debt obligation of, the covered financial company or any covered subsidiary;

(2) purchasing or guaranteeing against loss the assets of the covered financial company or any covered subsidiary, directly or through an entity established by the Corporation for such purpose;

(3) assuming or guaranteeing the obligations of the covered financial company or any covered subsidiary to 1 or more third parties;

(4) taking a lien on any or all assets of the covered financial company or any covered subsidiary, including a first priority lien on all unencumbered assets of the covered financial company or any covered subsidiary to secure repayment of any transactions conducted under this subsection;

(5) selling or transferring all, or any part, of such acquired assets, liabilities, or obligations of the covered financial company or any covered subsidiary; and

(6) making payments pursuant to subsections (b)(4), (d)(4), and (h)(5)(E) of section 210.

[Explanation at ¶ 520.]

[¶ 10,205] ACT SEC. 205. ORDERLY LIQUIDATION OF COVERED BROKERS AND DEALERS.

(a) APPOINTMENT OF SIPC AS TRUSTEE.—

(1) APPOINTMENT.—Upon the appointment of the Corporation as receiver for any covered broker or dealer, the Corporation shall appoint, without any need for court approval, the Securities Investor Protection Corporation to act as trustee for the liquidation under the Securities Investor Protection Act of 1970 (15 U.S.C. 78aaa et seq.) of the covered broker or dealer.

(2) ACTIONS BY SIPC.—

(A) FILING.—Upon appointment of SIPC under paragraph (1), SIPC shall promptly file with any Federal district court of competent jurisdiction specified in section 21 or 27 of the Securities Exchange Act of 1934 (15 U.S.C. 78u, 78aa), an application for a protective decree under the Securities Investor Protection Act of 1970 (15 U.S.C. 78aaa et seq.) as to the covered broker or dealer. The Federal district court shall accept and approve the filing, including outside of normal business hours, and shall immediately issue the protective decree as to the covered broker or dealer.

(B) ADMINISTRATION BY SIPC.—Following entry of the protective decree, and except as otherwise provided in this section, the determination of claims and the liquidation of assets retained in the receivership of the covered broker or dealer and not transferred to the bridge financial company shall be administered under the Securities Investor Protection Act of 1970 (15 U.S.C. 78aaa et seq.) by SIPC, as trustee for the covered broker or dealer.

(C) DEFINITION OF FILING DATE.—For purposes of the liquidation proceeding, the term "filing date" means the date on which the Corporation is appointed as receiver of the covered broker or dealer.

(D) DETERMINATION OF CLAIMS.—As trustee for the covered broker or dealer, SIPC shall determine and satisfy, consistent with this title and with the Securities Investor Protection Act of 1970 (15 U.S.C. 78aaa et seq.), all claims against the covered broker or dealer arising on or before the filing date.

(b) POWERS AND DUTIES OF SIPC.—

(1) IN GENERAL.—Except as provided in this section, upon its appointment as trustee for the liquidation of a covered broker or dealer, SIPC shall have all of the powers and duties provided by the Securities Investor Protection Act of 1970 (15 U.S.C. 78aaa et seq.), including, without limitation, all rights of action against third parties, and shall conduct such liquidation in accordance with the terms of the Securities Investor Protection Act of 1970 (15 U.S.C. 78aaa et seq.), except that SIPC shall have no powers or duties with respect to assets and liabilities transferred by the Corporation from the covered broker or dealer to any bridge financial company established in accordance with this title.

(2) LIMITATION OF POWERS.—The exercise by SIPC of powers and functions as trustee under subsection (a) shall not impair or impede the exercise of the powers and duties of the Corporation with regard to—

(A) any action, except as otherwise provided in this title—

(i) to make funds available under section 204(d);

(ii) to organize, establish, operate, or terminate any bridge financial company;

(iii) to transfer assets and liabilities;

(iv) to enforce or repudiate contracts; or

(v) to take any other action relating to such bridge financial company under section 210; or

(B) determining claims under subsection (e).

(3) PROTECTIVE DECREE.—SIPC and the Corporation, in consultation with the Commission, shall jointly determine the terms of the protective decree to be filed by SIPC with any court of competent jurisdiction under section 21 or 27 of the Securities Exchange Act of 1934 (15 U.S.C. 78u, 78aa), as required by subsection (a).

(4) QUALIFIED FINANCIAL CONTRACTS.—Notwithstanding any provision of the Securities Investor Protection Act of 1970 (15 U.S.C. 78aaa et seq.) to the contrary (including section 5(b)(2)(C) of that Act (15 U.S.C. 78eee(b)(2)(C))), the rights and obligations of any party to a qualified financial contract (as that term is defined in section 210(c)(8)) to which a covered broker or dealer for which the Corporation has been appointed receiver is a party shall be governed exclusively by section 210, including the limitations and restrictions contained in section 210(c)(10)(B).

(c) LIMITATION ON COURT ACTION.—Except as otherwise provided in this title, no court may take any action, including any action pursuant to the Securities Investor Protection Act of 1970 (15 U.S.C. 78aaa et seq.) or the Bankruptcy Code, to restrain or affect the exercise of powers or functions of the Corporation as receiver for a covered broker or dealer and any claims against the Corporation as such receiver shall be determined in accordance with subsection (e) and such claims shall be limited to money damages.

(d) ACTIONS BY CORPORATION AS RECEIVER.—

(1) IN GENERAL.—Notwithstanding any other provision of this title, no action taken by the Corporation as receiver with respect to a covered broker or dealer shall—

(A) adversely affect the rights of a customer to customer property or customer name securities;

(B) diminish the amount or timely payment of net equity claims of customers; or

(C) otherwise impair the recoveries provided to a customer under the Securities Investor Protection Act of 1970 (15 U.S.C. 78aaa et seq.).

(2) NET PROCEEDS.—The net proceeds from any transfer, sale, or disposition of assets of the covered broker or dealer, or proceeds thereof by the Corporation as receiver for the covered broker or dealer shall be for the benefit of the estate of the covered broker or dealer, as provided in this title.

(e) CLAIMS AGAINST THE CORPORATION AS RECEIVER.—Any claim against the Corporation as receiver for a covered broker or dealer for assets transferred to a bridge financial company established with respect to such covered broker or dealer—

(1) shall be determined in accordance with section 210(a)(2); and

(2) may be reviewed by the appropriate district or territorial court of the United States in accordance with section 210(a)(5).

(f) SATISFACTION OF CUSTOMER CLAIMS.—

(1) OBLIGATIONS TO CUSTOMERS.—Notwithstanding any other provision of this title, all obligations of a covered broker or dealer or of any bridge financial company established with respect to such covered broker or dealer to a customer relating to, or net equity claims based upon, customer property or customer name securities shall be promptly discharged by SIPC, the Corporation, or the bridge financial company, as applicable, by the delivery of securities or the making of payments to or for the account of such customer, in a manner and in an amount at least as beneficial to the customer as would have been the case had the actual proceeds realized from the liquidation of the covered broker or dealer under this title been distributed in a proceeding under the Securities Investor Protection Act of 1970 (15 U.S.C. 78aaa et seq.) without the appointment of the Corporation as receiver and without any transfer of assets or liabilities to a bridge financial company, and with a filing date as of the date on which the Corporation is appointed as receiver.

(2) SATISFACTION OF CLAIMS BY SIPC.—SIPC, as trustee for a covered broker or dealer, shall satisfy customer claims in the manner and amount provided under the Securities Investor Protection Act of 1970 (15 U.S.C. 78aaa et seq.), as if the appointment of the Corporation as receiver had not occurred, and with a filing date as of the date on which the Corporation is appointed as receiver. The Corporation shall satisfy customer claims, to the extent that a customer would have received more securities or cash with respect to the allocation of customer property had the covered financial company been subject to a proceeding under the Securities Investor Protection Act (15 U.S.C. 78aaa et seq.) without the appointment of the Corporation as receiver, and with a filing date as of the date on which the Corporation is appointed as receiver.

(g) PRIORITIES.—

(1) CUSTOMER PROPERTY.—As trustee for a covered broker or dealer, SIPC shall allocate customer property and deliver customer name securities in accordance with section 8(c) of the Securities Investor Protection Act of 1970 (15 U.S.C. 78fff-2(c)).

(2) OTHER CLAIMS.—All claims other than those described in paragraph (1) (including any unpaid claim by a customer for the allowed net equity claim of such customer from customer property) shall be paid in accordance with the priorities in section 210(b).

(h) RULEMAKING.—The Commission and the Corporation, after consultation with SIPC, shall jointly issue rules to implement this section.

[Explanation at ¶ 520.]

[¶ 10,206] ACT SEC. 206. MANDATORY TERMS AND CONDITIONS FOR ALL ORDERLY LIQUIDATION ACTIONS.

In taking action under this title, the Corporation shall—

(1) determine that such action is necessary for purposes of the financial stability of the United States, and not for the purpose of preserving the covered financial company;

(2) ensure that the shareholders of a covered financial company do not receive payment until after all other claims and the Fund are fully paid;

(3) ensure that unsecured creditors bear losses in accordance with the priority of claim provisions in section 210;

(4) ensure that management responsible for the failed condition of the covered financial company is removed (if such management has not already been removed at the time at which the Corporation is appointed receiver);

(5) ensure that the members of the board of directors (or body performing similar functions) responsible for the failed condition of the covered financial company are removed, if such members have not already been removed at the time the Corporation is appointed as receiver; and

(6) not take an equity interest in or become a shareholder of any covered financial company or any covered subsidiary.

[Explanation at ¶ 520.]

[¶ 10,207] ACT SEC. 207. DIRECTORS NOT LIABLE FOR ACQUIESCING IN APPOINTMENT OF RECEIVER.

The members of the board of directors (or body performing similar functions) of a covered financial company shall not be liable to the shareholders or creditors thereof for acquiescing in or consenting in good faith to the appointment of the Corporation as receiver for the covered financial company under section 203.

[Explanation at ¶ 510.]

[¶ 10,208] ACT SEC. 208. DISMISSAL AND EXCLUSION OF OTHER ACTIONS.

(a) IN GENERAL.—Effective as of the date of the appointment of the Corporation as receiver for the covered financial company under section 202 or the appointment of SIPC as trustee for a covered broker or dealer under section 205, as applicable, any case or proceeding commenced with respect to the covered financial company under the Bankruptcy Code or the Securities Investor Protection Act of 1970 (15 U.S.C. 78aaa et seq.) shall be dismissed, upon notice to the bankruptcy court (with respect to a case commenced under the Bankruptcy Code), and upon notice to SIPC (with respect to a covered broker or dealer) and no such case or proceeding may be commenced with respect to a covered financial company at any time while the orderly liquidation is pending.

(b) REVESTING OF ASSETS.—Effective as of the date of appointment of the Corporation as receiver, the assets of a covered financial company shall, to the extent they have vested in any entity other than the covered financial company as a result of any case or proceeding commenced with respect to the covered financial company under the Bankruptcy Code, the Securities Investor Protection Act of 1970 (15 U.S.C. 78aaa et seq.), or any similar provision of State liquidation or insolvency law applicable to the covered financial company, revest in the covered financial company.

(c) LIMITATION.—Notwithstanding subsections (a) and (b), any order entered or other relief granted by a bankruptcy court prior to the date of appointment of the Corporation as receiver shall continue with the same validity as if an orderly liquidation had not been commenced.

[Explanation at ¶ 505.]

[¶ 10,209] ACT SEC. 209. RULEMAKING; NON-CONFLICTING LAW.

The Corporation shall, in consultation with the Council, prescribe such rules or regulations as the Corporation considers necessary or appropriate to implement this title, including rules and regulations with respect to the rights, interests, and priorities of creditors, counterparties, security entitlement holders, or other persons with respect to any covered financial company or any assets or other property of or held by such covered financial company, and address the potential for conflicts of interest between or among individual receiverships established under this title or under the Federal Deposit Insurance Act. To the extent possible, the Corporation shall seek to harmonize applicable rules and regulations promulgated under this section with the insolvency laws that would otherwise apply to a covered financial company.

[Explanation at ¶ 505.]

[¶ 10,210] ACT SEC. 210. POWERS AND DUTIES OF THE CORPORATION.

(a) POWERS AND AUTHORITIES.—

(1) GENERAL POWERS.—

(A) SUCCESSOR TO COVERED FINANCIAL COMPANY.—The Corporation shall, upon appointment as receiver for a covered financial company under this title, succeed to—

(i) all rights, titles, powers, and privileges of the covered financial company and its assets, and of any stockholder, member, officer, or director of such company; and

(ii) title to the books, records, and assets of any previous receiver or other legal custodian of such covered financial company.

(B) OPERATION OF THE COVERED FINANCIAL COMPANY DURING THE PERIOD OF ORDERLY LIQUIDATION.—The Corporation, as receiver for a covered financial company, may—

(i) take over the assets of and operate the covered financial company with all of the powers of the members or shareholders, the directors, and the officers of the covered financial company, and conduct all business of the covered financial company;

(ii) collect all obligations and money owed to the covered financial company;

(iii) perform all functions of the covered financial company, in the name of the covered financial company;

(iv) manage the assets and property of the covered financial company, consistent with maximization of the value of the assets in the context of the orderly liquidation; and

(v) provide by contract for assistance in fulfilling any function, activity, action, or duty of the Corporation as receiver.

(C) FUNCTIONS OF COVERED FINANCIAL COMPANY OFFICERS, DIRECTORS, AND SHAREHOLDERS.—The Corporation may provide for the exercise of any function by any member or stockholder, director, or officer of any covered financial company for which the Corporation has been appointed as receiver under this title.

(D) ADDITIONAL POWERS AS RECEIVER.—The Corporation shall, as receiver for a covered financial company, and subject to all legally enforceable and perfected security interests and all legally enforceable security entitlements in respect of assets held by the covered financial company, liquidate, and wind-up the affairs of a covered financial company, including taking steps to realize upon the assets of the covered financial company, in such manner as the Corporation deems appropriate, including through the sale of assets, the transfer of assets to a bridge financial company established under subsection (h), or the exercise of any other rights or privileges granted to the receiver under this section.

(E) ADDITIONAL POWERS WITH RESPECT TO FAILING SUBSIDIARIES OF A COVERED FINANCIAL COMPANY.—

(i) IN GENERAL.—In any case in which a receiver is appointed for a covered financial company under section 202, the Corporation may appoint itself as receiver of any covered subsidiary of the covered financial company that is organized under Federal law or the laws of any State, if the Corporation and the Secretary jointly determine that—

(I) the covered subsidiary is in default or in danger of default;

(II) such action would avoid or mitigate serious adverse effects on the financial stability or economic conditions of the United States; and

(III) such action would facilitate the orderly liquidation of the covered financial company.

(ii) TREATMENT AS COVERED FINANCIAL COMPANY.—If the Corporation is appointed as receiver of a covered subsidiary of a covered financial company under clause (i), the covered subsidiary shall thereafter be considered a covered financial company under this title, and the Corporation shall thereafter have all the powers and rights with respect to that covered subsidiary as it has with respect to a covered financial company under this title.

(F) ORGANIZATION OF BRIDGE COMPANIES.—The Corporation, as receiver for a covered financial company, may organize a bridge financial company under subsection (h).

(G) MERGER; TRANSFER OF ASSETS AND LIABILITIES.—

(i) IN GENERAL.—Subject to clauses (ii) and (iii), the Corporation, as receiver for a covered financial company, may—

(I) merge the covered financial company with another company; or

(II) transfer any asset or liability of the covered financial company (including any assets and liabilities held by the covered financial company for security entitlement holders, any customer property, or any assets and liabilities associated with any trust or custody business) without obtaining any approval, assignment, or consent with respect to such transfer.

(ii) FEDERAL AGENCY APPROVAL; ANTITRUST REVIEW.—With respect to a transaction described in clause (i)(I) that requires approval by a Federal agency—

(I) the transaction may not be consummated before the 5th calendar day after the date of approval by the Federal agency responsible for such approval;

(II) if, in connection with any such approval, a report on competitive factors is required, the Federal agency responsible for such approval shall promptly notify the Attorney General of the United States of the proposed transaction, and the Attorney General shall provide the required report not later than 10 days after the date of the request; and

(III) if notification under section 7A of the Clayton Act is required with respect to such transaction, then the required waiting period shall end on the 15th day after the date on which the Attorney General and the Federal Trade Commission receive such notification, unless the waiting period is terminated earlier under subsection (b)(2) of such section 7A, or is extended pursuant to subsection (e)(2) of such section 7A.

(iii) SETOFF.—Subject to the other provisions of this title, any transferee of assets from a receiver, including a bridge financial company, shall be subject to such claims or rights as would prevail over the rights of such transferee in such assets under applicable noninsolvency law.

(H) PAYMENT OF VALID OBLIGATIONS.—The Corporation, as receiver for a covered financial company, shall, to the extent that funds are available, pay all valid obligations of the covered financial company that are due and payable at the time of the appointment of the Corporation as receiver, in accordance with the prescriptions and limitations of this title.

(I) APPLICABLE NONINSOLVENCY LAW.—Except as may otherwise be provided in this title, the applicable noninsolvency law shall be determined by the noninsolvency choice of law rules otherwise applicable to the claims, rights, titles, persons, or entities at issue.

(J) SUBPOENA AUTHORITY.—

(i) IN GENERAL.—The Corporation, as receiver for a covered financial company, may, for purposes of carrying out any power, authority, or duty with respect to the covered financial company (including determining any claim against the covered financial company and determining and realizing upon any asset of any person in the course of collecting money due the covered financial company), exercise any power established under section 8(n) of the Federal Deposit Insurance Act, as if the Corporation were the appropriate Federal banking agency for the covered financial company, and the covered financial company were an insured depository institution.

(ii) RULE OF CONSTRUCTION.—This subparagraph may not be construed as limiting any rights that the Corporation, in any capacity, might otherwise have to exercise any powers described in clause (i) or under any other provision of law.

(K) INCIDENTAL POWERS.—The Corporation, as receiver for a covered financial company, may exercise all powers and authorities specifically granted to receivers under this title, and such incidental powers as shall be necessary to carry out such powers under this title.

(L) UTILIZATION OF PRIVATE SECTOR.—In carrying out its responsibilities in the management and disposition of assets from the covered financial company, the Corporation, as receiver for a covered financial company, may utilize the services of private persons, including real estate and loan portfolio asset management, property management, auction marketing, legal, and brokerage services, if such services are available in the private sector, and the Corporation determines that utilization of such services is practicable, efficient, and cost effective.

(M) SHAREHOLDERS AND CREDITORS OF COVERED FINANCIAL COMPANY.—Notwithstanding any other provision of law, the Corporation, as receiver for a covered financial company, shall succeed by operation of law to the rights, titles, powers, and privileges described in subparagraph (A), and shall terminate all rights and claims that the stockholders and creditors of the covered financial company may have against the assets of the covered financial company or the Corporation arising out of their status as stockholders or creditors, except for their right to payment, resolution, or other satisfaction of their claims, as permitted under this section. The Corporation shall ensure that shareholders and unsecured creditors bear losses, consistent with the priority of claims provisions under this section.

(N) COORDINATION WITH FOREIGN FINANCIAL AUTHORITIES.—The Corporation, as receiver for a covered financial company, shall coordinate, to the maximum extent possible, with the appropriate foreign financial authorities regarding the orderly liquidation of any covered financial company that has assets or operations in a country other than the United States.

(O) RESTRICTION ON TRANSFERS.—

(i) SELECTION OF ACCOUNTS FOR TRANSFER.—If the Corporation establishes one or more bridge financial companies with respect to a covered broker or dealer, the Corporation shall transfer to one of such bridge financial companies, all customer accounts of the covered broker or dealer, and all associated customer name securities and customer property, unless the Corporation, after consulting with the Commission and SIPC, determines that—

(I) the customer accounts, customer name securities, and customer property are likely to be promptly transferred to another broker or dealer that is registered with the Commission under section 15(b) of the Securities Exchange Act of 1934 (15 U.S.C. 73o(b)) and is a member of SIPC; or

(II) the transfer of the accounts to a bridge financial company would materially interfere with the ability of the Corporation to avoid or mitigate serious adverse effects on financial stability or economic conditions in the United States.

(ii) TRANSFER OF PROPERTY.—SIPC, as trustee for the liquidation of the covered broker or dealer, and the Commission shall provide any and all reasonable assistance necessary to complete such transfers by the Corporation.

(iii) CUSTOMER CONSENT AND COURT APPROVAL NOT REQUIRED.—Neither customer consent nor court approval shall be required to transfer any customer accounts or associated customer name securities or customer property to a bridge financial company in accordance with this section.

(iv) NOTIFICATION OF SIPC AND SHARING OF INFORMATION.—The Corporation shall identify to SIPC the customer accounts and associated customer name securities and customer property transferred to the bridge financial company. The Corporation and SIPC shall cooperate in the sharing of any information necessary for each entity to discharge its obligations under this title and under the Securities Investor Protection Act of 1970 (15 U.S.C. 78aaa et seq.) including by providing access to the books and records of the covered financial company and any bridge financial company established in accordance with this title.

(2) DETERMINATION OF CLAIMS.—

(A) IN GENERAL.—The Corporation, as receiver for a covered financial company, shall report on claims, as set forth in section 203(c)(3). Subject to paragraph (4) of this subsection, the Corporation, as receiver for a covered financial company, shall determine claims in accordance with the requirements of this subsection and regulations prescribed under section 209.

(B) NOTICE REQUIREMENTS.—The Corporation, as receiver for a covered financial company, in any case involving the liquidation or winding up of the affairs of a covered financial company, shall—

(i) promptly publish a notice to the creditors of the covered financial company to present their claims, together with proof, to the receiver by a date specified in the notice, which shall be not earlier than 90 days after the date of publication of such notice; and

(ii) republish such notice 1 month and 2 months, respectively, after the date of publication under clause (i).

(C) MAILING REQUIRED.—The Corporation as receiver shall mail a notice similar to the notice published under clause (i) or (ii) of subparagraph (B), at the time of such publication, to any creditor shown on the books and records of the covered financial company—

(i) at the last address of the creditor appearing in such books;

(ii) in any claim filed by the claimant; or

(iii) upon discovery of the name and address of a claimant not appearing on the books and records of the covered financial company, not later than 30 days after the date of the discovery of such name and address.

(3) PROCEDURES FOR RESOLUTION OF CLAIMS.—

(A) DECISION PERIOD.—

(i) IN GENERAL.—Prior to the 180th day after the date on which a claim against a covered financial company is filed with the Corporation as receiver, or such later date as may be agreed as provided in clause (ii), the Corporation shall notify the claimant whether it allows or disallows the claim, in accordance with subparagraphs (B), (C), and (D).

(ii) EXTENSION OF TIME.—By written agreement executed not later than 180 days after the date on which a claim against a covered financial company is filed with the Corporation, the period described in clause (i) may be extended by written agreement between the claimant and the Corporation. Failure to notify the claimant of any disallowance within the time period set forth in clause (i), as it may be extended by agreement under this clause, shall be deemed to be a disallowance of such claim, and the claimant may file or continue an action in court, as provided in paragraph (4).

(iii) MAILING OF NOTICE SUFFICIENT.—The requirements of clause (i) shall be deemed to be satisfied if the notice of any decision with respect to any claim is mailed to the last address of the claimant which appears—

(I) on the books, records, or both of the covered financial company;

(II) in the claim filed by the claimant; or

(III) in documents submitted in proof of the claim.

(iv) CONTENTS OF NOTICE OF DISALLOWANCE.—If the Corporation as receiver disallows any claim filed under clause (i), the notice to the claimant shall contain—

(I) a statement of each reason for the disallowance; and

(II) the procedures required to file or continue an action in court, as provided in paragraph (4).

(B) ALLOWANCE OF PROVEN CLAIM.—The receiver shall allow any claim received by the receiver on or before the date specified in the notice under paragraph (2)(B)(i), which is proved to the satisfaction of the receiver.

(C) DISALLOWANCE OF CLAIMS FILED AFTER END OF FILING PERIOD.—

(i) IN GENERAL.—Except as provided in clause (ii), claims filed after the date specified in the notice published under paragraph (2)(B)(i) shall be disallowed, and such disallowance shall be final.

(ii) CERTAIN EXCEPTIONS.—Clause (i) shall not apply with respect to any claim filed by a claimant after the date specified in the notice published under paragraph (2)(B)(i), and such claim may be considered by the receiver under subparagraph (B), if—

(I) the claimant did not receive notice of the appointment of the receiver in time to file such claim before such date; and

(II) such claim is filed in time to permit payment of such claim.

(D) AUTHORITY TO DISALLOW CLAIMS.—

(i) IN GENERAL.—The Corporation may disallow any portion of any claim by a creditor or claim of a security, preference, setoff, or priority which is not proved to the satisfaction of the Corporation.

(ii) PAYMENTS TO UNDERSECURED CREDITORS.—In the case of a claim against a covered financial company that is secured by any property or other asset of such covered financial company, the receiver—

(I) may treat the portion of such claim which exceeds an amount equal to the fair market value of such property or other asset as an unsecured claim; and

(II) may not make any payment with respect to such unsecured portion of the claim, other than in connection with the disposition of all claims of unsecured creditors of the covered financial company.

(iii) EXCEPTIONS.—No provision of this paragraph shall apply with respect to—

(I) any extension of credit from any Federal reserve bank, or the Corporation, to any covered financial company; or

(II) subject to clause (ii), any legally enforceable and perfected security interest in the assets of the covered financial company securing any such extension of credit.

(E) LEGAL EFFECT OF FILING.—

(i) STATUTE OF LIMITATIONS TOLLED.—For purposes of any applicable statute of limitations, the filing of a claim with the receiver shall constitute a commencement of an action.

(ii) NO PREJUDICE TO OTHER ACTIONS.—Subject to paragraph (8), the filing of a claim with the receiver shall not prejudice any right of the claimant to continue any action which was filed before the date of appointment of the receiver for the covered financial company.

(4) JUDICIAL DETERMINATION OF CLAIMS.—

(A) IN GENERAL.—Subject to subparagraph (B), a claimant may file suit on a claim (or continue an action commenced before the date of appointment of the Corporation as receiver) in the district or territorial court of the United States for the district within which the principal place of business of the covered financial company is located (and such court shall have jurisdiction to hear such claim).

(B) TIMING.—A claim under subparagraph (A) may be filed before the end of the 60-day period beginning on the earlier of—

(i) the end of the period described in paragraph (3)(A)(i) (or, if extended by agreement of the Corporation and the claimant, the period described in paragraph (3)(A)(ii)) with respect to any claim against a covered financial company for which the Corporation is receiver; or

(ii) the date of any notice of disallowance of such claim pursuant to paragraph (3)(A)(i).

(C) STATUTE OF LIMITATIONS.—If any claimant fails to file suit on such claim (or to continue an action on such claim commenced before the date of appointment of the Corporation as receiver) prior to the end of the 60-day period described in subparagraph (B), the claim shall be deemed to be disallowed (other than any portion of such claim which was allowed by the receiver) as of the end of such period, such disallowance shall be final, and the claimant shall have no further rights or remedies with respect to such claim.

(5) EXPEDITED DETERMINATION OF CLAIMS.—

(A) PROCEDURE REQUIRED.—The Corporation shall establish a procedure for expedited relief outside of the claims process established under paragraph (3), for any claimant that alleges—

(i) having a legally valid and enforceable or perfected security interest in property of a covered financial company or control of any legally valid and enforceable security entitlement in respect of any asset held by the covered financial company for which the Corporation has been appointed receiver; and

(ii) that irreparable injury will occur if the claims procedure established under paragraph (3) is followed.

(B) DETERMINATION PERIOD.—Prior to the end of the 90-day period beginning on the date on which a claim is filed in accordance with the procedures established pursuant to subparagraph (A), the Corporation shall—

(i) determine—

(I) whether to allow or disallow such claim, or any portion thereof; or

(II) whether such claim should be determined pursuant to the procedures established pursuant to paragraph (3);

(ii) notify the claimant of the determination; and

(iii) if the claim is disallowed, provide a statement of each reason for the disallowance and the procedure for obtaining a judicial determination.

(C) PERIOD FOR FILING OR RENEWING SUIT.—Any claimant who files a request for expedited relief shall be permitted to file suit (or continue a suit filed before the date of appointment of the Corporation as receiver seeking a determination of the rights of the claimant with respect to such security interest (or such security entitlement) after the earlier of—

(i) the end of the 90-day period beginning on the date of the filing of a request for expedited relief; or

(ii) the date on which the Corporation denies the claim or a portion thereof.

(D) STATUTE OF LIMITATIONS.—If an action described in subparagraph (C) is not filed, or the motion to renew a previously filed suit is not made, before the end of the 30-day period beginning on the date on which such action or motion may be filed in accordance with subparagraph (C), the claim shall be deemed to be disallowed as of the end of such period (other than any portion of such claim which was allowed by the receiver), such disallowance shall be final, and the claimant shall have no further rights or remedies with respect to such claim.

(E) LEGAL EFFECT OF FILING.—

(i) STATUTE OF LIMITATIONS TOLLED.—For purposes of any applicable statute of limitations, the filing of a claim with the receiver shall constitute a commencement of an action.

(ii) NO PREJUDICE TO OTHER ACTIONS.—Subject to paragraph (8), the filing of a claim with the receiver shall not prejudice any right of the claimant to continue any action which was filed before the appointment of the Corporation as receiver for the covered financial company.

(6) AGREEMENTS AGAINST INTEREST OF THE RECEIVER.—No agreement that tends to diminish or defeat the interest of the Corporation as receiver in any asset acquired by the receiver under this section shall be valid against the receiver, unless such agreement—

(A) is in writing;

(B) was executed by an authorized officer or representative of the covered financial company, or confirmed in the ordinary course of business by the covered financial company; and

(C) has been, since the time of its execution, an official record of the company or the party claiming under the agreement provides documentation, acceptable to the receiver, of such agreement and its authorized execution or confirmation by the covered financial company.

(7) PAYMENT OF CLAIMS.—

(A) IN GENERAL.—Subject to subparagraph (B), the Corporation as receiver may, in its discretion and to the extent that funds are available, pay creditor claims, in such manner and amounts as are authorized under this section, which are—

(i) allowed by the receiver;

(ii) approved by the receiver pursuant to a final determination pursuant to paragraph (3) or (5), as applicable; or

(iii) determined by the final judgment of a court of competent jurisdiction.

(B) LIMITATION.—A creditor shall, in no event, receive less than the amount that the creditor is entitled to receive under paragraphs (2) and (3) of subsection (d), as applicable.

(C) PAYMENT OF DIVIDENDS ON CLAIMS.—The Corporation as receiver may, in its sole discretion, and to the extent otherwise permitted by this section, pay dividends on proven claims at any time, and no liability shall attach to the Corporation as receiver, by reason of any such payment or for failure to pay dividends to a claimant whose claim is not proved at the time of any such payment.

(D) RULEMAKING BY THE CORPORATION.—The Corporation may prescribe such rules, including definitions of terms, as the Corporation deems appropriate to establish an interest rate for or to make payments of post-insolvency interest to creditors holding proven claims against the receivership estate of a covered financial company, except that no such interest shall be paid until the Corporation as receiver has satisfied the principal amount of all creditor claims.

(8) SUSPENSION OF LEGAL ACTIONS.—

(A) IN GENERAL.—After the appointment of the Corporation as receiver for a covered financial company, the Corporation may request a stay in any judicial action or proceeding in which such covered financial company is or becomes a party, for a period of not to exceed 90 days.

(B) GRANT OF STAY BY ALL COURTS REQUIRED.—Upon receipt of a request by the Corporation pursuant to subparagraph (A), the court shall grant such stay as to all parties.

(9) ADDITIONAL RIGHTS AND DUTIES.—

(A) PRIOR FINAL ADJUDICATION.—The Corporation shall abide by any final, non-appealable judgment of any court of competent jurisdiction that was rendered before the appointment of the Corporation as receiver.

(B) RIGHTS AND REMEDIES OF RECEIVER.—In the event of any appealable judgment, the Corporation as receiver shall—

(i) have all the rights and remedies available to the covered financial company (before the date of appointment of the Corporation as receiver under section 202) and the Corporation, including removal to Federal court and all appellate rights; and

(ii) not be required to post any bond in order to pursue such remedies.

(C) NO ATTACHMENT OR EXECUTION.—No attachment or execution may be issued by any court upon assets in the possession of the Corporation as receiver for a covered financial company.

(D) LIMITATION ON JUDICIAL REVIEW.—Except as otherwise provided in this title, no court shall have jurisdiction over—

(i) any claim or action for payment from, or any action seeking a determination of rights with respect to, the assets of any covered financial company for which the Corporation has been appointed receiver, including any assets which the Corporation may acquire from itself as such receiver; or

(ii) any claim relating to any act or omission of such covered financial company or the Corporation as receiver.

(E) DISPOSITION OF ASSETS.—In exercising any right, power, privilege, or authority as receiver in connection with any covered financial company for which the Corporation is acting as receiver under this section, the Corporation shall, to the greatest extent practicable, conduct its operations in a manner that—

(i) maximizes the net present value return from the sale or disposition of such assets;

(ii) minimizes the amount of any loss realized in the resolution of cases;

(iii) mitigates the potential for serious adverse effects to the financial system;

(iv) ensures timely and adequate competition and fair and consistent treatment of offerors; and

(v) prohibits discrimination on the basis of race, sex, or ethnic group in the solicitation and consideration of offers.

(10) STATUTE OF LIMITATIONS FOR ACTIONS BROUGHT BY RECEIVER.—

(A) IN GENERAL.—Notwithstanding any provision of any contract, the applicable statute of limitations with regard to any action brought by the Corporation as receiver for a covered financial company shall be—

(i) in the case of any contract claim, the longer of—

(I) the 6-year period beginning on the date on which the claim accrues; or

(II) the period applicable under State law; and

(ii) in the case of any tort claim, the longer of—

(I) the 3-year period beginning on the date on which the claim accrues; or

(II) the period applicable under State law.

(B) DATE ON WHICH A CLAIM ACCRUES.—For purposes of subparagraph (A), the date on which the statute of limitations begins to run on any claim described in subparagraph (A) shall be the later of—

(i) the date of the appointment of the Corporation as receiver under this title; or

(ii) the date on which the cause of action accrues.

(C) REVIVAL OF EXPIRED STATE CAUSES OF ACTION.—

(i) IN GENERAL.—In the case of any tort claim described in clause (ii) for which the applicable statute of limitations under State law has expired not more than 5 years before the date of appointment of the Corporation as receiver for a covered financial company, the Corporation may bring an action as receiver on such claim without regard to the expiration of the statute of limitations.

(ii) CLAIMS DESCRIBED.—A tort claim referred to in clause (i) is a claim arising from fraud, intentional misconduct resulting in unjust enrichment, or intentional misconduct resulting in substantial loss to the covered financial company.

(11) AVOIDABLE TRANSFERS.—

(A) FRAUDULENT TRANSFERS.—The Corporation, as receiver for any covered financial company, may avoid a transfer of any interest of the covered financial company in property, or any obligation incurred by the covered financial company, that was made or incurred at or within 2 years before the date on which the Corporation was appointed receiver, if—

(i) the covered financial company voluntarily or involuntarily—

(I) made such transfer or incurred such obligation with actual intent to hinder, delay, or defraud any entity to which the covered financial company was or became, on or after the date on which such transfer was made or such obligation was incurred, indebted; or

(II) received less than a reasonably equivalent value in exchange for such transferor obligation; and

(ii) the covered financial company voluntarily or involuntarily—

(I) was insolvent on the date that such transfer was made or such obligation was incurred, or became insolvent as a result of such transfer or obligation;

(II) was engaged in business or a transaction, or was about to engage in business or a transaction, for which any property remaining with the covered financial company was an unreasonably small capital;

(III) intended to incur, or believed that the covered financial company would incur, debts that would be beyond the ability of the covered financial company to pay as such debts matured; or

(IV) made such transfer to or for the benefit of an insider, or incurred such obligation to or for the benefit of an insider, under an employment contract and not in the ordinary course of business.

(B) PREFERENTIAL TRANSFERS.—The Corporation as receiver for any covered financial company may avoid a transfer of an interest of the covered financial company in property—

(i) to or for the benefit of a creditor;

(ii) for or on account of an antecedent debt that was owed by the covered financial company before the transfer was made;

(iii) that was made while the covered financial company was insolvent;

(iv) that was made—

(I) 90 days or less before the date on which the Corporation was appointed receiver; or

(II) more than 90 days, but less than 1 year before the date on which the Corporation was appointed receiver, if such creditor at the time of the transfer was an insider; and

(v) that enables the creditor to receive more than the creditor would receive if—

(I) the covered financial company had been liquidated under chapter 7 of the Bankruptcy Code;

(II) the transfer had not been made; and

(III) the creditor received payment of such debt to the extent provided by the provisions of chapter 7 of the Bankruptcy Code.

(C) POST-RECEIVERSHIP TRANSACTIONS.—The Corporation as receiver for any covered financial company may avoid a transfer of property of the receivership that occurred after the Corporation was appointed receiver that was not authorized under this title by the Corporation as receiver.

(D) RIGHT OF RECOVERY.—To the extent that a transfer is avoided under subparagraph (A), (B), or (C), the Corporation may recover, for the benefit of the covered financial company, the property transferred or, if a court so orders, the value of such property (at the time of such transfer) from—

(i) the initial transferee of such transfer or the person for whose benefit such transfer was made; or

(ii) any immediate or mediate transferee of any such initial transferee.

(E) RIGHTS OF TRANSFEREE OR OBLIGEE.—The Corporation may not recover under subparagraph (D)(ii) from—

(i) any transferee that takes for value, including in satisfaction of or to secure a present or antecedent debt, in good faith, and without knowledge of the voidability of the transfer avoided; or

(ii) any immediate or mediate good faith transferee of such transferee.

(F) DEFENSES.—Subject to the other provisions of this title—

(i) a transferee or obligee from which the Corporation seeks to recover a transfer or to avoid an obligation under subparagraph (A), (B), (C), or (D) shall have the same defenses available to a transferee or obligee from which a trustee seeks to recover a transfer or avoid an obligation under sections 547, 548, and 549 of the Bankruptcy Code; and

(ii) the authority of the Corporation to recover a transfer or avoid an obligation shall be subject to subsections (b) and (c) of section 546, section 547(c), and section 548(c) of the Bankruptcy Code.

(G) RIGHTS UNDER THIS SECTION.—The rights of the Corporation as receiver under this section shall be superior to any rights of a trustee or any other party (other than a Federal agency) under the Bankruptcy Code.

(H) RULES OF CONSTRUCTION; DEFINITIONS.—For purposes of—

(i) subparagraphs (A) and (B)—

(I) the term "insider" has the same meaning as in section 101(31) of the Bankruptcy Code;

(II) a transfer is made when such transfer is so perfected that a bona fide purchaser from the covered financial company against whom applicable law permits such transfer to be perfected cannot acquire an interest in the property transferred that is superior to the interest in such property of the transferee, but if such transfer is not so perfected before the date on which the Corporation is appointed as receiver for the covered financial company, such transfer is made immediately before the date of such appointment; and

(III) the term "value" means property, or satisfaction or securing of a present or antecedent debt of the covered financial company, but does not include an unperformed promise to furnish support to the covered financial company; and

(ii) subparagraph (B)—

(I) the covered financial company is presumed to have been insolvent on and during the 90-day period immediately preceding the date of appointment of the Corporation as receiver; and

(II) the term "insolvent" has the same meaning as in section 101(32) of the Bankruptcy Code.

(12) SETOFF.—

(A) GENERALLY.—Except as otherwise provided in this title, any right of a creditor to offset a mutual debt owed by the creditor to any covered financial company that arose before the Corporation was appointed as receiver for the covered financial company against a claim of such creditor may be asserted if enforceable under applicable noninsolvency law, except to the extent that—

(i) the claim of the creditor against the covered financial company is disallowed;

(ii) the claim was transferred, by an entity other than the covered financial company, to the creditor—

(I) after the Corporation was appointed as receiver of the covered financial company; or

(II)(aa) after the 90-day period preceding the date on which the Corporation was appointed as receiver for the covered financial company; and

(bb) while the covered financial company was insolvent (except for a setoff in connection with a qualified financial contract); or

(iii) the debt owed to the covered financial company was incurred by the covered financial company—

(I) after the 90-day period preceding the date on which the Corporation was appointed as receiver for the covered financial company;

(II) while the covered financial company was insolvent; and

(III) for the purpose of obtaining a right of setoff against the covered financial company (except for a setoff in connection with a qualified financial contract).

(B) INSUFFICIENCY.—

(i) IN GENERAL.—Except with respect to a setoff in connection with a qualified financial contract, if a creditor offsets a mutual debt owed to the covered financial company against a claim of the covered financial company on or within the 90-day period preceding the date on which the Corporation is appointed as receiver for the covered financial company, the Corporation may recover from the creditor the amount so offset, to the extent that any insufficiency on the date of such setoff is less than the insufficiency on the later of—

(I) the date that is 90 days before the date on which the Corporation is appointed as receiver for the covered financial company; or

(II) the first day on which there is an insufficiency during the 90-day period preceding the date on which the Corporation is appointed as receiver for the covered financial company.

(ii) DEFINITION OF INSUFFICIENCY.—In this subparagraph, the term "insufficiency" means the amount, if any, by which a claim against the covered financial company exceeds a mutual debt owed to the covered financial company by the holder of such claim.

(C) INSOLVENCY.—The term "insolvent" has the same meaning as in section 101(32) of the Bankruptcy Code.

(D) PRESUMPTION OF INSOLVENCY.—For purposes of this paragraph, the covered financial company is presumed to have been insolvent on and during the 90-day period preceding the date of appointment of the Corporation as receiver.

(E) LIMITATION.—Nothing in this paragraph (12) shall be the basis for any right of setoff where no such right exists under applicable noninsolvency law.

(F) PRIORITY CLAIM.—Except as otherwise provided in this title, the Corporation as receiver for the covered financial company may sell or transfer any assets free and clear of the setoff rights of any party, except that such party shall be entitled to a claim, subordinate to the claims payable under subparagraphs (A), (B), (C), and (D) of subsection (b)(1), but senior to all other unsecured liabilities defined in subsection (b)(1)(E), in an amount equal to the value of such setoff rights.

(13) ATTACHMENT OF ASSETS AND OTHER INJUNCTIVE RELIEF.—Subject to paragraph (14), any court of competent jurisdiction may, at the request of the Corporation as receiver for a covered financial company, issue an order in accordance with Rule 65 of the Federal Rules of Civil Procedure, including an order placing the assets of any person designated by the Corporation under the control of the court and appointing a trustee to hold such assets.

(14) STANDARDS.—

(A) SHOWING.—Rule 65 of the Federal Rules of Civil Procedure shall apply with respect to any proceeding under paragraph (13), without regard to the requirement that the applicant show that the injury, loss, or damage is irreparable and immediate.

(B) STATE PROCEEDING.—If, in the case of any proceeding in a State court, the court determines that rules of civil procedure available under the laws of the State provide substantially similar protections of the right of the parties to due process as provided under Rule 65 (as modified with respect to such proceeding by subparagraph (A)), the relief sought by the Corporation pursuant to paragraph (14) may be requested under the laws of such State.

(15) TREATMENT OF CLAIMS ARISING FROM BREACH OF CONTRACTS EXECUTED BY THE CORPORATION AS RECEIVER.—Notwithstanding any other provision of this title, any final and non-appealable judgment for monetary damages entered against the Corporation as receiver for a covered financial company for the breach of an agreement executed or approved by the Corporation after the date of its appointment shall be paid as an administrative expense of the receiver. Nothing in this paragraph shall be construed to limit the power of a receiver to exercise any rights under contract or law, including to terminate, breach, cancel, or otherwise discontinue such agreement.

(16) ACCOUNTING AND RECORDKEEPING REQUIREMENTS.—

(A) IN GENERAL.—The Corporation as receiver for a covered financial company shall, consistent with the accounting and reporting practices and procedures established by the Corporation, maintain a full accounting of each receivership or other disposition of any covered financial company.

(B) ANNUAL ACCOUNTING OR REPORT.—With respect to each receivership to which the Corporation is appointed, the Corporation shall make an annual accounting or report, as appropriate, available to the Secretary and the Comptroller General of the United States.

(C) AVAILABILITY OF REPORTS.—Any report prepared pursuant to subparagraph (B) and section 203(c)(3) shall be made available to the public by the Corporation.

(D) RECORDKEEPING REQUIREMENT.—

(i) IN GENERAL.—The Corporation shall prescribe such regulations and establish such retention schedules as are necessary to maintain the documents and records of the Corporation generated in exercising the authorities of this title and the records of a covered financial company for which the Corporation is appointed receiver, with due regard for—

(I) the avoidance of duplicative record retention; and

(II) the expected evidentiary needs of the Corporation as receiver for a covered financial company and the public regarding the records of covered financial companies.

(ii) RETENTION OF RECORDS.—Unless otherwise required by applicable Federal law or court order, the Corporation may not, at any time, destroy any records that are subject to clause (i).

(iii) RECORDS DEFINED.—As used in this subparagraph, the terms "records" and "records of a covered financial company" mean any document, book, paper, map, photograph, microfiche, microfilm, computer or electronically-created record generated or maintained by the covered financial company in the course of and necessary to its transaction of business.

(b) PRIORITY OF EXPENSES AND UNSECURED CLAIMS.—

(1) IN GENERAL.—Unsecured claims against a covered financial company, or the Corporation as receiver for such covered financial company under this section, that are proven to the satisfaction of the receiver shall have priority in the following order:

(A) Administrative expenses of the receiver.

(B) Any amounts owed to the United States, unless the United States agrees or consents otherwise.

(C) Wages, salaries, or commissions, including vacation, severance, and sick leave pay earned by an individual (other than an individual described in subparagraph (G)), but only to the extent of $11,725 for each individual (as indexed for inflation, by regulation of the Corporation) earned not later than 180 days before the date of appointment of the Corporation as receiver.

(D) Contributions owed to employee benefit plans arising from services rendered not later than 180 days before the date of appointment of the Corporation as receiver, to the extent of the number of employees covered by each such plan, multiplied by $11,725 (as indexed for inflation, by regulation of the Corporation), less the aggregate amount paid to such employees under subparagraph (C), plus the aggregate amount paid by the receivership on behalf of such employees to any other employee benefit plan.

(E) Any other general or senior liability of the covered financial company (which is not a liability described under subparagraph (F), (G), or (H)).

(F) Any obligation subordinated to general creditors (which is not an obligation described under subparagraph (G) or (H)).

(G) Any wages, salaries, or commissions, including vacation, severance, and sick leave pay earned, owed to senior executives and directors of the covered financial company.

(H) Any obligation to shareholders, members, general partners, limited partners, or other persons, with interests in the equity of the covered financial company arising as a result of their status as shareholders, members, general partners, limited partners, or other persons with interests in the equity of the covered financial company.

(2) POST-RECEIVERSHIP FINANCING PRIORITY.—In the event that the Corporation, as receiver for a covered financial company, is unable to obtain unsecured credit for the covered financial company from commercial sources, the Corporation as receiver may obtain credit or incur debt on the part of the covered financial company, which shall have priority over any or all administrative expenses of the receiver under paragraph (1)(A).

(3) CLAIMS OF THE UNITED STATES.—Unsecured claims of the United States shall, at a minimum, have a higher priority than liabilities of the covered financial company that count as regulatory capital.

(4) CREDITORS SIMILARLY SITUATED.—All claimants of a covered financial company that are similarly situated under paragraph (1) shall be treated in a similar manner, except that the Corporation may take any action (including making payments, subject to subsection (o)(1)(D)(i)) that does not comply with this subsection, if—

(A) the Corporation determines that such action is necessary—

(i) to maximize the value of the assets of the covered financial company;

(ii) to initiate and continue operations essential to implementation of the receivership or any bridge financial company;

(iii) to maximize the present value return from the sale or other disposition of the assets of the covered financial company; or

(iv) to minimize the amount of any loss realized upon the sale or other disposition of the assets of the covered financial company; and

(B) all claimants that are similarly situated under paragraph (1) receive not less than the amount provided in paragraphs (2) and (3) of subsection (d).

(5) SECURED CLAIMS UNAFFECTED.—This section shall not affect secured claims or security entitlements in respect of assets or property held by the covered financial company, except to the extent that the security is insufficient to satisfy the claim, and then only with regard to the difference between the claim and the amount realized from the security.

(6) PRIORITY OF EXPENSES AND UNSECURED CLAIMS IN THE ORDERLY LIQUIDATION OF SIPC MEMBER.— Where the Corporation is appointed as receiver for a covered broker or dealer, unsecured claims against such covered broker or dealer, or the Corporation as receiver for such covered broker or

dealer under this section, that are proven to the satisfaction of the receiver under section 205(e), shall have the priority prescribed in paragraph (1), except that—

(A) SIPC shall be entitled to recover administrative expenses incurred in performing its responsibilities under section 205 on an equal basis with the Corporation, in accordance with paragraph (1)(A);

(B) the Corporation shall be entitled to recover any amounts paid to customers or to SIPC pursuant to section 205(f), in accordance with paragraph (1)(B);

(C) SIPC shall be entitled to recover any amounts paid out of the SIPC Fund to meet its obligations under section 205 and under the Securities Investor Protection Act of 1970 (15 U.S.C. 78aaa et seq.), which claim shall be subordinate to the claims payable under subparagraphs (A) and (B) of paragraph (1), but senior to all other claims; and

(D) the Corporation may, after paying any proven claims to customers under section 205 and the Securities Investor Protection Act of 1970 (15 U.S.C. 78aaa et seq.), and as provided above, pay dividends on other proven claims, in its discretion, and to the extent that funds are available, in accordance with the priorities set forth in paragraph (1).

(c) PROVISIONS RELATING TO CONTRACTS ENTERED INTO BEFORE APPOINTMENT OF RECEIVER.—

(1) AUTHORITY TO REPUDIATE CONTRACTS.—In addition to any other rights that a receiver may have, the Corporation as receiver for any covered financial company may disaffirm or repudiate any contract or lease—

(A) to which the covered financial company is a party;

(B) the performance of which the Corporation as receiver, in the discretion of the Corporation, determines to be burdensome; and

(C) the disaffirmance or repudiation of which the Corporation as receiver determines, in the discretion of the Corporation, will promote the orderly administration of the affairs of the covered financial company.

(2) TIMING OF REPUDIATION.—The Corporation, as receiver for any covered financial company, shall determine whether or not to exercise the rights of repudiation under this section within a reasonable period of time.

(3) CLAIMS FOR DAMAGES FOR REPUDIATION.—

(A) IN GENERAL.—Except as provided in paragraphs (4), (5), and (6) and in subparagraphs (C), (D), and (E) of this paragraph, the liability of the Corporation as receiver for a covered financial company for the disaffirmance or repudiation of any contract pursuant to paragraph (1) shall be—

(i) limited to actual direct compensatory damages; and

(ii) determined as of—

(I) the date of the appointment of the Corporation as receiver; or

(II) in the case of any contract or agreement referred to in paragraph (8), the date of the disaffirmance or repudiation of such contract or agreement.

(B) NO LIABILITY FOR OTHER DAMAGES.—For purposes of subparagraph (A), the term "actual direct compensatory damages" does not include—

(i) punitive or exemplary damages;

(ii) damages for lost profits or opportunity; or

(iii) damages for pain and suffering.

(C) MEASURE OF DAMAGES FOR REPUDIATION OF QUALIFIED FINANCIAL CONTRACTS.—In the case of any qualified financial contract or agreement to which paragraph (8) applies, compensatory damages shall be—

(i) deemed to include normal and reasonable costs of cover or other reasonable measures of damages utilized in the industries for such contract and agreement claims; and

(ii) paid in accordance with this paragraph and subsection (d), except as otherwise specifically provided in this subsection.

(D) MEASURE OF DAMAGES FOR REPUDIATION OR DISAFFIRMANCE OF DEBT OBLIGATION.—In the case of any debt for borrowed money or evidenced by a security, actual direct compensatory damages shall be no less than the amount lent plus accrued interest plus any accreted original issue discount as of the date the Corporation was appointed receiver of the covered financial company and, to the extent that an allowed secured claim is secured by property the value of which is greater than the amount of such claim and any accrued interest through the date of repudiation or disaffirmance, such accrued interest pursuant to paragraph (1).

(E) MEASURE OF DAMAGES FOR REPUDIATION OR DISAFFIRMANCE OF CONTINGENT OBLIGATION.— In the case of any contingent obligation of a covered financial company consisting of any obligation under a guarantee, letter of credit, loan commitment, or similar credit obligation, the Corporation may, by rule or regulation, prescribe that actual direct compensatory damages shall be no less than the estimated value of the claim as of the date the Corporation was appointed receiver of the covered financial company, as such value is measured based on the likelihood that such contingent claim would become fixed and the probable magnitude thereof.

(4) LEASES UNDER WHICH THE COVERED FINANCIAL COMPANY IS THE LESSEE.—

(A) IN GENERAL.—If the Corporation as receiver disaffirms or repudiates a lease under which the covered financial company is the lessee, the receiver shall not be liable for any damages (other than damages determined pursuant to subparagraph (B)) for the disaffirmance or repudiation of such lease.

(B) PAYMENTS OF RENT.—Notwithstanding subparagraph (A), the lessor under a lease to which subparagraph (A) would otherwise apply shall—

(i) be entitled to the contractual rent accruing before the later of the date on which—

(I) the notice of disaffirmance or repudiation is mailed; or

(II) the disaffirmance or repudiation becomes effective, unless the lessor is in default or breach of the terms of the lease;

(ii) have no claim for damages under any acceleration clause or other penalty provision in the lease; and

(iii) have a claim for any unpaid rent, subject to all appropriate offsets and defenses, due as of the date of the appointment which shall be paid in accordance with this paragraph and subsection (d).

(5) LEASES UNDER WHICH THE COVERED FINANCIAL COMPANY IS THE LESSOR.—

(A) IN GENERAL.—If the Corporation as receiver for a covered financial company repudiates an unexpired written lease of real property of the covered financial company under which the covered financial company is the lessor and the lessee is not, as of the date of such repudiation, in default, the lessee under such lease may either—

(i) treat the lease as terminated by such repudiation; or

(ii) remain in possession of the leasehold interest for the balance of the term of the lease, unless the lessee defaults under the terms of the lease after the date of such repudiation.

(B) PROVISIONS APPLICABLE TO LESSEE REMAINING IN POSSESSION.—If any lessee under a lease described in subparagraph (A) remains in possession of a leasehold interest pursuant to clause (ii) of subparagraph (A)—

(i) the lessee—

(I) shall continue to pay the contractual rent pursuant to the terms of the lease after the date of the repudiation of such lease; and

(II) may offset against any rent payment which accrues after the date of the repudiation of the lease, any damages which accrue after such date due to the nonperformance of any obligation of the covered financial company under the lease after such date; and

(ii) the Corporation as receiver shall not be liable to the lessee for any damages arising after such date as a result of the repudiation, other than the amount of any offset allowed under clause (i)(II).

(6) CONTRACTS FOR THE SALE OF REAL PROPERTY.—

(A) IN GENERAL.—If the receiver repudiates any contract (which meets the requirements of subsection (a)(6)) for the sale of real property, and the purchaser of such real property under such contract is in possession and is not, as of the date of such repudiation, in default, such purchaser may either—

(i) treat the contract as terminated by such repudiation; or

(ii) remain in possession of such real property.

(B) PROVISIONS APPLICABLE TO PURCHASER REMAINING IN POSSESSION.—If any purchaser of real property under any contract described in subparagraph (A) remains in possession of such property pursuant to clause (ii) of subparagraph (A)—

(i) the purchaser—

(I) shall continue to make all payments due under the contract after the date of the repudiation of the contract; and

(II) may offset against any such payments any damages which accrue after such date due to the nonperformance (after such date) of any obligation of the covered financial company under the contract; and

(ii) the Corporation as receiver shall—

(I) not be liable to the purchaser for any damages arising after such date as a result of the repudiation, other than the amount of any offset allowed under clause (i)(II);

(II) deliver title to the purchaser in accordance with the provisions of the contract; and

(III) have no obligation under the contract other than the performance required under subclause (II).

(C) ASSIGNMENT AND SALE ALLOWED.—

(i) IN GENERAL.—No provision of this paragraph shall be construed as limiting the right of the Corporation as receiver to assign the contract described in subparagraph (A) and sell the property, subject to the contract and the provisions of this paragraph.

(ii) NO LIABILITY AFTER ASSIGNMENT AND SALE.—If an assignment and sale described in clause (i) is consummated, the Corporation as receiver shall have no further liability under the contract described in subparagraph (A) or with respect to the real property which was the subject of such contract.

(7) PROVISIONS APPLICABLE TO SERVICE CONTRACTS.—

(A) SERVICES PERFORMED BEFORE APPOINTMENT.—In the case of any contract for services between any person and any covered financial company for which the Corporation has been appointed receiver, any claim of such person for services performed before the date of appointment shall be—

(i) a claim to be paid in accordance with subsections (a), (b), and (d); and

(ii) deemed to have arisen as of the date on which the receiver was appointed.

(B) SERVICES PERFORMED AFTER APPOINTMENT AND PRIOR TO REPUDIATION.—If, in the case of any contract for services described in subparagraph (A), the Corporation as receiver accepts performance by the other person before making any determination to exercise the right of repudiation of such contract under this section—

(i) the other party shall be paid under the terms of the contract for the services performed; and

(ii) the amount of such payment shall be treated as an administrative expense of the receivership.

(C) ACCEPTANCE OF PERFORMANCE NO BAR TO SUBSEQUENT REPUDIATION.—The acceptance by the Corporation as receiver for services referred to in subparagraph (B) in connection with a contract described in subparagraph (B) shall not affect the right of the Corporation as receiver to repudiate such contract under this section at any time after such performance.

(8) CERTAIN QUALIFIED FINANCIAL CONTRACTS.—

(A) RIGHTS OF PARTIES TO CONTRACTS.—Subject to subsection (a)(8) and paragraphs (9) and (10) of this subsection, and notwithstanding any other provision of this section, any other provision of Federal law, or the law of any State, no person shall be stayed or prohibited from exercising—

(i) any right that such person has to cause the termination, liquidation, or acceleration of any qualified financial contract with a covered financial company which arises upon the date of appointment of the Corporation as receiver for such covered financial company or at any time after such appointment;

(ii) any right under any security agreement or arrangement or other credit enhancement related to one or more qualified financial contracts described in clause (i); or

(iii) any right to offset or net out any termination value, payment amount, or other transfer obligation arising under or in connection with 1 or more contracts or agreements described in clause (i), including any master agreement for such contracts or agreements.

(B) APPLICABILITY OF OTHER PROVISIONS.—Subsection (a)(8) shall apply in the case of any judicial action or proceeding brought against the Corporation as receiver referred to in subparagraph (A), or the subject covered financial company, by any party to a contract or agreement described in subparagraph (A)(i) with such covered financial company.

(C) CERTAIN TRANSFERS NOT AVOIDABLE.—

(i) IN GENERAL.—Notwithstanding subsection (a)(11), (a)(12), or (c)(12), section 5242 of the Revised Statutes of the United States, or any other provision of Federal or State law relating to the avoidance of preferential or fraudulent transfers, the Corporation, whether acting as the Corporation or as receiver for a covered financial company, may not avoid any transfer of money or other property in connection with any qualified financial contract with a covered financial company.

(ii) EXCEPTION FOR CERTAIN TRANSFERS.—Clause (i) shall not apply to any transfer of money or other property in connection with any qualified financial contract with a covered financial company if the transferee had actual intent to hinder, delay, or defraud such company, the creditors of such company, or the Corporation as receiver appointed for such company.

(D) CERTAIN CONTRACTS AND AGREEMENTS DEFINED.—For purposes of this subsection, the following definitions shall apply:

(i) QUALIFIED FINANCIAL CONTRACT.—The term "qualified financial contract" means any securities contract, commodity contract, forward contract, repurchase agreement, swap agreement, and any similar agreement that the Corporation determines by regulation, resolution, or order to be a qualified financial contract for purposes of this paragraph.

(ii) SECURITIES CONTRACT.—The term "securities contract"—

(I) means a contract for the purchase, sale, or loan of a security, a certificate of deposit, a mortgage loan, any interest in a mortgage loan, a group or index of securities, certificates of deposit, or mortgage loans or interests therein (including any interest therein or based on the value thereof), or any option on any of the foregoing, including any option to purchase or sell any such security, certificate of deposit, mortgage loan, interest, group or index, or option, and including any repurchase or reverse repurchase transaction on any such security, certificate of deposit, mortgage loan, interest, group or index, or option (whether or not such repurchase or reverse repurchase transaction is a "repurchase agreement", as defined in clause (v));

(II) does not include any purchase, sale, or repurchase obligation under a participation in a commercial mortgage loan unless the Corporation determines by regulation, resolution, or order to include any such agreement within the meaning of such term;

(III) means any option entered into on a national securities exchange relating to foreign currencies;

(IV) means the guarantee (including by novation) by or to any securities clearing agency of any settlement of cash, securities, certificates of deposit, mortgage loans or interests therein, group or index of securities, certificates of deposit or mortgage loans or interests therein (including any interest therein or based on the value thereof) or an option on any of the foregoing, including any option to purchase or sell any such security, certificate of deposit, mortgage loan, interest, group or index, or option (whether or not such settlement is in connection with any agreement or transaction referred to in subclauses (I) through (XII) (other than subclause (II)));

(V) means any margin loan;

(VI) means any extension of credit for the clearance or settlement of securities transactions;

(VII) means any loan transaction coupled with a securities collar transaction, any prepaid securities forward transaction, or any total return swap transaction coupled with a securities sale transaction;

(VIII) means any other agreement or transaction that is similar to any agreement or transaction referred to in this clause;

(IX) means any combination of the agreements or transactions referred to in this clause;

(X) means any option to enter into any agreement or transaction referred to in this clause;

(XI) means a master agreement that provides for an agreement or transaction referred to in any of subclauses (I) through (X), other than subclause (II), together with all supplements to any such master agreement, without regard to whether the master agreement provides for an agreement or transaction that is not a securities contract under this clause, except that the master agreement shall be considered to be a securities contract under this clause only with respect to each agreement or transaction under the master agreement that is referred to in any of subclauses (I) through (X), other than subclause (II); and

(XII) means any security agreement or arrangement or other credit enhancement related to any agreement or transaction referred to in this clause, including any guarantee or reimbursement obligation in connection with any agreement or transaction referred to in this clause.

(iii) COMMODITY CONTRACT.—The term "commodity contract" means—

(I) with respect to a futures commission merchant, a contract for the purchase or sale of a commodity for future delivery on, or subject to the rules of, a contract market or board of trade;

(II) with respect to a foreign futures commission merchant, a foreign future;

(III) with respect to a leverage transaction merchant, a leverage transaction;

(IV) with respect to a clearing organization, a contract for the purchase or sale of a commodity for future delivery on, or subject to the rules of, a contract market or board of trade that is cleared by such clearing organization, or commodity option traded on, or subject to the rules of, a contract market or board of trade that is cleared by such clearing organization;

(V) with respect to a commodity options dealer, a commodity option;

(VI) any other agreement or transaction that is similar to any agreement or transaction referred to in this clause;

(VII) any combination of the agreements or transactions referred to in this clause;

(VIII) any option to enter into any agreement or transaction referred to in this clause;

(IX) a master agreement that provides for an agreement or transaction referred to in any of subclauses (I) through (VIII), together with all supplements to any such master agreement, without regard to whether the master agreement provides for an agreement or transaction that is not a commodity contract under this clause, except that the master agreement shall be considered to be a commodity contract under this clause only with respect to each agreement or transaction under the master agreement that is referred to in any of subclauses (I) through (VIII); or

(X) any security agreement or arrangement or other credit enhancement related to any agreement or transaction referred to in this clause, including any guarantee or reimbursement obligation in connection with any agreement or transaction referred to in this clause.

(iv) FORWARD CONTRACT.—The term "forward contract" means—

(I) a contract (other than a commodity contract) for the purchase, sale, or transfer of a commodity or any similar good, article, service, right, or interest which is presently or in the future becomes the subject of dealing in the forward contract trade, or product or byproduct thereof, with a maturity date that is more than 2 days after the date on which the contract is entered into, including a repurchase or reverse repurchase transaction (whether or not such repurchase or reverse repurchase transaction is a "repurchase agreement", as defined in clause (v)), consignment, lease, swap, hedge transaction, deposit, loan, option, allocated transaction, unallocated transaction, or any other similar agreement;

(II) any combination of agreements or transactions referred to in subclauses (I) and (III);

(III) any option to enter into any agreement or transaction referred to in subclause (I) or (II);

(IV) a master agreement that provides for an agreement or transaction referred to in subclause (I), (II), or (III), together with all supplements to any such master agreement, without regard to whether the master agreement provides for an agreement or transaction that is not a forward contract under this clause, except that the master agreement shall be considered to be a forward contract under this clause only with respect to each agreement or transaction under the master agreement that is referred to in subclause (I), (II), or (III); or

(V) any security agreement or arrangement or other credit enhancement related to any agreement or transaction referred to in subclause (I), (II), (III), or (IV), including any guarantee or reimbursement obligation in connection with any agreement or transaction referred to in any such subclause.

(v) REPURCHASE AGREEMENT.—The term "repurchase agreement" (which definition also applies to a reverse repurchase agreement)—

(I) means an agreement, including related terms, which provides for the transfer of one or more certificates of deposit, mortgage related securities (as such term is defined in section 3 of the Securities Exchange Act of 1934), mortgage loans, interests in mortgage-related securities or mortgage loans, eligible bankers' acceptances, qualified foreign government securities (which, for purposes of this clause, means a security that is a direct obligation of, or that is fully guaranteed by, the central government of a member of the Organization for Economic Cooperation and Development, as determined by regulation or order adopted by the Board of Governors), or securities that are direct obligations of, or that are fully guaranteed by, the United States or any agency of the United States against the transfer of funds by the transferee of such certificates of deposit, eligible bankers' acceptances, securities, mortgage loans, or interests with a simultaneous agreement by such transferee to transfer to the transferor thereof certificates of deposit, eligible bankers' acceptances, securities, mortgage loans, or interests as described above, at a date certain not later than 1 year after such transfers or on demand, against the transfer of funds, or any other similar agreement;

(II) does not include any repurchase obligation under a participation in a commercial mortgage loan, unless the Corporation determines, by regulation, resolution, or order to include any such participation within the meaning of such term;

(III) means any combination of agreements or transactions referred to in subclauses (I) and (IV);

(IV) means any option to enter into any agreement or transaction referred to in subclause (I) or (III);

(V) means a master agreement that provides for an agreement or transaction referred to in subclause (I), (III), or (IV), together with all supplements to any such master agreement, without regard to whether the master agreement provides for an agreement or transaction that is not a repurchase agreement under this clause, except that the master agreement shall be considered to be a repurchase agreement under this subclause only with respect to each agreement or transaction under the master agreement that is referred to in subclause (I), (III), or (IV); and

(VI) means any security agreement or arrangement or other credit enhancement related to any agreement or transaction referred to in subclause (I), (III), (IV), or (V), including any guarantee or reimbursement obligation in connection with any agreement or transaction referred to in any such subclause.

(vi) SWAP AGREEMENT.—The term "swap agreement" means—

(I) any agreement, including the terms and conditions incorporated by reference in any such agreement, which is an interest rate swap, option, future, or forward agreement, including a rate floor, rate cap, rate collar, cross-currency rate swap, and basis swap; a spot, same day-tomorrow, tomorrow-next, forward, or other foreign exchange, precious metals, or other commodity agreement; a currency swap, option, future, or forward agreement; an equity index or equity swap, option, future, or forward agreement; a debt index or debt swap, option, future, or forward agreement; a total return, credit spread or credit swap, option, future, or forward agreement; a commodity index or commodity swap, option, future, or forward agreement; weather swap, option, future, or forward agreement; an emissions swap, option, future, or forward agreement; or an inflation swap, option, future, or forward agreement;

(II) any agreement or transaction that is similar to any other agreement or transaction referred to in this clause and that is of a type that has been, is presently, or in the future becomes, the subject of recurrent dealings in the swap or other derivatives markets (including terms and conditions incorporated by reference in such agreement) and that is a forward, swap, future, option, or spot transaction on one or more rates, currencies, commodities, equity securities or other equity instruments, debt securities or other debt instruments, quantitative measures associated with an occurrence, extent of an occurrence, or contingency associated with a financial, commercial, or economic consequence, or economic or financial indices or measures of economic or financial risk or value;

(III) any combination of agreements or transactions referred to in this clause;

(IV) any option to enter into any agreement or transaction referred to in this clause;

(V) a master agreement that provides for an agreement or transaction referred to in subclause (I), (II), (III), or (IV), together with all supplements to any such master agreement, without regard to whether the master agreement contains an agreement or transaction that is not a swap agreement under this clause, except that the master agreement shall be considered to be a swap agreement under this clause only with respect to each agreement or transaction under the master agreement that is referred to in subclause (I), (II), (III), or (IV); and

(VI) any security agreement or arrangement or other credit enhancement related to any agreement or transaction referred to in any of subclauses (I) through

(V), including any guarantee or reimbursement obligation in connection with any agreement or transaction referred to in any such clause.

(vii) DEFINITIONS RELATING TO DEFAULT.—When used in this paragraph and paragraphs (9) and (10)—

(I) the term "default" means, with respect to a covered financial company, any adjudication or other official decision by any court of competent jurisdiction, or other public authority pursuant to which the Corporation has been appointed receiver; and

(II) the term "in danger of default" means a covered financial company with respect to which the Corporation or appropriate State authority has determined that—

(aa) in the opinion of the Corporation or such authority—

(AA) the covered financial company is not likely to be able to pay its obligations in the normal course of business; and

(BB) there is no reasonable prospect that the covered financial company will be able to pay such obligations without Federal assistance; or

(bb) in the opinion of the Corporation or such authority—

(AA) the covered financial company has incurred or is likely to incur losses that will deplete all or substantially all of its capital; and

(BB) there is no reasonable prospect that the capital will be replenished without Federal assistance.

(viii) TREATMENT OF MASTER AGREEMENT AS ONE AGREEMENT.—Any master agreement for any contract or agreement described in any of clauses (i) through (vi) (or any master agreement for such master agreement or agreements), together with all supplements to such master agreement, shall be treated as a single agreement and a single qualified financial contact. If a master agreement contains provisions relating to agreements or transactions that are not themselves qualified financial contracts, the master agreement shall be deemed to be a qualified financial contract only with respect to those transactions that are themselves qualified financial contracts.

(ix) TRANSFER.—The term "transfer" means every mode, direct or indirect, absolute or conditional, voluntary or involuntary, of disposing of or parting with property or with an interest in property, including retention of title as a security interest and foreclosure of the equity of redemption of the covered financial company.

(x) PERSON.—The term "person" includes any governmental entity in addition to any entity included in the definition of such term in section 1, title 1, United States Code.

(E) CLARIFICATION.—No provision of law shall be construed as limiting the right or power of the Corporation, or authorizing any court or agency to limit or delay, in any manner, the right or power of the Corporation to transfer any qualified financial contract or to disaffirm or repudiate any such contract in accordance with this subsection.

(F) WALKAWAY CLAUSES NOT EFFECTIVE.—

(i) IN GENERAL.—Notwithstanding the provisions of subparagraph (A) of this paragraph and sections 403 and 404 of the Federal Deposit Insurance Corporation Improvement Act of 1991, no walkaway clause shall be enforceable in a qualified financial contract of a covered financial company in default.

(ii) LIMITED SUSPENSION OF CERTAIN OBLIGATIONS.—In the case of a qualified financial contract referred to in clause (i), any payment or delivery obligations otherwise due from a party pursuant to the qualified financial contract shall be suspended from the time at which the Corporation is appointed as receiver until the earlier of—

(I) the time at which such party receives notice that such contract has been transferred pursuant to paragraph (10)(A); or

(II) 5:00 p.m. (eastern time) on the business day following the date of the appointment of the Corporation as receiver.

(iii) WALKAWAY CLAUSE DEFINED.—For purposes of this subparagraph, the term "walkaway clause" means any provision in a qualified financial contract that suspends, conditions, or extinguishes a payment obligation of a party, in whole or in part, or does not create a payment obligation of a party that would otherwise exist, solely because of the status of such party as a nondefaulting party in connection with the insolvency of a covered financial company that is a party to the contract or the appointment of or the exercise of rights or powers by the Corporation as receiver for such covered financial company, and not as a result of the exercise by a party of any right to offset, setoff, or net obligations that exist under the contract, any other contract between those parties, or applicable law.

(G) CERTAIN OBLIGATIONS TO CLEARING ORGANIZATIONS.—In the event that the Corporation has been appointed as receiver for a covered financial company which is a party to any qualified financial contract cleared by or subject to the rules of a clearing organization (as defined in paragraph (9)(D)), the receiver shall use its best efforts to meet all margin, collateral, and settlement obligations of the covered financial company that arise under qualified financial contracts (other than any margin, collateral, or settlement obligation that is not enforceable against the receiver under paragraph (8)(F)(i) or paragraph (10)(B)), as required by the rules of the clearing organization when due. Notwithstanding any other provision of this title, if the receiver fails to satisfy any such margin, collateral, or settlement obligations under the rules of the clearing organization, the clearing organization shall have the immediate right to exercise, and shall not be stayed from exercising, all of its rights and remedies under its rules and applicable law with respect to any qualified financial contract of the covered financial company, including, without limitation, the right to liquidate all positions and collateral of such covered financial company under the company's qualified financial contracts, and suspend or cease to act for such covered financial company, all in accordance with the rules of the clearing organization.

(H) RECORDKEEPING.—

(i) JOINT RULEMAKING.—The Federal primary financial regulatory agencies shall jointly prescribe regulations requiring that financial companies maintain such records with respect to qualified financial contracts (including market valuations) that the Federal primary financial regulatory agencies determine to be necessary or appropriate in order to assist the Corporation as receiver for a covered financial company in being able to exercise its rights and fulfill its obligations under this paragraph or paragraph (9) or (10).

(ii) TIME FRAME.—The Federal primary financial regulatory agencies shall prescribe joint final or interim final regulations not later than 24 months after the date of enactment of this Act.

(iii) BACK-UP RULEMAKING AUTHORITY.—If the Federal primary financial regulatory agencies do not prescribe joint final or interim final regulations within the time frame in clause (ii), the Chairperson of the Council shall prescribe, in consultation with the Corporation, the regulations required by clause (i).

(iv) CATEGORIZATION AND TIERING.—The joint regulations prescribed under clause (i) shall, as appropriate, differentiate among financial companies by taking into consideration their size, risk, complexity, leverage, frequency and dollar amount of qualified financial contracts, interconnectedness to the financial system, and any other factors deemed appropriate.

(9) TRANSFER OF QUALIFIED FINANCIAL CONTRACTS.—

(A) IN GENERAL.—In making any transfer of assets or liabilities of a covered financial company in default, which includes any qualified financial contract, the Corporation as receiver for such covered financial company shall either—

(i) transfer to one financial institution, other than a financial institution for which a conservator, receiver, trustee in bankruptcy, or other legal custodian has been appointed or which is otherwise the subject of a bankruptcy or insolvency proceeding—

(I) all qualified financial contracts between any person or any affiliate of such person and the covered financial company in default;

(II) all claims of such person or any affiliate of such person against such covered financial company under any such contract (other than any claim which, under the terms of any such contract, is subordinated to the claims of general unsecured creditors of such company);

(III) all claims of such covered financial company against such person or any affiliate of such person under any such contract; and

(IV) all property securing or any other credit enhancement for any contract described in subclause (I) or any claim described in subclause (II) or (III) under any such contract; or

(ii) transfer none of the qualified financial contracts, claims, property or other credit enhancement referred to in clause (i) (with respect to such person and any affiliate of such person).

(B) TRANSFER TO FOREIGN BANK, FINANCIAL INSTITUTION, OR BRANCH OR AGENCY THEREOF.—In transferring any qualified financial contracts and related claims and property under subparagraph (A)(i), the Corporation as receiver for the covered financial company shall not make such transfer to a foreign bank, financial institution organized under the laws of a foreign country, or a branch or agency of a foreign bank or financial institution unless, under the law applicable to such bank, financial institution, branch or agency, to the qualified financial contracts, and to any netting contract, any security agreement or arrangement or other credit enhancement related to one or more qualified financial contracts, the contractual rights of the parties to such qualified financial contracts, netting contracts, security agreements or arrangements, or other credit enhancements are enforceable substantially to the same extent as permitted under this section.

(C) TRANSFER OF CONTRACTS SUBJECT TO THE RULES OF A CLEARING ORGANIZATION.—In the event that the Corporation as receiver for a financial institution transfers any qualified financial contract and related claims, property, or credit enhancement pursuant to subparagraph (A)(i) and such contract is cleared by or subject to the rules of a clearing organization, the clearing organization shall not be required to accept the transferee as a member by virtue of the transfer.

(D) DEFINITIONS.—For purposes of this paragraph—

(i) the term "financial institution" means a broker or dealer, a depository institution, a futures commission merchant, a bridge financial company, or any other institution determined by the Corporation, by regulation, to be a financial institution; and

(ii) the term "clearing organization" has the same meaning as in section 402 of the Federal Deposit Insurance Corporation Improvement Act of 1991.

(10) NOTIFICATION OF TRANSFER.—

(A) IN GENERAL.—

(i) NOTICE.—The Corporation shall provide notice in accordance with clause (ii), if—

(I) the Corporation as receiver for a covered financial company in default or in danger of default transfers any assets or liabilities of the covered financial company; and

(II) the transfer includes any qualified financial contract.

(ii) TIMING.—The Corporation as receiver for a covered financial company shall notify any person who is a party to any contract described in clause (i) of such transfer not later than 5:00 p.m. (eastern time) on the business day following the date of the appointment of the Corporation as receiver.

(B) CERTAIN RIGHTS NOT ENFORCEABLE.—

(i) RECEIVERSHIP.—A person who is a party to a qualified financial contract with a covered financial company may not exercise any right that such person has to terminate, liquidate, or net such contract under paragraph (8)(A) solely by reason of or incidental to the appointment under this section of the Corporation as receiver for the covered financial company (or the insolvency or financial condition of the covered financial company for which the Corporation has been appointed as receiver)—

(I) until 5:00 p.m. (eastern time) on the business day following the date of the appointment; or

(II) after the person has received notice that the contract has been transferred pursuant to paragraph (9)(A).

(ii) NOTICE.—For purposes of this paragraph, the Corporation as receiver for a covered financial company shall be deemed to have notified a person who is a party to a qualified financial contract with such covered financial company, if the Corporation has taken steps reasonably calculated to provide notice to such person by the time specified in subparagraph (A).

(C) TREATMENT OF BRIDGE FINANCIAL COMPANY.—For purposes of paragraph (9), a bridge financial company shall not be considered to be a financial institution for which a conservator, receiver, trustee in bankruptcy, or other legal custodian has been appointed, or which is otherwise the subject of a bankruptcy or insolvency proceeding.

(D) BUSINESS DAY DEFINED.—For purposes of this paragraph, the term "business day" means any day other than any Saturday, Sunday, or any day on which either the New York Stock Exchange or the Federal Reserve Bank of New York is closed.

(11) DISAFFIRMANCE OR REPUDIATION OF QUALIFIED FINANCIAL CONTRACTS.—In exercising the rights of disaffirmance or repudiation of the Corporation as receiver with respect to any qualified financial contract to which a covered financial company is a party, the Corporation shall either—

(A) disaffirm or repudiate all qualified financial contracts between—

(i) any person or any affiliate of such person; and

(ii) the covered financial company in default; or

(B) disaffirm or repudiate none of the qualified financial contracts referred to in subparagraph (A) (with respect to such person or any affiliate of such person).

(12) CERTAIN SECURITY AND CUSTOMER INTERESTS NOT AVOIDABLE.—No provision of this subsection shall be construed as permitting the avoidance of any—

(A) legally enforceable or perfected security interest in any of the assets of any covered financial company, except in accordance with subsection (a)(11); or

(B) legally enforceable interest in customer property, security entitlements in respect of assets or property held by the covered financial company for any security entitlement holder.

(13) AUTHORITY TO ENFORCE CONTRACTS.—

(A) IN GENERAL.—The Corporation, as receiver for a covered financial company, may enforce any contract, other than a liability insurance contract of a director or officer, a financial institution bond entered into by the covered financial company, notwithstanding any provision of the contract providing for termination, default, acceleration, or exercise of rights upon, or solely by reason of, insolvency, the appointment of or the exercise of rights or powers by the Corporation as receiver, the filing of the petition pursuant to section 202(a)(1), or the issuance of the recommendations or determination, or any actions or events occurring in connection therewith or as a result thereof, pursuant to section 203.

(B) CERTAIN RIGHTS NOT AFFECTED.—No provision of this paragraph may be construed as impairing or affecting any right of the Corporation as receiver to enforce or recover under a liability insurance contract of a director or officer or financial institution bond under other applicable law.

(C) Consent requirement and ipso facto clauses.—

(i) In general.—Except as otherwise provided by this section, no person may exercise any right or power to terminate, accelerate, or declare a default under any contract to which the covered financial company is a party (and no provision in any such contract providing for such default, termination, or acceleration shall be enforceable), or to obtain possession of or exercise control over any property of the covered financial company or affect any contractual rights of the covered financial company, without the consent of the Corporation as receiver for the covered financial company during the 90 day period beginning from the appointment of the Corporation as receiver.

(ii) Exceptions.—No provision of this subparagraph shall apply to a director or officer liability insurance contract or a financial institution bond, to the rights of parties to certain qualified financial contracts pursuant to paragraph (8), or to the rights of parties to netting contracts pursuant to subtitle A of title IV of the Federal Deposit Insurance Corporation Improvement Act of 1991 (12 U.S.C. 4401 et seq.), or shall be construed as permitting the Corporation as receiver to fail to comply with otherwise enforceable provisions of such contract.

(D) Contracts to extend credit.—Notwithstanding any other provision in this title, if the Corporation as receiver enforces any contract to extend credit to the covered financial company or bridge financial company, any valid and enforceable obligation to repay such debt shall be paid by the Corporation as receiver, as an administrative expense of the receivership.

(14) Exception for federal reserve banks and corporation security interest.—No provision of this subsection shall apply with respect to—

(A) any extension of credit from any Federal reserve bank or the Corporation to any covered financial company; or

(B) any security interest in the assets of the covered financial company securing any such extension of credit.

(15) Savings clause.—The meanings of terms used in this subsection are applicable for purposes of this subsection only, and shall not be construed or applied so as to challenge or affect the characterization, definition, or treatment of any similar terms under any other statute, regulation, or rule, including the Gramm-Leach-Bliley Act, the Legal Certainty for Bank Products Act of 2000, the securities laws (as that term is defined in section 3(a)(47) of the Securities Exchange Act of 1934), and the Commodity Exchange Act.

(16) Enforcement of contracts guaranteed by the covered financial company.—

(A) In general.—The Corporation, as receiver for a covered financial company or as receiver for a subsidiary of a covered financial company (including an insured depository institution) shall have the power to enforce contracts of subsidiaries or affiliates of the covered financial company, the obligations under which are guaranteed or otherwise supported by or linked to the covered financial company, notwithstanding any contractual right to cause the termination, liquidation, or acceleration of such contracts based solely on the insolvency, financial condition, or receivership of the covered financial company, if—

(i) such guaranty or other support and all related assets and liabilities are transferred to and assumed by a bridge financial company or a third party (other than a third party for which a conservator, receiver, trustee in bankruptcy, or other legal custodian has been appointed, or which is otherwise the subject of a bankruptcy or insolvency proceeding) within the same period of time as the Corporation is entitled to transfer the qualified financial contracts of such covered financial company; or

(ii) the Corporation, as receiver, otherwise provides adequate protection with respect to such obligations.

(B) Rule of construction.—For purposes of this paragraph, a bridge financial company shall not be considered to be a third party for which a conservator, receiver, trustee in bankruptcy, or other legal custodian has been appointed, or which is otherwise the subject of a bankruptcy or insolvency proceeding.

(d) VALUATION OF CLAIMS IN DEFAULT.—

(1) IN GENERAL.—Notwithstanding any other provision of Federal law or the law of any State, and regardless of the method utilized by the Corporation for a covered financial company, including transactions authorized under subsection (h), this subsection shall govern the rights of the creditors of any such covered financial company.

(2) MAXIMUM LIABILITY.—The maximum liability of the Corporation, acting as receiver for a covered financial company or in any other capacity, to any person having a claim against the Corporation as receiver or the covered financial company for which the Corporation is appointed shall equal the amount that such claimant would have received if—

(A) the Corporation had not been appointed receiver with respect to the covered financial company; and

(B) the covered financial company had been liquidated under chapter 7 of the Bankruptcy Code, or any similar provision of State insolvency law applicable to the covered financial company.

(3) SPECIAL PROVISION FOR ORDERLY LIQUIDATION BY SIPC.—The maximum liability of the Corporation, acting as receiver or in its corporate capacity for any covered broker or dealer to any customer of such covered broker or dealer, with respect to customer property of such customer, shall be—

(A) equal to the amount that such customer would have received with respect to such customer property in a case initiated by SIPC under the Securities Investor Protection Act of 1970 (15 U.S.C. 78aaa et seq.); and

(B) determined as of the close of business on the date on which the Corporation is appointed as receiver.

(4) ADDITIONAL PAYMENTS AUTHORIZED.—

(A) IN GENERAL.—Subject to subsection (o)(1)(D)(i), the Corporation, with the approval of the Secretary, may make additional payments or credit additional amounts to or with respect to or for the account of any claimant or category of claimants of the covered financial company, if the Corporation determines that such payments or credits are necessary or appropriate to minimize losses to the Corporation as receiver from the orderly liquidation of the covered financial company under this section.

(B) LIMITATIONS.—

(i) PROHIBITION.—The Corporation shall not make any payments or credit amounts to any claimant or category of claimants that would result in any claimant receiving more than the face value amount of any claim that is proven to the satisfaction of the Corporation.

(ii) NO OBLIGATION.—Notwithstanding any other provision of Federal or State law, or the Constitution of any State, the Corporation shall not be obligated, as a result of having made any payment under subparagraph (A) or credited any amount described in subparagraph (A) to or with respect to, or for the account, of any claimant or category of claimants, to make payments to any other claimant or category of claimants.

(C) MANNER OF PAYMENT.—The Corporation may make payments or credit amounts under subparagraph (A) directly to the claimants or may make such payments or credit such amounts to a company other than a covered financial company or a bridge financial company established with respect thereto in order to induce such other company to accept liability for such claims.

(e) LIMITATION ON COURT ACTION.—Except as provided in this title, no court may take any action to restrain or affect the exercise of powers or functions of the receiver hereunder, and any remedy against the Corporation or receiver shall be limited to money damages determined in accordance with this title.

(f) LIABILITY OF DIRECTORS AND OFFICERS.—

(1) IN GENERAL.—A director or officer of a covered financial company may be held personally liable for monetary damages in any civil action described in paragraph (2) by, on behalf of, or at the request or direction of the Corporation, which action is prosecuted wholly or partially for the benefit of the Corporation—

(A) acting as receiver for such covered financial company;

(B) acting based upon a suit, claim, or cause of action purchased from, assigned by, or otherwise conveyed by the Corporation as receiver; or

(C) acting based upon a suit, claim, or cause of action purchased from, assigned by, or otherwise conveyed in whole or in part by a covered financial company or its affiliate in connection with assistance provided under this title.

(2) ACTIONS COVERED.—Paragraph (1) shall apply with respect to actions for gross negligence, including any similar conduct or conduct that demonstrates a greater disregard of a duty of care (than gross negligence) including intentional tortious conduct, as such terms are defined and determined under applicable State law.

(3) SAVINGS CLAUSE.—Nothing in this subsection shall impair or affect any right of the Corporation under other applicable law.

(g) DAMAGES.—In any proceeding related to any claim against a director, officer, employee, agent, attorney, accountant, or appraiser of a covered financial company, or any other party employed by or providing services to a covered financial company, recoverable damages determined to result from the improvident or otherwise improper use or investment of any assets of the covered financial company shall include principal losses and appropriate interest.

(h) BRIDGE FINANCIAL COMPANIES.—

(1) ORGANIZATION.—

(A) PURPOSE.—The Corporation, as receiver for one or more covered financial companies or in anticipation of being appointed receiver for one or more covered financial companies, may organize one or more bridge financial companies in accordance with this subsection.

(B) AUTHORITIES.—Upon the creation of a bridge financial company under subparagraph (A) with respect to a covered financial company, such bridge financial company may—

(i) assume such liabilities (including liabilities associated with any trust or custody business, but excluding any liabilities that count as regulatory capital) of such covered financial company as the Corporation may, in its discretion, determine to be appropriate;

(ii) purchase such assets (including assets associated with any trust or custody business) of such covered financial company as the Corporation may, in its discretion, determine to be appropriate; and

(iii) perform any other temporary function which the Corporation may, in its discretion, prescribe in accordance with this section.

(2) CHARTER AND ESTABLISHMENT.—

(A) ESTABLISHMENT.—Except as provided in subparagraph (H), where the covered financial company is a covered broker or dealer, the Corporation, as receiver for a covered financial company, may grant a Federal charter to and approve articles of association for one or more bridge financial company or companies, with respect to such covered financial company which shall, by operation of law and immediately upon issuance of its charter and approval of its articles of association, be established and operate in accordance with, and subject to, such charter, articles, and this section.

(B) MANAGEMENT.—Upon its establishment, a bridge financial company shall be under the management of a board of directors appointed by the Corporation.

(C) ARTICLES OF ASSOCIATION.—The articles of association and organization certificate of a bridge financial company shall have such terms as the Corporation may provide, and shall be executed by such representatives as the Corporation may designate.

(D) TERMS OF CHARTER; RIGHTS AND PRIVILEGES.—Subject to and in accordance with the provisions of this subsection, the Corporation shall—

(i) establish the terms of the charter of a bridge financial company and the rights, powers, authorities, and privileges of a bridge financial company granted by the charter or as an incident thereto; and

(ii) provide for, and establish the terms and conditions governing, the management (including the bylaws and the number of directors of the board of directors) and operations of the bridge financial company.

(E) TRANSFER OF RIGHTS AND PRIVILEGES OF COVERED FINANCIAL COMPANY.—

(i) IN GENERAL.—Notwithstanding any other provision of Federal or State law, the Corporation may provide for a bridge financial company to succeed to and assume any rights, powers, authorities, or privileges of the covered financial company with respect to which the bridge financial company was established and, upon such determination by the Corporation, the bridge financial company shall immediately and by operation of law succeed to and assume such rights, powers, authorities, and privileges.

(ii) EFFECTIVE WITHOUT APPROVAL.—Any succession to or assumption by a bridge financial company of rights, powers, authorities, or privileges of a covered financial company under clause (i) or otherwise shall be effective without any further approval under Federal or State law, assignment, or consent with respect thereto.

(F) CORPORATE GOVERNANCE AND ELECTION AND DESIGNATION OF BODY OF LAW.—To the extent permitted by the Corporation and consistent with this section and any rules, regulations, or directives issued by the Corporation under this section, a bridge financial company may elect to follow the corporate governance practices and procedures that are applicable to a corporation incorporated under the general corporation law of the State of Delaware, or the State of incorporation or organization of the covered financial company with respect to which the bridge financial company was established, as such law may be amended from time to time.

(G) CAPITAL.—

(i) CAPITAL NOT REQUIRED.—Notwithstanding any other provision of Federal or State law, a bridge financial company may, if permitted by the Corporation, operate without any capital or surplus, or with such capital or surplus as the Corporation may in its discretion determine to be appropriate.

(ii) NO CONTRIBUTION BY THE CORPORATION REQUIRED.—The Corporation is not required to pay capital into a bridge financial company or to issue any capital stock on behalf of a bridge financial company established under this subsection.

(iii) AUTHORITY.—If the Corporation determines that such action is advisable, the Corporation may cause capital stock or other securities of a bridge financial company established with respect to a covered financial company to be issued and offered for sale in such amounts and on such terms and conditions as the Corporation may, in its discretion, determine.

(iv) OPERATING FUNDS IN LIEU OF CAPITAL AND IMPLEMENTATION PLAN.—Upon the organization of a bridge financial company, and thereafter as the Corporation may, in its discretion, determine to be necessary or advisable, the Corporation may make available to the bridge financial company, subject to the plan described in subsection (n)(9), funds for the operation of the bridge financial company in lieu of capital.

(H) BRIDGE BROKERS OR DEALERS.—

(i) IN GENERAL.—The Corporation, as receiver for a covered broker or dealer, may approve articles of association for one or more bridge financial companies with respect to such covered broker or dealer, which bridge financial company or companies shall, by operation of law and immediately upon approval of its articles of association—

(I) be established and deemed registered with the Commission under the Securities Exchange Act of 1934 and a member of SIPC;

(II) operate in accordance with such articles and this section; and

(III) succeed to any and all registrations and memberships of the covered financial company with or in any self-regulatory organizations.

(ii) OTHER REQUIREMENTS.—Except as provided in clause (i), and notwithstanding any other provision of this section, the bridge financial company shall be subject to the Federal securities laws and all requirements with respect to being a member of a self-regulatory organization, unless exempted from any such requirements by the Commission, as is necessary or appropriate in the public interest or for the protection of investors.

(iii) TREATMENT OF CUSTOMERS.—Except as otherwise provided by this title, any customer of the covered broker or dealer whose account is transferred to a bridge financial company shall have all the rights, privileges, and protections under section 205(f) and under the Securities Investor Protection Act of 1970 (15 U.S.C. 78aaa et seq.), that such customer would have had if the account were not transferred from the covered financial company under this subparagraph.

(iv) OPERATION OF BRIDGE BROKERS OR DEALERS.—Notwithstanding any other provision of this title, the Corporation shall not operate any bridge financial company created by the Corporation under this title with respect to a covered broker or dealer in such a manner as to adversely affect the ability of customers to promptly access their customer property in accordance with applicable law.

(3) INTERESTS IN AND ASSETS AND OBLIGATIONS OF COVERED FINANCIAL COMPANY.—Notwithstanding paragraph (1) or (2) or any other provision of law—

(A) a bridge financial company shall assume, acquire, or succeed to the assets or liabilities of a covered financial company (including the assets or liabilities associated with any trust or custody business) only to the extent that such assets or liabilities are transferred by the Corporation to the bridge financial company in accordance with, and subject to the restrictions set forth in, paragraph (1)(B); and

(B) a bridge financial company shall not assume, acquire, or succeed to any obligation that a covered financial company for which the Corporation has been appointed receiver may have to any shareholder, member, general partner, limited partner, or other person with an interest in the equity of the covered financial company that arises as a result of the status of that person having an equity claim in the covered financial company.

(4) BRIDGE FINANCIAL COMPANY TREATED AS BEING IN DEFAULT FOR CERTAIN PURPOSES.—A bridge financial company shall be treated as a covered financial company in default at such times and for such purposes as the Corporation may, in its discretion, determine.

(5) TRANSFER OF ASSETS AND LIABILITIES.—

(A) AUTHORITY OF CORPORATION.—The Corporation, as receiver for a covered financial company, may transfer any assets and liabilities of a covered financial company (including any assets or liabilities associated with any trust or custody business) to one or more bridge financial companies, in accordance with and subject to the restrictions of paragraph (1).

(B) SUBSEQUENT TRANSFERS.—At any time after the establishment of a bridge financial company with respect to a covered financial company, the Corporation, as receiver, may transfer any assets and liabilities of such covered financial company as the Corporation may, in its discretion, determine to be appropriate in accordance with and subject to the restrictions of paragraph (1).

(C) TREATMENT OF TRUST OR CUSTODY BUSINESS.—For purposes of this paragraph, the trust or custody business, including fiduciary appointments, held by any covered financial company is included among its assets and liabilities.

(D) EFFECTIVE WITHOUT APPROVAL.—The transfer of any assets or liabilities, including those associated with any trust or custody business of a covered financial company, to a bridge financial company shall be effective without any further approval under Federal or State law, assignment, or consent with respect thereto.

(E) EQUITABLE TREATMENT OF SIMILARLY SITUATED CREDITORS.—The Corporation shall treat all creditors of a covered financial company that are similarly situated under subsection (b)(1), in a similar manner in exercising the authority of the Corporation under this subsection to transfer any assets or liabilities of the covered financial company to one or more bridge financial companies established with respect to such covered financial company, except that the Corporation may take any action (including making payments, subject to subsection (o)(1)(D)(i)) that does not comply with this subparagraph, if—

(i) the Corporation determines that such action is necessary—

(I) to maximize the value of the assets of the covered financial company;

(II) to maximize the present value return from the sale or other disposition of the assets of the covered financial company; or

(III) to minimize the amount of any loss realized upon the sale or other disposition of the assets of the covered financial company; and

(ii) all creditors that are similarly situated under subsection (b)(1) receive not less than the amount provided under paragraphs (2) and (3) of subsection (d).

(F) LIMITATION ON TRANSFER OF LIABILITIES.—Notwithstanding any other provision of law, the aggregate amount of liabilities of a covered financial company that are transferred to, or assumed by, a bridge financial company from a covered financial company may not exceed the aggregate amount of the assets of the covered financial company that are transferred to, or purchased by, the bridge financial company from the covered financial company.

(6) STAY OF JUDICIAL ACTION.—Any judicial action to which a bridge financial company becomes a party by virtue of its acquisition of any assets or assumption of any liabilities of a covered financial company shall be stayed from further proceedings for a period of not longer than 45 days (or such longer period as may be agreed to upon the consent of all parties) at the request of the bridge financial company.

(7) AGREEMENTS AGAINST INTEREST OF THE BRIDGE FINANCIAL COMPANY.—No agreement that tends to diminish or defeat the interest of the bridge financial company in any asset of a covered financial company acquired by the bridge financial company shall be valid against the bridge financial company, unless such agreement—

(A) is in writing;

(B) was executed by an authorized officer or representative of the covered financial company or confirmed in the ordinary course of business by the covered financial company; and

(C) has been on the official record of the company, since the time of its execution, or with which, the party claiming under the agreement provides documentation of such agreement and its authorized execution or confirmation by the covered financial company that is acceptable to the receiver.

(8) NO FEDERAL STATUS.—

(A) AGENCY STATUS.—A bridge financial company is not an agency, establishment, or instrumentality of the United States.

(B) EMPLOYEE STATUS.—Representatives for purposes of paragraph (1)(B), directors, officers, employees, or agents of a bridge financial company are not, solely by virtue of service in any such capacity, officers or employees of the United States. Any employee of the Corporation or of any Federal instrumentality who serves at the request of the Corporation as a representative for purposes of paragraph (1)(B), director, officer, employee, or agent of a bridge financial company shall not—

(i) solely by virtue of service in any such capacity lose any existing status as an officer or employee of the United States for purposes of title 5, United States Code, or any other provision of law; or

Act Sec. 210(h)(8)(B)(i) ¶10,210

(ii) receive any salary or benefits for service in any such capacity with respect to a bridge financial company in addition to such salary or benefits as are obtained through employment with the Corporation or such Federal instrumentality.

(9) FUNDING AUTHORIZED.—The Corporation may, subject to the plan described in subsection (n)(9), provide funding to facilitate any transaction described in subparagraph (A), (B), (C), or (D) of paragraph (13) with respect to any bridge financial company, or facilitate the acquisition by a bridge financial company of any assets, or the assumption of any liabilities, of a covered financial company for which the Corporation has been appointed receiver.

(10) EXEMPT TAX STATUS.—Notwithstanding any other provision of Federal or State law, a bridge financial company, its franchise, property, and income shall be exempt from all taxation now or hereafter imposed by the United States, by any territory, dependency, or possession thereof, or by any State, county, municipality, or local taxing authority.

(11) FEDERAL AGENCY APPROVAL; ANTITRUST REVIEW.—If a transaction involving the merger or sale of a bridge financial company requires approval by a Federal agency, the transaction may not be consummated before the 5th calendar day after the date of approval by the Federal agency responsible for such approval with respect thereto. If, in connection with any such approval a report on competitive factors from the Attorney General is required, the Federal agency responsible for such approval shall promptly notify the Attorney General of the proposed transaction and the Attorney General shall provide the required report within 10 days of the request. If a notification is required under section 7A of the Clayton Act with respect to such transaction, the required waiting period shall end on the 15th day after the date on which the Attorney General and the Federal Trade Commission receive such notification, unless the waiting period is terminated earlier under section 7A(b)(2) of the Clayton Act, or extended under section 7A(e)(2) of that Act.

(12) DURATION OF BRIDGE FINANCIAL COMPANY.—Subject to paragraphs (13) and (14), the status of a bridge financial company as such shall terminate at the end of the 2-year period following the date on which it was granted a charter. The Corporation may, in its discretion, extend the status of the bridge financial company as such for no more than 3 additional 1-year periods.

(13) TERMINATION OF BRIDGE FINANCIAL COMPANY STATUS.—The status of any bridge financial company as such shall terminate upon the earliest of—

(A) the date of the merger or consolidation of the bridge financial company with a company that is not a bridge financial company;

(B) at the election of the Corporation, the sale of a majority of the capital stock of the bridge financial company to a company other than the Corporation and other than another bridge financial company;

(C) the sale of 80 percent, or more, of the capital stock of the bridge financial company to a person other than the Corporation and other than another bridge financial company;

(D) at the election of the Corporation, either the assumption of all or substantially all of the liabilities of the bridge financial company by a company that is not a bridge financial company, or the acquisition of all or substantially all of the assets of the bridge financial company by a company that is not a bridge financial company, or other entity as permitted under applicable law; and

(E) the expiration of the period provided in paragraph (12), or the earlier dissolution of the bridge financial company, as provided in paragraph (15).

(14) EFFECT OF TERMINATION EVENTS.—

(A) MERGER OR CONSOLIDATION.—A merger or consolidation, described in paragraph (13)(A) shall be conducted in accordance with, and shall have the effect provided in, the provisions of applicable law. For the purpose of effecting such a merger or consolidation, the bridge financial company shall be treated as a corporation organized under the laws of the State of Delaware (unless the law of another State has been selected by the bridge financial company in accordance with paragraph (2)(F)), and the Corporation shall be treated as the sole shareholder thereof, notwithstanding any other provision of State or Federal law.

(B) CHARTER CONVERSION.—Following the sale of a majority of the capital stock of the bridge financial company, as provided in paragraph (13)(B), the Corporation may amend the charter of the bridge financial company to reflect the termination of the status of the bridge financial company as such, whereupon the company shall have all of the rights, powers, and privileges under its constituent documents and applicable Federal or State law. In connection therewith, the Corporation may take such steps as may be necessary or convenient to reincorporate the bridge financial company under the laws of a State and, notwithstanding any provisions of Federal or State law, such State-chartered corporation shall be deemed to succeed by operation of law to such rights, titles, powers, and interests of the bridge financial company as the Corporation may provide, with the same effect as if the bridge financial company had merged with the State-chartered corporation under provisions of the corporate laws of such State.

(C) SALE OF STOCK.—Following the sale of 80 percent or more of the capital stock of a bridge financial company, as provided in paragraph (13)(C), the company shall have all of the rights, powers, and privileges under its constituent documents and applicable Federal or State law. In connection therewith, the Corporation may take such steps as may be necessary or convenient to reincorporate the bridge financial company under the laws of a State and, notwithstanding any provisions of Federal or State law, the State-chartered corporation shall be deemed to succeed by operation of law to such rights, titles, powers and interests of the bridge financial company as the Corporation may provide, with the same effect as if the bridge financial company had merged with the State-chartered corporation under provisions of the corporate laws of such State.

(D) ASSUMPTION OF LIABILITIES AND SALE OF ASSETS.—Following the assumption of all or substantially all of the liabilities of the bridge financial company, or the sale of all or substantially all of the assets of the bridge financial company, as provided in paragraph (13)(D), at the election of the Corporation, the bridge financial company may retain its status as such for the period provided in paragraph (12) or may be dissolved at the election of the Corporation.

(E) AMENDMENTS TO CHARTER.—Following the consummation of a transaction described in subparagraph (A), (B), (C), or (D) of paragraph (13), the charter of the resulting company shall be amended to reflect the termination of bridge financial company status, if appropriate.

(15) DISSOLUTION OF BRIDGE FINANCIAL COMPANY.—

(A) IN GENERAL.—Notwithstanding any other provision of Federal or State law, if the status of a bridge financial company as such has not previously been terminated by the occurrence of an event specified in subparagraph (A), (B), (C), or (D) of paragraph (13)—

(i) the Corporation may, in its discretion, dissolve the bridge financial company in accordance with this paragraph at any time; and

(ii) the Corporation shall promptly commence dissolution proceedings in accordance with this paragraph upon the expiration of the 2-year period following the date on which the bridge financial company was chartered, or any extension thereof, as provided in paragraph (12).

(B) PROCEDURES.—The Corporation shall remain the receiver for a bridge financial company for the purpose of dissolving the bridge financial company. The Corporation as receiver for a bridge financial company shall wind up the affairs of the bridge financial company in conformity with the provisions of law relating to the liquidation of covered financial companies under this title. With respect to any such bridge financial company, the Corporation as receiver shall have all the rights, powers, and privileges and shall perform the duties related to the exercise of such rights, powers, or privileges granted by law to the Corporation as receiver for a covered financial company under this title and, notwithstanding any other provision of law, in the exercise of such rights, powers, and privileges, the Corporation shall not be subject to the direction or supervision of any State agency or other Federal agency.

(16) AUTHORITY TO OBTAIN CREDIT.—

(A) IN GENERAL.—A bridge financial company may obtain unsecured credit and issue unsecured debt.

(B) INABILITY TO OBTAIN CREDIT.—If a bridge financial company is unable to obtain unsecured credit or issue unsecured debt, the Corporation may authorize the obtaining of credit or the issuance of debt by the bridge financial company—

(i) with priority over any or all of the obligations of the bridge financial company;

(ii) secured by a lien on property of the bridge financial company that is not otherwise subject to a lien; or

(iii) secured by a junior lien on property of the bridge financial company that is subject to a lien.

(C) LIMITATIONS.—

(i) IN GENERAL.—The Corporation, after notice and a hearing, may authorize the obtaining of credit or the issuance of debt by a bridge financial company that is secured by a senior or equal lien on property of the bridge financial company that is subject to a lien, only if—

(I) the bridge financial company is unable to otherwise obtain such credit or issue such debt; and

(II) there is adequate protection of the interest of the holder of the lien on the property with respect to which such senior or equal lien is proposed to be granted.

(ii) HEARING.—The hearing required pursuant to this subparagraph shall be before a court of the United States, which shall have jurisdiction to conduct such hearing and to authorize a bridge financial company to obtain secured credit under clause (i).

(D) BURDEN OF PROOF.—In any hearing under this paragraph, the Corporation has the burden of proof on the issue of adequate protection.

(E) QUALIFIED FINANCIAL CONTRACTS.—No credit or debt obtained or issued by a bridge financial company may contain terms that impair the rights of a counterparty to a qualified financial contract upon a default by the bridge financial company, other than the priority of such counterparty's unsecured claim (after the exercise of rights) relative to the priority of the bridge financial company's obligations in respect of such credit or debt, unless such counterparty consents in writing to any such impairment.

(17) EFFECT ON DEBTS AND LIENS.—The reversal or modification on appeal of an authorization under this subsection to obtain credit or issue debt, or of a grant under this section of a priority or a lien, does not affect the validity of any debt so issued, or any priority or lien so granted, to an entity that extended such credit in good faith, whether or not such entity knew of the pendency of the appeal, unless such authorization and the issuance of such debt, or the granting of such priority or lien, were stayed pending appeal.

(i) SHARING RECORDS.—If the Corporation has been appointed as receiver for a covered financial company, other Federal regulators shall make all records relating to the covered financial company available to the Corporation, which may be used by the Corporation in any manner that the Corporation determines to be appropriate.

(j) EXPEDITED PROCEDURES FOR CERTAIN CLAIMS.—

(1) TIME FOR FILING NOTICE OF APPEAL.—The notice of appeal of any order, whether interlocutory or final, entered in any case brought by the Corporation against a director, officer, employee, agent, attorney, accountant, or appraiser of the covered financial company, or any other person employed by or providing services to a covered financial company, shall be filed not later than 30 days after the date of entry of the order. The hearing of the appeal shall be held not later than 120 days after the date of the notice of appeal. The appeal shall be decided not later than 180 days after the date of the notice of appeal.

(2) SCHEDULING.—The court shall expedite the consideration of any case brought by the Corporation against a director, officer, employee, agent, attorney, accountant, or appraiser of a

covered financial company or any other person employed by or providing services to a covered financial company. As far as practicable, the court shall give such case priority on its docket.

(3) JUDICIAL DISCRETION.—The court may modify the schedule and limitations stated in paragraphs (1) and (2) in a particular case, based on a specific finding that the ends of justice that would be served by making such a modification would outweigh the best interest of the public in having the case resolved expeditiously.

(k) FOREIGN INVESTIGATIONS.—The Corporation, as receiver for any covered financial company, and for purposes of carrying out any power, authority, or duty with respect to a covered financial company—

(1) may request the assistance of any foreign financial authority and provide assistance to any foreign financial authority in accordance with section 8(v) of the Federal Deposit Insurance Act, as if the covered financial company were an insured depository institution, the Corporation were the appropriate Federal banking agency for the company, and any foreign financial authority were the foreign banking authority; and

(2) may maintain an office to coordinate foreign investigations or investigations on behalf of foreign financial authorities.

(l) PROHIBITION ON ENTERING SECRECY AGREEMENTS AND PROTECTIVE ORDERS.—The Corporation may not enter into any agreement or approve any protective order which prohibits the Corporation from disclosing the terms of any settlement of an administrative or other action for damages or restitution brought by the Corporation in its capacity as receiver for a covered financial company.

(m) LIQUIDATION OF CERTAIN COVERED FINANCIAL COMPANIES OR BRIDGE FINANCIAL COMPANIES.—

(1) IN GENERAL.—Except as specifically provided in this section, and notwithstanding any other provision of law, the Corporation, in connection with the liquidation of any covered financial company or bridge financial company with respect to which the Corporation has been appointed as receiver, shall—

(A) in the case of any covered financial company or bridge financial company that is a stockbroker, but is not a member of the Securities Investor Protection Corporation, apply the provisions of subchapter III of chapter 7 of the Bankruptcy Code, in respect of the distribution to any customer of all customer name security and customer property and member property, as if such covered financial company or bridge financial company were a debtor for purposes of such subchapter; or

(B) in the case of any covered financial company or bridge financial company that is a commodity broker, apply the provisions of subchapter IV of chapter 7 the Bankruptcy Code, in respect of the distribution to any customer of all customer property and member property, as if such covered financial company or bridge financial company were a debtor for purposes of such subchapter.

(2) DEFINITIONS.—For purposes of this subsection—

(A) the terms "customer", "customer name security", and "customer property and member property" have the same meanings as in sections 741 and 761 of title 11, United States Code; and

(B) the terms "commodity broker" and "stockbroker" have the same meanings as in section 101 of the Bankruptcy Code.

(n) ORDERLY LIQUIDATION FUND.—

(1) ESTABLISHMENT.—There is established in the Treasury of the United States a separate fund to be known as the "Orderly Liquidation Fund", which shall be available to the Corporation to carry out the authorities contained in this title, for the cost of actions authorized by this title, including the orderly liquidation of covered financial companies, payment of administrative expenses, the payment of principal and interest by the Corporation on obligations issued under paragraph (5), and the exercise of the authorities of the Corporation under this title.

(2) PROCEEDS.—Amounts received by the Corporation, including assessments received under subsection (o), proceeds of obligations issued under paragraph (5), interest and other earnings from investments, and repayments to the Corporation by covered financial companies, shall be deposited into the Fund.

Act Sec. 210(n)(2) ¶10,210

(3) MANAGEMENT.—The Corporation shall manage the Fund in accordance with this subsection and the policies and procedures established under section 203(d).

(4) INVESTMENTS.—At the request of the Corporation, the Secretary may invest such portion of amounts held in the Fund that are not, in the judgment of the Corporation, required to meet the current needs of the Corporation, in obligations of the United States having suitable maturities, as determined by the Corporation. The interest on and the proceeds from the sale or redemption of such obligations shall be credited to the Fund.

(5) AUTHORITY TO ISSUE OBLIGATIONS.—

(A) CORPORATION AUTHORIZED TO ISSUE OBLIGATIONS.—Upon appointment by the Secretary of the Corporation as receiver for a covered financial company, the Corporation is authorized to issue obligations to the Secretary.

(B) SECRETARY AUTHORIZED TO PURCHASE OBLIGATIONS.—The Secretary may, under such terms and conditions as the Secretary may require, purchase or agree to purchase any obligations issued under subparagraph (A), and for such purpose, the Secretary is authorized to use as a public debt transaction the proceeds of the sale of any securities issued under chapter 31 of title 31, United States Code, and the purposes for which securities may be issued under chapter 31 of title 31, United States Code, are extended to include such purchases.

(C) INTEREST RATE.—Each purchase of obligations by the Secretary under this paragraph shall be upon such terms and conditions as to yield a return at a rate determined by the Secretary, taking into consideration the current average yield on outstanding marketable obligations of the United States of comparable maturity, plus an interest rate surcharge to be determined by the Secretary, which shall be greater than the difference between—

(i) the current average rate on an index of corporate obligations of comparable maturity; and

(ii) the current average rate on outstanding marketable obligations of the United States of comparable maturity.

(D) SECRETARY AUTHORIZED TO SELL OBLIGATIONS.—The Secretary may sell, upon such terms and conditions as the Secretary shall determine, any of the obligations acquired under this paragraph.

(E) PUBLIC DEBT TRANSACTIONS.—All purchases and sales by the Secretary of such obligations under this paragraph shall be treated as public debt transactions of the United States, and the proceeds from the sale of any obligations acquired by the Secretary under this paragraph shall be deposited into the Treasury of the United States as miscellaneous receipts.

(6) MAXIMUM OBLIGATION LIMITATION.—The Corporation may not, in connection with the orderly liquidation of a covered financial company, issue or incur any obligation, if, after issuing or incurring the obligation, the aggregate amount of such obligations outstanding under this subsection for each covered financial company would exceed—

(A) an amount that is equal to 10 percent of the total consolidated assets of the covered financial company, based on the most recent financial statement available, during the 30-day period immediately following the date of appointment of the Corporation as receiver (or a shorter time period if the Corporation has calculated the amount described under subparagraph (B)); and

(B) the amount that is equal to 90 percent of the fair value of the total consolidated assets of each covered financial company that are available for repayment, after the time period described in subparagraph (A).

(7) RULEMAKING.—The Corporation and the Secretary shall jointly, in consultation with the Council, prescribe regulations governing the calculation of the maximum obligation limitation defined in this paragraph.

(8) RULE OF CONSTRUCTION.—

(A) IN GENERAL.—Nothing in this section shall be construed to affect the authority of the Corporation under subsection (a) or (b) of section 14 or section 15(c)(5) of the Federal Deposit Insurance Act (12 U.S.C. 1824, 1825(c)(5)), the management of the Deposit Insurance Fund by the Corporation, or the resolution of insured depository institutions, provided that—

(i) the authorities of the Corporation contained in this title shall not be used to assist the Deposit Insurance Fund or to assist any financial company under applicable law other than this Act;

(ii) the authorities of the Corporation relating to the Deposit Insurance Fund, or any other responsibilities of the Corporation under applicable law other than this title, shall not be used to assist a covered financial company pursuant to this title; and

(iii) the Deposit Insurance Fund may not be used in any manner to otherwise circumvent the purposes of this title.

(B) VALUATION.—For purposes of determining the amount of obligations under this subsection—

(i) the Corporation shall include as an obligation any contingent liability of the Corporation pursuant to this title; and

(ii) the Corporation shall value any contingent liability at its expected cost to the Corporation.

(9) ORDERLY LIQUIDATION AND REPAYMENT PLANS.—

(A) ORDERLY LIQUIDATION PLAN.—Amounts in the Fund shall be available to the Corporation with regard to a covered financial company for which the Corporation is appointed receiver after the Corporation has developed an orderly liquidation plan that is acceptable to the Secretary with regard to such covered financial company, including the provision and use of funds, including taking any actions specified under section 204(d) and subsection (h)(2)(G)(iv) and (h)(9) of this section, and payments to third parties. The orderly liquidation plan shall take into account actions to avoid or mitigate potential adverse effects on low income, minority, or underserved communities affected by the failure of the covered financial company, and shall provide for coordination with the primary financial regulatory agencies, as appropriate, to ensure that such actions are taken. The Corporation may, at any time, amend any orderly liquidation plan approved by the Secretary with the concurrence of the Secretary.

(B) MANDATORY REPAYMENT PLAN.—

(i) IN GENERAL.—No amount authorized under paragraph (6)(B) may be provided by the Secretary to the Corporation under paragraph (5), unless an agreement is in effect between the Secretary and the Corporation that—

(I) provides a specific plan and schedule to achieve the repayment of the outstanding amount of any borrowing under paragraph (5); and

(II) demonstrates that income to the Corporation from the liquidated assets of the covered financial company and assessments under subsection (o) will be sufficient to amortize the outstanding balance within the period established in the repayment schedule and pay the interest accruing on such balance within the time provided in subsection (o)(1)(B).

(ii) CONSULTATION WITH AND REPORT TO CONGRESS.—The Secretary and the Corporation shall—

(I) consult with the Committee on Banking, Housing, and Urban Affairs of the Senate and the Committee on Financial Services of the House of Representatives on the terms of any repayment schedule agreement; and

(II) submit a copy of the repayment schedule agreement to the Committees described in subclause (I) before the end of the 30-day period beginning on the date on which any amount is provided by the Secretary to the Corporation under paragraph (5).

(10) IMPLEMENTATION EXPENSES.—

(A) IN GENERAL.—Reasonable implementation expenses of the Corporation incurred after the date of enactment of this Act shall be treated as expenses of the Council.

(B) REQUESTS FOR REIMBURSEMENT.—The Corporation shall periodically submit a request for reimbursement for implementation expenses to the Chairperson of the Council, who shall arrange for prompt reimbursement to the Corporation of reasonable implementation expenses.

(C) DEFINITION.—As used in this paragraph, the term "implementation expenses"—

(i) means costs incurred by the Corporation beginning on the date of enactment of this Act, as part of its efforts to implement this title that do not relate to a particular covered financial company; and

(ii) includes the costs incurred in connection with the development of policies, procedures, rules, and regulations and other planning activities of the Corporation consistent with carrying out this title.

(o) ASSESSMENTS.—

(1) RISK-BASED ASSESSMENTS.—

(A) ELIGIBLE FINANCIAL COMPANIES DEFINED.—For purposes of this subsection, the term "eligible financial company" means any bank holding company with total consolidated assets equal to or greater than $50,000,000,000 and any nonbank financial company supervised by the Board of Governors.

(B) ASSESSMENTS.—The Corporation shall charge one or more risk-based assessments in accordance with the provisions of subparagraph (D), if such assessments are necessary to pay in full the obligations issued by the Corporation to the Secretary under this title within 60 months of the date of issuance of such obligations.

(C) EXTENSIONS AUTHORIZED.—The Corporation may, with the approval of the Secretary, extend the time period under subparagraph (B), if the Corporation determines that an extension is necessary to avoid a serious adverse effect on the financial system of the United States.

(D) APPLICATION OF ASSESSMENTS.—To meet the requirements of subparagraph (B), the Corporation shall—

(i) impose assessments, as soon as practicable, on any claimant that received additional payments or amounts from the Corporation pursuant to subsection (b)(4), (d)(4), or (h)(5)(E), except for payments or amounts necessary to initiate and continue operations essential to implementation of the receivership or any bridge financial company, to recover on a cumulative basis, the entire difference between—

(I) the aggregate value the claimant received from the Corporation on a claim pursuant to this title (including pursuant to subsection (b)(4), (d)(4), and (h)(5)(E)), as of the date on which such value was received; and

(II) the value the claimant was entitled to receive from the Corporation on such claim solely from the proceeds of the liquidation of the covered financial company under this title; and

(ii) if the amounts to be recovered on a cumulative basis under clause (i) are insufficient to meet the requirements of subparagraph (B), after taking into account the considerations set forth in paragraph (4), impose assessments on—

(I) eligible financial companies; and

(II) financial companies with total consolidated assets equal to or greater than $50,000,000,000 that are not eligible financial companies.

(E) PROVISION OF FINANCING.—Payments or amounts necessary to initiate and continue operations essential to implementation of the receivership or any bridge financial company described in subparagraph (D)(i) shall not include the provision of financing, as defined by rule of the Corporation, to third parties.

(2) GRADUATED ASSESSMENT RATE.—The Corporation shall impose assessments on a graduated basis, with financial companies having greater assets and risk being assessed at a higher rate.

(3) NOTIFICATION AND PAYMENT.—The Corporation shall notify each financial company of that company's assessment under this subsection. Any financial company subject to assessment under this subsection shall pay such assessment in accordance with the regulations prescribed pursuant to paragraph (6).

(4) RISK-BASED ASSESSMENT CONSIDERATIONS.—In imposing assessments under paragraph (1)(D)(ii), the Corporation shall use a risk matrix. The Council shall make a recommendation to the Corporation on the risk matrix to be used in imposing such assessments, and the Corporation shall take into account any such recommendation in the establishment of the risk matrix to be used to impose such assessments. In recommending or establishing such risk matrix, the Council and the Corporation, respectively, shall take into account—

(A) economic conditions generally affecting financial companies so as to allow assessments to increase during more favorable economic conditions and to decrease during less favorable economic conditions;

(B) any assessments imposed on a financial company or an affiliate of a financial company that—

(i) is an insured depository institution, assessed pursuant to section 7 or 13(c)(4)(G) of the Federal Deposit Insurance Act;

(ii) is a member of the Securities Investor Protection Corporation, assessed pursuant to section 4 of the Securities Investor Protection Act of 1970 (15 U.S.C. 78ddd);

(iii) is an insured credit union, assessed pursuant to section 202(c)(1)(A)(i) of the Federal Credit Union Act (12 U.S.C. 1782(c)(1)(A)(i)); or

(iv) is an insurance company, assessed pursuant to applicable State law to cover (or reimburse payments made to cover) the costs of the rehabilitation, liquidation, or other State insolvency proceeding with respect to 1 or more insurance companies;

(C) the risks presented by the financial company to the financial system and the extent to which the financial company has benefitted, or likely would benefit, from the orderly liquidation of a financial company under this title, including—

(i) the amount, different categories, and concentrations of assets of the financial company and its affiliates, including both on-balance sheet and off-balance sheet assets;

(ii) the activities of the financial company and its affiliates;

(iii) the relevant market share of the financial company and its affiliates;

(iv) the extent to which the financial company is leveraged;

(v) the potential exposure to sudden calls on liquidity precipitated by economic distress;

(vi) the amount, maturity, volatility, and stability of the company's financial obligations to, and relationship with, other financial companies;

(vii) the amount, maturity, volatility, and stability of the liabilities of the company, including the degree of reliance on short-term funding, taking into consideration existing systems for measuring a company's risk-based capital;

(viii) the stability and variety of the company's sources of funding;

(ix) the company's importance as a source of credit for households, businesses, and State and local governments and as a source of liquidity for the financial system;

(x) the extent to which assets are simply managed and not owned by the financial company and the extent to which ownership of assets under management is diffuse; and

(xi) the amount, different categories, and concentrations of liabilities, both insured and uninsured, contingent and noncontingent, including both on-balance sheet and off-balance sheet liabilities, of the financial company and its affiliates;

(D) any risks presented by the financial company during the 10-year period immediately prior to the appointment of the Corporation as receiver for the covered financial company that contributed to the failure of the covered financial company; and

(E) such other risk-related factors as the Corporation, or the Council, as applicable, may determine to be appropriate.

(5) COLLECTION OF INFORMATION.—The Corporation may impose on covered financial companies such collection of information requirements as the Corporation deems necessary to carry out this subsection after the appointment of the Corporation as receiver under this title.

(6) RULEMAKING.—

(A) IN GENERAL.—The Corporation shall prescribe regulations to carry out this subsection. The Corporation shall consult with the Secretary in the development and finalization of such regulations.

(B) EQUITABLE TREATMENT.—The regulations prescribed under subparagraph (A) shall take into account the differences in risks posed to the financial stability of the United States by financial companies, the differences in the liability structures of financial companies, and the different bases for other assessments that such financial companies may be required to pay, to ensure that assessed financial companies are treated equitably and that assessments under this subsection reflect such differences.

(p) UNENFORCEABILITY OF CERTAIN AGREEMENTS.—

(1) IN GENERAL.—No provision described in paragraph (2) shall be enforceable against or impose any liability on any person, as such enforcement or liability shall be contrary to public policy.

(2) PROHIBITED PROVISIONS.—A provision described in this paragraph is any term contained in any existing or future standstill, confidentiality, or other agreement that, directly or indirectly—

(A) affects, restricts, or limits the ability of any person to offer to acquire or acquire;

(B) prohibits any person from offering to acquire or acquiring; or

(C) prohibits any person from using any previously disclosed information in connection with any such offer to acquire or acquisition of, all or part of any covered financial company, including any liabilities, assets, or interest therein, in connection with any transaction in which the Corporation exercises its authority under this title.

(q) OTHER EXEMPTIONS.—

(1) IN GENERAL.—When acting as a receiver under this title—

(A) the Corporation, including its franchise, its capital, reserves and surplus, and its income, shall be exempt from all taxation imposed by any State, county, municipality, or local taxing authority, except that any real property of the Corporation shall be subject to State, territorial, county, municipal, or local taxation to the same extent according to its value as other real property is taxed, except that, notwithstanding the failure of any person to challenge an assessment under State law of the value of such property, such value, and the tax thereon, shall be determined as of the period for which such tax is imposed;

(B) no property of the Corporation shall be subject to levy, attachment, garnishment, foreclosure, or sale without the consent of the Corporation, nor shall any involuntary lien attach to the property of the Corporation; and

(C) the Corporation shall not be liable for any amounts in the nature of penalties or fines, including those arising from the failure of any person to pay any real property, personal property, probate, or recording tax or any recording or filing fees when due; and

(D) the Corporation shall be exempt from all prosecution by the United States or any State, county, municipality, or local authority for any criminal offense arising under Federal, State, county, municipal, or local law, which was allegedly committed by the covered financial company, or persons acting on behalf of the covered financial company, prior to the appointment of the Corporation as receiver.

(2) LIMITATION.—Paragraph (1) shall not apply with respect to any tax imposed (or other amount arising) under the Internal Revenue Code of 1986.

(r) CERTAIN SALES OF ASSETS PROHIBITED.—

(1) PERSONS WHO ENGAGED IN IMPROPER CONDUCT WITH, OR CAUSED LOSSES TO, COVERED FINANCIAL COMPANIES.—The Corporation shall prescribe regulations which, at a minimum, shall prohibit the sale of assets of a covered financial company by the Corporation to—

(A) any person who—

(i) has defaulted, or was a member of a partnership or an officer or director of a corporation that has defaulted, on 1 or more obligations, the aggregate amount of which exceeds $1,000,000, to such covered financial company;

(ii) has been found to have engaged in fraudulent activity in connection with any obligation referred to in clause (i); and

(iii) proposes to purchase any such asset in whole or in part through the use of the proceeds of a loan or advance of credit from the Corporation or from any covered financial company;

(B) any person who participated, as an officer or director of such covered financial company or of any affiliate of such company, in a material way in any transaction that resulted in a substantial loss to such covered financial company; or

(C) any person who has demonstrated a pattern or practice of defalcation regarding obligations to such covered financial company.

(2) CONVICTED DEBTORS.—Except as provided in paragraph (3), a person may not purchase any asset of such institution from the receiver, if that person—

(A) has been convicted of an offense under section 215, 656, 657, 1005, 1006, 1007, 1008, 1014, 1032, 1341, 1343, or 1344 of title 18, United States Code, or of conspiring to commit such an offense, affecting any covered financial company; and

(B) is in default on any loan or other extension of credit from such covered financial company which, if not paid, will cause substantial loss to the Fund or the Corporation.

(3) SETTLEMENT OF CLAIMS.—Paragraphs (1) and (2) shall not apply to the sale or transfer by the Corporation of any asset of any covered financial company to any person, if the sale or transfer of the asset resolves or settles, or is part of the resolution or settlement, of 1 or more claims that have been, or could have been, asserted by the Corporation against the person.

(4) DEFINITION OF DEFAULT.—For purposes of this subsection, the term "default" means a failure to comply with the terms of a loan or other obligation to such an extent that the property securing the obligation is foreclosed upon.

(s) RECOUPMENT OF COMPENSATION FROM SENIOR EXECUTIVES AND DIRECTORS.—

(1) IN GENERAL.—The Corporation, as receiver of a covered financial company, may recover from any current or former senior executive or director substantially responsible for the failed condition of the covered financial company any compensation received during the 2-year period preceding the date on which the Corporation was appointed as the receiver of the covered financial company, except that, in the case of fraud, no time limit shall apply.

(2) COST CONSIDERATIONS.—In seeking to recover any such compensation, the Corporation shall weigh the financial and deterrent benefits of such recovery against the cost of executing the recovery.

(3) RULEMAKING.—The Corporation shall promulgate regulations to implement the requirements of this subsection, including defining the term "compensation" to mean any financial remuneration, including salary, bonuses, incentives, benefits, severance, deferred compensation, or golden parachute benefits, and any profits realized from the sale of the securities of the covered financial company.

[Explanation at ¶ 505, ¶ 520, ¶ 525, ¶ 530, ¶ 535, ¶ 540 and ¶ 545.]

[¶ 10,211] ACT SEC. 211. MISCELLANEOUS PROVISIONS.

(a) CLARIFICATION OF PROHIBITION REGARDING CONCEALMENT OF ASSETS FROM RECEIVER OR LIQUIDATING AGENT.—Section 1032(1) of title 18, United States Code, is amended by inserting "the Federal Deposit Insurance Corporation acting as receiver for a covered financial company, in accordance with title II of the Dodd-Frank Wall Street Reform and Consumer Protection Act," before "or the National Credit".

(b) CONFORMING AMENDMENT.—Section 1032 of title 18, United States Code, is amended in the section heading, by striking **"of financial institution"**.

(c) FEDERAL DEPOSIT INSURANCE CORPORATION IMPROVEMENT ACT OF 1991.—Section 403(a) of the Federal Deposit Insurance Corporation Improvement Act of 1991 (12 U.S.C. 4403(a)) is amended by inserting "section 210(c) of the Dodd-Frank Wall Street Reform and Consumer Protection Act, section 1367 of the Federal Housing Enterprises Financial Safety and Soundness Act of 1992 (12 U.S.C. 4617(d))," after "section 11(e) of the Federal Deposit Insurance Act,".

(d) FDIC INSPECTOR GENERAL REVIEWS.—

(1) SCOPE.—The Inspector General of the Corporation shall conduct, supervise, and coordinate audits and investigations of the liquidation of any covered financial company by the Corporation as receiver under this title, including collecting and summarizing—

(A) a description of actions taken by the Corporation as receiver;

(B) a description of any material sales, transfers, mergers, obligations, purchases, and other material transactions entered into by the Corporation;

(C) an evaluation of the adequacy of the policies and procedures of the Corporation under section 203(d) and orderly liquidation plan under section 210(n)(14);

(D) an evaluation of the utilization by the Corporation of the private sector in carrying out its functions, including the adequacy of any conflict-of-interest reviews; and

(E) an evaluation of the overall performance of the Corporation in liquidating the covered financial company, including administrative costs, timeliness of liquidation process, and impact on the financial system.

(2) FREQUENCY.—Not later than 6 months after the date of appointment of the Corporation as receiver under this title and every 6 months thereafter, the Inspector General of the Corporation shall conduct the audit and investigation described in paragraph (1).

(3) REPORTS AND TESTIMONY.—The Inspector General of the Corporation shall include in the semiannual reports required by section 5(a) of the Inspector General Act of 1978 (5 U.S.C. App.), a summary of the findings and evaluations under paragraph (1), and shall appear before the appropriate committees of Congress, if requested, to present each such report.

(4) FUNDING.—

(A) INITIAL FUNDING.—The expenses of the Inspector General of the Corporation in carrying out this subsection shall be considered administrative expenses of the receivership.

(B) ADDITIONAL FUNDING.—If the maximum amount available to the Corporation as receiver under this title is insufficient to enable the Inspector General of the Corporation to carry out the duties under this subsection, the Corporation shall pay such additional amounts from assessments imposed under section 210.

(5) TERMINATION OF RESPONSIBILITIES.—The duties and responsibilities of the Inspector General of the Corporation under this subsection shall terminate 1 year after the date of termination of the receivership under this title.

(e) TREASURY INSPECTOR GENERAL REVIEWS.—

(1) SCOPE.—The Inspector General of the Department of the Treasury shall conduct, supervise, and coordinate audits and investigations of actions taken by the Secretary related to the liquidation of any covered financial company under this title, including collecting and summarizing—

(A) a description of actions taken by the Secretary under this title;

(B) an analysis of the approval by the Secretary of the policies and procedures of the Corporation under section 203 and acceptance of the orderly liquidation plan of the Corporation under section 210; and

(C) an assessment of the terms and conditions underlying the purchase by the Secretary of obligations of the Corporation under section 210.

(2) FREQUENCY.—Not later than 6 months after the date of appointment of the Corporation as receiver under this title and every 6 months thereafter, the Inspector General of the Department of the Treasury shall conduct the audit and investigation described in paragraph (1).

(3) REPORTS AND TESTIMONY.—The Inspector General of the Department of the Treasury shall include in the semiannual reports required by section 5(a) of the Inspector General Act of 1978 (5 U.S.C. App.), a summary of the findings and assessments under paragraph (1), and shall appear before the appropriate committees of Congress, if requested, to present each such report.

(4) TERMINATION OF RESPONSIBILITIES.—The duties and responsibilities of the Inspector General of the Department of the Treasury under this subsection shall terminate 1 year after the date on which the obligations purchased by the Secretary from the Corporation under section 210 are fully redeemed.

(f) PRIMARY FINANCIAL REGULATORY AGENCY INSPECTOR GENERAL REVIEWS.—

(1) SCOPE.—Upon the appointment of the Corporation as receiver for a covered financial company supervised by a Federal primary financial regulatory agency or the Board of Governors under section 165, the Inspector General of the agency or the Board of Governors shall make a written report reviewing the supervision by the agency or the Board of Governors of the covered financial company, which shall—

(A) evaluate the effectiveness of the agency or the Board of Governors in carrying out its supervisory responsibilities with respect to the covered financial company;

(B) identify any acts or omissions on the part of agency or Board of Governors officials that contributed to the covered financial company being in default or in danger of default;

(C) identify any actions that could have been taken by the agency or the Board of Governors that would have prevented the company from being in default or in danger of default; and

(D) recommend appropriate administrative or legislative action.

(2) REPORTS AND TESTIMONY.—Not later than 1 year after the date of appointment of the Corporation as receiver under this title, the Inspector General of the Federal primary financial regulatory agency or the Board of Governors shall provide the report required by paragraph (1) to such agency or the Board of Governors, and along with such agency or the Board of Governors, as applicable, shall appear before the appropriate committees of Congress, if requested, to present the report required by paragraph (1). Not later than 90 days after the date of receipt of the report required by paragraph (1), such agency or the Board of Governors, as applicable, shall provide a written report to Congress describing any actions taken in response to the recommendations in the report, and if no such actions were taken, describing the reasons why no actions were taken.

[Explanation at ¶ 505 and ¶ 550.]

[¶ 10,212] ACT SEC. 212. PROHIBITION OF CIRCUMVENTION AND PREVENTION OF CONFLICTS OF INTEREST.

(a) NO OTHER FUNDING.—Funds for the orderly liquidation of any covered financial company under this title shall only be provided as specified under this title.

(b) LIMIT ON GOVERNMENTAL ACTIONS.—No governmental entity may take any action to circumvent the purposes of this title.

(c) CONFLICT OF INTEREST.—In the event that the Corporation is appointed receiver for more than 1 covered financial company or is appointed receiver for a covered financial company and receiver for any insured depository institution that is an affiliate of such covered financial company, the

Corporation shall take appropriate action, as necessary to avoid any conflicts of interest that may arise in connection with multiple receiverships.

[Explanation at ¶ 505 and ¶ 545.]

[¶ 10,213] ACT SEC. 213. BAN ON CERTAIN ACTIVITIES BY SENIOR EXECUTIVES AND DIRECTORS.

(a) PROHIBITION AUTHORITY.—The Board of Governors or, if the covered financial company was not supervised by the Board of Governors, the Corporation, may exercise the authority provided by this section.

(b) AUTHORITY TO ISSUE ORDER.—The appropriate agency described in subsection (a) may take any action authorized by subsection (c), if the agency determines that—

(1) a senior executive or a director of the covered financial company, prior to the appointment of the Corporation as receiver, has, directly or indirectly—

(A) violated—

(i) any law or regulation;

(ii) any cease-and-desist order which has become final;

(iii) any condition imposed in writing by a Federal agency in connection with any action on any application, notice, or request by such company or senior executive; or

(iv) any written agreement between such company and such agency;

(B) engaged or participated in any unsafe or unsound practice in connection with any financial company; or

(C) committed or engaged in any act, omission, or practice which constitutes a breach of the fiduciary duty of such senior executive or director;

(2) by reason of the violation, practice, or breach described in any subparagraph of paragraph (1), such senior executive or director has received financial gain or other benefit by reason of such violation, practice, or breach and such violation, practice, or breach contributed to the failure of the company; and

(3) such violation, practice, or breach—

(A) involves personal dishonesty on the part of such senior executive or director; or

(B) demonstrates willful or continuing disregard by such senior executive or director for the safety or soundness of such company.

(c) AUTHORIZED ACTIONS.—

(1) IN GENERAL.—The appropriate agency for a financial company, as described in subsection (a), may serve upon a senior executive or director described in subsection (b) a written notice of the intention of the agency to prohibit any further participation by such person, in any manner, in the conduct of the affairs of any financial company for a period of time determined by the appropriate agency to be commensurate with such violation, practice, or breach, provided such period shall be not less than 2 years.

(2) PROCEDURES.—The due process requirements and other procedures under section 8(e) of the Federal Deposit Insurance Act (12 U.S.C. 1818(e)) shall apply to actions under this section as if the covered financial company were an insured depository institution and the senior executive or director were an institution-affiliated party, as those terms are defined in that Act.

(d) REGULATIONS.—The Corporation and the Board of Governors, in consultation with the Council, shall jointly prescribe rules or regulations to administer and carry out this section, including rules, regulations, or guidelines to further define the term senior executive for the purposes of this section.

[Explanation at ¶ 505 and ¶ 545.]

[¶ 10,214] ACT SEC. 214. PROHIBITION ON TAXPAYER FUNDING.

(a) LIQUIDATION REQUIRED.—All financial companies put into receivership under this title shall be liquidated. No taxpayer funds shall be used to prevent the liquidation of any financial company under this title.

(b) RECOVERY OF FUNDS.—All funds expended in the liquidation of a financial company under this title shall be recovered from the disposition of assets of such financial company, or shall be the responsibility of the financial sector, through assessments.

(c) NO LOSSES TO TAXPAYERS.—Taxpayers shall bear no losses from the exercise of any authority under this title.

[Explanation at ¶ 545.]

[¶ 10,215] ACT SEC. 215. STUDY ON SECURED CREDITOR HAIRCUTS.

(a) STUDY REQUIRED.—The Council shall conduct a study evaluating the importance of maximizing United States taxpayer protections and promoting market discipline with respect to the treatment of fully secured creditors in the utilization of the orderly liquidation authority authorized by this Act. In carrying out such study, the Council shall—

(1) not be prejudicial to current or past laws or regulations with respect to secured creditor treatment in a resolution process;

(2) study the similarities and differences between the resolution mechanisms authorized by the Bankruptcy Code, the Federal Deposit Insurance Corporation Improvement Act of 1991, and the orderly liquidation authority authorized by this Act;

(3) determine how various secured creditors are treated in such resolution mechanisms and examine how a haircut (of various degrees) on secured creditors could improve market discipline and protect taxpayers;

(4) compare the benefits and dynamics of prudent lending practices by depository institutions in secured loans for consumers and small businesses to the lending practices of secured creditors to large, interconnected financial firms;

(5) consider whether credit differs according to different types of collateral and different terms and timing of the extension of credit; and

(6) include an examination of stakeholders who were unsecured or under-collateralized and seek collateral when a firm is failing, and the impact that such behavior has on financial stability and an orderly resolution that protects taxpayers if the firm fails.

(b) REPORT.—Not later than the end of the 1-year period beginning on the date of enactment of this Act, the Council shall issue a report to the Congress containing all findings and conclusions made by the Council in carrying out the study required under subsection (a).

[Explanation at ¶ 545.]

[¶ 10,216] ACT SEC. 216. STUDY ON BANKRUPTCY PROCESS FOR FINANCIAL AND NONBANK FINANCIAL INSTITUTIONS.

(a) STUDY.—

(1) IN GENERAL.—Upon enactment of this Act, the Board of Governors, in consultation with the Administrative Office of the United States Courts, shall conduct a study regarding the resolution of financial companies under the Bankruptcy Code, under chapter 7 or 11 thereof.

(2) ISSUES TO BE STUDIED.—Issues to be studied under this section include—

(A) the effectiveness of chapter 7 and chapter 11 of the Bankruptcy Code in facilitating the orderly resolution or reorganization of systemic financial companies;

(B) whether a special financial resolution court or panel of special masters or judges should be established to oversee cases involving financial companies to provide for the resolution of such companies under the Bankruptcy Code, in a manner that minimizes adverse impacts on financial markets without creating moral hazard;

(C) whether amendments to the Bankruptcy Code should be adopted to enhance the ability of the Code to resolve financial companies in a manner that minimizes adverse impacts on financial markets without creating moral hazard;

(D) whether amendments should be made to the Bankruptcy Code, the Federal Deposit Insurance Act, and other insolvency laws to address the manner in which qualified financial contracts of financial companies are treated; and

(E) the implications, challenges, and benefits to creating a new chapter or subchapter of the Bankruptcy Code to deal with financial companies.

(b) REPORTS TO CONGRESS.—Not later than 1 year after the date of enactment of this Act, and in each successive year until the fifth year after the date of enactment of this Act, the Administrative Office of the United States courts shall submit to the Committees on Banking, Housing, and Urban Affairs and the Judiciary of the Senate and the Committees on Financial Services and the Judiciary of the House of Representatives a report summarizing the results of the study conducted under subsection (a).

[Explanation at ¶ 510.]

[¶ 10,217] ACT SEC. 217. STUDY ON INTERNATIONAL COORDINATION RELATING TO BANKRUPTCY PROCESS FOR NONBANK FINANCIAL INSTITUTIONS.

(a) STUDY.—

(1) IN GENERAL.—The Board of Governors, in consultation with the Administrative Office of the United States Courts, shall conduct a study regarding international coordination relating to the resolution of systemic financial companies under the United States Bankruptcy Code and applicable foreign law.

(2) ISSUES TO BE STUDIED.—With respect to the bankruptcy process for financial companies, issues to be studied under this section include—

(A) the extent to which international coordination currently exists;

(B) current mechanisms and structures for facilitating international cooperation;

(C) barriers to effective international coordination; and

(D) ways to increase and make more effective international coordination of the resolution of financial companies, so as to minimize the impact on the financial system without creating moral hazard.

(b) REPORT TO CONGRESS.—Not later than 1 year after the date of enactment of this Act, the Administrative office of the United States Courts shall submit to the Committees on Banking, Housing, and Urban Affairs and the Judiciary of the Senate and the Committees on Financial Services and the Judiciary of the House of Representatives a report summarizing the results of the study conducted under subsection (a).

[Explanation at ¶ 510.]

TITLE III—TRANSFER OF POWERS TO THE COMPTROLLER OF THE CURRENCY, THE CORPORATION, AND THE BOARD OF GOVERNORS

[¶ 10,300] ACT SEC. 300. SHORT TITLE.

This title may be cited as the "Enhancing Financial Institution Safety and Soundness Act of 2010".

Title III—Transfer of Powers

[Explanation at ¶ 1005.]

[¶ 10,301] ACT SEC. 301. PURPOSES.

The purposes of this title are—

(1) to provide for the safe and sound operation of the banking system of the United States;

(2) to preserve and protect the dual system of Federal and State-chartered depository institutions;

(3) to ensure the fair and appropriate supervision of each depository institution, regardless of the size or type of charter of the depository institution; and

(4) to streamline and rationalize the supervision of depository institutions and the holding companies of depository institutions.

[Explanation at ¶ 1005.]

[¶ 10,302] ACT SEC. 302. DEFINITION.

In this title, the term "transferred employee" means, as the context requires, an employee transferred to the Office of the Comptroller of the Currency or the Corporation under section 322.

Subtitle A—Transfer of Powers and Duties

[¶ 10,311] ACT SEC. 311. TRANSFER DATE.

(a) TRANSFER DATE.—Except as provided in subsection (b), the term "transfer date" means the date that is 1 year after the date of enactment of this Act.

(b) EXTENSION PERMITTED.—

(1) NOTICE REQUIRED.—The Secretary, in consultation with the Comptroller of the Currency, the Director of the Office of Thrift Supervision, the Chairman of the Board of Governors, and the Chairperson of the Corporation, may extend the period under subsection (a) and designate a transfer date that is not later than 18 months after the date of enactment of this Act, if the Secretary transmits to the Committee on Banking, Housing, and Urban Affairs of the Senate and the Committee on Financial Services of the House of Representatives—

(A) a written determination that commencement of the orderly process to implement this title is not feasible by the date that is 1 year after the date of enactment of this Act;

(B) an explanation of why an extension is necessary to commence the process of orderly implementation of this title;

(C) the transfer date designated under this subsection; and

(D) a description of the steps that will be taken to initiate the process of an orderly and timely implementation of this title within the extended time period.

(2) PUBLICATION OF NOTICE.—Not later than 270 days after the date of enactment of this Act, the Secretary shall publish in the Federal Register notice of any transfer date designated under paragraph (1).

[Explanation at ¶ 1005.]

[¶ 10,312] ACT SEC. 312. POWERS AND DUTIES TRANSFERRED.

(a) EFFECTIVE DATE.—This section, and the amendments made by this section, shall take effect on the transfer date.

(b) FUNCTIONS OF THE OFFICE OF THRIFT SUPERVISION.—

(1) SAVINGS AND LOAN HOLDING COMPANY FUNCTIONS TRANSFERRED.—

(A) TRANSFER OF FUNCTIONS.—There are transferred to the Board of Governors all functions of the Office of Thrift Supervision and the Director of the Office of Thrift Supervision (including the authority to issue orders) relating to—

(i) the supervision of—

(I) any savings and loan holding company; and

(II) any subsidiary (other than a depository institution) of a savings and loan holding company; and

(ii) all rulemaking authority of the Office of Thrift Supervision and the Director of the Office of Thrift Supervision relating to savings and loan holding companies.

(B) POWERS, AUTHORITIES, RIGHTS, AND DUTIES.—The Board of Governors shall succeed to all powers, authorities, rights, and duties that were vested in the Office of Thrift Supervision and the Director of the Office of Thrift Supervision on the day before the transfer date relating to the functions and authority transferred under subparagraph (A).

(2) ALL OTHER FUNCTIONS TRANSFERRED.—

(A) BOARD OF GOVERNORS.—All rulemaking authority of the Office of Thrift Supervision and the Director of the Office of Thrift Supervision under section 11 of the Home Owners' Loan Act (12 U.S.C. 1468) relating to transactions with affiliates and extensions of credit to executive officers, directors, and principal shareholders and under section 5(q) of such Act relating to tying arrangements is transferred to the Board of Governors.

(B) COMPTROLLER OF THE CURRENCY.—Except as provided in paragraph (1) and subparagraph (A)—

(i) there are transferred to the Office of the Comptroller of the Currency and the Comptroller of the Currency—

(I) all functions of the Office of Thrift Supervision and the Director of the Office of Thrift Supervision, respectively, relating to Federal savings associations; and

(II) all rulemaking authority of the Office of Thrift Supervision and the Director of the Office of Thrift Supervision, respectively, relating to savings associations; and

(ii) the Office of the Comptroller of the Currency and the Comptroller of the Currency shall succeed to all powers, authorities, rights, and duties that were vested in the Office of Thrift Supervision and the Director of the Office of Thrift Supervision, respectively, on the day before the transfer date relating to the functions and authority transferred under clause (i).

(C) CORPORATION.—Except as provided in paragraph (1) and subparagraphs (A) and (B)—

(i) all functions of the Office of Thrift Supervision and the Director of the Office of Thrift Supervision relating to State savings associations are transferred to the Corporation; and

(ii) the Corporation shall succeed to all powers, authorities, rights, and duties that were vested in the Office of Thrift Supervision and the Director of the Office of Thrift Supervision on the day before the transfer date relating to the functions transferred under clause (i).

(c) CONFORMING AMENDMENTS.—Section 3 of the Federal Deposit Insurance Act (12 U.S.C. 1813) is amended—

(1) in subsection (q), by striking paragraphs (1) through (4) and inserting the following:

"(1) the Office of the Comptroller of the Currency, in the case of—

"(A) any national banking association;

"(B) any Federal branch or agency of a foreign bank; and

"(C) any Federal savings association;

"(2) the Federal Deposit Insurance Corporation, in the case of—

"(A) any State nonmember insured bank;

"(B) any foreign bank having an insured branch; and

"(C) any State savings association;

"(3) the Board of Governors of the Federal Reserve System, in the case of—

"(A) any State member bank;

"(B) any branch or agency of a foreign bank with respect to any provision of the Federal Reserve Act which is made applicable under the International Banking Act of 1978;

"(C) any foreign bank which does not operate an insured branch;

"(D) any agency or commercial lending company other than a Federal agency;

"(E) supervisory or regulatory proceedings arising from the authority given to the Board of Governors under section 7(c)(1) of the International Banking Act of 1978, including such proceedings under the Financial Institutions Supervisory Act of 1966;

"(F) any bank holding company and any subsidiary (other than a depository institution) of a bank holding company; and

"(G) any savings and loan holding company and any subsidiary (other than a depository institution) of a savings and loan holding company."; and

(2) in paragraphs (1) and (3) of subsection (u), by striking "(other than a bank holding company" and inserting "(other than a bank holding company or savings and loan holding company".

(d) CONSUMER PROTECTION.—Nothing in this section may be construed to limit or otherwise affect the transfer of powers under title X.

[Explanation at ¶ 1015.]

[¶ 10,313] ACT SEC. 313. ABOLISHMENT.

Effective 90 days after the transfer date, the Office of Thrift Supervision and the position of Director of the Office of Thrift Supervision are abolished.

[Explanation at ¶ 1010.]

[¶ 10,314] ACT SEC. 314. AMENDMENTS TO THE REVISED STATUTES.

(a) AMENDMENT TO SECTION 324.—Section 324 of the Revised Statutes of the United States (12 U.S.C. 1) is amended to read as follows:

"SEC. 324. COMPTROLLER OF THE CURRENCY.

"(a) OFFICE OF THE COMPTROLLER OF THE CURRENCY ESTABLISHED.—There is established in the Department of the Treasury a bureau to be known as the 'Office of the Comptroller of the Currency' which is charged with assuring the safety and soundness of, and compliance with laws and regulations, fair access to financial services, and fair treatment of customers by, the institutions and other persons subject to its jurisdiction.

"(b) COMPTROLLER OF THE CURRENCY.—

"(1) IN GENERAL.—The chief officer of the Office of the Comptroller of the Currency shall be known as the Comptroller of the Currency. The Comptroller of the Currency shall perform the duties of the Comptroller of the Currency under the general direction of the Secretary of the Treasury. The Secretary of the Treasury may not delay or prevent the issuance of any rule or the promulgation of any regulation by the Comptroller of the Currency, and may not intervene in any matter or proceeding before the Comptroller of the Currency (including agency enforcement actions), unless otherwise specifically provided by law.

"(2) ADDITIONAL AUTHORITY.—The Comptroller of the Currency shall have the same authority with respect to functions transferred to the Comptroller of the Currency under the Enhancing Financial Institution Safety and Soundness Act of 2010 as was vested in the Director of the Office of Thrift Supervision on the transfer date, as defined in section 311 of that Act.".

(b) SUPERVISION OF FEDERAL SAVINGS ASSOCIATIONS.—Chapter 9 of title VII of the Revised Statutes of the United States (12 U.S.C. 1 et seq.) is amended by inserting after section 327A (12 U.S.C. 4a) the following:

"SEC. 327B. DEPUTY COMPTROLLER FOR THE SUPERVISION AND EXAMINATION OF FEDERAL SAVINGS ASSOCIATIONS.

"The Comptroller of the Currency shall designate a Deputy Comptroller, who shall be responsible for the supervision and examination of Federal savings associations.".

(c) AMENDMENT TO SECTION 329.—Section 329 of the Revised Statutes of the United States (12 U.S.C. 11) is amended by inserting before the period at the end the following: "or any Federal savings association".

(d) EFFECTIVE DATE.—This section, and the amendments made by this section, shall take effect on the transfer date.

[Explanation at ¶1020.]

[¶10,315] ACT SEC. 315. FEDERAL INFORMATION POLICY.

Section 3502(5) of title 44, United States Code, is amended by inserting "Office of the Comptroller of the Currency," after "the Securities and Exchange Commission,".

[Explanation at ¶1025.]

[¶10,316] ACT SEC. 316. SAVINGS PROVISIONS.

(a) OFFICE OF THRIFT SUPERVISION.—

(1) EXISTING RIGHTS, DUTIES, AND OBLIGATIONS NOT AFFECTED.—Sections 312(b) and 313 shall not affect the validity of any right, duty, or obligation of the United States, the Director of the Office of Thrift Supervision, the Office of Thrift Supervision, or any other person, that existed on the day before the transfer date.

(2) CONTINUATION OF SUITS.—This title shall not abate any action or proceeding commenced by or against the Director of the Office of Thrift Supervision or the Office of Thrift Supervision before the transfer date, except that—

(A) for any action or proceeding arising out of a function of the Office of Thrift Supervision or the Director of the Office of Thrift Supervision transferred to the Board of Governors by this title, the Board of Governors shall be substituted for the Office of Thrift Supervision or the Director of the Office of Thrift Supervision as a party to the action or proceeding on and after the transfer date;

(B) for any action or proceeding arising out of a function of the Office of Thrift Supervision or the Director of the Office of Thrift Supervision transferred to the Office of the Comptroller of the Currency or the Comptroller of the Currency by this title, the Office of the Comptroller of the Currency or the Comptroller of the Currency shall be substituted for the Office of Thrift Supervision or the Director of the Office of Thrift Supervision, as the case may be, as a party to the action or proceeding on and after the transfer date; and

(C) for any action or proceeding arising out of a function of the Office of Thrift Supervision or the Director of the Office of Thrift Supervision transferred to the Corporation by this title, the Corporation shall be substituted for the Office of Thrift Supervision or the Director of the Office of Thrift Supervision as a party to the action or proceeding on and after the transfer date.

(b) CONTINUATION OF EXISTING OTS ORDERS, RESOLUTIONS, DETERMINATIONS, AGREEMENTS, REGULATIONS, ETC.—All orders, resolutions, determinations, agreements, and regulations, interpretative rules, other interpretations, guidelines, procedures, and other advisory materials, that have been issued, made, prescribed, or allowed to become effective by the Office of Thrift Supervision or the Director of the Office of Thrift Supervision, or by a court of competent jurisdiction, in the performance of functions that are transferred by this title and that are in effect on the day before the transfer date, shall continue in effect according to the terms of such orders, resolutions, determinations, agreements, and regulations, interpretative rules, other interpretations, guidelines, procedures, and other advisory materials, and shall be enforceable by or against—

(1) the Board of Governors, in the case of a function of the Office of Thrift Supervision or the Director of the Office of Thrift Supervision transferred to the Board of Governors, until modified,

terminated, set aside, or superseded in accordance with applicable law by the Board of Governors, by any court of competent jurisdiction, or by operation of law;

(2) the Office of the Comptroller of the Currency or the Comptroller of the Currency, in the case of a function of the Office of Thrift Supervision or the Director of the Office of Thrift Supervision transferred to the Office of the Comptroller of the Currency or the Comptroller of the Currency, respectively, until modified, terminated, set aside, or superseded in accordance with applicable law by the Office of the Comptroller of the Currency or the Comptroller of the Currency, by any court of competent jurisdiction, or by operation of law; and

(3) the Corporation, in the case of a function of the Office of Thrift Supervision or the Director of the Office of Thrift Supervision transferred to the Corporation, until modified, terminated, set aside, or superseded in accordance with applicable law by the Corporation, by any court of competent jurisdiction, or by operation of law.

(c) IDENTIFICATION OF REGULATIONS CONTINUED.—

(1) BY THE BOARD OF GOVERNORS.—Not later than the transfer date, the Board of Governors shall—

(A) identify the regulations continued under subsection (b) that will be enforced by the Board of Governors; and

(B) publish a list of the regulations identified under subparagraph (A) in the Federal Register.

(2) BY OFFICE OF THE COMPTROLLER OF THE CURRENCY.—Not later than the transfer date, the Office of the Comptroller of the Currency shall—

(A) after consultation with the Corporation, identify the regulations continued under subsection (b) that will be enforced by the Office of the Comptroller of the Currency; and

(B) publish a list of the regulations identified under subparagraph (A) in the Federal Register.

(3) BY THE CORPORATION.—Not later than the transfer date, the Corporation shall—

(A) after consultation with the Office of the Comptroller of the Currency, identify the regulations continued under subsection (b) that will be enforced by the Corporation; and

(B) publish a list of the regulations identified under subparagraph (A) in the Federal Register.

(d) STATUS OF REGULATIONS PROPOSED OR NOT YET EFFECTIVE.—

(1) PROPOSED REGULATIONS.—Any proposed regulation of the Office of Thrift Supervision, which the Office of Thrift Supervision in performing functions transferred by this title, has proposed before the transfer date but has not published as a final regulation before such date, shall be deemed to be a proposed regulation of the Office of the Comptroller of the Currency or the Board of Governors, as appropriate, according to the terms of the proposed regulation.

(2) REGULATIONS NOT YET EFFECTIVE.—Any interim or final regulation of the Office of Thrift Supervision, which the Office of Thrift Supervision, in performing functions transferred by this title, has published before the transfer date but which has not become effective before that date, shall become effective as a regulation of the Office of the Comptroller of the Currency or the Board of Governors, as appropriate, according to the terms of the interim or final regulation, unless modified, terminated, set aside, or superseded in accordance with applicable law by the Office of the Comptroller of the Currency or the Board of Governors, as appropriate, by any court of competent jurisdiction, or by operation of law.

[Explanation at ¶ 1030.]

[¶ 10,317] ACT SEC. 317. REFERENCES IN FEDERAL LAW TO FEDERAL BANKING AGENCIES.

On and after the transfer date, any reference in Federal law to the Director of the Office of Thrift Supervision or the Office of Thrift Supervision, in connection with any function of the Director of the Office of Thrift Supervision or the Office of Thrift Supervision transferred under section 312(b) or any other provision of this subtitle, shall be deemed to be a reference to the Comptroller of the Currency, the Office of the Comptroller of the Currency, the Chairperson of the Corporation, the Corporation, the Chairman of the Board of Governors, or the Board of Governors, as appropriate and consistent with the amendments made in subtitle E.

[Explanation at ¶1035.]

[¶10,318] ACT SEC. 318. FUNDING.

(a) COMPENSATION OF EXAMINERS.—Section 5240 of the Revised Statutes of the United States (12 U.S.C. 481 et seq.) is amended—

(1) in the second undesignated paragraph (12 U.S.C. 481), in the fourth sentence, by striking "without regard to the provisions of other laws applicable to officers or employees of the United States" and inserting the following: "set and adjusted subject to chapter 71 of title 5, United States Code, and without regard to the provisions of other laws applicable to officers or employees of the United States"; and

(2) in the third undesignated paragraph (12 U.S.C. 482), in the first sentence, by striking "shall fix" and inserting "shall, subject to chapter 71 of title 5, United States Code, fix".

(b) FUNDING OF OFFICE OF THE COMPTROLLER OF THE CURRENCY.—Chapter 4 of title LXII of the Revised Statutes is amended by inserting after section 5240 (12 U.S.C. 481, 482) the following:

"SEC. 5240A. The Comptroller of the Currency may collect an assessment, fee, or other charge from any entity described in section 3(q)(1) of the Federal Deposit Insurance Act (12 U.S.C. 1813(q)(1)), as the Comptroller determines is necessary or appropriate to carry out the responsibilities of the Office of the Comptroller of the Currency. In establishing the amount of an assessment, fee, or charge collected from an entity under this section, the Comptroller of the Currency may take into account the nature and scope of the activities of the entity, the amount and type of assets that the entity holds, the financial and managerial condition of the entity, and any other factor, as the Comptroller of the Currency determines is appropriate. Funds derived from any assessment, fee, or charge collected or payment made pursuant to this section may be deposited by the Comptroller of the Currency in accordance with the provisions of section 5234. Such funds shall not be construed to be Government funds or appropriated monies, and shall not be subject to apportionment for purposes of chapter 15 of title 31, United States Code, or any other provision of law. The authority of the Comptroller of the Currency under this section shall be in addition to the authority under section 5240.

"The Comptroller of the Currency shall have sole authority to determine the manner in which the obligations of the Office of the Comptroller of the Currency shall be incurred and its disbursements and expenses allowed and paid, in accordance with this section, except as provided in chapter 71 of title 5, United States Code (with respect to compensation).".

(c) FUNDING OF BOARD OF GOVERNORS.—Section 11 of the Federal Reserve Act (12 U.S.C. 248) is amended by adding at the end the following:

"(s) ASSESSMENTS, FEES, AND OTHER CHARGES FOR CERTAIN COMPANIES.—

"(1) IN GENERAL.—The Board shall collect a total amount of assessments, fees, or other charges from the companies described in paragraph (2) that is equal to the total expenses the Board estimates are necessary or appropriate to carry out the supervisory and regulatory responsibilities of the Board with respect to such companies.

"(2) COMPANIES.—The companies described in this paragraph are—

"(A) all bank holding companies having total consolidated assets of $50,000,000,000 or more;

"(B) all savings and loan holding companies having total consolidated assets of $50,000,000,000 or more; and

"(C) all nonbank financial companies supervised by the Board under section 113 of the Dodd-Frank Wall Street Reform and Consumer Protection Act.".

(d) CORPORATION EXAMINATION FEES.—Section 10(e) of the Federal Deposit Insurance Act (12 U.S.C. 1820(e)) is amended by striking paragraph (1) and inserting the following:

"(1) REGULAR AND SPECIAL EXAMINATIONS OF DEPOSITORY INSTITUTIONS.—The cost of conducting any regular examination or special examination of any depository institution under subsection (b)(2), (b)(3), or (d) or of any entity described in section 3(q)(2) may be assessed by the Corporation against the institution or entity to meet the expenses of the Corporation in carrying out such examinations.".

(e) EFFECTIVE DATE.—This section, and the amendments made by this section, shall take effect on the transfer date.

[Explanation at ¶ 1040.]

[¶ 10,319] ACT SEC. 319. CONTRACTING AND LEASING AUTHORITY.

Notwithstanding the Federal Property and Administrative Services Act of 1949 (41 U.S.C. 251 et seq.) or any other provision of law (except the full and open competition requirements of the Competition in Contracting Act), the Office of the Comptroller of the Currency may—

(1) enter into and perform contracts, execute instruments, and acquire real property (or property interest) as the Comptroller deems necessary to carry out the duties and responsibilities of the Office of the Comptroller of the Currency; and

(2) hold, maintain, sell, lease, or otherwise dispose of the property (or property interest) acquired under paragraph (1).

[Explanation at ¶ 1045.]

Subtitle B—Transitional Provisions

[¶ 10,321] ACT SEC. 321. INTERIM USE OF FUNDS, PERSONNEL, AND PROPERTY OF THE OFFICE OF THRIFT SUPERVISION.

(a) IN GENERAL.—Before the transfer date, the Office of the Comptroller of the Currency, the Corporation, and the Board of Governors shall—

(1) consult and cooperate with the Office of Thrift Supervision to facilitate the orderly transfer of functions to the Office of the Comptroller of the Currency, the Corporation, and the Board of Governors in accordance with this title;

(2) determine jointly, from time to time—

(A) the amount of funds necessary to pay any expenses associated with the transfer of functions (including expenses for personnel, property, and administrative services) during the period beginning on the date of enactment of this Act and ending on the transfer date;

(B) which personnel are appropriate to facilitate the orderly transfer of functions by this title; and

(C) what property and administrative services are necessary to support the Office of the Comptroller of the Currency, the Corporation, and the Board of Governors during the period beginning on the date of enactment of this Act and ending on the transfer date; and

(3) take such actions as may be necessary to provide for the orderly implementation of this title.

(b) AGENCY CONSULTATION.—When requested jointly by the Office of the Comptroller of the Currency, the Corporation, and the Board of Governors to do so before the transfer date, the Office of Thrift Supervision shall—

(1) pay to the Office of the Comptroller of the Currency, the Corporation, or the Board of Governors, as applicable, from funds obtained by the Office of Thrift Supervision through assessments, fees, or other charges that the Office of Thrift Supervision is authorized by law to impose, such amounts as the Office of the Comptroller of the Currency, the Corporation, and the Board of Governors jointly determine to be necessary under subsection (a);

(2) detail to the Office of the Comptroller of the Currency, the Corporation, or the Board of Governors, as applicable, such personnel as the Office of the Comptroller of the Currency, the Corporation, and the Board of Governors jointly determine to be appropriate under subsection (a); and

(3) make available to the Office of the Comptroller of the Currency, the Corporation, or the Board of Governors, as applicable, such property and provide to the Office of the Comptroller of

the Currency, the Corporation, or the Board of Governors, as applicable, such administrative services as the Office of the Comptroller of the Currency, the Corporation, and the Board of Governors jointly determine to be necessary under subsection (a).

(c) NOTICE REQUIRED.—The Office of the Comptroller of the Currency, the Corporation, and the Board of Governors shall jointly give the Office of Thrift Supervision reasonable prior notice of any request that the Office of the Comptroller of the Currency, the Corporation, and the Board of Governors jointly intend to make under subsection (b).

[Explanation at ¶ 1050 and ¶ 1055.]

[¶ 10,322] ACT SEC. 322. TRANSFER OF EMPLOYEES.

(a) IN GENERAL.—

(1) OFFICE OF THRIFT SUPERVISION EMPLOYEES.—

(A) IN GENERAL.—Except as provided in section 1064, all employees of the Office of Thrift Supervision shall be transferred to the Office of the Comptroller of the Currency or the Corporation for employment in accordance with this section.

(B) ALLOCATING EMPLOYEES FOR TRANSFER TO RECEIVING AGENCIES.—The Director of the Office of Thrift Supervision, the Comptroller of the Currency, and the Chairperson of the Corporation shall—

(i) jointly determine the number of employees of the Office of Thrift Supervision necessary to perform or support the functions that are transferred to the Office of the Comptroller of the Currency or the Corporation by this title; and

(ii) consistent with the determination under clause (i), jointly identify employees of the Office of Thrift Supervision for transfer to the Office of the Comptroller of the Currency or the Corporation.

(2) EMPLOYEES TRANSFERRED; SERVICE PERIODS CREDITED.—For purposes of this section, periods of service with a Federal home loan bank, a joint office of Federal home loan banks, or a Federal reserve bank shall be credited as periods of service with a Federal agency.

(3) APPOINTMENT AUTHORITY FOR EXCEPTED SERVICE TRANSFERRED.—

(A) IN GENERAL.—Except as provided in subparagraph (B), any appointment authority of the Office of Thrift Supervision under Federal law that relates to the functions transferred under section 312, including the regulations of the Office of Personnel Management, for filling the positions of employees in the excepted service shall be transferred to the Comptroller of the Currency or the Chairperson of the Corporation, as appropriate.

(B) DECLINING TRANSFERS ALLOWED.—The Comptroller of the Currency or the Chairperson of the Corporation may decline to accept a transfer of authority under subparagraph (A) (and the employees appointed under that authority) to the extent that such authority relates to positions excepted from the competitive service because of their confidential, policy-making, policy-determining, or policy-advocating character.

(4) ADDITIONAL APPOINTMENT AUTHORITY.—Notwithstanding any other provision of law, the Office of the Comptroller of the Currency and the Corporation may appoint transferred employees to positions in the Office of the Comptroller of the Currency or the Corporation, respectively.

(b) TIMING OF TRANSFERS AND POSITION ASSIGNMENTS.—Each employee to be transferred under subsection (a)(1) shall—

(1) be transferred not later than 90 days after the transfer date; and

(2) receive notice of the position assignment of the employee not later than 120 days after the effective date of the transfer of the employee.

(c) TRANSFER OF FUNCTIONS.—

(1) IN GENERAL.—Notwithstanding any other provision of law, the transfer of employees under this subtitle shall be deemed a transfer of functions for the purpose of section 3503 of title 5, United States Code.

(2) PRIORITY.—If any provision of this subtitle conflicts with any protection provided to a transferred employee under section 3503 of title 5, United States Code, the provisions of this subtitle shall control.

(d) EMPLOYEE STATUS AND ELIGIBILITY.—The transfer of functions and employees under this subtitle, and the abolishment of the Office of Thrift Supervision under section 313, shall not affect the status of the transferred employees as employees of an agency of the United States under any provision of law.

(e) EQUAL STATUS AND TENURE POSITIONS.—

(1) STATUS AND TENURE.—Each transferred employee from the Office of Thrift Supervision shall be placed in a position at the Office of the Comptroller of the Currency or the Corporation with the same status and tenure as the transferred employee held on the day before the date on which the employee was transferred.

(2) FUNCTIONS.—To the extent practicable, each transferred employee shall be placed in a position at the Office of the Comptroller of the Currency or the Corporation, as applicable, responsible for the same functions and duties as the transferred employee had on the day before the date on which the employee was transferred, in accordance with the expertise and preferences of the transferred employee.

(f) NO ADDITIONAL CERTIFICATION REQUIREMENTS.—An examiner who is a transferred employee shall not be subject to any additional certification requirements before being placed in a comparable position at the Office of the Comptroller of the Currency or the Corporation, if the examiner carries out examinations of the same type of institutions as an employee of the Office of the Comptroller of the Currency or the Corporation as the employee was responsible for carrying out before the date on which the employee was transferred.

(g) PERSONNEL ACTIONS LIMITED.—

(1) PROTECTION.—

(A) IN GENERAL.—Except as provided in paragraph (2), each affected employee shall not, during the 30-month period beginning on the transfer date, be involuntarily separated, or involuntarily reassigned outside his or her locality pay area.

(B) AFFECTED EMPLOYEES.—For purposes of this paragraph, the term "affected employee" means—

(i) an employee transferred from the Office of Thrift Supervision holding a permanent position on the day before the transfer date; and

(ii) an employee of the Office of the Comptroller of the Currency or the Corporation holding a permanent position on the day before the transfer date.

(2) EXCEPTIONS.—Paragraph (1) does not limit the right of the Office of the Comptroller of the Currency or the Corporation to—

(A) separate an employee for cause or for unacceptable performance;

(B) terminate an appointment to a position excepted from the competitive service because of its confidential policy-making, policy-determining, or policy-advocating character; or

(C) reassign an employee outside such employee's locality pay area when the Office of the Comptroller of the Currency or the Corporation determines that the reassignment is necessary for the efficient operation of the agency.

(h) PAY.—

(1) 30-MONTH PROTECTION.—Except as provided in paragraph (2), during the 30-month period beginning on the date on which the employee was transferred under this subtitle, a transferred employee shall be paid at a rate that is not less than the basic rate of pay, including any geographic differential, that the transferred employee received during the pay period immediately preceding the date on which the employee was transferred. Notwithstanding the preceding sentence, if the employee was receiving a higher rate of basic pay on a temporary basis (because of a temporary assignment, temporary promotion, or other temporary action) immediately

before the transfer, the Agency may reduce the rate of basic pay on the date the rate would have been reduced but for the transfer, and the protected rate for the remainder of the 30-month period will be the reduced rate that would have applied but for the transfer.

(2) EXCEPTIONS.—The Comptroller of the Currency or the Corporation may reduce the rate of basic pay of a transferred employee—

(A) for cause, including for unacceptable performance; or

(B) with the consent of the transferred employee.

(3) PROTECTION ONLY WHILE EMPLOYED.—This subsection shall apply to a transferred employee only during the period that the transferred employee remains employed by Office of the Comptroller of the Currency or the Corporation.

(4) PAY INCREASES PERMITTED.—Nothing in this subsection shall limit the authority of the Comptroller of the Currency or the Chairperson of the Corporation to increase the pay of a transferred employee.

(i) BENEFITS.—

(1) RETIREMENT BENEFITS FOR TRANSFERRED EMPLOYEES.—

(A) IN GENERAL.—

(i) CONTINUATION OF EXISTING RETIREMENT PLAN.—Each transferred employee shall remain enrolled in the retirement plan of the transferred employee, for as long as the transferred employee is employed by the Office of the Comptroller of the Currency or the Corporation.

(ii) EMPLOYER'S CONTRIBUTION.—The Comptroller of the Currency or the Chairperson of the Corporation, as appropriate, shall pay any employer contributions to the existing retirement plan of each transferred employee, as required under each such existing retirement plan.

(B) DEFINITION.—In this paragraph, the term "existing retirement plan" means, with respect to a transferred employee, the retirement plan (including the Financial Institutions Retirement Fund), and any associated thrift savings plan, of the agency from which the employee was transferred in which the employee was enrolled on the day before the date on which the employee was transferred.

(2) BENEFITS OTHER THAN RETIREMENT BENEFITS.—

(A) DURING FIRST YEAR.—

(i) EXISTING PLANS CONTINUE.—During the 1-year period following the transfer date, each transferred employee may retain membership in any employee benefit program (other than a retirement benefit program) of the agency from which the employee was transferred under this title, including any dental, vision, long term care, or life insurance program to which the employee belonged on the day before the transfer date.

(ii) EMPLOYER'S CONTRIBUTION.—The Office of the Comptroller of the Currency or the Corporation, as appropriate, shall pay any employer cost required to extend coverage in the benefit program to the transferred employee as required under that program or negotiated agreements.

(B) DENTAL, VISION, OR LIFE INSURANCE AFTER FIRST YEAR.—If, after the 1-year period beginning on the transfer date, the Office of the Comptroller of the Currency or the Corporation determines that the Office of the Comptroller of the Currency or the Corporation, as the case may be, will not continue to participate in any dental, vision, or life insurance program of an agency from which an employee was transferred, a transferred employee who is a member of the program may, before the decision takes effect and without regard to any regularly scheduled open season, elect to enroll in—

(i) the enhanced dental benefits program established under chapter 89A of title 5, United States Code;

(ii) the enhanced vision benefits established under chapter 89B of title 5, United States Code; and

(iii) the Federal Employees' Group Life Insurance Program established under chapter 87 of title 5, United States Code, without regard to any requirement of insurability.

(C) LONG TERM CARE INSURANCE AFTER 1ST YEAR.—If, after the 1-year period beginning on the transfer date, the Office of the Comptroller of the Currency or the Corporation determines that the Office of the Comptroller of the Currency or the Corporation, as appropriate, will not continue to participate in any long term care insurance program of an agency from which an employee transferred, a transferred employee who is a member of such a program may, before the decision takes effect, elect to apply for coverage under the Federal Long Term Care Insurance Program established under chapter 90 of title 5, United States Code, under the underwriting requirements applicable to a new active workforce member, as described in part 875 of title 5, Code of Federal Regulations (or any successor thereto).

(D) CONTRIBUTION OF TRANSFERRED EMPLOYEE.—

(i) IN GENERAL.—Subject to clause (ii), a transferred employee who is enrolled in a plan under the Federal Employees Health Benefits Program shall pay any employee contribution required under the plan.

(ii) COST DIFFERENTIAL.—The Office of the Comptroller of the Currency or the Corporation, as applicable, shall pay any difference in cost between the employee contribution required under the plan provided to transferred employees by the agency from which the employee transferred on the date of enactment of this Act and the plan provided by the Office of the Comptroller of the Currency or the Corporation, as the case may be, under this section.

(iii) FUNDS TRANSFER.—The Office of the Comptroller of the Currency or the Corporation, as the case may be, shall transfer to the Employees Health Benefits Fund established under section 8909 of title 5, United States Code, an amount determined by the Director of the Office of Personnel Management, after consultation with the Comptroller of the Currency or the Chairperson of the Corporation, as the case may be, and the Office of Management and Budget, to be necessary to reimburse the Fund for the cost to the Fund of providing any benefits under this subparagraph that are not otherwise paid for by a transferred employee under clause (i).

(E) SPECIAL PROVISIONS TO ENSURE CONTINUATION OF LIFE INSURANCE BENEFITS.—

(i) IN GENERAL.—An annuitant, as defined in section 8901 of title 5, United States Code, who is enrolled in a life insurance plan administered by an agency from which employees are transferred under this title on the day before the transfer date shall be eligible for coverage by a life insurance plan under sections 8706(b), 8714a, 8714b, or 8714c of title 5, United States Code, or by a life insurance plan established by the Office of the Comptroller of the Currency or the Corporation, as applicable, without regard to any regularly scheduled open season or any requirement of insurability.

(ii) CONTRIBUTION OF TRANSFERRED EMPLOYEE.—

(I) IN GENERAL.—Subject to subclause (II), a transferred employee enrolled in a life insurance plan under this subparagraph shall pay any employee contribution required by the plan.

(II) COST DIFFERENTIAL.—The Office of the Comptroller of the Currency or the Corporation, as the case may be, shall pay any difference in cost between the benefits provided by the agency from which the employee transferred on the date of enactment of this Act and the benefits provided under this section.

(III) FUNDS TRANSFER.—The Office of the Comptroller of the Currency or the Corporation, as the case may be, shall transfer to the Federal Employees' Group Life Insurance Fund established under section 8714 of title 5, United States Code, an amount determined by the Director of the Office of Personnel Management, after consultation with the Comptroller of the Currency or the Chairperson of the

Corporation, as the case may be, and the Office of Management and Budget, to be necessary to reimburse the Federal Employees' Group Life Insurance Fund for the cost to the Federal Employees' Group Life Insurance Fund of providing benefits under this subparagraph not otherwise paid for by a transferred employee under subclause (I).

(IV) CREDIT FOR TIME ENROLLED IN OTHER PLANS.—For any transferred employee, enrollment in a life insurance plan administered by the agency from which the employee transferred, immediately before enrollment in a life insurance plan under chapter 87 of title 5, United States Code, shall be considered as enrollment in a life insurance plan under that chapter for purposes of section 8706(b)(1)(A) of title 5, United States Code.

(j) INCORPORATION INTO AGENCY PAY SYSTEM.—Not later than 30 months after the transfer date, the Comptroller of the Currency and the Chairperson of the Corporation shall place each transferred employee into the established pay system and structure of the appropriate employing agency.

(k) EQUITABLE TREATMENT.—In administering the provisions of this section, the Comptroller of the Currency and the Chairperson of the Corporation—

(1) may not take any action that would unfairly disadvantage a transferred employee relative to any other employee of the Office of the Comptroller of the Currency or the Corporation on the basis of prior employment by the Office of Thrift Supervision;

(2) may take such action as is appropriate in an individual case to ensure that a transferred employee receives equitable treatment, with respect to the status, tenure, pay, benefits (other than benefits under programs administered by the Office of Personnel Management), and accrued leave or vacation time for prior periods of service with any Federal agency of the transferred employee;

(3) shall, jointly with the Director of the Office of Thrift Supervision, develop and adopt procedures and safeguards designed to ensure that the requirements of this subsection are met; and

(4) shall conduct a study detailing the position assignments of all employees transferred pursuant to subsection (a), describing the procedures and safeguards adopted pursuant to paragraph (3), and demonstrating that the requirements of this subsection have been met; and shall, not later than 365 days after the transfer date, submit a copy of such study to Congress.

(l) REORGANIZATION.—

(1) IN GENERAL.—If the Comptroller of the Currency or the Chairperson of the Corporation determines, during the 2-year period beginning 1 year after the transfer date, that a reorganization of the staff of the Office of the Comptroller of the Currency or the Corporation, respectively, is required, the reorganization shall be deemed a "major reorganization" for purposes of affording affected employees retirement under section 8336(d)(2) or 8414(b)(1)(B) of title 5, United States Code.

(2) SERVICE CREDIT.—For purposes of this subsection, periods of service with a Federal home loan bank or a joint office of Federal home loan banks shall be credited as periods of service with a Federal agency.

[Explanation at ¶ 1050 and ¶ 1060.]

[¶ 10,323] ACT SEC. 323. PROPERTY TRANSFERRED.

(a) PROPERTY DEFINED.—For purposes of this section, the term "property" includes all real property (including leaseholds) and all personal property, including computers, furniture, fixtures, equipment, books, accounts, records, reports, files, memoranda, paper, reports of examination, work papers, and correspondence related to such reports, and any other information or materials.

(b) PROPERTY OF THE OFFICE OF THRIFT SUPERVISION.—

(1) IN GENERAL.—No later than 90 days after the transfer date, all property of the Office of Thrift Supervision (other than property described under paragraph (b)(2)) that the Comptroller of the Currency and the Chairperson of the Corporation jointly determine is used, on the day

before the transfer date, to perform or support the functions of the Office of Thrift Supervision transferred to the Office of the Comptroller of the Currency or the Corporation under this title, shall be transferred to the Office of the Comptroller of the Currency or the Corporation in a manner consistent with the transfer of employees under this subtitle.

(2) PERSONAL PROPERTY.—All books, accounts, records, reports, files, memoranda, papers, documents, reports of examination, work papers, and correspondence of the Office of Thrift Supervision that the Comptroller of the Currency, the Chairperson of the Corporation, and the Chairman of the Board of Governors jointly determine is used, on the day before the transfer date, to perform or support the functions of the Office of Thrift Supervision transferred to the Board of Governors under this title shall be transferred to the Board of Governors in a manner consistent with the purposes of this title.

(c) CONTRACTS RELATED TO PROPERTY TRANSFERRED.—Each contract, agreement, lease, license, permit, and similar arrangement relating to property transferred to the Office of the Comptroller of the Currency or the Corporation by this section shall be transferred to the Office of the Comptroller of the Currency or the Corporation, as appropriate, together with the property to which it relates.

(d) PRESERVATION OF PROPERTY.—Property identified for transfer under this section shall not be altered, destroyed, or deleted before transfer under this section.

[Explanation at ¶ 1050 and ¶ 1065.]

[¶ 10,324] ACT SEC. 324. FUNDS TRANSFERRED.

The funds that, on the day before the transfer date, the Director of the Office of Thrift Supervision (in consultation with the Comptroller of the Currency, the Chairperson of the Corporation, and the Chairman of the Board of Governors) determines are not necessary to dispose of the affairs of the Office of Thrift Supervision under section 325 and are available to the Office of Thrift Supervision to pay the expenses of the Office of Thrift Supervision—

(1) relating to the functions of the Office of Thrift Supervision transferred under section 312(b)(2)(B), shall be transferred to the Office of the Comptroller of the Currency on the transfer date;

(2) relating to the functions of the Office of Thrift Supervision transferred under section 312(b)(2)(C), shall be transferred to the Corporation on the transfer date; and

(3) relating to the functions of the Office of Thrift Supervision transferred under section 312(b)(1)(A), shall be transferred to the Board of Governors on the transfer date.

[Explanation at ¶ 1050 and ¶ 1070.]

[¶ 10,325] ACT SEC. 325. DISPOSITION OF AFFAIRS.

(a) AUTHORITY OF DIRECTOR.—During the 90-day period beginning on the transfer date, the Director of the Office of Thrift Supervision—

(1) shall, solely for the purpose of winding up the affairs of the Office of Thrift Supervision relating to any function transferred to the Office of the Comptroller of the Currency, the Corporation, or the Board of Governors under this title—

(A) manage the employees of the Office of Thrift Supervision who have not yet been transferred and provide for the payment of the compensation and benefits of the employees that accrue before the date on which the employees are transferred under this title; and

(B) manage any property of the Office of Thrift Supervision, until the date on which the property is transferred under section 323; and

(2) may take any other action necessary to wind up the affairs of the Office of Thrift Supervision.

(b) STATUS OF DIRECTOR.—

(1) IN GENERAL.—Notwithstanding the transfer of functions under this subtitle, during the 90-day period beginning on the transfer date, the Director of the Office of Thrift Supervision shall retain and may exercise any authority vested in the Director of the Office of Thrift Supervision on the day before the transfer date, only to the extent necessary—

(A) to wind up the Office of Thrift Supervision; and

(B) to carry out the transfer under this subtitle during such 90-day period.

(2) OTHER PROVISIONS.—For purposes of paragraph (1), the Director of the Office of Thrift Supervision shall, during the 90-day period beginning on the transfer date, continue to be—

(A) treated as an officer of the United States; and

(B) entitled to receive compensation at the same annual rate of basic pay that the Director of the Office of Thrift Supervision received on the day before the transfer date.

[Explanation at ¶1050 and ¶1075.]

[¶10,326] ACT SEC. 326. CONTINUATION OF SERVICES.

Any agency, department, or other instrumentality of the United States, and any successor to any such agency, department, or instrumentality, that was, before the transfer date, providing support services to the Office of Thrift Supervision in connection with functions transferred to the Office of the Comptroller of the Currency, the Corporation or the Board of Governors under this title, shall—

(1) continue to provide such services, subject to reimbursement by the Office of the Comptroller of the Currency, the Corporation, or the Board of Governors, until the transfer of functions under this title is complete; and

(2) consult with the Comptroller of the Currency, the Chairperson of the Corporation, or the Chairman of the Board of Governors, as appropriate, to coordinate and facilitate a prompt and orderly transition.

[Explanation at ¶1080.]

[¶10,327] ACT SEC. 327. IMPLEMENTATION PLAN AND REPORTS.

(a) PLAN SUBMISSION.—Within 180 days of the enactment of the Dodd-Frank Wall Street Reform and Consumer Protection Act, the Board of Governors, the Corporation, the Office of the Comptroller of the Currency, and the Office of Thrift Supervision, shall jointly submit a plan to the Committee on Banking, Housing, and Urban Affairs of the Senate, the Committee on Financial Services of the House of Representatives, and the Inspectors General of the Department of the Treasury, the Corporation, and the Board of Governors detailing the steps the Board of Governors, the Corporation, the Office of the Comptroller of the Currency, and the Office of Thrift Supervision will take to implement the provisions of sections 301 through 326, and the provisions of the amendments made by such sections.

(b) INSPECTORS GENERAL REVIEW OF THE PLAN.—Within 60 days of receiving the plan required under subsection (a), the Inspectors General of the Department of the Treasury, the Corporation, and the Board of Governors shall jointly provide a written report to the Board of Governors, the Corporation, the Office of the Comptroller of the Currency, and the Office of Thrift Supervision and shall submit a copy to the Committee on Banking, Housing, and Urban Affairs of the Senate and the Committee on Financial Services of the House of Representatives detailing whether the plan conforms with the provisions of sections 301 through 326, and the provisions of the amendments made by such sections, including—

(1) whether the plan sufficiently takes into consideration the orderly transfer of personnel;

(2) whether the plan describes procedures and safeguards to ensure that the Office of Thrift Supervision employees are not unfairly disadvantaged relative to employees of the Office of the Comptroller of the Currency and the Corporation;

(3) whether the plan sufficiently takes into consideration the orderly transfer of authority and responsibilities;

(4) whether the plan sufficiently takes into consideration the effective transfer of funds;

(5) whether the plan sufficiently takes in consideration the orderly transfer of property; and

(6) any additional recommendations for an orderly and effective process.

(c) IMPLEMENTATION REPORTS.—Not later than 6 months after the date on which the Committee on Banking, Housing, and Urban Affairs of the Senate and the Committee on Financial Services of the House of Representatives receives the report required under subsection (b), and every 6 months thereafter until all aspects of the plan have been implemented, the Inspectors General of the Department of the Treasury, the Corporation, and the Board of Governors shall jointly provide a written report on the status of the implementation of the plan to the Board of Governors, the Corporation, the Office of the Comptroller of the Currency, and the Office of Thrift Supervision and shall submit a copy to the Committee on Banking, Housing, and Urban Affairs of the Senate and the Committee on Financial Services of the House of Representatives.

[Explanation at ¶ 1085.]

Subtitle C—Federal Deposit Insurance Corporation

[¶ 10,331] ACT SEC. 331. DEPOSIT INSURANCE REFORMS.

(a) SIZE DISTINCTIONS.—Section 7(b)(2) of the Federal Deposit Insurance Act (12 U.S.C. 1817(b)(2)) is amended—

(1) by striking subparagraph (D); and

(2) by redesignating subparagraph (C) as subparagraph (D).

(b) ASSESSMENT BASE.—The Corporation shall amend the regulations issued by the Corporation under section 7(b)(2) of the Federal Deposit Insurance Act (12 U.S.C. 1817(b)(2)) to define the term "assessment base" with respect to an insured depository institution for purposes of that section 7(b)(2), as an amount equal to—

(1) the average consolidated total assets of the insured depository institution during the assessment period; minus

(2) the sum of—

(A) the average tangible equity of the insured depository institution during the assessment period; and

(B) in the case of an insured depository institution that is a custodial bank (as defined by the Corporation, based on factors including the percentage of total revenues generated by custodial businesses and the level of assets under custody) or a banker's bank (as that term is used in section 5136 of the Revised Statutes (12 U.S.C. 24)), an amount that the Corporation determines is necessary to establish assessments consistent with the definition under section 7(b)(1) of the Federal Deposit Insurance Act (12 U.S.C. 1817(b)(1)) for a custodial bank or a banker's bank.

[Explanation at ¶ 1095.]

[¶ 10,332] ACT SEC. 332. ELIMINATION OF PROCYCLICAL ASSESSMENTS.

Section 7(e) of the Federal Deposit Insurance Act is amended—

(1) in paragraph (2)—

(A) by amending subparagraph (B) to read as follows:

"(B) LIMITATION.—The Board of Directors may, in its sole discretion, suspend or limit the declaration of payment of dividends under subparagraph (A).";

(B) by amending subparagraph (C) to read as follows:

"(C) NOTICE AND OPPORTUNITY FOR COMMENT.—The Corporation shall prescribe, by regulation, after notice and opportunity for comment, the method for the declaration, calculation, distribution, and payment of dividends under this paragraph"; and

(C) by striking subparagraphs (D) through (G); and

(2) in paragraph (4)(A) by striking "paragraphs (2)(D) and" and inserting "paragraphs (2) and".

[Explanation at ¶ 1095.]

[¶ 10,333] ACT SEC. 333. ENHANCED ACCESS TO INFORMATION FOR DEPOSIT INSURANCE PURPOSES.

(a) Section 7(a)(2)(B) of the Federal Deposit Insurance Act is amended by striking "agreement" and inserting "consultation".

(b) Section 7(b)(1)(E) of the Federal Deposit Insurance Act is amended—

(1) in clause (i), by striking "such as" and inserting "including"; and

(2) in clause (iii), by striking "Corporation" and inserting "Corporation, except as provided in section 7(a)(2)(B)".

[Explanation at ¶ 1095.]

[¶ 10,334] ACT SEC. 334. TRANSITION RESERVE RATIO REQUIREMENTS TO REFLECT NEW ASSESSMENT BASE.

(a) Section 7(b)(3)(B) of the Federal Deposit Insurance Act is amended to read as follows:

"(B) MINIMUM RESERVE RATIO.—The reserve ratio designated by the Board of Directors for any year may not be less than 1.35 percent of estimated insured deposits, or the comparable percentage of the assessment base set forth in paragraph (2)(C).".

(b) Section 3(y)(3) of the Federal Deposit Insurance Act is amended by inserting ", or such comparable percentage of the assessment base set forth in section 7(b)(2)(C)" before the period.

(c) For a period of not less than 5 years after the date of the enactment of this title, the Federal Deposit Insurance Corporation shall make available to the public the reserve ratio and the designated reserve ratio using both estimated insured deposits and the assessment base under section 7(b)(2)(C) of the Federal Deposit Insurance Act.

(d) RESERVE RATIO.—Notwithstanding the timing requirements of section 7(b)(3)(E)(ii) of the Federal Deposit Insurance Act, the Corporation shall take such steps as may be necessary for the reserve ratio of the Deposit Insurance Fund to reach 1.35 percent of estimated insured deposits by September 30, 2020.

(e) OFFSET.—In setting the assessments necessary to meet the requirements of subsection (d), the Corporation shall offset the effect of subsection (d) on insured depository institutions with total consolidated assets of less than $10,000,000,000.

[Explanation at ¶ 1095.]

[¶ 10,335] ACT SEC. 335. PERMANENT INCREASE IN DEPOSIT AND SHARE INSURANCE.

(a) PERMANENT INCREASE IN DEPOSIT INSURANCE.—Section 11(a)(1)(E) of the Federal Deposit Insurance Act (12 U.S.C. 1821(a)(1)(E)) is amended—

(1) by striking "$100,000" and inserting "$250,000"; and

(2) by adding at the end the following new sentences: "Notwithstanding any other provision of law, the increase in the standard maximum deposit insurance amount to $250,000 shall apply to depositors in any institution for which the Corporation was appointed as receiver or conservator on or after January 1, 2008, and before October 3, 2008. The Corporation shall take such actions as are necessary to carry out the requirements of this section with respect to such depositors, without regard to any time limitations under this Act. In implementing this and the preceding 2 sentences, any payment on a deposit claim made by the Corporation as receiver or conservator to a depositor above the standard maximum deposit insurance amount in effect at the time of the appointment of the Corporation as receiver or conservator shall be deemed to be part of the net amount due to the depositor under subparagraph (B)."

(b) PERMANENT INCREASE IN SHARE INSURANCE.—Section 207(k)(5) of the Federal Credit Union Act (12 U.S.C. 1787(k)(5)) is amended by striking "$100,000" and inserting "$250,000".

[Explanation at ¶ 1100.]

[¶ 10,336] ACT SEC. 336. MANAGEMENT OF THE FEDERAL DEPOSIT INSURANCE CORPORATION.

(a) IN GENERAL.—Section 2 of the Federal Deposit Insurance Act (12 U.S.C. 1812) is amended—

(1) in subsection (a)(1)(B), by striking "Director of the Office of Thrift Supervision" and inserting "Director of the Consumer Financial Protection Bureau";

(2) by amending subsection (d)(2) to read as follows:

"(2) ACTING OFFICIALS MAY SERVE.—In the event of a vacancy in the office of the Comptroller of the Currency or the office of Director of the Consumer Financial Protection Bureau and pending the appointment of a successor, or during the absence or disability of the Comptroller of the Currency or the Director of the Consumer Financial Protection Bureau, the acting Comptroller of the Currency or the acting Director of the Consumer Financial Protection Bureau, as the case may be, shall be a member of the Board of Directors in the place of the Comptroller or Director."; and

(3) in subsection (f)(2), by striking "Office of Thrift Supervision" and inserting "Consumer Financial Protection Bureau".

(b) EFFECTIVE DATE.—This section, and the amendments made by this section, shall take effect on the transfer date.

[Explanation at ¶1105.]

Subtitle D—Other Matters

[¶10,341] ACT SEC. 341. BRANCHING.

Notwithstanding the Federal Deposit Insurance Act (12 U.S.C. 1811 et seq.), the Bank Holding Company Act of 1956 (12 U.S.C. 1841 et seq.), or any other provision of Federal or State law, a savings association that becomes a bank may—

(1) continue to operate any branch or agency that the savings association operated immediately before the savings association became a bank; and

(2) establish, acquire, and operate additional branches and agencies at any location within any State in which the savings association operated a branch immediately before the savings association became a bank, if the law of the State in which the branch is located, or is to be located, would permit establishment of the branch if the bank were a State bank chartered by such State.

[Explanation at ¶1110.]

[¶10,342] ACT SEC. 342. OFFICE OF MINORITY AND WOMEN INCLUSION.

(a) OFFICE OF MINORITY AND WOMEN INCLUSION.—

(1) ESTABLISHMENT.—

(A) IN GENERAL.—Except as provided in subparagraph (B), not later than 6 months after the date of enactment of this Act, each agency shall establish an Office of Minority and Women Inclusion that shall be responsible for all matters of the agency relating to diversity in management, employment, and business activities.

(B) BUREAU.—The Bureau shall establish an Office of Minority and Women Inclusion not later than 6 months after the designated transfer date established under section 1062.

(2) TRANSFER OF RESPONSIBILITIES.—Each agency that, on the day before the date of enactment of this Act, assigned the responsibilities described in paragraph (1) (or comparable responsibilities) to another office of the agency shall ensure that such responsibilities are transferred to the Office.

(3) DUTIES WITH RESPECT TO CIVIL RIGHTS LAWS.—The responsibilities described in paragraph (1) do not include enforcement of statutes, regulations, or executive orders pertaining to civil rights, except each Director shall coordinate with the agency administrator, or the designee of the agency administrator, regarding the design and implementation of any remedies resulting from violations of such statutes, regulations, or executive orders.

(b) DIRECTOR.—

(1) IN GENERAL.—The Director of each Office shall be appointed by, and shall report to, the agency administrator. The position of Director shall be a career reserved position in the Senior Executive Service, as that position is defined in section 3132 of title 5, United States Code, or an equivalent designation.

(2) DUTIES.—Each Director shall develop standards for—

(A) equal employment opportunity and the racial, ethnic, and gender diversity of the workforce and senior management of the agency;

(B) increased participation of minority-owned and women-owned businesses in the programs and contracts of the agency, including standards for coordinating technical assistance to such businesses; and

(C) assessing the diversity policies and practices of entities regulated by the agency.

(3) OTHER DUTIES.—Each Director shall advise the agency administrator on the impact of the policies and regulations of the agency on minority-owned and women-owned businesses.

(4) RULE OF CONSTRUCTION.—Nothing in paragraph (2)(C) may be construed to mandate any requirement on or otherwise affect the lending policies and practices of any regulated entity, or to require any specific action based on the findings of the assessment.

(c) INCLUSION IN ALL LEVELS OF BUSINESS ACTIVITIES.—

(1) IN GENERAL.—The Director of each Office shall develop and implement standards and procedures to ensure, to the maximum extent possible, the fair inclusion and utilization of minorities, women, and minority-owned and women-owned businesses in all business and activities of the agency at all levels, including in procurement, insurance, and all types of contracts.

(2) CONTRACTS.—The procedures established by each agency for review and evaluation of contract proposals and for hiring service providers shall include, to the extent consistent with applicable law, a component that gives consideration to the diversity of the applicant. Such procedure shall include a written statement, in a form and with such content as the Director shall prescribe, that a contractor shall ensure, to the maximum extent possible, the fair inclusion of women and minorities in the workforce of the contractor and, as applicable, subcontractors.

(3) TERMINATION.—

(A) DETERMINATION.—The standards and procedures developed and implemented under this subsection shall include a procedure for the Director to make a determination whether an agency contractor, and, as applicable, a subcontractor has failed to make a good faith effort to include minorities and women in their workforce.

(B) EFFECT OF DETERMINATION.—

(i) RECOMMENDATION TO AGENCY ADMINISTRATOR.—Upon a determination described in subparagraph (A), the Director shall make a recommendation to the agency administrator that the contract be terminated.

(ii) ACTION BY AGENCY ADMINISTRATOR.—Upon receipt of a recommendation under clause (i), the agency administrator may—

(I) terminate the contract;

(II) make a referral to the Office of Federal Contract Compliance Programs of the Department of Labor; or

(III) take other appropriate action.

(d) APPLICABILITY.—This section shall apply to all contracts of an agency for services of any kind, including the services of financial institutions, investment banking firms, mortgage banking firms, asset management firms, brokers, dealers, financial services entities, underwriters, accountants, investment consultants, and providers of legal services. The contracts referred to in this subsection include all contracts for all business and activities of an agency, at all levels, including contracts for the issuance or guarantee of any debt, equity, or security, the sale of assets, the management of the assets of the agency, the making of equity investments by the agency, and the implementation by the agency of programs to address economic recovery.

(e) REPORTS.—Each Office shall submit to Congress an annual report regarding the actions taken by the agency and the Office pursuant to this section, which shall include—

(1) a statement of the total amounts paid by the agency to contractors since the previous report;

(2) the percentage of the amounts described in paragraph (1) that were paid to contractors described in subsection (c)(1);

(3) the successes achieved and challenges faced by the agency in operating minority and women outreach programs;

(4) the challenges the agency may face in hiring qualified minority and women employees and contracting with qualified minority-owned and women-owned businesses; and

(5) any other information, findings, conclusions, and recommendations for legislative or agency action, as the Director determines appropriate.

(f) DIVERSITY IN AGENCY WORKFORCE.—Each agency shall take affirmative steps to seek diversity in the workforce of the agency at all levels of the agency in a manner consistent with applicable law. Such steps shall include—

(1) recruiting at historically black colleges and universities, Hispanic-serving institutions, women's colleges, and colleges that typically serve majority minority populations;

(2) sponsoring and recruiting at job fairs in urban communities;

(3) placing employment advertisements in newspapers and magazines oriented toward minorities and women;

(4) partnering with organizations that are focused on developing opportunities for minorities and women to place talented young minorities and women in industry internships, summer employment, and full-time positions;

(5) where feasible, partnering with inner-city high schools, girls' high schools, and high schools with majority minority populations to establish or enhance financial literacy programs and provide mentoring; and

(6) any other mass media communications that the Office determines necessary.

(g) DEFINITIONS.—For purposes of this section, the following definitions shall apply:

(1) AGENCY.—The term "agency" means—

(A) the Departmental Offices of the Department of the Treasury;

(B) the Corporation;

(C) the Federal Housing Finance Agency;

(D) each of the Federal reserve banks;

(E) the Board;

(F) the National Credit Union Administration;

(G) the Office of the Comptroller of the Currency;

(H) the Commission; and

(I) the Bureau.

(2) AGENCY ADMINISTRATOR.—The term "agency administrator" means the head of an agency.

(3) MINORITY.—The term "minority" has the same meaning as in section 1204(c) of the Financial Institutions Reform, Recovery, and Enforcement Act of 1989 (12 U.S.C. 1811 note).

(4) MINORITY-OWNED BUSINESS.—The term "minority-owned business" has the same meaning as in section 21A(r)(4)(A) of the Federal Home Loan Bank Act (12 U.S.C. 1441a(r)(4)(A)), as in effect on the day before the transfer date.

(5) OFFICE.—The term "Office" means the Office of Minority and Women Inclusion established by an agency under subsection (a).

(6) WOMEN-OWNED BUSINESS.—The term "women-owned business" has the meaning given the term "women's business" in section 21A(r)(4)(B) of the Federal Home Loan Bank Act (12 U.S.C. 1441a(r)(4)(B)), as in effect on the day before the transfer date.

[Explanation at ¶1115.]

[¶10,343] ACT SEC. 343. INSURANCE OF TRANSACTION ACCOUNTS.

(a) BANKS AND SAVINGS ASSOCIATIONS.—

(1) AMENDMENTS.—Section 11(a)(1) of the Federal Deposit Insurance Act (12 U.S.C. 1821(a)(1)) is amended—

(A) in subparagraph (B)—

(i) by striking "The net amount" and inserting the following:

"(i) IN GENERAL.—Subject to clause (ii), the net amount"; and

(ii) by adding at the end the following new clauses:

"(ii) INSURANCE FOR NONINTEREST-BEARING TRANSACTION ACCOUNTS.—Notwithstanding clause (i), the Corporation shall fully insure the net amount that any depositor at an insured depository institution maintains in a noninterest-bearing transaction account. Such amount shall not be taken into account when computing the net amount due to such depositor under clause (i).

"(iii) NONINTEREST-BEARING TRANSACTION ACCOUNT DEFINED.—For purposes of this subparagraph, the term 'noninterest-bearing transaction account' means a deposit or account maintained at an insured depository institution—

"(I) with respect to which interest is neither accrued nor paid;

"(II) on which the depositor or account holder is permitted to make withdrawals by negotiable or transferable instrument, payment orders of withdrawal, telephone or other electronic media transfers, or other similar items for the purpose of making payments or transfers to third parties or others; and

"(III) on which the insured depository institution does not reserve the right to require advance notice of an intended withdrawal."; and

(B) in subparagraph (C), by striking "subparagraph (B)" and inserting "subparagraph (B)(i)".

(2) EFFECTIVE DATE.—The amendments made by paragraph (1) shall take effect on December 31, 2010.

(3) PROSPECTIVE REPEAL.—Effective January 1, 2013, section 11(a)(1) of the Federal Deposit Insurance Act (12 U.S.C. 1821(a)(1)), as amended by paragraph (1), is amended—

(A) in subparagraph (B)—

(i) by striking "DEPOSIT.—"and all that follows through "clause (ii), the net amount" and insert "DEPOSIT.—The net amount"; and

(ii) by striking clauses (ii) and (iii); and

(B) in subparagraph (C), by striking "subparagraph (B)(i)" and inserting "subparagraph (B)".

(b) CREDIT UNIONS.—

(1) AMENDMENTS.—Section 207(k)(1) of the Federal Credit Union Act (12 U.S.C. 1787(k)(1)) is amended—

(A) in subparagraph (A)—

(i) by striking "Subject to the provisions of paragraph (2), the net amount" and inserting the following:

"(i) NET AMOUNT OF INSURANCE PAYABLE.—Subject to clause (ii) and the provisions of paragraph (2), the net amount"; and

(ii) by adding at the end the following new clauses: "(ii).—"(iii).—".

"(ii) INSURANCE FOR NONINTEREST-BEARING TRANSACTION ACCOUNTS.—Notwithstanding clause (i), the Board shall fully insure the net amount that any member or depositor at an insured credit union maintains in a noninterest-bearing transaction account. Such amount shall not be taken into account when computing the net amount due to such member or depositor under clause (i).

"(iii) NONINTEREST-BEARING TRANSACTION ACCOUNT DEFINED.—For purposes of this subparagraph, the term 'noninterest-bearing transaction account' means an account or deposit maintained at an insured credit union—

"(I) with respect to which interest is neither accrued nor paid;

"(II) on which the account holder or depositor is permitted to make withdrawals by negotiable or transferable instrument, payment orders of withdrawal, telephone or other electronic media transfers, or other similar items for the purpose of making payments or transfers to third parties or others; and

"(III) on which the insured credit union does not reserve the right to require advance notice of an intended withdrawal."; and

(B) in subparagraph (B), by striking "subparagraph (A)" and inserting "subparagraph (A)(i)".

(2) EFFECTIVE DATE.—The amendments made by paragraph (1) shall take effect upon the date of the enactment of this Act

(3) PROSPECTIVE REPEAL.—Effective January 1, 2013, section 207(k)(1) of the Federal Credit Union Act (12 U.S.C. 1787(k)(1)), as amended by paragraph (1), is amended—

(A) in subparagraph (A)—

(i) by striking "(i) NET AMOUNT OF INSURANCE PAYABLE.—"and all that follows through "paragraph (2), the net amount" and inserting "Subject to the provisions of paragraph (2), the net amount"; and

(ii) by striking clauses (ii) and (iii); and

(B) in subparagraph (B), by striking "subparagraph (A)(i)" and inserting "subparagraph (A)".

[Explanation at ¶1120.]

Subtitle E—Technical and Conforming Amendments

[¶10,351] ACT SEC. 351. EFFECTIVE DATE.

Except as provided in section 364(a), the amendments made by this subtitle shall take effect on the transfer date.

[Explanation at ¶1005.]

[¶10,352] ACT SEC. 352. BALANCED BUDGET AND EMERGENCY DEFICIT CONTROL ACT OF 1985.

Section 256(h) of the Balanced Budget and Emergency Deficit Control Act of 1985 (2 U.S.C. 906(h)) is amended—

(1) in paragraph (4), by striking subparagraphs (C) and (G); and

(2) by redesignating subparagraphs (D), (E), (F), and (H) as subparagraphs (C), (D), (E), and (F), respectively.

[Explanation at ¶1125.]

[¶10,353] ACT SEC. 353. BANK ENTERPRISE ACT OF 1991.

Section 232(a) of the Bank Enterprise Act of 1991 (12 U.S.C. 1834(a)) is amended—

(1) in the subsection heading, by striking "BY FEDERAL RESERVE BOARD";

(2) in paragraph (1)—

(A) by striking "The Board of Governors of the Federal Reserve System," and inserting "The Comptroller of the Currency"; and

(B) by striking "section 7(b)(2)(H)" and inserting "section 7(b)(2)(E)";

(3) in paragraph (2)(A), by striking "Board" and inserting "Comptroller"; and

(4) in paragraph (3)—

(A) by redesignating subparagraphs (A) through (C) as subparagraphs (B) through (D), respectively; and

(B) by inserting before subparagraph (B) the following:

"(A) COMPTROLLER.—The term 'Comptroller' means the Comptroller of the Currency.".

[Explanation at ¶1130.]

[¶10,354] ACT SEC. 354. BANK HOLDING COMPANY ACT OF 1956.

The Bank Holding Company Act of 1956 (12 U.S.C. 1841 et seq.) is amended—

(1) in section 2(j)(3) (12 U.S.C. 1841(j)(3)), strike "Director of the Office of Thrift Supervision" and inserting "appropriate Federal banking agency";

(2) in section 4 (12 U.S.C. 1843)—

(A) in subsection (i)—

(i) in paragraph (4)—

(I) in subparagraph (A)—

(aa) in the subparagraph heading, by striking "TO DIRECTOR"; and

(bb) by striking "Board" and all that follows through the end of the subparagraph and inserting "Board shall solicit comments and recommendations from—

"(i) the Comptroller of the Currency, with respect to the acquisition of a Federal savings association; and

"(ii) the Federal Deposit Insurance Corporation, with respect to the acquisition of a State savings association.".

(II) in subparagraph (B), by striking "Director" each place that term appears and inserting "Comptroller of the Currency or the Federal Deposit Insurance Corporation, as applicable,";

(ii) in paragraph (5)—

(I) in subparagraph (B), by striking "Director with" and inserting "Comptroller of the Currency or the Federal Deposit Insurance Corporation, as applicable, with"; and

(II) by striking "Director" each place that term appears and inserting "Comptroller of the Currency or the Federal Deposit Insurance Corporation";

(iii) in paragraph (6), by striking "Director" and inserting "Comptroller of the Currency or the Federal Deposit Insurance Corporation, as applicable,"; and

(iv) by striking paragraph (7); and

(3) in section 5(f) (12 U.S.C. 1844(f))—

(A) by striking "subpena" each place that term appears and inserting "subpoena";

(B) by striking "subpenas" each place that term appears and inserting "subpoenas"; and

(C) by striking "subpenaed" and inserting "subpoenaed".

[Explanation at ¶1135.]

[¶10,355] ACT SEC. 355. BANK HOLDING COMPANY ACT AMENDMENTS OF 1970.

Section 106(b)(1) of the Bank Holding Company Act Amendments of 1970 (12 U.S.C. 1972(1)) is amended in the undesignated matter following subparagraph (E) by inserting "issue such regulations as are necessary to carry out this section, and, in consultation with the Comptroller of the Currency and the Federal Deposit Insurance Company, may" after "The Board may".

[Explanation at ¶ 1140.]

[¶ 10,356] ACT SEC. 356. BANK PROTECTION ACT OF 1968.

The Bank Protection Act of 1968 (12 U.S.C. 1881 et seq.) is amended—

(1) in section 2 (12 U.S.C. 1881), by striking "the term" and all that follows through the end of the section and inserting "the term 'Federal supervisory agency' means the appropriate Federal banking agency, as defined in section 3(q) of the Federal Deposit Insurance Act (12 U.S.C. 1813(q)).";

(2) in section 3 (12 U.S.C. 1882), by striking "and loan" each place that term appears; and

(3) in section 5 (12 U.S.C. 1884), by striking "and loan".

[Explanation at ¶ 1145.]

[¶ 10,357] ACT SEC. 357. BANK SERVICE COMPANY ACT.

The Bank Service Company Act (12 U.S.C. 1861 et seq.) is amended—

(1) in section 1(b)(4) (12 U.S.C. 1861(b)(4))—

(A) by inserting after "an insured bank," the following: "a savings association,";

(B) by striking "Director of the Office of Thrift Supervision" and inserting "appropriate Federal banking agency"; and

(C) by striking ", the Federal Savings and Loan Insurance Corporation,";

(2) in section 1(b)(5), by striking "term 'insured depository institution' has the same meaning as in section 3(c)" and inserting "terms 'depository institution' and 'savings association' have the same meanings as in section 3"; and

(3) in section 7(c)(2) (12 U.S.C. 1867(c)(2)), by inserting "each" after "notify".

[Explanation at ¶ 1150.]

[¶ 10,358] ACT SEC. 358. COMMUNITY REINVESTMENT ACT OF 1977.

The Community Reinvestment Act of 1977 (12 U.S.C. 2901 et seq.) is amended—

(1) in section 803 (12 U.S.C. 2902)—

(A) in paragraph (1)—

(i) in subparagraph (A), by inserting "and Federal savings associations (the deposits of which are insured by the Federal Deposit Insurance Corporation)" after "banks";

(ii) in subparagraph (B), by striking "and bank holding companies" and inserting ", bank holding companies, and savings and loan holding companies"; and

(iii) in subparagraph (C), by striking "; and" and inserting ", and State savings associations (the deposits of which are insured by the Federal Deposit Insurance Corporation)."; and

(B) by striking paragraph (2) (relating to the Office of Thrift Supervision), as added by section 744(q) of the Financial Institutions Reform, Recovery, and Enforcement Act of 1989 (Public Law 101-73; 103 Stat. 440); and

(2) in section 806 (12 U.S.C. 2905), by inserting ", except that the Comptroller of the Currency shall prescribe regulations applicable to savings associations and the Board of Governors shall prescribe regulations applicable to insured State member banks, bank holding companies and savings and loan holding companies," after "supervisory agency".

[Explanation at ¶ 1155.]

[¶ 10,359] ACT SEC. 359. CRIME CONTROL ACT OF 1990.

The Crime Control Act of 1990 is amended—

(1) in section 2539(c)(2) (28 U.S.C. 509 note)—

(A) by striking subparagraphs (C) and (D); and

(B) by redesignating subparagraphs (E) through (H) as subparagraphs (C) through (G), respectively; and

(2) in section 2554(b)(2) (Public Law 101-647; 104 Stat. 4890)—

(A) in subparagraph (A), by striking ", the Director of the Office of Thrift Supervision," and inserting "the Comptroller of the Currency"; and

(B) in subparagraph (B), by striking ", the Director" and all that follows through "Trust Corporation" and inserting "or the Federal Deposit Insurance Corporation".

[Explanation at ¶1160.]

[¶10,360] ACT SEC. 360. DEPOSITORY INSTITUTION MANAGEMENT INTERLOCKS ACT.

The Depository Institution Management Interlocks Act (12 U.S.C. 3201 et seq.) is amended—

(1) in section 207 (12 U.S.C. 3206)—

(A) in paragraph (1), by inserting before the comma at the end the following: "and Federal savings associations (the deposits of which are insured by the Federal Deposit Insurance Corporation)";

(B) in paragraph (2), by striking ", and bank holding companies" and inserting ", bank holding companies, and savings and loan holding companies";

(C) in paragraph (3), by striking "Corporation," and inserting "Corporation and State savings associations (the deposits of which are insured by the Federal Deposit Insurance Corporation),";

(D) by striking paragraph (4);

(E) by redesignating paragraphs (5) and (6) as paragraphs (4) and (5), respectively; and

(F) in paragraph (5), as so redesignated, by striking "through (5)" and inserting "through (4)";

(2) in section 209 (12 U.S.C. 3207)—

(A) in paragraph (1), by inserting before the comma at the end the following: "and Federal savings associations (the deposits of which are insured by the Federal Deposit Insurance Corporation)";

(B) in paragraph (2), by striking ", and bank holding companies" and inserting ", bank holding companies, and savings and loan holding companies";

(C) in paragraph (3), by striking "Corporation," and inserting "Corporation and State savings associations (the deposits of which are insured by the Federal Deposit Insurance Corporation),";

(D) by striking paragraph (4); and

(E) by redesignating paragraph (5) as paragraph (4); and

(3) in section 210(a) (12 U.S.C. 3208(a))—

(A) by striking "his" and inserting "the"; and

(B) by inserting "of the Attorney General" after "enforcement functions".

[Explanation at ¶1165.]

[¶10,361] ACT SEC. 361. EMERGENCY HOMEOWNERS' RELIEF ACT.

Section 110 of the Emergency Homeowners' Relief Act (12 U.S.C. 2709) is amended in the second sentence, by striking "Home Loan Bank Board, the Federal Savings and Loan Insurance Corporation" and inserting "Housing Finance Agency".

[Explanation at ¶1170.]

[¶10,362] ACT SEC. 362. FEDERAL CREDIT UNION ACT.

The Federal Credit Union Act (12 U.S.C. 1751 et seq.) is amended—

(1) in section 107(8) (12 U.S.C. 1757(8)), by striking "or the Federal Savings and Loan Insurance Corporation";

(2) in section 205 (12 U.S.C. 1785)—

(A) in subsection (b)(2)(G)(i), by striking "the Office of Thrift Supervision and"; and

(B) in subsection (i)(1), by striking "or the Federal Savings and Loan Insurance Corporation"; and

(3) in section 206(g)(7) (12 U.S.C. 1786(g)(7))—

(A) in subparagraph (A)—

(i) in clause (ii), by striking "(b)(8)" and inserting "(b)(9)";

(ii) in clause (v)—

(I) by striking "depository" and inserting "financial"; and

(II) by adding "and" at the end;

(iii) in clause (vi)—

(I) by striking "Board" and inserting "Agency"; and

(II) by striking "; and" and inserting a period; and

(iv) by striking clause (vii); and

(B) in subparagraph (D)—

(i) in clause (iii), by adding "and" at the end;

(ii) in clause (iv)—

(I) by striking "Board" and inserting "Agency"; and

(II) by striking "and" at the end; and

(iii) by striking clause (v).

[Explanation at ¶1175.]

[¶10,363] ACT SEC. 363. FEDERAL DEPOSIT INSURANCE ACT.

The Federal Deposit Insurance Act (12 U.S.C. 1811 et seq.) is amended—

(1) in section 3 (12 U.S.C. 1813)—

(A) in subsection (b)(1)(C), by striking "Director of the Office of Thrift Supervision" and inserting "Comptroller of the Currency";

(B) in subsection (1)(5), in the matter preceding subparagraph (A), by striking "Director of the Office of Thrift Supervision,"; and

(C) in subsection (z), by striking "the Director of the Office of Thrift Supervision,";

(2) in section 7 (12 U.S.C. 1817)—

(A) in subsection (a)—

(i) in paragraph (2)—

(I) in subparagraph (A)—

(aa) in the first sentence, by striking "the Director of the Office of Thrift Supervision,";

(bb) in the second sentence—

(AA) by striking "the Director of the Office of Thrift Supervision," and inserting "to"; and

(BB) by inserting "to" before "any Federal home"; and

(cc) by striking "Finance Board" each place that term appears and inserting "Finance Agency"; and

(II) in subparagraph (B), by striking "the Comptroller of the Currency, the Board of Governors of the Federal Reserve System, and the Director of the Office of Thrift Supervision," and inserting "the Comptroller of the Currency and the Board of Governors of the Federal Reserve System,";

(ii) in paragraph (3), in the first sentence, by striking "Comptroller of the Currency, the Chairman of the Board of Governors of the Federal Reserve System, and the Director of the Office of Thrift Supervision." and inserting "Comptroller of the Currency, and the Chairman of the Board of Governors of the Federal Reserve System.";

(iii) in paragraph (6), by striking "section 232(a)(3)(C)" and inserting "section 232(a)(3)(D)"; and

(iv) in paragraph (7), by striking ", the Director of the Office of Thrift Supervision,"; and

(B) in subsection (n)—

(i) in the heading, by striking "DIRECTOR OF THE OFFICE OF THRIFT SUPERVISION" and inserting "COMPTROLLER OF THE CURRENCY";

(ii) in the first sentence—

(I) by striking "the Director of the Office of Thrift Supervision" and inserting "the Comptroller of the Currency"; and

(II) by inserting "Federal" before "savings associations";

(iii) in the third sentence, by striking ", the Financing Corporation, and the Resolution Funding Corporation"; and

(iv) by striking "the Director" each place that term appears and inserting "the Comptroller";

(3) in section 8 (12 U.S.C. 1818)—

(A) in subsection (a)(8)(B)(ii), in the last sentence, by striking "Director of the Office of Thrift Supervision" each place that term appears and inserting "Comptroller of the Currency";

(B) in subsection (b)(3)—

(i) by inserting "any savings and loan holding company and any subsidiary (other than a depository institution) of a savings and loan holding company (as such terms are defined in section 10 of Home Owners' Loan Act)), any noninsured State member bank" after "Bank Holding Company Act of 1956,"; and

(ii) by inserting "or against a savings and loan holding company or any subsidiary thereof (other than a depository institution or a subsidiary of such depository institution)" before the period at the end;

(C) by striking paragraph (9) of subsection (b) and inserting the following new paragraph:

"(9) [Repealed]".

(D) in subsection (e)(7)—

(i) in subparagraph (A)—

(I) in clause (v), by inserting "and" after the semicolon;

(II) in clause (vi)—

(aa) by striking "Board" and inserting "Agency"; and

(bb) by striking "; and" and inserting a period; and

(III) by striking clause (vii); and

(ii) in subparagraph (D)—

(I) in clause (iii), by inserting "and" after the semicolon;

(II) in clause (iv)—

(aa) by striking "Board" and inserting "Agency"; and

(bb) by striking "; and" and inserting a period; and

(III) by striking clause (v);

(E) in subsection (j)—

(i) in paragraph (2), by striking ", or as a savings association under subsection (b)(9) of this section";

(ii) in paragraph (3), by inserting "or" after the semicolon;

(iii) in paragraph (4), by striking "; or" and inserting a comma; and

(iv) by striking paragraph (5);

(F) in subsection (o), by striking "Director of the Office of Thrift Supervision" and inserting "Comptroller of the Currency"; and

(G) in subsection (w)(3)(A), by striking "and the Office of Thrift Supervision";

(4) in section 10 (12 U.S.C. 1820)—

(A) in subsection (d)(5), by striking "or the Resolution Trust Corporation" each place that term appears; and

(B) in subsection (k)(5)(B)—

(i) in clause (ii), by inserting "and" after the semicolon;

(ii) in clause (iii), by striking "; and" and inserting a period; and

(iii) by striking clause (iv);

(5) in section 11 (12 U.S.C. 1821)—

(A) in subsection (c)—

(i) in paragraph (2)(A)(ii), by striking "(other than section 21A of the Federal Home Loan Bank Act)";

(ii) in paragraph (4), by striking "Except as otherwise provided in section 21A of the Federal Home Loan Bank Act and notwithstanding" and inserting "Notwithstanding";

(iii) in paragraph (6)—

(I) in the heading, by striking "DIRECTOR OF THE OFFICE OF THRIFT SUPERVISION" and inserting "COMPTROLLER OF THE CURRENCY";

(II) in subparagraph (A)—

(aa) by striking "or the Resolution Trust Corporation"; and

(bb) by striking "Director of the Office of Thrift Supervision" and inserting "Comptroller of the Currency"; and

(III) by amending subparagraph

(B) to read as follows:

"(B) RECEIVER.—The Corporation may, at the discretion of the Comptroller of the Currency, be appointed receiver and the Corporation may accept any such appointment.";

(iv) in paragraph (12)(A), by striking "or the Resolution Trust Corporation";

(B) in subsection (d)—

(i) in paragraph (17)(A), by striking "or the Director of the Office of Thrift Supervision"; and

(ii) in paragraph (18)(B), by striking "or the Director of the Office of Thrift Supervision";

(C) in subsection (m)—

(i) in paragraph (9), by striking "or the Director of the Office of Thrift Supervision, as appropriate";

(ii) in paragraph (16), by striking "or the Director of the Office of Thrift Supervision, as appropriate" each place that term appears; and

(iii) in paragraph (18), by striking "or the Director of the Office of Thrift Supervision, as appropriate" each place that term appears;

(D) in subsection (n)—

(i) in paragraph (1)(A)—

(I) by striking ", or the Director of the Office of Thrift Supervision, with respect to" and inserting "or"; and

(II) by striking "applicable,," and inserting "applicable,";

(ii) in paragraph (2)(A), by striking "or the Director of the Office of Thrift Supervision";

(iii) in paragraph (4)(D), by striking "and the Director of the Office of Thrift Supervision, as appropriate,";

(iv) in paragraph (4)(G), by striking "and the Director of the Office of Thrift Supervision, as appropriate,"; and

(v) in paragraph (12)(B)—

(I) by inserting "as" after "shall appoint the Corporation";

(II) by striking "or the Director of the Office of Thrift Supervision, as appropriate," each place such term appears;

(E) in subsection (p)—

(i) in paragraph (2)(B), by striking "the Corporation, the FSLIC Resolution Fund, or the Resolution Trust Corporation," and inserting "or the Corporation,"; and

(ii) in paragraph (3)(B), by striking ", the FSLIC Resolution Fund, the Resolution Trust Corporation,"; and

(F) in subsection (r), by striking "and the Resolution Trust Corporation";

(6) in section 13(k)(1)(A)(iv) (12 U.S.C. 1823(k)(1)(A)(iv)), by striking "Director of the Office of Thrift Supervision" and inserting "Comptroller of the Currency";

(7) in section 18 (12 U.S.C. 1828)—

(A) in subsection (c)(2)—

(i) in subparagraph (A), by inserting "or a Federal savings association" before the semicolon;

(ii) in subparagraph (B), by adding "and" at the end;

(iii) in subparagraph (C), by striking "(except" and all that follows through "; and" and inserting "or a State savings association."; and

(iv) by striking subparagraph (D);

(B) in subsection (g)(1), by striking "the Director of the Office of Thrift Supervision" and inserting "the Comptroller of the Currency";

(C) in subsection (i)(2)(C), by striking "Director of the Office of Thrift Supervision" and inserting "Corporation"; and

(D) in subsection (m)—

(i) in paragraph (1)—

(I) in subparagraph (A), by striking "and the Director of the Office of Thrift Supervision" and inserting "or the Comptroller of the Currency, as appropriate,"; and

(II) in subparagraph (B), by striking "and orders of the Director of the Office of Thrift Supervision" and inserting "of the Comptroller of the Currency and orders of the Corporation and the Comptroller of the Currency";

(ii) in paragraph (2)—

(I) in subparagraph (A), by striking "Director of the Office of Thrift Supervision" and inserting "Comptroller of the Currency, as appropriate,"; and

(II) in subparagraph (B)—

(aa) in the matter before clause (i), by striking "Director of the Office of Thrift Supervision" and inserting "Corporation or the Comptroller of the Currency, as appropriate,"; and

(bb) in the matter following clause (ii)—

(AA) in the first sentence, by striking "Director of the Office of Thrift Supervision" and inserting "Office of the Comptroller of the Currency, as appropriate,"; and

(BB) by striking the second sentence and inserting the following: "The Corporation or the Comptroller of the Currency, as appropriate, may take any other corrective measures with respect to the subsidiary, including the authority to require the subsidiary to terminate the activities or operations posing such risks, as the Corporation or the Comptroller of the Currency, respectively, may deem appropriate."; and

(iii) in paragraph (3)—

(I) in subparagraph (A), in the second sentence—

(aa) by inserting ", in the case of a Federal savings association," before "consult with"; and (bb) by striking "Director of the Office of Thrift Supervision" and inserting "Comptroller of the Currency"; and

(II) in subparagraph (B)—

(aa) in the subparagraph heading, by striking "DIRECTOR" and inserting "COMPTROLLER OF THE CURRENCY";

(bb) by striking "Office of Thrift Supervision" and inserting "Comptroller of the Currency";

(cc) by inserting a comma after "soundness"; and

(dd) by inserting "as to Federal savings associations" after "compliance";

(8) in section 19(e) (12 U.S.C. 1829(e))—

(A) in paragraph (1), by striking "Director of the Office of Thrift Supervision" and inserting "Board of Governors of the Federal Reserve System"; and

(B) in paragraph (2), by striking "Director of the Office of Thrift Supervision" and inserting "Board of Governors of the Federal Reserve System";

(9) in section 28 (12 U.S.C. 1831e)—

(A) in subsection (e)—

(i) in paragraph (2)—

(I) in subparagraph (A)(ii), by striking "Director of the Office of Thrift Supervision" and inserting "Comptroller of the Currency or the Corporation, as appropriate";

(II) in subparagraph (C), by striking "Director of the Office of Thrift Supervision" and inserting "Comptroller of the Currency or the Corporation, as appropriate,"; and

(III) in subparagraph (F), by striking "Director of the Office of Thrift Supervision" and inserting "Comptroller of the Currency or the Corporation, as appropriate"; and

(ii) in paragraph (3)—

(I) in subparagraph (A), by striking "Director of the Office of Thrift Supervision" and inserting "Comptroller of the Currency or the Corporation, as appropriate"; and

(II) in subparagraph (B), by striking "Director of the Office of Thrift Supervision" and inserting "Comptroller of the Currency or the Corporation, as appropriate,"; and

(B) in subsection (h)(2), by striking "Director of the Office of Thrift Supervision" and inserting "Comptroller of the Currency, of the Corporation,"; and

(10) in section 33(e) (12 U.S.C. 1831j(e)), by striking "Federal Housing Finance Board, the Comptroller of the Currency, and the Director of the Office of Thrift Supervision" and inserting "Federal Housing Finance Agency and the Comptroller of the Currency".

[Explanation at ¶1180.]

[¶10,364] ACT SEC. 364. FEDERAL HOME LOAN BANK ACT.

(a) REPEAL OF SECTION 18(C).—Effective 90 days after the transfer date, section 18(c) of the Federal Home Loan Bank Act (12 U.S.C. 1438(c)) is repealed.

(b) REPEAL OF SECTION 21A.—Section 21A of the Federal Home Loan Bank Act (12 U.S.C. 1441a) is repealed.

[Explanation at ¶1185.]

[¶10,365] ACT SEC. 365. FEDERAL HOUSING ENTERPRISES FINANCIAL SAFETY AND SOUNDNESS ACT OF 1992.

The Federal Housing Enterprises Financial Safety and Soundness Act of 1992 (12 U.S.C. 4501 et seq.) is amended—

(1) in section 1315(b) (12 U.S.C. 4515(b)), by striking "the Federal Deposit Insurance Corporation, and the Office of Thrift Supervision." and inserting "and the Federal Deposit Insurance Corporation."; and

(2) in section 1317(c) (12 U.S.C. 4517(c)), by striking "the Federal Deposit Insurance Corporation, or the Director of the Office of Thrift Supervision" and inserting "or the Federal Deposit Insurance Corporation".

[Explanation at ¶1190.]

[¶10,366] ACT SEC. 366. FEDERAL RESERVE ACT.

The Federal Reserve Act (12 U.S.C. 221 et seq.) is amended—

(1) in section 11(a)(2) (12 U.S.C. 248(a)(2))—

(A) by inserting "State savings associations that are insured depository institutions (as defined in section 3 of the Federal Deposit Insurance Act)," after "case of insured";

(B) by striking "Director of the Office of Thrift Supervision" and inserting "Comptroller of the Currency";

(C) by inserting "Federal" before "savings association which"; and

(D) by striking "savings and loan association" and inserting "savings association"; and

(2) in section 19(b) (12 U.S.C. 461(b))—

(A) in paragraph (1)(F), by striking "Director of the Office of Thrift Supervision" and inserting "Comptroller of the Currency"; and

(B) in paragraph (4)(B), by striking "Director of the Office of Thrift Supervision" and inserting "Comptroller of the Currency".

[Explanation at ¶1195.]

[¶10,367] ACT SEC. 367. FINANCIAL INSTITUTIONS REFORM, RECOVERY, AND ENFORCEMENT ACT OF 1989.

The Financial Institutions Reform, Recovery, and Enforcement Act of 1989 is amended—

(1) in section 203 (12 U.S.C. 1812 note), by striking subsection (b);

(2) in section 302(1) (12 U.S.C. 1467a note), by striking "Director of the Office of Thrift Supervision" and inserting "Comptroller of the Currency";

(3) in section 305 (12 U.S.C. 1464 note), by striking subsection (b);

(4) in section 308 (12 U.S.C. 1463 note)—

(A) in subsection (a), by striking "Director of the Office of Thrift Supervision" and inserting "Chairman of the Board of Governors of the Federal Reserve System, the Comptroller of the Currency, the Chairman of the National Credit Union Administration,"; and

(B) by adding at the end the following new subsection:

"(c) REPORTS.—The Secretary of the Treasury, the Chairman of the Board of Governors of the Federal Reserve System, the Comptroller of the Currency, the Chairman of the National Credit Union Administration, and the Chairperson of Board of Directors of the Federal Deposit Insurance Corporation shall each submit an annual report to the Congress containing a description of actions taken to carry out this section.";

(5) in section 402 (12 U.S.C. 1437 note)—

(A) in subsection (a), by striking "Director of the Office of Thrift Supervision" and inserting "Comptroller of the Currency";

(B) by striking subsection (b);

(C) in subsection (e)—

(i) in paragraph (1), by striking "Office of Thrift Supervision" and inserting "Comptroller of the Currency"; and

(ii) in each of paragraphs (2), (3), and (4), by striking "Director of the Office of Thrift Supervision" each place that term appears and inserting "Comptroller of the Currency"; and

(D) by striking "Federal Housing Finance Board" each place that term appears and inserting "Federal Housing Finance Agency";

(6) in section 1103(a) (12 U.S.C. 3332(a)), by striking "and the Resolution Trust Corporation";

(7) in section 1205(b) (12 U.S.C. 1818 note)—

(A) in paragraph (1)—

(i) by striking subparagraph (B); and

(ii) by redesignating subparagraphs (C) through (F) as subparagraphs (B) through (E), respectively; and

(B) in paragraph (2), by striking "paragraph (1)(F)" and inserting "paragraph (1)(E)";

(8) in section 1206 (12 U.S.C. 1833b)—

(A) by striking "Board, the Oversight Board of the Resolution Trust Corporation" and inserting "Agency, and"; and

(B) by striking ", and the Office of Thrift Supervision";

(9) in section 1216 (12 U.S.C. 1833e)—

(A) in subsection (a)—

(i) in paragraph (3), by adding "and" at the end;

(ii) in paragraph (4), by striking the semicolon at the end and inserting a period;

(iii) by striking paragraphs (2), (5), and (6); and

(iv) by redesignating paragraphs (3) and (4), as paragraphs (2) and (3), respectively;

(B) in subsection (c)—

(i) by striking "the Director of the Office of Thrift Supervision," and inserting "and"; and

(ii) by striking "the Thrift Depositor Protection Oversight Board of the Resolution Trust Corporation, and the Resolution Trust Corporation"; and

(C) in subsection (d)—

(i) by striking paragraphs (3), (5), and (6); and

(ii) by redesignating paragraphs (4), (7), and (8) as paragraphs (3), (4), and (5), respectively.

[Explanation at ¶ 1200.]

[¶ 10,368] ACT SEC. 368. FLOOD DISASTER PROTECTION ACT OF 1973.

Section 3(a)(5) of the Flood Disaster Protection Act of 1973 (42 U.S.C. 4003(a)(5)) is amended by striking ", the Office of Thrift Supervision".

[Explanation at ¶ 1205.]

[¶ 10,369] ACT SEC. 369. HOME OWNERS' LOAN ACT.

The Home Owners' Loan Act (12 U.S.C. 1461 et seq.) is amended—

(1) in section 1 (12 U.S.C. 1461), by striking the table of contents;

(2) in section 2 (12 U.S.C. 1462), as amended by this Act—

(A) by striking paragraphs (1) and (3);

(B) by redesignating paragraph (2) as paragraph (1);

(C) by redesignating paragraphs (4) through (9) as paragraphs (2) through (7), respectively; and

(D) by adding at the end the following:

"(8) BOARD.—The term 'Board', other than in the context of the Board of Directors of the Corporation, means the Board of Governors of the Federal Reserve System.

"(9) COMPTROLLER.—The term 'Comptroller' means the Comptroller of the Currency.";

(3) in section 3 (12 U.S.C. 1462a)—

(A) by striking the section heading and inserting the following:

"SEC. 3. ADMINISTRATIVE PROVISIONS.";

(B) by striking subsections (a), (b), (c), (d), (g), (h), (i), and (j);

(C) by redesignating subsections (e) and (f) as subsections (a) and (b), respectively;

(D) in subsection (a), as so redesignated—

(i) in the heading by striking "OF THE DIRECTOR"; and

(ii) in the matter preceding paragraph (1), by striking "The Director" and inserting "In accordance with subtitle A of title III of the Dodd-Frank Wall Street Reform and Consumer Protection Act, the appropriate Federal banking agency"; and

(E) in subsection (b), as so redesignated, by striking "Director" and inserting "appropriate Federal banking agency";

(4) in section 4 (12 U.S.C. 1463)—

(A) in subsection (a)—

(i) in the subsection heading, by striking "FEDERAL";

(ii) by striking paragraphs (1) and (2) and inserting the following:

"(1) EXAMINATION AND SAFE AND SOUND OPERATION.—

"(A) FEDERAL SAVINGS ASSOCIATIONS.—The Comptroller shall provide for the examination and safe and sound operation of Federal savings associations.

"(B) STATE SAVINGS ASSOCIATIONS.—The Corporation shall provide for the examination and safe and sound operation of State savings associations.

"(2) REGULATIONS FOR SAVINGS ASSOCIATIONS.—The Comptroller may prescribe regulations with respect to savings associations, as the Comptroller determines to be appropriate to carry out the purposes of this Act."; and

(iii) in paragraph (3), by striking "Director" each place that term appears and inserting "Comptroller and the Corporation";

(B) in subsection (b)—

(i) in paragraph (2)—

(I) in subparagraph (A), by adding "and" at the end;

(II) in subparagraph (B), by striking "; and" and inserting a period; and

(III) by striking subparagraph (C); and

(ii) by striking "Director" each place that term appears and inserting "Comptroller";

(C) in subsection (c)—

(i) by striking "All regulations and policies of the Director" and inserting "The regulations of the Comptroller and the policies of the Comptroller and the Corporation"; and

(ii) by striking "of the Currency";

(D) in subsection (e)(5), by striking "Director" and inserting "Comptroller";

(E) in subsection (f), by striking "Director" each place that term appears and inserting "appropriate Federal banking agency"; and

(F) in subsection (h), by striking "Director" each place that term appears and inserting "appropriate Federal banking agency";

(5) in section 5 (12 U.S.C. 1464)—

(A) in subsection (a), by striking "Director", each place such term appears and inserting "Comptroller of the Currency";

(B) in subsection (b), by striking "Director", each place such term appears and inserting "Comptroller of the Currency";

(C) in subsection (c)—

(i) in paragraph (5)—

(I) in subparagraph (A), by striking "Director" and inserting "appropriate Federal banking agency"; and

(II) in subparagraph (B)—

(aa) by striking "The Director" and inserting "The appropriate Federal banking agency"; and (bb) by striking "the Director" and inserting "the appropriate Federal banking agency";

(D) in subsection (d)—

(i) in paragraph (1)—

(I) in subparagraph (A)—

(aa) in the first sentence, by striking "Director" and inserting "appropriate Federal banking agency";

(bb) in the second sentence—

(AA) by striking "Director's own name and through the Director's own attorneys" and inserting "name of the appropriate Federal banking agency and through the attorneys of the appropriate Federal banking agency"; and

(BB) by striking "Director" each place that term appears and inserting "appropriate Federal banking agency"; and

(cc) in the third sentence, by striking "Director" each place that term appears and inserting "Comptroller";

(II) in subparagraph (B)—

(aa) in clauses (i) through (iv), by striking "Director" each place that term appears and inserting "appropriate Federal banking agency";

(III) in clause (v)—

(aa) in the matter preceding subclause (I), by striking "Director" and inserting "appropriate Federal banking agency";

(bb) in subclause (II), by striking "subpenas" and inserting "subpoenas"; and

(cc) in the matter following subclause (II), by striking "subpena" and inserting "subpoena";

(IV) in clause (vi)—

(aa) in the first sentence, by striking "Director" and inserting "appropriate Federal banking agency"; and

(bb) in the second sentence, by striking "Director" and inserting "Comptroller";

(V) in clause (vii)—

(aa) in the first sentence, by striking "subpena" and inserting "subpoena";

(bb) in the second sentence, by striking "subpenaed" and inserting "subpoenaed"; and

(cc) in the third sentence, by striking "Director" and inserting "appropriate Federal banking agency";

(ii) in paragraph (2)—

(I) in subparagraph (A)—

(aa) by striking "Director of the Office of Thrift Supervision" and inserting "appropriate Federal banking agency";

(bb) by striking "any insured savings association" and inserting "an insured savings association"; and

(cc) by striking "Director determines, in the Director's discretion" and inserting "appropriate Federal banking agency determines, in the discretion of the appropriate Federal banking agency";

(II) in subparagraph (B), by striking "Director" each place that term appears and inserting "appropriate Federal banking agency";

(III) in subparagraphs (C) and (D), by striking "Director" and inserting "appropriate Federal banking agency";

(IV) in subparagraph (E)—

(aa) in clause (ii)—

(AA) in the clause heading, by striking "OR RTC"; and

(BB) by striking "or the Resolution Trust Corporation, as appropriate," each place that term appears; and

(bb) by striking "Director" each place that term appears and inserting "appropriate Federal banking agency"; and

(iii) in paragraph (3)—

(I) in subparagraph (A), by striking "Director" each place that term appears and inserting "Comptroller"; and

(II) in subparagraph (B)—

(aa) in the subparagraph heading, by striking "OR RTC";

(bb) by striking "Corporation or the Resolution Trust"; and

(cc) by striking "Director" and inserting "Comptroller";

(iv) in paragraph (4), by striking "Director" and inserting "appropriate Federal banking agency";

(v) in paragraph (6)—

(I) in subparagraph (A), by striking "Director" and inserting "Comptroller"; and

(II) in subparagraphs (B) and (C), by striking "Director" each place that term appears and inserting "appropriate Federal banking agency";

(vi) in paragraph (7)—

(I) in subparagraphs (A), (B), and (D), by striking "Director" each place that term appears and inserting "appropriate Federal banking agency";

(II) in subparagraph (C), by striking "Director" and inserting "Federal Deposit Insurance Corporation or the Comptroller, as appropriate,"; and

(III) by striking subparagraph

(E) and inserting the following:

"(E) ADMINISTRATION BY THE COMPTROLLER AND THE CORPORATION.—The Comptroller may issue such regulations, and the appropriate Federal banking agency may issue such orders, including those issued pursuant to section 8 of the Federal Deposit Insurance Act, as may be necessary to administer and carry out this paragraph and to prevent evasion of this paragraph.";

(E) in subsection (e)(2), strike "Director" and insert "Comptroller";

(F) in subsection (i)—

(i) by striking "Director", each place such term appears, and inserting "Comptroller";

(ii) in paragraph (2), in the heading, by striking "DIRECTOR" and inserting "COMPTROLLER";

(iii) in paragraph (5)(A), by striking "of the Currency"; and

(iv) except as provided in clauses (i) through (iii), by striking "Director" each place such term appears and inserting "Comptroller";

(G) in subsection (o)—

(i) in paragraph (1), by striking "Director" and inserting "Comptroller"; and

(ii) in paragraph (2)(B), by striking "Director's determination" and inserting "determination of the Comptroller";

(H) in subsections (m), (n), (o), and (p), by striking "Director", each place such term appears, and inserting "Comptroller";

(I) in subsection (q)—

(i) in paragraph (6), by striking "of Governors of the Federal Reserve System";

(ii) by striking "Director" each place that term appears and inserting "Board"; and

(iii) by inserting "in consultation with the Comptroller and the Corporation," before "considers";

(J) in subsection (r)(3), by striking "Director" and inserting "Comptroller of the Currency";

(K) in subsection (s)—

(i) in paragraph (1), strike "Director" and insert "Comptroller of the Currency";

(ii) in paragraph (2), strike "Director" and insert "Comptroller of the Currency";

(iii) in paragraph (3), by striking "Director's discretion, the Director" and inserting "discretion of the appropriate Federal banking agency, the appropriate Federal banking agency,";

(iv) in paragraph (4), by striking "Director" each place that term appears and inserting "appropriate Federal banking agency"; and

(v) in paragraph (5)—

(I) by striking "Director", each place such term appears, and inserting "appropriate Federal banking agency"; and

(II) by striking "Director's approval" and inserting "approval of the appropriate Federal banking agency";

(L) in subsection (t)—

(i) in paragraph (1), by striking subparagraph (D);

(ii) by striking paragraph (3) and inserting the following:

"(3) [Repealed].";

(iii) in paragraph (5)—

(I) in subparagraph (B), by striking "Corporation, in its sole discretion" and inserting "appropriate Federal banking agency, in the sole discretion of the appropriate Federal banking agency"; and

(II) by striking subparagraph (D);

(iv) in paragraph (6)—

(I) by striking subparagraph (A) and inserting the following:

"(A) [Reserved].";

(II) in subparagraph (B), by striking "Director" each place that term appears and inserting "appropriate Federal banking agency";

(III) in subparagraph (C)—

(aa) in clause (i), by striking "Director's prior approval" and inserting "prior approval of the appropriate Federal banking agency";

(bb) in clause (ii), by striking "Director's discretion" and inserting "discretion of the appropriate Federal banking agency"; and

(cc) by striking "Director" each place that term appears and inserting "appropriate Federal banking agency";

(IV) in subparagraph (E), by striking "Director shall" and inserting "appropriate Federal banking agency may"; and

(V) in subparagraph (F), by striking "Director" and all that follows through the end of the subparagraph and inserting "appropriate Federal banking agency under this Act or any other provision of law.";

(v) in paragraph (7), by striking "Director" each place that term appears and inserting "appropriate Federal banking agency";

(vi) by striking paragraph (8) and inserting the following:

"(8) [Repealed].";

(vii) in paragraph (9)—

(I) in subparagraph (A), by striking "Director" and inserting "Comptroller";

(II) in subparagraph (C), by striking "of the Currency"; and

(III) by striking subparagraph (B) and redesignating subparagraphs (C) and (D) as subparagraphs (B) and (C), respectively; and

(viii) except as provided in clauses (i) through (vii), by striking "Director" each place that term appears and inserting "appropriate Federal banking agency";

(M) in subsection (u), by striking "Director" each place that term appears and inserting "appropriate Federal banking agency";

(N) in subsection (v)—

(i) in paragraph (2), by striking "Director's determinations" and inserting "determinations of the appropriate Federal banking agency"; and

(ii) by striking "Director" each place that term appears and inserting "appropriate Federal banking agency";

(O) in subsection (w)(1)—

(i) in subparagraph (A)(II), by striking "Director's intention" and inserting "intention of the Comptroller"; and

(ii) in subparagraph (B), by striking "Director's intention" and inserting "intention of the Comptroller"; and

(P) except as provided in subparagraphs (A) through (J), by striking "Director" each place that term appears and inserting "Comptroller";

(6) in section 8 (12 U.S.C. 1466a), by striking "Director" each place that term appears and inserting "Comptroller";

(7) in section 9 (12 U.S.C. 1467)—

(A) in subsection (a), by striking "assessed by the Director" and all that follows through the end of the subsection and inserting the following: "assessed by—

"(1) the Comptroller, against each such Federal savings association, as the Comptroller deems necessary or appropriate; and

"(2) the Corporation, against each such State savings association, as the Corporation deems necessary or appropriate.";

(B) in subsection (b), by striking "Director", each place such term appears, and inserting "Comptroller or Corporation, as appropriate";

(C) in subsection (e)—

(i) by striking "Only the Director" and inserting "The Comptroller"; and

(ii) by striking "Director's designee" and inserting "designee of the Comptroller";

(D) by striking subsection (f) and inserting the following:

"(f) [Reserved].";

(E) in subsection (g)—

(i) in paragraph (1), by striking "Director" and inserting "appropriate Federal banking agency"; and

(ii) in paragraph (2), by striking "Director, or the Corporation, as the case may be," and inserting "appropriate Federal banking agency for the savings association";

(F) in subsection (i), by striking "Director" each place that term appears and inserting "appropriate Federal banking agency";

(G) in subsection (j), by striking "Director's sole discretion" and inserting "sole discretion of the appropriate Federal banking agency";

(H) in subsection (k), by striking "Director may assess against institutions for which the Director is the appropriate Federal banking agency, as defined in section 3 of the Federal Deposit Insurance Act," and inserting "appropriate Federal banking agency may assess against an institution"; and

(I) except as provided in subparagraphs (A) through (G), by striking "Director" each place that term appears and inserting "appropriate Federal banking agency";

(8) in section 10 (12 U.S.C. 1467a)—

(A) in subsection (a)(1), by striking "Director" each place that term appears and inserting "appropriate Federal banking agency";

(B) in subsection (b)—

(i) in paragraph (2), by striking "and the regional office of the Director of the district in which its principal office is located,"; and

(ii) in paragraph (6), by striking "Director's own motion or application" and inserting "motion or application of the Board";

(C) in subsection (c)—

(i) in paragraph (2)(F), by striking "of Governors of the Federal Reserve System";

(ii) in paragraph (4)(B), in the subparagraph heading, by striking "BY DIRECTOR";

(iii) in paragraph (6)(D), in the subparagraph heading, by striking "BY DIRECTOR"; and

(iv) in paragraph (9)(E), by inserting "(in consultation with the appropriate Federal banking agency)" after "including a determination";

(D) in subsection (g)(5)(B), by striking "the Director's discretion" and inserting "the discretion of the Board";

(E) in subsection (1), by striking "Director" each place that term appears and inserting "appropriate Federal banking agency";

(F) in subsection (m), by striking "Director" and inserting "appropriate Federal banking agency";

(G) in subsection (p)—

(i) in paragraph (1)—

(I) by striking "Director determines" the 1st place such term appears and inserting "Board or the appropriate Federal banking agency for the savings association determines";

(II) by striking "Director may" and inserting "Board may"; and

(III) by striking "Director determines" the 2nd place such term appears and inserting "Board, in consultation with the appropriate Federal banking agency for the savings association determines"; and

(ii) in paragraph (2), by striking "Director", each place such term appears, and inserting "Board";

(H) in subsection (q), by striking "Director", each place such term appears, and inserting "Board";

(I) in subsection (r), by striking "Director", each place such term appears, and inserting "Board or appropriate Federal banking agency";

(J) in subsection (s)—

(i) in paragraph (2)—

(I) in subparagraph (B)(ii), by striking "Director's judgment" and inserting "judgment of the appropriate Federal banking agency for the savings association"; and

(II) by striking "Director" each place that term appears and inserting "appropriate Federal banking agency for the savings association"; and

(ii) in paragraph (4), by striking "Director" and inserting "Comptroller"; and

(K) except as provided in subparagraphs (A) through (J), by striking "Director" each place that term appears and inserting "Board";

(9) in section 11 (12 U.S.C. 1468), by striking "Director" each place that term appears and inserting "appropriate Federal banking agency";

(10) in section 12 (12 U.S.C. 1468a), by striking "the Director" and inserting "a Federal banking agency"; and

(11) in section 13 (12 U.S.C. 1468a) is amended by striking "Director" and inserting "a Federal banking agency".

[Explanation at ¶ 1210.]

[¶ 10,370] ACT SEC. 370. HOUSING ACT OF 1948.

Section 502(c) of the Housing Act of 1948 (12 U.S.C. 1701c(c)) is amended—

(1) in the matter preceding paragraph (1), by striking "and the Director of the Office of Thrift Supervision" and inserting ", the Comptroller of the Currency, and the Federal Deposit Insurance Corporation"; and

(2) in paragraph (3), by striking "Board" and inserting "Agency".

[Explanation at ¶1215.]

[¶10,371] ACT SEC. 371. HOUSING AND COMMUNITY DEVELOPMENT ACT OF 1992.

Section 543 of the Housing and Community Development Act of 1992 (Public Law 102-550; 106 Stat. 3798) is amended—

(1) in subsection (c)(1)—

(A) by striking subparagraphs (D) through (F); and

(B) by redesignating subparagraphs (G) and (H) as subparagraphs (D) and (E), respectively; and

(2) in subsection (f)—

(A) in paragraph (2), by striking "the Office of Thrift Supervision," each place that term appears; and

(B) in paragraph (3)—

(i) in the matter preceding subparagraph (A), by striking "the Office of Thrift Supervision,"; and

(ii) in subparagraph (D), by striking "Office of Thrift Supervision,".

[Explanation at ¶1220.]

[¶10,372] ACT SEC. 372. HOUSING AND URBAN-RURAL RECOVERY ACT OF 1983.

Section 469 of the Housing and Urban-Rural Recovery Act of 1983 (12 U.S.C. 1701p-1) is amended in the first sentence, by striking "Federal Home Loan Bank Board" and inserting "Federal Housing Finance Agency".

[Explanation at ¶1225.]

[¶10,373] ACT SEC. 373. NATIONAL HOUSING ACT.

Section 202(f) of the National Housing Act (12 U.S.C. 1708(f)) is amended—

(1) by striking paragraph (5) and inserting the following:

"(5) if the mortgagee is a national bank, a subsidiary or affiliate of such bank, a Federal savings association or a subsidiary or affiliate of a savings association, the Comptroller of the Currency;";

(2) in paragraph (6), by adding "and" at the end;

(3) in paragraph (7)—

(A) by inserting "or State savings association" after "State bank"; and

(B) by striking "; and" and inserting a period; and

(4) by striking paragraph (8).

[Explanation at ¶1230.]

[¶10,374] ACT SEC. 374. NEIGHBORHOOD REINVESTMENT CORPORATION ACT.

Section 606(c)(3) of the Neighborhood Reinvestment Corporation Act (42 U.S.C. 8105(c)(3)) is amended by striking "Federal Home Loan Bank Board" and inserting "Federal Housing Finance Agency".

[Explanation at ¶1235.]

[¶10,375] ACT SEC. 375. PUBLIC LAW 93-100.

Section 5(d) of Public Law 93-100 (12 U.S.C. 1470(a)) is amended—

(1) in paragraph (1), by striking "Federal Savings and Loan Insurance Corporation with respect to insured institutions, the Board of Governors of the Federal Reserve System with respect to State member insured banks, and the Federal Deposit Insurance Corporation with respect to State non-

member insured banks" and inserting "appropriate Federal banking agency, with respect to the institutions subject to the jurisdiction of each such agency,"; and

(2) in paragraph (2), by striking "supervisory" and inserting "banking".

[Explanation at ¶ 1240.]

[¶ 10,376] ACT SEC. 376. SECURITIES EXCHANGE ACT OF 1934.

The Securities Exchange Act of 1934 (15 U.S.C. 78a et seq.) is amended—

(1) in section 3(a)(34) (15 U.S.C. 78c(a)(34))—

(A) in subparagraph (A)—

(i) in clause (i), by striking "or a subsidiary or a department or division of any such bank" and inserting "a subsidiary or a department or division of any such bank, a Federal savings association (as defined in section 3(b)(2) of the Federal Deposit Insurance Act (12 U.S.C. 1813(b)(2))), the deposits of which are insured by the Federal Deposit Insurance Corporation, or a subsidiary or department or division of any such Federal savings association";

(ii) in clause (ii), by striking "or a subsidiary or a department or division of such subsidiary" and inserting "a subsidiary or a department or division of such subsidiary, or a savings and loan holding company";

(iii) in clause (iii), by striking "or a subsidiary or department or division thereof;" and inserting "a subsidiary or department or division of any such bank, a State savings association (as defined in section 3(b)(3) of the Federal Deposit Insurance Act (12 U.S.C. 1813(b)(3))), the deposits of which are insured by the Federal Deposit Insurance Corporation, or a subsidiary or a department or division of any such State savings association; and";

(iv) by striking clause (iv); and

(v) by redesignating clause (v) as clause (iv);

(B) in subparagraph (B)—

(i) in clause (i), by striking "or a subsidiary of any such bank" and inserting "a subsidiary of any such bank, a Federal savings association (as defined in section 3(b)(2) of the Federal Deposit Insurance Act (12 U.S.C. 1813(b)(2))), the deposits of which are insured by the Federal Deposit Insurance Corporation, or a subsidiary of any such Federal savings association";

(ii) in clause (ii), by striking "or a subsidiary of a bank holding company which is a bank other than a bank specified in clause (i), (iii), or (iv) of this subparagraph" and inserting "a subsidiary of a bank holding company that is a bank other than a bank specified in clause (i) or (iii) of this subparagraph, or a savings and loan holding company";

(iii) in clause (iii), by striking "or a subsidiary thereof;" and inserting "a subsidiary of any such bank, a State savings association (as defined in section 3(b)(3) of the Federal Deposit Insurance Act (12 U.S.C. 1813(b)(3))), the deposits of which are insured by the Federal Deposit Insurance Corporation, or a subsidiary of any such State savings association; and";

(iv) by striking clause (iv); and

(v) by redesignating clause (v) as clause (iv);

(C) in subparagraph (C)—

(i) in clause (i), by striking "bank" and inserting "bank or a Federal savings association (as defined in section 3(b)(2) of the Federal Deposit Insurance Act (12 U.S.C. 1813(b)(2))), the deposits of which are insured by the Federal Deposit Insurance Corporation";

(ii) in clause (ii), by striking "or a subsidiary of a bank holding company which is a bank other than a bank specified in clause (i), (iii), or (iv) of this subparagraph" and inserting "a subsidiary of a bank holding company that is a bank other than a bank specified in clause (i) or (iii) of this subparagraph, or a savings and loan holding company";

(iii) in clause (iii), by striking "System)" and inserting, "System) or a State savings association (as defined in section 3(b)(3) of the Federal Deposit Insurance Act (12 U.S.C.

1813(b)(3))), the deposits of which are insured by the Federal Deposit Insurance Corporation; and";

(iv) by striking clause (iv); and

(v) by redesignating clause (v) as clause (iv);

(D) in subparagraph (D)—

(i) in clause (i), by inserting after "bank" the following: "or a Federal savings association (as defined in section 3(b)(2) of the Federal Deposit Insurance Act (12 U.S.C. 1813(b)(2))), the deposits of which are insured by the Federal Deposit Insurance Corporation";

(ii) in clause (ii), by adding "and" at the end;

(iii) by striking clause (iii);

(iv) by redesignating clause (iv) as clause (iii); and

(v) in clause (iii), as so redesignated, by inserting after "bank" the following: "or a State savings association (as defined in section 3(b)(3) of the Federal Deposit Insurance Act (12 U.S.C. 1813(b)(3))), the deposits of which are insured by the Federal Deposit Insurance Corporation";

(E) in subparagraph (F)—

(i) in clause (i), by inserting after "bank" the following: "or a Federal savings association (as defined in section 3(b)(2) of the Federal Deposit Insurance Act (12 U.S.C. 1813(b)(2))), the deposits of which are insured by the Federal Deposit Insurance Corporation";

(ii) by striking clause (ii);

(iii) by redesignating clauses (iii), (iv), and (v) as clauses (ii), (iii), and (iv), respectively; and

(iv) in clause (iii), as so redesignated, by inserting before the semicolon the following: "or a State savings association (as defined in section 3(b)(3) of the Federal Deposit Insurance Act (12 U.S.C. 1813(b)(3))), the deposits of which are insured by the Federal Deposit Insurance Corporation";

(F) in subparagraph (G)—

(i) in clause (i), by inserting after "national bank" the following: ", a Federal savings association (as defined in section 3(b)(2) of the Federal Deposit Insurance Act), the deposits of which are insured by the Federal Deposit Insurance Corporation,";

(ii) in clause (iii)—

(I) by inserting after "bank)" the following: ", a State savings association (as defined in section 3(b)(3) of the Federal Deposit Insurance Act), the deposits of which are insured by the Federal Deposit Insurance Corporation,"; and

(II) by adding "and" at the end;

(iii) by striking clause (iv); and

(iv) by redesignating clause (v) as clause (iv); and

(G) in the undesignated matter following subparagraph (H), by striking ", and the term 'District of Columbia savings and loan association' means any association subject to examination and supervision by the Office of Thrift Supervision under section 8 of the Home Owners' Loan Act of 1933";

(2) in section 12(i) (15 U.S.C. 78l(i))—

(A) in paragraph (1), by inserting after "national banks" the following: "and Federal savings associations, the accounts of which are insured by the Federal Deposit Insurance Corporation";

(B) by striking "(3)" and all that follows through "vested in the Office of Thrift Supervision" and inserting "and (3) with respect to all other insured banks and State savings associations, the accounts of which are insured by the Federal Deposit Insurance Corporation, are vested in the Federal Deposit Insurance Corporation"; and

(C) in the second sentence, by striking "the Federal Deposit Insurance Corporation, and the Office of Thrift Supervision" and inserting "and the Federal Deposit Insurance Corporation";

(3) in section 15C(g)(1) (15 U.S.C. 78o-5(g)(1)), by striking "the Director of the Office of Thrift Supervision, the Federal Savings and Loan Insurance Corporation,"; and

(4) in section 23(b)(1) (15 U.S.C. 78w(b)(1)), by striking ", other than the Office of Thrift Supervision,".

[Explanation at ¶ 1245.]

[¶ 10,377] ACT SEC. 377. TITLE 18, UNITED STATES CODE.

Title 18, United States Code, is amended—

(1) in section 212(c)(2)—

(A) by striking subparagraph (C); and

(B) by redesignating subparagraphs (D) through (H) as subparagraphs (C) through (G), respectively;

(2) in section 657, by striking "Office of Thrift Supervision, the Resolution Trust Corporation,";

(3) in section 981(a)(1)(D)—

(A) by striking "Resolution Trust Corporation,"; and

(B) by striking "or the Office of Thrift Supervision";

(4) in section 982(a)(3)—

(A) by striking "Resolution Trust Corporation,"; and

(B) by striking "or the Office of Thrift Supervision";

(5) in section 1006—

(A) by striking "Office of Thrift Supervision,"; and

(B) by striking "the Resolution Trust Corporation,";

(6) in section 1014—

(A) by striking "the Office of Thrift Supervision"; and

(B) by striking "the Resolution Trust Corporation,"; and

(7) in section 1032(1)—

(A) by striking "the Resolution Trust Corporation,"; and

(B) by striking "or the Director of the Office of Thrift Supervision".

[Explanation at ¶ 1250.]

[¶ 10,378] ACT SEC. 378. TITLE 31, UNITED STATES CODE.

Title 31, United States Code, is amended—

(1) in section 321—

(A) in subsection (c)—

(i) in paragraph (1), by adding "and" at the end;

(ii) in paragraph (2), by striking "; and" and inserting a period; and

(iii) by striking paragraph (3); and

(B) by striking subsection (e); and

(2) in section 714(a), by striking "the Office of the Comptroller of the Currency, and the Office of Thrift Supervision." and inserting "and the Office of the Comptroller of the Currency.".

[Explanation at ¶ 1255.]

TITLE IV—REGULATION OF ADVISERS TO HEDGE FUNDS AND OTHERS

[¶ 10,401] ACT SEC. 401. SHORT TITLE.

This title may be cited as the "Private Fund Investment Advisers Registration Act of 2010".

[Explanation at ¶ 1505.]

[¶ 10,402] ACT SEC. 402. DEFINITIONS.

(a) INVESTMENT ADVISERS ACT OF 1940 DEFINITIONS.—Section 202(a) of the Investment Advisers Act of 1940 (15 U.S.C. 80b-2(a)) is amended by adding at the end the following:

"(29) The term 'private fund' means an issuer that would be an investment company, as defined in section 3 of the Investment Company Act of 1940 (15 U.S.C. 80a-3), but for section 3(c)(1) or 3(c)(7) of that Act.

"(30) The term 'foreign private adviser' means any investment adviser who—

"(A) has no place of business in the United States;

"(B) has, in total, fewer than 15 clients and investors in the United States in private funds advised by the investment adviser;

"(C) has aggregate assets under management attributable to clients in the United States and investors in the United States in private funds advised by the investment adviser of less than $25,000,000, or such higher amount as the Commission may, by rule, deem appropriate in accordance with the purposes of this title; and

"(D) neither—

"(i) holds itself out generally to the public in the United States as an investment adviser; nor

"(ii) acts as—

"(I) an investment adviser to any investment company registered under the Investment Company Act of 1940; or

"(II) a company that has elected to be a business development company pursuant to section 54 of the Investment Company Act of 1940 (15 U.S.C. 80a-53), and has not withdrawn its election.".

(b) OTHER DEFINITIONS.—As used in this title, the terms "investment adviser" and "private fund" have the same meanings as in section 202 of the Investment Advisers Act of 1940, as amended by this title.

[Explanation at ¶ 1510.]

[¶ 10,403] ACT SEC. 403. ELIMINATION OF PRIVATE ADVISER EXEMPTION; LIMITED EXEMPTION FOR FOREIGN PRIVATE ADVISERS; LIMITED INTRASTATE EXEMPTION.

Section 203(b) of the Investment Advisers Act of 1940 (15 U.S.C. 80b-3(b)) is amended—

(1) in paragraph (1), by inserting ", other than an investment adviser who acts as an investment adviser to any private fund," before "all of whose";

(2) by striking paragraph (3) and inserting the following:

"(3) any investment adviser that is a foreign private adviser;"; and

(3) in paragraph (5), by striking "or" at the end;

(4) in paragraph (6)—

(A) by striking "any investment adviser" and inserting "(A) any investment adviser";

(B) by redesignating subparagraphs (A) and (B) as clauses (i) and (ii), respectively; and

(C) in clause (ii) (as so redesignated), by striking the period at the end and inserting "; or"; and

(D) by adding at the end the following:

"(B) any investment adviser that is registered with the Commodity Futures Trading Commission as a commodity trading advisor and advises a private fund, provided that, if after the date of enactment of the Private Fund Investment Advisers Registration Act of 2010, the business of the advisor should become predominately the provision of securities-related advice, then such adviser shall register with the Commission.".

(5) by adding at the end the following:

"(7) any investment adviser, other than any entity that has elected to be regulated or is regulated as a business development company pursuant to section 54 of the Investment Company Act of 1940 (15 U.S.C. 80a-54), who solely advises—

"(A) small business investment companies that are licensees under the Small Business Investment Act of 1958;

"(B) entities that have received from the Small Business Administration notice to proceed to qualify for a license as a small business investment company under the Small Business Investment Act of 1958, which notice or license has not been revoked; or

"(C) applicants that are affiliated with 1 or more licensed small business investment companies described in subparagraph (A) and that have applied for another license under the Small Business Investment Act of 1958, which application remains pending.".

[Explanation at ¶ 1515.]

[¶ 10,404] ACT SEC. 404. COLLECTION OF SYSTEMIC RISK DATA; REPORTS; EXAMINATIONS; DISCLOSURES.

Section 204 of the Investment Advisers Act of 1940 (15 U.S.C. 80b-4) is amended—

(1) by redesignating subsections (b) and (c) as subsections (c) and (d), respectively; and

(2) by inserting after subsection (a) the following:

"(b) RECORDS AND REPORTS OF PRIVATE FUNDS.—

"(1) IN GENERAL.—The Commission may require any investment adviser registered under this title—

"(A) to maintain such records of, and file with the Commission such reports regarding, private funds advised by the investment adviser, as necessary and appropriate in the public interest and for the protection of investors, or for the assessment of systemic risk by the Financial Stability Oversight Council (in this subsection referred to as the 'Council'); and

"(B) to provide or make available to the Council those reports or records or the information contained therein.

"(2) TREATMENT OF RECORDS.—The records and reports of any private fund to which an investment adviser registered under this title provides investment advice shall be deemed to be the records and reports of the investment adviser.

"(3) REQUIRED INFORMATION.—The records and reports required to be maintained by an investment adviser and subject to inspection by the Commission under this subsection shall include, for each private fund advised by the investment adviser, a description of—

"(A) the amount of assets under management and use of leverage, including off-balance-sheet leverage;

"(B) counterparty credit risk exposure;

"(C) trading and investment positions;

"(D) valuation policies and practices of the fund;

"(E) types of assets held;

"(F) side arrangements or side letters, whereby certain investors in a fund obtain more favorable rights or entitlements than other investors;

"(G) trading practices; and

"(H) such other information as the Commission, in consultation with the Council, determines is necessary and appropriate in the public interest and for the protection of investors or for the assessment of systemic risk, which may include the establishment of different reporting requirements for different classes of fund advisers, based on the type or size of private fund being advised.

"(4) MAINTENANCE OF RECORDS.—An investment adviser registered under this title shall maintain such records of private funds advised by the investment adviser for such period or periods as the Commission, by rule, may prescribe as necessary and appropriate in the public interest and for the protection of investors, or for the assessment of systemic risk.

"(5) FILING OF RECORDS.—The Commission shall issue rules requiring each investment adviser to a private fund to file reports containing such information as the Commission deems necessary and appropriate in the public interest and for the protection of investors or for the assessment of systemic risk.

"(6) EXAMINATION OF RECORDS.—

"(A) PERIODIC AND SPECIAL EXAMINATIONS.—The Commission—

"(i) shall conduct periodic inspections of the records of private funds maintained by an investment adviser registered under this title in accordance with a schedule established by the Commission; and

"(ii) may conduct at any time and from time to time such additional, special, and other examinations as the Commission may prescribe as necessary and appropriate in the public interest and for the protection of investors, or for the assessment of systemic risk.

"(B) AVAILABILITY OF RECORDS.—An investment adviser registered under this title shall make available to the Commission any copies or extracts from such records as may be prepared without undue effort, expense, or delay, as the Commission or its representatives may reasonably request.

"(7) INFORMATION SHARING.—

"(A) IN GENERAL.—The Commission shall make available to the Council copies of all reports, documents, records, and information filed with or provided to the Commission by an investment adviser under this subsection as the Council may consider necessary for the purpose of assessing the systemic risk posed by a private fund.

"(B) CONFIDENTIALITY.—The Council shall maintain the confidentiality of information received under this paragraph in all such reports, documents, records, and information, in a manner consistent with the level of confidentiality established for the Commission pursuant to paragraph (8). The Council shall be exempt from section 552 of title 5, United States Code, with respect to any information in any report, document, record, or information made available, to the Council under this subsection.".

"(8) COMMISSION CONFIDENTIALITY OF REPORTS.—Notwithstanding any other provision of law, the Commission may not be compelled to disclose any report or information contained therein required to be filed with the Commission under this subsection, except that nothing in this subsection authorizes the Commission—

"(A) to withhold information from Congress, upon an agreement of confidentiality; or

"(B) prevent the Commission from complying with—

"(i) a request for information from any other Federal department or agency or any self-regulatory organization requesting the report or information for purposes within the scope of its jurisdiction; or

"(ii) an order of a court of the United States in an action brought by the United States or the Commission.

"(9) OTHER RECIPIENTS CONFIDENTIALITY.—Any department, agency, or self-regulatory organization that receives reports or information from the Commission under this subsection shall maintain the confidentiality of such reports, documents, records, and information in a manner consistent with the level of confidentiality established for the Commission under paragraph (8).

"(10) PUBLIC INFORMATION EXCEPTION.—

"(A) IN GENERAL.—The Commission, the Council, and any other department, agency, or self-regulatory organization that receives information, reports, documents, records, or information from the Commission under this subsection, shall be exempt from the provisions of section 552 of title 5, United States Code, with respect to any such report, document, record, or information. Any proprietary information of an investment adviser ascertained by the Commission from any report required to be filed with the Commission pursuant to this subsection shall be subject to the same limitations on public disclosure as any facts ascertained during an examination, as provided by section 210(b) of this title.

"(B) PROPRIETARY INFORMATION.—For purposes of this paragraph, proprietary information includes sensitive, non-public information regarding—

"(i) the investment or trading strategies of the investment adviser;

"(ii) analytical or research methodologies;

"(iii) trading data;

"(iv) computer hardware or software containing intellectual property; and

"(v) any additional information that the Commission determines to be proprietary.

"(11) ANNUAL REPORT TO CONGRESS.—The Commission shall report annually to Congress on how the Commission has used the data collected pursuant to this subsection to monitor the markets for the protection of investors and the integrity of the markets.".

[Explanation at ¶ 1520.]

[¶ 10,405] ACT SEC. 405. DISCLOSURE PROVISION AMENDMENT.

Section 210(c) of the Investment Advisers Act of 1940 (15 U.S.C. 80b-10(c)) is amended by inserting before the period at the end the following: "or for purposes of assessment of potential systemic risk".

[Explanation at ¶ 1520.]

[¶ 10,406] ACT SEC. 406. CLARIFICATION OF RULEMAKING AUTHORITY.

Section 211 of the Investment Advisers Act of 1940 (15 U.S.C. 80b-11) is amended—

(1) in subsection (a), by inserting before the period at the end of the first sentence the following: ", including rules and regulations defining technical, trade, and other terms used in this title, except that the Commission may not define the term 'client' for purposes of paragraphs (1) and (2) of section 206 to include an investor in a private fund managed by an investment adviser, if such private fund has entered into an advisory contract with such adviser"; and

(2) by adding at the end the following:

"(e) DISCLOSURE RULES ON PRIVATE FUNDS.—The Commission and the Commodity Futures Trading Commission shall, after consultation with the Council but not later than 12 months after the date of enactment of the Private Fund Investment Advisers Registration Act of 2010, jointly promulgate rules to establish the form and content of the reports required to be filed with the Commission under subsection 204(b) and with the Commodity Futures Trading Commission by investment advisers that are registered both under this title and the Commodity Exchange Act (7 U.S.C. 1a et seq.).".

[Explanation at ¶ 1525.]

[¶ 10,407] ACT SEC. 407. EXEMPTION OF AND REPORTING BY VENTURE CAPITAL FUND ADVISERS.

Section 203 of the Investment Advisers Act of 1940 (15 U.S.C. 80b-3) is amended by adding at the end the following:

"(l) EXEMPTION OF VENTURE CAPITAL FUND ADVISERS.—No investment adviser that acts as an investment adviser solely to 1 or more venture capital funds shall be subject to the registration requirements of this title with respect to the provision of investment advice relating to a venture capital fund. Not later than 1 year after the date of enactment of this subsection, the Commission shall issue final rules to define the term 'venture capital fund' for purposes of this subsection. The Commission shall require such advisers to maintain such records and provide to the Commission such annual or other reports as the Commission determines necessary or appropriate in the public interest or for the protection of investors.".

[Explanation at ¶ 1515.]

[¶ 10,408] ACT SEC. 408. EXEMPTION OF AND REPORTING BY CERTAIN PRIVATE FUND ADVISERS.

Section 203 of the Investment Advisers Act of 1940 (15 U.S.C. 80b-3) is amended by adding at the end the following:

"(m) EXEMPTION OF AND REPORTING BY CERTAIN PRIVATE FUND ADVISERS.—

"(1) IN GENERAL.—The Commission shall provide an exemption from the registration requirements under this section to any investment adviser of private funds, if each of such investment adviser acts solely as an adviser to private funds and has assets under management in the United States of less than $150,000,000.

"(2) REPORTING.—The Commission shall require investment advisers exempted by reason of this subsection to maintain such records and provide to the Commission such annual or other reports as the Commission determines necessary or appropriate in the public interest or for the protection of investors.

"(n) REGISTRATION AND EXAMINATION OF MIDSIZED PRIVATE FUND ADVISERS.—In prescribing regulations to carry out the requirements of this section with respect to investment advisers acting as investment advisers to mid-sized private funds, the Commission shall take into account the size, governance, and investment strategy of such funds to determine whether they pose systemic risk, and shall provide for registration and examination procedures with respect to the investment advisers of such funds which reflect the level of systemic risk posed by such funds.".

[Explanation at ¶ 1515.]

[¶ 10,409] ACT SEC. 409. FAMILY OFFICES.

(a) IN GENERAL.—Section 202(a)(11) of the Investment Advisers Act of 1940 (15 U.S.C. 80b-2(a)(11)) is amended by striking "or (G)" and inserting the following: "; (G) any family office, as defined by rule, regulation, or order of the Commission, in accordance with the purposes of this title; or (H)".

(b) RULEMAKING.—The rules, regulations, or orders issued by the Commission pursuant to section 202(a)(11)(G) of the Investment Advisers Act of 1940, as added by this section, regarding the definition of the term "family office" shall provide for an exemption that—

(1) is consistent with the previous exemptive policy of the Commission, as reflected in exemptive orders for family offices in effect on the date of enactment of this Act, and the grandfathering provisions in paragraph (3);

(2) recognizes the range of organizational, management, and employment structures and arrangements employed by family offices; and

(3) does not exclude any person who was not registered or required to be registered under the Investment Advisers Act of 1940 on January 1, 2010 from the definition of the term "family office", solely because such person provides investment advice to, and was engaged before January 1, 2010 in providing investment advice to—

(A) natural persons who, at the time of their applicable investment, are officers, directors, or employees of the family office who—

(i) have invested with the family office before January 1, 2010; and

(ii) are accredited investors, as defined in Regulation D of the Commission (or any successor thereto) under the Securities Act of 1933, or, as the Commission may prescribe by rule, the successors-in-interest thereto;

(B) any company owned exclusively and controlled by members of the family of the family office, or as the Commission may prescribe by rule;

(C) any investment adviser registered under the Investment Adviser Act of 1940 that provides investment advice to the family office and who identifies investment opportunities to the family office, and invests in such transactions on substantially the same terms as the family office invests, but does not invest in other funds advised by the family office, and whose assets as to which the family office directly or indirectly provides investment advice represent, in the aggregate, not more than 5 percent of the value of the total assets as to which the family office provides investment advice.

(c) ANTIFRAUD AUTHORITY.—A family office that would not be a family office, but for subsection (b)(3), shall be deemed to be an investment adviser for the purposes of paragraphs (1), (2) and (4) of section 206 of the Investment Advisers Act of 1940.

[Explanation at ¶ 1530.]

[¶ 10,410] ACT SEC. 410. STATE AND FEDERAL RESPONSIBILITIES; ASSET THRESHOLD FOR FEDERAL REGISTRATION OF INVESTMENT ADVISERS.

Section 203A(a) of the of the Investment Advisers Act of 1940 (15 U.S.C. 80b-3a(a)) is amended—

(1) by redesignating paragraph (2) as paragraph (3); and

(2) by inserting after paragraph (1) the following:

"(2) TREATMENT OF MID-SIZED INVESTMENT ADVISERS.—

"(A) IN GENERAL.—No investment adviser described in subparagraph (B) shall register under section 203, unless the investment adviser is an adviser to an investment company registered under the Investment Company Act of 1940, or a company which has elected to be a business development company pursuant to section 54 of the Investment Company Act of 1940, and has not withdrawn the election, except that, if by effect of this paragraph an investment adviser would be required to register with 15 or more States, then the adviser may register under section 203.

"(B) COVERED PERSONS.—An investment adviser described in this subparagraph is an investment adviser that—

"(i) is required to be registered as an investment adviser with the securities commissioner (or any agency or office performing like functions) of the State in which it maintains its principal office and place of business and, if registered, would be subject to examination as an investment adviser by any such commissioner, agency, or office; and

"(ii) has assets under management between—

"(I) the amount specified under subparagraph (A) of paragraph (1), as such amount may have been adjusted by the Commission pursuant to that subparagraph; and

"(II) $100,000,000, or such higher amount as the Commission may, by rule, deem appropriate in accordance with the purposes of this title.".

[Explanation at ¶ 1535.]

[¶ 10,411] ACT SEC. 411. CUSTODY OF CLIENT ASSETS.

The Investment Advisers Act of 1940 (15 U.S.C. 80b-1 et seq.) is amended by adding at the end the following new section:

"SEC. 223. CUSTODY OF CLIENT ACCOUNTS.

"An investment adviser registered under this title shall take such steps to safeguard client assets over which such adviser has custody, including, without limitation, verification of such assets by an independent public accountant, as the Commission may, by rule, prescribe.".

[Explanation at ¶ 1540.]

[¶ 10,412] ACT SEC. 412. COMPTROLLER GENERAL STUDY ON CUSTODY RULE COSTS.

The Comptroller General of the United States shall—

(1) conduct a study of—

(A) the compliance costs associated with the current Securities and Exchange Commission rules 204-2 (17 C.F.R. Parts 275.204-2) and rule 206(4)-2 (17 C.F.R. 275.206(4)-2) under the

Investment Advisers Act of 1940 regarding custody of funds or securities of clients by investment advisers; and

(B) the additional costs if subsection (b)(6) of rule 206(4)-2 (17 C.F.R. 275.206(4)2(b)(6)) relating to operational independence were eliminated; and

(2) submit a report to the Committee on Banking, Housing, and Urban Affairs of the Senate and the Committee on Financial Services of the House of Representatives on the results of such study, not later than 3 years after the date of enactment of this Act.

[Explanation at ¶ 1540 and ¶ 1560.]

[¶ 10,413] ACT SEC. 413. ADJUSTING THE ACCREDITED INVESTOR STANDARD.

(a) IN GENERAL.—The Commission shall adjust any net worth standard for an accredited investor, as set forth in the rules of the Commission under the Securities Act of 1933, so that the individual net worth of any natural person, or joint net worth with the spouse of that person, at the time of purchase, is more than $1,000,000 (as such amount is adjusted periodically by rule of the Commission), excluding the value of the primary residence of such natural person, except that during the 4-year period that begins on the date of enactment of this Act, any net worth standard shall be $1,000,000, excluding the value of the primary residence of such natural person.

(b) REVIEW AND ADJUSTMENT.—

(1) INITIAL REVIEW AND ADJUSTMENT.—

(A) INITIAL REVIEW.—The Commission may undertake a review of the definition of the term "accredited investor", as such term applies to natural persons, to determine whether the requirements of the definition, excluding the requirement relating to the net worth standard described in subsection (a), should be adjusted or modified for the protection of investors, in the public interest, and in light of the economy.

(B) ADJUSTMENT OR MODIFICATION.—Upon completion of a review under subparagraph (A), the Commission may, by notice and comment rulemaking, make such adjustments to the definition of the term "accredited investor", excluding adjusting or modifying the requirement relating to the net worth standard described in subsection (a), as such term applies to natural persons, as the Commission may deem appropriate for the protection of investors, in the public interest, and in light of the economy.

(2) SUBSEQUENT REVIEWS AND ADJUSTMENT.—

(A) SUBSEQUENT REVIEWS.—Not earlier than 4 years after the date of enactment of this Act, and not less frequently than once every 4 years thereafter, the Commission shall undertake a review of the definition, in its entirety, of the term "accredited investor", as defined in section 230.215 of title 17, Code of Federal Regulations, or any successor thereto, as such term applies to natural persons, to determine whether the requirements of the definition should be adjusted or modified for the protection of investors, in the public interest, and in light of the economy.

(B) ADJUSTMENT OR MODIFICATION.—Upon completion of a review under subparagraph (A), the Commission may, by notice and comment rulemaking, make such adjustments to the definition of the term "accredited investor", as defined in section 230.215 of title 17, Code of Federal Regulations, or any successor thereto, as such term applies to natural persons, as the Commission may deem appropriate for the protection of investors, in the public interest, and in light of the economy.

[Explanation at ¶ 1545.]

[¶ 10,414] ACT SEC. 414. RULE OF CONSTRUCTION RELATING TO THE COMMODITIES EXCHANGE ACT.

The Investment Advisers Act of 1940 (15 U.S.C. 80b-1 et seq.) is further amended by adding at the end the following new section:

¶ 10,413   Act Sec. 412(1)(B)

"SEC. 224. RULE OF CONSTRUCTION RELATING TO THE COMMODITIES EXCHANGE ACT.

"Nothing in this title shall relieve any person of any obligation or duty, or affect the availability of any right or remedy available to the Commodity Futures Trading Commission or any private party, arising under the Commodity Exchange Act (7 U.S.C. 1 et seq.) governing commodity pools, commodity pool operators, or commodity trading advisors.".

[Explanation at ¶1550.]

[¶10,415] ACT SEC. 415. GAO STUDY AND REPORT ON ACCREDITED INVESTORS.

The Comptroller General of the United States shall conduct a study on the appropriate criteria for determining the financial thresholds or other criteria needed to qualify for accredited investor status and eligibility to invest in private funds, and shall submit a report to the Committee on Banking, Housing, and Urban Affairs of the Senate and the Committee on Financial Services of the House of Representatives on the results of such study not later than 3 years after the date of enactment of this Act.

[Explanation at ¶1560.]

[¶10,416] ACT SEC. 416. GAO STUDY ON SELF-REGULATORY ORGANIZATION FOR PRIVATE FUNDS.

The Comptroller General of the United States shall—

(1) conduct a study of the feasibility of forming a self-regulatory organization to oversee private funds; and

(2) submit a report to the Committee on Banking, Housing, and Urban Affairs of the Senate and the Committee on Financial Services of the House of Representatives on the results of such study, not later than 1 year after the date of enactment of this Act.

[Explanation at ¶1560.]

[¶10,417] ACT SEC. 417. COMMISSION STUDY AND REPORT ON SHORT SELLING.

(a) STUDIES.—The Division of Risk, Strategy, and Financial Innovation of the Commission shall conduct—

(1) a study, taking into account current scholarship, on the state of short selling on national securities exchanges and in the over-the-counter markets, with particular attention to the impact of recent rule changes and the incidence of—

(A) the failure to deliver shares sold short; or

(B) delivery of shares on the fourth day following the short sale transaction; and

(2) a study of—

(A) the feasibility, benefits, and costs of requiring reporting publicly, in real time short sale positions of publicly listed securities, or, in the alternative, reporting such short positions in real time only to the Commission and the Financial Industry Regulatory Authority; and

(B) the feasibility, benefits, and costs of conducting a voluntary pilot program in which public companies will agree to have all trades of their shares marked "short", "market maker short", "buy", "buy-to-cover", or "long", and reported in real time through the Consolidated Tape.

(b) REPORTS.—The Commission shall submit a report to the Committee on Banking, Housing, and Urban Affairs of the Senate and the Committee on Financial Services of the House of Representatives—

(1) on the results of the study required under subsection (a)(1), including recommendations for market improvements, not later than 2 years after the date of enactment of this Act; and

(2) on the results of the study required under subsection (a)(2), not later than 1 year after the date of enactment of this Act.

[Explanation at ¶ 1560.]

[¶ 10,418] ACT SEC. 418. QUALIFIED CLIENT STANDARD.

Section 205(e) of the Investment Advisers Act of 1940 (15 U.S.C. 80b-5(e)) is amended by adding at the end the following: "With respect to any factor used in any rule or regulation by the Commission in making a determination under this subsection, if the Commission uses a dollar amount test in connection with such factor, such as a net asset threshold, the Commission shall, by order, not later than 1 year after the date of enactment of the Private Fund Investment Advisers Registration Act of 2010, and every 5 years thereafter, adjust for the effects of inflation on such test. Any such adjustment that is not a multiple of $100,000 shall be rounded to the nearest multiple of $100,000.".

[Explanation at ¶ 1555.]

[¶ 10,419] ACT SEC. 419. TRANSITION PERIOD.

Except as otherwise provided in this title, this title and the amendments made by this title shall become effective 1 year after the date of enactment of this Act, except that any investment adviser may, at the discretion of the investment adviser, register with the Commission under the Investment Advisers Act of 1940 during that 1-year period, subject to the rules of the Commission.

[Explanation at ¶ 1505.]

TITLE V—INSURANCE

Subtitle A—Federal Insurance Office

[¶ 10,501] ACT SEC. 501. SHORT TITLE.

This subtitle may be cited as the "Federal Insurance Office Act of 2010".

[Explanation at ¶ 2005.]

[¶ 10,502] ACT SEC. 502. FEDERAL INSURANCE OFFICE.

(a) ESTABLISHMENT OF OFFICE.—Subchapter I of chapter 3 of subtitle I of title 31, United States Code, is amended—

    (1) by redesignating section 312 as section 315;

    (2) by redesignating section 313 as section 312; and

    (3) by inserting after section 312 (as so redesignated) the following new sections:

"SEC. 313. FEDERAL INSURANCE OFFICE.

    "(a) ESTABLISHMENT.—There is established within the Department of the Treasury the Federal Insurance Office.

    "(b) LEADERSHIP.—The Office shall be headed by a Director, who shall be appointed by the Secretary of the Treasury. The position of Director shall be a career reserved position in the Senior Executive Service, as that position is defined under section 3132 of title 5, United States Code.

    "(c) FUNCTIONS.—

        "(1) AUTHORITY PURSUANT TO DIRECTION OF SECRETARY.—The Office, pursuant to the direction of the Secretary, shall have the authority—

            "(A) to monitor all aspects of the insurance industry, including identifying issues or gaps in the regulation of insurers that could contribute to a systemic crisis in the insurance industry or the United States financial system;

            "(B) to monitor the extent to which traditionally underserved communities and consumers, minorities (as such term is defined in section 1204(c) of the Financial Institutions Reform, Recovery, and Enforcement Act of 1989 (12 U.S.C. 1811 note)), and low- and moderate-income persons have access to affordable insurance products regarding all lines of insurance, except health insurance;

"(C) to recommend to the Financial Stability Oversight Council that it designate an insurer, including the affiliates of such insurer, as an entity subject to regulation as a nonbank financial company supervised by the Board of Governors pursuant to title I of the Dodd-Frank Wall Street Reform and Consumer Protection Act;

"(D) to assist the Secretary in administering the Terrorism Insurance Program established in the Department of the Treasury under the Terrorism Risk Insurance Act of 2002 (15 U.S.C. 6701 note);

"(E) to coordinate Federal efforts and develop Federal policy on prudential aspects of international insurance matters, including representing the United States, as appropriate, in the International Association of Insurance Supervisors (or a successor entity) and assisting the Secretary in negotiating covered agreements (as such term is defined in subsection (r));

"(F) to determine, in accordance with subsection (f), whether State insurance measures are preempted by covered agreements;

"(G) to consult with the States (including State insurance regulators) regarding insurance matters of national importance and prudential insurance matters of international importance; and

"(H) to perform such other related duties and authorities as may be assigned to the Office by the Secretary.

"(2) ADVISORY FUNCTIONS.—The Office shall advise the Secretary on major domestic and prudential international insurance policy issues.

"(3) ADVISORY CAPACITY ON COUNCIL.—The Director shall serve in an advisory capacity on the Financial Stability Oversight Council established under the Financial Stability Act of 2010.

"(d) SCOPE.—The authority of the Office shall extend to all lines of insurance except—

"(1) health insurance, as determined by the Secretary in coordination with the Secretary of Health and Human Services based on section 2791 of the Public Health Service Act (42 U.S.C. 300gg-91);

"(2) long-term care insurance, except long-term care insurance that is included with life or annuity insurance components, as determined by the Secretary in coordination with the Secretary of Health and Human Services, and in the case of long-term care insurance that is included with such components, the Secretary shall coordinate with the Secretary of Health and Human Services in performing the functions of the Office; and

"(3) crop insurance, as established by the Federal Crop Insurance Act (7 U.S.C. 1501 et seq.).

"(e) GATHERING OF INFORMATION.—

"(1) IN GENERAL.—In carrying out the functions required under subsection (c), the Office may—

"(A) receive and collect data and information on and from the insurance industry and insurers;

"(B) enter into information-sharing agreements;

"(C) analyze and disseminate data and information; and

"(D) issue reports regarding all lines of insurance except health insurance.

"(2) COLLECTION OF INFORMATION FROM INSURERS AND AFFILIATES.—

"(A) IN GENERAL.—Except as provided in paragraph (3), the Office may require an insurer, or any affiliate of an insurer, to submit such data or information as the Office may reasonably require in carrying out the functions described under subsection (c).

"(B) RULE OF CONSTRUCTION.—Notwithstanding any other provision of this section, for purposes of subparagraph (A), the term 'insurer' means any entity that writes insurance or reinsures risks and issues contracts or policies in 1 or more States.

Act Sec. 502(a)(3) ¶10,502

"(3) EXCEPTION FOR SMALL INSURERS.—Paragraph (2) shall not apply with respect to any insurer or affiliate thereof that meets a minimum size threshold that the Office may establish, whether by order or rule.

"(4) ADVANCE COORDINATION.—Before collecting any data or information under paragraph (2) from an insurer, or affiliate of an insurer, the Office shall coordinate with each relevant Federal agency and State insurance regulator (or other relevant Federal or State regulatory agency, if any, in the case of an affiliate of an insurer) and any publicly available sources to determine if the information to be collected is available from, and may be obtained in a timely manner by, such Federal agency or State insurance regulator, individually or collectively, other regulatory agency, or publicly available sources. If the Director determines that such data or information is available, and may be obtained in a timely manner, from such an agency, regulator, regulatory agency, or source, the Director shall obtain the data or information from such agency, regulator, regulatory agency, or source. If the Director determines that such data or information is not so available, the Director may collect such data or information from an insurer (or affiliate) only if the Director complies with the requirements of subchapter I of chapter 35 of title 44, United States Code (relating to Federal information policy; commonly known as the Paperwork Reduction Act), in collecting such data or information. Notwithstanding any other provision of law, each such relevant Federal agency and State insurance regulator or other Federal or State regulatory agency is authorized to provide to the Office such data or information.

"(5) CONFIDENTIALITY.—

"(A) RETENTION OF PRIVILEGE.—The submission of any nonpublicly available data and information to the Office under this subsection shall not constitute a waiver of, or otherwise affect, any privilege arising under Federal or State law (including the rules of any Federal or State court) to which the data or information is otherwise subject.

"(B) CONTINUED APPLICATION OF PRIOR CONFIDENTIALITY AGREEMENTS.—Any requirement under Federal or State law to the extent otherwise applicable, or any requirement pursuant to a written agreement in effect between the original source of any nonpublicly available data or information and the source of such data or information to the Office, regarding the privacy or confidentiality of any data or information in the possession of the source to the Office, shall continue to apply to such data or information after the data or information has been provided pursuant to this subsection to the Office.

"(C) INFORMATION-SHARING AGREEMENT.—Any data or information obtained by the Office may be made available to State insurance regulators, individually or collectively, through an information-sharing agreement that—

"(i) shall comply with applicable Federal law; and

"(ii) shall not constitute a waiver of, or otherwise affect, any privilege under Federal or State law (including the rules of any Federal or State court) to which the data or information is otherwise subject.

"(D) AGENCY DISCLOSURE REQUIREMENTS.—Section 552 of title 5, United States Code, shall apply to any data or information submitted to the Office by an insurer or an affiliate of an insurer.

"(6) SUBPOENAS AND ENFORCEMENT.—The Director shall have the power to require by subpoena the production of the data or information requested under paragraph (2), but only upon a written finding by the Director that such data or information is required to carry out the functions described under subsection (c) and that the Office has coordinated with such regulator or agency as required under paragraph (4). Subpoenas shall bear the signature of the Director and shall be served by any person or class of persons designated by the Director for that purpose. In the case of contumacy or failure to obey a subpoena, the subpoena shall be enforceable by order of any appropriate district court of the United States. Any failure to obey the order of the court may be punished by the court as a contempt of court.

"(f) PREEMPTION OF STATE INSURANCE MEASURES.—

"(1) STANDARD.—A State insurance measure shall be preempted pursuant to this section or section 314 if, and only to the extent that the Director determines, in accordance with this subsection, that the measure—

"(A) results in less favorable treatment of a non-United States insurer domiciled in a foreign jurisdiction that is subject to a covered agreement than a United States insurer domiciled, licensed, or otherwise admitted in that State; and

"(B) is inconsistent with a covered agreement.

"(2) DETERMINATION.—

"(A) NOTICE OF POTENTIAL INCONSISTENCY.—Before making any determination under paragraph (1), the Director shall—

"(i) notify and consult with the appropriate State regarding any potential inconsistency or preemption;

"(ii) notify and consult with the United States Trade Representative regarding any potential inconsistency or preemption;

"(iii) cause to be published in the Federal Register notice of the issue regarding the potential inconsistency or preemption, including a description of each State insurance measure at issue and any applicable covered agreement;

"(iv) provide interested parties a reasonable opportunity to submit written comments to the Office; and

"(v) consider any comments received.

"(B) SCOPE OF REVIEW.—For purposes of this subsection, any determination of the Director regarding State insurance measures, and any preemption under paragraph (1) as a result of such determination, shall be limited to the subject matter contained within the covered agreement involved and shall achieve a level of protection for insurance or reinsurance consumers that is substantially equivalent to the level of protection achieved under State insurance or reinsurance regulation.

"(C) NOTICE OF DETERMINATION OF INCONSISTENCY.—Upon making any determination under paragraph (1), the Director shall—

"(i) notify the appropriate State of the determination and the extent of the inconsistency;

"(ii) establish a reasonable period of time, which shall not be less than 30 days, before the determination shall become effective; and

"(iii) notify the Committees on Financial Services and Ways and Means of the House of Representatives and the Committees on Banking, Housing, and Urban Affairs and Finance of the Senate.

"(3) NOTICE OF EFFECTIVENESS.—Upon the conclusion of the period referred to in paragraph (2)(C)(ii), if the basis for such determination still exists, the determination shall become effective and the Director shall—

"(A) cause to be published a notice in the Federal Register that the preemption has become effective, as well as the effective date; and

"(B) notify the appropriate State.

"(4) LIMITATION.—No State may enforce a State insurance measure to the extent that such measure has been preempted under this subsection.

"(g) APPLICABILITY OF ADMINISTRATIVE PROCEDURES ACT.—Determinations of inconsistency made pursuant to subsection (f)(2) shall be subject to the applicable provisions of subchapter II of chapter 5 of title 5, United States Code (relating to administrative procedure), and chapter 7 of such title (relating to judicial review), except that in any action for judicial review of a determination of inconsistency, the court shall determine the matter de novo.

"(h) REGULATIONS, POLICIES, AND PROCEDURES.—The Secretary may issue orders, regulations, policies, and procedures to implement this section.

"(i) CONSULTATION.—The Director shall consult with State insurance regulators, individually or collectively, to the extent the Director determines appropriate, in carrying out the functions of the Office.

"(j) SAVINGS PROVISIONS.—Nothing in this section shall—

"(1) preempt—

"(A) any State insurance measure that governs any insurer's rates, premiums, underwriting, or sales practices;

"(B) any State coverage requirements for insurance;

"(C) the application of the antitrust laws of any State to the business of insurance; or

"(D) any State insurance measure governing the capital or solvency of an insurer, except to the extent that such State insurance measure results in less favorable treatment of a non-United State insurer than a United States insurer;

"(2) be construed to alter, amend, or limit any provision of the Consumer Financial Protection Agency Act of 2010; or

"(3) affect the preemption of any State insurance measure otherwise inconsistent with and preempted by Federal law.

"(k) RETENTION OF EXISTING STATE REGULATORY AUTHORITY.—Nothing in this section or section 314 shall be construed to establish or provide the Office or the Department of the Treasury with general supervisory or regulatory authority over the business of insurance.

"(l) RETENTION OF AUTHORITY OF FEDERAL FINANCIAL REGULATORY AGENCIES.—Nothing in this section or section 314 shall be construed to limit the authority of any Federal financial regulatory agency, including the authority to develop and coordinate policy, negotiate, and enter into agreements with foreign governments, authorities, regulators, and multinational regulatory committees and to preempt State measures to affect uniformity with international regulatory agreements.

"(m) RETENTION OF AUTHORITY OF UNITED STATES TRADE REPRESENTATIVE.—Nothing in this section or section 314 shall be construed to affect the authority of the Office of the United States Trade Representative pursuant to section 141 of the Trade Act of 1974 (19 U.S.C. 2171) or any other provision of law, including authority over the development and coordination of United States international trade policy and the administration of the United States trade agreements program.

"(n) ANNUAL REPORTS TO CONGRESS.—

"(1) SECTION 313(F) REPORTS.—Beginning September 30, 2011, the Director shall submit a report on or before September 30 of each calendar year to the President and to the Committees on Financial Services and Ways and Means of the House of Representatives and the Committees on Banking, Housing, and Urban Affairs and Finance of the Senate on any actions taken by the Office pursuant to subsection (f) (regarding preemption of inconsistent State insurance measures).

"(2) INSURANCE INDUSTRY.—Beginning September 30, 2011, the Director shall submit a report on or before September 30 of each calendar year to the President and to the Committee on Financial Services of the House of Representatives and the Committee on Banking, Housing, and Urban Affairs of the Senate on the insurance industry and any other information as deemed relevant by the Director or requested by such Committees.

"(o) REPORTS ON U.S. AND GLOBAL REINSURANCE MARKET.—The Director shall submit to the Committee on Financial Services of the House of Representatives and the Committee on Banking, Housing, and Urban Affairs of the Senate—

"(1) a report received not later than September 30, 2012, describing the breadth and scope of the global reinsurance market and the critical role such market plays in supporting insurance in the United States; and

"(2) a report received not later than January 1, 2013, and updated not later than January 1, 2015, describing the impact of part II of the Nonadmitted and Reinsurance Reform Act of

2010 on the ability of State regulators to access reinsurance information for regulated companies in their jurisdictions.

"(p) STUDY AND REPORT ON REGULATION OF INSURANCE.—

"(1) IN GENERAL.—Not later than 18 months after the date of enactment of this section, the Director shall conduct a study and submit a report to Congress on how to modernize and improve the system of insurance regulation in the United States.

"(2) CONSIDERATIONS.—The study and report required under paragraph (1) shall be based on and guided by the following considerations:

"(A) Systemic risk regulation with respect to insurance.

"(B) Capital standards and the relationship between capital allocation and liabilities, including standards relating to liquidity and duration risk.

"(C) Consumer protection for insurance products and practices, including gaps in State regulation.

"(D) The degree of national uniformity of State insurance regulation.

"(E) The regulation of insurance companies and affiliates on a consolidated basis.

"(F) International coordination of insurance regulation.

"(3) ADDITIONAL FACTORS.—The study and report required under paragraph (1) shall also examine the following factors:

"(A) The costs and benefits of potential Federal regulation of insurance across various lines of insurance (except health insurance).

"(B) The feasibility of regulating only certain lines of insurance at the Federal level, while leaving other lines of insurance to be regulated at the State level.

"(C) The ability of any potential Federal regulation or Federal regulators to eliminate or minimize regulatory arbitrage.

"(D) The impact that developments in the regulation of insurance in foreign jurisdictions might have on the potential Federal regulation of insurance.

"(E) The ability of any potential Federal regulation or Federal regulator to provide robust consumer protection for policyholders.

"(F) The potential consequences of subjecting insurance companies to a Federal resolution authority, including the effects of any Federal resolution authority—

"(i) on the operation of State insurance guaranty fund systems, including the loss of guaranty fund coverage if an insurance company is subject to a Federal resolution authority;

"(ii) on policyholder protection, including the loss of the priority status of policyholder claims over other unsecured general creditor claims;

"(iii) in the case of life insurance companies, on the loss of the special status of separate account assets and separate account liabilities; and

"(iv) on the international competitiveness of insurance companies.

"(G) Such other factors as the Director determines necessary or appropriate, consistent with the principles set forth in paragraph (2).

"(4) REQUIRED RECOMMENDATIONS.—The study and report required under paragraph (1) shall also contain any legislative, administrative, or regulatory recommendations, as the Director determines appropriate, to carry out or effectuate the findings set forth in such report.

"(5) CONSULTATION.—With respect to the study and report required under paragraph (1), the Director shall consult with the State insurance regulators, consumer organizations, representatives of the insurance industry and policyholders, and other organizations and experts, as appropriate.

"(q) USE OF EXISTING RESOURCES.—To carry out this section, the Office may employ personnel, facilities, and any other resource of the Department of the Treasury available to the Secretary and the Secretary shall dedicate specific personnel to the Office.

"(r) DEFINITIONS.—In this section and section 314, the following definitions shall apply:

"(1) AFFILIATE.—The term 'affiliate' means, with respect to an insurer, any person who controls, is controlled by, or is under common control with the insurer.

"(2) COVERED AGREEMENT.—The term 'covered agreement' means a written bilateral or multilateral agreement regarding prudential measures with respect to the business of insurance or reinsurance that—

"(A) is entered into between the United States and one or more foreign governments, authorities, or regulatory entities; and

"(B) relates to the recognition of prudential measures with respect to the business of insurance or reinsurance that achieves a level of protection for insurance or reinsurance consumers that is substantially equivalent to the level of protection achieved under State insurance or reinsurance regulation.

"(3) INSURER.—The term 'insurer' means any person engaged in the business of insurance, including reinsurance.

"(4) FEDERAL FINANCIAL REGULATORY AGENCY.—The term 'Federal financial regulatory agency' means the Department of the Treasury, the Board of Governors of the Federal Reserve System, the Office of the Comptroller of the Currency, the Office of Thrift Supervision, the Securities and Exchange Commission, the Commodity Futures Trading Commission, the Federal Deposit Insurance Corporation, the Federal Housing Finance Agency, or the National Credit Union Administration.

"(5) NON-UNITED STATES INSURER.—The term 'non-United States insurer' means an insurer that is organized under the laws of a jurisdiction other than a State, but does not include any United States branch of such an insurer.

"(6) OFFICE.—The term 'Office' means the Federal Insurance Office established by this section.

"(7) STATE INSURANCE MEASURE.—The term 'State insurance measure' means any State law, regulation, administrative ruling, bulletin, guideline, or practice relating to or affecting prudential measures applicable to insurance or reinsurance.

"(8) STATE INSURANCE REGULATOR.—The term 'State insurance regulator' means any State regulatory authority responsible for the supervision of insurers.

"(9) SUBSTANTIALLY EQUIVALENT TO THE LEVEL OF PROTECTION ACHIEVED.—The term 'substantially equivalent to the level of protection achieved' means the prudential measures of a foreign government, authority, or regulatory entity achieve a similar outcome in consumer protection as the outcome achieved under State insurance or reinsurance regulation.

"(10) UNITED STATES INSURER.—The term 'United States insurer' means—

"(A) an insurer that is organized under the laws of a State; or

"(B) a United States branch of a nonUnited States insurer."

"(s) AUTHORIZATION OF APPROPRIATIONS.—There are authorized to be appropriated for the Office for each fiscal year such sums as may be necessary.

"SEC. 314. COVERED AGREEMENTS.

"(a) AUTHORITY.—The Secretary and the United States Trade Representative are authorized, jointly, to negotiate and enter into covered agreements on behalf of the United States.

"(b) REQUIREMENTS FOR CONSULTATION WITH CONGRESS.—

"(1) IN GENERAL.—Before initiating negotiations to enter into a covered agreement under subsection (a), during such negotiations, and before entering into any such agreement, the Secretary and the United States Trade Representative shall jointly consult with the Committee on Financial Services and the Committee on Ways and Means of the House of Representatives and the Committee on Banking, Housing, and Urban Affairs and the Committee on Finance of the Senate.

"(2) SCOPE.—The consultation described in paragraph (1) shall include consultation with respect to—

"(A) the nature of the agreement;

"(B) how and to what extent the agreement will achieve the applicable purposes, policies, priorities, and objectives of section 313 and this section; and

"(C) the implementation of the agreement, including the general effect of the agreement on existing State laws.

"(c) SUBMISSION AND LAYOVER PROVISIONS.—A covered agreement under subsection (a) may enter into force with respect to the United States only if—

"(1) the Secretary and the United States Trade Representative jointly submit to the congressional committees specified in subsection (b)(1), on a day on which both Houses of Congress are in session, a copy of the final legal text of the agreement; and

"(2) a period of 90 calendar days beginning on the date on which the copy of the final legal text of the agreement is submitted to the congressional committees under paragraph (1) has expired.".

(b) DUTIES OF SECRETARY.—Section 321(a) of title 31, United States Code, is amended—

(1) in paragraph (7), by striking "; and" and inserting a semicolon;

(2) in paragraph (8)(C), by striking the period at the end and inserting "; and"; and

(3) by adding at the end the following new paragraph:

"(9) advise the President on major domestic and international prudential policy issues in connection with all lines of insurance except health insurance.".

(c) CLERICAL AMENDMENT.—The table of sections for subchapter I of chapter 3 of title 31, United States Code, is amended by striking the item relating to section 312 and inserting the following new items:

"Sec. 312. Terrorism and financial intelligence.
"Sec. 313. Federal Insurance Office.
"Sec. 314. Covered agreements.
"Sec. 315. Continuing in office.".

[Explanation at ¶ 2005 and ¶ 2010.]

Subtitle B—State-Based Insurance Reform

[¶ 10,511] ACT SEC. 511. SHORT TITLE.

This subtitle may be cited as the "Nonadmitted and Reinsurance Reform Act of 2010".

[Explanation at ¶ 2015.]

[¶ 10,512] ACT SEC. 512. EFFECTIVE DATE.

Except as otherwise specifically provided in this subtitle, this subtitle shall take effect upon the expiration of the 12-month period beginning on the date of the enactment of this subtitle.

[Explanation at ¶ 2015.]

PART I—NONADMITTED INSURANCE

[¶ 10,521] ACT SEC. 521. REPORTING, PAYMENT, AND ALLOCATION OF PREMIUM TAXES.

(a) HOME STATE'S EXCLUSIVE AUTHORITY.—No State other than the home State of an insured may require any premium tax payment for nonadmitted insurance.

(b) ALLOCATION OF NONADMITTED PREMIUM TAXES.—

(1) IN GENERAL.—The States may enter into a compact or otherwise establish procedures to allocate among the States the premium taxes paid to an insured's home State described in subsection (a).

(2) EFFECTIVE DATE.—Except as expressly otherwise provided in such compact or other procedures, any such compact or other procedures—

(A) if adopted on or before the expiration of the 330-day period that begins on the date of the enactment of this subtitle, shall apply to any premium taxes that, on or after such date of enactment, are required to be paid to any State that is subject to such compact or procedures; and

(B) if adopted after the expiration of such 330-day period, shall apply to any premium taxes that, on or after January 1 of the first calendar year that begins after the expiration of such 330-day period, are required to be paid to any State that is subject to such compact or procedures.

(3) REPORT.—Upon the expiration of the 330day period referred to in paragraph (2), the NAIC may submit a report to the Committee on Financial Services and the Committee on the Judiciary of the House of Representatives and the Committee on Banking, Housing, and Urban Affairs of the Senate identifying and describing any compact or other procedures for allocation among the States of premium taxes that have been adopted during such period by any States.

(4) NATIONWIDE SYSTEM.—The Congress intends that each State adopt nationwide uniform requirements, forms, and procedures, such as an interstate compact, that provide for the reporting, payment, collection, and allocation of premium taxes for nonadmitted insurance consistent with this section.

(c) ALLOCATION BASED ON TAX ALLOCATION REPORT.—To facilitate the payment of premium taxes among the States, an insured's home State may require surplus lines brokers and insureds who have independently procured insurance to annually file tax allocation reports with the insured's home State detailing the portion of the nonadmitted insurance policy premium or premiums attributable to properties, risks, or exposures located in each State. The filing of a nonadmitted insurance tax allocation report and the payment of tax may be made by a person authorized by the insured to act as its agent.

[Explanation at ¶ 2020.]

[¶ 10,522] ACT SEC. 522. REGULATION OF NONADMITTED INSURANCE BY INSURED'S HOME STATE.

(a) HOME STATE AUTHORITY.—Except as otherwise provided in this section, the placement of nonadmitted insurance shall be subject to the statutory and regulatory requirements solely of the insured's home State.

(b) BROKER LICENSING.—No State other than an insured's home State may require a surplus lines broker to be licensed in order to sell, solicit, or negotiate nonadmitted insurance with respect to such insured.

(c) ENFORCEMENT PROVISION.—With respect to section 521 and subsections (a) and (b) of this section, any law, regulation, provision, or action of any State that applies or purports to apply to nonadmitted insurance sold to, solicited by, or negotiated with an insured whose home State is another State shall be preempted with respect to such application.

(d) WORKERS' COMPENSATION EXCEPTION.—This section may not be construed to preempt any State law, rule, or regulation that restricts the placement of workers' compensation insurance or excess insurance for self-funded workers' compensation plans with a nonadmitted insurer.

[Explanation at ¶ 2025.]

[¶ 10,523] ACT SEC. 523. PARTICIPATION IN NATIONAL PRODUCER DATABASE.

After the expiration of the 2-year period beginning on the date of the enactment of this subtitle, a State may not collect any fees relating to licensing of an individual or entity as a surplus lines broker in the State unless the State has in effect at such time laws or regulations that provide for participation by the State in the national insurance producer database of the NAIC, or any other equivalent uniform national database, for the licensure of surplus lines brokers and the renewal of such licenses.

[Explanation at ¶ 2030.]

[¶ 10,524] ACT SEC. 524. UNIFORM STANDARDS FOR SURPLUS LINES ELIGIBILITY.

A State may not—

(1) impose eligibility requirements on, or otherwise establish eligibility criteria for, nonadmitted insurers domiciled in a United States jurisdiction, except in conformance with such requirements and criteria in sections 5A(2) and 5C(2)(a) of the Non-Admitted Insurance Model Act, unless the State has adopted nationwide uniform requirements, forms, and procedures developed in accordance with section 521(b) of this subtitle that include alternative nationwide uniform eligibility requirements; or

(2) prohibit a surplus lines broker from placing nonadmitted insurance with, or procuring nonadmitted insurance from, a nonadmitted insurer domiciled outside the United States that is listed on the Quarterly Listing of Alien Insurers maintained by the International Insurers Department of the NAIC.

[Explanation at ¶ 2035.]

[¶ 10,525] ACT SEC. 525. STREAMLINED APPLICATION FOR COMMERCIAL PURCHASERS.

A surplus lines broker seeking to procure or place nonadmitted insurance in a State for an exempt commercial purchaser shall not be required to satisfy any State requirement to make a due diligence search to determine whether the full amount or type of insurance sought by such exempt commercial purchaser can be obtained from admitted insurers if—

(1) the broker procuring or placing the surplus lines insurance has disclosed to the exempt commercial purchaser that such insurance may or may not be available from the admitted market that may provide greater protection with more regulatory oversight; and

(2) the exempt commercial purchaser has subsequently requested in writing the broker to procure or place such insurance from a nonadmitted insurer.

[Explanation at ¶ 2040.]

[¶ 10,526] ACT SEC. 526. GAO STUDY OF NONADMITTED INSURANCE MARKET.

(a) IN GENERAL.—The Comptroller General of the United States shall conduct a study of the nonadmitted insurance market to determine the effect of the enactment of this part on the size and market share of the nonadmitted insurance market for providing coverage typically provided by the admitted insurance market.

(b) CONTENTS.—The study shall determine and analyze—

(1) the change in the size and market share of the nonadmitted insurance market and in the number of insurance companies and insurance holding companies providing such business in the 18-month period that begins upon the effective date of this subtitle;

(2) the extent to which insurance coverage typically provided by the admitted insurance market has shifted to the nonadmitted insurance market;

(3) the consequences of any change in the size and market share of the nonadmitted insurance market, including differences in the price and availability of coverage available in both the admitted and nonadmitted insurance markets;

(4) the extent to which insurance companies and insurance holding companies that provide both admitted and nonadmitted insurance have experienced shifts in the volume of business between admitted and nonadmitted insurance; and

(5) the extent to which there has been a change in the number of individuals who have nonadmitted insurance policies, the type of coverage provided under such policies, and whether such coverage is available in the admitted insurance market.

(c) CONSULTATION WITH NAIC.—In conducting the study under this section, the Comptroller General shall consult with the NAIC.

(d) REPORT.—The Comptroller General shall complete the study under this section and submit a report to the Committee on Banking, Housing, and Urban Affairs of the Senate and the Committee on Financial Services of the House of Representatives regarding the findings of the study not later than 30 months after the effective date of this subtitle.

[Explanation at ¶ 2045.]

[¶ 10,527] ACT SEC. 527. DEFINITIONS.

For purposes of this part, the following definitions shall apply:

(1) ADMITTED INSURER.—The term "admitted insurer" means, with respect to a State, an insurer licensed to engage in the business of insurance in such State.

(2) AFFILIATE.—The term "affiliate" means, with respect to an insured, any entity that controls, is controlled by, or is under common control with the insured.

(3) AFFILIATED GROUP.—The term "affiliated group" means any group of entities that are all affiliated.

(4) CONTROL.—An entity has "control" over another entity if—

(A) the entity directly or indirectly or acting through 1 or more other persons owns, controls, or has the power to vote 25 percent or more of any class of voting securities of the other entity; or

(B) the entity controls in any manner the election of a majority of the directors or trustees of the other entity.

(5) EXEMPT COMMERCIAL PURCHASER.—The term "exempt commercial purchaser" means any person purchasing commercial insurance that, at the time of placement, meets the following requirements:

(A) The person employs or retains a qualified risk manager to negotiate insurance coverage.

(B) The person has paid aggregate nationwide commercial property and casualty insurance premiums in excess of $100,000 in the immediately preceding 12 months.

(C)(i) The person meets at least 1 of the following criteria:

(I) The person possesses a net worth in excess of $20,000,000, as such amount is adjusted pursuant to clause (ii).

(II) The person generates annual revenues in excess of $50,000,000, as such amount is adjusted pursuant to clause (ii).

(III) The person employs more than 500 full-time or full-time equivalent employees per individual insured or is a member of an affiliated group employing more than 1,000 employees in the aggregate.

(IV) The person is a not-for-profit organization or public entity generating annual budgeted expenditures of at least $30,000,000, as such amount is adjusted pursuant to clause (ii).

(V) The person is a municipality with a population in excess of 50,000 persons.

(ii) Effective on the fifth January 1 occurring after the date of the enactment of this subtitle and each fifth January 1 occurring thereafter, the amounts in subclauses (I), (II), and (IV) of clause (i) shall be adjusted to reflect the percentage change for such 5-year period in the Consumer Price Index for All Urban Consumers published by the Bureau of Labor Statistics of the Department of Labor.

(6) HOME STATE.—

(A) IN GENERAL.—Except as provided in subparagraph (B), the term "home State" means, with respect to an insured—

(i) the State in which an insured maintains its principal place of business or, in the case of an individual, the individual's principal residence; or

(ii) if 100 percent of the insured risk is located out of the State referred to in clause (i), the State to which the greatest percentage of the insured's taxable premium for that insurance contract is allocated.

(B) AFFILIATED GROUPS.—If more than 1 insured from an affiliated group are named insureds on a single nonadmitted insurance contract, the term "home State" means the home State, as determined pursuant to subparagraph (A), of the member of the affiliated group that has the largest percentage of premium attributed to it under such insurance contract.

(7) INDEPENDENTLY PROCURED INSURANCE.—The term "independently procured insurance" means insurance procured directly by an insured from a nonadmitted insurer.

(8) NAIC.—The term "NAIC" means the National Association of Insurance Commissioners or any successor entity.

(9) NONADMITTED INSURANCE.—The term "nonadmitted insurance" means any property and casualty insurance permitted to be placed directly or through a surplus lines broker with a nonadmitted insurer eligible to accept such insurance.

(10) NON-ADMITTED INSURANCE MODEL ACT.—The term "Non-Admitted Insurance Model Act" means the provisions of the Non-Admitted Insurance Model Act, as adopted by the NAIC on August 3, 1994, and amended on September 30, 1996, December 6, 1997, October 2, 1999, and June 8, 2002.

(11) NONADMITTED INSURER.—The term "nonadmitted insurer"—

(A) means, with respect to a State, an insurer not licensed to engage in the business of insurance in such State; but

(B) does not include a risk retention group, as that term is defined in section 2(a)(4) of the Liability Risk Retention Act of 1986 (15 U.S.C. 3901(a)(4)).

(12) PREMIUM TAX.—The term "premium tax" means, with respect to surplus lines or independently procured insurance coverage, any tax, fee, assessment, or other charge imposed by a government entity directly or indirectly based on any payment made as consideration for an insurance contract for such insurance, including premium deposits, assessments, registration fees, and any other compensation given in consideration for a contract of insurance.

(13) QUALIFIED RISK MANAGER.—The term "qualified risk manager" means, with respect to a policyholder of commercial insurance, a person who meets all of the following requirements:

(A) The person is an employee of, or third-party consultant retained by, the commercial policyholder.

(B) The person provides skilled services in loss prevention, loss reduction, or risk and insurance coverage analysis, and purchase of insurance.

(C) The person—

(i)(I) has a bachelor's degree or higher from an accredited college or university in risk management, business administration, finance, economics, or any other field determined by a State insurance commissioner or other State regulatory official or entity to demonstrate minimum competence in risk management; and

(II)(aa) has 3 years of experience in risk financing, claims administration, loss prevention, risk and insurance analysis, or purchasing commercial lines of insurance; or

(bb) has—

(AA) a designation as a Chartered Property and Casualty Underwriter (in this subparagraph referred to as "CPCU") issued by the American Institute for CPCU/Insurance Institute of America;

(BB) a designation as an Associate in Risk Management (ARM) issued by the American Institute for CPCU/Insurance Institute of America;

(CC) a designation as Certified Risk Manager (CRM) issued by the National Alliance for Insurance Education & Research;

(DD) a designation as a RIMS Fellow (RF) issued by the Global Risk Management Institute; or

(EE) any other designation, certification, or license determined by a State insurance commissioner or other State insurance regulatory official or entity to demonstrate minimum competency in risk management;

(ii)(I) has at least 7 years of experience in risk financing, claims administration, loss prevention, risk and insurance coverage analysis, or purchasing commercial lines of insurance; and

(II) has any 1 of the designations specified in subitems (AA) through (EE) of clause (i)(II)(bb);

(iii) has at least 10 years of experience in risk financing, claims administration, loss prevention, risk and insurance coverage analysis, or purchasing commercial lines of insurance; or

(iv) has a graduate degree from an accredited college or university in risk management, business administration, finance, economics, or any other field determined by a State insurance commissioner or other State regulatory official or entity to demonstrate minimum competence in risk management.

(14) REINSURANCE.—The term "reinsurance" means the assumption by an insurer of all or part of a risk undertaken originally by another insurer.

(15) SURPLUS LINES BROKER.—The term "surplus lines broker" means an individual, firm, or corporation which is licensed in a State to sell, solicit, or negotiate insurance on properties, risks, or exposures located or to be performed in a State with nonadmitted insurers.

(16) STATE.—The term "State" includes any State of the United States, the District of Columbia, the Commonwealth of Puerto Rico, Guam, the Northern Mariana Islands, the Virgin Islands, and American Samoa.

[Explanation at ¶ 2050.]

PART II—REINSURANCE

[¶ 10,531] ACT SEC. 531. REGULATION OF CREDIT FOR REINSURANCE AND REINSURANCE AGREEMENTS.

(a) CREDIT FOR REINSURANCE.—If the State of domicile of a ceding insurer is an NAIC-accredited State, or has financial solvency requirements substantially similar to the requirements necessary for NAIC accreditation, and recognizes credit for reinsurance for the insurer's ceded risk, then no other State may deny such credit for reinsurance.

(b) ADDITIONAL PREEMPTION OF EXTRATERRITORIAL APPLICATION OF STATE LAW.—In addition to the application of subsection (a), all laws, regulations, provisions, or other actions of a State that is not the domiciliary State of the ceding insurer, except those with respect to taxes and assessments on insurance companies or insurance income, are preempted to the extent that they—

(1) restrict or eliminate the rights of the ceding insurer or the assuming insurer to resolve disputes pursuant to contractual arbitration to the extent such contractual provision is not inconsistent with the provisions of title 9, United States Code;

(2) require that a certain State's law shall govern the reinsurance contract, disputes arising from the reinsurance contract, or requirements of the reinsurance contract;

(3) attempt to enforce a reinsurance contract on terms different than those set forth in the reinsurance contract, to the extent that the terms are not inconsistent with this part; or

(4) otherwise apply the laws of the State to reinsurance agreements of ceding insurers not domiciled in that State.

[Explanation at ¶ 2055.]

[¶ 10,532] ACT SEC. 532. REGULATION OF REINSURER SOLVENCY.

(a) DOMICILIARY STATE REGULATION.—If the State of domicile of a reinsurer is an NAIC-accredited State or has financial solvency requirements substantially similar to the requirements necessary for NAIC accreditation, such State shall be solely responsible for regulating the financial solvency of the reinsurer.

(b) NONDOMICILIARY STATES.—

(1) LIMITATION ON FINANCIAL INFORMATION REQUIREMENTS.—If the State of domicile of a reinsurer is an NAIC-accredited State or has financial solvency requirements substantially similar to the requirements necessary for NAIC accreditation, no other State may require the reinsurer to provide any additional financial information other than the information the reinsurer is required to file with its domiciliary State.

(2) RECEIPT OF INFORMATION.—No provision of this section shall be construed as preventing or prohibiting a State that is not the State of domicile of a reinsurer from receiving a copy of any financial statement filed with its domiciliary State.

[Explanation at ¶ 2060.]

[¶ 10,533] ACT SEC. 533. DEFINITIONS.

For purposes of this part, the following definitions shall apply:

(1) CEDING INSURER.—The term "ceding insurer" means an insurer that purchases reinsurance.

(2) DOMICILIARY STATE.—The terms "State of domicile" and "domiciliary State" mean, with respect to an insurer or reinsurer, the State in which the insurer or reinsurer is incorporated or entered through, and licensed.

(3) NAIC.—The term "NAIC" means the National Association of Insurance Commissioners or any successor entity.

(4) REINSURANCE.—The term "reinsurance" means the assumption by an insurer of all or part of a risk undertaken originally by another insurer.

(5) REINSURER.—

(A) IN GENERAL.—The term "reinsurer" means an insurer to the extent that the insurer—

(i) is principally engaged in the business of reinsurance;

(ii) does not conduct significant amounts of direct insurance as a percentage of its net premiums; and

(iii) is not engaged in an ongoing basis in the business of soliciting direct insurance.

(B) DETERMINATION.—A determination of whether an insurer is a reinsurer shall be made under the laws of the State of domicile in accordance with this paragraph.

(6) STATE.—The term "State" includes any State of the United States, the District of Columbia, the Commonwealth of Puerto Rico, Guam, the Northern Mariana Islands, the Virgin Islands, and American Samoa.

[Explanation at ¶ 2065.]

PART III—RULE OF CONSTRUCTION

[¶ 10,541] ACT SEC. 541. RULE OF CONSTRUCTION.

Nothing in this subtitle or the amendments made by this subtitle shall be construed to modify, impair, or supersede the application of the antitrust laws. Any implied or actual conflict between this subtitle and any amendments to this subtitle and the antitrust laws shall be resolved in favor of the operation of the antitrust laws.

[Explanation at ¶ 2070.]

[¶ 10,542] ACT SEC. 542. SEVERABILITY.

If any section or subsection of this subtitle, or any application of such provision to any person or circumstance, is held to be unconstitutional, the remainder of this subtitle, and the application of the provision to any other person or circumstance, shall not be affected.

[Explanation at ¶ 2075.]

TITLE VI—IMPROVEMENTS TO REGULATION OF BANK AND SAVINGS ASSOCIATION HOLDING COMPANIES AND DEPOSITORY INSTITUTIONS

[¶ 10,601] ACT SEC. 601. SHORT TITLE.

This title may be cited as the "Bank and Savings Association Holding Company and Depository Institution Regulatory Improvements Act of 2010".

[Explanation at ¶ 2505.]

[¶ 10,602] ACT SEC. 602. DEFINITION.

For purposes of this title, a company is a "commercial firm" if the annual gross revenues derived by the company and all of its affiliates from activities that are financial in nature (as defined in section 4(k) of the Bank Holding Company Act of 1956 (12 U.S.C. 1843(k))) and, if applicable, from the ownership or control of one or more insured depository institutions, represent less than 15 percent of the consolidated annual gross revenues of the company.

[Explanation at ¶ 2510.]

[¶ 10,603] ACT SEC. 603. MORATORIUM AND STUDY ON TREATMENT OF CREDIT CARD BANKS, INDUSTRIAL LOAN COMPANIES, AND CERTAIN OTHER COMPANIES UNDER THE BANK HOLDING COMPANY ACT OF 1956.

(a) MORATORIUM.—

(1) DEFINITIONS.—In this subsection—

(A) the term "credit card bank" means an institution described in section 2(c)(2)(F) of the Bank Holding Company Act of 1956 (12 U.S.C. 1841(c)(2)(F));

(B) the term "industrial bank" means an institution described in section 2(c)(2)(H) of the Bank Holding Company Act of 1956 (12 U.S.C. 1841(c)(2)(H)); and

(C) the term "trust bank" means an institution described in section 2(c)(2)(D) of the Bank Holding Company Act of 1956 (12 U.S.C. 1841(c)(2)(D)).

(2) MORATORIUM ON PROVISION OF DEPOSIT INSURANCE.—The Corporation may not approve an application for deposit insurance under section 5 of the Federal Deposit Insurance Act (12 U.S.C. 1815) that is received after November 23, 2009, for an industrial bank, a credit card bank, or a trust bank that is directly or indirectly owned or controlled by a commercial firm.

(3) CHANGE IN CONTROL.—

(A) IN GENERAL.—Except as provided in subparagraph (B), the appropriate Federal banking agency shall disapprove a change in control, as provided in section 7(j) of the Federal Deposit Insurance Act (12 U.S.C. 1817(j)), of an industrial bank, a credit card bank, or a trust bank if the change in control would result in direct or indirect control of the industrial bank, credit card bank, or trust bank by a commercial firm.

(B) EXCEPTIONS.—Subparagraph (A) shall not apply to a change in control of an industrial bank, credit card bank, or trust bank—

(i) that—

(I) is in danger of default, as determined by the appropriate Federal banking agency;

(II) results from the merger or whole acquisition of a commercial firm that directly or indirectly controls the industrial bank, credit card bank, or trust bank in a bona fide merger with or acquisition by another commercial firm, as determined by the appropriate Federal banking agency; or

(III) results from an acquisition of voting shares of a publicly traded company that controls an industrial bank, credit card bank, or trust bank, if, after the acquisition, the acquiring shareholder (or group of shareholders acting in concert) holds less than 25 percent of any class of the voting shares of the company; and

(ii) that has obtained all regulatory approvals otherwise required for such change of control under any applicable Federal or State law, including section 7(j) of the Federal Deposit Insurance Act (12 U.S.C. 1817(j)).

(4) SUNSET.—This subsection shall cease to have effect 3 years after the date of enactment of this Act.

(b) GOVERNMENT ACCOUNTABILITY OFFICE STUDY OF EXCEPTIONS UNDER THE BANK HOLDING COMPANY ACT OF 1956.—

(1) STUDY REQUIRED.—The Comptroller General of the United States shall carry out a study to determine whether it is necessary, in order to strengthen the safety and soundness of institutions or the stability of the financial system, to eliminate the exceptions under section 2 of the Bank Holding Company Act of 1956 (12 U.S.C. 1841) for institutions described in—

(A) section 2(a)(5)(E) of the Bank Holding Company Act of 1956 (12 U.S.C. 1841(a)(5)(E));

(B) section 2(a)(5)(F) of the Bank Holding Company Act of 1956 (12 U.S.C. 1841(a)(5)(F));

(C) section 2(c)(2)(D) of the Bank Holding Company Act of 1956 (12 U.S.C. 1841(c)(2)(D));

(D) section 2(c)(2)(F) of the Bank Holding Company Act of 1956 (12 U.S.C. 1841(c)(2)(F));

(E) section 2(c)(2)(H) of the Bank Holding Company Act of 1956 (12 U.S.C. 1841(c)(2)(H)); and

(F) section 2(c)(2)(B) of the Bank Holding Company Act of 1956 (12 U.S.C. 1841(c)(2)(B)).

(2) CONTENT OF STUDY.—

(A) IN GENERAL.—The study required under paragraph (1), with respect to the institutions referenced in each of subparagraphs (A) through (E) of paragraph (1), shall, to the extent feasible be based on information provided to the Comptroller General by the appropriate Federal or State regulator, and shall—

(i) identify the types and number of institutions excepted from section 2 of the Bank Holding Company Act of 1956 (12 U.S.C. 1841) under each of the subparagraphs described in subparagraphs (A) through (E) of paragraph (1);

(ii) generally describe the size and geographic locations of the institutions described in clause (i);

(iii) determine the extent to which the institutions described in clause (i) are held by holding companies that are commercial firms;

(iv) determine whether the institutions described in clause (i) have any affiliates that are commercial firms;

(v) identify the Federal banking agency responsible for the supervision of the institutions described in clause (i) on and after the transfer date;

(vi) determine the adequacy of the Federal bank regulatory framework applicable to each category of institution described in clause (i), including any restrictions (including limitations on affiliate transactions or cross-marketing) that apply to transactions

Act Sec. 603(b)(2)(A)(vi) ¶10,603

between an institution, the holding company of the institution, and any other affiliate of the institution; and

(vii) evaluate the potential consequences of subjecting the institutions described in clause (i) to the requirements of the Bank Holding Company Act of 1956, including with respect to the availability and allocation of credit, the stability of the financial system and the economy, the safe and sound operation of each category of institution, and the impact on the types of activities in which such institutions, and the holding companies of such institutions, may engage.

(B) SAVINGS ASSOCIATIONS.—With respect to institutions described in paragraph (1)(F), the study required under paragraph (1) shall—

(i) determine the adequacy of the Federal bank regulatory framework applicable to such institutions, including any restrictions (including limitations on affiliate transactions or cross-marketing) that apply to transactions between an institution, the holding company of the institution, and any other affiliate of the institution; and

(ii) evaluate the potential consequences of subjecting the institutions described in paragraph (1)(F) to the requirements of the Bank Holding Company Act of 1956, including with respect to the availability and allocation of credit, the stability of the financial system and the economy, the safe and sound operation of such institutions, and the impact on the types of activities in which such institutions, and the holding companies of such institutions, may engage.

(3) REPORT.—Not later than 18 months after the date of enactment of this Act, the Comptroller General shall submit to the Committee on Banking, Housing, and Urban Affairs of the Senate and the Committee on Financial Services of the House of Representatives a report on the study required under paragraph (1).

[Explanation at ¶ 2510 and ¶ 2515.]

[¶ 10,604] ACT SEC. 604. REPORTS AND EXAMINATIONS OF HOLDING COMPANIES; REGULATION OF FUNCTIONALLY REGULATED SUBSIDIARIES.

(a) REPORTS BY BANK HOLDING COMPANIES.—Sections 5(c)(1) of the Bank Holding Company Act of 1956 (12 U.S.C. 1844(c)(1)) is amended—

(1) by striking subclause (A)(ii) and inserting the following:

"(ii) compliance by the bank holding company or subsidiary with—

"(I) this Act;

"(II) Federal laws that the Board has specific jurisdiction to enforce against the company or subsidiary; and

"(III) other than in the case of an insured depository institution or functionally regulated subsidiary, any other applicable provision of Federal law.";

(2) by striking subparagraph (B) and inserting the following:

"(B) USE OF EXISTING REPORTS AND OTHER SUPERVISORY INFORMATION.—The Board shall, to the fullest extent possible, use—

"(i) reports and other supervisory information that the bank holding company or any subsidiary thereof has been required to provide to other Federal or State regulatory agencies;

"(ii) externally audited financial statements of the bank holding company or subsidiary;

"(iii) information otherwise available from Federal or State regulatory agencies; and

"(iv) information that is otherwise required to be reported publicly."; and

(3) by adding at the end the following:

"(C) AVAILABILITY.—Upon the request of the Board, the bank holding company or a subsidiary of the bank holding company shall promptly provide to the Board any information described in clauses (i) through (iii) of subparagraph (B).".

(b) EXAMINATIONS OF BANK HOLDING COMPANIES.—Section 5(c)(2) of the Bank Holding Company Act of 1956 (12 U.S.C. 1844(c)(2)) is amended to read as follows:

"(2) EXAMINATIONS.—

"(A) IN GENERAL.—Subject to subtitle B of the Consumer Financial Protection Act of 2010, the Board may make examinations of a bank holding company and each subsidiary of a bank holding company in order to—

"(i) inform the Board of—

"(I) the nature of the operations and financial condition of the bank holding company and the subsidiary;

"(II) the financial, operational, and other risks within the bank holding company system that may pose a threat to—

"(aa) the safety and soundness of the bank holding company or of any depository institution subsidiary of the bank holding company; or

"(bb) the stability of the financial system of the United States; and

"(III) the systems of the bank holding company for monitoring and controlling the risks described in subclause (II); and

"(ii) monitor the compliance of the bank holding company and the subsidiary with—

"(I) this Act;

"(II) Federal laws that the Board has specific jurisdiction to enforce against the company or subsidiary; and

"(III) other than in the case of an insured depository institution or functionally regulated subsidiary, any other applicable provisions of Federal law.

"(B) USE OF REPORTS TO REDUCE EXAMINATIONS.—For purposes of this paragraph, the Board shall, to the fullest extent possible, rely on—

"(i) examination reports made by other Federal or State regulatory agencies relating to a bank holding company and any subsidiary of a bank holding company; and

"(ii) the reports and other information required under paragraph (1).

"(C) COORDINATION WITH OTHER REGULATORS.—The Board shall—

"(i) provide reasonable notice to, and consult with, the appropriate Federal banking agency, the Securities and Exchange Commission, the Commodity Futures Trading Commission, or State regulatory agency, as appropriate, for a subsidiary that is a depository institution or a functionally regulated subsidiary of a bank holding company before commencing an examination of the subsidiary under this section; and

"(ii) to the fullest extent possible, avoid duplication of examination activities, reporting requirements, and requests for information.".

(c) AUTHORITY TO REGULATE FUNCTIONALLY REGULATED SUBSIDIARIES OF BANK HOLDING COMPANIES.—The Bank Holding Company Act of 1956 (12 U.S.C. 1841 et seq.) is amended—

(1) in section 5(c)(5)(B) (12 U.S.C. 1844(c)(5)(B)), by striking clause (v) and inserting the following:

"(v) an entity that is subject to regulation by, or registration with, the Commodity Futures Trading Commission, with respect to activities conducted as a futures commission merchant, commodity trading adviser, commodity pool, commodity pool operator, swap execution facility, swap data repository, swap dealer, major swap participant, and activities that are incidental to such commodities and swaps activities."; and

(2) by striking section 10A (12 U.S.C. 1848a).

(d) ACQUISITIONS OF BANKS.—Section 3(c) of the Bank Holding Company Act of 1956 (12 U.S.C. 1842(c)) is amended by adding at the end the following:

"(7) FINANCIAL STABILITY.—In every case, the Board shall take into consideration the extent to which a proposed acquisition, merger, or consolidation would result in greater or more concentrated risks to the stability of the United States banking or financial system.".

(e) ACQUISITIONS OF NONBANKS.—

(1) NOTICE PROCEDURES.—Section 4(j)(2)(A) of the Bank Holding Company Act of 1956 (12 U.S.C. 1843(j)(2)(A)) is amended by striking "or unsound banking practices" and inserting "unsound banking practices, or risk to the stability of the United States banking or financial system".

(2) ACTIVITIES THAT ARE FINANCIAL IN NATURE.—Section 4(k)(6)(B) of the Bank Holding Company Act of 1956 (12 U.S.C. 1843(k)(6)(B)) is amended to read as follows:

"(B) APPROVAL NOT REQUIRED FOR CERTAIN FINANCIAL ACTIVITIES.—

"(i) IN GENERAL.—Except as provided in subsection (j) with regard to the acquisition of a savings association and clause (ii), a financial holding company may commence any activity, or acquire any company, pursuant to paragraph (4) or any regulation prescribed or order issued under paragraph (5), without prior approval of the Board.

"(ii) EXCEPTION.—A financial holding company may not acquire a company, without the prior approval of the Board, in a transaction in which the total consolidated assets to be acquired by the financial holding company exceed $10,000,000,000.

"(iii) HART-SCOTT-RODINO FILING REQUIREMENT.—Solely for purposes of section 7A(c)(8) of the Clayton Act (15 U.S.C. 18a(c)(8)), the transactions subject to the requirements of this paragraph shall be treated as if the approval of the Board is not required.".

(f) BANK MERGER ACT TRANSACTIONS.—Section 18(c)(5) of the Federal Deposit Insurance Act (12 U.S.C. 1828(c)(5)) is amended, in the matter immediately following subparagraph (B), by striking "and the convenience and needs of the community to be served" and inserting "the convenience and needs of the community to be served, and the risk to the stability of the United States banking or financial system".

(g) REPORTS BY SAVINGS AND LOAN HOLDING COMPANIES.—Section 10(b)(2) of the Home Owners' Loan Act (12 U.S.C. 1467a(b)(2) is amended—

(1) by striking "Each savings" and inserting the following:

"(A) IN GENERAL.—Each savings"; and

(2) by adding at the end the following:

"(B) USE OF EXISTING REPORTS AND OTHER SUPERVISORY INFORMATION.—The Board shall, to the fullest extent possible, use—

"(i) reports and other supervisory information that the savings and loan holding company or any subsidiary thereof has been required to provide to other Federal or State regulatory agencies;

"(ii) externally audited financial statements of the savings and loan holding company or subsidiary;

"(iii) information that is otherwise available from Federal or State regulatory agencies; and

"(iv) information that is otherwise required to be reported publicly.

"(C) AVAILABILITY.—Upon the request of the Board, a savings and loan holding company or a subsidiary of a savings and loan holding company shall promptly provide to the Board any information described in clauses (i) through (iii) of subparagraph (B).".

(h) EXAMINATION OF SAVINGS AND LOAN HOLDING COMPANIES.—

(1) DEFINITIONS.—Section 2 of the Home Owners' Loan Act (12 U.S.C. 1462) is amended by adding at the end the following:

"(10) APPROPRIATE FEDERAL BANKING AGENCY.—The term 'appropriate Federal banking agency' has the same meaning as in section 3(q) of the Federal Deposit Insurance Act (12 U.S.C. 1813(q)).

"(11) FUNCTIONALLY REGULATED SUBSIDIARY.—The term 'functionally regulated subsidiary' has the same meaning as in section 5(c)(5) of the Bank Holding Company Act of 1956 (12 U.S.C. 1844(c)(5)).".

"(2) EXAMINATION.—Section 10(b) of the Home Owners' Loan Act (12 U.S.C. 1467a(b)) is amended by striking paragraph (4) and inserting the following:

"(4) EXAMINATIONS.—

"(A) IN GENERAL.—Subject to subtitle B of the Consumer Financial Protection Act of 2010, the Board may make examinations of a savings and loan holding company and each subsidiary of a savings and loan holding company system, in order to—

"(i) inform the Board of—

"(I) the nature of the operations and financial condition of the savings and loan holding company and the subsidiary;

"(II) the financial, operational, and other risks within the savings and loan holding company system that may pose a threat to—

"(aa) the safety and soundness of the savings and loan holding company or of any depository institution subsidiary of the savings and loan holding company; or

"(bb) the stability of the financial system of the United States; and

"(III) the systems of the savings and loan holding company for monitoring and controlling the risks described in subclause (II); and

"(ii) monitor the compliance of the savings and loan holding company and the subsidiary with—

"(I) this Act;

"(II) Federal laws that the Board has specific jurisdiction to enforce against the company or subsidiary; and

"(III) other than in the case of an insured depository institution or functionally regulated subsidiary, any other applicable provisions of Federal law.

"(B) USE OF REPORTS TO REDUCE EXAMINATIONS.—For purposes of this subsection, the Board shall, to the fullest extent possible, rely on—

"(i) the examination reports made by other Federal or State regulatory agencies relating to a savings and loan holding company and any subsidiary; and

"(ii) the reports and other information required under paragraph (2).

"(C) COORDINATION WITH OTHER REGULATORS.—The Board shall—

"(i) provide reasonable notice to, and consult with, the appropriate Federal banking agency, the Securities and Exchange Commission, the Commodity Futures Trading Commission, or State regulatory agency, as appropriate, for a subsidiary that is a depository institution or a functionally regulated subsidiary of a savings and loan holding company before commencing an examination of the subsidiary under this section; and

"(ii) to the fullest extent possible, avoid duplication of examination activities, reporting requirements, and requests for information.".

(i) DEFINITION OF THE TERM "SAVINGS AND LOAN HOLDING COMPANY".—Section 10(a)(1)(D)(ii) of the Home Owners' Loan Act (12 U.S.C. 1467a(a)(1)(D)(ii)) is amended to read as follows:

"(ii) EXCLUSION.—The term 'savings and loan holding company' does not include—

"(I) a bank holding company that is registered under, and subject to, the Bank Holding Company Act of 1956 (12 U.S.C. 1841 et seq.), or to any company directly or indirectly controlled by such company (other than a savings association);

"(II) a company that controls a savings association that functions solely in a trust or fiduciary capacity as described in section 2(c)(2)(D) of the Bank Holding Company Act of 1956 (12 U.S.C. 1841(c)(2)(D)); or

"(III) a company described in subsection (c)(9)(C) solely by virtue of such company's control of an intermediate holding company established pursuant to section 10A.".

(j) EFFECTIVE DATE.—The amendments made by this section shall take effect on the transfer date.

[Explanation at ¶ 2520, ¶ 2525 and ¶ 2530.]

[¶ 10,605] ACT SEC. 605. ASSURING CONSISTENT OVERSIGHT OF PERMISSIBLE ACTIVITIES OF DEPOSITORY INSTITUTION SUBSIDIARIES OF HOLDING COMPANIES.

(a) IN GENERAL.—The Federal Deposit Insurance Act (12 U.S.C. 1811 et seq.) is amended by inserting after section 25 the following new section:

"SEC. 26. ASSURING CONSISTENT OVERSIGHT OF SUBSIDIARIES OF HOLDING COMPANIES.

"(a) DEFINITIONS.—For purposes of this section:

"(1) BOARD.—The term 'Board' means the Board of Governors of the Federal Reserve System.

"(2) FUNCTIONALLY REGULATED SUBSIDIARY.—The term 'functionally regulated subsidiary' has the same meaning as in section 5(c)(5) of the Bank Holding Company Act.

"(3) LEAD INSURED DEPOSITORY INSTITUTION.—The term 'lead insured depository institution' has the same meaning as in section 2(o)(8) of the Bank Holding Company Act.

"(b) EXAMINATION REQUIREMENTS.—Subject to subtitle B of the Consumer Financial Protection Act of 2010, the Board shall examine the activities of a nondepository institution subsidiary (other than a functionally regulated subsidiary or a subsidiary of a depository institution) of a depository institution holding company that are permissible for the insured depository institution subsidiaries of the depository institution holding company in the same manner, subject to the same standards, and with the same frequency as would be required if such activities were conducted in the lead insured depository institution of the depository institution holding company.

"(c) STATE COORDINATION.—

"(1) CONSULTATION AND COORDINATION.—If a nondepository institution subsidiary is supervised by a State bank supervisor or other State regulatory authority, the Board, in conducting the examinations required in subsection (b), shall consult and coordinate with such State regulator.

"(2) ALTERNATING EXAMINATIONS PERMITTED.—The examinations required under subsection (b) may be conducted in joint or alternating manner with a State regulator, if the Board determines that an examination of a nondepository institution subsidiary conducted by the State carries out the purposes of this section.

"(d) APPROPRIATE FEDERAL BANKING AGENCY BACKUP EXAMINATION AUTHORITY.—

"(1) IN GENERAL.—In the event that the Board does not conduct examinations required under subsection (b) in the same manner, subject to the same standards, and with the same frequency as would be required if such activities were conducted by the lead insured depository institution subsidiary of the depository institution holding company, the appropriate Federal banking agency for the lead insured depository institution may recommend in writing (which shall include a written explanation of the concerns giving rise to the recommendation) that the Board perform the examination required under subsection (b).

"(2) EXAMINATION BY AN APPROPRIATE FEDERAL BANKING AGENCY.—If the Board does not, before the end of the 60-day period beginning on the date on which the Board receives a recommendation under paragraph (1), begin an examination as required under subsection (b) or provide a written explanation or plan to the appropriate Federal banking agency making such recommendation responding to the concerns raised by the appropriate Federal banking agency for the lead insured depository institution, the appropriate Federal banking agency for the lead insured depository institution may, subject to the Consumer Financial Protection Act of 2010, examine the activities that are permissible for a depository institution subsidiary conducted by such nondepository institution subsidiary (other than a functionally regulated subsidiary or a subsidiary of a depository institution) of the depository institution holding company as if the nondepository institution subsidiary were an insured depository institution for which the appropriate Federal banking agency of the lead insured depository institution was the appropriate Federal banking agency, to determine whether the activities—

"(A) pose a material threat to the safety and soundness of any insured depository institution subsidiary of the depository institution holding company;

"(B) are conducted in accordance with applicable Federal law; and

"(C) are subject to appropriate systems for monitoring and controlling the financial, operating, and other material risks of the activities that may pose a material threat to the safety and soundness of the insured depository institution subsidiaries of the holding company.

"(3) AGENCY COORDINATION WITH THE BOARD.—An appropriate Federal banking agency that conducts an examination pursuant to paragraph (2) shall coordinate examination of the activities of nondepository institution subsidiaries described in subsection (b) with the Board in a manner that—

"(A) avoids duplication;

"(B) shares information relevant to the supervision of the depository institution holding company;

"(C) achieves the objectives of subsection (b); and

"(D) ensures that the depository institution holding company and the subsidiaries of the depository institution holding company are not subject to conflicting supervisory demands by such agency and the Board.

"(4) FEE PERMITTED FOR EXAMINATION COSTS.—An appropriate Federal banking agency that conducts an examination or enforcement action pursuant to this section may collect an assessment, fee, or such other charge from the subsidiary as the appropriate Federal banking agency determines necessary or appropriate to carry out the responsibilities of the appropriate Federal banking agency in connection with such examination.

"(e) REFERRALS FOR ENFORCEMENT BY APPROPRIATE FEDERAL BANKING AGENCY.—

"(1) RECOMMENDATION OF ENFORCEMENT ACTION.—The appropriate Federal banking agency for the lead insured depository institution, based upon its examination of a nondepository institution subsidiary conducted pursuant to subsection (d), or other relevant information, may submit to the Board, in writing, a recommendation that the Board take enforcement action against such nondepository institution subsidiary, together with an explanation of the concerns giving rise to the recommendation, if the appropriate Federal banking agency determines (by a vote of its members, if applicable) that the activities of the nondepository institution subsidiary pose a material threat to the safety and soundness of any insured depository institution subsidiary of the depository institution holding company.

"(2) BACK-UP AUTHORITY OF THE APPROPRIATE FEDERAL BANKING AGENCY.—If, within the 60-day period beginning on the date on which the Board receives a recommendation under paragraph (1), the Board does not take enforcement action against the nondepository institution subsidiary or provide a plan for supervisory or enforcement action that is acceptable to the appropriate Federal banking agency that made the recommendation pursuant to paragraph (1), such agency may take the recommended enforcement action against the nondepository institution subsidiary, in the same manner as if the nondepository institution subsidiary were an insured depository institution for which the agency was the appropriate Federal banking agency.

"(f) COORDINATION AMONG APPROPRIATE FEDERAL BANKING AGENCIES.—Each Federal banking agency, prior to or when exercising authority under subsection (d) or (e) shall—

"(1) provide reasonable notice to, and consult with, the appropriate Federal banking agency or State bank supervisor (or other State regulatory agency) of the nondepository institution subsidiary of a depository institution holding company that is described in subsection (d) before commencing any examination of the subsidiary;

"(2) to the fullest extent possible—

"(A) rely on the examinations, inspections, and reports of the appropriate Federal banking agency or the State bank supervisor (or other State regulatory agency) of the subsidiary;

"(B) avoid duplication of examination activities, reporting requirements, and requests for information; and

"(C) ensure that the depository institution holding company and the subsidiaries of the depository institution holding company are not subject to conflicting supervisory demands by the appropriate Federal banking agencies.

"(g) RULE OF CONSTRUCTION.—No provision of this section shall be construed as limiting any authority of the Board, the Corporation, or the Comptroller of the Currency under any other provision of law.".

(b) EFFECTIVE DATE.—The amendment made by subsection (a) shall take effect on the transfer date.

[Explanation at ¶ 2535.]

[¶ 10,606] ACT SEC. 606. REQUIREMENTS FOR FINANCIAL HOLDING COMPANIES TO REMAIN WELL CAPITALIZED AND WELL MANAGED.

(a) AMENDMENT.—Section 4(1)(1) of the Bank Holding Company Act of 1956 (12 U.S.C. 1843(1)(1)) is amended—

(1) in subparagraph (B), by striking "and" at the end;

(2) by redesignating subparagraph (C) as subparagraph (D);

(3) by inserting after subparagraph (B) the following:

"(C) the bank holding company is well capitalized and well managed; and"; and

(4) in subparagraph (D)(ii), as so redesignated, by striking "subparagraphs (A) and (B)" and inserting "subparagraphs (A), (B), and (C)".

(b) HOME OWNERS' LOAN ACT AMENDMENT.—Section 10(c)(2) of the Home Owners' Loan Act (12 U.S.C. 1467a(c)(2)) is amended by adding at the end the following new subparagraph:

"(H) Any activity that is permissible for a financial holding company (as such term is defined under section 2(p) of the Bank Holding Company Act of 1956 (12 U.S.C. 1841(p)) to conduct under section 4(k) of the Bank Holding Company Act of 1956 if—

"(i) the savings and loan holding company meets all of the criteria to qualify as a financial holding company, and complies with all of the requirements applicable to a financial holding company, under sections 4(1) and 4(m) of the Bank Holding Company Act and section 804(c) of the Community Reinvestment Act of 1977 (12 U.S.C. 2903(c)) as if the savings and loan holding company was a bank holding company; and

"(ii) the savings and loan holding company conducts the activity in accordance with the same terms, conditions, and requirements that apply to the conduct of such activity by a bank holding company under the Bank Holding Company Act of 1956 and the Board's regulations and interpretations under such Act.".

(c) EFFECTIVE DATE.—The amendments made by this section shall take effect on the transfer date.

[Explanation at ¶ 2540.]

[¶ 10,607] ACT SEC. 607. STANDARDS FOR INTERSTATE ACQUISITIONS.

(a) ACQUISITION OF BANKS.—Section 3(d)(1)(A) of the Bank Holding Company Act of 1956 (12 U.S.C. 1842(d)(1)(A)) is amended by striking "adequately capitalized and adequately managed" and inserting "well capitalized and well managed".

(b) INTERSTATE BANK MERGERS.—Section 44(b)(4)(B) of the Federal Deposit Insurance Act (12 U.S.C. 1831u(b)(4)(B)) is amended by striking "will continue to be adequately capitalized and adequately managed" and inserting "will be well capitalized and well managed".

(c) EFFECTIVE DATE.—The amendments made by this section shall take effect on the transfer date.

[Explanation at ¶ 2540.]

[¶ 10,608] ACT SEC. 608. ENHANCING EXISTING RESTRICTIONS ON BANK TRANSACTIONS WITH AFFILIATES.

(a) AFFILIATE TRANSACTIONS.—Section 23A of the Federal Reserve Act (12 U.S.C. 371c) is amended—

(1) in subsection (b)—

(A) in paragraph (1), by striking subparagraph (D) and inserting the following:

"(D) any investment fund with respect to which a member bank or affiliate thereof is an investment adviser; and"; and

(B) in paragraph (7)—

(i) in subparagraph (A), by inserting before the semicolon at the end the following: ", including a purchase of assets subject to an agreement to repurchase";

(ii) in subparagraph (C), by striking ", including assets subject to an agreement to repurchase,";

(iii) in subparagraph (D)—

(I) by inserting "or other debt obligations" after "acceptance of securities"; and

(II) by striking "or" at the end; and

(iv) by adding at the end the following:

"(F) a transaction with an affiliate that involves the borrowing or lending of securities, to the extent that the transaction causes a member bank or a subsidiary to have credit exposure to the affiliate; or

"(G) a derivative transaction, as defined in paragraph (3) of section 5200(b) of the Revised Statutes of the United States (12 U.S.C. 84(b)), with an affiliate, to the extent that the transaction causes a member bank or a subsidiary to have credit exposure to the affiliate;";

(2) in subsection (c)—

(A) in paragraph (1)—

(i) in the matter preceding subparagraph (A), by striking "subsidiary" and all that follows through "time of the transaction" and inserting "subsidiary, and any credit exposure of a member bank or a subsidiary to an affiliate resulting from a securities borrowing or lending transaction, or a derivative transaction, shall be secured at all times"; and

(ii) in each of subparagraphs (A) through (D), by striking "or letter of credit" and inserting "letter of credit, or credit exposure";

(B) by striking paragraph (2);

(C) by redesignating paragraphs (3) through (5) as paragraphs (2) through (4), respectively;

(D) in paragraph (2), as so redesignated, by inserting before the period at the end ", or credit exposure to an affiliate resulting from a securities borrowing or lending transaction, or derivative transaction"; and

(E) in paragraph (3), as so redesignated—

(i) by inserting "or other debt obligations" after "securities"; and

(ii) by striking "or guarantee" and all that follows through "behalf of," and inserting "guarantee, acceptance, or letter of credit issued on behalf of, or credit exposure from a securities borrowing or lending transaction, or derivative transaction to,";

(3) in subsection (d)(4), in the matter preceding subparagraph (A), by striking "or issuing" and all that follows through "behalf of," and inserting "issuing a guarantee, acceptance, or letter of credit on behalf of, or having credit exposure resulting from a securities borrowing or lending transaction, or derivative transaction to,"; and

(4) in subsection (f)—

(A) in paragraph (2)—

(i) by striking "or order";

(ii) by striking "if it finds" and all that follows through the end of the paragraph and inserting the following: "if—

"(i) the Board finds the exemption to be in the public interest and consistent with the purposes of this section, and notifies the Federal Deposit Insurance Corporation of such finding; and

"(ii) before the end of the 60-day period beginning on the date on which the Federal Deposit Insurance Corporation receives notice of the finding under clause (i), the Federal Deposit Insurance Corporation does not object, in writing, to the finding, based on a determination that the exemption presents an unacceptable risk to the Deposit Insurance Fund.";

(iii) by striking the Board and inserting the following:

"(A) IN GENERAL.—The Board"; and

(iv) by adding at the end the following:

"(B) ADDITIONAL EXEMPTIONS.—

"(i) NATIONAL BANKS.—The Comptroller of the Currency may, by order, exempt a transaction of a national bank from the requirements of this section if—

"(I) the Board and the Office of the Comptroller of the Currency jointly find the exemption to be in the public interest and consistent with the purposes of this section and notify the Federal Deposit Insurance Corporation of such finding; and

"(II) before the end of the 60day period beginning on the date on which the Federal Deposit Insurance Corporation receives notice of the finding under subclause (I), the Federal Deposit Insurance Corporation does not object, in writing, to the finding, based on a determination that the exemption presents an unacceptable risk to the Deposit Insurance Fund.

"(ii) STATE BANKS.—The Federal Deposit Insurance Corporation may, by order, exempt a transaction of a State nonmember bank, and the Board may, by order, exempt a transaction of a State member bank, from the requirements of this section if—

"(I) the Board and the Federal Deposit Insurance Corporation jointly find that the exemption is in the public interest and consistent with the purposes of this section; and

"(II) the Federal Deposit Insurance Corporation finds that the exemption does not present an unacceptable risk to the Deposit Insurance Fund."; and

(B) by adding at the end the following:

"(4) AMOUNTS OF COVERED TRANSACTIONS.—The Board may issue such regulations or interpretations as the Board determines are necessary or appropriate with respect to the manner in which a netting agreement may be taken into account in determining the amount of a covered transaction between a member bank or a subsidiary and an affiliate, including the extent to which netting agreements between a member bank or a subsidiary and an affiliate may be taken into account in determining whether a covered transaction is fully secured for purposes of subsection (d)(4). An interpretation under this paragraph with respect to a specific member bank, subsidiary, or affiliate shall be issued jointly with the appropriate Federal banking agency for such member bank, subsidiary, or affiliate.".

(b) TRANSACTIONS WITH AFFILIATES.—Section 23B(e) of the Federal Reserve Act (12 U.S.C. 371c-1(e)) is amended—

(1) by striking the undesignated matter following subparagraph (B);

(2) by redesignating subparagraphs (A) and (B) as clauses (i) and (ii), respectively, and adjusting the clause margins accordingly;

(3) by redesignating paragraphs (1) and (2) as subparagraphs (A) and (B), respectively, and adjusting the subparagraph margins accordingly;

(4) by striking "The Board" and inserting the following:

"(1) IN GENERAL.—The Board";

(5) in paragraph (1)(B), as so redesignated—

(A) in the matter preceding clause (i), by inserting before "regulations" the following: "subject to paragraph (2), if the Board finds that an exemption or exclusion is in the public

Title VI—Bank and Thrift Regulatory Improvements

interest and is consistent with the purposes of this section, and notifies the Federal Deposit Insurance Corporation of such finding,"; and

(B) in clause (ii), by striking the comma at the end and inserting a period; and

(6) by adding at the end the following:

"(2) EXCEPTION.—The Board may grant an exemption or exclusion under this subsection only if, during the 60-day period beginning on the date of receipt of notice of the finding from the Board under paragraph (1)(B), the Federal Deposit Insurance Corporation does not object, in writing, to such exemption or exclusion, based on a determination that the exemption presents an unacceptable risk to the Deposit Insurance Fund.".

(c) HOME OWNERS' LOAN ACT.—Section 11 of the Home Owners' Loan Act (12 U.S.C. 1468) is amended by adding at the end the following:

"(d) EXEMPTIONS.—

"(1) FEDERAL SAVINGS ASSOCIATIONS.—The Comptroller of the Currency may, by order, exempt a transaction of a Federal savings association from the requirements of this section if—

"(A) the Board and the Office of the Comptroller of the Currency jointly find the exemption to be in the public interest and consistent with the purposes of this section and notify the Federal Deposit Insurance Corporation of such finding; and

"(B) before the end of the 60-day period beginning on the date on which the Federal Deposit Insurance Corporation receives notice of the finding under subparagraph (A), the Federal Deposit Insurance Corporation does not object, in writing, to the finding, based on a determination that the exemption presents an unacceptable risk to the Deposit Insurance Fund.

"(2) STATE SAVINGS ASSOCIATION.—The Federal Deposit Insurance Corporation may, by order, exempt a transaction of a State savings association from the requirements of this section if the Board and the Federal Deposit Insurance Corporation jointly find that—

"(A) the exemption is in the public interest and consistent with the purposes of this section; and

"(B) the exemption does not present an unacceptable risk to the Deposit Insurance Fund.".

(d) EFFECTIVE DATE.—The amendments made by this section shall take effect 1 year after the transfer date.

[Explanation at ¶ 2545.]

[¶ 10,609] ACT SEC. 609. ELIMINATING EXCEPTIONS FOR TRANSACTIONS WITH FINANCIAL SUBSIDIARIES.

(a) AMENDMENT.—Section 23A(e) of the Federal Reserve Act (12 U.S.C. 371e(e)) is amended—

(1) by striking paragraph (3); and

(2) by redesignating paragraph (4) as paragraph (3).

(b) PROSPECTIVE APPLICATION OF AMENDMENT.—The amendments made by this section shall apply with respect to any covered transaction between a bank and a subsidiary of the bank, as those terms are defined in section 23A of the Federal Reserve Act (12 U.S.C. 371c), that is entered into on or after the date of enactment of this Act.

(c) EFFECTIVE DATE.—The amendments made by this section shall take effect 1 year after the transfer date.

[Explanation at ¶ 2545.]

[¶ 10,610] ACT SEC. 610. LENDING LIMITS APPLICABLE TO CREDIT EXPOSURE ON DERIVATIVE TRANSACTIONS, REPURCHASE AGREEMENTS, REVERSE REPURCHASE AGREEMENTS, AND SECURITIES LENDING AND BORROWING TRANSACTIONS.

(a) NATIONAL BANKS.—Section 5200(b) of the Revised Statutes of the United States (12 U.S.C. 84(b)) is amended—

(1) in paragraph (1), by striking "shall include" and all that follows through the end of the paragraph and inserting the following: "shall include—

"(A) all direct or indirect advances of funds to a person made on the basis of any obligation of that person to repay the funds or repayable from specific property pledged by or on behalf of the person;

"(B) to the extent specified by the Comptroller of the Currency, any liability of a national banking association to advance funds to or on behalf of a person pursuant to a contractual commitment; and

"(C) any credit exposure to a person arising from a derivative transaction, repurchase agreement, reverse repurchase agreement, securities lending transaction, or securities borrowing transaction between the national banking association and the person;";

(2) in paragraph (2), by striking the period at the end and inserting "; and"; and

(3) by adding at the end the following:

"(3) the term 'derivative transaction' includes any transaction that is a contract, agreement, swap, warrant, note, or option that is based, in whole or in part, on the value of, any interest in, or any quantitative measure or the occurrence of any event relating to, one or more commodities, securities, currencies, interest or other rates, indices, or other assets.".

(b) SAVINGS ASSOCIATIONS.—Section 5(u)(3) of the Home Owners' Loan Act (12 U.S.C. 1464(u)(3)) is amended by striking "Director" each place that term appears and inserting "Comptroller of the Currency".

(c) EFFECTIVE DATE.—The amendments made by this section shall take effect 1 year after the transfer date.

[Explanation at ¶ 2550.]

[¶ 10,611] ACT SEC. 611. CONSISTENT TREATMENT OF DERIVATIVE TRANSACTIONS IN LENDING LIMITS.

(a) AMENDMENT.—Section 18 of the Federal Deposit Insurance Act (12 U.S.C. 1828) is amended by adding at the end the following:

"(y) STATE LENDING LIMIT TREATMENT OF DERIVATIVES TRANSACTIONS.—An insured State bank may engage in a derivative transaction, as defined in section 5200(b)(3) of the Revised Statutes of the United States (12 U.S.C. 84(b)(3)), only if the law with respect to lending limits of the State in which the insured State bank is chartered takes into consideration credit exposure to derivative transactions.".

(b) EFFECTIVE DATE.—The amendment made by this section shall take effect 18 months after the transfer date.

[Explanation at ¶ 2550.]

[¶ 10,612] ACT SEC. 612. RESTRICTION ON CONVERSIONS OF TROUBLED BANKS.

(a) CONVERSION OF A NATIONAL BANKING ASSOCIATION.—The Act entitled "An Act to provide for the conversion of national banking associations into and their merger or consolidation with State banks, and for other purposes." (12 U.S.C. 214 et seq.) is amended by adding at the end the following:

"SEC. 10. PROHIBITION ON CONVERSION.

"A national banking association may not convert to a State bank or State savings association during any period in which the national banking association is subject to a cease and desist order (or other formal enforcement order) issued by, or a memorandum of understanding entered into with, the Comptroller of the Currency with respect to a significant supervisory matter.".

(b) CONVERSION OF A STATE BANK OR SAVINGS ASSOCIATION.—Section 5154 of the Revised Statutes of the United States (12 U.S.C. 35) is amended by adding at the end the following: "The Comptroller of the Currency may not approve the conversion of a State bank or State savings association to a national banking association or Federal savings association during any period in which the State bank or State savings association is subject to a cease and desist order (or other formal enforcement order) issued by, or a memorandum of understanding entered into with, a State bank supervisor or the appropriate Federal banking agency with respect to a significant supervisory matter or a final enforcement action by a State Attorney General.".

(c) CONVERSION OF A FEDERAL SAVINGS ASSOCIATION.—Section 5(i) of the Home Owners' Loan Act (12 U.S.C. 1464(i)) is amended by adding at the end the following:

"(6) LIMITATION ON CERTAIN CONVERSIONS BY FEDERAL SAVINGS ASSOCIATIONS.—A Federal savings association may not convert to a State bank or State savings association during any period in which the Federal savings association is subject to a cease and desist order (or other formal enforcement order) issued by, or a memorandum of understanding entered into with, the Office of Thrift Supervision or the Comptroller of the Currency with respect to a significant supervisory matter.".

(d) EXCEPTION.—The prohibition on the approval of conversions under the amendments made by subsections (a), (b), and (c) shall not apply, if—

(1) the Federal banking agency that would be the appropriate Federal banking agency after the proposed conversion gives the appropriate Federal banking agency or State bank supervisor that issued the cease and desist order (or other formal enforcement order) or memorandum of understanding, as appropriate, written notice of the proposed conversion including a plan to address the significant supervisory matter in a manner that is consistent with the safe and sound operation of the institution;

(2) within 30 days of receipt of the written notice required under paragraph (1), the appropriate Federal banking agency or State bank supervisor that issued the cease and desist order (or other formal enforcement order) or memorandum of understanding, as appropriate, does not object to the conversion or the plan to address the significant supervisory matter;

(3) after conversion of the insured depository institution, the appropriate Federal banking agency after the conversion implements such plan; and

(4) in the case of a final enforcement action by a State Attorney General, approval of the conversion is conditioned on compliance by the insured depository institution with the terms of such final enforcement action.

(e) NOTIFICATION OF PENDING ENFORCEMENT ACTIONS.—

(1) COPY OF CONVERSION APPLICATION.—At the time an insured depository institution files a conversion application, the insured depository institution shall transmit a copy of the conversion application to—

(A) the appropriate Federal banking agency for the insured depository institution; and

(B) the Federal banking agency that would be the appropriate Federal banking agency of the insured depository institution after the proposed conversion.

(2) NOTIFICATION AND ACCESS TO INFORMATION.—Upon receipt of a copy of the application described in paragraph (1), the appropriate Federal banking agency for the insured depository institution proposing the conversion shall—

(A) notify the Federal banking agency that would be the appropriate Federal banking agency for the institution after the proposed conversion in writing of any ongoing supervisory or investigative proceedings that the appropriate Federal banking agency for the institution proposing to convert believes is likely to result, in the near term and absent the proposed conversion, in a cease and desist order (or other formal enforcement order) or memorandum of understanding with respect to a significant supervisory matter; and

(B) provide the Federal banking agency that would be the appropriate Federal banking agency for the institution after the proposed conversion access to all investigative and supervisory information relating to the proceedings described in subparagraph (A).

[Explanation at ¶ 2555.]

[¶ 10,613] ACT SEC. 613. DE NOVO BRANCHING INTO STATES.

(a) NATIONAL BANKS.—Section 5155(g)(1)(A) of the Revised Statutes of the United States (12 U.S.C. 36(g)(1)(A)) is amended to read as follows:

"(A) the law of the State in which the branch is located, or is to be located, would permit establishment of the branch, if the national bank were a State bank chartered by such State; and".

(b) STATE INSURED BANKS.—Section 18(d)(4)(A)(i) of the Federal Deposit Insurance Act (12 U.S.C. 1828(d)(4)(A)(i)) is amended to read as follows:

"(i) the law of the State in which the branch is located, or is to be located, would permit establishment of the branch, if the bank were a State bank chartered by such State; and".

[Explanation at ¶ 2560.]

[¶ 10,614] ACT SEC. 614. LENDING LIMITS TO INSIDERS.

(a) EXTENSIONS OF CREDIT.—Section 22(h)(9)(D)(i) of the Federal Reserve Act (12 U.S.C. 375b(9)(D)(i)) is amended—

(1) by striking the period at the end and inserting "; or";

(2) by striking "a person" and inserting "the person";

(3) by striking "extends credit by making" and inserting the following: "extends credit to a person by—

"(I) making"; and

(4) by adding at the end the following:

"(II) having credit exposure to the person arising from a derivative transaction (as defined in section 5200(b) of the Revised Statutes of the United States (12 U.S.C. 84(b))), repurchase agreement, reverse repurchase agreement, securities lending transaction, or securities borrowing transaction between the member bank and the person.".

(b) EFFECTIVE DATE.—The amendments made by this section shall take effect 1 year after the transfer date.

[Explanation at ¶ 2545.]

[¶ 10,615] ACT SEC. 615. LIMITATIONS ON PURCHASES OF ASSETS FROM INSIDERS.

(a) AMENDMENT TO THE FEDERAL DEPOSIT INSURANCE ACT.—Section 18 of the Federal Deposit Insurance Act (12 U.S.C. 1828) is amended by adding at the end the following:

"(z) GENERAL PROHIBITION ON SALE OF ASSETS.—

"(1) IN GENERAL.—An insured depository institution may not purchase an asset from, or sell an asset to, an executive officer, director, or principal shareholder of the insured depository institution, or any related interest of such person (as such terms are defined in section 22(h) of Federal Reserve Act), unless—

"(A) the transaction is on market terms; and

"(B) if the transaction represents more than 10 percent of the capital stock and surplus of the insured depository institution, the transaction has been approved in advance by a majority of the members of the board of directors of the insured depository institution who do not have an interest in the transaction.

"(2) RULEMAKING.—The Board of Governors of the Federal Reserve System may issue such rules as may be necessary to define terms and to carry out the purposes this subsection. Before proposing or adopting a rule under this paragraph, the Board of Governors of the Federal Reserve System shall consult with the Comptroller of the Currency and the Corporation as to the terms of the rule.".

(b) AMENDMENTS TO THE FEDERAL RESERVE ACT.—Section 22(d) of the Federal Reserve Act (12 U.S.C. 375) is amended to read as follows:

"(d) [Reserved]".

(c) EFFECTIVE DATE.—The amendments made by this section shall take effect on the transfer date.

[Explanation at ¶ 2545.]

[¶ 10,616] ACT SEC. 616. REGULATIONS REGARDING CAPITAL LEVELS.

(a) CAPITAL LEVELS OF BANK HOLDING COMPANIES.—Section 5(b) of the Bank Holding Company Act of 1956 (12 U.S.C. 1844(b)) is amended—

(1) by inserting after "orders" the following: ", including regulations and orders relating to the capital requirements for bank holding companies,"; and

(2) by adding at the end the following: "In establishing capital regulations pursuant to this subsection, the Board shall seek to make such requirements countercyclical, so that the amount of capital required to be maintained by a company increases in times of economic expansion and decreases in times of economic contraction, consistent with the safety and soundness of the company.".

(b) CAPITAL LEVELS OF SAVINGS AND LOAN HOLDING COMPANIES.—Section 10(g)(1) of the Home Owners' Loan Act (12 U.S.C. 1467a(g)(1)) is amended—

(1) by inserting after "orders" the following: ", including regulations and orders relating to capital requirements for savings and loan holding companies,"; and

(2) by inserting at the end the following: "In establishing capital regulations pursuant to this subsection, the appropriate Federal banking agency shall seek to make such requirements countercyclical so that the amount of capital required to be maintained by a company increases in times of economic expansion and decreases in times of economic contraction, consistent with the safety and soundness of the company.".

(c) CAPITAL LEVELS OF INSURED DEPOSITORY INSTITUTIONS.—Section 908(a)(1) of the International Lending Supervision Act of 1983 (12 U.S.C. 3907(a)(1)) is amended by adding at the end the following: "Each appropriate Federal banking agency shall seek to make the capital standards required under this section or other provisions of Federal law for insured depository institutions countercyclical so that the amount of capital required to be maintained by an insured depository institution increases in times of economic expansion and decreases in times of economic contraction, consistent with the safety and soundness of the insured depository institution."

(d) SOURCE OF STRENGTH.—The Federal Deposit Insurance Act (12 U.S.C. 1811 et seq.) is amended by inserting after section 38 (12 U.S.C. 1831o) the following:

"SEC. 38A. SOURCE OF STRENGTH.

"(a) HOLDING COMPANIES.—The appropriate Federal banking agency for a bank holding company or savings and loan holding company shall require the bank holding company or savings and loan holding company to serve as a source of financial strength for any subsidiary of the bank holding company or savings and loan holding company that is a depository institution.

"(b) OTHER COMPANIES.—If an insured depository institution is not the subsidiary of a bank holding company or savings and loan holding company, the appropriate Federal banking agency for the insured depository institution shall require any company that directly or indirectly controls the insured depository institution to serve as a source of financial strength for such institution.

"(c) REPORTS.—The appropriate Federal banking agency for an insured depository institution described in subsection (b) may, from time to time, require the company, or a company that directly or indirectly controls the insured depository institution, to submit a report, under oath, for the purposes of—

"(1) assessing the ability of such company to comply with the requirement under subsection (b); and

"(2) enforcing the compliance of such company with the requirement under subsection (b).

"(d) RULES.—Not later than 1 year after the transfer date, as defined in section 311 of the Enhancing Financial Institution Safety and Soundness Act of 2010, the appropriate Federal banking agencies shall jointly issue final rules to carry out this section.

"(e) DEFINITION.—In this section, the term 'source of financial strength' means the ability of a company that directly or indirectly owns or controls an insured depository institution to provide financial assistance to such insured depository institution in the event of the financial distress of the insured depository institution.".

(e) EFFECTIVE DATE.—The amendments made by this section shall take effect on the transfer date.

[Explanation at ¶ 2540 and ¶ 2565.]

[¶ 10,617] ACT SEC. 617. ELIMINATION OF ELECTIVE INVESTMENT BANK HOLDING COMPANY FRAMEWORK.

(a) AMENDMENT.—Section 17 of the Securities Exchange Act of 1934 (15 U.S.C. 78q) is amended—

(1) by striking subsection (i); and

(2) by redesignating subsections (j) and (k) as subsections (i) and (j), respectively.

(b) EFFECTIVE DATE.—The amendments made by this section shall take effect on the transfer date.

[Explanation at ¶ 2570.]

[¶ 10,618] ACT SEC. 618. SECURITIES HOLDING COMPANIES.

(a) DEFINITIONS.—In this section—

(1) the term "associated person of a securities holding company" means a person directly or indirectly controlling, controlled by, or under common control with, a securities holding company;

(2) the term "foreign bank" has the same meaning as in section 1(b)(7) of the International Banking Act of 1978 (12 U.S.C. 3101(7));

(3) the term "insured bank" has the same meaning as in section 3 of the Federal Deposit Insurance Act (12 U.S.C. 1813);

(4) the term "securities holding company"—

(A) means—

(i) a person (other than a natural person) that owns or controls 1 or more brokers or dealers registered with the Commission; and

(ii) the associated persons of a person described in clause (i); and

(B) does not include a person that is—

(i) a nonbank financial company supervised by the Board under title I;

(ii) an insured bank (other than an institution described in subparagraphs (D), (F), or (H) of section 2(c)(2) of the Bank Holding Company Act of 1956 (12 U.S.C. 1841(c)(2)) or a savings association;

(iii) an affiliate of an insured bank (other than an institution described in subparagraphs (D), (F), or (H) of section 2(c)(2) of the Bank Holding Company Act of 1956 (12 U.S.C. 1841(c)(2)) or an affiliate of a savings association;

(iv) a foreign bank, foreign company, or company that is described in section 8(a) of the International Banking Act of 1978 (12 U.S.C. 3106(a));

(v) a foreign bank that controls, directly or indirectly, a corporation chartered under section 25A of the Federal Reserve Act (12 U.S.C. 611 et seq.); or

(vi) subject to comprehensive consolidated supervision by a foreign regulator;

(5) the term "supervised securities holding company" means a securities holding company that is supervised by the Board of Governors under this section; and

(6) the terms "affiliate", "bank", "bank holding company", "company", "control", "savings association", and "subsidiary" have the same meanings as in section 2 of the Bank Holding Company Act of 1956.

(b) SUPERVISION OF A SECURITIES HOLDING COMPANY NOT HAVING A BANK OR SAVINGS ASSOCIATION AFFILIATE.—

(1) IN GENERAL.—A securities holding company that is required by a foreign regulator or provision of foreign law to be subject to comprehensive consolidated supervision may register with the Board of Governors under paragraph (2) to become a supervised securities holding company. Any securities holding company filing such a registration shall be supervised in accordance with this section, and shall comply with the rules and orders prescribed by the Board of Governors applicable to supervised securities holding companies.

(2) REGISTRATION AS A SUPERVISED SECURITIES HOLDING COMPANY.—

(A) REGISTRATION.—A securities holding company that elects to be subject to comprehensive consolidated supervision shall register by filing with the Board of Governors such information and documents as the Board of Governors, by regulation, may prescribe as necessary or appropriate in furtherance of the purposes of this section.

(B) EFFECTIVE DATE.—A securities holding company that registers under subparagraph (A) shall be deemed to be a supervised securities holding company, effective on the date that is 45 days after the date of receipt of the registration information and documents under subparagraph (A) by the Board of Governors, or within such shorter period as the Board of Governors, by rule or order, may determine.

(c) SUPERVISION OF SECURITIES HOLDING COMPANIES.—

(1) RECORDKEEPING AND REPORTING.—

(A) RECORDKEEPING AND REPORTING REQUIRED.—Each supervised securities holding company and each affiliate of a supervised securities holding company shall make and keep for periods determined by the Board of Governors such records, furnish copies of such records, and make such reports, as the Board of Governors determines to be necessary or appropriate to carry out this section, to prevent evasions thereof, and to monitor compliance by the supervised securities holding company or affiliate with applicable provisions of law.

(B) FORM AND CONTENTS.—

(i) IN GENERAL.—Any record or report required to be made, furnished, or kept under this paragraph shall—

(I) be prepared in such form and according to such specifications (including certification by a registered public accounting firm), as the Board of Governors may require; and

(II) be provided promptly to the Board of Governors at any time, upon request by the Board of Governors.

(ii) CONTENTS.—Records and reports required to be made, furnished, or kept under this paragraph may include—

(I) a balance sheet or income statement of the supervised securities holding company or an affiliate of a supervised securities holding company;

(II) an assessment of the consolidated capital and liquidity of the supervised securities holding company;

(III) a report by an independent auditor attesting to the compliance of the supervised securities holding company with the internal risk management and internal control objectives of the supervised securities holding company; and

(IV) a report concerning the extent to which the supervised securities holding company or affiliate has complied with the provisions of this section and any regulations prescribed and orders issued under this section.

(2) USE OF EXISTING REPORTS.—

(A) IN GENERAL.—The Board of Governors shall, to the fullest extent possible, accept reports in fulfillment of the requirements of this paragraph that a supervised securities holding company or an affiliate of a supervised securities holding company has been required to provide to another regulatory agency or a self-regulatory organization.

(B) AVAILABILITY.—A supervised securities holding company or an affiliate of a supervised securities holding company shall promptly provide to the Board of Governors, at the request of the Board of Governors, any report described in subparagraph (A), as permitted by law.

(3) EXAMINATION AUTHORITY.—

(A) FOCUS OF EXAMINATION AUTHORITY.—The Board of Governors may make examinations of any supervised securities holding company and any affiliate of a supervised securities holding company to carry out this subsection, to prevent evasions thereof, and to monitor compliance by the supervised securities holding company or affiliate with applicable provisions of law.

(B) DEFERENCE TO OTHER EXAMINATIONS.—For purposes of this subparagraph, the Board of Governors shall, to the fullest extent possible, use the reports of examination made by other appropriate Federal or State regulatory authorities with respect to any functionally regulated subsidiary or any institution described in subparagraph (D), (F), or (H) of section 2(c)(2) of the Bank Holding Company Act of 1956 (12 U.S.C. 1841(c)(2)).

(d) CAPITAL AND RISK MANAGEMENT.—

(1) IN GENERAL.—The Board of Governors shall, by regulation or order, prescribe capital adequacy and other risk management standards for supervised securities holding companies that are appropriate to protect the safety and soundness of the supervised securities holding companies and address the risks posed to financial stability by supervised securities holding companies.

(2) DIFFERENTIATION.—In imposing standards under this subsection, the Board of Governors may differentiate among supervised securities holding companies on an individual basis, or by category, taking into consideration the requirements under paragraph (3).

(3) CONTENT.—Any standards imposed on a supervised securities holding company under this subsection shall take into account—

(A) the differences among types of business activities carried out by the supervised securities holding company;

(B) the amount and nature of the financial assets of the supervised securities holding company;

(C) the amount and nature of the liabilities of the supervised securities holding company, including the degree of reliance on short-term funding;

(D) the extent and nature of the off-balance sheet exposures of the supervised securities holding company;

(E) the extent and nature of the transactions and relationships of the supervised securities holding company with other financial companies;

(F) the importance of the supervised securities holding company as a source of credit for households, businesses, and State and local governments, and as a source of liquidity for the financial system; and

(G) the nature, scope, and mix of the activities of the supervised securities holding company.

(4) NOTICE.—A capital requirement imposed under this subsection may not take effect earlier than 180 days after the date on which a supervised securities holding company is provided notice of the capital requirement.

(e) OTHER PROVISIONS OF LAW APPLICABLE TO SUPERVISED SECURITIES HOLDING COMPANIES.—

(1) FEDERAL DEPOSIT INSURANCE ACT.—Subsections (b), (c) through (s), and (u) of section 8 of the Federal Deposit Insurance Act (12 U.S.C. 1818) shall apply to any supervised securities holding company, and to any subsidiary (other than a bank or an institution described in subparagraph (D), (F), or (H) of section 2(c)(2) of the Bank Holding Company Act of 1956 (12 U.S.C. 1841(c)(2))) of a supervised securities holding company, in the same manner as such subsections apply to a bank holding company for which the Board of Governors is the appropriate Federal banking agency. For purposes of applying such subsections to a supervised securities holding company or a subsidiary (other than a bank or an institution described in subparagraph (D), (F), or (H) of section 2(c)(2) of the Bank Holding Company Act of 1956 (12 U.S.C. 1841(c)(2))) of a supervised securities holding company, the Board of Governors shall be deemed the appropriate Federal banking agency for the supervised securities holding company or subsidiary.

(2) BANK HOLDING COMPANY ACT OF 1956.—Except as the Board of Governors may otherwise provide by regulation or order, a supervised securities holding company shall be subject to the provisions of the Bank Holding Company Act of 1956 (12 U.S.C. 1841 et seq.) in the same manner and to the same extent a bank holding company is subject to such provisions, except that a supervised securities holding company may not, by reason of this paragraph, be deemed to be a bank holding company for purposes of section 4 of the Bank Holding Company Act of 1956 (12 U.S.C. 1843).

[Explanation at ¶ 2570 and ¶ 2580.]

[¶ 10,619] ACT SEC. 619. PROHIBITIONS ON PROPRIETARY TRADING AND CERTAIN RELATIONSHIPS WITH HEDGE FUNDS AND PRIVATE EQUITY FUNDS.

The Bank Holding Company Act of 1956 (12 U.S.C. 1841 et seq.) is amended by adding at the end the following:

"SEC. 13. PROHIBITIONS ON PROPRIETARY TRADING AND CERTAIN RELATIONSHIPS WITH HEDGE FUNDS AND PRIVATE EQUITY FUNDS.

"(a) IN GENERAL.—

"(1) PROHIBITION.—Unless otherwise provided in this section, a banking entity shall not—

"(A) engage in proprietary trading; or

"(B) acquire or retain any equity, partnership, or other ownership interest in or sponsor a hedge fund or a private equity fund.

"(2) NONBANK FINANCIAL COMPANIES SUPERVISED BY THE BOARD.—Any nonbank financial company supervised by the Board that engages in proprietary trading or takes or retains any equity, partnership, or other ownership interest in or sponsors a hedge fund or a private equity fund shall be subject, by rule, as provided in subsection (b)(2), to additional capital requirements for and additional quantitative limits with regards to such proprietary trading and taking or retaining any equity, partnership, or other ownership interest in or sponsorship of a hedge fund or a private equity fund, except that permitted activities as described in subsection (d) shall not be subject to the additional capital and additional quantitative limits except as provided in subsection (d)(3), as if the nonbank financial company supervised by the Board were a banking entity.

"(b) STUDY AND RULEMAKING.—

"(1) STUDY.—Not later than 6 months after the date of enactment of this section, the Financial Stability Oversight Council shall study and make recommendations on implementing the provisions of this section so as to—

"(A) promote and enhance the safety and soundness of banking entities;

Act Sec. 619 ¶10,619

"(B) protect taxpayers and consumers and enhance financial stability by minimizing the risk that insured depository institutions and the affiliates of insured depository institutions will engage in unsafe and unsound activities;

"(C) limit the inappropriate transfer of Federal subsidies from institutions that benefit from deposit insurance and liquidity facilities of the Federal Government to unregulated entities;

"(D) reduce conflicts of interest between the self-interest of banking entities and nonbank financial companies supervised by the Board, and the interests of the customers of such entities and companies;

"(E) limit activities that have caused undue risk or loss in banking entities and nonbank financial companies supervised by the Board, or that might reasonably be expected to create undue risk or loss in such banking entities and nonbank financial companies supervised by the Board;

"(F) appropriately accommodate the business of insurance within an insurance company, subject to regulation in accordance with the relevant insurance company investment laws, while protecting the safety and soundness of any banking entity with which such insurance company is affiliated and of the United States financial system; and

"(G) appropriately time the divestiture of illiquid assets that are affected by the implementation of the prohibitions under subsection (a).

"(2) RULEMAKING.—

"(A) IN GENERAL.—Unless otherwise provided in this section, not later than 9 months after the completion of the study under paragraph (1), the appropriate Federal banking agencies, the Securities and Exchange Commission, and the Commodity Futures Trading Commission, shall consider the findings of the study under paragraph (1) and adopt rules to carry out this section, as provided in subparagraph (B).

"(B) COORDINATED RULEMAKING.—

"(i) REGULATORY AUTHORITY.—The regulations issued under this paragraph shall be issued by—

"(I) the appropriate Federal banking agencies, jointly, with respect to insured depository institutions;

"(II) the Board, with respect to any company that controls an insured depository institution, or that is treated as a bank holding company for purposes of section 8 of the International Banking Act, any nonbank financial company supervised by the Board, and any subsidiary of any of the foregoing (other than a subsidiary for which an agency described in subclause (I), (III), or (IV) is the primary financial regulatory agency);

"(III) the Commodity Futures Trading Commission, with respect to any entity for which the Commodity Futures Trading Commission is the primary financial regulatory agency, as defined in section 2 of the Dodd-Frank Wall Street Reform and Consumer Protection Act; and

"(IV) the Securities and Exchange Commission, with respect to any entity for which the Securities and Exchange Commission is the primary financial regulatory agency, as defined in section 2 of the Dodd-Frank Wall Street Reform and Consumer Protection Act.

"(ii) COORDINATION, CONSISTENCY, AND COMPARABILITY.—In developing and issuing regulations pursuant to this section, the appropriate Federal banking agencies, the Securities and Exchange Commission, and the Commodity Futures Trading Commission shall consult and coordinate with each other, as appropriate, for the purposes of assuring, to the extent possible, that such regulations are comparable and provide for consistent application and implementation of the applicable provisions of this section to avoid providing advantages or imposing disadvantages to the companies affected by this subsection and to protect the safety and soundness of banking entities and nonbank financial companies supervised by the Board.

"(iii) COUNCIL ROLE.—The Chairperson of the Financial Stability Oversight Council shall be responsible for coordination of the regulations issued under this section.

"(c) EFFECTIVE DATE.—

"(1) IN GENERAL.—Except as provided in paragraphs (2) and (3), this section shall take effect on the earlier of—

"(A) 12 months after the date of the issuance of final rules under subsection (b); or

"(B) 2 years after the date of enactment of this section.

"(2) CONFORMANCE PERIOD FOR DIVESTITURE.—A banking entity or nonbank financial company supervised by the Board shall bring its activities and investments into compliance with the requirements of this section not later than 2 years after the date on which the requirements become effective pursuant to this section or 2 years after the date on which the entity or company becomes a nonbank financial company supervised by the Board. The Board may, by rule or order, extend this two-year period for not more than one year at a time, if, in the judgment of the Board, such an extension is consistent with the purposes of this section and would not be detrimental to the public interest. The extensions made by the Board under the preceding sentence may not exceed an aggregate of 3 years.

"(3) EXTENDED TRANSITION FOR ILLIQUID FUNDS.—

"(A) APPLICATION.—The Board may, upon the application of a banking entity, extend the period during which the banking entity, to the extent necessary to fulfill a contractual obligation that was in effect on May 1, 2010, may take or retain its equity, partnership, or other ownership interest in, or otherwise provide additional capital to, an illiquid fund.

"(B) TIME LIMIT ON APPROVAL.—The Board may grant 1 extension under subparagraph (A), which may not exceed 5 years.

"(4) DIVESTITURE REQUIRED.—Except as otherwise provided in subsection (d)(1)(G), a banking entity may not engage in any activity prohibited under subsection (a)(1)(B) after the earlier of—

"(A) the date on which the contractual obligation to invest in the illiquid fund terminates; and

"(B) the date on which any extensions granted by the Board under paragraph (3) expire.

"(5) ADDITIONAL CAPITAL DURING TRANSITION PERIOD.—Notwithstanding paragraph (2), on the date on which the rules are issued under subsection (b)(2), the appropriate Federal banking agencies, the Securities and Exchange Commission, and the Commodity Futures Trading Commission shall issue rules, as provided in subsection (b)(2), to impose additional capital requirements, and any other restrictions, as appropriate, on any equity, partnership, or ownership interest in or sponsorship of a hedge fund or private equity fund by a banking entity.

"(6) SPECIAL RULEMAKING.—Not later than 6 months after the date of enactment of this section, the Board shall issues rules to implement paragraphs (2) and (3).

"(d) PERMITTED ACTIVITIES.—

"(1) IN GENERAL.—Notwithstanding the restrictions under subsection (a), to the extent permitted by any other provision of Federal or State law, and subject to the limitations under paragraph (2) and any restrictions or limitations that the appropriate Federal banking agencies, the Securities and Exchange Commission, and the Commodity Futures Trading Commission, may determine, the following activities (in this section referred to as 'permitted activities') are permitted:

"(A) The purchase, sale, acquisition, or disposition of obligations of the United States or any agency thereof, obligations, participations, or other instruments of or issued by the Government National Mortgage Association, the Federal National Mortgage Association, the Federal Home Loan Mortgage Corporation, a Federal Home Loan

Bank, the Federal Agricultural Mortgage Corporation, or a Farm Credit System institution chartered under and subject to the provisions of the Farm Credit Act of 1971 (12 U.S.C. 2001 et seq.), and obligations of any State or of any political subdivision thereof.

"(B) The purchase, sale, acquisition, or disposition of securities and other instruments described in subsection (h)(4) in connection with underwriting or market-making-related activities, to the extent that any such activities permitted by this subparagraph are designed not to exceed the reasonably expected near term demands of clients, customers, or counterparties.

"(C) Risk-mitigating hedging activities in connection with and related to individual or aggregated positions, contracts, or other holdings of a banking entity that are designed to reduce the specific risks to the banking entity in connection with and related to such positions, contracts, or other holdings.

"(D) The purchase, sale, acquisition, or disposition of securities and other instruments described in subsection (h)(4) on behalf of customers.

"(E) Investments in one or more small business investment companies, as defined in section 102 of the Small Business Investment Act of 1958 (15 U.S.C. 662), investments designed primarily to promote the public welfare, of the type permitted under paragraph (11) of section 5136 of the Revised Statutes of the United States (12 U.S.C. 24), or investments that are qualified rehabilitation expenditures with respect to a qualified rehabilitated building or certified historic structure, as such terms are defined in section 47 of the Internal Revenue Code of 1986 or a similar State historic tax credit program.

"(F) The purchase, sale, acquisition, or disposition of securities and other instruments described in subsection (h)(4) by a regulated insurance company directly engaged in the business of insurance for the general account of the company and by any affiliate of such regulated insurance company, provided that such activities by any affiliate are solely for the general account of the regulated insurance company, if—

"(i) the purchase, sale, acquisition, or disposition is conducted in compliance with, and subject to, the insurance company investment laws, regulations, and written guidance of the State or jurisdiction in which each such insurance company is domiciled; and

"(ii) the appropriate Federal banking agencies, after consultation with the Financial Stability Oversight Council and the relevant insurance commissioners of the States and territories of the United States, have not jointly determined, after notice and comment, that a particular law, regulation, or written guidance described in clause (i) is insufficient to protect the safety and soundness of the banking entity, or of the financial stability of the United States.

"(G) Organizing and offering a private equity or hedge fund, including serving as a general partner, managing member, or trustee of the fund and in any manner selecting or controlling (or having employees, officers, directors, or agents who constitute) a majority of the directors, trustees, or management of the fund, including any necessary expenses for the foregoing, only if—

"(i) the banking entity provides bona fide trust, fiduciary, or investment advisory services;

"(ii) the fund is organized and offered only in connection with the provision of bona fide trust, fiduciary, or investment advisory services and only to persons that are customers of such services of the banking entity;

"(iii) the banking entity does not acquire or retain an equity interest, partnership interest, or other ownership interest in the funds except for a de minimis investment subject to and in compliance with paragraph (4);

"(iv) the banking entity complies with the restrictions under paragraphs (1) and (2) of subparagraph (f);

"(v) the banking entity does not, directly or indirectly, guarantee, assume, or otherwise insure the obligations or performance of the hedge fund or private equity fund or of any hedge fund or private equity fund in which such hedge fund or private equity fund invests;

"(vi) the banking entity does not share with the hedge fund or private equity fund, for corporate, marketing, promotional, or other purposes, the same name or a variation of the same name;

"(vii) no director or employee of the banking entity takes or retains an equity interest, partnership interest, or other ownership interest in the hedge fund or private equity fund, except for any director or employee of the banking entity who is directly engaged in providing investment advisory or other services to the hedge fund or private equity fund; and

"(viii) the banking entity discloses to prospective and actual investors in the fund, in writing, that any losses in such hedge fund or private equity fund are borne solely by investors in the fund and not by the banking entity, and otherwise complies with any additional rules of the appropriate Federal banking agencies, the Securities and Exchange Commission, or the Commodity Futures Trading Commission, as provided in subsection (b)(2), designed to ensure that losses in such hedge fund or private equity fund are borne solely by investors in the fund and not by the banking entity.

"(H) Proprietary trading conducted by a banking entity pursuant to paragraph (9) or (13) of section 4(c), provided that the trading occurs solely outside of the United States and that the banking entity is not directly or indirectly controlled by a banking entity that is organized under the laws of the United States or of one or more States.

"(I) The acquisition or retention of any equity, partnership, or other ownership interest in, or the sponsorship of, a hedge fund or a private equity fund by a banking entity pursuant to paragraph (9) or (13) of section 4(c) solely outside of the United States, provided that no ownership interest in such hedge fund or private equity fund is offered for sale or sold to a resident of the United States and that the banking entity is not directly or indirectly controlled by a banking entity that is organized under the laws of the United States or of one or more States.

"(J) Such other activity as the appropriate Federal banking agencies, the Securities and Exchange Commission, and the Commodity Futures Trading Commission determine, by rule, as provided in subsection (b)(2), would promote and protect the safety and soundness of the banking entity and the financial stability of the United States.

"(2) LIMITATION ON PERMITTED ACTIVITIES.—

"(A) IN GENERAL.—No transaction, class of transactions, or activity may be deemed a permitted activity under paragraph (1) if the transaction, class of transactions, or activity—

"(i) would involve or result in a material conflict of interest (as such term shall be defined by rule as provided in subsection (b)(2)) between the banking entity and its clients, customers, or counterparties;

"(ii) would result, directly or indirectly, in a material exposure by the banking entity to high-risk assets or high-risk trading strategies (as such terms shall be defined by rule as provided in subsection (b)(2));

"(iii) would pose a threat to the safety and soundness of such banking entity; or

"(iv) would pose a threat to the financial stability of the United States.

"(B) RULEMAKING.—The appropriate Federal banking agencies, the Securities and Exchange Commission, and the Commodity Futures Trading Commission shall issue regulations to implement subparagraph (A), as part of the regulations issued under subsection (b)(2).

"(3) CAPITAL AND QUANTITATIVE LIMITATIONS.—The appropriate Federal banking agencies, the Securities and Exchange Commission, and the Commodity Futures Trading Commission shall, as provided in subsection (b)(2), adopt rules imposing additional capital requirements and quantitative limitations, including diversification requirements, regarding the activities permitted under this section if the appropriate Federal banking agencies, the Securities and Exchange Commission, and the Commodity Futures Trading Commission determine that additional capital and quantitative limitations are appropriate to protect the safety and soundness of banking entities engaged in such activities.

"(4) DE MINIMIS INVESTMENT.—

"(A) IN GENERAL.—A banking entity may make and retain an investment in a hedge fund or private equity fund that the banking entity organizes and offers, subject to the limitations and restrictions in subparagraph (B) for the purposes of—

"(i) establishing the fund and providing the fund with sufficient initial equity for investment to permit the fund to attract unaffiliated investors; or

"(ii) making a de minimis investment.

"(B) LIMITATIONS AND RESTRICTIONS ON INVESTMENTS.—

"(i) REQUIREMENT TO SEEK OTHER INVESTORS.—A banking entity shall actively seek unaffiliated investors to reduce or dilute the investment of the banking entity to the amount permitted under clause (ii).

"(ii) LIMITATIONS ON SIZE OF INVESTMENTS.—Notwithstanding any other provision of law, investments by a banking entity in a hedge fund or private equity fund shall—

"(I) not later than 1 year after the date of establishment of the fund, be reduced through redemption, sale, or dilution to an amount that is not more than 3 percent of the total ownership interests of the fund;

"(II) be immaterial to the banking entity, as defined, by rule, pursuant to subsection (b)(2), but in no case may the aggregate of all of the interests of the banking entity in all such funds exceed 3 percent of the Tier 1 capital of the banking entity.

"(iii) CAPITAL.—For purposes of determining compliance with applicable capital standards under paragraph (3), the aggregate amount of the outstanding investments by a banking entity under this paragraph, including retained earnings, shall be deducted from the assets and tangible equity of the banking entity, and the amount of the deduction shall increase commensurate with the leverage of the hedge fund or private equity fund.

"(C) EXTENSION.—Upon an application by a banking entity, the Board may extend the period of time to meet the requirements under subparagraph (B)(ii)(I) for 2 additional years, if the Board finds that an extension would be consistent with safety and soundness and in the public interest.

"(e) ANTI-EVASION.—

"(1) RULEMAKING.—The appropriate Federal banking agencies, the Securities and Exchange Commission, and the Commodity Futures Trading Commission shall issue regulations, as part of the rulemaking provided for in subsection (b)(2), regarding internal controls and recordkeeping, in order to insure compliance with this section.

"(2) TERMINATION OF ACTIVITIES OR INVESTMENT.—Notwithstanding any other provision of law, whenever an appropriate Federal banking agency, the Securities and Exchange Commission, or the Commodity Futures Trading Commission, as appropriate, has reasonable cause to believe that a banking entity or nonbank financial company supervised by the Board under the respective agency's jurisdiction has made an investment or engaged in an activity in a manner that functions as an evasion of the requirements of this section (including through an abuse of any permitted activity) or otherwise violates the restrictions under this section, the appropriate Federal banking agency, the Securities and Exchange Commission, or the Commodity Futures Trading Commission, as appropriate, shall order, after due notice and opportunity for hearing, the banking entity or nonbank financial company supervised by the Board to terminate the activity and, as relevant, dispose of the investment. Nothing in this paragraph shall be construed to limit the inherent authority of any Federal agency or State regulatory authority to further restrict any investments or activities under otherwise applicable provisions of law.

"(f) Limitations on Relationships with Hedge Funds and Private Equity Funds.—

"(1) In General.—No banking entity that serves, directly or indirectly, as the investment manager, investment adviser, or sponsor to a hedge fund or private equity fund, or that organizes and offers a hedge fund or private equity fund pursuant to paragraph (d)(1)(G), and no affiliate of such entity, may enter into a transaction with the fund, or with any other hedge fund or private equity fund that is controlled by such fund, that would be a covered transaction, as defined in section 23A of the Federal Reserve Act (12 U.S.C. 371c), with the hedge fund or private equity fund, as if such banking entity and the affiliate thereof were a member bank and the hedge fund or private equity fund were an affiliate thereof.

"(2) Treatment as Member Bank.—A banking entity that serves, directly or indirectly, as the investment manager, investment adviser, or sponsor to a hedge fund or private equity fund, or that organizes and offers a hedge fund or private equity fund pursuant to paragraph (d)(1)(G), shall be subject to section 23B of the Federal Reserve Act (12 U.S.C. 371c-1), as if such banking entity were a member bank and such hedge fund or private equity fund were an affiliate thereof.

"(3) Permitted Services.—

"(A) In General.—Notwithstanding paragraph (1), the Board may permit a banking entity to enter into any prime brokerage transaction with any hedge fund or private equity fund in which a hedge fund or private equity fund managed, sponsored, or advised by such banking entity has taken an equity, partnership, or other ownership interest, if—

"(i) the banking entity is in compliance with each of the limitations set forth in subsection (d)(1)(G) with regard to a hedge fund or private equity fund organized and offered by such banking entity;

"(ii) the chief executive officer (or equivalent officer) of the banking entity certifies in writing annually (with a duty to update the certification if the information in the certification materially changes) that the conditions specified in subsection (d)(1)(g)(v) are satisfied; and

"(iii) the Board has determined that such transaction is consistent with the safe and sound operation and condition of the banking entity.

"(B) Treatment of Prime Brokerage Transactions.—For purposes of subparagraph (A), a prime brokerage transaction described in subparagraph (A) shall be subject to section 23B of the Federal Reserve Act (12 U.S.C. 371c-1) as if the counterparty were an affiliate of the banking entity.

"(4) Application to Nonbank Financial Companies Supervised by the Board.—The appropriate Federal banking agencies, the Securities and Exchange Commission, and the Commodity Futures Trading Commission shall adopt rules, as provided in subsection (b)(2), imposing additional capital charges or other restrictions for nonbank financial companies supervised by the Board to address the risks to and conflicts of interest of banking entities described in paragraphs (1), (2), and (3) of this subsection.

"(g) Rules of Construction.—

"(1) Limitation on Contrary Authority.—Except as provided in this section, notwithstanding any other provision of law, the prohibitions and restrictions under this section shall apply to activities of a banking entity or nonbank financial company supervised by the Board, even if such activities are authorized for a banking entity or nonbank financial company supervised by the Board.

"(2) Sale or Securitization of Loans.—Nothing in this section shall be construed to limit or restrict the ability of a banking entity or nonbank financial company supervised by the Board to sell or securitize loans in a manner otherwise permitted by law.

"(3) Authority of Federal Agencies and State Regulatory Authorities.—Nothing in this section shall be construed to limit the inherent authority of any Federal agency or State regulatory authority under otherwise applicable provisions of law.

"(h) DEFINITIONS.—In this section, the following definitions shall apply:

"(1) BANKING ENTITY.—The term 'banking entity' means any insured depository institution (as defined in section 3 of the Federal Deposit Insurance Act (12 U.S.C. 1813)), any company that controls an insured depository institution, or that is treated as a bank holding company for purposes of section 8 of the International Banking Act of 1978, and any affiliate or subsidiary of any such entity. For purposes of this paragraph, the term 'insured depository institution' does not include an institution that functions solely in a trust or fiduciary capacity, if—

"(A) all or substantially all of the deposits of such institution are in trust funds and are received in a bona fide fiduciary capacity;

"(B) no deposits of such institution which are insured by the Federal Deposit Insurance Corporation are offered or marketed by or through an affiliate of such institution;

"(C) such institution does not accept demand deposits or deposits that the depositor may withdraw by check or similar means for payment to third parties or others or make commercial loans; and

"(D) such institution does not—

"(i) obtain payment or payment related services from any Federal Reserve bank, including any service referred to in section 11A of the Federal Reserve Act (12 U.S.C. 248a); or

"(ii) exercise discount or borrowing privileges pursuant to section 19(b)(7) of the Federal Reserve Act (12 U.S.C. 461(b)(7)).

"(2) HEDGE FUND; PRIVATE EQUITY FUND.—The terms 'hedge fund' and 'private equity fund' mean an issuer that would be an investment company, as defined in the Investment Company Act of 1940 (15 U.S.C. 80a-1 et seq.), but for section 3(c)(1) or 3(c)(7) of that Act, or such similar funds as the appropriate Federal banking agencies, the Securities and Exchange Commission, and the Commodity Futures Trading Commission may, by rule, as provided in subsection (b)(2), determine.

"(3) NONBANK FINANCIAL COMPANY SUPERVISED BY THE BOARD.—The term 'nonbank financial company supervised by the Board' means a nonbank financial company supervised by the Board of Governors, as defined in section 102 of the Financial Stability Act of 2010.

"(4) PROPRIETARY TRADING.—The term 'proprietary trading', when used with respect to a banking entity or nonbank financial company supervised by the Board, means engaging as a principal for the trading account of the banking entity or nonbank financial company supervised by the Board in any transaction to purchase or sell, or otherwise acquire or dispose of, any security, any derivative, any contract of sale of a commodity for future delivery, any option on any such security, derivative, or contract, or any other security or financial instrument that the appropriate Federal banking agencies, the Securities and Exchange Commission, and the Commodity Futures Trading Commission may, by rule as provided in subsection (b)(2), determine.

"(5) SPONSOR.—The term to 'sponsor' a fund means—

"(A) to serve as a general partner, managing member, or trustee of a fund;

"(B) in any manner to select or to control (or to have employees, officers, or directors, or agents who constitute) a majority of the directors, trustees, or management of a fund; or

"(C) to share with a fund, for corporate, marketing, promotional, or other purposes, the same name or a variation of the same name.

"(6) TRADING ACCOUNT.—The term 'trading account' means any account used for acquiring or taking positions in the securities and instruments described in paragraph (4) principally for the purpose of selling in the near term (or otherwise with the intent to resell in order to profit from short-term price movements), and any such other accounts as the appropriate Federal banking agencies, the Securities and Exchange Commission, and the

Commodity Futures Trading Commission may, by rule as provided in subsection (b)(2), determine.

"(7) ILLIQUID FUND.—

"(A) IN GENERAL.—The term 'illiquid fund' means a hedge fund or private equity fund that—

"(i) as of May 1, 2010, was principally invested in, or was invested and contractually committed to principally invest in, illiquid assets, such as portfolio companies, real estate investments, and venture capital investments; and

"(ii) makes all investments pursuant to, and consistent with, an investment strategy to principally invest in illiquid assets. In issuing rules regarding this subparagraph, the Board shall take into consideration the terms of investment for the hedge fund or private equity fund, including contractual obligations, the ability of the fund to divest of assets held by the fund, and any other factors that the Board determines are appropriate.

"(B) HEDGE FUND.—For the purposes of this paragraph, the term 'hedge fund' means any fund identified under subsection (h)(2), and does not include a private equity fund, as such term is used in section 203(m) of the Investment Advisers Act of 1940 (15 U.S.C. 80b-3(m)).".

[Explanation at ¶ 2575.]

[¶ 10,620] ACT SEC. 620. STUDY OF BANK INVESTMENT ACTIVITIES.

(a) STUDY.—

(1) IN GENERAL.—Not later than 18 months after the date of enactment of this Act, the appropriate Federal banking agencies shall jointly review and prepare a report on the activities that a banking entity, as such term is defined in the Bank Holding Company Act of 1956 (12 U.S.C. 1841 et. seq.), may engage in under Federal and State law, including activities authorized by statute and by order, interpretation and guidance.

(2) CONTENT.—In carrying out the study under paragraph (1), the appropriate Federal banking agencies shall review and consider—

(A) the type of activities or investments;

(B) any financial, operational, managerial, or reputation risks associated with or presented as a result of the banking entity engaged in the activity or making the investment; and

(C) risk mitigation activities undertaken by the banking entity with regard to the risks.

(b) REPORT AND RECOMMENDATIONS TO THE COUNCIL AND TO CONGRESS.—The appropriate Federal banking agencies shall submit to the Council, the Committee on Financial Services of the House of Representatives, and the Committee on Banking, Housing, and Urban Affairs of the Senate the study conducted pursuant to subsection (a) no later than 2 months after its completion. In addition to the information described in subsection (a), the report shall include recommendations regarding—

(1) whether each activity or investment has or could have a negative effect on the safety and soundness of the banking entity or the United States financial system;

(2) the appropriateness of the conduct of each activity or type of investment by banking entities; and

(3) additional restrictions as may be necessary to address risks to safety and soundness arising from the activities or types of investments described in subsection (a).

[Explanation at ¶ 2580.]

[¶ 10,621] ACT SEC. 621. CONFLICTS OF INTEREST.

(a) IN GENERAL.—The Securities Act of 1933 (15 U.S.C. 77a et seq.) is amended by inserting after section 27A the following:

"SEC. 27B. CONFLICTS OF INTEREST RELATING TO CERTAIN SECURITIZATIONS.

"(a) IN GENERAL.—An underwriter, placement agent, initial purchaser, or sponsor, or any affiliate or subsidiary of any such entity, of an asset-backed security (as such term is defined in section 3 of the Securities and Exchange Act of 1934 (15 U.S.C. 78c), which for the purposes of this section shall include a synthetic asset-backed security), shall not, at any time for a period ending on the date that is one year after the date of the first closing of the sale of the asset-backed security, engage in any transaction that would involve or result in any material conflict of interest with respect to any investor in a transaction arising out of such activity.

"(b) RULEMAKING.—Not later than 270 days after the date of enactment of this section, the Commission shall issue rules for the purpose of implementing subsection (a).

"(c) EXCEPTION.—The prohibitions of subsection (a) shall not apply to—

"(1) risk-mitigating hedging activities in connection with positions or holdings arising out of the underwriting, placement, initial purchase, or sponsorship of an asset-backed security, provided that such activities are designed to reduce the specific risks to the underwriter, placement agent, initial purchaser, or sponsor associated with positions or holdings arising out of such underwriting, placement, initial purchase, or sponsorship; or

"(2) purchases or sales of asset-backed securities made pursuant to and consistent with—

"(A) commitments of the underwriter, placement agent, initial purchaser, or sponsor, or any affiliate or subsidiary of any such entity, to provide liquidity for the asset-backed security, or

"(B) bona fide market-making in the asset backed security.

"(d) RULE OF CONSTRUCTION.—This subsection shall not otherwise limit the application of section 15G of the Securities Exchange Act of 1934.".

(b) EFFECTIVE DATE.—Section 27B of the Securities Act of 1933, as added by this section, shall take effect on the effective date of final rules issued by the Commission under subsection (b) of such section 27B, except that subsections (b) and (d) of such section 27B shall take effect on the date of enactment of this Act.

[Explanation at ¶ 2585.]

[¶ 10,622] ACT SEC. 622. CONCENTRATION LIMITS ON LARGE FINANCIAL FIRMS.

The Bank Holding Company Act of 1956 (12 U.S.C. 1841 et seq.) is amended by adding at the end the following:

"SEC. 14. CONCENTRATION LIMITS ON LARGE FINANCIAL FIRMS.

"(a) DEFINITIONS.—In this section—

"(1) the term 'Council' means the Financial Stability Oversight Council;

"(2) the term 'financial company' means—

"(A) an insured depository institution;

"(B) a bank holding company;

"(C) a savings and loan holding company;

"(D) a company that controls an insured depository institution;

"(E) a nonbank financial company supervised by the Board under title I of the Dodd-Frank Wall Street Reform and Consumer Protection Act; and

"(F) a foreign bank or company that is treated as a bank holding company for purposes of this Act; and

"(3) the term 'liabilities' means—

"(A) with respect to a United States financial company—

"(i) the total risk-weighted assets of the financial company, as determined under the risk-based capital rules applicable to bank holding companies, as adjusted to reflect exposures that are deducted from regulatory capital; less

"(ii) the total regulatory capital of the financial company under the risk-based capital rules applicable to bank holding companies;

"(B) with respect to a foreign-based financial company—

"(i) the total risk-weighted assets of the United States operations of the financial company, as determined under the applicable risk-based capital rules, as adjusted to reflect exposures that are deducted from regulatory capital; less

"(ii) the total regulatory capital of the United States operations of the financial company, as determined under the applicable risk-based capital rules; and

"(C) with respect to an insurance company or other nonbank financial company supervised by the Board, such assets of the company as the Board shall specify by rule, in order to provide for consistent and equitable treatment of such companies.

"(b) CONCENTRATION LIMIT.—Subject to the recommendations by the Council under subsection (e), a financial company may not merge or consolidate with, acquire all or substantially all of the assets of, or otherwise acquire control of, another company, if the total consolidated liabilities of the acquiring financial company upon consummation of the transaction would exceed 10 percent of the aggregate consolidated liabilities of all financial companies at the end of the calendar year preceding the transaction.

"(c) EXCEPTION TO CONCENTRATION LIMIT.—With the prior written consent of the Board, the concentration limit under subsection (b) shall not apply to an acquisition—

"(1) of a bank in default or in danger of default;

"(2) with respect to which assistance is provided by the Federal Deposit Insurance Corporation under section 13(c) of the Federal Deposit Insurance Act (12 U.S.C. 1823(c)); or

"(3) that would result only in a de minimis increase in the liabilities of the financial company.

"(d) RULEMAKING AND GUIDANCE.—The Board shall issue regulations implementing this section in accordance with the recommendations of the Council under subsection (e), including the definition of terms, as necessary. The Board may issue interpretations or guidance regarding the application of this section to an individual financial company or to financial companies in general.

"(e) COUNCIL STUDY AND RULEMAKING.—

"(1) STUDY AND RECOMMENDATIONS.—Not later than 6 months after the date of enactment of this section, the Council shall—

"(A) complete a study of the extent to which the concentration limit under this section would affect financial stability, moral hazard in the financial system, the efficiency and competitiveness of United States financial firms and financial markets, and the cost and availability of credit and other financial services to households and businesses in the United States; and

"(B) make recommendations regarding any modifications to the concentration limit that the Council determines would more effectively implement this section.

"(2) RULEMAKING.—Not later than 9 months after the date of completion of the study under paragraph (1), and notwithstanding subsections (b) and (d), the Board shall issue final regulations implementing this section, which shall reflect any recommendations by the Council under paragraph (1)(B).".

[Explanation at ¶ 2590.]

[¶ 10,623] ACT SEC. 623. INTERSTATE MERGER TRANSACTIONS.

(a) INTERSTATE MERGER TRANSACTIONS.—Section 18(c) of the Federal Deposit Insurance Act (12 U.S.C. 1828(c)) is amended by adding at the end the following:

"(13)

(A) Except as provided in subparagraph (B), the responsible agency may not approve an application for an interstate merger transaction if the resulting insured depository institution (including all insured depository institutions which are affiliates of the resulting insured depository institution), upon consummation of the transaction, would control more than 10 percent of the total amount of deposits of insured depository institutions in the United States.

"(B) Subparagraph (A) shall not apply to an interstate merger transaction that involves 1 or more insured depository institutions in default or in danger of default, or with respect to which the Corporation provides assistance under section 13.

"(C) In this paragraph—

"(i) the term 'interstate merger transaction' means a merger transaction involving 2 or more insured depository institutions that have different home States and that are not affiliates; and

"(ii) the term 'home State' means—

"(I) with respect to a national bank, the State in which the main office of the bank is located;

"(II) with respect to a State bank or State savings association, the State by which the State bank or State savings association is chartered; and

"(III) with respect to a Federal savings association, the State in which the home office (as defined by the regulations of the Director of the Office of Thrift Supervision, or, on and after the transfer date, the Comptroller of the Currency) of the Federal savings association is located.".

(b) ACQUISITIONS BY BANK HOLDING COMPANIES.—

(1) IN GENERAL.—Section 4 of the Bank Holding Company Act of 1956 (12 U.S.C. 1843) is amended—

(A) in subsection (i), by adding at the end the following:

"(8) INTERSTATE ACQUISITIONS.—

"(A) IN GENERAL.—The Board may not approve an application by a bank holding company to acquire an insured depository institution under subsection (c)(8) or any other provision of this Act if—

"(i) the home State of such insured depository institution is a State other than the home State of the bank holding company; and

"(ii) the applicant (including all insured depository institutions which are affiliates of the applicant) controls, or upon consummation of the transaction would control, more than 10 percent of the total amount of deposits of insured depository institutions in the United States.

"(B) EXCEPTION.—Subparagraph (A) shall not apply to an acquisition that involves an insured depository institution in default or in danger of default, or with respect to which the Federal Deposit Insurance Corporation provides assistance under section 13 of the Federal Deposit Insurance Act (12 U.S.C. 1823)."; and

(B) in subsection (k)(6)(B), by striking "savings association" and inserting "insured depository institution".

(2) DEFINITIONS.—Section 2(o)(4) of the Bank Holding Company Act of 1956 (12 U.S.C. 1841(o)(4)) is amended—

(A) in subparagraph (B), by striking "and" at the end;

(B) in subparagraph (C)(ii), by striking the period at the end and inserting a semicolon; and

(C) by adding at the end the following:

"(D) with respect to a State savings association, the State by which the savings association is chartered; and

"(E) with respect to a Federal savings association, the State in which the home office (as defined by the regulations of the Director of the Office of Thrift Supervision, or, on and after the transfer date, the Comptroller of the Currency) of the Federal savings association is located.".

(c) ACQUISITIONS BY SAVINGS AND LOAN HOLDING COMPANIES.—Section 10(e)(2) of the Home Owners' Loan Act (12 U.S.C. 1467a(e)(2)) is amended—

(1) in paragraph (2)—

(A) in subparagraph (C), by striking "or" at the end;

(B) in subparagraph (D), by striking the period at the end and inserting ", or"; and

(C) by adding at the end the following:

"(E) in the case of an application by a savings and loan holding company to acquire an insured depository institution, if—

"(i) the home State of the insured depository institution is a State other than the home State of the savings and loan holding company;

"(ii) the applicant (including all insured depository institutions which are affiliates of the applicant) controls, or upon consummation of the transaction would control, more than 10 percent of the total amount of deposits of insured depository institutions in the United States; and

"(iii) the acquisition does not involve an insured depository institution in default or in danger of default, or with respect to which the Federal Deposit Insurance Corporation provides assistance under section 13 of the Federal Deposit Insurance Act (12 U.S.C. 1823)."; and

(2) by adding at the end the following:

"(7) DEFINITIONS.—For purposes of paragraph (2)(E)—

"(A) the terms 'default', 'in danger of default', and 'insured depository institution' have the same meanings as in section 3 of the Federal Deposit Insurance Act (12 U.S.C. 1813); and

"(B) the term 'home State' means—

"(i) with respect to a national bank, the State in which the main office of the bank is located;

"(ii) with respect to a State bank or State savings association, the State by which the savings association is chartered;

"(iii) with respect to a Federal savings association, the State in which the home office (as defined by the regulations of the Director of the Office of Thrift Supervision, or, on and after the transfer date, the Comptroller of the Currency) of the Federal savings association is located; and

"(iv) with respect to a savings and loan holding company, the State in which the amount of total deposits of all insured depository institution subsidiaries of such company was the greatest on the date on which the company became a savings and loan holding company.".

[Explanation at ¶ 2595.]

[¶ 10,624] ACT SEC. 624. QUALIFIED THRIFT LENDERS.

Section 10(m)(3) of the Home Owners' Loan Act (12 U.S.C. 1467a(m)(3)) is amended—

(1) by striking subparagraph (A) and inserting the following:

"(A) IN GENERAL.—A savings association that fails to become or remain a qualified thrift lender shall immediately be subject to the restrictions under subparagraph (B)."; and

(2) in subparagraph (B)(i), by striking subclause (III) and inserting the following:

"(III) DIVIDENDS.—The savings association may not pay dividends, except for dividends that—

"(aa) would be permissible for a national bank;

"(bb) are necessary to meet obligations of a company that controls such savings association; and

"(cc) are specifically approved by the Comptroller of the Currency and the Board after a written request submitted to the Comptroller of the Currency and the Board by the savings association not later than 30 days before the date of the proposed payment.

"(IV) REGULATORY AUTHORITY.—A savings association that fails to become or remain a qualified thrift lender shall be deemed to have violated section 5 of the Home Owners' Loan Act (12 U.S.C. 1464) and subject to actions authorized by section 5(d) of the Home Owners' Loan Act (12 U.S.C. 1464(d)).".

[Explanation at ¶ 2600.]

[¶ 10,625] ACT SEC. 625. TREATMENT OF DIVIDENDS BY CERTAIN MUTUAL HOLDING COMPANIES.

(a) IN GENERAL.—Section 10(o) of the Home Owners' Loan Act (12 U.S.C. 1467a(o) is amended by adding at the end the following:

"(11) DIVIDENDS.—

"(A) DECLARATION OF DIVIDENDS.—

"(i) ADVANCE NOTICE REQUIRED.—Each subsidiary of a mutual holding company that is a savings association shall give the appropriate Federal banking agency and the Board notice not later than 30 days before the date of a proposed declaration by the board of directors of the savings association of any dividend on the guaranty, permanent, or other nonwithdrawable stock of the savings association.

"(ii) INVALID DIVIDENDS.—Any dividend described in clause (i) that is declared without giving notice to the appropriate Federal banking agency and the Board under clause (i), or that is declared during the 30-day period preceding the date of a proposed declaration for which notice is given to the appropriate Federal banking agency and the Board under clause (i), shall be invalid and shall confer no rights or benefits upon the holder of any such stock.

"(B) WAIVER OF DIVIDENDS.—A mutual holding company may waive the right to receive any dividend declared by a subsidiary of the mutual holding company, if—

"(i) no insider of the mutual holding company, associate of an insider, or tax-qualified or non-tax-qualified employee stock benefit plan of the mutual holding company holds any share of the stock in the class of stock to which the waiver would apply; or

"(ii) the mutual holding company gives written notice to the Board of the intent of the mutual holding company to waive the right to receive dividends, not later than 30 days before the date of the proposed date of payment of the dividend, and the Board does not object to the waiver.

"(C) RESOLUTION INCLUDED IN WAIVER NOTICE.—A notice of a waiver under subparagraph (B) shall include a copy of the resolution of the board of directors of the mutual holding company, in such form and substance as the Board may determine, together with any supporting materials relied upon by the board of directors of the mutual holding company, concluding that the proposed dividend waiver is consistent with the fiduciary duties of the board of directors to the mutual members of the mutual holding company.

"(D) STANDARDS FOR WAIVER OF DIVIDEND.—The Board may not object to a waiver of dividends under subparagraph (B) if—

"(i) the waiver would not be detrimental to the safe and sound operation of the savings association;

"(ii) the board of directors of the mutual holding company expressly determines that a waiver of the dividend by the mutual holding company is consistent with the fiduciary duties of the board of directors to the mutual members of the mutual holding company; and

"(iii) the mutual holding company has, prior to December 1, 2009—

"(I) reorganized into a mutual holding company under subsection (o);

"(II) issued minority stock either from its mid-tier stock holding company or its subsidiary stock savings association; and

"(III) waived dividends it had a right to receive from the subsidiary stock savings association.

"(E) VALUATION.—

"(i) IN GENERAL.—The appropriate Federal banking agency shall consider waived dividends in determining an appropriate exchange ratio in the event of a full conversion to stock form.

"(ii) EXCEPTION.—In the case of a savings association that has reorganized into a mutual holding company, has issued minority stock from a mid-tier stock holding company or a subsidiary stock savings association of the mutual holding company, and has waived dividends it had a right to receive from a subsidiary savings association before December 1, 2009, the appropriate Federal banking agency shall not consider waived dividends in determining an appropriate exchange ratio in the event of a full conversion to stock form.".

(b) EFFECTIVE DATE.—The amendment made by subsection (a) shall take effect on the transfer date.

[Explanation at ¶ 2605.]

[¶ 10,626] ACT SEC. 626. INTERMEDIATE HOLDING COMPANIES.

The Home Owners' Loan Act (12 U.S.C. 1461 et seq.) is amended by inserting after section 10 (12 U.S.C. 1467a) the following new section:

"SEC. 10A. INTERMEDIATE HOLDING COMPANIES.

"(a) DEFINITION.—For purposes of this section:

"(1) FINANCIAL ACTIVITIES.—The term 'financial activities' means activities described in clauses (i) and (ii) of section 10(c)(9)(A).

"(2) GRANDFATHERED UNITARY SAVINGS AND LOAN HOLDING COMPANY.—The term 'grandfathered unitary savings and loan holding company' means a company described in section 10(c)(9)(C).

"(3) INTERNAL FINANCIAL ACTIVITIES.—The term 'internal financial activities' includes—

"(A) internal financial activities conducted by a grandfathered savings and loan holding company or any affiliate; and

"(B) internal treasury, investment, and employee benefit functions.

"(b) REQUIREMENT.—

"(1) IN GENERAL.—

"(A) ACTIVITIES OTHER THAN FINANCIAL ACTIVITIES.—If a grandfathered unitary savings and loan holding company conducts activities other than financial activities, the Board may require such company to establish and conduct all or a portion of such financial activities in or through an intermediate holding company, which shall be a savings and loan holding company, established pursuant to regulations of the Board, not later than 90 days (or such longer period as the Board may deem appropriate) after the transfer date.

"(B) OTHER ACTIVITIES.—Notwithstanding subparagraph (A), the Board shall require a grandfathered unitary savings and loan holding company to establish an intermediate holding company if the Board makes a determination that the establishment of such intermediate holding company is necessary—

"(i) to appropriately supervise activities that are determined to be financial activities; or

"(ii) to ensure that supervision by the Board does not extend to the activities of such company that are not financial activities.

"(2) INTERNAL FINANCIAL ACTIVITIES.—

"(A) TREATMENT OF INTERNAL FINANCIAL ACTIVITIES.—For purposes of this subsection, the internal financial activities of a grandfathered unitary savings and loan holding company shall not be required to be placed in an intermediate holding company.

"(B) GRANDFATHERED ACTIVITIES.—A grandfathered unitary savings and loan holding company may continue to engage in an internal financial activity, subject to review by the Board to determine whether engaging in such activity presents undue risk to the grandfathered unitary savings and loan holding company or to the financial stability of the United States, if—

"(i) the grandfathered unitary savings and loan holding company engaged in the activity during the year before the date of enactment of this section; and

"(ii) at least 2/3 of the assets or 2/3 of the revenues generated from the activity are from or attributable to the grandfathered unitary savings and loan holding company.

"(3) SOURCE OF STRENGTH.—A grandfathered unitary savings and loan holding company that directly or indirectly controls an intermediate holding company established under this section shall serve as a source of strength to its subsidiary intermediate holding company.

"(4) PARENT COMPANY REPORTS.—The Board, may from time to time, examine and require reports under oath from a grandfathered unitary savings and loan holding company that controls an intermediate holding company, and from the appropriate officers or directors of such company, solely for purposes of ensuring compliance with the provisions of this section, including assessing the ability of the company to serve as a source of strength to its subsidiary intermediate holding company as required under paragraph (3) and enforcing compliance with such requirement.

"(5) LIMITED PARENT COMPANY ENFORCEMENT.—

"(A) IN GENERAL.—In addition to any other authority of the Board, the Board may enforce compliance with the provisions of this subsection that are applicable to any company described in paragraph (1)(A) that controls an intermediate holding company under section 8 of the Federal Deposit Insurance Act, and a company described in paragraph (1)(A) shall be subject to such section (solely for purposes of this subparagraph) in the same manner and to the same extent as if the company described in paragraph (1)(A) were a savings and loan holding company.

"(B) APPLICATION OF OTHER ACT.—Any violation of this subsection by a grandfathered unitary savings and loan holding company that controls an intermediate holding company may also be treated as a violation of the Federal Deposit Insurance Act for purposes of subparagraph (A).

"(C) NO EFFECT ON OTHER AUTHORITY.—No provision of this paragraph shall be construed as limiting any authority of the Board or any other Federal agency under any other provision of law.

"(c) REGULATIONS.—The Board—

"(1) shall promulgate regulations to establish the criteria for determining whether to require a grandfathered unitary savings and loan holding company to establish an intermediate holding company under subsection (b); and

"(2) may promulgate regulations to establish any restrictions or limitations on transactions between an intermediate holding company or a parent of such company and its affiliates, as necessary to prevent unsafe and unsound practices in connection with transactions between the intermediate holding company, or any subsidiary thereof, and its parent company or affiliates that are not subsidiaries of the intermediate holding company, except that such regulations shall not restrict or limit any transaction in connection with the bona fide acquisition or lease by an unaffiliated person of assets, goods, or services.

"(d) RULES OF CONSTRUCTION.—

"(1) ACTIVITIES.—Nothing in this section shall be construed to require a grandfathered unitary savings and loan holding company to conform its activities to permissible activities.

"(2) PERMISSIBLE CORPORATE REORGANIZATION.—The formation of an intermediate holding company as required in subsection (b) shall be presumed to be a permissible corporate reorganization as described in section 10(c)(9)(D).".

[Explanation at ¶ 2610.]

[¶ 10,627] ACT SEC. 627. INTEREST-BEARING TRANSACTION ACCOUNTS AUTHORIZED.

(a) REPEAL OF PROHIBITION ON PAYMENT OF INTEREST ON DEMAND DEPOSITS.—

(1) FEDERAL RESERVE ACT.—Section 19(i) of the Federal Reserve Act (12 U.S.C. 371a) is amended to read as follows:

"(i) [Repealed]".

(2) HOME OWNERS' LOAN ACT.—The first sentence of section 5(b)(1)(B) of the Home Owners' Loan Act (12 U.S.C. 1464(b)(1)(B)) is amended by striking "savings association may not-" and all that follows through "(ii) permit any" and inserting "savings association may not permit any".

(3) FEDERAL DEPOSIT INSURANCE ACT.—Section 18(g) of the Federal Deposit Insurance Act (12 U.S.C. 1828(g)) is amended to read as follows:

"(g) [Repealed]".

(b) EFFECTIVE DATE.—The amendments made by subsection (a) shall take effect 1 year after the date of the enactment of this Act.

[Explanation at ¶ 2615.]

[¶ 10,628] ACT SEC. 628. CREDIT CARD BANK SMALL BUSINESS LENDING.

Section 2(c)(2)(F)(v) of the Bank Holding Company Act of 1956 (12 U.S.C. 1841(c)(2)(F)(v)) is amended by inserting before the period the following: ", other than credit card loans that are made to businesses that meet the criteria for a small business concern to be eligible for business loans under regulations established by the Small Business Administration under part 121 of title 13, Code of Federal Regulations".

[Explanation at ¶ 2620.]

TITLE VII—WALL STREET TRANSPARENCY AND ACCOUNTABILITY

[¶ 10,701] ACT SEC. 701. SHORT TITLE.

This title may be cited as the "Wall Street Transparency and Accountability Act of 2010".

Subtitle A—Regulation of Over-the-Counter Swaps Markets
PART I—REGULATORY AUTHORITY

[¶ 10,711] ACT SEC. 711. DEFINITIONS.

In this subtitle, the terms "prudential regulator", "swap", "swap dealer", "major swap participant", "swap data repository", "associated person of a swap dealer or major swap participant", "eligible contract participant", "swap execution facility", "security-based swap", "security-based swap dealer", "major security-based swap participant", and "associated person of a security-based swap dealer or major security-based swap participant" have the meanings given the terms in section 1a of the Commodity Exchange Act (7 U.S.C. 1a), including any modification of the meanings under section 721(b) of this Act.

[Explanation at ¶ 3010.]

[¶ 10,712] ACT SEC. 712. REVIEW OF REGULATORY AUTHORITY.

(a) CONSULTATION.—

(1) COMMODITY FUTURES TRADING COMMISSION.—Before commencing any rulemaking or issuing an order regarding swaps, swap dealers, major swap participants, swap data repositories, derivative clearing organizations with regard to swaps, persons associated with a swap dealer or major swap participant, eligible contract participants, or swap execution facilities pursuant to this subtitle, the Commodity Futures Trading Commission shall consult and coordinate to the extent possible with the Securities and Exchange Commission and the prudential regulators for the purposes of assuring regulatory consistency and comparability, to the extent possible.

(2) SECURITIES AND EXCHANGE COMMISSION.—Before commencing any rulemaking or issuing an order regarding security-based swaps, security-based swap dealers, major security-based swap participants, security-based swap data repositories, clearing agencies with regard to security-based swaps, persons associated with a security-based swap dealer or major security-based swap participant, eligible contract participants with regard to security-based swaps, or security-based swap execution facilities pursuant to subtitle B, the Securities and Exchange Commission shall consult and coordinate to the extent possible with the Commodity Futures Trading Commission and the prudential regulators for the purposes of assuring regulatory consistency and comparability, to the extent possible.

(3) PROCEDURES AND DEADLINE.—Such regulations shall be prescribed in accordance with applicable requirements of title 5, United States Code, and shall be issued in final form not later than 360 days after the date of enactment of this Act.

(4) APPLICABILITY.—The requirements of paragraphs (1) and (2) shall not apply to an order issued—

(A) in connection with or arising from a violation or potential violation of any provision of the Commodity Exchange Act (7 U.S.C. 1 et seq.);

(B) in connection with or arising from a violation or potential violation of any provision of the securities laws; or

(C) in any proceeding that is conducted on the record in accordance with sections 556 and 557 of title 5, United States Code.

(5) EFFECT.—Nothing in this subsection authorizes any consultation or procedure for consultation that is not consistent with the requirements of subchapter II of chapter 5, and chapter 7, of title 5, United States Code (commonly known as the "Administrative Procedure Act").

(6) RULES; ORDERS.—In developing and promulgating rules or orders pursuant to this subsection, each Commission shall consider the views of the prudential regulators.

(7) TREATMENT OF SIMILAR PRODUCTS AND ENTITIES.—

(A) IN GENERAL.—In adopting rules and orders under this subsection, the Commodity Futures Trading Commission and the Securities and Exchange Commission shall treat functionally or economically similar products or entities described in paragraphs (1) and (2) in a similar manner.

(B) EFFECT.—Nothing in this subtitle requires the Commodity Futures Trading Commission or the Securities and Exchange Commission to adopt joint rules or orders that treat functionally or economically similar products or entities described in paragraphs (1) and (2) in an identical manner.

(8) MIXED SWAPS.—The Commodity Futures Trading Commission and the Securities and Exchange Commission, after consultation with the Board of Governors, shall jointly prescribe such regulations regarding mixed swaps, as described in section la(47)(D) of the Commodity Exchange Act (7 U.S.C. la(47)(D)) and in section 3(a)(68)(D) of the Securities Exchange Act of 1934 (15 U.S.C. 78c(a)(68)(D)), as may be necessary to carry out the purposes of this title.

(b) LIMITATION.—

(1) COMMODITY FUTURES TRADING COMMISSION.—Nothing in this title, unless specifically provided, confers jurisdiction on the Commodity Futures Trading Commission to issue a rule, regulation, or order providing for oversight or regulation of—

    (A) security-based swaps; or

    (B) with regard to its activities or functions concerning security-based swaps—

        (i) security-based swap dealers;

        (ii) major security-based swap participants;

        (iii) security-based swap data repositories;

        (iv) associated persons of a security-based swap dealer or major security-based swap participant;

        (v) eligible contract participants with respect to security-based swaps; or

        (vi) swap execution facilities with respect to security-based swaps.

(2) SECURITIES AND EXCHANGE COMMISSION.—Nothing in this title, unless specifically provided, confers jurisdiction on the Securities and Exchange Commission or State securities regulators to issue a rule, regulation, or order providing for oversight or regulation of—

    (A) swaps; or

    (B) with regard to its activities or functions concerning swaps—

        (i) swap dealers;

        (ii) major swap participants;

        (iii) swap data repositories;

        (iv) persons associated with a swap dealer or major swap participant;

        (v) eligible contract participants with respect to swaps; or

        (vi) swap execution facilities with respect to swaps.

(3) PROHIBITION ON CERTAIN FUTURES ASSOCIATIONS AND NATIONAL SECURITIES ASSOCIATIONS.—

    (A) FUTURES ASSOCIATIONS.—Notwithstanding any other provision of law (including regulations), unless otherwise authorized by this title, no futures association registered under section 17 of the Commodity Exchange Act (7 U.S.C. 21) may issue a rule, regulation, or order for the oversight or regulation of, or otherwise assert jurisdiction over, for any purpose, any security-based swap, except that this subparagraph shall not limit the authority of a registered futures association to examine for compliance with, and enforce, its rules on capital adequacy.

    (B) NATIONAL SECURITIES ASSOCIATIONS.—Notwithstanding any other provision of law (including regulations), unless otherwise authorized by this title, no national securities association registered under section 15A of the Securities Exchange Act of 1934 (15 U.S.C. 78o-3) may issue a rule, regulation, or order for the oversight or regulation of, or otherwise assert jurisdiction over, for any purpose, any swap, except that this subparagraph shall not limit the authority of a national securities association to examine for compliance with, and enforce, its rules on capital adequacy.

(c) OBJECTION TO COMMISSION REGULATION.—

(1) FILING OF PETITION FOR REVIEW.—

    (A) IN GENERAL.—If either Commission referred to in this section determines that a final rule, regulation, or order of the other Commission conflicts with subsection (a)(7) or (b), then the complaining Commission may obtain review of the final rule, regulation, or order in the United States Court of Appeals for the District of Columbia Circuit by filing in the court, not later than 60 days after the date of publication of the final rule, regulation, or order, a written petition requesting that the rule, regulation, or order be set aside.

    (B) EXPEDITED PROCEEDING.—A proceeding described in subparagraph (A) shall be expedited by the United States Court of Appeals for the District of Columbia Circuit.

(2) TRANSMITTAL OF PETITION AND RECORD.—

(A) IN GENERAL.—A copy of a petition described in paragraph (1) shall be transmitted not later than 1 business day after the date of filing by the complaining Commission to the Secretary of the responding Commission.

(B) DUTY OF RESPONDING COMMISSION.—On receipt of the copy of a petition described in paragraph (1), the responding Commission shall file with the United States Court of Appeals for the District of Columbia Circuit—

(i) a copy of the rule, regulation, or order under review (including any documents referred to therein); and

(ii) any other materials prescribed by the United States Court of Appeals for the District of Columbia Circuit.

(3) STANDARD OF REVIEW.—The United States Court of Appeals for the District of Columbia Circuit shall—

(A) give deference to the views of neither Commission; and

(B) determine to affirm or set aside a rule, regulation, or order of the responding Commission under this subsection, based on the determination of the court as to whether the rule, regulation, or order is in conflict with subsection (a)(7) or (b), as applicable.

(4) JUDICIAL STAY.—The filing of a petition by the complaining Commission pursuant to paragraph (1) shall operate as a stay of the rule, regulation, or order until the date on which the determination of the United States Court of Appeals for the District of Columbia Circuit is final (including any appeal of the determination).

(d) JOINT RULEMAKING.—

(1) IN GENERAL.—Notwithstanding any other provision of this title and subsections (b) and (c), the Commodity Futures Trading Commission and the Securities and Exchange Commission, in consultation with the Board of Governors, shall further define the terms "swap", "security-based swap", "swap dealer", "security-based swap dealer", "major swap participant", "major security-based swap participant", "eligible contract participant", and "security-based swap agreement" in section la(47)(A)(v) of the Commodity Exchange Act (7 U.S.C. la(47)(A)(v)) and section 3(a)(78) of the Securities Exchange Act of 1934 (15 U.S.C. 78c(a)(78)).

(2) AUTHORITY OF THE COMMISSIONS.—

(A) IN GENERAL.—Notwithstanding any other provision of this title, the Commodity Futures Trading Commission and the Securities and Exchange Commission, in consultation with the Board of Governors, shall jointly adopt such other rules regarding such definitions as the Commodity Futures Trading Commission and the Securities and Exchange Commission determine are necessary and appropriate, in the public interest, and for the protection of investors.

(B) TRADE REPOSITORY RECORDKEEPING.—Notwithstanding any other provision of this title, the Commodity Futures Trading Commission and the Securities and Exchange Commission, in consultation with the Board of Governors, shall engage in joint rulemaking to jointly adopt a rule or rules governing the books and records that are required to be kept and maintained regarding security-based swap agreements by persons that are registered as swap data repositories under the Commodity Exchange Act, including uniform rules that specify the data elements that shall be collected and maintained by each repository.

(C) BOOKS AND RECORDS.—Notwithstanding any other provision of this title, the Commodity Futures Trading Commission and the Securities and Exchange Commission, in consultation with the Board of Governors, shall engage in joint rulemaking to jointly adopt a rule or rules governing books and records regarding security-based swap agreements, including daily trading records, for swap dealers, major swap participants, security-based swap dealers, and security-based swap participants.

(D) COMPARABLE RULES.—Rules and regulations prescribed jointly under this title by the Commodity Futures Trading Commission and the Securities and Exchange Commission shall be comparable to the maximum extent possible, taking into consideration differences in instruments and in the applicable statutory requirements.

(E) TRACKING UNCLEARED TRANSACTIONS.—Any rules prescribed under subparagraph (A) shall require the maintenance of records of all activities relating to security-based swap agreement transactions defined under subparagraph (A) that are not cleared.

(F) SHARING OF INFORMATION.—The Commodity Futures Trading Commission shall make available to the Securities and Exchange Commission information relating to security-based swap agreement transactions defined in subparagraph (A) that are not cleared.

(3) FINANCIAL STABILITY OVERSIGHT COUNCIL.—In the event that the Commodity Futures Trading Commission and the Securities and Exchange Commission fail to jointly prescribe rules pursuant to paragraph (1) or (2) in a timely manner, at the request of either Commission, the Financial Stability Oversight Council shall resolve the dispute—

(A) within a reasonable time after receiving the request;

(B) after consideration of relevant information provided by each Commission; and

(C) by agreeing with 1 of the Commissions regarding the entirety of the matter or by determining a compromise position.

(4) JOINT INTERPRETATION.—Any interpretation of, or guidance by either Commission regarding, a provision of this title, shall be effective only if issued jointly by the Commodity Futures Trading Commission and the Securities and Exchange Commission, after consultation with the Board of Governors, if this title requires the Commodity Futures Trading Commission and the Securities and Exchange Commission to issue joint regulations to implement the provision.

(e) GLOBAL RULEMAKING TIMEFRAME.—Unless otherwise provided in this title, or an amendment made by this title, the Commodity Futures Trading Commission or the Securities and Exchange Commission, or both, shall individually, and not jointly, promulgate rules and regulations required of each Commission under this title or an amendment made by this title not later than 360 days after the date of enactment of this Act.

(f) RULES AND REGISTRATION BEFORE FINAL EFFECTIVE DATES.—Beginning on the date of enactment of this Act and notwithstanding the effective date of any provision of this Act, the Commodity Futures Trading Commission and the Securities and Exchange Commission may, in order to prepare for the effective dates of the provisions of this Act—

(1) promulgate rules, regulations, or orders permitted or required by this Act;

(2) conduct studies and prepare reports and recommendations required by this Act;

(3) register persons under the provisions of this Act; and

(4) exempt persons, agreements, contracts, or transactions from provisions of this Act, under the terms contained in this Act,

provided, however, that no action by the Commodity Futures Trading Commission or the Securities and Exchange Commission described in paragraphs (1) through (4) shall become effective prior to the effective date applicable to such action under the provisions of this Act.

[Explanation at ¶ 3020.]

[¶ 10,713] ACT SEC. 713. PORTFOLIO MARGINING CONFORMING CHANGES.

(a) SECURITIES EXCHANGE ACT OF 1934.—Section 15(c)(3) of the Securities Exchange Act of 1934 (15 U.S.C. 78o(c)(3)) is amended by adding at the end the following:

"(C) Notwithstanding any provision of sections 2(a)(1)(C)(i) or 4d(a)(2) of the Commodity Exchange Act and the rules and regulations thereunder, and pursuant to an exemption granted by the Commission under section 36 of this title or pursuant to a rule or regulation, cash and securities may be held by a broker or dealer registered pursuant to subsection (b)(1) and also registered as a futures commission merchant pursuant to section 4f(a)(1) of the Commodity Exchange Act, in a portfolio margining account carried as a futures account subject to section 4d of the Commodity Exchange Act and the rules and regulations thereunder, pursuant to a portfolio margining program approved by the Commodity Futures Trading Commission, and subject to subchapter IV of chapter 7 of title 11 of the United States Code and the rules and regulations thereunder. The Commission shall consult with the Commodity Futures Trading Commission to adopt rules to ensure that such transactions and accounts are subject to comparable requirements to the extent practicable for similar products.".

(b) COMMODITY EXCHANGE ACT.—Section 4d of the Commodity Exchange Act (7 U.S.C. 6d) is amended by adding at the end the following:

"(h) Notwithstanding subsection (a)(2) or the rules and regulations thereunder, and pursuant to an exemption granted by the Commission under section 4(c) of this Act or pursuant to a rule or regulation, a futures commission merchant that is registered pursuant to section 4f(a)(1) of this Act and also registered as a broker or dealer pursuant to section 15(b)(1) of the Securities Exchange Act of 1934 may, pursuant to a portfolio margining program approved by the Securities and Exchange Commission pursuant to section 19(b) of the Securities Exchange Act of 1934, hold in a portfolio margining account carried as a securities account subject to section 15(c)(3) of the Securities Exchange Act of 1934 and the rules and regulations thereunder, a contract for the purchase or sale of a commodity for future delivery or an option on such a contract, and any money, securities or other property received from a customer to margin, guarantee or secure such a contract, or accruing to a customer as the result of such a contract. The Commission shall consult with the Securities and Exchange Commission to adopt rules to ensure that such transactions and accounts are subject to comparable requirements to the extent practical for similar products.".

(c) DUTY OF COMMODITY FUTURES TRADING COMMISSION.—Section 20 of the Commodity Exchange Act (7 U.S.C. 24) is amended by adding at the end the following:

"(c) The Commission shall exercise its authority to ensure that securities held in a portfolio margining account carried as a futures account are customer property and the owners of those accounts are customers for the purposes of subchapter IV of chapter 7 of title 11 of the United States Code.".

[Explanation at ¶ 3025.]

[¶ 10,714] ACT SEC. 714. ABUSIVE SWAPS.

The Commodity Futures Trading Commission or the Securities and Exchange Commission, or both, individually may, by rule or order—

(1) collect information as may be necessary concerning the markets for any types of—

(A) swap (as defined in section 1a of the Commodity Exchange Act (7 U.S.C. 1a)); or

(B) security-based swap (as defined in section 1a of the Commodity Exchange Act (7 U.S.C. 1a)); and

(2) issue a report with respect to any types of swaps or security-based swaps that the Commodity Futures Trading Commission or the Securities and Exchange Commission determines to be detrimental to—

(A) the stability of a financial market; or

(B) participants in a financial market.

[Explanation at ¶ 3015.]

[¶ 10,715] ACT SEC. 715. AUTHORITY TO PROHIBIT PARTICIPATION IN SWAP ACTIVITIES.

Except as provided in section 4 of the Commodity Exchange Act (7 U.S.C. 6), if the Commodity Futures Trading Commission or the Securities and Exchange Commission determines that the regulation of swaps or security-based swaps markets in a foreign country undermines the stability of the United States financial system, either Commission, in consultation with the Secretary of the Treasury, may prohibit an entity domiciled in the foreign country from participating in the United States in any swap or security-based swap activities.

[Explanation at ¶ 3015.]

[¶ 10,716] ACT SEC. 716. PROHIBITION AGAINST FEDERAL GOVERNMENT BAILOUTS OF SWAPS ENTITIES.

(a) PROHIBITION ON FEDERAL ASSISTANCE.—Notwithstanding any other provision of law (including regulations), no Federal assistance may be provided to any swaps entity with respect to any swap, security-based swap, or other activity of the swaps entity.

(b) DEFINITIONS.—In this section:

(1) FEDERAL ASSISTANCE.—The term "Federal assistance" means the use of any advances from any Federal Reserve credit facility or discount window that is not part of a program or facility with broad-based eligibility under section 13(3)(A) of the Federal Reserve Act, Federal Deposit Insurance Corporation insurance or guarantees for the purpose of—

(A) making any loan to, or purchasing any stock, equity interest, or debt obligation of, any swaps entity;

(B) purchasing the assets of any swaps entity;

(C) guaranteeing any loan or debt issuance of any swaps entity; or

(D) entering into any assistance arrangement (including tax breaks), loss sharing, or profit sharing with any swaps entity.

(2) SWAPS ENTITY.—

(A) IN GENERAL.—The term "swaps entity" means any swap dealer, security-based swap dealer, major swap participant, major security-based swap participant, that is registered under—

(i) the Commodity Exchange Act (7 U.S.C. 1 et seq.); or

(ii) the Securities Exchange Act of 1934 (15 U.S.C. 78a et seq.).

(B) EXCLUSION.—The term "swaps entity" does not include any major swap participant or major security-based swap participant that is an insured depository institution.

(c) AFFILIATES OF INSURED DEPOSITORY INSTITUTIONS.—The prohibition on Federal assistance contained in subsection (a) does not apply to and shall not prevent an insured depository institution from having or establishing an affiliate which is a swaps entity, as long as such insured depository institution is part of a bank holding company, or savings and loan holding company, that is supervised by the Federal Reserve and such swaps entity affiliate complies with sections 23A and 23B of the Federal Reserve Act and such other requirements as the Commodity Futures Trading Commission or the Securities Exchange Commission, as appropriate, and the Board of Governors of the Federal Reserve System, may determine to be necessary and appropriate.

(d) ONLY BONA FIDE HEDGING AND TRADITIONAL BANK ACTIVITIES PERMITTED.—The prohibition in subsection (a) shall apply to any insured depository institution unless the insured depository institution limits its swap or security-based swap activities to:

(1) Hedging and other similar risk mitigating activities directly related to the insured depository institution's activities.

(2) Acting as a swaps entity for swaps or security-based swaps involving rates or reference assets that are permissible for investment by a national bank under the paragraph designated as "Seventh." of section 5136 of the Revised Statutes of the United States (12 U.S.C. 24), other than as described in paragraph (3).

(3) LIMITATION ON CREDIT DEFAULT SWAPS.—Acting as a swaps entity for credit default swaps, including swaps or security-based swaps referencing the credit risk of asset-backed securities as defined in section 3(a)(77) of the Securities Exchange Act of 1934 (15 U.S.C. 78c(a)(77)) (as amended by this Act) shall not be considered a bank permissible activity for purposes of subsection (d)(2) unless such swaps or security-based swaps are cleared by a derivatives clearing organization (as such term is defined in section 1a of the Commodity Exchange Act (7 U.S.C. 1a)) or a clearing agency (as such term is defined in section 3 of the Securities Exchange Act (15 U.S.C. 78c)) that is registered, or exempt from registration, as a derivatives clearing organization under

the Commodity Exchange Act or as a clearing agency under the Securities Exchange Act, respectively.

(e) EXISTING SWAPS AND SECURITY-BASED SWAPS.—The prohibition in subsection (a) shall only apply to swaps or security-based swaps entered into by an insured depository institution after the end of the transition period described in subsection (f).

(f) TRANSITION PERIOD.—To the extent an insured depository institution qualifies as a "swaps entity" and would be subject to the Federal assistance prohibition in subsection (a), the appropriate Federal banking agency, after consulting with and considering the views of the Commodity Futures Trading Commission or the Securities Exchange Commission, as appropriate, shall permit the insured depository institution up to 24 months to divest the swaps entity or cease the activities that require registration as a swaps entity. In establishing the appropriate transition period to effect such divestiture or cessation of activities, which may include making the swaps entity an affiliate of the insured depository institution, the appropriate Federal banking agency shall take into account and make written findings regarding the potential impact of such divestiture or cessation of activities on the insured depository institution's (1) mortgage lending, (2) small business lending, (3) job creation, and (4) capital formation versus the potential negative impact on insured depositors and the Deposit Insurance Fund of the Federal Deposit Insurance Corporation. The appropriate Federal banking agency may consider such other factors as may be appropriate. The appropriate Federal banking agency may place such conditions on the insured depository institution's divestiture or ceasing of activities of the swaps entity as it deems necessary and appropriate. The transition period under this subsection may be extended by the appropriate Federal banking agency, after consultation with the Commodity Futures Trading Commission and the Securities and Exchange Commission, for a period of up to 1 additional year.

(g) EXCLUDED ENTITIES.—For purposes of this section, the term "swaps entity" shall not include any insured depository institution under the Federal Deposit Insurance Act or a covered financial company under title II which is in a conservatorship, receivership, or a bridge bank operated by the Federal Deposit Insurance Corporation.

(h) EFFECTIVE DATE.—The prohibition in subsection (a) shall be effective 2 years following the date on which this Act is effective.

(i) LIQUIDATION REQUIRED.—

(1) IN GENERAL.—

(A) FDIC INSURED INSTITUTIONS.—All swaps entities that are FDIC insured institutions that are put into receivership or declared insolvent as a result of swap or security-based swap activity of the swaps entities shall be subject to the termination or transfer of that swap or security-based swap activity in accordance with applicable law prescribing the treatment of those contracts. No taxpayer funds shall be used to prevent the receivership of any swap entity resulting from swap or security-based swap activity of the swaps entity.

(B) INSTITUTIONS THAT POSE A SYSTEMIC RISK AND ARE SUBJECT TO HEIGHTENED PRUDENTIAL SUPERVISION AS REGULATED UNDER SECTION 113.—All swaps entities that are institutions that pose a systemic risk and are subject to heightened prudential supervision as regulated under section 113, that are put into receivership or declared insolvent as a result of swap or security-based swap activity of the swaps entities shall be subject to the termination or transfer of that swap or security-based swap activity in accordance with applicable law prescribing the treatment of those contracts. No taxpayer funds shall be used to prevent the receivership of any swap entity resulting from swap or security-based swap activity of the swaps entity.

(C) NON-FDIC INSURED, NON-SYSTEMICALLY SIGNIFICANT INSTITUTIONS NOT SUBJECT TO HEIGHTENED PRUDENTIAL SUPERVISION AS REGULATED UNDER SECTION 113.—No taxpayer resources shall be used for the orderly liquidation of any swaps entities that are non-FDIC insured, non-systemically significant institutions not subject to heightened prudential supervision as regulated under section 113.

(2) RECOVERY OF FUNDS.—All funds expended on the termination or transfer of the swap or security-based swap activity of the swaps entity shall be recovered in accordance with applicable

law from the disposition of assets of such swap entity or through assessments, including on the financial sector as provided under applicable law.

(3) NO LOSSES TO TAXPAYERS.—Taxpayers shall bear no losses from the exercise of any authority under this title.

(j) PROHIBITION ON UNREGULATED COMBINATION OF SWAPS ENTITIES AND BANKING.—At no time following adoption of the rules in subsection (k) may a bank or bank holding company be permitted to be or become a swap entity unless it conducts its swap or security-based swap activity in compliance with such minimum standards set by its prudential regulator as are reasonably calculated to permit the swaps entity to conduct its swap or security-based swap activities in a safe and sound manner and mitigate systemic risk.

(k) RULES.—In prescribing rules, the prudential regulator for a swaps entity shall consider the following factors:

(1) The expertise and managerial strength of the swaps entity, including systems for effective oversight.

(2) The financial strength of the swaps entity.

(3) Systems for identifying, measuring and controlling risks arising from the swaps entity's operations.

(4) Systems for identifying, measuring and controlling the swaps entity's participation in existing markets.

(5) Systems for controlling the swaps entity's participation or entry into in new markets and products.

(l) AUTHORITY OF THE FINANCIAL STABILITY OVERSIGHT COUNCIL.—The Financial Stability Oversight Council may determine that, when other provisions established by this Act are insufficient to effectively mitigate systemic risk and protect taxpayers, that swaps entities may no longer access Federal assistance with respect to any swap, security-based swap, or other activity of the swaps entity. Any such determination by the Financial Stability Oversight Council of a prohibition of federal assistance shall be made on an institution-by-institution basis, and shall require the vote of not fewer than two-thirds of the members of the Financial Stability Oversight Council, which must include the vote by the Chairman of the Council, the Chairman of the Board of Governors of the Federal Reserve System, and the Chairperson of the Federal Deposit Insurance Corporation. Notice and hearing requirements for such determinations shall be consistent with the standards provided in title I.

(m) BAN ON PROPRIETARY TRADING IN DERIVATIVES.—An insured depository institution shall comply with the prohibition on proprietary trading in derivatives as required by section 619 of the Dodd-Frank Wall Street Reform and Consumer Protection Act.

[Explanation at ¶ 3030.]

[¶ 10,717] ACT SEC. 717. NEW PRODUCT APPROVAL CFTC—SEC PROCESS.

(a) AMENDMENTS TO THE COMMODITY EXCHANGE ACT.—Section 2(a)(1)(C) of the Commodity Exchange Act (7 U.S.C. 2(a)(1)(C)) is amended—

(1) in clause (i) by striking "This" and inserting "(I) Except as provided in subclause (II), this"; and

(2) by adding at the end of clause (i) the following:

"(II) This Act shall apply to and the Commission shall have jurisdiction with respect to accounts, agreements, and transactions involving, and may permit the listing for trading pursuant to section 5c(c) of, a put, call, or other option on 1 or more securities (as defined in section 2(a)(1) of the Securities Act of 1933 or section 3(a)(10) of the Securities Exchange Act of 1934 on the date of enactment of the Futures Trading Act of 1982), including any group or index of such securities, or any interest therein or based on the value thereof, that is exempted by the Securities and Exchange Commission pursuant to section 36(a)(1) of the Securities Exchange Act of 1934 with the condition that the Commission exercise concurrent jurisdiction over such put, call, or other option; provided, however, that nothing in this paragraph shall be construed to affect the jurisdiction and authority of the Securities and Exchange Commission over such put, call, or other option.".

(b) AMENDMENTS TO THE SECURITIES EXCHANGE ACT OF 1934.—The Securities Exchange Act of 1934 is amended by adding the following section after section 3A (15 U.S.C. 78c-1):

"SEC. 3B. SECURITIES-RELATED DERIVATIVES.

"(a) Any agreement, contract, or transaction (or class thereof) that is exempted by the Commodity Futures Trading Commission pursuant to section 4(c)(1) of the Commodity Exchange Act (7 U.S.C. 6(c)(1)) with the condition that the Commission exercise concurrent jurisdiction over such agreement, contract, or transaction (or class thereof) shall be deemed a security for purposes of the securities laws.

"(b) With respect to any agreement, contract, or transaction (or class thereof) that is exempted by the Commodity Futures Trading Commission pursuant to section 4(c)(1) of the Commodity Exchange Act (7 U.S.C. 6(c)(1)) with the condition that the Commission exercise concurrent jurisdiction over such agreement, contract, or transaction (or class thereof), references in the securities laws to the 'purchase' or 'sale' of a security shall be deemed to include the execution, termination (prior to its scheduled maturity date), assignment, exchange, or similar transfer or conveyance of, or extinguishing of rights or obligations under such agreement, contract, or transaction, as the context may require.".

(c) AMENDMENT TO SECURITIES EXCHANGE ACT OF 1934.—Section 19(b) of the Securities Exchange Act of 1934 (15 U.S.C. 78s(b)) is amended by adding at the end the following:

"(10) Notwithstanding paragraph (2), the time period within which the Commission is required by order to approve a proposed rule change or institute proceedings to determine whether the proposed rule change should be disapproved is stayed pending a determination by the Commission upon the request of the Commodity Futures Trading Commission or its Chairman that the Commission issue a determination as to whether a product that is the subject of such proposed rule change is a security pursuant to section 718 of the Wall Street Transparency and Accountability Act of 2010.".

(d) AMENDMENT TO COMMODITY EXCHANGE ACT.—Section 5c(c)(1) of the Commodity Exchange Act (7 U.S.C. 7a-2(c)(1)) is amended—

(1) by striking "Subject to paragraph (2)" and inserting the following:

"(A) ELECTION.—Subject to paragraph (2)"; and

(2) by adding at the end the following:

"(B) CERTIFICATION.—The certification of a product pursuant to this paragraph shall be stayed pending a determination by the Commission upon the request of the Securities and Exchange Commission or its Chairman that the Commission issue a determination as to whether the product that is the subject of such certification is a contract of sale of a commodity for future delivery, an option on such a contract, or an option on a commodity pursuant to section 718 of the Wall Street Transparency and Accountability Act of 2010.".

[Explanation at ¶ 3035.]

[¶ 10,718] ACT SEC. 718. DETERMINING STATUS OF NOVEL DERIVATIVE PRODUCTS.

(a) PROCESS FOR DETERMINING THE STATUS OF A NOVEL DERIVATIVE PRODUCT.—

(1) NOTICE.—

(A) IN GENERAL.—Any person filing a proposal to list or trade a novel derivative product that may have elements of both securities and contracts of sale of a commodity for future delivery (or options on such contracts or options on commodities) may concurrently provide notice and furnish a copy of such filing with the Securities and Exchange Commission and the Commodity Futures Trading Commission. Any such notice shall state that notice has been made with both Commissions.

(B) NOTIFICATION.—If no concurrent notice is made pursuant to subparagraph (A), within 5 business days after determining that a proposal that seeks to list or trade a novel derivative product may have elements of both securities and contracts of sale of a commodity for future delivery (or options on such contracts or options on commodities), the Securities and Exchange Commission or the Commodity Futures Trading Commission, as applicable, shall notify the other Commission and provide a copy of such filing to the other Commission.

(2) REQUEST FOR DETERMINATION.—

(A) IN GENERAL.—No later than 21 days after receipt of a notice under paragraph (1), or upon its own initiative if no such notice is received, the Commodity Futures Trading Commission may request that the Securities and Exchange Commission issue a determination as to whether a product is a security, as defined in section 3(a)(10) of the Securities Exchange Act of 1934 (15 U.S.C. 78c(a)(10)).

(B) REQUEST.—No later than 21 days after receipt of a notice under paragraph (1), or upon its own initiative if no such notice is received, the Securities and Exchange Commission may request that the Commodity Futures Trading Commission issue a determination as to whether a product is a contract of sale of a commodity for future delivery, an option on such a contract, or an option on a commodity subject to the Commodity Futures Trading Commission's exclusive jurisdiction under section 2(a)(1)(A) of the Commodity Exchange Act (7 U.S.C. 2(a)(1)(A)).

(C) REQUIREMENT RELATING TO REQUEST.—A request under subparagraph (A) or (B) shall be made by submitting such request, in writing, to the Securities and Exchange Commission or the Commodity Futures Trading Commission, as applicable.

(D) EFFECT.—Nothing in this paragraph shall be construed to prevent—

(i) the Commodity Futures Trading Commission from requesting that the Securities and Exchange Commission grant an exemption pursuant to section 36(a)(1) of the Securities Exchange Act of 1934 (15 U.S.C. 78mm(a)(1)) with respect to a product that is the subject of a filing under paragraph (1); or

(ii) the Securities and Exchange Commission from requesting that the Commodity Futures Trading Commission grant an exemption pursuant to section 4(c)(1) of the Commodity Exchange Act (7 U.S.C. 6(c)(1)) with respect to a product that is the subject of a filing under paragraph (1),

Provided, however, that nothing in this subparagraph shall be construed to require the Commodity Futures Trading Commission or the Securities and Exchange Commission to issue an exemption requested pursuant to this subparagraph; *provided further*, That an order granting or denying an exemption described in this subparagraph and issued under paragraph (3)(B) shall not be subject to judicial review pursuant to subsection (b).

(E) WITHDRAWAL OF REQUEST.—A request under subparagraph (A) or (B) may be withdrawn by the Commission making the request at any time prior to a determination being made pursuant to paragraph (3) for any reason by providing written notice to the head of the other Commission.

(3) DETERMINATION.—Notwithstanding any other provision of law, no later than 120 days after the date of receipt of a request—

(A) under subparagraph (A) or (B) of paragraph (2), unless such request has been withdrawn pursuant to paragraph (2)(E), the Securities and Exchange Commission or the Commodity Futures Trading Commission, as applicable, shall, by order, issue the determination requested in subparagraph (A) or (B) of paragraph (2), as applicable, and the reasons therefor; or

(B) under paragraph (2)(D), unless such request has been withdrawn, the Securities and Exchange Commission or the Commodity Futures Trading Commission, as applicable, shall grant an exemption or provide reasons for not granting such exemption, provided that any decision by the Securities and Exchange Commission not to grant such exemption shall not be reviewable under section 25 of the Securities Exchange Act of 1934 (15 U.S.C. 78y).

(b) JUDICIAL RESOLUTION.—

(1) IN GENERAL.—The Commodity Futures Trading Commission or the Securities and Exchange Commission may petition the United States Court of Appeals for the District of Columbia Circuit for review of a final order of the other Commission issued pursuant to subsection (a)(3)(A), with respect to a novel derivative product that may have elements of both securities

and contracts of sale of a commodity for future delivery (or options on such contracts or options on commodities) that it believes affects its statutory jurisdiction within 60 days after the date of entry of such order, a written petition requesting a review of the order. Any such proceeding shall be expedited by the Court of Appeals.

(2) TRANSMITTAL OF PETITION AND RECORD.—A copy of a petition described in paragraph (1) shall be transmitted not later than 1 business day after filing by the complaining Commission to the responding Commission. On receipt of the petition, the responding Commission shall file with the court a copy of the order under review and any documents referred to therein, and any other materials prescribed by the court.

(3) STANDARD OF REVIEW.—The court, in considering a petition filed pursuant to paragraph (1), shall give no deference to, or presumption in favor of, the views of either Commission.

(4) JUDICIAL STAY.—The filing of a petition by the complaining Commission pursuant to paragraph (1) shall operate as a stay of the order, until the date on which the determination of the court is final (including any appeal of the determination).

[Explanation at ¶ 3040.]

[¶ 10,719] ACT SEC. 719. STUDIES.

(a) STUDY ON EFFECTS OF POSITION LIMITS ON TRADING ON EXCHANGES IN THE UNITED STATES.—

(1) STUDY.—The Commodity Futures Trading Commission, in consultation with each entity that is a designated contract market under the Commodity Exchange Act, shall conduct a study of the effects (if any) of the position limits imposed pursuant to the other provisions of this title on excessive speculation and on the movement of transactions from exchanges in the United States to trading venues outside the United States.

(2) REPORT TO THE CONGRESS.—Within 12 months after the imposition of position limits pursuant to the other provisions of this title, the Commodity Futures Trading Commission, in consultation with each entity that is a designated contract market under the Commodity Exchange Act, shall submit to the Congress a report on the matters described in paragraph (1).

(3) REQUIRED HEARING.—Within 30 legislative days after the submission to the Congress of the report described in paragraph (2), the Committee on Agriculture of the House of Representatives shall hold a hearing examining the findings of the report.

(4) BIENNIAL REPORTING.—In addition to the study required in paragraph (1), the Chairman of the Commodity Futures Trading Commission shall prepare and submit to the Congress biennial reports on the growth or decline of the derivatives markets in the United States and abroad, which shall include assessments of the causes of any such growth or decline, the effectiveness of regulatory regimes in managing systemic risk, a comparison of the costs of compliance at the time of the report for market participants subject to regulation by the United States with the costs of compliance in December 2008 for the market participants, and the quality of the available data. In preparing the report, the Chairman shall solicit the views of, consult with, and address the concerns raised by, market participants, regulators, legislators, and other interested parties.

(b) STUDY ON FEASIBILITY OF REQUIRING USE OF STANDARDIZED ALGORITHMIC DESCRIPTIONS FOR FINANCIAL DERIVATIVES.—

(1) IN GENERAL.—The Securities and Exchange Commission and the Commodity Futures Trading Commission shall conduct a joint study of the feasibility of requiring the derivatives industry to adopt standardized computer-readable algorithmic descriptions which may be used to describe complex and standardized financial derivatives.

(2) GOALS.—The algorithmic descriptions defined in the study shall be designed to facilitate computerized analysis of individual derivative contracts and to calculate net exposures to complex derivatives. The algorithmic descriptions shall be optimized for simultaneous use by—

(A) commercial users and traders of derivatives;

(B) derivative clearing houses, exchanges and electronic trading platforms;

(C) trade repositories and regulator investigations of market activities; and

(D) systemic risk regulators.

The study will also examine the extent to which the algorithmic description, together with standardized and extensible legal definitions, may serve as the binding legal definition of derivative contracts. The study will examine the logistics of possible implementations of standardized algorithmic descriptions for derivatives contracts. The study shall be limited to electronic formats for exchange of derivative contract descriptions and will not contemplate disclosure of proprietary valuation models.

(3) INTERNATIONAL COORDINATION.—In conducting the study, the Securities and Exchange Commission and the Commodity Futures Trading Commission shall coordinate the study with international financial institutions and regulators as appropriate and practical.

(4) REPORT.—Within 8 months after the date of the enactment of this Act, the Securities and Exchange Commission and the Commodity Futures Trading Commission shall jointly submit to the Committees on Agriculture and on Financial Services of the House of Representatives and the Committees on Agriculture, Nutrition, and Forestry and on Banking, Housing, and Urban Affairs of the Senate a written report which contains the results of the study required by paragraphs (1) through (3).

(c) INTERNATIONAL SWAP REGULATION.—

(1) IN GENERAL.—The Commodity Futures Trading Commission and the Securities and Exchange Commission shall jointly conduct a study—

(A) relating to—

(i) swap regulation in the United States, Asia, and Europe; and

(ii) clearing house and clearing agency regulation in the United States, Asia, and Europe; and

(B) that identifies areas of regulation that are similar in the United States, Asia and Europe and other areas of regulation that could be harmonized

(2) REPORT.—Not later than 18 months after the date of enactment of this Act, the Commodity Futures Trading Commission and the Securities and Exchange Commission shall submit to the Committee on Agriculture, Nutrition, and Forestry and the Committee on Banking, Housing, and Urban Affairs of the Senate and the Committee on Agriculture and the Committee on Financial Services of the House of Representatives a report that includes a description of the results of the study under subsection (a), including—

(A) identification of the major exchanges and their regulator in each geographic area for the trading of swaps and security-based swaps including a listing of the major contracts and their trading volumes and notional values as well as identification of the major swap dealers participating in such markets;

(B) identification of the major clearing houses and clearing agencies and their regulator in each geographic area for the clearing of swaps and security-based swaps, including a listing of the major contracts and the clearing volumes and notional values as well as identification of the major clearing members of such clearing houses and clearing agencies in such markets;

(C) a description of the comparative methods of clearing swaps in the United States, Asia, and Europe; and

(D) a description of the various systems used for establishing margin on individual swaps, security-based swaps, and swap portfolios.

(d) STABLE VALUE CONTRACTS.—

(1) DETERMINATION.—

(A) STATUS.—Not later than 15 months after the date of the enactment of this Act, the Securities and Exchange Commission and the Commodity Futures Trading Commission shall, jointly, conduct a study to determine whether stable value contracts fall within the definition of a swap. In making the determination required under this subparagraph, the Commissions jointly shall consult with the Department of Labor, the Department of the Treasury, and the State entities that regulate the issuers of stable value contracts.

(B) REGULATIONS.—If the Commissions determine that stable value contracts fall within the definition of a swap, the Commissions jointly shall determine if an exemption for stable value contracts from the definition of swap is appropriate and in the public interest. The Commissions shall issue regulations implementing the determinations required under this paragraph. Until the effective date of such regulations, and notwithstanding any other provision of this title, the requirements of this title shall not apply to stable value contracts.

(C) LEGAL CERTAINTY.—Stable value contracts in effect prior to the effective date of the regulations described in subparagraph (B) shall not be considered swaps.

(2) DEFINITION.—For purposes of this subsection, the term "stable value contract" means any contract, agreement, or transaction that provides a crediting interest rate and guaranty or financial assurance of liquidity at contract or book value prior to maturity offered by a bank, insurance company, or other State or federally regulated financial institution for the benefit of any individual or commingled fund available as an investment in an employee benefit plan (as defined in section 3(3) of the Employee Retirement Income Security Act of 1974, including plans described in section 3(32) of such Act) subject to participant direction, an eligible deferred compensation plan (as defined in section 457(b) of the Internal Revenue Code of 1986) that is maintained by an eligible employer described in section 457(e)(1)(A) of such Code, an arrangement described in section 403(b) of such Code, or a qualified tuition program (as defined in section 529 of such Code).

[Explanation at ¶ 3050.]

[¶ 10,720] ACT SEC. 720. MEMORANDUM.

(a)(1) The Commodity Futures Trading Commission and the Federal Energy Regulatory Commission shall, not later than 180 days after the date of the enactment of this Act, negotiate a memorandum of understanding to establish procedures for—

(A) applying their respective authorities in a manner so as to ensure effective and efficient regulation in the public interest;

(B) resolving conflicts concerning overlapping jurisdiction between the 2 agencies; and

(C) avoiding, to the extent possible, conflicting or duplicative regulation.

(2) Such memorandum and any subsequent amendments to the memorandum shall be promptly submitted to the appropriate committees of Congress.

(b) The Commodity Futures Trading Commission and the Federal Energy Regulatory Commission shall, not later than 180 days after the date of the enactment of this section, negotiate a memorandum of understanding to share information that may be requested where either Commission is conducting an investigation into potential manipulation, fraud, or market power abuse in markets subject to such Commission's regulation or oversight. Shared information shall remain subject to the same restrictions on disclosure applicable to the Commission initially holding the information.

[Explanation at ¶ 3015.]

PART II—REGULATION OF SWAP MARKETS

[¶ 10,721] ACT SEC. 721. DEFINITIONS.

(a) IN GENERAL.—Section 1a of the Commodity Exchange Act (7 U.S.C. 1a) is amended—

(1) by redesignating paragraphs (2), (3) and (4), (5) through (17), (18) through (23), (24) through (28), (29), (30), (31) through (33), and (34) as paragraphs (6), (8) and (9), (11) through (23), (26) through (31), (34) through (38), (40), (41), (44) through (46), and (51), respectively;

(2) by inserting after paragraph (1) the following:

"(2) APPROPRIATE FEDERAL BANKING AGENCY.—The term 'appropriate Federal banking agency'—

"(A) has the meaning given the term in section 3 of the Federal Deposit Insurance Act (12 U.S.C. 1813);

"(B) means the Board in the case of a noninsured State bank; and

"(C) is the Farm Credit Administration for farm credit system institutions.

"(3) ASSOCIATED PERSON OF A SECURITY-BASED SWAP DEALER OR MAJOR SECURITY-BASED SWAP PARTICIPANT.—The term 'associated person of a security-based swap dealer or major security-based swap participant' has the meaning given the term in section 3(a) of the Securities Exchange Act of 1934 (15 U.S.C. 78c(a)).

"(4) ASSOCIATED PERSON OF A SWAP DEALER OR MAJOR SWAP PARTICIPANT.—

"(A) IN GENERAL.—The term 'associated person of a swap dealer or major swap participant' means a person who is associated with a swap dealer or major swap participant as a partner, officer, employee, or agent (or any person occupying a similar status or performing similar functions), in any capacity that involves—

"(i) the solicitation or acceptance of swaps; or

"(ii) the supervision of any person or persons so engaged.

"(B) EXCLUSION.—Other than for purposes of section 4s(b)(6), the term 'associated person of a swap dealer or major swap participant' does not include any person associated with a swap dealer or major swap participant the functions of which are solely clerical or ministerial.

"(5) BOARD.—The term 'Board' means the Board of Governors of the Federal Reserve System.";

(3) by inserting after paragraph (6) (as redesignated by paragraph (1)) the following:

"(7) CLEARED SWAP.—The term 'cleared swap' means any swap that is, directly or indirectly, submitted to and cleared by a derivatives clearing organization registered with the Commission.";

(4) in paragraph (9) (as redesignated by paragraph (1)), by striking "except onions" and all that follows through the period at the end and inserting the following: "except onions (as provided by the first section of Public Law 85-839 (7 U.S.C. 13-1)) and motion picture box office receipts (or any index, measure, value, or data related to such receipts), and all services, rights, and interests (except motion picture box office receipts, or any index, measure, value or data related to such receipts) in which contracts for future delivery are presently or in the future dealt in.";

(5) by inserting after paragraph (9) (as redesignated by paragraph (1)) the following:

"(10) COMMODITY POOL.—

"(A) IN GENERAL.—The term 'commodity pool' means any investment trust, syndicate, or similar form of enterprise operated for the purpose of trading in commodity interests, including any—

"(i) commodity for future delivery, security futures product, or swap;

"(ii) agreement, contract, or transaction described in section 2(c)(2)(C)(i) or section 2(c)(2)(D)(i);

"(iii) commodity option authorized under section 4c; or

"(iv) leverage transaction authorized under section 19.

"(B) FURTHER DEFINITION.—The Commission, by rule or regulation, may include within, or exclude from, the term 'commodity pool' any investment trust, syndicate, or similar form of enterprise if the Commission determines that the rule or regulation will effectuate the purposes of this Act.";

(6) by striking paragraph (11) (as redesignated by paragraph (1)) and inserting the following:

"(11) COMMODITY POOL OPERATOR.—

"(A) IN GENERAL.—The term 'commodity pool operator' means any person—

"(i) engaged in a business that is of the nature of a commodity pool, investment trust, syndicate, or similar form of enterprise, and who, in connection therewith, solicits, accepts, or receives from others, funds, securities, or property, either directly or through capital contributions, the sale of stock or other forms of securities, or otherwise, for the purpose of trading in commodity interests, including any—

"(I) commodity for future delivery, security futures product, or swap;

"(II) agreement, contract, or transaction described in section 2(c)(2)(C)(i) or section 2(c)(2)(D)(i);

"(III) commodity option authorized under section 4c; or

"(IV) leverage transaction authorized under section 19; or

"(ii) who is registered with the Commission as a commodity pool operator.

"(B) FURTHER DEFINITION.—The Commission, by rule or regulation, may include within, or exclude from, the term 'commodity pool operator' any person engaged in a business that is of the nature of a commodity pool, investment trust, syndicate, or similar form of enterprise if the Commission determines that the rule or regulation will effectuate the purposes of this Act.";

(7) in paragraph (12) (as redesignated by paragraph (1)), in subparagraph (A)—

(A) in clause (i)—

(i) in subclause (I), by striking "made or to be made on or subject to the rules of a contract market or derivatives transaction execution facility" and inserting ", security futures product, or swap";

(ii) by redesignating subclauses (II) and (III) as subclauses (III) and (IV);

(iii) by inserting after subclause (I) the following:

"(II) any agreement, contract, or transaction described in section 2(c)(2)(C)(i) or section 2(c)(2)(D)(i)"; and

(iv) in subclause (IV) (as so redesignated), by striking "or";

(B) in clause (ii), by striking the period at the end and inserting a semicolon; and

(C) by adding at the end the following:

"(iii) is registered with the Commission as a commodity trading advisor; or

"(iv) the Commission, by rule or regulation, may include if the Commission determines that the rule or regulation will effectuate the purposes of this Act.";

(8) in paragraph (17) (as redesignated by paragraph (1)), in subparagraph (A), in the matter preceding clause (i), by striking "paragraph (12)(A)" and inserting "paragraph (18)(A)";

(9) in paragraph (18) (as redesignated by paragraph (1))—

(A) in subparagraph (A)—

(i) in the matter following clause (vii)(III)—

(I) by striking "section 1a (11)(A)" and inserting "paragraph (17)(A)"; and

(II) by striking "$25,000,000" and inserting "$50,000,000"; and

(ii) in clause (xi), in the matter preceding subclause (I), by striking "total assets in an amount" and inserting "amounts invested on a discretionary basis, the aggregate of which is";

(10) by striking paragraph (22) (as redesignated by paragraph (1)) and inserting the following:

"(22) FLOOR BROKER.—

"(A) IN GENERAL.—The term 'floor broker' means any person—

"(i) who, in or surrounding any pit, ring, post, or other place provided by a contract market for the meeting of persons similarly engaged, shall purchase or sell for any other person—

"(I) any commodity for future delivery, security futures product, or swap; or

"(II) any commodity option authorized under section 4c; or

"(ii) who is registered with the Commission as a floor broker.

"(B) FURTHER DEFINITION.—The Commission, by rule or regulation, may include within, or exclude from, the term 'floor broker' any person in or surrounding any pit, ring, post, or other place provided by a contract market for the meeting of persons similarly engaged who trades for any other person if the Commission determines that the rule or regulation will effectuate the purposes of this Act.";

(11) by striking paragraph (23) (as redesignated by paragraph (1)) and inserting the following:

"(23) FLOOR TRADER.—

"(A) IN GENERAL.—The term 'floor trader' means any person—

"(i) who, in or surrounding any pit, ring, post, or other place provided by a contract market for the meeting of persons similarly engaged, purchases, or sells solely for such person's own account—

"(I) any commodity for future delivery, security futures product, or swap; or

"(II) any commodity option authorized under section 4c; or

"(ii) who is registered with the Commission as a floor trader.

"(B) FURTHER DEFINITION.—The Commission, by rule or regulation, may include within, or exclude from, the term 'floor trader' any person in or surrounding any pit, ring, post, or other place provided by a contract market for the meeting of persons similarly engaged who trades solely for such person's own account if the Commission determines that the rule or regulation will effectuate the purposes of this Act.";

(12) by inserting after paragraph (23) (as redesignated by paragraph (1)) the following:

"(24) FOREIGN EXCHANGE FORWARD.—The term 'foreign exchange forward' means a transaction that solely involves the exchange of 2 different currencies on a specific future date at a fixed rate agreed upon on the inception of the contract covering the exchange.

"(25) FOREIGN EXCHANGE SWAP.—The term 'foreign exchange swap' means a transaction that solely involves—

"(A) an exchange of 2 different currencies on a specific date at a fixed rate that is agreed upon on the inception of the contract covering the exchange; and

"(B) a reverse exchange of the 2 currencies described in subparagraph (A) at a later date and at a fixed rate that is agreed upon on the inception of the contract covering the exchange.";

(13) by striking paragraph (28) (as redesignated by paragraph (1)) and inserting the following:

"(28) FUTURES COMMISSION MERCHANT.—

"(A) IN GENERAL.—The term 'futures commission merchant' means an individual, association, partnership, corporation, or trust—

"(i) that—

"(I) is—

"(aa) engaged in soliciting or in accepting orders for—

"(AA) the purchase or sale of a commodity for future delivery;

"(BB) a security futures product;

"(CC) a swap;

"(DD) any agreement, contract, or transaction described in section 2(c)(2)(C)(i) or section 2(c)(2)(D)(i);

"(EE) any commodity option authorized under section 4c; or

"(FF) any leverage transaction authorized under section 19; or

"(bb) acting as a counterparty in any agreement, contract, or transaction described in section 2(c)(2)(C)(i) or section 2(c)(2)(D)(i); and

"(II) in or in connection with the activities described in items (aa) or (bb) of subclause (I), accepts any money, securities, or property (or extends credit in lieu thereof) to margin, guarantee, or secure any trades or contracts that result or may result therefrom; or

"(ii) that is registered with the Commission as a futures commission merchant.

"(B) FURTHER DEFINITION.—The Commission, by rule or regulation, may include within, or exclude from, the term 'futures commission merchant' any person who engages in soliciting or accepting orders for, or acting as a counterparty in, any agreement, contract, or transaction subject to this Act, and who accepts any money, securities, or property (or extends credit in lieu thereof) to margin, guarantee, or secure any trades or contracts that result or may result therefrom, if the Commission determines that the rule or regulation will effectuate the purposes of this Act.";

(14) in paragraph (30) (as redesignated by paragraph (1)), in subparagraph (B), by striking "state" and inserting "State";

(15) by striking paragraph (31) (as redesignated by paragraph (1)) and inserting the following:

"(31) INTRODUCING BROKER.—

"(A) IN GENERAL.—The term 'introducing broker' means any person (except an individual who elects to be and is registered as an associated person of a futures commission merchant)—

"(i) who—

"(I) is engaged in soliciting or in accepting orders for—

"(aa) the purchase or sale of any commodity for future delivery, security futures product, or swap;

"(bb) any agreement, contract, or transaction described in section 2(c)(2)(C)(i) or section 2(c)(2)(D)(i);

"(cc) any commodity option authorized under section 4c; or

"(dd) any leverage transaction authorized under section 19; and

"(II) does not accept any money, securities, or property (or extend credit in lieu thereof) to margin, guarantee, or secure any trades or contracts that result or may result therefrom; or

"(ii) who is registered with the Commission as an introducing broker.

"(B) FURTHER DEFINITION.—The Commission, by rule or regulation, may include within, or exclude from, the term 'introducing broker' any person who engages in soliciting or accepting orders for any agreement, contract, or transaction subject to this Act, and who does not accept any money, securities, or property (or extend credit in lieu thereof) to margin, guarantee, or secure any trades or contracts that result or may result therefrom, if the Commission determines that the rule or regulation will effectuate the purposes of this Act.";

(16) by inserting after paragraph (31) (as redesignated by paragraph (1)) the following:

"(32) MAJOR SECURITY-BASED SWAP PARTICIPANT.—The term 'major security-based swap participant' has the meaning given the term in section 3(a) of the Securities Exchange Act of 1934 (15 U.S.C. 78c(a)).

"(33) MAJOR SWAP PARTICIPANT.—

"(A) IN GENERAL.—The term 'major swap participant' means any person who is not a swap dealer, and—

"(i) maintains a substantial position in swaps for any of the major swap categories as determined by the Commission, excluding—

"(I) positions held for hedging or mitigating commercial risk; and

"(II) positions maintained by any employee benefit plan (or any contract held by such a plan) as defined in paragraphs (3) and (32) of section 3 of the Employee Retirement Income Security Act of 1974 (29 U.S.C. 1002) for the primary purpose of hedging or mitigating any risk directly associated with the operation of the plan;

"(ii) whose outstanding swaps create substantial counterparty exposure that could have serious adverse effects on the financial stability of the United States banking system or financial markets; or

"(iii)

(I) is a financial entity that is highly leveraged relative to the amount of capital it holds and that is not subject to capital requirements established by an appropriate Federal banking agency; and

"(II) maintains a substantial position in outstanding swaps in any major swap category as determined by the Commission.

"(B) DEFINITION OF SUBSTANTIAL POSITION.—For purposes of subparagraph (A), the Commission shall define by rule or regulation the term 'substantial position' at the threshold that the Commission determines to be prudent for the effective monitoring, management, and oversight of entities that are systemically important or can significantly impact the financial system of the United States. In setting the definition under this subparagraph, the Commission shall consider the person's relative position in uncleared as opposed to cleared swaps and may take into consideration the value and quality of collateral held against counterparty exposures.

"(C) SCOPE OF DESIGNATION.—For purposes of subparagraph (A), a person may be designated as a major swap participant for 1 or more categories of swaps without being classified as a major swap participant for all classes of swaps.

"(D) EXCLUSIONS.—The definition under this paragraph shall not include an entity whose primary business is providing financing, and uses derivatives for the purpose of hedging underlying commercial risks related to interest rate and foreign currency exposures, 90 percent or more of which arise from financing that facilitates the purchase or lease of products, 90 percent or more of which are manufactured by the parent company or another subsidiary of the parent company.";

(17) by inserting after paragraph (38) (as redesignated by paragraph (1)) the following:

"(39) PRUDENTIAL REGULATOR.—The term 'prudential regulator' means—

"(A) the Board in the case of a swap dealer, major swap participant, security-based swap dealer, or major security-based swap participant that is—

"(i) a State-chartered bank that is a member of the Federal Reserve System;

"(ii) a State-chartered branch or agency of a foreign bank;

"(iii) any foreign bank which does not operate an insured branch;

"(iv) any organization operating under section 25A of the Federal Reserve Act or having an agreement with the Board under section 225 of the Federal Reserve Act;

"(v) any bank holding company (as defined in section 2 of the Bank Holding Company Act of 1965 (12 U.S.C. 1841)), any foreign bank (as defined in section 1(b)(7) of the International Banking Act of 1978 (12 U.S.C. 3101(b)(7)) that is treated as a bank holding company under section 8(a) of the International Banking Act of 1978 (12 U.S.C. 3106(a)), and any subsidiary of such a company or foreign bank (other than a subsidiary that is described in subparagraph (A) or (B) or that is required to be registered with the Commission as a swap dealer or major swap participant under this Act or with the Securities and Exchange Commission as a security-based swap dealer or major security-based swap participant);

"(vi) after the transfer date (as defined in section 311 of the Dodd-Frank Wall Street Reform and Consumer Protection Act), any savings and loan holding company (as defined in section 10 of the Home Owners' Loan Act (12 U.S.C. 1467a)) and any subsidiary of such company (other than a subsidiary that is described in subparagraph (A) or (B) or that is required to be registered as a swap dealer or major swap participant with the Commission under this Act or with the Securities and Exchange Commission as a security-based swap dealer or major security-based swap participant); or

"(vii) any organization operating under section 25A of the Federal Reserve Act (12U.S.C. 611 et seq.) or having an agreement with the Board under section 25 of the Federal Reserve Act (12 U.S.C. 601 et seq.);

"(B) the Office of the Comptroller of the Currency in the case of a swap dealer, major swap participant, security-based swap dealer, or major security-based swap participant that is—

"(i) a national bank;

"(ii) a federally chartered branch or agency of a foreign bank; or

"(iii) any Federal savings association;

"(C) the Federal Deposit Insurance Corporation in the case of a swap dealer, major swap participant, security-based swap dealer, or major security-based swap participant that is—

"(i) a State-chartered bank that is not a member of the Federal Reserve System; or

"(ii) any State savings association;

"(D) the Farm Credit Administration, in the case of a swap dealer, major swap participant, security-based swap dealer, or major security-based swap participant that is an institution chartered under the Farm Credit Act of 1971 (12 U.S.C. 2001 et seq.); and

"(E) the Federal Housing Finance Agency in the case of a swap dealer, major swap participant, security-based swap dealer, or major security-based swap participant that is a regulated entity (as such term is defined in section 1303 of the Federal Housing Enterprises Financial Safety and Soundness Act of 1992).";

(18) in paragraph (40) (as redesignated by paragraph (1))—

(A) by striking subparagraph (B);

(B) by redesignating subparagraphs (C), (D), and (E) as subparagraphs (B), (C), and (F), respectively;

(C) in subparagraph (C) (as so redesignated), by striking "and"; and

(D) by inserting after subparagraph (C) (as so redesignated) the following:

"(D) a swap execution facility registered under section 5h;

"(E) a swap data repository registered under section 21; and";

(19) by inserting after paragraph (41) (as redesignated by paragraph (1)) the following:

"(42) SECURITY-BASED SWAP.—The term 'security-based swap' has the meaning given the term in section 3(a) of the Securities Exchange Act of 1934 (15 U.S.C. 78c(a)).

"(43) SECURITY-BASED SWAP DEALER.—The term 'security-based swap dealer' has the meaning given the term in section 3(a) of the Securities Exchange Act of 1934 (15 U.S.C. 78c(a)).";

(20) in paragraph (46) (as redesignated by paragraph (1)), by striking "subject to section 2(h)(7)" and inserting "subject to section 2(h)(5)";

(21) by inserting after paragraph (46) (as redesignated by paragraph (1)) the following:

"(47) SWAP.—

"(A) IN GENERAL.—Except as provided in subparagraph (B), the term 'swap' means any agreement, contract, or transaction—

"(i) that is a put, call, cap, floor, collar, or similar option of any kind that is for the purchase or sale, or based on the value, of 1 or more interest or other rates, currencies, commodities, securities, instruments of indebtedness, indices, quantitative measures, or other financial or economic interests or property of any kind;

"(ii) that provides for any purchase, sale, payment, or delivery (other than a dividend on an equity security) that is dependent on the occurrence, nonoccurrence, or the extent of the occurrence of an event or contingency associated with a potential financial, economic, or commercial consequence;

"(iii) that provides on an executory basis for the exchange, on a fixed or contingent basis, of 1 or more payments based on the value or level of 1 or more interest or other rates, currencies, commodities, securities, instruments of indebtedness, indices, quantitative measures, or other financial or economic interests or property of any kind, or any interest therein or based on the value thereof, and that transfers, as between the parties to the transaction, in whole or in part, the financial risk associated with a future change in any such value or level without also conveying a current or future direct or indirect ownership interest in an asset (including any enterprise or investment pool) or liability that incorporates the financial risk so transferred, including any agreement, contract, or transaction commonly known as—

"(I) an interest rate swap;

"(II) a rate floor;

"(III) a rate cap;

"(IV) a rate collar;

"(V) a cross-currency rate swap;

"(VI) a basis swap;

"(VII) a currency swap;

"(VIII) a foreign exchange swap;

"(IX) a total return swap;

"(X) an equity index swap;

"(XI) an equity swap;

"(XII) a debt index swap;

"(XIII) a debt swap;

"(XIV) a credit spread;

"(XV) a credit default swap;

"(XVI) a credit swap;

"(XVII) a weather swap;

"(XVIII) an energy swap;

"(XIX) a metal swap;

"(XX) an agricultural swap;

"(XXI) an emissions swap; and

"(XXII) a commodity swap;

"(iv) that is an agreement, contract, or transaction that is, or in the future becomes, commonly known to the trade as a swap;

"(v) including any security-based swap agreement which meets the definition of 'swap agreement' as defined in section 206A of the Gramm-Leach-Bliley Act (15 U.S.C. 78c note) of which a material term is based on the price, yield, value, or volatility of any security or any group or index of securities, or any interest therein; or

"(vi) that is any combination or permutation of, or option on, any agreement, contract, or transaction described in any of clauses (i) through (v).

"(B) EXCLUSIONS.—The term 'swap' does not include—

"(i) any contract of sale of a commodity for future delivery (or option on such a contract), leverage contract authorized under section 19, security futures product, or agreement, contract, or transaction described in section 2(c)(2)(C)(i) or section 2(c)(2)(D)(i);

"(ii) any sale of a nonfinancial commodity or security for deferred shipment or delivery, so long as the transaction is intended to be physically settled;

"(iii) any put, call, straddle, option, or privilege on any security, certificate of deposit, or group or index of securities, including any interest therein or based on the value thereof, that is subject to—

"(I) the Securities Act of 1933 (15 U.S.C. 77a et seq.); and

"(II) the Securities Exchange Act of 1934 (15 U.S.C. 78a et seq.);

"(iv) any put, call, straddle, option, or privilege relating to a foreign currency entered into on a national securities exchange registered pursuant to section 6(a) of the Securities Exchange Act of 1934 (15 U.S.C. 78f(a));

"(v) any agreement, contract, or transaction providing for the purchase or sale of 1 or more securities on a fixed basis that is subject to—

"(I) the Securities Act of 1933 (15 U.S.C. 77a et seq.); and

"(II) the Securities Exchange Act of 1934 (15 U.S.C. 78a et seq.);

"(vi) any agreement, contract, or transaction providing for the purchase or sale of 1 or more securities on a contingent basis that is subject to the Securities Act of 1933 (15 U.S.C. 77a et seq.) and the Securities Exchange Act of 1934 (15 U.S.C. 78a et seq.), unless the agreement, contract, or transaction predicates the purchase or sale on the occurrence of a bona fide contingency that might reasonably be expected to affect or be affected by the creditworthiness of a party other than a party to the agreement, contract, or transaction;

"(vii) any note, bond, or evidence of indebtedness that is a security, as defined in section 2(a)(1) of the Securities Act of 1933 (15 U.S.C. 77b(a)(1));

"(viii) any agreement, contract, or transaction that is—

"(I) based on a security; and

"(II) entered into directly or through an underwriter (as defined in section 2(a)(11) of the Securities Act of 1933 (15 U.S.C. 77b(a)(11)) by the issuer of such security for the purposes of raising capital, unless the agreement, contract, or transaction is entered into to manage a risk associated with capital raising;

"(ix) any agreement, contract, or transaction a counterparty of which is a Federal Reserve bank, the Federal Government, or a Federal agency that is expressly backed by the full faith and credit of the United States; and

"(x) any security-based swap, other than a security-based swap as described in subparagraph (D).

"(C) RULE OF CONSTRUCTION REGARDING MASTER AGREEMENTS.—

"(i) IN GENERAL.—Except as provided in clause (ii), the term 'swap' includes a master agreement that provides for an agreement, contract, or transaction that is a swap under subparagraph (A), together with each supplement to any master agreement, without regard to whether the master agreement contains an agreement, contract, or transaction that is not a swap pursuant to subparagraph (A).

"(ii) EXCEPTION.—For purposes of clause (i), the master agreement shall be considered to be a swap only with respect to each agreement, contract, or transaction covered by the master agreement that is a swap pursuant to subparagraph (A).

"(D) MIXED SWAP.—The term 'security-based swap' includes any agreement, contract, or transaction that is as described in section 3(a)(68)(A) of the Securities Exchange Act of 1934 (15 U.S.C. 78c(a)(68)(A)) and also is based on the value of 1 or more interest or other rates, currencies, commodities, instruments of indebtedness, indices, quantitative measures, other financial or economic interest or property of any kind (other than a single security or a narrow-based security index), or the occurrence, non-occurrence, or the extent of the occurrence of an event or contingency associated with a potential financial, economic, or commercial consequence (other than an event described in subparagraph (A)(iii)).

"(E) TREATMENT OF FOREIGN EXCHANGE SWAPS AND FORWARDS.—

"(i) IN GENERAL.—Foreign exchange swaps and foreign exchange forwards shall be considered swaps under this paragraph unless the Secretary makes a written determination under section 1b that either foreign exchange swaps or foreign exchange forwards or both—

"(I) should be not be regulated as swaps under this Act; and

"(II) are not structured to evade the Dodd-Frank Wall Street Reform and Consumer Protection Act in violation of any rule promulgated by the Commission pursuant to section 721(c) of that Act.

"(ii) CONGRESSIONAL NOTICE; EFFECTIVENESS.—The Secretary shall submit any written determination under clause (i) to the appropriate committees of Congress, including the Committee on Agriculture, Nutrition, and Forestry of the Senate and the Committee on Agriculture of the House of Representatives. Any such written determination by the Secretary shall not be effective until it is submitted to the appropriate committees of Congress.

"(iii) REPORTING.—Notwithstanding a written determination by the Secretary under clause (i), all foreign exchange swaps and foreign exchange forwards shall be reported to either a swap data repository, or, if there is no swap data repository that would accept such swaps or forwards, to the Commission pursuant to section 4r within such time period as the Commission may by rule or regulation prescribe.

"(iv) BUSINESS STANDARDS.—Notwithstanding a written determination by the Secretary pursuant to clause (i), any party to a foreign exchange swap or forward that is a swap dealer or major swap participant shall conform to the business conduct standards contained in section 4s(h).

"(v) SECRETARY.—For purposes of this subparagraph, the term 'Secretary' means the Secretary of the Treasury.

"(F) EXCEPTION FOR CERTAIN FOREIGN EXCHANGE SWAPS AND FORWARDS.—

"(i) REGISTERED ENTITIES.—Any foreign exchange swap and any foreign exchange forward that is listed and traded on or subject to the rules of a designated contract market or a swap execution facility, or that is cleared by a derivatives clearing organization, shall not be exempt from any provision of this Act or amendments made by the Wall Street Transparency and Accountability Act of 2010 prohibiting fraud or manipulation.

"(ii) RETAIL TRANSACTIONS.—Nothing in subparagraph (E) shall affect, or be construed to affect, the applicability of this Act or the jurisdiction of the Commission with respect to agreements, contracts, or transactions in foreign currency pursuant to section 2(c)(2).

"(48) SWAP DATA REPOSITORY.—The term 'swap data repository' means any person that collects and maintains information or records with respect to transactions or positions in, or the terms and conditions of, swaps entered into by third parties for the purpose of providing a centralized recordkeeping facility for swaps.

"(49) SWAP DEALER.—

"(A) IN GENERAL.—The term 'swap dealer' means any person who—

"(i) holds itself out as a dealer in swaps;

"(ii) makes a market in swaps;

"(iii) regularly enters into swaps with counterparties as an ordinary course of business for its own account; or

"(iv) engages in any activity causing the person to be commonly known in the trade as a dealer or market maker in swaps,

provided however, in no event shall an insured depository institution be considered to be a swap dealer to the extent it offers to enter into a swap with a customer in connection with originating a loan with that customer.

"(B) INCLUSION.—A person may be designated as a swap dealer for a single type or single class or category of swap or activities and considered not to be a swap dealer for other types, classes, or categories of swaps or activities.

"(C) EXCEPTION.—The term 'swap dealer' does not include a person that enters into swaps for such person's own account, either individually or in a fiduciary capacity, but not as a part of a regular business.

"(D) DE MINIMIS EXCEPTION.—The Commission shall exempt from designation as a swap dealer an entity that engages in a de minimis quantity of swap dealing in connection with transactions with or on behalf of its customers. The Commission shall promulgate regulations to establish factors with respect to the making of this determination to exempt.

"(50) SWAP EXECUTION FACILITY.—The term 'swap execution facility' means a trading system or platform in which multiple participants have the ability to execute or trade swaps by accepting bids and offers made by multiple participants in the facility or system, through any means of interstate commerce, including any trading facility, that—

"(A) facilitates the execution of swaps between persons; and

"(B) is not a designated contract market.".

(22) in paragraph (51) (as redesignated by paragraph (1)), in subparagraph (A)(i), by striking "partipants" and inserting "participants".

(b) AUTHORITY TO DEFINE TERMS.—The Commodity Futures Trading Commission may adopt a rule to define—

(1) the term "commercial risk"; and

(2) any other term included in an amendment to the Commodity Exchange Act (7 U.S.C. 1 et seq.) made by this subtitle.

(c) MODIFICATION OF DEFINITIONS.—To include transactions and entities that have been structured to evade this subtitle (or an amendment made by this subtitle), the Commodity Futures Trading Commission shall adopt a rule to further define the terms "swap", "swap dealer", "major swap participant", and "eligible contract participant".

(d) EXEMPTIONS.—Section 4(c)(1) of the Commodity Exchange Act (7 U.S.C. 6(c)(1)) is amended by striking "except that" and all that follows through the period at the end and inserting the following: "except that—

"(A) unless the Commission is expressly authorized by any provision described in this subparagraph to grant exemptions, with respect to amendments made by subtitle A of the Wall Street Transparency and Accountability Act of 2010—

"(i) with respect to—

"(I) paragraphs (2), (3), (4), (5), and (7), paragraph (18)(A)(vii)(III), paragraphs (23), (24), (31), (32), (38), (39), (41), (42), (46), (47), (48), and (49) of section 1a, and sections 2(a)(13), 2(c)(1)(D), 4a(a), 4a(b), 4d(c), 4d(d), 4r, 4s, 5b(a), 5b(b), 5(d), 5(g), 5(h), 5b(c), 5b(i), 8e, and 21; and

"(II) section 206(e) of the Gramm-Leach-Bliley Act (Public Law 106-102; 15 U.S.C. 78c note); and

"(ii) in sections 721(c) and 742 of the Dodd-Frank Wall Street Reform and Consumer Protection Act; and

"(B) the Commission and the Securities and Exchange Commission may by rule, regulation, or order jointly exclude any agreement, contract, or transaction from section 2(a)(1)(D) if the Commissions determine that the exemption would be consistent with the public interest.".

(e) CONFORMING AMENDMENTS.—

(1) Section 2(c)(2)(B)(i)(II) of the Commodity Exchange Act (7 U.S.C. 2(c)(2)(B)(i)(II)) is amended—

(A) in item (cc)—

(i) in subitem (AA), by striking "section 1a(20)" and inserting "section 1a"; and

(ii) in subitem (BB), by striking "section 1a(20)" and inserting "section la"; and

(B) in item (dd), by striking "section 1a(12)(A)(ii)" and inserting "section 1a(18)(A)(ii)".

(2) Section 4m(3) of the Commodity Exchange Act (7 U.S.C. 6m(3)) is amended by striking "section 1a(6)" and inserting "section 1a".

(3) Section 4q(a)(1) of the Commodity Exchange Act (7 U.S.C. 6o-1(a)(1)) is amended by striking "section 1a(4)" and inserting "section 1a(9)".

(4) Section 5(e)(1) of the Commodity Exchange Act (7 U.S.C. 7(e)(1)) is amended by striking "section 1a(4)" and inserting "section 1a(9)".

(5) Section 5a(b)(2)(F) of the Commodity Exchange Act (7 U.S.C. 7a(b)(2)(F)) is amended by striking "section 1a(4)" and inserting "section 1a(9)".

(6) Section 5b(a) of the Commodity Exchange Act (7 U.S.C. 7a-1(a)) is amended, in the matter preceding paragraph (1), by striking "section 1a(9)" and inserting "section la".

(7) Section 5c(c)(2)(B) of the Commodity Exchange Act (7 U.S.C. 7a-2(c)(2)(B)) is amended by striking "section 1a(4)" and inserting "section 1a(9)".

(8) Section 6(g)(5)(B)(i) of the Securities Exchange Act of 1934 (15 U.S.C. 78f(g)(5)(B)(i)) is amended—

(A) in subclause (I), by striking "section 1a(12)(B)(ii)" and inserting "section 1a(18)(B)(ii)"; and

(B) in subclause (II), by striking "section 1a(12)" and inserting "section 1a(18)".

(9) Section 402 of the Legal Certainty for Bank Products Act of 2000 (7 U.S.C. 27 et seq.) is amended—

(A) in subsection (a)(7), by striking "section 1a(20)" and inserting "section 1a";

(B) in subsection (b)(2), by striking "section 1a(12)" and inserting "section 1a"; and

(C) in subsection (c), by striking "section 1a(4)" and inserting "section 1a".

(10) The first section of Public Law 85-839 (7 U.S.C. 13-1) is amended in subsection (a), in the first sentence, by inserting "motion picture box office receipts (or any index, measure, value, or data related to such receipts) or" after "sale of".

(f) EFFECTIVE DATE.—Notwithstanding any other provision of this Act, the amendments made by subsection (a)(4) shall take effect on June 1, 2010.

[Explanation at ¶ 3010.]

[¶ 10,722] ACT SEC. 722. JURISDICTION.

(a) EXCLUSIVE JURISDICTION.—Section 2(a)(1) of the Commodity Exchange Act (7 U.S.C. 2(a)(1)) is amended—

(1) in subparagraph (A), in the first sentence—

(A) by inserting "the Wall Street Transparency and Accountability Act of 2010 (including an amendment made by that Act) and" after "otherwise provided in";

(B) by striking "(C) and (D)" and inserting "(C), (D), and (I)";

(C) by striking "(c) through (i) of this section" and inserting "(c) and (f)";

(D) by striking "contracts of sale" and inserting "swaps or contracts of sale"; and

(E) by striking "or derivatives transaction execution facility registered pursuant to section 5 or 5a" and inserting "pursuant to section 5 or a swap execution facility pursuant to section 5h"; and

(2) by adding at the end the following:

"(G)

(i) Nothing in this paragraph shall limit the jurisdiction conferred on the Securities and Exchange Commission by the Wall Street Transparency and Accountability Act of 2010 with regard to security-based swap agreements as defined pursuant to section 3(a)(78) of the Securities Exchange Act of 1934, and security-based swaps.

"(ii) In addition to the authority of the Securities and Exchange Commission described in clause (i), nothing in this subparagraph shall limit or affect any statutory authority of the Commission with respect to an agreement, contract, or transaction described in clause (i).

"(H) Notwithstanding any other provision of law, the Wall Street Transparency and Accountability Act of 2010 shall not apply to, and the Commodity Futures Trading Commission shall have no jurisdiction under such Act (or any amendments to the Commodity Exchange Act made by such Act) with respect to, any security other than a security-based swap.".

(b) REGULATION OF SWAPS UNDER FEDERAL AND STATE LAW.—Section 12 of the Commodity Exchange Act (7 U.S.C. 16) is amended by adding at the end the following:

"(h) REGULATION OF SWAPS AS INSURANCE UNDER STATE LAW.—A swap—

"(1) shall not be considered to be insurance; and

"(2) may not be regulated as an insurance contract under the law of any State.".

(c) AGREEMENTS, CONTRACTS, AND TRANSACTIONS TRADED ON AN ORGANIZED EXCHANGE.—Section 2(c)(2)(A) of the Commodity Exchange Act (7 U.S.C. 2(c)(2)(A)) is amended—

(1) in clause (i), by striking "or" at the end;

(2) by redesignating clause (ii) as clause (iii); and

(3) by inserting after clause (i) the following:

"(ii) a swap; or".

(d) APPLICABILITY.—Section 2 of the Commodity Exchange Act (7 U.S.C. 2) (as amended by section 723(a)(3)) is amended by adding at the end the following:

"(i) APPLICABILITY.—The provisions of this Act relating to swaps that were enacted by the Wall Street Transparency and Accountability Act of 2010 (including any rule prescribed or regulation promulgated under that Act), shall not apply to activities outside the United States unless those activities—

"(1) have a direct and significant connection with activities in, or effect on, commerce of the United States; or

"(2) contravene such rules or regulations as the Commission may prescribe or promulgate as are necessary or appropriate to prevent the evasion of any provision of this Act that was enacted by the Wall Street Transparency and Accountability Act of 2010.".

(e) FEDERAL ENERGY REGULATORY COMMISSION.—Section 2(a)(1) of the Commodity Exchange Act (7 U.S.C. 2(a)(1)) is amended by adding at the end the following:

"(I)

(i) Nothing in this Act shall limit or affect any statutory authority of the Federal Energy Regulatory Commission or a State regulatory authority (as defined in section 3(21) of the Federal Power Act (16 U.S.C. 796(21)) with respect to an agreement, contract, or transaction that is entered into pursuant to a tariff or rate schedule approved by the Federal Energy Regulatory Commission or a State regulatory authority and is—

"(I) not executed, traded, or cleared on a registered entity or trading facility; or

"(II) executed, traded, or cleared on a registered entity or trading facility owned or operated by a regional transmission organization or independent system operator.

"(ii) In addition to the authority of the Federal Energy Regulatory Commission or a State regulatory authority described in clause (i), nothing in this subparagraph shall limit or affect—

"(I) any statutory authority of the Commission with respect to an agreement, contract, or transaction described in clause (i); or

"(II) the jurisdiction of the Commission under subparagraph (A) with respect to an agreement, contract, or transaction that is executed, traded, or cleared on a registered entity or trading facility that is not owned or operated by a regional transmission organization or independent system operator (as defined by sections 3(27) and (28) of the Federal Power Act (16 U.S.C. 796(27), 796(28)).".

(f) PUBLIC INTEREST WAIVER.—Section 4(c) of the Commodity Exchange Act (7 U.S.C. 6(c)) (as amended by section 721(d)) is amended by adding at the end the following:

"(6) If the Commission determines that the exemption would be consistent with the public interest and the purposes of this Act, the Commission shall, in accordance with paragraphs (1) and (2), exempt from the requirements of this Act an agreement, contract, or transaction that is entered into—

"(A) pursuant to a tariff or rate schedule approved or permitted to take effect by the Federal Energy Regulatory Commission;

"(B) pursuant to a tariff or rate schedule establishing rates or charges for, or protocols governing, the sale of electric energy approved or permitted to take effect by the regulatory authority of the State or municipality having jurisdiction to regulate rates and charges for the sale of electric energy within the State or municipality; or

"(C) between entities described in section 201(f) of the Federal Power Act (16 U.S.C. 824(f)).".

(g) AUTHORITY OF FERC.—Nothing in the Wall Street Transparency and Accountability Act of 2010 or the amendments to the Commodity Exchange Act made by such Act shall limit or affect any statutory enforcement authority of the Federal Energy Regulatory Commission pursuant to section 222 of the Federal Power Act and section 4A of the Natural Gas Act that existed prior to the date of enactment of the Wall Street Transparency and Accountability Act of 2010.

(h) DETERMINATION.—The Commodity Exchange Act is amended by inserting after section 1a (7 U.S.C. 1a) the following:

"SEC. 1b. REQUIREMENTS OF SECRETARY OF THE TREASURY REGARDING EXEMPTION OF FOREIGN EXCHANGE SWAPS AND FOREIGN EXCHANGE FORWARDS FROM DEFINITION OF THE TERM 'SWAP'.

"(a) REQUIRED CONSIDERATIONS.—In determining whether to exempt foreign exchange swaps and foreign exchange forwards from the definition of the term 'swap', the Secretary of the Treasury (referred to in this section as the 'Secretary') shall consider—

"(1) whether the required trading and clearing of foreign exchange swaps and foreign exchange forwards would create systemic risk, lower transparency, or threaten the financial stability of the United States;

"(2) whether foreign exchange swaps and foreign exchange forwards are already subject to a regulatory scheme that is materially comparable to that established by this Act for other classes of swaps;

"(3) the extent to which bank regulators of participants in the foreign exchange market provide adequate supervision, including capital and margin requirements;

"(4) the extent of adequate payment and settlement systems; and

"(5) the use of a potential exemption of foreign exchange swaps and foreign exchange forwards to evade otherwise applicable regulatory requirements.

"(b) DETERMINATION.—If the Secretary makes a determination to exempt foreign exchange swaps and foreign exchange forwards from the definition of the term 'swap', the Secretary shall submit to the appropriate committees of Congress a determination that contains—

"(1) an explanation regarding why foreign exchange swaps and foreign exchange forwards are qualitatively different from other classes of swaps in a way that would make the foreign exchange swaps and foreign exchange forwards ill-suited for regulation as swaps; and

"(2) an identification of the objective differences of foreign exchange swaps and foreign exchange forwards with respect to standard swaps that warrant an exempted status.

"(c) EFFECT OF DETERMINATION.—A determination by the Secretary under subsection (b) shall not exempt any foreign exchange swaps and foreign exchange forwards traded on a designated contract market or swap execution facility from any applicable antifraud and antimanipulation provision under this title.".

[Explanation at ¶ 3015.]

[¶ 10,723] ACT SEC. 723. CLEARING.

(a) CLEARING REQUIREMENT.—

(1) IN GENERAL.—Section 2 of the Commodity Exchange Act (7 U.S.C. 2) is amended—

(A) by striking subsections (d), (e), (g), and (h); and

(B) by redesignating subsection (i) as subsection (g).

(2) SWAPS; LIMITATION ON PARTICIPATION.—Section 2 of the Commodity Exchange Act (7 U.S.C. 2) (as amended by paragraph (1)) is amended by inserting after subsection (c) the following:

"(d) SWAPS.—Nothing in this Act (other than subparagraphs (A), (B), (C), (D), (G), and (H) of subsection (a)(1), subsections (f) and (g), sections 1a, 2(a)(13), 2(c)(2)(A)(ii), 2(e), 2(h), 4(c), 4a, 4b, and 4b-1, subsections (a), (b), and (g) of section 4c, sections 4d, 4e, 4f, 4g, 4h, 4i, 4j, 4k, 41, 4m, 4n, 4o, 4p, 4r, 4s, 4t, 5, 5b, 5c, 5e, and 5h, subsections (c) and (d) of section 6, sections 6c, 6d, 8, 8a, and 9, subsections (e)(2), (f), and (h) of section 12, subsections (a) and (b) of section 13, sections 17, 20, 21, and 22(a)(4), and any other provision of this Act that is applicable to registered entities or Commission registrants) governs or applies to a swap.

"(e) LIMITATION ON PARTICIPATION.—It shall be unlawful for any person, other than an eligible contract participant, to enter into a swap unless the swap is entered into on, or subject to the rules of, a board of trade designated as a contract market under section 5.".

(3) MANDATORY CLEARING OF SWAPS.—Section 2 of the Commodity Exchange Act (7 U.S.C. 2) is amended by inserting after subsection (g) (as redesignated by paragraph (1)(B)) the following:

"(h) CLEARING REQUIREMENT.—

"(1) IN GENERAL.—

"(A) STANDARD FOR CLEARING.—It shall be unlawful for any person to engage in a swap unless that person submits such swap for clearing to a derivatives clearing organization that is registered under this Act or a derivatives clearing organization that is exempt from registration under this Act if the swap is required to be cleared.

"(B) OPEN ACCESS.—The rules of a derivatives clearing organization described in subparagraph (A) shall—

"(i) prescribe that all swaps (but not contracts of sale of a commodity for future delivery or options on such contracts) submitted to the derivatives clearing organization with the same terms and conditions are economically equivalent within the derivatives clearing organization and may be offset with each other within the derivatives clearing organization; and

"(ii) provide for non-discriminatory clearing of a swap (but not a contract of sale of a commodity for future delivery or option on such contract) executed bilaterally or on or through the rules of an unaffiliated designated contract market or swap execution facility.

"(2) COMMISSION REVIEW.—

"(A) COMMISSION-INITIATED REVIEW.—

"(i) The Commission on an ongoing basis shall review each swap, or any group, category, type, or class of swaps to make a determination as to whether the swap or group, category, type, or class of swaps should be required to be cleared.

"(ii) The Commission shall provide at least a 30-day public comment period regarding any determination made under clause (i).

"(B) SWAP SUBMISSIONS.—

"(i) A derivatives clearing organization shall submit to the Commission each swap, or any group, category, type, or class of swaps that it plans to accept for clearing, and provide notice to its members (in a manner to be determined by the Commission) of the submission.

"(ii) Any swap or group, category, type, or class of swaps listed for clearing by a derivative clearing organization as of the date of enactment of this subsection shall be considered submitted to the Commission.

"(iii) The Commission shall—

"(I) make available to the public submissions received under clauses (i) and (ii);

"(II) review each submission made under clauses (i) and (ii), and determine whether the swap, or group, category, type, or class of swaps described in the submission is required to be cleared; and

"(III) provide at least a 30-day public comment period regarding its determination as to whether the clearing requirement under paragraph (1)(A) shall apply to the submission.

"(C) DEADLINE.—The Commission shall make its determination under subparagraph (B)(iii) not later than 90 days after receiving a submission made under subparagraphs (B)(i) and (B)(ii), unless the submitting derivatives clearing organization agrees to an extension for the time limitation established under this subparagraph.

"(D) DETERMINATION.—

"(i) In reviewing a submission made under subparagraph (B), the Commission shall review whether the submission is consistent with section 5b(c)(2).

"(ii) In reviewing a swap, group of swaps, or class of swaps pursuant to subparagraph (A) or a submission made under subparagraph (B), the Commission shall take into account the following factors:

"(I) The existence of significant outstanding notional exposures, trading liquidity, and adequate pricing data.

"(II) The availability of rule framework, capacity, operational expertise and resources, and credit support infrastructure to clear the contract on terms that are consistent with the material terms and trading conventions on which the contract is then traded.

"(III) The effect on the mitigation of systemic risk, taking into account the size of the market for such contract and the resources of the derivatives clearing organization available to clear the contract.

"(IV) The effect on competition, including appropriate fees and charges applied to clearing.

"(V) The existence of reasonable legal certainty in the event of the insolvency of the relevant derivatives clearing organization or 1 or more of its clearing members with regard to the treatment of customer and swap counterparty positions, funds, and property.

"(iii) In making a determination under subparagraph (A) or (B)(iii) that the clearing requirement shall apply, the Commission may require such terms and conditions to the requirement as the Commission determines to be appropriate.

"(E) RULES.—Not later than 1 year after the date of the enactment of this subsection, the Commission shall adopt rules for a derivatives clearing organization's submission for review, pursuant to this paragraph, of a swap, or a group, category, type, or class of swaps, that it seeks to accept for clearing. Nothing in this subparagraph limits the Commission from making a determination under subparagraph (B)(iii) for swaps described in subparagraph (B)(ii).

"(3) STAY OF CLEARING REQUIREMENT.—

"(A) IN GENERAL.—After making a determination pursuant to paragraph (2)(B), the Commission, on application of a counterparty to a swap or on its own initiative, may stay the clearing requirement of paragraph (1) until the Commission completes a review of the terms of the swap (or the group, category, type, or class of swaps) and the clearing arrangement.

"(B) DEADLINE.—The Commission shall complete a review undertaken pursuant to subparagraph (A) not later than 90 days after issuance of the stay, unless the derivatives clearing organization that clears the swap, or group, category, type, or class of swaps agrees to an extension of the time limitation established under this subparagraph.

"(C) DETERMINATION.—Upon completion of the review undertaken pursuant to subparagraph (A), the Commission may—

"(i) determine, unconditionally or subject to such terms and conditions as the Commission determines to be appropriate, that the swap, or group, category, type, or class of swaps must be cleared pursuant to this subsection if it finds that such clearing is consistent with paragraph (2)(D); or

"(ii) determine that the clearing requirement of paragraph (1) shall not apply to the swap, or group, category, type, or class of swaps.

"(D) RULES.—Not later than 1 year after the date of the enactment of the Wall Street Transparency and Accountability Act of 2010, the Commission shall adopt rules for reviewing, pursuant to this paragraph, a derivatives clearing organization's clearing of a swap, or a group, category, type, or class of swaps, that it has accepted for clearing.

"(4) PREVENTION OF EVASION.—

"(A) IN GENERAL.—The Commission shall prescribe rules under this subsection (and issue interpretations of rules prescribed under this subsection) as determined by the Commission to be necessary to prevent evasions of the mandatory clearing requirements under this Act.

"(B) DUTY OF COMMISSION TO INVESTIGATE AND TAKE CERTAIN ACTIONS.—To the extent the Commission finds that a particular swap, group, category, type, or class of swaps would otherwise be subject to mandatory clearing but no derivatives clearing organization has listed the swap, group, category, type, or class of swaps for clearing, the Commission shall—

"(i) investigate the relevant facts and circumstances;

"(ii) within 30 days issue a public report containing the results of the investigation; and

"(iii) take such actions as the Commission determines to be necessary and in the public interest, which may include requiring the retaining of adequate margin or capital by parties to the swap, group, category, type, or class of swaps.

"(C) EFFECT ON AUTHORITY.—Nothing in this paragraph—

"(i) authorizes the Commission to adopt rules requiring a derivatives clearing organization to list for clearing a swap, group, category, type, or class of swaps if the clearing of the swap, group, category, type, or class of swaps would threaten the financial integrity of the derivatives clearing organization; and

"(ii) affects the authority of the Commission to enforce the open access provisions of paragraph (1)(B) with respect to a swap, group, category, type, or class of swaps that is listed for clearing by a derivatives clearing organization.

"(5) REPORTING TRANSITION RULES.—Rules adopted by the Commission under this section shall provide for the reporting of data, as follows:

"(A) Swaps entered into before the date of the enactment of this subsection shall be reported to a registered swap data repository or the Commission no later than 180 days after the effective date of this subsection.

"(B) Swaps entered into on or after such date of enactment shall be reported to a registered swap data repository or the Commission no later than the later of—

"(i) 90 days after such effective date; or

"(ii) such other time after entering into the swap as the Commission may prescribe by rule or regulation.

"(6) CLEARING TRANSITION RULES.—

"(A) Swaps entered into before the date of the enactment of this subsection are exempt from the clearing requirements of this subsection if reported pursuant to paragraph (5)(A).

"(B) Swaps entered into before application of the clearing requirement pursuant to this subsection are exempt from the clearing requirements of this subsection if reported pursuant to paragraph (5)(B).

"(7) EXCEPTIONS.—

"(A) IN GENERAL.—The requirements of paragraph (1)(A) shall not apply to a swap if 1 of the counterparties to the swap—

"(i) is not a financial entity;

"(ii) is using swaps to hedge or mitigate commercial risk; and

"(iii) notifies the Commission, in a manner set forth by the Commission, how it generally meets its financial obligations associated with entering into non-cleared swaps.

"(B) OPTION TO CLEAR.—The application of the clearing exception in subparagraph (A) is solely at the discretion of the counterparty to the swap that meets the conditions of clauses (i) through (iii) of subparagraph (A).

"(C) FINANCIAL ENTITY DEFINITION.—

"(i) IN GENERAL.—For the purposes of this paragraph, the term 'financial entity' means—

"(I) a swap dealer;

"(II) a security-based swap dealer;

"(III) a major swap participant;

"(IV) a major security-based swap participant;

"(V) a commodity pool;

"(VI) a private fund as defined in section 202(a) of the Investment Advisers Act of 1940 (15 U.S.C. 80-b-2(a));

"(VII) an employee benefit plan as defined in paragraphs (3) and (32) of section 3 of the Employee Retirement Income Security Act of 1974 (29 U.S.C. 1002);

"(VIII) a person predominantly engaged in activities that are in the business of banking, or in activities that are financial in nature, as defined in section 4(k) of the Bank Holding Company Act of 1956.

"(ii) EXCLUSION.—The Commission shall consider whether to exempt small banks, savings associations, farm credit system institutions, and credit unions, including—

"(I) depository institutions with total assets of $10,000,000,000 or less;

"(II) farm credit system institutions with total assets of $10,000,000,000 or less; or

"(III) credit unions with total assets of $10,000,000,000 or less.

"(iii) LIMITATION.—Such definition shall not include an entity whose primary business is providing financing, and uses derivatives for the purpose of hedging underlying commercial risks related to interest rate and foreign currency exposures, 90 percent or more of which arise from financing that facilitates the purchase or lease of products, 90 percent or more of which are manufactured by the parent company or another subsidiary of the parent company.

"(D) TREATMENT OF AFFILIATES.—

"(i) IN GENERAL.—An affiliate of a person that qualifies for an exception under subparagraph (A) (including affiliate entities predominantly engaged in providing financing for the purchase of the merchandise or manufactured goods of the person) may qualify for the exception only if the affiliate, acting on behalf of the person and as an agent, uses the swap to hedge or mitigate the commercial risk of the person or other affiliate of the person that is not a financial entity.

"(ii) PROHIBITION RELATING TO CERTAIN AFFILIATES.—The exception in clause (i) shall not apply if the affiliate is—

"(I) a swap dealer;

"(II) a security-based swap dealer;

"(III) a major swap participant;

"(IV) a major security-based swap participant;

"(V) an issuer that would be an investment company, as defined in section 3 of the Investment Company Act of 1940 (15 U.S.C. 80a-3), but for paragraph (1) or (7) of subsection (c) of that Act (15 U.S.C. 80a-3(c));

"(VI) a commodity pool; or

"(VII) a bank holding company with over $50,000,000,000 in consolidated assets.

"(iii) TRANSITION RULE FOR AFFILIATES.—An affiliate, subsidiary, or a wholly owned entity of a person that qualifies for an exception under subparagraph (A) and is predominantly engaged in providing financing for the purchase or lease of merchandise or manufactured goods of the person shall be exempt from the margin requirement described in section 4s(e) and the clearing requirement described in paragraph (1) with regard to swaps entered into to mitigate the risk of the financing activities for not less than a 2-year period beginning on the date of enactment of this clause.

"(E) ELECTION OF COUNTERPARTY.—

"(i) SWAPS REQUIRED TO BE CLEARED.—With respect to any swap that is subject to the mandatory clearing requirement under this subsection and entered into by a swap dealer or a major swap participant with a counterparty that is not a swap dealer, major swap participant, security-based swap dealer, or major security-based swap participant, the counterparty shall have the sole right to select the derivatives clearing organization at which the swap will be cleared.

"(ii) SWAPS NOT REQUIRED TO BE CLEARED.—With respect to any swap that is not subject to the mandatory clearing requirement under this subsection and entered into by a swap dealer or a major swap participant with a counterparty that is not a swap dealer, major swap participant, security-based swap dealer, or major security-based swap participant, the counterparty—

"(I) may elect to require clearing of the swap; and

"(II) shall have the sole right to select the derivatives clearing organization at which the swap will be cleared.

"(F) ABUSE OF EXCEPTION.—The Commission may prescribe such rules or issue interpretations of the rules as the Commission determines to be necessary to prevent abuse of the exceptions described in this paragraph. The Commission may also request information from those persons claiming the clearing exception as necessary to prevent abuse of the exceptions described in this paragraph.

"(8) TRADE EXECUTION.—

"(A) IN GENERAL.—With respect to transactions involving swaps subject to the clearing requirement of paragraph (1), counterparties shall—

"(i) execute the transaction on a board of trade designated as a contract market under section 5; or

"(ii) execute the transaction on a swap execution facility registered under 5h or a swap execution facility that is exempt from registration under section 5h(f) of this Act.

"(B) EXCEPTION.—The requirements of clauses (i) and (ii) of subparagraph (A) shall not apply if no board of trade or swap execution facility makes the swap available to trade or for swap transactions subject to the clearing exception under paragraph (7).".

(b) COMMODITY EXCHANGE ACT.—Section 2 of the Commodity Exchange Act (7 U.S.C. 2) is amended by adding at the end the following:

"(j) COMMITTEE APPROVAL BY BOARD.—Exemptions from the requirements of subsection (h)(1) to clear a swap and subsection (h)(8) to execute a swap through a board of trade or swap execution facility shall be available to a counterparty that is an issuer of securities that are registered under section 12 of the Securities Exchange Act of 1934 (15 U.S.C. 78l) or that is required to file reports pursuant to section 15(d) of the Securities Exchange Act of 1934 (15 U.S.C. 78o) only if an appropriate committee of the issuer's board or governing body has reviewed and approved its decision to enter into swaps that are subject to such exemptions.".

(c) GRANDFATHER PROVISIONS.—

(1) LEGAL CERTAINTY FOR CERTAIN TRANSACTIONS IN EXEMPT COMMODITIES.—Not later than 60 days after the date of enactment of this Act, a person may submit to the Commodity Futures Trading Commission a petition to remain subject to section 2(h) of the Commodity Exchange Act (7 U.S.C. 2(h)) (as in effect on the day before the date of enactment of this Act).

(2) CONSIDERATION; AUTHORITY OF COMMODITY FUTURES TRADING COMMISSION.—The Commodity Futures Trading Commission—

(A) shall consider any petition submitted under subparagraph (A) in a prompt manner; and

(B) may allow a person to continue operating subject to section 2(h) of the Commodity Exchange Act (7 U.S.C. 2(h)) (as in effect on the day before the date of enactment of this Act) for not longer than a 1-year period.

(3) AGRICULTURAL SWAPS.—

(A) IN GENERAL.—Except as provided in subparagraph (B), no person shall offer to enter into, enter into, or confirm the execution of, any swap in an agricultural commodity (as defined by the Commodity Futures Trading Commission).

(B) EXCEPTION.—Notwithstanding subparagraph (A), a person may offer to enter into, enter into, or confirm the execution of, any swap in an agricultural commodity pursuant to section 4(c) of the Commodity Exchange Act (7 U.S.C. 6(c)) or any rule, regulation, or order issued thereunder (including any rule, regulation, or order in effect as of the date of enactment of this Act) by the Commodity Futures Trading Commission to allow swaps under such terms and conditions as the Commission shall prescribe.

(4) REQUIRED REPORTING.—If the exception described in section 2(h)(8)(B) of the Commodity Exchange Act applies, the counterparties shall comply with any recordkeeping and transaction

reporting requirements that may be prescribed by the Commission with respect to swaps subject to section 2(h)(8)(B) of the Commodity Exchange Act.

[Explanation at ¶ 3060.]

[¶ 10,724] ACT SEC. 724. SWAPS; SEGREGATION AND BANKRUPTCY TREATMENT.

(a) SEGREGATION REQUIREMENTS FOR CLEARED SWAPS.—Section 4d of the Commodity Exchange Act (7 U.S.C. 6d) (as amended by section 732) is amended by adding at the end the following:

"(f) SWAPS.—

"(1) REGISTRATION REQUIREMENT.—It shall be unlawful for any person to accept any money, securities, or property (or to extend any credit in lieu of money, securities, or property) from, for, or on behalf of a swaps customer to margin, guarantee, or secure a swap cleared by or through a derivatives clearing organization (including money, securities, or property accruing to the customer as the result of such a swap), unless the person shall have registered under this Act with the Commission as a futures commission merchant, and the registration shall not have expired nor been suspended nor revoked.

"(2) CLEARED SWAPS.—

"(A) SEGREGATION REQUIRED.—A futures commission merchant shall treat and deal with all money, securities, and property of any swaps customer received to margin, guarantee, or secure a swap cleared by or though a derivatives clearing organization (including money, securities, or property accruing to the swaps customer as the result of such a swap) as belonging to the swaps customer.

"(B) COMMINGLING PROHIBITED.—Money, securities, and property of a swaps customer described in subparagraph (A) shall be separately accounted for and shall not be commingled with the funds of the futures commission merchant or be used to margin, secure, or guarantee any trades or contracts of any swaps customer or person other than the person for whom the same are held.

"(3) EXCEPTIONS.—

"(A) USE OF FUNDS.—

"(i) IN GENERAL.—Notwithstanding paragraph (2), money, securities, and property of swap customers of a futures commission merchant described in paragraph (2) may, for convenience, be commingled and deposited in the same account or accounts with any bank or trust company or with a derivatives clearing organization.

"(ii) WITHDRAWAL.—Notwithstanding paragraph (2), such share of the money, securities, and property described in clause (i) as in the normal course of business shall be necessary to margin, guarantee, secure, transfer, adjust, or settle a cleared swap with a derivatives clearing organization, or with any member of the derivatives clearing organization, may be withdrawn and applied to such purposes, including the payment of commissions, brokerage, interest, taxes, storage, and other charges, lawfully accruing in connection with the cleared swap.

"(B) COMMISSION ACTION.—Notwithstanding paragraph (2), in accordance with such terms and conditions as the Commission may prescribe by rule, regulation, or order, any money, securities, or property of the swaps customers of a futures commission merchant described in paragraph (2) may be commingled and deposited in customer accounts with any other money, securities, or property received by the futures commission merchant and required by the Commission to be separately accounted for and treated and dealt with as belonging to the swaps customer of the futures commission merchant.

"(4) PERMITTED INVESTMENTS.—Money described in paragraph (2) may be invested in obligations of the United States, in general obligations of any State or of any political subdivision of a State, and in obligations fully guaranteed as to principal and interest by the United States, or in any other investment that the Commission may by rule or regulation prescribe, and such investments shall be made in accordance with such rules and regulations and subject to such conditions as the Commission may prescribe.

"(5) COMMODITY CONTRACT.—A swap cleared by or through a derivatives clearing organization shall be considered to be a commodity contract as such term is defined in section 761 of title 11, United States Code, with regard to all money, securities, and property of any swaps customer received by a futures commission merchant or a derivatives clearing organization to margin, guarantee, or secure the swap (including money, securities, or property accruing to the customer as the result of the swap).

"(6) PROHIBITION.—It shall be unlawful for any person, including any derivatives clearing organization and any depository institution, that has received any money, securities, or property for deposit in a separate account or accounts as provided in paragraph (2) to hold, dispose of, or use any such money, securities, or property as belonging to the depositing futures commission merchant or any person other than the swaps customer of the futures commission merchant.".

(b) BANKRUPTCY TREATMENT OF CLEARED SWAPS.—Section 761 of title 11, United States Code, is amended—

(1) in paragraph (4), by striking subparagraph (F) and inserting the following:

"(F)

(i) any other contract, option, agreement, or transaction that is similar to a contract, option, agreement, or transaction referred to in this paragraph; and

"(ii) with respect to a futures commission merchant or a clearing organization, any other contract, option, agreement, or transaction, in each case, that is cleared by a clearing organization;"; and

(2) in paragraph (9)(A)(i), by striking "the commodity futures account" and inserting "a commodity contract account".

(c) SEGREGATION REQUIREMENTS FOR UNCLEARED SWAPS.—Section 4s of the Commodity Exchange Act (as added by section 731) is amended by adding at the end the following:

"(1) SEGREGATION REQUIREMENTS.—

"(1) SEGREGATION OF ASSETS HELD AS COLLATERAL IN UNCLEARED SWAP TRANSACTIONS.—

"(A) NOTIFICATION.—A swap dealer or major swap participant shall be required to notify the counterparty of the swap dealer or major swap participant at the beginning of a swap transaction that the counterparty has the right to require segregation of the funds or other property supplied to margin, guarantee, or secure the obligations of the counterparty.

"(B) SEGREGATION AND MAINTENANCE OF FUNDS.—At the request of a counterparty to a swap that provides funds or other property to a swap dealer or major swap participant to margin, guarantee, or secure the obligations of the counterparty, the swap dealer or major swap participant shall—

"(i) segregate the funds or other property for the benefit of the counterparty; and

"(ii) in accordance with such rules and regulations as the Commission may promulgate, maintain the funds or other property in a segregated account separate from the assets and other interests of the swap dealer or major swap participant.

"(2) APPLICABILITY.—The requirements described in paragraph (1) shall—

"(A) apply only to a swap between a counterparty and a swap dealer or major swap participant that is not submitted for clearing to a derivatives clearing organization; and

"(B)

(i) not apply to variation margin payments; or

"(ii) not preclude any commercial arrangement regarding—

"(I) the investment of segregated funds or other property that may only be invested in such investments as the Commission may permit by rule or regulation; and

"(II) the related allocation of gains and losses resulting from any investment of the segregated funds or other property.

"(3) USE OF INDEPENDENT THIRD-PARTY CUSTODIANS.—The segregated account described in paragraph (1) shall be—

"(A) carried by an independent third-party custodian; and

"(B) designated as a segregated account for and on behalf of the counterparty.

"(4) REPORTING REQUIREMENT.—If the counterparty does not choose to require segregation of the funds or other property supplied to margin, guarantee, or secure the obligations of the counterparty, the swap dealer or major swap participant shall report to the counterparty of the swap dealer or major swap participant on a quarterly basis that the back office procedures of the swap dealer or major swap participant relating to margin and collateral requirements are in compliance with the agreement of the counterparties.".

[Explanation at ¶ 3065.]

[¶ 10,725] ACT SEC. 725. DERIVATIVES CLEARING ORGANIZATIONS.

(a) REGISTRATION REQUIREMENT.—Section 5b of the Commodity Exchange Act (7 U.S.C. 7a-1) is amended by striking subsections (a) and (b) and inserting the following:

"(a) REGISTRATION REQUIREMENT.—

"(1) IN GENERAL.—Except as provided in paragraph (2), it shall be unlawful for a derivatives clearing organization, directly or indirectly, to make use of the mails or any means or instrumentality of interstate commerce to perform the functions of a derivatives clearing organization with respect to—

"(A) a contract of sale of a commodity for future delivery (or an option on the contract of sale) or option on a commodity, in each case, unless the contract or option is—

"(i) excluded from this Act by subsection (a)(1)(C)(i), (c), or (f) of section 2; or

"(ii) a security futures product cleared by a clearing agency registered with the Securities and Exchange Commission under the Securities Exchange Act of 1934 (15 U.S.C. 78a et seq.); or

"(B) a swap.

"(2) EXCEPTION.—Paragraph (1) shall not apply to a derivatives clearing organization that is registered with the Commission.

"(b) VOLUNTARY REGISTRATION.—A person that clears 1 or more agreements, contracts, or transactions that are not required to be cleared under this Act may register with the Commission as a derivatives clearing organization.".

(b) REGISTRATION FOR DEPOSITORY INSTITUTIONS AND CLEARING AGENCIES; EXEMPTIONS; COMPLIANCE OFFICER; ANNUAL REPORTS.—Section 5b of the Commodity Exchange Act (7 U.S.C. 7a-1) is amended by adding at the end the following:

"(g) EXISTING DEPOSITORY INSTITUTIONS AND CLEARING AGENCIES.—

"(1) IN GENERAL.—A depository institution or clearing agency registered with the Securities and Exchange Commission under the Securities Exchange Act of 1934 (15 U.S.C. 78a et seq.) that is required to be registered as a derivatives clearing organization under this section is deemed to be registered under this section to the extent that, before the date of enactment of this subsection—

"(A) the depository institution cleared swaps as a multilateral clearing organization; or

"(B) the clearing agency cleared swaps.

"(2) CONVERSION OF DEPOSITORY INSTITUTIONS.—A depository institution to which this subsection applies may, by the vote of the shareholders owning not less than 51 percent of the voting interests of the depository institution, be converted into a State corporation, partnership, limited liability company, or similar legal form pursuant to a plan of conversion, if the conversion is not in contravention of applicable State law.

"(3) SHARING OF INFORMATION.—The Securities and Exchange Commission shall make available to the Commission, upon request, all information determined to be relevant by the Securities and Exchange Commission regarding a clearing agency deemed to be registered with the Commission under paragraph (1).

"(h) EXEMPTIONS.—The Commission may exempt, conditionally or unconditionally, a derivatives clearing organization from registration under this section for the clearing of swaps if the Commission determines that the derivatives clearing organization is subject to comparable, comprehensive supervision and regulation by the Securities and Exchange Commission or the appropriate government authorities in the home country of the organization. Such conditions may include, but are not limited to, requiring that the derivatives clearing organization be available for inspection by the Commission and make available all information requested by the Commission.

"(i) DESIGNATION OF CHIEF COMPLIANCE OFFICER.—

"(1) IN GENERAL.—Each derivatives clearing organization shall designate an individual to serve as a chief compliance officer.

"(2) DUTIES.—The chief compliance officer shall—

"(A) report directly to the board or to the senior officer of the derivatives clearing organization;

"(B) review the compliance of the derivatives clearing organization with respect to the core principles described in subsection (c)(2);

"(C) in consultation with the board of the derivatives clearing organization, a body performing a function similar to the board of the derivatives clearing organization, or the senior officer of the derivatives clearing organization, resolve any conflicts of interest that may arise;

"(D) be responsible for administering each policy and procedure that is required to be established pursuant to this section;

"(E) ensure compliance with this Act (including regulations) relating to agreements, contracts, or transactions, including each rule prescribed by the Commission under this section;

"(F) establish procedures for the remediation of noncompliance issues identified by the compliance officer through any—

"(i) compliance office review;

"(ii) look-back;

"(iii) internal or external audit finding;

"(iv) self-reported error; or

"(v) validated complaint; and

"(G) establish and follow appropriate procedures for the handling, management response, remediation, retesting, and closing of noncompliance issues.

"(3) ANNUAL REPORTS.—

"(A) IN GENERAL.—In accordance with rules prescribed by the Commission, the chief compliance officer shall annually prepare and sign a report that contains a description of—

"(i) the compliance of the derivatives clearing organization of the compliance officer with respect to this Act (including regulations); and

"(ii) each policy and procedure of the derivatives clearing organization of the compliance officer (including the code of ethics and conflict of interest policies of the derivatives clearing organization).

"(B) REQUIREMENTS.—A compliance report under subparagraph (A) shall—

"(i) accompany each appropriate financial report of the derivatives clearing organization that is required to be furnished to the Commission pursuant to this section; and

"(ii) include a certification that, under penalty of law, the compliance report is accurate and complete.".

"(c) CORE PRINCIPLES FOR DERIVATIVES CLEARING ORGANIZATIONS.—Section 5b(c) of the Commodity Exchange Act (7 U.S.C. 7a-1(c)) is amended by striking paragraph (2) and inserting the following:

"(2) CORE PRINCIPLES FOR DERIVATIVES CLEARING ORGANIZATIONS.—

"(A) COMPLIANCE.—

"(i) IN GENERAL.—To be registered and to maintain registration as a derivatives clearing organization, a derivatives clearing organization shall comply with each core principle described in this paragraph and any requirement that the Commission may impose by rule or regulation pursuant to section 8a(5).

"(ii) DISCRETION OF DERIVATIVES CLEARING ORGANIZATION.—Subject to any rule or regulation prescribed by the Commission, a derivatives clearing organization shall have reasonable discretion in establishing the manner by which the derivatives clearing organization complies with each core principle described in this paragraph.

"(B) FINANCIAL RESOURCES.—

"(i) IN GENERAL.—Each derivatives clearing organization shall have adequate financial, operational, and managerial resources, as determined by the Commission, to discharge each responsibility of the derivatives clearing organization.

"(ii) MINIMUM AMOUNT OF FINANCIAL RESOURCES.—Each derivatives clearing organization shall possess financial resources that, at a minimum, exceed the total amount that would—

"(I) enable the organization to meet its financial obligations to its members and participants notwithstanding a default by the member or participant creating the largest financial exposure for that organization in extreme but plausible market conditions; and

"(II) enable the derivatives clearing organization to cover the operating costs of the derivatives clearing organization for a period of 1 year (as calculated on a rolling basis).

"(C) PARTICIPANT AND PRODUCT ELIGIBILITY.—

"(i) IN GENERAL.—Each derivatives clearing organization shall establish—

"(I) appropriate admission and continuing eligibility standards (including sufficient financial resources and operational capacity to meet obligations arising from participation in the derivatives clearing organization) for members of, and participants in, the derivatives clearing organization; and

"(II) appropriate standards for determining the eligibility of agreements, contracts, or transactions submitted to the derivatives clearing organization for clearing.

"(ii) REQUIRED PROCEDURES.—Each derivatives clearing organization shall establish and implement procedures to verify, on an ongoing basis, the compliance of each participation and membership requirement of the derivatives clearing organization.

"(iii) REQUIREMENTS.—The participation and membership requirements of each derivatives clearing organization shall—

"(I) be objective;

"(II) be publicly disclosed; and

"(III) permit fair and open access.

"(D) RISK MANAGEMENT.—

"(i) IN GENERAL.—Each derivatives clearing organization shall ensure that the derivatives clearing organization possesses the ability to manage the risks associated with discharging the responsibilities of the derivatives clearing organization through the use of appropriate tools and procedures.

"(ii) MEASUREMENT OF CREDIT EXPOSURE.—Each derivatives clearing organization shall—

"(I) not less than once during each business day of the derivatives clearing organization, measure the credit exposures of the derivatives clearing organization to each member and participant of the derivatives clearing organization; and

"(II) monitor each exposure described in subclause (I) periodically during the business day of the derivatives clearing organization.

"(iii) LIMITATION OF EXPOSURE TO POTENTIAL LOSSES FROM DEFAULTS.—Each derivatives clearing organization, through margin requirements and other risk control mechanisms, shall limit the exposure of the derivatives clearing organization to potential losses from defaults by members and participants of the derivatives clearing organization to ensure that—

"(I) the operations of the derivatives clearing organization would not be disrupted; and

"(II) nondefaulting members or participants would not be exposed to losses that nondefaulting members or participants cannot anticipate or control.

"(iv) MARGIN REQUIREMENTS.—The margin required from each member and participant of a derivatives clearing organization shall be sufficient to cover potential exposures in normal market conditions.

"(v) REQUIREMENTS REGARDING MODELS AND PARAMETERS.—Each model and parameter used in setting margin requirements under clause (iv) shall be—

"(I) risk-based; and

"(II) reviewed on a regular basis.

"(E) SETTLEMENT PROCEDURES.—Each derivatives clearing organization shall—

"(i) complete money settlements on a timely basis (but not less frequently than once each business day);

"(ii) employ money settlement arrangements to eliminate or strictly limit the exposure of the derivatives clearing organization to settlement bank risks (including credit and liquidity risks from the use of banks to effect money settlements);

"(iii) ensure that money settlements are final when effected;

"(iv) maintain an accurate record of the flow of funds associated with each money settlement;

"(v) possess the ability to comply with each term and condition of any permitted netting or offset arrangement with any other clearing organization;

"(vi) regarding physical settlements, establish rules that clearly state each obligation of the derivatives clearing organization with respect to physical deliveries; and

"(vii) ensure that each risk arising from an obligation described in clause (vi) is identified and managed.

"(F) TREATMENT OF FUNDS.—

"(i) REQUIRED STANDARDS AND PROCEDURES.—Each derivatives clearing organization shall establish standards and procedures that are designed to protect and ensure the safety of member and participant funds and assets.

"(ii) HOLDING OF FUNDS AND ASSETS.—Each derivatives clearing organization shall hold member and participant funds and assets in a manner by which to minimize the risk of loss or of delay in the access by the derivatives clearing organization to the assets and funds.

"(iii) PERMISSIBLE INVESTMENTS.—Funds and assets invested by a derivatives clearing organization shall be held in instruments with minimal credit, market, and liquidity risks.

"(G) DEFAULT RULES AND PROCEDURES.—

"(i) IN GENERAL.—Each derivatives clearing organization shall have rules and procedures designed to allow for the efficient, fair, and safe management of events during which members or participants—

"(I) become insolvent; or

"(II) otherwise default on the obligations of the members or participants to the derivatives clearing organization.

"(ii) DEFAULT PROCEDURES.—Each derivatives clearing organization shall—

"(I) clearly state the default procedures of the derivatives clearing organization;

"(II) make publicly available the default rules of the derivatives clearing organization; and

"(III) ensure that the derivatives clearing organization may take timely action—

"(aa) to contain losses and liquidity pressures; and

"(bb) to continue meeting each obligation of the derivatives clearing organization.

"(H) RULE ENFORCEMENT.—Each derivatives clearing organization shall—

"(i) maintain adequate arrangements and resources for—

"(I) the effective monitoring and enforcement of compliance with the rules of the derivatives clearing organization; and

"(II) the resolution of disputes;

"(ii) have the authority and ability to discipline, limit, suspend, or terminate the activities of a member or participant due to a violation by the member or participant of any rule of the derivatives clearing organization; and

"(iii) report to the Commission regarding rule enforcement activities and sanctions imposed against members and participants as provided in clause (ii).

"(I) SYSTEM SAFEGUARDS.—Each derivatives clearing organization shall—

"(i) establish and maintain a program of risk analysis and oversight to identify and minimize sources of operational risk through the development of appropriate controls and procedures, and automated systems, that are reliable, secure, and have adequate scalable capacity;

"(ii) establish and maintain emergency procedures, backup facilities, and a plan for disaster recovery that allows for—

"(I) the timely recovery and resumption of operations of the derivatives clearing organization; and

"(II) the fulfillment of each obligation and responsibility of the derivatives clearing organization; and

"(iii) periodically conduct tests to verify that the backup resources of the derivatives clearing organization are sufficient to ensure daily processing, clearing, and settlement.

"(J) REPORTING.—Each derivatives clearing organization shall provide to the Commission all information that the Commission determines to be necessary to conduct oversight of the derivatives clearing organization.

"(K) RECORDKEEPING.—Each derivatives clearing organization shall maintain records of all activities related to the business of the derivatives clearing organization as a derivatives clearing organization—

"(i) in a form and manner that is acceptable to the Commission; and

"(ii) for a period of not less than 5 years.

"(L) PUBLIC INFORMATION.—

"(i) IN GENERAL.—Each derivatives clearing organization shall provide to market participants sufficient information to enable the market participants to identify and evaluate accurately the risks and costs associated with using the services of the derivatives clearing organization.

"(ii) AVAILABILITY OF INFORMATION.—Each derivatives clearing organization shall make information concerning the rules and operating and default procedures governing the clearing and settlement systems of the derivatives clearing organization available to market participants.

"(iii) PUBLIC DISCLOSURE.—Each derivatives clearing organization shall disclose publicly and to the Commission information concerning—

"(I) the terms and conditions of each contract, agreement, and transaction cleared and settled by the derivatives clearing organization;

"(II) each clearing and other fee that the derivatives clearing organization charges the members and participants of the derivatives clearing organization;

"(III) the margin-setting methodology, and the size and composition, of the financial resource package of the derivatives clearing organization;

"(IV) daily settlement prices, volume, and open interest for each contract settled or cleared by the derivatives clearing organization; and

"(V) any other matter relevant to participation in the settlement and clearing activities of the derivatives clearing organization.

"(M) INFORMATION-SHARING.—Each derivatives clearing organization shall—

"(i) enter into, and abide by the terms of, each appropriate and applicable domestic and international information-sharing agreement; and

"(ii) use relevant information obtained from each agreement described in clause (i) in carrying out the risk management program of the derivatives clearing organization.

"(N) ANTITRUST CONSIDERATIONS.—Unless necessary or appropriate to achieve the purposes of this Act, a derivatives clearing organization shall not—

"(i) adopt any rule or take any action that results in any unreasonable restraint of trade; or

"(ii) impose any material anticompetitive burden.

"(O) GOVERNANCE FITNESS STANDARDS.—

"(i) GOVERNANCE ARRANGEMENTS.—Each derivatives clearing organization shall establish governance arrangements that are transparent—

"(I) to fulfill public interest requirements; and

"(II) to permit the consideration of the views of owners and participants.

"(ii) FITNESS STANDARDS.—Each derivatives clearing organization shall establish and enforce appropriate fitness standards for—

"(I) directors;

"(II) members of any disciplinary committee;

"(III) members of the derivatives clearing organization;

"(IV) any other individual or entity with direct access to the settlement or clearing activities of the derivatives clearing organization; and

"(V) any party affiliated with any individual or entity described in this clause.

"(P) CONFLICTS OF INTEREST.—Each derivatives clearing organization shall—

"(i) establish and enforce rules to minimize conflicts of interest in the decision-making process of the derivatives clearing organization; and

"(ii) establish a process for resolving conflicts of interest described in clause (i).

"(Q) COMPOSITION OF GOVERNING BOARDS.—Each derivatives clearing organization shall ensure that the composition of the governing board or committee of the derivatives clearing organization includes market participants.

"(R) LEGAL RISK.—Each derivatives clearing organization shall have a well-founded, transparent, and enforceable legal framework for each aspect of the activities of the derivatives clearing organization.".

(d) CONFLICTS OF INTEREST.—The Commodity Futures Trading Commission shall adopt rules mitigating conflicts of interest in connection with the conduct of business by a swap dealer or a major swap participant with a derivatives clearing organization, board of trade, or a swap execution facility that clears or trades swaps in which the swap dealer or major swap participant has a material debt or material equity investment.

(e) REPORTING REQUIREMENTS.—Section 5b of the Commodity Exchange Act (7 U.S.C. 7a-1) (as amended by subsection (b)) is amended by adding at the end the following:

"(k) REPORTING REQUIREMENTS.—

"(1) DUTY OF DERIVATIVES CLEARING ORGANIZATIONS.—Each derivatives clearing organization that clears swaps shall provide to the Commission all information that is determined by the Commission to be necessary to perform each responsibility of the Commission under this Act.

"(2) DATA COLLECTION AND MAINTENANCE REQUIREMENTS.—The Commission shall adopt data collection and maintenance requirements for swaps cleared by derivatives clearing organizations that are comparable to the corresponding requirements for—

"(A) swaps data reported to swap data repositories; and

"(B) swaps traded on swap execution facilities.

"(3) REPORTS ON SECURITY-BASED SWAP AGREEMENTS TO BE SHARED WITH THE SECURITIES AND EXCHANGE COMMISSION.—

"(A) IN GENERAL.—A derivatives clearing organization that clears security-based swap agreements (as defined in section 1a(47)(A)(v)) shall, upon request, open to inspection and examination to the Securities and Exchange Commission all books and records relating to such security-based swap agreements, consistent with the confidentiality and disclosure requirements of section 8.

"(B) JURISDICTION.—Nothing in this paragraph shall affect the exclusive jurisdiction of the Commission to prescribe recordkeeping and reporting requirements for a derivatives clearing organization that is registered with the Commission.

"(4) INFORMATION SHARING.—Subject to section 8, and upon request, the Commission shall share information collected under paragraph (2) with—

"(A) the Board;

"(B) the Securities and Exchange Commission;

"(C) each appropriate prudential regulator;

"(D) the Financial Stability Oversight Council;

"(E) the Department of Justice; and

"(F) any other person that the Commission determines to be appropriate, including—

"(i) foreign financial supervisors (including foreign futures authorities);

"(ii) foreign central banks; and

"(iii) foreign ministries.

"(5) CONFIDENTIALITY AND INDEMNIFICATION AGREEMENT.—Before the Commission may share information with any entity described in paragraph (4)—

"(A) the Commission shall receive a written agreement from each entity stating that the entity shall abide by the confidentiality requirements described in section 8 relating to the information on swap transactions that is provided; and

"(B) each entity shall agree to indemnify the Commission for any expenses arising from litigation relating to the information provided under section 8.

"(6) PUBLIC INFORMATION.—Each derivatives clearing organization that clears swaps shall provide to the Commission (including any designee of the Commission) information under paragraph (2) in such form and at such frequency as is required by the Commission to comply with the public reporting requirements contained in section 2(a)(13).".

(f) PUBLIC DISCLOSURE.—Section 8(e) of the Commodity Exchange Act (7 U.S.C. 12(e)) is amended in the last sentence—

(1) by inserting ", central bank and ministries," after "department" each place it appears; and

(2) by striking ". is a party." and inserting ", is a party.".

(g) LEGAL CERTAINTY FOR IDENTIFIED BANKING PRODUCTS.—

(1) REPEALS.—The Legal Certainty for Bank Products Act of 2000 (7 U.S.C. 27 et seq.) is amended—

(A) by striking sections 404 and 407 (7 U.S.C. 27b, 27e);

(B) in section 402 (7 U.S.C. 27), by striking subsection (d); and

(C) in section 408 (7 U.S.C. 27f)—

(i) in subsection (c)—

(I) by striking "in the case" and all that follows through "a hybrid" and inserting "in the case of a hybrid";

(II) by striking "; or" and inserting a period; and

(III) by striking paragraph (2);

(ii) by striking subsection (b); and

(iii) by redesignating subsection (c) as subsection (b).

(2) LEGAL CERTAINTY FOR BANK PRODUCTS ACT OF 2000.—Section 403 of the Legal Certainty for Bank Products Act of 2000 (7 U.S.C. 27a) is amended to read as follows:

"SEC. 403. EXCLUSION OF IDENTIFIED BANKING PRODUCT.

"(a) EXCLUSION.—Except as provided in subsection (b) or (c)—

"(1) the Commodity Exchange Act (7 U.S.C. 1 et seq.) shall not apply to, and the Commodity Futures Trading Commission shall not exercise regulatory authority under the Commodity Exchange Act (7 U.S.C. 1 et seq.) with respect to, an identified banking product; and

"(2) the definitions of 'security-based swap' in section 3(a)(68) of the Securities Exchange Act of 1934 and 'security-based swap agreement' in section 1a(47)(A)(v) of the Commodity Exchange Act and section 3(a)(78) of the Securities Exchange Act of 1934 do not include any identified bank product.

"(b) EXCEPTION.—An appropriate Federal banking agency may except an identified banking product of a bank under its regulatory jurisdiction from the exclusion in subsection (a) if the agency determines, in consultation with the Commodity Futures Trading Commission and the Securities and Exchange Commission, that the product—

"(1) would meet the definition of a 'swap' under section 1a(47) of the Commodity Exchange Act (7 U.S.C. 1a) or a 'security-based swap' under that section 3(a)(68) of the Securities Exchange Act of 1934; and

"(2) has become known to the trade as a swap or security-based swap, or otherwise has been structured as an identified banking product for the purpose of evading the provisions of the Commodity Exchange Act (7 U.S.C. 1 et seq.), the Securities Act of 1933 (15 U.S.C. 77a et seq.), or the Securities Exchange Act of 1934 (15 U.S.C. 78a et seq.).

"(c) EXCEPTION.—The exclusions in subsection (a) shall not apply to an identified bank product that—

"(1) is a product of a bank that is not under the regulatory jurisdiction of an appropriate Federal banking agency;

"(2) meets the definition of swap in section 1a(47) of the Commodity Exchange Act or security-based swap in section 3(a)(68) of the Securities Exchange Act of 1934; and

"(3) has become known to the trade as a swap or security-based swap, or otherwise has been structured as an identified banking product for the purpose of evading the provisions of the Commodity Exchange Act (7 U.S.C. 1 et seq.), the Securities Act of 1933 (15 U.S.C. 77a et seq.), or the Securities Exchange Act of 1934 (15 U.S.C. 78a et seq.).".

(h) REDUCING CLEARING SYSTEMIC RISK.—Section 5b(f)(1) of the Commodity Exchange Act (7 U.S.C. 7a-1(F)(i)) is amended by adding at the end the following: "In order to minimize systemic risk, under no circumstances shall a derivatives clearing organization be compelled to accept the counterparty credit risk of another clearing organization.".

[Explanation at ¶ 3070.]

[¶ 10,726] ACT SEC. 726. RULEMAKING ON CONFLICT OF INTEREST.

(a) IN GENERAL.—In order to mitigate conflicts of interest, not later than 180 days after the date of enactment of the Wall Street Transparency and Accountability Act of 2010, the Commodity Futures Trading Commission shall adopt rules which may include numerical limits on the control of, or the voting rights with respect to, any derivatives clearing organization that clears swaps, or swap execution facility or board of trade designated as a contract market that posts swaps or makes swaps available for trading, by a bank holding company (as defined in section 2 of the Bank Holding Company Act of 1956 (12 U.S.C. 1841)) with total consolidated assets of $50,000,000,000 or more, a nonbank financial company (as defined in section 102) supervised by the Board, an affiliate of such a bank holding company or nonbank financial company, a swap dealer, major swap participant, or associated person of a swap dealer or major swap participant.

(b) PURPOSES.—The Commission shall adopt rules if it determines, after the review described in subsection (a), that such rules are necessary or appropriate to improve the governance of, or to mitigate systemic risk, promote competition, or mitigate conflicts of interest in connection with a swap dealer or major swap participant's conduct of business with, a derivatives clearing organization, contract market, or swap execution facility that clears or posts swaps or makes swaps available for trading and in which such swap dealer or major swap participant has a material debt or equity investment.

(c) CONSIDERATIONS.—In adopting rules pursuant to this section, the Commodity Futures Trading Commission shall consider any conflicts of interest arising from the amount of equity owned by a single investor, the ability to vote, cause the vote of, or withhold votes entitled to be cast on any matters by the holders of the ownership interest, and the governance arrangements of any derivatives clearing organization that clears swaps, or swap execution facility or board of trade designated as a contract market that posts swaps or makes swaps available for trading.

[Explanation at ¶ 3045.]

[¶ 10,727] ACT SEC. 727. PUBLIC REPORTING OF SWAP TRANSACTION DATA.

Section 2(a) of the Commodity Exchange Act (7 U.S.C. 2(a)) is amended by adding at the end the following:

"(13) PUBLIC AVAILABILITY OF SWAP TRANSACTION DATA.—

"(A) DEFINITION OF REAL-TIME PUBLIC REPORTING.—In this paragraph, the term 'real-time public reporting' means to report data relating to a swap transaction, including price and volume, as soon as technologically practicable after the time at which the swap transaction has been executed.

"(B) PURPOSE.—The purpose of this section is to authorize the Commission to make swap transaction and pricing data available to the public in such form and at such times as the Commission determines appropriate to enhance price discovery.

"(C) GENERAL RULE.—The Commission is authorized and required to provide by rule for the public availability of swap transaction and pricing data as follows:

"(i) With respect to those swaps that are subject to the mandatory clearing requirement described in subsection (h)(1) (including those swaps that are excepted from the requirement pursuant to subsection (h)(7)), the Commission shall require real-time public reporting for such transactions.

"(ii) With respect to those swaps that are not subject to the mandatory clearing requirement described in subsection (h)(1), but are cleared at a registered derivatives clearing organization, the Commission shall require real-time public reporting for such transactions.

"(iii) With respect to swaps that are not cleared at a registered derivatives clearing organization and which are reported to a swap data repository or the Commission under subsection (h)(6), the Commission shall require real-time public reporting for such transactions, in a manner that does not disclose the business transactions and market positions of any person.

"(iv) With respect to swaps that are determined to be required to be cleared under subsection (h)(2) but are not cleared, the Commission shall require real-time public reporting for such transactions.

"(D) REGISTERED ENTITIES AND PUBLIC REPORTING.—The Commission may require registered entities to publicly disseminate the swap transaction and pricing data required to be reported under this paragraph.

"(E) RULEMAKING REQUIRED.—With respect to the rule providing for the public availability of transaction and pricing data for swaps described in clauses (i) and (ii) of subparagraph (C), the rule promulgated by the Commission shall contain provisions—

"(i) to ensure such information does not identify the participants;

"(ii) to specify the criteria for determining what constitutes a large notional swap transaction (block trade) for particular markets and contracts;

"(iii) to specify the appropriate time delay for reporting large notional swap transactions (block trades) to the public; and

"(iv) that take into account whether the public disclosure will materially reduce market liquidity.

"(F) TIMELINESS OF REPORTING.—Parties to a swap (including agents of the parties to a swap) shall be responsible for reporting swap transaction information to the appropriate registered entity in a timely manner as may be prescribed by the Commission.

"(G) REPORTING OF SWAPS TO REGISTERED SWAP DATA REPOSITORIES.—Each swap (whether cleared or uncleared) shall be reported to a registered swap data repository.

"(14) SEMIANNUAL AND ANNUAL PUBLIC REPORTING OF AGGREGATE SWAP DATA.—

"(A) IN GENERAL.—In accordance with subparagraph (B), the Commission shall issue a written report on a semiannual and annual basis to make available to the public information relating to—

"(i) the trading and clearing in the major swap categories; and

"(ii) the market participants and developments in new products.

"(B) USE; CONSULTATION.—In preparing a report under subparagraph (A), the Commission shall—

"(i) use information from swap data repositories and derivatives clearing organizations; and

"(ii) consult with the Office of the Comptroller of the Currency, the Bank for International Settlements, and such other regulatory bodies as may be necessary.

"(C) AUTHORITY OF THE COMMISSION.—

The Commission may, by rule, regulation, or order, delegate the public reporting responsibilities of the Commission under this paragraph in accordance with such terms and conditions as the Commission determines to be appropriate and in the public interest.".

[Explanation at ¶ 3075.]

[¶ 10,728] ACT SEC. 728. SWAP DATA REPOSITORIES.

The Commodity Exchange Act is amended by inserting after section 20 (7 U.S.C. 24) the following:

"SEC. 21. SWAP DATA REPOSITORIES.

"(a) REGISTRATION REQUIREMENT.—

"(1) REQUIREMENT; AUTHORITY OF DERIVATIVES CLEARING ORGANIZATION.—

"(A) IN GENERAL.—It shall be unlawful for any person, unless registered with the Commission, directly or indirectly to make use of the mails or any means or instrumentality of interstate commerce to perform the functions of a swap data repository.

"(B) REGISTRATION OF DERIVATIVES CLEARING ORGANIZATIONS.—A derivatives clearing organization may register as a swap data repository.

"(2) INSPECTION AND EXAMINATION.—Each registered swap data repository shall be subject to inspection and examination by any representative of the Commission.

"(3) COMPLIANCE WITH CORE PRINCIPLES.—

"(A) IN GENERAL.—To be registered, and maintain registration, as a swap data repository, the swap data repository shall comply with—

"(i) the requirements and core principles described in this section; and

"(ii) any requirement that the Commission may impose by rule or regulation pursuant to section 8a(5).

"(B) REASONABLE DISCRETION OF SWAP DATA REPOSITORY.—Unless otherwise determined by the Commission by rule or regulation, a swap data repository described in subparagraph (A) shall have reasonable discretion in establishing the manner in which the swap data repository complies with the core principles described in this section.

"(b) STANDARD SETTING.—

"(1) DATA IDENTIFICATION.—

"(A) IN GENERAL.—In accordance with subparagraph (B), the Commission shall prescribe standards that specify the data elements for each swap that shall be collected and maintained by each registered swap data repository.

"(B) REQUIREMENT.—In carrying out subparagraph (A), the Commission shall prescribe consistent data element standards applicable to registered entities and reporting counterparties.

"(2) DATA COLLECTION AND MAINTENANCE.—The Commission shall prescribe data collection and data maintenance standards for swap data repositories.

"(3) COMPARABILITY.—The standards prescribed by the Commission under this subsection shall be comparable to the data standards imposed by the Commission on derivatives clearing organizations in connection with their clearing of swaps.

"(c) DUTIES.—A swap data repository shall—

"(1) accept data prescribed by the Commission for each swap under subsection (b);

"(2) confirm with both counterparties to the swap the accuracy of the data that was submitted;

"(3) maintain the data described in paragraph (1) in such form, in such manner, and for such period as may be required by the Commission;

"(4)

(A) provide direct electronic access to the Commission (or any designee of the Commission, including another registered entity); and

"(B) provide the information described in paragraph (1) in such form and at such frequency as the Commission may require to comply with the public reporting requirements contained in section 2(a)(13);

"(5) at the direction of the Commission, establish automated systems for monitoring, screening, and analyzing swap data, including compliance and frequency of end user clearing exemption claims by individual and affiliated entities;

"(6) maintain the privacy of any and all swap transaction information that the swap data repository receives from a swap dealer, counterparty, or any other registered entity; and

"(7) on a confidential basis pursuant to section 8, upon request, and after notifying the Commission of the request, make available all data obtained by the swap data repository, including individual counterparty trade and position data, to—

"(A) each appropriate prudential regulator;

"(B) the Financial Stability Oversight Council;

"(C) the Securities and Exchange Commission;

"(D) the Department of Justice; and

"(E) any other person that the Commission determines to be appropriate, including—

"(i) foreign financial supervisors (including foreign futures authorities);

"(ii) foreign central banks; and

"(iii) foreign ministries; and

"(8) establish and maintain emergency procedures, backup facilities, and a plan for disaster recovery that allows for the timely recovery and resumption of operations and the fulfillment of the responsibilities and obligations of the organization.

"(d) CONFIDENTIALITY AND INDEMNIFICATION AGREEMENT.—Before the swap data repository may share information with any entity described in subsection (c)(7)—

"(1) the swap data repository shall receive a written agreement from each entity stating that the entity shall abide by the confidentiality requirements described in section 8 relating to the information on swap transactions that is provided; and

"(2) each entity shall agree to indemnify the swap data repository and the Commission for any expenses arising from litigation relating to the information provided under section 8.

"(e) DESIGNATION OF CHIEF COMPLIANCE OFFICER.—

"(1) IN GENERAL.—Each swap data repository shall designate an individual to serve as a chief compliance officer.

"(2) DUTIES.—The chief compliance officer shall—

"(A) report directly to the board or to the senior officer of the swap data repository;

"(B) review the compliance of the swap data repository with respect to the requirements and core principles described in this section;

"(C) in consultation with the board of the swap data repository, a body performing a function similar to the board of the swap data repository, or the senior officer of the swap data repository, resolve any conflicts of interest that may arise;

"(D) be responsible for administering each policy and procedure that is required to be established pursuant to this section;

"(E) ensure compliance with this Act (including regulations) relating to agreements, contracts, or transactions, including each rule prescribed by the Commission under this section;

"(F) establish procedures for the remediation of noncompliance issues identified by the chief compliance officer through any—

"(i) compliance office review;

"(ii) look-back;

"(iii) internal or external audit finding;

"(iv) self-reported error; or

"(v) validated complaint; and

"(G) establish and follow appropriate procedures for the handling, management response, remediation, retesting, and closing of noncompliance issues.

"(3) ANNUAL REPORTS.—

"(A) IN GENERAL.—In accordance with rules prescribed by the Commission, the chief compliance officer shall annually prepare and sign a report that contains a description of—

"(i) the compliance of the swap data repository of the chief compliance officer with respect to this Act (including regulations); and "(ii) each policy and procedure of the swap data repository of the chief compliance officer (including the code of ethics and conflict of interest policies of the swap data repository).

"(B) REQUIREMENTS.—A compliance report under subparagraph (A) shall—

"(i) accompany each appropriate financial report of the swap data repository that is required to be furnished to the Commission pursuant to this section; and

"(ii) include a certification that, under penalty of law, the compliance report is accurate and complete.

"(f) CORE PRINCIPLES APPLICABLE TO SWAP DATA REPOSITORIES.—

"(1) ANTITRUST CONSIDERATIONS.—Unless necessary or appropriate to achieve the purposes of this Act, a swap data repository shall not—

"(A) adopt any rule or take any action that results in any unreasonable restraint of trade; or

"(B) impose any material anticompetitive burden on the trading, clearing, or reporting of transactions.

"(2) GOVERNANCE ARRANGEMENTS.—Each swap data repository shall establish governance arrangements that are transparent—

"(A) to fulfill public interest requirements; and

"(B) to support the objectives of the Federal Government, owners, and participants.

"(3) CONFLICTS OF INTEREST.—Each swap data repository shall—

"(A) establish and enforce rules to minimize conflicts of interest in the decision-making process of the swap data repository; and

"(B) establish a process for resolving conflicts of interest described in subparagraph (A).

"(4) ADDITIONAL DUTIES DEVELOPED BY COMMISSION.—

"(A) IN GENERAL.—The Commission may develop 1 or more additional duties applicable to swap data repositories.

"(B) CONSIDERATION OF EVOLVING STANDARDS.—In developing additional duties under subparagraph (A), the Commission may take into consideration any evolving standard of the United States or the international community.

"(C) ADDITIONAL DUTIES FOR COMMISSION DESIGNEES.—The Commission shall establish additional duties for any registrant described in section la(48) in order to minimize conflicts of interest, protect data, ensure compliance, and guarantee the safety and security of the swap data repository.

"(g) REQUIRED REGISTRATION FOR SWAP DATA REPOSITORIES.—Any person that is required to be registered as a swap data repository under this section shall register with the Commission regardless of whether that person is also licensed as a bank or registered with the Securities and Exchange Commission as a swap data repository.

"(h) RULES.—The Commission shall adopt rules governing persons that are registered under this section.".

[Explanation at ¶ 3080.]

[¶ 10,729] ACT SEC. 729. REPORTING AND RECORDKEEPING.

The Commodity Exchange Act is amended by inserting after section 4q (7 U.S.C. 60-1) the following:

"SEC. 4r. REPORTING AND RECORDKEEPING FOR UNCLEARED SWAPS.

"(a) REQUIRED REPORTING OF SWAPS NOT ACCEPTED BY ANY DERIVATIVES CLEARING ORGANIZATION.—

"(1) IN GENERAL.—Each swap that is not accepted for clearing by any derivatives clearing organization shall be reported to—

"(A) a swap data repository described in section 21; or

"(B) in the case in which there is no swap data repository that would accept the swap, to the Commission pursuant to this section within such time period as the Commission may by rule or regulation prescribe.

"(2) TRANSITION RULE FOR PREENACTMENT SWAPS.—

"(A) SWAPS ENTERED INTO BEFORE THE DATE OF ENACTMENT OF THE WALL STREET TRANSPARENCY AND ACCOUNTABILITY ACT OF 2010.—Each swap entered into before the date of enactment of the Wall Street Transparency and Accountability Act of 2010, the terms of which have not expired as of the date of enactment of that Act, shall be reported to a registered swap data repository or the Commission by a date that is not later than—

"(i) 30 days after issuance of the interim final rule; or

"(ii) such other period as the Commission determines to be appropriate.

"(B) COMMISSION RULEMAKING.—The Commission shall promulgate an interim final rule within 90 days of the date of enactment of this section providing for the reporting of each swap entered into before the date of enactment as referenced in subparagraph (A).

"(C) EFFECTIVE DATE.—The reporting provisions described in this section shall be effective upon the enactment of this section.

"(3) REPORTING OBLIGATIONS.—

"(A) SWAPS IN WHICH ONLY 1 COUNTERPARTY IS A SWAP DEALER OR MAJOR SWAP PARTICIPANT.—With respect to a swap in which only 1 counterparty is a swap dealer or major swap participant, the swap dealer or major swap participant shall report the swap as required under paragraphs (1) and (2).

"(B) SWAPS IN WHICH 1 COUNTERPARTY IS A SWAP DEALER AND THE OTHER A MAJOR SWAP PARTICIPANT.—With respect to a swap in which 1 counterparty is a swap dealer and the other a major swap participant, the swap dealer shall report the swap as required under paragraphs (1) and (2).

"(C) OTHER SWAPS.—With respect to any other swap not described in subparagraph (A) or (B), the counterparties to the swap shall select a counterparty to report the swap as required under paragraphs (1) and (2).

"(b) DUTIES OF CERTAIN INDIVIDUALS.—Any individual or entity that enters into a swap shall meet each requirement described in subsection (c) if the individual or entity did not—

"(1) clear the swap in accordance with section 2(h)(1); or

"(2) have the data regarding the swap accepted by a swap data repository in accordance with rules (including timeframes) adopted by the Commission under section 21.

"(c) REQUIREMENTS.—An individual or entity described in subsection (b) shall—

"(1) upon written request from the Commission, provide reports regarding the swaps held by the individual or entity to the Commission in such form and in such manner as the Commission may request; and

"(2) maintain books and records pertaining to the swaps held by the individual or entity in such form, in such manner, and for such period as the Commission may require, which shall be open to inspection by—

"(A) any representative of the Commission;

"(B) an appropriate prudential regulator;

"(C) the Securities and Exchange Commission;

"(D) the Financial Stability Oversight Council; and

"(E) the Department of Justice.

"(d) IDENTICAL DATA.—In prescribing rules under this section, the Commission shall require individuals and entities described in subsection (b) to submit to the Commission a report that contains data that is not less comprehensive than the data required to be collected by swap data repositories under section 21.".

[Explanation at ¶ 3085.]

[¶ 10,730] ACT SEC. 730. LARGE SWAP TRADER REPORTING.

The Commodity Exchange Act (7 U.S.C. 1 et seq.) is amended by adding after section 4s (as added by section 731) the following:

"SEC. 4t. LARGE SWAP TRADER REPORTING.

"(a) PROHIBITION.—

"(1) IN GENERAL.—Except as provided in paragraph (2), it shall be unlawful for any person to enter into any swap that the Commission determines to perform a significant price discovery function with respect to registered entities if—

"(A) the person directly or indirectly enters into the swap during any 1 day in an amount equal to or in excess of such amount as shall be established periodically by the Commission; and

"(B) the person directly or indirectly has or obtains a position in the swap equal to or in excess of such amount as shall be established periodically by the Commission.

"(2) EXCEPTION.—Paragraph (1) shall not apply if—

"(A) the person files or causes to be filed with the properly designated officer of the Commission such reports regarding any transactions or positions described in subparagraphs (A) and (B) of paragraph (1) as the Commission may require by rule or regulation; and

"(B) in accordance with the rules and regulations of the Commission, the person keeps books and records of all such swaps and any transactions and positions in any related commodity traded on or subject to the rules of any designated contract market or swap execution facility, and of cash or spot transactions in, inventories of, and purchase and sale commitments of, such a commodity.

"(b) REQUIREMENTS.—

"(1) IN GENERAL.—Books and records described in subsection (a)(2)(B) shall—

"(A) show such complete details concerning all transactions and positions as the Commission may prescribe by rule or regulation;

"(B) be open at all times to inspection and examination by any representative of the Commission; and

"(C) be open at all times to inspection and examination by the Securities and Exchange Commission, to the extent such books and records relate to transactions in swaps (as that term is defined in section 1a(47)(A)(v)), and consistent with the confidentiality and disclosure requirements of section 8.

"(2) JURISDICTION.—Nothing in paragraph (1) shall affect the exclusive jurisdiction of the Commission to prescribe recordkeeping and reporting requirements for large swap traders under this section.

"(c) APPLICABILITY.—For purposes of this section, the swaps, futures, and cash or spot transactions and positions of any person shall include the swaps, futures, and cash or spot transactions and positions of any persons directly or indirectly controlled by the person.

"(d) SIGNIFICANT PRICE DISCOVERY FUNCTION.—In making a determination as to whether a swap performs or affects a significant price discovery function with respect to registered entities, the Commission shall consider the factors described in section 4a(a)(3).".

[Explanation at ¶ 3090.]

[¶ 10,731] ACT SEC. 731. REGISTRATION AND REGULATION OF SWAP DEALERS AND MAJOR SWAP PARTICIPANTS.

The Commodity Exchange Act (7 U.S.C. 1 et seq.) is amended by inserting after section 4r (as added by section 729) the following:

"SEC. 4s. REGISTRATION AND REGULATION OF SWAP DEALERS AND MAJOR SWAP PARTICIPANTS.

"(a) REGISTRATION.—

"(1) SWAP DEALERS.—It shall be unlawful for any person to act as a swap dealer unless the person is registered as a swap dealer with the Commission.

"(2) MAJOR SWAP PARTICIPANTS.—It shall be unlawful for any person to act as a major swap participant unless the person is registered as a major swap participant with the Commission.

"(b) REQUIREMENTS.—

"(1) IN GENERAL.—A person shall register as a swap dealer or major swap participant by filing a registration application with the Commission.

"(2) CONTENTS.—

"(A) IN GENERAL.—The application shall be made in such form and manner as prescribed by the Commission, and shall contain such information, as the Commission considers necessary concerning the business in which the applicant is or will be engaged.

"(B) CONTINUAL REPORTING.—A person that is registered as a swap dealer or major swap participant shall continue to submit to the Commission reports that contain such information pertaining to the business of the person as the Commission may require.

"(3) EXPIRATION.—Each registration under this section shall expire at such time as the Commission may prescribe by rule or regulation.

"(4) RULES.—Except as provided in subsections (d) and (e), the Commission may prescribe rules applicable to swap dealers and major swap participants, including rules that limit the activities of swap dealers and major swap participants.

"(5) TRANSITION.—Rules under this section shall provide for the registration of swap dealers and major swap participants not later than 1 year after the date of enactment of the Wall Street Transparency and Accountability Act of 2010.

"(6) STATUTORY DISQUALIFICATION.—Except to the extent otherwise specifically provided by rule, regulation, or order, it shall be unlawful for a swap dealer or a major swap participant to permit any person associated with a swap dealer or a major swap participant who is subject to a statutory disqualification to effect or be involved in effecting swaps on behalf of the swap dealer or major swap participant, if the swap dealer or major swap participant knew, or in the exercise of reasonable care should have known, of the statutory disqualification.

"(c) DUAL REGISTRATION.—

"(1) SWAP DEALER.—Any person that is required to be registered as a swap dealer under this section shall register with the Commission regardless of whether the person also is a depository institution or is registered with the Securities and Exchange Commission as a security-based swap dealer.

"(2) MAJOR SWAP PARTICIPANT.—Any person that is required to be registered as a major swap participant under this section shall register with the Commission regardless of whether the person also is a depository institution or is registered with the Securities and Exchange Commission as a major security-based swap participant.

"(d) RULEMAKINGS.—

"(1) IN GENERAL.—The Commission shall adopt rules for persons that are registered as swap dealers or major swap participants under this section.

"(2) EXCEPTION FOR PRUDENTIAL REQUIREMENTS.—

"(A) IN GENERAL.—The Commission may not prescribe rules imposing prudential requirements on swap dealers or major swap participants for which there is a prudential regulator.

"(B) APPLICABILITY.—Subparagraph (A) does not limit the authority of the Commission to prescribe rules as directed under this section.

"(e) CAPITAL AND MARGIN REQUIREMENTS.—

"(1) IN GENERAL.—

"(A) SWAP DEALERS AND MAJOR SWAP PARTICIPANTS THAT ARE BANKS.—Each registered swap dealer and major swap participant for which there is a prudential regulator shall meet such minimum capital requirements and minimum initial and variation margin requirements as the prudential regulator shall by rule or regulation prescribe under paragraph (2)(A).

"(B) SWAP DEALERS AND MAJOR SWAP PARTICIPANTS THAT ARE NOT BANKS.—Each registered swap dealer and major swap participant for which there is not a prudential regulator shall meet such minimum capital requirements and minimum initial and variation margin requirements as the Commission shall by rule or regulation prescribe under paragraph (2)(B).

"(2) RULES.—

"(A) SWAP DEALERS AND MAJOR SWAP PARTICIPANTS THAT ARE BANKS.—The prudential regulators, in consultation with the Commission and the Securities and Exchange Commission, shall jointly adopt rules for swap dealers and major swap participants, with respect to their activities as a swap dealer or major swap participant, for which there is a prudential regulator imposing—

"(i) capital requirements; and

"(ii) both initial and variation margin requirements on all swaps that are not cleared by a registered derivatives clearing organization.

"(B) SWAP DEALERS AND MAJOR SWAP PARTICIPANTS THAT ARE NOT BANKS.—The Commission shall adopt rules for swap dealers and major swap participants, with respect to their activities as a swap dealer or major swap participant, for which there is not a prudential regulator imposing—

"(i) capital requirements; and

"(ii) both initial and variation margin requirements on all swaps that are not cleared by a registered derivatives clearing organization.

"(C) CAPITAL.—In setting capital requirements for a person that is designated as a swap dealer or a major swap participant for a single type or single class or category of swap or activities, the prudential regulator and the Commission shall take into account the risks associated with other types of swaps or classes of swaps or categories of swaps engaged in and the other activities conducted by that person that are not otherwise subject to regulation applicable to that person by virtue of the status of the person as a swap dealer or a major swap participant.

"(3) STANDARDS FOR CAPITAL AND MARGIN.—

"(A) IN GENERAL.—To offset the greater risk to the swap dealer or major swap participant and the financial system arising from the use of swaps that are not cleared, the requirements imposed under paragraph (2) shall—

"(i) help ensure the safety and soundness of the swap dealer or major swap participant; and

"(ii) be appropriate for the risk associated with the non-cleared swaps held as a swap dealer or major swap participant.

"(B) RULE OF CONSTRUCTION.—

"(i) IN GENERAL.—Nothing in this section shall limit, or be construed to limit, the authority—

"(I) of the Commission to set financial responsibility rules for a futures commission merchant or introducing broker registered pursuant to section 4f(a) (except for section 4f(a)(3)) in accordance with section 4f(b); or

"(II) of the Securities and Exchange Commission to set financial responsibility rules for a broker or dealer registered pursuant to section 15(b) of the Securities Exchange Act of 1934 (15 U.S.C. 78o(b)) (except for section 15(b)(11) of that Act (15 U.S.C. 78o(b)(11)) in accordance with section 15(c)(3) of the Securities Exchange Act of 1934 (15 U.S.C. 78o(c)(3)).

"(ii) FUTURES COMMISSION MERCHANTS AND OTHER DEALERS.—A futures commission merchant, introducing broker, broker, or dealer shall maintain sufficient capital to comply with the stricter of any applicable capital requirements to which such futures commission merchant, introducing broker, broker, or dealer is subject to under this Act or the Securities Exchange Act of 1934 (15 U.S.C. 78a et seq.).

"(C) MARGIN REQUIREMENTS.—In prescribing margin requirements under this subsection, the prudential regulator with respect to swap dealers and major swap participants for which it is the prudential regulator and the Commission with respect to swap dealers and major swap participants for which there is no prudential regulator shall permit the use of noncash collateral, as the regulator or the Commission determines to be consistent with—

"(i) preserving the financial integrity of markets trading swaps; and

"(ii) preserving the stability of the United States financial system.

"(D) COMPARABILITY OF CAPITAL AND MARGIN REQUIREMENTS.—

"(i) IN GENERAL.—The prudential regulators, the Commission, and the Securities and Exchange Commission shall periodically (but not less frequently than annually) consult on minimum capital requirements and minimum initial and variation margin requirements.

"(ii) COMPARABILITY.—The entities described in clause (i) shall, to the maximum extent practicable, establish and maintain comparable minimum capital requirements and minimum initial and variation margin requirements, including the use of non cash collateral, for—

"(I) swap dealers; and

"(II) major swap participants.

"(f) REPORTING AND RECORDKEEPING.—

"(1) IN GENERAL.—Each registered swap dealer and major swap participant—

"(A) shall make such reports as are required by the Commission by rule or regulation regarding the transactions and positions and financial condition of the registered swap dealer or major swap participant;

"(B)

"(i) for which there is a prudential regulator, shall keep books and records of all activities related to the business as a swap dealer or major swap participant in such form and manner and for such period as may be prescribed by the Commission by rule or regulation; and

"(ii) for which there is no prudential regulator, shall keep books and records in such form and manner and for such period as may be prescribed by the Commission by rule or regulation;

"(C) shall keep books and records described in subparagraph (B) open to inspection and examination by any representative of the Commission; and

"(D) shall keep any such books and records relating to swaps defined in section 1a(47)(A)(v) open to inspection and examination by the Securities and Exchange Commission.

"(2) RULES.—The Commission shall adopt rules governing reporting and recordkeeping for swap dealers and major swap participants.

"(g) DAILY TRADING RECORDS.—

"(1) IN GENERAL.—Each registered swap dealer and major swap participant shall maintain daily trading records of the swaps of the registered swap dealer and major swap participant and all related records (including related cash or forward transactions) and recorded communications, including electronic mail, instant messages, and recordings of telephone calls, for such period as may be required by the Commission by rule or regulation.

"(2) INFORMATION REQUIREMENTS.—The daily trading records shall include such information as the Commission shall require by rule or regulation.

"(3) COUNTERPARTY RECORDS.—Each registered swap dealer and major swap participant shall maintain daily trading records for each counterparty in a manner and form that is identifiable with each swap transaction.

"(4) AUDIT TRAIL.—Each registered swap dealer and major swap participant shall maintain a complete audit trail for conducting comprehensive and accurate trade reconstructions.

"(5) RULES.—The Commission shall adopt rules governing daily trading records for swap dealers and major swap participants.

"(h) BUSINESS CONDUCT STANDARDS.—

"(1) IN GENERAL.—Each registered swap dealer and major swap participant shall conform with such business conduct standards as prescribed in paragraph (3) and as may be prescribed by the Commission by rule or regulation that relate to—

"(A) fraud, manipulation, and other abusive practices involving swaps (including swaps that are offered but not entered into);

"(B) diligent supervision of the business of the registered swap dealer and major swap participant;

"(C) adherence to all applicable position limits; and

"(D) such other matters as the Commission determines to be appropriate.

"(2) RESPONSIBILITIES WITH RESPECT TO SPECIAL ENTITIES.—

"(A) ADVISING SPECIAL ENTITIES.—A swap dealer or major swap participant that acts as an advisor to a special entity regarding a swap shall comply with the requirements of subparagraph (4) with respect to such Special Entity.

"(B) ENTERING OF SWAPS WITH RESPECT TO SPECIAL ENTITIES.—A swap dealer that enters into or offers to enter into swap with a Special Entity shall comply with the requirements of subparagraph (5) with respect to such Special Entity.

"(C) SPECIAL ENTITY DEFINED.—For purposes of this subsection, the term 'special entity' means—

"(i) a Federal agency;

"(ii) a State, State agency, city, county, municipality, or other political subdivision of a State;

"(iii) any employee benefit plan, as defined in section 3 of the Employee Retirement Income Security Act of 1974 (29 U.S.C. 1002);

"(iv) any governmental plan, as defined in section 3 of the Employee Retirement Income Security Act of 1974 (29 U.S.C. 1002); or

"(v) any endowment, including an endowment that is an organization described in section 501(c)(3) of the Internal Revenue Code of 1986.

"(3) BUSINESS CONDUCT REQUIREMENTS.—Business conduct requirements adopted by the Commission shall—

"(A) establish a duty for a swap dealer or major swap participant to verify that any counterparty meets the eligibility standards for an eligible contract participant;

"(B) require disclosure by the swap dealer or major swap participant to any counterparty to the transaction (other than a swap dealer, major swap participant, security-based swap dealer, or major security-based swap participant) of—

"(i) information about the material risks and characteristics of the swap;

"(ii) any material incentives or conflicts of interest that the swap dealer or major swap participant may have in connection with the swap; and

"(iii)

(I) for cleared swaps, upon the request of the counterparty, receipt of the daily mark of the transaction from the appropriate derivatives clearing organization; and

"(II) for uncleared swaps, receipt of the daily mark of the transaction from the swap dealer or the major swap participant;

"(C) establish a duty for a swap dealer or major swap participant to communicate in a fair and balanced manner based on principles of fair dealing and good faith; and

"(D) establish such other standards and requirements as the Commission may determine are appropriate in the public interest, for the protection of investors, or otherwise in furtherance of the purposes of this Act.

"(4) SPECIAL REQUIREMENTS FOR SWAP DEALERS ACTING AS ADVISORS.—

"(A) IN GENERAL.—It shall be unlawful for a swap dealer or major swap participant—

"(i) to employ any device, scheme, or artifice to defraud any Special Entity or prospective customer who is a Special Entity;

"(ii) to engage in any transaction, practice, or course of business that operates as a fraud or deceit on any Special Entity or prospective customer who is a Special Entity; or

"(iii) to engage in any act, practice, or course of business that is fraudulent, deceptive or manipulative.

"(B) DUTY.—Any swap dealer that acts as an advisor to a Special Entity shall have a duty to act in the best interests of the Special Entity.

"(C) REASONABLE EFFORTS.—Any swap dealer that acts as an advisor to a Special Entity shall make reasonable efforts to obtain such information as is necessary to make a reasonable determination that any swap recommended by the swap dealer is in the best interests of the Special Entity, including information relating to—

"(i) the financial status of the Special Entity;

"(ii) the tax status of the Special Entity;

"(iii) the investment or financing objectives of the Special Entity; and

"(iv) any other information that the Commission may prescribe by rule or regulation.

"(5) SPECIAL REQUIREMENTS FOR SWAP DEALERS AS COUNTERPARTIES TO SPECIAL ENTITIES.—

"(A) Any swap dealer or major swap participant that offers to enter or enters into a swap with a Special Entity shall—

"(i) comply with any duty established by the Commission for a swap dealer or major swap participant, with respect to a counterparty that is an eligible contract participant within the meaning of subclause (I) or (II) of clause (vii) of section la(18) of this Act, that requires the swap dealer or major swap participant to have a reasonable basis to believe that the counterparty that is a Special Entity has an independent representative that—

"(I) has sufficient knowledge to evaluate the transaction and risks;

"(II) is not subject to a statutory disqualification;

"(III) is independent of the swap dealer or major swap participant;

"(IV) undertakes a duty to act in the best interests of the counterparty it represents;

"(V) makes appropriate disclosures;

"(VI) will provide written representations to the Special Entity regarding fair pricing and the appropriateness of the transaction; and

"(VII) in the case of employee benefit plans subject to the Employee Retirement Income Security act of 1974, is a fiduciary as defined in section 3 of that Act (29 U.S.C. 1002); and

"(ii) before the initiation of the transaction, disclose to the Special Entity in writing the capacity in which the swap dealer is acting; and

"(B) the Commission may establish such other standards and requirements as the Commission may determine are appropriate in the public interest, for the protection of investors, or otherwise in furtherance of the purposes of this Act.

"(6) RULES.—The Commission shall prescribe rules under this subsection governing business conduct standards for swap dealers and major swap participants.

"(7) APPLICABILITY.—This section shall not apply with respect to a transaction that is—

"(A) initiated by a Special Entity on an exchange or swap execution facility; and

"(B) one in which the swap dealer or major swap participant does not know the identity of the counterparty to the transaction.

"(i) DOCUMENTATION STANDARDS.—

"(1) IN GENERAL.—Each registered swap dealer and major swap participant shall conform with such standards as may be prescribed by the Commission by rule or regulation that relate to timely and accurate confirmation, processing, netting, documentation, and valuation of all swaps.

"(2) RULES.—The Commission shall adopt rules governing documentation standards for swap dealers and major swap participants.

"(j) DUTIES.—Each registered swap dealer and major swap participant at all times shall comply with the following requirements:

"(1) MONITORING OF TRADING.—The swap dealer or major swap participant shall monitor its trading in swaps to prevent violations of applicable position limits.

"(2) RISK MANAGEMENT PROCEDURES.—The swap dealer or major swap participant shall establish robust and professional risk management systems adequate for managing the day-to-day business of the swap dealer or major swap participant.

"(3) DISCLOSURE OF GENERAL INFORMATION.—The swap dealer or major swap participant shall disclose to the Commission and to the prudential regulator for the swap dealer or major swap participant, as applicable, information concerning—

"(A) terms and conditions of its swaps;

"(B) swap trading operations, mechanisms, and practices;

"(C) financial integrity protections relating to swaps; and

"(D) other information relevant to its trading in swaps.

"(4) ABILITY TO OBTAIN INFORMATION.—The swap dealer or major swap participant shall—

"(A) establish and enforce internal systems and procedures to obtain any necessary information to perform any of the functions described in this section; and

"(B) provide the information to the Commission and to the prudential regulator for the swap dealer or major swap participant, as applicable, on request.

"(5) CONFLICTS OF INTEREST.—The swap dealer and major swap participant shall implement conflict-of-interest systems and procedures that—

"(A) establish structural and institutional safeguards to ensure that the activities of any person within the firm relating to research or analysis of the price or market for any commodity or swap or acting in a role of providing clearing activities or making determinations as to accepting clearing customers are separated by appropriate informational partitions within the firm from the review, pressure, or oversight of persons whose involvement in pricing, trading, or clearing activities might potentially bias their judgment or supervision and contravene the core principles of open access and the business conduct standards described in this Act; and

"(B) address such other issues as the Commission determines to be appropriate.

"(6) ANTITRUST CONSIDERATIONS.—Unless necessary or appropriate to achieve the purposes of this Act, a swap dealer or major swap participant shall not—

"(A) adopt any process or take any action that results in any unreasonable restraint of trade; or

"(B) impose any material anticompetitive burden on trading or clearing.

"(7) RULES.—The Commission shall prescribe rules under this subsection governing duties of swap dealers and major swap participants.

"(k) DESIGNATION OF CHIEF COMPLIANCE OFFICER.—

"(1) IN GENERAL.—Each swap dealer and major swap participant shall designate an individual to serve as a chief compliance officer.

"(2) DUTIES.—The chief compliance officer shall—

"(A) report directly to the board or to the senior officer of the swap dealer or major swap participant;

"(B) review the compliance of the swap dealer or major swap participant with respect to the swap dealer and major swap participant requirements described in this section;

"(C) in consultation with the board of directors, a body performing a function similar to the board, or the senior officer of the organization, resolve any conflicts of interest that may arise;

"(D) be responsible for administering each policy and procedure that is required to be established pursuant to this section;

"(E) ensure compliance with this Act (including regulations) relating to swaps, including each rule prescribed by the Commission under this section;

"(F) establish procedures for the remediation of noncompliance issues identified by the chief compliance officer through any—

"(i) compliance office review;

"(ii) look-back;

"(iii) internal or external audit finding;

"(iv) self-reported error; or

"(v) validated complaint; and

"(G) establish and follow appropriate procedures for the handling, management response, remediation, retesting, and closing of noncompliance issues.

"(3) ANNUAL REPORTS.—

"(A) IN GENERAL.—In accordance with rules prescribed by the Commission, the chief compliance officer shall annually prepare and sign a report that contains a description of—

"(i) the compliance of the swap dealer or major swap participant with respect to this Act (including regulations); and

"(ii) each policy and procedure of the swap dealer or major swap participant of the chief compliance officer (including the code of ethics and conflict of interest policies).

"(B) REQUIREMENTS.—A compliance report under subparagraph (A) shall—

"(i) accompany each appropriate financial report of the swap dealer or major swap participant that is required to be furnished to the Commission pursuant to this section; and

"(ii) include a certification that, under penalty of law, the compliance report is accurate and complete.".

[Explanation at ¶ 3095.]

[¶ 10,732] ACT SEC. 732. CONFLICTS OF INTEREST.

Section 4d of the Commodity Exchange Act (7 U.S.C. 6d) is amended—

(1) by redesignating subsection (c) as subsection (e); and

(2) by inserting after subsection (b) the following:

"(c) CONFLICTS OF INTEREST.—The Commission shall require that futures commission merchants and introducing brokers implement conflict-of-interest systems and procedures that—

"(1) establish structural and institutional safeguards to ensure that the activities of any person within the firm relating to research or analysis of the price or market for any commodity are separated by appropriate informational partitions within the firm from the review, pressure, or oversight of persons whose involvement in trading or clearing activities might potentially bias the judgment or supervision of the persons; and

"(2) address such other issues as the Commission determines to be appropriate.

"(d) DESIGNATION OF CHIEF COMPLIANCE OFFICER.—Each futures commission merchant shall designate an individual to serve as its Chief Compliance Officer and perform such duties and responsibilities as shall be set forth in regulations to be adopted by the Commission or rules to be adopted by a futures association registered under section 17.".

[Explanation at ¶ 3045.]

[¶ 10,733] ACT SEC. 733. SWAP EXECUTION FACILITIES.

The Commodity Exchange Act is amended by inserting after section 5g (7 U.S.C. 7b-2) the following:

"SEC. 5h. SWAP EXECUTION FACILITIES.

"(a) REGISTRATION.—

"(1) IN GENERAL.—No person may operate a facility for the trading or processing of swaps unless the facility is registered as a swap execution facility or as a designated contract market under this section.

"(2) DUAL REGISTRATION.—Any person that is registered as a swap execution facility under this section shall register with the Commission regardless of whether the person also is registered with the Securities and Exchange Commission as a swap execution facility.

"(b) TRADING AND TRADE PROCESSING.—

"(1) IN GENERAL.—Except as specified in paragraph (2), a swap execution facility that is registered under subsection (a) may—

"(A) make available for trading any swap; and

"(B) facilitate trade processing of any swap.

"(2) AGRICULTURAL SWAPS.—A swap execution facility may not list for trading or confirm the execution of any swap in an agricultural commodity (as defined by the Commission) except pursuant to a rule or regulation of the Commission allowing the swap under such terms and conditions as the Commission shall prescribe.

"(c) IDENTIFICATION OF FACILITY USED TO TRADE SWAPS BY CONTRACT MARKETS.—A board of trade that operates a contract market shall, to the extent that the board of trade also operates a swap execution facility and uses the same electronic trade execution system for listing and executing trades of swaps on or through the contract market and the swap execution facility, identify whether the electronic trading of such swaps is taking place on or through the contract market or the swap execution facility.

"(d) RULE-WRITING.—

"(1) The Securities and Exchange Commission and Commodity Futures Trading Commission may promulgate rules defining the universe of swaps that can be executed on a swap execution facility. These rules shall take into account the price and nonprice requirements of the counterparties to a swap and the goal of this section as set forth in subsection (e).

"(2) For all swaps that are not required to be executed through a swap execution facility as defined in paragraph (1), such trades may be executed through any other available means of interstate commerce.

"(3) The Securities and Exchange Commission and Commodity Futures Trading Commission shall update these rules as necessary to account for technological and other innovation.

"(e) RULE OF CONSTRUCTION.—The goal of this section is to promote the trading of swaps on swap execution facilities and to promote pre-trade price transparency in the swaps market.

"(f) CORE PRINCIPLES FOR SWAP EXECUTION FACILITIES.—

"(1) COMPLIANCE WITH CORE PRINCIPLES.—

"(A) IN GENERAL.—To be registered, and maintain registration, as a swap execution facility, the swap execution facility shall comply with—

"(i) the core principles described in this subsection; and

"(ii) any requirement that the Commission may impose by rule or regulation pursuant to section 8a(5).

"(B) REASONABLE DISCRETION OF SWAP EXECUTION FACILITY.—Unless otherwise determined by the Commission by rule or regulation, a swap execution facility described in subparagraph (A) shall have reasonable discretion in establishing the manner in which the swap execution facility complies with the core principles described in this subsection.

"(2) COMPLIANCE WITH RULES.—A swap execution facility shall—

"(A) establish and enforce compliance with any rule of the swap execution facility, including—

"(i) the terms and conditions of the swaps traded or processed on or through the swap execution facility; and

"(ii) any limitation on access to the swap execution facility;

"(B) establish and enforce trading, trade processing, and participation rules that will deter abuses and have the capacity to detect, investigate, and enforce those rules, including means—

"(i) to provide market participants with impartial access to the market; and

"(ii) to capture information that may be used in establishing whether rule violations have occurred;

"(C) establish rules governing the operation of the facility, including rules specifying trading procedures to be used in entering and executing orders traded or posted on the facility, including block trades; and

"(D) provide by its rules that when a swap dealer or major swap participant enters into or facilitates a swap that is subject to the mandatory clearing requirement of section 2(h), the swap dealer or major swap participant shall be responsible for compliance with the mandatory trading requirement under section 2(h)(8).

"(3) SWAPS NOT READILY SUSCEPTIBLE TO MANIPULATION.—The swap execution facility shall permit trading only in swaps that are not readily susceptible to manipulation.

"(4) MONITORING OF TRADING AND TRADE PROCESSING.—The swap execution facility shall—

"(A) establish and enforce rules or terms and conditions defining, or specifications detailing—

"(i) trading procedures to be used in entering and executing orders traded on or through the facilities of the swap execution facility; and

"(ii) procedures for trade processing of swaps on or through the facilities of the swap execution facility; and

"(B) monitor trading in swaps to prevent manipulation, price distortion, and disruptions of the delivery or cash settlement process through surveillance, compliance, and disciplinary practices and procedures, including methods for conducting real-time monitoring of trading and comprehensive and accurate trade reconstructions.

"(5) ABILITY TO OBTAIN INFORMATION.—The swap execution facility shall—

"(A) establish and enforce rules that will allow the facility to obtain any necessary information to perform any of the functions described in this section;

"(B) provide the information to the Commission on request; and

"(C) have the capacity to carry out such international information-sharing agreements as the Commission may require.

"(6) POSITION LIMITS OR ACCOUNTABILITY.—

"(A) IN GENERAL.—To reduce the potential threat of market manipulation or congestion, especially during trading in the delivery month, a swap execution facility that is a trading facility shall adopt for each of the contracts of the facility, as is necessary and appropriate, position limitations or position accountability for speculators.

"(B) POSITION LIMITS.—For any contract that is subject to a position limitation established by the Commission pursuant to section 4a(a), the swap execution facility shall—

"(i) set its position limitation at a level no higher than the Commission limitation; and

"(ii) monitor positions established on or through the swap execution facility for compliance with the limit set by the Commission and the limit, if any, set by the swap execution facility.

"(7) FINANCIAL INTEGRITY OF TRANSACTIONS.—The swap execution facility shall establish and enforce rules and procedures for ensuring the financial integrity of swaps entered on or through the facilities of the swap execution facility, including the clearance and settlement of the swaps pursuant to section 2(h)(1).

"(8) EMERGENCY AUTHORITY.—The swap execution facility shall adopt rules to provide for the exercise of emergency authority, in consultation or cooperation with the Commission, as is necessary and appropriate, including the authority to liquidate or transfer open positions in any swap or to suspend or curtail trading in a swap.

"(9) TIMELY PUBLICATION OF TRADING INFORMATION.—

"(A) IN GENERAL.—The swap execution facility shall make public timely information on price, trading volume, and other trading data on swaps to the extent prescribed by the Commission.

"(B) CAPACITY OF SWAP EXECUTION FACILITY.—The swap execution facility shall be required to have the capacity to electronically capture and transmit trade information with respect to transactions executed on the facility.

"(10) RECORDKEEPING AND REPORTING.—

"(A) IN GENERAL.—A swap execution facility shall—

"(i) maintain records of all activities relating to the business of the facility, including a complete audit trail, in a form and manner acceptable to the Commission for a period of 5 years;

"(ii) report to the Commission, in a form and manner acceptable to the Commission, such information as the Commission determines to be necessary or appropriate for the Commission to perform the duties of the Commission under this Act; and

"(iii) shall keep any such records relating to swaps defined in section la(47)(A)(v) open to inspection and examination by the Securities and Exchange Commission."

"(B) REQUIREMENTS.—The Commission shall adopt data collection and reporting requirements for swap execution facilities that are comparable to corresponding requirements for derivatives clearing organizations and swap data repositories.

"(11) ANTITRUST CONSIDERATIONS.—Unless necessary or appropriate to achieve the purposes of this Act, the swap execution facility shall not—

"(A) adopt any rules or taking any actions that result in any unreasonable restraint of trade; or

"(B) impose any material anticompetitive burden on trading or clearing.

"(12) CONFLICTS OF INTEREST.—The swap execution facility shall—

"(A) establish and enforce rules to minimize conflicts of interest in its decision-making process; and

"(B) establish a process for resolving the conflicts of interest.

"(13) FINANCIAL RESOURCES.—

"(A) IN GENERAL.—The swap execution facility shall have adequate financial, operational, and managerial resources to discharge each responsibility of the swap execution facility.

"(B) DETERMINATION OF RESOURCE ADEQUACY.—The financial resources of a swap execution facility shall be considered to be adequate if the value of the financial resources exceeds the total amount that would enable the swap execution facility to cover the operating costs of the swap execution facility for a 1-year period, as calculated on a rolling basis.

"(14) SYSTEM SAFEGUARDS.—The swap execution facility shall—

"(A) establish and maintain a program of risk analysis and oversight to identify and minimize sources of operational risk, through the development of appropriate controls and procedures, and automated systems, that—

"(i) are reliable and secure; and

"(ii) have adequate scalable capacity;

"(B) establish and maintain emergency procedures, backup facilities, and a plan for disaster recovery that allow for—

"(i) the timely recovery and resumption of operations; and

"(ii) the fulfillment of the responsibilities and obligations of the swap execution facility; and

"(C) periodically conduct tests to verify that the backup resources of the swap execution facility are sufficient to ensure continued—

"(i) order processing and trade matching;

"(ii) price reporting;

"(iii) market surveillance and

"(iv) maintenance of a comprehensive and accurate audit trail.

"(15) DESIGNATION OF CHIEF COMPLIANCE OFFICER.—

"(A) IN GENERAL.—Each swap execution facility shall designate an individual to serve as a chief compliance officer.

"(B) DUTIES.—The chief compliance officer shall—

"(i) report directly to the board or to the senior officer of the facility;

"(ii) review compliance with the core principles in this subsection;

"(iii) in consultation with the board of the facility, a body performing a function similar to that of a board, or the senior officer of the facility, resolve any conflicts of interest that may arise;

"(iv) be responsible for establishing and administering the policies and procedures required to be established pursuant to this section;

"(v) ensure compliance with this Act and the rules and regulations issued under this Act, including rules prescribed by the Commission pursuant to this section; and

"(vi) establish procedures for the remediation of noncompliance issues found during compliance office reviews, look backs, internal or external audit findings, self-reported errors, or through validated complaints.

"(C) REQUIREMENTS FOR PROCEDURES.—In establishing procedures under subparagraph (B)(vi), the chief compliance officer shall design the procedures to establish the handling, management response, remediation, retesting, and closing of noncompliance issues.

"(D) ANNUAL REPORTS.—

"(i) IN GENERAL.—In accordance with rules prescribed by the Commission, the chief compliance officer shall annually prepare and sign a report that contains a description of—

"(I) the compliance of the swap execution facility with this Act; and

"(II) the policies and procedures, including the code of ethics and conflict of interest policies, of the swap execution facility.

"(ii) REQUIREMENTS.—The chief compliance officer shall—

"(I) submit each report described in clause (i) with the appropriate financial report of the swap execution facility that is required to be submitted to the Commission pursuant to this section; and

"(II) include in the report a certification that, under penalty of law, the report is accurate and complete.

"(g) EXEMPTIONS.—The Commission may exempt, conditionally or unconditionally, a swap execution facility from registration under this section if the Commission finds that the facility is subject to comparable, comprehensive supervision and regulation on a consolidated basis by the Securities and Exchange Commission, a prudential regulator, or the appropriate governmental authorities in the home country of the facility.

"(h) RULES.—The Commission shall prescribe rules governing the regulation of alternative swap execution facilities under this section.".

[Explanation at ¶ 3100.]

[¶ 10,734] ACT SEC. 734. DERIVATIVES TRANSACTION EXECUTION FACILITIES AND EXEMPT BOARDS OF TRADE.

(a) IN GENERAL.—Sections 5a and 5d of the Commodity Exchange Act (7 U.S.C. 7a, 7a-3) are repealed.

(b) CONFORMING AMENDMENTS.—

(1) Section 2 of the Commodity Exchange Act (7 U.S.C. 2) is amended—

(A) in subsection (a)(1)(A), in the first sentence, by striking "or 5a"; and

(B) in paragraph (2) of subsection (g) (as redesignated by section 723(a)(1)(B)), by striking "section 5a of this Act" and all that follows through "5d of this Act" and inserting "section 5b of this Act".

(2) Section 6(g)(1)(A) of the Securities Exchange Act of 1934 (15 U.S.C. 78f(g)(1)(A)) is amended—

(A) by striking "that—"and all that follows through "(i) has been designated" and inserting "that has been designated";

(B) by striking "; or" and inserting "; and" and

(C) by striking clause (ii).

(c) ABILITY TO PETITION COMMISSION.—

(1) IN GENERAL.—Prior to the final effective dates in this title, a person may petition the Commodity Futures Trading Commission to remain subject to the provisions of section 5d of the Commodity Exchange Act, as such provisions existed prior to the effective date of this subtitle.

(2) CONSIDERATION OF PETITION.—The Commodity Futures Trading Commission shall consider any petition submitted under paragraph (1) in a prompt manner and may allow a person to continue operating subject to the provisions of section 5d of the Commodity Exchange Act for up to 1 year after the effective date of this subtitle.

[Explanation at ¶ 3105.]

[¶ 10,735] ACT SEC. 735. DESIGNATED CONTRACT MARKETS.

(a) CRITERIA FOR DESIGNATION.—Section 5 of the Commodity Exchange Act (7 U.S.C. 7) is amended by striking subsection (b).

(b) CORE PRINCIPLES FOR CONTRACT MARKETS.—Section 5 of the Commodity Exchange Act (7 U.S.C. 7) is amended by striking subsection (d) and inserting the following:

"(d) CORE PRINCIPLES FOR CONTRACT MARKETS.—

"(1) DESIGNATION AS CONTRACT MARKET.—

"(A) IN GENERAL.—To be designated, and maintain a designation, as a contract market, a board of trade shall comply with—

"(i) any core principle described in this subsection; and

"(ii) any requirement that the Commission may impose by rule or regulation pursuant to section 8a(5).

"(B) REASONABLE DISCRETION OF CONTRACT MARKET.—Unless otherwise determined by the Commission by rule or regulation, a board of trade described in subparagraph (A) shall have reasonable discretion in establishing the manner in which the board of trade complies with the core principles described in this subsection.

"(2) COMPLIANCE WITH RULES.—

"(A) IN GENERAL.—The board of trade shall establish, monitor, and enforce compliance with the rules of the contract market, including—

"(i) access requirements;

"(ii) the terms and conditions of any contracts to be traded on the contract market; and

"(iii) rules prohibiting abusive trade practices on the contract market.

"(B) CAPACITY OF CONTRACT MARKET.—The board of trade shall have the capacity to detect, investigate, and apply appropriate sanctions to any person that violates any rule of the contract market.

"(C) REQUIREMENT OF RULES.—The rules of the contract market shall provide the board of trade with the ability and authority to obtain any necessary information to perform any function described in this subsection, including the capacity to carry out such international information-sharing agreements as the Commission may require.

"(3) CONTRACTS NOT READILY SUBJECT TO MANIPULATION.—The board of trade shall list on the contract market only contracts that are not readily susceptible to manipulation.

"(4) PREVENTION OF MARKET DISRUPTION.—The board of trade shall have the capacity and responsibility to prevent manipulation, price distortion, and disruptions of the delivery or cash-settlement process through market surveillance, compliance, and enforcement practices and procedures, including—

"(A) methods for conducting real-time monitoring of trading; and

"(B) comprehensive and accurate trade reconstructions.

"(5) POSITION LIMITATIONS OR ACCOUNTABILITY.—

"(A) IN GENERAL.—To reduce the potential threat of market manipulation or congestion (especially during trading in the delivery month), the board of trade shall adopt for each contract of the board of trade, as is necessary and appropriate, position limitations or position accountability for speculators.

"(B) MAXIMUM ALLOWABLE POSITION LIMITATION.—For any contract that is subject to a position limitation established by the Commission pursuant to section 4a(a), the board of trade shall set the position limitation of the board of trade at a level not higher than the position limitation established by the Commission.

"(6) EMERGENCY AUTHORITY.—The board of trade, in consultation or cooperation with the Commission, shall adopt rules to provide for the exercise of emergency authority, as is necessary and appropriate, including the authority—

"(A) to liquidate or transfer open positions in any contract;

"(B) to suspend or curtail trading in any contract; and

"(C) to require market participants in any contract to meet special margin requirements.

"(7) AVAILABILITY OF GENERAL INFORMATION.—The board of trade shall make available to market authorities, market participants, and the public accurate information concerning—

"(A) the terms and conditions of the contracts of the contract market; and

"(B)

(i) the rules, regulations, and mechanisms for executing transactions on or through the facilities of the contract market; and

"(ii) the rules and specifications describing the operation of the contract market's—

"(I) electronic matching platform; or

"(II) trade execution facility.

"(8) DAILY PUBLICATION OF TRADING INFORMATION.—The board of trade shall make public daily information on settlement prices, volume, open interest, and opening and closing ranges for actively traded contracts on the contract market.

"(9) EXECUTION OF TRANSACTIONS.—

"(A) IN GENERAL.—The board of trade shall provide a competitive, open, and efficient market and mechanism for executing transactions that protects the price discovery process of trading in the centralized market of the board of trade.

"(B) RULES.—The rules of the board of trade may authorize, for bona fide business purposes—

"(i) transfer trades or office trades;

"(ii) an exchange of—

"(I) futures in connection with a cash commodity transaction;

"(II) futures for cash commodities; or

"(III) futures for swaps; or

"(iii) a futures commission merchant, acting as principal or agent, to enter into or confirm the execution of a contract for the purchase or sale of a commodity for future delivery if the contract is reported, recorded, or cleared in accordance with the rules of the contract market or a derivatives clearing organization.

"(10) TRADE INFORMATION.—The board of trade shall maintain rules and procedures to provide for the recording and safe storage of all identifying trade information in a manner that enables the contract market to use the information—

"(A) to assist in the prevention of customer and market abuses; and

"(B) to provide evidence of any violations of the rules of the contract market.

"(11) FINANCIAL INTEGRITY OF TRANSACTIONS.—The board of trade shall establish and enforce—

"(A) rules and procedures for ensuring the financial integrity of transactions entered into on or through the facilities of the contract market (including the clearance and settlement of the transactions with a derivatives clearing organization); and

"(B) rules to ensure—

"(i) the financial integrity of any—

"(I) futures commission merchant; and

"(II) introducing broker; and

"(ii) the protection of customer funds.

"(12) PROTECTION OF MARKETS AND MARKET PARTICIPANTS.—The board of trade shall establish and enforce rules—

"(A) to protect markets and market participants from abusive practices committed by any party, including abusive practices committed by a party acting as an agent for a participant; and

"(B) to promote fair and equitable trading on the contract market.

"(13) DISCIPLINARY PROCEDURES.—The board of trade shall establish and enforce disciplinary procedures that authorize the board of trade to discipline, suspend, or expel members or market participants that violate the rules of the board of trade, or similar methods for performing the same functions, including delegation of the functions to third parties.

"(14) DISPUTE RESOLUTION.—The board of trade shall establish and enforce rules regarding, and provide facilities for alternative dispute resolution as appropriate for, market participants and any market intermediaries.

"(15) GOVERNANCE FITNESS STANDARDS.—The board of trade shall establish and enforce appropriate fitness standards for directors, members of any disciplinary committee, members of the contract market, and any other person with direct access to the facility (including any party affiliated with any person described in this paragraph).

"(16) CONFLICTS OF INTEREST.—The board of trade shall establish and enforce rules—

"(A) to minimize conflicts of interest in the decision-making process of the contract market; and

"(B) to establish a process for resolving conflicts of interest described in subparagraph (A).

"(17) COMPOSITION OF GOVERNING BOARDS OF CONTRACT MARKETS.—The governance arrangements of the board of trade shall be designed to permit consideration of the views of market participants.

"(18) RECORDKEEPING.—The board of trade shall maintain records of all activities relating to the business of the contract market—

"(A) in a form and manner that is acceptable to the Commission; and

"(B) for a period of at least 5 years.

"(19) ANTITRUST CONSIDERATIONS.—Unless necessary or appropriate to achieve the purposes of this Act, the board of trade shall not—

"(A) adopt any rule or taking any action that results in any unreasonable restraint of trade; or

"(B) impose any material anticompetitive burden on trading on the contract market.

"(20) SYSTEM SAFEGUARDS.—The board of trade shall—

"(A) establish and maintain a program of risk analysis and oversight to identify and minimize sources of operational risk, through the development of appropriate controls and procedures, and the development of automated systems, that are reliable, secure, and have adequate scalable capacity;

"(B) establish and maintain emergency procedures, backup facilities, and a plan for disaster recovery that allow for the timely recovery and resumption of operations and the fulfillment of the responsibilities and obligations of the board of trade; and

"(C) periodically conduct tests to verify that backup resources are sufficient to ensure continued order processing and trade matching, price reporting, market surveillance, and maintenance of a comprehensive and accurate audit trail.

"(21) FINANCIAL RESOURCES.—

"(A) IN GENERAL.—The board of trade shall have adequate financial, operational, and managerial resources to discharge each responsibility of the board of trade.

"(B) DETERMINATION OF ADEQUACY.—The financial resources of the board of trade shall be considered to be adequate if the value of the financial resources exceeds the total amount that would enable the contract market to cover the operating costs of the contract market for a 1-year period, as calculated on a rolling basis.

"(22) DIVERSITY OF BOARD OF DIRECTORS.—The board of trade, if a publicly traded company, shall endeavor to recruit individuals to serve on the board of directors and the other decision-making bodies (as determined by the Commission) of the board of trade from among, and to have the composition of the bodies reflect, a broad and culturally diverse pool of qualified candidates.

"(23) SECURITIES AND EXCHANGE COMMISSION.—The board of trade shall keep any such records relating to swaps defined in section 1a(47)(A)(v) open to inspection and examination by the Securities and Exchange Commission.".

[Explanation at ¶3110.]

[¶10,736] ACT SEC. 736. MARGIN.

Section 8a(7) of the Commodity Exchange Act (7 U.S.C. 12a(7)) is amended—

(1) in subparagraph (C), by striking ", excepting the setting of levels of margin";

(2) by redesignating subparagraphs (D) through (F) as subparagraphs (E) through (G), respectively; and

(3) by inserting after subparagraph (C) the following:

"(D) margin requirements, provided that the rules, regulations, or orders shall—

"(i) be limited to protecting the financial integrity of the derivatives clearing organization;

"(ii) be designed for risk management purposes to protect the financial integrity of transactions; and

"(iii) not set specific margin amounts;".

[Explanation at ¶ 3110.]

[¶ 10,737] ACT SEC. 737. POSITION LIMITS.

(a) AGGREGATE POSITION LIMITS.—Section 4a(a) of the Commodity Exchange Act (7 U.S.C. 6a(a)) is amended—

(1) by inserting after "(a)" the following:

"(1) IN GENERAL.—";

(2) in the first sentence, by striking "on electronic trading facilities with respect to a significant price discovery contract" and inserting "swaps that perform or affect a significant price discovery function with respect to registered entities";

(3) in the second sentence—

(A) by inserting ", including any group or class of traders," after "held by any person"; and

(B) by striking "on an electronic trading facility with respect to a significant price discovery contract," and inserting "swaps traded on or subject to the rules of a designated contract market or a swap execution facility, or swaps not traded on or subject to the rules of a designated contract market or a swap execution facility that performs a significant price discovery function with respect to a registered entity,"; and

(4) by adding at the end the following:

"(2) ESTABLISHMENT OF LIMITATIONS.—

"(A) IN GENERAL.—In accordance with the standards set forth in paragraph (1) of this subsection and consistent with the good faith exception cited in subsection (b)(2), with respect to physical commodities other than excluded commodities as defined by the Commission, the Commission shall by rule, regulation, or order establish limits on the amount of positions, as appropriate, other than bona fide hedge positions, that may be held by any person with respect to contracts of sale for future delivery or with respect to options on the contracts or commodities traded on or subject to the rules of a designated contract market.

"(B) TIMING.—

"(i) EXEMPT COMMODITIES.—For exempt commodities, the limits required under subparagraph (A) shall be established within 180 days after the date of the enactment of this paragraph.

"(ii) AGRICULTURAL COMMODITIES.—For agricultural commodities, the limits required under subparagraph (A) shall be established within 270 days after the date of the enactment of this paragraph.

"(C) GOAL.—In establishing the limits required under subparagraph (A), the Commission shall strive to ensure that trading on foreign boards of trade in the same commodity will be subject to comparable limits and that any limits to be imposed by the Commission will not cause price discovery in the commodity to shift to trading on the foreign boards of trade.

"(3) SPECIFIC LIMITATIONS.—In establishing the limits required in paragraph (2), the Commission, as appropriate, shall set limits—

"(A) on the number of positions that may be held by any person for the spot month, each other month, and the aggregate number of positions that may be held by any person for all months; and

"(B) to the maximum extent practicable, in its discretion—

"(i) to diminish, eliminate, or prevent excessive speculation as described under this section;

"(ii) to deter and prevent market manipulation, squeezes, and corners;

"(iii) to ensure sufficient market liquidity for bona fide hedgers; and

"(iv) to ensure that the price discovery function of the underlying market is not disrupted.

"(4) SIGNIFICANT PRICE DISCOVERY FUNCTION.—In making a determination whether a swap performs or affects a significant price discovery function with respect to regulated markets, the Commission shall consider, as appropriate:

"(A) PRICE LINKAGE.—The extent to which the swap uses or otherwise relies on a daily or final settlement price, or other major price parameter, of another contract traded on a regulated market based upon the same underlying commodity, to value a position, transfer or convert a position, financially settle a position, or close out a position.

"(B) ARBITRAGE.—The extent to which the price for the swap is sufficiently related to the price of another contract traded on a regulated market based upon the same underlying commodity so as to permit market participants to effectively arbitrage between the markets by simultaneously maintaining positions or executing trades in the swaps on a frequent and recurring basis.

"(C) MATERIAL PRICE REFERENCE.—The extent to which, on a frequent and recurring basis, bids, offers, or transactions in a contract traded on a regulated market are directly based on, or are determined by referencing, the price generated by the swap.

"(D) MATERIAL LIQUIDITY.—The extent to which the volume of swaps being traded in the commodity is sufficient to have a material effect on another contract traded on a regulated market.

"(E) OTHER MATERIAL FACTORS.—Such other material factors as the Commission specifies by rule or regulation as relevant to determine whether a swap serves a significant price discovery function with respect to a regulated market.

"(5) ECONOMICALLY EQUIVALENT CONTRACTS.—

"(A) Notwithstanding any other provision of this section, the Commission shall establish limits on the amount of positions, including aggregate position limits, as appropriate, other than bona fide hedge positions, that may be held by any person with respect to swaps that are economically equivalent to contracts of sale for future delivery or to options on the contracts or commodities traded on or subject to the rules of a designated contract market subject to paragraph (2).

"(B) In establishing limits pursuant to subparagraph (A), the Commission shall—

"(i) develop the limits concurrently with limits established under paragraph (2), and the limits shall have similar requirements as under paragraph (3)(B); and

"(ii) establish the limits simultaneously with limits established under paragraph (2).

"(6) AGGREGATE POSITION LIMITS.—The Commission shall, by rule or regulation, establish limits (including related hedge exemption provisions) on the aggregate number or amount of positions in contracts based upon the same underlying commodity (as defined by the Commission) that may be held by any person, including any group or class of traders, for each month across—

"(A) contracts listed by designated contract markets;

"(B) with respect to an agreement contract, or transaction that settles against any price (including the daily or final settlement price) of 1 or more contracts listed for trading on a registered entity, contracts traded on a foreign board of trade that provides members or other participants located in the United States with direct access to its electronic trading and order matching system; and

"(C) swap contracts that perform or affect a significant price discovery function with respect to regulated entities.

"(7) EXEMPTIONS.—The Commission, by rule, regulation, or order, may exempt, conditionally or unconditionally, any person or class of persons, any swap or class of swaps, any contract of sale of a commodity for future delivery or class of such contracts, any option or class of options, or any transaction or class of transactions from any requirement it may establish under this section with respect to position limits.".

(b) CONFORMING AMENDMENTS.—Section 4a(b) of the Commodity Exchange Act (7 U.S.C. 6a(b)) is amended—

(1) in paragraph (1), by striking "or derivatives transaction execution facility or facilities or electronic trading facility" and inserting "or swap execution facility or facilities"; and

(2) in paragraph (2), by striking "or derivatives transaction execution facility or facilities or electronic trading facility" and inserting "or swap execution facility".

(c) BONA FIDE HEDGING TRANSACTION.—Section 4a(c) of the Commodity Exchange Act is amended—

(1) by inserting "(1)" after "(c)"; and

(2) by adding at the end the following:

"(2) For the purposes of implementation of subsection (a)(2) for contracts of sale for future delivery or options on the contracts or commodities, the Commission shall define what constitutes a bona fide hedging transaction or position as a transaction or position that—

"(A)

"(i) represents a substitute for transactions made or to be made or positions taken or to be taken at a later time in a physical marketing channel;

"(ii) is economically appropriate to the reduction of risks in the conduct and management of a commercial enterprise; and

"(iii) arises from the potential change in the value of—

"(I) assets that a person owns, produces, manufactures, processes, or merchandises or anticipates owning, producing, manufacturing, processing, or merchandising;

"(II) liabilities that a person owns or anticipates incurring; or

"(III) services that a person provides, purchases, or anticipates providing or purchasing; or

"(B) reduces risks attendant to a position resulting from a swap that—

"(i) was executed opposite a counterparty for which the transaction would qualify as a bona fide hedging transaction pursuant to subparagraph (A); or

"(ii) meets the requirements of subparagraph (A).".

(d) EFFECTIVE DATE.—This section and the amendments made by this section shall become effective on the date of the enactment of this section.

[Explanation at ¶ 3115.]

[¶ 10,738] ACT SEC. 738. FOREIGN BOARDS OF TRADE.

(a) IN GENERAL.—Section 4(b) of the Commodity Exchange Act (7 U.S.C. 6(b)) is amended—

(1) in the first sentence, by striking "The Commission" and inserting the following:

"(2) PERSONS LOCATED IN THE UNITED STATES.—

"(A) IN GENERAL.—The Commission";

(2) in the second sentence, by striking "Such rules and regulations" and inserting the following:

"(B) DIFFERENT REQUIREMENTS.—Rules and regulations described in subparagraph (A)";

(3) in the third sentence—

(A) by striking "No rule or regulation" and inserting the following:

"(C) PROHIBITION.—Except as provided in paragraphs (1) and (2), no rule or regulation";

(B) by striking "that (1) requires" and inserting the following: "that—

"(i) requires"; and

(C) by striking "market, or (2) governs" and inserting the following: "market; or

"(ii) governs"; and

(4) by inserting before paragraph (2) (as designated by paragraph (1)) the following:

"(1) FOREIGN BOARDS OF TRADE.—

"(A) REGISTRATION.—The Commission may adopt rules and regulations requiring registration with the Commission for a foreign board of trade that provides the members of the foreign board of trade or other participants located in the United States with direct access to the electronic trading and order matching system of the foreign board of trade, including rules and regulations prescribing procedures and requirements applicable to the registration of such foreign boards of trade. For purposes of this paragraph, 'direct access' refers to an explicit grant of authority by a foreign board of trade to an identified member or other participant located in the United States to enter trades directly into the trade matching system of the foreign board of trade. In adopting such rules and regulations, the commission shall consider—

"(i) whether any such foreign board of trade is subject to comparable, comprehensive supervision and regulation by the appropriate governmental authorities in the foreign board of trade's home country; and

"(ii) any previous commission findings that the foreign board of trade is subject to comparable comprehensive supervision and regulation by the appropriate government authorities in the foreign board of trade's home country.

"(B) LINKED CONTRACTS.—The Commission may not permit a foreign board of trade to provide to the members of the foreign board of trade or other participants located in the United States direct access to the electronic trading and order-matching system of the foreign board of trade with respect to an agreement, contract, or transaction that settles against any price (including the daily or final settlement price) of 1 or more contracts listed for trading on a registered entity, unless the Commission determines that—

"(i) the foreign board of trade makes public daily trading information regarding the agreement, contract, or transaction that is comparable to the daily trading information published by the registered entity for the 1 or more contracts against which the agreement, contract, or transaction traded on the foreign board of trade settles; and

"(ii) the foreign board of trade (or the foreign futures authority that oversees the foreign board of trade)—

"(I) adopts position limits (including related hedge exemption provisions) for the agreement, contract, or transaction that are comparable to the position limits (including related hedge exemption provisions) adopted by the registered entity for the 1 or more contracts against which the agreement, contract, or transaction traded on the foreign board of trade settles;

"(II) has the authority to require or direct market participants to limit, reduce, or liquidate any position the foreign board of trade (or the foreign futures authority that oversees the foreign board of trade) determines to be necessary to prevent or reduce the threat of price manipulation, excessive speculation as described in section 4a, price distortion, or disruption of delivery or the cash settlement process;

"(III) agrees to promptly notify the Commission, with regard to the agreement, contract, or transaction that settles against any price (including the daily or final settlement price) of 1 or more contracts listed for trading on a registered entity, of any change regarding—

"(aa) the information that the foreign board of trade will make publicly available;

"(bb) the position limits that the foreign board of trade or foreign futures authority will adopt and enforce;

"(cc) the position reductions required to prevent manipulation, excessive speculation as described in section 4a, price distortion, or disruption of delivery or the cash settlement process; and

"(dd) any other area of interest expressed by the Commission to the foreign board of trade or foreign futures authority;

"(IV) provides information to the Commission regarding large trader positions in the agreement, contract, or transaction that is comparable to the large trader position information collected by the Commission for the 1 or more contracts against which the agreement, contract, or transaction traded on the foreign board of trade settles; and

"(V) provides the Commission such information as is necessary to publish reports on aggregate trader positions for the agreement, contract, or transaction traded on the foreign board of trade that are comparable to such reports on aggregate trader positions for the 1 or more contracts against which the agreement, contract, or transaction traded on the foreign board of trade settles.

"(C) EXISTING FOREIGN BOARDS OF TRADE.—Subparagraphs (A) and (B) shall not be effective with respect to any foreign board of trade to which, prior to the date of enactment of this paragraph, the Commission granted direct access permission until the date that is 180 days after that date of enactment.".

(b) LIABILITY OF REGISTERED PERSONS TRADING ON A FOREIGN BOARD OF TRADE.—Section 4 of the Commodity Exchange Act (7 U.S.C. 6) is amended—

(1) in subsection (a), in the matter preceding paragraph (1), by inserting "or by subsection (e)" after "Unless exempted by the Commission pursuant to subsection (c)"; and

(2) by adding at the end the following:

"(e) LIABILITY OF REGISTERED PERSONS TRADING ON A FOREIGN BOARD OF TRADE.—

"(1) IN GENERAL.—A person registered with the Commission, or exempt from registration by the Commission, under this Act may not be found to have violated subsection (a) with respect to a transaction in, or in connection with, a contract of sale of a commodity for future delivery if the person—

"(A) has reason to believe that the transaction and the contract is made on or subject to the rules of a foreign board of trade that is—

"(i) legally organized under the laws of a foreign country;

"(ii) authorized to act as a board of trade by a foreign futures authority; and

"(iii) subject to regulation by the foreign futures authority; and

"(B) has not been determined by the Commission to be operating in violation of subsection (a).

"(2) RULE OF CONSTRUCTION.—Nothing in this subsection shall be construed as implying or creating any presumption that a board of trade, exchange, or market is located outside the United States, or its territories or possessions, for purposes of subsection (a).".

(c) CONTRACT ENFORCEMENT FOR FOREIGN FUTURES CONTRACTS.—Section 22(a) of the Commodity Exchange Act (7 U.S.C. 25(a)) (as amended by section 739) is amended by adding at the end the following:

"(6) CONTRACT ENFORCEMENT FOR FOREIGN FUTURES CONTRACTS.—A contract of sale of a commodity for future delivery traded or executed on or through the facilities of a board of trade, exchange, or market located outside the United States for purposes of section 4(a) shall not be void, voidable, or unenforceable, and a party to such a contract shall not be entitled to rescind or recover any payment made with respect to the contract, based on the failure of the foreign board of trade to comply with any provision of this Act.".

[Explanation at ¶ 3120.]

[¶ 10,739] ACT SEC. 739. LEGAL CERTAINTY FOR SWAPS.

Section 22(a) of the Commodity Exchange Act (7 U.S.C. 25(a)) is amended by striking paragraph (4) and inserting the following:

"(4) CONTRACT ENFORCEMENT BETWEEN ELIGIBLE COUNTERPARTIES.—

"(A) IN GENERAL.—No hybrid instrument sold to any investor shall be void, voidable, or unenforceable, and no party to a hybrid instrument shall be entitled to rescind, or recover any payment made with respect to, the hybrid instrument under this section or any other provision of Federal or State law, based solely on the failure of the hybrid instrument to comply with the terms or conditions of section 2(f) or regulations of the Commission.

"(B) SWAPS.—No agreement, contract, or transaction between eligible contract participants or persons reasonably believed to be eligible contract participants shall be void, voidable, or unenforceable, and no party to such agreement, contract, or transaction shall be entitled to rescind, or recover any payment made with respect to, the agreement, contract, or transaction under this section or any other provision of Federal or State law, based solely on the failure of the agreement, contract, or transaction—

"(i) to meet the definition of a swap under section 1a; or

"(ii) to be cleared in accordance with section 2(h)(1).

"(5) LEGAL CERTAINTY FOR LONG-TERM SWAPS ENTERED INTO BEFORE THE DATE OF ENACTMENT OF THE WALL STREET TRANSPARENCY AND ACCOUNTABILITY ACT OF 2010.—

"(A) EFFECT ON SWAPS.—Unless specifically reserved in the applicable swap, neither the enactment of the Wall Street Transparency and Accountability Act of 2010, nor any requirement under that Act or an amendment made by that Act, shall constitute a termination event, force majeure, illegality, increased costs, regulatory change, or similar event under a swap (including any related credit support arrangement) that would permit a party to terminate, renegotiate, modify, amend, or supplement 1 or more transactions under the swap.

"(B) POSITION LIMITS.—Any position limit established under the Wall Street Transparency and Accountability Act of 2010 shall not apply to a position acquired in good faith prior to the effective date of any rule, regulation, or order under the Act that establishes the position limit; provided, however, that such positions shall be attributed to the trader if the trader's position is increased after the effective date of such position limit rule, regulation, or order.".

[Explanation at ¶ 3105 and ¶ 3125.]

[¶ 10,740] ACT SEC. 740. MULTILATERAL CLEARING ORGANIZATIONS.

Sections 408 and 409 of the Federal Deposit Insurance Corporation Improvement Act of 1991 (12 U.S.C. 4421, 4422) are repealed.

[Explanation at ¶ 3070.]

[¶ 10,741] ACT SEC. 741. ENFORCEMENT.

(a) ENFORCEMENT AUTHORITY.—The Commodity Exchange Act is amended by inserting after section 4b (7 U.S.C. 6b) the following:

"SEC. 4b-1. ENFORCEMENT AUTHORITY.

"(a) COMMODITY FUTURES TRADING COMMISSION.—Except as provided in subsections (b), (c), and (d), the Commission shall have exclusive authority to enforce the provisions of subtitle A of the Wall Street Transparency and Accountability Act of 2010 with respect to any person.

"(b) PRUDENTIAL REGULATORS.—The prudential regulators shall have exclusive authority to enforce the provisions of section 4s(e) with respect to swap dealers or major swap participants for which they are the prudential regulator.

"(c) REFERRALS.—

"(1) PRUDENTIAL REGULATORS.—If the prudential regulator for a swap dealer or major swap participant has cause to believe that the swap dealer or major swap participant, or any affiliate or division of the swap dealer or major swap participant, may have engaged in conduct that constitutes a violation of the nonprudential requirements of this Act (including section 4s or rules adopted by the Commission under that section), the prudential regulator may promptly notify the Commission in a written report that includes—

"(A) a request that the Commission initiate an enforcement proceeding under this Act; and

"(B) an explanation of the facts and circumstances that led to the preparation of the written report.

"(2) COMMISSION.—If the Commission has cause to believe that a swap dealer or major swap participant that has a prudential regulator may have engaged in conduct that constitutes a violation of any prudential requirement of section 4s or rules adopted by the Commission under that section, the Commission may notify the prudential regulator of the conduct in a written report that includes—

"(A) a request that the prudential regulator initiate an enforcement proceeding under this Act or any other Federal law (including regulations); and

"(B) an explanation of the concerns of the Commission, and a description of the facts and circumstances, that led to the preparation of the written report.

"(d) BACKSTOP ENFORCEMENT AUTHORITY.—

"(1) INITIATION OF ENFORCEMENT PROCEEDING BY PRUDENTIAL REGULATOR.—If the Commission does not initiate an enforcement proceeding before the end of the 90-day period beginning on the date on which the Commission receives a written report under subsection (c)(1), the prudential regulator may initiate an enforcement proceeding.

"(2) INITIATION OF ENFORCEMENT PROCEEDING BY COMMISSION.—If the prudential regulator does not initiate an enforcement proceeding before the end of the 90-day period beginning on the date on which the prudential regulator receives a written report under subsection (c)(2), the Commission may initiate an enforcement proceeding.".

(b) CONFORMING AMENDMENTS.—

(1) Section 4b of the Commodity Exchange Act (7 U.S.C. 6b) is amended—

(A) in subsection (a)(2), by striking "or other agreement, contract, or transaction subject to paragraphs (1) and (2) of section 5a(g)," and inserting "or swap,";

(B) in subsection (b), by striking "or other agreement, contract or transaction subject to paragraphs (1) and (2) of section 5a(g)," and inserting "or swap,"; and

(C) by adding at the end the following:

"(e) It shall be unlawful for any person, directly or indirectly, by the use of any means or instrumentality of interstate commerce, or of the mails, or of any facility of any registered entity, in or in connection with any order to make, or the making of, any contract of sale of any commodity for future delivery (or option on such a contract), or any swap, on a group or index of securities (or any interest therein or based on the value thereof)—

"(1) to employ any device, scheme, or artifice to defraud;

"(2) to make any untrue statement of a material fact or to omit to state a material fact necessary in order to make the statements made, in the light of the circumstances under which they were made, not misleading; or

"(3) to engage in any act, practice, or course of business which operates or would operate as a fraud or deceit upon any person.".

(2) Section 4c(a)(1) of the Commodity Exchange Act (7 U.S.C. 6c(a)(1)) is amended by inserting "or swap," before "if the transaction is used or may be used".

(3) Section 6(c) of the Commodity Exchange Act (7 U.S.C. 9) is amended in the first sentence by inserting "or of any swap," before "or has willfully made".

(4) Section 6(d) of the Commodity Exchange Act (7 U.S.C. 13b) is amended in the first sentence, in the matter preceding the proviso, by inserting "or of any swap," before "or otherwise is violating".

(5) Section 6c(a) of the Commodity Exchange Act (7 U.S.C. 13a-1(a)) is amended in the matter preceding the proviso by inserting "or any swap" after "commodity for future delivery".

(6) Section 9 of the Commodity Exchange Act (7 U.S.C. 13) is amended—

(A) in subsection (a)—

(i) in paragraph (2), by inserting "or of any swap," before "or to corner"; and

(ii) in paragraph (4), by inserting "swap data repository," before "or futures association" and

(B) in subsection (e)(1)—

(i) by inserting "swap data repository," before "or registered futures association"; and

(ii) by inserting ", or swaps," before "on the basis".

(7) Section 9(a) of the Commodity Exchange Act (7 U.S.C. 13(a)) is amended by adding at the end the following:

"(6) Any person to abuse the end user clearing exemption under section 2(h)(4), as determined by the Commission.".

(8) Section 2(c)(2)(B) of the Commodity Exchange Act (7 U.S.C. 2(c)(2)(B)) is amended—

(A) by striking "(dd)," each place it appears;

(B) in clause (iii), by inserting ", and accounts or pooled investment vehicles described in clause (vi)," before "shall be subject to"; and

(C) by adding at the end the following:

"(vi) This Act applies to, and the Commission shall have jurisdiction over, an account or pooled investment vehicle that is offered for the purpose of trading, or that trades, any agreement, contract, or transaction in foreign currency described in clause (i).".

(9) Section 2(c)(2)(C) of the Commodity Exchange Act (7 U.S.C. 2(c)(2)(C)) is amended—

(A) by striking "(dd)," each place it appears;

(B) in clause (ii)(I), by inserting ", and accounts or pooled investment vehicles described in clause (vii)," before "shall be subject to"; and

(C) by adding at the end the following:

"(vii) This Act applies to, and the Commission shall have jurisdiction over, an account or pooled investment vehicle that is offered for the purpose of trading, or that trades, any agreement, contract, or transaction in foreign currency described in clause (i).".

(10) Section 1a(19)(A)(iv)(II) of the Commodity Exchange Act (7 U.S.C. 1a(19)(A)(iv)(II)) (as redesignated by section 721(a)(1)) is amended by inserting before the semicolon at the end the following: "provided, however, that for purposes of section 2(c)(2)(B)(vi) and section 2(c)(2)(C)(vii), the term 'eligible contract participant' shall not include a commodity pool in which any participant is not otherwise an eligible contract participant".

(11) Section 6(e) of the Commodity Exchange Act (7 U.S.C. 9a) is amended by adding at the end the following:

"(4) Any designated clearing organization that knowingly or recklessly evades or participates in or facilitates an evasion of the requirements of section 2(h) shall be liable for a civil money penalty in twice the amount otherwise available for a violation of section 2(h).

"(5) Any swap dealer or major swap participant that knowingly or recklessly evades or participates in or facilitates an evasion of the requirements of section 2(h) shall be liable for a civil money penalty in twice the amount otherwise available for a violation of section 2(h).".

(c) SAVINGS CLAUSE.—Notwithstanding any other provision of this title, nothing in this subtitle shall be construed as divesting any appropriate Federal banking agency of any authority it may have to establish or enforce, with respect to a person for which such agency is the appropriate Federal banking agency, prudential or other standards pursuant to authority granted by Federal law other than this title.

[Explanation at ¶ 3130.]

[¶ 10,742] ACT SEC. 742. RETAIL COMMODITY TRANSACTIONS.

(a) IN GENERAL.—Section 2(c) of the Commodity Exchange Act (7 U.S.C. 2(c)) is amended—

(1) in paragraph (1), by striking "5a (to the extent provided in section 5a(g)), 5b, 5d, or 12(e)(2)(B))" and inserting ", 5b, or 12(e)(2)(B))"; and

(2) in paragraph (2), by adding at the end the following:

"(D) RETAIL COMMODITY TRANSACTIONS.—

"(i) APPLICABILITY.—Except as provided in clause (ii), this subparagraph shall apply to any agreement, contract, or transaction in any commodity that is—

"(I) entered into with, or offered to (even if not entered into with), a person that is not an eligible contract participant or eligible commercial entity; and

"(II) entered into, or offered (even if not entered into), on a leveraged or margined basis, or financed by the offeror, the counterparty, or a person acting in concert with the offeror or counterparty on a similar basis.

"(ii) EXCEPTIONS.—This subparagraph shall not apply to—

"(I) an agreement, contract, or transaction described in paragraph (1) or subparagraphs (A), (B), or (C), including any agreement, contract, or transaction specifically excluded from subparagraph (A), (B), or (C);

"(II) any security;

"(III) a contract of sale that—

"(aa) results in actual delivery within 28 days or such other longer period as the Commission may determine by rule or regulation based upon the typical commercial practice in cash or spot markets for the commodity involved; or

"(bb) creates an enforceable obligation to deliver between a seller and a buyer that have the ability to deliver and accept delivery, respectively, in connection with the line of business of the seller and buyer; or

"(IV) an agreement, contract, or transaction that is listed on a national securities exchange registered under section 6(a) of the Securities Exchange Act of 1934 (15 U.S.C. 78f(a)); or

"(V) an identified banking product, as defined in section 402(b) of the Legal Certainty for Bank Products Act of 2000 (7 U.S.C.27(b)).

"(iii) ENFORCEMENT.—Sections 4(a), 4(b), and 4b apply to any agreement, contract, or transaction described in clause (i), as if the agreement, contract, or transaction was a contract of sale of a commodity for future delivery.

"(iv) ELIGIBLE COMMERCIAL ENTITY.—For purposes of this subparagraph, an agricultural producer, packer, or handler shall be considered to be an eligible commercial entity for any agreement, contract, or transaction for a commodity in connection with the line of business of the agricultural producer, packer, or handler.".

(b) GRAMM-LEACH-BLILEY ACT.—Section 206(a) of the Gramm-Leach-Bliley Act (Public Law 106-102; 15 U.S.C. 78c note) is amended, in the matter preceding paragraph (1), by striking "For purposes of" and inserting "Except as provided in subsection (e), for purposes of".

(c) CONFORMING AMENDMENTS RELATING TO RETAIL FOREIGN EXCHANGE TRANSACTIONS.—

(1) Section 2(c)(2)(B)(i)(II) of the Commodity Exchange Act (7 U.S.C. 2(c)(2)(B)(i)(II)) is amended—

(A) in item (aa), by inserting "United States" before "financial institution";

(B) by striking items (dd) and (ff);

(C) by redesignating items (ee) and (gg) as items (dd) and (ff), respectively; and

(D) in item (dd) (as so redesignated), by striking the semicolon and inserting "; or".

(2) Section 2(c)(2) of the Commodity Exchange Act (7 U.S.C. 2(c)(2)) (as amended by subsection (a)(2)) is amended by adding at the end the following:

"(E) PROHIBITION.—

"(i) DEFINITION OF FEDERAL REGULATORY AGENCY.—In this subparagraph, the term 'Federal regulatory agency' means—

"(I) the Commission;

"(II) the Securities and Exchange Commission;

"(III) an appropriate Federal banking agency;

"(IV) the National Credit Union Association; and

"(V) the Farm Credit Administration.

"(ii) PROHIBITION.—

"(I) IN GENERAL.—Except as provided in subclause (II), a person described in subparagraph (B)(i)(II) for which there is a Federal regulatory agency shall not offer to, or enter into with, a person that is not an eligible contract participant, any agreement, contract, or transaction in foreign currency described in subparagraph (B)(i)(I) except pursuant to a rule or regulation of a Federal regulatory agency allowing the agreement, contract, or transaction under such terms and conditions as the Federal regulatory agency shall prescribe.

"(II) EFFECTIVE DATE.—With regard to persons described in subparagraph (B)(i)(II) for which a Federal regulatory agency has issued a proposed rule concerning agreements, contracts, or transactions in foreign currency described in subparagraph (B)(i)(I) prior to the date of enactment of this subclause, subclause (I) shall take effect 90 days after the date of enactment of this subclause.

"(iii) REQUIREMENTS OF RULES AND REGULATIONS.—

"(I) IN GENERAL.—The rules and regulations described in clause (ii) shall prescribe appropriate requirements with respect to—

"(aa) disclosure;

"(bb) recordkeeping;

"(cc) capital and margin;

"(dd) reporting;

"(ee) business conduct;

"(ff) documentation; and

"(gg) such other standards or requirements as the Federal regulatory agency shall determine to be necessary.

"(II) TREATMENT.—The rules or regulations described in clause (ii) shall treat all agreements, contracts, and transactions in foreign currency described in subparagraph (B)(i)(I), and all agreements, contracts, and transactions in foreign currency that are functionally or economically similar to agreements, contracts, or transactions described in subparagraph (B)(i)(I), similarly.".

[Explanation at ¶ 3135.]

[¶ 10,743] ACT SEC. 743. OTHER AUTHORITY.

Unless otherwise provided by the amendments made by this subtitle, the amendments made by this subtitle do not divest any appropriate Federal banking agency, the Commodity Futures Trading Commission, the Securities and Exchange Commission, or other Federal or State agency of any authority derived from any other applicable law.

[Explanation at ¶ 3015.]

[¶ 10,744] ACT SEC. 744. RESTITUTION REMEDIES.

Section 6c(d) of the Commodity Exchange Act (7 U.S.C. 13a-1(d)) is amended by adding at the end the following:

"(3) EQUITABLE REMEDIES.—In any action brought under this section, the Commission may seek, and the court may impose, on a proper showing, on any person found in the action to have committed any violation, equitable remedies including—

"(A) restitution to persons who have sustained losses proximately caused by such violation (in the amount of such losses); and

"(B) disgorgement of gains received in connection with such violation.".

[Explanation at ¶ 3130.]

[¶ 10,745] ACT SEC. 745. ENHANCED COMPLIANCE BY REGISTERED ENTITIES.

(a) EFFECT OF INTERPRETATION.—Section 5c(a) of the Commodity Exchange Act (7 U.S.C. 7a-2(a)) is amended by striking paragraph (2) and inserting the following:

"(2) EFFECT OF INTERPRETATION.—An interpretation issued under paragraph (1) may provide the exclusive means for complying with each section described in paragraph (1).".

(b) NEW CONTRACTS, NEW RULES, AND RULE AMENDMENTS.—Section 5c of the Commodity Exchange Act (7 U.S.C. 7a-2) is amended by striking subsection (c) and inserting the following:

"(c) NEW CONTRACTS, NEW RULES, AND RULE AMENDMENTS.—

"(1) IN GENERAL.—A registered entity may elect to list for trading or accept for clearing any new contract, or other instrument, or may elect to approve and implement any new rule or rule amendment, by providing to the Commission (and the Secretary of the Treasury, in the case of a contract of sale of a government security for future delivery (or option on such a contract) or a rule or rule amendment specifically related to such a contract) a written certification that the new contract or instrument or clearing of the new contract or instrument, new rule, or rule amendment complies with this Act (including regulations under this Act).

"(2) RULE REVIEW.—The new rule or rule amendment described in paragraph (1) shall become effective, pursuant to the certification of the registered entity and notice of such certification to its members (in a manner to be determined by the Commission), on the date that is 10 business days after the date on which the Commission receives the certification (or such shorter period as determined by the Commission by rule or regulation) unless the Commission notifies the registered entity within such time that it is staying the certification because there exist novel or complex issues that require additional time to analyze, an inadequate explanation by the submitting registered entity, or a potential inconsistency with this Act (including regulations under this Act).

"(3) STAY OF CERTIFICATION FOR RULES.—

"(A) A notification by the Commission pursuant to paragraph (2) shall stay the certification of the new rule or rule amendment for up to an additional 90 days from the date of the notification.

"(B) A rule or rule amendment subject to a stay pursuant to subparagraph (A) shall become effective, pursuant to the certification of the registered entity, at the expiration of the period described in subparagraph (A) unless the Commission—

"(i) withdraws the stay prior to that time; or

"(ii) notifies the registered entity during such period that it objects to the proposed certification on the grounds that it is inconsistent with this Act (including regulations under this Act).

"(C) The Commission shall provide a not less than 30-day public comment period, within the 90-day period in which the stay is in effect as described in subparagraph (A), whenever the Commission reviews a rule or rule amendment pursuant to a notification by the Commission under this paragraph.

"(4) PRIOR APPROVAL.—

"(A) IN GENERAL.—A registered entity may request that the Commission grant prior approval to any new contract or other instrument, new rule, or rule amendment.

"(B) PRIOR APPROVAL REQUIRED.—Notwithstanding any other provision of this section, a designated contract market shall submit to the Commission for prior approval each rule amendment that materially changes the terms and conditions, as determined by the Commission, in any contract of sale for future delivery of a commodity specifically enumerated in section 1a(10) (or any option thereon) traded through its facilities if the rule amendment applies to contracts and delivery months which have already been listed for trading and have open interest.

"(C) DEADLINE.—If prior approval is requested under subparagraph (A), the Commission shall take final action on the request not later than 90 days after submission of the request, unless the person submitting the request agrees to an extension of the time limitation established under this subparagraph.

"(5) APPROVAL.—

"(A) RULES.—The Commission shall approve a new rule, or rule amendment, of a registered entity unless the Commission finds that the new rule, or rule amendment, is inconsistent with this subtitle (including regulations).

"(B) CONTRACTS AND INSTRUMENTS.—The Commission shall approve a new contract or other instrument unless the Commission finds that the new contract or other instrument would violate this Act (including regulations).

"(C) SPECIAL RULE FOR REVIEW AND APPROVAL OF EVENT CONTRACTS AND SWAPS CONTRACTS.—

"(i) EVENT CONTRACTS.—In connection with the listing of agreements, contracts, transactions, or swaps in excluded commodities that are based upon the occurrence, extent of an occurrence, or contingency (other than a change in the price, rate, value, or levels of a commodity described in section 1a(2)(i)), by a designated contract market or swap execution facility, the Commission may determine that such agreements, contracts, or transactions are contrary to the public interest if the agreements, contracts, or transactions involve—

"(I) activity that is unlawful under any Federal or State law;

"(II) terrorism;

"(III) assassination;

"(IV) war;

"(V) gaming; or

"(VI) other similar activity determined by the Commission, by rule or regulation, to be contrary to the public interest.

"(ii) PROHIBITION.—No agreement, contract, or transaction determined by the Commission to be contrary to the public interest under clause (i) may be listed or made available for clearing or trading on or through a registered entity.

"(iii) SWAPS CONTRACTS.—

"(I) IN GENERAL.—In connection with the listing of a swap for clearing by a derivatives clearing organization, the Commission shall determine, upon request or on its own motion, the initial eligibility, or the continuing qualification, of a derivatives clearing organization to clear such a swap under those criteria, conditions, or rules that the Commission, in its discretion, determines.

"(II) REQUIREMENTS.—Any such criteria, conditions, or rules shall consider—

"(aa) the financial integrity of the derivatives clearing organization; and

"(bb) any other factors which the Commission determines may be appropriate.

"(iv) DEADLINE.—The Commission shall take final action under clauses (i) and (ii) in not later than 90 days from the commencement of its review unless the party seeking to offer the contract or swap agrees to an extension of this time limitation.".

(c) VIOLATION OF CORE PRINCIPLES.—Section 5c of the Commodity Exchange Act (7 U.S.C. 7a-2) is amended by striking subsection (d).

[Explanation at ¶ 3140.]

[¶ 10,746] ACT SEC. 746. INSIDER TRADING.

Section 4c(a) of the Commodity Exchange Act (7 U.S.C. 6c(a)) is amended by adding at the end the following:

"(3) CONTRACT OF SALE.—It shall be unlawful for any employee or agent of any department or agency of the Federal Government who, by virtue of the employment or position of the employee or agent, acquires information that may affect or tend to affect the price of any commodity in interstate commerce, or for future delivery, or any swap, and which information has not been disseminated by the department or agency of the Federal Government holding or creating the information in a manner which makes it generally available to the trading public, or disclosed in a criminal, civil, or administrative hearing, or in a congressional, administrative, or Government Accountability Office report, hearing, audit, or investigation, to use the information in his personal capacity and for personal gain to enter into, or offer to enter into—

"(A) a contract of sale of a commodity for future delivery (or option on such a contract);

"(B) an option (other than an option executed or traded on a national securities exchange registered pursuant to section 6(a) of the Securities Exchange Act of 1934 (15 U.S.C. 78f(a)); or

"(C) a swap.

"(4) NONPUBLIC INFORMATION.—

"(A) IMPARTING OF NONPUBLIC INFORMATION.—It shall be unlawful for any employee or agent of any department or agency of the Federal Government who, by virtue of the employment or position of the employee or agent, acquires information that may affect or tend to affect the price of any commodity in interstate commerce, or for future delivery, or any swap, and which information has not been disseminated by the department or agency of the Federal Government holding or creating the information in a manner which makes it generally available to the trading public, or disclosed in a criminal, civil, or administrative hearing, or in a congressional, administrative, or Government Accountability Office report, hearing, audit, or investigation, to impart the information in his personal capacity and for personal gain with intent to assist another person, directly or indirectly, to use the information to enter into, or offer to enter into—

"(i) a contract of sale of a commodity for future delivery (or option on such a contract);

"(ii) an option (other than an option executed or traded on a national securities exchange registered pursuant to section 6(a) of the Securities Exchange Act of 1934 (15 U.S.C. 78f(a)); or

"(iii) a swap.

"(B) KNOWING USE.—It shall be unlawful for any person who receives information imparted by any employee or agent of any department or agency of the Federal Government as described in subparagraph (A) to knowingly use such information to enter into, or offer to enter into—

"(i) a contract of sale of a commodity for future delivery (or option on such a contract);

"(ii) an option (other than an option executed or traded on a national securities exchange registered pursuant to section 6(a) of the Securities Exchange Act of 1934 (15 U.S.C. 78f(a)); or

"(iii) a swap.

"(C) THEFT OF NONPUBLIC INFORMATION.—It shall be unlawful for any person to steal, convert, or misappropriate, by any means whatsoever, information held or created by any department or agency of the Federal Government that may affect or tend to affect the price of any commodity in interstate commerce, or for future delivery, or any swap, where such person knows, or acts in reckless disregard of the fact, that such information has not been disseminated by the department or agency of the Federal Government holding or creating the information in a manner which makes it generally available to the trading public, or disclosed in a criminal, civil, or administrative hearing, or in a congressional, administrative, or Government Accountability Office report, hearing, audit, or investigation, and to use such information, or to impart such information with the intent to assist another person, directly or indirectly, to use such information to enter into, or offer to enter into—

"(i) a contract of sale of a commodity for future delivery (or option on such a contract);

"(ii) an option (other than an option executed or traded on a national securities exchange registered pursuant to section 6(a) of the Securities Exchange Act of 1934 (15 U.S.C. 78f(a)); or

"(iii) a swap, provided, however, that nothing in this subparagraph shall preclude a person that has provided information concerning, or generated by, the person, its operations or activities, to any employee or agent of any department or agency of the Federal Government, voluntarily or as required by law, from using such information to enter into, or offer to enter into, a contract of sale, option, or swap described in clauses (i), (ii), or (iii).".

[Explanation at ¶ 3155.]

[¶ 10,747] ACT SEC. 747. ANTIDISRUPTIVE PRACTICES AUTHORITY.

Section 4c(a) of the Commodity Exchange Act (7 U.S.C. 6c(a)) (as amended by section 746) is amended by adding at the end the following:

"(5) DISRUPTIVE PRACTICES.—It shall be unlawful for any person to engage in any trading, practice, or conduct on or subject to the rules of a registered entity that—

"(A) violates bids or offers;

"(B) demonstrates intentional or reckless disregard for the orderly execution of transactions during the closing period; or

"(C) is, is of the character of, or is commonly known to the trade as, 'spoofing' (bidding or offering with the intent to cancel the bid or offer before execution).

"(6) RULEMAKING AUTHORITY.—The Commission may make and promulgate such rules and regulations as, in the judgment of the Commission, are reasonably necessary to prohibit the trading practices described in paragraph (5) and any other trading practice that is disruptive of fair and equitable trading.

"(7) USE OF SWAPS TO DEFRAUD.—It shall be unlawful for any person to enter into a swap knowing, or acting in reckless disregard of the fact, that its counterparty will use the swap as part of a device, scheme, or artifice to defraud any third party.".

[Explanation at ¶ 3155.]

[¶ 10,748] ACT SEC. 748. COMMODITY WHISTLEBLOWER INCENTIVES AND PROTECTION.

The Commodity Exchange Act (7 U.S.C. 1 et seq.) is amended by adding at the end the following:

"SEC. 23. COMMODITY WHISTLEBLOWER INCENTIVES AND PROTECTION.

"(a) DEFINITIONS.—In this section:

"(1) COVERED JUDICIAL OR ADMINISTRATIVE ACTION.—The term 'covered judicial or administrative action' means any judicial or administrative action brought by the Commission under this Act that results in monetary sanctions exceeding $1,000,000.

"(2) FUND.—The term 'Fund' means the Commodity Futures Trading Commission Customer Protection Fund established under subsection (g).

"(3) MONETARY SANCTIONS.—The term 'monetary sanctions', when used with respect to any judicial or administrative action means—

"(A) any monies, including penalties, disgorgement, restitution, and interest ordered to be paid; and

"(B) any monies deposited into a disgorgement fund or other fund pursuant to section 308(b) of the Sarbanes-Oxley Act of 2002 (15 U.S.C. 7246(b)), as a result of such action or any settlement of such action.

"(4) ORIGINAL INFORMATION.—The term 'original information' means information that—

"(A) is derived from the independent knowledge or analysis of a whistleblower;

"(B) is not known to the Commission from any other source, unless the whistleblower is the original source of the information; and

"(C) is not exclusively derived from an allegation made in a judicial or administrative hearing, in a governmental report, hearing, audit, or investigation, or from the news media, unless the whistleblower is a source of the information.

"(5) RELATED ACTION.—The term 'related action', when used with respect to any judicial or administrative action brought by the Commission under this Act, means any judicial or administrative action brought by an entity described in subclauses (I) through (VI) of subsection (h)(2)(C) that is based upon the original information provided by a whistleblower pursuant to subsection (a) that led to the successful enforcement of the Commission action.

"(6) SUCCESSFUL RESOLUTION.—The term 'successful resolution', when used with respect to any judicial or administrative action brought by the Commission under this Act, includes any settlement of such action.

"(7) WHISTLEBLOWER.—The term 'whistleblower' means any individual, or 2 or more individuals acting jointly, who provides information relating to a violation of this Act to the Commission, in a manner established by rule or regulation by the Commission.

"(b) AWARDS.—

"(1) IN GENERAL.—In any covered judicial or administrative action, or related action, the Commission, under regulations prescribed by the Commission and subject to subsection (c), shall pay an award or awards to 1 or more whistleblowers who voluntarily provided original information to the Commission that led to the successful enforcement of the covered judicial or administrative action, or related action, in an aggregate amount equal to—

"(A) not less than 10 percent, in total, of what has been collected of the monetary sanctions imposed in the action or related actions; and

"(B) not more than 30 percent, in total, of what has been collected of the monetary sanctions imposed in the action or related actions.

"(2) PAYMENT OF AWARDS.—Any amount paid under paragraph (1) shall be paid from the Fund.

"(c) DETERMINATION OF AMOUNT OF AWARD; DENIAL OF AWARD.—

"(1) DETERMINATION OF AMOUNT OF AWARD.—

"(A) DISCRETION.—The determination of the amount of an award made under subsection (b) shall be in the discretion of the Commission.

"(B) CRITERIA.—In determining the amount of an award made under subsection (b), the Commission—

"(i) shall take into consideration—

"(I) the significance of the information provided by the whistleblower to the success of the covered judicial or administrative action;

"(II) the degree of assistance provided by the whistleblower and any legal representative of the whistleblower in a covered judicial or administrative action;

"(III) the programmatic interest of the Commission in deterring violations of the Act (including regulations under the Act) by making awards to whistleblowers who provide information that leads to the successful enforcement of such laws; and

"(IV) such additional relevant factors as the Commission may establish by rule or regulation; and

"(ii) shall not take into consideration the balance of the Fund.

"(2) DENIAL OF AWARD.—No award under subsection (b) shall be made—

"(A) to any whistleblower who is, or was at the time the whistleblower acquired the original information submitted to the Commission, a member, officer, or employee of—

"(i) a appropriate regulatory agency;

"(ii) the Department of Justice;

"(iii) a registered entity;

"(iv) a registered futures association;

"(v) a self-regulatory organization as defined in section 3(a) of the Securities Exchange Act of 1934 (15 U.S.C. 78c(a)); or

"(vi) a law enforcement organization;

"(B) to any whistleblower who is convicted of a criminal violation related to the judicial or administrative action for which the whistleblower otherwise could receive an award under this section;

"(C) to any whistleblower who submits information to the Commission that is based on the facts underlying the covered action submitted previously by another whistleblower;

"(D) to any whistleblower who fails to submit information to the Commission in such form as the Commission may, by rule or regulation, require.

"(d) REPRESENTATION.—

"(1) PERMITTED REPRESENTATION.—Any whistleblower who makes a claim for an award under subsection (b) may be represented by counsel.

"(2) REQUIRED REPRESENTATION.—

"(A) IN GENERAL.—Any whistleblower who anonymously makes a claim for an award under subsection (b) shall be represented by counsel if the whistleblower submits the information upon which the claim is based.

"(B) DISCLOSURE OF IDENTITY.—Prior to the payment of an award, a whistleblower shall disclose the identity of the whistleblower and provide such other information as the Commission may require, directly or through counsel for the whistleblower.

"(e) NO CONTRACT NECESSARY.—No contract with the Commission is necessary for any whistleblower to receive an award under subsection (b), unless otherwise required by the Commission, by rule or regulation.

"(f) APPEALS.—

"(1) IN GENERAL.—Any determination made under this section, including whether, to whom, or in what amount to make awards, shall be in the discretion of the Commission.

"(2) APPEALS.—Any determination described in paragraph (1) may be appealed to the appropriate court of appeals of the United States not more than 30 days after the determination is issued by the Commission.

"(3) REVIEW.—The court shall review the determination made by the Commission in accordance with section 7064 of title 5, United States Code.

"(g) COMMODITY FUTURES TRADING COMMISSION CUSTOMER PROTECTION FUND.—

"(1) ESTABLISHMENT.—There is established in the Treasury of the United States a revolving fund to be known as the 'Commodity Futures Trading Commission Customer Protection Fund'.

"(2) USE OF FUND.—The Fund shall be available to the Commission, without further appropriation or fiscal year limitation, for—

"(A) the payment of awards to whistleblowers as provided in subsection (a); and

"(B) the funding of customer education initiatives designed to help customers protect themselves against fraud or other violations of this Act, or the rules and regulations thereunder.

"(3) DEPOSITS AND CREDITS.—There shall be deposited into or credited to the Fund:

"(A) MONETARY SANCTIONS.—Any monetary sanctions collected by the Commission in any covered judicial or administrative action that is not otherwise distributed to victims of a violation of this Act or the rules and regulations thereunder underlying such action, unless the balance of the Fund at the time the monetary judgment is collected exceeds $100,000,000.

"(B) ADDITIONAL AMOUNTS.—If the amounts deposited into or credited to the Fund under subparagraph (A) are not sufficient to satisfy an award made under subsection (b), there shall be deposited into or credited to the Fund an amount equal to the unsatisfied portion of the award from any monetary sanction collected by the Commission in any judicial or administrative action brought by the Commission under this Act that is based on information provided by a whistleblower.

"(C) INVESTMENT INCOME.—All income from investments made under paragraph (4).

"(4) INVESTMENTS.—

"(A) AMOUNTS IN FUND MAY BE INVESTED.—The Commission may request the Secretary of the Treasury to invest the portion of the Fund that is not, in the Commission's judgment, required to meet the current needs of the Fund.

"(B) ELIGIBLE INVESTMENTS.—Investments shall be made by the Secretary of the Treasury in obligations of the United States or obligations that are guaranteed as to principal and interest by the United States, with maturities suitable to the needs of the Fund as determined by the Commission.

"(C) INTEREST AND PROCEEDS CREDITED.—The interest on, and the proceeds from the sale or redemption of, any obligations held in the Fund shall be credited to, and form a part of, the Fund.

"(5) REPORTS TO CONGRESS.—Not later than October 30 of each year, the Commission shall transmit to the Committee on Agriculture, Nutrition, and Forestry of the Senate, and the Committee on Agriculture of the House of Representatives a report on—

"(A) the Commission's whistleblower award program under this section, including a description of the number of awards granted and the types of cases in which awards were granted during the preceding fiscal year;

"(B) customer education initiatives described in paragraph (2)(B) that were funded by the Fund during the preceding fiscal year;

"(C) the balance of the Fund at the beginning of the preceding fiscal year;

"(D) the amounts deposited into or credited to the Fund during the preceding fiscal year;

"(E) the amount of earnings on investments of amounts in the Fund during the preceding fiscal year;

"(F) the amount paid from the Fund during the preceding fiscal year to whistleblowers pursuant to subsection (b);

"(G) the amount paid from the Fund during the preceding fiscal year for customer education initiatives described in paragraph (2)(B);

"(H) the balance of the Fund at the end of the preceding fiscal year; and

"(I) a complete set of audited financial statements, including a balance sheet, income statement, and cash flow analysis.

"(h) PROTECTION OF WHISTLEBLOWERS.—

"(1) PROHIBITION AGAINST RETALIATION.—

"(A) IN GENERAL.—No employer may discharge, demote, suspend, threaten, harass, directly or indirectly, or in any other manner discriminate against, a whistleblower in the terms and conditions of employment because of any lawful act done by the whistleblower—

"(i) in providing information to the Commission in accordance with subsection (b); or

"(ii) in assisting in any investigation or judicial or administrative action of the Commission based upon or related to such information.

"(B) ENFORCEMENT.—

"(i) CAUSE OF ACTION.—An individual who alleges discharge or other discrimination in violation of subparagraph (A) may bring an action under this subsection in the appropriate district court of the United States for the relief provided in subparagraph (C), unless the individual who is alleging discharge or other discrimination in violation of subparagraph (A) is an employee of the Federal Government, in which case the individual shall only bring an action under section 1221 of title 5, United States Code.

"(ii) SUBPOENAS.—A subpoena requiring the attendance of a witness at a trial or hearing conducted under this subsection may be served at any place in the United States.

"(iii) STATUTE OF LIMITATIONS.—An action under this subsection may not be brought more than 2 years after the date on which the violation reported in subparagraph (A) is committed.

"(C) RELIEF.—Relief for an individual prevailing in an action brought under subparagraph (B) shall include—

"(i) reinstatement with the same seniority status that the individual would have had, but for the discrimination;

"(ii) the amount of back pay otherwise owed to the individual, with interest; and

"(iii) compensation for any special damages sustained as a result of the discharge or discrimination, including litigation costs, expert witness fees, and reasonable attorney's fees.

"(2) CONFIDENTIALITY.—

"(A) IN GENERAL.—Except as provided in subparagraphs (B) and (C), the Commission, and any officer or employee of the Commission, shall not disclose any information, including information provided by a whistleblower to the Commission, which could reasonably be expected to reveal the identity of a whistleblower, except in accordance with the provisions of section 552a of title 5, United States Code, unless and until required to be disclosed to a defendant or respondent in connection with a public proceeding instituted by the Commission or any entity described in subparagraph (C). For purposes of section 552 of title 5, United States Code, this paragraph shall be considered a statute described in subsection (b)(3)(B) of such section 552.

"(B) EFFECT.—Nothing in this paragraph is intended to limit the ability of the Attorney General to present such evidence to a grand jury or to share such evidence with potential witnesses or defendants in the course of an ongoing criminal investigation.

"(C) AVAILABILITY TO GOVERNMENT AGENCIES.—

"(i) IN GENERAL.—Without the loss of its status as confidential in the hands of the Commission, all information referred to in subparagraph (A) may, in the discretion of the Commission, when determined by the Commission to be necessary or appropriate to accomplish the purposes of this Act and protect customers and in accordance with clause (ii), be made available to—

"(I) the Department of Justice;

"(II) an appropriate department or agency of the Federal Government, acting within the scope of its jurisdiction;

"(III) a registered entity, registered futures association, or self-regulatory organization as defined in section 3(a) of the Securities Exchange Act of 1934 (15 U.S.C. 78c(a));

"(IV) a State attorney general in connection with any criminal investigation;

"(V) an appropriate department or agency of any State, acting within the scope of its jurisdiction; and

"(VI) a foreign futures authority.

"(ii) MAINTENANCE OF INFORMATION.—Each of the entities, agencies, or persons described in clause (i) shall maintain information described in that clause as confidential, in accordance with the requirements in subparagraph (A).

"(iii) STUDY ON IMPACT OF FOIA EXEMPTION ON COMMODITY FUTURES TRADING COMMISSION.—

"(I) STUDY.—The Inspector General of the Commission shall conduct a study—

"(aa) on whether the exemption under section 552(b)(3) of title 5, United States Code (known as the Freedom of Information Act) established in paragraph (2) (A) aids whistleblowers in disclosing information to the Commission;

"(bb) on what impact the exemption has had on the public's ability to access information about the Commission's regulation of commodity futures and option markets; and

"(cc) to make any recommendations on whether the Commission should continue to use the exemption.

"(II) REPORT.—Not later than 30 months after the date of enactment of this clause, the Inspector General shall—

"(aa) submit a report on the findings of the study required under this clause to the Committee on Banking, Housing, and Urban Affairs of the Senate and the Committee on Financial Services of the House of Representatives; and

"(bb) make the report available to the public through publication of a report on the website of the Commission.

"(3) RIGHTS RETAINED.—Nothing in this section shall be deemed to diminish the rights, privileges, or remedies of any whistleblower under any Federal or State law, or under any collective bargaining agreement.

"(i) RULEMAKING AUTHORITY.—The Commission shall have the authority to issue such rules and regulations as may be necessary or appropriate to implement the provisions of this section consistent with the purposes of this section.

"(j) IMPLEMENTING RULES.—The Commission shall issue final rules or regulations implementing the provisions of this section not later than 270 days after the date of enactment of the Wall Street Transparency and Accountability Act of 2010.

"(k) ORIGINAL INFORMATION.—Information submitted to the Commission by a whistleblower in accordance with rules or regulations implementing this section shall not lose its status as original information solely because the whistleblower submitted such information prior to the effective date of such rules or regulations, provided such information was submitted after the date of enactment of the Wall Street Transparency and Accountability Act of 2010.

"(l) AWARDS.—A whistleblower may receive an award pursuant to this section regardless of whether any violation of a provision of this Act, or a rule or regulation thereunder, underlying the judicial or administrative action upon which the award is based occurred prior to the date of enactment of the Wall Street Transparency and Accountability Act of 2010.

"(m) PROVISION OF FALSE INFORMATION.—A whistleblower who knowingly and willfully makes any false, fictitious, or fraudulent statement or representation, or who makes or uses any false writing or document knowing the same to contain any false, fictitious, or fraudulent statement or entry, shall not be entitled to an award under this section and shall be subject to prosecution under section 1001 of title 18, United States Code.

"(n) NONENFORCEABILITY OF CERTAIN PROVISIONS WAIVING RIGHTS AND REMEDIES OR REQUIRING ARBITRATION OF DISPUTES.—

"(1) WAIVER OF RIGHTS AND REMEDIES.—The rights and remedies provided for in this section may not be waived by any agreement, policy form, or condition of employment including by a predispute arbitration agreement.

"(2) PREDISPUTE ARBITRATION AGREEMENTS.—No predispute arbitration agreement shall be valid or enforceable, if the agreement requires arbitration of a dispute arising under this section.".

[Explanation at ¶ 3145.]

[¶ 10,749] ACT SEC. 749. CONFORMING AMENDMENTS.

(a) Section 4d of the Commodity Exchange Act (7 U.S.C. 6d) (as amended by section 724) is amended—

(1) in subsection (a)—

(A) in the matter preceding paragraph (1)—

(i) by striking "engage as" and inserting "be a"; and

(ii) by striking "or introducing broker" and all that follows through "or derivatives transaction execution facility";

(B) in paragraph (1), by striking "or introducing broker"; and

(C) in paragraph (2), by striking "if a futures commission merchant,"; and

(2) by adding at the end the following:

"(g) It shall be unlawful for any person to be an introducing broker unless such person shall have registered under this Act with the Commission as an introducing broker and such registration shall not have expired nor been suspended nor revoked.".

(b) Section 4m(3) of the Commodity Exchange Act (7 U.S.C. 6m(3)) is amended—

(1) by striking "(3) Subsection (1) of this section" and inserting the following:

"(3) EXCEPTION.—

"(A) IN GENERAL.—Paragraph (1)"; and

(2) by striking "to any investment trust" and all that follows through the period at the end and inserting the following: "to any commodity pool that is engaged primarily in trading commodity interests.

"(B) ENGAGED PRIMARILY.—For purposes of subparagraph (A), a commodity trading advisor or a commodity pool shall be considered to be 'engaged primarily' in the business of being a commodity trading advisor or commodity pool if it is or holds itself out to the public as being engaged primarily, or proposes to engage primarily, in the business of advising on commodity interests or investing, reinvesting, owning, holding, or trading in commodity interests, respectively.

"(C) COMMODITY INTERESTS.—For purposes of this paragraph, commodity interests shall include contracts of sale of a commodity for future delivery, options on such contracts, security futures, swaps, leverage contracts, foreign exchange, spot and forward contracts on physical commodities, and any monies held in an account used for trading commodity interests.".

(c) Section 5c of the Commodity Exchange Act (7 U.S.C. 7a-2) is amended—

(1) in subsection (a)(1)—

(A) by striking ", 5a(d),"; and

(B) by striking "and section (2)(h)(7) with respect to significant price discovery contracts,"; and

(2) in subsection (f)(1), by striking "section 4d(c) of this Act" and inserting "section 4d(e)".

(d) Section 5e of the Commodity Exchange Act (7 U.S.C. 7b) is amended by striking "or revocation of the right of an electronic trading facility to rely on the exemption set forth in section 2(h)(3) with respect to a significant price discovery contract,".

(e) Section 6(b) of the Commodity Exchange Act (7 U.S.C. 8(b)) is amended in the first sentence by striking ", or to revoke the right of an electronic trading facility to rely on the exemption set forth in section 2(h)(3) with respect to a significant price discovery contract,".

(f) Section 12(e)(2)(B) of the Commodity Exchange Act (7 U.S.C. 16(e)(2)(B)) is amended—

(1) by striking "section 2(c), 2(d), 2(f), or 2(g) of this Act" and inserting "section 2(c) or 2(f) of this Act"; and

(2) by striking "2(h) or".

(g) Section 17(r)(1) of the Commodity Exchange Act (7 U.S.C. 21(r)(1)) is amended by striking "section 4d(c) of this Act" and inserting "section 4d(e)".

(h) Section 22 of the Commodity Exchange Act is amended—

(1) in subsection (a)(1)(B), by—

(A) inserting "or any swap" after "commodity)"; and

(B) inserting "or any swap" after "such contract";

(2) in subsection (a)(1)(C), by adding at the end the following:

"(iv) a swap; or"; and

(3) in subsection (b)(1)(A), by striking "section 2(h)(7) or sections 5 through 5c" and inserting "section 5, 5b, 5c, 5h, or 21".

(i) Section 408(2)(C) of the Federal Deposit Insurance Corporation Improvement Act of 1991 (12 U.S.C. 4421(2)(C)) is amended—

(1) by striking "section 2(c), 2(d), 2(f), or (2)(g) of such Act" and inserting "section 2(c), 2(f), or 2(i) of that Act"; and

(2) by striking "2(h) or".

[¶ 10,750] ACT SEC. 750. STUDY ON OVERSIGHT OF CARBON MARKETS.

(a) INTERAGENCY WORKING GROUP.—There is established to carry out this section an interagency working group (referred to in this section as the "interagency group") composed of the following members or designees:

(1) The Chairman of the Commodity Futures Trading Commission (referred to in this section as the "Commission"), who shall serve as Chairman of the interagency group.

(2) The Secretary of Agriculture.

(3) The Secretary of the Treasury.

(4) The Chairman of the Securities and Exchange Commission.

(5) The Administrator of the Environmental Protection Agency.

(6) The Chairman of the Federal Energy Regulatory Commission.

(7) The Commissioner of the Federal Trade Commission.

(8) The Administrator of the Energy Information Administration.

(b) ADMINISTRATIVE SUPPORT.—The Commission shall provide the interagency group such administrative support services as are necessary to enable the interagency group to carry out the functions of the interagency group under this section.

(c) CONSULTATION.—In carrying out this section, the interagency group shall consult with representatives of exchanges, clearinghouses, self-regulatory bodies, major carbon market participants, consumers, and the general public, as the interagency group determines to be appropriate.

(d) STUDY.—The interagency group shall conduct a study on the oversight of existing and prospective carbon markets to ensure an efficient, secure, and transparent carbon market, including oversight of spot markets and derivative markets.

(e) REPORT.—Not later than 180 days after the date of enactment of this Act, the interagency group shall submit to Congress a report on the results of the study conducted under subsection (b), including recommendations for the oversight of existing and prospective carbon markets to ensure an efficient, secure, and transparent carbon market, including oversight of spot markets and derivative markets.

[Explanation at ¶ 3050.]

[¶ 10,751] ACT SEC. 751. ENERGY AND ENVIRONMENTAL MARKETS ADVISORY COMMITTEE.

Section 2(a) of the Commodity Exchange Act (7 U.S.C. 2(a)) (as amended by section 727) is amended by adding at the end the following:

"(15) ENERGY AND ENVIRONMENTAL MARKETS ADVISORY COMMITTEE.—

"(A) ESTABLISHMENT.—

"(i) IN GENERAL.—An Energy and Environmental Markets Advisory Committee is hereby established.

"(ii) MEMBERSHIP.—The Committee shall have 9 members.

"(iii) ACTIVITIES.—The Committee's objectives and scope of activities shall be—

"(I) to conduct public meetings;

"(II) to submit reports and recommendations to the Commission (including dissenting or minority views, if any); and

"(III) otherwise to serve as a vehicle for discussion and communication on matters of concern to exchanges, firms, end users, and regulators regarding energy and environmental markets and their regulation by the Commission.

"(B) REQUIREMENTS.—

"(i) IN GENERAL.—The Committee shall hold public meetings at such intervals as are necessary to carry out the functions of the Committee, but not less frequently than 2 times per year.

"(ii) MEMBERS.—Members shall be appointed to 3-year terms, but may be removed for cause by vote of the Commission.

"(C) APPOINTMENT.—The Commission shall appoint members with a wide diversity of opinion and who represent a broad spectrum of interests, including hedgers and consumers.

"(D) REIMBURSEMENT.—Members shall be entitled to per diem and travel expense reimbursement by the Commission.

"(E) FACA.—The Committee shall not be subject to the Federal Advisory Committee Act (5 U.S.C. App.).".

[Explanation at ¶ 3015.]

[¶ 10,752] ACT SEC. 752. INTERNATIONAL HARMONIZATION.

(a) In order to promote effective and consistent global regulation of swaps and security-based swaps, the Commodity Futures Trading Commission, the Securities and Exchange Commission, and the prudential regulators (as that term is defined in section 1a(39) of the Commodity Exchange Act), as appropriate, shall consult and coordinate with foreign regulatory authorities on the establishment of consistent international standards with respect to the regulation (including fees) of swaps, security-based swaps, swap entities, and security-based swap entities and may agree to such information-sharing arrangements as may be deemed to be necessary or appropriate in the public interest or for the protection of investors, swap counterparties, and security-based swap counterparties.

(b) In order to promote effective and consistent global regulation of contracts of sale of a commodity for future delivery and options on such contracts, the Commodity Futures Trading Commission shall consult and coordinate with foreign regulatory authorities on the establishment of consistent international standards with respect to the regulation of contracts of sale of a commodity for future delivery and options on such contracts, and may agree to such information-sharing arrangements as may be deemed necessary or appropriate in the public interest for the protection of users of contracts of sale of a commodity for future delivery.

[Explanation at ¶ 3150.]

[¶ 10,753] ACT SEC. 753. ANTI-MANIPULATION AUTHORITY.

(a) PROHIBITION REGARDING MANIPULATION AND FALSE INFORMATION.—Subsection (c) of section 6 of the Commodity Exchange Act (7 U.S.C. 9, 15) is amended to read as follows:

"(c) PROHIBITION REGARDING MANIPULATION AND FALSE INFORMATION.—

"(1) PROHIBITION AGAINST MANIPULATION.—It shall be unlawful for any person, directly or indirectly, to use or employ, or attempt to use or employ, in connection with any swap, or a contract of sale of any commodity in interstate commerce, or for future delivery on or subject to the rules of any registered entity, any manipulative or deceptive device or contrivance, in contravention of such rules and regulations as the Commission shall promulgate by not later than 1 year after the date of enactment of the Dodd-Frank Wall Street Reform and Consumer Protection Act, provided no rule or regulation promulgated by the Commission shall require any person to disclose to another person nonpublic information that may be material to the market price, rate, or level of the commodity transaction, except as necessary to make any statement made to the other person in or in connection with the transaction not misleading in any material respect.

"(A) SPECIAL PROVISION FOR MANIPULATION BY FALSE REPORTING.—Unlawful manipulation for purposes of this paragraph shall include, but not be limited to, delivering, or causing to be delivered for transmission through the mails or interstate commerce, by any means of communication whatsoever, a false or misleading or inaccurate report concerning crop or market information or conditions that affect or tend to affect the price of any commodity in interstate commerce, knowing, or acting in reckless disregard of the fact that such report is false, misleading or inaccurate.

"(B) EFFECT ON OTHER LAW.—Nothing in this paragraph shall affect, or be construed to affect, the applicability of section 9(a)(2).

"(C) GOOD FAITH MISTAKES.—Mistakenly transmitting, in good faith, false or misleading or inaccurate information to a price reporting service would not be sufficient to violate subsection (c)(1)(A).

"(2) PROHIBITION REGARDING FALSE INFORMATION.—It shall be unlawful for any person to make any false or misleading statement of a material fact to the Commission, including in any registration application or any report filed with the Commission under this Act, or any other information relating to a swap, or a contract of sale of a commodity, in interstate commerce, or for future delivery on or subject to the rules of any registered entity, or to omit to state in any such statement any material fact that is necessary to make any statement of a material fact made not misleading in any material respect, if the person knew, or reasonably should have known, the statement to be false or misleading.

"(3) OTHER MANIPULATION.—In addition to the prohibition in paragraph (1), it shall be unlawful for any person, directly or indirectly, to manipulate or attempt to manipulate the price of any swap, or of any commodity in interstate commerce, or for future delivery on or subject to the rules of any registered entity.

"(4) ENFORCEMENT.—

"(A) AUTHORITY OF COMMISSION.—If the Commission has reason to believe that any person (other than a registered entity) is violating or has violated this subsection, or any other provision of this Act (including any rule, regulation, or order of the Commission promulgated in accordance with this subsection or any other provision of this Act), the Commission may serve upon the person a complaint.

"(B) CONTENTS OF COMPLAINT.—A complaint under subparagraph (A) shall—

"(i) contain a description of the charges against the person that is the subject of the complaint; and

"(ii) have attached or contain a notice of hearing that specifies the date and location of the hearing regarding the complaint.

"(C) HEARING.—A hearing described in subparagraph (B)(ii)—

"(i) shall be held not later than 3 days after service of the complaint described in subparagraph (A);

"(ii) shall require the person to show cause regarding why—

"(I) an order should not be made—

"(aa) to prohibit the person from trading on, or subject to the rules of, any registered entity; and

"(bb) to direct all registered entities to refuse all privileges to the person until further notice of the Commission; and

"(II) the registration of the person, if registered with the Commission in any capacity, should not be suspended or revoked; and

"(iii) may be held before—

"(I) the Commission; or

"(II) an administrative law judge designated by the Commission, under which the administrative law judge shall ensure that all evidence is recorded in written form and submitted to the Commission.

"(5) SUBPOENA.—For the purpose of securing effective enforcement of the provisions of this Act, for the purpose of any investigation or proceeding under this Act, and for the purpose of any action taken under section 12(f), any member of the Commission or any Administrative Law Judge or other officer designated by the Commission (except as provided in paragraph (7)) may administer oaths and affirmations, subpoena witnesses, compel their attendance, take evidence, and require the production of any books, papers, correspondence, memoranda, or other records that the Commission deems relevant or material to the inquiry.

"(6) WITNESSES.—The attendance of witnesses and the production of any such records may be required from any place in the United States, any State, or any foreign country or jurisdiction at any designated place of hearing.

"(7) SERVICE.—A subpoena issued under this section may be served upon any person who is not to be found within the territorial jurisdiction of any court of the United States in such manner as the Federal Rules of Civil Procedure prescribe for service of process in a foreign country, except that a subpoena to be served on a person who is not to be found within the territorial jurisdiction of any court of the United States may be issued only on the prior approval of the Commission.

"(8) REFUSAL TO OBEY.—In case of contumacy by, or refusal to obey a subpoena issued to, any person, the Commission may invoke the aid of any court of the United States within the jurisdiction in which the investigation or proceeding is conducted, or where such person resides or transacts business, in requiring the attendance and testimony of witnesses and the production of books, papers, correspondence, memoranda, and other records. Such court may issue an order requiring such person to appear before the Commission or member or Administrative Law Judge or other officer designated by the Commission, there to produce records, if so ordered, or to give testimony touching the matter under investigation or in question.

"(9) FAILURE TO OBEY.—Any failure to obey such order of the court may be punished by the court as a contempt thereof. All process in any such case may be served in the judicial district wherein such person is an inhabitant or transacts business or wherever such person may be found.

"(10) EVIDENCE.—On the receipt of evidence under paragraph (4)(C)(iii), the Commission may—

"(A) prohibit the person that is the subject of the hearing from trading on, or subject to the rules of, any registered entity and require all registered entities to refuse the person all privileges on the registered entities for such period as the Commission may require in the order;

"(B) if the person is registered with the Commission in any capacity, suspend, for a period not to exceed 180 days, or revoke, the registration of the person;

"(C) assess such person—

"(i) a civil penalty of not more than an amount equal to the greater of—

"(I) $140,000; or

"(II) triple the monetary gain to such person for each such violation; or

"(ii) in any case of manipulation or attempted manipulation in violation of this subsection or section 9(a)(2), a civil penalty of not more than an amount equal to the greater of—

"(I) $1,000,000; or

"(II) triple the monetary gain to the person for each such violation; and

"(D) require restitution to customers of damages proximately caused by violations of the person.

"(11) ORDERS.—

"(A) NOTICE.—The Commission shall provide to a person described in paragraph (10) and the appropriate governing board of the registered entity notice of the order described in paragraph (10) by—

"(i) registered mail;

"(ii) certified mail; or

"(iii) personal delivery.

"(B) REVIEW.—

"(i) IN GENERAL.—A person described in paragraph (10) may obtain a review of the order or such other equitable relief as determined to be appropriate by a court described in clause (ii).

"(ii) PETITION.—To obtain a review or other relief under clause (i), a person may, not later than 15 days after notice is given to the person under clause (i), file a written petition to set aside the order with the United States Court of Appeals—

"(I) for the circuit in which the petitioner carries out the business of the petitioner; or

"(II) in the case of an order denying registration, the circuit in which the principal place of business of the petitioner is located, as listed on the application for registration of the petitioner.

"(C) PROCEDURE.—

"(i) DUTY OF CLERK OF APPROPRIATE COURT.—The clerk of the appropriate court under subparagraph (B)(ii) shall transmit to the Commission a copy of a petition filed under subparagraph (B)(ii).

"(ii) DUTY OF COMMISSION.—In accordance with section 2112 of title 28, United States Code, the Commission shall file in the appropriate court described in subparagraph (B)(ii) the record theretofore made.

"(iii) JURISDICTION OF APPROPRIATE COURT.—Upon the filing of a petition under subparagraph (B)(ii), the appropriate court described in subparagraph (B)(ii) may affirm, set aside, or modify the order of the Commission.".

(b) CEASE AND DESIST ORDERS, FINES.—Section 6(d) of the Commodity Exchange Act (7 U.S.C. 13b) is amended to read as follows:

"(d) If any person (other than a registered entity), is violating or has violated subsection (c) or any other provisions of this Act or of the rules, regulations, or orders of the Commission thereunder, the Commission may, upon notice and hearing, and subject to appeal as in other cases provided for in subsection (c), make and enter an order directing that such person shall cease and desist therefrom and, if such person thereafter and after the lapse of the period allowed for appeal of such order or after the affirmance of such order, shall knowingly fail or refuse to obey or comply with such order, such person, upon conviction thereof, shall be fined not more than the higher of $140,000 or triple the monetary gain to such person, or imprisoned for not more than 1 year, or both, except that if such knowing failure or refusal to obey or comply with such order involves any offense within subsection

(a) or (b) of section 9, such person, upon conviction thereof, shall be subject to the penalties of said subsection (a) or (b): Provided, That any such cease and desist order under this subsection against any respondent in any case of manipulation shall be issued only in conjunction with an order issued against such respondent under subsection (c).".

(c) MANIPULATIONS; PRIVATE RIGHTS OF ACTION.—Section 22(a)(1) of the Commodity Exchange Act (7 U.S.C. 25(a)(1)) is amended by striking subparagraph (D) and inserting the following:

"(D) who purchased or sold a contract referred to in subparagraph (B) hereof or swap if the violation constitutes—

"(i) the use or employment of, or an attempt to use or employ, in connection with a swap, or a contract of sale of a commodity, in interstate commerce, or for future delivery on or subject to the rules of any registered entity, any manipulative device or contrivance in contravention of such rules and regulations as the Commission shall promulgate by not later than 1 year after the date of enactment of the Dodd-Frank Wall Street Reform and Consumer Protection Act; or

"(ii) a manipulation of the price of any such contract or swap or the price of the commodity underlying such contract or swap.".

(d) EFFECTIVE DATE.—

(1) The amendments made by this section shall take effect on the date on which the final rule promulgated by the Commodity Futures Trading Commission pursuant to this Act takes effect.

(2) Paragraph (1) shall not preclude the Commission from undertaking prior to the effective date any rulemaking necessary to implement the amendments contained in this section.

[Explanation at ¶ 3155.]

[¶ 10,754] ACT SEC. 754. EFFECTIVE DATE.

Unless otherwise provided in this title, the provisions of this subtitle shall take effect on the later of 360 days after the date of the enactment of this subtitle or, to the extent a provision of this subtitle requires a rulemaking, not less than 60 days after publication of the final rule or regulation implementing such provision of this subtitle.

[Explanations at ¶ 3005, ¶ 3010, ¶ 3015, ¶ 3020, ¶ 3025, ¶ 3035 and ¶ 3040.]

Subtitle B—Regulation of Security-Based Swap Markets

[¶ 10,761] ACT SEC. 761. DEFINITIONS UNDER THE SECURITIES EXCHANGE ACT OF 1934.

(a) DEFINITIONS.—Section 3(a) of the Securities Exchange Act of 1934 (15 U.S.C. 78c(a)) is amended—

(1) in subparagraphs (A) and (B) of paragraph (5), by inserting "(not including security-based swaps, other than security-based swaps with or for persons that are not eligible contract participants)" after "securities" each place that term appears;

(2) in paragraph (10), by inserting "security-based swap," after "security future,";

(3) in paragraph (13), by adding at the end the following: "For security-based swaps, such terms include the execution, termination (prior to its scheduled maturity date), assignment, exchange, or similar transfer or conveyance of, or extinguishing of rights or obligations under, a security-based swap, as the context may require.";

(4) in paragraph (14), by adding at the end the following: "For security-based swaps, such terms include the execution, termination (prior to its scheduled maturity date), assignment, exchange, or similar transfer or conveyance of, or extinguishing of rights or obligations under, a security-based swap, as the context may require.";

(5) in paragraph (39)—

(A) in subparagraph (B)(i)—

(i) in subclause (I), by striking "or government securities dealer" and inserting "government securities dealer, security-based swap dealer, or major security-based swap participant"; and

(ii) in subclause (II), by inserting "security-based swap dealer, major security-based swap participant," after "government securities dealer,";

(B) in subparagraph (C), by striking "or government securities dealer" and inserting "government securities dealer, security-based swap dealer, or major security-based swap participant"; and

(C) in subparagraph (D), by inserting "security-based swap dealer, major security-based swap participant," after "government securities dealer,"; and

(6) by adding at the end the following:

"(65) ELIGIBLE CONTRACT PARTICIPANT.—The term 'eligible contract participant' has the same meaning as in section 1a of the Commodity Exchange Act (7 U.S.C. 1a).

"(66) MAJOR SWAP PARTICIPANT.—The term 'major swap participant' has the same meaning as in section 1a of the Commodity Exchange Act (7 U.S.C. 1a).

"(67) MAJOR SECURITY-BASED SWAP PARTICIPANT.—

"(A) IN GENERAL.—The term 'major security-based swap participant' means any person—

"(i) who is not a security-based swap dealer; and

"(ii)

(I) who maintains a substantial position in security-based swaps for any of the major security-based swap categories, as such categories are determined by the Commission, excluding both positions held for hedging or mitigating commercial risk and positions maintained by any employee benefit plan (or any contract held by such a plan) as defined in paragraphs (3) and (32) of section 3 of the Employee Retirement Income Security Act of 1974 (29 U.S.C. 1002) for the primary purpose of hedging or mitigating any risk directly associated with the operation of the plan;

"(II) whose outstanding security-based swaps create substantial counterparty exposure that could have serious adverse effects on the financial stability of the United States banking system or financial markets; or

"(III) that is a financial entity that—

"(aa) is highly leveraged relative to the amount of capital such entity holds and that is not subject to capital requirements established by an appropriate Federal banking agency; and

"(bb) maintains a substantial position in outstanding security-based swaps in any major security-based swap category, as such categories are determined by the Commission.

"(B) DEFINITION OF SUBSTANTIAL POSITION.—For purposes of subparagraph (A), the Commission shall define, by rule or regulation, the term 'substantial position' at the threshold that the Commission determines to be prudent for the effective monitoring, management, and oversight of entities that are systemically important or can significantly impact the financial system of the United States. In setting the definition under this subparagraph, the Commission shall consider the person's relative position in uncleared as opposed to cleared security-based swaps and may take into consideration the value and quality of collateral held against counterparty exposures.

"(C) SCOPE OF DESIGNATION.—For purposes of subparagraph (A), a person may be designated as a major security-based swap participant for 1 or more categories of security-based swaps without being classified as a major security-based swap participant for all classes of security-based swaps.

"(68) SECURITY-BASED SWAP.—

"(A) IN GENERAL.—Except as provided in subparagraph (B), the term 'security-based swap' means any agreement, contract, or transaction that—

"(i) is a swap, as that term is defined under section 1a of the Commodity Exchange Act (without regard to paragraph (47)(B)(x) of such section); and

"(ii) is based on—

"(I) an index that is a narrow-based security index, including any interest therein or on the value thereof;

"(II) a single security or loan, including any interest therein or on the value thereof; or

"(III) the occurrence, nonoccur-rence, or extent of the occurrence of an event relating to a single issuer of a security or the issuers of securities in a narrow-based security index, provided that such event directly affects the financial statements, financial condition, or financial obligations of the issuer.

"(B) RULE OF CONSTRUCTION REGARDING MASTER AGREEMENTS.—The term 'security-based swap' shall be construed to include a master agreement that provides for an agreement, contract, or transaction that is a security-based swap pursuant to subparagraph (A), together with all supplements to any such master agreement, without regard to whether the master agreement contains an agreement, contract, or transaction that is not a security-based swap pursuant to subparagraph (A), except that the master agreement shall be considered to be a security-based swap only with respect to each agreement, contract, or transaction under the master agreement that is a security-based swap pursuant to subparagraph (A).

"(C) EXCLUSIONS.—The term 'security-based swap' does not include any agreement, contract, or transaction that meets the definition of a security-based swap only because such agreement, contract, or transaction references, is based upon, or settles through the transfer, delivery, or receipt of an exempted security under paragraph (12), as in effect on the date of enactment of the Futures Trading Act of 1982 (other than any municipal security as defined in paragraph (29) as in effect on the date of enactment of the Futures Trading Act of 1982), unless such agreement, contract, or transaction is of the character of, or is commonly known in the trade as, a put, call, or other option.

"(D) MIXED SWAP.—The term 'security-based swap' includes any agreement, contract, or transaction that is as described in subparagraph (A) and also is based on the value of 1 or more interest or other rates, currencies, commodities, instruments of indebtedness, indices, quantitative measures, other financial or economic interest or property of any kind (other than a single security or a narrow-based security index), or the occurrence, non-occurrence, or the extent of the occurrence of an event or contingency associated with a potential financial, economic, or commercial consequence (other than an event described in subparagraph (A)(ii)(III)).

"(E) RULE OF CONSTRUCTION REGARDING USE OF THE TERM INDEX.—The term 'index' means an index or group of securities, including any interest therein or based on the value thereof.

"(69) SWAP.—The term 'swap' has the same meaning as in section 1a of the Commodity Exchange Act (7 U.S.C. 1a).

"(70) PERSON ASSOCIATED WITH A SECURITY-BASED SWAP DEALER OR MAJOR SECURITY-BASED SWAP PARTICIPANT.—

"(A) IN GENERAL.—The term 'person associated with a security-based swap dealer or major security-based swap participant' or 'associated person of a security-based swap dealer or major security-based swap participant' means—

"(i) any partner, officer, director, or branch manager of such security-based swap dealer or major security-based swap participant (or any person occupying a similar status or performing similar functions);

"(ii) any person directly or indirectly controlling, controlled by, or under common control with such security-based swap dealer or major security-based swap participant; or

"(iii) any employee of such security-based swap dealer or major security-based swap participant.

"(B) EXCLUSION.—Other than for purposes of section 15F(1)(2), the term 'person associated with a security-based swap dealer or major security-based swap participant' or 'associated person of a security-based swap dealer or major security-based swap participant' does not include any person associated with a security-based swap dealer or major security-based swap participant whose functions are solely clerical or ministerial.

"(71) SECURITY-BASED SWAP DEALER.—

"(A) IN GENERAL.—The term 'security-based swap dealer' means any person who—

"(i) holds themself out as a dealer in security-based swaps;

"(ii) makes a market in security-based swaps;

"(iii) regularly enters into security-based swaps with counterparties as an ordinary course of business for its own account; or

"(iv) engages in any activity causing it to be commonly known in the trade as a dealer or market maker in security-based swaps.

"(B) DESIGNATION BY TYPE OR CLASS.—A person may be designated as a security-based swap dealer for a single type or single class or category of security-based swap or activities and considered not to be a security-based swap dealer for other types, classes, or categories of security-based swaps or activities.

"(C) EXCEPTION.—The term 'security-based swap dealer' does not include a person that enters into security-based swaps for such person's own account, either individually or in a fiduciary capacity, but not as a part of regular business.

"(D) DE MINIMIS EXCEPTION.—The Commission shall exempt from designation as a security-based swap dealer an entity that engages in a de minimis quantity of security-based swap dealing in connection with transactions with or on behalf of its customers. The Commission shall promulgate regulations to establish factors with respect to the making of any determination to exempt.

"(72) APPROPRIATE FEDERAL BANKING AGENCY.—The term 'appropriate Federal banking agency' has the same meaning as in section 3(q) of the Federal Deposit Insurance Act (12 U.S.C. 1813(q)).

"(73) BOARD.—The term 'Board' means the Board of Governors of the Federal Reserve System.

"(74) PRUDENTIAL REGULATOR.—The term 'prudential regulator' has the same meaning as in section 1a of the Commodity Exchange Act (7 U.S.C. 1a).

"(75) SECURITY-BASED SWAP DATA REPOSITORY.—The term 'security-based swap data repository' means any person that collects and maintains information or records with respect to transactions or positions in, or the terms and conditions of, security-based swaps entered into by third parties for the purpose of providing a centralized recordkeeping facility for security-based swaps.

"(76) SWAP DEALER.—The term 'swap dealer' has the same meaning as in section 1a of the Commodity Exchange Act (7 U.S.C. 1a).

"(77) SECURITY-BASED SWAP EXECUTION FACILITY.—The term 'security-based swap execution facility' means a trading system or platform in which multiple participants have the ability to execute or trade security-based swaps by accepting bids and offers made by multiple participants in the facility or system, through any means of interstate commerce, including any trading facility, that—

"(A) facilitates the execution of security-based swaps between persons; and

"(B) is not a national securities exchange.

"(78) SECURITY-BASED SWAP AGREEMENT.—

"(A) IN GENERAL.—For purposes of sections 9, 10, 16, 20, and 21A of this Act, and section 17 of the Securities Act of 1933 (15 U.S.C. 77q), the term 'security-based swap agreement' means a swap agreement as defined in section 206A of the Gramm-Leach-Bliley Act (15 U.S.C. 78c note) of which a material term is based on the price, yield, value, or volatility of any security or any group or index of securities, or any interest therein.

"(B) EXCLUSIONS.—The term 'security-based swap agreement' does not include any security-based swap.".

(b) AUTHORITY TO FURTHER DEFINE TERMS.—The Securities and Exchange Commission may, by rule, further define—

(1) the term "commercial risk";

(2) any other term included in an amendment to the Securities Exchange Act of 1934 (15 U.S.C. 78c(a)) made by this subtitle; and

(3) the terms "security-based swap", "security-based swap dealer", "major security-based swap participant", and "eligible contract participant", with regard to security-based swaps (as such terms are defined in the amendments made by subsection (a)) for the purpose of including transactions and entities that have been structured to evade this subtitle or the amendments made by this subtitle.

[Explanation at ¶ 3010.]

[¶ 10,762] ACT SEC. 762. REPEAL OF PROHIBITION ON REGULATION OF SECURITY-BASED SWAP AGREEMENTS.

(a) REPEAL.—Sections 206B and 206C of the Gramm-Leach-Bliley Act (Public Law 106-102; 15 U.S.C. 78c note) are repealed.

(b) CONFORMING AMENDMENTS TO GRAMM-LEACH-BLILEY.—Section 206A(a) of the Gramm-Leach-Bliley Act (15 U.S.C. 78c note) is amended in the material preceding paragraph (1), by striking "Except as" and all that follows through "that—"and inserting the following: "Except as provided in subsection (b), as used in this section, the term 'swap agreement' means any agreement, contract, or transaction that—".

(c) CONFORMING AMENDMENTS TO THE SECURITIES ACT OF 1933.—

(1) Section 2A of the Securities Act of 1933 (15 U.S.C. 77b-1) is amended—

(A) by striking subsection (a) and reserving that subsection; and

(B) by striking "(as defined in section 206B of the Gramm-Leach-Bliley Act)" each place that such term appears and inserting "(as defined in section 3(a)(78) of the Securities Exchange Act of 1934)".

(2) Section 17 of the Securities Act of 1933 (15 U.S.C. 77q) is amended—

(A) in subsection (a)—

(i) by inserting "(including security-based swaps)" after "securities"; and

(ii) by striking "(as defined in section 206B of the Gramm-Leach-Bliley Act)" and inserting "(as defined in section 3(a)(78) of the Securities Exchange Act)"; and

(B) in subsection (d), by striking "206B of the Gramm-Leach-Bliley Act" and inserting "3(a)(78) of the Securities Exchange Act of 1934."

(d) CONFORMING AMENDMENTS TO THE SECURITIES EXCHANGE ACT OF 1934.—The Securities Exchange Act of 1934 (15 U.S.C. 78a et seq.) is amended—

(1) in section 3A (15 U.S.C. 78c-1)—

(A) by striking subsection (a) and reserving that subsection; and

(B) by striking "(as defined in section 206B of the Gramm-Leach-Bliley Act)" each place that the term appears;

(2) in section 9 (15 U.S.C. 78i)—

(A) in subsection (a), by striking paragraphs (2) through (5) and inserting the following:

"(2) To effect, alone or with 1 or more other persons, a series of transactions in any security registered on a national securities exchange, any security not so registered, or in connection with any security-based swap or security-based swap agreement with respect to such security creating actual or apparent active trading in such security, or raising or depressing the price of such security, for the purpose of inducing the purchase or sale of such security by others.

"(3) If a dealer, broker, security-based swap dealer, major security-based swap participant, or other person selling or offering for sale or purchasing or offering to purchase the security, a security-based swap, or a security-based swap agreement with respect to such security, to induce the purchase or sale of any security registered on a national securities exchange, any security not so registered, any security-based swap, or any security-based swap agreement with respect to such security by the circulation or dissemination in the ordinary course of business of information to the effect that the price of any such security will or is likely to rise or fall because of market operations of any 1 or more persons conducted for the purpose of raising or depressing the price of such security.

"(4) If a dealer, broker, security-based swap dealer, major security-based swap participant, or other person selling or offering for sale or purchasing or offering to purchase the security, a security-based swap, or security-based swap agreement with respect to such security, to make, regarding any security registered on a national securities exchange, any security not so registered, any security-based swap, or any security-based swap agreement with respect to such security, for the purpose of inducing the purchase or sale of such security, such security-based swap, or such security-based swap agreement any statement which was at the time and in the light of the circumstances under which it was made, false or misleading with respect to any material fact, and which that person knew or had reasonable ground to believe was so false or misleading.

"(5) For a consideration, received directly or indirectly from a broker, dealer, security-based swap dealer, major security-based swap participant, or other person selling or offering for sale or purchasing or offering to purchase the security, a security-based swap, or security-based swap agreement with respect to such security, to induce the purchase of any security registered on a national securities exchange, any security not so registered, any security-based swap, or any security-based swap agreement with respect to such security by the circulation or dissemination of information to the effect that the price of any such security will or is likely to rise or fall because of the market operations of any 1 or more persons conducted for the purpose of raising or depressing the price of such security."; and

(B) in subsection (i), by striking "(as defined in section 206B of the Gramm-Leach-Bliley Act)";

(3) in section 10 (15 U.S.C. 78j)—

(A) in subsection (b), by striking "(as defined in section 206B of the Gramm-Leach-Bliley Act)," each place that term appears; and

(B) in the matter following subsection (b), by striking "(as defined in section 206B of the Gramm-Leach-Bliley Act), in each place that such terms appear";

(4) in section 15 (15 U.S.C. 78o)—

(A) in subsection (c)(1)(A), by striking "(as defined in section 206B of the Gramm-Leach-Bliley Act),";

(B) in subparagraphs (B) and (C) of subsection (c)(1), by striking "(as defined in section 206B of the Gramm-Leach-Bliley Act)" each place that term appears;

(C) by redesignating subsection (i), as added by section 303(f) of the Commodity Futures Modernization Act of 2000 (Public Law 106-554; 114 Stat. 2763A-455)), as subsection (j); and

(D) in subsection (j), as redesignated by subparagraph (C), by striking "(as defined in section 206B of the Gramm-Leach-Bliley Act)";

(5) in section 16 (15 U.S.C. 78p)—

(A) in subsection (a)(2)(C), by striking "(as defined in section 206(b) of the Gramm-Leach-Bliley Act (15 U.S.C. 78c note))";

(B) in subsection (a)(3)(B), by inserting "or security-based swaps" after "security-based swap agreement";

(C) in the first sentence of subsection (b), by striking "(as defined in section 206B of the Gramm-Leach-Bliley Act)";

(D) in the third sentence of subsection (b), by striking "(as defined in section 206B of the Gramm-Leach Bliley Act)" and inserting "or a security-based swap"; and

(E) in subsection (g), by striking "(as defined in section 206B of the Gramm-Leach-Bliley Act)";

(6) in section 20 (15 U.S.C. 78t),

(A) in subsection (d), by striking "(as defined in section 206B of the Gramm-Leach-Bliley Act)"; and

(B) in subsection (f), by striking "(as defined in section 206B of the Gramm-Leach-Bliley Act)"; and

(7) in section 21A (15 U.S.C. 78u-1)—

(A) in subsection (a)(1), by striking "(as defined in section 206B of the Gramm-Leach-Bliley Act)"; and

(B) in subsection (g), by striking "(as defined in section 206B of the Gramm-Leach-Bliley Act)".

[Explanation at ¶3015.]

[¶10,763] ACT SEC. 763. AMENDMENTS TO THE SECURITIES EXCHANGE ACT OF 1934.

(a) CLEARING FOR SECURITY-BASED SWAPS.—The Securities Exchange Act of 1934 (15 U.S.C. 78a et seq.) is amended by inserting after section 3B (as added by section 717 of this Act):

"SEC. 3C. CLEARING FOR SECURITY-BASED SWAPS.

"(a) IN GENERAL.—

"(1) STANDARD FOR CLEARING.—It shall be unlawful for any person to engage in a security-based swap unless that person submits such security-based swap for clearing to a clearing agency that is registered under this Act or a clearing agency that is exempt from registration under this Act if the security-based swap is required to be cleared.

"(2) OPEN ACCESS.—The rules of a clearing agency described in paragraph (1) shall—

"(A) prescribe that all security-based swaps submitted to the clearing agency with the same terms and conditions are economically equivalent within the clearing agency and may be offset with each other within the clearing agency; and

"(B) provide for non-discriminatory clearing of a security-based swap executed bilaterally or on or through the rules of an unaffiliated national securities exchange or security-based swap execution facility.

"(b) COMMISSION REVIEW.—

"(1) COMMISSION-INITIATED REVIEW.—

"(A) The Commission on an ongoing basis shall review each security-based swap, or any group, category, type, or class of security-based swaps to make a determination that such security-based swap, or group, category, type, or class of security-based swaps should be required to be cleared.

"(B) The Commission shall provide at least a 30-day public comment period regarding any determination under subparagraph (A).

"(2) SWAP SUBMISSIONS.—

"(A) A clearing agency shall submit to the Commission each security-based swap, or any group, category, type, or class of security-based swaps that it plans to accept for clearing and provide notice to its members (in a manner to be determined by the Commission) of such submission.

"(B) Any security-based swap or group, category, type, or class of security-based swaps listed for clearing by a clearing agency as of the date of enactment of this subsection shall be considered submitted to the Commission.

"(C) The Commission shall—

"(i) make available to the public any submission received under subparagraphs (A) and (B);

"(ii) review each submission made under subparagraphs (A) and (B), and determine whether the security-based swap, or group, category, type, or class of security-based swaps, described in the submission is required to be cleared; and

"(iii) provide at least a 30-day public comment period regarding its determination whether the clearing requirement under subsection (a)(1) shall apply to the submission.

"(3) DEADLINE.—The Commission shall make its determination under paragraph (2)(C) not later than 90 days after receiving a submission made under paragraphs (2)(A) and (2)(B), unless the submitting clearing agency agrees to an extension for the time limitation established under this paragraph.

"(4) DETERMINATION.—

"(A) In reviewing a submission made under paragraph (2), the Commission shall review whether the submission is consistent with section 17A.

"(B) In reviewing a security-based swap, group of security-based swaps or class of security-based swaps pursuant to paragraph (1) or a submission made under paragraph (2), the Commission shall take into account the following factors:

"(i) The existence of significant outstanding notional exposures, trading liquidity and adequate pricing data.

"(ii) The availability of rule framework, capacity, operational expertise and resources, and credit support infrastructure to clear the contract on terms that are consistent with the material terms and trading conventions on which the contract is then traded.

"(iii) The effect on the mitigation of systemic risk, taking into account the size of the market for such contract and the resources of the clearing agency available to clear the contract.

"(iv) The effect on competition, including appropriate fees and charges applied to clearing.

"(v) The existence of reasonable legal certainty in the event of the insolvency of the relevant clearing agency or 1 or more of its clearing members with regard to the treatment of customer and security-based swap counterparty positions, funds, and property.

"(C) In making a determination under subsection (b)(1) or paragraph (2)(C) that the clearing requirement shall apply, the Commission may require such terms and conditions to the requirement as the Commission determines to be appropriate.

"(5) RULES.—Not later than 1 year after the date of the enactment of this section, the Commission shall adopt rules for a clearing agency's submission for review, pursuant to this subsection, of a security-based swap, or a group, category, type, or class of security-based swaps, that it seeks to accept for clearing. Nothing in this paragraph limits the Commission from making a determination under paragraph (2)(C) for security-based swaps described in paragraph (2)(B).

"(c) STAY OF CLEARING REQUIREMENT.—

"(1) IN GENERAL.—After making a determination pursuant to subsection (b)(2), the Commission, on application of a counterparty to a security-based swap or on its own initiative, may stay the clearing requirement of subsection (a)(1) until the Commission completes a review of the terms of the security-based swap (or the group, category, type, or class of security-based swaps) and the clearing arrangement.

"(2) DEADLINE.—The Commission shall complete a review undertaken pursuant to paragraph (1) not later than 90 days after issuance of the stay, unless the clearing agency that clears the security-based swap, or group, category, type, or class of security-based swaps, agrees to an extension of the time limitation established under this paragraph.

"(3) DETERMINATION.—Upon completion of the review undertaken pursuant to paragraph (1), the Commission may—

"(A) determine, unconditionally or subject to such terms and conditions as the Commission determines to be appropriate, that the security-based swap, or group, category, type, or class of security-based swaps, must be cleared pursuant to this subsection if it finds that such clearing is consistent with subsection (b)(4); or

"(B) determine that the clearing requirement of subsection (a)(1) shall not apply to the security-based swap, or group, category, type, or class of security-based swaps.

"(4) RULES.—Not later than 1 year after the date of the enactment of this section, the Commission shall adopt rules for reviewing, pursuant to this subsection, a clearing agency's clearing of a security-based swap, or a group, category, type, or class of security-based swaps, that it has accepted for clearing.

"(d) PREVENTION OF EVASION.—

"(1) IN GENERAL.—The Commission shall prescribe rules under this section (and issue interpretations of rules prescribed under this section), as determined by the Commission to be necessary to prevent evasions of the mandatory clearing requirements under this Act.

"(2) DUTY OF COMMISSION TO INVESTIGATE AND TAKE CERTAIN ACTIONS.—To the extent the Commission finds that a particular security-based swap or any group, category, type, or class of security-based swaps that would otherwise be subject to mandatory clearing but no clearing agency has listed the security-based swap or the group, category, type, or class of security-based swaps for clearing, the Commission shall—

"(A) investigate the relevant facts and circumstances;

"(B) within 30 days issue a public report containing the results of the investigation; and

"(C) take such actions as the Commission determines to be necessary and in the public interest, which may include requiring the retaining of adequate margin or capital by parties to the security-based swap or the group, category, type, or class of security-based swaps.

"(3) EFFECT ON AUTHORITY.—Nothing in this subsection—

"(A) authorizes the Commission to adopt rules requiring a clearing agency to list for clearing a security-based swap or any group, category, type, or class of security-based swaps if the clearing of the security-based swap or the group, category, type, or class of security-based swaps would threaten the financial integrity of the clearing agency; and

"(B) affects the authority of the Commission to enforce the open access provisions of subsection (a)(2) with respect to a security-based swap or the group, category, type, or class of security-based swaps that is listed for clearing by a clearing agency.

"(e) REPORTING TRANSITION RULES.—Rules adopted by the Commission under this section shall provide for the reporting of data, as follows:

"(1) Security-based swaps entered into before the date of the enactment of this section shall be reported to a registered security-based swap data repository or the Commission no later than 180 days after the effective date of this section.

"(2) Security-based swaps entered into on or after such date of enactment shall be reported to a registered security-based swap data repository or the Commission no later than the later of—

"(A) 90 days after such effective date; or

"(B) such other time after entering into the security-based swap as the Commission may prescribe by rule or regulation.

"(f) CLEARING TRANSITION RULES.—

"(1) Security-based swaps entered into before the date of the enactment of this section are exempt from the clearing requirements of this subsection if reported pursuant to subsection (e)(1).

"(2) Security-based swaps entered into before application of the clearing requirement pursuant to this section are exempt from the clearing requirements of this section if reported pursuant to subsection (e)(?).

"(g) EXCEPTIONS.—

"(1) IN GENERAL.—The requirements of subsection (a)(1) shall not apply to a security-based swap if 1 of the counterparties to the security-based swap—

"(A) is not a financial entity;

"(B) is using security-based swaps to hedge or mitigate commercial risk; and

"(C) notifies the Commission, in a manner set forth by the Commission, how it generally meets its financial obligations associated with entering into non-cleared security-based swaps.

"(2) OPTION TO CLEAR.—The application of the clearing exception in paragraph (1) is solely at the discretion of the counterparty to the security-based swap that meets the conditions of subparagraphs (A) through (C) of paragraph (1).

"(3) FINANCIAL ENTITY DEFINITION.—

"(A) IN GENERAL.—For the purposes of this subsection, the term 'financial entity' means—

"(i) a swap dealer;

"(ii) a security-based swap dealer;

"(iii) a major swap participant;

"(iv) a major security-based swap participant;

"(v) a commodity pool as defined in section 1a(10) of the Commodity Exchange Act;

"(vi) a private fund as defined in section 202(a) of the Investment Advisers Act of 1940 (15 U.S.C. 80-b-2(a));

"(vii) an employee benefit plan as defined in paragraphs (3) and (32) of section 3 of the Employee Retirement Income Security Act of 1974 (29 U.S.C. 1002);

"(viii) a person predominantly engaged in activities that are in the business of banking or financial in nature, as defined in section 4(k) of the Bank Holding Company Act of 1956.

"(B) EXCLUSION.—The Commission shall consider whether to exempt small banks, savings associations, farm credit system institutions, and credit unions, including—

"(i) depository institutions with total assets of $10,000,000,000 or less;

"(ii) farm credit system institutions with total assets of $10,000,000,000 or less; or

"(iii) credit unions with total assets of $10,000,000,000 or less.

"(4) TREATMENT OF AFFILIATES.—

"(A) IN GENERAL.—An affiliate of a person that qualifies for an exception under this subsection (including affiliate entities predominantly engaged in providing financing for the purchase of the merchandise or manufactured goods of the person) may qualify for the exception only if the affiliate, acting on behalf of the person and as an agent, uses the security-based swap to hedge or mitigate the commercial risk of the person or other affiliate of the person that is not a financial entity.

"(B) PROHIBITION RELATING TO CERTAIN AFFILIATES.—The exception in subparagraph (A) shall not apply if the affiliate is—

"(i) a swap dealer;

"(ii) a security-based swap dealer;

"(iii) a major swap participant;

"(iv) a major security-based swap participant;

"(v) an issuer that would be an investment company, as defined in section 3 of the Investment Company Act of 1940 (15 U.S.C. 80a-3), but for paragraph (1) or (7) of subsection (c) of that Act (15 U.S.C. 80a-3(c));

"(vi) a commodity pool; or

"(vii) a bank holding company with over $50,000,000,000 in consolidated assets.

"(C) TRANSITION RULE FOR AFFILIATES.—An affiliate, subsidiary, or a wholly owned entity of a person that qualifies for an exception under subparagraph (A) and is predominantly engaged in providing financing for the purchase or lease of merchandise or manufactured goods of the person shall be exempt from the margin requirement described in section 15F(e) and the clearing requirement described in subsection (a) with regard to security-based swaps entered into to mitigate the risk of the financing activities for not less than a 2-year period beginning on the date of enactment of this subparagraph.

"(5) ELECTION OF COUNTERPARTY.—

"(A) SECURITY-BASED SWAPS REQUIRED TO BE CLEARED.—With respect to any security-based swap that is subject to the mandatory clearing requirement under subsection (a) and entered into by a security-based swap dealer or a major security-based swap participant with a counterparty that is not a swap dealer, major swap participant, security-based swap dealer, or major security-based swap participant, the counterparty shall have the sole right to select the clearing agency at which the security-based swap will be cleared.

"(B) SECURITY-BASED SWAPS NOT REQUIRED TO BE CLEARED.—With respect to any security-based swap that is not subject to the mandatory clearing requirement under subsection (a) and entered into by a security-based swap dealer or a major security-based swap participant with a counterparty that is not a swap dealer, major swap participant, security-based swap dealer, or major security-based swap participant, the counterparty—

"(i) may elect to require clearing of the security-based swap; and

"(ii) shall have the sole right to select the clearing agency at which the security-based swap will be cleared.

"(6) ABUSE OF EXCEPTION.—The Commission may prescribe such rules or issue interpretations of the rules as the Commission determines to be necessary to prevent abuse of the exceptions described in this subsection. The Commission may also request information from those persons claiming the clearing exception as necessary to prevent abuse of the exceptions described in this subsection.

"(h) TRADE EXECUTION.—

"(1) IN GENERAL.—With respect to transactions involving security-based swaps subject to the clearing requirement of subsection (a)(1), counterparties shall—

"(A) execute the transaction on an exchange; or

"(B) execute the transaction on a security-based swap execution facility registered under section 3D or a security-based swap execution facility that is exempt from registration under section 3D(e).

"(2) EXCEPTION.—The requirements of subparagraphs (A) and (B) of paragraph (1) shall not apply if no exchange or security-based swap execution facility makes the security-based swap available to trade or for security-based swap transactions subject to the clearing exception under subsection (g).

"(i) BOARD APPROVAL.—Exemptions from the requirements of this section to clear a security-based swap or execute a security-based swap through a national securities exchange or security-based swap execution facility shall be available to a counterparty that is an issuer of securities that are registered under section 12 or that is required to file reports pursuant to section 15(d), only if an appropriate committee of the issuer's board or governing body has reviewed and approved the issuer's decision to enter into security-based swaps that are subject to such exemptions.

"(j) DESIGNATION OF CHIEF COMPLIANCE OFFICER.—

"(1) IN GENERAL.—Each registered clearing agency shall designate an individual to serve as a chief compliance officer.

"(2) DUTIES.—The chief compliance officer shall—

"(A) report directly to the board or to the senior officer of the clearing agency;

"(B) in consultation with its board, a body performing a function similar thereto, or the senior officer of the registered clearing agency, resolve any conflicts of interest that may arise;

"(C) be responsible for administering each policy and procedure that is required to be established pursuant to this section;

"(D) ensure compliance with this title (including regulations issued under this title) relating to agreements, contracts, or transactions, including each rule prescribed by the Commission under this section;

"(E) establish procedures for the remediation of noncompliance issues identified by the compliance officer through any—

"(i) compliance office review;

"(ii) look-back;

"(iii) internal or external audit finding;

"(iv) self-reported error; or

"(v) validated complaint; and

"(F) establish and follow appropriate procedures for the handling, management response, remediation, retesting, and closing of noncompliance issues.

"(3) ANNUAL REPORTS.—

"(A) IN GENERAL.—In accordance with rules prescribed by the Commission, the chief compliance officer shall annually prepare and sign a report that contains a description of—

"(i) the compliance of the registered clearing agency or security-based swap execution facility of the compliance officer with respect to this title (including regulations under this title); and

"(ii) each policy and procedure of the registered clearing agency of the compliance officer (including the code of ethics and conflict of interest policies of the registered clearing agency).

"(B) REQUIREMENTS.—A compliance report under subparagraph (A) shall—

"(i) accompany each appropriate financial report of the registered clearing agency that is required to be furnished to the Commission pursuant to this section; and

"(ii) include a certification that, under penalty of law, the compliance report is accurate and complete.".

(b) CLEARING AGENCY REQUIREMENTS.—Section 17A of the Securities Exchange Act of 1934 (15 U.S.C. 78q-1) is amended by adding at the end the following:

"(g) REGISTRATION REQUIREMENT.—It shall be unlawful for a clearing agency, unless registered with the Commission, directly or indirectly to make use of the mails or any means or instrumentality of interstate commerce to perform the functions of a clearing agency with respect to a security-based swap.

"(h) VOLUNTARY REGISTRATION.—A person that clears agreements, contracts, or transactions that are not required to be cleared under this title may register with the Commission as a clearing agency.

"(i) STANDARDS FOR CLEARING AGENCIES CLEARING SECURITY-BASED SWAP TRANSACTIONS.—To be registered and to maintain registration as a clearing agency that clears security-based swap transactions, a clearing agency shall comply with such standards as the Commission may establish by rule. In establishing any such standards, and in the exercise of its oversight of such a clearing agency pursuant to this title, the Commission may conform such standards or oversight to reflect evolving United States and international standards. Except where the Commission determines otherwise by rule or regulation, a clearing agency shall have reasonable discretion in establishing the manner in which it complies with any such standards.

"(j) RULES.—The Commission shall adopt rules governing persons that are registered as clearing agencies for security-based swaps under this title.

"(k) EXEMPTIONS.—The Commission may exempt, conditionally or unconditionally, a clearing agency from registration under this section for the clearing of security-based swaps if the Commission determines that the clearing agency is subject to comparable, comprehensive supervision and regulation by the Commodity Futures Trading Commission or the appropriate government authorities in the home country of the agency. Such conditions may include, but are not limited to, requiring that the clearing agency be available for inspection by the Commission and make available all information requested by the Commission.

"(l) EXISTING DEPOSITORY INSTITUTIONS AND DERIVATIVE CLEARING ORGANIZATIONS.—

"(1) IN GENERAL.—A depository institution or derivative clearing organization registered with the Commodity Futures Trading Commission under the Commodity Exchange Act that is required to be registered as a clearing agency under this section is deemed to be registered under this section solely for the purpose of clearing security-based swaps to the extent that, before the date of enactment of this subsection—

"(A) the depository institution cleared swaps as a multilateral clearing organization; or

"(B) the derivative clearing organization cleared swaps pursuant to an exemption from registration as a clearing agency.

"(2) CONVERSION OF DEPOSITORY INSTITUTIONS.—A depository institution to which this subsection applies may, by the vote of the shareholders owning not less than 51 percent of the voting interests of the depository institution, be converted into a State corporation, partnership, limited liability company, or similar legal form pursuant to a plan of conversion, if the conversion is not in contravention of applicable State law.

"(3) SHARING OF INFORMATION.—The Commodity Futures Trading Commission shall make available to the Commission, upon request, all information determined to be relevant by the Commodity Futures Trading Commission regarding a derivatives clearing organization deemed to be registered with the Commission under paragraph (1).

"(m) MODIFICATION OF CORE PRINCIPLES.—The Commission may conform the core principles established in this section to reflect evolving United States and international standards.".

(c) SECURITY-BASED SWAP EXECUTION FACILITIES.—The Securities Exchange Act of 1934 (15 U.S.C. 78a et seq.) is amended by inserting after section 3C (as added by subsection (a) of this section) the following:

"SEC. 3D. SECURITY-BASED SWAP EXECUTION FACILITIES.

"(a) REGISTRATION.—

"(1) IN GENERAL.—No person may operate a facility for the trading or processing of security-based swaps, unless the facility is registered as a security-based swap execution facility or as a national securities exchange under this section.

"(2) DUAL REGISTRATION.—Any person that is registered as a security-based swap execution facility under this section shall register with the Commission regardless of whether the person also is registered with the Commodity Futures Trading Commission as a swap execution facility.

"(b) TRADING AND TRADE PROCESSING.—A security-based swap execution facility that is registered under subsection (a) may—

"(1) make available for trading any security-based swap; and

"(2) facilitate trade processing of any security-based swap.

"(c) IDENTIFICATION OF FACILITY USED TO TRADE SECURITY-BASED SWAPS BY NATIONAL SECURITIES EXCHANGES.—A national securities exchange shall, to the extent that the exchange also operates a security-based swap execution facility and uses the same electronic trade execution system for listing and executing trades of security-based swaps on or through the exchange and the facility, identify whether electronic trading of such security-based swaps is taking place on or through the national securities exchange or the security-based swap execution facility.

"(d) CORE PRINCIPLES FOR SECURITY-BASED SWAP EXECUTION FACILITIES.—

"(1) COMPLIANCE WITH CORE PRINCIPLES.—

"(A) IN GENERAL.—To be registered, and maintain registration, as a security-based swap execution facility, the security-based swap execution facility shall comply with—

"(i) the core principles described in this subsection; and

"(ii) any requirement that the Commission may impose by rule or regulation.

"(B) REASONABLE DISCRETION OF SECURITY-BASED SWAP EXECUTION FACILITY.—Unless otherwise determined by the Commission, by rule or regulation, a security-based swap execution facility described in subparagraph (A) shall have reasonable discretion in establishing the manner in which it complies with the core principles described in this subsection.

"(2) COMPLIANCE WITH RULES.—A security-based swap execution facility shall—

"(A) establish and enforce compliance with any rule established by such security-based swap execution facility, including—

"(i) the terms and conditions of the security-based swaps traded or processed on or through the facility; and

"(ii) any limitation on access to the facility;

"(B) establish and enforce trading, trade processing, and participation rules that will deter abuses and have the capacity to detect, investigate, and enforce those rules, including means—

"(i) to provide market participants with impartial access to the market; and

"(ii) to capture information that may be used in establishing whether rule violations have occurred; and

"(C) establish rules governing the operation of the facility, including rules specifying trading procedures to be used in entering and executing orders traded or posted on the facility, including block trades.

"(3) SECURITY-BASED SWAPS NOT READILY SUSCEPTIBLE TO MANIPULATION.—The security-based swap execution facility shall permit trading only in security-based swaps that are not readily susceptible to manipulation.

"(4) MONITORING OF TRADING AND TRADE PROCESSING.—The security-based swap execution facility shall—

"(A) establish and enforce rules or terms and conditions defining, or specifications detailing—

"(i) trading procedures to be used in entering and executing orders traded on or through the facilities of the security-based swap execution facility; and

"(ii) procedures for trade processing of security-based swaps on or through the facilities of the security-based swap execution facility; and

"(B) monitor trading in security-based swaps to prevent manipulation, price distortion, and disruptions of the delivery or cash settlement process through surveillance, compliance, and disciplinary practices and procedures, including methods for conducting real-time monitoring of trading and comprehensive and accurate trade reconstructions.

"(5) ABILITY TO OBTAIN INFORMATION.—The security-based swap execution facility shall—

"(A) establish and enforce rules that will allow the facility to obtain any necessary information to perform any of the functions described in this subsection;

"(B) provide the information to the Commission on request; and

"(C) have the capacity to carry out such international information-sharing agreements as the Commission may require.

"(6) FINANCIAL INTEGRITY OF TRANSACTIONS.—The security-based swap execution facility shall establish and enforce rules and procedures for ensuring the financial integrity of security-based swaps entered on or through the facilities of the security-based swap execution facility, including the clearance and settlement of security-based swaps pursuant to section 3C(a)(1).

"(7) EMERGENCY AUTHORITY.—The security-based swap execution facility shall adopt rules to provide for the exercise of emergency authority, in consultation or cooperation with the Commission, as is necessary and appropriate, including the authority to liquidate or transfer open positions in any security-based swap or to suspend or curtail trading in a security-based swap.

"(8) TIMELY PUBLICATION OF TRADING INFORMATION.—

"(A) IN GENERAL.—The security-based swap execution facility shall make public timely information on price, trading volume, and other trading data on security-based swaps to the extent prescribed by the Commission.

"(B) CAPACITY OF SECURITY-BASED SWAP EXECUTION FACILITY.—The security-based swap execution facility shall be required to have the capacity to electronically capture and transmit and disseminate trade information with respect to transactions executed on or through the facility.

"(9) RECORDKEEPING AND REPORTING.—

"(A) IN GENERAL.—A security-based swap execution facility shall—

"(i) maintain records of all activities relating to the business of the facility, including a complete audit trail, in a form and manner acceptable to the Commission for a period of 5 years; and

"(ii) report to the Commission, in a form and manner acceptable to the Commission, such information as the Commission determines to be necessary or appropriate for the Commission to perform the duties of the Commission under this title.

"(B) REQUIREMENTS.—The Commission shall adopt data collection and reporting requirements for security-based swap execution facilities that are comparable to corresponding requirements for clearing agencies and security-based swap data repositories.

"(10) ANTITRUST CONSIDERATIONS.—Unless necessary or appropriate to achieve the purposes of this title, the security-based swap execution facility shall not—

"(A) adopt any rules or taking any actions that result in any unreasonable restraint of trade; or

"(B) impose any material anticompetitive burden on trading or clearing.

"(11) CONFLICTS OF INTEREST.—The security-based swap execution facility shall—

"(A) establish and enforce rules to minimize conflicts of interest in its decision-making process; and

"(B) establish a process for resolving the conflicts of interest.

"(12) FINANCIAL RESOURCES.—

"(A) IN GENERAL.—The security-based swap execution facility shall have adequate financial, operational, and managerial resources to discharge each responsibility of the security-based swap execution facility, as determined by the Commission.

"(B) DETERMINATION OF RESOURCE ADEQUACY.—The financial resources of a security-based swap execution facility shall be considered to be adequate if the value of the financial resources—

"(i) enables the organization to meet its financial obligations to its members and participants notwithstanding a default by the member or participant creating the largest financial exposure for that organization in extreme but plausible market conditions; and "(ii) exceeds the total amount that would enable the security-based swap execution facility to cover the operating costs of the security-based swap execution facility for a 1-year period, as calculated on a rolling basis.

"(13) SYSTEM SAFEGUARDS.—The security-based swap execution facility shall—

"(A) establish and maintain a program of risk analysis and oversight to identify and minimize sources of operational risk, through the development of appropriate controls and procedures, and automated systems, that—

"(i) are reliable and secure; and

"(ii) have adequate scalable capacity;

"(B) establish and maintain emergency procedures, backup facilities, and a plan for disaster recovery that allow for—

"(i) the timely recovery and resumption of operations; and

"(ii) the fulfillment of the responsibilities and obligations of the security-based swap execution facility; and

"(C) periodically conduct tests to verify that the backup resources of the security-based swap execution facility are sufficient to ensure continued—

"(i) order processing and trade matching;

"(ii) price reporting;

"(iii) market surveillance; and

"(iv) maintenance of a comprehensive and accurate audit trail.

"(14) DESIGNATION OF CHIEF COMPLIANCE OFFICER.—

"(A) IN GENERAL.—Each security-based swap execution facility shall designate an individual to serve as a chief compliance officer.

"(B) DUTIES.—The chief compliance officer shall—

"(i) report directly to the board or to the senior officer of the facility;

"(ii) review compliance with the core principles in this subsection;

"(iii) in consultation with the board of the facility, a body performing a function similar to that of a board, or the senior officer of the facility, resolve any conflicts of interest that may arise;

"(iv) be responsible for establishing and administering the policies and procedures required to be established pursuant to this section;

"(v) ensure compliance with this title and the rules and regulations issued under this title, including rules prescribed by the Commission pursuant to this section;

"(vi) establish procedures for the remediation of noncompliance issues found during—

"(I) compliance office reviews;

"(II) look backs;

"(III) internal or external audit findings;

"(IV) self-reported errors; or

"(V) through validated complaints; and

"(vii) establish and follow appropriate procedures for the handling, management response, remediation, retesting, and closing of noncompliance issues.

"(C) ANNUAL REPORTS.—

"(i) IN GENERAL.—In accordance with rules prescribed by the Commission, the chief compliance officer shall annually prepare and sign a report that contains a description of—

"(I) the compliance of the security-based swap execution facility with this title; and

"(II) the policies and procedures, including the code of ethics and conflict of interest policies, of the security-based security-based swap execution facility.

"(ii) REQUIREMENTS.—The chief compliance officer shall—

"(I) submit each report described in clause (i) with the appropriate financial report of the security-based swap execution facility that is required to be submitted to the Commission pursuant to this section; and

"(II) include in the report a certification that, under penalty of law, the report is accurate and complete.

"(e) EXEMPTIONS.—The Commission may exempt, conditionally or unconditionally, a security-based swap execution facility from registration under this section if the Commission finds that the facility is subject to comparable, comprehensive supervision and regulation on a consolidated basis by the Commodity Futures Trading Commission.

"(f) RULES.—The Commission shall prescribe rules governing the regulation of security-based swap execution facilities under this section.".

(d) SEGREGATION OF ASSETS HELD AS COLLATERAL IN SECURITY-BASED SWAP TRANSACTIONS.—The Securities Exchange Act of 1934 (15 U.S.C. 78a et seq.) is amended by inserting after section 3D (as added by subsection (b)) the following:

"SEC. 3E. SEGREGATION OF ASSETS HELD AS COLLATERAL IN SECURITY-BASED SWAP TRANSACTIONS.

"(a) REGISTRATION REQUIREMENT.—It shall be unlawful for any person to accept any money, securities, or property (or to extend any credit in lieu of money, securities, or property) from, for, or on behalf of a security-based swaps customer to margin, guarantee, or secure a security-based swap cleared by or through a clearing agency (including money, securities, or property accruing to the customer as the result of such a security-based swap), unless the person shall have registered under this title with the Commission as a broker, dealer, or security-based swap dealer, and the registration shall not have expired nor been suspended nor revoked.

"(b) CLEARED SECURITY-BASED SWAPS.—

"(1) SEGREGATION REQUIRED.—A broker, dealer, or security-based swap dealer shall treat and deal with all money, securities, and property of any security-based swaps customer received to margin, guarantee, or secure a security-based swap cleared by or though a clearing agency (including money, securities, or property accruing to the security-based swaps customer as the result of such a security-based swap) as belonging to the security-based swaps customer.

"(2) COMMINGLING PROHIBITED.—Money, securities, and property of a security-based swaps customer described in paragraph (1) shall be separately accounted for and shall not be commingled with the funds of the broker, dealer, or security-based swap dealer or be used to margin, secure, or guarantee any trades or contracts of any security-based swaps customer or person other than the person for whom the same are held.

"(c) EXCEPTIONS.—

"(1) USE OF FUNDS.—

"(A) IN GENERAL.—Notwithstanding subsection (b), money, securities, and property of a security-based swaps customer of a broker, dealer, or security-based swap dealer described in subsection (b) may, for convenience, be commingled and deposited in the same 1 or more accounts with any bank or trust company or with a clearing agency.

"(B) WITHDRAWAL.—Notwithstanding subsection (b), such share of the money, securities, and property described in subparagraph (A) as in the normal course of business shall be necessary to margin, guarantee, secure, transfer, adjust, or settle a cleared security-based swap with a clearing agency, or with any member of the clearing agency, may be withdrawn and applied to such purposes, including the payment of commissions, brokerage, interest, taxes, storage, and other charges, lawfully accruing in connection with the cleared security-based swap.

"(2) COMMISSION ACTION.—Notwithstanding subsection (b), in accordance with such terms and conditions as the Commission may prescribe by rule, regulation, or order, any money, securities, or property of the security-based swaps customer of a broker, dealer, or security-based swap dealer described in subsection (b) may be commingled and deposited as provided in this section with any other money, securities, or property received by the broker, dealer, or security-based swap dealer and required by the Commission to be separately accounted for and treated and dealt with as belonging to the security-based swaps customer of the broker, dealer, or security-based swap dealer.

"(d) PERMITTED INVESTMENTS.—Money described in subsection (b) may be invested in obligations of the United States, in general obligations of any State or of any political subdivision of a State, and in obligations fully guaranteed as to principal and interest by the United States, or in any other investment that the Commission may by rule or regulation prescribe, and such investments shall be made in accordance with such rules and regulations and subject to such conditions as the Commission may prescribe.

"(e) PROHIBITION.—It shall be unlawful for any person, including any clearing agency and any depository institution, that has received any money, securities, or property for deposit in a separate account or accounts as provided in subsection (b) to hold, dispose of, or use any such money, securities, or property as belonging to the depositing broker, dealer, or security-based swap dealer or any person other than the swaps customer of the broker, dealer, or security-based swap dealer.

"(f) SEGREGATION REQUIREMENTS FOR UNCLEARED SECURITY-BASED SWAPS.—

"(1) SEGREGATION OF ASSETS HELD AS COLLATERAL IN UNCLEARED SECURITY-BASED SWAP TRANSACTIONS.—

"(A) NOTIFICATION.—A security-based swap dealer or major security-based swap participant shall be required to notify the counterparty of the security-based swap dealer or major security-based swap participant at the beginning of a security-based swap transaction that the counterparty has the right to require segregation of the funds of other property supplied to margin, guarantee, or secure the obligations of the counterparty.

"(B) SEGREGATION AND MAINTENANCE OF FUNDS.—At the request of a counterparty to a security-based swap that provides funds or other property to a security-based swap dealer or major security-based swap participant to margin, guarantee, or secure the obligations of the counterparty, the security-based swap dealer or major security-based swap participant shall—

"(i) segregate the funds or other property for the benefit of the counterparty; and

"(ii) in accordance with such rules and regulations as the Commission may promulgate, maintain the funds or other property in a segregated account separate from the assets and other interests of the security-based swap dealer or major security-based swap participant.

"(2) APPLICABILITY.—The requirements described in paragraph (1) shall—

"(A) apply only to a security-based swap between a counterparty and a security-based swap dealer or major security-based swap participant that is not submitted for clearing to a clearing agency; and

"(B)

(i) not apply to variation margin payments; or

"(ii) not preclude any commercial arrangement regarding—

"(I) the investment of segregated funds or other property that may only be invested in such investments as the Commission may permit by rule or regulation; and

"(II) the related allocation of gains and losses resulting from any investment of the segregated funds or other property.

"(3) USE OF INDEPENDENT THIRD-PARTY CUSTODIANS.—The segregated account described in paragraph (1) shall be—

"(A) carried by an independent third-party custodian; and

"(B) designated as a segregated account for and on behalf of the counterparty.

"(4) REPORTING REQUIREMENT.—If the counterparty does not choose to require segregation of the funds or other property supplied to margin, guarantee, or secure the obligations of the counterparty, the security-based swap dealer or major security-based swap participant shall report to the counterparty of the security-based swap dealer or major security-based swap participant on a quarterly basis that the back office procedures of the security-based swap dealer or major security-based swap participant relating to margin and collateral requirements are in compliance with the agreement of the counterparties.

"(g) BANKRUPTCY.—A security-based swap, as defined in section 3(a)(68) shall be considered to be a security as such term is used in section 101(53A)(B) and subchapter III of title 11, United States Code. An account that holds a security-based swap, other than a portfolio margining account referred to in section 15(c)(3)(C) shall be considered to be a securities account, as that term is defined in section 741 of title 11, United States Code. The definitions of the terms 'purchase' and 'sale' in section 3(a)(13) and (14) shall be applied to the terms 'purchase' and 'sale', as used in section 741 of title 11, United States Code. The term 'customer', as defined in section 741 of title 11, United States Code, excludes any person, to the extent that such person has a claim based on any open repurchase agreement, open reverse repurchase agreement, stock borrowed agreement, non-cleared option, or non-cleared security-based swap except to the extent of any margin delivered to or by the customer with respect to which there is a customer protection requirement under section 15(c)(3) or a segregation requirement.".

(e) TRADING IN SECURITY-BASED SWAPS.—Section 6 of the Securities Exchange Act of 1934 (15 U.S.C. 78f) is amended by adding at the end the following:

"(l) SECURITY-BASED SWAPS.—It shall be unlawful for any person to effect a transaction in a security-based swap with or for a person that is not an eligible contract participant, unless such transaction is effected on a national securities exchange registered pursuant to subsection (b).".

(f) ADDITIONS OF SECURITY-BASED SWAPS TO CERTAIN ENFORCEMENT PROVISIONS.—Section 9(b) of the Securities Exchange Act of 1934 (15 U.S.C. 78i(b)) is amended by striking paragraphs (1) through (3) and inserting the following:

"(1) any transaction in connection with any security whereby any party to such transaction acquires—

"(A) any put, call, straddle, or other option or privilege of buying the security from or selling the security to another without being bound to do so;

"(B) any security futures product on the security; or

"(C) any security-based swap involving the security or the issuer of the security;

"(2) any transaction in connection with any security with relation to which such person has, directly or indirectly, any interest in any—

"(A) such put, call, straddle, option, or privilege;

"(B) such security futures product; or

"(C) such security-based swap; or

"(3) any transaction in any security for the account of any person who such person has reason to believe has, and who actually has, directly or indirectly, any interest in any—

"(A) such put, call, straddle, option, or privilege;

"(B) such security futures product with relation to such security; or

"(C) any security-based swap involving such security or the issuer of such security.".

(g) RULEMAKING AUTHORITY TO PREVENT FRAUD, MANIPULATION AND DECEPTIVE CONDUCT IN SECURITY-BASED SWAPS.—Section 9 of the Securities Exchange Act of 1934 (15 U.S.C. 78i) is amended by adding at the end the following:

"(j) It shall be unlawful for any person, directly or indirectly, by the use of any means or instrumentality of interstate commerce or of the mails, or of any facility of any national securities exchange, to effect any transaction in, or to induce or attempt to induce the purchase or sale of, any security-based swap, in connection with which such person engages in any fraudulent, deceptive, or manipulative act or practice, makes any fictitious quotation, or engages in any transaction, practice, or course of business which operates as a fraud or deceit upon any person. The Commission shall, for the purposes of this subsection, by rules and regulations define, and prescribe means reasonably designed to prevent, such transactions, acts, practices, and courses of business as are fraudulent, deceptive, or manipulative, and such quotations as are fictitious.".

(h) POSITION LIMITS AND POSITION ACCOUNTABILITY FOR SECURITY-BASED SWAPS.—The Securities Exchange Act of 1934 is amended by inserting after section 10A (15 U.S.C. 78j-1) the following:

"SEC. 10B. POSITION LIMITS AND POSITION ACCOUNTABILITY FOR SECURITY-BASED SWAPS AND LARGE TRADER REPORTING.

"(a) POSITION LIMITS.—As a means reasonably designed to prevent fraud and manipulation, the Commission shall, by rule or regulation, as necessary or appropriate in the public interest or for the protection of investors, establish limits (including related hedge exemption provisions) on the size of positions in any security-based swap that may be held by any person. In establishing such limits, the Commission may require any person to aggregate positions in—

"(1) any security-based swap and any security or loan or group of securities or loans on which such security-based swap is based, which such security-based swap references, or to which such security-based swap is related as described in paragraph (68) of section 3(a), and any other instrument relating to such security or loan or group or index of securities or loans; or

"(2) any security-based swap and—

"(A) any security or group or index of securities, the price, yield, value, or volatility of which, or of which any interest therein, is the basis for a material term of such security-based swap as described in paragraph (68) of section 3(a); and

"(B) any other instrument relating to the same security or group or index of securities described under subparagraph (A).

"(b) EXEMPTIONS.—The Commission, by rule, regulation, or order, may conditionally or unconditionally exempt any person or class of persons, any security-based swap or class of security-based swaps, or any transaction or class of transactions from any requirement the Commission may establish under this section with respect to position limits.

"(c) SRO RULES.—

"(1) IN GENERAL.—As a means reasonably designed to prevent fraud or manipulation, the Commission, by rule, regulation, or order, as necessary or appropriate in the public interest, for the protection of investors, or otherwise in furtherance of the purposes of this title, may direct a self-regulatory organization—

"(A) to adopt rules regarding the size of positions in any security-based swap that may be held by—

"(i) any member of such self-regulatory organization; or

"(ii) any person for whom a member of such self-regulatory organization effects transactions in such security-based swap; and

"(B) to adopt rules reasonably designed to ensure compliance with requirements prescribed by the Commission under this subsection.

"(2) REQUIREMENT TO AGGREGATE POSITIONS.—In establishing the limits under paragraph (1), the self-regulatory organization may require such member or person to aggregate positions in—

"(A) any security-based swap and any security or loan or group or narrow-based security index of securities or loans on which such security-based swap is based, which such security-based swap references, or to which such security-based swap is related as described in section 3(a)(68), and any other instrument relating to such security or loan or group or narrow-based security index of securities or loans; or

"(B)

"(i) any security-based swap; and

"(ii) any security-based swap and any other instrument relating to the same security or group or narrow-based security index of securities.

"(d) LARGE TRADER REPORTING.—The Commission, by rule or regulation, may require any person that effects transactions for such person's own account or the account of others in any securities-based swap or uncleared security-based swap and any security or loan or group or narrow-based security index of securities or loans as set forth in paragraphs (1) and (2) of subsection (a) under this section to report such information as the Commission may prescribe regarding any position or positions in any security-based swap or uncleared security-based swap and any security or loan or group or narrow-based security index of securities or loans and any other instrument relating to such security or loan or group or narrow-based security index of securities or loans as set forth in paragraphs (1) and (2) of subsection (a) under this section.".

(i) PUBLIC REPORTING AND REPOSITORIES FOR SECURITY-BASED SWAPS.—Section 13 of the Securities Exchange Act of 1934 (15 U.S.C. 78m) is amended by adding at the end the following:

"(m) PUBLIC AVAILABILITY OF SECURITY-BASED SWAP TRANSACTION DATA.—

"(1) IN GENERAL.—

"(A) DEFINITION OF REAL-TIME PUBLIC REPORTING.—In this paragraph, the term 'realtime public reporting' means to report data relating to a security-based swap transaction, including price and volume, as soon as technologically practicable after the time at which the security-based swap transaction has been executed.

"(B) PURPOSE.—The purpose of this subsection is to authorize the Commission to make security-based swap transaction and pricing data available to the public in such form and at such times as the Commission determines appropriate to enhance price discovery.

"(C) GENERAL RULE.—The Commission is authorized to provide by rule for the public availability of security-based swap transaction, volume, and pricing data as follows:

"(i) With respect to those security-based swaps that are subject to the mandatory clearing requirement described in section 3C(a)(1) (including those security-based swaps that are excepted from the requirement pursuant to section 3C(g)), the Commission shall require real-time public reporting for such transactions.

"(ii) With respect to those security-based swaps that are not subject to the mandatory clearing requirement described in section 3C(a)(1), but are cleared at a registered clearing agency, the Commission shall require real-time public reporting for such transactions.

"(iii) With respect to security-based swaps that are not cleared at a registered clearing agency and which are reported to a security-based swap data repository or the Commission under section 3C(a)(6), the Commission shall require real-time public reporting for such transactions, in a manner that does not disclose the business transactions and market positions of any person.

"(iv) With respect to security-based swaps that are determined to be required to be cleared under section 3C(b) but are not cleared, the Commission shall require real-time public reporting for such transactions.

"(D) REGISTERED ENTITIES AND PUBLIC REPORTING.—The Commission may require registered entities to publicly disseminate the security-based swap transaction and pricing data required to be reported under this paragraph.

"(E) RULEMAKING REQUIRED.—With respect to the rule providing for the public availability of transaction and pricing data for security-based swaps described in clauses (i) and (ii) of subparagraph (C), the rule promulgated by the Commission shall contain provisions

"(i) to ensure such information does not identify the participants;

"(ii) to specify the criteria for determining what constitutes a large notional security-based swap transaction (block trade) for particular markets and contracts;

"(iii) to specify the appropriate time delay for reporting large notional security-based swap transactions (block trades) to the public; and "(iv) that take into account whether the public disclosure will materially reduce market liquidity.

"(F) TIMELINESS OF REPORTING.—Parties to a security-based swap (including agents of the parties to a security-based swap) shall be responsible for reporting security-based swap transaction information to the appropriate registered entity in a timely manner as may be prescribed by the Commission.

"(G) REPORTING OF SWAPS TO REGISTERED SECURITY-BASED SWAP DATA REPOSITORIES.—Each security-based swap (whether cleared or uncleared) shall be reported to a registered security-based swap data repository.

"(H) REGISTRATION OF CLEARING AGENCIES.—A clearing agency may register as a security-based swap data repository.

"(2) SEMIANNUAL AND ANNUAL PUBLIC REPORTING OF AGGREGATE SECURITY-BASED SWAP DATA.—

"(A) IN GENERAL.—In accordance with subparagraph (B), the Commission shall issue a written report on a semiannual and annual basis to make available to the public information relating to—

"(i) the trading and clearing in the major security-based swap categories; and

"(ii) the market participants and developments in new products.

"(B) USE; CONSULTATION.—In preparing a report under subparagraph (A), the Commission shall—

"(i) use information from security-based swap data repositories and clearing agencies; and

"(ii) consult with the Office of the Comptroller of the Currency, the Bank for International Settlements, and such other regulatory bodies as may be necessary.

"(C) AUTHORITY OF COMMISSION.—The Commission may, by rule, regulation, or order, delegate the public reporting responsibilities of the Commission under this paragraph in accordance with such terms and conditions as the Commission determines to be appropriate and in the public interest.

"(n) SECURITY-BASED SWAP DATA REPOSITORIES.—

"(1) REGISTRATION REQUIREMENT.—It shall be unlawful for any person, unless registered with the Commission, directly or indirectly, to make use of the mails or any means or instrumentality of interstate commerce to perform the functions of a security-based swap data repository.

"(2) INSPECTION AND EXAMINATION.—Each registered security-based swap data repository shall be subject to inspection and examination by any representative of the Commission.

"(3) COMPLIANCE WITH CORE PRINCIPLES.—

"(A) IN GENERAL.—To be registered, and maintain registration, as a security-based swap data repository, the security-based swap data repository shall comply with—

"(i) the requirements and core principles described in this subsection; and

"(ii) any requirement that the Commission may impose by rule or regulation.

"(B) REASONABLE DISCRETION OF SECURITY-BASED SWAP DATA REPOSITORY.—Unless otherwise determined by the Commission, by rule or regulation, a security-based swap data repository described in subparagraph (A) shall have reasonable discretion in establishing the manner in which the security-based swap data repository complies with the core principles described in this subsection.

"(4) STANDARD SETTING.—

"(A) DATA IDENTIFICATION.—

"(i) IN GENERAL.—In accordance with clause (ii), the Commission shall prescribe standards that specify the data elements for each security-based swap that shall be collected and maintained by each registered security-based swap data repository.

"(ii) REQUIREMENT.—In carrying out clause (i), the Commission shall prescribe consistent data element standards applicable to registered entities and reporting counterparties.

"(B) DATA COLLECTION AND MAINTENANCE.—The Commission shall prescribe data collection and data maintenance standards for security-based swap data repositories.

"(C) COMPARABILITY.—The standards prescribed by the Commission under this subsection shall be comparable to the data standards imposed by the Commission on clearing agencies in connection with their clearing of security-based swaps.

"(5) DUTIES.—A security-based swap data repository shall—

"(A) accept data prescribed by the Commission for each security-based swap under subsection (b);

"(B) confirm with both counterparties to the security-based swap the accuracy of the data that was submitted;

"(C) maintain the data described in subparagraph (A) in such form, in such manner, and for such period as may be required by the Commission;

"(D)

(i) provide direct electronic access to the Commission (or any designee of the Commission, including another registered entity); and

"(ii) provide the information described in subparagraph (A) in such form and at such frequency as the Commission may require to comply with the public reporting requirements set forth in subsection (m);

"(E) at the direction of the Commission, establish automated systems for monitoring, screening, and analyzing security-based swap data;

"(F) maintain the privacy of any and all security-based swap transaction information that the security-based swap data repository receives from a security-based swap dealer, counterparty, or any other registered entity; and

"(G) on a confidential basis pursuant to section 24, upon request, and after notifying the Commission of the request, make available all data obtained by the security-based swap data repository, including individual counterparty trade and position data, to—

"(i) each appropriate prudential regulator;

"(ii) the Financial Stability Oversight Council;

"(iii) the Commodity Futures Trading Commission;

"(iv) the Department of Justice; and

"(v) any other person that the Commission determines to be appropriate, including—

"(I) foreign financial supervisors (including foreign futures authorities);

"(II) foreign central banks; and

"(III) foreign ministries.

"(H) CONFIDENTIALITY AND INDEMNIFICATION AGREEMENT.—Before the security-based swap data repository may share information with any entity described in subparagraph (G)—

"(i) the security-based swap data repository shall receive a written agreement from each entity stating that the entity shall abide by the confidentiality requirements described in section 24 relating to the information on security-based swap transactions that is provided; and

"(ii) each entity shall agree to indemnify the security-based swap data repository and the Commission for any expenses arising from litigation relating to the information provided under section 24.

"(6) DESIGNATION OF CHIEF COMPLIANCE OFFICER.—

"(A) IN GENERAL.—Each security-based swap data repository shall designate an individual to serve as a chief compliance officer.

"(B) DUTIES.—The chief compliance officer shall—

"(i) report directly to the board or to the senior officer of the security-based swap data repository;

"(ii) review the compliance of the security-based swap data repository with respect to the requirements and core principles described in this subsection;

"(iii) in consultation with the board of the security-based swap data repository, a body performing a function similar to the board of the security-based swap data repository, or the senior officer of the security-based swap data repository, resolve any conflicts of interest that may arise;

"(iv) be responsible for administering each policy and procedure that is required to be established pursuant to this section;

"(v) ensure compliance with this title (including regulations) relating to agreements, contracts, or transactions, including each rule prescribed by the Commission under this section;

"(vi) establish procedures for the remediation of noncompliance issues identified by the chief compliance officer through any—

"(I) compliance office review;

"(II) look-back;

"(III) internal or external audit finding;

"(IV) self-reported error; or

"(V) validated complaint; and

"(vii) establish and follow appropriate procedures for the handling, management response, remediation, retesting, and closing of noncompliance issues.

"(C) ANNUAL REPORTS.—

"(i) IN GENERAL.—In accordance with rules prescribed by the Commission, the chief compliance officer shall annually prepare and sign a report that contains a description of—

"(I) the compliance of the security-based swap data repository of the chief compliance officer with respect to this title (including regulations); and

"(II) each policy and procedure of the security-based swap data repository of the chief compliance officer (including the code of ethics and conflict of interest policies of the security-based swap data repository).

"(ii) REQUIREMENTS.—A compliance report under clause (i) shall—

"(I) accompany each appropriate financial report of the security-based swap data repository that is required to be furnished to the Commission pursuant to this section; and

"(II) include a certification that, under penalty of law, the compliance report is accurate and complete.

"(7) CORE PRINCIPLES APPLICABLE TO SECURITY-BASED SWAP DATA REPOSITORIES.—

"(A) ANTITRUST CONSIDERATIONS.—Unless necessary or appropriate to achieve the purposes of this title, the swap data repository shall not—

"(i) adopt any rule or take any action that results in any unreasonable restraint of trade; or

"(ii) impose any material anticompetitive burden on the trading, clearing, or reporting of transactions.

"(B) GOVERNANCE ARRANGEMENTS.—Each security-based swap data repository shall establish governance arrangements that are transparent—

"(i) to fulfill public interest requirements; and

"(ii) to support the objectives of the Federal Government, owners, and participants.

"(C) CONFLICTS OF INTEREST.—Each security-based swap data repository shall—

"(i) establish and enforce rules to minimize conflicts of interest in the decision-making process of the security-based swap data repository; and

"(ii) establish a process for resolving any conflicts of interest described in clause (i).

"(D) ADDITIONAL DUTIES DEVELOPED BY COMMISSION.—

"(i) IN GENERAL.—The Commission may develop 1 or more additional duties applicable to security-based swap data repositories.

"(ii) CONSIDERATION OF EVOLVING STANDARDS.—In developing additional duties under subparagraph (A), the Commission may take into consideration any evolving standard of the United States or the international community.

"(iii) ADDITIONAL DUTIES FOR COMMISSION DESIGNEES.—The Commission shall establish additional duties for any registrant described in section 13(m)(2)(C) in order to minimize conflicts of interest, protect data, ensure compliance, and guarantee the safety and security of the security-based swap data repository.

"(8) REQUIRED REGISTRATION FOR SECURITY-BASED SWAP DATA REPOSITORIES.—Any person that is required to be registered as a security-based swap data repository under this subsection shall register with the Commission, regardless of whether that person is also licensed under the Commodity Exchange Act as a swap data repository.

"(9) RULES.—The Commission shall adopt rules governing persons that are registered under this subsection.".

[Explanation at ¶ 3160.]

[¶ 10,764] ACT SEC. 764. REGISTRATION AND REGULATION OF SECURITY-BASED SWAP DEALERS AND MAJOR SECURITY-BASED SWAP PARTICIPANTS.

(a) IN GENERAL.—The Securities Exchange Act of 1934 (15 U.S.C. 78a et seq.) is amended by inserting after section 15E (15 U.S.C. 78o-7) the following:

"SEC. 15F. REGISTRATION AND REGULATION OF SECURITY-BASED SWAP DEALERS AND MAJOR SECURITY-BASED SWAP PARTICIPANTS.

"(a) REGISTRATION.—

"(1) SECURITY-BASED SWAP DEALERS.—It shall be unlawful for any person to act as a security-based swap dealer unless the person is registered as a security-based swap dealer with the Commission.

"(2) MAJOR SECURITY-BASED SWAP PARTICIPANTS.—It shall be unlawful for any person to act as a major security-based swap participant unless the person is registered as a major security-based swap participant with the Commission.

"(b) REQUIREMENTS.—

"(1) IN GENERAL.—A person shall register as a security-based swap dealer or major security-based swap participant by filing a registration application with the Commission.

"(2) CONTENTS.—

"(A) IN GENERAL.—The application shall be made in such form and manner as prescribed by the Commission, and shall contain such information, as the Commission considers necessary concerning the business in which the applicant is or will be engaged.

"(B) CONTINUAL REPORTING.—A person that is registered as a security-based swap dealer or major security-based swap participant shall continue to submit to the Commission reports that contain such information pertaining to the business of the person as the Commission may require.

"(3) EXPIRATION.—Each registration under this section shall expire at such time as the Commission may prescribe by rule or regulation.

"(4) RULES.—Except as provided in subsections (d) and (e), the Commission may prescribe rules applicable to security-based swap dealers and major security-based swap participants, including rules that limit the activities of non-bank security-based swap dealers and major security-based swap participants.

"(5) TRANSITION.—Not later than 1 year after the date of enactment of the Wall Street Transparency and Accountability Act of 2010, the Commission shall issue rules under this section to provide for the registration of security-based swap dealers and major security-based swap participants.

"(6) STATUTORY DISQUALIFICATION.—Except to the extent otherwise specifically provided by rule, regulation, or order of the Commission, it shall be unlawful for a security-based swap dealer or a major security-based swap participant to permit any person associated with a security-based swap dealer or a major security-based swap participant who is subject to a statutory disqualification to effect or be involved in effecting security-based swaps on behalf of the security-based swap dealer or major security-based swap participant, if the security-based swap dealer or major security-based swap participant knew, or in the exercise of reasonable care should have known, of the statutory disqualification.

"(c) DUAL REGISTRATION.—

"(1) SECURITY-BASED SWAP DEALER.—Any person that is required to be registered as a security-based swap dealer under this section shall register with the Commission, regardless of whether the person also is registered with the Commodity Futures Trading Commission as a swap dealer.

"(2) MAJOR SECURITY-BASED SWAP PARTICIPANT.—Any person that is required to be registered as a major security-based swap participant under this section shall register with the Commission, regardless of whether the person also is registered with the Commodity Futures Trading Commission as a major swap participant.

"(d) RULEMAKING.—

"(1) IN GENERAL.—The Commission shall adopt rules for persons that are registered as security-based swap dealers or major security-based swap participants under this section.

"(2) EXCEPTION FOR PRUDENTIAL REQUIREMENTS.—

"(A) IN GENERAL.—The Commission may not prescribe rules imposing prudential requirements on security-based swap dealers or major security-based swap participants for which there is a prudential regulator.

"(B) APPLICABILITY.—Subparagraph (A) does not limit the authority of the Commission to prescribe rules as directed under this section.

"(e) CAPITAL AND MARGIN REQUIREMENTS.—

"(1) IN GENERAL.—

"(A) SECURITY-BASED SWAP DEALERS AND MAJOR SECURITY-BASED SWAP PARTICIPANTS THAT ARE BANKS.—Each registered security-based swap dealer and major security-based swap participant for which there is not a prudential regulator shall meet such minimum capital requirements and minimum initial and variation margin requirements as the prudential regulator shall by rule or regulation prescribe under paragraph (2)(A).

"(B) SECURITY-BASED SWAP DEALERS AND MAJOR SECURITY-BASED SWAP PARTICIPANTS THAT ARE NOT BANKS.—Each registered security-based swap dealer and major security-based swap participant for which there is not a prudential regulator shall meet such minimum capital requirements and minimum initial and variation margin requirements as the Commission shall by rule or regulation prescribe under paragraph (2)(B).

"(2) RULES.—

"(A) SECURITY-BASED SWAP DEALERS AND MAJOR SECURITY-BASED SWAP PARTICIPANTS THAT ARE BANKS.—The prudential regulators, in consultation with the Commission and the Commodity Futures Trading Commission, shall adopt rules for security-based swap dealers and major security-based swap participants, with respect to their activities as a swap dealer or major swap participant, for which there is a prudential regulator imposing—

"(i) capital requirements; and

"(ii) both initial and variation margin requirements on all security-based swaps that are not cleared by a registered clearing agency.

"(B) SECURITY-BASED SWAP DEALERS AND MAJOR SECURITY-BASED SWAP PARTICIPANTS THAT ARE NOT BANKS.—The Commission shall adopt rules for security-based swap dealers and major security-based swap participants, with respect to their activities as a swap dealer or major swap participant, for which there is not a prudential regulator imposing—

"(i) capital requirements; and

"(ii) both initial and variation margin requirements on all swaps that are not cleared by a registered clearing agency.

"(C) CAPITAL.—In setting capital requirements for a person that is designated as a security-based swap dealer or a major security-based swap participant for a single type or single class or category of security-based swap or activities, the prudential regulator and the Commission shall take into account the risks associated with other types of security-based swaps or classes of security-based swaps or categories of security-based swaps engaged in and the other activities conducted by that person that are not otherwise subject to regulation applicable to that person by virtue of the status of the person.

"(3) STANDARDS FOR CAPITAL AND MARGIN.—

"(A) IN GENERAL.—To offset the greater risk to the security-based swap dealer or major security-based swap participant and the financial system arising from the use of security-based swaps that are not cleared, the requirements imposed under paragraph (2) shall —

"(i) help ensure the safety and soundness of the security-based swap dealer or major security-based swap participant; and

"(ii) be appropriate for the risk associated with the non-cleared security-based swaps held as a security-based swap dealer or major security-based swap participant.

"(B) RULE OF CONSTRUCTION.—

"(i) IN GENERAL.—Nothing in this section shall limit, or be construed to limit, the authority—

"(I) of the Commission to set financial responsibility rules for a broker or dealer registered pursuant to section 15(b) (except for section 15(b)(11) thereof) in accordance with section 15(c)(3); or

"(II) of the Commodity Futures Trading Commission to set financial responsibility rules for a futures commission merchant or introducing broker registered pursuant to section 4f(a) of the Commodity Exchange Act (except for section 4f(a)(3) thereof) in accordance with section 4f(b) of the Commodity Exchange Act.

"(ii) FUTURES COMMISSION MERCHANTS AND OTHER DEALERS.—A futures commission merchant, introducing broker, broker, or dealer shall maintain sufficient capital to comply with the stricter of any applicable capital requirements to which such futures commission merchant, introducing broker, broker, or dealer is subject to under this title or the Commodity Exchange Act.

"(C) MARGIN REQUIREMENTS.—In prescribing margin requirements under this subsection, the prudential regulator with respect to security-based swap dealers and major security-based swap participants that are depository institutions, and the Commission with respect to security-based swap dealers and major security-based swap participants that are not depository institutions shall permit the use of noncash collateral, as the regulator or the Commission determines to be consistent with—

"(i) preserving the financial integrity of markets trading security-based swaps; and

"(ii) preserving the stability of the United States financial system.

"(D) COMPARABILITY OF CAPITAL AND MARGIN REQUIREMENTS.—

"(i) IN GENERAL.—The prudential regulators, the Commission, and the Securities and Exchange Commission shall periodically (but not less frequently than annually) consult on minimum capital requirements and minimum initial and variation margin requirements.

"(ii) COMPARABILITY.—The entities described in clause (i) shall, to the maximum extent practicable, establish and maintain comparable minimum capital requirements and minimum initial and variation margin requirements, including the use of noncash collateral, for—

"(I) security-based swap dealers; and

"(II) major security-based swap participants.

"(f) REPORTING AND RECORDKEEPING.—

"(1) IN GENERAL.—Each registered security-based swap dealer and major security-based swap participant—

"(A) shall make such reports as are required by the Commission, by rule or regulation, regarding the transactions and positions and financial condition of the registered security-based swap dealer or major security-based swap participant;

"(B)

(i) for which there is a prudential regulator, shall keep books and records of all activities related to the business as a security-based swap dealer or major security-based swap participant in such form and manner and for such period as may be prescribed by the Commission by rule or regulation; and

"(ii) for which there is no prudential regulator, shall keep books and records in such form and manner and for such period as may be prescribed by the Commission by rule or regulation; and

"(C) shall keep books and records described in subparagraph (B) open to inspection and examination by any representative of the Commission.

"(2) RULES.—The Commission shall adopt rules governing reporting and recordkeeping for security-based swap dealers and major security-based swap participants.

"(g) DAILY TRADING RECORDS.—

"(1) IN GENERAL.—Each registered security-based swap dealer and major security-based swap participant shall maintain daily trading records of the security-based swaps of the registered security-based swap dealer and major security-based swap participant and all related records (including related cash or forward transactions) and recorded communications, including electronic mail, instant messages, and recordings of telephone calls, for such period as may be required by the Commission by rule or regulation.

"(2) INFORMATION REQUIREMENTS.—The daily trading records shall include such information as the Commission shall require by rule or regulation.

"(3) COUNTERPARTY RECORDS.—Each registered security-based swap dealer and major security-based swap participant shall maintain daily trading records for each counterparty in a manner and form that is identifiable with each security-based swap transaction.

"(4) AUDIT TRAIL.—Each registered security-based swap dealer and major security-based swap participant shall maintain a complete audit trail for conducting comprehensive and accurate trade reconstructions.

"(5) RULES.—The Commission shall adopt rules governing daily trading records for security-based swap dealers and major security-based swap participants.

"(h) BUSINESS CONDUCT STANDARDS.—

"(1) IN GENERAL.—Each registered security-based swap dealer and major security-based swap participant shall conform with such business conduct standards as prescribed in paragraph (3) and as may be prescribed by the Commission by rule or regulation that relate to—

"(A) fraud, manipulation, and other abusive practices involving security-based swaps (including security-based swaps that are offered but not entered into);

"(B) diligent supervision of the business of the registered security-based swap dealer and major security-based swap participant;

"(C) adherence to all applicable position limits; and

"(D) such other matters as the Commission determines to be appropriate.

"(2) RESPONSIBILITIES WITH RESPECT TO SPECIAL ENTITIES.—

"(A) ADVISING SPECIAL ENTITIES.—A security-based swap dealer or major security-based swap participant that acts as an advisor to special entity regarding a security-based swap shall comply with the requirements of paragraph (4) with respect to such special entity.

"(B) ENTERING OF SECURITY-BASED SWAPS WITH RESPECT TO SPECIAL ENTITIES.—A security-based swap dealer that enters into or offers to enter into security-based swap with a special entity shall comply with the requirements of paragraph (5) with respect to such special entity.

"(C) SPECIAL ENTITY DEFINED.—For purposes of this subsection, the term 'special entity' means—

"(i) a Federal agency;

"(ii) a State, State agency, city, county, municipality, or other political subdivision of a State or;

"(iii) any employee benefit plan, as defined in section 3 of the Employee Retirement Income Security Act of 1974 (29 U.S.C. 1002);

"(iv) any governmental plan, as defined in section 3 of the Employee Retirement Income Security Act of 1974 (29 U.S.C. 1002); or

"(v) any endowment, including an endowment that is an organization described in section 501(c)(3) of the Internal Revenue Code of 1986.

"(3) BUSINESS CONDUCT REQUIREMENTS.—Business conduct requirements adopted by the Commission shall—

"(A) establish a duty for a security-based swap dealer or major security-based swap participant to verify that any counterparty meets the eligibility standards for an eligible contract participant;

"(B) require disclosure by the security-based swap dealer or major security-based swap participant to any counterparty to the transaction (other than a security-based swap dealer, major security-based swap participant, security-based swap dealer, or major security-based swap participant) of—

"(i) information about the material risks and characteristics of the security-based swap;

"(ii) any material incentives or conflicts of interest that the security-based swap dealer or major security-based swap participant may have in connection with the security-based swap; and

"(iii)

"(I) for cleared security-based swaps, upon the request of the counterparty, receipt of the daily mark of the transaction from the appropriate derivatives clearing organization; and

"(II) for uncleared security-based swaps, receipt of the daily mark of the transaction from the security-based swap dealer or the major security-based swap participant;

"(C) establish a duty for a security-based swap dealer or major security-based swap participant to communicate in a fair and balanced manner based on principles of fair dealing and good faith; and

"(D) establish such other standards and requirements as the Commission may determine are appropriate in the public interest, for the protection of investors, or otherwise in furtherance of the purposes of this Act.

"(4) SPECIAL REQUIREMENTS FOR SECURITY-BASED SWAP DEALERS ACTING AS ADVISORS.—

"(A) IN GENERAL.—It shall be unlawful for a security-based swap dealer or major security-based swap participant—

"(i) to employ any device, scheme, or artifice to defraud any special entity or prospective customer who is a special entity;

"(ii) to engage in any transaction, practice, or course of business that operates as a fraud or deceit on any special entity or prospective customer who is a special entity; or

"(iii) to engage in any act, practice, or course of business that is fraudulent, deceptive, or manipulative.

"(B) DUTY.—Any security-based swap dealer that acts as an advisor to a special entity shall have a duty to act in the best interests of the special entity.

"(C) REASONABLE EFFORTS.—Any security-based swap dealer that acts as an advisor to a special entity shall make reasonable efforts to obtain such information as is necessary to make a reasonable determination that any security-based swap recommended by the security-based swap dealer is in the best interests of the special entity, including information relating to—

"(i) the financial status of the special entity;

"(ii) the tax status of the special entity;

"(iii) the investment or financing objectives of the special entity; and

"(iv) any other information that the Commission may prescribe by rule or regulation.

"(5) SPECIAL REQUIREMENTS FOR SECURITY-BASED SWAP DEALERS AS COUNTERPARTIES TO SPECIAL ENTITIES.—

"(A) IN GENERAL.—Any security-based swap dealer or major security-based swap participant that offers to or enters into a security-based swap with a special entity shall—

"(i) comply with any duty established by the Commission for a security-based swap dealer or major security-based swap participant, with respect to a counterparty that is an eligible contract participant within the meaning of subclause (I) or (II) of clause (vii) of section 1a(18) of the Commodity Exchange Act, that requires the security-based swap dealer or major security-based swap participant to have a reasonable basis to believe that the counterparty that is a special entity has an independent representative that—

"(I) has sufficient knowledge to evaluate the transaction and risks;

"(II) is not subject to a statutory disqualification;

"(III) is independent of the security-based swap dealer or major security-based swap participant;

"(IV) undertakes a duty to act in the best interests of the counterparty it represents;

"(V) makes appropriate disclosures;

"(VI) will provide written representations to the special entity regarding fair pricing and the appropriateness of the transaction; and

"(VII) in the case of employee benefit plans subject to the Employee Retirement Income Security act of 1974, is a fiduciary as defined in section 3 of that Act (29 U.S.C. 1002); and

"(ii) before the initiation of the transaction, disclose to the special entity in writing the capacity in which the security-based swap dealer is acting.

"(B) COMMISSION AUTHORITY.—The Commission may establish such other standards and requirements under this paragraph as the Commission may determine are appropriate in the public interest, for the protection of investors, or otherwise in furtherance of the purposes of this Act.

"(6) RULES.—The Commission shall prescribe rules under this subsection governing business conduct standards for security-based swap dealers and major security-based swap participants.

"(7) APPLICABILITY.—This subsection shall not apply with respect to a transaction that is—

"(A) initiated by a special entity on an exchange or security-based swaps execution facility; and

"(B) the security-based swap dealer or major security-based swap participant does not know the identity of the counterparty to the transaction."

"(i) DOCUMENTATION STANDARDS.—

"(1) IN GENERAL.—Each registered security-based swap dealer and major security-based swap participant shall conform with such standards as may be prescribed by the Commission, by rule or regulation, that relate to timely and accurate confirmation, processing, netting, documentation, and valuation of all security-based swaps.

"(2) RULES.—The Commission shall adopt rules governing documentation standards for security-based swap dealers and major security-based swap participants.

"(j) DUTIES.—Each registered security-based swap dealer and major security-based swap participant shall, at all times, comply with the following requirements:

"(1) MONITORING OF TRADING.—The security-based swap dealer or major security-based swap participant shall monitor its trading in security-based swaps to prevent violations of applicable position limits.

"(2) RISK MANAGEMENT PROCEDURES.—The security-based swap dealer or major security-based swap participant shall establish robust and professional risk management systems adequate for managing the day-to-day business of the security-based swap dealer or major security-based swap participant.

"(3) DISCLOSURE OF GENERAL INFORMATION.—The security-based swap dealer or major security-based swap participant shall disclose to the Commission and to the prudential regulator for the security-based swap dealer or major security-based swap participant, as applicable, information concerning—

"(A) terms and conditions of its security-based swaps;

"(B) security-based swap trading operations, mechanisms, and practices;

"(C) financial integrity protections relating to security-based swaps; and

"(D) other information relevant to its trading in security-based swaps.

"(4) ABILITY TO OBTAIN INFORMATION.—The security-based swap dealer or major security-based swap participant shall—

"(A) establish and enforce internal systems and procedures to obtain any necessary information to perform any of the functions described in this section; and

"(B) provide the information to the Commission and to the prudential regulator for the security-based swap dealer or major security-based swap participant, as applicable, on request.

"(5) CONFLICTS OF INTEREST.—The security-based swap dealer and major security-based swap participant shall implement conflict-of-interest systems and procedures that—

"(A) establish structural and institutional safeguards to ensure that the activities of any person within the firm relating to research or analysis of the price or market for any security-based swap or acting in a role of providing clearing activities or making determinations as to accepting clearing customers are separated by appropriate informational partitions within the firm from the review, pressure, or oversight of persons whose involvement in pricing, trading, or clearing activities might potentially bias their judgment or supervision and contravene the core principles of open access and the business conduct standards described in this title; and

"(B) address such other issues as the Commission determines to be appropriate.

"(6) ANTITRUST CONSIDERATIONS.—Unless necessary or appropriate to achieve the purposes of this title, the security-based swap dealer or major security-based swap participant shall not—

"(A) adopt any process or take any action that results in any unreasonable restraint of trade; or

"(B) impose any material anticompetitive burden on trading or clearing.

"(7) RULES.—The Commission shall prescribe rules under this subsection governing duties of security-based swap dealers and major security-based swap participants.

"(k) DESIGNATION OF CHIEF COMPLIANCE OFFICER.—

"(1) IN GENERAL.—Each security-based swap dealer and major security-based swap participant shall designate an individual to serve as a chief compliance officer.

"(2) DUTIES.—The chief compliance officer shall—

"(A) report directly to the board or to the senior officer of the security-based swap dealer or major security-based swap participant;

"(B) review the compliance of the security-based swap dealer or major security-based swap participant with respect to the security-based swap dealer and major security-based swap participant requirements described in this section;

"(C) in consultation with the board of directors, a body performing a function similar to the board, or the senior officer of the organization, resolve any conflicts of interest that may arise;

"(D) be responsible for administering each policy and procedure that is required to be established pursuant to this section;

"(E) ensure compliance with this title (including regulations) relating to security-based swaps, including each rule prescribed by the Commission under this section;

"(F) establish procedures for the remediation of noncompliance issues identified by the chief compliance officer through any—

"(i) compliance office review;

"(ii) look-back;

"(iii) internal or external audit finding;

"(iv) self-reported error; or

"(v) validated complaint; and

"(G) establish and follow appropriate procedures for the handling, management response, remediation, retesting, and closing of non-compliance issues.

"(3) ANNUAL REPORTS.—

"(A) IN GENERAL.—In accordance with rules prescribed by the Commission, the chief compliance officer shall annually prepare and sign a report that contains a description of—

"(i) the compliance of the security-based swap dealer or major swap participant with respect to this title (including regulations); and

"(ii) each policy and procedure of the security-based swap dealer or major security-based swap participant of the chief compliance officer (including the code of ethics and conflict of interest policies).

"(B) REQUIREMENTS.—A compliance report under subparagraph (A) shall—

"(i) accompany each appropriate financial report of the security-based swap dealer or major security-based swap participant that is required to be furnished to the Commission pursuant to this section; and

"(ii) include a certification that, under penalty of law, the compliance report is accurate and complete.

"(l) ENFORCEMENT AND ADMINISTRATIVE PROCEEDING AUTHORITY.—

"(1) PRIMARY ENFORCEMENT AUTHORITY.—

"(A) SECURITIES AND EXCHANGE COMMISSION.—Except as provided in subparagraph (B), (C), or (D), the Commission shall have primary authority to enforce subtitle B, and the amendments made by subtitle B of the Wall Street Transparency and Accountability Act of 2010, with respect to any person.

"(B) PRUDENTIAL REGULATORS.—The prudential regulators shall have exclusive authority to enforce the provisions of subsection (e) and other prudential requirements of this title (including risk management standards), with respect to security-based swap dealers or major security-based swap participants for which they are the prudential regulator.

"(C) REFERRAL.—

"(i) VIOLATIONS OF NONPRUDENTIAL REQUIREMENTS.—If the appropriate Federal banking agency for security-based swap dealers or major security-based swap participants that are depository institutions has cause to believe that such security-based swap dealer or major security-based swap participant may have engaged in conduct that constitutes a violation of the nonprudential requirements of this section or rules adopted by the Commission thereunder, the agency may recommend in writing to the Commission that the Commission initiate an enforcement proceeding as authorized under this title. The recommendation shall be accompanied by a written explanation of the concerns giving rise to the recommendation.

"(ii) VIOLATIONS OF PRUDENTIAL REQUIREMENTS.—If the Commission has cause to believe that a securities-based swap dealer or major securities-based swap participant that has a prudential regulator may have engaged in conduct that constitute a violation of the prudential requirements of subsection (e) or rules adopted thereunder, the Commission may recommend in writing to the prudential regulator that the prudential regulator initiate an enforcement proceeding as authorized under this title. The recommendation shall be accompanied by a written explanation of the concerns giving rise to the recommendation.

"(D) BACKSTOP ENFORCEMENT AUTHORITY.—

"(i) INITIATION OF ENFORCEMENT PROCEEDING BY PRUDENTIAL REGULATOR.—If the Commission does not initiate an enforcement proceeding before the end of the 90-day period beginning on the date on which the Commission receives a written report under subsection (C)(i), the prudential regulator may initiate an enforcement proceeding.

"(ii) INITIATION OF ENFORCEMENT PROCEEDING BY COMMISSION.—If the prudential regulator does not initiate an enforcement proceeding before the end of the 90-day period beginning on the date on which the prudential regulator receives a written report under subsection (C)(ii), the Commission may initiate an enforcement proceeding.

"(2) CENSURE, DENIAL, SUSPENSION; NOTICE AND HEARING.—The Commission, by order, shall censure, place limitations on the activities, functions, or operations of, or revoke the registration of any security-based swap dealer or major security-based swap participant that has registered with the Commission pursuant to subsection (b) if the Commission finds, on the record after notice and opportunity for hearing, that such censure, placing of limitations, or revocation is in the public interest and that such security-based swap dealer or major security-based swap participant, or any person associated with such security-based swap dealer or major security-based swap participant effecting or involved in effecting transactions in security-based swaps on behalf of such security-based swap dealer or major security-based swap participant, whether prior or subsequent to becoming so associated—

"(A) has committed or omitted any act, or is subject to an order or finding, enumerated in subparagraph (A), (D), or (E) of paragraph (4) of section 15(b);

"(B) has been convicted of any offense specified in subparagraph (B) of such paragraph (4) within 10 years of the commencement of the proceedings under this subsection;

"(C) is enjoined from any action, conduct, or practice specified in subparagraph (C) of such paragraph (4);

"(D) is subject to an order or a final order specified in subparagraph (F) or (H), respectively, of such paragraph (4); or

"(E) has been found by a foreign financial regulatory authority to have committed or omitted any act, or violated any foreign statute or regulation, enumerated in subparagraph (G) of such paragraph (4).

"(3) ASSOCIATED PERSONS.—With respect to any person who is associated, who is seeking to become associated, or, at the time of the alleged misconduct, who was associated or was seeking to become associated with a security-based swap dealer or major security-based swap participant for the purpose of effecting or being involved in effecting security-based swaps on behalf of such security-based swap dealer or major security-based swap participant, the Commission, by order, shall censure, place limitations on the activities or functions of such person, or suspend for a period not exceeding 12 months, or bar such person from being associated with a security-based swap dealer or major security-based swap participant, if the Commission finds, on the record after notice and opportunity for a hearing, that such censure, placing of limitations, suspension, or bar is in the public interest and that such person—

"(A) has committed or omitted any act, or is subject to an order or finding, enumerated in subparagraph (A), (D), or (E) of paragraph (4) of section 15(b);

"(B) has been convicted of any offense specified in subparagraph (B) of such paragraph (4) within 10 years of the commencement of the proceedings under this subsection;

"(C) is enjoined from any action, conduct, or practice specified in subparagraph (C) of such paragraph (4);

"(D) is subject to an order or a final order specified in subparagraph (F) or (H), respectively, of such paragraph (4); or

"(E) has been found by a foreign financial regulatory authority to have committed or omitted any act, or violated any foreign statute or regulation, enumerated in subparagraph (G) of such paragraph (4).

"(4) UNLAWFUL CONDUCT.—It shall be unlawful—

"(A) for any person as to whom an order under paragraph (3) is in effect, without the consent of the Commission, willfully to become, or to be, associated with a security-based swap dealer or major security-based swap participant in contravention of such order; or

"(B) for any security-based swap dealer or major security-based swap participant to permit such a person, without the consent of the Commission, to become or remain a person associated with the security-based swap dealer or major security-based swap participant in contravention of such order, if such security-based swap dealer or major security-based swap participant knew, or in the exercise of reasonable care should have known, of such order.".

(b) SAVINGS CLAUSE.—Notwithstanding any other provision of this title, nothing in this subtitle shall be construed as divesting any appropriate Federal banking agency of any authority it may have to establish or enforce, with respect to a person for which such agency is the appropriate Federal banking agency, prudential or other standards pursuant to authority by Federal law other than this title.

[Explanation at ¶ 3165.]

[¶ 10,765] ACT SEC. 765. RULEMAKING ON CONFLICT OF INTEREST.

(a) IN GENERAL.—In order to mitigate conflicts of interest, not later than 180 days after the date of enactment of the Wall Street Transparency and Accountability Act of 2010, the Securities and Exchange Commission shall adopt rules which may include numerical limits on the control of, or the voting rights with respect to, any clearing agency that clears security-based swaps, or on the control of any security-based swap execution facility or national securities exchange that posts or makes available for trading security-based swaps, by a bank holding company (as defined in section 2 of the Bank Holding Company Act of 1956 (12 U.S.C. 1841)) with total consolidated assets of $50,000,000,000 or more, a nonbank financial company (as defined in section 102) supervised by the Board of Governors of the Federal Reserve System, affiliate of such a bank holding company or nonbank financial company, a security-based swap dealer, major security-based swap participant, or person associated with a security-based swap dealer or major security-based swap participant.

(b) PURPOSES.—The Securities and Exchange Commission shall adopt rules if the Commission determines, after the review described in subsection (a), that such rules are necessary or appropriate to improve the governance of, or to mitigate systemic risk, promote competition, or mitigate conflicts of interest in connection with a security-based swap dealer or major security-based swap participant's conduct of business with, a clearing agency, national securities exchange, or security-based swap execution facility that clears, posts, or makes available for trading security-based swaps and in which such security-based swap dealer or major security-based swap participant has a material debt or equity investment.

(c) CONSIDERATIONS.—In adopting rules pursuant to this section, the Securities and Exchange Commission shall consider any conflicts of interest arising from the amount of equity owned by a single investor, the ability to vote, cause the vote of, or withhold votes entitled to be cast on any matters by the holders of the ownership interest, and the governance arrangements of any derivatives clearing organization that clears swaps, or swap execution facility or board of trade designated as a contract market that posts swaps or makes swaps available for trading.

[Explanation at ¶ 3045.]

[¶ 10,766] ACT SEC. 766. REPORTING AND RECORDKEEPING.

(a) IN GENERAL.—The Securities Exchange Act of 1934 (15 U.S.C. 78a et seq.) is amended by inserting after section 13 the following:

"SEC. 13A. REPORTING AND RECORDKEEPING FOR CERTAIN SECURITY-BASED SWAPS.

"(a) REQUIRED REPORTING OF SECURITY-BASED SWAPS NOT ACCEPTED BY ANY CLEARING AGENCY OR DERIVATIVES CLEARING ORGANIZATION.—

"(1) IN GENERAL.—Each security-based swap that is not accepted for clearing by any clearing agency or derivatives clearing organization shall be reported to—

"(A) a security-based swap data repository described in section 13(n); or

"(B) in the case in which there is no security-based swap data repository that would accept the security-based swap, to the Commission pursuant to this section within such time period as the Commission may by rule or regulation prescribe.

"(2) TRANSITION RULE FOR PREENACTMENT SECURITY-BASED SWAPS.—

"(A) SECURITY-BASED SWAPS ENTERED INTO BEFORE THE DATE OF ENACTMENT OF THE WALL STREET TRANSPARENCY AND ACCOUNTABILITY ACT OF 2010.—Each security-based swap entered into before the date of enactment of the Wall Street Transparency and Accountability Act of 2010, the terms of which have not expired as of the date of enactment of that Act, shall be reported to a registered security-based swap data repository or the Commission by a date that is not later than—

"(i) 30 days after issuance of the interim final rule; or

"(ii) such other period as the Commission determines to be appropriate.

"(B) COMMISSION RULEMAKING.—The Commission shall promulgate an interim final rule within 90 days of the date of enactment of this section providing for the reporting of each security-based swap entered into before the date of enactment as referenced in subparagraph (A).

"(C) EFFECTIVE DATE.—The reporting provisions described in this section shall be effective upon the date of the enactment of this section.

"(3) REPORTING OBLIGATIONS.—

"(A) SECURITY-BASED SWAPS IN WHICH ONLY 1 COUNTERPARTY IS A SECURITY-BASED SWAP DEALER OR MAJOR SECURITY-BASED SWAP PARTICIPANT.—With respect to a security-based swap in which only 1 counterparty is a security-based swap dealer or major security-based swap participant, the security-based swap dealer or major security-based swap participant shall report the security-based swap as required under paragraphs (1) and (2).

"(B) SECURITY-BASED SWAPS IN WHICH 1 COUNTERPARTY IS A SECURITY-BASED SWAP DEALER AND THE OTHER A MAJOR SECURITY-BASED SWAP PARTICIPANT.—With respect to a security-based swap in which 1 counterparty is a security-based swap dealer and the other a major security-based swap participant, the security-based swap dealer shall report the security-based swap as required under paragraphs (1) and (2).

"(C) OTHER SECURITY-BASED SWAPS.—With respect to any other security-based swap not described in subparagraph (A) or (B), the counterparties to the security-based swap shall select a counterparty to report the security-based swap as required under paragraphs (1) and (2).

"(b) DUTIES OF CERTAIN INDIVIDUALS.—Any individual or entity that enters into a security-based swap shall meet each requirement described in subsection (c) if the individual or entity did not—

"(1) clear the security-based swap in accordance with section 3C(a)(1); or

"(2) have the data regarding the security-based swap accepted by a security-based swap data repository in accordance with rules (including timeframes) adopted by the Commission under this title.

"(c) REQUIREMENTS.—An individual or entity described in subsection (b) shall—

"(1) upon written request from the Commission, provide reports regarding the security-based swaps held by the individual or entity to the Commission in such form and in such manner as the Commission may request; and

"(2) maintain books and records pertaining to the security-based swaps held by the individual or entity in such form, in such manner, and for such period as the Commission may require, which shall be open to inspection by—

"(A) any representative of the Commission;

"(B) an appropriate prudential regulator;

"(C) the Commodity Futures Trading Commission;

"(D) the Financial Stability Oversight Council; and

"(E) the Department of Justice.

"(d) IDENTICAL DATA.—In prescribing rules under this section, the Commission shall require individuals and entities described in subsection (b) to submit to the Commission a report that contains data that is not less comprehensive than the data required to be collected by security-based swap data repositories under this title.".

(b) BENEFICIAL OWNERSHIP REPORTING.—Section 13 of the Securities Exchange Act of 1934 (15 U.S.C. 78m) is amended—

(1) in subsection (d)(1), by inserting "or otherwise becomes or is deemed to become a beneficial owner of any of the foregoing upon the purchase or sale of a security-based swap that the Commission may define by rule, and" after "Alaska Native Claims Settlement Act,"; and

(2) in subsection (g)(1), by inserting "or otherwise becomes or is deemed to become a beneficial owner of any security of a class described in subsection (d)(1) upon the purchase or sale of a security-based swap that the Commission may define by rule" after "subsection (d)(1) of this section".

(c) REPORTS BY INSTITUTIONAL INVESTMENT MANAGERS.—Section 13(f)(1) of the Securities Exchange Act of 1934 (15 U.S.C. 78m(f)(1)) is amended by inserting "or otherwise becomes or is deemed to become a beneficial owner of any security of a class described in subsection (d)(1) upon the purchase or sale of a security-based swap that the Commission may define by rule," after "subsection (d)(1) of this section".

(d) ADMINISTRATIVE PROCEEDING AUTHORITY.—Section 15(b)(4) of the Securities Exchange Act of 1934 (15 U.S.C. 78o(b)(4)) is amended—

(1) in subparagraph (C), by inserting "security-based swap dealer, major security-based swap participant," after "government securities dealer,"; and

(2) in subparagraph (F), by striking "broker or dealer" and inserting "broker, dealer, security-based swap dealer, or a major security-based swap participant".

(e) SECURITY-BASED SWAP BENEFICIAL OWNERSHIP.—Section 13 of the Securities Exchange Act of 1934 (15 U.S.C. 78m) is amended by adding at the end the following:

"(o) BENEFICIAL OWNERSHIP.—For purposes of this section and section 16, a person shall be deemed to acquire beneficial ownership of an equity security based on the purchase or sale of a security-based swap, only to the extent that the Commission, by rule, determines after consultation with the prudential regulators and the Secretary of the Treasury, that the purchase or sale of the security-based swap, or class of security-based swap, provides incidents of ownership comparable to direct ownership of the equity security, and that it is necessary to achieve the purposes of this section that the purchase or sale of the security-based swaps, or class of security-based swap, be deemed the acquisition of beneficial ownership of the equity security.".

[Explanation at ¶ 3170.]

[¶ 10,767] ACT SEC. 767. STATE GAMING AND BUCKET SHOP LAWS.

Section 28(a) of the Securities Exchange Act of 1934 (15 U.S.C. 78bb(a)) is amended to read as follows:

"(a) LIMITATION ON JUDGMENTS.—

"(1) IN GENERAL.—No person permitted to maintain a suit for damages under the provisions of this title shall recover, through satisfaction of judgment in 1 or more actions, a total amount in excess of the actual damages to that person on account of the act complained of. Except as otherwise specifically provided in this title, nothing in this title shall affect the jurisdiction of the securities commission (or any agency or officer performing like functions) of any State over any security or any person insofar as it does not conflict with the provisions of this title or the rules and regulations under this title.

"(2) RULE OF CONSTRUCTION.—Except as provided in subsection (f), the rights and remedies provided by this title shall be in addition to any and all other rights and remedies that may exist at law or in equity.

"(3) STATE BUCKET SHOP LAWS.—No State law which prohibits or regulates the making or promoting of wagering or gaming contracts, or the operation of 'bucket shops' or other similar or related activities, shall invalidate—

"(A) any put, call, straddle, option, privilege, or other security subject to this title (except any security that has a pari-mutuel payout or otherwise is determined by the Commission, acting by rule, regulation, or order, to be appropriately subject to such laws), or apply to any activity which is incidental or related to the offer, purchase, sale, exercise, settlement, or closeout of any such security;

"(B) any security-based swap between eligible contract participants; or

"(C) any security-based swap effected on a national securities exchange registered pursuant to section 6(b).

"(4) OTHER STATE PROVISIONS.—No provision of State law regarding the offer, sale, or distribution of securities shall apply to any transaction in a security-based swap or a security futures product, except that this paragraph may not be construed as limiting any State antifraud law of general applicability. A security-based swap may not be regulated as an insurance contract under any provision of State law.".

[Explanation at ¶ 3175.]

[¶ 10,768] ACT SEC. 768. AMENDMENTS TO THE SECURITIES ACT OF 1933; TREATMENT OF SECURITY-BASED SWAPS.

(a) DEFINITIONS.—Section 2(a) of the Securities Act of 1933 (15 U.S.C. 77b(a)) is amended—

(1) in paragraph (1), by inserting "security-based swap," after "security future,";

(2) in paragraph (3), by adding at the end the following: "Any offer or sale of a security-based swap by or on behalf of the issuer of the securities upon which such security-based swap is based or is referenced, an affiliate of the issuer, or an underwriter, shall constitute a contract for sale of, sale of, offer for sale, or offer to sell such securities."; and

(3) by adding at the end the following:

"(17) The terms 'swap' and 'security-based swap' have the same meanings as in section 1a of the Commodity Exchange Act (7 U.S.C. 1a).

"(18) The terms 'purchase' or 'sale' of a security-based swap shall be deemed to mean the execution, termination (prior to its scheduled maturity date), assignment, exchange, or similar transfer or conveyance of, or extinguishing of rights or obligations under, a security-based swap, as the context may require.".

(b) REGISTRATION OF SECURITY-BASED SWAPS.—Section 5 of the Securities Act of 1933 (15 U.S.C. 77e) is amended by adding at the end the following:

"(d) Notwithstanding the provisions of section 3 or 4, unless a registration statement meeting the requirements of section 10(a) is in effect as to a security-based swap, it shall be unlawful for any person, directly or indirectly, to make use of any means or instruments of transportation or communication in interstate commerce or of the mails to offer to sell, offer to buy or purchase or sell a security-based swap to any person who is not an eligible contract participant as defined in section 1a(18) of the Commodity Exchange Act (7 U.S.C. 1a(18)).".

[Explanation at ¶ 3160.]

[¶ 10,769] ACT SEC. 769. DEFINITIONS UNDER THE INVESTMENT COMPANY ACT OF 1940.

Section 2(a) of the Investment Company Act of 1940 (15 U.S.C. 80a-2) is amended by adding at the end the following:

"(54) The terms 'commodity pool', 'commodity pool operator', 'commodity trading advisor', 'major swap participant', 'swap', 'swap dealer', and 'swap execution facility' have the same meanings as in section 1a of the Commodity Exchange Act (7 U.S.C. 1a).".

[Explanation at ¶ 3010.]

[¶ 10,770] ACT SEC. 770. DEFINITIONS UNDER THE INVESTMENT ADVISERS ACT OF 1940.

Section 202(a) of the Investment Advisers Act of 1940 (15 U.S.C. 80b-2) is amended by adding at the end the following:

"(29) The terms 'commodity pool', 'commodity pool operator', 'commodity trading advisor', 'major swap participant', 'swap', 'swap dealer', and 'swap execution facility' have the same meanings as in section 1a of the Commodity Exchange Act (7 U.S.C. 1a).".

[Explanation at ¶ 3010.]

[¶ 10,771] ACT SEC. 771. OTHER AUTHORITY.

Unless otherwise provided by its terms, this subtitle does not divest any appropriate Federal banking agency, the Securities and Exchange Commission, the Commodity Futures Trading Commission, or any other Federal or State agency, of any authority derived from any other provision of applicable law.

[Explanation at ¶ 3010 and ¶ 3015.]

[¶ 10,772] ACT SEC. 772. JURISDICTION.

(a) IN GENERAL.—Section 36 of the Securities Exchange Act of 1934 (15 U.S.C. 78mm) is amended by adding at the end the following:

"(c) DERIVATIVES.—Unless the Commission is expressly authorized by any provision described in this subsection to grant exemptions, the Commission shall not grant exemptions, with respect to amendments made by subtitle B of the Wall Street Transparency and Accountability Act of 2010, with respect to paragraphs (65), (66), (68), (69), (70), (71), (72), (73), (74), (75), (76), and (79) of section 3(a), and sections 10B(a), 10B(b), 10B(c), 13A, 15F, 17A(g), 17A(h), 17A(i), 17A(j), 17A(k), and 17A(l); provided that the Commission shall have exemptive authority under this title with respect to security-based swaps as to the same matters that the Commodity Futures Trading Commission has under the Wall Street Transparency and Accountability Act of 2010 with respect to swaps, including under section 4(c) of the Commodity Exchange Act.".

(b) RULE OF CONSTRUCTION.—Section 30 of the Securities Exchange Act of 1934 (15 U.S.C. 78dd) is amended by adding at the end the following:

"(c) RULE OF CONSTRUCTION.—No provision of this title that was added by the Wall Street Transparency and Accountability Act of 2010, or any rule or regulation thereunder, shall apply to any person insofar as such person transacts a business in security-based swaps without the jurisdiction of the United States, unless such person transacts such business in contravention of such rules and regulations as the Commission may prescribe as necessary or appropriate to prevent the evasion of any provision of this title that was added by the Wall Street Transparency and Accountability Act of 2010. This subsection shall not be construed to limit the jurisdiction of the Commission under any provision of this title, as in effect prior to the date of enactment of the Wall Street Transparency and Accountability Act of 2010.".

[Explanation at ¶ 3015.]

[¶ 10,773] ACT SEC. 773. CIVIL PENALTIES.

Section 21B of the Securities Exchange Act of 1934 (15 U.S.C. 78p-2) is amended by adding at the end the following:

"(f) SECURITY-BASED SWAPS.—

"(1) CLEARING AGENCY.—Any clearing agency that knowingly or recklessly evades or participates in or facilitates an evasion of the requirements of section 3C shall be liable for a civil money penalty in twice the amount otherwise available for a violation of section 3C.

"(2) SECURITY-BASED SWAP DEALER OR MAJOR SECURITY-BASED SWAP PARTICIPANT.—Any security-based swap dealer or major security-based swap participant that knowingly or recklessly evades or participates in or facilitates an evasion of the requirements of section 3C shall be liable for a civil money penalty in twice the amount otherwise available for a violation of section 3C.".

[Explanation at ¶3130.]

[¶10,774] ACT SEC. 774. EFFECTIVE DATE.

Unless otherwise provided, the provisions of this subtitle shall take effect on the later of 360 days after the date of the enactment of this subtitle or, to the extent a provision of this subtitle requires a rulemaking, not less than 60 days after publication of the final rule or regulation implementing such provision of this subtitle.

[Explanation at ¶3005, ¶3010, ¶3015, ¶3045, ¶3130, ¶3160, ¶3165 and ¶3175.]

TITLE VIII—PAYMENT, CLEARING, AND SETTLEMENT SUPERVISION

[¶10,801] ACT SEC. 801. SHORT TITLE.

This title may be cited as the "Payment, Clearing, and Settlement Supervision Act of 2010".

[Explanation at ¶3505.]

[¶10,802] ACT SEC. 802. FINDINGS AND PURPOSES.

(a) FINDINGS.—Congress finds the following:

(1) The proper functioning of the financial markets is dependent upon safe and efficient arrangements for the clearing and settlement of payment, securities, and other financial transactions.

(2) Financial market utilities that conduct or support multilateral payment, clearing, or settlement activities may reduce risks for their participants and the broader financial system, but such utilities may also concentrate and create new risks and thus must be well designed and operated in a safe and sound manner.

(3) Payment, clearing, and settlement activities conducted by financial institutions also present important risks to the participating financial institutions and to the financial system.

(4) Enhancements to the regulation and supervision of systemically important financial market utilities and the conduct of systemically important payment, clearing, and settlement activities by financial institutions are necessary—

(A) to provide consistency;

(B) to promote robust risk management and safety and soundness;

(C) to reduce systemic risks; and

(D) to support the stability of the broader financial system.

(b) PURPOSE.—The purpose of this title is to mitigate systemic risk in the financial system and promote financial stability by—

(1) authorizing the Board of Governors to promote uniform standards for the—

(A) management of risks by systemically important financial market utilities; and

(B) conduct of systemically important payment, clearing, and settlement activities by financial institutions;

(2) providing the Board of Governors an enhanced role in the supervision of risk management standards for systemically important financial market utilities;

(3) strengthening the liquidity of systemically important financial market utilities; and

(4) providing the Board of Governors an enhanced role in the supervision of risk management standards for systemically important payment, clearing, and settlement activities by financial institutions.

[Explanation at ¶ 3505.]

[¶ 10,803] ACT SEC. 803. DEFINITIONS.

In this title, the following definitions shall apply:

(1) APPROPRIATE FINANCIAL REGULATOR.—The term "appropriate financial regulator" means—

(A) the primary financial regulatory agency, as defined in section 2 of this Act;

(B) the National Credit Union Administration, with respect to any insured credit union under the Federal Credit Union Act (12 U.S.C. 1751 et seq.); and

(C) the Board of Governors, with respect to organizations operating under section 25A of the Federal Reserve Act (12 U.S.C. 611), and any other financial institution engaged in a designated activity.

(2) DESIGNATED ACTIVITY.—The term "designated activity" means a payment, clearing, or settlement activity that the Council has designated as systemically important under section 804.

(3) DESIGNATED CLEARING ENTITY.—The term "designated clearing entity" means a designated financial market utility that is a derivatives clearing organization registered under section 5b of the Commodity Exchange Act (7 U.S.C. 7a-1) or a clearing agency registered with the Securities and Exchange Commission under section 17A of the Securities Exchange Act of 1934 (15 U.S.C. 78q-1).

(4) DESIGNATED FINANCIAL MARKET UTILITY.—The term "designated financial market utility" means a financial market utility that the Council has designated as systemically important under section 804.

(5) FINANCIAL INSTITUTION.—

(A) IN GENERAL.—The term "financial institution" means—

(i) a depository institution, as defined in section 3 of the Federal Deposit Insurance Act (12 U.S.C. 1813);

(ii) a branch or agency of a foreign bank, as defined in section 1(b) of the International Banking Act of 1978 (12 U.S.C. 3101);

(iii) an organization operating under section 25 or 25A of the Federal Reserve Act (12 U.S.C. 601-604a and 611 through 631);

(iv) a credit union, as defined in section 101 of the Federal Credit Union Act (12 U.S.C. 1752);

(v) a broker or dealer, as defined in section 3 of the Securities Exchange Act of 1934 (15 U.S.C. 78c);

(vi) an investment company, as defined in section 3 of the Investment Company Act of 1940 (15 U.S.C. 80a-3);

(vii) an insurance company, as defined in section 2 of the Investment Company Act of 1940 (15 U.S.C. 80a-2);

(viii) an investment adviser, as defined in section 202 of the Investment Advisers Act of 1940 (15 U.S.C. 80b-2);

(ix) a futures commission merchant, commodity trading advisor, or commodity pool operator, as defined in section 1a of the Commodity Exchange Act (7 U.S.C. 1a); and

(x) any company engaged in activities that are financial in nature or incidental to a financial activity, as described in section 4 of the Bank Holding Company Act of 1956 (12 U.S.C. 1843(k)).

(B) EXCLUSIONS.—The term "financial institution" does not include designated contract markets, registered futures associations, swap data repositories, and swap execution facilities registered under the Commodity Exchange Act (7 U.S.C. 1 et seq.), or national securities exchanges, national securities associations, alternative trading systems, securities information processors solely with respect to the activities of the entity as a securities information processor, security-based swap data repositories, and swap execution facilities registered under the Securities Exchange Act of 1934 (15 U.S.C. 78a et seq.), or designated clearing entities, provided that the exclusions in this subparagraph apply only with respect to the activities that require the entity to be so registered.

(6) FINANCIAL MARKET UTILITY.—

(A) INCLUSION.—The term "financial market utility" means any person that manages or operates a multilateral system for the purpose of transferring, clearing, or settling payments, securities, or other financial transactions among financial institutions or between financial institutions and the person.

(B) EXCLUSIONS.—The term "financial market utility" does not include—

(i) designated contract markets, registered futures associations, swap data repositories, and swap execution facilities registered under the Commodity Exchange Act (7 U.S.C. 1 et seq.), or national securities exchanges, national securities associations, alternative trading systems, security-based swap data repositories, and swap execution facilities registered under the Securities Exchange Act of 1934 (15 U.S.C. 78a et seq.), solely by reason of their providing facilities for comparison of data respecting the terms of settlement of securities or futures transactions effected on such exchange or by means of any electronic system operated or controlled by such entities, provided that the exclusions in this clause apply only with respect to the activities that require the entity to be so registered; and

(ii) any broker, dealer, transfer agent, or investment company, or any futures commission merchant, introducing broker, commodity trading advisor, or commodity pool operator, solely by reason of functions performed by such institution as part of brokerage, dealing, transfer agency, or investment company activities, or solely by reason of acting on behalf of a financial market utility or a participant therein in connection with the furnishing by the financial market utility of services to its participants or the use of services of the financial market utility by its participants, provided that services performed by such institution do not constitute critical risk management or processing functions of the financial market utility.

(7) PAYMENT, CLEARING, OR SETTLEMENT ACTIVITY.—

(A) IN GENERAL.—The term "payment, clearing, or settlement activity" means an activity carried out by 1 or more financial institutions to facilitate the completion of financial transactions, but shall not include any offer or sale of a security under the Securities Act of 1933 (15 U.S.C. 77a et seq.), or any quotation, order entry, negotiation, or other pre-trade activity or execution activity.

(B) FINANCIAL TRANSACTION.—For the purposes of subparagraph (A), the term "financial transaction" includes—

(i) funds transfers;

(ii) securities contracts;

(iii) contracts of sale of a commodity for future delivery;

(iv) forward contracts;

(v) repurchase agreements;

(vi) swaps;

(vii) security-based swaps;

(viii) swap agreements;

(ix) security-based swap agreements;

(x) foreign exchange contracts;

(xi) financial derivatives contracts; and

(xii) any similar transaction that the Council determines to be a financial transaction for purposes of this title.

(C) INCLUDED ACTIVITIES.—When conducted with respect to a financial transaction, payment, clearing, and settlement activities may include—

(i) the calculation and communication of unsettled financial transactions between counterparties;

(ii) the netting of transactions;

(iii) provision and maintenance of trade, contract, or instrument information;

(iv) the management of risks and activities associated with continuing financial transactions;

(v) transmittal and storage of payment instructions;

(vi) the movement of funds;

(vii) the final settlement of financial transactions; and

(viii) other similar functions that the Council may determine.

(D) EXCLUSION.—Payment, clearing, and settlement activities shall not include public reporting of swap transaction data under section 727 or 763(i) of the Wall Street Transparency and Accountability Act of 2010.

(8) SUPERVISORY AGENCY.—

(A) IN GENERAL.—The term "Supervisory Agency" means the Federal agency that has primary jurisdiction over a designated financial market utility under Federal banking, securities, or commodity futures laws, as follows:

(i) The Securities and Exchange Commission, with respect to a designated financial market utility that is a clearing agency registered with the Securities and Exchange Commission.

(ii) The Commodity Futures Trading Commission, with respect to a designated financial market utility that is a derivatives clearing organization registered with the Commodity Futures Trading Commission.

(iii) The appropriate Federal banking agency, with respect to a designated financial market utility that is an institution described in section 3(q) of the Federal Deposit Insurance Act.

(iv) The Board of Governors, with respect to a designated financial market utility that is otherwise not subject to the jurisdiction of any agency listed in clauses (i), (ii), and (iii).

(B) MULTIPLE AGENCY JURISDICTION.—If a designated financial market utility is subject to the jurisdictional supervision of more than 1 agency listed in subparagraph (A), then such agencies should agree on 1 agency to act as the Supervisory Agency, and if such agencies cannot agree on which agency has primary jurisdiction, the Council shall decide which agency is the Supervisory Agency for purposes of this title.

(9) SYSTEMICALLY IMPORTANT AND SYSTEMIC IMPORTANCE.—The terms "systemically important" and "systemic importance" mean a situation where the failure of or a disruption to the functioning of a financial market utility or the conduct of a payment, clearing, or settlement activity could create, or increase, the risk of significant liquidity or credit problems spreading among financial institutions or markets and thereby threaten the stability of the financial system of the United States.

[Explanation at ¶ 3510 and ¶ 3530.]

[¶ 10,804] ACT SEC. 804. DESIGNATION OF SYSTEMIC IMPORTANCE.

(a) DESIGNATION.—

(1) FINANCIAL STABILITY OVERSIGHT COUNCIL.—The Council, on a nondelegable basis and by a vote of not fewer than ⅔ of members then serving, including an affirmative vote by the Chairperson of the Council, shall designate those financial market utilities or payment, clearing, or settlement activities that the Council determines are, or are likely to become, systemically important.

(2) CONSIDERATIONS.—In determining whether a financial market utility or payment, clearing, or settlement activity is, or is likely to become, systemically important, the Council shall take into consideration the following:

(A) The aggregate monetary value of transactions processed by the financial market utility or carried out through the payment, clearing, or settlement activity.

(B) The aggregate exposure of the financial market utility or a financial institution engaged in payment, clearing, or settlement activities to its counterparties.

(C) The relationship, interdependencies, or other interactions of the financial market utility or payment, clearing, or settlement activity with other financial market utilities or payment, clearing, or settlement activities.

(D) The effect that the failure of or a disruption to the financial market utility or payment, clearing, or settlement activity would have on critical markets, financial institutions, or the broader financial system.

(E) Any other factors that the Council deems appropriate.

(b) RESCISSION OF DESIGNATION.—

(1) IN GENERAL.—The Council, on a nondelegable basis and by a vote of not fewer than 2/3 of members then serving, including an affirmative vote by the Chairperson of the Council, shall rescind a designation of systemic importance for a designated financial market utility or designated activity if the Council determines that the utility or activity no longer meets the standards for systemic importance.

(2) EFFECT OF RESCISSION.—Upon rescission, the financial market utility or financial institutions conducting the activity will no longer be subject to the provisions of this title or any rules or orders prescribed under this title.

(c) CONSULTATION AND NOTICE AND OPPORTUNITY FOR HEARING.—

(1) CONSULTATION.—Before making any determination under subsection (a) or (b), the Council shall consult with the relevant Supervisory Agency and the Board of Governors.

(2) ADVANCE NOTICE AND OPPORTUNITY FOR HEARING.—

(A) IN GENERAL.—Before making any determination under subsection (a) or (b), the Council shall provide the financial market utility or, in the case of a payment, clearing, or settlement activity, financial institutions with advance notice of the proposed determination of the Council.

(B) NOTICE IN FEDERAL REGISTER.—The Council shall provide such advance notice to financial institutions by publishing a notice in the Federal Register.

(C) REQUESTS FOR HEARING.—Within 30 days from the date of any notice of the proposed determination of the Council, the financial market utility or, in the case of a payment, clearing, or settlement activity, a financial institution engaged in the designated activity may request, in writing, an opportunity for a written or oral hearing before the Council to demonstrate that the proposed designation or rescission of designation is not supported by substantial evidence.

(D) WRITTEN SUBMISSIONS.—Upon receipt of a timely request, the Council shall fix a time, not more than 30 days after receipt of the request, unless extended at the request of the financial market utility or financial institution, and place at which the financial market utility or financial institution may appear, personally or through counsel, to submit written materials, or, at the sole discretion of the Council, oral testimony or oral argument.

(3) EMERGENCY EXCEPTION.—

(A) WAIVER OR MODIFICATION BY VOTE OF THE COUNCIL.—The Council may waive or modify the requirements of paragraph (2) if the Council determines, by an affirmative vote of not fewer than 2/3 of members then serving, including an affirmative vote by the Chairperson of the Council, that the waiver or modification is necessary to prevent or mitigate an immediate threat to the financial system posed by the financial market utility or the payment, clearing, or settlement activity.

(B) NOTICE OF WAIVER OR MODIFICATION.—The Council shall provide notice of the waiver or modification to the financial market utility concerned or, in the case of a payment, clearing, or settlement activity, to financial institutions, as soon as practicable, which shall be no later than 24 hours after the waiver or modification in the case of a financial market utility and 3 business days in the case of financial institutions. The Council shall provide the notice to financial institutions by posting a notice on the website of the Council and by publishing a notice in the Federal Register.

(d) NOTIFICATION OF FINAL DETERMINATION.—

(1) AFTER HEARING.—Within 60 days of any hearing under subsection (c)(2), the Council shall notify the financial market utility or financial institutions of the final determination of the Council in writing, which shall include findings of fact upon which the determination of the Council is based.

(2) WHEN NO HEARING REQUESTED.—If the Council does not receive a timely request for a hearing under subsection (c)(2), the Council shall notify the financial market utility or financial institutions of the final determination of the Council in writing not later than 30 days after the expiration of the date by which a financial market utility or a financial institution could have requested a hearing. All notices to financial institutions under this subsection shall be published in the Federal Register.

(e) EXTENSION OF TIME PERIODS.—The Council may extend the time periods established in subsections (c) and (d) as the Council determines to be necessary or appropriate.

[Explanation at ¶ 3505 and ¶ 3510.]

[¶ 10,805] ACT SEC. 805. STANDARDS FOR SYSTEMICALLY IMPORTANT FINANCIAL MARKET UTILITIES AND PAYMENT, CLEARING, OR SETTLEMENT ACTIVITIES.

(a) AUTHORITY TO PRESCRIBE STANDARDS.—

(1) BOARD OF GOVERNORS.—Except as provided in paragraph (2), the Board of Governors, by rule or order, and in consultation with the Council and the Supervisory Agencies, shall prescribe risk management standards, taking into consideration relevant international standards and existing prudential requirements, governing—

(A) the operations related to the payment, clearing, and settlement activities of designated financial market utilities; and

(B) the conduct of designated activities by financial institutions.

(2) SPECIAL PROCEDURES FOR DESIGNATED CLEARING ENTITIES AND DESIGNATED ACTIVITIES OF CERTAIN FINANCIAL INSTITUTIONS.—

(A) CFTC AND COMMISSION.—The Commodity Futures Trading Commission and the Commission may each prescribe regulations, in consultation with the Council and the Board of Governors, containing risk management standards, taking into consideration relevant international standards and existing prudential requirements, for those designated clearing entities and financial institutions engaged in designated activities for which each is the Supervisory Agency or the appropriate financial regulator, governing—

(i) the operations related to payment, clearing, and settlement activities of such designated clearing entities; and

(ii) the conduct of designated activities by such financial institutions.

(B) REVIEW AND DETERMINATION.—The Board of Governors may determine that existing prudential requirements of the Commodity Futures Trading Commission, the Commission, or both (including requirements prescribed pursuant to subparagraph (A)) with respect to designated clearing entities and financial institutions engaged in designated activities for which the Commission or the Commodity Futures Trading Commission is the Supervisory Agency or the appropriate financial regulator are insufficient to prevent or mitigate significant liquidity, credit, operational, or other risks to the financial markets or to the financial stability of the United States.

(C) WRITTEN DETERMINATION.—Any determination by the Board of Governors under subparagraph (B) shall be provided in writing to the Commodity Futures Trading Commission or the Commission, as applicable, and the Council, and shall explain why existing prudential requirements, considered as a whole, are insufficient to ensure that the operations and activities of the designated clearing entities or the activities of financial institutions described in subparagraph (B) will not pose significant liquidity, credit, operational, or other risks to the financial markets or to the financial stability of the United States. The Board of

Governors' determination shall contain a detailed analysis supporting its findings and identify the specific prudential requirements that are insufficient.

(D) CFTC AND COMMISSION RESPONSE.—The Commodity Futures Trading Commission or the Commission, as applicable, shall within 60 days either object to the Board of Governors' determination with a detailed analysis as to why existing prudential requirements are sufficient, or submit an explanation to the Council and the Board of Governors describing the actions to be taken in response to the Board of Governors' determination.

(E) AUTHORIZATION.—Upon an affirmative vote by not fewer than 2/3 of members then serving on the Council, the Council shall either find that the response submitted under subparagraph (D) is sufficient, or require the Commodity Futures Trading Commission, or the Commission, as applicable, to prescribe such risk management standards as the Council determines is necessary to address the specific prudential requirements that are determined to be insufficient."

(b) OBJECTIVES AND PRINCIPLES.—The objectives and principles for the risk management standards prescribed under subsection (a) shall be to—

(1) promote robust risk management;

(2) promote safety and soundness;

(3) reduce systemic risks; and

(4) support the stability of the broader financial system.

(c) SCOPE.—The standards prescribed under subsection (a) may address areas such as—

(1) risk management policies and procedures;

(2) margin and collateral requirements;

(3) participant or counterparty default policies and procedures;

(4) the ability to complete timely clearing and settlement of financial transactions;

(5) capital and financial resource requirements for designated financial market utilities; and

(6) other areas that are necessary to achieve the objectives and principles in subsection (b).

(d) LIMITATION ON SCOPE.—Except as provided in subsections (e) and (f) of section 807, nothing in this title shall be construed to permit the Council or the Board of Governors to take any action or exercise any authority granted to the Commodity Futures Trading Commission under section 2(h) of the Commodity Exchange Act or the Securities and Exchange Commission under section 3C(a) of the Securities Exchange Act of 1934, including—

(1) the approval of, disapproval of, or stay of the clearing requirement for any group, category, type, or class of swaps that a designated clearing entity may accept for clearing;

(2) the determination that any group, category, type, or class of swaps shall be subject to the mandatory clearing requirement of section 2(h)(1) of the Commodity Exchange Act or section 3C(a)(1) of the Securities Exchange Act of 1934;

(3) the determination that any person is exempt from the mandatory clearing requirement of section 2(h)(1) of the Commodity Exchange Act or section 3C(a)(1) of the Securities Exchange Act of 1934; or

(4) any authority granted to the Commodity Futures Trading Commission or the Securities and Exchange Commission with respect to transaction reporting or trade execution.

(e) THRESHOLD LEVEL.—The standards prescribed under subsection (a) governing the conduct of designated activities by financial institutions shall, where appropriate, establish a threshold as to the level or significance of engagement in the activity at which a financial institution will become subject to the standards with respect to that activity.

(f) COMPLIANCE REQUIRED.—Designated financial market utilities and financial institutions subject to the standards prescribed under subsection (a) for a designated activity shall conduct their operations in compliance with the applicable risk management standards.

[Explanation at ¶ 3515.]

[¶ 10,806] ACT SEC. 806. OPERATIONS OF DESIGNATED FINANCIAL MARKET UTILITIES.

(a) FEDERAL RESERVE ACCOUNT AND SERVICES.—The Board of Governors may authorize a Federal Reserve Bank to establish and maintain an account for a designated financial market utility and provide the services listed in section 11A(b) of the Federal Reserve Act (12 U.S.C. 248a(b)) and deposit accounts under the first undesignated paragraph of section 13 of the Federal Reserve Act (12 U.S.C. 342) to the designated financial market utility that the Federal Reserve Bank is authorized under the Federal Reserve Act to provide to a depository institution, subject to any applicable rules, orders, standards, or guidelines prescribed by the Board of Governors.

(b) ADVANCES.—The Board of Governors may authorize a Federal Reserve bank under section 10B of the Federal Reserve Act (12 U.S.C. 347b) to provide to a designated financial market utility discount and borrowing privileges only in unusual or exigent circumstances, upon the affirmative vote of a majority of the Board of Governors then serving (or such other number in accordance with the provisions of section 11(r)(2) of the Federal Reserve Act (12 U.S.C. 248(r)(2)) after consultation with the Secretary, and upon a showing by the designated financial market utility that it is unable to secure adequate credit accommodations from other banking institutions. All such discounts and borrowing privileges shall be subject to such other limitations, restrictions, and regulations as the Board of Governors may prescribe. Access to discount and borrowing privileges under section 10B of the Federal Reserve Act as authorized in this section does not require a designated financial market utility to be or become a bank or bank holding company.

(c) EARNINGS ON FEDERAL RESERVE BALANCES.—A Federal Reserve Bank may pay earnings on balances maintained by or on behalf of a designated financial market utility in the same manner and to the same extent as the Federal Reserve Bank may pay earnings to a depository institution under the Federal Reserve Act, subject to any applicable rules, orders, standards, or guidelines prescribed by the Board of Governors.

(d) RESERVE REQUIREMENTS.—The Board of Governors may exempt a designated financial market utility from, or modify any, reserve requirements under section 19 of the Federal Reserve Act (12 U.S.C. 461) applicable to a designated financial market utility.

(e) CHANGES TO RULES, PROCEDURES, OR OPERATIONS.—

(1) ADVANCE NOTICE.—

(A) ADVANCE NOTICE OF PROPOSED CHANGES REQUIRED.—A designated financial market utility shall provide notice 60 days in advance notice to its Supervisory Agency of any proposed change to its rules, procedures, or operations that could, as defined in rules of each Supervisory Agency, materially affect, the nature or level of risks presented by the designated financial market utility.

(B) TERMS AND STANDARDS PRESCRIBED BY THE SUPERVISORY AGENCIES.—Each Supervisory Agency, in consultation with the Board of Governors, shall prescribe regulations that define and describe the standards for determining when notice is required to be provided under subparagraph (A).

(C) CONTENTS OF NOTICE.—The notice of a proposed change shall describe—

(i) the nature of the change and expected effects on risks to the designated financial market utility, its participants, or the market; and

(ii) how the designated financial market utility plans to manage any identified risks.

(D) ADDITIONAL INFORMATION.—The Supervisory Agency may require a designated financial market utility to provide any information necessary to assess the effect the proposed change would have on the nature or level of risks associated with the designated financial market utility's payment, clearing, or settlement activities and the sufficiency of any proposed risk management techniques.

(E) NOTICE OF OBJECTION.—The Supervisory Agency shall notify the designated financial market utility of any objection regarding the proposed change within 60 days from the later of—

(i) the date that the notice of the proposed change is received; or

(ii) the date any further information requested for consideration of the notice is received.

(F) CHANGE NOT ALLOWED IF OBJECTION.—A designated financial market utility shall not implement a change to which the Supervisory Agency has an objection.

(G) CHANGE ALLOWED IF NO OBJECTION WITHIN 60 DAYS.—A designated financial market utility may implement a change if it has not received an objection to the proposed change within 60 days of the later of—

(i) the date that the Supervisory Agency receives the notice of proposed change; or

(ii) the date the Supervisory Agency receives any further information it requests for consideration of the notice.

(H) REVIEW EXTENSION FOR NOVEL OR COMPLEX ISSUES.—The Supervisory Agency may, during the 60-day review period, extend the review period for an additional 60 days for proposed changes that raise novel or complex issues, subject to the Supervisory Agency providing the designated financial market utility with prompt written notice of the extension. Any extension under this subparagraph will extend the time periods under subparagraphs (E) and (G).

(I) CHANGE ALLOWED EARLIER IF NOTIFIED OF NO OBJECTION.—A designated financial market utility may implement a change in less than 60 days from the date of receipt of the notice of proposed change by the Supervisory Agency, or the date the Supervisory Agency receives any further information it requested, if the Supervisory Agency notifies the designated financial market utility in writing that it does not object to the proposed change and authorizes the designated financial market utility to implement the change on an earlier date, subject to any conditions imposed by the Supervisory Agency.

(2) EMERGENCY CHANGES.—

(A) IN GENERAL.—A designated financial market utility may implement a change that would otherwise require advance notice under this subsection if it determines that—

(i) an emergency exists; and

(ii) immediate implementation of the change is necessary for the designated financial market utility to continue to provide its services in a safe and sound manner.

(B) NOTICE REQUIRED WITHIN 24 HOURS.—The designated financial market utility shall provide notice of any such emergency change to its Supervisory Agency, as soon as practicable, which shall be no later than 24 hours after implementation of the change.

(C) CONTENTS OF EMERGENCY NOTICE.—In addition to the information required for changes requiring advance notice, the notice of an emergency change shall describe—

(i) the nature of the emergency; and

(ii) the reason the change was necessary for the designated financial market utility to continue to provide its services in a safe and sound manner.

(D) MODIFICATION OR RESCISSION OF CHANGE MAY BE REQUIRED.—The Supervisory Agency may require modification or rescission of the change if it finds that the change is not consistent with the purposes of this Act or any applicable rules, orders, or standards prescribed under section 805(a).

(3) COPYING THE BOARD OF GOVERNORS.—The Supervisory Agency shall provide the Board of Governors concurrently with a complete copy of any notice, request, or other information it issues, submits, or receives under this subsection.

(4) CONSULTATION WITH BOARD OF GOVERNORS.—Before taking any action on, or completing its review of, a change proposed by a designated financial market utility, the Supervisory Agency shall consult with the Board of Governors.

[Explanation at ¶ 3520.]

[¶ 10,807] ACT SEC. 807. EXAMINATION OF AND ENFORCEMENT ACTIONS AGAINST DESIGNATED FINANCIAL MARKET UTILITIES.

(a) EXAMINATION.—Notwithstanding any other provision of law and subject to subsection (d), the Supervisory Agency shall conduct examinations of a designated financial market utility at least once annually in order to determine the following:

(1) The nature of the operations of, and the risks borne by, the designated financial market utility.

(2) The financial and operational risks presented by the designated financial market utility to financial institutions, critical markets, or the broader financial system.

(3) The resources and capabilities of the designated financial market utility to monitor and control such risks.

(4) The safety and soundness of the designated financial market utility.

(5) The designated financial market utility's compliance with—

(A) this title; and

(B) the rules and orders prescribed under this title.

(b) SERVICE PROVIDERS.—Whenever a service integral to the operation of a designated financial market utility is performed for the designated financial market utility by another entity, whether an affiliate or non-affiliate and whether on or off the premises of the designated financial market utility, the Supervisory Agency may examine whether the provision of that service is in compliance with applicable law, rules, orders, and standards to the same extent as if the designated financial market utility were performing the service on its own premises.

(c) ENFORCEMENT.—For purposes of enforcing the provisions of this title, a designated financial market utility shall be subject to, and the appropriate Supervisory Agency shall have authority under the provisions of subsections (b) through (n) of section 8 of the Federal Deposit Insurance Act (12 U.S.C. 1818) in the same manner and to the same extent as if the designated financial market utility was an insured depository institution and the Supervisory Agency was the appropriate Federal banking agency for such insured depository institution.

(d) BOARD OF GOVERNORS INVOLVEMENT IN EXAMINATIONS.—

(1) BOARD OF GOVERNORS CONSULTATION ON EXAMINATION PLANNING.—The Supervisory Agency shall consult annually with the Board of Governors regarding the scope and methodology of any examination conducted under subsections (a) and (b). The Supervisory Agency shall lead all examinations conducted under subsections (a) and (b)

(2) BOARD OF GOVERNORS PARTICIPATION IN EXAMINATION.—The Board of Governors may, in its discretion, participate in any examination led by a Supervisory Agency and conducted under subsections (a) and (b).

(e) BOARD OF GOVERNORS ENFORCEMENT RECOMMENDATIONS.—

(1) RECOMMENDATION.—The Board of Governors may, after consulting with the Council and the Supervisory Agency, at any time recommend to the Supervisory Agency that such agency take enforcement action against a designated financial market utility in order to prevent or mitigate significant liquidity, credit, operational, or other risks to the financial markets or to the financial stability of the United States. Any such recommendation for enforcement action shall provide a detailed analysis supporting the recommendation of the Board of Governors.

(2) CONSIDERATION.—The Supervisory Agency shall consider the recommendation of the Board of Governors and submit a response to the Board of Governors within 60 days.

(3) BINDING ARBITRATION.—If the Supervisory Agency rejects, in whole or in part, the recommendation of the Board of Governors, the Board of Governors may refer the recommendation to the Council for a binding decision on whether an enforcement action is warranted.

(4) ENFORCEMENT ACTION.—Upon an affirmative vote by a majority of the Council in favor of the Board of Governors' recommendation under paragraph (3), the Council may require the Supervisory Agency to—

    (A) exercise the enforcement authority referenced in subsection (c); and

    (B) take enforcement action against the designated financial market utility.

(f) EMERGENCY ENFORCEMENT ACTIONS BY THE BOARD OF GOVERNORS.—

    (1) IMMINENT RISK OF SUBSTANTIAL HARM.—The Board of Governors may, after consulting with the Supervisory Agency and upon an affirmative vote by a majority the Council, take enforcement action against a designated financial market utility if the Board of Governors has reasonable cause to conclude that—

        (A) either—

            (i) an action engaged in, or contemplated by, a designated financial market utility (including any change proposed by the designated financial market utility to its rules, procedures, or operations that would otherwise be subject to section 806(e)) poses an imminent risk of substantial harm to financial institutions, critical markets, or the broader financial system of the United States; or

            (ii) the condition of a designated financial market utility poses an imminent risk of substantial harm to financial institutions, critical markets, or the broader financial system; and

        (B) the imminent risk of substantial harm precludes the Board of Governors' use of the procedures in subsection (e).

    (2) ENFORCEMENT AUTHORITY.—For purposes of taking enforcement action under paragraph (1), a designated financial market utility shall be subject to, and the Board of Governors shall have authority under the provisions of subsections (b) through (n) of section 8 of the Federal Deposit Insurance Act (12 U.S.C. 1818) in the same manner and to the same extent as if the designated financial market utility was an insured depository institution and the Board of Governors was the appropriate Federal banking agency for such insured depository institution.

[Explanation at ¶ 3525.]

[¶ 10,808] ACT SEC. 808. EXAMINATION OF AND ENFORCEMENT ACTIONS AGAINST FINANCIAL INSTITUTIONS SUBJECT TO STANDARDS FOR DESIGNATED ACTIVITIES.

(a) EXAMINATION.—The appropriate financial regulator is authorized to examine a financial institution subject to the standards prescribed under section 805(a) for a designated activity in order to determine the following:

    (1) The nature and scope of the designated activities engaged in by the financial institution.

    (2) The financial and operational risks the designated activities engaged in by the financial institution may pose to the safety and soundness of the financial institution.

    (3) The financial and operational risks the designated activities engaged in by the financial institution may pose to other financial institutions, critical markets, or the broader financial system.

    (4) The resources available to and the capabilities of the financial institution to monitor and control the risks described in paragraphs (2) and (3).

    (5) The financial institution's compliance with this title and the rules and orders prescribed under section 805(a).

(b) ENFORCEMENT.—For purposes of enforcing the provisions of this title, and the rules and orders prescribed under this section, a financial institution subject to the standards prescribed under section 805(a) for a designated activity shall be subject to, and the appropriate financial regulator shall have authority under the provisions of subsections (b) through (n) of section 8 of the Federal Deposit Insurance Act (12 U.S.C. 1818) in the same manner and to the same extent as if the financial institution was an insured depository institution and the appropriate financial regulator was the appropriate Federal banking agency for such insured depository institution.

(c) TECHNICAL ASSISTANCE.—The Board of Governors shall consult with and provide such technical assistance as may be required by the appropriate financial regulators to ensure that the rules and orders prescribed under this title are interpreted and applied in as consistent and uniform a manner as practicable.

(d) DELEGATION.—

(1) EXAMINATION.—

(A) REQUEST TO BOARD OF GOVERNORS.—The appropriate financial regulator may request the Board of Governors to conduct or participate in an examination of a financial institution subject to the standards prescribed under section 805(a) for a designated activity in order to assess the compliance of such financial institution with—

(i) this title; or

(ii) the rules or orders prescribed under this title.

(B) EXAMINATION BY BOARD OF GOVERNORS.—Upon receipt of an appropriate written request, the Board of Governors will conduct the examination under such terms and conditions to which the Board of Governors and the appropriate financial regulator mutually agree.

(2) ENFORCEMENT.—

(A) REQUEST TO BOARD OF GOVERNORS.—The appropriate financial regulator may request the Board of Governors to enforce this title or the rules or orders prescribed under this title against a financial institution that is subject to the standards prescribed under section 805(a) for a designated activity.

(B) ENFORCEMENT BY BOARD OF GOVERNORS.—Upon receipt of an appropriate written request, the Board of Governors shall determine whether an enforcement action is warranted, and, if so, it shall enforce compliance with this title or the rules or orders prescribed under this title and, if so, the financial institution shall be subject to, and the Board of Governors shall have authority under the provisions of subsections (b) through (n) of section 8 of the Federal Deposit Insurance Act (12 U.S.C. 1818) in the same manner and to the same extent as if the financial institution was an insured depository institution and the Board of Governors was the appropriate Federal banking agency for such insured depository institution.

(e) BACK-UP AUTHORITY OF THE BOARD OF GOVERNORS.—

(1) EXAMINATION AND ENFORCEMENT.—Notwithstanding any other provision of law, the Board of Governors may—

(A) conduct an examination of the type described in subsection (a) of any financial institution that is subject to the standards prescribed under section 805(a) for a designated activity; and

(B) enforce the provisions of this title or any rules or orders prescribed under this title against any financial institution that is subject to the standards prescribed under section 805(a) for a designated activity.

(2) LIMITATIONS.—

(A) EXAMINATION.—The Board of Governors may exercise the authority described in paragraph (1)(A) only if the Board of Governors has—

(i) reasonable cause to believe that a financial institution is not in compliance with this title or the rules or orders prescribed under this title with respect to a designated activity;

(ii) notified, in writing, the appropriate financial regulator and the Council of its belief under clause (i) with supporting documentation included;

(iii) requested the appropriate financial regulator to conduct a prompt examination of the financial institution;

(iv) either—

(I) not been afforded a reasonable opportunity to participate in an examination of the financial institution by the appropriate financial regulator within 30 days after the date of the Board's notification under clause (ii); or

(II) reasonable cause to believe that the financial institution's noncompliance with this title or the rules or orders prescribed under this title poses a substantial risk to other financial institutions, critical markets, or the broader financial system, subject to the Board of Governors affording the appropriate financial regulator a reasonable opportunity to participate in the examination; and

(v) obtained the approval of the Council upon an affirmative vote by a majority of the Council.

(B) ENFORCEMENT.—The Board of Governors may exercise the authority described in paragraph (1)(B) only if the Board of Governors has—

(i) reasonable cause to believe that a financial institution is not in compliance with this title or the rules or orders prescribed under this title with respect to a designated activity;

(ii) notified, in writing, the appropriate financial regulator and the Council of its belief under clause (i) with supporting documentation included and with a recommendation that the appropriate financial regulator take 1 or more specific enforcement actions against the financial institution;

(iii) either—

(I) not been notified, in writing, by the appropriate financial regulator of the commencement of an enforcement action recommended by the Board of Governors against the financial institution within 60 days from the date of the notification under clause (ii); or

(II) reasonable cause to believe that the financial institution's noncompliance with this title or the rules or orders prescribed under this title poses significant liquidity, credit, operational, or other risks to the financial markets or to the financial stability of the United States, subject to the Board of Governors notifying the appropriate financial regulator of the Board's enforcement action; and

(iv) obtained the approval of the Council upon an affirmative vote by a majority of the Council.

(3) ENFORCEMENT PROVISIONS.—For purposes of taking enforcement action under paragraph (1), the financial institution shall be subject to, and the Board of Governors shall have authority under the provisions of subsections (b) through (n) of section 8 of the Federal Deposit Insurance Act (12 U.S.C. 1818) in the same manner and to the same extent as if the financial institution was an insured depository institution and the Board of Governors was the appropriate Federal banking agency for such insured depository institution.

[Explanation at ¶ 3530.]

[¶ 10,809] ACT SEC. 809. REQUESTS FOR INFORMATION, REPORTS, OR RECORDS.

(a) INFORMATION TO ASSESS SYSTEMIC IMPORTANCE.—

(1) FINANCIAL MARKET UTILITIES.—The Council is authorized to require any financial market utility to submit such information as the Council may require for the sole purpose of assessing whether that financial market utility is systemically important, but only if the Council has reasonable cause to believe that the financial market utility meets the standards for systemic importance set forth in section 804.

(2) FINANCIAL INSTITUTIONS ENGAGED IN PAYMENT, CLEARING, OR SETTLEMENT ACTIVITIES.—The Council is authorized to require any financial institution to submit such information as the Council may require for the sole purpose of assessing whether any payment, clearing, or settlement activity engaged in or supported by a financial institution is systemically important, but only if the Council has reasonable cause to believe that the activity meets the standards for systemic importance set forth in section 804.

(b) REPORTING AFTER DESIGNATION.—

(1) DESIGNATED FINANCIAL MARKET UTILITIES.—The Board of Governors and the Council may each require a designated financial market utility to submit reports or data to the Board of Governors and the Council in such frequency and form as deemed necessary by the Board of Governors or the Council in order to assess the safety and soundness of the utility and the systemic risk that the utility's operations pose to the financial system.

(2) FINANCIAL INSTITUTIONS SUBJECT TO STANDARDS FOR DESIGNATED ACTIVITIES.—The Board of Governors and the Council may each require 1 or more financial institutions subject to the standards prescribed under section 805(a) for a designated activity to submit, in such frequency and form as deemed necessary by the Board of Governors or the Council, reports and data to the Board of Governors and the Council solely with respect to the conduct of the designated activity and solely to assess whether—

(A) the rules, orders, or standards prescribed under section 805(a) with respect to the designated activity appropriately address the risks to the financial system presented by such activity; and

(B) the financial institutions are in compliance with this title and the rules and orders prescribed under section 805(a) with respect to the designated activity.

(3) LIMITATION.—The Board of Governors may, upon an affirmative vote by a majority of the Council, prescribe regulations under this section that impose a recordkeeping or reporting requirement on designated clearing entities or financial institutions engaged in designated activities that are subject to standards that have been prescribed under section 805(a)(2).

(c) COORDINATION WITH APPROPRIATE FEDERAL SUPERVISORY AGENCY.—

(1) ADVANCE COORDINATION.—Before requesting any material information from, or imposing reporting or recordkeeping requirements on, any financial market utility or any financial institution engaged in a payment, clearing, or settlement activity, the Board of Governors or the Council shall coordinate with the Supervisory Agency for a financial market utility or the appropriate financial regulator for a financial institution to determine if the information is available from or may be obtained by the agency in the form, format, or detail required by the Board of Governors or the Council.

(2) SUPERVISORY REPORTS.—Notwithstanding any other provision of law, the Supervisory Agency, the appropriate financial regulator, and the Board of Governors are authorized to disclose to each other and the Council copies of its examination reports or similar reports regarding any financial market utility or any financial institution engaged in payment, clearing, or settlement activities.

(d) TIMING OF RESPONSE FROM APPROPRIATE FEDERAL SUPERVISORY AGENCY.—If the information, report, records, or data requested by the Board of Governors or the Council under subsection (c)(1) are not provided in full by the Supervisory Agency or the appropriate financial regulator in less than 15 days after the date on which the material is requested, the Board of Governors or the Council may request the information or impose recordkeeping or reporting requirements directly on such persons as provided in subsections (a) and (b) with notice to the agency.

(e) SHARING OF INFORMATION.—

(1) MATERIAL CONCERNS.—Notwithstanding any other provision of law, the Board of Governors, the Council, the appropriate financial regulator, and any Supervisory Agency are authorized to—

(A) promptly notify each other of material concerns about a designated financial market utility or any financial institution engaged in designated activities; and

(B) share appropriate reports, information, or data relating to such concerns.

(2) OTHER INFORMATION.—Notwithstanding any other provision of law, the Board of Governors, the Council, the appropriate financial regulator, or any Supervisory Agency may, under such terms and conditions as it deems appropriate, provide confidential supervisory information and other information obtained under this title to each other, and to the Secretary, Federal Reserve Banks, State financial institution supervisory agencies, foreign financial supervisors, foreign central banks, and foreign finance ministries, subject to reasonable assurances of confi-

dentiality, provided, however, that no person or entity receiving information pursuant to this section may disseminate such information to entities or persons other than those listed in this paragraph without complying with applicable law, including section 8 of the Commodity Exchange Act (7 U.S.C. 12).

(f) PRIVILEGE MAINTAINED.—The Board of Governors, the Council, the appropriate financial regulator, and any Supervisory Agency providing reports or data under this section shall not be deemed to have waived any privilege applicable to those reports or data, or any portion thereof, by providing the reports or data to the other party or by permitting the reports or data, or any copies thereof, to be used by the other party.

(g) DISCLOSURE EXEMPTION.—Information obtained by the Board of Governors, the Supervisory Agencies, or the Council under this section and any materials prepared by the Board of Governors, the Supervisory Agencies, or the Council regarding their assessment of the systemic importance of financial market utilities or any payment, clearing, or settlement activities engaged in by financial institutions, and in connection with their supervision of designated financial market utilities and designated activities, shall be confidential supervisory information exempt from disclosure under section 552 of title 5, United States Code. For purposes of such section 552, this subsection shall be considered a statute described in subsection (b)(3) of such section 552.

[Explanation at ¶ 3535.]

[¶ 10,810] ACT SEC. 810. RULEMAKING.

The Board of Governors, the Supervisory Agencies, and the Council are authorized to prescribe such rules and issue such orders as may be necessary to administer and carry out their respective authorities and duties granted under this title and prevent evasions thereof.

[Explanation at ¶ 3505.]

[¶ 10,811] ACT SEC. 811. OTHER AUTHORITY.

Unless otherwise provided by its terms, this title does not divest any appropriate financial regulator, any Supervisory Agency, or any other Federal or State agency, of any authority derived from any other applicable law, except that any standards prescribed by the Board of Governors under section 805 shall supersede any less stringent requirements established under other authority to the extent of any conflict.

[Explanation at ¶ 3505 and ¶ 3515.]

[¶ 10,812] ACT SEC. 812. CONSULTATION.

(a) CFTC.—The Commodity Futures Trading Commission shall consult with the Board of Governors—

(1) prior to exercising its authorities under sections 2(h)(2)(C), 2(h)(3)(A), 2(h)(3)(C), 2(h)(4)(A), and 2(h)(4)(B) of the Commodity Exchange Act, as amended by the Wall Street Transparency and Accountability Act of 2010;

(2) with respect to any rule or rule amendment of a derivatives clearing organization for which a stay of certification has been issued under section 745(b)(3) of the Wall Street Transparency and Accountability Act of 2010; and

(3) prior to exercising its rulemaking authorities under section 728 of the Wall Street Transparency and Accountability Act of 2010.

(b) SEC.—The Commission shall consult with the Board of Governors—

(1) prior to exercising its authorities under sections 3C(a)(2)(C), 3C(a)(3)(A), 3C(a)(3)(C), 3C(a)(4)(A), and 3C(a)(4)(B) of the Securities Exchange Act of 1934, as amended by the Wall Street Transparency and Accountability Act of 2010;

(2) with respect to any proposed rule change of a clearing agency for which an extension of the time for review has been designated under section 19(b)(2) of the Securities Exchange Act of 1934; and

(3) prior to exercising its rulemaking authorities under section 13(n) of the Securities Exchange Act of 1934, as added by section 763(i) of the Wall Street Transparency and Accountability Act of 2010.

[Explanation at ¶3515.]

[¶10,813] ACT SEC. 813. COMMON FRAMEWORK FOR DESIGNATED CLEARING ENTITY RISK MANAGEMENT.

The Commodity Futures Trading Commission and the Commission shall coordinate with the Board of Governors to jointly develop risk management supervision programs for designated clearing entities. Not later than 1 year after the date of enactment of this Act, the Commodity Futures Trading Commission, the Commission, and the Board of Governors shall submit a joint report to the Committee on Banking, Housing, and Urban Affairs and the Committee on Agriculture, Nutrition, and Forestry of the Senate, and the Committee on Financial Services and the Committee on Agriculture of the House of Representatives recommendations for—

(1) improving consistency in the designated clearing entity oversight programs of the Commission and the Commodity Futures Trading Commission;

(2) promoting robust risk management by designated clearing entities;

(3) promoting robust risk management oversight by regulators of designated clearing entities; and

(4) improving regulators' ability to monitor the potential effects of designated clearing entity risk management on the stability of the financial system of the United States.

[Explanation at ¶3515.]

[¶10,814] ACT SEC. 814. EFFECTIVE DATE.

This title is effective as of the date of enactment of this Act.

[Explanation at ¶3505, ¶3510, ¶3515, ¶3520, ¶3525, ¶3530 and ¶3535.]

TITLE IX—INVESTOR PROTECTIONS AND IMPROVEMENTS TO THE REGULATION OF SECURITIES

[¶10,901] ACT SEC. 901. SHORT TITLE.

This title may be cited as the "Investor Protection and Securities Reform Act of 2010".

Subtitle A—Increasing Investor Protection

[¶10,911] ACT SEC. 911. INVESTOR ADVISORY COMMITTEE ESTABLISHED.

Title I of the Securities Exchange Act of 1934 (15 U.S.C. 78a et seq.) is amended by adding at the end the following:

"SEC. 39. INVESTOR ADVISORY COMMITTEE.

"(a) ESTABLISHMENT AND PURPOSE.—

"(1) ESTABLISHMENT.—There is established within the Commission the Investor Advisory Committee (referred to in this section as the 'Committee').

"(2) PURPOSE.—The Committee shall—

"(A) advise and consult with the Commission on—

"(i) regulatory priorities of the Commission;

"(ii) issues relating to the regulation of securities products, trading strategies, and fee structures, and the effectiveness of disclosure;

"(iii) initiatives to protect investor interest; and

"(iv) initiatives to promote investor confidence and the integrity of the securities marketplace; and

"(B) submit to the Commission such findings and recommendations as the Committee determines are appropriate, including recommendations for proposed legislative changes.

"(b) MEMBERSHIP.—

"(1) IN GENERAL.—The members of the Committee shall be—

"(A) the Investor Advocate;

"(B) a representative of State securities commissions;

"(C) a representative of the interests of senior citizens; and

"(D) not fewer than 10, and not more than 20, members appointed by the Commission, from among individuals who—

"(i) represent the interests of individual equity and debt investors, including investors in mutual funds;

"(ii) represent the interests of institutional investors, including the interests of pension funds and registered investment companies;

"(iii) are knowledgeable about investment issues and decisions; and

"(iv) have reputations of integrity.

"(2) TERM.—Each member of the Committee appointed under paragraph (1)(B) shall serve for a term of 4 years.

"(3) MEMBERS NOT COMMISSION EMPLOYEES.—Members appointed under paragraph (1)(B) shall not be deemed to be employees or agents of the Commission solely because of membership on the Committee.

"(c) CHAIRMAN; VICE CHAIRMAN; SECRETARY; ASSISTANT SECRETARY.—

"(1) IN GENERAL.—The members of the Committee shall elect, from among the members of the Committee—

"(A) a chairman, who may not be employed by an issuer;

"(B) a vice chairman, who may not be employed by an issuer;

"(C) a secretary; and

"(D) an assistant secretary.

"(2) TERM.—Each member elected under paragraph (1) shall serve for a term of 3 years in the capacity for which the member was elected under paragraph (1).

"(d) MEETINGS.—

"(1) FREQUENCY OF MEETINGS.—The Committee shall meet—

"(A) not less frequently than twice annually, at the call of the chairman of the Committee; and

"(B) from time to time, at the call of the Commission.

"(2) NOTICE.—The chairman of the Committee shall give the members of the Committee written notice of each meeting, not later than 2 weeks before the date of the meeting.

"(e) COMPENSATION AND TRAVEL EXPENSES.—Each member of the Committee who is not a full-time employee of the United States shall—

"(1) be entitled to receive compensation at a rate not to exceed the daily equivalent of the annual rate of basic pay in effect for a position at level V of the Executive Schedule under section 5316 of title 5, United States Code, for each day during which the member is engaged in the actual performance of the duties of the Committee; and

"(2) while away from the home or regular place of business of the member in the performance of services for the Committee, be allowed travel expenses, including per diem in lieu of subsistence, in the same manner as persons employed intermittently in the Government service are allowed expenses under section 5703(b) of title 5, United States Code.

"(f) STAFF.—The Commission shall make available to the Committee such staff as the chairman of the Committee determines are necessary to carry out this section.

"(g) REVIEW BY COMMISSION.—The Commission shall—

"(1) review the findings and recommendations of the Committee; and

"(2) each time the Committee submits a finding or recommendation to the Commission, promptly issue a public statement—

"(A) assessing the finding or recommendation of the Committee; and

"(B) disclosing the action, if any, the Commission intends to take with respect to the finding or recommendation.

"(h) COMMITTEE FINDINGS.—Nothing in this section shall require the Commission to agree to or act upon any finding or recommendation of the Committee.

"(i) FEDERAL ADVISORY COMMITTEE ACT.—The Federal Advisory Committee Act (5 U.S.C. App.) shall not apply with respect to the Committee and its activities.

"(j) AUTHORIZATION OF APPROPRIATIONS.—There is authorized to be appropriated to the Commission such sums as are necessary to carry out this section.".

[Explanation at ¶ 4005 and ¶ 4010.]

[¶ 10,912] ACT SEC. 912. CLARIFICATION OF AUTHORITY OF THE COMMISSION TO ENGAGE IN INVESTOR TESTING.

Section 19 of the Securities Act of 1933 (15 U.S.C. 77s) is amended by adding at the end the following:

"(e) EVALUATION OF RULES OR PROGRAMS.—For the purpose of evaluating any rule or program of the Commission issued or carried out under any provision of the securities laws, as defined in section 3 of the Securities Exchange Act of 1934 (15 U.S.C. 78c), and the purposes of considering, proposing, adopting, or engaging in any such rule or program or developing new rules or programs, the Commission may—

"(1) gather information from and communicate with investors or other members of the public;

"(2) engage in such temporary investor testing programs as the Commission determines are in the public interest or would protect investors; and

"(3) consult with academics and consultants, as necessary to carry out this subsection.

"(f) RULE OF CONSTRUCTION.—For purposes of the Paperwork Reduction Act (44 U.S.C. 3501 et seq.), any action taken under subsection (e) shall not be construed to be a collection of information.".

[Explanation at ¶ 4015.]

[¶ 10,913] ACT SEC. 913. STUDY AND RULEMAKING REGARDING OBLIGATIONS OF BROKERS, DEALERS, AND INVESTMENT ADVISERS.

(a) DEFINITION.—For purposes of this section, the term "retail customer" means a natural person, or the legal representative of such natural person, who—

(1) receives personalized investment advice about securities from a broker or dealer or investment adviser; and

(2) uses such advice primarily for personal, family, or household purposes.

(b) STUDY.—The Commission shall conduct a study to evaluate—

(1) the effectiveness of existing legal or regulatory standards of care for brokers, dealers, investment advisers, persons associated with brokers or dealers, and persons associated with investment advisers for providing personalized investment advice and recommendations about securities to retail customers imposed by the Commission and a national securities association, and other Federal and State legal or regulatory standards; and

(2) whether there are legal or regulatory gaps, shortcomings, or overlaps in legal or regulatory standards in the protection of retail customers relating to the standards of care for brokers, dealers, investment advisers, persons associated with brokers or dealers, and persons associated with investment advisers for providing personalized investment advice about securities to retail customers that should be addressed by rule or statute.

(c) CONSIDERATIONS.—In conducting the study required under subsection (b), the Commission shall consider—

(1) the effectiveness of existing legal or regulatory standards of care for brokers, dealers, investment advisers, persons associated with brokers or dealers, and persons associated with investment advisers for providing personalized investment advice and recommendations about securities to retail customers imposed by the Commission and a national securities association, and other Federal and State legal or regulatory standards;

(2) whether there are legal or regulatory gaps, shortcomings, or overlaps in legal or regulatory standards in the protection of retail customers relating to the standards of care for brokers, dealers, investment advisers, persons associated with brokers or dealers, and persons associated with investment advisers for providing personalized investment advice about securities to retail customers that should be addressed by rule or statute;

(3) whether retail customers understand that there are different standards of care applicable to brokers, dealers, investment advisers, persons associated with brokers or dealers, and persons associated with investment advisers in the provision of personalized investment advice about securities to retail customers;

(4) whether the existence of different standards of care applicable to brokers, dealers, investment advisers, persons associated with brokers or dealers, and persons associated with investment advisers is a source of confusion for retail customers regarding the quality of personalized investment advice that retail customers receive;

(5) the regulatory, examination, and enforcement resources devoted to, and activities of, the Commission, the States, and a national securities association to enforce the standards of care for brokers, dealers, investment advisers, persons associated with brokers or dealers, and persons associated with investment advisers when providing personalized investment advice and recommendations about securities to retail customers, including—

(A) the effectiveness of the examinations of brokers, dealers, and investment advisers in determining compliance with regulations;

(B) the frequency of the examinations; and

(C) the length of time of the examinations;

(6) the substantive differences in the regulation of brokers, dealers, and investment advisers, when providing personalized investment advice and recommendations about securities to retail customers;

(7) the specific instances related to the provision of personalized investment advice about securities in which—

(A) the regulation and oversight of investment advisers provide greater protection to retail customers than the regulation and oversight of brokers and dealers; and

(B) the regulation and oversight of brokers and dealers provide greater protection to retail customers than the regulation and oversight of investment advisers;

(8) the existing legal or regulatory standards of State securities regulators and other regulators intended to protect retail customers;

(9) the potential impact on retail customers, including the potential impact on access of retail customers to the range of products and services offered by brokers and dealers, of imposing upon brokers, dealers, and persons associated with brokers or dealers—

(A) the standard of care applied under the Investment Advisers Act of 1940 (15 U.S.C. 80b-1 et seq.) for providing personalized investment advice about securities to retail customers of investment advisers, as interpreted by the Commission and the courts; and

(B) other requirements of the Investment Advisers Act of 1940 (15 U.S.C. 80b-1 et seq.);

(10) the potential impact of eliminating the broker and dealer exclusion from the definition of "investment adviser" under section 202(a)(11)(C) of the Investment Advisers Act of 1940 (15 U.S.C. 80b-2(a)(11)(C)), in terms of—

(A) the impact and potential benefits and harm to retail customers that could result from such a change, including any potential impact on access to personalized investment advice and recommendations about securities to retail customers or the availability of such advice and recommendations;

(B) the number of additional entities and individuals that would be required to register under, or become subject to, the Investment Advisers Act of 1940 (15 U.S.C. 80b-1 et seq.), and the additional requirements to which brokers, dealers, and persons associated with brokers and dealers would become subject, including—

(i) any potential additional associated person licensing, registration, and examination requirements; and

(ii) the additional costs, if any, to the additional entities and individuals; and

(C) the impact on Commission and State resources to—

(i) conduct examinations of registered investment advisers and the representatives of registered investment advisers, including the impact on the examination cycle; and

(ii) enforce the standard of care and other applicable requirements imposed under the Investment Advisers Act of 1940 (15 U.S.C. 80b-1 et seq.);

(11) the varying level of services provided by brokers, dealers, investment advisers, persons associated with brokers or dealers, and persons associated with investment advisers to retail customers and the varying scope and terms of retail customer relationships of brokers, dealers, investment advisers, persons associated with brokers or dealers, and persons associated with investment advisers with such retail customers;

(12) the potential impact upon retail customers that could result from potential changes in the regulatory requirements or legal standards of care affecting brokers, dealers, investment advisers, persons associated with brokers or dealers, and persons associated with investment advisers relating to their obligations to retail customers regarding the provision of investment advice, including any potential impact on—

(A) protection from fraud;

(B) access to personalized investment advice, and recommendations about securities to retail customers; or

(C) the availability of such advice and recommendations;

(13) the potential additional costs and expenses to—

(A) retail customers regarding and the potential impact on the profitability of their investment decisions; and

(B) brokers, dealers, and investment advisers resulting from potential changes in the regulatory requirements or legal standards affecting brokers, dealers, investment advisers, persons associated with brokers or dealers, and persons associated with investment advisers relating to their obligations, including duty of care, to retail customers; and

(14) any other consideration that the Commission considers necessary and appropriate in determining whether to conduct a rulemaking under subsection (f).

(d) REPORT.—

(1) IN GENERAL.—Not later than 6 months after the date of enactment of this Act, the Commission shall submit a report on the study required under subsection (b) to—

(A) the Committee on Banking, Housing, and Urban Affairs of the Senate; and

(B) the Committee on Financial Services of the House of Representatives.

(2) CONTENT REQUIREMENTS.—The report required under paragraph (1) shall describe the findings, conclusions, and recommendations of the Commission from the study required under subsection (b), including—

(A) a description of the considerations, analysis, and public and industry input that the Commission considered, as required under subsection (b), to make such findings, conclusions, and policy recommendations; and

(B) an analysis of whether any identified legal or regulatory gaps, shortcomings, or overlap in legal or regulatory standards in the protection of retail customers relating to the standards of care for brokers, dealers, investment advisers, persons associated with brokers or dealers, and persons associated with investment advisers for providing personalized investment advice about securities to retail customers.

(e) PUBLIC COMMENT.—The Commission shall seek and consider public input, comments, and data in order to prepare the report required under subsection (d).

(f) RULEMAKING.—The Commission may commence a rulemaking, as necessary or appropriate in the public interest and for the protection of retail customers (and such other customers as the Commission may by rule provide), to address the legal or regulatory standards of care for brokers, dealers, investment advisers, persons associated with brokers or dealers, and persons associated with investment advisers for providing personalized investment advice about securities to such retail customers. The Commission shall consider the findings conclusions, and recommendations of the study required under subsection (b).

(g) AUTHORITY TO ESTABLISH A FIDUCIARY DUTY FOR BROKERS AND DEALERS.—

(1) SECURITIES EXCHANGE ACT OF 1934.—Section 15 of the Securities Exchange Act of 1934 (15 U.S.C. 78o) is amended by adding at the end the following:

"(k) STANDARD OF CONDUCT.—

"(1) IN GENERAL.—Notwithstanding any other provision of this Act or the Investment Advisers Act of 1940, the Commission may promulgate rules to provide that, with respect to a broker or dealer, when providing personalized investment advice about securities to a retail customer (and such other customers as the Commission may by rule provide), the standard of conduct for such broker or dealer with respect to such customer shall be the same as the standard of conduct applicable to an investment adviser under section 211 of the Investment Advisers Act of 1940. The receipt of compensation based on commission or other standard compensation for the sale of securities shall not, in and of itself, be considered a violation of such standard applied to a broker or dealer. Nothing in this section shall require a broker or dealer or registered representative to have a continuing duty of care or loyalty to the customer after providing personalized investment advice about securities.

"(2) DISCLOSURE OF RANGE OF PRODUCTS OFFERED.—Where a broker or dealer sells only proprietary or other limited range of products, as determined by the Commission, the Commission may by rule require that such broker or dealer provide notice to each retail customer and obtain the consent or acknowledgment of the customer. The sale of only proprietary or other limited range of products by a broker or dealer shall not, in and of itself, be considered a violation of the standard set forth in paragraph (1).

"(l) OTHER MATTERS.—The Commission shall—

"(1) facilitate the provision of simple and clear disclosures to investors regarding the terms of their relationships with brokers, dealers, and investment advisers, including any material conflicts of interest; and

"(2) examine and, where appropriate, promulgate rules prohibiting or restricting certain sales practices, conflicts of interest, and compensation schemes for brokers, dealers, and investment advisers that the Commission deems contrary to the public interest and the protection of investors.".

(2) INVESTMENT ADVISERS ACT OF 1940.—Section 211 of the Investment Advisers Act of 1940, is further amended by adding at the end the following new subsections:

"(g) STANDARD OF CONDUCT.—

"(1) IN GENERAL.—The Commission may promulgate rules to provide that the standard of conduct for all brokers, dealers, and investment advisers, when providing personalized investment advice about securities to retail customers (and such other customers as the Commission may by rule provide), shall be to act in the best interest of the customer without regard to the financial or other interest of the broker, dealer, or investment adviser providing the advice. In accordance with such rules, any material conflicts of interest shall be disclosed and may be consented to by the customer. Such rules shall provide that such standard of conduct shall be no less stringent than the standard applicable to investment advisers under section 206(1) and (2) of this Act when providing personalized investment advice about securities, except the Commission shall not ascribe a meaning to the term 'customer' that would include an investor in a private fund managed by an investment adviser, where such private fund has entered into an advisory contract with such adviser. The receipt of compensation based on commission or fees shall not, in and of itself, be considered a violation of such standard applied to a broker, dealer, or investment adviser.

"(2) RETAIL CUSTOMER DEFINED.—For purposes of this subsection, the term 'retail customer' means a natural person, or the legal representative of such natural person, who—

"(A) receives personalized investment advice about securities from a broker, dealer, or investment adviser; and

"(B) uses such advice primarily for personal, family, or household purposes.

"(h) OTHER MATTERS.—The Commission shall—

"(1) facilitate the provision of simple and clear disclosures to investors regarding the terms of their relationships with brokers, dealers, and investment advisers, including any material conflicts of interest; and

"(2) examine and, where appropriate, promulgate rules prohibiting or restricting certain sales practices, conflicts of interest, and compensation schemes for brokers, dealers, and investment advisers that the Commission deems contrary to the public interest and the protection of investors.".

(h) HARMONIZATION OF ENFORCEMENT.—

(1) SECURITIES EXCHANGE ACT OF 1934.—Section 15 of the Securities Exchange Act of 1934, as amended by subsection (g)(1), is further amended by adding at the end the following new subsection:

"(m) HARMONIZATION OF ENFORCEMENT.—The enforcement authority of the Commission with respect to violations of the standard of conduct applicable to a broker or dealer providing personalized investment advice about securities to a retail customer shall include—

"(1) the enforcement authority of the Commission with respect to such violations provided under this Act; and

"(2) the enforcement authority of the Commission with respect to violations of the standard of conduct applicable to an investment adviser under the Investment Advisers Act of 1940, including the authority to impose sanctions for such violations, and

the Commission shall seek to prosecute and sanction violators of the standard of conduct applicable to a broker or dealer providing personalized investment advice about securities to a retail customer under this Act to same extent as the Commission prosecutes and sanctions violators of the standard of conduct applicable to an investment advisor under the Investment Advisers Act of 1940.".

(2) INVESTMENT ADVISERS ACT OF 1940.—Section 211 of the Investment Advisers Act of 1940, as amended by subsection (g)(2), is further amended by adding at the end the following new subsection:

"(i) HARMONIZATION OF ENFORCEMENT.—The enforcement authority of the Commission with respect to violations of the standard of conduct applicable to an investment adviser shall include—

"(1) the enforcement authority of the Commission with respect to such violations provided under this Act; and

"(2) the enforcement authority of the Commission with respect to violations of the standard of conduct applicable to a broker or dealer providing personalized investment advice about securities to a retail customer under the Securities Exchange Act of 1934, including the authority to impose sanctions for such violations, and

the Commission shall seek to prosecute and sanction violators of the standard of conduct applicable to an investment adviser under this Act to same extent as the Commission prosecutes and sanctions violators of the standard of conduct applicable to a broker or dealer providing personalized investment advice about securities to a retail customer under the Securities Exchange Act of 1934.".

[Explanation at ¶ 4020.]

[¶ 10,914] ACT SEC. 914. STUDY ON ENHANCING INVESTMENT ADVISER EXAMINATIONS.

(a) STUDY REQUIRED.—

(1) IN GENERAL.—The Commission shall review and analyze the need for enhanced examination and enforcement resources for investment advisers.

(2) AREAS OF CONSIDERATION.—The study required by this subsection shall examine—

(A) the number and frequency of examinations of investment advisers by the Commission over the 5 years preceding the date of the enactment of this subtitle;

(B) the extent to which having Congress authorize the Commission to designate one or more self-regulatory organizations to augment the Commission's efforts in overseeing investment advisers would improve the frequency of examinations of investment advisers; and

(C) current and potential approaches to examining the investment advisory activities of dually registered broker-dealers and investment advisers or affiliated broker-dealers and investment advisers.

(b) REPORT REQUIRED.—The Commission shall report its findings to the Committee on Financial Services of the House of Representatives and the Committee on Banking, Housing, and Urban Affairs of the Senate, not later than 180 days after the date of enactment of this subtitle, and shall use such findings to revise its rules and regulations, as necessary. The report shall include a discussion of regulatory or legislative steps that are recommended or that may be necessary to address concerns identified in the study.

[Explanation at ¶ 4040]

[¶ 10,915] ACT SEC. 915. OFFICE OF THE INVESTOR ADVOCATE.

Section 4 of the Securities Exchange Act of 1934 (15 U.S.C. 78d) is amended by adding at the end the following:

"(g) OFFICE OF THE INVESTOR ADVOCATE.—

"(1) OFFICE ESTABLISHED.—There is established within the Commission the Office of the Investor Advocate (in this subsection referred to as the 'Office').

"(2) INVESTOR ADVOCATE.—

"(A) IN GENERAL.—The head of the Office shall be the Investor Advocate, who shall—

"(i) report directly to the Chairman; and

"(ii) be appointed by the Chairman, in consultation with the Commission, from among individuals having experience in advocating for the interests of investors in securities and investor protection issues, from the perspective of investors.

"(B) COMPENSATION.—The annual rate of pay for the Investor Advocate shall be equal to the highest rate of annual pay for other senior executives who report to the Chairman of the Commission.

"(C) LIMITATION ON SERVICE.—An individual who serves as the Investor Advocate may not be employed by the Commission—

"(i) during the 2-year period ending on the date of appointment as Investor Advocate; or

"(ii) during the 5-year period beginning on the date on which, the person ceases to serve as the Investor Advocate.

"(3) STAFF OF OFFICE.—The Investor Advocate, after consultation with the Chairman of the Commission, may retain or employ independent counsel, research staff, and service staff, as the Investor Advocate deems necessary to carry out the functions, powers, and duties of the Office.

"(4) FUNCTIONS OF THE INVESTOR ADVOCATE.—The Investor Advocate shall—

"(A) assist retail investors in resolving significant problems such investors may have with the Commission or with self-regulatory organizations;

"(B) identify areas in which investors would benefit from changes in the regulations of the Commission or the rules of self-regulatory organizations;

"(C) identify problems that investors have with financial service providers and investment products;

"(D) analyze the potential impact on investors of—

"(i) proposed regulations of the Commission; and

"(ii) proposed rules of self-regulatory organizations registered under this title; and

"(E) to the extent practicable, propose to the Commission changes in the regulations or orders of the Commission and to Congress any legislative, administrative, or personnel changes that may be appropriate to mitigate problems identified under this paragraph and to promote the interests of investors.

"(5) ACCESS TO DOCUMENTS.—The Commission shall ensure that the Investor Advocate has full access to the documents of the Commission and any self-regulatory organization, as necessary to carry out the functions of the Office.

"(6) ANNUAL REPORTS.—

"(A) REPORT ON OBJECTIVES.—

"(i) IN GENERAL.—Not later than June 30 of each year after 2010, the Investor Advocate shall submit to the Committee on Banking, Housing, and Urban Affairs of the Senate and the Committee on Financial Services of the House of Representatives a report on the objectives of the Investor Advocate for the following fiscal year.

"(ii) CONTENTS.—Each report required under clause (i) shall contain full and substantive analysis and explanation.

"(B) REPORT ON ACTIVITIES.—

"(i) IN GENERAL.—Not later than December 31 of each year after 2010, the Investor Advocate shall submit to the Committee on Banking, Housing, and Urban Affairs of the Senate and the Committee on Financial Services of the House of Representatives a report on the activities of the Investor Advocate during the immediately preceding fiscal year.

"(ii) CONTENTS.—Each report required under clause (i) shall include—

"(I) appropriate statistical information and full and substantive analysis;

"(II) information on steps that the Investor Advocate has taken during the reporting period to improve investor services and the responsiveness of the Commission and self-regulatory organizations to investor concerns;

"(III) a summary of the most serious problems encountered by investors during the reporting period;

"(IV) an inventory of the items described in subclause (III) that includes—

"(aa) identification of any action taken by the Commission or the self-regulatory organization and the result of such action;

"(bb) the length of time that each item has remained on such inventory; and

"(cc) for items on which no action has been taken, the reasons for inaction, and an identification of any official who is responsible for such action;

"(V) recommendations for such administrative and legislative actions as may be appropriate to resolve problems encountered by investors; and

"(VI) any other information, as determined appropriate by the Investor Advocate.

"(iii) INDEPENDENCE.—Each report required under this paragraph shall be provided directly to the Committees listed in clause (i) without any prior review or comment from the Commission, any commissioner, any other officer or employee of the Commission, or the Office of Management and Budget.

"(iv) CONFIDENTIALITY.—No report required under clause (i) may contain confidential information.

"(7) REGULATIONS.—The Commission shall, by regulation, establish procedures requiring a formal response to all recommendations submitted to the Commission by the Investor Advocate, not later than 3 months after the date of such submission.".

[Explanation at ¶ 4025.]

[¶ 10,916] ACT SEC. 916. STREAMLINING OF FILING PROCEDURES FOR SELF-REGULATORY ORGANIZATIONS.

(a) FILING PROCEDURES.—Section 19(b) of the Securities Exchange Act of 1934 (15 U.S.C. 78s(b)) is amended by striking paragraph (2) (including the undesignated matter immediately following subparagraph (B)) and inserting the following:

"(2) APPROVAL PROCESS.—

"(A) APPROVAL PROCESS ESTABLISHED.—

"(i) IN GENERAL.—Except as provided in clause (ii), not later than 45 days after the date of publication of a proposed rule change under paragraph (1), the Commission shall—

"(I) by order, approve or disapprove the proposed rule change; or

"(II) institute proceedings under subparagraph (B) to determine whether the proposed rule change should be disapproved.

"(ii) EXTENSION OF TIME PERIOD.—The Commission may extend the period established under clause (i) by not more than an additional 45 days, if—

"(I) the Commission determines that a longer period is appropriate and publishes the reasons for such determination; or

"(II) the self-regulatory organization that filed the proposed rule change consents to the longer period.

"(B) PROCEEDINGS.—

"(i) NOTICE AND HEARING.—If the Commission does not approve or disapprove a proposed rule change under subparagraph (A), the Commission shall provide to the self-regulatory organization that filed the proposed rule change—

"(I) notice of the grounds for disapproval under consideration; and

"(II) opportunity for hearing, to be concluded not later than 180 days after the date of publication of notice of the filing of the proposed rule change.

"(ii) ORDER OF APPROVAL OR DISAPPROVAL.—

"(I) IN GENERAL.—Except as provided in subclause (II), not later than 180 days after the date of publication under paragraph (1), the Commission shall issue an order approving or disapproving the proposed rule change.

"(II) EXTENSION OF TIME PERIOD.—The Commission may extend the period for issuance under clause (I) by not more than 60 days, if—

"(aa) the Commission determines that a longer period is appropriate and publishes the reasons for such determination; or

"(bb) the self-regulatory organization that filed the proposed rule change consents to the longer period.

"(C) STANDARDS FOR APPROVAL AND DISAPPROVAL.—

"(i) APPROVAL.—The Commission shall approve a proposed rule change of a self-regulatory organization if it finds that such proposed rule change is consistent with the requirements of this title and the rules and regulations issued under this title that are applicable to such organization.

"(ii) DISAPPROVAL.—The Commission shall disapprove a proposed rule change of a self-regulatory organization if it does not make a finding described in clause (i).

"(iii) TIME FOR APPROVAL.—The Commission may not approve a proposed rule change earlier than 30 days after the date of publication under paragraph (1), unless the Commission finds good cause for so doing and publishes the reason for the finding.

"(D) RESULT OF FAILURE TO INSTITUTE OR CONCLUDE PROCEEDINGS.—A proposed rule change shall be deemed to have been approved by the Commission, if—

"(i) the Commission does not approve or disapprove the proposed rule change or begin proceedings under subparagraph (B) within the period described in subparagraph (A); or

"(ii) the Commission does not issue an order approving or disapproving the proposed rule change under subparagraph (B) within the period described in subparagraph (B)(ii).

"(E) PUBLICATION DATE BASED ON FEDERAL REGISTER PUBLISHING.—For purposes of this paragraph, if, after filing a proposed rule change with the Commission pursuant to paragraph (1), a self-regulatory organization publishes a notice of the filing of such proposed rule change, together with the substantive terms of such proposed rule change, on a publicly accessible website, the Commission shall thereafter send the notice to the Federal Register for publication thereof under paragraph (1) within 15 days of the date on which such website publication is made. If the Commission fails to send the notice for publication thereof within such 15 day period, then the date of publication shall be deemed to be the date on which such website publication was made.

"(F) RULEMAKING.—

"(i) IN GENERAL.—Not later than 180 days after the date of enactment of the Investor Protection and Securities Reform Act of 2010, after consultation with other regulatory agencies, the Commission shall promulgate rules setting forth the procedural requirements of the proceedings required under this paragraph.

"(ii) NOTICE AND COMMENT NOT REQUIRED.—The rules promulgated by the Commission under clause (i) are not required to include republication of proposed rule changes or solicitation of public comment.".

(b) CLARIFICATION OF FILING DATE.—

(1) RULE OF CONSTRUCTION.—Section 19(b) of the Securities Exchange Act of 1934 (15 U.S.C. 78s(b)) is amended by adding at the end the following:

"(10) RULE OF CONSTRUCTION RELATING TO FILING DATE OF PROPOSED RULE CHANGES.—

"(A) IN GENERAL.—For purposes of this subsection, the date of filing of a proposed rule change shall be deemed to be the date on which the Commission receives the proposed rule change.

"(B) EXCEPTION.—A proposed rule change has not been received by the Commission for purposes of subparagraph (A) if, not later than 7 business days after the date of receipt by the Commission, the Commission notifies the self-regulatory organization that such proposed rule change does not comply with the rules of the Commission relating to the required form of a proposed rule change, except that if the Commission determines that the proposed rule change is unusually lengthy and is complex or raises novel regulatory issues, the Commission shall inform the self-regulatory organization of such determination not later than 7 business days after the date of receipt by the Commission and, for the purposes of subparagraph (A), a proposed rule change has not been received by the Commission, if, not later than 21 days after the date of receipt by the Commission, the Commission notifies the self-regulatory organization that such proposed rule change does not comply with the rules of the Commission relating to the required form of a proposed rule change.".

(2) PUBLICATION.—Section 19(b)(1) of the Securities Exchange Act of 1934 (15 U.S.C. 78s(b)(1)) is amended by striking "upon" and inserting "as soon as practicable after the date of".

(c) EFFECTIVE DATE OF PROPOSED RULES.—Section 19(b)(3) of the Securities Exchange Act of 1934 (15 U.S.C. 78s(b)(3)) is amended—

(1) in subparagraph (A)—

(A) by striking "may take effect" and inserting "shall take effect"; and

(B) by inserting "on any person, whether or not the person is a member of the self-regulatory organization" after "charge imposed by the self-regulatory organization"; and

(2) in subparagraph (C)—

(A) by amending the second sentence to read as follows: "At any time within the 60-day period beginning on the date of filing of such a proposed rule change in accordance with the provisions of paragraph (1), the Commission summarily may temporarily suspend the change in the rules of the self-regulatory organization made thereby, if it appears to the Commission that such action is necessary or appropriate in the public interest, for the protection of investors, or otherwise in furtherance of the purposes of this title.";

(B) by inserting after the second sentence the following: "If the Commission takes such action, the Commission shall institute proceedings under paragraph (2)(B) to determine whether the proposed rule should be approved or disapproved."; and

(C) in the third sentence, by striking "the preceding sentence" and inserting "this subparagraph".

(d) CONFORMING CHANGE.—Section 19(b)(4)(D) of the Securities Exchange Act of 1934 (15 U.S.C. 78s(b)(4)(D)) is amended to read as follows:

"(D)

"(i) The Commission shall order the temporary suspension of any change in the rules of a clearing agency made by a proposed rule change that has taken effect under paragraph (3), if the appropriate regulatory agency for the clearing agency notifies the Commission not later than 30 days after the date on which the proposed rule change was filed of—

"(I) the determination by the appropriate regulatory agency that the rules of such clearing agency, as so changed, may be inconsistent with the safeguarding of securities or funds in the custody or control of such clearing agency or for which it is responsible; and

"(II) the reasons for the determination described in subclause (I).

"(ii) If the Commission takes action under clause (i), the Commission shall institute proceedings under paragraph (2)(B) to determine if the proposed rule change should be approved or disapproved.".

[Explanation at ¶4030.]

[¶10,917] ACT SEC. 917. STUDY REGARDING FINANCIAL LITERACY AMONG INVESTORS.

(a) IN GENERAL.—The Commission shall conduct a study to identify—

(1) the existing level of financial literacy among retail investors, including subgroups of investors identified by the Commission;

(2) methods to improve the timing, content, and format of disclosures to investors with respect to financial intermediaries, investment products, and investment services;

(3) the most useful and understandable relevant information that retail investors need to make informed financial decisions before engaging a financial intermediary or purchasing an investment product or service that is typically sold to retail investors, including shares of open-end companies, as that term is defined in section 5 of the Investment Company Act of 1940 (15 U.S.C. 80a-5) that are registered under section 8 of that Act;

(4) methods to increase the transparency of expenses and conflicts of interests in transactions involving investment services and products, including shares of open-end companies described in paragraph (3);

(5) the most effective existing private and public efforts to educate investors; and

(6) in consultation with the Financial Literacy and Education Commission, a strategy (including, to the extent practicable, measurable goals and objectives) to increase the financial literacy of investors in order to bring about a positive change in investor behavior.

(b) REPORT.—Not later than 2 years after the date of enactment of this Act, the Commission shall submit a report on the study required under subsection (a) to—

(1) the Committee on Banking, Housing, and Urban Affairs of the Senate; and

(2) the Committee on Financial Services of the House of Representatives.

[Explanation at ¶ 4040.]

[¶ 10,918] ACT SEC. 918. STUDY REGARDING MUTUAL FUND ADVERTISING.

(a) IN GENERAL.—The Comptroller General of the United States shall conduct a study on mutual fund advertising to identify—

(1) existing and proposed regulatory requirements for open-end investment company advertisements;

(2) current marketing practices for the sale of open-end investment company shares, including the use of past performance data, funds that have merged, and incubator funds;

(3) the impact of such advertising on consumers; and

(4) recommendations to improve investor protections in mutual fund advertising and additional information necessary to ensure that investors can make informed financial decisions when purchasing shares.

(b) REPORT.—Not later than 18 months after the date of enactment of this Act, the Comptroller General of the United States shall submit a report on the results of the study conducted under subsection (a) to—

(1) the Committee on Banking, Housing, and Urban Affairs of the United States Senate; and

(2) the Committee on Financial Services of the House of Representatives.

[Explanation at ¶ 4040.]

[¶ 10,919] ACT SEC. 919. CLARIFICATION OF COMMISSION AUTHORITY TO REQUIRE INVESTOR DISCLOSURES BEFORE PURCHASE OF INVESTMENT PRODUCTS AND SERVICES.

Section 15 of the Securities Exchange Act of 1934 (15 U.S.C. 78o) is amended by adding at the end the following:

"(n) DISCLOSURES TO RETAIL INVESTORS.—

"(1) IN GENERAL.—Notwithstanding any other provision of the securities laws, the Commission may issue rules designating documents or information that shall be provided by a broker or dealer to a retail investor before the purchase of an investment product or service by the retail investor.

"(2) CONSIDERATIONS.—In developing any rules under paragraph (1), the Commission shall consider whether the rules will promote investor protection, efficiency, competition, and capital formation.

"(3) FORM AND CONTENTS OF DOCUMENTS AND INFORMATION.—Any documents or information designated under a rule promulgated under paragraph (1) shall—

"(A) be in a summary format; and

"(B) contain clear and concise information about—

"(i) investment objectives, strategies, costs, and risks; and

"(ii) any compensation or other financial incentive received by a broker, dealer, or other intermediary in connection with the purchase of retail investment products.".

[Explanation at ¶ 4035.]

[¶ 10,919A] ACT SEC. 919A. STUDY ON CONFLICTS OF INTEREST.

(a) IN GENERAL.—The Comptroller General of the United States shall conduct a study—

(1) to identify and examine potential conflicts of interest that exist between the staffs of the investment banking and equity and fixed income securities analyst functions within the same firm; and

(2) to make recommendations to Congress designed to protect investors in light of such conflicts.

(b) CONSIDERATIONS.—In conducting the study under subsection (a), the Comptroller General shall—

(1) consider—

(A) the potential for investor harm resulting from conflicts, including consideration of the forms of misconduct engaged in by the several securities firms and individuals that entered into the Global Analyst Research Settlements in 2003 (also known as the "Global Settlement");

(B) the nature and benefits of the undertakings to which those firms agreed in enforcement proceedings, including firewalls between research and investment banking, separate reporting lines, dedicated legal and compliance staffs, allocation of budget, physical separation, compensation, employee performance evaluations, coverage decisions, limitations on soliciting investment banking business, disclosures, transparency, and other measures;

(C) whether any such undertakings should be codified and applied permanently to securities firms, or whether the Commission should adopt rules applying any such undertakings to securities firms; and

(D) whether to recommend regulatory or legislative measures designed to mitigate possible adverse consequences to investors arising from the conflicts of interest or to enhance investor protection or confidence in the integrity of the securities markets; and

(2) consult with State attorneys general, State securities officials, the Commission, the Financial Industry Regulatory Authority ("FINRA"), NYSE Regulation, investor advocates, brokers, dealers, retail investors, institutional investors, and academics.

(c) REPORT.—The Comptroller General shall submit a report on the results of the study required by this section to the Committee on Banking, Housing, and Urban Affairs of the Senate and the Committee on Financial Services of the House of Representatives, not later than 18 months after the date of enactment of this Act.

[Explanation at ¶ 4040.]

[¶ 10,919B] ACT SEC. 919B. STUDY ON IMPROVED INVESTOR ACCESS TO INFORMATION ON INVESTMENT ADVISERS AND BROKER-DEALERS.

(a) STUDY.—

(1) IN GENERAL.—Not later than 6 months after the date of enactment of this Act, the Commission shall complete a study, including recommendations, of ways to improve the access of investors to registration information (including disciplinary actions, regulatory, judicial, and arbitration proceedings, and other information) about registered and previously registered investment advisers, associated persons of investment advisers, brokers and dealers and their associated persons on the existing Central Registration Depository and Investment Adviser Registration Depository systems, as well as identify additional information that should be made publicly available.

(2) CONTENTS.—The study required by subsection (a) shall include an analysis of the advantages and disadvantages of further centralizing access to the information contained in the 2 systems, including—

(A) identification of those data pertinent to investors; and

(B) the identification of the method and format for displaying and publishing such data to enhance accessibility by and utility to investors.

(b) IMPLEMENTATION.—Not later than 18 months after the date of completion of the study required by subsection (a), the Commission shall implement any recommendations of the study.

[Explanation at ¶ 4040.]

[¶ 10,919C] ACT SEC. 919C. STUDY ON FINANCIAL PLANNERS AND THE USE OF FINANCIAL DESIGNATIONS.

(a) IN GENERAL.—The Comptroller General of the United States shall conduct a study to evaluate—

(1) the effectiveness of State and Federal regulations to protect investors and other consumers from individuals who hold themselves out as financial planners through the use of misleading titles, designations, or marketing materials;

(2) current State and Federal oversight structure and regulations for financial planners; and

(3) legal or regulatory gaps in the regulation of financial planners and other individuals who provide or offer to provide financial planning services to consumers.

(b) CONSIDERATIONS.—In conducting the study required under subsection (a), the Comptroller General shall consider—

(1) the role of financial planners in providing advice regarding the management of financial resources, including investment planning, income tax planning, education planning, retirement planning, estate planning, and risk management;

(2) whether current regulations at the State and Federal level provide adequate ethical and professional standards for financial planners;

(3) the possible risk posed to investors and other consumers by individuals who hold themselves out as financial planners or as otherwise providing financial planning services in connection with the sale of financial products, including insurance and securities;

(4) the possible risk posed to investors and other consumers by individuals who otherwise use titles, designations, or marketing materials in a misleading way in connection with the delivery of financial advice;

(6) the ability of investors and other consumers to understand licensing requirements and standards of care that apply to individuals who hold themselves out as financial planners or as otherwise providing financial planning services;

(7) the possible benefits to investors and other consumers of regulation and professional oversight of financial planners; and

(8) any other consideration that the Comptroller General deems necessary or appropriate to effectively execute the study required under subsection (a).

(c) RECOMMENDATIONS.—In providing recommendations for the appropriate regulation of financial planners and other individuals who provide or offer to provide financial planning services, in order to protect investors and other consumers of financial planning services, the Comptroller General shall consider—

(1) the appropriate structure for regulation of financial planners and individuals providing financial planning services; and

(2) the appropriate scope of the regulations needed to protect investors and other consumers, including but not limited to the need to establish competency standards, practice standards, ethical guidelines, disciplinary authority, and transparency to investors and other consumers.

(d) REPORT.—

(1) IN GENERAL.—Not later than 180 days after the date of enactment of this Act, the Comptroller General shall submit a report on the study required under subsection (a) to—

(A) the Committee on Banking, Housing, and Urban Affairs of the Senate;

(B) the Special Committee on Aging of the Senate; and

(C) the Committee on Financial Services of the House of Representatives.

(2) CONTENT REQUIREMENTS.—The report required under paragraph (1) shall describe the findings and determinations made by the Comptroller General in carrying out the study required under subsection (a), including a description of the considerations, analysis, and government, public, industry, nonprofit and consumer input that the Comptroller General considered to make such findings, conclusions, and legislative, regulatory, or other recommendations.

[Explanation at ¶ 4040.]

[¶ 10,919D] ACT SEC. 919D. OMBUDSMAN.

Section 4(g) of the Securities Exchange Act of 1934, as added by section 914, is amended by adding at the end the following:

"(8) OMBUDSMAN.—

"(A) APPOINTMENT.—Not later than 180 days after the date on which the first Investor Advocate is appointed under paragraph (2)(A)(i), the Investor Advocate shall appoint an Ombudsman, who shall report directly to the Investor Advocate.

"(B) DUTIES.—The Ombudsman appointed under subparagraph (A) shall—

"(i) act as a liaison between the Commission and any retail investor in resolving problems that retail investors may have with the Commission or with self-regulatory organizations;

"(ii) review and make recommendations regarding policies and procedures to encourage persons to present questions to the Investor Advocate regarding compliance with the securities laws; and

"(iii) establish safeguards to maintain the confidentiality of communications between the persons described in clause (ii) and the Ombudsman.

"(C) LIMITATION.—In carrying out the duties of the Ombudsman under subparagraph (B), the Ombudsman shall utilize personnel of the Commission to the extent practicable. Nothing in this paragraph shall be construed as replacing, altering, or diminishing the activities of any ombudsman or similar office of any other agency.

"(D) REPORT.—The Ombudsman shall submit a semiannual report to the Investor Advocate that describes the activities and evaluates the effectiveness of the Ombudsman during the preceding year. The Investor Advocate shall include the reports required under this section in the reports required to be submitted by the Inspector Advocate under paragraph (6).".

[Explanation at ¶ 4025.]

Subtitle B—Increasing Regulatory Enforcement and Remedies

[¶ 10,921] ACT SEC. 921. AUTHORITY TO RESTRICT MANDATORY PRE-DISPUTE ARBITRATION.

(a) AMENDMENT TO SECURITIES EXCHANGE ACT OF 1934.—Section 15 of the Securities Exchange Act of 1934 (15 U.S.C. 78o), as amended by this title, is further amended by adding at the end the following new subsection:

"(o) AUTHORITY TO RESTRICT MANDATORY PRE-DISPUTE ARBITRATION.—The Commission, by rule, may prohibit, or impose conditions or limitations on the use of, agreements that require customers or clients of any broker, dealer, or municipal securities dealer to arbitrate any future dispute between them arising under the Federal securities laws, the rules and regulations thereunder, or the rules of a self-regulatory organization if it finds that such prohibition, imposition of conditions, or limitations are in the public interest and for the protection of investors.".

(b) AMENDMENT TO INVESTMENT ADVISERS ACT OF 1940.—Section 205 of the Investment Advisers Act of 1940 (15 U.S.C. 80b-5) is amended by adding at the end the following new subsection:

"(f) AUTHORITY TO RESTRICT MANDATORY PRE-DISPUTE ARBITRATION.—The Commission, by rule, may prohibit, or impose conditions or limitations on the use of, agreements that require customers or clients of any investment adviser to arbitrate any future dispute between them arising under the Federal securities laws, the rules and regulations thereunder, or the rules of a self-regulatory organization if it finds that such prohibition, imposition of conditions, or limitations are in the public interest and for the protection of investors.".

[Explanation at ¶ 4050 and ¶ 4055.]

[¶ 10,922] ACT SEC. 922. WHISTLEBLOWER PROTECTION.

(a) IN GENERAL.—The Securities Exchange Act of 1934 (15 U.S.C. 78a et seq.) is amended by inserting after section 21E the following:

"SEC. 21F. SECURITIES WHISTLEBLOWER INCENTIVES AND PROTECTION.

"(a) DEFINITIONS.—In this section the following definitions shall apply:

"(1) COVERED JUDICIAL OR ADMINISTRATIVE ACTION.—The term 'covered judicial or administrative action' means any judicial or administrative action brought by the Commission under the securities laws that results in monetary sanctions exceeding $1,000,000.

"(2) FUND.—The term 'Fund' means the Securities and Exchange Commission Investor Protection Fund.

"(3) ORIGINAL INFORMATION.—The term 'original information' means information that—

"(A) is derived from the independent knowledge or analysis of a whistleblower;

"(B) is not known to the Commission from any other source, unless the whistleblower is the original source of the information; and

"(C) is not exclusively derived from an allegation made in a judicial or administrative hearing, in a governmental report, hearing, audit, or investigation, or from the news media, unless the whistleblower is a source of the information.

"(4) MONETARY SANCTIONS.—The term 'monetary sanctions', when used with respect to any judicial or administrative action, means—

"(A) any monies, including penalties, disgorgement, and interest, ordered to be paid; and

"(B) any monies deposited into a disgorgement fund or other fund pursuant to section 308(b) of the Sarbanes-Oxley Act of 2002 (15 U.S.C. 7246(b)), as a result of such action or any settlement of such action.

"(5) RELATED ACTION.—The term 'related action', when used with respect to any judicial or administrative action brought by the Commission under the securities laws, means any judicial or administrative action brought by an entity described in subclauses (I) through (IV) of subsection (h)(2)(D)(i) that is based upon the original information provided by a whistleblower pursuant to subsection (a) that led to the successful enforcement of the Commission action.

"(6) WHISTLEBLOWER.—The term 'whistleblower' means any individual who provides, or 2 or more individuals acting jointly who provide, information relating to a violation of the securities laws to the Commission, in a manner established, by rule or regulation, by the Commission.

"(b) AWARDS.—

"(1) IN GENERAL.—In any covered judicial or administrative action, or related action, the Commission, under regulations prescribed by the Commission and subject to subsection (c), shall pay an award or awards to 1 or more whistleblowers who voluntarily provided original information to the Commission that led to the successful enforcement of the covered judicial or administrative action, or related action, in an aggregate amount equal to—

"(A) not less than 10 percent, in total, of what has been collected of the monetary sanctions imposed in the action or related actions; and

"(B) not more than 30 percent, in total, of what has been collected of the monetary sanctions imposed in the action or related actions.

"(2) PAYMENT OF AWARDS.—Any amount paid under paragraph (1) shall be paid from the Fund.

"(c) DETERMINATION OF AMOUNT OF AWARD; DENIAL OF AWARD.—

"(1) DETERMINATION OF AMOUNT OF AWARD.—

"(A) DISCRETION.—The determination of the amount of an award made under subsection (b) shall be in the discretion of the Commission.

"(B) CRITERIA.—In determining the amount of an award made under subsection (b), the Commission—

"(i) shall take into consideration—

"(I) the significance of the information provided by the whistleblower to the success of the covered judicial or administrative action;

"(II) the degree of assistance provided by the whistleblower and any legal representative of the whistleblower in a covered judicial or administrative action;

"(III) the programmatic interest of the Commission in deterring violations of the securities laws by making awards to whistleblowers who provide information that lead to the successful enforcement of such laws; and

"(IV) such additional relevant factors as the Commission may establish by rule or regulation; and

"(ii) shall not take into consideration the balance of the Fund.

"(2) DENIAL OF AWARD.—No award under subsection (b) shall be made—

"(A) to any whistleblower who is, or was at the time the whistleblower acquired the original information submitted to the Commission, a member, officer, or employee of—

"(i) an appropriate regulatory agency;

"(ii) the Department of Justice;

"(iii) a self-regulatory organization;

"(iv) the Public Company Accounting Oversight Board; or

"(v) a law enforcement organization;

"(B) to any whistleblower who is convicted of a criminal violation related to the judicial or administrative action for which the whistleblower otherwise could receive an award under this section;

"(C) to any whistleblower who gains the information through the performance of an audit of financial statements required under the securities laws and for whom such submission would be contrary to the requirements of section 10A of the Securities Exchange Act of 1934 (15 U.S.C. 78j-1); or

"(D) to any whistleblower who fails to submit information to the Commission in such form as the Commission may, by rule, require.

"(d) REPRESENTATION.—

"(1) PERMITTED REPRESENTATION.—Any whistleblower who makes a claim for an award under subsection (b) may be represented by counsel.

"(2) REQUIRED REPRESENTATION.—

"(A) IN GENERAL.—Any whistleblower who anonymously makes a claim for an award under subsection (b) shall be represented by counsel if the whistleblower anonymously submits the information upon which the claim is based.

"(B) DISCLOSURE OF IDENTITY.—Prior to the payment of an award, a whistleblower shall disclose the identity of the whistleblower and provide such other information as the Commission may require, directly or through counsel for the whistleblower.

"(e) NO CONTRACT NECESSARY.—No contract with the Commission is necessary for any whistleblower to receive an award under subsection (b), unless otherwise required by the Commission by rule or regulation.

"(f) APPEALS.—Any determination made under this section, including whether, to whom, or in what amount to make awards, shall be in the discretion of the Commission. Any such determination, except the determination of the amount of an award if the award was made in accordance with subsection (b), may be appealed to the appropriate court of appeals of the United States not more than 30 days after the determination is issued by the Commission. The court shall review the determination made by the Commission in accordance with section 706 of title 5, United States Code.

"(g) INVESTOR PROTECTION FUND.—

"(1) FUND ESTABLISHED.—There is established in the Treasury of the United States a fund to be known as the 'Securities and Exchange Commission Investor Protection Fund'.

"(2) USE OF FUND.—The Fund shall be available to the Commission, without further appropriation or fiscal year limitation, for—

"(A) paying awards to whistleblowers as provided in subsection (b); and

"(B) funding the activities of the Inspector General of the Commission under section 4(i).

"(3) DEPOSITS AND CREDITS.—

"(A) IN GENERAL.—There shall be deposited into or credited to the Fund an amount equal to—

"(i) any monetary sanction collected by the Commission in any judicial or administrative action brought by the Commission under the securities laws that is not added to a disgorgement fund or other fund under section 308 of the Sarbanes-Oxley Act of 2002 (15 U.S.C. 7246) or otherwise distributed to victims of a violation of the securities laws, or the rules and regulations thereunder, underlying such action, unless the balance of the Fund at the time the monetary sanction is collected exceeds $300,000,000;

"(ii) any monetary sanction added to a disgorgement fund or other fund under section 308 of the Sarbanes-Oxley Act of 2002 (15 U.S.C. 7246) that is not distributed to the victims for whom the Fund was established, unless the balance of the disgorgement fund at the time the determination is made not to distribute the monetary sanction to such victims exceeds $200,000,000; and

"(iii) all income from investments made under paragraph (4).

"(B) ADDITIONAL AMOUNTS.—If the amounts deposited into or credited to the Fund under subparagraph (A) are not sufficient to satisfy an award made under subsection (b), there shall be deposited into or credited to the Fund an amount equal to the unsatisfied portion of the award from any monetary sanction collected by the Commission in the covered judicial or administrative action on which the award is based.

"(4) INVESTMENTS.—

"(A) AMOUNTS IN FUND MAY BE INVESTED.—The Commission may request the Secretary of the Treasury to invest the portion of the Fund that is not, in the discretion of the Commission, required to meet the current needs of the Fund.

"(B) ELIGIBLE INVESTMENTS.—Investments shall be made by the Secretary of the Treasury in obligations of the United States or obligations that are guaranteed as to principal and interest by the United States, with maturities suitable to the needs of the Fund as determined by the Commission on the record.

"(C) INTEREST AND PROCEEDS CREDITED.—The interest on, and the proceeds from the sale or redemption of, any obligations held in the Fund shall be credited to the Fund.

"(5) REPORTS TO CONGRESS.—Not later than October 30 of each fiscal year beginning after the date of enactment of this subsection, the Commission shall submit to the Committee on Banking, Housing, and Urban Affairs of the Senate, and the Committee on Financial Services of the House of Representatives a report on—

"(A) the whistleblower award program, established under this section, including—

"(i) a description of the number of awards granted; and

"(ii) the types of cases in which awards were granted during the preceding fiscal year;

"(B) the balance of the Fund at the beginning of the preceding fiscal year;

"(C) the amounts deposited into or credited to the Fund during the preceding fiscal year;

"(D) the amount of earnings on investments made under paragraph (4) during the preceding fiscal year;

"(E) the amount paid from the Fund during the preceding fiscal year to whistleblowers pursuant to subsection (b);

"(F) the balance of the Fund at the end of the preceding fiscal year; and

"(G) a complete set of audited financial statements, including—

"(i) a balance sheet;

"(ii) income statement; and

"(iii) cash flow analysis.

"(h) PROTECTION OF WHISTLEBLOWERS.—

"(1) PROHIBITION AGAINST RETALIATION.—

"(A) IN GENERAL.—No employer may discharge, demote, suspend, threaten, harass, directly or indirectly, or in any other manner discriminate against, a whistleblower in the terms and conditions of employment because of any lawful act done by the whistleblower—

"(i) in providing information to the Commission in accordance with this section;

"(ii) in initiating, testifying in, or assisting in any investigation or judicial or administrative action of the Commission based upon or related to such information; or

"(iii) in making disclosures that are required or protected under the Sarbanes-Oxley Act of 2002 (15 U.S.C. 7201 et seq.), the Securities Exchange Act of 1934 (15 U.S.C. 78a et seq.), including section 10A(m) of such Act (15 U.S.C. 78f(m)), section 1513(e) of title 18, United States Code, and any other law, rule, or regulation subject to the jurisdiction of the Commission.

"(B) ENFORCEMENT.—

"(i) CAUSE OF ACTION.—An individual who alleges discharge or other discrimination in violation of subparagraph (A) may bring an action under this subsection in the appropriate district court of the United States for the relief provided in subparagraph (C).

"(ii) SUBPOENAS.—A subpoena requiring the attendance of a witness at a trial or hearing conducted under this section may be served at any place in the United States.

"(iii) STATUTE OF LIMITATIONS.—

"(I) IN GENERAL.—An action under this subsection may not be brought—

"(aa) more than 6 years after the date on which the violation of subparagraph (A) occurred; or

"(bb) more than 3 years after the date when facts material to the right of action are known or reasonably should have been known by the employee alleging a violation of subparagraph (A).

"(II) REQUIRED ACTION WITHIN 10 YEARS.—Notwithstanding subclause (I), an action under this subsection may not in any circumstance be brought more than 10 years after the date on which the violation occurs.

"(C) RELIEF.—Relief for an individual prevailing in an action brought under subparagraph (B) shall include—

"(i) reinstatement with the same seniority status that the individual would have had, but for the discrimination;

"(ii) 2 times the amount of back pay otherwise owed to the individual, with interest; and

"(iii) compensation for litigation costs, expert witness fees, and reasonable attorneys' fees.

"(2) CONFIDENTIALITY.—

"(A) IN GENERAL.—Except as provided in subparagraphs (B) and (C), the Commission and any officer or employee of the Commission shall not disclose any information, including information provided by a whistleblower to the Commission, which could reasonably be expected to reveal the identity of a whistleblower, except in accordance with the provisions of section 552a of title 5, United States Code, unless and until required to be disclosed to a defendant or respondent in connection with a public proceeding instituted by the Commission or any entity described in subparagraph (C). For purposes of section 552 of title 5, United States Code, this paragraph shall be considered a statute described in subsection (b)(3)(B) of such section.

"(B) EXEMPTED STATUTE.—For purposes of section 552 of title 5, United States Code, this paragraph shall be considered a statute described in subsection (b)(3)(B) of such section 552.

"(C) RULE OF CONSTRUCTION.—Nothing in this section is intended to limit, or shall be construed to limit, the ability of the Attorney General to present such evidence to a grand jury or to share such evidence with potential witnesses or defendants in the course of an ongoing criminal investigation.

"(D) AVAILABILITY TO GOVERNMENT AGENCIES.—

"(i) IN GENERAL.—Without the loss of its status as confidential in the hands of the Commission, all information referred to in subparagraph (A) may, in the discretion of the Commission, when determined by the Commission to be necessary to accomplish the purposes of this Act and to protect investors, be made available to—

"(I) the Attorney General of the United States;

"(II) an appropriate regulatory authority;

"(III) a self-regulatory organization;

"(IV) a State attorney general in connection with any criminal investigation;

"(V) any appropriate State regulatory authority;

"(VI) the Public Company Accounting Oversight Board;

"(VII) a foreign securities authority; and

"(VIII) a foreign law enforcement authority.

"(ii) CONFIDENTIALITY.—

"(I) IN GENERAL.—Each of the entities described in subclauses (I) through (VI) of clause (i) shall maintain such information as confidential in accordance with the requirements established under subparagraph (A).

"(II) FOREIGN AUTHORITIES.—Each of the entities described in subclauses (VII) and (VIII) of clause (i) shall maintain such information in accordance with such assurances of confidentiality as the Commission determines appropriate.

"(3) RIGHTS RETAINED.—Nothing in this section shall be deemed to diminish the rights, privileges, or remedies of any whistleblower under any Federal or State law, or under any collective bargaining agreement.

"(i) PROVISION OF FALSE INFORMATION.—A whistleblower shall not be entitled to an award under this section if the whistleblower—

"(1) knowingly and willfully makes any false, fictitious, or fraudulent statement or representation; or

"(2) uses any false writing or document knowing the writing or document contains any false, fictitious, or fraudulent statement or entry.

"(j) RULEMAKING AUTHORITY.—The Commission shall have the authority to issue such rules and regulations as may be necessary or appropriate to implement the provisions of this section consistent with the purposes of this section.".

(b) PROTECTION FOR EMPLOYEES OF NATIONALLY RECOGNIZED STATISTICAL RATING ORGANIZATIONS.—Section 1514A(a) of title 18, United States Code, is amended—

(1) by inserting "or nationally recognized statistical rating organization (as defined in section 3(a) of the Securities Exchange Act of 1934 (15 U.S.C. 78c)," after "78o(d)),"; and

(2) by inserting "or nationally recognized statistical rating organization" after "such company".

(c) SECTION 1514A OF TITLE 18, UNITED STATES CODE.—

(1) STATUTE OF LIMITATIONS; JURY TRIAL.—Section 1514A(b)(2) of title 18, United States Code, is amended—

(A) in subparagraph (D)—

(i) by striking "90" and inserting "180"; and

(ii) by striking the period at the end and inserting ", or after the date on which the employee became aware of the violation."; and

(B) by adding at the end the following:

"(E) JURY TRIAL.—A party to an action brought under paragraph (1)(B) shall be entitled to trial by jury.".

(2) PRIVATE SECURITIES LITIGATION WITNESSES; NONENFORCEABILITY; INFORMATION.—Section 1514A of title 18, United States Code, is amended by adding at the end the following:

"(e) NONENFORCEABILITY OF CERTAIN PROVISIONS WAIVING RIGHTS AND REMEDIES OR REQUIRING ARBITRATION OF DISPUTES.—

"(1) WAIVER OF RIGHTS AND REMEDIES.—The rights and remedies provided for in this section may not be waived by any agreement, policy form, or condition of employment, including by a predispute arbitration agreement.

"(2) PREDISPUTE ARBITRATION AGREEMENTS.—No predispute arbitration agreement shall be valid or enforceable, if the agreement requires arbitration of a dispute arising under this section.".

(d) STUDY OF WHISTLEBLOWER PROTECTION PROGRAM.—

(1) STUDY.—The Inspector General of the Commission shall conduct a study of the whistleblower protections established under the amendments made by this section, including—

(A) whether the final rules and regulation issued under the amendments made by this section have made the whistleblower protection program (referred to in this subsection as the "program") clearly defined and user-friendly;

(B) whether the program is promoted on the website of the Commission and has been widely publicized;

(C) whether the Commission is prompt in—

(i) responding to—

(I) information provided by whistleblowers; and

(II) applications for awards filed by whistleblowers;

(ii) updating whistleblowers about the status of their applications; and

(iii) otherwise communicating with the interested parties;

(D) whether the minimum and maximum reward levels are adequate to entice whistleblowers to come forward with information and whether the reward levels are so high as to encourage illegitimate whistleblower claims;

(E) whether the appeals process has been unduly burdensome for the Commission;

(F) whether the funding mechanism for the Investor Protection Fund is adequate;

(G) whether, in the interest of protecting investors and identifying and preventing fraud, it would be useful for Congress to consider empowering whistleblowers or other individuals, who have already attempted to pursue the case through the Commission, to have a private right of action to bring suit based on the facts of the same case, on behalf of the Government and themselves, against persons who have committee securities fraud;

(H)(i) whether the exemption under section 552(b)(3) of title 5 (known as the Freedom of Information Act) established in section 21F(h)(2)(A) of the Securities Exchange Act of 1934, as added by this Act, aids whistleblowers in disclosing information to the Commission;

(ii) what impact the exemption described in clause (i) has had on the ability of the public to access information about the regulation and enforcement by the Commission of securities; and

(iii) any recommendations on whether the exemption described in clause (i) should remain in effect; and

(I) such other matters as the Inspector General deems appropriate.

(2) REPORT.—Not later than 30 months after the date of enactment of this Act, the Inspector General shall—

(A) submit a report on the findings of the study required under paragraph (1) to the Committee on Banking, Housing, and Urban Affairs of the Senate and the Committee on Financial Services of the House; and

(B) make the report described in subparagraph (A) available to the public through publication of the report on the website of the Commission.

[Explanation at ¶ 4060 and ¶ 4215.]

[¶ 10,923] ACT SEC. 923. CONFORMING AMENDMENTS FOR WHISTLEBLOWER PROTECTION.

(a) IN GENERAL.—

(1) SECURITIES ACT OF 1933.—Section 20(d)(3)(A) of the Securities Act of 1933 (15 U.S.C. 77t(d)(3)(A)) is amended by inserting "and section 21F of the Securities Exchange Act of 1934" after "the Sarbanes-Oxley Act of 2002".

(2) INVESTMENT COMPANY ACT OF 1940.—Section 42(e)(3)(A) of the Investment Company Act of 1940 (15 U.S.C. 80a-41(e)(3)(A)) is amended by inserting "and section 21F of the Securities Exchange Act of 1934" after "the Sarbanes-Oxley Act of 2002".

(3) INVESTMENT ADVISERS ACT OF 1940.—Section 209(e)(3)(A) of the Investment Advisers Act of 1940 (15 U.S.C. 80b-9(e)(3)(A)) is amended by inserting "and section 21F of the Securities Exchange Act of 1934" after "the Sarbanes-Oxley Act of 2002".

(b) SECURITIES EXCHANGE ACT.—

(1) SECTION 21.—Section 21(d)(3)(C)(i) of the Securities Exchange Act of 1934 (15 U.S.C. 78u(d)(3)(C)(i)) is amended by inserting "and section 21F of this title" after "the Sarbanes-Oxley Act of 2002".

(2) SECTION 21A.—Section 21A of the Securities Exchange Act of 1934 (15 U.S.C. 78u-1) is amended—

(A) in subsection (d)(1) by—

(i) striking "(subject to subsection (e))"; and

(ii) inserting "and section 21F of this title" after "the Sarbanes-Oxley Act of 2002";

(B) by striking subsection (e); and

(C) by redesignating subsections (f) and (g) as subsections (e) and (f), respectively.

[Explanation at ¶ 4060.]

[¶ 10,924] ACT SEC. 924. IMPLEMENTATION AND TRANSITION PROVISIONS FOR WHISTLEBLOWER PROTECTION.

(a) IMPLEMENTING RULES.—The Commission shall issue final regulations implementing the provisions of section 21F of the Securities Exchange Act of 1934, as added by this subtitle, not later than 270 days after the date of enactment of this Act.

(b) ORIGINAL INFORMATION.—Information provided to the Commission in writing by a whistleblower shall not lose the status of original information (as defined in section 21F(a)(3) of the Securities Exchange Act of 1934, as added by this subtitle) solely because the whistleblower provided the information prior to the effective date of the regulations, if the information is provided by the whistleblower after the date of enactment of this subtitle.

(c) AWARDS.—A whistleblower may receive an award pursuant to section 21F of the Securities Exchange Act of 1934, as added by this subtitle, regardless of whether any violation of a provision of the securities laws, or a rule or regulation thereunder, underlying the judicial or administrative action upon which the award is based, occurred prior to the date of enactment of this subtitle.

(d) ADMINISTRATION AND ENFORCEMENT.—The Securities and Exchange Commission shall establish a separate office within the Commission to administer and enforce the provisions of section 21F of the Securities Exchange Act of 1934 (as add by section 922(a)). Such office shall report annually to the Committee on Banking, Housing, and Urban Affairs of the Senate and the Committee on Financial Services of the House of Representatives on its activities, whistleblower complaints, and the response of the Commission to such complaints.

[Explanation at ¶ 4060.]

[¶ 10,925] ACT SEC. 925. COLLATERAL BARS.

(a) SECURITIES EXCHANGE ACT OF 1934.—

(1) SECTION 15.—Section 15(b)(6)(A) of the Securities Exchange Act of 1934 (15 U.S.C. 78o(b)(6)(A)) is amended by striking "12 months, or bar such person from being associated with a broker or dealer," and inserting "12 months, or bar any such person from being associated with a broker, dealer, investment adviser, municipal securities dealer, municipal advisor, transfer agent, or nationally recognized statistical rating organization,".

(2) SECTION 15B.—Section 15B(c)(4) of the Securities Exchange Act of 1934 (15 U.S.C. 78o-4(c)(4)) is amended by striking "twelve months or bar any such person from being associated with a municipal securities dealer," and inserting "12 months or bar any such person from being associated with a broker, dealer, investment adviser, municipal securities dealer, municipal advisor, transfer agent, or nationally recognized statistical rating organization,".

(3) SECTION 17A.—Section 17A(c)(4)(C) of the Securities Exchange Act of 1934 (15 U.S.C. 78q-1(c)(4)(C)) is amended by striking "twelve months or bar any such person from being associated with the transfer agent," and inserting "12 months or bar any such person from being associated with any transfer agent, broker, dealer, investment adviser, municipal securities dealer, municipal advisor, or nationally recognized statistical rating organization,".

(b) INVESTMENT ADVISERS ACT OF 1940.—Section 203(f) of the Investment Advisers Act of 1940 (15 U.S.C. 80b-3(f)) is amended by striking "twelve months or bar any such person from being associated with an investment adviser," and inserting "12 months or bar any such person from being associated with an investment adviser, broker, dealer, municipal securities dealer, municipal advisor, transfer agent, or nationally recognized statistical rating organization,".

[Explanation at ¶ 4065.]

[¶ 10,926] ACT SEC. 926. DISQUALIFYING FELONS AND OTHER "BAD ACTORS" FROM REGULATION D OFFERINGS.

Not later than 1 year after the date of enactment of this Act, the Commission shall issue rules for the disqualification of offerings and sales of securities made under section 230.506 of title 17, Code of Federal Regulations, that—

(1) are substantially similar to the provisions of section 230.262 of title 17, Code of Federal Regulations, or any successor thereto; and

(2) disqualify any offering or sale of securities by a person that—

(A) is subject to a final order of a State securities commission (or an agency or officer of a State performing like functions), a State authority that supervises or examines banks, savings associations, or credit unions, a State insurance commission (or an agency or officer of a State performing like functions), an appropriate Federal banking agency, or the National Credit Union Administration, that—

(i) bars the person from—

(I) association with an entity regulated by such commission, authority, agency, or officer;

(II) engaging in the business of securities, insurance, or banking; or

(III) engaging in savings association or credit union activities; or

(ii) constitutes a final order based on a violation of any law or regulation that prohibits fraudulent, manipulative, or deceptive conduct within the 10-year period ending on the date of the filing of the offer or sale; or

(B) has been convicted of any felony or misdemeanor in connection with the purchase or sale of any security or involving the making of any false filing with the Commission.

[Explanation at ¶ 4070.]

[¶ 10,927] ACT SEC. 927. EQUAL TREATMENT OF SELF-REGULATORY ORGANIZATION RULES.

Section 29(a) of the Securities Exchange Act of 1934 (15 U.S.C. 78cc(a)) is amended by striking "an exchange required thereby" and inserting "a self-regulatory organization,".

[Explanation at ¶ 4075.]

[¶ 10,928] ACT SEC. 928. CLARIFICATION THAT SECTION 205 OF THE INVESTMENT ADVISERS ACT OF 1940 DOES NOT APPLY TO STATE-REGISTERED ADVISERS.

Section 205(a) of the Investment Advisers Act of 1940 (15 U.S.C. 80b-5(a)) is amended, in the matter preceding paragraph (1)—

(1) by striking ", unless exempt from registration pursuant to section 203(b)," and inserting "registered or required to be registered with the Commission";

(2) by striking "make use of the mails or any means or instrumentality of interstate commerce, directly or indirectly, to"; and

(3) by striking "to" after "in any way".

[Explanation at ¶ 4080.]

[¶ 10,929] ACT SEC. 929. UNLAWFUL MARGIN LENDING.

Section 7(c)(1)(A) of the Securities Exchange Act of 1934 (15 U.S.C. 78g(c)(1)(A)) is amended by striking "; and" and inserting "; or".

[¶ 10,929A] ACT SEC. 929A. PROTECTION FOR EMPLOYEES OF SUBSIDIARIES AND AFFILIATES OF PUBLICLY TRADED COMPANIES.

Section 1514A of title 18, United States Code, is amended by inserting "including any subsidiary or affiliate whose financial information is included in the consolidated financial statements of such company" after "the Securities Exchange Act of 1934 (15 U.S.C. 78o(d))".

[Explanation at ¶ 4060.]

[¶ 10,929B] ACT SEC. 929B. FAIR FUND AMENDMENTS.

Section 308 of the Sarbanes-Oxley Act of 2002 (15 U.S.C. 7246(a)) is amended—

(1) by striking subsection (a) and inserting the following:

"(a) CIVIL PENALTIES TO BE USED FOR THE RELIEF OF VICTIMS.—If, in any judicial or administrative action brought by the Commission under the securities laws, the Commission obtains a civil penalty against any person for a violation of such laws, or such person agrees, in settlement of any such action, to such civil penalty, the amount of such civil penalty shall, on the motion or at the direction of the Commission, be added to and become part of a disgorgement fund or other fund established for the benefit of the victims of such violation.";

(2) in subsection (b)—

(A) by striking "for a disgorgement fund described in subsection (a)" and inserting "for a disgorgement fund or other fund described in subsection (a)"; and

(B) by striking "in the disgorgement fund" and inserting "in such fund"; and

(3) by striking subsection (e).

[Explanation at ¶ 4090.]

[¶ 10,929C] ACT SEC. 929C. INCREASING THE BORROWING LIMIT ON TREASURY LOANS.

Section 4(h) of the Securities Investor Protection Act of 1970 (15 U.S.C. 78ddd(h)) is amended in the first sentence, by striking "$1,000,000,000" and inserting "$2,500,000,000".

[Explanation at ¶ 4095.]

[¶ 10,929D] ACT SEC. 929D. LOST AND STOLEN SECURITIES.

Section 17(f)(1) of the Securities Exchange Act of 1934 (15 U.S.C. 78q(f)(1)) is amended—

(1) in subparagraph (A), by striking "missing, lost, counterfeit, or stolen securities" and inserting "securities that are missing, lost, counterfeit, stolen, or cancelled"; and

(2) in subparagraph (B), by striking "or stolen" and inserting "stolen, cancelled, or reported in such other manner as the Commission, by rule, may prescribe".

[Explanation at ¶ 4100.]

[¶ 10,929E] ACT SEC. 929E. NATIONWIDE SERVICE OF SUBPOENAS.

(a) SECURITIES ACT OF 1933.—Section 22(a) of the Securities Act of 1933 (15 U.S.C. 77v(a)) is amended by inserting after the second sentence the following: "In any action or proceeding instituted by the Commission under this title in a United States district court for any judicial district, a subpoena issued to compel the attendance of a witness or the production of documents or tangible things (or both) at a hearing or trial may be served at any place within the United States. Rule 45(c)(3)(A)(ii) of the Federal Rules of Civil Procedure shall not apply to a subpoena issued under the preceding sentence.".

(b) SECURITIES EXCHANGE ACT OF 1934.—Section 27 of the Securities Exchange Act of 1934 (15 U.S.C. 78aa) is amended by inserting after the third sentence the following: "In any action or proceeding instituted by the Commission under this title in a United States district court for any judicial district, a subpoena issued to compel the attendance of a witness or the production of documents or tangible things (or both) at a hearing or trial may be served at any place within the United States. Rule 45(c)(3) (A) (ii) of the Federal Rules of Civil Procedure shall not apply to a subpoena issued under the preceding sentence.".

(c) INVESTMENT COMPANY ACT OF 1940.—Section 44 of the Investment Company Act of 1940 (15 U.S.C. 80a-43) is amended by inserting after the fourth sentence the following: "In any action or proceeding instituted by the Commission under this title in a United States district court for any judicial district, a subpoena issued to compel the attendance of a witness or the production of documents or tangible things (or both) at a hearing or trial may be served at any place within the United States. Rule 45(c)(3)(A)(ii) of the Federal Rules of Civil Procedure shall not apply to a subpoena issued under the preceding sentence.".

(d) INVESTMENT ADVISERS ACT OF 1940.—Section 214 of the Investment Advisers Act of 1940 (15 U.S.C. 80b-14) is amended by inserting after the third sentence the following: "In any action or proceeding instituted by the Commission under this title in a United States district court for any judicial district, a subpoena issued to compel the attendance of a witness or the production of documents or tangible things (or both) at a hearing or trial may be served at any place within the United States. Rule 45(c)(3)(A)(ii) of the Federal Rules of Civil Procedure shall not apply to a subpoena issued under the preceding sentence.".

[Explanation at ¶ 4105.]

[¶ 10,929F] ACT SEC. 929F. FORMERLY ASSOCIATED PERSONS.

(a) MEMBER OR EMPLOYEE OF THE MUNICIPAL SECURITIES RULEMAKING BOARD.—Section 15B(c)(8) of the Securities Exchange Act of 1934 (15 U.S.C. 78o-4(c)(8)) is amended by striking "any member or employee" and inserting "any person who is, or at the time of the alleged violation or abuse was, a member or employee".

(b) PERSON ASSOCIATED WITH A GOVERNMENT SECURITIES BROKER OR DEALER.—Section 15C(c) of the Securities Exchange Act of 1934 (15 U.S.C. 78o-5(c)) is amended—

(1) in paragraph (1)(C), by striking "any person associated, or seeking to become associated," and inserting "any person who is, or at the time of the alleged misconduct was, associated or seeking to become associated"; and

(2) in paragraph (2)—

(A) in subparagraph (A), by inserting ", seeking to become associated, or, at the time of the alleged misconduct, associated or seeking to become associated" after "any person associated"; and

(B) in subparagraph (B), by inserting ", seeking to become associated, or, at the time of the alleged misconduct, associated or seeking to become associated" after "any person associated".

(c) PERSON ASSOCIATED WITH A MEMBER OF A NATIONAL SECURITIES EXCHANGE OR REGISTERED SECURITIES ASSOCIATION.—Section 21(a)(1) of the Securities Exchange Act of 1934 (15 U.S.C. 78u(a)(1)) is amended, in the first sentence, by inserting ", or, as to any act or practice, or omission to act, while associated with a member, formerly associated" after "member or a person associated".

(d) PARTICIPANT OF A REGISTERED CLEARING AGENCY.—Section 21(a)(1) of the Securities Exchange Act of 1934 (15 U.S.C. 78u(a)(1)) is amended, in the first sentence, by inserting "or, as to any act or practice, or omission to act, while a participant, was a participant," after "in which such person is a participant,".

(e) OFFICER OR DIRECTOR OF A SELF-REGULATORY ORGANIZATION.—Section 19(h)(4) of the Securities Exchange Act of 1934 (15 U.S.C. 78s(h)(4)) is amended—

(1) by striking "any officer or director" and inserting "any person who is, or at the time of the alleged misconduct was, an officer or director"; and

(2) by striking "such officer or director" and inserting "such person".

(f) OFFICER OR DIRECTOR OF AN INVESTMENT COMPANY.—Section 36(a) of the Investment Company Act of 1940 (15 U.S.C. 80a-35(a)) is amended—

(1) by striking "a person serving or acting" and inserting "a person who is, or at the time of the alleged misconduct was, serving or acting"; and

(2) by striking "such person so serves or acts" and inserting "such person so serves or acts, or at the time of the alleged misconduct, so served or acted".

(g) PERSON ASSOCIATED WITH A PUBLIC ACCOUNTING FIRM.—

(1) SARBANES-OXLEY ACT OF 2002 AMENDMENT.—Section 2(a)(9) of the Sarbanes-Oxley Act of 2002 (15 U.S.C. 7201(9)) is amended by adding at the end the following:

"(C) INVESTIGATIVE AND ENFORCEMENT AUTHORITY.—For purposes of sections 3(c), 101(c), 105, and 107(c) and the rules of the Board and Commission issued thereunder, except to the extent specifically excepted by such rules, the terms defined in subparagraph (A) shall include any person associated, seeking to become associated, or formerly associated with a public accounting firm, except that—

"(i) the authority to conduct an investigation of such person under section 105(b) shall apply only with respect to any act or practice, or omission to act, by the person while such person was associated or seeking to become associated with a registered public accounting firm; and

"(ii) the authority to commence a disciplinary proceeding under section 105(c)(1), or impose sanctions under section 105(c)(4), against such person shall apply only with respect to—

"(I) conduct occurring while such person was associated or seeking to become associated with a registered public accounting firm; or

"(II) non-cooperation, as described in section 105(b)(3), with respect to a demand in a Board investigation for testimony, documents, or other information relating to a period when such person was associated or seeking to become associated with a registered public accounting firm.".

(2) SECURITIES EXCHANGE ACT OF 1934 AMENDMENT.—Section 21(a)(1) of the Securities Exchange Act of 1934 (15 U.S.C. 78u(a)(1)) is amended by striking "or a person associated with such a firm" and inserting ", a person associated with such a firm, or, as to any act, practice, or omission to act, while associated with such firm, a person formerly associated with such a firm".

(h) SUPERVISORY PERSONNEL OF AN AUDIT FIRM.—Section 105(c)(6) of the Sarbanes-Oxley Act of 2002 (15 U.S.C. 7215(c)(6)) is amended—

(1) in subparagraph (A), by striking "the supervisory personnel" and inserting "any person who is, or at the time of the alleged failure reasonably to supervise was, a supervisory person"; and

(2) in subparagraph (B)—

(A) by striking "No associated person" and inserting "No current or former supervisory person"; and

(B) by striking "any other person" and inserting "any associated person".

(i) MEMBER OF THE PUBLIC COMPANY ACCOUNTING OVERSIGHT BOARD.—Section 107(d)(3) of the Sarbanes-Oxley Act of 2002 (15 U.S.C. 7217(d)(3)) is amended by striking "any member" and inserting "any person who is, or at the time of the alleged misconduct was, a member".

[Explanation at ¶4110.]

[¶10,929G] ACT SEC. 929G. STREAMLINED HIRING AUTHORITY FOR MARKET SPECIALISTS.

(a) APPOINTMENT AUTHORITY.—Section 3114 of title 5, United States Code, is amended by striking the section heading and all that follows through the end of subsection (a) and inserting the following:

"§3114. Appointment of candidates to certain positions in the competitive service by the Securities and Exchange Commission

"(a) APPLICABILITY.—This section applies with respect to any position of accountant, economist, and securities compliance examiner at the Commission that is in the competitive service, and any position at the Commission in the competitive service that requires specialized knowledge of financial and capital market formation or regulation, financial market structures or surveillance, or information technology.".

(b) CLERICAL AMENDMENT.—The table of sections for chapter 31 of title 5, United States Code, is amended by striking the item relating to section 3114 and inserting the following:

"3114. Appointment of candidates to positions in the competitive service by the Securities and Exchange Commission.".

(c) PAY AUTHORITY.—The Commission may set the rate of pay for experts and consultants appointed under the authority of section 3109 of title 5, United States Code, in the same manner in which it sets the rate of pay for employees of the Commission.

[Explanation at ¶ 4115.]

[¶ 10,929H] ACT SEC. 929H. SIPC REFORMS.

(a) INCREASING THE CASH LIMIT OF PROTECTION.—Section 9 of the Securities Investor Protection Act of 1970 (15 U.S.C. 78fff-3) is amended—

(1) in subsection (a)(1), by striking "$100,000 for each such customer" and inserting "the standard maximum cash advance amount for each such customer, as determined in accordance with subsection (d)"; and

(2) by adding the following new subsections:

"(d) STANDARD MAXIMUM CASH ADVANCE AMOUNT DEFINED.—For purposes of this section, the term 'standard maximum cash advance amount' means $250,000, as such amount may be adjusted after December 31, 2010, as provided under subsection (e).

"(e) INFLATION ADJUSTMENT.—

"(1) IN GENERAL.—Not later than January 1, 2011, and every 5 years thereafter, and subject to the approval of the Commission as provided under section 3(e)(2), the Board of Directors of SIPC shall determine whether an inflation adjustment to the standard maximum cash advance amount is appropriate. If the Board of Directors of SIPC determines such an adjustment is appropriate, then the standard maximum cash advance amount shall be an amount equal to—

"(A) $250,000 multiplied by—

"(B) the ratio of the annual value of the Personal Consumption Expenditures Chain-Type Price Index (or any successor index there-to), published by the Department of Commerce, for the calendar year preceding the year in which such determination is made, to the published annual value of such index for the calendar year preceding the year in which this subsection was enacted.

The index values used in calculations under this paragraph shall be, as of the date of the calculation, the values most recently published by the Department of Commerce.

"(2) ROUNDING.—If the standard maximum cash advance amount determined under paragraph (1) for any period is not a multiple of $10,000, the amount so determined shall be rounded down to the nearest $10,000.

"(3) PUBLICATION AND REPORT TO THE CONGRESS.—Not later than April 5 of any calendar year in which a determination is required to be made under paragraph (1)—

"(A) the Commission shall publish in the Federal Register the standard maximum cash advance amount; and

"(B) the Board of Directors of SIPC shall submit a report to the Congress stating the standard maximum cash advance amount.

"(4) IMPLEMENTATION PERIOD.—Any adjustment to the standard maximum cash advance amount shall take effect on January 1 of the year immediately succeeding the calendar year in which such adjustment is made.

"(5) INFLATION ADJUSTMENT CONSIDERATIONS.—In making any determination under paragraph (1) to increase the standard maximum cash advance amount, the Board of Directors of SIPC shall consider—

"(A) the overall state of the fund and the economic conditions affecting members of SIPC;

"(B) the potential problems affecting members of SIPC; and

"(C) such other factors as the Board of Directors of SIPC may determine appropriate.".

(b) LIQUIDATION OF A CARRYING BROKER-DEALER.—Section 5(a)(3) of the Securities Investor Protection Act of 1970 (15 U.S.C. 78eee(a)(3)) is amended—

(1) by striking the undesignated matter immediately following subparagraph (B);

(2) in subparagraph (A), by striking "any member of SIPC" and inserting "the member";

(3) in subparagraph (B), by striking the comma at the end and inserting a period;

(4) by striking "If SIPC" and inserting the following:

"(A) IN GENERAL.—SIPC may, upon notice to a member of SIPC, file an application for a protective decree with any court of competent jurisdiction specified in section 21(e) or 27 of the Securities Exchange Act of 1934, except that no such application shall be filed with respect to a member, the only customers of which are persons whose claims could not be satisfied by SIPC advances pursuant to section 9, if SIPC"; and

(5) by adding at the end the following:

"(B) CONSENT REQUIRED.—No member of SIPC that has a customer may enter into an insolvency, receivership, or bankruptcy proceeding, under Federal or State law, without the specific consent of SIPC, except as provided in title II of the Dodd-Frank Wall Street Reform and Consumer Protection Act.".

[Explanation at ¶ 4095.]

[¶ 10,929I] ACT SEC. 929I. PROTECTING CONFIDENTIALITY OF MATERIALS SUBMITTED TO THE COMMISSION.

(a) SECURITIES EXCHANGE ACT OF 1934.—Section 24 of the Securities Exchange Act of 1934 (15 U.S.C. 78x) is amended—

(1) in subsection (d), by striking "subsection (e)" and inserting "subsection (f)";

(2) by redesignating subsection (e) as subsection (f); and

(3) by inserting after subsection (d) the following:

"(e) RECORDS OBTAINED FROM REGISTERED PERSONS.—

"(1) IN GENERAL.—Except as provided in subsection (f), the Commission shall not be compelled to disclose records or information obtained pursuant to section 17(b), or records or information based upon or derived from such records or information, if such records or information have been obtained by the Commission for use in furtherance of the purposes of this title, including surveillance, risk assessments, or other regulatory and oversight activities.

"(2) TREATMENT OF INFORMATION.—For purposes of section 552 of title 5, United States Code, this subsection shall be considered a statute described in subsection (b)(3)(B) of such section 552. Collection of information pursuant to section 17 shall be an administrative action involving an agency against specific individuals or agencies pursuant to section 3518(c)(1) of title 44, United States Code.".

(b) INVESTMENT COMPANY ACT OF 1940.—Section 31 of the Investment Company Act of 1940 (15 U.S.C. 80a-30) is amended—

(1) by striking subsection (c) and inserting the following:

"(c) LIMITATIONS ON DISCLOSURE BY COMMISSION.—Notwithstanding any other provision of law, the Commission shall not be compelled to disclose any records or information provided to the Commission under this section, or records or information based upon or derived from such records or information, if such records or information have been obtained by the Commission for use in furtherance of the purposes of this title, including surveillance, risk assessments, or other regulatory and oversight activities. Nothing in this subsection authorizes the Commission to withhold information from the Congress or prevent the Commission from complying with a request for information from any other Federal department or agency requesting the information for purposes within the scope of jurisdiction of that department or agency, or complying with an order of a court of the United States in an action brought by the United States or the Commission. For purposes of section 552 of title 5, United States Code, this section shall be considered a statute described in subsection (b)(3)(B) of such section 552. Collection of information pursuant to section 31 shall be an administrative action involving an agency against specific individuals or agencies pursuant to section 3518(c)(1) of title 44, United States Code.";

(2) by striking subsection (d); and

(3) by redesignating subsections (e) and (f) as subsections (d) and (e), respectively.

(c) INVESTMENT ADVISERS ACT OF 1940.—Section 210 of the Investment Advisers Act of 1940 (15 U.S.C. 80b-10) is amended by adding at the end the following:

"(d) LIMITATIONS ON DISCLOSURE BY THE COMMISSION.—Notwithstanding any other provision of law, the Commission shall not be compelled to disclose any records or information provided to the Commission under section 204, or records or information based upon or derived from such records or information, if such records or information have been obtained by the Commission for use in furtherance of the purposes of this title, including surveillance, risk assessments, or other regulatory and oversight activities. Nothing in this subsection authorizes the Commission to withhold information from the Congress or prevent the Commission from complying with a request for information from any other Federal department or agency requesting the information for purposes within the scope of jurisdiction of that department or agency, or complying with an order of a court of the United States in an action brought by the United States or the Commission. For purposes of section 552 of title 5, United States Code, this subsection shall be considered a statute described in subsection (b)(3)(B) of such section 552. Collection of information pursuant to section 204 shall be an administrative action involving an agency against specific individuals or agencies pursuant to section 3518(c)(1) of title 44, United States Code.";

[Explanation at ¶ 4120.]

[¶ 10,929J] ACT SEC. 929J. EXPANSION OF AUDIT INFORMATION TO BE PRODUCED AND EXCHANGED.

Section 106 of the Sarbanes-Oxley Act of 2002 (15 U.S.C. 7216) is amended—

(1) by striking subsection (b) and inserting the following:

"(b) PRODUCTION OF DOCUMENTS.—

"(1) PRODUCTION BY FOREIGN FIRMS.—If a foreign public accounting firm performs material services upon which a registered public accounting firm relies in the conduct of an audit or interim review, issues an audit report, performs audit work, or conducts interim reviews, the foreign public accounting firm shall—

"(A) produce the audit work papers of the foreign public accounting firm and all other documents of the firm related to any such audit work or interim review to the Commission or the Board, upon request of the Commission or the Board; and

"(B) be subject to the jurisdiction of the courts of the United States for purposes of enforcement of any request for such documents.

"(2) OTHER PRODUCTION.—Any registered public accounting firm that relies, in whole or in part, on the work of a foreign public accounting firm in issuing an audit report, performing audit work, or conducting an interim review, shall—

"(A) produce the audit work papers of the foreign public accounting firm and all other documents related to any such work in response to a request for production by the Commission or the Board; and

"(B) secure the agreement of any foreign public accounting firm to such production, as a condition of the reliance by the registered public accounting firm on the work of that foreign public accounting firm.";

(2) by redesignating subsection (d) as subsection (g); and

(3) by inserting after subsection (c) the following:

"(d) SERVICE OF REQUESTS OR PROCESS.—

"(1) IN GENERAL.—Any foreign public accounting firm that performs work for a domestic registered public accounting firm shall furnish to the domestic registered public accounting firm a written irrevocable consent and power of attorney that designates the domestic registered public accounting firm as an agent upon whom may be served any request by the Commission or the Board under this section or upon whom may be served any process, pleadings, or other papers in any action brought to enforce this section.

"(2) SPECIFIC AUDIT WORK.—Any foreign public accounting firm that performs material services upon which a registered public accounting firm relies in the conduct of an audit or interim review, issues an audit report, performs audit work, or, performs interim reviews, shall designate to the Commission or the Board an agent in the United States upon whom may be served any request by the Commission or the Board under this section or upon whom may be served any process, pleading, or other papers in any action brought to enforce this section.

"(e) SANCTIONS.—A willful refusal to comply, in whole in or in part, with any request by the Commission or the Board under this section, shall be deemed a violation of this Act.

"(f) OTHER MEANS OF SATISFYING PRODUCTION OBLIGATIONS.—Notwithstanding any other provisions of this section, the staff of the Commission or the Board may allow a foreign public accounting firm that is subject to this section to meet production obligations under this section through alternate means, such as through foreign counterparts of the Commission or the Board.".

[Explanation at ¶ 4425.]

[¶ 10,929K] ACT SEC. 929K. SHARING PRIVILEGED INFORMATION WITH OTHER AUTHORITIES.

Section 24 of the Securities Exchange Act of 1934 (15 U.S.C. 78x) is amended—

(1) in subsection (d), as amended by subsection (d)(1)(A), by striking "subsection (f)" and inserting "subsection (g)";

(2) in subsection (e), as added by subsection (d)(1)(C), by striking "subsection (f)" and inserting "subsection (g)";

(3) by redesignating subsection (f) as subsection (g); and

(4) by inserting after subsection (e) the following:

"(f) SHARING PRIVILEGED INFORMATION WITH OTHER AUTHORITIES.—

"(1) PRIVILEGED INFORMATION PROVIDED BY THE COMMISSION.—The Commission shall not be deemed to have waived any privilege applicable to any information by transferring that information to or permitting that information to be used by—

"(A) any agency (as defined in section 6 of title 18, United States Code);

"(B) the Public Company Accounting Oversight Board;

"(C) any self-regulatory organization;

"(D) any foreign securities authority;

"(E) any foreign law enforcement authority; or

"(F) any State securities or law enforcement authority.

"(2) NONDISCLOSURE OF PRIVILEGED INFORMATION PROVIDED TO THE COMMISSION.—The Commission shall not be compelled to disclose privileged information obtained from any foreign securities authority, or foreign law enforcement authority, if the authority has in good faith determined and represented to the Commission that the information is privileged.

"(3) NONWAIVER OF PRIVILEGED INFORMATION PROVIDED TO THE COMMISSION.—

"(A) IN GENERAL.—Federal agencies, State securities and law enforcement authorities, self-regulatory organizations, and the Public Company Accounting Oversight Board shall not be deemed to have waived any privilege applicable to any information by transferring that information to or permitting that information to be used by the Commission.

"(B) EXCEPTION.—The provisions of subparagraph (A) shall not apply to a self-regulatory organization or the Public Company Accounting Oversight Board with respect to information used by the Commission in an action against such organization.

"(4) DEFINITIONS.—For purposes of this subsection—

"(A) the term 'privilege' includes any work-product privilege, attorney-client privilege, governmental privilege, or other privilege recognized under Federal, State, or foreign law;

"(B) the term 'foreign law enforcement authority' means any foreign authority that is empowered under foreign law to detect, investigate or prosecute potential violations of law; and

"(C) the term 'State securities or law enforcement authority' means the authority of any State or territory that is empowered under State or territory law to detect, investigate, or prosecute potential violations of law.".

[Explanation at ¶ 4120.]

[¶ 10,929L] ACT SEC. 929L. ENHANCED APPLICATION OF ANTIFRAUD PROVISIONS.

The Securities Exchange Act of 1934 (15 U.S.C. 78a et seq.) is amended—

(1) in section 9—

(A) by striking "registered on a national securities exchange" each place that term appears and inserting "other than a government security";

(B) in subsection (b), by striking "by use of any facility of a national securities exchange,"; and

(C) in subsection (c), by inserting after "unlawful for any" the following: "broker, dealer, or";

(2) in section 10(a)(1), by striking "registered on a national securities exchange" and inserting "other than a government security"; and

(3) in section 15(c)(1)(A), by striking "otherwise than on a national securities exchange of which it is a member".

[Explanation at ¶ 4125.]

[¶ 10,929M] ACT SEC. 929M. AIDING AND ABETTING AUTHORITY UNDER THE SECURITIES ACT AND THE INVESTMENT COMPANY ACT.

(a) UNDER THE SECURITIES ACT OF 1933.—Section 15 of the Securities Act of 1933 (15 U.S.C. 77o) is amended—

(1) by striking "Every person who" and inserting "(a) CONTROLLING PERSONS.—Every person who"; and

(2) by adding at the end the following:

"(b) PROSECUTION OF PERSONS WHO AID AND ABET VIOLATIONS.—For purposes of any action brought by the Commission under subparagraph (b) or (d) of section 20, any person that knowingly or recklessly provides substantial assistance to another person in violation of a provision of this Act, or of any rule or regulation issued under this Act, shall be deemed to be in violation of such provision to the same extent as the person to whom such assistance is provided.".

(b) UNDER THE INVESTMENT COMPANY ACT OF 1940.—Section 48 of the Investment Company Act of 1940 (15 U.S.C. 80a-48) is amended by redesignating subsection (b) as subsection (c) and inserting after subsection (a) the following:

"(b) For purposes of any action brought by the Commission under subsection (d) or (e) of section 42, any person that knowingly or recklessly provides substantial assistance to another person in violation of a provision of this Act, or of any rule or regulation issued under this Act, shall be deemed to be in violation of such provision to the same extent as the person to whom such assistance is provided.".

[Explanation at ¶ 4130.]

[¶ 10,929N] ACT SEC. 929N. AUTHORITY TO IMPOSE PENALTIES FOR AIDING AND ABETTING VIOLATIONS OF THE INVESTMENT ADVISERS ACT.

Section 209 of the Investment Advisers Act of 1940 (15 U.S.C. 80b-9) is amended by inserting at the end the following new subsection:

"(f) AIDING AND ABETTING.—For purposes of any action brought by the Commission under subsection (e), any person that knowingly or recklessly has aided, abetted, counseled, commanded, induced, or procured a violation of any provision of this Act, or of any rule, regulation, or order hereunder, shall be deemed to be in violation of such provision, rule, regulation, or order to the same extent as the person that committed such violation.".

[Explanation at ¶ 4130.]

[¶ 10,929O] ACT SEC. 929O. AIDING AND ABETTING STANDARD OF KNOWLEDGE SATISFIED BY RECKLESSNESS.

Section 20(e) of the Securities Exchange Act of 1934 (15 U.S.C. 78t(e)) is amended by inserting "or recklessly" after "knowingly".

[Explanation at ¶ 4130.]

[¶ 10,929P] ACT SEC. 929P. STRENGTHENING ENFORCEMENT BY THE COMMISSION.

(a) AUTHORITY TO IMPOSE CIVIL PENALTIES IN CEASE AND DESIST PROCEEDINGS.—

(1) UNDER THE SECURITIES ACT OF 1933.—Section 8A of the Securities Act of 1933 (15 U.S.C. 77h-1) is amended by adding at the end the following new subsection:

"(g) AUTHORITY TO IMPOSE MONEY PENALTIES.—

"(1) GROUNDS.—In any cease-and-desist proceeding under subsection (a), the Commission may impose a civil penalty on a person if the Commission finds, on the record, after notice and opportunity for hearing, that—

"(A) such person—

"(i) is violating or has violated any provision of this title, or any rule or regulation issued under this title; or

"(ii) is or was a cause of the violation of any provision of this title, or any rule or regulation thereunder; and

"(B) such penalty is in the public interest.

"(2) MAXIMUM AMOUNT OF PENALTY.—

"(A) FIRST TIER.—The maximum amount of a penalty for each act or omission described in paragraph (1) shall be $7,500 for a natural person or $75,000 for any other person.

"(B) SECOND TIER.—Notwithstanding subparagraph (A), the maximum amount of penalty for each such act or omission shall be $75,000 for a natural person or $375,000 for any other person, if the act or omission described in paragraph (1) involved fraud, deceit, manipulation, or deliberate or reckless disregard of a regulatory requirement.

"(C) THIRD TIER.—Notwithstanding subparagraphs (A) and (B), the maximum amount of penalty for each such act or omission shall be $150,000 for a natural person or $725,000 for any other person, if—

"(i) the act or omission described in paragraph (1) involved fraud, deceit, manipulation, or deliberate or reckless disregard of a regulatory requirement; and

"(ii) such act or omission directly or indirectly resulted in—

"(I) substantial losses or created a significant risk of substantial losses to other persons; or

"(II) substantial pecuniary gain to the person who committed the act or omission.

"(3) EVIDENCE CONCERNING ABILITY TO PAY.—In any proceeding in which the Commission may impose a penalty under this section, a respondent may present evidence of the ability of the respondent to pay such penalty. The Commission may, in its discretion, consider such evidence in determining whether such penalty is in the public interest. Such evidence may relate to the extent of the ability of the respondent to continue in business and the collectability of a penalty, taking into account any other claims of the United States or third parties upon the assets of the respondent and the amount of the assets of the respondent.".

(2) UNDER THE SECURITIES EXCHANGE ACT OF 1934.—Section 21B(a) of the Securities Exchange Act of 1934 (15 U.S.C. 78u-2(a)) is amended—

(A) by striking the matter following paragraph (4);

(B) in the matter preceding paragraph (1), by inserting after "opportunity for hearing," the following: "that such penalty is in the public interest and";

(C) by redesignating paragraphs (1) through (4) as subparagraphs (A) through (D), respectively, and adjusting the margins accordingly;

(D) by striking "In any proceeding" and inserting the following:

"(1) IN GENERAL.—In any proceeding"; and

(E) by adding at the end the following:

"(2) CEASE-AND-DESIST PROCEEDINGS.—In any proceeding instituted under section 21C against any person, the Commission may impose a civil penalty, if the Commission finds, on the record after notice and opportunity for hearing, that such person—

"(A) is violating or has violated any provision of this title, or any rule or regulation issued under this title; or

"(B) is or was a cause of the violation of any provision of this title, or any rule or regulation issued under this title.".

(3) UNDER THE INVESTMENT COMPANY ACT OF 1940.—Section 9(d)(1) of the Investment Company Act of 1940 (15 U.S.C. 80a-9(d)(1)) is amended—

(A) by striking the matter following subparagraph (C);

(B) in the matter preceding subparagraph (A), by inserting after "opportunity for hearing," the following: "that such penalty is in the public interest, and";

(C) by redesignating subparagraphs (A) through (C) as clauses (i) through (iii), respectively, and adjusting the margins accordingly;

(D) by striking "In any proceeding" and inserting the following:

"(A) IN GENERAL.—In any proceeding"; and

(E) by adding at the end the following:

"(B) CEASE-AND-DESIST PROCEEDINGS.—In any proceeding instituted pursuant to subsection (f) against any person, the Commission may impose a civil penalty if the Commission finds, on the record, after notice and opportunity for hearing, that such person—

"(i) is violating or has violated any provision of this title, or any rule or regulation issued under this title; or

"(ii) is or was a cause of the violation of any provision of this title, or any rule or regulation issued under this title.".

(4) UNDER THE INVESTMENT ADVISERS ACT OF 1940. Section 203(i)(1) of the Investment Advisers Act of 1940 (15 U.S.C. 80b-3(i)(1)) is amended—

(A) by striking the matter following subparagraph (D);

(B) in the matter preceding subparagraph (A), by inserting after "opportunity for hearing," the following: "that such penalty is in the public interest and";

(C) by redesignating subparagraphs (A) through (D) as clauses (i) through (iv), respectively, and adjusting the margins accordingly;

(D) by striking "In any proceeding" and inserting the following:

"(A) IN GENERAL.—In any proceeding"; and

(E) by adding at the end the following new subparagraph:

"(B) CEASE-AND-DESIST PROCEEDINGS.—In any proceeding instituted pursuant to subsection (k) against any person, the Commission may impose a civil penalty if the Commission finds, on the record, after notice and opportunity for hearing, that such person—

"(i) is violating or has violated any provision of this title, or any rule or regulation issued under this title; or

"(ii) is or was a cause of the violation of any provision of this title, or any rule or regulation issued under this title.".

(b) EXTRATERRITORIAL JURISDICTION OF THE ANTIFRAUD PROVISIONS OF THE FEDERAL SECURITIES LAWS.—

(1) UNDER THE SECURITIES ACT OF 1933.—Section 22 of the Securities Act of 1933 (15 U.S.C. 77v(a)) is amended by adding at the end the following new subsection:

"(c) EXTRATERRITORIAL JURISDICTION.—The district courts of the United States and the United States courts of any Territory shall have jurisdiction of an action or proceeding brought or instituted by the Commission or the United States alleging a violation of section 17(a) involving—

"(1) conduct within the United States that constitutes significant steps in furtherance of the violation, even if the securities transaction occurs outside the United States and involves only foreign investors; or

"(2) conduct occurring outside the United States that has a foreseeable substantial effect within the United States.".

(2) UNDER THE SECURITIES EXCHANGE ACT OF 1934.—Section 27 of the Securities Exchange Act of 1934 (15 U.S.C. 78aa) is amended—

(A) by striking "The district" and inserting the following:

"(a) IN GENERAL.—The district"; and

(B) by adding at the end the following new subsection:

"(b) EXTRATERRITORIAL JURISDICTION.—The district courts of the United States and the United States courts of any Territory shall have jurisdiction of an action or proceeding brought or instituted by the Commission or the United States alleging a violation of the antifraud provisions of this title involving—

"(1) conduct within the United States that constitutes significant steps in furtherance of the violation, even if the securities transaction occurs outside the United States and involves only foreign investors; or

"(2) conduct occurring outside the United States that has a foreseeable substantial effect within the United States.".

(3) UNDER THE INVESTMENT ADVISERS ACT OF 1940.—Section 214 of the Investment Advisers Act of 1940 (15 U.S.C. 80b-14) is amended—

(A) by striking "The district" and inserting the following:

"(a) IN GENERAL.—The district"; and

(B) by adding at the end the following new subsection:

"(b) EXTRATERRITORIAL JURISDICTION.—The district courts of the United States and the United States courts of any Territory shall have jurisdiction of an action or proceeding brought or instituted by the Commission or the United States alleging a violation of section 206 involving—

"(1) conduct within the United States that constitutes significant steps in furtherance of the violation, even if the violation is committed by a foreign adviser and involves only foreign investors; or

"(2) conduct occurring outside the United States that has a foreseeable substantial effect within the United States.".

(c) CONTROL PERSON LIABILITY UNDER THE SECURITIES EXCHANGE ACT OF 1934.—Section 20(a) of the Securities Exchange Act of 1934 (15 U.S.C. 78t(a)) is amended by inserting after "controlled person is liable" the following: "(including to the Commission in any action brought under paragraph (1) or (3) of section 21(d))".

[Explanation at ¶4135.]

[¶10,929Q] ACT SEC. 929Q. REVISION TO RECORDKEEPING RULE.

(a) INVESTMENT COMPANY ACT OF 1940 AMENDMENTS.—Section 31 of the Investment Company Act of 1940 (15 U.S.C. 80a-30) is amended—

(1) in subsection (a)(1), by adding at the end the following: "Each person having custody or use of the securities, deposits, or credits of a registered investment company shall maintain and preserve all records that relate to the custody or use by such person of the securities, deposits, or credits of the registered investment company for such period or periods as the Commission, by rule or regulation, may prescribe, as necessary or appropriate in the public interest or for the protection of investors."; and

(2) in subsection (b), by adding at the end the following:

"(4) RECORDS OF PERSONS WITH CUSTODY OR USE.—

"(A) IN GENERAL.—Records of persons having custody or use of the securities, deposits, or credits of a registered investment company that relate to such custody or use, are subject at any time, or from time to time, to such reasonable periodic, special, or other examinations and other information and document requests by representatives of the Commission, as the Commission deems necessary or appropriate in the public interest or for the protection of investors.

"(B) CERTAIN PERSONS SUBJECT TO OTHER REGULATION.—Any person that is subject to regulation and examination by a Federal financial institution regulatory agency (as such term is defined under section 212(c)(2) of title 18, United States Code) may satisfy any examination request, information request, or document request described under subparagraph (A), by providing to the Commission a detailed listing, in writing, of the securities, deposits, or credits of the registered investment company within the custody or use of such person.".

(b) INVESTMENT ADVISERS ACT OF 1940 AMENDMENT.—Section 204 of the Investment Advisers Act of 1940 (15 U.S.C. 80b-4) is amended by adding at the end the following new subsection:

"(d) RECORDS OF PERSONS WITH CUSTODY OR USE.—

"(1) IN GENERAL.—Records of persons having custody or use of the securities, deposits, or credits of a client, that relate to such custody or use, are subject at any time, or from time to time, to such reasonable periodic, special, or other examinations and other information and document requests by representatives of the Commission, as the Commission deems necessary or appropriate in the public interest or for the protection of investors.

"(2) CERTAIN PERSONS SUBJECT TO OTHER REGULATION.—Any person that is subject to regulation and examination by a Federal financial institution regulatory agency (as such term is defined under section 212(c)(2) of title 18, United States Code) may satisfy any examination request, information request, or document request described under paragraph (1), by providing the Commission with a detailed listing, in writing, of the securities, deposits, or credits of the client within the custody or use of such person.".

[Explanation at ¶4140.]

[¶10,929R] ACT SEC. 929R. BENEFICIAL OWNERSHIP AND SHORT-SWING PROFIT REPORTING.

(a) BENEFICIAL OWNERSHIP REPORTING.—Section 13 of the Securities Exchange Act of 1934 (15 U.S.C. 78m) is amended—

(1) in subsection (d)(1)—

(A) by inserting after "within ten days after such acquisition" the following: "or within such shorter time as the Commission may establish by rule"; and

(B) by striking "send to the issuer of the security at its principal executive office, by registered or certified mail, send to each exchange where the security is traded, and";

(2) in subsection (d)(2)—

(A) by striking "in the statements to the issuer and the exchange, and"; and

(B) by striking "shall be transmitted to the issuer and the exchange and";

(3) in subsection (g)(1), by striking "shall send to the issuer of the security and"; and

(4) in subsection (g)(2)—

(A) by striking "sent to the issuer and"; and

(B) by striking "shall be transmitted to the issuer and".

(b) SHORT-SWING PROFIT REPORTING.—Section 16(a) of the Securities Exchange Act of 1934 (15 U.S.C. 78p(a)) is amended—

(1) in paragraph (1), by striking "(and, if such security is registered on a national securities exchange, also with the exchange)"; and

(2) in paragraph (2)(B), by inserting after "officer" the following: ", or within such shorter time as the Commission may establish by rule".

[Explanation at ¶ 4145.]

[¶ 10,929S] ACT SEC. 929S. FINGERPRINTING.

Section 17(f)(2) of the Securities Exchange Act of 1934 (15 U.S.C. 78q(f)(2)) is amended—

(1) in the first sentence, by striking "and registered clearing agency," and inserting "registered clearing agency, registered securities information processor, national securities exchange, and national securities association"; and

(2) in the second sentence, by striking "or clearing agency," and inserting "clearing agency, securities information processor, national securities exchange, or national securities association,".

[Explanation at ¶ 4150.]

[¶ 10,929T] ACT SEC. 929T. EQUAL TREATMENT OF SELF-REGULATORY ORGANIZATION RULES.

Section 29(a) of the Securities Exchange Act of 1934 (15 U.S.C. 78cc(a)) is amended by striking "an exchange required thereby" and inserting "a self-regulatory organization,".

[Explanation at ¶ 4075.]

[¶ 10,929U] ACT SEC. 929U. DEADLINE FOR COMPLETING EXAMINATIONS, INSPECTIONS AND ENFORCEMENT ACTIONS.

The Securities Exchange Act of 1934 (15 U.S.C. 78a et seq.) is amended by inserting after section 4D the following new section:

"SEC. 4E. DEADLINE FOR COMPLETING ENFORCEMENT INVESTIGATIONS AND COMPLIANCE EXAMINATIONS AND INSPECTIONS.

"(a) ENFORCEMENT INVESTIGATIONS.—

"(1) IN GENERAL.—Not later than 180 days after the date on which Commission staff provide a written Wells notification to any person, the Commission staff shall either file an action against such person or provide notice to the Director of the Division of Enforcement of its intent to not file an action.

"(2) EXCEPTIONS FOR CERTAIN COMPLEX ACTIONS.—Notwithstanding paragraph (1), if the Director of the Division of Enforcement of the Commission or the Director's designee determines that a particular enforcement investigation is sufficiently complex such that a determination regarding the filing of an action against a person cannot be completed within the deadline specified in paragraph (1), the Director of the Division of Enforcement of the Commission or the Director's designee may, after providing notice to the Chairman of the Commission, extend such deadline as needed for one additional 180-day period. If after the additional 180-day period the Director of the Division of Enforcement of the Commission or the Director's designee determines that a particular enforcement investigation is sufficiently complex such that a determination regarding the filing of an action against a person cannot be completed within the additional 180-day period, the Director of the Division of Enforcement of the Commission or the Director's designee may, after providing notice to and receiving approval of the Commission, extend such deadline as needed for one or more additional successive 180-day periods.

"(b) COMPLIANCE EXAMINATIONS AND INSPECTIONS.—

"(1) IN GENERAL.—Not later than 180 days after the date on which Commission staff completes the on-site portion of its compliance examination or inspection or receives all records requested from the entity being examined or inspected, whichever is later, Commission staff shall provide the entity being examined or inspected with written notification indicating either that the examination or inspection has concluded, has concluded without findings, or that the staff requests the entity undertake corrective action.

"(2) EXCEPTION FOR CERTAIN COMPLEX ACTIONS.—Notwithstanding paragraph (1), if the head of any division or office within the Commission responsible for compliance examinations and inspections or his designee determines that a particular compliance examination or inspection is sufficiently complex such that a determination regarding concluding the examination or inspection, or regarding the staff requests the entity undertake corrective action, cannot be completed within the deadline specified in paragraph (1), the head of any division or office within the Commission responsible for compliance examinations and inspections or his designee may, after providing notice to the Chairman of the Commission, extend such deadline as needed for one additional 180-day period.".

[Explanation at ¶4155.]

[¶10,929V] ACT SEC. 929V. SECURITY INVESTOR PROTECTION ACT AMENDMENTS.

(a) INCREASING THE MINIMUM ASSESSMENT PAID BY SIPC MEMBERS.—Section 4(d)(1)(C) of the Securities Investor Protection Act of 1970 (15 U.S.C. 78ddd(d)(1)(C)) is amended by striking "$150 per annum" and inserting the following: "0.02 percent of the gross revenues from the securities business of such member of SIPC".

(b) INCREASING THE FINE FOR PROHIBITED ACTS UNDER SIPA.—Section 14(c) of the Securities Investor Protection Act of 1970 (15 U.S.C. 78jjj(c)) is amended—

(1) in paragraph (1), by striking "$50,000" and inserting "$250,000"; and

(2) in paragraph (2), by striking "$50,000" and inserting "$250,000".

(c) PENALTY FOR MISREPRESENTATION OF SIPC MEMBERSHIP OR PROTECTION.—Section 14 of the Securities Investor Protection Act of 1970 (15 U.S.C. 78jjj) is amended by adding at the end the following new subsection:

"(d) MISREPRESENTATION OF SIPC MEMBERSHIP OR PROTECTION.—

"(1) IN GENERAL.—Any person who falsely represents by any means (including, without limitation, through the Internet or any other medium of mass communication), with actual knowledge of the falsity of the representation and with an intent to deceive or cause injury to another, that such person, or another person, is a member of SIPC or that any person or account is protected or is eligible for protection under this Act or by SIPC, shall be liable for any damages caused thereby and shall be fined not more than $250,000 or imprisoned for not more than 5 years.

"(2) INJUNCTIONS.—Any court having jurisdiction of a civil action arising under this Act may grant temporary injunctions and final injunctions on such terms as the court deems reasonable to prevent or restrain any violation of paragraph (1). Any such injunction may be served anywhere in the United States on the person enjoined, shall be operative throughout the United States, and shall be enforceable, by proceedings in contempt or otherwise, by any United States court having jurisdiction over that person. The clerk of the court granting the injunction shall, when requested by any other court in which enforcement of the injunction is sought, transmit promptly to the other court a certified copy of all papers in the case on file in such clerk's office.".

[Explanation at ¶ 4095.]

[¶ 10,929W] ACT SEC. 929W. NOTICE TO MISSING SECURITY HOLDERS.

Section 17A of the Securities Exchange Act of 1934 (15 U.S.C. 78q-1) is amended by adding at the end the following new subsection:

"(g) DUE DILIGENCE FOR THE DELIVERY OF DIVIDENDS, INTEREST, AND OTHER VALUABLE PROPERTY RIGHTS.—

"(1) REVISION OF RULES REQUIRED.—The Commission shall revise its regulations in section 240.17Ad-17 of title 17, Code of Federal Regulations, as in effect on December 8, 1997, to extend the application of such section to brokers and dealers and to provide for the following:

"(A) A requirement that the paying agent provide a single written notification to each missing security holder that the missing security holder has been sent a check that has not yet been negotiated. The written notification may be sent along with a check or other mailing subsequently sent to the missing security holder but must be provided no later than 7 months after the sending of the not yet negotiated check.

"(B) An exclusion for paying agents from the notification requirements when the value of the not yet negotiated check is less than $25.

"(C) A provision clarifying that the requirements described in subparagraph (A) shall have no effect on State escheatment laws.

"(D) For purposes of such revised regulations—

"(i) a security holder shall be considered a 'missing security holder' if a check is sent to the security holder and the check is not negotiated before the earlier of the paying agent sending the next regularly scheduled check or the elapsing of 6 months after the sending of the not yet negotiated check; and

"(ii) the term 'paying agent' includes any issuer, transfer agent, broker, dealer, investment adviser, indenture trustee, custodian, or any other person that accepts payments from the issuer of a security and distributes the payments to the holders of the security.

"(2) RULEMAKING.—The Commission shall adopt such rules, regulations, and orders necessary to implement this subsection no later than 1 year after the date of enactment of this subsection. In proposing such rules, the Commission shall seek to minimize disruptions to current systems used by or on behalf of paying agents to process payment to account holders and avoid requiring multiple paying agents to send written notification to a missing security holder regarding the same not yet negotiated check.".

[Explanation at ¶ 4160.]

[¶ 10,929X] ACT SEC. 929X. SHORT SALE REFORMS.

(a) SHORT SALE DISCLOSURE.—Section 13(f) of the Securities Exchange Act of 1934 (15 U.S.C. 78m(f)) is amended by redesignating paragraphs (2), (3), (4), and (5) as paragraphs (3), (4), (5), and (6), respectively, and inserting after paragraph (1) the following:

"(2) The Commission shall prescribe rules providing for the public disclosure of the name of the issuer and the title, class, CUSIP number, aggregate amount of the number of short sales of each security, and any additional information determined by the Commission following the end of the reporting period. At a minimum, such public disclosure shall occur every month.".

(b) SHORT SELLING ENFORCEMENT.—Section 9 of the Securities Exchange Act of 1934 (15 U.S.C. 78i) is amended—

(1) by redesignating subsections (d), (e), (f), (g), (h), and (i) as subsections (e), (f), (g), (h), (i), and (j), respectively; and

(2) inserting after subsection (c), the following new subsection:

"(d) Transactions Relating to Short Sales of Securities.—It shall be unlawful for any person, directly or indirectly, by the use of the mails or any means or instrumentality of interstate commerce, or of any facility of any national securities exchange, or for any member of a national securities exchange to effect, alone or with one or more other persons, a manipulative short sale of any security. The Commission shall issue such other rules as are necessary or appropriate to ensure that the appropriate enforcement options and remedies are available for violations of this subsection in the public interest or for the protection of investors.".

(c) Investor Notification.—Section 15 of the Securities Exchange Act of 1934 (15 U.S.C. 78o) is amended—

(1) by redesignating subsections (e), (f), (g), (h), and (i) as subsections (f), (g), (h), (i), and (j), respectively; and

(2) inserting after subsection (d) the following new subsection:

"(e) Notices to Customers Regarding Securities Lending.—Every registered broker or dealer shall provide notice to its customers that they may elect not to allow their fully paid securities to be used in connection with short sales. If a broker or dealer uses a customer's securities in connection with short sales, the broker or dealer shall provide notice to its customer that the broker or dealer may receive compensation in connection with lending the customer's securities. The Commission, by rule, as it deems necessary or appropriate in the public interest and for the protection of investors, may prescribe the form, content, time, and manner of delivery of any notice required under this paragraph.".

[Explanation at ¶ 4165.]

[¶ 10,929Y] ACT SEC. 929Y. STUDY ON EXTRATERRITORIAL PRIVATE RIGHTS OF ACTION.

(a) In General.—The Securities and Exchange Commission of the United States shall solicit public comment and thereafter conduct a study to determine the extent to which private rights of action under the antifraud provisions of the Securities and Exchange Act of 1934 (15 U.S.C. 78u-4) should be extended to cover—

(1) conduct within the United States that constitutes a significant step in the furtherance of the violation, even if the securities transaction occurs outside the United States and involves only foreign investors; and

(2) conduct occurring outside the United States that has a foreseeable substantial effect within the United States.

(b) Contents.—The study shall consider and analyze, among other things—

(1) the scope of such a private right of action, including whether it should extend to all private actors or whether it should be more limited to extend just to institutional investors or otherwise;

(2) what implications such a private right of action would have on international comity;

(3) the economic costs and benefits of extending a private right of action for transnational securities frauds; and

(4) whether a narrower extraterritorial standard should be adopted.

(c) Report.—A report of the study shall be submitted and recommendations made to the Committee on Banking, Housing, and Urban Affairs of the Senate and the Committee on Financial Services of the House not later than 18 months after the date of enactment of this Act.

[Explanation at ¶ 4135.]

[¶ 10,929Z] ACT SEC. 929Z. GAO STUDY ON SECURITIES LITIGATION.

(a) Study.—The Comptroller General of the United States shall conduct a study on the impact of authorizing a private right of action against any person who aids or abets another person in violation of the securities laws. To the extent feasible, this study shall include—

(1) a review of the role of secondary actors in companies issuance of securities;

(2) the courts interpretation of the scope of liability for secondary actors under Federal securities laws after January 14, 2008; and

(3) the types of lawsuits decided under the Private Securities Litigation Act of 1995.

(b) REPORT.—Not later than 1 year after the date of enactment of this Act, the Comptroller General shall submit a report to Congress on the findings of the study required under subsection (a).

[Explanation at ¶ 4170.]

Subtitle C—Improvements to the Regulation of Credit Rating Agencies

[¶ 10,931] ACT SEC. 931. FINDINGS.

Congress finds the following:

(1) Because of the systemic importance of credit ratings and the reliance placed on credit ratings by individual and institutional investors and financial regulators, the activities and performances of credit rating agencies, including nationally recognized statistical rating organizations, are matters of national public interest, as credit rating agencies are central to capital formation, investor confidence, and the efficient performance of the United States economy.

(2) Credit rating agencies, including nationally recognized statistical rating organizations, play a critical "gatekeeper" role in the debt market that is functionally similar to that of securities analysts, who evaluate the quality of securities in the equity market, and auditors, who review the financial statements of firms. Such role justifies a similar level of public oversight and accountability.

(3) Because credit rating agencies perform evaluative and analytical services on behalf of clients, much as other financial "gatekeepers" do, the activities of credit rating agencies are fundamentally commercial in character and should be subject to the same standards of liability and oversight as apply to auditors, securities analysts, and investment bankers.

(4) In certain activities, particularly in advising arrangers of structured financial products on potential ratings of such products, credit rating agencies face conflicts of interest that need to be carefully monitored and that therefore should be addressed explicitly in legislation in order to give clearer authority to the Securities and Exchange Commission.

(5) In the recent financial crisis, the ratings on structured financial products have proven to be inaccurate. This inaccuracy contributed significantly to the mismanagement of risks by financial institutions and investors, which in turn adversely impacted the health of the economy in the United States and around the world. Such inaccuracy necessitates increased accountability on the part of credit rating agencies.

[Explanation at ¶ 4180.]

[¶ 10,932] ACT SEC. 932. ENHANCED REGULATION, ACCOUNTABILITY, AND TRANSPARENCY OF NATIONALLY RECOGNIZED STATISTICAL RATING ORGANIZATIONS.

(a) IN GENERAL.—Section 15E of the Securities Exchange Act of 1934 (15 U.S.C. 78o-7) is amended—

(1) in subsection (b)—

(A) in paragraph (1)(A), by striking "furnished" and inserting "filed" and by striking "furnishing" and inserting "filing";

(B) in paragraph (1)(B), by striking "furnishing" and inserting "filing"; and

(C) in the first sentence of paragraph (2), by striking "furnish to" and inserting "file with";

(2) in subsection (c)—

(A) in paragraph (2)—

(i) in the second sentence, by inserting "any other provision of this section, or" after "Notwithstanding"; and

(ii) by inserting after the period at the end the following: "Nothing in this paragraph may be construed to afford a defense against any action or proceeding brought by the Commission to enforce the antifraud provisions of the securities laws."; and

(B) by adding at the end the following:

"(3) INTERNAL CONTROLS OVER PROCESSES FOR DETERMINING CREDIT RATINGS.—

"(A) IN GENERAL.—Each nationally recognized statistical rating organization shall establish, maintain, enforce, and document an effective internal control structure governing the implementation of and adherence to policies, procedures, and methodologies for determining credit ratings, taking into consideration such factors as the Commission may prescribe, by rule.

"(B) ATTESTATION REQUIREMENT.—The Commission shall prescribe rules requiring each nationally recognized statistical rating organization to submit to the Commission an annual internal controls report, which shall contain—

"(i) a description of the responsibility of the management of the nationally recognized statistical rating organization in establishing and maintaining an effective internal control structure under subparagraph (A);

"(ii) an assessment of the effectiveness of the internal control structure of the nationally recognized statistical rating organization; and

"(iii) the attestation of the chief executive officer, or equivalent individual, of the nationally recognized statistical rating organization.";

(3) in subsection (d)—

(A) by inserting after "or revoke the registration of any nationally recognized statistical rating organization" the following: ", or with respect to any person who is associated with, who is seeking to become associated with, or, at the time of the alleged misconduct, who was associated or was seeking to become associated with a nationally recognized statistical rating organization, the Commission, by order, shall censure, place limitations on the activities or functions of such person, suspend for a period not exceeding 1 year, or bar such person from being associated with a nationally recognized statistical rating organization,";

(B) by inserting "bar" after "placing of limitations, suspension,";

(C) in paragraph (2), by striking "furnished to" and inserting "filed with";

(D) in paragraph (2), by redesignating subparagraphs (A) and (B) as clauses (i) and (ii), respectively, and adjusting the clause margins accordingly;

(E) by redesignating paragraphs (1) through (5) as subparagraphs (A) through (E), respectively, and adjusting the subparagraph margins accordingly;

(F) in the matter preceding subparagraph (A), as so redesignated, by striking "The Commission" and inserting the following:

"(1) IN GENERAL.—The Commission";

(G) in subparagraph (D), as so redesignated—

(i) by striking "furnish" and inserting "file"; and

(ii) by striking "or" at the end.

(H) in subparagraph (E), as so redesignated, by striking the period at the end and inserting a semicolon; and

(I) by adding at the end the following:

"(F) has failed reasonably to supervise, with a view to preventing a violation of the securities laws, an individual who commits such a violation, if the individual is subject to the supervision of that person.

"(2) SUSPENSION OR REVOCATION FOR PARTICULAR CLASS OF SECURITIES.—

"(A) IN GENERAL.—The Commission may temporarily suspend or permanently revoke the registration of a nationally recognized statistical rating organization with respect to a particular class or subclass of securities, if the Commission finds, on the record after notice and opportunity for hearing, that the nationally recognized statistical rating organization does not have adequate financial and managerial resources to consistently produce credit ratings with integrity.

"(B) CONSIDERATIONS.—In making any determination under subparagraph (A), the Commission shall consider—

"(i) whether the nationally recognized statistical rating organization has failed over a sustained period of time, as determined by the Commission, to produce ratings that are accurate for that class or subclass of securities; and

"(ii) such other factors as the Commission may determine.";

(4) in subsection (h), by adding at the end the following:

"(3) SEPARATION OF RATINGS FROM SALES AND MARKETING.—

"(A) RULES REQUIRED.—The Commission shall issue rules to prevent the sales and marketing considerations of a nationally recognized statistical rating organization from influencing the production of ratings by the nationally recognized statistical rating organization.

"(B) CONTENTS OF RULES.—The rules issued under subparagraph (A) shall provide for—

"(i) exceptions for small nationally recognized statistical rating organizations with respect to which the Commission determines that the separation of the production of ratings and sales and marketing activities is not appropriate; and

"(ii) suspension or revocation of the registration of a nationally recognized statistical rating organization, if the Commission finds, on the record, after notice and opportunity for a hearing, that—

"(I) the nationally recognized statistical rating organization has committed a violation of a rule issued under this subsection; and

"(II) the violation of a rule issued under this subsection affected a rating.

"(4) LOOK-BACK REQUIREMENT.—

"(A) REVIEW BY THE NATIONALLY RECOGNIZED STATISTICAL RATING ORGANIZATION.—Each nationally recognized statistical rating organization shall establish, maintain, and enforce policies and procedures reasonably designed to ensure that, in any case in which an employee of a person subject to a credit rating of the nationally recognized statistical rating organization or the issuer, underwriter, or sponsor of a security or money market instrument subject to a credit rating of the nationally recognized statistical rating organization was employed by the nationally recognized statistical rating organization and participated in any capacity in determining credit ratings for the person or the securities or money market instruments during the 1-year period preceding the date an action was taken with respect to the credit rating, the nationally recognized statistical rating organization shall—

"(i) conduct a review to determine whether any conflicts of interest of the employee influenced the credit rating; and

"(ii) take action to revise the rating if appropriate, in accordance with such rules as the Commission shall prescribe.

"(B) REVIEW BY COMMISSION.—

"(i) IN GENERAL.—The Commission shall conduct periodic reviews of the policies described in subparagraph (A) and the implementation of the policies at each nationally recognized statistical rating organization to ensure they are reasonably designed and implemented to most effectively eliminate conflicts of interest.

"(ii) TIMING OF REVIEWS.—The Commission shall review the code of ethics and conflict of interest policy of each nationally recognized statistical rating organization—

"(I) not less frequently than annually; and

"(II) whenever such policies are materially modified or amended.

"(5) REPORT TO COMMISSION ON CERTAIN EMPLOYMENT TRANSITIONS.—

"(A) REPORT REQUIRED.—Each nationally recognized statistical rating organization shall report to the Commission any case such organization knows or can reasonably be expected to know where a person associated with such organization within the previous 5 years obtains employment with any obligor, issuer, underwriter, or sponsor of a security or money market instrument for which the organization issued a credit rating during the 12-month period prior to such employment, if such employee—

"(i) was a senior officer of such organization;

"(ii) participated in any capacity in determining credit ratings for such obligor, issuer, underwriter, or sponsor; or

"(iii) supervised an employee described in clause (ii).

"(B) PUBLIC DISCLOSURE.—Upon receiving such a report, the Commission shall make such information publicly available.";

(5) in subsection (j)—

(A) by striking "Each" and inserting the following:

"(1) IN GENERAL.—Each"; and

(B) by adding at the end the following:

"(2) LIMITATIONS.—

"(A) IN GENERAL.—Except as provided in subparagraph (B), an individual designated under paragraph (1) may not, while serving in the designated capacity—

"(i) perform credit ratings;

"(ii) participate in the development of ratings methodologies or models;

"(iii) perform marketing or sales functions; or

"(iv) participate in establishing compensation levels, other than for employees working for that individual.

"(B) EXCEPTION.—The Commission may exempt a small nationally recognized statistical rating organization from the limitations under this paragraph, if the Commission finds that compliance with such limitations would impose an unreasonable burden on the nationally recognized statistical rating organization.

"(3) OTHER DUTIES.—Each individual designated under paragraph (1) shall establish procedures for the receipt, retention, and treatment of—

"(A) complaints regarding credit ratings, models, methodologies, and compliance with the securities laws and the policies and procedures developed under this section; and

"(B) confidential, anonymous complaints by employees or users of credit ratings.

"(4) COMPENSATION.—The compensation of each compliance officer appointed under paragraph (1) shall not be linked to the financial performance of the nationally recognized statistical rating organization and shall be arranged so as to ensure the independence of the officer's judgment.

"(5) ANNUAL REPORTS REQUIRED.—

"(A) ANNUAL REPORTS REQUIRED.—Each individual designated under paragraph (1) shall submit to the nationally recognized statistical rating organization an annual report on the compliance of the nationally recognized statistical rating organization with the securities laws and the policies and procedures of the nationally recognized statistical rating organization that includes—

"(i) a description of any material changes to the code of ethics and conflict of interest policies of the nationally recognized statistical rating organization; and

"(ii) a certification that the report is accurate and complete.

"(B) SUBMISSION OF REPORTS TO THE COMMISSION.—Each nationally recognized statistical rating organization shall file the reports required under subparagraph (A) together with the financial report that is required to be submitted to the Commission under this section.";

(6) in subsection (k), by striking "furnish to" and inserting "file with";

(7) in subsection (l)(2)(A)(i), by striking "furnished" and inserting "filed"; and

(8) by striking subsection (p) and inserting the following:

"(p) REGULATION OF NATIONALLY RECOGNIZED STATISTICAL RATING ORGANIZATIONS.—

"(1) ESTABLISHMENT OF OFFICE OF CREDIT RATINGS.—

"(A) OFFICE ESTABLISHED.—The Commission shall establish within the Commission an Office of Credit Ratings (referred to in this subsection as the 'Office') to administer the rules of the Commission—

"(i) with respect to the practices of nationally recognized statistical rating organizations in determining ratings, for the protection of users of credit ratings and in the public interest;

"(ii) to promote accuracy in credit ratings issued by nationally recognized statistical rating organizations; and

"(iii) to ensure that such ratings are not unduly influenced by conflicts of interest.

"(B) DIRECTOR OF THE OFFICE.—The head of the Office shall be the Director, who shall report to the Chairman.

"(2) STAFFING.—The Office established under this subsection shall be staffed sufficiently to carry out fully the requirements of this section. The staff shall include persons with knowledge of and expertise in corporate, municipal, and structured debt finance.

"(3) COMMISSION EXAMINATIONS.—

"(A) ANNUAL EXAMINATIONS REQUIRED.—The Office shall conduct an examination of each nationally recognized statistical rating organization at least annually.

"(B) CONDUCT OF EXAMINATIONS.—Each examination under subparagraph (A) shall include a review of—

"(i) whether the nationally recognized statistical rating organization conducts business in accordance with the policies, procedures, and rating methodologies of the nationally recognized statistical rating organization;

"(ii) the management of conflicts of interest by the nationally recognized statistical rating organization;

"(iii) implementation of ethics policies by the nationally recognized statistical rating organization;

"(iv) the internal supervisory controls of the nationally recognized statistical rating organization;

"(v) the governance of the nationally recognized statistical rating organization;

"(vi) the activities of the individual designated by the nationally recognized statistical rating organization under subsection (j)(1);

"(vii) the processing of complaints by the nationally recognized statistical rating organization; and

"(viii) the policies of the nationally recognized statistical rating organization governing the post-employment activities of former staff of the nationally recognized statistical rating organization.

"(C) INSPECTION REPORTS.—The Commission shall make available to the public, in an easily understandable format, an annual report summarizing—

"(i) the essential findings of all examinations conducted under subparagraph (A), as deemed appropriate by the Commission;

"(ii) the responses by the nationally recognized statistical rating organizations to any material regulatory deficiencies identified by the Commission under clause (i); and

"(iii) whether the nationally recognized statistical rating organizations have appropriately addressed the recommendations of the Commission contained in previous reports under this subparagraph.

"(4) RULEMAKING AUTHORITY.—The Commission shall—

"(A) establish, by rule, fines, and other penalties applicable to any nationally recognized statistical rating organization that violates the requirements of this section and the rules thereunder; and

"(B) issue such rules as may be necessary to carry out this section.

"(q) TRANSPARENCY OF RATINGS PERFORMANCE.—

"(1) RULEMAKING REQUIRED.—The Commission shall, by rule, require that each nationally recognized statistical rating organization publicly disclose information on the initial credit ratings determined by the nationally recognized statistical rating organization for each type of obligor, security, and money market instrument, and any subsequent changes to such credit ratings, for the purpose of allowing users of credit ratings to evaluate the accuracy of ratings and compare the performance of ratings by different nationally recognized statistical rating organizations.

"(2) CONTENT.—The rules of the Commission under this subsection shall require, at a minimum, disclosures that—

"(A) are comparable among nationally recognized statistical rating organizations, to allow users of credit ratings to compare the performance of credit ratings across nationally recognized statistical rating organizations;

"(B) are clear and informative for investors having a wide range of sophistication who use or might use credit ratings;

"(C) include performance information over a range of years and for a variety of types of credit ratings, including for credit ratings withdrawn by the nationally recognized statistical rating organization;

"(D) are published and made freely available by the nationally recognized statistical rating organization, on an easily accessible portion of its website, and in writing, when requested;

"(E) are appropriate to the business model of a nationally recognized statistical rating organization; and

"(F) each nationally recognized statistical rating organization include an attestation with any credit rating it issues affirming that no part of the rating was influenced by any other business activities, that the rating was based solely on the merits of the instruments being rated, and that such rating was an independent evaluation of the risks and merits of the instrument.

"(r) CREDIT RATINGS METHODOLOGIES.—The Commission shall prescribe rules, for the protection of investors and in the public interest, with respect to the procedures and methodologies, including qualitative and quantitative data and models, used by nationally recognized statistical rating organizations that require each nationally recognized statistical rating organization—

"(1) to ensure that credit ratings are determined using procedures and methodologies, including qualitative and quantitative data and models, that are—

"(A) approved by the board of the nationally recognized statistical rating organization, a body performing a function similar to that of a board; and

"(B) in accordance with the policies and procedures of the nationally recognized statistical rating organization for the development and modification of credit rating procedures and methodologies;

"(2) to ensure that when material changes to credit rating procedures and methodologies (including changes to qualitative and quantitative data and models) are made, that—

"(A) the changes are applied consistently to all credit ratings to which the changed procedures and methodologies apply;

"(B) to the extent that changes are made to credit rating surveillance procedures and methodologies, the changes are applied to then-current credit ratings by the nationally recognized statistical rating organization within a reasonable time period determined by the Commission, by rule; and

"(C) the nationally recognized statistical rating organization publicly discloses the reason for the change; and

"(3) to notify users of credit ratings—

"(A) of the version of a procedure or methodology, including the qualitative methodology or quantitative inputs, used with respect to a particular credit rating;

"(B) when a material change is made to a procedure or methodology, including to a qualitative model or quantitative inputs;

"(C) when a significant error is identified in a procedure or methodology, including a qualitative or quantitative model, that may result in credit rating actions; and

"(D) of the likelihood of a material change described in subparagraph (B) resulting in a change in current credit ratings.

"(s) TRANSPARENCY OF CREDIT RATING METHODOLOGIES AND INFORMATION REVIEWED.—

"(1) FORM FOR DISCLOSURES.—The Commission shall require, by rule, each nationally recognized statistical rating organization to prescribe a form to accompany the publication of each credit rating that discloses—

"(A) information relating to—

"(i) the assumptions underlying the credit rating procedures and methodologies;

"(ii) the data that was relied on to determine the credit rating; and

"(iii) if applicable, how the nationally recognized statistical rating organization used servicer or remittance reports, and with what frequency, to conduct surveillance of the credit rating; and

"(B) information that can be used by investors and other users of credit ratings to better understand credit ratings in each class of credit rating issued by the nationally recognized statistical rating organization.

"(2) FORMAT.—The form developed under paragraph (1) shall—

"(A) be easy to use and helpful for users of credit ratings to understand the information contained in the report;

"(B) require the nationally recognized statistical rating organization to provide the content described in paragraph (3)(B) in a manner that is directly comparable across types of securities; and

"(C) be made readily available to users of credit ratings, in electronic or paper form, as the Commission may, by rule, determine.

"(3) CONTENT OF FORM.—

"(A) QUALITATIVE CONTENT.—Each nationally recognized statistical rating organization shall disclose on the form developed under paragraph (1)—

"(i) the credit ratings produced by the nationally recognized statistical rating organization;

"(ii) the main assumptions and principles used in constructing procedures and methodologies, including qualitative methodologies and quantitative inputs and assumptions about the correlation of defaults across underlying assets used in rating structured products;

"(iii) the potential limitations of the credit ratings, and the types of risks excluded from the credit ratings that the nationally recognized statistical rating organization does not comment on, including liquidity, market, and other risks;

"(iv) information on the uncertainty of the credit rating, including—

"(I) information on the reliability, accuracy, and quality of the data relied on in determining the credit rating; and

"(II) a statement relating to the extent to which data essential to the determination of the credit rating were reliable or limited, including—

"(aa) any limits on the scope of historical data; and

"(bb) any limits in accessibility to certain documents or other types of information that would have better informed the credit rating;

"(v) whether and to what extent third party due diligence services have been used by the nationally recognized statistical rating organization, a description of the information that such third party reviewed in conducting due diligence services, and a description of the findings or conclusions of such third party;

"(vi) a description of the data about any obligor, issuer, security, or money market instrument that were relied upon for the purpose of determining the credit rating;

"(vii) a statement containing an overall assessment of the quality of information available and considered in producing a rating for an obligor, security, or money market instrument, in relation to the quality of information available to the nationally recognized statistical rating organization in rating similar issuances;

"(viii) information relating to conflicts of interest of the nationally recognized statistical rating organization; and

"(ix) such additional information as the Commission may require.

"(B) QUANTITATIVE CONTENT.—Each nationally recognized statistical rating organization shall disclose on the form developed under this subsection—

"(i) an explanation or measure of the potential volatility of the credit rating, including—

"(I) any factors that might lead to a change in the credit ratings; and

"(II) the magnitude of the change that a user can expect under different market conditions;

"(ii) information on the content of the rating, including—

"(I) the historical performance of the rating; and

"(II) the expected probability of default and the expected loss in the event of default;

"(iii) information on the sensitivity of the rating to assumptions made by the nationally recognized statistical rating organization, including—

"(I) 5 assumptions made in the ratings process that, without accounting for any other factor, would have the greatest impact on a rating if the assumptions were proven false or inaccurate; and

"(II) an analysis, using specific examples, of how each of the 5 assumptions identified under subclause (I) impacts a rating;

"(iv) such additional information as may be required by the Commission.

"(4) DUE DILIGENCE SERVICES FOR ASSET-BACKED SECURITIES.—

"(A) FINDINGS.—The issuer or underwriter of any asset-backed security shall make publicly available the findings and conclusions of any third-party due diligence report obtained by the issuer or underwriter.

"(B) CERTIFICATION REQUIRED.—In any case in which third-party due diligence services are employed by a nationally recognized statistical rating organization, an issuer, or an underwriter, the person providing the due diligence services shall provide to any nationally recognized statistical rating organization that produces a rating to which such services relate, written certification, as provided in subparagraph (C).

"(C) FORMAT AND CONTENT.—The Commission shall establish the appropriate format and content for the written certifications required under subparagraph (B), to ensure that providers of due diligence services have conducted a thorough review of data, documentation, and other relevant information necessary for a nationally recognized statistical rating organization to provide an accurate rating.

"(D) DISCLOSURE OF CERTIFICATION.—The Commission shall adopt rules requiring a nationally recognized statistical rating organization, at the time at which the nationally recognized statistical rating organization produces a rating, to disclose the certification described in subparagraph (B) to the public in a manner that allows the public to determine the adequacy and level of due diligence services provided by a third party.

"(t) CORPORATE GOVERNANCE, ORGANIZATION, AND MANAGEMENT OF CONFLICTS OF INTEREST.—

"(1) BOARD OF DIRECTORS.—Each nationally recognized statistical rating organization shall have a board of directors.

"(2) INDEPENDENT DIRECTORS.—

"(A) IN GENERAL.—At least ½ of the board of directors, but not fewer than 2 of the members thereof, shall be independent of the nationally recognized statistical rating agency. A portion of the independent directors shall include users of ratings from a nationally recognized statistical rating organization.

"(B) INDEPENDENCE DETERMINATION.—In order to be considered independent for purposes of this subsection, a member of the board of directors of a nationally recognized statistical rating organization—

"(i) may not, other than in his or her capacity as a member of the board of directors or any committee thereof—

"(I) accept any consulting, advisory, or other compensatory fee from the nationally recognized statistical rating organization; or

"(II) be a person associated with the nationally recognized statistical rating organization or with any affiliated company thereof; and

"(ii) shall be disqualified from any deliberation involving a specific rating in which the independent board member has a financial interest in the outcome of the rating.

"(C) COMPENSATION AND TERM.—The compensation of the independent members of the board of directors of a nationally recognized statistical rating organization shall not be linked to the business performance of the nationally recognized statistical rating organization, and shall be arranged so as to ensure the independence of their judgment. The term of office of the independent directors shall be for a pre-agreed fixed period, not to exceed 5 years, and shall not be renewable.

"(3) DUTIES OF BOARD OF DIRECTORS.—In addition to the overall responsibilities of the board of directors, the board shall oversee—

"(A) the establishment, maintenance, and enforcement of policies and procedures for determining credit ratings;

"(B) the establishment, maintenance, and enforcement of policies and procedures to address, manage, and disclose any conflicts of interest;

"(C) the effectiveness of the internal control system with respect to policies and procedures for determining credit ratings; and

"(D) the compensation and promotion policies and practices of the nationally recognized statistical rating organization.

"(4) TREATMENT OF NRSRO SUBSIDIARIES.—If a nationally recognized statistical rating organization is a subsidiary of a parent entity, the board of the directors of the parent entity may satisfy the requirements of this subsection by assigning to a committee of such board of directors the duties under paragraph (3), if—

"(A) at least ½ of the members of the committee (including the chairperson of the committee) are independent, as defined in this section; and

"(B) at least 1 member of the committee is a user of ratings from a nationally recognized statistical rating organization.

"(5) EXCEPTION AUTHORITY.—If the Commission finds that compliance with the provisions of this subsection present an unreasonable burden on a small nationally recognized statistical rating organization, the Commission may permit the nationally recognized statistical rating organization to delegate such responsibilities to a committee that includes at least one individual who is a user of ratings of a nationally recognized statistical rating organization.".

(b) CONFORMING AMENDMENT.—Section 3(a)(62) of the Securities Exchange Act of 1934 (15 U.S.C. 78c(a)(62)) is amended by striking subparagraph (A) and redesignating subparagraphs (B) and (C) as subparagraphs (A) and (B), respectively.

[Explanation at ¶ 4185.]

[¶ 10,933] ACT SEC. 933. STATE OF MIND IN PRIVATE ACTIONS.

(a) ACCOUNTABILITY.—Section 15E(m) of the Securities Exchange Act of 1934 (15 U.S.C. 78o-7(m)) is amended to read as follows:

"(m) ACCOUNTABILITY.—

"(1) IN GENERAL.—The enforcement and penalty provisions of this title shall apply to statements made by a credit rating agency in the same manner and to the same extent as such provisions apply to statements made by a registered public accounting firm or a securities analyst under the securities laws, and such statements shall not be deemed forwardlooking statements for the purposes of section 21E.

"(2) RULEMAKING.—The Commission shall issue such rules as may be necessary to carry out this subsection.".

(b) STATE OF MIND.—Section 21D(b)(2) of the Securities Exchange Act of 1934 (15 U.S.C. 78u-4(b)(2)) is amended—

(1) by striking "In any" and inserting the following:

"(A) IN GENERAL.—Except as provided in subparagraph (B), in any"; and

(2) by adding at the end the following:

"(B) EXCEPTION.—In the case of an action for money damages brought against a credit rating agency or a controlling person under this title, it shall be sufficient, for purposes of pleading any required state of mind in relation to such action, that the complaint state with particularity facts giving rise to a strong inference that the credit rating agency knowingly or recklessly failed—

"(i) to conduct a reasonable investigation of the rated security with respect to the factual elements relied upon by its own methodology for evaluating credit risk; or

"(ii) to obtain reasonable verification of such factual elements (which verification may be based on a sampling technique that does not amount to an audit) from other sources that the credit rating agency considered to be competent and that were independent of the issuer and underwriter.".

[Explanation at ¶ 4195.]

[¶ 10,934] ACT SEC. 934. REFERRING TIPS TO LAW ENFORCEMENT OR REGULATORY AUTHORITIES.

Section 15E of the Securities Exchange Act of 1934 (15 U.S.C. 78o-7), as amended by this subtitle, is amended by adding at the end the following:

"(u) DUTY TO REPORT TIPS ALLEGING MATERIAL VIOLATIONS OF LAW.—

"(1) DUTY TO REPORT.—Each nationally recognized statistical rating organization shall refer to the appropriate law enforcement or regulatory authorities any information that the nationally recognized statistical rating organization receives from a third party and finds credible that alleges that an issuer of securities rated by the nationally recognized statistical rating organization has committed or is committing a material violation of law that has not been adjudicated by a Federal or State court.

"(2) RULE OF CONSTRUCTION.—Nothing in paragraph (1) may be construed to require a nationally recognized statistical rating organization to verify the accuracy of the information described in paragraph (1).".

[Explanation at ¶ 4215.]

[¶ 10,935] ACT SEC. 935. CONSIDERATION OF INFORMATION FROM SOURCES OTHER THAN THE ISSUER IN RATING DECISIONS.

Section 15E of the Securities Exchange Act of 1934 (15 U.S.C. 78o-7), as amended by this subtitle, is amended by adding at the end the following:

"(v) INFORMATION FROM SOURCES OTHER THAN THE ISSUER.—In producing a credit rating, a nationally recognized statistical rating organization shall consider information about an issuer that the nationally recognized statistical rating organization has, or receives from a source other than the issuer or underwriter, that the nationally recognized statistical rating organization finds credible and potentially significant to a rating decision.".

[Explanation at ¶4200.]

[¶10,936] ACT SEC. 936. QUALIFICATION STANDARDS FOR CREDIT RATING ANALYSTS.

Not later than 1 year after the date of enactment of this Act, the Commission shall issue rules that are reasonably designed to ensure that any person employed by a nationally recognized statistical rating organization to perform credit ratings—

(1) meets standards of training, experience, and competence necessary to produce accurate ratings for the categories of issuers whose securities the person rates; and

(2) is tested for knowledge of the credit rating process.

[Explanation at ¶4205.]

[¶10,937] ACT SEC. 937. TIMING OF REGULATIONS.

Unless otherwise specifically provided in this subtitle, the Commission shall issue final regulations, as required by this subtitle and the amendments made by this subtitle, not later than 1 year after the date of enactment of this Act.

[Explanation at ¶4180.]

[¶10,938] ACT SEC. 938. UNIVERSAL RATINGS SYMBOLS.

(a) RULEMAKING.—The Commission shall require, by rule, each nationally recognized statistical rating organization to establish, maintain, and enforce written policies and procedures that—

(1) assess the probability that an issuer of a security or money market instrument will default, fail to make timely payments, or otherwise not make payments to investors in accordance with the terms of the security or money market instrument;

(2) clearly define and disclose the meaning of any symbol used by the nationally recognized statistical rating organization to denote a credit rating; and

(3) apply any symbol described in paragraph (2) in a manner that is consistent for all types of securities and money market instruments for which the symbol is used.

(b) RULE OF CONSTRUCTION.—Nothing in this section shall prohibit a nationally recognized statistical rating organization from using distinct sets of symbols to denote credit ratings for different types of securities or money market instruments.

[Explanation at ¶4210.]

[¶10,939] ACT SEC. 939. REMOVAL OF STATUTORY REFERENCES TO CREDIT RATINGS.

(a) FEDERAL DEPOSIT INSURANCE ACT.—The Federal Deposit Insurance Act (12 U.S.C. 1811 et seq.) is amended—

(1) in section 7(b)(1)(E)(i), by striking "credit rating entities, and other private economic" and insert "private economic, credit,";

(2) in section 28(d)—

(A) in the subsection heading, by striking "NOT OF INVESTMENT GRADE";

(B) in paragraph (1), by striking "not of investment grade" and inserting "that does not meet standards of credit-worthiness as established by the Corporation";

(C) in paragraph (2), by striking "not of investment grade";

(D) by striking paragraph (3);

(E) by redesignating paragraph (4) as paragraph (3); and

(F) in paragraph (3), as so redesignated—

(i) by striking subparagraph (A);

(ii) by redesignating subparagraphs (B) and (C) as subparagraphs (A) and (B), respectively; and

(iii) in subparagraph (B), as so redesignated, by striking "not of investment grade" and inserting "that does not meet standards of credit-worthiness as established by the Corporation"; and

(3) in section 28(e)—

(A) in the subsection heading, by striking "NOT OF INVESTMENT GRADE";

(B) in paragraph (1), by striking "not of investment grade" and inserting "that does not meet standards of credit-worthiness as established by the Corporation"; and

(C) in paragraphs (2) and (3), by striking "not of investment grade" each place that it appears and inserting "that does not meet standards of credit-worthiness established by the Corporation".

(b) FEDERAL HOUSING ENTERPRISES FINANCIAL SAFETY AND SOUNDNESS ACT OF 1992.—Section 1319 of the Federal Housing Enterprises Financial Safety and Soundness Act of 1992 (12 U.S.C. 4519) is amended by striking "that is a nationally recognized statistical rating organization, as such term is defined in section 3(a) of the Securities Exchange Act of 1934,".

(c) INVESTMENT COMPANY ACT OF 1940.—Section 6(a)(5)(A)(iv)(I) Investment Company Act of 1940 (15 U.S.C. 80a-6(a)(5)(A)(iv)(I)) is amended by striking "is rated investment grade by not less than 1 nationally recognized statistical rating organization" and inserting "meets such standards of credit-worthiness as the Commission shall adopt".

(d) REVISED STATUTES.—Section 5136A of title LXII of the Revised Statutes of the United States (12 U.S.C. 24a) is amended—

(1) in subsection (a)(2)(E), by striking "any applicable rating" and inserting "standards of credit-worthiness established by the Comptroller of the Currency";

(2) in the heading for subsection (a)(3) by striking "RATING OR COMPARABLE REQUIREMENT" and inserting "REQUIREMENT";

(3) subsection (a)(3), by amending subparagraph (A) to read as follows:

"(A) IN GENERAL.—A national bank meets the requirements of this paragraph if the bank is one of the 100 largest insured banks and has not fewer than 1 issue of outstanding debt that meets standards of credit-worthiness or other criteria as the Secretary of the Treasury and the Board of Governors of the Federal Reserve System may jointly establish.".

(4) in the heading for subsection (f), by striking "MAINTAIN PUBLIC RATING OR" and inserting "MEET STANDARDS OF CREDIT-WORTHINESS"; and

(5) in subsection (f)(1), by striking "any applicable rating" and inserting "standards of credit-worthiness established by the Comptroller of the Currency".

(e) SECURITIES EXCHANGE ACT OF 1934.—Section 3(a) Securities Exchange Act of 1934 (15 U.S.C. 78a(3)(a)) is amended—

(1) in paragraph (41), by striking "is rated in one of the two highest rating categories by at least one nationally recognized statistical rating organization" and inserting "meets standards of credit-worthiness as established by the Commission"; and

(2) in paragraph (53)(A), by striking "is rated in 1 of the 4 highest rating categories by at least 1 nationally recognized statistical rating organization" and inserting "meets standards of credit-worthiness as established by the Commission".

(f) WORLD BANK DISCUSSIONS.—Section 3(a)(6) of the amendment in the nature of a substitute to the text of H.R. 4645, as ordered reported from the Committee on Banking, Finance and Urban Affairs on September 22, 1988, as enacted into law by section 555 of Public Law 100-461, (22 U.S.C. 286hh(a)(6)), is amended by striking "credit rating" and inserting "credit-worthiness".

(g) EFFECTIVE DATE.—The amendments made by this section shall take effect 2 years after the date of enactment of this Act.

(h) STUDY AND REPORT.—

(1) IN GENERAL.—Commission shall undertake a study on the feasability and desirability of—

(A) standardizing credit ratings terminology, so that all credit rating agencies issue credit ratings using identical terms;

(B) standardizing the market stress conditions under which ratings are evaluated;

(C) requiring a quantitative correspondence between credit ratings and a range of default probabilities and loss expectations under standardized conditions of economic stress; and

(D) standardizing credit rating terminology across asset classes, so that named ratings correspond to a standard range of default probabilities and expected losses independent of asset class and issuing entity.

(2) REPORT.—Not later than 1 year after the date of enactment of this Act, the Commission shall submit to Congress a report containing the findings of the study under paragraph (1) and the recommendations, if any, of the Commission with respect to the study.

[Explanation at ¶ 4220.]

[¶ 10,939A] ACT SEC. 939A. REVIEW OF RELIANCE ON RATINGS.

(a) AGENCY REVIEW.—Not later than 1 year after the date of the enactment of this subtitle, each Federal agency shall, to the extent applicable, review—

(1) any regulation issued by such agency that requires the use of an assessment of the credit-worthiness of a security or money market instrument; and

(2) any references to or requirements in such regulations regarding credit ratings.

(b) MODIFICATIONS REQUIRED.—Each such agency shall modify any such regulations identified by the review conducted under subsection (a) to remove any reference to or requirement of reliance on credit ratings and to substitute in such regulations such standard of credit-worthiness as each respective agency shall determine as appropriate for such regulations. In making such determination, such agencies shall seek to establish, to the extent feasible, uniform standards of credit-worthiness for use by each such agency, taking into account the entities regulated by each such agency and the purposes for which such entities would rely on such standards of credit-worthiness.

(c) REPORT.—Upon conclusion of the review required under subsection (a), each Federal agency shall transmit a report to Congress containing a description of any modification of any regulation such agency made pursuant to subsection (b).

[Explanation at ¶ 4235.]

[¶ 10,939B] ACT SEC. 939B. ELIMINATION OF EXEMPTION FROM FAIR DISCLOSURE RULE.

Not later than 90 days after the date of enactment of this subtitle, the Securities Exchange Commission shall revise Regulation FD (17 C.F.R. 243.100) to remove from such regulation the exemption for entities whose primary business is the issuance of credit ratings (17 C.F.R. 243.100(b)(2)(iii)).

[Explanation at ¶ 4225.]

[¶ 10,939C] ACT SEC. 939C. SECURITIES AND EXCHANGE COMMISSION STUDY ON STRENGTHENING CREDIT RATING AGENCY INDEPENDENCE.

(a) STUDY.—The Commission shall conduct a study of—

(1) the independence of nationally recognized statistical rating organizations; and

(2) how the independence of nationally recognized statistical rating organizations affects the ratings issued by the nationally recognized statistical rating organizations.

(b) SUBJECTS FOR EVALUATION.—In conducting the study under subsection (a), the Commission shall evaluate—

(1) the management of conflicts of interest raised by a nationally recognized statistical rating organization providing other services, including risk management advisory services, ancillary assistance, or consulting services;

(2) the potential impact of rules prohibiting a nationally recognized statistical rating organization that provides a rating to an issuer from providing other services to the issuer; and

(3) any other issue relating to nationally recognized statistical rating organizations, as the Chairman of the Commission determines is appropriate.

(c) REPORT.—Not later than 3 years after the date of enactment of this Act, the Chairman of the Commission shall submit to the Committee on Banking, Housing, and Urban Affairs of the Senate and the Committee on Financial Services of the House of Representatives a report on the results of the study conducted under subsection (a), including recommendations, if any, for improving the integrity of ratings issued by nationally recognized statistical rating organizations.

[Explanation at ¶ 4235.]

[¶ 10,939D] ACT SEC. 939D. GOVERNMENT ACCOUNTABILITY OFFICE STUDY ON ALTERNATIVE BUSINESS MODELS.

(a) STUDY.—The Comptroller General of the United States shall conduct a study on alternative means for compensating nationally recognized statistical rating organizations in order to create incentives for nationally recognized statistical rating organizations to provide more accurate credit ratings, including any statutory changes that would be required to facilitate the use of an alternative means of compensation.

(b) REPORT.—Not later than 18 months after the date of enactment of this Act, the Comptroller General shall submit to the Committee on Banking, Housing, and Urban Affairs of the Senate and the Committee on Financial Services of the House of Representatives a report on the results of the study conducted under subsection (a), including recommendations, if any, for providing incentives to credit rating agencies to improve the credit rating process.

[Explanation at ¶ 4235.]

[¶ 10,939E] ACT SEC. 939E. GOVERNMENT ACCOUNTABILITY OFFICE STUDY ON THE CREATION OF AN INDEPENDENT PROFESSIONAL ANALYST ORGANIZATION.

(a) STUDY.—The Comptroller General of the United States shall conduct a study on the feasibility and merits of creating an independent professional organization for rating analysts employed by nationally recognized statistical rating organizations that would be responsible for—

(1) establishing independent standards for governing the profession of rating analysts;

(2) establishing a code of ethical conduct; and

(3) overseeing the profession of rating analysts.

(b) REPORT.—Not later than 1 year after the date of publication of the rules issued by the Commission pursuant to section 936, the Comptroller General shall submit to the Committee on Banking, Housing, and Urban Affairs of the Senate and the Committee on Financial Services of the House of Representatives a report on the results of the study conducted under subsection (a).

[Explanation at ¶ 4235.]

[¶ 10,939F] ACT SEC. 939F. STUDY AND RULEMAKING ON ASSIGNED CREDIT RATINGS.

(a) DEFINITION.—In this section, the term "structured finance product" means an asset-backed security, as defined in section 3(a)(77) of the Securities Exchange Act of 1934, as added by section 941, and any structured product based on an asset-backed security, as determined by the Commission, by rule.

(b) STUDY.—The Commission shall carry out a study of—

(1) the credit rating process for structured finance products and the conflicts of interest associated with the issuer-pay and the subscriber-pay models;

(2) the feasibility of establishing a system in which a public or private utility or a self-regulatory organization assigns nationally recognized statistical rating organizations to determine the credit ratings of structured finance products, including—

(A) an assessment of potential mechanisms for determining fees for the nationally recognized statistical rating organizations;

(B) appropriate methods for paying fees to the nationally recognized statistical rating organizations;

(C) the extent to which the creation of such a system would be viewed as the creation of moral hazard by the Federal Government; and

(D) any constitutional or other issues concerning the establishment of such a system;

(3) the range of metrics that could be used to determine the accuracy of credit ratings; and

(4) alternative means for compensating nationally recognized statistical rating organizations that would create incentives for accurate credit ratings.

(c) REPORT AND RECOMMENDATION.—Not later than 24 months after the date of enactment of this Act, the Commission shall submit to the Committee on Banking, Housing, and Urban Affairs of the Senate and the Committee on Financial Services of the House of Representatives a report that contains—

(1) the findings of the study required under subsection (b); and

(2) any recommendations for regulatory or statutory changes that the Commission determines should be made to implement the findings of the study required under subsection (b).

(d) RULEMAKING.—

(1) RULEMAKING.—After submission of the report under subsection (c), the Commission shall, by rule, as the Commission determines is necessary or appropriate in the public interest or for the protection of investors, establish a system for the assignment of nationally recognized statistical rating organizations to determine the initial credit ratings of structured finance products, in a manner that prevents the issuer, sponsor, or underwriter of the structured finance product from selecting the nationally recognized statistical rating organization that will determine the initial credit ratings and monitor such credit ratings. In issuing any rule under this paragraph, the Commission shall give thorough consideration to the provisions of section 15E(w) of the Securities Exchange Act of 1934, as that provision would have been added by section 939D of H.R. 4173 (111th Congress), as passed by the Senate on May 20, 2010, and shall implement the system described in such section 939D unless the Commission determines that an alternative system would better serve the public interest and the protection of investors.

(2) RULE OF CONSTRUCTION.—Nothing in this subsection may be construed to limit or suspend any other rulemaking authority of the Commission.

[Explanation at ¶4190.]

[¶10,939G] ACT SEC. 939G. EFFECT OF RULE 436(G).

Rule 436(g), promulgated by the Securities and Exchange Commission under the Securities Act of 1933, shall have no force or effect.

[Explanation at ¶4230.]

[¶10,939H] ACT SEC. 939H. SENSE OF CONGRESS.

It is the sense of Congress that the Securities and Exchange Commission should exercise the rulemaking authority of the Commission under section 15E(h)(2)(B) of the Securities Exchange Act of 1934 (15 U.S.C. 78o-7(h)(2)(B)) to prevent improper conflicts of interest arising from employees of nationally recognized statistical rating organizations providing services to issuers of securities that are unrelated to the issuance of credit ratings, including consulting, advisory, and other services.

[Explanation at ¶ 4180.]

Subtitle D—Improvements to the Asset-Backed Securitization Process

[¶ 10,941] ACT SEC. 941. REGULATION OF CREDIT RISK RETENTION.

(a) DEFINITION OF ASSET-BACKED SECURITY.—Section 3(a) of the Securities Exchange Act of 1934 (15 U.S.C. 78c(a)) is amended by adding at the end the following:

"(77) ASSET-BACKED SECURITY.—The term 'asset-backed security'—

"(A) means a fixed-income or other security collateralized by any type of self-liquidating financial asset (including a loan, a lease, a mortgage, or a secured or unsecured receivable) that allows the holder of the security to receive payments that depend primarily on cash flow from the asset, including—

"(i) a collateralized mortgage obligation;

"(ii) a collateralized debt obligation;

"(iii) a collateralized bond obligation;

"(iv) a collateralized debt obligation of asset-backed securities;

"(v) a collateralized debt obligation of collateralized debt obligations; and

"(vi) a security that the Commission, by rule, determines to be an asset-backed security for purposes of this section; and

"(B) does not include a security issued by a finance subsidiary held by the parent company or a company controlled by the parent company, if none of the securities issued by the finance subsidiary are held by an entity that is not controlled by the parent company.".

(b) CREDIT RISK RETENTION.—The Securities Exchange Act of 1934 (15 U.S.C. 78a et seq.) is amended by inserting after section 15F, as added by this Act, the following:

"SEC. 15G. CREDIT RISK RETENTION.

"(a) DEFINITIONS.—In this section—

"(1) the term 'Federal banking agencies' means the Office of the Comptroller of the Currency, the Board of Governors of the Federal Reserve System, and the Federal Deposit Insurance Corporation;

"(2) the term 'insured depository institution' has the same meaning as in section 3(c) of the Federal Deposit Insurance Act (12 U.S.C. 1813(c));

"(3) the term 'securitizer' means—

"(A) an issuer of an asset-backed security; or

"(B) a person who organizes and initiates an asset-backed securities transaction by selling or transferring assets, either directly or indirectly, including through an affiliate, to the issuer; and

"(4) the term 'originator' means a person who—

"(A) through the extension of credit or otherwise, creates a financial asset that collateralizes an asset-backed security; and

"(B) sells an asset directly or indirectly to a securitizer.

"(b) REGULATIONS REQUIRED.—

"(1) IN GENERAL.—Not later than 270 days after the date of enactment of this section, the Federal banking agencies and the Commission shall jointly prescribe regulations to require any securitizer to retain an economic interest in a portion of the credit risk for any asset that the securitizer, through the issuance of an asset-backed security, transfers, sells, or conveys to a third party.

"(2) RESIDENTIAL MORTGAGES.—Not later than 270 days after the date of the enactment of this section, the Federal banking agencies, the Commission, the Secretary of Housing and Urban Development, and the Federal Housing Finance Agency, shall jointly prescribe regulations to require any securitizer to retain an economic interest in a portion of the credit risk for any residential mortgage asset that the securitizer, through the issuance of an asset-backed security, transfers, sells, or conveys to a third party.

"(c) STANDARDS FOR REGULATIONS.—

"(1) STANDARDS.—The regulations prescribed under subsection (b) shall—

"(A) prohibit a securitizer from directly or indirectly hedging or otherwise transferring the credit risk that the securitizer is required to retain with respect to an asset;

"(B) require a securitizer to retain—

"(i) not less than 5 percent of the credit risk for any asset—

"(I) that is not a qualified residential mortgage that is transferred, sold, or conveyed through the issuance of an asset-backed security by the securitizer; or

"(II) that is a qualified residential mortgage that is transferred, sold, or conveyed through the issuance of an asset-backed security by the securitizer, if 1 or more of the assets that collateralize the asset-backed security are not qualified residential mortgages; or

"(ii) less than 5 percent of the credit risk for an asset that is not a qualified residential mortgage that is transferred, sold, or conveyed through the issuance of an asset-backed security by the securitizer, if the originator of the asset meets the underwriting standards prescribed under paragraph (2)(B);

"(C) specify—

"(i) the permissible forms of risk retention for purposes of this section;

"(ii) the minimum duration of the risk retention required under this section; and

"(iii) that a securitizer is not required to retain any part of the credit risk for an asset that is transferred, sold or conveyed through the issuance of an asset-backed security by the securitizer, if all of the assets that collateralize the asset-backed security are qualified residential mortgages;

"(D) apply, regardless of whether the securitizer is an insured depository institution;

"(E) with respect to a commercial mortgage, specify the permissible types, forms, and amounts of risk retention that would meet the requirements of subparagraph (B), which in the determination of the Federal banking agencies and the Commission may include—

"(i) retention of a specified amount or percentage of the total credit risk of the asset;

"(ii) retention of the first-loss position by a third-party purchaser that specifically negotiates for the purchase of such first loss position, holds adequate financial resources to back losses, provides due diligence on all individual assets in the pool before the issuance of the asset-backed securities, and meets the same standards for risk retention as the Federal banking agencies and the Commission require of the securitizer;

"(iii) a determination by the Federal banking agencies and the Commission that the underwriting standards and controls for the asset are adequate; and

"(iv) provision of adequate representations and warranties and related enforcement mechanisms; and

"(F) establish appropriate standards for retention of an economic interest with respect to collateralized debt obligations, securities collateralized by collateralized debt obligations, and similar instruments collateralized by other asset-backed securities; and

"(G) provide for—

"(i) a total or partial exemption of any securitization, as may be appropriate in the public interest and for the protection of investors;

"(ii) a total or partial exemption for the securitization of an asset issued or guaranteed by the United States, or an agency of the United States, as the Federal banking agencies and the Commission jointly determine appropriate in the public interest and for the protection of investors, except that, for purposes of this clause, the Federal National Mortgage Association and the Federal Home Loan Mortgage Corporation are not agencies of the United States;

"(iii) a total or partial exemption for any asset-backed security that is a security issued or guaranteed by any State of the United States, or by any political subdivision of a State or territory, or by any public instrumentality of a State or territory that is exempt from, the registration requirements of the Securities Act of 1933 by reason of section 3(a)(2) of that Act (15 U.S.C. 77c(a)(2)), or a security defined as a qualified scholarship funding bond in section 150(d)(2) of the Internal Revenue Code of 1986, as may be appropriate in the public interest and for the protection of investors; and

"(iv) the allocation of risk retention obligations between a securitizer and an originator in the case of a securitizer that purchases assets from an originator, as the Federal banking agencies and the Commission jointly determine appropriate.

"(2) ASSET CLASSES.—

"(A) ASSET CLASSES.—The regulations prescribed under subsection (b) shall establish asset classes with separate rules for securitizers of different classes of assets, including residential mortgages, commercial mortgages, commercial loans, auto loans, and any other class of assets that the Federal banking agencies and the Commission deem appropriate.

"(B) CONTENTS.—For each asset class established under subparagraph (A), the regulations prescribed under subsection (b) shall include underwriting standards established by the Federal banking agencies that specify the terms, conditions, and characteristics of a loan within the asset class that indicate a low credit risk with respect to the loan.

"(d) ORIGINATORS.—In determining how to allocate risk retention obligations between a securitizer and an originator under subsection (c)(1)(E)(iv), the Federal banking agencies and the Commission shall—

"(1) reduce the percentage of risk retention obligations required of the securitizer by the percentage of risk retention obligations required of the originator; and

"(2) consider—

"(A) whether the assets sold to the securitizer have terms, conditions, and characteristics that reflect low credit risk;

"(B) whether the form or volume of transactions in securitization markets creates incentives for imprudent origination of the type of loan or asset to be sold to the securitizer; and

"(C) the potential impact of the risk retention obligations on the access of consumers and businesses to credit on reasonable terms, which may not include the transfer of credit risk to a third party.

"(e) EXEMPTIONS, EXCEPTIONS, AND ADJUSTMENTS.—

"(1) IN GENERAL.—The Federal banking agencies and the Commission may jointly adopt or issue exemptions, exceptions, or adjustments to the rules issued under this section, including exemptions, exceptions, or adjustments for classes of institutions or assets relating to the risk retention requirement and the prohibition on hedging under subsection (c)(1).

"(2) APPLICABLE STANDARDS.—Any exemption, exception, or adjustment adopted or issued by the Federal banking agencies and the Commission under this paragraph shall—

"(A) help ensure high quality underwriting standards for the securitizers and originators of assets that are securitized or available for securitization; and

"(B) encourage appropriate risk management practices by the securitizers and originators of assets, improve the access of consumers and businesses to credit on reasonable terms, or otherwise be in the public interest and for the protection of investors.

"(3) CERTAIN INSTITUTIONS AND PROGRAMS EXEMPT.—

"(A) FARM CREDIT SYSTEM INSTITUTIONS.—Notwithstanding any other provision of this section, the requirements of this section shall not apply to any loan or other financial asset made, insured, guaranteed, or purchased by any institution that is subject to the supervision of the Farm Credit Administration, including the Federal Agricultural Mortgage Corporation.

"(B) OTHER FEDERAL PROGRAMS.—This section shall not apply to any residential, multifamily, or health care facility mortgage loan asset, or securitization based directly or indirectly on such an asset, which is insured or guaranteed by the United States or an agency of the United States. For purposes of this subsection, the Federal National Mortgage Association, the Federal Home Loan Mortgage Corporation, and the Federal home loan banks shall not be considered an agency of the United States.

"(4) EXEMPTION FOR QUALIFIED RESIDENTIAL MORTGAGES.—

"(A) IN GENERAL.—The Federal banking agencies, the Commission, the Secretary of Housing and Urban Development, and the Director of the Federal Housing Finance Agency shall jointly issue regulations to exempt qualified residential mortgages from the risk retention requirements of this subsection.

"(B) QUALIFIED RESIDENTIAL MORTGAGE.—The Federal banking agencies, the Commission, the Secretary of Housing and Urban Development, and the Director of the Federal Housing Finance Agency shall jointly define the term 'qualified residential mortgage' for purposes of this subsection, taking into consideration underwriting and product features that historical loan performance data indicate result in a lower risk of default, such as—

"(i) documentation and verification of the financial resources relied upon to qualify the mortgagor;

"(ii) standards with respect to—

"(I) the residual income of the mortgagor after all monthly obligations;

"(II) the ratio of the housing payments of the mortgagor to the monthly income of the mortgagor;

"(III) the ratio of total monthly installment payments of the mortgagor to the income of the mortgagor;

"(iii) mitigating the potential for payment shock on adjustable rate mortgages through product features and underwriting standards;

"(iv) mortgage guarantee insurance or other types of insurance or credit enhancement obtained at the time of origination, to the extent such insurance or credit enhancement reduces the risk of default; and

"(v) prohibiting or restricting the use of balloon payments, negative amortization, prepayment penalties, interest-only payments, and other features that have been demonstrated to exhibit a higher risk of borrower default.

"(C) LIMITATION ON DEFINITION.—The Federal banking agencies, the Commission, the Secretary of Housing and Urban Development, and the Director of the Federal Housing Finance Agency in defining the term 'qualified residential mortgage', as required by subparagraph (B), shall define that term to be no broader than the definition 'qualified mortgage' as the term is defined under section 129C(c)(2) of the Truth in Lending Act, as amended by the Consumer Financial Protection Act of 2010, and regulations adopted thereunder.

"(5) CONDITION FOR QUALIFIED RESIDENTIAL MORTGAGE EXEMPTION.—The regulations issued under paragraph (4) shall provide that an asset-backed security that is collateralized by tranches of other asset-backed securities shall not be exempt from the risk retention requirements of this subsection.

"(6) CERTIFICATION.—The Commission shall require an issuer to certify, for each issuance of an asset-backed security collateralized exclusively by qualified residential mortgages, that the issuer has evaluated the effectiveness of the internal supervisory controls of the issuer with respect to the process for ensuring that all assets that collateralize the asset-backed security are qualified residential mortgages.

"(f) ENFORCEMENT.—The regulations issued under this section shall be enforced by—

"(1) the appropriate Federal banking agency, with respect to any securitizer that is an insured depository institution; and

"(2) the Commission, with respect to any securitizer that is not an insured depository institution.

"(g) AUTHORITY OF COMMISSION.—The authority of the Commission under this section shall be in addition to the authority of the Commission to otherwise enforce the securities laws.

"(h) AUTHORITY TO COORDINATE ON RULEMAKING.—The Chairperson of the Financial Stability Oversight Council shall coordinate all joint rulemaking required under this section.

"(i) EFFECTIVE DATE OF REGULATIONS.—The regulations issued under this section shall become effective—

"(1) with respect to securitizers and originators of asset-backed securities backed by residential mortgages, 1 year after the date on which final rules under this section are published in the Federal Register; and

"(2) with respect to securitizers and originators of all other classes of asset-backed securities, 2 years after the date on which final rules under this section are published in the Federal Register.".

(c) STUDY ON RISK RETENTION.—

(1) STUDY.—The Board of Governors of the Federal Reserve System, in coordination and consultation with the Comptroller of the Currency, the Director of the Office of Thrift Supervision, the Chairperson of the Federal Deposit Insurance Corporation, and the Securities and Exchange Commission shall conduct a study of the combined impact on each individual class of asset-backed security established under section 15G(c)(2) of the Securities Exchange Act of 1934, as added by subsection (b), of—

(A) the new credit risk retention requirements contained in the amendment made by subsection (b), including the effect credit risk retention requirements have on increasing the market for Federally subsidized loans; and

(B) the Financial Accounting Statements 166 and 167 issued by the Financial Accounting Standards Board.

(2) REPORT.—Not later than 90 days after the date of enactment of this Act, the Board of Governors of the Federal Reserve System shall submit to Congress a report on the study conducted under paragraph (1). Such report shall include statutory and regulatory recommendations for eliminating any negative impacts on the continued viability of the asset-backed securitization markets and on the availability of credit for new lending identified by the study conducted under paragraph (1).

[Explanation at ¶ 4250 and ¶ 4255.]

[¶ 10,942] ACT SEC. 942. DISCLOSURES AND REPORTING FOR ASSET-BACKED SECURITIES.

(a) SECURITIES EXCHANGE ACT OF 1934.—Section 15(d) of the Securities Exchange Act of 1934 (15 U.S.C. 78o(d)) is amended—

(1) by striking "(d) Each" and inserting the following:

"(d) SUPPLEMENTARY AND PERIODIC INFORMATION.—

"(1) IN GENERAL.—Each";

(2) in the third sentence, by inserting after "securities of each class" the following: ", other than any class of asset-backed securities,"; and

(3) by adding at the end the following:

"(2) ASSET-BACKED SECURITIES.—

"(A) SUSPENSION OF DUTY TO FILE.—The Commission may, by rule or regulation, provide for the suspension or termination of the duty to file under this subsection for any class of asset-backed security, on such terms and conditions and for such period or periods as the Commission deems necessary or appropriate in the public interest or for the protection of investors.

"(B) CLASSIFICATION OF ISSUERS.—The Commission may, for purposes of this subsection, classify issuers and prescribe requirements appropriate for each class of issuers of asset-backed securities.".

(b) SECURITIES ACT OF 1933.—Section 7 of the Securities Act of 1933 (15 U.S.C. 77g) is amended by adding at the end the following:

"(c) DISCLOSURE REQUIREMENTS.—

"(1) IN GENERAL.—The Commission shall adopt regulations under this subsection requiring each issuer of an asset-backed security to disclose, for each tranche or class of security, information regarding the assets backing that security.

"(2) CONTENT OF REGULATIONS.—In adopting regulations under this subsection, the Commission shall—

"(A) set standards for the format of the data provided by issuers of an asset-backed security, which shall, to the extent feasible, facilitate comparison of such data across securities in similar types of asset classes; and

"(B) require issuers of asset-backed securities, at a minimum, to disclose asset-level or loan-level data, if such data are necessary for investors to independently perform due diligence, including—

"(i) data having unique identifiers relating to loan brokers or originators;

"(ii) the nature and extent of the compensation of the broker or originator of the assets backing the security; and

"(iii) the amount of risk retention by the originator and the securitizer of such assets.".

[Explanation at ¶ 4260.]

[¶ 10,943] ACT SEC. 943. REPRESENTATIONS AND WARRANTIES IN ASSET-BACKED OFFERINGS.

Not later than 180 days after the date of enactment of this Act, the Securities and Exchange Commission shall prescribe regulations on the use of representations and warranties in the market for asset-backed securities (as that term is defined in section 3(a)(77) of the Securities Exchange Act of 1934, as added by this subtitle) that—

(1) require each national recognized statistical rating organization to include in any report accompanying a credit rating a description of—

(A) the representations, warranties, and enforcement mechanisms available to investors; and

(B) how they differ from the representations, warranties, and enforcement mechanisms in issuances of similar securities; and

(2) require any securitizer (as that term is defined in section 15G(a) of the Securities Exchange Act of 1934, as added by this subtitle) to disclose fulfilled and unfulfilled repurchase requests across all trusts aggregated by the securitizer, so that investors may identify asset originators with clear underwriting deficiencies.

[¶ 10,944] ACT SEC. 944. EXEMPTED TRANSACTIONS UNDER THE SECURITIES ACT OF 1933.

(a) EXEMPTION ELIMINATED.—Section 4 of the Securities Act of 1933 (15 U.S.C. 77d) is amended—

(1) by striking paragraph (5); and

(2) by striking "(6) transactions" and inserting the following:

"(5) transactions".

(b) CONFORMING AMENDMENT.—Section 3(a)(4)(B)(vii)(I) of the Securities Exchange Act of 1934 (15 U.S.C. 78c(a)(4)(B)(vii)(I)) is amended by striking "4(6)" and inserting "4(5)".

[Explanation at ¶ 4265.]

[¶ 10,945] ACT SEC. 945. DUE DILIGENCE ANALYSIS AND DISCLOSURE IN ASSET-BACKED SECURITIES ISSUES.

Section 7 of the Securities Act of 1933 (15 U.S.C. 77g), as amended by this subtitle, is amended by adding at the end the following:

"(d) REGISTRATION STATEMENT FOR ASSET-BACKED SECURITIES.—Not later than 180 days after the date of enactment of this subsection, the Commission shall issue rules relating to the registration statement required to be filed by any issuer of an asset-backed security (as that term is defined in section 3(a)(77) of the Securities Exchange Act of 1934) that require any issuer of an asset-backed security—

"(1) to perform a review of the assets underlying the asset-backed security; and

"(2) to disclose the nature of the review under paragraph (1).".

[Explanation at ¶ 4270.]

[¶ 10,946] ACT SEC. 946. STUDY ON THE MACROECONOMIC EFFECTS OF RISK RETENTION REQUIREMENTS.

(a) STUDY REQUIRED.—The Chairman of the Financial Services Oversight Council shall carry out a study on the macroeconomic effects of the risk retention requirements under this subtitle, and the amendments made by this subtitle, with emphasis placed on potential beneficial effects with respect to stabilizing the real estate market. Such study shall include—

(1) an analysis of the effects of risk retention on real estate asset price bubbles, including a retrospective estimate of what fraction of real estate losses may have been averted had such requirements been in force in recent years;

(2) an analysis of the feasibility of minimizing real estate price bubbles by proactively adjusting the percentage of risk retention that must be borne by creditors and securitizers of real estate debt, as a function of regional or national market conditions;

(3) a comparable analysis for proactively adjusting mortgage origination requirements;

(4) an assessment of whether such proactive adjustments should be made by an independent regulator, or in a formulaic and transparent manner;

(5) an assessment of whether such adjustments should take place independently or in concert with monetary policy; and

(6) recommendations for implementation and enabling legislation.

(b) REPORT.—Not later than the end of the 180-day period beginning on the date of the enactment of this title, the Chairman of the Financial Services Oversight Council shall issue a report to the Congress containing any findings and determinations made in carrying out the study required under subsection (a).

[Explanation at ¶ 4275.]

Subtitle E—Accountability and Executive Compensation

[¶ 10,951] ACT SEC. 951. SHAREHOLDER VOTE ON EXECUTIVE COMPENSATION DISCLOSURES.

The Securities Exchange Act of 1934 (15 U.S.C. 78a et seq.) is amended by inserting after section 14 (15 U.S.C. 78n) the following:

"SEC. 14A. SHAREHOLDER APPROVAL OF EXECUTIVE COMPENSATION.

"(a) SEPARATE RESOLUTION REQUIRED.—

"(1) IN GENERAL.—Not less frequently than once every 3 years, a proxy or consent or authorization for an annual or other meeting of the shareholders for which the proxy solicitation rules of the Commission require compensation disclosure shall include a separate resolution subject to shareholder vote to approve the compensation of executives, as disclosed pursuant to section 229.402 of title 17, Code of Federal Regulations, or any successor thereto.

"(2) FREQUENCY OF VOTE.—Not less frequently than once every 6 years, a proxy or consent or authorization for an annual or other meeting of the shareholders for which the proxy solicitation rules of the Commission require compensation disclosure shall include a separate resolution subject to shareholder vote to determine whether votes on the resolutions required under paragraph (1) will occur every 1, 2, or 3 years.

"(3) EFFECTIVE DATE.—The proxy or consent or authorization for the first annual or other meeting of the shareholders occurring after the end of the 6-month period beginning on the date of enactment of this section shall include—

"(A) the resolution described in paragraph (1); and

"(B) a separate resolution subject to shareholder vote to determine whether votes on the resolutions required under paragraph (1) will occur every 1, 2, or 3 years.

"(b) SHAREHOLDER APPROVAL OF GOLDEN PARACHUTE COMPENSATION.—

"(1) DISCLOSURE.—In any proxy or consent solicitation material (the solicitation of which is subject to the rules of the Commission pursuant to subsection (a)) for a meeting of the shareholders occurring after the end of the 6-month period beginning on the date of enactment of this section, at which shareholders are asked to approve an acquisition, merger, consolidation, or proposed sale or other disposition of all or substantially all the assets of an issuer, the person making such solicitation shall disclose in the proxy or consent solicitation material, in a clear and simple form in accordance with regulations to be promulgated by the Commission, any agreements or understandings that such person has with any named executive officers of such issuer (or of the acquiring issuer, if such issuer is not the acquiring issuer) concerning any type of compensation (whether present, deferred, or contingent) that is based on or otherwise relates to the acquisition, merger, consolidation, sale, or other disposition of all or substantially all of the assets of the issuer and the aggregate total of all such compensation that may (and the conditions upon which it may) be paid or become payable to or on behalf of such executive officer.

"(2) SHAREHOLDER APPROVAL.—Any proxy or consent or authorization relating to the proxy or consent solicitation material containing the disclosure required by paragraph (1) shall include a separate resolution subject to shareholder vote to approve such agreements or understandings and compensation as disclosed, unless such agreements or understandings have been subject to a shareholder vote under subsection (a).

"(c) RULE OF CONSTRUCTION.—The shareholder vote referred to in subsections (a) and (b) shall not be binding on the issuer or the board of directors of an issuer, and may not be construed—

"(1) as overruling a decision by such issuer or board of directors;

"(2) to create or imply any change to the fiduciary duties of such issuer or board of directors;

"(3) to create or imply any additional fiduciary duties for such issuer or board of directors; or

"(4) to restrict or limit the ability of shareholders to make proposals for inclusion in proxy materials related to executive compensation.

"(d) DISCLOSURE OF VOTES.—Every institutional investment manager subject to section 13(f) shall report at least annually how it voted on any shareholder vote pursuant to subsections (a) and (b), unless such vote is otherwise required to be reported publicly by rule or regulation of the Commission.

"(e) EXEMPTION.—The Commission may, by rule or order, exempt an issuer or class of issuers from the requirement under subsection (a) or (b). In determining whether to make an exemption under this subsection, the Commission shall take into account, among other considerations, whether the requirements under subsections (a) and (b) disproportionately burdens small issuers.".

[Explanation at ¶ 4290 and ¶ 4295.]

[¶ 10,952] ACT SEC. 952. COMPENSATION COMMITTEE INDEPENDENCE.

(a) IN GENERAL.—The Securities Exchange Act of 1934 (15 U.S.C. 78 et seq.) is amended by inserting after section 10B, as added by section 753, the following:

"SEC. 10C. COMPENSATION COMMITTEES.

"(a) INDEPENDENCE OF COMPENSATION COMMITTEES.—

"(1) LISTING STANDARDS.—The Commission shall, by rule, direct the national securities exchanges and national securities associations to prohibit the listing of any equity security of an issuer, other than an issuer that is a controlled company, limited partnership, company in bankruptcy proceedings, open-ended management investment company that is registered under the Investment Company Act of 1940, or a foreign private issuer that provides annual disclosures to shareholders of the reasons that the foreign private issuer does not have an independent compensation committee, that does not comply with the requirements of this subsection.

"(2) INDEPENDENCE OF COMPENSATION COMMITTEES.—The rules of the Commission under paragraph (1) shall require that each member of the compensation committee of the board of directors of an issuer be—

"(A) a member of the board of directors of the issuer; and

"(B) independent.

"(3) INDEPENDENCE.—The rules of the Commission under paragraph (1) shall require that, in determining the definition of the term 'independence' for purposes of paragraph (2), the national securities exchanges and the national securities associations shall consider relevant factors, including—

"(A) the source of compensation of a member of the board of directors of an issuer, including any consulting, advisory, or other compensatory fee paid by the issuer to such member of the board of directors; and

"(B) whether a member of the board of directors of an issuer is affiliated with the issuer, a subsidiary of the issuer, or an affiliate of a subsidiary of the issuer.

"(4) EXEMPTION AUTHORITY.—The rules of the Commission under paragraph (1) shall permit a national securities exchange or a national securities association to exempt a particular relationship from the requirements of paragraph (2), with respect to the members of a compensation committee, as the national securities exchange or national securities association determines is appropriate, taking into consideration the size of an issuer and any other relevant factors.

"(b) INDEPENDENCE OF COMPENSATION CONSULTANTS AND OTHER COMPENSATION COMMITTEE ADVISERS.—

"(1) IN GENERAL.—The compensation committee of an issuer may only select a compensation consultant, legal counsel, or other adviser to the compensation committee after taking into consideration the factors identified by the Commission under paragraph (2).

"(2) RULES.—The Commission shall identify factors that affect the independence of a compensation consultant, legal counsel, or other adviser to a compensation committee of an issuer. Such factors shall be competitively neutral among categories of consultants, legal counsel, or other advisers and preserve the ability of compensation committees to retain the services of members of any such category, and shall include—

"(A) the provision of other services to the issuer by the person that employs the compensation consultant, legal counsel, or other adviser;

"(B) the amount of fees received from the issuer by the person that employs the compensation consultant, legal counsel, or other adviser, as a percentage of the total revenue of the person that employs the compensation consultant, legal counsel, or other adviser;

"(C) the policies and procedures of the person that employs the compensation consultant, legal counsel, or other adviser that are designed to prevent conflicts of interest;

"(D) any business or personal relationship of the compensation consultant, legal counsel, or other adviser with a member of the compensation committee; and

"(E) any stock of the issuer owned by the compensation consultant, legal counsel, or other adviser.

"(c) COMPENSATION COMMITTEE AUTHORITY RELATING TO COMPENSATION CONSULTANTS.—

"(1) AUTHORITY TO RETAIN COMPENSATION CONSULTANT.—

"(A) IN GENERAL.—The compensation committee of an issuer, in its capacity as a committee of the board of directors, may, in its sole discretion, retain or obtain the advice of a compensation consultant.

"(B) DIRECT RESPONSIBILITY OF COMPENSATION COMMITTEE.—The compensation committee of an issuer shall be directly responsible for the appointment, compensation, and oversight of the work of a compensation consultant.

"(C) RULE OF CONSTRUCTION.—This paragraph may not be construed—

"(i) to require the compensation committee to implement or act consistently with the advice or recommendations of the compensation consultant; or

"(ii) to affect the ability or obligation of a compensation committee to exercise its own judgment in fulfillment of the duties of the compensation committee.

"(2) DISCLOSURE.—In any proxy or consent solicitation material for an annual meeting of the shareholders (or a special meeting in lieu of the annual meeting) occurring on or after the date that is 1 year after the date of enactment of this section, each issuer shall disclose in the proxy or consent material, in accordance with regulations of the Commission, whether—

"(A) the compensation committee of the issuer retained or obtained the advice of a compensation consultant; and

"(B) the work of the compensation consultant has raised any conflict of interest and, if so, the nature of the conflict and how the conflict is being addressed.

"(d) AUTHORITY TO ENGAGE INDEPENDENT LEGAL COUNSEL AND OTHER ADVISERS.—

"(1) IN GENERAL.—The compensation committee of an issuer, in its capacity as a committee of the board of directors, may, in its sole discretion, retain and obtain the advice of independent legal counsel and other advisers.

"(2) DIRECT RESPONSIBILITY OF COMPENSATION COMMITTEE.—The compensation committee of an issuer shall be directly responsible for the appointment, compensation, and oversight of the work of independent legal counsel and other advisers.

"(3) RULE OF CONSTRUCTION.—This subsection may not be construed—

"(A) to require a compensation committee to implement or act consistently with the advice or recommendations of independent legal counsel or other advisers under this subsection; or

"(B) to affect the ability or obligation of a compensation committee to exercise its own judgment in fulfillment of the duties of the compensation committee.

"(e) COMPENSATION OF COMPENSATION CONSULTANTS, INDEPENDENT LEGAL COUNSEL, AND OTHER ADVISERS.—Each issuer shall provide for appropriate funding, as determined by the compensation committee in its capacity as a committee of the board of directors, for payment of reasonable compensation—

"(1) to a compensation consultant; and

"(2) to independent legal counsel or any other adviser to the compensation committee.

"(f) COMMISSION RULES.—

"(1) IN GENERAL.—Not later than 360 days after the date of enactment of this section, the Commission shall, by rule, direct the national securities exchanges and national securities associations to prohibit the listing of any security of an issuer that is not in compliance with the requirements of this section.

"(2) OPPORTUNITY TO CURE DEFECTS.—The rules of the Commission under paragraph (1) shall provide for appropriate procedures for an issuer to have a reasonable opportunity to cure any defects that would be the basis for the prohibition under paragraph (1), before the imposition of such prohibition.

"(3) EXEMPTION AUTHORITY.—

"(A) IN GENERAL.—The rules of the Commission under paragraph (1) shall permit a national securities exchange or a national securities association to exempt a category of issuers from the requirements under this section, as the national securities exchange or the national securities association determines is appropriate.

"(B) CONSIDERATIONS.—In determining appropriate exemptions under subparagraph (A), the national securities exchange or the national securities association shall take into account the potential impact of the requirements of this section on smaller reporting issuers.

"(g) CONTROLLED COMPANY EXEMPTION.—

"(1) IN GENERAL.—This section shall not apply to any controlled company.

"(2) DEFINITION.—For purposes of this section, the term 'controlled company' means an issuer—

"(A) that is listed on a national securities exchange or by a national securities association; and

"(B) that holds an election for the board of directors of the issuer in which more than 50 percent of the voting power is held by an individual, a group, or another issuer.".

(b) STUDY AND REPORT.—

(1) STUDY.—The Securities and Exchange Commission shall conduct a study and review of the use of compensation consultants and the effects of such use.

(2) REPORT.—Not later than 2 years after the date of the enactment of this Act, the Commission shall submit a report to Congress on the results of the study and review required by this subsection.

[Explanation at ¶ 4300.]

[¶ 10,953] ACT SEC. 953. EXECUTIVE COMPENSATION DISCLOSURES.

(a) DISCLOSURE OF PAY VERSUS PERFORMANCE.—Section 14 of the Securities Exchange Act of 1934 (15 U.S.C. 78n), as amended by this title, is amended by adding at the end the following:

"(i) DISCLOSURE OF PAY VERSUS PERFORMANCE.—The Commission shall, by rule, require each issuer to disclose in any proxy or consent solicitation material for an annual meeting of the shareholders of the issuer a clear description of any compensation required to be disclosed by the issuer under section 229.402 of title 17, Code of Federal Regulations (or any successor thereto), including information that shows the relationship between executive compensation actually paid and the financial performance of the issuer, taking into account any change in the value of the shares of stock and dividends of the issuer and any distributions. The disclosure under this subsection may include a graphic representation of the information required to be disclosed.".

(b) ADDITIONAL DISCLOSURE REQUIREMENTS.—

(1) IN GENERAL.—The Commission shall amend section 229.402 of title 17, Code of Federal Regulations, to require each issuer to disclose in any filing of the issuer described in section 229.10(a) of title 17, Code of Federal Regulations (or any successor thereto)—

(A) the median of the annual total compensation of all employees of the issuer, except the chief executive officer (or any equivalent position) of the issuer;

(B) the annual total compensation of the chief executive officer (or any equivalent position) of the issuer; and

(C) the ratio of the amount described in subparagraph (A) to the amount described in subparagraph (B).

(2) TOTAL COMPENSATION.—For purposes of this subsection, the total compensation of an employee of an issuer shall be determined in accordance with section 229.402(c)(2)(x) of title 17, Code of Federal Regulations, as in effect on the day before the date of enactment of this Act.

[Explanation at ¶ 4305.]

[¶ 10,954] ACT SEC. 954. RECOVERY OF ERRONEOUSLY AWARDED COMPENSATION.

The Securities Exchange Act of 1934 is amended by inserting after section 10C, as added by section 952, the following:

"SEC. 10D. RECOVERY OF ERRONEOUSLY AWARDED COMPENSATION POLICY.

"(a) LISTING STANDARDS.—The Commission shall, by rule, direct the national securities exchanges and national securities associations to prohibit the listing of any security of an issuer that does not comply with the requirements of this section.

"(b) RECOVERY OF FUNDS.—The rules of the Commission under subsection (a) shall require each issuer to develop and implement a policy providing—

"(1) for disclosure of the policy of the issuer on incentive-based compensation that is based on financial information required to be reported under the securities laws; and

"(2) that, in the event that the issuer is required to prepare an accounting restatement due to the material noncompliance of the issuer with any financial reporting requirement under the securities laws, the issuer will recover from any current or former executive officer of the issuer who received incentive-based compensation (including stock options awarded as compensation) during the 3-year period preceding the date on which the issuer is required to prepare an accounting restatement, based on the erroneous data, in excess of what would have been paid to the executive officer under the accounting restatement.".

[Explanation at ¶ 4305.]

[¶ 10,955] ACT SEC. 955. DISCLOSURE REGARDING EMPLOYEE AND DIRECTOR HEDGING.

Section 14 of the Securities Exchange Act of 1934 (15 U.S.C. 78n), as amended by this title, is amended by adding at the end the following:

"(j) DISCLOSURE OF HEDGING BY EMPLOYEES AND DIRECTORS.—The Commission shall, by rule, require each issuer to disclose in any proxy or consent solicitation material for an annual meeting of the shareholders of the issuer whether any employee or member of the board of directors of the issuer, or any designee of such employee or member, is permitted to purchase financial instruments (including prepaid variable forward contracts, equity swaps, collars, and exchange funds) that are designed to hedge or offset any decrease in the market value of equity securities—

"(1) granted to the employee or member of the board of directors by the issuer as part of the compensation of the employee or member of the board of directors; or

"(2) held, directly or indirectly, by the employee or member of the board of directors.".

[Explanation at ¶ 4315.]

[¶ 10,956] ACT SEC. 956. ENHANCED COMPENSATION STRUCTURE REPORTING.

(a) ENHANCED DISCLOSURE AND REPORTING OF COMPENSATION ARRANGEMENTS.—

(1) IN GENERAL.—Not later than 9 months after the date of enactment of this title, the appropriate Federal regulators jointly shall prescribe regulations or guidelines to require each covered financial institution to disclose to the appropriate Federal regulator the structures of all incentive-based compensation arrangements offered by such covered financial institutions sufficient to determine whether the compensation structure—

(A) provides an executive officer, employee, director, or principal shareholder of the covered financial institution with excessive compensation, fees, or benefits; or

(B) could lead to material financial loss to the covered financial institution.

(2) RULES OF CONSTRUCTION.—Nothing in this section shall be construed as requiring the reporting of the actual compensation of particular individuals. Nothing in this section shall be construed to require a covered financial institution that does not have an incentive-based payment arrangement to make the disclosures required under this subsection.

(b) PROHIBITION ON CERTAIN COMPENSATION ARRANGEMENTS.—Not later than 9 months after the date of enactment of this title, the appropriate Federal regulators shall jointly prescribe regulations or guidelines that prohibit any types of incentive-based payment arrangement, or any feature of any such arrangement, that the regulators determine encourages inappropriate risks by covered financial institutions—

(1) by providing an executive officer, employee, director, or principal shareholder of the covered financial institution with excessive compensation, fees, or benefits; or

(2) that could lead to material financial loss to the covered financial institution.

(c) STANDARDS.—The appropriate Federal regulators shall—

(1) ensure that any standards for compensation established under subsections (a) or (b) are comparable to the standards established under section of the Federal Deposit Insurance Act (12 U.S.C. 2 1831p-1) for insured depository institutions; and

(2) in establishing such standards under such subsections, take into consideration the compensation standards described in section 39(c) of the Federal Deposit Insurance Act (12 U.S.C. 1831p- 9 1(c)).

(d) ENFORCEMENT.—The provisions of this section and the regulations issued under this section shall be enforced under section 505 of the Gramm-Leach-Bliley Act and, for purposes of such section, a violation of this section or such regulations shall be treated as a violation of subtitle A of title V of such Act.

(e) DEFINITIONS.—As used in this section—

(1) the term "appropriate Federal regulator" means the Board of Governors of the Federal Reserve System, the Office of the Comptroller of the Currency, the Board of Directors of the Federal Deposit Insurance Corporation, the Director of the Office of Thrift Supervision, the National Credit Union Administration Board, the Securities and Exchange Commission, the Federal Housing Finance Agency; and

(2) the term "covered financial institution" means—

(A) a depository institution or depository institution holding company, as such terms are defined in section 3 of the Federal Deposit Insurance Act (12 U.S.C. 1813);

(B) a broker-dealer registered under section 15 of the Securities Exchange Act of 1934 (15 U.S.C. 78o);

(C) a credit union, as described in section 19(b)(1)(A)(iv) of the Federal Reserve Act;

(D) an investment advisor, as such term is defined in section 202(a)(11) of the Investment Advisers Act of 1940 (15 U.S.C. 80b-2(a)(11));

(E) the Federal National Mortgage Association;

(F) the Federal Home Loan Mortgage Corporation; and

(G) any other financial institution that the appropriate Federal regulators, jointly, by rule, determine should be treated as a covered financial institution for purposes of this section.

(f) EXEMPTION FOR CERTAIN FINANCIAL INSTITUTIONS.—The requirements of this section shall not apply to covered financial institutions with assets of less than $1,000,000,000.

[Explanation at ¶ 4320.]

[¶ 10,957] ACT SEC. 957. VOTING BY BROKERS.

Section 6(b) of the Securities Exchange Act of 1934 (15 U.S.C. 78f(b)) is amended—

(1) in paragraph (9)—

(A) in subparagraph (A), by redesignating clauses (i) through (v) as subclauses (I) through (V), respectively, and adjusting the margins accordingly;

(B) by redesignating subparagraphs (A) through (D) as clauses (i) through (iv), respectively, and adjusting the margins accordingly;

(C) by inserting "(A)" after "(9)"; and

(D) in the matter immediately following clause (iv), as so redesignated, by striking "As used" and inserting the following:

"(B) As used".

(2) by adding at the end the following:

"(10)

(A) The rules of the exchange prohibit any member that is not the beneficial owner of a security registered under section 12 from granting a proxy to vote the security in connection with a shareholder vote described in subparagraph (B), unless the beneficial owner of the security has instructed the member to vote the proxy in accordance with the voting instructions of the beneficial owner.

"(B) A shareholder vote described in this subparagraph is a shareholder vote with respect to the election of a member of the board of directors of an issuer, executive compensation, or any other significant matter, as determined by the Commission, by rule, and does not include a vote with respect to the uncontested election of a member of the board of directors of any investment company registered under the Investment Company Act of 1940 (15 U.S.C. 80b-1 et seq.).

"(C) Nothing in this paragraph shall be construed to prohibit a national securities exchange from prohibiting a member that is not the beneficial owner of a security registered under section 12 from granting a proxy to vote the security in connection with a shareholder vote not described in subparagraph (A).".

[Explanation at ¶ 4325.]

Subtitle F—Improvements to the Management of the Securities and Exchange Commission

[¶ 10,961] ACT SEC. 961. REPORT AND CERTIFICATION OF INTERNAL SUPERVISORY CONTROLS.

(a) ANNUAL REPORTS AND CERTIFICATION.—Not later than 90 days after the end of each fiscal year, the Commission shall submit a report to the Committee on Banking, Housing, and Urban Affairs of the Senate and the Committee on Financial Services of the House of Representatives on the conduct by the Commission of examinations of registered entities, enforcement investigations, and review of corporate financial securities filings.

(b) CONTENTS OF REPORTS.—Each report under subsection (a) shall contain—

(1) an assessment, as of the end of the most recent fiscal year, of the effectiveness of—

(A) the internal supervisory controls of the Commission; and

(B) the procedures of the Commission applicable to the staff of the Commission who perform examinations of registered entities, enforcement investigations, and reviews of corporate financial securities filings;

(2) a certification that the Commission has adequate internal supervisory controls to carry out the duties of the Commission described in paragraph (1)(B); and

(3) a summary by the Comptroller General of the United States of the review carried out under subsection (d).

(c) CERTIFICATION.—

(1) SIGNATURE.—The certification under subsection (b)(2) shall be signed by the Director of the Division of Enforcement, the Director of the Division of Corporation Finance, and the Director of the Office of Compliance Inspections and Examinations (or the head of any successor division or office).

(2) CONTENT OF CERTIFICATION.—Each individual described in paragraph (1) shall certify that the individual—

(A) is directly responsible for establishing and maintaining the internal supervisory controls of the Division or Office of which the individual is the head;

(B) is knowledgeable about the internal supervisory controls of the Division or Office of which the individual is the head;

(C) has evaluated the effectiveness of the internal supervisory controls during the 90-day period ending on the final day of the fiscal year to which the report relates; and

(D) has disclosed to the Commission any significant deficiencies in the design or operation of internal supervisory controls that could adversely affect the ability of the Division or Office to consistently conduct inspections, or investigations, or reviews of filings with professional competence and integrity.

(d) NEW DIRECTOR OR ACTING DIRECTOR.—Notwithstanding subsection (a), if the Director of the Division of Enforcement, the Director of the Division of Corporate Finance, or the Director of the Office of Compliance Inspections and Examinations has served as Director of the Division or Office for less than 90 days on the date on which a report is required to be submitted under subsection (a), the Commission may submit the report on the date on which the Director has served as Director for 90 days. If there is no Director of the Division of Enforcement, the Division of Corporate Finance, or the Office of Compliance Inspections and Examinations, on the date on which a report is required to be submitted under subsection (a), the Acting Director of the Division or Office may make the certification required under subsection (c).

(e) REVIEW BY THE COMPTROLLER GENERAL.—

(1) REPORT.—The Comptroller General of the United States shall submit to the Committee on Banking, Housing, and Urban Affairs of the Senate and the Committee on Financial Services of the House of Representatives a report that contains a review of the adequacy and effectiveness of the internal supervisory control structure and procedures described in subsection (b)(1), not less frequently than once every 3 years, at a time to coincide with the publication of the reports of the Commission under this section.

(2) AUTHORITY TO HIRE EXPERTS.—The Comptroller General of the United States may hire independent consultants with specialized expertise in any area relevant to the duties of the Comptroller General described in this section, in order to assist the Comptroller General in carrying out such duties.

[Explanation at ¶ 4350 and ¶ 4355.]

[¶ 10,962] ACT SEC. 962. TRIENNIAL REPORT ON PERSONNEL MANAGEMENT.

(a) TRIENNIAL REPORT REQUIRED.—Once every 3 years, the Comptroller General of the United States shall submit a report to the Committee on Banking, Housing, and Urban Affairs of the Senate and the Committee on Financial Services of the House of Representatives on the quality of personnel management by the Commission.

(b) CONTENTS OF REPORT.—Each report under subsection (a) shall include—

(1) an evaluation of—

(A) the effectiveness of supervisors in using the skills, talents, and motivation of the employees of the Commission to achieve the goals of the Commission;

(B) the criteria for promoting employees of the Commission to supervisory positions;

(C) the fairness of the application of the promotion criteria to the decisions of the Commission;

(D) the competence of the professional staff of the Commission;

(E) the efficiency of communication between the units of the Commission regarding the work of the Commission (including communication between divisions and between subunits of a division) and the efforts by the Commission to promote such communication;

(F) the turnover within subunits of the Commission, including the consideration of supervisors whose subordinates have an unusually high rate of turnover;

(G) whether there are excessive numbers of low-level, mid-level, or senior-level managers;

(H) any initiatives of the Commission that increase the competence of the staff of the Commission;

(I) the actions taken by the Commission regarding employees of the Commission who have failed to perform their duties and circumstances under which the Commission has issued to employees a notice of termination; and

(J) such other factors relating to the management of the Commission as the Comptroller General determines are appropriate;

(2) an evaluation of any improvements made with respect to the areas described in paragraph (1) since the date of submission of the previous report; and

(3) recommendations for how the Commission can use the human resources of the Commission more effectively and efficiently to carry out the mission of the Commission.

(c) CONSULTATION.—In preparing the report under subsection (a), the Comptroller General shall consult with current employees of the Commission, retired employees and other former employees of the Commission, the Inspector General of the Commission, persons that have business before the Commission, any union representing the employees of the Commission, private management consultants, academics, and any other source that the Comptroller General deems appropriate.

(d) REPORT BY COMMISSION.—Not later than 90 days after the date on which the Comptroller General submits each report under subsection (a), the Commission shall submit to the Committee on Banking, Housing, and Urban Affairs of the Senate and the Committee on Financial Services of the House of Representatives a report describing the actions taken by the Commission in response to the recommendations contained in the report under subsection (a).

(e) REIMBURSEMENTS FOR COST OF REPORTS.—

(1) REIMBURSEMENTS REQUIRED.—The Commission shall reimburse the Government Accountability Office for the full cost of making the reports under this section, as billed therefor by the Comptroller General.

(2) CREDITING AND USE OF REIMBURSEMENTS.—Such reimbursements shall—

(A) be credited to the appropriation account "Salaries and Expenses, Government Accountability Office" current when the payment is received; and

(B) remain available until expended.

(f) AUTHORITY TO HIRE EXPERTS.—The Comptroller General of the United States may hire independent consultants with specialized expertise in any area relevant to the duties of the Comptroller General described in this section, in order to assist the Comptroller General in carrying out such duties.

[Explanation at ¶ 4355.]

[¶ 10,963] ACT SEC. 963. ANNUAL FINANCIAL CONTROLS AUDIT.

(a) REPORTS OF COMMISSION.—

(1) ANNUAL REPORTS REQUIRED.—Not later than 6 months after the end of each fiscal year, the Commission shall publish and submit to Congress a report that—

(A) describes the responsibility of the management of the Commission for establishing and maintaining an adequate internal control structure and procedures for financial reporting; and

(B) contains an assessment of the effectiveness of the internal control structure and procedures for financial reporting of the Commission during that fiscal year.

(2) ATTESTATION.—The reports required under paragraph (1) shall be attested to by the Chairman and chief financial officer of the Commission.

(b) REPORT BY COMPTROLLER GENERAL.—

(1) REPORT REQUIRED.—Not later than 6 months after the end of the first fiscal year after the date of enactment of this Act, the Comptroller General of the United States shall submit a report to Congress that assesses—

(A) the effectiveness of the internal control structure and procedures of the Commission for financial reporting; and

(B) the assessment of the Commission under subsection (a)(1)(B).

(2) ATTESTATION.—The Comptroller General shall attest to, and report on, the assessment made by the Commission under subsection (a).

(c) REIMBURSEMENTS FOR COST OF REPORTS.—

(1) REIMBURSEMENTS REQUIRED.—The Commission shall reimburse the Government Accountability Office for the full cost of making the reports under subsection (b), as billed therefor by the Comptroller General.

(2) CREDITING AND USE OF REIMBURSEMENTS.—Such reimbursements shall—

(A) be credited to the appropriation account "Salaries and Expenses, Government Accountability Office" current when the payment is received; and

(B) remain available until expended.

[Explanation at ¶ 4355.]

[¶ 10,964] ACT SEC. 964. REPORT ON OVERSIGHT OF NATIONAL SECURITIES ASSOCIATIONS.

(a) REPORT REQUIRED.—Not later than 2 years after the date of enactment of this Act, and every 3 years thereafter, the Comptroller General of the United States shall submit to the Committee on Banking, Housing, and Urban Affairs of the Senate and the Committee on Financial Services of the House of Representatives a report that includes an evaluation of the oversight by the Commission of national securities associations registered under section 15A of the Securities Exchange Act of 1934 (15 U.S.C. 78o-3) with respect to—

(1) the governance of such national securities associations, including the identification and management of conflicts of interest by such national securities associations, together with an analysis of the impact of any conflicts of interest on the regulatory enforcement or rulemaking by such national securities associations;

(2) the examinations carried out by the national securities associations, including the expertise of the examiners;

(3) the executive compensation practices of such national securities associations;

(4) the arbitration services provided by the national securities associations;

(5) the review performed by national securities associations of advertising by the members of the national securities associations;

(6) the cooperation with and assistance to State securities administrators by the national securities associations to promote investor protection;

(7) how the funding of national securities associations is used to support the mission of the national securities associations, including—

   (A) the methods of funding;

   (B) the sufficiency of funds;

   (C) how funds are invested by the national securities association pending use; and

   (D) the impact of the methods, sufficiency, and investment of funds on regulatory enforcement by the national securities associations;

(8) the policies regarding the employment of former employees of national securities associations by regulated entities;

(9) the ongoing effectiveness of the rules of the national securities associations in achieving the goals of the rules;

(10) the transparency of governance and activities of the national securities associations; and

(11) any other issue that has an impact, as determined by the Comptroller General, on the effectiveness of such national securities associations in performing their mission and in dealing fairly with investors and members;

(b) REIMBURSEMENTS FOR COST OF REPORTS.—

   (1) REIMBURSEMENTS REQUIRED.—The Commission shall reimburse the Government Accountability Office for the full cost of making the reports under subsection (a), as billed therefor by the Comptroller General.

   (2) CREDITING AND USE OF REIMBURSEMENTS.—Such reimbursements shall—

      (A) be credited to the appropriation account "Salaries and Expenses, Government Accountability Office" current when the payment is received; and

      (B) remain available until expended.

[Explanation at ¶ 4355.]

[¶ 10,965] ACT SEC. 965. COMPLIANCE EXAMINERS.

Section 4 of the Securities Exchange Act of 1934 (15 U.S.C. 78d) is amended by adding at the end the following:

"(h) EXAMINERS.—

   "(1) DIVISION OF TRADING AND MARKETS.—The Division of Trading and Markets of the Commission, or any successor organizational unit, shall have a staff of examiners who shall—

      "(A) perform compliance inspections and examinations of entities under the jurisdiction of that Division; and

      "(B) report to the Director of that Division.

   "(2) DIVISION OF INVESTMENT MANAGEMENT.—The Division of Investment Management of the Commission, or any successor organizational unit, shall have a staff of examiners who shall—

      "(A) perform compliance inspections and examinations of entities under the jurisdiction of that Division; and

      "(B) report to the Director of that Division.".

[Explanation at ¶ 4360.]

[¶ 10,966] ACT SEC. 966. SUGGESTION PROGRAM FOR EMPLOYEES OF THE COMMISSION.

The Securities Exchange Act of 1934 (15 U.S.C. 78a et seq.) is amended by inserting after section 4C (15 U.S.C. 78d-3) the following:

"SEC. 4D. ADDITIONAL DUTIES OF INSPECTOR GENERAL.

"(a) SUGGESTION SUBMISSIONS BY COMMISSION EMPLOYEES.—

"(1) HOTLINE ESTABLISHED.—The Inspector General of the Commission shall establish and maintain a telephone hotline or other electronic means for the receipt of—

"(A) suggestions by employees of the Commission for improvements in the work efficiency, effectiveness, and productivity, and the use of the resources, of the Commission; and

"(B) allegations by employees of the Commission of waste, abuse, misconduct, or mismanagement within the Commission.

"(2) CONFIDENTIALITY.—The Inspector General shall maintain as confidential—

"(A) the identity of any individual who provides information by the means established under paragraph (1), unless the individual requests otherwise, in writing; and

"(B) at the request of any such individual, any specific information provided by the individual.

"(b) CONSIDERATION OF REPORTS.—The Inspector General shall consider any suggestions or allegations received by the means established under subsection (a)(1), and shall recommend appropriate action in relation to such suggestions or allegations.

"(c) RECOGNITION.—The Inspector General may recognize any employee who makes a suggestion under subsection (a)(1) (or by other means) that would or does—

"(1) increase the work efficiency, effectiveness, or productivity of the Commission; or

"(2) reduce waste, abuse, misconduct, or mismanagement within the Commission.

"(d) REPORT.—The Inspector General of the Commission shall submit to Congress an annual report containing a description of—

"(1) the nature, number, and potential benefits of any suggestions received under subsection (a);

"(2) the nature, number, and seriousness of any allegations received under subsection (a);

"(3) any recommendations made or actions taken by the Inspector General in response to substantiated allegations received under subsection (a); and

"(4) any action the Commission has taken in response to suggestions or allegations received under subsection (a).

"(e) FUNDING.—The activities of the Inspector General under this subsection shall be funded by the Securities and Exchange Commission Investor Protection Fund established under section 21F.".

[Explanation at ¶4365.]

[¶10,967] ACT SEC. 967. COMMISSION ORGANIZATIONAL STUDY AND REFORM.

(a) STUDY REQUIRED.—

(1) IN GENERAL.—Not later than the end of the 90-day period beginning on the date of the enactment of this subtitle, the Securities and Exchange Commission (hereinafter in this section referred to as the "SEC") shall hire an independent consultant of high caliber and with expertise in organizational restructuring and the operations of capital markets to examine the internal operations, structure, funding, and the need for comprehensive reform of the SEC, as well as the SEC's relationship with and the reliance on self-regulatory organizations and other entities relevant to the regulation of securities and the protection of securities investors that are under the SEC's oversight.

(2) SPECIFIC AREAS FOR STUDY.—The study required under paragraph (1) shall, at a minimum, include the study of—

(A) the possible elimination of unnecessary or redundant units at the SEC;

(B) improving communications between SEC offices and divisions;

(C) the need to put in place a clear chain-of-command structure, particularly for enforcement examinations and compliance inspections;

(D) the effect of high-frequency trading and other technological advances on the market and what the SEC requires to monitor the effect of such trading and advances on the market;

(E) the SEC's hiring authorities, workplace policies, and personal practices, including—

(i) whether there is a need to further streamline hiring authorities for those who are not lawyers, accountants, compliance examiners, or economists;

(ii) whether there is a need for further pay reforms;

(iii) the diversity of skill sets of SEC employees and whether the present skill set diversity efficiently and effectively fosters the SEC's mission of investor protection; and

(iv) the application of civil service laws by the SEC;

(F) whether the SEC's oversight and reliance on self-regulatory organizations promotes efficient and effective governance for the securities markets; and

(G) whether adjusting the SEC's reliance on self-regulatory organizations is necessary to promote more efficient and effective governance for the securities markets.

(b) CONSULTANT REPORT.—Not later than the end of the 150-day period after being retained, the independent consultant hired pursuant to subsection (a)(1) shall issue a report to the SEC and the Congress containing—

(1) a detailed description of any findings and conclusions made while carrying out the study required under subsection (a)(1); and

(2) recommendations for legislative, regulatory, or administrative action that the consultant determines appropriate to enable the SEC and other entities on which the consultant reports to perform their statutorily or otherwise mandated missions.

(c) SEC REPORT.—Not later than the end of the 6-month period beginning on the date the consultant issues the report under subsection (b), and every 6-months thereafter during the 2-year period following the date on which the consultant issues such report, the SEC shall issue a report to the Committee on Financial Services of the House of Representatives and the Committee on Banking, Housing, and Urban Affairs of the Senate describing the SEC's implementation of the regulatory and administrative recommendations contained in the consultant's report.

[Explanation at ¶ 4355.]

[¶ 10,968] ACT SEC. 968. STUDY ON SEC REVOLVING DOOR.

(a) GOVERNMENT ACCOUNTABILITY OFFICE STUDY.—The Comptroller General of the United States shall conduct a study that will—

(1) review the number of employees who leave the Securities and Exchange Commission to work for financial institutions regulated by such Commission;

(2) determine how many employees who leave the Securities and Exchange Commission worked on cases that involved financial institutions regulated by such Commission;

(3) review the length of time employees work for the Securities and Exchange Commission before leaving to be employed by financial institutions regulated by such Commission;

(4) review existing internal controls and make recommendations on strengthening such controls to ensure that employees of the Securities and Exchange Commission who are later employed by financial institutions did not assist such institutions in violating any rules or regulations of the Commission during the course of their employment with such Commission;

(5) determine if greater post-employment restrictions are necessary to prevent employees of the Securities and Exchange Commission from being employed by financial institutions after employment with such Commission;

(6) determine if the volume of employees of the Securities and Exchange Commission who are later employed by financial institutions has led to inefficiencies in enforcement;

(7) determine if employees of the Securities and Exchange Commission who are later employed by financial institutions assisted such institutions in circumventing Federal rules and regulations while employed by such Commission;

(8) review any information that may address the volume of employees of the Securities and Exchange Commission who are later employed by financial institutions, and make recommendations to Congress; and

(9) review other additional issues as may be raised during the course of the study conducted under this subsection.

(b) REPORT.—Not later than 1 year after the date of the enactment of this subtitle, the Comptroller General of the United States shall submit to the Committee on Financial Services of the House of Representatives and the Committee on Banking, Housing, and Urban Affairs of the Senate a report on the results of the study required by subsection (a).

[Explanation at ¶4355.]

Subtitle G—Strengthening Corporate Governance

[¶10,971] ACT SEC. 971. PROXY ACCESS.

(a) PROXY ACCESS.—Section 14(a) of the Securities Exchange Act of 1934 (15 U.S.C. 78n(a)) is amended—

(1) by inserting "(1)" after "(a)"; and

(2) by adding at the end the following:

"(2) The rules and regulations prescribed by the Commission under paragraph (1) may include—

"(A) a requirement that a solicitation of proxy, consent, or authorization by (or on behalf of) an issuer include a nominee submitted by a shareholder to serve on the board of directors of the issuer; and

"(B) a requirement that an issuer follow a certain procedure in relation to a solicitation described in subparagraph (A).".

(b) REGULATIONS.—The Commission may issue rules permitting the use by a shareholder of proxy solicitation materials supplied by an issuer of securities for the purpose of nominating individuals to membership on the board of directors of the issuer, under such terms and conditions as the Commission determines are in the interests of shareholders and for the protection of investors.

(c) EXEMPTIONS.—The Commission may, by rule or order, exempt an issuer or class of issuers from the requirement made by this section or an amendment made by this section. In determining whether to make an exemption under this subsection, the Commission shall take into account, among other considerations, whether the requirement in the amendment made by subsection (a) disproportionately burdens small issuers.

[Explanation at ¶4290 and ¶4330.]

[¶10,972] ACT SEC. 972. DISCLOSURES REGARDING CHAIRMAN AND CEO STRUCTURES.

The Securities Exchange Act of 1934 (15 U.S. C. 78a et seq.) is amended by inserting after section 14A, as added by this title, the following:

"SEC. 14B. CORPORATE GOVERNANCE.

"Not later than 180 days after the date of enactment of this subsection, the Commission shall issue rules that require an issuer to disclose in the annual proxy sent to investors the reasons why the issuer has chosen—

"(1) the same person to serve as chairman of the board of directors and chief executive officer (or in equivalent positions); or

"(2) different individuals to serve as chairman of the board of directors and chief executive officer (or in equivalent positions of the issuer).".

[Explanation at ¶ 4335.]

Subtitle H—Municipal Securities

[¶ 10,975] ACT SEC. 975. REGULATION OF MUNICIPAL SECURITIES AND CHANGES TO THE BOARD OF THE MSRB.

(a) REGISTRATION OF MUNICIPAL SECURITIES DEALERS AND MUNICIPAL ADVISORS.—Section 15B(a) of the Securities Exchange Act of 1934 (15 U.S.C. 78o-4(a)) is amended—

    (1) in paragraph (1)—

        (A) by inserting "(A)" after "(1)"; and

        (B) by adding at the end the following:

"(B) It shall be unlawful for a municipal advisor to provide advice to or on behalf of a municipal entity or obligated person with respect to municipal financial products or the issuance of municipal securities, or to undertake a solicitation of a municipal entity or obligated person, unless the municipal advisor is registered in accordance with this subsection.";

    (2) in paragraph (2), by inserting "or municipal advisor" after "municipal securities dealer" each place that term appears;

    (3) in paragraph (3), by inserting "or municipal advisor" after "municipal securities dealer" each place that term appears;

    (4) in paragraph (4), by striking "dealer, or municipal securities dealer or class of brokers, dealers, or municipal securities dealers" and inserting "dealer, municipal securities dealer, or municipal advisor, or class of brokers, dealers, municipal securities dealers, or municipal advisors"; and

    (5) by adding at the end the following:

"(5) No municipal advisor shall make use of the mails or any means or instrumentality of interstate commerce to provide advice to or on behalf of a municipal entity or obligated person with respect to municipal financial products, the issuance of municipal securities, or to undertake a solicitation of a municipal entity or obligated person, in connection with which such municipal advisor engages in any fraudulent, deceptive, or manipulative act or practice.".

(b) MUNICIPAL SECURITIES RULEMAKING BOARD.—Section 15B(b) of the Securities Exchange Act of 1934 (15 U.S.C. 78o-4(b)) is amended—

    (1) in paragraph (1)—

        (A) in the first sentence, by striking "Not later than" and all that follows through "appointed by the Commission" and inserting "The Municipal Securities Rulemaking Board shall be composed of 15 members, or such other number of members as specified by rules of the Board pursuant to paragraph (2)(B),";

        (B) by striking the second sentence and inserting the following: "The members of the Board shall serve as members for a term of 3 years or for such other terms as specified by rules of the Board pursuant to paragraph (2)(B), and shall consist of (A) 8 individuals who are independent of any municipal securities broker, municipal securities dealer, or municipal advisor, at least 1 of whom shall be representative of institutional or retail investors in municipal securities, at least 1 of whom shall be representative of municipal entities, and at least 1 of whom shall be a member of the public with knowledge of or experience in the municipal industry (which members are hereinafter referred to as 'public representatives'); and (B) 7 individuals who are associated with a broker, dealer, municipal securities dealer, or municipal advisor, including at least 1 individual who is associated with and representative of brokers, dealers, or municipal securities dealers that are not banks or subsidiaries or departments or divisions of banks (which members are hereinafter referred to as 'broker-dealer representatives'), at least 1 individual who is associated with and representative of municipal securities dealers which are banks or subsidiaries or departments or divisions of banks (which members are hereinafter referred to as 'bank representatives'), and at least 1 individual who is associated with a municipal advisor (which members are hereinafter referred to as 'advisor representatives' and, together with the broker-dealer representatives and the bank representatives, are referred to as 'regulated representatives'). Each member of the board shall be knowledgeable of matters related to the municipal securities markets."; and

    (C) in the third sentence, by striking "initial";

  (2) in paragraph (2)—

    (A) in the matter preceding subparagraph (A)—

      (i) by inserting before the period at the end of the first sentence the following: "and advice provided to or on behalf of municipal entities or obligated persons by brokers, dealers, municipal securities dealers, and municipal advisors with respect to municipal financial products, the issuance of municipal securities, and solicitations of municipal entities or obligated persons undertaken by brokers, dealers, municipal securities dealers, and municipal advisors"; and

      (ii) by striking the second sentence;

    (B) in subparagraph (A)—

      (i) in the matter preceding clause (i)—

        (I) by inserting ", and no broker, dealer, municipal securities dealer, or municipal advisor shall provide advice to or on behalf of a municipal entity or obligated person with respect to municipal financial products or the issuance of municipal securities," after "sale of, any municipal security"; and

        (II) by inserting "and municipal entities or obligated persons" after "protection of investors";

      (ii) in clause (i), by striking "municipal securities brokers and municipal securities dealers" each place that term appears and inserting "municipal securities brokers, municipal securities dealers, and municipal advisors";

      (iii) in clause (ii), by adding "and" at the end;

      (iv) in clause (iii), by striking "; and" and inserting a period; and

      (v) by striking clause (iv);

    (C) by amending subparagraph (B) to read as follows:

"(B) establish fair procedures for the nomination and election of members of the Board and assure fair representation in such nominations and elections of public representatives, broker dealer representatives, bank representatives, and advisor representatives. Such rules—

"(i) shall provide that the number of public representatives of the Board shall at all times exceed the total number of regulated representatives and that the membership shall at all times be as evenly divided in number as possible between public representatives and regulated representatives;

"(ii) shall specify the length or lengths of terms members shall serve;

"(iii) may increase the number of members which shall constitute the whole Board, provided that such number is an odd number; and

"(iv) shall establish requirements regarding the independence of public representatives.".

    (D) in subparagraph (C)—

      (i) by inserting "and municipal financial products" after "municipal securities" the first two times that term appears;

      (ii) by inserting ", municipal entities, obligated persons," before "and the public interest";

      (iii) by striking "between" and inserting "among";

      (iv) by striking "issuers, municipal securities brokers, or municipal securities dealers, to fix" and inserting "municipal entities, obligated persons, municipal securities brokers, municipal securities dealers, or municipal advisors, to fix"; and

      (v) by striking "brokers or municipal securities dealers, to regulate" and inserting "brokers, municipal securities dealers, or municipal advisors, to regulate";

    (E) in subparagraph (D)—

      (i) by inserting "and advice concerning municipal financial products" after "transactions in municipal securities";

(ii) by striking "That no" and inserting "that no";

(iii) by inserting "municipal advisor," before "or person associated"; and

(iv) by striking "a municipal securities broker or municipal securities dealer may be compelled" and inserting "a municipal securities broker, municipal securities dealer, or municipal advisor may be compelled";

(F) in subparagraph (E)—

(i) by striking "municipal securities brokers and municipal securities dealers" and inserting "municipal securities brokers, municipal securities dealers, and municipal advisors"; and

(ii) by striking "municipal securities broker or municipal securities dealer" and inserting "municipal securities broker, municipal securities dealer, or municipal advisor";

(G) in subparagraph (G), by striking "municipal securities brokers and municipal securities dealers" and inserting "municipal securities brokers, municipal securities dealers, and municipal advisors";

(H) in subparagraph (J)—

(i) by striking "municipal securities broker and each municipal securities dealer" and inserting "municipal securities broker, municipal securities dealer, and municipal advisor"; and

(ii) by striking the period at the end of the second sentence and inserting ", which may include charges for failure to submit to the Board, or to any information system operated by the Board, within the prescribed timeframes, any items of information or documents required to be submitted under any rule issued by the Board.";

(I) in subparagraph (K)—

(i) by inserting "broker, dealer, or" before "municipal securities dealer" each place that term appears; and

(ii) by striking "municipal securities investment portfolio" and inserting "related account of a broker, dealer, or municipal securities dealer"; and

(J) by adding at the end the following:

"(L) with respect to municipal advisors—

"(i) prescribe means reasonably designed to prevent acts, practices, and courses of business as are not consistent with a municipal advisor's fiduciary duty to its clients;

"(ii) provide continuing education requirements for municipal advisors;

"(iii) provide professional standards; and

"(iv) not impose a regulatory burden on small municipal advisors that is not necessary or appropriate in the public interest and for the protection of investors, municipal entities, and obligated persons, provided that there is robust protection of investors against fraud.";

(3) by redesignating paragraph (3) as paragraph (7); and

(4) by inserting after paragraph (2) the following:

"(3) The Board, in conjunction with or on behalf of any Federal financial regulator or self-regulatory organization, may—

"(A) establish information systems; and

"(B) assess such reasonable fees and charges for the submission of information to, or the receipt of information from, such systems from any persons which systems may be developed for the purposes of serving as a repository of information from municipal market participants or otherwise in furtherance of the purposes of the Board, a Federal financial regulator, or a self-regulatory organization, except that the Board—

"(i) may not charge a fee to municipal entities or obligated persons to submit documents or other information to the Board or charge a fee to any person to obtain, directly from the Internet site of the Board, documents or information submitted by municipal entities, obligated persons, brokers, dealers, municipal securities dealers, or municipal advisors, including documents submitted under the rules of the Board or the Commission; and

"(ii) shall not be prohibited from charging commercially reasonable fees for automated subscription-based feeds or similar services, or for charging for other data or document-based services customized upon request of any person, made available to commercial enterprises, municipal securities market professionals, or the general public, whether delivered through the Internet or any other means, that contain all or part of the documents or information, subject to approval of the fees by the Commission under section 19(b).

"(4) The Board may provide guidance and assistance in the enforcement of, and examination for, compliance with the rules of the Board to the Commission, a registered securities association under section 15A, or any other appropriate regulatory agency, as applicable.

"(5) The Board, the Commission, and a registered securities association under section 15A, or the designees of the Board, the Commission, or such association, shall meet not less frequently than 2 times a year—

"(A) to describe the work of the Board, the Commission, and the registered securities association involving the regulation of municipal securities; and

"(B) to share information about—

"(i) the interpretation of the Board, the Commission, and the registered securities association of Board rules; and

"(ii) examination and enforcement of compliance with Board rules.".

(c) DISCIPLINE OF BROKERS, DEALERS, MUNICIPAL SECURITIES DEALERS AND MUNICIPAL ADVISORS; FIDUCIARY DUTY OF MUNICIPAL ADVISORS.—Section 15B(c) of the Securities Exchange Act of 1934 (15 U.S.C. 78o-4(c)) is amended—

(1) in paragraph (1), by inserting ", and no broker, dealer, municipal securities dealer, or municipal advisor shall make use of the mails or any means or instrumentality of interstate commerce to provide advice to or on behalf of a municipal entity or obligated person with respect to municipal financial products, the issuance of municipal securities, or to undertake a solicitation of a municipal entity or obligated person," after "any municipal security";

(2) by adding at the end of paragraph (1) the following: "A municipal advisor and any person associated with such municipal advisor shall be deemed to have a fiduciary duty to any municipal entity for whom such municipal advisor acts as a municipal advisor, and no municipal advisor may engage in any act, practice, or course of business which is not consistent with a municipal advisor's fiduciary duty or that is in contravention of any rule of the Board.".

(3) in paragraph (2), by inserting "or municipal advisor" after "municipal securities dealer" each place that term appears;

(4) in paragraph (3)—

(A) by inserting "or municipal entities or obligated person" after "protection of investors" each place that term appears; and

(B) by inserting "or municipal advisor" after "municipal securities dealer" each place that term appears;

(5) in paragraph (4), by inserting "or municipal advisor" after "municipal securities dealer or obligated person" each place that term appears;

(6) in paragraph (6)(B), by inserting "or municipal entities or obligated person" after "protection of investors";

(7) in paragraph (7)—

(A) in subparagraph (A)—

(i) in clause (i), by striking "; and" and inserting a semicolon;

(ii) in clause (ii), by striking the period and inserting "; and"; and

(iii) by adding at the end the following:

"(iii) the Commission, or its designee, in the case of municipal advisors.".

(B) in subparagraph (B), by inserting "or municipal entities or obligated person" after "protection of investors"; and

(8) by adding at the end the following:

"(9)

(A) Fines collected by the Commission for violations of the rules of the Board shall be equally divided between the Commission and the Board.

"(B) Fines collected by a registered securities association under section 15A(7) with respect to violations of the rules of the Board shall be accounted for by such registered securities association separately from other fines collected under section 15A(7) and shall be allocated between such registered securities association and the Board, and such allocation shall require the registered securities association to pay to the Board ⅓ of all fines collected by the registered securities association reasonably allocable to violations of the rules of the Board, or such other portion of such fines as may be directed by the Commission upon agreement between the registered securities association and the Board.".

(d) ISSUANCE OF MUNICIPAL SECURITIES.—Section 15B(d)(2) of the Securities Exchange Act of 1934 (15 U.S.C. 78o-4(d)) is amended—

(1) by striking "through a municipal securities broker or municipal securities dealer or otherwise" and inserting "through a municipal securities broker, municipal securities dealer, municipal advisor, or otherwise"; and

(2) by inserting "or municipal advisors" before "to furnish".

(e) DEFINITIONS.—Section 15B of the Securities Exchange Act of 1934 (15 U.S.C. 78o-4) is amended by adding at the end the following:

"(e) DEFINITIONS.—For purposes of this section—

"(1) the term 'Board' means the Municipal Securities Rulemaking Board established under subsection (b)(1);

"(2) the term 'guaranteed investment contract' includes any investment that has specified withdrawal or reinvestment provisions and a specifically negotiated or bid interest rate, and also includes any agreement to supply investments on 2 or more future dates, such as a forward supply contract;

"(3) the term 'investment strategies' includes plans or programs for the investment of the proceeds of municipal securities that are not municipal derivatives, guaranteed investment contracts, and the recommendation of and brokerage of municipal escrow investments;

"(4) the term 'municipal advisor'—

"(A) means a person (who is not a municipal entity or an employee of a municipal entity) that—

"(i) provides advice to or on behalf of a municipal entity or obligated person with respect to municipal financial products or the issuance of municipal securities, including advice with respect to the structure, timing, terms, and other similar matters concerning such financial products or issues; or

"(ii) undertakes a solicitation of a municipal entity;

"(B) includes financial advisors, guaranteed investment contract brokers, third-party marketers, placement agents, solicitors, finders, and swap advisors, if such persons are described in any of clauses (i) through (iii) of subparagraph (A); and

"(C) does not include a broker, dealer, or municipal securities dealer serving as an underwriter (as defined in section 2(a)(11) of the Securities Act of 1933) (15 U.S.C. 77b(a)(11)), any investment adviser registered under the Investment Advisers Act of 1940, or persons associated with such investment advisers who are providing investment advice, any commodity trading advisor registered under the Commodity Exchange Act or persons associated with a commodity trading advisor who are providing advice related to swaps, attorneys offering legal advice or providing services that are of a traditional legal nature, or engineers providing engineering advice;

"(5) the term 'municipal financial product' means municipal derivatives, guaranteed investment contracts, and investment strategies;

"(6) the term 'rules of the Board' means the rules proposed and adopted by the Board under subsection (b)(2);

"(7) the term 'person associated with a municipal advisor' or 'associated person of an advisor' means—

"(A) any partner, officer, director, or branch manager of such municipal advisor (or any person occupying a similar status or performing similar functions);

"(B) any other employee of such municipal advisor who is engaged in the management, direction, supervision, or performance of any activities relating to the provision of advice to or on behalf of a municipal entity or obligated person with respect to municipal financial products or the issuance of municipal securities; and

"(C) any person directly or indirectly controlling, controlled by, or under common control with such municipal advisor;

"(8) the term 'municipal entity' means any State, political subdivision of a State, or municipal corporate instrumentality of a State, including—

"(A) any agency, authority, or instrumentality of the State, political subdivision, or municipal corporate instrumentality;

"(B) any plan, program, or pool of assets sponsored or established by the State, political subdivision, or municipal corporate instrumentality or any agency, authority, or instrumentality thereof; and

"(C) any other issuer of municipal securities;

"(9) the term 'solicitation of a municipal entity or obligated person' means a direct or indirect communication with a municipal entity or obligated person made by a person, for direct or indirect compensation, on behalf of a broker, dealer, municipal securities dealer, municipal advisor, or investment adviser (as defined in section 202 of the Investment Advisers Act of 1940) that does not control, is not controlled by, or is not under common control with the person undertaking such solicitation for the purpose of obtaining or retaining an engagement by a municipal entity or obligated person of a broker, dealer, municipal securities dealer, or municipal advisor for or in connection with municipal financial products, the issuance of municipal securities, or of an investment adviser to provide investment advisory services to or on behalf of a municipal entity; and

"(10) the term 'obligated person' means any person, including an issuer of municipal securities, who is either generally or through an enterprise, fund, or account of such person, committed by contract or other arrangement to support the payment of all or part of the obligations on the municipal securities to be sold in an offering of municipal securities.".

(f) REGISTERED SECURITIES ASSOCIATION.—Section 15A(b) of the Securities Exchange Act of 1934 (15 U.S.C. 78o-3(b)) is amended by adding at the end the following:

"(15) The rules of the association provide that the association shall—

"(A) request guidance from the Municipal Securities Rulemaking Board in interpretation of the rules of the Municipal Securities Rulemaking Board; and

"(B) provide information to the Municipal Securities Rulemaking Board about the enforcement actions and examinations of the association under section 15B(b)(2)(E), so that the Municipal Securities Rulemaking Board may—

"(i) assist in such enforcement actions and examinations; and

"(ii) evaluate the ongoing effectiveness of the rules of the Board.".

(g) REGISTRATION AND REGULATION OF BROKERS AND DEALERS.—Section 15 of the Securities Exchange Act of 1934 is amended—

(1) in subsection (b)(4), by inserting "municipal advisor," after "municipal securities dealer" each place that term appears; and

(2) in subsection (c), by inserting "broker, dealer, or" before "municipal securities dealer" each place that term appears.

(h) ACCOUNTS AND RECORDS, REPORTS, EXAMINATIONS OF EXCHANGES, MEMBERS, AND OTHERS.—Section 17(a)(1) of the Securities Exchange Act of 1934 is amended by inserting "municipal advisor," after "municipal securities dealer".

(i) EFFECTIVE DATE.—This section, and the amendments made by this section, shall take effect on October 1, 2010.

[Explanation at ¶ 4380, ¶ 4385, ¶ 4390 and ¶ 4395.]

[¶ 10,976] ACT SEC. 976. GOVERNMENT ACCOUNTABILITY OFFICE STUDY OF INCREASED DISCLOSURE TO INVESTORS.

(a) STUDY.—The Comptroller General of the United States shall conduct a study and review of the disclosure required to be made by issuers of municipal securities.

(b) SUBJECTS FOR EVALUATION.—In conducting the study under subsection (a), the Comptroller General of the United States shall—

(1) broadly describe—

(A) the size of the municipal securities markets and the issuers and investors; and

(B) the disclosures provided by issuers to investors;

(2) compare the amount, frequency, and quality of disclosures that issuers of municipal securities are required by law to provide for the benefit of municipal securities holders, including the amount of and frequency of disclosures actually provided by issuers of municipal securities, with the amount of and frequency of disclosures that issuers of corporate securities provide for the benefit of corporate securities holders, taking into account the differences between issuers of municipal securities and issuers of corporate securities;

(3) evaluate the costs and benefits to various types of issuers of municipal securities of requiring issuers of municipal bonds to provide additional financial disclosures for the benefit of investors;

(4) evaluate the potential benefit to investors from additional financial disclosures by issuers of municipal bonds; and

(5) make recommendations relating to disclosure requirements for municipal issuers, including the advisability of the repeal or retention of section 15B(d) of the Securities Exchange Act of 1934 (15 U.S.C. 78o-4(d)) (commonly known as the "Tower Amendment").

(c) REPORT.—Not later than 24 months after the date of enactment of this Act, the Comptroller General of the United States shall submit a report to Congress on the results of the study conducted under subsection (a), including recommendations for how to improve disclosure by issuers of municipal securities.

[Explanation at ¶ 4410.]

[¶ 10,977] ACT SEC. 977. GOVERNMENT ACCOUNTABILITY OFFICE STUDY ON THE MUNICIPAL SECURITIES MARKETS.

(a) STUDY.—The Comptroller General of the United States shall conduct a study of the municipal securities markets.

(b) REPORT.—Not later than 18 months after the date of enactment of this Act, the Comptroller General of the United States shall submit a report to the Committee on Banking, Housing, and Urban Affairs of the Senate, and the Committee on Financial Services of the House of Representatives, with copies to the Special Committee on Aging of the Senate and the Commission, on the results of the study conducted under subsection (a), including—

(1) an analysis of the mechanisms for trading, quality of trade executions, market transparency, trade reporting, price discovery, settlement clearing, and credit enhancements;

(2) the needs of the markets and investors and the impact of recent innovations;

(3) recommendations for how to improve the transparency, efficiency, fairness, and liquidity of trading in the municipal securities markets, including with reference to items listed in paragraph (1); and

(4) potential uses of derivatives in the municipal securities markets.

(c) RESPONSES.—Not later than 180 days after receipt of the report required under subsection (b), the Commission shall submit a response to the Committee on Banking, Housing, and Urban Affairs of the Senate, and the Committee on Financial Services of the House of Representatives, with a copy to the Special Committee on Aging of the Senate, stating the actions the Commission has taken in response to the recommendations contained in such report.

[Explanation at ¶ 4410.]

[¶ 10,978] ACT SEC. 978. FUNDING FOR GOVERNMENTAL ACCOUNTING STANDARDS BOARD.

(a) AMENDMENT TO THE SECURITIES ACT OF 1933.—Section 19 of the Securities Act of 1933 (15 U.S.C. 77s), as amended by section 912, is further amended by adding at the end the following:

"(g) FUNDING FOR THE GASB.—

"(1) IN GENERAL.—The Commission may, subject to the limitations imposed by section 15B of the Securities Exchange Act of 1934 (15 U.S.C. 78o-4), require a national securities association registered under the Securities Exchange Act of 1934 to establish—

"(A) a reasonable annual accounting support fee to adequately fund the annual budget of the Governmental Accounting Standards Board (referred to in this subsection as the 'GASB'); and

"(B) rules and procedures, in consultation with the principal organizations representing State governors, legislators, local elected officials, and State and local finance officers, to provide for the equitable allocation, assessment, and collection of the accounting support fee established under subparagraph (A) from the members of the association, and the remittance of all such accounting support fees to the Financial Accounting Foundation.

"(2) ANNUAL BUDGET.—For purposes of this subsection, the annual budget of the GASB is the annual budget reviewed and approved according to the internal procedures of the Financial Accounting Foundation.

"(3) USE OF FUNDS.—Any fees or funds collected under this subsection shall be used to support the efforts of the GASB to establish standards of financial accounting and reporting recognized as generally accepted accounting principles applicable to State and local governments of the United States.

"(4) LIMITATION ON FEE.—The annual accounting support fees collected under this subsection for a fiscal year shall not exceed the recoverable annual budgeted expenses of the GASB (which may include operating expenses, capital, and accrued items).

"(5) RULES OF CONSTRUCTION.—

"(A) FEES NOT PUBLIC MONIES.—Accounting support fees collected under this subsection and other receipts of the GASB shall not be considered public monies of the United States.

"(B) LIMITATION ON AUTHORITY OF THE COMMISSION.—Nothing in this subsection shall be construed to—

"(i) provide the Commission or any national securities association direct or indirect oversight of the budget or technical agenda of the GASB; or

"(ii) affect the setting of generally accepted accounting principles by the GASB.

"(C) NONINTERFERENCE WITH STATES.—Nothing in this subsection shall be construed to impair or limit the authority of a State or local government to establish accounting and financial reporting standards.".

(b) STUDY OF FUNDING FOR GOVERNMENTAL ACCOUNTING STANDARDS BOARD.—

(1) STUDY.—The Comptroller General of the United States shall conduct a study that evaluates—

(A) the role and importance of the Governmental Accounting Standards Board in the municipal securities markets; and

(B) the manner and the level at which the Governmental Accounting Standards Board has been funded.

(2) CONSULTATION.—In conducting the study required under paragraph (1), the Comptroller General shall consult with the principal organizations representing State governors, legislators, local elected officials, and State and local finance officers.

(3) REPORT.—Not later than 180 days after the date of enactment of this Act, the Comptroller General shall submit to the Committee on Banking, Housing, and Urban Affairs of the Senate and the Committee on Financial Services of the House of Representatives a report on the study required under paragraph (1).

[Explanation at ¶ 4405 and ¶ 4410.]

[¶ 10,979] ACT SEC. 979. COMMISSION OFFICE OF MUNICIPAL SECURITIES.

(a) IN GENERAL.—There shall be in the Commission an Office of Municipal Securities, which shall—

(1) administer the rules of the Commission with respect to the practices of municipal securities brokers and dealers, municipal securities advisors, municipal securities investors, and municipal securities issuers; and

(2) coordinate with the Municipal Securities Rulemaking Board for rulemaking and enforcement actions as required by law.

(b) DIRECTOR OF THE OFFICE.—The head of the Office of Municipal Securities shall be the Director, who shall report to the Chairman.

(c) STAFFING.—

(1) IN GENERAL.—The Office of Municipal Securities shall be staffed sufficiently to carry out the requirements of this section.

(2) REQUIREMENT.—The staff of the Office of Municipal Securities shall include individuals with knowledge of and expertise in municipal finance.

[Explanation at ¶ 4400.]

Subtitle I—Public Company Accounting Oversight Board, Portfolio Margining, and Other Matters

[¶ 10,981] ACT SEC. 981. AUTHORITY TO SHARE CERTAIN INFORMATION WITH FOREIGN AUTHORITIES.

(a) DEFINITION.—Section 2(a) of the Sarbanes-Oxley Act of 2002 (15 U.S.C. 7201(a)) is amended by adding at the end the following:

"(17) FOREIGN AUDITOR OVERSIGHT AUTHORITY.—The term 'foreign auditor oversight authority' means any governmental body or other entity empowered by a foreign government to conduct inspections of public accounting firms or otherwise to administer or enforce laws related to the regulation of public accounting firms.".

(b) AVAILABILITY TO SHARE INFORMATION.—Section 105(b)(5) of the Sarbanes-Oxley Act of 2002 (15 U.S.C. 7215(b)(5)) is amended by adding at the end the following:

"(C) AVAILABILITY TO FOREIGN OVERSIGHT AUTHORITIES.—Without the loss of its status as confidential and privileged in the hands of the Board, all information referred to in subparagraph (A) that relates to a public accounting firm that a foreign government has empowered a foreign auditor oversight authority to inspect or otherwise enforce laws with respect to, may, at the discretion of the Board, be made available to the foreign auditor oversight authority, if—

"(i) the Board finds that it is necessary to accomplish the purposes of this Act or to protect investors;

"(ii) the foreign auditor oversight authority provides—

"(I) such assurances of confidentiality as the Board may request;

"(II) a description of the applicable information systems and controls of the foreign auditor oversight authority; and

"(III) a description of the laws and regulations of the foreign government of the foreign auditor oversight authority that are relevant to information access; and

"(iii) the Board determines that it is appropriate to share such information.".

(c) CONFORMING AMENDMENT.—Section 105(b)(5)(A) of the Sarbanes-Oxley Act of 2002 (15 U.S.C. 7215(b)(5)(A)) is amended by striking "subparagraph (B)" and inserting "subparagraphs (B) and (C)".

[Explanation at ¶4420 and ¶4430.]

[¶10,982] ACT SEC. 982. OVERSIGHT OF BROKERS AND DEALERS.

(a) DEFINITIONS.—

(1) DEFINITIONS AMENDED.—Title I of the Sarbanes-Oxley Act of 2002 (15 U.S.C. 7201 et seq.) is amended by adding at the end the following new section:

"SEC. 110. DEFINITIONS.

"For the purposes of this title, the following definitions shall apply:

"(1) AUDIT.—The term 'audit' means an examination of the financial statements, reports, documents, procedures, controls, or notices of any issuer, broker, or dealer by an independent public accounting firm in accordance with the rules of the Board or the Commission, for the purpose of expressing an opinion on the financial statements or providing an audit report.

"(2) AUDIT REPORT.—The term 'audit report' means a document, report, notice, or other record—

"(A) prepared following an audit performed for purposes of compliance by an issuer, broker, or dealer with the requirements of the securities laws; and

"(B) in which a public accounting firm either—

"(i) sets forth the opinion of that firm regarding a financial statement, report, notice, or other document, procedures, or controls; or

"(ii) asserts that no such opinion can be expressed.

"(3) BROKER.—The term 'broker' means a broker (as such term is defined in section 3(a)(4) of the Securities Exchange Act of 1934 (15 U.S.C. 78c(a)(4))) that is required to file a balance sheet, income statement, or other financial statement under section 17(e)(1)(A) of such Act (15 U.S.C. 78q(e)(1)(A)), where such balance sheet, income statement, or financial statement is required to be certified by a registered public accounting firm.

"(4) DEALER.—The term 'dealer' means a dealer (as such term is defined in section 3(a)(5) of the Securities Exchange Act of 1934 (15 U.S.C. 78c(a)(5))) that is required to file a balance sheet, income statement, or other financial statement under section 17(e)(1)(A) of such Act (15 U.S.C. 78q(e)(1)(A)), where such balance sheet, income statement, or financial statement is required to be certified by a registered public accounting firm.

"(5) PROFESSIONAL STANDARDS.—The term 'professional standards' means—

"(A) accounting principles that are—

"(i) established by the standard setting body described in section 19(b) of the Securities Act of 1933, as amended by this Act, or prescribed by the Commission under section 19(a) of that Act (15 U.S.C. 17a(s)) or section 13(b) of the Securities Exchange Act of 1934 (15 U.S.C. 78a(m)); and

"(ii) relevant to audit reports for particular issuers, brokers, or dealers, or dealt with in the quality control system of a particular registered public accounting firm; and

"(B) auditing standards, standards for attestation engagements, quality control policies and procedures, ethical and competency standards, and independence standards (including rules implementing title II) that the Board or the Commission determines—

"(i) relate to the preparation or issuance of audit reports for issuers, brokers, or dealers; and

"(ii) are established or adopted by the Board under section 103(a), or are promulgated as rules of the Commission.

"(6) SELF-REGULATORY ORGANIZATION.—The term 'self-regulatory organization' has the same meaning as in section 3(a) of the Securities Exchange Act of 1934 (15 U.S.C. 78c(a)).".

(2) CONFORMING AMENDMENT.—Section 2(a) of the Sarbanes-Oxley Act of 2002 (15 U.S.C. 7201(a)) is amended in the matter preceding paragraph (1), by striking "In this" and inserting "Except as otherwise specifically provided in this Act, in this".

(b) ESTABLISHMENT AND ADMINISTRATION OF THE PUBLIC COMPANY ACCOUNTING OVERSIGHT BOARD.—Section 101 of the Sarbanes-Oxley Act of 2002 (15 U.S.C. 7211) is amended—

(1) by striking "issuers" each place that term appears and inserting "issuers, brokers, and dealers"; and

(2) in subsection (a)—

(A) by striking "public companies" and inserting "companies"; and

(B) by striking "for companies the securities of which are sold to, and held by and for, public investors".

(c) REGISTRATION WITH THE BOARD.—Section 102 of the Sarbanes-Oxley Act of 2002 (15 U.S.C. 7212) is amended—

(1) in subsection (a)—

(A) by striking "Beginning 180" and all that follows through "101(d), it" and inserting "It"; and

(B) by striking "issuer" and inserting "issuer, broker, or dealer";

(2) in subsection (b)—

(A) in paragraph (2)(A), by striking "issuers" and inserting "issuers, brokers, and dealers"; and

(B) by striking "issuer" each place that term appears and inserting "issuer, broker, or dealer".

(d) AUDITING AND INDEPENDENCE.—Section 103(a) of the Sarbanes-Oxley Act of 2002 (15 U.S.C. 7213(a)) is amended—

(1) in paragraph (1), by striking "and such ethics standards" and inserting "such ethics standards, and such independence standards";

(2) in paragraph (2)(A)(iii), by striking "describe in each audit report" and inserting "in each audit report for an issuer, describe"; and

(3) in paragraph (2)(B)(i), by striking "issuers" and inserting "issuers, brokers, and dealers".

(e) INSPECTIONS OF REGISTERED PUBLIC ACCOUNTING FIRMS.—

(1) AMENDMENTS.—Section 104(a) of the Sarbanes-Oxley Act of 2002 (15 U.S.C. 7214(a)) is amended—

(A) by striking "The Board shall" and inserting the following:

"(1) INSPECTIONS GENERALLY.—The Board shall"; and

(B) by adding at the end the following:

"(2) INSPECTIONS OF AUDIT REPORTS FOR BROKERS AND DEALERS.—

"(A) The Board may, by rule, conduct and require a program of inspection in accordance with paragraph (1), on a basis to be determined by the Board, of registered public accounting firms that provide one or more audit reports for a broker or dealer. The Board, in establishing such a program, may allow for differentiation among classes of brokers and dealers, as appropriate.

"(B) If the Board determines to establish a program of inspection pursuant to subparagraph (A), the Board shall consider in establishing any inspection schedules whether differing schedules would be appropriate with respect to registered public accounting firms that issue audit reports only for one or more brokers or dealers that do not receive, handle, or hold customer securities or cash or are not a member of the Securities Investor Protection Corporation.

"(C) Any rules of the Board pursuant to this paragraph shall be subject to prior approval by the Commission pursuant to section 107(b) before the rules become effective, including an opportunity for public notice and comment.

"(D) Notwithstanding anything to the contrary in section 102 of this Act, a public accounting firm shall not be required to register with the Board if the public accounting firm is exempt from the inspection program which may be established by the Board under subparagraph (A).".

(2) CONFORMING AMENDMENT.—Section 17(e)(1)(A) of the Securities Exchange Act of 1934 (15 U.S.C. 78q(e)(1)(A)) is amended by striking "registered public accounting firm" and inserting "independent public accounting firm, or by a registered public accounting firm if the firm is required to be registered under the Sarbanes-Oxley Act of 2002,".

(f) INVESTIGATIONS AND DISCIPLINARY PROCEEDINGS.—Section 105(c)(7)(B) of the Sarbanes-Oxley Act of 2002 (15 U.S.C. 7215(c)(7)(B)) is amended—

(1) in the subparagraph heading, by inserting ", BROKER, OR DEALER" after "ISSUER";

(2) by striking "any issuer" each place that term appears and inserting "any issuer, broker, or dealer"; and

(3) by striking "an issuer under this subsection" and inserting "a registered public accounting firm under this subsection".

(g) FOREIGN PUBLIC ACCOUNTING FIRMS.—Section 106(a) of the Sarbanes-Oxley Act of 2002 (15 U.S.C. 7216(a)) is amended—

(1) in paragraph (1), by striking "issuer" and inserting "issuer, broker, or dealer"; and

(2) in paragraph (2), by striking "issuers" and inserting "issuers, brokers, or dealers".

(h) FUNDING.—Section 109 of the Sarbanes-Oxley Act of 2002 (15 U.S.C. 7219) is amended—

(1) in subsection (c)(2), by striking "subsection (i)" and inserting "subsection (j)";

(2) in subsection (d)—

(A) in paragraph (2), by striking "allowing for differentiation among classes of issuers, as appropriate" and inserting "and among brokers and dealers, in accordance with subsection (h), and allowing for differentiation among classes of issuers, brokers and dealers, as appropriate"; and

(B) by adding at the end the following:

"(3) BROKERS AND DEALERS.—The Board shall begin the allocation, assessment, and collection of fees under paragraph (2) with respect to brokers and dealers with the payment of support fees to fund the first full fiscal year beginning after the date of enactment of the Investor Protection and Securities Reform Act of 2010.";

(3) by redesignating subsections (h), (i), and (j) as subsections (i), (j), and (k), respectively; and

(4) by inserting after subsection (g) the following:

"(h) ALLOCATION OF ACCOUNTING SUPPORT FEES AMONG BROKERS AND DEALERS.—

"(1) OBLIGATION TO PAY.—Each broker or dealer shall pay to the Board the annual accounting support fee allocated to such broker or dealer under this section.

"(2) ALLOCATION.—Any amount due from a broker or dealer (or from a particular class of brokers and dealers) under this section shall be allocated among brokers and dealers and payable by the broker or dealer (or the brokers and dealers in the particular class, as applicable).

"(3) PROPORTIONALITY.—The amount due from a broker or dealer shall be in proportion to the net capital of the broker or dealer (before or after any adjustments), compared to the total net capital of all brokers and dealers (before or after any adjustments), in accordance with rules issued by the Board.".

(i) REFERRAL OF INVESTIGATIONS TO A SELF-REGULATORY ORGANIZATION.—Section 105(b)(4)(B) of the Sarbanes-Oxley Act of 2002 (15 U.S.C. 7215(b)(4)(B)) is amended—

(1) by redesignating clauses (ii) and (iii) as clauses (iii) and (iv), respectively; and

(2) by inserting after clause (i) the following:

"(ii) to a self-regulatory organization, in the case of an investigation that concerns an audit report for a broker or dealer that is under the jurisdiction of such self-regulatory organization;".

(j) USE OF DOCUMENTS RELATED TO AN INSPECTION OR INVESTIGATION.—Section 105(b)(5)(B)(ii) of the Sarbanes-Oxley Act of 2002 (15 U.S.C. 7215(b)(5)(B)(ii)) is amended—

(1) in subclause (III), by striking "and" at the end;

(2) in subclause (IV), by striking the comma and inserting "; and"; and

(3) by inserting after subclause (IV) the following:

"(V) a self-regulatory organization, with respect to an audit report for a broker or dealer that is under the jurisdiction of such self-regulatory organization,".

[Explanation at ¶4420 and ¶4435.]

[¶10,983] ACT SEC. 983. PORTFOLIO MARGINING.

(a) ADVANCES.—Section 9(a)(1) of the Securities Investor Protection Act of 1970 (15 U.S.C. 78fff3(a)(1)) is amended by inserting "or options on commodity futures contracts" after "claim for securities".

(b) DEFINITIONS.—Section 16 of the Securities Investor Protection Act of 1970 (15 U.S.C. 78lll) is amended—

(1) by striking paragraph (2) and inserting the following:

"(2) CUSTOMER.—

"(A) IN GENERAL.—The term 'customer' of a debtor means any person (including any person with whom the debtor deals as principal or agent) who has a claim on account of securities received, acquired, or held by the debtor in the ordinary course of its business as a broker or dealer from or for the securities accounts of such person for safekeeping, with a view to sale, to cover consummated sales, pursuant to purchases, as collateral, security, or for purposes of effecting transfer.

"(B) INCLUDED PERSONS.—The term 'customer' includes—

"(i) any person who has deposited cash with the debtor for the purpose of purchasing securities;

"(ii) any person who has a claim against the debtor for cash, securities, futures contracts, or options on futures contracts received, acquired, or held in a portfolio margining account carried as a securities account pursuant to a portfolio margining program approved by the Commission; and

"(iii) any person who has a claim against the debtor arising out of sales or conversions of such securities.

"(C) EXCLUDED PERSONS.—The term 'customer' does not include any person, to the extent that—

"(i) the claim of such person arises out of transactions with a foreign subsidiary of a member of SIPC; or

"(ii) such person has a claim for cash or securities which by contract, agreement, or understanding, or by operation of law, is part of the capital of the debtor, or is subordinated to the claims of any or all creditors of the debtor, notwithstanding that some ground exists for declaring such contract, agreement, or understanding void or voidable in a suit between the claimant and the debtor.";

(2) in paragraph (4)—

(A) in subparagraph (C), by striking "and" at the end;

(B) by redesignating subparagraph (D) as subparagraph (E); and

(C) by inserting after subparagraph (C) the following:

"(D) in the case of a portfolio margining account of a customer that is carried as a securities account pursuant to a portfolio margining program approved by the Commission, a futures contract or an option on a futures contract received, acquired, or held by or for the account of a debtor from or for such portfolio margining account, and the proceeds thereof; and";

(3) in paragraph (9), in the matter following subparagraph (L), by inserting after "Such term" the following: "includes revenues earned by a broker or dealer in connection with a transaction in the portfolio margining account of a customer carried as securities accounts pursuant to a portfolio margining program approved by the Commission. Such term"; and

(4) in paragraph (11)—

(A) in subparagraph (A)—

(i) by striking "filing date, all" and all that follows through the end of the subparagraph and inserting the following: "filing date—

"(i) all securities positions of such customer (other than customer name securities reclaimed by such customer); and

"(ii) all positions in futures contracts and options on futures contracts held in a portfolio margining account carried as a securities account pursuant to a portfolio margining program approved by the Commission, including all property collateralizing such positions, to the extent that such property is not otherwise included herein; minus"; and

(B) in the matter following subparagraph (C), by striking "In determining" and inserting the following: "A claim for a commodity futures contract received, acquired, or held in a portfolio margining account pursuant to a portfolio margining program approved by the Commission or a claim for a security futures contract, shall be deemed to be a claim with respect to such contract as of the filing date, and such claim shall be treated as a claim for cash. In determining".

[Explanation at ¶ 4095 and ¶ 4455.]

[¶ 10,984] ACT SEC. 984. LOAN OR BORROWING OF SECURITIES.

(a) RULEMAKING AUTHORITY.—Section 10 of the Securities Exchange Act of 1934 (15 U.S.C. 78j) is amended by adding at the end the following:

"(c)

(1) To effect, accept, or facilitate a transaction involving the loan or borrowing of securities in contravention of such rules and regulations as the Commission may prescribe as necessary or appropriate in the public interest or for the protection of investors.

"(2) Nothing in paragraph (1) may be construed to limit the authority of the appropriate Federal banking agency (as defined in section 3(q) of the Federal Deposit Insurance Act (12 U.S.C. 1813(q))), the National Credit Union Administration, or any other Federal department or agency having a responsibility under Federal law to prescribe rules or regulations restricting transactions involving the loan or borrowing of securities in order to protect the safety and soundness of a financial institution or to protect the financial system from systemic risk.".

(b) RULEMAKING REQUIRED.—Not later than 2 years after the date of enactment of this Act, the Commission shall promulgate rules that are designed to increase the transparency of information available to brokers, dealers, and investors, with respect to the loan or borrowing of securities.

[Explanation at ¶ 4460.]

[¶ 10,985] ACT SEC. 985. TECHNICAL CORRECTIONS TO FEDERAL SECURITIES LAWS.

(a) SECURITIES ACT OF 1933.—The Securities Act of 1933 (15 U.S.C. 77a et seq.) is amended—

(1) in section 3(a)(4) (15 U.S.C. 77c(a)(4)), by striking "individual;" and inserting "individual,";

(2) in section 18 (15 U.S.C. 77r)—

(A) in subsection (b)(1)(C), by striking "is a security" and inserting "a security"; and

(B) in subsection (c)(2)(B)(i), by striking "State, or" and inserting "State or";

(3) in section 19(d)(6)(A) (15 U.S.C. 77s(d)(6)(A)), by striking "in paragraph (1) of (3)" and inserting "in paragraph (1) or (3)"; and

(4) in section 27A(c)(1)(B)(ii) (15 U.S.C. 77z-2(c)(1)(B)(ii)), by striking "business entity;" and inserting "business entity,";

(b) SECURITIES EXCHANGE ACT OF 1934.—The Securities Exchange Act of 1934 (15 U.S.C. 78a et seq.) is amended—

(1) in section 2 (15 U.S.C. 78b), by striking "affected" and inserting "effected";

(2) in section 3 (15 U.S.C. 78c)—

(A) in subsection (a)(55)(A), by striking "section 3(a)(12) of the Securities Exchange Act of 1934" and inserting "section 3(a)(12) of this title"; and

(B) in subsection (g), by striking "company, account person, or entity" and inserting "company, account, person, or entity";

(3) in section 10A(i)(1)(B) (15 U.S.C. 78j-1(i)(1)(B))—

(A) in the subparagraph heading, by striking "MINIMUS" and inserting "MINIMIS"; and

(B) in clause (i), by striking "nonaudit" and inserting "non-audit";

(4) in section 13(b)(1) (15 U.S.C. 78m(b)(1)), by striking "earning statement" and inserting "earnings statement";

(5) in section 15 (15 U.S.C. 78o)—

(A) in subsection (b)(1)—

(i) in subparagraph (B), by striking "The order granting" and all that follows through "from such membership."; and

(ii) in the undesignated matter immediately following subparagraph (B), by inserting after the first sentence the following: "The order granting registration shall not be effective until such broker or dealer has become a member of a registered securities association, or until such broker or dealer has become a member of a national securities exchange, if such broker or dealer effects transactions solely on that exchange, unless the Commission has exempted such broker or dealer, by rule or order, from such membership.";

(6) in section 15C(a)(2) (15 U.S.C. 78o-5(a)(2))—

(A) by redesignating clauses (i) and (ii) as subparagraphs (A) and (B), respectively, and adjusting the subparagraph margins accordingly;

(B) in subparagraph (B), as so redesignated, by striking "The order granting" and all that follows through "from such membership."; and

(C) in the matter following subparagraph (B), as so redesignated, by inserting after the first sentence the following: "The order granting registration shall not be effective until such government securities broker or government securities dealer has become a member of a national securities exchange registered under section 6 of this title, or a securities association registered under section 15A of this title, unless the Commission has exempted such government securities broker or government securities dealer, by rule or order, from such membership.";

(7) in section 17(b)(1)(B) (15 U.S.C. 78q(b)(1)(B)), by striking "15A(k) gives" and inserting "15A(k), give"; and

(8) in section 21C(c)(2) (15 U.S.C. 78u-3(c)(2)), by striking "paragraph (1) subsection" and inserting "Paragraph (1)".

(c) TRUST INDENTURE ACT OF 1939.—The Trust Indenture Act of 1939 (15 U.S.C. 77aaa et seq.) is amended—

(1) in section 304(b) (15 U.S.C. 77ddd(b)), by striking "section 2 of such Act" and inserting "section 2(a) of such Act"; and

(2) in section 317(a)(1) (15 U.S.C. 77qqq(a)(1)), by striking ", in the" and inserting "in the".

(d) INVESTMENT COMPANY ACT OF 1940.—The Investment Company Act of 1940 (15 U.S.C. 80a-1 et seq.) is amended—

(1) in section 2(a)(19) (15 U.S.C. 80a-2(a)(19)), in the matter following subparagraph (B)(vii)—

(A) by striking "clause (vi)" each place that term appears and inserting "clause (vii)"; and

(B) in each of subparagraphs (A)(vi) and (B)(vi), by adding "and" at the end of subclause (III);

(2) in section 9(b)(4)(B) (15 U.S.C. 80a-9(b)(4)(B)), by adding "or" after the semicolon at the end;

(3) in section 12(d)(1)(J) (15 U.S.C. 80a-12(d)(1)(J)), by striking "any provision of this subsection" and inserting "any provision of this paragraph";

(4) in section 17(f) (15 U.S.C. 80a-17(f))—

(A) in paragraph (4), by striking "No such member" and inserting "No member of a national securities exchange"; and

(B) in paragraph (6), by striking "company may serve" and inserting "company, may serve"; and

(5) in section 61(a)(3)(B)(iii) (15 U.S.C. 80a-60(a)(3)(B)(iii))—

(A) by striking "paragraph (1) of section 205" and inserting "section 205(a)(1)"; and

(B) by striking "clause (A) or (B) of that section" and inserting "paragraph (1) or (2) of section 205(b)".

(e) INVESTMENT ADVISERS ACT OF 1940.—The Investment Advisers Act of 1940 (15 U.S.C. 80b-1 et seq.) is amended—

(1) in section 203 (15 U.S.C. 80b-3)—

(A) in subsection (c)(1)(A), by striking "principal business office and" and inserting "principal office, principal place of business, and"; and

(B) in subsection (k)(4)(B), in the matter following clause (ii), by striking "principal place of business" and inserting "principal office or place of business";

(2) in section 206(3) (15 U.S.C. 80b-6(3)), by adding "or" after the semicolon at the end;

(3) in section 213(a) (15 U.S.C. 80b-13(a)), by striking "principal place of business" and inserting "principal office or place of business"; and

(4) in section 222 (15 U.S.C. 80b-18a), by striking "principal place of business" each place that term appears and inserting "principal office and place of business".

[Explanation at ¶ 4450.]

[¶ 10,986] ACT SEC. 986. CONFORMING AMENDMENTS RELATING TO REPEAL OF THE PUBLIC UTILITY HOLDING COMPANY ACT OF 1935.

(a) SECURITIES EXCHANGE ACT OF 1934.—The Securities Exchange Act of 1934 (15 U.S.C. 78 et seq.) is amended—

(1) in section 3(a)(47) (15 U.S.C. 78c(a)(47)), by striking "the Public Utility Holding Company Act of 1935 (15 U.S.C. 79a et seq.),";

(2) in section 12(k) (15 U.S.C. 78l(k)), by amending paragraph (7) to read as follows:

"(7) DEFINITION.—For purposes of this subsection, the term 'emergency' means—

"(A) a major market disturbance characterized by or constituting—

"(i) sudden and excessive fluctuations of securities prices generally, or a substantial threat thereof, that threaten fair and orderly markets; or

"(ii) a substantial disruption of the safe or efficient operation of the national system for clearance and settlement of transactions in securities, or a substantial threat thereof; or

"(B) a major disturbance that substantially disrupts, or threatens to substantially disrupt—

"(i) the functioning of securities markets, investment companies, or any other significant portion or segment of the securities markets; or

"(ii) the transmission or processing of securities transactions."; and

(3) in section 21(h)(2) (15 U.S.C. 78u(h)(2)), by striking "section 18(c) of the Public Utility Holding Company Act of 1935,".

(b) TRUST INDENTURE ACT OF 1939.—The Trust Indenture Act of 1939 (15 U.S.C. 77aaa et seq.) is amended—

(1) in section 303 (15 U.S.C. 77ccc), by striking paragraph (17) and inserting the following:

"(17) The terms 'Securities Act of 1933' and 'Securities Exchange Act of 1934' shall be deemed to refer, respectively, to such Acts, as amended, whether amended prior to or after the enactment of this title.";

(2) in section 308 (15 U.S.C. 77hhh), by striking "Securities Act of 1933, the Securities Exchange Act of 1934, or the Public Utility Holding Company Act of 1935" each place that term appears and inserting "Securities Act of 1933 or the Securities Exchange Act of 1934";

(3) in section 310 (15 U.S.C. 77jjj), by striking subsection (c);

(4) in section 311 (15 U.S.C. 77kkk), by striking subsection (c);

(5) in section 323(b) (15 U.S.C. 77www(b)), by striking "Securities Act of 1933, or the Securities Exchange Act of 1934, or the Public Utility Holding Company Act of 1935" and inserting "Securities Act of 1933 or the Securities Exchange Act of 1934"; and

(6) in section 326 (15 U.S.C. 77zzz), by striking "Securities Act of 1933, or the Securities Exchange Act of 1934, or the Public Utility Holding Company Act of 1935," and inserting "Securities Act of 1933 or the Securities Exchange Act of 1934".

(c) INVESTMENT COMPANY ACT OF 1940.—The Investment Company Act of 1940 (15 U.S.C. 80a-1 et seq.) is amended—

(1) in section 2(a)(44) (15 U.S.C. 80a-2(a)(44)), by striking "'Public Utility Holding Company Act of 1935',";

(2) in section 3(c) (15 U.S.C. 80a-3(c)), by striking paragraph (8) and inserting the following:

"(8) [Repealed]";

(3) in section 38(b) (15 U.S.C. 80a-37(b)), by striking "the Public Utility Holding Company Act of 1935,"; and

(4) in section 50 (15 U.S.C. 80a-49), by striking "the Public Utility Holding Company Act of 1935,".

(d) INVESTMENT ADVISERS ACT OF 1940.—Section 202(a)(21) of the Investment Advisers Act of 1940 (15 U.S.C. 80b-2(a)(21)) is amended by striking "'Public Utility Holding Company Act of 1935',".

[Explanation at ¶ 4450.]

[¶ 10,987] ACT SEC. 987. AMENDMENT TO DEFINITION OF MATERIAL LOSS AND NONMATERIAL LOSSES TO THE DEPOSIT INSURANCE FUND FOR PURPOSES OF INSPECTOR GENERAL REVIEWS.

(a) IN GENERAL.—Section 38(k) of the Federal Deposit Insurance Act (U.S.C. 1831o(k)) is amended—

(1) in paragraph (2), by striking subparagraph (B) and inserting the following:

"(B) MATERIAL LOSS DEFINED.—The term 'material loss' means any estimated loss in excess of—

"(i) $200,000,000, if the loss occurs during the period beginning on January 1, 2010, and ending on December 31, 2011;

"(ii) $150,000,000, if the loss occurs during the period beginning on January 1, 2012, and ending on December 31, 2013; and

"(iii) $50,000,000, if the loss occurs on or after January 1, 2014, provided that if the inspector general of a Federal banking agency certifies to the Committee on Banking, Housing, and Urban Affairs of the Senate and the Committee on Financial Services of the House of Representatives that the number of projected failures of depository institutions that would require material loss reviews for the following 12 months will be greater than 30 and would hinder the effectiveness of its oversight functions, then the definition of 'material loss' shall be $75,000,000 for a duration of 1 year from the date of the certification.";

(2) in paragraph (4)(A) by striking "the report" and inserting "any report on losses required under this subsection,";

(3) by striking paragraph (6);

(4) by redesignating paragraph (5) as paragraph (6); and

(5) by inserting after paragraph (4) the following:

"(5) LOSSES THAT ARE NOT MATERIAL.—

"(A) SEMIANNUAL REPORT.—For the 6-month period ending on March 31, 2010, and each 6-month period thereafter, the Inspector General of each Federal banking agency shall—

"(i) identify losses that the Inspector General estimates have been incurred by the Deposit Insurance Fund during that 6month period, with respect to the insured depository institutions supervised by the Federal banking agency;

"(ii) for each loss incurred by the Deposit Insurance Fund that is not a material loss, determine—

"(I) the grounds identified by the Federal banking agency or State bank supervisor for appointing the Corporation as receiver under section 11(c)(5); and

"(II) whether any unusual circumstances exist that might warrant an in-depth review of the loss; and

"(iii) prepare and submit a written report to the appropriate Federal banking agency and to Congress on the results of any determination by the Inspector General, including—

"(I) an identification of any loss that warrants an in-depth review, together with the reasons why such review is warranted, or, if the Inspector General determines that no review is warranted, an explanation of such determination; and

"(II) for each loss identified under subclause (I) that warrants an in-depth review, the date by which such review, and a report on such review prepared in a manner consistent with reports under paragraph (1)(A), will be completed and submitted to the Federal banking agency and Congress.

"(B) DEADLINE FOR SEMIANNUAL REPORT.—The Inspector General of each Federal banking agency shall—

"(i) submit each report required under paragraph (A) expeditiously, and not later than 90 days after the end of the 6month period covered by the report; and

"(ii) provide a copy of the report required under paragraph (A) to any Member of Congress, upon request.".

(b) TECHNICAL AND CONFORMING AMENDMENT.—The heading for subsection (k) of section 38 of the Federal Deposit Insurance Act (U.S.C. 1831o(k)) is amended to read as follows:

"(k) REVIEWS REQUIRED WHEN DEPOSIT INSURANCE FUND INCURS LOSSES.—".

[Explanation at ¶ 4465.]

[¶ 10,988] ACT SEC. 988. AMENDMENT TO DEFINITION OF MATERIAL LOSS AND NONMATERIAL LOSSES TO THE NATIONAL CREDIT UNION SHARE INSURANCE FUND FOR PURPOSES OF INSPECTOR GENERAL REVIEWS.

(a) IN GENERAL.—Section 216(j) of the Federal Credit Union Act (12 U.S.C. 1790d(j)) is amended to read as follows:

"(j) REVIEWS REQUIRED WHEN SHARE INSURANCE FUND EXPERIENCES LOSSES.—

"(1) IN GENERAL.—If the Fund incurs a material loss with respect to an insured credit union, the Inspector General of the Board shall—

"(A) submit to the Board a written report reviewing the supervision of the credit union by the Administration (including the implementation of this section by the Administration), which shall include—

"(i) a description of the reasons why the problems of the credit union resulted in a material loss to the Fund; and

"(ii) recommendations for preventing any such loss in the future; and

"(B) submit a copy of the report under subparagraph (A) to—

"(i) the Comptroller General of the United States;

"(ii) the Corporation;

"(iii) in the case of a report relating to a State credit union, the appropriate State supervisor; and

"(iv) to any Member of Congress, upon request.

"(2) MATERIAL LOSS DEFINED.—For purposes of determining whether the Fund has incurred a material loss with respect to an insured credit union, a loss is material if it exceeds the sum of—

"(A) $25,000,000; and

"(B) an amount equal to 10 percent of the total assets of the credit union on the date on which the Board initiated assistance under section 208 or was appointed liquidating agent.

"(3) PUBLIC DISCLOSURE REQUIRED.—

"(A) IN GENERAL.—The Board shall disclose a report under this subsection, upon request under section 552 of title 5, United States Code, without excising—

"(i) any portion under section 552(b)(5) of title 5, United States Code; or

"(ii) any information about the insured credit union (other than trade secrets) under section 552(b)(8) of title 5, United States Code.

"(B) RULE OF CONSTRUCTION.—Subparagraph (A) may not be construed as requiring the agency to disclose the name of any customer of the insured credit union (other than an institution-affiliated party), or information from which the identity of such customer could reasonably be ascertained.

"(4) LOSSES THAT ARE NOT MATERIAL.—

"(A) SEMIANNUAL REPORT.—For the 6-month period ending on March 31, 2010, and each 6-month period thereafter, the Inspector General of the Board shall—

"(i) identify any losses that the Inspector General estimates were incurred by the Fund during such 6-month period, with respect to insured credit unions;

"(ii) for each loss to the Fund that is not a material loss, determine—

"(I) the grounds identified by the Board or the State official having jurisdiction over a State credit union for appointing the Board as the liquidating agent for any Federal or State credit union; and

"(II) whether any unusual circumstances exist that might warrant an in-depth review of the loss; and

"(iii) prepare and submit a written report to the Board and to Congress on the results of the determinations of the Inspector General that includes—

"(I) an identification of any loss that warrants an in-depth review, and the reasons such review is warranted, or if the Inspector General determines that no review is warranted, an explanation of such determination; and

"(II) for each loss identified in subclause (I) that warrants an in-depth review, the date by which such review, and a report on the review prepared in a manner consistent with reports under paragraph (1)(A), will be completed.

"(B) DEADLINE FOR SEMIANNUAL REPORT.—The Inspector General of the Board shall—

"(i) submit each report required under subparagraph (A) expeditiously, and not later than 90 days after the end of the 6-month period covered by the report; and

"(ii) provide a copy of the report required under subparagraph (A) to any Member of Congress, upon request.

"(5) GAO REVIEW.—The Comptroller General of the United States shall, under such conditions as the Comptroller General determines to be appropriate—

"(A) review each report made under paragraph (1), including the extent to which the Inspector General of the Board complied with the requirements under section 8L of the Inspector General Act of 1978 (5 U.S.C. App.) with respect to each such report; and

"(B) recommend improvements to the supervision of insured credit unions (including improvements relating to the implementation of this section).".

[Explanation at ¶ 4465.]

[¶ 10,989] ACT SEC. 989. GOVERNMENT ACCOUNTABILITY OFFICE STUDY ON PROPRIETARY TRADING.

(a) DEFINITIONS.—In this section—

(1) the term "covered entity" means—

(A) an insured depository institution, an affiliate of an insured depository institution, a bank holding company, a financial holding company, or a subsidiary of a bank holding company or a financial holding company, as those terms are defined in the Bank Holding Company Act of 1956 (12 U.S.C. 1841 et seq.); and

(B) any other entity, as the Comptroller General of the United States may determine; and

(2) the term "proprietary trading" means the act of a covered entity investing as a principal in securities, commodities, derivatives, hedge funds, private equity firms, or such other financial products or entities as the Comptroller General may determine.

(b) STUDY.—

(1) IN GENERAL.—The Comptroller General of the United States shall conduct a study regarding the risks and conflicts associated with proprietary trading by and within covered entities, including an evaluation of—

(A) whether proprietary trading presents a material systemic risk to the stability of the United States financial system, and if so, the costs and benefits of options for mitigating such systemic risk;

(B) whether proprietary trading presents material risks to the safety and soundness of the covered entities that engage in such activities, and if so, the costs and benefits of options for mitigating such risks;

(C) whether proprietary trading presents material conflicts of interest between covered entities that engage in proprietary trading and the clients of the institutions who use the firm to execute trades or who rely on the firm to manage assets, and if so, the costs and benefits of options for mitigating such conflicts of interest;

(D) whether adequate disclosure regarding the risks and conflicts of proprietary trading is provided to the depositors, trading and asset management clients, and investors of covered entities that engage in proprietary trading, and if not, the costs and benefits of options for the improvement of such disclosure; and

(E) whether the banking, securities, and commodities regulators of institutions that engage in proprietary trading have in place adequate systems and controls to monitor and contain any risks and conflicts of interest related to proprietary trading, and if not, the costs and benefits of options for the improvement of such systems and controls.

(2) CONSIDERATIONS.—In carrying out the study required under paragraph (1), the Comptroller General shall consider—

(A) current practice relating to proprietary trading;

(B) the advisability of a complete ban on proprietary trading;

(C) limitations on the scope of activities that covered entities may engage in with respect to proprietary trading;

(D) the advisability of additional capital requirements for covered entities that engage in proprietary trading;

(E) enhanced restrictions on transactions between affiliates related to proprietary trading;

(F) enhanced accounting disclosures relating to proprietary trading;

(G) enhanced public disclosure relating to proprietary trading; and

(H) any other options the Comptroller General deems appropriate.

(c) REPORT TO CONGRESS.—Not later than 15 months after the date of enactment of this Act, the Comptroller General shall submit a report to Congress on the results of the study conducted under subsection (b).

(d) ACCESS BY COMPTROLLER GENERAL.—For purposes of conducting the study required under subsection (b), the Comptroller General shall have access, upon request, to any information, data, schedules, books, accounts, financial records, reports, files, electronic communications, or other papers, things, or property belonging to or in use by a covered entity that engages in proprietary trading, and to the officers, directors, employees, independent public accountants, financial advisors, staff, and agents and representatives of a covered entity (as related to the activities of the agent or representative on behalf of the covered entity), at such reasonable times as the Comptroller General may request. The Comptroller General may make and retain copies of books, records, accounts, and other records, as the Comptroller General deems appropriate.

(e) CONFIDENTIALITY OF REPORTS.—

(1) IN GENERAL.—Except as provided in paragraph (2), the Comptroller General may not disclose information regarding—

(A) any proprietary trading activity of a covered entity, unless such information is disclosed at a level of generality that does not reveal the investment or trading position or strategy of the covered entity for any specific security, commodity, derivative, or other investment or financial product; or

(B) any individual interviewed by the Comptroller General for purposes of the study under subsection (b), unless such information is disclosed at a level of generality that does not reveal—

(i) the name of or identifying details relating to such individual; or

(ii) in the case of an individual who is an employee of a third party that provides professional services to a covered entity believed to be engaged in proprietary trading, the name of or any identifying details relating to such third party.

(2) EXCEPTIONS.—The Comptroller General may disclose the information described in paragraph (1)—

(A) to a department, agency, or official of the Federal Government, for official use, upon request;

(B) to a committee of Congress, upon request; and

(C) to a court, upon an order of such court.

[Explanation at ¶ 4470.]

[¶ 10,989A] ACT SEC. 989A. SENIOR INVESTOR PROTECTIONS.

(a) DEFINITIONS.—As used in this section—

(1) the term "eligible entity" means—

(A) a securities commission (or any agency or office performing like functions) of a State that the Office determines has adopted rules on the appropriate use of designations in the offer or sale of securities or the provision of investment advice that meet or exceed the minimum requirements of the NASAA Model Rule on the Use of Senior-Specific Certifications and Professional Designations (or any successor thereto);

(B) the insurance commission (or any agency or office performing like functions) of any State that the Office determines has—

(i) adopted rules on the appropriate use of designations in the sale of insurance products that, to the extent practicable, conform to the minimum requirements of the National Association of Insurance Commissioners Model Regulation on the Use of Senior-Specific Certifications and Professional Designations in the Sale of Life Insurance and Annuities (or any successor thereto); and

(ii) adopted rules with respect to fiduciary or suitability requirements in the sale of annuities that meet or exceed the minimum requirements established by the Suitability in Annuity Transactions Model Regulation of the National Association of Insurance Commissioners (or any successor thereto); or

(C) a consumer protection agency of any State, if—

(i) the securities commission (or any agency or office performing like functions) of the State is eligible under subparagraph (A); or

(ii) the insurance commission (or any agency or office performing like functions) of the State is eligible under subparagraph (B);

(2) the term "financial product" means a security, an insurance product (including an insurance product that pays a return, whether fixed or variable), a bank product, and a loan product;

(3) the term "misleading designation"—

(A) means a certification, professional designation, or other purported credential that indicates or implies that a salesperson or adviser has special certification or training in advising or servicing seniors; and

(B) does not include a certification, professional designation, license, or other credential that—

(i) was issued by or obtained from an academic institution having regional accreditation;

(ii) meets the standards for certifications and professional designations out-lined by the NASAA Model Rule on the Use of Senior-Specific Certifications and Professional Designations (or any successor thereto) or by the Model Regulations on the Use of Senior-Specific Certifications and Professional Designations in the Sale of Life Insurance and Annuities, adopted by the National Association of Insurance Commissioners (or any successor thereto); or

(iii) was issued by or obtained from a State;

(4) the term "misleading or fraudulent marketing" means the use of a misleading designation by a person that sells to or advises a senior in connection with the sale of a financial product;

(5) the term "NASAA" means the North American Securities Administrators Association;

(6) the term "Office" means the Office of Financial Literacy of the Bureau;

(7) the term "senior" means any individual who has attained the age of 62 years or older; and

(8) the term "State" has the same meaning as in section 3 of the Securities Exchange Act of 1934 (15 U.S.C. 78c(a)).

(b) GRANTS TO STATES FOR ENHANCED PROTECTION OF SENIORS FROM BEING MISLED BY FALSE DESIGNATIONS.—The Office shall establish a program under which the Office may make grants to States or eligible entities—

(1) to hire staff to identify, investigate, and prosecute (through civil, administrative, or criminal enforcement actions) cases involving misleading or fraudulent marketing;

(2) to fund technology, equipment, and training for regulators, prosecutors, and law enforcement officers, in order to identify salespersons and advisers who target seniors through the use of misleading designations;

(3) to fund technology, equipment, and training for prosecutors to increase the successful prosecution of salespersons and advisers who target seniors with the use of misleading designations;

(4) to provide educational materials and training to regulators on the appropriateness of the use of designations by salespersons and advisers in connection with the sale and marketing of financial products;

(5) to provide educational materials and training to seniors to increase awareness and understanding of misleading or fraudulent marketing;

(6) to develop comprehensive plans to combat misleading or fraudulent marketing of financial products to seniors; and

(7) to enhance provisions of State law to provide protection for seniors against misleading or fraudulent marketing.

(c) APPLICATIONS.—A State or eligible entity desiring a grant under this section shall submit an application to the Office, in such form and in such a manner as the Office may determine, that includes—

(1) a proposal for activities to protect seniors from misleading or fraudulent marketing that are proposed to be funded using a grant under this section, including—

(A) an identification of the scope of the problem of misleading or fraudulent marketing in the State;

(B) a description of how the proposed activities would—

(i) protect seniors from misleading or fraudulent marketing in the sale of financial products, including by proactively identifying victims of misleading and fraudulent marketing who are seniors;

(ii) assist in the investigation and prosecution of those using misleading or fraudulent marketing; and

(iii) discourage and reduce cases of misleading or fraudulent marketing; and

(C) a description of how the proposed activities would be coordinated with other State efforts; and

(2) any other information, as the Office determines is appropriate.

(d) PERFORMANCE OBJECTIVES AND REPORTING REQUIREMENTS.—The Office may establish such performance objectives and reporting requirements for States and eligible entities receiving a grant under this section as the Office determines are necessary to carry out and assess the effectiveness of the program under this section.

(e) MAXIMUM AMOUNT.—The amount of a grant under this section may not exceed—

(1) $500,000 for each of 3 consecutive fiscal years, if the recipient is a State, or an eligible entity of a State, that has adopted rules—

(A) on the appropriate use of designations in the offer or sale of securities or investment advice that meet or exceed the minimum requirements of the NASAA Model Rule on the Use of Senior-Specific Certifications and Professional Designations (or any successor thereto);

(B) on the appropriate use of designations in the sale of insurance products that, to the extent practicable, conform to the minimum requirements of the National Association of Insurance Commissioners Model Regulation on the Use of Senior-Specific Certifications and Professional Designations in the Sale of Life Insurance and Annuities (or any successor thereto); and

(C) with respect to fiduciary or suitability requirements in the sale of annuities that meet or exceed the minimum requirements established by the Suitability in Annuity Transactions Model Regulation of the National Association of Insurance Commissioners (or any successor thereto); and

(2) $100,000 for each of 3 consecutive fiscal years, if the recipient is a State, or an eligible entity of a State, that has adopted—

(A) rules on the appropriate use of designations in the offer or sale of securities or investment advice that meet or exceed the minimum requirements of the NASAA Model Rule on the Use of Senior-Specific Certifications and Professional Designations (or any successor thereto); or

(B) rules—

(i) on the appropriate use of designations in the sale of insurance products that, to the extent practicable, conform to the minimum requirements of the National Association of Insurance Commissioners Model Regulation on the Use of Senior-Specific Certifications and Professional Designations in the Sale of Life Insurance and Annuities (or any successor thereto); and

(ii) with respect to fiduciary or suitability requirements in the sale of annuities that meet or exceed the minimum requirements established by the Suitability in Annuity Transactions Model Regulation of the National Association of Insurance Commissioners (or any successor thereto).

(f) SUBGRANTS.—A State or eligible entity that receives a grant under this section may make a subgrant, as the State or eligible entity determines is necessary to carry out the activities funded using a grant under this section.

(g) REAPPLICATION.—A State or eligible entity that receives a grant under this section may reapply for a grant under this section, notwithstanding the limitations on grant amounts under subsection (e).

(h) AUTHORIZATION OF APPROPRIATIONS.—There are authorized to be appropriated to carry out this section, $8,000,000 for each of fiscal years 2011 through 2015.

[Explanation at ¶ 4475.]

[¶ 10,989B] ACT SEC. 989B. DESIGNATED FEDERAL ENTITY INSPECTORS GENERAL INDEPENDENCE.

Section 8G of the Inspector General Act of 1978 (5 U.S.C. App.) is amended—

(1) in subsection (a)(4)—

(A) in the matter preceding subparagraph (A), by inserting "the board or commission of the designated Federal entity, or in the event the designated Federal entity does not have a board or commission," after "means";

(B) in subparagraph (A), by striking "and" after the semicolon; and

(C) by adding after subparagraph (B) the following:

"(C) with respect to the Federal Labor Relations Authority, such term means the members of the Authority (described under section 7104 of title 5, United States Code);

"(D) with respect to the National Archives and Records Administration, such term means the Archivist of the United States;

"(E) with respect to the National Credit Union Administration, such term means the National Credit Union Administration Board (described under section 102 of the Federal Credit Union Act (12 U.S.C. 1752a);

"(F) with respect to the National Endowment of the Arts, such term means the National Council on the Arts;

"(G) with respect to the National Endowment for the Humanities, such term means the National Council on the Humanities; and

"(H) with respect to the Peace Corps, such term means the Director of the Peace Corps;"; and

(2) in subsection (h), by inserting "if the designated Federal entity is not a board or commission, include" after "designated Federal entities and".

[Explanation at ¶ 4480.]

[¶ 10,989C] ACT SEC. 989C. STRENGTHENING INSPECTOR GENERAL ACCOUNTABILITY.

Section 5(a) of the Inspector General Act of 1978 (5 U.S.C. App.) is amended—

(1) in paragraph (12), by striking "and" after the semicolon;

(2) in paragraph (13), by striking the period and inserting a semicolon; and

(3) by adding at the end the following:

"(14)

(A) an appendix containing the results of any peer review conducted by another Office of Inspector General during the reporting period; or

"(B) if no peer review was conducted within that reporting period, a statement identifying the date of the last peer review conducted by another Office of Inspector General;

"(15) a list of any outstanding recommendations from any peer review conducted by another Office of Inspector General that have not been fully implemented, including a statement describing the status of the implementation and why implementation is not complete; and

"(16) a list of any peer reviews conducted by the Inspector General of another Office of the Inspector General during the reporting period, including a list of any outstanding recommendations made from any previous peer review (including any peer review conducted before the reporting period) that remain outstanding or have not been fully implemented.".

[Explanation at ¶ 4480.]

[¶ 10,989D] ACT SEC. 989D. REMOVAL OF INSPECTORS GENERAL OF DESIGNATED FEDERAL ENTITIES.

Section 8G(e) of the Inspector General Act of 1978 (5 U.S.C. App.) is amended—

(1) by redesignating the sentences following "(e)" as paragraph (2); and

(2) by striking "(e)" and inserting the following:

"(e)

(1) In the case of a designated Federal entity for which a board or commission is the head of the designated Federal entity, a removal under this subsection may only be made upon the written concurrence of a ⅔ majority of the board or commission.".

[Explanation at ¶ 4480.]

[¶ 10,989E] ACT SEC. 989E. ADDITIONAL OVERSIGHT OF FINANCIAL REGULATORY SYSTEM.

(a) COUNCIL OF INSPECTORS GENERAL ON FINANCIAL OVERSIGHT.—

(1) ESTABLISHMENT AND MEMBERSHIP.—There is established a Council of Inspectors General on Financial Oversight (in this section referred to as the "Council of Inspectors General") chaired by the Inspector General of the Department of the Treasury and composed of the inspectors general of the following:

(A) The Board of Governors of the Federal Reserve System.

(B) The Commodity Futures Trading Commission.

(C) The Department of Housing and Urban Development.

(D) The Department of the Treasury.

(E) The Federal Deposit Insurance Corporation.

(F) The Federal Housing Finance Agency.

(G) The National Credit Union Administration.

(H) The Securities and Exchange Commission.

(I) The Troubled Asset Relief Program (until the termination of the authority of the Special Inspector General for such program under section 121(k) of the Emergency Economic Stabilization Act of 2008 (12 U.S.C. 5231(k))).

(2) DUTIES.—

(A) MEETINGS.—The Council of Inspectors General shall meet not less than once each quarter, or more frequently if the chair considers it appropriate, to facilitate the sharing of information among inspectors general and to discuss the ongoing work of each inspector general who is a member of the Council of Inspectors General, with a focus on concerns that may apply to the broader financial sector and ways to improve financial oversight.

(B) ANNUAL REPORT.—Each year the Council of Inspectors General shall submit to the Council and to Congress a report including—

(i) for each inspector general who is a member of the Council of Inspectors General, a section within the exclusive editorial control of such inspector general that highlights the concerns and recommendations of such inspector general in such inspector general's ongoing and completed work, with a focus on issues that may apply to the broader financial sector; and

(ii) a summary of the general observations of the Council of Inspectors General based on the views expressed by each inspector general as required by clause (i), with a focus on measures that should be taken to improve financial oversight.

(3) WORKING GROUPS TO EVALUATE COUNCIL.—

(A) CONVENING A WORKING GROUP.—The Council of Inspectors General may, by majority vote, convene a Council of Inspectors General Working Group to evaluate the effectiveness and internal operations of the Council.

(B) PERSONNEL AND RESOURCES.—The inspectors general who are members of the Council of Inspectors General may detail staff and resources to a Council of Inspectors General Working Group established under this paragraph to enable it to carry out its duties.

(C) REPORTS.—A Council of Inspectors General Working Group established under this paragraph shall submit regular reports to the Council and to Congress on its evaluations pursuant to this paragraph.

(b) RESPONSE TO REPORT BY COUNCIL.—The Council shall respond to the concerns raised in the report of the Council of Inspectors General under subsection (a)(2)(B) for such year.

[Explanation at ¶ 4480.]

[¶ 10,989F] ACT SEC. 989F. GAO STUDY OF PERSON TO PERSON LENDING.

(a) STUDY.—

(1) IN GENERAL.—The Comptroller General of the United States shall conduct a study of person to person lending to determine the optimal Federal regulatory structure.

(2) CONSULTATION.—In conducting the study required under paragraph (1), the Comptroller General shall consult with Federal banking agencies, the Commission, consumer groups, outside experts, and the person to person lending industry.

(3) CONTENT OF STUDY.—The study required under paragraph (1) shall include an examination of—

(A) the regulatory structure as it exists on the date of enactment of this Act, as determined by the Commission, with particular attention to—

(i) the application of the Securities Act of 1933 to person to person lending platforms;

(ii) the posting of consumer loan information on the EDGAR database of the Commission; and

(iii) the treatment of privately held person to person lending platforms as public companies;

(B) the State and other Federal regulators responsible for the oversight and regulation of person to person lending markets;

(C) any Federal, State, or local government or private studies of person to person lending completed or in progress on the date of enactment of this Act;

(D) consumer privacy and data protections, minimum credit standards, anti-money laundering and risk management in the regulatory structure as it exists on the date of enactment of this Act, and whether additional or alternative safeguards are needed; and

(E) the uses of person to person lending.

(b) REPORT.—

(1) IN GENERAL.—Not later than 1 year after the date of enactment of this Act, the Comptroller General shall submit a report on the study required under subsection (a) to the Committee on Banking, Housing, and Urban Affairs of the Senate and the Committee on Financial Services of the House of Representatives.

(2) CONTENT OF REPORT.—The report required under paragraph (1) shall include alternative regulatory options, including—

(A) the involvement of other Federal agencies; and

(B) alternative approaches by the Commission and recommendations on whether the alternative approaches are effective.

[Explanation at ¶ 4485.]

[¶ 10,989G] ACT SEC. 989G. EXEMPTION FOR NONACCELERATED FILERS.

(a) EXEMPTION.—Section 404 of the Sarbanes-Oxley Act of 2002 is amended by adding at the end the following:

"(c) EXEMPTION FOR SMALLER ISSUERS.—Subsection (b) shall not apply with respect to any audit report prepared for an issuer that is neither a 'large accelerated filer' nor an 'accelerated filer' as those terms are defined in Rule 12b-2 of the Commission (17 C.F.R. 240.12b-2).".

(b) STUDY.—The Securities and Exchange Commission shall conduct a study to determine how the Commission could reduce the burden of complying with section 404(b) of the Sarbanes-Oxley Act of 2002 for companies whose market capitalization is between $75,000,000 and $250,000,000 for the relevant reporting period while maintaining investor protections for such companies. The study shall also consider whether any such methods of reducing the compliance burden or a complete exemption for such companies from compliance with such section would encourage companies to list on exchanges in the United States in their initial public offerings. Not later than 9 months after the date of the enactment of this subtitle, the Commission shall transmit a report of such study to Congress.

[Explanation at ¶ 4490.]

[¶ 10,989H] ACT SEC. 989H. CORRECTIVE RESPONSES BY HEADS OF CERTAIN ESTABLISHMENTS TO DEFICIENCIES IDENTIFIED BY INSPECTORS GENERAL.

The Chairman of the Board of Governors of the Federal Reserve System, the Chairman of the Commodity Futures Trading Commission, the Chairman of the National Credit Union Administration, the Director of the Pension Benefit Guaranty Corporation, and the Chairman of the Securities and Exchange Commission shall each—

(1) take action to address deficiencies identified by a report or investigation of the Inspector General of the establishment concerned; or

(2) certify to both Houses of Congress that no action is necessary or appropriate in connection with a deficiency described in paragraph (1).

[Explanation at ¶ 4480.]

[¶ 10,989I] ACT SEC. 989I. GAO STUDY REGARDING EXEMPTION FOR SMALLER ISSUERS.

(a) STUDY REGARDING EXEMPTION FOR SMALLER ISSUERS.—The Comptroller General of the United States shall carry out a study on the impact of the amendments made by this Act to section 404(b) of the Sarbanes-Oxley Act of 2002 (15 U.S.C. 7262(b)), which shall include an analysis of—

(1) whether issuers that are exempt from such section 404(b) have fewer or more restatements of published accounting statements than issuers that are required to comply with such section 404(b);

(2) the cost of capital for issuers that are exempt from such section 404(b) compared to the cost of capital for issuers that are required to comply with such section 404(b);

(3) whether there is any difference in the confidence of investors in the integrity of financial statements of issuers that comply with such section 404(b) and issuers that are exempt from compliance with such section 404(b);

(4) whether issuers that do not receive the attestation for internal controls required under such section 404(b) should be required to disclose the lack of such attestation to investors; and

(5) the costs and benefits to issuers that are exempt from such section 404(b) that voluntarily have obtained the attestation of an independent auditor.

(b) REPORT.—Not later than 3 years after the date of enactment of this Act, the Comptroller General shall submit to the Committee on Banking, Housing, and Urban Affairs of the Senate and the Committee on Financial Services of the House of Representatives a report on the results of the study required under subsection (a).

[Explanation at ¶ 4490.]

[¶ 10,989J] ACT SEC. 989J. FURTHER PROMOTING THE ADOPTION OF THE NAIC MODEL REGULATIONS THAT ENHANCE PROTECTION OF SENIORS AND OTHER CONSUMERS.

(a) IN GENERAL.—The Commission shall treat as exempt securities described under section 3(a)(8) of the Securities Act of 1933 (15 U.S.C. 77c(a)(8)) any insurance or endowment policy or annuity contract or optional annuity contract—

(1) the value of which does not vary according to the performance of a separate account;

(2) that—

(A) satisfies standard nonforfeiture laws or similar requirements of the applicable State at the time of issue; or

(B) in the absence of applicable standard nonforfeiture laws or requirements, satisfies the Model Standard Nonforfeiture Law for Life Insurance or Model Standard Nonforfeiture Law for Individual Deferred Annuities, or any successor model law, as published by the National Association of Insurance Commissioners; and

(3) that is issued—

(A) on and after June 16, 2013, in a State, or issued by an insurance company that is domiciled in a State, that—

(i) adopts rules that govern suitability requirements in the sale of an insurance or endowment policy or annuity contract or optional annuity contract, which shall substantially meet or exceed the minimum requirements established by the Suitability in Annuity Transactions Model Regulation adopted by the National Association of Insurance Commissioners in March 2010; and

(ii) adopts rules that substantially meet or exceed the minimum requirements of any successor modifications to the model regulations described in subparagraph (A) within 5 years of the adoption by the Association of any further successors thereto; or

(B) by an insurance company that adopts and implements practices on a nationwide basis for the sale of any insurance or endowment policy or annuity contract or optional annuity contract that meet or exceed the minimum requirements established by the National Association of Insurance Commissioners Suitability in Annuity Transactions Model Regulation (Model 275), and any successor thereto, and is therefore subject to examination by the State of domicile of the insurance company, or by any other State where the insurance company conducts sales of such products, for the purpose of monitoring compliance under this section.

(b) RULE OF CONSTRUCTION.—Nothing in this section shall be construed to affect whether any insurance or endowment policy or annuity contract or optional annuity contract that is not described in this section is or is not an exempt security under section 3(a)(8) of the Securities Act of 1933 (15 U.S.C. 77c(a)(8)).

[Explanation at ¶ 4495.]

Subtitle J—Securities and Exchange Commission Match Funding

[¶ 10,991] ACT SEC. 991. SECURITIES AND EXCHANGE COMMISSION MATCH FUNDING.

(a) MATCH FUNDING AUTHORITY.—

(1) AMENDMENTS.—Section 31 of the Securities Exchange Act of 1934 (15 U.S.C. 78ee) is amended—

(A) by striking subsection (a) and inserting the following:

"(a) RECOVERY OF COSTS OF ANNUAL APPROPRIATION.—The Commission shall, in accordance with this section, collect transaction fees and assessments that are designed to recover the costs to the Government of the annual appropriation to the Commission by Congress.";

(B) in subsection (e)(2), by striking "September 30" and inserting "September 25";

(C) in subsection (g), by striking "April 30 of the fiscal year preceding the fiscal year to which such rate applies" and inserting "30 days after the date on which an Act making a regular appropriation to the Commission for such fiscal year is enacted";

(D) by striking subsection (j) and inserting the following:

"(j) ADJUSTMENTS TO FEE RATES.—

"(1) ANNUAL ADJUSTMENT.—Subject to subsections (i)(1)(B) and (k), for each fiscal year, the Commission shall by order adjust each of the rates applicable under subsections (b) and (c) for such fiscal year to a uniform adjusted rate that, when applied to the baseline estimate of the aggregate dollar amount of sales for such fiscal year, is reasonably likely to produce aggregate fee collections under this section (including assessments collected under subsection (d) of this section) that are equal to the regular appropriation to the Commission by Congress for such fiscal year.

"(2) MID-YEAR ADJUSTMENT.—Subject to subsections (i)(1)(B) and (k), for each fiscal year, the Commission shall determine, by March 1 of such fiscal year, whether, based on the actual aggregate dollar volume of sales during the first 5 months of such fiscal year, the baseline estimate of the aggregate dollar volume of sales used under paragraph (1) for such fiscal year is reasonably likely to be 10 percent (or more) greater or less than the actual aggregate dollar volume of sales for such fiscal year. If the Commission so determines, the Commission shall by order, no later than March 1, adjust each of the rates applicable under subsections (b) and (c) for such fiscal year to a uniform adjusted rate that, when applied to the revised estimate of the aggregate dollar amount of sales for the remainder of such fiscal year, is reasonably likely to produce aggregate fee collections under this section (including fees collected during such five-month period and assessments collected under subsection (d) of this section) that are equal to the regular appropriation to the Commission by Congress for such fiscal year. In making such revised estimate, the Commission shall, after consultation with the Congressional Budget Office and the Office of Management and Budget, use the same methodology required by subsection (1).

"(3) REVIEW.—In exercising its authority under this subsection, the Commission shall not be required to comply with the provisions of section 553 of title 5, United States Code. An adjusted rate prescribed under paragraph (1) or (2) and published under subsection (g) shall not be subject to judicial review.

"(4) EFFECTIVE DATE.—

"(A) ANNUAL ADJUSTMENT.—Subject to subsections (i)(1)(B) and (k), an adjusted rate prescribed under paragraph (1) shall take effect on the later of—

"(i) the first day of the fiscal year to which such rate applies; or

"(ii) 60 days after the date on which an Act making a regular appropriation to the Commission for such fiscal year is enacted.

"(B) MID-YEAR ADJUSTMENT.—An adjusted rate prescribed under paragraph (2) shall take effect on April 1 of the fiscal year to which such rate applies.";

(E) in subsection (k), by striking "30 days" and inserting "60 days"; and

(F) in subsection (l), by striking "DEFINITIONS.—"and all that follows through "SALES.—The baseline" and inserting "BASELINE ESTIMATE OF THE AGGREGATE DOLLAR AMOUNT OF SALES.—The baseline".

(2) EFFECTIVE DATE.—The amendments made by this subsection shall take effect on the later of—

(A) October 1, 2011; or

(B) the date of enactment of an Act making a regular appropriation to the Commission for fiscal year 2012.

(b) AMENDMENTS TO REGISTRATION FEE PROVISIONS.—

(1) SECTION 6(B) OF THE SECURITIES ACT OF 1933.—Section 6(b) of the Securities Act of 1933 (15 U.S.C. 77f(b)) is amended—

(A) by striking "offsetting" each place that term appears and inserting "fee";

(B) by striking paragraphs (1), (3), (4), (6), (8), and (9);

(C) by redesignating paragraph (2) as paragraph (1);

(D) by redesignating paragraph (5) as paragraph (2);

(E) by redesignating paragraph (7) as paragraph (3);

(F) by redesignating paragraph (10) as paragraph (5);

(G) by redesignating paragraph (11) as paragraph (6);

(H) in paragraph (1), as so redesignated, by striking "paragraph (5) or (6)." and inserting "paragraph (2).";

(I) in paragraph (2), as so redesignated—

(i) by striking "of the fiscal years 2003 through 2011" and inserting "fiscal year"; and

(ii) by striking "paragraph (2)" and inserting "paragraph (1)";

(J) by inserting after paragraph (3), as so redesignated, the following:

"(4) REVIEW AND EFFECTIVE DATE.—In exercising its authority under this subsection, the Commission shall not be required to comply with the provisions of section 553 of title 5, United States Code. An adjusted rate prescribed under paragraph (2) and published under paragraph (5) shall not be subject to judicial review. An adjusted rate prescribed under paragraph (2) shall take effect on the first day of the fiscal year to which such rate applies.";

(K) in paragraph (5), as redesignated, by striking "April 30" and inserting "August 31";

(L) in paragraph (6), as so redesignated—

(i) by striking "of the fiscal years 2002 through 2011" and inserting "fiscal year"; and

(ii) by inserting at the end of the table in subparagraph (A) the following:

"2012	$425,000,000
2013	$455,000,000
2014	$485,000,000
2015	$515,000,000
2016	$550,000,000
2017	$585,000,000
2018	$620,000,000
2019	$660,000,000
2020	$205,000,000
2021 and each fiscal year thereafter	An amount that is equal to the target fee collection amount for the prior fiscal year, adjusted by the rate of inflation.".

(2) SECTION 13(E) OF THE SECURITIES EXCHANGE ACT OF 1934.—Section 13(e) of the Securities Exchange Act of 1934 (15 U.S.C. 78m(e)) is amended—

(A) in paragraph (3), by striking "paragraphs (5) and (6)" and inserting "paragraph (4)";

(B) by striking paragraphs (4), (5), and (6);

(C) by inserting after paragraph (3) the following:

"(4) ANNUAL ADJUSTMENT.—For each fiscal year, the Commission shall by order adjust the rate required by paragraph (3) for such fiscal year to a rate that is equal to the rate (expressed in dollars per million) that is applicable under section 6(b) of the Securities Act of 1933 for such fiscal year.

"(5) FEE COLLECTIONS.—Fees collected pursuant to this subsection for fiscal year 2012 and each fiscal year thereafter shall be deposited and credited as general revenue of the Treasury and shall not be available for obligation.

"(6) EFFECTIVE DATE; PUBLICATION.—In exercising its authority under this subsection, the Commission shall not be required to comply with the provisions of section 553 of title 5, United States Code. An adjusted rate prescribed under paragraph (4) shall be published and take effect in accordance with section 6(b) of the Securities Act of 1933 (15 U.S.C. 77f(b))."; and

(D) by striking paragraphs (8), (9), and (10).

(3) SECTION 14(G) OF THE SECURITIES EXCHANGE ACT OF 1934.—Section 14(g) of the Securities Exchange Act of 1934 (15 U.S.C. 78n(g)) is amended—

(A) in paragraph (1), by striking "paragraphs (5) and (6)" each time that term appears and inserting "paragraph (4)";

(B) in paragraph (3), by striking "paragraphs (5) and (6)" and inserting "paragraph (4)";

(C) by striking paragraphs (4), (5), and (6);

(D) by inserting after paragraph (3) the following:

"(4) ANNUAL ADJUSTMENT.—For each fiscal year, the Commission shall by order adjust the rate required by paragraphs (1) and (3) for such fiscal year to a rate that is equal to the rate (expressed in dollars per million) that is applicable under section 6(b) of the Securities Act of 1933 (15 U.S.C. 77f(b)) for such fiscal year.

"(5) FEE COLLECTION.—Fees collected pursuant to this subsection for fiscal year 2012 and each fiscal year thereafter shall be deposited and credited as general revenue of the Treasury and shall not be available for obligation.

"(6) REVIEW; EFFECTIVE DATE; PUBLICATION.—In exercising its authority under this subsection, the Commission shall not be required to comply with the provisions of section 553 of title 5, United States Code. An adjusted rate prescribed under paragraph (4) shall be published and take effect in accordance with section 6(b) of the Securities Act of 1933 (15 U.S.C. 77f(b)).";

(E) by striking paragraphs (8), (9), and (10); and

(F) by redesignating paragraph (11) as paragraph (8).

(4) EFFECTIVE DATE.—The amendments made by this subsection shall take effect on October 1, 2011, except that for fiscal year 2012, the Commission shall publish the rate established under section 6(b) of the Securities Act of 1933 (15 U.S.C. 77f(b)), as amended by this Act, on August 31, 2011.

(c) AUTHORIZATION OF APPROPRIATIONS.—Section 35 of the Securities Exchange Act of 1934 (15 U.S.C. 78kk) is amended to read as follows:

"SEC. 35. AUTHORIZATION OF APPROPRIATIONS.

"In addition to any other funds authorized to be appropriated to the Commission, there are authorized to be appropriated to carry out the functions, powers, and duties of the Commission—

"(1) for fiscal year 2011, $1,300,000,000;

"(2) for fiscal year 2012, $1,500,000,000;

"(3) for fiscal year 2013, $1,750,000,000;

"(4) for fiscal year 2014, $2,000,000,000; and

"(5) for fiscal year 2015, $2,250,000,000.".

(d) TRANSMITTAL OF BUDGET REQUESTS.—

(1) AMENDMENT.—Section 31 of the Securities Exchange Act of 1934 (15 U.S.C. 78ee) is amended by adding at the end the following:

"(m) TRANSMITTAL OF COMMISSION BUDGET REQUESTS.—

"(1) BUDGET REQUIRED.—For fiscal year 2012, and each fiscal year thereafter, the Commission shall prepare and submit a budget to the President. Whenever the Commission submits a budget estimate or request to the President or the Office of Management and Budget, the Commission shall concurrently transmit copies of the estimate or request to the Committee on Appropriations of the Senate, the Committee on Appropriations of the House of Representatives, the Committee on Banking, Housing, and Urban Affairs of the Senate, and the Committee on Financial Services of the House of Representatives.

"(2) SUBMISSION TO CONGRESS.—The President shall submit each budget submitted under paragraph (1) to Congress, in unaltered form, together with the annual budget for the Administration submitted by the President.

"(3) CONTENTS.—The Commission shall include in each budget submitted under paragraph (1)—

"(A) an itemization of the amount of funds necessary to carry out the functions of the Commission.

"(B) an amount to be designated as contingency funding to be used by the Commission to address unanticipated needs; and

"(C) a designation of any activities of the Commission for which multi-year budget authority would be suitable.".

(2) BUDGET OF THE PRESIDENT.—For fiscal year 2012, and each fiscal year thereafter, the annual budget for the Administration submitted by the President to Congress shall reflect the amendments made by this section.

(e) SECURITIES AND EXCHANGE COMMISSION RESERVE FUND.—

(1) AMENDMENT.—Section 4 of the Securities Exchange Act of 1934 (15 U.S.C. 78d), as amended by this Act, is amended by adding at the end the following:

"(i) SECURITIES AND EXCHANGE COMMISSION RESERVE FUND.—

"(1) RESERVE FUND ESTABLISHED.—There is established in the Treasury of the United States a separate fund, to be known as the 'Securities and Exchange Commission Reserve Fund' (referred to in this subsection as the 'Reserve Fund').

"(2) RESERVE FUND AMOUNTS.—

"(A) IN GENERAL.—Except as provided in subparagraph (B), any registration fees collected by the Commission under section 6(b) of the Securities Act of 1933 (15 U.S.C. 77f(b)) or section 24(f) of the Investment Company Act of 1940 (15 U.S.C. 80a-24(f)) shall be deposited into the Reserve Fund.

"(B) LIMITATIONS.—For any 1 fiscal year—

"(i) the amount deposited in the Fund may not exceed $50,000,000; and

"(ii) the balance in the Fund may not exceed $100,000,000.

"(C) EXCESS FEES.—Any amounts in excess of the limitations described in subparagraph (B) that the Commission collects from registration fees under section 6(b) of the Securities Act of 1933 (15 U.S.C. 77f(b)) or section 24(f) of the Investment Company Act of 1940 (15 U.S.C. 80a-24(f)) shall be deposited in the General Fund of the Treasury of the United States and shall not be available for obligation by the Commission.

"(3) USE OF AMOUNTS IN RESERVE FUND.—The Commission may obligate amounts in the Reserve Fund, not to exceed a total of $100,000,000 in any 1 fiscal year, as the Commission determines is necessary to carry out the functions of the Commission. Any amounts in the reserve fund shall remain available until expended. Not later than 10 days after the date on which the Commission obligates amounts under this paragraph, the Commission shall notify Congress of the date, amount, and purpose of the obligation.

"(4) RULE OF CONSTRUCTION.—Amounts collected and deposited in the Reserve Fund shall not be construed to be Government funds or appropriated monies and shall not be subject to apportionment for the purpose of chapter 15 of title 31, United States Code, or under any other authority.".

(2) EFFECTIVE DATE.—The amendment made by this subsection shall take effect on October 1, 2011.

[Explanation at ¶ 4350 and ¶ 4370.]

TITLE X—BUREAU OF CONSUMER FINANCIAL PROTECTION

[¶ 11,001] ACT SEC. 1001. SHORT TITLE.

This title may be cited as the "Consumer Financial Protection Act of 2010".

[Explanation at ¶ 4505.]

[¶ 11,002] ACT SEC. 1002. DEFINITIONS.

Except as otherwise provided in this title, for purposes of this title, the following definitions shall apply:

(1) AFFILIATE.—The term "affiliate" means any person that controls, is controlled by, or is under common control with another person.

(2) BUREAU.—The term "Bureau" means the Bureau of Consumer Financial Protection.

(3) BUSINESS OF INSURANCE.—The term "business of insurance" means the writing of insurance or the reinsuring of risks by an insurer, including all acts necessary to such writing or reinsuring and the activities relating to the writing of insurance or the reinsuring of risks conducted by persons who act as, or are, officers, directors, agents, or employees of insurers or who are other persons authorized to act on behalf of such persons.

(4) CONSUMER.—The term "consumer" means an individual or an agent, trustee, or representative acting on behalf of an individual.

(5) CONSUMER FINANCIAL PRODUCT OR SERVICE.—The term "consumer financial product or service" means any financial product or service that is described in one or more categories under—

(A) paragraph (15) and is offered or provided for use by consumers primarily for personal, family, or household purposes; or

(B) clause (i), (iii), (ix), or (x) of paragraph (15)(A), and is delivered, offered, or provided in connection with a consumer financial product or service referred to in subparagraph (A).

(6) COVERED PERSON.—The term "covered person" means—

(A) any person that engages in offering or providing a consumer financial product or service; and

(B) any affiliate of a person described in subparagraph (A) if such affiliate acts as a service provider to such person.

(7) CREDIT.—The term "credit" means the right granted by a person to a consumer to defer payment of a debt, incur debt and defer its payment, or purchase property or services and defer payment for such purchase.

(8) DEPOSIT-TAKING ACTIVITY.—The term "deposit-taking activity" means—

(A) the acceptance of deposits, maintenance of deposit accounts, or the provision of services related to the acceptance of deposits or the maintenance of deposit accounts;

(B) the acceptance of funds, the provision of other services related to the acceptance of funds, or the maintenance of member share accounts by a credit union; or

(C) the receipt of funds or the equivalent thereof, as the Bureau may determine by rule or order, received or held by a covered person (or an agent for a covered person) for the purpose of facilitating a payment or transferring funds or value of funds between a consumer and a third party.

(9) DESIGNATED TRANSFER DATE.—The term "designated transfer date" means the date established under section 1062.

(10) DIRECTOR.—The term "Director" means the Director of the Bureau.

(11) ELECTRONIC CONDUIT SERVICES.—The term "electronic conduit services"—

(A) means the provision, by a person, of electronic data transmission, routing, intermediate or transient storage, or connections to a telecommunications system or network; and

(B) does not include a person that provides electronic conduit services if, when providing such services, the person—

(i) selects or modifies the content of the electronic data;

(ii) transmits, routes, stores, or provides connections for electronic data, including financial data, in a manner that such financial data is differentiated from other types of data of the same form that such person transmits, routes, or stores, or with respect to which, provides connections; or

(iii) is a payee, payor, correspondent, or similar party to a payment transaction with a consumer.

(12) ENUMERATED CONSUMER LAWS.—Except as otherwise specifically provided in section 1029, subtitle G or subtitle H, the term "enumerated consumer laws" means—

(A) the Alternative Mortgage Transaction Parity Act of 1982 (12 U.S.C. 3801 et seq.);

(B) the Consumer Leasing Act of 1976 (15 U.S.C. 1667 et seq.);

(C) the Electronic Fund Transfer Act (15 U.S.C. 1693 et seq.), except with respect to section 920 of that Act;

(D) the Equal Credit Opportunity Act (15 U.S.C. 1691 et seq.);

(E) the Fair Credit Billing Act (15 U.S.C. 1666 et seq.);

(F) the Fair Credit Reporting Act (15 U.S.C. 1681 et seq.), except with respect to sections 615(e) and 628 of that Act (15 U.S.C. 1681m(e), 1681w);

(G) the Home Owners Protection Act of 1998 (12 U.S.C. 4901 et seq.);

(H) the Fair Debt Collection Practices Act (15 U.S.C. 1692 et seq.);

(I) subsections (b) through (f) of section 43 of the Federal Deposit Insurance Act (12 U.S.C. 1831t(c)-(f));

(J) sections 502 through 509 of the Gramm-Leach-Bliley Act (15 U.S.C. 6802-6809) except for section 505 as it applies to section 501(b);

(K) the Home Mortgage Disclosure Act of 1975 (12 U.S.C. 2801 et seq.);

(L) the Home Ownership and Equity Protection Act of 1994 (15 U.S.C. 1601 note);

(M) the Real Estate Settlement Procedures Act of 1974 (12 U.S.C. 2601 et seq.);

(N) the S.A.F.E. Mortgage Licensing Act of 2008 (12 U.S.C. 5101 et seq.);

(O) the Truth in Lending Act (15 U.S.C. 1601 et seq.);

(P) the Truth in Savings Act (12 U.S.C. 4301 et seq.);

(Q) section 626 of the Omnibus Appropriations Act, 2009 (Public Law 111-8); and

(R) the Interstate Land Sales Full Disclosure Act (15 U.S.C. 1701).

(13) FAIR LENDING.—The term "fair lending" means fair, equitable, and nondiscriminatory access to credit for consumers.

(14) FEDERAL CONSUMER FINANCIAL LAW.—The term "Federal consumer financial law" means the provisions of this title, the enumerated consumer laws, the laws for which authorities are transferred under subtitles F and H, and any rule or order prescribed by the Bureau under this title, an enumerated consumer law, or pursuant to the authorities transferred under subtitles F and H. The term does not include the Federal Trade Commission Act.

(15) FINANCIAL PRODUCT OR SERVICE.—

(A) IN GENERAL.—The term "financial product or service" means—

(i) extending credit and servicing loans, including acquiring, purchasing, selling, brokering, or other extensions of credit (other than solely extending commercial credit to a person who originates consumer credit transactions);

(ii) extending or brokering leases of personal or real property that are the functional equivalent of purchase finance arrangements, if—

(I) the lease is on a non-operating basis;

(II) the initial term of the lease is at least 90 days; and

(III) in the case of a lease involving real property, at the inception of the initial lease, the transaction is intended to result in ownership of the leased property to be transferred to the lessee, subject to standards prescribed by the Bureau;

(iii) providing real estate settlement services, except such services excluded under subparagraph (C), or performing appraisals of real estate or personal property;

(iv) engaging in deposit-taking activities, transmitting or exchanging funds, or otherwise acting as a custodian of funds or any financial instrument for use by or on behalf of a consumer;

(v) selling, providing, or issuing stored value or payment instruments, except that, in the case of a sale of, or transaction to reload, stored value, only if the seller exercises substantial control over the terms or conditions of the stored value provided to the consumer where, for purposes of this clause—

(I) a seller shall not be found to exercise substantial control over the terms or conditions of the stored value if the seller is not a party to the contract with the consumer for the stored value product, and another person is principally responsible for establishing the terms or conditions of the stored value; and

(II) advertising the nonfinancial goods or services of the seller on the stored value card or device is not in itself an exercise of substantial control over the terms or conditions;

(vi) providing check cashing, check collection, or check guaranty services;

(vii) providing payments or other financial data processing products or services to a consumer by any technological means, including processing or storing financial or banking data for any payment instrument, or through any payments systems or network used for processing payments data, including payments made through an online banking system or mobile telecommunications network, except that a person shall not be deemed to be a covered person with respect to financial data processing solely because the person—

(I) is a merchant, retailer, or seller of any nonfinancial good or service who engages in financial data processing by transmitting or storing payments data about a consumer exclusively for purpose of initiating payments instructions by the consumer to pay such person for the purchase of, or to complete a commercial transaction for, such nonfinancial good or service sold directly by such person to the consumer; or

(II) provides access to a host server to a person for purposes of enabling that person to establish and maintain a website;

(viii) providing financial advisory services (other than services relating to securities provided by a person regulated by the Commission or a person regulated by a State securities Commission, but only to the extent that such person acts in a regulated capacity) to consumers on individual financial matters or relating to proprietary financial products or services (other than by publishing any bona fide newspaper, news magazine, or business or financial publication of general and regular circulation, including publishing market data, news, or data analytics or investment information or recommendations that are not tailored to the individual needs of a particular consumer), including—

(I) providing credit counseling to any consumer; and

(II) providing services to assist a consumer with debt management or debt settlement, modifying the terms of any extension of credit, or avoiding foreclosure;

(ix) collecting, analyzing, maintaining, or providing consumer report information or other account information, including information relating to the credit history of consumers, used or expected to be used in connection with any decision regarding the offering or provision of a consumer financial product or service, except to the extent that—

(I) a person—

(aa) collects, analyzes, or maintains information that relates solely to the transactions between a consumer and such person;

(bb) provides the information described in item (aa) to an affiliate of such person; or

(cc) provides information that is used or expected to be used solely in any decision regarding the offering or provision of a product or service that is not a consumer financial product or service, including a decision for employment, government licensing, or a residential lease or tenancy involving a consumer; and

(II) the information described in subclause (I)(aa) is not used by such person or affiliate in connection with any decision regarding the offering or provision of a consumer financial product or service to the consumer, other than credit described in section 1027(a)(2)(A);

(x) collecting debt related to any consumer financial product or service; and

(xi) such other financial product or service as may be defined by the Bureau, by regulation, for purposes of this title, if the Bureau finds that such financial product or service is—

(I) entered into or conducted as a subterfuge or with a purpose to evade any Federal consumer financial law; or

(II) permissible for a bank or for a financial holding company to offer or to provide under any provision of a Federal law or regulation applicable to a bank or a financial holding company, and has, or likely will have, a material impact on consumers.

(B) RULE OF CONSTRUCTION.—

(i) IN GENERAL.—For purposes of subparagraph (A)(xi)(II), and subject to clause (ii) of this subparagraph, the following activities provided to a covered person shall not, for purposes of this title, be considered incidental or complementary to a financial activity permissible for a financial holding company to engage in under any provision of a Federal law or regulation applicable to a financial holding company:

(I) Providing information products or services to a covered person for identity authentication.

(II) Providing information products or services for fraud or identify theft detection, prevention, or investigation.

(III) Providing document retrieval or delivery services.

(IV) Providing public records information retrieval.

(V) Providing information products or services for anti-money laundering activities.

(ii) LIMITATION.—Nothing in clause (i) may be construed as modifying or limiting the authority of the Bureau to exercise any—

(I) examination or enforcement powers authority under this title with respect to a covered person or service provider engaging in an activity described in subparagraph (A)(ix); or

(II) powers authorized by this title to prescribe rules, issue orders, or take other actions under any enumerated consumer law or law for which the authorities are transferred under subtitle F or H.

(C) EXCLUSIONS.—The term "financial product or service" does not include—

(i) the business of insurance; or

(ii) electronic conduit services.

(16) FOREIGN EXCHANGE.—The term "foreign exchange" means the exchange, for compensation, of currency of the United States or of a foreign government for currency of another government.

(17) INSURED CREDIT UNION.—The term "insured credit union" has the same meaning as in section 101 of the Federal Credit Union Act (12 U.S.C. 1752).

(18) PAYMENT INSTRUMENT.—The term "payment instrument" means a check, draft, warrant, money order, traveler's check, electronic instrument, or other instrument, payment of funds, or monetary value (other than currency).

(19) PERSON.—The term "person" means an individual, partnership, company, corporation, association (incorporated or unincorporated), trust, estate, cooperative organization, or other entity.

(20) PERSON REGULATED BY THE COMMODITY FUTURES TRADING COMMISSION.—The term "person regulated by the Commodity Futures Trading Commission" means any person that is registered, or required by statute or regulation to be registered, with the Commodity Futures Trading Commission, but only to the extent that the activities of such person are subject to the jurisdiction of the Commodity Futures Trading Commission under the Commodity Exchange Act.

(21) PERSON REGULATED BY THE COMMISSION.—The term "person regulated by the Commission" means a person who is—

(A) a broker or dealer that is required to be registered under the Securities Exchange Act of 1934;

(B) an investment adviser that is registered under the Investment Advisers Act of 1940;

(C) an investment company that is required to be registered under the Investment Company Act of 1940, and any company that has elected to be regulated as a business development company under that Act;

(D) a national securities exchange that is required to be registered under the Securities Exchange Act of 1934;

(E) a transfer agent that is required to be registered under the Securities Exchange Act of 1934;

(F) a clearing corporation that is required to be registered under the Securities Exchange Act of 1934;

(G) any self-regulatory organization that is required to be registered with the Commission;

(H) any nationally recognized statistical rating organization that is required to be registered with the Commission;

(I) any securities information processor that is required to be registered with the Commission;

(J) any municipal securities dealer that is required to be registered with the Commission;

(K) any other person that is required to be registered with the Commission under the Securities Exchange Act of 1934; and

(L) any employee, agent, or contractor acting on behalf of, registered with, or providing services to, any person described in any of subparagraphs (A) through (K), but only to the extent that any person described in any of subparagraphs (A) through (K), or the employee, agent, or contractor of such person, acts in a regulated capacity.

(22) PERSON REGULATED BY A STATE INSURANCE REGULATOR.—The term "person regulated by a State insurance regulator" means any person that is engaged in the business of insurance and subject to regulation by any State insurance regulator, but only to the extent that such person acts in such capacity.

(23) PERSON THAT PERFORMS INCOME TAX PREPARATION ACTIVITIES FOR CONSUMERS.—The term "person that performs income tax preparation activities for consumers" means—

(A) any tax return preparer (as defined in section 7701(a)(36) of the Internal Revenue Code of 1986), regardless of whether compensated, but only to the extent that the person acts in such capacity;

(B) any person regulated by the Secretary under section 330 of title 31, United States Code, but only to the extent that the person acts in such capacity; and

(C) any authorized IRS e-file Providers (as defined for purposes of section 7216 of the Internal Revenue Code of 1986), but only to the extent that the person acts in such capacity.

(24) PRUDENTIAL REGULATOR.—The term "prudential regulator" means—

(A) in the case of an insured depository institution or depository institution holding company (as defined in section 3 of the Federal Deposit Insurance Act), or subsidiary of such institution or company, the appropriate Federal banking agency, as that term is defined in section 3 of the Federal Deposit Insurance Act; and

(B) in the case of an insured credit union, the National Credit Union Administration.

(25) RELATED PERSON.—The term "related person"—

(A) shall apply only with respect to a covered person that is not a bank holding company (as that term is defined in section 2 of the Bank Holding Company Act of 1956), credit union, or depository institution;

(B) shall be deemed to mean a covered person for all purposes of any provision of Federal consumer financial law; and

(C) means—

(i) any director, officer, or employee charged with managerial responsibility for, or controlling shareholder of, or agent for, such covered person;

(ii) any shareholder, consultant, joint venture partner, or other person, as determined by the Bureau (by rule or on a case-by-case basis) who materially participates in the conduct of the affairs of such covered person; and

(iii) any independent contractor (including any attorney, appraiser, or accountant) who knowingly or recklessly participates in any—

(I) violation of any provision of law or regulation; or

(II) breach of a fiduciary duty.

(26) SERVICE PROVIDER.—

(A) IN GENERAL.—The term "service provider" means any person that provides a material service to a covered person in connection with the offering or provision by such covered person of a consumer financial product or service, including a person that—

(i) participates in designing, operating, or maintaining the consumer financial product or service; or

(ii) processes transactions relating to the consumer financial product or service (other than unknowingly or incidentally transmitting or processing financial data in a manner that such data is undifferentiated from other types of data of the same form as the person transmits or processes).

(B) EXCEPTIONS.—The term "service provider" does not include a person solely by virtue of such person offering or providing to a covered person—

(i) a support service of a type provided to businesses generally or a similar ministerial service; or

(ii) time or space for an advertisement for a consumer financial product or service through print, newspaper, or electronic media.

(C) RULE OF CONSTRUCTION.—A person that is a service provider shall be deemed to be a covered person to the extent that such person engages in the offering or provision of its own consumer financial product or service.

(27) STATE.—The term "State" means any State, territory, or possession of the United States, the District of Columbia, the Commonwealth of Puerto Rico, the Commonwealth of the Northern Mariana Islands, Guam, American Samoa, or the United States Virgin Islands or any federally recognized Indian tribe, as defined by the Secretary of the Interior under section 104(a) of the Federally Recognized Indian Tribe List Act of 1994 (25 U.S.C. 479a-1(a)).

(28) STORED VALUE.—

(A) IN GENERAL.—The term "stored value" means funds or monetary value represented in any electronic format, whether or not specially encrypted, and stored or capable of storage on electronic media in such a way as to be retrievable and transferred electronically, and includes a prepaid debit card or product, or any other similar product, regardless of whether the amount of the funds or monetary value may be increased or reloaded.

(B) EXCLUSION.—Notwithstanding subparagraph (A), the term "stored value" does not include a special purpose card or certificate, which shall be defined for purposes of this paragraph as funds or monetary value represented in any electronic format, whether or not specially encrypted, that is—

(i) issued by a merchant, retailer, or other seller of nonfinancial goods or services;

(ii) redeemable only for transactions with the merchant, retailer, or seller of nonfinancial goods or services or with an affiliate of such person, which affiliate itself is a merchant, retailer, or seller of nonfinancial goods or services;

(iii) issued in a specified amount that, except in the case of a card or product used solely for telephone services, may not be increased or reloaded;

(iv) purchased on a prepaid basis in exchange for payment; and

(v) honored upon presentation to such merchant, retailer, or seller of nonfinancial goods or services or an affiliate of such person, which affiliate itself is a merchant, retailer, or seller of nonfinancial goods or services, only for any nonfinancial goods or services.

(29) TRANSMITTING OR EXCHANGING FUNDS.—The term "transmitting or exchanging funds" means receiving currency, monetary value, or payment instruments from a consumer for the purpose of exchanging or transmitting the same by any means, including transmission by wire, facsimile, electronic transfer, courier, the Internet, or through bill payment services or through other businesses that facilitate third-party transfers within the United States or to or from the United States.

[Explanation at ¶4510.]

Subtitle A—Bureau of Consumer Financial Protection

[¶11,011] ACT SEC. 1011. ESTABLISHMENT OF THE BUREAU OF CONSUMER FINANCIAL PROTECTION.

(a) BUREAU ESTABLISHED.—There is established in the Federal Reserve System, an independent bureau to be known as the "Bureau of Consumer Financial Protection", which shall regulate the offering and provision of consumer financial products or services under the Federal consumer financial laws. The Bureau shall be considered an Executive agency, as defined in section 105 of title 5, United States Code. Except as otherwise provided expressly by law, all Federal laws dealing with public or Federal contracts, property, works, officers, employees, budgets, or funds, including the provisions of chapters 5 and 7 of title 5, shall apply to the exercise of the powers of the Bureau.

(b) DIRECTOR AND DEPUTY DIRECTOR.—

(1) IN GENERAL.—There is established the position of the Director, who shall serve as the head of the Bureau.

(2) APPOINTMENT.—Subject to paragraph (3), the Director shall be appointed by the President, by and with the advice and consent of the Senate.

(3) QUALIFICATION.—The President shall nominate the Director from among individuals who are citizens of the United States.

(4) COMPENSATION.—The Director shall be compensated at the rate prescribed for level II of the Executive Schedule under section 5313 of title 5, United States Code.

(5) DEPUTY DIRECTOR.—There is established the position of Deputy Director, who shall—

(A) be appointed by the Director; and

(B) serve as acting Director in the absence or unavailability of the Director.

(c) TERM.—

(1) IN GENERAL.—The Director shall serve for a term of 5 years.

(2) EXPIRATION OF TERM.—An individual may serve as Director after the expiration of the term for which appointed, until a successor has been appointed and qualified.

(3) REMOVAL FOR CAUSE.—The President may remove the Director for inefficiency, neglect of duty, or malfeasance in office.

(d) SERVICE RESTRICTION.—No Director or Deputy Director may hold any office, position, or employment in any Federal reserve bank, Federal home loan bank, covered person, or service provider during the period of service of such person as Director or Deputy Director.

(e) OFFICES.—The principal office of the Bureau shall be in the District of Columbia. The Director may establish regional offices of the Bureau, including in cities in which the Federal reserve banks, or branches of such banks, are located, in order to carry out the responsibilities assigned to the Bureau under the Federal consumer financial laws.

[Explanation at ¶ 4515.]

[¶ 11,012] ACT SEC. 1012. EXECUTIVE AND ADMINISTRATIVE POWERS.

(a) POWERS OF THE BUREAU.—The Bureau is authorized to establish the general policies of the Bureau with respect to all executive and administrative functions, including—

(1) the establishment of rules for conducting the general business of the Bureau, in a manner not inconsistent with this title;

(2) to bind the Bureau and enter into contracts;

(3) directing the establishment and maintenance of divisions or other offices within the Bureau, in order to carry out the responsibilities under the Federal consumer financial laws, and to satisfy the requirements of other applicable law;

(4) to coordinate and oversee the operation of all administrative, enforcement, and research activities of the Bureau;

(5) to adopt and use a seal;

(6) to determine the character of and the necessity for the obligations and expenditures of the Bureau;

(7) the appointment and supervision of personnel employed by the Bureau;

(8) the distribution of business among personnel appointed and supervised by the Director and among administrative units of the Bureau;

(9) the use and expenditure of funds;

(10) implementing the Federal consumer financial laws through rules, orders, guidance, interpretations, statements of policy, examinations, and enforcement actions; and

(11) performing such other functions as may be authorized or required by law.

(b) DELEGATION OF AUTHORITY.—The Director of the Bureau may delegate to any duly authorized employee, representative, or agent any power vested in the Bureau by law.

(c) AUTONOMY OF THE BUREAU.—

(1) COORDINATION WITH THE BOARD OF GOVERNORS.—Notwithstanding any other provision of law applicable to the supervision or examination of persons with respect to Federal consumer financial laws, the Board of Governors may delegate to the Bureau the authorities to examine persons subject to the jurisdiction of the Board of Governors for compliance with the Federal consumer financial laws.

(2) AUTONOMY.—Notwithstanding the authorities granted to the Board of Governors under the Federal Reserve Act, the Board of Governors may not—

(A) intervene in any matter or proceeding before the Director, including examinations or enforcement actions, unless otherwise specifically provided by law;

(B) appoint, direct, or remove any officer or employee of the Bureau; or

(C) merge or consolidate the Bureau, or any of the functions or responsibilities of the Bureau, with any division or office of the Board of Governors or the Federal reserve banks.

(3) RULES AND ORDERS.—No rule or order of the Bureau shall be subject to approval or review by the Board of Governors. The Board of Governors may not delay or prevent the issuance of any rule or order of the Bureau.

(4) RECOMMENDATIONS AND TESTIMONY.—No officer or agency of the United States shall have any authority to require the Director or any other officer of the Bureau to submit legislative recommendations, or testimony or comments on legislation, to any officer or agency of the United States for approval, comments, or review prior to the submission of such recommendations, testimony, or comments to the Congress, if such recommendations, testimony, or com-

ments to the Congress include a statement indicating that the views expressed therein are those of the Director or such officer, and do not necessarily reflect the views of the Board of Governors or the President.

(5) CLARIFICATION OF AUTONOMY OF THE BUREAU IN LEGAL PROCEEDINGS.—The Bureau shall not be liable under any provision of law for any action or inaction of the Board of Governors, and the Board of Governors shall not be liable under any provision of law for any action or inaction of the Bureau.

[Explanation at ¶ 4520.]

[¶ 11,013] ACT SEC. 1013. ADMINISTRATION.

(a) PERSONNEL.—

(1) APPOINTMENT.—

(A) IN GENERAL.—The Director may fix the number of, and appoint and direct, all employees of the Bureau, in accordance with the applicable provisions of title 5, United States Code.

(B) EMPLOYEES OF THE BUREAU.—The Director is authorized to employ attorneys, compliance examiners, compliance supervision analysts, economists, statisticians, and other employees as may be deemed necessary to conduct the business of the Bureau. Unless otherwise provided expressly by law, any individual appointed under this section shall be an employee as defined in section 2105 of title 5, United States Code, and subject to the provisions of such title and other laws generally applicable to the employees of an Executive agency.

(C) WAIVER AUTHORITY.—

(i) IN GENERAL.—In making any appointment under subparagraph (A), the Director may waive the requirements of chapter 33 of title 5, United States Code, and the regulations implementing such chapter, to the extent necessary to appoint employees on terms and conditions that are consistent with those set forth in section 11(1) of the Federal Reserve Act (12 U.S.C. 248(1)), while providing for—

(I) fair, credible, and transparent methods of establishing qualification requirements for, recruitment for, and appointments to positions;

(II) fair and open competition and equitable treatment in the consideration and selection of individuals to positions;

(III) fair, credible, and transparent methods of assigning, reassigning, detailing, transferring, and promoting employees.

(ii) VETERANS PREFERENCES.—In implementing this subparagraph, the Director shall comply with the provisions of section 2302(b)(11), regarding veterans' preference requirements, in a manner consistent with that in which such provisions are applied under chapter 33 of title 5, United States Code. The authority under this subparagraph to waive the requirements of that chapter 33 shall expire 5 years after the date of enactment of this Act.

(2) COMPENSATION.—Notwithstanding any otherwise applicable provision of title 5, United States Code, concerning compensation, including the provisions of chapter 51 and chapter 53, the following provisions shall apply with respect to employees of the Bureau:

(A) The rates of basic pay for all employees of the Bureau may be set and adjusted by the Director.

(B) The Director shall at all times provide compensation (including benefits) to each class of employees that, at a minimum, are comparable to the compensation and benefits then being provided by the Board of Governors for the corresponding class of employees.

(C) All such employees shall be compensated (including benefits) on terms and conditions that are consistent with the terms and conditions set forth in section 11(1) of the Federal Reserve Act (12 U.S.C. 248(1)).

(3) BUREAU PARTICIPATION IN FEDERAL RESERVE SYSTEM RETIREMENT PLAN AND FEDERAL RESERVE SYSTEM THRIFT PLAN.—

(A) EMPLOYEE ELECTION.—Employees appointed to the Bureau may elect to participate in either—

(i) both the Federal Reserve System Retirement Plan and the Federal Reserve System Thrift Plan, under the same terms on which such participation is offered to employees of the Board of Governors who participate in such plans and under the terms and conditions specified under section 1064(i)(1)(C); or

(ii) the Civil Service Retirement System under chapter 83 of title 5, United States Code, or the Federal Employees Retirement System under chapter 84 of title 5, United States Code, if previously covered under one of those Federal employee retirement systems.

(B) ELECTION PERIOD.—Bureau employees shall make an election under this paragraph not later than 1 year after the date of appointment by, or transfer under subtitle F to, the Bureau. Participation in, and benefit accruals under, any other retirement plan established or maintained by the Federal Government shall end not later than the date on which participation in, and benefit accruals under, the Federal Reserve System Retirement Plan and Federal Reserve System Thrift Plan begin.

(C) EMPLOYER CONTRIBUTION.—The Bureau shall pay an employer contribution to the Federal Reserve System Retirement Plan, in the amount established as an employer contribution under the Federal Employees Retirement System, as established under chapter 84 of title 5, United States Code, for each Bureau employee who elects to participate in the Federal Reserve System Retirement Plan. The Bureau shall pay an employer contribution to the Federal Reserve System Thrift Plan for each Bureau employee who elects to participate in such plan, as required under the terms of such plan.

(D) CONTROLLED GROUP STATUS.—The Bureau is the same employer as the Federal Reserve System (as comprised of the Board of Governors and each of the 12 Federal reserve banks prior to the date of enactment of this Act) for purposes of subsections (b), (c), (m), and (o) of section 414 of the Internal Revenue Code of 1986, (26 U.S.C. 414).

(4) LABOR-MANAGEMENT RELATIONS.—Chapter 71 of title 5, United States Code, shall apply to the Bureau and the employees of the Bureau.

(5) AGENCY OMBUDSMAN.—

(A) ESTABLISHMENT REQUIRED.—Not later than 180 days after the designated transfer date, the Bureau shall appoint an ombudsman.

(B) DUTIES OF OMBUDSMAN.—The ombudsman appointed in accordance with subparagraph (A) shall—

(i) act as a liaison between the Bureau and any affected person with respect to any problem that such party may have in dealing with the Bureau, resulting from the regulatory activities of the Bureau; and

(ii) assure that safeguards exist to encourage complainants to come forward and preserve confidentiality.

(b) SPECIFIC FUNCTIONAL UNITS.—

(1) RESEARCH.—The Director shall establish a unit whose functions shall include researching, analyzing, and reporting on—

(A) developments in markets for consumer financial products or services, including market areas of alternative consumer financial products or services with high growth rates and areas of risk to consumers;

(B) access to fair and affordable credit for traditionally underserved communities;

(C) consumer awareness, understanding, and use of disclosures and communications regarding consumer financial products or services;

(D) consumer awareness and understanding of costs, risks, and benefits of consumer financial products or services;

(E) consumer behavior with respect to consumer financial products or services, including performance on mortgage loans; and

(F) experiences of traditionally underserved consumers, including un-banked and under-banked consumers.

(2) COMMUNITY AFFAIRS.—The Director shall establish a unit whose functions shall include providing information, guidance, and technical assistance regarding the offering and provision of consumer financial products or services to traditionally underserved consumers and communities.

(3) COLLECTING AND TRACKING COMPLAINTS.—

(A) IN GENERAL.—The Director shall establish a unit whose functions shall include establishing a single, toll-free telephone number, a website, and a database or utilizing an existing database to facilitate the centralized collection of, monitoring of, and response to consumer complaints regarding consumer financial products or services. The Director shall coordinate with the Federal Trade Commission or other Federal agencies to route complaints to such agencies, where appropriate.

(B) ROUTING CALLS TO STATES.—To the extent practicable, State agencies may receive appropriate complaints from the systems established under subparagraph (A), if—

(i) the State agency system has the functional capacity to receive calls or electronic reports routed by the Bureau systems;

(ii) the State agency has satisfied any conditions of participation in the system that the Bureau may establish, including treatment of personally identifiable information and sharing of information on complaint resolution or related compliance procedures and resources; and

(iii) participation by the State agency includes measures necessary to provide for protection of personally identifiable information that conform to the standards for protection of the confidentiality of personally identifiable information and for data integrity and security that apply to the Federal agencies described in subparagraph (D).

(C) REPORTS TO THE CONGRESS.—The Director shall present an annual report to Congress not later than March 31 of each year on the complaints received by the Bureau in the prior year regarding consumer financial products and services. Such report shall include information and analysis about complaint numbers, complaint types, and, where applicable, information about resolution of complaints.

(D) DATA SHARING REQUIRED.—To facilitate preparation of the reports required under subparagraph (C), supervision and enforcement activities, and monitoring of the market for consumer financial products and services, the Bureau shall share consumer complaint information with prudential regulators, the Federal Trade Commission, other Federal agencies, and State agencies, subject to the standards applicable to Federal agencies for protection of the confidentiality of personally identifiable information and for data security and integrity. The prudential regulators, the Federal Trade Commission, and other Federal agencies shall share data relating to consumer complaints regarding consumer financial products and services with the Bureau, subject to the standards applicable to Federal agencies for protection of confidentiality of personally identifiable information and for data security and integrity.

(c) OFFICE OF FAIR LENDING AND EQUAL OPPORTUNITY.—

(1) ESTABLISHMENT.—The Director shall establish within the Bureau the Office of Fair Lending and Equal Opportunity.

(2) FUNCTIONS.—The Office of Fair Lending and Equal Opportunity shall have such powers and duties as the Director may delegate to the Office, including—

(A) providing oversight and enforcement of Federal laws intended to ensure the fair, equitable, and nondiscriminatory access to credit for both individuals and communities that are enforced by the Bureau, including the Equal Credit Opportunity Act and the Home Mortgage Disclosure Act;

(B) coordinating fair lending efforts of the Bureau with other Federal agencies and State regulators, as appropriate, to promote consistent, efficient, and effective enforcement of Federal fair lending laws;

(C) working with private industry, fair lending, civil rights, consumer and community advocates on the promotion of fair lending compliance and education; and

(D) providing annual reports to Congress on the efforts of the Bureau to fulfill its fair lending mandate.

(3) ADMINISTRATION OF OFFICE.—There is established the position of Assistant Director of the Bureau for Fair Lending and Equal Opportunity, who—

(A) shall be appointed by the Director; and

(B) shall carry out such duties as the Director may delegate to such Assistant Director.

(d) OFFICE OF FINANCIAL EDUCATION.—

(1) ESTABLISHMENT.—The Director shall establish an Office of Financial Education, which shall be responsible for developing and implementing initiatives intended to educate and empower consumers to make better informed financial decisions.

(2) OTHER DUTIES.—The Office of Financial Education shall develop and implement a strategy to improve the financial literacy of consumers that includes measurable goals and objectives, in consultation with the Financial Literacy and Education Commission, consistent with the National Strategy for Financial Literacy, through activities including providing opportunities for consumers to access—

(A) financial counseling, including community-based financial counseling, where practicable;

(B) information to assist with the evaluation of credit products and the understanding of credit histories and scores;

(C) savings, borrowing, and other services found at mainstream financial institutions;

(D) activities intended to—

(i) prepare the consumer for educational expenses and the submission of financial aid applications, and other major purchases;

(ii) reduce debt; and

(iii) improve the financial situation of the consumer;

(E) assistance in developing long-term savings strategies; and

(F) wealth building and financial services during the preparation process to claim earned income tax credits and Federal benefits.

(3) COORDINATION.—The Office of Financial Education shall coordinate with other units within the Bureau in carrying out its functions, including—

(A) working with the Community Affairs Office to implement the strategy to improve financial literacy of consumers; and

(B) working with the research unit established by the Director to conduct research related to consumer financial education and counseling.

(4) REPORT.—Not later than 24 months after the designated transfer date, and annually thereafter, the Director shall submit a report on its financial literacy activities and strategy to improve financial literacy of consumers to—

(A) the Committee on Banking, Housing, and Urban Affairs of the Senate; and

(B) the Committee on Financial Services of the House of Representatives.

(5) MEMBERSHIP IN FINANCIAL LITERACY AND EDUCATION COMMISSION.—Section 513(c)(1) of the Financial Literacy and Education Improvement Act (20 U.S.C. 9702(c)(1)) is amended—

(A) in subparagraph (B), by striking "and" at the end;

(B) by redesignating subparagraph (C) as subparagraph (D); and

(C) by inserting after subparagraph (B) the following new subparagraph:

"(C) the Director of the Bureau of Consumer Financial Protection; and".

(6) CONFORMING AMENDMENT.—Section 513(d) of the Financial Literacy and Education Improvement Act (20 U.S.C. 9702(d)) is amended by adding at the end the following: "The Director of the Bureau of Consumer Financial Protection shall serve as the Vice Chairman.".

(7) STUDY AND REPORT ON FINANCIAL LITERACY PROGRAM.—

(A) IN GENERAL.—The Comptroller General of the United States shall conduct a study to identify—

(i) the feasibility of certification of persons providing the programs or performing the activities described in paragraph (2), including recognizing outstanding programs, and developing guidelines and resources for community-based practitioners, including—

(I) a potential certification process and standards for certification;

(II) appropriate certifying entities;

(III) resources required for funding such a process; and

(IV) a cost-benefit analysis of such certification;

(ii) technological resources intended to collect, analyze, evaluate, or promote financial literacy and counseling programs;

(iii) effective methods, tools, and strategies intended to educate and empower consumers about personal finance management; and

(iv) recommendations intended to encourage the development of programs that effectively improve financial education outcomes and empower consumers to make better informed financial decisions based on findings.

(B) REPORT.—Not later than 1 year after the date of enactment of this Act, the Comptroller General of the United States shall submit a report on the results of the study conducted under this paragraph to the Committee on Banking, Housing, and Urban Affairs of the Senate and the Committee on Financial Services of the House of Representatives.

(e) OFFICE OF SERVICE MEMBER AFFAIRS.—

(1) IN GENERAL.—The Director shall establish an Office of Service Member Affairs, which shall be responsible for developing and implementing initiatives for service members and their families intended to—

(A) educate and empower service members and their families to make better informed decisions regarding consumer financial products and services;

(B) coordinate with the unit of the Bureau established under subsection (b)(3), in order to monitor complaints by service members and their families and responses to those complaints by the Bureau or other appropriate Federal or State agency; and

(C) coordinate efforts among Federal and State agencies, as appropriate, regarding consumer protection measures relating to consumer financial products and services offered to, or used by, service members and their families.

(2) COORDINATION.—

(A) REGIONAL SERVICES.—The Director is authorized to assign employees of the Bureau as may be deemed necessary to conduct the business of the Office of Service Member Affairs, including by establishing and maintaining the functions of the Office in regional offices of the Bureau located near military bases, military treatment facilities, or other similar military facilities.

(B) AGREEMENTS.—The Director is authorized to enter into memoranda of understanding and similar agreements with the Department of Defense, including any branch or agency as authorized by the department, in order to carry out the business of the Office of Service Member Affairs.

(3) DEFINITION.—As used in this subsection, the term "service member" means any member of the United States Armed Forces and any member of the National Guard or Reserves.

(f) TIMING.—The Office of Fair Lending and Equal Opportunity, the Office of Financial Education, and the Office of Service Member Affairs shall each be established not later than 1 year after the designated transfer date.

(g) OFFICE OF FINANCIAL PROTECTION FOR OLDER AMERICANS.—

(1) ESTABLISHMENT.—Before the end of the 180-day period beginning on the designated transfer date, the Director shall establish the Office of Financial Protection for Older Americans, the functions of which shall include activities designed to facilitate the financial literacy of individuals who have attained the age of 62 years or more (in this subsection, referred to as "seniors") on protection from unfair, deceptive, and abusive practices and on current and future financial choices, including through the dissemination of materials to seniors on such topics.

(2) ASSISTANT DIRECTOR.—The Office of Financial Protection for Older Americans (in this subsection referred to as the "Office") shall be headed by an assistant director.

(3) DUTIES.—The Office shall—

(A) develop goals for programs that provide seniors financial literacy and counseling, including programs that—

(i) help seniors recognize warning signs of unfair, deceptive, or abusive practices, protect themselves from such practices;

(ii) provide one-on-one financial counseling on issues including long-term savings and later-life economic security; and

(iii) provide personal consumer credit advocacy to respond to consumer problems caused by unfair, deceptive, or abusive practices;

(B) monitor certifications or designations of financial advisors who advise seniors and alert the Commission and State regulators of certifications or designations that are identified as unfair, deceptive, or abusive;

(C) not later than 18 months after the date of the establishment of the Office, submit to Congress and the Commission any legislative and regulatory recommendations on the best practices for—

(i) disseminating information regarding the legitimacy of certifications of financial advisers who advise seniors;

(ii) methods in which a senior can identify the financial advisor most appropriate for the senior's needs; and

(iii) methods in which a senior can verify a financial advisor's credentials;

(D) conduct research to identify best practices and effective methods, tools, technology and strategies to educate and counsel seniors about personal finance management with a focus on—

(i) protecting themselves from unfair, deceptive, and abusive practices;

(ii) long-term savings; and

(iii) planning for retirement and long-term care;

(E) coordinate consumer protection efforts of seniors with other Federal agencies and State regulators, as appropriate, to promote consistent, effective, and efficient enforcement; and

(F) work with community organizations, non-profit organizations, and other entities that are involved with educating or assisting seniors (including the National Education and Resource Center on Women and Retirement Planning).

[Explanation at ¶ 4525.]

[¶ 11,014] ACT SEC. 1014. CONSUMER ADVISORY BOARD.

(a) ESTABLISHMENT REQUIRED.—The Director shall establish a Consumer Advisory Board to advise and consult with the Bureau in the exercise of its functions under the Federal consumer financial laws, and to provide information on emerging practices in the consumer financial products or services industry, including regional trends, concerns, and other relevant information.

(b) MEMBERSHIP.—In appointing the members of the Consumer Advisory Board, the Director shall seek to assemble experts in consumer protection, financial services, community development, fair lending and civil rights, and consumer financial products or services and representatives of depository institutions that primarily serve underserved communities, and representatives of communities that have been significantly impacted by higher-priced mortgage loans, and seek representation of the interests of covered persons and consumers, without regard to party affiliation. Not fewer than 6 members shall be appointed upon the recommendation of the regional Federal Reserve Bank Presidents, on a rotating basis.

(c) MEETINGS.—The Consumer Advisory Board shall meet from time to time at the call of the Director, but, at a minimum, shall meet at least twice in each year.

(d) COMPENSATION AND TRAVEL EXPENSES.—Members of the Consumer Advisory Board who are not full-time employees of the United States shall—

(1) be entitled to receive compensation at a rate fixed by the Director while attending meetings of the Consumer Advisory Board, including travel time; and

(2) be allowed travel expenses, including transportation and subsistence, while away from their homes or regular places of business.

[Explanation at ¶4530.]

[¶11,015] ACT SEC. 1015. COORDINATION.

The Bureau shall coordinate with the Commission, the Commodity Futures Trading Commission, the Federal Trade Commission, and other Federal agencies and State regulators, as appropriate, to promote consistent regulatory treatment of consumer financial and investment products and services.

[Explanation at ¶4535.]

[¶11,016] ACT SEC. 1016. APPEARANCES BEFORE AND REPORTS TO CONGRESS.

(a) APPEARANCES BEFORE CONGRESS.—The Director of the Bureau shall appear before the Committee on Banking, Housing, and Urban Affairs of the Senate and the Committee on Financial Services and the Committee on Energy and Commerce of the House of Representatives at semi-annual hearings regarding the reports required under subsection (b).

(b) REPORTS REQUIRED.—The Bureau shall, concurrent with each semi-annual hearing referred to in subsection (a), prepare and submit to the President and to the Committee on Banking, Housing, and Urban Affairs of the Senate and the Committee on Financial Services and the Committee on Energy and Commerce of the House of Representatives, a report, beginning with the session following the designated transfer date. The Bureau may also submit such report to the Committee on Commerce, Science, and Transportation of the Senate.

(c) CONTENTS.—The reports required by subsection (b) shall include—

(1) a discussion of the significant problems faced by consumers in shopping for or obtaining consumer financial products or services;

(2) a justification of the budget request of the previous year;

(3) a list of the significant rules and orders adopted by the Bureau, as well as other significant initiatives conducted by the Bureau, during the preceding year and the plan of the Bureau for rules, orders, or other initiatives to be undertaken during the upcoming period;

(4) an analysis of complaints about consumer financial products or services that the Bureau has received and collected in its central database on complaints during the preceding year;

(5) a list, with a brief statement of the issues, of the public supervisory and enforcement actions to which the Bureau was a party during the preceding year;

(6) the actions taken regarding rules, orders, and supervisory actions with respect to covered persons which are not credit unions or depository institutions;

(7) an assessment of significant actions by State attorneys general or State regulators relating to Federal consumer financial law;

(8) an analysis of the efforts of the Bureau to fulfill the fair lending mission of the Bureau; and

(9) an analysis of the efforts of the Bureau to increase workforce and contracting diversity consistent with the procedures established by the Office of Minority and Women Inclusion.

[Explanation at ¶ 4540.]

[¶ 11,017] ACT SEC. 1017. FUNDING; PENALTIES AND FINES.

(a) TRANSFER OF FUNDS FROM BOARD OF GOVERNORS.—

(1) IN GENERAL.—Each year (or quarter of such year), beginning on the designated transfer date, and each quarter thereafter, the Board of Governors shall transfer to the Bureau from the combined earnings of the Federal Reserve System, the amount determined by the Director to be reasonably necessary to carry out the authorities of the Bureau under Federal consumer financial law, taking into account such other sums made available to the Bureau from the preceding year (or quarter of such year).

(2) FUNDING CAP.—

(A) IN GENERAL.—Notwithstanding paragraph (1), and in accordance with this paragraph, the amount that shall be transferred to the Bureau in each fiscal year shall not exceed a fixed percentage of the total operating expenses of the Federal Reserve System, as reported in the Annual Report, 2009, of the Board of Governors, equal to—

(i) 10 percent of such expenses in fiscal year 2011;

(ii) 11 percent of such expenses in fiscal year 2012; and

(iii) 12 percent of such expenses in fiscal year 2013, and in each year thereafter.

(B) ADJUSTMENT OF AMOUNT.—The dollar amount referred to in subparagraph (A)(iii) shall be adjusted annually, using the percent increase, if any, in the employment cost index for total compensation for State and local government workers published by the Federal Government, or the successor index thereto, for the 12-month period ending on September 30 of the year preceding the transfer.

(C) REVIEWABILITY.—Notwithstanding any other provision in this title, the funds derived from the Federal Reserve System pursuant to this subsection shall not be subject to review by the Committees on Appropriations of the House of Representatives and the Senate.

(3) TRANSITION PERIOD.—Beginning on the date of enactment of this Act and until the designated transfer date, the Board of Governors shall transfer to the Bureau the amount estimated by the Secretary needed to carry out the authorities granted to the Bureau under Federal consumer financial law, from the date of enactment of this Act until the designated transfer date.

(4) BUDGET AND FINANCIAL MANAGEMENT.—

(A) FINANCIAL OPERATING PLANS AND FORECASTS.—The Director shall provide to the Director of the Office of Management and Budget copies of the financial operating plans and forecasts of the Director, as prepared by the Director in the ordinary course of the operations of the Bureau, and copies of the quarterly reports of the financial condition and results of operations of the Bureau, as prepared by the Director in the ordinary course of the operations of the Bureau.

(B) FINANCIAL STATEMENTS.—The Bureau shall prepare annually a statement of—

(i) assets and liabilities and surplus or deficit;

(ii) income and expenses; and

(iii) sources and application of funds.

(C) FINANCIAL MANAGEMENT SYSTEMS.—The Bureau shall implement and maintain financial management systems that comply substantially with Federal financial management systems requirements and applicable Federal accounting standards.

(D) ASSERTION OF INTERNAL CONTROLS.—The Director shall provide to the Comptroller General of the United States an assertion as to the effectiveness of the internal controls that apply to financial reporting by the Bureau, using the standards established in section 3512(c) of title 31, United States Code.

(E) RULE OF CONSTRUCTION.—This subsection may not be construed as implying any obligation on the part of the Director to consult with or obtain the consent or approval of the Director of the Office of Management and Budget with respect to any report, plan, forecast, or other information referred to in subparagraph (A) or any jurisdiction or oversight over the affairs or operations of the Bureau.

(F) FINANCIAL STATEMENTS.—The financial statements of the Bureau shall not be consolidated with the financial statements of either the Board of Governors or the Federal Reserve System.

(5) AUDIT OF THE BUREAU.—

(A) IN GENERAL.—The Comptroller General shall annually audit the financial transactions of the Bureau in accordance with the United States generally accepted government auditing standards, as may be prescribed by the Comptroller General of the United States. The audit shall be conducted at the place or places where accounts of the Bureau are normally kept. The representatives of the Government Accountability Office shall have access to the personnel and to all books, accounts, documents, papers, records (including electronic records), reports, files, and all other papers, automated data, things, or property belonging to or under the control of or used or employed by the Bureau pertaining to its financial transactions and necessary to facilitate the audit, and such representatives shall be afforded full facilities for verifying transactions with the balances or securities held by depositories, fiscal agents, and custodians. All such books, accounts, documents, records, reports, files, papers, and property of the Bureau shall remain in possession and custody of the Bureau. The Comptroller General may obtain and duplicate any such books, accounts, documents, records, working papers, automated data and files, or other information relevant to such audit without cost to the Comptroller General, and the right of access of the Comptroller General to such information shall be enforceable pursuant to section 716(c) of title 31, United States Code.

(B) REPORT.—The Comptroller General shall submit to the Congress a report of each annual audit conducted under this subsection. The report to the Congress shall set forth the scope of the audit and shall include the statement of assets and liabilities and surplus or deficit, the statement of income and expenses, the statement of sources and application of funds, and such comments and information as may be deemed necessary to inform Congress of the financial operations and condition of the Bureau, together with such recommendations with respect thereto as the Comptroller General may deem advisable. A copy of each report shall be furnished to the President and to the Bureau at the time submitted to the Congress.

(C) ASSISTANCE AND COSTS.—For the purpose of conducting an audit under this subsection, the Comptroller General may, in the discretion of the Comptroller General, employ by contract, without regard to section 3709 of the Revised Statutes of the United States (41 U.S.C. 5), professional services of firms and organizations of certified public accountants for temporary periods or for special purposes. Upon the request of the Comptroller General, the Director of the Bureau shall transfer to the Government Accountability Office from funds available, the amount requested by the Comptroller General to cover the full costs of any audit and report conducted by the Comptroller General. The Comptroller General shall credit funds transferred to the account established for salaries and expenses of the Government Accountability Office, and such amount shall be available upon receipt and without fiscal year limitation to cover the full costs of the audit and report.

(b) CONSUMER FINANCIAL PROTECTION FUND.—

(1) SEPARATE FUND IN FEDERAL RESERVE ESTABLISHED.—There is established in the Federal Reserve a separate fund, to be known as the "Bureau of Consumer Financial Protection Fund" (referred to in this section as the "Bureau Fund"). The Bureau Fund shall be maintained and

established at a Federal reserve bank, in accordance with such requirements as the Board of Governors may impose.

(2) FUND RECEIPTS.—All amounts transferred to the Bureau under subsection (a) shall be deposited into the Bureau Fund.

(3) INVESTMENT AUTHORITY.—

(A) AMOUNTS IN BUREAU FUND MAY BE INVESTED.—The Bureau may request the Board of Governors to direct the investment of the portion of the Bureau Fund that is not, in the judgment of the Bureau, required to meet the current needs of the Bureau.

(B) ELIGIBLE INVESTMENTS.—Investments authorized by this paragraph shall be made in obligations of the United States or obligations that are guaranteed as to principal and interest by the United States, with maturities suitable to the needs of the Bureau Fund, as determined by the Bureau.

(C) INTEREST AND PROCEEDS CREDITED.—The interest on, and the proceeds from the sale or redemption of, any obligations held in the Bureau Fund shall be credited to the Bureau Fund.

(c) USE OF FUNDS.—

(1) IN GENERAL.—Funds obtained by, transferred to, or credited to the Bureau Fund shall be immediately available to the Bureau and under the control of the Director, and shall remain available until expended, to pay the expenses of the Bureau in carrying out its duties and responsibilities. The compensation of the Director and other employees of the Bureau and all other expenses thereof may be paid from, obtained by, transferred to, or credited to the Bureau Fund under this section.

(2) FUNDS THAT ARE NOT GOVERNMENT FUNDS.—Funds obtained by or transferred to the Bureau Fund shall not be construed to be Government funds or appropriated monies.

(3) AMOUNTS NOT SUBJECT TO APPORTIONMENT.—Notwithstanding any other provision of law, amounts in the Bureau Fund and in the Civil Penalty Fund established under subsection (d) shall not be subject to apportionment for purposes of chapter 15 of title 31, United States Code, or under any other authority.

(d) PENALTIES AND FINES.—

(1) ESTABLISHMENT OF VICTIMS RELIEF FUND.—There is established in the Federal Reserve a separate fund, to be known as the "Consumer Financial Civil Penalty Fund" (referred to in this section as the "Civil Penalty Fund"). The Civil Penalty Fund shall be maintained and established at a Federal reserve bank, in accordance with such requirements as the Board of Governors may impose. If the Bureau obtains a civil penalty against any person in any judicial or administrative action under Federal consumer financial laws, the Bureau shall deposit into the Civil Penalty Fund, the amount of the penalty collected.

(2) PAYMENT TO VICTIMS.—Amounts in the Civil Penalty Fund shall be available to the Bureau, without fiscal year limitation, for payments to the victims of activities for which civil penalties have been imposed under the Federal consumer financial laws. To the extent that such victims cannot be located or such payments are otherwise not practicable, the Bureau may use such funds for the purpose of consumer education and financial literacy programs.

(e) AUTHORIZATION OF APPROPRIATIONS; ANNUAL REPORT.—

(1) DETERMINATION REGARDING NEED FOR APPROPRIATED FUNDS.—

(A) IN GENERAL.—The Director is authorized to determine that sums available to the Bureau under this section will not be sufficient to carry out the authorities of the Bureau under Federal consumer financial law for the upcoming year.

(B) REPORT REQUIRED.—When making a determination under subparagraph (A), the Director shall prepare a report regarding the funding of the Bureau, including the assets and liabilities of the Bureau, and the extent to which the funding needs of the Bureau are anticipated to exceed the level of the amount set forth in subsection (a)(2). The Director shall submit the report to the President and to the Committee on Appropriations of the Senate and the Committee on Appropriations of the House of Representatives.

(2) AUTHORIZATION OF APPROPRIATIONS.—If the Director makes the determination and submits the report pursuant to paragraph (1), there are hereby authorized to be appropriated to the Bureau, for the purposes of carrying out the authorities granted in Federal consumer financial law, $200,000,000 for each of fiscal years 2010, 2011, 2012, 2013, and 2014.

(3) APPORTIONMENT.—Notwithstanding any other provision of law, the amounts in paragraph (2) shall be subject to apportionment under section 1517 of title 31, United States Code, and restrictions that generally apply to the use of appropriated funds in title 31, United States Code, and other laws.

(4) ANNUAL REPORT.—The Director shall prepare and submit a report, on an annual basis, to the Committee on Appropriations of the Senate and the Committee on Appropriations of the House of Representatives regarding the financial operating plans and forecasts of the Director, the financial condition and results of operations of the Bureau, and the sources and application of funds of the Bureau, including any funds appropriated in accordance with this subsection.

[Explanation at ¶ 4545.]

[¶ 11,018] ACT SEC. 1018. EFFECTIVE DATE.
This subtitle shall become effective on the date of enactment of this Act.

[Explanation at ¶ 4515.]

Subtitle B—General Powers of the Bureau

[¶ 11,021] ACT SEC. 1021. PURPOSE, OBJECTIVES, AND FUNCTIONS.

(a) PURPOSE.—The Bureau shall seek to implement and, where applicable, enforce Federal consumer financial law consistently for the purpose of ensuring that all consumers have access to markets for consumer financial products and services and that markets for consumer financial products and services are fair, transparent, and competitive.

(b) OBJECTIVES.—The Bureau is authorized to exercise its authorities under Federal consumer financial law for the purposes of ensuring that, with respect to consumer financial products and services—

(1) consumers are provided with timely and understandable information to make responsible decisions about financial transactions;

(2) consumers are protected from unfair, deceptive, or abusive acts and practices and from discrimination;

(3) outdated, unnecessary, or unduly burdensome regulations are regularly identified and addressed in order to reduce unwarranted regulatory burdens;

(4) Federal consumer financial law is enforced consistently, without regard to the status of a person as a depository institution, in order to promote fair competition; and

(5) markets for consumer financial products and services operate transparently and efficiently to facilitate access and innovation.

(c) FUNCTIONS.—The primary functions of the Bureau are—

(1) conducting financial education programs;

(2) collecting, investigating, and responding to consumer complaints;

(3) collecting, researching, monitoring, and publishing information relevant to the functioning of markets for consumer financial products and services to identify risks to consumers and the proper functioning of such markets;

(4) subject to sections 1024 through 1026, supervising covered persons for compliance with Federal consumer financial law, and taking appropriate enforcement action to address violations of Federal consumer financial law;

(5) issuing rules, orders, and guidance implementing Federal consumer financial law; and

(6) performing such support activities as may be necessary or useful to facilitate the other functions of the Bureau.

[Explanation at ¶ 4550.]

[¶ 11,022] ACT SEC. 1022. RULEMAKING AUTHORITY.

(a) IN GENERAL.—The Bureau is authorized to exercise its authorities under Federal consumer financial law to administer, enforce, and otherwise implement the provisions of Federal consumer financial law.

(b) RULEMAKING, ORDERS, AND GUIDANCE.—

(1) GENERAL AUTHORITY.—The Director may prescribe rules and issue orders and guidance, as may be necessary or appropriate to enable the Bureau to administer and carry out the purposes and objectives of the Federal consumer financial laws, and to prevent evasions thereof.

(2) STANDARDS FOR RULEMAKING.—In prescribing a rule under the Federal consumer financial laws—

(A) the Bureau shall consider—

(i) the potential benefits and costs to consumers and covered persons, including the potential reduction of access by consumers to consumer financial products or services resulting from such rule; and

(ii) the impact of proposed rules on covered persons, as described in section 1026, and the impact on consumers in rural areas;

(B) the Bureau shall consult with the appropriate prudential regulators or other Federal agencies prior to proposing a rule and during the comment process regarding consistency with prudential, market, or systemic objectives administered by such agencies; and

(C) if, during the consultation process described in subparagraph (B), a prudential regulator provides the Bureau with a written objection to the proposed rule of the Bureau or a portion thereof, the Bureau shall include in the adopting release a description of the objection and the basis for the Bureau decision, if any, regarding such objection, except that nothing in this clause shall be construed as altering or limiting the procedures under section 1023 that may apply to any rule prescribed by the Bureau.

(3) EXEMPTIONS.—

(A) IN GENERAL.—The Bureau, by rule, may conditionally or unconditionally exempt any class of covered persons, service providers, or consumer financial products or services, from any provision of this title, or from any rule issued under this title, as the Bureau determines necessary or appropriate to carry out the purposes and objectives of this title, taking into consideration the factors in subparagraph (B).

(B) FACTORS.—In issuing an exemption, as permitted under subparagraph (A), the Bureau shall, as appropriate, take into consideration—

(i) the total assets of the class of covered persons;

(ii) the volume of transactions involving consumer financial products or services in which the class of covered persons engages; and

(iii) existing provisions of law which are applicable to the consumer financial product or service and the extent to which such provisions provide consumers with adequate protections.

(4) EXCLUSIVE RULEMAKING AUTHORITY.—

(A) IN GENERAL.—Notwithstanding any other provisions of Federal law and except as provided in section 1061(b)(5), to the extent that a provision of Federal consumer financial law authorizes the Bureau and another Federal agency to issue regulations under that provision of law for purposes of assuring compliance with Federal consumer financial law and any regulations thereunder, the Bureau shall have the exclusive authority to prescribe rules subject to those provisions of law.

(B) DEFERENCE.—Notwithstanding any power granted to any Federal agency or to the Council under this title, and subject to section 1061(b)(5)(E), the deference that a court affords to the Bureau with respect to a determination by the Bureau regarding the meaning or interpretation of any provision of a Federal consumer financial law shall be applied as if the Bureau were the only agency authorized to apply, enforce, interpret, or administer the provisions of such Federal consumer financial law.

(c) MONITORING.—

(1) IN GENERAL.—In order to support its rulemaking and other functions, the Bureau shall monitor for risks to consumers in the offering or provision of consumer financial products or services, including developments in markets for such products or services.

(2) CONSIDERATIONS.—In allocating its resources to perform the monitoring required by this section, the Bureau may consider, among other factors—

(A) likely risks and costs to consumers associated with buying or using a type of consumer financial product or service;

(B) understanding by consumers of the risks of a type of consumer financial product or service;

(C) the legal protections applicable to the offering or provision of a consumer financial product or service, including the extent to which the law is likely to adequately protect consumers;

(D) rates of growth in the offering or provision of a consumer financial product or service;

(E) the extent, if any, to which the risks of a consumer financial product or service may disproportionately affect traditionally underserved consumers; or

(F) the types, number, and other pertinent characteristics of covered persons that offer or provide the consumer financial product or service.

(3) SIGNIFICANT FINDINGS.—

(A) IN GENERAL.—The Bureau shall publish not fewer than 1 report of significant findings of its monitoring required by this subsection in each calendar year, beginning with the first calendar year that begins at least 1 year after the designated transfer date.

(B) CONFIDENTIAL INFORMATION.—The Bureau may make public such information obtained by the Bureau under this section as is in the public interest, through aggregated reports or other appropriate formats designed to protect confidential information in accordance with paragraphs (4), (6), (8), and (9).

(4) COLLECTION OF INFORMATION.—

(A) IN GENERAL.—In conducting any monitoring or assessment required by this section, the Bureau shall have the authority to gather information from time to time regarding the organization, business conduct, markets, and activities of covered persons and service providers.

(B) METHODOLOGY.—In order to gather information described in subparagraph (A), the Bureau may—

(i) gather and compile information from a variety of sources, including examination reports concerning covered persons or service providers, consumer complaints, voluntary surveys and voluntary interviews of consumers, surveys and interviews with covered persons and service providers, and review of available databases; and

(ii) require covered persons and service providers participating in consumer financial services markets to file with the Bureau, under oath or otherwise, in such form and within such reasonable period of time as the Bureau may prescribe by rule or order, annual or special reports, or answers in writing to specific questions, furnishing information described in paragraph (4), as necessary for the Bureau to fulfill the monitoring, assessment, and reporting responsibilities imposed by Congress.

(C) LIMITATION.—The Bureau may not use its authorities under this paragraph to obtain records from covered persons and service providers participating in consumer financial services markets for purposes of gathering or analyzing the personally identifiable financial information of consumers.

(5) LIMITED INFORMATION GATHERING.—In order to assess whether a nondepository is a covered person, as defined in section 1002, the Bureau may require such nondepository to file with the Bureau, under oath or otherwise, in such form and within such reasonable period of time as the Bureau may prescribe by rule or order, annual or special reports, or answers in writing to specific questions.

(6) CONFIDENTIALITY RULES.—

(A) RULEMAKING.—The Bureau shall prescribe rules regarding the confidential treatment of information obtained from persons in connection with the exercise of its authorities under Federal consumer financial law.

(B) ACCESS BY THE BUREAU TO REPORTS OF OTHER REGULATORS.—

(i) EXAMINATION AND FINANCIAL CONDITION REPORTS.—Upon providing reasonable assurances of confidentiality, the Bureau shall have access to any report of examination or financial condition made by a prudential regulator or other Federal agency having jurisdiction over a covered person or service provider, and to all revisions made to any such report.

(ii) PROVISION OF OTHER REPORTS TO THE BUREAU.—In addition to the reports described in clause (i), a prudential regulator or other Federal agency having jurisdiction over a covered person or service provider may, in its discretion, furnish to the Bureau any other report or other confidential supervisory information concerning any insured depository institution, credit union, or other entity examined by such agency under authority of any provision of Federal law.

(C) ACCESS BY OTHER REGULATORS TO REPORTS OF THE BUREAU.—

(i) EXAMINATION REPORTS.—Upon providing reasonable assurances of confidentiality, a prudential regulator, a State regulator, or any other Federal agency having jurisdiction over a covered person or service provider shall have access to any report of examination made by the Bureau with respect to such person, and to all revisions made to any such report.

(ii) PROVISION OF OTHER REPORTS TO OTHER REGULATORS.—In addition to the reports described in clause (i), the Bureau may, in its discretion, furnish to a prudential regulator or other agency having jurisdiction over a covered person or service provider any other report or other confidential supervisory information concerning such person examined by the Bureau under the authority of any other provision of Federal law.

(7) REGISTRATION.—

(A) IN GENERAL.—The Bureau may prescribe rules regarding registration requirements applicable to a covered person, other than an insured depository institution, insured credit union, or related person.

(B) REGISTRATION INFORMATION.—Subject to rules prescribed by the Bureau, the Bureau may publicly disclose registration information to facilitate the ability of consumers to identify covered persons that are registered with the Bureau.

(C) CONSULTATION WITH STATE AGENCIES.—In developing and implementing registration requirements under this paragraph, the Bureau shall consult with State agencies regarding requirements or systems (including coordinated or combined systems for registration), where appropriate.

(8) PRIVACY CONSIDERATIONS.—In collecting information from any person, publicly releasing information held by the Bureau, or requiring covered persons to publicly report information, the Bureau shall take steps to ensure that proprietary, personal, or confidential consumer informa-

tion that is protected from public disclosure under section 552(b) or 552a of title 5, United States Code, or any other provision of law, is not made public under this title.

(9) CONSUMER PRIVACY.—

(A) IN GENERAL.—The Bureau may not obtain from a covered person or service provider any personally identifiable financial information about a consumer from the financial records of the covered person or service provider, except—

(i) if the financial records are reasonably described in a request by the Bureau and the consumer provides written permission for the disclosure of such information by the covered person or service provider to the Bureau; or

(ii) as may be specifically permitted or required under other applicable provisions of law and in accordance with the Right to Financial Privacy Act of 1978 (12 U.S.C. 3401 et seq.).

(B) TREATMENT OF COVERED PERSON OR SERVICE PROVIDER.—With respect to the application of any provision of the Right to Financial Privacy Act of 1978, to a disclosure by a covered person or service provider subject to this subsection, the covered person or service provider shall be treated as if it were a "financial institution", as defined in section 1101 of that Act (12 U.S.C. 3401).

(d) ASSESSMENT OF SIGNIFICANT RULES.—

(1) IN GENERAL.—The Bureau shall conduct an assessment of each significant rule or order adopted by the Bureau under Federal consumer financial law. The assessment shall address, among other relevant factors, the effectiveness of the rule or order in meeting the purposes and objectives of this title and the specific goals stated by the Bureau. The assessment shall reflect available evidence and any data that the Bureau reasonably may collect.

(2) REPORTS.—The Bureau shall publish a report of its assessment under this subsection not later than 5 years after the effective date of the subject rule or order.

(3) PUBLIC COMMENT REQUIRED.—Before publishing a report of its assessment, the Bureau shall invite public comment on recommendations for modifying, expanding, or eliminating the newly adopted significant rule or order.

[Explanation at ¶ 4555.]

[¶ 11,023] ACT SEC. 1023. REVIEW OF BUREAU REGULATIONS.

(a) REVIEW OF BUREAU REGULATIONS.—On the petition of a member agency of the Council, the Council may set aside a final regulation prescribed by the Bureau, or any provision thereof, if the Council decides, in accordance with subsection (c), that the regulation or provision would put the safety and soundness of the United States banking system or the stability of the financial system of the United States at risk.

(b) PETITION.—

(1) PROCEDURE.—An agency represented by a member of the Council may petition the Council, in writing, and in accordance with rules prescribed pursuant to subsection (f), to stay the effectiveness of, or set aside, a regulation if the member agency filing the petition—

(A) has in good faith attempted to work with the Bureau to resolve concerns regarding the effect of the rule on the safety and soundness of the United States banking system or the stability of the financial system of the United States; and

(B) files the petition with the Council not later than 10 days after the date on which the regulation has been published in the Federal Register.

(2) PUBLICATION.—Any petition filed with the Council under this section shall be published in the Federal Register and transmitted contemporaneously with filing to the Committee on Banking, Housing, and Urban Affairs of the Senate and the Committee on Financial Services of the House of Representatives.

(c) STAYS AND SET ASIDES.—

(1) STAY.—

(A) IN GENERAL.—Upon the request of any member agency, the Chairperson of the Council may stay the effectiveness of a regulation for the purpose of allowing appropriate consideration of the petition by the Council.

(B) EXPIRATION.—A stay issued under this paragraph shall expire on the earlier of—

(i) 90 days after the date of filing of the petition under subsection (b); or

(ii) the date on which the Council makes a decision under paragraph (3).

(2) NO ADVERSE INFERENCE.—After the expiration of any stay imposed under this section, no inference shall be drawn regarding the validity or enforceability of a regulation which was the subject of the petition.

(3) VOTE.—

(A) IN GENERAL.—The decision to issue a stay of, or set aside, any regulation under this section shall be made only with the affirmative vote in accordance with subparagraph (B) of 2/3 of the members of the Council then serving.

(B) AUTHORIZATION TO VOTE.—A member of the Council may vote to stay the effectiveness of, or set aside, a final regulation prescribed by the Bureau only if the agency or department represented by that member has—

(i) considered any relevant information provided by the agency submitting the petition and by the Bureau; and

(ii) made an official determination, at a public meeting where applicable, that the regulation which is the subject of the petition would put the safety and soundness of the United States banking system or the stability of the financial system of the United States at risk.

(4) DECISIONS TO SET ASIDE.—

(A) EFFECT OF DECISION.—A decision by the Council to set aside a regulation prescribed by the Bureau, or provision thereof, shall render such regulation, or provision thereof, unenforceable.

(B) TIMELY ACTION REQUIRED.—The Council may not issue a decision to set aside a regulation, or provision thereof, which is the subject of a petition under this section after the expiration of the later of—

(i) 45 days following the date of filing of the petition, unless a stay is issued under paragraph (1); or

(ii) the expiration of a stay issued by the Council under this section.

(C) SEPARATE AUTHORITY.—The issuance of a stay under this section does not affect the authority of the Council to set aside a regulation.

(5) DISMISSAL DUE TO INACTION.—A petition under this section shall be deemed dismissed if the Council has not issued a decision to set aside a regulation, or provision thereof, within the period for timely action under paragraph (4)(B).

(6) PUBLICATION OF DECISION.—Any decision under this subsection to issue a stay of, or set aside, a regulation or provision thereof shall be published by the Council in the Federal Register as soon as practicable after the decision is made, with an explanation of the reasons for the decision.

(7) RULEMAKING PROCEDURES INAPPLICABLE.—The notice and comment procedures under section 553 of title 5, United States Code, shall not apply to any decision under this section of the Council to issue a stay of, or set aside, a regulation.

(8) JUDICIAL REVIEW OF DECISIONS BY THE COUNCIL.—A decision by the Council to set aside a regulation prescribed by the Bureau, or provision thereof, shall be subject to review under chapter 7 of title 5, United States Code.

(d) APPLICATION OF OTHER LAW.—Nothing in this section shall be construed as altering, limiting, or restricting the application of any other provision of law, except as otherwise specifically provided in this section, including chapter 5 and chapter 7 of title 5, United States Code, to a regulation which is the subject of a petition filed under this section.

(e) SAVINGS CLAUSE.—Nothing in this section shall be construed as limiting or restricting the Bureau from engaging in a rulemaking in accordance with applicable law.

(f) IMPLEMENTING RULES.—The Council shall prescribe procedural rules to implement this section.

[Explanation at ¶ 4560.]

[¶ 11,024] ACT SEC. 1024. SUPERVISION OF NONDEPOSITORY COVERED PERSONS.

(a) SCOPE OF COVERAGE.—

(1) APPLICABILITY.—Notwithstanding any other provision of this title, and except as provided in paragraph (3), this section shall apply to any covered person who—

(A) offers or provides origination, brokerage, or servicing of loans secured by real estate for use by consumers primarily for personal, family, or household purposes, or loan modification or foreclosure relief services in connection with such loans;

(B) is a larger participant of a market for other consumer financial products or services, as defined by rule in accordance with paragraph (2);

(C) the Bureau has reasonable cause to determine, by order, after notice to the covered person and a reasonable opportunity for such covered person to respond, based on complaints collected through the system under section 1013(b)(3) or information from other sources, that such covered person is engaging, or has engaged, in conduct that poses risks to consumers with regard to the offering or provision of consumer financial products or services;

(D) offers or provides to a consumer any private education loan, as defined in section 140 of the Truth in Lending Act (15 U.S.C. 1650), notwithstanding section 1027(a)(2)(A) and subject to section 1027(a)(2)(C); or

(E) offers or provides to a consumer a payday loan.

(2) RULEMAKING TO DEFINE COVERED PERSONS SUBJECT TO THIS SECTION.—The Bureau shall consult with the Federal Trade Commission prior to issuing a rule, in accordance with paragraph (1)(B), to define covered persons subject to this section. The Bureau shall issue its initial rule not later than 1 year after the designated transfer date.

(3) RULES OF CONSTRUCTION.—

(A) CERTAIN PERSONS EXCLUDED.—This section shall not apply to persons described in section 1025(a) or 1026(a).

(B) ACTIVITY LEVELS.—For purposes of computing activity levels under paragraph (1) or rules issued thereunder, activities of affiliated companies (other than insured depository institutions or insured credit unions) shall be aggregated.

(b) SUPERVISION.—

(1) IN GENERAL.—The Bureau shall require reports and conduct examinations on a periodic basis of persons described in subsection (a)(1) for purposes of—

(A) assessing compliance with the requirements of Federal consumer financial law;

(B) obtaining information about the activities and compliance systems or procedures of such person; and

(C) detecting and assessing risks to consumers and to markets for consumer financial products and services.

(2) RISK-BASED SUPERVISION PROGRAM.—The Bureau shall exercise its authority under paragraph (1) in a manner designed to ensure that such exercise, with respect to persons described in

subsection (a)(1), is based on the assessment by the Bureau of the risks posed to consumers in the relevant product markets and geographic markets, and taking into consideration, as applicable—

    (A) the asset size of the covered person;

    (B) the volume of transactions involving consumer financial products or services in which the covered person engages;

    (C) the risks to consumers created by the provision of such consumer financial products or services;

    (D) the extent to which such institutions are subject to oversight by State authorities for consumer protection; and

    (E) any other factors that the Bureau determines to be relevant to a class of covered persons.

(3) COORDINATION.—To minimize regulatory burden, the Bureau shall coordinate its supervisory activities with the supervisory activities conducted by prudential regulators and the State bank regulatory authorities, including establishing their respective schedules for examining persons described in subsection (a)(1) and requirements regarding reports to be submitted by such persons.

(4) USE OF EXISTING REPORTS.—The Bureau shall, to the fullest extent possible, use—

    (A) reports pertaining to persons described in subsection (a)(1) that have been provided or required to have been provided to a Federal or State agency; and

    (B) information that has been reported publicly.

(5) PRESERVATION OF AUTHORITY.—Nothing in this title may be construed as limiting the authority of the Director to require reports from persons described in subsection (a)(1), as permitted under paragraph (1), regarding information owned or under the control of such person, regardless of whether such information is maintained, stored, or processed by another person.

(6) REPORTS OF TAX LAW NONCOMPLIANCE.—The Bureau shall provide the Commissioner of Internal Revenue with any report of examination or related information identifying possible tax law noncompliance.

(7) REGISTRATION, RECORDKEEPING AND OTHER REQUIREMENTS FOR CERTAIN PERSONS.—

    (A) IN GENERAL.—The Bureau shall prescribe rules to facilitate supervision of persons described in subsection (a)(1) and assessment and detection of risks to consumers.

    (B) RECORDKEEPING.—The Bureau may require a person described in subsection (a)(1), to generate, provide, or retain records for the purposes of facilitating supervision of such persons and assessing and detecting risks to consumers.

    (C) REQUIREMENTS CONCERNING OBLIGATIONS.—The Bureau may prescribe rules regarding a person described in subsection (a)(1), to ensure that such persons are legitimate entities and are able to perform their obligations to consumers. Such requirements may include background checks for principals, officers, directors, or key personnel and bonding or other appropriate financial requirements.

    (D) CONSULTATION WITH STATE AGENCIES.—In developing and implementing requirements under this paragraph, the Bureau shall consult with State agencies regarding requirements or systems (including coordinated or combined systems for registration), where appropriate.

(c) ENFORCEMENT AUTHORITY.—

(1) THE BUREAU TO HAVE ENFORCEMENT AUTHORITY.—Except as provided in paragraph (3) and section 1061, with respect to any person described in subsection (a)(1), to the extent that Federal law authorizes the Bureau and another Federal agency to enforce Federal consumer financial law, the Bureau shall have exclusive authority to enforce that Federal consumer financial law.

(2) REFERRAL.—Any Federal agency authorized to enforce a Federal consumer financial law described in paragraph (1) may recommend in writing to the Bureau that the Bureau initiate an enforcement proceeding, as the Bureau is authorized by that Federal law or by this title.

(3) COORDINATION WITH THE FEDERAL TRADE COMMISSION.—

(A) IN GENERAL.—The Bureau and the Federal Trade Commission shall negotiate an agreement for coordinating with respect to enforcement actions by each agency regarding the offering or provision of consumer financial products or services by any covered person that is described in subsection (a)(1), or service providers thereto. The agreement shall include procedures for notice to the other agency, where feasible, prior to initiating a civil action to enforce any Federal law regarding the offering or provision of consumer financial products or services.

(B) CIVIL ACTIONS.—Whenever a civil action has been filed by, or on behalf of, the Bureau or the Federal Trade Commission for any violation of any provision of Federal law described in subparagraph (A), or any regulation prescribed under such provision of law—

(i) the other agency may not, during the pendency of that action, institute a civil action under such provision of law against any defendant named in the complaint in such pending action for any violation alleged in the complaint; and

(ii) the Bureau or the Federal Trade Commission may intervene as a party in any such action brought by the other agency, and, upon intervening—

(I) be heard on all matters arising in such enforcement action; and

(II) file petitions for appeal in such actions.

(C) AGREEMENT TERMS.—The terms of any agreement negotiated under subparagraph (A) may modify or supersede the provisions of subparagraph (B).

(D) DEADLINE.—The agencies shall reach the agreement required under subparagraph (A) not later than 6 months after the designated transfer date.

(d) EXCLUSIVE RULEMAKING AND EXAMINATION AUTHORITY.—Notwithstanding any other provision of Federal law and except as provided in section 1061, to the extent that Federal law authorizes the Bureau and another Federal agency to issue regulations or guidance, conduct examinations, or require reports from a person described in subsection (a)(1) under such law for purposes of assuring compliance with Federal consumer financial law and any regulations thereunder, the Bureau shall have the exclusive authority to prescribe rules, issue guidance, conduct examinations, require reports, or issue exemptions with regard to a person described in subsection (a)(1), subject to those provisions of law.

(e) SERVICE PROVIDERS.—A service provider to a person described in subsection (a)(1) shall be subject to the authority of the Bureau under this section, to the same extent as if such service provider were engaged in a service relationship with a bank, and the Bureau were an appropriate Federal banking agency under section 7(c) of the Bank Service Company Act (12 U.S.C. 1867(c)). In conducting any examination or requiring any report from a service provider subject to this subsection, the Bureau shall coordinate with the appropriate prudential regulator, as applicable.

(f) PRESERVATION OF FARM CREDIT ADMINISTRATION AUTHORITY.—No provision of this title may be construed as modifying, limiting, or otherwise affecting the authority of the Farm Credit Administration.

[Explanation at ¶ 4565.]

[¶ 11,025] ACT SEC. 1025. SUPERVISION OF VERY LARGE BANKS, SAVINGS ASSOCIATIONS, AND CREDIT UNIONS.

(a) SCOPE OF COVERAGE.—This section shall apply to any covered person that is—

(1) an insured depository institution with total assets of more than $10,000,000,000 and any affiliate thereof; or

(2) an insured credit union with total assets of more than $10,000,000,000 and any affiliate thereof.

(b) SUPERVISION.—

(1) IN GENERAL.—The Bureau shall have exclusive authority to require reports and conduct examinations on a periodic basis of persons described in subsection (a) for purposes of—

(A) assessing compliance with the requirements of Federal consumer financial laws;

(B) obtaining information about the activities subject to such laws and the associated compliance systems or procedures of such persons; and

(C) detecting and assessing associated risks to consumers and to markets for consumer financial products and services.

(2) COORDINATION.—To minimize regulatory burden, the Bureau shall coordinate its supervisory activities with the supervisory activities conducted by prudential regulators and the State bank regulatory authorities, including consultation regarding their respective schedules for examining such persons described in subsection (a) and requirements regarding reports to be submitted by such persons.

(3) USE OF EXISTING REPORTS.—The Bureau shall, to the fullest extent possible, use—

(A) reports pertaining to a person described in subsection (a) that have been provided or required to have been provided to a Federal or State agency; and

(B) information that has been reported publicly.

(4) PRESERVATION OF AUTHORITY.—Nothing in this title may be construed as limiting the authority of the Director to require reports from a person described in subsection (a), as permitted under paragraph (1), regarding information owned or under the control of such person, regardless of whether such information is maintained, stored, or processed by another person.

(5) REPORTS OF TAX LAW NONCOMPLIANCE.—The Bureau shall provide the Commissioner of Internal Revenue with any report of examination or related information identifying possible tax law noncompliance.

(c) PRIMARY ENFORCEMENT AUTHORITY.—

(1) THE BUREAU TO HAVE PRIMARY ENFORCEMENT AUTHORITY.—To the extent that the Bureau and another Federal agency are authorized to enforce a Federal consumer financial law, the Bureau shall have primary authority to enforce that Federal consumer financial law with respect to any person described in subsection (a).

(2) REFERRAL.—Any Federal agency, other than the Federal Trade Commission, that is authorized to enforce a Federal consumer financial law may recommend, in writing, to the Bureau that the Bureau initiate an enforcement proceeding with respect to a person described in subsection (a), as the Bureau is authorized to do by that Federal consumer financial law.

(3) BACKUP ENFORCEMENT AUTHORITY OF OTHER FEDERAL AGENCY.—If the Bureau does not, before the end of the 120-day period beginning on the date on which the Bureau receives a recommendation under paragraph (2), initiate an enforcement proceeding, the other agency referred to in paragraph (2) may initiate an enforcement proceeding, including performing follow up supervisory and support functions incidental thereto, to assure compliance with such proceeding.

(d) SERVICE PROVIDERS.—A service provider to a person described in subsection (a) shall be subject to the authority of the Bureau under this section, to the same extent as if the Bureau were an appropriate Federal banking agency under section 7(c) of the Bank Service Company Act 12 U.S.C. 1867(c). In conducting any examination or requiring any report from a service provider subject to this subsection, the Bureau shall coordinate with the appropriate prudential regulator.

(e) SIMULTANEOUS AND COORDINATED SUPERVISORY ACTION.—

(1) EXAMINATIONS.—A prudential regulator and the Bureau shall, with respect to each insured depository institution, insured credit union, or other covered person described in subsection (a) that is supervised by the prudential regulator and the Bureau, respectively—

(A) coordinate the scheduling of examinations of the insured depository institution, insured credit union, or other covered person described in subsection (a);

(B) conduct simultaneous examinations of each insured depository institution or insured credit union, unless such institution requests examinations to be conducted separately;

(C) share each draft report of examination with the other agency and permit the receiving agency a reasonable opportunity (which shall not be less than a period of 30 days after the date of receipt) to comment on the draft report before such report is made final; and

(D) prior to issuing a final report of examination or taking supervisory action, take into consideration concerns, if any, raised in the comments made by the other agency.

(2) COORDINATION WITH STATE BANK SUPERVISORS.—The Bureau shall pursue arrangements and agreements with State bank supervisors to coordinate examinations, consistent with paragraph (1).

(3) AVOIDANCE OF CONFLICT IN SUPERVISION.—

(A) REQUEST.—If the proposed supervisory determinations of the Bureau and a prudential regulator (in this section referred to collectively as the "agencies") are conflicting, an insured depository institution, insured credit union, or other covered person described in subsection (a) may request the agencies to coordinate and present a joint statement of coordinated supervisory action.

(B) JOINT STATEMENT.—The agencies shall provide a joint statement under subparagraph (A), not later than 30 days after the date of receipt of the request of the insured depository institution, credit union, or covered person described in subsection (a).

(4) APPEALS TO GOVERNING PANEL.—

(A) IN GENERAL.—If the agencies do not resolve the conflict or issue a joint statement required by subparagraph (B), or if either of the agencies takes or attempts to take any supervisory action relating to the request for the joint statement without the consent of the other agency, an insured depository institution, insured credit union, or other covered person described in subsection (a) may institute an appeal to a governing panel, as provided in this subsection, not later than 30 days after the expiration of the period during which a joint statement is required to be filed under paragraph (3)(B).

(B) COMPOSITION OF GOVERNING PANEL.—The governing panel for an appeal under this paragraph shall be composed of—

(i) a representative from the Bureau and a representative of the prudential regulator, both of whom—

(I) have not participated in the material supervisory determinations under appeal; and

(II) do not directly or indirectly report to the person who participated materially in the supervisory determinations under appeal; and

(ii) one individual representative, to be determined on a rotating basis, from among the Board of Governors, the Corporation, the National Credit Union Administration, and the Office of the Comptroller of the Currency, other than any agency involved in the subject dispute.

(C) CONDUCT OF APPEAL.—In an appeal under this paragraph—

(i) the insured depository institution, insured credit union, or other covered person described in subsection (a)—

(I) shall include in its appeal all the facts and legal arguments pertaining to the matter; and

(II) may, through counsel, employees, or representatives, appear before the governing panel in person or by telephone; and

(ii) the governing panel—

(I) may request the insured depository institution, insured credit union, or other covered person described in subsection (a), the Bureau, or the prudential regulator to produce additional information relevant to the appeal; and

(II) by a majority vote of its members, shall provide a final determination, in writing, not later than 30 days after the date of filing of an informationally complete appeal, or such longer period as the panel and the insured depository institution, insured credit union, or other covered person described in subsection (a) may jointly agree.

(D) PUBLIC AVAILABILITY OF DETERMINATIONS.—A governing panel shall publish all information contained in a determination by the governing panel, with appropriate redactions of information that would be subject to an exemption from disclosure under section 552 of title 5, United States Code.

(E) PROHIBITION AGAINST RETALIATION.—The Bureau and the prudential regulators shall prescribe rules to provide safeguards from retaliation against the insured depository institution, insured credit union, or other covered person described in subsection (a) instituting an appeal under this paragraph, as well as their officers and employees.

(F) LIMITATION.—The process provided in this paragraph shall not apply to a determination by a prudential regulator to appoint a conservator or receiver for an insured depository institution or a liquidating agent for an insured credit union, as the case may be, or a decision to take action pursuant to section 38 of the Federal Deposit Insurance Act (12 U.S.C. 1831o) or section 212 of the Federal Credit Union Act (112 U.S.C. 1790a), as applicable.

(G) EFFECT ON OTHER AUTHORITY.—Nothing in this section shall modify or limit the authority of the Bureau to interpret, or take enforcement action under, any Federal consumer financial law, or the authority of a prudential regulator to interpret or take enforcement action under any other provision of Federal law for safety and soundness purposes.

[Explanation at ¶ 4570.]

[¶ 11,026] ACT SEC. 1026. OTHER BANKS, SAVINGS ASSOCIATIONS, AND CREDIT UNIONS.

(a) SCOPE OF COVERAGE.—This section shall apply to any covered person that is—

(1) an insured depository institution with total assets of $10,000,000,000 or less; or

(2) an insured credit union with total assets of $10,000,000,000 or less.

(b) REPORTS.—The Director may require reports from a person described in subsection (a), as necessary to support the role of the Bureau in implementing Federal consumer financial law, to support its examination activities under subsection (c), and to assess and detect risks to consumers and consumer financial markets.

(1) USE OF EXISTING REPORTS.—The Bureau shall, to the fullest extent possible, use—

(A) reports pertaining to a person described in subsection (a) that have been provided or required to have been provided to a Federal or State agency; and

(B) information that has been reported publicly.

(2) PRESERVATION OF AUTHORITY.—Nothing in this subsection may be construed as limiting the authority of the Director from requiring from a person described in subsection (a), as permitted under paragraph (1), information owned or under the control of such person, regardless of whether such information is maintained, stored, or processed by another person.

(3) REPORTS OF TAX LAW NONCOMPLIANCE.—The Bureau shall provide the Commissioner of Internal Revenue with any report of examination or related information identifying possible tax law noncompliance.

(c) EXAMINATIONS.—

(1) IN GENERAL.—The Bureau may, at its discretion, include examiners on a sampling basis of the examinations performed by the prudential regulator to assess compliance with the requirements of Federal consumer financial law of persons described in subsection (a).

(2) AGENCY COORDINATION.—The prudential regulator shall—

(A) provide all reports, records, and documentation related to the examination process for any institution included in the sample referred to in paragraph (1) to the Bureau on a timely and continual basis;

(B) involve such Bureau examiner in the entire examination process for such person; and

(C) consider input of the Bureau concerning the scope of an examination, conduct of the examination, the contents of the examination report, the designation of matters requiring attention, and examination ratings.

(d) ENFORCEMENT.—

(1) IN GENERAL.—Except for requiring reports under subsection (b), the prudential regulator is authorized to enforce the requirements of Federal consumer financial laws and, with respect to a covered person described in subsection (a), shall have exclusive authority (relative to the Bureau) to enforce such laws.

(2) COORDINATION WITH PRUDENTIAL REGULATOR.—

(A) REFERRAL.—When the Bureau has reason to believe that a person described in subsection (a) has engaged in a material violation of a Federal consumer financial law, the Bureau shall notify the prudential regulator in writing and recommend appropriate action to respond.

(B) RESPONSE.—Upon receiving a recommendation under subparagraph (A), the prudential regulator shall provide a written response to the Bureau not later than 60 days thereafter.

(e) SERVICE PROVIDERS.—A service provider to a substantial number of persons described in subsection (a) shall be subject to the authority of the Bureau under section 1025 to the same extent as if the Bureau were an appropriate Federal bank agency under section 7(c) of the Bank Service Company Act (12 U.S.C. 1867(c)). When conducting any examination or requiring any report from a service provider subject to this subsection, the Bureau shall coordinate with the appropriate prudential regulator.

[Explanation at ¶ 4575.]

[¶ 11,027] ACT SEC. 1027. LIMITATIONS ON AUTHORITIES OF THE BUREAU; PRESERVATION OF AUTHORITIES.

(a) EXCLUSION FOR MERCHANTS, RETAILERS, AND OTHER SELLERS OF NONFINANCIAL GOODS OR SERVICES.—

(1) SALE OR BROKERAGE OF NONFINANCIAL GOOD OR SERVICE.—The Bureau may not exercise any rulemaking, supervisory, enforcement or other authority under this title with respect to a person who is a merchant, retailer, or seller of any nonfinancial good or service and is engaged in the sale or brokerage of such nonfinancial good or service, except to the extent that such person is engaged in offering or providing any consumer financial product or service, or is otherwise subject to any enumerated consumer law or any law for which authorities are transferred under subtitle F or H.

(2) OFFERING OR PROVISION OF CERTAIN CONSUMER FINANCIAL PRODUCTS OR SERVICES IN CONNECTION WITH THE SALE OR BROKERAGE OF NONFINANCIAL GOOD OR SERVICE.—

(A) IN GENERAL.—Except as provided in subparagraph (B), and subject to subparagraph (C), the Bureau may not exercise any rulemaking, supervisory, enforcement, or other authority under this title with respect to a merchant, retailer, or seller of nonfinancial goods or services, but only to the extent that such person—

(i) extends credit directly to a consumer, in a case in which the good or service being provided is not itself a consumer financial product or service (other than credit described in this subparagraph), exclusively for the purpose of enabling that consumer to purchase such nonfinancial good or service directly from the merchant, retailer, or seller;

(ii) directly, or through an agreement with another person, collects debt arising from credit extended as described in clause (i); or

(iii) sells or conveys debt described in clause (i) that is delinquent or otherwise in default.

(B) APPLICABILITY.—Subparagraph (A) does not apply to any credit transaction or collection of debt, other than as described in subparagraph (C)(i), arising from a transaction described in subparagraph (A)—

(i) in which the merchant, retailer, or seller of nonfinancial goods or services assigns, sells or otherwise conveys to another person such debt owed by the consumer (except for a sale of debt that is delinquent or otherwise in default, as described in subparagraph (A)(iii));

(ii) in which the credit extended significantly exceeds the market value of the nonfinancial good or service provided, or the Bureau otherwise finds that the sale of the nonfinancial good or service is done as a subterfuge, so as to evade or circumvent the provisions of this title; or

(iii) in which the merchant, retailer, or seller of nonfinancial goods or services regularly extends credit and the credit is subject to a finance charge.

(C) LIMITATIONS.—

(i) IN GENERAL.—Notwithstanding subparagraph (B), subparagraph (A) shall apply with respect to a merchant, retailer, or seller of nonfinancial goods or services that is not engaged significantly in offering or providing consumer financial products or services.

(ii) EXCEPTION.—Subparagraph (A) and clause (i) of this subparagraph do not apply to any merchant, retailer, or seller of nonfinancial goods or services—

(I) if such merchant, retailer, or seller of nonfinancial goods or services is engaged in a transaction described in subparagraph (B)(i) or (B)(ii); or

(II) to the extent that such merchant, retailer, or seller is subject to any enumerated consumer law or any law for which authorities are transferred under subtitle F or H, but the Bureau may exercise such authority only with respect to that law.

(D) RULES.—

(i) AUTHORITY OF OTHER AGENCIES.—No provision of this title shall be construed as modifying, limiting, or superseding the supervisory or enforcement authority of the Federal Trade Commission or any other agency (other than the Bureau) with respect to credit extended, or the collection of debt arising from such extension, directly by a merchant or retailer to a consumer exclusively for the purpose of enabling that consumer to purchase nonfinancial goods or services directly from the merchant or retailer.

(ii) SMALL BUSINESSES.—A merchant, retailer, or seller of nonfinancial goods or services that would otherwise be subject to the authority of the Bureau solely by virtue of the application of subparagraph (B)(iii) shall be deemed not to be engaged significantly in offering or providing consumer financial products or services under subparagraph (C)(i), if such person—

(I) only extends credit for the sale of nonfinancial goods or services, as described in subparagraph (A)(i);

(II) retains such credit on its own accounts (except to sell or convey such debt that is delinquent or otherwise in default); and

(III) meets the relevant industry size threshold to be a small business concern, based on annual receipts, pursuant to section 3 of the Small Business Act (15 U.S.C. 632) and the implementing rules thereunder.

(iii) INITIAL YEAR.—A merchant, retailer, or seller of nonfinancial goods or services shall be deemed to meet the relevant industry size threshold described in clause (ii)(III) during the first year of operations of that business concern if, during that year, the receipts of that business concern reasonably are expected to meet that size threshold.

(iv) OTHER STANDARDS FOR SMALL BUSINESS.—With respect to a merchant, retailer, or seller of nonfinancial goods or services that is a classified on a basis other than annual receipts for the purposes of section 3 of the Small Business Act (15 U.S.C. 632) and the implementing rules thereunder, such merchant, retailer, or seller shall be deemed to meet the relevant industry size threshold described in clause (ii)(III) if such merchant, retailer, or seller meets the relevant industry size threshold to be a small business concern based on the number of employees, or other such applicable measure, established under that Act.

(E) EXCEPTION FROM STATE ENFORCEMENT.—To the extent that the Bureau may not exercise authority under this subsection with respect to a merchant, retailer, or seller of nonfinancial goods or services, no action by a State attorney general or State regulator with respect to a claim made under this title may be brought under subsection 1042(a), with respect to an activity described in any of clauses (i) through (iii) of subparagraph (A) by such merchant, retailer, or seller of nonfinancial goods or services.

(b) EXCLUSION FOR REAL ESTATE BROKERAGE ACTIVITIES.—

(1) REAL ESTATE BROKERAGE ACTIVITIES EXCLUDED.—Without limiting subsection (a), and except as permitted in paragraph (2), the Bureau may not exercise any rulemaking, supervisory, enforcement, or other authority under this title with respect to a person that is licensed or registered as a real estate broker or real estate agent, in accordance with State law, to the extent that such person—

(A) acts as a real estate agent or broker for a buyer, seller, lessor, or lessee of real property;

(B) brings together parties interested in the sale, purchase, lease, rental, or exchange of real property;

(C) negotiates, on behalf of any party, any portion of a contract relating to the sale, purchase, lease, rental, or exchange of real property (other than in connection with the provision of financing with respect to any such transaction); or

(D) offers to engage in any activity, or act in any capacity, described in subparagraph (A), (B), or (C).

(2) DESCRIPTION OF ACTIVITIES.—The Bureau may exercise rulemaking, supervisory, enforcement, or other authority under this title with respect to a person described in paragraph (1) when such person is—

(A) engaged in an activity of offering or providing any consumer financial product or service, except that the Bureau may exercise such authority only with respect to that activity; or

(B) otherwise subject to any enumerated consumer law or any law for which authorities are transferred under subtitle F or H, but the Bureau may exercise such authority only with respect to that law.

(c) EXCLUSION FOR MANUFACTURED HOME RETAILERS AND MODULAR HOME RETAILERS.—

(1) IN GENERAL.—The Director may not exercise any rulemaking, supervisory, enforcement, or other authority over a person to the extent that—

(A) such person is not described in paragraph (2); and

(B) such person—

(i) acts as an agent or broker for a buyer or seller of a manufactured home or a modular home;

(ii) facilitates the purchase by a consumer of a manufactured home or modular home, by negotiating the purchase price or terms of the sales contract (other than providing financing with respect to such transaction); or

(iii) offers to engage in any activity described in clause (i) or (ii).

(2) DESCRIPTION OF ACTIVITIES.—A person is described in this paragraph to the extent that such person is engaged in the offering or provision of any consumer financial product or service or is otherwise subject to any enumerated consumer law or any law for which authorities are transferred under subtitle F or H.

(3) DEFINITIONS.—For purposes of this subsection, the following definitions shall apply:

(A) Manufactured home.—The term "manufactured home" has the same meaning as in section 603 of the National Manufactured Housing Construction and Safety Standards Act of 1974 (42 U.S.C. 5402).

(B) Modular home.—The term "modular home" means a house built in a factory in 2 or more modules that meet the State or local building codes where the house will be located, and where such modules are transported to the building site, installed on foundations, and completed.

(d) Exclusion for Accountants and Tax Preparers.—

(1) In general.—Except as permitted in paragraph (2), the Bureau may not exercise any rulemaking, supervisory, enforcement, or other authority over—

(A) any person that is a certified public accountant, permitted to practice as a certified public accounting firm, or certified or licensed for such purpose by a State, or any individual who is employed by or holds an ownership interest with respect to a person described in this subparagraph, when such person is performing or offering to perform—

(i) customary and usual accounting activities, including the provision of accounting, tax, advisory, or other services that are subject to the regulatory authority of a State board of accountancy or a Federal authority; or

(ii) other services that are incidental to such customary and usual accounting activities, to the extent that such incidental services are not offered or provided—

(I) by the person separate and apart from such customary and usual accounting activities; or

(II) to consumers who are not receiving such customary and usual accounting activities; or

(B) any person, other than a person described in subparagraph (A) that performs income tax preparation activities for consumers.

(2) Description of activities.—

(A) In general.—Paragraph (1) shall not apply to any person described in paragraph (1)(A) or (1)(B) to the extent that such person is engaged in any activity which is not a customary and usual accounting activity described in paragraph (1)(A) or incidental thereto but which is the offering or provision of any consumer financial product or service, except to the extent that a person described in paragraph (1)(A) is engaged in an activity which is a customary and usual accounting activity described in paragraph (1)(A), or incidental thereto.

(B) Not a customary and usual accounting activity.—For purposes of this subsection, extending or brokering credit is not a customary and usual accounting activity, or incidental thereto.

(C) Rule of construction.—For purposes of subparagraphs (A) and (B), a person described in paragraph (1)(A) shall not be deemed to be extending credit, if such person is only extending credit directly to a consumer, exclusively for the purpose of enabling such consumer to purchase services described in clause (i) or (ii) of paragraph (1)(A) directly from such person, and such credit is—

(i) not subject to a finance charge; and

(ii) not payable by written agreement in more than 4 installments.

(D) Other limitations.—Paragraph (1) does not apply to any person described in paragraph (1)(A) or (1)(B) that is otherwise subject to any enumerated consumer law or any law for which authorities are transferred under subtitle F or H.

(e) Exclusion for Practice of Law.—

(1) In general.—Except as provided under paragraph (2), the Bureau may not exercise any supervisory or enforcement authority with respect to an activity engaged in by an attorney as part of the practice of law under the laws of a State in which the attorney is licensed to practice law.

(2) RULE OF CONSTRUCTION.—Paragraph (1) shall not be construed so as to limit the exercise by the Bureau of any supervisory, enforcement, or other authority regarding the offering or provision of a consumer financial product or service described in any subparagraph of section 1002(5)—

(A) that is not offered or provided as part of, or incidental to, the practice of law, occurring exclusively within the scope of the attorney-client relationship; or

(B) that is otherwise offered or provided by the attorney in question with respect to any consumer who is not receiving legal advice or services from the attorney in connection with such financial product or service.

(3) EXISTING AUTHORITY.—Paragraph (1) shall not be construed so as to limit the authority of the Bureau with respect to any attorney, to the extent that such attorney is otherwise subject to any of the enumerated consumer laws or the authorities transferred under subtitle F or H.

(f) EXCLUSION FOR PERSONS REGULATED BY A STATE INSURANCE REGULATOR.—

(1) IN GENERAL.—No provision of this title shall be construed as altering, amending, or affecting the authority of any State insurance regulator to adopt rules, initiate enforcement proceedings, or take any other action with respect to a person regulated by a State insurance regulator. Except as provided in paragraph (2), the Bureau shall have no authority to exercise any power to enforce this title with respect to a person regulated by a State insurance regulator.

(2) DESCRIPTION OF ACTIVITIES.—Paragraph (1) does not apply to any person described in such paragraph to the extent that such person is engaged in the offering or provision of any consumer financial product or service or is otherwise subject to any enumerated consumer law or any law for which authorities are transferred under subtitle F or H.

(3) STATE INSURANCE AUTHORITY UNDER GRAMM-LEACH-BLILEY.—Notwithstanding paragraph (2), the Bureau shall not exercise any authorities that are granted a State insurance authority under section 505(a)(6) of the Gramm-Leach-Bliley Act with respect to a person regulated by a State insurance authority.

(g) EXCLUSION FOR EMPLOYEE BENEFIT AND COMPENSATION PLANS AND CERTAIN OTHER ARRANGEMENTS UNDER THE INTERNAL REVENUE CODE OF 1986.—

(1) PRESERVATION OF AUTHORITY OF OTHER AGENCIES.—No provision of this title shall be construed as altering, amending, or affecting the authority of the Secretary of the Treasury, the Secretary of Labor, or the Commissioner of Internal Revenue to adopt regulations, initiate enforcement proceedings, or take any actions with respect to any specified plan or arrangement.

(2) ACTIVITIES NOT CONSTITUTING THE OFFERING OR PROVISION OF ANY CONSUMER FINANCIAL PRODUCT OR SERVICE.—For purposes of this title, a person shall not be treated as having engaged in the offering or provision of any consumer financial product or service solely because such person is—

(A) a specified plan or arrangement;

(B) engaged in the activity of establishing or maintaining, for the benefit of employees of such person (or for members of an employee organization), any specified plan or arrangement; or

(C) engaged in the activity of establishing or maintaining a qualified tuition program under section 529(b)(1) of the Internal Revenue Code of 1986 offered by a State or other prepaid tuition program offered by a State.

(3) LIMITATION ON BUREAU AUTHORITY.—

(A) IN GENERAL.—Except as provided under subparagraphs (B) and (C), the Bureau may not exercise any rulemaking or enforcement authority with respect to products or services that relate to any specified plan or arrangement.

(B) BUREAU ACTION PURSUANT TO AGENCY REQUEST.—

(i) AGENCY REQUEST.—The Secretary and the Secretary of Labor may jointly issue a written request to the Bureau regarding implementation of appropriate consumer protection standards under this title with respect to the provision of services relating to any specified plan or arrangement.

(ii) AGENCY RESPONSE.—In response to a request by the Bureau, the Secretary and the Secretary of Labor shall jointly issue a written response, not later than 90 days after receipt of such request, to grant or deny the request of the Bureau regarding implementation of appropriate consumer protection standards under this title with respect to the provision of services relating to any specified plan or arrangement.

(iii) SCOPE OF BUREAU ACTION.—Subject to a request or response pursuant to clause (i) or clause (ii) by the agencies made under this subparagraph, the Bureau may exercise rulemaking authority, and may act to enforce a rule prescribed pursuant to such request or response, in accordance with the provisions of this title. A request or response made by the Secretary and the Secretary of Labor under this subparagraph shall describe the basis for, and scope of, appropriate consumer protection standards to be implemented under this title with respect to the provision of services relating to any specified plan or arrangement.

(C) DESCRIPTION OF PRODUCTS OR SERVICES.—To the extent that a person engaged in providing products or services relating to any specified plan or arrangement is subject to any enumerated consumer law or any law for which authorities are transferred under subtitle F or H, subparagraph (A) shall not apply with respect to that law.

(4) SPECIFIED PLAN OR ARRANGEMENT.—For purposes of this subsection, the term "specified plan or arrangement" means any plan, account, or arrangement described in section 220, 223, 401(a), 403(a), 403(b), 408, 408A, 529, or 530 of the Internal Revenue Code of 1986, or any employee benefit or compensation plan or arrangement, including a plan that is subject to title I of the Employee Retirement Income Security Act of 1974, or any prepaid tuition program offered by a State.

(h) PERSONS REGULATED BY A STATE SECURITIES COMMISSION.—

(1) IN GENERAL.—No provision of this title shall be construed as altering, amending, or affecting the authority of any securities commission (or any agency or office performing like functions) of any State to adopt rules, initiate enforcement proceedings, or take any other action with respect to a person regulated by any securities commission (or any agency or office performing like functions) of any State. Except as permitted in paragraph (2) and subsection (f), the Bureau shall have no authority to exercise any power to enforce this title with respect to a person regulated by any securities commission (or any agency or office performing like functions) of any State, but only to the extent that the person acts in such regulated capacity.

(2) DESCRIPTION OF ACTIVITIES.—Paragraph (1) shall not apply to any person to the extent such person is engaged in the offering or provision of any consumer financial product or service, or is otherwise subject to any enumerated consumer law or any law for which authorities are transferred under subtitle F or H.

(i) EXCLUSION FOR PERSONS REGULATED BY THE COMMISSION.—

(1) IN GENERAL.—No provision of this title may be construed as altering, amending, or affecting the authority of the Commission to adopt rules, initiate enforcement proceedings, or take any other action with respect to a person regulated by the Commission. The Bureau shall have no authority to exercise any power to enforce this title with respect to a person regulated by the Commission.

(2) CONSULTATION AND COORDINATION.—Notwithstanding paragraph (1), the Commission shall consult and coordinate, where feasible, with the Bureau with respect to any rule (including any advance notice of proposed rulemaking) regarding an investment product or service that is the same type of product as, or that competes directly with, a consumer financial product or service that is subject to the jurisdiction of the Bureau under this title or under any other law. In carrying out this paragraph, the agencies shall negotiate an agreement to establish procedures for such coordination, including procedures for providing advance notice to the Bureau when the Commission is initiating a rulemaking.

(j) EXCLUSION FOR PERSONS REGULATED BY THE COMMODITY FUTURES TRADING COMMISSION.—

(1) IN GENERAL.—No provision of this title shall be construed as altering, amending, or affecting the authority of the Commodity Futures Trading Commission to adopt rules, initiate enforcement proceedings, or take any other action with respect to a person regulated by the Commodity Futures Trading Commission. The Bureau shall have no authority to exercise any power to enforce this title with respect to a person regulated by the Commodity Futures Trading Commission.

(2) CONSULTATION AND COORDINATION.—Notwithstanding paragraph (1), the Commodity Futures Trading Commission shall consult and coordinate with the Bureau with respect to any rule (including any advance notice of proposed rulemaking) regarding a product or service that is the same type of product as, or that competes directly with, a consumer financial product or service that is subject to the jurisdiction of the Bureau under this title or under any other law.

(k) EXCLUSION FOR PERSONS REGULATED BY THE FARM CREDIT ADMINISTRATION.—

(1) IN GENERAL.—No provision of this title shall be construed as altering, amending, or affecting the authority of the Farm Credit Administration to adopt rules, initiate enforcement proceedings, or take any other action with respect to a person regulated by the Farm Credit Administration. The Bureau shall have no authority to exercise any power to enforce this title with respect to a person regulated by the Farm Credit Administration.

(2) DEFINITION.—For purposes of this subsection, the term "person regulated by the Farm Credit Administration" means any Farm Credit System institution that is chartered and subject to the provisions of the Farm Credit Act of 1971 (12 U.S.C. 2001 et seq.).

(l) EXCLUSION FOR ACTIVITIES RELATING TO CHARITABLE CONTRIBUTIONS.—

(1) IN GENERAL.—The Director and the Bureau may not exercise any rulemaking, supervisory, enforcement, or other authority, including authority to order penalties, over any activities related to the solicitation or making of voluntary contributions to a tax-exempt organization as recognized by the Internal Revenue Service, by any agent, volunteer, or representative of such organizations to the extent the organization, agent, volunteer, or representative thereof is soliciting or providing advice, information, education, or instruction to any donor or potential donor relating to a contribution to the organization.

(2) LIMITATION.—The exclusion in paragraph (1) does not apply to other activities not described in paragraph (1) that are the offering or provision of any consumer financial product or service, or are otherwise subject to any enumerated consumer law or any law for which authorities are transferred under subtitle F or H.

(m) INSURANCE.—The Bureau may not define as a financial product or service, by regulation or otherwise, engaging in the business of insurance.

(n) LIMITED AUTHORITY OF THE BUREAU.—Notwithstanding subsections (a) through (h) and (1), a person subject to or described in one or more of such provisions—

(1) may be a service provider; and

(2) may be subject to requests from, or requirements imposed by, the Bureau regarding information in order to carry out the responsibilities and functions of the Bureau and in accordance with section 1022, 1052, or 1053.

(o) NO AUTHORITY TO IMPOSE USURY LIMIT.—No provision of this title shall be construed as conferring authority on the Bureau to establish a usury limit applicable to an extension of credit offered or made by a covered person to a consumer, unless explicitly authorized by law.

(p) ATTORNEY GENERAL.—No provision of this title, including section 1024(c)(1), shall affect the authorities of the Attorney General under otherwise applicable provisions of law.

(q) SECRETARY OF THE TREASURY.—No provision of this title shall affect the authorities of the Secretary, including with respect to prescribing rules, initiating enforcement proceedings, or taking other actions with respect to a person that performs income tax preparation activities for consumers.

(r) DEPOSIT INSURANCE AND SHARE INSURANCE.—Nothing in this title shall affect the authority of the Corporation under the Federal Deposit Insurance Act or the National Credit Union Administration

Board under the Federal Credit Union Act as to matters related to deposit insurance and share insurance, respectively.

(s) FAIR HOUSING ACT.—No provision of this title shall be construed as affecting any authority arising under the Fair Housing Act.

[Explanation at ¶ 4580.]

[¶ 11,028] ACT SEC. 1028. AUTHORITY TO RESTRICT MANDATORY PRE-DISPUTE ARBITRATION.

(a) STUDY AND REPORT.—The Bureau shall conduct a study of, and shall provide a report to Congress concerning, the use of agreements providing for arbitration of any future dispute between covered persons and consumers in connection with the offering or providing of consumer financial products or services.

(b) FURTHER AUTHORITY.—The Bureau, by regulation, may prohibit or impose conditions or limitations on the use of an agreement between a covered person and a consumer for a consumer financial product or service providing for arbitration of any future dispute between the parties, if the Bureau finds that such a prohibition or imposition of conditions or limitations is in the public interest and for the protection of consumers. The findings in such rule shall be consistent with the study conducted under subsection (a).

(c) LIMITATION.—The authority described in subsection (b) may not be construed to prohibit or restrict a consumer from entering into a voluntary arbitration agreement with a covered person after a dispute has arisen.

(d) EFFECTIVE DATE.—Notwithstanding any other provision of law, any regulation prescribed by the Bureau under subsection (b) shall apply, consistent with the terms of the regulation, to any agreement between a consumer and a covered person entered into after the end of the 180-day period beginning on the effective date of the regulation, as established by the Bureau.

[Explanation at ¶ 4585.]

[¶ 11,029] ACT SEC. 1029. EXCLUSION FOR AUTO DEALERS.

(a) SALE, SERVICING, AND LEASING OF MOTOR VEHICLES EXCLUDED.—Except as permitted in subsection (b), the Bureau may not exercise any rulemaking, supervisory, enforcement or any other authority, including any authority to order assessments, over a motor vehicle dealer that is predominantly engaged in the sale and servicing of motor vehicles, the leasing and servicing of motor vehicles, or both.

(b) CERTAIN FUNCTIONS EXCEPTED.—Subsection (a) shall not apply to any person, to the extent that such person—

(1) provides consumers with any services related to residential or commercial mortgages or self-financing transactions involving real property;

(2) operates a line of business—

(A) that involves the extension of retail credit or retail leases involving motor vehicles; and

(B) in which—

(i) the extension of retail credit or retail leases are provided directly to consumers; and

(ii) the contract governing such extension of retail credit or retail leases is not routinely assigned to an unaffiliated third party finance or leasing source; or

(3) offers or provides a consumer financial product or service not involving or related to the sale, financing, leasing, rental, repair, refurbishment, maintenance, or other servicing of motor vehicles, motor vehicle parts, or any related or ancillary product or service.

(c) PRESERVATION OF AUTHORITIES OF OTHER AGENCIES.—Except as provided in subsections (b) and (d), nothing in this title, including subtitle F, shall be construed as modifying, limiting, or superseding the operation of any provision of Federal law, or otherwise affecting the authority of the Board of

Governors, the Federal Trade Commission, or any other Federal agency, with respect to a person described in subsection (a).

(d) FEDERAL TRADE COMMISSION AUTHORITY.—Notwithstanding section 18 of the Federal Trade Commission Act, the Federal Trade Commission is authorized to prescribe rules under sections 5 and 18(a)(1)(B) of the Federal Trade Commission Act. in accordance with section 553 of title 5, United States Code, with respect to a person described in subsection (a).

(e) COORDINATION WITH OFFICE OF SERVICE MEMBER AFFAIRS.—The Board of Governors and the Federal Trade Commission shall coordinate with the Office of Service Member Affairs, to ensure that—

(1) service members and their families are educated and empowered to make better informed decisions regarding consumer financial products and services offered by motor vehicle dealers, with a focus on motor vehicle dealers in the proximity of military installations; and

(2) complaints by service members and their families concerning such motor vehicle dealers are effectively monitored and responded to, and where appropriate, enforcement action is pursued by the authorized agencies.

(f) DEFINITIONS.—For purposes of this section, the following definitions shall apply:

(1) MOTOR VEHICLE.—The term "motor vehicle" means—

(A) any self-propelled vehicle designed for transporting persons or property on a street, highway, or other road;

(B) recreational boats and marine equipment;

(C) motorcycles;

(D) motor homes, recreational vehicle trailers, and slide-in campers, as those terms are defined in sections 571.3 and 575.103 (d) of title 49, Code of Federal Regulations, or any successor thereto; and

(E) other vehicles that are titled and sold through dealers.

(2) MOTOR VEHICLE DEALER.—The term "motor vehicle dealer" means any person or resident in the United States, or any territory of the United States, who—

(A) is licensed by a State, a territory of the United States, or the District of Columbia to engage in the sale of motor vehicles; and

(B) takes title to, holds an ownership in, or takes physical custody of motor vehicles.

[Explanation at ¶ 4590.]

[¶ 11,029A] ACT SEC. 1029A. EFFECTIVE DATE.

This subtitle shall become effective on the designated transfer date, except that sections 1022, 1024, and 1025(e) shall become effective on the date of enactment of this Act.

[Explanation at ¶ 4550.]

Subtitle C—Specific Bureau Authorities

[¶ 11,031] ACT SEC. 1031. PROHIBITING UNFAIR, DECEPTIVE, OR ABUSIVE ACTS OR PRACTICES.

(a) IN GENERAL.—The Bureau may take any action authorized under subtitle E to prevent a covered person or service provider from committing or engaging in an unfair, deceptive, or abusive act or practice under Federal law in connection with any transaction with a consumer for a consumer financial product or service, or the offering of a consumer financial product or service.

(b) RULEMAKING.—The Bureau may prescribe rules applicable to a covered person or service provider identifying as unlawful unfair, deceptive, or abusive acts or practices in connection with any transaction with a consumer for a consumer financial product or service, or the offering of a consumer financial product or service. Rules under this section may include requirements for the purpose of preventing such acts or practices.

(c) UNFAIRNESS.—

(1) IN GENERAL.—The Bureau shall have no authority under this section to declare an act or practice in connection with a transaction with a consumer for a consumer financial product or service, or the offering of a consumer financial product or service, to be unlawful on the grounds that such act or practice is unfair, unless the Bureau has a reasonable basis to conclude that—

(A) the act or practice causes or is likely to cause substantial injury to consumers which is not reasonably avoidable by consumers; and

(B) such substantial injury is not outweighed by countervailing benefits to consumers or to competition.

(2) CONSIDERATION OF PUBLIC POLICIES.—In determining whether an act or practice is unfair, the Bureau may consider established public policies as evidence to be considered with all other evidence. Such public policy considerations may not serve as a primary basis for such determination.

(d) ABUSIVE.—The Bureau shall have no authority under this section to declare an act or practice abusive in connection with the provision of a consumer financial product or service, unless the act or practice—

(1) materially interferes with the ability of a consumer to understand a term or condition of a consumer financial product or service; or

(2) takes unreasonable advantage of—

(A) a lack of understanding on the part of the consumer of the material risks, costs, or conditions of the product or service;

(B) the inability of the consumer to protect the interests of the consumer in selecting or using a consumer financial product or service; or

(C) the reasonable reliance by the consumer on a covered person to act in the interests of the consumer.

(e) CONSULTATION.—In prescribing rules under this section, the Bureau shall consult with the Federal banking agencies, or other Federal agencies, as appropriate, concerning the consistency of the proposed rule with prudential, market, or systemic objectives administered by such agencies.

(f) CONSIDERATION OF SEASONAL INCOME.—The rules of the Bureau under this section shall provide, with respect to an extension of credit secured by residential real estate or a dwelling, if documented income of the borrower, including income from a small business, is a repayment source for an extension of credit secured by residential real estate or a dwelling, the creditor may consider the seasonality and irregularity of such income in the underwriting of and scheduling of payments for such credit.

[Explanation at ¶ 4595]

[¶ 11,032] ACT SEC. 1032. DISCLOSURES.

(a) IN GENERAL.—The Bureau may prescribe rules to ensure that the features of any consumer financial product or service, both initially and over the term of the product or service, are fully, accurately, and effectively disclosed to consumers in a manner that permits consumers to understand the costs, benefits, and risks associated with the product or service, in light of the facts and circumstances.

(b) MODEL DISCLOSURES.—

(1) IN GENERAL.—Any final rule prescribed by the Bureau under this section requiring disclosures may include a model form that may be used at the option of the covered person for provision of the required disclosures.

(2) FORMAT.—A model form issued pursuant to paragraph (1) shall contain a clear and conspicuous disclosure that, at a minimum—

(A) uses plain language comprehensible to consumers;

(B) contains a clear format and design, such as an easily readable type font; and

(C) succinctly explains the information that must be communicated to the consumer.

(3) CONSUMER TESTING.—Any model form issued pursuant to this subsection shall be validated through consumer testing.

(c) BASIS FOR RULEMAKING.—In prescribing rules under this section, the Bureau shall consider available evidence about consumer awareness, understanding of, and responses to disclosures or communications about the risks, costs, and benefits of consumer financial products or services.

(d) SAFE HARBOR.—Any covered person that uses a model form included with a rule issued under this section shall be deemed to be in compliance with the disclosure requirements of this section with respect to such model form.

(e) TRIAL DISCLOSURE PROGRAMS.—

(1) IN GENERAL.—The Bureau may permit a covered person to conduct a trial program that is limited in time and scope, subject to specified standards and procedures, for the purpose of providing trial disclosures to consumers that are designed to improve upon any model form issued pursuant to subsection (b)(1), or any other model form issued to implement an enumerated statute, as applicable.

(2) SAFE HARBOR.—The standards and procedures issued by the Bureau shall be designed to encourage covered persons to conduct trial disclosure programs. For the purposes of administering this subsection, the Bureau may establish a limited period during which a covered person conducting a trial disclosure program shall be deemed to be in compliance with, or may be exempted from, a requirement of a rule or an enumerated consumer law.

(3) PUBLIC DISCLOSURE.—The rules of the Bureau shall provide for public disclosure of trial disclosure programs, which public disclosure may be limited, to the extent necessary to encourage covered persons to conduct effective trials.

(f) COMBINED MORTGAGE LOAN DISCLOSURE.—Not later than 1 year after the designated transfer date, the Bureau shall propose for public comment rules and model disclosures that combine the disclosures required under the Truth in Lending Act and sections 4 and 5 of the Real Estate Settlement Procedures Act of 1974, into a single, integrated disclosure for mortgage loan transactions covered by those laws, unless the Bureau determines that any proposal issued by the Board of Governors and the Secretary of Housing and Urban Development carries out the same purpose.

[Explanation at ¶ 4600.]

[¶ 11,033] ACT SEC. 1033. CONSUMER RIGHTS TO ACCESS INFORMATION.

(a) IN GENERAL.—Subject to rules prescribed by the Bureau, a covered person shall make available to a consumer, upon request, information in the control or possession of the covered person concerning the consumer financial product or service that the consumer obtained from such covered person, including information relating to any transaction, series of transactions, or to the account including costs, charges and usage data. The information shall be made available in an electronic form usable by consumers.

(b) EXCEPTIONS.—A covered person may not be required by this section to make available to the consumer—

(1) any confidential commercial information, including an algorithm used to derive credit scores or other risk scores or predictors;

(2) any information collected by the covered person for the purpose of preventing fraud or money laundering, or detecting, or making any report regarding other unlawful or potentially unlawful conduct;

(3) any information required to be kept confidential by any other provision of law; or

(4) any information that the covered person cannot retrieve in the ordinary course of its business with respect to that information.

(c) NO DUTY TO MAINTAIN RECORDS.—Nothing in this section shall be construed to impose any duty on a covered person to maintain or keep any information about a consumer.

(d) STANDARDIZED FORMATS FOR DATA.—The Bureau, by rule, shall prescribe standards applicable to covered persons to promote the development and use of standardized formats for information, including through the use of machine readable files, to be made available to consumers under this section.

(e) CONSULTATION.—The Bureau shall, when prescribing any rule under this section, consult with the Federal banking agencies and the Federal Trade Commission to ensure, to the extent appropriate, that the rules—

(1) impose substantively similar requirements on covered persons;

(2) take into account conditions under which covered persons do business both in the United States and in other countries; and

(3) do not require or promote the use of any particular technology in order to develop systems for compliance.

[Explanation at ¶ 4605.]

[¶ 11,034] ACT SEC. 1034. RESPONSE TO CONSUMER COMPLAINTS AND INQUIRIES.

(a) TIMELY REGULATOR RESPONSE TO CONSUMERS.—The Bureau shall establish, in consultation with the appropriate Federal regulatory agencies, reasonable procedures to provide a timely response to consumers, in writing where appropriate, to complaints against, or inquiries concerning, a covered person, including—

(1) steps that have been taken by the regulator in response to the complaint or inquiry of the consumer;

(2) any responses received by the regulator from the covered person; and

(3) any follow-up actions or planned follow-up actions by the regulator in response to the complaint or inquiry of the consumer.

(b) TIMELY RESPONSE TO REGULATOR BY COVERED PERSON.—A covered person subject to supervision and primary enforcement by the Bureau pursuant to section 1025 shall provide a timely response, in writing where appropriate, to the Bureau, the prudential regulators, and any other agency having jurisdiction over such covered person concerning a consumer complaint or inquiry, including—

(1) steps that have been taken by the covered person to respond to the complaint or inquiry of the consumer;

(2) responses received by the covered person from the consumer; and

(3) follow-up actions or planned follow-up actions by the covered person to respond to the complaint or inquiry of the consumer.

(c) PROVISION OF INFORMATION TO CONSUMERS.—

(1) IN GENERAL.—A covered person subject to supervision and primary enforcement by the Bureau pursuant to section 1025 shall, in a timely manner, comply with a consumer request for information in the control or possession of such covered person concerning the consumer financial product or service that the consumer obtained from such covered person, including supporting written documentation, concerning the account of the consumer.

(2) EXCEPTIONS.—A covered person subject to supervision and primary enforcement by the Bureau pursuant to section 1025, a prudential regulator, and any other agency having jurisdiction over a covered person subject to supervision and primary enforcement by the Bureau pursuant to section 1025 may not be required by this section to make available to the consumer—

(A) any confidential commercial information, including an algorithm used to derive credit scores or other risk scores or predictors;

(B) any information collected by the covered person for the purpose of preventing fraud or money laundering, or detecting or making any report regarding other unlawful or potentially unlawful conduct;

(C) any information required to be kept confidential by any other provision of law; or

(D) any nonpublic or confidential information, including confidential supervisory information.

(d) AGREEMENTS WITH OTHER AGENCIES.—The Bureau shall enter into a memorandum of understanding with any affected Federal regulatory agency regarding procedures by which any covered person, and the prudential regulators, and any other agency having jurisdiction over a covered person, including the Secretary of the Department of Housing and Urban Development and the Secretary of Education, shall comply with this section.

[Explanation at ¶4610.]

[¶11,035] ACT SEC. 1035. PRIVATE EDUCATION LOAN OMBUDSMAN.

(a) ESTABLISHMENT.—The Secretary, in consultation with the Director, shall designate a Private Education Loan Ombudsman (in this section referred to as the "Ombudsman") within the Bureau, to provide timely assistance to borrowers of private education loans.

(b) PUBLIC INFORMATION.—The Secretary and the Director shall disseminate information about the availability and functions of the Ombudsman to borrowers and potential borrowers, as well as institutions of higher education, lenders, guaranty agencies, loan servicers, and other participants in private education student loan programs.

(c) FUNCTIONS OF OMBUDSMAN.—The Ombudsman designated under this subsection shall—

(1) in accordance with regulations of the Director, receive, review, and attempt to resolve informally complaints from borrowers of loans described in subsection (a), including, as appropriate, attempts to resolve such complaints in collaboration with the Department of Education and with institutions of higher education, lenders, guaranty agencies, loan servicers, and other participants in private education loan programs;

(2) not later than 90 days after the designated transfer date, establish a memorandum of understanding with the student loan ombudsman established under section 141(f) of the Higher Education Act of 1965 (20 U.S.C. 1018(f)), to ensure coordination in providing assistance to and serving borrowers seeking to resolve complaints related to their private education or Federal student loans;

(3) compile and analyze data on borrower complaints regarding private education loans; and

(4) make appropriate recommendations to the Director, the Secretary, the Secretary of Education, the Committee on Banking, Housing, and Urban Affairs and the Committee on Health, Education, Labor, and Pensions of the Senate and the Committee on Financial Services and the Committee on Education and Labor of the House of Representatives.

(d) ANNUAL REPORTS.—

(1) IN GENERAL.—The Ombudsman shall prepare an annual report that describes the activities, and evaluates the effectiveness of the Ombudsman during the preceding year.

(2) SUBMISSION.—The report required by paragraph (1) shall be submitted on the same date annually to the Secretary, the Secretary of Education, the Committee on Banking, Housing, and Urban Affairs and the Committee on Health, Education, Labor, and Pensions of the Senate and the Committee on Financial Services and the Committee on Education and Labor of the House of Representatives.

(e) DEFINITIONS.—For purposes of this section, the terms "private education loan" and "institution of higher education" have the same meanings as in section 140 of the Truth in Lending Act (15 U.S.C. 1650).

[Explanation at ¶ 4615.]

[¶ 11,036] ACT SEC. 1036. PROHIBITED ACTS.

(a) IN GENERAL.—It shall be unlawful for—

(1) any covered person or service provider—

(A) to offer or provide to a consumer any financial product or service not in conformity with Federal consumer financial law, or otherwise commit any act or omission in violation of a Federal consumer financial law; or

(B) to engage in any unfair, deceptive, or abusive act or practice;

(2) any covered person or service provider to fail or refuse, as required by Federal consumer financial law, or any rule or order issued by the Bureau thereunder—

(A) to permit access to or copying of records;

(B) to establish or maintain records; or

(C) to make reports or provide information to the Bureau; or

(3) any person to knowingly or recklessly provide substantial assistance to a covered person or service provider in violation of the provisions of section 1031, or any rule or order issued thereunder, and notwithstanding any provision of this title, the provider of such substantial assistance shall be deemed to be in violation of that section to the same extent as the person to whom such assistance is provided.

(b) EXCEPTION.—No person shall be held to have violated subsection (a)(1) solely by virtue of providing or selling time or space to a covered person or service provider placing an advertisement.

[Explanation at ¶ 4620]

[¶ 11,037] ACT SEC. 1037. EFFECTIVE DATE.

This subtitle shall take effect on the designated transfer date.

[Explanation at ¶ 4595.]

Subtitle D—Preservation of State Law

[¶ 11,041] ACT SEC. 1041. RELATION TO STATE LAW.

(a) IN GENERAL.—

(1) RULE OF CONSTRUCTION.—This title, other than sections 1044 through 1048, may not be construed as annulling, altering, or affecting, or exempting any person subject to the provisions of this title from complying with, the statutes, regulations, orders, or interpretations in effect in any State, except to the extent that any such provision of law is inconsistent with the provisions of this title, and then only to the extent of the inconsistency.

(2) GREATER PROTECTION UNDER STATE LAW.—For purposes of this subsection, a statute, regulation, order, or interpretation in effect in any State is not inconsistent with the provisions of this title if the protection that such statute, regulation, order, or interpretation affords to consumers is greater than the protection provided under this title. A determination regarding whether a statute, regulation, order, or interpretation in effect in any State is inconsistent with the provisions of this title may be made by the Bureau on its own motion or in response to a nonfrivolous petition initiated by any interested person.

(b) RELATION TO OTHER PROVISIONS OF ENUMERATED CONSUMER LAWS THAT RELATE TO STATE LAW.—No provision of this title, except as provided in section 1083, shall be construed as modifying, limiting, or superseding the operation of any provision of an enumerated consumer law that relates to the application of a law in effect in any State with respect to such Federal law.

(c) ADDITIONAL CONSUMER PROTECTION REGULATIONS IN RESPONSE TO STATE ACTION.—

(1) NOTICE OF PROPOSED RULE REQUIRED.—The Bureau shall issue a notice of proposed rulemaking whenever a majority of the States has enacted a resolution in support of the establishment or modification of a consumer protection regulation by the Bureau.

(2) BUREAU CONSIDERATIONS REQUIRED FOR ISSUANCE OF FINAL REGULATION.—Before prescribing a final regulation based upon a notice issued pursuant to paragraph (1), the Bureau shall take into account whether—

(A) the proposed regulation would afford greater protection to consumers than any existing regulation;

(B) the intended benefits of the proposed regulation for consumers would outweigh any increased costs or inconveniences for consumers, and would not discriminate unfairly against any category or class of consumers; and

(C) a Federal banking agency has advised that the proposed regulation is likely to present an unacceptable safety and soundness risk to insured depository institutions.

(3) EXPLANATION OF CONSIDERATIONS.—The Bureau—

(A) shall include a discussion of the considerations required in paragraph (2) in the Federal Register notice of a final regulation prescribed pursuant to this subsection; and

(B) whenever the Bureau determines not to prescribe a final regulation, shall publish an explanation of such determination in the Federal Register, and provide a copy of such explanation to each State that enacted a resolution in support of the proposed regulation, the Committee on Banking, Housing, and Urban Affairs of the Senate, and the Committee on Financial Services of the House of Representatives.

(4) RESERVATION OF AUTHORITY.—No provision of this subsection shall be construed as limiting or restricting the authority of the Bureau to enhance consumer protection standards established pursuant to this title in response to its own motion or in response to a request by any other interested person.

(5) RULE OF CONSTRUCTION.—No provision of this subsection shall be construed as exempting the Bureau from complying with subchapter II of chapter 5 of title 5, United States Code.

(6) DEFINITION.—For purposes of this subsection, the term "consumer protection regulation" means a regulation that the Bureau is authorized to prescribe under the Federal consumer financial laws.

[Explanation at ¶ 4625.]

[¶ 11,042] ACT SEC. 1042. PRESERVATION OF ENFORCEMENT POWERS OF STATES.

(a) IN GENERAL.—

(1) ACTION BY STATE.—Except as provided in paragraph (2), the attorney general (or the equivalent thereof) of any State may bring a civil action in the name of such State in any district court of the United States in that State or in State court that is located in that State and that has jurisdiction over the defendant, to enforce provisions of this title or regulations issued under this title, and to secure remedies under provisions of this title or remedies otherwise provided under other law. A State regulator may bring a civil action or other appropriate proceeding to enforce the provisions of this title or regulations issued under this title with respect to any entity that is State-chartered, incorporated, licensed, or otherwise authorized to do business under State law (except as provided in paragraph (2)), and to secure remedies under provisions of this title or remedies otherwise provided under other provisions of law with respect to such an entity.

(2) ACTION BY STATE AGAINST NATIONAL BANK OR FEDERAL SAVINGS ASSOCIATION TO ENFORCE RULES.—

(A) IN GENERAL.—Except as permitted under subparagraph (B), the attorney general (or equivalent thereof) of any State may not bring a civil action in the name of such State against a national bank or Federal savings association to enforce a provision of this title.

(B) ENFORCEMENT OF RULES PERMITTED.—The attorney general (or the equivalent thereof) of any State may bring a civil action in the name of such State against a national bank or Federal savings association in any district court of the United States in the State or in State court that is located in that State and that has jurisdiction over the defendant to enforce a regulation prescribed by the Bureau under a provision of this title and to secure remedies under provisions of this title or remedies otherwise provided under other law.

(3) RULE OF CONSTRUCTION.—No provision of this title shall be construed as modifying, limiting, or superseding the operation of any provision of an enumerated consumer law that relates to the authority of a State attorney general or State regulator to enforce such Federal law.

(b) CONSULTATION REQUIRED.—

(1) NOTICE.—

(A) IN GENERAL.—Before initiating any action in a court or other administrative or regulatory proceeding against any covered person as authorized by subsection (a) to enforce any provision of this title, including any regulation prescribed by the Bureau under this title, a State attorney general or State regulator shall timely provide a copy of the complete complaint to be filed and written notice describing such action or proceeding to the Bureau and the prudential regulator, if any, or the designee thereof.

(B) EMERGENCY ACTION.—If prior notice is not practicable, the State attorney general or State regulator shall provide a copy of the complete complaint and the notice to the Bureau and the prudential regulator, if any, immediately upon instituting the action or proceeding.

(C) CONTENTS OF NOTICE.—The notification required under this paragraph shall, at a minimum, describe—

(i) the identity of the parties;

(ii) the alleged facts underlying the proceeding; and

(iii) whether there may be a need to coordinate the prosecution of the proceeding so as not to interfere with any action, including any rulemaking, undertaken by the Bureau, a prudential regulator, or another Federal agency.

(2) BUREAU RESPONSE.—In any action described in paragraph (1), the Bureau may—

(A) intervene in the action as a party;

(B) upon intervening—

(i) remove the action to the appropriate United States district court, if the action was not originally brought there; and

(ii) be heard on all matters arising in the action; and

(C) appeal any order or judgment, to the same extent as any other party in the proceeding may.

(c) REGULATIONS.—The Bureau shall prescribe regulations to implement the requirements of this section and, from time to time, provide guidance in order to further coordinate actions with the State attorneys general and other regulators.

(d) PRESERVATION OF STATE AUTHORITY.—

(1) STATE CLAIMS.—No provision of this section shall be construed as altering, limiting, or affecting the authority of a State attorney general or any other regulatory or enforcement agency or authority to bring an action or other regulatory proceeding arising solely under the law in effect in that State.

(2) STATE SECURITIES REGULATORS.—No provision of this title shall be construed as altering, limiting, or affecting the authority of a State securities commission (or any agency or office performing like functions) under State law to adopt rules, initiate enforcement proceedings, or take any other action with respect to a person regulated by such commission or authority.

(3) STATE INSURANCE REGULATORS.—No provision of this title shall be construed as altering, limiting, or affecting the authority of a State insurance commission or State insurance regulator under State law to adopt rules, initiate enforcement proceedings, or take any other action with respect to a person regulated by such commission or regulator.

[Explanation at ¶ 4630.]

[¶ 11,043] ACT SEC. 1043. PRESERVATION OF EXISTING CONTRACTS.

This title, and regulations, orders, guidance, and interpretations prescribed, issued, or established by the Bureau, shall not be construed to alter or affect the applicability of any regulation, order, guidance, or interpretation prescribed, issued, and established by the Comptroller of the Currency or the Director of the Office of Thrift Supervision regarding the applicability of State law under Federal banking law to any contract entered into on or before the date of enactment of this Act, by national banks, Federal savings associations, or subsidiaries thereof that are regulated and supervised by the Comptroller of the Currency or the Director of the Office of Thrift Supervision, respectively.

[Explanation at ¶ 4635.]

[¶ 11,044] ACT SEC. 1044. STATE LAW PREEMPTION STANDARDS FOR NATIONAL BANKS AND SUBSIDIARIES CLARIFIED.

(a) IN GENERAL.—Chapter one of title LXII of the Revised Statutes of the United States (12 U.S.C. 21 et seq.) is amended by inserting after section 5136B the following new section:

"SEC. 5136C. STATE LAW PREEMPTION STANDARDS FOR NATIONAL BANKS AND SUBSIDIARIES CLARIFIED.

"(a) DEFINITIONS.—For purposes of this section, the following definitions shall apply:

"(1) NATIONAL BANK.—The term 'national bank' includes—

"(A) any bank organized under the laws of the United States; and

"(B) any Federal branch established in accordance with the International Banking Act of 1978.

"(2) STATE CONSUMER FINANCIAL LAWS.—The term 'State consumer financial law' means a State law that does not directly or indirectly discriminate against national banks and that directly and specifically regulates the manner, content, or terms and conditions of any financial transaction (as may be authorized for national banks to engage in), or any account related thereto, with respect to a consumer.

"(3) OTHER DEFINITIONS.—The terms 'affiliate', 'subsidiary', 'includes', and 'including' have the same meanings as in section 3 of the Federal Deposit Insurance Act.

"(b) PREEMPTION STANDARD.—

"(1) IN GENERAL.—State consumer financial laws are preempted, only if—

"(A) application of a State consumer financial law would have a discriminatory effect on national banks, in comparison with the effect of the law on a bank chartered by that State;

"(B) in accordance with the legal standard for preemption in the decision of the Supreme Court of the United States in Barnett Bank of Marion County, N. A. v. Nelson, Florida Insurance Commissioner, et al., 517 U.S. 25 (1996), the State consumer financial law prevents or significantly interferes with the exercise by the national bank of its powers; and any preemption determination under this subparagraph may be made by a court, or by regulation or order of the Comptroller of the Currency on a case-by-case basis, in accordance with applicable law; or

"(C) the State consumer financial law is preempted by a provision of Federal law other than this title.

"(2) SAVINGS CLAUSE.—This title and section 24 of the Federal Reserve Act (12 U.S.C. 371) do not preempt, annul, or affect the applicability of any State law to any subsidiary or affiliate of a national bank (other than a subsidiary or affiliate that is chartered as a national bank).

"(3) CASE-BY-CASE BASIS.—

"(A) DEFINITION.—As used in this section the term 'case-by-case basis' refers to a determination pursuant to this section made by the Comptroller concerning the impact of a particular State consumer financial law on any national bank that is subject to that law, or the law of any other State with substantively equivalent terms.

"(B) CONSULTATION.—When making a determination on a case-by-case basis that a State consumer financial law of another State has substantively equivalent terms as one that the Comptroller is preempting, the Comptroller shall first consult with the Bureau of Consumer Financial Protection and shall take the views of the Bureau into account when making the determination.

"(4) RULE OF CONSTRUCTION.—This title does not occupy the field in any area of State law.

"(5) STANDARDS OF REVIEW.—

"(A) PREEMPTION.—A court reviewing any determinations made by the Comptroller regarding preemption of a State law by this title or section 24 of the Federal Reserve Act (12 U.S.C. 371) shall assess the validity of such determinations, depending upon the thoroughness evident in the consideration of the agency, the validity of the reasoning of the agency, the consistency with other valid determinations made by the agency, and other factors which the court finds persuasive and relevant to its decision.

"(B) SAVINGS CLAUSE.—Except as provided in subparagraph (A), nothing in this section shall affect the deference that a court may afford to the Comptroller in making determinations regarding the meaning or interpretation of title LXII of the Revised Statutes of the United States or other Federal laws.

"(6) COMPTROLLER DETERMINATION NOT DELEGABLE.—Any regulation, order, or determination made by the Comptroller of the Currency under paragraph (1)(B) shall be made by the Comptroller, and shall not be delegable to another officer or employee of the Comptroller of the Currency.

"(c) SUBSTANTIAL EVIDENCE.—No regulation or order of the Comptroller of the Currency prescribed under subsection (b)(1)(B), shall be interpreted or applied so as to invalidate, or otherwise declare inapplicable to a national bank, the provision of the State consumer financial law, unless substantial evidence, made on the record of the proceeding, supports the specific finding regarding the preemption of such provision in accordance with the legal standard of the decision of the Supreme Court of the United States in Barnett Bank of Marion County, N.A. v. Nelson, Florida Insurance Commissioner, et al., 517 U.S. 25 (1996).

"(d) PERIODIC REVIEW OF PREEMPTION DETERMINATIONS.—

"(1) IN GENERAL.—The Comptroller of the Currency shall periodically conduct a review, through notice and public comment, of each determination that a provision of Federal law preempts a State consumer financial law. The agency shall conduct such review within the 5-year period after prescribing or otherwise issuing such determination, and at least once during each 5-year period thereafter. After conducting the review of, and inspecting the comments made on, the determination, the agency shall publish a notice in the Federal Register announcing the decision to continue or rescind the determination or a proposal to amend the determination. Any such notice of a proposal to amend a determination and the subsequent resolution of such proposal shall comply with the procedures set forth in subsections (a) and (b) of section 5244 of the Revised Statutes of the United States (12 U.S.C. 43 (a), (b)).

"(2) REPORTS TO CONGRESS.—At the time of issuing a review conducted under paragraph (1), the Comptroller of the Currency shall submit a report regarding such review to the Committee on Financial Services of the House of Representatives and the Committee on Banking, Housing, and Urban Affairs of the Senate. The report submitted to the respective committees shall address whether the agency intends to continue, rescind, or propose to amend any determination that a provision of Federal law preempts a State consumer financial law, and the reasons therefor.

"(e) APPLICATION OF STATE CONSUMER FINANCIAL LAW TO SUBSIDIARIES AND AFFILIATES.—Notwithstanding any provision of this title or section 24 of Federal Reserve Act (12 U.S.C. 371), a State consumer financial law shall apply to a subsidiary or affiliate of a national bank (other than a subsidiary or affiliate that is chartered as a national bank) to the same extent that the State consumer financial law applies to any person, corporation, or other entity subject to such State law.

"(f) PRESERVATION OF POWERS RELATED TO CHARGING INTEREST.—No provision of this title shall be construed as altering or otherwise affecting the authority conferred by section 5197 of the Revised Statutes of the United States (12 U.S.C. 85) for the charging of interest by a national bank at the rate allowed by the laws of the State, territory, or district where the bank is located, including with respect to the meaning of 'interest' under such provision.

"(g) TRANSPARENCY OF OCC PREEMPTION DETERMINATIONS.—The Comptroller of the Currency shall publish and update no less frequently than quarterly, a list of preemption determinations by the Comptroller of the Currency then in effect that identifies the activities and practices covered by each determination and the requirements and constraints determined to be preempted.".

(b) CLERICAL AMENDMENT.—The table of sections for chapter one of title LXII of the Revised Statutes of the United States is amended by inserting after the item relating to section 5136B the following new item:

"Sec. 5136C. State law preemption standards for national banks and subsidiaries clarified.".

[Explanation at ¶ 4640.]

[¶ 11,045] ACT SEC. 1045. CLARIFICATION OF LAW APPLICABLE TO NONDEPOSITORY INSTITUTION SUBSIDIARIES.

Section 5136C of the Revised Statutes of the United States (as added by this subtitle) is amended by adding at the end the following:

"(h) CLARIFICATION OF LAW APPLICABLE TO NONDEPOSITORY INSTITUTION SUBSIDIARIES AND AFFILIATES OF NATIONAL BANKS.—

"(1) DEFINITIONS.—For purposes of this subsection, the terms 'depository institution', 'subsidiary', and 'affiliate' have the same meanings as in section 3 of the Federal Deposit Insurance Act.

"(2) RULE OF CONSTRUCTION.—No provision of this title or section 24 of the Federal Reserve Act (12 U.S.C. 371) shall be construed as preempting, annulling, or affecting the applicability of State law to any subsidiary, affiliate, or agent of a national bank (other than a subsidiary, affiliate, or agent that is chartered as a national bank).".

[Explanation at ¶ 4645.]

[¶ 11,046] ACT SEC. 1046. STATE LAW PREEMPTION STANDARDS FOR FEDERAL SAVINGS ASSOCIATIONS AND SUBSIDIARIES CLARIFIED.

(a) IN GENERAL.—The Home Owners' Loan Act (12 U.S.C. 1461 et seq.) is amended by inserting after section 5 the following new section:

"SEC. 6. STATE LAW PREEMPTION STANDARDS FOR FEDERAL SAVINGS ASSOCIATIONS CLARIFIED.

"(a) IN GENERAL.—Any determination by a court or by the Director or any successor officer or agency regarding the relation of State law to a provision of this Act or any regulation or order prescribed under this Act shall be made in accordance with the laws and legal standards applicable to national banks regarding the preemption of State law.

"(b) PRINCIPLES OF CONFLICT PREEMPTION APPLICABLE.—Notwithstanding the authorities granted under sections 4 and 5, this Act does not occupy the field in any area of State law.".

(b) CLERICAL AMENDMENT.—The table of sections for the Home Owners' Loan Act (12 U.S.C. 1461 et seq.) is amended by striking the item relating to section 6 and inserting the following new item:

"Sec. 6. State law preemption standards for Federal savings associations and subsidiaries clarified.".

Title X—Consumer Financial Protection

[Explanation at ¶ 4650.]

[¶ 11,047] ACT SEC. 1047. VISITORIAL STANDARDS FOR NATIONAL BANKS AND SAVINGS ASSOCIATIONS.

(a) NATIONAL BANKS.—Section 5136C of the Revised Statutes of the United States (as added by this subtitle) is amended by adding at the end the following:

"(i) VISITORIAL POWERS.—

"(1) IN GENERAL.—In accordance with the decision of the Supreme Court of the United States in Cuomo v. Clearing House Assn., L. L. C. (129 S. Ct. 2710 (2009)), no provision of this title which relates to visitorial powers or otherwise limits or restricts the visitorial authority to which any national bank is subject shall be construed as limiting or restricting the authority of any attorney general (or other chief law enforcement officer) of any State to bring an action against a national bank in a court of appropriate jurisdiction to enforce an applicable law and to seek relief as authorized by such law.

"(j) ENFORCEMENT ACTIONS.—The ability of the Comptroller of the Currency to bring an enforcement action under this title or section 5 of the Federal Trade Commission Act does not preclude any private party from enforcing rights granted under Federal or State law in the courts.".

(b) SAVINGS ASSOCIATIONS.—Section 6 of the Home Owners' Loan Act (as added by this title) is amended by adding at the end the following:

"(c) VISITORIAL POWERS.—The provisions of sections 5136C(i) of the Revised Statutes of the United States shall apply to Federal savings associations, and any subsidiary thereof, to the same extent and in the same manner as if such savings associations, or subsidiaries thereof, were national banks or subsidiaries of national banks, respectively."

"(d) ENFORCEMENT ACTIONS.—The ability of the Comptroller of the Currency to bring an enforcement action under this Act or section 5 of the Federal Trade Commission Act does not preclude any private party from enforcing rights granted under Federal or State law in the courts.".

[Explanation at ¶ 4655.]

[¶ 11,048] ACT SEC. 1048. EFFECTIVE DATE.

This subtitle shall become effective on the designated transfer date.

[Explanation at ¶ 4625.]

Subtitle E—Enforcement Powers

[¶ 11,051] ACT SEC. 1051. DEFINITIONS.

For purposes of this subtitle, the following definitions shall apply:

(1) BUREAU INVESTIGATION.—The term "Bureau investigation" means any inquiry conducted by a Bureau investigator for the purpose of ascertaining whether any person is or has been engaged in any conduct that is a violation, as defined in this section.

(2) BUREAU INVESTIGATOR.—The term "Bureau investigator" means any attorney or investigator employed by the Bureau who is charged with the duty of enforcing or carrying into effect any Federal consumer financial law.

(3) CUSTODIAN.—The term "custodian" means the custodian or any deputy custodian designated by the Bureau.

(4) DOCUMENTARY MATERIAL.—The term "documentary material" includes the original or any copy of any book, document, record, report, memorandum, paper, communication, tabulation, chart, logs, electronic files, or other data or data compilations stored in any medium.

(5) VIOLATION.—The term "violation" means any act or omission that, if proved, would constitute a violation of any provision of Federal consumer financial law.

[Explanation at ¶4660.]

[¶11,052] ACT SEC. 1052. INVESTIGATIONS AND ADMINISTRATIVE DISCOVERY.

(a) JOINT INVESTIGATIONS.—

(1) IN GENERAL.—The Bureau or, where appropriate, a Bureau investigator, may engage in joint investigations and requests for information, as authorized under this title.

(2) FAIR LENDING.—The authority under paragraph (1) includes matters relating to fair lending, and where appropriate, joint investigations with, and requests for information from, the Secretary of Housing and Urban Development, the Attorney General of the United States, or both.

(b) SUBPOENAS.—

(1) IN GENERAL.—The Bureau or a Bureau investigator may issue subpoenas for the attendance and testimony of witnesses and the production of relevant papers, books, documents, or other material in connection with hearings under this title.

(2) FAILURE TO OBEY.—In the case of contumacy or refusal to obey a subpoena issued pursuant to this paragraph and served upon any person, the district court of the United States for any district in which such person is found, resides, or transacts business, upon application by the Bureau or a Bureau investigator and after notice to such person, may issue an order requiring such person to appear and give testimony or to appear and produce documents or other material.

(3) CONTEMPT.—Any failure to obey an order of the court under this subsection may be punished by the court as a contempt thereof.

(c) DEMANDS.—

(1) IN GENERAL.—Whenever the Bureau has reason to believe that any person may be in possession, custody, or control of any documentary material or tangible things, or may have any information, relevant to a violation, the Bureau may, before the institution of any proceedings under the Federal consumer financial law, issue in writing, and cause to be served upon such person, a civil investigative demand requiring such person to—

(A) produce such documentary material for inspection and copying or reproduction in the form or medium requested by the Bureau;

(B) submit such tangible things;

(C) file written reports or answers to questions;

(D) give oral testimony concerning documentary material, tangible things, or other information; or

(E) furnish any combination of such material, answers, or testimony.

(2) REQUIREMENTS.—Each civil investigative demand shall state the nature of the conduct constituting the alleged violation which is under investigation and the provision of law applicable to such violation.

(3) PRODUCTION OF DOCUMENTS.—Each civil investigative demand for the production of documentary material shall—

(A) describe each class of documentary material to be produced under the demand with such definiteness and certainty as to permit such material to be fairly identified;

(B) prescribe a return date or dates which will provide a reasonable period of time within which the material so demanded may be assembled and made available for inspection and copying or reproduction; and

(C) identify the custodian to whom such material shall be made available.

(4) PRODUCTION OF THINGS.—Each civil investigative demand for the submission of tangible things shall—

(A) describe each class of tangible things to be submitted under the demand with such definiteness and certainty as to permit such things to be fairly identified;

(B) prescribe a return date or dates which will provide a reasonable period of time within which the things so demanded may be assembled and submitted; and

(C) identify the custodian to whom such things shall be submitted.

(5) DEMAND FOR WRITTEN REPORTS OR ANSWERS.—Each civil investigative demand for written reports or answers to questions shall—

(A) propound with definiteness and certainty the reports to be produced or the questions to be answered;

(B) prescribe a date or dates at which time written reports or answers to questions shall be submitted; and

(C) identify the custodian to whom such reports or answers shall be submitted.

(6) ORAL TESTIMONY.—Each civil investigative demand for the giving of oral testimony shall—

(A) prescribe a date, time, and place at which oral testimony shall be commenced; and

(B) identify a Bureau investigator who shall conduct the investigation and the custodian to whom the transcript of such investigation shall be submitted.

(7) SERVICE.—Any civil investigative demand issued, and any enforcement petition filed, under this section may be served—

(A) by any Bureau investigator at any place within the territorial jurisdiction of any court of the United States; and

(B) upon any person who is not found within the territorial jurisdiction of any court of the United States—

(i) in such manner as the Federal Rules of Civil Procedure prescribe for service in a foreign nation; and

(ii) to the extent that the courts of the United States have authority to assert jurisdiction over such person, consistent with due process, the United States District Court for the District of Columbia shall have the same jurisdiction to take any action respecting compliance with this section by such person that such district court would have if such person were personally within the jurisdiction of such district court.

(8) METHOD OF SERVICE.—Service of any civil investigative demand or any enforcement petition filed under this section may be made upon a person, including any legal entity, by—

(A) delivering a duly executed copy of such demand or petition to the individual or to any partner, executive officer, managing agent, or general agent of such person, or to any agent of such person authorized by appointment or by law to receive service of process on behalf of such person;

(B) delivering a duly executed copy of such demand or petition to the principal office or place of business of the person to be served; or

(C) depositing a duly executed copy in the United States mails, by registered or certified mail, return receipt requested, duly addressed to such person at the principal office or place of business of such person.

(9) PROOF OF SERVICE.—

(A) IN GENERAL.—A verified return by the individual serving any civil investigative demand or any enforcement petition filed under this section setting forth the manner of such service shall be proof of such service.

(B) RETURN RECEIPTS.—In the case of service by registered or certified mail, such return shall be accompanied by the return post office receipt of delivery of such demand or enforcement petition.

(10) PRODUCTION OF DOCUMENTARY MATERIAL.—The production of documentary material in response to a civil investigative demand shall be made under a sworn certificate, in such form as the demand designates, by the person, if a natural person, to whom the demand is directed or, if

not a natural person, by any person having knowledge of the facts and circumstances relating to such production, to the effect that all of the documentary material required by the demand and in the possession, custody, or control of the person to whom the demand is directed has been produced and made available to the custodian.

(11) SUBMISSION OF TANGIBLE THINGS.—The submission of tangible things in response to a civil investigative demand shall be made under a sworn certificate, in such form as the demand designates, by the person to whom the demand is directed or, if not a natural person, by any person having knowledge of the facts and circumstances relating to such production, to the effect that all of the tangible things required by the demand and in the possession, custody, or control of the person to whom the demand is directed have been submitted to the custodian.

(12) SEPARATE ANSWERS.—Each reporting requirement or question in a civil investigative demand shall be answered separately and fully in writing under oath, unless it is objected to, in which event the reasons for the objection shall be stated in lieu of an answer, and it shall be submitted under a sworn certificate, in such form as the demand designates, by the person, if a natural person, to whom the demand is directed or, if not a natural person, by any person responsible for answering each reporting requirement or question, to the effect that all information required by the demand and in the possession, custody, control, or knowledge of the person to whom the demand is directed has been submitted.

(13) TESTIMONY.—

(A) IN GENERAL.—

(i) OATH AND RECORDATION.—The examination of any person pursuant to a demand for oral testimony served under this subsection shall be taken before an officer authorized to administer oaths and affirmations by the laws of the United States or of the place at which the examination is held. The officer before whom oral testimony is to be taken shall put the witness on oath or affirmation and shall personally, or by any individual acting under the direction of and in the presence of the officer, record the testimony of the witness.

(ii) TRANSCRIPTION.—The testimony shall be taken stenographically and transcribed.

(iii) TRANSMISSION TO CUSTODIAN.—After the testimony is fully transcribed, the officer investigator before whom the testimony is taken shall promptly transmit a copy of the transcript of the testimony to the custodian.

(B) PARTIES PRESENT.—Any Bureau investigator before whom oral testimony is to be taken shall exclude from the place where the testimony is to be taken all other persons, except the person giving the testimony, the attorney for that person, the officer before whom the testimony is to be taken, an investigator or representative of an agency with which the Bureau is engaged in a joint investigation, and any stenographer taking such testimony.

(C) LOCATION.—The oral testimony of any person taken pursuant to a civil investigative demand shall be taken in the judicial district of the United States in which such person resides, is found, or transacts business, or in such other place as may be agreed upon by the Bureau investigator before whom the oral testimony of such person is to be taken and such person.

(D) ATTORNEY REPRESENTATION.—

(i) IN GENERAL.—Any person compelled to appear under a civil investigative demand for oral testimony pursuant to this section may be accompanied, represented, and advised by an attorney.

(ii) AUTHORITY.—The attorney may advise a person described in clause (i), in confidence, either upon the request of such person or upon the initiative of the attorney, with respect to any question asked of such person.

(iii) OBJECTIONS.—A person described in clause (i), or the attorney for that person, may object on the record to any question, in whole or in part, and such person shall briefly state for the record the reason for the objection. An objection may properly be made, received, and entered upon the record when it is claimed that such person is entitled to refuse to answer the question on grounds of any constitutional or other legal right or privilege, including the privilege against self-incrimination, but such person shall not otherwise object to or refuse to answer any question, and such person or attorney shall not otherwise interrupt the oral examination.

(iv) REFUSAL TO ANSWER.—If a person described in clause (i) refuses to answer any question—

(I) the Bureau may petition the district court of the United States pursuant to this section for an order compelling such person to answer such question; and

(II) if the refusal is on grounds of the privilege against self-incrimination, the testimony of such person may be compelled in accordance with the provisions of section 6004 of title 18, United States Code.

(E) TRANSCRIPTS.—For purposes of this subsection—

(i) after the testimony of any witness is fully transcribed, the Bureau investigator shall afford the witness (who may be accompanied by an attorney) a reasonable opportunity to examine the transcript;

(ii) the transcript shall be read to or by the witness, unless such examination and reading are waived by the witness;

(iii) any changes in form or substance which the witness desires to make shall be entered and identified upon the transcript by the Bureau investigator, with a statement of the reasons given by the witness for making such changes;

(iv) the transcript shall be signed by the witness, unless the witness in writing waives the signing, is ill, cannot be found, or refuses to sign; and

(v) if the transcript is not signed by the witness during the 30-day period following the date on which the witness is first afforded a reasonable opportunity to examine the transcript, the Bureau investigator shall sign the transcript and state on the record the fact of the waiver, illness, absence of the witness, or the refusal to sign, together with any reasons given for the failure to sign.

(F) CERTIFICATION BY INVESTIGATOR.—The Bureau investigator shall certify on the transcript that the witness was duly sworn by him or her and that the transcript is a true record of the testimony given by the witness, and the Bureau investigator shall promptly deliver the transcript or send it by registered or certified mail to the custodian.

(G) COPY OF TRANSCRIPT.—The Bureau investigator shall furnish a copy of the transcript (upon payment of reasonable charges for the transcript) to the witness only, except that the Bureau may for good cause limit such witness to inspection of the official transcript of his testimony.

(H) WITNESS FEES.—Any witness appearing for the taking of oral testimony pursuant to a civil investigative demand shall be entitled to the same fees and mileage which are paid to witnesses in the district courts of the United States.

(d) CONFIDENTIAL TREATMENT OF DEMAND MATERIAL.—

(1) IN GENERAL.—Documentary materials and tangible things received as a result of a civil investigative demand shall be subject to requirements and procedures regarding confidentiality, in accordance with rules established by the Bureau.

(2) DISCLOSURE TO CONGRESS.—No rule established by the Bureau regarding the confidentiality of materials submitted to, or otherwise obtained by, the Bureau shall be intended to prevent disclosure to either House of Congress or to an appropriate committee of the Congress, except that the Bureau is permitted to adopt rules allowing prior notice to any party that owns or otherwise provided the material to the Bureau and had designated such material as confidential.

(e) PETITION FOR ENFORCEMENT.—

(1) IN GENERAL.—Whenever any person fails to comply with any civil investigative demand duly served upon him under this section, or whenever satisfactory copying or reproduction of material requested pursuant to the demand cannot be accomplished and such person refuses to surrender such material, the Bureau, through such officers or attorneys as it may designate, may

file, in the district court of the United States for any judicial district in which such person resides, is found, or transacts business, and serve upon such person, a petition for an order of such court for the enforcement of this section.

(2) SERVICE OF PROCESS.—All process of any court to which application may be made as provided in this subsection may be served in any judicial district.

(f) PETITION FOR ORDER MODIFYING OR SETTING ASIDE DEMAND.—

(1) IN GENERAL.—Not later than 20 days after the service of any civil investigative demand upon any person under subsection (b), or at any time before the return date specified in the demand, whichever period is shorter, or within such period exceeding 20 days after service or in excess of such return date as may be prescribed in writing, subsequent to service, by any Bureau investigator named in the demand, such person may file with the Bureau a petition for an order by the Bureau modifying or setting aside the demand.

(2) COMPLIANCE DURING PENDENCY.—The time permitted for compliance with the demand in whole or in part, as determined proper and ordered by the Bureau, shall not run during the pendency of a petition under paragraph (1) at the Bureau, except that such person shall comply with any portions of the demand not sought to be modified or set aside.

(3) SPECIFIC GROUNDS.—A petition under paragraph (1) shall specify each ground upon which the petitioner relies in seeking relief, and may be based upon any failure of the demand to comply with the provisions of this section, or upon any constitutional or other legal right or privilege of such person.

(g) CUSTODIAL CONTROL.—At any time during which any custodian is in custody or control of any documentary material, tangible things, reports, answers to questions, or transcripts of oral testimony given by any person in compliance with any civil investigative demand, such person may file, in the district court of the United States for the judicial district within which the office of such custodian is situated, and serve upon such custodian, a petition for an order of such court requiring the performance by such custodian of any duty imposed upon him by this section or rule promulgated by the Bureau.

(h) JURISDICTION OF COURT.—

(1) IN GENERAL.—Whenever any petition is filed in any district court of the United States under this section, such court shall have jurisdiction to hear and determine the matter so presented, and to enter such order or orders as may be required to carry out the provisions of this section.

(2) APPEAL.—Any final order entered as described in paragraph (1) shall be subject to appeal pursuant to section 1291 of title 28, United States Code.

[Explanation at ¶ 4665.]

[¶ 11,053] ACT SEC. 1053. HEARINGS AND ADJUDICATION PROCEEDINGS.

(a) IN GENERAL.—The Bureau is authorized to conduct hearings and adjudication proceedings with respect to any person in the manner prescribed by chapter 5 of title 5, United States Code in order to ensure or enforce compliance with—

(1) the provisions of this title, including any rules prescribed by the Bureau under this title; and

(2) any other Federal law that the Bureau is authorized to enforce, including an enumerated consumer law, and any regulations or order prescribed thereunder, unless such Federal law specifically limits the Bureau from conducting a hearing or adjudication proceeding and only to the extent of such limitation.

(b) SPECIAL RULES FOR CEASE-AND-DESIST PROCEEDINGS.—

(1) ORDERS AUTHORIZED.—

(A) IN GENERAL.—If, in the opinion of the Bureau, any covered person or service provider is engaging or has engaged in an activity that violates a law, rule, or any condition imposed in writing on the person by the Bureau, the Bureau may, subject to sections 1024, 1025, and 1026, issue and serve upon the covered person or service provider a notice of charges in respect thereof.

(B) CONTENT OF NOTICE.—The notice under subparagraph (A) shall contain a statement of the facts constituting the alleged violation or violations, and shall fix a time and place at which a hearing will be held to determine whether an order to cease and desist should issue against the covered person or service provider, such hearing to be held not earlier than 30 days nor later than 60 days after the date of service of such notice, unless an earlier or a later date is set by the Bureau, at the request of any party so served.

(C) CONSENT.—Unless the party or parties served under subparagraph (B) appear at the hearing personally or by a duly authorized representative, such person shall be deemed to have consented to the issuance of the cease-and-desist order.

(D) PROCEDURE.—In the event of consent under subparagraph (C), or if, upon the record, made at any such hearing, the Bureau finds that any violation specified in the notice of charges has been established, the Bureau may issue and serve upon the covered person or service provider an order to cease and desist from the violation or practice. Such order may, by provisions which may be mandatory or otherwise, require the covered person or service provider to cease and desist from the subject activity, and to take affirmative action to correct the conditions resulting from any such violation.

(2) EFFECTIVENESS OF ORDER.—A cease-and-desist order shall become effective at the expiration of 30 days after the date of service of an order under paragraph (1) upon the covered person or service provider concerned (except in the case of a cease-and-desist order issued upon consent, which shall become effective at the time specified therein), and shall remain effective and enforceable as provided therein, except to such extent as the order is stayed, modified, terminated, or set aside by action of the Bureau or a reviewing court.

(3) DECISION AND APPEAL.—Any hearing provided for in this subsection shall be held in the Federal judicial district or in the territory in which the residence or principal office or place of business of the person is located unless the person consents to another place, and shall be conducted in accordance with the provisions of chapter 5 of title 5 of the United States Code. After such hearing, and within 90 days after the Bureau has notified the parties that the case has been submitted to the Bureau for final decision, the Bureau shall render its decision (which shall include findings of fact upon which its decision is predicated) and shall issue and serve upon each party to the proceeding an order or orders consistent with the provisions of this section. Judicial review of any such order shall be exclusively as provided in this subsection. Unless a petition for review is timely filed in a court of appeals of the United States, as provided in paragraph (4), and thereafter until the record in the proceeding has been filed as provided in paragraph (4), the Bureau may at any time, upon such notice and in such manner as the Bureau shall determine proper, modify, terminate, or set aside any such order. Upon filing of the record as provided, the Bureau may modify, terminate, or set aside any such order with permission of the court.

(4) APPEAL TO COURT OF APPEALS.—Any party to any proceeding under this subsection may obtain a review of any order served pursuant to this subsection (other than an order issued with the consent of the person concerned) by the filing in the court of appeals of the United States for the circuit in which the principal office of the covered person is located, or in the United States Court of Appeals for the District of Columbia Circuit, within 30 days after the date of service of such order, a written petition praying that the order of the Bureau be modified, terminated, or set aside. A copy of such petition shall be forthwith transmitted by the clerk of the court to the Bureau, and thereupon the Bureau shall file in the court the record in the proceeding, as provided in section 2112 of title 28 of the United States Code. Upon the filing of such petition, such court shall have jurisdiction, which upon the filing of the record shall except as provided in the last sentence of paragraph (3) be exclusive, to affirm, modify, terminate, or set aside, in whole or in part, the order of the Bureau. Review of such proceedings shall be had as provided in chapter 7 of title 5 of the United States Code. The judgment and decree of the court shall be final, except that the same shall be subject to review by the Supreme Court of the United States, upon certiorari, as provided in section 1254 of title 28 of the United States Code.

(5) NO STAY.—The commencement of proceedings for judicial review under paragraph (4) shall not, unless specifically ordered by the court, operate as a stay of any order issued by the Bureau.

(c) SPECIAL RULES FOR TEMPORARY CEASE-AND-DESIST PROCEEDINGS.—

(1) IN GENERAL.—Whenever the Bureau determines that the violation specified in the notice of charges served upon a person, including a service provider, pursuant to subsection (b), or the continuation thereof, is likely to cause the person to be insolvent or otherwise prejudice the interests of consumers before the completion of the proceedings conducted pursuant to subsection (b), the Bureau may issue a temporary order requiring the person to cease and desist from any such violation or practice and to take affirmative action to prevent or remedy such insolvency or other condition pending completion of such proceedings. Such order may include any requirement authorized under this subtitle. Such order shall become effective upon service upon the person and, unless set aside, limited, or suspended by a court in proceedings authorized by paragraph (2), shall remain effective and enforceable pending the completion of the administrative proceedings pursuant to such notice and until such time as the Bureau shall dismiss the charges specified in such notice, or if a cease-and-desist order is issued against the person, until the effective date of such order.

(2) APPEAL.—Not later than 10 days after the covered person or service provider concerned has been served with a temporary cease-and-desist order, the person may apply to the United States district court for the judicial district in which the residence or principal office or place of business of the person is located, or the United States District Court for the District of Columbia, for an injunction setting aside, limiting, or suspending the enforcement, operation, or effectiveness of such order pending the completion of the administrative proceedings pursuant to the notice of charges served upon the person under subsection (b), and such court shall have jurisdiction to issue such injunction.

(3) INCOMPLETE OR INACCURATE RECORDS.—

(A) TEMPORARY ORDER.—If a notice of charges served under subsection (b) specifies, on the basis of particular facts and circumstances, that the books and records of a covered person or service provider are so incomplete or inaccurate that the Bureau is unable to determine the financial condition of that person or the details or purpose of any transaction or transactions that may have a material effect on the financial condition of that person, the Bureau may issue a temporary order requiring—

(i) the cessation of any activity or practice which gave rise, whether in whole or in part, to the incomplete or inaccurate state of the books or records; or

(ii) affirmative action to restore such books or records to a complete and accurate state, until the completion of the proceedings under subsection (b)(1).

(B) EFFECTIVE PERIOD.—Any temporary order issued under subparagraph (A)—

(i) shall become effective upon service; and

(ii) unless set aside, limited, or suspended by a court in proceedings under paragraph (2), shall remain in effect and enforceable until the earlier of—

(I) the completion of the proceeding initiated under subsection (b) in connection with the notice of charges; or

(II) the date the Bureau determines, by examination or otherwise, that the books and records of the covered person or service provider are accurate and reflect the financial condition thereof.

(d) SPECIAL RULES FOR ENFORCEMENT OF ORDERS.—

(1) IN GENERAL.—The Bureau may in its discretion apply to the United States district court within the jurisdiction of which the principal office or place of business of the person is located, for the enforcement of any effective and outstanding notice or order issued under this section, and such court shall have jurisdiction and power to order and require compliance herewith.

(2) EXCEPTION.—Except as otherwise provided in this subsection, no court shall have jurisdiction to affect by injunction or otherwise the issuance or enforcement of any notice or order or to review, modify, suspend, terminate, or set aside any such notice or order.

(e) RULES.—The Bureau shall prescribe rules establishing such procedures as may be necessary to carry out this section.

[Explanation at ¶ 4670.]

[¶ 11,054] ACT SEC. 1054. LITIGATION AUTHORITY.

(a) IN GENERAL.—If any person violates a Federal consumer financial law, the Bureau may, subject to sections 1024, 1025, and 1026, commence a civil action against such person to impose a civil penalty or to seek all appropriate legal and equitable relief including a permanent or temporary injunction as permitted by law.

(b) REPRESENTATION.—The Bureau may act in its own name and through its own attorneys in enforcing any provision of this title, rules thereunder, or any other law or regulation, or in any action, suit, or proceeding to which the Bureau is a party.

(c) COMPROMISE OF ACTIONS.—The Bureau may compromise or settle any action if such compromise is approved by the court.

(d) NOTICE TO THE ATTORNEY GENERAL.—

(1) IN GENERAL.—When commencing a civil action under Federal consumer financial law, or any rule thereunder, the Bureau shall notify the Attorney General and, with respect to a civil action against an insured depository institution or insured credit union, the appropriate prudential regulator.

(2) NOTICE AND COORDINATION.—

(A) NOTICE OF OTHER ACTIONS.—In addition to any notice required under paragraph (1), the Bureau shall notify the Attorney General concerning any action, suit, or proceeding to which the Bureau is a party, except an action, suit, or proceeding that involves the offering or provision of consumer financial products or services.

(B) COORDINATION.—In order to avoid conflicts and promote consistency regarding litigation of matters under Federal law, the Attorney General and the Bureau shall consult regarding the coordination of investigations and proceedings, including by negotiating an agreement for coordination by not later than 180 days after the designated transfer date. The agreement under this subparagraph shall include provisions to ensure that parallel investigations and proceedings involving the Federal consumer financial laws are conducted in a manner that avoids conflicts and does not impede the ability of the Attorney General to prosecute violations of Federal criminal laws.

(C) RULE OF CONSTRUCTION.—Nothing in this paragraph shall be construed to limit the authority of the Bureau under this title, including the authority to interpret Federal consumer financial law.

(e) APPEARANCE BEFORE THE SUPREME COURT.—The Bureau may represent itself in its own name before the Supreme Court of the United States, provided that the Bureau makes a written request to the Attorney General within the 10-day period which begins on the date of entry of the judgment which would permit any party to file a petition for writ of certiorari, and the Attorney General concurs with such request or fails to take action within 60 days of the request of the Bureau.

(f) FORUM.—Any civil action brought under this title may be brought in a United States district court or in any court of competent jurisdiction of a state in a district in which the defendant is located or resides or is doing business, and such court shall have jurisdiction to enjoin such person and to require compliance with any Federal consumer financial law.

(g) TIME FOR BRINGING ACTION.—

(1) IN GENERAL.—Except as otherwise permitted by law or equity, no action may be brought under this title more than 3 years after the date of discovery of the violation to which an action relates.

(2) LIMITATIONS UNDER OTHER FEDERAL LAWS.—

(A) IN GENERAL.—An action arising under this title does not include claims arising solely under enumerated consumer laws.

(B) BUREAU AUTHORITY.—In any action arising solely under an enumerated consumer law, the Bureau may commence, defend, or intervene in the action in accordance with the requirements of that provision of law, as applicable.

(C) TRANSFERRED AUTHORITY.—In any action arising solely under laws for which authorities were transferred under subtitles F and H, the Bureau may commence, defend, or intervene in the action in accordance with the requirements of that provision of law, as applicable.

[Explanation at ¶ 4675.]

[¶ 11,055] ACT SEC. 1055. RELIEF AVAILABLE.

(a) ADMINISTRATIVE PROCEEDINGS OR COURT ACTIONS.—

(1) JURISDICTION.—The court (or the Bureau, as the case may be) in an action or adjudication proceeding brought under Federal consumer financial law, shall have jurisdiction to grant any appropriate legal or equitable relief with respect to a violation of Federal consumer financial law, including a violation of a rule or order prescribed under a Federal consumer financial law.

(2) RELIEF.—Relief under this section may include, without limitation—

(A) rescission or reformation of contracts;

(B) refund of moneys or return of real property;

(C) restitution;

(D) disgorgement or compensation for unjust enrichment;

(E) payment of damages or other monetary relief;

(F) public notification regarding the violation, including the costs of notification;

(G) limits on the activities or functions of the person; and

(H) civil money penalties, as set forth more fully in subsection (c).

(3) NO EXEMPLARY OR PUNITIVE DAMAGES.—Nothing in this subsection shall be construed as authorizing the imposition of exemplary or punitive damages.

(b) RECOVERY OF COSTS.—In any action brought by the Bureau, a State attorney general, or any State regulator to enforce any Federal consumer financial law, the Bureau, the State attorney general, or the State regulator may recover its costs in connection with prosecuting such action if the Bureau, the State attorney general, or the State regulator is the prevailing party in the action.

(c) CIVIL MONEY PENALTY IN COURT AND ADMINISTRATIVE ACTIONS.—

(1) IN GENERAL.—Any person that violates, through any act or omission, any provision of Federal consumer financial law shall forfeit and pay a civil penalty pursuant to this subsection.

(2) PENALTY AMOUNTS.—

(A) FIRST TIER.—For any violation of a law, rule, or final order or condition imposed in writing by the Bureau, a civil penalty may not exceed $5,000 for each day during which such violation or failure to pay continues.

(B) SECOND TIER.—Notwithstanding paragraph (A), for any person that recklessly engages in a violation of a Federal consumer financial law, a civil penalty may not exceed $25,000 for each day during which such violation continues.

(C) THIRD TIER.—Notwithstanding subparagraphs (A) and (B), for any person that knowingly violates a Federal consumer financial law, a civil penalty may not exceed $1,000,000 for each day during which such violation continues.

(3) MITIGATING FACTORS.—In determining the amount of any penalty assessed under paragraph (2), the Bureau or the court shall take into account the appropriateness of the penalty with respect to—

    (A) the size of financial resources and good faith of the person charged;

    (B) the gravity of the violation or failure to pay;

    (C) the severity of the risks to or losses of the consumer, which may take into account the number of products or services sold or provided;

    (D) the history of previous violations; and

    (E) such other matters as justice may require.

(4) AUTHORITY TO MODIIFY OR REMIT PENALTY.—The Bureau may compromise, modify, or remit any penalty which may be assessed or had already been assessed under paragraph (2). The amount of such penalty, when finally determined, shall be exclusive of any sums owed by the person to the United States in connection with the costs of the proceeding, and may be deducted from any sums owing by the United States to the person charged.

(5) NOTICE AND HEARING.—No civil penalty may be assessed under this subsection with respect to a violation of any Federal consumer financial law, unless—

    (A) the Bureau gives notice and an opportunity for a hearing to the person accused of the violation; or

    (B) the appropriate court has ordered such assessment and entered judgment in favor of the Bureau.

[Explanation at ¶4680.]

[¶11,056] ACT SEC. 1056. REFERRALS FOR CRIMINAL PROCEEDINGS.

If the Bureau obtains evidence that any person, domestic or foreign, has engaged in conduct that may constitute a violation of Federal criminal law, the Bureau shall transmit such evidence to the Attorney General of the United States, who may institute criminal proceedings under appropriate law. Nothing in this section affects any other authority of the Bureau to disclose information.

[Explanation at ¶4685.]

[¶11,057] ACT SEC. 1057. EMPLOYEE PROTECTION.

(a) IN GENERAL.—No covered person or service provider shall terminate or in any other way discriminate against, or cause to be terminated or discriminated against, any covered employee or any authorized representative of covered employees by reason of the fact that such employee or representative, whether at the initiative of the employee or in the ordinary course of the duties of the employee (or any person acting pursuant to a request of the employee), has—

(1) provided, caused to be provided, or is about to provide or cause to be provided, information to the employer, the Bureau, or any other State, local, or Federal, government authority or law enforcement agency relating to any violation of, or any act or omission that the employee reasonably believes to be a violation of, any provision of this title or any other provision of law that is subject to the jurisdiction of the Bureau, or any rule, order, standard, or prohibition prescribed by the Bureau;

(2) testified or will testify in any proceeding resulting from the administration or enforcement of any provision of this title or any other provision of law that is subject to the jurisdiction of the Bureau, or any rule, order, standard, or prohibition prescribed by the Bureau;

(3) filed, instituted, or caused to be filed or instituted any proceeding under any Federal consumer financial law; or

(4) objected to, or refused to participate in, any activity, policy, practice, or assigned task that the employee (or other such person) reasonably believed to be in violation of any law, rule, order, standard, or prohibition, subject to the jurisdiction of, or enforceable by, the Bureau.

(b) DEFINITION OF COVERED EMPLOYEE.—For the purposes of this section, the term "covered employee" means any individual performing tasks related to the offering or provision of a consumer financial product or service.

(c) PROCEDURES AND TIMETABLES.—

(1) COMPLAINT.—

(A) IN GENERAL.—A person who believes that he or she has been discharged or otherwise discriminated against by any person in violation of subsection (a) may, not later than 180 days after the date on which such alleged violation occurs, file (or have any person file on his or her behalf) a complaint with the Secretary of Labor alleging such discharge or discrimination and identifying the person responsible for such act.

(B) ACTIONS OF SECRETARY OF LABOR.—Upon receipt of such a complaint, the Secretary of Labor shall notify, in writing, the person named in the complaint who is alleged to have committed the violation, of—

(i) the filing of the complaint;

(ii) the allegations contained in the complaint;

(iii) the substance of evidence supporting the complaint; and

(iv) opportunities that will be afforded to such person under paragraph (2).

(2) INVESTIGATION BY SECRETARY OF LABOR.—

(A) IN GENERAL.—Not later than 60 days after the date of receipt of a complaint filed under paragraph (1), and after affording the complainant and the person named in the complaint who is alleged to have committed the violation that is the basis for the complaint an opportunity to submit to the Secretary of Labor a written response to the complaint and an opportunity to meet with a representative of the Secretary of Labor to present statements from witnesses, the Secretary of Labor shall—

(i) initiate an investigation and determine whether there is reasonable cause to believe that the complaint has merit; and

(ii) notify the complainant and the person alleged to have committed the violation of subsection (a), in writing, of such determination.

(B) NOTICE OF RELIEF AVAILABLE.—If the Secretary of Labor concludes that there is reasonable cause to believe that a violation of subsection (a) has occurred, the Secretary of Labor shall, together with the notice under subparagraph (A)(ii), issue a preliminary order providing the relief prescribed by paragraph (4)(B).

(C) REQUEST FOR HEARING.—Not later than 30 days after the date of receipt of notification of a determination of the Secretary of Labor under this paragraph, either the person alleged to have committed the violation or the complainant may file objections to the findings or preliminary order, or both, and request a hearing on the record. The filing of such objections shall not operate to stay any reinstatement remedy contained in the preliminary order. Any such hearing shall be conducted expeditiously, and if a hearing is not requested in such 30-day period, the preliminary order shall be deemed a final order that is not subject to judicial review.

(3) GROUNDS FOR DETERMINATION OF COMPLAINTS.—

(A) IN GENERAL.—The Secretary of Labor shall dismiss a complaint filed under this subsection, and shall not conduct an investigation otherwise required under paragraph (2), unless the complainant makes a prima facie showing that any behavior described in paragraphs (1) through (4) of subsection (a) was a contributing factor in the unfavorable personnel action alleged in the complaint.

(B) REBUTTAL EVIDENCE.—Notwithstanding a finding by the Secretary of Labor that the complainant has made the showing required under subparagraph (A), no investigation otherwise required under paragraph (2) shall be conducted, if the employer demonstrates, by clear and convincing evidence, that the employer would have taken the same unfavorable personnel action in the absence of that behavior.

(C) EVIDENTIARY STANDARDS.—The Secretary of Labor may determine that a violation of subsection (a) has occurred only if the complainant demonstrates that any behavior described in paragraphs (1) through (4) of subsection (a) was a contributing factor in the unfavorable personnel action alleged in the complaint. Relief may not be ordered under subparagraph (A) if the employer demonstrates by clear and convincing evidence that the employer would have taken the same unfavorable personnel action in the absence of that behavior.

(4) ISSUANCE OF FINAL ORDERS; REVIEW PROCEDURES.—

(A) TIMING.—Not later than 120 days after the date of conclusion of any hearing under paragraph (2), the Secretary of Labor shall issue a final order providing the relief prescribed by this paragraph or denying the complaint. At any time before issuance of a final order, a proceeding under this subsection may be terminated on the basis of a settlement agreement entered into by the Secretary of Labor, the complainant, and the person alleged to have committed the violation.

(B) PENALTIES.—

(i) ORDER OF SECRETARY OF LABOR.—If, in response to a complaint filed under paragraph (1), the Secretary of Labor determines that a violation of subsection (a) has occurred, the Secretary of Labor shall order the person who committed such violation—

(I) to take affirmative action to abate the violation;

(II) to reinstate the complainant to his or her former position, together with compensation (including back pay) and restore the terms, conditions, and privileges associated with his or her employment; and

(III) to provide compensatory damages to the complainant.

(ii) PENALTY.—If an order is issued under clause (i), the Secretary of Labor, at the request of the complainant, shall assess against the person against whom the order is issued, a sum equal to the aggregate amount of all costs and expenses (including attorney fees and expert witness fees) reasonably incurred, as determined by the Secretary of Labor, by the complainant for, or in connection with, the bringing of the complaint upon which the order was issued.

(C) PENALTY FOR FRIVOLOUS CLAIMS.—If the Secretary of Labor finds that a complaint under paragraph (1) is frivolous or has been brought in bad faith, the Secretary of Labor may award to the prevailing employer a reasonable attorney fee, not exceeding $1,000, to be paid by the complainant.

(D) DE NOVO REVIEW.—

(i) FAILURE OF THE SECRETARY TO ACT.—If the Secretary of Labor has not issued a final order within 210 days after the date of filing of a complaint under this subsection, or within 90 days after the date of receipt of a written determination, the complainant may bring an action at law or equity for de novo review in the appropriate district court of the United States having jurisdiction, which shall have jurisdiction over such an action without regard to the amount in controversy, and which action shall, at the request of either party to such action, be tried by the court with a jury.

(ii) PROCEDURES.—A proceeding under clause (i) shall be governed by the same legal burdens of proof specified in paragraph (3). The court shall have jurisdiction to grant all relief necessary to make the employee whole, including injunctive relief and compensatory damages, including—

(I) reinstatement with the same seniority status that the employee would have had, but for the discharge or discrimination;

(II) the amount of back pay, with interest; and

(III) compensation for any special damages sustained as a result of the discharge or discrimination, including litigation costs, expert witness fees, and reasonable attorney fees.

(E) OTHER APPEALS.—Unless the complainant brings an action under subparagraph (D), any person adversely affected or aggrieved by a final order issued under subparagraph (A) may file a petition for review of the order in the United States Court of Appeals for the circuit in which the violation with respect to which the order was issued, allegedly occurred or the circuit in which the complainant resided on the date of such violation, not later than 60 days after the date of the issuance of the final order of the Secretary of Labor under subparagraph (A). Review shall conform to chapter 7 of title 5, United States Code. The commencement of proceedings under this subparagraph shall not, unless ordered by the court, operate as a stay of the order. An order of the Secretary of Labor with respect to which review could have been obtained under this subparagraph shall not be subject to judicial review in any criminal or other civil proceeding.

(5) FAILURE TO COMPLY WITH ORDER.—

(A) ACTIONS BY THE SECRETARY.—If any person has failed to comply with a final order issued under paragraph (4), the Secretary of Labor may file a civil action in the United States district court for the district in which the violation was found to have occurred, or in the United States district court for the District of Columbia, to enforce such order. In actions brought under this paragraph, the district courts shall have jurisdiction to grant all appropriate relief including injunctive relief and compensatory damages.

(B) CIVIL ACTIONS TO COMPEL COMPLIANCE.—A person on whose behalf an order was issued under paragraph (4) may commence a civil action against the person to whom such order was issued to require compliance with such order. The appropriate United States district court shall have jurisdiction, without regard to the amount in controversy or the citizenship of the parties, to enforce such order.

(C) AWARD OF COSTS AUTHORIZED.—The court, in issuing any final order under this paragraph, may award costs of litigation (including reasonable attorney and expert witness fees) to any party, whenever the court determines such award is appropriate.

(D) MANDAMUS PROCEEDINGS.—Any nondiscretionary duty imposed by this section shall be enforceable in a mandamus proceeding brought under section 1361 of title 28, United States Code.

(d) UNENFORCEABILITY OF CERTAIN AGREEMENTS.—

(1) NO WAIVER OF RIGHTS AND REMEDIES.—Except as provided under paragraph (3), and notwithstanding any other provision of law, the rights and remedies provided for in this section may not be waived by any agreement, policy, form, or condition of employment, including by any predispute arbitration agreement.

(2) NO PREDISPUTE ARBITRATION AGREEMENTS.—Except as provided under paragraph (3), and notwithstanding any other provision of law, no predispute arbitration agreement shall be valid or enforceable to the extent that it requires arbitration of a dispute arising under this section.

(3) EXCEPTION.—Notwithstanding paragraphs (1) and (2), an arbitration provision in a collective bargaining agreement shall be enforceable as to disputes arising under subsection (a)(4), unless the Bureau determines, by rule, that such provision is inconsistent with the purposes of this title.

[Explanation at ¶ 4690.]

[¶ 11,058] ACT SEC. 1058. EFFECTIVE DATE.

This subtitle shall become effective on the designated transfer date.

[Explanation at ¶ 4660.]

Subtitle F—Transfer of Functions and Personnel; Transitional Provisions

[¶ 11,061] ACT SEC. 1061. TRANSFER OF CONSUMER FINANCIAL PROTECTION FUNCTIONS.

(a) DEFINED TERMS.—For purposes of this subtitle—

(1) the term "consumer financial protection functions" means—

(A) all authority to prescribe rules or issue orders or guidelines pursuant to any Federal consumer financial law, including performing appropriate functions to promulgate and review such rules, orders, and guidelines; and

(B) the examination authority described in subsection (c)(1), with respect to a person described in subsection 1025(a); and

(2) the terms "transferor agency" and "transferor agencies" mean, respectively—

(A) the Board of Governors (and any Federal reserve bank, as the context requires), the Federal Deposit Insurance Corporation, the Federal Trade Commission, the National Credit Union Administration, the Office of the Comptroller of the Currency, the Office of Thrift Supervision, and the Department of Housing and Urban Development, and the heads of those agencies; and

(B) the agencies listed in subparagraph (A), collectively.

(b) IN GENERAL.—Except as provided in subsection (c), consumer financial protection functions are transferred as follows:

(1) BOARD OF GOVERNORS.—

(A) TRANSFER OF FUNCTIONS.—All consumer financial protection functions of the Board of Governors are transferred to the Bureau.

(B) BOARD OF GOVERNORS AUTHORITY.—The Bureau shall have all powers and duties that were vested in the Board of Governors, relating to consumer financial protection functions, on the day before the designated transfer date.

(2) COMPTROLLER OF THE CURRENCY.—

(A) TRANSFER OF FUNCTIONS.—All consumer financial protection functions of the Comptroller of the Currency are transferred to the Bureau.

(B) COMPTROLLER AUTHORITY.—The Bureau shall have all powers and duties that were vested in the Comptroller of the Currency, relating to consumer financial protection functions, on the day before the designated transfer date.

(3) DIRECTOR OF THE OFFICE OF THRIFT SUPERVISION.—

(A) TRANSFER OF FUNCTIONS.—All consumer financial protection functions of the Director of the Office of Thrift Supervision are transferred to the Bureau.

(B) DIRECTOR AUTHORITY.—The Bureau shall have all powers and duties that were vested in the Director of the Office of Thrift Supervision, relating to consumer financial protection functions, on the day before the designated transfer date.

(4) FEDERAL DEPOSIT INSURANCE CORPORATION.—

(A) TRANSFER OF FUNCTIONS.—All consumer financial protection functions of the Federal Deposit Insurance Corporation are transferred to the Bureau.

(B) CORPORATION AUTHORITY.—The Bureau shall have all powers and duties that were vested in the Federal Deposit Insurance Corporation, relating to consumer financial protection functions, on the day before the designated transfer date.

(5) FEDERAL TRADE COMMISSION.—

(A) TRANSFER OF FUNCTIONS.—The authority of the Federal Trade Commission under an enumerated consumer law to prescribe rules, issue guidelines, or conduct a study or issue a report mandated under such law shall be transferred to the Bureau on the designated transfer date. Nothing in this title shall be construed to require a mandatory transfer of any employee of the Federal Trade Commission.

(B) BUREAU AUTHORITY.—

(i) IN GENERAL.—The Bureau shall have all powers and duties under the enumerated consumer laws to prescribe rules, issue guidelines, or to conduct studies or issue reports mandated by such laws, that were vested in the Federal Trade Commission on the day before the designated transfer date.

(ii) FEDERAL TRADE COMMISSION ACT.—Subject to subtitle B, the Bureau may enforce a rule prescribed under the Federal Trade Commission Act by the Federal Trade Commission with respect to an unfair or deceptive act or practice to the extent that such rule applies to a covered person or service provider with respect to the offering or provision of a consumer financial product or service as if it were a rule prescribed under section 1031 of this title.

(C) AUTHORITY OF THE FEDERAL TRADE COMMISSION.—

(i) IN GENERAL.—No provision of this title shall be construed as modifying, limiting, or otherwise affecting the authority of the Federal Trade Commission (including its authority with respect to affiliates described in section 1025(a)(1)) under the Federal Trade Commission Act or any other law, other than the authority under an enumerated consumer law to prescribe rules, issue official guidelines, or conduct a study or issue a report mandated under such law.

(ii) COMMISSION AUTHORITY RELATING TO RULES PRESCRIBED BY THE BUREAU.—Subject to subtitle B, the Federal Trade Commission shall have authority to enforce under the Federal Trade Commission Act (15 U.S.C. 41 et seq.) a rule prescribed by the Bureau under this title with respect to a covered person subject to the jurisdiction of the Federal Trade Commission under that Act, and a violation of such a rule by such a person shall be treated as a violation of a rule issued under section 18 of that Act (15 U.S.C. 57a) with respect to unfair or deceptive acts or practices.

(D) COORDINATION.—To avoid duplication of or conflict between rules prescribed by the Bureau under section 1031 of this title and the Federal Trade Commission under section 18(a)(1)(B) of the Federal Trade Commission Act that apply to a covered person or service provider with respect to the offering or provision of consumer financial products or services, the agencies shall negotiate an agreement with respect to rulemaking by each agency, including consultation with the other agency prior to proposing a rule and during the comment period.

(E) DEFERENCE.—No provision of this title shall be construed as altering, limiting, expanding, or otherwise affecting the deference that a court affords to the—

(i) Federal Trade Commission in making determinations regarding the meaning or interpretation of any provision of the Federal Trade Commission Act, or of any other Federal law for which the Commission has authority to prescribe rules; or

(ii) Bureau in making determinations regarding the meaning or interpretation of any provision of a Federal consumer financial law (other than any law described in clause (i)).

(6) NATIONAL CREDIT UNION ADMINISTRATION.—

(A) TRANSFER OF FUNCTIONS.—All consumer financial protection functions of the National Credit Union Administration are transferred to the Bureau.

(B) NATIONAL CREDIT UNION ADMINISTRATION AUTHORITY.—The Bureau shall have all powers and duties that were vested in the National Credit Union Administration, relating to consumer financial protection functions, on the day before the designated transfer date.

(7) DEPARTMENT OF HOUSING AND URBAN DEVELOPMENT.—

(A) TRANSFER OF FUNCTIONS.—All consumer protection functions of the Secretary of the Department of Housing and Urban Development relating to the Real Estate Settlement Procedures Act of 1974 (12 U.S.C. 2601 et seq.), the Secure and Fair Enforcement for Mortgage Licensing Act of 2008 (12 U.S.C. 5102 et seq.), and the Interstate Land Sales Full Disclosure Act (15 U.S.C. 1701 et seq.) are transferred to the Bureau.

(B) AUTHORITY OF THE DEPARTMENT OF HOUSING AND URBAN DEVELOPMENT.—The Bureau shall have all powers and duties that were vested in the Secretary of the Department of Housing and Urban Development relating to the Real Estate Settlement Procedures Act of

1974 (12 U.S.C. 2601 et seq.), the Secure and Fair Enforcement for Mortgage Licensing Act of 2008 (12 U.S.C. 5101 et seq.), and the Interstate Land Sales Full Disclosure Act (15 U.S.C. 1701 et seq.), on the day before the designated transfer date.

(c) AUTHORITIES OF THE PRUDENTIAL REGULATORS.—

(1) EXAMINATION.—A transferor agency that is a prudential regulator shall have—

(A) authority to require reports from and conduct examinations for compliance with Federal consumer financial laws with respect to a person described in section 1025(a), that is incidental to the backup and enforcement procedures provided to the regulator under section 1025(c); and

(B) exclusive authority (relative to the Bureau) to require reports from and conduct examinations for compliance with Federal consumer financial laws with respect to a person described in section 1026(a), except as provided to the Bureau under subsections (b) and (c) of section 1026.

(2) ENFORCEMENT.—

(A) LIMITATION.—The authority of a transferor agency that is a prudential regulator to enforce compliance with Federal consumer financial laws with respect to a person described in section 1025(a), shall be limited to the backup and enforcement procedures in described in section 1025(c).

(B) EXCLUSIVE AUTHORITY.—A transferor agency that is a prudential regulator shall have exclusive authority (relative to the Bureau) to enforce compliance with Federal consumer financial laws with respect to a person described in section 1026(a), except as provided to the Bureau under subsections (b) and (c) of section 1026.

(C) STATUTORY ENFORCEMENT.—For purposes of carrying out the authorities under, and subject to the limitations of, subtitle B, each prudential regulator may enforce compliance with the requirements imposed under this title, and any rule or order prescribed by the Bureau under this title, under—

(i) the Federal Credit Union Act (12 U.S.C. 1751 et seq.), by the National Credit Union Administration Board with respect to any covered person or service provider that is an insured credit union, or service provider thereto, or any affiliate of an insured credit union, who is subject to the jurisdiction of the Board under that Act; and

(ii) section 8 of the Federal Deposit Insurance Act (12 U.S.C. 1818), by the appropriate Federal banking agency, as defined in section 3(q) of the Federal Deposit Insurance Act (12 U.S.C. 1813(q)), with respect to a covered person or service provider that is a person described in section 3(q) of that Act and who is subject to the jurisdiction of that agency, as set forth in sections 3(q) and 8 of the Federal Deposit Insurance Act; or

(iii) the Bank Service Company Act (12 U.S.C. 1861 et seq.).

(d) EFFECTIVE DATE.—Subsections (b) and (c) shall become effective on the designated transfer date.

[Explanation at ¶ 4695.]

[¶ 11,062] ACT SEC. 1062. DESIGNATED TRANSFER DATE.

(a) IN GENERAL.—Not later than 60 days after the date of enactment of this Act, the Secretary shall—

(1) in consultation with the Chairman of the Board of Governors, the Chairperson of the Corporation, the Chairman of the Federal Trade Commission, the Chairman of the National Credit Union Administration Board, the Comptroller of the Currency, the Director of the Office of Thrift Supervision, the Secretary of the Department of Housing and Urban Development, and the Director of the Office of Management and Budget, designate a single calendar date for the transfer of functions to the Bureau under section 1061; and

(2) publish notice of that designated date in the Federal Register.

(b) CHANGING DESIGNATION.—The Secretary—

(1) may, in consultation with the Chairman of the Board of Governors, the Chairperson of the Federal Deposit Insurance Corporation, the Chairman of the Federal Trade Commission, the Chairman of the National Credit Union Administration Board, the Comptroller of the Currency, the Director of the Office of Thrift Supervision, the Secretary of the Department of Housing and Urban Development, and the Director of the Office of Management and Budget, change the date designated under subsection (a); and

(2) shall publish notice of any changed designated date in the Federal Register.

(c) PERMISSIBLE DATES.—

(1) IN GENERAL.—Except as provided in paragraph (2), any date designated under this section shall be not earlier than 180 days, nor later than 12 months, after the date of enactment of this Act.

(2) EXTENSION OF TIME.—The Secretary may designate a date that is later than 12 months after the date of enactment of this Act if the Secretary transmits to appropriate committees of Congress—

(A) a written determination that orderly implementation of this title is not feasible before the date that is 12 months after the date of enactment of this Act;

(B) an explanation of why an extension is necessary for the orderly implementation of this title; and

(C) a description of the steps that will be taken to effect an orderly and timely implementation of this title within the extended time period.

(3) EXTENSION LIMITED.—In no case may any date designated under this section be later than 18 months after the date of enactment of this Act.

[Explanation at ¶ 4700.]

[¶ 11,063] ACT SEC. 1063. SAVINGS PROVISIONS.

(a) BOARD OF GOVERNORS.—

(1) EXISTING RIGHTS, DUTIES, AND OBLIGATIONS NOT AFFECTED.—Section 1061(b)(1) does not affect the validity of any right, duty, or obligation of the United States, the Board of Governors (or any Federal reserve bank), or any other person that—

(A) arises under any provision of law relating to any consumer financial protection function of the Board of Governors transferred to the Bureau by this title; and

(B) existed on the day before the designated transfer date.

(2) CONTINUATION OF SUITS.—No provision of this Act shall abate any proceeding commenced by or against the Board of Governors (or any Federal reserve bank) before the designated transfer date with respect to any consumer financial protection function of the Board of Governors (or any Federal reserve bank) transferred to the Bureau by this title, except that the Bureau, subject to sections 1024, 1025, and 1026, shall be substituted for the Board of Governors (or Federal reserve bank) as a party to any such proceeding as of the designated transfer date.

(b) FEDERAL DEPOSIT INSURANCE CORPORATION.—

(1) EXISTING RIGHTS, DUTIES, AND OBLIGATIONS NOT AFFECTED.—Section 1061(b)(4) does not affect the validity of any right, duty, or obligation of the United States, the Federal Deposit Insurance Corporation, the Board of Directors of that Corporation, or any other person, that—

(A) arises under any provision of law relating to any consumer financial protection function of the Federal Deposit Insurance Corporation transferred to the Bureau by this title; and

(B) existed on the day before the designated transfer date.

(2) CONTINUATION OF SUITS.—No provision of this Act shall abate any proceeding commenced by or against the Federal Deposit Insurance Corporation (or the Board of Directors of that Corporation) before the designated transfer date with respect to any consumer financial protection function of the Federal Deposit Insurance Corporation transferred to the Bureau by this title,

except that the Bureau, subject to sections 1024, 1025, and 1026, shall be substituted for the Federal Deposit Insurance Corporation (or Board of Directors) as a party to any such proceeding as of the designated transfer date.

(c) FEDERAL TRADE COMMISSION.—Section 1061(b)(5) does not affect the validity of any right, duty, or obligation of the United States, the Federal Trade Commission, or any other person, that—

(1) arises under any provision of law relating to any consumer financial protection function of the Federal Trade Commission transferred to the Bureau by this title; and

(2) existed on the day before the designated transfer date.

(d) NATIONAL CREDIT UNION ADMINISTRATION.—

(1) EXISTING RIGHTS, DUTIES, AND OBLIGATIONS NOT AFFECTED.—Section 1061(b)(6) does not affect the validity of any right, duty, or obligation of the United States, the National Credit Union Administration, the National Credit Union Administration Board, or any other person, that—

(A) arises under any provision of law relating to any consumer financial protection function of the National Credit Union Administration transferred to the Bureau by this title; and

(B) existed on the day before the designated transfer date.

(2) CONTINUATION OF SUITS.—No provision of this Act shall abate any proceeding commenced by or against the National Credit Union Administration (or the National Credit Union Administration Board) before the designated transfer date with respect to any consumer financial protection function of the National Credit Union Administration transferred to the Bureau by this title, except that the Bureau, subject to sections 1024, 1025, and 1026, shall be substituted for the National Credit Union Administration (or National Credit Union Administration Board) as a party to any such proceeding as of the designated transfer date.

(e) OFFICE OF THE COMPTROLLER OF THE CURRENCY.—

(1) EXISTING RIGHTS, DUTIES, AND OBLIGATIONS NOT AFFECTED.—Section 1061(b)(2) does not affect the validity of any right, duty, or obligation of the United States, the Comptroller of the Currency, the Office of the Comptroller of the Currency, or any other person, that—

(A) arises under any provision of law relating to any consumer financial protection function of the Comptroller of the Currency transferred to the Bureau by this title; and

(B) existed on the day before the designated transfer date.

(2) CONTINUATION OF SUITS.—No provision of this Act shall abate any proceeding commenced by or against the Comptroller of the Currency (or the Office of the Comptroller of the Currency) with respect to any consumer financial protection function of the Comptroller of the Currency transferred to the Bureau by this title before the designated transfer date, except that the Bureau, subject to sections 1024, 1025, and 1026, shall be substituted for the Comptroller of the Currency (or the Office of the Comptroller of the Currency) as a party to any such proceeding as of the designated transfer date.

(f) OFFICE OF THRIFT SUPERVISION.—

(1) EXISTING RIGHTS, DUTIES, AND OBLIGATIONS NOT AFFECTED.—Section 1061(b)(3) does not affect the validity of any right, duty, or obligation of the United States, the Director of the Office of Thrift Supervision, the Office of Thrift Supervision, or any other person, that—

(A) arises under any provision of law relating to any consumer financial protection function of the Director of the Office of Thrift Supervision transferred to the Bureau by this title; and

(B) that existed on the day before the designated transfer date.

(2) CONTINUATION OF SUITS.—No provision of this Act shall abate any proceeding commenced by or against the Director of the Office of Thrift Supervision (or the Office of Thrift Supervision) with respect to any consumer financial protection function of the Director of the Office of Thrift Supervision transferred to the Bureau by this title before the designated transfer date, except that the Bureau, subject to sections 1024, 1025, and 1026, shall be substituted for the Director (or the Office of Thrift Supervision) as a party to any such proceeding as of the designated transfer date.

(g) DEPARTMENT OF HOUSING AND URBAN DEVELOPMENT.—

(1) EXISTING RIGHTS, DUTIES, AND OBLIGATIONS NOT AFFECTED.—Section 1061(b)(7) shall not affect the validity of any right, duty, or obligation of the United States, the Secretary of the Department of Housing and Urban Development (or the Department of Housing and Urban Development), or any other person, that—

(A) arises under any provision of law relating to any function of the Secretary of the Department of Housing and Urban Development with respect to the Real Estate Settlement Procedures Act of 1974 (12 U.S.C. 2601 et seq.), the Secure and Fair Enforcement for Mortgage Licensing Act of 2008 (12 U.S.C. 5102 et seq.), or the Interstate Land Sales Full Disclosure Act (15 U.S.C. 1701 et seq) transferred to the Bureau by this title; and

(B) existed on the day before the designated transfer date.

(2) CONTINUATION OF SUITS.—This title shall not abate any proceeding commenced by or against the Secretary of the Department of Housing and Urban Development (or the Department of Housing and Urban Development) with respect to any consumer financial protection function of the Secretary of the Department of Housing and Urban Development transferred to the Bureau by this title before the designated transfer date, except that the Bureau, subject to sections 1024, 1025, and 1026, shall be substituted for the Secretary of the Department of Housing and Urban Development (or the Department of Housing and Urban Development) as a party to any such proceeding as of the designated transfer date.

(h) CONTINUATION OF EXISTING ORDERS, RULINGS, DETERMINATIONS, AGREEMENTS, AND RESOLUTIONS.—

(1) IN GENERAL.—Except as provided in paragraph (2) and under subsection (i), all orders, resolutions, determinations, agreements, and rulings that have been issued, made, prescribed, or allowed to become effective by any transferor agency or by a court of competent jurisdiction, in the performance of consumer financial protection functions that are transferred by this title and that are in effect on the day before the designated transfer date, shall continue in effect, and shall continue to be enforceable by the appropriate transferor agency, according to the terms of those orders, resolutions, determinations, agreements, and rulings, and shall not be enforceable by or against the Bureau.

(2) EXCEPTION FOR ORDERS APPLICABLE TO PERSONS DESCRIBED IN SECTION 1025(A).—All orders, resolutions, determinations, agreements, and rulings that have been issued, made, prescribed, or allowed to become effective by any transferor agency or by a court of competent jurisdiction, in the performance of consumer financial protection functions that are transferred by this title and that are in effect on the day before the designated transfer date with respect to any person described in section 1025(a), shall continue in effect, according to the terms of those orders, resolutions, determinations, agreements, and rulings, and shall be enforceable by or against the Bureau or transferor agency.

(i) IDENTIFICATION OF RULES AND ORDERS CONTINUED.—Not later than the designated transfer date, the Bureau—

(1) shall, after consultation with the head of each transferor agency, identify the rules and orders that will be enforced by the Bureau; and

(2) shall publish a list of such rules and orders in the Federal Register.

(j) STATUS OF RULES PROPOSED OR NOT YET EFFECTIVE.—

(1) PROPOSED RULES.—Any proposed rule of a transferor agency which that agency, in performing consumer financial protection functions transferred by this title, has proposed before the designated transfer date, but has not been published as a final rule before that date, shall be deemed to be a proposed rule of the Bureau.

(2) RULES NOT YET EFFECTIVE.—Any interim or final rule of a transferor agency which that agency, in performing consumer financial protection functions transferred by this title, has published before the designated transfer date, but which has not become effective before that date, shall become effective as a rule of the Bureau according to its terms.

[Explanation at ¶ 4705.]

[¶ 11,064] ACT SEC. 1064. TRANSFER OF CERTAIN PERSONNEL.

(a) IN GENERAL.—

(1) CERTAIN FEDERAL RESERVE SYSTEM EMPLOYEES TRANSFERRED.—

(A) IDENTIFYING EMPLOYEES FOR TRANSFER.—The Bureau and the Board of Governors shall—

(i) jointly determine the number of employees of the Board of Governors necessary to perform or support the consumer financial protection functions of the Board of Governors that are transferred to the Bureau by this title; and

(ii) consistent with the number determined under clause (i), jointly identify employees of the Board of Governors for transfer to the Bureau, in a manner that the Bureau and the Board of Governors, in their sole discretion, determine equitable.

(B) IDENTIFIED EMPLOYEES TRANSFERRED.—All employees of the Board of Governors identified under subparagraph (A)(ii) shall be transferred to the Bureau for employment.

(C) FEDERAL RESERVE BANK EMPLOYEES.—Employees of any Federal reserve bank who are performing consumer financial protection functions on behalf of the Board of Governors shall be treated as employees of the Board of Governors for purposes of subparagraphs (A) and (B).

(2) CERTAIN FDIC EMPLOYEES TRANSFERRED.—

(A) IDENTIFYING EMPLOYEES FOR TRANSFER.—The Bureau and the Board of Directors of the Federal Deposit Insurance Corporation shall—

(i) jointly determine the number of employees of that Corporation necessary to perform or support the consumer financial protection functions of the Corporation that are transferred to the Bureau by this title; and

(ii) consistent with the number determined under clause (i), jointly identify employees of the Corporation for transfer to the Bureau, in a manner that the Bureau and the Board of Directors of the Corporation, in their sole discretion, determine equitable.

(B) IDENTIFIED EMPLOYEES TRANSFERRED.—All employees of the Corporation identified under subparagraph (A)(ii) shall be transferred to the Bureau for employment.

(3) CERTAIN NCUA EMPLOYEES TRANSFERRED.—

(A) IDENTIFYING EMPLOYEES FOR TRANSFER.—The Bureau and the National Credit Union Administration Board shall—

(i) jointly determine the number of employees of the National Credit Union Administration necessary to perform or support the consumer financial protection functions of the National Credit Union Administration that are transferred to the Bureau by this title; and

(ii) consistent with the number determined under clause (i), jointly identify employees of the National Credit Union Administration for transfer to the Bureau, in a manner that the Bureau and the National Credit Union Administration Board, in their sole discretion, determine equitable.

(B) IDENTIFIED EMPLOYEES TRANSFERRED.—All employees of the National Credit Union Administration identified under subparagraph (A)(ii) shall be transferred to the Bureau for employment.

(4) CERTAIN OFFICE OF THE COMPTROLLER OF THE CURRENCY EMPLOYEES TRANSFERRED.—

(A) IDENTIFYING EMPLOYEES FOR TRANSFER.—The Bureau and the Comptroller of the Currency shall—

(i) jointly determine the number of employees of the Office of the Comptroller of the Currency necessary to perform or support the consumer financial protection functions of the Office of the Comptroller of the Currency that are transferred to the Bureau by this title; and

(ii) consistent with the number determined under clause (i), jointly identify employees of the Office of the Comptroller of the Currency for transfer to the Bureau, in a manner that the Bureau and the Office of the Comptroller of the Currency, in their sole discretion, determine equitable.

(B) IDENTIFIED EMPLOYEES TRANSFERRED.—All employees of the Office of the Comptroller of the Currency identified under subparagraph (A)(ii) shall be transferred to the Bureau for employment.

(5) CERTAIN OFFICE OF THRIFT SUPERVISION EMPLOYEES TRANSFERRED.—

(A) IDENTIFYING EMPLOYEES FOR TRANSFER.—The Bureau and the Director of the Office of Thrift Supervision shall—

(i) jointly determine the number of employees of the Office of Thrift Supervision necessary to perform or support the consumer financial protection functions of the Office of Thrift Supervision that are transferred to the Bureau by this title; and

(ii) consistent with the number determined under clause (i), jointly identify employees of the Office of Thrift Supervision for transfer to the Bureau, in a manner that the Bureau and the Office of Thrift Supervision, in their sole discretion, determine equitable.

(B) IDENTIFIED EMPLOYEES TRANSFERRED.—All employees of the Office of Thrift Supervision identified under subparagraph (A)(ii) shall be transferred to the Bureau for employment.

(6) CERTAIN EMPLOYEES OF DEPARTMENT OF HOUSING AND URBAN DEVELOPMENT TRANSFERRED.—

(A) IDENTIFYING EMPLOYEES FOR TRANSFER.—The Bureau and the Secretary of the Department of Housing and Urban Development shall—

(i) jointly determine the number of employees of the Department of Housing and Urban Development necessary to perform or support the consumer protection functions of the Department that are transferred to the Bureau by this title; and

(ii) consistent with the number determined under clause (i), jointly identify employees of the Department of Housing and Urban Development for transfer to the Bureau in a manner that the Bureau and the Secretary of the Department of Housing and Urban Development, in their sole discretion, deem equitable.

(B) IDENTIFIED EMPLOYEES TRANSFERRED.—All employees of the Department of Housing and Urban Development identified under subparagraph (A)(ii) shall be transferred to the Bureau for employment.

(7) CONSUMER EDUCATION, FINANCIAL LITERACY, CONSUMER COMPLAINTS, AND RESEARCH FUNCTIONS.—The Bureau and each of the transferor agencies (except the Federal Trade Commission) shall jointly determine the number of employees and the types and grades of employees necessary to perform the functions of the Bureau under subtitle A, including consumer education, financial literacy, policy analysis, responses to consumer complaints and inquiries, research, and similar functions. All employees jointly identified under this paragraph shall be transferred to the Bureau for employment.

(8) AUTHORITY OF THE PRESIDENT TO RESOLVE DISPUTES.—

(A) ACTION AUTHORIZED.—In the event that the Bureau and a transferor agency are unable to reach an agreement under paragraphs (1) through (7) by the designated transfer date, the President, or the designee thereof, may issue an order or directive to the transferor agency to effect the transfer of personnel and property under this subtitle.

(B) TRANSMITTAL TO CONGRESS REQUIRED.—If an order or directive is issued under subparagraph (A), the President shall transmit a copy of the written determination made with respect to such order or directive, including an explanation for the need for the order or directive, to the Committee on Banking, Housing, and Urban Affairs and the Committee on Appropriations of the Senate and the Committee on Financial Services and the Committee on Appropriations of the House of Representatives.

(C) SUNSET.—The authority provided in this paragraph shall terminate 3 years after the designated transfer date.

(9) APPOINTMENT AUTHORITY FOR EXCEPTED SERVICE AND SENIOR EXECUTIVE SERVICE TRANSFERRED.—

(A) IN GENERAL.—In the case of an employee occupying a position in the excepted service or the Senior Executive Service, any appointment authority established pursuant to law or regulations of the Office of Personnel Management for filling such positions shall be transferred, subject to subparagraph (B).

(B) DECLINING TRANSFERS ALLOWED.—An agency or entity may decline to make a transfer of authority under subparagraph (A) (and the employees appointed pursuant thereto) to the extent that such authority relates to positions excepted from the competitive service because of their confidential, policy-making, policy-determining, or policy-advocating character, and non-career positions in the Senior Executive Service (within the meaning of section 3132(a)(7) of title 5, United States Code).

(b) TIMING OF TRANSFERS AND POSITION ASSIGNMENTS.—Each employee to be transferred under this section shall—

(1) be transferred not later than 90 days after the designated transfer date; and

(2) receive notice of a position assignment not later than 120 days after the effective date of his or her transfer.

(c) TRANSFER OF FUNCTION.—

(1) IN GENERAL.—Notwithstanding any other provision of law, the transfer of employees shall be deemed a transfer of functions for the purpose of section 3503 of title 5, United States Code.

(2) PRIORITY OF THIS TITLE.—If any provisions of this title conflict with any protection provided to transferred employees under section 3503 of title 5, United States Code, the provisions of this title shall control.

(d) EQUAL STATUS AND TENURE POSITIONS.—

(1) EMPLOYEES TRANSFERRED FROM THE FEDERAL RESERVE SYSTEM, FDIC, HUD, NCUA, OCC, AND OTS.—Each employee transferred to the Bureau from the Board of Governors, a Federal reserve bank, the Federal Deposit Insurance Corporation, the Department of Housing and Urban Development, the National Credit Union Administration, the Office of the Comptroller of the Currency, or the Office of Thrift Supervision shall be placed in a position at the Bureau with the same status and tenure as that employee held on the day before the designated transfer date.

(2) EMPLOYEES TRANSFERRED FROM THE FEDERAL RESERVE SYSTEM.—For purposes of determining the status and position placement of a transferred employee, any period of service with the Board of Governors or a Federal reserve bank shall be credited as a period of service with a Federal agency.

(e) ADDITIONAL CERTIFICATION REQUIREMENTS LIMITED.—Examiners transferred to the Bureau are not subject to any additional certification requirements before being placed in a comparable examiner position at the Bureau examining the same types of institutions as they examined before they were transferred.

(f) PERSONNEL ACTIONS LIMITED.—

(1) 2-YEAR PROTECTION.—Except as provided in paragraph (2), each transferred employee holding a permanent position on the day before the designated transfer date may not, during the 2-year period beginning on the designated transfer date, be involuntarily separated, or involuntarily reassigned outside his or her locality pay area.

(2) EXCEPTIONS.—Paragraph (1) does not limit the right of the Bureau—

(A) to separate an employee for cause or for unacceptable performance;

(B) to terminate an appointment to a position excepted from the competitive service because of its confidential policy-making, policy-determining, or policy-advocating character; or

(C) to reassign a supervisory employee outside of his or her locality pay area when the Bureau determines that the reassignment is necessary for the efficient operation of the Bureau.

(g) PAY.—

(1) 2-YEAR PROTECTION.—

(A) IN GENERAL.—Except as provided in paragraph (2), each transferred employee shall, during the 2-year period beginning on the designated transfer date, receive pay at a rate equal to not less than the basic rate of pay (including any geographic differential) that the employee received during the pay period immediately preceding the date of transfer.

(B) LIMITATION.—Notwithstanding subparagraph (A), if the employee was receiving a higher rate of basic pay on a temporary basis (because of a temporary assignment, temporary promotion, or other temporary action) immediately before the date of transfer, the Bureau may reduce the rate of basic pay on the date on which the rate would have been reduced but for the transfer, and the protected rate for the remainder of the 2-year period shall be the reduced rate that would have applied, but for the transfer.

(2) EXCEPTIONS.—Paragraph (1) does not limit the right of the Bureau to reduce the rate of basic pay of a transferred employee—

(A) for cause;

(B) for unacceptable performance; or

(C) with the consent of the employee.

(3) PROTECTION ONLY WHILE EMPLOYED.—Paragraph (1) applies to a transferred employee only while that employee remains employed by the Bureau.

(4) PAY INCREASES PERMITTED.—Paragraph (1) does not limit the authority of the Bureau to increase the pay of a transferred employee.

(h) REORGANIZATION.—

(1) BETWEEN 1ST AND 3RD YEAR.—

(A) IN GENERAL.—If the Bureau determines, during the 2-year period beginning 1 year after the designated transfer date, that a reorganization of the staff of the Bureau is required—

(i) that reorganization shall be deemed a "substantial reorganization" for purposes of affording affected employees retirement under section 8336(d)(2) or 8414(b)(1)(B) of title 5, United States Code;

(ii) before the reorganization occurs, all employees in the same locality pay area as defined by the Office of Personnel Management shall be placed in a uniform position classification system; and

(iii) any resulting reduction in force shall be governed by the provisions of chapter 35 of title 5, United States Code, except that the Bureau shall—

(I) establish competitive areas (as that term is defined in regulations issued by the Office of Personnel Management) to include at a minimum all employees in the same locality pay area as defined by the Office of Personnel Management;

(II) establish competitive levels (as that term is defined in regulations issued by the Office of Personnel Management) without regard to whether the particular employees have been appointed to positions in the competitive service or the excepted service; and

(III) afford employees appointed to positions in the excepted service (other than to a position excepted from the competitive service because of its confidential policy-making, policy-determining, or policy-advocating character) the same assignment rights to positions within the Bureau as employees appointed to positions in the competitive service.

(B) SERVICE CREDIT FOR REDUCTIONS IN FORCE.—For purposes of this paragraph, periods of service with a Federal home loan bank, a joint office of the Federal home loan banks, the Board of Governors, a Federal reserve bank, the Federal Deposit Insurance Corporation, or the National Credit Union Administration shall be credited as periods of service with a Federal agency.

(2) AFTER 3RD YEAR.—

(A) IN GENERAL.—If the Bureau determines, at any time after the 3-year period beginning on the designated transfer date, that a reorganization of the staff of the Bureau is required, any resulting reduction in force shall be governed by the provisions of chapter 35 of title 5, United States Code, except that the Bureau shall establish competitive levels (as that term is defined in regulations issued by the Office of Personnel Management) without regard to types of appointment held by particular employees transferred under this section.

(B) SERVICE CREDIT FOR REDUCTIONS IN FORCE.—For purposes of this paragraph, periods of service with a Federal home loan bank, a joint office of the Federal home loan banks, the Board of Governors, a Federal reserve bank, the Federal Deposit Insurance Corporation, or the National Credit Union Administration shall be credited as periods of service with a Federal agency.

(i) BENEFITS.—

(1) RETIREMENT BENEFITS FOR TRANSFERRED EMPLOYEES.—

(A) IN GENERAL.—

(i) CONTINUATION OF EXISTING RETIREMENT PLAN.—Unless an election is made under clause (iii) or subparagraph (B), each employee transferred pursuant to this subtitle shall remain enrolled in the existing retirement plan of that employee as of the date of transfer, through any period of continuous employment with the Bureau.

(ii) EMPLOYER CONTRIBUTION.—The Bureau shall pay any employer contributions to the existing retirement plan of each transferred employee, as required under that plan.

(iii) OPTION TO ELECT INTO THE FEDERAL RESERVE SYSTEM RETIREMENT PLAN AND FEDERAL RESERVE SYSTEM THRIFT PLAN.—Any employee transferred pursuant to this subtitle may, during the 1-year period beginning 6 months after the designated transfer date, elect to end their participation and benefit accruals under their existing retirement plan or plans and elect to participate in both the Federal Reserve System Retirement Plan and the Federal Reserve System Thrift Plan, through any period of continuous employment with the Bureau, under the same terms as are applicable to Federal Reserve System transferred employees, as provided in subparagraph (C). An election of coverage by the Federal Reserve System Retirement Plan and the Federal Reserve System Thrift Plan shall begin on the day following the end of the 18-month period beginning on the designated transfer date, and benefit accruals under the existing retirement plan of the transferred employee shall end on the last day of the 18-month period beginning on the designated transfer date If an employee elects to participate in the Federal Reserve System Retirement Plan and the Federal Reserve System Thrift Plan, all of the service of the employee that was creditable under their existing retirement plan shall be transferred to the Federal Reserve System Retirement Plan on the day following the end of the 18-month period beginning on the designated transfer date.

(iv) BUREAU CONTRIBUTION.—The Bureau shall pay an employer contribution to the Federal Reserve System Retirement Plan, in the amount established as an employer contribution under the Federal Employees Retirement System, as established under chapter 84 of title 5, United States Code, for each Bureau employee who elects to participate in the Federal Reserve System Retirement Plan under this subparagraph. The Bureau shall pay an employer contribution to the Federal Reserve System Thrift Plan for each Bureau employee who elects to participate in such plan, as required under the terms of the Federal Reserve System Thrift Plan.

(v) ADDITIONAL FUNDING.—The Bureau shall transfer to the Federal Reserve System Retirement Plan an amount determined by the Board of Governors, in consultation with the Bureau, to be necessary to reimburse the Federal Reserve System Retirement Plan for the costs to such plan of providing benefits to employees electing coverage under the Federal Reserve System Retirement Plan under subparagraph (iii), and who were transferred to the Bureau from outside of the Federal Reserve System.

(vi) OPTION TO ELECT INTO THRIFT PLAN CREATED BY THE BUREAU.—If the Bureau chooses to establish a thrift plan, the employees transferred pursuant to this subtitle shall have the option to elect, under such terms and conditions as the Bureau may establish, coverage under such a thrift plan established by the Bureau. Transferred employees may not remain in the thrift plan of the agency from which the employee transferred under this subtitle, if the employee elects to participate in a thrift plan established by the Bureau.

(B) OPTION FOR EMPLOYEES TRANSFERRED FROM FEDERAL RESERVE SYSTEM TO BE SUBJECT TO THE FEDERAL EMPLOYEE RETIREMENT PROGRAM.—

(i) ELECTION.—Any Federal Reserve System transferred employee who was enrolled in the Federal Reserve System Retirement Plan on the day before the date of his or her transfer to the Bureau may, during the 1-year period beginning 6 months after the designated transfer date, elect to be subject to the Federal Employee Retirement Program.

(ii) EFFECTIVE DATE OF COVERAGE.—An election of coverage by the Federal Employee Retirement Program under this subparagraph shall begin on the day following the end of the 18-month period beginning on the designated transfer date, and benefit accruals under the existing retirement plan of the Federal Reserve System transferred employee shall end on the last day of the 18-month period beginning on the designated transfer date.

(C) BUREAU PARTICIPATION IN FEDERAL RESERVE SYSTEM RETIREMENT PLAN.—

(i) BENEFITS PROVIDED.—Federal Reserve System employees transferred pursuant to this subtitle shall continue to be eligible to participate in the Federal Reserve System Retirement Plan and Federal Reserve System Thrift Plan through any period of continuous employment with the Bureau, unless the employee makes an election under subparagraph (A)(vi) or (B). The retirement benefits, formulas, and features offered to the Federal Reserve System transferred employees shall be the same as those offered to employees of the Board of Governors who participate in the Federal Reserve System Retirement Plan and the Federal Reserve System Thrift Plan, as amended from time to time.

(ii) LIMITATION.—The Bureau shall not have responsibility or authority—

(I) to amend an existing retirement plan (including the Federal Reserve System Retirement Plan or Federal Reserve System Thrift Plan);

(II) for administering an existing retirement plan (including the Federal Reserve System Retirement Plan or Federal Reserve System Thrift Plan); or

(III) for ensuring the plans comply with applicable laws, fiduciary rules, and related responsibilities.

(iii) TAX QUALIFIED STATUS.—Notwithstanding any other provision of law, providing benefits to Federal Reserve System employees transferred to the Bureau pursuant to this subtitle, and to employees who elect coverage pursuant to subparagraph (A)(iii) or under section 1013(a)(2)(B), shall not cause any existing retirement plan (including the Federal Reserve System Retirement Plan and the Federal Reserve System Thrift Plan) to lose its tax-qualified status under sections 401(a) and 501(a) of the Internal Revenue Code of 1986.

(iv) BUREAU CONTRIBUTION.—The Bureau shall pay any employer contributions to the existing retirement plan (including the Federal Reserve System Retirement Plan and the Federal Reserve System Thrift Plan) for each Federal Reserve System transferred employee participating in those plans, as required under the plan, after the designated transfer date.

(v) CONTROLLED GROUP STATUS.—The Bureau is the same employer as the Federal Reserve System (as comprised of the Board of Governors and each of the 12 Federal reserve banks prior to the date of enactment of this Act) for purposes of subsections (b), (c), (m), and (o) of section 414 of the Internal Revenue Code of 1986 (26 U.S.C. 414).

(D) DEFINITIONS.—For purposes of this paragraph—

(i) the term "existing retirement plan" means, with respect to an employee transferred pursuant to this subtitle, the retirement plan (including the Financial Institutions Retirement Fund) and any associated thrift savings plan, of the agency from which the employee was transferred under this subtitle, in which the employee was enrolled on the day before the date on which the employee was transferred;

(ii) the term "Federal Employee Retirement Program" means either the Civil Service Retirement System established under chapter 83 of title 5, United States Code, or the Federal Employees Retirement System established under chapter 84 of title 5, United States Code, depending upon the service history of the individual;

(iii) the term "Federal Reserve System transferred employee" means a transferred employee who is an employee of the Board of Governors or a Federal reserve bank on the day before the designated transfer date, and who is transferred to the Bureau on the designated transfer date pursuant to this subtitle;

(iv) the term "Federal Reserve System Retirement Plan" means the Retirement Plan for Employees of the Federal Reserve System; and

(v) the term "Federal Reserve System Thrift Plan" means the Thrift Plan for Employees of the Federal Reserve System.

(2) BENEFITS OTHER THAN RETIREMENT BENEFITS FOR TRANSFERRED EMPLOYEES.—

(A) DURING 1ST YEAR.—

(i) EXISTING PLANS CONTINUE.—Each employee transferred pursuant to this subtitle may, for 1 year after the designated transfer date, retain membership in any other employee benefit program of the agency or bank from which the employee transferred, including a medical, dental, vision, long term care, or life insurance program, to which the employee belonged on the day before the designated transfer date.

(ii) EMPLOYER CONTRIBUTION.—The Bureau shall reimburse the agency or bank from which an employee was transferred for any cost incurred by that agency or bank in continuing to extend coverage in the benefit program to the employee, as required under that program or negotiated agreements.

(B) MEDICAL, DENTAL, VISION, OR LIFE INSURANCE AFTER FIRST YEAR.—If, at the end of the 1-year period beginning on the designated transfer date, the Bureau has not established its own, or arranged for participation in another entity's, medical, dental, vision, or life insurance program, an employee transferred pursuant to this subtitle who was a member of such a program at the agency or Federal reserve bank from which the employee transferred may, before the coverage of that employee ends under subparagraph (A)(i), elect to enroll, without regard to any regularly scheduled open season, in—

(i) the enhanced dental benefits program established under chapter 89A of title 5, United States Code;

(ii) the enhanced vision benefits established under chapter 89B of title 5, United States Code;

(iii) the Federal Employees Group Life Insurance Program established under chapter 87 of title 5, United States Code, without regard to any requirement of insurability; and

(iv) the Federal Employees Health Benefits Program established under chapter 89 of title 5, United States Code.

(C) LONG TERM CARE INSURANCE AFTER 1ST YEAR.—If, at the end of the 1-year period beginning on the designated transfer date, the Bureau has not established its own, or arranged for participation in another entity's, long term care insurance program, an employee transferred pursuant to this subtitle who was a member of such a program at the agency or Federal reserve bank from which the employee transferred may, before the coverage of that employee ends under subparagraph (A)(i), elect to apply for coverage under the Federal Long Term Care Insurance Program established under chapter 90 of title 5, United States Code, under the underwriting requirements applicable to a new active workforce member (as defined in part 875 of title 5, Code of Federal Regulations).

(D) EMPLOYEE CONTRIBUTION.—An individual enrolled in the Federal Employees Health Benefits program shall pay any employee contribution required by the plan.

(E) ADDITIONAL FUNDING.—The Bureau shall transfer to the Federal Employees Health Benefits Fund established under section 8909 of title 5, United States Code, an amount determined by the Director of the Office of Personnel Management, after consultation with the Bureau and the Office of Management and Budget, to be necessary to reimburse the Fund for the cost to the Fund of providing benefits under this paragraph.

(F) CREDIT FOR TIME ENROLLED IN OTHER PLANS.—For employees transferred under this title, enrollment in a health benefits plan administered by a transferor agency or a Federal reserve bank, as the case may be, immediately before enrollment in a health benefits plan under chapter 89 of title 5, United States Code, shall be considered as enrollment in a health benefits plan under that chapter for purposes of section 8905(b)(1)(A) of title 5, United States Code.

(G) SPECIAL PROVISIONS TO ENSURE CONTINUATION OF LIFE INSURANCE BENEFITS.—

(i) IN GENERAL.—An annuitant (as defined in section 8901(3) of title 5, United States Code) who is enrolled in a life insurance plan administered by a transferor agency on the day before the designated transfer date shall be eligible for coverage by a life insurance plan under sections 8706(b), 8714a, 8714b, and 8714c of title 5, United States Code, or in a life insurance plan established by the Bureau, without regard to any regularly scheduled open season and requirement of insurability.

(ii) EMPLOYEE CONTRIBUTION.—An individual enrolled in a life insurance plan under this subparagraph shall pay any employee contribution required by the plan.

(iii) ADDITIONAL FUNDING.—The Bureau shall transfer to the Employees' Life Insurance Fund established under section 8714 of title 5, United States Code, an amount determined by the Director of the Office of Personnel Management, after consultation with the Bureau and the Office of Management and Budget, to be necessary to reimburse the Fund for the cost to the Fund of providing benefits under this subparagraph not otherwise paid for by the employee under clause (ii).

(iv) CREDIT FOR TIME ENROLLED IN OTHER PLANS.—For employees transferred under this title, enrollment in a life insurance plan administered by a transferor agency immediately before enrollment in a life insurance plan under chapter 87 of title 5, United States Code, shall be considered as enrollment in a life insurance plan under that chapter for purposes of section 8706(b)(1)(A) of title 5, United States Code.

(3) OPM RULES.—The Office of Personnel Management shall issue such rules as are necessary to carry out this subsection.

(j) IMPLEMENTATION OF UNIFORM PAY AND CLASSIFICATION SYSTEM.—Not later than 2 years after the designated transfer date, the Bureau shall implement a uniform pay and classification system for all employees transferred under this title.

(k) EQUITABLE TREATMENT.—In administering the provisions of this section, the Bureau—

(1) shall take no action that would unfairly disadvantage transferred employees relative to each other based on their prior employment by the Board of Governors, the Federal Deposit Insurance Corporation, the Department of Housing and Urban Development, the National Credit Union Administration, the Office of the Comptroller of the Currency, the Office of Thrift Supervision, a Federal reserve bank, a Federal home loan bank, or a joint office of the Federal home loan banks; and

(2) may take such action as is appropriate in individual cases so that employees transferred under this section receive equitable treatment, with respect to the status, tenure, pay, benefits (other than benefits under programs administered by the Office of Personnel Management), and

accrued leave or vacation time of those employees, for prior periods of service with any Federal agency, including the Board of Governors, the Corporation, the Department of Housing and Urban Development, the National Credit Union Administration, the Office of the Comptroller of the Currency, the Office of Thrift Supervision, a Federal reserve bank, a Federal home loan bank, or a joint office of the Federal home loan banks.

(l) IMPLEMENTATION.—In implementing the provisions of this section, the Bureau shall coordinate with the Office of Personnel Management and other entities having expertise in matters related to employment to ensure a fair and orderly transition for affected employees.

[Explanation at ¶ 4710.]

[¶ 11,065] ACT SEC. 1065. INCIDENTAL TRANSFERS.

(a) INCIDENTAL TRANSFERS AUTHORIZED.—The Director of the Office of Management and Budget, in consultation with the Secretary, shall make such additional incidental transfers and dispositions of assets and liabilities held, used, arising from, available, or to be made available, in connection with the functions transferred by this title, as the Director may determine necessary to accomplish the purposes of this title.

(b) SUNSET.—The authority provided in this section shall terminate 5 years after the date of enactment of this Act.

[Explanation at ¶ 4715.]

[¶ 11,066] ACT SEC. 1066. INTERIM AUTHORITY OF THE SECRETARY.

(a) IN GENERAL.—The Secretary is authorized to perform the functions of the Bureau under this subtitle until the Director of the Bureau is confirmed by the Senate in accordance with section 1011.

(b) INTERIM ADMINISTRATIVE SERVICES BY THE DEPARTMENT OF THE TREASURY.—The Department of the Treasury may provide administrative services necessary to support the Bureau before the designated transfer date.

[Explanation at ¶ 4720.]

[¶ 11,067] ACT SEC. 1067. TRANSITION OVERSIGHT.

(a) PURPOSE.—The purpose of this section is to ensure that the Bureau—

(1) has an orderly and organized startup;

(2) attracts and retains a qualified workforce; and

(3) establishes comprehensive employee training and benefits programs.

(b) REPORTING REQUIREMENT.—

(1) IN GENERAL.—The Bureau shall submit an annual report to the Committee on Banking, Housing, and Urban Affairs of the Senate and the Committee on Financial Services of the House of Representatives that includes the plans described in paragraph (2).

(2) PLANS.—The plans described in this paragraph are as follows:

(A) TRAINING AND WORKFORCE DEVELOPMENT PLAN.—The Bureau shall submit a training and workforce development plan that includes, to the extent practicable—

(i) identification of skill and technical expertise needs and actions taken to meet those requirements;

(ii) steps taken to foster innovation and creativity;

(iii) leadership development and succession planning; and

(iv) effective use of technology by employees.

(B) WORKPLACE FLEXIBILITIES PLAN.—The Bureau shall submit a workforce flexibility plan that includes, to the extent practicable—

(i) telework;

(ii) flexible work schedules;

(iii) phased retirement;

(iv) reemployed annuitants;

(v) part-time work;

(vi) job sharing;

(vii) parental leave benefits and childcare assistance;

(viii) domestic partner benefits;

(ix) other workplace flexibilities; or

(x) any combination of the items described in clauses (i) through (ix).

(C) RECRUITMENT AND RETENTION PLAN.—The Bureau shall submit a recruitment and retention plan that includes, to the extent practicable, provisions relating to—

(i) the steps necessary to target highly qualified applicant pools with diverse backgrounds;

(ii) streamlined employment application processes;

(iii) the provision of timely notification of the status of employment applications to applicants; and

(iv) the collection of information to measure indicators of hiring effectiveness.

(c) EXPIRATION.—The reporting requirement under subsection (b) shall terminate 5 years after the date of enactment of this Act.

(d) RULE OF CONSTRUCTION.—Nothing in this section may be construed to affect—

(1) a collective bargaining agreement, as that term is defined in section 7103(a)(8) of title 5, United States Code, that is in effect on the date of enactment of this Act; or

(2) the rights of employees under chapter 71 of title 5, United States Code.

(e) PARTICIPATION IN EXAMINATIONS.—In order to prepare the Bureau to conduct examinations under section 1025 upon the designated transfer date, the Bureau and the applicable prudential regulator may agree to include, on a sampling basis, examiners on examinations of the compliance with Federal consumer financial law of institutions described in section 1025(a) conducted by the prudential regulators prior to the designated transfer date.

[Explanation at ¶ 4725.]

Subtitle G—Regulatory Improvements

[¶ 11,071] ACT SEC. 1071. SMALL BUSINESS DATA COLLECTION.

(a) IN GENERAL.—The Equal Credit Opportunity Act (15 U.S.C. 1691 et seq.) is amended by inserting after section 704A the following:

"SEC. 704B. SMALL BUSINESS LOAN DATA COLLECTION.

"(a) PURPOSE.—The purpose of this section is to facilitate enforcement of fair lending laws and enable communities, governmental entities, and creditors to identify business and community development needs and opportunities of women-owned, minority-owned, and small businesses.

"(b) INFORMATION GATHERING.—Subject to the requirements of this section, in the case of any application to a financial institution for credit for women-owned, minority-owned, or small business, the financial institution shall—

"(1) inquire whether the business is a women-owned, minority-owned, or small business, without regard to whether such application is received in person, by mail, by telephone, by electronic mail or other form of electronic transmission, or by any other means, and whether or not such application is in response to a solicitation by the financial institution; and

"(2) maintain a record of the responses to such inquiry, separate from the application and accompanying information.

"(c) RIGHT TO REFUSE.—Any applicant for credit may refuse to provide any information requested pursuant to subsection (b) in connection with any application for credit.

"(d) NO ACCESS BY UNDERWRITERS.—

"(1) LIMITATION.—Where feasible, no loan underwriter or other officer or employee of a financial institution, or any affiliate of a financial institution, involved in making any determination concerning an application for credit shall have access to any information provided by the applicant pursuant to a request under subsection (b) in connection with such application.

"(2) LIMITED ACCESS.—If a financial institution determines that a loan underwriter or other officer or employee of a financial institution, or any affiliate of a financial institution, involved in making any determination concerning an application for credit should have access to any information provided by the applicant pursuant to a request under subsection (b), the financial institution shall provide notice to the applicant of the access of the underwriter to such information, along with notice that the financial institution may not discriminate on the basis of such information.

"(e) FORM AND MANNER OF INFORMATION.—

"(1) IN GENERAL.—Each financial institution shall compile and maintain, in accordance with regulations of the Bureau, a record of the information provided by any loan applicant pursuant to a request under subsection (b).

"(2) ITEMIZATION.—Information compiled and maintained under paragraph (1) shall be itemized in order to clearly and conspicuously disclose—

"(A) the number of the application and the date on which the application was received;

"(B) the type and purpose of the loan or other credit being applied for;

"(C) the amount of the credit or credit limit applied for, and the amount of the credit transaction or the credit limit approved for such applicant;

"(D) the type of action taken with respect to such application, and the date of such action;

"(E) the census tract in which is located the principal place of business of the women-owned, minority-owned, or small business loan applicant;

"(F) the gross annual revenue of the business in the last fiscal year of the women-owned, minority-owned, or small business loan applicant preceding the date of the application;

"(G) the race, sex, and ethnicity of the principal owners of the business; and

"(H) any additional data that the Bureau determines would aid in fulfilling the purposes of this section.

"(3) NO PERSONALLY IDENTIFIABLE INFORMATION.—In compiling and maintaining any record of information under this section, a financial institution may not include in such record the name, specific address (other than the census tract required under paragraph (1)(E)), telephone number, electronic mail address, or any other personally identifiable information concerning any individual who is, or is connected with, the women-owned, minority-owned, or small business loan applicant.

"(4) DISCRETION TO DELETE OR MODIFY PUBLICLY AVAILABLE DATA.—The Bureau may, at its discretion, delete or modify data collected under this section which is or will be available to the public, if the Bureau determines that the deletion or modification of the data would advance a privacy interest.

"(f) AVAILABILITY OF INFORMATION.—

"(1) SUBMISSION TO BUREAU.—The data required to be compiled and maintained under this section by any financial institution shall be submitted annually to the Bureau.

"(2) AVAILABILITY OF INFORMATION.—Information compiled and maintained under this section shall be—

"(A) retained for not less than 3 years after the date of preparation;

"(B) made available to any member of the public, upon request, in the form required under regulations prescribed by the Bureau;

"(C) annually made available to the public generally by the Bureau, in such form and in such manner as is determined by the Bureau, by regulation.

"(3) COMPILATION OF AGGREGATE DATA.—The Bureau may, at its discretion—

"(A) compile and aggregate data collected under this section for its own use; and

"(B) make public such compilations of aggregate data.

"(g) BUREAU ACTION.—

"(1) IN GENERAL.—The Bureau shall prescribe such rules and issue such guidance as may be necessary to carry out, enforce, and compile data pursuant to this section.

"(2) EXCEPTIONS.—The Bureau, by rule or order, may adopt exceptions to any requirement of this section and may, conditionally or unconditionally, exempt any financial institution or class of financial institutions from the requirements of this section, as the Bureau deems necessary or appropriate to carry out the purposes of this section.

"(3) GUIDANCE.—The Bureau shall issue guidance designed to facilitate compliance with the requirements of this section, including assisting financial institutions in working with applicants to determine whether the applicants are women-owned, minority-owned, or small businesses for purposes of this section.

"(h) DEFINITIONS.—For purposes of this section, the following definitions shall apply:

"(1) FINANCIAL INSTITUTION.—The term 'financial institution' means any partnership, company, corporation, association (incorporated or unincorporated), trust, estate, cooperative organization, or other entity that engages in any financial activity.

"(2) SMALL BUSINESS.—The term 'small business' has the same meaning as the term 'small business concern' in section 3 of the Small Business Act (15 U.S.C. 632).

"(3) SMALL BUSINESS LOAN.—The term 'small business loan' means a loan made to a small business.

"(4) MINORITY.—The term 'minority' has the same meaning as in section 1204(c)(3) of the Financial Institutions Reform, Recovery, and Enforcement Act of 1989.

"(5) MINORITY-OWNED BUSINESS.—The term 'minority-owned business' means a business—

"(A) more than 50 percent of the ownership or control of which is held by 1 or more minority individuals; and

"(B) more than 50 percent of the net profit or loss of which accrues to 1 or more minority individuals.

"(6) WOMEN-OWNED BUSINESS.—The term 'women-owned business' means a business—

"(A) more than 50 percent of the ownership or control of which is held by 1 or more women; and

"(B) more than 50 percent of the net profit or loss of which accrues to 1 or more women.".

(b) TECHNICAL AND CONFORMING AMENDMENTS.—Section 701(b) of the Equal Credit Opportunity Act (15 U.S.C. 1691(b)) is amended—

(1) in paragraph (3), by striking "or" at the end;

(2) in paragraph (4), by striking the period at the end and inserting "; or"; and

(3) by inserting after paragraph (4), the following:

"(5) to make an inquiry under section 704B, in accordance with the requirements of that section.".

(c) CLERICAL AMENDMENT.—The table of sections for title VII of the Consumer Credit Protection Act is amended by inserting after the item relating to section 704A the following new item:

"704B. Small business loan data collection.".

(d) EFFECTIVE DATE.—This section shall become effective on the designated transfer date.

[Explanation at ¶ 4730.]

[¶ 11,072] ACT SEC. 1072. ASSISTANCE FOR ECONOMICALLY VULNERABLE INDIVIDUALS AND FAMILIES.

(a) HERA AMENDMENTS.—Section 1132 of the Housing and Economic Recovery Act of 2008 (12 U.S.C. 1701x note) is amended—

(1) in subsection (a), by inserting in each of paragraphs (1), (2), (3), and (4) "or economically vulnerable individuals and families" after "homebuyers" each place that term appears;

(2) in subsection (b)(1), by inserting "or economically vulnerable individuals and families" after "homebuyers";

(3) in subsection (c)(1)—

(A) in subparagraph (A), by striking "or" at the end;

(B) in subparagraph (B), by striking the period at the end and inserting "; or"; and

(C) by adding at the end the following:

"(C) a nonprofit corporation that—

"(i) is exempt from taxation under section 501(c)(3) of the Internal Revenue Code of 1986; and

"(ii) specializes or has expertise in working with economically vulnerable individuals and families, but whose primary purpose is not provision of credit counseling services."; and

(4) in subsection (d)(1), by striking "not more than 5".

(b) APPLICABILITY.—Amendments made by subsection (a) shall not apply to programs authorized by section 1132 of the Housing and Economic Recovery Act of 2008 (12 U.S.C. 1701x note) that are funded with appropriations prior to fiscal year 2011.

[Explanation at ¶ 4735.]

[¶ 11,073] ACT SEC. 1073. REMITTANCE TRANSFERS.

(a) TREATMENT OF REMITTANCE TRANSFERS.—The Electronic Fund Transfer Act (15 U.S.C. 1693 et seq.) is amended—

(1) in section 902(b) (15 U.S.C. 1693(b)), by inserting "and remittance" after "electronic fund";

(2) in section 904(c) (15 U.S.C. 1693b(c)), in the first sentence, by inserting "or remittance transfers" after "electronic fund transfers";

(3) by redesignating sections 919, 920, 921, and 922 as sections 920, 921, 922, and 923, respectively; and

(4) by inserting after section 918 the following:

"SEC. 919. REMITTANCE TRANSFERS.

"(a) DISCLOSURES REQUIRED FOR REMITTANCE TRANSFERS.—

"(1) IN GENERAL.—Each remittance transfer provider shall make disclosures as required under this section and in accordance with rules prescribed by the Board. Disclosures required under this section shall be in addition to any other disclosures applicable under this title.

"(2) DISCLOSURES.—Subject to rules prescribed by the Board, a remittance transfer provider shall provide, in writing and in a form that the sender may keep, to each sender requesting a remittance transfer, as applicable to the transaction—

"(A) at the time at which the sender requests a remittance transfer to be initiated, and prior to the sender making any payment in connection with the remittance transfer, a disclosure describing—

"(i) the amount of currency that will be received by the designated recipient, using the values of the currency into which the funds will be exchanged;

"(ii) the amount of transfer and any other fees charged by the remittance transfer provider for the remittance transfer; and

"(iii) any exchange rate to be used by the remittance transfer provider for the remittance transfer, to the nearest 1/100th of a point; and

"(B) at the time at which the sender makes payment in connection with the remittance transfer—

"(i) a receipt showing—

"(I) the information described in subparagraph (A);

"(II) the promised date of delivery to the designated recipient; and

"(III) the name and either the telephone number or the address of the designated recipient, if either the telephone number or the address of the designated recipient is provided by the sender; and

"(ii) a statement containing—

"(I) information about the rights of the sender under this section regarding the resolution of errors; and

"(II) appropriate contact information for—

"(aa) the remittance transfer provider; and

"(bb) the State agency that regulates the remittance transfer provider and the Board, including the toll-free telephone number established under section 1013 of the Consumer Financial Protection Act of 2010.

"(3) REQUIREMENTS RELATING TO DISCLOSURES.—With respect to each disclosure required to be provided under paragraph (2) a remittance transfer provider shall—

"(A) provide an initial notice and receipt, as required by subparagraphs (A) and (B) of paragraph (2), and an error resolution statement, as required by subsection (d), that clearly and conspicuously describe the information required to be disclosed therein; and

"(B) with respect to any transaction that a sender conducts electronically, comply with the Electronic Signatures in Global and National Commerce Act (15 U.S.C. 7001 et seq.).

"(4) EXCEPTION FOR DISCLOSURES OF AMOUNT RECEIVED.—

"(A) IN GENERAL.—Subject to the rules prescribed by the Board, and except as provided under subparagraph (B), the disclosures required regarding the amount of currency that will be received by the designated recipient shall be deemed to be accurate, so long as the disclosures provide a reasonably accurate estimate of the foreign currency to be received. This paragraph shall apply only to a remittance transfer provider who is an insured depository institution, as defined in section 3 of the Federal Deposit Insurance Act (12 U.S.C. 1813), or an insured credit union, as defined in section 101 of the Federal Credit Union Act (12 U.S.C. 1752), and if—

"(i) a remittance transfer is conducted through a demand deposit, savings deposit, or other asset account that the sender holds with such remittance transfer provider; and

"(ii) at the time at which the sender requests the transaction, the remittance transfer provider is unable to know, for reasons beyond its control, the amount of currency that will be made available to the designated recipient.

"(B) DEADLINE.—The application of subparagraph (A) shall terminate 5 years after the date of enactment of the Consumer Financial Protection Act of 2010, unless the Board determines that termination of such provision would negatively affect the ability of remittance transfer providers described in subparagraph (A) to send remittances to locations in foreign countries, in which case, the Board may, by rule, extend the application of subparagraph (A) to not longer than 10 years after the date of enactment of the Consumer Financial Protection Act of 2010.

"(5) EXEMPTION AUTHORITY.—The Board may, by rule, permit a remittance transfer provider to satisfy the requirements of—

"(A) paragraph (2)(A) orally, if the transaction is conducted entirely by telephone;

"(B) paragraph (2)(B), in the case of a transaction conducted entirely by telephone, by mailing the disclosures required under such subparagraph to the sender, not later than 1 business day after the date on which the transaction is conducted, or by including such documents in the next periodic statement, if the telephone transaction is conducted through a demand deposit, savings deposit, or other asset account that the sender holds with the remittance transfer provider;

"(C) subparagraphs (A) and (B) of paragraph (2) together in one written disclosure, but only to the extent that the information provided in accordance with paragraph (3)(A) is accurate at the time at which payment is made in connection with the subject remittance transfer; and

"(D) paragraph (2)(A), without compliance with section 101(c) of the Electronic Signatures in Global Commerce Act, if a sender initiates the transaction electronically and the information is displayed electronically in a manner that the sender can keep.

"(6) STOREFRONT AND INTERNET NOTICES.—

"(A) IN GENERAL.—

"(i) PROMINENT POSTING.—Subject to subparagraph (B), the Board may prescribe rules to require a remittance transfer provider to prominently post, and timely update, a notice describing a model remittance transfer for one or more amounts, as the Board may determine, which notice shall show the amount of currency that will be received by the designated recipient, using the values of the currency into which the funds will be exchanged.

"(ii) ONSITE DISPLAYS.—The Board may require the notice prescribed under this subparagraph to be displayed in every physical storefront location owned or controlled by the remittance transfer provider.

"(iii) INTERNET NOTICES.—Subject to paragraph (3), the Board shall prescribe rules to require a remittance transfer provider that provides remittance transfers via the Internet to provide a notice, comparable to a storefront notice described in this subparagraph, located on the home page or landing page (with respect to such remittance transfer services) owned or controlled by the remittance transfer provider.

"(iv) RULEMAKING AUTHORITY.—In prescribing rules under this subparagraph, the Board may impose standards or requirements regarding the provision of the storefront and Internet notices required under this subparagraph and the provision of the disclosures required under paragraphs (2) and (3).

"(B) STUDY AND ANALYSIS.—Prior to proposing rules under subparagraph (A), the Board shall undertake appropriate studies and analyses, which shall be consistent with section 904(a)(2), and may include an advanced notice of proposed rulemaking, to determine whether a storefront notice or Internet notice facilitates the ability of a consumer—

"(i) to compare prices for remittance transfers; and

"(ii) to understand the types and amounts of any fees or costs imposed on remittance transfers.

"(b) FOREIGN LANGUAGE DISCLOSURES.—The disclosures required under this section shall be made in English and in each of the foreign languages principally used by the remittance transfer provider, or any of its agents, to advertise, solicit, or market, either orally or in writing, at that office.

"(c) REGULATIONS REGARDING TRANSFERS TO CERTAIN NATIONS.—If the Board determines that a recipient nation does not legally allow, or the method by which transactions are made in the recipient country do not allow, a remittance transfer provider to know the amount of currency that will be received by the designated recipient, the Board may prescribe rules (not later than 18 months after the date of enactment of the Consumer Financial Protection Act of 2010) addressing the issue, which rules shall include standards for a remittance transfer provider to provide—

"(1) a receipt that is consistent with subsections (a) and (b); and

"(2) a reasonably accurate estimate of the foreign currency to be received, based on the rate provided to the sender by the remittance transfer provider at the time at which the transaction was initiated by the sender.

"(d) REMITTANCE TRANSFER ERRORS.—

"(1) ERROR RESOLUTION.—

"(A) IN GENERAL.—If a remittance transfer provider receives oral or written notice from the sender within 180 days of the promised date of delivery that an error occurred with respect to a remittance transfer, including the amount of currency designated in subsection (a)(3)(A) that was to be sent to the designated recipient of the remittance transfer, using the values of the currency into which the funds should have been exchanged, but was not made available to the designated recipient in the foreign country, the remittance transfer provider shall resolve the error pursuant to this subsection and investigate the reason for the error.

"(B) REMEDIES.—Not later than 90 days after the date of receipt of a notice from the sender pursuant to subparagraph (A), the remittance transfer provider shall, as applicable to the error and as designated by the sender—

"(i) refund to the sender the total amount of funds tendered by the sender in connection with the remittance transfer which was not properly transmitted;

"(ii) make available to the designated recipient, without additional cost to the designated recipient or to the sender, the amount appropriate to resolve the error;

"(iii) provide such other remedy, as determined appropriate by rule of the Board for the protection of senders; or

"(iv) provide written notice to the sender that there was no error with an explanation responding to the specific complaint of the sender.

"(2) RULES.—The Board shall establish, by rule issued not later than 18 months after the date of enactment of the Consumer Financial Protection Act of 2010, clear and appropriate standards for remittance transfer providers with respect to error resolution relating to remittance transfers, to protect senders from such errors. Standards prescribed under this paragraph shall include appropriate standards regarding record keeping, as required, including documentation—

"(A) of the complaint of the sender;

"(B) that the sender provides the remittance transfer provider with respect to the alleged error; and

"(C) of the findings of the remittance transfer provider regarding the investigation of the alleged error that the sender brought to their attention.

"(3) CANCELLATION AND REFUND POLICY RULES.—Not later than 18 months after the date of enactment of the Consumer Financial Protection Act of 2010, the Board shall issue final rules regarding appropriate remittance transfer cancellation and refund policies for consumers.

"(e) APPLICABILITY OF THIS TITLE.—

"(1) IN GENERAL.—A remittance transfer that is not an electronic fund transfer, as defined in section 903, shall not be subject to any of the provisions of sections 905 through 913. A remittance transfer that is an electronic fund transfer, as defined in section 903, shall be subject to all provisions of this title, except for section 908, that are otherwise applicable to electronic fund transfers under this title.

"(2) RULE OF CONSTRUCTION.—Nothing in this section shall be construed—

"(A) to affect the application to any transaction, to any remittance provider, or to any other person of any of the provisions of subchapter II of chapter 53 of title 31, United States Code, section 21 of the Federal Deposit Insurance Act (12 U.S.C. 1829b), or chapter 2 of title I of Public Law 91-508 (12 U.S.C. 1951-1959), or any regulations promulgated thereunder; or

"(B) to cause any fund transfer that would not otherwise be treated as such under paragraph (1) to be treated as an electronic fund transfer, or as otherwise subject to this title, for the purposes of any of the provisions referred to in subparagraph (A) or any regulations promulgated thereunder.

"(f) ACTS OF AGENTS.—

"(1) IN GENERAL.—A remittance transfer provider shall be liable for any violation of this section by any agent, authorized delegate, or person affiliated with such provider, when such agent, authorized delegate, or affiliate acts for that remittance transfer provider.

"(2) OBLIGATIONS OF REMITTANCE TRANSFER PROVIDERS.—The Board shall prescribe rules to implement appropriate standards or conditions of, liability of a remittance transfer provider, including a provider who acts through an agent or authorized delegate. An agency charged with enforcing the requirements of this section, or rules prescribed by the Board under this section, may consider, in any action or other proceeding against a remittance transfer provider, the extent to which the provider had established and maintained policies or procedures for compliance, including policies, procedures, or other appropriate oversight measures designed to assure compliance by an agent or authorized delegate acting for such provider.

"(g) DEFINITIONS.—As used in this section—

"(1) the term 'designated recipient' means any person located in a foreign country and identified by the sender as the authorized recipient of a remittance transfer to be made by a remittance transfer provider, except that a designated recipient shall not be deemed to be a consumer for purposes of this Act;

"(2) the term 'remittance transfer'—

"(A) means the electronic (as defined in section 106(2) of the Electronic Signatures in Global and National Commerce Act (15 U.S.C. 7006(2))) transfer of funds requested by a sender located in any State to a designated recipient that is initiated by a remittance transfer provider, whether or not the sender holds an account with the remittance transfer provider or whether or not the remittance transfer is also an electronic fund transfer, as defined in section 903; and

"(B) does not include a transfer described in subparagraph (A) in an amount that is equal to or lesser than the amount of a small-value transaction determined, by rule, to be excluded from the requirements under section 906(a);

"(3) the term 'remittance transfer provider' means any person or financial institution that provides remittance transfers for a consumer in the normal course of its business, whether or not the consumer holds an account with such person or financial institution; and

"(4) the term 'sender' means a consumer who requests a remittance provider to send a remittance transfer for the consumer to a designated recipient.".

(b) AUTOMATED CLEARINGHOUSE SYSTEM.—

(1) EXPANSION OF SYSTEM.—The Board of Governors shall work with the Federal reserve banks and the Department of the Treasury to expand the use of the automated clearinghouse system and other payment mechanisms for remittance transfers to foreign countries, with a focus on countries that receive significant remittance transfers from the United States, based on—

(A) the number, volume, and size of such transfers;

(B) the significance of the volume of such transfers relative to the external financial flows of the receiving country, including—

(i) the total amount transferred; and

(ii) the total volume of payments made by United States Government agencies to beneficiaries and retirees living abroad;

(C) the feasibility of such an expansion; and

(D) the ability of the Federal Reserve System to establish payment gateways in different geographic regions and currency zones to receive remittance transfers and route them through the payments systems in the destination countries.

(2) REPORT TO CONGRESS.—Not later than one calendar year after the date of enactment of this Act, and on April 30 biennially thereafter during the 10-year period beginning on that date of enactment, the Board of Governors shall submit a report to the Committee on Banking, Housing, and Urban Affairs of the Senate and the Committee on Financial Services of the House of Representatives on the status of the automated clearinghouse system and its progress in complying with the requirements of this subsection. The report shall include an analysis of adoption rates of International ACH Transactions rules and formats, the efficacy of increasing adoption rates, and potential recommendations to increase adoption.

(c) EXPANSION OF FINANCIAL INSTITUTION PROVISION OF REMITTANCE TRANSFERS.—

(1) PROVISION OF GUIDELINES TO INSTITUTIONS.—Each of the Federal banking agencies and the National Credit Union Administration shall provide guidelines to financial institutions under the jurisdiction of the agency regarding the offering of low-cost remittance transfers and no-cost or low-cost basic consumer accounts, as well as agency services to remittance transfer providers.

(2) ASSISTANCE TO FINANCIAL LITERACY COMMISSION.—As part of its duties as members of the Financial Literacy and Education Commission, the Bureau, the Federal banking agencies, and the National Credit Union Administration shall assist the Financial Literacy and Education Commission in executing the Strategy for Assuring Financial Empowerment (or the "SAFE Strategy"), as it relates to remittances.

(d) FEDERAL CREDIT UNION ACT CONFORMING AMENDMENT.—Paragraph (12) of section 107 of the Federal Credit Union Act (12 U.S.C. 1757) is amended to read as follows:

"(12) in accordance with regulations prescribed by the Board—

"(A) to sell, to persons in the field of membership, negotiable checks (including travelers checks), money orders, and other similar money transfer instruments (including international and domestic electronic fund transfers and remittance transfers, as defined in section 919 of the Electronic Fund Transfer Act); and

"(B) to cash checks and money orders for persons in the field of membership for a fee;".

(e) REPORT ON FEASIBILITY OF AND IMPEDIMENTS TO USE OF REMITTANCE HISTORY IN CALCULATION OF CREDIT SCORE.—Before the end of the 365-day period beginning on the date of enactment of this Act, the Director shall submit a report to the President, the Committee on Banking, Housing, and Urban Affairs of the Senate, and the Committee on Financial Services of the House of Representatives regarding—

(1) the manner in which the remittance history of a consumer could be used to enhance the credit score of the consumer;

(2) the current legal and business model barriers and impediments that impede the use of the remittance history of the consumer to enhance the credit score of the consumer; and

(3) recommendations on the manner in which maximum transparency and disclosure to consumers of exchange rates for remittance transfers subject to this title and the amendments made by this title may be accomplished, whether or not such exchange rates are known at the time of origination or payment by the consumer for the remittance transfer, including disclosure to the sender of the actual exchange rate used and the amount of currency that the recipient of the remittance transfer received, using the values of the currency into which the funds were exchanged, as contained in sections 919(a)(2)(D) and 919(a)(3) of the Electronic Fund Transfer Act (as amended by this section).

Title X—Consumer Financial Protection   **1211**

[Explanation at ¶ 4740.]

[¶ 11,074] ACT SEC. 1074. DEPARTMENT OF THE TREASURY STUDY ON ENDING THE CONSERVATORSHIP OF FANNIE MAE, FREDDIE MAC, AND REFORMING THE HOUSING FINANCE SYSTEM.

(a) STUDY REQUIRED.—

(1) IN GENERAL.—The Secretary of the Treasury shall conduct a study of and develop recommendations regarding the options for ending the conservatorship of the Federal National Mortgage Association (in this section referred to as "Fannie Mae") and the Federal Home Loan Mortgage Corporation (in this section referred to as "Freddie Mac"), while minimizing the cost to taxpayers, including such options as—

(A) the gradual wind-down and liquidation of such entities;

(B) the privatization of such entities;

(C) the incorporation of the functions of such entities into a Federal agency;

(D) the dissolution of Fannie Mae and Freddie Mac into smaller companies; or

(E) any other measures the Secretary determines appropriate.

(2) ANALYSES.—The study required under paragraph (1) shall include an analysis of—

(A) the role of the Federal Government in supporting a stable, well-functioning housing finance system, and whether and to what extent the Federal Government should bear risks in meeting Federal housing finance objectives;

(B) how the current structure of the housing finance system can be improved;

(C) how the housing finance system should support the continued availability of mortgage credit to all segments of the market;

(D) how the housing finance system should be structured to ensure that consumers continue to have access to 30-year, fixed rate, prepayable mortgages and other mortgage products that have simple terms that can be easily understood;

(E) the role of the Federal Housing Administration and the Department of Veterans Affairs in a future housing system;

(F) the impact of reforms of the housing finance system on the financing of rental housing;

(G) the impact of reforms of the housing finance system on secondary market liquidity;

(H) the role of standardization in the housing finance system;

(I) how housing finance systems in other countries offer insights that can help inform options for reform in the United States; and

(J) the options for transition to a reformed housing finance system.

(b) REPORT AND RECOMMENDATIONS.—Not later than January 31, 2011, the Secretary of the Treasury shall submit the report and recommendations required under subsection (a) to the Committee on Banking, Housing, and Urban Affairs of the Senate and the Committee on Financial Services of the House of Representatives.

[Explanation at ¶ 4745.]

[¶ 11,075] ACT SEC. 1075. REASONABLE FEES AND RULES FOR PAYMENT CARD TRANSACTIONS.

(a) IN GENERAL.—The Electronic Fund Transfer Act (15 U.S.C. 1693 et seq.) is amended—

(1) by redesignating sections 920 and 921 as sections 921 and 922, respectively; and

(2) by inserting after section 919 the following:

"SEC. 920. REASONABLE FEES AND RULES FOR PAYMENT CARD TRANSACTIONS.

"(a) REASONABLE INTERCHANGE TRANSACTION FEES FOR ELECTRONIC DEBIT TRANSACTIONS.—

"(1) REGULATORY AUTHORITY OVER INTERCHANGE TRANSACTION FEES.—The Board may prescribe regulations, pursuant to section 553 of title 5, United States Code, regarding any interchange transaction fee that an issuer may receive or charge with respect to an electronic debit transaction, to implement this subsection (including related definitions), and to prevent circumvention or evasion of this subsection.

"(2) REASONABLE INTERCHANGE TRANSACTION FEES.—The amount of any interchange transaction fee that an issuer may receive or charge with respect to an electronic debit transaction shall be reasonable and proportional to the cost incurred by the issuer with respect to the transaction.

"(3) RULEMAKING REQUIRED.—

"(A) IN GENERAL.—The Board shall prescribe regulations in final form not later than 9 months after the date of enactment of the Consumer Financial Protection Act of 2010, to establish standards for assessing whether the amount of any interchange transaction fee described in paragraph (2) is reasonable and proportional to the cost incurred by the issuer with respect to the transaction.

"(B) INFORMATION COLLECTION.—The Board may require any issuer (or agent of an issuer) or payment card network to provide the Board with such information as may be necessary to carry out the provisions of this subsection and the Board, in issuing rules under subparagraph (A) and on at least a bi-annual basis thereafter, shall disclose such aggregate or summary information concerning the costs incurred, and interchange transaction fees charged or received, by issuers or payment card networks in connection with the authorization, clearance or settlement of electronic debit transactions as the Board considers appropriate and in the public interest.

"(4) CONSIDERATIONS; CONSULTATION.—In prescribing regulations under paragraph (3)(A), the Board shall—

"(A) consider the functional similarity between—

"(i) electronic debit transactions; and

"(ii) checking transactions that are required within the Federal Reserve bank system to clear at par;

"(B) distinguish between—

"(i) the incremental cost incurred by an issuer for the role of the issuer in the authorization, clearance, or settlement of a particular electronic debit transaction, which cost shall be considered under paragraph (2); and

"(ii) other costs incurred by an issuer which are not specific to a particular electronic debit transaction, which costs shall not be considered under paragraph (2); and

"(C) consult, as appropriate, with the Comptroller of the Currency, the Board of Directors of the Federal Deposit Insurance Corporation, the Director of the Office of Thrift Supervision, the National Credit Union Administration Board, the Administrator of the Small Business Administration, and the Director of the Bureau of Consumer Financial Protection.

"(5) ADJUSTMENTS TO INTERCHANGE TRANSACTION FEES FOR FRAUD PREVENTION COSTS.—

"(A) ADJUSTMENTS.—The Board may allow for an adjustment to the fee amount received or charged by an issuer under paragraph (2), if—

"(i) such adjustment is reasonably necessary to make allowance for costs incurred by the issuer in preventing fraud in relation to electronic debit transactions involving that issuer; and

"(ii) the issuer complies with the fraud-related standards established by the Board under subparagraph (B), which standards shall—

"(I) be designed to ensure that any fraud-related adjustment of the issuer is limited to the amount described in clause (i) and takes into account any fraud-related reimbursements (including amounts from charge-backs) received from consumers, merchants, or payment card networks in relation to electronic debit transactions involving the issuer; and

"(II) require issuers to take effective steps to reduce the occurrence of, and costs from, fraud in relation to electronic debit transactions, including through the development and implementation of cost-effective fraud prevention technology.

"(B) RULEMAKING REQUIRED.—

"(i) IN GENERAL.—The Board shall prescribe regulations in final form not later than 9 months after the date of enactment of the Consumer Financial Protection Act of 2010, to establish standards for making adjustments under this paragraph.

"(ii) FACTORS FOR CONSIDERATION.—In issuing the standards and prescribing regulations under this paragraph, the Board shall consider—

"(I) the nature, type, and occurrence of fraud in electronic debit transactions;

"(II) the extent to which the occurrence of fraud depends on whether authorization in an electronic debit transaction is based on signature, PIN, or other means;

"(III) the available and economical means by which fraud on electronic debit transactions may be reduced;

"(IV) the fraud prevention and data security costs expended by each party involved in electronic debit transactions (including consumers, persons who accept debit cards as a form of payment, financial institutions, retailers and payment card networks);

"(V) the costs of fraudulent transactions absorbed by each party involved in such transactions (including consumers, persons who accept debit cards as a form of payment, financial institutions, retailers and payment card networks);

"(VI) the extent to which interchange transaction fees have in the past reduced or increased incentives for parties involved in electronic debit transactions to reduce fraud on such transactions; and

"(VII) such other factors as the Board considers appropriate.

"(6) EXEMPTION FOR SMALL ISSUERS.—

"(A) IN GENERAL.—This subsection shall not apply to any issuer that, together with its affiliates, has assets of less than $10,000,000,000, and the Board shall exempt such issuers from regulations prescribed under paragraph (3)(A).

"(B) DEFINITION.—For purposes of this paragraph, the term "issuer" shall be limited to the person holding the asset account that is debited through an electronic debit transaction.

"(7) EXEMPTION FOR GOVERNMENT-ADMINISTERED PAYMENT PROGRAMS AND RELOADABLE PREPAID CARDS.—

"(A) IN GENERAL.—This subsection shall not apply to an interchange transaction fee charged or received with respect to an electronic debit transaction in which a person uses—

"(i) a debit card or general-use prepaid card that has been provided to a person pursuant to a Federal, State or local government-administered payment program, in which the person may only use the debit card or general-use prepaid card to transfer or debit funds, monetary value, or other assets that have been provided pursuant to such program; or

"(ii) a plastic card, payment code, or device that is—

"(I) linked to funds, monetary value, or assets which are purchased or loaded on a prepaid basis;

"(II) not issued or approved for use to access or debit any account held by or for the benefit of the card holder (other than a subaccount or other method of recording or tracking funds purchased or loaded on the card on a prepaid basis);

"(III) redeemable at multiple, unaffiliated merchants or service providers, or automated teller machines;

"(IV) used to transfer or debit funds, monetary value, or other assets; and

"(V) reloadable and not marketed or labeled as a gift card or gift certificate.

"(B) EXCEPTION.—Notwithstanding subparagraph (A), after the end of the 1-year period beginning on the effective date provided in paragraph (9), this subsection shall apply to an interchange transaction fee charged or received with respect to an electronic debit transaction described in subparagraph (A)(i) in which a person uses a general-use prepaid card, or an electronic debit transaction described in subparagraph (A)(ii), if any of the following fees may be charged to a person with respect to the card:

"(i) A fee for an overdraft, including a shortage of funds or a transaction processed for an amount exceeding the account balance.

"(ii) A fee imposed by the issuer for the first withdrawal per month from an automated teller machine that is part of the issuer's designated automated teller machine network.

"(C) DEFINITION.—For purposes of subparagraph (B), the term 'designated automated teller machine network' means either—

"(i) all automated teller machines identified in the name of the issuer; or

"(ii) any network of automated teller machines identified by the issuer that provides reasonable and convenient access to the issuer's customers.

"(D) REPORTING.—Beginning 12 months after the date of enactment of the Consumer Financial Protection Act of 2010, the Board shall annually provide a report to the Congress regarding —

"(i) the prevalence of the use of general-use prepaid cards in Federal, State or local government-administered payment programs; and

"(ii) the interchange transaction fees and cardholder fees charged with respect to the use of such general-use prepaid cards.

"(8) REGULATORY AUTHORITY OVER NETWORK FEES.—

"(A) IN GENERAL.—The Board may prescribe regulations, pursuant to section 553 of title 5, United States Code, regarding any network fee.

"(B) LIMITATION.—The authority under subparagraph (A) to prescribe regulations shall be limited to regulations to ensure that—

"(i) a network fee is not used to directly or indirectly compensate an issuer with respect to an electronic debit transaction; and

"(ii) a network fee is not used to circumvent or evade the restrictions of this subsection and regulations prescribed under such subsection.

"(C) RULEMAKING REQUIRED.—The Board shall prescribe regulations in final form before the end of the 9-month period beginning on the date of the enactment of the Consumer Financial Protection Act of 2010, to carry out the authorities provided under subparagraph (A).

"(9) EFFECTIVE DATE.—This subsection shall take effect at the end of the 12-month period beginning on the date of the enactment of the Consumer Financial Protection Act of 2010.

"(b) LIMITATION ON PAYMENT CARD NETWORK RESTRICTIONS.—

"(1) PROHIBITIONS AGAINST EXCLUSIVITY ARRANGEMENTS.—

"(A) NO EXCLUSIVE NETWORK.—The Board shall, before the end of the 1-year period beginning on the date of the enactment of the Consumer Financial Protection Act of 2010, prescribe regulations providing that an issuer or payment card network shall not directly or through any agent, processor, or licensed member of a payment card network, by contract, requirement, condition, penalty, or otherwise, restrict the number of payment card networks on which an electronic debit transaction may be processed to—

"(i) 1 such network; or

"(ii) 2 or more such networks which are owned, controlled, or otherwise operated by—

"(I) affiliated persons; or

"(II) networks affiliated with such issuer.

"(B) NO ROUTING RESTRICTIONS.—The Board shall, before the end of the 1-year period beginning on the date of the enactment of the Consumer Financial Protection Act of 2010, prescribe regulations providing that an issuer or payment card network shall not, directly or through any agent, processor, or licensed member of the network, by contract, requirement, condition, penalty, or otherwise, inhibit the ability of any person who accepts debit cards for payments to direct the routing of electronic debit transactions for processing over any payment card network that may process such transactions.

"(2) LIMITATION ON RESTRICTIONS ON OFFERING DISCOUNTS FOR USE OF A FORM OF PAYMENT.—

"(A) IN GENERAL.—A payment card network shall not, directly or through any agent, processor, or licensed member of the network, by contract, requirement, condition, penalty, or otherwise, inhibit the ability of any person to provide a discount or in-kind incentive for payment by the use of cash, checks, debit cards, or credit cards to the extent that—

"(i) in the case of a discount or in-kind incentive for payment by the use of debit cards, the discount or in-kind incentive does not differentiate on the basis of the issuer or the payment card network;

"(ii) in the case of a discount or in-kind incentive for payment by the use of credit cards, the discount or in-kind incentive does not differentiate on the basis of the issuer or the payment card network; and

"(iii) to the extent required by Federal law and applicable State law, such discount or in-kind incentive is offered to all prospective buyers and disclosed clearly and conspicuously.

"(B) LAWFUL DISCOUNTS.—For purposes of this paragraph, the network may not penalize any person for the providing of a discount that is in compliance with Federal law and applicable State law.

"(3) LIMITATION ON RESTRICTIONS ON SETTING TRANSACTION MINIMUMS OR MAXIMUMS.—

"(A) IN GENERAL.—A payment card network shall not, directly or through any agent, processor, or licensed member of the network, by contract, requirement, condition, penalty, or otherwise, inhibit the ability—

"(i) of any person to set a minimum dollar value for the acceptance by that person of credit cards, to the extent that—

"(I) such minimum dollar value does not differentiate between issuers or between payment card networks; and

"(II) such minimum dollar value does not exceed $10.00; or

"(ii) of any Federal agency or institution of higher education to set a maximum dollar value for the acceptance by that Federal agency or institution of higher education of credit cards, to the extent that such maximum dollar value does not differentiate between issuers or between payment card networks.

"(B) INCREASE IN MINIMUM DOLLAR AMOUNT.—The Board may, by regulation prescribed pursuant to section 553 of title 5, United States Code, increase the amount of the dollar value listed in subparagraph (A)(i)(II).

"(4) RULE OF CONSTRUCTION:.—No provision of this subsection shall be construed to authorize any person—

"(A) to discriminate between debit cards within a payment card network on the basis of the issuer that issued the debit card; or

"(B) to discriminate between credit cards within a payment card network on the basis of the issuer that issued the credit card.

"(c) DEFINITIONS.—For purposes of this section, the following definitions shall apply:

"(1) AFFILIATE.—The term 'affiliate' means any company that controls, is controlled by, or is under common control with another company.

"(2) DEBIT CARD.—The term 'debit card'—

"(A) means any card, or other payment code or device, issued or approved for use through a payment card network to debit an asset account (regardless of the purpose for which the account is established), whether authorization is based on signature, PIN, or other means;

"(B) includes a general-use prepaid card, as that term is defined in section 915(a)(2)(A); and

"(C) does not include paper checks.

"(3) CREDIT CARD.—The term 'credit card' has the same meaning as in section 103 of the Truth in Lending Act.

"(4) DISCOUNT.—The term 'discount'—

"(A) means a reduction made from the price that customers are informed is the regular price; and

"(B) does not include any means of increasing the price that customers are informed is the regular price.

"(5) ELECTRONIC DEBIT TRANSACTION.—The term 'electronic debit transaction' means a transaction in which a person uses a debit card.

"(6) FEDERAL AGENCY.—The term 'Federal agency' means—

"(A) an agency (as defined in section 101 of title 31, United States Code); and

"(B) a Government corporation (as defined in section 103 of title 5, United States Code).

"(7) INSTITUTION OF HIGHER EDUCATION.—The term 'institution of higher education' has the same meaning as in 101 and 102 of the Higher Education Act of 1965 (20 U.S.C. 1001, 1002).

"(8) INTERCHANGE TRANSACTION FEE.—The term 'interchange transaction fee' means any fee established, charged or received by a payment card network for the purpose of compensating an issuer for its involvement in an electronic debit transaction.

"(9) ISSUER.—The term 'issuer' means any person who issues a debit card, or credit card, or the agent of such person with respect to such card.

"(10) NETWORK FEE.—The term 'network fee' means any fee charged and received by a payment card network with respect to an electronic debit transaction, other than an interchange transaction fee.

"(11) PAYMENT CARD NETWORK.—The term 'payment card network' means an entity that directly, or through licensed members, processors, or agents, provides the proprietary services, infrastructure, and software that route information and data to conduct debit card or credit card transaction authorization, clearance, and settlement, and that a person uses in order to accept as a form of payment a brand of debit card, credit card or other device that may be used to carry out debit or credit transactions.

"(d) ENFORCEMENT.—

"(1) IN GENERAL.—Compliance with the requirements imposed under this section shall be enforced under section 918.

"(2) EXCEPTION.—Sections 916 and 917 shall not apply with respect to this section or the requirements imposed pursuant to this section.".

(b) AMENDMENT TO THE FOOD AND NUTRITION ACT OF 2008.—Section 7(h)(10) of the Food and Nutrition Act of 2008 (7 U.S.C. 2016(h)(10)) is amended to read as follows:

"(10) FEDERAL LAW NOT APPLICABLE.—Section 920 of the Electronic Fund Transfer Act shall not apply to electronic benefit transfer or reimbursement systems under this Act.".

(c) AMENDMENT TO THE FARM SECURITY AND RURAL INVESTMENT ACT OF 2002.—Section 4402 of the Farm Security and Rural Investment Act of 2002 (7 U.S.C. 3007) is amended by adding at the end the following new subsection:

"(f) FEDERAL LAW NOT APPLICABLE.—Section 920 of the Electronic Fund Transfer Act shall not apply to electronic benefit transfer systems established under this section.".

(d) AMENDMENT TO THE CHILD NUTRITION ACT OF 1966.—Section 11 of the Child Nutrition Act of 1966 (42 U.S.C. 1780) is amended by adding at the end the following:

"(c) FEDERAL LAW NOT APPLICABLE.—Section 920 of the Electronic Fund Transfer Act shall not apply to electronic benefit transfer systems established under this Act or the Richard B. Russell National School Lunch Act (42 U.S.C. 1751 et seq.).".

[Explanation at ¶ 4750.]

[¶ 11,076] ACT SEC. 1076. REVERSE MORTGAGE STUDY AND REGULATIONS.

(a) STUDY.—Not later than 1 year after the designated transfer date, the Bureau shall conduct a study on reverse mortgage transactions.

(b) REGULATIONS.—

(1) IN GENERAL.—If the Bureau determines through the study required under subsection (a) that conditions or limitations on reverse mortgage transactions are necessary or appropriate for accomplishing the purposes and objectives of this title, including protecting borrowers with respect to the obtaining of reverse mortgage loans for the purpose of funding investments, annuities, and other investment products and the suitability of a borrower in obtaining a reverse mortgage for such purpose.

(2) IDENTIFIED PRACTICES AND INTEGRATED DISCLOSURES.—The regulations prescribed under paragraph (1) may, as the Bureau may so determine—

(A) identify any practice as unfair, deceptive, or abusive in connection with a reverse mortgage transaction; and

(B) provide for an integrated disclosure standard and model disclosures for reverse mortgage transactions, consistent with section 4302(d), that combines the relevant disclosures required under the Truth in Lending Act (15 U.S.C. 1601 et seq.) and the Real Estate Settlement Procedures Act, with the disclosures required to be provided to consumers for Home Equity Conversion Mortgages under section 255 of the National Housing Act.

(c) RULE OF CONSTRUCTION.—This section shall not be construed as limiting the authority of the Bureau to issue regulations, orders, or guidance that apply to reverse mortgages prior to the completion of the study required under subsection (a).

[Explanation at ¶ 4755.]

[¶ 11,077] ACT SEC. 1077. REPORT ON PRIVATE EDUCATION LOANS AND PRIVATE EDUCATIONAL LENDERS.

(a) REPORT.—Not later than 2 years after the date of enactment of this Act, the Director and the Secretary of Education, in consultation with the Commissioners of the Federal Trade Commission, and the Attorney General of the United States, shall submit a report to the Committee on Banking, Housing, and Urban Affairs and the Committee on Health, Education, Labor, and Pensions of the Senate and the Committee on Financial Services and the Committee on Education and Labor of the House of Representatives, on private education loans (as that term is defined in section 140 of the Truth in Lending Act (15 U.S.C. 1650)) and private educational lenders (as that term is defined in such section).

(b) CONTENT.—The report required by this section shall examine, at a minimum—

(1) the growth and changes of the private education loan market in the United States;

(2) factors influencing such growth and changes;

(3) the extent to which students and parents of students rely on private education loans to finance postsecondary education and the private education loan indebtedness of borrowers;

(4) the characteristics of private education loan borrowers, including—

(A) the types of institutions of higher education that they attend;

(B) socioeconomic characteristics (including income and education levels, racial characteristics, geographical background, age, and gender);

(C) what other forms of financing borrowers use to pay for education;

(D) whether they exhaust their Federal loan options before taking out a private loan;

(E) whether such borrowers are dependent or independent students (as determined under part F of title IV of the Higher Education Act of 1965) or parents of such students;

(F) whether such borrowers are students enrolled in a program leading to a certificate, license, or credential other than a degree, an associates degree, a baccalaureate degree, or a graduate or professional degree; and

(G) if practicable, employment and repayment behaviors;

(5) the characteristics of private educational lenders, including whether such creditors are for-profit, non-profit, or institutions of higher education;

(6) the underwriting criteria used by private educational lenders, including the use of cohort default rate (as such term is defined in section 435(m) of the Higher Education Act of 1965);

(7) the terms, conditions, and pricing of private education loans;

(8) the consumer protections available to private education loan borrowers, including the effectiveness of existing disclosures and requirements and borrowers' awareness and understanding about terms and conditions of various financial products;

(9) whether Federal regulators and the public have access to information sufficient to provide them with assurances that private education loans are provided in accord with the Nation's fair lending laws and that allows public officials to determine lender compliance with fair lending laws; and

(10) any statutory or legislative recommendations necessary to improve consumer protections for private education loan borrowers and to better enable Federal regulators and the public to ascertain private educational lender compliance with fair lending laws.

[Explanation at ¶ 4760.]

[¶ 11,078] ACT SEC. 1078. STUDY AND REPORT ON CREDIT SCORES.

(a) STUDY.—The Bureau shall conduct a study on the nature, range, and size of variations between the credit scores sold to creditors and those sold to consumers by consumer reporting agencies that compile and maintain files on consumers on a nationwide basis (as defined in section 603(p) of the Fair Credit Reporting Act; 15 U.S.C. 1681a(p)), and whether such variations disadvantage consumers.

(b) REPORT TO CONGRESS.—The Bureau shall submit a report to Congress on the results of the study conducted under subsection (a) not later than 1 year after the date of enactment of this Act.

[Explanation at ¶ 4765.]

[¶ 11,079] ACT SEC. 1079. REVIEW, REPORT, AND PROGRAM WITH RESPECT TO EXCHANGE FACILITATORS.

(a) REVIEW.—The Director shall review all Federal laws and regulations relating to the protection of consumers who use exchange facilitators for transactions primarily for personal, family, or household purposes.

(b) REPORT.—Not later than 1 year after the designated transfer date, the Director shall submit to Congress a report describing—

(1) recommendations for legislation to ensure the appropriate protection of consumers who use exchange facilitators for transactions primarily for personal, family, or household purposes;

(2) recommendations for updating the regulations of Federal departments and agencies to ensure the appropriate protection of such consumers; and

(3) recommendations for regulations to ensure the appropriate protection of such consumers.

(c) PROGRAM.—Not later than 2 years after the date of the submission of the report under subsection (b), the Bureau shall, consistent with subtitle B, propose regulations or otherwise establish a program to protect consumers who use exchange facilitators.

(d) EXCHANGE FACILITATOR DEFINED.—In this section, the term "exchange facilitator" means a person that—

(1) facilitates, for a fee, an exchange of like kind property by entering into an agreement with a taxpayer by which the exchange facilitator acquires from the taxpayer the contractual rights to sell the taxpayer's relinquished property and transfers a replacement property to the taxpayer as a qualified intermediary (within the meaning of Treasury Regulations section 1.1031(k)-1(g)(4)) or enters into an agreement with the taxpayer to take title to a property as an exchange accommodation titleholder (within the meaning of Revenue Procedure 2000-37) or enters into an agreement with a taxpayer to act as a qualified trustee or qualified escrow holder (within the meaning of Treasury Regulations section 1.1031(k)-1(g)(3));

(2) maintains an office for the purpose of soliciting business to perform the services described in paragraph (1); or

(3) advertises any of the services described in paragraph (1) or solicits clients in printed publications, direct mail, television or radio advertisements, telephone calls, facsimile transmissions, or other electronic communications directed to the general public for purposes of providing any such services.

[Explanation at ¶ 4770.]

[¶ 11,079A] ACT SEC. 1079A. FINANCIAL FRAUD PROVISIONS.

(a) SENTENCING GUIDELINES.—

(1) SECURITIES FRAUD.—

(A) DIRECTIVE.—Pursuant to its authority under section 994 of title 28, United States Code, and in accordance with this paragraph, the United States Sentencing Commission shall review and, if appropriate, amend the Federal Sentencing Guidelines and policy statements applicable to persons convicted of offenses relating to securities fraud or any other similar provision of law, in order to reflect the intent of Congress that penalties for the offenses under the guidelines and policy statements appropriately account for the potential and actual harm to the public and the financial markets from the offenses.

(B) REQUIREMENTS.—In making any amendments to the Federal Sentencing Guidelines and policy statements under subparagraph (A), the United States Sentencing Commission shall—

(i) ensure that the guidelines and policy statements, particularly section 2B1.1(b)(14) and section 2B1.1(b)(17) (and any successors thereto), reflect—

(I) the serious nature of the offenses described in subparagraph (A);

(II) the need for an effective deterrent and appropriate punishment to prevent the offenses; and

(III) the effectiveness of incarceration in furthering the objectives described in subclauses (I) and (II);

(ii) consider the extent to which the guidelines appropriately account for the potential and actual harm to the public and the financial markets resulting from the offenses;

(iii) ensure reasonable consistency with other relevant directives and guidelines and Federal statutes;

(iv) make any necessary conforming changes to guidelines; and

(v) ensure that the guidelines adequately meet the purposes of sentencing, as set forth in section 3553(a)(2) of title 18, United States Code.

(2) FINANCIAL INSTITUTION FRAUD.—

(A) DIRECTIVE.—Pursuant to its authority under section 994 of title 28, United States Code, and in accordance with this paragraph, the United States Sentencing Commission shall review and, if appropriate, amend the Federal Sentencing Guidelines and policy statements applicable to persons convicted of fraud offenses relating to financial institutions or federally related mortgage loans and any other similar provisions of law, to reflect the intent of Congress that the penalties for the offenses under the guidelines and policy statements ensure appropriate terms of imprisonment for offenders involved in substantial bank frauds or other frauds relating to financial institutions.

(B) REQUIREMENTS.—In making any amendments to the Federal Sentencing Guidelines and policy statements under subparagraph (A), the United States Sentencing Commission shall—

(i) ensure that the guidelines and policy statements reflect—

(I) the serious nature of the offenses described in subparagraph (A);

(II) the need for an effective deterrent and appropriate punishment to prevent the offenses; and

(III) the effectiveness of incarceration in furthering the objectives described in subclauses (I) and (II);

(ii) consider the extent to which the guidelines appropriately account for the potential and actual harm to the public and the financial markets resulting from the offenses;

(iii) ensure reasonable consistency with other relevant directives and guidelines and Federal statutes;

(iv) make any necessary conforming changes to guidelines; and

(v) ensure that the guidelines adequately meet the purposes of sentencing, as set forth in section 3553(a)(2) of title 18, United States Code.

(b) EXTENSION OF STATUTE OF LIMITATIONS FOR SECURITIES FRAUD VIOLATIONS.—

(1) IN GENERAL.—Chapter 213 of title 18, United States Code, is amended by adding at the end the following:

"§ 3301. Securities fraud offenses

"(a) DEFINITION.—In this section, the term 'securities fraud offense' means a violation of, or a conspiracy or an attempt to violate—

"(1) section 1348;

"(2) section 32(a) of the Securities Exchange Act of 1934 (15 U.S.C. 78ff(a));

"(3) section 24 of the Securities Act of 1933 (15 U.S.C. 77x);

"(4) section 217 of the Investment Advisers Act of 1940 (15 U.S.C. 80b-17);

"(5) section 49 of the Investment Company Act of 1940 (15 U.S.C. 80a-48); or

"(6) section 325 of the Trust Indenture Act of 1939 (15 U.S.C. 77yyy).

"(b) LIMITATION.—No person shall be prosecuted, tried, or punished for a securities fraud offense, unless the indictment is found or the information is instituted within 6 years after the commission of the offense.".

(2) TECHNICAL AND CONFORMING AMENDMENT.—The table of sections for chapter 213 of title 18, United States Code, is amended by adding at the end the following:

"3301. Securities fraud offenses.".

(c) AMENDMENTS TO THE FALSE CLAIMS ACT RELATING TO LIMITATIONS ON ACTIONS.—Section 3730(h) of title 31, United States Code, is amended—

(1) in paragraph (1), by striking "or agent on behalf of the employee, contractor, or agent or associated others in furtherance of other efforts to stop 1 or more violations of this subchapter" and inserting "agent or associated others in furtherance of an action under this section or other efforts to stop 1 or more violations of this subchapter"; and

(2) by adding at the end the following:

"(3) LIMITATION ON BRINGING CIVIL ACTION.—A civil action under this subsection may not be brought more than 3 years after the date when the retaliation occurred.".

[Explanation at ¶ 4775.]

Subtitle H—Conforming Amendments

[¶ 11,081] ACT SEC. 1081. AMENDMENTS TO THE INSPECTOR GENERAL ACT.

Effective on the date of enactment of this Act, the Inspector General Act of 1978 (5 U.S.C. App. 3) is amended—

(1) in section 8G(a)(2), by inserting "and the Bureau of Consumer Financial Protection" after "Board of Governors of the Federal Reserve System";

(2) in section 8G(c), by adding at the end the following: "For purposes of implementing this section, the Chairman of the Board of Governors of the Federal Reserve System shall appoint the Inspector General of the Board of Governors of the Federal Reserve System and the Bureau of Consumer Financial Protection. The Inspector General of the Board of Governors of the Federal Reserve System and the Bureau of Consumer Financial Protection shall have all of the authorities and responsibilities provided by this Act with respect to the Bureau of Consumer Financial Protection, as if the Bureau were part of the Board of Governors of the Federal Reserve System."; and

(3) in section 8G(g)(3), by inserting "and the Bureau of Consumer Financial Protection" after "Board of Governors of the Federal Reserve System" the first place that term appears.

[Explanation at ¶ 4780.]

[¶ 11,082] ACT SEC. 1082. AMENDMENTS TO THE PRIVACY ACT OF 1974.

Effective on the date of enactment of this Act, section 552a of title 5, United States Code, is amended by adding at the end the following:

"(w) APPLICABILITY TO BUREAU OF CONSUMER FINANCIAL PROTECTION.—Except as provided in the Consumer Financial Protection Act of 2010, this section shall apply with respect to the Bureau of Consumer Financial Protection.".

[Explanation at ¶ 4785.]

[¶ 11,083] ACT SEC. 1083. AMENDMENTS TO THE ALTERNATIVE MORTGAGE TRANSACTION PARITY ACT OF 1982.

(a) IN GENERAL.—The Alternative Mortgage Transaction Parity Act of 1982 (12 U.S.C. 3801 et seq.) is amended—

(1) in section 803 (12 U.S.C. 3802(1)), by striking "1974" and all that follows through "described and defined" and inserting the following: "1974), in which the interest rate or finance charge may be adjusted or renegotiated, described and defined"; and

(2) in section 804 (12 U.S.C. 3803)—

(A) in subsection (a)—

(i) in each of paragraphs (1), (2), and (3), by inserting after "transactions made" each place that term appears "on or before the designated transfer date, as determined under section 1062 of the Consumer Financial Protection Act of 2010,";

(ii) in paragraph (2), by striking "and" at the end;

(iii) in paragraph (3), by striking the period at the end and inserting "; and"; and

(iv) by adding at the end the following new paragraph:

"(4) with respect to transactions made after the designated transfer date, only in accordance with regulations governing alternative mortgage transactions, as issued by the Bureau of Consumer Financial Protection for federally chartered housing creditors, in accordance with the rulemaking authority granted to the Bureau of Consumer Financial Protection with regard to federally chartered housing creditors under provisions of law other than this section.";

(B) by striking subsection (c) and inserting the following:

"(c) PREEMPTION OF STATE LAW.—An alternative mortgage transaction may be made by a housing creditor in accordance with this section, notwithstanding any State constitution, law, or regulation that prohibits an alternative mortgage transaction. For purposes of this subsection, a State constitution, law, or regulation that prohibits an alternative mortgage transaction does not include any State constitution, law, or regulation that regulates mortgage transactions generally, including any restriction on prepayment penalties or late charges."; and

(C) by adding at the end the following:

"(d) BUREAU ACTIONS.—The Bureau of Consumer Financial Protection shall—

"(1) review the regulations identified by the Comptroller of the Currency and the National Credit Union Administration, (as those rules exist on the designated transfer date), as applicable under paragraphs (1) through (3) of subsection (a);

"(2) determine whether such regulations are fair and not deceptive and otherwise meet the objectives of the Consumer Financial Protection Act of 2010; and

"(3) promulgate regulations under subsection (a)(4) after the designated transfer date.

"(e) DESIGNATED TRANSFER DATE.—As used in this section, the term 'designated transfer date' means the date determined under section 1062 of the Consumer Financial Protection Act of 2010.".

(b) EFFECTIVE DATE.—This section and the amendments made by this section shall become effective on the designated transfer date.

(c) RULE OF CONSTRUCTION.—The amendments made by subsection (a) shall not affect any transaction covered by the Alternative Mortgage Transaction Parity Act of 1982 (12 U.S.C. 3801 et seq.) and entered into on or before the designated transfer date.

[Explanation at ¶ 4790.]

[¶ 11,084] ACT SEC. 1084. AMENDMENTS TO THE ELECTRONIC FUND TRANSFER ACT.

The Electronic Fund Transfer Act (15 U.S.C. 1693 et seq.) is amended—

(1) by striking "Board" each place that term appears and inserting "Bureau", except in subsections (a) and (e) of section 904 (as amended in paragraph (3) of this section) and in 918 (15 U.S.C. 1693o) (as so designated by the Credit Card Act of 2009) and section 920 (as added by section 1076);

(2) in section 903 (15 U.S.C. 1693a)—

(A) by redesignating paragraphs (3) through (11) as paragraphs (4) through (12), respectively; and

(B) by inserting after paragraph (3) the following:

"(4) the term 'Bureau' means the Bureau of Consumer Financial Protection;";

(3) in section 904 (15 U.S.C. 1693b)—

(A) in subsection (a), by striking "(a) PRESCRIPTION BY BOARD.—The Board shall prescribe regulations to carry out the purposes of this title." and inserting the following:

"(a) PRESCRIPTION BY THE BUREAU AND THE BOARD.—

"(1) IN GENERAL.—Except as provided in paragraph (2), the Bureau shall prescribe rules to carry out the purposes of this title.

"(2) AUTHORITY OF THE BOARD.—The Board shall have sole authority to prescribe rules—

"(A) to carry out the purposes of this title with respect to a person described in section 1029(a) of the Consumer Financial Protection Act of 2010; and

"(B) to carry out the purposes of section 920."; and

(B) by adding at the end the following new subsection:

"(e) DEFERENCE.—No provision of this title may be construed as altering, limiting, or otherwise affecting the deference that a court affords to—

"(1) the Bureau in making determinations regarding the meaning or interpretation of any provision of this title for which the Bureau has authority to prescribe regulations; or

"(2) the Board in making determinations regarding the meaning or interpretation of section 920.".

(4) in section 916(d) (15 U.S.C. 1693m) (as so designated by the Credit CARD Act of 2009)—

(A) in the subsection heading, by striking "OF BOARD OR APPROVAL OF DULY AUTHORIZED OFFICIAL OR EMPLOYEE OF FEDERAL RESERVE SYSTEM";

(B) by inserting "Bureau or the" before "Board" each place that term appears; and

(C) by inserting "Bureau of Consumer Financial Protection or the" before "Federal Reserve System"; and

(5) in section 918 (15 U.S.C. 1693o) (as so designated by the Credit CARD Act of 2009)—

(A) in subsection (a)—

(i) by striking "Compliance" and inserting "Subject to subtitle B of the Consumer Financial Protection Act of 2010, compliance";

(ii) by striking paragraphs (1) and (2), and inserting the following:

"(1) section 8 of the Federal Deposit Insurance Act, by the appropriate Federal banking agency, as defined in section 3(q) of the Federal Deposit Insurance Act (12 U.S.C. 1813(q)), with respect to—

"(A) national banks, Federal savings associations, and Federal branches and Federal agencies of foreign banks;

"(B) member banks of the Federal Reserve System (other than national banks), branches and agencies of foreign banks (other than Federal branches, Federal agencies, and insured State branches of foreign banks), commercial lending companies owned or controlled by foreign banks, and organizations operating under section 25 or 25A of the Federal Reserve Act; and

"(C) banks and State savings associations insured by the Federal Deposit Insurance Corporation (other than members of the Federal Reserve System), and insured State branches of foreign banks;";

(iii) by redesignating paragraphs (3) through (5) as paragraphs (2) through (4), respectively;

(iv) in paragraph (2) (as so redesignated), by striking the period at the end and inserting a semicolon;

(v) in paragraph (3) (as so redesignated), by striking "and" at the end;

(vi) in paragraph (4) (as so redesignated), by striking the period at the end and inserting "and"; and

(vii) by adding at the end the following:

"(5) subtitle E of the Consumer Financial Protection Act of 2010, by the Bureau, with respect to any person subject to this title, except that the Bureau shall not have authority to enforce the requirements of section 920 or any regulations prescribed by the Board under section 920.";

(B) in subsection (b), by inserting "any of paragraphs (1) through (4) of" before "subsection (a)" each place that term appears; and

(C) by striking subsection (c) and inserting the following:

"(c) OVERALL ENFORCEMENT AUTHORITY OF THE FEDERAL TRADE COMMISSION.—Except to the extent that enforcement of the requirements imposed under this title is specifically committed to some other Government agency under any of paragraphs (1) through (4) of subsection (a), and subject to subtitle B of the Consumer Financial Protection Act of 2010, the Federal Trade Commission shall be authorized to enforce such requirements. For the purpose of the exercise by the Federal Trade Commission of its functions and powers under the Federal Trade Commission Act, a violation of any requirement imposed under this title shall be deemed a violation of a requirement imposed under that Act. All of the functions and powers of the Federal Trade Commission under the Federal Trade Commission Act are available to the Federal Trade Commission to enforce compliance by any person subject to the jurisdiction of the Federal Trade Commission with the requirements imposed under this title, irrespective of whether that person is engaged in commerce or meets any other jurisdictional tests under the Federal Trade Commission Act.".

[Explanation at ¶ 4795.]

[¶ 11,085] ACT SEC. 1085. AMENDMENTS TO THE EQUAL CREDIT OPPORTUNITY ACT.

The Equal Credit Opportunity Act (15 U.S.C. 1691 et seq.) is amended—

(1) by striking "Board" each place that term appears, other than in section 703(f) (as added by this section) and section 704(a)(4) (15 U.S.C. 1691c(a)(4)), and inserting "Bureau";

(2) in section 702 (15 U.S.C. 1691a), by striking subsection (c) and inserting the following:

"(c) The term 'Bureau' means the Bureau of Consumer Financial Protection.";

(3) in section 703 (15 U.S.C. 1691b)—

(A) by striking the section heading and inserting the following:

"SEC. 703. PROMULGATION OF REGULATIONS BY THE BUREAU.";

(B) by striking "(a) REGULATIONS.—";

(C) by striking subsection (b);

(D) by redesignating paragraphs (1) through (5) as subsections (a) through (e), respectively;

(E) in subsection (c), as so redesignated, by striking "paragraph (2)" and inserting "subsection (b)"; and

(F) by adding at the end the following:

"(f) BOARD AUTHORITY.—Notwithstanding subsection (a), the Board shall prescribe regulations to carry out the purposes of this title with respect to a person described in section 1029(a) of the Consumer Financial Protection Act of 2010. These regulations may contain but are not limited to such classifications, differentiation, or other provision, and may provide for such adjustments and exceptions for any class of transactions, as in the judgment of the Board are necessary or proper to effectuate the purposes of this title, to prevent circumvention or evasion thereof, or to facilitate or substantiate compliance therewith.

"(g) DEFERENCE.—Notwithstanding any power granted to any Federal agency under this title, the deference that a court affords to a Federal agency with respect to a determination made by such agency relating to the meaning or interpretation of any provision of this title that is subject to the jurisdiction of such agency shall be applied as if that agency were the only agency authorized to apply, enforce, interpret, or administer the provisions of this title";

(4) in section 704 (15 U.S.C. 1691c)—

(A) in subsection (a)—

(i) by striking "Compliance" and inserting "Subject to subtitle B of the Consumer Protection Financial Protection Act of 2010";

(ii) by striking paragraphs (1) and (2) and inserting the following:

"(1) section 8 of the Federal Deposit Insurance Act, by the appropriate Federal banking agency, as defined in section 3(q) of the Federal Deposit Insurance Act (12 U.S.C. 1813(q)), with respect to—

"(A) national banks, Federal savings associations, and Federal branches and Federal agencies of foreign banks;

"(B) member banks of the Federal Reserve System (other than national banks), branches and agencies of foreign banks (other than Federal branches, Federal agencies, and insured State branches of foreign banks), commercial lending companies owned or controlled by foreign banks, and organizations operating under section 25 or 25A of the Federal Reserve Act; and

"(C) banks and State savings associations insured by the Federal Deposit Insurance Corporation (other than members of the Federal Reserve System), and insured State branches of foreign banks;";

(iii) by redesignating paragraphs (3) through (9) as paragraphs (2) through (8), respectively;

(iv) in paragraph (7) (as so redesignated), by striking "and" at the end;

(v) in paragraph (8) (as so redesignated), by striking the period at the end, and inserting "; and"; and

(vi) by adding at the end the following:

"(9) Subtitle E of the Consumer Financial Protection Act of 2010, by the Bureau, with respect to any person subject to this title.";

(B) by striking subsection (c) and inserting the following:

"(c) OVERALL ENFORCEMENT AUTHORITY OF FEDERAL TRADE COMMISSION.—Except to the extent that enforcement of the requirements imposed under this title is specifically committed to some other Government agency under any of paragraphs (1) through (8) of subsection (a), and subject to subtitle B of the Consumer Financial Protection Act of 2010, the Federal Trade Commission shall be authorized to enforce such requirements. For the purpose of the exercise by the Federal Trade Commission of its functions and powers under the Federal Trade Commission Act (15 U.S.C. 41 et seq.), a violation of any requirement imposed under this subchapter shall be deemed a violation of a requirement imposed under that Act. All of the functions and powers of the Federal Trade Commission under the Federal Trade Commission Act are available to the Federal Trade Commission to enforce compliance by any person with the requirements imposed under this title, irrespective of whether that person is engaged in commerce or meets any other jurisdictional tests under the Federal Trade Commission Act, including the power to enforce any rule prescribed by the Bureau under this title in the same manner as if the violation had been a violation of a Federal Trade Commission trade regulation rule."; and

(C) in subsection (d), by striking "Board" and inserting "Bureau";

(5) in section 706(e) (15 U.S.C. 1691e(e))—

(A) in the subsection heading—

(i) by striking "BOARD" each place that term appears and inserting "BUREAU"; and

(ii) by striking "FEDERAL RESERVE SYSTEM" and inserting "BUREAU OF CONSUMER FINANCIAL PROTECTION"; and

(B) by striking "Federal Reserve System" and inserting "Bureau of Consumer Financial Protection";

(6) in section 706(g) (15 U.S.C. 1691e(g)), by striking "(3)" and inserting "(9)"; and

(7) in section 706(f) (15 U.S.C. 1691e(f)), by striking "two years from" each place that term appears and inserting "5 years after".

[Explanation at ¶ 4800.]

[¶ 11,086] ACT SEC. 1086. AMENDMENTS TO THE EXPEDITED FUNDS AVAILABILITY ACT.

(a) AMENDMENT TO SECTION 603.—Section 603(d)(1) of the Expedited Funds Availability Act (12 U.S.C. 4002) is amended by inserting after "Board" the following ", jointly with the Director of the Bureau of Consumer Financial Protection,".

(b) AMENDMENTS TO SECTION 604.—Section 604 of the Expedited Funds Availability Act (12 U.S.C. 4003) is amended—

(1) by inserting after "Board" each place that term appears, other than in subsection (f), the following: ", jointly with the Director of the Bureau of Consumer Financial Protection,"; and

(2) in subsection (f), by striking "Board." each place that term appears and inserting the following: "Board, jointly with the Director of the Bureau of Consumer Financial Protection.".

(c) AMENDMENTS TO SECTION 605.—Section 605 of the Expedited Funds Availability Act (12 U.S.C. 4004) is amended—

(1) by inserting after "Board" each place that term appears, other than in the heading for section 605(f)(1), the following: ", jointly with the Director of the Bureau of Consumer Financial Protection,"; and

(2) in subsection (f)(1), in the paragraph heading, by inserting "AND BUREAU" after "BOARD".

(d) AMENDMENTS TO SECTION 609.—Section 609 of the Expedited Funds Availability Act (12 U.S.C. 4008) is amended:

(1) in subsection (a), by inserting after "Board" the following ", jointly with the Director of the Bureau of Consumer Financial Protection,"; and

(2) by striking subsection (e) and inserting the following:

"(e) CONSULTATIONS.—In prescribing regulations under subsections (a) and (b), the Board and the Director of the Bureau of Consumer Financial Protection, in the case of subsection (a), and the Board, in the case of subsection (b), shall consult with the Comptroller of the Currency, the Board of Directors of the Federal Deposit Insurance Corporation, and the National Credit Union Administration Board.".

(e) EXPEDITED FUNDS AVAILABILITY IMPROVEMENTS.—Section 603 of the Expedited Funds Availability Act (12 U.S.C. 4002) is amended—

(1) in subsection (a)(2)(D), by striking "$100" and inserting "$200"; and

(2) in subsection (b)(3)(C), in the subparagraph heading, by striking "$100" and inserting "$200"; and

(3) in subsection (c)(1)(B)(iii), in the clause heading, by striking "$100" and inserting "$200".

(f) REGULAR ADJUSTMENTS FOR INFLATION.—Section 607 of the Expedited Funds Availability Act (12 U.S.C. 4006) is amended by adding at the end the following:

"(f) ADJUSTMENTS TO DOLLAR AMOUNTS FOR INFLATION.—The dollar amounts under this title shall be adjusted every 5 years after December 31, 2011, by the annual percentage increase in the Consumer Price Index for Urban Wage Earners and Clerical Workers, as published by the Bureau of Labor Statistics, rounded to the nearest multiple of $25.".

[Explanation at ¶ 4805.]

[¶ 11,087] ACT SEC. 1087. AMENDMENTS TO THE FAIR CREDIT BILLING ACT.

The Fair Credit Billing Act (15 U.S.C. 1666-1666j) is amended by striking "Board" each place that term appears, other than in section 105(i) (as added by this subtitle) and inserting "Bureau".

[Explanation at ¶ 4810.]

[¶ 11,088] ACT SEC. 1088. AMENDMENTS TO THE FAIR CREDIT REPORTING ACT AND THE FAIR AND ACCURATE CREDIT TRANSACTIONS ACT OF 2003.

(a) FAIR CREDIT REPORTING ACT.—The Fair Credit Reporting Act (15 U.S.C. 1681 et seq.) is amended—

(1) in section 603 (15 U.S.C. 1681a)—

(A) by redesignating subsections (w) and (x) as subsections (x) and (y), respectively; and

(B) by inserting after subsection (v) the following:

"(w) The term 'Bureau' means the Bureau of Consumer Financial Protection."; and

(2) except as otherwise specifically provided in this subsection—

(A) by striking "Federal Trade Commission" each place that term appears and inserting "Bureau";

(B) by striking "FTC" each place that term appears and inserting "Bureau";

(C) by striking "the Commission" each place that term appears, other than sections 615(e) (15 U.S.C. 1681m(e)) and 628(a)(1) (15 U.S.C. 1681w(a)(1)), and inserting "the Bureau"; and

(D) by striking "The Federal banking agencies, the National Credit Union Administration, and the Commission shall jointly" each place that term appears, other than section 615(e)(1) (15 U.S.C. 1681m(e)) and section 628(a)(1) (15 U.S.C. 1681w(a)(1)), and inserting "The Bureau shall";

(3) in section 603(k)(2) (15 U.S.C. 1681a(k)(2)), by striking "Board of Governors of the Federal Reserve System" and inserting "Bureau";

(4) in section 604(g) (15 U.S.C. 1681b(g))—

(A) in paragraph (3), by striking subparagraph (C) and inserting the following:

"(C) as otherwise determined to be necessary and appropriate, by regulation or order, by the Bureau or the applicable State insurance authority (with respect to any person engaged in providing insurance or annuities)."; and

(B) by striking paragraph (5) and inserting the following:

"(5) REGULATIONS AND EFFECTIVE DATE FOR PARAGRAPH (2).—

"(A) REGULATIONS REQUIRED.—The Bureau may, after notice and opportunity for comment, prescribe regulations that permit transactions under paragraph (2) that are determined to be necessary and appropriate to protect legitimate operational, transactional, risk, consumer, and other needs (and which shall include permitting actions necessary for administrative verification purposes), consistent with the intent of paragraph (2) to restrict the use of medical information for inappropriate purposes.";

(5) in section 605(h)(2)(A) (15 U.S.C. 1681c(h)(2)(A)), by striking "with respect to the entities that are subject to their respective enforcement authority under section 621" and inserting ", in consultation with the Federal banking agencies, the National Credit Union Administration, and the Federal Trade Commission,".

(6) in section 611(e)(2) (15 U.S.C. 1681i(e)), by striking paragraph (2) and inserting the following:

"(2) EXCLUSION.—Complaints received or obtained by the Bureau pursuant to its investigative authority under the Consumer Financial Protection Act of 2010 shall not be subject to paragraph (1).";

(7) in section 615(d)(2)(B) (15 U.S.C. 1681m(d)(2)(B)), by striking "the Federal banking agencies" and inserting "the Federal Trade Commission, the Federal banking agencies,";

(8) in section 615(e)(1) (15 U.S.C. 1681m(e)(1)), by striking "and the Commission" and inserting "the Federal Trade Commission, the Commodity Futures Trading Commission, and the Securities and Exchange Commission";

(9) in section 615(h)(6) (15 U.S.C. 1681m(h)(6)), by striking subparagraph (A) and inserting the following:

"(A) RULES REQUIRED.—The Bureau shall prescribe rules to carry out this subsection.";

(10) in section 621 (15 U.S.C. 1681s)—

(A) by striking subsection (a) and inserting the following:

"(a) ENFORCEMENT BY FEDERAL TRADE COMMISSION.—

"(1) IN GENERAL.—The Federal Trade Commission shall be authorized to enforce compliance with the requirements imposed by this title under the Federal Trade Commission Act (15 U.S.C. 41 et seq.), with respect to consumer reporting agencies and all other persons subject thereto, except to the extent that enforcement of the requirements imposed under this title is specifically committed to some other Government agency under any of subparagraphs (A) through (G) of subsection (b)(1), and subject to subtitle B of the Consumer Financial Protection Act of 2010, subsection (b). For the purpose of the exercise by the Federal Trade Commission of its functions and powers under the Federal Trade Commission Act, a violation of any requirement or prohibition imposed under this title shall constitute an unfair or deceptive act or practice in commerce, in violation of section 5(a) of the Federal Trade Commission Act (15 U.S.C. 45(a)), and shall be subject to enforcement by the Federal Trade Commission under section 5(b) of that Act with respect to any consumer reporting agency or person that is subject to enforcement by the Federal Trade Commission pursuant to this subsection, irrespective of whether that person is engaged in commerce or meets any other jurisdictional tests under the Federal Trade Commission Act. The Federal Trade Commission shall have such procedural, investigative, and enforcement powers, including the power to issue procedural rules in enforcing compliance with the requirements imposed under this title and to require the filing of reports, the production of documents, and the appearance of witnesses, as though the applicable terms and conditions of the Federal Trade Commission Act were part of this title. Any person violating any of the provisions of this title shall be subject to the penalties and entitled to the privileges and immunities provided in the Federal Trade Commission Act as though the applicable terms and provisions of such Act are part of this title.

"(2) PENALTIES.—

"(A) KNOWING VIOLATIONS.—Except as otherwise provided by subtitle B of the Consumer Financial Protection Act of 2010, in the event of a knowing violation, which constitutes a pattern or practice of violations of this title, the Federal Trade Commission may commence a civil action to recover a civil penalty in a district court of the United States against any person that violates this title. In such action, such person shall be liable for a civil penalty of not more than $2,500 per violation.

"(B) DETERMINING PENALTY AMOUNT.—In determining the amount of a civil penalty under subparagraph (A), the court shall take into account the degree of culpability, any history of such prior conduct, ability to pay, effect on ability to continue to do business, and such other matters as justice may require.

"(C) LIMITATION.—Notwithstanding paragraph (2), a court may not impose any civil penalty on a person for a violation of section 623(a)(1), unless the person has been enjoined from committing the violation, or ordered not to commit the violation, in an action or proceeding brought by or on behalf of the Federal Trade Commission, and has violated the injunction or order, and the court may not impose any civil penalty for any violation occurring before the date of the violation of the injunction or order.";

(B) by striking subsection (b) and inserting the following:

"(b) ENFORCEMENT BY OTHER AGENCIES.—

"(1) IN GENERAL.—Subject to subtitle B of the Consumer Financial Protection Act of 2010, compliance with the requirements imposed under this title with respect to consumer reporting agencies, persons who use consumer reports from such agencies, persons who furnish information to such agencies, and users of information that are subject to section 615(d) shall be enforced under—

"(A) section 8 of the Federal Deposit Insurance Act (12 U.S.C. 1818), by the appropriate Federal banking agency, as defined in section 3(q) of the Federal Deposit Insurance Act (12 U.S.C. 1813(q)), with respect to—

"(i) any national bank or State savings association, and any Federal branch or Federal agency of a foreign bank;

"(ii) any member bank of the Federal Reserve System (other than a national bank), a branch or agency of a foreign bank (other than a Federal branch, Federal agency, or insured State branch of a foreign bank), a commercial lending company owned or controlled by a foreign bank, and any organization operating under section 25 or 25A of the Federal Reserve Act; and

"(iii) any bank or Federal savings association insured by the Federal Deposit Insurance Corporation (other than a member of the Federal Reserve System) and any insured State branch of a foreign bank;

"(B) the Federal Credit Union Act (12 U.S.C. 1751 et seq.), by the Administrator of the National Credit Union Administration with respect to any Federal credit union;

"(C) subtitle IV of title 49, United States Code, by the Secretary of Transportation, with respect to all carriers subject to the jurisdiction of the Surface Transportation Board;

"(D) the Federal Aviation Act of 1958 (49 U.S.C. App. 1301 et seq.), by the Secretary of Transportation, with respect to any air carrier or foreign air carrier subject to that Act;

"(E) the Packers and Stockyards Act, 1921 (7 U.S.C. 181 et seq.) (except as provided in section 406 of that Act), by the Secretary of Agriculture, with respect to any activities subject to that Act;

"(F) the Commodity Exchange Act, with respect to a person subject to the jurisdiction of the Commodity Futures Trading Commission;

"(G) the Federal securities laws, and any other laws that are subject to the jurisdiction of the Securities and Exchange Commission, with respect to a person that is subject to the jurisdiction of the Securities and Exchange Commission; and

"(H) subtitle E of the Consumer Financial Protection Act of 2010, by the Bureau, with respect to any person subject to this title.

"(2) INCORPORATED DEFINITIONS.—The terms used in paragraph (1) that are not defined in this title or otherwise defined in section 3(s) of the Federal Deposit Insurance Act (12 U.S.C. 1813(s)) have the same meanings as in section 1(b) of the International Banking Act of 1978 (12 U.S.C. 3101).";

(C) in subsection (c)(2)—

(i) by inserting "and the Federal Trade Commission" before "or the appropriate"; and

(ii) by inserting "and the Federal Trade Commission" before "or appropriate" each place that term appears;

(D) in subsection (c)(4), by inserting before "or the appropriate" each place that term appears the following: ", the Federal Trade Commission,";

(E) by striking subsection (e) and inserting the following:

"(e) REGULATORY AUTHORITY.—

"(1) IN GENERAL.—The Bureau shall prescribe such regulations as are necessary to carry out the purposes of this title, except with respect to sections 615(e) and 628. The Bureau may prescribe regulations as may be necessary or appropriate to administer and carry out the purposes and objectives of this title, and to prevent evasions thereof or to facilitate compliance therewith. Except as provided in section 1029(a) of the Consumer Financial Protection Act of 2010, the regulations prescribed by the Bureau under this title shall apply to any person that is subject to this title, notwithstanding the enforcement authorities granted to other agencies under this section.

"(2) DEFERENCE.—Notwithstanding any power granted to any Federal agency under this title, the deference that a court affords to a Federal agency with respect to a determination made by such agency relating to the meaning or interpretation of any provision of this title that is subject to the jurisdiction of such agency shall be applied as if that agency were the only agency authorized to apply, enforce, interpret, or administer the provisions of this title The regulations prescribed by the Bureau under this title shall apply to any person that is subject to this title, notwithstanding the enforcement authorities granted to other agencies under this section."; and

(F) in subsection (f)(2), by striking "the Federal banking agencies" and insert "the Federal Trade Commission, the Federal banking agencies,";

(11) in section 623 (15 U.S.C. 1681s-2)—

(A) in subsection (a)(7), by striking subparagraph (D) and inserting the following:

"(D) MODEL DISCLOSURE.—

"(i) DUTY OF BUREAU.—The Bureau shall prescribe a brief model disclosure that a financial institution may use to comply with subparagraph (A), which shall not exceed 30 words.

"(ii) USE OF MODEL NOT REQUIRED.—No provision of this paragraph may be construed to require a financial institution to use any such model form prescribed by the Bureau.

"(iii) COMPLIANCE USING MODEL.—A financial institution shall be deemed to be in compliance with subparagraph (A) if the financial institution uses any model form prescribed by the Bureau under this subparagraph, or the financial institution uses any such model form and rearranges its format.";

(B) in subsection (a)(8), by inserting ", in consultation with the Federal Trade Commission, the Federal banking agencies, and the National Credit Union Administration," before "shall jointly"; and

(C) by striking subsection (e) and inserting the following:

"(e) ACCURACY GUIDELINES AND REGULATIONS REQUIRED.—

"(1) GUIDELINES.—The Bureau shall, with respect to persons or entities that are subject to the enforcement authority of the Bureau under section 621—

"(A) establish and maintain guidelines for use by each person that furnishes information to a consumer reporting agency regarding the accuracy and integrity of the information relating to consumers that such entities furnish to consumer reporting agencies, and update such guidelines as often as necessary; and

"(B) prescribe regulations requiring each person that furnishes information to a consumer reporting agency to establish reasonable policies and procedures for implementing the guidelines established pursuant to subparagraph (A).

"(2) CRITERIA.—In developing the guidelines required by paragraph (1)(A), the Bureau shall—

"(A) identify patterns, practices, and specific forms of activity that can compromise the accuracy and integrity of information furnished to consumer reporting agencies;

"(B) review the methods (including technological means) used to furnish information relating to consumers to consumer reporting agencies;

"(C) determine whether persons that furnish information to consumer reporting agencies maintain and enforce policies to ensure the accuracy and integrity of information furnished to consumer reporting agencies; and

"(D) examine the policies and processes that persons that furnish information to consumer reporting agencies employ to conduct reinvestigations and correct inaccurate information relating to consumers that has been furnished to consumer reporting agencies.";

(12) in section 628(a)(1) (15 U.S.C. 1681w(a)(1)), by striking "Not later than" and all that follows through "Exchange Commission," and inserting "The Federal Trade Commission, the Securities and Exchange Commission, the Commodity Futures Trading Commission, the Federal banking agencies, and the National Credit Union Administration, with respect to the entities that are subject to their respective enforcement authority under section 621,"; and

(13) in section 628(a)(3) (15 U.S.C. 1681w(a)(3)), by striking "the Federal banking agencies, the National Credit Union Administration, the Commission, and the Securities and Exchange Commission" and inserting "the agencies identified in paragraph (1)".

(b) FAIR AND ACCURATE CREDIT TRANSACTIONS ACT OF 2003.—The Fair and Accurate Credit Transactions Act of 2003 (Public Law 108-159) is amended—

(1) in section 112(b) (15 U.S.C. 1681c-1 note), by striking "Commission" and inserting "Bureau";

(2) in section 211(d) (15 U.S.C. 1681j note), by striking "Commission" each place that term appears and inserting "Bureau";

(3) in section 214(b) (15 U.S.C. 1681s-3 note), by striking paragraph (1) and inserting the following:

"(1) IN GENERAL.—Regulations to carry out section 624 of the Fair Credit Reporting Act (15 U.S.C. 1681s-3), shall be prescribed, as described in paragraph (2), by—

"(A) the Commodity Futures Trading Commission, with respect to entities subject to its enforcement authorities;

"(B) the Securities and Exchange Commission, with respect to entities subject to its enforcement authorities; and

"(C) the Bureau, with respect to other entities subject to this Act."; and

(4) in section 214(e)(1) (15 U.S.C. 1681s-3 note), by striking "Commission" and inserting "Bureau".

[Explanation at ¶ 4815.]

[¶ 11,089] ACT SEC. 1089. AMENDMENTS TO THE FAIR DEBT COLLECTION PRACTICES ACT.

The Fair Debt Collection Practices Act (15 U.S.C. 1692 et seq.) is amended—

(1) by striking "Commission" each place that term appears and inserting "Bureau";

(2) in section 803 (15 U.S.C. 1692a)—

(A) by striking paragraph (1) and inserting the following:

"(1) The term 'Bureau' means the Bureau of Consumer Financial Protection.";

(3) in section 814 (15 U.S.C. 16921)—

(A) by striking subsection (a) and inserting the following:

"(a) FEDERAL TRADE COMMISSION.—The Federal Trade Commission shall be authorized to enforce compliance with this title, except to the extent that enforcement of the requirements imposed under this title is specifically committed to another Government agency under any of paragraphs (1) through (5) of subsection (b), subject to subtitle B of the Consumer Financial Protection Act of 2010. For purpose of the exercise by the Federal Trade Commission of its functions and powers under the Federal Trade Commission Act (15 U.S.C. 41 et seq.), a violation of this title shall be deemed an unfair or deceptive act or practice in violation of that Act. All of the functions and powers of the Federal Trade Commission under the Federal Trade Commission Act are available to the Federal Trade Commission to enforce compliance by any person with this title, irrespective of whether that person is engaged in commerce or meets any other jurisdictional tests under the Federal Trade Commission Act, including the power to enforce the provisions of this title, in the same manner as if the violation had been a violation of a Federal Trade Commission trade regulation rule."; and

(B) in subsection (b)—

(i) by striking "Compliance" and inserting "Subject to subtitle B of the Consumer Financial Protection Act of 2010, compliance";

(ii) by striking paragraphs (1) and (2) and inserting the following:

"(1) section 8 of the Federal Deposit Insurance Act, by the appropriate Federal banking agency, as defined in section 3(q) of the Federal Deposit Insurance Act (12 U.S.C. 1813(q)), with respect to—

"(A) national banks, Federal savings associations, and Federal branches and Federal agencies of foreign banks;

"(B) member banks of the Federal Reserve System (other than national banks), branches and agencies of foreign banks (other than Federal branches, Federal agencies, and insured State branches of foreign banks), commercial lending companies owned or controlled by foreign banks, and organizations operating under section 25 or 25A of the Federal Reserve Act; and

"(C) banks and State savings associations insured by the Federal Deposit Insurance Corporation (other than members of the Federal Reserve System), and insured State branches of foreign banks;";

(iii) by redesignating paragraphs (3) through (6), as paragraphs (2) through (5), respectively;

(iv) in paragraph (4) (as so redesignated), by striking "and" at the end;

(v) in paragraph (5) (as so redesignated), by striking the period at the end and inserting "; and"; and

(vi) by inserting before the undesignated matter at the end the following:

"(6) subtitle E of the Consumer Financial Protection Act of 2010, by the Bureau, with respect to any person subject to this title.".

(4) in subsection (d), by striking "Neither the Commission" and all that follows through the end of the subsection and inserting the following: "Except as provided in section 1029(a) of the Consumer Financial Protection Act of 2010, the Bureau may prescribe rules with respect to the collection of debts by debt collectors, as defined in this title.".

[Explanation at ¶ 4820.]

[¶ 11,090] ACT SEC. 1090. AMENDMENTS TO THE FEDERAL DEPOSIT INSURANCE ACT.

The Federal Deposit Insurance Act (12 U.S.C. 1811 et seq.) is amended—

(1) in section 8(t) (12 U.S.C. 1818(t)), by adding at the end the following:

"(6) REFERRAL TO BUREAU OF CONSUMER FINANCIAL PROTECTION.—Subject to subtitle B of the Consumer Financial Protection Act of 2010, each appropriate Federal banking agency shall make a referral to the Bureau of Consumer Financial Protection when the Federal banking agency has a reasonable belief that a violation of an enumerated consumer law, as defined in the Consumer Financial Protection Act of 2010, has been committed by any insured depository institution or institution-affiliated party within the jurisdiction of that appropriate Federal banking agency."; and

(2) in section 43 (12 U.S.C. 1831t)—

(A) in subsection (c), by striking "Federal Trade Commission" and inserting "Bureau";

(B) in subsection (d), by striking "Federal Trade Commission" and inserting "Bureau";

(C) in subsection (e)—

(i) in paragraph (2), by striking "Federal Trade Commission" and inserting "Bureau"; and

(ii) by adding at the end the following new paragraph:

"(5) BUREAU.—The term 'Bureau' means the Bureau of Consumer Financial Protection."; and

(D) in subsection (f)—

(i) by striking paragraph (1) and inserting the following:

"(1) LIMITED ENFORCEMENT AUTHORITY.—Compliance with the requirements of subsections (b), (c), and (e), and any regulation prescribed or order issued under such subsection, shall be enforced under the Consumer Financial Protection Act of 2010, by the Bureau, subject to subtitle B of the Consumer Financial Protection Act of 2010, and under the Federal Trade Commission Act (15 U.S.C. 41 et seq.) by the Federal Trade Commission."; and

(ii) in paragraph (2), by striking subparagraph (C) and inserting the following:

"(C) LIMITATION ON STATE ACTION WHILE FEDERAL ACTION PENDING.—If the Bureau or Federal Trade Commission has instituted an enforcement action for a violation of this section, no appropriate State supervisory agency may, during the pendency of such action, bring an action under this section against any defendant named in the complaint of the Bureau or Federal Trade Commission for any violation of this section that is alleged in that complaint.".

[Explanation at ¶ 4825.]

[¶ 11,091] ACT SEC. 1091. AMENDMENT TO FEDERAL FINANCIAL INSTITUTIONS EXAMINATION COUNCIL ACT OF 1978.

Section 1004(a)(4) of the Federal Financial Institutions Examination Council Act of 1978 (12 U.S.C. 3303(a)(4)) is amended by striking "Director, Office of Thrift Supervision" and inserting "Director of the Consumer Financial Protection Bureau".

[Explanation at ¶ 4830.]

[¶ 11,092] ACT SEC. 1092. AMENDMENTS TO THE FEDERAL TRADE COMMISSION ACT.

Section 18(f) of the Federal Trade Commission Act (15 U.S.C. 57a(f)) is amended—

(1) by striking the subsection heading and inserting the following:

"(f) DEFINITIONS OF BANKS, SAVINGS AND LOAN INSTITUTIONS, AND FEDERAL CREDIT UNIONS.—".

(2) by striking paragraph (1) and inserting the following:

"(1) [Repealed.]";

(3) by striking paragraphs (5) through (7);

(4) in paragraph (2)—

(A) by striking "(2) ENFORCEMENT" and all that follows through "in the case of" and inserting the following:

"(2) DEFINITION.—For purposes of this Act, the term 'bank' means";

(B) in subparagraph (A), by striking ", by the division" and all that follows through "Currency";

(C) in subparagraph (B)—

(i) by striking ", by the division" and all that follows through "System"; and

(ii) by striking "25(a)" and inserting "25A"; and

(D) in subparagraph (C)—

(i) by striking "(other" and inserting "(other than"; and

(ii) by striking ", by the division" and all that follows through "Corporation";

(5) in paragraph (3), by striking "Compliance" and all that follows through "as defined in" and inserting the following: "For purposes of this Act, the term "savings and loan institution" has the same meaning as in"; and

(6) in paragraph (4), by striking "Compliance" and all that follows through "credit unions under" and inserting the following: "For purposes of this Act, the term "Federal credit union" has the same meaning as in".

[Explanation at ¶ 4835.]

[¶ 11,093] ACT SEC. 1093. AMENDMENTS TO THE GRAMM-LEACH-BLILEY ACT.

Title V of the Gramm-Leach-Bliley Act (15 U.S.C. 6801 et seq.) is amended—

(1) in section 501(b) (15 U.S.C. 6801(b)), by inserting ", other than the Bureau of Consumer Financial Protection," after "505(a)";

(2) in section 502(e)(5) (15 U.S.C. 6802(e)(5)), by inserting "the Bureau of Consumer Financial Protection" after "(including";

(3) in section 504(a) (15 U.S.C. 6804(a))—

(A) by striking paragraphs (1) and (2) and inserting the following:

"(1) RULEMAKING.—

"(A) IN GENERAL.—Except as provided in subparagraph (C), the Bureau of Consumer Financial Protection and the Securities and Exchange Commission shall have authority to prescribe such regulations as may be necessary to carry out the purposes of this subtitle with respect to financial institutions and other persons subject to their respective jurisdiction under section 505 (and notwithstanding subtitle B of the Consumer Financial Protection Act of 2010), except that the Bureau of Consumer Financial Protection shall not have authority to prescribe regulations with respect to the standards under section 501.

"(B) CFTC.—The Commodity Futures Trading Commission shall have authority to prescribe such regulations as may be necessary to carry out the purposes of this subtitle with respect to financial institutions and other persons subject to the jurisdiction of the Commodity Futures Trading Commission under section 5g of the Commodity Exchange Act.

"(C) FEDERAL TRADE COMMISSION AUTHORITY.—Notwithstanding the authority of the Bureau of Consumer Financial Protection under subparagraph (A), the Federal Trade Commission shall have authority to prescribe such regulations as may be necessary to carry out the purposes of this subtitle with respect to any financial institution that is a person described in section 1029(a) of the Consumer Financial Protection Act of 2010.

"(D) RULE OF CONSTRUCTION.—Nothing in this paragraph shall be construed to alter, affect, or otherwise limit the authority of a State insurance authority to adopt regulations to carry out this subtitle.

"(2) COORDINATION, CONSISTENCY, AND COMPARABILITY.—Each of the agencies authorized under paragraph (1) to prescribe regulations shall consult and coordinate with the other such agencies and, as appropriate, and with representatives of State insurance authorities designated by the National

Association of Insurance Commissioners, for the purpose of assuring, to the extent possible, that the regulations prescribed by each such agency are consistent and comparable with the regulations prescribed by the other such agencies."; and

(B) in paragraph (3), by striking ", and shall be issued in final form not later than 6 months after the date of enactment of this Act";

(4) in section 505(a) (15 U.S.C. 6805(a))—

(A) by striking "This subtitle" and all that follows through "as follows:" and inserting "Subject to subtitle B of the Consumer Financial Protection Act of 2010, this subtitle and the regulations prescribed thereunder shall be enforced by the Bureau of Consumer Financial Protection, the Federal functional regulators, the State insurance authorities, and the Federal Trade Commission with respect to financial institutions and other persons subject to their jurisdiction under applicable law, as follows:";

(B) in paragraph (1)—

(i) in the matter preceding subparagraph (A), by inserting "by the appropriate Federal banking agency, as defined in section 3(q) of the Federal Deposit Insurance Act," after "Act,";

(ii) in subparagraph (A), by striking ", by the Office of the Comptroller of the Currency";

(iii) in subparagraph (B), by striking ", by the Board of Governors of the Federal Reserve System";

(iv) in subparagraph (C), by striking ", by the Board of Directors of the Federal Deposit Insurance Corporation"; and

(v) in subparagraph (D), by striking ", by the Director of the Office of Thrift Supervision"; and

(C) by adding at the end the following:

"(8) Under subtitle E of the Consumer Financial Protection Act of 2010, by the Bureau of Consumer Financial Protection, in the case of any financial institution and other covered person or service provider that is subject to the jurisdiction of the Bureau and any person subject to this subtitle, but not with respect to the standards under section 501.";

(5) in section 505(b)(1) (15 U.S.C. 6805(b)(1)), by inserting ", other than the Bureau of Consumer Financial Protection," after "subsection (a)"; and

(6) in section 507(b) (15 U.S.C. 6807), by striking "Federal Trade Commission" and inserting "Bureau of Consumer Financial Protection".

[Explanation at ¶ 4840.]

[¶ 11,094] ACT SEC. 1094. AMENDMENTS TO THE HOME MORTGAGE DISCLOSURE ACT OF 1975.

The Home Mortgage Disclosure Act of 1975 (12 U.S.C. 2801 et seq.) is amended—

(1) by striking "Board" each place that term appears, other than in sections 303, 304(h), 305(b) (as amended by this section), and 307(a) (as amended by this section) and inserting "Bureau".

(2) in section 303 (12 U.S.C. 2802)—

(A) by redesignating paragraphs (1) through (6) as paragraphs (2) through (7), respectively; and

(B) by inserting before paragraph (2) the following:

"(1) the term 'Bureau' means the Bureau of Consumer Financial Protection;";

(3) in section 304 (12 U.S.C. 2803)—

(A) in subsection (b)—

(i) in paragraph (4), by inserting "age," before "and gender";

(ii) in paragraph (3), by striking "and" at the end;

(iii) in paragraph (4), by striking the period at the end and inserting a semicolon; and

(iv) by adding at the end the following:

"(5) the number and dollar amount of mortgage loans grouped according to measurements of—

"(A) the total points and fees payable at origination in connection with the mortgage as determined by the Bureau, taking into account 15 U.S.C. 1602(aa)(4);

"(B) the difference between the annual percentage rate associated with the loan and a benchmark rate or rates for all loans;

"(C) the term in months of any prepayment penalty or other fee or charge payable on repayment of some portion of principal or the entire principal in advance of scheduled payments; and

"(D) such other information as the Bureau may require; and

"(6) the number and dollar amount of mortgage loans and completed applications grouped according to measurements of—

"(A) the value of the real property pledged or proposed to be pledged as collateral;

"(B) the actual or proposed term in months of any introductory period after which the rate of interest may change;

"(C) the presence of contractual terms or proposed contractual terms that would allow the mortgagor or applicant to make payments other than fully amortizing payments during any portion of the loan term;

"(D) the actual or proposed term in months of the mortgage loan;

"(E) the channel through which application was made, including retail, broker, and other relevant categories;

"(F) as the Bureau may determine to be appropriate, a unique identifier that identifies the loan originator as set forth in section 1503 of the S.A.F.E. Mortgage Licensing Act of 2008;

"(G) as the Bureau may determine to be appropriate, a universal loan identifier;

"(H) as the Bureau may determine to be appropriate, the parcel number that corresponds to the real property pledged or proposed to be pledged as collateral;

"(I) the credit score of mortgage applicants and mortgagors, in such form as the Bureau may prescribe; and

"(J) such other information as the Bureau may require.";

(B) by striking subsection (h) and inserting the following:

"(h) SUBMISSION TO AGENCIES.—

"(1) IN GENERAL.—The data required to be disclosed under subsection (b) shall be submitted to the Bureau or to the appropriate agency for the institution reporting under this title, in accordance with rules prescribed by the Bureau. Notwithstanding the requirement of subsection (a)(2)(A) for disclosure by census tract, the Bureau, in consultation with other appropriate agencies described in paragraph (2) and, after notice and comment, shall develop regulations that—

"(A) prescribe the format for such disclosures, the method for submission of the data to the appropriate agency, and the procedures for disclosing the information to the public;

"(B) require the collection of data required to be disclosed under subsection (b) with respect to loans sold by each institution reporting under this title;

"(C) require disclosure of the class of the purchaser of such loans;

"(D) permit any reporting institution to submit in writing to the Bureau or to the appropriate agency such additional data or explanations as it deems relevant to the decision to originate or purchase mortgage loans; and

"(E) modify or require modification of itemized information, for the purpose of protecting the privacy interests of the mortgage applicants or mortgagors, that is or will be available to the public.

"(2) OTHER APPROPRIATE AGENCIES.—The appropriate agencies described in this paragraph are—

"(A) the appropriate Federal banking agencies, as defined in section 3(q) of the Federal Deposit Insurance Act (12 U.S.C. 1813(q)), with respect to the entities that are subject to the jurisdiction of each such agency, respectively;

"(B) the Federal Deposit Insurance Corporation for banks insured by the Federal Deposit Insurance Corporation (other than members of the Federal Reserve System), mutual savings banks, insured State branches of foreign banks, and any other depository institution described in section 303(2)(A) which is not otherwise referred to in this paragraph;

"(C) the National Credit Union Administration Board with respect to credit unions; and

"(D) the Secretary of Housing and Urban Development with respect to other lending institutions not regulated by the agencies referred to in subparagraph (A) or (B).

"(3) RULES FOR MODIFICATIONS UNDER PARAGRAPH (1).—

"(A) APPLICATION.—A modification under paragraph (1)(E) shall apply to information concerning—

"(i) credit score data described in subsection (b)(6)(I), in a manner that is consistent with the purpose described in paragraph (1)(E); and

"(ii) age or any other category of data described in paragraph (5) or (6) of subsection (b), as the Bureau determines to be necessary to satisfy the purpose described in paragraph (1)(E), and in a manner consistent with that purpose.

"(B) STANDARDS.—The Bureau shall prescribe standards for any modification under paragraph (1)(E) to effectuate the purposes of this title, in light of the privacy interests of mortgage applicants or mortgagors. Where necessary to protect the privacy interests of mortgage applicants or mortgagors, the Bureau shall provide for the disclosure of information described in subparagraph (A) in aggregate or other reasonably modified form, in order to effectuate the purposes of this title.";

(C) in subsection (i), by striking "subsection (b)(4)" and inserting "subsections (b)(4), (b)(5), and (b)(6)";

(D) in subsection (j)—

(i) by striking paragraph (3) and inserting the following:

"(3) CHANGE OF FORM NOT REQUIRED.—A depository institution meets the disclosure requirement of paragraph (1) if the institution provides the information required under such paragraph in such formats as the Bureau may require"; and

(ii) in paragraph (2)(A), by striking "in the format in which such information is maintained by the institution" and inserting "in such formats as the Bureau may require";

(E) in subsection (m), by striking paragraph (2) and inserting the following:

"(2) FORM OF INFORMATION.—In complying with paragraph (1), a depository institution shall provide the person requesting the information with a copy of the information requested in such formats as the Bureau may require."; and

(F) by adding at the end the following:

"(n) TIMING OF CERTAIN DISCLOSURES.—The data required to be disclosed under subsection (b) shall be submitted to the Bureau or to the appropriate agency for any institution reporting under this title, in accordance with regulations prescribed by the Bureau. Institutions shall not be required to report new data under paragraph (5) or (6) of subsection (b) before the first January 1 that occurs after the end of the 9-month period beginning on the date on which regulations are issued by the Bureau in final form with respect to such disclosures.";

(4) in section 305 (12 U.S.C. 2804)—

(A) by striking subsection (b) and inserting the following:

"(b) POWERS OF CERTAIN OTHER AGENCIES.—

"(1) IN GENERAL.—Subject to subtitle B of the Consumer Financial Protection Act of 2010, compliance with the requirements of this title shall be enforced—

"(A) under section 8 of the Federal Deposit Insurance Act, the appropriate Federal banking agency, as defined in section 3(q) of the Federal Deposit Insurance Act (12 U.S.C. 1813(q)), with respect to—

"(i) any national bank or Federal savings association, and any Federal branch or Federal agency of a foreign bank;

"(ii) any member bank of the Federal Reserve System (other than a national bank), branch or agency of a foreign bank (other than a Federal branch, Federal agency, and insured State branch of a foreign bank), commercial lending company owned or controlled by a foreign bank, and any organization operating under section 25 or 25A of the Federal Reserve Act; and

"(iii) any bank or State savings association insured by the Federal Deposit Insurance Corporation (other than a member of the Federal Reserve System), any mutual savings bank as, defined in section 3(f) of the Federal Deposit Insurance Act (12 U.S.C. 1813(f)), any insured State branch of a foreign bank, and any other depository institution not referred to in this paragraph or subparagraph (B) or (C);

"(B) under subtitle E of the Consumer Financial Protection Act of 2010, by the Bureau, with respect to any person subject to this subtitle;

"(C) under the Federal Credit Union Act, by the Administrator of the National Credit Union Administration with respect to any insured credit union; and

"(D) with respect to other lending institutions, by the Secretary of Housing and Urban Development.

"(2) INCORPORATED DEFINITIONS.—The terms used in paragraph (1) that are not defined in this title or otherwise defined in section 3(s) of the Federal Deposit Insurance Act (12 U.S.C. 1813(s)) shall have the same meanings as in section 1(b) of the International Banking Act of 1978 (12 U.S.C. 3101)."; and

(B) by adding at the end the following:

"(d) OVERALL ENFORCEMENT AUTHORITY OF THE BUREAU OF CONSUMER FINANCIAL PROTECTION.—Subject to subtitle B of the Consumer Financial Protection Act of 2010, enforcement of the requirements imposed under this title is committed to each of the agencies under subsection (b). To facilitate research, examinations, and enforcement, all data collected pursuant to section 304 shall be available to the entities listed under subsection (b). The Bureau may exercise its authorities under the Consumer Financial Protection Act of 2010 to exercise principal authority to examine and enforce compliance by any person with the requirements of this title.";

(5) in section 306 (12 U.S.C. 2805(b)), by striking subsection (b) and inserting the following:

"(b) EXEMPTION AUTHORITY.—The Bureau may, by regulation, exempt from the requirements of this title any State-chartered depository institution within any State or subdivision thereof, if the agency determines that, under the law of such State or subdivision, that institution is subject to requirements that are substantially similar to those imposed under this title, and that such law contains adequate provisions for enforcement. Notwithstanding any other provision of this subsection, compliance with the requirements imposed under this subsection shall be enforced by the Office of the Comptroller of the Currency under section 8 of the Federal Deposit Insurance Act, in the case of national banks and Federal savings associations, the deposits of which are insured by the Federal Deposit Insurance Corporation."; and

(6) by striking section 307 (12 U.S.C. 2806) and inserting the following:

"SEC. 307. COMPLIANCE IMPROVEMENT METHODS.

"(a) IN GENERAL.—

"(1) CONSULTATION REQUIRED.—The Director of the Bureau of Consumer Financial Protection, with the assistance of the Secretary, the Director of the Bureau of the Census, the Board of Governors of the Federal Reserve System, the Federal Deposit Insurance Corporation, and such other persons as the Bureau deems appropriate, shall develop or assist in the improvement of, methods of matching addresses and census tracts to facilitate compliance by depository institutions in as economical a manner as possible with the requirements of this title.

"(2) AUTHORIZATION OF APPROPRIATIONS.—There are authorized to be appropriated, such sums as may be necessary to carry out this subsection.

"(3) CONTRACTING AUTHORITY.—The Director of the Bureau of Consumer Financial Protection is authorized to utilize, contract with, act through, or compensate any person or agency in order to carry out this subsection.

"(b) RECOMMENDATIONS TO CONGRESS.—The Director of the Bureau of Consumer Financial Protection shall recommend to the Committee on Banking, Housing, and Urban Affairs of the Senate and the Committee on Financial Services of the House of Representatives, such additional legislation as the Director of the Bureau of Consumer Financial Protection deems appropriate to carry out the purpose of this title.".

[Explanation at ¶ 4845.]

[¶ 11,095] ACT SEC. 1095. AMENDMENTS TO THE HOMEOWNERS PROTECTION ACT OF 1998.

Section 10 of the Homeowners Protection Act of 1998 (12 U.S.C. 4909) is amended—

(1) in subsection (a)—

(A) by striking "Compliance" and all that follows through the end of paragraph (1) and inserting the following: "Subject to subtitle B of the Consumer Financial Protection Act of 2010, compliance with the requirements imposed under this Act shall be enforced under—

"(1) section 8 of the Federal Deposit Insurance Act, by the appropriate Federal banking agency (as defined in section 3(q) of that Act), with respect to—

"(A) insured depository institutions (as defined in section 3(c)(2) of that Act);

"(B) depository institutions described in clause (i), (ii), or (iii) of section 19(b)(1)(A) of the Federal Reserve Act which are not insured depository institutions (as defined in section 3(c)(2) of the Federal Deposit Insurance Act); and

"(C) depository institutions described in clause (v) or (vi) of section 19(b)(1)(A) of the Federal Reserve Act which are not insured depository institutions (as defined in section 3(c)(2) of the Federal Deposit Insurance Act);";

(B) in paragraph (2), by striking "and" at the end;

(C) in paragraph (3), by striking the period at the end and inserting "; and"; and

(D) by adding at the end the following:

"(4) subtitle E of the Consumer Financial Protection Act of 2010, by the Bureau of Consumer Financial Protection, with respect to any person subject to this Act."; and

(2) in subsection (b)(2), by inserting before the period at the end the following: ", subject to subtitle B of the Consumer Financial Protection Act of 2010".

[Explanation at ¶ 4850.]

[¶ 11,096] ACT SEC. 1096. AMENDMENTS TO THE HOME OWNERSHIP AND EQUITY PROTECTION ACT OF 1994.

The Home Ownership and Equity Protection Act of 1994 (15 U.S.C. 1601 note) is amended—

(1) in section 158(a), by striking "Board of Governors of the Federal Reserve System, in consultation with the Consumer Advisory Council of the Board" and inserting "Bureau, in consultation with the Advisory Board to the Bureau"; and

(2) in section 158(b), by striking "Board of Governors of the Federal Reserve System" and inserting "Bureau".

[Explanation at ¶ 4855.]

[¶ 11,097] ACT SEC. 1097. AMENDMENTS TO THE OMNIBUS APPROPRIATIONS ACT, 2009.

Section 626 of the Omnibus Appropriations Act, 2009 (15 U.S.C. 1638 note) is amended—

(1) by striking subsection (a) and inserting the following:

"(a)

(1) The Bureau of Consumer Financial Protection shall have authority to prescribe rules with respect to mortgage loans in accordance with section 553 of title 5, United States Code. Such rulemaking shall relate to unfair or deceptive acts or practices regarding mortgage loans, which may include unfair or deceptive acts or practices involving loan modification and foreclosure rescue services. Any violation of a rule prescribed under this paragraph shall be treated as a violation of a rule prohibiting unfair, deceptive, or abusive acts or practices under the Consumer Financial Protection Act of 2010 and a violation of a rule under section 18 of the Federal Trade Commission Act (15 U.S.C. 57a) regarding unfair or deceptive acts or practices.

"(2) The Bureau of Consumer Financial Protection shall enforce the rules issued under paragraph (1) in the same manner, by the same means, and with the same jurisdiction, powers, and duties, as though all applicable terms and provisions of the Consumer Financial Protection Act of 2010 were incorporated into and made part of this subsection.

"(3) Subject to subtitle B of the Consumer Financial Protection Act of 2010, the Federal Trade Commission shall enforce the rules issued under paragraph (1), in the same manner, by the same means, and with the same jurisdiction, as though all applicable terms and provisions of the Federal Trade Commission Act were incorporated into and made part of this section."; and

(2) in subsection (b)—

(A) by striking paragraph (1) and inserting the following:

"(1) Except as provided in paragraph (6), in any case in which the attorney general of a State has reason to believe that an interest of the residents of the State has been or is threatened or adversely affected by the engagement of any person subject to a rule prescribed under subsection (a) in practices that violate such rule, the State, as parens patriae, may bring a civil action on behalf of its residents in an appropriate district court of the United States or other court of competent jurisdiction—

"(A) to enjoin that practice;

"(B) to enforce compliance with the rule;

"(C) to obtain damages, restitution, or other compensation on behalf of the residents of the State; or

"(D) to obtain penalties and relief provided under the Consumer Financial Protection Act of 2010, the Federal Trade Commission Act, and such other relief as the court deems appropriate.";

(B) in paragraphs (2) and (3), by striking "the primary Federal regulator" each time the term appears and inserting "the Bureau of Consumer Financial Protection or the Commission, as appropriate";

(C) in paragraph (3), by inserting "and subject to subtitle B of the Consumer Financial Protection Act of 2010," after "paragraph (2),"; and

(D) in paragraph (6), by striking "the primary Federal regulator" each place that term appears and inserting "the Bureau of Consumer Financial Protection or the Commission".

[Explanation at ¶ 4860.]

[¶ 11,098] ACT SEC. 1098. AMENDMENTS TO THE REAL ESTATE SETTLEMENT PROCEDURES ACT OF 1974.

The Real Estate Settlement Procedures Act of 1974 (12 U.S.C. 2601 et seq.) is amended—

(1) in section 3 (12 U.S.C. 2602)—

(A) in paragraph (7), by striking "and" at the end;

(B) in paragraph (8), by striking the period at the end and inserting "; and"; and

(C) by adding at the end the following:

"(9) the term 'Bureau' means the Bureau of Consumer Financial Protection.";

(2) in section 4 (12 U.S.C. 2603)—

(A) in subsection (a), by striking the first sentence and inserting the following: "The Bureau shall publish a single, integrated disclosure for mortgage loan transactions (including real estate settlement cost statements) which includes the disclosure requirements of this section and section 5, in conjunction with the disclosure requirements of the Truth in Lending Act that, taken together, may apply to a transaction that is subject to both or either provisions of law. The purpose of such model disclosure shall be to facilitate compliance with the disclosure requirements of this title and the Truth in Lending Act, and to aid the borrower or lessee in understanding the transaction by utilizing readily understandable language to simplify the technical nature of the disclosures.";

(B) by striking "Secretary" each place that term appears and inserting "Bureau"; and

(C) by striking "form" each place that term appears and inserting "forms";

(3) in section 5 (12 U.S.C. 2604)—

(A) by striking "Secretary" each place that term appears and inserting "Bureau"; and

(B) in subsection (a), by striking the first sentence and inserting the following: "The Bureau shall prepare and distribute booklets jointly addressing compliance with the requirements of the Truth in Lending Act and the provisions of this title, in order to help persons borrowing money to finance the purchase of residential real estate better to understand the nature and costs of real estate settlement services.";

(4) in section 6(j)(3) (12 U.S.C. 2605(j)(3))—

(A) by striking "Secretary" and inserting "Bureau"; and

(B) by striking ", by regulations that shall take effect not later than April 20, 1991,";

(5) in section 7(b) (12 U.S.C. 2606(b)) by striking "Secretary" and inserting "Bureau";

(6) in section 8(c)(5) (12 U.S.C. 2607(c)(5)), by striking "Secretary" and inserting "Bureau";

(7) in section 8(d) (12 U.S.C. 2607(d))—

(A) in the subsection heading, by inserting "BUREAU AND" before "SECRETARY"; and

(B) by striking paragraph (4), and inserting the following:

"(4) The Bureau, the Secretary, or the attorney general or the insurance commissioner of any State may bring an action to enjoin violations of this section. Except, to the extent that a person is subject to the jurisdiction of the Bureau, the Secretary, or the attorney general or the insurance commissioner of any State, the Bureau shall have primary authority to enforce or administer this section, subject to subtitle B of the Consumer Financial Protection Act of 2010.";

(8) in section 10(c) (12 U.S.C. 2609(c) and (d)), by striking "Secretary" and inserting "Bureau";

(9) in section 16 (12 U.S.C. 2614), by inserting "the Bureau," before "the Secretary";

(10) in section 18 (12 U.S.C. 2616), by striking "Secretary" each place that term appears and inserting "Bureau"; and

(11) in section 19 (12 U.S.C. 2617)—

(A) in the section heading by striking **"SECRETARY"** and inserting **"BUREAU"**;

(B) in subsection (a), by striking "Secretary" each place that term appears and inserting "Bureau"; and

(C) in subsections (b) and (c), by striking "the Secretary" each place that term appears and inserting "the Bureau".

[Explanation at ¶ 4865 and ¶ 4870.]

[¶ 11,098A] ACT SEC. 1098A. AMENDMENTS TO THE INTERSTATE LAND SALES FULL DISCLOSURE ACT.

The Interstate Land Sales Full Disclosure Act (15 U.S.C. 1701 et seq.) is amended—

(1) by striking "Secretary" each place that term appears and inserting "Director";

(2) by striking "Department of Housing and Urban Development" each place that term appears and inserting "Bureau of Consumer Financial Protection";

(3) by striking "Department" each place that term appears and inserting "Bureau";

(4) in section 1402 (15 U.S.C. 1701)—

(A) by striking paragraph (1) and inserting the following:

"(1) 'Director' means the Director of the Bureau of Consumer Financial Protection;";

(B) in paragraph (10), by striking "and" at the end;

(C) in paragraph (11), by striking the period at the end and inserting "; and"; and

(D) by adding at the end the following:

"(12) 'Bureau' means the Bureau of Consumer Financial Protection."; and

(5) in section 1416(a) (15 U.S.C. 1715(a)), by striking "Secretary of Housing and Urban Development" and inserting "Director of the Bureau of Consumer Financial Protection".

[Explanation at ¶ 4870.]

[¶ 11,099] ACT SEC. 1099. AMENDMENTS TO THE RIGHT TO FINANCIAL PRIVACY ACT OF 1978.

The Right to Financial Privacy Act of 1978 (12 U.S.C. 3401 et seq.) is amended—

(1) in section 1101—

(A) in paragraph (6)—

(i) in subparagraph (A), by inserting "and" after the semicolon;

(ii) in subparagraph (B), by striking "and" at the end; and

(iii) by striking subparagraph (C); and

(B) in paragraph (7), by striking subparagraph (B), and inserting the following:

"(B) the Bureau of Consumer Financial Protection;";

(2) in section 1112(e) (12 U.S.C. 3412(e)), by striking "and the Commodity Futures Trading Commission is permitted" and inserting "the Commodity Futures Trading Commission, and the Bureau of Consumer Financial Protection is permitted"; and

(3) in section 1113 (12 U.S.C. 3413), by adding at the end the following new subsection:

"(r) DISCLOSURE TO THE BUREAU OF CONSUMER FINANCIAL PROTECTION.—Nothing in this title shall apply to the examination by or disclosure to the Bureau of Consumer Financial Protection of financial records or information in the exercise of its authority with respect to a financial institution.".

[Explanation at ¶ 4875.]

[¶ 11,100] ACT SEC. 1100. AMENDMENTS TO THE SECURE AND FAIR ENFORCEMENT FOR MORTGAGE LICENSING ACT OF 2008.

The S.A.F.E. Mortgage Licensing Act of 2008 (12 U.S.C. 5101 et seq.) is amended—

(1) by striking "a Federal banking agency" each place that term appears, other than in paragraphs (7) and (11) of section 1503 and section 1507(a)(1), and inserting "the Bureau";

(2) by striking "Federal banking agencies" each place that term appears and inserting "Bureau"; and

(3) by striking "Secretary" each place that term appears and inserting "Director";

(4) in section 1503 (12 U.S.C. 5102)—

(A) by redesignating paragraphs (2) through (12) as (3) through (13), respectively;

(B) by striking paragraph (1) and inserting the following:

"(1) BUREAU.—The term 'Bureau' means the Bureau of Consumer Financial Protection.

"(2) FEDERAL BANKING AGENCY.—The term 'Federal banking agency' means the Board of Governors of the Federal Reserve System, the Office of the Comptroller of the Currency, the National Credit Union Administration, and the Federal Deposit Insurance Corporation."; and

(C) by striking paragraph (10), as so designated by this section, and inserting the following:

"(10) DIRECTOR.—The term 'Director' means the Director of the Bureau of Consumer Financial Protection."; and

(5) in section 1507 (12 U.S.C. 5106)—

(A) in subsection (a)—

(i) by striking paragraph (1) and inserting the following:

"(1) IN GENERAL.—The Bureau shall develop and maintain a system for registering employees of a depository institution, employees of a subsidiary that is owned and controlled by a depository institution and regulated by a Federal banking agency, or employees of an institution regulated by the Farm Credit Administration, as registered loan originators with the Nationwide Mortgage Licensing System and Registry. The system shall be implemented before the end of the 1-year period beginning on the date of enactment of the Consumer Financial Protection Act of 2010."; and

(ii) in paragraph (2)—

(I) by striking "appropriate Federal banking agency and the Farm Credit Administration" and inserting "Bureau"; and

(II) by striking "employees's identity" and inserting "identity of the employee"; and

(B) in subsection (b), by striking "through the Financial Institutions Examination Council, and the Farm Credit Administration", and inserting "and the Bureau of Consumer Financial Protection";

(6) in section 1508 (12 U.S.C. 5107)—

(A) by striking the section heading and inserting the following: "**SEC. 1508. BUREAU OF CONSUMER FINANCIAL PROTECTION BACKUP AUTHORITY TO ESTABLISH LOAN ORIGINATOR LICENSING SYSTEM.**"; and

(B) by adding at the end the following:

"(f) REGULATION AUTHORITY.—

"(1) IN GENERAL.—The Bureau is authorized to promulgate regulations setting minimum net worth or surety bond requirements for residential mortgage loan originators and minimum requirements for recovery funds paid into by loan originators.

"(2) CONSIDERATIONS.—In issuing regulations under paragraph (1), the Bureau shall take into account the need to provide originators adequate incentives to originate affordable and sustainable mortgage loans, as well as the need to ensure a competitive origination market that maximizes consumer access to affordable and sustainable mortgage loans.";

(7) by striking section 1510 (12 U.S.C. 5109) and inserting the following:

"SEC. 1510. FEES.

"The Bureau, the Farm Credit Administration, and the Nationwide Mortgage Licensing System and Registry may charge reasonable fees to cover the costs of maintaining and providing access to information from the Nationwide Mortgage Licensing System and Registry, to the extent that such fees are not charged to consumers for access to such system and registry.";

(8) by striking section 1513 (12 U.S.C. 5112) and inserting the following:

"SEC. 1513. LIABILITY PROVISIONS.

"The Bureau, any State official or agency, or any organization serving as the administrator of the Nationwide Mortgage Licensing System and Registry or a system established by the Director under section 1509, or any officer or employee of any such entity, shall not be subject to any civil action or proceeding for monetary damages by reason of the good faith action or omission of any officer or employee of any such entity, while acting within the scope of office or employment, relating to the collection, furnishing, or dissemination of information concerning persons who are loan originators or are applying for licensing or registration as loan originators."; and

(9) in section 1514 (12 U.S.C. 5113) in the section heading, by striking "**UNDER HUD BACKUP LICENSING SYSTEM**" and inserting "**BY THE BUREAU**".

[Explanation at ¶ 4880.]

[¶ 11,100A] ACT SEC. 1100A. AMENDMENTS TO THE TRUTH IN LENDING ACT.

The Truth in Lending Act (15 U.S.C. 1601 et seq.) is amended—

(1) in section 103 (15 U.S.C. 1602)—

(A) by redesignating subsections (b) through (bb) as subsections (c) through (cc), respectively; and

(B) by inserting after subsection (a) the following:

Title X—Consumer Financial Protection 1243

"(b) BUREAU.—The term 'Bureau' means the Bureau of Consumer Financial Protection.";

(2) by striking "Board" each place that term appears, other than in section 140(d) and sections 105(i) and 108(a), as amended by this section, and inserting "Bureau";

(3) by striking "Federal Trade Commission" each place that term appears, other than in section 108(c) and section 129(m), as amended by this Act, and other than in the context of a reference to the Federal Trade Commission Act, and inserting "Bureau";

(4) in section 105(a) (15 U.S.C. 1604(a)), in the second sentence—

(A) by striking "Except in the case of a mortgage referred to in section 103(aa), these regulations may contain such" and inserting "Except with respect to the provisions of section 129 that apply to a mortgage referred to in section 103(aa), such regulations may contain such additional requirements,"; and

(B) by inserting "all or" after "exceptions for";

(5) in section 105(b) (15 U.S.C. 1604(b)), by striking the first sentence and inserting the following: "The Bureau shall publish a single, integrated disclosure for mortgage loan transactions (including real estate settlement cost statements) which includes the disclosure requirements of this title in conjunction with the disclosure requirements of the Real Estate Settlement Procedures Act of 1974 that, taken together, may apply to a transaction that is subject to both or either provisions of law. The purpose of such model disclosure shall be to facilitate compliance with the disclosure requirements of this title and the Real Estate Settlement Procedures Act of 1974, and to aid the borrower or lessee in understanding the transaction by utilizing readily understandable language to simplify the technical nature of the disclosures.";

(6) in section 105(f)(1) (15 U.S.C. 1604(f)(1)), by inserting "all or" after "from all or part of this title";

(7) in section 105 (15 U.S.C. 1604), by adding at the end the following:

"(i) AUTHORITY OF THE BOARD TO PRESCRIBE RULES.—Notwithstanding subsection (a), the Board shall have authority to prescribe rules under this title with respect to a person described in section 1029(a) of the Consumer Financial Protection Act of 2010. Regulations prescribed under this subsection may contain such classifications, differentiations, or other provisions, as in the judgment of the Board are necessary or proper to effectuate the purposes of this title, to prevent circumvention or evasion thereof, or to facilitate compliance therewith.";

(8) in section 108 (15 U.S.C. 1604), by adding at the end the following:

(A) by striking subsection (a) and inserting the following:

"(a) ENFORCING AGENCIES.—Subject to subtitle B of the Consumer Financial Protection Act of 2010, compliance with the requirements imposed under this title shall be enforced under—

"(1) section 8 of the Federal Deposit Insurance Act, by the appropriate Federal banking agency, as defined in section 3(q) of the Federal Deposit Insurance Act (12 U.S.C. 1813(q)), with respect to—

"(A) national banks, Federal savings associations, and Federal branches and Federal agencies of foreign banks;

"(B) member banks of the Federal Reserve System (other than national banks), branches and agencies of foreign banks (other than Federal branches, Federal agencies, and insured State branches of foreign banks), commercial lending companies owned or controlled by foreign banks, and organizations operating under section 25 or 25A of the Federal Reserve Act; and

"(C) banks and State savings associations insured by the Federal Deposit Insurance Corporation (other than members of the Federal Reserve System), and insured State branches of foreign banks;

"(2) the Federal Credit Union Act, by the Director of the National Credit Union Administration, with respect to any Federal credit union;

"(3) the Federal Aviation Act of 1958, by the Secretary of Transportation, with respect to any air carrier or foreign air carrier subject to that Act;

"(4) the Packers and Stockyards Act, 1921 (except as provided in section 406 of that Act), by the Secretary of Agriculture, with respect to any activities subject to that Act;

Act Sec. 1100A(8)(A) ¶11,100A

"(5) the Farm Credit Act of 1971, by the Farm Credit Administration with respect to any Federal land bank, Federal land bank association, Federal intermediate credit bank, or production credit association; and

"(6) subtitle E of the Consumer Financial Protection Act of 2010, by the Bureau, with respect to any person subject to this title."; and

(B) by striking subsection (c) and inserting the following:

"(c) OVERALL ENFORCEMENT AUTHORITY OF THE FEDERAL TRADE COMMISSION.—Except to the extent that enforcement of the requirements imposed under this title is specifically committed to some other Government agency under any of paragraphs (1) through (5) of subsection (a), and subject to subtitle B of the Consumer Financial Protection Act of 2010, the Federal Trade Commission shall be authorized to enforce such requirements. For the purpose of the exercise by the Federal Trade Commission of its functions and powers under the Federal Trade Commission Act, a violation of any requirement imposed under this title shall be deemed a violation of a requirement imposed under that Act. All of the functions and powers of the Federal Trade Commission under the Federal Trade Commission Act are available to the Federal Trade Commission to enforce compliance by any person with the requirements under this title, irrespective of whether that person is engaged in commerce or meets any other jurisdictional tests under the Federal Trade Commission Act."; and

(9) in section 129 (15 U.S.C. 1639), by striking subsection (m) and inserting the following:

"(m) CIVIL PENALTIES IN FEDERAL TRADE COMMISSION ENFORCEMENT ACTIONS.—For purposes of enforcement by the Federal Trade Commission, any violation of a regulation issued by the Bureau pursuant to subsection (1)(2) shall be treated as a violation of a rule promulgated under section 18 of the Federal Trade Commission Act (15 U.S.C. 57a) regarding unfair or deceptive acts or practices."; and

(10) in chapter 5 (15 U.S.C. 1667 et seq.)—

(A) by striking "the Board" each place that term appears and inserting "the Bureau"; and

(B) by striking "The Board" each place that term appears and inserting "The Bureau".

[Explanation at ¶ 4885.]

[¶ 11,100B] ACT SEC. 1100B. AMENDMENTS TO THE TRUTH IN SAVINGS ACT.

The Truth in Savings Act (12 U.S.C. 4301 et seq.) is amended—

(1) by striking "Board" each place that term appears, other than in section 272(b) (12 U.S.C. 4311), and inserting "Bureau";

(2) in section 270(a) (12 U.S.C. 4309)—

(A) by striking "Compliance" and all that follows through the end of paragraph (1) and inserting: "Subject to subtitle B of the Consumer Financial Protection Act of 2010, compliance with the requirements imposed under this subtitle shall be enforced under—

"(1) section 8 of the Federal Deposit Insurance Act by the appropriate Federal banking agency (as defined in section 3(q) of that Act), with respect to—

"(A) insured depository institutions (as defined in section 3(c)(2) of that Act);

"(B) depository institutions described in clause (i), (ii), or (iii) of section 19(b)(1)(A) of the Federal Reserve Act which are not insured depository institutions (as defined in section 3(c)(2) of the Federal Deposit Insurance Act); and

"(C) depository institutions described in clause (v) or (vi) of section 19(b)(1)(A) of the Federal Reserve Act which are not insured depository institutions (as defined in section 3(c)(2) of the Federal Deposit Insurance Act);";

(B) in paragraph (2), by striking the period at the end and inserting "; and"; and

(C) by adding at the end the following:

"(3) subtitle E of the Consumer Financial Protection Act of 2010, by the Bureau, with respect to any person subject to this subtitle.";

(3) in section 272(b) (12 U.S.C. 4311(b)), by striking "regulation prescribed by the Board" each place that term appears and inserting "regulation prescribed by the Bureau"; and

(4) in section 274 (12 U.S.C. 4313), by striking paragraph (4) and inserting the following:

"(4) BUREAU.—The term 'Bureau' means the Bureau of Consumer Financial Protection.".

[Explanation at ¶ 4890.]

[¶ 11,100C] ACT SEC. 1100C. AMENDMENTS TO THE TELEMARKETING AND CONSUMER FRAUD AND ABUSE PREVENTION ACT.

(a) AMENDMENTS TO SECTION 3.—Section 3 of the Telemarketing and Consumer Fraud and Abuse Prevention Act (15 U.S.C. 6102) is amended by striking subsections (b) and (c) and inserting the following:

"(b) RULEMAKING AUTHORITY.—The Commission shall have authority to prescribe rules under subsection (a), in accordance with section 553 of title 5, United States Code. In prescribing a rule under this section that relates to the provision of a consumer financial product or service that is subject to the Consumer Financial Protection Act of 2010, including any enumerated consumer law thereunder, the Commission shall consult with the Bureau of Consumer Financial Protection regarding the consistency of a proposed rule with standards, purposes, or objectives administered by the Bureau of Consumer Financial Protection.

"(c) VIOLATIONS.—Any violation of any rule prescribed under subsection (a)—

"(1) shall be treated as a violation of a rule under section 18 of the Federal Trade Commission Act regarding unfair or deceptive acts or practices; and

"(2) that is committed by a person subject to the Consumer Financial Protection Act of 2010 shall be treated as a violation of a rule under section 1031 of that Act regarding unfair, deceptive, or abusive acts or practices.".

(b) AMENDMENTS TO SECTION 4.—Section 4(d) of the Telemarketing and Consumer Fraud and Abuse Prevention Act (15 U.S.C. 6103(d)) is amended by inserting after "Commission" each place that term appears the following: "or the Bureau of Consumer Financial Protection".

(c) AMENDMENTS TO SECTION 5.—Section 5(c) of the Telemarketing and Consumer Fraud and Abuse Prevention Act (15 U.S.C. 6104(c)) is amended by inserting after "Commission" each place that term appears the following: "or the Bureau of Consumer Financial Protection".

(d) AMENDMENT TO SECTION 6.—Section 6 of the Telemarketing and Consumer Fraud and Abuse Prevention Act (15 U.S.C. 6105) is amended by adding at the end the following:

"(d) ENFORCEMENT BY BUREAU OF CONSUMER FINANCIAL PROTECTION.—Except as otherwise provided in sections 3(d), 3(e), 4, and 5, and subject to subtitle B of the Consumer Financial Protection Act of 2010, this Act shall be enforced by the Bureau of Consumer Financial Protection under subtitle E of the Consumer Financial Protection Act of 2010, with respect to the offering or provision of a consumer financial product or service subject to that Act.".

[Explanation at ¶ 4895.]

[¶ 11,100D] ACT SEC. 1100D. AMENDMENTS TO THE PAPERWORK REDUCTION ACT.

(a) DESIGNATION AS AN INDEPENDENT AGENCY.—Section 2(5) of the Paperwork Reduction Act (44 U.S.C. 3502(5)) is amended by inserting "the Bureau of Consumer Financial Protection, the Office of Financial Research," after "the Securities and Exchange Commission,".

(b) COMPARABLE TREATMENT.—Section 3513 of title 44, United States Code, is amended by adding at the end the following:

"(c) COMPARABLE TREATMENT.—Notwithstanding any other provision of law, the Director shall treat or review a rule or order prescribed or proposed by the Director of the Bureau of Consumer Financial Protection on the same terms and conditions as apply to any rule or order prescribed or proposed by the Board of Governors of the Federal Reserve System.".

[Explanation at ¶ 4900.]

[¶ 11,100E] **ACT SEC. 1100E. ADJUSTMENTS FOR INFLATION IN THE TRUTH IN LENDING ACT.**

(a) CAPS.—

(1) CREDIT TRANSACTIONS.—Section 104(3) of the Truth in Lending Act (15 U.S.C. 1603(3)) is amended by striking "$25,000" and inserting "$50,000".

(2) CONSUMER LEASES.—Section 181(1) of the Truth in Lending Act (15 U.S.C. 1667(1)) is amended by striking "$25,000" and inserting "$50,000".

(b) ADJUSTMENTS FOR INFLATION.—On and after December 31, 2011, the Bureau shall adjust annually the dollar amounts described in sections 104(3) and 181(1) of the Truth in Lending Act (as amended by this section), by the annual percentage increase in the Consumer Price Index for Urban Wage Earners and Clerical Workers, as published by the Bureau of Labor Statistics, rounded to the nearest multiple of $100, or $1,000, as applicable.

[Explanation at ¶ 4905.]

[¶ 11,100F] **ACT SEC. 1100F. USE OF CONSUMER REPORTS.**

Section 615 of the Fair Credit Reporting Act (15 U.S.C. 1681m) is amended—

(1) in subsection (a)—

(A) by redesignating paragraphs (2) and (3) as paragraphs (3) and (4), respectively;

(B) by inserting after paragraph (1) the following:

"(2) provide to the consumer written or electronic disclosure—

"(A) of a numerical credit score as defined in section 609(f)(2)(A) used by such person in taking any adverse action based in whole or in part on any information in a consumer report; and

"(B) of the information set forth in subparagraphs (B) through (E) of section 609(f)(1);"; and

(C) in paragraph (4) (as so redesignated), by striking "paragraph (2)" and inserting "paragraph (3)"; and

(2) in subsection (h)(5)—

(A) in subparagraph (C), by striking "; and" and inserting a semicolon;

(B) in subparagraph (D), by striking the period and inserting "; and"; and

(C) by inserting at the end the following:

"(E) include a statement informing the consumer of—

"(i) a numerical credit score as defined in section 609(f)(2)(A), used by such person in making the credit decision described in paragraph (1) based in whole or in part on any information in a consumer report; and

"(ii) the information set forth in subparagraphs (B) through (E) of section 609(f)(1).".

[Explanation at ¶ 4910.]

[¶ 11,100G] **ACT SEC. 1100G. SMALL BUSINESS FAIRNESS AND REGULATORY TRANSPARENCY.**

(a) PANEL REQUIREMENT.—Section 609(d) of title 5, United States Code, is amended by striking "means the" and all that follows and inserting the following: "means—

"(1) the Environmental Protection Agency;

"(2) the Consumer Financial Protection Bureau of the Federal Reserve System; and

"(3) the Occupational Safety and Health Administration of the Department of Labor.".

(b) INITIAL REGULATORY FLEXIBILITY ANALYSIS.—Section 603 of title 5, United States Code, is amended by adding at the end the following:

"(d)

(1) For a covered agency, as defined in section 609(d)(2), each initial regulatory flexibility analysis shall include a description of—

"(A) any projected increase in the cost of credit for small entities;

"(B) any significant alternatives to the proposed rule which accomplish the stated objectives of applicable statutes and which minimize any increase in the cost of credit for small entities; and

"(C) advice and recommendations of representatives of small entities relating to issues described in subparagraphs (A) and (B) and subsection (b).

"(2) A covered agency, as defined in section 609(d)(2), shall, for purposes of complying with paragraph (1)(C)—

"(A) identify representatives of small entities in consultation with the Chief Counsel for Advocacy of the Small Business Administration; and

"(B) collect advice and recommendations from the representatives identified under subparagraph (A) relating to issues described in subparagraphs (A) and (B) of paragraph (1) and subsection (b).".

(c) FINAL REGULATORY FLEXIBILITY ANALYSIS.—Section 604(a) of title 5, United States Code, is amended—

(1) in paragraph (4), by striking "and" at the end;

(2) in paragraph (5), by striking the period at the end and inserting "; and"; and

(3) by adding at the end the following:

"(6) for a covered agency, as defined in section 609(d)(2), a description of the steps the agency has taken to minimize any additional cost of credit for small entities.".

[Explanation at ¶4915.]

[¶11,100H] ACT SEC. 1100H. EFFECTIVE DATE.

Except as otherwise provided in this subtitle and the amendments made by this subtitle, this subtitle and the amendments made by this subtitle, other than sections 1081 and 1082, shall become effective on the designated transfer date.

[Explanation at ¶4780.]

TITLE XI—FEDERAL RESERVE SYSTEM PROVISIONS

[¶11,101] ACT SEC. 1101. FEDERAL RESERVE ACT AMENDMENTS ON EMERGENCY LENDING AUTHORITY.

(a) FEDERAL RESERVE ACT.—The third undesignated paragraph of section 13 of the Federal Reserve Act (12 U.S.C. 343) (relating to emergency lending authority) is amended—

(1) by inserting "(3)(A)" before "In unusual";

(2) by striking "individual, partnership, or corporation" the first place that term appears and inserting the following: "participant in any program or facility with broad-based eligibility";

(3) by striking "exchange for an individual or a partnership or corporation" and inserting "exchange,";

(4) by striking "such individual, partnership, or corporation" and inserting the following: "such participant in any program or facility with broad-based eligibility";

(5) by striking "for individuals, partnerships, corporations" and inserting "for any participant in any program or facility with broad-based eligibility"; and

(6) by striking "may prescribe." and inserting the following: "may prescribe.

"(B)

"(i) As soon as is practicable after the date of enactment of this subparagraph, the Board shall establish, by regulation, in consultation with the Secretary of the Treasury, the policies and procedures governing emergency lending under this paragraph. Such policies and procedures shall be designed to ensure that any emergency lending program or facility is for the purpose of providing liquidity to the financial system, and not to aid a failing financial company, and that the security for emergency loans is sufficient to protect taxpayers from losses and that any such program is terminated in a timely and orderly fashion. The policies and procedures established by the Board shall require that a Federal reserve bank assign, consistent with sound risk management practices and to ensure protection for the taxpayer, a lendable value to all collateral for a loan executed by a Federal reserve bank under this paragraph in determining whether the loan is secured satisfactorily for purposes of this paragraph.

"(ii) The Board shall establish procedures to prohibit borrowing from programs and facilities by borrowers that are insolvent. Such procedures may include a certification from the chief executive officer (or other authorized officer) of the borrower, at the time the borrower initially borrows under the program or facility (with a duty by the borrower to update the certification if the information in the certification materially changes), that the borrower is not insolvent. A borrower shall be considered insolvent for purposes of this subparagraph, if the borrower is in bankruptcy, resolution under title II of the Dodd-Frank Wall Street Reform and Consumer Protection Act, or any other Federal or State insolvency proceeding.

"(iii) A program or facility that is structured to remove assets from the balance sheet of a single and specific company, or that is established for the purpose of assisting a single and specific company avoid bankruptcy, resolution under title II of the Dodd-Frank Wall Street Reform and Consumer Protection Act, or any other Federal or State insolvency proceeding, shall not be considered a program or facility with broad-based eligibility.

"(iv) The Board may not establish any program or facility under this paragraph without the prior approval of the Secretary of the Treasury.

"(C) The Board shall provide to the Committee on Banking, Housing, and Urban Affairs of the Senate and the Committee on Financial Services of the House of Representatives—

"(i) not later than 7 days after the Board authorizes any loan or other financial assistance under this paragraph, a report that includes—

"(I) the justification for the exercise of authority to provide such assistance;

"(II) the identity of the recipients of such assistance;

"(III) the date and amount of the assistance, and form in which the assistance was provided; and

"(IV) the material terms of the assistance, including—

"(aa) duration;

"(bb) collateral pledged and the value thereof;

"(cc) all interest, fees, and other revenue or items of value to be received in exchange for the assistance;

"(dd) any requirements imposed on the recipient with respect to employee compensation, distribution of dividends, or any other corporate decision in exchange for the assistance; and

"(ee) the expected costs to the taxpayers of such assistance; and

"(ii) once every 30 days, with respect to any outstanding loan or other financial assistance under this paragraph, written updates on—

"(I) the value of collateral;

"(II) the amount of interest, fees, and other revenue or items of value received in exchange for the assistance; and

"(III) the expected or final cost to the taxpayers of such assistance.

"(D) The information required to be submitted to Congress under subparagraph (C) related to—

"(i) the identity of the participants in an emergency lending program or facility commenced under this paragraph;

"(ii) the amounts borrowed by each participant in any such program or facility;

"(iii) identifying details concerning the assets or collateral held by, under, or in connection with such a program or facility, shall be kept confidential, upon the written request of the Chairman of the Board, in which case such information shall be made available only to the Chairpersons or Ranking Members of the Committees described in subparagraph (C).

"(E) If an entity to which a Federal reserve bank has provided a loan under this paragraph becomes a covered financial company, as defined in section 201 of the Dodd-Frank Wall Street Reform and Consumer Protection Act, at any time while such loan is outstanding, and the Federal reserve bank incurs a realized net loss on the loan, then the Federal reserve bank shall have a claim equal to the amount of the net realized loss against the covered entity, with the same priority as an obligation to the Secretary of the Treasury under section 210(b) of the Dodd-Frank Wall Street Reform and Consumer Protection Act.".

(b) CONFORMING AMENDMENT.—Section 507(a)(2) of title 11, United States Code, is amended by inserting "unsecured claims of any Federal reserve bank related to loans made through programs or facilities authorized under section 13(3) of the Federal Reserve Act (12 U.S.C. 343)," after "this title,".

(c) REFERENCES.—On and after the date of enactment of this Act, any reference in any provision of Federal law to the third undesignated paragraph of section 13 of the Federal Reserve Act (12 U.S.C. 343) shall be deemed to be a reference to section 13(3) of the Federal Reserve Act, as so designated by this section.

[Explanation at ¶ 5010.]

[¶ 11,102] ACT SEC. 1102. AUDITS OF SPECIAL FEDERAL RESERVE CREDIT FACILITIES.

(a) AUDITS.—Section 714 of title 31, United States Code, is amended by adding at the end the following:

"(f) AUDITS OF CREDIT FACILITIES OF THE FEDERAL RESERVE SYSTEM.—

"(1) DEFINITIONS.—In this subsection, the following definitions shall apply:

"(A) CREDIT FACILITY.—The term 'credit facility' means a program or facility, including any special purpose vehicle or other entity established by or on behalf of the Board of Governors of the Federal Reserve System or a Federal reserve bank, authorized by the Board of Governors under section 13(3) of the Federal Reserve Act (12 U.S.C. 343), that is not subject to audit under subsection (e).

"(B) COVERED TRANSACTION.—The term 'covered transaction' means any open market transaction or discount window advance that meets the definition of 'covered transaction' in section 11(s) of the Federal Reserve Act.

"(2) AUTHORITY FOR AUDITS AND EXAMINATIONS.—Subject to paragraph (3), and notwithstanding any limitation in subsection (b) on the auditing and oversight of certain functions of the Board of Governors of the Federal Reserve System or any Federal reserve bank, the Comptroller General of the United States may conduct audits, including onsite examinations, of the Board of Governors, a Federal reserve bank, or a credit facility, if the Comptroller General determines that such audits are appropriate, solely for the purposes of assessing, with respect to a credit facility or a covered transaction—

"(A) the operational integrity, accounting, financial reporting, and internal controls governing the credit facility or covered transaction;

"(B) the effectiveness of the security and collateral policies established for the facility or covered transaction in mitigating risk to the relevant Federal reserve bank and taxpayers;

"(C) whether the credit facility or the conduct of a covered transaction inappropriately favors one or more specific participants over other institutions eligible to utilize the facility; and

"(D) the policies governing the use, selection, or payment of third-party contractors by or for any credit facility or to conduct any covered transaction.

"(3) REPORTS AND DELAYED DISCLOSURE.—

"(A) REPORTS REQUIRED.—A report on each audit conducted under paragraph (2) shall be submitted by the Comptroller General to the Congress before the end of the 90-day period beginning on the date on which such audit is completed.

"(B) CONTENTS.—The report under subparagraph (A) shall include a detailed description of the findings and conclusions of the Comptroller General with respect to the matters described in paragraph (2) that were audited and are the subject of the report, together with such recommendations for legislative or administrative action relating to such matters as the Comptroller General may determine to be appropriate.

"(C) DELAYED RELEASE OF CERTAIN INFORMATION.—

"(i) IN GENERAL.—The Comptroller General shall not disclose to any person or entity, including to Congress, the names or identifying details of specific participants in any credit facility or covered transaction, the amounts borrowed by or transferred by or to specific participants in any credit facility or covered transaction, or identifying details regarding assets or collateral held or transferred by, under, or in connection with any credit facility or covered transaction, and any report provided under subparagraph (A) shall be redacted to ensure that such names and details are not disclosed.

"(ii) DELAYED RELEASE.—The nondisclosure obligation under clause (i) shall expire with respect to any participant on the date on which the Board of Governors, directly or through a Federal reserve bank, publicly discloses the identity of the subject participant or the identifying details of the subject assets, collateral, or transaction.

"(iii) GENERAL RELEASE.—The Comptroller General shall release a nonredacted version of any report on a credit facility 1 year after the effective date of the termination by the Board of Governors of the authorization for the credit facility. For purposes of this clause, a credit facility shall be deemed to have terminated 24 months after the date on which the credit facility ceases to make extensions of credit and loans, unless the credit facility is otherwise terminated by the Board of Governors.

"(iv) EXCEPTIONS.—The nondisclosure obligation under clause (i) shall not apply to the credit facilities Maiden Lane, Maiden Lane II, and Maiden Lane III.

"(v) RELEASE OF COVERED TRANSACTION INFORMATION.—The Comptroller General shall release a nonredacted version of any report regarding covered transactions upon the release of the information regarding such covered transactions by the Board of Governors of the Federal Reserve System, as provided in section 11(s) of the Federal Reserve Act.".

(b) ACCESS TO RECORDS.—Section 714(d) of title 31, United States Code, is amended—

(1) in paragraph (2), by inserting "or any person or entity described in paragraph (3)(A)" after "used by an agency";

(2) in paragraph (3), by inserting "or (f)" after "subsection (e)" each place that term appears;

(3) in clauses (i) and (ii) of paragraph (3)(A), by inserting "or the Federal Reserve banks" after "by the Board" each place that term appears;

(4) in paragraph (3)(A)(ii), by inserting "participating in or" after "any entity"; and

(5) in paragraph (3)(B), by adding at the end the following: "The Comptroller General may make and retain copies of books, accounts, and other records provided under subparagraph (A) as the Comptroller General deems appropriate. The Comptroller General shall provide to any person or entity described in subparagraph (A) a current list of officers and employees to whom, with proper identification, records and property may be made available, and who may make notes or copies necessary to carry out a audit or examination under this subsection.".

[Explanation at ¶ 5015.]

[¶ 11,103] ACT SEC. 1103. PUBLIC ACCESS TO INFORMATION.

(a) IN GENERAL.—Section 2B of the Federal Reserve Act (12 U.S.C. 225b) is amended by adding at the end the following:

"(c) PUBLIC ACCESS TO INFORMATION.—The Board shall place on its home Internet website, a link entitled 'Audit', which shall link to a webpage that shall serve as a repository of information made available to the public for a reasonable period of time, not less than 6 months following the date of release of the relevant information, including—

"(1) the reports prepared by the Comptroller General under section 714 of title 31, United States Code;

"(2) the annual financial statements prepared by an independent auditor for the Board in accordance with section 11B;

"(3) the reports to the Committee on Banking, Housing, and Urban Affairs of the Senate required under section 13(3) (relating to emergency lending authority); and

"(4) such other information as the Board reasonably believes is necessary or helpful to the public in understanding the accounting, financial reporting, and internal controls of the Board and the Federal reserve banks.".

(b) FEDERAL RESERVE TRANSPARENCY AND RELEASE OF INFORMATION.—Section 11 of the Federal Reserve Act (12 U.S.C. 248) is amended by adding at the end the following new subsection:

"(s) FEDERAL RESERVE TRANSPARENCY AND RELEASE OF INFORMATION.—

"(1) IN GENERAL.—In order to ensure the disclosure in a timely manner consistent with the purposes of this Act of information concerning the borrowers and counterparties participating in emergency credit facilities, discount window lending programs, and open market operations authorized or conducted by the Board or a Federal reserve bank, the Board of Governors shall disclose, as provided in paragraph (2)—

"(A) the names and identifying details of each borrower, participant, or counterparty in any credit facility or covered transaction;

"(B) the amount borrowed by or transferred by or to a specific borrower, participant, or counterparty in any credit facility or covered transaction;

"(C) the interest rate or discount paid by each borrower, participant, or counterparty in any credit facility or covered transaction; and

"(D) information identifying the types and amounts of collateral pledged or assets transferred in connection with participation in any credit facility or covered transaction.

"(2) MANDATORY RELEASE DATE.—In the case of—

"(A) a credit facility, the Board shall disclose the information described in paragraph (1) on the date that is 1 year after the effective date of the termination by the Board of the authorization of the credit facility; and

"(B) a covered transaction, the Board shall disclose the information described in paragraph (1) on the last day of the eighth calendar quarter following the calendar quarter in which the covered transaction was conducted.

"(3) EARLIER RELEASE DATE AUTHORIZED.—The Chairman of the Board may publicly release the information described in paragraph (1) before the relevant date specified in paragraph (2), if the Chairman determines that such disclosure would be in the public interest and would not harm the effectiveness of the relevant credit facility or the purpose or conduct of covered transactions.

"(4) DEFINITIONS.—For purposes of this subsection, the following definitions shall apply:

"(A) CREDIT FACILITY.—The term 'credit facility' has the same meaning as in section 714(f)(1)(A) of title 31, United States Code.

"(B) COVERED TRANSACTION.—The term 'covered transaction' means—

"(i) any open market transaction with a nongovernmental third party conducted under the first undesignated paragraph of section 14 or subparagraph (a), (b), or (c) of the 2nd undesignated paragraph of such section, after the date of enactment of the Dodd-Frank Wall Street Reform and Consumer Protection Act; and

"(ii) any advance made under section 10B after the date of enactment of that Act.

"(5) TERMINATION OF CREDIT FACILITY BY OPERATION OF LAW.—A credit facility shall be deemed to have terminated as of the end of the 24-month period beginning on the date on which the credit facility ceases to make extensions of credit and loans, unless the credit facility is otherwise terminated by the Board before such date.

"(6) CONSISTENT TREATMENT OF INFORMATION.—Except as provided in this subsection or section 13(3)(D), or in section 714(f)(3)(C) of title 31, United States Code, the information described in paragraph (1) and information concerning the transactions described in section 714(f) of such title, shall be confidential, including for purposes of section 552(b)(3) of title 5 of such Code, until the relevant mandatory release date described in paragraph (2), unless the Chairman of the Board determines that earlier disclosure of such information would be in the public interest and would not harm the effectiveness of the relevant credit facility or the purpose of conduct of the relevant transactions.

"(7) PROTECTION OF PERSONAL PRIVACY.—This subsection and section 13(3)(C), section 714(f)(3)(C) of title 31, United States Code, and subsection (a) or (c) of section 1109 of the Dodd-Frank Wall Street Reform and Consumer Protection Act shall not be construed as requiring any disclosure of nonpublic personal information (as defined for purposes of section 502 of the Gramm-Leach-Bliley Act (12 U.S.C. 6802)) concerning any individual who is referenced in collateral pledged or assets transferred in connection with a credit facility or covered transaction, unless the person is a borrower, participant, or counterparty under the credit facility or covered transaction.

"(8) STUDY OF FOIA EXEMPTION IMPACT.—

"(A) STUDY.—The Inspector General of the Board of Governors of the Federal Reserve System shall—

"(i) conduct a study on the impact that the exemption from section 552(b)(3) of title 5 (known as the Freedom of Information Act) established under paragraph (6) has had on the ability of the public to access information about the administration by the Board of Governors of emergency credit facilities, discount window lending programs, and open market operations; and

"(ii) make any recommendations on whether the exemption described in clause (i) should remain in effect.

"(B) REPORT.—Not later than 30 months after the date of enactment of this section, the Inspector General of the Board of Governors of the Federal Reserve System shall submit a report on the findings of the study required under subparagraph (A) to the Committee on Banking, Housing, and Urban Affairs of the Senate and the Committee on Financial Services of the House of Representatives, and publish the report on the website of the Board.

"(9) RULE OF CONSTRUCTION.—Nothing in this section is meant to affect any pending litigation or lawsuit filed under section 552 of title 5, United States Code (popularly known as the Freedom of Information Act), on or before the date of enactment of the Dodd-Frank Wall Street Reform and Consumer Protection Act.".

[Explanations at ¶ 5010, ¶ 5015, ¶ 5020, ¶ 5025 and ¶ 5030.]

[¶ 11,104] ACT SEC. 1104. LIQUIDITY EVENT DETERMINATION.

(a) DETERMINATION AND WRITTEN RECOMMENDATION.—

(1) DETERMINATION REQUEST.—The Secretary may request the Corporation and the Board of Governors to determine whether a liquidity event exists that warrants use of the guarantee program authorized under section 1105.

(2) REQUIREMENTS OF DETERMINATION.—Any determination pursuant to paragraph (1) shall—

(A) be written; and

(B) contain an evaluation of the evidence that—

(i) a liquidity event exists;

(ii) failure to take action would have serious adverse effects on financial stability or economic conditions in the United States; and

(iii) actions authorized under section 1105 are needed to avoid or mitigate potential adverse effects on the United States financial system or economic conditions.

(b) PROCEDURES.—Notwithstanding any other provision of Federal or State law, upon the determination of both the Corporation (upon a vote of not fewer than ⅔ of the members of the Corporation then serving) and the Board of Governors (upon a vote of not fewer than ⅔ of the members of the Board of Governors then serving) under subsection (a) that a liquidity event exists that warrants use of the guarantee program authorized under section 1105, and with the written consent of the Secretary—

(1) the Corporation shall take action in accordance with section 1105(a); and

(2) the Secretary (in consultation with the President) shall take action in accordance with section 1105(c).

(c) DOCUMENTATION AND REVIEW.—

(1) DOCUMENTATION.—The Secretary shall—

(A) maintain the written documentation of each determination of the Corporation and the Board of Governors under this section; and

(B) provide the documentation for review under paragraph (2).

(2) GAO REVIEW.—The Comptroller General of the United States shall review and report to Congress on any determination of the Corporation and the Board of Governors under subsection (a), including—

(A) the basis for the determination; and

(B) the likely effect of the actions taken.

(d) REPORT TO CONGRESS.—On the earlier of the date of a submission made to Congress under section 1105(c), or within 30 days of the date of a determination under subsection (a), the Secretary shall provide written notice of the determination of the Corporation and the Board of Governors to the Committee on Banking, Housing, and Urban Affairs of the Senate and the Committee on Financial Services of the House of Representatives, including a description of the basis for the determination.

[Explanation at ¶ 5035.]

[¶ 11,105] ACT SEC. 1105. EMERGENCY FINANCIAL STABILIZATION.

(a) IN GENERAL.—Upon the written determination of the Corporation and the Board of Governors under section 1104, the Corporation shall create a widely available program to guarantee obligations of solvent insured depository institutions or solvent depository institution holding companies (including any affiliates thereof) during times of severe economic distress, except that a guarantee of obligations under this section may not include the provision of equity in any form.

(b) RULEMAKING AND TERMS AND CONDITIONS.—

(1) POLICIES AND PROCEDURES.—As soon as is practicable after the date of enactment of this Act, the Corporation shall establish, by regulation, and in consultation with the Secretary, policies and procedures governing the issuance of guarantees authorized by this section. Such policies and procedures may include a requirement of collateral as a condition of any such guarantee.

(2) TERMS AND CONDITIONS.—The terms and conditions of any guarantee program shall be established by the Corporation, with the concurrence of the Secretary.

(c) DETERMINATION OF GUARANTEED AMOUNT.—

(1) IN GENERAL.—In connection with any program established pursuant to subsection (a) and subject to paragraph (2) of this subsection, the Secretary (in consultation with the President) shall

determine the maximum amount of debt outstanding that the Corporation may guarantee under this section, and the President may transmit to Congress a written report on the plan of the Corporation to exercise the authority under this section to issue guarantees up to that maximum amount and a request for approval of such plan. The Corporation shall exercise the authority under this section to issue guarantees up to that specified maximum amount upon passage of the joint resolution of approval, as provided in subsection (d). Absent such approval, the Corporation shall issue no such guarantees.

(2) ADDITIONAL DEBT GUARANTEE AUTHORITY.—If the Secretary (in consultation with the President) determines, after a submission to Congress under paragraph (1), that the maximum guarantee amount should be raised, and the Council concurs with that determination, the President may transmit to Congress a written report on the plan of the Corporation to exercise the authority under this section to issue guarantees up to the increased maximum debt guarantee amount. The Corporation shall exercise the authority under this section to issue guarantees up to that specified maximum amount upon passage of the joint resolution of approval, as provided in subsection (d). Absent such approval, the Corporation shall issue no such guarantees.

(d) RESOLUTION OF APPROVAL.—

(1) ADDITIONAL DEBT GUARANTEE AUTHORITY.—A request by the President under this section shall be considered granted by Congress upon adoption of a joint resolution approving such request. Such joint resolution shall be considered in the Senate under expedited procedures.

(2) FAST TRACK CONSIDERATION IN SENATE.—

(A) RECONVENING.—Upon receipt of a request under subsection (c), if the Senate has adjourned or recessed for more than 2 days, the majority leader of the Senate, after consultation with the minority leader of the Senate, shall notify the Members of the Senate that, pursuant to this section, the Senate shall convene not later than the second calendar day after receipt of such message.

(B) PLACEMENT ON CALENDAR.—Upon introduction in the Senate, the joint resolution shall be placed immediately on the calendar.

(C) FLOOR CONSIDERATION.—

(i) IN GENERAL.—Notwithstanding Rule XXII of the Standing Rules of the Senate, it is in order at any time during the period beginning on the 4th day after the date on which Congress receives a request under subsection (c), and ending on the 7th day after that date (even though a previous motion to the same effect has been disagreed to) to move to proceed to the consideration of the joint resolution, and all points of order against the joint resolution (and against consideration of the joint resolution) are waived. The motion to proceed is not debatable. The motion is not subject to a motion to postpone. A motion to reconsider the vote by which the motion is agreed to or disagreed to shall not be in order. If a motion to proceed to the consideration of the resolution is agreed to, the joint resolution shall remain the unfinished business until disposed of.

(ii) DEBATE.—Debate on the joint resolution, and on all debatable motions and appeals in connection therewith, shall be limited to not more than 10 hours, which shall be divided equally between the majority and minority leaders or their designees. A motion further to limit debate is in order and not debatable. An amendment to, or a motion to postpone, or a motion to proceed to the consideration of other business, or a motion to recommit the joint resolution is not in order.

(iii) VOTE ON PASSAGE.—The vote on passage shall occur immediately following the conclusion of the debate on the joint resolution, and a single quorum call at the conclusion of the debate if requested in accordance with the rules of the Senate.

(iv) RULINGS OF THE CHAIR ON PROCEDURE.—Appeals from the decisions of the Chair relating to the application of the rules of the Senate, as the case may be, to the procedure relating to a joint resolution shall be decided without debate.

(3) RULES.—

(A) COORDINATION WITH ACTION BY HOUSE OF REPRESENTATIVES.—If, before the passage by the Senate of a joint resolution of the Senate, the Senate receives a joint resolution, from the House of Representatives, then the following procedures shall apply:

(i) The joint resolution of the House of Representatives shall not be referred to a committee.

(ii) With respect to a joint resolution of the Senate—

(I) the procedure in the Senate shall be the same as if no joint resolution had been received from the other House; but

(II) the vote on passage shall be on the joint resolution of the House of Representatives.

(B) TREATMENT OF JOINT RESOLUTION OF HOUSE OF REPRESENTATIVES.—If the Senate fails to introduce or consider a joint resolution under this section, the joint resolution of the House of Representatives shall be entitled to expedited floor procedures under this subsection.

(C) TREATMENT OF COMPANION MEASURES.—If, following passage of the joint resolution in the Senate, the Senate then receives the companion measure from the House of Representatives, the companion measure shall not be debatable.

(D) RULES OF THE SENATE.—This subsection is enacted by Congress—

(i) as an exercise of the rulemaking power of the Senate, and as such it is deemed a part of the rules of the Senate, but applicable only with respect to the procedure to be followed in the Senate in the case of a joint resolution, and it supersedes other rules, only to the extent that it is inconsistent with such rules; and

(ii) with full recognition of the constitutional right of the Senate to change the rules (so far as relating to the procedure of the Senate) at any time, in the same manner, and to the same extent as in the case of any other rule of the Senate.

(4) DEFINITION.—As used in this subsection, the term "joint resolution" means only a joint resolution—

(A) that is introduced not later than 3 calendar days after the date on which the request referred to in subsection (c) is received by Congress;

(B) that does not have a preamble;

(C) the title of which is as follows: "Joint resolution relating to the approval of a plan to guarantee obligations under section 1105 of the Dodd-Frank Wall Street Reform and Consumer Protection Act"; and

(D) the matter after the resolving clause of which is as follows: "That Congress approves the obligation of any amount described in section 1105(c) of the Dodd-Frank Wall Street Reform and Consumer Protection Act.".

(e) FUNDING.—

(1) FEES AND OTHER CHARGES.—The Corporation shall charge fees and other assessments to all participants in the program established pursuant to this section, in such amounts as are necessary to offset projected losses and administrative expenses, including amounts borrowed pursuant to paragraph (3), and such amounts shall be available to the Corporation.

(2) EXCESS FUNDS.—If, at the conclusion of the program established under this section, there are any excess funds collected from the fees associated with such program, the funds shall be deposited in the General Fund of the Treasury.

(3) AUTHORITY OF CORPORATION.—The Corporation—

(A) may borrow funds from the Secretary of the Treasury and issue obligations of the Corporation to the Secretary for amounts borrowed, and the amounts borrowed shall be available to the Corporation for purposes of carrying out a program established pursuant to this section, including the payment of reasonable costs of administering the program, and the obligations issued shall be repaid in full with interest through fees and charges paid by participants in accordance with paragraphs (1) and (4), as applicable; and

(B) may not borrow funds from the Deposit Insurance Fund established pursuant to section 11(a)(4) of the Federal Deposit Insurance Act.

(4) BACKUP SPECIAL ASSESSMENTS.—To the extent that the funds collected pursuant to paragraph (1) are insufficient to cover any losses or expenses, including amounts borrowed pursuant to paragraph (3), arising from a program established pursuant to this section, the Corporation shall impose a special assessment solely on participants in the program, in amounts necessary to address such insufficiency, and which shall be available to the Corporation to cover such losses or expenses.

(5) AUTHORITY OF THE SECRETARY.—The Secretary may purchase any obligations issued under paragraph (3)(A). For such purpose, the Secretary may use the proceeds of the sale of any securities issued under chapter 31 of title 31, United States Code, and the purposes for which securities may be issued under that chapter 31 are extended to include such purchases, and the amount of any securities issued under that chapter 31 for such purpose shall be treated in the same manner as securities issued under section 208(n)(5)(E).

(f) RULE OF CONSTRUCTION.—For purposes of this section, a guarantee of deposits held by insured depository institutions shall not be treated as a debt guarantee program.

(g) DEFINITIONS.—For purposes of this section, the following definitions shall apply:

(1) COMPANY.—The term "company" means any entity other than a natural person that is incorporated or organized under Federal law or the laws of any State.

(2) DEPOSITORY INSTITUTION HOLDING COMPANY.—The term "depository institution holding company" has the same meaning as in section 3 of the Federal Deposit Insurance Act (12 U.S.C. 1813).

(3) LIQUIDITY EVENT.—The term "liquidity event" means—

(A) an exceptional and broad reduction in the general ability of financial market participants—

(i) to sell financial assets without an unusual and significant discount; or

(ii) to borrow using financial assets as collateral without an unusual and significant increase in margin; or

(B) an unusual and significant reduction in the ability of financial market participants to obtain unsecured credit.

(4) SOLVENT.—The term "solvent" means that the value of the assets of an entity exceed its obligations to creditors.

[Explanation at ¶ 5035.]

[¶ 11,106] ACT SEC. 1106. ADDITIONAL RELATED AMENDMENTS.

(a) SUSPENSION OF PARALLEL FEDERAL DEPOSIT INSURANCE ACT AUTHORITY.—Effective upon the date of enactment of this section, the Corporation may not exercise its authority under section 13(c)(4)(G)(i) of the Federal Deposit Insurance Act (12 U.S.C. 1823(c)(4)(G)(i)) to establish any widely available debt guarantee program for which section 1105 would provide authority.

(b) FEDERAL DEPOSIT INSURANCE ACT.—Section 13(c)(4)(G) of the Federal Deposit Insurance Act (12 U.S.C. 1823(c)(4)(G)) is amended—

(1) in clause (i)—

(A) in subclause (I), by inserting "for which the Corporation has been appointed receiver" before "would have serious"; and

(B) in the undesignated matter following subclause (II), by inserting "for the purpose of winding up the insured depository institution for which the Corporation has been appointed receiver" after "provide assistance under this section"; and

(2) in clause (v)(I), by striking "The" and inserting "Not later than 3 days after making a determination under clause (i), the".

(c) EFFECT OF DEFAULT ON AN FDIC GUARANTEE.—If an insured depository institution or depository institution holding company (as those terms are defined in section 3 of the Federal Deposit Insurance Act) participating in a program under section 1105, or any participant in a debt guarantee program established pursuant to section 13(c)(4)(G)(i) of the Federal Deposit Insurance Act defaults on any obligation guaranteed by the Corporation after the date of enactment of this Act, the Corporation shall—

(1) appoint itself as receiver for the insured depository institution that defaults; and

(2) with respect to any other participating company that is not an insured depository institution that defaults—

(A) require—

(i) consideration of whether a determination shall be made, as provided in section 203 to resolve the company under section 202; and

(ii) the company to file a petition for bankruptcy under section 301 of title 11, United States Code, if the Corporation is not appointed receiver pursuant to section 202 within 30 days of the date of default; or

(B) file a petition for involuntary bankruptcy on behalf of the company under section 303 of title 11, United States Code.

[Explanation at ¶ 5035.]

[¶ 11,107] ACT SEC. 1107. FEDERAL RESERVE ACT AMENDMENTS ON FEDERAL RESERVE BANK GOVERNANCE.

The 5th subparagraph of the 4th undesignated paragraph of section 4 of the Federal Reserve Act (12 U.S.C. 341) is amended by striking the 2nd sentence and inserting the following: "The president shall be the chief executive officer of the bank and shall be appointed by the Class B and Class C directors of the bank, with the approval of the Board of Governors of the Federal Reserve System, for a term of 5 years; and all other executive officers and all employees of the bank shall be directly responsible to the president.".

[Explanation at ¶ 5040.]

[¶ 11,108] ACT SEC. 1108. FEDERAL RESERVE ACT AMENDMENTS ON SUPERVISION AND REGULATION POLICY.

(a) ESTABLISHMENT OF THE POSITION OF VICE CHAIRMAN FOR SUPERVISION.—

(1) POSITION ESTABLISHED.—The second undesignated paragraph of section 10 of the Federal Reserve Act (12 U.S.C. 242) (relating to the Chairman and Vice Chairman of the Board) is amended by striking the third sentence and inserting the following: "Of the persons thus appointed, 1 shall be designated by the President, by and with the advice and consent of the Senate, to serve as Chairman of the Board for a term of 4 years, and 2 shall be designated by the President, by and with the advice and consent of the Senate, to serve as Vice Chairmen of the Board, each for a term of 4 years, 1 of whom shall serve in the absence of the Chairman, as provided in the fourth undesignated paragraph of this section, and 1 of whom shall be designated Vice Chairman for Supervision. The Vice Chairman for Supervision shall develop policy recommendations for the Board regarding supervision and regulation of depository institution holding companies and other financial firms supervised by the Board, and shall oversee the supervision and regulation of such firms.".

(2) EFFECTIVE DATE.—The amendment made by subsection (a) takes effect on the date of enactment of this title and applies to individuals who are designated by the President on or after that date to serve as Vice Chairman of Supervision.

(b) APPEARANCES BEFORE CONGRESS.—Section 10 of the Federal Reserve Act (12 U.S.C. 241 et seq.) is amended by adding at the end the following:

"(12) APPEARANCES BEFORE CONGRESS.—The Vice Chairman for Supervision shall appear before the Committee on Banking, Housing, and Urban Affairs of the Senate and the Committee on Financial Services of the House of Representatives and at semi-annual hearings regarding the efforts, activities, objectives, and plans of the Board with respect to the conduct of supervision and regulation of depository institution holding companies and other financial firms supervised by the Board.".

(c) BOARD RESPONSIBILITY TO SET SUPERVISION AND REGULATORY POLICY.—Section 11 of the Federal Reserve Act (12 U.S.C. 248) (relating to enumerated powers of the Board) is amended by adding at the end of subsection (k) (relating to delegation) the following: "The Board of Governors may not delegate to a Federal reserve bank its functions for the establishment of policies for the supervision and regulation of depository institution holding companies and other financial firms supervised by the Board of Governors.".

(d) EXERCISE OF FEDERAL RESERVE AUTHORITY.—

(1) NO DECISIONS BY FEDERAL RESERVE BANK PRESIDENTS.—No provision of title I relating to the authority of the Board of Governors shall be construed as conferring any decision-making authority on presidents of Federal reserve banks.

(2) VOTING DECISIONS BY BOARD.—The Board of Governors shall not delegate the authority to make any voting decision that the Board of Governors is authorized or required to make under title I of this Act in contravention of section 11(k) of the Federal Reserve Act.

[Explanation at ¶ 5040.]

[¶ 11,109] ACT SEC. 1109. GAO AUDIT OF THE FEDERAL RESERVE FACILITIES; PUBLICATION OF BOARD ACTIONS.

(a) GAO AUDIT.—

(1) IN GENERAL.—Notwithstanding section 714(b) of title 31, United States Code, or any other provision of law, the Comptroller General of the United States (in this subsection referred to as the "Comptroller General") shall conduct a one-time audit of all loans and other financial assistance provided during the period beginning on December 1, 2007 and ending on the date of enactment of this Act by the Board of Governors or a Federal reserve bank under the Asset-Backed Commercial Paper Money Market Mutual Fund Liquidity Facility, the Term Asset-Backed Securities Loan Facility, the Primary Dealer Credit Facility, the Commercial Paper Funding Facility, the Term Securities Lending Facility, the Term Auction Facility, Maiden Lane, Maiden Lane II, Maiden Lane III, the agency Mortgage-Backed Securities program, foreign currency liquidity swap lines, and any other program created as a result of section 13(3) of the Federal Reserve Act (as so designated by this title).

(2) ASSESSMENTS.—In conducting the audit under paragraph (1), the Comptroller General shall assess—

(A) the operational integrity, accounting, financial reporting, and internal controls of the credit facility;

(B) the effectiveness of the security and collateral policies established for the facility in mitigating risk to the relevant Federal reserve bank and taxpayers;

(C) whether the credit facility inappropriately favors one or more specific participants over other institutions eligible to utilize the facility;

(D) the policies governing the use, selection, or payment of third-party contractors by or for any credit facility; and

(E) whether there were conflicts of interest with respect to the manner in which such facility was established or operated.

(3) TIMING.—The audit required by this subsection shall be commenced not later than 30 days after the date of enactment of this Act, and shall be completed not later than 12 months after that date of enactment.

(4) REPORT REQUIRED.—The Comptroller General shall submit a report on the audit conducted under paragraph (1) to the Congress not later than 12 months after the date of enactment of this Act, and such report shall be made available to—

(A) the Speaker of the House of Representatives;

(B) the majority and minority leaders of the House of Representatives;

(C) the majority and minority leaders of the Senate;

(D) the Chairman and Ranking Member of the Committee on Banking, Housing, and Urban Affairs of the Senate and of the Committee on Financial Services of the House of Representatives; and

(E) any member of Congress who requests it.

(b) AUDIT OF FEDERAL RESERVE BANK GOVERNANCE.—

(1) AUDIT.—

(A) IN GENERAL.—Not later than 1 year after the date of enactment of this Act, the Comptroller General shall complete an audit of the governance of the Federal reserve bank system.

(B) REQUIRED EXAMINATIONS.—The audit required under subparagraph (A) shall—

(i) examine the extent to which the current system of appointing Federal reserve bank directors effectively represents "the public, without discrimination on the basis of race, creed, color, sex or national origin, and with due but not exclusive consideration to the interests of agriculture, commerce, industry, services, labor, and consumers" in the selection of bank directors, as such requirement is set forth under section 4 of the Federal Reserve Act;

(ii) examine whether there are actual or potential conflicts of interest created when the directors of Federal reserve banks, which execute the supervisory functions of the Board of Governors of the Federal Reserve System, are elected by member banks;

(iii) examine the establishment and operations of each facility described in subsection (a)(1) and each Federal reserve bank involved in the establishment and operations thereof; and

(iv) identify changes to selection procedures for Federal reserve bank directors, or to other aspects of Federal reserve bank governance, that would—

(I) improve how the public is represented;

(II) eliminate actual or potential conflicts of interest in bank supervision;

(III) increase the availability of information useful for the formation and execution of monetary policy; or

(IV) in other ways increase the effectiveness or efficiency of reserve banks.

(2) REPORT REQUIRED.—A report on the audit conducted under paragraph (1) shall be submitted by the Comptroller General to the Congress before the end of the 90-day period beginning on the date on which such audit is completed, and such report shall be made available to—

(A) the Speaker of the House of Representatives;

(B) the majority and minority leaders of the House of Representatives;

(C) the majority and minority leaders of the Senate;

(D) the Chairman and Ranking Member of the Committee on Banking, Housing, and Urban Affairs of the Senate and of the Committee on Financial Services of the House of Representatives; and

(E) any member of Congress who requests it.

(c) PUBLICATION OF BOARD ACTIONS.—Notwithstanding any other provision of law, the Board of Governors shall publish on its website, not later than December 1, 2010, with respect to all loans and other financial assistance provided during the period beginning on December 1, 2007 and ending on the date of enactment of this Act under the Asset-Backed Commercial Paper Money Market Mutual Fund Liquidity Facility, the Term Asset-Backed Securities Loan Facility, the Primary Dealer Credit Facility, the Commercial Paper Funding Facility, the Term Securities Lending Facility, the Term Auction Facility, Maiden Lane, Maiden Lane II, Maiden Lane III, the agency Mortgage-Backed Securities program, foreign currency liquidity swap lines, and any other program created as a result of section 13(3) of the Federal Reserve Act (as so designated by this title)—

(1) the identity of each business, individual, entity, or foreign central bank to which the Board of Governors or a Federal reserve bank has provided such assistance;

(2) the type of financial assistance provided to that business, individual, entity, or foreign central bank;

(3) the value or amount of that financial assistance;

(4) the date on which the financial assistance was provided;

(5) the specific terms of any repayment expected, including the repayment time period, interest charges, collateral, limitations on executive compensation or dividends, and other material terms; and

(6) the specific rationale for each such facility or program.

[Explanation at ¶ 5020.]

TITLE XII—IMPROVING ACCESS TO MAINSTREAM FINANCIAL INSTITUTIONS

[¶ 11,201] ACT SEC. 1201. SHORT TITLE.

This title may be cited as the "Improving Access to Mainstream Financial Institutions Act of 2010".

[Explanation at ¶ 5505.]

[¶ 11,202] ACT SEC. 1202. PURPOSE.

The purpose of this title is to encourage initiatives for financial products and services that are appropriate and accessible for millions of Americans who are not fully incorporated into the financial mainstream.

[Explanation at ¶ 5505.]

[¶ 11,203] ACT SEC. 1203. DEFINITIONS.

In this title, the following definitions shall apply:

(1) ACCOUNT.—The term "account" means an agreement between an individual and an eligible entity under which the individual obtains from or through the entity 1 or more banking products and services, and includes a deposit account, a savings account (including a money market savings account), an account for a closed-end loan, and other products or services, as the Secretary deems appropriate.

(2) COMMUNITY DEVELOPMENT FINANCIAL INSTITUTION.—The term "community development financial institution" has the same meaning as in section 103(5) of the Community Development Banking and Financial Institutions Act of 1994 (12 U.S.C. 4702(5)).

(3) ELIGIBLE ENTITY.—The term "eligible entity" means—

(A) an organization described in section 501(c)(3) of the Internal Revenue Code of 1986, and exempt from tax under section 501(a) of such Code;

(B) a federally insured depository institution;

(C) a community development financial institution;

(D) a State, local, or tribal government entity; or

(E) a partnership or other joint venture comprised of 1 or more of the entities described in subparagraphs (A) through (D), in accordance with regulations prescribed by the Secretary under this title.

(4) FEDERALLY INSURED DEPOSITORY INSTITUTION.—The term "federally insured depository institution" means any insured depository institution (as that term is defined in section 3 of the Federal Deposit Insurance Act (12 U.S.C. 1813)) and any insured credit union (as that term is defined in section 101 of the Federal Credit Union Act (12 U.S.C. 1752)).

¶ 11,201   Act Sec. 1109(c)(2)

[Explanation at ¶ 5510 and ¶ 5520.]

[¶ 11,204] ACT SEC. 1204. EXPANDED ACCESS TO MAINSTREAM FINANCIAL INSTITUTIONS.

(a) IN GENERAL.—The Secretary is authorized to establish a multiyear program of grants, cooperative agreements, financial agency agreements, and similar contracts or undertakings to promote initiatives designed—

(1) to enable low- and moderate-income individuals to establish one or more accounts in a federally insured depository institution that are appropriate to meet the financial needs of such individuals; and

(2) to improve access to the provision of accounts, on reasonable terms, for low- and moderate-income individuals.

(b) PROGRAM ELIGIBILITY AND ACTIVITIES.—

(1) IN GENERAL.—The Secretary shall restrict participation in any program established under subsection (a) to an eligible entity. Subject to regulations prescribed by the Secretary under this title, 1 or more eligible entities may participate in 1 or several programs established under subsection (a).

(2) ACCOUNT ACTIVITIES.—Subject to regulations prescribed by the Secretary, an eligible entity may, in participating in a program established under subsection (a), offer or provide to low- and moderate-income individuals products and services relating to accounts, including—

(A) small-dollar value loans; and

(B) financial education and counseling relating to conducting transactions in and managing accounts.

[Explanation at ¶ 5510.]

[¶ 11,205] ACT SEC. 1205. LOW-COST ALTERNATIVES TO SMALL DOLLAR LOANS.

(a) GRANTS AUTHORIZED.—The Secretary is authorized to establish multiyear demonstration programs by means of grants, cooperative agreements, financial agency agreements, and similar contracts or undertakings, with eligible entities to provide low-cost, small loans to consumers that will provide alternatives to more costly small dollar loans.

(b) TERMS AND CONDITIONS.—

(1) IN GENERAL.—Loans under this section shall be made on terms and conditions, and pursuant to lending practices, that are reasonable for consumers.

(2) FINANCIAL LITERACY AND EDUCATION OPPORTUNITIES.—

(A) IN GENERAL.—Each eligible entity awarded a grant under this section shall promote and take appropriate steps to ensure the provision of financial literacy and education opportunities, such as relevant counseling services, educational courses, or wealth building programs, to each consumer provided with a loan pursuant to this section.

(B) AUTHORITY TO EXPAND ACCESS.—As part of the grants, agreements, and undertakings established under this section, the Secretary may implement reasonable measures or programs designed to expand access to financial literacy and education opportunities, including relevant counseling services, educational courses, or wealth building programs to be provided to individuals who obtain loans from eligible entities under this section.

[Explanation at ¶ 5515.]

[¶ 11,206] ACT SEC. 1206. GRANTS TO ESTABLISH LOAN-LOSS RESERVE FUNDS.

The Community Development Banking and Financial Institutions Act of 1994 (12 U.S.C. 4701 et seq.) is amended by adding at the end the following:

"SEC. 122. GRANTS TO ESTABLISH LOAN-LOSS RESERVE FUNDS.

"(a) PURPOSES.—The purposes of this section are—

"(1) to make financial assistance available from the Fund in order to help community development financial institutions defray the costs of operating small dollar loan programs, by providing the amounts necessary for such institutions to establish their own loan loss reserve funds to mitigate some of the losses on such small dollar loan programs; and

"(2) to encourage community development financial institutions to establish and maintain small dollar loan programs that would help give consumers access to mainstream financial institutions and combat high cost small dollar lending.

"(b) GRANTS.—

"(1) LOAN-LOSS RESERVE FUND GRANTS.—The Fund shall make grants to community development financial institutions or to any partnership between such community development financial institutions and any other federally insured depository institution with a primary mission to serve targeted investment areas, as such areas are defined under section 103(16), to enable such institutions or any partnership of such institutions to establish a loan-loss reserve fund in order to defray the costs of a small dollar loan program established or maintained by such institution.

"(2) MATCHING REQUIREMENT.—A community development financial institution or any partnership of institutions established pursuant to paragraph (1) shall provide non-Federal matching funds in an amount equal to 50 percent of the amount of any grant received under this section.

"(3) USE OF FUNDS.—Any grant amounts received by a community development financial institution or any partnership between or among such institutions under paragraph (1)—

"(A) may not be used by such institution to provide direct loans to consumers;

"(B) may be used by such institution to help recapture a portion or all of a defaulted loan made under the small dollar loan program of such institution; and

"(C) may be used to designate and utilize a fiscal agent for services normally provided by such an agent.

"(4) TECHNICAL ASSISTANCE GRANTS.—The Fund shall make technical assistance grants to community development financial institutions or any partnership between or among such institutions to support and maintain a small dollar loan program. Any grant amounts received under this paragraph may be used for technology, staff support, and other costs associated with establishing a small dollar loan program.

"(c) DEFINITIONS.—For purposes of this section—

"(1) the term 'consumer reporting agency that compiles and maintains files on consumers on a nationwide basis' has the same meaning given such term in section 603(p) of the Fair Credit Reporting Act (15 U.S.C. 1681a(p)); and

"(2) the term 'small dollar loan program' means a loan program wherein a community development financial institution or any partnership between or among such institutions offers loans to consumers that—

"(A) are made in amounts not exceeding $2,500;

"(B) must be repaid in installments;

"(C) have no pre-payment penalty;

"(D) the institution has to report payments regarding the loan to at least 1 of the consumer reporting agencies that compiles and maintains files on consumers on a nationwide basis; and

"(E) meet any other affordability requirements as may be established by the Administrator.".

[Explanation at ¶ 5520.]

[¶ 11,207] ACT SEC. 1207. PROCEDURAL PROVISIONS.

An eligible entity desiring to participate in a program or obtain a grant under this title shall submit an application to the Secretary, in such form and containing such information as the Secretary may require.

[Explanation at ¶ 5510.]

[¶ 11,208] ACT SEC. 1208. AUTHORIZATION OF APPROPRIATIONS.

(a) AUTHORIZATION TO THE SECRETARY.—There are authorized to be appropriated to the Secretary, such sums as are necessary to both administer and fund the programs and projects authorized by this title, to remain available until expended.

(b) AUTHORIZATION TO THE FUND.—There is authorized to be appropriated to the Fund for each fiscal year beginning in fiscal year 2010, an amount equal to the amount of the administrative costs of the Fund for the operation of the grant program established under this title.

[Explanation at ¶ 5525.]

[¶ 11,209] ACT SEC. 1209. REGULATIONS.

(a) IN GENERAL.—The Secretary is authorized to promulgate regulations to implement and administer the grant programs and undertakings authorized by this title.

(b) REGULATORY AUTHORITY.—Regulations prescribed under this section may contain such classifications, differentiations, or other provisions, and may provide for such adjustments and exceptions for any class of grant programs, undertakings, or eligible entities, as, in the judgment of the Secretary, are necessary or proper to effectuate the purposes of this title, to prevent circumvention or evasion of this title, or to facilitate compliance with this title.

[Explanation at ¶ 5525.]

[¶ 11,210] ACT SEC. 1210. EVALUATION AND REPORTS TO CONGRESS.

For each fiscal year in which a program or project is carried out under this title, the Secretary shall submit a report to the Committee on Banking, Housing, and Urban Affairs of the Senate and the Committee on Financial Services of the House of Representatives containing a description of the activities funded, amounts distributed, and measurable results, as appropriate and available.

[Explanation at ¶ 5525.]

TITLE XIII—PAY IT BACK ACT

[¶ 11,301] ACT SEC. 1301. SHORT TITLE.

This title may be cited as the "Pay It Back Act".

[Explanation at ¶ 6005.]

[¶ 11,302] ACT SEC. 1302. AMENDMENT TO REDUCE TARP AUTHORIZATION.

Section 115(a) of the Emergency Economic Stabilization Act of 2008 (12 U.S.C. 5225(a)) is amended—

(1) in paragraph (3)—

(A) by striking ", $700,000,000,000, as such amount is reduced by $1,259,000,000, as such amount is reduced by $1,244,000,000" and inserting "$475,000,000,000"; and

(B) by striking "outstanding at any one time"; and

(2) by adding at the end the following:

"(4) For purposes of this subsection, the amount of authority considered to be exercised by the Secretary shall not be reduced by—

"(A) any amounts received by the Secretary before, on, or after the date of enactment of the Pay It Back Act from repayment of the principal of financial assistance by an entity that has received financial assistance under the TARP or any other program enacted by the Secretary under the authorities granted to the Secretary under this Act;

"(B) any amounts committed for any guarantees pursuant to the TARP that became or become uncommitted; or

"(C) any losses realized by the Secretary.

"(5) No authority under this Act may be used to incur any obligation for a program or initiative that was not initiated prior to June 25, 2010.".

[Explanation at ¶ 6010.]

[¶ 11,303] ACT SEC. 1303. REPORT.

Section 106 of the Emergency Economic Stabilization Act of 2008 (12 U.S.C. 5216) is amended by inserting at the end the following:

"(f) REPORT.—The Secretary of the Treasury shall report to Congress every 6 months on amounts received and transferred to the general fund under subsection (d).".

[Explanation at ¶ 6015.]

[¶ 11,304] ACT SEC. 1304. AMENDMENTS TO HOUSING AND ECONOMIC RECOVERY ACT OF 2008.

(a) SALE OF FANNIE MAE OBLIGATIONS AND SECURITIES BY THE TREASURY; DEFICIT REDUCTION.—Section 304(g)(2) of the Federal National Mortgage Association Charter Act (12 U.S.C. 1719(g)(2)) is amended—

(1) by redesignating subparagraph (C) as subparagraph (D); and

(2) by inserting after subparagraph (B) the following:

"(C) DEFICIT REDUCTION.—The Secretary of the Treasury shall deposit in the General Fund of the Treasury any amounts received by the Secretary from the sale of any obligation acquired by the Secretary under this subsection, where such amounts shall be—

"(i) dedicated for the sole purpose of deficit reduction; and

"(ii) prohibited from use as an offset for other spending increases or revenue reductions.".

(b) SALE OF FREDDIE MAC OBLIGATIONS AND SECURITIES BY THE TREASURY; DEFICIT REDUCTION.—Section 306(1)(2) of the Federal Home Loan Mortgage Corporation Act (12 U.S.C. 1455(1)(2)) is amended—

(1) by redesignating subparagraph (C) as subparagraph (D); and

(2) by inserting after subparagraph (B) the following:

"(C) DEFICIT REDUCTION.—The Secretary of the Treasury shall deposit in the General Fund of the Treasury any amounts received by the Secretary from the sale of any obligation acquired by the Secretary under this subsection, where such amounts shall be—

"(i) dedicated for the sole purpose of deficit reduction; and

"(ii) prohibited from use as an offset for other spending increases or revenue reductions.".

(c) SALE OF FEDERAL HOME LOAN BANKS OBLIGATIONS BY THE TREASURY; DEFICIT REDUCTION.—Section 11(l)(2) of the Federal Home Loan Bank Act (12 U.S.C. 1431(1)(2)) is amended—

(1) by redesignating subparagraph (C) as subparagraph (D); and

(2) by inserting after subparagraph (B) the following:

"(C) DEFICIT REDUCTION.—The Secretary of the Treasury shall deposit in the General Fund of the Treasury any amounts received by the Secretary from the sale of any obligation acquired by the Secretary under this subsection, where such amounts shall be—

"(i) dedicated for the sole purpose of deficit reduction; and "(ii) prohibited from use as an offset for other spending increases or revenue reductions.".

(d) REPAYMENT OF FEES.—Any periodic commitment fee or any other fee or assessment paid by the Federal National Mortgage Association or Federal Home Loan Mortgage Corporation to the Secretary of the Treasury as a result of any preferred stock purchase agreement, mortgage-backed security purchase program, or any other program or activity authorized or carried out pursuant to the authorities granted to the Secretary of the Treasury under section 1117 of the Housing and Economic Recovery Act of 2008 (Public Law 110-289; 122 Stat. 2683), including any fee agreed to by contract between the Secretary and the Association or Corporation, shall be deposited in the General Fund of the Treasury where such amounts shall be—

(1) dedicated for the sole purpose of deficit reduction; and

(2) prohibited from use as an offset for other spending increases or revenue reductions.

[Explanation at ¶ 6015.]

[¶ 11,305] ACT SEC. 1305. FEDERAL HOUSING FINANCE AGENCY REPORT.

The Director of the Federal Housing Finance Agency shall submit to Congress a report on the plans of the Agency to continue to support and maintain the Nation's vital housing industry, while at the same time guaranteeing that the American taxpayer will not suffer unnecessary losses.

[Explanation at ¶ 6020.]

[¶ 11,306] ACT SEC. 1306. REPAYMENT OF UNOBLIGATED ARRA FUNDS.

(a) REJECTION OF ARRA FUNDS BY STATE.—Section 1607 of the American Recovery and Reinvestment Act of 2009 (Public Law 111-5; 123 Stat. 305) is amended by adding at the end the following:

"(d) STATEWIDE REJECTION OF FUNDS.—If funds provided to any State in any division of this Act are not accepted for use by the Governor of the State pursuant to subsection (a) or by the State legislature pursuant to subsection (b), then all such funds shall be—

"(1) rescinded; and

"(2) deposited in the General Fund of the Treasury where such amounts shall be—

"(A) dedicated for the sole purpose of deficit reduction; and

"(B) prohibited from use as an offset for other spending increases or revenue reductions.".

(b) WITHDRAWAL OR RECAPTURE OF UNOBLIGATED FUNDS.—Title XVI of the American Recovery and Reinvestment Act of 2009 (Public Law 111-5; 123 Stat. 302) is amended by adding at the end the following:

"SEC. 1613. WITHDRAWAL OR RECAPTURE OF UNOBLIGATED FUNDS.

"Notwithstanding any other provision of this Act, if the head of any executive agency withdraws or recaptures for any reason funds appropriated or otherwise made available under this division, and such funds have not been obligated by a State to a local government or for a specific project, such recaptured funds shall be—

"(1) rescinded; and

"(2) deposited in the General Fund of the Treasury where such amounts shall be—

"(A) dedicated for the sole purpose of deficit reduction; and

"(B) prohibited from use as an offset for other spending increases or revenue reductions.".

(c) RETURN OF UNOBLIGATED FUNDS BY END OF 2012.—Section 1603 of the American Recovery and Reinvestment Act of 2009 (Public Law 111-5; 123 Stat. 302) is amended by—

(1) striking "All funds" and inserting "(a) IN GENERAL.—All funds"; and

(2) adding at the end the following:

"(b) REPAYMENT OF UNOBLIGATED FUNDS.—Any discretionary appropriations made available in this division that have not been obligated as of December 31, 2012, are hereby rescinded, and such amounts shall be deposited in the General Fund of the Treasury where such amounts shall be—

"(1) dedicated for the sole purpose of deficit reduction; and

"(2) prohibited from use as an offset for other spending increases or revenue reductions.

"(c) PRESIDENTIAL WAIVER AUTHORITY.—

"(1) IN GENERAL.—The President may waive the requirements under subsection (b), if the President determines that it is not in the best interest of the Nation to rescind a specific unobligated amount after December 31, 2012.

"(2) REQUESTS.—The head of an executive agency may also apply to the President for a waiver from the requirements under subsection (b).".

[Explanation at ¶ 6025.]

TITLE XIV—MORTGAGE REFORM AND ANTI-PREDATORY LENDING ACT

[¶ 11,400] ACT SEC. 1400. SHORT TITLE; DESIGNATION AS ENUMERATED CONSUMER LAW.

(a) SHORT TITLE.—This title may be cited as the "Mortgage Reform and Anti-Predatory Lending Act".

(b) DESIGNATION AS ENUMERATED CONSUMER LAW UNDER THE PURVIEW OF THE BUREAU OF CONSUMER FINANCIAL PROTECTION.—Subtitles A, B, C, and E and sections 1471, 1472, 1475, and 1476, and the amendments made by such subtitles and sections, shall be enumerated consumer laws, as defined in section 1002, and come under the purview of the Bureau of Consumer Financial Protection for purposes of title X, including the transfer of functions and personnel under subtitle F of title X and the savings provisions of such subtitle.

(c) REGULATIONS; EFFECTIVE DATE.—

(1) REGULATIONS.—The regulations required to be prescribed under this title or the amendments made by this title shall—

(A) be prescribed in final form before the end of the 18-month period beginning on the designated transfer date; and

(B) take effect not later than 12 months after the date of issuance of the regulations in final form.

(2) EFFECTIVE DATE ESTABLISHED BY RULE.—Except as provided in paragraph (3), a section, or provision thereof, of this title shall take effect on the date on which the final regulations implementing such section, or provision, take effect.

(3) EFFECTIVE DATE.—A section of this title for which regulations have not been issued on the date that is 18 months after the designated transfer date shall take effect on such date.

[Explanation at ¶ 6505.]

Subtitle A—Residential Mortgage Loan Origination Standards

[¶ 11,401] ACT SEC. 1401. DEFINITIONS.

Section 103 of the Truth in Lending Act (15 U.S.C. 1602) is amended by adding at the end the following new subsection:

"(cc) DEFINITIONS RELATING TO MORTGAGE ORIGINATION AND RESIDENTIAL MORTGAGE LOANS.—

"(1) COMMISSION.—Unless otherwise specified, the term 'Commission' means the Federal Trade Commission.

"(2) MORTGAGE ORIGINATOR.—The term 'mortgage originator'—

"(A) means any person who, for direct or indirect compensation or gain, or in the expectation of direct or indirect compensation or gain—

"(i) takes a residential mortgage loan application;

"(ii) assists a consumer in obtaining or applying to obtain a residential mortgage loan; or

"(iii) offers or negotiates terms of a residential mortgage loan;

"(B) includes any person who represents to the public, through advertising or other means of communicating or providing information (including the use of business cards, stationery, brochures, signs, rate lists, or other promotional items), that such person can or will provide any of the services or perform any of the activities described in subparagraph (A);

"(C) does not include any person who is (i) not otherwise described in subparagraph (A) or (B) and who performs purely administrative or clerical tasks on behalf of a person who is described in any such subparagraph, or (ii) an employee of a retailer of manufactured homes who is not described in clause (i) or (iii) of subparagraph (A) and who does not advise a consumer on loan terms (including rates, fees, and other costs);

"(D) does not include a person or entity that only performs real estate brokerage activities and is licensed or registered in accordance with applicable State law, unless such person or entity is compensated by a lender, a mortgage broker, or other mortgage originator or by any agent of such lender, mortgage broker, or other mortgage originator;

"(E) does not include, with respect to a residential mortgage loan, a person, estate, or trust that provides mortgage financing for the sale of 3 properties in any 12-month period to purchasers of such properties, each of which is owned by such person, estate, or trust and serves as security for the loan, provided that such loan—

"(i) is not made by a person, estate, or trust that has constructed, or acted as a contractor for the construction of, a residence on the property in the ordinary course of business of such person, estate, or trust;

"(ii) is fully amortizing;

"(iii) is with respect to a sale for which the seller determines in good faith and documents that the buyer has a reasonable ability to repay the loan;

"(iv) has a fixed rate or an adjustable rate that is adjustable after 5 or more years, subject to reasonable annual and lifetime limitations on interest rate increases; and

"(v) meets any other criteria the Board may prescribe;

"(F) does not include the creditor (except the creditor in a table-funded transaction) under paragraph (1), (2), or (4) of section 129B(c); and

"(G) does not include a servicer or servicer employees, agents and contractors, including but not limited to those who offer or negotiate terms of a residential mortgage loan for purposes of renegotiating, modifying, replacing and subordinating principal of existing mortgages where borrowers are behind in their payments, in default or have a reasonable likelihood of being in default or falling behind.

"(3) NATIONWIDE MORTGAGE LICENSING SYSTEM AND REGISTRY.—The term 'Nationwide Mortgage Licensing System and Registry' has the same meaning as in the Secure and Fair Enforcement for Mortgage Licensing Act of 2008.

"(4) OTHER DEFINITIONS RELATING TO MORTGAGE ORIGINATOR.—For purposes of this subsection, a person 'assists a consumer in obtaining or applying to obtain a residential mortgage loan' by, among other things, advising on residential mortgage loan terms (including rates, fees, and other costs), preparing residential mortgage loan packages, or collecting information on behalf of the consumer with regard to a residential mortgage loan.

"(5) RESIDENTIAL MORTGAGE LOAN.—The term 'residential mortgage loan' means any consumer credit transaction that is secured by a mortgage, deed of trust, or other equivalent consensual security interest on a dwelling or on residential real property that includes a dwelling, other than a consumer credit transaction under an open end credit plan or, for purposes of sections 129B and 129C and section 128(a) (16), (17), (18), and (19), and sections 128(f) and 130(k), and any regulations promulgated thereunder, an extension of credit relating to a plan described in section 101(53D) of title 11, United States Code.

"(6) SECRETARY.—The term 'Secretary', when used in connection with any transaction or person involved with a residential mortgage loan, means the Secretary of Housing and Urban Development.

"(7) SERVICER.—The term 'servicer' has the same meaning as in section 6(i)(2) of the Real Estate Settlement Procedures Act of 1974 (12 U.S.C. 2605(i)(2)).".

[Explanation at ¶ 6515.]

[¶ 11,402] ACT SEC. 1402. RESIDENTIAL MORTGAGE LOAN ORIGINATION.

(a) IN GENERAL.—Chapter 2 of the Truth in Lending Act (15 U.S.C. 1631 et seq.) is amended—

(1) by redesignating the 2nd of the 2 sections designated as section 129 (15 U.S.C. 1639a) (relating to duty of servicers of residential mortgages) as section 129A; and

(2) by inserting after section 129A (as so redesignated) the following new section:

"§ 129B. Residential mortgage loan origination

"(a) FINDING AND PURPOSE.—

"(1) FINDING.—The Congress finds that economic stabilization would be enhanced by the protection, limitation, and regulation of the terms of residential mortgage credit and the practices related to such credit, while ensuring that responsible, affordable mortgage credit remains available to consumers.

"(2) PURPOSE.—It is the purpose of this section and section 129C to assure that consumers are offered and receive residential mortgage loans on terms that reasonably reflect their ability to repay the loans and that are understandable and not unfair, deceptive or abusive.

"(b) DUTY OF CARE.—

"(1) STANDARD.—Subject to regulations prescribed under this subsection, each mortgage originator shall, in addition to the duties imposed by otherwise applicable provisions of State or Federal law—

"(A) be qualified and, when required, registered and licensed as a mortgage originator in accordance with applicable State or Federal law, including the Secure and Fair Enforcement for Mortgage Licensing Act of 2008; and

"(B) include on all loan documents any unique identifier of the mortgage originator provided by the Nationwide Mortgage Licensing System and Registry.

"(2) COMPLIANCE PROCEDURES REQUIRED.—The Board shall prescribe regulations requiring depository institutions to establish and maintain procedures reasonably designed to assure and monitor the compliance of such depository institutions, the subsidiaries of such institutions, and the employees of such institutions or subsidiaries with the requirements of this section and the registration procedures established under section 1507 of the Secure and Fair Enforcement for Mortgage Licensing Act of 2008.".

(b) CLERICAL AMENDMENT.—The table of sections for chapter 2 of the Truth in Lending Act is amended by inserting after the item relating to section 129 the following new items:

"129A. Fiduciary duty of servicers of pooled residential mortgages.

"129B. Residential mortgage loan origination.".

[Explanation at ¶ 6520.]

[¶ 11,403] ACT SEC. 1403. PROHIBITION ON STEERING INCENTIVES.

Section 129B of the Truth in Lending Act (as added by section 1402(a)) is amended by inserting after subsection (b) the following new subsection:

"(c) PROHIBITION ON STEERING INCENTIVES.—

"(1) IN GENERAL.—For any residential mortgage loan, no mortgage originator shall receive from any person and no person shall pay to a mortgage originator, directly or indirectly, compensation that varies based on the terms of the loan (other than the amount of the principal).

"(2) RESTRUCTURING OF FINANCING ORIGINATION FEE.—

"(A) IN GENERAL.—For any mortgage loan, a mortgage originator may not receive from any person other than the consumer and no person, other than the consumer, who knows or has reason to know that a consumer has directly compensated or will directly compensate a mortgage originator may pay a mortgage originator any origination fee or charge except bona fide third party charges not retained by the creditor, mortgage originator, or an affiliate of the creditor or mortgage originator.

"(B) EXCEPTION.—Notwithstanding subparagraph (A), a mortgage originator may receive from a person other than the consumer an origination fee or charge, and a person other than the consumer may pay a mortgage originator an origination fee or charge, if—

"(i) the mortgage originator does not receive any compensation directly from the consumer; and

"(ii) the consumer does not make an upfront payment of discount points, origination points, or fees, however denominated (other than bona fide third party charges not retained by the mortgage originator, creditor, or an affiliate of the creditor or originator), except that the Board may, by rule, waive or provide exemptions to this clause if the Board determines that such waiver or exemption is in the interest of consumers and in the public interest.

"(3) REGULATIONS.—The Board shall prescribe regulations to prohibit—

"(A) mortgage originators from steering any consumer to a residential mortgage loan that—

"(i) the consumer lacks a reasonable ability to repay (in accordance with regulations prescribed under section 129C(a)); or

"(ii) has predatory characteristics or effects (such as equity stripping, excessive fees, or abusive terms);

"(B) mortgage originators from steering any consumer from a residential mortgage loan for which the consumer is qualified that is a qualified mortgage (as defined in section 129C(b)(2)) to a residential mortgage loan that is not a qualified mortgage;

"(C) abusive or unfair lending practices that promote disparities among consumers of equal credit worthiness but of different race, ethnicity, gender, or age; and

"(D) mortgage originators from—

"(i) mischaracterizing the credit history of a consumer or the residential mortgage loans available to a consumer;

"(ii) mischaracterizing or suborning the mischaracterization of the appraised value of the property securing the extension of credit; or

"(iii) if unable to suggest, offer, or recommend to a consumer a loan that is not more expensive than a loan for which the consumer qualifies, discouraging a consumer from seeking a residential mortgage loan secured by a consumer's principal dwelling from another mortgage originator.

"(4) RULES OF CONSTRUCTION.—No provision of this subsection shall be construed as—

"(A) permitting any yield spread premium or other similar compensation that would, for any residential mortgage loan, permit the total amount of direct and indirect compensation from all sources permitted to a mortgage originator to vary based on the terms of the loan (other than the amount of the principal);

"(B) limiting or affecting the amount of compensation received by a creditor upon the sale of a consummated loan to a subsequent purchaser;

"(C) restricting a consumer's ability to finance, at the option of the consumer, including through principal or rate, any origination fees or costs permitted under this subsection, or the mortgage originator's right to receive such fees or costs (including compensation) from any person, subject to paragraph (2)(B), so long as such fees or costs do not vary based on the terms of the loan (other than the amount of the principal) or the consumer's decision about whether to finance such fees or costs; or

"(D) prohibiting incentive payments to a mortgage originator based on the number of residential mortgage loans originated within a specified period of time.".

[Explanation at ¶ 6525.]

[¶ 11,404] ACT SEC. 1404. LIABILITY.

Section 129B of the Truth in Lending Act is amended by inserting after subsection (c) (as added by section 1403) the following new subsection:

"(d) LIABILITY FOR VIOLATIONS.—

"(1) IN GENERAL.—For purposes of providing a cause of action for any failure by a mortgage originator, other than a creditor, to comply with any requirement imposed under this section and any regulation prescribed under this section, section 130 shall be applied with respect to any such failure by substituting 'mortgage originator' for 'creditor' each place such term appears in each such subsection.

"(2) MAXIMUM.—The maximum amount of any liability of a mortgage originator under paragraph (1) to a consumer for any violation of this section shall not exceed the greater of actual damages or an amount equal to 3 times the total amount of direct and indirect compensation or gain accruing to the mortgage originator in connection with the residential mortgage loan involved in the violation, plus the costs to the consumer of the action, including a reasonable attorney's fee.".

[Explanation at ¶ 6530.]

[¶ 11,405] ACT SEC. 1405. REGULATIONS.

(a) DISCRETIONARY REGULATORY AUTHORITY.—Section 129B of the Truth in Lending Act is amended by inserting after subsection (d) (as added by section 1404) the following new subsection:

"(e) DISCRETIONARY REGULATORY AUTHORITY.—

"(1) IN GENERAL.—The Board shall, by regulations, prohibit or condition terms, acts or practices relating to residential mortgage loans that the Board finds to be abusive, unfair, deceptive, predatory, necessary or proper to ensure that responsible, affordable mortgage credit remains available to consumers in a manner consistent with the purposes of this section and section 129C, necessary or proper to effectuate the purposes of this section and section 129C, to prevent circumvention or evasion thereof, or to facilitate compliance with such sections, or are not in the interest of the borrower.

"(2) APPLICATION.—The regulations prescribed under paragraph (1) shall be applicable to all residential mortgage loans and shall be applied in the same manner as regulations prescribed under section 105.

"(f) Section 129B and any regulations promulgated thereunder do not apply to an extension of credit relating to a plan described in section 101(53D) of title 11, United States Code.".

(b) DISCLOSURES.—Notwithstanding any other provision of this title, in order to improve consumer awareness and understanding of transactions involving residential mortgage loans through the use of disclosures, the Board may, by rule, exempt from or modify disclosure requirements, in whole or in part, for any class of residential mortgage loans if the Board determines that such exemption or modification is in the interest of consumers and in the public interest.

[Explanation at ¶ 6535.]

[¶ 11,406] ACT SEC. 1406. STUDY OF SHARED APPRECIATION MORTGAGES.

(a) STUDY.—The Secretary of Housing and Urban Development, in consultation with the Secretary of the Treasury and other relevant agencies, shall conduct a comprehensive study to determine prudent statutory and regulatory requirements sufficient to provide for the widespread use of shared appreciation mortgages to strengthen local housing markets, provide new opportunities for affordable homeownership, and enable homeowners at risk of foreclosure to refinance or modify their mortgages.

(b) REPORT.—Not later than the expiration of the 6-month period beginning on the date of the enactment of this Act, the Secretary of Housing and Urban Development shall submit a report to the Congress on the results of the study, which shall include recommendations for the regulatory and legislative requirements referred to in subsection (a).

[Explanation at ¶ 6540.]

Subtitle B—Minimum Standards For Mortgages

[¶ 11,411] ACT SEC. 1411. ABILITY TO REPAY.

(a) IN GENERAL.—

(1) RULE OF CONSTRUCTION.—No regulation, order, or guidance issued by the Bureau under this title shall be construed as requiring a depository institution to apply mortgage underwriting standards that do not meet the minimum underwriting standards required by the appropriate prudential regulator of the depository institution.

(2) AMENDMENT TO TRUTH IN LENDING ACT.—Chapter 2 of the Truth in Lending Act (15 U.S.C. 1631 et seq.) is amended by inserting after section 129B (as added by section 1402(a)) the following new section:

"§ 129C. Minimum standards for residential mortgage loans

"(a) ABILITY TO REPAY.—

"(1) IN GENERAL.—In accordance with regulations prescribed by the Board, no creditor may make a residential mortgage loan unless the creditor makes a reasonable and good faith determination based on verified and documented information that, at the time the loan is consummated, the consumer has a reasonable ability to repay the loan, according to its terms, and all applicable taxes, insurance (including mortgage guarantee insurance), and assessments.

"(2) MULTIPLE LOANS.—If the creditor knows, or has reason to know, that 1 or more residential mortgage loans secured by the same dwelling will be made to the same consumer, the creditor shall make a reasonable and good faith determination, based on verified and documented information, that the consumer has a reasonable ability to repay the combined payments of all loans on the same dwelling according to the terms of those loans and all applicable taxes, insurance (including mortgage guarantee insurance), and assessments.

"(3) BASIS FOR DETERMINATION.—A determination under this subsection of a consumer's ability to repay a residential mortgage loan shall include consideration of the consumer's credit history, current income, expected income the consumer is reasonably assured of receiving, current obligations, debt-to-income ratio or the residual income the consumer will have after paying non-mortgage debt and mortgage-related obligations, employment status, and other financial resources other than the consumer's equity in the dwelling or real property that secures repayment of the loan. A creditor shall determine the ability of the consumer to repay using a payment schedule that fully amortizes the loan over the term of the loan.

"(4) INCOME VERIFICATION.—A creditor making a residential mortgage loan shall verify amounts of income or assets that such creditor relies on to determine repayment ability, including expected income or assets, by reviewing the consumer's Internal Revenue Service Form W-2, tax returns, payroll receipts, financial institution records, or other third-party documents that provide reasonably reliable evidence of the consumer's income or assets. In order to safeguard against fraudulent reporting, any consideration of a consumer's income history in making a determination under this subsection shall include the verification of such income by the use of—

"(A) Internal Revenue Service transcripts of tax returns; or

"(B) a method that quickly and effectively verifies income documentation by a third party subject to rules prescribed by the Board.

"(5) EXEMPTION.—With respect to loans made, guaranteed, or insured by Federal departments or agencies identified in subsection (b)(3)(B)(ii), such departments or agencies may exempt refinancings under a streamlined refinancing from this income verification requirement as long as the following conditions are met:

"(A) The consumer is not 30 days or more past due on the prior existing residential mortgage loan.

"(B) The refinancing does not increase the principal balance outstanding on the prior existing residential mortgage loan, except to the extent of fees and charges allowed by the department or agency making, guaranteeing, or insuring the refinancing.

"(C) Total points and fees (as defined in section 103(aa)(4), other than bona fide third party charges not retained by the mortgage originator, creditor, or an affiliate of the creditor or mortgage originator) payable in connection with the refinancing do not exceed 3 percent of the total new loan amount.

"(D) The interest rate on the refinanced loan is lower than the interest rate of the original loan, unless the borrower is refinancing from an adjustable rate to a fixed-rate loan, under guidelines that the department or agency shall establish for loans they make, guarantee, or issue.

"(E) The refinancing is subject to a payment schedule that will fully amortize the refinancing in accordance with the regulations prescribed by the department or agency making, guaranteeing, or insuring the refinancing.

"(F) The terms of the refinancing do not result in a balloon payment, as defined in subsection (b)(2)(A)(ii).

"(G) Both the residential mortgage loan being refinanced and the refinancing satisfy all requirements of the department or agency making, guaranteeing, or insuring the refinancing.

"(6) NONSTANDARD LOANS.—

"(A) VARIABLE RATE LOANS THAT DEFER REPAYMENT OF ANY PRINCIPAL OR INTEREST.—For purposes of determining, under this subsection, a consumer's ability to repay a variable rate residential mortgage loan that allows or requires the consumer to defer the repayment of any principal or interest, the creditor shall use a fully amortizing repayment schedule.

"(B) INTEREST-ONLY LOANS.—For purposes of determining, under this subsection, a consumer's ability to repay a residential mortgage loan that permits or requires the payment of interest only, the creditor shall use the payment amount required to amortize the loan by its final maturity.

"(C) CALCULATION FOR NEGATIVE AMORTIZATION.—In making any determination under this subsection, a creditor shall also take into consideration any balance increase that may accrue from any negative amortization provision.

"(D) CALCULATION PROCESS.—For purposes of making any determination under this subsection, a creditor shall calculate the monthly payment amount for principal and interest on any residential mortgage loan by assuming—

"(i) the loan proceeds are fully disbursed on the date of the consummation of the loan;

"(ii) the loan is to be repaid in substantially equal monthly amortizing payments for principal and interest over the entire term of the loan with no balloon payment, unless the loan contract requires more rapid repayment (including balloon payment), in which case the calculation shall be made (I) in accordance with regulations prescribed by the Board, with respect to any loan which has an annual percentage rate that does not exceed the average prime offer rate for a comparable transaction, as of the date the interest rate is set, by 1.5 or more percentage points for a first lien residential mortgage loan; and by 3.5 or more percentage points for a subordinate lien residential mortgage loan; or (II) using the contract's repayment schedule, with respect to a loan which has an annual percentage rate, as of the date the interest rate is set, that is at least 1.5 percentage points above the average prime offer rate for a first lien residential mortgage loan; and 3.5 percentage points above the average prime offer rate for a subordinate lien residential mortgage loan; and

"(iii) the interest rate over the entire term of the loan is a fixed rate equal to the fully indexed rate at the time of the loan closing, without considering the introductory rate.

"(E) REFINANCE OF HYBRID LOANS WITH CURRENT LENDER.—In considering any application for refinancing an existing hybrid loan by the creditor into a standard loan to be made by the same creditor in any case in which there would be a reduction in monthly payment and the mortgagor has not been delinquent on any payment on the existing hybrid loan, the creditor may—

"(i) consider the mortgagor's good standing on the existing mortgage;

"(ii) consider if the extension of new credit would prevent a likely default should the original mortgage reset and give such concerns a higher priority as an acceptable underwriting practice; and

"(iii) offer rate discounts and other favorable terms to such mortgagor that would be available to new customers with high credit ratings based on such underwriting practice.

"(7) FULLY-INDEXED RATE DEFINED.—For purposes of this subsection, the term 'fully indexed rate' means the index rate prevailing on a residential mortgage loan at the time the loan is made plus the margin that will apply after the expiration of any introductory interest rates.

"(8) REVERSE MORTGAGES AND BRIDGE LOANS.—This subsection shall not apply with respect to any reverse mortgage or temporary or bridge loan with a term of 12 months or less, including to any loan to purchase a new dwelling where the consumer plans to sell a different dwelling within 12 months.

"(9) SEASONAL INCOME.—If documented income, including income from a small business, is a repayment source for a residential mortgage loan, a creditor may consider the seasonality and irregularity of such income in the underwriting of and scheduling of payments for such credit.".

(b) CLERICAL AMENDMENT.—The table of sections for chapter 2 of the Truth in Lending Act is amended by inserting after the item relating to section 129B (as added by section 1402(b)) the following new item:

"129C. Minimum standards for residential mortgage loans.".

[Explanation at ¶ 6545.]

[¶ 11,412] ACT SEC. 1412. SAFE HARBOR AND REBUTTABLE PRESUMPTION.

Section 129C of the Truth in Lending Act is amended by inserting after subsection (a) (as added by section 1411) the following new subsection:

"(b) PRESUMPTION OF ABILITY TO REPAY.—

"(1) IN GENERAL.—Any creditor with respect to any residential mortgage loan, and any assignee of such loan subject to liability under this title, may presume that the loan has met the requirements of subsection (a), if the loan is a qualified mortgage.

"(2) DEFINITIONS.—For purposes of this subsection, the following definitions shall apply:

"(A) QUALIFIED MORTGAGE.—The term 'qualified mortgage' means any residential mortgage loan—

"(i) for which the regular periodic payments for the loan may not—

"(I) result in an increase of the principal balance; or

"(II) except as provided in subparagraph (E), allow the consumer to defer repayment of principal;

"(ii) except as provided in subparagraph (E), the terms of which do not result in a balloon payment, where a 'balloon payment' is a scheduled payment that is more than twice as large as the average of earlier scheduled payments;

"(iii) for which the income and financial resources relied upon to qualify the obligors on the loan are verified and documented;

"(iv) in the case of a fixed rate loan, for which the underwriting process is based on a payment schedule that fully amortizes the loan over the loan term and takes into account all applicable taxes, insurance, and assessments;

"(v) in the case of an adjustable rate loan, for which the underwriting is based on the maximum rate permitted under the loan during the first 5 years, and a payment schedule that fully amortizes the loan over the loan term and takes into account all applicable taxes, insurance, and assessments;

"(vi) that complies with any guidelines or regulations established by the Board relating to ratios of total monthly debt to monthly income or alternative measures of ability to pay regular expenses after payment of total monthly debt, taking into account the income levels of the borrower and such other factors as the Board may determine relevant and consistent with the purposes described in paragraph (3)(B)(i);

"(vii) for which the total points and fees (as defined in subparagraph (C)) payable in connection with the loan do not exceed 3 percent of the total loan amount;

"(viii) for which the term of the loan does not exceed 30 years, except as such term may be extended under paragraph (3), such as in high-cost areas; and

"(ix) in the case of a reverse mortgage (except for the purposes of subsection (a) of section 129C, to the extent that such mortgages are exempt altogether from those requirements), a reverse mortgage which meets the standards for a qualified mortgage, as set by the Board in rules that are consistent with the purposes of this subsection.

"(B) AVERAGE PRIME OFFER RATE.—The term 'average prime offer rate' means the average prime offer rate for a comparable transaction as of the date on which the interest rate for the transaction is set, as published by the Board..

"(C) POINTS AND FEES.—

"(i) IN GENERAL.—For purposes of subparagraph (A), the term 'points and fees' means points and fees as defined by section 103(aa)(4) (other than bona fide third party charges not retained by the mortgage originator, creditor, or an affiliate of the creditor or mortgage originator).

"(ii) COMPUTATION.—For purposes of computing the total points and fees under this subparagraph, the total points and fees shall exclude either of the amounts described in the following subclauses, but not both:

"(I) Up to and including 2 bona fide discount points payable by the consumer in connection with the mortgage, but only if the interest rate from which the mortgage's interest rate will be discounted does not exceed by more than 1 percentage point the average prime offer rate.

"(II) Unless 2 bona fide discount points have been excluded under subclause (I), up to and including 1 bona fide discount point payable by the consumer in connection with the mortgage, but only if the interest rate from which the mortgage's interest rate will be discounted does not exceed by more than 2 percentage points the average prime offer rate.

"(iii) BONA FIDE DISCOUNT POINTS DEFINED.—For purposes of clause (ii), the term 'bona fide discount points' means loan discount points which are knowingly paid by the consumer for the purpose of reducing, and which in fact result in a bona fide reduction of, the interest rate or time-price differential applicable to the mortgage.

"(iv) INTEREST RATE REDUCTION.—Subclauses (I) and (II) of clause (ii) shall not apply to discount points used to purchase an interest rate reduction unless the amount of the interest rate reduction purchased is reasonably consistent with established industry norms and practices for secondary mortgage market transactions.

"(D) SMALLER LOANS.—The Board shall prescribe rules adjusting the criteria under subparagraph (A)(vii) in order to permit lenders that extend smaller loans to meet the requirements of the presumption of compliance under paragraph (1). In prescribing such rules, the Board shall consider the potential impact of such rules on rural areas and other areas where home values are lower.

"(E) BALLOON LOANS.—The Board may, by regulation, provide that the term 'qualified mortgage' includes a balloon loan—

"(i) that meets all of the criteria for a qualified mortgage under subparagraph (A) (except clauses (i)(II), (ii), (iv), and (v) of such subparagraph);

"(ii) for which the creditor makes a determination that the consumer is able to make all scheduled payments, except the balloon payment, out of income or assets other than the collateral;

"(iii) for which the underwriting is based on a payment schedule that fully amortizes the loan over a period of not more than 30 years and takes into account all applicable taxes, insurance, and assessments; and

"(iv) that is extended by a creditor that—

"(I) operates predominantly in rural or underserved areas;

"(II) together with all affiliates, has total annual residential mortgage loan originations that do not exceed a limit set by the Board;

"(III) retains the balloon loans in portfolio; and

"(IV) meets any asset size threshold and any other criteria as the Board may establish, consistent with the purposes of this subtitle.

"(3) REGULATIONS.—

"(A) IN GENERAL.—The Board shall prescribe regulations to carry out the purposes of this subsection.

"(B) REVISION OF SAFE HARBOR CRITERIA.—

"(i) IN GENERAL.—The Board may prescribe regulations that revise, add to, or subtract from the criteria that define a qualified mortgage upon a finding that such regulations are necessary or proper to ensure that responsible, affordable mortgage credit remains available to consumers in a manner consistent with the purposes of this section, necessary and appropriate to effectuate the purposes of this section and section 129B, to prevent circumvention or evasion thereof, or to facilitate compliance with such sections.

"(ii) LOAN DEFINITION.—The following agencies shall, in consultation with the Board, prescribe rules defining the types of loans they insure, guarantee, or administer, as the case may be, that are qualified mortgages for purposes of paragraph (2)(A), and such rules may revise, add to, or subtract from the criteria used to define a qualified mortgage under paragraph (2)(A), upon a finding that such rules are consistent with the purposes of this section and section 129B, to prevent circumvention or evasion thereof, or to facilitate compliance with such sections:

"(I) The Department of Housing and Urban Development, with regard to mortgages insured under the National Housing Act (12 U.S.C. 1707 et seq.).

"(II) The Department of Veterans Affairs, with regard to a loan made or guaranteed by the Secretary of Veterans Affairs.

"(III) The Department of Agriculture, with regard loans guaranteed by the Secretary of Agriculture pursuant to 42 U.S.C. 1472(h).

"(IV) The Rural Housing Service, with regard to loans insured by the Rural Housing Service.".

[Explanation at ¶ 6550.]

[¶ 11,413] ACT SEC. 1413. DEFENSE TO FORECLOSURE.

Section 130 of the Truth in Lending Act (15 U.S.C. 1640) is amended by adding at the end the following new subsection:

"(k) DEFENSE TO FORECLOSURE.—

"(1) IN GENERAL.—Notwithstanding any other provision of law, when a creditor, assignee, or other holder of a residential mortgage loan or anyone acting on behalf of such creditor, assignee, or holder, initiates a judicial or nonjudicial foreclosure of the residential mortgage loan, or any other action to collect the debt in connection with such loan, a consumer may assert a violation by a creditor of paragraph (1) or (2) of section 129B(c), or of section 129C(a), as a matter of defense by recoupment or set off without regard for the time limit on a private action for damages under subsection (e).

"(2) AMOUNT OF RECOUPMENT OR SETOFF.—

"(A) IN GENERAL.—The amount of recoupment or set-off under paragraph (1) shall equal the amount to which the consumer would be entitled under subsection (a) for damages for a valid claim brought in an original action against the creditor, plus the costs to the consumer of the action, including a reasonable attorney's fee.

"(B) SPECIAL RULE.—Where such judgment is rendered after the expiration of the applicable time limit on a private action for damages under subsection (e), the amount of recoupment or set-off under paragraph (1) derived from damages under subsection (a)(4) shall not exceed the amount to which the consumer would have been entitled under subsection (a)(4) for damages computed up to the day preceding the expiration of the applicable time limit.".

[Explanation at ¶ 6555.]

[¶ 11,414] ACT SEC. 1414. ADDITIONAL STANDARDS AND REQUIREMENTS.

(a) IN GENERAL.—Section 129C of the Truth in Lending Act is amended by inserting after subsection (b) (as added by this title) the following new subsections:

"(c) PROHIBITION ON CERTAIN PREPAYMENT PENALTIES.—

"(1) PROHIBITED ON CERTAIN LOANS.—

"(A) IN GENERAL.—A residential mortgage loan that is not a 'qualified mortgage', as defined under subsection (b)(2), may not contain terms under which a consumer must pay a prepayment penalty for paying all or part of the principal after the loan is consummated.

"(B) EXCLUSIONS.—For purposes of this subsection, a 'qualified mortgage' may not include a residential mortgage loan that—

"(i) has an adjustable rate; or

"(ii) has an annual percentage rate that exceeds the average prime offer rate for a comparable transaction, as of the date the interest rate is set—

"(I) by 1.5 or more percentage points, in the case of a first lien residential mortgage loan having a original principal obligation amount that is equal to or less than the amount of the maximum limitation on the original principal obligation of mortgage in effect for a residence of the applicable size, as of the date of such interest rate set, pursuant to the 6th sentence of section 305(a)(2) the Federal Home Loan Mortgage Corporation Act (12 U.S.C. 1454(a)(2));

"(II) by 2.5 or more percentage points, in the case of a first lien residential mortgage loan having a original principal obligation amount that is more than the amount of the maximum limitation on the original principal obligation of mortgage in effect for a residence of the applicable size, as of the date of such interest rate set, pursuant to the 6th sentence of section 305(a)(2) the Federal Home Loan Mortgage Corporation Act (12 U.S.C. 1454(a)(2)); and

"(III) by 3.5 or more percentage points, in the case of a subordinate lien residential mortgage loan.

"(2) PUBLICATION OF AVERAGE PRIME OFFER RATE AND APR THRESHOLDS.—The Board—
"(A) shall publish, and update at least weekly, average prime offer rates;
"(B) may publish multiple rates based on varying types of mortgage transactions; and
"(C) shall adjust the thresholds established under subclause (I), (II), and (III) of paragraph (1)(B)(ii) as necessary to reflect significant changes in market conditions and to effectuate the purposes of the Mortgage Reform and Anti-Predatory Lending Act.

"(3) PHASED-OUT PENALTIES ON QUALIFIED MORTGAGES.—A qualified mortgage (as defined in subsection (b)(2)) may not contain terms under which a consumer must pay a prepayment penalty for paying all or part of the principal after the loan is consummated in excess of the following limitations:
"(A) During the 1-year period beginning on the date the loan is consummated, the prepayment penalty shall not exceed an amount equal to 3 percent of the outstanding balance on the loan.
"(B) During the 1-year period beginning after the period described in subparagraph (A), the prepayment penalty shall not exceed an amount equal to 2 percent of the outstanding balance on the loan.
"(C) During the 1-year period beginning after the 1-year period described in subparagraph (B), the prepayment penalty shall not exceed an amount equal to 1 percent of the outstanding balance on the loan.
"(D) After the end of the 3-year period beginning on the date the loan is consummated, no prepayment penalty may be imposed on a qualified mortgage.

"(4) OPTION FOR NO PREPAYMENT PENALTY REQUIRED.—A creditor may not offer a consumer a residential mortgage loan product that has a prepayment penalty for paying all or part of the principal after the loan is consummated as a term of the loan without offering the consumer a residential mortgage loan product that does not have a prepayment penalty as a term of the loan.

"(d) SINGLE PREMIUM CREDIT INSURANCE PROHIBITED.—No creditor may finance, directly or indirectly, in connection with any residential mortgage loan or with any extension of credit under an open end consumer credit plan secured by the principal dwelling of the consumer, any credit life, credit disability, credit unemployment, or credit property insurance, or any other accident, loss-of-income, life, or health insurance, or any payments directly or indirectly for any debt cancellation or suspension agreement or contract, except that—
"(1) insurance premiums or debt cancellation or suspension fees calculated and paid in full on a monthly basis shall not be considered financed by the creditor; and
"(2) this subsection shall not apply to credit unemployment insurance for which the unemployment insurance premiums are reasonable, the creditor receives no direct or indirect compensation in connection with the unemployment insurance premiums, and the unemployment insurance premiums are paid pursuant to another insurance contract and not paid to an affiliate of the creditor.

"(e) ARBITRATION.—
"(1) IN GENERAL.—No residential mortgage loan and no extension of credit under an open end consumer credit plan secured by the principal dwelling of the consumer may include terms which require arbitration or any other nonjudicial procedure as the method for resolving any controversy or settling any claims arising out of the transaction.
"(2) POST CONTROVERSY AGREEMENTS.—Subject to paragraph (3), paragraph (1) shall not be construed as limiting the right of the consumer and the creditor or any assignee to agree to arbitration or any other nonjudicial procedure as the method for resolving any controversy at any time after a dispute or claim under the transaction arises.
"(3) NO WAIVER OF STATUTORY CAUSE OF ACTION.—No provision of any residential mortgage loan or of any extension of credit under an open end consumer credit plan secured by the principal dwelling of the consumer, and no other agreement between the consumer and the

creditor relating to the residential mortgage loan or extension of credit referred to in paragraph (1), shall be applied or interpreted so as to bar a consumer from bringing an action in an appropriate district court of the United States, or any other court of competent jurisdiction, pursuant to section 130 or any other provision of law, for damages or other relief in connection with any alleged violation of this section, any other provision of this title, or any other Federal law.

"(f) MORTGAGES WITH NEGATIVE AMORTIZATION.—No creditor may extend credit to a borrower in connection with a consumer credit transaction under an open or closed end consumer credit plan secured by a dwelling or residential real property that includes a dwelling, other than a reverse mortgage, that provides or permits a payment plan that may, at any time over the term of the extension of credit, result in negative amortization unless, before such transaction is consummated—

"(1) the creditor provides the consumer with a statement that—

"(A) the pending transaction will or may, as the case may be, result in negative amortization;

"(B) describes negative amortization in such manner as the Board shall prescribe;

"(C) negative amortization increases the outstanding principal balance of the account; and

"(D) negative amortization reduces the consumer's equity in the dwelling or real property; and

"(2) in the case of a first-time borrower with respect to a residential mortgage loan that is not a qualified mortgage, the first-time borrower provides the creditor with sufficient documentation to demonstrate that the consumer received homeownership counseling from organizations or counselors certified by the Secretary of Housing and Urban Development as competent to provide such counseling.".

(b) CONFORMING AMENDMENT RELATING TO ENFORCEMENT.—Section 108(a) of the Truth in Lending Act (15 U.S.C. 1607(a)) is amended by inserting after paragraph (6) the following new paragraph:

"(7) sections 21B and 21C of the Securities Exchange Act of 1934, in the case of a broker or dealer, other than a depository institution, by the Securities and Exchange Commission.".

(c) PROTECTION AGAINST LOSS OF ANTI-DEFICIENCY PROTECTION.—Section 129C of the Truth in Lending Act is amended by inserting after subsection (f) (as added by subsection (a)) the following new subsection:

"(g) PROTECTION AGAINST LOSS OF ANTI-DEFICIENCY PROTECTION.—

"(1) DEFINITION.—For purposes of this subsection, the term 'anti-deficiency law' means the law of any State which provides that, in the event of foreclosure on the residential property of a consumer securing a mortgage, the consumer is not liable, in accordance with the terms and limitations of such State law, for any deficiency between the sale price obtained on such property through foreclosure and the outstanding balance of the mortgage.

"(2) NOTICE AT TIME OF CONSUMMATION.—In the case of any residential mortgage loan that is, or upon consummation will be, subject to protection under an anti-deficiency law, the creditor or mortgage originator shall provide a written notice to the consumer describing the protection provided by the anti-deficiency law and the significance for the consumer of the loss of such protection before such loan is consummated.

"(3) NOTICE BEFORE REFINANCING THAT WOULD CAUSE LOSS OF PROTECTION.—In the case of any residential mortgage loan that is subject to protection under an anti-deficiency law, if a creditor or mortgage originator provides an application to a consumer, or receives an application from a consumer, for any type of refinancing for such loan that would cause the loan to lose the protection of such anti-deficiency law, the creditor or mortgage originator shall provide a written notice to the consumer describing the protection provided by the anti-deficiency law and the significance for the consumer of the loss of such protection before any agreement for any such refinancing is consummated.".

(d) POLICY REGARDING ACCEPTANCE OF PARTIAL PAYMENT.—Section 129C of the Truth in Lending Act is amended by inserting after subsection (g) (as added by subsection (c)) the following new subsection:

"(h) POLICY REGARDING ACCEPTANCE OF PARTIAL PAYMENT.—In the case of any residential mortgage loan, a creditor shall disclose prior to settlement or, in the case of a person becoming a creditor with respect to an existing residential mortgage loan, at the time such person becomes a creditor—

"(1) the creditor's policy regarding the acceptance of partial payments; and

"(2) if partial payments are accepted, how such payments will be applied to such mortgage and if such payments will be placed in escrow.

"(i) TIMESHARE PLANS.—This section and any regulations promulgated under this section do not apply to an extension of credit relating to a plan described in section 101(53D) of title 11, United States Code.".

[Explanation at ¶ 6560.]

[¶ 11,415] ACT SEC. 1415. RULE OF CONSTRUCTION.

Except as otherwise expressly provided in section 129B or 129C of the Truth in Lending Act (as added by this title), no provision of such section 129B or 129C shall be construed as superseding, repealing, or affecting any duty, right, obligation, privilege, or remedy of any person under any other provision of the Truth in Lending Act or any other provision of Federal or State law.

[Explanation at ¶ 6565.]

[¶ 11,416] ACT SEC. 1416. AMENDMENTS TO CIVIL LIABILITY PROVISIONS.

(a) INCREASE IN AMOUNT OF CIVIL MONEY PENALTIES FOR CERTAIN VIOLATIONS.—Section 130(a) of the Truth in Lending Act (15 U.S.C. 1640(a)) is amended—

(1) in paragraph (2)(A)(ii)—

(A) by striking "$100" and inserting "$200"; and

(B) by striking "$1,000" and inserting "$2,000";

(2) in paragraph (2)(B), by striking "$500,000" and inserting "$1,000,000"; and

(3) in paragraph (4), by inserting ", paragraph (1) or (2) of section 129B(c), or section 129C(a)" after "section 129".

(b) STATUTE OF LIMITATIONS EXTENDED FOR SECTION 129 VIOLATIONS.—Section 130(e) of the Truth in Lending Act (15 U.S.C. 1640(e)) is amended—

(1) in the first sentence, by striking "Any action" and inserting "Except as provided in the subsequent sentence, any action"; and

(2) by inserting after the first sentence the following new sentence: "Any action under this section with respect to any violation of section 129, 129B, or 129C may be brought in any United States district court, or in any other court of competent jurisdiction, before the end of the 3-year period beginning on the date of the occurrence of the violation.".

[Explanation at ¶ 6570.]

[¶ 11,417] ACT SEC. 1417. LENDER RIGHTS IN THE CONTEXT OF BORROWER DECEPTION.

Section 130 of the Truth in Lending Act (15 U.S.C. 1640) is amended by adding after subsection (k) (as added by this title) the following new subsection:

"(1) EXEMPTION FROM LIABILITY AND RESCISSION IN CASE OF BORROWER FRAUD OR DECEPTION.—In addition to any other remedy available by law or contract, no creditor or assignee shall be liable to an obligor under this section, if such obligor, or co-obligor has been convicted of obtaining by actual fraud such residential mortgage loan.".

[Explanation at ¶ 6575.]

[¶ 11,418] ACT SEC. 1418. SIX-MONTH NOTICE REQUIRED BEFORE RESET OF HYBRID ADJUSTABLE RATE MORTGAGES.

(a) IN GENERAL.—Chapter 2 of the Truth in Lending Act (15 U.S.C. 1631 et seq.) is amended by inserting after section 128 the following new section:

"§ 128A. Reset of hybrid adjustable rate mortgages

"(a) HYBRID ADJUSTABLE RATE MORTGAGES DEFINED.—For purposes of this section, the term 'hybrid adjustable rate mortgage' means a consumer credit transaction secured by the consumer's principal residence with a fixed interest rate for an introductory period that adjusts or resets to a variable interest rate after such period.

"(b) NOTICE OF RESET AND ALTERNATIVES.—During the 1-month period that ends 6 months before the date on which the interest rate in effect during the introductory period of a hybrid adjustable rate mortgage adjusts or resets to a variable interest rate or, in the case of such an adjustment or resetting that occurs within the first 6 months after consummation of such loan, at consummation, the creditor or servicer of such loan shall provide a written notice, separate and distinct from all other correspondence to the consumer, that includes the following:

"(1) Any index or formula used in making adjustments to or resetting the interest rate and a source of information about the index or formula.

"(2) An explanation of how the new interest rate and payment would be determined, including an explanation of how the index was adjusted, such as by the addition of a margin.

"(3) A good faith estimate, based on accepted industry standards, of the creditor or servicer of the amount of the monthly payment that will apply after the date of the adjustment or reset, and the assumptions on which this estimate is based.

"(4) A list of alternatives consumers may pursue before the date of adjustment or reset, and descriptions of the actions consumers must take to pursue these alternatives, including—

"(A) refinancing;

"(B) renegotiation of loan terms;

"(C) payment forbearances; and

"(D) pre-foreclosure sales.

"(5) The names, addresses, telephone numbers, and Internet addresses of counseling agencies or programs reasonably available to the consumer that have been certified or approved and made publicly available by the Secretary of Housing and Urban Development or a State housing finance authority (as defined in section 1301 of the Financial Institutions Reform, Recovery, and Enforcement Act of 1989).

"(6) The address, telephone number, and Internet address for the State housing finance authority (as so defined) for the State in which the consumer resides.

"(c) SAVINGS CLAUSE.—The Board may require the notice in paragraph (b) or other notice consistent with this Act for adjustable rate mortgage loans that are not hybrid adjustable rate mortgage loans.".

(b) CLERICAL AMENDMENT.—The table of sections for chapter 2 of the Truth in Lending Act is amended by inserting after the item relating to section 128 the following new item:

"128A. Reset of hybrid adjustable rate mortgages.".

[Explanation at ¶ 6580.]

[¶ 11,419] ACT SEC. 1419. REQUIRED DISCLOSURES.

Section 128(a) of Truth in Lending Act (15 U.S.C. 1638(a)) is amended by adding at the end the following new paragraphs:

"(16) In the case of a variable rate residential mortgage loan for which an escrow or impound account will be established for the payment of all applicable taxes, insurance, and assessments—

"(A) the amount of initial monthly payment due under the loan for the payment of principal and interest, and the amount of such initial monthly payment including the monthly payment deposited in the account for the payment of all applicable taxes, insurance, and assessments; and

"(B) the amount of the fully indexed monthly payment due under the loan for the payment of principal and interest, and the amount of such fully indexed monthly payment including the monthly payment deposited in the account for the payment of all applicable taxes, insurance, and assessments.

"(17) In the case of a residential mortgage loan, the aggregate amount of settlement charges for all settlement services provided in connection with the loan, the amount of charges that are included in the loan and the amount of such charges the borrower must pay at closing, the approximate amount of the wholesale rate of funds in connection with the loan, and the aggregate amount of other fees or required payments in connection with the loan.

"(18) In the case of a residential mortgage loan, the aggregate amount of fees paid to the mortgage originator in connection with the loan, the amount of such fees paid directly by the consumer, and any additional amount received by the originator from the creditor.

"(19) In the case of a residential mortgage loan, the total amount of interest that the consumer will pay over the life of the loan as a percentage of the principal of the loan. Such amount shall be computed assuming the consumer makes each monthly payment in full and on-time, and does not make any over-payments.".

[Explanation at ¶ 6585.]

[¶ 11,420] ACT SEC. 1420. DISCLOSURES REQUIRED IN MONTHLY STATEMENTS FOR RESIDENTIAL MORTGAGE LOANS.

Section 128 of the Truth in Lending Act (15 U.S.C. 1638) is amended by adding at the end the following new subsection:

"(f) PERIODIC STATEMENTS FOR RESIDENTIAL MORTGAGE LOANS.—

"(1) IN GENERAL.—The creditor, assignee, or servicer with respect to any residential mortgage loan shall transmit to the obligor, for each billing cycle, a statement setting forth each of the following items, to the extent applicable, in a conspicuous and prominent manner:

"(A) The amount of the principal obligation under the mortgage.

"(B) The current interest rate in effect for the loan.

"(C) The date on which the interest rate may next reset or adjust.

"(D) The amount of any prepayment fee to be charged, if any.

"(E) A description of any late payment fees.

"(F) A telephone number and electronic mail address that may be used by the obligor to obtain information regarding the mortgage.

"(G) The names, addresses, telephone numbers, and Internet addresses of counseling agencies or programs reasonably available to the consumer that have been certified or approved and made publicly available by the Secretary of Housing and Urban Development or a State housing finance authority (as defined in section 1301 of the Financial Institutions Reform, Recovery, and Enforcement Act of 1989).

"(H) Such other information as the Board may prescribe in regulations.

"(2) DEVELOPMENT AND USE OF STANDARD FORM.—The Board shall develop and prescribe a standard form for the disclosure required under this subsection, taking into account that the statements required may be transmitted in writing or electronically.

"(3) EXCEPTION.—Paragraph (1) shall not apply to any fixed rate residential mortgage loan where the creditor, assignee, or servicer provides the obligor with a coupon book that provides the obligor with substantially the same information as required in paragraph (1).".

[Explanation at ¶ 6590.]

[¶ 11,421] ACT SEC. 1421. REPORT BY THE GAO.

(a) REPORT REQUIRED.—The Comptroller General of the United States shall conduct a study to determine the effects the enactment of this Act will have on the availability and affordability of credit for consumers, small businesses, homebuyers, and mortgage lending, including the effect—

(1) on the mortgage market for mortgages that are not within the safe harbor provided in the amendments made by this subtitle;

(2) on the ability of prospective homebuyers to obtain financing;

(3) on the ability of homeowners facing resets or adjustments to refinance—for example, do they have fewer refinancing options due to the unavailability of certain loan products that were available before the enactment of this Act;

(4) on minorities' ability to access affordable credit compared with other prospective borrowers;

(5) on home sales and construction;

(6) of extending the rescission right, if any, on adjustable rate loans and its impact on litigation;

(7) of State foreclosure laws and, if any, an investor's ability to transfer a property after foreclosure;

(8) of expanding the existing provisions of the Home Ownership and Equity Protection Act of 1994;

(9) of prohibiting prepayment penalties on high-cost mortgages; and

(10) of establishing counseling services under the Department of Housing and Urban Development and offered through the Office of Housing Counseling.

(b) REPORT.—Before the end of the 1-year period beginning on the date of the enactment of this Act, the Comptroller General shall submit a report to the Congress containing the findings and conclusions of the Comptroller General with respect to the study conducted pursuant to subsection (a).

(c) EXAMINATION RELATED TO CERTAIN CREDIT RISK RETENTION PROVISIONS.—The report required by subsection (b) shall also include an analysis by the Comptroller General of the effect on the capital reserves and funding of lenders of credit risk retention provisions for non-qualified mortgages, including an analysis of the exceptions and adjustments authorized in section 129C(b)(3) of the Truth in Lending Act and a recommendation on whether a uniform standard is needed.

(d) ANALYSIS OF CREDIT RISK RETENTION PROVISIONS.—The report required by subsection (b) shall also include—

(1) an analysis by the Comptroller General of whether the credit risk retention provisions have significantly reduced risks to the larger credit market of the repackaging and selling of securitized loans on a secondary market; and

(2) recommendations to the Congress on adjustments that should be made, or additional measures that should be undertaken.

[Explanation at ¶ 6595.]

[¶ 11,422] ACT SEC. 1422. STATE ATTORNEY GENERAL ENFORCEMENT AUTHORITY.

Section 130(e) of the Truth in Lending Act (15 U.S.C. 1640(e)) is amended by striking "section 129 may also" and inserting "section 129, 129B, 129C, 129D, 129E, 129F, 129G, or 129H of this Act may also".

[Explanation at ¶ 6600.]

Subtitle C—High-Cost Mortgages

[¶ 11,431] ACT SEC. 1431. DEFINITIONS RELATING TO HIGH-COST MORTGAGES.

(a) HIGH-COST MORTGAGE DEFINED.—Section 103(aa) of the Truth in Lending Act (15 U.S.C. 1602(aa)) is amended by striking all that precedes paragraph (2) and inserting the following:

"(aa) HIGH-COST MORTGAGE.—

"(1) DEFINITION.—

"(A) IN GENERAL.—The term 'high-cost mortgage', and a mortgage referred to in this subsection, means a consumer credit transaction that is secured by the consumer's principal dwelling, other than a reverse mortgage transaction, if—

"(i) in the case of a credit transaction secured—

"(I) by a first mortgage on the consumer's principal dwelling, the annual percentage rate at consummation of the transaction will exceed by more than 6.5 percentage points (8.5 percentage points, if the dwelling is personal property and the transaction is for less than $50,000) the average prime offer rate, as defined in section 129C(b)(2)(B), for a comparable transaction; or

"(II) by a subordinate or junior mortgage on the consumer's principal dwelling, the annual percentage rate at consummation of the transaction will exceed by more than 8.5 percentage points the average prime offer rate, as defined in section 129C(b)(2)(B), for a comparable transaction;

"(ii) the total points and fees payable in connection with the transaction, other than bona fide third party charges not retained by the mortgage originator, creditor, or an affiliate of the creditor or mortgage originator, exceed—

"(I) in the case of a transaction for $20,000 or more, 5 percent of the total transaction amount; or

"(II) in the case of a transaction for less than $20,000, the lesser of 8 percent of the total transaction amount or $1,000 (or such other dollar amount as the Board shall prescribe by regulation); or

"(iii) the credit transaction documents permit the creditor to charge or collect prepayment fees or penalties more than 36 months after the transaction closing or such fees or penalties exceed, in the aggregate, more than 2 percent of the amount prepaid.

"(B) INTRODUCTORY RATES TAKEN INTO ACCOUNT.—For purposes of subparagraph (A)(i), the annual percentage rate of interest shall be determined based on the following interest rate:

"(i) In the case of a fixed-rate transaction in which the annual percentage rate will not vary during the term of the loan, the interest rate in effect on the date of consummation of the transaction.

"(ii) In the case of a transaction in which the rate of interest varies solely in accordance with an index, the interest rate determined by adding the index rate in effect on the date of consummation of the transaction to the maximum margin permitted at any time during the loan agreement.

"(iii) In the case of any other transaction in which the rate may vary at any time during the term of the loan for any reason, the interest charged on the transaction at the maximum rate that may be charged during the term of the loan.

"(C) MORTGAGE INSURANCE.—For the purposes of computing the total points and fees under paragraph (4), the total points and fees shall exclude—

"(i) any premium provided by an agency of the Federal Government or an agency of a State;

"(ii) any amount that is not in excess of the amount payable under policies in effect at the time of origination under section 203(c)(2)(A) of the National Housing Act (12 U.S.C. 1709(c)(2)(A)), provided that the premium, charge, or fee is required to be refundable on a pro-rated basis and the refund is automatically issued upon notification of the satisfaction of the underlying mortgage loan; and

"(iii) any premium paid by the consumer after closing.".

(b) ADJUSTMENT OF PERCENTAGE POINTS.—Section 103(aa)(2) of the Truth in Lending Act (15 U.S.C. 1602(aa)(2)) is amended by striking subparagraph (B) and inserting the following new subparagraph:

"(B) An increase or decrease under subparagraph (A)—

"(i) may not result in the number of percentage points referred to in paragraph (1)(A)(i)(I) being less than 6 percentage points or greater than 10 percentage points; and

"(ii) may not result in the number of percentage points referred to in paragraph (1)(A)(i)(II) being less than 8 percentage points or greater than 12 percentage points.".

(c) POINTS AND FEES DEFINED.—

(1) IN GENERAL.—Section 103(aa)(4) of the Truth in Lending Act (15 U.S.C. 1602(aa)(4)) is amended—

(A) by striking subparagraph (B) and inserting the following:

"(B) all compensation paid directly or indirectly by a consumer or creditor to a mortgage originator from any source, including a mortgage originator that is also the creditor in a table-funded transaction;";

(B) by redesignating subparagraph (D) as subparagraph (G); and

(C) by inserting after subparagraph (C) the following new subparagraphs:

"(D) premiums or other charges payable at or before closing for any credit life, credit disability, credit unemployment, or credit property insurance, or any other accident, loss-of-income, life or health insurance, or any payments directly or indirectly for any debt cancellation or suspension agreement or contract, except that insurance premiums or debt cancellation or suspension fees calculated and paid in full on a monthly basis shall not be considered financed by the creditor;

"(E) the maximum prepayment fees and penalties which may be charged or collected under the terms of the credit transaction;

"(F) all prepayment fees or penalties that are incurred by the consumer if the loan refinances a previous loan made or currently held by the same creditor or an affiliate of the creditor; and".

(2) CALCULATION OF POINTS AND FEES FOR OPEN-END CONSUMER CREDIT PLANS.—Section 103(aa) of the Truth in Lending Act (15 U.S.C. 1602(aa)) is amended—

(A) by redesignating paragraph (5) as paragraph (6); and

(B) by inserting after paragraph (4) the following new paragraph:

"(5) CALCULATION OF POINTS AND FEES FOR OPEN-END CONSUMER CREDIT PLANS.—In the case of open-end consumer credit plans, points and fees shall be calculated, for purposes of this section and section 129, by adding the total points and fees known at or before closing, including the maximum prepayment penalties which may be charged or collected under the terms of the credit transaction, plus the minimum additional fees the consumer would be required to pay to draw down an amount equal to the total credit line.".

(d) BONA FIDE DISCOUNT LOAN DISCOUNT POINTS.—Section 103 of the Truth in Lending Act (15 U.S.C. 1602) is amended by inserting after subsection (cc) (as added by section 1401) the following new subsection:

"(dd) BONA FIDE DISCOUNT POINTS AND PREPAYMENT PENALTIES.—For the purposes of determining the amount of points and fees for purposes of subsection (aa), either the amounts described in paragraph (1) or (2) of the following paragraphs, but not both, shall be excluded:

"(1) Up to and including 2 bona fide discount points payable by the consumer in connection with the mortgage, but only if the interest rate from which the mortgage's interest rate will be discounted does not exceed by more than 1 percentage point—

"(A) the average prime offer rate, as defined in section 129C; or

"(B) if secured by a personal property loan, the average rate on a loan in connection with which insurance is provided under title I of the National Housing Act (12 U.S.C. 1702 et seq.).

"(2) Unless 2 bona fide discount points have been excluded under paragraph (1), up to and including 1 bona fide discount point payable by the consumer in connection with the mortgage, but only if the interest rate from which the mortgage's interest rate will be discounted does not exceed by more than 2 percentage points—

"(A) the average prime offer rate, as defined in section 129C; or

"(B) if secured by a personal property loan, the average rate on a loan in connection with which insurance is provided under title I of the National Housing Act (12 U.S.C. 1702 et seq.).

"(3) For purposes of paragraph (1), the term 'bona fide discount points' means loan discount points which are knowingly paid by the consumer for the purpose of reducing, and which in fact result in a bona fide reduction of, the interest rate or time-price differential applicable to the mortgage.

"(4) Paragraphs (1) and (2) shall not apply to discount points used to purchase an interest rate reduction unless the amount of the interest rate reduction purchased is reasonably consistent with established industry norms and practices for secondary mortgage market transactions.".

[Explanation at ¶ 6605.]

[¶ 11,432] ACT SEC. 1432. AMENDMENTS TO EXISTING REQUIREMENTS FOR CERTAIN MORTGAGES.

(a) PREPAYMENT PENALTY PROVISIONS.—Section 129(c)(2) of the Truth in Lending Act (15 U.S.C. 1639(c)(2)) is hereby repealed.

(b) NO BALLOON PAYMENTS.—Section 129(e) of the Truth in Lending Act (15 U.S.C. 1639(e)) is amended to read as follows:

"(e) NO BALLOON PAYMENTS.—No high-cost mortgage may contain a scheduled payment that is more than twice as large as the average of earlier scheduled payments. This subsection shall not apply when the payment schedule is adjusted to the seasonal or irregular income of the consumer.".

[Explanation at ¶ 6610.]

[¶ 11,433] ACT SEC. 1433. ADDITIONAL REQUIREMENTS FOR CERTAIN MORTGAGES.

(a) ADDITIONAL REQUIREMENTS FOR CERTAIN MORTGAGES.—Section 129 of the Truth in Lending Act (15 U.S.C. 1639) is amended—

(1) by redesignating subsections (j), (k), (l) and (m) as subsections (n), (o), (p), and (q) respectively; and

(2) by inserting after subsection (i) the following new subsections:

"(j) RECOMMENDED DEFAULT.—No creditor shall recommend or encourage default on an existing loan or other debt prior to and in connection with the closing or planned closing of a high-cost mortgage that refinances all or any portion of such existing loan or debt.

"(k) LATE FEES.—

"(1) IN GENERAL.—No creditor may impose a late payment charge or fee in connection with a high-cost mortgage—

"(A) in an amount in excess of 4 percent of the amount of the payment past due;

"(B) unless the loan documents specifically authorize the charge or fee;

"(C) before the end of the 15-day period beginning on the date the payment is due, or in the case of a loan on which interest on each installment is paid in advance, before the end of the 30-day period beginning on the date the payment is due; or

"(D) more than once with respect to a single late payment.

"(2) COORDINATION WITH SUBSEQUENT LATE FEES.—If a payment is otherwise a full payment for the applicable period and is paid on its due date or within an applicable grace period, and the only delinquency or insufficiency of payment is attributable to any late fee or delinquency charge assessed on any earlier payment, no late fee or delinquency charge may be imposed on such payment.

"(3) FAILURE TO MAKE INSTALLMENT PAYMENT.—If, in the case of a loan agreement the terms of which provide that any payment shall first be applied to any past due principal balance, the consumer fails to make an installment payment and the consumer subsequently resumes making installment payments but has not paid all past due installments, the creditor may impose a separate late payment charge or fee for any principal due (without deduction due to late fees or related fees) until the default is cured.

"(l) ACCELERATION OF DEBT.—No high-cost mortgage may contain a provision which permits the creditor to accelerate the indebtedness, except when repayment of the loan has been accelerated by default in payment, or pursuant to a due-on-sale provision, or pursuant to a material violation of some other provision of the loan document unrelated to payment schedule.

"(m) RESTRICTION ON FINANCING POINTS AND FEES.—No creditor may directly or indirectly finance, in connection with any high-cost mortgage, any of the following:

"(1) Any prepayment fee or penalty payable by the consumer in a refinancing transaction if the creditor or an affiliate of the creditor is the noteholder of the note being refinanced.

"(2) Any points or fees.".

(b) PROHIBITIONS ON EVASIONS.—Section 129 of the Truth in Lending Act (15 U.S.C. 1639) is amended by inserting after subsection (q) (as so redesignated by subsection (a)(1)) the following new subsection:

"(r) PROHIBITIONS ON EVASIONS, STRUCTURING OF TRANSACTIONS, AND RECIPROCAL ARRANGEMENTS.—A creditor may not take any action in connection with a high-cost mortgage—

"(1) to structure a loan transaction as an open-end credit plan or another form of loan for the purpose and with the intent of evading the provisions of this title; or

"(2) to divide any loan transaction into separate parts for the purpose and with the intent of evading provisions of this title.".

(c) MODIFICATION OR DEFERRAL FEES.—Section 129 of the Truth in Lending Act (15 U.S.C. 1639) is amended by inserting after subsection (r) (as added by subsection (b) of this section) the following new subsection:

"(s) MODIFICATION AND DEFERRAL FEES PROHIBITED.—A creditor, successor in interest, assignee, or any agent of any of the above, may not charge a consumer any fee to modify, renew, extend, or amend a high-cost mortgage, or to defer any payment due under the terms of such mortgage.".

(d) PAYOFF STATEMENT.—Section 129 of the Truth in Lending Act (15 U.S.C. 1639) is amended by inserting after subsection (s) (as added by subsection (c) of this section) the following new subsection:

"(t) PAYOFF STATEMENT.—

"(1) FEES.—

"(A) IN GENERAL.—Except as provided in subparagraph (B), no creditor or servicer may charge a fee for informing or transmitting to any person the balance due to pay off the outstanding balance on a high-cost mortgage.

"(B) TRANSACTION FEE.—When payoff information referred to in subparagraph (A) is provided by facsimile transmission or by a courier service, a creditor or servicer may charge a processing fee to cover the cost of such transmission or service in an amount not to exceed an amount that is comparable to fees imposed for similar services provided in connection with consumer credit transactions that are secured by the consumer's principal dwelling and are not high-cost mortgages.

"(C) FEE DISCLOSURE.—Prior to charging a transaction fee as provided in subparagraph (B), a creditor or servicer shall disclose that payoff balances are available for free pursuant to subparagraph (A).

"(D) MULTIPLE REQUESTS.—If a creditor or servicer has provided payoff information referred to in subparagraph (A) without charge, other than the transaction fee allowed by subparagraph (B), on 4 occasions during a calendar year, the creditor or servicer may thereafter charge a reasonable fee for providing such information during the remainder of the calendar year.

"(2) PROMPT DELIVERY.—Payoff balances shall be provided within 5 business days after receiving a request by a consumer or a person authorized by the consumer to obtain such information.".

(e) PRE-LOAN COUNSELING REQUIRED.—Section 129 of the Truth in Lending Act (15 U.S.C. 1639) is amended by inserting after subsection t) (as added by subsection (d) of this section) the following new subsection:

"(u) PRE-LOAN COUNSELING.—

"(1) IN GENERAL.—A creditor may not extend credit to a consumer under a high-cost mortgage without first receiving certification from a counselor that is approved by the Secretary of Housing and Urban Development, or at the discretion of the Secretary, a State housing finance authority, that the consumer has received counseling on the advisability of the mortgage. Such counselor shall not be employed by the creditor or an affiliate of the creditor or be affiliated with the creditor.

"(2) DISCLOSURES REQUIRED PRIOR TO COUNSELING.—No counselor may certify that a consumer has received counseling on the advisability of the high-cost mortgage unless the counselor can verify that the consumer has received each statement required (in connection with such loan) by this section or the Real Estate Settlement Procedures Act of 1974 with respect to the transaction.

"(3) REGULATIONS.—The Board may prescribe such regulations as the Board determines to be appropriate to carry out the requirements of paragraph (1).".

(f) CORRECTIONS AND UNINTENTIONAL VIOLATIONS.—Section 129 of the Truth in Lending Act (15 U.S.C. 1639) is amended by inserting after subsection (u) (as added by subsection (e)) the following new subsection:

"(v) CORRECTIONS AND UNINTENTIONAL VIOLATIONS.—A creditor or assignee in a high-cost mortgage who, when acting in good faith, fails to comply with any requirement under this section will not be deemed to have violated such requirement if the creditor or assignee establishes that either—

"(1) within 30 days of the loan closing and prior to the institution of any action, the consumer is notified of or discovers the violation, appropriate restitution is made, and whatever adjustments are necessary are made to the loan to either, at the choice of the consumer—

"(A) make the loan satisfy the requirements of this chapter; or

"(B) in the case of a high-cost mortgage, change the terms of the loan in a manner beneficial to the consumer so that the loan will no longer be a high-cost mortgage; or

"(2) within 60 days of the creditor's discovery or receipt of notification of an unintentional violation or bona fide error and prior to the institution of any action, the consumer is notified of the compliance failure, appropriate restitution is made, and whatever adjustments are necessary are made to the loan to either, at the choice of the consumer—

"(A) make the loan satisfy the requirements of this chapter; or

"(B) in the case of a high-cost mortgage, change the terms of the loan in a manner beneficial so that the loan will no longer be a highcost mortgage.".

[Explanation at ¶ 6615.]

Subtitle D—Office of Housing Counseling

[¶ 11,441] ACT SEC. 1441. SHORT TITLE.

This subtitle may be cited as the "Expand and Preserve Home Ownership Through Counseling Act".

[Explanation at ¶ 6620.]

[¶ 11,442] ACT SEC. 1442. ESTABLISHMENT OF OFFICE OF HOUSING COUNSELING.

Section 4 of the Department of Housing and Urban Development Act (42 U.S.C. 3533) is amended by adding at the end the following new subsection:

"(g) OFFICE OF HOUSING COUNSELING.—

"(1) ESTABLISHMENT.—There is established, in the Department, the Office of Housing Counseling.

"(2) DIRECTOR.—There is established the position of Director of Housing Counseling. The Director shall be the head of the Office of Housing Counseling and shall be appointed by, and shall report to, the Secretary. Such position shall be a career-reserved position in the Senior Executive Service.

"(3) FUNCTIONS.—

"(A) IN GENERAL.—The Director shall have primary responsibility within the Department for all activities and matters relating to homeownership counseling and rental housing counseling, including—

"(i) research, grant administration, public outreach, and policy development relating to such counseling; and

"(ii) establishment, coordination, and administration of all regulations, requirements, standards, and performance measures under programs and laws administered by the Department that relate to housing counseling, homeownership counseling (including maintenance of homes), mortgage-related counseling (including home equity conversion mortgages and credit protection options to avoid foreclosure), and rental housing counseling, including the requirements, standards, and performance measures relating to housing counseling.

"(B) SPECIFIC FUNCTIONS.—The Director shall carry out the functions assigned to the Director and the Office under this section and any other provisions of law. Such functions shall include establishing rules necessary for—

"(i) the counseling procedures under section 106(g)(1) of the Housing and Urban Development Act of 1968 (12 U.S.C. 1701x(h)(1));

"(ii) carrying out all other functions of the Secretary under section 106(g) of the Housing and Urban Development Act of 1968, including the establishment, operation, and publication of the availability of the toll-free telephone number under paragraph (2) of such section;

"(iii) contributing to the distribution of home buying information booklets pursuant to section 5 of the Real Estate Settlement Procedures Act of 1974 (12 U.S.C. 2604);

"(iv) carrying out the certification program under section 106(e) of the Housing and Urban Development Act of 1968 (12 U.S.C. 1701x(e));

"(v) carrying out the assistance program under section 106(a)(4) of the Housing and Urban Development Act of 1968, including criteria for selection of applications to receive assistance;

"(vi) carrying out any functions regarding abusive, deceptive, or unscrupulous lending practices relating to residential mortgage loans that the Secretary considers appropriate, which shall include conducting the study under section 6 of the Expand and Preserve Home Ownership Through Counseling Act;

"(vii) providing for operation of the advisory committee established under paragraph (4) of this subsection;

"(viii) collaborating with community-based organizations with expertise in the field of housing counseling; and

"(ix) providing for the building of capacity to provide housing counseling services in areas that lack sufficient services, including underdeveloped areas that lack basic water and sewer systems, electricity services, and safe, sanitary housing.

"(4) ADVISORY COMMITTEE.—

"(A) IN GENERAL.—The Secretary shall appoint an advisory committee to provide advice regarding the carrying out of the functions of the Director.

"(B) MEMBERS.—Such advisory committee shall consist of not more than 12 individuals, and the membership of the committee shall equally represent the mortgage and real estate industry, including consumers and housing counseling agencies certified by the Secretary.

"(C) TERMS.—Except as provided in subparagraph (D), each member of the advisory committee shall be appointed for a term of 3 years. Members may be reappointed at the discretion of the Secretary.

"(D) TERMS OF INITIAL APPOINTEES.—As designated by the Secretary at the time of appointment, of the members first appointed to the advisory committee, 4 shall be appointed for a term of 1 year and 4 shall be appointed for a term of 2 years.

"(E) PROHIBITION OF PAY; TRAVEL EXPENSES.—Members of the advisory committee shall serve without pay, but shall receive travel expenses, including per diem in lieu of subsistence, in accordance with applicable provisions under subchapter I of chapter 57 of title 5, United States Code.

"(F) ADVISORY ROLE ONLY.—The advisory committee shall have no role in reviewing or awarding housing counseling grants.

"(5) SCOPE OF HOMEOWNERSHIP COUNSELING.—In carrying out the responsibilities of the Director, the Director shall ensure that homeownership counseling provided by, in connection with, or pursuant to any function, activity, or program of the Department addresses the entire process of homeownership, including the decision to purchase a home, the selection and purchase of a home, issues arising during or affecting the period of ownership of a home (including refinancing, default and foreclosure, and other financial decisions), and the sale or other disposition of a home.".

[Explanation at ¶ 6620.]

[¶ 11,443] ACT SEC. 1443. COUNSELING PROCEDURES.

(a) IN GENERAL.—Section 106 of the Housing and Urban Development Act of 1968 (12 U.S.C. 1701x) is amended by adding at the end the following new subsection:

"(g) PROCEDURES AND ACTIVITIES.—

"(1) COUNSELING PROCEDURES.—

"(A) IN GENERAL.—The Secretary shall establish, coordinate, and monitor the administration by the Department of Housing and Urban Development of the counseling procedures for homeownership counseling and rental housing counseling provided in connection with any program of the Department, including all requirements, standards, and performance measures that relate to homeownership and rental housing counseling.

"(B) HOMEOWNERSHIP COUNSELING.—For purposes of this subsection and as used in the provisions referred to in this subparagraph, the term 'homeownership counseling' means counseling related to homeownership and residential mortgage loans. Such term includes counseling related to homeownership and residential mortgage loans that is provided pursuant to—

"(i) section 105(a)(20) of the Housing and Community Development Act of 1974 (42 U.S.C. 5305(a)(20));

"(ii) in the United States Housing Act of 1937—

"(I) section 9(e) (42 U.S.C. 1437g(e));

"(II) section 8(y)(1)(D) (42 U.S.C. 1437f(y)(1)(D));

"(III) section 18(a)(4)(D) (42 U.S.C. 1437p(a)(4)(D));

"(IV) section 23(c)(4) (42 U.S.C. 1437u(c)(4));

"(V) section 32(e)(4) (42 U.S.C. 1437z-4(e)(4));

"(VI) section 33(d)(2)(B) (42 U.S.C. 1437z-5(d)(2)(B));

"(VII) sections 302(b)(6) and 303(b)(7) (42 U.S.C. 1437aaa-1(b)(6), 1437aaa-2(b)(7)); and

"(VIII) section 304(c)(4) (42 U.S.C. 1437aaa-3(c)(4));

"(iii) section 302(a)(4) of the American Homeownership and Economic Opportunity Act of 2000 (42 U.S.C. 1437f note);

"(iv) sections 233(b)(2) and 258(b) of the Cranston-Gonzalez National Affordable Housing Act (42 U.S.C. 12773(b)(2), 12808(b));

"(v) this section and section 101(e) of the Housing and Urban Development Act of 1968 (12 U.S.C. 1701x, 1701w(e));

"(vi) section 220(d)(2)(G) of the Low-Income Housing Preservation and Resident Homeownership Act of 1990 (12 U.S.C. 4110(d)(2)(G));

"(vii) sections 422(b)(6), 423(b)(7), 424(c)(4), 442(b)(6), and 443(b)(6) of the Cranston-Gonzalez National Affordable Housing Act (42 U.S.C. 12872(b)(6), 12873(b)(7), 12874(c)(4), 12892(b)(6), and 12893(b)(6));

"(viii) section 491(b)(1)(F)(iii) of the McKinney-Vento Homeless Assistance Act (42 U.S.C. 11408(b)(1)(F)(iii));

"(ix) sections 202(3) and 810(b)(2)(A) of the Native American Housing and Self-Determination Act of 1996 (25 U.S.C. 4132(3), 4229(b)(2)(A));

"(x) in the National Housing Act—

"(I) in section 203 (12 U.S.C. 1709), the penultimate undesignated paragraph of paragraph (2) of subsection (b), subsection (c)(2)(A), and subsection (r)(4);

"(II) subsections (a) and (c)(3) of section 237 (12 U.S.C. 1715z-2); and

"(III) subsections (d)(2)(B) and (m)(1) of section 255 (12 U.S.C. 1715z-20);

"(xi) section 502(h)(4)(B) of the Housing Act of 1949 (42 U.S.C. 1472(h)(4)(B));

"(xii) section 508 of the Housing and Urban Development Act of 1970 (12 U.S.C. 1701z-7); and

"(xiii) section 106 of the Energy Policy Act of 1992 (42 U.S.C. 12712 note).

"(C) RENTAL HOUSING COUNSELING.—For purposes of this subsection, the term 'rental housing counseling' means counseling related to rental of residential property, which may include counseling regarding future homeownership opportunities and providing referrals for renters and prospective renters to entities providing counseling and shall include counseling related to such topics that is provided pursuant to—

"(i) section 105(a)(20) of the Housing and Community Development Act of 1974 (42 U.S.C. 5305(a)(20));

"(ii) in the United States Housing Act of 1937—

"(I) section 9(e) (42 U.S.C. 1437g(e));

"(II) section 18(a)(4)(D) (42 U.S.C. 1437p(a)(4)(D));

"(III) section 23(c)(4) (42 U.S.C. 1437u(c)(4));

"(IV) section 32(e)(4) (42 U.S.C. 1437z-4(e)(4));

"(V) section 33(d)(2)(B) (42 U.S.C. 1437z-5(d)(2)(B)); and

"(VI) section 302(b)(6) (42 U.S.C. 1437aaa-1(b)(6));

"(iii) section 233(b)(2) of the Cranston-Gonzalez National Affordable Housing Act (42 U.S.C. 12773(b)(2));

"(iv) section 106 of the Housing and Urban Development Act of 1968 (12 U.S.C. 1701x);

"(v) section 422(b)(6) of the Cranston-Gonzalez National Affordable Housing Act (42 U.S.C. 12872(b)(6));

"(vi) section 491(b)(1)(F)(iii) of the McKinney-Vento Homeless Assistance Act (42 U.S.C. 11408(b)(1)(F)(iii));

"(vii) sections 202(3) and 810(b)(2)(A) of the Native American Housing and Self-Determination Act of 1996 (25 U.S.C. 4132(3), 4229(b)(2)(A)); and

"(viii) the rental assistance program under section 8 of the United States Housing Act of 1937 (42 U.S.C. 1437f).

"(2) STANDARDS FOR MATERIALS.—The Secretary, in consultation with the advisory committee established under subsection (g)(4) of the Department of Housing and Urban Development Act, shall establish standards for materials and forms to be used, as appropriate, by organizations providing homeownership counseling services, including any recipients of assistance pursuant to subsection (a)(4).

"(3) MORTGAGE SOFTWARE SYSTEMS.—

"(A) CERTIFICATION.—The Secretary shall provide for the certification of various computer software programs for consumers to use in evaluating different residential mortgage loan proposals. The Secretary shall require, for such certification, that the mortgage software systems take into account—

"(i) the consumer's financial situation and the cost of maintaining a home, including insurance, taxes, and utilities;

"(ii) the amount of time the consumer expects to remain in the home or expected time to maturity of the loan; and

"(iii) such other factors as the Secretary considers appropriate to assist the consumer in evaluating whether to pay points, to lock in an interest rate, to select an adjustable or fixed rate loan, to select a conventional or government-insured or guaranteed loan and to make other choices during the loan application process.

If the Secretary determines that available existing software is inadequate to assist consumers during the residential mortgage loan application process, the Secretary shall arrange for the development by private sector software companies of new mortgage software systems that meet the Secretary's specifications.

"(B) USE AND INITIAL AVAILABILITY.—Such certified computer software programs shall be used to supplement, not replace, housing counseling. The Secretary shall provide that such programs are initially used only in connection with the assistance of housing counselors certified pursuant to subsection (e).

"(C) AVAILABILITY.—After a period of initial availability under subparagraph (B) as the Secretary considers appropriate, the Secretary shall take reasonable steps to make mortgage software systems certified pursuant to this paragraph widely available through the Internet and at public locations, including public libraries, senior-citizen centers, public housing sites, offices of public housing agencies that administer rental housing assistance vouchers, and housing counseling centers.

"(D) BUDGET COMPLIANCE.—This paragraph shall be effective only to the extent that amounts to carry out this paragraph are made available in advance in appropriations Acts.

"(4) NATIONAL PUBLIC SERVICE MULTIMEDIA CAMPAIGNS TO PROMOTE HOUSING COUNSELING.—

"(A) IN GENERAL.—The Director of Housing Counseling shall develop, implement, and conduct national public service multimedia campaigns designed to make persons facing mortgage foreclosure, persons considering a subprime mortgage loan to purchase a home, elderly persons, persons who face language barriers, low-income persons, minorities, and other potentially vulnerable consumers aware that it is advisable, before seeking or maintaining a residential mortgage loan, to obtain homeownership counseling from an unbiased and reliable sources and that such homeownership counseling is available, including through programs sponsored by the Secretary of Housing and Urban Development.

"(B) CONTACT INFORMATION.—Each segment of the multimedia campaign under subparagraph (A) shall publicize the toll-free telephone number and website of the Department of Housing and Urban Development through which persons seeking housing counseling can locate a housing counseling agency in their State that is certified by the Secretary of Housing and Urban Development and can provide advice on buying a home, renting, defaults, foreclosures, credit issues, and reverse mortgages.

"(C) AUTHORIZATION OF APPROPRIATIONS.—There are authorized to be appropriated to the Secretary, not to exceed $3,000,000 for fiscal years 2009, 2010, and 2011, for the development, implementation, and conduct of national public service multimedia campaigns under this paragraph.

"(D) FORECLOSURE RESCUE EDUCATION PROGRAMS.—

"(i) IN GENERAL.—Ten percent of any funds appropriated pursuant to the authorization under subparagraph (C) shall be used by the Director of Housing Counseling to conduct an education program in areas that have a high density of foreclosure. Such program shall involve direct mailings to persons living in such areas describing—

"(I) tips on avoiding foreclosure rescue scams;

"(II) tips on avoiding predatory lending mortgage agreements;

"(III) tips on avoiding for-profit foreclosure counseling services; and

"(IV) local counseling resources that are approved by the Department of Housing and Urban Development.

"(ii) PROGRAM EMPHASIS.—In conducting the education program described under clause (i), the Director of Housing Counseling shall also place an emphasis on serving communities that have a high percentage of retirement communities or a high percentage of low-income minority communities.

"(iii) TERMS DEFINED.—For purposes of this subparagraph:

"(I) HIGH DENSITY OF FORECLOSURES.—An area has a 'high density of foreclosures' if such area is one of the metropolitan statistical areas (as that term is defined by the Director of the Office of Management and Budget) with the highest home foreclosure rates.

"(II) HIGH PERCENTAGE OF RETIREMENT COMMUNITIES.—An area has a 'high percentage of retirement communities' if such area is one of the metropolitan statistical areas (as that term is defined by the Director of the Office of Management and Budget) with the highest percentage of residents aged 65 or older.

"(III) HIGH PERCENTAGE OF LOW-INCOME MINORITY COMMUNITIES.—An area has a 'high percentage of low-income minority communities' if such area contains a higherthan-normal percentage of residents who are both minorities and low-income, as defined by the Director of Housing Counseling.

"(5) EDUCATION PROGRAMS.—The Secretary shall provide advice and technical assistance to States, units of general local government, and nonprofit organizations regarding the establishment and operation of, including assistance with the development of content and materials for, educational programs to inform and educate consumers, particularly those most vulnerable with respect to residential mortgage loans (such as elderly persons, persons facing language barriers, low-income persons, minorities, and other potentially vulnerable consumers), regarding home mortgages, mortgage refinancing, home equity loans, home repair loans, and where appropriate by region, any requirements and costs associated with obtaining flood or other disaster-specific insurance coverage.".

(b) CONFORMING AMENDMENTS TO GRANT PROGRAM FOR HOMEOWNERSHIP COUNSELING ORGANIZATIONS.—Section 106(c)(5)(A)(ii) of the Housing and Urban Development Act of 1968 (12 U.S.C. 1701x(c)(5)(A)(ii)) is amended—

(1) in subclause (III), by striking "and" at the end;

(2) in subclause (IV) by striking the period at the end and inserting "; and"; and

(3) by inserting after subclause (IV) the following new subclause:

"(V) notify the housing or mortgage applicant of the availability of mortgage software systems provided pursuant to subsection (g)(3).".

[Explanation at ¶ 6625.]

[¶ 11,444] ACT SEC. 1444. GRANTS FOR HOUSING COUNSELING ASSISTANCE.

Section 106(a) of the Housing and Urban Development Act of 1968 (12 U.S.C. 1701x(a)) is amended by adding at the end the following new paragraph:

"(4) HOMEOWNERSHIP AND RENTAL COUNSELING ASSISTANCE.—

"(A) IN GENERAL.—The Secretary shall make financial assistance available under this paragraph to HUD-approved housing counseling agencies and State housing finance agencies.

"(B) QUALIFIED ENTITIES.—The Secretary shall establish standards and guidelines for eligibility of organizations (including governmental and nonprofit organizations) to receive assistance under this paragraph, in accordance with subparagraph (D).

"(C) DISTRIBUTION.—Assistance made available under this paragraph shall be distributed in a manner that encourages efficient and successful counseling programs and that ensures adequate distribution of amounts for rural areas having traditionally low levels of access to such counseling services, including areas with insufficient access to the Internet. In distributing such assistance, the Secretary may give priority consideration to entities serving areas with the highest home foreclosure rates.

"(D) LIMITATION ON DISTRIBUTION OF ASSISTANCE.—

"(i) IN GENERAL.—None of the amounts made available under this paragraph shall be distributed to—

"(I) any organization which has been convicted for a violation under Federal law relating to an election for Federal office; or

"(II) any organization which employs applicable individuals.

"(ii) DEFINITION OF APPLICABLE INDIVIDUALS.—In this subparagraph, the term 'applicable individual' means an individual who—

"(I) is—

"(aa) employed by the organization in a permanent or temporary capacity;

"(bb) contracted or retained by the organization; or

"(cc) acting on behalf of, or with the express or apparent authority of, the organization; and

"(II) has been convicted for a violation under Federal law relating to an election for Federal office.

"(E) GRANTMAKING PROCESS.—In making assistance available under this paragraph, the Secretary shall consider appropriate ways of streamlining and improving the processes for grant application, review, approval, and award.

"(F) AUTHORIZATION OF APPROPRIATIONS.—There are authorized to be appropriated $45,000,000 for each of fiscal years 2009 through 2012 for—

"(i) the operations of the Office of Housing Counseling of the Department of Housing and Urban Development;

"(ii) the responsibilities of the Director of Housing Counseling under paragraphs (2) through (5) of subsection (g); and

"(iii) assistance pursuant to this paragraph for entities providing homeownership and rental counseling.".

[Explanation at ¶ 6630.]

[¶ 11,445] ACT SEC. 1445. REQUIREMENTS TO USE HUD-CERTIFIED COUNSELORS UNDER HUD PROGRAMS.

Section 106(e) of the Housing and Urban Development Act of 1968 (12 U.S.C. 1701x(e)) is amended—

(1) by striking paragraph (1) and inserting the following new paragraph:

"(1) REQUIREMENT FOR ASSISTANCE.—An organization may not receive assistance for counseling activities under subsection (a)(1)(iii), (a)(2), (a)(4), (c), or (d) of this section, or under section 101(e), unless the organization, or the individuals through which the organization provides such counseling, has been certified by the Secretary under this subsection as competent to provide such counseling.";

(2) in paragraph (2)—

(A) by inserting "and for certifying organizations" before the period at the end of the first sentence; and

(B) in the second sentence by striking "for certification" and inserting ", for certification of an organization, that each individual through which the organization provides counseling shall demonstrate, and, for certification of an individual,";

(3) in paragraph (3), by inserting "organizations and" before "individuals";

(4) by redesignating paragraph (3) as paragraph (5); and

(5) by inserting after paragraph (2) the following new paragraphs:

"(3) REQUIREMENT UNDER HUD PROGRAMS.—Any homeownership counseling or rental housing counseling (as such terms are defined in subsection (g)(1)) required under, or provided in connection with, any program administered by the Department of Housing and Urban Development shall be provided only by organizations or counselors certified by the Secretary under this subsection as competent to provide such counseling.

"(4) OUTREACH.—The Secretary shall take such actions as the Secretary considers appropriate to ensure that individuals and organizations providing homeownership or rental housing counseling are aware of the certification requirements and standards of this subsection and of the training and certification programs under subsection (f).".

[Explanation at ¶ 6635.]

[¶ 11,446] ACT SEC. 1446. STUDY OF DEFAULTS AND FORECLOSURES.

The Secretary of Housing and Urban Development shall conduct an extensive study of the root causes of default and foreclosure of home loans, using as much empirical data as are available. The study shall also examine the role of escrow accounts in helping prime and nonprime borrowers to avoid defaults and foreclosures, and the role of computer registries of mortgages, including those used for trading mortgage loans. Not later than 12 months after the date of the enactment of this Act, the Secretary shall submit to the Congress a preliminary report regarding the study. Not later than 24 months after such date of enactment, the Secretary shall submit a final report regarding the results of the study, which shall include any recommended legislation relating to the study, and recommendations for best practices and for a process to identify populations that need counseling the most.

[Explanation at ¶ 6640.]

[¶ 11,447] ACT SEC. 1447. DEFAULT AND FORECLOSURE DATABASE.

(a) ESTABLISHMENT.—The Secretary of Housing and Urban Development and the Director of the Bureau, in consultation with the Federal agencies responsible for regulation of banking and financial institutions involved in residential mortgage lending and servicing, shall establish and maintain a database of information on foreclosures and defaults on mortgage loans for one- to four-unit residential properties and shall make such information publicly available, subject to subsection (e).

(b) CENSUS TRACT DATA.—Information in the database may be collected, aggregated, and made available on a census tract basis.

(c) REQUIREMENTS.—Information collected and made available through the database shall include—

(1) the number and percentage of such mortgage loans that are delinquent by more than 30 days;

(2) the number and percentage of such mortgage loans that are delinquent by more than 90 days;

(3) the number and percentage of such properties that are real estate-owned;

(4) number and percentage of such mortgage loans that are in the foreclosure process;

(5) the number and percentage of such mortgage loans that have an outstanding principal obligation amount that is greater than the value of the property for which the loan was made; and

(6) such other information as the Secretary of Housing and Urban Development and the Director of the Bureau consider appropriate.

(d) RULE OF CONSTRUCTION.—Nothing in this section shall be construed to encourage discriminatory or unsound allocation of credit or lending policies or practices.

(e) PRIVACY AND CONFIDENTIALITY.—In establishing and maintaining the database described in subsection (a), the Secretary of Housing and Urban Development and the Director of the Bureau shall—

(1) be subject to the standards applicable to Federal agencies for the protection of the confidentiality of personally identifiable information and for data security and integrity;

(2) implement the necessary measures to conform to the standards for data integrity and security described in paragraph (1); and

(3) collect and make available information under this section, in accordance with paragraphs (5) and (6) of section 1022(c) and the rules prescribed under such paragraphs, in order to protect privacy and confidentiality.

[Explanation at ¶ 6645.]

[¶ 11,448] ACT SEC. 1448. DEFINITIONS FOR COUNSELING-RELATED PROGRAMS.

Section 106 of the Housing and Urban Development Act of 1968 (12 U.S.C. 1701x), as amended by the preceding provisions of this subtitle, is amended by adding at the end the following new subsection:

"(h) DEFINITIONS.—For purposes of this section:

"(1) NONPROFIT ORGANIZATION.—The term 'nonprofit organization' has the meaning given such term in section 104(5) of the Cranston-Gonzalez National Affordable Housing Act (42 U.S.C. 12704(5)), except that subparagraph (D) of such section shall not apply for purposes of this section.

"(2) STATE.—The term 'State' means each of the several States, the Commonwealth of Puerto Rico, the District of Columbia, the Commonwealth of the Northern Mariana Islands, Guam, the Virgin Islands, American Samoa, the Trust Territories of the Pacific, or any other possession of the United States.

"(3) UNIT OF GENERAL LOCAL GOVERNMENT.—The term 'unit of general local government' means any city, county, parish, town, township, borough, village, or other general purpose political subdivision of a State.

"(4) HUD-APPROVED COUNSELING AGENCY.—The term 'HUD-approved counseling agency' means a private or public nonprofit organization that is—

"(A) exempt from taxation under section 501(c) of the Internal Revenue Code of 1986; and

"(B) certified by the Secretary to provide housing counseling services.

"(5) STATE HOUSING FINANCE AGENCY.—The term 'State housing finance agency' means any public body, agency, or instrumentality specifically created under State statute that is authorised to finance activities designed to provide housing and related facilities throughout an entire State through land acquisition, construction, or rehabilitation.".

[Explanation at ¶ 6650.]

[¶ 11,449] ACT SEC. 1449. ACCOUNTABILITY AND TRANSPARENCY FOR GRANT RECIPIENTS.

Section 106 of the Housing and Urban Development Act of 1968 (12 U.S.C. 1701x), as amended by the preceding provisions of this subtitle, is amended by adding at the end the following:

"(i) ACCOUNTABILITY FOR RECIPIENTS OF COVERED ASSISTANCE.—

"(1) TRACKING OF FUNDS.—The Secretary shall—

"(A) develop and maintain a system to ensure that any organization or entity that receives any covered assistance uses all amounts of covered assistance in accordance with this section, the regulations issued under this section, and any requirements or conditions under which such amounts were provided; and

"(B) require any organization or entity, as a condition of receipt of any covered assistance, to agree to comply with such requirements regarding covered assistance as the Secretary shall establish, which shall include—

"(i) appropriate periodic financial and grant activity reporting, record retention, and audit requirements for the duration of the covered assistance to the organization or entity to ensure compliance with the limitations and requirements of this section, the regulations under this section, and any requirements or conditions under which such amounts were provided; and

"(ii) any other requirements that the Secretary determines are necessary to ensure appropriate administration and compliance.

"(2) MISUSE OF FUNDS.—If any organization or entity that receives any covered assistance is determined by the Secretary to have used any covered assistance in a manner that is materially in violation of this section, the regulations issued under this section, or any requirements or conditions under which such assistance was provided—

"(A) the Secretary shall require that, within 12 months after the determination of such misuse, the organization or entity shall reimburse the Secretary for such misused amounts and return to the Secretary any such amounts that remain unused or uncommitted for use; and

"(B) such organization or entity shall be ineligible, at any time after such determination, to apply for or receive any further covered assistance.

The remedies under this paragraph are in addition to any other remedies that may be available under law.

"(3) COVERED ASSISTANCE.—For purposes of this subsection, the term 'covered assistance' means any grant or other financial assistance provided under this section.".

[Explanation at ¶ 6655.]

[¶ 11,450] ACT SEC. 1450. UPDATING AND SIMPLIFICATION OF MORTGAGE INFORMATION BOOKLET.

Section 5 of the Real Estate Settlement Procedures Act of 1974 (12 U.S.C. 2604) is amended—

(1) in the section heading, by striking "SPECIAL" and inserting "HOME BUYING";

(2) by striking subsections (a) and (b) and inserting the following new subsections:

"(a) PREPARATION AND DISTRIBUTION.—The Director of the Bureau of Consumer Financial Protection (hereafter in this section referred to as the 'Director') shall prepare, at least once every 5 years, a booklet to help consumers applying for federally related mortgage loans to understand the nature and costs of real estate settlement services. The Director shall prepare the booklet in various languages and cultural styles, as the Director determines to be appropriate, so that the booklet is understandable and accessible to homebuyers of different ethnic and cultural backgrounds. The Director shall distribute such booklets to all lenders that make federally related mortgage loans. The Director shall also distribute to such lenders lists, organized by location, of homeownership counselors certified under section 106(e) of the Housing and Urban Development Act of 1968 (12 U.S.C. 1701x(e)) for use in complying with the requirement under subsection (c) of this section.

"(b) CONTENTS.—Each booklet shall be in such form and detail as the Director shall prescribe and, in addition to such other information as the Director may provide, shall include in plain and understandable language the following information:

"(1) A description and explanation of the nature and purpose of the costs incident to a real estate settlement or a federally related mortgage loan. The description and explanation shall provide general information about the mortgage process as well as specific information concerning, at a minimum—

"(A) balloon payments;

"(B) prepayment penalties;

"(C) the advantages of prepayment; and

"(D) the trade-off between closing costs and the interest rate over the life of the loan.

"(2) An explanation and sample of the uniform settlement statement required by section 4.

"(3) A list and explanation of lending practices, including those prohibited by the Truth in Lending Act or other applicable Federal law, and of other unfair practices and unreasonable or unnecessary charges to be avoided by the prospective buyer with respect to a real estate settlement.

"(4) A list and explanation of questions a consumer obtaining a federally related mortgage loan should ask regarding the loan, including whether the consumer will have the ability to repay the loan, whether the consumer sufficiently shopped for the loan, whether the loan terms include prepayment penalties or balloon payments, and whether the loan will benefit the borrower.

"(5) An explanation of the right of rescission as to certain transactions provided by sections 125 and 129 of the Truth in Lending Act.

"(6) A brief explanation of the nature of a variable rate mortgage and a reference to the booklet entitled 'Consumer Handbook on Adjustable Rate Mortgages', published by the Director, or to any suitable substitute of such booklet that the Director may subsequently adopt pursuant to such section.

"(7) A brief explanation of the nature of a home equity line of credit and a reference to the pamphlet required to be provided under section 127A of the Truth in Lending Act.

"(8) Information about homeownership counseling services made available pursuant to section 106(a)(4) of the Housing and Urban Development Act of 1968 (12 U.S.C. 1701x(a)(4)), a recommendation that the consumer use such services, and notification that a list of certified providers of homeownership counseling in the area, and their contact information, is available.

"(9) An explanation of the nature and purpose of escrow accounts when used in connection with loans secured by residential real estate and the requirements under section 10 of this Act regarding such accounts.

"(10) An explanation of the choices available to buyers of residential real estate in selecting persons to provide necessary services incidental to a real estate settlement.

"(11) An explanation of a consumer's responsibilities, liabilities, and obligations in a mortgage transaction.

"(12) An explanation of the nature and purpose of real estate appraisals, including the difference between an appraisal and a home inspection.

"(13) Notice that the Office of Housing of the Department of Housing and Urban Development has made publicly available a brochure regarding loan fraud and a World Wide Web address and toll-free telephone number for obtaining the brochure.

The booklet prepared pursuant to this section shall take into consideration differences in real estate settlement procedures that may exist among the several States and territories of the United States and among separate political subdivisions within the same State and territory.";

(3) in subsection (c), by inserting at the end the following new sentence: "Each lender shall also include with the booklet a reasonably complete or updated list of homeownership counselors who are certified pursuant to section 106(e) of the Housing and Urban Development Act of 1968 (12 U.S.C. 1701x(e)) and located in the area of the lender."; and

(4) in subsection (d), by inserting after the period at the end of the first sentence the following: "The lender shall provide the booklet in the version that is most appropriate for the person receiving it."

[Explanation at ¶ 6660.]

[¶ 11,451] ACT SEC. 1451. HOME INSPECTION COUNSELING.

(a) PUBLIC OUTREACH.—

(1) IN GENERAL.—The Secretary of Housing and Urban Development (in this section referred to as the "Secretary") shall take such actions as may be necessary to inform potential homebuyers of the availability and importance of obtaining an independent home inspection. Such actions shall include—

(A) publication of the HUD/FHA form HUD 92564-CN entitled "For Your Protection: Get a Home Inspection", in both English and Spanish languages;

(B) publication of the HUD/FHA booklet entitled "For Your Protection: Get a Home Inspection", in both English and Spanish languages;

(C) development and publication of a HUD booklet entitled "For Your Protection—Get a Home Inspection" that does not reference FHA-insured homes, in both English and Spanish languages; and

(D) publication of the HUD document entitled "Ten Important Questions To Ask Your Home Inspector", in both English and Spanish languages.

(2) AVAILABILITY.—The Secretary shall make the materials specified in paragraph (1) available for electronic access and, where appropriate, inform potential homebuyers of such availability through home purchase counseling public service announcements and toll-free telephone hotlines of the Department of Housing and Urban Development. The Secretary shall give special emphasis to reaching first-time and low-income homebuyers with these materials and efforts.

(3) UPDATING.—The Secretary may periodically update and revise such materials, as the Secretary determines to be appropriate.

(b) REQUIREMENT FOR FHA-APPROVED LENDERS.—Each mortgagee approved for participation in the mortgage insurance programs under title II of the National Housing Act shall provide prospective homebuyers, at first contact, whether upon pre-qualification, pre-approval, or initial application, the materials specified in subparagraphs (A), (B), and (D) of subsection (a)(1).

(c) REQUIREMENTS FOR HUD-APPROVED COUNSELING AGENCIES.—Each counseling agency certified pursuant by the Secretary to provide housing counseling services shall provide each of their clients, as part of the home purchase counseling process, the materials specified in subparagraphs (C) and (D) of subsection (a)(1).

(d) TRAINING.—Training provided the Department of Housing and Urban Development for housing counseling agencies, whether such training is provided directly by the Department or otherwise, shall include—

(1) providing information on counseling potential homebuyers of the availability and importance of getting an independent home inspection;

(2) providing information about the home inspection process, including the reasons for specific inspections such as radon and lead-based paint testing;

(3) providing information about advising potential homebuyers on how to locate and select a qualified home inspector; and

(4) review of home inspection public outreach materials of the Department.

[Explanation at ¶ 6665.]

[¶ 11,452] ACT SEC. 1452. WARNINGS TO HOMEOWNERS OF FORECLOSURE RESCUE SCAMS.

(a) ASSISTANCE TO NRC.—Notwithstanding any other provision of law, of any amounts made available for any fiscal year pursuant to section 106(a)(4)(F) of the Housing and Urban Development Act of 1968 (12 U.S.C. 1701x(a)(4)(F)) (as added by section 1444), 10 percent shall be used only for assistance to the Neighborhood Reinvestment Corporation for activities, in consultation with servicers of residential mortgage loans, to provide notice to borrowers under such loans who are delinquent with respect to payments due under such loans that makes such borrowers aware of the dangers of fraudulent activities associated with foreclosure.

(b) NOTICE.—The Neighborhood Reinvestment Corporation, in consultation with servicers of residential mortgage loans, shall use the amounts provided pursuant to subsection (a) to carry out activities to inform borrowers under residential mortgage loans—

(1) that the foreclosure process is complex and can be confusing;

(2) that the borrower may be approached during the foreclosure process by persons regarding saving their home and they should use caution in any such dealings;

(3) that there are Federal Government and nonprofit agencies that may provide information about the foreclosure process, including the Department of Housing and Urban Development;

(4) that they should contact their lender immediately, contact the Department of Housing and Urban Development to find a housing counseling agency certified by the Department to assist in avoiding foreclosure, or visit the Department's website regarding tips for avoiding foreclosure; and

(5) of the telephone number of the loan servicer or successor, the telephone number of the Department of Housing and Urban Development housing counseling line, and the Uniform Resource Locators (URLs) for the Department of Housing and Urban Development Web sites for housing counseling and for tips for avoiding foreclosure.

[Explanation at ¶ 6670.]

Subtitle E—Mortgage Servicing

[¶ 11,461] ACT SEC. 1461. ESCROW AND IMPOUND ACCOUNTS RELATING TO CERTAIN CONSUMER CREDIT TRANSACTIONS.

(a) IN GENERAL.—Chapter 2 of the Truth in Lending Act (15 U.S.C. 1631 et seq.) is amended by inserting after section 129C (as added by section 1411) the following new section:

"§ 129D. Escrow or impound accounts relating to certain consumer credit transactions

"(a) IN GENERAL.—Except as provided in subsection (b), (c), (d), or (e), a creditor, in connection with the consummation of a consumer credit transaction secured by a first lien on the principal dwelling of the consumer, other than a consumer credit transaction under an open end credit plan or a reverse mortgage, shall establish, before the consummation of such transaction, an escrow or impound account for the payment of taxes and hazard insurance, and, if applicable, flood insurance, mortgage insurance, ground rents, and any other required periodic payments or premiums with respect to the property or the loan terms, as provided in, and in accordance with, this section.

"(b) WHEN REQUIRED.—No impound, trust, or other type of account for the payment of property taxes, insurance premiums, or other purposes relating to the property may be required as a condition of a real property sale contract or a loan secured by a first deed of trust or mortgage on the principal dwelling of the consumer, other than a consumer credit transaction under an open end credit plan or a reverse mortgage, except when—

"(1) any such impound, trust, or other type of escrow or impound account for such purposes is required by Federal or State law;

"(2) a loan is made, guaranteed, or insured by a State or Federal governmental lending or insuring agency;

"(3) the transaction is secured by a first mortgage or lien on the consumer's principal dwelling having an original principal obligation amount that—

"(A) does not exceed the amount of the maximum limitation on the original principal obligation of mortgage in effect for a residence of the applicable size, as of the date such interest rate set, pursuant to the sixth sentence of section 305(a)(2) the Federal Home Loan Mortgage Corporation Act (12 U.S.C. 1454(a)(2)), and the annual percentage rate will exceed the average prime offer rate as defined in section 129C by 1.5 or more percentage points; or

"(B) exceeds the amount of the maximum limitation on the original principal obligation of mortgage in effect for a residence of the applicable size, as of the date such interest rate set, pursuant to the sixth sentence of section 305(a)(2) the Federal Home Loan Mortgage Corporation Act (12 U.S.C. 1454(a)(2)), and the annual percentage rate will exceed the average prime offer rate as defined in section 129C by 2.5 or more percentage points; or

"(4) so required pursuant to regulation.

"(c) EXEMPTIONS.—The Board may, by regulation, exempt from the requirements of subsection (a) a creditor that—

"(1) operates predominantly in rural or underserved areas;

"(2) together with all affiliates, has total annual mortgage loan originations that do not exceed a limit set by the Board;

"(3) retains its mortgage loan originations in portfolio; and

"(4) meets any asset size threshold and any other criteria the Board may establish, consistent with the purposes of this subtitle.

"(d) DURATION OF MANDATORY ESCROW OR IMPOUND ACCOUNT.—An escrow or impound account established pursuant to subsection (b) shall remain in existence for a minimum period of 5 years, beginning with the date of the consummation of the loan, unless and until—

"(1) such borrower has sufficient equity in the dwelling securing the consumer credit transaction so as to no longer be required to maintain private mortgage insurance;

"(2) such borrower is delinquent;

"(3) such borrower otherwise has not complied with the legal obligation, as established by rule; or

"(4) the underlying mortgage establishing the account is terminated.

"(e) LIMITED EXEMPTIONS FOR LOANS SECURED BY SHARES IN A COOPERATIVE OR IN WHICH AN ASSOCIATION MUST MAINTAIN A MASTER INSURANCE POLICY.—Escrow accounts need not be established for loans secured by shares in a cooperative. Insurance premiums need not be included in escrow accounts for loans secured by dwellings or units, where the borrower must join an association as a condition of ownership, and that association has an obligation to the dwelling or unit owners to maintain a master policy insuring the dwellings or units.

"(f) CLARIFICATION ON ESCROW ACCOUNTS FOR LOANS NOT MEETING STATUTORY TEST.—For mortgages not covered by the requirements of subsection (b), no provision of this section shall be construed as precluding the establishment of an impound, trust, or other type of account for the payment of property taxes, insurance premiums, or other purposes relating to the property—

"(1) on terms mutually agreeable to the parties to the loan;

"(2) at the discretion of the lender or servicer, as provided by the contract between the lender or servicer and the borrower; or

"(3) pursuant to the requirements for the escrowing of flood insurance payments for regulated lending institutions in section 102(d) of the Flood Disaster Protection Act of 1973.

"(g) ADMINISTRATION OF MANDATORY ESCROW OR IMPOUND ACCOUNTS.—

"(1) IN GENERAL.—Except as may otherwise be provided for in this title or in regulations prescribed by the Board, escrow or impound accounts established pursuant to subsection (b) shall be established in a federally insured depository institution or credit union.

"(2) ADMINISTRATION.—Except as provided in this section or regulations prescribed under this section, an escrow or impound account subject to this section shall be administered in accordance with—

"(A) the Real Estate Settlement Procedures Act of 1974 and regulations prescribed under such Act;

"(B) the Flood Disaster Protection Act of 1973 and regulations prescribed under such Act; and

"(C) the law of the State, if applicable, where the real property securing the consumer credit transaction is located.

"(3) APPLICABILITY OF PAYMENT OF INTEREST.—If prescribed by applicable State or Federal law, each creditor shall pay interest to the consumer on the amount held in any impound, trust, or escrow account that is subject to this section in the manner as prescribed by that applicable State or Federal law.

"(4) PENALTY COORDINATION WITH RESPA.—Any action or omission on the part of any person which constitutes a violation of the Real Estate Settlement Procedures Act of 1974 or any regulation prescribed under such Act for which the person has paid any fine, civil money penalty, or other damages shall not give rise to any additional fine, civil money penalty, or other damages under this section, unless the action or omission also constitutes a direct violation of this section.

"(h) DISCLOSURES RELATING TO MANDATORY ESCROW OR IMPOUND ACCOUNT.—In the case of any impound, trust, or escrow account that is required under subsection (b), the creditor shall disclose by written notice to the consumer at least 3 business days before the consummation of the consumer credit transaction giving rise to such account or in accordance with timeframes established in prescribed regulations the following information:

"(1) The fact that an escrow or impound account will be established at consummation of the transaction.

"(2) The amount required at closing to initially fund the escrow or impound account.

"(3) The amount, in the initial year after the consummation of the transaction, of the estimated taxes and hazard insurance, including flood insurance, if applicable, and any other required periodic payments or premiums that reflects, as appropriate, either the taxable assessed value of the real property securing the transaction, including the value of any improvements on the property or to be constructed on the property (whether or not such construction will be financed from the proceeds of the transaction) or the replacement costs of the property.

"(4) The estimated monthly amount payable to be escrowed for taxes, hazard insurance (including flood insurance, if applicable) and any other required periodic payments or premiums.

"(5) The fact that, if the consumer chooses to terminate the account in the future, the consumer will become responsible for the payment of all taxes, hazard insurance, and flood insurance, if applicable, as well as any other required periodic payments or premiums on the property unless a new escrow or impound account is established.

"(6) Such other information as the Board determines necessary for the protection of the consumer.

"(i) DEFINITIONS.—For purposes of this section, the following definitions shall apply:

"(1) FLOOD INSURANCE.—The term 'flood insurance' means flood insurance coverage provided under the national flood insurance program pursuant to the National Flood Insurance Act of 1968.

"(2) HAZARD INSURANCE.—The term 'hazard insurance' shall have the same meaning as provided for 'hazard insurance', 'casualty insurance', 'homeowner's insurance', or other similar term under the law of the State where the real property securing the consumer credit transaction is located.".

(b) EXEMPTIONS AND MODIFICATIONS.—The Board may prescribe rules that revise, add to, or subtract from the criteria of section 129D(b) of the Truth in Lending Act if the Board determines that such rules are in the interest of consumers and in the public interest.

(c) CLERICAL AMENDMENT.—The table of sections for chapter 2 of the Truth in Lending Act is amended by inserting after the item relating to section 129C (as added by section 1411) the following new item:

"129D. Escrow or impound accounts relating to certain consumer credit transactions.".

[Explanation at ¶ 6675.]

[¶ 11,462] ACT SEC. 1462. DISCLOSURE NOTICE REQUIRED FOR CONSUMERS WHO WAIVE ESCROW SERVICES.

Section 129D of the Truth in Lending Act (as added by section 1461) is amended by adding at the end the following new subsection:

"(j) DISCLOSURE NOTICE REQUIRED FOR CONSUMERS WHO WAIVE ESCROW SERVICES.—

"(1) IN GENERAL.—If—

"(A) an impound, trust, or other type of account for the payment of property taxes, insurance premiums, or other purposes relating to real property securing a consumer credit transaction is not established in connection with the transaction; or

"(B) a consumer chooses, and provides written notice to the creditor or servicer of such choice, at any time after such an account is established in connection with any such transaction and in accordance with any statute, regulation, or contractual agreement, to close such account,

the creditor or servicer shall provide a timely and clearly written disclosure to the consumer that advises the consumer of the responsibilities of the consumer and implications for the consumer in the absence of any such account.

"(2) DISCLOSURE REQUIREMENTS.—Any disclosure provided to a consumer under paragraph (1) shall include the following:

"(A) Information concerning any applicable fees or costs associated with either the nonestablishment of any such account at the time of the transaction, or any subsequent closure of any such account.

"(B) A clear and prominent statement that the consumer is responsible for personally and directly paying the non-escrowed items, in addition to paying the mortgage loan payment, in the absence of any such account, and the fact that the costs for taxes, insurance, and related fees can be substantial.

"(C) A clear explanation of the consequences of any failure to pay non-escrowed items, including the possible requirement for the forced placement of insurance by the creditor or servicer and the potentially higher cost (including any potential commission payments to the servicer) or reduced coverage for the consumer in the event of any such creditor-placed insurance.

"(D) Such other information as the Board determines necessary for the protection of the consumer.".

[Explanation at ¶ 6680.]

[¶ 11,463] ACT SEC. 1463. REAL ESTATE SETTLEMENT PROCEDURES ACT OF 1974 AMENDMENTS.

(a) SERVICER PROHIBITIONS.—Section 6 of the Real Estate Settlement Procedures Act of 1974 (12 U.S.C. 2605) is amended by adding at the end the following new subsections:

"(k) SERVICER PROHIBITIONS.—

"(1) IN GENERAL.—A servicer of a federally related mortgage shall not—

"(A) obtain force-placed hazard insurance unless there is a reasonable basis to believe the borrower has failed to comply with the loan contract's requirements to maintain property insurance;

"(B) charge fees for responding to valid qualified written requests (as defined in regulations which the Bureau of Consumer Financial Protection shall prescribe) under this section;

"(C) fail to take timely action to respond to a borrower's requests to correct errors relating to allocation of payments, final balances for purposes of paying off the loan, or avoiding foreclosure, or other standard servicer's duties;

"(D) fail to respond within 10 business days to a request from a borrower to provide the identity, address, and other relevant contact information about the owner or assignee of the loan; or

"(E) fail to comply with any other obligation found by the Bureau of Consumer Financial Protection, by regulation, to be appropriate to carry out the consumer protection purposes of this Act.

"(2) FORCE-PLACED INSURANCE DEFINED.—For purposes of this subsection and subsections (1) and (m), the term 'force-placed insurance' means hazard insurance coverage obtained by a servicer of a federally related mortgage when the borrower has failed to maintain or renew hazard insurance on such property as required of the borrower under the terms of the mortgage.

"(l) REQUIREMENTS FOR FORCE-PLACED INSURANCE.—A servicer of a federally related mortgage shall not be construed as having a reasonable basis for obtaining force-placed insurance unless the requirements of this subsection have been met.

"(1) WRITTEN NOTICES TO BORROWER.—A servicer may not impose any charge on any borrower for force-placed insurance with respect to any property securing a federally related mortgage unless—

"(A) the servicer has sent, by first-class mail, a written notice to the borrower containing—

"(i) a reminder of the borrower's obligation to maintain hazard insurance on the property securing the federally related mortgage;

"(ii) a statement that the servicer does not have evidence of insurance coverage of such property;

"(iii) a clear and conspicuous statement of the procedures by which the borrower may demonstrate that the borrower already has insurance coverage; and

"(iv) a statement that the servicer may obtain such coverage at the borrower's expense if the borrower does not provide such demonstration of the borrower's existing coverage in a timely manner;

"(B) the servicer has sent, by first-class mail, a second written notice, at least 30 days after the mailing of the notice under subparagraph (A) that contains all the information described in each clause of such subparagraph; and

"(C) the servicer has not received from the borrower any demonstration of hazard insurance coverage for the property securing the mortgage by the end of the 15-day period beginning on the date the notice under subparagraph (B) was sent by the servicer.

"(2) SUFFICIENCY OF DEMONSTRATION.—A servicer of a federally related mortgage shall accept any reasonable form of written confirmation from a borrower of existing insurance coverage, which shall include the existing insurance policy number along with the identity of, and contact information for, the insurance company or agent, or as otherwise required by the Bureau of Consumer Financial Protection.

"(3) TERMINATION OF FORCE-PLACED INSURANCE.—Within 15 days of the receipt by a servicer of confirmation of a borrower's existing insurance coverage, the servicer shall—

"(A) terminate the force-placed insurance; and

"(B) refund to the consumer all force-placed insurance premiums paid by the borrower during any period during which the borrower's insurance coverage and the force-placed insurance coverage were each in effect, and any related fees charged to the consumer's account with respect to the force-placed insurance during such period.

"(4) CLARIFICATION WITH RESPECT TO FLOOD DISASTER PROTECTION ACT.—No provision of this section shall be construed as prohibiting a servicer from providing simultaneous or concurrent notice of a lack of flood insurance pursuant to section 102(e) of the Flood Disaster Protection Act of 1973.

"(m) LIMITATIONS ON FORCE-PLACED INSURANCE CHARGES.—All charges, apart from charges subject to State regulation as the business of insurance, related to force-placed insurance imposed on the borrower by or through the servicer shall be bona fide and reasonable.".

(b) INCREASE IN PENALTY AMOUNTS.—Section 6(f) of the Real Estate Settlement Procedures Act of 1974 (12 U.S.C. 2605(f)) is amended—

(1) in paragraphs (1)(B) and (2)(B), by striking "$1,000" each place such term appears and inserting "$2,000"; and

(2) in paragraph (2)(B)(i), by striking "$500,000" and inserting "$1,000,000".

(c) DECREASE IN RESPONSE TIMES.—Section 6(e) of the Real Estate Settlement Procedures Act of 1974 (12 U.S.C. 2605(e)) is amended—

(1) in paragraph (1)(A), by striking "20 days" and inserting "5 days";

(2) in paragraph (2), by striking "60 days" and inserting "30 days"; and

(3) by adding at the end the following new paragraph:

"(4) LIMITED EXTENSION OF RESPONSE TIME.—The 30-day period described in paragraph (2) may be extended for not more than 15 days if, before the end of such 30-day period, the servicer notifies the borrower of the extension and the reasons for the delay in responding.".

(d) PROMPT REFUND OF ESCROW ACCOUNTS UPON PAYOFF.—Section 6(g) of the Real Estate Settlement Procedures Act of 1974 (12 U.S.C. 2605(g)) is amended by adding at the end the following new sentence: "Any balance in any such account that is within the servicer's control at the time the loan is paid off shall be promptly returned to the borrower within 20 business days or credited to a similar account for a new mortgage loan to the borrower with the same lender.".

[Explanation at ¶ 6685.]

[¶ 11,464] ACT SEC. 1464. TRUTH IN LENDING ACT AMENDMENTS.

(a) REQUIREMENTS FOR PROMPT CREDITING OF HOME LOAN PAYMENTS.—Chapter 2 of the Truth in Lending Act (15 U.S.C. 1631 et seq.) is amended by inserting after section 129E (as added by section 1472) the following new section:

"§ 129F. Requirements for prompt crediting of home loan payments

"(a) IN GENERAL.—In connection with a consumer credit transaction secured by a consumer's principal dwelling, no servicer shall fail to credit a payment to the consumer's loan account as of the date of receipt, except when a delay in crediting does not result in any charge to the consumer or in the reporting of negative information to a consumer reporting agency, except as required in subsection (b).

"(b) EXCEPTION.—If a servicer specifies in writing requirements for the consumer to follow in making payments, but accepts a payment that does not conform to the requirements, the servicer shall credit the payment as of 5 days after receipt.".

(b) REQUESTS FOR PAYOFF AMOUNTS.—Chapter 2 of the Truth in Lending Act (15 U.S.C. 1631 et seq.), as amended by this title, is amended by inserting after section 129F (as added by subsection (a)) the following new section:

"§ 129G. Requests for payoff amounts of home loan

"A creditor or servicer of a home loan shall send an accurate payoff balance within a reasonable time, but in no case more than 7 business days, after the receipt of a written request for such balance from or on behalf of the borrower.".

[Explanation at ¶ 6690.]

[¶ 11,465] ACT SEC. 1465. ESCROWS INCLUDED IN REPAYMENT ANALYSIS.

Section 128(b) of the Truth in Lending Act (15 U.S.C. 1638(b)) is amended by adding at the end the following new paragraph:

"(4) REPAYMENT ANALYSIS REQUIRED TO INCLUDE ESCROW PAYMENTS.—

"(A) IN GENERAL.—In the case of any consumer credit transaction secured by a first mortgage or lien on the principal dwelling of the consumer, other than a consumer credit transaction under an open end credit plan or a reverse mortgage, for which an impound, trust, or other type of account has been or will be established in connection with the transaction for the payment of property taxes, hazard and flood (if any) insurance premiums, or other periodic payments or premiums with respect to the property, the information required to be provided under subsection (a) with respect to the number, amount, and due dates or period of payments scheduled to repay the total of payments shall take into account the amount of any monthly payment to such account for each such repayment in accordance with section 10(a)(2) of the Real Estate Settlement Procedures Act of 1974.

"(B) ASSESSMENT VALUE.—The amount taken into account under subparagraph (A) for the payment of property taxes, hazard and flood (if any) insurance premiums, or other periodic payments or premiums with respect to the property shall reflect the taxable assessed value of the real property securing the transaction after the consummation of the transaction, including the value of any improvements on the property or to be constructed on the property (whether or not such construction will be financed from the proceeds of the transaction), if known, and the replacement costs of the property for hazard insurance, in the initial year after the transaction.".

[Explanation at ¶ 6695.]

Subtitle F—Appraisal Activities

[¶ 11,471] ACT SEC. 1471. PROPERTY APPRAISAL REQUIREMENTS.

Chapter 2 of the Truth in Lending Act (15 U.S.C. 1631 et seq.) is amended by inserting after 129G (as added by section 1464(b)) the following new section:

"§ 129H. Property appraisal requirements

"(a) IN GENERAL.—A creditor may not extend credit in the form of a higher-risk mortgage to any consumer without first obtaining a written appraisal of the property to be mortgaged prepared in accordance with the requirements of this section.

"(b) APPRAISAL REQUIREMENTS.—

"(1) PHYSICAL PROPERTY VISIT.—Subject to the rules prescribed under paragraph (4), an appraisal of property to be secured by a higher-risk mortgage does not meet the requirement of this section unless it is performed by a certified or licensed appraiser who conducts a physical property visit of the interior of the mortgaged property.

"(2) SECOND APPRAISAL UNDER CERTAIN CIRCUMSTANCES.—

"(A) IN GENERAL.—If the purpose of a higher-risk mortgage is to finance the purchase or acquisition of the mortgaged property from a person within 180 days of the purchase or acquisition of such property by that person at a price that was lower than the current sale price of the property, the creditor shall obtain a second appraisal from a different certified or licensed appraiser. The second appraisal shall include an analysis of the difference in sale prices, changes in market conditions, and any improvements made to the property between the date of the previous sale and the current sale.

"(B) NO COST TO APPLICANT.—The cost of any second appraisal required under subparagraph (A) may not be charged to the applicant.

"(3) CERTIFIED OR LICENSED APPRAISER DEFINED.—For purposes of this section, the term 'certified or licensed appraiser' means a person who—

"(A) is, at a minimum, certified or licensed by the State in which the property to be appraised is located; and

"(B) performs each appraisal in conformity with the Uniform Standards of Professional Appraisal Practice and title XI of the Financial Institutions Reform, Recovery, and Enforcement Act of 1989, and the regulations prescribed under such title, as in effect on the date of the appraisal.

"(4) REGULATIONS.—

"(A) IN GENERAL.—The Board, the Comptroller of the Currency, the Federal Deposit Insurance Corporation, the National Credit Union Administration Board, the Federal Housing Finance Agency, and the Bureau shall jointly prescribe regulations to implement this section.

"(B) EXEMPTION.—The agencies listed in subparagraph (A) may jointly exempt, by rule, a class of loans from the requirements of this subsection or subsection (a) if the agencies determine that the exemption is in the public interest and promotes the safety and soundness of creditors.

"(c) FREE COPY OF APPRAISAL.—A creditor shall provide 1 copy of each appraisal conducted in accordance with this section in connection with a higher-risk mortgage to the applicant without charge, and at least 3 days prior to the transaction closing date.

"(d) CONSUMER NOTIFICATION.—At the time of the initial mortgage application, the applicant shall be provided with a statement by the creditor that any appraisal prepared for the mortgage is for the sole use of the creditor, and that the applicant may choose to have a separate appraisal conducted at the expense of the applicant.

"(e) VIOLATIONS.—In addition to any other liability to any person under this title, a creditor found to have willfully failed to obtain an appraisal as required in this section shall be liable to the applicant or borrower for the sum of $2,000.

"(f) HIGHER-RISK MORTGAGE DEFINED.—For purposes of this section, the term 'higher-risk mortgage' means a residential mortgage loan, other than a reverse mortgage loan that is a qualified mortgage, as defined in section 129C, secured by a principal dwelling—

"(1) that is not a qualified mortgage, as defined in section 129C; and

"(2) with an annual percentage rate that exceeds the average prime offer rate for a comparable transaction, as defined in section 129C, as of the date the interest rate is set—

"(A) by 1.5 or more percentage points, in the case of a first lien residential mortgage loan having an original principal obligation amount that does not exceed the amount of the maximum limitation on the original principal obligation of mortgage in effect for a residence of the applicable size, as of the date of such interest rate set, pursuant to the sixth sentence of section 305(a)(2) the Federal Home Loan Mortgage Corporation Act (12 U.S.C. 1454(a)(2));

"(B) by 2.5 or more percentage points, in the case of a first lien residential mortgage loan having an original principal obligation amount that exceeds the amount of the maximum limitation on the original principal obligation of mortgage in effect for a residence of the applicable size, as of the date of such interest rate set, pursuant to the sixth sentence of section 305(a)(2) the Federal Home Loan Mortgage Corporation Act (12 U.S.C. 1454(a)(2)); and

"(C) by 3.5 or more percentage points for a subordinate lien residential mortgage loan.".

[Explanation at ¶ 6700.]

[¶ 11,472] ACT SEC. 1472. APPRAISAL INDEPENDENCE REQUIREMENTS.

(a) IN GENERAL.—Chapter 2 of the Truth in Lending Act (15 U.S.C. 1631 et seq.) is amended by inserting after section 129D (as added by section 1461(a)) the following new section:

"§ 129E. Appraisal independence requirements

"(a) IN GENERAL.—It shall be unlawful, in extending credit or in providing any services for a consumer credit transaction secured by the principal dwelling of the consumer, to engage in any act or practice that violates appraisal independence as described in or pursuant to regulations prescribed under this section.

"(b) APPRAISAL INDEPENDENCE.—For purposes of subsection (a), acts or practices that violate appraisal independence shall include—

"(1) any appraisal of a property offered as security for repayment of the consumer credit transaction that is conducted in connection with such transaction in which a person with an interest in the underlying transaction compensates, coerces, extorts, colludes, instructs, induces, bribes, or intimidates a person, appraisal management company, firm, or other entity conducting or involved in an appraisal, or attempts, to compensate, coerce, extort, collude, instruct, induce, bribe, or intimidate such a person, for the purpose of causing the appraised value assigned, under the appraisal, to the property to be based on any factor other than the independent judgment of the appraiser;

"(2) mischaracterizing, or suborning any mischaracterization of, the appraised value of the property securing the extension of the credit;

"(3) seeking to influence an appraiser or otherwise to encourage a targeted value in order to facilitate the making or pricing of the transaction; and

"(4) withholding or threatening to withhold timely payment for an appraisal report or for appraisal services rendered when the appraisal report or services are provided for in accordance with the contract between the parties.

"(c) EXCEPTIONS.—The requirements of subsection (b) shall not be construed as prohibiting a mortgage lender, mortgage broker, mortgage banker, real estate broker, appraisal management company, employee of an appraisal management company, consumer, or any other person with an interest in a real estate transaction from asking an appraiser to undertake 1 or more of the following:

"(1) Consider additional, appropriate property information, including the consideration of additional comparable properties to make or support an appraisal.

"(2) Provide further detail, substantiation, or explanation for the appraiser's value conclusion.

"(3) Correct errors in the appraisal report.

"(d) PROHIBITIONS ON CONFLICTS OF INTEREST.—No certified or licensed appraiser conducting, and no appraisal management company procuring or facilitating, an appraisal in connection with a consumer credit transaction secured by the principal dwelling of a consumer may have a direct or indirect interest, financial or otherwise, in the property or transaction involving the appraisal.

"(e) MANDATORY REPORTING.—Any mortgage lender, mortgage broker, mortgage banker, real estate broker, appraisal management company, employee of an appraisal management company, or any other person involved in a real estate transaction involving an appraisal in connection with a consumer credit transaction secured by the principal dwelling of a consumer who has a reasonable basis to believe an appraiser is failing to comply with the Uniform Standards of Professional Appraisal Practice, is violating applicable laws, or is otherwise engaging in unethical or unprofessional conduct, shall refer the matter to the applicable State appraiser certifying and licensing agency.

"(f) NO EXTENSION OF CREDIT.—In connection with a consumer credit transaction secured by a consumer's principal dwelling, a creditor who knows, at or before loan consummation, of a violation of the appraisal independence standards established in subsections (b) or (d) shall not extend credit based on such appraisal unless the creditor documents that the creditor has acted with reasonable diligence to determine that the appraisal does not materially misstate or misrepresent the value of such dwelling.

"(g) RULES AND INTERPRETIVE GUIDELINES.—

"(1) IN GENERAL.—Except as provided under paragraph (2), the Board, the Comptroller of the Currency, the Federal Deposit Insurance Corporation, the National Credit Union Administration Board, the Federal Housing Finance Agency, and the Bureau may jointly issue rules, interpretive guidelines, and general statements of policy with respect to acts or practices that violate appraisal independence in the provision of mortgage lending services for a consumer credit transaction secured by the principal dwelling of the consumer and mortgage brokerage services for such a transaction, within the meaning of subsections (a), (b), (c), (d), (e), (f), (h), and (i).

"(2) INTERIM FINAL REGULATIONS.—The Board shall, for purposes of this section, prescribe interim final regulations no later than 90 days after the date of enactment of this section defining with specificity acts or practices that violate appraisal independence in the provision of mortgage lending services for a consumer credit transaction secured by the principal dwelling of the consumer or mortgage brokerage services for such a transaction and defining any terms in this section or such regulations. Rules prescribed by the Board under

Act Sec. 1472(a) ¶11,472

this paragraph shall be deemed to be rules prescribed by the agencies jointly under paragraph (1).

"(h) APPRAISAL REPORT PORTABILITY.—Consistent with the requirements of this section, the Board, the Comptroller of the Currency, the Federal Deposit Insurance Corporation, the National Credit Union Administration Board, the Federal Housing Finance Agency, and the Bureau may jointly issue regulations that address the issue of appraisal report portability, including regulations that ensure the portability of the appraisal report between lenders for a consumer credit transaction secured by a 1-4 unit single family residence that is the principal dwelling of the consumer, or mortgage brokerage services for such a transaction.

"(i) CUSTOMARY AND REASONABLE FEE.—

"(1) IN GENERAL.—Lenders and their agents shall compensate fee appraisers at a rate that is customary and reasonable for appraisal services performed in the market area of the property being appraised. Evidence for such fees may be established by objective third-party information, such as government agency fee schedules, academic studies, and independent private sector surveys. Fee studies shall exclude assignments ordered by known appraisal management companies.

"(2) FEE APPRAISER DEFINITION.—For purposes of this section, the term 'fee appraiser' means a person who is not an employee of the mortgage loan originator or appraisal management company engaging the appraiser and is—

"(A) a State licensed or certified appraiser who receives a fee for performing an appraisal and certifies that the appraisal has been prepared in accordance with the Uniform Standards of Professional Appraisal Practice; or

"(B) a company not subject to the requirements of section 1124 of the Financial Institutions Reform, Recovery, and Enforcement Act of 1989 (12 U.S.C. 3331 et seq.) that utilizes the services of State licensed or certified appraisers and receives a fee for performing appraisals in accordance with the Uniform Standards of Professional Appraisal Practice.

"(3) EXCEPTION FOR COMPLEX ASSIGNMENTS.—In the case of an appraisal involving a complex assignment, the customary and reasonable fee may reflect the increased time, difficulty, and scope of the work required for such an appraisal and include an amount over and above the customary and reasonable fee for non-complex assignments.

"(j) SUNSET.—Effective on the date the interim final regulations are promulgated pursuant to subsection (g), the Home Valuation Code of Conduct announced by the Federal Housing Finance Agency on December 23, 2008, shall have no force or effect.

"(k) PENALTIES.—

"(1) FIRST VIOLATION.—In addition to the enforcement provisions referred to in section 130, each person who violates this section shall forfeit and pay a civil penalty of not more than $10,000 for each day any such violation continues.

"(2) SUBSEQUENT VIOLATIONS.—In the case of any person on whom a civil penalty has been imposed under paragraph (1), paragraph (1) shall be applied by substituting '$20,000' for '$10,000' with respect to all subsequent violations.

"(3) ASSESSMENT.—The agency referred to in subsection (a) or (c) of section 108 with respect to any person described in paragraph (1) shall assess any penalty under this subsection to which such person is subject.".

(b) CLERICAL AMENDMENT.—The table of sections for chapter 2 of the Truth in Lending Act is amended by inserting after the item relating to section 129D (as added by section 1461(c)) the following new items:

"129E. Appraisal independence requirements.

"129F. Requirements for prompt crediting of home loan payments.

"129G. Requests for payoff amounts of home loan.

"129H. Property appraisal requirements.".

(c) DEFERENCE.—Section 105 of the Truth in Lending Act (15 U.S.C. 1604) is amended by adding at the end the following:

"(h) DEFERENCE.—Notwithstanding any power granted to any Federal agency under this title, the deference that a court affords to the Bureau with respect to a determination made by the Bureau relating to the meaning or interpretation of any provision of this title, other than section 129E or 129H, shall be applied as if the Bureau were the only agency authorized to apply, enforce, interpret, or administer the provisions of this title.".

(d) CONFORMING AMENDMENTS IN TITLE X NOT APPLICABLE TO SECTIONS 129E AND 129H.—Notwithstanding section 1099A, the term "Board" in sections 129E and 129H, as added by this subtitle, shall not be substituted by the term "Bureau".

[Explanation at ¶ 6705.]

[¶ 11,473] ACT SEC. 1473. AMENDMENTS RELATING TO APPRAISAL SUBCOMMITTEE OF FFIEC, APPRAISER INDEPENDENCE MONITORING, APPROVED APPRAISER EDUCATION, APPRAISAL MANAGEMENT COMPANIES, APPRAISER COMPLAINT HOTLINE, AUTOMATED VALUATION MODELS, AND BROKER PRICE OPINIONS.

(a) THRESHOLD LEVELS.—Section 1112(b) of the Financial Institutions Reform, Recovery, and Enforcement Act of 1989 (12 U.S.C. 3341(b)) is amended by inserting before the period the following: ", and receives concurrence from the Bureau of Consumer Financial Protection that such threshold level provides reasonable protection for consumers who purchase 1-4 unit single-family residences".

(b) ANNUAL REPORT OF APPRAISAL SUBCOMMITTEE.—Section 1103(a) of the Financial Institutions Reform, Recovery, and Enforcement Act of 1989 (12 U.S.C. 3332(a)) is amended at the end by inserting the following new paragraph:

"(5) transmit an annual report to the Congress not later than June 15 of each year that describes the manner in which each function assigned to the Appraisal Subcommittee has been carried out during the preceding year. The report shall also detail the activities of the Appraisal Subcommittee, including the results of all audits of State appraiser regulatory agencies, and provide an accounting of disapproved actions and warnings taken in the previous year, including a description of the conditions causing the disapproval and actions taken to achieve compliance.".

(c) OPEN MEETINGS.—Section 1104(b) of the Financial Institutions Reform, Recovery, and Enforcement Act of 1989 (12 U.S.C. 3333(b)) is amended—

(1) by inserting "in public session after notice in the Federal Register, but may close certain portions of these meetings related to personnel and review of preliminary State audit reports," after "shall meet"; and

(2) by adding after the final period the following: "The subject matter discussed in any closed or executive session shall be described in the Federal Register notice of the meeting.".

(d) REGULATIONS.—Section 1106 of the Financial Institutions Reform, Recovery, and Enforcement Act of 1989 (12 U.S.C. 3335) is amended—

(1) by inserting "prescribe regulations in accordance with chapter 5 of title 5, United States Code (commonly referred to as the Administrative Procedures Act) after notice and opportunity for comment," after "hold hearings"; and

(2) at the end by inserting "Any regulations prescribed by the Appraisal Subcommittee shall (unless otherwise provided in this title) be limited to the following functions: temporary practice, national registry, information sharing, and enforcement. For purposes of prescribing regulations, the Appraisal Subcommittee shall establish an advisory committee of industry participants, including appraisers, lenders, consumer advocates, real estate agents, and government agencies, and hold meetings as necessary to support the development of regulations.".

(e) APPRAISAL REVIEWS AND COMPLEX APPRAISALS.—

(1) SECTION 1110.—Section 1110 of the Financial Institutions Reform, Recovery, and Enforcement Act of 1989 (12 U.S.C. 3339) is amended—

(A) in paragraph (1), by striking "and";

(B) in paragraph (2), by striking the period at the end and inserting "; and"; and

(C) by inserting after paragraph (2) the following:

"(3) that such appraisals shall be subject to appropriate review for compliance with the Uniform Standards of Professional Appraisal Practice.".

(2) SECTION 1113.—Section 1113 of the Financial Institutions and Reform, Recovery, and Enforcement Act of 1989 (12 U.S.C. 3342) is amended by inserting before the period the following: ", where a complex 1-to-4 unit single family residential appraisal means an appraisal for which the property to be appraised, the form of ownership, the property characteristics, or the market conditions are atypical".

(f) APPRAISAL MANAGEMENT SERVICES.—

(1) SUPERVISION OF THIRD PARTY PROVIDERS OF APPRAISAL MANAGEMENT SERVICES.—Section 1103(a) of the Financial Institutions Reform, Recovery, and Enforcement Act of 1989 (12 U.S.C. 3332(a)) (as previously amended by this section) is amended—

(A) by amending paragraph (1) to read as follows:

"(1) monitor the requirements established by States—

"(A) for the certification and licensing of individuals who are qualified to perform appraisals in connection with federally related transactions, including a code of professional responsibility; and

"(B) for the registration and supervision of the operations and activities of an appraisal management company;"; and

(B) by adding at the end the following new paragraph:

"(6) maintain a national registry of appraisal management companies that either are registered with and subject to supervision of a State appraiser certifying and licensing agency or are operating subsidiaries of a Federally regulated financial institution.".

(2) APPRAISAL MANAGEMENT COMPANY MINIMUM REQUIREMENTS.—Title XI of the Financial Institutions Reform, Recovery, and Enforcement Act of 1989 (12 U.S.C. 3331 et seq.) is amended by adding at the end the following new section (and amending the table of contents accordingly):

"SEC. 1124. APPRAISAL MANAGEMENT COMPANY MINIMUM REQUIREMENTS.

"(a) IN GENERAL.—The Board of Governors of the Federal Reserve System, the Comptroller of the Currency, the Federal Deposit Insurance Corporation, the National Credit Union Administration Board, the Federal Housing Finance Agency, and the Bureau of Consumer Financial Protection shall jointly, by rule, establish minimum requirements to be applied by a State in the registration of appraisal management companies. Such requirements shall include a requirement that such companies—

"(1) register with and be subject to supervision by a State appraiser certifying and licensing agency in each State in which such company operates;

"(2) verify that only licensed or certified appraisers are used for federally related transactions;

"(3) require that appraisals coordinated by an appraisal management company comply with the Uniform Standards of Professional Appraisal Practice; and

"(4) require that appraisals are conducted independently and free from inappropriate influence and coercion pursuant to the appraisal independence standards established under section 129E of the Truth in Lending Act.

"(b) RELATION TO STATE LAW.—Nothing in this section shall be construed to prevent States from establishing requirements in addition to any rules promulgated under subsection (a).

"(c) FEDERALLY REGULATED FINANCIAL INSTITUTIONS.—The requirements of subsection (a) shall apply to an appraisal management company that is a subsidiary owned and controlled by a financial institution and regulated by a Federal financial institution regulatory agency. An appraisal management company that is a subsidiary owned and controlled by a financial institution regulated by a Federal financial institution regulatory agency shall not be required to register with a State.

"(d) REGISTRATION LIMITATIONS.—An appraisal management company shall not be registered by a State or included on the national registry if such company, in whole or in part, directly or indirectly, is owned by any person who has had an appraiser license or certificate refused, denied, cancelled, surrendered in lieu of revocation, or revoked in any State. Additionally, each person that owns more than 10 percent of an appraisal management company shall be of good moral character, as determined by the State appraiser certifying and licensing agency, and shall submit to a background investigation carried out by the State appraiser certifying and licensing agency.

"(e) REPORTING.—The Board of Governors of the Federal Reserve System, the Comptroller of the Currency, the Federal Deposit Insurance Corporation, the National Credit Union Administration Board, the Federal Housing Finance Agency, and the Bureau of Consumer Financial Protection shall jointly promulgate regulations for the reporting of the activities of appraisal management companies to the Appraisal Subcommittee in determining the payment of the annual registry fee.

"(f) EFFECTIVE DATE.—

"(1) IN GENERAL.—No appraisal management company may perform services related to a federally related transaction in a State after the date that is 36 months after the date on which the regulations required to be prescribed under subsection (a) are prescribed in final form unless such company is registered with such State or subject to oversight by a Federal financial institutions regulatory agency.

"(2) EXTENSION OF EFFECTIVE DATE.—Subject to the approval of the Council, the Appraisal Subcommittee may extend by an additional 12 months the requirements for the registration and supervision of appraisal management companies if it makes a written finding that a State has made substantial progress in establishing a State appraisal management company registration and supervision system that appears to conform with the provisions of this title.".

(3) STATE APPRAISER CERTIFYING AND LICENSING AGENCY AUTHORITY.—Section 1117 of the Financial Institutions Reform, Recovery, and Enforcement Act of 1989 (12 U.S.C. 3346) is amended by adding at the end the following: "The duties of such agency may additionally include the registration and supervision of appraisal management companies and the addition of information about the appraisal management company to the national registry.".

(4) APPRAISAL MANAGEMENT COMPANY DEFINITION.—Section 1121 of the Financial Institutions Reform, Recovery, and Enforcement Act of 1989 (12 U.S.C. 3350) is amended by adding at the end the following:

"(11) APPRAISAL MANAGEMENT COMPANY.—The term 'appraisal management company' means, in connection with valuing properties collateralizing mortgage loans or mortgages incorporated into a securitization, any external third party authorized either by a creditor of a consumer credit transaction secured by a consumer's principal dwelling or by an underwriter of or other principal in the secondary mortgage markets, that oversees a network or panel of more than 15 certified or licensed appraisers in a State or 25 or more nationally within a given year—

"(A) to recruit, select, and retain appraisers;

"(B) to contract with licensed and certified appraisers to perform appraisal assignments;

"(C) to manage the process of having an appraisal performed, including providing administrative duties such as receiving appraisal orders and appraisal reports, submitting completed appraisal reports to creditors and underwriters, collecting fees from creditors and underwriters for services provided, and reimbursing appraisers for services performed; or

"(D) to review and verify the work of appraisers.".

(g) STATE AGENCY REPORTING REQUIREMENT.—Section 1109(a) of the Financial Institutions Reform, Recovery, and Enforcement Act of 1989 (12 U.S.C. 3338(a)) is amended—

(1) by striking "and" after the semicolon in paragraph (1);

(2) by redesignating paragraph (2) as paragraph (4); and

(3) by inserting after paragraph (1) the following new paragraphs:

"(2) transmit reports on the issuance and renewal of licenses and certifications, sanctions, disciplinary actions, license and certification revocations, and license and certification suspensions on a timely basis to the national registry of the Appraisal Subcommittee;

"(3) transmit reports on a timely basis of supervisory activities involving appraisal management companies or other third-party providers of appraisals and appraisal management services, including investigations initiated and disciplinary actions taken; and".

(h) REGISTRY FEES MODIFIED.—

(1) IN GENERAL.—Section 1109(a) of the Financial Institutions Reform, Recovery, and Enforcement Act of 1989 (12 U.S.C. 3338(a)) is amended—

(A) by amending paragraph (4) (as modified by section 1473(g)) to read as follows:

"(4) collect—

"(A) from such individuals who perform or seek to perform appraisals in federally related transactions, an annual registry fee of not more than $40, such fees to be transmitted by the State agencies to the Council on an annual basis; and

"(B) from an appraisal management company that either has registered with a State appraiser certifying and licensing agency in accordance with this title or operates as a subsidiary of a federally regulated financial institution, an annual registry fee of—

"(i) in the case of such a company that has been in existence for more than a year, $25 multiplied by the number of appraisers working for or contracting with such company in such State during the previous year, but where such $25 amount may be adjusted, up to a maximum of $50, at the discretion of the Appraisal Subcommittee, if necessary to carry out the Subcommittee's functions under this title; and

"(ii) in the case of such a company that has not been in existence for more than a year, $25 multiplied by an appropriate number to be determined by the Appraisal Subcommittee, and where such number will be used for determining the fee of all such companies that were not in existence for more than a year, but where such $25 amount may be adjusted, up to a maximum of $50, at the discretion of the Appraisal Subcommittee, if necessary to carry out the Subcommittee's functions under this title."; and

(B) by amending the matter following paragraph (4), as redesignated, to read as follows:

"Subject to the approval of the Council, the Appraisal Subcommittee may adjust the dollar amount of registry fees under paragraph (4)(A), up to a maximum of $80 per annum, as necessary to carry out its functions under this title. The Appraisal Subcommittee shall consider at least once every 5 years whether to adjust the dollar amount of the registry fees to account for inflation. In implementing any change in registry fees, the Appraisal Subcommittee shall provide flexibility to the States for multi-year certifications and licenses already in place, as well as a transition period to implement the changes in registry fees. In establishing the amount of the annual registry fee for an appraisal management company, the Appraisal Subcommittee shall have the discretion to impose a minimum annual registry fee for an appraisal management company to protect against the under reporting of the number of appraisers working for or contracted by the appraisal management company.".

(2) INCREMENTAL REVENUES.—Incremental revenues collected pursuant to the increases required by this subsection shall be placed in a separate account at the United States Treasury, entitled the "Appraisal Subcommittee Account".

(i) GRANTS AND REPORTS.—Section 1109(b) of the Financial Institutions Reform, Recovery, and Enforcement Act of 1989 (12 U.S.C. 3338(b)) is amended—

(1) by striking "and" after the semicolon in paragraph (3);

(2) by striking the period at the end of paragraph (4) and inserting a semicolon;

(3) by adding at the end the following new paragraphs:

"(5) to make grants to State appraiser certifying and licensing agencies, in accordance with policies to be developed by the Appraisal Subcommittee, to support the efforts of such agencies to comply with this title, including—

"(A) the complaint process, complaint investigations, and appraiser enforcement activities of such agencies; and

"(B) the submission of data on State licensed and certified appraisers and appraisal management companies to the National appraisal registry, including information affirming that the appraiser or appraisal management company meets the required qualification criteria and formal and informal disciplinary actions; and

"(6) to report to all State appraiser certifying and licensing agencies when a license or certification is surrendered, revoked, or suspended.".

Obligations authorized under this subsection may not exceed 75 percent of the fiscal year total of incremental increase in fees collected and deposited in the "Appraisal Subcommittee Account" pursuant to subsection (h).

(j) CRITERIA.—Section 1116 of the Financial Institutions Reform, Recovery, and Enforcement Act of 1989 (12 U.S.C. 3345) is amended—

(1) in subsection (c), by inserting "whose criteria for the licensing of a real estate appraiser currently meet or exceed the minimum criteria issued by the Appraisal Qualifications Board of The Appraisal Foundation for the licensing of real estate appraisers" before the period at the end; and

(2) by striking subsection (e) and inserting the following new subsection:

"(e) MINIMUM QUALIFICATION REQUIREMENTS.—Any requirements established for individuals in the position of 'Trainee Appraiser' and 'Supervisory Appraiser' shall meet or exceed the minimum qualification requirements of the Appraiser Qualifications Board of The Appraisal Foundation. The Appraisal Subcommittee shall have the authority to enforce these requirements.".

(k) MONITORING OF STATE APPRAISER CERTIFYING AND LICENSING AGENCIES.—Section 1118 of the Financial Institutions Reform, Recovery, and Enforcement Act of 1989 (12 U.S.C. 3347) is amended—

(1) by amending subsection (a) to read as follows:

"(a) IN GENERAL.—The Appraisal Subcommittee shall monitor each State appraiser certifying and licensing agency for the purposes of determining whether such agency—

"(1) has policies, practices, funding, staffing, and procedures that are consistent with this title;

"(2) processes complaints and completes investigations in a reasonable time period;

"(3) appropriately disciplines sanctioned appraisers and appraisal management companies;

"(4) maintains an effective regulatory program; and

"(5) reports complaints and disciplinary actions on a timely basis to the national registries on appraisers and appraisal management companies maintained by the Appraisal Subcommittee.

The Appraisal Subcommittee shall have the authority to remove a State licensed or certified appraiser or a registered appraisal management company from a national registry on an interim basis, not to exceed 90 days, pending State agency action on licensing, certification, registration, and disciplinary proceedings. The Appraisal Subcommittee and all agencies, instrumentalities, and Federally recognized entities under this title shall not recognize appraiser certifications and licenses from States whose appraisal policies, practices, funding, staffing, or procedures are found to be inconsistent with this title. The Appraisal Subcommittee shall have the authority to impose sanctions, as described in this section, against a State agency that fails to have an effective appraiser regulatory program. In determining whether such a program is effective, the Appraisal Subcommittee shall include an analysis of the licensing and certification of appraisers, the registration of appraisal management companies, the issuance of temporary licenses and certifications for appraisers, the receiving and tracking of submitted complaints against appraisers and appraisal management companies, the investigation of complaints, and enforcement actions against appraisers and appraisal management companies. The Appraisal Subcommittee shall have the authority to impose interim actions and suspensions against a State agency as an alternative to, or in advance of, the derecognition of a State agency.".

(2) in subsection (b)(2), by inserting after "authority" the following: "or sufficient funding".

(l) RECIPROCITY.—Subsection (b) of section 1122 of the Financial Institutions Reform, Recovery, and Enforcement Act of 1989 (12 U.S.C. 3351(b)) is amended to read as follows:

"(b) RECIPROCITY.—Notwithstanding any other provisions of this title, a federally related transaction shall not be appraised by a certified or licensed appraiser unless the State appraiser certifying or licensing agency of the State certifying or licensing such appraiser has in place a policy of issuing a reciprocal certification or license for an individual from another State when—

"(1) the appraiser licensing and certification program of such other State is in compliance with the provisions of this title; and

"(2) the appraiser holds a valid certification from a State whose requirements for certification or licensing meet or exceed the licensure standards established by the State where an individual seeks appraisal licensure.".

(m) CONSIDERATION OF PROFESSIONAL APPRAISAL DESIGNATIONS.—Section 1122(d) of the Financial Institutions Reform, Recovery, and Enforcement Act of 1989 (12 U.S.C. 3351(d)) is amended by striking "shall not exclude" and all that follows through the end of the subsection and inserting the following: "may include education achieved, experience, sample appraisals, and references from prior clients. Membership in a nationally recognized professional appraisal organization may be a criteria considered, though lack of membership therein shall not be the sole bar against consideration for an assignment under these criteria.".

(n) APPRAISER INDEPENDENCE.—Section 1122 of the Financial Institutions Reform, Recovery, and Enforcement Act of 1989 (12 U.S.C. 3351) is amended by adding at the end the following new subsection:

"(g) APPRAISER INDEPENDENCE MONITORING.—The Appraisal Subcommittee shall monitor each State appraiser certifying and licensing agency for the purpose of determining whether such agency's policies, practices, and procedures are consistent with the purposes of maintaining appraiser independence and whether such State has adopted and maintains effective laws, regulations, and policies aimed at maintaining appraiser independence.".

(o) APPRAISER EDUCATION.—Section 1122 of the Financial Institutions Reform, Recovery, and Enforcement Act of 1989 (12 U.S.C. 3351) is amended by inserting after subsection (g) (as added by subsection (1) of this section) the following new subsection:

"(h) APPROVED EDUCATION.—The Appraisal Subcommittee shall encourage the States to accept courses approved by the Appraiser Qualification Board's Course Approval Program.".

(p) APPRAISAL COMPLAINT HOTLINE.—Section 1122 of the Financial Institutions Reform, Recovery, and Enforcement Act of 1989 (12 U.S.C. 3351), as amended by this section, is amended by adding at the end the following new subsection:

"(i) APPRAISAL COMPLAINT NATIONAL HOTLINE.—If, 6 months after the date of the enactment of this subsection, the Appraisal Subcommittee determines that no national hotline exists to receive complaints of non-compliance with appraisal independence standards and Uniform Standards of Professional Appraisal Practice, including complaints from appraisers, individuals, or other entities concerning the improper influencing or attempted improper influencing of appraisers or the appraisal process, the Appraisal Subcommittee shall establish and operate such a national hotline, which shall include a toll-free telephone number and an email address. If the Appraisal Subcommittee operates such a national hotline, the Appraisal Subcommittee shall refer complaints for further action to appropriate governmental bodies, including a State appraiser certifying and licensing agency, a financial institution regulator, or other appropriate legal authorities. For complaints referred to State appraiser certifying and licensing agencies or to Federal regulators, the Appraisal Subcommittee shall have the authority to follow up such complaint referrals in order to determine the status of the resolution of the complaint.".

(q) AUTOMATED VALUATION MODELS.—Title XI of the Financial Institutions Reform, Recovery, and Enforcement Act of 1989 (12 U.S.C. 3331 et seq.), as amended by this section, is amended by adding at the end the following new section (and amending the table of contents accordingly):

"SEC. 1125. AUTOMATED VALUATION MODELS USED TO ESTIMATE COLLATERAL VALUE FOR MORTGAGE LENDING PURPOSES.

"(a) IN GENERAL.—Automated valuation models shall adhere to quality control standards designed to—

"(1) ensure a high level of confidence in the estimates produced by automated valuation models;

"(2) protect against the manipulation of data;

"(3) seek to avoid conflicts of interest;

"(4) require random sample testing and reviews; and

"(5) account for any other such factor that the agencies listed in subsection (b) determine to be appropriate.

"(b) ADOPTION OF REGULATIONS.—The Board, the Comptroller of the Currency, the Federal Deposit Insurance Corporation, the National Credit Union Administration Board, the Federal Housing Finance Agency, and the Bureau of Consumer Financial Protection, in consultation with the staff of the Appraisal Subcommittee and the Appraisal Standards Board of the Appraisal Foundation, shall promulgate regulations to implement the quality control standards required under this section.

"(c) ENFORCEMENT.—Compliance with regulations issued under this subsection shall be enforced by—

"(1) with respect to a financial institution, or subsidiary owned and controlled by a financial institution and regulated by a Federal financial institution regulatory agency, the Federal financial institution regulatory agency that acts as the primary Federal supervisor of such financial institution or subsidiary; and

"(2) with respect to other participants in the market for appraisals of 1-to-4 unit single family residential real estate, the Federal Trade Commission, the Bureau of Consumer Financial Protection, and a State attorney general.

"(d) AUTOMATED VALUATION MODEL DEFINED.—For purposes of this section, the term 'automated valuation model' means any computerized model used by mortgage originators and secondary market issuers to determine the collateral worth of a mortgage secured by a consumer's principal dwelling.".

(r) BROKER PRICE OPINIONS.—Title XI of the Financial Institutions Reform, Recovery, and Enforcement Act of 1989 (12 U.S.C. 3331 et seq.), as amended by this section, is amended by adding at the end the following new section (and amending the table of contents accordingly):

"SEC. 1126. BROKER PRICE OPINIONS.

"(a) GENERAL PROHIBITION.—In conjunction with the purchase of a consumer's principal dwelling, broker price opinions may not be used as the primary basis to determine the value of a piece of property for the purpose of a loan origination of a residential mortgage loan secured by such piece of property.

"(b) BROKER PRICE OPINION DEFINED.—For purposes of this section, the term 'broker price opinion' means an estimate prepared by a real estate broker, agent, or sales person that details the probable selling price of a particular piece of real estate property and provides a varying level of detail about the property's condition, market, and neighborhood, and information on comparable sales, but does not include an automated valuation model, as defined in section 1125(c).".

(s) AMENDMENTS TO APPRAISAL SUBCOMMITTEE.—Section 1011 of the Federal Financial Institutions Examination Council Act of 1978 (12 U.S.C. 3310) is amended—

(1) in the first sentence, by adding before the period the following: ", the Bureau of Consumer Financial Protection, and the Federal Housing Finance Agency"; and

(2) by inserting at the end the following: "At all times at least one member of the Appraisal Subcommittee shall have demonstrated knowledge and competence through licensure, certification, or professional designation within the appraisal profession.".

(t) TECHNICAL CORRECTIONS.—

(1) Section 1119(a)(2) of the Financial Institutions Reform, Recovery, and Enforcement Act of 1989 (12 U.S.C. 3348(a)(2)) is amended by striking "council," and inserting "Council,".

(2) Section 1121(6) of the Financial Institutions Reform, Recovery, and Enforcement Act of 1989 (12 U.S.C. 3350(6)) is amended by striking "Corporations," and inserting "Corporation,".

(3) Section 1121(8) of the Financial Institutions Reform, Recovery, and Enforcement Act of 1989 (12 U.S.C. 3350(8)) is amended by striking "council" and inserting "Council".

(4) Section 1122 of the Financial Institutions Reform, Recovery, and Enforcement Act of 1989 (12 U.S.C. 3351) is amended—

(A) in subsection (a)(1) by moving the left margin of subparagraphs (A), (B), and (C) 2 ems to the right; and

(B) in subsection (c)—

(i) by striking "Federal Financial Institutions Examination Council" and inserting "Financial Institutions Examination Council"; and

(ii) by striking "the council's functions" and inserting "the Council's functions".

[Explanation at ¶ 6710.]

[¶ 11,474] ACT SEC. 1474. EQUAL CREDIT OPPORTUNITY ACT AMENDMENT.

Subsection (e) of section 701 of the Equal Credit Opportunity Act (15 U.S.C. 1691) is amended to read as follows:

"(e) COPIES FURNISHED TO APPLICANTS.—

"(1) IN GENERAL.—Each creditor shall furnish to an applicant a copy of any and all written appraisals and valuations developed in connection with the applicant's application for a loan that is secured or would have been secured by a first lien on a dwelling promptly upon completion, but in no ease later than 3 days prior to the closing of the loan, whether the creditor grants or denies the applicant's request for credit or the application is incomplete or withdrawn.

"(2) WAIVER.—The applicant may waive the 3 day requirement provided for in paragraph (1), except where otherwise required in law.

"(3) REIMBURSEMENT.—The applicant may be required to pay a reasonable fee to reimburse the creditor for the cost of the appraisal, except where otherwise required in law.

"(4) FREE COPY.—Notwithstanding paragraph (3), the creditor shall provide a copy of each written appraisal or valuation at no additional cost to the applicant.

"(5) NOTIFICATION TO APPLICANTS.—At the time of application, the creditor shall notify an applicant in writing of the right to receive a copy of each written appraisal and valuation under this subsection.

"(6) VALUATION DEFINED.—For purposes of this subsection, the term 'valuation' shall include any estimate of the value of a dwelling developed in connection with a creditor's decision to provide credit, including those values developed pursuant to a policy of a government sponsored enterprise or by an automated valuation model, a broker price opinion, or other methodology or mechanism.".

[Explanation at ¶ 6715.]

[¶ 11,475] ACT SEC. 1475. REAL ESTATE SETTLEMENT PROCEDURES ACT OF 1974 AMENDMENT RELATING TO CERTAIN APPRAISAL FEES.

Section 4 of the Real Estate Settlement Procedures Act of 1974 is amended by adding at the end the following new subsection:

"(c) The standard form described in subsection (a) may include, in the case of an appraisal coordinated by an appraisal management company (as such term is defined in section 1121(11) of the Financial Institutions Reform, Recovery, and Enforcement Act of 1989 (12 U.S.C. 3350(11))), a clear disclosure of—

"(1) the fee paid directly to the appraiser by such company; and

"(2) the administration fee charged by such company.".

[Explanation at ¶ 6720.]

[¶ 11,476] ACT SEC. 1476. GAO STUDY ON THE EFFECTIVENESS AND IMPACT OF VARIOUS APPRAISAL METHODS, VALUATION MODELS AND DISTRIBUTIONS CHANNELS, AND ON THE HOME VALUATION CODE OF CONDUCT AND THE APPRAISAL SUBCOMMITTEE.

(a) IN GENERAL.—The Government Accountability Office shall conduct a study on—

(1) the effectiveness and impact of—

(A) appraisal methods, including the cost approach, the comparative sales approach, the income approach, and others that may be available;

(B) appraisal valuation models, including licensed and certified appraisals, broker-priced opinions, and automated valuation models; and

(C) appraisal distribution channels, including appraisal management companies, independent appraisal operations within mortgage originators, and fee-for-service appraisers;

(2) the Home Valuation Code of Conduct; and

(3) the Appraisal Subcommittee's functions pursuant to title XI of the Financial Institutions Reform, Recovery, and Enforcement Act of 1989.

(b) STUDY.—Not later than—

(1) 12 months after the date of enactment of this Act, the Government Accountability Office shall submit a study to the Committee on Banking, Housing, and Urban Affairs of the Senate and the Committee on Financial Services of the House of Representatives; and

(2) 90 days after the date of enactment of this Act, the Government Accountability Office shall provide a report on the status of the study and any preliminary findings to the Committee on Banking, Housing, and Urban Affairs of the Senate and the Committee on Financial Services of the House of Representatives.

(c) CONTENT OF STUDY.—The study required by this section shall include an examination of the following:

(1) APPRAISAL APPROACHES, VALUATION MODELS, AND DISTRIBUTION CHANNELS.—

(A) The prevalence, alone or in combination, of certain appraisal approaches, models, and channels in purchase-money and refinance mortgage transactions.

(B) The accuracy of these approaches, models, and channels in assessing the property as collateral.

(C) Whether and how these approaches, models, and channels contributed to price speculation during the previous cycle.

(D) The costs to consumers of these approaches, models, and channels.

(E) The disclosure of fees to consumers in the appraisal process.

(F) To what extent the usage of these approaches, models, and channels may be influenced by a conflict of interest between the mortgage lender and the appraiser and the mechanism by which the lender selects and compensates the appraiser.

(G) The suitability of these approaches, models, and channels in rural versus urban areas.

(2) HOME VALUATION CODE OF CONDUCT (HVCC).—

(A) How the HVCC affects mortgage lenders' selection of appraisers.

(B) How the HVCC affects State regulation of appraisers and appraisal distribution channels.

(C) How the HVCC affects the quality and cost of appraisals and the length of time to obtain an appraisal.

(D) How the HVCC affects mortgage brokers, small businesses, and consumers.

Act Sec. 1476(c)(2)(D) ¶ 11,476

(d) ADDITIONAL STUDY REQUIRED.—

(1) IN GENERAL.—Not later than 18 months after the date of enactment of this Act, the Government Accountability Office shall submit a study to the Committee on Banking, Housing, and Urban Affairs of the Senate and the Committee on Financial Services of the House of Representatives.

(2) CONTENT OF ADDITIONAL STUDY.—The study required under paragraph (1) shall include—

(A) an examination of—

(i) the Appraisal Subcommittee's ability to monitor and enforce State and Federal certification requirements and standards, including by providing a summary with a statistical breakdown of enforcement actions taken during the last 10 years;

(ii) whether existing Federal financial institutions regulatory agency exemptions on appraisals for federally related transactions needs to be revised; and

(iii) whether new means of data collection, such as the establishment of a national repository, would benefit the Appraisal Subcommittee's ability to perform its functions; and

(B) recommendations from this examination for administrative and legislative action at the Federal and State level.

[Explanation at ¶ 6725.]

Subtitle G—Mortgage Resolution and Modification

[¶ 11,481] ACT SEC. 1481. MULTIFAMILY MORTGAGE RESOLUTION PROGRAM.

(a) ESTABLISHMENT.—The Secretary of Housing and Urban Development shall develop a program under this subsection to ensure the protection of current and future tenants and at-risk multifamily properties, where feasible, based on criteria that may include—

(1) creating sustainable financing of such properties, that may take into consideration such factors as—

(A) the rental income generated by such properties; and

(B) the preservation of adequate operating reserves;

(2) maintaining the level of Federal, State, and city subsidies in effect as of the date of the enactment of this Act;

(3) providing funds for rehabilitation; and

(4) facilitating the transfer of such properties, when appropriate and with the agreement of owners, to responsible new owners and ensuring affordability of such properties.

(b) COORDINATION.—The Secretary of Housing and Urban Development may, in carrying out the program developed under this section, coordinate with the Secretary of the Treasury, the Federal Deposit Insurance Corporation, the Board of Governors of the Federal Reserve System, the Federal Housing Finance Agency, and any other Federal Government agency that the Secretary considers appropriate.

(c) DEFINITION.—For purposes of this section, the term "multifamily properties" means a residential structure that consists of 5 or more dwelling units.

(d) PREVENTION OF QUALIFICATION FOR CRIMINAL APPLICANTS.—

(1) IN GENERAL.—No person shall be eligible to begin receiving assistance from the Making Home Affordable Program authorized under the Emergency Economic Stabilization Act of 2008 (12 U.S.C. 5201 et seq.), or any other mortgage assistance program authorized or funded by that Act, on or after 60 days after the date of the enactment of this Act, if such person, in connection with a mortgage or real estate transaction, has been convicted, within the last 10 years, of any one of the following:

(A) Felony larceny, theft, fraud, or forgery.

(B) Money laundering.

(C) Tax evasion.

(2) PROCEDURES.—The Secretary shall establish procedures to ensure compliance with this subsection.

(3) REPORT.—The Secretary shall report to the Committee on Financial Services of the House of Representatives and the Committee on Banking, Housing, and Urban Affairs of the Senate regarding the implementation of this provision. The report shall also describe the steps taken to implement this subsection.

[Explanation at ¶ 6730.]

[¶ 11,482] ACT SEC. 1482. HOME AFFORDABLE MODIFICATION PROGRAM GUIDELINES.

(a) NET PRESENT VALUE INPUT DATA.—The Secretary of the Treasury (in this section referred to as the "Secretary") shall revise the supplemental directives and other guidelines for the Home Affordable Modification Program of the Making Home Affordable initiative of the Secretary of the Treasury, authorized under the Emergency Economic Stabilization Act of 2008 (Public Law 110-343), to require each mortgage servicer participating in such program to provide each borrower under a mortgage whose request for a mortgage modification under the Program is denied with all borrower-related and mortgage-related input data used in any net present value (NPV) analyses performed in connection with the subject mortgage. Such input data shall be provided to the borrower at the time of such denial.

(b) WEB-BASED SITE FOR NPV CALCULATOR AND APPLICATION.—

(1) NPV CALCULATOR.—In carrying out the Home Affordable Modification Program, the Secretary shall establish and maintain a site on the World Wide Web that provides a calculator for net present value analyses of a mortgage, based on the Secretary's methodology for calculating such value, that mortgagors can use to enter information regarding their own mortgages and that provides a determination after entering such information regarding a mortgage of whether such mortgage would be accepted or rejected for modification under the Program, using such methodology.

(2) DISCLOSURE.—Such Web site shall also prominently disclose that each mortgage servicer participating in such Program may use a method for calculating net present value of a mortgage that is different than the method used by such calculator.

(3) APPLICATION.—The Secretary shall make a reasonable effort to include on such World Wide Web site a method for homeowners to apply for a mortgage modification under the Home Affordable Modification Program.

(c) PUBLIC AVAILABILITY OF NPV METHODOLOGY, COMPUTER MODEL, AND VARIABLES.—The Secretary shall make publicly available, including by posting on a World Wide Web site of the Secretary—

(1) the Secretary's methodology and computer model, including all formulae used in such computer model, used for calculating net present value of a mortgage that is used by the calculator established pursuant to subsection (b); and

(2) all non-proprietary variables used in such net present value analysis.

[Explanation at ¶ 6735.]

[¶ 11,483] ACT SEC. 1483. PUBLIC AVAILABILITY OF INFORMATION OF MAKING HOME AFFORDABLE PROGRAM.

(a) REVISIONS TO PROGRAM GUIDELINES.—The Secretary of the Treasury (in this section referred to as the "Secretary") shall revise the guidelines for the Home Affordable Modification Program of the Making Home Affordable initiative of the Secretary of the Treasury, authorized under the Emergency Economic Stabilization Act of 2008 (Public Law 110-343), to provide that the data being collected by the Secretary from each mortgage servicer and lender participating in the Program is made public in accordance with subsection (b).

(b) PUBLIC AVAILABILITY.—Data shall be made available according to the following guidelines:

(1) Not more than 14 days after each monthly deadline for submission of data by mortgage servicers and lenders participating in the Program, reports shall be made publicly available by

means of a World Wide Web site of the Secretary, and by submitting a report to the Congress, that shall includes the following information:

> (A) The number of requests for mortgage modifications under the Program that the servicer or lender has received.
>
> (B) The number of requests for mortgage modifications under the Program that the servicer or lender has processed.
>
> (C) The number of requests for mortgage modifications under the Program that the servicer or lender has approved.
>
> (D) The number of requests for mortgage modifications under the Program that the servicer or lender has denied.

(2) Not more than 60 days after each monthly deadline for submission of data by mortgage servicers and lenders participating in the Program, the Secretary shall make data tables available to the public at the individual record level. The Secretary shall issue regulations prescribing—

> (A) the procedures for disclosing such data to the public; and
>
> (B) such deletions as the Secretary may determine to be appropriate to protect any privacy interest of any mortgage modification applicant, including the deletion or alteration of the applicant's name and identification number.

[Explanation at ¶ 6740.]

[¶ 11,484] ACT SEC. 1484. PROTECTING TENANTS AT FORECLOSURE EXTENSION AND CLARIFICATION.

The Protecting Tenants at Foreclosure Act is amended—

(1) in section 702 (12 U.S.C. 5220 note)—

> (A) in subsection (a)(2), by striking ", as of the date of such notice of foreclosure"; and
>
> (B) in subsection (c), by inserting after the period the following: "For purposes of this section, the date of a notice of foreclosure shall be deemed to be the date on which complete title to a property is transferred to a successor entity or person as a result of an order of a court or pursuant to provisions in a mortgage, deed of trust, or security deed."; and

(2) in section 704 (12 U.S.C. 5201 note), by striking "2012" and inserting "2014".

[Explanation at ¶ 6745.]

Subtitle H—Miscellaneous Provisions

[¶ 11,491] ACT SEC. 1491. SENSE OF CONGRESS REGARDING THE IMPORTANCE OF GOVERNMENT-SPONSORED ENTERPRISES REFORM TO ENHANCE THE PROTECTION, LIMITATION, AND REGULATION OF THE TERMS OF RESIDENTIAL MORTGAGE CREDIT.

(a) FINDINGS.—The Congress finds as follows:

(1) The Government-sponsored enterprises, Federal National Mortgage Association (Fannie Mae) and the Federal Home Loan Mortgage Corporation (Freddie Mac), were chartered by Congress to ensure a reliable and affordable supply of mortgage funding, but enjoy a dual legal status as privately owned corporations with Government mandated affordable housing goals.

(2) In 1996, the Department of Housing and Urban Development required that 42 percent of Fannie Mae's and Freddie Mac's mortgage financing should go to borrowers with income levels below the median for a given area.

(3) In 2004, the Department of Housing and Urban Development revised those goals, increasing them to 56 percent of their overall mortgage purchases by 2008, and additionally mandated that 12 percent of all mortgage purchases by Fannie Mae and Freddie Mac be "special affordable" loans made to borrowers with incomes less than 60 percent of an area's median income, a target that ultimately increased to 28 percent for 2008.

Title XIV—Mortgage Reform

(4) To help fulfill those mandated affordable housing goals, in 1995 the Department of Housing and Urban Development authorized Fannie Mae and Freddie Mac to purchase subprime securities that included loans made to low-income borrowers.

(5) After this authorization to purchase subprime securities, subprime and near-prime loans increased from 9 percent of securitized mortgages in 2001 to 40 percent in 2006, while the market share of conventional mortgages dropped from 78.8 percent in 2003 to 50.1 percent by 2007 with a corresponding increase in subprime and Alt-A loans from 10.1 percent to 32.7 percent over the same period.

(6) In 2004 alone, Fannie Mae and Freddie Mac purchased $175,000,000,000 in subprime mortgage securities, which accounted for 44 percent of the market that year, and from 2005 through 2007, Fannie Mae and Freddie Mac purchased approximately $1,000,000,000,000 in subprime and Alt-A loans, while Fannie Mae's acquisitions of mortgages with less than 10 percent down payments almost tripled.

(7) According to data from the Federal Housing Finance Agency (FHFA) for the fourth quarter of 2008, Fannie Mae and Freddie Mac own or guarantee 75 percent of all newly originated mortgages, and Fannie Mae and Freddie Mac currently own 13.3 percent of outstanding mortgage debt in the United States and have issued mortgage-backed securities for 31.0 percent of the residential debt market, a combined total of 44.3 percent of outstanding mortgage debt in the United States.

(8) On September 7, 2008, the FHFA placed Fannie Mae and Freddie Mac into conservatorship, with the Treasury Department subsequently agreeing to purchase at least $200,000,000,000 of preferred stock from each enterprise in exchange for warrants for the purchase of 79.9 percent of each enterprise's common stock.

(9) The conservatorship for Fannie Mae and Freddie Mac has potentially exposed taxpayers to upwards of $5,300,000,000,000 worth of risk.

(10) The hybrid public-private status of Fannie Mae and Freddie Mac is untenable and must be resolved to assure that consumers are offered and receive residential mortgage loans on terms that reasonably reflect their ability to repay the loans and that are understandable and not unfair, deceptive, or abusive.

(b) SENSE OF THE CONGRESS.—It is the sense of the Congress that efforts to enhance by the protection, limitation, and regulation of the terms of residential mortgage credit and the practices related to such credit would be incomplete without enactment of meaningful structural reforms of Fannie Mae and Freddie Mac.

[Explanation at ¶ 6750.]

[¶ 11,492] ACT SEC. 1492. GAO STUDY REPORT ON GOVERNMENT EFFORTS TO COMBAT MORTGAGE FORECLOSURE RESCUE SCAMS AND LOAN MODIFICATION FRAUD.

(a) STUDY.—The Comptroller General of the United States shall conduct a study of the current inter-agency efforts of the Secretary of the Treasury, the Secretary of Housing and Urban Development, the Attorney General, and the Federal Trade Commission to crackdown on mortgage foreclosure rescue scams and loan modification fraud in order to advise the Congress to the risks and vulnerabilities of emerging schemes in the loan modification arena.

(b) REPORT.—

(1) IN GENERAL.—The Comptroller General shall submit a report to the Congress on the study conducted under subsection (a) containing such recommendations for legislative and administrative actions as the Comptroller General may determine to be appropriate in addition to the recommendations required under paragraph (2).

(2) SPECIFIC TOPICS.—The report made under paragraph (1) shall include—

(A) an evaluation of the effectiveness of the inter-agency task force current efforts to combat mortgage foreclosure rescue scams and loan modification fraud scams;

(B) specific recommendations on agency or legislative action that are essential to properly protect homeowners from mortgage foreclosure rescue scams and loan modification fraud scams; and

(C) the adequacy of financial resources that the Federal Government is allocating to—

(i) crackdown on loan modification and foreclosure rescue scams; and

(ii) the education of homeowners about fraudulent scams relating to loan modification and foreclosure rescues.

[¶ 11,493] ACT SEC. 1493. REPORTING OF MORTGAGE DATA BY STATE.

(a) IN GENERAL.—Section 104(a) of the Helping Families Save Their Homes Act of 2009 (division A of Public Law 111-22) is amended—

(1) in paragraph (2), by striking "resulting" and inserting "in each State that result";

(2) in paragraph (3), by inserting "each State for" after "modifications in"; and

(3) in paragraph (4), by inserting "in each State" after "total number of loans".

(b) CONFORMING AMENDMENT.—Section 104(b)(1)(A) of such Act is amended by adding at the end the following sentence: "Not later than 60 days after the date of the enactment of the Dodd-Frank Wall Street Reform and Consumer Protection Act, the Comptroller of the Currency and the Director of the Office of Thrift Supervision shall update such requirements to reflect amendments made to this section by such Act.".

[Explanation at ¶ 6755.]

[¶ 11,494] ACT SEC. 1494. STUDY OF EFFECT OF DRYWALL PRESENCE ON FORECLOSURES.

(a) STUDY.—The Secretary of Housing and Urban Development, in consultation with the Secretary of the Treasury, shall conduct a study of the effect on residential mortgage loan foreclosures of—

(1) the presence in residential structures subject to such mortgage loans of drywall that was imported from China during the period beginning with 2004 and ending at the end of 2007; and

(2) the availability of property insurance for residential structures in which such drywall is present.

(b) REPORT.—Not later than the expiration of the 120-day period beginning on the date of the enactment of this Act, the Secretary of Housing and Urban Development shall submit to the Congress a report on the study conducted under subsection (a) containing its findings, conclusions, and recommendations.

[Explanation at ¶ 6760.]

[¶ 11,495] ACT SEC. 1495. DEFINITION.

For purposes of this title, the term "designated transfer date" means the date established under section 1062 of this Act.

[¶ 11,496] ACT SEC. 1496. EMERGENCY MORTGAGE RELIEF.

(a) EMERGENCY HOMEOWNERS' RELIEF FUND.—Effective October 1, 2010, and notwithstanding any other provision of law, there is hereby made available to the Secretary of Housing and Urban Development such sums as are necessary to provide $1,000,000,000 in assistance through the Emergency Homeowners' Relief Fund, which such Secretary shall establish pursuant to section 107 of the Emergency Housing Act of 1975 (12 U.S.C. 2706), as such Act is amended by this section, for use for emergency mortgage assistance in accordance with title I of such Act.

(b) REAUTHORIZATION OF EMERGENCY MORTGAGE RELIEF PROGRAM.—Title I of the Emergency Housing Act of 1975 is amended—

(1) in section 103 (12 U.S.C. 2702)—

(A) in paragraph (2)—

(i) by striking "have indicated" and all that follows through "regulation of the holder" and insert "have certified";

(ii) by striking "(such as the volume of delinquent loans in its portfolio)"; and

(iii) by striking ", except that such statement" and all that follows through "purposes of this title"; and

(B) in paragraph (4), by inserting "or medical conditions" after "adverse economic conditions";

(2) in section 104 (12 U.S.C. 2703)—

(A) in subsection (b), by striking ", but such assistance" and all that follows through the period at the end and inserting the following: ". The amount of assistance provided to a homeowner under this title shall be an amount that the Secretary determines is reasonably necessary to supplement such amount as the homeowner is capable of contributing toward such mortgage payment, except that the aggregate amount of such assistance provided for any homeowner shall not exceed $50,000.";

(B) in subsection (d), by striking "interest on a loan or advance" and all that follows through the end of the subsection and inserting the following: "(1) the rate of interest on any loan or advance of credit insured under this title shall be fixed for the life of the loan or advance of credit and shall not exceed the rate of interest that is generally charged for mortgages on single-family housing insured by the Secretary of Housing and Urban Development under title II of the National Housing Act at the time such loan or advance of credit is made, and (2) no interest shall be charged on interest which is deferred on a loan or advance of credit made under this title. In establishing rates, terms and conditions for loans or advances of credit made under this title, the Secretary shall take into account a homeowner's ability to repay such loan or advance of credit."; and

(C) in subsection (e), by inserting after the period at the end of the first sentence the following: "Any eligible homeowner who receives a grant or an advance of credit under this title may repay the loan in full, without penalty, by lump sum or by installment payments at any time before the loan becomes due and payable.";

(3) in section 105 (12 U.S.C. 2704)—

(A) by striking subsection (b);

(B) in subsection (e)—

(i) by inserting "and emergency mortgage relief payments made under section 106" after "insured under this section"; and

(ii) by striking "$1,500,000,000 at any one time" and inserting "$3,000,000,000";

(C) by redesignating subsections (c), (d), and (e) as subsections (b), (c), and (d), respectively; and

(D) by adding at the end the following new subsection:

"(e) The Secretary shall establish underwriting guidelines or procedures to allocate amounts made available for loans and advances insured under this section and for emergency relief payments made under section 106 based on the likelihood that a mortgagor will be able to resume mortgage payments, pursuant to the requirement under section 103(5).";

(4) in section 107—

(A) by striking "(a)"; and

(B) by striking subsection (b);

(5) in section 108 (12 U.S.C. 2707), by adding at the end the following new subsection:

"(d) COVERAGE OF EXISTING PROGRAMS.—The Secretary shall allow funds to be administered by a State that has an existing program that is determined by the Secretary to provide substantially similar assistance to homeowners. After such determination is made such State shall not be required to modify such program to comply with the provisions of this title.";

(6) in section 109 (12 U.S.C. 2708)—

(A) in the section heading, by striking "AUTHORIZATION AND";

(B) by striking subsection (a);

(C) by striking "(b)"; and

(D) by striking "1977" and inserting "2011";

(7) by striking sections 110, 111, and 113 (12 U.S.C. 2709, 2710, 2712); and

(8) by redesignating section 112 (12 U.S.C. 2711) as section 110.

[Explanation at ¶ 6765.]

[¶ 11,497] ACT SEC. 1497. ADDITIONAL ASSISTANCE FOR NEIGHBORHOOD STABILIZATION PROGRAM.

(a) IN GENERAL.—Effective October 1, 2010, out of funds in the Treasury not otherwise appropriated, there is hereby made available to the Secretary of Housing and Urban Development $1,000,000,000, and the Secretary of Housing and Urban Development shall use such amounts for assistance to States and units of general local government for the redevelopment of abandoned and foreclosed homes, in accordance with the same provisions applicable under the second undesignated paragraph under the heading "Community Planning and Development—Community Development Fund" in title XII of division A of the American Recovery and Reinvestment Act of 2009 (Public Law 111-5; 123 Stat. 217) to amounts made available under such second undesignated paragraph, except as follows:

(1) Notwithstanding the matter of such second undesignated paragraph that precedes the first proviso, amounts made available by this section shall remain available until expended.

(2) The 3rd, 4th, 5th, 6th, 7th, and 15th provisos of such second undesignated paragraph shall not apply to amounts made available by this section.

(3) Amounts made available by this section shall be allocated based on a funding formula for such amounts established by the Secretary in accordance with section 2301(b) of the Housing and Economic Recovery Act of 2008 (42 U.S.C. 5301 note), except that—

(A) notwithstanding paragraph (2) of such section 2301(b), the formula shall be established not later than 30 days after the date of the enactment of this Act;

(B) notwithstanding such section 2301(b), each State shall receive, at a minimum, not less than 0.5 percent of funds made available under this section;

(C) the Secretary may establish a minimum grant amount for direct allocations to units of general local government located within a State, which shall not exceed $1,000,000;

(D) each State and local government receiving grant amounts shall establish procedures to create preferences for the development of affordable rental housing for properties assisted with amounts made available by this section; and

(E) the Secretary may use not more than 2 percent of the funds made available under this section for technical assistance to grantees.

(4) Paragraph (1) of section 2301(c) of the Housing and Economic Recovery Act of 2008 shall not apply to amounts made available by this section.

(5) The fourth proviso from the end of such second undesignated paragraph shall be applied to amounts made available by this section by substituting "2013" for "2012".

(6) Notwithstanding section 2301(a) of the Housing and Economic Recovery Act of 2008, the term "State" means any State, as defined in section 102 of the Housing and Community Development Act of 1974 (42 U.S.C. 5302), and the District of Columbia, for purposes of this section and this title, as applied to amounts made available by this section.

(7)(A) None of the amounts made available by this section shall be distributed to—

(i) any organization which has been convicted for a violation under Federal law relating to an election for Federal office; or

(ii) any organization which employs applicable individuals.

(B) In this paragraph, the term "applicable individual" means an individual who—

(i) is—

(I) employed by the organization in a permanent or temporary capacity;

(II) contracted or retained by the organization; or

(III) acting on behalf of, or with the express or apparent authority of, the organization; and

(ii) has been convicted for a violation under Federal law relating to an election for Federal office.

(8) An eligible entity receiving a grant under this section shall, to the maximum extent feasible, provide for the hiring of employees who reside in the vicinity, as such term is defined by the Secretary, of projects funded under this section or contract with small businesses that are owned and operated by persons residing in the vicinity of such projects.

(b) ADDITIONAL AMENDMENTS.—

(1) SECTION 2301.—Section 2301(f)(3)(A)(ii) of the Housing and Economic Recovery Act of 2008 (42 U.S.C. 5301(f)(3)(A)(ii))—

(A) is amended by striking "for the purchase and redevelopment of abandoned and foreclosed upon homes or residential properties that will be used"; and

(B) shall apply with respect to any unexpended or unobligated balances, including recaptured and reallocated funds made available under this Act, section 2301 of the Housing and Economic Recovery Act of 2008 (42 U.S.C. 5301), and the heading "Community Planning and Development—Community Development Fund" in title XII of division A of the American Recovery and Reinvestment Act of 2009 (Public Law 111-5; 123 Stat. 217).

(2) NOTICE OF FORECLOSURE.—For any amounts made available under this section, under division B, title III of the Housing and Economic Recovery Act of 2008 (42 U.S.C. 5301), or under the heading "Community Planning and Development— Community Development Fund" in title XII of division A of the American Recovery and Reinvestment Act of 2009 (Public Law 111-5; 123 Stat. 217), the date of a notice of foreclosure shall be deemed to be the date on which complete title to a property is transferred to a successor entity or person as a result of an order of a court or pursuant to provisions in a mortgage, deed of trust, or security deed.

[Explanation at ¶ 6770.]

[¶ 11,498] ACT SEC. 1498. LEGAL ASSISTANCE FOR FORECLOSURE-RELATED ISSUES.

(a) ESTABLISHMENT.—The Secretary of Housing and Urban Development (hereafter in this section referred to as the "Secretary") shall establish a program for making grants for providing a full range of foreclosure legal assistance to low- and moderate-income homeowners and tenants related to home ownership preservation, home foreclosure prevention, and tenancy associated with home foreclosure.

(b) COMPETITIVE ALLOCATION.—The Secretary shall allocate amounts made available for grants under this section to State and local legal organizations on the basis of a competitive process. For purposes of this subsection "State and local legal organizations" are those State and local organizations whose primary business or mission is to provide legal assistance.

(c) PRIORITY TO CERTAIN AREAS.—In allocating amounts in accordance with subsection (b), the Secretary shall give priority consideration to State and local legal organizations that are operating in the 125 metropolitan statistical areas (as that term is defined by the Director of the Office of Management and Budget) with the highest home foreclosure rates.

(d) LEGAL ASSISTANCE.—

(1) IN GENERAL.—Any State or local legal organization that receives financial assistance pursuant to this section may use such amounts only to assist—

(A) homeowners of owner-occupied homes with mortgages in default, in danger of default, or subject to or at risk of foreclosure; and

(B) tenants at risk of or subject to eviction as a result of foreclosure of the property in which such tenant resides.

(2) COMMENCE USE WITHIN 90 DAYS.—Any State or local legal organization that receives financial assistance pursuant to this section shall begin using any financial assistance received under this section within 90 days after receipt of the assistance.

(3) PROHIBITION ON CLASS ACTIONS.—No funds provided to a State or local legal organization under this section may be used to support any class action litigation.

(4) LIMITATION ON LEGAL ASSISTANCE.—Legal assistance funded with amounts provided under this section shall be limited to mortgage-related default, eviction, or foreclosure proceedings, without regard to whether such foreclosure is judicial or nonjudicial.

(5) EFFECTIVE DATE.—Notwithstanding any other provision of this Act, this subsection shall take effect on the date of the enactment of this Act.

(e) LIMITATION ON DISTRIBUTION OF ASSISTANCE.—

(1) IN GENERAL.—None of the amounts made available under this section shall be distributed to—

(A) any organization which has been convicted for a violation under Federal law relating to an election for Federal office; or

(B) any organization which employs applicable individuals.

(2) DEFINITION OF APPLICABLE INDIVIDUALS.—In this subsection, the term "applicable individual" means an individual who—

(A) is—

(i) employed by the organization in a permanent or temporary capacity;

(ii) contracted or retained by the organization; or

(iii) acting on behalf of, or with the express or apparent authority of, the organization; and

(B) has been convicted for a violation under Federal law relating to an election for Federal office.

(f) AUTHORIZATION OF APPROPRIATIONS.—There are authorized to be appropriated to the Secretary $35,000,000 for each of fiscal years 2011 through 2012 for grants under this section.

[Explanation at ¶ 6775.]

TITLE XV—MISCELLANEOUS PROVISIONS

[¶ 11,501] ACT SEC. 1501. RESTRICTIONS ON USE OF UNITED STATES FUNDS FOR FOREIGN GOVERNMENTS; PROTECTION OF AMERICAN TAXPAYERS.

The Bretton Woods Agreements Act (22 U.S.C. 286 et seq.) is amended by adding at the end the following:

"SEC. 68. RESTRICTIONS ON USE OF UNITED STATES FUNDS FOR FOREIGN GOVERNMENTS; PROTECTION OF AMERICAN TAXPAYERS.

"(a) IN GENERAL.—The Secretary of the Treasury shall instruct the United States Executive Director at the International Monetary Fund—

"(1) to evaluate, prior to consideration by the Board of Executive Directors of the Fund, any proposal submitted to the Board for the Fund to make a loan to a country if—

"(A) the amount of the public debt of the country exceeds the gross domestic product of the country as of the most recent year for which such information is available; and

"(B) the country is not eligible for assistance from the International Development Association.

"(2) OPPOSITION TO LOANS UNLIKELY TO BE REPAID IN FULL.—If any such evaluation indicates that the proposed loan is not likely to be repaid in full, the Secretary of the Treasury shall instruct the United States Executive Director at the Fund to use the voice and vote of the United States to oppose the proposal.

"(b) REPORTS TO CONGRESS.—Within 30 days after the Board of Executive Directors of the Fund approves a proposal described in subsection (a), and annually thereafter by June 30, for the duration of any program approved under such proposals, the Secretary of the Treasury shall report in writing to the Committee on Financial Services of the House of Representatives and the Committee on Foreign Relations and the Committee on Banking, Housing, and Urban Affairs of the Senate assessing the likelihood that loans made pursuant to such proposals will be repaid in full, including—

"(1) the borrowing country's current debt status, including, to the extent possible, its maturity structure, whether it has fixed or floating rates, whether it is indexed, and by whom it is held;

"(2) the borrowing country's external and internal vulnerabilities that could potentially affect its ability to repay; and

"(3) the borrowing country's debt management strategy.".

[Explanation at ¶ 7005 and ¶ 7015.]

[¶ 11,502] ACT SEC. 1502. CONFLICT MINERALS.

(a) SENSE OF CONGRESS ON EXPLOITATION AND TRADE OF CONFLICT MINERALS ORIGINATING IN THE DEMOCRATIC REPUBLIC OF THE CONGO.—It is the sense of Congress that the exploitation and trade of conflict minerals originating in the Democratic Republic of the Congo is helping to finance conflict characterized by extreme levels of violence in the eastern Democratic Republic of the Congo, particularly sexual- and gender-based violence, and contributing to an emergency humanitarian situation therein, warranting the provisions of section 13(p) of the Securities Exchange Act of 1934, as added by subsection (b).

(b) DISCLOSURE RELATING TO CONFLICT MINERALS ORIGINATING IN THE DEMOCRATIC REPUBLIC OF THE CONGO.—Section 13 of the Securities Exchange Act of 1934 (15 U.S.C. 78m), as amended by this Act, is amended by adding at the end the following new subsection:

"(p) DISCLOSURES RELATING TO CONFLICT MINERALS ORIGINATING IN THE DEMOCRATIC REPUBLIC OF THE CONGO.—

"(1) REGULATIONS.—

"(A) IN GENERAL.—Not later than 270 days after the date of the enactment of this subsection, the Commission shall promulgate regulations requiring any person described in paragraph (2) to disclose annually, beginning with the person's first full fiscal year that begins after the date of promulgation of such regulations, whether conflict minerals that are necessary as described in paragraph (2)(B), in the year for which such reporting is required, did originate in the Democratic Republic of the Congo or an adjoining country and, in cases in which such conflict minerals did originate in any such country, submit to the Commission a report that includes, with respect to the period covered by the report—

"(i) a description of the measures taken by the person to exercise due diligence on the source and chain of custody of such minerals, which measures shall include an independent private sector audit of such report submitted through the Commission that is conducted in accordance with standards established by the Comptroller General of the United States, in accordance with rules promulgated by the Commission, in consultation with the Secretary of State; and

"(ii) a description of the products manufactured or contracted to be manufactured that are not DRC conflict free ('DRC conflict free' is defined to mean the products that do not contain minerals that directly or indirectly finance or benefit armed groups in the Democratic Republic of the Congo or an adjoining country), the entity that conducted the independent private sector audit in accordance with clause (i), the facilities used to process the conflict minerals, the country of origin of the conflict minerals, and the efforts to determine the mine or location of origin with the greatest possible specificity.

"(B) CERTIFICATION.—The person submitting a report under subparagraph (A) shall certify the audit described in clause (i) of such subparagraph that is included in such report. Such a certified audit shall constitute a critical component of due diligence in establishing the source and chain of custody of such minerals.

"(C) Unreliable determination.—If a report required to be submitted by a person under subparagraph (A) relies on a determination of an independent private sector audit, as described under subparagraph (A)(i), or other due diligence processes previously determined by the Commission to be unreliable, the report shall not satisfy the requirements of the regulations promulgated under subparagraph (A)(i).

"(D) DRC conflict free.—For purposes of this paragraph, a product may be labeled as 'DRC conflict free' if the product does not contain conflict minerals that directly or indirectly finance or benefit armed groups in the Democratic Republic of the Congo or an adjoining country.

"(E) Information available to the public.—Each person described under paragraph (2) shall make available to the public on the Internet website of such person the information disclosed by such person under subparagraph (A).

"(2) Person described.—A person is described in this paragraph if—

"(A) the person is required to file reports with the Commission pursuant to paragraph (1)(A); and

"(B) conflict minerals are necessary to the functionality or production of a product manufactured by such person.

"(3) Revisions and waivers.—The Commission shall revise or temporarily waive the requirements described in paragraph (1) if the President transmits to the Commission a determination that—

"(A) such revision or waiver is in the national security interest of the United States and the President includes the reasons therefor; and

"(B) establishes a date, not later than 2 years after the initial publication of such exemption, on which such exemption shall expire.

"(4) Termination of disclosure requirements.—The requirements of paragraph (1) shall terminate on the date on which the President determines and certifies to the appropriate congressional committees, but in no case earlier than the date that is one day after the end of the 5-year period beginning on the date of the enactment of this subsection, that no armed groups continue to be directly involved and benefitting from commercial activity involving conflict minerals.

"(5) Definitions.—For purposes of this subsection, the terms 'adjoining country', 'appropriate congressional committees', 'armed group', and 'conflict mineral' have the meaning given those terms under section 1502 of the Dodd-Frank Wall Street Reform and Consumer Protection Act.".

(c) Strategy and Map to Address Linkages Between Conflict Minerals and Armed Groups.—

(1) Strategy.—

(A) In general.—Not later than 180 days after the date of the enactment of this Act, the Secretary of State, in consultation with the Administrator of the United States Agency for International Development, shall submit to the appropriate congressional committees a strategy to address the linkages between human rights abuses, armed groups, mining of conflict minerals, and commercial products.

(B) Contents.—The strategy required by subparagraph (A) shall include the following:

(i) A plan to promote peace and security in the Democratic Republic of the Congo by supporting efforts of the Government of the Democratic Republic of the Congo, including the Ministry of Mines and other relevant agencies, adjoining countries, and the international community, in particular the United Nations Group of Experts on the Democratic Republic of Congo, to—

(I) monitor and stop commercial activities involving the natural resources of the Democratic Republic of the Congo that contribute to the activities of armed groups and human rights violations in the Democratic Republic of the Congo; and

(II) develop stronger governance and economic institutions that can facilitate and improve transparency in the cross-border trade involving the natural resources of the Democratic Republic of the Congo to reduce exploitation by armed groups and promote local and regional development.

(ii) A plan to provide guidance to commercial entities seeking to exercise due diligence on and formalize the origin and chain of custody of conflict minerals used in their products and on their suppliers to ensure that conflict minerals used in the products of such suppliers do not directly or indirectly finance armed conflict or result in labor or human rights violations.

(iii) A description of punitive measures that could be taken against individuals or entities whose commercial activities are supporting armed groups and human rights violations in the Democratic Republic of the Congo.

(2) MAP.—

(A) IN GENERAL.—Not later than 180 days after the date of the enactment of this Act, the Secretary of State shall, in accordance with the recommendation of the United Nations Group of Experts on the Democratic Republic of the Congo in their December 2008 report—

(i) produce a map of mineral-rich zones, trade routes, and areas under the control of armed groups in the Democratic Republic of the Congo and adjoining countries based on data from multiple sources, including—

(I) the United Nations Group of Experts on the Democratic Republic of the Congo;

(II) the Government of the Democratic Republic of the Congo, the governments of adjoining countries, and the governments of other Member States of the United Nations; and

(III) local and international nongovernmental organizations;

(ii) make such map available to the public; and

(iii) provide to the appropriate congressional committees an explanatory note describing the sources of information from which such map is based and the identification, where possible, of the armed groups or other forces in control of the mines depicted.

(B) DESIGNATION.—The map required under subparagraph (A) shall be known as the "Conflict Minerals Map", and mines located in areas under the control of armed groups in the Democratic Republic of the Congo and adjoining countries, as depicted on such Conflict Minerals Map, shall be known as "Conflict Zone Mines".

(C) UPDATES.—The Secretary of State shall update the map required under subparagraph (A) not less frequently than once every 180 days until the date on which the disclosure requirements under paragraph (1) of section 13(p) of the Securities Exchange Act of 1934, as added by subsection (b), terminate in accordance with the provisions of paragraph (4) of such section 13(p).

(D) PUBLICATION IN FEDERAL REGISTER.—The Secretary of State shall add minerals to the list of minerals in the definition of conflict minerals under section 1502, as appropriate. The Secretary shall publish in the Federal Register notice of intent to declare a mineral as a conflict mineral included in such definition not later than one year before such declaration.

(d) REPORTS.—

(1) BASELINE REPORT.—Not later than 1 year after the date of the enactment of this Act and annually thereafter until the termination of the disclosure requirements under section 13(p) of the Securities Exchange Act of 1934, the Comptroller General of the United States shall submit to appropriate congressional committees a report that includes an assessment of the rate of sexual- and gender-based violence in war-torn areas of the Democratic Republic of the Congo and adjoining countries.

(2) REGULAR REPORT ON EFFECTIVENESS.—Not later than 2 years after the date of the enactment of this Act and annually thereafter, the Comptroller General of the United States shall submit to the appropriate congressional committees a report that includes the following:

(A) An assessment of the effectiveness of section 13(p) of the Securities Exchange Act of 1934, as added by subsection (b), in promoting peace and security in the Democratic Republic of the Congo and adjoining countries.

(B) A description of issues encountered by the Securities and Exchange Commission in carrying out the provisions of such section 13(p).

(C)(i) A general review of persons described in clause (ii) and whether information is publicly available about—

(I) the use of conflict minerals by such persons; and

(II) whether such conflict minerals originate from the Democratic Republic of the Congo or an adjoining country.

(ii) A person is described in this clause if—

(I) the person is not required to file reports with the Securities and Exchange Commission pursuant to section 13(p)(1)(A) of the Securities Exchange Act of 1934, as added by subsection (b); and

(II) conflict minerals are necessary to the functionality or production of a product manufactured by such person.

(3) REPORT ON PRIVATE SECTOR AUDITING.—Not later than 30 months after the date of the enactment of this Act, and annually thereafter, the Secretary of Commerce shall submit to the appropriate congressional committees a report that includes the following:

(A) An assessment of the accuracy of the independent private sector audits and other due diligence processes described under section 13(p) of the Securities Exchange Act of 1934.

(B) Recommendations for the processes used to carry out such audits, including ways to—

(i) improve the accuracy of such audits; and

(ii) establish standards of best practices.

(C) A listing of all known conflict mineral processing facilities worldwide.

(e) DEFINITIONS.—For purposes of this section:

(1) ADJOINING COUNTRY.—The term "adjoining country", with respect to the Democratic Republic of the Congo, means a country that shares an internationally recognized border with the Democratic Republic of the Congo.

(2) APPROPRIATE CONGRESSIONAL COMMITTEES.—The term "appropriate congressional committees" means—

(A) the Committee on Appropriations, the Committee on Foreign Affairs, the Committee on Ways and Means, and the Committee on Financial Services of the House of Representatives; and

(B) the Committee on Appropriations, the Committee on Foreign Relations, the Committee on Finance, and the Committee on Banking, Housing, and Urban Affairs of the Senate.

(3) ARMED GROUP.—The term "armed group" means an armed group that is identified as perpetrators of serious human rights abuses in the annual Country Reports on Human Rights Practices under sections 116(d) and 502B(b) of the Foreign Assistance Act of 1961 (22 U.S.C. 2151n(d) and 2304(b)) relating to the Democratic Republic of the Congo or an adjoining country.

(4) CONFLICT MINERAL.—The term "conflict mineral" means—

(A) columbite-tantalite (coltan), cassiterite, gold, wolframite, or their derivatives; or

(B) any other mineral or its derivatives determined by the Secretary of State to be financing conflict in the Democratic Republic of the Congo or an adjoining country.

(5) UNDER THE CONTROL OF ARMED GROUPS.—The term "under the control of armed groups" means areas within the Democratic Republic of the Congo or adjoining countries in which armed groups—

(A) physically control mines or force labor of civilians to mine, transport, or sell conflict minerals;

(B) tax, extort, or control any part of trade routes for conflict minerals, including the entire trade route from a Conflict Zone Mine to the point of export from the Democratic Republic of the Congo or an adjoining country; or

(C) tax, extort, or control trading facilities, in whole or in part, including the point of export from the Democratic Republic of the Congo or an adjoining country.

[Explanation at ¶ 7020.]

[¶ 11,503] ACT SEC. 1503. REPORTING REQUIREMENTS REGARDING COAL OR OTHER MINE SAFETY.

(a) REPORTING MINE SAFETY INFORMATION.—Each issuer that is required to file reports pursuant to section 13(a) or 15(d) of the Securities Exchange Act of 1934 (15 U.S.C. 78m, 78o) and that is an operator, or that has a subsidiary that is an operator, of a coal or other mine shall include, in each periodic report filed with the Commission under the securities laws on or after the date of enactment of this Act, the following information for the time period covered by such report:

(1) For each coal or other mine of which the issuer or a subsidiary of the issuer is an operator—

(A) the total number of violations of mandatory health or safety standards that could significantly and substantially contribute to the cause and effect of a coal or other mine safety or health hazard under section 104 of the Federal Mine Safety and Health Act of 1977 (30 U.S.C. 814) for which the operator received a citation from the Mine Safety and Health Administration;

(B) the total number of orders issued under section 104(b) of such Act (30 U.S.C. 814(b));

(C) the total number of citations and orders for unwarrantable failure of the mine operator to comply with mandatory health or safety standards under section 104(d) of such Act (30 U.S.C. 814(d));

(D) the total number of flagrant violations under section 110(b)(2) of such Act (30 U.S.C. 820(b)(2));

(E) the total number of imminent danger orders issued under section 107(a) of such Act (30 U.S.C. 817(a));

(F) the total dollar value of proposed assessments from the Mine Safety and Health Administration under such Act (30 U.S.C. 801 et seq.); and

(G) the total number of mining-related fatalities.

(2) A list of such coal or other mines, of which the issuer or a subsidiary of the issuer is an operator, that receive written notice from the Mine Safety and Health Administration of—

(A) a pattern of violations of mandatory health or safety standards that are of such nature as could have significantly and substantially contributed to the cause and effect of coal or other mine health or safety hazards under section 104(e) of such Act (30 U.S.C. 814(e)); or

(B) the potential to have such a pattern.

(3) Any pending legal action before the Federal Mine Safety and Health Review Commission involving such coal or other mine.

(b) REPORTING SHUTDOWNS AND PATTERNS OF VIOLATIONS.—Beginning on and after the date of enactment of this Act, each issuer that is an operator, or that has a subsidiary that is an operator, of a coal or other mine shall file a current report with the Commission on Form 8-K (or any successor form) disclosing the following regarding each coal or other mine of which the issuer or subsidiary is an operator:

(1) The receipt of an imminent danger order issued under section 107(a) of the Federal Mine Safety and Health Act of 1977 (30 U.S.C. 817(a)).

(2) The receipt of written notice from the Mine Safety and Health Administration that the coal or other mine has—

(A) a pattern of violations of mandatory health or safety standards that are of such nature as could have significantly and substantially contributed to the cause and effect of coal or other mine health or safety hazards under section 104(e) of such Act (30 U.S.C. 814(e)); or

(B) the potential to have such a pattern.

(c) RULE OF CONSTRUCTION.—Nothing in this section shall be construed to affect any obligation of a person to make a disclosure under any other applicable law in effect before, on, or after the date of enactment of this Act.

(d) COMMISSION AUTHORITY.—

(1) ENFORCEMENT.—A violation by any person of this section, or any rule or regulation of the Commission issued under this section, shall be treated for all purposes in the same manner as a violation of the Securities Exchange Act of 1934 (15 U.S.C. 78a et seq.) or the rules and regulations issued thereunder, consistent with the provisions of this section, and any such person shall be subject to the same penalties, and to the same extent, as for a violation of such Act or the rules or regulations issued thereunder.

(2) RULES AND REGULATIONS.—The Commission is authorized to issue such rules or regulations as are necessary or appropriate for the protection of investors and to carry out the purposes of this section.

(e) DEFINITIONS.—In this section—

(1) the terms "issuer" and "securities laws" have the meaning given the terms in section 3 of the Securities Exchange Act of 1934 (15 U.S.C. 78c);

(2) the term "coal or other mine" means a coal or other mine, as defined in section 3 of the Federal Mine Safety and Health Act of 1977 (30 U.S.C. 802), that is subject to the provisions of such Act (30 U.S.C. 801 et seq.); and

(3) the term "operator" has the meaning given the term in section 3 of the Federal Mine Safety and Health Act of 1977 (30 U.S.C. 802).

(f) EFFECTIVE DATE.—This section shall take effect on the day that is 30 days after the date of enactment of this Act.

[Explanation at ¶ 7025.]

[¶ 11,504] ACT SEC. 1504. DISCLOSURE OF PAYMENTS BY RESOURCE EXTRACTION ISSUERS.

Section 13 of the Securities Exchange Act of 1934 (15 U.S.C. 78m), as amended by this Act, is amended by adding at the end the following:

"(q) DISCLOSURE OF PAYMENTS BY RESOURCE EXTRACTION ISSUERS.—

"(1) DEFINITIONS.—In this subsection—

"(A) the term 'commercial development of oil, natural gas, or minerals' includes exploration, extraction, processing, export, and other significant actions relating to oil, natural gas, or minerals, or the acquisition of a license for any such activity, as determined by the Commission;

"(B) the term 'foreign government' means a foreign government, a department, agency, or instrumentality of a foreign government, or a company owned by a foreign government, as determined by the Commission;

"(C) the term 'payment'—

"(i) means a payment that is—

"(I) made to further the commercial development of oil, natural gas, or minerals; and

"(II) not de minimis; and

"(ii) includes taxes, royalties, fees (including license fees), production entitlements, bonuses, and other material benefits, that the Commission, consistent with the guidelines of the Extractive Industries Transparency Initiative (to the extent practicable), determines are part of the commonly recognized revenue stream for the commercial development of oil, natural gas, or minerals;

"(D) the term 'resource extraction issuer' means an issuer that—

"(i) is required to file an annual report with the Commission; and

"(ii) engages in the commercial development of oil, natural gas, or minerals;

"(E) the term 'interactive data format' means an electronic data format in which pieces of information are identified using an interactive data standard; and

"(F) the term 'interactive data standard' means standardized list of electronic tags that mark information included in the annual report of a resource extraction issuer.

"(2) DISCLOSURE.—

"(A) INFORMATION REQUIRED.—Not later than 270 days after the date of enactment of the Dodd-Frank Wall Street Reform and Consumer Protection Act, the Commission shall issue final rules that require each resource extraction issuer to include in an annual report of the resource extraction issuer information relating to any payment made by the resource extraction issuer, a subsidiary of the resource extraction issuer, or an entity under the control of the resource extraction issuer to a foreign government or the Federal Government for the purpose of the commercial development of oil, natural gas, or minerals, including—

"(i) the type and total amount of such payments made for each project of the resource extraction issuer relating to the commercial development of oil, natural gas, or minerals; and

"(ii) the type and total amount of such payments made to each government.

"(B) CONSULTATION IN RULEMAKING.—In issuing rules under subparagraph (A), the Commission may consult with any agency or entity that the Commission determines is relevant.

"(C) INTERACTIVE DATA FORMAT.—The rules issued under subparagraph (A) shall require that the information included in the annual report of a resource extraction issuer be submitted in an interactive data format.

"(D) INTERACTIVE DATA STANDARD.—

"(i) IN GENERAL.—The rules issued under subparagraph (A) shall establish an interactive data standard for the information included in the annual report of a resource extraction issuer.

"(ii) ELECTRONIC TAGS.—The interactive data standard shall include electronic tags that identify, for any payments made by a resource extraction issuer to a foreign government or the Federal Government—

"(I) the total amounts of the payments, by category;

"(II) the currency used to make the payments;

"(III) the financial period in which the payments were made;

"(IV) the business segment of the resource extraction issuer that made the payments;

"(V) the government that received the payments, and the country in which the government is located;

"(VI) the project of the resource extraction issuer to which the payments relate; and

"(VII) such other information as the Commission may determine is necessary or appropriate in the public interest or for the protection of investors.

"(E) INTERNATIONAL TRANSPARENCY EFFORTS.—To the extent practicable, the rules issued under subparagraph (A) shall support the commitment of the Federal Government to international transparency promotion efforts relating to the commercial development of oil, natural gas, or minerals.

"(F) EFFECTIVE DATE.—With respect to each resource extraction issuer, the final rules issued under subparagraph (A) shall take effect on the date on which the resource extraction issuer is required to submit an annual report relating to the fiscal year of the resource extraction issuer that ends not earlier than 1 year after the date on which the Commission issues final rules under subparagraph (A).

"(3) PUBLIC AVAILABILITY OF INFORMATION.—

"(A) IN GENERAL.—To the extent practicable, the Commission shall make available online, to the public, a compilation of the information required to be submitted under the rules issued under paragraph (2)(A).

"(B) OTHER INFORMATION.—Nothing in this paragraph shall require the Commission to make available online information other than the information required to be submitted under the rules issued under paragraph (2)(A).

"(4) AUTHORIZATION OF APPROPRIATIONS.—There are authorized to be appropriated to the Commission such sums as may be necessary to carry out this subsection.".

[Explanation at ¶ 7030.]

[¶ 11,505] ACT SEC. 1505. STUDY BY THE COMPTROLLER GENERAL.

(a) IN GENERAL.—Not later than 1 year after the date of enactment of this Act, the Comptroller General of the United States shall issue a report assessing the relative independence, effectiveness, and expertise of presidentially appointed inspectors general and inspectors general of designated Federal entities, as such term is defined under section 8G of the Inspector General Act of 1978, and the effects on independence of the amendments to the Inspector General Act of 1978 made by this Act.

(b) REPORT.—The report required by subsection (a) shall be issued to the Committees on Financial Services and Oversight and Government Reform of the House of Representatives and the Committees on Banking, Housing, and Urban Affairs and Homeland Security and Governmental Affairs of the Senate.

[Explanation at ¶ 7035.]

[¶ 11,506] ACT SEC. 1506. STUDY ON CORE DEPOSITS AND BROKERED DEPOSITS.

(a) STUDY.—The Corporation shall conduct a study to evaluate—

(1) the definition of core deposits for the purpose of calculating the insurance premiums of banks;

(2) the potential impact on the Deposit Insurance Fund of revising the definitions of brokered deposits and core deposits to better distinguish between them;

(3) an assessment of the differences between core deposits and brokered deposits and their role in the economy and banking sector of the United States;

(4) the potential stimulative effect on local economies of redefining core deposits; and

(5) the competitive parity between large institutions and community banks that could result from redefining core deposits.

(b) REPORT TO CONGRESS.—Not later than 1 year after the date of enactment of this Act, the Corporation shall submit to the Committee on Banking, Housing, and Urban Affairs of the Senate and the Committee on Financial Services of the House of Representatives a report on the results of the study under subsection (a) that includes legislative recommendations, if any, to address concerns arising in connection with the definitions of core deposits and brokered deposits.

[Explanation at ¶ 7040.]

TITLE XVI—SECTION 1256 CONTRACTS

[¶ 11,601] ACT SEC. 1601. CERTAIN SWAPS, ETC., NOT TREATED AS SECTION 1256 CONTRACTS.

(a) IN GENERAL.—Subsection (b) of section 1256 of the Internal Revenue Code of 1986 is amended—

(1) by redesignating paragraphs (1) through (5) as subparagraphs (A) through (E), respectively, and by indenting such subparagraphs (as so redesignated) accordingly,

(2) by striking "For purposes of" and inserting the following:

"(1) IN GENERAL.—For purposes of", and

(3) by striking the last sentence and inserting the following new paragraph:

"(2) EXCEPTIONS.—The term 'section 1256 contract' shall not include—

"(A) any securities futures contract or option on such a contract unless such contract or option is a dealer securities futures contract, or

"(B) any interest rate swap, currency swap, basis swap, interest rate cap, interest rate floor, commodity swap, equity swap, equity index swap, credit default swap, or similar agreement.".

(b) EFFECTIVE DATE.—The amendments made by this section shall apply to taxable years beginning after the date of the enactment of this Act.

[Explanation at ¶ 7005 and ¶ 7010.]

[¶50,001] Conference Committee Explanatory Statement

Joint Explanatory Statement of the Committee of Conference. Conference Committee Report No. 111-517, to accompany H.R. 4173, pages 864—879. June 29, 2010.

The managers on the part of the House and the Senate at the conference on the disagreeing votes of the two Houses on the amendment of the Senate to the bill H.R. 4173, to provide for financial regulatory reform, to protect consumers and investors, to enhance Federal understanding of insurance issues, to regulate the over-the-counter derivatives markets, and for other purposes, submit the following joint statement to the House and the Senate in explanation of the effect of the action agreed upon by the managers and recommended in the accompanying conference report:

The Senate amendment struck all of the House bill after the enacting clause and inserted a substitute text.

The House recedes from its disagreement to the amendment of the Senate with an amendment that is a substitute for the House bill and the Senate amendment. The differences between the House bill, the Senate amendment, and the substitute agreed to in conference are noted below, except for clerical corrections, conforming changes made necessary by agreements reached by the conferees, and minor drafting and clarifying changes.

[¶50,011] Title I - Financial Stability

Title I, which establishes a specific framework for ensuring financial stability, consists of three subtitles. Subtitle A establishes a Financial Stability Oversight Council to monitor potential threats to the financial system and provide for more stringent regulation of nonbank financial companies and financial activities that the Council determines, based on consideration of risk-related factors, pose risks to financial stability. Subtitle B establishes an Office of Financial Research that supports the Council by collecting information, conducting research, and analyzing data. Subtitle C provides a specific, more stringent supervisory framework for regulating large, interconnected bank holding companies, non-bank financial companies that the Council subjects to more stringent regulation, and activities and practices that the Council determines may pose systemic threats.

[¶50,021] Title II - Orderly Liquidation Authority

Title II establishes an orderly liquidation authority that may be used only if the Secretary of the Treasury (in consultation with the President), based on the written recommendation of two other federal regulators, agrees that doing so is necessary to mitigate serious adverse effects on financial stability in the United States. When the authority is used, the FDIC is appointed receiver and must liquidate the company in a manner that mitigates significant risks to financial stability and minimizes moral hazard. All costs of an orderly liquidation under this title are borne first by shareholders and unsecured creditors, and, if necessary, by risk-based assessments on large financial companies. Taxpayers specifically are protected from losses associated with use of this authority.

[¶50,031] Title III - Transfer of Powers to the Comptroller of the Currency, the Corporation, and the Board of Governors

Prudential Regulator Restructuring

Title III of the conference report transfers the functions of the Office of Thrift Supervision to the Office of the Comptroller of the Currency, which will now supervise federal thrifts, to the Federal Deposit Insurance Corporation ("FDIC"), which will supervise state-chartered thrifts, and to the Federal Reserve Board, which will supervise thrift holding companies.

The conference report also protects employees affected by the regulatory streamlining by preserving pay and benefits, and protecting them from involuntary separation or relocation for a period of time. Title III requires comprehensive coordination of the integration of the agencies, and reporting to the House Financial Services Committee and Senate Banking Committee regarding the implementation of the merger.

Federal Deposit Insurance Reforms

The title revises the FDIC's assessment base for deposit insurance, maintaining the risk-based nature of the assessment structure but transitioning to a broader assessment base for bank premiums based on total assets (minus tangible equity). The conference report also includes additional reforms that will enhance FDIC's ability to manage the Deposit Insurance Fund.

The title makes permanent the increase in deposit insurance to $250,000, and makes the increase retroactive to January 1, 2008. Full insurance of noninterest-bearing transaction accounts is also extended for an additional two years and a comparable program is authorized for credit unions.

Office of Minority and Women Inclusion

The title requires the establishment of offices of Minority and Women Inclusion by the Treasury Department, and the financial regulators, to coordinate technical assistance to minority-owned and women-owned businesses and to promote diversity in the workforce of the regulators.

[¶50,041] Title IV: Regulation of Advisers to Hedge Funds and Others

The conference report eliminates the "private adviser" exemption in the Investment Advisers Act of 1940 ("IAA") thus registering advisers to private funds with the U.S. Securities and Exchange Commission ("SEC"). It expands the advisers' reporting requirements to the SEC as necessary or appropriate in the public interest and for the protection of investors or for the assessment of risk by the Financial Stability Oversight Council. The SEC is authorized to take into account the size, governance, and investment strategy of an adviser to the fund to determine if the fund poses a systemic risk. The conference report also amends the IAA to allow the SEC to require investment advisers to disclose the identity, investments, or affairs of their clients for purposes of systemic risk.

The report includes exemptions for certain private fund advisers. It provides an exemption from registration requirements for advisers of private funds, each with less than $150 million in assets under management, while maintaining reporting requirements as directed by the SEC; an SEC reporting requirement for advisers to venture capital funds, as defined by the SEC and otherwise exempt from the framework; and an exemption for Family Offices. The conference report raises the assets threshold for federal regulation of investment advisers from $30 million to $100 million. Those advisers who qualify to register with their home state must register with the SEC should the adviser operate in more than 15 states.

Finally, the report clarifies the SEC's authority to make rules necessary for the exercise of the powers conferred upon the SEC by the IAA. The SEC must adjust for the effects of inflation any dollar amount measures used in making determinations of the qualified client standard.

Advisers must comply with the new provisions within one year of enactment of the conference report, though the report allows advisers to register earlier with the SEC.

[¶50,051] Title V-Insurance

Subtitle A, the Federal Insurance Office Act of 2010, creates a Federal Insurance Office (FIO) in the Treasury Department to provide the Executive Branch and the Congress with a source of information on the national insurance marketplace. FIO is not a federal regulator or supervisor of insurance. Rather, its functions include collecting information about the insurance industry; monitoring for systemic risk in the insurance industry, including serving in an advisory capacity to the Financial Stability Oversight Council; and administering the Terrorism Risk Insurance Program. Further, FIO will consult with the states regarding insurance matters of national importance and prudential insurance matters of international importance. FIO will also coordinate federal efforts and develop federal policy on prudential aspects of international insurance matters, including representing the United States in international insurance fora, and assisting the Treasury Secretary in negotiations of international insurance agreements with respect to the business of insurance or reinsurance. FIO will have a narrow and limited preemption power over state insurance measures that are inconsistent with such international insurance agreements.

The Federal Insurance Office Act of 2010 expressly provides the Secretary of the Treasury, jointly with the USTR, the authority to negotiate and enter into international insurance agreements. To assure uniform, national application of prudential measures such as reinsurance collateral requirements, the Federal Insurance Office Act provides the Director with the authority to identify and narrowly preempt state insurance measures inconsistent with a defined category of international insurance agreements.

Subtitle B, the Nonadmitted and Reinsurance Reform Act of 2010, will reform and modernize two important sectors of the commercial insurance marketplace, nonadmitted insurance (also known as 'surplus lines' insurance) and reinsurance. Specifically, the Nonadmitted and Reinsurance Reform Act of 2010 creates a uniform system for nonadmitted insurance premium tax payments based upon the home state of the policyholder, encourages the states to develop a compact or other procedural mechanism for uniform tax allocation, and establishes regulatory deference for the home state of the insured. The Act adopts uniform eligibility requirements for nonadmitted insurers as developed and promulgated by the National Association of Insurance Commissioners (NAIC) in the Nonadmitted Insurance Model Act. The Nonadmitted and Reinsurance Reform Act of 2010 will allow direct access to the nonadmitted insurance markets for certain sophisticated commercial purchasers. The Nonadmitted and Reinsurance Reform Act also streamlines the regulation of reinsurance by applying single state regulation for financial solvency and credit for reinsurance. Credit for reinsurance determinations will be controlled by the state of domicile of the ceding insurer. Reinsurance solvency regulation will be controlled by the state of domicile of the reinsurer provided such state is NAIC-accredited or has financial solvency requirements substantially similar to the requirements necessary for NAIC accreditation. Under the Act, non-domiciliary states are specifically prohibited from applying their reinsurance laws in an extra-territorial manner.

[¶50,061] Title VI-Improvements to Regulation of Bank and Savings Association Holding Companies and Depository Institutions

Title VI improves prudential regulation of banks, saving associations, and their holding companies. The improvements include significant limitations on proprietary trading and sponsoring or investing in hedge funds or private equity funds by banking entities through the Volcker rule, better supervision of nonbank subsidiaries of holding companies, enhanced restrictions on transactions with affiliates, limits on derivatives and securities lending credit exposure, and a requirement that any company that controls an insured depository institution serve as a source of financial strength to the institution.

[¶50,071] Title VII-Wall Street Transparency and Accountability

The conference report establishes a new regulatory framework to cover a broad range of participants and institutions in the over-the-counter derivatives market. The Commodity Futures Trading Commission ("CFTC") and the Securities and Exchange Commission ("SEC") are authorized to write rules for the swaps and security-based swaps markets, respectively. The Commissions shall consult and coordinate on rules and include the prudential regulators, to the extent possible, to assure regulatory consistency and comparability. The Commissions will register participants in the market including dealers, major participants, clearing agencies and organizations, exchanges, swap execution facilities, and trade repositories. Exemptions and exclusions from registration will apply as outlined in the report or at the discretion of the regulators. The Commissions will have enforcement authority in their jurisdictions while the prudential regulators maintain exclusive authority to enforce provisions for capital and margin for banks and branches or agencies of foreign banks.

The report provides definitions for terms used in the Commodity Exchange Act and Securities Exchange Act of 1934. The regulatory framework outlines provisions for:

• Mandatory clearing of swaps and security-based swaps for those trades that are eligible for clearing as determined by both the clearing houses and the regulators;

• Mandatory trading on an exchange or swap (or security based swap) execution facility should the transactions be cleared and a facility will accept it for trading;

• Public trade reporting of all cleared and uncleared swaps and security-based swaps;

• Regulators have authority to impose capital on dealers and major swap participants;

• Regulators have authority to impose margin requirements only on dealers and major participants for uncleared swaps, adding safeguards to the system by ensuring dealers and major swap participants have adequate financial resources to meet obligations;

• Position limits on swaps contracts that perform or affect a significant price discovery function and requirements to aggregate limits across markets; and

¶50,071

- Prohibitions against market manipulation.

The report includes a prohibition of federal assistance to swaps and security-based swap entities, including federal deposit insurance, access to the Federal Reserve discount window or Federal Reserve credit facility, to swaps entities in connection with their trading in swaps or securities-based swaps.

The report establishes a code of conduct for all registered swap dealers and major swap participants requiring them to disclose to the swap entity the material risks and characteristics of a swap and any conflicts of interest or material incentives. When acting as counterparties to a pension fund, endowment fund, or state or local government, dealers are to have a reasonable basis to believe that the fund or governmental entity has an independent representative advising them.

The report requires a number of studies, including studies on international swap regulation, the regulation of carbon markets, stable value contracts, and the effect of position limits on exchanges.

[¶50,081] Title VIII - Payment, Clearing, and Settlement Supervision

Title VIII establishes a specific framework for promoting uniform risk-management standards for systemically important financial market utilities (FMUs) and systemically important payment, clearing, and settlement (PCS) activities conducted by financial institutions. The Board of Governors of the Federal Reserve System (Board), the Securities and Exchange Commission (SEC), or the Commodity Futures Trading Commission (CFTC), as appropriate, is primarily responsible for establishing and enforcing risk-management standards for FMUs and PCS activities that the Council identifies as systemically important. If the Board determines that the standards imposed by the SEC or the CFTC or the enforcement actions of such agencies are insufficient, then the Council can require the SEC or CFTC to impose additional standards or take additional enforcement actions.

[¶50,091] Title IX-Investor Protections and

Improvements to the Regulation of Securities

Subtitle A-Increasing Investor Protection establishes mechanisms to assist investors in their dealings with the SEC by creating an Office of Investor Advocate and an Ombudsman. It also creates an Investor Advisory Committee at the SEC, and clarifies the authority of the SEC to engage in investor testing. Subtitle A directs the SEC to study the standards of care applicable to broker-dealers and investment advisers giving investment advice to retail customers, and it authorizes the SEC to promulgate rules imposing a fiduciary duty on broker-dealers and investment advisers to protect retail customers. In addition, the subtitle streamlines filing procedures for self-regulatory organizations. Subtitle A also clarifies the authority of the SEC to require investor disclosures before purchase of investment products and services. Finally, the subtitle requires studies on the enhancement of investment adviser examinations, financial literacy, mutual fund advertising, conflicts of interest, improved investor access to information on investment advisers and broker-dealers, and financial planners and the use of financial designations.

Subtitle B-Increasing Regulatory Enforcement and Remedies strengthens the SEC's authority to conduct investigations, impose liability on control persons, and assess penalties for violations of the securities laws. It also makes clear that the intent standard in SEC enforcement actions for aiding and abetting is recklessness, and it requires a study regarding the issue of aiding and abetting liability in private actions. Under subtitle B, the SEC has the authority to restrict pre-dispute mandatory arbitration. The subtitle further enhances incentives and protections for whistleblowers providing information leading to successful SEC enforcement actions. Awards to whistleblowers will range from 10 percent to 30 percent of the amounts collected by the SEC in actions where the SEC obtained monetary sanctions exceeding $1 million. The subtitle also works to protect the confidentiality of whistleblowers.

The subtitle further enhances the ability of the SEC to ban violators from all parts of the securities industry, disqualifies felons and other bad actors from using the Regulation D offering exemption, and provides for the equal treatment of self-regulatory organization (SRO) rules. It streamlines SRO rule filing procedures by requiring the SEC to complete the process of reviewing and taking action on proposed SRO rules within specified time frames. The subtitle enhances the ability of the SEC to issue subpoenas, bring cases against individuals, and share information with other authorities. It also updates the law governing the Securities Investor Protection Corporation (SIPC). These reforms include increasing the minimum assessments on SIPC members; raising penalties for fraud; and establishing civil and criminal penalties against any person who misrepresents membership in SIPC. Subtitle B gives the SEC authority to enhance public reporting of aggregate information on short selling, prohibits manipulative short sales, and requires notification to customers that they may choose not to allow their securities to be used in connection with short sales. The subtitle further establishes procedures to notify investors about missing securities, and it requires the SEC to complete investigations and examinations within certain time frames, subject to exceptions for complex cases. Finally, the subtitle requires a study regarding the issue of aiding and abetting liability in private actions for securities fraud.

Subtitle C- Improvement to the Regulation of Credit Rating Agencies gives broader powers to the SEC to regulate nationally recognized statistical rating organizations ("NRSROs"). A new Office of Credit Ratings ("Office") is required to examine NRSROs at least once a year and make key findings public. The Office will write new rules, including requiring NRSROs to (1) set up internal controls over the process for determining credit ratings; (2) establish an independent board of directors; (3) make greater disclosures to the public and investors; and (4) develop universal ratings across asset classes and types of issuer. The report also gives the Office the authority to deregister an NRSRO for providing bad ratings over time. New professional standards are established that require ratings analysts to pass qualifying exams and have continuing education.

The report includes provisions to address conflicts of interest. It prohibits compliance officers from working on ratings, methodologies, or sales and prevents other employees from both marketing ratings services and performing the ratings of securities. The subtitle includes on additional conflict of interest mitigation including a new requirement for NRSROs to conduct a one-year look-back review when an NRSRO employee goes to work for an obligor or underwriter of a security or money market instrument subject to a rating by that NRSRO; and report to the SEC when certain employees of the NRSRO go to work for an entity that the NRSRO has rated in the previous twelve months. The SEC shall make such reports publicly available.

To reduce the reliance on ratings, the report amends several statutes to remove references to credit ratings, credit rating agencies and NRSROs. The subtitle includes a requirement that all Federal agencies review their regulations, policies and practices that reference credit ratings, credit rating agencies, and NRSROs. After identifying where the agency relies on or makes these references, the agencies shall modify their regulations by striking these references and substituting a standard of creditworthiness to be established by the agencies.

New provisions address information gathering. NRSROs must consider information in their ratings that comes to their attention from a source other than the organizations being rated, if they find it credible. In addition, the subtitle includes an elimination of the credit rating agency exemption from Regulation Fair Disclosure, commonly known as Reg FD.

The report also addresses liability measures for the NRSRO. The report allows investors to bring private rights of action against credit rating agencies for a knowing or reckless failure to conduct a reasonable investigation of the facts or to obtain analysis from an independent source. The report also nullifies Rule 436(g) which provides an exemption for credit ratings provided by NRSROs from being considered a part of the registration statement prepared or certified by a person under the "expert liability" regime of Section 7 and Section 11 of the Securities Act of 1933. The subtitle requires all references to "furnish" be replaced with the word "file" in existing law. Information that is "furnished" to the SEC is subject to a lower standard of accuracy and liability than information "filed" with the SEC.

The report also directs the SEC to establish a system that prohibits issuers of structured finance from selecting the NRSRO that will provide the initial credit rating. The system would mandate that initial rating assignments for structured finance securities be made on a random or semi-random basis, unless the SEC determines, after study, that an alternative system of assigning ratings would better protect investors and serve the public interest.

Subtitle D-Improvements to Asset-Backed Securitization Process requires securitizers to retain an economic interest in a material portion of the credit risk for any asset that securitizers transfer, sell, or convey to a third party. Risk retention requirements and exemptions will be determined by regulators, which will include setting risk retention requirements for different asset classes that are securitized and allocating risk retention obligations between securitizers and originators. An exemption is provided for qualified residential mortgages, as defined by the regulators, but which can be no broader than the definition of qualified mortgage in Title XIV. Regulators may tailor risk retention requirements as appropriate to the structure of collateralized debt obligations and other complex asset-backed securities. Subtitle D also requires enhanced disclosure by issuers of asset-backed securities, including data related to the underlying loans or assets. Express exemptions are provided for the Farm Credit System and any residential, multifamily, or health care facility mortgage loan asset or securitization which is insured or guaranteed by the United States or an agency of the United States. Regulators also are required to issue total or partial exemptions from risk retention and disclosure requirements for municipal securities and for securitizations of assets issued or guaranteed by federal agencies, as long as the exemption is in the public interest and for the protection of investors.

Subtitle E: Accountability and Executive Compensation is designed to address shareholder rights and executive compensation practices. In this subtitle, Congress provides shareholders in a public company with a vote on executive compensation and additional disclosures involving compensation practices. Under the conference report, at least every three years shareholders can cast an advisory vote to approve the compensation of executives and, where appropriate, golden parachutes for executives. Also under this subtitle, (i) board committees that set compensation policy will consist only of directors who are independent; (ii) companies will tell shareholders about the relationship between the executive compensation the company paid and the company's financial performance; (iii) companies will be required to have a policy to recover money erroneously paid to executives based on financials that later have to be restated due to an accounting error; and (iv) companies will be required to disclose in the annual proxy statement whether employees or members of the board may hedge or offset any decrease in the market value of equity securities granted. This subtitle also requires federal financial regulators to monitor incentive-based payment arrangements of federally regulated financial institutions larger than $1 billion and prohibit incentive-based payment arrangements that the regulators determine jointly could threaten financial institutions' safety and soundness or could have serious adverse effects on economic conditions or financial stability. Finally, subtitle E prohibits brokers who are not beneficial owners of a security from voting through company proxies unless the beneficial owner has instructed the broker to vote on the owner's behalf.

Subtitle F- Improvements to the Management of the Securities and Exchange Commission requires several reports designed to assess SEC performance and provide recommendations for improvements. These involve assessment of the management of the SEC related to internal supervisory controls, personnel management, financial controls, and oversight of national securities associations. Subtitle F also creates a suggestion program for SEC employees and requires the Divisions of Trading and Markets and Investment Management to have examiners on their staffs. It requires the SEC to hire a consultant to study the SEC's operations and determine whether there is a need for comprehensive reform. Finally, Subtitle F requires the GAO to study issues surrounding employees who leave the SEC to work in the securities industry.

Subtitle G- Strengthening Corporate Governance authorizes the SEC to write rules allowing shareholders to nominate candidates for an issuer's board of directors, and to have such candidates listed on the issuer's own proxy materials. In writing such rules, the SEC must consider the burden on small issuers, and may issue exemptions from proxy access rules. Issuers must also disclose why the issuer has chosen to have a single person, or different individuals, serve as CEO and Chairman of the board of the company.

Subtitle H- Municipal Securities requires the registration of municipal financial advisors and subjects them to rules to be promulgated by the Municipal Securities Rulemaking Board (MSRB), which will be enforced by the SEC. An Office of Municipal Securities is created within the SEC. The MSRB will be reconstituted, so that a majority of members are independent of the municipal securities industry. Municipal advisors will have a fiduciary duty to municipal entities. Subtitle H calls for studies of municipal securities markets, and ways to increase disclosure to investors. It also provides a certain source of funding for the Government Accounting Standards Board.

Subtitle I-Public Company Accounting Oversight Board, Portfolio Margining, and Other Matters subtitle I allows the Public Company Accounting Oversight Board (PCAOB) to examine the auditors of broker-dealers. It further authorizes the PCAOB to share information with

¶50,091

foreign authorities. The conference report also authorizes portfolio margining for accounts that hold both securities and futures. In response to problems related to securities borrowing and lending, the conference report requires more transparency. It also raises the dollar threshold that triggers a full "material loss review" by federal banking regulators' inspectors general. Subtitle I improves the coordination, activities, flexibility, and accountability of inspectors general at Federal financial agencies. Subtitle I also exempts small issuers (those with less than $75,000,000 in market capitalization) from the external audit of internal controls requirements of Sarbanes-Oxley Section 404(b), and requires studies on the impact of such an exemption and the exemption for mid-sized companies. The subtitle also creates an exemption for certain annuities from federal securities regulation. Further, it makes numerous technical and conforming changes to Federal securities laws.

Subtitle J: Securities and Exchange Commission Match Funding maintains the role of the Appropriations Committees in setting the Securities and Exchange Commission's annual budgets on and after FY2012. Transaction fee receipts would be treated as offsetting collections equal to the amount of the appropriation. Any excess collections would go to the Treasury as general revenue and not offset any current or future appropriations. Subtitle J sets annual registration fee targets that will produce $5 billion of revenues over ten years that will go to the Treasury general fund. It also requires SEC's budget to be submitted to Congress concurrent with the earliest submission to the Office of Management and Budget and submitted unaltered by the President; builds in flexibility for multi-year budget authority and unanticipated needs; and authorizes graduated funding level increases for the SEC for FYs 2011-2015.

[¶50,101] Title X-Bureau of Consumer Financial Protection

Title X establishes the Bureau of Consumer Financial Protection (Bureau), which will be an independent bureau within the Federal Reserve System. It will be run by a Director who is Presidentially appointed and Senate confirmed. The Bureau will have the authority and accountability to ensure that existing consumer protection laws and regulations are comprehensive, fair, and vigorously enforced.

The Bureau will have authority to issue rules applicable to all financial institutions, including depository institutions that offer financial products and services to consumers. It will also have authority to issue rules under existing consumer banking statutes, including the Truth in Lending Act, the Equal Credit Opportunity Act, and the Real Estate Settlement Procedures Act. Furthermore, the Bureau will have authority to regulate unfair, deceptive and abusive practices and consumer products that it identifies (UDAP authority). The Bureau also may issue regulations relating to disclosures about consumer financial products and services.

Title X also establishes the Bureau as the federal agency with examination and enforcement authority over very large banks and non-bank financial institutions for compliance with the consumer protection laws. The prudential regulators will retain this authority for insured depository institutions and credit unions with assets of $10 billion or less. Exclusions from supervision and enforcement are provided for nonfinancial companies, including merchants, retailers, attorneys, accountants, and real estate brokers, that finance the purchase of their nonfinancial consumer products and services under certain conditions and where the nonfinancial company is not significantly engaged in such financing. There is also an exclusion from the authority of the Bureau for automobile dealers, for which the Federal Reserve Board will continue to write regulations under the enumerated federal consumer laws, to be enforced by the Federal Trade Commission (FTC). The FTC will also be able to write rules proscribing unfair or deceptive acts or practices with regard to auto dealers under the procedures set out under the Administrative Procedures Act.

The conference report also revises the standard the OCC will use to preempt state consumer protection laws. It codifies the standard in the 1996 Supreme Court case *Barnett Bank of Marion County, N.A. v. Nelson* to allow for the preemption of State consumer financial laws that prevent or significantly interfere with national banks' exercise of their powers. State Attorneys General also are given authority to enforce the UDAP and other authorities of the Bureau against banks and savings associations.

To address consumer protection and fair lending matters, Title X establishes the Office of Fair Lending and Equal Opportunity within the Bureau. This Office will oversee the enforcement of federal laws intended to ensure fair, equitable and nondiscriminatory access to credit for individuals and communities, including the Equal Credit Opportunity Act (ECOA) and Home Mortgage Disclosure Act (HMDA). The Office will promote coordination of fair lending enforcement efforts with other federal agencies and State regulators, as appropriate, to provide consistent, efficient and effective enforcement of federal fair lending laws.

The Bureau will also include an Office for Financial Education and an Office for the Financial Protection of Older Americans. In addition, Title X provides for enhanced data collection required by HMDA and ECOA.

[¶50,111] Title XI -Federal Reserve System Provisions

Liquidity Programs

The Federal Reserve will be able to make 13(3) emergency loans only through widely available programs approved by the Secretary of the Treasury, and not to individual firms. FDIC programs to guarantee short-term debt during financial crises will be limited to solvent depository institutions and their holding companies, and can be created only after meeting several conditions including Congressional approval.

Federal Reserve Governance and Oversight

The Government Accountability Office will conduct an audit of Federal Reserve 13(3) emergency lending since December 1, 2007, and the Federal Reserve will publish details about such lending on December 1, 2010. The GAO will have ongoing audit authority over Federal Reserve discount window and open market operation transactions, and emergency lending. The Federal Reserve will publicly disclose data on discount window and open market operations, and details about emergency lending, after a delay that will allow these tools to function effectively.

The position of Vice Chairman for Supervision on the Federal Reserve Board of Governors is established, and the Federal Reserve is formally prohibited from delegating its functions for establishing regulatory or supervisory policy to Federal Reserve banks. The presidents of each Federal Reserve Bank will be elected by the directors selected to represent the public (Class B and C directors), and the directors representing the member banks (Class A directors) will no longer be authorized to vote.

[¶50,121] Title XII-Improving Access to Mainstream Financial Institutions

This title will expand access to safe and affordable bank accounts, credit and financial information for low-income, minority and other underserved families. Specifically, the title would address the following challenges facing low- and moderate-income families with three authorized programs:

* authorizes a program to help low- and moderate-income individuals open low-cost checking or savings accounts at banks or credit unions;

* increases access to objective advice through non-profits and others aiding in offering financial advice to consumers; and

* creates a pool of capital to enable community development financial institutions (CDFIs) to establish and maintain small dollar loan programs, creating an alternative to pay day or car title loans in local communities.

[¶50,131] Title XIII-Pay It Back Act

Title XIII, the TARP Pay it Back Act, reduces the amount authorized under the Troubled Asset Repurchase Program to $475 billion, from the original $700 billion; prohibits Treasury from using repaid TARP funds; and prohibits Treasury from initiating new programs under TARP.

[¶50,141] Title XIV-Mortgage Reform and Anti-Predatory Lending Act

Title XIV enacts the Mortgage Reform and Anti-Predatory Lending Act. It sets minimum standards for mortgages by requiring lenders to establish that consumers have a reasonable ability to repay at the time the mortgage is consummated. It provides that certain high-quality, low-cost loans (defined as Qualified Mortgages) are presumed to meet this standard.

The Act also prohibits financial incentives (including payments known as "yield spread premiums") that may encourage mortgage originators, including mortgage brokers and loan officers of lending institutions, to steer consumers to higher-cost and more abusive mortgages. In addition, it prohibits prepayment penalties for any adjustable rate mortgage and other mortgages that do not meet the definition of Qualified Mortgage; limits prepayment penalties charged to borrowers who wish to prepay their mortgages (typically to refinance on more affordable terms); bans single premium credit insurance and prohibits mandatory arbitration clauses; and includes protections for renters of foreclosed properties. Finally, title XIV authorizes funds to provide legal assistance to homeowners and renters who are experiencing problems related to foreclosure.

Title XIV enhances and expands the scope of consumer protections for high-cost loans under the Home Ownership and Equity Protection Act (HOEPA) and requires additional disclosures to consumers. This title revises the benchmarks for determining loans subject to the heightened HOEPA standards. It also prohibits the financing of points and fees; excessive fees for payoff information, modifications, or late payments; and practices that increase the risk of foreclosure, such as balloon payments, encouraging a borrower to default, and call provisions. The title adds a requirement for pre-loan counseling.

The Act establishes an Office of Housing Counseling at HUD that will carry out and coordinate homeownership and rental housing counseling programs; requires the launch of a national public-service, multimedia campaign to promote housing counseling and the establishment of a website and toll-free hotline; authorizes the issuance of homeownership and rental housing counseling grants to HUD-approved housing counseling agencies and State housing finance agencies; and requires HUD to update the Mortgage Information Booklet to provide consumers with a greater understanding of the terms of the home buying process. Additionally, the title requires increased information to consumers about the need for home inspections and ways to avoid foreclosure scams.

Moreover, Title XIV requires all higher-cost mortgage borrowers to have escrow accounts established. It also requires lenders to provide written disclosures about the need to pay taxes and insurance premiums to all borrowers if they opt out of creating escrow accounts. With respect to mortgage servicing reforms, Title XIV updates the Real Estate Settlement Procedures Act to create new consumer protections related to force-placed insurance, swifter responses to inquiries, increased penalties, prompt crediting of payments, and the timely receipt of payoff statement quotes.

Concerning appraisal practices, Title XIV prohibits lenders from making a higher-cost mortgage without first obtaining a written appraisal. Lenders must additionally provide mortgage applicants with copies of any and all written appraisal reports and valuations developed in connection with a mortgage transaction at least 3 days before the scheduled closing date on the property. Title XIV further creates enforceable Federal appraisal independence standards with penalties within the Truth in Lending Act. These standards prohibit the parties involved in a real estate transaction from influencing the independent judgment of an appraiser through collusion, coercion, and bribery, among other activities. The bill also reforms the Federal oversight of the State appraisal regulatory system.

The Act provides $1 billion for "Emergency Mortgage Relief," in the form of loans to homeowners who lose their jobs, to help make mortgage payments while the homeowner is out of work. The Act also provides $1 billion for a third round of funding for the Neighborhood Stabilization Program to enable state and local governments to finance the purchase and redevelopment of foreclosed homes and residential properties. In addition, the Act authorizes a HUD-administered grant-making program to help entities that provide legal assistance to low- and moderateincome recipients on home ownership preservation, foreclosure prevention, and the rights of tenants associated with home foreclosure.

[¶50,151] Title XV- Miscellaneous Provisions

Title XV of the conference report includes:

Restrictions on use of U.S. Funds for Foreign Governments

The conference report [r]equires the Administration to evaluate any proposed loan by the IMF to a middle-income country if that country's public debt exceeds its annual Gross Domestic Product, and to oppose the loan if it cannot certify to Congress that the loan is likely to be repaid.

Extractive Industries Transparency

The conference report requires public disclosure to the SEC of any payment relating to the commercial development of oil, natural gas, and minerals made by any person to the U.S. or a foreign government, and includes as a "payment" taxes, royalties, fees, licenses, production entitlements, bonuses, and other material benefits, as determined by the Securities and Exchange Commission.

The conference report amends the Securities Exchange Act of 1934 to require the SEC to issue rules requiring each resource extraction issuer (an issuer that engages in the commercial development of oil, natural gas, or minerals) to include in an annual report information relating to any payment made by the issuer, a subsidiary or partner, or an entity under its control to the US or a foreign government for the purpose of such commercial development. Requires such rules, to the extent practicable, to support the U.S. commitment to international transparency promotion efforts relating to such commercial development.

Conflict Minerals

The conference report requires disclosure to the SEC by all persons otherwise required to file with the SEC for whom minerals originating in the Democratic Republic of Congo and adjoining countries are necessary to the functionality or production of a product manufactured by such person. Such a public disclosure report by the person must describe the measures taken to exercise due diligence on the source and chain of custody of such materials, the products manufactured, and other matters; requires an independent audit of the report.

The conference report requires that the Department of State, in consultation with others, submit to Congress a strategy to address the illicit minerals trade in the region, and a map to address linkages between conflict minerals and armed groups.

Section 1503 requires mining companies to disclose mining safety violations that are material to investors.

[¶50,161] Title XVI-Section 1256 Contracts

The title contains a provision to address the recharacterization of income as a result of increased exchange-trading of derivatives contracts by clarifying that section 1256 of the Internal Revenue Code does not apply to certain derivatives contracts transacted on exchanges.

Compliance with clause 9 of Rule XXI

Pursuant to clause 9 of rule XXI of the Rules of the House of Representatives, neither this conference report nor the accompanying joint statement of managers contains any congressional earmarks, limited tax benefits, or limited tariff benefits as defined in clause 9 of rule XXI.

[¶54,000] Senate Report No. 111-176
Report of the House Committee on Banking, Housing, and Urban Affairs to accompany S. 3217. Senate Report 111-176.
April 30, 2010

Senate Report 111-176. April 30, 2010

The Committee on Banking, Housing, and Urban Affairs, having considered the original bill (S. 3217) to promote the financial stability of the United States by improving accountability and transparency in the financial system, to end "too big to fail", to protect the American taxpayer by ending bailouts, to protect consumers from abusive financial services practices, and for other purposes, having considered the same, reports favorably thereon without amendment and recommends that the bill do pass.

CONTENTS

I. Introduction
II. Purpose and Scope of the Legislation
III. Background and Need for Legislation
IV. History of the Legislation
V. Section-by-Section Analysis of Bill
VI. Hearing Record
VII. Committee Consideration
VIII. Congressional Budget Office Cost Estimate
IX. Regulatory Impact Statement
X. Changes In Existing Law (Cordon Rule)
XI. Minority Views

I. Introduction

On March 22, 2010, the Senate Committee on Banking, Housing, and Urban Affairs marked up and ordered to be reported the "Restoring American Financial Stability Act of 2010 (RAFSA)." RAFSA is a direct and comprehensive response to the financial crisis that nearly crippled the U.S. economy beginning in 2008. The primary purpose of RAFSA is to promote the financial stability of the United States. It seeks to achieve that goal through multiple measures designed to improve accountability, resiliency, and transparency in the financial system by: establishing an early warning system to detect and address emerging threats to financial stability and the economy, enhancing consumer and investor protections, strengthening the supervision of large complex financial organizations and providing a mechanism to liquidate such companies should they fail without any losses to the taxpayer, and regulating the massive over-the-counter derivatives market.

[¶54,005] II. Purpose and Scope of the Legislation

FINANCIAL STABILITY

Title I establishes a new framework to prevent a recurrence or mitigate the impact of financial crises that could cripple financial markets and damage the economy. A new Financial Stability Oversight Council (Council) chaired by the Treasury Secretary and comprised of key regulators would monitor emerging risks to U.S. financial stability, recommend heightened prudential standards for large, interconnected financial companies, and require nonbank financial companies to be supervised by the Federal Reserve if their failure would pose a risk to U.S. financial stability.

The Federal Reserve would establish and implement the heightened prudential standards and would have additional authority to require (with Council approval) a large financial company to restrict or divest activities that present grave threats to U.S. financial stability. With respect to bank holding companies, the heightened prudential standards would increase in stringency gradually as appropriate in relation to the company's size, leverage, and other measures of risk for those that have assets of $50 billion or more. This graduated approach to the application of the heightened prudential standards is intended to avoid identification of any bank holding company as systemically significant. These heightened prudential standards would also apply to the nonbank financial companies supervised by the Federal Reserve.

A new Office of Financial Research within the Treasury Department would support the Council's work through financial data collection, research, and analysis.

When Treasury Secretary Timothy Geithner presented the Administration's financial reform proposal at a Committee hearing on June 18, 2009, he highlighted several shortcomings of the current supervisory framework that left the government ill-equipped to handle the recent financial crisis: overall capital and liquidity standards were too low; regulatory requirements failed to account for the harm that could be inflicted on the financial system and economy by the failure of large, interconnected and highly leveraged financial institutions; and investment banks and other types of nonbank financial firms operated with inadequate government oversight.[1] FDIC Chairman Sheila Bair testified on July 23, 2009 that the "existence of one regulatory scheme for insured institutions and a much less effective regulatory scheme for non-bank entities created the conditions for arbitrage that permitted the development of risk and harmful products and services outside regulated entities. . . . The performance of the regulatory system in the current crisis underscores the weakness of monitoring systemic risk through the lens of individual financial institutions and argues for the needs to assess emerging risks using a system-wide perspective."[2]

These and other witnesses at Committee hearings relating to the financial crisis and financial reform have made the case for the type of framework established in this title to promote U.S. financial stability. Treasury Secretary Geithner called for the creation of a council of regulators chaired by the Secretary to identify emerging risks in financial institutions and markets, determine where gaps in supervision exist, and facilitate coordination of policy and resolution of disputes. He argued for new authority for the Federal Reserve to set stricter prudential standards for large, interconnected financial firms that could threaten financial stability, including financial firms that do not own banks.[3] Federal Reserve Chairman Ben Bernanke called for a new prudential approach focusing on the stability of the financial system as a whole, with formal mechanisms to identify and deal with emerging systemic risks, and for more stringent capital and liquidity standards for large and complex financial firms.[4] FDIC Chairman Sheila Bair recommended establishing an interagency council that would bring a macro-prudential perspective to regulation and set or harmonize prudential standards for financial firms to mitigate systemic risk.[5] At the July hearing, SEC Chairman Mary Schapiro also testified in favor of establishing such a council with similar membership and authorities.[6] Federal Reserve Board Governor Daniel Tarullo testified at the same hearing that there was substantial merit in establishing a council of regulators to conduct macroprudential oversight and coordinate oversight of the financial system as a whole.[7] Former Comptroller of the Currency Eugene Ludwig argued at a September hearing that no single regulatory agency would be well suited to handle this function alone.[8]

At a February 12, 2010 hearing, several witnesses spoke in favor of the creation of an independent National Institute of Finance (Institute). While the Office of Financial Research (Office) would be established in the Treasury Department under this title, the Office is very similar in key respects to the proposed Institute. Like the Institute, the Office would support the council of regulators charged with monitoring emerging risks to financial stability. The Office would not supervise financial institutions but would have regulatory authority with respect to data collection. The Office's structure is modeled on the proposed Institute, with two main components to fulfill its primary functions—the Data Center and Research and Analysis Center. The structure and funding of the Office are intended to ensure that the Office, like the Institute, would have the resources and ability to provide objective, unbiased assessments of the risks facing the financial system.

ENDING "TOO BIG TO FAIL" BAILOUTS THROUGH THE ORDERLY LIQUIDATION AUTHORITY

Title II establishes an orderly liquidation authority to give the U.S. government a viable alternative to the undesirable choice it faced during the financial crisis between bankruptcy of a large, complex financial company that would disrupt markets and damage the economy, and bailout of such financial company that would expose taxpayers to losses and undermine market discipline. The new orderly liquidation authority would allow the FDIC, which has extensive experience as receiver for failed banking institutions, including large institutions, to safely unwind a failing nonbank financial com-

---

[1] Testimony of Timothy Geithner, Secretary of the Treasury, to the Banking Committee, June 18, 2009.

[2] Testimony of Sheila Bair, Chairman of the Federal Deposit Insurance Corporation to the Banking Committee, July 23, 2009.

[3] Testimony of Timothy Geithner, Secretary of the Treasury, to the Banking Committee, June 18, 2009.

[4] Testimony of Ben Bernanke, Federal Reserve Board Chairman, to the Banking Committee, July 22, 2009.

[5] Testimonies of Sheila Bair, Chairman of the Federal Deposit Insurance Corporation, to the Banking Committee, May 6 and July 23, 2009.

[6] Testimony of Mary Schapiro, Chairman of the Securities and Exchange Commission, to the Banking Committee, July 23, 2009.

[7] Testimony of Daniel Tarullo, Federal Reserve Board Governor, to the Banking Committee, July 23, 2009.

[8] Testimony of Eugene Ludwig, former Comptroller of the Currency, to the Banking Committee, September 29, 2009.

pany or bank holding company, an option that was not available during the financial crisis. Once a failing financial company is placed under this authority, liquidation is the only option; the failing financial company may not be kept open or rehabilitated. The financial company's business operations and assets will be sold off or liquidated, the culpable management of the company will be discharged, shareholders will have their investments wiped out, and unsecured creditors and counterparties will bear losses.

There is a strong presumption that the bankruptcy process will continue to be used to close and unwind failing financial companies, including large, complex ones. The orderly liquidation authority could be used if and only if the failure of the financial company would threaten U.S. financial stability. Therefore the threshold for triggering the orderly liquidation authority is very high: (1) a recommendation by a two thirds vote of the Board of the Governors of the Federal Reserve System; (2) a recommendation by a two thirds vote of the FDIC; (3) a determination and approval by the Secretary of the Treasury after consultation with the President; and (4) a review and determination by a judicial panel.

In order to protect taxpayers, large financial companies will contribute $50 billion over a period of 5 to 10 years to a fund held at the Treasury. This fund may only be used by the FDIC in the orderly liquidation of a failing financial company with the approval of the Treasury Secretary, and may not be used for any other purpose. The FDIC must first rely on these industry contributions if liquidity support is necessary to safely unwind the failing financial company and prevent a "fire sale" of assets that could further threaten financial stability. The fund would help avoid damaging "pro-cyclical" effects by allowing large financial companies to contribute gradually when they can most afford to pay, not when a crisis has already erupted. If additional liquidity is necessary, the FDIC may obtain financing from the Treasury but only if such financing can be repaid by the proceeds of the assets of the failed financial company. Additional assessments on large financial companies may be imposed if necessary to ensure 100 percent repayment of any funds obtained from the Treasury, and any financial company that received payments greater than what it otherwise would have received in bankruptcy will be assessed at a substantially higher rate. Taxpayers will bear no losses from the use of the orderly liquidation authority.

The Committee hearing record provides significant support for establishing an orderly liquidation authority for large, complex bank holding companies and nonbank financial companies. On February 4, 2009, former Federal Reserve Chairman Paul Volcker gave the recommendations of the "Group of 30" (an international body of senior representatives from the public and private sectors and academia dealing with economic and financial issues), which included a call for U.S. legislation to establish a regime to manage the resolution of failed non-depository financial institutions comparable to the process for depository institutions. The recommendations called for applying this regime "only to those few organizations whose failure might reasonably be considered to pose a threat to the financial system."[9] On June 18, 2009, Treasury Secretary Timothy Geithner presented the Administration's financial reform proposal, which called for a new authority modeled on the FDIC's existing authority for banks and thrifts to address the failure of a bank holding company or nonbank financial company when the stability of the financial system is at risk.

In testimony submitted on July 23 of 2009, FDIC Chairman Sheila Bair noted that large financial firms have been "given access to the credit markets at favorable terms without consideration of the firms' risk profile.... Investors and creditors believe their exposure is minimal since they also believe the government will not allow these firms to fail." In her July statement and in testimony on March 19 and May 6, Chairman Bair discussed the limitations of current bankruptcy procedures as applied to large and complex bank holding companies and nonbank financial companies, and advocated for a new statutory authority for the credible orderly unwinding of such companies modeled on the FDIC's existing authorities. Chairman Bair argued that the resolution authority must be able to allocate losses among creditors in accordance with an established claims priority "where stockholders and creditors, not the government, are in a first loss position." The testimony also discussed the merits of building up a fund over time in advance of a failure to provide working capital or to cover unanticipated losses in an orderly liquidation.[10] This type of "pre-funding" would enable the government to impose charges

---

[9] Testimony of Paul Volcker, former Federal Reserve Board Chairman, to the Banking Committee, February 4, 2009.

[10] Testimonies of Sheila Bair, Chairman of the Federal Deposit Insurance Corporation, to the Banking Committee, March 19, May 6, and July 23, 2009.

on large or complex financial companies consistent with the risks they pose to the financial system, provide economic incentives for a financial company against excessive and dangerous growth, and avoid large charges during times of economic stress that would have undesirable "pro-cyclical" effects.

In his July 23, 2009 testimony, Federal Reserve Board Governor Daniel Tarullo also argued for a new resolution authority as a "third option between the choices of bankruptcy and bailout." The testimony argued that allowing losses to be imposed on creditors and shareholders "is critical to addressing the too-big-to-fail problem and the resulting moral hazard effects."[11] Former Comptroller of the Currency Eugene Ludwig also urged the Congress at a September 29, 2009 hearing to create a new resolution function for large, complex financial companies with financing provided by large financial companies.[12]

LIQUIDITY PROGRAMS

Title XI eliminates the ability of either the Federal Reserve or the Federal Deposit Insurance Corporation to rescue an individual financial firm that is failing, while preserving the ability of both regulators to provide needed liquidity and confidence in financial markets during times of severe distress. That is to say, this Title ends the potential for either regulator to come to the rescue of a future AIG, while reconfiguring the weapons in their financial crisis arsenals to increase accountability without diminishing their effectiveness.

The Federal Reserve's emergency lending authority, under section 13(3) of the Federal Reserve Act, in the past allowed the Federal Reserve to make loans to individual entities like AIG. While such lending played an important role in ending the recent financial crisis, it also created potential moral hazard. If the Federal Reserve were to retain authority to make emergency loans to individual firms, then large, interconnected firms might increase their risk-taking behavior, since the Federal Reserve would be there to bail them out in a future financial crisis.

By eliminating the ability to lend to individual institutions, and by requiring all emergency lending to be done through widely-available liquidity facilities that will be approved by the Treasury, monitored through periodic reports to Congress and by Comptroller General audits, and backed by collateral sufficient to protect taxpayers from loss, emergency lending by the Federal Reserve will not be a source of moral hazard.

During the recent crisis the Federal Deposit Insurance Corporation (FDIC) used the "systemic risk exception" to its normal bank receivership rules to establish the Temporary Liquidity Guarantee Program (TLGP) on an *ad hoc* basis.

By paying a TLGP insurance fee, federally insured depositories and U.S. bank, financial and thrift holding companies were able to issue unsecured short-term debt with a federal government guarantee.[13] Many firms used this program, and its existence helped them to roll over needed short-term financing after a period in which the outstanding volume of financial commercial paper contracted sharply and discount rates spiked upward.[14] At its peak usage level in May 2009 the TLGP insured approximately $345 billion in outstanding debt. As of December 2009 the debt guarantee program had assessed $10.3 billion in guarantee fees.[15]

Under the TLGP, the FDIC also established a program to guarantee non-interest bearing transaction accounts that exceed the deposit insurance limit. Participating insured depositories pay an annualized risk-based assessment ranging from 15 to 25 basis points on transaction account amounts that exceed the current FDIC insurance amount of $250,000.

This Title allows the FDIC to guarantee short-term debt during financial crises, but limits the guarantees to *solvent* banks and bank holding companies, restricts the conditions under which such support may be offered, increases accountability of the guarantee program, and eliminates the possibility that taxpayers will pay for any losses from the program.

---

[11] Testimony of Daniel Tarullo, Federal Reserve Board Governor, to the Banking Committee, July 23, 2009.

[12] Testimony of Eugene Ludwig, former Comptroller of the Currency, to the Banking Committee, September 29, 2009.

[13] The fees charged increase with the maturity of the debt, rising from 12.5 basis points for three-month debt to 100 basis points for debt with maturities of one year or more, with additional charges added under certain conditions. Eligible entities include: (1) FDIC-insured depository institutions; (2) U.S. bank holding companies; (3) U.S. financial holding companies; and (4) U.S. savings and loan holding companies that either engage only in activities that are permissible for financial holding companies under section 4(k) of the Bank Holding Company Act (BHCA) or have an insured depository institution subsidiary that is the subject of an application under section 4(c)(8) of the BHCA regarding activities closely related to banking. See http://www.fdic.gov/regulations/resources/tlgp/index.html.

[14] For data on outstanding volumes of financial commercial paper and discount rates for AA financial commercial paper *see* http://www.federalreserve.gov/releases/cp/.

[15] For data on outstanding volumes guaranteed *see* http://www.fdic.gov/regulations/resources/tlgp/reports.html.

¶ 54,005

Under this Title no guarantee can be offered unless the Board of Governors of the Federal Reserve and the FDIC jointly agree that a liquidity event—essentially a breakdown in the ability of borrowers to access credit markets in a normal fashion—exists. The FDIC may then set up a facility to guarantee debt, following policies and procedures determined by regulation. The regulation is to be written in consultation with the Treasury. The terms and conditions of the guarantees must be approved by the Secretary of the Treasury.

The Secretary will determine a maximum amount of guarantees, and the President will request Congress to allow that amount. If the President does not submit the request, the guarantees will not be made. Congress has 5 days under an expedited procedure to disapprove the request. Fees for the guarantees are set to cover all expected costs. If there are losses, they are recouped from those firms that received guarantees. Firms that default on guarantees will be put into receivership, resolution or bankruptcy. Any FDIC aid to an individual firm under the "systemic risk exception" will henceforth only be possible if the firm has been placed in receivership, and therefore the FDIC will no longer be able to provide "open bank assistance" using this exception.

Hence FDIC debt guarantees will be available to help ease liquidity problems during financial crises, but will not be a source of moral hazard since the FDIC may guarantee only the debt of solvent institutions. Moreover, taxpayers are protected from any loss by the recoupment requirements.

Title XI also makes important changes to Federal Reserve governance. It establishes the position of Vice Chairman for Supervision on the Federal Reserve Board of Governors. The Vice Chairman will have the responsibility to develop policy recommendations on supervision and regulation for the Board, and will report twice each year to Congress. The Federal Reserve is also given formal responsibility to identify, measure, monitor, and mitigate risks to U.S. financial stability. In addition, the Federal Reserve is formally prohibited from delegating its functions for establishing regulatory or supervisory policy to Federal Reserve banks.

To eliminate potential conflicts of interest at Federal Reserve banks, the Federal Reserve Act is amended to state that no company, or subsidiary or affiliate of a company, that is supervised by the Board of Governors can vote for Federal Reserve Bank directors; and the officers, directors and employees of such companies and their affiliates cannot serve as directors. In addition, to increase the accountability of the Federal Reserve Bank of New York president, who plays a key role in formulating and executing monetary policy, this reserve bank officer will be appointed by the President, by and with the advice and consent of the Senate, rather than by the bank's board of directors.

"THE VOLCKER RULE"

Section 619 of Title VII prohibits or restricts certain types of financial activity—in banks, bank holding companies, other companies that control an insured depository institution, their subsidiaries, or nonbank financial companies supervised by the Board of Governors—that are high-risk or which create significant conflicts of interest between these institutions and their customers.

Banks, bank holding companies, other companies that control an insured depository institution, their subsidiaries, or nonbank financial companies supervised by the Board of Governors will be prohibited from proprietary trading, sponsoring and investing in hedge funds and private equity funds, and from having certain financial relationships with those hedge funds or private equity funds for which they serve as investment manager or investment adviser. A nonbank financial institution supervised by the Board of Governors that engages in proprietary trading, or sponsoring or investing in hedge funds and private equity funds will be subject to Board rules imposing capital requirements related to, or quantitative limits on, these activities.[16]

The incentive for firms to engage in these activities is clear: when things go well, high-risk behavior can produce high returns. In good times these profits allow firms to grow rapidly, and encourage additional risk-taking. However, when things do not go well, these same activities can produce outsize losses.

When losses from high-risk activities are significant, they can threaten the safety and soundness of individual firms and contribute to overall financial instability. Moreover, when the losses accrue to insured depositories or their holding companies, they can cause taxpayer

---

[16] These firms will be supervised by the Board of Governors because their failure could threaten overall financial stability.

losses. In addition, when banks engage in these activities for their own accounts, there is an increased likelihood that they will find that their interests conflict with those of their customers.

The prohibitions in section 619 therefore will reduce potential taxpayer losses at institutions protected by the federal safety net, and reduce threats to financial stability, by lowering their exposure to risk. Conflicts of interest will be reduced, for example, by eliminating the possibility that firms will favor inside funds when placing funds for clients. The prohibitions also will prevent firms protected by the federal safety net, which have a lower cost of funds, from directing those funds to high-risk uses. Moreover, they will restrict high-risk activity in those nonbank financial firms that pose threats to financial stability.

The prohibitions also will reduce the scale, complexity, and interconnectedness of those banks that are now actively engaged in proprietary trading, or have hedge fund or private equity exposure. They will reduce the possibility that banks will be too big or too complex to resolve in an orderly manner should they fail.

In testimony submitted to the Committee, Neal Wolin, Deputy Secretary of the Treasury, stated that "Proprietary trading, by definition, is not done for the benefit of customers or clients. Rather, it is conducted solely for the benefit of the bank itself. It is therefore difficult to justify an arrangement in which the federal safety net redounds to the benefit of such activities." Wolin noted that the role of proprietary trading and ownership of hedge funds, and their associated high risk, contributed to the crisis when banks were forced to bail out those operations. Wolin testified, "Major firms saw their hedge funds and proprietary trading operations suffer large losses in the financial crisis. Some of these firms 'bailed out' their troubled hedge funds, depleting the firm's capital at precisely the moment it was needed most."[17]

Paul Volcker, former Federal Reserve Board Chairman, discussed the benefits to the market from the prohibition and the impact on systemic risk: "Curbing the proprietary interests of commercial banks is in the interest of fair and open competition as well as protecting the provision of essential financial services." Volcker added that the proposal was "particularly designed to help deal with the problem of "too big to fail' and the related moral hazard that looms so large as an aftermath of the emergency rescues of financial institutions[.]"[18]

THE BUREAU OF CONSUMER FINANCIAL PROTECTION

The Committee has documented in numerous hearings over the years the failure of the federal banking and other regulators to address significant consumer protection issues detrimental to both consumers and the safety and soundness of the banking system.[19] These failures, which are described in more detail below, led to what has become known as the Great Recession in which millions of Americans have lost jobs; millions of American families have lost trillions of dollars in net worth; millions of Americans have lost their homes; and millions of Americans have lost their retirement, college, and other savings.

Structural Problems with Current Consumer Regulation

The current system of consumer protection suffers from a number of serious structural flaws that undermine its effectiveness, including a lack of focus resulting from conflicting regulatory missions, fragmentation, and regulatory arbitrage.

To begin with, placing consumer protection regulation and enforcement within safety and soundness regulators does not lead to better coordination of the two functions, as some would argue. As has been made amply apparent, when these two functions are put in the same agency, consumer protection fails to get the attention or focus it needs. Protecting consumers is not the banking agencies' priority, nor should it be. The primary mission of these regulators "in law and practice," as Assistant Secretary of the Treasury Michael Barr testified, is to ensure the safe and sound operations of the banks. Because of this, former Director of the Office of Thrift Supervision (OTS) Ellen Seidman testified, "[consumer] compliance has always had a hard time competing with safety and soundness for the attention

---

[17] Testimony by Neal Wolin, Deputy Secretary of the Treasury, to the Senate Banking Committee, 2/2/10.

[18] Testimony by Paul Volcker, former Federal Reserve Board Chairman and Chairman of the President's Economic Recovery Advisory Board, to the Senate Banking Committee, 2/2/10.

[19] "The need could not be clearer. Today's consumer protection regime just experienced massive failure. It could not stem a plague of abusive and unaffordable mortgages and exploitative credit cards despite clear warning signs. It cost millions of responsible consumers their homes, their savings, and their dignity. And it contributed to the near-collapse of our financial system. We did not have just a financial crisis; we had a consumer crisis." Testimony of Michael Barr, Assistant Secretary of the Treasury for Financial Institutions, to the Senate Committee on Banking, Housing, and Urban Affairs, July 14, 2009.

of regulators . . . ."[20] In fact, as Assistant Secretary Barr pointed out, bank regulators conduct consumer protection supervision with an eye toward bank safety and soundness by, for example, trying to protect the banks from reputation and litigation risks rather than examining how products and services affect consumers. "Managing risks to the bank does not and cannot protect consumers effectively. This approach judges a bank's conduct toward consumers by its effect on the bank, not . . . on consumers."[21]

This may lead, as some witnesses before the Committee testified, to an emphasis by the regulators on the short term profitability of the banks at the expense of consumer protection.[22]

The current system is also too fragmented to be effective. There are seven different federal regulators involved in consumer rule writing or enforcement. Gene Dodaro, Acting Comptroller General, testified that "the fragmented U.S. regulatory structure contributed to failures by the existing regulators to adequately protect consumers and ensure financial stability."[23] This undermines accountability.

This fragmentation led to regulatory arbitrage between federal regulators and the states, while the lack of any effective supervision on nondepositories led to a "race to the bottom" in which the institutions with the least effective consumer regulation and enforcement attracted more business, putting pressure on regulated institutions to lower standards to compete effectively, "and on their regulators to let them."[24]

A More Effective Approach

This legislation creates the Bureau of Consumer Financial Protection (CFPB), a new, streamlined independent consumer entity housed within the Federal Reserve System. The CFPB will be focused on ensuring that consumers get clear and effective disclosures in plain English and in a timely fashion so that they will be empowered to shop for and choose the best consumer financial products and services for them.

The new CFPB will establish a basic, minimum federal level playing field for all banks and, for the first time, nondepository financial companies that sell consumer financial products and services to American families. It will do so without creating an undue burden on banks, credits unions, or nondepository providers of these products and services.

The CFPB will help protect consumers from unfair, deceptive, and abusive acts that so often trap them in unaffordable financial products. The CFPB will stop regulatory arbitrage. It will write rules and enforce those rules consistently, without regard to whether a mortgage, credit card, auto loan, or any other consumer financial product or service is sold by a bank, a credit union, a mortgage broker, an auto dealer, or any other nondepository financial company. This way, a consumer can shop and compare products based on quality, price, and convenience without having to worry about getting trapped by the fine print into an abusive deal.

The legislation ends the fragmentation of the current system by combining the authority of the seven federal agencies involved in consumer financial protection in the CFPB, thereby ensuring accountability.

The CFPB will have enough flexibility to address future problems as they arise. Creating an agency that only had the authority to address the problems of the past, such as mortgages, would be too short-sighted. Experience has shown that consumer protections must adapt to new practices and new industries.

Mortgage Crisis

> The fundamental story of the current turmoil is relatively easy to tell. It began early in this decade with a weakening of underwriting standards for subprime mortgages in the U.S. Subprime, alt-A and other mortgage products [which] were sold to people who could not afford them and in some cases in violation of legal standards.[25]
>
> —Eugene Ludwig

This financial crisis was precipitated by the proliferation of poorly underwritten mortgages with abusive terms, followed by a broad fall in housing prices as those mortgages went into default and led to increasing foreclosures. These subprime and nontraditional mortgages were

---

[20] Testimony of Ellen Seidman, former Director of the Office of Thrift Supervision, to the Banking Committee, March 2, 2009.

[21] Testimony of Michael Barr, July 14, 2009.

[22] Testimony of Patricia McCoy, George J. and Helen M. England Professor of Law, University of Connecticut to the Banking Committee, hearing on March 3, 2009 and testimony of Travis Plunkett, Legislative Director of the Consumer Federation of America to the Banking Committee, July 14, 2009.

[23] Testimony of Gene Dodaro, Acting Comptroller General of the United States, February 4, 2009.

[24] Testimony of Michael Barr, July 14, 2009.

[25] Testimony of Eugene Ludwig to the Banking Committee, October 16, 2008.

¶54,005

characterized by relatively low initial interest rates that allowed borrowers to obtain loans for which they might not otherwise qualify.[26] However, after 2 or 3 years, the rates would jump up significantly—by as much as 30 to 40 percent or more, according to the testimony of Michael Calhoun, President of the Center for Responsible Lending (CRL).[27] The great majority of the payment-option adjustable rate mortgages (option ARMs) resulted in significant negative amortization, so that many borrowers owed more on their mortgages after several years than when the mortgages were initially sold.

According to testimony heard in the Committee in late 2006,[28] and again in early 2007,[29] many of these loans were made with little or no regard for a borrower's understanding of the terms of, or their ability to repay, the loans. At a September 20, 2006 Subcommittee hearing, Subcommittee Chairman Bunning said "it is not clear that borrowers understand [the] risks" associated with these mortgages, a conclusion borne out both by a study by the Federal Reserve Board and the Consumer Federation of America (CFA). As Allen Fishbein, then Director of Housing Policy at the CFA, testified:

> Consumers today face a dizzying array of mortgage products that are marketed and promoted under a range of products names. While the number of products has exploded, there appears to be little understanding by many borrowers about key features in today's mortgages and how to compare or even understand the differences between these products.

A 2004 Consumer Federation of America survey found that most consumers cannot calculate the payment change for an adjustable rate mortgage . . . . all respondents underestimated the annual increase in the cost of monthly mortgage payments if the interest rate [increased] from 6 percent to 8 percent . . . . Younger, poorer, and less formally educated respondents underestimated by as much as 50 percent.[30]

Fishbein also cited a Federal Reserve study of ARM borrowers that found that 35 percent of them did not know the maximum amount their interest rate could increase at one time; 44 percent did not know the maximum rate they could be charged; and 17 percent did not know the frequency with which the rate could change.[31]

Finally, Fishbein cited a focus group of exotic mortgage borrowers organized by Public Opinion Strategies. It found that these consumers were "surprised by the magnitude of the payment shock" once rate sheets with the various mortgage option terms were shown to them. Lower-income borrowers, in particular, called the payment increases "shocking." Fishbein explained that these lower-income borrowers "were less informed about the payment increases and debt risks of non-traditional mortgages, with some noting they "wish they had known more.'"[32]

In that same hearing, Senator Sarbanes said that:

---

[26] It is important to note that the vast majority of subprime mortgages were used to refinance existing mortgages rather than to purchase a home. According to data collected by the Center for Responsible Lending ("Subprime Lending: A Net Drain on Homeownership," CRL Issue Paper #14, March 27, 2007), 62% of subprime loans made from 1998 through 2006 were refinances; only 9% were for first time home purchase loans (11% in 2006 was the highest figure). In other words, even before the foreclosure crisis hit, subprime loans did not make a substantial contribution to new homeownership. Rather, they put existing homeowners at greatly increased risk of losing their homes. Indeed, according to CRL, as of early 2007, there was a net loss in homeownership of over 900,000 households, a figure that has certainly increased greatly since the CRL paper was written. FDIC Vice Chair Marty Gruenberg made this point in a speech in New York on January 8, 2008, when he said:
"[i]t has been said that a lot of these homes were bought on a speculative basis and people who did that don't deserve help. That is true of some. But it is important to understand that the majority of subprime mortgages were refinancings of existing homes. In other words, these were homes in which the homeowner was living, with mortgages that the homeowner was paying and could afford. In many cases the homeowner was encouraged or induced to refinance into one of these subprime mortgages with exploding interest rates that the homeowner couldn't afford."

[27] Testimony of Michael Calhoun, President of the Center for Responsible Lending, to the Subcommittee on Housing, Transportation, and Community Development of the Banking Committee, June 26, 2007.

[28] The Housing and Transportation and Economic Policy Subcommittees of the Banking Committee held two hearings on the issues arising from the increase in nontraditional mortgage lending: September 13, 2006 and September 20, 2006.

[29] See Banking Committee Hearings on February 7 and March 22, 2007.

[30] Testimony of Allen Fishbein, Director of Housing Policy at the Consumer Federation of America, to the joint Subcommittees, September 20, 2006. Mr. Fishbein is currently Assistant Director for Policy Analysis, Consumer Education and Research at the Federal Reserve Board.

[31] Testimony to the joint Subcommittee hearing, September 20, 2006 citing January, 2006 Federal Reserve Study, written by Brian Buck and Karen Pence, "Do Homeowners Know Their House Values and Mortgage Terms?"

[32] Testimony of Allen Fishbein, September 20, 2006.

Too often . . . loans have been made without the careful consideration as to the long-term sustainability of the mortgage. Loans are being made without the lender documenting that the borrower will be able to afford the loan after the expected payment shock hits without depending on rising incomes or increased appreciation.

Several months later, as the problem worsened, Chairman Dodd noted in a March 22, 2007 hearing that:

. . . a sort of frenzy gripped the market over the past several years as many [mortgage] brokers and lenders started selling these complicated mortgages to low-income borrowers, many with less than perfect credit, who *they knew or should have known* . . . would not be able to afford to repay these loans when the higher payments kicked in. (emphasis added).

Underscoring this point, the General Counsel of Countrywide Financial Corporation, one of the biggest subprime lenders in 2007, acknowledged in response to a question from Chairman Dodd that "about 60 percent of the people who do qualify for the hybrid ARMs would not be able to qualify at the fully indexed rate"[33] (that is, at the rate a borrower would have to pay after the loan reset, even assuming interest rates did not rise). Another witness, Jennie Haliburton, an elderly resident of Philadelphia, Pennsylvania who lived on a fixed income of social security benefits, had been sold such a mortgage and was facing a jump in her mortgage payment to 70 percent of her income. The Department of Housing and Urban Development considers payments by consumers of more than 50% of income for shelter to put those consumers at "high risk" of losing their homes.

This testimony clearly demonstrates that the lenders were aware that borrowers would need to refinance their loans or sell their homes when the mortgages reset, thereby generating additional fees for the brokers and lenders. This was, in the words of Martin Eakes, Chief Operating Officer of the Self-Help Credit Union, "a devil's choice."[34]

The Committee heard some discussion as to what institutions were most responsible for originating these loans. There is little doubt that nondepository financial companies were among the largest sellers of subprime and exotic mortgages. However, insured depositories and their subsidiaries were heavily involved in these markets. According to data compiled by Federal Reserve Board Economists, 36 percent of all higher-priced loans in 2005 and 31 percent in 2006 were made by insured depositories and their subsidiaries. Those numbers jump to 48 percent and 44 percent when bank affiliates are included.[35] This illustrates that being under the supervision of a federal prudential regulator did not guarantee that mortgage underwriting practices were any stronger, or consumer protections any more robust. As noted, the regulators allowed this deterioration in underwriting standards to take place in part to prevent the institutions they regulate from getting priced out of the market.

Unfortunately, many of these mortgages were packaged by big Wall Street banks into mortgage-backed securities (MBS) and sold in pieces all over the world. Because of the unaffordable and abusive terms of the loans, these mortgages became delinquent at the highest rates since mortgage performance data started being collected over 30 years ago, leading, in turn, to increasing foreclosures, decreasing housing demand, and a widespread decline in housing prices. Once housing prices fell, families who might otherwise have been able to refinance their mortgages were unable to do so because they found themselves "underwater," owing more on their mortgages than the home is worth at that time.

As a result, the MBS into which these now non-performing mortgages were bundled lost significant value, helping lead to the systemic collapse from which we are currently suffering.

Effect on Minorities

The mortgage lending system is deeply flawed . . . . The crisis is having a disproportionate impact on African American families, Latino families, low income families. And that disproportionate impact is

---

[33] See Banking Committee hearings on March 22, 2008.

[34] Testimony of Martin Eakes, Chief Operating Officer of the Self-Help Credit Union, to the Committee, February 7, 2007.

[35] Neil Bhutta and Glenn Canner, "Did CRA Cause the Mortgage Market Meltdown," Federal Reserve Bank of Minneapolis, March 9, 2009.

not explained away by factors that would ordinarily justify such a problem.[36]

—Wade Henderson

Regrettably, the Committee heard a lot of testimony outlining how mortgage originators targeted minorities for subprime mortgages even when these borrowers might have qualified for lower cost prime mortgages. In fact, according to a study conducted by the *Wall Street Journal*, as many as 61 percent of those receiving subprime loans "went to people with credit scores high enough to often qualify for conventional loans with far better terms."[37] Under the Home Mortgage Disclosure Act (HMDA), the Federal Reserve collects data on "high cost" mortgage lending, defined as mortgage loans which are 3 points above the Treasury rate. According to HMDA data released in 2007 by the Federal Reserve, 54 percent of African-Americans and 47 percent of Hispanics received high cost mortgages in 2006. Only 18 percent of non-Hispanic whites received high cost mortgages. The Federal Reserve study found that borrower related factors, such as income, accounted for only one sixth of this disparity. CRL did a study of the 2004 HMDA data which controls for other significant risk factors used to determine loan pricing, such as income and credit scores. The CRL study found that African-Americans were more likely to receive higher-rate home-purchase and refinance loans than similarly-situated white borrowers, and that Latino borrowers were more likely to receive higher-rate home purchase loans than similarly-situated non-Latino white borrowers.[38]

Failure of the Safety and Soundness Regulators

It has become clear that a major cause of the most calamitous worldwide recession since the Great Depression was the simple failure of federal regulators to stop abusive lending, particularly unsustainable home mortgage lending.[39]

—Travis Plunkett

Underlying this whole chain of events leading to the financial crisis was the spectacular failure of the prudential regulators to protect average American homeowners from risky, unaffordable, "exploding" adjustable rate mortgages, interest only mortgages, and negative amortization mortgages. These regulators "routinely sacrificed consumer protection for short-term profitability of banks,"[40] undercapitalized mortgage firms and mortgage brokers, and Wall Street investment firms, despite the fact that so many people were raising the alarm about the problems these loans would cause.

In 1994, Congress enacted the "Home Ownership and Equity Protection Act" (HOEPA) which states that:

> the Board, by regulation or order, shall prohibit acts or practices in connection with—
>
> (a) Mortgage loans that the Board finds to be unfair, deceptive, or designed to evade the provisions of this section; and
>
> (b) Refinancing of mortgage loans that the Board finds to be associated with abusive lending practices or that are otherwise not in the interests of borrower.

As early as late 2003 and early 2004, Federal Reserve staff began to "'observe deterioration of credit standards'" in the origination of non-traditional mortgages.[41] Yet, the Federal Reserve Board failed to meet its responsibilities under HOEPA, despite persistent calls for action.

As Professor McCoy noted in her testimony to the Committee, "federal banking regulators added fuel to the crisis by allowing reckless loans to flourish." Professor McCoy points out that the regulators had "ample authority" to prohibit banks from extending credit without proof of a borrower's ability to pay. Yet, she notes, "they refused to exercise their substantial powers of rule-making, formal enforcement, and sanctions to crack down on the proliferation of poorly underwritten loans until it was too late."[42]

Finally, in July of 2008, long after the marketplace had shut down the availability of sub-

---

[36] Testimony of Wade Henderson, President and CEO of the Leadership Conference on Civil Rights, to the Subcommittee on Housing, Transportation, and Community Development hearing, June 26, 2007.

[37] "Subprime Debacle Traps Even Very Credit-Worthy," *Wall Street Journal*, December 3, 2007.

[38] CRL, "Unfair Lending: The Effect of Race and Ethnicity on the Price of Subprime Mortgages," May 31, 2006.

[39] Testimony of Travis Plunkett, Legislative Director of the Consumer Federation of America to the Banking Committee, July 14, 2009.

[40] Testimony of Patricia McCoy to the Banking Committee, March 3, 2009.

[41] Banking Committee document, "Mortgage Market Turmoil: A Chronology of Regulatory Neglect" prepared by the staff of the Banking Committee, March 22, 2007.

[42] Testimony to the Banking Committee, March 3, 2009.

prime and exotic mortgage credit, and much of prime mortgage credit not directly supported by federal intervention, the Federal Reserve Board issued rules that would likely prevent a repeat of the same kinds of problems that led to the current crisis.

Where federal regulators refused to act, the states stepped into the breach. In 1999, North Carolina became the first State to enact a comprehensive anti-predatory law. Other States followed suit as the devastating results of predatory mortgage lending became apparent through increased foreclosures and disinvestment.

Unfortunately, rather than supporting these anti-predatory lending laws, federal regulators preempted them. In 1996, the OTS preempted all State lending laws. The OCC promulgated a rule in 2004 that, likewise, exempted all national banks from State lending laws, including the anti-predatory lending laws. At a hearing on the OCC's preemption rule, Comptroller Hawke acknowledged, in response to questioning from Senator Sarbanes, that one reason Hawke issued the preemption rule was to attract additional charters, which helps to bolster the budget of the OCC.[43]

Two recent studies by the Center for Community Capital at the University of North Carolina document the damage created by this preemption regulation. The two studies found that:

(1) States with strong anti-predatory lending laws exhibited significantly lower foreclosure risk than other States. A typical State law reduced neighborhood default rates by as much as 18 percent;

(2) Loans made by lenders covered by tougher State laws had fewer risky features and better underwriting practices to ensure that borrowers could repay;

(3) Mortgage defaults increased more significantly among exempt OCC lenders in States with strong anti-predatory lending laws than among lenders that were still subject to tougher State laws. For example, default rates of fixed-rate refinance mortgages made by national banks not subject to State laws were 41 percent more likely to default and purchase-money mortgages made by these banks were 7 percent more likely to default than loans those banks made prior to preemption; and

(4) Risky lending by national banks more than doubled in some loan categories (fixed-rate refinances) after preemption than before, 11 percent to 29 percent.[44]

In remarkably prescient testimony, Martin Eakes warned in 2004 that the OCC's action on preemption "plants the seeds for long-term trouble in the national banking system." He went on to say:

Abusive practices may well be profitable in the short term, but are ticking time bombs waiting to explode the safety and soundness of national banks in the years ahead. The OCC has not only done a tremendous disservice to hundreds of thousands of borrowers, but has also sown the seeds for future stress on the banking system.[45]

In sum, the Federal Reserve and other federal regulators failed to use their authority to deal with mortgage and other consumer abuses in a timely way, and the OCC and the OTS actively created an environment where abusive mortgage lending could flourish without State controls.

Other Consumer Financial Products and Services

Though the problems in the mortgage market have received most of the public's attention, consumers have long faced problems with many other consumer financial products and services without adequate federal rules and enforcement. Abusive lending, high and hidden fees, unfair and deceptive practices, confusing disclosures, and other anti-consumer practices have been a widespread feature in commonly available consumer financial products such as credit cards. These problems have been documented in numerous hearings before the Banking Committee and other Congressional Committees over the years.

Credit Cards. For example, credit card companies have long been known to provide extremely confusing disclosures, making it nearly impossible for consumers to understand the

---

[43] Banking Committee hearing, April 7, 2004.

[44] "The APL Effect: The Impacts of State Anti-Predatory Lending Laws on Foreclosures," by Lei Ding, et al; University of North Carolina, March 23, 2010 and "The Preemption Effect: The Impact of Federal Preemption of State Anti-Predatory Lending Laws on the Foreclosure Crisis," by Lei Ding et al, March 23, 2010.

[45] Testimony of Martin Eakes to the Banking Committee, April 7, 2004.

terms for which they are signing up. Card companies have engaged in extremely aggressive marketing, such that from 1999 to 2007 creditor marketing and credit extension increased at about two times the rate as credit card debt taken on by consumers.[46]

Moreover, typical credit card companies and banks engaged in a number of abusive pricing practices, including double-cycle billing, universal default, retroactive changes in interest rates, over the limit fees even where the consumer was not notified that a charge put him or her over the allotted credit limit, and arbitrary rate increases.

Despite the growing problems, federal banking regulators did very little. As Adam Levitin, Associate Professor of Law at Georgetown University Law Center explained to the Committee at a February, 2009 hearing,

> The current regulatory regime for credit cards is inadequate and incapable of keeping pace with credit card industry innovation. The agencies with jurisdiction over credit cards lack regulatory motivation and have conflicting missions . . . .[47]

To illustrate this point, research shows that from 1997 to 2007 the OCC took just 9 formal enforcement actions regarding violations of the Truth in Lending Act with regards to credit cards or other consumer lending.[48] In fact, the Comptroller of the Currency wrote a letter objecting to certain parts of the Federal Reserve Board's proposed regulation on credit cards on safety and soundness grounds.[49]

Even after President Obama signed the Credit Card Accountability, Responsibility, and Disclosures Act (CARD Act) into law, credit card companies sought ways to structure products to get around the new rules, highlighting the difficulty of combating new problems with additional laws, while underscoring the importance of creating a dedicated consumer entity that can respond quickly and effectively to these new threats to consumers.

Overdrafts. Similar problems have been revealed by the Committee's examination of overdraft fees.[50] Overdraft coverage for a fee is a form of short term credit that financial institutions extend to consumers to cover overdrafts on check, ACH, debit and AMT transactions. Historically, financial institutions covered overdrafts for a fee on an ad hoc basis. With the growth in specially designed software programs and in consumer use of debit cards, overdraft coverage for a fee has become more prevalent.

A consumer normally qualifies for overdraft coverage if his or her account has been open for a specified period (usually six months), and there are regular deposits into the account. If those criteria are met, most financial institutions automatically enroll consumers in overdraft coverage without the consumer's knowledge or choice. "Consumers do not apply for . . . this credit, do not receive information on the cost to borrow [these funds], are not warned when a transaction is about to initiate an overdraft, and are not given the choice of whether to borrow the funds at an exorbitant price or simply cancel the transaction."[51]

Once overdraft coverage for a fee has been added to an account, some financial institutions do not allow consumers the option of eliminating the coverage, although other more consumer friendly alternatives like overdraft lines of credit or linking checking and savings accounts are available.

Many consumers who are enrolled in these programs without their knowledge find themselves subject to high fees of up to $35 per transaction even if the overdraft is only a few cents. In some cases, consumers have been charged multiple fees in one day without being notified until days later. Most institutions also charge an additional fee for each day the account remains overdrawn. Some financial institutions will even rearrange the order in which they process purchases, charging for a later, larger purchase first so that th ey can charge repeated overdraft coverage fees for earlier, smaller purchases.

The result has been that American consumers paid $24 billion in overdraft fees in 2008[52]

---

[46] Testimony of Travis Plunkett to the Banking Committee, February 12, 2009.

[47] Testimony of Levitin, Associate Professor of Law at Georgetown University Law Center to the Banking Committee, February 12, 2009.

[48] Testimony of Michael Calhoun to the U.S. House of Representatives Committee on Financial Services, September 30, 2009.

[49] Letter from Comptroller of the Currency John Dugan to the Board of Governors of the Federal Reserve System, August 18, 2008.

[50] Banking Committee hearing, November 17, 2009.

[51] Testimony of Jean Ann Fox, Director of Financial Services at Consumer Federation of America to the Banking Committee, November 17, 2009.

[52] Testimony of Michael Calhoun, November 17, 2009.

and $38.5 billion in overdraft fees in 2009.[53] CRL also found that nearly $1 billion of those fees would come from young adults and that $4.5 billion would come from senior citizens.

In addition, the Federal Deposit Insurance Corporation (FDIC) found that a small percentage (12%) of consumers overdraw their account five times per year or more. For these consumers, overdraft coverage is a form of high cost short term credit similar to a payday loan. For example, a consumer repaying a $20 point of sale debit overdraft in two weeks is effectively paying an APR of 3,520%.[54]

For many years, the Federal Reserve and other regulators have been aware of the abusive nature of overdraft coverage programs. In fact, an Interagency Guidance in 2005 called overdraft coverage programs "abusive and misleading." Nonetheless, the Federal Reserve has only issued modest rule after modest rule to address these programs. Despite years of concerns raised, it was not until November of last year that the Federal Reserve adopted another modest rule on overdraft coverage that would prohibit financial institutions from charging any consumer a fee for overdrafts on ATM and debit card transactions, unless the consumer opts in to the overdraft service for those types of transactions. Much more needs to be done in this area to protect consumers and rein in abusive practices.

Debt Collection. The Committee has similar concerns regarding the record of abusive, deceptive and unfair practices by debt collectors. The Fair Debt Collection Practices Act (FDCPA) was passed by Congress to regulate debt collection activities and behavior, but despite the existence of the act, debt collection abuses proliferate. In the last five years, consumers have filed nearly half a million complaints with the Federal Trade Commission about debt collection practices. These complaints include numerous reports of behavior in violation of the act, including: debt collectors threatening violence, using profane or harassing language, bombarding consumers with continuous calls, telling neighbors or family about what is owed, calling late at night, and falsely threatening arrest, seizure of property or deportation. The FTC receives more complaints from consumers about debt collectors than any other industry. Despite these complaints, in the last five years, the FTC has only filed nine debt collection cases.

In addition to concerns about debt collection tactics, the Committee is concerned that consumers have little ability to dispute the validity of a debt that is being collected in error. The FDCPA provides that, if a consumer disputes a debt, the collector is required to obtain verification of the debt and provide it to the consumer before renewing its collection efforts. The FDCPA does not, however, specify what constitutes "verification of the debt," with the result that many collectors currently do little more than confirm that their information accurately reflects what they received from the creditor. The limited information debt collectors obtain in verifying debts is unlikely to dissuade them from continuing their attempts to collect from the wrong consumer or the wrong amount, so that an aggrieved consumer has virtually no protection against erroneous efforts to collect.

Debt collectors who are unsuccessful in collecting on a debt may use attorneys to file frequent lawsuits that they are not prepared to litigate, and which may not be factually valid, with the expectation that a large number of consumers will default or will not be prepared to defend themselves. Abuses in these suits have been documented in numerous press reports[55] and by the FTC as well as by consumer advocates. The FTC found that "the vast majority of debt collection suits filed in recent years has posed considerable challenges to the smooth and efficient operations of the courts."[56] This deluge of debt collection suits means the following abusive debt collection practices can occur: filing collection suits against the wrong people; filing suits past the statute of limitations; collection attorneys not having any proof of the debt sued upon and falsely swearing they do; suing for more than is legally owed; and laundering a time-barred debt with a new judgment. Most of these cases result in default judgment, often with little or no evidence to support the debt, because the debtor is intimidated and does not show up. Once a creditor obtains a judgment, the effects can be sustained and devastating, regardless of whether the consumer actually owed on the underlying debt. Despite the FDCPA, the FTC in February of 2009 issued a report stating that debt

---

[53] Julianne Pepitone, "Bank overdraft fees to total $38.5 billion," *CNNMoney.com*, http://money.cnn.com/2009/08/10/news/companies/bank_overdraft_fees_Moebs/index.htm. August 10, 2009.

[54] *FDIC Study of Bank Overdraft Programs*, November, 2008.

[55] "Debtors' Hell" 4-Part Series, *Boston Globe*, July 30–August 2, 2006.

[56] "Collecting Consumer Debts: The Challenges Of Change," Federal Trade Commission, February 2009, p. 55.

collection litigation practices appear to raise substantial consumer protection concerns.

Payday Lending. Payday loans are small, short-term cash advances made at extremely high interest rates. Typically, a borrower writes a personal check for $100-$500, plus a fee, payable to the lender. The loan is secured by the borrower's personal check or some form of electronic access to the borrower's bank account, and the full amount of the loan plus interest must be repaid on the borrower's next payday to keep the personal check required to secure the loan from bouncing.

The average loan amount for a payday loan is $325, and finance charges are generally calculated as a fee per hundred dollars borrowed. This fee is usually $15 to $30 per $100 borrowed. The average interest rate for a payday loan is between 391% and 782% APR for a two-week loan. Payday loans cost consumers over $4.2 billion in fees each year.

Cash-strapped consumers who must borrow money this way are usually in significant debt or living on the financial edge. A loan can become even more expensive for the borrower who does not have the funds to repay the loan at the end of two weeks and obtains a rollover or loan extension. Many borrowers must devote 25 to 50 percent of their take-home income to repay the payday loan, leaving them with inadequate resources to meet their other obligations. This often leads to a succession of new payday loans for that family.[57] An additional fee is attached each time the loan is extended through a rollover transaction. The high rates make it difficult for many borrowers to repay the loan, thus putting many consumers on a perpetual debt treadmill where they extend the loan several times over. For example, if a payday loan of $100 for 14 days with a fee of $15 were rolled over three times, it would cost the borrower $60 to borrow $100 for 56 days. Loan fees can quickly mount and could eventually become greater than the amount actually borrowed. The typical payday borrower renews his or her loan multiple times before being able to pay the loan in full, and ends up paying $793 for a $325 loan.[58]

If the borrower defaults on the loan, serious financial consequences can occur. Loans secured by personal checks or electronic access to the borrower's bank account can endanger the banking status of borrowers. The lender can deposit the customer's personal check, which would result in additional fees from the bank for insufficient funds if it did not clear the borrower's checking account and could result in the consumer being identified as a writer of bad checks. Requiring consumers to turn over a post-dated check can subject consumers to coercion or harassment by illegal threats or coercive collection practices. For example, consumers have reported being threatened with jail for passing a bad check, even when the law specifically says they cannot be prosecuted if the check bounces.

Auto Dealer Lending. Auto loans constitute the largest category of consumer credit outside of mortgages. Today, there is more outstanding auto debt ($850 billion) than there is credit card debt in this country. Auto dealers finance 79% of the purchases of cars in the United States. Auto dealers actively market and price borrowers' loans. They also routinely mark up loan rates that are higher than the borrower would need to pay to qualify for the credit, and, like mortgage brokers or bankers, the auto dealers collect a significant portion of the excess finance charges that result from that markup, similar to a yield spread premium.[59] In addition, auto dealers often charge origination fees and may use the financing transaction as a way to sell other unrelated products (warranties and credit insurance, for example) to unsuspecting buyers. Unlike a mortgage broker, however, auto dealers are the legal creditors.

As with mortgages, borrowers are simply unaware of the incentives pushing the auto dealers to charge buyers higher interest rates. Auto dealers have a history of abusive and discriminatory lending. In a letter to Chairman Dodd and Ranking Member Shelby, the Leadership Conference on Civil Rights (LCCR) explains that:

> detailed research by academics earlier this decade on millions of auto loans revealed that auto dealers were far more likely to mark up the loan rates of minorities. Class actions revealed discrimination at GM, Toyota, Ford dealerships, among others. As a result, courts ordered most major car finance companies to cap rates . . . though the orders expire soon.[60]

In meetings with Banking Committee staff, the National Automobile Dealers Association

---

[57] Leslie Parish and Uriah King, *Phantom Demand*, Center for Responsible Lending, July 9, 2009.

[58] King, Uriah, Parrish, Leslie, and Tanki, Ozlem. "Financial Quicksand." *Center for Responsible Lending*. November 30, 2006.

[59] Raj Date and Brian Reed, *Auto Race to the Bottom; Free Markets and Consumer Protection in Auto Finance*, November 16, 2009.

[60] Letter to Chairman Dodd and Ranking Member Shelby from the Leadership Conference on Civil Rights, December

(NADA) argued that the current rate cap imposed by the courts mitigate the need for CFPB rulemaking to protect consumers. To the contrary, this history of discriminatin indicates the need for careful oversight into the future, particularly as the court orders expire over the next several years.

As with mortgage bankers and brokers, auto dealers use an "originate to sell" model which results in the car dealers receiving upfront compensation for originating the loans, without regard to the ongoing performance of the loan. And, unlike mortgages, very few people ever refinance car loans, even if they find out that they have been charged above-market rates. As a result, auto dealers have a significant incentive to steer borrowers to the highest rate loans they can, without borrowers ever being aware of the backdoor transaction.

In addition to minorities and lower-income borrowers, military personnel are among those whom are frequently exploited by auto dealers. For that reason, Clifford Stanley, the Under Secretary of Defense for Personnel and Readiness, "welcome[s] and encourage[s] CFP[B] protections" for service members and their families "with regard to unscrupulous automobile sales and financing practices. . . ." Under Secretary Stanley writes that the oversight of auto financing by the CFPB for service members will help reduce concerns they have about their well-being. He goes on to say:

> The Department of Defense fully believes that personal financial readiness of our troops and families equates to mission readiness.[61]

Similarly, The Military Coalition, a consortium of nationally prominent military and veterans organizations representing more than 5.5 million current and former service members and their families supports CFPB regulation of auto dealers with regard to auto lending. In a letter to the Chairman and Ranking Member, the Coalition notes that auto financing is "the most significant financial obligation for the majority of service members." It goes on to say that "including auto dealers financing . . . in the financial reform bill will provide greater protections for our service members and their families" by protecting them from reported abuses such as bait and switch financing, falsification of loan documents, failure to pay off liens, and packing loans with other products.[62]

Access to automobile financing on fair terms is very important to American families, particularly to low-income families. Studies indicate that access to a reliable automobile is an important factor for finding and keeping jobs, especially as more and more jobs are being created outside of city centers. Writing in *New England Community Developments*, Signe-Mary McKernan and Caroline Ratcliffe of the Urban Institute note that:

> providing low-income families with less burdensome auto-financing alternatives and helping them avoid the subprime loan market can lead to better credit scores and increase the likelihood that low-income families become integrated into the formal financial sector.[63]

However, despite the abuses in this sector, and the urgent need for better consumer protections, the federal government has not done enough to address these issues. "Given the widespread nature of the problem [with auto lending] revealed in the academic studies and private litigation, the current structure has failed to effectively police auto finance."[64] That is one of the reasons, according to the LCCR, the CFPB is needed.

STRENGTHENING AND CONSOLIDATING PRUDENTIAL SUPERVISION

Title III seeks to increase the accountability of the banking regulators by establishing clearer lines of responsibility and to reduce the regulatory arbitrage in the financial regulatory system whereby financial companies "shop" for the most lenient regulators and regulatory framework. "One clear lesson learned from the recent crisis was that competition among different gov-

---

(Footnote Continued)

3, 2009. The letter explains that "minority car buyers pay significantly higher dealer markups [for auto loans] than non-minority car buyers *with the same credit scores*." (Emphasis in original).

[61] Letter from Under Secretary of Defense to Clifford Stanley to Assistant Secretary of the Treasury, Michael Barr, February 26, 2010.

[62] Letter to Chairman Dodd and Ranking Member Shelby from The Military Coalition, April 15, 2010. The Coalition includes 31 members, including the Veterans of Foreign Wars, the Military Order of the Purple Heart, the National Guard Association of the U.S., the Non Commissioned Officers Association of the U.S.A., the Iraq and Afghanistan Veterans of America, and others.

[63] Signe-Mary McKernan and Caroline Ratcliffe, "Asset Building for Today's Stability and Tomorrow's Security," *New England Community Developments*, Federal Reserve Bank of Boston, 2009, Issue 2.

[64] Letter to Chairman Dodd and Senator Shelby by the LCCR, December 3, 2009.

ernment agencies responsible for regulating similar financial firms led to reduced regulation in important parts of the financial system. The presence of multiple federal supervisors of firms that could easily change their charter led to weaker regulation and became a serious structural problem within our supervisory system."[65]

Need to Consolidate Fragmented Banking Supervision

Title III rationalizes the fragmented structure of banking supervision in the U.S. by abolishing one of the multiple banking regulators, consolidating supervision of state banks in a single federal regulator, and consolidating supervision of smaller bank holding companies (those with assets of less than $50 billion) so that the regulator for the bank or thrift will also regulate the holding company. For the largest bank and thrift holding companies, the Board will be the consolidated holding company supervisor. The Board will thus focus its supervisory responsibilities on the larger, more interconnected bank and thrift holding companies (which will include, but not be limited to, those companies whose failures potentially pose risk to U.S. financial stability) where its experience in capital and global markets can best be applied. By consolidating its supervision over these holding companies, the Board can pursue risks wherever they may emerge within the company (including its subsidiaries) and will ultimately be responsible for the sound operation of the entire organization.

The Committee heard repeated testimony that the U.S. financial regulatory system is more a product of history and responses to various crises, than deliberate design. According to the GAO, it has not kept pace with major developments in the financial marketplace. In testimony before the Committee on September 29, 2009, the GAO testified in favor of decreasing fragmentation in the system (beyond the Administration's proposal to abolish the OTS), reducing the potential for differing regulatory treatment, and improving regulatory independence.[66]

At the same hearing, former Comptroller of the Currency, Eugene Ludwig, testified that, "We must dramatically streamline the current alphabet soup of regulators", citing the needless burden on financial institutions of the duplicative and inefficient system, the fertile ground that multiple regulatory agencies create for regulatory arbitrage, and the serious gaps between regulatory responsibilities.[67]

The Committee heard testimony from Richard Carnell, Fordham Law School professor and former Treasury Assistant Secretary for Financial Institutions, that our current bank regulatory structure is needlessly complex and costly for banks. He maintained that its overlapping jurisdictions and responsibilities undercut regulators' accountability. And, it encourages regulators to compete with each other for "regulatory clientele" thereby creating an incentive for laxity in supervision.[68]

These sentiments were echoed by Martin Baily, senior fellow with the Brookings Institution, and former Chairman of the Council of Economic Advisers, who testified about the need for increased accountability among regulators. In speaking about competition among regulators Baily said, "The serious danger in regulatory competition is that it allows a race to the bottom as financial institutions seek out the most lenient regulator that will let them do the risky things they want to try, betting with other people's money."[69]

The Committee also heard testimony that the number of banking regulators could be reduced by creating a single federal regulator for state chartered banks, in contrast to the current scheme in which the Federal Reserve and the FDIC each supervise certain state banks. According to Comptroller of the Currency, John Dugan, "Today there is virtually no difference in the regulation applicable to state banks at the federal level based on membership in the [Federal Reserve] System and thus no real reason to have two different federal regulators. It would be simpler to have one. Opportunities for regulatory arbitrage—resulting, for example, from differences in the way federal activities restrictions are administered by one or the other regulator—would be reduced. Policy would be streamlined." Dugan went on to state the importance of ensuring the FDIC maintain a window into day-to-day banking supervision, which would be less

---

[65] "Financial Regulatory Reform: A New Foundation", Administration's White Paper, June 2009.

[66] Testimony of Richard J. Hillman, Managing Director Financial Markets and Community Investment, GAO, to the Banking Committee, 9/29/09.

[67] Testimony of Eugene Ludwig to the Banking Committee, 9/29/09.

[68] Testimony of Richard Carnell to the Banking Committee, September 29, 2009.

[69] Testimony of Martin Baily to the Banking Committee, September 29, 2009.

¶ 54,005

of a problem for the Board if it maintained holding company supervision.[70]

Dugan identified further opportunity for regulatory consolidation. He testified there was little need for separate holding company regulation where the bank is small or where it is the holding company's only, or dominant, asset. "Elimination of a separate holding company regulator thus would eliminate duplication, promote simplicity and accountability, and reduce unnecessary compliance burden for institutions as well. The case is harder and more challenging for the very largest bank holding companies engaged in complex capital market activities, especially where the company is engaged in many, or predominantly, nonbanking activities, such as securities and insurance." In those cases, Dugan recommended maintaining the role of the Board as the holding company supervisor.[71]

In his September 2009 testimony, Baily echoed Dugan's remarks that there was no good case for the Board to continue to supervise smaller bank holding companies. That regulation should be moved to the prudential regulator. Indeed public data from the banking regulators from year end 2009 demonstrate that in almost all instances of banking organizations with less than $50 billion in assets, the vast majority of assets are in the depository institution. According to Federal Reserve Board Governor Daniel Tarullo, "When a bank holding company is essentially a shell, with negligible activities or ownership stakes outside the bank itself, holding company regulation can be less intensive and more modest in scope."[72]

Title III adopts a number of these recommendations for consolidating bank supervision to enhance the accountability of individual regulators, reduce the opportunities for depository institutions to shop for the most lenient regulator, reduce regulatory gaps in supervision, and limit inefficiencies, duplication and needless regulatory burdens on the industry. Title III does so by abolishing the OTS in accordance with the Administration's financial reform proposal.

Abolishing the OTS

The OTS is responsible for regulating state and federal thrifts, as well as their holding companies.[73] The thrift charter suffered disproportionate losses during the financial crisis. According to FDIC data, 95 percent of failed institution assets in 2008 were attributable to thrifts regulated by the OTS. These losses were predominantly attributed to the failures of Washington Mutual and Indy Mac Bank.[74] From the start of 2008 through the present, 73 percent of failed institution assets were attributable to thrifts regulated by the OTS, even though the agency supervised only 12 percent of all bank and thrift assets at the beginning of this period.

In its White Paper on reforming the financial regulatory system, the Administration argues that advances in the financial services industry have decreased the need for federal thrifts as a specialized class of depository institutions focused on mortgage lending.[75] Additionally, the White Paper points out that the thrift charter "created opportunities for private sector arbitrage" of the regulatory system and that its focus on residential mortgage lending made it particu-

---

[70] Testimony of John Dugan to the Banking Committee, August 4, 2009.

[71] Id.

[72] Testimony of Daniel Tarullo to the Banking Committee, August 4, 2009.

[73] The OTS currently regulates 694 federal thrifts and 63 state thrifts.

[74] In its reports of the Washington Mutual and IndyMac failures, the inspectors general offices of the Treasury and FDIC cited numerous shortcomings with OTS supervision. With over $300 billion in total assets, Washington Mutual was OTS's largest regulated institution and represented as much as 15 percent of OTS's total assessment revenue from 2003 to 2008. The inspectors general found that, despite the multiple findings by OTS examiners of weaknesses at Washington Mutual, the OTS consistently gave the bank a high composite rating (CAMELS—capital, assets, management, earnings, liquidity, and sensitivity to risk) and Washington Mutual was thus considered well-capitalized until its closure. They further concluded that OTS did not adequately ensure that the thrift's management corrected examiner-identified weaknesses, that the agency failed to take formal enforcement action until it was too late, and that the OTS never instituted corrective measures under "prompt corrective action" (PCA) to minimize losses to the Deposit Insurance Fund because the OTS never properly downgraded the bank's CAMELS rating that would have triggered PCA. Evaluation of Federal Regulatory Oversight of Washington Mutual Bank, Report No. EVAL-10-002, April 2010.

In the case of IndyMac, the Treasury Inspector General found that the OTS did not identify or sufficiently address the core weaknesses that ultimately caused the thrift to fail until it was too late. As in the case of Washington Mutual, the Inspector General found that the OTS gave IndyMac inflated CAMELS ratings, and, that it failed to follow up with bank management to ensure that corrective actions were taken. The Inspector General also found that the OTS waited too long to bring an enforcement action against the bank. Material Loss Review of IndyMac Bank, FSB (OIG-09-032).

[75] "Financial Regulatory Reform: A New Foundation", June 2009.

larly susceptible to the housing downturn.[76] The fragility of the charter is borne out by the statistics, including the fact that total assets of OTS-supervised thrifts declined by 36 percent between 2006 and 2009, compared to an increase of 11 percent in all FDIC-insured banks and thrifts for the same time period.

Thus the bill does not permit the chartering of any new federal thrifts and disbands the OTS. Title III apportions the responsibility to regulate thrifts and thrift holding companies among the FDIC, the OCC and the Federal Reserve, and ensures that all OTS employees are transferred to the FDIC and the OCC.

Consolidating Federal Supervision of State Banks and Smaller Bank Holding Companies

It also consolidates federal supervision for state banks in the FDIC. As of yearend 2009, the FDIC regulated 4,941 state banks ranging in size from less than one billion dollars in assets to more than $100 billion in assets, compared to the 844 banks the Federal Reserve supervised. In addition to the state banks the FDIC supervises, the agency has on-site dedicated examiners at the largest banks. The FDIC also conducts targeted supervisory activities at specific Federal Reserve regulated banks over $10 billion. These institutions present complex risk profiles and activities and operations that include international operations, securitization activities, and trading books with material derivatives exposures. Thus, the FDIC has ample experience in supervising banks of all sizes, including large, complex organizations.

And Title III gives the prudential regulators—the FDIC and the OCC—the responsibility for supervising the holding companies of smaller, less complex organizations where nearly all of the assets in the holding companies are concentrated in the depository institutions these agencies already regulate. The Board, however, will retain its supervisory responsibility for the larger bank holding companies and for the larger thrift holding companies, thus ensuring that the Board continues to have a window into day-to-day supervision.

Focusing the Federal Reserve System on its Core Functions

The crisis exposed the shortcomings of the Federal Reserve System—mainly that it has too many responsibilities to execute well.[77][78] Currently, the Federal Reserve is responsible for conducting monetary policy, policing the payment system, serving as the lender of last resort, supervising state member banks, regulating all bank holding companies, and writing most of the consumer financial protection rules.

Chairman Dodd and other members of the Committee repeatedly expressed concerns during hearings about the many responsibilities of the Federal Reserve and about the need to preserve the Federal Reserve's primary focus on its core function of monetary policy. The Chairman also expressed concerns that so many diverse functions could ultimately threaten the independence of the Federal Reserve's monetary policy. Chairman Dodd said, "Some have expressed a concern—which I share, by the way—about overextending the Fed when they have not properly managed their existing authority, particularly in the area of protecting consumers."[79] The Chairman also said, "I worry that over the years loading up the Federal Reserve with too many piecemeal responsibilities has left important duties without proper attention and exposed the Fed to dangerous politicization that threatens the very independence of this institution."[80] Ranking Member Shelby stated, "The Federal Reserve already handled monetary policy, bank regulation, holding company regulation, payment systems oversight, international banking regulation, consumer protection, and the lender-of-last-resort function. These responsibilities conflict at times, and some receive more attention than

---

[76] Id. The OTS was also the consolidated supervisor of AIG because AIG was a thrift holding company. To date, AIG's failure has cost the U.S.government over $180 billion.

[77] The Committee heard testimony about the failures of the Federal Reserve in executing its consumer protection functions, as well as in identifying the risks in bank holding companies. Martin Eakes, CEO of Self-Help and CEO of the Center for Responsible Lending, testified to the Committee in November 2008, "The Board has been derelict in the duty to address predatory lending practices. In spite of the rampant abuses in the subprime market and all the damage imposed on consumers by predatory lending—billions of dollars in lost wealth—the Board has never implemented a single discretionary rule under HOEPA outside of the high cost context. To put it bluntly, the Board has simply not done its job."

[78] Speaking to its failures in identifying risk, Orice Williams, Director of Financial Markets and Community Investment at the Government Accountability Office, testified to the Committee in March 2009, "Although for some period, the Federal Reserve analyzed financial stability issues for systemically important institutions it supervises, it did not assess the risks on an integrated basis or identify many of the issues that just a few months later led to the near failure of some of these institutions and to severe instability in the overall financial system."

[79] Statement of Chairman Chris Dodd, hearing of the Banking Committee, 12/3/09.

[80] Statement of Chairman Chris Dodd, hearing of the Banking Committee, 2/4/09.

others. I do not believe that we can reasonably expect the Fed or any other agency [to] effectively play so many roles."[81]

In response to a question from Ranking Member Shelby, Former Federal Reserve Chairman Paul Volcker agreed that the Federal Reserve's conduct of monetary policy could be undermined if the Fed assumed additional responsibilities.[82] Chairman Volcker further testified, "You will have a different Federal Reserve if the Federal Reserve is going to do the main regulation or all the regulation from a prudential standpoint. And you'll have to consider whether that's a wise thing to do, given their primary—what's considered now their primary responsibilities for monetary policy. They obviously have important regulatory functions now, and maybe those functions have not been pursued with sufficient avidity all the time. But if you're going to give them the whole responsibility, for which there are arguments, I do think you have to consider whether that's consistent with the degree of independence that they have to focus on monetary policy."[83]

To narrow the focus of the Federal Reserve to its core functions, the bill strips it of its consumer protection functions,[84] and its role in supervising a relatively small number of state banks, as well as smaller bank holding companies. However, the Committee was persuaded that because of the Federal Reserve's expertise and its other unique functions, it should play an expanded role in maintaining financial stability.[85] Thus, Title III assigns the Federal Reserve the responsibility for the supervision of bank and thrift holding companies with assets over $50 billion. (Other aspects of the bill that address financial stability enhance the Federal Reserve's oversight of systemically important payment systems, direct the Federal Reserve to apply heightened prudential standards to large bank holding companies, and give the Federal Reserve supervisory responsibilities over designated nonbank financial companies.) To ensure the Federal Reserve can focus on these and its other essential responsibilities, the bill assigns the regulation of state member banks and smaller bank holding companies to other federal regulators. The bill therefore strikes an important balance in providing the Federal Reserve with enhanced authority to maintain financial stability, while at the same time, reducing its responsibilities for areas that are not central to its mission.

Finally, it should be noted that Title III leaves intact the Federal Reserve's ability to obtain information needed for the conduct of monetary policy. Section 11 of the Federal Reserve Act gives the Board of Governors authority to require any depository institution to provide "such reports of its liabilities and assets as the Board may determine to be necessary or desirable to enable the Board to discharge its responsibility to monitor and control monetary and credit aggregates." This information may be obtained from any bank, savings and loan association, or credit union, and does not depend on the chartering agency or regulator of the depository. In addition, section 21 of the Federal Reserve Act provides that the Board may conduct special examinations of any Federal Reserve member bank. Members include all national banks and state banks that elect to become members of their district Federal Reserve bank. These provisions of the Federal Reserve Act remain unchanged. Therefore the Federal Reserve will retain extensive powers to gather the data it needs to conduct monetary policy, including data from banks that it does not supervise.

REGULATION OF OVER-THE-COUNTER DERIVATIVES AND SYSTEMICALLY SIGNIFICANT PAYMENT, CLEARING, AND SETTLEMENT FUNCTIONS

> Making derivatives safer is a very important part of solving too-big-to-fail.[86] — Chairman Ben Bernanke

---

[81] Ranking Member Richard Shelby, Banking Committee hearing, 6/18/09.

[82] Banking Committee hearing, "Modernizing The U.S. Financial Regulatory System," 2/4/09.

[83] Testimony of Former Federal Reserve Board Chairman Paul Volcker to the Banking Committee, February 9, 2009.

[84] In proposing to take away the Federal Reserve's authority to write and enforce consumer protection rules Secretary Geithner called this authority a "preoccupation and distraction" for the Federal Reserve in testimony to the Banking Committee, June 18, 2009. Martin Baily, Senior Fellow of Economic Studies at the Brookings Institution, stated in testimony during a hearing in September 2009 that the Federal Reserve Board's added focus on consumer protection took time from properly doing the rest of its job: "I think the thing that the Federal Reserve has done well is monetary policy . . . they certainly haven't done a great job on prudential regulation and I don't see—what is the point of the Chairman of the Federal Reserve sitting around worrying about details of credit card regulation? That is what he is doing right now, and I think that is a mistake and not a good use of his time."

[85] "The Fed has several missions, and monetary policy is the primary one," said Alice Rivlin, a Brookings Institution scholar and former Fed vice chairman. "But they also have a mission to stabilize the banking system, and we're in the process of expanding our view of what the banking system is." Washington Post, 7/17/08.

[86] Testimony of Ben Bernanke, Federal Reserve Board Chairman, to the Senate Banking Committee, 12/3/09.

¶ 54,005

Many factors led to the unraveling of this country's financial sector and the government intervention to correct it, but a major contributor to the financial crisis was the unregulated over-the-counter ("OTC") derivatives market. Derivatives can trade either over-the-counter where contracts are often customized and privately negotiated between counterparties, or through regulated central clearinghouses and exchanges that establish rules for trading contracts among many different counterparties.

Massive growth in bilateral, unregulated derivatives trading: At the time of the crisis in December, 2008, the global over-the-counter derivatives market stood at $592 trillion.[87] The top five derivatives dealers in the United States accounted for 96 percent of outstanding over-the-counter contracts made by the leading bank holding companies, according to the OCC. As such, this market was dominated by the too-big-to-fail financial companies that trade derivatives with financial and non-financial users. The dangers posed by the OTC derivatives market have been known for many years. In 1994, the GAO produced a report, titled, "Financial Derivatives: Actions Needed to Protect the Financial System." At the time of their report, the GAO determined the size of the derivatives market to be $12.1 trillion. Included in GAO's findings in 1994 were concerns about risks to taxpayers arising from the interconnectedness between dealers and end users: "the rapid growth and increasing complexity of derivatives activities increase risks to the financial system, participants, and U.S. taxpayers;" and "relationships between the 15 major U.S. dealers that handle most derivatives activities, end users, and the exchange-traded markets makes the failure of any one of them potentially damaging to the entire financial market."[88] By the time of the 2008 crisis, the derivatives market had grown to be almost fifty times as large from when GAO raised a red flag. Much of this growth has been attributed to the Commodities Futures Modernization Act of 2000 which explicitly exempted OTC derivatives, to a large extent, from regulation by the Commodity Futures Trading Commission ("CFTC") and limited the SEC's authority to regulate certain types of OTC derivatives. By 2008, 59 percent of derivatives were traded over-the-counter, or away from regulated exchanges, compared to 41 percent in 1998.

According to the Obama Administration, "the downside of this lax regulatory regime . . . became disastrously clear during the recent financial crisis . . . many institutions and investors had substantial positions in credit default swaps—particularly tied to asset backed securities . . . excessive risk taking by AIG and certain monoline insurance companies that provided protection against declines in the value of such asset backed securities, as well as poor counterparty credit risk management by many banks, saddled our financial system with an enormous—and largely unrecognized—level of risk." "[T]he sheer volume of these contracts overwhelmed some firms that had promised to provide payment on the CDS and left institutions with losses that they believed they had been protected against. Lacking authority to regulate the OTC derivatives market, regulators were unable to identify or mitigate the enormous systemic threat that had developed."[89]

OTC contracts can be more flexible than standardized contracts, but they suffer from greater counterparty and operational risks and less transparency. Information on prices and quantities is opaque. This can lead to inefficient pricing and risk assessment for derivatives users and leave regulators ill-informed about risks building up throughout the financial system. Lack of transparency in the massive OTC market intensified systemic fears during the crisis about interrelated derivatives exposures from counterparty risk. These counterparty risk concerns played an important role in freezing up credit markets around the failures of Bear Stearns, AIG, and Lehman Brothers.

Hidden leverage due to under-collateralization: Although over-the-counter derivatives can be used to manage risk and increase liquidity, they also increase leverage in the financial system; traders can take large speculative positions on a relatively small capital base because there are no regulatory requirements for margin or capital. The ability of derivatives to hide leverage was evident in problems faced by financial companies such as Bear Stearns and Lehman as well as non-financial derivatives participants such as the government of Greece—Chairman Gensler recently stated that higher capital requirements for derivatives would have prevented Greece from using currency swaps to hide debt.[90] When users

---

[87] Bank for International Settlements, press release, 5/19/09.

[88] U.S. Government Accountability Office, "Financial Derivatives: Actions Needed to Protect the Financial System," GGD-94-133 May 18, 1994.

[89] Obama Administration white paper, *Financial Regulatory Reform: A New Foundation,* June 2009.

[90] Associated Press, *U.S. Warns EU Derivatives Ban Won't Work,* 3/16/10.

¶ 54,005

negotiate margin bilaterally, they "will act in their own interest to manage their risk. These actions may not take into account the spillover risk throughout the system."[91] For example, the markets generally considered AIG Financial Products ("AIGFP") an extremely low risk counterparty because its parent company was rated AAA. This high rating allowed AIGFP to hold lower capital/margin against its derivatives portfolio. Had market participants or regulators demanded more capital, the company would have had less incentive to enter into such large positions as the projected return on investment would have been lower. Even if AIGFP had such large positions, the company would have had more funds to apply to the losses. Had information been more readily available to regulators and counterparties about the scope of AIGFP's credit default swap positions, regulators and market participants might have detected the systemic implications of AIGFP's book.

The dangers of under-collateralization were recently identified by the International Monetary Fund ("IMF") and the Wall Street Journal:

The main risk posed by this gigantic pool is the hidden leverage. Put simply, a bank may have a large derivatives position but avoid posting cash upfront with its trading partner as others do.

This "under-collateralization" makes the system prone to runs because, when instability arrives, all banks rush to collect what they are owed on derivatives—and try to delay paying out what they themselves owe. Witness the Lehman Brothers collapse. And the numbers aren't small.

On Tuesday, the International Monetary Fund released a paper estimating that five large U.S. derivatives dealers were potentially under-collateralized by between $500 billion and $275 billion as of September 2009. The IMF gets to that range using firms' net derivatives liabilities, a figure showing how much banks owe on derivatives trades adjusted for netting and collateral posting.

Putting nearly all derivatives through clearinghouses, with tough margin rules, could do away with most of the under-collateralization. The IMF says getting there could be very costly for the banks. But consider it a bill they should have paid years ago.[92]

Counterparty credit exposure in the derivatives market was largely seen as a source of systemic risk during the failures of both Bear Stearns and Lehman Brothers, and would have brought down AIG but for a massive collateral payment made with taxpayer money. It created the dangerous interconnections that spread and amplified risk across the entire financial system. More collateral in the system, through margin requirements, will help protect taxpayers and the economy from bailing out companies' risky derivatives positions in the future. In testimony before the Senate Banking Committee, Federal Reserve Chairman Bernanke described margin requirements for derivatives users as "an appropriate cost of protecting against counterparty risk."[93]

Need to reduce systemic risk build-up and risk transmission in the derivatives market: Chairman Gensler of the Commodity Futures Trading Commission described the flaws of bilaterally-negotiated margin as follows: "Even though individual transactions with a financial counterparty may seem insignificant, in aggregate, they can affect the health of the entire system."[94] "One of the lessons that emerged from this recent crisis was that institutions were not just 'too big to fail,' but rather too interconnected as well. By mandating the use of central clearinghouses, institutions would become much less interconnected, mitigating risk and increasing transparency. Throughout this entire financial crisis, trades that were carried out through regulated exchanges and clearinghouses continued to be cleared and settled."[95]

In July of 2008, during a hearing on derivatives regulation before the Senate Banking Committee, Patrick Parkinson, deputy director of the Division of Research and Statistics for the Board of Governors of the Federal Reserve System, testified to the danger present in the OTC derivatives market: "weaknesses in the infrastructure for the credit derivatives markets and other OTC derivatives markets have created operational risks that could undermine the effectiveness of counterparty risk-management practices."[96] In June of 2009, A. Patricia White, the associate

---

[91] Acharya, et al., *The Ultimate Financial Innovation*, 2008.
[92] Wall Street Journal, 4/13/10.
[93] Chairman Bernanke, Senate Banking Committee testimony, 12/3/09.
[94] Chairman Gensler, Senate Agriculture Committee testimony, 11/18/09.
[95] Chairman Gensler, Senate Banking Committee testimony, 6/22/09.
[96] Testimony before the Subcommittee on Securities, Insurance, and Investment of the Senate Committee on Banking, Housing, and Urban Affairs, 7/9/08.

director of the Division of Research and Statistics for the Board of Governors of the Federal Reserve System, testified about unregulated derivatives' ability to spread harm through the system and the need to combat such risk. Ms. White said, "OTC derivatives appear to have amplified or transmitted shocks. An important objective of regulatory initiatives related to OTC derivatives is to ensure that improvements to the infrastructure supporting these products reduce the likelihood of such transmissions and make the financial system as a whole more resilient to future shocks. Centralized clearing of standardized OTC products is a key component of efforts to mitigate such systemic risk."[97] While the systemic risk presented by the unregulated OTC derivatives market has long been known, it was realized in 2008 with devastating consequences. Now it must be addressed to restore stability and confidence in the financial system.

Creating a Safer Derivatives Market to Protect Taxpayers Against Future Bailouts

As a key element of reducing systemic risk and protecting taxpayers in the future, protections must include comprehensive regulation and rules for how the OTC derivatives market operates. Increasing the use of central clearinghouses, exchanges, appropriate margining, capital requirements, and reporting will provide safeguards for American taxpayers and the financial system as a whole.

Under Title VII, for the first time, over-the-counter derivatives will be regulated by the SEC and the CFTC, more transactions will be required to clear through central clearing houses and trade on exchanges, un-cleared swaps will be subject to margin requirements, swap dealers and major swap participants will be subject to capital requirements, and all trades will be reported so that regulators can monitor risks in this vast, complex market. Under Title VIII, the Federal Reserve will be granted the authority to regulate and examine systemically important payment, clearing, and settlement functions. The overall result would be reduced costs and risks to taxpayers, end users, and the system as a whole. The language in these titles is based on proposals drafted by the Obama Administration and includes all of the key regulatory features for derivatives market reform that have been endorsed by the G20: more central clearing, exchange trading, capital, margin, and transparency.

G20 Steering Group Letter, 3/31/10: "Standardized over-the-counter derivatives contracts should be traded on exchanges or electronic platforms, where appropriate, cleared through central clearing counterparties by 2012 at the latest, and reported to trade repositories."[98]

G20 Leaders' Statement, The Pittsburgh Summit, 9/25/09: "Improving over-the-counter derivatives markets: All standardized OTC derivative contracts should be traded on exchanges or electronic trading platforms, where appropriate, and cleared through central counterparties by end-2012 at the latest. OTC derivative contracts should be reported to trade repositories. Non-centrally cleared contracts should be subject to higher capital requirements. We ask the FSB and its relevant members to assess regularly implementation and whether it is sufficient to improve transparency in the derivatives markets, mitigate systemic risk, and protect against market abuse."[99]

The combination of these new regulatory tools will provide market participants and investors with more confidence during times of crisis, taxpayers with protection against the need to pay for mistakes made by companies, derivatives users with more price transparency and liquidity, and regulators with more information about the risks in the system.

Central clearing, margin, and capital requirements as a systemic risk management tool: "The main tool for regulating contagion and systemic risk is liquidity reserves (margin)."[100] In the OTC market, margin requirements are set bilaterally and do not take account of the counterparty risk that each trade imposes on the rest of the system, thereby allowing systemically important exposures to build up without sufficient capital to mitigate associated risks. The problem of under-collateralization is especially apparent in bank transactions with non-financial firms and regulators should address this problem through the new margin requirements for uncleared deriva-

---

[97] Testimony before the Subcommittee on Securities, Insurance, and Investment of the Senate Committee on Banking, Housing, and Urban Affairs, 6/22/09.

[98] G20 Steering Group Letter, 3/31/10.

[99] G20 Leaders' Statement, The Pittsburgh Summit, 9/25/09, http://www.pittsburghsummit.gov/mediacenter/129639.htm.

[100] Rama Conti, Columbia University, Credit Derivatives: Systemic Risk and Policy Options, 2009.

tives established in the legislation. According to the Comptroller of the Currency, "Banks held collateral against 64 percent of total net current credit exposure ('NCCE') at the end of the third quarter. Bank credit exposures to banks/securities firms and hedge funds are very well secured. Banks hold collateral against 90 percent of their exposure to banks and securities firms, and 219 percent of their exposure to hedge funds. The high coverage of hedge fund exposures occurs because banks take 'initial margin' on transactions with hedge funds, in addition to fully securing any current credit exposure. Coverage of corporate, monoline and sovereign exposures is much less."[101]

With appropriate collateral and margin requirements, a central clearing organization can substantially reduce counterparty risk and provide an organized mechanism for clearing transactions. For uncleared swaps, regulators should establish margin requirements. In addition, regulators should also impose capital requirements on swap dealers and major swap participants. While large losses are to be expected in derivatives trading, if those positions are fully margined there will be no loss to counterparties and the overall financial system and none of the uncertainty about potential exposures that contributed to the panic in 2008.

Exchange trading as a price transparency mechanism: "While central clearing would mitigate counterparty risk, central clearing alone is not enough. Exchange trading is also essential in order to provide price discovery, transparency, and meaningful regulatory oversight of trading and intermediaries," said Former CFTC Chairman Brooksley Born.[102] Exchange trading can provide pre- and post-trade transparency for end users, market participants, and regulators. When swaps are executed on the basis of robust price information, rather than privately quoted, the cost of those transactions can be reduced over time. "The relative opaqueness of the OTC market implies that bid/ask spreads are in many cases not being set as competitively as they would be on exchanges. This entails a loss in market efficiency," wrote Stanford University Professor Darrel Duffie.[103] Trading more derivatives on regulated exchanges should be encouraged because it will result in more price transparency, efficiency in execution, and liquidity. In order to allow the OTC market to adapt to more exchange-trading, the legislation provides for "alternative swap execution facilities" ("ASEF") to fulfill the exchange-trading mandate. The absence of an exchange trading mandate provides "supra-normal returns paid to the dealers in the closed OTC derivatives market [and] are effectively a tax on other market participants, especially investors who trade on open, public exchanges," according to International Risk Analytics co-founder Christopher Whalen.[104] Resistance to price transparency in the financial markets has been overcome in the past, as noted by Duffie: "About 6 years ago, a post-trade reporting system known as TRACE was forced by U.S. regulation into the OTC markets for corporate and municipal bonds, which operate in a manner that is otherwise similar to the OTC derivatives markets. Dealers resisted the introduction of TRACE, claiming that more price transparency would reduce the incentives of dealers to make markets and in the end reduce market liquidity. So far, empirical evidence appearing in the academic literature has not given much support to these claims."[105]

Allow for some customized, bilateral contracts: Some parts of the OTC market may not be suitable for clearing and exchange trading due to individual business needs of certain users. Those users should retain the ability to engage in customized, uncleared contracts while bringing in as much of the OTC market under the centrally cleared and exchange-traded framework as possible. Also, OTC (contracts not cleared centrally) should still be subject to reporting, capital, and margin requirements so that regulators have the tools to monitor and discourage potentially risky activities, except in very narrow circumstances. These exceptions should be crafted very narrowly with an understanding that every company, regardless of the type of business they are engaged in, has a strong commercial incentive to evade regulatory requirements. "Every firm has reasons why its contracts are 'exceptional' and should trade privately; in reality, most derivatives contracts are standardized—or standardizable—and could trade on exchanges," said Joe

---

[101] Comptroller of the Currency, *Quarterly Report on Bank Trading and Derivatives Activities,* 12/18/09.

[102] Former CFTC Chairman Brooksley Born, Joint Economic Committee testimony, 12/1/09.

[103] Stanford University Professor Darrel Duffie, *The Road Ahead for the Fed,* 2009.

[104] International Risk Analytics co-founder Christopher Whalen, Senate Banking Committee testimony, 6/22/09.

[105] Stanford University Professor Darrel Duffie, *Pew Research,* 2009.

Dear, Chief Investment Officer of the California Public Employees' Retirement System.[106]

Therefore, the legislation permits regulators to exempt contracts from the clearing and exchange trading requirement based on these narrow criteria: one counterparty is not a swap/security-based swap dealer or major swap/security-based swap participant and does not meet the eligibility requirements of a clearinghouse. If no clearinghouse, board of trade, exchange, or alternative swap execution facility accepts the contract for clearing or trading, then the contract must be exempt from the clearing and exchange trading requirements. The regulators may also exempt swaps from the margin requirement for uncleared swaps under the following narrow criteria: one counterparty is not a swap/security-based swap dealer or major swap/security-based swap participant, using the swap as part of an effective hedge under generally accepted accounting principles, and predominantly engaged in activities that are not financial in nature. Regulators must notify the Financial Stability Oversight Council before issuing any permissive exemptions.

In providing exemptions, regulators should minimize making distinctions between the types of firms involved in the market or the types of products the firms are engaged in and instead evaluate the nature of the firm's derivatives activity: "[T]wo complementary regulatory regimes must be implemented: one focused on the dealers that make the markets in derivatives and one focused on the markets themselves—including regulated exchanges, electronic trading systems and clearing houses ... These two regimes should apply no matter which type of firm, method of trading or type of derivative or swap is involved," testified Chairman Gensler.[107] To achieve the objectives of regulatory reform in the OTC market,"it is critical that similar products and activities be subject to similar regulations and oversight."[108] In determining whether to bring non-swap dealers into the regulatory framework, regulators should focus on counterparty credit exposure. It was counterparty credit risk that played a critical role in exacerbating the 2008 crisis. Regulators would measure credit exposure by evaluating the value of collateral held against such exposure. According to the Office of the Comptroller of the Currency, "the first step to measuring credit exposure in derivative contracts involves identifying those contracts where a bank would lose value if the counterparty to a contract defaulted today . . . A more risk sensitive measure of credit exposure would also consider the value of collateral held against counterparty exposures."[109]

INVESTOR PROTECTION

Title IX addresses a number of securities issues, including provisions that respond to significant aspects of the financial crisis caused by poor securitization practices (Subtitle D); erroneous credit ratings (Subtitle C); ineffective SEC regulation of Madoff Securities, Lehman Brothers and other firms (Subtitle F); and executive compensation practices that promoted excessive risk-taking (Subtitle E). In connection with the crisis, concerns have also been raised that investors need more protection; shareholders need a greater voice in corporate governance; the SEC needs more authority; the SEC should be self-funded; and the municipal securities markets need improved regulation, which are addressed here as well.

Significant aspects of the financial crisis involved securities. Serious and far reaching problems were caused by poor and risky securitization practices; erroneous credit ratings; ineffective SEC regulation of investment banks such as Lehman Brothers and broker dealers such as Madoff; and excessive compensation incentives that promoted excessive risk taking. During the crisis, it became apparent that investors needed better protection, shareholders needed more voice in corporate governance, the municipal securities markets needed improved regulation, and the SEC needs assistance. Title IX addresses these and other investor protection and related securities issues.

Credit ratings that vastly understated the risks of complex mortgage-backed securities encouraged the build-up of excessive leverage and credit risk throughout the financial system in the years before the crisis. With the onset of the crisis, the ratings of many mortgage-backed bonds were sharply downgraded, fuelling widespread uncertainty about asset values and amplifying problems in residential mortgage markets into a global financial panic. The rating agencies' errors can be attributed to overreliance on math-

---

[106] Chief Investment Officer of the California Public Employees' Retirement System Joe Dear, National Press Club speech, 11/3/09.

[107] Chairman Gensler, Senate Banking Committee testimony, 6/22/09.

[108] Obama Administration white paper, *Financial Regulatory Reform: A New Foundation*, June 2009.

[109] Comptroller of the Currency, *Quarterly Report on Bank Trading and Derivatives Activities*, 12/18/09.

¶54,005

ematical risk models based on inadequate data and to conflicts of interest in the process of rating complex structured securities, where the rating agencies actually advised the issuers on how to obtain AAA ratings, without which the securities could not have been sold.

This legislation will improve the regulation and performance of credit rating agencies by enhancing SEC oversight authority and requiring more robust internal supervision of the ratings process. In addition, rating agencies will be required to disclose more data about assumptions and methodologies underlying ratings, in order to permit investors to better understand credit ratings and their limitations. Due diligence investigations into the facts underlying ratings will be encouraged. Rating agencies will be held accountable for failures to produce ratings with integrity, both by allowing the SEC to suspend rating agencies that consistently fail to produce accurate ratings and by lowering the pleading standard for private lawsuits alleging that a rating agency knowingly or recklessly failed to conduct a reasonable investigation of the factual elements of the rated security, or failed to obtain reasonable verification of such factual elements from independent sources that it considered to be competent. Finally, the legislation requires financial regulators to review and remove unnecessary references to credit ratings in their regulations.

Excesses and abuses in the securitization process played a major role in the crisis. Under the "originate to distribute" model, loans were made expressly to be sold into securitization pools, which meant that the lenders did not expect to bear the credit risk of borrower default. This led to significant deterioration in credit and loan underwriting standards, particularly in residential mortgages. Moreover, investors in asset-backed securities could not assess the risks of the underlying assets, particularly when those assets were resecuritized into complex instruments like collateralized debt obligations. With the onset of the crisis, there was widespread uncertainty regarding the true financial condition of holders of asset-backed securities, freezing interbank lending and constricting the general flow of credit. Complexity and opacity in securitization markets prolonged and deepened the crisis, and have made recovery efforts much more difficult.

This title requires securitizers to retain an economic interest in a material portion of the credit risk for any asset that securitizers transfer, sell, or convey to a third party. This "skin in the game" requirement will create incentives that encourage sound lending practices, restore investor confidence, and permit securitization markets to resume their important role as sources of credit for households and businesses.

Congress is empowering shareholders in a public company to have a greater voice on executive compensation and to have more fairness in compensation affairs. Under the new legislation, each publicly traded company would give its shareholders the right to cast advisory votes on whether they approve of its executive compensation. The board committee that sets compensation policy would consist only of directors who are independent. The company would tell shareholders about the relationship between the executive compensation it paid and its financial performance. The company would be required to have a policy to recover money that it erroneously paid to executives based on financials that later had to be restated due to an accounting error.

Management nominees for directors of public companies could generally serve on the board only if they won a majority of the votes in an uncontested election. Also, the S.E.C. would have the authority to allow shareholders to have more power in governing the public companies in which they own stock. If the S.E.C. gives shareholders proxy access, a shareholder who has owned an amount of stock for a period of time, as specified by the S.E.C., could choose a candidate to nominate for election to the board of directors on the company's proxy.

Investors would have new sources of assistance. The new Office of Investor Advocate housed within the SEC would help retail investors with problems they have with the SEC or self-regulatory organizations. Securities broker-dealers, such as Bernard L. Madoff Investment Securities, would have to use auditors that are subject to the inspections and discipline by a rigorous regulator, the Public Company Accounting Oversight Board, which would better protect investor accounts. Larger investors would have to post margin collateral based on the net positions in their securities and futures portfolio. An Investment Advisory Committee is created in the law to give advice to the SEC from its members, which would include representatives of mutual fund, stock and bond investors, senior citizens, State securities regulators, and others. The law increases the amount of money available to the Securities Investor Protection Corporation to pay off valid claims of customers of defunct broker-dealers.

The SEC would get more power, assistance and money at its disposal to be an effective securities markets regulator. The SEC would have new authority to impose limitation on mandatory arbitration; to bar someone who violated the securities laws while working for one type of registered securities firm, such as a broker-dealer, from working for other types of securities firms, such as investment advisers; to require that securities firms give new disclosures to investors before they buy investment products. The SEC would have more help in identifying securities law violations through a new, robust whistleblower program designed to motivate people who know of securities law violations to tell the SEC. It also expands existing whistleblower law. In light of recent failures of the SEC, the GAO will also provide assistance through studies and recommendations to improve the agency's internal supervisory controls, management and financial controls. The SEC has asked to be unfettered by the Congressional appropriation process and the new law would allow the agency to be self-funded.

A major lesson from the crisis is the importance of transparency in financial markets. The $3 trillion municipal securities market is subject to less supervision than corporate securities markets, and market participants generally have less information upon which to base investment decisions. During the crisis, a number of municipalities suffered losses from complex derivatives products that were marketed by unregulated financial intermediaries. This title requires a range of municipal financial advisors to register with the SEC and comply with regulations issued by the Municipal Securities Rulemaking Board (MSRB). The composition of the MSRB will be changed so that representatives of the public—including investors and municipalities—make up a majority of the board. In addition, the title establishes an Office of Municipal Securities within the SEC and contains a number of studies on ways to improve disclosure, accounting standards, and transparency in the municipal bond market.

REGULATION OF PRIVATE FUNDS

Title IV requires advisers to large hedge funds to register with the Securities and Exchange Commission, in order to close a significant gap in financial regulation. Because hedge funds are currently unregulated, no precise data regarding the size and scope of hedge fund activities are available, but the common estimate is that the funds had at least $2 trillion in capital before the crisis. Their impact on the financial system can be magnified by extensive use of leverage—their trades can move markets. While hedge funds are generally not thought to have caused the current financial crisis, information regarding their size, strategies, and positions could be crucial to regulatory attempts to deal with a future crisis. The case of Long-Term Capital Management, a hedge fund that was rescued through Federal Reserve intervention in 1998 because of concerns that it was "too-interconnected-to-fail," shows that the activities of even a single hedge fund may have systemic consequences.

Hedge fund registration was part of the Treasury's Department's regulatory reform proposal, and has been endorsed by many witnesses before the Committee, including Mr. James Chanos, Chairman of the Coalition of Private Investment Companies, who testified that "private funds (or their advisers) should be required to register with the SEC.... Registration will bring with it the ability of the SEC to conduct examinations and bring administrative proceedings against registered advisers, funds, and their personnel. The SEC also will have the ability to bring civil enforcement actions and to levy fines and penalties for violations."[110] Other supporters of the title include a range of industry groups, institutional investors, the Group of Thirty, the G-20, and the Investors' Working Group.

In addition to SEC registration, this title requires private funds—hedge funds with more than $100 million in assets under management—to disclose information regarding their investment positions and strategies. The required disclosures include information on fund size, use of leverage, counterparty credit risk exposure, trading and investment positions, valuation policies, types of assets held, and any other information that the SEC, in consultation with the Financial Stability Oversight Council, determines is necessary and appropriate to protect investors or assess systemic risk. The Council will have access to this information to monitor potential systemic risk, while the SEC will use it to protect investors and market integrity.

[¶54,010] III. Background and Need for Legislation

The statistics alone reveal the terrible toll the financial crisis exacted on the U.S. economy.

---

[110] Testimony of James Chanos, Chairman, Coalition of Private Investment Companies, to the Senate Banking Committee, 7/15/09.

From the start of the crisis through March 2010, more than 8 million jobs were lost.[111] Unemployment in the United States reached 10.1% in October 2009, the highest rate of unemployment since 1983, and as of March 2010 was holding at 9.7%; prior to the economic collapse, in October 2008, the unemployment rate was just 6.6%.[112] American household wealth fell by more than $13 trillion from the peak value of American wealth in 2007 to the height of the crisis at the end of 2008. Even after several months of recovery, household wealth is still down $11 trillion, or almost 17%, from its 2007 peak.[113] Home prices have dropped 30.2% from their 2006 peak,[114] and retirement assets dropped by more than 20%. Real Gross Domestic Product in the United States in the fourth quarter of 2008, and the first and second quarters of 2009 decreased by an annual rate of about 5.4%, 6.4%, and 0.7%, respectively, from the previous periods, and Real GDP through 2009 had not reached the levels seen prior to the economic collapse.[115] More than 7 million homes in America have entered foreclosure since the beginning of 2007.[116]

Behind the statistics are hardworking men and women whose lives have been shattered, small businesses that have been shuttered, retirement funds that have evaporated, and families who have lost their homes. While some of the most prominent American financial institutions have been destroyed or badly weakened, it is the millions of American families, who did nothing wrong, who have suffered the most. Indeed, the financial crisis has torn at the very fiber of our middle class.

This devastation was made possible by a long-standing failure of our regulatory structure to keep pace with the changing financial system and prevent the sort of dangerous risk-taking that led us to this point, propelled by greed, excess, and irresponsibility. The United States' financial regulatory structure, constructed in a piecemeal fashion over many decades, remains hopelessly inadequate to handle the complexities of modern finance. In January 2009, the GAO added the U.S. financial regulatory system to its list of high-risk areas of government operations because of its fragmented and outdated structure.[117]

Rather than taking measures to strengthen the financial services sector, some of our regulators actively embraced deregulation, pushed for lower capital standards, ignored calls for greater consumer protections and allowed the companies they supervised to use complex financial instruments to manage risk that neither they nor the companies really understood. Moreover, many actors in the financial system—the "shadow" banking system—have escaped any form of meaningful regulation. As former Comptroller of the Currency Eugene Ludwig testified, "The paradigm of the last decade has been the conviction that un- or under-regulated financial services sectors would produce more wealth, net-net. If the system got sick, the thinking went, it could be made well through massive injections of liquidity. This paradigm has not merely shifted—it has imploded."[118]

The financial crisis can trace its origins to a downturn in the housing market that in turn exposed a raft of unsound lending practices. These practices ultimately led to the failure of a number of companies heavily involved in making or investing in subprime loans. On April 2, 2007, New Century Financial Corporation, a leading subprime mortgage lender, filed for Chapter 11 bankruptcy. Quickly, the first signs of trouble in the housing market came to Wall Street. In June of 2007, Bear Stearns suspended redemptions from one of its funds and in July of 2007, Bear Stearns liquidated two of its hedge funds that were heavily invested in mortgage-backed securities. On August 6, a large retail mortgage lender, American Home Mortgage Investment Corporation, filed for Chapter 11 bankruptcy. In December of 2007, the Federal Reserve, after announcing several cuts to interest rates of both the federal funds rate and the primary credit rate over the previous months, announced the creation of a Term Auction Facility to address pressures in the short-term funding markets. In March of 2008, the Federal Reserve announced an additional short-term lending fa-

---

[111] Bureau of Labor Statistics, database of seasonally adjusted total nonfarm payroll, www.bls.gov.

[112] Bureau of Labor Statistics, database of seasonally adjusted unemployment rate, 16 years and older, www.bls.gov.

[113] The Federal Reserve, Flow of Funds report, 3/11/10, www.federalreserve.gov.

[114] S&P/Case-Shiller Home Prices Indices, 20-City Composite, press release, 3/30/10, www.standardandpoors.com.

[115] Bureau of Economic Analysis, Gross Domestic Product: Fourth Quarter 2009 press release, 3/26/10, www.bea.gov.

[116] Reuters News, January 29, 2008; January 15, 2009; January 14, 2010; March 11, 2010.

[117] GAO, High Risk Series: An Update, GAO-09-271 (Washington, D.C.: Jan. 2009).

[118] Testimony before the Senate Committee on Banking, Housing, and Urban Affairs, 10/16/08.

cility, the Term Securities Lending Facility to promote liquidity in the financial markets.[119]

On March 14, 2008, the first major shock wave spread across Wall Street when the Federal Reserve announced the bailout of Bear Stearns through an arrangement with JPMorgan Chase. Bear Stearns, whose assets were concentrated in mortgage-backed securities, faced a major liquidity crisis as it failed to find buyers for its now-toxic assets. Just days later, on March 16, JPMorgan Chase agreed to buy all of Bear Stearns with assistance from the Federal Reserve.[120]

In the months that followed the crisis grew more severe. On July 11, 2008, the OTS closed IndyMac BankFSB, a large thrift saddled with nonperforming mortgages. IndyMac had relied on an "originate-to-distribute" model of mortgage lending,[121] under which it originated loans or brought them from others, and then packaged them together in securities and sold them on the secondary market to banks, thrifts, or Wall Street investment banks.[122] By securitizing and selling its loans, IndyMac could shift the risk of borrower defaults onto others. This business model led to significant deterioration in its credit and loan underwriting standards. Accordingly,, when housing prices declined and the secondary market collapsed IndyMac was left with a large number of nonperforming mortgages in its portfolio which was the primary cause of its failure.[123]

Later in July 2008, regulators and lawmakers made several moves to stabilize government-sponsored entities Fannie Mae and Freddie Mac; the Federal Reserve authorized emergency lending by the Federal Reserve Bank of New York (FRBNY) and; the Securities and Exchange Commission temporarily prohibited naked short-selling in securities; President Bush signed into law the Housing and Economic Recovery Act of 2008 which allowed the Treasury Department to purchase GSE obligations and created a new regulatory regime for the entities—the Federal Housing Finance Agency (FHFA). Ultimately, on September 7, FHFA placed both Fannie Mae and Freddie Mac into government conservatorship.[124]

September 15, 2008 saw two more icons of Wall Street collapse and ushered in a period of extraordinary government intervention to prevent a complete financial meltdown, the depths of which, according to Federal Reserve Board Chairman Ben Bernanke, "could have rivaled or surpassed the Great Depression."[125] Bank of America announced its plan to purchase Merrill Lynch, and Lehman Brothers filed for bankruptcy, unable to find a buyer. The following day, the Federal Reserve authorized the FRBNY to provide the American International Group with up to $85 billion of emergency lending (the FRBNY was authorized to lend an additional $37.8 billion to AIG on October 6 and later the Treasury Department would purchase $40 billion of AIG preferred shares through the TARP program). On September 17, the SEC announced a ban on short-selling of all stocks of financial sector companies. On September 21, the Federal Reserve accepted applications from investment banking companies Goldman Sachs and Morgan Stanley to become bank holding companies, allowing them access to the federal safety net.

---

[119] Federal Reserve Bank of St. Louis, "The Financial Crisis—A Timeline of Events and Policy Actions."

[120] Ibid.

[121] In an "originate-to-distribute" model, for the most part, the originator of mortgages sells the mortgages to a person who packages the loans into securities and sells the securities to investors. By selling the mortgages, the originator thus gets more funds to make more loans. However, the ability to sell the mortgages without retaining any risk, also frees up the originator to make risky loans, even those without regard to the borrower's ability to repay. In the years leading up to the crisis, the originator was not penalized for failing to ensure that the borrower was actually qualified for the loan, and the buyer of the securitized debt had little detailed information about the underlying quality of the loans.

[122] Material Loss Review of IndyMac Bank, FSB (OIG-09-032); Office of Inspector General, U.S. Department of Treasury.

[123] "The primary causes of IndyMac's failure were largely associated with its business strategy of originating and securitizing Alt-A loans on a large scale. This strategy resulted in rapid growth and a high concentration of risky assets." *Id.* "IndyMac's aggressive growth strategy, use of Alt-A and other nontraditional loan products, insufficient underwriting, credit concentrations in residential real estate in the California and Florida markets, and heavy reliance on costly funds borrowed from the Federal Home Loan Bank (FHLB) and from brokered deposits, led to its demise when the mortgage market declined in 2007. IndyMac often made loans without verification of the borrower's income or assets, and to borrowers with poor credit histories. Appraisals obtained by IndyMac on underlying collateral were often questionable as well. As an Alt-A lender, IndyMac's business model was to offer loan products to fit the borrower's needs, using an extensive array of risky option-adjustable-rate-mortgages (option ARMs), subprime loans, 80/20 loans, and other nontraditional products. Ultimately, loans were made to many borrowers who simply could not afford to make their payments." *Id.*

[124] Federal Reserve Bank of St. Louis, "The Financial Crisis—A Timeline of Events and Policy Actions."

[125] Speech to the 43rd Annual Alexander Hamilton Awards Dinner, Center for the Study of the Presidency and Congress, Washington, D.C., 4/8/10.

¶ 54,010

From September 12 to October 10, the Dow Jones Industrial Average dropped 26%. Major bank failures continued, with the OTS closing Washington Mutual on September 25, and facilitating its acquisition by JPMorgan Chase. Wachovia bank also faced collapse, forcing it to find a buyer; ultimately Wells Fargo purchased the bank on October 12.[126]

While Wall Street was reeling, lawmakers worked to craft an emergency measure to stabilize the markets and halt the momentum of the crisis. On September 20, Treasury Secretary Henry Paulson delivered to Capitol Hill his proposal for the Emergency Economic Stabilization Act. Nine days later, the House of Representatives voted down a modified version of the Treasury Department proposal. On that day, the Dow Jones Industrial Average fell by more than 750 points.[127] The Senate later acted to pass a further modified measure including comprehensive oversight, help for homeowners, and corporate governance requirements not included in the Treasury Department proposal. The bill was signed into law by President Bush on October 3, 2008, establishing the $700 billion Troubled Asset Relief Program (TARP).

As a result of the crisis, in addition to the losses of homes, family savings, and jobs, the government became a reluctant, but major shareholder of private banks, automobile companies, and other giants of the economy. The TARP program was enacted to provide the government with a critical tool needed to wrest the economy from a free-fall. But with the passage of TARP, the Congress granted the Treasury Department extraordinary powers and a staggering sum of taxpayer money to address a crisis that was brought on by the failures of the very banks that benefited from the program and by the government regulators that failed at their jobs. While this extent of government intervention was necessary to avert a complete collapse of the U.S. economy, our nation should never again be put in the position of having to bail out big companies.

The consequences of the crisis could not be more evident, from the failures on Wall Street to the devastation on Main Street and across the globe. Its myriad causes however, are buried in a patchwork of problems touching on almost every aspect of the financial services sector. Throughout the course of its work over the past 40 months, the Committee probed and evaluated the causes of the economic downfall in order to develop a legislative response that prevents a recurrence of the same problems and that creates a new regulatory framework that can respond to the challenges of a 21st century marketplace.

Causes of the Financial Crisis

The crisis was first triggered by the downturn in the national housing market, leading to an overall housing slump. This slump brought into focus the prevalence of unsound lending practices, including predatory lending tactics, most often in the subprime market. Many of these practices, and the products that ultimately spread the risks associated with these practices, existed in what came to be known as the shadow banking system, a structure that eluded regulation and oversight despite its prevalence in the financial marketplace.

Though the market for subprime mortgages was less than 1% of global financial assets, the faults in the system allowed the turmoil in the housing market to spill over into other sectors. Faults in the system included a securitization process that fueled excessive risk taking by permitting mortgage originators to quickly sell the unsuitable loans they made, and thereby transfer the risks to someone else; credit rating agencies that gave inflated ratings to securities backed by risky mortgage loans; and the use of unregulated derivatives products based on these faulty loans that only served to spread and magnify the risk. The system operated on a wholesale misunderstanding of, or complete disregard for the risks inherent in the underlying assets and the complex instruments they were backing. Explaining the rise in complex financial products and their danger to the financial system, Eugene Ludwig testified to the Committee, "Technology, plus globalization, plus finance has created something quite new, often called 'financial technology.' Its emergence is a bit like the discovery of fire—productive and transforming when used with care, but enormously destructive when mishandled."[128]

Gaps in the regulatory structure allowed these risks and products to flourish outside the view of those responsible for overseeing the financial system. Many major market participants, such as AIG, were not subject to meaningful oversight by federal regulators. Additionally, no financial regulator was responsible for assessing the impact the failure of a single firm might have

---

[126] Federal Reserve Bank of St. Louis, "The Financial Crisis—A Timeline of Events and Policy Actions."

[127] Dow Jones Indexes, Index Data, *www.djaverages.com*.

[128] Testimony before the Senate Committee on Banking, Housing, and Urban Affairs, 10/16/08.

¶54,010

on the state of the financial system. Indeed, as the crisis grew more severe, the interconnected relationships among financial companies increased the pressure on those already struggling to survive, which only served to accelerate the downfall of some firms. For example, as AIG's position worsened, it was required to post more collateral to its counterparties and to increase its capital holdings as required by regulators.

Fueling the loss of confidence in the system was the failure of regulators and market participants to fully understand the extent of the obligations of these teetering firms, thus making an orderly shutdown of these companies nearly impossible. When Lehman Brothers declared bankruptcy, the markets panicked and the crisis escalated. With no other means to resolve large, complex and interconnected financial firms, the government was left with few options other than to provide massive assistance to prop up failing companies in an effort to prevent the crisis from spiraling into a great depression.

Despite initial efforts of the government, credit markets froze and the U.S problem spread across the globe. The crisis on Wall Street soon spilled over onto Main Street, touching the lives of most Americans and devastating many.

[¶54,015] IV. History of the Legislation

From the beginning of the 110th Congress, the work of the Senate Committee on Banking, Housing and Urban Affairs focused on the problems in the housing market that started with the spread of predatory lending and culminated in the turmoil in the credit markets that led to the economic crisis of 2008 and 2009. This work led to the drafting and committee passage of the Restoring American Financial Stability Act in March 2010.

The Committee's first official examination of the housing crisis began with a hearing in February 2007, titled "Preserving the American Dream: Predatory Lending Practices and Home Foreclosures" which featured testimony from representatives of the mortgage industry, consumer advocates, and victims of predatory lending. The next month, the Committee followed up with a hearing to explore problems in the mortgage market—"Mortgage Market Turmoil: Causes and Consequences." The hearing featured testimony from federal and state banking regulators as well as representatives from industry and consumers.

As the crisis evolved and leading up to Committee passage of RAFSA, the Committee held nearly 80 hearings to both examine the causes of the housing and economic crisis and assess how best to stabilize the nation's financial services industry and capital markets, while lessening the impact of the crisis on Main Street Americans. In the immediate aftermath of the collapse of Bear Stearns, the Committee held 8 hearings on the "Turmoil in the U.S. Credit Markets" and the foreclosure crisis. Upon the collapse of Lehman Brothers, the Committee held another series of hearings on the economic turmoil, including on the Bush Administration's proposed legislation that eventually became the "Emergency Economic Stabilization Act of 2008." The Committee has held a series of oversight hearings on the implementation of that Act since its passage as well as on other extraordinary measures the financial regulatory agencies have taken, including the Federal Reserve, to stabilize the economy.

Beginning in February 2009, the Committee began its first of more than 50 hearings to assess the types of reforms needed to protect the economy from another devastating financial crisis. The Committee held comprehensive hearings on how to end the abuses and loopholes that led the country into the current crisis. Hearings explored all specific elements of the financial reform legislation, as well as specific regulatory failures that contributed to the crisis.

With an eye toward drafting comprehensive legislation, the Committee held hearings on prudential bank supervision, systemic risk, ending taxpayer bailouts of companies perceived to be "too big to fail," consumer protection, derivatives regulation, investor protection, private investment pools, insurance regulation and government-sponsored entities. Throughout its examinations, the Committee took testimony from regulators, policy experts, industry representatives, and consumer advocates.

In looking at the consequences of the crisis, the Committee examined how the crisis affected sectors all across the financial services industry and the Main Street economy. Areas covered, aside from the overall state of the banking, housing and securities industries, included the impact on community banks and credit unions, manufacturing, international aspects of regulation, consumers, and the effect on homeownership.

To learn from the mistakes of the past, the Committee thoroughly examined factors that led to the crisis. These hearings began with investigations into the problems associated with subprime and predatory lending, and continued with hearings including the failure of AIG, investment fraud including the Bernard Madoff and Allen Stanford cases, the actions of credit ratings agencies, failures of regulators, problems of risk management oversight, and the role of securitization in the financial crisis.

In the spring of 2009, the Obama Administration released a set of its proposals for financial regulatory reform. On June 18, 2009, the Committee held a hearing, "The Administration's Proposal to Modernize the Financial Regulatory System," to examine the President's ideas for reforms, including testimony from Treasury Secretary Timothy Geithner. This hearing was followed by two hearings on additional proposals from the Administration in the start of 2010, titled "Prohibiting Certain High-Risk Investment Activities by Banks and Bank Holding Companies" and "Implications of the 'Volcker Rules' for Financial Stability." These hearings included testimony from Deputy Secretary Neal S. Wolin and Presidential Economic Recovery Advisory Board Chairman and former Federal Reserve Board Chairman Paul Volcker.

On November 10, 2009, Banking Committee Chairman Christopher Dodd introduced to his colleagues a discussion draft of financial reform legislation, based on the Committee's extensive hearing record, numerous briefings and meetings, as well as the Administration's proposal. Introducing the draft, Chairman Dodd said:

> It is the job of this Congress to restore responsibility and accountability in our financial system to give Americans confidence that there is a system in place that works for and protects them . . . . The financial crisis exposed a financial regulatory structure that was the product of historic accident, created piece by piece over decades with little thought given to how it would function as a whole, and unable to prevent threats to our economic security . . . . I will not stand for attempts to protect a broken status quo, particularly when those attempts are made by some of the same special interests who caused this mess in the first place.

The Committee convened on November 19, 2009, to begin consideration of the Restoring American Financial Stability Act of 2009. The Committee met only to receive opening statements from members. Based on the opening statements, the Chairman decided to postpone further consideration of the legislation, pending the outcome of various bipartisan working groups the Chairman assembled to consider significant aspects of the legislation.

On March 16, 2010, following more than 80 hearings with testimony from hundreds of experts and months of negotiations with both Republicans and Democrats on the Banking Committee, Chairman Dodd unveiled the financial reform proposal that he would introduce to the Committee. One week later, on March 22, the Committee met and passed the bill by a vote of 13 to 10, as amended with a single manager's amendment. No additional amendments were offered.

[¶54,020] V. Section-by-Section Analysis

Title I—Financial Stability

[¶54,021] Section 101. Short title

The title may be cited as the "Financial Stability Act of 2010."

[¶54,022] Section 102. Definitions

This section defines various terms used in the title, including "bank holding company," "member agency," "nonbank financial company," "Office of Financial Research," and "significant nonbank financial company." "Nonbank financial companies" are defined as companies substantially engaged in activities that are financial in nature (as defined in section 4(k) of the Bank Holding Company Act of 1956), excluding bank holding companies and their subsidiaries. "Nonbank financial companies supervised by the Board of Governors" refer to those nonbank financial companies that the Financial Stability Oversight Council ("Council") has determined shall be supervised by the Board of Governors of the Federal Reserve System ("Board of Governors") under section 113 and subject to prudential standards authorized under this title.

This section requires the Board of Governors to establish by rulemaking the criteria for determining whether a company is substantially engaged in financial activities to qualify as a nonbank financial company. It is intended that commercial companies, such as manufacturers, retailers, and others, would not be considered to be nonbank financial companies generally, and this provision is intended to provide certainty by mandating the establishment of the criteria through the public notice and comment process required for rulemaking.

This section provides that the Board of Governors will define the term "significant bank holding company" and "significant nonbank financial company" through rulemaking. It is not intended that securities or futures exchanges regulated by the SEC and the CFTC that act as administrators of marketplaces be considered a "significant nonbank financial company," which term is used in this title with respect to counterparty exposure, to the extent the exchanges do not act as a counterparty (and thus do not create credit exposures).

This section also clarifies that with respect to foreign nonbank financial companies, references to "company" and "subsidiary" include only the United States activities and subsidiaries of such foreign companies.

Subtitle A—Financial Stability Oversight Council

[¶ 54,040] Section 111. Financial Stability Oversight Council established

This section establishes the Council, consisting of the following voting members: (1) the Secretary of the Treasury, who will serve as the Chairperson ("Chairperson") of the Council, (2) the Chairman of the Board of Governors ("Board of Governors") of the Federal Reserve System, (3) the Comptroller of the Currency, (4) the Director of the Bureau of Consumer Financial Protection, (5) Director of the Federal Housing Finance Agency, (6) the Chairman of the Securities and Exchange Commission, (7) the Chairperson of the Federal Deposit Insurance Corporation ("FDIC"), (8) the Chairperson of the Commodity Futures Trading Commission, and (9) an independent member (appointed by the President, with the advice and consent of the Senate) having insurance expertise.

The Director of the Office of Financial Research (which is established under subtitle B) will serve in an advisory capacity as a nonvoting member. The Council will meet at the call of the Chairperson or majority of the members then serving, but not less frequently than quarterly. Any employee of the Federal government may be detailed to the Council, and any department or agency of the United States may provide the Council such support services the Council may determine advisable.

[¶ 54,041] Section 112. Council authority

This section enumerates the purposes of the Council, which include: (1) identifying risks to the financial stability of the United States that could arise from the material financial distress or failure of large, interconnected bank holding companies or nonbank financial companies; (2) promoting market discipline, by eliminating expectations on the part of shareholders, creditors, and counterparties of such companies that the government will shield them from losses in the event of failure; and (3) responding to emerging threats to the stability of the United States financial markets.

The duties of the Council include: (1) collecting information from member agencies and other regulatory agencies, and, if necessary to assess risks to the United States financial system, directing the Office of Financial Research to collect information from bank holding companies and nonbank financial companies; (2) providing direction to, and requesting data and analyses from, the Office of Financial Research to support the work of the Council; (3) monitoring the financial services marketplace to identify threats to U.S. financial stability; (4) facilitating information sharing among the member agencies; (5) recommending to member agencies general supervisory priorities and principles reflecting the outcome of discussions among the member agencies; (6) identifying gaps in regulation that could pose risks to U.S. financial stability; (7) requiring supervision by the Board of Governors for nonbank financial companies that may pose risks to the financial stability of the U.S. in the event of their material financial distress or failure; (8) making recommendations to the Board of Governors concerning the establishment of heightened prudential standards for risk-based capital, leverage, liquidity, contingent capital, resolution plans and credit exposure reports, concentration limits, enhanced public disclosures, and overall risk management for nonbank financial companies and large, interconnected bank holding companies supervised by the Board of Governors; (9) identifying systemically important financial market utilities and payments, clearing, and settlement system activities and subjecting them to prudential standards established by the Board of Governors; (10) making recommendations to primary financial regulatory agencies to apply new or heightened standards and safeguards for financial activities or practices that could create or increase risks of significant liquidity, credit, or other problems spreading among bank holding companies, nonbank financial companies, and United States financial markets; (11) providing a forum for discussion and analysis of emerging market developments and financial regulatory issues, and for resolution of jurisdictional disputes among member agencies; and (12) reporting to and testifying before Congress.

The section also authorizes the Council to request and receive data from the Office of Financial Research and member agencies to carry out the provisions of this title. The Council, acting through the Office of Financial Research, may also require the submission of reports from financial companies to help assess whether a financial company, activity, or market poses a threat to U.S. financial stability. Before requiring such reports, the Council, acting through the Office of Financial Research, shall coordinate with the appropriate member agency (including the Office of National Insurance established in the Treasury Department under Title V of this Act) or primary financial regulatory agency and shall rely, whenever possible, on information already available from these agencies. In the case of a foreign nonbank financial company or a foreign-based bank holding company, it is intended that the Council, acting through the Office of Financial Research, consult to the extent appropriate with the applicable foreign regulator for the company.

[¶ 54,042] **Section 113. Authority to require supervision and regulation of certain nonbank financial companies**

This section authorizes the Council, by a vote of not fewer than ⅔ of members then serving, including an affirmative vote by the Chairperson, to determine that a nonbank financial company will be supervised by the Board of Governors and subject to heightened prudential standards, if the Council determines that material financial distress at such company would pose a threat to the financial stability of the United States. Each determination will be based on a consideration of enumerated factors by the Council, including, among others: the degree of leverage (a typical mutual fund could be an example of a nonbank financial company with a low degree of leverage); amount and nature of financial assets; amount and types of liabilities (which could be different types of liabilities based on, for example, their maturity, volatility, or stability), including degree of reliance on short-term funding; extent and type of off-balance-sheet exposures; extent to which assets are managed rather than owned and to which ownership of assets under management is diffuse; the operation of, or ownership interest in, any clearing, settlement, or payment business of the company; and any other risk-related factors that the Council deems appropriate. Size alone should not be dispositive in the Council's determination; in its consideration of the enumerated factors, the Council should also take into account other indicia of the overall risk posed to U.S. financial stability, including the extent of the nonbank financial company's interconnections with other significant financial companies and the complexity of the nonbank financial company. It is not intended that a Council determination be based on the exchange functions of securities or futures exchanges regulated by the SEC and the CFTC, to the extent that as part of these functions the exchanges act as administrators of marketplaces and not as counterparties. Further, it is not intended that the activities of securities and futures exchanges overseen by the SEC and the CFTC that consist of, or occur prior to, trade execution be considered a "clearing, settlement or payment business," provided that such activities do not include functioning as a counterparty.

The Council will provide written notice to each nonbank financial company of its proposed determination and the company would have the opportunity for a hearing before the Council to contest the proposed determination. The Council will consult with the primary federal regulatory agency of each nonbank financial company or subsidiary of the company before making any final determination. The section provides for judicial review of the final determination of the Council. In case of a foreign nonbank financial company, it is intended that the Council consult to the extent appropriate with the applicable foreign regulator for the company.

[¶ 54,043] **Section 114. Registration of nonbank financial companies supervised by the Board of Governors**

This section directs a nonbank financial company to register with the Board of Governors if a final determination is made by the Council under section 113 that such company is to be supervised by the Board of Governors.

[¶ 54,044] **Section 115. Enhanced supervision and prudential standards for nonbank financial companies supervised by the Board of Governors and certain bank holding companies**

This section authorizes the Council to make recommendations to the Board of Governors concerning the establishment and refinement of prudential standards and reporting and disclosure requirements for nonbank financial companies supervised by the Board of Governors pursuant to a determination under section 113 and large, interconnected bank holding companies. Such standards and requirements must be more stringent than those applicable to other nonbank financial companies and bank holding companies that do not present similar risks to the financial stability of the United States, and they must increase in stringency as appropriate in relation to certain characteristics of the company, including its size and complexity. The Council may only recommend standards for bank holding companies with total consolidated assets of $50 billion or more, and the Council may recommend an asset threshold greater than $50 billion for the applicability of any particular standard. The prudential standards may include risk-based capital requirements, leverage limits, liquidity requirements, a contingent capital requirement, resolution plan and credit exposure report requirements, concentration limits, enhanced public disclosures, and overall risk management requirements.

The section enumerates the factors that the Council shall consider in making its recommendation, which include those factors considered in determining whether a nonbank financial company should be subject to supervision and prudential standards by the Board of Governors under section 113, among them the amounts and types of assets and liabilities, degree of leverage, and extent of off-balance sheet exposures. In making its recommendation, it is intended that the Council take into account the nature of the business of different types of nonbank financial companies as well as any existing regulatory regime applicable to different types of nonbank financial companies; the Committee recognizes that not all standards and requirements may be applicable universally. With respect to the contingent capital requirement, the Council shall conduct a study of the feasibility, benefits, costs, and structure of such a requirement and report to Congress not later than two years after the date of enactment of this Act.

[¶ 54,045] *Section 116. Reports*

Under this section, the Council, acting through the Office of Financial Research, may require reports from nonbank financial companies supervised by the Board of Governors pursuant to a section 113 determination and bank holding companies with total consolidated assets of $50 billion or more and their subsidiaries, but must use existing reports to the fullest extent possible.

[¶ 54,046] *Section 117. Treatment of certain companies that cease to be bank holding companies*

This section is intended to ensure that a bank holding company that could pose a risk to U.S. financial stability if it experienced material financial distress would remain supervised by the Board of Governors and subject to the prudential standards authorized under this title even if it sells or closes its bank. The section applies to any entity or a successor entity that (1) was a bank holding company having total consolidated assets equal to or greater than $50 billion as of January 1, 2010, and (2) received financial assistance under or participated in the Capital Purchase Program established under the Troubled Asset Relief Program. If such entity ceases to be a bank holding company at any time after January 1, 2010, then the entity will be treated as a nonbank financial company supervised by the Board of Governors as if the Council had made a determination under section 113. The entity may request a hearing and appeal to the Council its treatment as a nonbank financial company supervised by the Board of Governors.

[¶ 54,047] *Section 118. Council funding*

Any expenses of the Council will be treated as expenses of, and paid by, the Office of Financial Research. (The Council will have only one member for which it incurs salary and benefit expenses, the independent member having insurance expertise. All other members of the Council, and any employees detailed to the Council, will be paid by their respective agencies or departments.)

[¶ 54,048] *Section 119. Resolution of supervisory jurisdictional disputes among member agencies*

This section authorizes a dispute resolution function for the Council. The Council shall resolve disputes among member agencies about the respective jurisdiction over a particular financial company, activity, or product if the agencies cannot resolve the dispute without the Council's intervention. The section prescribes the procedures for dispute resolution and makes the Council's written decision binding on the member agencies that are parties to the dispute.

[¶ 54,049] *Section 120. Additional standards applicable to activities or practices for financial stability purposes*

This section authorizes the Council to issue recommendations to the primary financial regulatory agencies to apply new or heightened prudential standards and safeguards, including those enumerated in section 115, for a financial activity or practice conducted by bank holding companies or nonbank financial companies under the agencies' jurisdiction. The Council would make such recommendation if it deter-

¶ 54,045

mines that the conduct of the activity or practice could create or increase the risk of significant liquidity, credit, or other problems spreading among bank holding companies and nonbank financial companies or U.S. financial markets. The section requires the Council to consult with the primary financial regulatory agencies, provide notice and opportunity for comment on any proposed recommendations, and consider the effect of any recommendation on costs to long-term economic growth. The Council may recommend specific actions to apply to the conduct of a financial activity or practice, including limits on scope or additional capital and risk management requirements.

The Council may inform the primary financial regulatory agency of any Council determination that a bank holding company or nonbank financial company, activity, or practice no longer requires any heightened standards implemented under this title. The primary financial regulatory agency may determine whether to keep such standards in effect, and shall promulgate regulations to establish a procedure by which entities under its jurisdiction may appeal the determination of the primary financial regulatory agency.

[¶ 54,050] *Section 121. Mitigation of risks to financial stability*

This section is intended to provide additional authority for regulators to address grave threats to U.S. financial stability if the prudential standards established under this title would not otherwise do so. The section authorizes the Board of Governors, if it determines that a nonbank financial company supervised by the Board of Governors pursuant to a determination under section 113 or a bank holding company with total consolidated assets of $50 billion or more poses a grave threat to the financial stability of the United States, to require such company to comply with conditions on the conduct of certain activities, terminate certain activities, or, if the Board of Governors determines that such action is inadequate to mitigate a threat to the financial stability of the United States, sell or transfer assets to unaffiliated entities, with an affirmative vote of 2/3 of the Council members then serving and after notice and opportunity for hearing. The Board of Governors and the Council will take into consideration the factors set forth in section 113(a) and (b) in any determination or decision under this section.

Subtitle B—Office of Financial Research

[¶ 54,060] *Section 151. Definitions*

[¶ 54,061] *Section 152. Office of Financial Research established*

This section establishes within the Treasury Department the Office of Financial Research, ("Office") headed by a Director appointed by the President and confirmed by the Senate. The Director shall serve for a term of 6 years. This section provides the Director with certain authorities to manage the Office and also authorizes a fellowship program to be established.

[¶ 54,062] *Section 153. Purpose and duties of the Office*

The purpose of the Office is to support the Council in fulfilling the purposes and duties of the Council and to support member agencies of the Council by (1) collecting data on behalf of the Council and providing such data to the Council and member agencies; (2) standardizing the types and formats of data reported and collected; (3) performing applied research and essential long-term research; (4) developing tools for risk measurement and monitoring; (5) performing other related services; (6) making the results of the activities of the Office available to financial regulatory agencies, and (7) assisting member agencies in determining the types and formats of data where member agencies are authorized by this Act to collect data. This section provides the Office with certain administrative authorities and rulemaking authority regarding data collection and standardization, requires the Director to testify annually before Congress, and authorizes the Director to provide additional reports to Congress. Testimony provided by the Director is not subject to review or approval by any other Federal agency or officer.

[¶ 54,063] *Section 154. Organizational structure; responsibilities of primary programmatic units*

This section establishes within the Office, to carry out the programmatic responsibilities of the Office, the Data Center and the Research and Analysis Center. The Data Center shall, on behalf of the Council, collect, validate, and maintain all data necessary to carry out the duties of the Data Center. The data assembled shall be obtained from member agencies of the Council, commercial data providers, publicly available data sources, and financial entities. The Data Center shall prepare and publish a financial company reference database, financial instrument reference database, and formats and standards for Office data, but shall not publish any confidential data. The Research and Analysis Center shall, on behalf of the Council, develop and maintain independent analytical capabilities and computing resources to (1) develop and maintain metrics and reporting systems for risks to the financial stability of the United States, (2) monitor, investigate, and report on changes in system-wide risk levels and patterns to the Council and Congress, (3) conduct, coordinate, and sponsor research to support and improve regulation of financial entities and markets, (4) evaluate and report on stress tests or other stability-related evaluations of financial entities overseen by the member agencies, (5) maintain expertise in such areas as may be necessary to support specific requests for advice and assistance from financial regulators, (6) investigate disruptions and failures in the financial markets, report findings, and make recommendations to the Council based on those findings, (7) conduct studies and provide advice on the impact of policies related to systemic risk, and (8) promote best practices for financial risk management. Not later than 2 years after the date of enactment of this Act, and not later than 120 days after the end of each fiscal year thereafter, the Office shall submit a report to Congress that assesses the state of the United States financial system, including an analysis of any threats to the financial stability of the United States, the status of the efforts of the Office in meeting the mission of the Office, and key findings from the research and analysis of the financial system by the Office.

[¶ 54,064] *Section 155. Funding*

This section provides authority to fund the Office through assessments on nonbank financial companies supervised by the Board of Governors pursuant to a determination under section 113 and bank holding companies with total consolidated assets of $50 billion or more. The Board of Governors shall provide i nterim funding during the 2-year period following the date of enactment of this Act, and subsequent to the 2-year period the Secretary of Treasury shall establish by regulation, with the approval of the Council, an assessment schedule applicable to such companies that takes into account differences among such companies based on considerations for establishing the prudential standards for such companies under section 115.

[¶ 54,065] *Section 156. Transition oversight*

The purpose of this section is to ensure that the Office has an orderly and organized startup, attracts and retains a qualified workforce, and establishes comprehensive employee training and benefits programs. The Office shall submit an annual report to the Senate Banking Committee and the House Financial Services Committee that includes a training and workforce development plan, workplace flexibilities plan, and recruitment and retention plan. The reporting requirement shall terminate 5 years after the date of enactment of the Act. Nothing in this section shall be construed to affect a collective bargaining agreement or the rights of employees under chapter 71 of title 5, United States Code.

Subtitle C—Additional Board of Governors Authority for Certain Nonbank Financial Companies and Bank Holding Companies

[¶ 54,080] *Section 161. Reports by and examination of nonbank financial companies by the Board of Governors*

The Board of Governors may require reports from nonbank financial companies supervised by the Board of Governors pursuant to a determination under section 113 and any subsidiaries of such companies, and may examine them to determine the nature of the operations and financial condition of the company and its subsidiaries; the financial, operational, and other risks within the company that may pose a threat to the safety and soundness of the company or the stability of the U.S. financial system; the systems for monitoring and controlling such risks; and compliance with the requirements of this subtitle.

To the fullest extent possible, the Board of Governors shall rely on reports and information that such companies and their subsidiaries have provided to other Federal and State regulatory agencies, and on reports of examination of functionally regulated subsidiaries made by their primary regulators (or in case of foreign nonbank financial companies, reports provided to home country supervisor to the extent appropriate).

[¶ 54,081] *Section 162. Enforcement*

Nonbank financial companies supervised by the Board of Governors will be subject to the enforcement provisions under section 8 of the Federal Deposit Insurance Act.

If the Board of Governors determines that a depository institution or functionally regulated subsidiary does not comply with the regulations of the Board of Governors or otherwise poses a threat to the financial stability of the U.S., the Board of Governors may recommend in writing to the primary financial regulatory agency for the subsidiary that the agency initiate a supervisory action or an enforcement proceeding. If the agency does not initiate an action within 60 days, the Board of Governors may take the recommended supervisory or enforcement action.

[¶ 54,082] Section 163. Acquisitions

A nonbank financial company supervised by the Board of Governors pursuant to a determination under section 113 shall be treated as a bank holding company for purposes of section 3 of the Bank Holding Company Act which governs bank acquisitions. A nonbank financial company supervised by the Board of Governors or a bank holding company with total consolidated assets of $50 billion or more shall not acquire direct or indirect ownership or control of any voting shares of a company engaged in nonbanking activities having total consolidated assets of $10 billion or more without providing advanced written notice to the Board of Governors.

In addition to other criteria under the Bank Holding Company Act for reviewing acquisitions, the Board of Governors shall consider the extent to which a proposed acquisition would result in greater or more concentrated risks to global or U.S. financial stability of the global or U.S. economy.

[¶ 54,083] Section 164. Prohibition against management interlocks between certain financial holding companies

A nonbank financial company supervised by the Board of Governors pursuant to a determination under section 113 shall be treated as a bank holding company for purposes of the Depository Institutions Management Interlocks Act. It is not intended that a registered investment company sponsored by a nonbank financial company be deemed unaffiliated with its sponsor for the purpose of this section.

[¶ 54,084] Section 165. Enhanced supervision and prudential standards for nonbank financial companies supervised by the Board of Governors and certain bank holding companies

This section directs the Board of Governors to establish prudential standards and reporting and disclosure requirements for nonbank financial companies supervised by the Board of Governors pursuant to a determination under section 113 and large, interconnected bank holding companies with total consolidated assets of $50 billion or more. The standards and requirements shall be more stringent than those applicable to other nonbank financial companies and bank holding companies that do not present similar risks to the financial stability of the United States, and increase in stringency as appropriate in relation to certain characteristics of the company, including its size and complexity. The Board of Governors may adopt an asset threshold greater than $50 billion for the applicability of any particular standard. The prudential standards will include risk-based capital requirements, leverage limits, liquidity requirements, a contingent capital requirement, resolution plan and credit exposure report requirements, concentration limits, enhanced public disclosures, and overall risk management requirements. The section enumerates the factors that the Board of Governors shall consider in setting the standards, which include those factors considered in determining whether a nonbank financial company should be subject to supervision and prudential standards by the Board of Governors under section 113, among them the amounts and types of assets and liabilities, degree of leverage, and extent of off-balance sheet exposures. It requires that each nonbank financial company supervised by the Board of Governors as well as bank holding company with total consolidated assets of $10 billion or more that is a publicly traded company to establish a risk committee to be responsible for oversight of enterprise-wide risk management practices of the company.

With respect to the resolution plan requirement authorized in this section, if the Board of Governors and the FDIC jointly determine that the resolution plan of a company is not credible and would not facilitate an orderly resolution under the bankruptcy code, such company would have to resubmit resolution plans to correct deficiencies. Failure to resubmit a plan correcting deficiencies within a certain timeframe would result in the imposition of more stringent capital, leverage, or liquidity requirements, or restrictions on the growth, activities, or operations of the company. If, two years after the imposition of these requirements or restrictions, the company still has not resubmitted a plan that corrects the deficiencies, the Board of Governors and the FDIC, in consultation with the Council, may direct the company to divest certain assets or operations in order to facilitate an orderly resolution under the bankruptcy code in the event of failure.

[¶ 54,085] **Section 166. Early remediation requirements**

The Board of Governors, in consultation with the Council and the FDIC, shall by regulation establish requirements to provide for early remediation of financial distress of a nonbank financial company supervised by the Board of Governors pursuant to a determination under section 113 or a large, interconnected bank holding company with total consolidated assets of $50 billion or more. This provision does not authorize the provision of any financial assistance from the Federal government. Instead, the purpose of this provision is to establish a series of specific remedial actions to be taken by such company if it is experiencing financial distress, in order to minimize the probability that the company will become insolvent and the potential harm of such insolvency to the financial stability of the United States. It is intended that the requirements established under this section take into account the structure and operations of, and any existing regulatory regime applicable to, different types of nonbank financial companies, including whether certain structures impose legal or structural limits on the ability of the nonbank financial company to hold capital.

[¶ 54,086] **Section 167. Affiliation**

Nothing in this subtitle shall be construed to require a nonbank financial company supervised by the Board of Governors pursuant to a determination under section 113 or a company that controls such nonbank financial company to conform it's activities to the requirements of section 4 of the Bank Holding Company Act. If such company engages in activities that are not financial in nature, the Board of Governors may require such company to establish and conduct its financial activities in an intermediate holding company.

[¶ 54,087] **Section 168. Regulations**

Except as otherwise specified in this subtitle, the Board of Governors shall issue final regulations to implement this subtitle no later than 18 months after the transfer date.

[¶ 54,088] **Section 169. Avoiding duplication**

The Board of Governors shall take any action it deems appropriate to avoid imposing requirements that are duplicative of applicable requirements under other provisions of law.

[¶ 54,089] **Section 170. Safe harbor**

The Board of Governors shall promulgate regulations on behalf of, and in consultation with, the Council setting forth the criteria for exempting certain types or classes of nonbank financial companies from supervision by the Board of Governors pursuant to a determination under section 113. It is intended that such regulations take into account potential duplication between the requirements under this title and Title VIII of this Act for financial market utilities. The Board of Governors, in consultation with the Council, shall review such regulations no less frequently than every 5 years, and based upon the review, the Board of Governors may update such regulations, and such updates will not take effect until 2 years after publication in final form. The Chairpersons of the Board of Governors and the Council shall submit a joint report to the Senate Banking Committee and the House Financial Services Committee not later than 30 days after issuing the regulations or updates, and such report shall include at a minimum the rationale for exemption and empirical evidence to support the criteria for exemption.

Title II—Orderly Liquidation Authority

[¶ 54,100] **Section 201. Definitions**

This section defines various terms used in this title. Financial companies are defined as (1) bank holding companies, (2) nonbank financial companies supervised by the Board of Governors of the Federal Reserve System (Board of Governors) pursuant to a determination under section 113 of this Act, (3) other companies predominantly engaged in activities that the Board of Governors has determined are financial in nature, or incidental to activities that are financial in nature, for purposes of section 4(k) of the Bank Holding Company Act of 1956, and (4) subsidiaries of any of the companies included in (1), (2), and (3) other than an insured depository institution or insurance company (but it is not intended that an investment company required to be registered under the Investment Company Act of 1940 would be deemed to be a subsidiary of a company included in (1) (2), and (3) by reason of the provision by such company of services to the investment company, unless such company (including through all of its affiliates) owns 25 percent or more of the shares of the investment company). An "insurance company" is any entity that is engaged in the business of insurance, subject to regulation by a State insurance regulator, and covered by a State law that is designed to specifically deal with the rehabilitation, liquidation, or insolvency of an insurance company. A mutual insurance holding company organized and operating under State insurance laws may be considered an insurance company for the purpose of this title. A "covered financial company" is a financial company for which a determination has been made to use the orderly liquidation authority under section 203.A "covered broker or dealer" is a covered financial company that is a broker dealer registered with the Securities and Exchange Commission ("SEC") under section 15(b) of the Securities Exchange Act of 1934 and is a member of Securities Investor Protection Corporation ("SIPC").

[¶54,101] Section 202. Orderly Liquidation Authority Panel

This section establishes an Orderly Liquidation Authority Panel ("Panel") composed of 3 judges from the United States Bankruptcy Court for the District of Delaware. Subsequent to a determination by the Secretary of the Treasury ("Secretary") under section 203, the Secretary, upon notice to the Federal Deposit Insurance Corporation ("FDIC") and the covered financial company, shall petition the Panel for an order authorizing the Secretary to appoint the FDIC as receiver. The Panel, after notice to the covered financial company and a hearing in which the covered financial company may oppose the petition, shall determine within 24 hours of receipt of the petition whether the determination of the Secretary is supported by substantial evidence. If the Panel determines that the determination of the Secretary (1) is supported by substantial evidence, the Panel shall issue an order immediately authorizing the Secretary to appoint the Corporation as receiver of the covered financial company, and (2) is not supported by substantial evidence, the Panel shall immediately provide the Secretary with a written statement of its reasons and afford the Secretary with an opportunity to amend and refile the petition with the Panel. The decision of the Panel may be appealed to the United States Court of Appeals not later than 30 days after the date on which the decision of the Panel is rendered, and the decision of the Court of Appeals may be appealed to the Supreme Court not later than 30 days after the date of the final decision of the Court of Appeals.

This section also requires the following studies: a study each by the Administrative Office of the United States Courts and the Comptroller General of the United States regarding the bankruptcy and orderly liquidation process for financial companies under the Bankruptcy Code, and a study by the Comptroller General of the United States regarding international coordination relating to the orderly liquidation of financial companies under the Bankruptcy Code.

[¶54,102] Section 203. Systemic risk determination

This section establishes the process for triggering the use of the orderly liquidation authority. The process includes several steps intended to make the use of this authority very rare. There is a strong presumption that the Bankruptcy Code will continue to apply to most failing financial companies (other than insured depository institutions and insurance companies which have their own separate resolution processes), including large financial companies.

To trigger the orderly liquidation authority, the Board of Governors and the Board of Directors of the FDIC must each, by a two-thirds vote of its members then serving, provide a written recommendation to the Secretary that includes: (1) an evaluation of whether a financial company is in default or in danger of default; (2) a description of the effects that the failure of the financial company would have on financial stability in the United States; and (3) a recommendation regarding the nature and extent of actions that should be taken under this title. (The Secretary may request the Board of Governors and the FDIC to consider making the recommendation, or the Board of Governors and the FDIC may make the recommendation on their own initiative.)

In the case of a covered broker or dealer, or in which the largest U.S. subsidiary of a covered financial company is a covered broker or dealer, the SEC and the Board of Governors must each, by a two-thirds vote of its members then serving, provide a written recommendation to the Secretary as described above. (The Secretary of the Treasury may request the Board of Governors and the SEC to consider making the recommendation, or the Board of Governors and the SEC may make the recommendation on their own initiative.)

Upon receiving such recommendations, the Secretary (in consultation with the President) may make a written determination that: (1) the financial company is in default or in danger of default; (2) the failure of the financial company and its resolution under otherwise applicable law would have serious adverse effects on U.S. financial stability; (3) no viable private sector alternative is available to prevent default; (4) any effect on the claims or interests of creditors, counterparties, and shareholders as a result of actions taken under this title has been taken into account; (5) any action under section 204 would avoid or mitigate such adverse effects; and (6) a Federal regulatory agency has ordered the financial company to convert all of its convertible debt instruments that are subject to the regulatory order. The Secretary would take into consideration the effectiveness of the action in mitigating adverse effects on the financial system, any cost to the Treasury, and the potential to increase excessive risk taking on the part of creditors, counterparties, and shareholders in the covered financial company.

The Secretary shall provide written notice of the determination to Congress within 24 hours. The FDIC shall submit a report to Congress within 60 days of its appointment as receiver on the covered financial company and update the information contained in the report at least quarterly. The Government Accountability Office will review and report on the Secretary's determination.

The FDIC shall establish policies and procedures acceptable to the Secretary governing the use of funds available to the FDIC to carry out this title.

If an insurance company that is a covered financial company or subsidiary or affiliate of a covered financial company, its liquidation or rehabilitation shall be conducted as provided under state law. The FDIC shall have backup authority to file appropriate judicial action in state court to place such a company into liquidation under state law if the state regulator fails to act within 60 days.

[¶54,103] Section 204. Orderly liquidation

This section provides a strong presumption that, in the exercise of orderly liquidation authority: (1) creditors and shareholders will bear losses, (2) management responsible for the company's financial condition are not retained, and (3) the FDIC and other agencies (where applicable) take steps to ensure that management and other parties responsible for the failed company's financial condition bear losses through actions for damages, restitution, and compensation clawbacks. The section provides that the FDIC act as receiver of the covered financial company upon appointment of the Corporation under section 202. The FDIC, as receiver, must consult with primary financial regulatory agencies of: (1) the covered financial company and its covered subsidiaries to ensure an orderly liquidation; and (2) any subsidiaries that are not covered subsidiaries to coordinate the appropriate treatment of any such solvent subsidiaries and the separate resolution of any such insolvent subsidiaries under other governmental authority, as appropriate. The FDIC shall consult with the SEC and the SIPC in the case of a covered financial company that is a broker dealer and member of SIPC. The FDIC may consult with or acquire the services of outside experts to assist in the orderly liquidation process.

The FDIC may make funds available to the receivership for the orderly liquidation of the covered financial company subject to the mandatory terms and conditions set forth in section 206 and the orderly liquidation plan described in section 210(n)(14).

[¶54,104] Section 205. Orderly liquidation of covered brokers and dealers

This section authorizes the application of orderly liquidation authority, if necessary, to a SIPC-member broker or dealer while generally preserving SIPC's powers and duties under the Securities Investor Protection Act of 1970 ("SIPA") with respect to the liquidation of such entity. The section provides that the FDIC shall appoint SIPC, without any need for court approval, to act as trustee for liquidation under the SIPA of a covered broker or dealer. The subsection prescribes the powers, duties, and limitation of powers of SIPC as trustee. Except as otherwise provide in this title, no court may take any action, including an action pursuant to the SIPA or the Bankruptcy Code, to restrain or affect the powers or functions of the FDIC as receiver of the covered broker or dealer.

[¶54,105] Section 206. Mandatory terms and conditions for all orderly liquidation actions

The FDIC shall take action under this title only if it determines that such actions are necessary for financial stability and not for the purpose of preserving the covered financial company. The FDIC must also ensure that shareholders would not receive any payment until after all other claims are fully paid, that unsecured creditors bear losses in accordance with the claims priority provisions in section 210, and that management responsible for the company's failure is removed (if it has not already been removed at the time of the FDIC's appointment as receiver).

[¶ 54,106] Section 207. Directors not liable for acquiescing in appointment of receiver

This section exempts the board of directors of a covered financial company from liability to the company's shareholders or creditors for acquiescing or consenting in good faith to appointment of a receiver under section 202.

[¶ 54,107] Section 208. Dismissal and exclusion of other actions

This section provides that the appointment of the FDIC as receiver under section 202 for a covered financial company or the appointment of SIPC as trustee for a covered broker or dealer under section 205 shall result in the dismissal of any existing bankruptcy or insolvency case or proceeding and prevent the commencement of any such case or proceeding while the orderly liquidation is pending.

[¶ 54,108] Section 209. Rulemaking; non-conflicting law

This section requires the FDIC, in consultation with the Council, to prescribe such rules or regulations as considered necessary or appropriate to implement this title. To the extent possible, the FDIC shall seek to harmonize applicable rules and regulations promulgated under this section with the insolvency laws that would otherwise apply to a covered financial company.

[¶ 54,109] Section 210. Powers and duties of the corporation

Subsection (a). Powers and authorities

This subsection defines the powers and authorities of the FDIC as receiver of a covered financial company, including its powers and duties: (1) to succeed to the rights, title, powers, and privileges of the covered financial company and its stockholders, members, officers, and directors; (2) to operate the company with all the powers of shareholders, members, directors, and officers; (3) to liquidate the company through sale of assets or transfer of assets to a bridge financial company established under subsection (h); (4) to merge the company with another company or transferring assets or liabilities; (5) to pay valid obligations that come due, to the extent that funds are available; (6) to exercise subpoena powers; (7) to utilize private sector services to manage and dispose of assets; (8) to terminate rights and claims of stockholders and creditors (except for the right to payment of claims consistent with the priority of claims provision under this section); and (9) to determine and pay claims. The subsection also prescribes the FDIC's authorities to avoid fraudulent or preferential transfers of interests of the covered financial company.

Subsection (b). Priority of expenses and unsecured claims

This section defines the priority of expenses and unsecured claims against the covered financial company or the FDIC as receiver for such company. All claimants of a covered financial company that are similarly situated in the expenses and claims priority shall be treated in a similar manner except in cases where the FDIC determines that doing otherwise would maximize the value of the company's assets or maximize the present value of the proceeds (or minimize the amount of any loss) from disposing of the assets of the company. Creditors who receive more than they would otherwise receive if all similarly situated creditors were treated in a similar manner would be subject to a substantially higher assessment rate under subsection (o)(1)(E)(ii). All claimants that are similarly situated in the expenses and claims priority shall not receive less than the maximum liability amount defined in subsection (d). The section also defines the priority of expenses and unsecured claims in those cases where the FDIC is appointed receiver for a covered broker or dealer.

Subsection (c). Provisions relating to contracts entered into before appointment of receiver

This subsection authorizes the FDIC to repudiate and enforce contracts and handle the financial company's qualified financial contracts (including derivatives). A counterparty to a qualified financial contract would be stayed from terminating, liquidating, or netting the contract (solely by reason of the appointment of a receiver) until 5:00 PM on the fifth business day after the date that the FDIC was appointed receiver. (The length of the stay differs from that authorized under the Federal Deposit Insurance Act with respect to an insured depository institution. Under the Federal Deposit Insurance Act, the stay would last until 5:00 PM one business day following the date that the FDIC was appointed receiver.)

Subsection (d). Valuation of claims in default

This subsection establishes the FDIC's maximum liability for claims against the covered financial company (or FDIC as receiver) as the amount that the claimant would have received if the FDIC had not been appointed receiver with respect to the covered financial company and the company was liquidated under chapter 7 of the

U.S. Bankruptcy Code or any State insolvency law. The subsection also authorizes the FDIC, as receiver and with the Secretary's approval, to make additional payments to claimants only if the FDIC determines this to be necessary to minimize losses to the FDIC as receiver from the orderly liquidation of the covered financial company. Creditors who receive such additional payments would be subject to a substantially higher assessment rate under subsection (o)(1)(E)(ii).

Subsection (e). Limitation on court action

This subsection precludes a court from taking action to restrain or affect the powers or functions of the FDIC when it is exercising its powers as receiver, except as otherwise provided in the title.

Subsection (f). Liability of directors and officers

This subsection provides that FDIC may take actions to hold directors and officers of a covered financial company personally liable for monetary damages with respect to gross negligence.

Subsection (g). Damages

This subsection provides that recoverable damages in claims brought against directors, officers, or employees of a covered financial company for improper investment or use of company assets include principal losses and appropriate interest.

Subsection (h). Bridge financial companies

This subsection authorizes the FDIC, as receiver, to establish one or more bridge financial companies. Such bridge financial companies may assume liabilities and purchase assets of the covered financial company, and perform other temporary functions that the FDIC may prescribe.

Subsection (i). Sharing records

This subsection requires other Federal regulators to make available to the FDIC all records relating to the covered financial company.

Subsection (j). Expedited procedures for certain claims

This subsection expedites federal courts' consideration of cases brought by the FDIC against a covered financial company's directors, officers, employees, or agents.

Subsection (k). Foreign investigations

This subsection authorizes the FDIC, as receiver, to request assistance from, and provide assistance to, any foreign financial authority.

Subsection (l). Prohibition on entering secrecy agreements and protective orders

This subsection prohibits the FDIC from entering into any agreement that prohibits it from disclosing the terms of any settlement of any action brought by the FDIC as receiver of a covered financial company.

Subsection (m). Liquidation of certain covered financial companies or bridge financial companies

This subsection provides that the FDIC, as receiver, in liquidating any covered financial company or bridge financial company that is either (1) a stockbroker that is not a member of SIPC, or (2) a commodity broker, will apply the applicable liquidation provisions of the bankruptcy code pertaining to "stockbrokers" and "commodity brokers" (as such terms are defined in subchapters III and IV, respectively, of chapter 7 of chapter 7 of the U.S. Bankruptcy Code).

Subsection (n). Orderly Liquidation Fund

This subsection creates the Orderly Liquidation Fund ("Fund') in the Treasury Department that will be available to the FDIC to carry out the authorities in this title. The sole purpose of the Fund is to allow the FDIC to carry out the orderly liquidation of a covered financial company as authorized by this title; the Fund may not be used for any other purpose. The FDIC shall manage the Fund consistent with the policies and procedures acceptable to the Secretary of Treasury that are established under section 203(d), and invest amounts held in the Fund that are not required to meet the FDIC's current needs in obligations of the United States.

The target size of the Fund shall be $50 billion, adjusted on a periodic basis for inflation. The FDIC shall impose assessments as provided in subsection (o) to capitalize the Fund and reach the target size during an "initial capitalization period" of not less than 5 years or greater than 10 years from the date of enactment. (The FDIC, with the approval of the Secretary of the Treasury, may extend the initial capitalization period if the Fund incurs a loss from the failure of a covered financial company before the initial capitalization period expires.) Except as provided in subsection (o), FDIC shall suspend assessments when the initial capitalization period expires. The intention of this subsection and subsection (o) is to require large financial firms, rather than taxpayers, to serve as the first source of liquidity in winding down the failed financial company.

The FDIC may issue obligations to the Secretary of the Treasury. FDIC may not issue or incur any obligation that would result in total obligations outstanding that exceed the sum of (1) the amount of cash and cash equivalents held in the Fund, and (2) the amount that is equal to 90 percent of the fair value of assets from each covered financial company that are available to repay the FDIC (the "maximum obligation limitation"). It is intended that the determination of the amount available to the FDIC under (2) above be limited to what the assets of the covered financial company, calculated on a consolidated basis, can support. The FDIC and the Secretary shall jointly prescribe rules, in consultation with the Council, governing the calculation of the maximum obligation limitation.

The FDIC may issue obligations only after the cash and cash equivalents of the Fund have been drawn down to facilitate the orderly liquidation of a covered financial company.

Amounts in the Fund shall be available to the FDIC with regard to a covered financial company for which the FDIC has been appointed receiver after the FDIC has developed an orderly liquidation plan acceptable to the Secretary of the Treasury. The FDIC may amend an approved plan at any time, with the concurrence of the Secretary.

Subsection (o). Risk-based assessments

This subsection requires the FDIC to charge risk-based assessments to eligible financial companies during the initial capitalization period until the FDIC determines that the Fund has reached the target size. Eligible financial companies include bank holding companies with total consolidated assets equal to or greater than $50 billion and nonbank financial companies supervised by the Board of Governors pursuant to a determination under section 113 of Title I.

The FDIC must charge additional risk-based assessments if: (1) the Fund falls below the target size after the initial capitalization period in order to restore the Fund to the target size over a period determined by the FDIC; (2) the FDIC is appointed receiver for a covered financial company and the Fund incurs a loss during the initial capitalization period; or (3) such assessments are necessary to pay in full obligations issued to the Secretary of the Treasury within 60 months of their issuance (unless the FDIC requests, and the Secretary approves, an extension in order to avoid as serious adverse effect on the U.S. financial system). If required, any such additional risk-based assessments shall be imposed on (1) eligible financial companies and financial companies with total assets equal to or greater than $50 billion that are not eligible financial companies, and (2) any financial company, at a substantially higher rate than would otherwise be assessed, that benefitted from the orderly liquidation under this title by receiving payments or credit pursuant to subsections (b)(4), (d)(4), and (h)(5). The subsection outlines the risk factors that the FDIC shall consider in imposing risk-based assessments to capitalize the Fund as well as any additional assessments that may be required.

The FDIC shall prescribe regulations to carry out this subsection in consultation with the Secretary and the Council, and such regulations shall take into account the differences in risks posed by different financial companies, the differences in the liability structure of financial companies, and the different bases for other assessments that such financial companies may be required to pay, to ensure that assessed financial companies are treated equitably and that assessments under this subsection reflect such differences. It is intended that the risk-based assessments may vary among different types or classes of financial companies in accordance with the risks posed to the financial stability of the United States. For instance, certain types of financial companies such as insurance companies and other financial companies that may present lower risk to U.S. financial stability (as indicated, for example, by higher capital, lower leverage, or similar measures of risk as appropriate depending on the nature of the business of the financial companies) relative to other types of financial companies should be assessed at a lower rate. Furthermore, the FDIC should consider the impact of potential assessment on the ability of certain tax-exempt entities to carry out their legally required charitable and educational missions, such as the ability of not-for-profit fraternal benefit societies to carry out their state and federally required missions to serve their members and communities.

Subsection (p). Unenforceability of certain agreements

This subsection prohibits enforceability of any term contained in any existing or future standstill, confidentiality, or other agreement that affects or restricts the ability of a person to acquire, that prohibits a person from offering to acquire, or that prohibits a person from using previously disclosed information in connection with an offer to acquire, all or part of a covered financial company.

Subsection (q). Other exemptions

This subsection provides certain exemptions to the FDIC from taxes and levies when acting as a receiver for a covered financial company.

Subsection (r). Certain sales of assets prohibited

This subsection requires the FDIC to prescribe regulations prohibiting the sale of assets of a covered financial company to certain persons found to have been engaged in fraudulent activity or participated in transactions causing substantial losses to a covered financial company or who are convicted debtors.

[¶54,110] Section 211. Miscellaneous provisions

This section makes a conforming change relating to concealment of assets from the FDIC acting as receiver for a covered financial company, and makes a conforming change to the netting provisions contained in the Federal Deposit Insurance Corporation Improvement Act of 1991 by expanding the exceptions to include section 210(c) of this Act and section 1367 of HERA (12 U.S.C. 4617(d)).

Title III—Transfer of Powers to the Comptroller of the Currency, the Corporation, and the Board of Governors

[¶54,120] Section 301. Short title and purposes

The short title is "Enhancing Financial Institution Safety and Soundness Act of 2010." Among the purposes of the title are to provide for the safe and sound operation of the banking system; to preserve and protect the dual banking system of federal and state chartered depository institutions; and to streamline and rationalize the supervision of depository institutions and their holding companies.

[¶54,121] Section 302. Definitions

Defines the term "transferred employee" to refer to those employees who are transferred from the Office of Thrift Supervision ("OTS") to the Office of the Comptroller of the Currency ("OCC") or the Federal Deposit Insurance Corporation ("FDIC").

Subtitle A—Transfer of Powers and Duties

[¶54,140] Section 311. Transfer date

The "transfer date" is the date that is 1 year after the date of enactment or another date not later than 18 months if so designated by the Secretary of the Treasury. The transfer date is the date upon which various functions are transferred from the OTS to the Federal Reserve Board ("Board"), the OCC, and the FDIC. Additionally, certain functions of the Board are transferred to the OCC and FDIC. The transfer of personnel, property and funding are also keyed to the transfer date.

[¶54,141] Section 312. Powers and duties transferred

This section transfers all functions of the OTS to the Board, the OCC, and the FDIC. It also transfers from the Board to the OCC and the FDIC, supervisory authority over the holding companies of smaller banks. And, it transfers from the Board to the FDIC, the supervision of insured state member banks.

As a result of these various transfers, the Board will regulate the larger, more complex bank and thrift holding companies—i.e., those with total consolidated assets of $50 billion or more. The OCC will retain its authority over all national banks regardless of their size and will also supervise federal thrifts. The OCC will become a holding company regulator for the smaller bank and thrift holding companies (under $50 billion) where the majority of depository institution assets are in national banks or federal thrifts. The FDIC will regulate all insured state banks regardless of their size—including those that are members of the Federal Reserve System—and all state savings associations. The FDIC will also supervise the smaller holding companies (under $50 billion) where the majority of depository institution assets are in insured state banks or state thrifts.

The Board will retain its authority to issue rules under the Bank Holding Company Act and will also have the authority to issue rules under the Home Owners Loan Act with respect to savings and loan holding companies. When issuing rules under these acts that apply to bank and thrift holding companies with less than $50 billion in assets, the Board must consult with the OCC and the FDIC. The OCC and FDIC will jointly write the rules that apply to thrifts.

This section amends the definition of "appropriate federal banking agency" in section 3(q) of the Federal Deposit Insurance Act which indicates the allocation of regulatory responsibility among the federal banking agencies by type of company—such as a national bank, a state member bank, a federal savings association. The definition is amended to reflect the new responsibilities of the Board, FDIC, and OCC. In addition to the description above, the Board will maintain its supervision of uninsured state member banks and various foreign bank-related entities.

This section also requires the OCC, Board and FDIC to issue a joint regulation specifying how the $50 billion will be calculated and at what frequency to determine the appropriate holding company regulator. In terms of the frequency of the assessment, it can be no less than 2 years, unless with respect to a particular institution there is a transaction outside the ordinary course of business, such as a merger or acquisition. In issuing the regulations, the agencies are directed to avoid disruptive transfers of regulatory authority.

[¶ 54,142] *Section 313. Abolishment*

This section abolishes the OTS.

[¶ 54,143] *Section 314. Amendments to the revised statutes*

This section clarifies the mission and authorities of the OCC.

[¶ 54,144] *Section 315. Federal information policy*

This section clarifies that the OCC is an independent agency for purposes of Federal information policy.

[¶ 54,145] *Section 316. Savings provisions*

This section preserves the existing rights, duties and obligations of the OTS, the Board, and the Federal Reserve banks that existed on the day before the transfer date. This section also preserves existing law suits by or against the OTS, the Board, and the Federal Reserve banks, but states that as of the transfer date, law suits against the OTS in connection with functions transferred to the OCC, the FDIC, or Board, are transferred to these agencies as appropriate. In addition, as of the transfer date, law suits against the Board or a Federal Reserve bank in connection with functions transferred to the OCC or the FDIC are transferred to these agencies as appropriate.

This section also continues all of the existing orders, regulations, determinations, agreements, procedures, interpretations and advisory materials of the OTS and those of the Board that relate to the Board's functions that have been transferred.

[¶ 54,146] *Section 317. References in Federal law to Federal banking agencies*

This section provides that references in Federal law to the OTS with respect to functions that are transferred shall be deemed references to the OCC, FDIC, or Board, as appropriate. In addition, references in Federal law to the Board and the Federal Reserve banks with respect to their functions that are transferred shall be deemed references to the OCC or the FDIC, as appropriate.

[¶ 54,147] *Section 318. Funding*

This section allows the Comptroller to collect an assessment, fee, or other charge from any entity the OCC supervises as necessary to carry out its responsibilities including with respect to holding companies, federal thrifts, and nonbank affiliates (that are not functionally regulated) that engage in bank permissible activities. The OCC's supervision of these nonbank affiliates is provided under a new section 6 of the Bank Holding Company Act of 1956 which is added in Title VI of this Act. In establishing the amount of an assessment, fee, or other charge collected from an entity, the OCC may take into account the funds transferred to the OCC (under a new arrangement with the FDIC), the nature and scope of the activities of the entity, the amount and types of assets held by the entity, the financial and managerial condition of the entity, and any other factor that the OCC deems appropriate.

This section also authorizes the FDIC to charge for its supervision of nonbank affiliates under new section 6 of the Bank Holding Company Act.

This section requires the OCC to submit to the FDIC a proposal to promote parity in the examination fees state and federal depository institutions having total consolidated assets of less than $50,000,000,000 pay for their supervision.

Currently, the FDIC and the Board do not charge state banks for their federal supervision. (These agencies share examination responsibilities with the states, and thus lower the costs to the states of supervising these entities. While the states charge for supervision, the FDIC and Board do not.) The FDIC pays for supervision of state banks from the Deposit Insurance Fund

(DIF). Both state and federal depository institutions pay insurance premiums into the DIF. Thus, national banks and federal thrifts help defray the costs associated with the FDIC's supervision of state nonmember banks. This subsidy will only grow when the FDIC assumes the supervision of all state banks and state thrifts, as well as most of their holding companies, if the FDIC continues to rely on the DIF to fund supervision.

The funding disparity can also exacerbate regulatory arbitrage according to testimony the Committee received. The OCC must assess its banks for examination fees whereas the FDIC and the Board have other means to fund their supervision of state banks. [footnote to Ludwig's testimony, September 29, 2009] Thus promoting parity in examination fees should reduce the arbitrage in the system and the subsidy for federal supervision of state banks by national banks and federal thrifts.

Under this section, the OCC's proposal will recommend a transfer from the FDIC to the OCC of a percentage of the amount that the OCC estimates is necessary or appropriate to carry out its supervisory responsibilities of federal depository institutions having total consolidated assets of less than $50,000,000,000. The FDIC is directed to assist the OCC in collecting data relative to the supervision of State depository institutions to develop the proposal.

Not later than 60 days after receipt of the proposal, the FDIC Board must vote on the proposal and promptly implement a plan to periodically transfer to the OCC a percentage of the amount that the OCC estimates is necessary or appropriate to carry out the its supervisory responsibilities for national banks and federal thrifts having total consolidated assets of less than $50,000,000,000, as approved by the FDIC Board. Not later than 30 days after the FDIC Board's vote, the FDIC must submit to the Senate Banking Committee and House Financial Services Committee a report describing the OCC's proposal and the decision resulting from the FDIC Board's vote. If, by 2 years after the date of enactment of this Act, the FDIC Board has failed to approve a plan, the Financial Stability Oversight Council shall approve a plan using the dispute resolution procedures under section 119.

The section also requires the Board to collect assessments, fees, and charges from (1) bank holding companies and savings and loan holding companies that have total consolidated assets equal to or greater than $50 billion, and (2) all nonbank financial companies supervised by the Board under section 113 of this Act, that are equal to the total expenses incurred by the Board to carry out its responsibilities with respect to such companies. Charging holding companies for the Board's supervision will result in savings by the taxpayer.

[¶ 54,148] *Section 319. Contracting and leasing authority*

This section clarifies the contracting and leasing authorities of the Office of the Comptroller of the Currency.

Subtitle B—Transitional Provisions

[¶ 54,160] *Section 321. Interim use of funds, personnel, and property*

This section provides for the orderly transfer of functions (1) from the OTS to the OCC, FDIC and the Board; and (2) from the Board to the OCC and FDIC, with specific reference to funds, personnel and property.

[¶ 54,161] *Section 322. Transfer of employees*

This section states that all employees of the OTS are transferred to OCC or the FDIC. The OTS, OCC and FDIC must jointly identify the employees necessary to carry out the duties transferred from the OTS to the OCC and the FDIC. The Board, OCC and FDIC must jointly identify the employees necessary to carry out the duties transferred from the Board (including the Federal Reserve banks) to the OCC or the FDIC.

Under this section, relevant employees are transferred within 90 days of the transfer date. The section also describes the extent to which employees' status, tenure, pay, retirement and health care benefits are protected, and describes employee protections from involuntary separation and reassignments outside locality pay area. It also provides that not later than 2 years from the transfer date, the OCC and FDIC must each place the transferred employees into the established pay and classification systems of the OCC and FDIC. In addition, this section provides that the OCC and FDIC may not take any action that would unfairly disadvantage a transferred employee relative to other OCC and FDIC employees on the basis of their prior employment by the OTS.

[¶ 54,162] *Section 323. Property transferred*

This section provides that property of the OTS is transferred to the OCC and FDIC. The OCC, FDIC and Board, will jointly determine which property of the Board should be transferred and to which of the agencies.

[¶ 54,163] Section 324. Funds transferred

This section provides that except to the extent necessary to dispose of the affairs of the OTS, all funds available to the OTS are transferred to the OCC, FDIC, or Board, in a manner commensurate with the functions that are transferred to these agencies.

[¶ 54,164] Section 325. Disposition of affairs

This section describes the authority of the Director of the OTS and the Chairman of the Board during the 90 day period beginning on the transfer date, to manage employees and property that have not yet been transferred, and to take actions necessary to wind up matters relating to any function transferred to another agency.

[¶ 54,165] Section 326. Continuation of services

This section states that any agency, department or instrumentality of the U.S. that was providing support services to the OTS or the Board, in connection with functions transferred to another agency, shall continue to provide such services until the transfer of functions is complete, and consult with the OCC, FDIC, or Board, as appropriate, to coordinate and facilitate a prompt and orderly transition.

Subtitle C—Federal Deposit Insurance Corporation

[¶ 54,180] Section 331. Deposit insurance reform

This section amends the Federal Deposit Insurance Act to repeal the provision that states no institution may be denied the lowest-risk category solely because of its size. This section also directs the FDIC, unless it makes a written determination discussed below, to amend its regulations to define the term "assessment base" of an insured depository institution for purposes of deposit insurance assessments as the average total assets of the insured depository institution during the assessment period, minus the sum of (1) the average tangible equity of the insured depository institution during the assessment period and (2) the average long-term unsecured debt of the insured depository institution during the assessment period.

If, not later than 1 year after the date of enactment of this Act, the FDIC submits to the Senate Banking Committee and House Financial Services Committee, in writing, a finding that such an amendment to its regulations regarding the definition of the term "assessment base" would reduce the effectiveness of the FDIC's risk-based assessment system or increase the risk of loss to the Deposit Insurance Fund, the FDIC may retain the definition of the term "assessment base", as in effect on the day before the date of enactment of this Act, or establish, by rule, a definition of the term "assessment base" that the FDIC deems appropriate.

There is concern that the new assessment base will create an additional burden on insured depository institutions that support asset growth through increased reliance on Federal Home Loan Bank advances. Based on its current risk-based assessment rate regulations, the FDIC imposes an upward adjustment on an institution's deposit insurance assessment rate if the institution has secured liabilities, including Federal Home Loan Bank advances, in excess of a certain threshold. This section would now direct the FDIC to include assets funded by secured liabilities (including Federal Home Loan Bank advances) in an institution's assessment base. Therefore, the Committee recommends that the FDIC also review and adjust its risk-based assessment rate regulations, if warranted, to ensure that the assessment appropriately reflects the risk posed by an insured depository institution as a result of the changes to the assessment base.

[¶ 54,181] Section 332. Management of the Federal Deposit Insurance Corporation

This section replaces the position of the OTS on the FDIC Board of Directors with the Director of the Consumer Financial Protection Bureau.

Subtitle D—Termination of Federal Thrift Charter

[¶ 54,200] Section 341. Termination of federal savings associations

This section provides that upon the date of enactment of this Act, neither the Director of the OTS nor the OCC may issue a charter for a federal savings association.[129]

---

[129] "Congress created the federal thrift charter in the Home Owners' Loan Act of 1933 in response to the extensive failures of state-chartered thrifts and the collapse of the broader financial system during the Great Depression. The

While this provision would not allow the establishment of any new federal thrifts, it does not affect the state thrift charter. Nor does it impose any new limits on existing federal thrifts or their owners. It would not require the divestiture of any thrift and it protects the status of existing unitary thrift holding companies.

[¶ 54,201] **Section 342. Branching**

This section states that a savings association that becomes a bank may continue to operate its branches.

Title IV—Private Fund Investment Advisers Registration Act of 2010

[¶54,220] **Section 401. Short title**

Section 401 provides the title of the Act as the "Private Fund Investment Advisers Registration Act of 2010".

[¶54,221] **Section 402. Definitions**

Section 402 defines the terms "private fund" and "foreign private adviser." "Private funds" are issuers that would be regulated investment companies, but for sections 3(c)(1) or 3(c)(7) of the Investment Company Act of 1940 (which provide exemptions for issuers with fewer than 100 shareholders or where all shareholders are qualified purchasers).

"Foreign private advisers" are those that have no place of business in the United States; do not hold themselves out generally to the public in the United States as investment advisers; and have fewer than 15 U.S. clients with less than $25 million in assets under management.

[¶54,222] **Section 403. Elimination of private adviser exemption; limited exemption for foreign private advisers; limited intrastate exemption**

Section 403 would require advisers to large hedge funds to register with the SEC, making them subject to record keeping, examination, and disclosure requirements. The rationale for the provision is that the unregulated status of large hedge funds constitutes a serious regulatory gap. No precise data regarding the size and scope of hedge fund activities are available, but the common estimate is that the funds had about $2 trillion under management before the crisis, and that amount may be magnified by leverage. They are significant participants in many financial markets; their trades and strategies can affect prices. While hedge funds are generally not thought to have caused the current financial crisis, information regarding their size, strategies, and positions could be crucial to regulatory attempts to deal with a future crisis. The case of Long-Term Capital Management, a hedge fund that was rescued through Federal Reserve intervention in 1998 because of concerns that it was "too-interconnected-to-fail," indicates that the activities of even a single hedge fund may have systemic consequences.

Section 403 was included in the Treasury's Department's regulatory reform proposal for hedge funds.[130] Former SEC Chairman Arthur Levitt wrote in testimony for the Senate Banking Committee that he would "recommend placing hedge funds under SEC regulation in the context of their role as money managers and investment advisers."[131] Advocates such as the AFL-CIO[132], CalPERS,[133] and the Investment Adviser Associ-

---

(Footnote Continued)

rationale for federal thrifts as a specialized class of depository institutions focused on residential mortgage lending made sense at the time but the case for such specialized institutions has weakened considerably in recent years. Moreover, over the past few decades, the powers of thrifts and banks have substantially converged.

As securitization markets for residential mortgages have grown, commercial banks have increased their appetite for mortgage lending, and the Federal Home Loan Bank System has expanded its membership base. Accordingly, the need for a special class of mortgage-focused depository institutions has fallen. Moreover, the fragility of thrifts has become readily apparent during the financial crisis. In part because thrifts are required by law to focus more of their lending on residential mortgages, thrifts were more vulnerable to the housing downturn that the United States has been experiencing since 2007. The availability of the federal thrift charter has created opportunities for private sector arbitrage of our financial regulatory system." "Financial Regulatory Reform: A New Foundation," Administration's White Paper, introduced June 17, 2009.

[130] FACT SHEET: *Administration's Regulatory Reform Agenda Moves Forward; Legislation for the Registration of Hedge Funds Delivered to Capitol Hill*, U.S. Department of the Treasury, Press Release, July 15, 2009, www.financialstability.gov.

[131] *Enhancing Investor Protection and the Regulation of Securities Markets—Part II: Testimony before the U.S. Senate Committee on Banking, Housing, and Urban Affairs*, 111th Congress, 1st session, p.9 (2009) (Testimony of Mr. Arthur Levitt).

[132] *Enhancing Investor Protection and the Regulation of Securities Markets—Part I: Testimony before the U.S. Senate Committee on Banking, Housing, and Urban Affairs*, 111th Congress, 1st session (2009) (Testimony of Mr. Damon Silvers).

[133] *Regulating Hedge Funds and Other Private Investment Pools: Testimony before the Subcommittee on Securities, Insurance, and Investment of the U.S. Senate Committee on Banking, Housing, and Urban Affairs*, 111th Congress, 1st session (2009) (Testimony of Mr. Joseph Dear).

ation[134] also support placing hedge funds under SEC regulation via the Investment Advisers Act of 1940. Expert panels such as the Group of Thirty,[135] the G-20,[136] the Investor's Working Group,[137] and the Congressional Oversight Panel[138] also support this provision, as do industry groups such as the Alternative Investment Management Association,[139] the Private Equity Council,[140] and the Coalition of Private Investment Companies (CPIC). Mr. James Chanos, Chairman of the CPIC, testified before the Committee that "private funds (or their advisers) should be required to register with the SEC. . . . Registration will bring with it the ability of the SEC to conduct examinations and bring administrative proceedings against registered advisers, funds, and their personnel. The SEC also will have the ability to bring civil enforcement actions and to levy fines and penalties for violations."[141] Former SEC Chief Accountant Lynn Turner also supported this provision in testimony.[142]

A significant number of hedge funds are already registered with the SEC, on a voluntary basis. Hedge Fund Research reports that nearly 55 percent of the hedge fund firms located in the United States are currently registered with the SEC, and that SEC-registered hedge fund firms manage nearly 71 percent of all US-based hedge fund capital.

Section 403 eliminates the exemption in section 203(b)(3) of the Investment Advisers Act of 1940 for advisers with fewer than 15 clients. Under current law, a hedge fund is counted as a single client, allowing hedge fund advisers to escape the obligation to register with the SEC. The Section adds an exemption for foreign private advisers, as defined in this Act. The Section adds a limited intrastate exemption, and an exemption for Small Business Investment Companies licensed by (or in the process of obtaining a license from) the Small Business Administration.

[¶54,223] Section 404. Collection of systemic risk data; reports; examinations; disclosures

Section 404 authorizes the SEC to require advisers to private funds to file specific reports, which the SEC shall share with the Financial Stability Oversight Council. The filings shall describe the amount of assets under management, use of leverage, counterparty credit risk exposure, trading and investment positions, valuation policies, types of assets held, and other information that the SEC, in consultation with the Council, determines is necessary and appropriate to protect investors or assess systemic risk. Reporting requirements may be tailored to the type or size of the private fund. Frequency of reporting is at the SEC's discretion.

Paul Schott Stevens, President of the Investment Company Institute, testified before the Committee that "the Capital Markets Regulator should require nonpublic reporting of information, such as investment positions and strategies that could bear on systemic risk and adversely impact other market participants."[143] Richard Ketchum, Chairman of FINRA, said "The absence of transparency about hedge funds and their investment positions is a concern."[144] Hedge fund industry groups also support this provision, including the Managed Funds Associ-

---

[134] *Enhancing Investor Protection and the Regulation of Securities Markets—Part II: Testimony before the U.S. Senate Committee on Banking, Housing, and Urban Affairs*, 111th Congress, 1st session (2009) (Testimony of Mr. David Tittsworth).

[135] *Financial Reform: A Framework for Financial Stability*, Group of Thirty, January 15, 2009.

[136] *Enhancing Sound Regulation and Strengthening Transparency*, G20 Working Group 1, March 25, 2009.

[137] *U.S. Financial Regulatory Reform: An Investor's Perspective*, Investor's Working Group, July 2009.

[138] *Special Report on Regulatory Reform*, Congressional Oversight Panel, January 2009.

[139] Alternative Investment Management Association (January 23, 2009) "AIMA Supports US Regulatory Reform Proposals", Press Release, www.aima.org.

[140] *Capital Markets Regulatory Reform: Strengthening Investor Protection, Enhancing Oversight of Private Pools of Capital, and Creating a National Insurance Office: Testimony before the U.S. House Committee on Financial Services*, 111th Congress, 1st session (2009) (Testimony of Mr. Douglas Lowenstein).

[141] *Regulating Hedge Funds and Other Private Investment Pools: Testimony before the Subcommittee on Securities, Insurance, and Investment of the U.S. Senate Committee on Banking, Housing, and Urban Affairs*, 111th Congress, 1st session, p.17 (2009) (Testimony of Mr. James Chanos).

[142] *Enhancing Investor Protection and the Regulation of Securities Markets—Part I: Testimony before the U.S. Senate Committee on Banking, Housing, and Urban Affairs*, 111th Congress, 1st session (2009) (Testimony of Mr. Lynn Turner).

[143] *Enhancing Investor Protection and the Regulation of Securities Markets—Part I: Testimony before the U.S. Senate Committee on Banking, Housing, and Urban Affairs*, 111th Congress, 1st session, p.12 (2009) (Testimony of Mr. Paul Schott Stevens).

[144] *Enhancing Investor Protection and the Regulation of Securities Markets—Part II: Testimony before the U.S. Senate Committee on Banking, Housing, and Urban Affairs*, 111th Congress, 1st session, p.5 (2009) (Testimony of Mr. Richard Ketchum).

ation,[145] the Coalition of Private Investment Companies,[146] and the Private Equity Council.[147]

Section 404 requires the SEC to make available to the Financial Stability Oversight Council any private fund records it receives that the Council considers necessary to assess the systemic risk posed by a private fund. These records must be kept confidential: the Council must observe the same standards of confidentiality that apply to the SEC. Private fund records, including those containing proprietary information, are not subject to disclosure pursuant to the Freedom of Information Act.

This section also directs the SEC to report annually to Congress on how it has used information collected from private funds to monitor markets for the protection of investors and market integrity.

[¶54,224] Section 405. Disclosure provision eliminated

Section 405 authorizes the SEC to require investment advisers to disclose the identity, investments, or affairs of any client, if necessary to assess potential systemic risk.

[¶54,225] Section 406. Clarification of rulemaking authority

Section 406 clarifies the SEC's authority to define technical, trade, and other terms used in the title, except that the SEC may not define "client" to mean investors in a fund, rather than the fund itself, for purposes of Section 206 (1) and (2) of the Advisers Act, which governs fraud. The clarification avoids potential conflicts between the fiduciary duty an adviser owes to a private fund and to the individual investors in the fund (if those investors are defined as clients of the adviser). Actions in the best interest of the fund may not always be in the best interests of each individual investor. The section also directs the SEC and CFTC to jointly promulgate rules regarding the form and content of reporting by firms that are registered with both agencies.

[¶54,226] Section 407. Exemptions of venture capital fund advisers

The Committee believes that venture capital funds, a subset of private investment funds specializing in long-term equity investment in small or start-up businesses, do not present the same risks as the large private funds whose advisers are required to register with the SEC under this title. Their activities are not interconnected with the global financial system, and they generally rely on equity funding, so that losses that may occur do not ripple throughout world markets but are borne by fund investors alone. Terry McGuire, Chairman of the National Venture Capital Association, wrote in congressional testimony that "venture capital did not contribute to the implosion that occurred in the financial system in the last year, nor does it pose a future systemic risk to our world financial markets or retail investors."[148] Section 407 directs the SEC to define "venture capital fund" and provides that no investment adviser shall become subject to registration requirements for providing investment advice to a venture capital fund.

[¶54,227] Section 408. Exemption of and record keeping by private equity fund advisers

The Committee believes that private equity funds characterized by long-term equity investments in operating businesses do not present the same risks as the large private funds whose advisers are required to register with the SEC under this title. Private equity investments are characterized by long-term commitments of equity capital—investors generally do not have redemption rights that could force the funds into disorderly liquidations of their positions. Private equity funds use limited or no leverage at the fund level, which means that their activities do not pose risks to the wider markets through credit or counterparty relationships. Accordingly, Section 408 directs the SEC to define "private equity fund" and provides an exemption

---

[145] *Enhancing Investor Protection and the Regulation of Securities Markets—Part II: Testimony before the U.S. Senate Committee on Banking, Housing, and Urban Affairs*, 111th Congress, 1st session, (2009) (Testimony of Mr. Richard Baker).

[146] *Regulating Hedge Funds and Other Private Investment Pools: Testimony before the Subcommittee on Securities, Insurance, and Investment of the U.S. Senate Committee on Banking, Housing, and Urban Affairs*, 111th Congress, 1st session (2009) (Testimony of Mr. James Chanos).

[147] *Capital Markets Regulatory Reform: Strengthening Investor Protection, Enhancing Oversight of Private Pools of Capital, and Creating a National Insurance Office: Testimony before the U.S. House Committee on Financial Services*, 111th Congress, 1st session (2009) (Testimony of Mr. Douglas Lowenstein).

[148] *Capital Markets Regulatory Reform: Strengthening Investor Protection, Enhancing Oversight of Private Pools of Capital, and Creating a National Insurance Office: Testimony before the U.S. House Committee on Financial Services*, 111th Congress, 1st session, p.15 (2009) (Testimony of Mr. Terry McGuire).

from registration for advisers to private equity funds.

Informed observers believe that in some cases the line between hedge funds and private equity may not be clear, and that the activities of the two types of funds may overlap. We expect the SEC to define the term "private equity fund" in a way to exclude firms that call themselves "private equity" but engage in activities that either raise significant potential systemic risk concerns or are more characteristic of traditional hedge funds. The section requires advisers to private equity funds to maintain such records, and provide to the SEC such annual or other reports, as the SEC determines necessary and appropriate in the public interest and for the protection of investors.

[¶54,228] **Section 409. Family offices**

Family offices provide investment advice in the course of managing the investments and financial affairs of one or more generations of a single family. Since the enactment of the Investment Advisers Act of 1940, the SEC has issued orders to family offices declaring that those family offices are not investment advisers within the intent of the Act (and thus not subject to the registration and other requirements of the Act). The Committee believes that family offices are not investment advisers intended to be subject to registration under the Advisers Act. The Advisers Act is not designed to regulate the interactions of family members, and registration would unnecessarily intrude on the privacy of the family involved. Accordingly, Section 409 directs the SEC to define "family office" and excludes family offices from the definition of investment adviser Section 202(a)(11) of the Advisers Act.

Section 409 directs the SEC to adopt rules of general applicability defining "family offices" for purposes of the exemption. The rules shall provide for an exemption that is consistent with the SEC's previous exemptive policy and that takes into account the range of organizational and employment structures employed by family offices. The Committee recognizes that many family offices have become professional in nature and may have officers, directors, and employees who are not family members, and who may be employed by the family office itself or by an affiliated entity. Such persons (and other persons who may provide services to the family office) may co-invest with family members, enabling them to share in the profits of investments they oversee, and better aligning the interests of such persons with those of the family members served by the family office. The Committee expects that such arrangements would not automatically exclude a family office from the definition.

[¶54,229] **Section 410. State and federal responsibilities; asset threshold for federal registration of investment advisers**

Section 410 increases the asset threshold above which investment advisers must register with the SEC from $25,000,000 to $100,000,000. States will have responsibility for regulating advisers with less than $100,000,000 in assets under management. The Committee expects that the SEC, by concentrating its examination and enforcement resources on the largest investment advisers, will improve its record in uncovering major cases of investment fraud, and that the States will provide more effective surveillance of smaller funds. In a letter to Chairman Dodd and Ranking Member Shelby, the North American Securities Administrators Association stated that "State securities regulators are ready to accept the increased responsibility for the oversight of investment advisers with up to $100 million in assets under management. The state system of investment adviser regulation has worked well with the $25 million threshold since it was mandated in 1996 and states have developed an effective regulatory structure and enhanced technology to oversee investment advisers.... An increase in the threshold would allow the SEC to focus on larger investment advisers while the smaller advisers would continue to be subject to strong state regulation and oversight."[149]

In a letter to Senate Banking Committee staff in October 2009, Professor Mercer Bullard stated, "I support the $100 million threshold. This merely restores the distribution of advisers between the SEC and states that existed at the time they were split by [the National Securities Markets Improvement Act]."

[¶54,230] **Section 411. Custody of client assets**

Section 411 requires registered investment advisers to comply with SEC rules for the safeguarding of client assets and to use independent public accountants to verify assets. The SEC has recently adopted new rules imposing heightened

---

[149] North American Securities Administrators Association, letter to Chairman Dodd and Ranking Member Shelby, November 17, 2009.

standards for custody of client assets. Mr. James Chanos, Chairman of the Coalition of Private Investment Companies, wrote in testimony for the Committee that "Any new private fund legislation should include provisions to reduce the risks of Ponzi schemes and theft by requiring money managers to keep client assets at a qualified custodian, and by requiring investment funds to be audited by independent public accounting firms that are overseen by the PCAOB."[150]

Professor John Coffee wrote in testimony for the Senate Banking Committee that "the custodian requirement largely removes the ability of an investment adviser to pay the proceeds invested by new investors to old investors. The custodian will take the instructions to buy or sell securities, but not to remit the proceeds of sales to the adviser or to others (except in return for share redemptions by investors). At a stroke, this requirement eliminates the ability of the manager to 'recycle' funds from new to old investors."[151] SEC Inspector General H. David Kotz also supports this provision.[152]

[¶54,231] **Section 412. Adjusting the accredited investor standard for inflation**

Accredited investor status, defined in SEC regulations under the Securities Act of 1933, is required to invest in hedge funds and other private securities offerings. Accredited investors are presumed to be sophisticated, and not in need of the investor protections afforded by the registration and disclosure requirements that apply to public offerings. For individuals, the accredited investor thresholds are dollar amounts for annual income ($200,000 or $300,000 for an individual and spouse) and net worth ($1 million, which may include the value of a person's primary residence). These amounts have not been adjusted since 1982; some observers believe that because of inflation and real estate price appreciation many individuals who now meet the accredited investor standard may lack the degree of financial expertise that was implied by the thresholds when they were established nearly three decades ago. The North American Securities Administrators Association wrote in a 2007 comment letter to the SEC that "NASAA has long advocated for adjusting the definition of accredited investor' in light of inflation and has expressed concern at the length of time the thresholds contained in the definition have not been adjusted . . . [I]nflation has seriously eroded the efficacy of the existing thresholds in the definition of accredited investor' since their adoption in 1982. NASAA further supports an inflation adjustment every five years."[153]

Section 412 requires the SEC to increase the dollar thresholds for accredited investor status, to take into account price inflation since the current figures were established. The Section also directs the SEC to adjust those figures at least every five years to reflect the percentage increase in the cost of living. This provision is intended to increase investor protection by limiting participation in private securities offerings to investors who are capable of evaluating the risks of such offerings.

[¶54,232] **Section 413. GAO study and report on accredited investors**

Section 413 directs the GAO to submit a report on the appropriate criteria for accredited investor status and eligibility to invest in private funds. The goal of the exemptions for accredited investors is to identify a category of investors who have sufficient knowledge and expertise to fend for themselves in making investment decisions. Currently, this category is identified by salary or wealth. However, we recognize that these are imperfect standards. For example, a person's wealth may include a valuable primary residence but little liquid cash, or a wealthy person may be a widow or widower with a large inheritance, but little investment expertise. Accordingly, we ask the GAO to determine whether other measures would be more appropriate.

---

[150] *Regulating Hedge Funds and Other Private Investment Pools: Testimony before the Subcommittee on Securities, Insurance, and Investment of the U.S. Senate Committee on Banking, Housing, and Urban Affairs*, 111th Congress, 1st session, p. 18 (2009) (Testimony of Mr. James Chanos).

[151] *Madoff Investment Securities Fraud: Regulatory and Oversight Concerns and the Need for Reform: Testimony before the U.S. Senate Committee on Banking, Housing, and Urban Affairs*, 111th Congress, 1st session, pp. 8,10 (2009) (Testimony of Professor John Coffee).

[152] SEC Inspector General H. David Kotz, letter to Senator Dodd, October 29, 2009.

[153] North American Securities Administrators Association, comment letter in response to SEC proposed rule *Revisions of Limited Offering Exemptions in Regulation D*, Release No. 33 8828; IC-27922; File No. S7-18-07, October 26, 2007.

[¶ 54,233] *Section 414. GAO study on self-regulatory organization for private funds*

Section 414 directs the GAO to study the feasibility of creating a self-regulatory organization to oversee private funds—which can include hedge funds, private equity funds, and venture capital funds.

[¶ 54,234] *Section 415. Commission study and report on short selling*

Section 415 directs the Office of Risk, Strategy, and Financial Innovation of the SEC to conduct a study on the current state of short selling, the impact of recent SEC rules, the recent incidence of failures to deliver, the practice of delivering shares sold short on the fourth day following the trade, and consideration of real time reporting of short positions.

[¶ 54,235] *Section 416. Transition period*

Section 416 provides that the title becomes effective one year after the date of enactment of this Act, but advisers to private funds may voluntarily register with the SEC during that 1-year period.

Title V—Insurance

Subtitle A—Office of National Insurance

[¶ 54,240] *Section 501. Short title*

[¶ 54,241] *Section 502. Establishment of Office of National Insurance*

This section establishes the Office of National Insurance ("Office") within the Department of the Treasury. The Office, to be headed by a career Senior Executive Service Director appointed by the Secretary of the Treasury ("Secretary"), will have the authority to: (1) monitor all aspects of the insurance industry; (2) recommend to the Financial Stability Oversight Council ("Council") that the Council designate an insurer, including its affiliates, as an entity subject to regulation by the Board of Governors as a nonbank financial company as defined in Title I of the Restoring American Financial Stability Act, (3) assist the Secretary in administering the Terrorism Risk Insurance Program; (4) coordinate Federal efforts and establish Federal policy on prudential aspects of international insurance matters; (5) determine whether State insurance measures are preempted by International Insurance Agreements on Prudential Measures; and (6) consult with the States regarding insurance matters of national importance and prudential insurance matters of international importance. The authority of the Office extends to all lines of insurance except health insurance and crop insurance.

In carrying out its functions, the Office may collect data and information on the insurance industry and insurers, as well as issue reports. It may require an insurer or an affiliate to submit data or information reasonably required to carry out functions of the Office, although the Office may establish an exception to data submission requirements for insurers meeting a minimum size threshold. Before collecting any data or information directly from an insurer, the Office must first coordinate with each relevant State insurance regulator (or other relevant Federal or State regulatory agency, in the case of an affiliate) to determine whether the information is available from such State insurance regulator or other regulatory agency. The Office will have power to require by subpoena that an insurer produce the data or information requested, but only upon a written finding by the Director that the data or information is required to carry out its functions and that it has coordinated with relevant regulator or agency as required. The subpoena authority is intended to be an option of last resort that would very rarely be used, since it is expected that the relevant regulator or agency and the insurers would cooperate with reasonable requests for data or information by the Office. Any non-publicly available data and information submitted to the Office will be subject to confidentiality provisions: privileges are not waived; any requirements regarding privacy or confidentiality will continue to apply; and information contained in examination reports will be considered subject to the applicable exemption under the Freedom of Information Act for this type of information.

The Director will determine whether a State insurance measure is preempted because it: (a) results in less favorable treatment of a non-United States insurer domiciled in a foreign jurisdiction that is subject to an International Insurance Agreement on Prudential Measures than a United States insurer domiciled, licensed, or otherwise admitted in that State and (b) is inconsistent with an International Insurance Agreement on Prudential Measures. However, the savings clause provides that nothing in this section preempts any State insurance measure that governs any insurer's rates, premiums, underwriting or sales practices, State coverage requirements for insurance, application of State antitrust laws to the business of insurance, or any State insurance measure governing the capital or solvency of an insurer (except to the extent such measure results in less favorable treatment of a non-United States insurer than a United States insurer). The savings clause is intended to shield these important State consumer protection measures from preemption.

An "International Insurance Agreement on Prudential Measures" is defined as a written bilateral or multilateral agreement entered into between the United States and a foreign government, authority, or regulatory entity regarding prudential measures applicable to the business of insurance or reinsurance. Before making a determination of inconsistency, the Director will notify and consult with the appropriate State, publish a notice in the Federal Register, and give interested parties the opportunity to submit comments. Upon making the determination, the Director will notify the appropriate State and Congress, and establish a reasonable period of time before the preemption will become effective. At the conclusion of that period, if the basis for the determination still exists, the Director will publish a notice in the Federal Register that the preemption has become effective and notify the appropriate State.

The Director will consult with State insurance regulators, to the extent the Director determines appropriate, in carrying out the functions of the Office. The Director may also consult on insurance matters with Indian Tribes (as defined in Section 4(e) of the Indian Self-Determination and Education Assistance Act, as amended (25 U.S.C. 450b(e))) regarding insurance entities wholly owned by Indian Tribes. Nothing in this section will be construed to give the Office or the Treasury Department general supervisory or regulatory authority over the business of insurance.

The Director must submit a report to the President and to Congress by September 30th of each year on the insurance industry and any actions taken by the Office regarding preemption of inconsistent State insurance measures.

The Director must also conduct a study and submit a report to Congress within 18 months of the enactment of this section on how to modernize and improve the system of insurance regulation in the United States. The study and report must be guided by the following six considerations: (1) systemic risk regulation with respect to insurance; (2) capital standards and the relationship between capital allocation and liabilities; (3) consumer protection for insurance products and practices; (4) degree of national uniformity of state insurance regulation; (5) regulation of insurance companies and affiliates on a consolidated basis; and (6) international coordination of insurance regulation. The study and report must also examine additional factors as set forth in this section.

This section also authorizes the Secretary of the Treasury to negotiate and enter into International Insurance Agreements on Prudential Measures on behalf of the United States. However, nothing in this section will be construed to affect the development and coordination of the United States international trade policy or the administration of the United States trade agreements program. The Secretary will consult with the United States Trade Representative on the negotiation of International Insurance Agreements on Prudential Measures, including prior to initiating and concluding any such agreements.

Subtitle B—State-Based Insurance Reform

[¶ 54,260] *Section 511. Short title*

This subtitle may be cited as the "Nonadmitted and Reinsurance Reform Act of 2009".

[¶ 54,261] *Section 512. Effective date*

Part I—Nonadmitted Insurance

[¶ 54,265] *Sec. 521. Reporting, payment, and allocation of premium taxes*

Gives the home State of the insured (policyholder) sole regulatory authority over the collection and allocation of premium tax obligations related to nonadmitted insurance (also known as surplus lines insurance). States are authorized to enter into a compact or other agreement to establish uniform allocation and remittance procedures. Insured's home State may require surplus lines brokers and insureds to file tax allocation reports detailing portion of premiums attributable to properties, risks, or exposures located in each state.

[¶ 54,266] *Sec. 522. Regulation of nonadmitted insurance by insured's home state*

Unless otherwise provided, insured's home State has sole regulatory authority over nonadmitted insurance, including broker licensing.

[¶ 54,267] *Sec. 523. Participation in national producer database*

State may not collect fees relating to licensing of nonadmitted brokers unless the State participates in the national insurance producer database of the National Association of Insurance Commissioners (NAIC) within 2 years of enactment of this subtitle.

[¶54,268] *Sec. 524. Uniform standards for surplus lines eligibility*

Streamlines eligibility requirements for nonadmitted insurance providers with the eligibility requirements set forth in the NAIC's Nonadmitted Insurance Model Act.

[¶54,269] *Sec. 525. Streamlined application for commercial purchasers*

Allows exempt commercial purchasers, as defined in section 527, easier access to the nonadmitted marketplace by waiving certain requirements.

[¶54,270] *Sec. 526. GAO study of nonadmitted insurance market*

The Comptroller General shall conduct a study of the nonadmitted insurance market to determine the effect of the enactment of this part on the size and market share of the nonadmitted market. The Comptroller General shall consult with the NAIC and produce this report within 30 months after the effective date.

[¶54,271] *Sec. 527. Definitions*

Among others, defines Exempt Commercial Purchasers and details the qualifications necessary to qualify as such for the purposes of section 525.

Part II—Reinsurance

[¶54,275] *Sec. 531. Regulation of credit for reinsurance and reinsurance agreements*

Prohibits non-domiciliary States from denying credit for reinsurance if the State of domicile of a ceding insurer is an NAIC-accredited State or has solvency requirements substantially similar to those required for NAIC accreditation. Prohibits non-domiciliary States from restricting or eliminating the rights of reinsurers to resolve disputes pursuant to contractual arbitration clauses, prohibits non-domiciliary States from ignoring or eliminating contractual agreements on choice of law determinations, and prohibits non-domiciliary States from enforcing reinsurance contracts on terms different from those set forth in the reinsurance contract.

[¶54,276] *Sec. 532. Solvency regulation*

State of domicile of the reinsurer is solely responsible for regulating the financial solvency of the reinsurer. Non-domiciliary States may not require reinsurer to provide any additional financial information other than the information required by State of domicile. Non-domiciliary States are required to be provided with copies of the financial information that is required to be filed with the State of domicile.

[¶54,277] *Sec. 533. Definitions*

Among others, defines a reinsurer and clarifies how an insurer could be determined as a reinsurer under the laws of the state of domicile.

Part III—Rule of Construction

[¶54,280] *Sec. 541. Rule of construction*

Clarifies that this subtitle will not modify, impair, or supersede the application of antitrust laws, confirms that any potential conflict between this subtitle and the antitrust laws will be resolved in favor of the operation of the antitrust laws.

[¶54,281] *Sec. 542. Severability*

States that if any section, subsection, or application of this subtitle is held to be unconstitutional, the remainder of the subtitle shall not be affected.

Title VI—Bank and Savings Association Holding Company and Depository Institution Regulatory Improvements Act of 2009

[¶54,290] **Section 601. Short title**

The short title of this section is the "Bank and Savings Association Holding Company and Depository Institution Regulatory Improvements Act of 2010."

[¶54,291] **Section 602. Definitions**

This section defines the term "commercial firm" as any entity that derives not less than 15 percent of the consolidated annual gross revenues of the entity, including all affiliates of the entity, from engaging in activities that are not financial in nature or incidental to activities that are financial in nature, as provided in section

¶54,291

4(k) of the Bank Holding Company Act of 1956 (12 U.S.C. 1843(k)).

[¶54,292] Section 603. Moratorium and study on treatment of credit card banks, industrial loan companies, trust banks and certain other companies as bank holding companies under the Bank Holding Company Act

This section imposes a three-year moratorium on the ability of the Federal Deposit Insurance Corporation to approve a new application for deposit insurance for an industrial loan company, credit card bank, or trust bank that is owned or controlled by a commercial firm. During this period, the appropriate Federal banking agency may not approve a change in control of an industrial bank, a credit card bank, or a trust bank if the change in control would result in direct or indirect control of the industrial bank, credit card bank, or trust bank by a commercial firm, unless the bank is in danger of default, or unless the change in control results from the merger or whole acquisition of a commercial firm that directly or indirectly controls the industrial bank, credit card bank, or trust bank in a bona fide merger with or acquisition by another commercial firm.

In addition, this section provides that within 18 months of enactment of this Act, the Comptroller General must submit a report to Congress analyzing whether it is necessary to eliminate the exceptions in the Bank Holding Company Act of 1956 (BHCA) for credit card banks, industrial loan companies, trust banks, thrifts, and certain other companies, in order to strengthen the safety and soundness of these institutions or the stability of the financial system.

The Treasury Department's legislative proposal for financial reform includes a provision that would have eliminated the exceptions in the BHCA for credit card banks, industrial loan companies, trust banks and certain other limited purpose banks.[154] Under this proposal, firms owning such companies, including commercial firms, would have been subject to regulation as bank holding companies. As a consequence, these firms would have been required to divest of certain financial businesses in accordance with BHCA activity limitations, and would have been subject to new capital requirements. The Committee is seeking additional information through the GAO to determine whether this new supervisory regime should be applied to firms that own credit card banks, industrial loan companies, trust banks, or other limited purpose banks.

[¶54,293] Section 604. Reports and examinations of bank holding companies; regulation of functionally regulated subsidiaries

This section removes limitations on the ability of the appropriate Federal banking agency (AFBA) for a bank or savings and loan holding company to obtain reports from, examine, and regulate all subsidiaries of the holding company. The Committee agrees with testimony provided by Governor Daniel K. Tarullo, on behalf of the Board of Governors of the Federal Reserve System (Federal Reserve) "that to be fully effective, consolidated supervisors need the information and ability to identify and address risk throughout an organization."[155] For this reason, this section removes the so-called Fed-lite provisions of the Gramm-Leach-Bliley Act that placed limitations on the ability of the Federal Reserve to examine, obtain reports from, or take actions to identify or address risks with respect to subsidiaries of a bank holding company that are supervised by other agencies. However, this section also requires the AFBA for the holding company to coordinate with other Federal and state regulators of subsidiaries of the holding company, to the fullest extent possible, to avoid duplication of examination activities, reporting requirements, and requests for information.

While the Committee supports consolidated regulation, it also supports coordinated regulation. Accordingly, section 604(b) requires the AFBA for a bank holding company to give prior notice to, and to consult with, the primary regulator of a subsidiary before commencing an examination of that subsidiary. The section contains an identical requirement with respect to the examination by the AFBA for a savings and loan holding company of a subsidiary of a savings and loan holding company. Other provisions in section 604 specifically require the holding company regulator to rely "to the fullest extent possible" on reports and supervisory information that are available from sources other than the subsidiary itself, including information

---

[154] FACT SHEET: ADMINISTRATION'S REGULATORY REFORM AGENDA MOVES FORWARD; Legislation for Strengthening Investor Protection Delivered to Capitol Hill, U.S. Department of the Treasury, Press Release, July 10, 2009, www.financialstability.gov.

[155] Strengthening and Streamlining Prudential Bank Supervision—Part I: Testimony of Daniel K. Tarullo, Member Board of Governors of the Federal Reserve System, before the U.S. Senate Committee on Banking, Housing, and Urban Affairs, 111th Congress, 2nd session, p.13 (August 4, 2009).

that is "otherwise available" from other Federal or State regulators of the subsidiary. These provisions effectively require that the holding company regulator provide notice to and consult with the primary regulator, *e.g.*, the appropriate Federal banking agency for a depository institution, to identify the information it wants and ascertain whether that information already is available from the primary regulator. In addition, section 604 specifically requires the AFBA for the holding company to coordinate with other Federal and state regulators of subsidiaries of the holding company, "to the fullest extent possible, to avoid duplication of examination activities, reporting requirements, and requests for information."

This section also requires the AFBA for the holding company to consider risks to the stability of the United States banking or financial system when reviewing bank holding company proposals to engage in mergers, acquisitions, or nonbank activities or financial holding company proposals to engage in activities that are financial in nature. A financial holding company also may not engage in certain activities that are financial in nature without the approval of the AFBA for the holding company if they involve the acquisition of assets that exceed $25 billion.

In addition, the section amends the Home Owners' Loan Act to clarify the authority of the AFBA of a savings and loan holding company to examine and require reports from the savings and loan holding company and all of its subsidiaries. It also directs the AFBA to coordinate its supervisory activities with other Federal and state regulators of the holding company subsidiaries.

[¶ 54,294] Section 605. Assuring consistent oversight of permissible activities of depository institution subsidiaries of holding companies

This section requires the "lead Federal banking agency" for each depository institution holding company to examine the bank permissible activities of each non-depository institution subsidiary (other than a functionally regulated subsidiary) of the depository institution holding company to determine whether the activities present safety and soundness risks to any depository institution subsidiary of the holding company. For purposes of this section, "lead Federal banking agency" is defined as (1) the Office of the Comptroller of the Currency for holding companies with Federally-chartered depository institution subsidiaries, or where total consolidated assets in its Federally-chartered depository institution subsidiaries exceed those in its State-chartered depository institution subsidiaries or (2) the Federal Deposit Insurance Corporation for holding companies with state-chartered depository institution subsidiaries, or where total consolidated assets in its state-chartered depository institution subsidiaries exceed those in its Federally-chartered depository institution subsidiaries. The "lead Federal banking agency" can recommend that the Federal Reserve take enforcement action against a non-depository subsidiary where the Board is the holding company regulator. If the Federal Reserve does not take enforcement action within 60-days of receiving the recommendation, the "lead Federal banking agency" may take enforcement action against the non-depository institution.

This provision addresses the problem of the uneven supervisory standards under today's regulatory regime, applicable to depository and non-depository subsidiaries holding companies, highlighted by John C. Dugan, Comptroller of the Currency, in his testimony before the Committee. Changes made by this section are consistent with the recommendation of Comptroller Dugan that where subsidiaries are engaged in the same business as is conducted, or could be conducted, by an affiliated bank mortgage or other consumer lending, for example the prudential supervisor already has the resources and expertise needed to examine the activity. Affiliated companies would then be made subject to the same standards and examined with the same frequency as the affiliated bank. This approach also would ensure that the placement of an activity in a holding company structure could not be used to arbitrage between different supervisory regimes or approaches.[156]

[¶ 54,295] Section 606. Requirements for financial holding companies to remain well capitalized and well managed

This section amends the BHCA to require all financial holding companies engaging in expanded financial activities to remain well capitalized and well managed.

---

[156] *Strengthening and Streamlining Prudential Bank Supervision—Part I: Testimony of John C. Dugan, Comptroller of the Currency, before the U.S. Senate Committee on Banking, Housing, and Urban Affairs*, 111th Congress, 2nd session, p.17 (August 4, 2009).

[¶54,296] **Section 607. Standards for interstate acquisitions and mergers**

This section raises the capital and management standards for bank holding companies engaging in interstate bank acquisitions by requiring them to be well capitalized and well managed. In addition, interstate mergers of banks will only be permitted if the resulting bank is well capitalized and well managed.

[¶54,297] **Section 608. Enhancing existing restrictions on bank transactions with affiliates**

This section amends section 23A of the Federal Reserve Act by, among other things, defining an investment fund, for which a member bank is an investment adviser, as an affiliate of the member bank.

It also adds credit exposure from a securities borrowing or lending transaction or derivative transaction to the list of inter-affiliate "covered transactions" in section 23A. The Federal Reserve is provided the discretion to define "credit exposure." In addition, the Federal Reserve may issue regulations or interpretations with respect to the manner in which a netting agreement may be taken into account in determining the amount of a covered transaction between a member bank or a subsidiary and an affiliate, including the extent to which netting agreements between a member bank or a subsidiary and an affiliate may be taken into account in determining whether a covered transaction is fully secured for purposes of subsection (d)(4) of section 23A.

This provision represents a second attempt by Congress to address the credit exposure to banks from affiliate derivative transactions. Section 121 of the Gramm-Leach-Bliley Act provided that "not later than 18 months after November 12, 1999, the Federal Reserve shall adopt final rules under this section [23A of the Federal Reserve Act] to address as covered transactions credit exposure arising out of derivative transactions between member banks and their affiliates."[157] In 2002, the Federal Reserve announced that it "expects to issue, in the near future, a proposed rule that would invite public comment on how to treat as covered transactions under section 23A certain derivative transactions that are the functional equivalent of a loan by a member bank to an affiliate or the functional equivalent of an asset purchase by a member bank from an affiliate."[158] However, the proposed rule was not issued.

The bank regulatory framework must address bank credit exposure to affiliates from derivative transactions to limit a bank's exposure to loss in the event of the failure of an affiliate. Over the last two years, the Committee has heard testimony regarding the damage to the U.S. economy caused by derivatives. Inter-affiliate derivative transactions are a major source of intra-firm complexity among the largest depository institutions. Moreover, tight limits on traditional credit exposures of banks to affiliates, such as loans, and no limits on nontraditional credit exposures of banks to affiliates, such as derivatives, have created a perverse incentive for banks to engage with their affiliates in these more complex, volatile and opaque transaction forms.

Placing limits on derivative transactions will result in greater transparency and disclosure of derivative transactions between banks and their affiliates, a reduction in the volume of internal risk-shifting transactions, and in the simplification of the internal structures of our major financial firms.

[¶54,298] **Section 609. Eliminating exceptions for transactions with financial subsidiaries**

This section amends section 23A of the Federal Reserve Act by eliminating the special treatment for transactions with financial subsidiaries.

[¶54,299] **Section 610. Lending limits applicable to credit exposure on derivative transactions, repurchase agreements, reverse repurchase agreements, and securities lending and borrowing transactions**

This section tightens national bank lending limits by treating credit exposures on derivatives, repurchase agreements, and reverse repurchase agreements as extensions of credit for the purposes of national bank lending limits. Accordingly, banks must take into account these exposures for purposes of the affiliate transaction limitations described in section 608, the insider transaction limits described in section 614, but also for purposes of lending limits that apply to non-affiliated third parties.

---

[157] Pub. L. 106-102, Title I, section 121(b), 113 Stat. 1378 (November 12, 1999).

[158] 69 Fed Reg. 239 (December 12, 2002).

[¶54,300] Section 611. Application of national bank lending limits to insured state banks

This section requires all insured depository institutions to comply with national bank lending limits. This legislation applies national bank lending limits to insured state banks for several reasons. First, lending limits restrict the percentage of a bank's capital that can be loaned to a single borrower and are one of the core safety and soundness laws applicable to bank operations. In almost all similar areas involving safety and soundness (capital adequacy, affiliate transaction limits, limits on loans to executive officers, and limits on loans to insiders) there is a uniform Federal standard that applies to all insured depository institutions. It is the view of the Committee that, as a matter of good public policy, banks should be subject to a uniform Federal standard with respect to lending limits, and should not compete on the basis of differences in safety and soundness regulation. A second reason relates to section 610 of the legislation that requires exposure from derivatives transactions to be included in Federal lending limits. State bank lending limits typically do not address derivatives. This section addresses the Committee's concern that if uniform restrictions in this area do not apply across the banking sector, risky derivative activities could migrate to state banks, or national banks may seek state charters to escape from regulation in this area. This section includes a 2-year transition period to ensure that state banks have adequate time to implement these new limits.

[¶54,301] Section 612. Restriction on conversions of troubled banks and savings associations

This section prohibits conversions from a national bank charter to a state bank or savings association charter or vice versa during any time in which a bank or savings association is subject to a cease and desist order, other formal enforcement action, or memorandum of understanding. It also prohibits the conversion of a federal savings association to a national or state bank or state savings association under these circumstances.

As Governor Daniel K. Tarullo noted in his testimony to the Committee, on behalf of the Federal Reserve, "while institutions may engage in charter conversions for a variety of sound business reasons, conversions that are motivated by a hope of escaping current or prospective supervisory actions by the institution's existing supervisor undermine the efficacy of the prudential supervisory framework."[159] The Federal Financial Institutions Examination Council (FFIEC) recently issued a Statement on Regulatory Conversions declaring that supervisors will only consider applications undertaken for legitimate reasons and will not entertain regulatory conversion applications that undermine the supervisory process.[160] This section codifies this important principle.

[¶54,302] Section 613. De novo branching into states

This section expands the ability of a national bank or state bank to establish a de novo branch in another state. In the age of Internet transactions, such branching restrictions are anachronistic and ineffectual.

[¶54,303] Section 614. Lending limits to insiders

This section expands the type of transactions subject to insider lending limits to include derivatives transactions, repurchase agreements, reverse repurchase agreements, and securities lending or borrowing transactions. This section is consistent with this legislation's expansion of affiliate transaction limits in section 608, and lending limits applicable to non-affiliated third parties in section 610, and to include such exposures.

[¶54,304] Section 615. Limitations on purchases of assets from insiders

This section prohibits insured depository institutions from entering into asset purchase or sales transactions with its executive officers, directors, or principal shareholders or a related interest unless the transaction is on market terms and, if the transaction represents more than ten percent of the capital and surplus of the institution, has been approved in advance by a majority of the disinterested members of the board.

This section replaces and expands a similar provision in section 22(d) of the Federal Reserve

---

[159] *Strengthening and Streamlining Prudential Bank Supervision—Part I: Testimony of Daniel K. Tarullo, Member Board of Governors of the Federal Reserve System, before the U.S. Senate Committee on Banking, Housing, and Urban Affairs*, 111th Congress, 2nd session, p. 13 (August 4, 2009).

[160] Federal Financial Institutions Examination Council (2009), "FFIEC Issues Statement on Regulatory Conversions, press release, July 1, www.ffiec.gov/press/pr070109.htm.

Act (12 U.S.C. 375) that simply restricts purchases and sales transactions between a member bank and its directors.

[¶54,305] Section 616. Rules regarding capital levels of holding companies

This section clarifies that the Federal Reserve may adopt rules governing the capital levels of bank and savings and loan holding companies. According to testimony provided to the Committee by John C. Dugan, Comptroller of the Currency, under the current regulatory system, "thrift holding companies, unlike bank holding companies, are not subject to consolidated regulation for example, no consolidated capital requirements apply at the holding company level. This difference between bank and thrift holding company regulation created arbitrage opportunities for companies that were able to take on greater risk under a less rigorous regulatory regime."[161] This section provides the Federal Reserve with the same authority to prescribe capital standards for savings and loan holding companies that it currently has for bank holding companies. It is the intent of the Committee that in issuing regulations relating to capital requirements of bank holding companies and savings and loan holding companies under this section, the Federal Reserve should take into account the regulatory accounting practices and procedures applicable to, and capital structure of, holding companies that are insurance companies (including mutuals and fraternals), or have subsidiaries that are insurance companies.

This section also directs the AFBA for a bank or savings and loan holding company to require the company to serve as a source of financial strength for any insured depository institution that the company owns or controls. If an insured depository institution is not the subsidiary of a bank or savings and loan holding company, the AFBA for the insured depository institution must require any company that owns or controls the insured depository institution to serve as a source of financial strength for the institution. The AFBA for such an insured depository institution may, from time to time, require the company, or a company that directly or indirectly controls the depository to submit a report, under oath, for the purposes of assessing the ability of the company to comply with the source of strength requirement, and for purposes of enforcing the company's compliance with the source of strength requirement. It is the intent of the Committee that such companies will be permitted to provide financial reporting to the AFBA utilizing the accounting method they currently employ in reporting their financial information. More specifically, nothing in this provision is intended to mandate that insurance companies otherwise subject to alternative regulatory accounting practices and procedures use GAAP reporting.

[¶54,306] Section 617. Elimination of elective investment bank holding company framework

This section eliminates the elective Investment Bank Holding Company Framework in the Securities Exchange Act of 1934. This repeals the current supervised investment bank holding company program under which the Securities and Exchange Commission may supervise a non-bank securities firm that is required by a foreign regulator to be subject to consolidated supervision by a U.S. regulator and replaces this program with the supervisory regime described in section 618.

[¶54,307] Section 618. Securities holding companies

This section permits a securities holding company, not otherwise regulated by an AFBA, that is required by a foreign regulator to be subject to comprehensive consolidated supervision to register with the Federal Reserve to become a "supervised securities holding company." To qualify, a securities holding company must own or control one or more brokers or dealers registered with the Securities and Exchange Commission, and cannot be a nonbank financial company supervised by the Board, an affiliate of an insured bank or savings association, a foreign bank, or subject to comprehensive consolidated supervision by a foreign regulator. This section describes the manner in which the Board must supervise and regulate "supervised securities holding companies," including through issuance of regulations that prescribe capital adequacy and other risk management standards to protect the safety and soundness of the company and to address risks posed to financial stability by such companies.

---

[161] *Strengthening and Streamlining Prudential Bank Supervision—Part I: Testimony of John C. Dugan, Comptroller of the Currency, before the U.S. Senate Committee on Banking, Housing, and Urban Affairs,* 111th Congress, 2nd session, p.7 (August 4, 2009).

[¶54,308] **Section 619. Restrictions on capital market activity by banks and bank holding companies**

The intent of this section is to prohibit or restrict certain types of financial activity—in banks, bank holding companies, other companies that control an insured depository institution, their subsidiaries, or nonbank financial companies supervised by the Board of Governors—that are high-risk or which create significant conflicts of interest between these institutions and their customers. The prohibitions and restrictions are intended to limit threats to the safety and soundness of the institutions, to limit threats to financial stability, and eliminate any economic subsidy to high-risk activities that is provided by access to lower-cost capital because of participation in the regulatory safety net.

Subject to recommendations and modifications by the Financial Stability Oversight Council, an insured depository institution, a company that controls an insured depository institution or is treated as a bank holding company for purposes of the Bank Holding Company Act, and any subsidiary of such institution or company, will be prohibited from proprietary trading, sponsoring and investing in hedge funds and private equity funds, and from having certain financial relationships with those hedge funds or private equity funds for which they serve as investment manager or investment adviser. A nonbank financial institution supervised by the Board of Governors that engages in proprietary trading, or sponsoring or investing in hedge funds and private equity funds will be subject to Board rules imposing capital requirements relate to, or quantitative limits on, these activities. These prohibitions and restrictions will be subject to certain exemptions.

The Council recommendations and modifications will be included in a study to assess the extent to which the prohibitions, limitations and requirements of section 619 will promote several goals, including: the safety and soundness of depositories and their affiliates; protecting taxpayers from loss; limiting the inappropriate transfer of economic subsidies from institutions that benefit from deposit insurance and liquidity facilities of the Federal government to unregulated entities; reducing inappropriate conflicts of interest between depositories and their affiliates, or financial companies supervised by the Board of Governors, and their customers; affecting the cost of credit or other financial services, limiting undue risk or loss in financial institutions; and appropriately accommodating the business of insurance within insurance companies subject to State insurance company investment laws.

The Council study is included to assure that the prohibitions included in section 619 work effectively. It is not the intent of the section to interfere inadvertently with longstanding, traditional banking activities that do not produce high levels of risk or significant conflicts of interest. For that reason the Council is given some latitude to make needed modifications to definitions and provisions in order to prevent undesired outcomes. However, it is intended that the Council will determine how to effectively implement the prohibitions and restrictions of the section, and not to weaken them.

The Council will have six months to write the study, and the appropriate Federal bank agencies will have nine months in which to issue regulations that reflect the recommendations of the Council.

Paul Volcker, chairman of the President's Economic Recovery Advisory Board and former chairman of Board of Governors of the Federal Reserve, has strongly advocated that beneficiaries of the federal financial safety net be prohibited from engaging in high-risk activities. In the statement he submitted to the Senate Committee on Banking, Housing and Urban Affairs on February 2, Mr. Volcker argued that there is no public policy rationale for subsidizing high risk activities:

> The basic point is that there has been, and remains, a strong public interest in providing a "safety net"—in particular, deposit insurance and the provision of liquidity in emergencies—for commercial banks carrying out essential services. There is not, however, a similar rationale for public funds—taxpayer funds—protecting and supporting essentially proprietary and speculative activities. Hedge funds, private equity funds, and trading activities unrelated to customer needs and continuing banking relationships should stand on their own, without the subsidies implied by public support for depository institutions.

He also went on to note that these high-risk activities produce unacceptable conflicts of interest in insured and regulated institutions:

> . . . I want to note the strong conflicts of interest inherent in the participation of commercial banking organizations in proprietary or private investment activity. That is especially evident for banks conducting substantial investment manage-

ment activities, in which they are acting explicitly or implicitly in a fiduciary capacity. When the bank itself is a "customer", i.e., it is trading for its own account, it will almost inevitably find itself, consciously or inadvertently, acting at cross purposes to the interests of an unrelated commercial customer of a bank. "Inside" hedge funds and equity funds with outside partners may generate generous fees for the bank without the test of market pricing, and those same "inside" funds may be favored over outside competition in placing funds for clients. More generally, proprietary trading activity should not be able to profit from knowledge of customer trades.

At the same hearing Deputy Treasury Secretary Neal Wolin emphasized the volatility and riskiness of the activities that are prohibited under section 619. In his statement he noted that:

Major firms saw their hedge funds and proprietary trading operations suffer large losses in the financial crisis. Some of these firms "bailed out" their troubled hedge funds, depleting the firm's capital at precisely the moment it was needed most. The complexity of owning such entities has also made it more difficult for the market, investors, and regulators to understand risks in major financial firms, and for their managers to mitigate such risks. Exposing the taxpayer to potential risks from these activities is ill-advised.

[¶54,309] Section 620. Concentration limits on large financial firms

Subject to recommendations from the Financial Stability Oversight Council, a financial company may not merge or consolidate with, acquire all or substantially all of the assets of, or otherwise acquire control of, another company, if the total consolidated liabilities of the acquiring financial company upon consummation of the transaction would exceed 10 percent of the aggregate consolidated liabilities of all financial companies at the end of the calendar year preceding the transaction.

The Council recommendations will be included in a study of the extent to which the concentration limit under section 620 would affect financial stability, moral hazard in the financial system, the efficiency and competitiveness of United States financial firms and financial markets, and the cost and availability of credit and other financial services to households and businesses in the United States. The intent is to have the Council determine how to effectively implement the concentration limit, and not whether to do so.

The Council will have six months to write the study, and the Board of Governors of the Federal Reserve will have nine months in which to issue regulations that reflect the recommendations and modifications of the Council.

Title VII—Over-the-Counter Derivatives Markets Act of 2009

[¶54,320] Section 701. Short title

[¶54,321] Section 701. Findings and purposes

This section describes the findings and purposes of the Over-the-Counter Derivatives Markets Act of 2009. In order to mitigate costs and risks to taxpayers and the financial system, this Act establishes regulations for the over-the-counter derivatives market including requirements for clearing, exchange trading, capital, margin, and reporting.

Subtitle A—Regulation of Swap Markets

[¶54,340] Section 711. Definitions

This section adds new definitions to the Commodity Exchange Act and directs the Commodity Futures Trading Commission ("CFTC") and Securities and Exchange Commission ("SEC") to jointly adopt uniform interpretations. The defined terms include "swap," "swap dealer," "swap repository," and "major swap participant."

This section also establishes guidelines for joint CFTC and SEC rulemaking authority under this Act. This section requires that rules and regulations prescribed jointly under this Act by the CFTC and SEC shall be uniform and shall treat functionally or economically equivalent products similarly. This section authorizes the CFTC and SEC to prescribe rules defining "swap" and "security-based swap" to prevent evasions of this Act. This section also requires the CFTC and SEC to prescribe joint rules in a timely manner and authorizes the Financial Stability Oversight Council to resolve disputes if the CFTC and SEC fail to jointly prescribe rules.

[¶54,341] Section 712. Jurisdiction

This section removes limitations on the CFTC's jurisdiction with respect to certain derivatives transactions, including swap transactions between "eligible contract participants."

[¶ 54,342] Section 713. Clearing

Subsection (a). Clearing requirement

This subsection requires clearing of all swaps that are accepted for clearing by a registered derivatives clearing organization unless one of the parties to the swap qualifies for an exemption. This subsection requires cleared swaps that are accepted for trading to be executed on a designated contract market or on a registered alternative swap execution facility. The CFTC may exempt a party to a swap from the clearing and exchange trading requirement if one of the counterparties to the swap is not a swap dealer or major swap participant and does not meet the eligibility requirements of any derivatives clearing organization that clears the swap. The CFTC must consult the Financial Stability Oversight Council before issuing an exemption. Requires a party to a swap to submit the swap for clearing if a counterparty requests that such swap be cleared and the swap is accepted for clearing by a registered derivatives clearing organization.

This subsection requires derivatives clearing organizations to seek approval from the CFTC prior to clearing any group or category of swaps and directs the CFTC and SEC to jointly adopt rules to further identify any group or category of swaps acceptable for clearing based on specified criteria; authorizes the CFTC and SEC jointly to prescribe rules or issue interpretations as necessary to prevent evasions of section 2(j) of the Commodity Exchange Act; and requires parties who enter into non-cleared swaps to report such transactions to a swap repository or the CFTC.

Subsection (b). Derivatives clearing organizations

This subsection requires derivatives clearing organizations that clear swaps to register with the CFTC, and directs the CFTC and SEC (in consultation with the appropriate federal banking agencies) to jointly adopt uniform rules governing entities registered as derivatives clearing organizations for swaps under this subsection and entities registered as clearing agencies for security-based swaps under the Securities Exchange Act of 1934 ("Exchange Act"). This subsection also permits dual registration of a derivatives clearing organization with the CFTC and SEC or appropriate banking agency, authorizes the CFTC to exempt from registration under this subsection a derivatives clearing organization that is subject to comparable, comprehensive supervision and regulation on a consolidated basis by another regulator, and provides transition for existing clearing agencies. This subsection specifies core regulatory principles for derivatives clearing organizations, including standards for minimum financial resources, participant and product eligibility, risk management, settlement procedures, safety of member or participant funds and assets, rules and procedures for defaults, rule enforcement, system safeguards, reporting, recordkeeping, disclosure, information sharing, antitrust considerations, governance arrangements, conflict of interest mitigation, board composition, and legal risk. This subsection also requires a derivatives clearing organization to provide the CFTC with all information necessary for the CFTC to perform its responsibilities.

Subsection (c). Legal certainty for identified banking products

This subsection clarifies that the Federal banking agencies, rather than the CFTC or SEC, retain regulatory authority with respect to identified banking products, unless a Federal banking agency, in consultation with the CFTC and SEC, determines that a product has been structured as an identified banking product for the purpose of evading the provisions of the Commodity Exchange Act, Securities Act of 1933, or Exchange Act.

[¶ 54,343] Section 714. Public reporting of aggregate swap data

This section directs the CFTC (or a derivatives clearing organization or swap repository designated by the CFTC) to make available to the public, in a manner that does not disclose the business transactions or market positions of any person, aggregate data on swap trading volumes and positions.

[¶ 54,344] Section 715. Swap repositories

This section describes the duties of a swap repository as accepting, maintaining, and making available swap data as prescribed by the CFTC; makes registration with the CFTC voluntary for swap repositories; and subjects registered swap repositories to CFTC inspection and examination. This section also directs the CFTC and SEC to jointly adopt uniform rules governing entities that register with the CFTC as swap repositories and entities that register with the SEC as security-based swap repositories, and authorizes the CFTC to exempt from registration any swap repository subject to comparable, comprehensive supervision or regulation by another regulator.

[¶ 54,345] Section 716. Reporting and recordkeeping

This section requires reporting and recordkeeping by any person who enters into a swap that is not cleared through a registered derivatives clearing organization or reported to a swap repository.

[¶ 54,346] Section 717. Registration and regulation of swap dealers and major swap participants

This section requires swap dealers and major swap participants to register with the CFTC, directs the CFTC and SEC to jointly adopt rules to mitigate conflicts, and directs the CFTC and SEC to jointly prescribe uniform rules for entities that register with the CFTC as swap dealers or major swap participants and entities that register with the SEC as security-based swap dealers or major security-based swap participants. This section also requires a registered swap dealer or major swap participant to (1) meet such minimum capital and margin requirements as the primary financial regulatory agency (for banks) or CFTC and SEC (for nonbanks) shall jointly prescribe; (2) meet reporting and recordkeeping requirements; (3) conform with business conduct standards; (4) conform with documentation and back office standards; and (5) comply with requirements relating to position limits, disclosure, conflicts of interest, and antitrust considerations. The Commission may exempt swap dealers and major swap participants from the margin requirement according to certain criteria and pursuant to consultation with the Financial Stability Oversight Council. If a party requests margin for an exempt swap, the exemption shall not apply. Regulators may permit the use of non-cash collateral to meet margin requirements.

[¶ 54,347] Section 718. Segregation of assets held as collateral in swap transactions

For cleared swaps, this section requires that swap dealers, futures commission merchants, and derivatives clearing organizations segregate funds held to margin, guarantee, or secure the obligations of a counterparty under a cleared swap in a manner that protects their property. In addition, counterparties to an un-cleared swap will be able to request that any margin posted in the transaction be held by an independent third party custodian. Assets must be segregated on a non-discriminatory basis and may not be rehypothecated.

[¶ 54,348] Section 719. Conflicts of interest

This section also directs the CFTC to require futures commission merchants and introducing brokers to implement conflict-of-interest systems and procedures relating to research activities and trading.

[¶ 54,349] Section 720. Alternative swap execution facilities

This section defines alternative swap execution facility and requires a facility for the trading of swaps to register with the CFTC as an alternative swap execution facility ("ASEF"), subject to certain criteria relating to deterrence of abuses, trading procedures, and financial integrity of transactions. This section also establishes core regulatory principles for ASEFs relating to enforcement, anti-manipulation, monitoring, information collection and disclosure, position limits, emergency powers, recordkeeping and reporting, antitrust considerations, and conflicts of interest. This section directs the CFTC and SEC to jointly prescribe rules governing the regulation of alternative swap execution facilities, and authorizes the CFTC to exempt from registration under this section an alternative swap execution facility that is subject to comparable, comprehensive supervision and regulation by another regulator.

[¶ 54,350] Section 721. Derivatives transaction execution facilities and exempt boards of trade

This section repeals the existing provisions of the Commodity Exchange Act relating to derivatives transaction execution facilities and exempt boards of trade.

[¶ 54,351] Section 722. Designated contract markets

This section requires a board of trade, in order to maintain designation as a contract market, to demonstrate that it provides a competitive, open, and efficient market for trading; has adequate financial, operational, and managerial resources; and has established robust system safeguards to help ensure resiliency.

[¶ 54,352] Section 723. Margin

This section authorizes the CFTC to set margin levels for registered entities.

[¶ 54,353] *Section 724. Position limits*

This section authorizes the CFTC to establish aggregate position limits across commodity contracts listed by designated contract markets, commodity contracts traded on a foreign board of trade that provides participants located in the United States with direct access to its electronic trading and order matching system, and swap contracts that perform or affect a significant price discovery function with respect to regulated markets.

[¶ 54,354] *Section 725. Enhanced authority over registered entities*

This section enhances the CFTC's authority to establish mechanisms for complying with regulatory principles and to review and approve new contracts and rules for registered entities.

[¶ 54,355] *Section 726. Foreign boards of trade*

This section authorizes the CFTC to adopt rules and regulations requiring registration by, and prescribing registration requirements and procedures for, a foreign board of trade that provides members or other participants located in the United States direct access to the foreign board of trade's electronic trading and order matching system. This section also prohibits foreign boards of trade from providing members or other participants located in the United States with direct access to the electronic trading and order matching systems of the foreign board of trade with respect to a contract that settles against the price of a contract listed for trading on a CFTC-registered entity unless the foreign board of trade meets, in the CFTC's determination, certain standards of comparability to the requirements applicable to U.S. boards of trade. This section also provides legal certainty for certain contracts traded on or through a foreign board of trade.

[¶ 54,356] *Section 727. Legal certainty for swaps*

This section clarifies that no hybrid instrument sold to any investor and no transaction between eligible contract participants shall be void based solely on the failure of the instrument or transaction to comply with statutory or regulatory terms, conditions, or definitions.

[¶ 54,357] *Section 728. FDICIA amendments*

Makes conforming amendments to the Federal Deposit Insurance Corporation Improvement Act of 1991 ("FDICIA") to reflect that the definition of "over-the-counter derivative instrument" under FDICIA no longer includes swaps or security-based swaps.

[¶ 54,358] *Section 729. Primary enforcement authority*

This section clarifies that the CFTC shall have primary enforcement authority for all provisions of Subtitle A of this Act, other than new Section 4s(e) of the Commodity Exchange Act (as added by Section 717 of this Act, relating to capital and margin requirements for swap dealers and major swap participants), for which the primary financial regulatory agency shall have exclusive enforcement authority with respect to banks and branches or agencies of foreign banks that are swap dealers or major swap participants. This section also provides the primary financial regulatory agency with backstop enforcement authority with respect to the non-prudential requirements of the new Section 4s of the Commodity Exchange Act (relating to registration and regulation of swap dealers and major swap participants) if the CFTC does not initiate an enforcement proceeding within 90 days of a written recommendation by the primary financial regulatory agency.

[¶ 54,359] *Section 730. Enforcement*

This section clarifies the enforcement authority of the CFTC with respect to swaps and swap repositories, and of the primary financial regulatory agency with respect to swaps, swap dealers, major swap participants, swap repositories, alternative swap execution facilities, and derivatives clearing organizations.

[¶ 54,360] *Section 731. Retail commodity transactions*

This section clarifies CFTC jurisdiction with respect to certain retail commodity transactions.

[¶ 54,361] *Section 732. Large swap trader reporting*

This section requires reporting and recordkeeping with respect to large swap positions in the regulated markets.

[¶ 54,362] *Section 733. Other authority*

This section clarifies that this title, unless otherwise provided by its terms, does not divest any appropriate federal banking agency, the CFTC, the SEC, or other federal or state agency of any authority derived from any other applicable law.

[¶ 54,363] **Section 734. Antitrust**

This section clarifies that nothing in this title shall be construed to modify, impair, or supersede antitrust law.

Subtitle B—Regulation of Security-Based Swap Markets

[¶ 54,380] **Section 751. Definitions under the Securities Exchange Act of 1934**

This section adds new definitions to the Securities Exchange Act of 1934 and directs the CFTC and SEC to jointly adopt uniform interpretations. The defined terms include "security-based swap," "security-based swap dealer," "security-based swap repository," "mixed swap," and "major security-based swap participant."

This section also establishes guidelines for joint CFTC and SEC rulemaking authority under this Act. This section requires that rules and regulations prescribed jointly under this Act by the CFTC and SEC shall be uniform and shall treat functionally or economically equivalent products similarly. This section authorizes the CFTC and SEC to prescribe rules defining "swap" and "security-based swap" to prevent evasions of this Act. This section also requires the CFTC and SEC to prescribe joint rules in a timely manner and authorizes the Financial Stability Oversight Council to resolve disputes if the CFTC and SEC fail to jointly prescribe rules.

[¶ 54,381] **Section 752. Repeal of prohibition on regulation of security-based swaps**

This section repeals provisions enacted as part of the Gramm-Leach-Bliley Act and the Commodity Futures Modernization Act that prohibit the SEC from regulating security-based swaps.

[¶ 54,382] **Section 753. Amendments to the Securities Exchange Act of 1934**

Subsection (a). Clearing for security-based swaps

This subsection requires clearing of all security-based swaps that are accepted for clearing by a registered clearing agency unless one of the parties to the swap qualifies for an exemption. This subsection requires cleared security-based swaps that are accepted for trading to be executed on a registered national securities exchange or on a registered alternative swap execution facility. The SEC may exempt a security-based swap from the clearing and exchange trading requirement if one of the counterparties to the swap is not a security-based swap dealer or major swap participant and does not meet the eligibility requirements of any clearing agency that clears the swap. The SEC must consult the Financial Stability Oversight Council before issuing an exemption. Requires a party to a security-based swap to submit the swap for clearing if a counterparty requests that the swap be cleared and the swap is accepted for clearing by a registered clearing agency.

This subsection requires clearing agencies to seek approval from the SEC prior to clearing any group or category of security-based swaps and directs the CFTC and SEC to jointly adopt rules to further identify any group or category of security-based swaps acceptable for clearing based on specified criteria; authorizes the CFTC and SEC jointly to prescribe rules or issue interpretations as necessary to prevent evasions of section 3A of the Exchange Act; requires parties who enter into non-cleared swaps to report such transactions to a swap repository or the CFTC; and directs the SEC and CFTC to jointly adopt uniform rules governing entities registered with the CFTC as derivatives clearing organizations for swaps and with the SEC as clearing agencies for security-based swaps.

Subsection (b). Alternative swap execution facilities

This subsection defines alternative swap execution facility and requires facilities for the trading of security-based swaps to register with the SEC as ASEFs, subject to certain criteria relating to deterrence of abuses, trading procedures, and financial integrity of transactions. This subsection also establishes core regulatory principles for ASEFs relating to enforcement, anti-manipulation, monitoring, information collection and disclosure, position limits, emergency powers, recordkeeping and reporting, antitrust considerations, and conflicts of interest. This subsection directs the SEC and CFTC to jointly prescribe rules governing the regulation of alternative swap execution facilities, and authorizes the SEC to exempt from registration under this subsection an alternative swap execution facility that is subject to comparable, comprehensive supervision and regulation by another regulator.

Subsection (c). Trading in security-based swap agreements

This subsection prohibits parties who are not eligible contract participants (as defined in the Commodity Exchange Act) from effecting security-based swap transactions off of a registered national securities exchange.

Subsection (d). Registration and regulation of swap dealers and major swap participants

This subsection requires security-based swap dealers and major security-based swap participants to register with the SEC, and directs the SEC and CFTC to jointly prescribe uniform rules for entities that register with the SEC as security-based swap dealers or major security-based swap participants and entities that register with the CFTC as swap dealers or major swap participants. This subsection also requires security-based swap dealers and major security-based swap participants to (1) meet such minimum capital and margin requirements as the primary financial regulatory agency (for banks) or CFTC and SEC (for nonbanks) shall jointly prescribe; (2) meet reporting and recordkeeping requirements; (3) conform with business conduct standards; (4) conform with documentation and back office standards; and (5) comply with requirements relating to position limits, disclosure, conflicts of interest, and antitrust considerations. The Commission may exempt security-based swap dealers and major swap participants from the margin requirement according to certain criteria and pursuant consultation with the Financial Stability Oversight Council. If a party requests margin for an exempt swap, the exemption shall not apply. Regulators may permit the use of non-cash collateral to meet margin requirements.

Subsection (e). Additions of security-based swaps to certain enforcement provisions

This subsection adds security-based swaps to the Exchange Act's list of financial instruments that a person may not use to manipulate security prices.

Subsection (f). Rulemaking authority to prevent fraud, manipulation, and deceptive conduct in security-based swaps

This subsection prohibits fraudulent, manipulative, and deceptive acts involving security-based swaps and security-based swap agreements, and directs the SEC to prescribe rules and regulations to define and prevent such conduct.

Subsection (g). Position limits and position accountability for security-based swaps and large trader reporting

As a means to prevent fraud and manipulation, this subsection authorizes the SEC to (1) establish limits on the aggregate number or amount of positions that any person or persons may hold across security-based swaps that perform or affect a significant price discovery function with respect to regulated markets; (2) exempt from such limits any person, class of persons, transaction, or class of transactions; and (3) direct a self-regulatory organization to adopt rules relating to position limits for security-based swaps. This subsection also requires reporting and recordkeeping with respect to large security-based swap positions in regulated markets.

Subsection (h). Public reporting and repositories for security-based swap agreements

This subsection requires the SEC or its designee to make available to the public, in a manner that does not disclose the business transactions and market positions of any person, aggregate data on security-based swap trading volumes and positions. This subsection also describes the duties of a security-based swap repository as accepting and maintaining security-based swap data as prescribed by the SEC, makes SEC registration for security-based swap repositories voluntary, and subjects registered security-based swap repositories to SEC inspection and examination. This subsection directs the SEC and CFTC to jointly adopt uniform rules governing entities that register with the SEC as security-based swap repositories and entities that register with the CFTC as swap repositories and authorizes the SEC to exempt from registration any security-based swap repository subject to comparable, comprehensive supervision or regulation by another regulator.

[¶ 54,383] *Section 754. Segregation of assets held as collateral in security-based swap transactions*

For cleared swaps, this section requires that security-based swap dealers or clearing agencies segregate funds held to margin, guarantee, or secure the obligations of a counterparty in a manner that protects their property. In addition, counterparties to an un-cleared swap will be able to request that any margin posted in the transaction be held by an independent third party custodian. Assets must be segregated on a non-discriminatory bases and may not be rehypothecated.

[¶ 54,384] *Section 755. Reporting and recordkeeping*

This section requires reporting and recordkeeping by any person who enters into a security-based swap that is not cleared with a registered clearing agency or reported to a security-based swap repository. This section also includes security-based swaps within the scope of

¶54,384

certain reporting requirements under Sections 13 and 16 of the Exchange Act.

[¶ 54,385] Section 756. State gaming and bucket shop laws

This section clarifies the applicability of certain state laws to security-based swaps.

[¶ 54,386] Section 757. Amendments to the Securities Act of 1933; treatment of security-based swaps

This section amends the Securities Act of 1933 to include security-based swaps within the definition of "security." This section also amends Section 5 of the Securities Act of 1933 to prohibit offers to sell or purchase a security-based swap without an effective registration statement to any person other than an eligible contract participant (as defined in the Commodity Exchange Act).

[¶ 54,387] Section 758. Other authority

This section clarifies that this title, unless otherwise provided by its terms, does not divest any appropriate federal banking agency, the SEC, the CFTC, or other federal or state agency of any authority derived from any other applicable law.

[¶ 54,388] Section 758. Jurisdiction

This section clarifies that the SEC shall not have authority to grant exemptions from the provisions of this Act, except as expressly authorized by this Act; provides the SEC with express authorization to use any authority granted under subsection (a) to exempt any person or transaction from any provision of this title that applies to such person or transaction solely because a security-based swap is a security under section 3(a).

Subtitle C—Other Provisions

[¶ 54,400] Section 761. International harmonization

This section requires regulators to consult and coordinate with international authorities on the establishment of consistent standards for the regulation of swaps and security-based swaps.

[¶ 54,401] Section 762. Interagency cooperation

This section establishes a SEC-CFTC Joint Advisory Committee to monitor and develop solutions emerging in the swaps and security-based swaps markets, a SEC-CFTC Joint Enforcement Task Force to improve market oversight, a SEC-CFTC-Federal Reserve Trading and Markets Fellowship Program to provide cross-training among agency staff about the interaction between financial markets activity and the real economy, SEC-CFTC cross-agency enforcement training and education, and detailing of staff between the SEC and CFTC.

[¶ 54,402] Section 763. Study and report on implementation

This section requires the GAO to conduct on study on the implementation of this Act within one year of the date of enactment.

[¶ 54,403] Section 764. Recommendations for changes to insolvency laws

This section requires the SEC, CFTC, and FIRA to make recommendations to Congress within 180 days of enactment regarding Federal insolvency laws and their impact on various swaps and security-based swaps activity.

[¶ 54,404] Section 765. Effective date

This section specifies that this title shall become effective 180 days after the date of enactment.

Title VIII—Payment, Clearing, and Settlement Supervision Act of 2009

[¶ 54,420] Section 801. Short title

[¶ 54,421] Section 802. Findings and purposes

This section describes the findings and purposes of the Payment, Clearing, and Settlement Supervision Act of 2009. In order to mitigate systemic risk in the financial system and promote financial stability, this Act provides the Financial Stability Oversight Council a role in identifying systemically important financial market utilities and the Board of Governors of the Federal Reserve System ("Board") with an enhanced role in supervising risk management standards for systemically important financial market utilities and for systemically important payment, clearing, and settlement activities conducted by financial institutions.

¶ 54,385

[¶ 54,422] *Section 803. Definitions*

[¶ 54,423] *Section 804. Designation of systemic importance*

This section authorizes the Financial Stability Oversight Council to designate financial market utilities or payment, clearing, or settlement activities as systemically important, and establishes procedures and criteria for making and rescinding such a designation. Criteria for designation and rescission of designation include the aggregate monetary value of transactions processed and the effect that a failure of a financial market utility or payment, clearing, or settlement activity would have on counterparties and the financial system.

[¶ 54,424] *Section 805. Standards for systemically important financial market utilities and payment, clearing, or settlement activities*

This section authorizes the Board, in consultation with the Financial Stability Oversight Council and the appropriate supervisory agencies, to prescribe risk management standards governing the operations of designated financial market utilities and the conduct of designated payment, clearing, and settlement activities by financial institutions. This section also establishes the objectives, principles, and scope of such standards.

[¶ 54,425] *Section 806. Operations of designated financial market utilities*

This section authorizes a Federal Reserve bank to establish and maintain an account for a designated financial market utility and allows the Board to modify or provide an exemption from reserve requirements that would otherwise be applicable to the designated financial market utility. This section requires a designated financial market utility to provide advance notice of and obtain approval of material changes to its rules, procedures, or operations.

[¶ 54,426] *Section 807. Examination and enforcement actions against designated financial market utilities*

This section requires the supervisory agency to conduct safety and soundness examinations of a designated financial market utility at least annually and authorizes the supervisory agency to take enforcement actions against the utility. This section also allows the Board to participate in examinations by, and make recommendations to, other supervisors and designates the Board as the supervisory agency for designated financial market utilities that do not otherwise have a supervisory agency. The Board is also authorized to take enforcement actions against a designated financial market utility if there is an imminent risk of substantial harm to financial institutions or the broader financial system.

[¶ 54,427] *Section 808. Examination and enforcement actions against financial institutions engaged in designated activities*

This section authorizes the primary financial regulatory agency to examine a financial institution engaged in designated payment, clearing, or settlement activities and to enforce the provisions of this Act and the rules prescribed by the Board against such an institution. This section also requires the Board to collaborate with the primary financial regulatory agency to ensure consistent application of the Board's rules. The Board is granted back-up authority to conduct examinations and take enforcement actions if it has reasonable cause to believe a violation of its rules or of this Act has occurred.

[¶ 54,428] *Section 809. Requests for information, reports, or records*

This section authorizes the Financial Stability Oversight Council to collect information from financial market utilities and financial institutions engaged in payment, clearing, or settlement activities in order to assess systemic importance. Upon a designation by the Financial Stability Oversight Council, the Board may require submission of reports or data by systemically important financial market utilities or financial institutions engaged in activities designated to be systemically important. This section also facilitates sharing of relevant information and coordination among financial regulators, with protections for confidential information.

[¶ 54,429] *Section 810. Rulemaking*

This section authorizes the Board and the Financial Stability Oversight Council to prescribe such rules and issue such orders as may be necessary to administer and carry out the purposes of this title and prevent evasions thereof.

[¶ 54,430] *Section 811. Other authority*

This section clarifies that this Act, unless otherwise provided by its terms, does not divest any appropriate financial regulatory agency, supervisory agency, or other Federal or State agency of any authority derived from any other applicable law.

[¶ 54,431] Section 812. Effective date

This section specifies that this Act shall be effective as of the date of enactment.

Title IX—Investor Protections

Subtitle A

[¶ 54,440] Section 911. Investor Advisory Committee established

Section 911 establishes within the SEC the Investor Advisory Committee to assist the SEC by advising and consulting on regulatory priorities; issues relating to securities, trading, fee structures and the effectiveness of disclosures; investor protection; and initiatives to promote investor confidence. The Committee shall be composed of the Investor Advocate, a representative of state securities commissions because of the important work that States have performed in protecting investors, a representative of the interests of senior citizens who are sometimes targeted for securities frauds, and between 12 and 22 members who represent the interests of individual investors, institutional investors, and pension fund investors.

The Committee shall elect from among themselves a Chairman, Vice Chairman, Secretary, and Assistant Secretary, each of whom shall serve a 3 year term. The Committee shall meet at least twice per year. The SEC shall provide the Committee with the staff necessary to fulfill its mission. The SEC must publicly respond to Committee findings and recommendations by assessing them and disclosing any action the SEC intends to take. It is expected that the responses will be made shortly after the Committee acts.

In June of 2009, the SEC formed an Investor Advisory Committee. This legislation gives the Investor Advisory Committee a statutory foundation and sets congressional prerogatives for the Committee's composition and function.

The proposal for this Committee was included in the Treasury Department legislative proposal for financial reform.[162] AARP supports the statutory establishment of this Committee. On November 19, 2009, the AARP wrote in a letter to Senators Dodd and Shelby, "AARP also supports additional powers granted to the SEC to strengthen its work on behalf of investors, including explicit authority to establish an Investor Advisory Committee."[163]

[¶ 54,441] Section 912. Clarification of authority of the commission to engage in consumer testing

Section 912 clarifies the SEC's authority to gather information from and communicate with investors and engage in such temporary programs as the SEC determines are in the public interest for the purpose of evaluating any rule or program of the SEC.

In the past, the SEC has carried out consumer testing programs, but there have been questions of the legality of this practice. This legislative language gives clear authority to the SEC for these activities.

This proposal is included in the Treasury Department's legislative language for financial reform[164]. The AARP told the Committee that it "supports the explicit authority granted to the SEC to test rules or programs by gathering information and communicating with investors and other members of the public. This type of testing has the very real potential to improve the clarity and usefulness of the disclosures that our securities regulatory scheme relies upon."[165] Mr. James Hamilton, Principal Analyst, CCH Federal Securities Law Reporter has said "The SEC can better evaluate the effectiveness of investor disclosures if it can meaningfully engage in consumer testing of those disclosures. The SEC should be better enabled to engage in field testing, consumer outreach and testing of disclosures to individual investors, including by providing budgetary support for those activities."[166]

---

[162] FACT SHEET: ADMINISTRATION'S REGULATORY REFORM AGENDA MOVES FORWARD; Legislation for Strengthening Investor Protection Delivered to Capitol Hill, U.S. Department of the Treasury, Press Release, July 10, 2009, www.financialstability.gov.

[163] AARP, letter to Senators Dodd and Shelby, November 19, 2009.

[164] FACT SHEET: ADMINISTRATION'S REGULATORY REFORM AGENDA MOVES FORWARD; Legislation for Strengthening Investor Protection Delivered to Capitol Hill, U.S. Department of the Treasury, Press Release, July 10, 2009, www.financialstability.gov.

[165] AARP, letter to Senators Dodd and Shelby, November 19, 2009.

[166] Obama Reform Proposal Would Enhance SEC Investor Protection Role, Jim Hamilton's World of Securities Regulation, jimhamiltonblog.blogspot.com, June 17, 2009.

[¶ 54,442] **Section 913. Study and rulemaking regarding obligations of brokers, dealers, and investment advisers**

Section 913 was authored by Senators Johnson and Crapo. It directs the SEC to conduct a study of the effectiveness of existing legal or regulatory standards of care for brokers, dealers, and investment advisers for providing personalized investment advice and recommendations about securities to retail customers imposed by the SEC and FINRA, and whether there are legal or regulatory gaps or overlap in legal or regulatory standards in the protection of retail customers. The section also requires the SEC to issue a report within one year that considers public input. If this study identifies any gaps or overlap in the legal or regulatory standards in the protection of retail customers relating to the standards of care for brokers, dealers, and investment advisers, the SEC shall commence a rulemaking within two years to address such regulatory gaps and overlap that can be addressed by rule, using its existing authority under the Securities Exchange Act of 1934 and the Investment Advisers Act of 1940.

[¶ 54,443] **Section 914. Creation of Office of the Investor Advocate**

Section 914 was authored by Senator Akaka. Section 914 creates the Office of the Investor Advocate within the Securities and Exchange Commission (SEC). The Committee believes it is necessary to create an office of the Investor Advocate within the SEC to strengthen the institution and ensure that the interests of retail investors are better represented. The Investor Advocate is tasked with assisting retail investors to resolve significant problems with the SEC or the self-regulatory organizations (SROs). The Investor Advocate's mission includes identifying areas where investors would benefit from changes in SEC or SRO policies and problems that investors have with financial service providers and investment products. The Investor Advocate will recommend policy changes to the SEC and Congress in the interests of investors. The Taxpayer Advocate within the Internal Revenue Service has contributed significantly to the improvement of policies that have benefited taxpayers. A similar office in the SEC has a tremendous potential to similarly benefit retail investors. The Investor Advocate, with its independent reporting lines, would help to ensure that the interests of retail investors are built into rulemaking proposals from the outset and that agency priorities reflect the issues that confront average investors. The Investor Advocate will increase transparency and accountability at the SEC and be equipped to act in response to feedback from investors and potentially avoid situations such as the mishandling of tips that could have exposed Ponzi schemes much earlier. The Investor Advocate, and staff of the Office of the Investor Advocate, shall maintain the same level of confidentiality for any document or information made available under this section as is required of any member, officer, or employee of the SEC. In this regard, the Investor Advocate and staff in the Office of the Investor Advocate are subject to the same statutory and regulatory restrictions on, and applicable penalties for, the unauthorized disclosure or use of any nonpublic information that apply to any member, officer, or employee of the SEC.

[¶ 54,444] **Section 915. Streamlining of filing procedures for self-regulatory organizations**

Section 915 requires the SEC to approve a proposed SRO rule or institute a proceeding to consider whether the rule should be disapproved within 45 days. The SEC can extend this period by 45 days if appropriate. If the SEC does not approve the rule within this period then it must provide a hearing within 180 days of the rule proposal publication. The SEC must approve or disapprove the rule during this same period, or it can extend this period by 60 days if necessary. If the SEC does not follow these time restrictions, the rule is deemed to have been approved. The SEC has 7 days after the receipt of the proposal to notify the SRO if the proposed rule change does not comply with the rules of the SEC relating to the required form of a proposed rule change.

The Committee recognizes that in the modern securities markets it is important that the SEC operate efficiently and responsively. The Committee has heard concerns about current SEC processes for action on rule changes by exchanges and other self-regulatory organizations.

The Committee expects that the changes will encourage the SEC to employ a more transparent and rapid process for consideration of rule changes.

Nothing in the Section diminishes the SEC's authority to reject an improperly filed rule, disapprove a rule that is not consistent with the Exchange Act, or diminishes the applicable public notice and comment period.

Nasdaq OMX, NYSE Euronext, International Securities Exchange and Chicago Board Options Exchange have written jointly by letter dated

November 24, 2009 in strong support of this provision because "it would streamline the Securities and Exchange Commission's (SEC) process for making a determination on an exchange rule proposal." They explained, "As Self Regulatory Organizations (SROs), we are subject to the regulatory authority of the SEC, which includes the requirement that we submit all proposed rule changes to the SEC for approval. Although the SEC has made progress in increasing the number of rule proposals that may be submitted for immediate effectiveness, the process that rule proposals that are not subject to immediate effectiveness must undergo remains a point of frustration for SROs. The current process enables the SEC to use internal interpretations to avoid what should be reasonable timelines to move rule filings toward a determination of approval or denial. This process not only delays transparency and public input, it provides a significant competitive advantage to our less regulated competitors, which do not have to seek regulatory approval before changing their rules."

[¶ 54,445] *Section 916. Study regarding financial literacy among investors*

Section 916 was authored by Senator Akaka. This Section directs the SEC to study and issue a report on the existing level of financial literacy among retail investors. The SEC will have to develop an investor financial literacy strategy. The strategy is intended to bring about positive behavioral change in investors. The study will identify: (1) the existing level of financial literacy among retail investors; (2) methods to improve the timing, content, and format of disclosures to investors with respect to financial intermediaries, investment products, and investment services; (3) the most useful and understandable relevant information that retail investors need to make informed financial decisions; (4) methods to increase the transparency of expenses and conflicts of interests in transactions involving investment services and products; (5) the most effective existing private and public efforts to educate investors; and (6) in consultation with the Financial Literacy and Education Commission, a strategy to increase the financial literacy of investors in order to bring about a positive change in investor behavior.

The AARP also supported the study of financial literacy in a letter to Senators Dodd and Shelby.[167]

[¶ 54,446] *Section 917. Study regarding mutual fund advertising*

Section 917 directs the GAO to conduct a study and issue a report on mutual fund advertising to examine: (1) existing and proposed regulatory requirements for open-end investment company advertisements; (2) current marketing practices for the sale of open-end investment company shares, including the use of past performance data, funds that have merged, and incubator funds; (3) the impact of such advertising on consumers; and (4) recommendations to improve investor protections in mutual fund advertising and additional information necessary to ensure that investors can make informed financial decisions when purchasing shares.

[¶ 54,447] *Section 918. Clarification of commission authority to require investor disclosures before purchase of investment products and services*

Section 918 was authored by Senator Akaka. Section 918 clarifies the SEC's authority to require investor disclosures before the purchase of investment company shares. This section will give the SEC the authority to require broker-dealers to disclose to clients their compensation for sales of open- and closed-end mutual funds. The Committee believes that investors must be provided with relevant, meaningful, and timely disclosures about financial products and services from which they can make better informed investment decisions. The Committee encourages the SEC to use the consumer testing authorized under Section 912 and the study on financial literacy under Section 916 to inform its scope of disclosures.

Mr. James Hamilton, Principal Analyst, CCH Federal Securities Law Reporter, said "legislation should authorize the SEC to require that certain disclosures (including a summary prospectus) be provided to investors at or before the point of sale, if the SEC finds that such disclosures would improve investor understanding of the particular financial products, and their costs and risks. Currently, most prospectuses (including the mutual fund summary prospectus) are delivered with the confirmation of sale, after the sale has taken place. Without slowing the pace of transactions in modern capital markets, the SEC should require that adequate information is

---

[167] AARP, letter to Senators Dodd and Shelby, November 19, 2009.

given to investor to make informed investment decisions."[168]

Mr. Travis Plunkett, Legislative Director of the Consumer Federation of America, also supports this provision. In testimony for the House Financial Services Committee, he wrote "we also strongly support requiring pre-sale disclosure to assist mutual fund investors to make more informed investment decisions. While mutual funds are subject to more robust disclosure requirements than many competing investment products and services, the disclosures typically do not arrive until three days after the sale. This makes them essentially useless in helping investors to assess the risks and costs of the fund, as well as the uses for which it may be most appropriate."[169] AARP also supports this provision.[170] The Committee encourages that Securities and Exchange Commission to use the consumer testing authorized under Section 912 and the study on financial literacy under Section 916 to inform its scope of disclosures.

[¶ 54,448] *Section 919. Study on conflicts of interest*

Section 919 directs the GAO to conduct a study and make recommendations regarding potential conflicts of interest between securities underwriting and securities analysis functions within firms. In this study, the GAO will consider potential harm to investors of these conflicts, the nature and benefit of the undertakings to which the firms agreed as part of the Global Settlement, whether any of these undertakings should be codified, and whether to recommend regulatory or legislative measures to mitigate harm to investors caused by these conflicts of interest. The GAO will consult with the SEC, FINRA, investor advocates, retail investors, institutional investors, academics, and State securities officials in performing this study. This issue has been a subject of public concern for many years. On March 15, 2010, the U.S. District Court in New York rejected a proposal by the SEC and 12 securities firms to change the legal settlement put in place with the Global Research Analyst Settlements to end abuses on Wall Street that would have allowed employees in investment-banking and research departments at Wall Street firms to "communicate with each other . . . outside of the presence" of lawyers or compliance-department officials responsible for policing employee conduct—an activity strictly prohibited by the settlement. The 2003 Global Settlement resolved a major securities scandal, in which 10 of the largest securities firms and two individual analysts were charged with issuing misleading or fraudulent analyst recommendations and fines of $1.4 billion were assessed.

Title V of the Sarbanes-Oxley Act of 2002 (P.L. 107-204) addressed aspects of this issue by amending the Securities Exchange Act of 1934 to require the SEC, or upon the authorization and direction of the SEC, a registered securities association or national securities exchange, to adopt rules reasonably designed to address conflicts of interest that can arise when securities analysts recommend equity securities in research reports and public appearances.

[¶ 54,449] *Section 919A. Study on improved access to information on investment advisers and broker-dealers*

Senator Brown (OH) authored Section 919A. This Section directs the SEC to study and make recommendations on ways to improve the access of investors to registration information about registered and previously registered investment advisers, associated persons of investment advisers, brokers and dealers and their associated persons on the existing Central Registration Depository and Investment Adviser Registration Depository systems, as well as identify additional information that should be made publicly available.

[¶ 54,450] *Section 919B. Study on financial planners and the use of financial designations*

Senator Kohl authored Section 919B. This Section directs the GAO to conduct a study to evaluate and make recommendations on the effectiveness of State and Federal regulations to protect consumers from misleading financial advisor designations; current State and Federal oversight structure and regulations for financial planners; and legal or regulatory gaps in the regulation of financial planners and other individuals who provide or offer to provide financial planning services to consumers.

Senator Kohl has said that "Financial planners provide advice on a wide range of issues,

---

[168] *Obama Administration Would Enhance SEC's Investor Protection Role*, Mr. James Hamilton, CCH Financial Crisis Newsletter, June 18, 2009, www.financialcrisisupdate.com.

[169] *Community and Consumer Advocates' Perspectives on the Obama Administration's Financial Regulatory Reform Proposals:* Testimony before the U.S. House Committee on Financial Services, 111th Congress, 1st session, p.24 (2009) (Testimony of Mr. Travis Plunkett).

[170] AARP, letter to Senators Dodd and Shelby, November 19, 2009.

including home ownership, saving for college and selecting appropriate investment products. Because this advice will have a lasting impact on the financial health of the consumer, it is important that the service provider meets certain standards. Currently, different states' laws govern financial planners, with no standard code of conduct, training requirements or conflict of interest disclosure requirements. Additionally, there is little accountability for financial planners that take advantage of consumers. Both consumers and financial planners will benefit from standardizing rules and increased oversight at the federal level."[171] Marilyn Mohrman-Gillis, Managing Director, Public Policy, Certified Financial Planner Board of Standards, Inc. said "we recognize that the study is certainly a first step in Congress recognizing the need for reform."

Subtitle B

[¶ 54,460] Section 921. Authority to issue rules to restrict mandatory predispute arbitration

Section 921 gives the SEC the authority to conduct a rulemaking to prohibit, or impose conditions or limitations on the use of, agreements that require customers or clients of any broker, dealer, or municipal securities dealer to arbitrate any dispute between them. This provision was included in the Treasury Department's legislative proposal.[172]

There have been concerns over the past several years that mandatory pre-dispute arbitration is unfair to the investors. In a letter to Chairman Dodd and Ranking Member Shelby, AARP expressed support for this provision. In listing some of the problems with mandatory pre-dispute arbitration, the letter identified "high upfront costs; limited access to documents and other key information; limited knowledge upon which to base the choice of arbitrator; the absence of a requirement that arbitrators follow the law or issue written decisions; and extremely limited grounds for appeal."[173]

The North American Securities Administrators Association also supports this provision, stating in testimony that a "major step toward improving the integrity of the arbitration system is the removal of the mandatory industry arbitrator. This mandatory industry arbitrator, with their industry ties, automatically puts the investor at an unfair disadvantage."[174] The Consumer Federation of America,[175] AARP,[176] and the Public Investors Arbitration Bar Association support this approach.[177]

[¶ 54,461] Section 922. Whistleblower protection

The Whistleblower Program, established and administered by the Securities and Exchange Commission, is intended to provide monetary rewards to those who contribute "original information" that lead to recoveries of monetary sanctions of $1,000,000 or more in criminal and civil proceedings. The genesis of the program is found in President Obama's June 2009 financial regulatory reform proposal.[178] A similar provision was included in the House of Representatives financial reform bill (H.R. 4173).

The Whistleblower Program aims to motivate those with inside knowledge to come forward and assist the Government to identify and prosecute persons who have violated securities laws and recover money for victims of financial fraud. In a testimony for the Senate Banking Committee, Certified Fraud Examiner and Madoff whistleblower Harry Markopolos testified in support of creating a strong Whistleblower Program. He cited statistics showing the efficiency of Whistleblower Programs: "whistleblower tips detected 54.1% of uncovered fraud schemes in public companies.

---

[171] Senator Kohl, letter to Senator Dodd, February 22, 2010.

[172] FACT SHEET: ADMINISTRATION'S REGULATORY REFORM AGENDA MOVES FORWARD; Legislation for Strengthening Investor Protection Delivered to Capitol Hill, U.S. Department of the Treasury, Press Release, July 10, 2009, www.financialstability.gov.

[173] AARP, letter to Senators Dodd and Shelby, November 19, 2009.

[174] Enhancing Investor Protection and the Regulation of Securities Markets—Part II: Testimony before the U.S. Senate Committee on Banking, Housing, and Urban Affairs, 111th Congress, 1st session, p.18 (2009) (Testimony of Mr. Fred Joseph).

[175] Consumer Federation of America (November 10, 2009), "CFA Applauds Introduction of Senator Dodd's Financial Reform Package," Press release, www.consumerfed.org.

[176] AARP, letter to Senators Dodd and Shelby, November 19, 2009.

[177] The following article references the Public Investors Arbitration Bar Association's support for this provision: "Death Knell For Mandatory Arbitration," Helen Kearney, On Wall Street, August 1, 2009.

[178] Fact Sheet: Administration's Regulatory Reform Agenda Moves Forward; Legislation for Strengthening Investor Protection Delivered to Capitol Hill, U.S. Department of the Treasury, Press Release, July 10, 2009. Available at http://www.financialstability.gov.

External auditors, and the SEC exam teams would certainly be considered external auditors, detected a mere 4.1% of uncovered fraud schemes. Whistleblower tips were 13 times more effective than external audits, hence my recommendation to the SEC to encourage the submission of whistleblower tips."[179] In his letter to Senator Dodd, SEC Inspector General David Kotz also recommended a similar Whistleblower Program.[180]

Recognizing that whistleblowers often face the difficult choice between telling the truth and the risk of committing "career suicide", the program provides for amply rewarding whistleblower(s), with between 10% and 30% of any monetary sanctions that are collected based on the "original information" offered by the whistleblower. The program is modeled after a successful IRS Whistleblower Program enacted into law in 2006. The reformed IRS program, which, too, has a similar minimum-maximum award levels and an appeals process,[181] is credited to have reinvigorated the earlier, largely ineffective, IRS Whistleblower Program. The Committee feels the critical component of the Whistleblower Program is the minimum payout that any individual could look towards in determining whether to take the enormous risk of blowing the whistle in calling attention to fraud.

We also note a recent report of the current SEC insider-trading Whistleblower Program by the Office of Inspector General of SEC. Since the inception of the program in 1989, there have been a total of only seven payouts to five whistleblowers for a meager total of $159,537.[182] In the report, the Inspector General recommends several important guidelines that any current or future SEC Whistleblower Programs should follow, including: development of specific criteria for bounty awards (including a provision to award whistleblowers that partly rely upon public information), development of tips and complaints tracking systems, incorporating best practices from DOJ and IRS's Whistleblower Programs, and establishment of a timeframe for the new policies.

"Original information" is defined as information that is derived from the independent analysis or knowledge of the whistleblower, and is not derived from an allegation in court or government reports, and is not exclusively from news media. In circumstances when bits and pieces of the whistleblower's information were known to the media prior to the emergence of the whistleblower, and that for the purposes of the SEC enforcement[183] the critical components of the information was supplied by the whistleblower, the intent of the Committee is to require the SEC to reward such person(s) in accordance with the degree of assistance that was provided. The rewards are to be from the Investor Protection Fund, which receives funds from sanctions collected based on civil enforcement and from other funds within SEC that are otherwise not distributed to investors (i.e., unused disgorgement funds). Whenever a whistleblower or whistleblowers tip leads the SEC to collect sanctions and penalties that are determined to be distributed to the victims of the fraud, the intent of the Committee is to reward the whistleblower prior or at the same time as paying such victims, recognizing that were it not for the whistleblower's actions, there would have been no discovery of the harm to the investors and no collection of any sanctions for their benefit.

The SEC has discretion in determining the amount and whether or not a whistleblower is eligible to be awarded. In cases when whistleblowers feel that the SEC had abused its discretion in determining the amount of the award, they have the right to appeal, within 30 days of the decision to a court of appeals. The court is to review the determination in accordance with section 706 of title 5 of U.S. Code. The Committee feels that this review process will significantly contribute to make the program reliable for persons who are contemplating whether or not to blow the whistle on fraud. It will add to the notion of enforceable payout. The Committee, having heard from several parties involved in whistleblower related cases, has determined that enforceability and relatively pre-

---

[179] "Oversight of the SEC's Failure to Identify the Bernard L. Madoff Ponzi Scheme and How to Improve SEC Performance: Testimony before the U.S. Senate Committee on Banking, Housing, and Urban Affairs", 111th Congress, 1st session, p.33 (2009) (Testimony of Mr. Harry Markopolos).

[180] Inspector General H. David Kotz, letter to Senator Dodd, October 29, 2009.

[181] Like the IRS program, the new SEC Whistleblower Program provides for an appeals process, the appropriate court of appeals will review the determination made by the Commission in accordance with section 706 of title 5 of U.S. Code (i.e., abuse of discretion).

[182] "Assessment of the SEC's Bounty Program", Office of Inspector General, U.S. Securities and Exchange Commission, Report No. 474. March 29, 2010.

[183] Same would apply to cases when SEC forwards criminal cases to DOJ that lead to penalties and sanctions.

¶54,461

dictable level of payout will go a long way to motivate potential whistleblowers to come forward and help the Government identify and prosecute fraudsters. Whistleblowers who are employees of an appropriate regulatory agency, DOJ, SROs, PCAOB, accountants in certain circumstances, or a law enforcement organization are generally not eligible for an award. Also not eligible are whistleblowers who are convicted of a criminal violation related to the case at hand.

The Committee intends for this program to be used actively with ample rewards to promote the integrity of the financial markets.

The program also requires the SEC to annually report back to Congress, among other things, with details regarding the number and types of awards granted. It also provides for various protections for whistleblowers, specifically barring employers to discharge, demote, suspend, threaten, harass directly or indirectly, or in any other manner discriminate. The provision also makes it unlawful to knowingly and willfully make any false, fictitious or fraudulent statement or representation, or use any false writing or document knowing the writing or document contains any false, fictitious, or fraudulent statement or entry. Following the enactment of the Act, the SEC will have 270 days to issue final regulations implementing the provisions of the Act.

[¶ 54,462] Section 923. Conforming amendments for whistleblower protection

Section 923 contains conforming amendments for whistleblower protection.

[¶ 54,464] Section 924. Implementation and transition provisions for whistleblower protection

Section 924 contains implementation and transition provisions for whistleblower provisions. The section directs the SEC to issue final regulations implementing the provisions of section 21F of the Securities Exchange Act of 1934 within 270 days within enactment of the Act.

[¶ 54,465] Section 925. Collateral bars

Section 925 gives the SEC the authority to bar individuals from being associated with various registered securities market participants after violating the law while associated in only one area. This provision is included in the Treasury Department's legislative proposal.[184] The Committee finds that this provision is necessary because, under current rules, individuals could be barred from one registered entity for violations, such as fraud, but then work in another industry where they could prey upon other investors.

[¶ 54,466] Section 926. Authority of state regulators over regulation D offerings

Section 926 restores certain authority of States over Regulation D offerings. This provision will give the States the authority over certain securities sales that are not subject to the '33 Act requirements due to their size and scope, as determined by the SEC.

The North American Securities Administrators Association described why this provision is needed: "These offerings also enjoy an exemption from registration under federal securities law, so they receive virtually no regulatory scrutiny even where the promoters or broker-dealers have a criminal or disciplinary history. As a result, Rule 506 offerings have become the favorite vehicle under Regulation D, and many of them are fraudulent. Although Congress preserved the states' authority to take enforcement actions for fraud in the offer and sale of all 'covered' securities, including Rule 506 offerings, this power is no substitute for a state's ability to scrutinize offerings for signs of potential abuse and to ensure that disclosure is adequate before harm is done to investors."[185] In light of the growing popularity of Rule 506 offerings and the expansive reading of the exemption given by certain courts, NASAA believes the time has come for Congress to reinstate state regulatory oversight of all Rule 506 offerings by repealing Subsection 18(b)4(D) of the Securities Act of 1933."[186]

---

[184] FACT SHEET: ADMINISTRATION'S REGULATORY REFORM AGENDA MOVES FORWARD; Legislation for Strengthening Investor Protection Delivered to Capitol Hill, U.S. Department of the Treasury, Press Release, July 10, 2009, www.financialstability.gov.

[185] North American Securities Administrators Association, Inc., letter to Chairman Dodd and Ranking Member Shelby, November 17, 2009.

[186] Pro-Investor Legislative Agenda for the 111th Congress, North American Securities Administrators Association, January, 2009, www.nasaa.org.

The Committee also heard from interested parties stating that the SEC is adequately capable of reviewing these filings, however we note, in the words of Jennifer Johnson, that "the SEC simply does not have the resources, even if it had the will, to police smaller private placements. State regulators, on the other hand, as 'local cops on the beat,' are well positioned to fill this regulatory gap. While states currently have enforcement powers under NSMIA . . . they may not become aware of serious problems involving Rule 506 offerings until after injured investors contact them. While states may be able to prosecute the perpetrators of fraud, they cannot prophylactically protect future victims."[187]

The Committee is concerned to protect investors who, under current regulatory scheme and practice, lack regulatory protections. There is a particular concern to protect investors from recidivist perpetrators of securities fraud. This Section does not resolve other current issues involving the SEC's administration of Regulation D, several of which are highlighted in the SEC Office of Inspector General audit report on "Regulation D Exemption Process," March 31, 2009 (e.g., the SEC "should develop a process to assess and better ensure issuers' compliance with Regulation D and take appropriate action when . . . [it] finds companies have materially misused the Regulation D exemptions").

[¶ 54,467] *Section 927. Equal treatment of self-regulatory organization rules*

Section 927 provides equal treatment for the rules of all SROs under Section 29(a), which voids any condition, stipulation, or provision binding any person to waive compliance with any provision of the Exchange Act, any rule or regulation thereunder, or any rule of an exchange.

[¶ 54,468] *Section 928. Clarification that Section 205 of the Investment Advisers Act of 1940 does not apply to state-registered advisers*

Section 928 clarifies that Sec. 205 of the Advisers Act (performance fees and advisory contracts) does not apply to state-registered investment advisors. This is a clarification from the National Securities Markets Improvement Act that these restrictions on investment adviser contracts do not apply to state-registered advisers.

[¶ 54,469] *Section 929. Unlawful margin lending*

Under previous law, it was unlawful for any member of a national securities exchange or any broker or dealer to provide margin lending to or for any customer on any non-exempt security unless the loan met margin regulations provided for in Chapter 2B of Title 15 of the U.S. Code and was properly collateralized. Section 929 provides that either of these two infractions is unlawful by itself.

[¶ 54,470] *Section 929A. Protection for employees of subsidiaries and affiliates of publicly traded companies*

Amends Section 806 of the Sarbanes-Oxley Act of 2002 to make clear that subsidiaries and affiliates of issuers may not retaliate against whistleblowers, eliminating a defense often raised by issuers in actions brought by whistleblowers. Section 806 of the Sarbanes-Oxley Act creates protections for whistleblowers who report securities fraud and other violations. The language of the statute may be read as providing a remedy only for retaliation by the issuer, and not by subsidiaries of an issuer. This clarification would eliminate a defense now raised in a substantial number of actions brought by whistleblowers under the statute.

[¶ 54,471] *Section 929B. Fair Fund amendments*

Amends Section 308 of the Sarbanes-Oxley Act of 2002 to permit the SEC use penalties obtained from a defendant for the benefit of victims even if the SEC does not obtain disgorgement from the defendant (e.g., because defendant did not benefit from its securities law violation that nonetheless harmed investors). Under the Fair Fund provisions of the Sarbanes-Oxley Act, the SEC must obtain disgorgement from a defendant before the SEC can use penalties obtained from the defendant in a Fair Fund for the benefit of victims of the defendant's violation of the securities laws, or a rule or regulation thereunder. This section would revise the Fair Fund provisions to permit the SEC to use penalties obtained from a defendant for the benefit of victims even if the SEC does not obtain an order requiring the defendant to pay disgorgement. In some cases, a defendant may engage in a securities law violation that harms investors,

---

[187] Johnson, Jennifer, 2010. "Private Placements: A regulatory Black Hole". Delaware Journal of Corporate Law. Vol. 34, p. 195.

but the SEC cannot obtain disgorgement from the defendant because, for example, the defendant did not benefit from the violation.

[¶ 54,472] **Section 929C. Increasing the borrowing limit on treasury loans**

Section 929C updates Securities Investor Protection Act, including borrowing of funds, distinction between securities and cash insurance, portfolio margin, and liquidation. This line of credit has not been increased since SIPA was enacted in 1970. SEC staff believes an increase is necessary to provide the Securities Investor Protection Corporation (SIPC) with sufficient resources in the event of the failure of a large broker-dealer. This line of credit is used in the event that SIPC asks for a loan from the SEC and the SEC determines that such a loan is necessary "for the protection of customers of brokers or dealers and the maintenance of confidence in the United States securities markets." SEC staff also support eliminating the distinction in the statute between claims for cash and claims for securities. Section 21 of the Glass-Steagall Act, 12 USC 378, prevents broker-dealers (and any entity other than a bank) from accepting deposits. Staff believes that the distinction between claims for cash and claims for securities has become blurred in recent years and that the distinction can be confusing to customers.

Subtitle C

[¶ 54,480] **Section 931. Findings**

This section contains Congressional findings that credit ratings are systemically important; relied upon by individual and institutional investors and regulators; and central to capital formation, investor confidence and economic efficiency. Credit rating agencies play a gatekeeper role in financial markets that justifies the same level of oversight and accountability that applies to securities analysts, auditors, and investment banks. Inaccurate ratings, generated in part by conflicts of interest in the process of rating structured financial products, contributed to the mismanagement of risk by large financial institutions and investors, which set the stage for global financial panic.

[¶ 54,481] **Section 932. Enhanced regulation, accountability, and transparency of nationally recognized statistical ratings organizations**

This section provides for enhanced regulation of nationally recognized statistical ratings organizations (NRSROs), greater accountability on the part of NRSROs that fail to produce accurate ratings, and more disclosure to permit investors to better understand credit ratings and their limitations. The section builds upon the principles of the Credit Rating Agency Reform Act of 2006, which introduced the NRSRO designation and sought to improve ratings performance through a combination of regulatory oversight and competition.

Enhanced Regulation

Paragraph (1) of Section 932 provides that each NRSRO shall establish, maintain, enforce, and document an effective internal control structure governing the implementation of and adherence to policies, procedures, and methodologies for determining credit ratings, taking into consideration such factors as the SEC may prescribe, by rule. This provision also calls for an annual report containing an assessment of the effectiveness and a CEO attestation on the internal controls. In support of this provision, Ms. Rita Bolger, Senior Vice President and Associate General Counsel of Standard & Poor's, wrote in testimony for the Senate Banking Committee that "a regulatory regime should provide for effective oversight of registered agencies' compliance with their policies and procedures through robust, periodic inspections. Such oversight must avoid interfering in the analytical process and methodologies, and refrain from second-guessing rating opinions. External interference in ratings analytics undermines investor confidence in the independence of the rating opinion and heightens moral hazard risk in influencing a rating outcome."[188]

Section 932 also gives the SEC the authority to fine an NRSRO for violations of law or regulation. Under previous law, the SEC could not fine NRSROs, but could only censure, place limitations on the activities, functions, or operations of, suspend for a period not exceeding 12 months, or revoke the registration of any NRSRO. Under this provision the SEC retains these abilities. Lynn Turner, former Chief Accountant of the SEC, supports this provision. He wrote in testimony for the Senate Banking Committee

---

[188] *Enhancing Investor Protection and the Regulation of Securities Markets—Part II: Testimony before the U.S. Senate Committee on Banking, Housing, and Urban Affairs,* 111th Congress, 1st session, p. 11 (2009) (Testimony of Ms. Rita Bolger).

that "the SEC should be given the authority to fine the agencies or their employees who fail to adequately protect investors."[189]

Section 932 attempts to eliminate the effect of the inherent conflict of interest in the issuer-pays model of the credit rating industry. Under this model, issuers of debt have the incentive to use the rating agency that provides the highest rating. A conflict of interest thus arises because rating agencies want to provide the highest rating to keep the issuer's business and are less willing to publish a lower rating. The section addresses this conflict by directing the SEC to write rules preventing sales and marketing considerations from influencing the production of ratings. Violation of these rules will lead to suspension or revocation of NRSRO status if the violation affects a rating.

Section 932 addresses the role of the NRSRO compliance officer, a position created by the Credit Rating Agency Reform Act of 2006. The section prohibits NRSRO compliance officers from participating in production of ratings, the development of ratings methodologies, or the setting of compensation for NRSRO employees. The section allows the SEC to provide exemptions for small NRSROs if the SEC finds that compliance would impose an unreasonable burden.

Section 932 also directs NRSRO compliance officers to establish procedures for the receipt, retention, and treatment of complaints about the rating agency or its ratings. Finally, the section directs the compliance officer to submit to the NRSRO an annual report on its compliance with the securities laws, and its related policies and procedures. The NRSRO must submit this report to the SEC.

Paragraph 6 of Section 932 establishes the Office of Credit Ratings within the SEC. The Office shall administer the rules of the SEC with respect to NRSROs to protect investors and the public interest, to promote accuracy in credit ratings, and to prevent conflicts of interest from unduly influencing credit ratings. The Director of the Office will report to the Chairman of the SEC. The Office will be adequately staffed to fulfill its statutory role and will include persons with knowledge of and expertise in corporate, municipal, and structured debt.

The Committee believes that the unique nature of NRSRO oversight warrants an independent office within the SEC. The fact that there will be a dedicated Office within the SEC to focus on NRSROs should improve the quality and efficiency of the regulation. Many advocated for a separate Office within the SEC to carry out the regulation of NRSROs because of the NRSRO's unique and distinct role from the other entities overseen by the SEC. Mr. Deven Sharma, President of Standard & Poor's, supports "creating a dedicated office within the SEC to oversee NRSROs."[190]

The Office of Credit Ratings shall conduct annual examinations of each NRSRO. Each examination will include a review of the policies, procedures, and rating methodologies of the NRSRO and whether the NRSRO follows these; the management of conflicts of interest by the NRSRO; the implementation of ethics policies; the internal supervisory controls of the NRSRO; the governance of the NRSRO; the activities of the NRSRO compliance officer; the processing of complaints by the NRSRO; and the policies of the NRSRO governing the post-employment activities of former staff.

The SEC will make public, in an easily understandable format, an annual report summarizing the essential findings of all NRSRO examinations that year. The report shall include the responses of NRSROs to material regulatory deficiencies identified by the SEC and to recommendations made by the SEC.

Many interested parties believe that, given the rating agencies' important role in the financial markets, it is appropriate and desirable for the SEC to examine them as they would other securities firms. Mr. Lynn Turner, former Chief Accountant of the SEC wrote in congressional testimony that "the SEC has insufficient authority over the credit ratings agencies despite the roles those firms played in Enron and now the sub-prime crisis. This deficiency needs to be remedied by giving the SEC the authority to inspect credit ratings, just as Congress gave the PCAOB the ability to inspect independent au-

---

[189] *Enhancing Investor Protection and the Regulation of Securities Markets—Part I: Testimony before the U.S. Senate Committee on Banking, Housing, and Urban Affairs*, 111th Congress, 1st session, p. 11 (2009) (Testimony of Mr. Lynn Turner).

[190] *Reforming Credit Rating Agencies: Testimony before the U.S. House Committee on Financial Services*, 111th Congress, 1st session, p.12 (2009) (Testimony of Mr. Deven Sharma).

dits."[191] Ms. Barbara Roper, Director of Investor Protection at the Consumer Federation of America, wrote in testimony that "the agency should have authority to examine individual ratings engagements to determine not only that analysts are following company practices and procedures but that those practices and procedures are adequate to develop an accurate rating. Congress would need to ensure that any such oversight function was adequately funded and staffed."[192] Standard & Poor's President Deven Sharma wrote in testimony that S&P supports "empowering the SEC to conduct frequent reviews of NRSROs to ensure that NRSROs follow their internal controls and policies for determining ratings and managing conflicts of interest."[193]

Accountability

Paragraph (2) of Section 932 provides that the SEC may temporarily suspend or permanently revoke the registration of an NRSRO with respect to a particular class or subclass of securities, if the SEC finds, on the record after notice and opportunity for hearing, that NRSRO does not have adequate financial and managerial resources to consistently produce credit ratings with integrity. In determining whether an NRSRO lacks such resources, the SEC shall consider an NRSRO's failure to consistently produce accurate ratings over a sustained period of time.

Subsection (q) of Paragraph 6 of Section 932 directs the SEC to require that each NRSRO publicly disclose information on the initial credit ratings published by the NRSRO for each type of obligor, security, and money market instrument and any subsequent changes to such credit ratings. The purpose of this disclosure is to allow users of credit ratings to compare the performance and accuracy of ratings issued by different NRSROs. Disclosures would be clear and informative for investors with varying levels of financial sophistication.

This provision seeks to address the lack of market competition in the credit rating industry by allowing investors to compare NRSRO performance. Industry analysts often identify the lack of competition as one reason why the industry performed poorly in rating securities, such as mortgage-backed securities, and thus contributed to the economic crisis of 2008. To portray the concentrated market for credit ratings, Sean Egan, Managing Director of Egan-Jones Ratings Co., noted that S&P and Moody's control over 90% of the revenues in the ratings industry.[194] This provision will make rating performance public—the goal is to foster market competition by forcing ratings firms to compete on the basis of their rating accuracy. In support of this proposal, Mr. George Miller, Executive Director of the American Securitization Forum, wrote in congressional testimony "we support the publication in a format reasonably accessible to investors of a record of all ratings actions for securitization instruments for which ratings are published. We believe that publication of these data will enable investors and other market participants to evaluate and compare the performance, stability and quality of ratings judgments over time."[195] Ms. Rita Bolger, on behalf of Standard & Poor's, an NRSRO, supports this performance disclosure. She wrote in congressional testimony that a way to promote sound rating oversight would be to "require registered rating agencies to publicly issue performance measurement statistics over the short, medium, and long term, and across asset classes and geographies."[196]

Finally, this subsection makes accommodation for subscriber-pay NRSROs, by mandating that the disclosure be appropriate to the business model of an NRSRO. For these NRSROs, the publication of rating performance would likely be unsustainable because they rely on credit rating users to pay them for ratings.

During the markup of this legislation, the Committee adopted an amendment proposed by Senator Bennet that would require that at least one-half the members of NRSRO boards be independent directors. Independent directors are de-

---

[191] *Enhancing Investor Protection and the Regulation of Securities Markets—Part I: Testimony before the U.S. Senate Committee on Banking, Housing, and Urban Affairs*, 111th Congress, 1st session, p. 11 (2009) (Testimony of Mr. Lynn Turner).

[192] *Enhancing Investor Protection and the Regulation of Securities Markets—Part II: Testimony before the U.S. Senate Committee on Banking, Housing, and Urban Affairs*, 111th Congress, 1st session, p.9 (2009) (Testimony of Ms. Barbara Roper).

[193] *Reforming Credit Rating Agencies: Testimony before the U.S. House Committee on Financial Services*, 111th Congress, 1st session, p.12 (2009) (Testimony of Mr. Deven Sharma).

[194] *Examining the Role of Credit Rating Agencies in the Capital Markets: Testimony before the U.S. Senate Committee on Banking, Housing, and Urban Affairs*, 109th Congress, 2nd session, p.1 (2005) (Testimony of Mr. Sean Egan).

[195] *Securitization of Assets: Problems and Solutions: Testimony before the U.S. Senate Committee on Banking, Housing, and Urban Affairs*, 111th Congress, 1st session, p.25 (2009) (Testimony of Mr. George Miller).

[196] *Enhancing Investor Protection and the Regulation of Securities Markets—Part II: Testimony before the U.S. Senate Committee on Banking, Housing, and Urban Affairs*, 111th Congress, 1st session, p.9 (2009) (Testimony of Ms. Rita Bolger).

¶54,481

fined as those who do not accept consulting, advisory, or other fees from the NRSRO; are not associated with the NRSRO or an affiliate; and do not participate in any deliberation involving a rating in which the independent director has a financial interest. The NRSRO board must be responsible for establishing, maintaining, and enforcing policies and procedures for determining credit ratings; preventing conflicts of interests; the internal control systems; and compensation practices. The provision authorizes the SEC to grant an exemption from independence rules for small NRSROs where compliance would present an unreasonable burden, provided that the responsibilities of the board are delegated to a committee including at least one user of NRSRO ratings.

Disclosure

Subsection (r) of Paragraph 6 of Section 932 directs the SEC to prescribe rules to require each NRSRO to ensure that credit ratings are determined using procedures and methodologies that are approved by the board of directors or senior credit officer. The SEC's rules must require that material changes to ratings procedures and methodologies be applied consistently and publicly disclosed. Such changes must be applied to all credit ratings to which they apply within a reasonable time period, to be determined by the SEC.

The rules will also require each NRSRO to notify users of credit ratings when a material change is made to a procedure or methodology, and when a significant error is identified in a procedure or methodology that may result in credit rating actions. Ms. Rita Bolger, Senior Vice President and Associate General Counsel of Standard & Poor's, wrote in testimony for the Senate Banking Committee that "with greater transparency of credit rating agency methodologies, investors would be in a better position to assess the opinions."[197]

Subsection (s) of Paragraph 6 of Section 932 directs the SEC to require NRSROs, by rule, to publish a form with each rating that discloses qualitative and quantitative information that is intended to enable investors and users of credit ratings to better understand the main principles and assumptions that underlie the rating. The disclosures shall be easy to use, directly comparable across different classes of securities, and may be provided in either paper or electronic form, as the SEC may, by rule, determine.

The qualitative content of the form shall include the credit ratings produced; the main assumptions and principles used in constructing procedures and methodologies (including qualitative methodologies and quantitative inputs and assumptions about the correlation of defaults across obligors used in rating structured products); the potential limitations of the credit ratings and the types of risks excluded from the credit ratings that the NRSRO does not comment on; information on the uncertainty of the credit rating including information on the reliability, accuracy, and quality of the data relied on in determining the credit rating; a statement on the reliability and limitations of the data relied upon and any other data accessibility limitations; and whether and to what extent third party due diligence services have been used by the NRSRO, including a description of the information that such third party reviewed in conducting due diligence services and a description of the findings or conclusions of such third party.

The form shall include an overall assessment of the quality of information available and considered in producing a rating in relation to the quality of information available to the NRSRO in rating similar issuances; information relating to conflicts of interest of the nationally recognized statistical rating organization; and such additional information as the SEC may require.

The quantitative content will include an explanation or measure of the potential volatility of the credit rating (including any factors that might lead to a change in the credit ratings), information on the sensitivity of the rating to assumptions made by the NRSRO, and the extent of the change that a user can expect under different market conditions. In addition, the disclosures will include information on the historical performance of the rating and the expected probability of default and the expected loss in the event of default.

These substantial disclosures will give investors and other market participants far more information about the credit risk of a debt issue and the reliability of ratings. Dr. William Irving, Portfolio Manager at Fidelity Investments, wrote in congressional testimony that the Committee should "facilitate greater transparency of the methodology and assumptions used by the rating agencies to determine credit ratings. In particular, there should be public disclosure of the

---

[197] *Enhancing Investor Protection and the Regulation of Securities Markets—Part II: Testimony before the U.S. Senate Committee on Banking, Housing, and Urban Affairs*, 111th Congress, 1st session, p.9 (2009) (Testimony of Ms. Rita Bolger).

main assumptions behind rating methodologies and models. Furthermore, when those models change or errors are discovered, the market should be notified."[198] Mr. George Miller, Executive Director of the American Securitization Forum, added that he "strongly supports enhanced disclosure of securitization ratings methods and processes, including information relating to the use of ratings models and key assumptions utilized by those models."[199] The Council of Institutional Investors wrote in a letter to Senator Dodd that it supports these reforms designed to "improve the transparency of rating methodologies and assumptions and make rating agencies truly accountable to the investors that depend on them."[200]

Another disclosure that the NRSROs will have to make regards due diligence services. Subsection (s) provides the findings and conclusions of any third-party due diligence report obtained by the issuer or underwriter of an asset-backed security shall be made public, in a format to be determined by the SEC. The disclosures shall be in a manner that allows the public to determine the adequacy and level of due diligence services provided by a third party. Many analysts point to the decline of due diligence as a factor that contributed to the poor performance of asset-backed securities during the crisis. Professor John Coffee described the effect of poor due diligence in the credit rating industry in testimony for the Senate Banking Committee: "Unlike other gatekeepers, the credit rating agencies do not perform due diligence or make its performance a precondition of their ratings. In contrast, accountants are, quite literally, bean counters who do conduct audits. But the credit rating agencies do not make any significant effort to verify the facts on which their models rely (as they freely conceded to this Committee in earlier testimony here). Rather, they simply accept the representations and data provided them by issuers, loan originators and underwriters. The problem this presents is obvious and fundamental: no model, however well designed, can outperform its information inputs—Garbage, In; Garbage Out.... Ultimately, unless the users of credit ratings believe that ratings are based on the real facts and not just a hypothetical set of facts, the credibility of ratings, particularly in the field of structured finance, will remain tarnished, and private housing finance in the U.S. will remain starved and underfunded because it will be denied access to the broader capital markets."[201] Ms. Barbara Roper, Director of Investor Protection at the Consumer Federation of America, also believes that this provision is important. She wrote in congressional testimony that new legislation should address "lack of due diligence regarding information on which ratings are based."[202]

[¶ 54,482] Section 933. State of mind in private actions

Section 933 was introduced by Senator Reed. It provides that the enforcement and penalty provisions applicable to statements made by a credit rating agency shall apply in the same manner and to the same extent as to statements made by a registered public accounting firm or a securities analyst, and such statements shall not be deemed forward looking statements. In actions for money damages brought against a credit rating agency or a controlling person, it shall be sufficient for pleading any required state of mind in relation to such action, that the complaint state facts giving rise to a strong inference that the credit rating agency knowingly or recklessly failed to conduct a reasonable investigation of the factual elements of the rated security, or failed to obtain reasonable verification of such factual elements from independent sources that it considered to be competent.

Section 933 specifies that, for purposes of passing the pleading test of the Private Securities Litigation Reform Act, plaintiffs need not plead that the CRA "knowingly or recklessly" engaged in a deceptive misrepresentation or omission in communicating with investors, but instead requires only that they plead that the CRA "knowingly or recklessly failed ... to conduct a reasonable investigation ... with respect to ... factual elements ... or to obtain reasonable verification of such ... elements ... "

---

[198] *Securitization of Assets: Problems and Solutions: Testimony before the U.S. Senate Committee on Banking, Housing, and Urban Affairs*, 111th Congress, 1st session, p.12 (2009) (Testimony of Dr. William Irving).

[199] *Securitization of Assets: Problems and Solutions: Testimony before the U.S. Senate Committee on Banking, Housing, and Urban Affairs*, 111th Congress, 1st session, p.25 (2009) (Testimony of Mr. George Miller).

[200] Mr. Jeff Mahoney, Council of Institutional Investors, letter to Senator Dodd, p. 3, November 18, 2009.

[201] *Examining Proposals to Enhance the Regulation of Credit Rating Agencies: Testimony before the U.S. Senate Committee on Banking, Housing, and Urban Affairs*, 111th Congress, 1st session, pp.1-2 (2009) (Testimony of Professor John Coffee).

[202] *Enhancing Investor Protection and the Regulation of Securities Markets—Part II: Testimony before the U.S. Senate Committee on Banking, Housing, and Urban Affairs*, 111th Congress, 1st session, p.8 (2009) (Testimony of Ms. Barbara Roper).

The Section permits plaintiffs to more easily pass the motion to dismiss stage of litigation. It does not change the ultimate standard used by a fact-finder in determining whether the basic elements of 10b-5 have been met.

Columbia University Law Professor John C. Coffee testified before the Committee that this provision "struck a very sensible compromise in my judgment. It created a standard of liability for the rating agencies, but one with which they easily could comply (if they tried)." He opined that this "language does not truly expose rating agencies to any serious risk of liability—at least if they either conduct a reasonable investigation themselves or obtain verification from others (such as a due diligence firm) that they reasonably believed to be competent and independent . . . so that a rating agency would be fully protected when it received such a certification from an independent due diligence firm that covered the basic factual elements in its model."

Professor Coffee further testified, "The case for this limited litigation threat is that it is unsafe and unsound to let rating agencies remain willfully ignorant. Over the last decade, they have essentially been issuing hypothetical ratings in structured finance transactions based on hypothetical assumed facts provided them by issuers and underwriters. Such conduct is inherently reckless; the damage that it caused is self-evident, and the proposed language would end this state of affairs (without creating anything approaching liability for negligence)."[203]

[¶ 54,483] *Section 934. Referring tips to law enforcement or regulatory authorities*

Section 934 provides that each NRSRO will refer to the appropriate law enforcement or regulatory authorities any information that the NRSRO receives and finds credible that alleges that an issuer of securities rated by the NRSRO has committed or is committing a violation of law that has not been adjudicated by a Federal or State court. This is in effect a mandatory whistleblowing provision, and exceptions could be created to cover circumstances when the compliance officer concluded that the information was false or unreliable. This provision requires the NRSRO to determine whether it feels the information is credible, but does not require the NRSRO to undertake extensive fact finding or analysis or to determine whether a violation of law has occurred.

[¶ 54,484] *Section 935. Consideration of information from sources other than the issuer in rating decisions*

Section 935 provides that NRSROs must consider information about an issuer that the NRSRO has, or receives from a source other than the issuer, that the NRSRO finds credible and potentially significant to a rating decision. The Section does not require an NRSRO to initiate a search for such information. The information is expected to be evaluated on its own merits as to whether it indeed should affect the rating. The Committee believes that if the NRSRO possesses credible information that is significant to a rating decision about an issuer, it should consider it even if it has not undertaken to independently verify information it has received from an issuer.

NRSROs use data received from issuers in formulating a rating and may not undertake to verify it. For example, one NRSRO states:

While [the NRSRO] has obtained information from sources it believes to be reliable, [the NRSRO] does not perform an audit and undertakes no duty of due diligence or independent verification of any information it receives.

This type of disclosure and policy may create the appearance that the NRSRO could receive credible, material information about the creditworthiness of an issuer from an outside source but choose not to consider it in formulating a rating. Such information could come from a highly credible press report, information from a knowledgeable industry insider, views from a former employee or other source.

Mr. James Gellert, Chairman of Rapid Ratings International, Inc., wrote in congressional testimony that "we believe that, if a rating agency's business model is to provide qualitative assessments of an entity or pool of assets collateralizing a structured product, it should take into account all data it can reasonably attain and qualify as being reliable."[204]

---

[203] *Enhancing Investor Protection and the Regulation of Securities Markets—Part I: Testimony before the U.S. Senate Committee on Banking, Housing, and Urban Affairs*, 111th Congress, 1st session (2009) (Testimony of Professor John Coffee).

[204] *Examining Proposals to Enhance the Regulation of Credit Rating Agencies: Testimony before the U.S. Senate Committee on Banking, Housing, and Urban Affairs*, 111th Congress, 1st session, p.18 (2009) (Testimony of Mr. James Gellert).

[¶ 54,485] **Section 936. Qualification standards for credit rating analysts**

Section 936 directs the SEC to issue rules reasonably designed to ensure that any person employed by an NRSRO to perform credit ratings meets standards of training, experience, and competence necessary to produce accurate ratings; and is tested for knowledge of the credit rating process.

Following the devastating impact on investors, the economy, and families that erroneous ratings had during the credit crisis, the Committee feels there is need to improve the analysis underlying credit ratings. This requirement is intended to improve the quality of ratings by increasing the skills of those who formulate them. This section would require credit rating analysts to meet high professional standards for their industry, just as investment advisers, registered representatives, and auditors do for theirs.

Mr. Mark Froeba testified before the Committee about concerns that "Every rating agency employs 'rating analysts' but there are no independent standards governing this 'profession': there are no minimum educational requirements, there is no common code of ethical conduct, and there is no continuing education obligation. Even where each agency has its own standards for these things, the standards differ widely from agency to agency. One agency may assign a senior analyst with a PhD in statistics to rate a complex transaction; another might assign a junior analyst with a BA in international relations to the same transaction. The staffing decision might appear to investors as yet another tool to manipulate the rating outcome."[205]

[¶ 54,486] **Section 937. Timing of regulations**

Section 937 directs the SEC to issue final regulations within 1 year of the date of enactment of the Act.

[¶ 54,487] **Section 938. Universal ratings symbols**

Section 938 was introduced by Senator Menendez. It requires NRSROs to clearly define any symbols used to denote a credit rating, and apply any such symbols in a consistent manner to all types of securities and money market instruments to which they are applied. The Committee believes that an NRSRO's credit rating symbol should have the same meaning about creditworthiness when it is applied to any issuer—the same symbol should not have different meaning depending on the issuer. This Section does not dictate the meaning of any credit rating—whether it refers to an issuer's likelihood of default, ability to pay on time, or other factors. Also, this Section does not prevent an NRSRO from using distinct sets of symbols to denote credit ratings for different types of securities.

Some observers have expressed concerns that some rating agencies apply stricter standards to municipal debt than to corporate debt. Consumer Federation of America and Americans for Financial Reform stated, "Most municipal bonds are rated on a different, more conservative rating scale than corporate bonds. This dual system employed by the largest rating agencies ends up costing state and local governments and their taxpayers over a billion dollars a year, a cost these governments can ill afford. Bond issuers, be they corporate bond issuers or municipal bond issuers, should be rated on the same standard—the likelihood of default."[206] They recommended that the legislation require each NRSRO to: (1) establish, maintain and enforce written policies and procedures designed to assess the risk that investors in securities and money market instruments may not receive payment in accordance with the terms of such securities and instruments, (2) define clearly any credit rating symbols used by the organization, and (3) apply such credit rating symbols in a consistent manner for all types of securities and money market instruments."[207] The National Association of State Treasurers stated that "Bond ratings have a direct impact on the interest rates at which governments can issue their bonds to finance the construction of critically-need infrastructure, and the ratings given to these bonds by the major credit ratings agencies play a large role in determining the cost that taxpayers assume when their governments invest in infrastructure . . . We believe that ratings applied to municipal bonds should indicate the same risk as the identical rating applied to a corporate bond, while also recognizing the need for rela-

---

[205] *Examining Proposals to Enhance the Regulation of Credit Rating Agencies: Testimony before the U.S. Senate Committee on Banking, Housing, and Urban Affairs,* 111th Congress, 1st session (2009) (Testimony of Mr. Mark Froeba).

[206] Consumer Federation of America, Letter to Senators Dodd and Shelby, November 24, 2009.

[207] Letter to Chairman Dodd and Ranking Member Shelby, November 24, 2009.

tive ratings among municipal issuers. We further believe that ratings should measure the ability of an issuer to meet its obligation to investors as promised in the bond documents, such obligation primarily being to pay its debt service on time and in full."[208]

[¶ 54,488] Section 939. Government Accountability Office study and federal agency review of required uses of nationally recognized statistical rating organization ratings

Section 939 directs the GAO to study the scope of Federal and State laws and regulations with respect to the regulation of securities markets, banking, insurance, and other areas that require the use of ratings issued by NRSROs. Consulting with a range of regulators and market participants, GAO shall evaluate the necessity of such rating requirements and the potential impact on markets and investors of removing them. Within 2 years of the date of enactment of this Act, the GAO shall report to Congress with recommendations on which ratings requirements, if any, could be removed with minimal disruption to the markets and whether the financial markets and investors would benefit from the rescission of the ratings requirements identified by the study.

Within one year of the completion of GAO's report, the SEC and other financial regulators shall review rating requirements in their regulations, and shall remove such rating requirements, unless they determine that there is no reasonable alternative standard of creditworthiness to replace a credit rating, and that removing the rating requirement would be inconsistent with the purposes of the statute that authorized the regulation and not in the public interest.

Currently, there are numerous instances in government rules and regulations that require the use of NRSRO ratings. This gives the ratings a tacit government sanction. Many observers have recommended to the Senate Banking Committee to enact policy to remove these references to ratings. Professor Lawrence White advised "Eliminate regulatory reliance on ratings—eliminate the force of law that has been accorded to these third-party judgments. The institutional participants in the bond markets could then more readily (with appropriate oversight by financial regulators) make use of a wider set of providers of information, and the bond information market would be opened to new ideas and new entry in a way that has not been possible for over 70 years."

One concern is that the reliance on ratings has become so prevalent that the abrupt removal of ratings could cause unintended consequences and negative effects in the market. Therefore, the Committee provides for a GAO study of the reliance on ratings. Supporting the caution behind this approach, Mr. George Miller, Executive Director of the American Securitization Forum, wrote in congressional testimony "ASF believes that credit ratings are an important part of existing regulatory regimes, and that steps aimed at reducing or eliminating the use of ratings in regulation should be considered carefully, to avoid undue disruption to market function and efficiency." The Investor's Working Group[209] and Mr. Andrew Davidson[210] also support the ultimate goal of reducing the reliance on ratings. The studies would identify those requirements for NRSRO ratings for which there is a necessity and those requirements which could be removed with minimal disruption to the markets over a sufficiently long time period to fully explore possible unintended consequences, alternative measures of creditworthiness and other factors which can ultimately lead to strengthening the financial markets.

[¶ 54,489] Section 939A. Securities and Exchange Commission study on strengthening credit rating agency independence

Section 939A directs the SEC to conduct a study of the independence of NRSROs, evaluate the management of conflicts of interest by NRSROs, and evaluate the potential impact of rules prohibiting an NRSRO that provided a rating to an issuer from providing other services to the issuer. The Committee intends this study to include an identification of the types and scope of services provided by NRSROs and which of these services raises a potential for raising a conflict that could change a rating and to cover other relevant issues identified by GAO.

---

[208] Letter dated November 17, 2009.

[209] U.S. Financial Regulatory Reform: An Investor's Perspective, Investor's Working Group, July 2009.

[210] Securitization of Assets: Problems and Solutions: Testimony before the U.S. Senate Committee on Banking, Housing, and Urban Affairs, 111th Congress, 1st session (2009) (Testimony of Mr. Andrew Davidson).

[¶ 54,490] **Section 939B. Government Accountability Office study on alternative business models**

Section 939B directs the GAO to conduct a study on alternative means of compensating NRSROs in order to create incentives for NRSROs to provide more accurate ratings and any statutory changes that would be required to facilitate these changes. The GAO will submit this report, with recommendations, within one year of passage of the Act. The predominant NRSRO business model involves the issuer paying for the rating, while a small number of NRSROs rely on subscription fees from users. The Committee asks the GAO to analyze which model is likely to produce the most accurate ratings.

The Committee recognizes that conflicts of interest exist for NRSROs and is interested in an analysis of how and whether they are effectively managed so that they do not unfairly influence ratings decisions. The study should include any recommendations for legislative, regulatory or voluntary industry action. Mr. Stephen Joynt, President and CEO of Fitch, testified "The majority of Fitch's revenues are fees paid by issuers for assigning and maintaining ratings. This is supplemented by fees paid by a variety of market participants for research subscriptions. The primary benefit of this model is that it enables Fitch to be in a position to offer analytical coverage on every asset class in every capital market—and to make our rating opinions freely available to the market in realtime, thus enabling the market to freely and fully assess the quality of our work. Fitch has long acknowledged the potential conflicts of being an issuer-paid rating agency. Fitch believes that the potential conflicts of interest in the 'issuer pays' model have been, and continue to be, effectively managed through a broad range of policies, procedures and organizational structures aimed at reinforcing the objectivity, integrity and independence of its credit ratings, combined with enhanced and ongoing regulatory oversight."

Mark Froeba, Principal at PF2 Securities Evaluations, Inc. and former Senior Vice President at Moody's, testified that "there are those who believe that real rating agency reform requires a return to an investor-pay model. But there may be a third way, a business model that preserves the issuer-pay 'delivery system' (the issuer still gets the bill for the rating) but incorporates the incentives of the investor-pay model. . . . These and other reforms are necessary not only to restore investor confidence in ratings but also to prevent future ratings-related financial crises."[211]

[¶ 54,491] **Section 939C. Government Accountability Office study on the creation of an independent professional analysts organization**

Section 939C directs the GAO to conduct a study on the feasibility and merits of creating an independent professional organization for NRSRO rating analysts that would establish independent standards for governing the rating analyst profession, establishing a code of ethical conduct, and overseeing the rating analyst profession. The GAO shall submit a report to the relevant congressional committees within one year of passage of the Act. In the aftermath of the devastating financial crisis caused in part by poor credit ratings, the Committee is interested in exploring means to increase the skills of the professionals who produce credit ratings. This Section directs the GAO to explore the potential impact of an independent professional analysts organization. Mark Froeba, Principal at PF2 Securities Evaluations, Inc. and former Senior Vice President at Moody's, testified that he recommended the creation of "an independent professional organization for rating analysts. Every rating agency employs 'rating analysts' but there are no independent standards governing this 'profession': there are no minimum educational requirements, there is no common code of ethical conduct, and there is no continuing education obligation. Even where each agency has its own standards for these things, the standards differ widely from agency to agency. One agency may assign a senior analyst with a PhD in statistics to rate a complex transaction; another might assign a junior analyst with a BA in international relations to the same transaction . . . Creating one independent professional organization to which rating analysts from all rating agencies must belong will ensure uniform standards especially ethical standards—across all the rating agencies. It would also provide a forum external to the agencies where rating analysts might bring confidential complaints about ethical concerns. An independent organization could track and report the nature and number of these complaints and alert regulators if there are patterns in the complaints, problems at particular agencies, and even whether there are problems with particular managers at one rating agency. Finally, such an

---

[211] *Examining Proposals to Enhance the Regulation of Credit Rating Agencies: Testimony before the U.S. Senate Committee on Banking, Housing, and Urban Affairs*, 111th Congress, 1st session, p.18 (2009) (Testimony of Mr. Mark Froeba).

organization should have the power to discipline analysts for unethical behavior."[212]

Subtitle D

[¶ 54,500] *Section 941. Regulation of credit risk retention*

This section requires securitizers, defined as those who issue, organize, or initiate asset-backed securities, to retain an economic interest in a material portion of the credit risk for any asset that securitizers transfer, sell, or convey to a third party. The provision intends to create incentives that will prevent a recurrence of the excesses and abuses that preceded the crisis, restore investor confidence in asset-backed finance, and permit securitization markets to resume their important role as sources of credit for households and businesses.

The Committee's investigation into the causes of the financial crisis identified abuses of the securitization process as a major contributing factor. Two problems emerged in the crisis. First, under the "originate to distribute" model, loans were expressly to be sold into securitization pools, which meant that the lenders did not expect to bear the credit risk of borrower default. This led to significant deterioration in credit and loan underwriting standards, particularly in residential mortgages. According to the testimony of Dr. William Irving, Portfolio Manager of Fidelity Investments:

> Without a doubt, securitization played a role in this crisis. Most importantly, the "originate-to-distribute" model of credit provision seemed to spiral out of control. Under this model, intermediaries found a way to lend money profitably without worrying if the loans were paid back. The loan originator, the warehouse facilitator, the security designer, the credit rater, and the marketing and product-placement professionals all received a fee for their part in helping to create and distribute the securities. These fees were generally linked to the size of the transaction and most of them were paid up front. So long as there were willing buyers, this situation created enormous incentive to originate mortgage loans solely for the purpose of realizing that up-front intermediation profit.[213]

Second, it proved impossible for investors in asset-backed securities to assess the risks of the underlying assets, particularly when those assets were resecuritized into complex instruments like collateralized debt obligations (CDOs) and CDO-squared. With the onset of the crisis, there was widespread uncertainty regarding the true financial condition of holders of asset-backed securities, freezing interbank lending and constricting the general flow of credit. Complexity and opacity in securitization markets created the conditions that allowed the financial shock from the subprime mortgage sector to spread into a global financial crisis, as Professor Patricia A. McCoy testified before the Committee:

> General investor panic is [another] reason for contagion. Even in transactions involving no nonprime collateral, concerns about the nonprime crisis had a ripple effect, making it hard for companies and cities across-the-board to secure financing. Banks did not want to lend to other banks out of fear that undisclosed nonprime losses might be lurking on their books. Investors did not want to buy other types of securitized bonds, such as those backed by student loans or car loans, because they lost faith in ratings and could not assess the quality of the underlying collateral.[214]

Section 941 directs the Federal banking agencies and the SEC to jointly prescribe regulations to require any securitizer to retain a material portion of the credit risk of any asset that the securitizer, through the issuance of an asset-backed security, transfers, sells, or conveys to a third party. When securitizers retain a material amount of risk, they have "skin in the game," aligning their economic interests with those of investors in asset-backed securities. Securitizers who retain risk have a strong incentive to monitor the quality of the assets they purchase from originators, package into securities, and sell.

The regulations will prohibit securitizers from hedging or otherwise transferring the credit risk they are required to retain. The prohibition does not extend to hedging risks other

---

[212] *Examining Proposals to Enhance the Regulation of Credit Rating Agencies: Testimony before the U.S. Senate Committee on Banking, Housing, and Urban Affairs*, 111th Congress, 1st session, p.18 (2009) (Testimony of Mr. Mark Froeba).

[213] *Securitization of Assets: Problems and Solutions: Testimony before the U.S. Senate Committee on Banking, Housing, and Urban Affairs*, 111th Congress, 1st session, (2009) (Testimony of Dr. William Irving).

[214] *Securitization of Assets: Problems and Solutions: Testimony before the U.S. Senate Committee on Banking, Housing, and Urban Affairs*, 111th Congress, 1st session, (2009) (Testimony of Patricia A. McCoy).

than credit risk (such as interest rate risk) associated with the retained assets or position. Originators (defined as persons who through the extension of credit or otherwise create financial assets that collateralize an asset-backed security, and sell assets to a securitizer) will come under increasing market discipline because securitizers who retain risk will be unwilling to purchase poor-quality assets. Thus, the bill does not require that the regulations impose risk retention obligations on originators. Risk retention may be divided between securitizers and originators only if the regulators consider that assets being securitized do not have characteristics of low credit risk, that conditions in securitization markets are creating incentives for imprudent origination, and that allocating part of the risk retention obligation to originators would not prevent consumers and businesses from obtaining credit on reasonable terms.

There is broad support for risk retention by securitizers. The provision was included in the Treasury Department's 2009 legislative proposal.[215] Mr. George Miller, Executive Director of the American Securitization Forum, testified before the Committee that "we support the concept of requiring retention of a meaningful economic interest in securitized loans as a means of creating a better alignment of incentives among transaction participants."[216] The Group of Thirty recommended risk retention as part of broad financial reform:

> The healthy redevelopment of securitized credit markets requires a restoration of market confidence in the adequacy and sustainability of credit underwriting standards. To help achieve this, regulators should require regulated financial institutions to retain a meaningful portion of the credit risk they are packaging into securitized and other structured credit products.[217]

The Consumer Federation of America[218], CalPERS[219], and the Investor's Working Group[220] also support this provision.

The Committee believes that implementation of risk retention obligations should recognize the differences in securitization practices for various asset classes. Witnesses before the Committee and a number of market participants have indicated that a "one size fits all" approach to risk retention may adversely affect certain securitization markets. For example, Mr. J. Christopher Hoeffel of the Commercial Mortgage Securities Association testified that "[P]olicymakers must ensure that any regulatory reforms are tailored to address the specific needs of each securitization asset class. Again, CMSA does not oppose these [risk retention] measures *per se*, but emphasizes that they should be tailored to reflect key differences between the different asset-backed securities markets."[221] Accordingly, the bill requires that the initial joint rulemaking include separate components addressing individual asset classes—home mortgages, commercial mortgages, commercial loans, auto loans, and any other asset class that the regulators deem appropriate. The Committee expects that these regulations will recognize differences in the assets securitized, in existing risk management practices, and in the structure of asset-backed securities, and that regulators will make appropriate adjustments to the amount of risk retention required.

In addition, the risk retention rules may provide a total or partial exemption for any securitization, as may be appropriate in the public interest and for the protection of investors. The Committee expects that asset-backed securities backed by the full faith and credit of the United States, or where the underlying assets were guaranteed by an agency of the United States, would qualify for such an exemption.

---

[215] *Title IX—Additional Improvements to Financial Markets Regulation Subtitle D*, U.S. Department of the Treasury, 2009, www.financialstability.gov.

[216] *Securitization of Assets: Problems and Solutions: Testimony before the U.S. Senate Committee on Banking, Housing, and Urban Affairs*, 111th Congress, 1st session, p.19 (2009) (Testimony of Mr. George Miller).

[217] *Financial Reform: A Framework for Financial Stability*, Group of Thirty, p. 49, January 15, 2009.

[218] *Enhancing Investor Protection and the Regulation of Securities Markets—Part II: Testimony before the U.S. Senate Committee on Banking, Housing, and Urban Affairs*, 111th Congress, 1st session (2009) (Testimony of Ms. Barbara Roper).

[219] *Regulating Hedge Funds and Other Private Investment Pools: Testimony before the Subcommittee on Securities, Insurance, and Investment of the U.S. Senate Committee on Banking, Housing, and Urban Affairs*, 111th Congress, 1st session, (2009) (Testimony of Mr. Joseph Dear).

[220] *U.S. Financial Regulatory Reform: An Investor's Perspective*, Investor's Working Group, July 2009.

[221] [*Securitization of Assets: Problems and Solutions: Testimony before the U.S. Senate Committee on Banking, Housing, and Urban Affairs*, 111th Congress, 1st session, (2009) (Testimony of Mr. J. Christopher Hoeffel).]

¶54,500

The section provides a baseline risk retention amount of 5 percent of the credit risk in any securitized asset. The figure may be set higher at the regulators' discretion, or it may be reduced below 5 percent when the assets securitized meet standards of low credit risk to be established by rule for the various asset classes. The Committee believes that regulators should have flexibility in setting risk retention levels, to encourage recovery of securitization markets and to accommodate future market developments and innovations, but that in all cases the amount of risk retained should be material, in order to create meaningful incentives for sound and sustainable securitization practices.

The section also authorizes regulators to make exemptions, exceptions, or adjustments to the risk retention rules, provided that any such exemptions, exceptions, or adjustments help ensure high underwriting standards, encourage appropriate risk management practices, improve access to credit on reasonable terms, or are otherwise in the public interest.

[¶ 54,501] *Section 942. Disclosures and reporting for asset-backed securities*

Section 942 seeks to improve transparency in asset-backed securities. It directs the SEC to adopt regulations requiring each issuer of an asset-backed security to disclose, for each tranche or class of security, information regarding the assets backing that security. These disclosures shall be in a format that facilitates comparison of such data across securities in similar types of asset classes. Issuers of asset-backed securities shall disclose asset-level or loan-level data necessary for investors to independently perform due diligence. This data would include data having unique identifiers relating to loan brokers or originators, the nature and extent of the compensation of the broker or originator of the assets backing the security, and the amount of risk retention by the originator or the securitizer of such assets. The Committee does not expect that disclosure of data about individual borrowers would be required in cases such as securitizations of credit card or automobile loans or leases, where asset pools typically include many thousands of credit agreements, where individual loan data would not be useful to investors, and where disclosure might raise privacy concerns.

Mr. George Miller, Executive Director of the American Securitization Forum, wrote in testimony for the Committee that "ASF supports increased transparency and standardization in the securitization markets, and related improvements to the securitization market infrastructure.... ASF believes that every mortgage loan should be assigned a unique identification number at origination, which would facilitate the identification and tracking of individual loans as they are sold or financed in the secondary market, including via RMBS securitization."[222] The Investor's Working Group wrote in a report that "the SEC should develop a regulatory regime for such asset-backed securities that would require issuers to make prospectuses available for potential investors in advance of their purchasing decisions. These prospectuses should disclose important information about the securities, including the terms of the offering, information about the sponsor, the issuer and the trust, and details about the collateral supporting the securities. Such new rules would give investors critical information they need to perform due diligence on offerings prior to investing. It would also create better opportunities for due diligence by the underwriters of such securities, thus adding additional levels of oversight of the quality and appropriateness of structured offerings."[223] Professor Patricia McCoy wrote in testimony "the SEC should require securitizers to provide investors with all of the loan-level data they need to assess the risks involved.... In addition, the SEC should require securitizers and servicers to provide loan-level information on a monthly basis on the performance of each loan and the incidence of loan modifications and recourse."[224] CalPERS[225], Mr. Andrew Davidson[226], and Dr. William Irving[227] also supported enhanced disclosure in testimony before the Committee.

---

[222] *Securitization of Assets: Problems and Solutions: Testimony before the U.S. Senate Committee on Banking, Housing, and Urban Affairs*, 111th Congress, 1st session, p.18 (2009) (Testimony of Mr. George Miller).

[223] *U.S. Financial Regulatory Reform: An Investor's Perspective*, Investor's Working Group, p.14, July 2009.

[224] *Securitization of Assets: Problems and Solutions: Testimony before the U.S. Senate Committee on Banking, Housing, and Urban Affairs*, 111th Congress, 1st session, p.13 (2009) (Testimony of Professor Patricia McCoy).

[225] *Regulating Hedge Funds and Other Private Investment Pools: Testimony before the Subcommittee on Securities, Insurance, and Investment of the U.S. Senate Committee on Banking, Housing, and Urban Affairs*, 111th Congress, 1st session (2009) (Testimony of Mr. Joseph Dear).

[226] *Securitization of Assets: Problems and Solutions: Testimony before the U.S. Senate Committee on Banking, Housing, and Urban Affairs*, 111th Congress, 1st session (2009) (Testimony of Mr. Andrew Davidson).

[227] *Securitization of Assets: Problems and Solutions: Testimony before the U.S. Senate Committee on Banking, Housing, and Urban Affairs*, 111th Congress, 1st session, p. (2009) (Testimony of Dr. William Irving).

[¶ 54,502] Section 943. Representations and warranties in asset-backed offerings

This section directs the SEC to prescribe regulations on the use of representations and warranties in the market for asset-backed securities that require each NRSRO to include in any report accompanying a credit rating a description of the representations, warranties, and enforcement mechanisms available to investors and how they differ from the representations, warranties, and enforcement mechanisms in issuances of similar securities. The SEC will also prescribe rules to require any originator to disclose fulfilled repurchase requests across all trusts aggregated by the originator, so that investors may identify asset originators with clear underwriting deficiencies.

This provision was included in the Treasury Department's legislative proposal.[228] Moody's Investor Services described the use of representations and warranties and pointed out weaknesses in their current usage:

> [T]he seller or originator in structured securities makes representations and warranties regarding the characteristics of the loans they sell into securitizations. In light of recent events, typical representations and warranties should be strengthened. In addition to other matters, the seller could provide representations and warranties to investors as to the quality and accuracy of all information presented to investors, rating agencies and other market participants. The value of representations and warranties is diminished when made by entities that are not financially strong, as such entities may be less able to fulfill their obligation to repurchase loans that breach the representations and warranties.[229]

The Committee believes that enhanced disclosure will allow investors to better evaluate representations and warranties and create incentives for issuers to insist that originators back up their representations and warranties with real financial resources.

[¶ 54,503] Section 944. Exempted transactions under the Securities Act of 1933

Section 944 removes the Securities Act of 1933 exemption of transactions involving offers or sales of one or more promissory notes directly secured by a first lien on a single parcel of real estate upon which is located a dwelling or other residential or commercial structure.

[¶ 54,504] Section 945. Due diligence analysis and disclosure in asset-backed securities issues

Section 945 directs the SEC to issue rules that require any issuer of an asset-backed security to perform a due diligence analysis of the assets underlying the asset-backed security; and to disclose the nature of this analysis. Professor John Coffee, in congressional testimony, called for action to "re-introduce due diligence into the securities offering process."[230]

Subtitle E

[¶ 54,520] Section 951. Shareholder vote on executive compensation disclosures

Section 951 provides that any proxy or consent or authorization for an annual or other meeting of the shareholders will include a separate resolution subject to shareholder advisory vote to approve the compensation of executives. The Committee believes that shareholders, as the owners of the corporation, have a right to express their opinion collectively on the appropriateness of executive pay. The vote must be tabulated and reported, but the result is not binding on the board or management.

In crafting this Section, there was consideration of alternative time intervals, such as votes every three years, and of whether votes after the first year should be triggered only by a failure to receive a minimum percentage of votes in support of the compensation plan. This provision would not preclude an issuer from seeking more specific shareholder opinion through separate

---

[228] Title IX—Additional Improvements to Financial Markets Regulation Subtitle D, U.S. Department of the Treasury, 2009, www.financialstability.gov.

[229] Moody's Proposes Enhancements to Non-Prime RMBS Securitization, Moody's, Special Report, p.2, September 25, 2007.

[230] Enhancing Investor Protection and the Regulation of Securities Markets—Part I: Testimony before the U.S. Senate Committee on Banking, Housing, and Urban Affairs, 111th Congress, 1st session, p.53 (2009) (Testimony of Professor John Coffee).

votes on cash compensation, golden parachute policy, severance or other aspects of compensation.

A "say on pay" proposal was included in the Treasury Department's legislative proposal. The economic crisis revealed instances in which corporate executives received very high compensation despite the very poor performance by their firms. For example, Mr. Charles O. Prince III, the former chief executive of Citigroup, "collected $110 million while presiding over the evaporation of roughly $64 billion in market value. He left Citigroup in November with an exit package worth $68 million, including $29.5 million in accumulated stock, a $1.7 million pension, an office and assistant, and a car and a driver. Citigroup's board also awarded him a cash bonus for 2007 worth about $10 million, largely based on his performance in 2006 when the bank's results were better. Citigroup has announced write-offs worth roughly $20 billion and its share has plummeted over 60 percent from last year's high."[231]

Ms. Ann Yerger, representing the Council of Institutional Investors, wrote in congressional testimony for the Committee that "the Council believes an annual, advisory shareowner vote on executive compensation would efficiently and effectively provide boards with useful information about whether investors view the company's compensation practices to be in shareowners' best interests. Nonbinding shareowner votes on pay would serve as a direct referendum on the decisions of the compensation committee and would offer a more targeted way to signal shareowner discontent than withholding votes from committee members. They might also induce compensation committees to be more careful about doling out rich rewards, to avoid the embarrassment of shareowner rejection at the ballot box. In addition, compensation committees looking to actively rein in executive compensation could use the results of advisory shareowner votes to stand up to excessively demanding officers or compensation consultants."[232]

The UK has implemented "say on pay" policy. Professor John Coates in testimony for the Senate Banking Committee stated that the UK's experience has been positive; "different researchers have conducted several investigations of this kind ... These findings suggest that say-on-pay legislation would have a positive impact on corporate governance in the U.S. While the two legal contexts are not identical, there is no evidence in the existing literature to suggest that the differences would turn what would be a good idea in the UK into a bad one in the U.S."

Other observers who support "say on pay" include the Consumer Federation of America, AFSCME, and the Investor's Working Group.

[¶ 54,521] Section 952. Compensation committee independence

Section 952 directs the SEC to direct the national securities exchanges and national securities associations to prohibit the listing of any security of an issuer that does not comply with independent compensation committee standards. In determining whether a director is independent, the national securities exchanges should consider the source of compensation of a member of the board of directors of an issuer, including any consulting, advisory, or other compensatory fee paid by the issuer to such member of the board of directors; and whether a member of the board of directors of an issuer is affiliated with the issuer, a subsidiary of the issuer, or an affiliate of a subsidiary of the issuer. Any compensation counsel or adviser shall be independent.

The issuer's proxy or consent materials must disclose whether the compensation committee has used the advice of a compensation consultant and whether the committee has raised any conflict of interest. However, the provision does not require the use of compensation consultants. The Section also directs the SEC to conduct a study of the use of compensation consultants and their impact. The Treasury Department's legislative proposal included an independent compensation committee.

The Council of Institutional Investors wrote in a letter to Senator Dodd "Compensation committees and their external consultants play a key role in the pay-setting process. Conflicts of interest contribute to a ratcheting up effect for executive pay, however, and should thus be minimized and disclosed. Reforms included in the discussion draft would help ensure that compensation committees are free of conflicts and receive unbiased advice."

---

[231] "Chiefs' Pay Under Fire At Capitol," The New York Times, March 8, 2008.
[232] *Protecting Shareholders and Enhancing Public Confidence by Improving Corporate Governance: Testimony before the Subcommittee on Securities, Insurance, and Investment of the U.S. Senate Committee on Banking, Housing, and Urban Affairs*, 111th Congress, 1st session, (2009) (Testimony of Ms. Ann Yerger).

[¶ 54,522] **Section 953. Executive compensation disclosures**

Section 953 directs the SEC to require each issuer to disclose in the annual proxy statement of the issuer a clear description of any compensation required to be disclosed under the SEC executive compensation forms and information that shows the relationship between executive compensation and the financial performance of the issuers, taking into account the change in the value of the shares, dividends and distributions. It has become apparent that a significant concern of shareholders is the relationship between executive pay and the company's financial performance for the benefit of shareholders. Shareholders are keenly interested when executive compensation is increasing sharply at the same time as financial performance is falling.

The Committee believes that these disclosures will add to corporate responsibility as firms will have to more clearly disclose and explain executive pay. Ms. Ann Yerger wrote in congressional testimony on behalf of the Council of Institutional Investors "of primary concern to the Council is full and clear disclosure of executive pay. As U.S. Supreme Court Justice Louis Brandeis noted, 'sunlight is the best disinfectant.' Transparency of executive pay enables shareowners to evaluate the performance of the compensation committee and board in setting executive pay, to assess pay-for-performance links and to optimize their role of overseeing executive compensation through such means as proxy voting."

This disclosure about the relationship between executive compensation and the financial performance of the issuer may include a clear graphic comparison of the amount of executive compensation and the financial performance of the issuer or return to investors and may take many forms. For example, a graph could have a horizontal axis of a number of years and a vertical axis with two scales, one for executive compensation and a second for financial performance of the issuer for each year.

[¶ 54,523] **Section 954. Recovery of erroneously awarded compensation**

Section 954 requires public companies to have a policy to recover money that they erroneously paid in incentive compensation to executives as a result of material noncompliance with accounting rules. This is money that the executive would not have received if the accounting was done properly and was not entitled to. This provision creates Section 10D of the Securities Exchange Act of 1934, which requires the SEC to direct the national securities exchanges and national securities associations to prohibit the listing of issuers who do not develop and implement a policy providing that, in the event that the issuer is required to prepare an accounting restatement due to the material noncompliance, the issuer will recover from any current or former executive officer of the issuer any compensation in excess of what would have been paid to the executive officer had correct accounting procedures been followed. This policy is required to apply to executive officers, a very limited number of employees, and is not required to apply to other employees. It does not require adjudication of misconduct in connection with the problematic accounting that required restatement.

The Committee believes it is unfair to shareholders for corporations to allow executives to retain compensation that they were awarded erroneously. This proposal will clarify that all issuers must have a policy in place to recover compensation based on inaccurate accounting so that shareholders do not have to embark on costly legal expenses to recoup their losses or so that executives must return monies that should belong to the shareholders. The Investor's Working Group wrote "federal clawback provisions on unearned executive pay should be strengthened."[233]

[¶ 54,524] **Section 955. Disclosure regarding employee and director hedging**

Section 955 directs the SEC to require each issuer to disclose in the annual proxy statement whether the employees or members of the board of the issuer are permitted to purchase financial instruments that are designed to hedge or offset any decrease in the market value of equity securities granted to employees by the issuer as part of an employee compensation. This will allow shareholders to know if executives are allowed to purchase financial instruments to effectively avoid compensation restrictions that they hold stock long-term, so that they will receive their compensation even in the case that their firm does not perform. Dr. Carr Bettis has written that derivatives instruments "provide a mechanism that insiders can use to trade on inside information prior to adverse corporate events without

---

[233] *U.S. Financial Regulatory Reform: An Investor's Perspective*, Investor's Working Group, July 2009.

the level of transparency typically associated with open market sales."[234]

[¶ 54,525] Section 956. Excessive compensation by holding companies of depository institutions

Section 956 amends Section 5 of the Bank Holding Company Act of 1956 to establish standards prohibiting as an unsafe and unsound practice any compensation plan of a bank holding company that provides an executive officer, employee, director, or principal shareholder with excessive compensation, fees, or benefits; or could lead to material financial loss to the bank holding company. This applies regulatory authority currently applicable to banks to their holding companies.

[¶ 54,526] Section 957. Voting by brokers

Section 957 amends the Securities Exchange Act of 1934 so that brokers who are not beneficial owners of a security cannot vote through company proxies unless the beneficial owner has instructed the broker to do so. The final vote tallies should reflect the wishes of the beneficial owners of the stock and not be affected by the wishes of the broker that holds the shares.

Subtitle F

[¶ 54,540] Section 961. Report and certification of internal supervisory controls

Section 961 directs the SEC to submit a report on SEC's conduct of examinations of registered entities, enforcement investigations, and review of corporate financial securities filings to the House Financial Services and Senate Banking Committees. Each report should contain an assessment of the SEC's internal supervisory controls and examination staff procedures; a certification of adequate supervisory controls by the Directors of the Divisions of Enforcement, Division of Corporation Finance, and Office of Compliance Inspection and Examinations; and a review by the U.S. Comptroller General attesting to the adequacy and effectiveness of the internal supervisory control structure and procedures.

The purpose of this Section is to promote complete and consistent performance of SEC staff examinations, investigations and reviews, and appropriate supervision of these activities, through internal supervisory controls. There have been numerous examples where securities misconduct has flourished and investors have been harmed due to failure to follow reasonable procedures. For example, the Inspector General found that the Enforcement Office of the Chief Accountant received numerous complaints alleging financial fraud committed by a public company over 21.2 years which were "not reviewed, analyzed or investigated" because "the referral procedures for monitoring the progress of referrals of complaints . . . were not followed in the 2005-2007 time period. For example, regular meetings to decide the disposition of referrals were being held." (SEC Office of Inspector General Report of Investigation, "Failure to Timely Investigate Allegations of Financial Fraud," February 26, 2010).

The massive fraud perpetrated by Bernard L. Madoff through a Ponzi scheme cost investors a tremendous amount of money and went undetected through failures in SEC exams and investigations. This illustrates the need for such internal supervisory controls. The failure of the SEC (or of FINRA) to identify the fraud before Mr. Madoff confessed to his sons and to law enforcement seriously damaged investor confidence in the effectiveness and competence of regulators. The Inspector General of the SEC, Mr. David Kotz, testified before the Committee about his study of the SEC's failure to find the Madoff fraud. The study found "that the SEC received more than ample information in the form of detailed and substantive complaints over the years to warrant a thorough and comprehensive examination and/or investigation of Bernard Madoff and BMIS for operating a Ponzi scheme, and that despite three examinations and two investigations being conducted, a thorough and competent investigation or examination was never performed. The OIG found that between June 1992 and December 2008 when Madoff confessed, the SEC received six substantive complaints that raised significant red flags concerning Madoff's hedge fund operations and should have led to questions about whether Madoff was actually engaged in trading. Finally, the SEC was also aware of two articles regarding Madoff's investment operations that appeared in reputable publications in 2001 and questioned Madoff's unusually consistent returns." [IG Report pages 20-21]

---

[234] See Bettis, Bizjak and Kalpathy, "Insiders' Use of Hedging Instruments: An Empirical Examination," March 2009.

Inspector General Kotz's comprehensive study found that on several occasions during more than a decade, the SEC failed to perform what appear to be rudimentary procedures that could or would have uncovered the Ponzi scheme. The Inspector General reported that the "complaints all contained specific information and could not have been fully and adequately resolved without thoroughly examining and investigating Madoff for operating a Ponzi scheme." [Page 22]. For example, the Inspector General retained an expert to assist in the investigation and was told that "the most critical step in examining or investigating a potential Ponzi scheme is to verify the subject's trading through an independent third party." The OIG investigation "found the SEC conducted two investigations and three examinations . . . based upon the detailed and credible complaints that raised the possibility that Madoff was misrepresenting his trading and could have been operating a Ponzi scheme. Yet, at no time did the SEC ever verify Madoff's trading through an independent third-party." The OIG found that the examinations were "too narrowly focused." The OIG found that "the examination teams . . . caught Madoff in contradictions and inconsistencies. However they either disregarded these concerns or simply asked Madoff about them. Even when Madoff's answers were seemingly implausible, the SEC examiners accepted them at face value." [page 23]

"In the first of the two OCIE examinations, the examiners drafted a letter to the National Association of Securities Dealers . . . seeking independent trade data, but they never sent the letter, claiming that it would have been too time-consuming to review the data they would have obtained. The OIG's expert opined that had the letter to the NASD been sent, the data would have provided the information necessary to reveal the Ponzi scheme. In the second examination, the OCIE Assistant Director sent a document request to a financial institution that Madoff claimed he used to clear his trades, requesting trading done by or on behalf of particular Madoff feeder funds during a specific time period, and received a response that there was no transaction activity in Madoff's account for that period. However, the Assistant Director did not determine that the response required any follow-up . . . Both examinations concluded with numerous unresolved questions and without any significant attempt to examine the possibility that Madoff was misrepresenting his trading and operating a Ponzi scheme." [page 24]

The "Enforcement staff almost immediately caught Madoff in lies and misrepresentations, but failed to follow up on inconsistencies. . . . When Madoff provided evasive or contradictory answers to important questions in testimony, they simply accepted as plausible his explanations . . . They reached out to the NASD and asked for information on whether Madoff had options positions on a certain date, but when they received a report that there were in fact no options positions on that date, they did not take further steps. An Enforcement staff attorney made several attempts to obtain documentation from European counterparties (another independent third-party) and although a letter was drafted, the Enforcement staff decided not to send it. Had any of these efforts been fully executed, they would have led to Madoff's Ponzi scheme being uncovered."

In addition, the incidents of courts overturning SEC rulemakings in recent years calls into question whether the process by which the SEC is promulgating final rules should be reexamined and refined. The SEC's process for reaching settlement recommendations may need to be reexamined also, in light of the recent decision of the Federal District Court in New York that rejected as inadequate a proposed $33 million settlement involving charges of securities fraud against Bank of America which it said "does not comport with the most elementary notions of justice and morality . . . [and] suggests a rather cynical relationship between the parties: the SEC gets to claim that it is exposing wrongdoing on the part of the Bank of America in a high-profile merger; the Bank's management gets to claim that they have been coerced into an onerous settlement by overzealous regulators. And all of this is done at the expense, not only of the shareholders, but also of the truth."[235] Internationally renowned Columbia University Professor John C. Coffee has expressed concerns about what he has seen as "dysfunction in SEC enforcement practices."[236] Recently, the SEC Office of Inspector General Report of Investigation published a report, "Investigation of the SEC's Response to Concerns Regarding Robert Allen Stanford's Alleged Ponzi Scheme" which found that over eight years an SEC office "dutifully conducted examinations of Stanford in 1997, 1998, 2002 and 2004, concluding in each case that Stanford's CDs were likely a Ponzi scheme or a similar

---

[235] The case is Securities and Exchange Commission v. Bank of America Corp., 09-cv-06829, U.S. District Court, Southern District of New York (Manhattan).

[236] The End of Phony Deterrence? 'SEC v. Bank of America', John C. Coffee, Jr., *New York Law Journal*, September 17, 2009.

¶ 54,540

fraudulent scheme.... [while the] Examination group made multiple effort after each examination to convince ... [Enforcement] to open and conduct an investigation of Stanford, no meaningful effort was made by Enforcement to investigate the potential fraud or to bring an actions to attempt to stop it until late 2005.

[¶ 54,541] *Section 962. Triennial report on personnel management*

Section 962 directs the GAO to submit a triennial report to the Committee on Banking, Housing, and Urban Affairs of the Senate and the Committee on Financial Services of the House of Representatives on personnel management by the SEC. In the wake of the financial crisis, it is clear that the SEC, along with other federal regulators, did not perform its duties as intended. The study would review several areas that have been implicated, including supervision, competence, communication, turnover, and other areas, with recommendations for improvements. Within 90 days the SEC will submit a report to these congressional Committees describing what actions it has taken in response to the GAO report.

The SEC has been receiving increased amounts of funds and is expected to continue to do so. It is critical that these funds be used efficiently and not wasted. These studies will promote the effective use of resources.

Mr. Damon Silvers, Associate General Counsel of the AFL-CIO, wrote in congressional testimony that "The Commission should look at more intensive recruiting efforts aimed at more experienced private sector lawyers who may be looking for public service opportunities."[237]

The Investor's Working Group wrote in their regulatory reform report "Regulators should acquire deeper knowledge and expertise. The speed with which financial products and services have proliferated and grown more complex has outpaced regulators' ability to monitor the financial waterfront. Staffing levels failed to keep pace with the growing work load, and many agencies lack staff with the necessary expertise to grapple with emerging issues. Political appointees and senior civil service staff should have a wide range of financial backgrounds.

Compensation should be sufficient to attract top-notch talent. In addition, continuing education and training should be dramatically expanded and officially mandated to help regulators keep pace with innovation."[238]

The reports should address key management issues. Renowned Columbia University Law School Professor John C. Coffee said an important "issue is how to change the SEC's culture."[239] Senator Merkley at the Madoff IG hearing asked about SEC employees involved, "Was there a general culture of a lack of curiosity, a lack of wanting to inconvenience big players ... What are the managerial issues?"[240] Information in the SEC Inspector General's report on the Madoff investigation raises concerns about whether some employees who had been promoted to serve as mid-level supervisors had the necessary judgment, commitment or temperament to be effective supervisors. This suggests questions about the appropriateness of how employees are promoted to supervisory positions. One indication of a supervisor's ineffectiveness may be high turnover among subordinates. Related to this issue, the Committee notes that the Division of Enforcement will eliminate the position of branch chief. The stated purpose "is to streamline our management structure ... by redeploying our branch chiefs ... to the heart-and-soul function of the SEC—conducting investigations. This flattening of our management structure will increase the resources dedicated to our investigative efforts, and will operate as a check on the extra process, duplication, unnecessary internal review and the inevitable drag on decision-making that happens in any overly-managed organization." The Committee sees this as a positive step, which suggests the question of whether there are excessive numbers of low- or mid-level managers in other divisions and similar steps should be taken to improve the effectiveness and better use the resources of those divisions.

Members of the Committee noted that it was some SEC employees' apparent incompetence that allowed the Madoff fraud to continue for so long—a case of incompetence and not lack of resources or legal authority. For example, Senator Menendez said that "the SEC staff was, from everything I've read of your report, grossly un-

---

[237] *Enhancing Investor Protection and the Regulation of Securities Markets—Part I: Testimony before the U.S. Senate Committee on Banking, Housing, and Urban Affairs*, 111th Congress, 1st session, pp. 5–6 (2009) (Testimony of Mr. Damon A. Silvers).

[238] *U.S. Financial Regulatory Reform: An Investor's Perspective*, Investor's Working Group, p. 10, July 2009.

[239] *The End of Phony Deterrence? 'SEC v. Bank of America'*, John C. Coffee, Jr., *New York Law Journal*, September 17, 2009.

[240] "Oversight of the SEC's Failure to Identify the Bernard L. Madoff Ponzi Scheme and How to Improve SEC Performance: Testimony before the U.S. Senate Committee on Banking, Housing, and Urban Affairs", 111th Congress, 1st session, p. 33 (2009) (Statement of Senator Jeff Merkley).

trained, uncoordinated and lazy in their investigations." He asked "who's held accountable for these grossly incompetent performances?"[241] This raises a concern to review SEC response to employees who fail to perform their duties. The IG report also identifies a concern that SEC-regulated entities have on many occasions brought informally to the attention of the Committee in other contexts, that different offices within the Commission do not communicate effectively or, at times, willingly, with each other to share expertise. Former SEC Chairman William Donaldson embarked upon a project to "tear down the silos" and promote more communication. Some regulated entities have informally complained to the Committee that the SEC inspectors arrive on their premises with a limited knowledge of the business they are about to inspect, and ask the employees of the regulated entity to teach them how their businesses operate. It would be appropriate for formal reviews of the efficiency of communication between units of the Commission.

Since the concerns identified here, and related ones, have faced the Commission for many years, the Committee feels it is important to have periodic studies by and recommendations from the GAO with the goal of sustaining improvements at the Commission.

[¶ 54,542] Section 963. Annual financial controls audit

Section 963 directs the SEC to submit an annual report to Congress that describes the responsibility of the management of the SEC for establishing and maintaining an adequate internal control structure and procedures for financial reporting; and contains an assessment of the effectiveness of the internal control structure and procedures for financial reporting of the SEC during that fiscal year. This is intended to improve the quality of the SEC's internal financial control structure.

The SEC administers the requirements under Section 404 of the Sarbanes-Oxley Act of 2002 that public companies report on the effectiveness of their internal control structure and procedures for financial reporting. Public companies need effective internal controls in order to produce accurate financial reports, confidently plan their financial activities, and inspire the confidence of investors in the integrity of public companies and in the securities markets.

As the Federal regulator of compliance with these requirements, it is appropriate for the SEC itself to be an example and have an effective internal financial control structure and for that to be attested to. Unfortunately, the SEC has been found to have material weaknesses in its own internal financial controls.

The GAO has reviewed the SEC's internal financial controls since 2004. In many of these reviews, the GAO has found that the SEC has material weaknesses and needs improvement in their internal control structure. GAO stated in November of 2009 that "in GAO's opinion, SEC did not have effective internal control over financial reporting as of September 30, 2009 . . . . During this year's audit, we identified six significant deficiencies that collectively represent a material weakness in SEC's internal control over financial reporting. The significant deficiencies involve SEC's internal control over (1) information security, (2) financial reporting process, (3) fund balance with Treasury, (4) registrant deposits, (5) budgetary resources, and (6) risk assessment and monitoring processes. These internal control weaknesses give rise to significant management challenges that have reduced assurance that data processed by SEC's information systems are reliable and appropriately protected; impaired management's ability to prepare its financial statements without extensive compensating manual procedures; and resulted in unsupported entries and errors in the general ledger."[242] Similarly, the GAO has found that the SEC did not have effective internal controls over financial reporting as of September 30, 2004, 2005, and 2007. In light of these persistent shortcomings and the importance of the SEC, an annual review is appropriate and beneficial.

[¶ 54,543] Section 964. Report on oversight of national securities associations

Section 964 provides that, once every three years, the GAO shall study and submit a report to Congress on the SEC's oversight of national securities associations (NSA). The report is intended to promote regular and effective oversight by the SEC of the NSA and to inform the Congress in its oversight role of the Nation's securities markets. Such oversight is important

---

[241] "Oversight of the SEC's Failure to Identify the Bernard L. Madoff Ponzi Scheme and How to Improve SEC Performance: Testimony before the U.S. Senate Committee on Banking, Housing, and Urban Affairs", 111th Congress, 1st session, p. 33 (2009) (Statement of Senator Robert Menendez).

[242] Securities and Exchange Commission's Financial Statements for Fiscal Years 2009 and 2008, GAO, "Highlights", November 2009.

to assist and promote the NSA's performance of its mission and fair dealing with investors and members and to evaluate any public concerns that arise.

It is the Committee's intent that the SEC should oversee specifically several important functions which have been discussed in connection with the current market situation. These matters include an evaluation of governance, including the identification and management of conflicts of interest, such as those existing when an executive of a broker-dealer sits on an NSA board and the NSA enforces its rules on such firms; examinations, including the evaluation of the expertise of staff; executive compensation practices; the extent of cooperation with and responsiveness in providing assistance to State securities administrators; funding; arbitration services, which may include enforcement of discovery rules and fairness of selection process for arbitrators on the panel, and NSA review of member advertising.

Former SEC Chief Accountant Lynn Turner testified on March 10, 2009 that:

FINRA has been a useful participant in the capital markets. It has provided resources that otherwise would not have been available to regulate and police the markets. Yet serious questions have arisen that need to be considered when improving the effectiveness and efficiency of regulation.

Currently the Board of FINRA includes representatives from those who are being regulated. This is an inherent conflict and raises the question of whose interest the Board of FINRA serves. To address this concern, consideration should be given to establishing an independent board, much like what Congress did when it established the Public Company Accounting Oversight Board.

In addition, the arbitration system at FINRA has been shown to favor the industry, much to the detriment of investors. While arbitration in some instances can be a benefit, in others it has been shown to be costly, time consuming, and biased to those who are constantly involved with it. Accordingly, FINRA's system of arbitration should be made optional, and investors given the opportunity to pursue their case in a court of law if they so desire to do so.

Finally careful consideration should be given to whether or not FINRA should be given expanded powers over investment advisors as well as broker dealers. FINRA's drop in fines and penalties in recent years, and lack of transparency in their annual report to the public, raises questions about its effectiveness as an enforcement agency and regulator. And with broker dealers involved in providing investment advice, it is important that all who do so are governed by the same set of regulations, ensuring adequate protection for the investing public.

The Committee has received letters from groups that have raised numerous concerns about the performance of FINRA, expressing concern that they "have failed to prevent virtually all of the major securities scandals since the 1980s," their compensation packages for the organization's senior executives are "outrageous" for their large size, they failed to warn the public about auction rate securities and other reasons. The Committee believes it is necessary for the GAO to conduct a study and issue a report on the SEC oversight of national securities associations at least every three years given their important role in the market and the concerns which have arisen or persisted for many years.

[¶ 54,544] *Section 965. Compliance examiners*

Section 965 directs the SEC Divisions of Trading and Markets and of Investment Management each to have a staff of examiners to perform compliance inspections and examinations of entities under their jurisdictions and report to the Director of the Division. This is intended to improve the effectiveness of the SEC. This will provide each Division internally with experts in inspections and in the regulations of that Division, who are closely acquainted with and have access to the staff who write and interpret those regulations.

The Inspector General's report on the Madoff investigation and the testimony of Mr. Harry Markopolos, for example, were critical of the competence and training of the examiners, including their unwillingness to ask for information or expertise from someone in another SEC division. Mr. David G. Tittsworth, Executive Director of the Investment Adviser Association, wrote in testimony for the Senate Banking Committee that "the SEC can and should improve its inspection program."[243] Informal information presented to the Committee from regulated entities has indicated that the Office of Compliance Inspection and Examinations sometimes sends staff on examinations who have lacked requisite expertise to examine complex registered financial or securities firms. As a result, the quality of the exams appears to have suffered, the staff may have taken undue amounts of time to perform inspections because they relied excessively on the employees of the firms being examined to teach them about the business, and the reputation of the agency has suffered.

[¶ 54,545] Section 966. Suggestion program for employees of the commission

Section 966 directs the SEC Inspector General to establish a hotline for SEC employees to submit suggestions for improvements in the efficiency, effectiveness, productivity and use of resources of the SEC, as well as allegations of waste, abuse, misconduct or mismanagement within the SEC. The Inspector General shall maintain as confidential the identity of a person who provides information unless he or she requests otherwise in writing and any specific information at the person's request. The Inspector General will report to Congress annually on the nature, number and potential benefits of the suggestions of any suggestions; the nature, number and seriousness of any allegations; the Inspector General's recommendations and actions taken in response to the allegations; and actions the SEC has taken in response to the suggestions and allegations.

The SEC would benefit by having more meritorious suggestions from its employees on how to improve efficiency and productivity. This is particularly important when the SEC will be receiving larger budgets and after a period of increased public concerns about the agency's ineffective use of resources raised in Madoff, restacking, and in other situations. It is not clear that the current system for attracting suggestions to improve productivity has been producing a robust crop of meritorious suggestions.

The Committee expects that there will be review and appropriate action on meritorious suggestions. The Inspector General may recognize an employee who makes a suggestion that would or does increase efficiency, effectiveness or productivity at the SEC or reduces waste, abuse, misconduct or mismanagement. The costs of this Suggestion Program shall be funded by the SEC Investor Protection Fund. Nothing in this section limits other statutory authorities of the Inspector General.

This Program is placed within the Office of the Inspector General, which has a tradition of analyzing agency activity to prevent abuse and promote effective operations. The IG already has a formal system in place for receiving employee complaints which can be adapted to receive suggestions. Further, the Office of Inspector General has a reputation for keeping employee confidences and is not in the normal chain of command in the SEC, so that employees may feel more confident that they can offer suggestions confidentially and without the risk of retaliation by a supervisor. The Inspector General is sufficiently independent from the daily SEC staff interactions for employees to trust his impartiality in deciding rewards. The Office of IG will have few potential conflicts of interest in reviewing suggestions compared to other SEC offices. The Committee observes that the SEC already has the authority to run a suggestion program and has discretion to make cash awards, so it would not need legislative authority to do so.

The Committee has considered whether a Suggestion Program must offer monetary rewards that are sufficiently large to motivate employees to make meritorious and valuable suggestions, and to overcome fears of offending or annoying a supervisor or of retribution. The Committee hopes that the Suggestion Program would motivate employees to produce meaningful suggestions for the benefit of the SEC.

Subtitle G

[¶ 54,560] Section 971. Election of directors by majority vote in uncontested elections

Section 971 provides that if a majority of a public company's shares are voted against or withheld from a nominee for director who runs uncontested, or without an opponent, he or she should be required to resign, unless the board unanimously finds it is in the best interest of the shareholders for him or her to serve and publishes its reasoning. It does this by requiring the SEC to direct the national securities exchanges and national securities associations to prohibit the listing of any security of an issuer who has on their board members that did not receive a

---

[243] *Enhancing Investor Protection and the Regulation of Securities Markets—Part II: Testimony before the U.S. Senate Committee on Banking, Housing, and Urban Affairs,* 111th Congress, 1st session (2009) (Testimony of Mr. David Tittsworth).

majority vote in uncontested board elections, subject to an exception if the directors unanimously voted that it is in the best interests of the shareholders that the director serve.

The Committee believes that in the uncommon circumstance where a majority of shareholders voting in an uncontested election prefer that a nominee not serve on the board, it is fair and appropriate for their wishes to be honored. Currently, an uncontested nominee who receives even one vote would be elected as a director of many companies.

The Committee has received many views on this matter. Former SEC Chief Accountant Lynn Turner testified that Congress should "[r]equire majority voting for directors and those who can't get a majority of the votes of investors they are to represent should be required to step down."[244] Ms. Barbara Roper, Director of Investor Protection of the Consumer Federation of America also testified in favor of requiring "mandatory majority voting for directors."[245] The Council of Institutional Investors, a nonprofit association of public, union and corporate pension funds with combined assets that exceed $3 trillion, favors majority voting stating: "Currently, the accountability of directors at most US companies is severely weakened by the fact that shareowners do not have a meaningful vote in director elections. Under most state laws, including Delaware, the default standard for uncontested elections is a plurality vote, which means that a director is elected even if a majority of the shares are withheld from the nominee. The Council has long believed that a plurality standard for the uncontested election of directors is inherently unfair and undemocratic and should be replaced by a majority vote standard. In recent years, many companies, including more than two-thirds of the S&P 500 have agreed with the Council and have voluntarily adopted majority voting standards. At most public companies, however, plurality voting still remains the rule. For example, nearly three-quarters of the companies in the Russell 3000 continue to use a straight plurality voting standard for director elections. The benefits of moving to a majority voting standard are many: it would democratize the corporate electoral process; put real voting power in the hands of investors; and make boards more representative of shareowners. Simply stated,

Section 971, if enacted, would eliminate a fundamental flaw in the US governance model."[246]

The Committee has also heard from those who are concerned and believe that some directors who fail to receive the vote of a majority of shareholders should nonetheless serve on the board. Such an individual might be, for example, the board's only financial expert or a person with unique expertise.

The Committee has taken this type of concern into account. The legislation would allow a director who received less than a majority of votes to serve on the board if the remaining board members unanimously vote at a board meeting that it is in the best interests of the issuer and its shareholders not to accept the resignation. When the issuer publishes this decision, it should include a specific discussion of the board's analysis in reaching that conclusion. Such publication may be made in a filing made with the SEC.

[¶ 54,561] *Section 972. Proxy access*

Section 972 was introduced by Senator Schumer. It gives the SEC the authority to require issuers to allow shareholders to put Board nominees on the company proxy. It does not require the SEC to engage in rulemaking. The authority gives the SEC wide latitude in setting the terms of such proxy access.

The Committee intentionally did not specify that shareholders must have held a certain number of shares or have held shares for a particular period of time to be eligible to use the proxy. If the SEC proposes rules, interested persons can offer their views on the appropriateness of proposed regulatory terms in the public comment process.

The Committee feels that it is proper for shareholders, as the owners of the corporation, to have the right to nominate candidates for the Board using the issuer's proxy under limited circumstances.

Former SEC Chairman Richard Breeden testified before the Committee in favor of one form of proxy access and recommended to "Allow the five (or ten) largest shareholders of any public company who have owned shares for more than one year to nominate up to three directors for

---

[244] *Enhancing Investor Protection and the Regulation of Securities Markets—Part I: Testimony before the U.S. Senate Committee on Banking, Housing, and Urban Affairs*, 111th Congress, 1st session (2009) (Testimony of Mr. Lynn Turner).

[245] *Enhancing Investor Protection and the Regulation of Securities Markets—Part II: Testimony before the U.S. Senate Committee on Banking, Housing, and Urban Affairs*, 111th Congress, 1st session (2009) (Testimony of Ms. Barbara Roper).

[246] Letter to Chairman Dodd, March 19, 2010.

inclusion on any public company's proxy statement. Overly entrenched boards have widely failed to protect shareholder interests for the simple reason that they sometimes think more about their own tenure than the interests of the people they are supposed to be protecting . . . This provision would give 'proxy access' to shareholder candidates without the cost and distraction of hostile proxy contests. At the same time, any such nomination would require support from a majority of shares held by the largest holders, thereby protecting against narrow special interest campaigns. This reform would make it easier for the largest shareowners to get boards to deal with excessive risks, poor performance, excessive compensation and other issues that impair shareholder interests." Ms. Barbara Roper, Director of Investor Protection of Consumer Federation of America, testified before the Committee and recommended "improved proxy access for shareholders." Mr. Jeff Mahoney, General Counsel of the Council of Institutional Investors, wrote in a letter to Chairman Dodd that "the only way that shareowners can present alternative director candidates at a U.S. public company is by waging a full-blown election contest. For most investors, that is onerous and prohibitively expensive. A measured right for investors to place their nominees for directors on the company's proxy card would overcome these obstacles, invigorating board elections and making directors more responsive, thoughtful and vigilant." Former SEC Chief Accountant Lynn Turner testified before the Committee that "Congress should move to adopt legislation that would: . . . Give investors who own the company, the same equal access to the proxy as management currently has." A coalition of state public officials in charge of public investments, AFSCME, CalPERS, and the Investor's Working Group also support proxy access.

[¶ 54,562] *Section 973. Disclosures regarding Chairman and CEO structures*

Section 973 directs the SEC to issue rules that require an issuer to disclose the reasons that it has chosen the same person or elected to have different people serve in the offices of Chairman of the Board of Directors and Chief Executive Officer of the issuer.

The Committee has received strong views on the merits of one or the other model and on whether to prohibit a public company from having the same individual serve as Chairman and as CEO. For example, Mr. Joseph Dear, Chief Investment Officer of the California Public Employees' Retirement System, on behalf of the Council of Institutional Investors, wrote in testimony for the Senate Banking Committee that "Boards of directors should be encouraged to separate the role of chair and CEO, or explain why they have adopted another method to assure independent leadership of the board."

The Committee feels this is an important matter, and recognizes that different public companies may have good reasons for having the same person as CEO and Chairman or different persons in these two positions. Accordingly, the legislation asks public companies to disclose to shareholders the reasons why it has chosen its governance method. The legislation does not endorse or prohibit either method.

Subtitle H

[¶ 54,580] *Section 975. Regulation of municipal securities and changes to the board of the MSRB*

Section 975 strengthens oversight of municipal securities and broadens current municipal securities market protections to cover previously unregulated market participants and previously unregulated financial transactions with states, counties, cities and other municipal entities. This section establishes municipal advisors as a new category of SEC registrant. Such municipal advisors provide advice to municipal entities on the issuance of municipal securities, the use of municipal derivatives, and investment advice relating to bond proceeds.

Mr. Timothy Ryan, President and CEO of SIFMA, in testimony before the Committee, said: "we feel it is important to level the regulatory playing field by increasing the Municipal Securities Rulemaking Board's authority to encompass the regulation of financial advisors, investment brokers and other intermediaries in the municipal market to create a comprehensive regulatory framework that prohibits fraudulent and manipulative practices; requires fair treatment of investors, state and local government issuers of municipal bonds and other market participants; ensures rigorous standards of professional qualifications; and promotes market efficiencies."[247] Mr. Ronald A. Stack, Chair of the Municipal Securities Rulemaking Board (MSRB), wrote in testimony for the Senate Banking Committee:

---

[247] *Enhancing Investor Protection and the Regulation of Securities Markets—Part I: Testimony before the U.S. Senate Committee on Banking, Housing, and Urban Affairs*, 111th Congress, 1st session, pp. 9-10 (2009) (Testimony of Mr. Timothy Ryan).

Investors in the municipal securities market would be best served by subjecting unregulated market professionals to a comprehensive body of rules that (i) prohibit fraudulent and manipulative practices, (ii) require the fair treatment of investors, issuers, and other market participants, (iii) mandate full transparency, (iv) restrict real and perceived conflicts of interests, (v) ensure rigorous standards of professional qualifications, and (vi) promote market efficiencies.[248]

The U.S. Council of Mayors[249] also testified in support of this policy.

The SEC recently proposed new rules under the Investment Advisers Act of 1940 relating to the provision by registered investment advisers of investment advisory services to municipal entities in which, among other things, the SEC proposed prohibiting investment advisers from making payments to unrelated persons for solicitation of municipal entities for investment advisory services on behalf of investment advisers. Rather than effectively prohibiting such third-party solicitation for investment advisory services, this section would provide that activities of a municipal advisor, broker, dealer or municipal securities dealer to solicit a municipal entity to engage an unrelated investment adviser to provide investment advisory services to a municipal entity or to engage to undertake underwriting, financial advisory or other activities for a municipal entity in connection with the issuance of municipal securities, would be subject to regulation by the MSRB. These activities of municipal advisors are currently unregulated in most respects and would become subject to regulation by the MSRB to the same extent as would such activities undertaken by brokers, dealers and municipal securities dealers with respect to their transactions in municipal securities. Thus, the MSRB would be authorized to establish qualification requirements, continuing education and operational standards, and fair practice, disclosure, conflict of interest and other rules with respect to municipal advisors in the same manner as for brokers, dealers and municipal securities dealers.

Section 975 authorizes the MSRB to make rules regulating municipal advisors, including financial advisors, brokers of guaranteed investment contracts and other investments, swap and other municipal derivatives advisors, and certain third party solicitors of municipal entities. The Committee believes that giving MSRB rulemaking authority in this area is an efficient use of regulatory resources, particularly since the SEC currently has very few staff with expertise in municipal securities. Not only does the MSRB have greater resources in terms of personnel and experience in the municipal market. The Board has an existing, comprehensive set of rules on key issues such as pay-to-play and fair dealing. Therefore, the Committee is of the view that consistency would be important to ensure common standards. As a baseline for rulemaking with respect to municipal advisors, the MSRB has an extensive understanding of the municipal securities market and has put in place a mature body of comprehensive regulation that (i) prohibits fraudulent and manipulative practices, (ii) requires the fair treatment of investors, issuers and other market participants, (iii) mandates full transparency, (iv) restricts real and perceived conflicts of interests, including prohibiting pay-to-play practices, (v) ensures rigorous standards of professional qualifications, and (vi) promotes market efficiencies. The rules for municipal advisory activities would apply equally to broker-dealers acting as financial advisors and to non-affiliated financial advisors. The Committee also notes that the MSRB has made important contributions to the transparency of the municipal market with its EMMA online reporting system.

The SEC has general oversight authority over the MSRB, and would enforce the municipal advisor rules issued pursuant to this section. The MSRB's rulemaking process, including a public comment process and SEC approval of all new rules, provides another layer of protection regarding the appropriateness of rules written by the MSRB. The section creates an expanded role for the MSRB in supporting SEC examinations and enforcement; gives the MSRB a share of fines collected by the SEC and FINRA; and gives the MSRB authority to be an information repository for the systemic risk regulator.

This section also modifies the composition of the MSRB, in light of the expansion of the Board's jurisdiction and to avoid conflicts of interest. Under current law, 10 of the 15 board members represent the securities dealers and underwriters that are regulated by the MSRB. With the expansion of the MSRB's jurisdiction to in-

---

[248] *Enhancing Investor Protection and the Regulation of Securities Markets—Part II: Testimony before the U.S. Senate Committee on Banking, Housing, and Urban Affairs*, 111th Congress, 1st session, p. 25 (2009) (Testimony of Mr. Ronald A. Stack).

[249] *Legislative Proposals to Improve the Efficiency and Oversight of Municipal Finance: Testimony before the U.S. House Committee on Financial Services*, 111th Congress, 1st session (2009) (Testimony of The Honorable Thomas C. Leppert).

¶54,580

clude municipal advisors, it is appropriate to provide for majority public representation. The section provides that the MSRB shall include 8 individuals who are not associated with broker-dealers, municipal advisors, or municipal securities dealers, and 7 individuals who are associated with broker-dealers, municipal advisors, or municipal securities dealers. The 8 public members will include at least one investor representative, one representative of municipalities, and a member of the public with knowledge or experience in the municipal securities field. As reconstituted under this Section, the MSRB would not be dominated by members having exclusive legal obligations to investors, given the requirement for majority public membership as well as required representation of regulated municipal advisors. Further, the section would establish an explicit MSRB statutory mandate to protect municipal entities, as well as investors.

The Section also provides that the MSRB, in conjunction with or on behalf of other Federal financial regulators or self-regulatory organizations, may establish information systems and assess reasonable fees to support those information systems.

[¶ 54,581] Section 976. Government Accountability Office study of increased disclosure to investors

Section 976 directs the GAO to conduct a study and review of the disclosure required to be made by issuers of municipal securities and report on the findings. The GAO will describe the size of the municipal securities markets and the issuers and investors; compare the disclosure regimes applicable to issuers of municipal versus corporate bonds; evaluate the costs and benefits to issuers of municipal securities of requiring additional financial disclosures to investors; and make recommendations relating to the repeal of the Tower Amendment, which bars the MSRB and the SEC from imposing disclosure requirements on municipal issuers.

The Committee believes that to improve investor protection there is merit in considering the revocation of the Tower Amendment, but that this move is significant and deserves a deliberate study before action is taken. In support of repealing the Tower Amendment, former SEC Chief Accountant Lynn Turner wrote in testimony for the Senate Banking Committee "there is a gap in regulation of the municipal securities market as a result of what is known as the Tower Amendment. Recent SEC enforcement actions such as with the City of San Diego, the problems in the auction rate securities, and the lurking problems with pension obligation bonds, all cry out for greater regulation and transparency in these markets. As a result, these token regulated markets now amount to trillions of dollars and significant risks. Accordingly, as former Chairman Cox recommended, I believe Section 15B(d)—Issuance of Municipal Securities—of the Securities Act of 1934 should be deleted."[250] The Investment Company Institute,[251] Municipal Market Advisers,[252] and former SEC Chairman Arthur Levitt[253] support increased disclosure by municipalities.

[¶ 54,582] Section 977. Government Accountability Office study on the municipal securities markets

Section 977 directs the GAO to conduct a study and issue a report on the municipal securities markets, to include an analysis of the mechanisms for trading, reporting, and settling transactions; the needs of the markets and investors and the impact of recent innovations; potential uses of derivatives in the municipal markets; and recommendations to improve the transparency, efficiency, fairness, and liquidity of the municipal securities market. The GAO shall submit its report to the Committee on Banking, Housing, and Urban Affairs of the Senate, the Financial Services Committee of the House of Representatives, with a copy to the Special Committee on Aging of the Senate, within 180 days of the enactment of this Act.

[¶ 54,583] Section 978. Study of funding for Government Accounting Standards Board

Section 978 requires the SEC to study the funding of the Government Accounting Stan-

---

[250] *Enhancing Investor Protection and the Regulation of Securities Markets—Part I: Testimony before the U.S. Senate Committee on Banking, Housing, and Urban Affairs*, 111th Congress, 1st session, p. 11 (2009) (Testimony of Mr. Lynn Turner).

[251] *Enhancing Investor Protection and the Regulation of Securities Markets—Part I: Testimony before the U.S. Senate Committee on Banking, Housing, and Urban Affairs*, 111th Congress, 1st session (2009) (Testimony of Mr. Paul Schott Stevens).

[252] *Enhancing Investor Protection and the Regulation of Securities Markets—Part I: Testimony before the U.S. Senate Committee on Banking, Housing, and Urban Affairs*, 111th Congress, 1st session (2009) (Testimony of Mr. Thomas G. Doe).

[253] *Enhancing Investor Protection and the Regulation of Securities Markets—Part II: Testimony before the U.S. Senate Committee on Banking, Housing, and Urban Affairs*, 111th Congress, 1st session (2009) (Testimony of Mr. Arthur Levitt).

dards Board (GASB). GASB establishes accounting principles that are used by many states and local governments. As a result, GASB plays an important role in the municipal securities market by providing the foundation for financial reporting that investors rely on to make investment decisions. GASB is currently funded by voluntary contributions from states, local governments, and the financial community, and through the sale of its publications, to meet its annual budget of less than $8 million.

The Committee is concerned that such voluntary funding arrangements can cause undue uncertainty and potentially lead to the compromise of the GASB standard setting process. The Banking Committee faced and solved a similar problem in 2002, when the Financial Accounting Standards Board, which had been relying on voluntary contributions and materials sales, was given a secure funding mechanism through Section 109 of the Sarbanes-Oxley Act.

The municipal securities market is an important component of the Nation's capital markets, as it finances infrastructure and other government needs, while at the same time providing generally low-risk investment opportunities to Americans. There are over 50,000 issuers of municipal securities, with more than $2.8 trillion of United States municipal securities outstanding. In 2008, over $450 billion of new municipal securities were issued and nearly $5 trillion in municipal securities were traded.

In this regard, the Committee is concerned that the current funding mechanism may not ensure that GASB can produce high-quality, unbiased, and transparent governmental accounting and financial reporting standards.

This section requires the SEC to conduct a study that evaluates: the role and importance of GASB in the municipal securities markets; the manner in which GASB is funded and how such manner of funding affects the financial information available to securities investors; the advisability of changes to the manner in which GASB is funded; and whether legislative changes to the manner in which GASB is funded are necessary for the benefit of investors and in the public interest. In conducting the study, the SEC shall consult with State and local government officers.

In considering the "advisability" of changes to the funding, the Committee expects the SEC to evaluate alternative methods, including methods that would provide GASB with certainty about its income to meet its budget. In addition, the SEC may consider whether it would be feasible or efficient for a private entity, such as a self-regulatory organization, to assess a fee from its members that underwrite municipal securities offerings or whether it would be appropriate to assess fees on secondary market transactions. The SEC is required to submit the study to the Committee on Banking, Housing, and Urban Affairs of the Senate and the Committee on Financial Services of the House of Representatives within 270 days of the date of enactment.

[¶ 54,584] *Section 979. Commission Office of Municipal Securities*

Section 979 establishes an Office of Municipal Securities in the SEC to administer the Commission's rules with respect to municipal securities dealers, advisors, investors, and issuers. The Director of the Office shall report to the Chairman of the Commission. The Office shall coordinate with the MSRB for rulemaking and enforcement actions, and shall have sufficient staff to carry out the requirements of this section, including individuals with knowledge and expertise in municipal finance. The Committee is concerned that the SEC has reduced the number of staff in its municipal securities office over the past few decades, and expects that the creation of the Office will allow the SEC to devote increased supervisory attention to the municipal market.

Subtitle I

[¶ 54,600] *Section 981. Authority to share certain information with foreign authorities*

Section 102(a) of the Sarbanes-Oxley Act of 2002 ("the Act") makes it unlawful for any public accounting firm to prepare or issue, or participate in the preparation or issuance, of any audit reports with respect to any issuer without being registered with the Public Company Accounting Oversight Board ("PCAOB"). As of January 1, 2010, 2,349 firms were registered with the PCAOB, including 936 firms in 88 non-U.S. jurisdictions. Many of those non-U.S. firms regularly provide audit reports for issuers and are therefore inspected by the PCAOB on a regular basis. As of March 31, 2010, the Board had conducted 226 non-U.S. inspections located in 33 jurisdictions.

In conducting inspections abroad, the Board has sought to coordinate and cooperate with local authorities. The Board has said that its cooperative efforts have been impeded by the Board's inability to share with its non-U.S. counterparts confidential information related to the Board's oversight activities. The list of authorities that may receive such information is limited to the SEC, the Attorney General of the United States, appropriate federal functional regulators, state attorneys general in connection with criminal investigations, and appropriate state regulatory agencies (such as state boards of accountancy). These provisions, therefore, limit the PCAOB's ability to share such information with other regulators, including non-U.S. regulators.

A significant number of non-U.S. audit regulators have cited this limitation as a reason for not cooperating with PCAOB inspections and discouraging or prohibiting PCAOB-registered firms in their jurisdictions from cooperating. For example, the EU Directive on statutory audits permits cooperation only if reciprocal working relationships have been established between the member state's audit regulator and the PCAOB. The European Commission has asserted that these working relationships require that the PCAOB and the EU member state's auditor regulator be able to engage in a mutual exchange of inspection related information including audit working papers.

Section 981 will allow the PCAOB to share confidential inspection and investigative information with foreign audit oversight authorities under specified circumstances. The sharing may occur if (1) the PCAOB makes a finding that it is necessary to accomplish the purposes of the Act of to protect investors in U.S. issuers; (2) the foreign authority has: provided the assurances of confidentiality requested by the PCAOB, described its information systems and controls; described its jurisdiction's laws and regulations that are relevant to information access and (3) the PCAOB determines it is appropriate to share such information. The information about information controls and relevant law is to assist the PCAOB in making an independent determination that the foreign authority has the capability and authority to keep the information confidential in its jurisdiction. The PCAOB may rely on additional information in making the determination that the information will be kept confidential and used no more extensively than the same manner that the U.S. and State entities identified in Section 105(b)(5)(B) of the Act may use the information, which is an important consideration of determining the appropriateness of such sharing.

Thus, the bill requires the Board to consider whether applicable foreign laws and the respective foreign auditor oversight authority offer protections comparable to those provided under the Act. This would require the PCAOB to consider not only the foreign auditor oversight authority's willingness to maintain the confidentiality of the information, but also its ability to do so, both as a matter of the law in its jurisdiction and as a matter of the security of its information technology systems. The Committee believes that the Board could accept an assurance of confidentiality as adequate even in circumstances where the foreign auditor oversight authority could disclose the information to relevant law enforcement or regulatory authorities in its jurisdiction, so long as any such authorities are also committed and able to comply with confidentiality limitations comparable to those that apply to the U.S. and state entities with which the Board shares information under Section 105(b)(5)(B) of the Act.

The Chairman of the PCAOB has written to the Chairman and Ranking Member asking for legislation "to allow the PCAOB to share with a foreign audit oversight authority, upon receiving appropriate assurances of confidentiality, the inspection and investigative information related to the public accounting firms within that authority's jurisdiction . . . [in order to] facilitate the Board's and foreign authorities' efforts to fulfill their inspection mandates. This recommendation enjoys widespread investor and profession support."[254]

[¶ 54,601] *Section 982. Oversight of brokers and dealers*

Section 982 provides the Public Company Accounting Oversight Board ("PCAOB") with the authority to write professional standards related to audits of SEC-registered brokers and dealers, to inspect those audits, and, when appropriate, to investigate and bring disciplinary proceedings related to those audits. This Section provides the PCAOB with authority over audits of registered brokers and dealers that is generally comparable to its existing authority over audits of issuers. This authority permits it to write standards for, inspect, investigate, and bring disciplinary actions arising out of, any audit of a registered broker or dealer. It enables the PCAOB to use its inspection and disciplinary processes to identify auditors that lack expertise or fail to exercise care in broker and dealer audits, identify and address deficiencies in their practices, and, where appropriate, suspend or bar them from conducting such audits.

---

[254] Letter from the Honorable Mark W. Olson, July 7, 2009.

¶ 54,601

Currently, every SEC-registered broker and dealer is required by section 17(e)(1)(A) of the Securities Exchange Act of 1934 (15 U.S.C. 78q(e)(1)(A)) to file with the SEC a balance sheet and income statement certified by a public accounting firm that is registered with the PCAOB. However, the PCAOB's authority to write professional standards, inspect audits, investigate audit deficiencies, and bring disciplinary proceedings for audit deficiencies extends to audits of "issuers," as defined in section 2(a)(7) of the Sarbanes-Oxley Act of 2002 (15 U.S.C. 7201(7)). Therefore, the PCAOB does not have the authority to regulate and inspect audits of brokers and dealers unless a broker or dealer is an issuer (which is typically not the case) or its financial statements are part of the consolidated financial statements of an issuer.

Under the current situation, where auditors of brokers and dealers register with the PCAOB but their audits of brokers and dealers are not subject to the PCAOB's standard setting, inspection and disciplinary authority, investors may expect that PCAOB-registered auditors of brokers and dealers are subject to inspections and oversight when, in fact, the PCAOB has no authority to govern the conduct or monitor the quality of their audit work.

In a July 7, 2009 letter to Chairman Dodd and Ranking Member Shelby, Chairman Mark Olson of the PCAOB recommended that Congress consider amending the Sarbanes-Oxley Act to grant the PCAOB authority to inspect audits of brokers and dealers and to take action where deficiencies occur. The Securities Investor Protection Corporation has supported granting the PCAOB full oversight of audits of brokers and dealers, and feels that the PCAOB's new oversight authority should apply to audits of all registered brokers and dealers and not only those that perform a clearing function or carry customer accounts.

The Section requires the PCAOB to allocate, assess and collect its support fees among brokers and dealers as well as issuers. The Committee expects that the PCAOB will reasonably estimate the amounts required to fund the portions of its programs devoted to the oversight of audits of brokers and dealers, as contrasted to the oversight of audits of issuers, in deciding the total amounts to be allocated to, assessed, and collected from all brokers and dealers. The Committee notes that the implementation of a program for PCAOB inspections of auditors of brokers and dealers is not intended to and should not affect the PCAOB's program for the inspections of auditors of issuers. Cost accounting for each program is not required.

An example of the type of harm that might be avoided in the future by extending PCAOB authority is the investor reliance on the fraudulent audit of the broker-dealer Bernard L. Madoff Investment Securities LLC by Friehling & Horowitz, a firm that was not registered with the PCAOB.

Columbia University Law Professor John C. Coffee testified before the Banking Committee on March 10, 2009: "From this perspective focused on prevention, rather than detection, the most obvious lesson is that the SEC's recent strong tilt towards deregulation contributed to, and enabled, the Madoff fraud in two important respects. First, Bernard L. Madoff Investment Securities LLC ('BMIS') was audited by a fly-by-night auditing firm with only one active accountant who had neither registered with the Public Company Accounting Oversight Board ('PCAOB') nor even participated in New York State's peer review program for auditors."

Professor Coffee noted that the Sarbanes-Oxley Act "required broker-dealers to use a PCAOB-registered auditor. Nonetheless, until the Madoff scandal exploded, the SEC repeatedly exempted privately held broker-dealers from the obligation to use such a PCAOB-registered auditor and permitted any accountant to suffice. Others also exploited this exemption. For example, in the Bayou Hedge Fund fraud, which was the last major Ponzi scheme before Madoff, the promoters simply invented a fictitious auditing firm and forged certifications in its name. Had auditors been required to have been registered with PCAOB, this would not have been feasible because careful investors would have been able to detect that the fictitious firm was not registered . . . At the end of 2008, the SEC quietly closed the barn door by failing to renew this exemption—but only after $50 billion worth of horses had been stolen."

[¶ 54,602] *Section 983. Portfolio margining*

Section 983 amends the Securities Investor Protection Act of 1970 ("SIPA"), which protects customers from certain losses caused by the insolvency of their broker-dealer. Under SIPA, claims of customers take priority over claims of general unsecured creditors with respect to customer property held by an insolvent broker-dealer. Under current law, the protections of SIPA do not extend to futures contracts other than security futures. As a result, customers currently are effectively precluded from including securities and related futures in a single securities account.

The Section will enable customers to benefit from hedging activities by facilitating the inclusion of both securities and related futures products in a single "portfolio margining account" provided for under rules of self-regulatory organizations approved by the Securities and Exchange Commission (the "SEC"). A portfolio margining account can be margined based upon the net risk of the positions in the account.

Section 983 is consistent with a recommendation of the SEC and CFTC in their Joint Report on Harmonization of Regulation released on October 16, 2009. The agencies recommended giving customers the choice of whether to put related futures in a securities account or their related securities derivatives in a futures account. Customer choice is facilitated by extending SIPC insurance to futures in a securities portfolio margining account. The Section is also supported by each of the U.S. exchanges that trade options.

Section 983 amends the definitions of "customer," "customer property," and "net equity" in Section 16 of SIPA to provide that the owner of a portfolio margining account would be given the priority of a customer under SIPA with respect to any futures contracts or options on futures contracts permitted under SEC-approved rules to be carried in the account. Similarly, the customer's "net equity" in the account would include such futures and options on futures, and they would be treated along with cash and securities in the account as securities customer property. The definition of "net equity" is further amended to clarify that a customer's claim for either a commodity futures contract or a security futures contract will be treated as a claim for cash rather than as a claim for a security. The Section also amends the definition of "gross revenues from the securities business" to specifically include revenues earned by a broker or dealer in connection with transactions in portfolio margining accounts carried as securities accounts.

[¶ 54,603] *Section 984. Loan or borrowing of securities*

During the period preceding the crisis, a number of financial institutions used securities lending programs as a basis for leveraged and risky trading activities. This Section directs the SEC to write rules that are designed to increase the transparency of information available to brokers, dealers, and investors with respect to loaned or borrowed securities within two years of the date of enactment of this Act. The Section also makes it unlawful for any person to effect, accept, or facilitate a transaction involving the loan or borrowing of securities in contravention of such rules as the SEC may prescribe. The SEC is encouraged to act in a shorter period of time if necessary in the public interest.

[¶ 54,604] *Section 985. Technical corrections to federal securities laws*

[¶ 54,605] *Section 986. Conforming amendments relating to the repeal of the Public Utility Holding Company Act of 1935*

[¶ 54,606] *Section 987. Amendment to definition of material loss and nonmaterial losses to the Deposit Insurance Fund for purposes of Inspector General reviews*

Section 987 amends the definition of material loss and adds "nonmaterial losses" definition to the Deposit Insurance Fund for purposes of Inspector General Reviews. The Inspectors General (IG) of Federal Banking Regulators are required to conduct a Material Loss Review for each depository institutions that fails and costs the Deposit Insurance Fund $25 million and more. The Senate Banking Committee has heard from the IGs that due to the rise in bank failures they are severely strained by the amount of Material Loss Reviews they must produce. In their communications to the Banking Committee the IGs from Federal Reserve, Treasury and FDIC have claimed to have hired more personnel to reduce the backlog accumulated during the financial crisis; however, the number of bank failures has also been more than they've expected, and such, the volume of workload has remained strenuously high. Because of this, and the understanding that most of the bank failures seemed have occurred due to similar reasons (exposure to failing mortgages) the Committee is proposing an increase in the dollar amount that the Deposit Insurance Fund must lose to trigger a Material Loss Review. The change will follow this schedule: it will rise from the current $25,000,000 to $100,000,000 for the period of September 30, 2009 to December 31, 2010 and cascade down to $75,000,000 for the period of January 1, 2011 to December 31, 2011, and rest on $50,000,000 for January 1, 2012 and after. In bank failures that do not meet the materiality threshold (and thus are "nonmaterial losses" to the Deposit Insurance Fund), the IGs could still conduct a Material Loss Review if, based on their preliminary assessment, such a report would be helpful.

For every 6 month period after March 31, 2010, the IGs must prepare and submit a written report to the appropriate Federal banking agency and to Congress on whether any losses deemed to be nonmaterial exhibit unusual circumstances and deserve an in-depth review of the loss.

[¶ 54,607] *Section 988. Amendment to definition of material loss and nonmaterial losses to the National Credit Union Share Insurance Fund for purposes of Inspector General reviews*

Section 988 does for credit unions what Section 987 does for other insured depository institutions. The Section defines a material loss for the National Credit Union Share Insurance Fund for purposes of Inspectors General reviews. If the Fund incurs a material loss with respect to an insured credit union, the Inspector General of the NCUA Board will submit to the Board a written report reviewing the supervision of the credit union by the Administration. For the purposes of this provision, a material loss is defined as an amount exceeding the sum of $25,000,000 or an amount equal to 10 percent of the total assets of the credit union on the date on which the Board initiated assistance. The GAO, under its discretion, could review each of these reports and recommend improvements to the supervision of insured credit unions.

For every 6 months period after March 31, 2010, the Board IG must prepare and submit a written report to the appropriate Federal banking agency and to Congress on whether any losses deemed to be nonmaterial exhibit unusual circumstances and deserve an in-depth review of the loss.

[¶ 54,608] *Section 989. Government Accountability Office study on proprietary trading*

Section 989A was authored by Senator Merkley. Section 989 directs the GAO to conduct a study on proprietary trading by financial institutions and the implication of this practice on systemic risk. This will include an evaluation of whether proprietary trading presents a material systemic risk to the stability of the United States financial system; whether proprietary trading presents material risks to the safety and soundness of the covered entities that engage in such activities; whether proprietary trading presents material conflicts of interest between covered entities that engage in proprietary trading and the clients of the institutions who use the firm to execute trades or who rely on the firm to manage assets; whether adequate disclosure regarding the risks and conflicts of proprietary trading is provided to the depositors, trading and asset management clients, and investors of covered entities that engage in proprietary trading; and whether the banking, securities, and commodities regulators of institutions that engage in proprietary trading have in place adequate systems and controls to monitor and contain any risks and conflicts of interest related to proprietary trading. The GAO will submit a report to Congress on the results of this study within 15 months of passage of the Act.

[¶ 54,609] *Section 989A. Senior investor protection*

Section 989A was authored by Senator Kohl. Section 989A defines the terms "misleading designation", "financial product", "misleading or fraudulent marketing" and "senior" for the purposes of protecting senior citizens from investment frauds. The Section directs the Office of Financial Literacy within Bureau of Consumer Financial Protection to establish a program to provide grants of up to $500,000 per fiscal year to individual States to investigate and prosecute misleading and fraudulent marketing practices or to develop educational materials and training to reduce misleading and fraudulent marketing of financial products toward seniors. States may use the grants for staff, technology, equipment, training and educational materials. To receive these grants, states must adopt rules on the appropriate use of designations in the offer or sale of securities or investment advice; on fiduciary or suitability requirements in the sale of securities; on the use of designations in the sale of insurance products; and on insurer conduct related to the sale of annuity products. This Section authorizes $8 million to be appropriated for these purposes for fiscal years 2010 through 2014.

This section is intended to protect seniors from less than scrupulous financial advisors who prey on the elderly by touting misleading or fraudulent "senior designations." Often these deceptive designations can be obtained online and require little or no training to acquire. The new grant program will provide needed resources to state fraud enforcement agencies fighting fraud. The grant application process will incentivize states to crack down against the misleading use of senior designations by encouraging them to adopt the North American Securities Administrators Association (NASAA)'s and the National Association of Insurance Commission's (NAIC) newly developed model rules on the use of senior designations for the sale of securities and insurance products. The grant also calls for improved suitability standards for the sales of annuity products, with provisions that are likely to be reflected in the new suitability standards that are being developed by the NAIC. This section has been endorsed by organizations such as the AARP, North American Securities Administrators Association (NASAA), National Organization for Competency Assurance (NOCA), The American College, Financial Planners Association, Fund Democracy, Consumer Federation of America, Alliance for Retired Americans, National Association of Personal Financial Advisors (NAPFA), Older Women's League (OWL) and Financial Certified Planners Board of Standards (CFP Board).

[¶ 54,610] *Section 989B. Changes in appointment of certain Inspectors General*

Senator Menendez authored this Section, which provides for presidential appointment of the Inspectors General of the Federal Reserve Board of Governors, the CFTC, the NCUA, the PBGC, the SEC, and the Bureau of Consumer Financial Protection with Senate approval. The provision is intended to increase the stature of the Inspectors General within their agencies. This Section strengthens also the subpoena authority.

Subtitle J

[¶ 54,620] *Section 991. Securities and Exchange Commission self-funding*

Section 991 provides for the SEC to become a self-funded organization. Each year the SEC will submit a budget request to Congress and the Treasury. The Treasury will deposit this money into an account for use by the SEC. The SEC will set its fees and assessments at a level meant to fully repay Treasury. If the SEC does not recoup sufficient funds, then the SEC is not obligated to fully repay Treasury. Any collections in excess of 25% of the next year's budget request must be paid to Treasury.

The Council of Institutional Investors,[255] former SEC Chief Accountant Mr. Lynn Turner,[256] the Investment Adviser Association,[257] and the Investor's Working Group[258] support this policy.

Title X—Bureau of Consumer Financial Protection

[¶ 54,640] *Section 1001. Short title*

Section 1001 establishes the name of this title to be the Consumer Financial Protection Act of 2010.

[¶ 54,641] *Section 1002. Definitions*

Section 1002 provides the definitions for key terms in Title X.

Paragraph 1 defines the term "affiliate."

Paragraph 2 explains that "Bureau" means the Bureau of Consumer Financial Protection.

Paragraph 3 defines the term "business of insurance."

Paragraph 4 defines the term "consumer."

Paragraph 5 makes clear that financial products or services defined in the Act that are offered or provided for use by consumers primarily for personal, family, or household purposes are considered to be "consumer financial products or services" for purposes of this Act. The definition of "consumer financial product or service" in this paragraph is a subset of the defined term "financial product or serve" in paragraph 13, and includes all activities that are part of the broader definition, which excludes the "business of insurance" under paragraph 13(B). In addition, other key financial activities that are central to consumers are also included in this definition. These include, among others listed, the servicing of mortgage loans and debt collection services where the financial service being provided is the result of a contract between the lender and the servicer or debt collector. For example, mortgage servicers typically provide services to the owners of the mortgages. Nonetheless, this service is included in the definition of "consumer financial product or service" because of its obvious impact on consumers. A number of other financial activities of a similar nature are included in this definition.

The Committee intends, however, that a financial institution's exercise of bona fide trust or fiduciary powers would not be subject to the

---

[255] Mr. Jeff Mahoney, Council of Institutional Investors, letter to Senator Dodd, p.3, November 18, 2009.

[256] *Enhancing Investor Protection and the Regulation of Securities Markets—Part I: Testimony before the U.S. Senate Committee on Banking, Housing, and Urban Affairs,* 111th Congress, 1st session (2009) (Testimony of Mr. Lynn Turner).

[257] *Enhancing Investor Protection and the Regulation of Securities Markets—Part II: Testimony before the U.S. Senate Committee on Banking, Housing, and Urban Affairs,* 111th Congress, 1st session (2009) (Testimony of Mr. David Tittsworth).

[258] *U.S. Financial Regulatory Reform: An Investor's Perspective,* Investor's Working Group, July 2009.

jurisdiction of the Bureau. In addition, financial products and services delivered for establishing a trust, or to a trust itself, would not be for use by a consumer primarily for personal, family, or household purposes.

Paragraph 6 defines "covered person" as any person engaged in offering or providing a consumer financial product or service and an affiliate of such a person that provides a material service in connection with the provision of such consumer financial product or service is subject to the regulatory authority of and, in some cases, to examinations by, the CFPB under this title.

Paragraph 7 defines the term "credit."

Paragraph 8 defines "deposit-taking activity."

Paragraph 9 defines the term "designated transfer date."

Paragraph 10 defines the term "Director."

Paragraph 11 defines the term "enumerated consumer laws."

Paragraph 12 defines the term "Federal consumer financial law."

Paragraph 13 defines the term "financial product or service" and is modeled on the activities that are permissible for a bank or a bank holding company, such as under section 4(k) of the Bank Holding Company Act and implementing regulations. However, it is more narrowly drawn in this Act in that the list does not include insurance or securities activities. The paragraph describes the activities, products, and services that are defined as a "financial product or service" in the context of this legislation. The legislation does not intend to capture as "covered persons" companies that engage in financial data processing activities, as defined in paragraph 13, where the company acts as a mere conduit for such data, provides services to a person that enables that person to establish and maintain a web site simply as a conduit, or merchants that provide for electronic payments for the sale of their nonfinancial goods or services.

Paragraph 14 defines the term "foreign exchange."

Paragraph 15 defines the term "insured credit union."

Paragraph 16 defines the term "payment instrument."

Paragraph 17 defines the term "person."

Paragraph 18 defines the term "person regulated by the Commodity Futures Trading Commission."

Paragraph 19 defines the term "person regulated by the Commission."

Paragraph 20 defines the term "person regulated by a State insurance regulator."

Paragraph 21 defines the term "person that performs income tax preparation activities for consumers."

Paragraph 22 defines the term "prudential regulator."

Paragraph 23 defines the term "related person."

Paragraph 24 defines the term "service provider" and is designed to create authority that is generally comparable to the authority that federal banking regulators have under the Bank Service Company Act. It is included in this Act in order to ensure that material outsourced services by a covered person in connection with the offering or provision of a consumer financial product or service are subject to the regulation and supervision of the CFPB for the activities that could be done directly by the covered person. Without such authority, covered persons could remove many important functions that bear directly on consumers from the CFPB's oversight simply by contracting those functions out to service providers, thereby escaping the jurisdiction of the CFPB and leading to significant regulatory arbitrage. Companies that merely provide general support or ministerial services to a broad range of businesses, or space for advertising either in print or in an electronic medium, are not intended to be defined as service providers for the purposes of this Act.

Paragraph 25 defines the term "State."

Paragraph 26 defines the term "stored value."

Paragraph 27 defines the term "transmitting or exchanging money." This paragraph is not intended to capture a mere conduit, such as a telecommunications company that provides a network over which a money service business sends funds. The paragraph is intended to cover the companies that are receiving currency directly from a consumer, not as a consequence of receiving it from the money service business for further transmission to a recipient.

¶54,641

Subtitle A—Bureau of Consumer Financial Protection.

[¶ 54,660] Section 1011. Establishment of the Bureau

This section creates the Bureau of Consumer Financial Protection (the Bureau) in the Federal Reserve System; it establishes the Bureau's authority to regulate the offering and provision of consumer financial products and services. This section also establishes the positions of the Director and Deputy Director of the Bureau. The Director is appointed by the President and confirmed by the Senate for a 5-year term and subject to removal for cause.

[¶ 54,661] Section 1012. Executive and administrative powers

Section 1012 authorizes the Bureau to establish general policies with respect to all executive and administrative functions of the Bureau. It provides that the Director may delegate to any authorized employee, representative, or agent any power vested in the Bureau. The section makes clear that the Bureau is to operate without any interference by the Board of Governors of the Federal Reserve including with regards to rule writing, issuance of orders, examinations, enforcement actions, and appointment or removal of employees of the Bureau. These provisions are modeled on similar statutes governing the Office of the Comptroller of the Currency and the Office of Thrift Supervision, which are located within the Department of Treasury.

This section also establishes that, like other federal financial services regulators, any Bureau testimony, legislative recommendations, or comments on legislation are not subject to review or approval by other agencies. The Bureau must make clear that any such communications do not reflect the views of the President or Board of Governors.

[¶ 54,662] Section 1013. Administration

This section authorizes the Director to appoint and employ officials and professional staff, and to establish in the Bureau functional units for research, community affairs, and consumer complaints. The Committee expects these functions to ensure that the Bureau has a robust knowledge of the markets for consumer financial products and services in order to meet its purposes and objectives in as efficient and effective manner as possible. The Committee also expects the Bureau to work with other federal agencies, such as the Federal Trade Commission (FTC), to make use of the FTC's existing consumer complaints collection infrastructure where efficient and advantageous in facilitating complaint monitoring, response, and referrals. Section 1013 also establishes within the Bureau an Office of Fair Lending and Equal Opportunity and an Office of Financial Literacy. Evidence of discriminatory pricing in the provision of auto loans, certain terms of mortgage loans, and other products indicate the importance of tracking this information. Likewise, a more effective effort to improve financial literacy should play a crucial role in improving consumer protection.

[¶ 54,663] Section 1014. Consumer Advisory Board

Section 1014 requires the Director to create a Consumer Advisory Board and to consult with it on matters pertaining to the Bureau's functions and authorities. This panel is modeled on the Consumer Advisory Council of the Federal Reserve Board and is intended to bring a broad spectrum of perspectives together to advise the Director. This provision requires the Director to appoint 6 members to the Consumer Advisory Board who have been recommended by the Federal Reserve Bank Presidents. The provision requires that members are appointed without regard to party affiliation, just like the members of the advisory committees to the Federal Reserve, the SEC, the FDIC, the FDA, and many other federal advisory committees. This is important because, as the GAO found in 2004, when a federal advisory committee is viewed as politicized, the value of its work can be jeopardized.

[¶ 54,664] Section 1015. Coordination

This section requires the Bureau to coordinate with the SEC and CFTC and Federal agencies and State regulators to promote consistent regulatory treatment of consumer financial and investment products and services.

[¶ 54,665] Section 1016. Appearances before and reports to Congress

This section requires the Director to appear before Congress at semi-annual hearings and, concurrently, to prepare and submit a report to the President and Congress concerning the Bureau's budget and regulation, supervision, and enforcement activities. This provision is modeled on the semi-annual monetary report and testimony requirement imposed on the Federal Reserve. The Committee expects that this requirement will ensure the ongoing accountability of the Bureau to the Committee and the Congress.

[¶ 54,666] **Section 1017. Funding; penalties and fines**

Section 1017 requires the Federal Reserve Board to transfer the amount determined by the Director to to be reasonably necessary for the Bureau's annual budget, not to exceed a specified percentage of the total operating expenses of the Federal Reserve System as reported in the 2009 Annual Report of the Board of Governors. The Bureau's funding is capped at 12 percent for fiscal year 2013 and each year thereafter, except that the cap is to be adjusted for inflation, and will be subject to annual audits and reports to Congress by the GAO. This funding is needed to perform the following key functions: examinations and enforcement over larger banks, mortgage market companies, and other large covered nondepository companies; registration and reporting by nondepository companies that are subject to the Bureau's examination authority; analytical support, monitoring and research, industry guidance and rulemaking; operation of a nationwide consumer complaint center; and consumer financial education. The mortgage market consists of more than 25,000 lenders, servicers, brokers, and loan modification firms that would be subject to Bureau supervision and enforcement. The Treasury estimates that there are more than 75,000 nonbank, non-mortgage firms offering or providing consumer financial products or services, of which the agency would supervise a percentage. In order to conduct thorough supervision of these firms comparable to bank consumer compliance supervision will require an adequate budget.

The Committee finds that the assurance of adequate funding, independent of the Congressional appropriations process, is absolutely essential to the independent operations of any financial regulator. This was a hard learned lesson from the difficulties faced by the Office of Federal Housing Enterprise Oversight (OFHEO), which was subject to repeated Congressional pressure because it was forced to go through the annual appropriations process. It is widely acknowledged that this helped limit OFHEO's effectiveness. For that reason, ensuring that OFHEO's successor agency—the Federal Housing Finance Agency—would not be subject to appropriations was a high priority for the Committee and the Congress in the Housing and Economic Recovery Act of 2008. The budget established in this Act will ensure that the Bureau has the funds to perform its mission. By comparison with other financial regulatory bodies, the CFPB budget is modest, as the chart below illustrates.

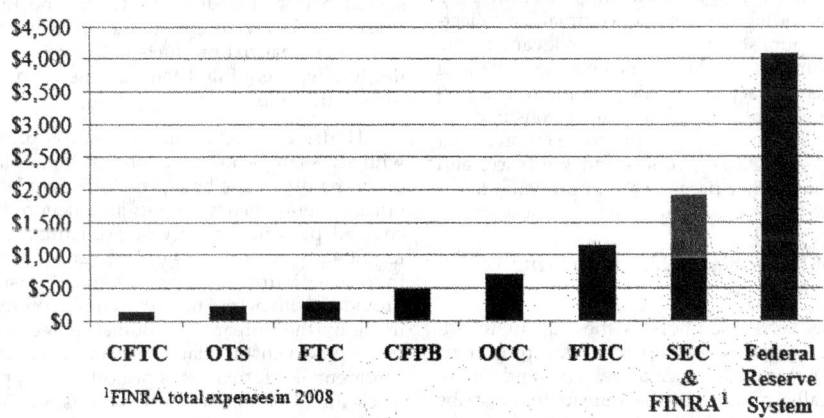

This section also establishes within the Federal Reserve Board a special fund for receipts which can be invested under certain guidelines and which are to be used to pay for Bureau expenses. Finally, section 1017 creates a victims' relief fund for civil penalties obtained by the Bureau.

[¶ 54,667] **Section 1018. Effective date**

This section provides that this subtitle shall become effective on the date of enactment of this Act.

Subtitle B—General Powers of the Bureau

[¶ 54,680] **Section 1021. Purpose, objectives, and functions**

This section mandates that the purpose of the Bureau is to implement and enforce, where applicable, Federal consumer financial laws to ensure that markets for consumer financial products and services are fair, transparent and competitive.

The Bureau is authorized to act to ensure that consumers are provided with accurate, timely, and understandable information in order to make effective decisions about financial transactions; to protect consumers from unfair, deceptive, or abusive acts and practices and from discrimination; to reduce unwarranted regulatory burdens; to ensure that Federal consumer financial law is enforced consistently in order to promote fair competition; and to ensure that markets for consumer financial products and services operate transparently and efficiently to facilitate access and innovation.

This section further establishes the Bureau's functions with regard to regulation, supervision and enforcement, including: conducting financial education programs; collecting, investigating and responding to consumer complaints; collecting and publishing information relevant to the functioning of markets for consumer financial products and services; supervising covered persons for compliance with Federal consumer financial law, and taking appropriate enforcement action; issuing rules, orders and guidance; and performing other necessary support activities to facilitate the Bureau's functions.

[¶ 54,681] **Section 1022. Rulemaking authorities**

This section authorizes the Bureau to administer, enforce and implement the provisions of Federal consumer financial law and, more specifically, authorizes the Bureau to prescribe rules and issue orders and guidance as may be necessary to carry out the purposes, and prevent evasions of, those laws. Under this section, the Bureau must, when prescribing rules, consider potential benefits and costs to consumers and covered persons, and consult with prudential regulators regarding consistency with safety and soundness considerations and other objectives of such agencies. This consultation would have to take place prior to the Bureau proposing a rule as well as during the public comment process. If during such consultation process a prudential regulator provides the Bureau with a written objection to the proposed rule, the Bureau is required to include in the adopting release a description of the objection and the basis for the Bureau's decision regarding such objection. The Bureau is authorized under this section to exempt classes of covered persons, service providers, or consumer financial products or services, from provisions of this title.

This section requires the Bureau to monitor for risks to consumers in the offering or provision of consumer financial products or services. In monitoring for risks, the Bureau is authorized to consider factors including likely risks and costs to consumers associated with buying or using a type of consumer financial product or service, the extent to which the law is likely to adequately protect consumers, and the extent to which the risks of a consumer financial product or service may disproportionately affect traditionally underserved consumers. The Bureau is further granted authority to gather and compile information regarding the organization, business conduct, markets, and activities of persons operating in consumer financial services markets, and to make such information public, as is in the public interest.

The Committee considers the monitoring and information gathering function to be an essential part of the Bureau's work. The Bureau must stay closely attuned to the marketplace for consumer financial products and services in order to effectively fulfill the purposes and objectives of this title.

Under this section, the Bureau is provided with access to the examination and financial condition reports made by a prudential regulator or other Federal agency having jurisdiction over a covered person. Similarly, a prudential regulator, State regulator or other Federal agency having jurisdiction over a covered person is provided with access to any examination reports made by the Bureau. The Bureau is required to take steps to ensure that proprietary, personal or confidential information is protected from public disclosure. In addition, the Bureau is required to assess the efficacy of its rules.

[¶ 54,682] **Section 1023. Review of Bureau regulations**

This section provides for a process by which the Financial Stability Oversight Council may set aside a final regulation promulgated by the Bureau if, in the view of two-thirds of the Council, the regulation would put the safety and soundness of the banking system or the stability of the financial system at risk. Under this section, an agency represented by a member of the Council may petition the Council to stay the effectiveness of, or set aside, a regulation if the member agency filing the petition has attempted to work with the Bureau to resolve concerns regarding the effect of the rule on financial stability or safety and soundness of the banking system. Such petition is required to be filed with the Council not later than 10 days after the regulation has been published in the Federal Register. A decision by the Council to set aside a regulation prescribed by the Bureau shall render such regulation unenforceable.

Any such decision by the Council would be required to be done within certain specified time limits. A decision to issue a stay of, or set aside, a regulation is required to be published in the Federal Register as soon as practicable after the decision is made, with an explanation of the reasons for the decision. A decision by the Council to set aside a regulation prescribed by the Bureau is subject to judicial review.

This provision is designed to ensure that consumer protection regulations do not put the safety and soundness of the banking system or the stability of the financial system at risk. This provision is in addition to the significant consultation requirements included in Section 1022.

The Committee notes that there was no evidence provided during its hearings that consumer protection regulation would put safety and soundness at risk. To the contrary, there has been significant evidence and extensive testimony that the opposite was the case. Specifically, it was the failure by the prudential regulators to give sufficient consideration to consumer protection that helped bring the financial system down. In fact, it was the organizations that promote consumer protection that were urging that underwriting standards be tightened for both consumer protection and safety and soundness reasons, and it was the prudential regulators who ignored these calls.

For example, in testimony before the Committee (June 26, 2007), David Berenbaum from the National Community Reinvestment Coalition said, "For the past 5 years, community groups, consumer protection groups, fair lending groups, and all of our members in the National Community Reinvestment Coalition have been sounding an alarm about poor underwriting—underwriting that not only endangered communities, their tax bases, their municipal governments, their ability to have sound services and celebrate homeownership—but [underwriting that] was going to impact on the safety and soundness of our banking institutions themselves. Those cries for action fell on deaf ears, and here we are today."

An article in the *American Banker* ("Do Safety and Soundness and Consumer Protection Really Conflict?," by Cheyenne Hopkins, March 30, 2010) calls the banking industry argument that such a conflict exists "shaky." The article quotes Kevin Jacques who worked for 10 years in the Office of the Comptroller of the Currency, who said, " . . . I cannot recall a meeting I sat in where we worried about consumer protection and looked at safety and soundness and said the two are in conflict . . .." A former New York Federal Reserve Bank official, Brad Sabel, agreed with this assessment, saying "In my experience I do not recall seeing a case where a consumer protection regulation was found to pose a threat to safe and sound operations of the banks."

Nonetheless, the Committee included this provision in order to reassure that the Bureau cannot put the safety and soundness or the stability of the financial system at risk.

[¶ 54,683] *Section 1024. Supervision of nondepository covered persons*

Section 1024 establishes the scope of the Bureau's supervisory authority over certain nondepository institutions (nondepository covered persons). Oversight of these companies has largely been left to the States, and they are not currently subject to regular Federal consumer compliance examinations comparable to examinations of their depository institution competitors. According to one Treasury official, "The federal government spends at least 15 times more on consumer compliance and enforcement for banks and credit unions than for nonbanks—even though there are at least five times as many nonbanks as there are banks and credit unions." The Federal Trade Commission has approximately 70 staff members assigned to perform enforcement and monitoring functions for approximately 100,000 nondepository financial service providers nationwide. The FTC's authority to issue rules regarding unfair and deceptive practices is constrained by procedural requirements, and it does not have authority to conduct compliance exams, as bank regulators do. For that reason, it has brought fewer than 25 lawsuits in the last five years against mortgage originators, payday lenders and debt collectors.

The authority provided to the Bureau in this section will establish for the first time consistent Federal oversight of nondepository institutions, based on the Bureau's assessment of the risks posed to consumers and other criteria set forth in this section. Banks and other nondepository companies that provide consumer financial products or services should be held to the same minimum standards for complying with Federal consumer financial laws regardless of their corporate structure. Specifically, the Bureau will have the authority to supervise all participants in the consumer mortgage arena, including mortgage originators, brokers, and servicers and consumer mortgage modification and foreclosure relief services. These entities contributed to the housing crisis that led to the near collapse of the financial system. The Bureau will also have the authority to supervise larger nondepository institutions that offer or provide other consumer financial products and services. Larger nondepositories will be defined through a Bureau rulemaking and in consultation with the Federal Trade Commission. Nondepository covered persons that are subject to the Bureau's supervision authority will be required to register with the Bureau. This section does not apply to depository institutions.

Specifically, the Bureau will have the authority to supervise all participants in the consumer mortgage arena, including mortgage originators, brokers, and servicers and consumer mortgage modification and foreclosure relief services. These entities contributed to the housing crisis that led to the near collapse of the financial system. The Bureau will also have the authority to supervise larger nondepository institutions that offer or provide other consumer financial products and services. Larger nondepositories will be defined through a Bureau rule making and in consultation with the Federal Trade Commission. Nondepository covered persons that are subject to the Bureau's supervision authority will be required to register with the Bureau. This section does not apply to depository institutions.

The Bureau will have the authority to require reports from and to conduct periodic examinations of nondepository covered persons described in section 1026(a) to assess compliance with Federal consumer financial laws, to obtain information about activities and compliance systems, and to detect and assess risks to consumers and markets for consumer financial products and services. The Bureau will exercise its authority by establishing a risk-based supervision program based on an assessment of the risks posed to consumers in certain product and geographic markets. In establishing the risk-based supervisory program, the Bureau will consider the asset size of the nondepository covered person, the volume of consumer financial product and service transactions it is engaged in, the risks to consumers of those products and services, and the extent to which the institution is overseen by State regulators.

Section 1024 provides that the Bureau's enforcement authority over larger nondepository covered persons, other than mortgage entities described in section 1024(a)(1)(A), is exclusive, although other Federal agencies may recommend (in writing) enforcement actions to the Bureau. Pursuant to a Memorandum of Understanding, the Bureau and the FTC will coordinate enforcement action of nondepository mortgage actors, including civil actions.

[¶ 54,684] Section 1025. Supervision of very large banks, savings associations, and credit unions

Section 1025 grants the Bureau primary examination and enforcement authority over all insured depository institutions and credit unions with more than $10 billion in assets. This authority extends to the affiliates and service providers of these large depositories. The current consumer protection system divides jurisdiction and authority for consumer protection between many federal regulators, whose mission is not focused on consumer protection. The result has been that banks could choose the least restrictive consumer compliance supervisor. The fragmented regulatory structure also resulted in finger pointing among regulators and inaction when problems with consumer products and services arose. The authority granted to the Bureau under this section creates one federal regulator with consolidated consumer protection authority over the largest depository institutions, leaving regulatory arbitrage and inter-agency finger pointing in the past.

Specifically, the Bureau will have the authority to require reports from and to conduct periodic examinations of the largest depository institutions to assess compliance with Federal consumer financial laws, to obtain information about activities and compliance systems, and to detect and assess risks to consumers and markets for consumer financial products and services. In order to minimize regulatory burden, the Bureau is required to coordinate examination and enforcement activities with the appropriate prudential regulator, including coordinating the scheduling of examinations, conducting simultaneous examinations unless the financial institution requests otherwise, sharing draft reports, requiring reasonable opportunity (30 days) to comment, and requiring that concerns raised by the prudential regulator be considered prior to issuing a final report. The Bureau must also pursue arrangements and agreements with State bank supervisors to coordinate examinations where appropriate.

Section 1025 also provides that any conflicts between regulators may be resolved by a governing panel. If the proposed supervisory determinations of the Bureau and the prudential regulator conflict, the examined financial institution may request that the agencies coordinate and present a joint statement of coordinated supervisory action. The agencies have 30 days to comply. If the agencies do not issue a joint statement, the financial institution may appeal to a governing panel 30 days after the joint statement is due. The governing panel would consist of a representative of the Board of Governors, the FDIC, the NCUA or OCC on a rotating basis (as long as that agency is not involved in the dispute) and a representative of the Bureau and the prudential regulator. The panel would have 30 days to provide a final determination to the financial institution.

[¶ 54,685] *Section 1026. Other banks, savings associations, and credit unions*

Section 1026 provides that an insured depository institution or credit union with $10 billion in assets or less will continue to be examined for consumer compliance by its prudential regulator. The Bureau is authorized to ride along on a sample of examinations conducted by the prudential regulators, which will assist the Bureau in understanding the operations of smaller banks and credit unions. The Bureau would not have authority to take enforcement action. Section 1026 provides the Bureau access to reports by banks and credit unions under the $10 billion threshold to help it better understand the markets for consumer financial products and services, and to ensure that it is a fair and consistent market-wide rule writer.

[¶ 54,686] *Section 1027. Limitations on authorities of the Bureau; preservation of authorities*

Section 1027 lays out the limits on the Bureau's authority with regard to certain entities and product types. These limitations make clear that the Bureau does not have authority over commercial transactions or the sale of nonfinancial goods or services.

Subsection (a) makes clear that the Bureau may not exercise any authority with respect to a merchant, retailer, seller or broker of nonfinancial good or service. However, the Bureau would have authority if such a person is significantly engaged in offering or providing any consumer financial product or service or is otherwise subject to an enumerated consumer law or other law that is transferred to the Bureau's authority. This subsection also allows a merchant to extend credit to a consumer for the purchase of a nonfinancial good or service without coming under the authority of the Bureau under this title. This has been described as allowing local merchants to "extend a tab" to a customer. Merchants may also collect these debts (or hire someone to do so), or sell such debts, if delinquent, without being subject to the Bureau's authority over those activities. This limitation would not extend to merchants who, for example, extend credit which exceeds the market value of the good or service offered or provided or who regularly extend credit that is subject to a finance charge and payable by written agreement in more than 4 installments.

Under this subsection, the Bureau would have no authority to issue rules or take enforcement action against merchants, retailers, or sellers of nonfinancial goods or services that are not engaged significantly in offering or providing consumer financial products or services. This makes clear that the Committee intends to exclude persons and businesses such as dentists, doctors, and small Main Street retailers that simply allow their customers to pay bills over time from the new authority of the Bureau. Such persons typically are not engaged significantly in offering or providing consumer financial products or services.

Finally, for the purposes of this section (a), the term "finance charge" is expected to be interpreted consistent with the current rules that implement the Truth in Lending Act, including appropriate exclusions from that term for charges for unanticipated late payment, delinquency, or default.

Subsection (b) clarifies that real estate brokerage activities are not covered by the Bureau except to the extent that a real estate broker is engaged in the offering of a consumer financial product or service or is otherwise subject to an enumerated consumer law or transferred authority.

Subsection (c) clarifies that retailers of manufactured housing and modular homes are not covered by the Bureau, except to the extent that a retailer is engaged in offering or providing a consumer financial product or service or is otherwise covered by a Federal consumer financial law.

Subsection (d) clarifies that accountants and tax preparers are not covered by the Bureau for certain activities.

Subsection (e) clarifies that attorneys are not covered by the Bureau to the extent they are engaged in the practice of law under the law of the State in which they are licensed. However, this exception to the Bureau's coverage does not extend to an attorney who is engaged in the offering of a consumer financial product or service or is otherwise subject to an enumerated consumer law or transferred authority.

Subsection (f) clarifies that persons regulated by a State insurance regulator are not covered by the Bureau except to the extent that such persons are engaged in the offering of a consumer financial product or service or are otherwise covered by a Federal consumer financial law.

Subsection (g) clarifies the authority of the Bureau with regards to employee benefit plans and certain other arrangements under the Internal Revenue Code of 1986, such as IRAs, certain education savings accounts, and others. The subsection preserves the authority of other existing agencies that regulate these programs. The subsection also prohibits the Bureau from exercising any authority with respect to these plans except in very limited circumstances. Any rulemaking could be done only after a joint request by the Secretary of Labor and the Secretary of the Treasury.

Subsection (h) clarifies that persons regulated by a State securities commission are not covered by the Bureau except to the extent that such persons are engaged in the offering of a consumer financial product or service or are otherwise subject to an enumerated consumer law or transferred authority.

Subsection (i) clarifies that persons regulated by the SEC are not covered by the Bureau. However, the SEC is required to consult and coordinate with the Bureau with respect to any rule for the same type of product as, or competes directly with, a consumer financial product or service that is subject to the Bureau's jurisdiction. This is to ensure equivalent regulatory treatment and prevent regulatory arbitrage.

Subsection (j) clarifies that persons regulated by the CFTC are not covered by the Bureau. As in subsection (i), coordination and consultation are required for rule making regarding products of the same type or that compete with each other and fall under the Bureau's jurisdiction.

Subsection (k) clarifies that the Bureau has no authority with respect to a person regulated by the Farm Credit Administration.

Subsection (l) clarifies that activities relating to charitable contributions are not covered by the Bureau. However, activities not involving charitable contributions that are the offering or provision of any consumer financial product or service are covered.

Subsection (m) clarifies that the Bureau may not define engaging in the business of insurance as a financial product or service.

Subsection (n) clarifies that a number of persons that are described above may be a service provider and subject to certain requests for information.

Subsection (o) clarifies that nothing in this title shall be construed as conferring authority on the Bureau to establish a usury limit on an extension of credit or made by a covered person to a consumer unless explicitly authorized by law.

Subsection (p) preserves the authorities of the Attorney General of the United States.

Subsection (q) preserves the authorities of the Secretary of the Treasury with regards to a person who performs income tax preparation activities for consumers.

Subsection (r) preserves the authority of the FDIC and NCUA with regards to deposit and share insurance.

[¶ 54,687] *Section 1028. Authority to restrict mandatory pre-dispute arbitration*

The Committee is concerned that consumers have little leverage to bargain over arbitration procedures when they sign a contract for a consumer financial product or service. The Bureau is therefore required by this section to conduct a study and provide a report to Congress on the use of mandatory pre-dispute arbitration agreements as they pertain to the offering or provision of consumer financial products or services. This section grants the Bureau authority to prohibit or impose conditions and limitations on certain arbitration agreements between a covered person and a consumer consistent with the results of the study if it is in the public interest. Additionally, the Bureau is prohibited from restricting consumers from entering into voluntary arbitration agreements after a dispute has arisen.

The bill empowers the Bureau to take a range of steps, which could include a prohibition, or could instead be to impose conditions or limitations. In addition, the Bureau may choose to focus on pre-dispute mandatory arbitration provisions in contracts for certain types of consumer financial products or services, such as mortgage loans. The Bureau has to justify any rule by finding it is in the public interest and for the protection of consumers.

[¶ 54,688] *Section 1029. Effective date*

This section provides that this subtitle become effective on the designated transfer date.

Subtitle C—Specific Bureau Authorities

[¶ 54,700] *Section 1031. Prohibiting unfair, deceptive, or abusive acts or practices*

This section authorizes the Bureau to prevent a covered person from engaging in or committing an unfair, deceptive or abusive act or practice in connection with a transaction with a consumer for a consumer financial product or service, or the offering thereof. The Bureau is authorized to prescribe rules to identify such acts or practices. In prescribing rules, the Bureau is required to consult with the Federal banking agencies, or other Federal agencies, as appropriate, concerning the consistency of the proposed rule with prudential, market, or systemic objectives administered by such agencies.

Current law prohibits unfair or deceptive acts or practices. The addition of "abusive" will ensure that the Bureau is empowered to cover practices where providers unreasonably take advantage of consumers. The Bureau could define acts or practices as abusive only if it has a factual basis to show that the act or practice either: (1) materially interferes with the ability of a consumer to understand a term or condition of a consumer financial product or service; or (2) takes unreasonable advantage of consumers' lack of understanding of material risks, costs, or conditions of the product, inability to protect their interests in selecting or using the product, or reasonable reliance on a covered person to act in the consumers' interest.

[¶ 54,701] *Section 1032. Disclosures*

This section helps ensure that consumers receive effective disclosures relevant to the purchase of consumer financial products or services. Under this section, the Bureau is granted rulemaking authority to ensure that information relevant to the purchase of such products or services is disclosed to the consumer in plain language in a manner that permits consumers to understand the costs, benefits, and risks associated with the product or service. In prescribing rules, the Bureau is required to consider available evidence about consumer awareness, understanding of, and responses to disclosures or communications about the risks, costs, and benefits of consumer financial products or services. The Bureau is granted the authority to provide a model form of such disclosure standards, and a safe harbor is provided for covered persons that use model forms included with a rule issued under this section.

Under this section, a procedure is established to allow the Bureau to permit a covered person to conduct a trial disclosure program for the purpose of improving on any model disclosure forms issued to consumers to implement an enumerated consumer law. The Bureau is required to propose for public comment rules and model forms that combine Truth in Lending Act (TILA) and Real Estate Settlement Procedures Act (RESPA) disclosures.

[¶ 54,702] *Section 1033. Consumer rights to access information*

This section ensures that consumers are provided with access to their own financial information. This section requires the Bureau to prescribe rules requiring a covered person to make available to consumers information concerning their purchase and possession of a consumer financial product or service, including costs, charges, and usage data. The information is required to be made available upon a consumer's request in an electronic form usable by the consumer.

Under this section, a covered person may not be required to make available any confidential or proprietary information, any information collected by the covered person for antifraud or antimoney laundering purposes, or any information that the covered person cannot retrieve in the ordinary course of business. This section does not impose a duty on covered persons to maintain or keep any information about a consumer.

[¶ 54,703] *Section 1034. Response to consumer complaints and inquiries*

Section 1034 requires the Bureau to establish procedures, in consultation with the appropriate Federal regulatory agencies, for providing a timely response to consumer complaints or inquiries which include steps taken by the regulator in response to the complaint or inquiry, any responses received by the regulator from the institution, and any follow-up plans or actions by the regulator in response to the consumer complaint or inquiry.

In addition, this section requires very large banks and credit unions (as defined in section 1025) subject to supervision and primary enforcement by the Bureau to provide a timely response to the Bureau, the prudential regulators, and any other related agency concerning a consumer complaint or inquiry. This includes steps taken by the institution in response to the complaint or inquiry, responses received by the institution from the consumer, and any follow-up plans or actions by the institution in response to the consumer complaint or inquiry.

Section 1034 also requires these very large depository institutions to comply in a timely manner with a consumer request for information in the control or possession of the institution concerning the account of the consumer, not including any confidential commercial information, such as algorithms used to derive credit scores, information collected for the purpose of preventing fraud or other unlawful or potentially unlawful conduct, information required to be kept confidential by any other provision of law, or any nonpublic or confidential information, including confidential supervisory information.

Finally, this section requires the Bureau to enter into a Memorandum of Understanding with the appropriate Federal regulatory agencies to establish procedures by which very large depository institutions and relevant agencies shall comply with this section.

[¶ 54,704] *Section 1035. Private Education Loan Ombudsman*

Section 1035 requires the Secretary of the Treasury, in consultation with the Director, to designate a Private Education Loan Ombudsman within the Bureau to provide timely assistance to borrowers of private education loans, and to disseminate information about the availability and functions of the Ombudsman to borrowers, potential borrowers, and related institutions, agencies, and participants.

This section requires the Ombudsman to receive, review, and attempt to informally resolve complaints from borrowers of private student loans. It also ensures coordination with the student loan ombudsman established under the Higher Education Act of 1965 by requiring a Memorandum of Understanding no later than 90 days after the designated transfer date. The Private Education Loan Ombudsman will also compile and analyze data on borrower complaints regarding private education loans, and make recommendations to the Director, the Secretary of Treasury, the Secretary of Education, and relevant Congressional Committees.

Finally, the Ombudsman is required to prepare an annual report describing and evaluating its activities during the preceding year, and to submit the report on a consistent annual date to the Secretary of the Treasury, the Secretary of Education, and relevant Congressional Committees.

[¶ 54,705] *Section 1036. Prohibited acts*

This section prohibits by law certain activities such as the selling or advertising of consumer financial products or services which are not in conformity with the sections of this title, the failure or refusal to provide information to the Bureau as required by law, and knowingly or recklessly providing substantial assistance to another person in violation of section 1031.

[¶ 54,706] *Section 1037. Effective date*

This section provides that this subtitle become effective on the designated transfer date.

Subtitle D—Preservation of State Law

[¶ 54,720] *Section 1041. Relation to State law*

Section 1041 confirms that the Consumer Financial Protection Act (CFP Act) will not preempt State law if the State law provides greater protection for consumers. Federal consumer financial laws have historically established only minimum standards and have not precluded the States from enacting more protective standards. This title maintains that status quo.

A strong and independent Bureau with a clear mission to keep consumer protections up-to-date with the changing marketplace will reduce the incentive for State action and increase uniformity. The Gramm-Leach-Bliley Act of 1999 set federal financial privacy standards and gave the States the authority to go further. Only three States have used that power, and banks' operations have not been impaired. If States can continue to provide new consumer protections as problems arise, and the Bureau has the authority to follow the market and keep Federal protection up-to-date, then the Bureau will be in a position to set a strong, consistent standard that will satisfy the States.

Additionally, State initiatives can be an important signal to Congress and Federal regulators of the need for Federal action. States are much closer to abuses and are able to move more quickly when necessary to address them. If States were not allowed to take the initiative to enact laws providing greater protection for consumers, the Federal Government would lose an important source of information and reason to adjust standards over time.

For that reason, section 1041 also requires the Bureau to propose a rule making when a majority of the States has enacted a resolution requesting a new or modified consumer protection regulation by the Bureau. As part of the rule making, the Bureau is required to consult with federal banking agencies to determine whether the proposed regulation presents an unacceptable safety and soundness risk. The Bureau must also make public in the Federal Register its determination to act or not to act on the States' request.

[¶ 54,721] *Section 1042. Preservation of enforcement powers of States*

Section 1042 grants authority to State attorneys general to enforce this Act against Federal and State chartered entities. State regulators are also authorized to take appropriate action against State chartered entities. The section also clarifies that the CFP Act does not limit any provision of any enumerated consumer law that relates to State authority to enforce Federal law. State attorneys general and regulators are directed to consult or notify the Bureau and the prudential regulators, when practicable, before initiating an enforcement action pursuant to this section. This section also confirms that the CFP Act has no impact on the authority of State securities or State insurance regulators regarding their enforcement actions or rulemaking activities.

[¶ 54,722] *Section 1043. Preservation of existing contracts*

Section 1043 makes clear that the CFP Act shall not be construed to affect the applicability of any rule, order, guidance or interpretation by the OCC or OTS regarding the preemption of State law by a Federal banking law to any contract entered into by banks, thrifts, or affiliates and subsidiaries thereof, prior to the date of enactment of the CFP Act. This section is intended to provide stability to existing contracts.

[¶ 54,723] *Section 1044. State law preemption standards for national banks and subsidiaries clarified*

Section 1044 amends the National Bank Act to clarify the preemption standard relating to State consumer financial laws as applied to national banks. This section does not alter the preemption standards for State laws of general applicability to business conduct. State consumer financial laws are defined as laws that directly and specifically regulate the manner, content, or terms and conditions of financial transactions or accounts with respect to consumers. The standard for preempting State consumer financial law would return to what it had been for decades, those recognized by the Supreme Court in *Barnett Bank v. Nelson*, 517 U.S. 25 (1996 *Barnett*), undoing broader standards adopted by rules, orders, and interpretations issued by the OCC in 2004.

Specifically, this section sets out the three circumstances under which a State consumer financial law can be preempted: (1) when the State law would have a discriminatory effect on national banks or federal thrifts in comparison with the effect of the law on a bank or thrift chartered in that State; (2) if the State law, as described in the standard established by the Supreme Court in *Barnett*, "prevents or significantly interferes with a national bank's exercise of its power;" or (3) the State law is preempted by another Federal law. A preemption determination pursuant to *Barnett* can be made by either a court or by the OCC on a case-by-case basis. The term "case-by-case basis" is defined to permit the OCC to make a single determination concerning multiple States' consumer financial laws, so long as the law contains substantively equivalent terms.

Prior to making a determination under the *Barnett* standard, the OCC must follow certain procedures when making a preemption determination. Prior to making such a determination the OCC must first consult with, and consider the views of, the Bureau. The determination by the OCC must also be based on substantial evidence supporting the finding that the provision meets the *Barnett* standard. After consulting with the Bureau, the OCC must make a written finding that a federal law provides a relevant substantive standard that would protect consumers if the State law was to be preempted. The federal standard does not have to be as strong as the State law that is being preempted.

Section 1044 clarifies that nothing affects the deference that a court may afford to the OCC under the *Chevron* doctrine when interpreting Federal laws administered by that agency, except for preemption determinations. For a preemption determination, a reviewing court must assess the validity of the agency's preemption claim based on certain factors, as the court finds to be persuasive and relevant.

Section 1044 does not alter or affect existing laws regarding the charging of interest by national banks

Finally, the OCC is required to periodically publish a list of its preemption determinations.

[¶ 54,724] Section 1045. Clarification of law applicable to nondepository institutions subsidiaries

Section 1045 clarifies that State law applies to State-chartered nondepository institution subsidiaries, affiliates, and agents of national banks, other than entities that are themselves chartered as national banks. Such entities are generally chartered by the States and therefore should be subject to State law.

[¶ 54,725] Section 1046. State law preemption standards for federal savings associations and subsidiaries clarified

Section 1046 amends the Home Owners' Loan Act to clarify that State law preemption standards for Federal savings associations and their subsidiaries shall be made in accordance with the standard applicable to national banks.

[¶ 54,726] Section 1047. Visitorial standards for national banks and savings associations

Section 1047 clarifies that a State attorney general may bring a judicial action against a national bank or Federal savings association to enforce Federal law, as permitted by such law, or nonpreempted State law, which is consistent with the provisions of the National Bank Act and Home Owners' Loan Act relating to visitorial powers. The United States Supreme Court affirmed this when it overturned a Federal preemption of States to enforce valid State laws against national banks in *Cuomo v. Clearing House Association*, 557 U.S. (2009) (Cuomo). The Court held that the National Bank Act generally preempts "vistorial" supervisory powers by States over national banks, but that law enforcement powers are separate and not preempted by the National Bank Act. A State attorney general is required to consult with the OCC before bringing an action against a national bank or Federal savings association.

[¶ 54,727] Section 1048. Effective date

Section 1048 provides that this subtitle becomes effective on the designated transfer date.

Subtitle E—Enforcement Powers

[¶ 54,740] Section 1051. Definitions

Section 1051 defines certain key terms for the purposes of this subtitle.

[¶ 54,741] Section 1052. Investigations and administrative discovery

Section 1052 provides the authority to the Bureau to issue subpoenas for documents and testimony. It also authorizes demands of materials and provides for confidential treatment of demanded material. Section 1052 provides for petitions to modify or set aside a demand, and for custodial control and district court jurisdiction.

[¶ 54,742] Section 1053. Hearings and adjudication proceedings

Section 1053 provides the authority to the Bureau to conduct hearings and adjudication proceedings with special rules for cease-and-desist proceedings, temporary cease-and-desist proceedings, and for enforcement of orders in the United States District Court.

[¶ 54,743] Section 1054. Litigation authority

Section 1054 provides the authority to the Bureau to commence civil action against a person who violates a provision of this title or any enumerated consumer law, rule or order.

[¶ 54,744] Section 1055. Relief available

Section 1055 provides for relief for consumers through administrative proceedings and court actions for violations of this title, including civil money penalties.

[¶ 54,745] Section 1056. Referrals for criminal proceedings

Section 1056 authorizes the Bureau to transmit evidence of conduct that may constitute a violation of Federal criminal law to the Attorney General of the United States.

[¶ 54,746] Section 1057. Employee protection

Section 1057 provides protection against firings of or discrimination against employees who provide information or testimony to the Bureau regarding violations of this title.

[¶ 54,747] *Section 1058. Effective date*

Section 1058 provides that this subtitle becomes effective on the designated transfer date.

Subtitle F—Transfer of Functions and Personnel and Transitional Provisions

[¶ 54,760] *Section 1061. Transfer of consumer financial protection functions*

Section 1061 transfers functions relating to consumer financial protection from the Federal banking agencies (Federal Reserve, OCC, OTS and FDIC) and NCUA, the Department of Housing and Urban Development and the Federal Trade Commission to the Bureau.

[¶ 54,761] *Section 1062. Designated transfer date*

Section 1062 identifies the date of transfer of functions to the Bureau as between 6 and 18 months after the date of enactment of the CFP Act and subject to a six month extension. It also requires that the transfer of functions be completed not later than 2 years after the date of enactment of the CFP Act.

[¶ 54,762] *Section 1063. Savings provision*

Section 1063 clarifies that existing rights, duties, obligations, orders, and rules of the Federal banking agencies, the NCUA, the Department of Housing and Urban Development and the Federal Trade Commission are not affected by the transfer.

[¶ 54,763] *Section 1064. Transfer of certain personnel*

Section 1064 provides for the transfer of personnel from various agencies to the Bureau and establishes employment and pay protection for two years. It also provides for continuation of benefits.

[¶ 54,764] *Section 1065. Incidental transfers*

Section 1065 authorizes the Director of the Office of Management and Budget, in consultation with the Secretary of the Treasury, to make additional incidental transfers of assets and liabilities of the various agencies. The authority in this section terminates after 5 years.

[¶ 54,765] *Section 1066. Interim authority of the Secretary*

Section 1066 provides the Secretary of the Treasury authority to perform the functions of the Bureau under the CFP Act until the Director of the Bureau is confirmed by the Senate.

[¶ 54,766] *Section 1067. Transition oversight*

Section 1067 ensures an orderly and organized creation of the Bureau. It also requires the Bureau to submit an annual report to Congress, which shall include plans for the recruitment of a qualified workforce and a training and development program.

Subtitle G—Regulatory Improvements

[¶ 54,780] *Section 1071. Collection of deposit account data*

Section 1071 authorizes the collection of deposit account data in order to promote awareness and understanding of the access of individuals and communities to financial services, and to identify business development needs and opportunities. In developing the rules prescribed under Section 1071, the Bureau should coordinate with the Federal banking regulators and the National Credit Union Administration regarding the type and form of the deposit account data, as well as the method of collection, making every effort to avoid duplicative data collection requirements and minimize additional regulatory burden. Where substantially similar data is collected by the appropriate Federal banking regulator or the National Credit Union Administration, the Bureau should use this data. This section becomes effective on the designated transfer date.

[¶ 54,781] *Section 1072. Small business data collection*

Section 1072 authorizes the Bureau to collect data on small businesses to facilitate enforcement of fair lending laws and to enable communities, governmental entities and creditors to identify business and community development needs and opportunities for women-owned and minority-owned small businesses. This section becomes effective on the designated transfer date.

¶ 54,781

[¶ 54,782] **Section 1073. GAO study on the effectiveness and impact of various appraisal methods**

Section 1073 requires the GAO to conduct a study on various appraisal methods and the extent to which the usage of such methods impacts costs to consumers, conflicts of interest and home price speculation.

[¶ 54,783] **Section 1074. Prohibition on certain prepayment penalties**

Section 1074 prohibits prepayment penalties on all residential mortgage loans that are not a qualified mortgage and restricts them on qualified mortgages. Qualified mortgages are defined to include residential mortgages that meet certain criteria, in particular with respect to the application of prepayment penalties.

[¶ 54,784] **Section 1075. Assistance for economically vulnerable individuals and families**

Section 1075 amends the Financial Education and Counseling Grant Program established in the Housing and Economic Recovery Act of 2008 by expanding the target audience beyond "potential homebuyers" to "economically vulnerable individuals and families" and deletes the 5 organization limit.

[¶ 54,785] **Section 1076. Remittance transfers**

Section 1076 amends the Electronic Fund Transfer Act to establish minimum protections for remittances sent by consumers in the United States to other countries (remittance transfers). Immigrants send substantial portions of their earnings to family members abroad. These senders of remittance transfers are not currently provided with adequate protections under federal or state law. They face significant problems with their remittance transfers, including being overcharged or not having the funds reach intended recipients. This section will require disclosures about the costs of sending remittance transfers to be displayed in storefronts and to be provided to senders prior to and after a transaction. An error resolution process for remittance transfers is also established.

Specifically, this section will allow consumers to compare costs by requiring remittance providers to post, on a daily basis, a model transfer for the amounts of $100 and $200 in their storefronts showing the amount of currency, including fees, which would be received by the recipient of a remittance. It also will require consumers sending remittances to be provided with simple disclosures describing the amount of currency for the designated recipient and a promised date of delivery. In addition, it establishes an error resolution process for remittances that are not properly transmitted.

Subtitle H—Conforming Amendments

[¶ 54,800] **Section 1081. Amendments to the Inspector General Act**

Section 1081 makes conforming amendments to the Inspector General Act to provide the Bureau with oversight by the Inspector General of the Board of Governors. This section becomes effective on the date of enactment of this Act.

[¶ 54,801] **Section 1082. Amendments to the Privacy Act of 1974**

Section 1082 makes conforming amendments to the Privacy Act. This section becomes effective on the date of enactment of this Act.

[¶ 54,802] **Section 1083. Amendments to the Alternative Mortgage Transaction Parity Act of 1982**

Section 1083 makes conforming amendments to the Alternative Mortgage Transaction Parity Act. The Alternative Mortgage Parity Act was passed in 1982 to preempt State laws and constitutions that prohibited adjustable rate mortgage (ARM) loans for Federally-chartered and State chartered entities. It also preempted State laws with respect to all "alternative" mortgages, including negative amortization loans and interest only loans. States were unable to regulate terms for mortgages which have proved to have had significant difficulty. The amendment continues to preempt State laws that would prohibit adjustable rate mortgages, but removes this preemption of other types of "alternative" mortgages or features, permitting States to legislate in this area.

[¶ 54,803] **Section 1084. Amendments to the Electronic Fund Transfer Act**

Section 1084 makes conforming amendments to the Electronic Fund Transfer Act.

[¶ 54,804] **Section 1085. Amendments to the Equal Credit Opportunity Act**

Section 1085 makes conforming amendments to the Equal Credit Opportunity Act.

[¶ 54,805] **Section 1086. Amendments to the Expedited Funds Availability Act**

Section 1086 makes conforming amendments to the Expedited Funds Availability Act. It also increases the next-day funds availability amount under the Expedited Funds Availability Act from $100 to $200, and allows future adjustments for inflation.

[¶ 54,806] **Section 1087. Amendments to the Fair Credit Billing Act**

Section 1087 makes conforming amendments to the Fair Credit Billing Act.

[¶ 54,807] **Section 1088. Amendments to the Fair Credit Reporting Act and the Fair and Accurate Credit Transactions Act**

Section 1088 makes conforming amendments to the Fair Credit Reporting Act and the Fair and Accurate Credit Transaction Act.

[¶ 54,808] **Section 1089. Amendments to the Fair Debt Collection Practices Act**

Section 1089 makes conforming amendments to the Fair Debt Collection Practices Act.

[¶ 54,809] **Section 1090. Amendments to the Federal Deposit Insurance Act**

Section 1090 makes conforming amendments to the Federal Deposit Insurance Act.

[¶ 54,810] **Section 1091. Amendments to the Gramm-Leach-Bliley Act**

Section 1091 makes conforming amendments to the Gramm-Leach-Bliley Act.

[¶ 54,811] **Section 1092. Amendments to the Home Mortgage Disclosure Act**

Section 1092 makes conforming and other amendments to the Home Mortgage Disclosure Act. The amendments require new data fields to be reported to the Bureau, including borrower age, total points and fees information, loan pricing, prepayment penalty information, house value for loan to value ratios, period of introductory interest rate, interest-only or negative amortization information, terms of the loan, channel of origination, unique originator ID from the Secure and Fair Enforcement for Mortgage Licensing Act, universal loan identifier, parcel number to permit geocoding, and credit score.

[¶ 54,812] **Section 1093. Amendments to the Home Owners Protection Act of 1998**

Section 1093 makes conforming amendments to the Home Owners Protection Act.

[¶ 54,813] **Section 1094. Amendments to the Home Ownership and Equity Protection Act of 1994**

Section 1094 makes conforming amendments to the Home Ownership and Equity Protection Act.

[¶ 54,814] **Section 1095. Amendments to the Omnibus Appropriations Act, 2009**

Section 1095 makes conforming amendments to the Omnibus Appropriations Act, 2009.

[¶ 54,815] **Section 1096. Amendments to the Real Estate Settlement Procedures Act**

Section 1096 makes conforming amendments to the Real Estate Settlement Procedures Act.

[¶ 54,816] **Section 1097. Amendments to the Right to Financial Privacy Act of 1978**

Section 1097 makes conforming amendments to the Right to Financial Privacy Act.

[¶ 54,817] **Section 1098. Amendments to the Secure and Fair Enforcement for Mortgage Licensing Act of 2008**

Section 1098 makes conforming amendments to the Secure and Fair Enforcement for Mortgage Licensing Act of 2008.

[¶ 54,818] **Section 1099. Amendments to the Truth in Lending Act**

Section 1099 makes conforming amendments to the Truth in Lending Act.

[¶ 54,819] **Section 1100. Amendments to the Truth in Savings Act**

Section 1100 makes conforming amendments to the Truth in Savings Act.

[¶ 54,820] **Section 1101. Amendments to the Telemarketing and Consumer Fraud and Abuse Prevention Act**

Section 1101 makes conforming amendments to the Telemarketing and Consumer Fraud and Abuse Prevention Act.

[¶ 54,821] **Section 1102. Amendments to the Paperwork Reduction Act**

Section 1102 makes conforming amendments to the Paperwork Reduction Act.

[¶ 54,822] **Section 1103. Adjustment for inflation in the Truth in Lending Act**

Section 1103 amends the Truth in Lending Act to cover transactions of up to $50,000 and allows future adjustments for inflation.

[¶ 54,823] **Section 1104. Effective date**

Section 1104 provides that Sections 1083 through 1102 become effective on the designated transfer date.

Title XI—Federal Reserve System Provisions

[¶ 54,840] **Section 1151. Federal Reserve Act amendment on emergency lending authority**

This section amends Section 13(3) of the Federal Reserve Act which governs emergency lending. Emergency lending to an individual entity is no longer permitted. The Board of Governors now is authorized to lend to a participant in any program or facility with broad-based eligibility. Policies and procedures governing emergency lending must be established by regulation, in consultation with the Secretary of the Treasury. The Treasury Secretary must approve the establishment of any lending program. Lending programs must be designed to provide liquidity and not to aid a failing financial company. Collateral or other security for loans must be sufficient to protect taxpayers from losses.

The Board of Governors must report to the Senate Committee on Banking, Housing and Urban Affairs and the House Committee on Financial Services on any 13(3) lending program within 7 days after it is initiated, and periodically thereafter. The identities of recipients of emergency lending will be disclosed within 1 year of receipt of assistance, unless the Federal Reserve reports to Congress that disclosure would reduce the effectiveness of the program or facility or have other serious adverse effects, in which case the identities of recipients will be disclosed no later than 1 year after the program terminates. The GAO will report to Congress evaluating whether a determination not to disclose recipient identities within a year is reasonable.

[¶ 54,841] **Section 1152. Reviews of special Federal Reserve credit facilities**

This section amends Section 714 of Title 31, United States Code, to establish Comptroller General audits of emergency lending by the Board of Governors of the Federal Reserve under Section 13(3) of the Federal Reserve Act.

[¶ 54,842] **Section 1153. Public access to information**

This section amends Section 2B of the Federal Reserve Act. The Comptroller General audits of 13(3) lending established under Section 1152 of this Act, the annual financial statements prepared by an independent auditor for the Board of Governors, and reports to the Senate Committee on Banking, Housing and Urban Affairs on 13(3) lending established under Section 1151 of this Act will be displayed on a webpage that will be accessed by an "Audit" link on the Board of Governors website. The required information will be made available within 6 months of the date of release.

[¶ 54,843] **Sections 1154-1155. Emergency financial stabilization debt guarantees**

The FDIC will be able to guarantee the debt of *solvent* insured depositories and their holding companies under very strict conditions. The Board of Governors of the Federal Reserve and the Financial Stability Oversight Council must determine that there is a "liquidity event" that failure to take action would have serious adverse effects on financial stability or economic conditions, and that guarantees are needed to avoid or mitigate the adverse effects. The determination must be in writing and is subject to GAO audit. The FDIC may then set up a facility to guarantee debt, following policies and procedures determined by regulation, but the terms and conditions of the guarantees must be approved by the Secretary of the Treasury.

The Secretary will determine a maximum amount of guarantees, and the President may request Congress to allow that amount. If the President does not submit the request, the guarantees will not be made. Congress has 5 days to disapprove the request. Fees for the guarantees are set to cover all expected costs. If there are losses, they are recouped from those firms that received guarantees.

[¶ 54,844] Section 1156. Additional related amendments

The FDIC may not exercise its systemic risk authority to establish any widely available debt guarantee program for which Section 1155 would provide authority.

If any firm defaults on a debt guarantee provided under section 1155, the FDIC shall appoint itself receiver of the company if it is an insured depository. If the defaulting firm is not an insured depository, the FDIC shall pursue one of two alternatives. Under the first alternative the FDIC will require consideration that the company be put into the resolution mechanism pursuant to Section 203, and require that the company file for bankruptcy if the FDIC is not appointed receiver within 30 days. Under the second alternative the FDIC will file a petition for involuntary bankruptcy on behalf of the defaulting company.

[¶ 54,845] Section 1157. Changes to Federal Reserve governance

The Federal Reserve Act is amended to state that a member of the Board of Governors of the Federal Reserve shall serve as Vice Chairman for Supervision. The Vice Chairman, who will be designated by the President, by and with the advice and consent of the Senate, will develop policy recommendations regarding supervision and regulation for the Board, and will appear before Congress semi-annually to report on the efforts, objectives and plans of the Board with respect to the conduct of supervision and regulation.

The Federal Reserve Act is amended to give the Board of Governors of the Federal Reserve a formal responsibility to identify, measure, monitor, and mitigate risks to U.S. financial stability.

The Federal Reserve Act is amended to state explicitly that the Board of Governors of the Federal Reserve may not delegate to a Federal reserve bank its functions for establishing supervisory and regulatory policy for bank holding companies and other financial firms supervised by the Board.

To eliminate potential conflicts of interest at Federal reserve banks, the Federal Reserve Act is amended to state that no company, or subsidiary or affiliate of a company that is supervised by the Board of Governors can vote for Federal reserve bank directors; and the officers, directors and employees of such companies and their affiliates cannot serve as directors.

The Federal Reserve Act is amended to state that the Federal Reserve Bank of New York president, who is currently appointed by the district board of directors, will be appointed by the President, by and with the advice and consent of the Senate.

Title XII—Improving Access to Mainstream Financial Institutions

[¶ 54,860] Section 1201. Short title

This section establishes the name of the title to be the "Improving Access to Mainstream Financial Institutions Act."

[¶ 54,861] Section 1202. Purpose

This section establishes the purpose of this title to encourage initiatives for financial products and services that are appropriate and accessible for millions of Americans who are not fully incorporated into the financial mainstream. The Committee is concerned about lack of access to mainstream financial institutions for significant numbers of unbanked or underbanked individuals. About one in four families are unbanked or underbanked. Many are low- and moderate-income families that cannot afford to have their earnings diminished by reliance on high-cost and often predatory financial products and services. Underbanked consumers rely on non-traditional forms of credit including payday lenders, title lenders, or refund anticipation loans for financial needs. The unbanked are unable to save securely for education expenses, a down payment on a first home, or other future financial needs.

[¶ 54,862] Section 1203. Definitions

[¶ 54,863] Section 1204. Expanded access to mainstream financial institutions

Section 1204 authorizes programs intended to assist low- and moderate-income individuals establish bank or credit union accounts. This section authorizes the Treasury Secretary to establish a multiyear program of grants, cooperative agreements, financial agency agreements, and similar contracts or undertakings to promote initiatives designed to expand access to mainstream financial institutions by low and moderate income individuals. Entities eligible under this program include: 501(c)(3) organizations;

federally insured depository institutions; community development financial institutions; State, local, or tribal government entities; and partnerships or other joint ventures comprised of one or more of these such entities. An eligible entity may, in participating in a program established by the Secretary under this section, offer or provide to low and moderate income individuals products or services including small-dollar value loans and financial education and counseling.

[¶54,864] Section 1205. Low-cost alternatives to payday loans

Section 1205 will encourage the development of small, affordable loans as an alternative to more costly, predatory, payday loans. This section authorizes the Secretary to establish multiyear demonstration programs by means of grants, cooperative agreements, financial agency agreements, and similar contracts or undertakings with eligible entities to provide low-cost small loans to consumers that will provide alternatives to payday loans. Loans under this section are required to be made on terms and conditions and pursuant to lending practices that are reasonable for consumers. The authorization of a grant program under this section is intended to encourage the further development of affordable small loans that will assist working families by providing access to reasonable credit and providing financial education opportunities. Entities awarded a grant under this section are required to promote financial literacy and education opportunities, such as relevant counseling services, educational courses, or wealth building programs, to each consumer provided with a loan pursuant to this section.

[¶54,865] Section 1206. Grants to establish loan-loss reserve funds

Section 1206 will enable Community Development Financial Institutions to establish and maintain small dollar loan programs by establishing a grant program within the CDFI Fund to encourage affordable small dollar lending through loan-loss reserve funds and provision of technical assistance. This section directs the CDFI Fund to make grants to CDFIs to establish loan-loss reserve funds to help CDFIs defray the costs of operating small dollar loan programs in order to help provide consumers access to mainstream financial institutions and provide payday loan alternatives. Loan-loss reserve funds enable financial institutions to maintain the necessary capital to offer small dollar loans in a prudentially sound manner. A CDFI receiving grants under this program must provide matching funds equal to 50% of the amount of any grant received under this section. Grants received by a CDFI under this section may not be used to provide direct loans to consumers, and may be used to help recapture a portion or all of a defaulted loan made under the small dollar loan program.

This section further requires the Fund to provide technical assistance grants to CDFIs to support and maintain small dollar loan programs. Technical assistance grants help financial institutions defray the initial fixed costs of establishing a small dollar loan program and effectively implement grant activities.

This section sets requirements for the terms and conditions of loans made by participating institutions to ensure affordability and help underserved consumers improve their financial condition. Small dollar loan programs are defined as loan programs where a CDFI offers loans to consumers that do not exceed $2500; are required to be paid in installments; have no prepayment penalty; report to at least one national consumer reporting agency; and meet any other affordability requirement established by the Administrator of the Fund.

[¶54,866] Section 1207. Procedural provisions

This section requires an eligible entity desiring to participate in a program or obtain a grant under this title to submit an application to the Secretary.

[¶54,867] Section 1208. Authorization of appropriations

This section authorizes to be appropriated to the Secretary, such sums necessary to administer and fund the programs and projects authorized by this title. It further authorizes to be appropriated to the Fund for each fiscal year beginning in FY 2010, an amount equal to the amount of the administrative costs of the Fund for the operation of the grant program established under this title.

[¶54,868] Section 1209. Regulations

This section authorizes the Secretary to promulgate regulations to implement and administer the grant programs and undertakings authorized by this title, including limiting the eligibility of entities as deemed appropriate for certain activities authorized in Section 1204.

[¶54,869] **Section 1210. Evaluation and reports to Congress**

This section requires the Secretary to submit a report to the Senate Committee on Banking, Housing and Urban Affairs and the House Financial Services Committee containing a description of the activities funded, amounts distributed, and measurable results, as appropriate and available.

[¶54,900] **VI. Hearing Record**

Since the beginning of the 110th Congress, the Committee on Banking, Housing, and Urban Affairs has held 79 hearings on topics surrounding the housing and economic crisis and financial regulatory reform.

Preserving the American Dream: Predatory Lending Practices and Home Foreclosures

Wednesday, February 7, 2007

Witnesses: The Reverend Jesse Jackson, President and Founder, RainbowPUSH Coalition; Mr. Harry H. Dinham, President, National Association of Mortgage Brokers; Mr. Hilary Shelton, Executive Director, National Association for the Advancement of Colored People; Mr. Martin Eakes, Chief Executive Officer, Self-Help Credit Union and the Center for Responsible Lending; Ms. Jean Constantine-Davis, Senior Attorney, AARP; Mr. Douglas G. Duncan, Senior Vice President of Research and Business Development, and Chief Economist, Mortgage Bankers Association; Ms. Delores King, Consumer; Ms. Amy Womble, Consumer.

Mortgage Market Turmoil: Causes and Consequences

Thursday, March 22, 2007

Witnesses:

Panel 1: Mr. Emory W. Rushton, Senior Deputy Comptroller and Chief National Bank Examiner, Office of the Comptroller of the Currency; Mr. Joseph A. Smith, North Carolina Commissioner of Banks and Chairman, Conference of State Bank Supervisors; Mr. Roger T. Cole, Director, Division of Banking Supervision and Regulation, Board of Governors of the Federal Reserve System; Mr. Scott M. Polakoff, Senior Deputy Director and Chief Operating Officer, Office of Thrift Supervision; Ms. Sandra Thompson, Director of the Division of Supervision and Consumer Protection, Federal Deposit Insurance Corporation.

Panel 2: Mr. Brendan McDonagh, Chief Executive Officer, HSBC Finance Corporation; Mr. Sandy Samuels, Executive Managing Director, Countrywide Financial Corporation; Mr. Laurent Bossard, Chief Executive Officer, WMC Mortgage; Mr. L. Andrew Pollock, President, First Franklin Financial Corporation; Ms. Janis Bowdler, Senior Policy Analyst, National Council of La Raza; Mr. Irv Ackelsberg, Consumer Attorney; Ms. Jennie Haliburton, Consumer; Mr. Al Ynigues, Borrower.

Subprime Mortgage Market Turmoil: Examining the Role of Securitization

Tuesday, April 17, 2007

Witnesses: Mr. Gyan Sinha, Senior Managing Director and Head of ABS and CDO Research, Bear Stearns & Co. Inc.; Mr. David Sherr, Managing Director and Head of Securitized Products, Lehman Brothers; Ms. Susan Barnes, Managing Director of Ratings Services, Standard and Poor's; Mr. Warren Kornfeld, Managing Director, Residential Mortgage-Backed Securities Rating Group, Moody's Investors Service; Mr. Kurt Eggert, Professor of Law, Chapman University School of Law; Mr. Christopher L. Peterson, Assistant Professor of Law, Levin College of Law, University of Florida.

Ending Mortgage Abuse: Safeguarding Homebuyers

Tuesday, June 26, 2007

Witnesses: Mr. David Berenbaum, Executive Vice President, National Community Reinvestment Coalition; Professor Anthony Yezer, Department of Economics, George Washington University; Ms. Denise Leonard, Chairman and CEO, Constitution Financial Group, Inc. on behalf of the National Association of Mortgage Brokers; Mr. John Robbins, Chairman, Mortgage Bankers Association; Mr. Wade Henderson, President and CEO, Leadership Conference on Civil Rights; Mr. Alan Hummel, Senior Vice President and Chief Appraiser, Forsythe Appraisals, LLC on behalf of the Appraisal Institute; Mr. Pat V. Combs, President, National Association of REALTORS; Mr. Michael D. Calhoun, President, Center For Responsible Lending.

The State of the Securities Markets

Tuesday, July 31, 2007

Witnesses: Honorable Christopher Cox, Chairman, Securities and Exchange Commission.

The Role and Impact of Credit Rating Agencies on the Subprime Credit Markets

Wednesday, September 26, 2007

Witnesses

Panel 1: Honorable Christopher Cox, Chairman, Securities and Exchange Commission.

Panel 2: Mr. John Coffee, Adolf A. Berle Professor of Law, Columbia Law School; Dr. Lawrence J. White, Leonard E. Imperatore Professor of Economics, New York University; Mr. Micheal Kanef, Group Managing Director, Assett Finance Group, Moody's Financial Services; Ms. Vickie A. Tillman, Executive Vice President for Credit Market Services, Standard & Poor's.

Strengthening our Economy: Foreclosure Prevention and Neighborhood Preservation

Thursday, January 31, 2008

Witnesses

Panel 1: Honorable Sheila Bair, Chairman, Federal Deposit Insurance Corporation; Robert Steel, Under Secretary of Treasury for Domestic Finance, Department of the Treasury.

Panel 2: Doris Koo, President and CEO, Enterprise Community Partners, Inc; Michael Barr, Senior Fellow, Center for American Progress, and Professor of Law, University of Michigan Law School; Mr. Wade Henderson, President and CEO, Leadership Conference on Civil Rights; Mr. Alex Pollock, Resident Fellow, American Enterprise Institute.

The State of the United States Economy and Financial Markets

Thursday, February 14, 2008

Witnesses: Honorable Henry M. Paulson, Secretary of the Treasury; Honorable Christopher Cox, Chairman, Securities and Exchange Commission; Honorable Ben S. Bernanke, Chairman, Board of Governors of the Federal Reserve System.

The State of the Banking Industry

Tuesday, March 4, 2008

Witnesses: Honorable Sheila Bair, Chairman, Federal Deposit Insurance Corporation; Honorable John C. Dugan, Comptroller of the Currency, United States Treasury; Honorable John M. Reich, Director, Office of Thrift Supervision; Honorable JoAnn Johnson, Chairman, National Credit Union Administration; Honorable Donald Kohn, Vice Chairman, Board of Governors, Federal Reserve System; Mr. Thomas B. Gronstal, Superintendent of Banking, State of Iowa.

Turmoil in U.S. Credit Markets: Examining the Recent Actions of Federal Financial Regulators

Thursday, April 3, 2008

Witnesses

Panel 1: The Honorable Ben S. Bernanke, Chairman, Board of Governors of the Federal Reserve System; Honorable Christopher Cox, Chairman, Securities and Exchange Commission; Robert Steel, Under Secretary of Treasury for Domestic Finance, Department of the Treasury; Mr. Timothy F. Geithner, President, Federal Reserve Bank of New York.

Panel 2: Mr. James Dimon, Chairman and Chief Executive Officer, JP Morgan Chase; Mr. Alan D. Schwartz, President and Chief Executive Officer, The Bear Stearns Companies, Inc.

Restoring the American Dream: Solutions to Predatory Lending and the Foreclosure Crisis

Monday, April 7, 2008

Witnesses: The Honorable Michael Nutter, Mayor of Philadelphia, Pennsylvania; Ms. Yajaira Rivera, Philadelphia, Pennsylvania; Ms. Christina Anderson-Jones, Philadelphia, Pennsylvania; Ph.D. Ira Goldstein, Director, Policy and Information Services, The Reinvestment Fund; Mr. Brian A. Hudson, Sr., Executive Director, Pennsylvania House Finance Agency.

Turmoil in U.S. Credit Markets: Examining Proposals to Mitigate Foreclosures and Restore Liquidity to the Mortgage Markets

Thursday, April 10, 2008

Witnesses: Dr. Lawrence H. Summers, Charles W. Eliot University Professor, Harvard University; Dr. Dean Baker, Co-Director, Center for Economic and Policy Research; Ms. Ellen Harnick, Senior Policy Counsel, Center for Responsible Lending; Mr. Scott Stern, Chief Executive Officer, Lenders One, Incorporated; Dr. Douglas Elmendorf, Senior Fellow, The Brookings Institution.

Turmoil in U.S. Credit Markets Impact on the Cost and Availability of Student Loans

Tuesday, April 15, 2008

Witnesses: John (Jack) F. Remondi, Vice Chairman and Chief Financial Officer, Sallie Mae, Inc.; Mr. Tom Deutsch, Deputy Executive Director, American Securitization Forum; Ms. Patricia McGuire, President, Trinity Washington University; Ms. Sarah Flanagan, Vice President for Policy Development, National Association of Independent Colleges and Universities; Mark Kantrowitz, Publisher, FinAid.org.

Turmoil in U.S. Credit Markets: Examining Proposals to Mitigate Foreclosures and Restore Liquidity to the Mortgage Markets

Wednesday, April 16, 2008

Witnesses: Honorable Brian D. Montgomery, Federal Housing Commissioner and Assistant Secretary, Department of Housing and

¶54,900

Urban Development; Mr. Art Murton, Director, Division of Insurance and Research, Federal Deposit Insurance Corporation; Mr. Scott M. Polakoff, Senior Deputy Director and Chief Operating Officer, Office of Thrift Supervision.

Turmoil in U.S. Credit Markets: The Role of the Credit Rating Agencies

Tuesday, April 22, 2008

Witnesses

Panel 1: Honorable Christopher Cox, Chairman, Securities and Exchange Commission.

Panel 2: Professor John C. Coffee, Jr., Adolf A. Berle Professor of Law, Columbia University Law School; Dr. Arturo Cifuentes, Managing Director, R.W. Pressprich & Co.; Mr. Stephen W. Joynt, President and Chief Executive Officer, Fitch Ratings; Ms. Claire Robinson, Senior Managing Director, Moody's Investors Service; Ms. Vickie A. Tillman, Executive Vice President for Credit Market Services, Standard & Poor's.

Turmoil in U.S. Credit Markets: Examining the U.S. Regulatory Framework for Assessing Sovereign Investments

Thursday, April 24, 2008

Witnesses

Panel 1: Mr. Scott Alvarez, General Counsel, Board of Governors of the Federal Reserve System; Mr. Ethiopis Tafara, Director, Office of International Affairs, Securities and Exchange Commission.

Panel 2: Mr. David Marchick, Managing Director, The Carlyle Group; Mr. Paul Rose, Assistant Professor of Law, Moritz College of Law, Ohio State University; Ms. Jeanne S. Archibald, Partner, Hogan and Hartson LLP; Mr. Dennis Johnson, Director of Corporate Governance, California Public Employees' Retirement System.

Turmoil in the U.S. Credit Markets: Examining the Regulation of Investment Banks by the U.S. Securities and Exchange Commission

Wednesday, May 7, 2008

Witnesses

Panel 1: Mr. Erik Sirri, Director, Division of Market Regulation, Securities and Exchange Commission.

Panel 2: Honorable Arthur Levitt, Former Chairman, U.S. Securities and Exchange Commission; Mr. David Ruder, Former Chairman, U.S. Securities and Exchange Commission.

The State of the Banking Industry: Part II

Thursday, June 5, 2008

Witnesses: Honorable Sheila Bair, Chairman, Federal Deposit Insurance Corporation; Honorable John C. Dugan, Comptroller of the Currency, United States Treasury; Honorable John M. Reich, Director, Office of Thrift Supervision; Honorable JoAnn Johnson, Chairman, National Credit Union Administration; Honorable Donald Kohn, Vice Chairman, Board of Governors, Federal Reserve System; Mr. Timothy J. Karsky, Commissioner/Chairman, North Dakota Department of Financial Institutions/Conference of State Bank Supervisors.

Risk Management and its Implications for Systemic Risk

Thursday, June 19, 2008

Witnesses: Honorable Donald Kohn, Vice Chairman, Board of Governors, Federal Reserve System; Dr. Erik Sirri, Director, Division of Trading and Markets, U.S. Securities and Exchange Commission; Mr. Scott M. Polakoff, Deputy Director, Office of Thrift Supervision; Mr. Richard Bookstaber, Financial Author; Professor Richard Herring, Jacob Safra Professor of International Banking and Co-Director of the Wharton Financial Institutions Center, Wharton School, University of Pennsylvania; Mr. Kevin Blakely, President and Chief Executive Officer, Risk Management Association.

Reducing Risks and Improving Oversight in the OTC Credit Derivatives Market

Wednesday, July 9, 2008

Witnesses: Mr. Patrick Parkinson, Deputy Director, Division of Research and Statistics, Board of Governors of the Federal Reserve System; Mr. James Overdahl, Senior Economist, U.S. Securities and Exchange Commission; Ms. Kathryn E. Dick, Deputy Comptroller for Credit and Market Risk, Office of the Comptroller of the Currency; Dr. Darrell Duffie, Dean Witter Distinguished Professor of Finance, Stanford University, Graduate School of Business; Mr. Craig Donohue, Chief Executive Officer, Chicago Mercantile Exchange Group; Mr. Edward J. Rosen, Cleary Gottlieb Steen & Hamilton LLP, Outside Counsel to The Clearing Corporation; Mr. Robert G. Pickel, Executive Director and Chief Executive Officer, International Swaps and Derivatives Association, Inc.

Recent Developments in U.S. Financial Markets and Regulatory Responses to Them

Tuesday, July 15, 2008

Witnesses: Honorable Henry M. Paulson, Secretary of the Treasury; The Honorable Ben S. Bernanke, Chairman, Board of Governors of the

Federal Reserve System; Honorable Christopher Cox, Chairman, Securities and Exchange Commission.

State of the Insurance Industry: Examining the Current Regulatory and Oversight Structure

Tuesday, July 29, 2008

Witnesses

Panel 1: Honorable Steven M. Goldman, Commissioner, New Jersey Department of Banking and Insurance, on behalf of the National Association of Insurance Commissioners; Mr. Travis B. Plunkett, Legislative Director, Consumer Federation of America; Mr. Alessandro Iuppa, Senior Vice President, Zurich North America, on behalf of the American Insurance Association; Mr. John L. Pearson, Chairman, President, and Chief Executive Officer, The Baltimore Life Insurance Company, on behalf of the American Council of Life Insurers.

Panel 2: Mr. George A. Steadman, President and Chief Operating Officer, Rutherfoord Inc., on behalf of the Council of Insurance Agents & Brokers; Mr. Thomas Minkler, President, Clark-Mortenson Agency, Inc., on behalf of the Independent Insurance Agents & Brokers of America; Mr. Franklin Nutter, President, Reinsurance Association of America; Mr. Richard Bouhan, Executive Director, National Association of Professional Surplus Lines Offices.

Transparency in Accounting: Proposed Changes to Accounting for Off-Balance Sheet Entities

Thursday, September 18, 2008

Witnesses

Panel 1: Mr. Lawrence Smith, Board Member, Financial Accounting Standards Board (FASB); Mr. John White, Director, Office of Corporate Finance, Securities and Exchange Commission; Mr. James Kroeker, Deputy Chief Accountant for Accounting, U.S. Securities and Exchange Commission.

Panel 2: Professor Joseph Mason, Hermann Moyse Jr. Endowed Chair of Banking, E.J. Ourso College of Business, Louisiana State University; Mr. Donald Young, Managing Director, Young and Company LLC, and former FASB Board Member; Ms. Elizabeth Mooney, Analyst, Capital Strategy Research, The Capital Group; Mr. George Miller, Executive Director, American Securitization Forum.

Turmoil in US Credit Markets Recent Actions Regarding Government Sponsored Entities, Investment Banks and Other Financial Institutions

Tuesday, September 23, 2008

Witnesses: Honorable Henry M. Paulson, Secretary of the Treasury; The Honorable Ben S. Bernanke, Chairman, Board of Governors of the Federal Reserve System; Honorable Christopher Cox, Chairman, Securities and Exchange Commission; Honorable James B. Lockhart, III, Director, Federal Housing Finance Agency.

Turmoil in the U.S. Credit Markets: The Genesis of the Current Economic Crisis

Thursday, October 16, 2008

Witnesses: Honorable Arthur Levitt, Jr., Senior Advisor, The Carlyle Group; Honorable Eugene A. Ludwig, Chief Executive Officer, Promontory Financial Group; Honorable Jim Rokakis, Treasurer, Cuyahoga County, Ohio; Honorable Marc H. Morial, President and CEO, National Urban League; Mr. Eric Stein, Senior Vice President, Center for Responsible Lending.

Turmoil in the U.S. Credit Markets: Examining Recent Regulatory Responses

Thursday, October 23, 2008

Witnesses: Honorable Sheila Bair, Chairman, Federal Deposit Insurance Corporation; Honorable Neel Kashkari, Interim Assistant Secretary for Financial Stability and Assistant Secretary for International Affairs, U.S. Department of the Treasury; Honorable James B. Lockhart, III, Director, Federal Housing Finance Agency; Honorable Elizabeth A. Duke, Governor, Board of Governors of the Federal Reserve System; Honorable Brian D. Montgomery, Federal Housing Commissioner and Assistant Secretary, Department of Housing and Urban Development.

Oversight of the Emergency Economic Stabilization Act: Examining Financial Institution Use of Funding Under the Capital Purchase Program

Thursday, November 13, 2008

Witnesses: Ms. Anne Finucane, Global Corporate Affairs Executive, Bank of America; Mr. Barry L. Zubrow, Executive Vice President, Chief Risk Officer, JPMorgan Chase; Mr. Jon Campbell, Executive Vice President, Chief Executive Officer of the Minnesota Region, Wells Fargo Bank; Mr. Gregory Palm, Executive Vice President and General Counsel, The Goldman Sachs Group, Inc.; Mr. Martin Eakes, Chief Executive Officer, Self-Help Credit Union and the Center for Responsible Lending; Nancy M. Zirkin, Director of Public Policy, Leadership Conference on Civil

Rights; Dr. Susan M. Wachter, Worley Professor of Financial Management, Wharton School of Business, University of Pennsylvania.

Examining the State of the Domestic Automobile Industry

Tuesday, November 18, 2008

Witnesses

Panel 1: Honorable Debbie Stabenow (D-MI), United States Senator.

Panel 2: Mr. Ron Gettelfinger, President, International Union, United Automobile, Aerospace and Agricultural Implement Workers of America; Mr. Alan Mulally, President and Chief Executive Officer, Ford Motor Company; Mr. Robert Nardelli, Chairman and Chief Executive Officer, Chrysler LLC; Mr. G. Richard Wagoner, Jr., Chairman and Chief Executive Officer, General Motors; Dr. Peter Morici, Professor, Robert H. Smith School of Business, University of Maryland.

The State of the Domestic Automobile Industry: Part II

Thursday, December 4, 2008

Witnesses

Panel 1: Mr. Gene L. Dodaro, Acting Comptroller General, United States Government Accountability Office.

Panel 2: Mr. Ron Gettelfinger, President, International Union, United Automobile, Aerospace and Agricultural Implement Workers of America; Mr. Alan Mulally, President and Chief Executive Officer, Ford Motor Company; Mr. Robert Nardelli, Chairman and Chief Executive Officer, Chrysler LLC; Mr. G. Richard Wagoner, Jr., Chairman and Chief Executive Officer, General Motors; Mr. Keith Wandell, President, Johnson Controls, Inc.; Mr. James Fleming, President, Connecticut Automotive Retailers Association; Dr. Mark Zandi, Chief Economist and Cofounder, Moody's Economy.com.

Madoff Investment Securities Fraud: Regulatory and Oversight Concerns and the Need for Reform

Tuesday, January 27, 2009

Witnesses: Professor John C. Coffee, Jr., Adolf A. Berle Professor of Law, Columbia University Law School; Dr. Henry A. Backe, Jr., Orthopedic Surgeon, Fairfield, Connecticut; Ms. Lori Richards, Director, Office of Compliance Inspections and Examinations, U.S. Securities and Exchange Commission; Ms. Linda Thomsen, Director, Division of Enforcement, U.S. Securities and Exchange Commission; Mr. Stephen Luparello, Interim Chief Executive Officer, Financial Industry Regulatory Authority; Mr. Stephen Harbeck, Interim Chief Executive Officer, Financial Industry Regulatory Authority.

Modernizing the U.S. Financial Regulatory System

Wednesday, February 4, 2009

Witnesses

Panel 1: Honorable Paul A. Volcker, Chair of the President's Economic Recovery Advisory Board, Former Chairman, Board of Governors of the Federal Reserve System.

Panel 2: Mr. Gene L. Dodaro, Acting Comptroller General, United States Government Accountability Office.

Pulling Back the TARP: Oversight of the Financial Rescue Program

Thursday, February 5, 2009

Witnesses: Mr. Gene L. Dodaro, Acting Comptroller General, United States Government Accountability Office; Honorable Neil M. Barofsky, Special Inspector General, Troubled Asset Relief Program; Professor Elizabeth Warren, Chair, Congressional Oversight Panel for the Troubled Asset Relief Program.

Oversight of the Financial Rescue Program: A New Plan for the TARP

Tuesday, February 10, 2009

Witnesses: Honorable Timothy Geithner, Secretary, United States Department of the Treasury.

Modernizing Consumer Protection in the Financial Regulatory System: Strengthening Credit Card Protections

Thursday, February 12, 2009

Witnesses: Mr. Travis B. Plunkett, Legislative Director, Consumer Federation of America; Mr. James C. Sturdevant, Esq., The Sturdevant Law Firm; Mr. Kenneth J. Clayton, Senior Vice President and General Counsel, Card Policy Council, American Bankers Association; Lawrence M. Ausubel, Professor of Economics, University of Maryland; Mr. Todd Zywicki, Professor, George Mason University School of Law; Mr. Adam J. Levitin, Associate Professor of Law, Georgetown University Law Center.

Homeowner Affordability and Stability Plan

Thursday, February 26, 2009

¶ 54,900

Witnesses: Honorable Shaun Donovan, Secretary, U.S. Department of Housing and Urban Development.

Consumer Protections in Financial Services: Past Problems, Future Solutions

Tuesday, March 3, 2009

Witnesses: Mr. Steve Bartlett, President and CEO, Financial Services Roundtable; Honorable Ellen Seidman, Senior Fellow of New America Foundation, Executive Vice President of ShoreBank Corporation; Professor Patricia McCoy, George J. & Helen M. England Professor of Law, University of Connecticut School of Law.

American International Group: Examining What Went Wrong, Government Intervention, and Implications for Future Regulation

Thursday, March 5, 2009

Witnesses: Honorable Donald Kohn, Vice Chairman, Board of Governors, Federal Reserve System; Mr. Scott M. Polakoff, Senior Deputy Director and Chief Operating Officer, Office of Thrift Supervision; Mr. Eric Dinallo, Superintendent, New York State Insurance Department.

Enhancing Investor Protection and the Regulation of Securities Markets

Tuesday, March 10, 2009

Witnesses: Mr. John Coffee, Adolf A. Berle Professor of Law, Columbia Law School; Mr. Lynn E. Turner, Former Chief Accountant, U.S. Securities and Exchange Commission; Mr. Timothy Ryan, President and CEO, Securities Industry and Financial Markets Association; Mr. Paul Schott Stevens, President and CEO, Investment Company Institute: Professor Mercer Bullard, Associate Professor and President, University of Mississippi School of Law and Fund Democracy; Mr. Robert G. Pickel, Executive Director and Chief Executive Officer, International Swaps and Derivatives Association, Inc.; Mr. Damon Silvers, Associate General Counsel, AFL-CIO; Thomas G. Doe, CEO, Municipal Market Advisors.

Perspectives on Modernizing Insurance Regulation

Tuesday, March 17, 2009

Witnesses: Mr. Michael McRaith, Director of Insurance, Illinois Department of Financial and Professional Regulation, on behalf of the National Association of Insurance Commissioners; Honorable Frank Keating, President and Chief Executive Officer, The American Council of Life Insurers; Mr. William R. Berkley, Chairman and Chief Executive Officer, W. R. Berkley Corporation, on behalf of the American Insurance Association; Mr. Spencer Houldin, President, Ericson Insurance Services, on behalf of the Independent Insurance Agents and Brokers of America; Mr. John Hill, President and Chief Operating Officer, Magna Carta Companies, on behalf of the National Association of Mutual Insurance Companies; Mr. Frank Nutter, President, The Reinsurance Association of America; Mr. Robert Hunter, Director of Insurance, The Consumer Federation of America.

Lessons Learned in Risk Management Oversight at Federal Financial Regulators

Wednesday, March 18, 2009

Witnesses: Mr. Scott M. Polakoff, Acting Director, Office of Thrift Supervision; Ms. Orice Williams, Director, Financial Markets and Community Investment, Government Accountability Office; Mr. Roger Cole, Director, Division of Banking Supervision and Regulation, Federal Reserve Board; Mr. Timothy Long, Senior Deputy Comptroller, Bank Supervision Policy and Chief National Bank Examiner, Office of the Comptroller of the Currency; Dr. Erik Sirri, Director, Division of Trading and Markets, U.S. Securities and Exchange Commission.

Modernizing Bank Supervision and Regulation

Thursday, March 19, 2009

Witnesses: Honorable John C. Dugan, Comptroller of the Currency, Office of the Comptroller of the Currency; Honorable Daniel K. Tarullo, Member, Board of Governors of the Federal Reserve System; Honorable Sheila Bair, Chairman, Federal Deposit Insurance Corporation; Honorable Michael E. Fryzel, Chairman, National Credit Union Administration; Mr. Scott M. Polakoff, Acting Director, Office of Thrift Supervision; Mr. Joseph A. Smith, North Carolina Commissioner of Banks and Chairman, Conference of State Bank Supervisors; Mr. George Reynolds, Chairman, National Association of State Credit Union Supervisors and Senior Deputy Commissioner, Georgia Department of Banking and Finance.

Current Issues in Deposit Insurance

Thursday, March 19, 2009

Witnesses

Panel 1: Mr. Art Murton, Director, Division of Insurance and Research, Federal Deposit Insurance Corporation; Mr. David M. Marquis, Executive Director, National Credit Union Administration.

Panel 2: Mr. William Grant, Chairman & CEO, First United Bank and Trust, Oakland, Ma-

¶ 54,900

ryland, on behalf of the American Bankers Association; Mr. Terry West, President and CEO, VyStar Credit Union in Jacksonville, Florida, on behalf of the Credit Union National Association; Mr. Steve Verdier, Senior Vice President, Independent Community Bankers of America; Mr. David J. Wright, CEO, Services Credit Union, Yankton, South Dakota, on behalf of the National Association of Federal Credit Unions.

Modernizing Bank Supervision and Regulation, Part II

Tuesday, March 24, 2009

Witnesses: Mr. William Attridge, President, Chief Executive Officer and Chief Operating Officer, Connecticut River Community Bank, on behalf of the Independent Community Bankers of America; Mr. Daniel A. Mica, President and Chief Executive Officer, Credit Union National Association; Mr. Aubrey Patterson, Chairman and Chief Executive Officer, BancorpSouth, Inc., on behalf of the American Bankers Association; Mr. Christopher Whalen, Managing Director, Institutional Risk Analytics; Ms. Gail Hillebrand, Senior Attorney, Consumers Union of U.S., Inc.

Enhancing Investor Protection and the Regulation of Securities Markets—Part II

Thursday, March 26, 2009

Witnesses

Panel 1: Honorable Mary Schapiro, Chairman, U.S. Securities and Exchange Commission; Honorable Fred Joseph, President, North American Securities Administrators Association.

Panel 2: Honorable Richard C. Breeden, Former Chairman, U.S. Securities and Exchange Commission; Honorable Arthur Levitt, Former Chairmen, U.S. Securities and Exchange Commission; Honorable Paul S. Atkins, Former Commissioner, U.S. Securities and Exchange Commission.

Panel 3: Mr. Richard Ketchum, Chairman and CEO, FINRA; Mr. Ronald A. Stack, Chair, Municipal Securities Rulemaking Board; Honorable Richard Baker, President and CEO, Managed Funds Association; Mr. James Chanos, Chairman, Coalition of Private Investment Companies; Ms. Barbara Roper, Director of Investor Protection, Consumer Federation of America; Mr. David G. Tittsworth, Executive Director and Executive Vice President, Investment Adviser Association; Ms. Rita Bolger, Senior Vice President and Associate General Counsel, Standard & Poor's, Global Regulatory Affairs; President Daniel Curry, President, DBRS, Inc.

Lessons from the New Deal

Tuesday, March 31, 2009

Witnesses

Panel 1: Honorable Christina Romer, Chair, Council of Economic Advisors.

Panel 2: Dr. James K. Galbraith, Lloyd M. Bentsen Chair, Lyndon B. Johnson School of Public Affairs, University of Texas at Austin; Dr. J. Bradford DeLong, Professor of Economics, University of California Berkeley; Dr. Allan M. Winkler, Professor of History, Miami (Ohio) University; Dr. Lee E. Ohanian, Professor, University of California, Los Angeles.

Regulating and Resolving Institutions Considered 'Too Big to Fail'

Wednesday, May 6, 2009

Witnesses

Panel 1: Honorable Sheila Bair, Chairman, Federal Deposit Insurance Corporation; Mr. Gary Stern, President, Federal Reserve Bank of Minneapolis.

Panel 2: Honorable Peter Wallison, Arthur F. Burns Fellow in Financial Policy Studies, American Enterprise Institute; Honorable Martin N. Baily, Senior Fellow, Economic Studies, The Brookings Institution; Mr. Raghuram G. Rajan, Eric J. Gleacher Distinguished Service Professor of Finance, University of Chicago Booth School of Business.

Strengthening the S.E.C.'s Vital Enforcement Responsibilities

Thursday, May 7, 2009

Witnesses: Mr. Richard Hillman, Managing Director, Financial Markets and Community Investment, U.S. Government Accountability Office; Robert Khuzami, Esq., Director, Division of Enforcement, U.S. Securities and Exchange Commission; Professor Mercer Bullard, Associate Professor of Law, University of Mississippi School of Law; Mr. Bruce Hiler, Partner and Head of Securities Enforcement Group, Cadwalader, Wickersham and Taft LLP.

Manufacturing and the Credit Crisis

Wednesday, May 13, 2009

Witnesses

Panel 1: Mr. Leo Gerard, President, United Steelworkers; Mr. David Marchick, Managing Director, The Carlyle Group.

Panel 2: Mr. Eugene Haffely, CEO, Assembly and Test Worldwide, Inc.; Lieutenant General Larry Farrell, (USAF, Retired) President, National Defense Industrial Association; Mr. Wil-

¶54,900

liam Gaskin, President, Precision Metalforming Association.

Oversight of the Troubled Assets Relief Program

Wednesday, May 20, 2009

Witnesses: Honorable Timothy Geithner, Secretary, United States Department of the Treasury.

The State of the Domestic Automobile Industry: Impact of Federal Assistance

Wednesday, June 10, 2009

Witnesses: Mr. Ron Bloom, Senior Advisor on the Auto Industry, U.S. Department of the Treasury; The Honorable Edward Montgomery, White House Director of Recovery for Auto Communities and Workers, The White House.

The Administration's Proposal to Modernize the Financial Regulatory System

Thursday, June 18, 2009

Witnesses: Honorable Timothy Geithner, Secretary, United States Department of the Treasury.

Over-the-Counter Derivatives: Modernizing Oversight to Increase Transparency and Reduce Risks

Monday, June 22, 2009

Witnesses

Panel 1: Honorable Mary Schapiro, Chairman, U.S. Securities and Exchange Commission; Honorable Gary Gensler, Chairman, U.S. Commodity Futures Trading Commission; Ms. A. Patricia White, Associate Director of the Division of Research and Statistics, Board of Governors of the Federal Reserve System.

Panel 2: Dr. Henry Hu, Allan Shivers Chair in the Law of Banking and Finance, University of Texas School of Law; Mr. Kenneth C. Griffin, Founder, President, and Chief Executive Officer, Citadel Investment Group, L.L.C.; Mr. Robert G. Pickel, Executive Director and Chief Executive Officer, International Swaps and Derivatives Association, Inc.; Mr. Christopher Whalen, Managing Director, Institutional Risk Analytics.

The Effects of the Economic Crisis on Community Banks and Credit Unions in Rural Communities

Wednesday, July 8, 2009

Witnesses: Mr. Jack Hopkins, President and Chief Executive Officer, CorTrust Bank National Association, Sioux Falls, SD on behalf of the Independent Community Bankers of America; Mr. Frank Michael, President and CEO, Allied Credit Union, Stockton, CA on behalf of the Credit Union National Association; Mr. Arthur Johnson, Chairman and CEO, United Bank of Michigan, Grand Rapids, MI on behalf of the American Bankers Association; Mr. Ed Templeton, President and CEO, SRP Federal Credit Union, North Augusta, SC; Mr. Peter Skillern, Executive Director, Community Reinvestment Association of North Carolina.

Creating a Consumer Financial Protection Agency: A Cornerstone of America's New Economic Foundation

Tuesday, July 14, 2009

Witnesses

Panel 1: Honorable Michael S. Barr, Assistant Secretary for Financial Institutions, U.S. Department of the Treasury.

Panel 2: Honorable Richard Blumenthal, Attorney General, State of Connecticut; Mr. Edward Yingling, President and CEO, American Bankers Association; Mr. Travis B. Plunkett, Legislative Director, Consumer Federation of America; Honorable Peter Wallison, Arthur F. Burns Fellow in Financial Policy Studies, American Enterprise Institute; Mr. Sendhil Mullainathan, Professor of Economics, Harvard University.

Regulating Hedge Funds and Other Private Investment Pools

Wednesday, July 15, 2009

Witnesses

Panel 1: Mr. Andrew J. Donohue, Director of the Division of Investment Management, U.S. Securities and Exchange Commission.

Panel 2: Mr. Dinakar Singh, Founder and Chief Executive Officer, TPG Axon Capital; Mr. James Chanos, Chairman, Coalition of Private Investment Companies; Mr. Trevor R. Loy, General Partner, Flywheel Ventures; Mr. Mark B. Tresnowski, Managing Director and General Counsel, Madison Dearborn Partners, LLC; Mr. Richard Bookstaber, Financial Author; Mr. Joseph Dear, Chief Investment Officer, California Public Employees' Retirement System.

Preserving Homeownership: Progress Needed to Prevent Foreclosures

Thursday, July 16, 2009

Witnesses

Panel 1: Honorable Herbert M. Allison, Jr., Assistant Secretary for Financial Stability, U.S. Department of the Treasury; Honorable William Apgar, Senior Advisor to the Secretary for Mort-

¶54,900

gage Finance, U.S. Department of Housing and Urban Development.

Panel 2: Ms. Joan Carty, President and CEO, The Housing Development Fund in Bridgeport, CT; Ms. Mary Coffin, Head of Mortgage Servicing, Wells Fargo; Ms. Diane E. Thompson, Of Counsel, National Consumer Law Center; Mr. Allen Jones, Default Management Executive, Bank of America Home Loans; Mr. Curtis Glovier, Managing Director, Fortress Investment Group; Mr. Paul S. Willen, Senior Economist and Policy Advisor, Federal Reserve Bank of Boston; Mr. Thomas Perretta, Consumer, State of Connecticut.

Establishing a Framework for Systemic Risk Regulation

Thursday, July 23, 2009

Witnesses

Panel 1: Honorable Sheila Bair, Chairman, Federal Deposit Insurance Corporation; Honorable Mary Schapiro, Chairman, U.S. Securities and Exchange Commission; Honorable Daniel K. Tarullo, Member, Board of Governors of the Federal Reserve System.

Panel 2: Ms. Alice Rivlin, Senior Fellow, Economic Studies, Brookings Institution; Dr. Allan H. Meltzer, Professor of Political Economy, Tepper School of Business, Carnegie Mellon University; Mr. Vincent Reinhart, Resident Scholar, American Enterprise Institute; Mr. Paul Schott Stevens, President and CEO, Investment Company Institute.

Regulatory Modernization: Perspectives on Insurance

Tuesday, July 28, 2009

Witnesses: Mr. Travis B. Plunkett, Legislative Director, Consumer Federation of America; Mr. Baird Webel, Specialist in Financial Economics, Congressional Research Service; Professor Hal Scott, Nomura Professor of International Financial Systems, Harvard Law School; Professor Martin Grace, James S. Kemper Professor of Risk Management, Department of Risk Management and Insurance, Georgia State University.

Protecting Shareholders and Enhancing Public Confidence by Improving Corporate Governance

Wednesday, July 29, 2009

Witnesses: Ms. Meredith B. Cross, Director of the Division of Corporate Finance, U.S. Securities and Exchange Commission; Professor John C. Coates IV, John F. Cogan, Jr. Professor of Law and Economics, Harvard Law School; Ms. Ann Yerger, Executive Director, Council of Institutional Investors; Mr. John J. Castellani, President, The Business Roundtable; Professor J.W. Verret, Assistant Professor of Law, George Mason University School of Law; Mr. Richard C. Ferlauto, Director of Corporate Governance and Pension Investment, American Federation of State, County and Municipal Employees.

Strengthening and Streamlining Prudential Bank Supervision

Tuesday, August 4, 2009

Witnesses

Panel 1: Honorable Sheila Bair, Chairman, Federal Deposit Insurance Corporation; Honorable John C. Dugan, Comptroller of the Currency, Office of the Comptroller of the Currency; Honorable Daniel K. Tarullo, Member, Board of Governors of the Federal Reserve System; Mr. John Bowman, Acting Director, Office of Thrift Supervision.

Panel 2: Honorable Eugene A. Ludwig, Chief Executive Officer, Promontory Financial Group; Honorable Richard S. Carnell, Associate Professor, Fordham University School of Law; Honorable Martin N. Baily, Senior Fellow, Economic Studies, The Brookings Institution.

Examining Proposals to Enhance the Regulation of Credit Rating Agencies

Wednesday, August 5, 2009

Witnesses

Panel 1: Mr. Michael S. Barr, Assistant Secretary-Designate for Financial Institutions, U.S. Department of the Treasury.

Panel 2: Professor John C. Coffee, Jr., Adolf A. Berle Professor of Law, Columbia University Law School; Dr. Lawrence J. White, Leonard E. Imperatore Professor of Economics, New York University; Mr. Stephen W. Joynt, President and Chief Executive Officer, Fitch Ratings; Mr. James Gellert, President and CEO, Rapid Ratings; Mr. Mark Froeba, Principal, PF2 Securities Evaluations, Inc

Alleged Stanford Financial Group Fraud: Regulatory and Oversight Concerns and the Need for Reform

Monday, August 17, 2009

Witnesses

Panel 1: Mr. Craig Nelson, Investor, Stanford Securities, Alabama; Mr. Troy Lillie, Investor, Stanford Securities, Louisiana; Ms. Leyla Wydler, Former Vice President and Financial Advisor, Stanford Financial Group; Professor Onnig Dombalagian, George Denegre Professor of Law, Tulane University Law School.

¶54,900

Panel 2: Ms. Rose Romero, Regional Director, U.S. Securities and Exchange Commission; Mr. Daniel M. Sibears, Executive Vice President, Member Regulation Programs, Financial Industry Regulatory Authority (FINRA).

Oversight of the SEC's Failure to Identify the Bernard L. Madoff Ponzi Scheme and How to Improve SEC Performance

Thursday, September 10, 2009

Witnesses

Panel 1: H. David Kotz, Esq., Inspector General, U.S. Securities and Exchange Commission.

Panel 2: Mr. Harry Markopolos, Chartered Financial Analyst and Certified Fraud Examiner; Robert Khuzami, Esq., Director, Division of Enforcement, U.S. Securities and Exchange Commission; John Walsh, Esq., Acting Director, Office of Compliance Inspections and Examinations, U.S. Securities and Exchange Commission.

Helping Homeowners Avoid Foreclosure

Monday, September 21, 2009

Witnesses

Panel 1: Honorable Shaun Donovan, Secretary, U.S. Department of Housing and Urban Development.

Panel 2: Honorable Anne Milgram, Attorney General of New Jersey; Ms. Marge Della Vecchia, Executive Director, New Jersey Housing and Mortgage Finance Agency; Ms. Phyllis Salowe-Kaye, Executive Director, New Jersey Citizen Action Board; Mr. Mario Vargas, Executive Director, New Jersey Puerto Rican Action Board; Mr. Edward Heaton, Homeowner from Springfield, New Jersey; Mr. Bryan Bolton, Senior Vice President, Loss Mitigation, CitiMortgage.

Emergency Economic Stabilization Act: One Year Later

Thursday, September 24, 2009

Witnesses

Panel 1: Honorable Herbert M. Allison, Jr., Assistant Secretary for Financial Stability (TARP), U.S. Department of the Treasury.

Panel 2: Honorable Neil M. Barofsky, Special Inspector General, Troubled Asset Relief Program; Mr. Gene L. Dodaro, Acting Comptroller General, United States Government Accountability Office; Professor Elizabeth Warren, Chair, Congressional Oversight Panel for the Troubled Asset Relief Program.

Strengthening and Streamlining Prudential Bank Supervision

Tuesday, September 29, 2009

Witnesses: Honorable Eugene A. Ludwig, Chief Executive Officer, Promontory Financial Group; Honorable Martin N. Baily, Senior Fellow, Economic Studies, The Brookings Institution; Honorable Richard S. Carnell, Associate Professor, Fordham University School of Law; Mr. Richard Hillman, Managing Director, Financial Markets and Community Investment, U.S. Government Accountability Office.

International Cooperation to Modernize Financial Regulation

Wednesday, September 30, 2009

Witnesses: Ms. Kathleen L. Casey, Commissioner, U.S. Securities and Exchange Commission; Mr. Mark Sobel, Acting Assistant Secretary for International Affairs, U.S. Department of the Treasury; Honorable Daniel K. Tarullo, Member, Board of Governors of the Federal Reserve System.

Securitization of Assets: Problems and Solutions

Wednesday, October 7, 2009

Witnesses: Professor Patricia McCoy, George J. & Helen M. England Professor of Law, University of Connecticut School of Law; Mr. George P. Miller, Executive Director, American Securitization Forum; Mr. Andrew Davidson, President, Andrew Davidson & Co.; Mr. J. Christopher Hoeffel, Executive Committee Member, Commercial Mortgage Securities Association; Dr. William Irving, Portfolio Manager, Fidelity Investments.

Future of the Mortgage Market and the Housing Enterprises

Thursday, October 8, 2009

Witnesses

Panel 1: Mr. Edward J. DeMarco, Acting Director, Federal Housing Finance Agency.

Panel 2: Mr. William Shear, Director, Financial Markets and Community Investment, U.S. Government Accountability Office; Mr. Andrew Jakabovics, Associate Director for Housing and Economics, Center for American Progress Action Fund; Dr. Susan M. Wachter, Worley Professor of Financial Management, Wharton School of Business, University of Pennsylvania; Honorable Peter Wallison, Arthur F. Burns Fellow in Financial Policy Studies, American Enterprise Institute.

Restoring Credit to Manufacturers

Friday, October 9, 2009

Witnesses: Mr. David Andrea, Vice President, Industry Analysis and Economics, Motor and Equipment Manufacturers Association; Mr.

¶54,900

Robert C. Kiener, Director of Member Outreach, Precision Machined Products Association; Mr. Stephen P. Wilson, Chairman and CEO, LCNB National Bank.

Examining the State of the Banking Industry

Wednesday, October 14, 2009

Witnesses: Honorable Sheila Bair, Chairman, Federal Deposit Insurance Corporation; Honorable John C. Dugan, Comptroller of the Currency, Office of the Comptroller of the Currency; Honorable Daniel K. Tarullo, Member, Board of Governors of the Federal Reserve System; Honorable Deborah Matz, Chairman, National Credit Union Administration; Mr. Timothy T. Ward, Deputy Director, Examinations, Supervision, and Consumer Protection, Office of Thrift Supervision; Mr. Joseph A. Smith, North Carolina Commissioner of Banks and Chairman, Conference of State Bank Supervisors; Mr. Thomas J. Candon, Deputy Commissioner, Vermont Department of Banking, Insurance, Securities and Health Care Administration, National Association of State Credit Union Supervisors.

The State of the Nation's Housing Market

Tuesday, October 20, 2009

Witnesses

Panel 1: Honorable Johnny Isakson (R-GA).

Panel 2: Honorable Shaun Donovan, Secretary, U.S. Department of Housing and Urban Development.

Panel 3: Ms. Diane Randall, Executive Director, Partnership for Strong Communities; Mr. Ronald Phipps, First Vice President, National Association of Realtors; Mr. Emile J. Brinkmann, Chief Economist and Senior Vice President for Research and Economics, Mortgage Bankers Association; Mr. David Crowe, Chief Economist, National Association of Home Builders.

Dark Pools, Flash Orders, High Frequency Trading, and Other Market Structure Issues

Wednesday, October 28, 2009

Witnesses

Panel 1: Honorable Edward Kaufman, United States Senator.

Panel 2: James A. Brigagliano, Esq., Co-Acting Director of the Division of Trading and Markets, U.S. Securities and Exchange Commission; Mr. Frank Hatheway, Senior Vice President and Chief Economist, NASDAQ OMX; William O'Brien, Esq., Chief Executive Officer, Direct Edge; Mr. Christopher Nagy, Managing Director of Order Routing Sales & Strategy, Ameritrade; Mr. Daniel Mathisson, Managing Director and Head of Advanced Execution Services, Credit Suisse; Mr. Robert C. Gasser, President and Chief Executive Officer, Investment Technology Group; Mr. Peter Driscoll, Chairman, Security Traders Association; Mr. Adam C. Sussman, Director of Research, TABB Group.

Protecting Consumers from Abusive Overdraft Fees: The Fairness and Accountability in Receiving Overdraft Coverage Act

Tuesday, November 17, 2009

Witnesses: Mr. Mario Livieri, Consumer, State of Connecticut; Mr. Michael D. Calhoun, President, Center For Responsible Lending; Mr. Frank Pollack, President and CEO, Pentagon Federal Credit Union; Mr. John Carey, Chief Administrative Officer, Citibank NA; Ms. Jean Ann Fox, Director of Financial Services, Consumer Federation of America.

Hearing on the nomination of The Honorable Ben S. Bernanke

Thursday, December 3, 2009

Witnesses: The Honorable Ben S. Bernanke, Chairman, Board of Governors of the Federal Reserve System.

Prohibiting Certain High-Risk Investment Activities by Banks and Bank Holding Companies

Tuesday, February 2, 2010

Witnesses: Honorable Paul Volcker, Chairman, President's Economic Recovery Advisory Board; Honorable Neal S. Wolin, Deputy Secretary, U.S. Department of the Treasury.

Implications of the 'Volcker Rules' for Financial Stability

Thursday, February 4, 2010

Witnesses: Mr. Gerald Corrigan, Managing Director, Goldman Sachs; Professor Simon Johnson, Ronald A. Kurtz Professor of Entrepreneurship, Sloan School of Management, Massachusetts Institute of Technology; Mr. John Reed, Retired Chairman, Citigroup; Professor Hal Scott, Nomura Professor of International Financial Systems, Harvard Law School; Mr. Barry L. Zubrow, Executive Vice President, Chief Risk Officer, JPMorgan Chase.

Equipping Financial Regulators with the Tools Necessary to Monitor Systemic Risk

Friday, February 12, 2010

Witnesses

¶ 54,900

Panel 1: Honorable Daniel K. Tarullo, Member, Board of Governors of the Federal Reserve System.

Panel 2: Honorable Allan I. Mendelowitz, Founding Member, Committee to Establish the National Institute of Finance; Professor John C. Liechty, Associate Professor of Marketing and Statistics, Smeal College of Business, Pennsylvania State University; Professor Robert Engle, Stern School of Business, New York University; Mr. Stephen C. Horne, Vice President, Master Data Management and Integration Services, Dow Jones Business & Relationship Intelligence.

Restoring Credit to Main Street: Proposals to Fix Small Business Borrowing and Lending Problems

Tuesday, March 2, 2010

Witnesses

Panel 1: Honorable Carl Levin (D-MI), United States Senator; Honorable Debbie Stabenow (D-MI), United States Senator.

Panel 2: Mr. Arthur Johnson, Chairman and CEO, United Bank of Michigan, Grand Rapids, MI on behalf of the American Bankers Association; Mr. Eric Gillett, Vice Chairman and CEO, Sutton Bank, Attica, OH on behalf of the Independent Community Bankers Association; Mr. Raj Date, Executive Director, Cambridge Winter Center for Financial Institutions Policy.

[¶54,905] VII. Committee Consideration

The Committee on Banking, Housing, and Urban Affairs met in open session on March 22, 2010, and by a vote of 13-10 ordered the bill reported, as amended.

[¶54,910] VIII. Congressional Budget Office Cost Estimate

Section 11(b) of the Standing Rules of the Senate, and Section 403 of the Congressional Budget Impoundment and Control Act, require that each committee report on a bill contain a statement estimating the cost and regulatory impact of the proposed legislation. The Congressional Budget Office has provided the following cost estimate.

S. 3217—Restoring American Financial Stability Act of 2010

Summary: S. 3217 would grant new federal regulatory powers and reassign existing regulatory authority among federal agencies with the aim of reducing the likelihood and severity of financial crises.

The legislation would establish a program to facilitate the resolution of large financial institutions that become insolvent or are in danger of becoming insolvent when their failure is determined to threaten the stability of the nation's financial system (such institutions are known as systemically important firms). The program would be funded by fees assessed on certain large financial companies; an Orderly Liquidation Fund (OLF) of $50 billion would be accumulated, and in the event of a costly resolution, the fund would be replenished over time with future assessments.

A second new program would expand the authority of the Federal Deposit Insurance Corporation (FDIC) to provide government guarantees on a broad array of financial obligations of banks and bank holding companies if federal officials determine that market conditions are impeding the normal provision of financing to creditworthy borrowers (known as a liquidity crisis). Under the bill, participants in the program would be charged fees designed to recover the costs of the government guarantees.

Other provisions of S. 3217 would change how financial institutions and securities markets are regulated, create a new Bureau of Consumer Financial Protection (BCFP), broaden the authority of the Commodity Futures Trading Commission (CFTC) and the Securities and Exchange Commission (SEC), establish a grant program to encourage the use of traditional banking services, expand the supervision of firms that settle payments between financial institutions, and make many other changes to current laws.

Under the legislation, as under current law, there is some probability that, at some point in the future, large financial firms will become insolvent and liquidity crises will arise, and that those financial problems will present significant risks to the nation's broader economy. The cost of addressing those problems under current law is unknown and would depend on how the Administration and the Congress chose to proceed when faced with financial crises in the future; they could, for example, change laws, create new programs, appropriate additional funds, and assess new fees. Depending on the effectiveness of the new regulatory initiatives and new authorities to resolve and support a broad variety of financial institutions contained in S. 3217, enacting this legislation could change the timing, severity, and federal cost of averting and resolving future financial crises. However, CBO has not determined whether the estimated costs under the bill would be smaller or larger than the costs of alternative approaches to addressing future financial crises and the risks they pose to the economy as a whole.

Estimated Federal Budgetary Impacts

CBO estimates that enacting S. 3217 would increase revenues by $32.4 billion over the 2011-2015 period and by $75.4 billion over the 2011-2020 period and increase direct spending by $25.8 billion and $54.4 billion, respectively, over the same periods. In total, CBO estimates those changes would decrease budget deficits by $6.6 billion over the 2011-2015 period and by $21.0 billion over the 2011-2020 period. In addition, CBO estimates that implementing the bill would increase spending subject to appropriation by $4.6 billion over the 2011-2015 period and $13.2 billion over the 2011-2020 period. Because enacting the legislation would affect direct spending and revenues, pay-as-you-go procedures apply.

Under S. 3217, the estimated reduction in budget deficits over the 2011-2020 period stems largely from industry assessments required to capitalize the OLF established by the bill to resolve systemically important firms. Those collections exceed the expected cost of liquidations during the capitalization period. After that time, a growing share of the budgetary resources for future liquidation activities would be derived from interest credited on balances in the OLF (with additional assessments collected only as needed to cover losses). Such intragovernmental interest payments are not budgetary receipts and do not affect the federal deficit. Thus, CBO estimates that the expenses of the OLF would ultimately exceed income from new assessments paid by financial firms, resulting in an increase in the deficit in those later years. Pursuant to section 311 of the Concurrent Resolution on the Budget for Fiscal Year 2009 (S. Con Res. 70), CBO estimates that the bill would increase projected deficits by more than $5 billion in at least one of the four consecutive 10-year periods starting in 2021.

Mandates

The bill would impose intergovernmental and private-sector mandates, as defined in the Unfunded Mandates Reform Act (UMRA), on banks and other private and public entities that participate in financial markets. The bill also would impose intergovernmental mandates by prohibiting states from taxing and regulating certain insurance products issued by companies based in other states and by preempting certain state laws. Because the costs of complying with some of the mandates would depend on future regulations that would be established under the bill, and because CBO has limited information about the extent to which public entities enter into swaps with unregulated entities, CBO cannot determine whether the aggregate costs of the intergovernmental mandates would exceed the annual threshold established in UMRA ($70 million in 2010, adjusted annually for inflation). However, CBO estimates that the cost of the mandates on private-sector entities would well exceed the annual threshold established in UMRA for such mandates ($141 million in 2010, adjusted annually for inflation) because the amount of fees collected would be more than that amount.

Page Reference Guide:

Sections

Major Provisions

Estimated Costs to the Federal Government

Basis of Estimate: Changes in Direct Spending and Revenues; Changes in Spending Subject to Appropriation

Pay-As-You-Go Considerations

Intergovernmental and Private-Sector Impact

Abbreviations used in the cost estimate:

BCFP—Bureau of Consumer Financial Protection

CFTC—Commodity Futures Trading Commission

DIF—Deposit Insurance Fund

FDIC—Federal Deposit Insurance Corporation

FSOC—Financial Stability Oversight Council

GAO—Government Accountability Office

OCC—Office of the Comptroller of the Currency

OFR—Office of Financial Research

OLF—Orderly Liquidation Fund

OTS—Office of Thrift Supervision

PCAOB—Public Company Accounting Oversight Board

SEC—Securities and Exchange Commission

SIPC—Securities Investor Protection Corporation

Major provisions:

Title I would establish the Financial Stability Oversight Council and the Office of Financial Research (OFR), both of which would be funded by assessments on certain financial and nonfinancial entities starting two years after the bill's enactment. For the first two years after enactment, the Federal Reserve would fund those activities.

Title II would establish a new program for resolving certain financial firms that are insolvent or in danger of becoming insolvent. The bill would create a fund, the OLF, from which the costs of liquidation would be paid. The FDIC would be directed to assess fees on private firms to build a $50 billion balance in the OLF within 10 years of the bill's enactment.

Title III would abolish the Office of Thrift Supervision (OTS) and change the regulatory oversight of banks, thrifts, and related holding companies by transferring authorities and employees among the remaining regulatory agencies.

Titles IV, VII, and IX would change and broaden the authority of the SEC to oversee activities and entities associated with the national securities exchanges.

Title V would establish an Office of National Insurance and set national standards for how states may regulate and collect taxes for a type of insurance that covers unique or atypical risks—known as "surplus lines" or "nonadmitted insurance." The bill also would establish national standards for how states regulate reinsurance—often referred to as insurance for insurance companies.

Titles VI would modify the regulation of bank, thrift, and securities holding companies.

Title VII would change and broaden the authority of the CFTC to regulate certain derivatives transactions on over-the-counter markets.

Title VIII would broaden the supervision of certain firms that settle payments between financial institutions.

Title X would establish the BCFP as an independent agency within the Federal Reserve to enforce federal laws that affect how banks and nonfinancial institutions make financial products available to consumers for their personal use. The BCFP would be funded by transfers from the Federal Reserve.

Title XI would establish a program to guarantee obligations of certain financial entities when federal officials determine that the economy faces a liquidity crisis. This title also would make changes to certain lending activities of the Federal Reserve.

Title XII would establish several grant programs to encourage certain individuals to increase their use of the federally insured banking system and community-based financial institutions.

Estimated cost to the Federal Government: The estimated budgetary impact of S. 3217 is shown in the following table. The cost of this legislation fall within budget functions 370 (commerce and housing credit), 450 (community and regional development), and 800 (general government).

TABLE 1.—ESTIMATED BUDGETARY IMPACT OF S. 3217, THE RESTORING AMERICAN FINANCIAL STABILITY ACT OF 2010

	By fiscal year, in billions of dollars—											
	2011	2012	2013	2014	2015	2016	2017	2018	2019	2020	2011-2015	2011-2020
CHANGES IN DIRECT SPENDING												
Estimated Budget Authority	4.0	6.3	5.6	5.1	5.4	5.6	5.5	5.3	5.8	6.5	26.4	55.2
Estimated Outlays	3.6	6.3	5.4	5.1	5.4	5.6	5.5	5.3	5.8	6.5	25.8	54.4
CHANGES IN REVENUES												
Estimated Revenues	1.8	6.4	7.9	8.0	8.3	8.5	8.8	8.9	8.7	8.1	32.4	75.4
NET CHANGES IN THE BUDGET DEFICIT FROM CHANGES IN DIRECT SPENDING AND REVENUES												
Estimated Impact on Deficit[a]	1.8	-0.1	-2.6	-2.9	-2.9	-2.9	-3.3	-3.7	-2.9	-1.6	-6.6	-21.0
CHANGES IN SPENDING SUBJECT TO APPROPRIATION												
Estimated Authorization Level	0.7	0.7	0.9	1.0	1.2	1.3	1.5	1.7	1.9	2.2	4.4	13.1
Estimated Outlays	0.8	0.7	0.9	1.0	1.2	1.3	1.5	1.7	1.9	2.2	4.6	13.2

[a] Positive numbers indicate increases in deficits; negative numbers indicate decreases in deficits.

Basis of estimate: For this estimate, CBO assumes that S. 3217 will be enacted before the end of fiscal year 2010, that the necessary amounts will be appropriated in each year, and that spending will follow historical patterns for activities of the FDIC, the Federal Reserve, and other agencies.

CBO estimates that the net decrease in the deficit as a result of the changes in revenues and direct spending would total $21.0 billion over the 2011-2020 period. Most of that amount, about $17.6 billion, would be generated by the assessments to build up the OLF and the spending of a portion of those funds.

About $4.9 billion of the net deficit decrease related to changes in direct spending and revenues would result from providing the SEC permanent authority to collect and spend certain fees and reclassifying discretionary spending and offsetting collections for the SEC as direct spending and revenues. Revenues from the fees would exceed the SEC's outlays. (Under current law, the SEC's authority to collect and spend fees is provided in annual appropriation acts; fee collections are recorded as offsetting collections, that is, a credit against the agency's spending). Fees collected by the SEC have historically exceeded the agency's spending; those excess collections currently offset discretionary spending in other areas of the budget. Consequently, changing the budgetary treatment of the SEC's spending and receipts would increase discretionary spending by removing that offset. CBO estimates that such spending would increase by about $11.8 billion over the 2011-2020 period. The $4.9 billion in net savings from the change in direct spending and revenues would be less than the increase in discretionary outlays because the SEC fees under S. 3217 would be lower than those projected under current law.

Changes in Direct Spending and Revenues

CBO estimates that enacting the legislation would increase revenues by $75.4 billion over the 2011-2020 period (see Table 2). About $43.9 billion of those revenues would be generated by assessments imposed by the FDIC, with the remainder arising from other activities under the bill. Specifically:

• Several provisions of the bill, most importantly those establishing the BCFP and reassigning supervisory responsibilities over financial institutions among the various regulators, would increase the net earnings of the Federal Reserve, which are recorded in the budget as revenues.

• Reclassification of fees collected by the SEC also would increase revenues, as would additional fees collected by the Public Company Accounting Oversight Board (PCAOB) and the Securities Investor Protection Corporation (SIPC).

CBO estimates that enacting the legislation would increase direct spending by $54.4 billion over the 2011-2020 period (see Table 2). About $19.4 billion of that amount would result from allowing the SEC to spend certain fees without annual appropriation action. Additional costs would be incurred by establishing the BCFP, the Financial Stability Oversight Council, and the OFR; broadening the regulatory duties of the PCAOB; increasing the amount the SIPC may borrow from the Treasury; authorizing the FDIC to provide loan guarantees to financial institutions; and creating a program to make awards to individuals providing certain information to the SEC.

TABLE 2.—NET CHANGES IN THE BUDGET DEFICIT FROM CHANGES IN DIRECT SPENDING AND REVENUES UNDER THE RESTORING AMERICAN FINANCIAL STABILITY ACT OF 2010

	By fiscal year, in billions of dollars—											
	2011	2012	2013	2014	2015	2016	2017	2018	2019	2020	2011-2015	2011-2020
NET CHANGES IN THE BUDGET DEFICIT FROM CHANGES IN DIRECT SPENDING AND REVENUES[a]												
Orderly Liquidation Authority	2.4	0.2	-2.1	-2.8	-2.7	-2.6	-2.9	-3.3	-2.5	-1.2	-5.0	-17.6
Securities and Exchange Commission Regulation	-0.7	-0.5	-0.4	-0.4	-0.5	-0.5	-0.5	-0.5	-0.5	-0.5	-2.5	-4.9
Consumer Financial Protection	*	0.1	0.1	0.4	0.4	0.4	0.4	0.4	0.4	0.5	1.0	3.2
Emergency Financial Stability	*	0.1	0.1	0.1	0.1	0.1	0.1	0.1	0.1	0.1	0.4	0.8
Changes Among Financial Regulators	*	-0.2	-0.4	-0.5	-0.5	-0.5	-0.5	-0.6	-0.6	-0.6	-1.5	-4.3
Other Financial Oversight and Protection	*	0.1	0.1	0.2	0.2	0.2	0.1	0.1	0.1	0.1	0.7	1.3
Financial Stability Oversight	*	*	*	0.1	0.1	*	*	*	*	*	0.3	0.4
Other Provisions Affecting the Federal Reserve	*	*	*	*	*	*	*	*	*	*	*	0.1
Total Net Change in the Budget Deficit	1.8	-0.1	-2.6	-2.9	-2.9	-2.9	-3.3	-3.7	-2.9	-1.6	-6.6	-21.0
CHANGES IN REVENUES												
Orderly Liquidation Authority[b]	0	4.2	5.2	5.1	5.2	5.2	5.2	5.1	4.8	4.0	19.7	43.9
Securities and Exchange Commission Regulation	1.8	1.9	2.1	2.2	2.3	2.5	2.7	2.9	2.9	3.0	10.3	24.4

	By fiscal year, in billions of dollars—											
	2011	2012	2013	2014	2015	2016	2017	2018	2019	2020	2011-2015	2011-2020
Consumer Financial Protection	0	0	0.1	0.1	0.1	0.2	0.2	0.2	0.2	0.2	0.4	1.2
Changes Among Financial Regulators	0	0.2	0.5	0.5	0.5	0.5	0.6	0.6	0.6	0.6	1.7	4.6
Other Financial Oversight and Protection	0	*	*	*	*	0.1	0.1	0.2	0.2	0.2	0.1	0.8
Financial Stability Oversight	0	0	0.1	0.1	0.1	0.1	0.1	0.1	0.1	0.1	0.2	0.5
Other Provisions Affecting the Federal Reserve	*	*	*	*	*	*	*	*	*	*	*	-0.1
Total Revenues	1.8	6.4	7.9	8.0	8.3	8.5	8.8	8.9	8.7	8.1	32.4	75.4
CHANGES IN DIRECT SPENDING												
Orderly Liquidation Authority:												
Estimated Budget Authority	2.4	4.4	3.1	2.3	2.4	2.5	2.2	1.8	2.3	2.9	14.6	26.3
Estimated Outlays	2.4	4.4	3.1	2.3	2.4	2.5	2.2	1.8	2.3	2.9	14.6	26.3
Securities and Exchange Commission Regulation:												
Estimated Budget Authority	1.5	1.5	1.7	1.8	1.9	2.1	2.3	2.4	2.5	2.5	8.3	20.1
Estimated Outlays	1.1	1.5	1.6	1.7	1.9	2.0	2.2	2.4	2.5	2.5	7.8	19.4
Consumer Financial Protection:												
Estimated Budget Authority	0.1	0.1	0.3	0.6	0.6	0.6	0.6	0.6	0.6	0.6	1.5	4.6
Estimated Outlays	*	0.1	0.2	0.5	0.6	0.6	0.6	0.6	0.6	0.6	1.4	4.5
Emergency Financial Stability:												
Estimated Budget Authority	*	0.1	0.1	0.1	0.1	0.1	0.1	0.1	0.1	0.1	0.4	0.8
Estimated Outlays	*	0.1	0.1	0.1	0.1	0.1	0.1	0.1	0.1	0.1	0.4	0.8
Changes Among Financial Regulators:												
Estimated Budget Authority	*	0.1	0.1	*	*	*	*	*	*	*	0.2	0.3
Estimated Outlays	*	0.1	0.1	*	*	*	*	*	*	*	0.2	0.3
Other Financial Oversight and Protection:												
Estimated Budget Authority	*	0.1	0.1	0.3	0.3	0.3	0.3	0.3	0.3	0.3	0.8	2.2
Estimated Outlays	*	0.1	0.1	0.3	0.3	0.3	0.3	0.3	0.3	0.3	0.8	2.2
Financial Stability Oversight:												
Estimated Budget Authority	*	0.1	0.3	0.1	0.1	0.1	0.1	0.1	0.1	0.1	0.5	0.9
Estimated Outlays	*	*	0.1	0.2	0.2	0.1	0.1	0.1	0.1	0.1	0.5	0.9
Total Changes in Direct Spending:												
Estimated Budget Authority	4.0	6.3	5.6	5.1	5.4	5.6	5.5	5.3	5.8	6.5	26.4	55.2
Estimated Outlays	3.6	6.3	5.4	5.1	5.4	5.6	5.5	5.3	5.8	6.5	25.8	54.4

a Positive numbers indicate increases in deficits; negative numbers indicate decreases in deficits.
b The legislation could affect federal tax receipts under the Internal Revenue Code. However, there are a number of uncertainties regarding potential effects of the use of a bridge financial company by the Federal Deposit Insurance Corporation on the tax attributes of a failed financial institution. It is not possible to determine whether the use of a bridge financial company would provide a tax result that is more or less favorable than bankruptcy, which is the current-law alternative. Therefore, the staff of the Joint Committee on Taxation is not currently able to estimate the changes in tax revenue that would result from this provision of the bill.
Note—* = between –$50 million and $50 million. Components may not sum to totals because of rounding.

Orderly Liquidation Authority

Title II would create new government mechanisms for liquidating systemically important financial firms that are in default or in danger of default. CBO estimates that implementing those provisions would, on balance, reduce the deficit by $17.6 billion over the 2011-2020 period.

Under conditions outlined in the bill, the FDIC would be authorized to enter into various arrangements necessary to liquidate such firms, including organizing bridge banks that would be exempt from federal and state taxation. Funding for those transactions would come from an Orderly Liquidation Fund (OLF) established by the legislation and built up from compulsory assessments paid by private firms (which would be classified as revenues) and interest earned on fund balances (which would be invested in Treasury securities). If fund balances were insufficient to finance transactions that the FDIC deemed appropriate, necessary amounts would be borrowed from the Treasury up to a specified amount. Amounts borrowed would be based on a formula tied to the value of the assets of the liquidated firms and would be repaid through future assessments.

The bill would direct the FDIC to assess upfront fees sufficient to establish the OLF at the level of $50 billion within 10 years after enactment but would allow the agency to extend that deadline if any losses to the fund are incurred during that period. The size of the fund would be adjusted periodically for inflation.

CBO's estimate of the cost of the resolution authorities provided under the bill represents the difference between the expected values of spending by the OLF to resolve insolvent firms and assessments collected by the OLF. Those expected values represent a weighted average of various scenarios regarding the potential frequency and magnitude of systemic financial problems. Although the estimate reflects CBO's best judgment on the basis of historical experience, the cost of the program would depend on future economic and financial events that are inherently unpredictable. Moreover, the timing of the cash flows associated with resolving insolvent firms is also difficult to predict. It might take several years, for example, to replenish the funds spent to liquidate a complex financial institution. As a result, some of the proceeds from asset sales or cost-recovery fees related to financial problems emerging in any 10-year period might be collected beyond that period. All told, actual spending and assessments in each year would probably vary significantly from the estimated amounts—either higher or lower than the expected-value estimate provided for each year.

Although the probability that the federal government would have to liquidate a financial institution in any year is small, the potential costs of such a liquidation could be large. Measured on an expected-value basis, CBO estimates that net direct spending for potential liquidation activities, which includes recoveries from the sale of assets acquired from liquidated institutions but excludes revenues from assessments, would be $26.3 billion through 2020. As a result, the expected timeframe for fully capitalizing the fund is longer than 10 years. CBO's estimate of assessments reflects the effects of the interest earnings of the OLF (an estimated $7 billion), which would reduce the amount that firms would have to pay to capitalize the fund, and assumes that the FDIC would adjust the size of the fund every year to account for inflation. CBO estimates that revenues from assessments paid to capitalize the fund and cover any losses would total about $44 billion through 2020, net of effects on payroll and income taxes.[1] Under CBO's estimate, the OLF would have a balance of about $45 billion at the end of 2020, including the value of assets acquired in the course of liquidating financial institutions.

Securities and Exchange Commission Regulation

Titles IV, VII, and IX would change and expand the regulatory activities of the SEC. The bill also would grant that agency permanent authority to collect and spend certain fees; under current law, this authority is provided in annual appropriation acts. Based on information from the agency, CBO estimates that enacting those provisions would increase direct spending by $19.4 billion over the 2011-2020 period. Of that amount, CBO estimates that $16.9 billion would support the agency's current activities. The balance, $2.5 billion, would be incurred to carry out the new and expanded authorities under the bill. CBO estimates that enacting the provisions also would increase revenues by $24.4 billion over the 2011-2020 period. Taken together, CBO estimates that the provisions would decrease deficits by $4.9 billion over the 2011-2020 period.

Most of that decrease in the deficit—about $4.3 billion—would be from fees collected that would be unavailable to the agency for spending. The reduction in budget deficits from changes in direct spending and revenues would probably be accompanied by increases in discretionary spending, as discussed later in this estimate.

Reclassification of Fees. Under the bill, the SEC's authority to collect fees would be permanent rather than being provided through annual appropriation action as is the case under current law. The bill would authorize the SEC to assess fees for securities trading activities sufficient to cover the agency's annual operating expenses, plus an additional amount to maintain a reserve that would be limited to 25 percent of the following year's budget. The bill also would authorize the SEC to collect fees to register securities in amounts sufficient to meet targets set in the legislation. Those collections would be recorded in the budget as revenues; amounts collected by the SEC that exceed annual spending limits plus the reserve amount would not be available for the agency to spend. CBO assumes that the agency would set fees at levels sufficient to meet its budgetary, statutory, and reserve requirements each year.

---

[1] The total amount collected from assessments is estimated to be about $58 billion through 2020. But such assessments would become an additional business expense for companies required to pay them. Those additional expenses would result in decreases in taxable income somewhere in the economy, which would produce a loss of government revenue from income and payroll taxes that would partially offset the revenue collected from the assessment itself.

¶54,910

Additional Regulatory Authority. The bill also would broaden the SEC's authority to regulate activities and entities associated with the securities markets. Among other things, the bill would require advisers to private funds and organizations that trade in or facilitate certain derivatives transactions to register with the SEC, and it would broaden the SEC's oversight of credit rating agencies and advisers for municipal issues. CBO estimates that those additional activities would cost about $2.5 billion over the 10-year period. CBO estimates that more than 800 staff positions would be added over several years to meet the agency's additional regulatory authority (a 22-percent increase over current staffing levels). This estimate assumes that the SEC generally would follow its regular examination cycle and established examination procedures for regulating advisers to private funds.

Consumer Financial Protection

Title X would establish the Bureau of Consumer Financial Protection as an autonomous entity within the Federal Reserve. The bureau would enforce federal laws related to consumer financial protection by establishing rules and issuing orders and guidance. CBO estimates that creating the BCFP would increase budget deficits by $3.2 billion over the 2011-2020 period.

The bureau would be authorized to:

- Examine and regulate insured depository institutions and credit unions with more than $10 billion in assets;

- Request reports from insured depository institutions and credit unions with $10 billion in assets or less, and participate in the examinations performed by the regulators of those institutions; and

- Supervise large nondepository institutions, mortgage lenders, brokers, and financial service providers.

The bureau would coordinate examinations with other federal or state regulators of the institutions. Similar functions and the personnel who now perform those duties at federal agencies and the Federal Reserve would be transferred to the new bureau.

The bill would require the Board of Governors of the Federal Reserve to fund the BCFP through transfers from the earnings of the Federal Reserve. The amounts transferred would be limited to a percentage, starting at 10 percent in 2011 and increasing to 12 percent in 2013 and thereafter, of the 2009 total operating expenses of the Federal Reserve, adjusted annually for inflation. In CBO's judgment, the costs of the BCFP should be reported as expenditures in the federal budget (rather than a reduction in revenues) because the BCFP would be independent of the Federal Reserve and its activities would be separate and distinct from the Federal Reserve's responsibilities for monetary policy and financial regulation. Therefore, CBO estimates that the provisions of title X would increase direct spending by $4.5 billion over the 2011-2020 period. That estimate is based on the Federal Reserve's reported 2008 operating expenses, the most recent information available.

Based on information from the Federal Reserve, CBO estimates that about 515 staff positions would be transferred from the Federal Reserve to the BCFP to carry out the new regulatory authorities. CBO estimates that this transfer of staff would reduce the Federal Reserve's operating expenses by $1.2 billion over the 2011-2020 period, increasing remittances from the Federal Reserve to the Treasury (which are recorded in the federal budget as revenues) by that amount.

Emergency Financial Stability

In 2008, the FDIC established a temporary program to guarantee certain obligations of insured depository institutions, holding companies that include insured depository institutions, and some affiliates of those firms. (The program remains open to some new participants, and significant potential liabilities remain from existing participants.) Participants pay an upfront fee set to offset expected losses, and any shortfall will be recovered through an assessment on all FDIC-insured institutions. Conversely, in the event that any excess fees are collected, those amounts will revert to the Deposit Insurance Fund (DIF) and may be spent or used to reduce future deposit insurance premiums. The program provides two types of guarantees: one program, which expires in December 2012, is for newly issued, senior unsecured debt, and the other, which expires in December 2010, is for amounts in certain non-interest-bearing accounts.

Title XI would provide a new statutory framework for similar, but potentially much broader, assistance. Under the bill, the FDIC would be authorized to establish a guarantee program if the Federal Reserve, the Secretary of the Treasury, and the FDIC determine that a liquidity crisis warrants use of such authority. Although the types of firms eligible to participate would be similar to those eligible under the existing FDIC program, the bill would not limit the types or duration of financial obligations that could be guaranteed. Firms still would be required to pay an upfront fee for the guarantees, but any shortfall would be recovered solely from program participants rather than all FDIC-insured institutions. In addition, any excess fees would be deposited in the U.S. Treasury and would not be available to be spent.

CBO's estimate of the cost of those provisions reflects the expected value of the costs of such guarantees relative to the expected value of the costs that would be incurred under current law. CBO expects that, in the absence of this legislation, the FDIC would respond to any future liquidity crises by implementing guarantee programs similar to those it adopted in 2008. The costs of this program, like those that would result from implementing the liquidation authorities in title II, would depend on circumstances that are difficult to predict. In addition, cash flows over the 10-year period would depend, as for title II, on the lag between potential spending for losses and the collection of fees to offset those costs. Therefore, while this estimate reflects CBO's best judgment regarding expected costs, the actual costs would probably vary significantly from the amount estimated for any given year.

Based on historical experience, we expect that the probability of systemic liquidity problems in any year is small. In the event of liquidity crises, however, the legislation would authorize the FDIC to take a broader range of actions that could generate losses that would take some time to recover. In particular, CBO expects that limiting the recourse for cost-recovery fees to program participants would cause the FDIC to recoup losses over a long period of time to avoid placing large burdens on a small set of firms. Altogether, CBO estimates that enacting those provisions would increase net direct spending by $0.8 billion over the 2011-2020 period relative to current law.

Changes Among Financial Regulators

Title III would change the regulatory regime for supervising banks, thrifts, and related holding companies. It would abolish the Office of Thrift Supervision (OTS) and reduce the number of firms regulated by the Federal Reserve. Supervision of firms with consolidated assets of less than $50 billion that currently are regulated by the OTS and the Federal Reserve would be transferred to the Office of the Comptroller of the Currency (OCC) or the FDIC, depending on each firm's charter. The Federal Reserve would continue regulating bank holding companies with assets totaling above $50 billion and also would supervise thrift holding companies exceeding that threshold. Other provisions would direct agencies to complete the transition within 18 months after enactment; authorize spending of unobligated balances held by the OTS for transition and other costs; and allow the OCC to enter into agreements without regard to existing laws governing the disposition of real or personal property. Finally, the bill would require all of those agencies, including the Federal Reserve, to charge fees to cover supervisory expenses.

CBO estimates that implementing those provisions would reduce the deficit by an estimated $4.3 billion over the next 10 years. CBO expects that changes in costs that would result from transferring personnel among the banking agencies would have no net budgetary impact because they would be offset by corresponding changes in the amounts collected from regulated institutions. The net budgetary impact of this title would result from:

• Collecting fees from firms currently regulated by the Federal Reserve, which CBO estimates would average about $500 million a year or a total of $4.6 billion over the 2011-2020 period;

• Spending of the unobligated balances held by the OTS over the 2011-2020 period, which CBO estimates would total about $150 million, net of certain existing liabilities; and

• Financing the acquisition of buildings and other property for OCC operations, which CBO estimates would result in a net increase in direct spending of $150 million over the next 10 years.

This title would change direct spending and revenues because of the way banking agencies are funded. Under current law, costs incurred by the OCC, OTS, and FDIC are recorded in the budget as direct spending and are offset by receipts from annual fees or insurance premiums. The budgetary effects of the Federal Reserve's activities are recorded as changes in revenues (governmental receipts). After accounting for changes in agency workloads and the implementation of new supervisory fees, CBO estimates that most of the budgetary impact of those changes would be recorded in the budget as an increase in revenues.

Other Financial Oversight and Protections

The bill would change the authorities of the PCAOB and SIPC, which provide oversight and various protections in the financial markets. The bill also would establish a program to give awards to individuals who provide information to the SEC about violations of securities laws. CBO estimates that taken together, those provisions would increase budget deficits by $1.3 billion over the 2011-2020 period.

¶54,910

In particular, the bill would establish a whistleblower program at the SEC that would award a portion of penalties collected in certain proceedings brought for violation of securities laws to individuals providing information leading to the imposition of the penalties. Based on information from the SEC, CBO estimates that this program would cost about $100 million per year once the regulations are in place. We estimate that enacting the award program would increase direct spending by $0.9 billion over the 2011-2020 period.

The bill would expand the authority of the PCAOB to oversee the auditors of brokers and dealers that are registered with the SEC; those provisions also would increase fees collected by the PCAOB to support examination activities. Based on information from the PCAOB, CBO estimates that the additional oversight and examination requirements would increase the agency's costs by about $25 million per year and that the agency would increase fees charged to brokers and dealers to cover those additional costs. CBO estimates that enacting the PCAOB provisions would increase direct spending by $0.2 billion over the 2011-2020 period and increase revenues, net of income and payroll tax offsets, by a similar amount over the same period. The net effect on the deficit as a result of the PCAOB provisions would be less than $0.1 billion.

The bill would raise the amount that SIPC would be authorized to borrow from the Treasury. Under current law, SIPC makes payments from fee collections and reserves to investors that are harmed when a brokerage firm fails and customers' assets are missing. In the event collections and reserves are insufficient to cover the losses, SIPC is authorized to borrow up to $1 billion from the Treasury; the bill would raise that borrowing limit to $2.5 billion. SIPC would repay any amounts borrowed by raising fees paid by brokers and dealers that are registered with the SEC; such fees are recorded in the budget as revenues.

Based on information from SIPC, CBO estimates that the agency would probably exercise some of the additional borrowing authority provided in this title during the next 10 years. We estimate that borrowing additional funds would increase direct spending by about $1.0 billion over the 2011-2020 period. Further, we estimate that SIPC would recover that cost by raising fees, thus increasing revenues over the same period by $0.7 billion; CBO estimates that the net effect of this provision would be to raise budget deficits by $0.3 billion over the 2011-2020 period.

Financial Stability Oversight

Title I would establish a new council and office in the Department of the Treasury to oversee the financial markets. The Financial Stability Oversight Council, led by the Secretary of the Treasury, would be responsible for identifying risks to the financial stability of the United States, facilitating information sharing and setting oversight priorities among regulators, and potentially directing the Federal Reserve to supervise additional financial institutions that it does not currently regulate. The council would rely upon the OFR, also established in the bill, to collect information on financial markets and to provide independent research.

Based on amounts spent by other councils and agencies that provide similar levels of analysis and support, CBO estimates that that those new functions would cost about $75 million annually. We expect that the office would steadily expand its staff and budget over a three- to four-year period before it reached that level of effort. We estimate that those functions would cost $0.3 billion over the 2011-2015 period and $0.7 billion over the 2011-2020 period.

Title I also would allow the OFR to enter into enhanced-use lease arrangements with nonfederal partners to acquire new facilities. Based on the experience of other agencies with similar authorities, CBO expects that such leases would involve significant federal commitments. We estimate that the OFR would use its enhanced-use leasing authorities to build one general-purpose office building at a net cost of $0.2 billion over the 2011-2015 and 2011-2020 periods. CBO expects that the remaining construction costs would be covered by fee collections after 2020.

To fund the OFR and the council, the legislation would establish a Financial Research Fund within the Treasury. For the first two years after enactment, the costs of the council and the OFR would be paid by the Federal Reserve. In CBO's judgment, those costs should be recorded as expenditures in the federal budget because, like the BCFP, the council and the OFR would be independent of the Federal Reserve and their activities would be distinct from the Federal Reserve's responsibilities for monetary policy and financial regulation. Starting in 2013, the Secretary of the Treasury would collect an assessment from certain bank holding companies and nonbank financial companies supervised by the Federal Reserve that would be sufficient to cover the operating expenses of the OFR and the council.

¶ 54,910

CBO estimates that collecting the assessment, net of income and payroll tax offsets, would increase revenues by $0.2 billion over the 2011-2015 period and $0.5 billion over the 2011-2020 period. On balance, we estimate that enacting title I would increase budget deficits by $0.3 billion over the 2011-2015 period and $0.4 billion over the 2011-2020 period.

Other Provisions Affecting the Federal Reserve

CBO estimates that the requirements in a number of titles would result in incremental costs to the Federal Reserve, thereby reducing remittances to the Treasury (which are recorded in the budget as revenues). Based on information from the Federal Reserve, CBO estimates that those provisions would reduce revenues by about $0.1 billion over the 2011-2020 period. CBO expects the costs under title I to occur only in the first few years; in all other cases, the costs are expected to be ongoing. The key provisions of this sort are:

• The Chairman of the Board of Governors would be a member of the Financial Stability Oversight Council, and Federal Reserve staff could be assigned to support the work of the council.

• Under title VI, the Federal Reserve would incur costs to supervise any qualifying securities holding companies that elect to be supervised by the Federal Reserve. Additionally, the Federal Reserve would develop, in conjunction with other federal banking agencies, the regulations to implement restrictions regarding investments by banking organizations in private equity funds and hedge funds and the proprietary trading activities of banking organizations.

• Title VII would expand the rule-making requirements for the Federal Reserve related to capital and margin requirements for swap dealers and major swap participants that are banks.

• Title VIII would likely increase the workload of the Federal Reserve to supervise systemically important entities that are involved in settling payments between financial institutions.

Changes in Spending Subject to Appropriation

CBO estimates that implementing the legislation would increase spending subject to appropriation by about $4.6 billion over the 2011-2015 period (see Table 3). Most of this additional spending would result from the proposed reclassification of fees and spending by the SEC, leading to a reduction in discretionary spending by the SEC and a greater reduction in discretionary offsetting collections from SEC fees.

Reclassification of SEC Fees and Spending

Enacting the bill would change the budgetary classification of fees collected by the SEC from offsetting collections (amounts netted against discretionary appropriations) to revenues. In addition, because the legislation would authorize the SEC to spend all the fees it collects without further appropriation, the need to appropriate funds for the SEC's operations would be eliminated. Historically, fees collected by the SEC have exceeded the agency's authorized spending limits.

CBO estimates that the proposed reclassification of fees and spending would reduce discretionary spending by $5.7 billion over the 2011-2015 period and reduce offsetting collections by $9.6 billion over the same period. Taken together, those reductions would increase net spending subject to appropriation by about $4.0 billion over the 2011-2015 period and by $11.8 billion over the 2011-2020 period because the reduction in amounts that offset spending would exceed the reduction in authorized spending levels. (As described on page 10, the new permanent authority to levy fees and spend the proceeds would decrease deficits by an estimated $2.5 billion over the 2011-2015 period and by $4.9 billion over the 2011-2020 period.)

TABLE 3.—CHANGES IN SPENDING SUBJECT TO APPROPRIATION UNDER THE RESTORING AMERICAN FINANCIAL STABILITY ACT OF 2010

	By fiscal year in millions of dollars—					
	2011	2012	2013	2014	2015	2011-2015
CHANGES IN SPENDING SUBJECT TO APPROPRIATION						
Reclassification of SEC Fees and Spending:						
Spending:						
Estimated Authorization Level	-1,117	-1,139	-1,167	-1,198	-1,233	-5,854
Estimated Outlays	-949	-1,136	-1,163	-1,193	-1,228	-5,669
Offsetting Collections:						

	By fiscal year in millions of dollars—					
	2011	2012	2013	2014	2015	2011-2015
Estimated Authorization Level	1,733	1,733	1,885	2,052	2,235	9,638
Estimated Outlays	1,733	1,733	1,885	2,052	2,235	9,638
Total Reclassification of SEC Fees and Spending:						
Estimated Authorization Level	616	594	718	854	1,002	3,784
Estimated Outlays	784	597	722	859	1,007	3,969
Regulation of Over-the-Counter Derivatives:						
Estimated Authorization Level	18	55	75	76	77	301
Estimated Outlays	16	51	73	76	77	293
Access to Mainstream Financial Institutions:						
Estimated Authorization Level	57	57	58	59	60	291
Estimated Outlays	15	57	58	59	59	248
Federal Insurance Office:						
Estimated Authorization Level	2	2	2	2	2	10
Estimated Outlays	1	2	2	2	2	9
Grants to Prevent Misleading Marketing:						
Authorization Level	8	8	8	8	8	40
Estimated Outlays	1	3	7	7	8	26
Reports:						
Estimated Authorization Level	8	3	1	1	1	14
Estimated Outlays	7	4	1	1	1	14
Total Changes:						
Estimated Authorization Level	709	719	862	1,000	1,150	4,440
Estimated Outlays	824	714	862	1,004	1,154	4,558

Note: Components may not sum to totals because of rounding

Regulation of Over-the-Counter Derivatives

Title VII would require certain derivatives transactions to take place on registered exchanges and would place new registration and reporting requirements on entities that trade in or facilitate such transactions. This title would broaden the authority of the CFTC to regulate entities and activities related to those transactions.

Based on information from the CFTC, CBO estimates that implementing those broader authorities would cost $293 million over the 2011-2015 period, assuming appropriation of the necessary amounts. CBO estimates that the agency would add 235 employees by fiscal year 2013 to write regulations and to undertake the additional oversight and enforcement activities required under the bill. That would amount to a roughly 40 percent increase over 2010 staffing levels.

Access to Mainstream Financial Institutions

Title XII would authorize the appropriation of such sums as may be necessary to establish several programs aimed at increasing access to and usage of traditional banking services in lieu of alternative financial services such as nonbank money orders and check cashing, rent-to-own agreements, and payday lending. Based on pilot programs operated by the private sector and information collected by the FDIC, CBO estimates that this effort would cost $248 million over the 2011-2015 period, assuming appropriation of the necessary amounts.

Federal Insurance Office

Title V would establish the Federal Insurance Office within the Department of the Treasury to monitor the insurance industry and to coordinate federal policy on insurance issues. The bill also would authorize the Secretary of the Treasury to enter into international agreements to harmonize regulations on the insurance industry. Based on information from the Treasury, CBO estimates that implementing those provisions would cost $9 million over the 2011-2015 period, subject to the appropriation of the necessary amounts.

Grants To Prevent Misleading Marketing

Title IX would authorize the appropriation of $8 million in each of fiscal years 2011 through 2015 for grants to states to protect elderly citizens from misleading marketing of financial products. CBO estimates that implementing this provision would cost $26 million over the 2011-2015 period.

Reports

The bill would require the Government Accountability Office (GAO) to prepare more than 20 reports on a wide range of topics, including financial literacy, oversight of financial planners, and disclosures by issuers of municipal securities. The bill also would require GAO to audit the BCFP annually. Based on information from the agency, CBO estimates that each report would cost, on average, $500,000 and would be completed within the time allotted in the bill. CBO estimates that implementing the reporting provisions in the bill would cost $14 million over the 2011-2015 period, assuming appropriation of the necessary amounts.

Pay-as-you-go considerations: The Statutory Pay-As-You-Go Act of 2010 establishes budget reporting and enforcement procedures for legislation affecting direct spending or revenues. The net changes in outlays and revenues that are subject to those pay-as-you-go procedures are shown in the following table.

CBO ESTIMATE OF PAY-AS-YOU-GO EFFECTS FOR S. 3217, THE RESTORING AMERICAN FINANCIAL STABILITY ACT OF 2010, AS ORDERED REPORTED BY THE SENATE COMMITTEE ON BANKING, HOUSING, AND URBAN AFFAIRS ON MARCH 22, 2010

	By fiscal year, in billions of dollars—										
	2011	2012	2013	2014	2015	2016	2017	2018	2019	2020	2011-2015	2011-2020
	NET INCREASE OR DECREASE (–) IN THE DEFICIT										
Statutory Pay-as-You-Go Impact[a]	1.8	–0.1	–2.6	–2.9	–2.9	–2.9	–3.3	–3.7	–2.9	–1.6	–6.6	–21.0

[a] Positive numbers indicate increases in deficits; negative numbers indicate decreases in deficits.

Intergovernmental and private-sector impact: The bill would impose intergovernmental and private-sector mandates, as defined in UMRA, on banks and other private and public entities that participate in financial markets. The bill also would impose intergovernmental mandates by prohibiting states from taxing and regulating certain insurance products issued by companies based in other states and by preempting certain state laws. Because the costs of complying with some of the mandates would depend on future regulations that would be established under the bill, and because CBO has limited information about the extent to which public entities enter into swaps with unregulated entities, CBO cannot determine whether the aggregate costs of the intergovernmental mandates would exceed the annual threshold established in UMRA ($70 million in 2010, adjusted annually for inflation). However, CBO estimates that the total amount of fees alone that would be collected from private entities would well exceed the annual threshold established in UMRA for private-sector mandates ($141 million in 2010, adjusted annually for inflation).

Mandates That Apply to Both Intergovernmental and Private-Sector Entities

Some mandates in the bill would affect both public and private entities, including pension funds and public finance authorities. The cost of complying with the mandates is uncertain and would depend on the nature of future regulations and the range of entities subject to them.

Consumer Financial Protection. The bill would authorize the BCFP to regulate banks and credit unions with assets over $10 million, all mortgage-related businesses (housing finance agencies, lenders, servicers, mortgage brokers, and foreclosure operators), and all large nonbank financial companies (such as payday lenders, debt collectors, and consumer reporting agencies). The BCFP would enforce federal laws related to consumer protection by establishing rules and issuing orders and guidance. Bank and nonbank entities that offer financial services or products would be required to make disclosures to customers and submit information to the BCFP. The bill also would require certain financial institutions to maintain records regarding deposit accounts of customers and would prohibit prepayment penalties for residential mortgage loans.

Regulation of Over-the-Counter Derivatives Markets. The bill would impose several requirements on public and private entities such as pension funds, swap dealers, and other participants in derivatives markets. For example, the bill would place new requirements on derivatives; require reporting by entities that gather trading information about swaps, organizations that clear derivatives, facilities that execute swaps, pension funds, and swap dealers; and

¶54,910

establish capital requirements for pension funds, swap dealers and major swap participants.

Regulation of Financial Securities. The bill would require entities (including public finance authorities) that sell products such as mortgage-backed securities to hold at least 5 percent of the credit risk of each asset that they securitize. Under the bill, the BCFP could exempt classes of assets from the retention requirement. The bill also would require issuers of securities to disclose information to the SEC about the underlying assets and to analyze the quality of those assets.

Mandates That Apply Only to Intergovernmental Entities

Prohibition on Investments by Small Public Entities. The bill would impose a mandate on public entities that invest more than $25 million but less than $50 million by prohibiting them from entering into swaps with entities that are not federally regulated.

The costs of complying with this mandate would be equal to the difference between the cost of entering into a swap with an unregulated entity and the cost of entering into one with a regulated entity, but because CBO has limited information about the extent to which public entities enter into such arrangements, we have no basis for estimating the cost of complying with this mandate.

Prohibition on Taxation of Surplus Lines. The bill would establish national standards for how states may regulate, collect, and allocate taxes for a type of insurance that covers unique or atypical risks—known as surplus lines or non-admitted insurance. The bill also would establish national standards for how states regulate reinsurance. As defined in UMRA, the direct costs of a mandate include any amounts that state and local governments would be prohibited from raising in revenues as a result of the mandate. The direct costs of this mandate would be the amount of taxes on premiums for surplus lines issued by out-of-state brokers that states would be precluded from collecting.

While there is some uncertainty surrounding the amount of tax that states currently collect, the portion of the surplus lines market that would be affected, and the flexibility available to states after enactment of the bill, CBO estimates that forgone revenues would total less than $50 million, annually, beginning one year after enactment. For the purpose of estimating the direct cost of the mandate, CBO considered the taxes that the industry estimates it is paying and the revenues that states, as a whole, would no longer be able to collect as a result of the bill.

Prohibition on Fees for Licensing Brokers. The bill would prohibit states from collecting licensing fees from brokers of surplus lines unless states participate in a national database of insurance brokers. CBO estimates that the costs of participating in the database would be small.

Regulation of Reinsurance. The bill would prohibit states other than the state where a reinsurer is incorporated and licensed from regulating the financial solvency of that reinsurer, if that state is accredited by the National Association of Insurance Commissioners. The bill also would limit the way states regulate insurers that purchase reinsurance. Those mandates would impose no direct costs on states.

Preemption of State Laws. The bill would preempt state laws that affect the offer, sale, or distribution of swaps as well as consumer protection and insurance laws. The preemptions would be mandates as defined in UMRA, but they would impose no duty on states that would result in additional spending.

Mandates That Apply Only to Private Entities

Orderly Liquidation Fund. Under the bill, the largest financial companies would be required to pay assessments totaling up to $50 billion into the OLF over the 10 years after the bill's enactment. Those companies also would have to submit plans to regulators for how they could be liquidated in the event of a failure. Because of the target size of the fund, CBO estimates that the cost of complying with the mandates would greatly exceed the annual threshold for private-sector mandates in each of the first five years the mandate is in effect.

Security and Exchange Commission Fees. The bill would increase the amount of fees collected by the SEC, and such an increase would impose a mandate on participants in securities markets. The cost of the mandate would be the incremental increase in such fees compared to current law. CBO estimates that increase would total at least $650 million over the first five years that the mandate is in effect.

Financial Stability Oversight. The Financial Stability Oversight Council would have the authority to require the Federal Reserve to supervise nonbank companies that may pose risks to the financial stability of the United States. The council also would have the authority to require a large bank holding company that poses a risk to the financial stability of the United States to meet certain conditions and to terminate certain activities. In addition, the Federal Reserve would be required to establish standards for nonbank financial companies and large bank holding companies regarding capital and liquidity requirements, leverage and concentration limits, credit exposure, and remediation. The cost of complying with these mandates is uncertain and would depend on the details of future regulations.

Beginning two years after the bill's enactment, certain bank holding companies and nonbank financial companies supervised by the Federal Reserve would be required to pay an assessment to the Secretary of the Treasury to cover the operating expenses of the Council and the Office of Financial Research. Based on information from the Treasury Department, CBO estimates that the cost of complying with the mandate would total about $70 million per year.

Regulation of Certain Financial Companies. The regulation of some financial companies (including some banks, thrifts, and related holding companies) would be transferred to different federal agencies, including the OCC and the FDIC. Companies that are currently regulated by the Federal Reserve would be required to pay new fees and meet the requirements of their new regulator. CBO estimates that the amount of additional fees paid by those companies would amount to about $500 million per year.

Federal regulators would be required to implement rules for banks, their affiliates and bank holding companies, and other financial companies to prohibit proprietary trading, sponsoring, and investing in hedge funds and private equity funds, and limiting relationships with hedge funds and private equity funds. Because the requirements on such companies would depend on future rules and regulations, CBO cannot estimate the cost of complying with the mandates.

Companies supervised by the Federal Reserve also would be prohibited from voting for directors of the Federal Reserve Banks. CBO expects there would be no cost to comply with that mandate.

Regulation of Financial Market Utilities. The legislation would require persons who manage or carry out payment, clearing, and settlement activities among financial institutions to meet uniform standards that would be established by the Federal Reserve regarding the management of risks and clearing and settlement activities. The cost of complying with the standards would depend on those future regulations.

Office of National Insurance. The bill would require insurance companies to provide data and information to the Office of National Insurance, which would also have subpoena authority. The cost of the mandates would be small.

Regulation of Securities Markets. The bill would broaden the SEC's authority to regulate entities and activities associated with securities markets.

Regulation of Advisers to Hedge Funds. The bill would require hedge fund advisers that manage over $100 million in assets to register with the SEC. According to industry experts, the expenses for those advisers to prepare for the registration process would probably average less than $30,000 per firm. Based on information from the SEC regarding the number of firms that could be affected by the requirement, CBO estimates that the cost of the mandate would fall below the annual threshold established in UMRA.

Mandatory Arbitration. The bill would authorize the SEC to prohibit mandatory predispute arbitration agreements between brokers, dealers, municipal financial advisers and their clients. Based upon information from industry sources, CBO expects that if the SEC were to impose such a mandate, the incremental cost to those entities of using the court system instead of arbitration could be significant.

Deficiencies in Regulation. The bill would require the SEC to establish regulations to address any deficiencies it finds in the regulation of brokers, dealers, and investment advisers. The cost of the mandates, if any, would depend on future rules and regulations.

Other Financial Oversight and Protections. The cost of each of the following mandates on securities markets would be small, relative to the annual threshold. The bill would:

• Change the makeup of the Municipal Securities Regulatory Board and require municipal securities advisers to register with the SEC;

• Require auditors of broker-dealers to register with PCAOB and allow it to charge higher regulatory fees;

• Require members of a compensation committee for companies that issue securities to be independent; require companies to provide for an annual nonbinding vote on executive pay and disclose to shareholder the relationship between executive pay and performance; and require companies to have a compliance officer;

• Place additional requirements on the election of directors to the board of a company; and

• Require credit rating agencies to provide public disclosures about methods used to determine credit ratings and the performance of those ratings; to meet education requirements for analysts; and to institute policies to address conflicts of interest.

Previous CBO estimates: CBO has transmitted several cost estimates for bills ordered reported by the House Committee on Financial Services containing provisions that are similar to provisions in the Restoring American Financial Stability Act of 2010. CBO also published estimates of the direct spending and revenue effects of the Wall Street Reform and Consumer Protection Act of 2009, which consolidated and amended the individual bills and contained additional provisions.

On December 9, 2009, CBO transmitted an estimate for the Wall Street Reform and Consumer Protection Act of 2009 as ordered reported by the House Committee on Rules on December 8, 2009. Earlier, on December 4, 2009, CBO published an estimate for the Wall Street Reform and Consumer Protection as introduced on December 2, 2009.

On July 30, 2009, CBO transmitted an estimate for H.R. 3269, the Corporate and Financial Institution Compensation Fairness Act of 2009, as ordered reported by the House Committee on Financial Services on July 28, 2009. H.R. 3269 contains provisions that are similar to subtitle E of title IX of the Restoring American Financial Stability Act.

On November 3, 2009, CBO transmitted an estimate for H.R. 3795, the Over-the-Counter Derivatives Markets Act of 2009, as ordered reported by the House Committee on Financial Services on October 15, 2009. On November 6, 2009, CBO transmitted an estimate for H.R. 3795, the Derivatives Markets Transparency and Accountability Act of 2009, as reported by the House Committee on Agriculture on October 21, 1998. Both House bills contain provisions that are similar to title VII of the Senate bill.

On November 13, 2009, CBO transmitted an estimate for H.R. 3818, the Private Fund Investment Advisers Registration Act of 2009, as ordered reported by the House Committee on Financial Services on October 27, 2009. H.R. 3818 contains provisions that are similar to title IV of the Senate bill.

On December 3, 2009, CBO transmitted an estimate for H.R. 3126, the Consumer Financial Protection Agency Act of 2009, as ordered reported by the House Committee on Financial Services on October 22, 2009. H.R. 3126 contains provisions that are similar to title X of the Senate bill.

On December 3, 2009, CBO transmitted an estimate for H.R. 3890, the Accountability and Transparency in Rating Agencies Act, as ordered reported by the House Committee on Financial Services on October 22, 2009. H.R. 3890 contains provisions that are similar to subtitle C of title IX of the Senate bill.

On March 11, 2010, CBO transmitted an estimate for H.R. 2609, the Federal Insurance Act of 2009, as ordered reported by the House Committee on Financial Services on December 2, 2009. H.R. 2609 is nearly identical to subtitle A of title V of the Senate bill.

Estimate prepared by: Federal Costs: Kathleen Gramp, Susan Willie, Matthew Pickford, Daniel Hoople, and Wendy Kiska; Federal Revenues: Barbara Edwards; Impact on State, Local, and Tribal Governments: Elizabeth Cove Delisle; Impact on the Private Sector: Paige Piper/Bach, Brian Prest, and Sam Wice.

Estimate approved by: Theresa Gullo, Deputy Assistant Director for Budget Analysis.

[¶54,915] IX. Regulatory Impact Statement

In accordance with paragraph 11(b), rule XXVI, of the Standing Rules of the Senate, the Committee makes the following statement concerning the regulatory impact of the bill.

NUMBER OF PERSONS COVERED

The reported bill would promote the financial stability of the United States through multiple measures designed to work together to improve accountability, resiliency, and transparency in the financial system by: establishing an early warning system to detect and address emerging threats to financial stability and the economy, enhancing consumer and investor protections, strengthening the supervision of large complex financial companies and providing a mechanism to liquidate such companies should they fail without any losses to the taxpayer, and regulating the massive over-the-counter derivatives market.

Among those who would benefit from the provisions in the reported bill include the participants in the U.S. financial system, such as consumers of financial products who would be empowered to make more informed choices through better disclosures, and investors in the capital markets who would be better protected through greater transparency and improved corporate governance. Taxpayers would be protected as well, by ending the possibility that individual companies could be bailed out as they were in 2008 during the financial crisis when regulators did not have the ability to liquidate large, interconnected financial companies in an orderly way. A large, complex financial company that fails will either go through bankruptcy, or in the rare, exceptional case where the bankruptcy of such financial company would threaten financial stability, the company will be liquidated in an orderly fashion by the FDIC with funding from the financial services industry, not from the taxpayers.

Under the reported bill, those who provide financial services would benefit as well since the bill seeks to ensure that financial companies operate in a safer, sounder manner through tougher oversight and accountability without jeopardizing the financial system through risky, irresponsible practices. Companies such as AIG, Lehman Brothers, and Bear Stearns would likely not have collapsed and put the entire financial system in jeopardy had they been under appropriately stringent supervision that limited the dangerous financial activities in which they engaged.

Regulated financial companies will continue to be regulated, with the larger, more complex and interconnected financial companies facing increasingly stringent supervision. (Smaller banks, on the other hand, should not be subject to additional regulation.) While the overall thrust of the reported bill is to close gaps in regulations and provide robust supervision to rein in abusive practices by the weakly regulated or unregulated financial companies that led to the financial crisis, some financial companies may see their regulations rationalized and streamlined through the consolidation of holding company and prudential supervision that aims to reduce unnecessary duplication. Certain financial companies that previously have not been subject to robust regulation (or any regulation in some cases), including some Wall Street firms and those financial companies operating within the unregulated "shadow" banking system, will be subject to supervision for the first time or become subject to tougher oversight so that their risky activities do not trigger another financial crisis.

ECONOMIC IMPACT

By promoting financial stability through a broad range of improvements, it is anticipated that the reported bill would have a positive economic impact overall by building a solid foundation upon which the financial system and the economy of the United States could continue to grow in a sustainable fashion, with reduced likelihood of, and mitigated impact from, any potential financial crises.

The costs of the last financial crisis to American workers, homeowners, and economy have been enormous: 8 million jobs were lost, more than 7 million homes entered foreclosure, and $13 trillion in American household wealth vanished. The reported bill seeks to improve the financial architecture of the U.S. to minimize or eliminate the likelihood of the recurrence of a financial crisis of such proportions. While no legislation could eliminate altogether economic cycles and periods of financial instability, the strengthened infrastructure for the financial system contemplated by the reported bill is intended to make the system more resilient and resistant to the adverse effects of financial instability.

A number of provisions in the reported bill would impact the U.S. economy positively. For instance, the comprehensive regulation and rules for how the OTC derivatives market operates would protect taxpayers and inject greater transparency into U.S. markets, attracting foreign investment and increasing U.S. competitiveness. Increasing the use of central clearinghouses and exchanges as well as setting appropriate margining, capital, and reporting requirements will provide safeguards for American taxpayers and the financial system as a whole. The overall result would be reduced costs and risks to taxpayers, end users, and the financial system as a whole.

The provision to prohibit banks and bank holding companies from proprietary trading and sponsoring and investing in hedge funds and private equity funds also would serve to protect taxpayers and reduce risks in the financial system. When losses from high-risk activities are significant, they can threaten the safety and soundness of individual banks and contribute to overall financial instability. Moreover, when the losses accrue to insured depositories or their holding companies, they can cause taxpayer losses. In addition, when banks engage in these activities for their own accounts, there is an increased likelihood that they will find that their interests conflict with those of their customers. This prohibition therefore will reduce potential taxpayer losses at financial companies protected by the federal safety net, and reduce threats to financial stability, by lowering the financial companies' exposure to risk. The provision also would prevent financial companies protected by the federal safety net, which have a lower cost of funds, from directing those funds to high-risk uses.

The creation of the Consumer Financial Protection Bureau (CFPB) would provide a level playing field for banks and nonbank financial companies that sell financial products and services to consumers, subjecting them to uniform rules and consistent enforcement for the benefit of consumers. It will do so without creating an undue burden on banks and credit unions. The CFPB would enable consumers to get clear and effective disclosures in plain English and in a timely fashion so that they can shop for the best consumer financial products and services. The CFPB would stop regulatory arbitrage—it will write rules and enforce those rules consistently, without regard to whether a mortgage, a credit card, an auto loan, or any other consumer financial product or service is made by a bank, a credit union, a mortgage broker, an auto dealer, or any other nonbank financial company, so that a consumer can shop and compare products based on quality, price, and convenience without having to worry about getting trapped by fine print into an abusive deal. The CFPB would have been able to head off the subprime mortgage crisis that directly led to the financial crisis, because the CFPB would have been able to see and take action against the proliferation of poorly underwritten mortgages with abusive terms. The CFPB therefore serves to provide another safeguard for the U.S. economy, taxpayers, and consumers.

Several provisions in the bill work together to strengthen the supervisory infrastructure of the U.S. financial system, reduce the likelihood that an individual financial company would become systemically dangerous, and protect taxpayers from losses if a financial company fails. The Financial Stability Oversight Council and the Office of Financial Research would monitor the financial system for emerging risks. The Federal Reserve would provide supervision to unregulated financial companies that the Council determines could threaten financial stability, and impose heightened prudential standards—"speed bumps"—such as capital, liquidity, and leverage requirements. If a financial company fails but its bankruptcy would threaten the financial system, instead of bailing out such company with taxpayer dollars, the FDIC would be able to step in and liquidate the company with funds from the largest, riskiest financial companies and then recover any losses from a broader set of large, risky financial companies, if there are any losses after selling off the assets of the failed company in an orderly fashion to avoid a "fire sale." Taxpayers thus would not be at risk from the failure of a financial company, and no financial company would be too big to fail.

PRIVACY

The reported bill is not expected to have an adverse impact on the personal privacy of individuals.

PAPERWORK

The reported bill seeks to minimize any increase in paperwork requirements. A number of provisions require regulators, before they can require reports or obtain information from financial companies, to first consult with and obtain such reports or information from other regulators or other sources to avoid unnecessary duplication and administrative burden.

[¶54,920] X. Changes in Existing Law (Cordon Rule)

On March 22, 2010 the Committee unanimously approved a motion by Senator Dodd to waive the Cordon rule. Thus, in the opinion of the Committee, it is necessary to dispense with the requirement of section 12 of rule XXVI of the Standing Rules of the Senate in order to expedite the business of the Senate.

[¶54,925] XI. Minority Views

MINORITY VIEWS OF SENATOR SHELBY, SENATOR BENNETT, SENATOR BUNNING, AND SENATOR VITTER

April 30, 2010

Background

Chairman Christopher J. Dodd submitted the *"Restoring Financial Stability Act of 2010"* (the "bill" or the "reported bill") to the Senate Committee on Banking, Housing and Urban Affairs ("Committee") on March 15, 2010. Although this bill has been improved since a discussion draft was first introduced in November of 2009, we cannot support it in its current form. On March 22, the bill was voted out of Committee without the support of any Republican members. The Committee did not hold a legislative hearing on the bill. A review of the hearing list set forth in the majority report reveals that the Committee did not hold substantive hearings on most of the provisions in this bill. Although the Committee prepared this legislation to address the causes of the financial crisis of 2008, the Committee has not conducted a single investigation into any aspect of the crisis. Furthermore, although the Committee authorized the creation of the Financial Crisis Inquiry Commission (S. 386) to study the causes of the crisis, the Commission will not report back to Congress with its findings and recommendations until later this year. None of the Commission's work informed the Committee's consideration of the reported bill. As a process matter, we believe that the Committee has yet to conduct the factual inquiries and develop the legislative record for a bill of this importance. We also note that the reported version of the bill differed in several substantive instances from the bill that the Committee approved. The discussion below is based on the bill that was actually approved by the Committee.

We offer these dissenting views on the reported bill because of our strong belief that the bill contains serious flaws and will undermine the long-term health of the U.S. economy. The reported bill's shortcomings include its: institutionalization of government bailouts; creation of vast and unaccountable new bureaucracies with unprecedented power and scope; faulty financial regulatory structure; imposition of costly and unnecessary regulation on American businesses; abrogation of the bankruptcy code in favor of a resolution process based not on law and precedent, but rather on the whims of un-elected regulators; authorization of data collection and monitoring of American consumers that undermines traditional civil liberties; creation of barriers-to-entry in financial services that will further concentrate market-share in the largest financial institutions; over-reliance on the judgment of regulators; proliferation of costly and needless litigation; mandating of significant new costs on small businesses; establishment of new barriers to capital formation by small businesses; slanting of corporate government rules in favor of special-interest investors; and failure to address the massive problems at Fannie Mae and Freddie Mac.

A detailed explanation of the reasons for Republican opposition to the reported bill is set forth in this document.

Title I: Financial Stability

Title I of the reported bill establishes a council of federal financial regulators, the Financial Stability Oversight Council ("FSOC" or "Council"), for systemic risk regulation (Section 111). The overall mission and structure of the FSOC is sound. The FSOC would formally bring together for the first time all federal financial regulators to improve financial regulation, maintain and monitor financial stability, promote market discipline, and coordinate the response of the federal government to future financial crises. The FSOC will enable coordination and communication across the U.S. financial regulatory system.

The particular authorities granted to the FSOC, however, are troubling because they entrench "too big to fail" financial institutions as a permanent part of the U.S. financial system, thereby perpetuating the unfair advantages these large institutions enjoy over their smaller competitors and increasing the risk of U.S. financial system instability. The FSOC is empowered to designate bank holding companies with over $50 billion in consolidated assets for heightened regulation by the Federal Reserve ("Fed") (Sections 115 and 165). The FSOC also can designate nonbank financial companies for regulation by the Fed.

The definition of a "nonbank financial company" is broad. The term includes all companies, other than bank holding companies, organized in the U.S. or a U.S. state that are substantially engaged in activities that are financial in nature. All such companies whose material financial distress in the judgment of at least two thirds of the FSOC would "pose a threat to the financial stability of the United States" would be subject to the FSOC designation and Fed regulation (Section 113). The FSOC systemic designation and follow-on Fed regulation could apply to broker-dealers, hedge funds, pension funds, insurance companies, and savings and loan holding companies (Sections 113 and 165).

This special designation for nonbank financial companies and large bank holding companies will result in these financial institutions receiving unfair marketplace advantages. Market participants will interpret this special regulation as an implicit government guaranty that prevents these firms from failing. These expectations will be reinforced by the expanded authorities that the reported bill grants to regulators to support designated financial institutions, including the ability, as provided in Titles II and XI, to subsidize creditors, lend against questionable collateral, and issue debt guarantees. The implicit stamp of approval that designated financial institutions will receive from this regulatory restructure will allow them to obtain a lower cost of funds and other unfair advantages. These advantages will lead to higher shareholder profits and lower counterparty risk. Such firms will grow larger and subsume smaller firms who do not have these advantages. As these large firms grow, the ability of the government to resolve them without taxpayer support diminishes. If a financial institution grows too large and constitutes too much of some aspect of financial intermediation, the U.S. economy may not be able to withstand its liquidation. For example, the Federal government has had difficulty addressing Fannie Mae and Freddie Mac because they comprised a majority stake of the U.S. housing finance market. The reported bill may replicate this phenomenon for the rest of the U.S. financial marketplace.

In addition, the reported bill establishes a $50 billion fund intended to be used in the resolution of a select group of large financial institutions. The select group that contributes to the fund will be perceived by markets as having special protection and will receive unfair funding advantages. Indeed, Treasury Secretary Timothy Geithner warned that " . . . standing fund would create expectations that the government would step in to protect shareholders and creditors from losses. In essence, a standing fund would be viewed as a form of insurance for those stakeholders."[259]

Title I of the reported bill also establishes the Office of Financial Research ("OFR") (Section 151). The office is fundamentally flawed, as it poses a grave danger to the civil liberties of the American people. It has an independent and unaccountable head with the authority to collect any and all information from any and all financial companies (Section 153). The office even has subpoena power (Section 153). No branch of government has oversight of this office (Section 152). Given the private and personal nature of information being collected and monitored by this office, judicial oversight should be mandated.

Advocates for the Office of Financial Research claim $500 million will be used to purchase servers adequate to store and analyze data on all financial transactions in the United States. An additional $500 million will be required to staff and operate the office. The unrealistic expectation is that this office will identify future asset bubbles and work with financial regulators to mitigate them before the pre-identified risks manifest as financial instability events. But that is not the entirety of the mission.

The advocates of the office openly claim that the office will result in cost savings for Wall Street financial institutions. The claim is that standardizing data reporting will dramatically reduce back office costs (costs associated with verifying details of trades with counter parties) and costs associated with maintaining reference databases (legal entity and financial instrument databases). The reported bill requires the office to share data with Wall Street financial institutions. Morgan Stanley estimates that implementation of a program like the OFR will result in a 20% to 30% savings in its operational costs.[260]

Title II: Orderly Liquidation Authority

Title II of the reported bill would institutionalize bailouts by granting the Executive Branch and federal regulatory agencies permanent authority to rescue firms and their creditors and shareholders. Rather than curtailing the ability of the federal government to bail out companies, this legislation would set the stage for repeated and potentially larger government bailouts in the future. The limited tools that regulators used during the recent crisis, often at the very edge of, if not beyond, their statutory authorities, would be augmented with new and broader authorities that explicitly empower regulators to bail out firms and their creditors and shareholders.[261]

The centerpiece of these new bailout authorities is the reported bill's new resolution authority. It would authorize the Secretary of the Treasury to place any financial company into an administrative resolution process with the Federal Deposit Insurance Corporation ("FDIC") serving as the receiver (Section 203). As the receiver, the FDIC, with the consent of the Secretary of the Treasury, is explicitly authorized to pay creditors and shareholders of the company more than they would be entitled to receive in bankruptcy (Section 210(d)(4)). Paying creditors and shareholders more than they are entitled to is the very definition of a bailout. The reported

---

[259] Press Release, United States Department of the Treasury, October 29, 2009.

[260] "FAQs: Role of the NIF, Value and Cost." *Committee to Establish the National Institute of Finance.* 10 Mar. 2010. <http://www.ce-nif.org/faqs-role-of-the-nif/role-of-the-nif-value-and-cost>.

[261] Despite clear legislative language to the contrary, the FDIC has interpreted the systemic risk exception under the Federal Deposit Insurance Act (12 U.S.C. 1823(c)(4)(G)) as authorizing the FDIC to provide broad financial assistance to financial institutions, including billions of dollars in debt guarantees. Similarly, although Section 13(3) of the Federal Reserve Act prohibits the Board of Governors from making equity investments in partnerships and corporations, the Board of Governors has interpreted its lending authority as authorizing it to lend to special purpose vehicles that invest in assets of failed firms, even though such lending has the economic characteristics of equity.

¶54,925

bill states that the FDIC should conduct resolutions with "a strong presumption" that creditors and shareholders bear losses (Section 204). It does not mandate that they take all of the losses.

The reported bill claims that it is "protecting taxpayers from bailouts," but it notably does not claim to end bailouts. Instead, it grants the FDIC the authority to impose assessments on financial companies to pay for bailouts of creditors and shareholders. Thus, the reported bill provides a permanent source of funding for bailouts while claiming that it protects taxpayers. According to the Congressional Budget Office ("CBO"), however, the assessments would be tax deductible.[262] As a result, taxpayers are directly on the hook to cover the costs of a resolution. To the extent the assessments actually are paid by financial companies, the American public still picks up the tab. First, CBO has indicated that the assessments will result in reduced compensation for employees at assessed companies.[263] Second, the assessments will be passed down (like all business taxes) to the consumers in the form of higher prices. It does not matter whether the funds to pay creditors and shareholders additional amounts come directly from taxpayers in the form of taxes or indirectly from the public in the form of assessments on financial companies. The end result is the same: the American people will pay for the losses of the investors of large financial institutions.

By establishing a mechanism to bail out creditors and shareholders, the reported bill will worsen the too big to fail problem that plagues our financial markets. If creditors and shareholders know that the FDIC will bail them out using this resolution authority, they will impose far less market discipline on these firms (such as imposing conditions on the firm before they invest, removing management, or selling their interests in the firm). After all, if the government will be there to ensure that creditors and shareholders do not take losses if the company fails, any funds that investors spend to monitor their investments would needlessly reduce their ultimate profits. And, because investors will abstain from disciplining these too big to fail firms, the firms will attract ever larger amounts of capital, allowing them to grow bigger and giving them a competitive advantage over their smaller competitors who investors believe are not too big to fail. Moreover, investors will have incentives to take greater risks, as they will reap all of the gains while losses will be transferred to other firms by the resolution authority. In total, this is the same recipe that produced the colossal failures of Fannie Mae and Freddie Mac, necessitating a government rescue that has cost taxpayers more than $127 billion to date.[264] Accordingly, far from ending bailouts, the reported bill's resolution authority actually will make our financial system less safe, more susceptible to crises, and more dependent on bailouts.

The reported bill's resolution authority also suffers from numerous technical problems. The bill does not provide any mechanism for ensuring that the resolution authority is not used to bail out creditors and shareholders of non-financial firms. Presently, the reported bill would allow a non-financial firm to be resolved under its resolution authority if (1) it is a subsidiary of a financial company, or (2) the Secretary of the Treasury determines that the company was "primarily" engaged in activities that are financial in nature. The Secretary's determination on whether a company is "primarily" engaged in financial activities is not reviewable, leaving the door open for misuse of the resolution authority. No evidence has been presented to the Committee that supports the use of the resolution authority to resolve non-financial companies.

Further, the reported bill does not provide any check on the FDIC as receiver for a covered financial company. There are no provisions that would permit the removal of the FDIC as receiver if the FDIC performs poorly in executing its duties under this title.

In addition, the reported bill does not guard against the use of the resolution authority to bail out politically influential creditors and shareholders. The FDIC, with the consent of the Treasury Secretary, can treat similarly situated creditors and shareholders differently, including paying some creditors and shareholders 100 percent (or more) of their claims while paying others only the amount they would have received in bankruptcy. This would allow the FDIC and the Treasury Secretary to bail out politically favored creditors and shareholders such

---

[262] Congressional Budget Office, Cost Estimate: S. 3217 Restoring American Financial Stability Act of 2010, April 21, 2010.

[263] Id.

[264] Federal National Mortgage Association. (2009) 12/31/2009 SEC Form 10-K Annual Report. ("When Treasury provides the additional funds that have been requested, we will have received an aggregate of $75.2 billion from Treasury. The aggregate liquidation preference on the senior preferred stock will be $76.2 billion, which will require an annualized dividend of approximately $7.6 billion.") Federal Home Loan Mortgage Corp. (2010). 2/24/2010 SEC Form 10-Q Quarterly Report. ("To date, we have received an aggregate of $50.7 billion in funding under the Purchase Agreement.")

as foreign governments or politically influential investors.

Finally, the reported bill contains no provisions to ensure that the directors, senior executives, and regulators of any financial company placed into resolution are held accountable. For example, there are no provisions that address the priority of the claims of directors and senior executives. In addition, the bill lacks any provisions requiring an evaluation of the performance of the primary regulators of a covered financial company to hold the regulatory staff accountable for any failings in their supervision of a covered financial company.

Title III: Transfer of Powers to the Comptroller of the Currency, the Corporation, and the Board of Governors

Title III of the reported bill creates a cumbersome financial regulatory structure that reinforces expectations that large financial institutions are too big to fail and that contains significant gaps in regulatory oversight. By stripping the Fed of all banking regulatory authority except for bank holding companies with assets of more than $50 billion, the reported bill signals to market participants that large financial institutions have a special regulator, the Fed, which will not allow any of those institutions to fail. These expectations are reinforced by the fact that the Fed has the authority, and has demonstrated recently the willingness, to provide funding through the discount window and Section 13(3) of the Federal Reserve Act to prevent its regulated entities from failing.

The reported bill also contains a significant regulatory gap because it does not automatically apply heightened regulatory standards to large savings and loan holding companies in Section 165 as it does for large bank holding companies. The majority claims heightened regulatory standards are needed for our largest financial institutions. Yet their reported bill exempts savings and loan holding companies from Section 165. In fact, it is possible to read Section 165 as a prohibition on applying heightened standards developed for large bank holding companies to savings and loan holding companies. This is of particular concern given the fact that several savings and loans holding companies are among the largest financial institutions in the country and contributed to financial instability, including American International Group ("AIG") and G.E. Capital. For these and all other savings and loan holding companies, the majority relies on the wisdom and judgment of future regulators to determine through a Financial Stability Oversight Council vote whether to apply heightened regulatory standards. A superior approach would be to apply heightened regulatory standards to all holding companies with an insured depository institution. In addition, the construct in the reported bill is unworkable for savings and loan holding companies that also undertake significant commercial activities. The Fed is not an appropriate regulator for commercial activities. The reported bill fails to clarify or address the regulation of savings and loan holding companies.

Title IV: Regulation of Advisers to Hedge Funds and Others

Title IV of the reported bill has identified hedge funds as potential systemic risks. To address these risks, the bill imposes a requirement that hedge fund advisers with more than $100 million under management register with the Securities and Exchange Commission ("SEC" or "Commission"). Hedge funds have not been identified as a cause of the financial crisis and investors in failed funds were not bailed out.

Regulators should have better information about hedge funds, but hedge fund advisor registration is not the appropriate approach, and the SEC is not the proper regulator to carry out systemic risk oversight. The SEC's responsibilities are protecting investors, facilitating capital formation, and maintaining fair, orderly, and efficient markets. The SEC is not a systemic risk regulator, and when it tried to be with the Consolidated Supervised Entity program, it failed.[265]

---

[265] Of the firms regulated by the SEC under its Consolidated Supervised Entities ("CSE") program, one collapsed and its creditors were bailed out by the Fed (Bear Stearns), one failed and was sold in bankruptcy (Lehman Brothers), one was rescued in a merger (Merrill Lynch), and two converted to bank holding companies to obtain a rescue from the Fed's discount window (Goldman Sachs and Morgan Stanley). The CSE program never was authorized by Congress. It was created by the SEC in 2005 to provide consolidated regulation to those select firms to allow them to avoid consolidated supervision under European Union regulation. The record of the SEC's CSEs programs must certainly stand as among the greatest regulatory failures in financial history, especially if one considers that the financial crisis started in September 2007 with the failure of two investment funds sponsored by Bear Stearns. Its record should serve as a reminder of the systemic problems and financial crises that flawed regulatory structures and agencies can produce. While well conceived regulation can enhance markets, poorly conceived regulation, especially when the regulation involves a captured regulator, can have devastating effects on the overall economy, financial stability, and the financial well-being of millions of Americans.

It is likely that investors will treat SEC registration as an SEC seal of approval. Fraudulent hedge fund advisors likely will use registration as a marketing tool.[266] Investor protection is an important job for the SEC, but its resources are not endless, and the SEC notoriously is unable to inspect its current stable of advisors on a regular basis.[267] Hedge funds are open only to wealthy investors on the theory that those investors can hire people to advise them about investments and that, ultimately, they can afford to lose money. Investors who do not meet the wealth threshold or who choose to invest in more closely regulated vehicles can invest in public investment companies. Limited SEC resources should not be diverted from regulated public investment companies, such as mutual funds, in order to monitor hedge fund advisors, as the reported bill proposes to do. If the SEC is spending its resources in this manner, it will not be long before investors that do not meet the accredited investor threshold start demanding to be allowed to invest in hedge funds. It will be hard to counter the argument that they should have access to investments on which the SEC is spending its investigative resources.

The reported bill also exempts venture capital and private equity advisors, but delegates to the SEC the difficult task of defining what those terms mean. The SEC, as part of its failed attempt several years ago to require hedge fund advisors to register, distinguished hedge funds from other types of funds by looking to the length of the investor lock-up period. In order to avoid registration, some hedge funds simply extended their lock-up periods beyond the two year cut-off. Investors' ability to exit a fund with which they were dissatisfied was thus curtailed. The reported bill may perpetuate this problem.

The reported bill is not the right way to achieve the objective of giving the appropriate regulator the information necessary to assess the potential systemic risks posed by large hedge funds, and it threatens to divert the SEC from its core mission.

Title V: Insurance

Title V would establish an Office of National Insurance ("ONI"). This office would remedy the lack of insurance expertise in the Executive Branch revealed during the insurance crises triggered by the September 11, 2001 terrorist attacks and by the failure of AIG in 2008. As was revealed during the Committee's March 5, 2009 hearing on the Fed's rescue of AIG, the problems at AIG were not limited to the company's derivatives operations in its Financial Products division. As discussed further in Title VI, there were also serious problems with several of AIG's insurance companies due to the collapse of their massive securities lending operation. In light of the serious ramifications that the failure of an insurance company can have on our financial system, as demonstrated by the collapse of AIG, we believe that among the issues that the reported bill presently mandates the director of ONI to study, there should be a study of the adequacy of state guaranty funds to handle the failure of large, interconnected, and international insurance companies.

Title VI: Improvements to Regulation of Bank and Savings Association Holding Companies and Depository Institutions

Title VI of the reported bill contains improvements to the regulation of bank and savings and loan holding companies and depository institutions. What notably is lacking in Title VI is any provision to enhance regulatory oversight of large insurance companies. During the financial crisis, several prominent insurance companies received a Federal bailout through the TARP program. In addition, the collapse of AIG revealed serious shortcomings in the regulation of large, interconnected, and international insurance companies. The failure of AIG was due, in large part, to the massive securities lending operation that several state-regulated AIG insurance companies ran collectively. Documents submitted at the Committee's sole hearing on AIG indicated that several of these insurance companies

---

[266] Bernard Madoff used the fact that the SEC had inspected his firm as a way to reassure skeptical investors. See SEC Office of Investigations, Investigation of Failure of the SEC to Uncover Bernard Madoff's Ponzi Scheme—Public Version, Aug. 31, 2009, at 427 (available at: http://www.sec.gov/news/studies/2009/oig-509.pdf) ("In addition, private entities who conducted due diligence stated that Madoff represented to them that the SEC had examined his operations when they raised issues with him about his strategy and returns.").

[267] See, e.g., Testimony by Mary Schapiro, Chairman of the Securities and Exchange Commission, before the Subcommittee on Financial Services and General Government of the House Committee on Appropriations (Mar. 17, 2010) (available at: http://www.sec.gov/news/testimony/2010/ts031710mls.htm) ("It is important to note, however, that even with an increase in the number of exams these additional resources will enable us to conduct, we anticipate examining only nine percent of SEC registered investment advisers and 17 percent of investment company complexes in FY2011.").

would have been insolvent had not the Fed recapitalized them as part of its bailout. The record revealed that the problems at AIG were well-known by its regulators at the Office of Thrift Supervision and by state insurance commissioners, but they failed to take sufficient action to prevent the collapse of the company.[268] In addition, it has recently been revealed that Treasury Secretary Geithner was informed personally by AIG of the company's problems weeks before AIG received a bailout from the Fed.[269] The Secretary also failed to take preventive action. While insurance regulation is a complex matter and our state system largely has functioned well for nearly two hundred years, the size and international reach of many insurance companies has raised legitimate questions, including whether reforms are needed to reflect changes in the marketplace. The failure of the reported bill to include provisions to ensure the proper oversight of large, interconnected, and international insurance companies like AIG is a glaring omission.

It is also worth noting that the reported bill remains silent with respect to the implementation of prompt corrective action during the economic downturn. Enacted as part of the Federal Deposit Insurance Corporation Improvement Act of 1991, prompt corrective action was designed to protect the Deposit Insurance Fund by requiring regulators to resolve failing banks before they incur substantial losses. An examination of the material loss reviews for the FDIC's resolution of banks over the past 3 years reveals that the resolution of banks regularly results in losses of 20 to 30 percent of assets.[270] Under prompt corrective action, regulators are required to close any bank whose capital falls below 2 percent of tangible net equity. The Committee has yet to hold a single hearing on the effectiveness of regulators in implementing prompt corrective action despite the substantial risks to the taxpayers involved.

The Committee also has failed to develop a record to demonstrate a link between proprietary trading and financial instability during the housing and credit market crisis. Yet, the reported bill contains a broad prohibition on proprietary trading. Insured depository institutions benefit from a government provided deposit insurance subsidy so robust activity restrictions, including proprietary trading limitations, may be warranted. But, the policy rationale for extending a proprietary trading ban beyond insured depositories is less compelling as non-insured depository institutions should not benefit from the government subsidies provided by the FDIC.

Title VII: Improvements to Regulation of Over-the-Counter Derivatives Markets

In addressing the regulation of the U.S. over-the-counter ("OTC") derivatives market, the reported bill is flawed in its objectives and the mechanics for achieving those objectives. Rather than focusing on the key goals of regulatory access and authority and greater use of central clearing, the bill attempts to restructure dramatically the OTC derivatives market. It does so without adequate regard for potentially severe unintended consequences, which include increasing systemic risk and outsourcing jobs to markets overseas, harming the U.S. economy.

The reported bill, despite its purported commitment to regulatory transparency, does not even reach significant segments of the OTC derivatives market. For example, a large percentage of the OTC market consists of foreign exchange derivatives which are explicitly carved out of the bill. Similarly, the definition of a "swap," which determines the bill's coverage, omits a category of swaps that, before now, has been included in the definition.[271] Rather than casting a wide net and then making appropriate exclusions, the bill leaves significant portions of the OTC swaps market in the dark.

The bill will have deleterious effects in the derivatives markets and in the marketplace as a whole. The highly international swaps market, which already is well established in Europe and Asia, may simply move offshore and beyond U.S. regulators' reach to a jurisdiction with a

---

[268] Senate Committee on Banking, Housing, and Urban Affairs, "American International Group: Examining what went wrong, government intervention, and implications for future regulation," March 5, 2009.

[269] Sorkin, Andrew Ross, "Too Big To Fail" p. 207, 235, (Viking 2010).

[270] Under Section 38(k) of the Federal Deposit Insurance Act, the inspector general for the appropriate Federal banking agency must make a written report reviewing the agencies supervision and implementation of prompt corrective action whenever the Deposit Insurance Fund incurs a material loss with respect to an insured depository institution. The term "material loss" is defined as a loss that exceeds the greater of $25 million or 2 percent of an institution's total assets at the time the FDIC was appointed receiver.

[271] Specifically, the Gramm-Leach-Bliley Act treated as a "swap agreement" any agreement, contract, or transaction that "provides for the purchase or sale, on a fixed or contingent basis, of any commodity, currency, instrument, interest, right, service, good, article, or property of any kind." These are not "swaps" in the reported bill.

¶ 54,925

more rational regulatory regime.[272] Corporations that currently use derivatives to manage their risk and may not be able to access foreign markets may choose simply not to manage their risk at all. Unhedged corporate risks will result in higher prices and greater price volatility for consumers, and less innovation and capital investment. Companies that cannot withstand a large unhedged risk may fail, resulting in large job losses. Alternatively, corporations may continue to use derivatives subject to the bill's strict requirements for collateral. Setting aside collateral in the required amounts will cause companies, already having a difficult time raising capital, to forgo other valuable uses of their capital. The effect on the real economy and the job market would be substantial. One estimate suggests that mandatory clearing and margining would force companies to set aside $900 billion in capital that would otherwise be used to build factories, hire workers, and fund research and development.[273]

The reported bill, by imposing bank-style capital requirements that are as strict or stricter for non-bank entities, likely will drive some of these entities out of the market and concentrate the market further among the dealers who already have established a powerful foothold in the market. Capital requirements are not necessary for non-banks that do not have access to federal deposit insurance or another form of federally subsidized insurance in the event of default.

The reported bill is rooted in a presumption that central clearing is always risk-reducing. While central clearing can reduce risk and should be encouraged, its abilities to do so should not be overstated. First, some clearinghouses may be stronger than others. A clearinghouse that is poorly run and poorly regulated may not be a strong counterparty. Second, even a well-regulated clearinghouse is not a riskless counterparty.[274] Third, there is no basis for the bill's categorical claim that there is "a greater risk to the swap dealer or major swap participant and to the financial system arising from the use of swaps that are not centrally cleared" that warrants "substantially higher capital requirements" for swaps that are not centrally cleared. Fourth, specialized dealers in bilateral markets can monitor and manage the risks of complex, illiquid derivatives contracts and complex, opaque counterparties more effectively than all-purpose clearinghouses that are designed to clear standardized liquid contracts among clearing members.

Moreover, most participants in the OTC market, such as hedge funds and commercial end users, do not clear directly through a clearinghouse. As a result, even when they clear a derivative, they do not directly face the clearinghouse. Instead, they clear through a firm that is a member of the clearinghouse. Such indirect access to clearinghouses exposes a market participant to credit risk associated with that clearing member and its other customers. In the event of the failure of the clearing member or one of its customers, other customer assets may be at risk. Certain protections can be put in place to minimize the likelihood of loss for non-defaulting customers, but some level of risk remains. As the CME Group notes, "While the policies applicable to the segregation of customer monies for products traded in regulated markets are specifically designed to protect customers from the consequences of a clearing member's failure, they do not always provide complete protection should the default be caused by another customer at the firm."[275]

The reported bill improperly delegates significant policy decisions to regulators and raises the possibility of arbitrary implementation. For example, market participants' statuses as "major

---

[272] Less-established overseas markets, such as Malaysia, have also expressed interest in attracting OTC derivatives trades. See, e.g., Financial Times, "Malaysia bourse plans derivatives boost" (April 27, 2010) (available at: http://www.ft.com/cms/s/0/5fdb7ab8-5222-11df-8b09-00144feab49a.html).

[273] See, e.g., Keybridge Research, An Analysis of the Business Roundtable's Survey on Over-the-Counter Derivatives (Apr. 14, 2010) (available at: http://www.businessroundtable.org/sites/default/files/BRT%20OTC%20Derivatives%20Survey%20284%20014% 2010%29.pdf) (finding that "a 3% margin requirement on OTC derivatives could be expected to reduce capital spending by $5 to $6 billion per year, leading to a loss of 100,000 to 120,000 jobs, including both direct and indirect effects"); Letter from the Natural Gas Supply Association and the National Corn Growers Association to Senate Majority Leader Reid, Senator Lincoln, and Senator Chambliss (April 15, 2010) (available at: http://www.ngsa.org/newsletter/pdfs/2010%20Press%20Releases/16-Corn%20Growers%20Join%20Drumbeat%20Against%20Mandatory%20Clearing.pdf).

[274] For example, last year, the Federal Reserve Board of Governors assigned a 20 percent risk weighting to ICE Trust, which is the same risk weighting that the individual members of the clearinghouse typically get. See letter from the Federal Reserve Board of Governors to Cleary, Gottlieb, Steen and Hamilton LLP (June 5, 2009) (available at: http://www.federalreserve.gov/boarddocs/legalint/BHClChangeInControl/2009/20090605.pdf) ("Exposures to ICE Trust in the form of Margin and [Guaranty Fund] Contributions are not materially riskier than exposures to the participants themselves, and the exposures to ICE Trust, therefore, need not be subject to higher risk weights.").

[275] CME Group, CME Clearing Financial Safeguards (available at: http://www.cmegroup.com/clearing/files/financialsafeguards.pdf)

swap participants" would turn on the judgment of regulators, who would have an incentive to make their regulatory reach extend as far as possible. Moreover, because a "major swap participant" is defined, in part, by whether a person would cause his or her counterparties "significant credit losses," a person's status will depend, in part, on how well its counterparties manage risk. This approach will undermine, rather than enhance, market discipline.

The bill, in trying to address systemic risk concerns, gives rise to a new set of concerns. As soon as one clearinghouse starts clearing a swap, there will be a presumptive mandate to clear the swap. In other words, clearinghouses' profit-driven, competitive decisions on when to start clearing which products would drive the clearing mandate. Moreover, the bill would require the SEC and the Commodity Futures Trading Commission ("CFTC") to identify swaps that clearinghouses had not asked for permission to clear that, in the judgment of the SEC and CFTC, should be accepted for clearing. By allowing the regulators to force clearinghouses to accept swaps for clearing, the bill could force clearinghouses to accept for clearing swaps the risks of which they do not understand. Pressuring clearinghouses into clearing in this manner could sow the seeds for a clearinghouse failure sometime in the future.

The reported bill makes it very difficult for anyone to get an exemption from clearing and exchange trading requirements. It allows the SEC and CFTC, with prior approval by the FSOC, to exempt a swap if one of the parties is not a swap dealer or major swap participant and does not meet the eligibility requirements of a clearing organization. Faced with the prospect of a long, burdensome exemptive process, the bill will dissuade corporations from using swaps to offset their risks. Even if a corporation succeeds in getting an exemption from the clearing requirement, it will be subject to margin requirements unless it can obtain an exemption. Exemptions only will be available for swaps that fit within the narrow and technically complex Generally Accepted Accounting Principles hedging category.

The reported bill requires that cleared swaps also be traded on an exchange or exchange-like facility. This requirement will effect a significant change in market structure. End users will face higher, not lower, costs as their dealers will find it more difficult to lay off the risk that they take on. Indeed, the exchange trading requirement may cause dealers to retain more risk on their books. Other markets have been allowed to develop in a manner that serves the interests of investors. Proponents of an exchange trading requirement cite improved price transparency. Exchange trading is not necessary for transparency, however. Through a system like the TRACE system employed in the corporate bond market, valuable post-trade transparency can be communicated to investors for use in assessing execution quality, marking their books, and assessing pricing in future transactions. SEC Chairman Mary Schapiro and independent academics have embraced a TRACE-like solution for the OTC derivatives market.[276]

Title VIII: Payment, Clearing, and Settlement Supervision

Title VIII of the reported bill would give the Council broad power to identify financial market utilities and payment, clearing or settlement activities that it deems to be now, or likely to become, systemically important. Those entities and activities would then be subject to risk regulation by the Fed's Board of Governors. This title is another example of the bill's inclination to leave difficult decisions to regulators. Forcing regulators to determine when someone or something ought to be regulated is an inappropriate delegation of Congressional power. Moreover, a regulator charged with the task of identifying regulatory targets has every incentive to cast its net wide to obtain additional jurisdiction and avoid accusations of regulatory timidity in the event of a future problem.

The egregiousness of this title's delegation of Congressional decision-making derives largely from the broad manner in which key terms are defined. "Payment, clearing and settlement activities," for example, include any "activity carried out by 1 or more financial institutions to facilitate the completion of financial transactions." Such an activity is "systemically important" if "the failure of or disruption to [that activity] could create, or increase, the risk of significant liquidity or credit problems spreading among financial institutions or markets and thereby threaten the stability of the financial system." With definitions like these guiding the

---

[276] See "Stronger regulation would help bring financial swaps out of the shadows," Washington Post OpEd by Mary Schapiro (April 2, 2010) (available at: http://www.washingtonpost.com/wp-dyn/content/article/2010/04/01/AR2010040102801.html), and the statement of the Shadow Financial Regulatory Committee on Derivatives, Clearing and Exchange-Trading (April 26, 2010) (available at: http://www.aei.org/docLib/Statement%20No.%20293-%20Derivatives-%20Clearing%20and%20Exchange%20Trading.pdf).

Council, it could decide to assign any aspect of the financial market to the Fed.

Once an entity or activity is identified, the Fed is given broad authority to set risk management standards that can address any areas that the Fed deems necessary to promote risk management and safety and soundness, reduce systemic risks, and support the stability of the broader financial system. In other words, this title gives the Fed unfettered discretion to regulate entities and activities that the Council determines "are, or are likely to become, systemically important." Private enterprises that are deemed to be of systemic importance will have to get preapproval from the Fed before making any material changes in their operations.

Lack of regulatory accountability contributed to the recent financial crisis. This title exacerbates the problem by allowing the Council to bring the Fed into significant sectors of the financial system as a back-up regulator. If a problem arises, both the Fed and the relevant supervisory agency will have someone else to blame. A more sensible approach would be for Congress to identify the existing financial market utilities and payment, clearing and settlement activities that merit greater oversight and provide the appropriate regulator with the appropriate authority. The Council could be given the authority to identify additional systemically important utilities and activities and make regulatory recommendations to Congress.

Title IX: Investor Protections and Improvements to the Regulation of Securities

Title IX of the reported bill is a "Christmas tree" of amendments to the securities laws, many of which are not related to the recent crisis and will not help to prevent another crisis. In addition, many were not the subject of Committee hearings. Some of these issues are important and warrant consideration by Congress and the SEC in the future. Considering them now as part of this bill is a distraction from the issues that are central to the bill and deserve Congress's undivided attention. Some of the issues that appear in Title IX have been on special interest wish lists for many years. The reported bill offers a convenient vehicle to pass them into law without the scrutiny they deserve.

Subtitle A establishes a permanent investment advisory committee at the SEC to advise the Commission on setting and implementing its regulatory priorities and promoting investor confidence. The intention may be good, but the statute implements it in a manner that ensures that special interests that may not serve investors' interests have a seat at the SEC rulemaking table. It also establishes an Office of Investor Advocate to serve the same function as the SEC's existing Office of Investor Education and Advocacy.

Subtitle B relates to enforcement issues. It includes a provision to protect and reward SEC whistleblowers. The value of whistleblowers was illustrated vividly by the role of Harry Markopolos in identifying the Madoff fraud, even though his warnings to the SEC went unheeded. Nevertheless, as established in the bill, the whistleblower provision does not afford the SEC with appropriate discretion and would force the SEC to devote considerable resources to defending its decisions with respect to whistleblower awards. For example, the bill would require the SEC to pay whistleblowers not less than ten percent of the monetary sanctions collected and would allow dissatisfied whistleblowers to appeal to the United States Court of Appeals.

Subtitle B also rolls back the National Securities Market Improvement Act by giving state regulators a role in regulating Regulation D offerings and by instituting a lengthy pre-approval process for such offerings which are available only to accredited investors. Legitimate entrepreneurs will be unable to fund their projects or will be forced to struggle through a slow and unpredictable bureaucratic process before they can raise money. At a time when the economy is weak and jobs are scarce, financial reform legislation should attempt to encourage capital formation and innovation, not discourage it by erecting new obstacles for our entrepreneurs.

Subtitle C attempts to address credit rating agencies. The bill's approach only would aggravate the over-reliance problem, however, undermining one of the key recommendations of the Treasury white paper on financial reform.[277] The bill also undermines the objectives of the 2006 Credit Rating Agency Reform Act, which focused on increasing competition, improving disclosure, and addressing conflicts of interest. The reported bill cites the systemic importance of, and investor reliance on, credit ratings as a justification for giving the SEC a new role, monitoring the accuracy of credit ratings. Excessive investor reliance on credit ratings was at the root

---

[277] See "Financial Reform: A New Foundation," U.S. Department of Treasury (available at: http://www.financialstability.gov/docs/regs/FinalReport 1web.pdf), page 44, "We propose several initiatives . . . reducing the incentives for over-reliance on credit ratings."

of the recent crisis. Encouraging greater reliance on credit ratings by promising that the SEC will identify and punish inaccurate rating agencies is exactly the opposite of what a financial reform bill ought to achieve. Reducing investors' perceptions that the SEC is looking over the shoulders of the credit rating agencies to ensure that they are doing a good job would help to encourage investors to do their own due diligence. Some of the bill's attempts to address conflicts of interest, such as imposing strict independence requirements for boards of directors and qualification standards for credit rating analysts, will discourage competition by setting up barriers to entry for credit rating agencies considering registering as nationally recognized statistical rating organizations. The bill also includes a new liability standard for *all* credit rating agencies, which will make credit rating agencies an easy target for lawsuits. This provision also is likely to harm competition and the value of credit ratings.

The reported bill also threatens a healthy return of the securitization markets. The centerpiece of Subtitle D is a five percent risk retention requirement for securitizations. The requirement is a one-size-fits-all solution in a very diverse securitization marketplace. In combination with accounting and bank capital rule changes, a risk retention requirement could force the entire securitization to be retained on bank balance sheets for accounting and capital purposes. Securitizations would then become economically unworkable. The bill would permit less than five percent risk retention in cases in which the originator complies with underwriting standards set by the SEC, along with the bank regulators. A more sensible approach would direct bank regulators to set underwriting standards that include a down payment requirement for all residential mortgages.[278] The SEC, a disclosure regulator, should focus its efforts on improving disclosure about the underlying assets in a securitization pool to enable investors to conduct due diligence, rather than instilling in investors a sense of complacency by an arbitrary risk retention requirement.

Subtitle E addresses executive compensation in a number of unproductive ways. First, it requires public companies to have annual votes on executive compensation. This one-size-fits-all solution imposed at the federal level tramples over state corporate law, forces shareholders to pay for something that they may not want, and exacerbates short-term thinking. The subtitle also imposes a requirement on public companies to disclose the ratio of the median employee compensation to the chief executive officer's compensation. Although provisions like this appeal to popular notions that chief executive officer salaries are too high, they do not provide material information to investors who are trying to make a reasoned assessment of how executive compensation levels are set. Existing SEC disclosures already do this. More generally, the subtitle's prescriptive approach hinders corporations from devising policies that work for the unique circumstances of their corporations.

Subtitle G likewise forces all public corporations to adopt uniform approaches to corporate governance regardless of whether those approaches would serve the needs of shareholders and without regard for the central role of states in establishing corporate governance standards. Subtitle G imposes a majority voting requirement for directors of public corporations, without any evidence that majority voting benefits shareholders. In fact, AIG, Washington Mutual, Lehman Brothers, Citigroup, Merrill Lynch, Bank of America, and Wachovia all required majority voting *before* the financial crisis. Special interest groups hope that the majority voting requirement will work in conjunction with the bill's proxy access requirement to give them special access to corporate boardrooms. Proxy access is designed to permit shareholders to put their nominees for the board on the company ballot at the company's expense. Mandating proxy access raises investor protection concerns because all shareholders are forced to fund campaigns by one shareholder to gain representation on the board and because directors are supposed to represent the interests of the shareholders as a whole, not particular special interests. Despite these concerns, some shareholders already are able to choose to implement proxy access. Changes in state law have made it possible for shareholders to tailor proxy access provisions that work for their particular corporations. A federal proxy access mandate is not needed and would deprive shareholders of the very voice it purports to give them.

Subtitle H of the reported bill deals with municipal securities, an area that warrants attention. Nevertheless, the subtitle includes some

---

[278] *See* John C. Dugan, Comptroller of the Currency, Speech before the American Securitization Forum (Feb. 2, 2010) (available at: http://www.occ.treas.gov/ftp/release/2010-13a.pdf) ("But while lax underwriting is plainly a fundamental problem that needs to be addressed, mandatory risk retention for securitizers is an imprecise and indirect way to do that, and is by no means guaranteed to work. How much retained risk is enough? And what type of retained risk would work best—first loss, vertical slice, or some other kind of structure?").

troubling features. Fines collected for enforcement violations would be shared between the SEC and the Municipal Securities Rulemaking Board. Allowing these entities to profit from their enforcement actions provides them with a profit motive for bringing cases, which would harm the credibility of the agency.

Subtitle I of the bill would, among other things, expand the mission of the Public Company Accounting Oversight Board ("PCAOB") to include overseeing auditors of broker-dealers. Because the PCAOB is still working on fulfilling its initial mission, a large influx of new registrants will pose additional resource challenges. To minimize this burden, the legislation should not extend to auditors of Introducing Brokers, who do not handle customer funds.

Subtitle J of the bill would remove the SEC from the appropriations process and permit it to fund itself through the fees and assessments that it collects. It could set its budget at any level that it determined proper and exceed that budget at its discretion. In the event the SEC spends more than its budget, it is permitted, but not required, to notify Congress of the amount of additional money and anticipated uses of that money. In the wake of some of the largest regulatory failures in the SEC's history and the embarrassing scandal involving senior SEC officials repeatedly downloading pornography on government computers during the height of the financial crisis, it is surprising that Congress would decide to make the SEC less accountable. Additional resources are warranted for the SEC's important responsibilities, but they should be accompanied by a responsibility to account to Congress for how those resources are spent.

Title X: Bureau of Consumer Financial Protection

Title X creates a massive new entity whose power and autonomy have no current equivalent anywhere else in the Federal government. The Bureau of Consumer Financial Protection ("Bureau") will have no meaningful coordination with the safety and soundness regulators to ensure that banks will not fail or be critically weakened as a result of a consumer rule. Indeed, the Bureau would have the authority to trump the safety and soundness regulators, thereby creating instability in our nation's financial system. The manner in which the legislation separates safety and soundness and consumer protection regulation is similar to the regulatory structure of Fannie Mae and Freddie Mac. In that instance, the Department of Housing and Urban Development (HUD) set consumer standards while the Office of Federal Housing Enterprise Oversight regulated for safety and soundness. Ultimately, the consumer standards set by HUD undermined the solvency of Fannie and Freddie. Fannie and Freddie are currently the largest recipients of bailout funds.

Under the reported bill, the Bureau would regulate every aspect of financial transactions. The Bureau would have enormous reach into Main Street companies like orthodontists, home repair and renovation contractors, and anyone else who extends credit in more than four installments. It would set lending standards; determine what type of documents lenders could use; and require banks to make a certain percentage of their loans to specific, politically favored borrowers (i.e., housing authorities or "green" businesses). The Bureau could force all lenders to use the same lending forms and terms and conditions.

The reported bill provides the Bureau with an enormous taxpayer-provided funding source without executive or congressional oversight of its budget. The legislation states that the budget for the new Bureau shall be 12 percent of the overall operating budget of the Federal Reserve System for fiscal year 2009. This would allow the Bureau to command approximately $650 million of Fed resources. Currently, the Office of the Comptroller of the Currency ("OCC") has an overall operating budget of $750 million, and the OCC handles both consumer protection supervision and prudential supervision.

The reported bill also undermines more than a century of precedent on preemption with respect to national banks. Presently, state laws that conflict with the National Bank Act are preempted because Congress has long sought to create a national financial market and ensure the efficient regulation of national banks. The reported bill, however, effectively eliminates preemption and allows states to set their own regulations under certain circumstances. Furthermore, the bill requires the OCC and the courts to determine on a case-by-case basis which state laws are pre-empted, which will create significant legal uncertainty and generate unnecessary litigation. In addition, the bill would allow State Attorneys General to bring class action suits against national banks, usurping the responsibility of federal regulators and creating even more needless litigation.

Finally, the Bureau poses a threat to Americans' civil liberties. Under Section 1022, the new Bureau would collect any information it chooses from businesses and consumers, including personal characteristics and financial information. Americans could be required to provide the new consumer agency with written answers, under oath, to any question posed by the Bureau regarding their personal financial information. The Bureau would have the authority to monitor transactions such as personal deposit account activity, credit card usage, and how much an individual spends on groceries. This is a massive new grant of authority for an entity whose budget is derived from taxpayer funds.

Title XI: Federal Reserve System Provisions

During the recent financial crisis, the FDIC put American taxpayers at risk by guaranteeing *trillions* of dollars of private debt. Title XI of this bill seeks to institutionalize such guarantees, under the rubric of "emergency financial stabilization" authority, providing permanent authority to put taxpayer resources at risk to insure private debt whenever the Fed and FDIC deem it appropriate. No regulator should be allowed to expose taxpayers to trillions of dollars of risk without express approval from Congress.

During the crisis, the Fed contributed to creating moral hazard by vastly expanding use of its discount window to fund a variety of financial market participants, including some over which it had no oversight. The Fed also created new lending facilities to direct liquidity and credit to markets that were deemed most stressed and systemically important. The Fed ballooned its balance sheet from a pre-crisis level of around $800 billion to over $2.2 *trillion*. Those resources are not free. Those resources are liabilities of the Fed, created through the Fed's money creation powers, and are therefore also liabilities of taxpayers. This bill seeks to institutionalize Fed support to whichever market segment it and the Treasury deem to be in need of liquidity. The Fed may make loans and take collateral that the Fed finds is to its "satisfaction."

The Fed does need to perform its lender of last resort function but should only do so to *briefly* assist firms who are solvent and in need of liquidity that cannot readily be obtained in the open market. The lender of last resort function of a central bank does not involve long-term loans to insolvent firms based on questionable collateral. Yet, this bill seeks to enshrine the Fed's ability to lend to "any program or facility with broad-based eligibility," taking as collateral whatever satisfies the Fed. The broad-based and vague language governing the Fed's emergency lending authorities is an invitation for future governments to avoid hard decisions and shift them to the Fed. With trillions of dollars of taxpayer resources likely to be on the line, the language in the bill governing the Fed's emergency lending power is far too loose.

Furthermore, the reported bill expands and codifies the FDIC's broad ability to guarantee the debt of depositories and of depository holding companies in a loosely defined "liquidity event." The amounts of the guarantees are unlimited. The President may, or may not, submit a report to Congress on the FDIC's plan to issue guarantees. Most troubling, however, is that there is no requirement that a company that receives guarantees and defaults on its obligations be taken into an FDIC receivership, bankruptcy, or resolution. Thus, the FDIC and Treasury could prop up whatever companies they choose. Moreover, there is ample room to grant debt guarantees in routine stressful, yet not crisis, circumstances given the broad definitions.

We believe that the Treasury Secretary and the Fed should be required to enter into an "Accord" to establish clear rules on the use of 13(3) of the Federal Reserve Act and the Fed's balance for fiscal purposes.

Title XII: Improving Access to Mainstream Financial Institutions

Title XII was inserted quietly into the Dodd bill at the last minute as part of the manager's amendment during the Committee mark-up. It was not considered by the Committee. Title XII creates a grant program that would give certain financial institutions, and others, taxpayer dollars to "recapture a portion or all of a defaulted loan" (Section 1206). The purpose of the grant program is to encourage certain financial institutions, and others, to get low- and moderate-income individuals to establish accounts at their institutions. We do not support using taxpayer dollars to pay financial institutions to attract new customers, and then cover the losses if the new customers default on the loans. This is an iteration of "heads Wall Street wins, tails the taxpayer loses." This is replicating on a smaller scale the precise practices that led to the bailouts of Fannie Mae and Freddie Mac.

Government sponsored entities

Fannie Mae and Freddie Mac played major roles in the financial crisis. Combined, these two institutions represent nearly $5.5 trillion in business, and they have been in conservatorship since September 6, 2008.[279] Despite this, the reported bill does nothing to address the future of the Government Sponsored Enterprises.

In doing so, the reported bill leaves uncertainty in the secondary mortgage market. As Fannie Mae and Freddie Mac have such a large influence on the market, private sector investment will not achieve optimal levels until investors are certain as to the future of these institutions. By remaining silent on their futures, the reported bill prevents the private sector from fully committing to the secondary mortgage market. Without a properly functioning secondary mortgage market, additional pressure falls upon the GSEs, the Federal Housing Administration, the Veterans Administration and Ginnie Mae. This additional pressure grows these entities, concentrating risk with the taxpayer rather than in the private sector, and increases the difficulty of reforming Fannie Mae and Freddie Mac.

Despite this, the reported bill takes no interim steps to protect taxpayers. On December 24, 2009, the Treasury Department and the Federal Housing Finance Administration ("FHFA") announced that the Preferred Stock Purchase program would be amended to "allow the cap on Treasury's funding commitment under these agreements to increase as necessary to accommodate any cumulative reduction in net worth over the next three years." It further allowed Fannie Mae and Freddie Mac higher portfolio holdings than previously mandated.[280]

The reported bill also does nothing to increase the accountability of Fannie Mae and Freddie Mac, nor those operating them. The President has yet to nominate anyone to officially run the FHFA, who acts as conservator, and the Office of Special Inspector General of FHFA remains vacant. Thus, there is no one politically accountable to the public for the operation of these multi-trillion dollar entities. By remaining silent on any interim taxpayer protections or oversight provisions, the reported bill allows for the continued unlimited bailout of Fannie Mae and Freddie Mac.

If nothing is to be done to address the future of the GSEs in the reported bill, it would be useful to establish new investigative over-sight that would provide regular updates to the Congress and to the American people. Limits governing the taxpayer funding available to Fannie and Freddie and the portfolio holdings of these institutions should be reestablished. A process to ensure that future agreements of this nature are approved by Congress also should be established. Finally, a deadline should be given to the President for the submission of a plan outlining his ideas for the ultimate reform of Fannie Mae and Freddie Mac to ensure that the timeline does not continue to slip.

Variation between the bill as reported and the specific changes to the bill approved by Committee action

The reported bill contains numerous substantive changes that were not approved by the Committee. Among these are:

1. Reducing the number of hours from 48 to 24 that the Secretary has to provide a report to Congress following the appointment of the FDIC as receiver for a financial company (Section 203(c));

2. Removing the provision that made the consent of a company's directors or shareholders to the appointment of a receiver constitute a company being "in default or in danger of default" (Section 203(c));

3. Prohibiting the FDIC from taking equity interest in a covered financial company (Section 206);

4. Removing language that made liquidation of a covered financial company optional and replacing it with language that makes liquidation mandatory (Section 210);

5. Removing language that gave the FDIC the discretion to put an institution into bankruptcy or resolution if it defaulted on a debt guarantee provided under Title VI and replacing it with language that makes such action mandatory (Section 1156); and

6. Changing language to allow the Fed to lend to "participants" rather than "programs" under Section 13(3) of the Federal Reserve Act (Section 1151).

These are non-technical changes that should have been made only through direct Committee action.

Conclusion

We are disappointed in the Committee's decision to report the bill in its current form for Senate consideration. Even the bill's proponents recognize that the reported bill is rife with substantive and technical problems. We believe that

---

[279] Monthly Summary Report, February 2010, Fannie Mae, and Monthly Volume Report, February 2010, Freddie Mac.

[280] Press Release: "Treasury Issues Update on Status of Support for Housing Programs," U.S. Treasury Department, December 24, 2010.

the reported bill's deficiencies are so significant that it will be impossible to correct them on the Senate floor. We would readily support a properly designed bipartisan financial reform bill. Unfortunately, the reported bill is not such a bill. In fact, with respect to the bill's treatment of the problems of too big to fail and bailouts, the bill's language promises a future clouded with moral hazards in financial markets, with unfair and undemocratic funding advantages for a select few large financial institutions, and with institutionalized bailout authorities. In the aftermath of the economic crisis of 2008, we believe that it is the responsibility of Congress to take action to prevent such a crisis from occurring again. This bill not only fails in that regard, it in fact makes future crises more likely.

[¶ 55,000] House Report No. 111-94
Report of the Committee on Financial Services
to accompany H.R. 1728.

House Report 111-94, May 4, 2010.

The Committee on Financial Services, to whom was referred the bill (H.R. 1728) to amend the Truth in Lending Act to reform consumer mortgage practices and provide accountability for such practices, to provide certain minimum standards for consumer mortgage loans, and for other purposes, having considered the same, report favorably thereon with an amendment and recommend that the bill as amended do pass.

AMENDMENT

* * *

[¶ 55,000A] PURPOSE AND SUMMARY

H.R. 1728, the Mortgage Reform and Anti-Predatory Lending Act, is intended to reform mortgage lending practices to avert a recurrence of the current situation of unprecedented levels of defaults and foreclosures rates. The bill is fashioned after similar legislation that passed the House in November 2007 (H.R. 3915), but has been updated and contains a number of new provisions.

As reported, Titles I and II of H.R. 1728 set minimum standards for mortgages requiring that consumers must have a reasonable ability to repay at the time the mortgage is consummated and that mortgage refinancings must provide a net tangible benefit to the consumer. Under the bill, securitizers and other participants in the secondary mortgage market would for the first time under federal law be liable for supporting irresponsible lending. It provides that certain high-quality, low-cost loans (defined as Qualified Mortgages) will be presumed to meet these Federal standards. This is a limited safe harbor for these loans because the presumption can be rebutted.

The bill also prohibits financial incentives (including payments known as "yield spread premiums") that encourage mortgage originators, including mortgage brokers and loan officers of lending institutions, to steer consumers to higher-cost and more abusive mortgages. In addition, it prohibits prepayment penalties for any adjustable rate mortgage and other mortgages that do not meet the definition of Qualified Mortgage, limits prepayment penalties charged to borrowers who wish to close out their loans, typically to refinance on more affordable terms, bans single premium credit insurance and prohibits mandatory arbitration clauses; and includes protections for renters of foreclosed properties. Finally, there are provisions to provide legal assistance to homeowners and tenants facing foreclosure.

H.R. 1728 requires creditors to retain an economic interest in a material portion of the credit risk for certain mortgages they originate. Another provision authorizes the Banking Agencies to address through rulemaking abusive mortgage terms and practices that may arise in the future. The bill permits consumers to obtain redress directly from firms involved in "securitizing" mortgages, unless the securitizer has performed appropriate due diligence to comply with the ability to repay and net tangible benefit standards and effected a modification or refinancing that provides the borrower with a loan that satisfies these standards.

Title III of H.R. 1728 expands the scope of and enhances consumer protections for high-cost loans under the Home Ownership and Equity Protection Act (HOEPA) and requires additional disclosures to consumers. This title revises the benchmark for determining these triggers from Treasuries securities to the "average prime offer rate," which is determined by the Federal Reserve. In addition, it lowers the points and fee trigger from 8 percent to 5 percent for transactions of $20,000 or more and including additional costs and fees in the trigger; prohibits the financing of points and fees; prohibits excessive fees for payoff information, modifications, or late payments; prohibits practices that increase the risk of foreclosure, such as balloon payments, encouraging a borrower to default, and call provisions; and requires pre-loan counseling.

Title IV of the bill establishes an Office of Housing Counseling at HUD that will carry out and coordinate homeownership and rental housing counseling programs; requires the launch of a national public service, multimedia campaign to promote housing counseling and the establishment of a website and toll-free hotline; authorizes the issuance of homeownership and rental housing counseling grants to HUD-approved housing counseling agencies and State

¶ 55,000A

housing finance agencies; and requires HUD to update the Mortgage Information Booklet to provide consumers with a greater understanding of the terms of the home buying process. Additionally, the bill requires increased information to consumers about the need for home inspections and ways to avoid foreclosure scams.

Titles V and VI of H.R. 1728 offer a comprehensive, balanced, and progressive set of solutions aimed at stopping or mitigating a number of abusive and deceptive practices related to escrow accounts, mortgage servicing, and appraisal practices. The two titles also build on the provisions previously incorporated by an amendment on the House floor into H.R. 3915.

Regarding the escrow provisions contained in Title V, H.R. 1728 requires all subprime borrowers to have accounts established in conjunction with their mortgages to provide protection against tax liens and the forced placement of insurance, among other things. In addition, the bill requires lenders to provide written disclosures about the need to pay taxes and insurance premiums to all borrowers if they opt out of creating escrow accounts. To ensure that lenders alert borrowers to all costs involved in a transaction, the bill requires the inclusion of escrow payments for taxes and insurance in any repayment analysis provided to consumers at the time of a quote on a mortgage.

With respect to mortgage servicing reforms, the Title V of H.R. 1728 also updates the Real Estate Settlement Procedures Act (RESPA) and the Truth in Lending Act (TILA) to create new consumer protections. These protections include detailing when the servicer can impose force-placed insurance, mandating swifter responses to consumer written inquiries, increasing penalties for violations of RESPA, requiring the prompt crediting of payments, and mandating that borrowers receive payoff statement quotes within a reasonable amount of time after a request.

Concerning appraisal practices, Title VI of H.R. 1728 prohibits the lender from making a subprime mortgage without first obtaining a written appraisal of the physical property. The bill also protects these loan applicants against loan flipping by requiring a second written appraisal, free of charge, if another loan on the property occurred in the past six months. Lenders must additionally provide mortgage applicants with copies of any and all written appraisal reports and valuations developed in connection with a mortgage transaction at least 3 days before the scheduled closing date on the property.

H.R. 1728 further creates enforceable Federal appraisal independence standards with penalties within TILA and amends the Financial Institutions Reform, Recovery, and Enforcement Act (FIRREA) to require the Appraisal Subcommittee to monitor the effectiveness of State appraiser agencies in maintaining appraisal independence. These standards prohibit the parties involved in a real estate transaction from influencing the independent judgment of an appraiser through collusion, coercion, and bribery, among other activities. In addition to other stipulations, they require appraisers to have no direct or indirect interest in the property or transaction involving the appraisal.

Moreover, the bill's changes will provide the Appraisal Subcommittee with a consumer protection mandate and more authority to monitor the performance of State appraiser agencies. The Appraisal Subcommittee is also required to describe its activities in greater detail in an annual report to the Congress. Many of the additional appraisal changes are designed to strengthen licensing and education standards, as well as to establish a Federal grant program to the States.

The modifications to appraisal regulation found in H.R. 1728 also create a system for registering and supervising appraisal management companies, ensure the establishment of a national hotline for collecting appraisal complaints, provide for the production of reliable results by automated valuation models, and bar the use of broker price opinions as the sole basis for determining the value of a property for purchase mortgage loans. Finally, Title VI amends RESPA to require the separate disclosure of fees paid to appraisal management companies and appraisers.

[¶55,001] BACKGROUND AND NEED FOR LEGISLATION

Mortgage crisis

It is now well documented that the explosive growth in subprime and Alt-A mortgage lending in the early part of this decade led many Americans to obtain mortgage credit that they could not afford. As a result, the country is facing an unprecedented foreclosure crisis and foreclosure rates are expected to increase.

This crisis can be traced in part to the movement of lenders and mortgage originators away from traditional commonsense underwriting practices during the real estate boom, giving rise to risky, exotic mortgages and practices such as "no doc" lending and allowing loans with "negative amortization" features, and to the proliferation of subprime mortgages, especially in refinancing. Many observers comment that the growth of mortgage securitization and the market in mortgage-backed securities—investment instruments backed by pools of loans purchased by investment firms—increased the number of lenders and propelled the sale of subprime products. Investors' demand for high-yield mortgage bonds in turn may have driven brokers and lenders to push borrowers to high-risk loans, loosening underwriting standards. Government data and academic studies have suggested that a disproportionate amount of higher priced subprime lending was concentrated in the minority population and in minority neighborhoods.

In general, subprime mortgages are loans that have more costly terms and conditions than "prime" mortgages (e.g., they may have higher interest rates, additional fees, prepayment penalties, or other features). Many subprime loans were made to borrowers who, due to weakened credit histories, pose higher credit risks. These borrowers may have lower credit scores than prime borrowers or higher debt to income ratios on their properties. In other cases, subprime borrowers may actually have qualified for prime loans, but did not receive them, for various reasons ranging from the benign (such as an inability to produce full income documentation) to predatory practices such as loan steering.

Subprime lenders included banks, bank affiliates, and non-bank mortgage companies. According to Mortgage Bankers Association (MBA), more than half of subprime mortgages were made by mortgage brokers and lenders with no Federal supervision; a quarter were made by finance companies that are affiliates of bank holding companies and indirectly regulated by the Federal Reserve Board; and the rest were made by institutions directly regulated by Federal financial regulators such as banks, thrifts, and credit unions.

Additional controversy surrounded so-called subprime payment option adjustable rate mortgages (ARMs) in which the interest rate starts at a low "teaser" level and then ratchets upward after a set period, often two or three years. The term "hybrid" refers to the blend of fixed-rate and adjustable-rate characteristics found in such ARMs. Like other adjustable-rate products, hybrid ARMs transfer some interest rate risk from the lender to the consumer, thus allowing the lender to offer a lower initial rate.

Hybrid ARMs are referred to by their initial fixed period and adjustment periods, for example 3/1 for an ARM with a 3-year fixed period and subsequent 1-year rate adjustment periods. Two products that have drawn particular attention are 2/28s and 3/27s. For these loans, the rate resets every six months after the initial teaser rate period for the remaining 28 or 27 years of the loan at a margin over a particular designated short-term interest rate, such as the London Interbank Offered Rate (LIBOR). Interest-only, no-principal balloon loans often result in even steeper increases as a result of deferred unpaid principal.

Many of these loans also had prepayment penalties that may extend beyond the low initial payment period. When these loans reset, consumers may face penalties for refinancing or have a very short time in which to refinance. Prepayment penalties can, however, sometimes provide consumers with lower interest rates because they provide a more stable revenue stream and thus increase the value of the loan on the secondary market.

The number of hybrid ARMs and other subprime loans—and their share of the mortgage market—has significantly increased in the past few years. According to press reports, in 1998, the percentage of hybrids relative to 30-year fixed-rate mortgages was less than 2 percent. By 2004, this percentage had risen to 27.5 percent. Origination volumes of subprime mortgages grew from $100 billion in 2001 to $800 billion in 2005. Many homeowners took out these loans because they couldn't afford the monthly payments that came with a 30-year fixed-rate loan. They were counting on having the value of their homes appreciate and then refinancing. Instead, home prices throughout the country have plummeted. In a period of declining home values, the principal amounts of many loans became greater than the value of the underlying assets, making refinancing difficult.

Many of these loans began to "reset" in 2007 from their two- and three-year teaser rates to significantly higher monthly payments for homeowners, pushing many borrowers into foreclosure. Foreclosures not only harm homeowners, who can lose their homes and the equity in them and suffer from tarnished credit records, but also can have negative effects on the broader community and the economy. Foreclosures can trigger domino effects that result in housing abandonment, declining property values in surrounding neighborhoods, and loss of property tax revenue to states and localities. Many observers also have cited the widespread apprehension over exposure to subprime mortgage-backed

¶ 55,001

bonds as the root cause of the ongoing credit crisis.

Congress has enacted a number of consumer protection laws in the financial sector over the last few decades. These statutes include TILA, the Fair Credit Reporting Act (FCRA), the Fair Debt Collection Practices Act (FDCPA), and the Equal Credit Opportunity Act (ECOA). Most of these statutes have sought to address particular consumer problems in particular sub-sectors. TILA, for example, requires that consumers receive critical disclosures in a uniform manner before entering into credit transactions. In response to reports of predatory lending practices in home equity lending in the early 1990s, Congress enacted HOEPA in 1994, which covers home equity loans but not purchase-money mortgages. Loans classified as 'high-cost home loans' under HOEPA because of their high annual percentage rates (APRs) or points and fees trigger certain prohibitions or disclosures or both.

In July 2008, the Federal Reserve adopted final rules to address unfair, abusive or deceptive home mortgage lending practices and to restrict certain other mortgage practices. The rules also establish advertising standards and require certain mortgage disclosures to be given to consumers earlier in a transaction. The Federal Reserve's action adds four key protections to a newly defined category of "higher-priced mortgage loans" secured by a consumer's principal dwelling.

The four protections adopted for the newly defined category of higher-priced mortgage loans will:

• Prohibit a lender from making a loan without regard to borrowers' ability to repay the loan from income and assets other than the home's value. A lender complies, in part, by assessing repayment ability based on the highest scheduled payment in the first seven years of the loan. To show that a lender violated this prohibition, a borrower does not need to demonstrate that it is part of a "pattern or practice;"

• Require creditors to verify the income and assets they rely upon to determine repayment ability;

• Ban any prepayment penalty if the payment can change in the initial four years. For other higher-priced loans, a prepayment penalty period cannot last for more than two years; and

• Require creditors to establish escrow accounts for property taxes and homeowner's insurance for all first-lien mortgage loans.

While the Federal Reserve's rules addressed some of the practices that led to the current crisis, H.R. 1728 will compliment the Federal Reserve's rule and provide additional protections to mortgage borrowers.

Many States have enacted statutes modeled after HOEPA. Currently, at least thirty States, the District of Columbia, and roughly a dozen municipalities have enacted either comprehensive statutes or other limited statutory protections aimed at predatory lending practices, some addressing a specific practice, some generally tracking HOEPA, and others going far beyond it.

As more families face foreclosure, the need for affordable legal assistance for homeowners and tenants increases. Throughout the country, legal assistance organizations report a dramatic increase in unmet need for foreclosure-related legal services. Given this urgent need, the bill provides for grants to state and local legal organizations to provide legal assistance to low and moderate income homeowners and tenants with foreclosure-related issues.

Affordable housing advocates report that at least 20 percent of properties in foreclosure were rental properties and roughly 40 percent of families facing eviction due to foreclosure are tenants. To address this unintended impact of the foreclosure crisis, the bill allows bona fide tenants to remain in their residence, pursuant to their lease, following foreclosure on the property, except in certain limited circumstance.

Escrows

An escrow is a trust account set up in a borrower's name to ensure the timely payment of specified obligations affiliated with a property. Current Federal law permits all consumers to voluntarily establish escrow accounts with their lender or mortgage servicer to cover property taxes, hazard insurance, and certain other periodic expenses related to the property or the contract. The administration of these accounts is covered by RESPA and, if applicable, State law.

Borrowers with escrows pay an additional amount on their mortgage each month to fund the account. In addition to any principal and interest payments, lenders collect a pro-rata assessment of the total expected annual outlays for taxes and insurance using RESPA's established guidelines. Lenders then use these collected sums to guarantee the timely payment of property tax bills and insurance premiums. In a way, an escrow serves as a safety net to protect the lender and the borrower from tax liens and property losses.

In analyzing the recent problems related to the fallout in the subprime lending industry, some experts have noted that subprime borrowers, even though they are more likely to need budgeting assistance given their weaker credit histories, are less likely than prime borrowers to have escrows. In its 2006 benchmarking studies, for example, the Mortgage Bankers Association found that approximately 50 percent of all first lien subprime mortgages had escrows, compared to 71 percent of prime loans. Other experts have suggested that the number of subprime borrowers with escrows is significantly lower.

In 2004, Fannie Mae updated its policies on escrows in its Selling and Servicing Guides. While it continued to allow the waiver of an escrow account requirement in certain instances, the updated policy recommends against waiving escrows for a borrower with a blemished credit record. In doing so, the enterprise noted that the borrower may find it difficult to maintain homeownership if he or she faces the need to make large lump-sum payments for taxes and/or insurance and any other periodic payment items.

In early 2007, the Federal banking regulators also issued guidance on disclosure notices for consumers who opt out of escrow services. The guidance laid out fundamental consumer protection principles for underwriting, including that consumers should be informed of their responsibilities to pay taxes and insurance, in addition to their loan payments, if not escrowed, and the fact that the costs for taxes and insurance costs can be substantial. Fannie Mae has adopted similar escrow opt-out disclosure policies, too.

Issues related to escrows have also arisen as part of the homebuying and refinancing process. Some mortgage originators, at the time of a payment quote, provide consumers only with details on principal and interest amounts. As a result, borrowers may underestimate the monthly payment actually needed to own a home. Moreover, because some quotes contain information regarding additional fees associated with a property like taxes and insurance premiums and some do not, borrowers sometimes lack the information needed to make accurate comparisons between different mortgage offers.

In its commentary in a rule promulgated last summer under the Home Ownership and Equity Protection Act (HOEPA), the Federal Reserve Board noted that "[c]onsumers in the subprime market tend to shop based on monthly payment amounts, rather than on interest rates. So creditors who are active in the subprime market, and who can quote low monthly payments to a prospective borrower, have a competitive advantage over creditors who quote higher monthly payments." Both apples-to-apples comparisons of payments and more realistic expectations of monthly obligations are better accomplished by mortgage offers containing four payment obligations: principal, interest, taxes, and insurance, otherwise known as PITI.

As a result of its findings, the Federal Reserve Board's recent HOEPA regulations require a creditor to establish an escrow account for taxes and insurance for subprime borrowers. These escrow accounts must remain in place for at least 12 months before a consumer can cancel them. The final rule also adopted changes to advertising practices to require the prominent disclosure that taxes and insurance are not included in promotional quotes.

Mortgage servicing

While much of the recent attention related to mitigating predatory lending practices has focused on the mortgage origination and underwriting process, the problems of abusive and deceptive lending also extends into mortgage servicing, which occurs after the consummation of a home loan. The problems that homeowners have encountered with loan servicing have received media attention.[1]

Under RESPA, servicers are the entities responsible for servicing a loan. Typically, servicers are large corporations servicing millions of mortgage loans at any one time. Servicers generally have no legal relationship with the owners or assignees of the loan and make their income from a small percentage earned on each payment made on the loan. Servicers may also earn income from the float from escrow accounts they maintain for borrowers to cover the required payments for property insurance on the loan.

---

[1] See Gretchen Morgenson, "Can These Mortgages Be Saved," *New York Times*, September 30, 2007, and Jack Guttentag, "Loan Servicers, the Lesser-Known Predators," *Washington Post*, November 3, 2007.

Unfortunately, in recent years, some servicers have discovered that greater profits can be obtained by squeezing borrowers in a variety of ways. One problematic method used to increase revenue by servicers is the forced placement of insurance without a reasonable basis for doing so. The 2004 agreement between Ocwen Federal Bank and the Office of Thrift Supervision and the 2003 settlement between Fairbanks Capital Holding Corporation and the Federal Trade Commission and the Department of Housing and Urban Development (HUD) both resulted in internal servicing reforms to improve the process for the forced placement of insurance.

Force-placed insurance is a product obtained by lenders to protect their interest in the property in the event the borrower fails to maintain or renew hazard and flood insurance as required under the terms of the mortgage contract. Force-placed insurance generally costs at least twice the amount of standard homeowners insurance, even though it generally only covers the replacement value of the underlying collateral. By comparison, homeowners insurance would cover not only the costs of repairing or replacing the home, but also the contents of the home itself.

Another practice that raises the concerns of consumer advocates relates to the prompt crediting of payments. A servicer may sometimes hold a payment past the due date in order to impose a late charge. Servicers may also profit from the float that occurs when the borrower makes less than a full payment. In such instances, the servicer will deposit the partial payment into a suspense account rather than crediting the consumer's account for the amount paid.

There are still many other concerns related to mortgage servicing. A lender may refuse to provide a pay-off amount on a loan, thus limiting a borrower's ability to satisfy the obligation (and potentially to refinance into a cheaper loan). Servicers may also postpone refunding balances in escrow accounts or charge excessive fees, including when responding to borrower requests to correct errors. RESPA establishes affirmative obligations on servicers to answer questions and address concerns consumers have about the status of their loans and their escrow accounts after the consumer has sent a "qualified written request." Some servicers, however, will game the system by failing to respond adequately to each such request, forcing the consumer to make repeated inquiries, yet charging amounts for each response.

Finally, servicers currently have no enforceable obligation to provide consumers with information about the true owner of the mortgage. A recent court case held that a consumer's attempt to rescind a loan under the Truth in Lending Act was ineffective when the rescission notice was served on the servicer, because the servicer was not an agent for the holder (even though the servicer is clearly an agent for purposes of receiving payments on the loan).

In its July 2008 HOEPA rulemaking, the Federal Reserve addressed several of the most problematic mortgage servicing issues, including those related to the prompt crediting of mortgage payments and the timely provision of pay-off statements. In response to the growing need to expeditiously help troubled borrowers to modify their loans, the HOPE Now coalition has also adopted best practices aimed at shortening the response times for processing requests. More, however, could be done to help protect consumer interests in the area of mortgage servicing.

Appraisals

Obtaining an appraisal is a key step in the mortgage underwriting process. It helps to verify a property's value for the buyer, seller, lender, investor, and others. For the process to work as intended, appraisers must act as unbiased arbiters. In other words, they ought to have independence in making their determinations of a property's worth.

In recent years, however, the appraisal process has experienced increased stress. According to the Appraisal Institute, appraiser-related mortgage fraud continues largely because:

• Unscrupulous third parties pressure appraisers to meet predetermined values;

• Appraiser regulators provide inadequate oversight over licensed appraisers;

• Too little attention is paid to improving appraisal quality; and

• Appraisals, in some areas of lending, have been reduced from an important safeguard role to merely a "speed bump" in the process of closing a loan.

Moreover, the October Research Corporation released a study in December 2006 finding that 90 percent of appraisers were pressured to raise property valuations to enable the completion of a transaction.[2] Such pressure can come from mortgage brokers, real estate agents/brokers, consumers, lenders, and appraisal management companies. The survey also found that 75 percent of appraisers reported "negative ramifications" if they did not cooperate by altering their appraisals.

Faulty appraisals can have real consequences: Individuals who obtained an overvalued appraisal may later encounter difficulty in refinancing or selling a home because the true value of the property used as collateral is less than the original mortgage.

The problems of inflated appraisals have also increasingly attracted the attention of enforcement officials. In January 2006, for example, State attorneys general announced a settlement with Ameriquest Mortgage Company. Among other things, the company agreed to take reasonable steps to ensure the accuracy of appraisals and enhance the independence of the appraisal process. The Ohio Attorney General additionally has filed and settled several cases against mortgage originators since the start of 2007 regarding violations of the State's new appraisal independence law.

Furthermore, New York Attorney General Andrew Cuomo filed a lawsuit on November 1, 2007 against one of the nation's largest real estate appraisal management companies (eAppraiseIT) and its parent corporation for colluding with a lender to inflate the appraised values of homes.[3] As part of his examinations of the appraisal industry, the New York Attorney General also identified problems with the loan purchased by Fannie Mae and Freddie Mac. As a result, he finalized an agreement known as the Home Valuation Code of Conduct to promote appraiser independence. The agreement became effective on May 1, 2009.

Interest in enacting laws aimed at protecting the independence of appraisers has blossomed in recent years. Since the start of the decade, 25 States have passed such laws. Many of these laws aim to protect appraiser independence by ensuring that no one with an interest in a transaction involving an appraisal can influence or attempt to influence an appraiser through coercion, extortion, compensation, instruction, inducement, intimidation, bribery, or nonpayment for services rendered. Many State legislatures around the nation also have similar bills under consideration.

Currently, no Federal statute specifically requires appraisal independence in the private mortgage markets, but the members of the Appraisal Subcommittee (ASC) have issued regulations and guidance to address this issue. These requirements, however, only apply to federally regulated banks, thrifts, and credit unions, as well as the parties affiliated with these federally regulated depositories.

In its 2008 HOEPA rulemaking, the Federal Reserve Board took further steps to address this issue. In its final rule, the Board determined that "[e]ncouraging an appraiser to overstate or understate the value of a consumer's dwelling causes consumers substantial injury." As a result, the Board adopted a standard "to prohibit creditors and mortgage brokers and their affiliates from coercing, influencing, or otherwise encouraging appraisers to misstate or misrepresent the value of a consumer's principal dwelling."

While this rule established a national standard for appraisal independence, to date Congress has not adopted a national law in this area to cover the vast majority of mortgage transactions. Moreover, the Federal Reserve rulemaking incorporated only some of the independence terms found in the growing field of State appraisal laws.

In the wake of the savings and loan crisis, the Congress established the ASC and housed it within the Financial Institutions Examination Council (FIEC) as part of the Financial Institutions Reform, Recovery, and Enforcement Act (FIRREA). Members of the ASC presently include the Federal Reserve Board, the Office of the Comptroller of the Currency, the Office of Thrift Supervision, the Federal Deposit Insurance Corporation, the National Credit Union Association, and the Department of Housing and Urban Development (HUD). Although it worked with New York Attorney General Cuomo to modify the Home Valuation Code of Conduct for Fannie Mae and Freddie Mac and this agreement has significant implications for the entities currently regulated by the members of the ASC, the Federal Housing Finance Agency currently does not belong to the ASC. A formal membership on the ASC by this agency might have facilitated the agreement's adoption.

The ASC presently works to ensure that real estate appraisers, who perform appraisals in real estate transactions that could expose the United States government to financial loss, are suffi-

---

[2] National Appraisal Survey, October Research Corporation, December 2006. *www.octoberresearch.com*

[3] *http://www.oag.state.ny.us/press/2007/nov/nov1a_07.html*

¶55,001

ciently trained and tested to assure competency, independence, and high ethical judgment according to the Uniform Standards of Professional Appraisal Practice, or USPAP. The ASC also monitors the work of the Appraisal Foundation, a nonprofit educational corporation established by the U.S. appraisal industry.

The ASC additionally monitors appraisers using State-based laws and enforcement agencies. A survey of State appraisal regulators by the Government Accountability Office in 2003 reported resource limitations as the primary impediment in carrying out their oversight responsibilities.[4] One of the critiques about the current oversight system often made by the Appraisal Institute and other professional appraisal organizations is that the ASC's 2006 annual report found that more than 60 percent of the State appraisal agencies failed to uphold their responsibilities in conducting enforcement activities. The ASC's 2007 report also found 18 instances in which a State failed to investigate and resolve complaints in a timely manner.

Moreover, the *Associated Press* reached similar conclusions in August 2008 about the effectiveness of current system to oversee appraisers and appraisals. After its 6-month investigation, which included the review of thousands of State and Federal documents and interviews with more than 35 real estate appraisers across the country, the *Associated Press* concluded that "the system is crippled by both the bumbling of its policemen and their inability to effectively punish those caught committing fraud." The study also found more than two dozen States and U.S. territories unable to investigate and resolve appraisal complaints within the one-year Federal deadline. The study additionally observed that both State appraisal boards and the ASC are chronically understaffed, many with only one full-time investigator to handle the hundreds of complaints that arrive each year.

The Congress has not taken any significant legislative action since establishing the ASC in 1989 to address newly identified shortcomings related to appraisal regulation. For example, the ASC presently lacks the authority to issue rules and enforce its own standards, and relies instead on policy statements. It additionally does not have a consumer protection mandate and provides very limited information in its annual report to the Congress. Short of decertifying a State's appraisal enforcement program for nonconformance with FIRREA, the ASC also lacks the power to pursue incremental improvements in State regulatory performance, like the prompt corrective action regime used by Federal banking regulators for monitoring depository institutions. The ASC also cannot make grants to the State appraisal regulators to improve their functioning.

Another problem with appraisals relates to consumer access. Under current Federal law, creditors must promptly furnish a borrower with a copy of the appraisal report used in connection with the application for a mortgage. Under regulations, a creditor may either routinely provide a copy of the appraisal report used in connection with a loan or send it within 30 days of receiving a written request. The receipt of the property appraisal typically comes at or after closing on the home loan. As a result, the consumer often cannot examine this document related to a purchase before the completion of the transaction.

In addition, sometimes the appraisal used to close the loan may not be the only appraisal performed in connection with the transaction. If an earlier appraisal comes in that is below the one needed to make the mortgage, then an originator may order another appraisal in order to "hit" the sales price and close the transaction. Borrowers affected by such a situation would only have access to the second appraisal report with the higher value instead of both appraisal reports.

Appraisal reforms could also help to address problems related to property flipping, which occurs when a recently acquired home is resold shortly thereafter for a profit, typically after undergoing some renovations and sometimes with an artificially inflated value. While the practice has been around for a long time, it has become increasingly popular and profitable during the last decade because of low interest rates and surging home prices. A number of reality television shows have even surfaced on the topic, such as Bravo's "Flipping Out", A&E's "Flip This House", and TLC's "Flip That House".

Many industry observers have further expressed concern that an individual flipping a property can often find an appraiser to inflate the home's value. Concern about property flipping scams has caused entities like the Federal Housing Administration to protect consumers by adopting regulatory reforms that involve appraisal reforms.

---

[4] http://www.gao.gov/htext/d04580t.html

In response to the implementation of the Home Valuation Code of Conduct, concerns about the oversight of the operations of appraisal management companies (AMCs) have also grown. Generally, AMCs are external third-party entities that manage the appraisal process for a mortgage originator. According to some estimates, AMCs are now involved in more than 60 percent of appraisals, and their market share is expected to grow as the Home Valuation Code of Conduct is implemented and mortgage originators seek outside parties to comply with the agreement's appraisal independence stipulations.

AMCs, however, are subject to little direct oversight. Only in recent months have three States—Utah, Arkansas, and New Mexico — adopted laws requiring their registration and supervision. The ASC also currently has no explicit statutory authority with respect to AMCs. Moreover, there have been instances in places like Florida and New Hampshire where individuals who have lost their appraisal licenses or certifications have turned around and opened AMCs to manage the work of other appraisers.

Critics have also warned that that the growth of AMCs may lead to a decline in appraisal quality. In testimony before the Financial Services Committee in March, Mr. Jim Amorin on behalf of the Appraisal Institute observed: "With many AMCs taking as much as 60 percent of the fee as their 'management' cost, many highly qualified appraisers are reluctant to perform mortgage appraisals for such entities." Because all appraisal fees are disclosed in a single line on closing documents, consumers and regulators currently lack the information needed to determine whether the growth of AMCs has led to low-cost, lower-quality appraisals.

Finally, in testimony before the Financial Services Committee during the 111th Congress, entities like the National Community Reinvestment Coalition and the Appraisal Institute have raised additional concerns about other methods for home valuation. For example, witnesses questioned the reliability of and confidence in the automated valuation models often used to develop estimates of home values. They also raised apprehensions about the quality of home value estimates developed by real estate brokers that are used for collateral purposes, particularly for purchase mortgages.

[¶55,002] HEARINGS

The Subcommittee on Financial Institutions and Consumer Credit held a hearing on March 11, 2009 entitled "Mortgage Lending Reform: A Comprehensive Review of the American Mortgage System." The following witnesses testified: Panel One: Ms. Sandra F. Braunstein, Director, Division of Consumer and Community Affairs, Board of Governors of the Federal Reserve System, Mr. Steven L. Antonakes, Commissioner, Massachusetts Division of Banks, on behalf of Conference of State Bank Supervisors; Panel Two: Mr. David Berenbaum, Executive Vice President, National Community Reinvestment Coalition, Ms. Julia Gordon, Senior Policy Counsel, Center for Responsible Lending, Ms. Margot Saunders, Counsel, National Consumer Law Center, Ms. Stephanie Jones, Executive Director, National Urban League Policy Institute, Ms. Graciela Aponte, Analyst, National Council of La Raza, Mr. Donald C. Lampe, Partner, Womble Carlyle Sandridge & Rice, PLLC; Panel Three: Mr. Michael Middleton, President and CEO, Community Bank of Tri-County, on behalf of the American Bankers Association, Mr. David G. Kittle, Chairman, Mortgage Bankers Association, Mr. Marc S. Savitt, President, National Association of Mortgage Brokers, Mr. Charles McMillan, President, National Association of Realtors, Mr. Jim Amorin, President, Appraisal Institute, Mr. Joe J. Robson, Chairman of the Board, National Association of Home Builders, Mr. Laurence E. Platt, Partner, K&L Gates, on behalf of the Securities Industry and Financial Markets Association.

The Committee on Financial Services held a hearing on April 23, 2009 entitled "H.R. 1728: Mortgage Reform and Anti-Predatory Lending Act". The following witnesses testified: Panel One: Ms. Sandra Braunstein, Director of the Division of Consumer and Community Affairs, Board of Governors of the Federal Reserve System, Mr. Steven L. Antonakes, Commissioner of Banks for the Commonwealth of Massachusetts on behalf of the Conference of State Bank Supervisors; Panel Two: Mr. John Taylor, President and Chief Executive Officer, National Community Reinvestment Coalition, Mr. Michael D. Calhoun, President, Center for Responsible Lending, Ms. Margot Saunders, Counsel, National Consumer Law Center, Mr. Eric Rodriguez, Vice President of Public Policy, National Council of La Raza, Mr. Hilary O. Shelton, Vice President for Advocacy and Director, Washington Bureau, NAACP; Panel Three: Mr. G. Gary Berner, Executive Vice President, Commercial Real Estate, First Niagara Bank on behalf of American Bankers Association, The Honorable John H. Dalton, President, Housing Policy Council, The Financial Services Roundtable, Mr. David G. Kittle, Chairman, Mortgage Bankers Association, Mr. Michael S. Menzies, Sr., President and Chief Executive Officer, Easton Bank and Trust Company on behalf of Independent Community Bankers Association, The Honorable T. Timothy Ryan, Jr., President and Chief Executive Officer, Securities Industry and Financial Markets Association, Ms. Denise M. Leonard, Vice President, Government Affairs, National Association of Mortgage Brokers, Mr. Charles McMillan, President, National Association of Realtors, Mr. Jim Amorin, President, Appraisal Institute, Mr. Jim Arbury, Senior Vice President, Government Affairs, on behalf of the National Multi Housing Council and the National Apartment Association.

[¶55,003] COMMITTEE CONSIDERATION

The Committee on Financial Services met in open session on April 28, 2009, and on April 29, 2009, ordered H.R. 1728, the Mortgage Reform and Anti-Predatory Lending Act, as amended, favorably reported to the House by a record vote of 49 yeas and 21 nays.

[¶55,004] COMMITTEE VOTES

Clause 3(b) of rule XIII of the Rules of the House of Representatives requires the Committee to list the record votes on the motion to report legislation and amendments thereto. A motion by Mr. Frank to report the bill to the House with a favorable recommendation was agreed to by a record vote of 49 yeas and 21 nays (Record vote no. FC-28). The names of Members voting for and against follow:

* * *

[Not reproduced—CCH.]

The following other amendments were also considered by the Committee:

An amendment by Mr. Sherman (and Mr. Green), No. 1, relating to the definition of mortgage originator-real estate brokerage activities, was agreed to by a voice vote.

An amendment by Mr. Sherman, No. 2, relating to the definition of mortgage originator—five or fewer properties, was offered and withdrawn.

An amendment by Mr. Grayson, No. 3, relating to time shares, was agreed to by a voice vote.

An amendment by Mr. Donnelly, No. 4, relating to the definition of mortgage originator and exclusion of bona fide discount points, was agreed to by a voice vote.

An amendment by Mr. Carson, No. 5, relating to foreclosure rescue education programs, was agreed to, as modified, by a voice vote.

An amendment by Mrs. Biggert, No. 6, making technical corrections to housing counseling, was agreed to by a voice vote.

An amendment by Mr. Kanjorski (and Mrs. Biggert), No. 7, regarding appraisals, was agreed to by a voice vote.

An amendment by Ms. Waters, No. 8, regarding housing counseling-minorities, was agreed to by a voice vote.

An amendment by Ms. Velazquez, No. 10, regarding home inspection counseling, was agreed to, as modified, by a voice vote.

An amendment by Mr. Paulson, No. 11, relating to examining certain credit risk retention provisions, was agreed to by a voice vote.

An amendment by Ms. Bean, No. 12, regarding closing document inspection by borrowers, was offered and withdrawn.

An amendment by Mr. Ellison, No. 13, regarding fiduciary duties of mortgage brokers, was offered and withdrawn.

An amendment by Mr. Moore (KS), No. 14, regarding residential mortgage loan origination purposes, was agreed to, reconsidered, and withdrawn.

An amendment by Mr. Hodes, No. 16, regarding State attorney general enforcement authority, was agreed to by a voice vote.

An amendment by Ms. Waters (and Mr. Meeks), No. 18, prohibiting prepayment penalties, was not agreed to by a voice vote.

An amendment by Mr. Neugebauer, No. 19, requiring full recourse mortgage loans for civil actions, was not agreed to by a voice vote.

An amendment by Mr. Sherman, No. 20, regarding the definition of mortgage originator, was agreed to by a voice vote.

An amendment by Ms. Bean (and Mr. Castle), No. 21, regarding safe harbor and rebuttable presumption, as amended by an amendment by Mr. Lance (and Mr. Miller (CA)), No. 21a, was agreed to by a voice vote.

An amendment by Mrs. Biggert (and Mr. Hinojosa and Mr. Neugebauer), No. 22, regarding RESPA and TILA disclosure improvement, as amended by an amendment by Mr. Neugebauer,

No. 22a, (as modified) was agreed to by a voice vote.

An amendment by Mr. Moore (KS), No. 23, regarding residential mortgage loan origination findings, was agreed to by a voice vote.

An amendment by Mr. Frank, No. 28, the first manager's amendment was agreed to by a voice vote. An amendment offered by Mr. Miller (CA), No. 28a, to the amendment was offered and withdrawn.

An amendment by Ms. Waters, No. 30, regarding excessive points and fees, was agreed to by a voice vote.

An amendment by Mr. Royce, No. 31, striking assignee and securitizer liability, was not agreed to by a voice vote.

An amendment by Mr. Ellison, No. 32, regarding tenant protection, was offered and withdrawn.

An amendment by Mr. Ellison, No. 33, regarding tenant protection, was agreed to by a voice vote.

An amendment by Mr. Hensarling, No. 38, expressing the Sense of the Congress regarding the importance of government sponsored enterprises reform, as modified, was agreed to by a voice vote.

An amendment by Mrs. Bachmann, No. 40, regarding a limitation on assistance, was agreed to by a voice vote.

An amendment by Ms. Moore (WI), No. 41, regarding foreclosure rescue fraud, was offered and withdrawn.

[¶55,005] COMMITTEE OVERSIGHT FINDINGS

Pursuant to clause 3(c)(1) of rule XIII of the Rules of the House of Representatives, the Committee has held hearings and made findings that are reflected in this report.

[¶55,006] PERFORMANCE GOALS AND OBJECTIVES

Pursuant to clause 3(c)(4) of rule XIII of the Rules of the House of Representatives, the Committee establishes the following performance related goals and objectives for this legislation:

H.R. 1728 is intended to reform mortgage lending practices to avert a recurrence of the current situation of unprecedented levels of defaults and foreclosures rates.

[¶55,007] NEW BUDGET AUTHORITY, ENTITLEMENT AUTHORITY, AND TAX EXPENDITURES

In compliance with clause 3(c)(2) of rule XIII of the Rules of the House of Representatives, the Committee adopts as its own the estimate of new budget authority, entitlement authority, or tax expenditures or revenues contained in the cost estimate prepared by the Director of the Congressional Budget Office pursuant to section 402 of the Congressional Budget Act of 1974.

[¶55,008] COMMITTEE COST ESTIMATE

The Committee adopts as its own the cost estimate prepared by the Director of the Congressional Budget Office pursuant to section 402 of the Congressional Budget Act of 1974.

[¶55,009] CONGRESSIONAL BUDGET OFFICE ESTIMATE

Pursuant to clause 3(c)(3) of rule XIII of the Rules of the House of Representatives, the following is the cost estimate provided by the Congressional Budget Office pursuant to section 402 of the Congressional Budget Act of 1974:

MAY 4, 2009.

Hon. BARNEY FRANK,

Chairman, Committee on Financial Services, House of Representatives, Washington, DC.

DEAR MR. CHAIRMAN: The Congressional Budget Office has prepared the enclosed cost estimate for H.R. 1728, the Mortgage Reform and Anti-Predatory Lending Act.

If you wish further details on this estimate, we will be pleased to provide them. The CBO staff contact is Susan Willie.

Sincerely,

DOUGLAS W. ELMENDORF.

Enclosure.

H.R. 1728—Mortgage Reform and Anti-Predatory Lending Act

Summary: H.R. 1728 would amend the Truth in Lending Act to reform consumer mortgage practices, establish minimum standards for consumer mortgage loans, and provide other protections to borrowers and investors. The bill also would broaden the oversight of professional appraisers and require the Government Accountability Office to conduct a study on the effects of H.R. 1728 on the availability of credit for homebuyers. The bill would require the Board of Governors of the Federal Reserve (Federal Reserve), in consultation with other agencies that regulate the financial industry, to prescribe regulations and forms to implement the new requirements.

H.R. 1728 would authorize the appropriation of $323 million over the 2009-2014 period for the Department of Housing and Urban Development (HUD) to support efforts to provide homeownership counseling and legal assistance to certain homeowners and tenants. In addition, CBO estimates that $80 million would be required over the 2009-2014 period for HUD to establish an Office of Housing Counseling. In total, CBO estimates that implementing H.R. 1728 would cost $403 million over the 2009-2014 period, subject to appropriation of the necessary amounts.

CBO estimates that enacting H.R. 1728 would increase revenues by $13 million over the 2009-2014 period and by $28 million over the 2009-2019 period. We estimate that direct spending would increase by corresponding amounts over the same time periods.

H.R. 1728 would impose intergovernmental and private-sector mandates, as defined in the Unfunded Mandates Reform Act (UMRA), on participants in the mortgage industry. While the costs of some of the mandates are likely to be small, the costs to comply with other mandates are uncertain. Consequently, CBO cannot determine whether the aggregate costs to comply with the mandates in the bill would exceed the annual thresholds established in UMRA for intergovernmental or private-sector mandates ($69 million and $139 million in 2009, respectively, adjusted annually for inflation).

Estimated cost to the Federal Government: The estimated budgetary impact of H.R. 1728 is shown in the following table. The costs of this legislation fall within budget function 370 (commerce and housing credit).

	By fiscal year, in millions of dollars—						
	2009	2010	2011	2012	2013	2014	2009-2014
CHANGES IN SPENDING SUBJECT TO APPROPRIATION							
Public Service Campaign:							
Authorization Level	3	0	0	0	0	0	3
Estimated Outlays	*	2	1	0	0	0	3
Housing Counseling Grants:							
Authorization Level	45	45	45	45	0	0	180
Estimated Outlays	1	38	49	45	40	7	180
Administrative Support for Office of Counseling:							
Estimated Authorization Level	16	16	16	16	16	16	96
Estimated Outlays	*	16	16	16	16	16	80
Legal Assistance:							
Authorization Level	35	35	35	35	0	0	140
Estimated Outlays	1	30	38	35	31	5	140
Total Changes:							
Estimated Authorization Level	99	96	96	96	16	16	419
Estimated Outlays	2	86	104	96	87	28	403
CHANGES IN REVENUES							
Estimated Revenues	*	2	2	3	3	3	13
CHANGES IN DIRECT SPENDING							
Estimated Budget Authority	*	2	2	3	3	3	13
Estimated Outlays	*	2	2	3	3	3	13

Note: * = less than $500,000.

Basis of Estimate: For this estimate, CBO assumes that H.R. 1728 will be enacted around July 2009 and that the necessary amounts will be appropriated for each year.

Spending Subject to Appropriation: CBO estimates that implementing H.R. 1728 would cost $403 million over the 2009-2014 period, subject to appropriation of the necessary amounts.

Public Service Campaign, Grants for Housing Counseling, and Administrative Support for the Office of Counseling. Title IV would establish the Office of Housing Counseling within HUD to support various activities related to providing counseling on homeownership and renting. Section 403 would authorize the appropriation of $3 million over the 2009-2011 period to support a national campaign to publicize the existence of counseling for home buyers, homeowners, and renters. In addition, section 404 would authorize the appropriation of $45 million annually over the 2009-2012 period to provide grants to states, local governments, and nonprofit organizations to support counseling services. In total, CBO estimates that implementing those provisions would cost $183 million over the 2009-2014 period.

In addition, based on information from HUD, CBO expects that funds for additional personnel, contractors, and information technology would be necessary to run the Office of Housing Counseling. We estimate that support would cost $80 million over the 2009-2014 period.

Legal Assistance for Foreclosure-Related Issues. Section 216 would authorize the appropriation of $35 million annually for fiscal years 2009 through 2012 for grants to provide legal assistance to low- and moderate-income homeowners and tenants related to home foreclosure prevention. Assuming appropriation of the authorize amounts, CBO estimates that implementing this section would cost $140 million over the 2009-2014 period.

Revenues and Direct Spending: CBO estimates that enacting H.R. 1728 would increase both revenues and direct spending by $28 million over the 2009-2019 period, as shown in the following table.

Appraisal Monitoring. Section 603 would expand the monitoring and oversight responsibilities of the Appraisal Subcommittee (ASC) of the Federal Financial Institutions Examination Council. The ASC is responsible for ensuring that real estate appraisals used in certain transactions are performed according to uniform standards by appraisers that are certified and licensed by states. To do this, the ASC monitors the activities of the state agencies that are responsible for licensing real estate appraisers. The ASC is authorized to collect fees from licensed and certified appraisers to offset the costs of its operations.

	By Fiscal year, in millions of dollars—											
	2009	2010	2011	2012	2013	2014	2015	2016	2017	2018	2019	2009-2014	2009-2019
	CHANGES IN REVENUES												
Net Revenues	*	2	2	3	3	3	3	3	3	3	3	13	28
	CHANGES IN DIRECT SPENDING												
Estimated Budget Authority	*	2	2	3	3	3	3	3	3	3	3	13	28
Estimated Outlays	*	2	2	3	3	3	3	3	3	3	3	13	28

Note: * = less than $500,000.

H.R. 1728 would authorize the ASC to monitor companies that retain or contract with appraisers and manage the process of having an appraisal performed (appraisal management companies). The bill would require those companies to be registered with a state (or be subject to oversight by a financial regulatory agency) in order to provide appraisal services on transactions undertaken through federally regulated financial institutions. As a result, the ASC would be required to develop regulations that states must follow in licensing appraisal management companies. Further, the ASC would be required to maintain a registry of appraisal management companies that are registered with a state licensing agency. The bill would authorize the ASC to collect fees from this new group of licensed entities.

Other provisions of the bill would authorize the ASC to make grants to states to improve their compliance with ASC regulations and would require the ASC to establish a complaint hotline.

Licensed and certified appraisers pay a fee, capped at $25 annually, to the ASC to support its operations. H.R. 1728 would raise the upper limit for the fee to $40, and would authorize the ASC to charge fees to appraisal management companies that are registered with a state licensing agency. Based on information from the ASC, CBO estimates that enacting the new fees would increase federal revenues by $13 million over the 2009-2014 period, and by $28 million over the 2009-2019 period, net of income and payroll tax effects.

Based on information from the ASC, CBO estimates that enacting H.R. 1728 would increase direct spending by $13 million over the 2009-2014 period and by $28 million over the 2009-2019 period to provide grants to states to improve their ability to comply with the requirements of the bill.

Spending by Federal Bank Regulators. According to Federal Reserve and other federal financial regulatory agencies, implementing H.R. 1728 would not have a significant effect on their workload or budgets. Any additional direct spending by the Office of the Comptroller of the Currency, the Office of Thrift Supervision, and the National Credit Union Administration would be offset by income from annual fees covering their administrative expenses. Similarly, the Federal Deposit Insurance Corporation would recover any added costs when it adjusts the premiums paid by insured depository institutions. Budgetary effects of spending by the Federal Reserve are recorded as changes in revenues, but current law requires the Federal Reserve to recover direct and indirect costs incurred in providing such services. Thus, CBO estimates that the additional activities of the agencies that regulate banks would have no significant net effect on direct spending or revenues.

Penalties. Under this legislation, certain civil penalties (which are recorded as revenues) currently applicable under the Truth in Lending Act would be increased and new civil penalties would be created for violations under this bill. CBO estimates that any increase in revenues resulting from those civil penalties would not be significant.

Intergovernmental and private-sector impact: H.R. 1728 contains several intergovernmental and private-sector mandates, as defined in UMRA, by placing new restrictions on entities that securitize mortgages, and on entities that purchase foreclosed properties. The bill also would impose intergovernmental mandates by preempting certain state property and securities laws. In addition, the bill would impose private-sector mandates by establishing new requirements for creditors, loan originators, mortgage servicers, real estate appraisers, and other entities that participate in the mortgage industry.

While the costs of some of the mandates are likely to be small (for example, the preemptions of state law), the costs to comply with other mandates are uncertain for several reasons. Many industry participants, including public entities, already comply with some of the bill's requirements. In addition, the cost of some of the requirements would depend on federal regulations to be issued under the bill, and the scope of those regulations is uncertain. Lastly, CBO does not have sufficient information about current business practices or how the requirements in the bill would affect industry income. Consequently, CBO cannot determine whether the aggregate costs to comply with the mandates in the bill would exceed the annual thresholds established in UMRA for intergovernmental or private-sector mandates ($69 million and $139 million in 2009, respectively, adjusted annually for inflation).

The bill also would authorize grants to support state agencies that license and certify appraisers, which would benefit state, local, and tribal governments.

Estimate prepared by: Federal Spending: Chad Chirico and Susan Willie; Federal Revenues: Barbara Edwards; Impact on State, Local, and Tribal Governments: Elizabeth Cove Delise; Impact on the Private Sector: Marin Randall.

Estimate approved by: Theresa Gullo, Deputy Assistant Director for Budget Analysis; Frank J. Sammartino, Acting Assistant Director for Tax Analysis.

[¶55,010] FEDERAL MANDATES STATEMENT

The Committee adopts as its own the estimate of Federal mandates prepared by the Director of the Congressional Budget Office pursuant to section 423 of the Unfunded Mandates Reform Act.

[¶55,011] ADVISORY COMMITTEE STATEMENT

No advisory committees within the meaning of section 5(b) of the Federal Advisory Committee Act were created by this legislation.

[¶ 55,012] CONSTITUTIONAL AUTHORITY STATEMENT

Pursuant to clause 3(d)(1) of rule XIII of the Rules of the House of Representatives, the Committee finds that the Constitutional Authority of Congress to enact this legislation is provided by Article 1, section 8, clause 1 (relating to the general welfare of the United States) and clause 3 (relating to the power to regulate interstate commerce).

[¶ 55,013] APPLICABILITY TO LEGISLATIVE BRANCH

The Committee finds that the legislation does not relate to the terms and conditions of employment or access to public services or accommodations within the meaning of section 102(b)(3) of the Congressional Accountability Act.

[¶ 55,014] EARMARK IDENTIFICATION

H.R. 1728 does not contain any congressional earmarks, limited tax benefits, or limited tariff benefits as defined in clause 9 of rule XXI.

[¶ 55,015] SECTION-BY-SECTION ANALYSIS OF THE LEGISLATION

Section 1. Short Title; Table of Contents

This section establishes the short title of the bill as the 'Mortgage Reform and Anti-Predatory Lending Act' (the Act).

TITLE I—RESIDENTIAL MORTGAGE LOAN ORIGINATION STANDARDS

[¶ 55,016] Section 101. Definitions

This section establishes definitions for various terms, including: 'Federal banking agencies,' 'mortgage originator,' 'nationwide mortgage licensing system,' 'residential mortgage loan,' 'securitization vehicle,' 'securitizer,' and 'servicer.'

[¶ 55,017] Section 102. Residential mortgage loan origination

Subsection (a) of this section is a Findings and Purpose provision in which Congress finds that economic stabilization would be enhanced by the protection, limitation, and regulation of the terms of residential mortgage credit and the practices related to such credit, while ensuring that responsible, affordable mortgage credit remains available to consumers. It is the purpose of the new sections 129B and 129C of the Truth in Lending Act to assure that consumers are offered and receive residential mortgage loans on terms that reasonably reflect their ability to repay the loans and that are understandable and not unfair, deceptive or abusive.

Subsection (b) of this section provides that all mortgage originators (including mortgage brokers and depository institutions that originate mortgages, and their loan officers) will be subject to a Federal duty of care that requires (1) licensing and registration under State or Federal law (including subtitle A of title I of this Act), (2) diligently working to present the consumer with a range of residential mortgage loan products for which the consumer likely qualifies and are appropriate to the consumer's existing circumstances (i.e., consumer has reasonable ability to repay and, in the case of refinancings, receives net tangible benefit and loan does not have predatory characteristics), (3) making full, complete, and timely disclosures to consumers, (4) certifying to creditors compliance with mortgage origination requirements under this section, and (5) including in all loan documents any unique identifier of the mortgage originator. Mortgage originators are not required, however, to present residential mortgage loan products of creditors that do not accept consumer referrals or applications from the mortgage originator, and creditors are not required to offer products that the creditor does not offer to the general public. The Act expressly does not create an agency or fiduciary relationship, but mortgage originators are free to become an agent or a fiduciary if they so desire. The Federal banking agencies, in consultation with the Secretary and the Federal Trade Commission (Commission), will jointly prescribe regulations to further define the Federal duty of care. The Federal banking agencies will prescribe regulations requiring depository institutions to establish procedures for monitoring compliance with the requirements of this section and the registration procedures of section 106 of the Act.

[¶55,018] Section 103. Prohibition on steering incentives

This section provides that for any mortgage loan, the total amount of direct and indirect compensation from all sources permitted to a mortgage originator may not vary based on the terms of the loan (other than amount of principal). In addition, the Federal banking agencies, in consultation with the Secretary and the Commission, will jointly prescribe regulations to prohibit (1) mortgage originators from steering any consumer to a residential mortgage loan that the consumer lacks a reasonable ability to repay, that does not provide net tangible benefit, or that has predatory characteristics, (2) mortgage originators from steering any consumer from a qualified mortgage (prime loan) to a loan that is not a qualified mortgage, (3) abusive or unfair lending practices that promote disparities among consumers of equal creditworthiness but of different race, ethnicity, gender, or age, and (4) mortgage originators from assessing excessive points and fees to a consumer for the origination of a residential mortgage loan based on such consumer's decision to finance all or part of the payment through the rate for such points and fees. However, nothing in the Act should be construed as permitting yield spread premiums or other similar incentive compensation, affecting the mechanism for providing the total amount of direct and indirect compensation permitted to a mortgage originator, restricting a consumer's ability to finance origination fees if they were disclosed to the consumer and do not vary with the consumer's decision to finance such fees, or prohibiting incentive payments to a mortgage originator based on the number of loans originated.

[¶55,019] Section 104. Liability

This section provides that a cause of action will exist under section 130(a) and 130(b) of the Truth in Lending Act (TILA) for a mortgage originator's failure to comply with this section. The maximum liability of a mortgage originator for violation of this section will not exceed the greater of actual damages or an amount equal to three times the total amount of direct and indirect mortgage originator fees, plus the consumer's costs including reasonable attorney's fees.

[¶55,020] Section 105. Regulations

This section provides the Federal banking agencies discretionary regulatory authority to issue joint regulations to prohibit or condition terms, acts or practices relating to residential mortgage loans that the agencies find to be abusive, unfair, deceptive, predatory, inconsistent with reasonable underwriting standards, necessary or proper to effectuate the purposes of this section and section 129C, to prevent circumvention or evasion thereof, or to facilitate compliance with such sections, or are not in the interest of the borrower. The section makes clear that this new authority will not prevent regulations adopted by the Federal Reserve concerning mortgage lending (73 Fed. Reg. 44522 (July 30, 2008)) will take effect as decided by the Federal Reserve with such exceptions or revisions as the Federal Reserve determines necessary.

This section also provides that regulations under this title will be promulgated within 12 months of the enactment of the Act and take effect no later than 18 months after the enactment of the Act.

[¶55,021] Section 106. RESPA and TILA Disclosure Improvement

This section requires HUD and the Federal Reserve, not later than six months after the date of enactment, to jointly issue for public comment proposed regulations providing for compatible disclosures for borrowers to receive at the time of mortgage application and at the time of closing. The statute requires the disclosures to meet both the requirements of the TILA and RESPA. The section also suspends the rulemaking HUD issued relating to RESPA (73 Fed. Reg. 26204 (Nov. 17, 2008)) until the joint regulations are issued by the Federal Reserve and HUD.

TITLE II—MINIMUM STANDARDS FOR MORTGAGES

[¶55,025] Section 201. Ability to Repay

This section provides that no creditor may make a residential mortgage loan unless the creditor makes a reasonable and good faith determination based on verified and documented information that, at the time the loan is consummated, the consumer has a reasonable ability to repay the loan (including all applicable taxes, insurance, and assessments). The Federal banking agencies, in consultation with the Commission, will jointly prescribe regulations regarding this provision. A determination of reasonable ability to repay will include consideration of a consumer's credit history, current income, expected income the consumer is reasonably assured of receiving, current obligations, debt-to-income ratio, employment status, and other financial resources other than the consumer's equity in the real property securing the loan.

[¶55,026] Section 202. Net Tangible Benefit for Refinancing of Residential Mortgage Loans

This section provides that no creditor may extend credit for refinancing unless the creditor reasonably and in good faith determines, at the time the loan is consummated and on the basis of information known by or obtained in good faith by the creditor, that the refinanced loan will provide a net tangible benefit to the consumer. The refinanced loan will not be considered to provide net tangible benefit if the costs of the loan, including points, fees, and other charges, exceed the amount of newly advanced principal without any corresponding changes in the terms of the refinanced loan that are advantageous to the consumer. The Federal banking agencies will jointly prescribe regulations further defining the term 'net tangible benefit.'

[¶55,027] Section 203. Safe harbor and rebuttable presumption

This section provides that any creditor, assignee or securitizer may presume that a mortgage loan meets the minimum standards (reasonable ability to repay and net tangible benefit) if it is a 'qualified mortgage.' Qualified mortgages are loans—

- that do not allow a consumer to defer repayment of principal or interest, or is not otherwise deemed a "non-traditional mortgage" under guidance, advisories, or regulations prescribed by the Federal Banking Agencies;
- that do not provide for a repayment schedule that results in negative amortization at any time;
- for which the terms are fully amortizing and which does not result in a balloon payment (where a balloon payment is a scheduled payment that is more than twice as large as the average of earlier scheduled payments);
- which have an annual percentage rate that does not exceed the average prime offer rate for a comparable transaction (set by the Federal Reserve), as of the date the interest rate is set—

- by 1.5 or more percentage points for residential mortgage loans with principal amounts that do not exceed the conforming loan limits in section 305(a)(2) of the Federal Home Loan Mortgage Corporation Act (Freddie Mac); and

- by 2.5 or more percentage points for residential mortgage loans with principal amounts that exceed the Freddie Mac conforming loan limit.

- for which the income and financial resources relied upon to qualify the obligors on the loan are verified and documented;

- in the case of a fixed rate loan, for which the underwriting process is based on a payment schedule that fully amortizes the loan over the loan term and takes into account all applicable taxes, insurance and assessments;

- in the case of an adjustable rate loan, for which the underwriting is based on the maximum rate permitted under the loan during the first seven years, and a payment schedule that fully amortizes the loan over the loan term and takes into account all applicable taxes, insurance and assessments;

- that do not cause the consumer's total monthly debts, including amounts under the loan, to exceed a debt-to-income ratio or ratios prescribed by the Banking Agencies;

- for which the total points and fees payable in connection with the loan do not exceed two percent of the total loan amount, where "points and fees" means points and fees as defined by Section 103(aa)(4) of the Truth in Lending Act (15 U.S.C. 1602(aa)(4)), as amended by this legislation; and

- for which the term of the loan does not exceed 30 years.

The Federal banking agencies may jointly prescribe regulations to revise, add to, or subtract from these safe harbor provisions to the extent necessary and appropriate to effectuate the purposes of section 129B and 129C, to prevent circumvention or evasion thereof, or to facilitate compliance with such section. In addition, HUD, the Secretary of Veterans Affairs, Secretary of Agriculture, the Federal Housing Finance Agency and the Rural Housing Service each are authorized to prescribe rules defining the types of loans they guarantee, insure, or administer, as the case may be, that are Qualified Mortgages.

[¶55,028] Section 204. Liability

This section provides that a consumer has a cause of action against a creditor for rescission of the loan and the consumer's costs for a loan that violates the minimum standards for reasonable ability to repay or net tangible benefits as set forth by regulation. A creditor will not be liable for such rescission if the creditor provides a cure to make the loan conform to the minimum standards within 90 days of receiving notice from the consumer. In addition, for a loan that violates the minimum standards, a consumer has an individual cause of action against any assignee or securitizer for rescission of the loan and the consumer's costs. An assignee or securitizer that has exercised reasonable due diligence in complying with the ability to repay and net tangible benefit standards is not liable for violations of these standards if it provides a cure to make the loan conform to the minimum standards within 90 days of receiving notice from the consumer.

If any creditor, assignee or securitizer and a consumer fail to agree on a cure, or if the consumer fails to accept a cure, the creditor, assignee, or securitizer may provide the cure and the consumer may challenge the adequacy of the cure within six months of the cure. If a creditor, assignee, or securitizer cannot provide rescission, they can provide the financial equivalent of a rescission. Liability of a creditor, assignee, or securitizer will apply for three years after consummation of the loan or, for a variable rate loan or a negative amortization loan, the earlier of one year after the loan resets or six years after consummation of the loan. Liability will not apply to pools of loans, including the securitization vehicle, or investors in pools of loans. It is not intended that liability will apply to trustees or titleholders who in their capacity hold loans solely for the benefit of the securitization vehicle.

Securitizers are responsible for providing in any agreement providing for the transfer, conveyance, or the establishment of a securitization vehicle that they have the right and ability to (i) identify and obtain access to the loans, (ii) acquire the loans in the event of a violation of an ability to repay or net tangible benefit standard, and (iii) provide to the consumer any and all remedies provided for under the statute. Securitizers subject to a remedy under this section will be subject to additional exemplary or punitive damages not to exceed the original principal balance of the loan.

Servicers are required to provide a written notice to a consumer about the creditor, assignee and securitizers relating to that loan upon request, whenever there is a change in ownership of the loan and on a regular basis (not less than annually). In addition, the Federal Reserve will promulgate rules to govern the rescission process established for violations of the ability to repay and net tangible benefit standards.

[¶55,029] Section 205. Defense to foreclosure

This section provides that, when the holder (including the securitization vehicle) of a residential mortgage loan or anyone acting on such holder's behalf initiates a judicial or non-judicial foreclosure, (1) a consumer who has a rescission right under this section may assert such right as a defense or counterclaim to foreclosure against the holder to forestall such foreclosure, or (2) if the foreclosure proceeding begins after the rescission right expires, the consumer may seek actual damages plus costs against the creditor or any assignee or securitizer. Such holder, anyone acting on behalf of such holder, or any other applicable third party may sell or assign a residential mortgage loan to a creditor, any assignee, or any securitizer, or their designee, to effect a rescission or a cure.

[¶55,030] Section 206. Additional standards and requirements

This section prohibits prepayment penalties on loans that are not qualified mortgages as defined in section 203 of the Act and adjustable rate mortgages that are qualified mortgages. For qualified mortgages that are not ARMs, phased out penalties are permitted provided that all remaining prepayment penalties expire three months before a loan resets.

Single-premium credit insurance and mandatory arbitration on mortgage loans are prohibited. Securitizers must reserve the right in any document or contract establishing pools of loans to obtain access to such loans and to provide for and obtain a remedy under this title. Negative amortization loans to a first-time borrower are prohibited unless the creditor makes certain disclosures to the consumer and the consumer has received homeownership counseling from a HUD-certified organization or counselor.

[¶ 55,031] **Section 207. Rule of construction**

This section provides that, except as otherwise expressly provided, no provisions of new TILA sections 129A and 129B added by the Act will be construed as superseding, repealing, or affecting any duty, right, obligation, privilege, or remedy of any person under any other provision of TILA or any other provision of Federal or State law.

[¶ 55,032] **Section 208. Effect on State laws**

This section provides that the provisions of section 204 of the Act will supersede any State law to the extent that it provides additional remedies against any assignee, securitizer, or securitization vehicle for a violation of section 201 or 202 of the Act or any other State law other than a provision of such law the terms of which address the specific subject matter of sections 201 and 202 of the Act, and the remedies in section 204 of the Act will constitute the sole remedies against any assignee, securitizer, or securitization vehicle for those violations. No provision of this section will be construed as limiting the application of any state law or the availability of remedies, including equitable remedies such as injunctive relief, against creditors, even if they also act as assignees or securitizers or against assignees, securitizers or securitization vehicles for their own participation in or direction of the credit or underwriting decisions of the creditor in making mortgages. It also shall not be construed as limiting the application of state laws or the availability of remedies under State law against an assignee, securitizer or securitization vehicle other than laws the terms of which address the specific subject matter of sections 201 and 202 of the Act.

[¶ 55,033] **Section 209. Regulations**

This section provides that regulations under this title will be promulgated within 12 months of the enactment of the Act, and take effect no later than 18 months after the enactment of the Act.

[¶ 55,034] **Section 210. Amendments to civil liability provisions**

This section doubles the amount of certain statutory civil liability penalties currently applicable under TILA and extends the statute of limitations from one year to three years.

[¶ 55,035] **Section 211. Lender rights in the context of borrower deception**

This provision provides that no creditor, assignee, or securitizer shall be liable to an obligor under section 129B and 129C if the obligor or co-obligor knowingly or willfully and with actual knowledge furnished material information known to be false for the purpose of obtaining such residential mortgage loan.

[¶ 55,036] **Section 212. Six-month notice required before reset of hybrid adjustable rate mortgages**

This section requires a notice to consumers in connection with adjustable rate mortgage loans at least six months before the expiration of a fixed introductory rate that explains the rate adjustment process and the consumer's alternatives.

[¶ 55,037] **Section 213. Credit risk retention**

This section requires the Federal banking agencies to prescribe regulations to require creditors that make residential mortgage loans that are not qualified mortgages, as defined by section 203, to retain an economic interest in a material portion of the credit risk for any loans they transfer, sell or convey. The regulations must prohibit creditors from hedging or otherwise transferring the credit risk, require creditors to retain at least 5 percent of the credit risk on any particular loan, specify the permissible forms of the risk to be held (e.g., first loss position or pro rata vertical slice) and the minimum duration of the required risk retention. The Federal banking agencies have the discretion to apply the risk retention requirements to securitizers in addition to or in place of creditors if the agencies determine such change would help ensure high quality underwriting standards for mortgage lenders and facilitate appropriate risk management practices by mortgage lenders or improve access of consumers to mortgage credit on reasonable terms.

[¶ 55,038] **Section 214. Required disclosures**

This section provides additional required disclosures under TILA. A creditor must disclose the maximum amount of regular payment a consumer has to make on a variable rate or otherwise variable payment mortgage. For a residential mortgage loan with an escrow or impound account for the payment of taxes, insurance, and assessments, a creditor must disclose that mortgage payments will be increased to cover taxes and insurance and the monthly dollar amount a consumer will pay to cover taxes and insurance in the first year of the mortgage. For a variable rate residential mortgage with an escrow or impound account, a creditor is required to disclose (1) the amount of initial monthly payment for principal and interest; (2) the amount of initial monthly payment including the amount deposited in an escrow or impound to pay for taxes, insurance, and assessments; (3) the amount of the fully indexed monthly payment for principal and interest; and (4) the amount of fully indexed monthly payment deposited in an escrow or impound to pay for taxes, insurance, and assessments. For all residential mortgages, a creditor must disclose the aggregate amount of settlement charges, the amount of charges included in a mortgage, the amount of charges a consumer must pay at closing, the approximate amount of the wholesale rate of funds, the aggregate amount of other fees or required payments, the aggregate amount of fees paid to a mortgage originator, the amount of fees paid directly by a consumer, and any additional amounts received by a mortgage originator from a creditor based on the interest rate of the loan. For all residential mortgage loans, the aggregate amount of fees paid to the mortgage originator in connection with the loan.

[¶55,039] Section 215. Disclosures required in monthly statements for residential mortgage loans

This section requires the new disclosures for monthly statements for all residential mortgage loans that require information about the remaining balance, interest and fees incurred on the account. The Federal banking agencies shall jointly prescribe a standard form for this disclosure.

[¶55,040] Section 216. Legal assistance for foreclosure-related issues

This section authorizes funds for foreclosure-related legal assistance. The funds will be administered by HUD and distributed through a competitive grant process to state and local legal organizations to provide legal assistance to low- and moderate-income homeowners and tenants with foreclosure related issues, including civil litigation. In allocating these funds, HUD shall give priority consideration to state and local legal organizations that are operating in the 100 metropolitan statistical areas with the highest home foreclosure rates. No funds authorized by this section may be used for class action lawsuits. Organizations eligible for the funding are state and local organizations whose primary business or mission is to provide legal assistance. No funds under this subsection may be distributed to any organization which has been or which employs an individual who has been indicted for a violation under Federal law relating to an election for Federal office.

[¶55,041] Section 217. Effective date

This section provides that the amendments made by this title shall apply to transactions consummated on or after the effective date of the regulations specified in section 209.

[¶55,042] Section 218. Report by the GAO

This section directs the Government Accountability Office to conduct a study to determine the effects of the bill on the availability and affordability of credit for homebuyers and mortgage lending, and submit a report to Congress within one year of enactment. The report will also include an analysis of the effect on the capital reserves and funding of lenders of credit risk retention provisions for non-qualified mortgages.

[¶55,043] Section 219. State Attorney General enforcement authority

This section extends the current authority of State attorneys general to enforce HOEPA violations to authorize State attorneys general to enforce violations of section 129B and 129C of TILA (the sections creating the new standards under this Act) and section 219 of this Act.

[¶55,044] Section 220. Tenant protections

This section allows bona fide tenants to remain in their residence, pursuant to their lease, following a foreclosure on the property except when the successor in interest or subsequent purchaser will occupy the unit as a primary residence. If the lease is to be terminated for subsequent occupancy by the successor in interest or purchaser, the tenant must receive notice to vacate at least 90 days before the effective date of such notice. A lease or tenancy is bona fide if it is the result of arms-length transaction and if the rent is not substantially less than fair market rent or is reduced or subsidized due to a Federal, state, or local subsidy.

The section also provides similar protections for section 8 tenants. In addition, for section 8 tenancies, during the initial term of the lease, the foreclosure cannot constitute good cause for termination of the lease. In subsequent lease terms, the lease may be terminated for good cause if the successor in interest or subsequent purchaser will occupy the unit as a primary residence or if the unit is unmarketable while occupied. If the lease is to be terminated, the tenant must receive notice to vacate at least 90 days before the effective date of such notice.

Also, the immediate successor in interest shall assume such interest subject to the lease between the prior owner and the housing assistance payment contract between the prior owner and the public housing agency for the occupied unit. If a public housing agency is unable to make payments under the contract to the immediate successor in interest after foreclosure, due to action or inaction by the successor in interest, including rejection of payments or failure to maintain the unit, then after reasonable steps to notify the owner, the agency may use the funds that would have been used to pay rent to pay for utilities that perhaps: were the responsibility of the owner or for the family's reasonable moving costs.

TITLE III—HIGH-COST MORTGAGES

[¶ 55,045] Section 301. Definitions relating to high-cost mortgages

This section expands the scope of the Home Ownership and Equity Protection Act (HOEPA) by revising the high-cost mortgage definition in 15 USC 1602(aa) in several respects. The new definition would cover purchase money loans, construction loans, and open-end loans, all of which specifically are excluded by the existing definition, that meet certain definitional triggers.

The new definition also would change the existing triggers for determining whether a loan is a high-cost mortgage. HOEPA currently has two triggers—one based on the amount by which the APR exceeds a benchmark rate, and another based on the level of the total points and fees payable in connection with the loan transaction. This section changes the benchmark against which to determine the APR trigger from the yield on Treasury securities to the "average prime offer rate," which is determined, and updated at least weekly, by the Federal Reserve. This section also lowers the number of percentage points by which the APR at consummation must exceed the benchmark in order to be a high-cost mortgage, includes separate APR triggers for first lien and subordinate lien loans, and specifies how to determine the APR for variable rate loans. This section also lowers the points-and-fees trigger from 8 percent to 5 percent of the total transaction amount (or, for mortgages less than $20,000, the lesser of 8 percent of the total transaction or $1,000). This section adds a third trigger by providing that a mortgage is a high-cost mortgage if the creditor may charge or collect prepayment penalties more than 36 months after the transaction closing or may charge prepayments penalties that exceed, in the aggregate, 2 percent of the amount prepaid.

This section revises the definition of points and fees to include all compensation paid directly or indirectly by a consumer or creditor to a mortgage originator from any source (including a mortgage originator that originates a loan in the name of the creditor in a table-funded transaction), certain insurance premiums, prepayment penalty charges under the loan, and prepayment penalties actually charged in a refinance by the original creditor or the original creditor's affiliate.

Finally, this section excludes certain bona fide discount points (up to two points for near-market interest rate loans) from the determination of the amount of points and fees that trigger HOEPA protections.

[¶ 55,046] Section 302. Amendments to existing requirements for certain mortgages

Section 206 bans prepayment penalties for any mortgage that is not a Qualified Mortgage. Because all high-cost mortgages subject to HOEPA (HOEPA loans) will, by definition, not be Qualified Mortgages, this section conforms HOEPA to section 206 by banning prepayment penalties on HOEPA loans. This section also revises the balloon payment prohibition in HOEPA to provide that no high-cost mortgage may contain a scheduled payment that is more than twice as large as the average of earlier scheduled payments, unless the payment schedule is adjusted to the seasonal or irregular income of the consumer.

[¶ 55,047] Section 303. Additional Requirements for Certain Mortgages

This section prohibits creditors from encouraging that borrowers default on an existing loan or other debt in connection with the planned refinancing of all or any portion of such existing loan or debt with a high-cost mortgage. This section also places amount, timing, frequency, and other restrictions on late fees for high-cost mortgages, including by prohibiting a creditor from charging more than one fee on the same delinquent payment and by capping a late fee at 4 percent of the amount of the past-due payment. This section also prohibits a creditor from unilaterally accelerating a high-cost mortgage, except in cases of default, pursuant to a due-on-sale provision, or pursuant to material violation of provisions of the loan document not related to the payment schedule. Finally, this section prohibits a creditor from directly or indirectly financing points and fees for high-cost mortgages if the creditor or its affiliate is the noteholder of the note being refinanced.

This section prohibits a creditor from structuring a mortgage transaction to evade the HOEPA protections that apply to high-cost mortgages, such as by structuring the loan in another form or dividing the loan transaction into separate parts with intent to evade HOEPA.

This section prohibits a creditor from charging a consumer any fee to modify, renew, extend, or amend a high-cost mortgage, or to defer any payment due under the mortgage terms, unless such adjustment results in a lower APR on the mortgage and the fee amount is comparable to fees imposed for similar transactions.

This section generally prohibits a creditor or servicer from charging a fee to any person for informing or transmitting to them the payoff amount for a high-cost mortgage and requires that payoff balance information be provided within 5 business days of the consumer's request. This section includes limited exceptions that allow the creditor to charge service fees for providing a payoff statement by facsimile or courier service (provided that the creditor meets specified requirements) or for providing payoff statements to the same consumer more than 4 times during a calendar year.

This section prohibits flipping, which is defined as making a high-cost mortgage that refinances an existing mortgage when the new, high-cost mortgage does not have a net tangible benefit, as defined in rules promulgated under Title II, to the consumer consider all the circumstances.

Finally, this section permits a creditor or assignee, prior to the institution of any legal action, (1) to correct violations and non-bona fide errors within 30 days of the loan closing and (2) to correct bona fide errors within 60 days of the creditor's discovery or receipt of notification of the error. To avoid liability, a creditor must make appropriate restitution and make whatever adjustments are necessary to either, at the choice of the consumer, make the loan satisfy the applicable requirements of TILA (including requirements of the Act), or, for a high-cost mortgage, change the terms of the loan so that the loan will no longer be a high-cost mortgage.

[¶55,048] **Section 304. Regulations**

This Federal Reserve Board must publish final regulations to implement this title by the effective date of the Act may prescribe regulations encouraging or requiring creditors to provide consumer mortgage education to prospective customers or direct such customers to qualified consumer mortgage education or counseling program.

[¶55,049] **Section 305. Effective date**

The amendments made by this title will take effect at the end of the 6-month period beginning on the date of enactment and will apply to HOEPA loans for which an application is received by a creditor after the end of such period.

TITLE IV—OFFICE OF HOUSING COUNSELING

[¶55,055] **Section 401. Short title**

This section provides that this title may be cited as the 'Expand and Preserve Home Ownership Through Counseling Act.'

[¶55,056] **Section 402. Establishment of Office of Housing Counseling**

This section establishes the Office of Housing Counseling, headed by a Director of Housing Counseling (Director) appointed by the Secretary. The Director will be responsible for all homeownership and rental housing counseling programs for HUD, and will establish, coordinate and administer all regulations, requirements, standards, and performance measures under the programs that relate to housing counseling, homeownership counseling, mortgage-related counseling, and rental housing counseling. The Director shall establish rules for (1) counseling procedures, (2) carrying out all other related functions, including establishing a toll-free number, (3) information booklets, (4) carrying out the certification of counseling service providers, (5) providing assistance in the provision of counseling services, (6) carrying out functions the Secretary deems appropriate with regard to unscrupulous lending practices in the home mortgage business, (7) support the advisory committee created under this act, (8) collaborate with community-based organizations, and (9) provide for building capacity to provide housing counseling services in areas that lack sufficient services. The Secretary shall appoint an advisory committee composed of no more than 12 individuals representing the mortgage and real estate industry, including consumers and housing counseling agencies. Advisory committee members appointed by the Secretary will serve 3-year terms, except that initially, four will be appointed for 1-year terms and four will be appointed for 2-year terms. The Secretary may reappoint members at his discretion. Members will not be paid, but may receive travel expenses. The advisory committee has no role in reviewing or awarding housing counseling grants. Counseling services will cover the entire process of homeownership, including refinancing and foreclosure.

This section directs the Secretary to establish, coordinate, and monitor all HUD counseling procedures, including requirements, standards, and performance measures that relate to homeownership and rental housing. 'Homeownership counseling' is defined as counseling related to homeownership and residential mortgage loans. 'Rental housing counseling' is defined as counseling related to rental of residential property, which may include counseling regarding future homeownership opportunities and providing referral for renters and prospective renters to entities providing counseling. The Secretary shall establish standards for materials and forms used by counseling service providers, and provide for the certification of various computer software programs for consumers to use in evaluating different residential mortgage loan proposals. The mortgage software system shall take into account (1) the consumer's financial situation and the cost of maintaining a home, including insurance, taxes, and utilities, (2) the amount of time the consumer expects to remain in the home or expected time to maturity of the loan, and (3) any other factors to assist the consumer in making choices during the loan application process. The certified software programs shall be used to supplement, not replace, housing counseling, and the software programs initially will be used only in connection with the assistance of certified housing counselors. Additionally, the certification program for mortgage software systems will be implemented only to the extent that funds are made available in advance in appropriations Acts. The Secretary shall develop, implement, and conduct national public service multimedia campaigns to make potentially vulnerable consumers aware of the existence of homeownership counseling. 10 percent of the multimedia campaign funds shall be used to distribute literature on ways to avoid foreclosure rescue scams, predatory lending agreements, for-profit foreclosure counseling services, and to provide a list of local HUD-approved counseling resources. Appropriations not to exceed $3 million are authorized for national public service multimedia campaigns for fiscal years 2009, 2010, and 2011. The Secretary shall provide advice and technical assistance to States, units of local government, and non-profit organizations regarding provisions of counseling services.

[¶55,057] Section 404. Grants for housing counseling assistance

This section directs the Secretary to make financial assistance available for homeownership or rental counseling to HUD-approved counseling agencies and State housing finance agencies. The Secretary shall establish standards and guidelines for assistance eligibility. Appropriations of $45 million are authorized for each of fiscal years 2009 through 2012 for the operations of the Office of Housing Counseling; homeownership and rental counseling assistance grants; and the establishment of materials and forms standards, computer software certification, and the national public service multimedia campaigns created in section 403 of the Act. This amount is meant to be in addition to the amounts currently authorized and appropriated for housing counseling activities. In making funds available, the Secretary will consider ways to streamline and improve the process for grant application, review, approval, and award. No funds under this section may be distributed to any organization which has been or which employs an individual who has been indicted for a violation under Federal law relating to an election for Federal office.

[¶55,058] Section 405. Requirements to use HUD-certified counselors under HUD programs

This section requires any homeownership counseling or rental housing counseling administered by HUD to be provided solely by organizations or counselors certified by the Secretary.

[¶55,059] **Section 406. Study of defaults and foreclosures**

This section directs the Secretary to submit to Congress not later than 12 months after the enactment of the Act a preliminary report on the root causes of default and foreclosure of home loans and the role of escrow accounts in helping prime and nonprime borrowers to avoid defaults and foreclosures. No later than 24 months after the enactment of the Act, the Secretary will submit a final report regarding the results of the study, which will include any recommended legislation relating to the study and recommendations for best practices and for a process to identify populations that need counseling the most.

[¶55,060] **Section 407. Definitions for counseling-related programs**

This section provides definitions of "nonprofit organization," "State," "unit of general local government," "HUD-approved counseling agency," and "State housing finance agency."

[¶55,061] **Section 408. Updating and simplification of mortgage information booklet**

This section directs the Secretary to prepare a booklet at least once every 5 years to help consumers applying for federally related mortgage loans to understand the nature and costs of real estate settlement services. The Secretary must include specific topics in the information booklet in plain and understandable language, including explanation of (1) costs incident to real estate settlement or Federally related mortgage loan (including at a minimum balloon payments, prepayment penalties, and trade-off between closing costs and the interest rate over the life of the loan); (2) the uniform settlement statement; (3) unfair lending practices and unreasonable or unnecessary charges to be avoided by the prospective buyer with respect to a real estate settlement; (4) questions that the consumer should ask about a loan; (5) the right of rescission; (6) variable rate mortgages; (7) home equity line of credit; (8) the availability and the value of homeownership counseling services; (9) escrow accounts; (10) available choices for providers of incidental services; (11) the buyer's responsibilities, liabilities, and obligations; (12) appraisals; and (13) HUD brochure regarding loan fraud.

[¶55,062] **Section 409. Home inspection counseling.**

This section requires HUD to publish outreach materials in both English and Spanish entitled "For Your Protection: Get a Home Inspection" and "Ten Important Questions To Ask Your Home Inspector". HUD must make these materials available for electronic access and through toll free telephone hotlines and public service announcements, and include the materials as part of any home purchase counseling.

HUD is required to make special efforts to reach first-time and low-income homebuyers, to require FHA approved mortgagees to provide these materials to prospective homebuyers at first contact, and to require HUD-approved housing counseling agencies to provide this information to clients as part of the home purchase counseling process.

HUD training of HUD-approved housing counseling agencies must include information about the home inspection process, including the reasons for specific inspections such as radon and lead based paint testing.

TITLE V—MORTGAGE SERVICING

[¶55,065] **Section 501. Escrow and impound accounts relating to certain consumer credit transactions**

This section establishes a new section in the Truth in Lending Act (TILA) to require that specified first-lien mortgages have an escrow account established at the time of consummation of the transaction to cover taxes and hazard insurance, and, if applicable, mortgage insurance, ground rents, and any other required periodic payments or premiums with respect to the property or loan terms.

The instances in which an escrow account must be established include (1) when required by Federal or State law; (2) when a loan is made, guaranteed, or insured by a State or Federal lending or insuring agency; (3) when the rate on the first lien on the consumer's principal dwelling, as of the date the interest rate is set, exceeds the average prime offer rate for a comparable transaction by 1.5 percentage points; or (4) when required pursuant to regulation.

Escrow accounts established pursuant to this section, unless the underlying mortgage is terminated, must remain in existence for a minimum of 5 years and until the borrower has enough equity to no longer meet the requirements of maintaining private mortgage insurance, or such other period provided in regulations to address situations such as a borrower's delinquency. These standards exceed the 12-month period provided for in the Federal Reserve Board's 2008 rulemaking under the Home Ownership and Equity Protection Act (HOEPA).

Consistent with the HOEPA rulemaking, a limited exemption of the escrow account requirement is provided for loans secured by shares in a cooperative and for certain condominium units. For mortgages not meeting the specified tests established under the law, clarifications are further provided that nothing precludes the establishment of an escrow account on terms mutually agreeable to the parties to the loan, at the discretion of the servicer or lender pursuant to the contract, or pursuant to the Flood Disaster Protection Act (FDPA).

Servicers must administer such accounts in accordance with the Real Estate Settlement Procedures Act (RESPA), FDPA, and, if applicable, the law of the State where the real property securing the transaction is located, including making interest payments on the escrow account if required under such laws. The account must also be maintained in a federally insured depository institution, and the amounts escrowed must reflect the actual property value (land and improvements thereto). Clarification is also provided that any violation of RESPA for a mandated escrow established under TILA does not also result in additional penalties under TILA unless the action or omission also constitutes a direct violation of TILA.

Consumers with mortgages covered by this section must also receive specific written disclosures about the establishment of an escrow account at least 3 business days before loan consummation or in accordance with timeframes established in prescribed regulations.

The Federal banking regulators and the Federal Trade Commission (FTC) have 180 days to adopt final regulations to implement the section. These regulations become effective and apply to all covered mortgages beginning one year after the publication of final rules.

[¶55,066] Section 502. Disclosure notice required for consumers who opt out of escrow services

This section amends the new section of TILA established by section 501 to require all consumers, regardless of whether they must have an escrow account established at the time the loan is consummated, to receive specified written disclosures advising them of the responsibilities of the consumer and implications for the consumer in the absence of any such account. The Federal banking regulators and the FTC have 180 days to adopt final regulations to implement these new disclosure requirements. These regulations become effective 180 days after the publication of final rules.

[¶55,067] Section 503. Real Estate Settlement Procedures Act of 1974 amendments

This section updates section 6 of RESPA and establishes new consumer protections related to servicer prohibitions, the administration of force-placed insurance, increased penalty amounts, servicer response times, and escrow account refunds.

Servicer prohibitions

The section prohibits mortgage servicers from obtaining force-placed hazard insurance unless they have a reasonable basis to believe that the borrower has failed to comply with the requirement to maintain property insurance. It also bars servicers from charging fees for responding to valid qualified written requests placed by the borrower, with regulations promulgated to determine the interpretation of what constitutes a valid qualified written request. The section further prohibits mortgage servicers from failing to take timely action to respond to a borrower's requests to correct errors relating to the allocation of payments, obtain final balances for purposes of paying off the loan, or avoid foreclosure.

The section additionally requires a servicer to respond within 10 business days to a request from a borrower to provide the identity of and contact information for the owner/assignee of the loan. Finally, the section requires servicers to comply with any other obligation to protect consumers established by the Secretary of the Department of Housing and Urban Development (HUD) via rulemaking.

Force-placed insurance

The section further establishes a definition for force-placed insurance.

The procedures for the forced placement of hazard insurance require the servicer initially to send, by first-class mail, a written notice with certain disclosures about the need to obtain hazard insurance. After at least 30 days, the servicer must send a second notice by first-class mail containing the same disclosures. The servicer may then force place insurance if it has not received demonstration from the borrower in writing of any insurance coverage 15 days after sending the second notice. The borrower's response must include the existing insurance policy number along with the identity of and contact information for the insurance company or agent.

The section requires the servicer to terminate force-placed insurance within 15 days of the receipt of confirmation of a borrower's existing hazard insurance coverage. The section also requires lenders to refund amounts to the consumer for force-placed insurance that overlap in time with the hazard insurance obtained directly by the homeowner. It additionally allows for the concurrent administration of notices required by FDPA for the forced placement of flood insurance.

The section additionally requires that all charges for force-placed insurance to be bona fide and reasonable in amount.

Increase in penalties

The section doubles the maximum statutory RESPA penalties in individual cases from $1,000 to $2,000, and in class action cases from $500,000 to $1,000,000. The changes apply to all RESPA violations.

Response times

The section mandates decreases in response times to qualified written requests made pursuant to RESPA. Specifically, these changes require a servicer to acknowledge receipt of a qualified written request within 5 days (down from 20 days) and complete action on the inquiry within 30 days (down from 60 days) except that this 30-day period may be extended for not more than 15 days if the servicer notifies the borrower of the extension within the initial 30-day period and details the reasons for the delay in responding.

Prompt refund of escrow accounts

The section finally requires the prompt refund of escrow accounts that are within the servicer's control within 20 business days of a loan's payoff. Alternatively, borrowers may roll over existing escrowed amounts for a similar account established by a new mortgage with the same lender.

[¶55,068] Section 504. Truth in Lending Act amendments

This section amends TILA to require the prompt crediting of mortgage payments and the timely provision to consumers of mortgage payoff amounts.

Requirements for prompt crediting of home loan payments

Consistent with the final HOEPA regulations adopted by the Federal Reserve Board in 2008, the section amends TILA to require servicers to credit payments made in connection with a credit transaction secured by a consumer's principal dwelling as of the date of receipt, except when a delay in crediting does not result in any charge to the consumer or in the reporting of negative information to a consumer reporting agency. For consumers who do not follow specified written requirements when making payments, an exception is provided to require the servicer to credit the payment as of 5 days after receipt.

Requests for payoff amounts

The section amends TILA to require a creditor or servicer of a home loan to send an accurate payoff balance within a reasonable time, but in no case more than 7 business days after the receipt of a written request for such balance from or on behalf of the borrower.

[¶55,069] Section 505. Escrows required in repayment analysis

The section amends TILA to require the inclusion of escrow payments for taxes and insurance in any monthly repayment analysis provided to consumers. The change will allow all consumers to make apples-to-apples comparisons in the mortgage quotes they receive and improve consumer understanding of the total costs of homeownership.

TITLE VI—APPRAISAL ACTIVITIES

[¶55,075] Section 601. Property appraisal requirements

This section modifies TILA to require lenders to obtain a written appraisal, resulting from an interior assessment of a physical property visit made by a qualified appraiser, of the covered property before extending credit in the form of a subprime mortgage. If the purpose of the covered mortgage is to finance the purchase or acquisition of the mortgaged property within 180 days of the purchase or acquisition of such property at a price that was lower than the current sale price of the property, this section also directs lenders to obtain a second appraisal at no cost to the applicant.

Also, this section entitles covered applicants to 1 free copy of each such appraisal provided at least 3 days prior to the transaction closing date and requires certain notifications about the limits of appraisals. Creditors found to have willfully failed to obtain an appraisal for a subprime mortgage are liable to the applicant or borrower for the sum of $2,000. The section defines a subprime mortgage consistent with metrics established by the Federal Reserve Board in its 2008 HOEPA rulemaking for first- and subordinate-liens on a residential mortgage loan.

[¶55,076] Section 602. Unfair and deceptive practices and acts relating to certain consumer transactions

The section creates a Federal unfair and deceptive practices standard for appraisals within TILA, with rules written and interpretative guidelines issued by the Federal banking regulators and the FTC. Specifically, this section prohibits the compensation, coercion, extortion, collusion, instruction, inducement, bribing, or intimidation or attempting any of the aforementioned activities for the purpose of causing the appraised value assigned to the property to be based on any fact other than the independent judgment of the appraiser.

This section further prohibits the mischaracterization of an appraised value, efforts to influence an appraiser to hit a targeted value, and withholding timely payment for an appraisal report. The bar against such withholding, however, is not intended to apply when an appraiser has breached the terms of a contract in the performance of duties. Exceptions are provided to permit valid communications about the property itself, to correct errors, and to obtain further detail about the appraiser's value conclusion.

The section additionally creates a statutory requirement that certified and licensed appraisers and appraisal management companies (AMCs) have no direct or indirect interest, financial or otherwise, in either the property or in the transaction involving the appraisal. The interest-in-property prohibition shall apply equally to both fee-for-service and staff appraisers. The interest-in-the-transaction bar, however, should not be construed as to prohibit work by staff appraisers within a financial institution or other organization, if such an entity has established firewalls, consistent with those outlined in the Home Valuation Code of Conduct, between the origination group and the appraisal unit designed to ensure the independence of appraisal results and reviews.

Moreover, the section establishes a requirement for those parties who have a reasonable basis to believe an appraiser is violating applicable laws or otherwise engaging in unethical or unprofessional conduct to report such matters to the applicable State appraisal agency. In addition, the section prohibits a creditor from extending credit in connection with a consumer credit transaction secured by a consumer's principal dwelling if the creditor knows of a violation of appraisal independence standards, unless the creditor documents that the creditor has acted with reasonable diligence to determine that the appraisal does not materially misstate or misrepresent the value of such dwelling.

This section establishes sanctions in addition to those already provided under TILA. These penalties are up to $10,000 for first violations and $20,000 for subsequent violations.

[¶55,077] Section 603. Amendments relating to Appraisal Subcommittee of the Financial Institutions Examination Council, appraiser independence, and approved appraiser education

This section generally supplements, strengthens, and modifies the existing appraisal requirements contained in Title XI of the Financial Institutions Reform, Recovery, and Enforcement Act of 1989 (FIRREA)

Appraisal Subcommittee reforms

Subsection (a) adds consumer protection to the mission and functions of the Appraisal Subcommittee (ASC). The section also requires the ASC to monitor the efforts of States and Federal banking regulators to protect consumers from improper appraisal practices and the predations of unlicensed appraisers in mortgage transactions. In order to reconcile this new consumer protection mandate with the existing safety-and-soundness mission of the ASC, the section amends the criteria and procedures by which Federal banking regulators establish the threshold below which a written appraisal by a certified or licensed appraiser is not required.

The Federal Reports Elimination and Sunset Act of 1995 (P.L. 104-66) effectively ended the ASC's annual reporting requirement as of May 15, 2000, although the ASC has continued in since then to produce such a document for Congress. Subsection (b) definitively reinstates the requirement that the ASC submit an annual report to Congress. This subsection additionally requires the ASC in its annual report to describe in greater detail its activities and the work of State appraisal agencies. The subsection further requires the ASC to provide information about the results of all audits of State appraisal agencies and details about disapprovals and warnings issued to State appraisal agencies.

Subsection (c) codifies the decision of the ASC to open its meetings to the general public.

Subsection (d) authorizes the panel to issue binding rules and regulations after public notice and opportunity for comment in several new areas: temporary practice, national registry, information sharing, and enforcement. The term "enforcement" covers the actions the ASC may take in evaluating State appraisal agencies and the gamut of sanctions that the ASC may impose against such agencies.

Subsection (e) statutorily defines what constitutes a complex transaction requiring the use of a certified appraiser in lieu of a licensed appraiser, consistent with Uniform Standards of Professional Appraisal Practice. The subsection also requires all appraisals performed at a property within a State to be prepared by appraisers licensed or certified in the State where the property is located. The subsection additionally requires all appraisal reviews by a lender, AMC, or other third-party organization to be performed by an appraiser who is duly licensed or certified by a State appraisal board.

Subsection (g) requires State appraisal agencies to transmit reports on sanctions, disciplinary actions, revocations, and suspensions to the ASC on a timely basis. These reports apply to both individuals and AMCs.

To account for inflation since the enactment of FIRREA in 1989, subsection (h) updates registry fee amounts annually paid by licensed and certified appraisers to support the activities of the ASC. The subsection additionally establishes a program for collecting fees from AMCs to support the additional work of the ASC. The subsection further requires the ASC to consider at least once every 5 years whether to adjust the dollar amounts for inflation and provides administrative flexibility to allow for the implementation of such adjustments in fee amounts. The incremental revenues raised by the fee increases are placed in the Appraisal Subcommittee Account within the U.S. Treasury.

Subsection (i) allows the ASC to use the amounts placed in the Appraisal Subcommittee Account to make grants to State appraisal agencies to help defray costs related to the complaint process, complaint investigations, and appraiser enforcement activities. The ASC may also use this funding to provide grants to States for the submission of data. It also requires the national registry to report to State appraisal agencies when a license or certification is surrendered, revoked, or suspended.

Subsection (k) improves the ability of the ASC to oversee State appraisal agencies in a number of ways. First, it adds funding and staffing to the list of criteria against which the ASC must evaluate a State appraisal agency. It also requires the ASC to evaluate whether a State appraisal agency processes complaints and completes its examinations in a reasonable time period, whether a state appropriately disciplines sanctioned appraisers and AMCs, whether a state maintains an effective regulatory program, and whether a State appraisal agency reports claims and disciplinary actions to the national registry on a timely basis. The subsection further permits the ASC to impose interim sanctions and suspensions.

Subsection (n) requires the ASC to monitor each State appraisal agency for the purpose of determining whether such agency's policies, practices, and procedures are consistent with the purpose of maintaining appraiser independence and whether such State has adopted and maintains effective laws, regulations, and policies aimed at maintaining appraiser independence.

Finally, Subsection (s) expands the membership of the ASC to include the Federal Housing Finance Agency. The subsection also requires that at all times at least one member of the Appraisal Subcommittee shall be a certified or licensed appraiser.

Appraisal management company registration and supervision

In response to the growth of and concerns about AMCs, subsection (f) creates a State-by-State system for registering and supervising AMCs, with oversight of the States conducted by the ASC, and it generally requires the system to be in place within 3 years of enactment. The subsection provides for the establishment of minimum standards to be applied in the registration of AMCs. The subsection also ensures that those who complete appraisal fraud or those who lose their appraisal licenses or certifications cannot turn around and establish an AMC. The amendment additionally puts in place a parallel Federal system of oversight for an AMC that operates as a subsidiary of a financial institution overseen by a Federal banking regulator. The section also incorporates a definition for appraisal management company.

Appraiser education and licensing

Subsections (j), (l), (m) and (o) generally make a variety of changes to appraiser licensing and educational standards. Subsection (j) expands the ability of the ASC to set minimum licensing standards for appraisers in addition to its existing authority to establish minimum certification standards. The subsection also permits the establishment of minimum requirements for trainee appraisers and supervisory appraisers.

Subsection (l) provides for reciprocity in State appraiser licenses and certifications. To promote greater professionalism and advanced training within the appraisal industry, subsection (m) codifies language now found in the selling guides for government-sponsored enterprises to allow for special consideration of appraisers who have obtained special designations or training from professional appraisal organizations. Finally, subsection (o) requires the ASC to encourage State appraisal agencies to accept courses and seminars approved by the Appraiser Qualification Board's Course Approval Program for educational training requirements.

Appraisal complaint national hotline

If no national hotline exists to receive complaints about non-compliance with appraisal independence standards within one year of enactment, subsection (p) requires the ASC to put in place a national hotline, which shall consist of a toll-free phone number and an e-mail address. The ASC must refer complaints received by the national hotline to the appropriate State or Federal regulator, or other appropriate legal authorities. In order to determine the status of the resolution of the complaint, the subsection also provides the ASC with the authority to follow up on referrals made to State appraisal agencies and Federal banking regulators.

The Committee intends that the ASC will not need to establish a national hotline if the national hotline provided for in the Home Valuation Code of Conduct becomes operative within the 1 year after enactment timeframe established under the Act. If, however, such a national hotline ceases to exist, then the ASC will establish and maintain a national hotline at that point in time.

Automated valuation model quality control standards

To enhance confidence in the results produced by automated valuation models used to develop estimates of home values, subsection (q) establishes minimum standards and requires the development and enforcement of rules by Federal banking regulators and the Appraisal Subcommittee.

Broker price opinion limitations

To address concerns about the quality of home value estimates developed by real estate brokers that are used for collateral purposes, subsection (r) codifies a policy recently adopted by Freddie Mac to prohibit the use of broker price opinions as a sole method for determining the value of a purchase mortgage loan.

Technical corrections

Subsection (t) makes several technical corrections to title XI of FIRREA to fix drafting errors.

[¶55,078] ***Section 604. Study required on improvements in appraisal process and compliance programs***

This section requires the Comptroller General to conduct a comprehensive study within 18 months of enactment of this Act on possible improvements in the appraisal process generally, and on the consistency in, the effectiveness of, and possible improvements to State compliance efforts and programs in accordance with FIRREA specifically. The study by the Government Accountability Office will also examine current exemptions to the use of certified appraisers issued by the Federal banking regulators and, in light of the new consumer protection mission of the ASC, explore the existing threshold levels below which Federal banking regulators do not require a written appraisal.

The section also requires a review of the quality of appraisals produced through different mechanisms and different distribution channels. It additionally mandates an analysis and statistical breakdown of the enforcement actions taken during the last decade against different types of appraisers. Finally, the study must examine the need to create a national repository to collect data related to real estate property collateral valuations performed in the United States.

[¶55,079] Section 605. Equal Credit Opportunity Act amendment

This section amends the Equal Credit Opportunity Act to provide mortgage applicants with access to a written appraisal report no later than 3 days before closing. This set of changes is generally consistent with the requirements of the Home Valuation Code of Conduct. The section also requires creditors to provide applicants with access to any other valuation report developed in conjunction with a mortgage transaction.

[¶55,080] Section 606. Real Estate Settlement Procedures Act of 1974 amendment relating to certain appraisal fees

This section modifies RESPA to require the disclosure to consumers of the fees paid to licensed and certified appraisers, as well the fees paid to AMCs. These disclosures will help interested parties, including Federal and State regulators and other appropriate authorities, to make better determinations about the quality of appraisals facilitated by an AMC.

TITLE VII—SENSE OF CONGRESS REGARDING THE IMPORTANCE OF GOVERNMENT SPONSORED ENTERPRISES REFORM

[¶55,085] Section 701. Sense of Congress regarding the importance of Government-sponsored enterprises reform to enhance the protection, limitation and regulation of the terms of residential mortgage credit

This section provides findings and a sense of Congress that efforts to enhance by the protection, limitation, and regulation of the terms of residential mortgage credit and the practices related to such credit would be incomplete without enactment of meaningful structural reforms of Fannie Mae and Freddie Mac.

CHANGES IN EXISTING LAW MADE BY THE BILL, AS REPORTED

* * *

[¶55,096] DISSENTING VIEWS

Economists agree that the roots of the current problems in the mortgage market can be traced to earlier this decade, when falling interest rates encouraged lenders to significantly relax—and in some cases abandon—sound underwriting criteria when qualifying borrowers for mortgages. Lenders pushed the envelope as they raised loan-to-value ratios to grow near term profits. As a result, borrowers who at one time might have been denied credit or granted limited credit found themselves able to borrow larger sums, and they took advantage of this opportunity to buy larger, more expensive houses than they otherwise would have been able to afford.

As a consequence of low interest rates and weak underwriting standards, home ownership rates rose from the 64 percent range in the 35 years prior to 1995 to an all-time high of 69 percent in 2004. The growing demand for houses caused home prices to skyrocket: according to the National Association of Realtors, the national median home price went from $110,500 in 1995 to $190,000 ten years later. Economists have pointed out that compared to other economic fundamentals, such as rental prices or incomes, these soaring housing prices were simply unsustainable.

Despite the higher risk associated with mortgages to borrowers with checkered credit histories, the opportunities to earn higher rates of return from subprime mortgages induced many lenders to further loosen their underwriting standards during the period 2005 to 2007, introducing even more risk into the system. Instead of protecting themselves against this increased risk by requiring borrowers to make higher down payments, lenders engineered new loans that permitted borrowers to buy with little or no money down, and compensated for this increased risk by charging these borrowers higher interest rates and fees. Lenders further eroded the integrity of the underwriting process by permitting borrowers to sign up for so-called "low documentation" or "no documentation" loans, which became known in the mortgage industry as "liar loans," so named because they

¶55,079

often featured loan applications characterized by misstated or falsified income.

As long as housing prices continued to rise, the risks inherent in such shoddy underwriting practices remained hidden. Borrowers who had stretched to purchase homes that they otherwise could not afford either refinanced their mortgages against home price appreciation or sold to other buyers and paid off their mortgages. Investors in securities collateralized by subprime residential mortgages believed their risk was limited: even if risky borrowers defaulted, home price appreciation all but guaranteed that the houses that secured the underlying mortgages could either be resold to other buyers through voluntary sales or, if necessary, foreclosed upon and resold at auction with only minimal impairment of the collateral securing the loan.

H.R. 1728, the "Mortgage Reform and Anti-Predatory Lending Act," attempts to correct past excesses in the mortgage market by establishing new standards for mortgage origination and imposing greater legal liability on the secondary mortgage market. This is not the first time the Committee has considered comprehensive mortgage reform legislation. In the 110th Congress, H.R. 3915 was reported favorably out of the Committee and passed the House by a vote of 291-127, although no action was taken in the Senate. Included in Title I of H.R. 3915 was the S.A.F.E. Act, which created a national licensing and registration regime for all mortgage loan originators. The S.A.F.E. Act later became law as part of the Housing and Economic Recovery Act of 2008 (Public Law 110-289), and has, according to testimony by state regulators at the Committee's legislative hearing on H.R. 1728, already begun to yield significant benefits in combating mortgage fraud and weeding bad actors out of the industry. Many Republicans supported H.R. 3915 on the ground that it struck the right balance by protecting consumers from unscrupulous originators without constricting the ability of the secondary market to fund suitable loan products for credit-worthy borrowers or increasing the cost of mortgage credit.

Unfortunately, while it carries over many of the useful reforms contained in H.R. 3915, H.R. 1728 strikes a far different balance than that earlier legislation, one that will undermine the mortgage market just as Americans are starting to see preliminary signs of a possible housing bottom. H.R. 1728 lacks the clarity needed to provide meaningful protection to consumers. Rather than focusing on basic underwriting standards, as the Federal Reserve has done in promulgating comprehensive regulations to combat abusive lending practices under the Home Ownership and Equity Protection Act (HOEPA), H.R. 1728 imposes new and untested mandates and duties that regulators and industry participants do not know how to implement, if they can be implemented at all, and that may end up punishing the very consumers the Majority wants to protect.

The Fed's HOEPA rules, which are set to go into effect in October 2009, will bring an end to the shoddy underwriting standards that plagued the subprime market. Indeed, Chairman Frank has previously acknowledged that "the Federal Reserve . . . has adopted regulations . . . so that the predatory and deceptive lending practices that led to the subprime crisis will be prohibited." But rather than allow the Fed's carefully vetted regulations to take effect, the Majority has chosen to superimpose onto those rules its own set of policy prescriptions, which seem likely only to inject legal uncertainty into the lending process, thereby raising the costs and reducing the availability of mortgage credit to consumers.

At the only legislative hearing that the Majority convened to consider H.R. 1728's complex and far-reaching provisions, representatives of the Federal Reserve, consumer advocacy groups, and affected industries expressed a number of concerns about various aspects of this bill. The director of the Federal Reserve's consumer affairs division, Sandra Braunstein, testified that the bill seemed "intended to drive the market into 30-year fixed loans," which "could have the consequence of very much limiting the kinds of products that become available when the markets reset." Even after the Committee adopted an amendment to expand the scope of the safe harbor and include certain prime ARMs within its coverage, the bill is still constructed in a way to expose to legal liability many safe and sustainable mortgage products, which will result in most lenders simply choosing not to offer those products. Interestingly, some of the most pointed criticism of H.R. 1728 came from consumer groups. Margot Saunders of the National Consumer Law Center, testifying on behalf of a coalition of consumer advocacy and labor organizations from across the country, called the bill "convoluted" and "virtually impossible as a mechanism to solve the current problem."

One of the changes to last Congress' legislation that has drawn the most concern is a new "credit risk retention" requirement that would force loan originators to hold 5 percent of any mortgage that does not fit the bill's narrow safe harbor. While there was general consensus at the legislative hearing on H.R. 1728 that requiring

¶55,096

lenders to retain more "skin in the game" was a worthy concept, there was general confusion as to how the execution of that concept in the bill language would work in practice, particularly for smaller non-bank lenders that do not enjoy the same reliable sources of funding as depository institutions. The Majority attempted to address those concerns through an amendment offered at the mark-up giving the Federal banking regulators greater discretion in writing rules to implement the "credit risk retention" requirement, but serious questions remain as to whether the requirement is either workable or necessary in light of the bill's other reforms imposing more stringent mortgage underwriting criteria.

Like H.R. 3915, H.R. 1728 contains provisions imposing liability on assignees and securitizers for loans that violate the "ability to repay" and "net tangible benefit" standards, giving consumers a cause of action for rescission of the loan and costs, unless the assignee or securitizer provides a cure to make the loan conform to the minimum standards within 90 days of receiving notice from the consumer. These liability provisions are considerably more stringent than H.R. 3915's, and eliminate one of the protections that H.R. 3915 offered to assignees: under H.R. 3915, assignees and securitizers could avoid liability if they could show that they had policies against buying loans that were outside the safe harbor, had exercised "reasonable due diligence" to adhere to such policies, and had obtained representations and warranties from the seller of the loans that the loans did not violate these minimum standards. Moreover, the Committee adopted an amendment authorizing suits by state Attorneys General to enforce H.R. 1728's provisions, magnifying the already substantial legal risks faced by participants in the mortgage market under the bill.

As if creating new avenues for additional litigation were not enough, H.R. 1728 provides a taxpayer subsidy for such activity by authorizing a $140 million fund for state and local legal organizations to provide foreclosure-related legal assistance to homeowners in default or foreclosure or tenants facing eviction due to foreclosure. Fortunately, the Committee adopted—with Chairman Frank's support—an amendment offered by Mrs. Bachmann that would render groups like ACORN ineligible for these legal assistance funds. The Bachmann amendment is identical to language signed into law in the Housing and Economic Recovery Act of 2008 (HERA) which barred any group indicted for federal election fraud from receiving housing counseling funds. Republicans will strongly oppose any attempt to remove or modify the Bachmann amendment as H.R. 1728 moves through the legislative process.

Finally, H.R. 1728 includes so-called "tenant protection" provisions creating new federal requirements that purchasers of foreclosed properties honor both private leases and Section 8 vouchers. While well-intentioned, these provisions could have a chilling effect on efforts to promote purchases of foreclosed properties and on owner participation in the Section 8 program, by making such participation more onerous. Currently, foreclosure is grounds for termination of a lease in the majority of states. While we share the Majority's concern for tenants facing eviction, we are not convinced that the provisions in H.R. 1728 are the most prudent way to provide tenant protections. It is important to note that a Section 8 tenant does not lose the government housing subsidy if his or her building goes into foreclosure. In fact, many new owners of these properties may well opt to renew existing Section 8 tenants or voluntarily agree to allow them to stay for the remainder of their Housing Assistance Payment (HAP) contract, but mandating owner adherence to a contract to which they were not a party is a dangerous precedent to set. It could also have the unintended consequence of discouraging sales of foreclosed properties, thereby frustrating the effectiveness of government policies designed to reduce the inventory of such properties and potentially prolonging the housing downturn. Mr. Neugebauer offered an amendment to strike these misguided restrictions from the bill, but it was defeated on a largely party-line vote.

Because we believe that the Majority's failure to remedy the many problems with H.R. 1728 identified during the Committee's consideration of the legislation will likely result in further damage to a fragile mortgage market in need of greater certainty—not untested and ill-defined mandates from Washington—we must reluctantly oppose it.

SPENCER BACHUS.

JEB HENSARLING.

RANDY NEUGEBAUER.

ERIK PAULSEN.

SCOTT GARRETT.

[¶56,001] Dodd-Lincoln Letter on Title VII (June 30, 2010)
United States Senate
WASHINGTON, DC 20510

June 30, 2010

The Honorable Chairman Barney Frank
Financial Services Committee
United States House of Representatives
2129 Rayburn House Office Building
Washington, DC 20515

The Honorable Chairman Colin Peterson
Committee on Agriculture
United States House of Representatives
1301 Longworth House Office Building
Washington, DC 20515

Dear Chairmen Frank and Peterson:

Whether swaps are used by an airline hedging its fuel costs or a global manufacturing company hedging interest rate risk, derivatives are an important tool businesses use to manage costs and market volatility. This legislation will preserve that tool. Regulators, namely the Commodity Futures Trading Commission (CFTC), the Securities and Exchange Commission (SEC), and the prudential regulators, must not make hedging so costly it becomes prohibitively expensive for end users to manage their risk. This letter seeks to provide some additional background on legislative intent on some, but not all, of the various sections of Title VII of H.R. 4173, the Dodd-Frank Act.

The legislation does not authorize the regulators to impose margin on end users, those exempt entities that use swaps to hedge or mitigate commercial risk. If regulators raise the costs of end user transactions, they may create more risk. It is imperative that the regulators do not unnecessarily divert working capital from our economy into margin accounts, in a way that would discourage hedging by end users or impair economic growth.

Again, Congress clearly stated in this bill that the margin and capital requirements are not to be imposed on end users, nor can the regulators require clearing for end user trades. Regulators are charged with establishing rules for the capital requirements, as well as the margin requirements for all uncleared trades, but rules may not be set in a way that requires the imposition of margin requirements on the end user side of a lawful transaction. In cases where a Swap Dealer enters into an uncleared swap with an end user, margin on the dealer side of the transaction should reflect the counterparty risk of the transaction. Congress strongly encourages regulators to establish margin requirements for such swaps or security-based swaps in a manner that is consistent with the Congressional intent to protect end users from burdensome costs.

In harmonizing the different approaches taken by the House and Senate in their respective derivatives titles, a number of provisions were deleted by the Conference Committee to avoid redundancy and to streamline the regulatory framework. However, a consistent Congressional directive throughout all drafts of this legislation, and in Congressional debate, has been to protect end users from burdensome costs associated with margin requirements and mandatory clearing. Accordingly, changes made in Conference to the section of the bill regulating capital and margin requirements for Swap Dealers and Major Swap Participants should not be construed as changing this important Congressional interest in protecting end users. In fact, the House offer amending the capital and margin provisions of Sections 731 and 764 expressly stated that the strike to the base text was made "to eliminate redundancy." Capital and margin standards should be set to mitigate risk in our financial system, not punish those who are trying to hedge their own commercial risk.

Congress recognized that the individualized credit arrangements worked out between counterparties in a bilateral transaction can be important components of business risk management. That is why Congress specifically mandates that regulators permit the use of non-cash collateral for counterparty arrangements with Swap Dealers and Major Swap Participants to permit flexibility. Mitigating risk is one of the most important reasons for passing this legislation.

Congress determined that clearing is at the heart of reform - bringing transactions and counterparties into a robust, conservative and transparent risk management framework. Congress also acknowledged that clearing may not be suitable for every transaction or every counterparty. End users who hedge their risks may find it challenging to use a standard derivative contracts to exactly match up their risks with counterparties willing to purchase their specific exposures. Standardized derivative contracts may not be suitable for every transaction. Congress recognized that imposing the clearing and exchange trading requirement on commercial end-users could raise transaction costs where there is a substantial public interest in keeping such costs low (i.e., to provide consumers with stable, low prices, promote investment, and create jobs.)

Congress recognized this concern and created a robust end user clearing exemption for those entities that are using the swaps market to hedge or mitigate commercial risk. These entities could be anything ranging from car companies to airlines or energy companies who produce and distribute power to farm machinery manufacturers. They also include captive finance affiliates, finance arms that are hedging in support of manufacturing or other commercial companies. The end user exemption also may apply to our smaller financial entities - credit unions, community banks, and farm credit institutions. These entities did not get us into this crisis and should not be punished for Wall Street's excesses. They help to finance jobs and provide lending for communities all across this nation. That is why Congress provided regulators the authority to exempt these institutions.

This is also why we narrowed the scope of the Swap Dealer and Major Swap Participant definitions. We should not inadvertently pull in entities that are appropriately managing their risk. In implementing the Swap Dealer and Major Swap Participant provisions, Congress expects the regulators to maintain through rulemaking that the definition of Major Swap Participant does not capture companies simply because they use swaps to hedge risk in their ordinary course of business. Congress does not intend to regulate end-users as Major Swap Participants or Swap Dealers just because they use swaps to hedge or manage the commercial risks associated with their business. For example, the Major Swap Participant and Swap Dealer definitions are not intended to include an electric or gas utility that purchases commodities that are used either as a source of fuel to produce electricity or to supply gas to retail customers and that uses swaps to hedge or manage the commercial risks associated with its business. Congress incorporated a de minimis exception to the Swap Dealer definition to ensure that smaller institutions that are responsibly managing their commercial risk are not inadvertently pulled into additional regulation.

Just as Congress has heard the end user community, regulators must carefully take into consideration the impact of regulation and capital and margin on these entities.

It is also imperative that regulators do not assume that all over-the-counter transactions share the same risk profile. While uncleared swaps should be looked at closely, regulators must carefully analyze the risk associated with cleared and uncleared swaps and apply that analysis when setting capital standards for Swap Dealers and Major Swap Participants. As regulators set capital and margin standards on Swap Dealers or Major Swap Participants, they must set the appropriate standards relative to the risks associated with trading. Regulators must carefully consider the potential burdens that Swap Dealers and Major Swap Participants may impose on end user counterparties - especially if those requirements will discourage the use of swaps by end users or harm economic growth. Regulators should seek to impose margins to the extent they are necessary to ensure the safety and soundness of the Swap Dealers and Major Swap Participants.

Congress determined that end users must be empowered in their counterparty relationships, especially relationships with swap dealers. This is why Congress explicitly gave to end users the option to clear swaps contracts, the option to choose their clearinghouse or clearing agency, and the option to segregate margin with an independent 3rd party custodian.

In implementing the derivatives title, Congress encourages the CFTC to clarify through rulemaking that the exclusion from the definition of swap for "any sale of a nonfinancial commodity or security for deferred shipment or delivery, so long as the transaction is intended to be physically settled" is intended to be consistent with the forward contract exclusion that is currently in the Commodity Exchange Act and the CFTC's established policy and orders on this subject, including situations where commercial parties agree to "book-out" their physical delivery obligations under a forward contract.

Congress recognized that the capital and margin requirements in this bill could have an impact on swaps contracts currently in existence. For this reason, we provided legal certainty to those contracts currently in existence, providing that no contract could be terminated, renegotiated, modified, amended, or supplemented (unless otherwise specified in the contract) based on the implementation of any requirement in this Act, including requirements on Swap Dealers and Major Swap Participants. It is imperative that we provide certainty to these existing contracts for the sake of our economy and financial system.

Regulators must carefully follow Congressional intent in implementing this bill. While Congress may not have the expertise to set specific standards, we have laid out our criteria and guidelines for implementing reform. It is imperative that these standards are not punitive to the end users, that we encourage the management of commercial risk, and that we build a strong but responsive framework for regulating the derivatives market.

Sincerely,

Chairman Christopher Dodd

Senate Committee on Banking, Housing, and Urban Affairs

United States Senate

Chairman Blanche Lincoln

Senate Committee on Agriculture, Nutrition, and Forestry

United States Senate

¶60,001 Effective Dates

Dodd-Frank Wall Street Reform and Consumer Protection Act

The table below lists provisions in the Dodd-Frank Wall Street Reform and Consumer Protection Act containing effective dates, together with a description of the subject matter involved. Generally, provisions of the Act are effective July 22, 2010—one day after the date of enactment. The list also shows the relevant sections of the Act and the paragraph number where the law text is located. Compliance dates for prescribed rules and regulations, as well as mandated studies and reports, also are included.

Act Sec.	Law Text ¶	Act Provision Subject	Effective Date
4	10,004	Effective date of Act	July 22, 2010 (1 day after the date of enactment), except as otherwise specifically provided in the Act or amendments made by the Act
		Title I—Financial Stability	
111	10,111	Establishment of Financial Stability Oversight Council	Date of enactment of Act
155(d)	10,155	Office of Financial Research—Permanent self-funding—Regulations establishing assessment schedule	2 years after date of enactment
165(d)(8)	10,165	Enhanced supervision and prudential standards for nonbank financial companies supervised by the Board of Governors and certain bank holding companies—Resolution plan and credit exposure reports—Issuance of final rules	Not later than 18 months after date of enactment
165(e)(7)	10,165	Enhanced supervision and prudential standards for nonbank financial companies supervised by the Board of Governors and certain bank holding companies—Concentration limits—Regulations limiting risk	3 years after date of enactment
165(h)(4)	10,165	Enhanced supervision and prudential standards for nonbank financial companies supervised by the Board of Governors and certain bank holding companies—Risk committee—Final rules	Not later than 1 year after transfer date; to take effect not later than 15 months after transfer date
168	10,168	Regulations	Not later than 18 months after transfer date

Act Sec.	Law Text ¶	Act Provision Subject	Effective Date
171(b)(4)(A)	10,171	Leverage and risk-based capital requirements—Minimum capital requirements—Phase-in periods—Debt or equity instruments issued on or after May 19, 2010	May 19, 2010
171(b)(4)(B)	10,171	Leverage and risk-based capital requirements—Minimum capital requirements—Phase-in periods—Debt or equity instruments issued before May 19, 2010	Regulatory capital deductions phased in incrementally over 3-year period, with phase-in period to begin on January 1, 2013, except as otherwise provided
171(b)(4)(D)	10,171	Leverage and risk-based capital requirements—Minimum capital requirements—Phase-in periods—Depository institution holding companies not supervised by the Board of Governors of the Federal Reserve System as of May 19, 2010	5 years after date of enactment
171(b)(4)(E)	10,171	Leverage and risk-based capital requirements—Minimum capital requirements—Phase-in periods—Bank holding company subsidiaries of foreign banking organizations that have relied on Supervision and Regulation Letter SR-01-1 issued by the Board of Governors of the Federal Reserve System as in effect on May 19, 2010	5 years after date of enactment, except as otherwise provided
171(b)(6)	10,171	Leverage and risk-based capital requirements—Minimum capital requirements—Study and report on small institutions access to capital	Not later than 18 months after date of enactment
Title II—Orderly Liquidation Authority			
202(b)	10,202	Judicial review—Establishment and transmittal of rules and procedures	Not later than 6 months after date of enactment
202(e)	10,202	Study of bankruptcy and orderly liquidation process for financial companies—Reports	Not later than 1 year after date of enactment; in each successive year until the third year; and every fifth year after date of enactment
202(f)	10,202	Study of international coordination relating to bankruptcy process for financial companies—Report	Not later than 1 year after date of enactment
202(g)(3)	10,202	Study of prompt corrective action implementation by the appropriate federal agencies—Report to council	Not later than 1 year after date of enactment
202(g)(4)	10,202	Study of prompt corrective action implementation by the appropriate federal agencies—Council report of action	Not later than 6 months after date of receipt of report

Act Sec.	Law Text ¶	Act Provision Subject	Effective Date
203(c)(2)	10,203	Systemic risk determination—Report to Congress	Not later than 24 hours after date of appointment of Federal Deposit Insurance Corporation as receiver for a covered financial company
203(c)(3)	10,203	Systemic risk determination—Reports to Congress and the public	Not later than 60 days after date of appointment of Federal Deposit Insurance Corporation as receiver for a covered financial company
208(a)	10,208	Dismissal and exclusion of other actions, generally	Date of appointment of Federal Deposit Insurance Corporation as receiver for covered financial company or appointment of the Securities Investor Protection Corporation as trustee for a covered broker or dealer
208(b)	10,208	Dismissal and exclusion of other actions, revesting of assets	Effective as of date of appointment of the Federal Deposit Insurance Corporation as receiver
210(c)(8)(H)	10,210	Powers and Duties of the Federal Deposit Insurance Corporation—Recordkeeping regulations	Joint final or interim final regulations to be prescribed not later than 24 months after date of enactment
211(d)(2)	10,211	FDIC Inspector General reviews	Not later than 6 months after date of appointment of Federal Deposit Insurance Corporation as receiver, and every 6 months thereafter
211(d)(5)	10,211	FDIC Inspector General reviews—Termination of responsibilities	1 year after date of termination of receivership
211(e)(2)	10,211	Treasury Inspector General reviews	Not later than 6 months after date of appointment of Federal Deposit Insurance Corporation as receiver, and every 6 months thereafter

¶60,001

Act Sec.	Law Text ¶	Act Provision Subject	Effective Date
211(e)(4)	10,211	Treasury Inspector General reviews—Termination of responsibilities	1 year after date obligations purchased by the Secretary of the Treasury from the Federal Deposit Insurance Corporation under are fully redeemed
211(f)(2)	10,211	Primary financial regulatory agency inspector general reviews—Report	Not later than 1 year after date of appointment of Federal Deposit Insurance Corporation as receiver
211(f)(2)	10,211	Primary financial regulatory agency inspector general reviews—Report to Congress by Federal primary financial regulatory or Board of Governors	Not later than 90 days after date of receipt of Inspector General report
215	10,215	Study on secured creditor haircuts—Report	Not later than end of 1-year period beginning on date of enactment
216(a)	10,216	Study on bankruptcy process for financial and nonbank financial institutions	Upon enactment
216(b)	10,216	Study on bankruptcy process for financial and nonbank financial institutions—Reports to Congress	Not later than 1 year after date of enactment, and in each successive year until fifth year after date of enactment
217(b)	10,217	Study on international coordination relating to bankruptcy process for nonbank financial institutions—Report	Not later than 1 year after date of enactment
		Title III—Transfer of Powers to the Comptroller of the Currency, the Corporation, and the Board of Governors	
311	10,311	Transfer date	One year after date of enactment
312	10,312	Transfer of powers to the comptroller of the currency, the corporation, and the board of governors—Powers and Duties Transferred	Transfer Date—One year after date of enactment
313	10,313	Abolishment of Office of Thrift Supervision and position of Director of the Office of Thrift Supervision	90 days after transfer date (one year and 90 days after date of enactment)
314	10,314	Amendments to National Bank Act relating to Comptroller of the Currency	Transfer Date—One year after date of enactment
316(c)	10,316	Savings provisions—Identification of regulations continued	Transfer Date—One year after date of enactment

¶60,001

Act Sec.	Law Text ¶	Act Provision Subject	Effective Date
318(e)	10,318	Funding	Transfer Date—One year after date of enactment
322	10,322	Transfer of employees—Timing of transfers and position assignments	Not later than 90 days after transfer date
322(g)	10,322	Transfer of employees—Personnel actions limited	30-month period beginning on transfer date
322(h)	10,322	Transfer of employees—Pay	30-month period beginning on date employee was transferred
322(i)(2)(A)	10,322	Transfer of employees—Benefits other than retirement benefits—Continuation of existing plans	1-year period following transfer date
322(i)(2)(B)	10,322	Transfer of certain personnel—Benefits other than retirement benefits for transferred employees—Dental, vision, or life insurance after first year	After 1-year period beginning on transfer date
322(i)(2)(C)	10,322	Transfer of certain personnel—Benefits other than retirement benefits for transferred employees—Long term care insurance after first year	After 1-year period beginning on transfer date
322(j)	10,322	Transfer of certain personnel—Incorporation into agency pay system	Not later than 2 years after transfer date
322(l)	10,322	Reorganization determination	2-year period beginning 1 year after transfer date
325(a)	10,325	Disposition of affairs—Authority of Director	90-day period beginning on transfer date
325(b)	10,325	Disposition of affairs—Status of Director	90-day period beginning on transfer date
327(a)	10,327	Implementation of plan and report—Plan submission	Within 180 days of enactment
327(b)	10,327	Implementation of plan and report—Inspectors General review of plan and report	Within 60 days of receiving plan
327(c)	10,327	Implementation of plan and report—Implementation reports	Not later than 6 months after Inspectors General report received, and every 6 months thereafter
334(c)	10,334	Transition reserve ratio requirements to reflect new assessment base—Public availability	Period of not less than 5 years after date of enactment
336	10,336	Management of the Federal Deposit Insurance Corporation	Transfer Date—One year after date of enactment
343(a)(1)	10,343	Insurance of transaction accounts—Banks and savings associations	December 31, 2010
343(a)(3)	10,343	Insurance of transaction accounts—Banks and savings associations—Prospective Repeal	January 1, 2013
343(b)(1)	10,343	Insurance of transaction accounts—Credit Unions	Date of enactment

Act Sec.	Law Text ¶	Act Provision Subject	Effective Date
343(b)(3)	10,343	Insurance of transaction accounts—Credit Unions—Prospective repeal	January 1, 2013
351	10,351	Technical and Conforming Amendments (Title III, Subtitle E, Sections 351–378)	Transfer Date—One year after date of enactment, except as provided in section 364(a)
364(a)	10,364	Repeal of Federal Home Loan Bank Act provisions relating to quarters and facilities for Director of the Office of Thrift Supervision	90 days after transfer date (one year and 90 days after date of enactment)
		Title IV—Regulation of Advisers to Hedge Funds and Others	
406	10,406	Promulgation of rules to establish form and content of reports to be filed by investment advisers	Not later than 12 months after date of enactment
407	10,407	Exemption of and reporting by venture capital fund advisers—Issuance of final rules to define term "venture capital fund"	Not later than 1 year after date of enactment
412	10,412	Comptroller General study on custody rule costs—Report	Not later than 3 years after date of enactment
413(a)	10,413	Adjusting the accredited investor standard—Net worth standard	4-year period beginning on date of enactment
413(b)	10,413	Adjusting the accredited investor standard—Review and adjustment—Subsequent reviews	Not earlier than 4 years after date of enactment, and not less frequently than once every 4 years thereafter
415	10,415	GAO study and report on accredited investors	Not later than 3 years after date of enactment
416	10,416	GAO study on self-regulatory organization for private funds—Report	Not later than 1 year after date of enactment
417(a)(1)	10,417	Commission study and report on short selling—Study on the state of short selling on national securities exchanges and in the over-the-counter markets	Not later than 2 years after date of enactment
417(a)(2)	10,417	Commission study and report on short selling—Study on reporting and conduction voluntary pilot program	Not later than 1 year after date of enactment

¶60,001

Act Sec.	Law Text ¶	Act Provision Subject	Effective Date
419	10,419	Transition period—Title IV and amendments made by Title IV	Except where otherwise provided, 1 year after date of enactment, except that any investment adviser may register with the Securities and Exchange Commission under the Investment Advisers Act of 1940 during that 1-year period, subject to rules of the Commission
		Title V—Insurance	
502	10,502	Reports on U.S. and global reinsurance market—Breadth and scope	September 30, 2012
502	10,502	Reports on U.S. and global reinsurance market—Impact of Part II of the Nonadmitted and Reinsurance Reform Act of 2010	January 1, 2013, and updated by January 1, 2015
502	10,502	Study and report on regulation of insurance	Not later than 18 months after date of enactment
512	10,512	State Based Insurance Reform—Nonadmitted and Reinsurance Reform Act of 2010 (Title V, Subtitle B, Sections 511—542)	Upon expiration of 12-month period beginning on date of enactment of Subtitle B of Title V, except as otherwise specifically provided

Act Sec.	Law Text ¶	Act Provision Subject	Effective Date
521(b)(2)	10,521	Nonadmitted insurance—Allocation of nonadmitted premium taxes—State compacts	If compact adopted on or before expiration of 330-day period that begins on date of enactment of Subtitle B of Title V, compact applies to any premium taxes that, on or after such date of enactment, are required to be paid to any State that is subject to the compact; if compact adopted after expiration of 330-day period, compact applies to any premium taxes that, on or after January 1 of the first calendar year that begins after expiration of the 330-day period, are required to be paid to any State that is subject to the compact
521(b)(3)	10,521	Nonadmitted insurance—Allocation of nonadmitted premium taxes—State compacts—Report	Upon expiration of 330-day period that begins on date of enactment of Subtitle B of Title V
523	10,523	Participation in national producer database—License fee collection prohibition	After expiration of 2-year period beginning on date of enactment
526(d)	10,526	GAO Study of Nonadmitted Insurance Market—Report	Not later than 30 months after effective date of Subtitle B of Title V
527(5)(c)(ii)	10,527	Adjustment of amounts relating to "exempt commercial purchaser" definition criteria	Effective on the fifth January 1 occurring after the date of the enactment of this subtitle and each fifth January 1 occurring thereafter

Title VI—Improvements to Regulation of Bank and Savings Association Holding Companies and Depository Institutions

Effective Dates

Act Sec.	Law Text ¶	Act Provision Subject	Effective Date
603(a)(2)	10,603	Moratorium and study on treatment of credit card banks, industrial loan companies, and certain other companies under the Bank Holding Company Act of 1956—Moratorium on provision of deposit insurance	November 23, 2009
603(a)(4)	10,603	Moratorium and study on treatment of credit card banks, industrial loan companies, and certain other companies under the Bank Holding Company Act of 1956—Sunset	3 years after date of enactment
603(b)	10,603	Government Accountability Office study of exceptions under the bank holding company act—Report	Not later than 18 months after date of enactment
604	10,604	Reports and examinations of holding companies; regulation of functionally regulated subsidiaries	Transfer Date—One year after date of enactment
605	10,605	Assuring consistent oversight of permissible activities of depository institution subsidiaries of holding companies	Transfer Date—One year after date of enactment
606	10,606	Requirements for financial holding companies to remain well capitalized and well managed	Transfer Date—One year after date of enactment
607	10,607	Standards for interstate acquisitions	Transfer Date—One year after date of enactment
608	10,608	Enhancing existing restrictions on bank transactions with affiliates	1 year after transfer date—Two years after date of enactment
609	10,609	Eliminating exceptions for transactions with financial subsidiaries	1 year after transfer date—Two years after date of enactment
610	10,610	Lending limits applicable to credit exposure on derivative transactions, repurchase agreements, reverse repurchase agreements, and securities lending and borrowing transactions	1 year after transfer date—Two years after date of enactment
611	10,611	Consistent treatment of derivative transactions in lending limits	18 months after transfer date—One year and 18 months after date of enactment
614	10,614	Lending limits to insiders	1 year after transfer date—Two years after date of enactment
615	10,615	Limitations on purchases of assets from insiders	Transfer Date—One year after date of enactment
616(d)	10,616	Regulations regarding capital levels of holding companies—Issuance of final rules to carry out amendment to Federal Deposit Insurance Act relating to source of strength	Not later than 1 year after transfer date—Two years after date of enactment

¶60,001

Act Sec.	Law Text ¶	Act Provision Subject	Effective Date
616(e)	10,616	Regulations regarding capital levels of holding companies—Amendments	Transfer Date—One year after date of enactment
617	10,617	Elimination of elective investment bank holding company framework	Transfer Date—One year after date of enactment
618(b)(2)(B)	10,618	Securities holding companies—Comprehensive consolidated supervision—Effective date of registration	45 days after date of receipt of the registration information and documents
619	10,619	Prohibitions on proprietary trading and certain relationships with hedge funds and private equity funds—Study	Not later than 6 months after date of enactment
619	10,619	Prohibitions on proprietary trading and certain relationships with hedge funds and private equity funds—Rulemaking	Not later than 9 months after completion of study
619	10,619	Prohibitions on proprietary trading and certain relationships with hedge funds and private equity funds—Provisions other than study and rulemaking provisions	Earlier of 12 months after date of issuance of final rules, or 2 years after date of enactment
619	10,619	Prohibitions on proprietary trading and certain relationships with hedge funds and private equity funds—Special rulemaking	Not later than 6 months after date of enactment
620(a)	10,620	Study on bank investment activities	Not later than 18 months after date of enactment
620(b)	10,620	Study on bank investment activities—Report and recommendations	No later than 2 months after completion of study
621(a)	10,612	Conflicts of interest relating to certain securitizations—Rulemaking by Securities and Exchange Commission to implement provisions	Not later than 270 days after date of enactment
621(b)	10,621	Conflicts of interest relating to certain securitizations	On effective date of final rules issued by the Securities and Exchange Commission
621(b)	10,621	Conflicts of interest relating to certain securitizations—Provisions relating to rulemaking and rule of construction	Date of enactment
622	10,622	Concentration limits on large financial firms—Study and recommendations	Not later than 6 months after date of enactment
622	10,622	Concentration limits on large financial firms—Rulemaking	Not later than 9 months after date of completion of study
625	10,625	Treatment of dividends by certain mutual holding companies	Transfer Date—One year after date of enactment

¶60,001

Act Sec.	Law Text ¶	Act Provision Subject	Effective Date
626	10,626	Intermediate Holding Companies—Activities other than financial activities by grandfathered unitary savings and loan holding company—Regulations	Not later than 90 days (or such longer period as deemed appropriate) after transfer date
627	10,627	Interest-bearing transaction accounts authorized	1 year after date of enactment
		Title VII—Wall Street Transparency and Accountability	
712(a)	10,712	Review of regulatory authority—Regulations	Issued in final form not later than 360 days after date of enactment
712(e)	10,712	Global rulemaking timeframe	Not later than 360 days after date of enactment
712(f)	10,712	Review of regulatory authority—Rules and registration before final effective dates to prepare for effective dates	Beginning on date of enactment, provided no action by the Commodity Futures Trading Commission or the Securities and Exchange Commission shall become effective prior to effective date applicable to such action under the provisions Act
716(h)	10,716	Prohibition against Federal Government bailouts of swaps entities	2 years following date on which Act is effective
721(f)	10,721	Regulation of swap markets—Commodity Exchange Act amendments—Definitions—"Commodity"	June 1, 2010
723	10,723	Adoption of rules for a derivatives clearing organization's submission for review of a swap; adoption of rules for reviewing derivatives clearing organization's clearing of a swap	Not later than 1 year after date of enactment
729	10,729	Reporting and recordkeeping for uncleared swaps	Upon enactment
734	10,734	Swap execution facilities—Ability to petition Commodity Futures Trading Commission to remain subject to provisions of section 5d of the Commodity Exchange Act	Prior to final effective dates in Title VII; Commodity Futures Trading Commission may allow a person to continue operating subject to provisions of section 5d of Commodity Exchange Act for up to 1 year after effective date of Subtitle A of Title VII.
737	10,737	Position limits	Date of enactment

¶60,001

Act Sec.	Law Text ¶	Act Provision Subject	Effective Date
738	10,738	Foreign boards of trade—Registration—Linked contracts	Not effective with respect to foreign board of trade to which, prior to the date of enactment, the Commission granted direct access permission until the date that is 180 days after date of enactment.
742	10,742	Agreements, contracts or transactions in foreign currency offered to, or entered into with, a person that is not an eligible contract participant or which a Federal regulatory agency has issued a proposed rule prior to date of enactment	90 days after date of enactment
748	10,748	Commodity whistleblower incentives and protection—Study on impact of FOIA exemption on Commodity Futures Trading Commission—Report	Not later than 30 months after date of enactment
748	10,748	Commodity whistleblower incentives and protection—Implementing rules	Not later than 270 days after date of enactment of the Wall Street Transparency and Accountability Act of 2010
753	10,753	Anti-manipulation authority amendments	Date on which final rule promulgated by the Commodity Futures Trading Commission takes effect
754	10,754	Provisions relating to the regulation of over-the-counter swaps markets (Subtitle A of Title VII)	Unless otherwise provided, later of 360 days after date of enactment or, to the extent a provision requires a rulemaking, not less than 60 days after publication of the final rule or regulation
763	10,763	Adoption of rules for clearing agency's submission for review of a security-based swap; adoption of rules for reviewing a clearing agency's clearing of a security-based swap	Not later than 1 year after date of the enactment
764	10,764	Issuance of rules to provide for the registration of security-based swap dealers and major security-based swap participants	Not later than 1 year after date of enactment of the Wall Street Transparency and Accountability Act of 2010

Effective Dates

Act Sec.	Law Text ¶	Act Provision Subject	Effective Date
766	10,766	Reporting and recordkeeping for certain security-based swaps—Promulgation of interim final rule	Within 90 days of date of enactment
766	10,766	Reporting and recordkeeping for certain security-based swaps—Reporting provisions	Date of enactment
774	10,774	Provisions relating to regulation of security-based swap markets (Subtitle B of Title VII)	Unless otherwise provided, later of 360 days after date of enactment or, to the extent a provision requires a rulemaking, not less than 60 days after publication of final rule or regulation
		Title VIII—Payment, Clearing, and Settlement Supervision	
813	10,813	Common framework for designated clearing entity risk management—Report	Not later than 1 year after date of enactment
814	10,814	Effective date of Title VIII provisions	Date of enactment
		Title IX—Investor Protections and Improvements to the Regulation of Securities	
913	10,913	Study and rulemaking regarding obligations of brokers, dealers, and investment advisers—Report	Not later than 6 months after date of enactment
914	10,914	Study on enhancing investment adviser examinations—Report	Not later than 180 days after date of enactment
916	10,916	Streamlining of filing procedures for self-regulatory organizations—Rulemaking	Not later than 180 days after date of enactment
917	10,917	Study regarding financial literacy among investors—Report	Not later than 2 years after date of enactment
918	10,918	Study regarding mutual fund advertising—Report	Not later than 18 months after date of enactment
919A	10,919	Study on conflicts of interest—Report	Not later than 18 months after date of enactment
919B	10,919	Study on improved investor access to information on investment advisers and broker-dealers	Not later than 6 months after date of enactment; implementation of recommendations not later than 18 months after date of completion of study

¶60,001

Act Sec.	Law Text ¶	Act Provision Subject	Effective Date
919C	10,919	Study on financial planners and the use of financial designations—Report	Not later than 180 days after date of enactment
922(a)	10,922	Whistleblower award program—Reports to Congress	Not later than October 30 of each fiscal year beginning after date of enactment
922(d)	10,922	Study of whistleblower protection programs—Study and report	Not later than 30 months after date of enactment
924	10,924	Implementation and transition provisions for whistleblower protection—Implementing rules	Not later than 270 days after date of enactment
926	10,926	Disqualifying felons and other "bad actors" from Regulation D offerings—Rules	Not later than 1 year after date of enactment
929H	10,929	Securities Investor Protection Act reforms—Determination of inflation adjustment to the standard maximum cash advance amount	Not later than January 1, 2011, and every 5 years thereafter; adjustment effective on January 1 of the year immediately succeeding the calendar year in which adjustment is made
929W	10,929	Notice to missing security holders—Due diligence for the delivery of dividends, interest, and other valuable property rights—Rules	Not later than 1 year after date of enactment
929Y	10,929	Study on extraterritorial private rights of action—Report	Not later than 18 months after date of enactment
929Z	10,929	GAO study on securities litigation—Report	Not later than 1 year after date of enactment
936	10,936	Qualification standards for credit rating analysts—Issuance of rules by Securities and Exchange Commission	Not later than 1 year after date of enactment
937	10,937	Timing of regulations	Not later than 1 year after date of enactment
939(g)	10,939	Removal of statutory references to credit ratings	2 years after date of enactment
939(h)	10,939	Securities and Exchange Commission report to Congress containing findings of study on the feasibility and desirability of standardizing credit ratings terminology	Not later than 1 year after date of enactment
939A	10,939	Agency review of reliance on ratings	Not later than 1 year after date of enactment
939B	10,939	Elimination of exemption from fair disclosure rule	Not later than 90 days after date of enactment
939C	10,939	Securities and Exchange Commission study on strengthening credit rating agency independence—Report	Not later than 3 years after date of enactment

Effective Dates   1565

Act Sec.	Law Text ¶	Act Provision Subject	Effective Date
939D	10,939	Government accountability office study on alternative business models—Report	Not later than 18 months after date of enactment
939E	10,939	Government Accountability Office study on the creation of an independent professional analyst organization—Report	Not later than 1 year after date of publication of rules issued by the Securities and Exchange Commission
939F	10,939	Study and rulemaking on assigned credit ratings—Report and recommendation	Not later than 24 months after date of enactment
941(b)	10,941	Credit risk retention—Regulations	Required to be prescribed not later than 270 days after date of enactment; effective with respect to securitizers and originators of asset-backed securities backed by residential mortgages, 1 year after the date final rules are published in the Federal Register; effective with respect to securitizers and originators of all other classes of asset-backed securities, 2 years after the date final rules are published in the Federal Register
941(c)	10,941	Credit risk retention study—Report	Not later than 90 days after date of enactment
943	10,943	Representations and warranties in asset-backed offerings—Securities and Exchange Commission to prescribe regulations	Not later than 180 days after date of enactment
946	10,946	Study on the macroeconomic effects of risk retention requirements—Report	Not later than the end of the 180-day period beginning on date of enactment
951	10,951	Shareholder vote on executive compensation disclosures—Inclusion in proxy or consent or authorization for an annual or other meeting of resolution approving compensation of executives	Proxy or consent or authorization for the first annual or other meeting of shareholders occurring after the end of the 6-month period beginning on the date of enactment

¶60,001

Act Sec.	Law Text ¶	Act Provision Subject	Effective Date
952(a)	10,952	Compensation committees—Authority of Securities and Exchange Commission, by rule, to direct the national securities exchanges and national securities associations to prohibit the listing of any security of an issuer that is not in compliance with requirements	Not later than 360 days after date of enactment
952(b)	10,952	Compensation consultants—Study and report	Not later than 2 years after date of enactment
956	10,956	Enhanced disclosure and reporting of compensation arrangements—Regulations required to be prescribed	Not later than 9 months after date of enactment
963(a)	10,963	Annual financial controls audit—Reports of Securities and Exchange Commission	Not later than 6 months after the end of each fiscal year
963(b)	10,963	Annual financial controls audit—Report by Comptroller General	Not later than 6 months after the end of the first fiscal year after date of enactment
964	10,964	Report on oversight of national securities associations	Not later than 2 years after date of enactment, and every 3 years thereafter
965(a)	10,965	Securities and Exchange Commission organizational study and reform—Hiring of independent consultant	Not later than the end of the 90-day period beginning on date of enactment
965(b)	10,965	Securities and Exchange Commission organizational study and reform—Consultant report	Not later than the end of the 150-day period after being retained
965(c)	10,965	Securities and Exchange Commission organizational study and reform—SEC report	Not later than the end of the 6-month period beginning on the date the consultant issues required report, and every 6-months thereafter during the 2-year period following the date on which the consultant issues report
966	10,966	Study on SEC revolving door—Report	Not later than 1 year after date of enactment
975	10,975	Amendments relating to the regulation of municipal securities and changes to the board of the Municipal Securities Rule	October 1, 2010
976	10,976	Government Accountability Office study of increased disclosure to investors—Report	Not later than 24 months after date of enactment
977	10,977	Government Accountability Office study on the municipal securities markets—Report	Not later than 18 months after date of enactment

¶60,001

Act Sec.	Law Text ¶	Act Provision Subject	Effective Date
978	10,978	Study of funding for governmental accounting standards board—Report	Not later than 180 days after date of enactment
984	10,984	Loan or borrowing of securities—Rulemaking	Not later than 2 years after date of enactment
989(c)	10,989	Government Accountability Office study on proprietary trading—Report	Not later than 15 months after date of enactment
989F	10,989	GAO study of person to person lending—Report	Not later than 1 year after date of enactment
989G	10,989	Exemption for nonaccelerated filers—Study and report	Not later than 9 months after date of enactment
989I	10,989	GAO study regarding exemption for smaller issuers	Not later than 3 years after date of enactment
991(a)(2)	10,991	Securities and Exchange Commission match funding—Match funding authority amendments	Later of October 1, 2011; or the date of enactment of an Act making a regular appropriation to the Securities and Exchange Commission for fiscal year 2012.
991(b)(4)	10,991	Securities and Exchange Commission match funding—Amendments to registration fee provisions	October 1, 2011, except that for fiscal year 2012, the Commission shall publish the rate established under section 6(b) of the Securities Act of 1933 (15 U.S.C. 77f(b)), as amended by the Investor Protection and Securities Reform Act of 2010 (Title IX), on August 31, 2011.
991(e)(2)	10,991	Securities and Exchange Commission match funding—Securities and Exchange Commission reserve fund	October 1, 2011
		Title X—Bureau of Consumer Financial Protection	
1013(d)(4)	11,013	Report by Director of Bureau of Consumer Financial Protection on Bureau's financial literacy activities and strategy to improve financial literacy of consumers	Not later than 24 months after designated transfer date, and annually thereafter
1013(d)(7)	11,013	Comptroller General study and report on financial literacy program	Not later than 1 year after date of enactment
1013(f)	11,013	Establishment of the Office of Fair Lending and Equal Opportunity, the Office of Financial Education, and the Office of Service Member Affairs	Not later than 1 year after designated transfer date

¶60,001

Act Sec.	Law Text ¶	Act Provision Subject	Effective Date
1013(g)	11,013	Establishment of Office of Financial Protection for Older Americans	Before end of 180-day period beginning on designated transfer date
1013(g)(3)(C)	11,013	Office of Financial Protection for Older Americans submission of recommendations on best practices for any legislative and regulatory disseminating information and methods relating to financial advisors for seniors	Not later than 18 months after date of establishment of Office
1016(b)	11,016	Reports by Bureau of Consumer Financial Protection	Concurrent with each semi-annual hearing beginning with the session following designated transfer date
1017(a)(1)	11,017	Funding—Transfer of funds from Board of Governors	Each year (or quarter of such year), beginning on designated transfer date, and each quarter thereafter
1017(a)(3)	11,017	Funding—Transfer of funds from Board of Governors—Transition Period	Beginning on the date of enactment until designated transfer date
1018	11,018	Bureau of Consumer Financial Protection (Subtitle A of Title X)	Date of enactment
1022	11,022	Rulemaking authority	Date of enactment
1022(d)	11,022	Assessment of significant rules—Reports	Not later than 5 years after effective date of the subject rule or order
1024	11,024	Supervision of nondepository covered persons	Date of enactment
1024(a)(2)	11,024	Supervision of nondepository covered persons—rulemaking to define covered persons subject to this section—Issuance of initial rule	Not later than 1 year after designated transfer date
1025(e)	11,025	Supervision of very large banks, savings associations, and credit unions—Simultaneous and coordinated supervisory action	Date of enactment
1028	11,028	Regulations prohibiting or imposing conditions or limitations on use of arbitration agreements	Applicable to any agreement entered into after the end of the 180-day period beginning on the effective date of the regulation, as established by the Bureau
1029A	11,029	General powers of Bureau (Subtitle B)	Transfer date (except as otherwise provided)
1032	11,032	Combined mortgage loan disclosure—Proposed rules	Not later than 1 year after designated transfer date

¶60,001

Act Sec.	Law Text ¶	Act Provision Subject	Effective Date
1035	11,035	Private education loan ombudsman—Memorandum of understanding with student loan ombudsman	Not later than 90 days after designated transfer date
1037	11,037	Specific Bureau Authorities (Subtitle C of Title X)	Designated transfer date
1044	11,044	Periodic review of preemption determinations—Reports to Congress	At time of issuing review within the 5-year period after prescribing or otherwise issuing of a preemption determination, and at least once during each 5-year period thereafter
1048	11,048	Preservation of State Law (Subtitle D of Title X)	Designated transfer date
1058	11,058	Enforcement Powers (Subtitle E of Title X)	Designated transfer date
1061(d)	11,061	Transfer of consumer financial protection functions, and authorities of the prudential regulators	Designated transfer date
1062(a)	11,062	Designated transfer date—Designation of single calendar date for transfer of functions to Bureau of Consumer Financial Protection	
1062(c)(1)	11,062	Designated transfer date—Permissible dates	Not earlier than 180 days, nor later than 9 months, after date of enactment
1062(c)(2)	11,062	Designated transfer date—Extension of time	A date that is later than 12 months after date of enactment, but no later than 18 months after date of enactment
1064(a)(8)	11,064	Transfer of certain personnel—Authority of President to resolve disputes—Sunset	3 years after designated transfer date
1064(b)	11,064	Transfer of certain personnel—Timing of transfers and position assignments	Not later than 90 days after designated transfer date
1064(f)	11,064	Transfer of certain personnel—Personnel actions limited	2-year period beginning on designated transfer date
1064(g)	11,064	Transfer of certain personnel—Pay protection	2-year period beginning on designated transfer date
1064(h)(1)(A)	11,064	Transfer of certain personnel—Reorganization	2-year period beginning 1 year after designated transfer date
1064(i)	11,064	Transfer of certain personnel—Benefits—Option to elect into Federal Reserve System Retirement Plan and Federal Reserve System Thrift Plan	1-year period beginning 6 months after designated transfer date

¶60,001

Act Sec.	Law Text ¶	Act Provision Subject	Effective Date
1064(i)(2)(A)	11,064	Transfer of certain personnel—Benefits other than retirement benefits for transferred employees—Continuation of existing plans	1 year after designated transfer date
1064(i)(2)(B)	11,064	Transfer of certain personnel—Benefits other than retirement benefits for transferred employees—Medical, dental, vision, or life insurance after first year	At end of 1-year period beginning on designated transfer date
1064(i)(2)(C)	11,064	Transfer of certain personnel—Benefits other than retirement benefits for transferred employees—Long term care insurance after first year	At end of 1-year period beginning on designated transfer date
1064(j)	11,064	Transfer of certain personnel—Implementation of uniform pay and classification system	Not later than 2 years after designated transfer date
1065(b)	11,065	Incidental transfers authorization—Sunset	5 years after date of enactment
1067(c)	11,067	Transition oversight—Reporting requirements—Expiration	5 years after the date of enactment
1071(d)	11,071	Small business data collection	Designated transfer date
1073	11,073	Remittance transfers—Disclosures—Exceptions for disclosure of amount received—Deadline	5 years after date of enactment of Consumer Financial Protection Act of 2010
1073(a)(4)	11,073	Remittance transfers—Disclosures—Exceptions for disclosure of amount received—Deadline extension	Not longer than 10 years after date of enactment of Consumer Financial Protection Act of 2010
1073(a)(4)	11,073	Remittance transfers—Regulations regarding transfers to certain nations	Not later than 18 months after date of enactment of Consumer Financial Protection Act of 2010
1073(a)(4)	11,073	Remittance transfers—Remittance transfer errors—Error resolution—Rules	Not later than 18 months after date of enactment of Consumer Financial Protection Act of 2010
1073(a)(4)	11,073	Remittance transfers—Remittance transfer errors—Cancellation and refund policy rules	Not later than 18 months after date of enactment of Consumer Financial Protection Act of 2010
1073(b)(2)	11,073	Remittance transfers—Automated clearinghouse system—Report to Congress	Not later than one calendar year after date of enactment, and on April 30 biennially thereafter during 10-year period beginning on date of enactment

¶60,001

Effective Dates

Act Sec.	Law Text ¶	Act Provision Subject	Effective Date
1074	11,074	Department of the Treasury study on ending the conservatorship of Fannie Mae, Freddie Mac, and reforming the housing finance system—Report and recommendations	Not later than January 31, 2011
1075(a)(2)	11,075	Reasonable interchange transaction fees for electronic debit transactions	At end of 12-month period beginning on date of enactment of Consumer Financial Protection Act of 2010
1075(a)(2)	11,075	Reasonable fees and rules for payment card transactions—Regulations establishing standards for assessing reasonableness of interchange transaction fees	Not later than 9 months after date of enactment of Consumer Financial Protection Act of 2010
1075(a)(2)	11,075	Reasonable fees and rules for payment card transactions—Regulations establishing standards for making adjustments	Not later than 9 months after date of enactment of Consumer Financial Protection Act of 2010
1075(a)(2)	11,075	Reasonable fees and rules for payment card transactions—Annual report of Federal Reserve Board	Beginning 12 months after date of enactment of Consumer Financial Protection Act of 2010
1075(a)(2)	11,075	Limitation on payment card network restrictions—Prohibitions against exclusivity arrangements—Regulations	Before end of 1-year period beginning on date of enactment of Consumer Financial Protection Act of 2010
1075(a)(2)	11,075	Limitation on payment card network restrictions—No routing restrictions—Regulations	Before end of 1-year period beginning on date of enactment of Consumer Financial Protection Act of 2010
1076(a)	11,076	Reverse mortgage study and regulations	Not later than 1 year after designated transfer date
1077	11,077	Report on private education loans and private educational lenders	Not later than 2 years after date of enactment
1078	11,078	Study and report on credit scores	Not later than 1 year after date of enactment
1079(b)	11,079	Review, report, and program with respect to exchange facilitators—Report to Congress	Not later than 1 year after designated transfer date
1079(c)	11,079	Review, report, and program with respect to exchange facilitators—Regulations to be proposed or program otherwise established	Not later than 2 years after submission of report to Congress
1081	11,081	Amendments to the Inspector General Act	Date of enactment
1082	11,082	Amendments to the Privacy Act of 1974	Date of enactment

¶60,001

Act Sec.	Law Text ¶	Act Provision Subject	Effective Date
1083(b)	11,083	Amendments to the Alternative Mortgage Transaction Parity Act of 1982	Designated transfer date
1100E	11,100	Adjustments for inflation in the Truth in Lending Act	On and after December 31, 2011
1100H	11,100	Effective date of conforming amendments not otherwise provided for	Designated transfer date
Title XI—Federal Reserve System Provisions			
1101	11,101	Federal Reserve Act amendments on emergency lending authority—Issuance of regulation establishing policies and procedures governing emergency lending	As soon as is practicable after date of enactment
1102	11,102	Reviews of special Federal Reserve credit facilities—Report to Congress	Before end of 90-day period beginning on date on which review is completed
1104(d)	11,104	Liquidity event determination—Determination and written recommendation—Report to Congress	Earlier of date of submission made to Congress, or within 30 days of date of a determination
1105	11,105	Emergency financial stabilization—Rulemaking	As soon as is practicable after date of enactment
1106(a)	11,106	Suspension of parallel Federal Deposit Insurance Act authority	Upon date of enactment of section
1108(a)(2)	11,108	Federal Reserve Act amendments on supervision and regulation policy—Establishment of the position of vice chairman for supervision	Date of enactment of Title XI
1109(a)(3)	11,109	Audit of federal reserve facilities	Commenced not later than 30 days after date of enactment, and completed not later than 12 months after date of enactment
1109(a)(4)	11,109	Report on audit of federal reserve facilities	12 months after date of enactment
1109(b)(1)	11,109	Audit of federal reserve bank governance	Not later than 1 year after date of enactment
1109(b)(2)	11,109	Audit of federal reserve bank governance—Report	Before the end of the 90-day period beginning on date on which audit is completed
1109(c)	11,109	Audit of federal reserve bank governance—Publication of Board actions	Not later than December 1, 2010
Title XII—Improving Access to Mainstream Financial Institutions			

Effective Dates

Act Sec.	Law Text ¶	Act Provision Subject	Effective Date
1210	11,210	Evaluation and reports to Congress	Each fiscal year
		Title XIII—Pay it Back Act	
1303	11,303	Amendment to Emergency Economic Stabilization Act of 2008—Report	Every 6 months
		Title XIV—Mortgage Reform and Anti-Predatory Lending Act	
1400(c)(1)	11,400	Regulations required to be prescribed under Title XIV	To be prescribed in final form before the end of the 18-month period beginning on designated transfer date; to take effect not later than 12 months after date of issuance of the regulations in final form
1400(c)(2)	11,400	Regulations—Effective date established by rule	Date on which final regulations implementing section, or provision, takes effect
1400(c)(3)	11,400	Regulations—Effective date of section for which regulations not issued	18 months after designated transfer date
1406	11,406	Study of shared appreciation mortgages—Report	Not later than expiration of 6-month period beginning on date of enactment
1421(b)	11,421	Report by GAO	Before the end of 1-year period beginning on date of enactment
1446	11,446	Study of defaults and foreclosures—Preliminary report	Not later than 12 months after the date of enactment
1446	11,446	Study of defaults and foreclosures—Final report	Not later than 24 months after date of enactment
1472(a)	11,472	Appraisal independence requirements—Interim final regulations	No later than 90 days after date of enactment
1472(a)	11,472	Home Valuation Code of Conduct sunset	Date interim final regulations are promulgated
1473(b)	11,473	Appraisal management companies—Annual report	June 15 of each year
1473(f)(2)	11,473	Appraisal management company minimum requirements—Prohibiting performance of services related to a federally related transaction in a State unless registered	After date that is 36 months after date on which the required regulations are prescribed in final form; may be extended by additional 12 months

¶60,001

1574 Dodd-Frank Wall Street Reform and Consumer Protection Act

Act Sec.	Law Text ¶	Act Provision Subject	Effective Date
1476(b)(1)	11,476	GAO study on the effectiveness and impact of various appraisal methods, valuation models and distributions channels, and on the Home Valuation Code of conduct and the Appraisal Subcommittee	12 months after date of enactment
1476(b)(2)	11,476	GAO study on the effectiveness and impact of various appraisal methods, valuation models and distributions channels, and on the Home Valuation Code of conduct and the Appraisal Subcommittee—Report	90 days after date of enactment
1476(d)	11,476	Additional study relating to appraisals and Appraisal Subcommittee functions	Not later than 18 months after date of enactment
1483	11,483	Public availability of information of making home affordable program—Availability of data tables to public—Issuance of regulations prescribing procedures for disclosing data	Not more than 60 days after each monthly deadline for submission of data by mortgage servicers and lenders participating in program
1494(b)	11,494	Study of effect of drywall presence on residential mortgage loan foreclosures—Report	Not later than expiration of 120-day period beginning on date of enactment
1497	11,497	Additional assistance for Neighborhood Stabilization Program	October 1, 2010
1498(d)	11,498	Legal assistance for foreclosure-related issues	Date of enactment
		Title XV—Miscellaneous Provisions	
1502(b)	11,502	Congo conflict minerals—Disclosure—Promulgation of regulations	Not later than 270 days after date of enactment
1502(d)(1)	11,502	Congo conflict minerals—Baseline report	Not later than 1 year after date of enactment and annually thereafter
1502(d)(2)	11,502	Congo conflict minerals—Regular report on effectiveness	Not later than 2 years after date of enactment and annually thereafter
1502(d)(3)	11,502	Congo conflict minerals—Regular report on effectiveness	Not later than 30 months after date of enactment and annually thereafter
1503(b)	11,503	Reporting requirements regarding coal or other mine safety—Reporting shutdowns and patterns of violations	Beginning on and after date of enactment
1503(f)	11,503	Provisions relating to reporting requirements regarding coal or other mine safety	30 days after date of enactment

¶60,001

Act Sec.	Law Text ¶	Act Provision Subject	Effective Date
1504	11,504	Disclosure of payments by resource extraction issuers—Final rules	Not later than 270 days after date of enactment
1504	11,504	Disclosure of payments by resource extraction issuers—Final rules—Effective date with respect to resource extraction issuers	Date on which resource extraction issuer is required to submit annual report relating to fiscal year of the resource extraction issuer that ends not earlier than 1 year after date on which final rules issued
1505(a)	11,505	Study and report by the Comptroller General relating to inspectors general	Not later than 1 year after date of enactment
1506(b)	11,506	Study on core deposits and brokered deposits—Report	Not later than 1 year after date of enactment
		Title XVI—Section 1256 Contracts	
1601	11,601	Certain swaps not treated as section 1256 contracts under the Internal Revenue Code	Applicable to taxable years beginning after date of enactment

¶60,001

¶61,001 Table of Statutes Added, Amended or Repealed

Dodd-Frank Wall Street Reform and Consumer Protection Act

The following table lists all existing sections of the federal banking and securities laws that were added, amended or repealed by the Dodd-Frank Wall Street Reform and Consumer Protection Act. The first column indicates the law section that was amended with a note indicating if the law section was added, stricken or repealed. The second column indicates the Dodd-Frank Act section. The third column indicates the Dodd-Frank Act paragraph number. The fourth column indicates the explanation paragraph number.

Administrative Procedure (5 USC)

Law Sec./Note	Dodd-Frank Act Sec.	Act Par. (¶)	Exp Par. (¶)
552a(w) (added)	1082	11,082	4785

Alternative Mortgage Transaction Parity Act of 1982

Law Sec./Note	Dodd-Frank Act Sec.	Act Par. (¶)	Exp Par. (¶)
803(1)	1083(a)(1)	11,083	4790
804(a) and (c)	1083(a)(2)	11,083	4790
804(d) and (e) (added)	1083(a)(2)	11,083	4790

Analysis of Regulatory Functions (5 USC)

Law Sec./Note	Dodd-Frank Act Sec.	Act Par. (¶)	Exp Par. (¶)
609(a)	1100G(c)	11,100G	4915
609(d) (added)	1100G(b)	11,100G	4915
609(g)	1100G(a)	11,100G	4915

Bank Enterprise Act of 1991

Law Sec./Note	Dodd-Frank Act Sec.	Act Par. (¶)	Exp Par. (¶)
232(a)	353	10,353	1130

Bank Holding Company Act Amendments of 1970

Law Sec./Note	Dodd-Frank Act Sec.	Act Par. (¶)	Exp Par. (¶)
106(b)(1)	355	10,355	1140

Bank Holding Company Act of 1956

Law Sec./Note	Dodd-Frank Act Sec.	Act Par. (¶)	Exp Par. (¶)
2(c)(2)(F)(v)	628	10,628	2620
2(j)(3)	354(1)	10,354	1135
2(o)(4)	623(b)(2)	10,623	2595
3(c)(7) (added)	604(d)	10,604	2520, 2525, 2530, 2555, 2560, 2570, 2590, 2595, 2600, 2610, 2620
3(d)(1)(A)	607(a)	10,607	2540
4(i)	354(2)	10,354	1135
4(i)(8) (added)	623(b)(1)	10,623	2595
4(j)(2)(A)	604(e)(1)	10,604	2520, 2525, 2530, 2555, 2560, 2570, 2590, 2595, 2600, 2610, 2620
4(k)(6)(B)	604(e)(2)	10,604	2520, 2525, 2530, 2555, 2560, 2570, 2590, 2595, 2600, 2610, 2620
4(l)(1)	606(a)	10,606	2540
5(b)	616(a)	10,616	2540
5(c)(1)	604(a)	10,604	2520, 2525, 2530, 2555, 2560, 2570, 2590, 2595, 2600, 2610, 2620
5(c)(2)	604(b)	10,604	2520, 2525, 2530, 2555, 2560, 2570, 2590, 2595, 2600, 2610, 2620
5(c)(5)	604(c)(1)	10,604	2520, 2525, 2530, 2555, 2560, 2570, 2590, 2595, 2600, 2610, 2620
5(f)	354(3)	10,354	1135
10A (stricken)	604(c)(2)	10,604	2520, 2525, 2530, 2555, 2560, 2570, 2590, 2595, 2600, 2610, 2620
13 (added)	619(a)	10,619	2575
14 (added)	622(a)	10,622	2590

Bank Protection Act of 1968

Law Sec./Note	Dodd-Frank Act Sec.	Act Par. (¶)	Exp Par. (¶)
2	356(1)	10,356	1145
3	356(2)	10,356	1145

Bank Service Company Act

Law Sec./Note	Dodd-Frank Act Sec.	Act Par. (¶)	Exp Par. (¶)
1(b)(4)	357(1)	10,357	1150
1(b)(5)	357(2)	10,357	1150
7(c)(2)	357(3)	10,357	1150

Commodity Exchange Act

Law Sec./Note	Dodd-Frank Act Sec.	Act Par. (¶)	Exp Par. (¶)
1a(2), (3), (4), and (5) (added)	721(a)(2)	10,721	3010
1a(7) (added)	721(a)(3)	10,721	3010
1a(9)	721(a)(4)	10,721	3010
1a(10) (added)	721(a)(5)	10,721	3010
1a(11) (stricken)	721(a)(6)	10,721	3010
1a(19)(A)(iv)(II)	741(b)(10)	10,741	3130
1b (added)	722(h)	10,722	3015
2	734(b)(1)	10,734	3110
2(a)(1)	722(a)	10,722	3015
2(a)(1)	722(e)	10,722	3015
2(a)(1)(C)	717(a)	10,717	3035
2(a)(15) (added)	751	10,751	3015
2(c)	742(a)	10,742	3135
2(c)(2)(A)	722(c)	10,722	3015
2(c)(2)(B)	741(b)(8)	10,741	3130
2(c)(2)(B)(i)(II)	721(e)(1)	10,721	3010
2(c)(2)(B)(i)(II)	742(c)(1)	10,742	3135
2(c)(2)(C)	741(b)(9)	10,741	3130
2(c)(2)(E) (added)	742(c)(2)	10,742	3135
2(d) and (e) (added)	723(a)(2)	10,723	3060
2(h) (added)	723(a)(3)	10,723	3060
2(i) (added)	722(d)	10,722	3015
2(j) (added)	723(b)	10,723	3060
2a(13) and (14) (added)	727	10,727	3075
4	738(b)	10,738	3120
4(b)	738(a)	10,738	3120
4(c)	722(f)	10,722	3015
4(c)(1)	721(d)	10,721	3010
4a(a)	737(a)	10,737	3115
4a(b)	737(b)	10,737	3115
4a(c)	737(c)	10,737	3115
4b	741(b)(1)	10,741	3130
4b-1 (added)	741(a)	10,741	3130
4c(a)(1)	741(b)(2)	10,741	3130
4c(a)(3) and (4) (added)	746	10,746	3155
4c(a)(5), (6), and (7) (added)	747	10,747	3155
4d	713(b)	10,713	3025
4d	749(a)	10,749	
4d(f) (added)	724(a)	10,724	3065
4m(3)	721(e)(2)	10,721	3010
4m(3)	749(b)	10,749	
4q(a)(1)	721(e)(3)	10,721	3010
4r (added)	729	10,729	3085
4s (added)	731	10,731	3095
4s(l) (added)	724(c)	10,724	3065
4t (added)	730	10,730	3090
5(b) (stricken)	735(a)	10,735	3110
5(e)(1)	721(e)(4)	10,721	3010
5a(b)(2)(F)	721(e)(5)	10,721	3010
5a (repealed)	734(a)	10,734	3105
5b(a)	721(e)(6)	10,721	3010

Law Sec./Note	Dodd-Frank Act Sec.	Act Par. (¶)	Exp Par. (¶)
5b(a) and (b)	725(a)	10,725	3070
5b(c)(2)	725(c)	10,725	3070
5b(f)(1)	725(h)	10,725	3070
5b(g), (h), and (i) (added)	725(b)	10,725	3070
5b(k) (added)	725(e)	10,725	3070
5c	749(c)	10,749	
5c(c)(1)	717(d)	10,717	3035
5c(c)(2)(B)	721(e)(7)	10,721	3010
5c(d) (stricken)	745(c)	10,745	3140
5d (repealed)	734(a)	10,734	3105
5e	749(d)	10,749	
5h (added)	733	10,733	3100
6(b)	749(e)	10,749	
6(c)	741(b)(3)	10,741	3130
6(c)	753(a)	10,753	3155
6(d)	741(b)(4)	10,741	3130
6(d)	753(b)	10,753	3155
6(e)	741(b)(11)	10,741	3130
6(g)(1)(A)	734(b)(2)	10,734	3110
6(g)(5)(B)(i)	721(e)(8)	10,721	3010
6c(a)	741(b)(5)	10,741	3130
6c(d)(3) (added)	744	10,744	3130
8(e)	725(f)	10,725	3070
8a(7)	736	10,736	3110
9	741(b)(6)	10,741	3130
9(a)	741(b)(7)	10,741	3130
12	722(b)	10,722	3015
12(e)(2)(B)	749(f)	10,749	
17(r)(1)	749(g)	10,749	
20(c) (added)	713(c)	10,713	3025
21 (added)	728	10,728	3080
22	749(h)	10,749	
22(a)(6) (added)	738(c)	10,738	3120
23 (added)	748	10,748	3145

Community Reinvestment Act of 1977

Law Sec./Note	Dodd-Frank Act Sec.	Act Par. (¶)	Exp Par. (¶)
803	358(1)	10,358	1155
806	358(2)	10,358	1155

Crime Control Act of 1990

Law Sec./Note	Dodd-Frank Act Sec.	Act Par. (¶)	Exp Par. (¶)
2501	211(b)	10,211	505, 550
2501(a)(1)	211(a)	10,211	505, 550

¶61,001

Table of Statutes Added, Amended or Repealed

Crimes and Criminal Procedure (18 USC)

Law Sec./Note	Dodd-Frank Act Sec.	Act Par. (¶)	Exp Par. (¶)
212(c)(2)	377(1)	10,377	1250

Depository Institution Management Interlocks Act

Law Sec./Note	Dodd-Frank Act Sec.	Act Par. (¶)	Exp Par. (¶)
207	360(1)	10,360	1165
209	360(2)	10,360	1165

Electronic Fund Transfer Act

Law Sec./Note	Dodd-Frank Act Sec.	Act Par. (¶)	Exp Par. (¶)
902(b)	1073(a)(1)	11,073	4740
904(a)	1084(3)	11,084	4795
904(c)	1073(a)(2)	11,073	4740
916(d)	1084(4)	11,084	4795
918(a) and (b)	1084(5)	11,084	4795
919 (added)	1073(a)(4	11,073	4740

Emergency Economic Stabilization Act of 2008

Law Sec./Note	Dodd-Frank Act Sec.	Act Par. (¶)	Exp Par. (¶)
106(f) (added)	1303	11,303	6015
115(a)	1302	11,302	6010

Emergency Housing Act of 1975

Law Sec./Note	Dodd-Frank Act Sec.	Act Par. (¶)	Exp Par. (¶)
103	1496(b)(1)	11,496	6765
104	1496(b)(2)	11,496	6765
105	1496(b)(3)	11,496	6765
107	1496(b)(4)	11,496	6765
108	1496(b)(5)	11,496	6765
109	1496(b)(6)	11,496	6765
110, 111, and 113 (stricken)	1496(b)(7)	11,496	6765

Equal Credit Opportunity Act

Law Sec./Note	Dodd-Frank Act Sec.	Act Par. (¶)	Exp Par. (¶)
701(b)	1071(b)	11,071	4730
701(e)	1474	11,474	6715

¶61,001

Law Sec./Note	Dodd-Frank Act Sec.	Act Par. (¶)	Exp Par. (¶)
702(c)	1085(2)	11,085	4800
703	1085(3)	11,085	4800
704(a), (c) and (d)	1085(4)	11,085	4800
704B (added)	1071(a)	11,071	4730
706(e)	1085(5)	11,085	4800
706(f)	1085(7)	11,085	4800
706(g)	1085(6)	11,085	4800

Expedited Funds Availability Act

Law Sec./Note	Dodd-Frank Act Sec.	Act Par. (¶)	Exp Par. (¶)
603(a)(2)(D), (b)(3)(C), and (c)(1)(B)(iii)	1086(e)	11,086	4805
603(d)(1)	1086(a)	11,086	4805
604	1086(b)	11,086	4805
605	1086(c)	11,086	4805
607(f) (added)	1086(f)	11,086	4805
609(a) and (e)	1086(d)	11,086	4805

Fair Credit Reporting Act

Law Sec./Note	Dodd-Frank Act Sec.	Act Par. (¶)	Exp Par. (¶)
603(k)(2)	1088(a)(3)	11,088	4815
603(w), (x) and (y)	1088(a)(1)	11,088	4815
604(g)	1088(a)(4)	11,088	4815
605(h)(2)(A)	1088(a)(5)	11,088	4815
611(e)(2)	1088(a)(6)	11,088	4815
615(a)	1100F(1)	11,100F	4910
615(d)(2)(B)	1088(a)(7)	11,088	4815
615(e)(1)	1088(a)(8)	11,088	4815
615(h)(5)	1100F(2)	11,100F	4910
615(h)(6)	1088(a)(9)	11,088	4815
621(a), (b), (c)(2), (c)(4), (e), and (f)	1088(a)(10)	11,088	4815
623(a)(7), (a)(8) and (e)	1088(a)(11)	11,088	4815
628(a)(1)	1088(a)(12)	11,088	4815
628(a)(3)	1088(a)(13)	11,088	4815

Fair Debt Collection Practices Act

Law Sec./Note	Dodd-Frank Act Sec.	Act Par. (¶)	Exp Par. (¶)
803(a)	1089(2)	11,089	4820
814(a) and (b)	1089(3)	11,089	4820
814(d)	1089(4)	11,089	4820

Federal Deposit Insurance Act

Law Sec./Note	Dodd-Frank Act Sec.	Act Par. (¶)	Exp Par. (¶)
2(a), (d), (f)	336	10,336	1105
3(b), (l), and (z)	363(1)	10,363	1180
3(q) and (u)	312(c)	10,312	1015
3(y)(3)	334(b)	10,334	1095
7(a) and (n)	363(2)	10,363	1180
7(a)(2)(B)	333(a)	10,333	1095
7(b)(1)(e)	333(b)	10,333	1095
7(b)(1)(E)(i)	939(a)(1)	10,939	4180
7(b)(2)	331(a)	10,331	1095
7(b)(3)(B)	334(a)	10,334	1095
7(e)	332	10,332	1095
8(a), (b), (e), (j), (o), and (w)	363(3)	10,363	1180
8(t)(6) (added)	1090(1)	11,090	4825
10(e)	318(d)	10,318	1040
10(d) and (k)	363(4)	10,363	1180
11(a)(1(E)	335(a)	10,335	1100
11(a)(1)	343(a)(1)	10,343	1120
11(a)(1)	343(a)(3)	10,343	1120
11(c)	363(5)(A)	10,363	1180
11(d)	363(5)(B)	10,363	1180
11(m)	363(5)(C)	10,363	1180
11(n)	363(5)(D)	10,363	1180
11(p)	363(5)(E)	10,363	1180
12(k)	363(6)	10,363	1180
13(c)(4)(G) (added)	1106(b)	11,106	5035
18(c)(2), (g)(1), (i)(2)(C) and (m)	363(7)	10,363	1180
18(c)(5)	604(f)	10,604	2520, 2525, 2530, 2555, 2560, 2570, 2590, 2595, 2600, 2610, 2620
18(c)(13) (added)	623(a)	10,623	2595
18(d)(4)(A)(i)	613(b)	10,613	2560
18(g) (repealed)	627(a)(3)	10,627	2615
18(y) (added)	611(a)	10,611	2550
18(z) (added)	615(a)	10,615	2545
28(d)	939(a)(2)	10,939	4180
28(e)	939(a)(3)	10,939	4180
28(e) and (h)	363(9)	10,363	1180
38A (added)	616(d)	10,616	2540
43(c), (d), (e) and (f)	1090(2)	11,090	4825
44(b)(4)(B)	607(b)	10,607	2540

Federal Deposit Insurance Corporation Improvement Act of 1991

Law Sec./Note	Dodd-Frank Act Sec.	Act Par. (¶)	Exp Par. (¶)
403(a)	211(c)	10,211	505, 550
408(2)(C)	749(i)	10,749	
408 (repealed)	740	10,740	3070
409 (repealed)	740	10,740	3070

¶61,001

Federal Financial Institutions Examination Council Act of 1978

Law Sec./Note	Dodd-Frank Act Sec.	Act Par. (¶)	Exp Par. (¶)
1004(a)(4)	1091	11,091	4830
1011	1473(s)	11,473	6710

Federal Home Loan Bank Act

Law Sec./Note	Dodd-Frank Act Sec.	Act Par. (¶)	Exp Par. (¶)
11(l)(2)	1304(c)	11,304	6015
18(c) (repealed)	364(a)	10,364	1185
21A (repealed)	364(b)	10,364	1185

Federal Reserve Act

Law Sec./Note	Dodd-Frank Act Sec.	Act Par. (¶)	Exp Par. (¶)
2B(c) (added)	1103(a)	11,103	5010, 5015, 5020, 5025, 5030
4	1107	11,107	5040
10(12) (added)	1108(b)	11,108	5040
11(a)(2)	366(1)	10,366	1195
11(s) (added)	318(c)	10,318	1040
11(s) (added)	1103(b)	11,103	5010, 5015, 5020, 5025, 5030
13	1101(a)	11,101	5010
19(b)	366(2)	10,366	1195
19(i) (repealed)	627(a)(1)	10,627	2615
22(d)	615(b)	10,615	2545
22(h)(9)(D)(i)	614(a)	10,614	2545
23A(b), (c), (d)(4), and (f)	608(a)	10,608	2545
23A(e)	609(a)	10,609	2545
23B(e)	608(b)	10,608	2545

Federal Trade Commission Act

Law Sec./Note	Dodd-Frank Act Sec.	Act Par. (¶)	Exp Par. (¶)
18(f)	1092	11,092	4835

Financial Institutions Reform, Recovery, and Enforcement Act of 1989

Law Sec./Note	Dodd-Frank Act Sec.	Act Par. (¶)	Exp Par. (¶)
1206	367(8)	10,367	1200
1216	367(9)	10,367	1200
1103(a)	1473(b)	11,473	6710
1103(a)	1473(f)(1)	11,473	6710

¶61,001

Law Sec./Note	Dodd-Frank Act Sec.	Act Par. (¶)	Exp Par. (¶)
1104(b)	1473(c)	11,473	6710
1106	1473(d)	11,473	6710
1109(a)	1473(g)	11,473	6710
1109(a)	1473(h)	11,473	6710
1109(b)	1473(i)	11,473	6710
1110	1473(e)	11,473	6710
1112(b)	1473(a)	11,473	6710
1116	1473(j)	11,473	6710
1117	1473(f)(3)	11,473	6710
1118	1473(k)	11,473	6710
1121	1473(f)(4)	11,473	6710
1121(6)	1473(t)(2)	11,473	6710
1121(8)	1473(t)(3)	11,473	6710
1122	1473(l)	11,473	6710
1122	1473(t)(4)	11,473	6710
1122(d)	1473(m)	11,473	6710
1122(g) (added)	1473(n)	11,473	6710
1122(h) (added)	1473(o)	11,473	6710
1122(i) (added)	1473(p)	11,473	6710
1124 (added)	1473(f)(2)	11,473	6710
1125 (added)	1473(q)	11,473	6710
1126 (added)	1473(r)	11,473	6710

Gramm-Leach-Bliley Act

Law Sec./Note	Dodd-Frank Act Sec.	Act Par. (¶)	Exp Par. (¶)
206(a)	742(b)	10,742	3135
206A(a)	762(b)	10,762	3015
206B (repealed)	762(a)	10,762	3015
206C (repealed)	762(a)	10,762	3015
501(b)	1093(1)	11,093	4840
502(e)(5)	1093(2)	11,093	4840
504(a)	1093(3)	11,093	4840
505(a)	1093(4)	11,093	4840
505(b)(1)	1093(5)	11,093	4840
507(b)	1093(6)	11,093	4840

Home Mortgage Disclosure Act of 1975

Law Sec./Note	Dodd-Frank Act Sec.	Act Par. (¶)	Exp Par. (¶)
304(b), (h), (i), (j), (m)	1094(3)	11,094	4845
304(n) (added)	1094(3)	11,094	4845
305(d) (added)	1094(4)	11,094	4845

Home Owners' Loan Act

Law Sec./Note	Dodd-Frank Act Sec.	Act Par. (¶)	Exp Par. (¶)
1	369(1)	10,369	1210

¶61,001

1586   Dodd-Frank Wall Street Reform and Consumer Protection Act

Law Sec./Note	Dodd-Frank Act Sec.	Act Par. (¶)	Exp Par. (¶)
2	369(2)	10,369	1210
2	604(h)(1)	10,604	2520, 2525, 2530, 2555, 2560, 2570, 2590, 2595, 2600, 2610, 2620
3	369(3)	10,369	1210
4	369(4)	10,369	1210
5(a)	369(5)(A)	10,369	1210
5(b)	369(5)(B)	10,369	1210
5(b)(1)(B)	627(a)(2)	10,627	2615
5(c)	369(5)(C)	10,369	1210
5(d)	369(5)(D)	10,369	1210
5(e)	369(5)(E)	10,369	1210
5(i)	369(5)(F)	10,369	1210
5(i)(6) (added)	612(c)	10,612	2555
5(m), (n), (o) and (p)	369(5)(H)	10,369	1210
5(o)	369(5)(G)	10,369	1210
5(q)	369(5)(I)	10,369	1210
5(r)(3)	369(5)(J)	10,369	1210
5(s)	369(5)(K)	10,369	1210
5(t)	369(5)(L)	10,369	1210
5(u)	369(5)(M)	10,369	1210
5(u)(3)	610(b)	10,610	2550
5(v)	369(5)(N)	10,369	1210
5(w)	369(5)(O)	10,369	1210
6 (added)	1046	11,046	4650
6 (c) and (d)	1047(b)	11,047	4655
8	369(6)	10,369	1210
9	369(7)	10,369	1210
10	369(8)	10,369	1210
10(a)(2)(D)(ii)	604(i)	10,604	2520, 2525, 2530, 2555, 2560, 2570, 2590, 2595, 2600, 2610, 2620
10(b)(2)	604(g)	10,604	2520, 2525, 2530, 2555, 2560, 2570, 2590, 2595, 2600, 2610, 2620
10(b)(4)	604(h)(2)	10,604	2520, 2525, 2530, 2555, 2560, 2570, 2590, 2595, 2600, 2610, 2620
10(c)(2)	606(b)	10,606	2540
10(e)(2)	623(c)	10,623	2595
10(g)(1)	616(b)	10,616	2540
10(m)(3)	624	10,624	2600
10(o)(11) (added)	625(a)	10,625	2605
10A (added)	626	10,626	2610
11	369(9)	10,369	1210
11(d) (added)	608(c)	10,608	2545
12	369(10)	10,369	1210
13	369(11)	10,369	1210

Homeowners Protection Act of 1998

Law Sec./Note	Dodd-Frank Act Sec.	Act Par. (¶)	Exp Par. (¶)
10(a)	1095(1)	11,095	4850

¶61,001

Law Sec./Note	Dodd-Frank Act Sec.	Act Par. (¶)	Exp Par. (¶)
10(b)(2)	1095(2)	11,095	4850

Housing and Economic Recovery Act of 2008

Law Sec./Note	Dodd-Frank Act Sec.	Act Par. (¶)	Exp Par. (¶)
2301(f)(3)(A)(ii)	1497(b)	11,497	6770

Housing and Urban Development Act of 1968

Law Sec./Note	Dodd-Frank Act Sec.	Act Par. (¶)	Exp Par. (¶)
106(a)(4) (added)	1444	11,444	6630
106(c)(5)(A)(ii)	1443(b)	11,443	6625
106(e)	1445	11,445	6635
106(g) (added)	1443(a)	11,443	6625
106(h) (added)	1448	11,448	6650
106(i) (added)	1449	11,449	6655

International Lending Supervision Act of 1983

Law Sec./Note	Dodd-Frank Act Sec.	Act Par. (¶)	Exp Par. (¶)
908(a)(1)	616(c)	10,616	2540

Investment Advisers Act of 1940

Law Sec./Note	Dodd-Frank Act Sec.	Act Par. (¶)	Exp Par. (¶)
202(a)	402(a)	10,402	1510
202(a)(11)	409(a)	10,409	1530
202(a)(21)	986(d)	10,986	4450
202(a)(29) (added)	402(a)	10,402	1510
202(a)(29) (added)	770	10,770	3010
202(a)(30) (added)	402(a)	10,402	1510
203	985(e)(1)	10,985	4450
203(b)(1)	403(1)	10,403	1515
203(b)(3)	403(2)	10,403	1515
203(b)(5)	403(3)	10,403	1515
203(b)(6)	403(4)	10,403	1515
203(b)(7) (added)	403(5)	10,403	1515
203(f)	925(h)	10,925	4065
203(i)(1)	929P(a)(4)	10,929P	4135
203(l) (added)	407	10,407	1515
203(m) (added)	408	10,408	1515
203(n) (added)	408	10,408	1515
203A(a)	410	10,410	1535
204	404	10,404	1520
204(d) (added)	929Q(b)	10,929Q	4140

¶61,001

Dodd-Frank Wall Street Reform and Consumer Protection Act

Law Sec./Note	Dodd-Frank Act Sec.	Act Par. (¶)	Exp Par. (¶)
205(a)	928	10,928	4080
205(e)	418	10,418	1555
205(f) (added)	921(b)	10,921	4050, 4055
206(3)	985(e)(2)	10,985	4450
209(e)(3)(A)	923(a)(3)	10,923	4060
209(f) (added)	929N	10,929N	4130
210(c)	405	10,405	1520
210(d) (added)	929I(c)	10,929I	4120
211(a)	406(1)	10,406	1525
211(e) (added)	406(2)	10,406	1525
211(g) and (h) (added)	913(g)(2)	10,913	4020
211(i) (added)	913(h)(2)	10,913	4020
213(a)	985(e)(3)	10,985	4450
214	929E(d)	10,929E	4105
214	929P(b)(3)	10,929P	4135
222	985(e)(4)	10,985	4450
223 (added)	411	10,411	1540
224 (added)	414	10,414	1550

Investment Company Act of 1940

Law Sec./Note	Dodd-Frank Act Sec.	Act Par. (¶)	Exp Par. (¶)
2(a)(19)	985(d)(1)	10,985	4450
2(a)(44)	986(c)(1)	10,986	4450
2(a)(54) (added)	769	10,769	3010
3(c)	986(c)(2)	10,986	4450
6(a)(5)(A)(iv)(I)	939(c)	10,939	4180
9(b)(4)(B)	985(d)(2)	10,985	4450
9(d)(1)	929P(a)(3)	10,929P	4135
12(d)(1)(J)	985(d)(3)	10,985	4450
17(f)	985(d)(4)	10,985	4450
31	929I(b)(1)	10,929I	4120
31	929Q(a)	10,929Q	4140
31(d) (stricken)	929I(b)(2)	10,929I	4120
36(a)	929F(f)	10,929F	4110
38(b)	986(c)(3)	10,986	4450
42(e)(3)(A)	923(a)(2)	10,923	4060
44	929E(c)	10,929E	4105
48	929M(b)	10,929M	4130
50	986(c)(4)	10,986	4450
61(a)(3)(B)(iii)	985(d)(5)	10,985	4450

Legal Certainty for Bank Products Act of 2000

Law Sec./Note	Dodd-Frank Act Sec.	Act Par. (¶)	Exp Par. (¶)
402(a)(7)	721(e)(9)(A)	10,721	3010
402(b)(2)	721(e)(9)(B)	10,721	3010
402(c)	721(e)(9)(C)	10,721	3010
402(d) (stricken)	721(g)(1)(B)	10,721	3010
403	721(g)(2)	10,721	3010

¶61,001

Law Sec./Note	Dodd-Frank Act Sec.	Act Par. (¶)	Exp Par. (¶)
404 (stricken)	721(g)(1)(A)	10,721	3010
407 (stricken)	721(g)(1)(A)	10,721	3010

National Banks (12 USC/Revised Statutes)

Law Sec./Note	Dodd-Frank Act Sec.	Act Par. (¶)	Exp Par. (¶)
24a(2)(E) (USC)	939(d)(1)	10,939	4180
24a(a)(3) (USC)	939(d)(2)	10,939	4180
24a(a)(3)(A) (USC)	939(d)(3)	10,939	4180
24a(f) (USC)	939(d)(4)	10,939	4180
24a(f)(1) (USC)	939(d)(5)	10,939	4180
35 (USC)	612(b)	10,612	2555
36(g)(1)(A) (USC)	613(a)(3)	10,613	2560
84(b)(1) and (b)(2) (USC)	610(a)	10,610	2550
84(b)(3) (added) (USC)	610(a)(3)	10,610	2550
214d (added) (USC)	612(a)	10,612	2555
324 (USC)	314(a)	10,314	1020
327B (added) (USC)	314(b)	10,314	1020
329 (USC)	314(c)	10,314	1020
5136C (added) (RS)	1044	11,044	4640
5136C(h) (added) (RS)	1045	11,045	4645
5136C(i)-(j) (added) (RS)	1047(a)	11,047	4655

Protecting Tenants at Foreclosure Act of 2009

Law Sec./Note	Dodd-Frank Act Sec.	Act Par. (¶)	Exp Par. (¶)
702	1484(1)	11,484	6745
704	1484(2)	11,484	6745

Real Estate Settlement Procedures Act of 1974

Law Sec./Note	Dodd-Frank Act Sec.	Act Par. (¶)	Exp Par. (¶)
3(7), (8)	1098(1)	11,098	4865
3(9) (added)	1098(1)	11,098	4865
4	1475	11,475	6720
4(a)	1098(2)	11,098	4865
5	1450	11,450	6660
6	1463(a)	11,463	6685
6(e)	1463(c)	11,463	6685
6(f)	1463(b)	11,463	6685
6(g)	1463(d)	11,463	6685
6(j)(3)	1098(4)	11,098	4865
7(b)	1098(5)	11,098	4865
8(c)(5)	1098(6)	11,098	4865
8(d)	1098(7)	11,098	4865
10(c) and (d)	1098(8)	11,098	4865
16	1098(9)	11,098	4865
18	1098(10)	11,098	4865

¶61,001

Law Sec./Note	Dodd-Frank Act Sec.	Act Par. (¶)	Exp Par. (¶)
19(a), (b) and (c)	1098(11)	11,098	4865

Right to Financial Privacy Act of 1978

Law Sec./Note	Dodd-Frank Act Sec.	Act Par. (¶)	Exp Par. (¶)
1101(6) and (7)	1099(1)	11,099	4875
1112(e)	1099(2)	11,099	4875
1113(r) (added)	1099(3)	11,099	4875

S.A.F.E. Mortgage Licensing Act of 2008

Law Sec./Note	Dodd-Frank Act Sec.	Act Par. (¶)	Exp Par. (¶)
1507(a) and (b)	1100(5)	11,100	4880
1508(f) (added)	1100(6)	11,100	4880
1510	1100(7)	11,100	4880
1513	1100(8)	11,100	4880
1514	1100(9)	11,100	4880

Sarbanes-Oxley Act of 2002

Law Sec./Note	Dodd-Frank Act Sec.	Act Par. (¶)	Exp Par. (¶)
2(a)	982(a)(2)	10,982	4420, 4435
2(a)(9)	929F(g)(1)	10,929F	4110
2(a)(17) (added)	981(a)	10,981	4420, 4430
101	982(b)	10,982	4420, 4435
102	982(c)	10,982	4420, 4435
103(a)	982(d)	10,982	4420, 4435
104(a)	982(e)(1)	10,982	4420, 4435
105(b)(4)(B)	982(i)	10,982	4420, 4435
105(b)(5)(A)	981(c)	10,981	4420, 4430
105(b)(5)(B)(ii)	982(j)	10,982	4420, 4435
105(b)(5)(C) (added)	981(b)	10,981	4420, 4430
105(c)(6)	929F(h)	10,929F	4110
105(c)(7)(B)	982(f)	10,982	4420, 4435
106	929J	10,929J	4420, 4425
106(a)	982(g)	10,982	4420, 4435
106(d), (e), and (f) (added)	929J(3)	10,929J	4420, 4425
107(d)(3)	929F(i)	10,929F	4110
109	982(h)	10,982	4420, 4435
110 (added)	982(a)(1)	10,982	4420, 4435
308	929B	10,929B	4090
404(c) (added)	989G(a)	10,989G	4490

¶61,001

Savings Associations, P.L. 93-100

Law Sec./Note	Dodd-Frank Act Sec.	Act Par. (¶)	Exp Par. (¶)
5(d)	375	10,375	1240

Securities Act of 1933

Law Sec./Note	Dodd-Frank Act Sec.	Act Par. (¶)	Exp Par. (¶)
2(a)	768(a)	10,768	3160
2A	762(c)(1)	10,762	3015
3(a)(4)	985(a)(1)	10,985	4450
4	944(a)	10,944	4265
5(d) (added)	768(b)	10,768	3160
6(b)	991(b)(1)	10,991	4350, 4370
7(c) (added)	942(b)	10,942	4260
7(d) (added)	945	10,945	4270
8A(g) (added)	929P(a)(1)	10,929P	4135
15	929M(a)(1)	10,929M	4130
15(b) (added)	929M(a)(2)	10,929M	4130
17	762(c)(2)	10,762	3015
18	985(a)(2)	10,985	4450
19(d)(6)(A)	985(a)(3)	10,985	4450
19(e) and (f) (added)	912	10,912	4015
19(g) (added)	978(a)	10,978	4405, 4410
20(d)(3)(A)	923(a)(1)	10,923	4060
22(a)	929E(a)	10,929E	4110
22(c) (added)	929P(b)(1)	10,929P	4135
27A(c)(1)(B)(ii)	985(a)(4)	10,985	4450
27B (added)	621	10,621	2585

Securities Exchange Act of 1934

Law Sec./Note	Dodd-Frank Act Sec.	Act Par. (¶)	Exp Par. (¶)
2	985(b)(1)	10,985	4450
3	985(b)(2)	10,985	4450
3(a)	939(e)	10,939	4180
3(a)(4)(B)(vii)(I)	944(b)	10,944	4265
3(a)(5)	761(a)(1)	10,761	3010
3(a)(10)	761(a)(2)	10,761	3010
3(a)(13)	761(a)(3)	10,761	3010
3(a)(14)	761(a)(4)	10,761	3010
3(a)(34)	376(1)	10,376	1245
3(a)(39)	761(a)(5)	10,761	3010
3(a)(47)	986(a)(1)	10,986	4450
3(a)(53)	939(e)(2)	10,939	4220
3(a)(62)	932(b)	10,932	4185
3(a)(65) (added)	761(a)(6)	10,761	3010
3(a)(66) (added)	761(a)(6)	10,761	3010
3(a)(67) (added)	761(a)(6)	10,761	3010
3(a)(68) (added)	761(a)(6)	10,761	3010
3(a)(69) (added)	761(a)(6)	10,761	3010

Law Sec./Note	Dodd-Frank Act Sec.	Act Par. (¶)	Exp Par. (¶)
3(a)(70) (added)	761(a)(6)	10,761	3010
3(a)(71) (added)	761(a)(6)	10,761	3010
3(a)(72) (added)	761(a)(6)	10,761	3010
3(a)(73) (added)	761(a)(6)	10,761	3010
3(a)(74) (added)	761(a)(6)	10,761	3010
3(a)(75) (added)	761(a)(6)	10,761	3010
3(a)(76) (added)	761(a)(6)	10,761	3010
3(a)(77) (added)	761(a)(6)	10,761	3010
3(a)(77) (added)	941(a)	10,941	4250
3(a)(78) (added)	761(a)(6)	10,761	3010
3A	762(d)(1)	10,762	3015
3B (added)	717(b)	10,717	3035
3C (added)	763(a)	10,763	3160
3D (added)	763(c)	10,763	3160
3E (added)	763(d)	10,763	3160
4(g)(8) (added)	919D	10,919D	4025, 4035, 4040
4(g) (added)	915	10,915	4025
4(h) (added)	965	10,965	4360
4(i) (added)	991(e)(1)	10,991	4350, 4370
4D (added)	966	10,966	4365
4E (added)	929U	10,929U	4155
6(b)(9)	957(1)	10,957	4325
6(b)(9)(10)(A) (added)	957(2)	10,957	4325
6(g)(5)(B)(i)	721	10,721	3010
6(l) (added)	763(e)	10,763	3160
7(c)(1)(A)	929	10,929	4085, 4145
9	929X(b)	10,929X	4085, 4145
9	929L(1)	10,929L	4125
9(a)(2), (3), (4), and (5)	762(d)(2)(A)	10,762	3015
9(b)(1) through (3)	763(f)	10,763	3160
9(i)	762(d)(2)(B)	10,762	3015
9(j) (added)	763(g)	10,763	3160
10	762(d)(3)	10,762	3015
10(a)(1)	929L(2)	10,929L	4125
10(c)(1) and (2) (added)	984(a)	10,984	4460
10A(i)(1)(B)	985(b)(3)	10,985	4450
10B (added)	763(h)	10,763	3160
10C (added)	952(a)	10,952	4300
10D (added)	954	10,954	4310
12(i)	376(2)	10,376	1245
12(k)(7)	986(a)(2)	10,986	4450
13	766(b)	10,766	3170
13	929R(a)	10,929R	4145
13(b)(1)	985(b)(4)	10,985	4450
13(e)	991(b)(2)	10,991	4350, 4370
13(f)	929X(a)	10,929X	4085, 4145
13(f)(1)	766(c)	10,766	3170
13(m) and (n) (added)	763(i)	10,763	3160
13(o) (added)	766(e)	10,766	3170
13(p) (added)	1502(b)	11,502	7020
13(q) (added)	1504	11,504	7030
13A (added)	766(a)	10,766	3170
14(a)	971(a)(1)	10,971	4290
14(a)(2) (added)	971(a)(2)	10,971	4290
14(g)	991(b)(3)	10,991	4350, 4370

Table of Statutes Added, Amended or Repealed

Law Sec./Note	Dodd-Frank Act Sec.	Act Par. (¶)	Exp Par. (¶)
14(i) (added)	953(a)	10,953	4305
14(j) (added)	955	10,955	4315
14A (added)	951	10,951	4290
14B (added)	972	10,972	4335
15	762(d)(4)	10,762	3015
15	929X(c)	10,929X	4165
15	975(g)	10,975	4380, 4385, 4390, 4395
15	985(b)(5)	10,985	4450
15(b)(4)	766(d)	10,766	3170
15(b)(6)(A)	925(a)(1)	10,925	4065
15(c)(1)(A)	929L(3)	10,929L	4135
15(c)(1)(B)	762(d)(4)(B)	10,762	3015
15(c)(1)(C)	762(d)(4)(C)	10,762	3015
15(c)(3)	713(a)	10,713	3025
15(d)	942(a)	10,942	4260
15(k) and (l) (added)	913(g)(1)	10,913	4020
15(k) (added)	173(c)	10,173	240
15(l) (added)	173(c)	10,173	240
15(m) (added)	913(h)(1)	10,913	4020
15(n) (added)	919	10,919	4035
15(o) (added)	921(a)	10,921	4050, 4055
15A(b)(15) (added)	975(f)	10,975	4380, 4385, 4390, 4395
15B(a)	975(a)	10,975	4380, 4385, 4390, 4395
15B(b)	975(b)	10,975	4380, 4385, 4390, 4395
15B(c)	975(c)	10,975	4380, 4385, 4390, 4395
15B(c)(4)	925(a)(2)	10,925	4065
15B(c)(8)	929F(a)	10,929F	4110
15B(d)(2)	975(d)	10,975	4380, 4385, 4390, 4395
15B(e) (added)	975(e)	10,975	4380, 4385, 4390, 4395
15C(a)(2)	985(b)(6)	10,985	4450
15C(c)	929F(b)	10,929F	4110
15C(g)(1)	376(3)	10,376	1245
15E	932(a)	10,932	4185
15E(m)	933(a)	10,933	4195
15E(u) (added)	934	10,934	4215
15E(v) (added)	935	10,935	4200
15F (added)	764(a)	10,764	3165
15G (added)	941(b)	10,941	4250
16	762(d)(5)	10,762	3015
16(a)	929R(b)	10,929R	4145
17(a)(1)	975(h)	10,975	4380, 4385, 4390, 4395
17(b)(1)(B)	985(b)(7)	10,985	4450
17(e)(1)(A)	982(e)(2)	10,982	4420, 4435
17(f)(1)	929D	10,929D	4100
17(f)(2)	929S	10,929S	4150
17(i) (stricken)	617	10,617	2570
17(i), (j) and (k)	617(a)	10,617	2570
17A(c)(4)(C)	925(a)(3)	10,925	4065
17A(g) through (m) (added)	763(b)	10,763	3160
17A(g) (added)	929W	10,929W	4160
19(b)	916(a)	10,916	4030
19(b)(1)	916(b)(2)	10,916	4030
19(b)(3)	916(c)	10,916	4030
19(b)(4)(D)	916(d)	10,916	4030

¶61,001

Law Sec./Note	Dodd-Frank Act Sec.	Act Par. (¶)	Exp Par. (¶)
19(b)(10) (added)	717(c)	10,717	3035
19(b)(10) (added)	916(b)(1)	10,916	4030
19(h)(4)	929F(e)	10,929F	4110
20	762(d)(6)	10,762	3015
20(a)	929P(c)	10,929P	4135
20(e)	929O	10,929O	4130
21(a)(1)	929F(c)	10,929F	4110
21(a)(1)	929F(d)	10,929F	4110
21(a)(1)	929F(g)(2)	10,929F	4110
21(d)(3)(C)(i)	923(b)(1)	10,923	4060
21(h)(2)	986(a)(3)	10,986	4450
21A	762(d)(7)	10,762	3015
21A	923(b)(2)	10,923	4060
21B(a)	929P(a)(2)	10,929P	4135
21B(f) (added)	773	10,773	3130
21C(c)(2)	985(b)(8)	10,985	4450
21D(b)(2)	933(b)	10,933	4195
21F (added)	922(a)	10,922	4060, 4215
23(b)(1)	376(4)	10,376	1245
24	929I(a)	10,929I	4120
24	929K	10,929K	4120
27	929E(b)	10,929E	4105
27	929P(b)(2)	10,929P	4135
28(a)	767	10,767	3175
29(a)	927	10,927	4075
29(a)	929T	10,929T	4075
30(c) (added)	772(b)	10,772	3015
31	991(a)(1)	10,991	4370
35	991(c)	10,991	4350, 4370
36(c)	772(a)	10,772	3015
39	911	10,911	3015

Securities Investor Protection Act of 1970

Law Sec./Note	Dodd-Frank Act Sec.	Act Par. (¶)	Exp Par. (¶)
4(d)(1)(C)	929V(a)	10,929V	4095
4(h)	929C	10,929C	4095
5(a)(3)	929H(b)	10,929H	4095
9(a)(1)	983(a)	10,983	4095, 4455
9(a)(1)	929H(a)(1)	10,929H	4095
9(d) and (e) (added)	929H(a)(2)	10,929H	4095
14(c)	929V(b)	10,929V	4095
14(d) (added)	929V(c)	10,929V	4095
16	983(b)	10,983	4095, 4455

Telemarketing and Consumer Fraud and Abuse Prevention Act

Law Sec./Note	Dodd-Frank Act Sec.	Act Par. (¶)	Exp Par. (¶)
3	1100C(a)	11,100C	4895
4(d)	1100C(b)	11,100C	4895

Law Sec./Note	Dodd-Frank Act Sec.	Act Par. (¶)	Exp Par. (¶)
5(c)	1100C(c)	11,100C	4895
6(d) (added)	1100C(d)	11,100C	4895

Trust Indenture Act of 1939

Law Sec./Note	Dodd-Frank Act Sec.	Act Par. (¶)	Exp Par. (¶)
303(17)	986(b)(1)	10,986	4450
304(b)	985(c)(1)	10,985	4450
308	986(b)(2)	10,986	4450
310	986(b)(3)	10,986	4450
311	986(b)(4)	10,986	4450
317(a)(1)	985(c)(2)	10,985	4450
323(b)	986(b)(5)	10,986	4450
326	986(b)(6)	10,986	4450

Truth in Lending Act

Law Sec./Note	Dodd-Frank Act Sec.	Act Par. (¶)	Exp Par. (¶)
103(aa)	1431(c)(2)	11,431	6605
103(aa)(1)	1431(a)	11,431	6605
103(aa)(2)	1431(b)	11,431	6605
103(aa)(4)	1431(c)(1)	11,431	6605
103(cc) (added)	1401	11,401	6515
103(dd) (added)	1431(d)	11,431	6605
104(3)	1100E(1)	11,100E	4905
105(a)	1100A(4)	11,100A	4885
105(b)	1100A(5)	11,100A	4885
105(f)(1)	1100A(6)	11,100A	4885
105(h) (added)	1472(c)	11,472	6705
105(i) (added)	1100A(7)	11,100A	4885
108(a) and (c)	1100A(8)	11,100A	4885
108(a)(7) (added)	1414(b)	11,414	6560
128(a) (added)	1419	11,419	6585
128(b)(4) (added)	1465	11,465	6695
128(f) (added)	1420	11,420	6590
128A (added)	1418	11,418	6580
129(c)(2) (repealed)	1432(a)	11,432	6610
129(e)	1432(b)	11,432	6610
129(m)	1100A(9)	11,100A	4885
129(r) (added)	1433(b)	11,433	6615
129(s) (added)	1433(c)	11,433	6615
129(t) (added)	1433(d)	11,433	6615
129(u) (added)	1433(c)	11,433	6615
129(v) (added)	1433(f)	11,433	6615
129B (added)	1402(a)(2)	11,402	6520
129B (added)	1402(b)	11,402	6520
129C (added)	1411(a)(2)	11,411	6545
129C (added)	1411(b)	11,411	6545
129D (added)	1461(a)	11,461	6675
129D (added)	1461(c)	11,461	6675

¶61,001

Law Sec./Note	Dodd-Frank Act Sec.	Act Par. (¶)	Exp Par. (¶)
129E (added)	1472(a)	11,472	6705
129F (added)	1464(a)	11,464	6690
129G (added)	1464(b)	11,464	6690
129G (added)	1472(b)	11,472	6705
129H (added)	1471	11,471	6700
130(a)	1416(a)	11,416	6570
130(e)	1416(b)	11,416	6570
130(e)	1422	11,422	660
130(k) (added)	1413	11,413	6555
130(l) (added)	1417	11,417	6575
181(1)	1100E(2)	11,100E	4905

Truth in Savings Act

Law Sec./Note	Dodd-Frank Act Sec.	Act Par. (¶)	Exp Par. (¶)
270(a)(1)	1100B(2)	11,100B	4890
272(b)	1100B(3)	11,100B	4890
274(4)	1100B(4)	11,100B	4890

¶62,001 Table of Act Sections Not Amending Existing Laws

Dodd-Frank Wall Street Reform and Consumer Protection Act

The following table lists all sections of the Dodd-Frank Wall Street Reform and Consumer Protection Act of 2010 that do not amend existing federal banking and securities laws.

	Paragraph
Sec. 1. Short Title; Table of Contents	¶10,001
Sec. 2. Definitions	¶10,002
Sec. 3. Severability	¶10,003
Sec. 4. Effective date	¶10,004
Sec. 5. Budgetary Effects	¶10,005
Sec. 6. Antitrust Savings Clause	¶10,006
TITLE I—FINANCIAL STABILITY	
Sec. 101. Short Title	¶10,101
Sec. 102. Definitions	¶10,102
Subtitle A—Financial Stability Oversight Council	
Sec. 111. Financial Stability Oversight Council Established	¶10,111
Sec. 112. Council Authority	¶10,112
Sec. 113. Authority to Require Supervision and Regulation of Certain Nonbank Financial Companies	¶10,113
Sec. 114. Registration of Nonbank Financial Companies Supervised by the Board of Governors	¶10,114
Sec. 115. Enhanced Supervision and Prudential Standards for Nonbank Financial Companies Supervised by the Board of Governors and Certain Bank Holding Companies	¶10,115
Sec. 116. Reports	¶10,116
Sec. 117. Treatment of Certain Companies that Cease to be Bank Holding Companies	¶10,117
Sec. 118. Council Funding	¶10,118
Sec. 119. Resolution of Supervisory Jurisdictional Disputes Among Member Agencies	¶10,119
Sec. 120. Additional Standards Applicable to Activities or Practices for Financial Stability Purposes	¶10,120
Sec. 121. Mitigation of Risks to Financial Stability	¶10,121
Sec. 122. Gao Audit of Council	¶10,122
Sec. 123. Study of the Effects of Size and Complexity of Financial Institutions on Capital Market Efficiency and Economic Growth	¶10,123
Subtitle B—Office of Financial Research	
Sec. 151. Definitions	¶10,151
Sec. 152. Office of Financial Research Established	¶10,152
Sec. 153. Purpose and Duties of the Office	¶10,153
Sec. 154. Organizational Structure; Responsibilities of Primary Programmatic Units	¶10,154
Sec. 155. Funding	¶10,155
Sec. 156. Transition Oversight	¶10,156

	Paragraph
Subtitle C—Additional Board of Governors Authority for Certain Nonbank Financial Companies and Bank Holding Companies	
Sec. 161. Reports by and Examinations of Nonbank Financial Companies by the Board of Governors	¶ 10,161
Sec. 162. Enforcement	¶ 10,162
Sec. 163. Acquisitions	¶ 10,163
Sec. 164. Prohibition Against Management Interlocks Between Certain Financial Companies	¶ 10,164
Sec. 165. Enhanced Supervision and Prudential Standards for Nonbank Financial Companies Supervised by the Board of Governors and Certain Bank Holding Companies	¶ 10,165
Sec. 166. Early Remediation Requirements	¶ 10,166
Sec. 167. Affiliations	¶ 10,167
Sec. 168. Regulations	¶ 10,168
Sec. 169. Avoiding Duplication	¶ 10,169
Sec. 170. Safe Harbor	¶ 10,170
Sec. 171. Leverage and Risk-Based Capital Requirements	¶ 10,171
Sec. 172. Examination and Enforcement Actions for Insurance and Orderly Liquidation Purposes	¶ 10,172
Sec. 174. Studies and Reports on Holding Company Capital Requirements	¶ 10,174
Sec. 175. International Policy Coordination	¶ 10,175
Sec. 176. Rule of Construction	¶ 10,176
TITLE II—ORDERLY LIQUIDATION AUTHORITY	
Sec. 201. Definitions	¶ 10,201
Sec. 202. Judicial Review	¶ 10,202
Sec. 203. Systemic Risk Determination	¶ 10,203
Sec. 204. Orderly Liquidation of Covered Financial Companies	¶ 10,204
Sec. 205. Orderly Liquidation of Covered Brokers and Dealers	¶ 10,205
Sec. 206. Mandatory Terms and Conditions for All Orderly Liquidation Actions	¶ 10,206
Sec. 207. Directors Not Liable for Acquiescing in Appointment of Receiver	¶ 10,207
Sec. 208. Dismissal and Exclusion of Other Actions	¶ 10,208
Sec. 209. Rulemaking; Non-Conflicting Law	¶ 10,209
Sec. 210. Powers and Duties of the Corporation	¶ 10,210
Sec. 212. Prohibition of Circumvention and Prevention of Conflicts of Interest	¶ 10,212
Sec. 213. Ban on Certain Activities by Senior Executives And Directors	¶ 10,213
Sec. 214. Prohibition on Taxpayer Funding	¶ 10,214
Sec. 215. Study on Secured Creditor Haircuts	¶ 10,215
Sec. 216. Study on Bankruptcy Process for Financial and Nonbank Financial Institutions	¶ 10,216
Sec. 217. Study on International Coordination Relating to Bankruptcy Process for Nonbank Financial Institutions	¶ 10,217
TITLE III—TRANSFER OF POWERS TO THE COMPTROLLER OF THE CURRENCY, THE CORPORATION, AND THE BOARD OF GOVERNORS	
Sec. 300. Short Title	¶ 10,300
Sec. 301. Purposes	¶ 10,301
Sec. 302. Definition	¶ 10,302
Subtitle A—Transfer of Powers and Duties	
Sec. 311. Transfer Date	¶ 10,311
Sec. 313. Abolishment	¶ 10,313
Sec. 316. Savings Provisions	¶ 10,316
Sec. 317. References in Federal Law to Federal Banking Agencies	¶ 10,317

	Paragraph
Sec. 319. Contracting and Leasing Authority	¶ 10,319

Subtitle B—Transitional Provisions

Sec. 321. Interim Use of Funds, Personnel, and Property of the Office of Thrift Supervision	¶ 10,321
Sec. 322. Transfer of Employees	¶ 10,322
Sec. 323. Property Transferred	¶ 10,323
Sec. 324. Funds Transferred	¶ 10,324
Sec. 325. Disposition of Affairs	¶ 10,325
Sec. 326. Continuation of Services	¶ 10,326
Sec. 327. Implementation Plan and Reports	¶ 10,327

Subtitle D—Other Matters

Sec. 341. Branching	¶ 10,341
Sec. 342. Office of Minority and Women Inclusion	¶ 10,342

Subtitle E—Technical and Conforming Amendments

Sec. 351. Effective Date	¶ 10,351
Sec. 352. Balanced Budget and Emergency Deficit Control Act of 1985	¶ 10,352
Sec. 359. Crime Control Act of 1990	¶ 10,359
Sec. 361. Emergency Homeowners' Relief Act	¶ 10,361
Sec. 362. Federal Credit Union Act	¶ 10,362
Sec. 365. Federal Housing Enterprises Financial Safety and Soundness Act of 1992	¶ 10,365
Sec. 368. Flood Disaster Protection Act of 1973	¶ 10,368
Sec. 370. Housing Act of 1948	¶ 10,370
Sec. 371. Housing and Community Development Act of 1992	¶ 10,371
Sec. 372. Housing and Urban-Rural Recovery Act of 1983	¶ 10,372
Sec. 373. National Housing Act	¶ 10,373
Sec. 374. Neighborhood Reinvestment Corporation Act	¶ 10,374
Sec. 378. Title 31, United States Code	¶ 10,378

TITLE IV—REGULATION OF ADVISERS TO HEDGE FUNDS AND OTHERS

Sec. 401. Short Title	¶ 10,401
Sec. 412. Comptroller General Study on Custody Rule Costs	¶ 10,412
Sec. 413. Adjusting the Accredited Investor Standard	¶ 10,413
Sec. 415. GAO Study and Report on Accredited Investors	¶ 10,415
Sec. 416. GAO Study on Self-Regulatory Organization for Private Funds	¶ 10,416
Sec. 417. Commission Study and Report on Shortselling	¶ 10,417
Sec. 419. Transition Period	¶ 10,419

TITLE V—INSURANCE

Subtitle A—Federal Insurance Office

Sec. 501. Short Title	¶ 10,501
Sec. 502. Federal Insurance Office	¶ 10,502

Subtitle B—State-Based Insurance Reform

Sec. 511. Short Title	¶ 10,511

Part I—Nonadmitted Insurance

Sec. 521. Reporting, Payment, and Allocation of Premium Taxes	¶ 10,521
Sec. 522. Regulation of Nonadmitted Insurance by Insured's Home State	¶ 10,522
Sec. 523. Participation in National Producer Database	¶ 10,523
Sec. 524. Uniform Standards for Surplus Lines Eligibility	¶ 10,524
Sec. 525. Streamlined Application for Commercial Purchasers	¶ 10,525
Sec. 526. GAO Study of Nonadmitted Insurance Market	¶ 10,526
Sec. 527. Definitions	¶ 10,527

Part II—Reinsurance

Sec. 531. Regulation of Credit for Reinsurance and Reinsurance Agreements	¶ 10,531

¶ 62,001

	Paragraph
Sec. 532. Regulation of Reinsurer Solvency	¶ 10,532
Sec. 533. Definitions	¶ 10,533

Part III—Rule Of Construction

Sec. 541. Rule of Construction	¶ 10,541
Sec. 542. Severability	¶ 10,542

TITLE VI—IMPROVEMENTS TO REGULATION OF BANK AND SAVINGS ASSOCIATION HOLDING COMPANIES AND DEPOSITORY INSTITUTIONS

Sec. 601. Short Title	¶ 10,601
Sec. 602. Definition	¶ 10,602
Sec. 603. Moratorium and Study on Treatment of Credit Card Banks, Industrial Loan Companies, and Certain Other Companies Under the Bank Holding Company Act of 1956	¶ 10,603
Sec. 618. Securities Holding Companies	¶ 10,618
Sec. 620. Study of Bank Investment Activities	¶ 10,620

TITLE VII—WALL STREET TRANSPARENCY AND ACCOUNTABILITY

Subtitle A—Regulation of Over-the-Counter Swaps Markets

Part I—Regulatory Authority

Sec. 711. Definitions	¶ 10,711
Sec. 712. Review of Regulatory Authority	¶ 10,712
Sec. 714. Abusive Swaps	¶ 10,714
Sec. 715. Authority to Prohibit Participation in Swap Activities	¶ 10,715
Sec. 716. Prohibition Against Federal Government Bailouts of Swaps Entities	¶ 10,716
Sec. 718. Determining Status of Novel Derivative Products	¶ 10,718
Sec. 719. Studies	¶ 10,719
Sec. 720. Memorandum	¶ 10,720

Part II—Regulation Of Swap Markets

Sec. 726. Rulemaking on Conflict of Interest	¶ 10,726
Sec. 743. Other Authority	¶ 10,743
Sec. 750. Study on Oversight of Carbon Markets	¶ 10,750
Sec. 752. International Harmonization	¶ 10,752
Sec. 754. Effective Date	¶ 10,754

Subtitle B—Regulation of Security-Based Swap Markets

Sec. 765. Rulemaking on Conflict of Interest	¶ 10,765
Sec. 771. Other Authority	¶ 10,771
Sec. 774. Effective Date	¶ 10,774

TITLE VIII—PAYMENT, CLEARING, AND SETTLEMENT SUPERVISION

Sec. 801. Short Title	¶ 10,801
Sec. 802. Findings and Purposes	¶ 10,802
Sec. 803. Definitions	¶ 10,803
Sec. 804. Designation of Systemic Importance	¶ 10,804
Sec. 805. Standards for Systemically Important Financial Market Utilities and Payment, Clearing, or Settlement Activities	¶ 10,805
Sec. 806. Operations of Designated Financial Market Utilities	¶ 10,806
Sec. 807. Examination of and Enforcement Actions Against Designated Financial Market Utilities	¶ 10,807
Sec. 808. Examination of and Enforcement Actions Against Financial Institutions Subject to Standards for Designated Activities	¶ 10,808
Sec. 809. Requests for Information, Reports, or Records	¶ 10,809
Sec. 810. Rulemaking	¶ 10,810
Sec. 811. Other Authority	¶ 10,811
Sec. 812. Consultation	¶ 10,812

	Paragraph
Sec. 813. Common Framework for Designated Clearing Entity Risk Management	¶10,813
Sec. 814. Effective Date	¶10,814

TITLE IX—INVESTOR PROTECTIONS AND IMPROVEMENTS TO THE REGULATION OF SECURITIES

	Paragraph
Sec. 901. Short Title	¶10,901

Subtitle A—Increasing Investor Protection

	Paragraph
Sec. 914. Study on Enhancing Investment Adviser Examinations	¶10,914
Sec. 917. Study Regarding Financial Literacy Among Investors	¶10,917
Sec. 918. Study Regarding Mutual Fund Advertising	¶10,918
Sec. 919A. Study on Conflicts of Interest	¶10,919A
Sec. 919B. Study on Improved Investor Access to Information on Investment Advisers and Broker-Dealers	¶10,919B
Sec. 919C. Study on Financial Planners and the Use of Financial Designations	¶10,919C

Subtitle B—Increasing Regulatory Enforcement and Remedies

	Paragraph
Sec. 924. Implementation and Transition Provisions for Whistleblower Protection	¶10,924
Sec. 926. Disqualifying Felons and Other "Bad Actors" From Regulation D Offerings	¶10,926
Sec. 929A. Protection for Employees of Subsidiaries and Affiliates of Publicly Traded Companies	¶10,929A
Sec. 929G. Streamlined Hiring Authority for Market Specialists	¶10,929G
Sec. 929Y. Study on Extraterritorial Private Rights of Action	¶10,929Y
Sec. 929Z. GAO Study on Securities Litigation	¶10,929Z

Subtitle C—Improvements to the Regulation of Credit Rating Agencies

	Paragraph
Sec. 931. Findings	¶10,931
Sec. 936. Qualification Standards for Credit Rating Analysts	¶10,936
Sec. 937. Timing of Regulations	¶10,937
Sec. 938. Universal Ratings Symbols	¶10,938
Sec. 939A. Review of Reliance on Ratings	¶10,939A
Sec. 939B. Elimination Of Exemption From Fair Disclosure Rule	¶10,939B
Sec. 939C. Securities and Exchange Commission Study on Strengthening Credit Rating Agency Independence	¶10,939C
Sec. 939D. Government Accountability Office Study on Alternative Business Models	¶10,939D
Sec. 939E. Government Accountability Office Study on the Creation of an Independent Professional Analyst Organization	¶10,939E
Sec. 939F. Study and Rulemaking on Assigned Credit Ratings	¶10,939F
Sec. 939G. Effect of Rule 436(G)	¶10,939G
Sec. 939H. Sense of Congress	¶10,939H

Subtitle D—Improvements to the Asset-Backed Securitization Process

	Paragraph
Sec. 943. Representations and Warranties in Asset-Backed Offerings	¶10,943
Sec. 946. Study on the Macroeconomic Effects of Risk Retention Requirements	¶10,946

Subtitle E—Accountability and Executive Compensation

	Paragraph
Sec. 956. Enhanced Compensation Structure Reporting	¶10,956

Subtitle F—Improvements to the Management of the Securities and Exchange Commission

	Paragraph
Sec. 962. Triennial Report on Personnel Management	¶10,962
Sec. 963. Annual Financial Controls Audit	¶10,963
Sec. 964. Report on Oversight of National Securities Associations	¶10,964
Sec. 967. Commission Organizational Study and Reform	¶10,967
Sec. 968. Study on Sec Revolving Door	¶10,968

Subtitle H—Municipal Securities

¶62,001

	Paragraph
Sec. 976. Government Accountability Office Study of Increased Disclosure to Investors	¶ 10,976
Sec. 977. Government Accountability Office Study on the Municipal Securities Markets	¶ 10,977
Sec. 979. Commission Office of Municipal Securities	¶ 10,979

Subtitle I—Public Company Accounting Oversight Board, Portfolio Margining, and Other Matters

Sec. 987. Amendment to Definition of Material Loss and Nonmaterial Losses to the Deposit Insurance Fund for Purposes of Inspector General Reviews	¶ 10,987
Sec. 988. Amendment to Definition of Material Loss and Nonmaterial Losses to the National Credit Union Share Insurance Fund for Purposes of Inspector General Reviews	¶ 10,988
Sec. 989. Government Accountability Office Study on Proprietary Trading	¶ 10,989
Sec. 989A. Senior Investor Protections	¶ 10,989A
Sec. 989B. Designated Federal Entity Inspectors General Independence	¶ 10,989B
Sec. 989C. Strengthening Inspector General Accountability	¶ 10,989C
Sec. 989D. Removal of Inspectors General of Designated Federal Entities	¶ 10,989D
Sec. 989E. Additional Oversight of Financial Regulatory System	¶ 10,989E
Sec. 989F. GAO Study Of Person To Person Lending	¶ 10,989F
Sec. 989H. Corrective Responses by Heads of Certain Establishments to Deficiencies Identified by Inspectors General	¶ 10,989H
Sec. 989I. GAO Study Regarding Exemption for Smaller Issuers	¶ 10,989I
Sec. 989J. Further Promoting the Adoption of the Naic Model Regulations That Enhance Protection of Seniors and Other Consumers	¶ 10,989J

TITLE X—BUREAU OF CONSUMER FINANCIAL PROTECTION

Sec. 1001. Short Title	¶ 11,001
Sec. 1002. Definitions	¶ 11,002

Subtitle A—Bureau of Consumer Financial Protection

Sec. 1011. Establishment of the Bureau of Consumer Financial Protection	¶ 11,011
Sec. 1012. Executive and Administrative Powers	¶ 11,012
Sec. 1013. Administration	¶ 11,013
Sec. 1014. Consumer Advisory Board	¶ 11,014
Sec. 1015. Coordination	¶ 11,015
Sec. 1016. Appearances Before and Reports to Congress	¶ 11,016
Sec. 1017. Funding; Penalties and Fines	¶ 11,017
Sec. 1018. Effective Date	¶ 11,018

Subtitle B—General Powers of the Bureau

Sec. 1021. Purpose, Objectives, and Functions	¶ 11,021
Sec. 1022. Rulemaking Authority	¶ 11,022
Sec. 1023. Review of Bureau Regulations	¶ 11,023
Sec. 1024. Supervision of Nondepository Covered Persons	¶ 11,024
Sec. 1025. Supervision of Very Large Banks, Savings Associations, and Credit Unions	¶ 11,025
Sec. 1026. Other Banks, Savings Associations, and Credit Unions	¶ 11,026
Sec. 1027. Limitations on Authorities of the Bureau; Preservation of Authorities	¶ 11,027
Sec. 1028. Authority to Restrict Mandatory Pre-Dispute Arbitration	¶ 11,028
Sec. 1029. Exclusion for Auto Dealers	¶ 11,029
Sec. 1029A. Effective Date	¶ 11,029A

Subtitle C—Specific Bureau Authorities

Sec. 1031. Prohibiting Unfair, Deceptive, or Abusive Acts or Practices	¶ 11,031
Sec. 1032. Disclosures	¶ 11,032

	Paragraph
Sec. 1033. Consumer Rights to Access Information	¶ 11,033
Sec. 1034. Response to Consumer Complaints and Inquiries	¶ 11,034
Sec. 1035. Private Education Loan Ombudsman	¶ 11,035
Sec. 1036. Prohibited Acts	¶ 11,036
Sec. 1037. Effective Date	¶ 11,037

Subtitle D—Preservation of State Law

Sec. 1041. Relation to State Law	¶ 11,041
Sec. 1042. Preservation of Enforcement Powers of States	¶ 11,042
Sec. 1043. Preservation of Existing Contracts	¶ 11,043
Sec. 1048. Effective Date	¶ 11,048

Subtitle E—Enforcement Powers

Sec. 1051. Definitions	¶ 11,051
Sec. 1052. Investigations and Administrative Discovery	¶ 11,052
Sec. 1053. Hearings and Adjudication Proceedings	¶ 11,053
Sec. 1054. Litigation Authority	¶ 11,054
Sec. 1055. Relief Available	¶ 11,055
Sec. 1056. Referrals for Criminal Proceedings	¶ 11,056
Sec. 1057. Employee Protection	¶ 11,057
Sec. 1058. Effective Date	¶ 11,058

Subtitle F—Transfer of Functions and Personnel; Transitional Provisions

Sec. 1061. Transfer of Consumer Financial Protection Functions	¶ 11,061
Sec. 1062. Designated Transfer Date	¶ 11,062
Sec. 1063. Savings Provisions	¶ 11,063
Sec. 1064. Transfer of Certain Personnel	¶ 11,064
Sec. 1065. Incidental Transfers	¶ 11,065
Sec. 1066. Interim Authority of the Secretary	¶ 11,066
Sec. 1067. Transition Oversight	¶ 11,067

Subtitle G—Regulatory Improvements

Sec. 1072. Assistance for Economically Vulnerable Individuals and Families	¶ 11,072
Sec. 1074. Department of the Treasury Study on Ending the Conservatorship of Fannie Mae, Freddie Mac, and Reforming the Housing Finance System	¶ 11,074
Sec. 1076. Reverse Mortgage Study and Regulations	¶ 11,076
Sec. 1077. Report on Private Education Loans and Private Educational Lenders	¶ 11,077
Sec. 1078. Study and Report on Credit Scores	¶ 11,078
Sec. 1079. Review, Report, and Program With Respect to Exchange Facilitators	¶ 11,079
Sec. 1079A. Financial Fraud Provisions	¶ 11,079A

TITLE XI—FEDERAL RESERVE SYSTEM PROVISIONS

Sec. 1104. Liquidity Event Determination	¶ 11,104
Sec. 1105. Emergency Financial Stabilization	¶ 11,105
Sec. 1109. GAO Audit of the Federal Reserve Facilities; Publication of Board Actions	¶ 11,109

TITLE XII—IMPROVING ACCESS TO MAINSTREAM FINANCIAL INSTITUTIONS

Sec. 1201. Short Title	¶ 11,201
Sec. 1202. Purpose	¶ 11,202
Sec. 1203. Definitions	¶ 11,203
Sec. 1204. Expanded Access to Mainstream Financial Institutions	¶ 11,204
Sec. 1205. Low-Cost Alternatives to Small Dollar Loans	¶ 11,205
Sec. 1207. Procedural Provisions	¶ 11,207
Sec. 1208. Authorization of Appropriations	¶ 11,208
Sec. 1209. Regulations	¶ 11,209
Sec. 1210. Evaluation and Reports to Congress	¶ 11,210

	Paragraph
TITLE XIII—PAY IT BACK ACT	
Sec. 1301. Short Title	¶ 11,301
Sec. 1305. Federal Housing Finance Agency Report	¶ 11,305
Sec. 1306. Repayment of Unobligated Arra Funds	¶ 11,306
TITLE XIV—MORTGAGE REFORM AND ANTI-PREDATORY LENDING ACT	
Sec. 1400. Short Title; Designation as Enumerated Consumer Law	¶ 11,400
Subtitle A—Residential Mortgage Loan Origination Standards	
Sec. 1403. Prohibition on Steering Incentives	¶ 11,403
Sec. 1404. Liability	¶ 11,404
Sec. 1405. Regulations	¶ 11,405
Sec. 1406. Study of Shared Appreciation Mortgages	¶ 11,406
Subtitle B—Minimum Standards For Mortgages	
Sec. 1411. Ability to Repay	¶ 11,411
Sec. 1412. Safe Harbor and Rebuttable Presumption	¶ 11,412
Sec. 1415. Rule of Construction	¶ 11,415
Sec. 1418. Six-Month Notice Required Before Reset of Hybrid Adjustable Rate Mortgages	¶ 11,418
Sec. 1418. Six-Month Notice Required Before Reset of Hybrid Adjustable Rate Mortgages	¶ 11,418
Sec. 1421. Report by the GAO	¶ 11,421
Subtitle D—Office of Housing Counseling	
Sec. 1441. Short Title	¶ 11,441
Sec. 1442. Establishment of Office of Housing Counseling	¶ 11,442
Sec. 1446. Study of Defaults and Foreclosures	¶ 11,446
Sec. 1447. Default and Foreclosure Database	¶ 11,447
Sec. 1451. Home Inspection Counseling	¶ 11,451
Sec. 1452. Warnings to Homeowners of Foreclosure Rescue Scams	¶ 11,452
Subtitle E—Mortgage Servicing	
Sec. 1461. Escrow and Impound Accounts Relating to Certain Consumer Credit Transactions	¶ 11,461
Sec. 1462. Disclosure Notice Required for Consumers Who Waive Escrow Services	¶ 11,462
Sec. 1464. Truth in Lending Act Amendments	¶ 11,464
Subtitle F—Appraisal Activities	
Sec. 1471. Property Appraisal Requirements	¶ 11,471
Sec. 1476. GAO Study on the Effectiveness and Impact of Various Appraisal Methods, Valuation Models and Distributions Channels, and on the Home Valuation Code of Conduct and the Appraisal Subcommittee	¶ 11,476
Subtitle G—Mortgage Resolution and Modification	
Sec. 1481. Multifamily Mortgage Resolution Program	¶ 11,481
Sec. 1482. Home Affordable Modification Program Guidelines	¶ 11,482
Sec. 1483. Public Availability of Information of Making Home Affordable Program	¶ 11,483
Subtitle H—Miscellaneous Provisions	
Sec. 1491. Sense of Congress Regarding the Importance of Government-Sponsored Enterprises Reform to Enhance the Protection, Limitation, and Regulation of the Terms of Residential Mortgage Credit	¶ 11,491
Sec. 1492. GAO Study Report on Government Efforts to Combat Mortgage Foreclosure Rescue Scams and Loan Modification Fraud	¶ 11,492
Sec. 1493. Reporting of Mortgage Data by State	¶ 11,493
Sec. 1494. Study of Effect of Drywall Presence on Foreclosures	¶ 11,494
Sec. 1495. Definition	¶ 11,495
Sec. 1496. Emergency Mortgage Relief	¶ 11,496

Paragraph

Sec. 1497. Additional Assistance for Neighborhood Stabilization Program . . . . ¶11,497
Sec. 1498. Legal Assistance for Foreclosure-Related Issues . . . . ¶11,498

TITLE XV—MISCELLANEOUS PROVISIONS

Sec. 1501. Restrictions on Use of United States Funds for Foreign Governments;
    Protection of American Taxpayers . . . . ¶11,501
Sec. 1503. Reporting Requirements Regarding Coal Or Other Mine Safety . . . . ¶11,503
Sec. 1505. Study by the Comptroller General . . . . ¶11,505
Sec. 1506. Study on Core Deposits and Brokered Deposits . . . . ¶11,506

TITLE XVI—SECTION 1256 CONTRACTS

Sec. 1601. Certain Swaps, Etc., Not Treated as Section 1256 Contracts . . . . ¶11,601

TOPICAL INDEX

References are to paragraph (¶) numbers.

A

Abusive or unfair lending practices
. Steering incentives . . . 6525
Accredited Investors
. GAO study . . . 1545
. Review and adjustment . . . 1545
Advisers (see Investment advisers)
Aiding and abetting
. Comptroller General study . . . 4170
. SEC Enforcement authority . . . 4130
Alternative Mortgage Transaction Parity Act
. Amendment . . . 4790
Analysts
. Credit rating agencies . . . 4205
Annual percentage rate
. Higher-risk mortgage . . . 6700
Anti-competitive payment card practices
. Contract provisions . . . 4750
. Exceptions . . . 4750
Appraisals
. Appraisal approaches study . . . 6725
. Appraisal management company . . . 6710
. Appraisal subcommittee
. . Appraisal management services . . . 6710
. . Automation valuation models . . . 6710
. . Definitions . . . 6710
. . FIRREA . . . 6710
. . Grants . . . 6710
. . National hotline . . . 6710
. . Regulations . . . 6710
. Appraisal valuation models study . . . 6725
. Appraiser regulatory programs
. . Enforcement actions against . . . 6710
. . Investigation of complaints . . . 6710
. . Issuance of temporary appraiser licenses and certifications . . . 6710
. . Licensing and certification of appraisers . . . 6710
. . Receiving and tracking of complaints against appraisers . . . 6710
. . Registration of appraisal management companies . . . 6710
Arbitration
. Arbitration agreements . . . 4585
. Mandatory arbitration . . . 4055
. Residential mortgage loans . . . 6560
Asset-backed securities (see Securitization)
Automated valuation models
. Definition and enforcement . . . 6710
. GAO study . . . 6725
Availability and affordability of credit
. GAO study . . . 6595

B

Balloon payment terms
. High-cost mortgages . . . 6610
. Limitations on . . . 6545

Banking entity
. Ban on proprietary trading . . . 2575
. Capital and quantitative limits . . . 2575
. Definitions . . . 2575
. Permitted activities . . . 2575
Bankruptcy
. Covered entities . . . 505
. Non-covered entities . . . 510
Books and records (see Recordkeeping and reporting)
Bridge financial companies (see Financial companies)
Broker-dealers
. Arbitration . . . 4055
. Audits
. . PCAOB oversight . . . 4435
. Definitions
. . Broker . . . 4435
. . Dealer . . . 4435
. Fiduciary standards . . . 4020
. Financial company as a broker-dealer (see Financial companies)
. Margin lending restrictions . . . 4085
. Standards of care study . . . 4020
Brokered deposits
. Study . . . 7040
Broker-priced opinions
. GAO study . . . 6725
Bureau of Consumer Financial Protection (BCFP)
. Annual operational reports . . . 4725
. Arbitration agreements . . . 4585
. Civil investigative demands . . . 4665
. Consumer access to information . . . 4605, 4610
. Consumer Advisory Board . . . 4530
. Contracts, effectiveness of existing . . . 4635
. Creation . . . 4515
. Credit score discrepancies study . . . 4765
. Delegation of authority . . . 4520
. Disclosure to consumers . . . 4600
. . Consumer access to information . . . 4605, 4610
. . Disclosure trials . . . 4600
. . Model disclosure forms . . . 4600
. . Mortgage loan disclosure . . . 4600
. . Privacy . . . 4785
. Employees . . . 4525, 4710, 4565
. Enforcement . . . 4570, 4575, 4660, 4670, 4675, 4685
. Exchange facilitators study . . . 4770
. Exemptions from regulation . . . 4555, 4580, 4590
. Functions . . . 4550
. Funding . . . 4545
. Hearings . . . 4670
. Independence . . . 4520
. Initial regulatory flexibility analysis . . . 4915
. Inspector general . . . 4780
. Interagency cooperation . . . 4710, 4535, 4565, 4570, 4665, 4895
. Interim operations . . . 4720
. Investigations . . . 4665
. Litigation
. . Civil suits . . . 4675
. . Criminal prosecution . . . 4685
. . Legal and equitable relief . . . 4680

BUR

Topical Index

References are to paragraph (¶) numbers.

Bureau of Consumer Financial Protection (BCFP)—continued
. Model mortgage loan transaction form . . . 4865
. Objectives . . . 4550
. Offices . . . 4525
. Ombudsman . . . 4525, 4615
. Oversight of . . . 4560
. Prohibited actions . . . 4620
. Registration . . . 4555, 4565
. Reverse mortgage transactions study . . . 4755
. Rulemaking . . . 4555, 4600, 4605, 4730
. Semi-annual reports . . . 4540
. Structure . . . 4515
. Supervisory activities
. . Larger institutions . . . 4570
. . Smaller institutions . . . 4575
. Transfer of authority to
. . Assets and liabilities . . . 4715
. . Date . . . 7400
. . In general . . . 4695
. . Savings provisions . . . 7405
. Unfair, deceptive or abusive practices . . . 4595
. Units
. . Community affairs . . . 4525
. . Complaints . . . 4525
. . Research . . . 4525
. Whistleblowers
. . Covered employees . . . 4690
. . Procedures . . . 4690
. . Relief . . . 4690
. Women-owned, minority-owned and small business lending . . . 4730

C

Cancelled securities
. Report to SEC and Federal Reserve . . . 4100
Capital gains
. Derivative contracts . . . 7010
Carbon markets
. Interagency study . . . 3050
Cease-and-desist proceedings
. Bureau of Consumer Financial Protection . . . 4670
. Penalties . . . 4135
Ceding insurer
. Reinsurance . . . 2055
Charter conversion
. National banks, state banks, federal saving associations . . . 2555
Clawbacks (see Executive compensation; Clawbacks)
Clearing and settlement
. Designations of systemic importance
. . Considerations . . . 3510
. . Notice and hearing . . . 3510
. . Rescission . . . 3510
. Financial institutions
. . Defined . . . 3510
. . Examination of financial institutions . . . 3530
. Financial market utilities
. . Defined . . . 3510
. . Examination and enforcement . . . 3525
. . Federal Reserve accounts and services . . . 3520
. . Operations and procedures . . . 3520
. Financial Stability Oversight Council (see Financial Stability Oversight Council; Clearing and settlement)

Clearing and settlement—continued
. Joint risk management programs for clearing agencies . . . 3515
. Reports and information requests . . . 3535
. Risk management standards . . . 3515
. Systemic importance . . . 3510
Clearing swaps
. Derivatives clearing organizations . . . 3060
. Exceptions . . . 3060
Collateral bars
. SEC imposition . . . 4065
Commercial end user
. Exemption from registration . . . 3095
Commercial firm
. Intermediate holding companies . . . 2610
Commodities Futures Trading Commission (CFTC)
. Clearing swaps
. . Exceptions . . . 3060, 3070
. . Procedure . . . 3060
. Commodity pool operators . . . 1550
. Conflicts of interest . . . 3045
. Derivatives clearing organizations
. . Registration . . . 3070
. . Reporting . . . 3070
. Energy and Environmental Markets Committee . . . 3015
. Enforcement . . . 3130
. Fair and Accurate Credit Transactions Act of 2003 (FACT Act) . . . 4815
. Foreign boards of trade
. . Registration . . . 3120
. Inspector general . . . 4480
. Interagency cooperation . . . 3020, 3040, 3095, 3145
. Jurisdiction
. . Retail commodity transactions . . . 3135
. Large swap traders . . . 3090
. Major swap participants
. . Registration . . . 3095
. Rulemaking
. . Business conduct standards . . . 3095
. . Capital and margin requirements . . . 3095, 3105
. . Clearing . . . 3095
. . Consultation . . . 3020, 3035
. . Disruptive practices . . . 3155
. . Fraud . . . 3155
. . Joint rulemaking . . . 3020
. . Manipulative practices . . . 3155
. . Position limits . . . 3115
. . Registered entities . . . 3140
. . Swap transaction data repositories . . . 3080
. . Swap transaction reporting . . . 3095
. . Securities futures . . . 3035
. . Significant price discovery . . . 3090
. Swap dealers
. . Registration . . . 3095
. Swap execution facilities
. . Registration . . . 3100
. Swap transaction and pricing reporting . . . 3075
. Swap transaction data repositories
. . Registration . . . 3080
. Swaps
. . Jurisdiction . . . 3015
. Termination of investment activities . . . 2575
. Trading advisors . . . 1550
. Uncleared swaps . . . 3085
. Whistleblowers . . . 3145

CAN

References are to paragraph (¶) numbers.

Community development financial institution (CDFI)
. Funding and oversight . . . 5525
. Loan-loss reserve fund grants . . . 5520
. Small dollar loan programs . . . 5505
. Technical assistance grants . . . 5520

Compensation consultants
. SEC study . . . 4300

Conflict minerals
. Department of State strategy . . . 7020
. Disclosure . . . 7020
. Linkages to human rights abuses . . . 7020
. Manufacturer reporting . . . 7020

Conflicts of interest
. Comptroller General study of securities firms . . . 4040
. Credit ratings . . . 4190
. Regulated securities and derivatives entities . . . 3045
. Securitization . . . 2585

Consumer Advisory Board
. Board members . . . 4530

Consumer financial laws (see Bureau of Consumer Financial Protection (BCFP); Litigation)

Consumer Financial Protection Act of 2010
. In general . . . 4505

Consumer Financial Protection Fund
. Funding . . . 4545

Consumer lending laws
. Abusive or unfair lending practices . . . 6525
. Amendment . . . 6510
. Anti-deficiency protection . . . 6560
. Appraisal independence . . . 6705
. Arbitration . . . 6560
. Balloon loans . . . 6550
. Balloon payment . . . 6545
. Class actions . . . 6570
. Credit insurance . . . 6560
. Definitions
. . Average prime offer rate . . . 6550
. . Bona fide discount points . . . 6550
. . Points and fees . . . 6550
. . Qualified mortgage . . . 6550
. Disclosure
. . Waiver of escrow services . . . 6680
. Emergency Homeowners' Relief Fund (Relief Fund) . . . 6765
. Executive agencies (see Bureau of Consumer Financial Protection (BCFP))
. Federally-related mortgages . . . 6685
. Force-placed hazard insurance . . . 6685
. Foreclosure . . . 6555, 6745
. High-cost mortgages (see High-cost mortgages)
. Home inspection information . . . 6665
. Home loan payments . . . 6690
. Hybrid adjustable rate mortgages . . . 6580
. Interest rate resets . . . 6580
. Lender rights . . . 6575
. Minimum loan standards
. . Documented information . . . 6545
. . Reasonably ability to repay loan . . . 6545
. . Verification of the consumer's income . . . 6545
. Monthly statement disclosures . . . 6590
. Mortgage information booklet . . . 6660
. Mortgage modification
. . Analysis . . . 6735
. . Requests . . . 6740
. Mortgage originator maximum liability . . . 6530

Consumer lending laws—continued
. Multifamily properties . . . 6730
. Negative amortization . . . 6560
. Net present value (NVP) . . . 6735
. Nonstandard loans . . . 6545
. Partial payments . . . 6560
. Payoff balance . . . 6690
. Payoff statement . . . 6690
. Prepayment penalty . . . 6560
. Property appraisal requirements . . . 6700
. Qualified mortgage . . . 6550
. Real estate settlement form . . . 6720
. Regulation of fraud . . . 6535
. Repayment disclosures . . . 6695
. Required disclosure . . . 6585
. Reverse mortgages . . . 6545
. Second appraisals . . . 6700
. Standard monthly statement disclosure forms . . . 6590
. State enforcement . . . 6600
. Statute of limitations . . . 6570
. Violation reporting . . . 4825

Contingent capital
. Contingent capital requirement study by Financial Stability Oversight Council . . . 125
. Definition . . . 125
. Nonbank financial companies . . . 215

Control person liability
. SEC standing . . . 4135

Core deposits
. Study . . . 7040

Council of Inspectors General on Financial Oversight
. Establishment and functions . . . 4480

Credit facility information
. Timely disclosure . . . 5030

Credit insurance
. Ban . . . 6560

Credit rating agencies
. Analysts . . . 4205
. Background and Congressional findings . . . 4180
. Conflicts of interest . . . 4190
. Credit Rating Agency Board . . . 4190
. Director independence . . . 4185
. Disclosure . . . 4185
. Internal controls report . . . 4185
. Litigation . . . 4195
. Private right of action . . . 4195
. Professional standards . . . 4205
. Regulation FD exemption . . . 4225
. Removal of statutory protection . . . 4220
. Reports and records
. . Credit rating agencies . . . 4185
. . Credit rating agency internal controls . . . 4185
. . NRSRO credit rating form . . . 4185
. Section 11 liability . . . 4230
. Studies
. . Credit rating agency compensation and incentive . . . 4235
. . Credit rating agency independence . . . 4235
. . Credit rating process for structured finance products . . . 4190
. . Credit rating terminology . . . 4220
. . Federal agency reliance on credit rating agencies . . . 4235

Topical Index

References are to paragraph (¶) numbers.

Credit rating agencies—continued
. Studies—continued
. . Professional organization for ratings analysts . . . 4235
. . Standardized credit rating terminology . . . 4220
. . Third party credit rating due diligence . . . 4185, 4200
. . Uniform rating system . . . 4210
. . Whistleblowers . . . 4215

Credit rating terminology
. SEC study . . . 4220

Credit score discrepancies
. Study of . . . 4765

Credit transactions and consumer leases
. Limit on coverage raised . . . 4905

Creditors
. Limitation on recovery . . . 530
. Priority . . . 530
. Qualified Financial Contracts . . . 530

D

Debit cards
. Restriction of interchange fees . . . 4750

Default and disclosure database
. Maintained by HUD . . . 6645

Definitions
. Adjoining country . . . 7020
. Admitted insurer . . . 2050
. Affiliate . . . 2545
. Anti-deficiency law . . . 6560
. Appropriate financial regulator . . . 3530
. Audit . . . 4435
. Audit report . . . 4435
. Banking entity . . . 2575
. Bona fide discount points . . . 6605
. Broker price options . . . 6710
. Ceding insurer . . . 2065
. Commercial development of oil, natural gas, or minerals . . . 7030
. Commercial firm . . . 2510
. Community development financial institution (CDFI) . . . 5520
. Concentration limits . . . 2590
. Conflict minerals . . . 7020
. Consumer . . . 4510
. Consumer financial product or service . . . 4510
. Consumer Financial Protection Act of 2010 . . . 4510
. Counterparty credit risk . . . 3005
. Covered assistance . . . 6655
. Covered person . . . 4510
. Covered transactions . . . 2545, 5015, 5030
. Credit . . . 4510
. Credit default swaps . . . 3005
. Credit facility . . . 5010, 5030
. Customer . . . 4455
. Customer property . . . 4455
. Deposit-taking activity . . . 4510
. Designated clearing entity . . . 3510
. Designated transfer date . . . 4510
. Eligible entity . . . 5510
. Enumerated consumer laws . . . 4510
. Federal banking agencies . . . 4255
. Federal consumer financial law . . . 4510
. Fee appraiser . . . 6705
. Financial company . . . 2590
. Financial institution . . . 3510

Definitions—continued
. Financial market utility . . . 3510
. Financial product or service . . . 4510
. Grandfathered unitary savings and loan holding companies . . . 2610
. Gross revenues from the securities business . . . 4455
. Hedge funds . . . 2575
. Illiquid funds . . . 2575
. Liquidity event . . . 5035
. Material loss . . . 4465
. Misleading designation . . . 4475
. Misleading or fraudulent marketing . . . 4475
. Nationwide Mortgage Licensing System and Registry . . . 6515
. Net equity . . . 4455
. Nonadmitted insurer . . . 2050
. Open-end consumer credit plans . . . 6605
. Payment, clearing and settlement activity . . . 3510
. Prepayment penalties . . . 6605
. Private equity funds . . . 2575
. Private Fund . . . 1510
. Professional standards . . . 4435
. Property appraisals . . . 6705
. Proprietary trading . . . 2575
. Prudential regulators . . . 4510
. Qualified appraiser . . . 6700
. Qualified mortgage . . . 6550
. Reinsurer . . . 2065
. Related person . . . 4510
. Remittance transfer . . . 4240
. Rental housing counseling . . . 6625
. Residential mortgage loan . . . 6515
. Residential mortgage loan origination standards . . . 6515
. Secretary . . . 6515
. Senior investor . . . 4475
. Small dollar loan program . . . 5520
. Source of financial strength . . . 2565
. Sponsoring . . . 2575
. State . . . 4510
. State licensed appraiser . . . 6710
. Stored value . . . 4510
. Surplus lines broker . . . 2050
. Swaps . . . 3010
. Trading account . . . 2575

Department of Housing and Urban Development (HUD)
. Certification of counselors . . . 6635
. Counseling programs
. . Definitions . . . 6650
. Default and disclosure database . . . 6645
. Housing counseling grants . . . 6630
. Mortgage software . . . 6625
. Office of Housing Counseling advisory committee . . . 6620

Deposit insurance
. Permanent increase . . . 1100
. Standard deposit insurance . . . 1100

Deposit insurance assessments
. Assessment base . . . 1095
. Enhance access to information . . . 1095
. Procyclical Assessments . . . 1095
. Reserve ratio
. . Risk-focused assessment base . . . 1095
. . Small banks . . . 1095
. . Target date . . . 1095

CRE

References are to paragraph (¶) numbers.

Deposit insurance assessments—continued
. Risk category . . . 1095
Deposit insurance reform
. Technical amendments . . . 1090
Depository institutions
. Federal Reserve examination powers . . . 2535
. Source of financial strength . . . 2565
Derivatives
. Capital gains . . . 7010
. Derivatives clearing organizations (see Derivatives; Derivatives clearing organizations)
. . Clearing swaps . . . 3060
. . Core principles . . . 3070
. . Foreign bank offerings . . . 3070
. . Registration . . . 3070
. . Reporting . . . 3070
. . Rule changes . . . 3140
. . Swap transaction data repositories . . . 3080
. Derivatives market
. . Definitions . . . 3005
. Derivatives transaction execution facilities . . . 3105
. Extensions of credit . . . 2545
. Lending limits . . . 2550
. Novel derivative products . . . 3040
. Over-the-counter (OTC) derivatives background . . . 3005
. Tax treatment of derivatives contracts . . . 7010
Designated contract market
. Core principles . . . 3110
. Registration . . . 3100
. Rule changes . . . 3140
Directors and officers
. Clawbacks (see Executive compensation; Clawbacks)
. Executive compensation (see Executive compensation)
. Liability
. . Personal . . . 535
. . Removal . . . 535
. Restrictions
. . Asset purchases . . . 535
. . Industry ban . . . 535
Disclosure
. Credit facilities (see Federal Reserve; Credit facility information disclosure)
. Credit rating agencies . . . 4185
. Disclosure of Chair and CEO roles . . . 4335
. Disclosure to consumers
. . BCFP authority . . . 4600
. . Bureau of Consumer Financial Protection (see Bureau of Consumer Financial Protection (BCFP); Disclosure to consumers)
. . Conflict minerals (see Conflict minerals)
. . Investment products and services . . . 4035
. . Model forms . . . 4600
. . Monthly statement disclosures . . . 6590
. . Remittance transfer service providers . . . 4240
. . Repayment disclosures . . . 6695
. . Residential mortgages . . . 6585
. . Standard monthly statement disclosure forms . . . 6590
. . Trial disclosures . . . 4600
. Escrow
. . Accounts . . . 6675
. . Waiver of escrow services . . . 6680

Disclosure—continued
. Executive compensation (see Executive compensation; Proxy statements)
. Integrated model disclosure form . . . 4865
. Issuer disclosures study
. . Issuer disclosures . . . 4410
. Mortgage lending default and disclosure database . . . 6645
. Public credit rating organization disclosure of methodologies and rating information . . . 4185
. Reports and records (see Recordkeeping and reporting)
. SEC information sharing . . . 4120
. Short selling . . . 4165
Distribution channels
. GAO study . . . 6725
Dividends
. Mutual holding companies . . . 2605
. Savings associations . . . 2600
Duty of care
. Mortgage originators . . . 6520

E

Economically vulnerable persons
. Financial education and counseling . . . 4735
Education loans and lenders
. Study of . . . 4760
Electronic Fund Transfer Act (EFTA)
. Amendment . . . 4795
. Interchange fees . . . 4750
. Remittance transfers . . . 4740
Emergency lending programs
. Eligibility, limitations, approval and reporting process . . . 5010
Emergency mortgage relief
. Emergency mortgage assistance . . . 6765
Equal Credit Opportunity Act (ECOA)
. Amendment . . . 4800, 6715
Escrow accounts
. Administration . . . 6675
. Conditions . . . 6675
. Disclosure . . . 6675
. HUD study . . . 6640
. Waiver of escrow services . . . 6680
Exchange facilitators
. Study of . . . 4770
Exchange ratio
. Conversion . . . 2605
Executive compensation
. Clawbacks . . . 4310
. Compensation committee independence . . . 4300
. Hedging . . . 4315
. In general . . . 4290
. Incentive-based compensation . . . 4320
. Non-binding vote . . . 4295
. Proxy statements
. . Executive compensation and performance disclosure . . . 4305
. . Shareholder proxy access . . . 4330
. Reports and records
. . Disclosure of Chair and CEO roles . . . 4335

EXE

References are to paragraph (¶) numbers.

Executive compensation—continued
- Reports and records—continued
  - Institutional investment advisor votes on executive compensation . . . 4295
- SEC rulemaking
  - Beneficial ownership and proxy voting . . . 4325
  - Chair and CEO bifurcation . . . 4335
  - Compensation committee independence . . . 4300
  - Executive compensation and performance disclosure . . . 4305
  - Hedging disclosure . . . 4315
  - Shareholder proxy access . . . 4330
- Self-regulatory organizations
  - Compensation committee independence and listing . . . 4300
- Studies
  - Compensation consultant impact . . . 4300
  - Compensation consultants . . . 4300
  - Internal controls . . . 4355
  - Personnel management practices . . . 4355
  - Revolving door . . . 4355
  - SEC oversight of SROs . . . 4355
  - Securities regulation, independent study of . . . 4355
  - Supervisory controls evaluation . . . 4355

Exempt Boards of Trade (EBOTs)
- Repeal of Commodity Exchange Act provisions . . . 3105

Exemptions
- Affiliate transaction exemptions . . . 2545
- BCFP authority . . . 4580
- Commercial purchasers . . . 2040
- Commodity trading advisers . . . 1515
- Foreign private funds . . . 1515
- Funds below $ 150 Million . . . 1505
- Intrastate clients . . . 1515
- Qualified client standard . . . 1555
- Savings and loan holding company exemptions . . . 2540
- Small business investment companies . . . 1515
- Venture capital funds . . . 1505

Expedited Funds Availability Act
- Next day funds . . . 4805

F

Fair and Accurate Credit Transactions Act of 2003 (FACT Act)
- Regulatory authority divided . . . 4815

Fair Credit Billing Act
- Amendment . . . 4810

Fair Credit Reporting Act (FCRA)
- Adverse action reporting to consumer . . . 4910
- Regulatory authority divided . . . 4815

Fair Debt Collection Practices Act (FDCPA)
- Amendment . . . 4820

Fannie Mae (see Government Sponsored Enterprise (GSE))

Farm Credit Administration
- Registration of regulated institution employees . . . 4880

Federal Credit Union Act
- Inspector general reviews . . . 4465
- Material losses . . . 4465

Federal Deposit Insurance Act (FDIA)
- Federal Reserve enforcement powers . . . 200
- Material losses . . . 4465
- Violation of consumer law reporting . . . 4825

Federal Deposit Insurance Corporation (FDIC)
- Affiliate transaction exemptions . . . 2545
- Assessment base . . . 1095
- Board of directors . . . 1105, 1090
- Bridge companies . . . 540
- Change in control applications . . . 2510
- Claims against covered financial company . . . 530
- Corporation employees . . . 1105
- Industrial banking . . . 2510
- Interagency cooperation . . . 220
- Issuance of securities . . . 545
- Limitations on liability . . . 530
- Liquidity guarantee programs . . . 5035
- Moratorium on deposit insurance applications . . . 2510
- Orderly liquidation authority . . . 520
- Receiver
  - Appointment as receiver . . . 510
  - Duties and powers . . . 525

Federal Energy Regulatory Commission (FERC)
- Swaps . . . 3015

Federal Financial Institutions Examination Council Act of 1978
- Amendment . . . 4830

Federal financial regulatory agencies
- Retention of authority . . . 2010

Federal Housing Finance Agency (FHFA)
- Housing industry report . . . 6020

Federal Insurance Office (FIO)
- Collection of information . . . 2010
- Confidentiality . . . 2010
- Director . . . 2010
- Information sharing . . . 2010
- Subpoena power . . . 2010

Federal Insurance Office Act of 2010 (see Federal Insurance Office (FIO))

Federal Reserve
- Additional powers, in general . . . 190
- Audit of 2007 - 2010 Federal Reserve credit facilities . . . 5020
- Backup enforcement authority . . . 4570
- Back-up enforcement authority . . . 3530
- Bank holding company supervision . . . 135
- Bureau of Consumer Financial Protection (BCFP), relation to . . . 4520, 4525
- Bureau of Consumer Financial Protection funding . . . 4545
- Capital and risk management standards . . . 2570
- Consumer protection supervision . . . 4575
- Covered transactions . . . 2545
- Credit facility information disclosure
  - Content . . . 5030
  - Timing . . . 5030
- Depository institutions subsidiaries
  - Enforcement and funding . . . 2535
  - Examination . . . 2535
  - State regulation and examination . . . 2535
- Emergency lending programs
  - Eligibility . . . 5010
  - Limitations . . . 5010

EXE

Topical Index

References are to paragraph (¶) numbers.

Federal Reserve—continued
. Emergency lending programs—continued
.. Losses . . . 5010
.. Treasury Department approval . . . 5010
. Examination of nonbank financial companies . . . 200
. Examination powers, nonbank financial companies . . . 195
. Financial holding companies
.. Acquisitions . . . 2530
.. Capital requirements . . . 2540
.. Examination . . . 2520
. Financial market utilities
.. Examination . . . 3525
.. Federal Reserve accounts and services . . . 3520
.. Imminent risk . . . 3525
.. Rules, procedures and operations . . . 3520
. Functionally regulated subsidiaries . . . 2525
. Governance
.. Non-delegation . . . 5040
.. Officers . . . 5040
.. Supervision and regulation . . . 5040
. Governance audit . . . 5020
. Holding companies
.. Functionally regulated subsidiaries . . . 2525
. Inspector General oversight of the Bureau of Consumer Financial Protection . . . 4780
. Interagency cooperation . . . 195, 220, 2575, 3535, 4320
. Intermediate holding companies . . . 225, 2610
. International policy coordination . . . 250
. Investment bank holding companies . . . 2570
. Joint risk management program . . . 3515
. Nonbank financial companies reporting . . . 195
. Posting of public information . . . 5025
. Prudential standards for nonbank financial companies . . . 215
. Qualified mortgage regulation . . . 6550
. Residential mortgage loan regulation . . . 6520, 6535
. Review of credit facilities . . . 5015
. Risk management standards . . . 3510
. Rulemaking
.. Concentration limits . . . 215
.. Early remediation of financial distress . . . 220
.. Exemption of certain nonbank holding companies . . . 230
.. In general . . . 190
.. Intermediate holding companies . . . 225
.. Nonbank financial company and covered financial company reporting . . . 215
.. Short-term debt and leverage limits . . . 215
. Securities holding companies
.. Registration and discipline . . . 2570
. Standard monthly statement disclosure forms . . . 6590
. Supervision of nonbank financial companies . . . 120, 125, 2575
. Systemic risk . . . 5005
. Termination of investment activities . . . 2575
. Wind down of a nonbank financial company . . . 150

Federal Trade Commission
. Consumer financial protection authority . . . 4695
. Enforcement authority . . . 4800
. Federal Trade Commission Act amendment . . . 4835

Fees
. Backup assessments . . . 5035
. Bank examination fees . . . 2535
. Deposit Insurance Assessments . . . 1095
. Liquidity event guarantee program . . . 5035

Fees—continued
. Market information systems fee assessment . . . 4395
. MSRB . . . 4395
. nonadmitted brokers . . . 530
. Pay It Back Act . . . 6015
. pro cyclical assessments. . . . 1095
. SEC funding . . . 4370
. SIPC . . . 4455
. State appraisal registry fee . . . 6710

Financial companies
. Bridge financial companies
.. Avoidable Transfers . . . 525
.. Formation and funding . . . 540
. Concentration limits . . . 2590
. Liquidation . . . 520
. Risk-based assessment . . . 545
. Transfer of assets . . . 525

Financial Institutions Reform, Recovery and Enforcement Act of 1989 (FIRREA)
. Appraisal management services . . . 6710
. Qualified appraiser . . . 6700

Financial literacy of investors (see also Retail banking)
. SEC study . . . 4040

Financial market utility
. Operations
.. Advanced notice of proposed changes . . . 3520
.. Emergency changes . . . 3520
.. Federal Reserve account and services . . . 3520

Financial planners
. Comptroller General study . . . 4040

Financial services industry
. Reform impact study by Financial Stability Oversight Council Chair . . . 105

Financial Stability Act of 2010
. In general . . . 105

Financial Stability Oversight Council
. Bureau of Consumer Financial Protection oversight . . . 4560
. Clearing and settlement . . . 3505
. Examination . . . 3525
. Financial institutions . . . 3505
. Financial market utilities . . . 3505
. Grave threat determination . . . 150
. In general . . . 105
. Interagency cooperation . . . 140
. International policy coordination . . . 250
. Joint risk management program . . . 3515
. Membership and structure . . . 110
. Nonbank financial companies (see Nonbank financial companies)
. Non-binding dispute resolution . . . 140
. Notice and hearing . . . 3510
. Office of Financial Research . . . 115
. Permitted activities . . . 2575
. Purpose and duties . . . 115
. Reports and records
.. Bank and nonbank financial condition reporting requirements . . . 130, 175
.. Financial market utility reporting . . . 3535
.. Systemic importance . . . 3535
. Risk management standards . . . 3515
. Studies
.. Analysis and recommendations . . . 115
.. Macroeconomic effects of risk retention . . . 4275

FIN

References are to paragraph (¶) numbers.

Financial Stability Oversight Council—continued
. Studies—continued
. . Prudential standards . . . 145, 3505
. Systemic importance . . . 3510

Flood Disaster Protection Act of 1973
. Escrow accounts . . . 6675

Force-placed hazard insurance
. Limitations on . . . 6685

Foreclosure
. Foreclosure rescue scams
. . Bureau of Consumer Financial Protection rulemaking authority . . . 4860
. . In general . . . 6670
. HUD study . . . 6640
. Neighborhood Stabilization program . . . 6770
. Recoupment or set-off . . . 6555

Foreign entities
. Foreign banks
. . Limitations on U.S. presence . . . 240
. . U.S. intermediate holding companies of foreign banks study by Comptroller General . . . 245
. Foreign boards of trade
. . Conditions for registration . . . 3120
. Foreign broker-dealers
. . Limitations on registration . . . 240
. Foreign government
. . Definitions . . . 7030
. Foreign private Adviser
. . Definitions . . . 1510
. Foreign securities regulators
. . Foreign auditor oversight authority . . . 4430
. . Privileged information . . . 4120

Fraud
. Bureau of Consumer Financial Protection . . . 4595, 4620
. Fair Funds
. . Fair Funds . . . 4090
. Formerly associated persons . . . 4110
. Increased penalties . . . 4775
. Mortgage assistance . . . 6730
. Off-exchange trading . . . 4125
. Recovery of assets . . . 525
. Residential mortgages . . . 6575
. Securities fraud offences . . . 4775
. Short sales . . . 4165
. SIPA . . . 4095
. Swaps . . . 3130, 3150
. Transnational securities fraud . . . 4135

Freddie Mac (see Government Sponsored Enterprise (GSE))

Futures
. Futures commission merchant (FCM)
. . Portfolio margining . . . 3025
. . Registration . . . 3065
. Jurisdiction . . . 3035

G

Government Accountability Office (GAO)
. Accredited Investors study . . . 1545
. Appraisal approaches study . . . 6725
. Appraisal valuation models study . . . 6725
. Automated valuation models study . . . 6725
. Availability and affordability of credit study . . . 6595
. Broker-priced opinions study . . . 6725

Government Accountability Office (GAO)—continued
. Credit rating agency compensation and incentive study . . . 4235
. Distribution channels study . . . 6725
. Home Valuation Code of Conduct (HVCC) study . . . 6725
. Insurance market study . . . 2045
. Licensed and certified appraisals study . . . 6725
. Loan modification fraud study . . . 6755
. Mortgage foreclosure scams study . . . 6755
. Professional organization for ratings analysts study . . . 4235
. Review of Federal Reserve credit facilities . . . 5015

Government Sponsored Enterprise (GSE)
. Fannie Mae . . . 6750
. Freddie Mac . . . 6750
. Sense of Congress . . . 6750
. Treasury Department wind down study . . . 4745

Governmental Accounting Standards Board (GASB)
. Comptroller General study of role and funding . . . 4410
. Funding . . . 4405

Gramm-Leach-Bliley Act
. Amendment . . . 4840

Grandfathered unitary savings and loan holding company
. Regulation and reporting . . . 2610

Grants to states
. Investor protection . . . 4475

GSE/FHL bank obligations
. Restriction on use . . . 6015

H

HAMP (see Homeowner protection; Home Affordable Modification Program (HAMP))

Hedge exempt positions
. Limits on . . . 3115

Hedge funds and private equity funds
. Advisers
. . Registration . . . 1515
. . Reports and records . . . 1520
. Capital and quantitative limits . . . 2575
. Definitions . . . 2575
. Prime brokerage transactions . . . 2575

Helping Families Save Their Homes Act
. State reporting . . . 6755

High-cost mortgages (see Mortgages)

Higher-risk mortgage (see Mortgages)

Holding companies
. Bank holding companies
. . Acquisition of a nonbank financial company . . . 205
. . Bank Holding Company Act exceptions GAO study . . . 2515
. . Federal Reserve examination powers . . . 2520
. . Liquidation . . . 135
. Financial holding companies
. . Acquisitions and mergers . . . 2540
. . Capital requirements . . . 2540
. . Functionally regulated subsidiaries . . . 2525
. . Source of financial strength . . . 2565
. Securities holding company
. . Registration and recordkeeping . . . 2570

FLO

References are to paragraph (¶) numbers.

Homeowner protection
. Home Affordable Modification Program (HAMP)
. . Guidelines . . . 6735
. . Mortgage modification . . . 6740
. Home inspection counseling
. . Materials . . . 6665
. . Training . . . 6665
. Home Mortgage Disclosure Act (HMDA)
. . New reporting data . . . 4845
. Home Ownership and Equity Protection Act
. . Amendment . . . 4855
. Home Valuation Code of Conduct (HVCC)
. . GAO study . . . 6725
. Homeowners Protection Act
. . Amendment . . . 4850
. Homeownership counseling
. . Certification of counselors . . . 6635
. . Definitions . . . 6625
. Housing counseling grants
. . HUD administered . . . 6630
. Housing counseling programs
. . Accountability . . . 6655
. . Covered assistance . . . 6655
. . Definitions . . . 6650
. . Economically vulnerable persons . . . 7535
. . Foreclosure grants . . . 6775
. . Grant limitations . . . 6775
. . Home foreclosure prevention . . . 6775
. . Home inspection counseling . . . 6665
. . Legal assistance . . . 6775
. . Mortgage information booklet . . . 6660
. . Training . . . 6665

Human rights
. Conflict minerals . . . 7020
. Resource extraction . . . 7030
. Strategy and Map to Address Linkages . . . 7020

Hybrid adjustable rate mortgages
. Resetting . . . 6580

Hybrid capital instruments
. Study of use by banks and bank holding companies by Comptroller General . . . 245

Hybrid instruments
. Legal validity of . . . 3125

I

Improving Access to Mainstream Financial Institutions Act of 2010 (see Retail banking)

Industrial banking
. Moratorium on deposit insurance applications . . . 2510

Insider lending
. Extensions of credit . . . 2545
. Sale of assets . . . 2545

Inspectors general
. Bank and credit union deposit insurance fund losses . . . 4465
. Bureau of Consumer Financial Protection . . . 4780
. Nonmaterial Loss Report . . . 4465
. SEC and CFTC . . . 4365, 4480
. Study of effectiveness . . . 7035

Insurance industry
. Definitions
. . Nonadmitted insurance . . . 2050
. . Reinsurance . . . 2065

Insurance industry—continued
. Exempt commercial purchasers . . . 2040
. Federal Insurance Office (FIO)
. . Creation . . . 2005
. . Functions . . . 2010
. Financial solvency . . . 2060
. Licensure of brokers . . . 2030
. National Association of Insurance Commissioners (NAIC) . . . 2030
. National Producer Database . . . 2030
. Nonadmitted insurance . . . 2035
. Reinsurance . . . 2055
. State action . . . 515
. State licensure of brokers . . . 2025
. State regulation . . . 2015
. Surplus lines insurance . . . 2020

Insurance market study
. GAO study . . . 2045

Integrated model disclosure form
. Mortgage loan transactions . . . 4865

Interchange fees
. Limitations on . . . 4750

Intermediate holding companies
. Formation . . . 2610
. Nonbank financial company affiliate . . . 225

International loans
. Standards and evaluation . . . 7015

International swap regulation
. Harmonization . . . 3150
. Joint CFTC and SEC study . . . 3050

Interstate Land Sales Full Disclosure Act
. Amendment . . . 4870

Investment advisers
. Commodity pool operators . . . 1550
. Contractual term restrictions . . . 4080
. Custody of client assets . . . 1540
. Examinations and enforcement resources
. . SEC study . . . 4040
. Family offices . . . 1530
. Fiduciary standards . . . 4020
. Private fund advisers
. . In general . . . 1505
. . Registration . . . 1515
. . Reports and records . . . 1520
. Qualified client standard . . . 1555
. Registration
. . Commodity trading advisers . . . 1515
. . Foreign private funds exemption . . . 1515
. . Funds below $150 Million exemption . . . 1505
. . Intrastate client exemption . . . 1515
. . Small business investment companies exemption . . . 1515
. . Transition period . . . 1505
. . Venture capital fund exemption . . . 1505
. Reports and records
. . Client confidentiality exception . . . 1520
. . In general . . . 1520
. . Proprietary information . . . 1520
. Standards of care study . . . 4020
. State oversight of mid-sized advisers . . . 1535
. Trading advisors . . . 1550
. Transition period . . . 1505

Investment bank holding companies
. Abolished . . . 2570

INV

References are to paragraph (¶) numbers.

Investor access to adviser and broker-dealer registration and discipline records
. SEC study . . . 4040
Investor Advisory Committee
. Composition . . . 4010
. Duties . . . 4010
Investor Advocate
. Duties and obligations . . . 4025
. Ombudsman . . . 4025
. Reports
. . Annual activities review and recommendations . . . 4025
. . Objectives . . . 4025
Investor protection
. In general . . . 4005
. Regulatory structure . . . 4450
Investor Protection Fund
. Whistleblowers . . . 4060
IRC Section 1256
. Exclusion of certain derivatives contracts . . . 7010
Issuer disclosures
. Comptroller General study . . . 4410
Issuers
. Asset-backed security reporting . . . 4260
. Due diligence reporting for asset-backed securities . . . 4270

L

Leverage capital requirements
. Minimum requirements . . . 235
Licensed and certified appraisals
. GAO study . . . 6725
Liquidation (see Receivership)
Loan defaults
. HUD study . . . 6640
Loan modification fraud
. Bureau of Consumer Financial Protection rulemaking authority . . . 4860
. GAO study . . . 6755
Lost, counterfeit or stolen securities
. Report to SEC and Federal Reserve . . . 4100

M

Macroeconomic effects of risk retention
. Financial Stability Oversight Council study (see Financial Stability Oversight Council; Studies)
Manipulative acts
. Securities lending and borrowing . . . 4460
. Swaps . . . 3155
Margin lending
. Restricted . . . 4085
Market participants
. Fingerprinting . . . 4150
Mergers and acquisitions
. Banks and depository institutions . . . 2595
Mine safety
. Periodic reports . . . 7025
Miscellaneous provisions
. In general . . . 7005

Missing securities holders
. Notice to . . . 4160
Monitoring consumer financial products and services markets (see Bureau of Consumer Financial Protection (BCFP); Rulemaking)
Mortgages
. High-cost mortgages
. . Adjustment of percentage points . . . 6605
. . Balloon payments . . . 6610
. . Bona fide discount points . . . 6605
. . Debt acceleration . . . 6615
. . Deferral fees . . . 6615
. . Definitions . . . 6605
. . Evasions . . . 6615
. . Fees . . . 6605
. . Financing . . . 6615
. . Introductory rates . . . 6605
. . Late payment charge . . . 6615
. . Modification . . . 6615
. . Mortgage insurance . . . 6605
. . Payoff statement . . . 6615
. . Pre-loan counseling . . . 6615
. . Prepayment penalties . . . 6605
. . Reverse mortgages . . . 6610
. . Structuring . . . 6615
. . Unintentional violations . . . 6615
. Higher-risk mortgage
. . Definitions . . . 6700
. Mortgage foreclosure scams
. . GAO study . . . 6755
. Mortgage information booklet
. . Federally-related mortgages . . . 6660
. Mortgage insurance programs
. . Home inspection information . . . 6665
. Mortgage origination
. . Maximum liability . . . 6530
. Mortgage originator
. . Definitions . . . 6515
. Mortgage Reform and Anti-Predatory Lending Act of 2007
. . Background . . . 6505
. . Enumerated consumer laws . . . 6510
. Mortgage software
. . HUD certification . . . 6625
. Mortgage-related products
. . Exemption revoked . . . 4265
Motor vehicle dealers
. Exemptions from regulation . . . 4590
Multifamily Mortgage Resolution Program
. Criminal applicants . . . 6730
. Multifamily properties . . . 6730
Municipal securities
. Broker dealers discipline . . . 4390
. Municipal adviser registration . . . 4385
. Municipal securities markets study by the Comptroller General . . . 4410
. Municipal Securities Rulemaking Board
. . Composition . . . 4395
. . Fees . . . 4395
. . Municipal securities . . . 4380
. . Office of Municipal Securities . . . 4400
. . Rulemaking authority . . . 4395
Mutual fund advertising
. Comptroller General study . . . 4040
Mutual holding companies
. Dividends . . . 2605

References are to paragraph (¶) numbers.

N

National Association of Insurance Commissioners (NAIC)
. State adoption of model rules . . . 4495

National banks
. Charter conversions . . . 2555

National Credit Union Administration Board
. Nonmaterial Loss Report . . . 4465

Nationally recognized statistical ratings organizations (NRSROs) (see Credit rating agencies)

Nationwide Mortgage Licensing System and Registry
. Farm Credit Administration institutions covered . . . 4880

Negative amortization
. Limitations on . . . 6560

Neighborhood Reinvestment Corporation (NRC)
. Foreclosure rescue scams . . . 6670

Neighborhood stabilization program
. Redevelopment . . . 6770

Next day funds
. Increased amount . . . 4805

Nonadmitted Insurance Model Act (see Insurance Industry)

Nonadmitted insurer
. Eligibility . . . 2035
. Quarterly listing of alien insurers . . . 2035

Nonbank financial companies
. Acquisitions . . . 205
. Capital and quantitative limits . . . 2575
. Examination by Federal Reserve . . . 200
. Exemption from Federal Reserve supervision . . . 230
. Intermediate holding company . . . 225
. Oversight . . . 120
. Permitted activities . . . 2575
. Prudential standards . . . 125
. Reporting of financial condition . . . 195
. Resolution plan . . . 215
. Risk committee . . . 215
. Shared management with bank holding companies . . . 210
. Subject to regulation . . . 120
. Supervised by the Board
. . Capital and quantitative limits . . . 2575
. . Definitions . . . 2575
. Treatment as a bank holding company . . . 210

Nondepository institution
. Federal Reserve examination powers . . . 2535

Non-domiciliary states
. Reinsurance . . . 2055

Nonstandard loans
. Residential mortgage loans . . . 6545

O

Office of Fair Lending and Equal Opportunity (see Bureau of Consumer Financial Protection (BCFP))

Office of Financial Education (see Bureau of Consumer Financial Protection (BCFP))

Office of Financial Literacy
. Purpose . . . 4475

Office of Financial Projection for Older Americans (see Bureau of Consumer Financial Protection (BCFP))

Office of Financial Research
. Data Center . . . 175
. Establishment and function . . . 165
. Financial Research Fund . . . 180
. In general . . . 160
. Purpose, powers and duties . . . 170
. Relation to Financial Stability Oversight Council . . . 115, 170
. Research and Analysis Center . . . 175

Office of Housing Counseling (OFC)
. Definitions
. . Homeownership counseling . . . 6625
. . Rental housing counseling . . . 6625
. Establishment . . . 6620
. Foreclosure rescue education . . . 6625
. National public service campaign . . . 6625

Office of Service Member Affairs (see Bureau of Consumer Financial Protection (BCFP))

Office of the Comptroller of the Currency
. Bank Savings Association Holding Company and Depository Institution Regulatory Improvement Act of 2010 . . . 2505

Office of Thrift Supervision
. Abolished . . . 2505

Open-end consumer credit plans
. Escrow or impound accounts . . . 6675

Orderly liquidation authority
. Appeals of receivership . . . 510
. Assets
. . Avoidable Transfers . . . 525
. . creditors . . . 525
. . Transfer of assets . . . 540
. Orderly liquidation plan . . . 545
. Systemic risk . . . 515
. Too big to fail . . . 505

Over-the-counter (OTC) derivatives (see Derivatives)

P

Paperwork Reduction Act
. Amendment . . . 4900

Pay It Back Act
. GSE (Government-sponsored enterprises) . . . 6015
. Troubled Asset Relief Program (TARP) . . . 6005
. Unused funds . . . 6025

Payment of interest on demand deposits
. Repealed . . . 2615

Payment, Clearing and Settlement Supervision Act (see Clearing and Settlement)

Person-to-person lending
. Study . . . 4485

Portfolio margining
. Regulation of . . . 3025

Position limits
. CFTC study . . . 3050
. Regulation of . . . 3115

POS

Topical Index

References are to paragraph (¶) numbers.

Prepayment penalties
. Residential mortgage loans . . . 6560

Private funds (see Hedge funds and private equity; Investment advisers)

Private loan ombudsman
. Bureau of Consumer Financial Protection . . . 4615

Private right of action
. Credit rating agencies . . . 4195
. Swap manipulation . . . 3155

Professional organization for ratings analysts
. GAO study . . . 4235

Property appraisals
. Appraisal independence . . . 6705
. Certified and licensed appraisers . . . 6700, 6705
. Customary and reasonable fees . . . 6705
. National registry of appraisal management companies . . . 6710
. Physical property visit . . . 6700
. Regulations . . . 6710
. Regulatory agencies . . . 6700
. Written appraisal . . . 6700

Protecting Tenants at Foreclosure Act of 2009
. Foreclosure . . . 6745

Proxy statements
. Executive compensation and performance disclosure . . . 4305
. Shareholder proxy access . . . 4330

Prudential regulators
. Consumer financial protection authority . . . 4695
. Security-based swaps . . . 3165
. Swaps . . . 3070, 3125
. Violation of consumer law reporting . . . 4825

Prudential standards
. Financial Stability Oversight Council recommendations (see Financial Stability Oversight Council; Studies; Prudential standards)
. Nonbank financial companies . . . 215

Public Company Accounting Oversight Board (PCAOB)
. Assessments . . . 4435
. Broker-dealer auditors . . . 4435
. In general . . . 4420
. Information sharing . . . 4430
. Referral to SROs . . . 4435

Public information
. Federal Reserve . . . 5025

Q

Qualified client standard
. Advisers Act exemption . . . 1555

Qualified mortgage
. Credit risk retention . . . 4255
. Higher-risk mortgage . . . 6700

R

Real estate settlement form
. Contents . . . 4600, 6720

Real Estate Settlement Procedures Act of 1974 (RESPA)
. Amendment . . . 6685
. Escrow accounts . . . 6675

Real Estate Settlement Procedures Act of 1974 (RESPA)—continued
. Increased penalty amounts . . . 6685
. Integrated model disclosure form . . . 4865
. Real estate settlement form . . . 4600, 6720

Receivership
. Appeals of receivership . . . 510
. Assets
. . Avoidable Transfers . . . 525
. . creditors . . . 525
. . Transfer of assets . . . 540
. Orderly liquidation plan . . . 545
. Systemic risk . . . 515
. Too big to fail . . . 505

Recordkeeping and reporting
. Advisers . . . 1520
. Appraisal management companies . . . 6710
. Asset-backed securities . . . 4260
. Bank holding company reports and records . . . 2520
. Beneficial ownership . . . 4145
. Bureau of Consumer Financial Protection
. . Record keeping requirements . . . 4565, 4570, 4575
. Cancelled securities . . . 4100
. Charter conversion requests . . . 2555
. Credit exposure report for nonbank financial companies . . . 215
. Credit rating agencies . . . 4185
. Credit rating agency internal controls . . . 4185
. Custody, maintenance and production of records . . . 4140
. Derivatives clearing organizations . . . 3070
. Disclosure of Chair and CEO roles . . . 4335
. Due diligence for asset-backed securities . . . 4270
. Foreign boards of trade . . . 3120
. Institutional investment manager vote on executive compensation . . . 4295
. Intermediate holding companies . . . 2610
. Large swap traders . . . 3090
. Major security-based swap participants . . . 3165
. Mine safety . . . 7025
. Mortgage modification data . . . 6755
. National registry of appraisal management companies reporting . . . 6710
. NRSRO credit rating form . . . 4185
. Resolution plan for nonbank financial companies . . . 215
. Resource extraction . . . 7030
. Securities holding companies . . . 2570
. Security-based swap dealers . . . 3165
. Short sales . . . 4165
. Short-swing profits . . . 4145
. Source of financial strength . . . 2565
. Swap transactions, real-time reporting . . . 3075, 3095
. Systemic importance assessment . . . 3535
. Systemic risk analysis . . . 130, 175
. Tax allocation reports . . . 2020
. U.S. financial system assessment . . . 175
. Uncleared swaps . . . 3085, 3170
. Women-owned, minority-owned and small business lending data . . . 4730

Recoupment
. Foreclosure . . . 6555

Registration
. Appraiser regulatory programs . . . 6710
. Bureau of Consumer Financial Protection (BCFP) . . . 4555, 4565

Topical Index

References are to paragraph (¶) numbers.

Registration—continued
. Derivatives clearing organizations . . . 3070
. Designated contract market . . . 3100
. Farm Credit Administration regulated institution employees . . . 4880
. Foreign boards of trade . . . 3120
. Futures commission merchant (FCM) . . . 3065
. Investment advisers
. . Commodity trading advisers . . . 1515
. . Foreign private funds exemption . . . 1515
. . Funds below $ 150 Million exemption . . . 1505
. . Intrastate client exemption . . . 1515
. . Small business investment companies exemption . . . 1515
. . Transition period . . . 1505
. . Venture capital fund exemption . . . 1505
. Providers of consumer financial products . . . 4555
. Securities holding companies . . . 2570
. Swap related
. . Major security-based swap participants . . . 3165
. . Major swap participants . . . 3095
. . Security-based swap dealers . . . 3165
. . Swap data repositories . . . 3080
. . Swap dealers . . . 3095
. . Swap execution facilities . . . 3100

Regulation D
. "Bad actor" bar . . . 4070

Regulation FD
. Credit rating agencies not exempt . . . 4225

Remittance transfer service providers
. Disclosure to consumers . . . 4240
. Exceptions . . . 4240

Rental housing counseling
. Certification of counselors . . . 6635

Repayment analysis
. Repayment disclosures . . . 6695

Residential mortgage loan origination
. Fiduciary standards . . . 6520
. Regulation . . . 6520

Resource extraction issuer
. Definitions . . . 7030
. Payments to foreign governments . . . 7030

Retail banking
. Bank Savings Association Holding Company and Depository Institution Regulatory Improvement Act of 2010
. . Creation . . . 2505
. Community development financial institution (CDFI) . . . 5520
. Improving Access to Mainstream Financial Institutions Act of 2010
. . Creation . . . 5505
. . Eligible entity . . . 5510
. . Loan-loss reserve fund grants . . . 5520
. . Specified account activities . . . 5510
. . Technical assistance grants . . . 5520
. Lending limits . . . 2550
. Payday loans . . . 5515
. Saving association branches . . . 1110
. Small dollar loan programs . . . 5520
. Small dollar loans . . . 5515

Reverse mortgages
. Escrow or impound accounts . . . 6675
. High-cost mortgages . . . 6610
. Minimum standards inapplicable . . . 6545

Right to Financial Privacy Act
. Bureau of Consumer Financial Protection exception . . . 4875

Risk committee
. Nonbank financial companies . . . 215

Risk management policies and procedures
. Designated clearing entities . . . 3515

Risk management standards
. Financial market utilities . . . 3515
. Payment, clearing and settlement activities . . . 3515

Risk-based capital requirements
. Minimum requirements . . . 235

S

S.A.F.E. Mortgage Licensing Act of 2008 (S.A.F.E. Act) (see Mortgages; Mortgage Reform and Anti-Predatory Lending Act)

Sarbanes-Oxley Act of 2002
. Fair Fund provisions . . . 4090
. Information sharing . . . 4430
. Small issuer reporting exemption . . . 4490
. Whistleblowers . . . 4060

Savings association
. Branching . . . 1110
. Charter conversions . . . 2555
. Dividends . . . 2600

Section 11 liability (see Credit rating agencies; Section 11 liability)

Securities and Exchange Commission (SEC)
. Broker dealers discipline . . . 4390
. Brokers, dealers and investment advisers standards of care study . . . 4020
. Collateral bars . . . 4065
. Conflicts of interest . . . 3045
. Credit Rating Agency Board (see Credit rating agencies; Credit Rating Agency Board)
. Disclosure of confidential information . . . 4120
. Employee hotline . . . 4365
. Enforcement
. . Aiding and abetting . . . 4130
. . Cease-and-desist proceedings . . . 4135
. . Control person liability . . . 4135
. . Fair Funds . . . 4090
. . Formerly associated persons . . . 4110
. . In general . . . 4050
. . Investigation time limit and extension . . . 4155
. . Off-exchange trading . . . 4125
. . Reckless conduct . . . 4130
. . Short sales . . . 4165
. . Subpoena power . . . 4105
. . Transnational fraud . . . 4135
. Examination staff . . . 4360
. Fair and Accurate Credit Transactions Act of 2003 (FACT Act) . . . 4815
. Funding . . . 4370
. GASB funding . . . 4405
. Hotline report by SEC Inspector General . . . 4360
. Inspector general . . . 4480
. Interagency cooperation . . . 3020, 3035, 3040, 3095, 3145, 4320
. Internal controls study of the SEC . . . 4355
. Investor Advisory Committee . . . 4010
. Investor testing . . . 4015

SEC

References are to paragraph (¶) numbers.

Securities and Exchange Commission (SEC)— continued
- Major security-based swap participants
  - Registration . . . 3165
- Market specialists . . . 4115
- MSRB . . . 4395
- Municipal adviser registration . . . 4385
- Municipal securities . . . 4380
- Office of Credit Rating . . . 4185
- Office of Municipal Securities . . . 4400
- Office of the Investor Advocate (see Investor Advocate)
- Organization . . . 4350
- Personnel management practices study by Comptroller General . . . 4355
- Post-SEC-employment study by Comptroller General . . . 4355
- Remedies
  - In general . . . 4050
- Reserve fund . . . 4370
- Rulemaking
  - Asset-backed security representations and warranties . . . 4260
  - Authority to define technical terms . . . 1525
  - Beneficial ownership and proxy voting . . . 4325
  - Business conduct standards . . . 3165
  - Capital and margin requirements . . . 3095, 3165
  - Chair and CEO bifurcation . . . 4335
  - Clearing . . . 3095
  - Compensation committee independence . . . 4300
  - Credit rating agencies . . . 4180, 4185, 4210
  - Credit rating system . . . 4190
  - Custody and maintenance of records . . . 4140
  - Due diligence reporting . . . 4270
  - Executive compensation and performance disclosure . . . 4305
  - Hedging disclosure . . . 4315
  - Investor testing . . . 4015
  - Issuance of joint agency rules . . . 1525
  - Mandatory arbitration . . . 4055
  - Notice to missing securities holders . . . 4160
  - Pre-purchase disclosure . . . 4035
  - Regulation D "bad actors" . . . 4070
  - Shareholder proxy access . . . 4330
  - Standards of care . . . 4020
  - Transition rules . . . 3170
- Sarbanes-Oxley compliance burdens . . . 4490
- Securities futures . . . 3035
- Securities regulation, independent study of . . . 4355
- Security-based swap dealers
  - Registration . . . 3165
- SRO oversight study by Comptroller General . . . 4355
- SRO rule changes . . . 4030
- Supervisory controls study . . . 4355
- Swaps
  - Jurisdiction . . . 3015
- Termination of investment activities . . . 2575
- Whistleblowers . . . 4060

Securities Investor Protection Act of 1970 (SIPA)
- Consumer rights . . . 520
- Maximum cash advance . . . 4095
- Member assessments . . . 4095
- Penalties . . . 4095
- Portfolio margining accounts . . . 4455
- Securities Investor Protection Corporation
  - Liquidation . . . 520
  - SEC loans to . . . 4095

Securities lending
- Fraud . . . 4460

Securitization
- Conflicts of interest . . . 2585
- Exemption . . . 4255
- Hedging prohibition . . . 4255
- In general . . . 4250
- Real estate mortgage notes . . . 4265
- Risk retention . . . 4255

Security-based swaps (see Swaps; Security-based swaps)

Self-regulatory organizations (SROs)
- Compensation committee independence and listing . . . 4300
- Equal treatment of rules . . . 4075
- Fingerprinting . . . 4150
- Proxy voting . . . 4325
- SEC review of rule changes . . . 4030

Set-off
- Foreclosure . . . 6555

Shared appreciation mortgages
- HUD study . . . 6540

Short selling
- Disclosure . . . 4165

Stable value contracts
- Joint CFTC and SEC study . . . 3050

Standardizing algorithmic descriptions
- Joint CFTC and SEC study . . . 3050

Standards of professional appraisal practice
- National hotline . . . 6710

State enforcement
- Appraisal management company minimum requirements . . . 6710
- Appraiser minimum qualifications . . . 6710
- Appraiser registry fees . . . 6710
- Certifying and licensing authority . . . 6710
- National registry of appraisal management companies reporting . . . 6710
- Residential mortgage loans . . . 6600

State regulation
- Adjustable rate mortgages . . . 4790
- Charter conversions . . . 2555
- Collection and allocation of premium tax obligations . . . 2020
- Consumer financial protection laws . . . 4625
- De novo branching . . . 2560
- Depository institutions subsidiaries . . . 2535
- Enforcement of consumer financial protection laws
  - In general . . . 4630
  - Visitorial authority . . . 4655
- Home state regulation . . . 2025
- Insurance industry . . . 515
- Insurer solvency . . . 2060
- Interest only loans . . . 4790
- Investment adviser contracts . . . 4080
- Licensure of insurance brokers . . . 2030
- Model insurance regulations . . . 4495
- Negative amortized loans . . . 4790

References are to paragraph (¶) numbers.

State regulation—continued
. Nonadmitted and Reinsurance Reform Act of 2010 . . . 2015
. Non-domiciliary states . . . 2055
. Preemption
. . Consumer financial laws . . . 4640, 4645, 4650
. . Insurance . . . 2010
. . Securities-based swaps . . . 3175
. . Regulation D bar . . . 4070
. Securities-based swaps . . . 3175
. Senior citizen investors . . . 4475
. State oversight of mid-sized advisers . . . 1535

State-chartered banks
. Charter conversions . . . 2555

Statistical rating organizations (see Credit rating agencies)

Statute of limitations
. Receivership . . . 525
. Whistleblowers . . . 4215

Steering incentives
. Regulations . . . 6525

Studies and reports
. Accredited investors . . . 1545, 1560
. Adviser examinations and enforcement resources . . . 4040
. Aiding and abetting . . . 4170
. Appraisal subcommittee . . . 6710
. Appraisal valuation models, licensed and certified appraisals, broker-priced opinions, automated valuation models . . . 6725
. Asset-backed securities and risk retention . . . 4255
. Audit of 2007 - 2010 Federal Reserve credit facilities . . . 5020
. Audit of Financial Stability Oversight Council by GAO . . . 110
. Availability and affordability of credit . . . 6595
. Bank Holding Company Act exceptions . . . 2515
. Bank investment activities . . . 2580
. Bankruptcy, effect on . . . 510
. Brokers, dealers and investment advisers standards of care . . . 4020
. Bureau of Consumer Financial Protection operational plans . . . 4725
. Bureau of Consumer Financial Protection semi-annual report . . . 4540, 4555
. Carbon markets . . . 3050
. Compensation consultant impact . . . 4300
. Congo conflict minerals . . . 7020
. Contingent capital . . . 125
. Core deposits and brokered deposits . . . 7040
. Council of Inspectors General on Financial Oversight . . . 4055
. Credit facility reviews . . . 5015
. Credit rating agency compensation and incentive . . . 4235
. Credit rating agency independence . . . 4235
. Credit rating process for structured finance products . . . 4190
. Credit score discrepancies . . . 4765
. Custody of client assets . . . 1560
. Effect of drywall on foreclosure . . . 6760
. Exchange facilitators . . . 4770
. Fannie Mae and Freddie Mac wind down . . . 4745
. FDIC Inspector General . . . 550
. Federal agency reliance on credit rating agencies . . . 4235
. Federal Insurance Office (FIO) . . . 2010

Studies and reports—continued
. Federal Reserve . . . 550
. Federal Reserve Bank governance . . . 5020
. Federal Reserve emergency lending programs . . . 5010
. FHA . . . 6020
. Financial literacy of investors . . . 4040
. Financial market utilities . . . 3535
. Financial planners . . . 4040
. Financial reform impact . . . 105
. Five-year review of BCFP rules . . . 4555
. Foreclosure rescue . . . 6755
. GASB role and funding . . . 4410
. Hybrid capital instruments use by banks and bank holding companies . . . 245
. Inspectors general . . . 7035
. Insurance market study . . . 2045
. Internal conflicts of interest within securities firms . . . 4040
. International swap regulation . . . 3050
. Investor access to adviser and broker-dealer registration and discipline records . . . 4040
. Investor Advocate annual activities review and recommendations . . . 4025
. Investor Advocate objectives . . . 4025
. Issuer disclosures . . . 4410
. Liquidation status reports . . . 515
. Loan defaults, foreclosures and escrow accounts . . . 6640
. Loan modification fraud . . . 6755
. Macroeconomic effects of risk retention . . . 4275
. Mortgage foreclosure scams . . . 6755
. Municipal securities markets . . . 4410
. Mutual fund advertising . . . 4040
. Nonbank financial company condition reports . . . 195
. Nonmaterial Loss Report . . . 4465
. Office of Financial Research additional reports . . . 170
. Person-to-person lending . . . 4485
. Position limits . . . 3050
. Private education loans and lenders . . . 4760
. Professional organization for ratings analysts . . . 4235
. Proprietary trading . . . 4470
. Proprietary trading ban study . . . 2575
. Prudential standards recommendations . . . 145
. Reverse mortgage transactions . . . 4755
. Review of Treasury Secretary's determinations . . . 515
. Sarbanes-Oxley compliance burdens . . . 4490
. SEC hotline . . . 4360
. SEC internal controls . . , 4355
. SEC oversight of SROs . . . 4355
. SEC personnel management practices . . . 4355
. SEC Revolving door . . . 4355
. Secured creditor haircuts . . . 545
. Securities regulation . . . 4355
. Shared appreciation mortgages . . . 6540
. Short selling . . . 1560
. Small issuer compliance reporting exemption . . . 4490
. SRO for private funds . . . 1560
. Stable value contracts . . . 3050
. Standardized credit rating terminology . . . 4220
. Standardizing algorithmic descriptions . . . 3050
. Supervisory controls evaluation . . . 4355
. Swap data . . . 3075
. Treasury . . . 550
. Troubled Asset Relief Program (TARP) . . . 6015

Studies and reports—continued
. U.S. intermediate holding companies of foreign banks . . . 245
. Whistleblowers . . . 4060

Subpoena power
. BCFP . . . 4665
. Office of Financial Research . . . 170
. SEC nationwide service . . . 4105

Swaps
. Banking products . . . 3070
. Bankruptcy . . . 3065
. Customer funds . . . 3065
. Designated contract market . . . 3100, 3105
. Energy related . . . 3015
. Foreign exchange swaps . . . 3015
. In general . . . 3015
. Major security-based swap participants
.. Capital and margin requirements . . . 3165
.. Registration . . . 3165
.. Reporting . . . 3170
. Major swap participants
.. Registration . . . 3095
. Mandatory clearing of swaps . . . 3060
. Pre-existing agreements . . . 3125
. Regulatory enforcement . . . 3130
. Security-based . . . 3015
. Security-based swaps
.. Beneficial ownership reporting . . . 3170
.. Dealer capital and margin requirements . . . 3165
.. Dealer registration . . . 3165
.. Dealer reporting . . . 3170
.. Definitions . . . 3010
.. In general . . . 3160
. Segregation of funds . . . 3065
. Swap dealer registration . . . 3095
. Swap entities
.. Federal assistance . . . 3030
. Swap execution facilities . . . 3100
.. Core principles . . . 3110
.. Registration . . . 3100

Systemic risk
. Bank holding company . . . 135
. Capital requirements . . . 235
. Concentration limits . . . 2590
. Conflicts of interest . . . 3045
. Conflicts of interest related to securitization . . . 2585
. Credit exposure report for nonbank financial companies . . . 215
. Early remediation of financial distress . . . 220
. Emergency enforcement action . . . 3525
. Federal Reserve . . . 5005
. Financial holding companies (see Holding companies; Financial holding companies)
. Financial market utilities . . . 3510
. Financial Stability Oversight Council (see Financial Stability Oversight Council)
. Grandfathered unitary savings and loan holding company . . . 2610
. Grave threat to financial stability by nonbank financial company . . . 150
. Hedge funds and private funds . . . 2575
. In general . . . 105
. Insurance industry . . . 2010
. Interstate mergers and acquisitions . . . 2595
. Liquidation of financial companies . . . 515
. Monitoring bank and nonbank financial companies . . . 130

Systemic risk—continued
. Nonbank financial companies (see Nonbank financial companies)
. Off-balance sheet activities . . . 215
. Payment, clearing and settlement activities . . . 3510
. Position limits . . . 3090
. Proprietary trading . . . 2575, 4470
. Prudential standards (see Prudential standards)
. Recordkeeping and reporting . . . 3535
. Reserve ratio . . . 1095
. Resolution plan for nonbank financial companies . . . 215
. Retail banking . . . 2505
. Risk management standards . . . 3515
. Risk profiles . . . 3095
. Securities lending . . . 4460
. Securitization (see Securitization)
. Short-term debt and leverage limits . . . 215
. State regulation of insurer solvency . . . 2060
. Systemic importance . . . 3510
. Temporary Liquidity Guarantee Program (TLGP) . . . 5035
. Too big to fail . . . 505

T

Taxation
. Section 1256 contracts
.. Exclusion of derivatives . . . 7010

Telemarketing and Consumer Fraud and Abuse Prevention Act (TCFAPA)
. Amendment . . . 4895

Temporary Liquidity Guarantee Program (TLGP).
. Conditions for . . . 5035

Thrifts (see Savings Associations)

Treasury Department
. Federal Insurance Office (FIO)
.. Creation . . . 2005
.. Structure and purpose . . . 2010
. Federal Reserve emergency lending programs . . . 5010
. Financial Research Fund . . . 180
. FIO
.. Rules of construction . . . 2070
.. Severability . . . 2075
. Home Affordable Modification Program (HAMP) (see Homeowner protection; Home Affordable Modification Program (HAMP))
. Housing and Economic Recovery Act of 2008 . . . 6770
. Office of Financial Research . . . 165
. Securities and Exchange Commission Reserve Fund . . . 4370
. Troubled Asset Relief Program (TARP) (see Troubled Asset Relief Program (TARP))

Treasury Secretary
. Appointment of receivers . . . 515
. Bureau of Consumer Financial Protection, interim Director . . . 4720
. Community Development Banking and Financial Institutions Fund (CDFI fund) oversight . . . 5525
. Covered agreements . . . 2010
. IMF loan proposals . . . 7015
. International policy coordination . . . 250

References are to paragraph (¶) numbers.

Troubled Asset Relief Program (TARP)
. Pay It Back Act . . . 6005
. TARP proceeds reporting . . . 6015
. TARP programs . . . 6010
. Unused funds . . . 6025
. Wind down . . . 6010

Truth in Lending Act (TILA)
. Appraisal independence . . . 6705
. Civil money penalties . . . 6570
. Conforming amendments . . . 4885
. Definitions
. . Bona fide discount points . . . 6605
. . High-cost mortgages . . . 6605
. . Open-end consumer credit plans . . . 6605
. . Prepayment penalties . . . 6605
. Escrow or impound accounts . . . 6675
. Overview . . . 6505
. Property appraisal requirements . . . 6700
. Repayment analysis . . . 6695
. Residential loan payments . . . 6690
. Rule of construction . . . 6565
. Violations of appraisal standards . . . 6705

Truth in Savings Act
. Amendment . . . 4890

U

Uniform Standards of Professional Appraisal and Practice
. Qualified appraiser . . . 6700

United States Trade Representative
. Retention of authority . . . 2010

V

Victims Relief Fund
. Funding . . . 4545

Volcker rule
. "Source of strength" . . . 2565
. Bank holding companies . . . 2570
. Banking activities
. . Limitations . . . 2575
. . Permitted . . . 2575

Volcker rule—continued
. Banking activities—continued
. . Prohibited . . . 2575
. Capital limits . . . 2575
. Compliance
. . Internal controls . . . 2575
. . Recordkeeping . . . 2575
. Definitions . . . 2575
. . Banking entity . . . 2575
. . Hedge funds . . . 2575
. . Illiquid funds . . . 2575
. . Private equity funds . . . 2575
. . Proprietary trading . . . 2575
. . Sponsoring . . . 2575
. . Trading accounts . . . 2575
. Derivative transactions in lending limits . . . 2550
. Fund investments . . . 2575
. Hedge fund exposure (see Hedge funds and private equity funds)
. Illiquid funds . . . 2575
. Limitations on business relationships
. . Prime brokerage transactions . . . 2575
. . Transactions with affiliates . . . 2575
. Proprietary trading . . . 2575
. Quantitative limits . . . 2575
. Regulations . . . 2575
. Securitization (see Securitization; Conflicts of interest)
. Termination of activities and investments . . . 2575

W

Waiver of SRO rules
. Contract provisions void . . . 4075

Wells notice
. Investigation time limit and extension . . . 4155

Whistleblowers (see also Bureau of Consumer Financial Protection (BCFP); Securities and Exchange Commission (SEC))
. Commodities industry . . . 3145
. Credit rating agencies . . . 4215

Women-owned, minority-owned and small business
. Lending data . . . 4730